Chr_____ _____3

fr. Cliff & Wilma

700
FAMILY
RECIPES

700
FAMILY
RECIPES

Edited by Norma MacMillan and Wendy James
Consultant Gill Edden

Forum House Publishing,
Toronto, Canada

Published by Forum House Publishing
Toronto, Canada

The material in this book has previously appeared in
The Complete Cook and the *100 Recipes in Colour* series

Printed in Singapore

Acknowledgements
Photographs were supplied by Editions Atlas, Editions Atlas/Cedus,
Editions Atlas/Zadora, Cadbury, Flour Advisory Board, Gales Honey,
Archivio IGDA, Lavinia Press Agency, Orbis GmbH, Pasta Information
Centre, Tate & Lyle Refineries Ltd., Wales Tourist Board.

Contents

Hungarian cabbage soup

Overall timing 2 hours

Freezing Suitable: add flour and soured cream when reheating.

To serve 4

8 oz	Onions	225 g
1	Garlic clove	1
3 tbsp	Oil	3x15 ml
12 oz	Stewing beef	350 g
12 oz	Canned sauerkraut	350 g
½ teasp	Fennel seeds	2.5 ml
½ teasp	Coarse salt	2.5 ml
3½ pints	Stock	2 litres
4 oz	Streaky bacon	125 g
2	Frankfurters	2
1 tbsp	Paprika	15 ml
2 tbsp	Plain flour	2x15 ml
4 tbsp	Water	4x15 ml
2 tbsp	Soured cream	2x15 ml

Peel and slice onions; peel and crush garlic. Heat 2 tbsp (2x15 ml) oil in large saucepan. Add onions and garlic and fry over moderate heat till golden. Cut beef into small cubes, add to pan and brown all over.

Add drained canned sauerkraut, fennel seeds and coarse salt to the pan. Cover with the stock (made with 2 stock cubes if necessary) and simmer gently for 1 hour or till meat is tender.

Derind and roughly chop the bacon. Fry bacon in remaining oil in a frying pan till crisp, then add the sliced frankfurters and paprika. Cook for 5 minutes, then remove and add to the saucepan.

Blend flour with cold water in a bowl till smooth, then stir into the soup mixture and cook for a further 5 minutes. Stir in the soured cream, adjust the seasoning and serve at once with slices of black bread.

Savoury dumpling soup

Overall timing 2½ hours

Freezing Suitable: add dumplings after reheating

To serve 6–8

1	Onion	1
4 oz	Carrots	125 g
3 oz	Parsnips	75 g
5	Stalks of celery	5
3 oz	Butter	75 g
2 tbsp	Plain flour	2x15 ml
3 pints	Chicken stock	1.7 litres
1 lb	Cooked chicken joints	450 g
Dumplings		
4 oz	Fresh breadcrumbs	125 g
2 oz	Streaky bacon	50 g
4 oz	Calf's liver	125 g
4 oz	Minced beef	125 g
1	Onion	1
1	Egg	1
½ teasp	Dried marjoram	2.5 ml
	Salt and pepper	
1 tbsp	Chopped parsley	15 ml

First make dumplings. Soak breadcrumbs in ½ pint (300 ml) water for 15 minutes. Derind and chop bacon and fry till crisp. Mince liver. Add beef, squeezed out breadcrumbs, chopped onion, drained bacon, egg, marjoram, seasoning and parsley. Shape into small dumplings.

Peel and chop onion, carrots and parsnips; chop celery. Melt butter, add onions and cook for 2–3 minutes. Add carrots, celery and parsnips, cover and cook till tender. Sieve vegetables and return to pan. Stir in flour then 1 pint (560 ml) stock. Simmer until thickened. Add remaining stock.

Skin, bone and chop chicken. Add to soup with dumplings and simmer for 15 minutes.

Scotch broth

Overall timing 2½ hours

Freezing Not suitable

To serve 4

4 oz	Pearl barley	125 g
2 lb	Scrag end of neck of lamb	900 g
2 oz	Butter	50 g
2	Onions	2
4	Stalks of celery	4
1 tbsp	Plain flour	15 ml
4 pints	Water	2.2 litres
1 teasp	Sugar	5 ml
	Salt and pepper	
1 lb	Potatoes	450 g
4	Carrots	4
1	Leek	1

Wash the barley and drain thoroughly. Wipe and trim the lamb and cut into pieces. Melt the butter in a saucepan or flameproof casserole. Add the lamb and fry over a high heat till browned on all sides.

Peel and chop the onions; trim and slice the celery. Add to the meat and fry till transparent. Add the barley and cook for 2 minutes. Sprinkle in the flour and cook, stirring, till flour begins to brown. Gradually add the water and bring to the boil, stirring constantly. Add the sugar, salt and pepper. Cover and simmer for about 1½ hours.

Peel and quarter the potatoes; scrape and slice the carrots. Add to the soup and simmer for a further 30 minutes.

Wash and finely chop the leek and add to the soup. Simmer for 3 minutes more. Taste and adjust the seasoning. Serve immediately with toast or granary rolls and butter.

Tregaron broth

Overall timing 1 hour

Freezing Not suitable

To serve 6

1 lb	Streaky bacon	450 g
1 lb	Shin beef	450 g
1 oz	Butter	25 g
1	Large leek	1
1 lb	Potatoes	450 g
8 oz	Carrots	225 g
8 oz	Parsnips	225 g
1	Small swede	1
3 pints	Water	1.7 litres
1	Small white cabbage	1
2 oz	Fine or medium oatmeal	50 g
	Salt and pepper	

Derind the bacon and cut into 1 inch (2.5 cm) pieces. Trim the beef and cut into chunks. Melt the butter in a large saucepan and fry the bacon and beef for 5 minutes.

Meanwhile, trim and slice the leek. Peel the potatoes, carrots, parsnips and swede. Cut into chunks. Add vegetables to pan and fry for 5 minutes. Add the water and bring to the boil.

Shred the cabbage and add to the pan with the oatmeal and seasoning. Cover and simmer for 45 minutes. Adjust the seasoning to taste before serving.

Shin of beef soup

Overall timing 4 hours

Freezing Not suitable

To serve 6–8

3 lb	Shin of beef on bone	1.4 kg
	Plain flour	
	Salt and pepper	
1	Onion	1
4	Stalks of celery	4
1	Leek	1
3	Carrots	3
2	Turnips	2
1 lb	Potatoes	450 g
1 lb	White cabbage	450 g
	Sprig of parsley	
	Sprig of thyme	
2 teasp	Powdered mustard	2x5 ml
4	Slices of toast	4

Wipe beef; slash meat through to bone several times. Make a stiff paste of flour and water and use to seal ends of bone to keep in the marrow. Place in large saucepan with 3 pints (1.7 litres) water, salt and pepper. Bring to the boil, skim off scum, cover and simmer for 3 hours.

Peel and chop onion; trim and chop celery and leek; scrape and slice carrots; peel turnips and potatoes and cut into chunks; shred cabbage.

Add vegetables to beef with herbs and cook for a further 30 minutes.

Lift out meat and cut into cubes and slices, reserving the bone. Remove vegetables with a draining spoon and place in serving dish with meat. Keep hot to serve as main course. Pour stock into a warmed soup tureen and keep hot.

Preheat grill. Scoop out marrow from bone. Mix with salt, pepper and mustard and spread on toast. Grill till bubbling, then serve with soup.

Turkish soup with meatballs

Overall timing 1¾ hours

Freezing Not suitable

To serve 4–6

1	Knuckle of veal	1
1 lb	Shin of beef	450 g
1	Large onion	1
2	Large carrots	2
1	Stalk of celery	1
	Parsley stalks	
	Salt and pepper	
2	Eggs	2
3 tbsp	Lemon juice	3x15 ml
Meatballs		
1 lb	Minced beef	450 g
4 oz	Cooked long grain rice	125 g
1	Egg	1
1 tbsp	Chopped parsley	15 ml
¼ teasp	Grated nutmeg	1.25 ml
	Salt and pepper	
1 oz	Butter	25 g
2 tbsp	Oil	2x15 ml

Chop knuckle in half lengthways. Dice beef. Peel and chop onion and carrots; chop celery. Put meat and vegetables into a saucepan with 4 pints (2.2 litres) water, parsley stalks and seasoning. Cover and simmer for 45 minutes.

Meanwhile, mix beef with rice, egg, parsley, nutmeg and seasoning to a stiff paste and shape into small balls.

Heat butter and oil in a frying pan. Add meatballs and fry till browned all over.

Strain stock, discarding meat and vegetables. Return to pan and bring back to boil. Add meatballs and simmer for 15 minutes.

Put the eggs and lemon juice into a tureen and gradually stir in soup.

Manhattan clam chowder

Overall timing 2 hours

Freezing Suitable

To serve 8

4 oz	Streaky bacon	125 g
2 tbsp	Oil	2x15 ml
3	Large onions	3
2	Large tomatoes	2
2	Leeks	2
1	Stalk of celery	1
1	Carrot	1
2	Potatoes	2
1½ pints	Fish stock	850 ml
2	Sprigs of parsley	2
1	Bay leaf	1
¼ teasp	Grated nutmeg	1.25 ml
	Salt and pepper	
¾ pint	Milk	400 ml
1 lb	Canned clams	450 g
1 oz	Butter	25 g
1 oz	Plain flour	25 g
2 teasp	Worcestershire sauce	2x5 ml
¼ teasp	Tabasco sauce	1.25 ml

Derind and dice bacon. Heat oil in a saucepan, add bacon and cook gently. Peel and slice onions and add to pan. Cook till transparent.

Blanch and peel tomatoes. Finely chop leeks and celery. Peel and finely chop carrot and potatoes. Add to pan and cook for 2–3 minutes. Add stock, parsley, bay leaf, nutmeg and seasoning. Cover and simmer for 10 minutes.

Discard parsley and bay leaf. Purée soup in blender, return to rinsed-out pan and add milk and drained clams. Simmer gently for 4 minutes.

Knead butter and flour to a paste. Stir into soup in tiny pieces. Cook for 2–3 minutes until thick. Stir in Worcestershire and Tabasco sauces and serve.

American fish chowder

Overall timing 1½ hours

Freezing Suitable

To serve 4

2 lb	Mixed white fish	900 g
2 oz	Streaky bacon	50 g
1 tbsp	Oil	15 ml
1	Large onion	1
4	Medium potatoes	4
4	Carrots	4
4	Stalks of celery	4
1 tbsp	Chopped parsley	15 ml
14 oz	Can of tomatoes	397 g
1½ pints	Fish stock or water	850 ml
2 tbsp	Tomato ketchup	2x15 ml
2 tbsp	Worcestershire sauce	2x15 ml
	Dried thyme	
	Salt and pepper	

Skin and bone fish and cut into bite-size pieces. Derind and dice bacon.

Heat oil in a saucepan and fry bacon till crisp. Remove from pan. Peel and chop onion and add to pan. Cook gently till transparent.

Peel and chop potatoes and carrots. Finely chop celery. Add to pan with chopped parsley, tomatoes and their juice, fish stock or water, tomato ketchup, Worcestershire sauce, a pinch of thyme and seasoning. Cover and simmer gently for about 45 minutes.

Add the fish pieces and bacon, cover and cook for a further 15 minutes.

Cantonese fish soup

Overall timing 35 minutes plus marination

Freezing Not suitable

To serve 6

12 oz	White fish fillets	350 g
2 tbsp	Soy sauce	2x15 ml
2 teasp	Dry sherry	2x5 ml
3 tbsp	Oil	3x15 ml
2	Medium onions	2
4	Shallots	4
2	Medium carrots	2
3	Stalks of celery	3
2½ pints	Chicken stock	1.5 litres
2 oz	Long grain rice	50 g
	Salt and pepper	

Cut across the fillets into thin strips and put into a bowl. Add the soy sauce, sherry and 1 tbsp (15 ml) of the oil. Mix well and leave to marinate in a cool place for 1 hour.

Peel and chop the onions and two of the shallots. Peel and dice the carrots. Trim and chop the celery. Heat remaining oil in a large saucepan, add prepared vegetables, cover and cook gently for 5 minutes. Add the stock and bring to the boil. Stir in rice and salt, bring back to the boil, cover and simmer for 10 minutes.

Add the fish and marinating juices and cook for a further 10 minutes. Taste and adjust seasoning. Pour into soup bowls and garnish with remaining shallots, peeled and finely chopped.

Provençal cod soup

Overall timing 1 hour

Freezing Not suitable

To serve 4

1	Large onion	1
1	Leek	1
1	Large tomato	1
2 tbsp	Oil	2x15 ml
1	Stalk of fresh fennel (optional)	1
2	Garlic cloves	2
2½ pints	Water	1.5 litres
	Bouquet garni	
	Orange rind	
¼ teasp	Saffron	1.25 ml
	Salt and pepper	
1¾ lb	Potatoes	750 g
1 lb	Cod fillets	450 g
4	Thick slices of bread	4
1 tbsp	Chopped parsley	15 ml

Peel and slice onion. Trim and finely chop leek. Blanch, peel and chop tomato. Heat oil in a large saucepan. Add onion, leek and tomato and cook, stirring, for 5 minutes.

Chop fennel, if using. Peel and crush garlic. Add water, bouquet garni, fennel, a strip of orange rind, garlic, saffron and pepper. Bring to the boil.

Peel and thickly slice potatoes. Add to pan and cook for 10 minutes. Chop cod fillets into pieces and add with seasoning. Cook for a further 15 minutes.

Remove cod and potatoes with a draining spoon and place in warmed serving dish. Put the slices of bread in a warmed soup tureen and pour the cooking juices over. Sprinkle with parsley. Serve soup and cod together or as separate courses.

Cock-a-leekie

Overall timing 2¼ hours

Freezing Suitable

To serve 6

2 lb	Leeks	900 g
1 oz	Butter	25 g
3 lb	Ovenready chicken	1.4 kg
3 pints	Stock or water	1.7 litres
	Bouquet garni	
	Salt and pepper	
4 oz	Prunes (optional)	125 g

Wash, trim and slice leeks. Melt butter in a frying pan, add leeks and fry quickly for 5 minutes. Put into a saucepan with the chicken, giblets, stock (made with cubes if necessary) or water, bouquet garni, salt and pepper. Bring to the boil, cover and simmer for 1½ hours.

Stone prunes and add to pan, if using. Cook for 30 minutes longer. Discard bouquet garni.

Remove chicken from pan. Cut the meat into strips, discarding skin and bones. Return meat to pan. Taste and adjust seasoning. Serve with baps or oatcakes.

Chicken, lemon and egg drop soup

Overall timing 2 hours 10 minutes

Freezing Suitable: add eggs after reheating

To serve 6

1 lb	Knuckle of veal	450 g
3½ pints	Water	2 litres
3 lb	Boiling chicken with giblets	1.4 kg
1	Lemon	1
2	Onions	2
2	Cloves	2
	Salt and pepper	
2	Eggs	2

Place knuckle in saucepan with the water. Bring to the boil, then cover and simmer for 1 hour.

Meanwhile, chop the chicken into joints and remove skin if liked. Wash giblets. Grate the rind of the lemon and squeeze out the juice. Reserve both. Peel onions and spike each with a clove. Add chicken, giblets, lemon rind, spiked onions and seasoning to pan. Cover and cook gently for 1 hour till chicken is tender.

Strain the stock into a clean pan. Cut meats into small pieces, discarding bones, skin, giblets and onions. Skim stock, add meats and bring to the boil. Stir in lemon juice, then taste and adjust seasoning.

Beat the eggs in a small bowl. Remove saucepan from heat and pour soup into tureen. Drizzle egg in a thin stream into soup, stirring continuously. Serve.

Chicken noodle soup

Overall timing 10 minutes

Freezing Not suitable

To serve 4

2½ pints	Chicken stock	1.5 litres
3 oz	Fine egg noodles	75 g
2 tbsp	Lemon juice	2x15 ml
	Salt and pepper	
2 tbsp	Chopped parsley	2x15 ml

Put the stock into a large saucepan. Bring to the boil and add the noodles. Boil for 3–4 minutes till tender.

Add the lemon juice and seasoning and sprinkle with chopped parsley. Serve with a side dish of grated mature Cheddar cheese.

Bacon dumpling soup

Overall timing 2¾ hours

Freezing Suitable: add dumplings to stock after thawing

To serve 4

12 oz	Stale white bread	350 g
½ pint	Milk	300 ml
2 oz	Lean bacon rashers	50 g
1 oz	Butter	25 g
1	Onion	1
1	Garlic clove	1
1 tbsp	Chopped parsley	15 ml
¼ teasp	Dried marjoram	1.25 ml
	Salt and pepper	
3	Eggs	3
4 oz	Self-raising flour	125 g
2 pints	Stock	1.1 litres

Remove crusts from bread, then soak in milk for 2 hours. Derind and chop bacon. Fry in butter till crisp.

Peel and finely chop onion. Peel and crush garlic. Put both into bowl with bread, bacon, parsley and marjoram. Season and add eggs. Mix together well. Sift in flour and stir until absorbed.

Heat the stock in a large saucepan. Make the bacon mixture into 1 inch (2.5 cm) balls and roll them in a little flour so they don't fall apart when cooking. Add the dumplings to the stock and simmer for 15 minutes. Serve hot.

Pea and bacon soup

Overall timing 2¾ hours plus overnight soaking

Freezing Suitable

To serve 6

12 oz	Dried whole green peas	350 g
4 pints	Water	2.3 litres
2 lb	Knuckle of smoked bacon	900 g
	Salt and pepper	

Put peas in a saucepan and cover with the cold water. Leave to soak overnight.

Add the bacon knuckle to the pan and bring to the boil. Skim off any scum. Cover and simmer for 1½–2 hours till the bacon and peas are tender.

Remove and drain the bacon joint. Discard the skin and bone and cut the meat into small cubes. Reserve one third of the peas. Purée the remaining peas in a blender or by pressing through a sieve. Return the puréed peas and reserved whole peas to the saucepan. Bring to the boil, stirring occasionally.

Add the diced bacon, and season to taste. Pour into a warmed tureen and serve with crispbread.

Turkey vegetable soup

Overall timing 1¼ hours

Freezing Not suitable

To serve 6

1	Large carrot	1
1	Large onion	1
1	Stalk of celery	1
2	Turkey wings	2
2½ pints	Water	1.5 litres
	Salt and pepper	
8 oz	Waxy potatoes	225 g
2	Leeks	2
4	Thick slices of bread	4
3 oz	Butter	75 g

Peel and chop carrot and onion. Trim and chop the celery. Wipe the turkey wings and put into a saucepan with the prepared vegetables, water and seasoning. Bring to the boil, skim off any scum, cover and simmer for 45 minutes.

Peel potatoes and cut into ½ inch (12.5 mm) cubes. Trim and slice leeks.

Lift turkey wings out of pan with a draining spoon and leave to cool slightly. Add potatoes and leeks to the soup and simmer for 5 minutes till vegetables are tender.

Remove the skin and bones from the turkey wings and cut the flesh into strips. Add to the soup and reheat gently.

Meanwhile, remove the crusts from bread and cut into cubes. Melt butter in a frying pan, add the bread and fry till golden all over. Drain croûtons on kitchen paper.

Taste soup and adjust seasoning. Pour into a warmed tureen and sprinkle with croûtons. Serve immediately.

Swiss cream of barley soup

Overall timing 2¾ hours

Freezing Not suitable

To serve 4–6

2	Large onions	2
3	Cloves	3
1	Calf's foot	1
4 oz	Pearl barley	125 g
	Bay leaf	
3 pints	Water	1.7 litres
	Salt and pepper	
12 oz	Carrots	350 g
4	Stalks of celery	4
2	Small leeks	2
4 oz	Smoked streaky bacon rashers	125 g
2 oz	Lard	50 g
2	Egg yolks	2
¼ pint	Carton of single cream	150 ml
1 tbsp	Chopped chives	15 ml

Peel one of the onions and spike with cloves. Wash calf's foot, chop in half lengthways and put into a saucepan with the barley, spiked onion and bay leaf. Add the water and seasoning, then cover and simmer for 2 hours.

Meanwhile, scrape and dice carrots. Peel and chop remaining onion. Trim and chop celery and leeks. Derind and dice bacon. Melt lard in a large saucepan. Add bacon and vegetables and fry for 10 minutes till golden.

Remove spiked onion and bay leaf from stock and discard. Lift calf's foot out of stock and remove the meat, discarding skin and bones. Add meat to stock with the vegetables. Bring to the boil and simmer for 10 minutes till vegetables are tender.

Put the egg yolks and cream into a tureen and beat together with a fork. Season the soup to taste and gradually stir into tureen. Sprinkle with chives and serve.

Spicy bortsch

Overall timing 2½ hours

Freezing Suitable

To serve 6

1	Carrot	1
1 lb	Parsnips	450 g
4	Tomatoes	4
1	Onion	1
9	Cloves	9
1 lb	Beef bones	450 g
1 lb	Stewing beef	450 g
½ teasp	Salt	2.5 ml
1 teasp	Sugar	5 ml
6	Peppercorns	6
1	Bay leaf	1
2½ pints	Cold water	1.5 litres
1½ lb	Raw beetroots	700 g
4 oz	Red or green cabbage	125 g

Peel and chop carrot and parsnips. Chop tomatoes. Peel onion and spike with cloves. Crack bones; dice beef.

Put vegetables, bones and beef into a large saucepan with salt, sugar, peppercorns, bay leaf and water. Bring to the boil, cover and simmer for 2 hours or until meat is tender. Remove bones, onion and bay leaf.

Peel and coarsely grate beetroots. Chop cabbage. Add to pan and simmer, uncovered, for a further 12–15 minutes.

Florentine minestrone

Overall timing 2¾ hours plus soaking

Freezing Suitable: add cabbage and macaroni after reheating

To serve 4

8 oz	Dried haricot beans	225 g
2	Large carrots	2
2	Stalks of celery	2
1	Garlic clove	1
2	Onions	2
4 tbsp	Oil	4x15 ml
1½ teasp	Dried mixed herbs	7.5 ml
14 oz	Can of tomatoes	397 g
8 oz	Cabbage	225 g
4 oz	Short macaroni	125 g
	Salt and pepper	

Place beans in large saucepan and cover with cold water. Bring to the boil and boil for 2 minutes. Remove from heat, cover and soak for 2 hours.

Drain beans, return to pan, cover with boiling water and simmer for 2 hours.

Peel and chop carrots; chop celery. Peel and crush garlic. Peel and slice onions. In a large saucepan, heat oil and fry vegetables until golden.

Drain beans, reserving cooking liquor. Purée half the beans. Add beans, whole and puréed, to fried vegetables with cooking liquor, herbs and tomatoes. Bring to the boil. Shred cabbage and add to boiling soup with macaroni and seasoning. Simmer for 20 minutes.

Tuscan vegetable soup

Overall timing 2 hours plus overnight soaking

Freezing Not suitable

To serve 6

8 oz	Dried beans	225 g
1¼ lb	Cabbage	600 g
1	Onion	1
1	Large leek	1
1	Stalk of celery	1
1	Carrot	1
1	Garlic clove	1
3 tbsp	Oil	3x15 ml
1	Bay leaf	1
3	Sprigs of oregano	3
	Sprig of rosemary	
	Salt and pepper	
2 tbsp	Tomato purée	2x15 ml
3 pints	Light stock	1.7 litres

Soak beans in cold water overnight. The next day, drain beans, put into a large saucepan and cover with fresh cold water. Bring to the boil and simmer for about 1½ hours till tender.

Meanwhile, shred cabbage. Peel and thinly slice onion; trim and slice leek and celery. Scrape and chop carrot. Peel and crush garlic. Heat oil in a large saucepan and fry vegetables, except cabbage, with garlic and herbs till lightly browned. Add cabbage and seasoning and fry for a further 5 minutes.

Remove herbs from pan and add the tomato purée, drained beans and stock. Bring to the boil and simmer for a further 15 minutes. Taste and adjust the seasoning and pour into warmed individual bowls.

Watercress soup

Overall timing 40 minutes

Freezing Suitable: add cream after thawing

To serve 4

1	Large onion	1
2	Large floury potatoes	2
1 oz	Butter	25 g
3	Bunches of watercress	3
1¾ pints	Chicken stock	1 litre
	Salt and pepper	
4 fl oz	Double cream	113 ml

Peel and finely chop onion. Peel and chop or grate potatoes. Melt butter in a saucepan, add onions and potatoes and turn till coated in butter. Cover and cook gently for 10 minutes.

Wash, dry and chop watercress leaves and stalks, reserving some whole leaves. Add to pan with stock and bring to boil. Cover and simmer for 15 minutes.

Rub soup through sieve or purée in blender. Return to pan, add reserved watercress leaves and reheat. Taste and adjust seasoning. Serve immediately with side dish of whipped cream, or cool, stir in cream and chill well before serving.

Rice and cabbage soup

Overall timing 45 minutes

Freezing Not suitable

To serve 6–8

1	Large onion	1
8 oz	Streaky bacon	225 g
1	Garlic clove	1
2 oz	Butter	50 g
8 oz	Long grain rice	225 g
3 pints	Light stock	1.7 litres
	Salt and pepper	
	Bouquet garni	
1 lb	Green cabbage	450 g
4 oz	Cheese	125 g

Peel and chop the onion; derind and finely dice the bacon. Peel and crush garlic. Melt the butter in a saucepan and add the onion, bacon and garlic. Fry gently for 5 minutes without browning.

Add the rice and cook, stirring, for 2 minutes till coated with butter. Add the stock, seasoning and bouquet garni. Bring to the boil and simmer for 15 minutes.

Meanwhile, coarsely shred the cabbage. Add to the pan, bring to the boil again and simmer for 5 minutes.

Remove pan from the heat and discard the bouquet garni. Grate cheese, stir into soup and adjust seasoning. Pour into a tureen and serve immediately with rye bread.

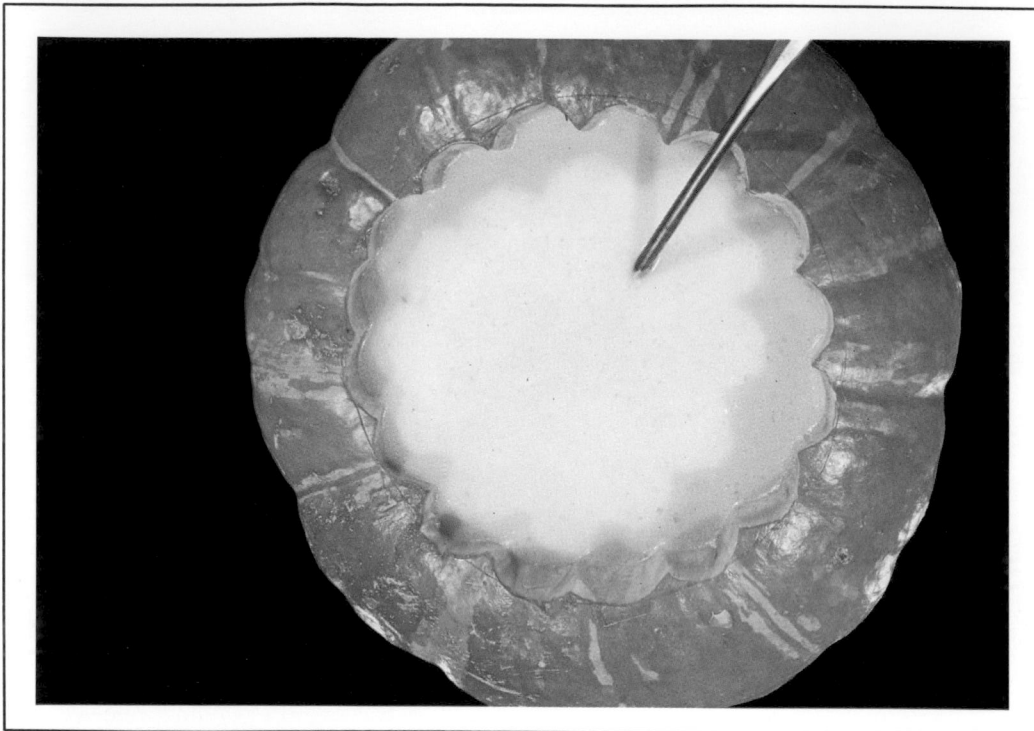

Pumpkin soup

Overall timing 50 minutes

Freezing Not suitable

To serve 6

2 lb	Pumpkin or other squash	900 g
½ pint	Water	300 ml
	Salt and pepper	
1½ pints	Milk	850 ml
1 teasp	Sugar	5 ml
¼ teasp	Grated nutmeg	1.25 ml
1	Egg yolk	1
4 tbsp	Single cream	4x15 ml

Prepare the squash, discarding fibrous centre and seeds. Cut the flesh into chunks, put into a saucepan with the water and salt and bring to the boil. Simmer for about 30 minutes till tender, then purée in a blender or food mill. Place purée in saucepan with milk, sugar and nutmeg. Heat through gently till almost boiling, stirring occasionally.

Beat the egg yolk and cream together in a bowl and pour in a little of the hot soup, stirring constantly. Pour back into the pan and stir over a low heat for 3 minutes – do not boil. Taste and adjust seasoning, then serve immediately with toasted rye bread.

Onion soup with wine

Overall timing 45 minutes

Freezing Suitable: pour soup over bread and add cheese after reheating

To serve 4

3	Large onions	3
2 oz	Butter	50 g
1 tbsp	Plain flour	15 ml
½ teasp	Brown sugar	2.5 ml
2½ pints	Water	1.5 litres
8	Slices of French bread	8
2 tbsp	Dry white wine	2x15 ml
	Salt and pepper	
2 oz	Gruyère or Cheddar cheese	50 g

Peel and slice onions. Melt half the butter in a large saucepan and cook onions till transparent. Sprinkle onions with flour. Cook, stirring, until flour colours. Add sugar, then gradually stir in water. Simmer for 20 minutes.

Preheat the oven to 450°F (230°C) Gas 8.

Fry bread in remaining butter. Place bread slices in bottom of individual bowls or oven-proof soup tureen. Add wine and seasoning, then pour soup over bread. Grate cheese and sprinkle it into the bowls. Bake for 5–10 minutes to melt the cheese.

Mushroom soup

Overall timing 30 minutes

Freezing Not suitable

To serve 4

2	Stalks of celery	2
8 oz	Mushrooms	225 g
2 teasp	Oil	2x5 ml
12 oz	Cooked chicken meat	350 g
1 tbsp	Soy sauce	15 ml
1 tbsp	Dry sherry	15 ml
8	Water chestnuts	8
1¾ pints	Chicken stock	1 litre
4 oz	Bean sprouts	125 g
	Salt and pepper	
1	Egg	1

Finely chop celery. Thinly slice mushrooms. Heat oil in a saucepan and stir-fry vegetables for 5 minutes.

Cut chicken into small pieces and sprinkle with soy sauce and sherry. Quarter or dice water chestnuts.

Add stock to pan with water chestnuts. Bring to the boil, then add chicken and soaking juices. Simmer for 10 minutes. Add bean sprouts and cook for 2 minutes. Taste and adjust seasoning.

Beat egg. Remove pan from heat and trickle in beaten egg, stirring constantly. Divide soup between individual soup bowls and serve.

Chicken vermicelli soup

Overall timing 40 minutes

Freezing Not suitable

To serve 6

1 oz	Chinese dried mushrooms	25 g
2½ pints	Chicken stock	1.5 litres
6 oz	Cooked chicken meat	175 g
2	Lettuce leaves	2
4	Eggs	4
	Salt and pepper	
1 oz	Butter	25 g
2 oz	Chinese vermicelli	50 g
2 tbsp	Dry sherry	2x15 ml

Soak mushrooms in warm water for 30 minutes. Drain, discard woody stalks and put into saucepan with stock. Bring to the boil and simmer for 10 minutes.

Meanwhile, cut chicken into strips. Shred lettuce. Beat eggs with seasoning. Melt half butter in frying pan, add half egg mixture and make a thin omelette. Remove from pan and reserve. Use remaining butter and egg mixture to make another omelette. Roll up both omelettes and cut into thin slices.

Add noodles and chicken to saucepan and simmer for 2 minutes. Remove from heat and add sherry, omelette strips and lettuce. Serve immediately.

Pumpkin rice soup

Overall timing 1 hour

Freezing Not suitable

To serve 6

1	Large onion	1
1	Stalk of celery	1
1	Large carrot	1
2 oz	Streaky bacon rashers	50 g
2 oz	Butter	50 g
1½ lb	Pumpkin	700 g
3 pints	Chicken stock	1.7 litres
1	Garlic clove	1
	Salt and pepper	
6 oz	Long grain rice	175 g
3 tbsp	Grated Parmesan cheese	3x15 ml

Peel the onion, trim the celery and scrape the carrot. Derind the bacon. Finely chop vegetables and bacon. Melt the butter in a saucepan, add the vegetables and bacon and fry for 5 minutes, stirring occasionally.

Scrape the seeds and fibrous centre out of the pumpkin. Cut into chunks, leaving the skin on, and add to the pan. Fry, stirring, for a further 5 minutes.

Add the stock (made with cubes if necessary), peeled and crushed garlic and seasoning and bring to the boil. Simmer for 10 minutes.

Wash the rice and add to the soup. Bring to the boil and simmer for 15–20 minutes till the rice is tender.

Stir in the Parmesan and adjust the seasoning. Pour into warmed serving bowls and serve immediately with bread sticks or fresh crusty rolls and butter.

Minestrone

Overall timing 2¼ hours

Freezing Not suitable

To serve 8

2 oz	Smoked bacon	50 g
1	Onion	1
1	Small leek	1
4 tbsp	Olive oil	4x15 ml
1	Garlic clove	1
1 tbsp	Chopped parsley	15 ml
2	Sage leaves	2
3	Carrots	3
1	Courgette	1
2	Large potatoes	2
3	Stalks of celery	3
1	Large tomato	1
12 oz	Savoy cabbage	350 g
3	Basil leaves	3
3½ pints	Hot stock	1.7 litres
1 tbsp	Tomato purée	15 ml
	Salt and pepper	
14 oz	Can of white beans	397 g
4 oz	Short-cut macaroni	125 g
	Grated Parmesan cheese	

Derind and chop the bacon. Place in saucepan and fry till fat runs.

Peel and finely chop the onion; trim and chop the leek. Add oil to saucepan and heat, then add onion, leek, peeled and crushed garlic, parsley and chopped sage. Cover and sweat for 10 minutes.

Meanwhile, peel the remaining vegetables, as necessary, and chop them. Add prepared vegetables and chopped basil to pan and cook, stirring, for 5 minutes. Gradually add stock, tomato purée, salt and pepper and bring to the boil. Drain the canned beans and add. Cover tightly and cook gently for 1¼ hours.

Add macaroni and cook for 20 minutes more. Serve with Parmesan cheese.

Majorcan vegetable and bread soup

Overall timing 1½ hours

Freezing Not suitable

To serve 6

8 oz	Continental lentils	225 g
3 pints	Water	1.7 litres
4 oz	Streaky bacon rashers	125 g
1 lb	Fresh broad beans	450 g
1 lb	Fresh peas	450 g
1 lb	Cabbage	450 g
8 oz	Fresh spinach	225 g
	Salt and pepper	.
18	Thin slices of brown bread	18

Wash and pick over the lentils and put into a saucepan with the water. Bring to the boil and simmer for 45 minutes.

Meanwhile, derind and dice the bacon. Shell the beans and peas. Shred the cabbage and spinach.

Rub the lentils with their cooking liquor through a sieve or purée in a blender. Return to the saucepan and add seasoning, bacon and vegetables and bring to the boil. Simmer for about 25 minutes till the vegetables are tender.

Taste and adjust the seasoning. Arrange three slices of bread in each soup bowl and pour the soup over. Serve immediately.

Irish celery soup

Overall timing 35 minutes

Freezing Suitable: add cream when reheating

To serve 4

1 lb	Celery	450 g
2	Potatoes	2
2	Onions	2
2 oz	Butter	50 g
	Salt and pepper	
1	Bay leaf	1
1	Garlic clove	1
	Grated nutmeg	
1¾ pints	Chicken stock	1 litre
¼ pint	Carton of single cream	150 ml

Cut off base of celery, then wash and chop stalks and leaves. Peel and finely chop potatoes and onions. Melt butter in saucepan over a low heat. Add celery stalks and leaves, potatoes and onions, cover and cook for 5 minutes, stirring to prevent colouring.

Sprinkle with salt and pepper, add the bay leaf, peeled and crushed garlic, pinch of nutmeg and hot stock (made with 2 cubes if necessary). Cover and simmer for 20 minutes.

Remove bay leaf. Push soup through sieve into a bowl, or liquidize, then return to saucepan and add the cream. Heat through without boiling. Adjust seasoning, then serve with croûtons (diced bread fried in oil till brown).

Gazpacho

Overall timing 20 minutes plus chilling

Freezing Suitable

To serve 6

1¼ lb	Tomatoes	600 g
½	Cucumber	½
1	Large onion	1
1	Green or red pepper	1
2	Garlic cloves	2
4 oz	Fresh white breadcrumbs	125 g
3 tbsp	Olive oil	3x15 ml
1 tbsp	Wine vinegar	15 ml
1	Sprig of parsley or mint	1
	Salt and pepper	
2 pints	Water	1.1 litres

Blanch, peel and chop the tomatoes. Peel, deseed and chop the cucumber. Peel and chop the onion. Deseed and chop the pepper; peel and chop the garlic.

Place all the vegetables in a blender with breadcrumbs, oil, vinegar, parsley or mint, salt and pepper and 1 pint (560 ml) of the water. Blend to a purée.

Place purée in a large bowl and stir in the remaining water. Cover and chill for 3 hours.

Before serving, add a few ice cubes. Serve with side dishes of chopped onion, hard-boiled eggs, tomatoes, peppers and croûtons.

Creamy cauliflower soup

Overall timing 35 minutes

Freezing Not suitable

To serve 4

1	Large cauliflower	1
1	Small onion	1
	Salt and pepper	
2 oz	Butter	50 g
2 oz	Plain flour	50 g
¾ pint	Milk	400 ml
	Lamb seasoning salt	
½ teasp	Dried mixed herbs	2.5 ml
¼ teasp	Grated nutmeg	1.25 ml
1	Egg yolk	1
4 tbsp	Single cream	4 x 15 ml
	Fresh dill	

Trim cauliflower, separate into florets and wash. Peel and finely chop onion. Put cauliflower and onion into pan of boiling salted water, cover and cook for 10 minutes. Drain, saving ¾ pint (400 ml) cooking liquor. Mash half cauliflower and onion.

Melt butter in a large saucepan. Stir in flour, then milk and reserved cooking liquor. Add a pinch of lamb seasoning salt, the herbs, nutmeg and pulped and whole cauliflower and onion. Simmer for 7 minutes. Taste and adjust seasoning.

Mix egg yolk and cream in warmed tureen. Pour in soup and serve garnished with dill.

Courgette and egg soup

Overall timing 30 minutes

Freezing Not suitable

To serve 4

1 lb	Courgettes	450 g
1 oz	Lard	25 g
3 tbsp	Olive oil	3 x 15 ml
1	Garlic clove	1
1¾ pints	Boiling water	1 litre
	Salt and pepper	
2	Eggs	2
10	Basil leaves (optional)	10
2 tbsp	Chopped parsley	2 x 15 ml
2 oz	White Cheshire or Wensleydale cheese	50 g
Garnish		
1 oz	White Cheshire or Wensleydale cheese	25 g
	Croûtons	

Wash courgettes, trim ends, then dice them. Heat the lard, oil and peeled, garlic clove in a saucepan or flameproof casserole. Cook over a moderate heat till the garlic turns golden, then discard it.

Add diced courgettes to pan and cook for a few minutes. Add the boiling water and a pinch of salt, cover and cook gently for about 15 minutes.

Break eggs into a warmed soup tureen and add chopped basil, parsley and salt and pepper. Grate or crumble in the cheese. Beat well with a fork.

Gradually add about a quarter of the soup and mix well, then pour in the rest. Garnish with more grated or crumbled cheese and freshly made croûtons.

Chicory soup

Overall timing 25 minutes

Freezing Suitable: add vermouth after reheating

To serve 4

4	Heads of chicory	4
2½ oz	Butter	65 g
2 teasp	Caster sugar	2x5 ml
1¾ pints	Chicken stock	1 litre
2 teasp	Plain flour	2x5 ml
3 fl oz	Dry vermouth	90 ml
	Salt and pepper	

Chop chicory. Melt 2 oz (50 g) of the butter in a saucepan and fry chicory over a gentle heat for about 5 minutes. Tilt pan, add sugar and allow to caramelize. Add stock, cover and simmer for 10 minutes.

Mix remaining butter with the flour to a smooth paste. Stir paste a little at a time into the soup. Return to the boil and simmer for 2–3 minutes.

Add vermouth and seasoning and cook, uncovered, for 1–2 minutes more. Pour into serving bowls and garnish with freshly made, hot croûtons.

Cheese soup

Overall timing 30 minutes

Freezing Not suitable

To serve 4–6

1	Onion	1
3 oz	Butter	75 g
1½ pints	Light stock	850 ml
¼ pint	Dry white wine	150 ml
4 teasp	Cornflour	4x5 ml
½ pint	Milk	300 ml
	Salt and white pepper	
4 oz	Cheddar cheese	125 g
4 oz	Parmesan cheese	125 g
	Croûtons	

Peel and finely chop the onion. Melt the butter in a saucepan, add onion and fry till transparent. Stir in the stock and wine and bring to the boil slowly.

Blend the cornflour with a little water and add to the pan, stirring constantly. Bring back to the boil, stirring, and cook for 3 minutes. Add the milk, salt, pepper and grated cheese. Stir over a very low heat till the cheese has completely melted. Taste and adjust seasoning, then pour into a warmed tureen. Serve immediately garnished with lots of croûtons.

Bean soup

Overall timing 30 minutes

Freezing Suitable: add soured cream after thawing

To serve 4

4 oz	Streaky bacon	125 g
1	Red pepper	1
1	Green pepper	1
1¾ pints	Strong beef stock	1 litre
12 oz	Can of butter beans	340 g
	Tabasco sauce	
	Salt	
4 tbsp	Soured cream	4x15 ml

Derind and chop bacon and fry it lightly in a frying pan till the fat runs. Place in a deep saucepan.

Deseed and finely chop half the red and green peppers and add to the pan with the stock (made up with 3 stock cubes if necessary) and drained beans. Bring to the boil and simmer for 20 minutes.

Add Tabasco sauce and salt to taste.

Slice remaining peppers and blanch for 5 minutes in boiling water. Drain well.

Remove soup from the heat and stir in the soured cream. Garnish with pepper slices and serve with a bowl of grated cheese and fresh wholemeal bread.

Barley and mushroom soup

Overall timing 3 hours 50 minutes

Freezing Suitable: add butter and cream after reheating

To serve 4

3 oz	Pearl barley	75 g
	Salt	
2	Carrots	2
2	Celery stalks	2
1	Leek	1
1	Onion	1
2	Bay leaves	2
10	Black peppercorns	10
1	Sprig of parsley	1
1½ oz	Dried mushrooms	40 g
2 tbsp	Vinegar	2x15 ml
2 oz	Butter	50 g
¼ pint	Carton of single cream	150 ml

Wash barley, then cook in lightly salted, boiling water for 2½ hours till very soft and gelatinous.

Meanwhile, scrape and chop carrots. Wash and slice celery and leek. Peel and quarter onion. Put all vegetables into a saucepan with bay leaves, salt, peppercorns, parsley, mushrooms and 9 fl oz (250 ml) water. Cover and simmer gently for 1 hour.

Strain stock into a bowl. Reserve mushrooms and discard remaining vegetables. Slice mushrooms and return to pan with strained stock.

Drain barley and crush with a potato masher, or partly liquidize in a blender. Add barley and vinegar to stock, heat through and season.

Cut butter into small pieces and put in bottom of a warmed soup tureen. Pour in soup, stir in cream and serve.

Brussels sprout soup

Overall timing 1¼ hours

Freezing Suitable: add cream and egg yolk mixture when reheating

To serve 4

1 lb	Brussels sprouts	450 g
3 oz	Butter	75 g
1¾ pints	Hot beef stock	1 litre
	Salt	
1 oz	Plain flour	25 g
	Grated nutmeg	
6 tbsp	Single cream	6x15 ml
1	Egg yolk	1

Trim sprouts. Cut a cross in base of each. Melt 2 oz (50 g) butter in a saucepan, add sprouts and cook for 3 minutes, stirring continuously. Add stock and salt. Cover and cook for 40 minutes.

Sieve sprouts into a bowl, or liquidize.

Melt remaining butter in a pan. Add flour and cook, stirring, for 3 minutes. Remove pan from heat and gradually add sprout purée. Return to heat and cook for 10 minutes over low heat. Season with salt and pinch of nutmeg.

Mix cream with egg yolk. Off heat, stir cream mixture into soup to thicken.

Avocado soup

Overall timing 15 minutes plus chilling if serving cold

Freezing Suitable: add cream after thawing

To serve 4

1¾ pints	Chicken stock	1 litre
2	Ripe avocados	2
1 tbsp	Lemon juice	15 ml
1	Egg yolk	1
3 tbsp	Single cream	3x15 ml
	Salt and pepper	

Heat chicken stock (made up with 4 cubes if necessary) in a saucepan to boiling point.

Cut open avocados and lift out stones. If intending to serve soup cold, cut eight very thin slices, sprinkle with lemon juice to prevent discoloration and set aside. Scoop out remaining avocado flesh, place in a bowl and mash well with the egg yolk and cream.

Remove stock from heat. Gradually add the avocado mixture, whisking vigorously. Add salt and pepper to taste. Do not reheat.

Serve hot with fried croûtons. If serving cold, chill the soup for at least 1 hour, then serve garnished with reserved avocado slices.

Pipérade

Overall timing 1 hour

Freezing Not suitable

To serve 4

1 lb	Ripe tomatoes	450 g
2	Green peppers	2
2	Onions	2
1	Garlic clove	1
5 tbsp	Oil	5x15 ml
	Salt and pepper	
$\frac{1}{4}$ teasp	Dried marjoram	1.25 ml
	Tabasco sauce	
8	Eggs	8

Blanch, peel and chop tomatoes. Deseed and chop peppers. Peel and slice onions. Peel and crush garlic.

Heat oil in frying pan. Add onions and garlic and cook till golden. Add peppers and tomatoes and cook over a high heat for 5 minutes. Season with salt, pepper, marjoram and Tabasco. Reduce heat, cover and simmer for 30 minutes or until the mixture is reduced to a purée.

Lightly beat eggs in a bowl. Season and pour over vegetable purée. Cook over increased heat, stirring, for 2–3 minutes till creamy. Serve with buttered toast and a green salad.

Baked eggs in potatoes

Overall timing 2 hours

Freezing Not suitable

To serve 4

4x10oz	Potatoes	4x275g
2oz	Butter	50g
	Salt and pepper	
2oz	Cheese	50g
4	Small eggs	4
4 tbsp	Double cream	4x15ml
2 teasp	Chopped chives	2x5ml

Preheat the oven to 400°F (200°C) Gas 6.

Scrub and dry the potatoes and push a metal skewer lengthways through each one. Place on a baking tray and rub a little of the butter over the skins. Bake for 1–1¼ hours.

Remove from the oven. Increase the temperature to 450°F (230°C) Gas 8.

Cut a slice lengthways off each potato and scoop out the insides, leaving a shell about ½ inch (12.5mm) thick. Mash the scooped-out potato (plus any from the lids) in a bowl with the remaining butter and seasoning. Grate cheese and beat into potato mixture.

Press the mixture back into the potato shells, leaving a hollow in the centre large enough for an egg. Place on baking tray. Carefully break an egg into each potato. Season and spoon the cream over. Return to the oven and bake for 8–10 minutes till the eggs are lightly set. Sprinkle the chives over and serve hot.

Curried eggs

Overall timing 35 minutes

Freezing Not suitable

To serve 4

6	Eggs	6
2	Onions	2
2 oz	Butter	50 g
2 teasp	Curry powder	2x5 ml
1 pint	Chicken stock	560 ml
1 teasp	Cornflour	5 ml
4 fl oz	Carton of single cream or top of milk	120 ml
	Salt and pepper	

Place eggs in a saucepan of cold water. Bring to the boil and simmer for 8 minutes, then drain.

Peel and finely chop onions. Melt butter in a frying pan, add onions, cover and cook until golden over a low heat (about 15 minutes).

Sprinkle with curry powder and cook for 2 minutes, stirring. Pour in the stock and simmer for 10 minutes. Mix cornflour and cream or milk together well, then stir into curry mixture with seasoning. Heat gently but do not boil.

Shell eggs and cut in half lengthways. Remove yolks with a spoon and mash yolks and a little of the curry mixture together with a fork. Spoon back into egg whites. Place eggs in curry sauce and heat through without boiling. Serve with rice or hot buttered toast.

Deep-fried eggs

Overall timing 15 minutes

Freezing Not suitable

To serve 4

	Oil for frying	
8	Eggs	8
	Salt and pepper	
2	Tomatoes	2
	Sprigs of parsley	

Half-fill a shallow frying pan with oil and heat to 370°F (188°C) or until a cube of bread browns in 1 minute. Swirl fat round with a spoon. Break an egg into a cup and carefully slide into the hot oil. Cook for 1–2 minutes, basting with the hot oil all the time and turning the egg once or twice.

Remove from pan with a draining spoon and drain on kitchen paper. Sprinkle with salt and pepper. Keep hot while you fry remaining eggs in the same way. Garnish with tomato wedges and parsley sprigs and serve hot with toast.

Lettuce and egg pipérade ✓

Overall timing 15 minutes

Freezing Not suitable

To serve 4

1	Onion	1
1	Small round lettuce	1
2 oz	Butter	50 g
1 tbsp	Chopped parsley	15 ml
4 oz	Frozen peas	125 g
4	Eggs	4
	Salt and pepper	
8 oz	Hot mashed potatoes	225 g

celery instead of peas

Peel and finely chop the onion. Wash, trim and shred lettuce.

Melt the butter in a frying pan. Add onion and cook till transparent. Add shredded lettuce, parsley and peas. Cook, stirring, for 5 minutes.

Lightly beat eggs in a bowl and season. Stir into pan, reduce heat and cook, stirring, until egg is lightly scrambled. Remove from heat and arrange on warmed serving dish.

Pipe or spoon mashed potato round the edge of the dish and serve immediately.

Egg and cheese sandwiches

Overall timing 30 minutes

Freezing Not suitable

To serve 4

1	Small onion	1
4 oz	Butter	125 g
2 oz	Mushrooms	50 g
4 tbsp	Dry white wine	4x15 ml
4 tbsp	Chicken stock	4x15 ml
	Salt and pepper	
4 oz	Cooked ham	125 g
6 oz	Cheddar cheese	175 g
8	Slices of bread	8
	Paprika	
4	Eggs	4

Peel and finely chop onion. Melt 1 oz (25 g) of the butter in a pan and cook onion till transparent. Slice mushrooms, add to pan and cook for 3 minutes. Add wine and stock and cook over a high heat until most of the liquid evaporates. Season with salt and pepper.

Preheat the oven to 400°F (200°C) Gas 6.

Cut the ham and cheese into thin slices. Butter the bread and place four slices in a shallow ovenproof dish, buttered side down. Divide cheese, ham, mushrooms and onion between them and sprinkle with a little paprika. Cover with remaining bread slices, buttered side up. Bake for 10 minutes until crisp and golden.

Meanwhile, melt remaining butter in a frying pan. Break eggs one at a time into a cup, then slide into the pan when butter is frothy. Cook for 2–3 minutes. Remove eggs from pan with an egg slice. Place on top of sandwiches, sprinkle with salt and pepper and serve.

Egg and pea scramble

Overall timing 50 minutes

Freezing Not suitable

To serve 2–4

2 lb	Fresh peas	900 g
1	Onion	1
2 oz	Streaky bacon rashers	50 g
2 oz	Butter	50 g
	Salt and pepper	
2 oz	Cheese	50 g
4	Eggs	4
2 oz	Fresh breadcrumbs	50 g

Shell peas. Peel and thinly slice the onion; derind and dice the bacon. Melt the butter in a saucepan and gently fry the onion and bacon till transparent.

Add the peas and salt and enough water to half cover them. Bring to the boil, then cover and simmer for 15–20 minutes till the peas are tender and most of the liquid has evaporated.

Grate cheese. Lightly beat the eggs in a bowl with the breadcrumbs and pepper. Pour over the peas and cook, stirring gently, till the eggs are lightly set. Serve immediately.

Eggs florentine

Overall timing 45 minutes

Freezing Not suitable

To serve 4

2 lb	Spinach	900 g
2 oz	Butter	50 g
	Salt	
¼ teasp	Grated nutmeg	1.25 ml
1½ oz	Plain flour	40 g
¾ pint	Milk	400 ml
3 oz	Cheese	75 g
	Cayenne pepper	
½ teasp	Made mustard	2.5 ml
8	Hard-boiled eggs	8
2 tbsp	Fresh white breadcrumbs	2x15 ml

Preheat the oven to 425°F (220°C) Gas 7.

Wash spinach well in several changes of water. Remove any coarse stalks. Put into saucepan with only the water that still clings to the spinach after washing. Cook for 5–10 minutes till tender. Stir in ½ oz (15 g) of the butter and season with salt and grated nutmeg, then spread over the bottom of a greased ovenproof dish.

Melt remaining butter in a pan. Stir in the flour and cook for 1 minute. Gradually add the milk, bring to the boil, stirring, and cook for 2 minutes.

Grate cheese. Reserve 2 tbsp (2x15 ml) for the topping and stir the rest into the sauce with a pinch each of salt and cayenne and the mustard.

Shell eggs and arrange on top of spinach. Pour sauce over eggs. Mix reserved grated cheese and breadcrumbs and sprinkle over the top. Bake for 10 minutes till cheese is bubbly and golden. Serve immediately.

Eggs in a nest

Overall timing 50 minutes

Freezing Not suitable

To serve 4

2 lb	Potatoes	900 g
	Salt and pepper	
½ pint	Milk	300 ml
3 oz	Butter	75 g
8	Eggs	8
2 tbsp	Dried breadcrumbs	2x15 ml
	Grated nutmeg	
	Parsley	

Peel the potatoes. Put into a pan of salted water, bring to the boil and cook for 25 minutes. Drain.

Preheat the oven to 425°F (220°C) Gas 7. Grease ovenproof dish.

Add milk to the potatoes and return to low heat. Mash the potatoes and beat in 2 oz (50 g) of the butter until smooth and creamy. Season to taste.

Spread creamed potatoes in ovenproof dish. Using the back of a spoon, hollow out eight "nests" for the eggs. Break an egg into each of the "nests". Sprinkle with breadcrumbs, dot with remaining butter and season with salt, pepper and nutmeg.

Bake for 8–9 minutes or until the eggs are lightly set. Garnish with parsley.

Eggs with sausages

Overall timing 15 minutes

Freezing Not suitable

To serve 2–4

1 tbsp	Oil	15 ml
12	Chipolatas	12
1 oz	Butter	25 g
4	Eggs	4
3 tbsp	Tomato ketchup	3x15 ml
	Pepper	

Heat the oil in a frying pan. Cook the chipolatas till golden all over, then remove from the pan.

Melt butter in the pan, break in the eggs and place chipolatas over whites. Fry for 2–3 minutes, then spoon ketchup around the edge of the pan. Sprinkle with pepper and serve with toast and grilled tomatoes.

Variation

Sprinkle grated cheese over the eggs and chipolatas and grill until the cheese has melted and is golden brown.

Eggs in mushroom sauce

Overall timing 30 minutes

Freezing Not suitable

To serve 6

12 oz	Mushrooms	350 g
6	Large eggs	6
1 tbsp	Oil	15 ml
1	Garlic clove	1
14 oz	Can of tomatoes	397 g
2 teasp	Chopped parsley	2x5 ml
	Salt and pepper	
2 oz	Butter	50 g
4 oz	Cheese	125 g
1 tbsp	Plain flour	15 ml

Wipe, trim and thickly slice the mushrooms. Hard-boil the eggs for 10 minutes.

Meanwhile, heat the oil in a frying pan. Add peeled garlic and fry till golden. Discard garlic. Add the mushrooms and fry over a high heat for 3–4 minutes. Sieve canned tomatoes and their juice and add to the pan with the parsley, salt and pepper. Cook for about 10 minutes.

Cool the eggs quickly by running cold water over them. Cut eggs in half lengthways. Scoop out yolks and place in a bowl.

Soften the butter and grate the cheese. Add to the egg yolks with the flour and seasoning. Mix well with a fork. Shape the mixture into 12 balls about 1 inch (2.5 cm) in diameter, using floured hands. Place one ball in each egg half.

Add egg halves to pan and spoon a little sauce over them. Cover and cook for a further 5 minutes. Divide between warmed serving dishes. Serve immediately with crusty bread.

Flamenco eggs

Overall timing 45 minutes

Freezing Not suitable

To serve 4–6

1	Onion	1
4 oz	Back bacon	125 g
2 tbsp	Oil	2x15 ml
8 oz	Can of tomatoes	227 g
2	Potatoes	2
1	Small red pepper	1
2 oz	Runner beans	50 g
2 tbsp	Frozen peas	2x15 ml
2 tbsp	Canned asparagus tips	2x15 ml
6 oz	Chorizo or other spicy sausage	175 g
3 tbsp	Dry sherry	3x15 ml
	Salt and pepper	
6	Eggs	6

Peel and finely chop onion. Derind and dice bacon.

Heat oil in a saucepan or flameproof casserole. Add onion and bacon and cook till golden. Add tomatoes, mashing them into the onion/bacon mixture till well combined.

Peel potatoes and cut into small dice. Wash, deseed and chop pepper. Wash beans. Top and tail them and remove strings. Cut into short lengths. Add potatoes, pepper, beans and peas to pan and cook for 10 minutes.

Add asparagus tips, sliced sausage and sherry. Season and cook for a further 5 minutes.

Break eggs carefully on top of the mixture. Cook for 5 minutes more or until the eggs are lightly set.

Roe and egg toasts

Overall timing 30 minutes

Freezing Not suitable

To serve 6

12 oz	Soft herring roes	350 g
	Salt and pepper	
3 oz	Butter	75 g
2 tbsp	Plain flour	2x15 ml
½ pint	Milk	300 ml
2	Anchovy fillets	2
3	Hard-boiled eggs	3
1 tbsp	Lemon juice	15 ml
6	Slices of bread	6
6 oz	Smoked cod's roe	175 g

Poach soft roes in boiling salted water for 5 minutes. Drain and chop.

Melt 2 oz (50 g) of the butter in a saucepan, stir in the flour and cook for 1 minute. Gradually add the milk and bring to the boil, stirring.

Pound the anchovy fillets in a bowl. Shell the eggs and cut in half. Sieve the yolks and stir into the sauce with the anchovies, soft roes, lemon juice and seasoning. Heat through.

Preheat the grill. Toast the bread, spread with remaining butter and arrange on the grill pan. Spread the soft roe mixture over. Finely chop the egg whites and use to decorate the toast. Cut the smoked cod's roe into 12 thin slices and place two on each piece of toast. Grill for 2–3 minutes till bubbling and golden. Serve hot.

Egg and ham moulds

Overall timing 20 minutes

Freezing Not suitable

To serve 4

2 oz	Softened butter	50 g
6 oz	Cooked ham	175 g
8	Eggs	8
	Salt	
1	Tomato	1

Grease 8 dariole moulds with the butter. Finely chop the ham and press onto the bottoms and sides of the moulds. Carefully break an egg into each mould and sprinkle with salt.

Put moulds into heatproof dish containing a little boiling water, cover and cook for 8–10 minutes till eggs are lightly set.

Run a knife blade around the inside of each mould and invert on to a warmed serving plate. Garnish with tomato slices and serve with a green salad.

Tomatoes and eggs American style

Overall timing 20 minutes

Freezing Not suitable

To serve 4–6

8 oz	Streaky bacon rashers	225 g
6	Large tomatoes	6
½ pint	Milk	300 ml
	Salt and pepper	
6	Eggs	6

Preheat the grill. Derind the bacon and arrange on the grill pan. Grill till crisp and golden. Remove and keep hot.

Wipe the tomatoes and cut in half. Place the tomatoes cut sides down on the grill pan and brush with a little fat from the bacon. Grill about 3 inches (7.5 cm) below heat for 3–4 minutes.

Meanwhile, pour the milk into a frying pan, add a pinch of salt and heat till simmering. Break an egg on to a saucer, then slide it into the milk. Repeat with remaining eggs. Cover and poach for 3 minutes.

Turn the tomatoes over, brush with bacon fat and grill for 2 more minutes. Arrange stalk halves cut sides up in a warmed serving dish and season. Lift the eggs out of the milk with a draining spoon and drain on kitchen paper. Place one on each tomato half and cover with the remaining halves. Arrange the bacon round the tomatoes and serve immediately with plenty of hot buttered toast.

Spinach flan

Overall timing 50 minutes

Freezing Not suitable

To serve 6

12 oz	Wholemeal shortcrust pastry	350 g
2 lb	Spinach	900 g
	Salt and pepper	
½ teasp	Grated nutmeg	2.5 ml
	Bunch of marjoram	
4 oz	Streaky bacon	125 g
3 oz	Butter	75 g
1	Onion	1
1 oz	Sultanas	25 g
4 tbsp	Single cream	4 x 15 ml
6 oz	Mozzarella cheese	175 g

Preheat the oven to 400°F (200°C) Gas 6.

Roll out dough and line 9 inch (23 cm) flan tin. Bake blind for 30 minutes.

Meanwhile, cook spinach with salt and nutmeg for 10 minutes. Drain and chop. Chop marjoram and add to spinach.

Derind and chop bacon. Melt half butter in a frying pan and fry bacon till crisp. Scatter bacon over base of flan.

Add remaining butter to pan. Peel and finely chop onion and fry till transparent. Add spinach mixture, three-quarters of sultanas, cream and seasoning. Cook for 5 minutes. Spread in flan case.

Slice cheese and arrange on top. Sprinkle with rest of sultanas and bake for 10 minutes.

Prawn scrambled eggs

Overall timing 15 minutes

Freezing Not suitable

To serve 4

2 oz	Butter	50 g
8 oz	Shelled prawns	225 g
8	Large eggs	8
	Salt and pepper	

Melt half the butter in a saucepan, add prawns and fry gently for 3–4 minutes.

Break the eggs into a bowl, add seasoning and beat lightly with a fork. Pour on to the prawns and stir gently but evenly till the eggs are lightly set.

Remove from the heat, quickly stir in the remaining butter and season to taste. Divide between warmed serving dishes and serve immediately with hot toast.

Italian shredded omelette

Overall timing 35 minutes

Freezing Not suitable

To serve 4

1	Small onion	1
1	Garlic clove	1
1	Stalk of celery	1
1	Carrot	1
2 oz	Streaky bacon rashers	50 g
1 tbsp	Oil	15 ml
14 oz	Can of tomatoes	397 g
	Salt and pepper	
9	Eggs	9
1 teasp	Chopped fresh mint	5 ml
3 tbsp	Chopped parsley	3x15 ml
2 oz	Butter	50 g

Peel and finely chop the onion. Peel and crush the garlic. Trim and chop the celery. Scrape and thinly slice the carrot. Derind and finely chop the bacon.

Heat the oil in a saucepan, add the bacon and vegetables and fry gently for 5 minutes. Add the tomatoes and juice, garlic and seasoning, bring to the boil and simmer for 20 minutes, stirring to break up the tomatoes.

Meanwhile, lightly beat the eggs in a bowl with the mint, parsley and seasoning. Melt one-third of the butter in a frying pan. Add one-third of the egg mixture and cook over a moderate heat, drawing the liquid into the centre as the mixture begins to set. When set, slide the omelette on to a board. Make two more omelettes in the same way.

Roll the omelettes loosely and cut into strips about ½ inch (12.5 mm) wide. Add to the tomato sauce and heat through for 3 minutes. Season to taste and pour into a warmed serving dish.

Minted cheese omelette

Overall timing 20 minutes

Freezing Not suitable

To serve 2

10	Fresh mint leaves	10
6	Eggs	6
1 oz	Fresh breadcrumbs	25 g
4 oz	Cheese	125 g
	Salt and pepper	
1 tbsp	Chopped parsley	15 ml
1 oz	Butter	25 g

Wash, dry and roughly chop the mint leaves. Lightly beat the eggs in a bowl with the breadcrumbs, grated cheese and seasoning. Stir in the parsley and mint and leave to stand for 5 minutes.

Melt the butter in a frying pan and pour in the egg mixture (or only half if making two omelettes). Tip the pan so that the bottom is coated and cook over a moderate heat until lightly set.

Using a large fish slice, carefully turn the omelette over and cook for 2 minutes more. Serve with tomato salad and wholemeal rolls.

Prawn omelette in béchamel sauce

Overall timing 40 minutes

Freezing Not suitable

To serve 2

1	Small onion	1
1	Small carrot	1
1	Stalk of celery	1
½ pint	Milk	300 ml
1	Bay leaf	1
2½ oz	Butter	65 g
2 tbsp	Plain flour	2x15 ml
6 oz	Shelled prawns	175 g
2 tbsp	Single cream	2x15 ml
	Salt and pepper	
6	Eggs	6
2 teasp	Chopped parsley	2x5 ml

Peel and roughly chop the onion and carrot. Trim and chop the celery. Put the milk into a saucepan with the bay leaf and prepared vegetables, cover and bring to the boil. Remove from heat and leave to infuse for 10 minutes.

Melt 2 oz (50 g) of the butter in a saucepan, add the flour and cook for 1 minute. Gradually add the strained milk and bring to the boil, stirring constantly. Cook, stirring, for 2 minutes. Reduce heat, stir in prawns, cream and seasoning. Heat without boiling.

Lightly beat the eggs in a bowl with a pinch of salt. Melt remaining butter in a frying pan, pour in the eggs and cook until set.

Spoon half the prawn sauce into the centre of the omelette and fold two sides over. Turn out of pan, placing join side down on warmed serving dish. Pour the remaining sauce round. Make a cut along the top of the omelette to expose the filling, sprinkle the parsley over and serve immediately with a tossed green salad.

Liver omelettes

Overall timing 15 minutes

Freezing Not suitable

To serve 4

4 oz	Chicken livers	125 g
4 oz	Butter	125 g
2	Sage leaves	2
	Salt and pepper	
3 tbsp	Marsala or sherry	3x15 ml
8	Eggs	8
	Sprigs of parsley	

Trim, wipe and finely chop the livers.

Melt 1 oz (25 g) of the butter in a saucepan and add livers. Chop sage and add to pan with seasoning. Stir-fry for 5 minutes. Pour Marsala or sherry over and cook till it has almost evaporated. Remove pan from heat.

Beat eggs in a bowl with a little seasoning. Melt a quarter of the remaining butter in an omelette or small frying pan. When it begins to foam, pour in a quarter of the egg mixture. Tilt pan so mixture runs evenly over the bottom. As the omelette begins to set underneath, place a quarter of the liver mixture along the centre and fold the sides of the omelette over the filling.

Slide omelette on to a warmed serving dish and keep hot. Make three more omelettes in the same way. Garnish with parsley and serve with sauté potatoes.

Chervil omelette

Overall timing 15 minutes

Freezing Not suitable

To serve 4

8	Eggs	8
	Salt and pepper	
3 tbsp	Chopped fresh chervil	3x15 ml
1 tbsp	Chopped parsley	15 ml
2 oz	Butter	50 g

Break the eggs into a bowl. Season with salt and pepper, add herbs and beat together lightly.

Melt one-quarter of the butter in an omelette pan over a high heat. When the butter begins to froth, pour in a quarter of the egg mixture. As the omelette starts to set, run a spatula round the edge to loosen it and tilt pan to let uncooked egg run underneath. When firm at the edges but still runny in the centre, fold omelette over and slide on to a warmed serving plate. Keep it hot while you make three more omelettes in the same way. Serve with a tomato salad.

Omelette forestière

Overall timing 25 minutes

Freezing Not suitable

To serve 2

4 oz	Thick streaky bacon rashers	125 g
4 oz	Button mushrooms	125 g
2	Small potatoes	2
2 oz	Butter	50 g
4–6	Eggs	4–6
1 tbsp	Chopped parsley	15 ml
	Salt and pepper	

Derind bacon, then cut into thin strips. Thinly slice mushrooms. Peel and thinly slice potatoes. Melt the butter in a frying pan, add potatoes and bacon and fry till tender and golden all over. Add mushrooms and cook for 5 minutes more.

Meanwhile, lightly beat the eggs in a bowl with parsley and seasoning. Pour over the ingredients in the frying pan. Cook for a few minutes, lifting the edges to ensure the underneath is evenly cooked. Fold over and slide on to warmed serving plate. Serve immediately.

Devilled liver omelettes

Overall timing 20 minutes

Freezing Not suitable

To serve 2

2	Bacon rashers	2
4 oz	Chicken livers	125 g
	Salt and pepper	
1 tbsp	Plain flour	15 ml
2 oz	Mushrooms	50 g
2 oz	Butter	50 g
1 teasp	Tomato purée	5 ml
½ teasp	Worcestershire sauce	2.5 ml
½ teasp	French mustard	2.5 ml
6	Eggs	6
1 teasp	Chopped chives	5 ml

Derind and chop the bacon. Trim and chop the livers and toss in seasoned flour. Slice the mushrooms.

Melt half the butter in a saucepan, add the bacon and fry till light brown. Add the chicken livers and stir-fry till browned. Add the mushrooms, tomato purée, Worcestershire sauce, mustard and seasoning. Mix well, then cover and cook for 3 minutes.

Heat the remaining butter in an omelette pan. Lightly beat the eggs with seasoning and add to pan. Cook until almost set, then spoon the liver mixture over and sprinkle with the chives. Fold omelette, cut in half and place on two warmed plates. Serve hot with granary bread and a tomato and cucumber salad.

Cheese dishes

Anchovy brochettes

Overall timing 30 minutes

Freezing Not suitable

To serve 2

4	Large slices of white bread	4
4 oz	Mozzarella or Gouda cheese	125 g
3 oz	Butter	75 g
	Salt and pepper	
8	Anchovy fillets	8
4 tbsp	Milk	4x15 ml

Preheat the oven to 400°F (200°C) Gas 6.

Cut bread and cheese into small squares. Thread alternately on to four skewers. Arrange in an ovenproof dish so that each end of the skewer is supported by the rim.

Melt half of the butter and brush generously over the brochettes. Season with salt and pepper. Bake for about 15–20 minutes, basting occasionally with butter in dish. The brochettes should be golden brown.

Meanwhile, melt remaining butter in a saucepan. Mash anchovies and add to butter. Gradually add milk and mix well together over gentle heat. Bring to boiling point.

Pour hot anchovy sauce over brochettes and serve immediately.

Welsh rarebit

Overall timing 30 minutes

Freezing Not suitable

To serve 4

8	Slices of bread	8
3 oz	Butter	75 g
12 oz	Cheddar cheese	350 g
½ teasp	Ground mace	2.5 ml
	Pinch of powdered mustard	
5 tbsp	Beer	5x15 ml
	Pepper	

Preheat the oven to 400°F (200°C) Gas 6.

Toast the bread, and butter the slices while still hot. Place on baking tray.

Cut the cheese into small cubes and put in a saucepan with mace, mustard and beer. Cook over a low heat, stirring with a wooden spoon, until cheese melts and is thick and creamy. Spread mixture over toast. Sprinkle generously with pepper and bake for 10 minutes. Serve immediately.

Cheese flan

Overall timing 1½ hours

Freezing Suitable: reheat in 425°F (220°C) Gas 7 oven for 10–15 minutes

To serve 4–6

5 oz	Butter	150 g
¼ pint	Water	150 ml
	Salt and pepper	
8 oz	Self-raising flour	225 g
2	Medium-size onions	2
1 tbsp	Plain flour	15 ml
4 fl oz	Milk	120 ml
3	Eggs	3
¼ teasp	Grated nutmeg	1.25 ml
	Cayenne pepper	
4 oz	Cheddar cheese	125 g
4 oz	Gruyère cheese	125 g

Melt 4 oz (125 g) of the butter. Cool slightly, then stir in 3 tbsp (3x15 ml) of the water and salt. Sift self-raising flour into a bowl. Slowly add butter mixture and mix until smooth. Chill for 30 minutes.

Preheat the oven to 350°F (180°C) Gas 4.

Peel and chop onions. Melt remaining butter in a saucepan and fry onions for 10 minutes until soft. Cool.

Mix plain flour and a little of the milk in a bowl, then add the rest of the milk and the remaining water. Separate the eggs. Mix the yolks into the flour and milk mixture. Season with salt, pepper, nutmeg and a pinch of cayenne. Beat egg whites till stiff, then fold into yolk mixture.

Roll out dough and use to line a greased 9 inch (23 cm) flan tin. Spread onions over bottom of flan, then grate both sorts of cheese on top. Cover with egg and milk mixture.

Bake for 15 minutes. Reduce heat to 325°F (170°C) Gas 3 and bake for a further 45 minutes. Serve hot.

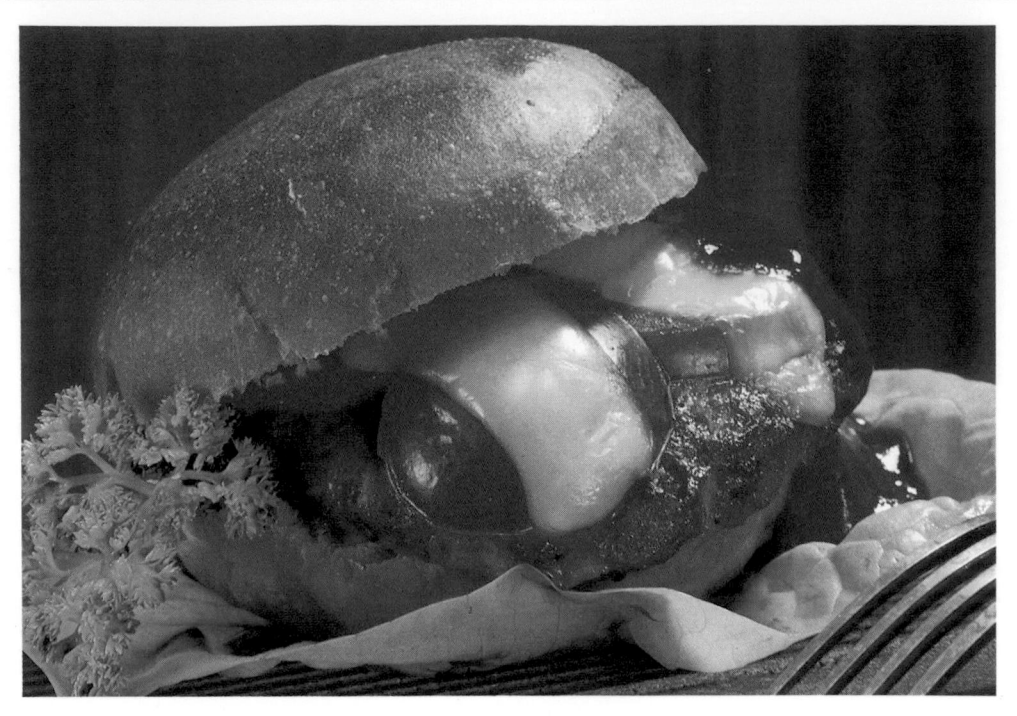

Cheeseburgers

Overall timing 30 minutes

Freezing Not suitable

To serve 4

1	Large onion	1
1 lb	Minced beef	450 g
3 tbsp	Fresh breadcrumbs	3x15 ml
4 tbsp	Milk	4x15 ml
	Salt	
	Paprika	
1 teasp	Powdered mustard	5 ml
	Oil	
4	Small tomatoes	4
4	Slices of Cheddar cheese	4
4	Buns	4

Preheat the grill.

Peel and finely chop onion. In a large bowl, mix together the onion, minced beef, breadcrumbs and milk. Season with salt, a pinch of paprika and mustard. Leave for 10 minutes.

Make 4 hamburgers from the mixture. Brush with oil. Cook for 5 minutes on each side under the grill.

Remove from heat. Top the burgers with slices of tomato and strips of cheese. Put back under the grill till the cheese melts. Serve in warm buns.

Cheese soufflé

Overall timing 45 minutes

Freezing Not suitable

To serve 4–6

3 oz	Butter	75 g
4	Eggs	4
2 oz	Cornflour	50 g
1 pint	Milk	560 ml
	Salt and pepper	
	Paprika	
	Grated nutmeg	
4 oz	Gruyère, Parmesan or mature Cheddar cheese	125 g

Preheat the oven to 400°F (200°C) Gas 6.

Grease a 7 inch (18 cm) diameter soufflé dish with 1 oz (25 g) of the butter, and tie with paper collar if liked. Separate the eggs.

Melt the remaining butter in a saucepan, stir in cornflour and cook for 1 minute. Gradually add the milk, stirring all the time until the sauce thickens. Season with salt and pepper and a pinch of both paprika and grated nutmeg. Take pan off heat and allow mixture to cool slightly.

Finely grate cheese and stir into sauce. Add egg yolks one at a time to the sauce, beating well.

In a large bowl, whisk egg whites till they hold stiff peaks, then carefully fold into the sauce with a metal spoon.

Pour soufflé mixture into prepared dish. Bake just above centre of oven for about 25 minutes or until risen and golden. Remove from oven and serve immediately with a crisp green salad, dressed with herb vinaigrette.

Cheesy tapioca fritters

Overall timing 1 hour

Freezing Not suitable

To serve 6

1	Medium-size onion	1
4 oz	Flaked tapioca	125 g
1½ pints	Milk	850 ml
1	Bay leaf	1
	Salt and pepper	
3	Eggs	3
6 oz	Cheese	175 g
½ teasp	Powdered mustard	2.5 ml
	Oil for deep frying	
	Sprigs of parsley	

Peel and finely chop the onion. Put into a saucepan with the tapioca, milk and bay leaf. Season and bring to the boil, stirring. Cook for about 30 minutes, stirring occasionally, till thick and creamy. Remove from the heat.

Separate the eggs and beat the yolks one at a time into the mixture. Grate the cheese and add to the mixture with mustard. Mix well and leave to cool.

Heat oil in a deep-fryer to 340°F (170°C).

Whisk the egg whites till stiff but not dry, then fold into the tapioca mixture with a metal spoon. Drop a few large spoonfuls of the mixture into the oil and fry for 3–4 minutes till crisp and golden. Drain on kitchen paper. Sprinkle with salt and serve hot, garnished with parsley.

Croque monsieur

Overall timing 20 minutes

Freezing Not suitable

To serve 4

8	Slices of bread	8
	Butter	
8	Slices of Gruyere or Cheddar cheese	8
4	Slices of cooked ham	4
	Extra grated cheese (optional)	

Preheat the grill.

Butter four slices of bread. Place a slice of cheese on each of the unbuttered slices of bread. Cover with the ham, then top with the rest of the sliced cheese. Place the buttered bread on top, buttered sides up.

Grill the sandwiches, buttered sides up, until golden brown. Turn and spread the other sides with butter. Continue grilling until golden. Sprinkle with a little extra grated cheese, if liked, and grill until the cheese has melted.

Variation

For a Croque milady, add sliced tomato to the sandwich and top with fried eggs.

Gnocchi

Overall timing 50 minutes plus cooling

Freezing Suitable: bake from frozen, allowing 1 hour

To serve 4

1½ pints	Milk	850 ml
6 oz	Coarse semolina	175 g
	Salt and pepper	
	Grated nutmeg	
6 oz	Grated Parmesan cheese	175 g
1	Egg yolk	1
2 tbsp	Milk	2x15 ml

Heat milk just to boiling in a saucepan, then sprinkle on semolina. Season with salt, pepper and nutmeg. Cook gently, stirring, for 4–5 minutes till mixture becomes solid. Remove pan from heat and beat in 4 oz (125 g) of the cheese. Pour into a greased Swiss roll tin. Leave in a cool place (not the refrigerator) for 45 minutes to 1 hour till cold.

Preheat the oven to 400°F (200°C) Gas 6.

Cut the cooled mixture into about 20 rounds, 2½ inches (6.5 cm) in diameter. Arrange the rounds, overlapping them, in a greased round ovenproof dish. Beat egg yolk and milk and pour over. Sprinkle with the rest of the cheese and bake for 30 minutes till golden brown. Serve immediately.

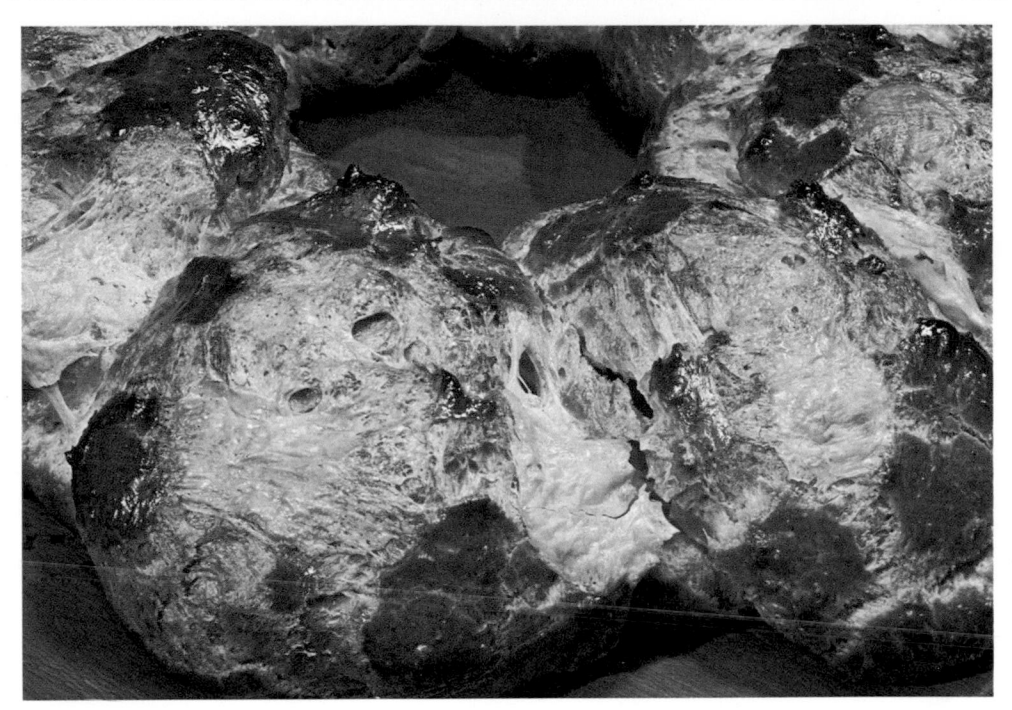

Gougère

Overall timing 1½ hours

Freezing Not suitable

To serve 6

7 fl oz	Water	200 ml
½ teasp	Salt	2.5 ml
4 oz	Butter	125 g
3½ oz	Plain flour	100 g
4	Eggs	4
8 oz	Gruyère cheese	225 g

Preheat oven to 400°F (200°C) Gas 6.

Put water and salt into a saucepan, with 3 oz (75 g) of the butter, chopped. Bring to the boil, stirring to melt the butter. Remove from heat and quickly add the flour all at once, stirring well. Return pan to heat and beat till the paste is smooth and leaves the sides of the pan cleanly. Remove from heat and allow to cool slightly.

Add three of the eggs, one at a time, beating well between additions. Grate 5 oz (150 g) of the cheese and stir into the paste.

With a large spoon, make a ring of the paste on a greased baking tray. Beat the remaining egg and brush over paste. Dice remaining cheese and place on top of the paste with tiny pieces of the remaining butter.

Bake for 20 minutes, then lower heat to 375°F (190°C) Gas 5, and bake for a further 20–25 minutes. Serve hot.

Deep-fried Mozzarella sandwiches

Overall timing 20 minutes

Freezing Not suitable

To serve 4

8	Slices of bread	8
4	Slices of Mozzarella cheese	4
	Plain flour	
1	Egg	1
	Oil for deep frying	

Remove the crusts from the bread. Make four sandwiches with the cheese and coat all over with flour. Beat the egg in a shallow dish. Dip in the sandwiches so the sides and edges are all coated.

Heat oil in a deep-fryer to 360°F (180°C). Deep fry the sandwiches until they are golden brown. Drain on kitchen paper and serve hot, with salad.

Italian deep-fried cheese

Overall timing 1¼ hours plus chilling

Freezing Not suitable

To serve 2

½	Onion	½
1 oz	Butter	25 g
2 oz	Long grain rice	50 g
4 fl oz	Chicken stock	120 ml
1 teasp	Grated Parmesan cheese	5 ml
	Pinch of grated nutmeg	
	Salt and pepper	
1 oz	Lean cooked ham	25 g
1½ oz	Mozzarella cheese	40 g
1	Egg	1
1 oz	Fine fresh breadcrumbs	25 g
	Oil for deep frying	

Peel and finely chop onion. Melt butter in a saucepan and fry onion till transparent.

Add rice and stir over a low heat for 2 minutes. Stir in stock, cover and bring to the boil. Simmer gently for 15–20 minutes till rice is tender. Remove from heat and stir in Parmesan, nutmeg and seasoning. Leave to cool completely.

Meanwhile, chop ham finely. Cut Mozzarella into four sticks about 1½ inches (4 cm) long and ½ inch (12.5 mm) thick. Break egg on to a plate and beat lightly with a fork. Spread breadcrumbs on another plate.

Beat a little egg and the ham into rice. Put 2 tbsp (2x15 ml) rice mixture in palm of one hand. Place a cheese stick on top and cover with more rice. Pat into a cylinder shape about 2½ inches (6.5 cm) long and 1 inch (2.5 cm) thick. Brush beaten egg over croquette, then coat with breadcrumbs. Shape and coat three more croquettes. Chill for 1 hour.

Heat oil in a deep-fryer to 360°F (180°C). Fry the croquettes for 5–6 minutes till golden. Drain on kitchen paper and serve hot.

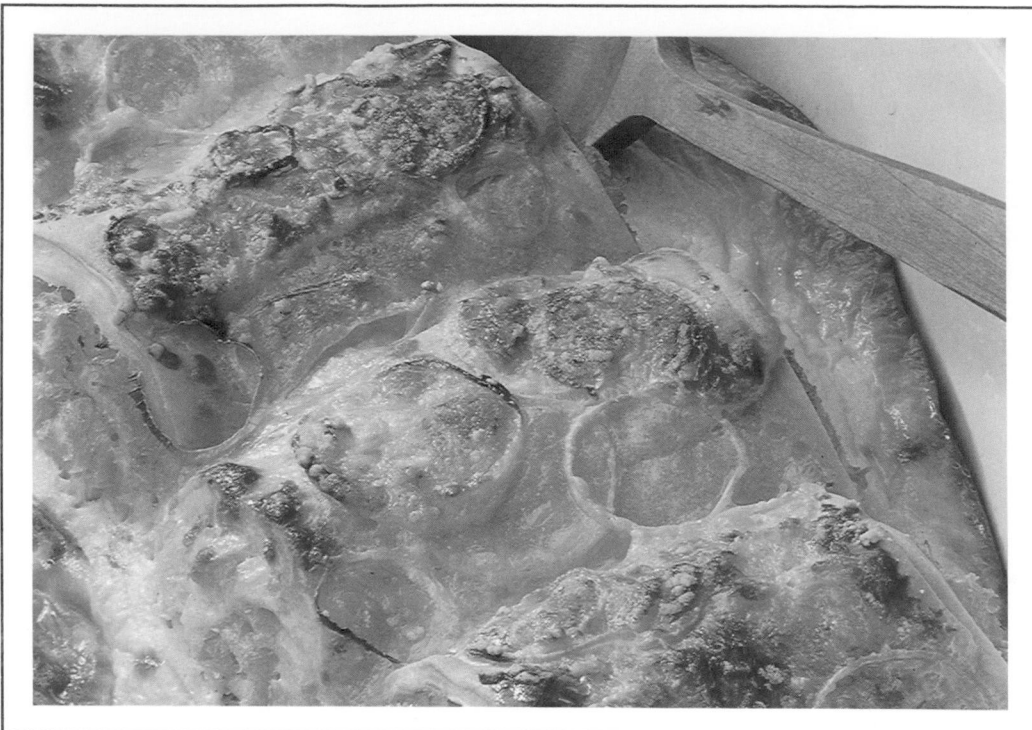

Sauerkraut cheese rolls

Overall timing 1½ hours

Freezing Not suitable

To serve 6

8 oz	Plain flour	225 g
	Salt	
8 oz	Cream cheese	225 g
5 oz	Butter	150 g
2	Eggs	2
¼ pint	Carton of soured cream	150 ml
	Grated nutmeg	
1	Small onion	1
3 oz	Cheese	75 g
Filling		
4 oz	Streaky bacon	125 g
1 lb	Can of sauerkraut	454 g
1 tbsp	Sugar	15 ml
	Salt and pepper	
1	Bay leaf	1

Sift flour and salt into bowl and rub in cream cheese and 4 oz (125 g) butter. Knead till smooth, then chill for 30 minutes.

Meanwhile, for the filling, derind and chop bacon. Place in saucepan and cook till golden, then add sauerkraut, sugar, seasoning and bay leaf. Cover and cook gently for 30 minutes. Remove bay leaf. Cool.

Preheat oven to 400°F (200°C) Gas 6.

Roll out dough to rectangle 18x10 inches (45x25 cm). Spoon filling over dough, leaving border. Beginning at long edge, roll up, then cut roll into six smaller rolls. Arrange rolls in greased ovenproof dish.

Beat eggs with soured cream, salt and nutmeg. Pour over the rolls. Peel and slice onion. Grate cheese. Top rolls with onion rings, cheese and remaining butter. Bake for 40 minutes.

Three-cheese savouries

Overall timing 10 minutes plus chilling

Freezing Not suitable

To serve 6

4 oz	Danish blue cheese	125 g
3	Petits suisses cheeses	3
4 oz	Gruyère cheese	125 g
2 tbsp	Chopped fresh herbs	2 x 15 ml
4 oz	Dried breadcrumbs	125 g

Mash Danish blue and Petits suisses cheeses together in a bowl with a fork. Grate Gruyère and add to bowl with herbs. Mix well together.

Shape into flat cakes or cylinders and coat in breadcrumbs. Place on a plate and chill for 3 hours before serving with toast, crisp biscuits or French bread.

Variation

Use a mixture of cream, cottage and curd cheeses, and flavour with 2 cloves of crushed garlic creamed with salt. Make into shapes (use biscuit or scone cutters) and coat in breadcrumbs or finely chopped parsley. Or use prepared pepper for steak which is a combination of pepper and mustard. Chill as above before serving.

Basque cod casserole

Overall timing 1 hour

Freezing Not suitable

To serve 4–6

1 lb	Cod fillets	450 g
	Bouquet garni	
	Salt and pepper	
4	Large potatoes	4
2	Hard-boiled eggs	2
3	Tomatoes	3
3 oz	Butter	75 g
3	Garlic cloves	3
2 oz	Black olives	50 g
2 tbsp	Capers	2x15 ml
1 tbsp	Chopped parsley	15 ml
2 tbsp	Lemon juice	2x15 ml

Place cod in a saucepan and cover with water. Add bouquet garni and seasoning and bring slowly to the boil. Remove pan from heat and leave to cool.

Meanwhile, cook unpeeled potatoes in boiling salted water for 30 minutes. Drain well, then peel and slice potatoes. Shell and slice eggs. Blanch, peel and chop tomatoes.

Melt 1 oz (25 g) butter in a pan and fry tomatoes. Season with salt and pepper.

Preheat the oven to 400°F (200°C) Gas 6.

Arrange egg slices around side of greased soufflé dish and make layers of the potatoes, drained and chopped fish, and the peeled and crushed garlic. Spread tomatoes over top. Dot with remaining butter and bake for 20 minutes.

Garnish with black olives, capers and chopped parsley and sprinkle with lemon juice. Serve hot or cold.

Baked cod with rosemary

Overall timing 45 minutes

Freezing Not suitable

To serve 4–6

2½ lb	End piece of cod	1.1 kg
4 tbsp	Oil	4x15 ml
8	Anchovy fillets	8
	Fresh rosemary	
4	Basil leaves (optional)	4
2 tbsp	Dried breadcrumbs	2x15 ml
	Salt and pepper	

Ask your fishmonger to remove bones from cod, leaving two halves attached at one side. Scale fish, using a descaler or the blunt side of a knife.

Preheat the oven to 350°F (180°C) Gas 4.

Heat half the oil in a flameproof casserole, add the chopped anchovies and heat through. Mash anchovies well, then transfer to a bowl. Put a little of the mashed anchovy mixture inside the fish, together with a few sprigs of fresh rosemary and the basil leaves, if using.

Place fish in the casserole and pour the remaining anchovy mixture and oil over. Add a little more rosemary and sprinkle with breadcrumbs, salt and pepper. Bake for about 30 minutes till the fish is cooked and the top is golden. Serve with boiled potatoes and a green vegetable or salad.

Grilled cod with bacon

Overall timing 25 minutes

Freezing Not suitable

To serve 2

2	Large cod fillets	2
2 tbsp	Oil	2x15 ml
	Salt and pepper	
2 oz	Thin streaky bacon rashers	50 g
1 oz	Butter	25 g
1 tbsp	Lemon juice	15 ml
	Sprigs of parsley	
	Lemon wedges	

Preheat the grill.

Brush the cod fillets with oil and season with salt and pepper. Place under a fairly hot grill and cook for about 15 minutes, turning fillets over halfway through cooking time.

Remove rind from the bacon, then grill or fry. Drain on kitchen paper.

Melt the butter in a small saucepan, taking care not to colour it. Arrange the fish and bacon on warmed serving plates. Pour the butter over and sprinkle with lemon juice. Garnish with parsley sprigs and lemon wedges. Serve with boiled potatoes tossed in butter and sprinkled with chopped parsley, and a crisp lettuce salad.

Cod croquettes

Overall timing 45 minutes

Freezing Suitable: bake cooked croquettes from frozen in 375°F (190°C) Gas 5 oven for 30 minutes

To serve 4–6

1 lb	Cooked cod fillets	450 g
1 lb	Mashed potatoes	450 g
	Salt and pepper	
	Grated nutmeg	
1	Egg	1
	Dried breadcrumbs	
	Oil for deep frying	
	Lettuce leaves	
1	Lemon	1

Finely mince cod, then mix with potatoes in a large bowl. Season well with salt, pepper and a pinch of nutmeg. Make small round or oval shapes of the mixture.

Lightly beat egg in a bowl. Dip croquettes in egg, then breadcrumbs.

Heat oil in deep-fryer to 360°F (180°C). Add croquettes and fry for about 5 minutes till golden. Remove croquettes and drain on kitchen paper. Pile them up on a bed of lettuce with pieces of lemon between. Serve with tomato sauce (see page 19).

Cod with onions and leeks

Overall timing 35 minutes

Freezing Not suitable

To serve 4–6

1¾ lb	Cod fillets	750 g
3 tbsp	Lemon juice	3x15 ml
	Salt	
2	Large onions	2
2	Leeks	2
3 tbsp	Oil	3x15 ml
¼ pint	Dry cider	150 ml
2 tbsp	Chopped parsley	2x15 ml

Place cod fillets in a bowl with lemon juice and salt.

Peel and chop onions. Trim and chop leeks. Heat oil in a frying pan and cook onions and leeks gently till softened.

Add cod fillets, with any juices, and cider to pan and cook for 15 minutes till fish is cooked through. Sprinkle with parsley before serving with mashed potatoes.

Mustard-topped cod

Overall timing 35 minutes

Freezing Not suitable

To serve 4

1¾ lb	Cod fillets	750 g
1	Onion	1
1 tbsp	Vinegar	15 ml
1	Bay leaf	1
6	Peppercorns	6
3 oz	Butter	75 g
2 tbsp	Powdered English mustard	2x15 ml
1 teasp	Sea-salt	5 ml
	Sprigs of parsley	
	Lemon slices	

Cut cod into large pieces. Place in a saucepan and cover with water. Peel and halve the onion and add to the pan with the vinegar, bay leaf and peppercorns. Bring to the boil over a high heat, then simmer for 20 minutes.

Melt the butter with the mustard and salt in a small saucepan. Mix well and simmer for 2–3 minutes, being careful not to let mixture stick or burn.

Remove pieces of cod from the saucepan with a draining spoon and place on a warmed serving plate. Spoon a little of the mustard mixture on to each piece of fish or serve in a separate dish. Garnish with a few sprigs of parsley and lemon slices. Serve with plain boiled rice and peas.

Whiting curls

Overall timing 50 minutes

Freezing Not suitable

To serve 2

2	Small whiting	2
	Salt and pepper	
4 tbsp	Plain flour	4x15 ml
	Oil for deep frying	
1	Lemon	1
	Sprigs of parsley	

Scale and dry the whiting. Place one on its side on a board and hold it firmly by the tail. Using a sharp knife in a sawing action cut between the flesh and the back-bone to just behind the head.

Turn the fish over and repeat the action on the other side to expose the backbone. Cut off the backbone just behind the head with kitchen scissors. Repeat with the other whiting.

Curl fish, pushing tail through skin at far side of mouth to hold in place. Lightly coat each fish with seasoned flour. Shake off any excess.

Heat the oil in a deep-fryer to 340°F (170°C). Fry the whiting for about 10 minutes till tender and golden brown. Drain on kitchen paper and arrange the fish on a warmed serving dish. Garnish with parsley and lemon and serve immediately, with tartare sauce.

Hake au gratin

Overall timing 30 minutes

Freezing Not suitable

To serve 4

1	Small onion	1
2 tbsp	Chopped parsley	2x15 ml
1¾ lb	Hake steaks	750 g
	Salt and pepper	
	Grated nutmeg	
2 tbsp	Lemon juice	2x15 ml
1 oz	Butter	25 g
4 oz	Cheese	125 g
2 oz	Fresh breadcrumbs	50 g

Preheat oven to 375°F (190°C) Gas 5.

Peel and chop onion and place in a shallow ovenproof dish with half the parsley and the fish steaks. Season with salt and pepper and a pinch of nutmeg. Sprinkle the lemon juice over the fish and dot with butter. Grate the cheese and mix with the breadcrumbs and remaining parsley. Sprinkle over the fish. Bake for about 20 minutes.

Remove from oven and baste with liquid in dish. Bake for another 10 minutes until topping is golden. Serve immediately with jacket-baked potatoes.

Coley with spicy sauce

Overall timing 1 hour

Freezing Not suitable

To serve 4

4	Onions	4
4–6	Garlic cloves	4–6
1 lb	Tomatoes	450 g
1	Lemon	1
¼ pint	Oil	150 ml
¼ teasp	Cayenne	1.25 ml
4	Coley steaks	4
	Salt	
	Chopped parsley	

Peel and slice onions. Peel and crush garlic. Blanch, peel and chop tomatoes. Cut four thin slices from lemon and squeeze juice from remainder.

Heat oil in a saucepan. Add onions, garlic and tomatoes and cook gently for about 25 minutes.

Add cayenne and mix in well. Place coley steaks on top of mixture in pan. Sprinkle with salt and lemon juice, cover with lid and cook for a further 15 minutes, turning the fish steaks once.

Arrange coley steaks on a bed of rice on warmed serving dish. Spoon tomato mixture on top and garnish with lemon slices and chopped parsley.

Baked coley

Overall timing 1 hour

Freezing Not suitable

To serve 4

3 lb	Piece of coley	1.4 kg
1	Strip of bacon fat	1
2 oz	Butter	50 g
	Salt and pepper	
4	Smoked bacon rashers	4
1	Large can of flageolet beans	1
$\frac{1}{4}$ teasp	Dried sage	1.25 ml
$\frac{1}{4}$ pint	Chicken stock	150 ml

Preheat the oven to 425°F (220°C) Gas 7.

Roll up the coley and tie as you would a piece of beef, with the bacon fat wrapped round. Reserve a knob of butter and use most of the rest to grease a roasting tin. Place coley in it. Dot with more butter, season, then bake for 30 minutes.

Derind and chop bacon. Melt reserved knob of butter in saucepan and fry bacon till crisp. Drain can of beans and add to pan with sage and stock. Cook over a low heat for 10 minutes.

Put coley on a warmed serving plate. Arrange beans and bacon round coley and serve with parsleyed new potatoes.

Plaice and chips

Overall timing 35 minutes plus 30 minutes soaking

Freezing Not suitable

To serve 4

2 lb	Waxy potatoes	900 g
2	Whole plaice, halved and boned	2
	Salt and pepper	
4 tbsp	Plain flour	4x15 ml
	Oil for frying	
	Lemon wedges	
	Sprigs of parsley	
Coating batter		
8 oz	Plain flour	225 g
½ teasp	Salt	2.5 ml
2	Eggs	2
2 tbsp	Oil	2x15 ml
6 tbsp	Cold water	6x15 ml

Peel the potatoes and cut into chips. Soak in cold water for 30 minutes.

Wipe the fish. Season the flour and lightly coat the fish.

To make the batter, sift flour and salt into a bowl. Separate eggs. Add yolks, oil and water to flour and beat till smooth.

Heat oil in a deep-fryer to 360°F (180°C). Drain the chips and dry well. Fry, in batches, for 4–5 minutes till tender but not brown. Remove and drain on kitchen paper.

Reduce the temperature of the oil to 340°F (170°C). Whisk the egg whites till stiff but not dry and fold into the batter. Coat the plaice with batter.

Fry the plaice, one at a time if necessary, for 2–3 minutes each side till crisp and golden. Drain on kitchen paper and keep hot, uncovered.

Increase the temperature of the oil to 360°F (180°C) again, put the chips in the basket and fry till crisp and golden. Drain on kitchen paper and pile into a warmed serving dish.

Garnish plaice with lemon wedges and sprigs of parsley. Serve immediately.

Fried plaice ✓

Overall timing 30 minutes

Freezing Not suitable

To serve 6

3 oz	Unsalted butter	75 g
2 tbsp	Chopped parsley	2x15 ml
1 tbsp	Lemon juice	15 ml
	Salt and pepper	
3 tbsp	Plain flour	3x15 ml
3	Whole plaice, halved and boned	3
2	Eggs	2
4 oz	Golden breadcrumbs	125 g
	Oil for frying	
	Lemon slices	
	Sprigs of parsley	

Mash the butter with the chopped parsley and lemon juice. Shape into a roll and chill.

Season the flour and lightly coat the plaice. Beat the eggs in a shallow dish. Spread the breadcrumbs on a plate. Dip the fish into the egg so that it covers both sides. Dip into the crumbs, pressing them on lightly till evenly coated.

Heat the oil in a large frying pan and add two or three of the coated fillets, skin side up. Fry gently for 3–5 minutes, then turn the fish carefully and cook for a further 3–5 minutes till the fish is tender and the coating crisp. Lift out of the pan with a fish slice and drain on kitchen paper. Arrange on a warmed serving dish and keep hot while the rest of the fish is cooked.

Garnish with slices of parsley butter, lemon slices and sprigs of parsley. Serve with chips or sauté potatoes.

Baked plaice au gratin

Overall timing 45 minutes

Freezing Not suitable

To serve 4

1½ lb	Plaice fillets	700 g
1	Small onion	1
2	Tomatoes	2
1 tbsp	Olive oil	15 ml
2	Bay leaves	2
	Salt and pepper	
1 tbsp	Chopped parsley	15 ml
¼ pint	Dry white wine or milk	150 ml
3 tbsp	Dried breadcrumbs	3x15 ml
1 oz	Cheese	25 g
1 oz	Butter	25 g

Preheat the oven to 350°F (180°C) Gas 4.

Remove the skin from the plaice fillets. Peel and finely chop the onion; blanch, peel and slice the tomatoes.

Sprinkle the oil into a shallow baking dish and add the chopped onion. Arrange half the plaice fillets on top with the sliced tomatoes and bay leaves. Sprinkle with salt, pepper and the chopped parsley. Cover with the remaining fish. Pour the white wine or milk over. Grate the cheese and sprinkle on top with the breadcrumbs. Dot with the butter.

Bake for about 25 minutes till golden brown on top. Serve immediately with creamed potatoes and runner beans.

Skate with capers

Overall timing 25 minutes

Freezing Not suitable

To serve 2

2x8 oz	Pieces of skate	2x225 g
	Salt and pepper	
1½ teasp	Vinegar	7.5 ml
1½ oz	Butter	40 g
1 tbsp	Capers	15 ml
1 tbsp	Chopped parsley	15 ml
1½ tbsp	Lemon juice	22.5 ml
2 tbsp	Single cream	2x15 ml

Put the skate into a saucepan. Cover with cold water and add a little salt and a few drops of vinegar. Bring to the boil, then remove from the heat, cover and leave to stand for 10 minutes.

Drain and dry the skate; remove the skin. Place on a warmed serving dish and keep hot.

Melt the butter in a small saucepan and stir in remaining vinegar, the capers, parsley, lemon juice, cream and seasoning. Cook for 2–3 minutes, without boiling, till heated through. Pour over the skate. Serve with boiled or steamed potatoes and a tossed green salad.

Grilled herrings with parsley butter

Overall timing 20 minutes

Freezing Not suitable

To serve 4

4 oz	Unsalted butter	125 g
2 tbsp	Chopped parsley	2x15 ml
1 tbsp	Lemon juice	15 ml
4	Cleaned whole herrings	4
1 tbsp	Oil	15 ml
	Salt and pepper	
1	Lemon	1
	Sprigs of parsley	

Mash butter with chopped parsley and lemon juice. Form into a roll, wrap in greaseproof paper and chill till ready to use.

Preheat the grill.

Brush herrings with oil and season. Place on grill pan and cook for 7 minutes on each side.

Arrange herrings on serving plate. Garnish with lemon, pats of chilled butter and parsley sprigs.

Fishermen's herrings

Overall timing 35 minutes plus chilling

Freezing Not suitable

To serve 6

12	Smoked herring fillets	12
1	Onion	1
4	Small gherkins	4
4 oz	Can of herring roes	113 g
1 tbsp	French mustard	15 ml
¼ pint	Oil	150 ml
	Pepper	

Put the herring fillets into a bowl, cover with boiling water and leave for 20 minutes.

Drain herring fillets, rinse and dry on kitchen paper. Peel onion and cut into thin rings. Slice gherkins. ·

Drain and chop the roes and put into a bowl with the mustard. Beat to a smooth paste with a wooden spoon. Gradually trickle in all but 2 tbsp (2x15 ml) of the oil, beating well after each addition. Add pepper to taste.

Spread roe sauce over bottom of a serving dish and arrange herring fillets on top. Brush with remaining oil and decorate with onion rings and gherkins. Chill for at least 30 minutes, then serve with potato and beetroot salads garnished with snipped chives.

Herrings with mustard sauce

Overall timing 20 minutes

Freezing Not suitable

To serve 4

4	Cleaned fresh whole herrings	4
2 tbsp	Oil	2x15 ml
2 tbsp	Plain flour	2x15ml
	Salt and pepper	
Sauce		
1 oz	Butter	25 g
1 tbsp	Plain flour	15 ml
½ pint	Stock	300 ml
½ teasp	Pepper	2.5 ml
1 tbsp	Prepared mustard	15 ml
2 tbsp	Single cream	2x15 ml

Preheat grill.

Wash herrings and pat dry on kitchen paper. Brush with oil and coat lightly with seasoned flour. Grill for 7 minutes on each side.

Meanwhile, make the sauce. Melt the butter in a saucepan. Stir in the flour and cook for 1 minute. Add the stock (made with a stock cube if necessary), bring to the boil and cook, stirring, for 3 minutes. Add pepper. Remove from heat and stir in mustard and cream.

Arrange herrings on warmed serving plates and spoon mustard sauce over.

Poached kippers

Overall timing 20 minutes

Freezing Not suitable

To serve 4

8	Kipper fillets	8
3 oz	Butter	75 g
2 teasp	Lemon juice	2x5 ml
½ teasp	Pepper	2.5 ml
	Sprigs of parsley	
	Lemon wedges	

Place kipper fillets in a large saucepan with the skins facing up. Cover with cold water and slowly bring to the boil.

As soon as the water boils, remove from heat, drain well and place on a warmed serving dish with the skin side down. Garnish with parsley.

Melt the butter and stir in the lemon juice and pepper. Pour over kippers at the table and serve with boiled new potatoes and lemon wedges.

Marinated kipper fillets

Overall timing 15 minutes plus marination

Freezing Not suitable

To serve 6

1	Carrot	1
2	Onions	2
1 lb	Kipper fillets	450 g
	Sprigs of thyme	
4–5	Bay leaves	4–5
4–5	Cloves	4–5
$\frac{1}{4}$ pint	Oil	150 ml
4 tbsp	Wine vinegar or lemon juice	4x15 ml
Garnish		
	Hard-boiled eggs	
	Lemon slices	
	Chopped parsley	
	Capers	

Peel and slice the carrot and onions. Place kipper fillets in a glass or pottery bowl, layered with slices of carrot, onion rings, sprigs of fresh thyme, bay leaves and cloves. Pour oil and wine vinegar or lemon juice over and leave for 24 hours in a cool place.

Drain the kippers and place in a serving dish. Garnish with slices of hard-boiled egg and lemon, chopped parsley and capers. Serve with cold potato and onion salad.

Rollmops

Overall timing 30 minutes plus 48 hours soaking and 4 days standing

Freezing Not suitable

To serve 6

4	Filleted fresh herrings	4
2 pints	Water	1.1 litre
8 oz	Salt	225 g
2 tbsp	Capers	2x15 ml
2	Onions	2
1	Large gherkin	1
4 teasp	Made mustard	4x5 ml
Marinade		
½ pint	Cider vinegar	300 ml
½ pint	Water	300 ml
1	Bay leaf	1
10	Black peppercorns	10
2	Cloves	2
5	Juniper berries	5
1 teasp	Mustard seed	5 ml

Soak herrings in half water and salt for 24 hours. Drain and repeat.

Put all marinade ingredients into a pan. Bring to the boil and boil for 5 minutes. Cool.

Chop capers. Peel onions and cut into rings. Quarter gherkin lengthways. Drain and rinse herrings. Lay skin down and spread with mustard. Sprinkle with capers and onion rings. Add gherkin and roll up. Pour over marinade. Leave 4 days before eating.

Marinated sprats

Overall timing 45 minutes plus overnight marination

Freezing Not suitable

To serve 6

2 lb	Sprats	900 g
	Salt and pepper	
3 oz	Plain flour	75 g
	Oil for frying	
1	Large onion	1
8	Sage leaves	8
6 tbsp	Vinegar	6x15 ml
4 tbsp	Water	4x15 ml

Clean the fish through the gills. Rinse and drain thoroughly. Season the flour and use to coat the fish. Heat 1 inch (2.5 cm) oil in a deep frying pan and fry the floured sprats, a few at a time, for about 4 minutes till crisp and golden. Drain on kitchen paper, then put into a shallow serving dish.

Peel and slice the onion. Heat 2 tbsp (2x15 ml) oil in frying pan, add the onion and fry gently till transparent. Add the sage leaves, vinegar and water and bring to the boil. Boil for 3 minutes, then remove from the heat and season.

Pour the hot marinade over the sprats. Cover and leave to marinate in a cool place overnight. Serve cold with crusty bread and butter.

Scrowled sprats

Overall timing 30 minutes plus salting

Freezing Not suitable

To serve 4

1 lb	Fresh sprats or pilchards	450 g
	Salt	
2	Sprigs of rosemary	2
2 oz	Butter	50 g
	Lemon wedges	

Cover the sprats or pilchards with salt and leave overnight.

The next day, rinse off the salt. Cut off the heads and tails, then slit each fish along the belly and remove the insides, including the backbone. Do this under cold running water. Dry the fish with kitchen paper.

Strip the rosemary leaves from the sprig. Melt the butter. Arrange the fish on the grill rack and sprinkle with the butter and rosemary. Grill until cooked, turning once. Serve with lemon wedges.

Mackerel in mushroom sauce

Overall timing 40 minutes

Freezing Not suitable

To serve 4

8 oz	Button mushrooms	225 g
2	Onions	2
1	Garlic clove	1
12 oz	Tomatoes	350 g
5 tbsp	Oil	5x15 ml
	Salt and pepper	
2 tbsp	White wine vinegar	2x15 ml
2 lb	Mackerel fillets	900 g
2 tbsp	Plain flour	2x15 ml

Slice mushrooms. Peel and finely chop onions. Peel and crush garlic. Wash tomatoes and cut into ½ inch (12.5 mm) thick slices.

Heat 2 tbsp (2x15 ml) of the oil in a saucepan. Add onions, mushrooms and garlic and fry for 10 minutes, stirring frequently. Season. Stir in the vinegar and boil rapidly till it evaporates.

Coat fillets with seasoned flour. Heat the remaining oil in a large frying pan, add the fillets and fry for 5 minutes on each side. Drain, arrange on a warmed serving dish and keep hot.

Add tomato slices to frying pan and fry for 2 minutes. Spoon mushroom mixture over fillets. Season tomatoes and arrange on top. Serve immediately with minted peas.

Bream with mushrooms

Overall timing 1 hour

Freezing Not suitable

To serve 2

2 lb	Bream or other whole fish	900 g
4 oz	Button mushrooms	125 g
1	Small onion	1
	Salt and pepper	
4 fl oz	Water	120 ml
1 teasp	Chopped parsley	5 ml
	Pinch of dried thyme	
1 oz	Butter	25 g
1	Lemon	1

Preheat the oven to 400°F (200°C) Gas 6.

Clean fish, but don't remove head. Trim tail and fins, and wash well. Dry on kitchen paper.

Thinly slice button mushrooms. Peel and finely chop onion. Cover bottom of ovenproof dish with most of mushrooms and onion and place the fish on top. Season with salt and pepper, and pour in the water. Sprinkle fish with parsley, thyme and remaining mushrooms and onion.

Melt butter and pour over fish. Cover dish with foil or a lid and bake for 40 minutes, basting frequently with juices in dish. Turn fish over halfway through cooking time and remove foil for last 10 minutes. The fish is cooked when the flesh becomes opaque.

Garnish with lemon and serve with boiled new potatoes.

Haddock creole

Overall timing 1 hour

Freezing Not suitable

To serve 4

1	Onion	1
1	Garlic clove	1
1	Red pepper	1
1	Green pepper	1
1 oz	Butter	25 g
2 tbsp	Oil	2x15 ml
14 oz	Can of tomatoes	397 g
	Salt and pepper	
2 lb	Haddock fillets	900 g
3 tbsp	Lemon juice	3x15 ml
	Chopped parsley	

Preheat the oven to 375°F (190°C) Gas 5.

Peel and chop onion and garlic. Deseed and slice peppers. Heat the butter and oil in a pan. Add onion, garlic and peppers and fry gently for 10 minutes.

Add tomatoes and mash with a wooden spoon to break them up. Season with salt and pepper. Bring to the boil and simmer gently for 10 minutes.

Place half tomato mixture in ovenproof dish, add haddock and season with salt and pepper. Sprinkle with lemon juice and cover with remaining tomato mixture.

Cover with lid or foil and bake for about 25 minutes. Sprinkle with chopped parsley and serve with plain boiled rice.

Haddock with potatoes and onions

Overall timing 45 minutes

Freezing Not suitable

To serve 4

2	Large onions	2
4	Potatoes	4
4 oz	Butter	125 g
2 lb	Haddock fillets	900 g
2 tbsp	Plain flour	2x15 ml
	Salt and pepper	
1 tbsp	Chopped parsley	15 ml
1 tbsp	Vinegar	15 ml

Peel and thinly slice the onions and potatoes. Melt half the butter in a frying pan, add the onions and cook till transparent.

Add remaining butter and potato slices and fry for 15 minutes, turning occasionally.

Meanwhile, wipe the haddock and pat dry with kitchen paper. Cut into small pieces and coat with seasoned flour. Add to pan and cook for a further 15 minutes, stirring from time to time.

Season with salt and pepper. Add parsley and vinegar and cook over a high heat till vinegar evaporates. Serve immediately with grilled tomatoes.

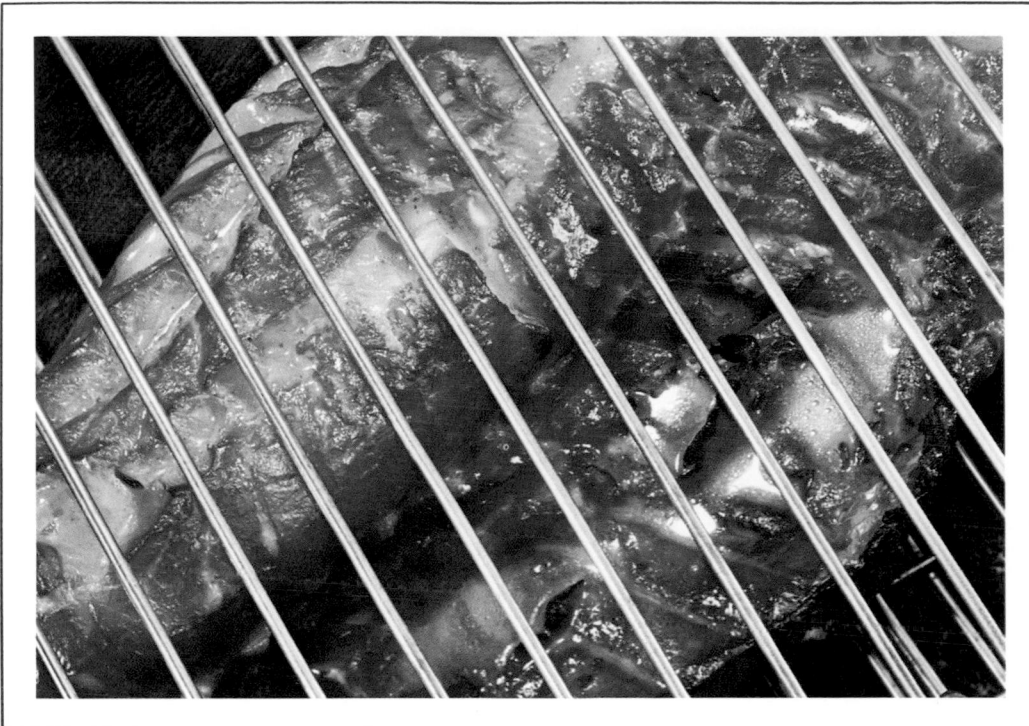

Barbecued haddock

Overall timing 20 minutes plus marination

Freezing Not suitable

To serve 2

1½ tbsp	Oil	22.5 ml
1½ teasp	Lemon juice	7.5 ml
1 tbsp	Soft brown sugar	15 ml
¼ teasp	Chilli powder	1.25 ml
½ teasp	Worcestershire sauce	2.5 ml
1 teasp	Tomato purée	5 ml
1 lb	Smoked haddock	450 g

Mix together oil, lemon juice, sugar, chilli powder, Worcestershire sauce and tomato purée in a shallow dish. Add the haddock, cover and marinate in the refrigerator for 1 hour, turning fish once or twice.

Preheat the grill.

Remove fish from marinade and place on a large piece of foil on the grill pan. Grill for 5–7 minutes on each side, brushing with marinade from time to time.

Alternatively, place the fish in a fish holder and barbecue over charcoal.

Trout with almonds

Overall timing 20 minutes

Freezing Not suitable

To serve 2

2	Trout, cleaned	2
1 oz	Plain flour	25 g
2 oz	Butter	50 g
2 tbsp	Chopped parsley	2x15 ml
2 oz	Flaked almonds	50 g
	Salt and pepper	
2	Lemon slices	2

Dust trout with flour. Melt butter in frying pan. Add trout and cook gently on one side for 5 minutes.

Turn trout over with a fish slice. Add half the parsley, the almonds and seasoning. Cook for a further 7–8 minutes till fish is tender and almonds are golden brown (turn them as they cook).

Place fish on warmed serving plates and spoon over almonds. Garnish with lemon slices and remaining chopped parsley. Serve with boiled potatoes and a mixed salad.

Welsh trout

Overall timing 45 minutes

Freezing Not suitable

To serve 2

1 teasp	Chopped fresh sage	5 ml
1 teasp	Chopped fresh rosemary	5 ml
1 teasp	Chopped fresh thyme	5 ml
1 tbsp	Chopped parsley	15 ml
	Salt and pepper	
2 oz	Butter	50 g
2x1 lb	Trout, cleaned	2x450 g
4	Streaky bacon rashers	4

Preheat the oven to 350°F (180°C) Gas 4.

Beat the herbs and seasoning into the butter and spread half inside each fish. Derind and stretch the bacon. Wrap two rashers around each fish, securing with wooden cocktail sticks.

Place the trout in a greased ovenproof dish, cover with foil and bake for about 25 minutes till tender.

Remove the cocktail sticks, place the trout on a warmed serving dish and garnish with lemon slices and sprigs of parsley. Surround with lettuce leaves, mustard and cress and tomato wedges and serve immediately.

Salmon cakes

Overall timing 25 minutes

Freezing Suitable: fry straight from frozen

To serve 4

1 lb	Boiled potatoes	450 g
2 tbsp	Milk	2x15 ml
1 oz	Butter	25 g
7½ oz	Can of salmon	212 g
2	Lemons	2
	Salt and pepper	
2	Eggs	2
2 tbsp	Plain flour	2x15 ml
4 tbsp	Dried breadcrumbs	4x15 ml
¼ pint	Oil	150 ml
	Lettuce leaves	

Mash the boiled potatoes with the milk and butter. Drain canned salmon and discard skin and bones. Mash flesh and add to potatoes.

Squeeze juice from one of the lemons. Add to salmon with seasoning to taste. Mix well and bind with one of the eggs.

Lightly beat remaining egg. Spread flour and dried breadcrumbs on separate plates. Divide salmon mixture into eight and shape into flat patties. Dip first in flour, then egg, then coat lightly with dried breadcrumbs.

Heat oil in frying pan. Add patties and fry for 5 minutes on each side until crisp and golden. Remove from pan with a draining spoon and arrange on serving plate. Serve immediately, garnished with lettuce leaves and the remaining lemon, cut into wedges.

Salmon pie

Overall timing 2 hours

Freezing Not suitable

To serve 6–8

1 lb	Frozen puff pastry	450 g
12 oz	Frozen spinach	350 g
1 lb	Canned salmon	450 g
1	Egg	1
8 oz	Long grain rice	225 g
3 tbsp	Single cream	3x15 ml
2 tbsp	Lemon juice	2x15 ml
	Salt and pepper	
3	Hard-boiled eggs	3

Thaw pastry and spinach. Drain and flake salmon. Separate egg. Cook rice, then mix with egg yolk, cream, lemon juice and seasoning.

Preheat the oven to 425°F (220°C) Gas 7. Roll out dough to two rectangles, one 9x14 inches (23x36cm), the other 11x16 inches (28x41cm). Put smallest one on damp baking tray.

Spread half rice over dough, leaving a border. Cover with half spinach and the salmon. Arrange hard-boiled eggs along centre and cover with remaining spinach and rice. Brush pastry border with lightly beaten egg white.

Place remaining dough over filling, seal edges and glaze with egg white.

Bake for 20 minutes. Reduce temperature to 350°F (180°C) Gas 4 and cook for a further 20 minutes.

Fish kebabs

Overall timing 25 minutes

Freezing Not suitable

To serve 4

1½ lb	Thick firm white fish	700 g
3 tbsp	Plain flour	3x15 ml
	Salt and pepper	
2	Eggs	2
1 teasp	Curry powder	5 ml
4 tbsp	Dried breadcrumbs	4x15 ml
8	Tomatoes	8
1 tbsp	Oil	15 ml

Preheat the grill.

Cut the fish into chunks and roll in seasoned flour to coat. Beat the eggs with the curry powder. Dip the floured fish pieces in the egg, then in the breadcrumbs, pressing the crumbs on to the fish. Cut the tomatoes into quarters. Thread fish and tomato pieces alternately on to greased skewers. Brush with oil.

Cook under the grill for 7–10 minutes till the fish is tender. Turn skewers over from time to time. Serve at once.

Indonesian fish curry

Overall timing 40 minutes

Freezing Not suitable

To serve 4

1½ lb	Cod or coley fillets	700 g
	Salt and pepper	
2 tbsp	Plain flour	2x15 ml
1	Onion	1
1	Large cooking apple	1
1 tbsp	Lemon juice	15 ml
2 oz	Butter	50 g
2 tbsp	Oil	2x15 ml
2 tbsp	Curry powder	2x15 ml
1 pint	Stock	560 ml
2 tbsp	Sultanas	2x15 ml
2 tbsp	Cornflour	2x15 ml
2 oz	Split almonds	50 g

Cut fish into pieces, sprinkle with salt and coat with the flour. Peel and slice onion. Peel, core and slice apple and sprinkle with the lemon juice.

Heat the butter and oil in a flameproof casserole. Add curry powder and onion and fry for 5 minutes. Add fish and cook for a few minutes on all sides. Add apple slices and cook for 3 minutes.

Pour stock into casserole and add sultanas. Blend cornflour with a little stock or water and stir in. Bring to the boil and simmer for 10–15 minutes.

Add almonds and cook for a further 2 minutes. Taste and adjust seasoning and serve.

Fish lasagne

Overall timing 1¼ hours

Freezing Suitable: reheat from frozen in 350°F (180°C) Gas 4 oven for 1 hour

To serve 4

1½ lb	Prepared mackerel	700 g
1	Onion	1
3 fl oz	Oil	90 ml
2	Garlic cloves	2
2 tbsp	Tomato purée	2x15 ml
	Salt and pepper	
1 lb	Fresh peas	450 g
4 oz	Mushrooms	125 g
8 oz	Lasagne	225 g
2 tbsp	Grated Parmesan cheese	2x15 ml
2 tbsp	Chopped parsley	2x15 ml

Cut fish into large pieces. Peel and chop onion. Heat 3 tbsp (3x15 ml) of oil in saucepan, add onion and fry until golden. Add fish and cook for 5 minutes, turning once.

Peel and crush garlic. Stir tomato purée into ¼ pint (150 ml) of water and add to pan with half garlic and seasoning. Cover and cook gently for 10 minutes.

Shell peas. Slice mushrooms. Heat 2 tbsp (2x15 ml) of oil in another saucepan, add peas, mushrooms and other half of garlic and cook for 5 minutes. Add 3 fl oz (90 ml) of water and seasoning, cover and cook for 10 minutes.

Meanwhile, cook lasagne in boiling salted water for 10–15 minutes or till tender. Drain thoroughly.

Preheat oven to 350°F (180°C) Gas 4.

Remove fish from pan and cut into pieces, discarding bones. Return to pan with mushroom mixture. Gradually stir in Parmesan and parsley.

Line greased ovenproof dish with one-third of lasagne, cover with one-third of fish mixture and sprinkle with a little oil. Repeat layers, finishing with fish mixture. Sprinkle with oil and bake for 20 minutes.

Cheesy fish croquettes

Overall timing 40 minutes

Freezing Suitable: reheat from frozen in 375°F (190°C) Gas 5 oven for 30 minutes

To serve 2

8 oz	White fish fillets	225 g
½ pint	Milk	300 ml
1	Small onion	1
2 oz	Butter	50 g
2 oz	Plain flour	50 g
1	Hard-boiled egg	1
1 tbsp	Grated Parmesan cheese	15 ml
	Salt and pepper	
	Oil for frying	

Place the fish fillets in a large frying pan with the milk. Cover and cook over a moderate heat for about 10 minutes till fish is tender. Lift fish out of milk. Discard skin and any bones, then mash flesh. Reserve fish and milk.

Peel and finely chop the onion. Melt the butter in clean frying pan and fry onion till transparent. Add the flour and cook for 2 minutes, stirring. Gradually stir in the reserved milk and bring to the boil.

Remove pan from heat and add the reserved fish. Shell and finely chop the hard-boiled egg and add to the sauce with the Parmesan and seasoning. Spread the mixture thickly on to a plate, cover and chill till firm.

Divide the mixture into four and shape on a well floured board into round patties about ½ inch (12.5 mm) thick.

Heat oil in deep-fryer to 340°F (170°C) and fry the croquettes for 5 minutes till crisp and golden. Drain on kitchen paper and serve hot.

Baked fish steaks

Overall timing 30 minutes

Freezing Not suitable

To serve 4

4	Cod steaks	4
	Salt and pepper	
¼ pint	Dry white wine or cider	150 ml
2 oz	Butter	50 g
2 tbsp	Chopped fresh coriander (optional)	2x15 ml
2 tbsp	Lemon or lime juice	2x15 ml

Preheat the oven to 425°F (220°C) Gas 7.

Wash and dry cod steaks. Place in a greased baking dish and sprinkle well with salt and pepper. Add the wine or cider and dot with butter.

Cover dish with foil and bake in centre of oven for about 25 minutes.

Sprinkle with chopped coriander, if used, and lemon or lime juice. Serve with mashed potatoes.

Fish in piquant sauce

Overall timing 1 hour

Freezing Not suitable

To serve 6

4 oz	Streaky bacon rashers	125 g
2 lb	Centre cut steak from large firm-fleshed fish	900 g
4 teasp	Olive oil	4x5 ml
1 oz	Butter	25 g
	Salt and pepper	
½ pint	Fish or chicken stock	300 ml
2 tbsp	Tomato purée	2x15 ml
3 tbsp	Lemon juice	3x15 ml

Derind and stretch the bacon rashers then wrap them round the fish, securing with cocktail sticks.

Heat the oil and butter in a flameproof casserole, add the fish and brown all over. Add salt, pepper, stock, tomato purée and lemon juice. Bring to the boil, cover tightly and simmer gently for 40 minutes, turning fish once.

Remove the fish from the casserole and discard bacon. Cut the fish into thick slices, place on a warmed serving dish and keep hot.

Taste the cooking liquor and adjust seasoning. Thicken if liked with ½ oz (15 g) each of butter and flour mashed together, then pour over the fish.

Tuna and pea casserole

Overall timing 40 minutes

Freezing Not suitable

To serve 4

1 lb	Waxy potatoes	450 g
	Salt and pepper	
8 oz	Frozen peas	225 g
7 oz	Can of tuna	198 g
2 oz	Butter	50 g
1	Onion	1
4 tbsp	Plain flour	4x15 ml
½ pint	Chicken stock	300 ml
½ pint	Milk	300 ml
4 oz	Cheddar cheese	125 g
2 tbsp	Fresh breadcrumbs	2x15 ml

Peel and dice potatoes. Cook in boiling salted water till tender. Add the peas and cook for a further 3 minutes.

Preheat the oven to 400°F (200°C) Gas 6.

Drain the potatoes and peas and put into an ovenproof dish. Drain and flake the tuna and stir into the vegetables.

Melt the butter in a saucepan. Peel and finely chop the onion and fry in the butter till pale golden. Add the flour and cook for 1 minute. Gradually stir in the stock and milk and bring to the boil, stirring. Grate the cheese. Add 3 oz (75 g) of the cheese and seasoning to the pan and stir. Pour over tuna mixture.

Mix the remaining cheese with the breadcrumbs and sprinkle over the top. Bake for 20 minutes.

Tuna stuffed loaf

Overall timing 50 minutes

Freezing Not suitable

To serve 4

2	Small round crusty loaves	2
1	Onion	1
4 oz	Button mushrooms	125 g
2 oz	Butter	50 g
2 tbsp	Plain flour	2x15 ml
10½ oz	Can of condensed mushroom soup	298 g
2	Egg yolks	2
2 tbsp	Single cream	2x15 ml
2x7 oz	Cans of tuna	2x198 g
2 tbsp	Lemon juice	2x15 ml
	Salt and pepper	
½ teasp	Paprika	2.5 ml
2	Lemon slices	2

Preheat the oven to 400°F (200°C) Gas 6.

Hollow out each loaf with a sharp knife to leave a thick shell. Place on a baking tray.

Peel and chop the onion. Wipe and thickly slice the mushrooms. Melt the butter in a saucepan, add the onion and fry till transparent. Add the mushrooms and fry for 2 minutes. Stir in the flour and cook for 1 minute. Gradually add the mushroom soup and bring to the boil, stirring constantly. Simmer for 2 minutes, then remove from the heat and allow to cool slightly.

Beat the egg yolks and cream into the mushroom sauce. Drain and flake the tuna and add to the sauce with the lemon juice. Season to taste.

Divide the hot tuna stuffing between the loaves and sprinkle with the paprika. Bake in the centre of the oven for about 25 minutes till bubbling and golden.

Arrange the loaves on a warmed serving dish and garnish each with a slice of lemon. Serve immediately.

Prawns ravigote

Overall timing 20 minutes plus marination

Freezing Not suitable

To serve 2

1	Stalk of celery	1
$\frac{1}{2}$	Red pepper	$\frac{1}{2}$
$\frac{1}{2}$	Green pepper	$\frac{1}{2}$
8 oz	Large shelled prawns	225 g
1 teasp	Chopped fresh herbs	5 ml
$\frac{1}{2}$	Round lettuce	$\frac{1}{2}$
1	Hard-boiled egg	1
Marinade		
1 tbsp	Soured cream	15 ml
4 tbsp	Thick mayonnaise	4x15 ml
1 tbsp	Lemon juice	15 ml
1 tbsp	White wine vinegar	15 ml
$\frac{1}{2}$ teasp	Made mustard	2.5 ml
	Salt and pepper	

To make marinade, mix the soured cream and mayonnaise in a bowl. Gradually add the lemon juice and vinegar, a few drops at a time, stirring constantly. Stir in the mustard and season to taste.

Trim the celery and cut into thin strips. Deseed and thinly slice the peppers. Place the prepared vegetables in a bowl and add the chopped prawns and herbs. Pour the marinade over, toss lightly and leave to marinate for 30 minutes.

Wash and dry the lettuce and line serving dish with the leaves. Spoon the prawn salad into the centre.

Shell the egg, cut in half and remove yolk. Slice the white; press yolk through a sieve. Use to garnish the salad.

Prawns magenta

Overall timing 40 minutes

Freezing Not suitable

To serve 2

2	Stalks of celery	2
1	Large carrot	1
1	Small leek	1
2 tbsp	Olive oil	2x15 ml
8 oz	Prawns	225 g
¼ pint	Dry white wine	150 ml
8 oz	Can of tomatoes	225 g
	Salt and pepper	
3	Fresh basil leaves	3
1 oz	Butter	25 g

Trim the celery and cut into thin sticks. Peel the carrot and cut into sticks. Trim and thinly slice the leek.

Heat the oil in a saucepan, add the prepared vegetables, cover and cook over a low heat for 10 minutes to release the flavours without browning vegetables.

Shell the prawns and add to the pan with the white wine and tomatoes and juice. Season, cover and cook over a low heat for 10 minutes, shaking pan occasionally.

Add the whole basil leaves and butter, adjust the seasoning and serve hot with boiled rice.

Roast pork with stuffing balls

Overall timing 2¼ hours

Freezing Not suitable

To serve 6

2½ lb	Rolled boned hindloin of pork	1.1 kg
	Oil	
	Salt	
Stuffing balls		
1	Onion	1
2 oz	Butter	50 g
4 oz	Fresh breadcrumbs	125 g
2 teasp	Dried sage	2x5 ml
	Salt and pepper	
2	Eggs	2
1 oz	Lard	25 g

Preheat the oven to 450°F (230°C) Gas 8.

Score the skin on the joint, then rub it well with oil and sprinkle with salt. Place in a roasting tin and roast for 20 minutes. Reduce the temperature to 375°F (190°C) Gas 5, and continue roasting for 1½ hours.

Meanwhile, make the stuffing balls. Peel and chop the onion. Melt the butter in a frying pan and fry the onion till golden. Tip the onion into a bowl and add the breadcrumbs, sage and seasoning. Bind with the eggs, then shape into small balls.

About 45 minutes before the pork has finished cooking, melt the lard in an oven-proof dish in the oven. Arrange the stuffing balls in the dish and place on a shelf below the pork. Turn once during the cooking.

Transfer the pork to a warmed serving platter and surround with the stuffing balls.

Roast pork with oranges

Overall timing 2¼ hours

Freezing Not suitable

To serve 6–8

3 lb	Rolled spare rib of pork	1.4 kg
1 oz	Butter	25 g
	Salt and pepper	
5	Oranges	5
2 tbsp	Lemon juice	2x15 ml
¼ pint	Hot water	150 ml
6	Sugar lumps	6
1 tbsp	Wine vinegar	15 ml
2 teasp	Arrowroot	2x5 ml

Preheat the oven to 450°F (230°C) Gas 8.

Place pork in a roasting tin. Spread butter over lean parts and rub salt and pepper into skin. Roast for 20 minutes.

Meanwhile, squeeze juice from two oranges.

Peel remaining oranges. Cut two into slices and one into segments.

Remove pork from tin and keep warm. Pour off any fat from tin and add orange and lemon juices and water. Stir well, scraping any sediment from bottom of tin. Reduce oven temperature to 400°F (200°C) Gas 6.

Replace meat in tin and roast for a further 1½ hours, basting occasionally.

Meanwhile, put sugar lumps into a saucepan with 1 tbsp (15 ml) water. Stir till dissolved, then boil rapidly, without stirring, till golden. Remove from heat and stir in vinegar. Return to heat and stir till caramel dissolves.

Place pork on a warmed serving dish. Stir cooking liquor from tin into caramel. Blend arrowroot with 2 tbsp (2x15 ml) water and add to caramel. Bring to the boil, stirring. Add the sliced and segmented oranges. Heat through for 1–2 minutes.

Cut pork into thick slices and arrange the pieces of orange around. Serve the sauce separately in a warmed sauceboat.

Cowboy's pork and beans

Overall timing 50 minutes

Freezing Not suitable

To serve 4

1½ lb	Belly of pork rashers	700 g
1	Large onion	1
2 tbsp	Oil	2x15 ml
2	Garlic cloves	2
¼ teasp	Chilli powder	1.25 ml
2 tbsp	Black treacle	2x15 ml
1 tbsp	Vinegar	15 ml
½ teasp	Powdered mustard	2.5 ml
2 tbsp	Tomato ketchup	2x15 ml
½ pint	Chicken stock	300 ml
	Salt and pepper	
2x14 oz	Cans of haricot beans	2x397 g

Preheat the oven to 425°F (220°C) Gas 7.

Cut the pork into ½ inch (12.5 mm) pieces, discarding any bones. Place in roasting tin with no extra fat. Cook in the oven for about 20 minutes till crisp and golden.

Meanwhile, peel and finely chop the onion. Heat the oil in a flameproof casserole and fry the onion till transparent. Peel and crush the garlic and add to the pan with the chilli powder. Fry, stirring, for 2 minutes.

Stir in the treacle, vinegar, mustard, ketchup and chicken stock. Bring to the boil, season and simmer for 5 minutes.

Drain and rinse the canned beans and add to the sauce.

Remove the pork from the oven and reduce the temperature to 350°F (180°C) Gas 4. Add the pork pieces to the beans with 1 tbsp (15 ml) of the fat from the tin. Put the casserole in the oven and cook for about 15 minutes, stirring once, till liquid is reduced by half. Taste and adjust the seasoning, then serve immediately with a tomato and onion salad and crusty bread.

Country pork with parsnips

Overall timing 2¼ hours

Freezing Not suitable

To serve 4–6

2½ lb	Piece of belly pork	1.1 kg
	Salt and pepper	
1 tbsp	Oil	15 ml
2 oz	Butter	50 g
2	Onions	2
2 lb	Parsnips	900 g
½ pint	Stock	300 ml
	Bouquet garni	
1 tbsp	Plain flour	15 ml
¼ pint	Dry white wine	150 ml

Preheat the oven to 400°F (200°C) Gas 6.

Wipe the pork and score the rind with a sharp knife. Rub salt and oil into the rind. Melt the butter in a roasting tin, place the pork in it and roast in the centre of the oven for 1 hour.

Meanwhile, peel and chop the onions. Peel and slice the parsnips.

Remove the roasting tin from the oven and arrange the onions and parsnips around the pork. Pour in the stock (made with cubes if necessary), add the bouquet garni and return to the oven. Roast for a further 45 minutes, basting the parsnips occasionally.

Discard the bouquet garni. Place the pork on a warmed serving dish and arrange the parsnips around it. Keep hot.

Pour all but 2 tbsp (2x15 ml) of the juices from the roasting tin into a jug. Sprinkle the flour into the tin and cook for 1 minute, stirring. Gradually add the reserved cooking liquor and the wine and bring to the boil, stirring constantly. Taste and adjust seasoning and spoon over the parsnips.

Meatballs and spinach

Overall timing 45 minutes

Freezing Not suitable

To serve 4

1 lb	Minced pork	450 g
1 tbsp	Chopped chives	15 ml
1	Egg	1
2 tbsp	Soy sauce	2x15 ml
4 tbsp	Oil	4x15 ml
2 tbsp	Dry sherry	2x15 ml
$\frac{1}{4}$ pint	Water	150 ml
2 lb	Spinach	900 g
1 teasp	Cornflour	5 ml
	Salt and pepper	

Pound minced pork with chives, egg and half the soy sauce till mixture binds together. Shape into eight balls.

Heat half the oil in a frying pan, add the meatballs and fry over a medium heat for 10 minutes, turning till browned. Add the remaining soy sauce, the sherry and water, bring to the boil, cover and simmer for 15 minutes.

Meanwhile, shred the spinach. Heat the remaining oil in another frying pan, add the spinach and stir-fry over a high heat for 3 minutes.

Blend the cornflour with 1 tbsp (15 ml) cold water and add to the meatballs. Bring to the boil, stirring till thickened. Season to taste.

Arrange the spinach on a warmed serving dish and place the meatballs on top. Spoon the sauce over the meatballs and serve with a side dish of soy sauce.

Braised pork with plum sauce

Overall timing 1¾ hours

Freezing Not suitable

To serve 6

2 oz	Lard	50 g
	Salt and pepper	
2½ lb	Boned and rolled loin of pork	1.1 kg
½ pint	Light stock	300 ml
3	Sage leaves	3
2 lb	Small potatoes	900 g
1½ lb	Red plums	700 g
2 oz	Sugar	50 g
1 tbsp	Chopped parsley	15 ml

Preheat the oven to 400°F (200°C) Gas 6.

Melt lard in a roasting tin. Season pork and fry quickly over a high heat till browned on all sides. Pour off the fat and reserve. Add the stock and sage leaves, cover the tin with foil and braise in the oven for 45 minutes.

Meanwhile, peel potatoes. Put into a saucepan, cover with cold salted water and bring to the boil. Drain.

Remove meat from oven and strain stock into a saucepan. Add reserved fat to roasting tin with the potatoes, return to the oven and cook uncovered for a further 50 minutes, basting the meat and potatoes occasionally.

Meanwhile, wash plums. Halve 1 lb (450 g) of them and discard stones. Add to the stock with the sugar. Bring to the boil, then cover and simmer for 10–15 minutes, stirring occasionally. Poach the rest of the plums whole in a little water till tender.

Remove meat from tin, carve into thick slices and arrange on a warmed serving plate. Arrange the potatoes and whole poached plums around the meat. Sprinkle with parsley. Lightly mash remaining plums and pour into a warmed sauceboat.

Iowa skillet chops

Overall timing 1 hour

Freezing Suitable

To serve 4

8	Pork loin chops	8
	Salt and pepper	
3 tbsp	Oil	3x15 ml
1 lb 12 oz	Can of tomatoes	794 g
1 tbsp	Tomato purée	15 ml
1 tbsp	Worcestershire sauce	15 ml
1	Onion	1
11½ oz	Can of sweetcorn kernels	326 g
1 tbsp	Arrowroot (optional)	15 ml
	Sprigs of parsley	

Sprinkle chops with salt and pepper. Heat oil in a frying pan and cook chops in two batches for 2 minutes on each side. When all chops are cooked, return first batch to pan. Remove from heat.

Purée the tomatoes with juice, tomato purée and Worcestershire sauce in a blender, then pour over chops. Finely chop the onion and add with the drained corn (use some of the corn water if the mixture is too thick). Bring back to the boil and add salt and pepper.

Cover the pan and cook over moderate heat for 25 minutes. Remove lid to reduce sauce a little and cook for a further 10 minutes. Thicken with arrowroot, if you like, blended with a little hot water, and cook till clear. Garnish with parsley and serve straight from the pan.

Barbecued pork chops

Overall timing 20 minutes plus marination

Freezing Not suitable

To serve 4

4	Pork spare rib chops	4
Marinade		
1	Large onion	1
2 tbsp	Lemon juice or vinegar	2x15 ml
2 tbsp	Oil	2x15 ml
½ teasp	Powdered mustard	2.5 ml
2 teasp	Worcestershire sauce	2x5 ml
½ teasp	Salt	2.5 ml
½ teasp	Freshly ground black pepper	2.5 ml
1 teasp	Granulated sugar	5 ml
½ teasp	Paprika	2.5 ml

Place pork chops in bowl. Peel and grate the onion and place in a jug. Add rest of marinade ingredients and mix well, then pour over chops. Leave to marinate for 1 hour in a cool place, turning chops at least twice.

Preheat the grill.

Cook the chops under the grill (or on a barbecue), occasionally brushing them with the reserved marinade. Serve with mixed salad, dressed with vinaigrette flavoured with fresh dill or other herb of choice.

Chinese spare ribs

Overall timing 45 minutes

Freezing Not suitable

To serve 4

1½ lb	Pork spare ribs	700 g
2 tbsp	Oil	2x15 ml
1 tbsp	Hoisin sauce	15 ml
1 tbsp	Soy sauce	15 ml
Sauce		
½ inch	Piece of root ginger	12.5 mm
1	Green pepper	1
2	Garlic cloves	2
2 tbsp	Oil	2x15 ml
1 tbsp	Soy sauce	15 ml
2 tbsp	Dry sherry	2x15 ml
2 tbsp	Tomato purée	2x15 ml
2 tbsp	Vinegar	2x15 ml
2 tbsp	Sugar	2x15 ml
1 tbsp	Cornflour	15 ml
4 tbsp	Pineapple juice	4x15 ml
3 tbsp	Water	3x15 ml

Separate the pork into ribs. Cook in boiling water for 15 minutes, then drain and dry on kitchen paper.

Heat oil in frying pan. Add ribs and stir in hoisin and soy sauces. Cook gently for 20 minutes.

Meanwhile, prepare sauce. Shred ginger. Deseed pepper and cut into thin strips. Peel and crush garlic. Heat oil in a saucepan, add garlic, ginger and pepper and stir-fry for 2 minutes. Remove from heat and stir in soy sauce, sherry, tomato purée, vinegar and sugar. Blend cornflour with fruit juice and water and add to the pan. Bring to the boil and cook for 2 minutes, stirring constantly.

Place ribs in a warmed serving dish. Pour sauce over and serve immediately with boiled rice.

Braised pork chops

Overall timing 55 minutes

Freezing Not suitable

To serve 2

4	Pork chops	4
	Salt and pepper	
2	Cooking apples	2
2	Onions	2
1 oz	Butter	25 g
3 fl oz	Water	90 ml
2 teasp	Worcestershire sauce	2x5 ml
	Fresh parsley	

Season chops with salt and pepper. Peel and core apples and cut into wedges. Peel onions and cut into rings.

Melt butter in frying pan and brown the chops on all sides. Add water and Worcestershire sauce, cover and cook for 10 minutes.

Turn chops over. Add apples and onions. Reduce heat, cover and cook for a further 30 minutes.

Garnish with parsley and serve with creamed potatoes.

Sweetbread bake

Overall timing 50 minutes

Freezing Not suitable

To serve 2

2 oz	Button mushrooms	50 g
8 oz	Prepared lambs' sweetbreads	225 g
	Salt and pepper	
2 tbsp	Plain flour	2x15 ml
1 oz	Butter	25 g
5 tbsp	Chicken stock	5x15 ml
1	Small egg	1
5 tbsp	Plain yogurt	5x15 ml
2 oz	Cheese	50 g
	Chopped parsley	

Preheat the oven to 375°F (190°C) Gas 5.

Slice the mushrooms. Cut the sweetbreads into $\frac{1}{4}$ inch (6 mm) thick slices. Season the flour and toss the sweetbreads in it till lightly coated.

Melt butter in a frying pan, add the sweetbreads and mushrooms and fry for about 10 minutes till golden. Add the stock and seasoning and simmer for 5 minutes.

Meanwhile, beat the egg with yogurt, grated cheese and seasoning.

Arrange the sweetbreads and mushrooms in an ovenproof dish and pour the yogurt mixture over. Bake for 20 minutes till lightly set and golden. Sprinkle with parsley and serve hot.

Orange pork rolls

Overall timing 1 hour

Freezing Not suitable

To serve 6

6x4oz	Slices of lean pork	6x125g
1	Onion	1
3oz	Butter	75g
4oz	Fresh breadcrumbs	125g
2 tbsp	Chopped parsley	2x15ml
1 teasp	Dried mixed herbs	5ml
	Salt and pepper	
1	Large orange	1
1	Egg	1
2 tbsp	Plain flour	2x15ml
¼ pint	Cider	150ml
¼ pint	Chicken stock	150ml

Preheat the oven to 375°F (190°C) Gas 5.

Place slices of pork between damp grease-proof and beat till very thin. Peel and finely chop onion. Melt 1oz (25g) of the butter in a frying pan and fry onion till golden. Add breadcrumbs, parsley, herbs and seasoning. Cook for 2 minutes, then remove from the heat.

Grate orange rind into stuffing, add egg and mix well. Divide stuffing between pork slices. Roll them up carefully, turning sides in to cover stuffing, and secure with wooden cock-tail sticks.

Arrange rolls in roasting tin and dot with remaining butter. Squeeze orange and pour juice over. Cook in the oven for about 35 minutes, basting occasionally, till pork is tender.

Place pork rolls on a warmed serving dish and keep hot. Sprinkle flour into roasting tin and stir over heat for 1 minute. Gradually add cider and stock and bring to the boil, stirring. Season to taste, pour into a sauce boat and serve with the pork rolls.

Sweet and sour pork

Overall timing 40 minutes plus marination

Freezing Suitable

To serve 4

1 lb	Lean pork	450 g
2 tbsp	Dry sherry	2x15 ml
	Salt and pepper	
1	Egg	1
3 tbsp	Plain flour	3x15 ml
3 tbsp	Oil	3x15 ml
2	Carrots	2
2	Onions	2
1	Large cucumber	1
1	Garlic clove	1
4 tbsp	Tomato ketchup	4x15 ml
2 teasp	Soy sauce	2x5 ml
2 tbsp	Vinegar	2x15 ml
1 tbsp	Brown sugar	15 ml
1 tbsp	Cornflour	15 ml
½ pint	Water	300 ml

Cut meat into ½ inch (12.5 mm) cubes. Put into a bowl with sherry and seasoning and marinate for 30 minutes.

Lightly beat egg. Dip pork cubes in egg, then coat with flour. Heat oil in a large frying pan. Fry pork for 8 minutes till golden brown on all sides. Remove from pan.

Peel and chop carrots, onions and cucumber. Peel and crush garlic. Add all to frying pan and stir-fry for 5 minutes over fairly high heat. Reduce heat to moderate. Add ketchup, soy sauce, vinegar, sugar, cornflour dissolved in water and reserved marinade to the pan. Bring to the boil and cook for 3 minutes, stirring.

Return pork to pan and cook for 3 minutes more till heated through. Serve with plain boiled rice and side dishes of tomato wedges, chunks of cucumber and a little desiccated coconut for sprinkling over the finished dish.

Roast pork with turnips

Overall timing 2¼ hours

Freezing Not suitable

To serve 6

2½ lb	Rolled hindloin of pork	1.1 kg
1	Garlic clove	1
2 oz	Butter	50 g
	Salt and pepper	
2 lb	Small turnips	900 g
2 teasp	Caster sugar	2x5 ml
¾ pint	Light stock	400 ml
1 tbsp	Plain flour	15 ml
1 tbsp	Chopped parsley	15 ml

Preheat the oven to 425°F (220°C) Gas 7.

Peel the garlic clove, cut in half and rub all over the pork. Place the pork in a roasting tin and spread the butter over. Sprinkle with salt and pepper and roast in the centre of the oven for 20 minutes. Reduce the temperature to 375°F (190°C) Gas 5 and cook for a further 40 minutes.

Meanwhile, peel and halve or quarter the turnips according to size. Put into a saucepan, cover with cold salted water and bring to the boil. Drain, then dry on kitchen paper.

Arrange the turnips round the pork. Sprinkle with the sugar and add the stock (made with a cube if necessary). Cover with foil and roast for 30 minutes. Remove the foil, turn the turnips over and cook for a further 15 minutes. Test pork for doneness and cook a little longer if necessary.

Place the pork in a warmed serving dish and carve into thick slices. Arrange the turnips on the dish and keep hot.

Pour off liquid from tin and reserve. Sprinkle the flour into the tin and cook, stirring, for 1 minute. Gradually add the reserved liquid and bring to the boil, stirring constantly. Adjust seasoning. Sprinkle the parsley over the turnips and serve.

Polish-style pork with sauerkraut

Overall timing 1 hour

Freezing Not suitable

To serve 6

3 tbsp	Oil	3x15ml
6	Pork loin chops	6
1	Large onion	1
1	Garlic clove	1
	Salt and pepper	
2lb	Sauerkraut	900g
1	Bay leaf	1
½ pint	Chicken stock	300ml
1	Large dessert apple	1
1 teasp	Cumin seeds	5ml

Heat the oil in flameproof casserole and fry the chops till browned on both sides. Remove from the pan and reserve.

Peel and finely chop the onion; peel and crush the garlic. Add both to the casserole and fry till transparent. Season, and add the drained sauerkraut and bay leaf. Arrange the chops on top. Pour the stock over, bring to the boil and simmer for 15 minutes.

Meanwhile, peel, core and dice the apple. Add to the pan with cumin seeds and stir well, then simmer for a further 15 minutes till the chops are tender.

Taste and adjust the seasoning. Discard the bay leaf. Serve with creamed potatoes, buttered carrots and thin slices of wholemeal bread.

Pork and beans

Overall timing 2¾ hours plus overnight soaking

Freezing Not suitable

To serve 4

1 lb	Dried butter beans	450 g
1	Onion	1
12	Cloves	12
2	Garlic cloves	2
2½ pints	Boiling water	1.5 litres
4 tbsp	Oil	4x15 ml
	Salt and pepper	
1 lb	Piece of smoked streaky bacon or belly of pork	450 g

Put the beans in a large saucepan of cold water and soak overnight.

The next day, bring to the boil and cook beans for 15 minutes. Drain.

Peel onion, spike with the cloves and add to pan with peeled garlic, boiling water, oil, pepper and bacon or belly pork, derinded and cut into thick rashers if easier to handle. Cover and simmer for 1½ hours. Taste and add salt, then cook for a further 30 minutes.

Remove spiked onion and garlic. Remove meat and beans from pan with a draining spoon and place in warmed serving dish. Keep hot.

Reduce cooking liquor to about ¼ pint (150 ml) by boiling fast, uncovered. Pour over beans and serve.

Frankfurter fritters

Overall timing 30 minutes

Freezing Not suitable

To serve 6

5 oz	Plain flour	150 g
	Salt and pepper	
1	Egg	1
1 tbsp	Oil	15 ml
4 fl oz	Beer	120 ml
	Oil for frying	
16	Frankfurters	16
2	Egg whites	2

Sift 4 oz (125 g) of the flour into a bowl with 1½ teasp (7.5 ml) salt and make a well in the centre. Add the whole egg and oil and mix with a wooden spoon. Gradually add the beer and mix to a smooth batter.

Heat the oil in a deep-fryer to 340°F (170°C).

Season the remaining flour. Cut the frankfurters in half and toss in flour. Whisk the egg whites till stiff but not dry and fold into the batter. Dip each frankfurter half into the batter and fry in the oil for about 3 minutes till crisp and golden. Drain on kitchen paper and serve hot.

Pork and sausage stew

Overall timing 1¾ hours

Freezing Not suitable

To serve 6

1½ lb	Onions	700 g
2 oz	Lard	50 g
6	Thin cut pork loin chops	6
1 lb	Coarse pork sausages	450 g
2 tbsp	Plain flour	2x15 ml
¾ pint	Chicken stock	400 ml
3 tbsp	Tomato purée	3x15 ml
	Salt and pepper	

Peel and thinly slice the onions. Heat the lard in a flameproof casserole, add the onions and fry gently for 10 minutes till pale golden.

Meanwhile, wipe the chops and remove the bones and any excess fat. Twist the sausages in half.

Sprinkle flour over the onions and cook for 1 minute. Gradually add the stock (made with a cube if necessary) and bring to the boil, stirring. Stir in the tomato purée.

Add the chops and sausages. Bring to the boil, cover and simmer for 1¼ hours, or cook in the centre of the oven preheated to 350°F (180°C) Gas 4 for 1¼ hours.

Adjust the seasoning to taste, then serve immediately with buttered pasta and a green salad.

Belgian pork chops

Overall timing 40 minutes

Freezing Not suitable

To serve 4

4	Pork chops	4
	Salt and pepper	
2 tbsp	Plain flour	2x15 ml
3 tbsp	Oil	3x15 ml
4	Onions	4
¼ pint	Beer	150 ml
¼ pint	Chicken stock	150 ml
1½ lb	Brussels sprouts	700 g
1 oz	Butter	25 g
2 teasp	Cornflour	2x5 ml

Coat the chops with seasoned flour. Heat oil in frying pan and cook chops for 3 minutes on each side.

Peel and thinly slice onions. Add to pan and cook for 5 minutes. Pour in beer and stock, season and simmer for 15 minutes.

Meanwhile, trim sprouts and cook in boiling water till just tender. Drain well, toss with butter and keep hot.

Remove chops from pan and place on warmed serving plate. Surround with sprouts. Mix cornflour with a little cold water and add to pan. Bring to the boil and cook for 2 minutes. Pour sauce over chops.

Porkburgers

Overall timing 25 minutes

Freezing Suitable: cook from frozen

To serve 6

1½ lb	Lean pork	700 g
	Salt and pepper	
1	Onion	1
1 teasp	Dried thyme	5 ml
1 tbsp	Oil	15 ml
	Lemon slices	

Mince the pork twice till fine and add plenty of salt and pepper. Peel and finely chop the onion and add to the pork with the dried thyme. Mix well with a wooden spoon.

Divide the meat into six portions and shape into thick burgers about 4 inches (10 cm) in diameter.

Brush a heavy-based frying pan or griddle with oil and heat well. Add the burgers and fry for about 10–15 minutes. Turn burgers carefully with a fish slice and cook for a further 5–10 minutes according to taste.

Garnish with lemon slices and serve with an endive and tomato salad or with chips.

Kidney-stuffed roast pork

Overall timing 3½ hours

Freezing Not suitable

To serve 6–8

1	Calf's kidney	1
4 lb	Boned loin of pork	1.8 kg
	Sprig of thyme	
	Salt and pepper	
6 oz	Butter	175 g
1½ lb	Cooked potatoes	700 g
3 tbsp	Oil	3 x 15 ml
1 lb	Button mushrooms	450 g
1 tbsp	Chopped parsley	15 ml

Preheat the oven to 375°F (190°C) Gas 5.

Prepare kidney. Spread out the pork loin and put kidney in the centre with thyme and seasoning. Roll meat tightly round kidney and tie at regular intervals with string. Place meat in roasting tin with 2 oz (50 g) of the butter. Roast for 3 hours, basting occasionally.

Meanwhile, slice cooked potatoes. Melt 2 oz (50 g) of the butter with the oil in a frying pan, add the potatoes and fry until golden.

Halve mushrooms. Melt remaining butter in another frying pan and cook the mushrooms for 5 minutes, shaking the pan from time to time.

Place meat on warmed serving plate. Surround with drained potatoes and mushrooms and garnish with chopped parsley. Serve with gravy made from roasting juices.

Pork cassoulet

Overall timing 3¼ hours plus soaking

Freezing Not suitable

To serve 6

1 lb	Dried haricot beans	450 g
1	Pig's trotter	1
4 oz	Pork rind	125 g
2	Garlic cloves	2
2	Carrots	2
2	Onions	2
	Bouquet garni	
8 oz	Italian salami	225 g
	Salt and pepper	
2 tbsp	Oil	2x15 ml
14 oz	Can of tomatoes	397 g
1 oz	Fresh breadcrumbs	25 g

Soak beans overnight.

Quarter trotter lengthways. Chop pork rind. Add to beans with peeled garlic, carrots, one onion and bouquet garni. Cover with water, cover and simmer for 1¼ hours.

Peel salami, prick and add to pan with seasoning. Cook for 15 minutes.

Chop remaining onion. Heat oil in a saucepan and fry onion till transparent. Add 1 pint (560 ml) water, tomatoes and seasoning. Simmer for 10 minutes.

Preheat the oven to 350°F (180°C) Gas 4.

Drain beans, reserving pork rind. Add sausage and trotter to other pan. Line deep ovenproof dish with pork rind. Add layers of beans and meat mixture; top with crumbs. Bake for 30 minutes.

Rib and bean stew

Overall timing 1½ hours plus soaking

Freezing Not suitable

To serve 4–6

8 oz	Dried borlotti beans	225 g
2	Carrots	2
2	Stalks of celery	2
2	Bay leaves	2
2 lb	Pork spare ribs	900 g
2	Large onions	2
4 tbsp	Oil	4x15 ml
14 oz	Can of tomatoes	397 g
4 tbsp	Tomato purée	4x15 ml
1 tbsp	Sugar	15 ml
¾ pint	Chicken stock	400 ml
	Salt and pepper	

Soak beans overnight, then drain and cover with fresh water. Slice carrots and celery and add to beans with bay leaves. Simmer for 1 hour.

Separate ribs. Peel and finely chop onions. Heat oil in saucepan and fry onions till transparent. Add ribs and brown all over. Add tomatoes, tomato purée, sugar and stock and bring to the boil.

Drain beans and add to meat. Season and simmer for 15 minutes till meat is tender and cooking liquor is thick.

Pork and treacle casserole

Overall timing 1¾ hours

Freezing Not suitable

To serve 6

1 lb	Lean boned pork	450 g
1½ lb	Thick belly of pork rashers	700 g
	Salt and pepper	
2 tbsp	Plain flour	2x15 ml
3	Large onions	3
2	Garlic cloves	2
2 oz	Lard	50 g
3 tbsp	Treacle	3x15 ml
2 tbsp	Tomato purée	2x15 ml
14 oz	Can of tomatoes	397 g
¾ pint	Beef stock	400 ml

Preheat the oven to 350°F (180°C) Gas 4.

Wipe and trim the boned pork and cut into cubes. Remove any bones from the belly of pork but leave rind on. Cut pork into 1 inch (2.5 cm) pieces. Toss in seasoned flour. Peel and slice the onions; peel and crush the garlic.

Heat the lard in a flameproof casserole, add the pork and fry over a high heat till browned all over. Remove with a draining spoon and reserve.

Add the onions to the pan and fry till transparent. Pour off any excess fat. Stir in the treacle, tomato purée and garlic. Return the pork to the pan and stir till coated. Add the canned tomatoes and juice, stock (made with a cube if necessary) and seasoning and bring to the boil, stirring to break up the tomatoes. Cover and cook in the centre of the oven for 45 minutes.

Remove the lid and stir the casserole. Cook uncovered for a further 30 minutes till the pork is tender.

Adjust seasoning to taste and serve immediately with buttered noodles.

Pork brochettes

Overall timing 30 minutes

Freezing Not suitable

To serve 4

1 lb	Lean pork	450 g
4 oz	Belly pork rashers	125 g
2	Pigs' kidneys	2
12	Bay leaves	12
	Oil	
	Salt and pepper	

Cut lean pork into 1 inch (2.5 cm) cubes. Remove rind from the belly pork rashers and chop them. Wash and dry kidneys. Cut them open, remove the fat and cut each into four.

Preheat grill.

Arrange bay leaves, meat cubes, belly pork and kidney pieces on skewers. Brush with a little oil and season liberally.

Grill for about 20 minutes, turning skewers occasionally. Serve with boiled rice and peas or a mixed salad with French dressing.

Baked pork chops

Overall timing 40 minutes

Freezing Not suitable

To serve 4

4	Pork chops	4
	Salt and pepper	
2 tbsp	Oil	2x15 ml
1 lb	Cooking apples	450 g
1 oz	Butter	25 g
1 tbsp	Chopped fresh rosemary	15 ml
¼ pint	Stock	150 ml

Preheat the oven to 400°F (200°C) Gas 6.

Season chops with salt and pepper. Heat oil in a flameproof casserole and brown the chops for 2 minutes on each side.

Peel, core and slice apples. Arrange in casserole round the chops and dot with the butter. Sprinkle with rosemary, add stock (made with ½ stock cube if liked) and cover casserole.

Bake in the centre of the oven for about 30 minutes, removing lid for last 10 minutes of cooking time. Serve with creamed potatoes and salad.

Pork chops with bananas

Overall timing 30 minutes

Freezing Not suitable

To serve 4

1 oz	Butter	25 g
4	Pork chops	4
3	Small, firm bananas	3
	Salt and pepper	
	Pinch of cayenne pepper	
1	Lemon	1
	Sprigs of parsley	
1 teasp	Plain flour	5 ml
¼ pint	Stock	150 ml

Melt the butter in a frying pan over medium heat. Add the chops and cook for 10–12 minutes on each side depending on thickness.

Five minutes before the chops are cooked, peel bananas and cut in half lengthways. Add to the frying pan and sprinkle with salt, pepper and cayenne.

Lift out the pork chops and bananas and arrange on a warmed serving dish. Garnish with lemon and parsley.

Stir the flour into the pan juices and add the stock gradually. Simmer for 2–3 minutes, then pour this gravy into a small serving jug.

Serve with plain boiled rice which will provide a contrast to the sweeter meat and bananas.

Pot roast pork with apples

Overall timing 1½ hours

Freezing Not suitable

To serve 4–6

2 oz	Butter	50 g
3¼ lb	Rolled pork	1.5 kg
	Salt and pepper	
2 tbsp	Cinnamon	2x15 ml
8	Granny Smith apples	8

Preheat oven to 400°F (200°C) Gas 6.

Melt 1 oz (25 g) butter in a flameproof casserole. Roll pork joint in a mixture of salt, pepper and half the cinnamon, then brown on all sides. Cover casserole and cook on the middle shelf of the oven for about 1 hour, turning joint over halfway through.

Peel and core apples and cut into quarters. Put into a saucepan with remaining butter and cinnamon. Cover and cook for about 10 minutes over a low heat, shaking the pan to prevent sticking.

Arrange the apples around the roast 15 minutes before the end of cooking time.

Remove pork from casserole; slice and place on warmed serving plate. Surround with apples. Make gravy from cooking juices and serve separately.

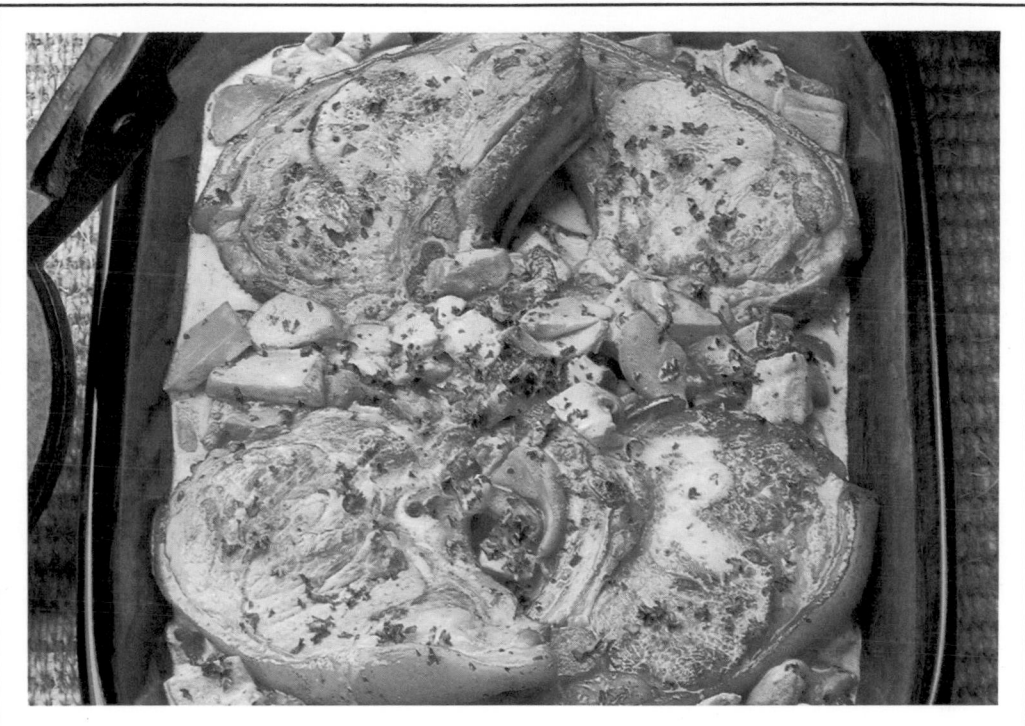

Russian pork chop casserole

Overall timing 30 minutes

Freezing Not suitable

To serve 4

1 lb	Potatoes	450 g
2 tbsp	Oil	2x15 ml
4	Pork rib chops	4
	Salt and pepper	
3 tbsp	Water	3x15 ml
4 oz	Button mushrooms	125 g
1 teasp	Garlic salt	5 ml
¼ pint	Carton of soured cream	150 ml
2 tbsp	Chopped parsley	2x15 ml

Peel potatoes and cut them into very small, thin pieces. Melt the oil in a flameproof casserole and fry the potatoes for 5 minutes. Remove from pan with draining spoon.

Season chops with salt and pepper. Add to casserole and cook for 1 minute on each side. Drain off excess fat. Add water, cover and cook for 10 minutes.

Slice mushrooms. Add to casserole with fried potatoes and garlic salt and cook for a further 10 minutes. Stir in soured cream and 1 tbsp (15 ml) of the chopped parsley. Heat through. Sprinkle with remaining parsley just before serving.

Scandinavian pork

Overall timing 2½ hours plus soaking

Freezing Not suitable

To serve 6–8

8 oz	Plump prunes	225 g
1	Large cooking apple	1
2 tbsp	Lemon juice	2x15 ml
3 lb	Piece of belly of pork	1.4 kg
	Salt and pepper	
1 tbsp	Oil	15 ml
½ pint	Stock	300 ml
2 tbsp	Plain flour	2x15 ml
	Sprigs of parsley	

Soak prunes in ½ pint (300 ml) hot water for 1 hour.

Preheat the oven to 375°F (190°C) Gas 5.

Drain prunes, reserving soaking water, and remove stones. Peel, core and slice apple. Toss in lemon juice to prevent browning and add to prunes.

Season pork. Place apple and prunes along the centre, then roll up lengthways and tie into a neat shape with fine string. Place in a roasting tin and rub oil into skin. Sprinkle with salt and roast for 45 minutes.

Pour prune soaking liquor and stock over pork. Reduce the temperature to 350°F (180°C) Gas 4 and roast for a further 1¼ hours.

Place the meat on a warmed serving dish, discard the string and keep hot. Drain pan juices into a small saucepan and skim off any fat. Blend flour to a smooth paste with 4 tbsp (4x15 ml) cold water. Add to meat juices and bring to the boil, stirring constantly. Simmer for 4–5 minutes. Carve pork into thick slices and garnish with sprigs of parsley. Serve with gravy.

Pork with bananas and peanuts

Overall timing 1¾ hours

Freezing Not suitable

To serve 4

12 oz	Onions	350 g
2	Garlic cloves	2
4 tbsp	Oil	4x15 ml
2 lb	Pork (top of belly)	900 g
3 oz	Rice	75 g
14 oz	Can of tomatoes	397 g
1	Chicken stock cube	1
¼ teasp	Paprika	1.25 ml
¼ teasp	Ground cinnamon	1.25 ml
8 oz	Potatoes	225 g
2	Bananas	2
2 oz	Salted peanuts	50 g
	Salt	

Peel and chop onions. Peel and crush garlic. Heat 2 tbsp (2x15 ml) of the oil in saucepan. Add onions and garlic and fry until browned.

Cut pork into cubes and add to pan with rice. Cook till rice has absorbed oil, stirring frequently to prevent sticking. Add a little water if necessary to prevent burning. Remove from heat.

Pour juice from canned tomatoes into jug. Crumble in stock cube and make up to ¾ pint (400 ml) with boiling water. Chop tomatoes and add to pan with stock mixture, paprika and cinnamon. Cover and simmer gently for 20 minutes.

Meanwhile, peel and cube potatoes. Heat remaining oil in a frying pan and fry potatoes over a low heat for about 10 minutes. Add them to the pan. Peel and slice bananas and stir into the stew with the peanuts. Cook for 10 minutes. Taste and add salt if necessary.

Pork chops with wine sauce

Overall timing 30 minutes

Freezing Not suitable

To serve 2

1 oz	Butter	25 g
2	Pork chops	2
	Salt and pepper	
1	Small onion	1
3 tbsp	Dry white wine	3x15 ml
3 tbsp	Water	3x15 ml
1½ teasp	Tomato purée	7.5 ml
4	Gherkins	4
1 teasp	Chopped parsley	5 ml
½ teasp	Made mustard	2.5 ml

Melt the butter in the frying pan and cook the pork chops gently for 10–12 minutes on each side. Season. Place on warmed serving dish and keep warm.

Peel and finely chop onion. Add to pan and fry till transparent. Stir in wine, water, tomato purée and seasoning and bring to the boil, stirring. Simmer for 3 minutes.

Remove pan from heat. Thinly slice two of the gherkins and stir into the sauce with the parsley and mustard. Pour sauce over chops. Garnish with remaining gherkins, cut into fan shapes, and serve with macaroni or noodles.

Beef

Beef pot roast

Overall timing 3 hours plus marination

Freezing Suitable: reheat, in sauce, in 400°F (200°C) Gas 6 oven for 1 hour

To serve 8–10

4lb	Braising beef	1.8kg
	Salt and pepper	
6oz	Pork fat with rind	175g
1	Large onion	1
3	Carrots	3
3	Stalks of celery	3
1	Garlic clove	1
	Sprigs of parsley	
2	Bay leaves	2
	Sprigs of thyme	
½ pint	Red or white wine	300ml
1oz	Butter	25g
2 tbsp	Oil	2x15ml
1	Pig's trotter	1
4fl oz	Water	120ml
1 tbsp	Tomato purée	15ml

Season the beef. Slice the pork fat. Wrap the fat around the beef and secure with string. Peel and chop the onion and carrots. Trim and chop the celery. Peel and crush the garlic. Tie the parsley, bay leaves and thyme together with string (or use a bouquet garni).

Put the beef in a bowl and add the prepared vegetables, herbs, wine and seasoning. Marinate overnight.

The next day, drain the beef, reserving the marinade. Pat the beef dry with kitchen paper. Melt the butter with the oil in a flameproof casserole and brown the beef on all sides.

Split the trotter and add to the casserole with the marinade, water and tomato purée. Bring to the boil, then cover and simmer for 2½ hours.

Transfer the beef to a warmed serving platter and keep hot. Strain the cooking liquor, discarding the trotter and vegetables, and return to the casserole. Boil the liquor till reduced, then pour into sauceboat. Serve beef with sauce, and carrots and button onions.

Salt beef

Overall timing 3½ hours plus 2 weeks salting

Freezing Not suitable

To serve 8–10

2 lb	Coarse salt	900 g
4 oz	Sugar	125 g
1 tbsp	Saltpetre	15 ml
1 oz	Pickling spice	25 g
4	Bay leaves	4
1	Sprig of thyme	1
5 lb	Silverside or brisket of beef	2.3 kg
3	Large onions	3
5	Cloves	5
1	Stalk of celery	1
1 teasp	Black peppercorns	5 ml
1 lb	Medium carrots	450 g
2	Medium turnips	2
1 lb	Leeks	450 g

Put salt, sugar and saltpetre into a large saucepan with pickling spices tied in muslin. Add bay leaves, thyme and 8 pints (4.5 litres) water and heat gently, stirring, till sugar and salt have dissolved. Bring to the boil, then pour into bowl and cool.

Add meat to bowl, making sure that salt solution covers it. Cover with clean tea-towel and leave to soak in cold place for up to 2 weeks. Turn meat occasionally.

To cook, remove from pickle and wash under cold running water. Put into a large saucepan with one onion, peeled and spiked with cloves. Chop celery and add to pan with peppercorns. Cover with cold water and bring to the boil slowly. Skim, reduce heat, cover and simmer for 2½ hours.

Meanwhile, peel and chop carrots and turnips. Peel remaining onions and slice thickly. Chop leeks. Add vegetables to pan, bring back to the boil and simmer for 30 minutes. Use strained cooking liquor to make a sauce.

Beef and bean casserole

Overall timing 3 hours plus soaking

Freezing Suitable: reheat from frozen in 325°F (170°C) Gas 3 oven

To serve 4–6

8 oz	Dried haricot beans	225 g
2	Onions	2
2 tbsp	Oil	2x15 ml
1 lb	Stewing beef	450 g
¼ teasp	Chilli powder	1.25 ml
1 teasp	Curry powder	5 ml
2 tbsp	Plain flour	2x15 ml
½ pint	Beef stock	300 ml
14 oz	Can of tomatoes	397 g
2 tbsp	Tomato purée	2x15 ml
2 teasp	Sugar	2x5 ml
	Salt and pepper	
1	Large cooking apple	1
2 oz	Sultanas	50 g

Put beans in a large saucepan and cover with cold water. Bring to the boil. Boil for 2 minutes, then remove from the heat, cover and leave to soak for 2 hours.

Preheat the oven to 325°F (170°C) Gas 3.

Peel and chop onions. Heat oil in a flame-proof casserole and fry onions for 3 minutes. Cut beef into chunks. Add to pan and fry quickly till brown. Stir in the chilli and curry powder and flour. Fry for 2 minutes.

Gradually add stock and bring to the boil, stirring. Add the tomatoes with their juice and tomato purée. Drain beans and add to casserole with the sugar and seasoning. Cover and cook in the oven for 2 hours.

Peel, core and chop apple. Stir into casserole with sultanas and cook for a further 30 minutes. Taste and adjust seasoning. Serve with crusty bread.

Beef and mushroom stuffed tomatoes

Overall timing 1¼ hours

Freezing Not suitable

To serve 3–4

6	Large tomatoes	6
1	Onion	1
1 oz	Butter	25 g
1 lb	Lean minced beef	450 g
4 oz	Mushrooms	125 g
1 tbsp	Chopped parsley	15 ml
6 tbsp	Dry white wine	6x15 ml
	Salt and pepper	
1 oz	Fresh breadcrumbs	25 g
	Lemon wedges	

Preheat the oven to 350°F (180°C) Gas 4.

Halve the tomatoes and scoop out the flesh. Chop the flesh. Peel and chop the onion. Melt the butter in a frying pan and fry the onion till transparent. Add the beef and fry for 5 minutes.

Chop the mushrooms and add to the pan with the parsley, chopped tomato flesh, wine and seasoning. Cover and cook for 10 minutes.

Stir in the breadcrumbs. Spoon the mixture into the tomato halves. Arrange in an ovenproof dish and bake for 25–30 minutes till the tops are brown and crisp. Garnish with lemon wedges and serve with mashed potatoes.

Beef and split pea stew

Overall timing 2 hours plus soaking

Freezing Not suitable

To serve 6

12 oz	Split peas	350 g
1	Onion	1
1½ lb	Braising steak	700 g
1 oz	Butter	25 g
2 tbsp	Oil	2x15 ml
2	Large carrots	2
	Bouquet garni	
¼ teasp	Grated nutmeg	1.25 ml
1½ pints	Beef stock	850 ml
	Salt and pepper	
8 oz	Potatoes	225 g
8 oz	Fresh spinach	225 g

Wash and pick over the split peas and put into a saucepan of cold water. Bring to the boil and boil for 2 minutes. Remove from the heat, cover and leave to soak for 2 hours.

Peel and chop the onion. Cut the meat into bite-size pieces. Heat the butter and oil in a flameproof casserole and fry the onion and meat till lightly browned.

Drain the split peas and add to the meat. Scrape the carrots, slice thinly and add to the pan with the bouquet garni, grated nutmeg and stock. Add seasoning and bring to the boil. Reduce the heat, cover and simmer for 1 hour.

Peel and dice the potatoes. Chop the spinach and add both to the meat. Cook for a further 30 minutes. Taste and adjust the seasoning. Serve with creamed potatoes and a green vegetable or boiled rice, or with crusty bread for a lighter meal.

Beef and vegetable stew

Overall timing 2 hours

Freezing Suitable: simmer for 30 minutes only; add vegetables after reheating in 350°F (180°C) Gas 4 oven for 45 minutes

To serve 6–8

2 lb	Stewing steak	900 g
	Salt and pepper	
4 tbsp	Plain flour	4x15 ml
1 lb	Onions	450 g
3 tbsp	Oil	3x15 ml
1¼ pints	Beef stock	700 g
2 tbsp	Tomato purée	2x15 ml
	Bay leaf	
1 lb	Carrots	450 g
1 lb	Potatoes	450 g
1 lb	Parsnips	450 g
8 oz	Frozen peas	225 g

Wipe and trim the meat and cut into 1½ inch (4 cm) cubes. Season the flour and toss the pieces of meat in it till evenly coated. Peel and slice the onions.

Heat the oil in a heavy-based saucepan and fry the onions till transparent. Add the meat and fry till browned all over, then add any remaining flour. Gradually add the stock (made with cubes if necessary) and bring to the boil, stirring constantly. Add the tomato purée, bay leaf and seasoning, cover and simmer for 1 hour.

Scrape the carrots and peel the potatoes and parsnips. Cut all into chunks and add to the meat. Cover and simmer for a further 30 minutes. Taste and adjust seasoning.

Stir in the peas and simmer for 10 minutes, then serve.

Beef carbonnade

Overall timing 2–2½ hours

Freezing Suitable

To serve 4

2¼ lb	Braising beef	1 kg
3 oz	Butter	75 g
8 oz	Onions	225 g
1 tbsp	Plain flour	15 ml
1 tbsp	Brown sugar	15 ml
1 tbsp	Wine vinegar	15 ml
18 fl oz	Stout	500 ml
	Salt and pepper	
1	Bouquet garni	1

Trim off any fat, then cut meat into large thin slices. Melt 2 oz (50 g) of the butter in a flameproof casserole. Add the meat and brown over a high heat. Remove beef from pan and put aside.

Peel and finely chop onions. Add onions to pan with remaining butter. Reduce heat, cover and cook for 10 minutes without burning.

Sprinkle flour into pan with the brown sugar and stir with a wooden spoon. Add vinegar, then the stout and stir until thick.

Replace beef in pan, season with salt and pepper and add bouquet garni. Cover and simmer for about 1½–2 hours over a low heat or cook in the oven at 350°F (180°C) Gas 4. Discard bouquet garni before serving, with mashed potatoes and endive salad.

Pot au feu

Overall timing 4 hours

Freezing Not suitable

To serve 6

1	Onion	1
2	Cloves	2
2	Stalks of celery	2
1 tbsp	Chopped parsley	15 ml
4 pints	Water	2.2 litres
	Salt and pepper	
1	Cow heel	1
$\frac{1}{2}$	Boiling chicken	$\frac{1}{2}$
2	Leeks	2
1	Carrot	1
2	Potatoes	2

Peel onion and spike with cloves. Chop celery. Put into a flameproof casserole with the parsley, water and seasoning. Bring to the boil, then add cow heel and chicken. Reduce heat and simmer for 3 hours, skimming occasionally.

Remove cow heel and chicken from pan. Cut meat off bones in small chunks. Trim and thinly slice leeks. Peel and slice carrot. Peel and chop potatoes.

Strain stock and return to pan. Add meat and vegetables. Bring back to the boil, then reduce heat and simmer for 30 minutes. Serve hot with toasted bread.

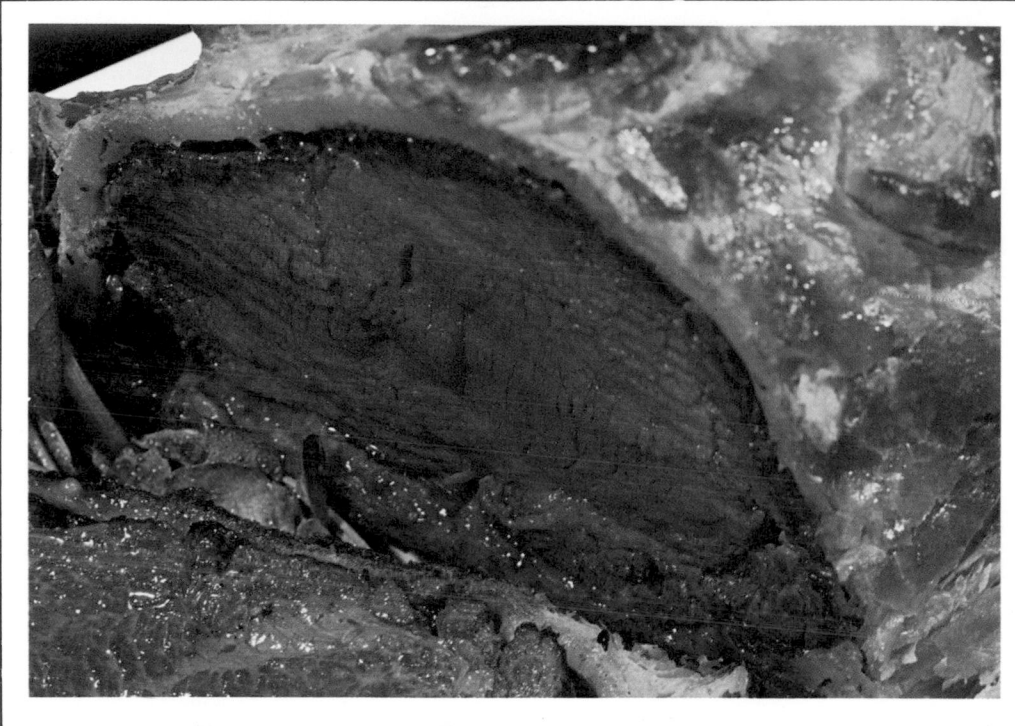

Boeuf en croûte

Overall timing 1½ hours plus cooling and chilling

Freezing Not suitable

To serve 6

1 lb	Frozen puff pastry	454 g
3 lb	Fillet of beef	1.4 kg
1	Garlic clove	1
1 oz	Softened butter	25 g
	Salt and pepper	
1 teasp	Dried thyme	5 ml
4 oz	Smooth liver pâté	125 g
1	Egg	1

Thaw pastry. Preheat the oven to 425°F (220°C) Gas 7.

Trim meat of all fat, then tie into a neat shape with fine string. Make tiny slits in meat with tip of a sharp knife and insert slivers of peeled garlic. Spread butter over beef, season and sprinkle with half the thyme. Place in roasting tin and roast for 10 minutes. Take meat out of tin, place on a wire rack and leave to cool completely.

Remove string from meat. Roll out dough to a large rectangle just over twice the size of the meat. Place meat on one half of dough rectangle and brush dough edges with water. Spread pâté over top of meat and sprinkle with remaining thyme. Fold dough over to enclose meat and seal edges. Trim round three sides and, if liked, make a hole in the top. Make a funnel from foil and place in hole if liked. Place on dampened baking tray.

Cut decorative shapes out of dough trimmings, dip them into beaten egg and arrange on dough. Glaze all over with egg and chill for 1 hour.

Preheat oven to 425°F (220°C) Gas 7. Bake for 35 minutes till pastry is well risen and golden. Place on a warmed serving dish, garnish with watercress and serve, cut into thick slices.

Bohemian goulash

Overall timing 2¼ hours

Freezing Suitable: add cream after reheating

To serve 4

8 oz	Boned shoulder of lamb	225 g
8 oz	Belly pork	225 g
8 oz	Chuck steak	225 g
2 oz	Butter	50 g
2	Onions	2
3	Garlic cloves	3
2 teasp	Paprika	2x5 ml
	Bouquet garni	
1 tbsp	Tomato purée	15 ml
	Salt and pepper	
¼ pint	Carton of soured cream	150 ml

Cut meats into chunks. Melt the butter in a flameproof casserole and brown the meats on all sides.

Peel and slice the onions. Peel and crush the garlic. Add both to the casserole and cook gently till golden brown. Stir in the paprika and cook for 2 minutes.

Add bouquet garni, tomato purée and seasoning. Cover with water and bring to the boil. Cover and simmer for 1½–2 hours.

Discard bouquet garni; adjust seasoning. Stir in soured cream and serve with boiled new potatoes and a crisp green salad.

Chilli con carne

Overall timing 3¼ hours plus overnight soaking

Freezing Suitable

To serve 4–6

8 oz	Dried brown or red beans	225 g
1¾ pints	Water	1 litre
2 lb	Braising steak	900 g
1	Onion	1
1 tbsp	Pork dripping or olive oil	15 ml
1 oz	Butter	25 g
	Salt and pepper	
1 teasp	Chilli powder	5 ml
1 tbsp	Sweet paprika	15 ml
8 oz	Canned tomatoes	225 g
2 teasp	Cornflour (optional)	2x5 ml

Soak beans in water overnight. The next day, place water and beans in saucepan, cover and cook gently for 1½ hours.

Cut the beef into 1 inch (2.5 cm) cubes. Peel and chop onion. Heat the dripping or oil and butter in frying pan. Add the beef. Cook till brown, then add the onion and cook till transparent.

Mix the meat and onion in with the cooked beans and season with salt, pepper, chilli powder and paprika. Cover and cook gently for 1 hour.

Add the drained tomatoes, cover and cook for 30 minutes more. Adjust seasoning. If you wish to thicken the sauce, blend the cornflour with a little water and add it to the mixture. Cook for a few minutes, then serve from the cooking pot with plain boiled rice or chunks of wholemeal bread and a crisp green salad.

Corned beef hash

Overall timing 1 hour

Freezing Not suitable

To serve 4

2	Medium-size onions	2
6 tbsp	Oil *or*	6x15 ml
2 oz	Dripping	50 g
1	Stalk of celery	1
1	Large carrot	1
1 lb	Corned beef	450 g
	Salt and pepper	
$\frac{1}{2}$ teasp	Powdered mustard	2.5 ml
1 lb	Potatoes	450 g
1 pint	Beef stock	560 ml

Peel and thinly slice onions. Heat oil or dripping in saucepan. Add the onions and cook gently till transparent.

Finely chop celery. Peel and grate or dice carrot. Cut corned beef into 1 inch (2.5 cm) cubes. Add all of these to onions and cook for a few minutes, then season with salt, pepper and mustard (add more if a stronger taste is preferred). Cook gently for 5 minutes.

Meanwhile, peel potatoes and cut into chunks. Add to pan with boiling stock and cook for 20 minutes. Serve in warm bowls topped with fried or poached eggs, and with lots of fresh bread to mop up the juices.

Corned beef patties

Overall timing 30 minutes

Freezing Suitable: cook from frozen

To serve 4

12 tbsp	Fresh breadcrumbs	12x15 ml
3 tbsp	Warm milk	3x15 ml
1 lb	Corned beef	450 g
2	Eggs	2
2 tbsp	Grated Parmesan cheese	2x15 ml
	Grated rind of ½ lemon	
	Plain flour	
2 oz	Butter	50 g
1 tbsp	Oil	15 ml
	Lemon wedges	
	Sprigs of parsley	

Soak 4 tbsp (4x15 ml) breadcrumbs in the milk. Cut off any excess fat from the edge of the corned beef and discard. Mash beef in a bowl with a fork, then add squeezed-out breadcrumbs, 1 egg, the cheese and lemon rind. Mix well.

With well floured hands, make patties from the mixture, then coat with flour. Lightly beat remaining egg. Using two forks, dip the patties first into beaten egg, then into remaining breadcrumbs.

Heat butter and oil in a large frying pan. Add the patties and cook over a moderate heat till brown on both sides. Remove from pan and drain on kitchen paper. Garnish with lemon wedges and parsley.

Danish meatballs

Overall timing 40 minutes

Freezing Suitable: fry meatballs after thawing, or fry from frozen, allowing 25 minutes

To serve 4

4 oz	Fresh breadcrumbs	125 g
¼ pint	Milk	150 ml
1	Small onion	1
8 oz	Minced beef	225 g
8 oz	Minced pork	225 g
	Salt and pepper	
½ teasp	Ground allspice	2.5 ml
1	Egg	1
2 tbsp	Plain flour	2x15 ml
2 oz	Butter	50 g
3 tbsp	Oil	3x15 ml
8	Lettuce leaves	8
2	Pickled beetroot	2
4 tbsp	Pickled red cabbage	4x15 ml

Put fresh breadcrumbs into a bowl with the milk and soak for 10 minutes.

Peel onion and grate into a large bowl. Add the beef and pork, squeezed out breadcrumbs, salt, pepper and allspice. Mix well and bind together with the beaten egg. Shape mixture into eight balls and coat lightly with flour.

Heat butter and oil in a frying pan. Add meatballs and fry gently for 15 minutes till brown all over and cooked through.

Meanwhile, wash and dry lettuce leaves and arrange in a shallow basket or serving dish. Drain and dice pickled beetroot.

Remove meatballs from pan with a draining spoon and drain on kitchen paper. Put one meatball on each lettuce leaf and spoon a little drained pickled cabbage and beetroot around. Serve with a lettuce, tomato and olive salad.

Flemish hotpot

Overall timing 3¾ hours

Freezing Not suitable

To serve 6

2	Pig's trotters	2
1 lb	Piece of belly of pork	450 g
1 lb	Beef flank	450 g
5 pints	Water	2.8 litres
1 tbsp	Salt	15 ml
2	Bay leaves	2
12	Peppercorns	12
3	Onions	3
4	Cloves	4
1½ lb	Potatoes	700 g
1 lb	Carrots	450 g
1 lb	Cabbage *or*	450 g
12 oz	Spinach	350 g

Split trotters lengthways, then halve each half. Cut belly of pork into 3x2 inch (7.5x5 cm) strips. Roll up beef and tie with string. Put water into a large pan and add meats with salt, bay leaves and peppercorns. Peel onions and spike one with cloves. Add it to pan and bring to the boil. Skim and simmer for 2 hours.

Remove meats from pan. Strain stock and return to pan with meats.

Peel and chop potatoes. Scrape and thickly slice carrots. Chop cabbage or spinach. Quarter remaining onions. Bring stock to the boil and add vegetables. Simmer for 20–25 minutes till vegetables are tender.

Lift meats out of stock. Remove string from beef and carve into thick slices. Strain off 1 pint (560 ml) of the stock and reserve.

Taste the soup and adjust the seasoning. Pour into a warmed tureen and serve immediately. Serve the meats after the soup with reserved stock thickened and made into gravy.

Beef with onions

Overall timing 1½ hours

Freezing Suitable

To serve 4

1½ lb	Chuck steak	700 g
12 oz	Onions	350 g
1 oz	Butter	25 g
1 tbsp	Oil	15 ml
1 tbsp	Plain flour	15 ml
½ pint	Beef stock	300 ml
1	Garlic clove	1
½ teasp	Ground cumin	2.5 ml
	Pinch of dried marjoram	
2 tbsp	Wine vinegar	2x15 ml
	Salt and pepper	

Cut meat across the grain into thin finger-length strips. Peel onions, slice crossways and separate rings. Heat the butter and oil in frying pan. Add the onion rings and cook, covered, over a low heat till transparent. Turn them over frequently so that they cook evenly but do not brown. Remove from pan.

Increase heat, put strips of meat into pan and brown them. Return onion rings. Sprinkle with flour and stir. When flour begins to colour, stir in stock, peeled and crushed garlic, cumin, marjoram, wine vinegar and seasoning. Cover and simmer for 1 hour. Serve with potatoes or rice and a crisp mixed salad.

Beef paprika

Overall timing 2¼ hours

Freezing Suitable

To serve 6

2 lb	Stewing beef	900 g
2 oz	Pork dripping	50 g
8 oz	Onions	225 g
2	Garlic cloves	2
1 tbsp	Plain flour	15 ml
1 pint	Beef stock	560 ml
½ teasp	Dried marjoram	2.5 ml
½ teasp	Caraway seed	2.5 ml
	Brown sugar	
2 teasp	Paprika	2 x 5 ml
	Salt and pepper	

Cube beef. Heat dripping in a large saucepan or flameproof casserole. Add beef and fry till brown on all sides. Peel and chop onions and garlic. Add to pan and cook till transparent.

Sprinkle in flour and stir into mixture. Add stock, marjoram, caraway seed, a pinch of sugar, paprika and seasoning. Cover tightly and cook gently for 1¾–2 hours.

Goulash

Overall timing 2¼ hours

Freezing Suitable

To serve 6

2 lb	Stewing beef	900 g
2 oz	Pork dripping	50 g
8 oz	Onions	225 g
2	Garlic cloves	2
1 tbsp	Plain flour	15 ml
1	Beef stock cube	1
1 pint	Boiling water	560 ml
	Salt and pepper	
½ teasp	Dried marjoram	2.5 ml
½ teasp	Caraway seed	2.5 ml
	Brown sugar	
½ teasp	Paprika	2.5 ml
8 oz	Potatoes	225 g
2	Green peppers	2
5	Tomatoes	5
¼ pint	Red wine	150 ml
¼ pint	Carton of soured cream (optional)	150 ml

Cube beef. Heat dripping in a large saucepan. Add beef and fry till meat is brown on all sides. Peel and chop onions and garlic. Add to meat and cook till transparent.

Sprinkle in flour and stir into mixture. Mix stock cube into boiling water and pour over meat. Season with salt, pepper, marjoram, caraway seed, a pinch of sugar and paprika. Cover tightly and cook gently for 1¼ hours.

Peel and roughly chop the potatoes. Deseed and slice peppers. Blanch, peel and chop tomatoes. Add all to pan, cover and cook for a further 25 minutes.

Add wine and check seasoning. Bring to simmering point and stir in soured cream, if using, or serve it separately.

Spicy meatballs

Overall timing 30 minutes

Freezing Not suitable

To serve 4–6

1	Small onion	1
1	Garlic clove	1
1½ lb	Lean minced beef	700 g
1	Egg	1
1 oz	Fresh white breadcrumbs	25 g
	Salt and pepper	
½ teasp	Ground allspice	2.5 ml
	Oil for frying	

Peel and finely chop the onion; peel and crush the garlic. Put with rest of ingredients (except for the oil) into a bowl and mix well together. Shape mixture into walnut-sized balls.

Fry the meatballs in shallow oil for about 15 minutes, turning once. Arrange on a warmed serving plate and serve with rice or pasta, and a tomato sauce or gravy.

Beef and carrot fry-up

Overall timing 45 minutes

Freezing Suitable

To serve 4

1 lb	Carrots	450 g
2	Leeks	2
2 oz	Butter	50 g
9 fl oz	White wine or beef stock	250 ml
	Salt and pepper	
1 lb	Minced beef	450 g
½ teasp	Worcestershire sauce	2.5 ml

Scrape carrots and chop into 1 inch (2.5 cm) pieces. Trim, wash and chop leeks into ½ inch (1.25 cm) slices. Melt half the butter in a frying pan or saucepan and fry chopped carrots for 3 minutes. Pour in white wine or stock, cover and cook over a low heat for 20 minutes.

Add the leeks, season with salt and pepper and cook for a further 15 minutes, or until tender.

Meanwhile, put mince in bowl and mix in salt and pepper with a fork. Roughly shape mince into 1 inch (2.5 cm) pieces. Melt remaining butter in another frying pan and fry meat for about 15 minutes until lightly browned and no longer pink in the middle. Stir from time to time.

Reduce any excess liquid in vegetable pan by boiling rapidly for a minute or two. Add meat and sprinkle with Worcestershire sauce. Serve from the pan, with creamy mashed potatoes and a green vegetable.

Mustardy beef rissoles

Overall timing 25 minutes

Freezing Suitable: fry from frozen for 15 minutes

To serve 4

2	Large onions	2
1	Carrot	1
1 lb	Minced beef	450 g
1 tbsp	Chopped parsley	15 ml
1	Egg	1
2 teasp	Mustard seeds	2x5 ml
	Salt and pepper	
3 tbsp	Plain flour	3x15 ml
4 tbsp	Oil	4x15 ml
	Sprigs of parsley	

Peel and finely chop the onions. Peel and finely grate the carrot. Put into a bowl with the minced beef, parsley and egg.

Roughly grind the mustard seed in a mortar or pepper mill and add to the beef with plenty of salt and pepper. Mix with a fork till the ingredients are well blended. Shape into 12 balls and coat with seasoned flour.

Heat the oil in a frying pan and fry the meatballs for about 10 minutes till crisp and golden on all sides. Drain on kitchen paper and arrange on a warmed serving plate. Garnish with sprigs of parsley.

Hamburgers

Overall timing 10 minutes

Freezing Suitable: cook after thawing

To serve 4

1 lb	Finely minced beef	450 g
2	Onions	2
	Salt and pepper	
3 tbsp	Oil	3x15 ml
4	Rolls or buns	4
2 oz	Butter	50 g
1 tbsp	French mustard	15 ml

Put the mince into a large bowl. Peel and finely chop one of the onions and add to the beef with plenty of seasoning. Mix. Divide into four portions and shape each into a thick burger.

Preheat a frying pan or griddle and brush lightly with 1 tbsp (15 ml) oil. Fry the burgers for about 5 minutes, then turn carefully and cook for a further 3–5 minutes.

While the hamburgers are cooking, peel and slice the second onion into rings. Heat the remaining oil in another frying pan and cook the onion till golden.

Meanwhile, halve and lightly toast the rolls, then spread cut sides with the butter mixed with the French mustard.

Place a hamburger in each roll and top with fried onions. Serve immediately.

Hamburgers with eggs

Overall timing 10 minutes

Freezing Not suitable

To serve 2

2	Onions	2
8 oz	Finely minced beef	225 g
	Salt and pepper	
2 teasp	Oil	2x5 ml
2	Tomatoes	2
2 oz	Butter	50 g
2	Eggs	2
	Cayenne	
	Watercress	

Peel the onions. Finely chop half of one and cut the other half and the second onion into rings. Mix the chopped onion with the beef and season. Divide in half and shape into burgers.

Heat the oil in a frying pan and fry the burgers for about 5 minutes on each side. Add the tomatoes halfway through the cooking.

Meanwhile, melt 1 oz (25 g) butter in another frying pan and fry the onion rings till crisp. Remove from the pan and keep hot.

Add the eggs to the pan with the remaining butter and fry till set.

Top each burger with an egg and arrange on warmed plates with the onions and tomatoes. Sprinkle a little cayenne over the eggs. Keep hot.

Put the watercress into the pan with the butter and fry quickly. Use to garnish the burgers.

Neapolitan beef

Overall timing 2½ hours

Freezing Not suitable

To serve 4

2 oz	Back bacon	50 g
2 oz	Belly pork fat	50 g
1 tbsp	Chopped parsley	15 ml
1 tbsp	Seedless raisins	15 ml
	Salt and pepper	
1 lb	Top rump of beef	450 g
1	Onion	1
1	Garlic clove	1
2 tbsp	Oil	2x15 ml
14 oz	Can of tomatoes	397 g
½ pint	Beef stock	300 ml
12 oz	Rigatoni	350 g
2 tbsp	Grated Parmesan cheese	2x15 ml

Chop or finely mince bacon and pork fat and mix with parsley to form a smooth paste. Work in raisins and seasoning. With a larding needle, make several deep holes in meat and firmly stuff paste into them. Tie meat into a neat roll with string.

Peel and finely chop onion. Peel and crush garlic. Heat oil in flameproof casserole, add onion and garlic and fry till transparent. Add the meat roll and fry, turning frequently, to seal. Press tomatoes and their juice through a sieve and add to casserole with the stock and seasoning. Mix well, cover and simmer for 1½ hours or till tender.

Meanwhile, cook rigatoni in boiling salted water till tender. Drain and keep hot.

Lift meat out of casserole, remove string and slice. Arrange on a warmed serving dish and arrange rigatoni round meat. Taste sauce and adjust seasoning. Spoon sauce over meat and rigatoni. Sprinkle with Parmesan. Serve immediately.

Pot roast beef with milk

Overall timing 3 hours plus overnight marination

Freezing Not suitable

To serve 6–8

3 lb	Silverside of beef	1.4 kg
1	Large onion	1
1	Large carrot	1
4	Stalks of celery	4
4	Fresh basil leaves	4
	Salt and pepper	
¾ pint	Milk	400 ml
2 tbsp	Brandy (optional)	2x15 ml
14 oz	Can of tomatoes	397 g
2 tbsp	Tomato purée	2x15 ml
8 oz	Pickling onions	225 g
1 oz	Butter	25 g

Tie the meat into a neat shape. Put into a flameproof casserole. Peel and chop the onion and carrot. Wash, trim and chop the celery. Add to the meat with the basil leaves, salt, pepper, milk and brandy (if used), cover and marinate in a cool place overnight.

The next day, preheat the oven to 325°F (170°C) Gas 3. Stir the tomatoes with juice and tomato purée into the casserole. Cover and cook in oven for 2 hours.

Meanwhile, peel the small onions and blanch in boiling water for 5 minutes. Melt butter in a frying pan and fry onions till golden. Add to casserole and cook for further 30 minutes.

Remove the meat from the casserole and discard the string. Place the meat on a warmed serving dish and keep hot.

Purée the cooking liquor in a blender or rub through a sieve, setting aside the button onions. Put purée and onions into saucepan and reheat. Meanwhile, cut the meat into slices. Taste and adjust the seasoning of the sauce and pour around the meat.

Hungarian beef

Overall timing 2½ hours

Freezing Suitable: reheat in 325°F (170°C) Gas 3 oven for 20 minutes, then add vegetables

To serve 4

1½ lb	Braising steak	700 g
2 oz	Lard	50 g
2	Onions	2
1 tbsp	Paprika	15 ml
½ teasp	Caraway seeds	2.5 ml
¾ pint	Beef stock	400 ml
	Salt and pepper	
2	Green peppers	2
8 oz	Tomatoes	225 g
1 lb	Potatoes	450 g

Preheat the oven to 325°F (170°C) Gas 3.

Cut steak into four equal-size pieces. Melt half the lard in a flameproof casserole, add the steaks and brown quickly on both sides. Remove from casserole and reserve.

Peel and chop the onions. Add remaining lard to casserole and fry onions gently for about 10 minutes till golden, stirring frequently. Remove casserole from the heat and stir in the paprika, mixing well. Add the caraway seeds, one-third of the stock, the steak and seasoning. Cover and cook in the oven for 1½ hours.

Meanwhile, deseed and slice peppers. Blanch, peel and chop tomatoes. Peel and thinly slice potatoes. Remove casserole from oven and stir in remaining stock, peppers, tomatoes and potatoes. Cover and cook for a further 30 minutes till potatoes are tender. Taste and adjust seasoning.

Lift out meat and place in individual deep serving plates. Spoon vegetables and sauce over.

Steak and eggs

Overall timing 10 minutes

Freezing Not suitable

To serve 4

3 oz	Butter	75 g
4	Thick steaks	4
4	Eggs	4
	Salt and pepper	
	Sprigs of parsley	

Melt 2 oz (50 g) of the butter in a frying pan. Add the steaks and fry for about 3 minutes on each side or until browned and cooked to your taste.

Meanwhile, melt the remaining butter in another frying pan and fry the eggs until just set. Use buttered poaching rings to make the eggs the same shape as the steaks, if possible.

Place the steaks on a warmed serving plate and top with the eggs. Pour the steak cooking juices over and season. Garnish with parsley.

Yugoslav kebabs

Overall timing 25 minutes plus marination

Freezing Suitable: reheat in 400°F (200°C) Gas 6 oven for 25 minutes

To serve 6

1	Onion	1
1½ lb	Finely minced beef	700 g
4 tbsp	Red wine	4x15 ml
	Salt and pepper	
1	Egg	1
2 tbsp	Oil	2x15 ml
Garnish		
	Lemons	
	Tomato slices	
	Onion rings	

Peel and finely chop the onion and add to the mince with the red wine and plenty of seasoning. Mix well and leave to marinate for 1 hour.

Preheat the grill. Add the egg to the mince and mix together. Divide the mixture into 18 portions and shape each into a croquette. Thread three on to each of six skewers.

Grill the kebabs for 10–15 minutes, turning and basting with oil.

Arrange the kebabs on a warmed serving dish and serve with lemons cut into halves or wedges, tomato slices, onion rings and jacket baked potatoes.

Steamed steak and kidney pudding

Overall timing 5¾ hours

Freezing Suitable: steam from frozen for 2½–3 hours

To serve 6

1½ lb	Chuck or blade steak	700 g
8 oz	Ox kidney	225 g
1	Large onion	1
	Salt and pepper	
3 tbsp	Plain flour	3x15 ml
12 oz	Self-raising flour	350 g
6 oz	Shredded suet	175 g
½ pint	Cold beef stock	300 ml

Cut the meat into 1½ inch (4 cm) cubes. Trim the kidney, removing any core, and cut into 1 inch (2.5 cm) cubes. Peel and thinly slice the onion. Season plain flour and use to coat the steak, kidney and onion.

Sift the self-raising flour and 1½ teasp (7.5 ml) salt into a bowl and stir in the suet and enough cold water to mix to a soft but not sticky dough. Knead lightly till smooth.

Roll out on a floured surface to a round, big enough to line a 3 pint (1.7 litre) pudding basin (about 14 inches/35 cm in diameter). Cut out one-quarter of the dough round and reserve. Lift the large piece and place it in the basin, curving it so it fits neatly, and sealing the edges together. Place the meat mixture in the basin and add the cold stock to come half-way up the meat.

Roll out the reserved dough to a round slightly larger than the top of the basin. Brush the top edge of the dough lining with water and cover with the dough lid. Seal the edges well.

Cover with greased, pleated greaseproof paper and pleated foil, or a pudding cloth and secure with string. Steam for 5 hours, topping up with boiling water as required.

Texan stew

Overall timing 2¼ hours

Freezing Suitable

To serve 4

1½ lb	Braising beef	700 g
1 oz	Butter	25 g
1 tbsp	Oil	15 ml
1 pint	Stock	560 ml
2	Green peppers	2
4	Tomatoes	4
11½ oz	Can of sweetcorn kernels	326 g
10 oz	Can of peas and carrots	280 g
	Salt and pepper	
2 teasp	Cornflour	2x5 ml

Chop meat into 1 inch (2.5cm) cubes. Heat butter and oil in saucepan, add meat and cook for 10 minutes till brown all over. Pour in stock (made with 2 stock cubes if necessary) and cook, covered, for 1½ hours over a gentle heat.

Wash, deseed and cut green peppers into strips. Blanch, peel and chop tomatoes. Drain corn and peas and carrots. Add vegetables to meat and season well with salt and pepper. Cook, covered, for 15 minutes over a moderate heat.

Blend cornflour with a little water in a cup. Stir into saucepan, then bring to boil again, stirring until thickened. Serve stew in warmed bowls.

Beef and horseradish loaf

Overall timing 1 hour

Freezing Suitable: reheat in 375°F (190°C) Gas 5 oven for 30 minutes

To serve 4

¼ pint	Strong beef stock	150 ml
4 oz	Fresh breadcrumbs	125 g
1 lb	Minced beef	450 g
1	Large onion	1
1 tbsp	Grated horseradish	15 ml
3	Eggs	3
2 tbsp	Sweet sherry	2x15 ml
	Salt and pepper	

Preheat the oven to 350°F (180°C) Gas 4.

Put the stock (made with a double quantity of cubes if necessary) in a saucepan and bring to the boil. Sprinkle in the breadcrumbs and stir till the crumbs have absorbed all the stock.

Put minced beef into a bowl with the breadcrumb mixture. Peel and finely chop onion and add to meat with the grated horseradish, eggs, sherry and seasoning. Mix well with a wooden spoon until all ingredients are well blended.

Grease ovenproof dish and press in the mixture. Smooth the top and bake in the centre of the oven for 45 minutes. Serve hot with boiled potatoes and buttered carrots.

Tripe and onions French style

Overall timing 1 hour 50 minutes

Freezing Not suitable

To serve 4

1	Large carrot	1
1½ lb	Onions	700 g
2	Stalks of celery	2
3 pints	Cold water	1.7 litres
	Bay leaf	
6	Peppercorns	6
1 tbsp	Lemon juice	15 ml
1½ lb	Dressed tripe	700 g
3 oz	Butter	75 g
	Salt and pepper	
2 tbsp	Chopped parsley	2x15 ml
2 tbsp	White wine vinegar	2x15 ml

Peel and chop carrot and one of the onions. Trim and chop celery. Put into a saucepan with water, bay leaf, peppercorns and lemon juice. Bring to the boil and simmer for 30 minutes. Strain and return to pan.

Cut tripe into pieces. Place in pan with stock and bring to the boil. Skim off any scum, cover and simmer for 1¼ hours till tender.

Peel and slice remaining onions. Melt butter in a frying pan, add the onions and fry gently till golden.

Drain the tripe thoroughly, discarding the stock, and cut into thin strips. Add to the onions with plenty of seasoning and fry over a moderate heat for 10 minutes, stirring frequently. Add the parsley and vinegar and mix lightly. Season to taste and pour into a warmed serving dish. Serve immediately with crusty bread.

Italian-style tripe

Overall timing 2½ hours plus soaking

Freezing Not suitable

To serve 6

4 oz	Dried broad beans	125 g
1½ lb	Blanket tripe	700 g
8 oz	Honeycomb tripe	225 g
2 oz	Streaky bacon	50 g
1	Sprig of sage	1
1 lb	Ripe tomatoes	450 g
1	Onion	1
1	Carrot	1
1	Stalk of celery	1
2 oz	Butter	50 g
	Salt and pepper	
¾ pint	Stock	400 ml
4 tbsp	Grated Parmesan cheese	4x15 ml

Soak beans in cold water overnight.

The next day, wash and drain both types of tripe. Shred the blanket tripe and cut the honeycomb tripe into squares. Derind and finely chop the bacon. Wash the sage. Blanch, peel and deseed the tomatoes and cut into small pieces. Peel and finely chop the onion and carrot. Wash and slice the celery.

Melt the butter in a saucepan and fry the bacon and onion till just golden. Add the celery, carrot and sage and fry for 5 minutes longer.

Add the two types of tripe and the tomatoes. Season. Add the stock (made with cubes if necessary) and bring to the boil. Cover the saucepan and simmer over a low heat for about 1 hour, stirring frequently to prevent the sauce from sticking to the saucepan.

Drain beans, rinse and add to the pan. Cover and simmer for 1 hour more.

Taste and adjust seasoning and sprinkle with the grated Parmesan.

Lamb

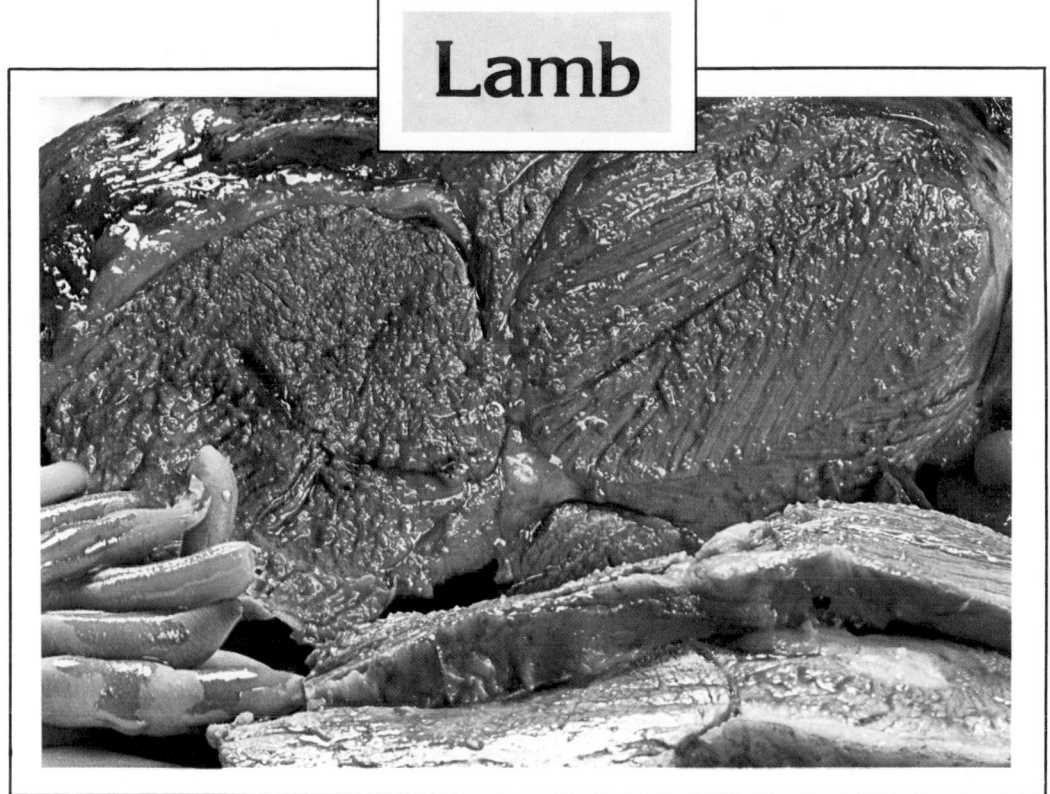

Roast lamb with garlic

Overall timing 2 hours

Freezing Not suitable

To serve 6

2–3	Garlic cloves	2–3
3½ lb	Leg of lamb	1.6 kg
1 oz	Butter or dripping	25 g
	Salt and pepper	

Preheat the oven to 350°F (180°C) Gas 4.

Peel the garlic cloves and cut each into thin slivers. Place lamb in roasting tin with the thickest fat uppermost. Using a sharp, thin bladed knife, make incisions about 1 inch (2.5 cm) deep in the meat. Insert a sliver of garlic into each incision, pressing it down so it is level with the surface of the meat.

Spread the softened butter or dripping over the lamb and season well. Roast for 1¾ hours or until the juices run clear when a skewer is inserted into the thickest part of the meat.

Transfer meat to warmed serving plate and make the gravy in the usual way. Serve with green beans and tomatoes.

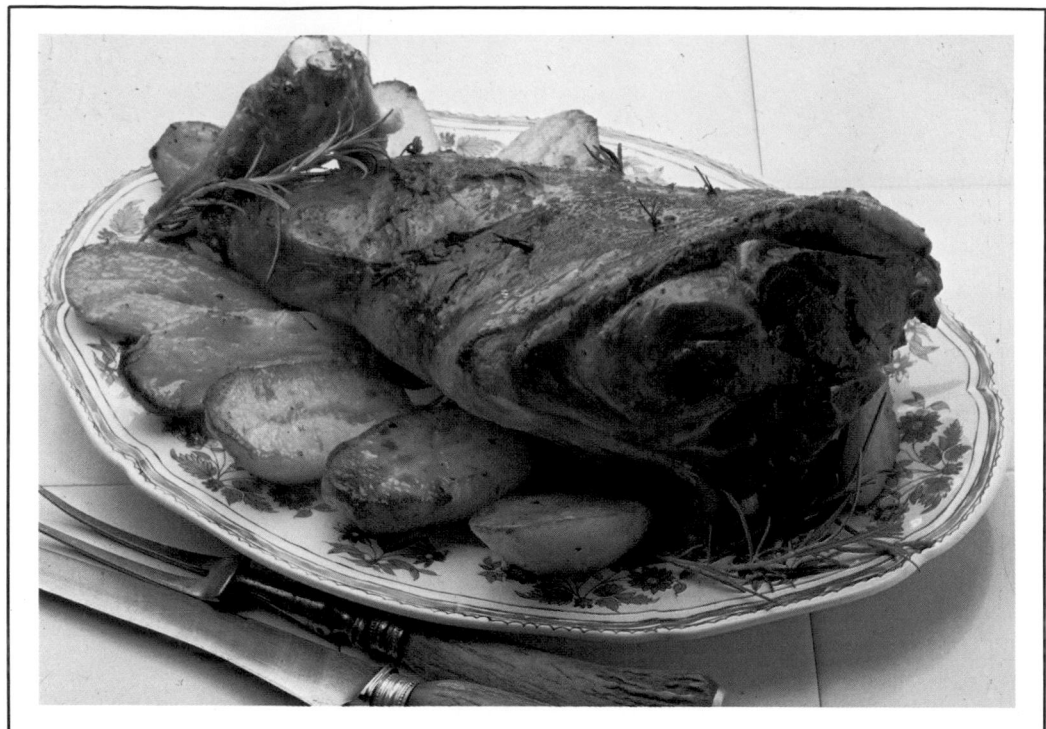

New Zealand roast lamb

Overall timing 3–3½ hours

Freezing Not suitable

To serve 4–6

4 lb	Leg of lamb	1.8 kg
2 tbsp	Oil	2x15 ml
	Fresh rosemary *or*	
2 teasp	Dried rosemary	2x5 ml
	Salt and pepper	
¼ pint	Water	150 ml
2 lb	Potatoes	900 g

Preheat oven to 350°F (180°C) Gas 4.

Place lamb in roasting tin, then rub the oil into the skin. Either make small slits in the meat and insert fresh rosemary leaves, or sprinkle surface with dried rosemary, then season well. Add water to the tin and cook for 3–3½ hours – the meat should almost be falling off the bone.

Meanwhile, peel, parboil and dry the potatoes. Add them to the roasting tin 1½ hours before end of cooking time and turn them till coated in fat. Turn again once during roasting.

Beanpot with lamb

Overall timing 2 hours 50 minutes plus overnight soaking

Freezing Not suitable

To serve 4

8 oz	Dried haricot beans	225 g
½ teasp	Salt	2.5 ml
1 oz	Dripping	25 g
1 lb	Chump lamb chops	450 g
1	Onion	1
4 tbsp	Tomato purée	4x15 ml
½ teasp	Ground cumin	2.5 ml
1	Bay leaf	1
½ teasp	Dried rosemary	2.5 ml
½ teasp	Garlic salt	2.5 ml
	Brown sugar	
½ teasp	Vinegar	2.5 ml
1 tbsp	Chopped chives	15 ml

Soak beans in 2½ pints (1.5 litres) water overnight. Next day, transfer beans and water to a saucepan, add salt and cook for 1 hour.

Melt dripping in a flameproof casserole and brown chops well on all sides. Peel and chop onion and add to casserole. Cook till transparent. Add beans and water, tomato purée, cumin, bay leaf, rosemary and garlic salt. Cover and cook for 1 hour.

Uncover and cook for a further 20 minutes till meat is tender.

Just before serving, stir in a pinch of sugar and the vinegar and sprinkle with chopped chives.

Minted lamb meatballs

Overall timing 30 minutes

Freezing Suitable: fry after thawing

To serve 4

1¼ lb	Minced lamb	600 g
4	Garlic cloves	4
2 tbsp	Chopped fresh mint	2x15 ml
1	Egg	1
	Salt and pepper	
1 teasp	Ground coriander	5 ml
	Plain flour	
2 tbsp	Oil	2x15 ml
	Mint or coriander leaves	

Place the lamb in a bowl with the peeled and finely chopped garlic, chopped mint, egg, salt, pepper and coriander and mix with a wooden spoon till well combined. Make little balls of the mixture, flouring your hands so it doesn't stick, and roll the balls in the flour to coat.

Heat oil in a frying pan, add meat balls and cook over a moderate heat for 8–10 minutes on each side till well browned. Drain on kitchen paper, then garnish with mint or coriander leaves and serve with rice.

Lamb curry

Overall timing 1½ hours

Freezing Suitable

To serve 2

1 lb	Boned lamb	450 g
1	Onion	1
1 oz	Butter	25 g
1 tbsp	Oil	15 ml
1 teasp	Curry powder	5 ml
	Salt and pepper	
1½ tbsp	Plain flour	22.5 ml
8 fl oz	Stock	220 ml
½ teasp	Tomato purée	2.5 ml
	Bouquet garni	
1	Tomato	1
½	Green pepper	½
2 oz	Button mushrooms	50 g
6 oz	New potatoes	175 g

Cut meat into cubes. Peel and chop onion. Heat butter and oil in a frying pan and fry onion till transparent.

Add curry powder and cook, stirring, for 2 minutes. Add meat and cook till golden on all sides. Season with salt and pepper, sprinkle with flour and stir over a high heat for a few minutes.

Reduce heat and stir in stock and tomato purée. Add bouquet garni and bring to the boil, stirring. Cover and cook gently for 40 minutes, stirring occasionally.

Chop tomato; deseed and slice pepper; halve or slice larger mushrooms. Scrub potatoes but don't peel; cut into chunks.

Add prepared vegetables to pan and cook for a further 20 minutes. Discard bouquet garni before serving, with plain boiled rice.

Casseroled lamb

Overall timing 2 hours

Freezing Not suitable

To serve 6

1	Carrot	1
1	Onion	1
1	Stalk of celery	1
4	Spring onions	4
3 oz	Streaky bacon	75 g
1	Garlic clove	1
2 tbsp	Oil	2x15 ml
3 tbsp	Chopped parsley	3x15 ml
2½ lb	Boned shoulder of lamb	1.1 kg
2 oz	Mushrooms	50 g
½ pint	Dry cider	300 ml
¼ pint	Stock	150 ml
	Salt and pepper	
1 lb	Potatoes	450 g

Peel and chop carrot and onion. Trim and chop celery and spring onions. Derind and chop bacon. Peel and crush garlic. Heat oil in flameproof casserole, add bacon, onion, spring onions, celery, carrot, garlic and parsley and fry till lightly browned.

Tie meat into shape, if necessary, add to casserole and brown on all sides over high heat. Chop mushrooms. Add to casserole with cider, stock and seasoning. Cover and cook for 1 hour over low heat.

Meanwhile, peel and quarter potatoes. Add to casserole and cook, covered, for a further 30 minutes. Taste and adjust seasoning then serve with broccoli.

Stuffed shoulder of lamb

Overall timing 2 hours

Freezing Not suitable

To serve 6

2	Onions	2
3 oz	Butter	75 g
12 oz	Sausagemeat	350 g
2 tbsp	Chopped parsley	2x15 ml
	Salt and pepper	
2½ lb	Boned shoulder of lamb	1.1 kg
7 fl oz	Dry white wine	200 ml
7 fl oz	Stock	200 ml
	Bouquet garni	
2½ lb	New potatoes	1.1 kg
2	Tomatoes	2

Peel and chop onions. Melt 1 oz (25 g) of butter in a frying pan, add onions and fry until golden.

Add to the sausagemeat with the parsley and seasoning.

Spread the lamb out, skin side down, on a board and season. Shape stuffing mixture into a large ball and place on lamb. Fold meat around stuffing to make a ball and tie firmly with string.

Melt 1 oz (25 g) of butter in a flameproof casserole and brown meat all over. Add wine, stock (made with cubes if necessary), bouquet garni, salt and pepper. Cover and cook slowly for 1 hour.

Meanwhile, scrape potatoes. Melt remaining butter in a frying pan, add potatoes and fry until golden brown. Arrange around the meat and cook uncovered for 20 minutes.

Blanch and peel tomatoes. Add to casserole and cook for 10 minutes more.

Remove bouquet garni. Place meat on warmed serving dish and remove string. Arrange potatoes and tomatoes around. Keep hot.

Transfer cooking liquor to a saucepan. Thicken with ½ oz (15 g) each of butter and flour mashed together. Serve this gravy separately.

Moussaka

Overall timing 2¼ hours

Freezing Suitable: bake from frozen in 375°F (190°C) Gas 5 oven for 1½ hours; add cheese sauce and bake 30 minutes more

To serve 6

1 lb	Onions	450 g
4	Garlic cloves	4
¼ pint	Oil	150 ml
1 tbsp	Chopped parsley	15 ml
2 lb	Minced lamb	900 g
4	Tomatoes	4
2 tbsp	Tomato purée	2x15 ml
	Salt and pepper	
¼ pint	Stock	150 ml
2 oz	Fresh breadcrumbs	50 g
2 lb	Aubergines	900 g
1 oz	Plain flour	25 g
2	Egg yolks	2
¾ pint	Thick white sauce	400 ml
4 oz	Strong cheese	125 g

Peel and chop onions; peel and crush garlic. Heat 1 tbsp (15 ml) oil in saucepan and fry onions, parsley, garlic and lamb till browned. Peel and quarter tomatoes and add to pan with tomato purée, seasoning and stock. Cover and simmer for 45 minutes. Remove from heat and stir in breadcrumbs.

Preheat oven to 350°F (180°C) Gas 4.

Thinly slice aubergines. Dust lightly with flour. Heat remaining oil in frying pan and brown aubergines. Drain on kitchen paper.

Arrange two-thirds of aubergines to cover bottom and sides of greased casserole. Add meat mixture, then top with remaining aubergines. Stir beaten egg yolks into sauce with half cheese, grated. Pour sauce over aubergines. Cover with rest of grated cheese. Put casserole in a roasting tin containing a little water. Bake for 1 hour.

Lamb kebabs with prunes

Overall timing 50 minutes

Freezing Not suitable

To serve 4

12	Prunes	12
¼ pint	Red wine	150 ml
1 lb	Lean lamb cut from the leg	450 g
3 tbsp	Oil	3x15 ml
	Salt and pepper	
½ teasp	Dried thyme	2.5 ml
2	Firm tomatoes	2
1	Medium onion	1
3	Thick rashers of streaky bacon	3

Put the prunes into a saucepan, add the red wine and bring to the boil. Remove from the heat and leave to soak for 30 minutes.

Cut lamb into 12 large cubes. Place in bowl with oil, seasoning and thyme. Cover and leave for 30 minutes.

Meanwhile, quarter the tomatoes. Peel the onion and cut through the root into eight wedges. Derind bacon and cut each rasher into four. Preheat the grill.

Drain the prunes, reserving the wine. Make a slit in each prune and remove the stone. Thread the lamb, prunes, tomatoes, bacon and onion on to four skewers. Brush the kebabs with the lamb marinade and the wine from the prunes, then sprinkle with salt and pepper. Grill for about 15 minutes, turning occasionally, till the lamb is tender. Arrange on a warmed serving dish and serve with boiled rice.

Lamb steaks with beans

Overall timing 45 minutes

Freezing Not suitable

To serve 4

1½ lb	Green beans	700 g
2 oz	Butter	50 g
	Salt and pepper	
4 fl oz	Meat stock	120 ml
5 tbsp	Oil	5x15 ml
2	Slices of white bread	2
¼ teasp	Garlic salt	1.25 ml
4	Lamb steaks	4
1 teasp	Mustard seed	5 ml
2 tbsp	Chopped parsley	2x15 ml
2	Tomatoes	2
	Sprigs of parsley	

Top and tail beans and remove strings. Break or cut into short lengths. Melt the butter in a saucepan. Add the beans and cook for a few minutes. Season with salt and pour in the stock. Cook for 10–15 minutes till just tender.

Meanwhile, heat half the oil in a frying pan. Halve the slices of bread and lightly brown them on both sides in the oil. Remove from pan and keep warm.

Add rest of oil to pan and heat. Sprinkle garlic salt over the lamb steaks. Cook the steaks for 5 minutes on each side. Sprinkle with salt, then with pepper mixed with ground mustard seed.

Mix chopped parsley into beans and spread over bottom of warmed serving dish. Put the lamb steaks on the bread and place on top of the beans. Garnish with tomatoes, cut into eighths, and a few parsley sprigs.

Mutton casserole

Overall timing 2 hours

Freezing Not suitable

To serve 4

2 lb	Lean mutton or lamb	900 g
1	Onion	1
1 oz	Butter	25 g
2 tbsp	Oil	2x15 ml
5 tbsp	Dry white wine or sherry	5x15 ml
	Salt and pepper	
4 oz	Streaky bacon	125 g
1	Garlic clove	1
3 tbsp	Chopped parsley	3x15 ml
$\frac{1}{4}$ pint	Light stock	150 ml

Wipe and trim the meat and cut into neat pieces. Peel and finely chop the onion. Heat the butter and oil in a flameproof casserole, add the onion and fry for 5 minutes, stirring.

Add the meat and fry till browned on all sides. Add the white wine or sherry, salt and pepper.

Derind and finely chop the bacon. Add to the mutton with the peeled and crushed garlic, 2 tbsp (2x15 ml) of parsley and the stock (made with a cube if necessary). Stir, then cover and simmer for about $1\frac{1}{2}$ hours till the mutton is tender.

Taste and adjust the seasoning. Sprinkle with the remaining parsley and serve immediately with boiled potatoes and buttered carrots.

Braised lamb with green beans

Overall timing 1¾ hours

Freezing Suitable: cook for only 1 hour; reheat from frozen in 400°F (200°C) Gas 6 oven for 1½ hours

To serve 4

1½ lb	Green beans	700 g
2 tbsp	Oil	2x15 ml
2 lb	Scrag end of lamb chops	900 g
2	Large onions	2
14 oz	Can of tomatoes	397 g
	Salt and pepper	
¼ teasp	Ground allspice	1.25 ml
¼ teasp	Grated nutmeg	1.25 ml
2	Red peppers	2

Preheat oven to 350°F (180°C) Gas 4.

Wash, top and tail beans and, if necessary, remove strings. Cut into 2 inch (5 cm) lengths. Spread over the bottom of large ovenproof dish.

Heat oil in a large frying pan. Trim lamb, removing excess fat. Fry in oil until brown on all sides. Drain and arrange on top of beans in casserole.

Peel onions and cut into wedges. Fry in oil until golden. With a spoon, break up the tomatoes in their juice. Add to onions with salt, pepper, allspice and nutmeg, stir well and cook for 5 minutes.

Deseed and slice peppers and add to casserole with tomato mixture. Cover tightly and cook in oven for 1½ hours. Serve with boiled rice.

Navarin

Overall timing 1¾ hours

Freezing Not suitable

To serve 6

2 oz	Butter	50 g
2½ lb	Middle neck of lamb	1.1 kg
4	Small onions	4
1 tbsp	Plain flour	15 ml
¾ pint	Stock	400 ml
3 tbsp	Tomato purée	3x15 ml
	Bouquet garni	
	Salt and pepper	
1 lb	Carrots	450 g
1 lb	Turnips	450 g
1 lb	Potatoes	450 g
8 oz	Frozen peas	225 g
1 tbsp	Chopped parsley	15 ml

Melt butter in flameproof casserole, add lamb and brown on all sides. Peel and quarter the onions. Add to casserole and fry gently for 5 minutes.

Sprinkle flour over and cook, stirring, for 2 minutes. Gradually stir in the stock, then add tomato purée, bouquet garni and seasoning and bring to the boil. Cover and simmer gently for 45 minutes.

Scrape and chop carrots. Peel turnips and cut into cubes. Add to casserole and cook for 15 minutes.

Meanwhile, peel potatoes and cut into chunks. Add to casserole and cook, covered, for 20 minutes. Add peas and cook for a further 10 minutes. Remove bouquet garni and adjust seasoning. Garnish with parsley and serve hot.

Summer casserole of lamb

Overall timing 1 hour

Freezing Suitable: add potatoes, beans and peas after reheating

To serve 6

8 oz	Button onions	225 g
1 oz	Butter	25 g
1 tbsp	Oil	15 ml
2½ lb	Middle neck lamb chops	1.1 kg
6	New carrots	6
2	Garlic cloves	2
1 tbsp	Plain flour	15 ml
4	Tomatoes	4
2 tbsp	Tomato purée	2x15 ml
¾ pint	Stock	400 ml
	Bouquet garni	
	Salt and pepper	
1 lb	New potatoes	450 g
2 oz	Green beans	50 g
2 oz	Peas	50 g

Peel button onions. Heat butter and oil in flameproof casserole and fry onions for 5 minutes. Remove from pan and reserve. Add chops and brown on all sides over a high heat.

Scrape carrots and halve if liked. Add to pan with peeled and crushed garlic and cook for 5 minutes. Sprinkle flour over and cook, stirring, for 3 minutes.

Blanch, peel and chop tomatoes. Add to the pan with tomato purée, stock, bouquet garni and seasoning. Cover and simmer for 30 minutes.

Scrape potatoes and add to the casserole. Cook for a further 10 minutes. Top and tail beans and cut into short lengths. Add to pan with peas and reserved onions. Cover and cook for a further 10 minutes. Taste and adjust seasoning if necessary. Discard bouquet garni and serve.

Dolma kara

Overall timing 1¾ hours

Freezing Not suitable

To serve 6

2 tbsp	Oil	2x15 ml
2	Onions	2
1 lb	Boned lamb	450 g
4 oz	Canned chickpeas	125 g
½ pint	Stock	300 ml
	Salt and pepper	
2 tbsp	Tomato purée	2x15 ml
8 oz	Minced cooked lamb	225 g
2 oz	Cooked rice	50 g
1	Egg	1
1 teasp	Lemon juice	5 ml
2 tbsp	Chopped parsley	2x15 ml
	Ground cinnamon	
1 lb	Courgettes	450 g

Heat oil in a saucepan. Peel and chop one of the onions and fry till tender. Cut the lamb into small pieces and add to the pan. Cook for 5–10 minutes.

Add the drained chickpeas, stock, salt, pepper and tomato purée. Cover and simmer for 30 minutes.

Preheat the oven to 375°F (190°C) Gas 5.

Mix the cooked lamb with the cooked rice, remaining onion, peeled and finely chopped, egg, lemon juice, half the parsley, seasoning and a pinch of cinnamon.

Trim courgettes, then cut them in half lengthways. Scoop out the seeds with a teaspoon. Blanch courgettes in boiling salted water for 5 minutes. Drain, then stuff the courgettes with the rice and lamb mixture.

Put the lamb and chickpea stew in an oven-proof dish and place stuffed courgettes on top. Cover with foil and bake for 40 minutes. Serve hot sprinkled with remaining parsley.

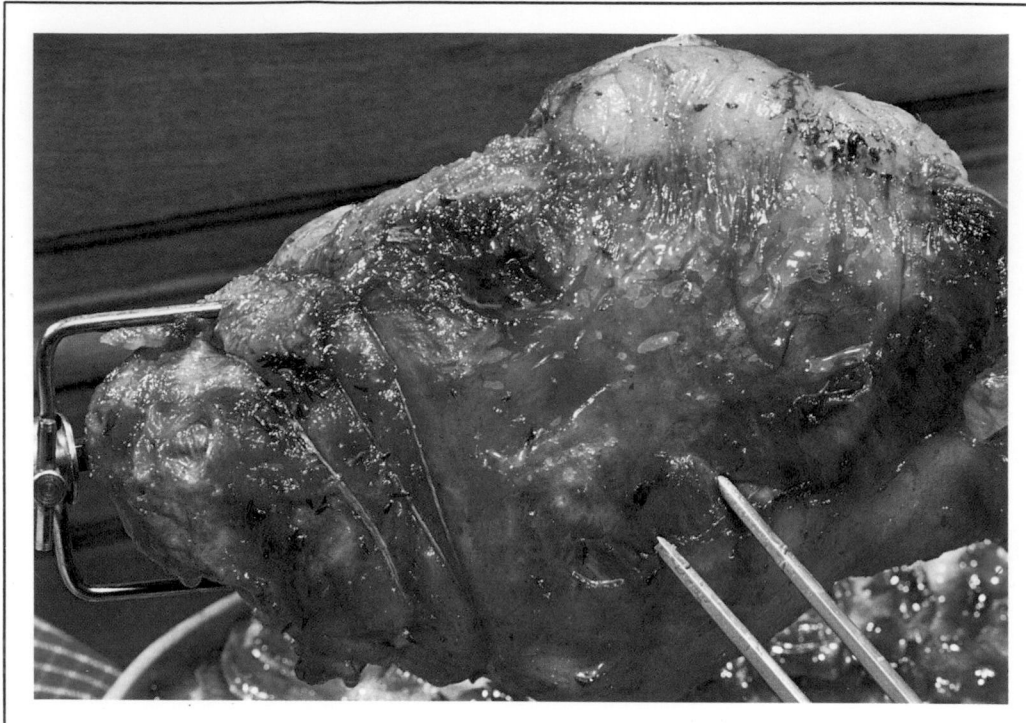

Brittany roast lamb

Overall timing 2½ hours

Freezing Not suitable

To serve 6

3	Garlic cloves	3
4 lb	Leg of lamb	1.8 kg
4 oz	Butter	125 g
	Salt and pepper	
3 lb	Waxy potatoes	1.4 kg
1 teasp	Dried thyme	5 ml

Preheat the oven to 375°F (190°C) Gas 5.

Peel the garlic cloves and slice very thinly. Make incisions through the skin of the lamb and push the garlic into them. Rub half the butter over the lamb and season well.

Grease ovenproof dish with 1 oz (25 g) butter. Peel potatoes and cut into slices about ⅛ inch (3 mm) thick. Arrange half over bottom of dish. Sprinkle with half the thyme and seasoning and dot with half the remaining butter. Repeat layer.

Place dish centrally on shelf below centre of the oven. Place the lamb directly on to the oven shelf above the potatoes so the juices will run on to the potatoes. Roast for 1¾–2 hours till the juices are only slightly pink when thickest part of meat is pierced with a fine skewer.

Place the lamb on a warmed serving dish and carve. Serve the potatoes from the ovenproof dish with a separate dish of cauliflower and whole green beans.

Lamb with broad beans and potatoes

Overall timing 1½ hours

Freezing Not suitable

To serve 6

4	Tomatoes	4
4 oz	Streaky bacon rashers	125 g
2	Onions	2
2	Garlic cloves	2
2 tbsp	Oil	2x15 ml
6	Lamb blade chops	6
½ pint	Stock	300 ml
1 tbsp	Lemon juice	15 ml
½ teasp	Dried thyme	2.5 ml
	Salt and pepper	
1½ lb	Shelled broad beans	700 g
1½ lb	Potatoes	700 g

Blanch, peel and chop tomatoes. Derind and chop bacon. Peel and slice onions. Peel and crush garlic. Heat oil in a flameproof casserole and fry onion and garlic till transparent. Add the chops and bacon and brown on all sides.

Add tomatoes, stock, lemon juice, thyme and seasoning. Cover and simmer for 30 minutes.

Blanch beans in boiling water for 5 minutes, then drain. Peel and slice the potatoes. Add potatoes to casserole and cook for 10 minutes. Add beans and cook for a further 15 minutes. Serve immediately.

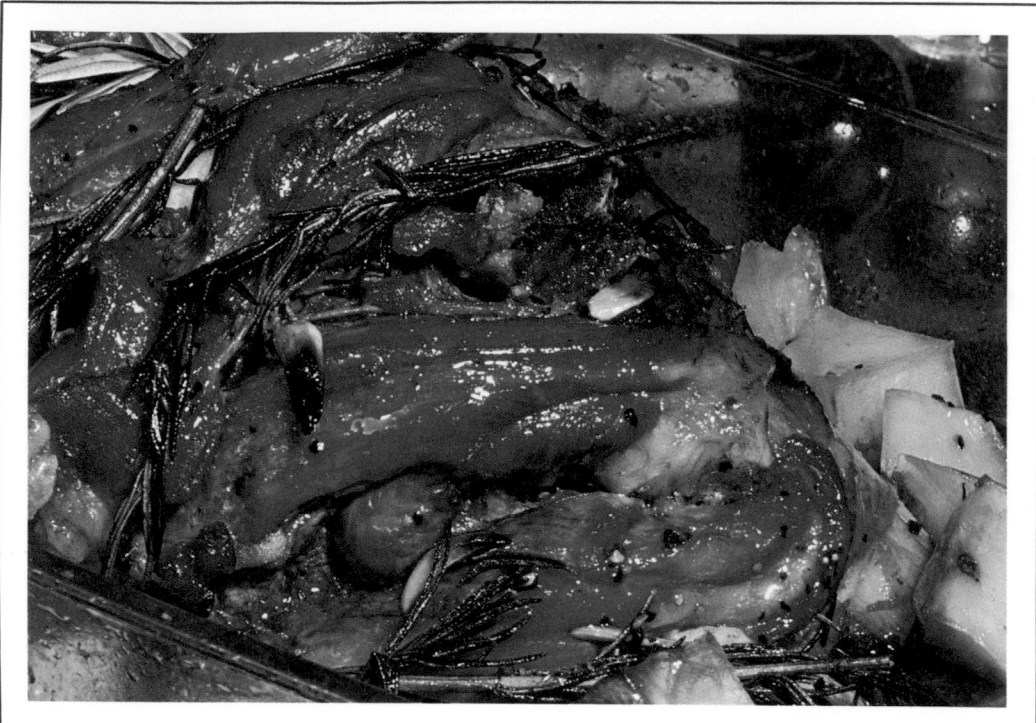

Italian-style roast lamb

Overall timing 1½ hours

Freezing Not suitable

To serve 4

2 lb	Chump end of loin of lamb	900 g
	Sprigs of rosemary	
2 lb	Potatoes	900 g
2 tbsp	Oil	2x15 ml
3 oz	Butter	75 g
1	Garlic clove	1
	Salt and pepper	

Preheat the oven to 350°F (180°C) Gas 4.

Slash through the chops, leaving the loin joined at the bottom. Place sprigs of rosemary in the slashes. Peel potatoes and cut into chunks.

Heat oil and butter in roasting tin. Add the meat and arrange potatoes around it. Peel and crush garlic and add to the lamb and potatoes with salt and pepper. Roast for 45 minutes–1 hour, basting occasionally and turning potatoes halfway through cooking. Serve with a mixed salad or a seasonal green vegetable and gravy.

Sweet sour lamb riblets

Overall timing 1¼ hours plus overnight marination

Freezing Not suitable

To serve 4

1	Onion	1
2	Garlic cloves	2
2 tbsp	Honey	2x15 ml
1 tbsp	Oil	15 ml
4 tbsp	Soy sauce	4x15 ml
¼ pint	Dry sherry	150 ml
1 teasp	Ground ginger	5 ml
2 oz	Caster sugar	50 g
1 teasp	Ground allspice	5 ml
2½ lb	Breast of lamb riblets	1.1 kg

Peel and slice onion. Peel and crush garlic. Put into a bowl with the honey, oil, soy sauce, sherry, ginger, sugar and allspice. Add the breast riblets, cover and marinate overnight in the refrigerator, turning occasionally.

The next day, preheat the oven to 375°F (190°C) Gas 5.

Put the meat into a roasting tin and spoon the marinade over. Bake for 1 hour, basting frequently with the marinade. Serve with plain boiled rice.

Turkish lamb stew

Overall timing 2¾ hours plus overnight soaking

Freezing Not suitable

To serve 6

12 oz	Dried chickpeas	350 g
	Bouquet garni	
2 lb	Boned shoulder of lamb	900 g
1	Onion	1
1	Garlic clove	1
2 oz	Butter	50 g
3 tbsp	Oil	3x15 ml
1 teasp	Ground cumin	5 ml
1 teasp	Ground cinnamon	5 ml
	Sprig of rosemary	
1	Bay leaf	1
	Salt and pepper	
14 oz	Can of tomatoes	397 g
2 tbsp	Lemon juice	2x15 ml
1 tbsp	Chopped parsley	15 ml

Soak chickpeas in water to cover overnight. The next day, drain chickpeas and put into saucepan. Cover with boiling water and add bouquet garni. Cover and simmer for 1 hour.

Cut the lamb into large pieces. Peel and chop the onion. Peel and crush garlic. Heat the butter and oil in flameproof casserole and fry the onion, garlic, cumin and cinnamon for 5 minutes. Add meat pieces to pan and brown on all sides.

Drain chickpeas and add to casserole with the rosemary, bay leaf, seasoning and tomatoes. Cover and cook gently for 1½ hours. Adjust seasoning and sprinkle with lemon juice and parsley just before serving.

Lamb with cauliflower

Overall timing 1½ hours

Freezing Not suitable

To serve 6

1	Small cauliflower	1
½ pint	Water	300 ml
	Salt and pepper	
8 oz	Tomatoes	225 g
1	Large onion	1
2	Garlic cloves	2
2 tbsp	Oil	2x15 ml
2 lb	Breast of lamb riblets	900 g
¼ pint	Tomato juice	150 ml

Trim cauliflower and divide into florets. Bring water and ½ teasp (2.5 ml) salt to the boil in a saucepan, add cauliflower and cook for 5 minutes. Drain, reserving cooking liquor.

Blanch, peel and chop tomatoes. Peel and chop onion. Peel and crush garlic. Heat the oil and garlic in a saucepan, add onion and cook till transparent. Season meat, add to pan and brown quickly on all sides over a high heat, turning frequently to prevent the riblets burning.

Add tomatoes to pan with reserved cooking liquor and tomato juice. Bring to the boil. Add pepper and cook, covered, for 1 hour.

Add cauliflower and cook for a further 15 minutes. Adjust seasoning, then serve with boiled potatoes.

French lamb hot-pot

Overall timing 1¾ hours

Freezing Not suitable

To serve 4

4 oz	Streaky bacon	125 g
2	Onions	2
1 oz	Butter	25 g
2 tbsp	Oil	2x15 ml
2½ lb	Neck of lamb chops	1.1 kg
1 tbsp	Plain flour	15 ml
¾ pint	Light stock	400 ml
1 lb	Turnips	450 g
1 lb	Potatoes	450 g
2	Garlic cloves	2
1 teasp	Caster sugar	5 ml
	Bouquet garni	
	Salt and pepper	
4	Large tomatoes	4

Derind the bacon and cut into strips. Peel onions and slice into thin rings. Heat the butter and oil in a saucepan and fry the bacon and onions. Add lamb and fry over a high heat till browned on both sides. Sprinkle in the flour and cook, stirring, till it browns. Gradually add the stock and bring to the boil.

Peel the turnips and potatoes and cut into quarters. Add to the pan with the peeled and crushed garlic, sugar, bouquet garni and seasoning. Cover and simmer for 1¼ hours.

Remove bouquet garni. Add the tomatoes and cook for a further 15 minutes. Taste and adjust the seasoning. Arrange the meat and vegetables on a warmed serving dish and spoon the cooking liquor over. Serve immediately.

Shepherds' pie

Overall timing 1 hour

Freezing Not suitable

To serve 4

2 lb	Potatoes	900 g
	Salt and pepper	
1	Large onion	1
3 tbsp	Oil	3x15 ml
1	Garlic clove	1
1 lb	Minced cooked lamb	450 g
2 oz	Butter	50 g
¼ pint	Milk	150 ml
3 oz	Cheese	75 g

Peel and halve potatoes. Cook in boiling salted water for 25–30 minutes.

Peel and finely chop onion. Heat oil in a frying pan, add onion and cook for about 10 minutes. Peel and crush garlic. Add garlic and meat to pan and cook for about 5 minutes, stirring.

Preheat the oven to 425°F (220°C) Gas 7.

Drain potatoes and mash with half the butter and the milk. Season to taste. Cover bottom of ovenproof dish with half of the mashed potato, cover with the meat, then spread or pipe the remaining potato on top.

Grate cheese. Sprinkle over potato, dot with remaining butter and bake for about 15 minutes till the top is browned. Serve with green salad.

Lamb stew

Overall timing 2 hours

Freezing Suitable: add potatoes after reheating

To serve 4

2 oz	Butter	50 g
1 tbsp	Oil	15 ml
2½ lb	Middle neck lamb chops	1.1 kg
2 tbsp	Plain flour	2x15 ml
½ pint	Stock or water	300 ml
8 oz	Turnips	225 g
2	Onions	2
8 oz	Carrots	225 g
1	Stalk of celery	1
	Bouquet garni	
	Salt and pepper	
1 lb	Potatoes	450 g

Heat the butter and oil in a flameproof casserole, add the chops and brown well on all sides. Sprinkle flour over and cook, stirring, for 3 minutes. Gradually stir in stock or water.

Peel and chop turnips and onions. Peel carrots and cut into pieces lengthways. Add to casserole with celery stalk, bouquet garni and seasoning. Cover and cook for 1½ hours over low heat.

Peel potatoes and cut into large chunks. Add to casserole and cook, covered, for a further 20 minutes. Discard bouquet garni before serving.

Russian lamb burgers

Overall timing 30 minutes

Freezing Suitable: coat with flour and fry after thawing

To serve 2

1 oz	Fresh breadcrumbs	25 g
2 tbsp	Milk	2x15 ml
8 oz	Minced shoulder of lamb	225 g
1 oz	Gruyère cheese	25 g
1	Small egg	1
	Salt and pepper	
1 tbsp	Plain flour	15 ml
1 oz	Butter	25 g
8 oz	Can of tomatoes	226 g

Put breadcrumbs in a large bowl with the milk and soak for a few minutes. Add the lamb, grated cheese, egg and seasoning and mix well. Divide the mixture into four and shape into patties. Coat lightly with flour.

Melt butter in a frying pan and fry for 5 minutes on each side. Remove from pan with a spatula and place on a warmed serving dish. Keep hot.

Heat tomatoes in a saucepan. Drain and arrange on serving dish with the burgers. Serve a hot tomato sauce separately, if liked, and mashed potatoes topped with crisp fried breadcrumbs and bacon bits.

Shoulder of lamb with turnips

Overall timing 2 hours

Freezing Not suitable

To serve 6

3 lb	Boned shoulder of lamb	1.4 kg
	Salt and pepper	
1	Carrot	1
1	Onion	1
3 oz	Butter	75 g
	Bouquet garni	
$\frac{1}{4}$ pint	Stock	150 ml
2 lb	Turnips	900 g
8 oz	Buttons onions	225 g

Preheat the oven to 350°F (180°C) Gas 4.

Season the lamb inside and out. Roll up and tie firmly with string into a neat shape. Peel and thinly slice carrot and onion.

Melt the butter in flameproof casserole, add onion and carrot and fry till golden. Add lamb and brown on all sides. Season and add bouquet garni and stock. Cover and cook in centre of oven for 1 hour.

Peel turnips and button onions. Place in a saucepan of cold salted water and bring to the boil. Drain and dry on kitchen paper. Arrange turnips and onions around the meat and adjust seasoning. Return to oven and cook for a further 45 minutes.

Remove bouquet garni and string. Transfer lamb to warmed serving plate and surround with turnips and onions.

Greek lamb stew with spinach

Overall timing 1½ hours

Freezing Not suitable

To serve 6

2 lb	Middle neck of lamb	900 g
1	Large onion	1
2 tbsp	Oil	2x15 ml
1 oz	Butter	25 g
1 lb	Ripe tomatoes	450 g
2 tbsp	Tomato purée	2x15 ml
	Dried oregano	
	Salt and pepper	
1 pint	Hot water or stock	560 ml
1¼ lb	Spinach	600 g

Cut the lamb into bite-size pieces. Peel and thinly slice the onion. Heat the oil and butter in a flameproof casserole, add the lamb and onion and fry over a moderate heat for about 10 minutes till browned, stirring occasionally.

Blanch, peel and chop the tomatoes. Add to the pan with the tomato purée, a pinch of oregano, seasoning and water or stock. Mix well and bring to the boil. Cover and simmer for 1½ hours till the lamb is tender.

Wash spinach and shred finely. Add to the pan, stir, cover and cook for a further 10 minutes. Taste and adjust the seasoning. Pour into a warmed serving dish and serve.

Lamb with potatoes and onions

Overall timing 2½ hours

Freezing Not suitable

To serve 8

4½ lb	Leg of lamb	2 kg
4 oz	Butter	125 g
	Salt and pepper	
1 lb	Onions	450 g
2 lb	Potatoes	900 g
¾ pint	Stock	400 ml
	Sprigs of rosemary	
	Bouquet garni	

Preheat the oven to 350°F (180°C) Gas 4.

Place meat in roasting tin, spread with half the butter and season. Roast for 1¼ hours.

Peel and slice the onions. Peel and quarter potatoes. Melt remaining butter in frying pan, add onions and potatoes and fry till golden brown. Add stock, rosemary, bouquet garni and seasoning and cook for 5 minutes, stirring occasionally.

Arrange potato mixture around meat and roast for a further 45 minutes till meat is tender.

Remove bouquet garni. Place lamb on warmed serving dish and surround with potato mixture. Serve with green vegetables.

Stuffed breast of lamb

Overall timing 2½ hours

Freezing Not suitable

To serve 8

1 or 2	Boned breasts of lamb	1 or 2
2 lb	Potatoes	900 g
1½ lb	Small carrots	700 g
4	Turnips	4
2	Stalks of celery	2
4	Leeks	4
1	Onion	1
4	Cloves	4
2 oz	Butter	50 g
1 pint	Stock	560 ml
	Bouquet garni	
Stuffing		
3	Lambs' kidneys	3
8 oz	Streaky bacon	225 g
8 oz	Sausagemeat	225 g
½ teasp	Ground allspice	2.5 ml
3 tbsp	Chopped parsley	3x15 ml
1 teasp	Dried marjoram	5 ml
1	Egg	1
	Salt and pepper	

Preheat the oven to 325°F (170°C) Gas 3.

Prepare and finely chop kidneys. Derind and chop bacon. Mix all stuffing ingredients.

Cut a deep pocket in lamb and fill with stuffing. Sew up opening. If using two breasts, place together with skin side out and sew around sides.

Peel potatoes and carrots. Peel and halve turnips. Chop celery and leeks. Peel onion and spike with cloves. Melt butter in flameproof casserole, add meat and brown all over. Remove. Add vegetables and fry for 2 minutes. Return meat and add stock, bouquet garni and salt. Cover and cook in oven for 2 hours.

Slice meat. Arrange vegetables around meat, discarding onion. Boil stock till reduced by half. Strain over vegetables.

Lamb with vegetables

Overall timing 2 hours

Freezing Not suitable

To serve 6

1½ lb	Best end of neck of lamb	700 g
2 pints	Water	1.1 litres
1 lb	Small swedes	450 g
8 oz	Carrots	225 g
2	Large leeks	2
	Salt and pepper	
1 lb	Waxy potatoes	450 g
1 tbsp	Chopped parsley	15 ml
2 tbsp	Plain flour	2x15 ml

Wipe and trim the lamb, removing the skin. Put into a large saucepan with the water and bring slowly to the boil.

Meanwhile, peel the swedes thickly and cut into quarters. Scrape and thickly slice the carrots. Wash and trim the leeks; slice the white parts and reserve the green.

Add the prepared vegetables to the pan with salt and pepper and bring back to the boil. Cover and simmer for 1 hour.

Peel the potatoes and cut into quarters. Add to the pan and simmer for 20 minutes.

Shred the green part of the leeks and add to the pan with the parsley. Simmer for 5 minutes.

Remove the meat from the pan and keep hot. Blend the flour to a smooth paste with 5 tbsp (5x15 ml) water. Add to the cooking liquor and bring to the boil, stirring constantly. Simmer for 3 minutes. Taste and adjust the seasoning, then pour into a warmed serving dish. Arrange the meat on top and serve.

Lamb cutlets with garlic and anchovy

Overall timing 40 minutes

Freezing Not suitable

To serve 4

2 lb	Best end of neck lamb cutlets	900 g
2	Garlic cloves	2
5 tbsp	Oil	5x15 ml
	Salt and pepper	
	Sprigs of rosemary	
2	Anchovy fillets	2
3 tbsp	White wine vinegar	3x15 ml

Trim cutlets of all fat. Peel and crush one garlic clove. Heat the oil in a large frying pan. Add the garlic and cutlets. Fry quickly on both sides till golden, then season, reduce heat and cook for a further 10–15 minutes.

Put a few pieces of fresh rosemary, the remaining garlic clove, peeled, and the anchovies in a mortar. Pound with a pestle, gradually mixing in the vinegar. Add garlic mixture to pan and cook till the liquid reduces by half.

Arrange cutlets on warmed serving dish and spoon cooking juices over. Garnish with remaining rosemary sprigs.

Lamb fricassee

Overall timing 1¼ hours

Freezing Not suitable

To serve 4

1½ lb	Boned shoulder of lamb	700 g
1	Onion	1
1	Stalk of celery	1
2 oz	Butter	50 g
1 tbsp	Plain flour	15 ml
¼ pint	Milk	150 ml
¼ pint	Stock	150 ml
1	Carrot	1
2	Sprigs of parsley	2
2	Sprigs of basil	2
2	Sprigs of sage	2
	Salt and pepper	
2	Egg yolks	2
1 tbsp	Lemon juice	15 ml

Cut the lamb into neat pieces. Peel and chop the onion. Trim and chop the celery. Melt half the butter in a flameproof casserole. Add onion and celery and fry over low heat for 5 minutes without browning.

Stir in the flour and fry until golden. Gradually add milk and stock, stirring constantly. Bring to the boil, then remove from heat.

Scrape and chop carrot. Tie in a piece of muslin with parsley, basil and sage. Add to casserole with remaining butter, the lamb and seasoning. Stir well. Cover and cook gently for 1 hour, stirring occasionally. Remove muslin bag.

Beat the egg yolks in a bowl and blend with the lemon juice. Stir gently into the fricassee until blended; do not boil. Taste and adjust seasoning, then serve with creamed potatoes and minted peas.

Paprika lamb stew

Overall timing 2 hours

Freezing Suitable

To serve 6

2	Green peppers	2
2	Onions	2
1	Garlic clove	1
2 oz	Bacon rashers	50 g
2 tbsp	Oil	2x15 ml
2 lb	Boned shoulder of lamb	900 g
14 oz	Can of tomatoes	397 g
2 tbsp	Tomato purée	2x15 ml
1 teasp	Paprika	5 ml
1 teasp	Sugar	5 ml
1 pint	Stock	560 ml
	Salt and pepper	
¼ pint	Carton of soured cream	150 ml

Deseed the peppers and cut into strips. Peel and finely chop the onions. Peel and crush the garlic. Derind and dice the bacon. Heat the oil in a flameproof casserole, add the onions, garlic and bacon and fry over a high heat till golden.

Cut the meat into cubes and add to casserole. Brown on all sides. Stir in peppers, tomatoes and their juice, tomato purée, paprika, sugar, stock and seasoning. Cover and cook gently for 1½ hours till meat is tender.

Taste and adjust seasoning and serve with boiled potatoes and soured cream for everyone to spoon on top of the stew.

Piquant kidneys

Overall timing 30 minutes

Freezing Not suitable

To serve 2

8 oz	Lamb's kidneys	225 g
2	Streaky bacon rashers	2
1	Onion	1
8 oz	Long macaroni	225 g
	Salt and pepper	
1 oz	Butter	25 g
1½ teasp	Plain flour	7.5 ml
½ pint	Beef stock	300 ml
1½ teasp	Tomato purée	7.5 ml
¼ teasp	Dried sage	1.25 ml

Prepare and thinly slice kidneys. Derind and dice bacon. Peel and chop onion. Cook macaroni in boiling salted water for 15 minutes till tender.

Meanwhile, melt butter in frying pan and fry kidneys for 3 minutes, stirring from time to time. Remove from pan.

Add bacon and onion to pan and fry gently till golden. Sprinkle flour over and cook, stirring, for 2 minutes. Add stock, tomato purée, sage and seasoning. Bring to the boil, stirring, then return kidneys to pan, reduce heat and simmer for 15 minutes.

Drain macaroni and arrange in warmed serving dish. Spoon kidneys and sauce over and serve hot with crisp lettuce and cucumber salad.

Kidneys in their jackets

Overall timing 45 minutes

Freezing Not suitable

To serve 4

8	Lamb kidneys in their suet	8
4	Slices of bread	4
	Salt and pepper	
1	Tomato	1
	Sprigs of parsley	

Preheat the oven to 400°F (200°C) Gas 6.

Place kidneys in their suet in a roasting tin. Bake for about 35 minutes till the fat is crisp and golden.

Pour a little of the melted fat from the roasting tin into a frying pan and fry the bread till golden on both sides. Arrange slices in warmed individual dishes.

Cut a deep cross in the top of the kidneys and open out like petals. Season inside and place on top of fried bread. Wash tomatoes and cut into wedges. Arrange with parsley sprigs on top of kidneys. Serve with sauté or mashed potatoes.

Kidney brochettes

Overall timing 25 minutes

Freezing Not suitable

To serve 4

4 oz	Unsalted butter	125 g
2 tbsp	Chopped parsley	2x15 ml
1 tbsp	Lemon juice	15 ml
1 lb	Lambs' kidneys	450 g
3	Tomatoes	3
1 teasp	Dried rosemary	5 ml
2 tbsp	Oil	2x15 ml
	Salt and pepper	

Mash the butter with the parsley and lemon juice until well combined. Form into a roll, wrap in greaseproof paper and chill until firm.

Preheat the grill.

Prepare kidneys and cut in half. Cut tomatoes into thin wedges. Thread kidneys and tomato wedges alternately on skewers. Sprinkle with rosemary and brush with oil.

Grill for 10–15 minutes, turning once. Season and garnish with pats of parsley butter. Serve immediately with matchstick chips and sprigs of watercress.

Swiss liver kebabs

Overall timing 35 minutes

Freezing Not suitable

To serve 4

1 lb	Calf's or lamb's liver	450 g
	Salt and pepper	
10	Sage leaves	10
10	Streaky bacon rashers	10
2 oz	Butter	50 g

Preheat the grill.

Cut the liver into 20 bite-size lengths. Season. Wash and dry sage leaves. Derind and stretch the bacon rashers, then cut in half. Wrap bacon rashers round liver pieces, including a sage leaf in alternate rolls. Thread on to four oiled skewers.

Melt the butter in the bottom of the grill pan. Balance the skewers across the pan and brush butter over. Grill for 10–15 minutes till cooked and crisp, turning frequently and brushing with butter. Serve immediately with boiled new potatoes.

Liver and bacon

Overall timing 20 minutes

Freezing Not suitable

To serve 4

4	Slices of lamb's or calf's liver	4
	Salt and pepper	
2 tbsp	Plain flour	2x15 ml
2 oz	Butter	50 g
8	Bacon rashers	8
1 tbsp	Chopped parsley	15 ml
1 tbsp	Lemon juice	15 ml

Trim and wipe the liver. Dust with seasoned flour.

Melt half the butter in a large frying pan, add the bacon rashers and fry till crisp and golden. Remove from pan and keep hot.

Melt the remaining butter in pan, add the liver and fry over a moderate heat for 3–4 minutes on each side.

Arrange liver on serving plate and put bacon on top. Add the parsley and lemon juice to the pan and bring to the boil. Season and spoon over liver. Serve immediately with watercress, matchstick chips and grilled whole tomatoes.

Liver and onions

Overall timing 20 minutes

Freezing Not suitable

To serve 6

1½ lb	Onions	700 g
6	Slices of calf's or lamb's liver	6
	Salt and pepper	
3 tbsp	Plain flour	3x15 ml
3 oz	Butter	75 g
2 tbsp	Chopped parsley (optional)	2x15 ml

Peel and slice onions. Trim and wipe liver. Season the flour and use to coat the liver.

Melt the butter in a large frying pan. Add the onions and fry till golden. Add liver slices and fry for 3–4 minutes on each side. Stir in parsley, if using.

Transfer to a warmed serving dish and top with fried onions. Spoon pan juices over. Serve with boiled potatoes and parsleyed baby carrots.

Liver and bacon kebabs

Overall timing 25 minutes

Freezing Not suitable

To serve 4

12 oz	Piece of lamb's liver	350 g
6 oz	Piece of streaky bacon	175 g
4 oz	Button mushrooms	125 g
2 oz	Melted butter	50 g
2 oz	Fine breadcrumbs	50 g
½ teasp	Paprika	2.5 ml
	Salt	
	Lemon slices	

Wipe and trim the liver and cut into 1 inch (2.5 cm) cubes. Derind the bacon; cut it into thick rashers, then into squares. Wipe and trim the mushrooms.

Preheat the grill. Line the grill pan with foil.

Thread the bacon, liver and mushrooms on to four skewers. Brush with melted butter. Mix the breadcrumbs, paprika and salt together on a plate. Turn the kebabs in the crumbs till evenly coated. Arrange on the grill pan and grill for about 15 minutes, turning the kebabs frequently and brushing them with the fat that runs from the bacon.

Arrange the kebabs on a warmed serving dish and serve immediately with lemon slices for squeezing, and saffron rice.

Brains Milan-style

Overall timing 15 minutes plus soaking and cooling

Freezing Not suitable

To serve 4

4	Lambs' brains	4
2 teasp	Vinegar	2x5 ml
	Salt and pepper	
	Bouquet garni	
4 tbsp	Plain flour	4x15 ml
1	Egg	1
4 tbsp	Fresh breadcrumbs	4x15 ml
2 oz	Butter	50 g
	Sage leaves	
	Lemon wedges	

Put the brains in a bowl of cold water with 1 teasp (5 ml) of the vinegar. Soak for 15 minutes.

Drain the brains. Holding them under running water, carefully pull away membranes and blood vessels. Put the brains into a saucepan and cover with cold water. Add the remaining vinegar, salt and bouquet garni. Bring to the boil, then remove from the heat. Leave to cool in the liquid.

Drain the brains and dry on kitchen paper. Break into small pieces and coat with the flour. Beat the egg. Dip the brains into the egg, then coat with the breadcrumbs.

Melt the butter in a frying pan till foaming. Add the brains and cook for 5 minutes till brown on all sides. Garnish with sage leaves and serve with lemon wedges.

Braised stuffed hearts

Overall timing 2 hours

Freezing Not suitable

To serve 6–8

1	Onion	1
2 oz	Butter	50 g
4 oz	Long-grain rice	125 g
¾ pint	Stock	400 ml
2	Calves' hearts *or*	2
4	Lambs' hearts	4
1	Lemon	1
2 tbsp	Chopped parsley	2x15 ml
1 tbsp	Chopped fresh sage	15 ml
1	Egg	1
	Salt and pepper	
8 oz	Streaky bacon rashers	225 g
2 tbsp	Dry sherry	2x15 ml

Preheat the oven to 350°F (180°C) Gas 4.

Peel and chop onion. Melt half the butter in a pan and fry onion till golden. Add rice and ½ pint (300 ml) of the stock. Bring to the boil, cover and simmer for 20 minutes till tender. Remove from the heat.

Prepare hearts, using kitchen scissors to cut through pockets inside. Wash well and dry with kitchen paper. Grate rind and squeeze juice from lemon. Add both to pan with parsley, sage, egg and seasoning. Mix well and spoon into hearts.

Derind bacon rashers and stretch with the back of a knife. Wrap around the hearts, tying them on with fine string.

Melt remaining butter in flameproof casserole and brown hearts all over. Pour over remaining stock, add sherry, cover and cook in the oven for 1 hour.

Remove string and slice hearts. Arrange on serving dish, garnish with sage and serve.

Hearts casseroled with potatoes and onions

Overall timing 1¾ hours

Freezing Not suitable

To serve 4

2	Calves' hearts or	2
4	Lambs' hearts	4
4 oz	Butter	125 g
1 pint	Beef stock	560 ml
	Bouquet garni	
6 oz	Streaky bacon	175 g
8 oz	Button onions	225 g
2 lb	Potatoes	900 g
2 tbsp	Oil	2x15 ml
	Salt and pepper	
2 tbsp	Redcurrant jelly	2x15 ml
1 tbsp	Chopped parsley	15 ml

Prepare hearts. Melt 2 oz (50 g) butter in saucepan, add hearts and brown on all sides. Pour in stock, add bouquet garni, cover and simmer for 1½ hours until tender.

Meanwhile, derind bacon and cut into strips. Peel onions. Peel and chop potatoes. Cook onions in boiling salted water for 5 minutes, then add potatoes and cook for a further 5 minutes. Drain well.

Melt remaining butter with oil in frying pan. Add bacon and fry till golden. Add potatoes, onions and seasoning and cook till golden brown, turning occasionally.

Remove hearts from pan and place on warmed serving dish. Keep hot. Reduce liquid in pan to about ¼ pint (150 ml), then stir in redcurrant jelly. Pour over vegetables in frying pan and cook for 2 minutes. Arrange vegetables around hearts. Spoon over cooking juices and serve sprinkled with parsley.

Sweetbread kebabs

Overall timing 35 minutes plus marination

Freezing Not suitable

To serve 4

1 lb	Prepared lambs' sweetbreads	450 g
4	Thick streaky bacon rashers	4
6 tbsp	Oil	6x15 ml
1 tbsp	Lemon juice	15 ml
	Salt and pepper	
$\frac{1}{2}$	Lemon	$\frac{1}{2}$
	Sprigs of parsley	

Cut the sweetbreads in half. Derind the bacon and cut into 1 inch (2.5 cm) pieces. Thread the sweetbreads and bacon alternately on to four greased skewers.

Mix the oil, lemon juice and seasoning in a shallow dish. Add the kebabs, turning them to coat with the marinade. Leave in a cool place for 1 hour.

Preheat the grill. Place each kebab on a piece of foil, shaping the foil into a dish so it will hold the marinade, and pour the marinade over. Arrange the kebabs on the grill pan and grill for 15–20 minutes, turning frequently in the marinade, till the sweetbreads are tender.

Arrange the kebabs on a warmed serving dish and pour the marinade over. Garnish with the lemon and parsley and serve immediately with crusty bread.

Honey-glazed bacon

Overall timing 1½ hours plus overnight soaking

Freezing Not suitable

To serve 6–8

4 lb	Collar bacon	1.8 kg
	Whole cloves	
2 tbsp	Clear honey	2x15 ml
3 tbsp	Soft brown sugar	3x15 ml
2	Granny Smith apples	2
2 oz	Butter	50 g

Put bacon into a large saucepan. Cover with cold water and leave to soak overnight.

The next day, drain the bacon. Return it to the same pan and cover with fresh water. Bring to the boil. Remove any scum. Reduce heat, cover and simmer gently for 1 hour.

Preheat the oven to 350°F (180°C) Gas 4.

Remove bacon from pan, allow to cool slightly then cut off the rind. Score fat in a lattice pattern and put a clove in the centre of each "diamond". Put in a roasting tin.

Gently heat honey and sugar in a small saucepan until melted. Brush over the surface of the bacon. Cook in the oven for 20 minutes, basting from time to time. Take care not to let the glaze burn.

Five minutes before the joint is cooked, peel, core and slice apples into ¼ inch (6 mm) thick rings. Melt butter in a frying pan and fry the apple rings on both sides until lightly golden and tender.

Serve bacon joint on a dish surrounded by apple rings.

Ham roasted in stout

Overall timing 2½ hours plus cooling

Freezing Suitable: slice meat and cover with sauce; reheat from frozen in moderate oven

To serve 6

3 lb	Lightly salted ham or bacon (collar, slipper, or gammon)	1.4 kg
2	Onions	2
½ pint	Stout	300 ml
1 oz	Butter	25 g
1 oz	Plain flour	25 g
¼ teasp	Crushed caraway seed	1.25 ml
	Pepper	

Preheat the oven to 400°F (200°C) Gas 4.

If using bacon joint, remove rind. Place ham or bacon in an ovenproof dish. Peel onions and slice into rings. Cover ham with onion rings. Pour stout over. Roast for 2 hours, turning meat once during cooking.

Remove meat from dish and place on warmed serving dish. Keep hot. Sieve cooking liquor, cool quickly and skim fat from surface. Place liquor in measuring jug and make up to ½ pint (300 ml) with water if necessary.

Melt butter in saucepan. Stir in flour and allow to brown lightly. Gradually add cooking liquor and simmer, stirring, till thickened. Season with crushed caraway seed and black pepper. Cook for 5 minutes, then pour over the roast and serve.

Bacon and cabbage casserole

Overall timing 1¼ hours

Freezing Not suitable

To serve 4

1	Medium-size white cabbage	1
2	Onions	2
1 oz	Lard	25 g
8 oz	Back bacon	225 g
1 lb	Minced beef	450 g
1 teasp	Caraway seeds	5 ml
¼ pint	Beef stock	150 ml
	Salt and pepper	
2 oz	Butter	50 g
8 oz	Streaky bacon rashers	225 g

Preheat the oven to 375°F (190°C) Gas 5.

Discard any marked outer leaves of the cabbage. Save two or three good ones. Cut the remaining cabbage in half. Remove the core, then shred the cabbage. Put with reserved leaves into a saucepan of cold water. Bring to the boil and drain. Set aside.

Peel and chop the onions. Melt the lard in a large saucepan, add the onions and cook gently for 3–4 minutes. Derind and chop back bacon. Add to the saucepan. Cook for 2–3 minutes. Add the minced beef and cook, stirring, until brown. Add the caraway seeds, stock and seasoning. Simmer for 10 minutes.

Melt the butter in a small saucepan. Put half of the shredded cabbage in the bottom of an ovenproof dish and pour the melted butter over. Spread the mince mixture evenly over the cabbage. Cover with remaining shredded cabbage and top with whole leaves. Arrange the streaky bacon rashers over the top of the cabbage. Bake for 45 minutes.

Frankfurters with apple purée

Overall timing 20 minutes

Freezing Suitable: add frankfurters when reheating

To serve 4

8	Dessert apples	8
½ pint	Sweet white wine or cider	300 ml
	Salt and pepper	
4 oz	Butter	100 g
8	Frankfurters	8

Peel, core and chop apples. Place in a saucepan with the wine or cider. Cover and cook over a low heat till the apples are soft, then beat until pulpy with a wooden spoon. Season to taste.

Melt butter in a frying pan, add the frankfurters, cover and cook gently over low heat till heated through.

Put apple purée on a warmed serving dish, place the frankfurters on top and serve immediately with crusty bread or jacket potatoes.

Bacon with lentils

Overall timing 2½ hours plus 3 hours soaking

Freezing Not suitable

To serve 6

2¼ lb	Middle cut bacon hock	1 kg
1	Carrot	1
2	Onions	2
1	Garlic clove	1
	Bouquet garni	
8	Peppercorns	8
1 lb	Continental lentils	450 g
	Salt and pepper	

Put bacon joint in a large saucepan and cover with cold water. Soak for 3 hours, changing the water several times.

Drain the bacon joint and cover with fresh water. Peel and slice the carrot; peel and quarter the onions; peel and halve the garlic. Add to the bacon with the bouquet garni and peppercorns. Bring to the boil, cover and simmer for 45 minutes.

Remove bouquet garni. Wash and pick over lentils. Add to bacon, cover and cook for a further hour till lentils are tender. Adjust seasoning, then arrange on warmed dish and serve with mustard.

Sausage surprise

Overall timing 35 minutes

Freezing Not suitable

To serve 4–6

2 lb	Potatoes	900 g
	Salt and pepper	
1 lb	Chipolatas	450 g
½ pint	Milk	300 ml
2 oz	Butter	50 g
6 oz	Cheese	175 g
½ teasp	Grated nutmeg	2.5 ml

Preheat the grill. Peel the potatoes and cut into quarters. Cook in boiling salted water for about 10 minutes till tender.

Meanwhile, grill the chipolatas for about 15 minutes, turning occasionally till well browned.

Drain the potatoes in a colander. Add the milk to the pan and bring just to the boil. Return the potatoes to the pan with the butter and mash till smooth.

Grate cheese and beat 4 oz (125 g) into potatoes with nutmeg and seasoning. Spread the mixture in a flameproof dish and push the chipolatas diagonally into the potato so that the tops are just showing.

Sprinkle the remaining cheese over and grill for about 5 minutes till golden.

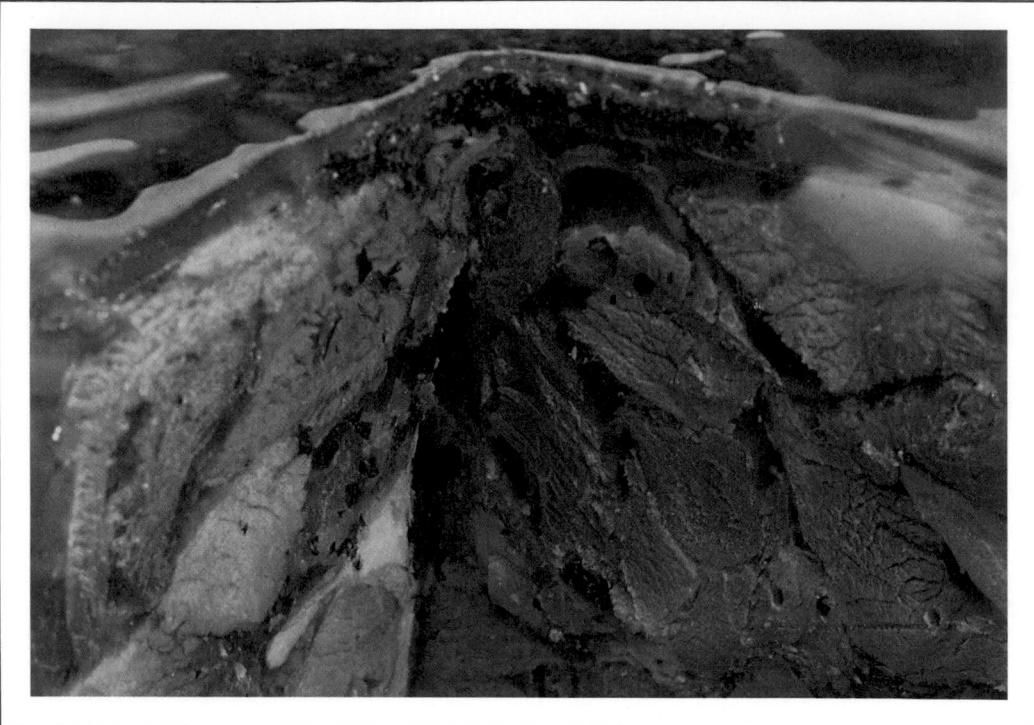

Savoury mould

Overall timing 2½ hours plus setting

Freezing Not suitable

To serve 8–10

2 lb	Collar bacon	900 g
1	Onion	1
1	Clove	1
1	Stalk of celery	1
2	Garlic cloves	2
	Bouquet garni	
	Salt and pepper	
5 tbsp	Chopped parsley	5 x 15 ml
1 tbsp	White wine vinegar	15 ml
2 teasp	Powdered gelatine	2 x 5 ml
1 teasp	Dried tarragon	5 ml
1 teasp	Dried chervil	5 ml
2	Egg whites	2
	Cucumber peel	
1	Red pepper	1
1 oz	Stoned black olives	25 g

Put bacon in a pan, cover with water and bring to the boil. Drain. Peel onion and spike with clove. Chop celery. Peel garlic. Add vegetables to pan with 3½ pints (2 litres) water, the bouquet garni and seasoning. Bring to the boil and simmer for 1 hour.

Soak parsley in vinegar.

Lift bacon joint out of pan. Remove meat from bone and chop. Reduce cooking liquor to ½ pint (300 ml) by boiling fast. Strain cooking liquor and return to pan. Add gelatine and herbs. Lightly beat egg whites and add. Leave for 30 minutes, then bring nearly to the boil, whisking. Remove from heat and pour through a scalded jelly bag or several layers of muslin.

Spoon a little jelly into wet pudding basin. Chill till set.

Chop cucumber peel. Deseed and slice pepper. Arrange decoratively in basin with olives. Add a little more jelly and chill again till set. Arrange bacon pieces and parsley in layers in basin. Pour remaining jelly over, cover and chill overnight.

Sausage and vegetable stew

Overall timing $3\frac{1}{4}$ hours

Freezing Not suitable

To serve 6

1	White cabbage	1
3	Carrots	3
1	Leek	1
1	Bacon knuckle	1
1	Pig's knuckle	1
$3\frac{1}{2}$ pints	Water	2 litres
	Salt and pepper	
2	Large potatoes	2
8 oz	Sausages	225 g

Shred cabbage. Peel and chop carrots. Trim and slice leek. Put vegetables into a pan with the knuckles, water and seasoning. Bring to the boil, then cover and cook for $2\frac{1}{2}$ hours.

Remove knuckles from pan and cut meat from bones. Peel potatoes and cut into large chunks. Cut sausages in half. Add meat, potatoes and sausages to pan and cook for a further 30 minutes. Taste and adjust seasoning before serving.

Sausages in cider sauce

Overall timing 50 minutes

Freezing Not suitable

To serve 4

1 lb	Boned pork chops	450 g
8	Pork chipolatas	8
1 oz	Lard	25 g
1	Large onion	1
1	Carrot	1
1	Stalk of celery	1
4	Large tomatoes	4
1	Garlic clove	1
$\frac{1}{4}$ pint	Dry cider	150 ml
	Salt and pepper	
1 oz	Butter	25 g
12 oz	Long grain rice	350 g
$1\frac{1}{2}$ pints	Chicken stock	850 ml
3 tbsp	Grated Parmesan cheese	3x15 ml

Cut the pork chops into bite-size pieces. Twist each chipolata in half to make 16 small sausages. Melt the lard in a frying pan and fry the pork and sausages gently, turning frequently, for 10 minutes.

Meanwhile, peel and chop the onion and carrot. Trim and chop the celery. Quarter the tomatoes. Peel and crush the garlic. Add the vegetables to the frying pan with the cider and seasoning. Cover and simmer for 20 minutes.

Melt the butter in a saucepan, add the rice and fry, stirring, for 2 minutes. Add the stock and bring to the boil, stirring. Cover and simmer for about 15 minutes till rice is tender and liquid is absorbed.

Remove the rice from the heat and stir in the cheese. Taste and adjust the seasoning and fluff with a fork. Pile into a warmed serving dish and arrange sausages and pork on top. Spoon cider sauce over and serve immediately with a mixed salad.

Roast ginger chicken

Overall timing 1¼ hours

Freezing Not suitable

To serve 4

1	Cooking apple	1
1 inch	Piece of root ginger	2.5 cm
4 oz	Cooked long grain rice	125 g
5 oz	Carton of natural yogurt	141 g
3 oz	Softened butter	75 g
	Salt and pepper	
3 lb	Ovenready chicken	1.4 kg

Preheat the oven to 400°F (200°C) Gas 6.

Peel, core and grate apple. Grate or finely chop ginger and add to apple with rice, yogurt, 2 oz (50 g) of the butter and seasoning. Mix well together. Use to stuff chicken.

Place chicken on its side in a roasting tin and dot with remaining butter. Roast for 15 minutes, then turn chicken on to its other side and roast for 15 minutes. Turn chicken on to its back and continue roasting for a further 30 minutes or until tender. Baste frequently.

Remove chicken from roasting tin and place on warmed serving dish. Serve with gravy made from pan juices, green or mixed salad and sauté or creamed potatoes.

Alsatian chicken

Overall timing 1½ hours

Freezing Not suitable

To serve 4–6

8	Chicken legs and wings	8
1	Garlic clove	1
2 oz	Streaky bacon	50 g
4 tbsp	Oil	4x15 ml
2	Onions	2
8 fl oz	Dry white wine	225 ml
4 oz	Mushrooms	125 g
2	Bay leaves	2
2 tbsp	Chopped parsley	2x15 ml
2 tbsp	Chopped chives	2x15 ml
	Salt and pepper	
1 tbsp	Arrowroot	15 ml
¼ pint	Carton of single cream	150 ml
	Sprigs of fresh parsley	

Rub chicken all over with halved garlic clove. Derind and dice bacon. Fry in flameproof casserole till brown. Add oil and when hot brown chicken pieces on all sides.

Peel and finely chop onions. Add to casserole and brown. Pour in half of wine, cover and cook for 35 minutes.

Slice mushrooms and add to casserole with bay leaves, half the chopped parsley and chives and seasoning. Cover and cook for 10 minutes.

Discard bay leaves. Take out chicken pieces with a draining spoon and place on a warmed serving dish. Keep hot. If there's a lot of liquid in casserole, boil till reduced by half. Mix arrowroot with remaining wine and stir into pan juices. Cook, stirring, till sauce thickens, then gradually stir in cream. When hot (it must not boil) pour sauce over chicken. Garnish with remaining chopped parsley and chives and parsley sprigs.

Cheesy chicken rolls

Overall timing 45 minutes

Freezing Not suitable

To serve 6

6	Large chicken breasts	6
	Salt and pepper	
2 teasp	Made mustard	2x5 ml
6	Thin slices of Derby cheese	6
6	Thin streaky bacon rashers	6
	Plain flour	
2 oz	Butter	50 g
2 tbsp	Oil	2x15 ml
½ pint	Light ale	300 ml
12	Stoned green olives	12

Remove skin and bones from chicken breasts. Season underside of chicken breasts and spread with mustard, then place a slice of cheese on each. Roll up and wrap a rasher of bacon around. Tie rolls firmly with string and coat lightly in flour.

Heat butter and oil in flameproof casserole. Lightly brown chicken rolls all over. Add beer, taking care that it does not fill more than half the casserole. Add more seasoning if required. Cover and simmer for 10 minutes.

Meanwhile, scald olives in boiling water. Drain well and add to casserole. Cover and simmer for 10 minutes more. Carefully remove string from chicken rolls and serve with rice or potatoes.

Chicken with turnips

Overall timing 1 hour

Freezing Not suitable

To serve 6

8 oz	Button onions	225 g
6	Saffron strands	6
3 lb	Ovenready chicken	1.4 kg
1½ lb	Small turnips	700 g
8 oz	Courgettes	225 g
2 oz	Butter	50 g
2 tbsp	Oil	2x15 ml
½ pint	Chicken stock	300 ml
4	Bay leaves	4
	Salt and pepper	

Blanch and peel onions. Soak saffron in 2 tbsp (2x15 ml) warm water. Cut chicken into 12 portions. Peel and chop turnips. Slice courgettes.

Heat butter and oil in frying pan and brown chicken pieces all over. Remove from pan with a draining spoon. Add onions and turnips and fry for 3 minutes, then add courgettes and fry for a further 2 minutes till browned.

Return chicken to pan with saffron and soaking water, stock, bay leaves and seasoning. Cover and simmer for 20 minutes till chicken is tender.

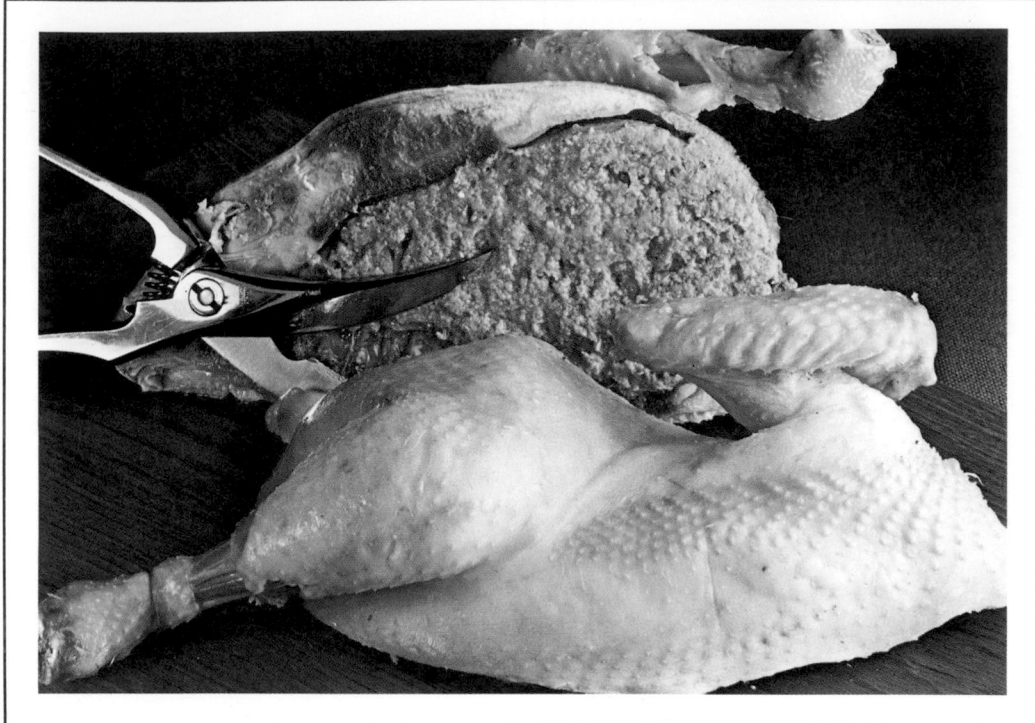

Lombardy chicken

Overall timing 2¼ hours

Freezing Not suitable

To serve 4

2 oz	Breadcrumbs	50 g
¼ pint	Milk	150 ml
4 oz	Cooked ham	125 g
3 lb	Chicken with giblets	1.4 kg
4 oz	Sausagemeat	125 g
2 tbsp	Chopped parsley	2x15 ml
1	Egg	1
2 oz	Grated Parmesan cheese	50 g
2 tbsp	Dry vermouth	2x15 ml
	Salt and pepper	
1	Stalk of celery	1
1	Carrot	1
1	Onion	1
2 teasp	Arrowroot	2x5 ml

Soak breadcrumbs in milk. Mince or finely chop ham, and liver and heart from giblets. Place in a bowl with the sausagemeat, parsley, egg, Parmesan, vermouth, salt and pepper. Squeeze liquid out of the breadcrumbs and add them to the mixture. Mix well together.

Wipe chicken and stuff with the mixture, leaving a little space for expansion. Close opening with a small skewer or by sewing with thick thread.

Half fill a large saucepan with lightly salted water and bring to the boil. Chop celery and carrot. Peel and quarter onion. Add them all to the pan and bring back to the boil.

Add the chicken and the rest of the giblets. Cover and simmer for 1¾ hours or until chicken is tender.

Lift chicken out of the stock and keep warm on serving dish. Dissolve the arrowroot in a little of the strained stock, then add a further ½ pint (300 ml) stock. Cook, stirring, until thick and clear.

Chicken à la king

Overall timing 35 minutes

Freezing Suitable

To serve 4

1 lb	Cooked boneless chicken	450 g
1	Onion	1
1	Large green pepper	1
2 oz	Butter	50 g
2 oz	Plain flour	50 g
2 tbsp	Cold milk	2x15 ml
½ pint	Warm milk	300 ml
	Salt and pepper	
	Grated nutmeg	
2 tbsp	Sherry	2x15 ml

Cut chicken into small pieces. Peel and finely chop onion. Deseed pepper and finely chop half of it.

Melt the butter in a saucepan and gently fry onion and pepper till onion is transparent.

Stir in the flour with a wooden spoon, then the cold milk. Remove from heat and gradually add the warm milk. Bring to the boil. Season with salt, pepper and a pinch of nutmeg. Reduce heat and simmer gently for 15 minutes.

Add chicken and sherry and cook for 5 minutes more. Stir frequently during this time to prevent mixture sticking.

Meanwhile, slice the remaining pepper and blanch in boiling water for 5 minutes.

Place chicken and sauce on a warmed serving plate and surround with the pepper slices. Serve with boiled rice or noodles.

Mustard chicken casserole

Overall timing 1 hour

Freezing Not suitable

To serve 4

3½ lb	Ovenready chicken	1.6 kg
1	Onion	1
4 tbsp	Oil	4x15 ml
	Salt and pepper	
1 lb	Potatoes	450 g
2 oz	Back bacon	50 g
1 tbsp	Vinegar	15 ml
2	Cloves	2
1	Bay leaf	1
¼ teasp	Grated nutmeg	1.25 ml
1 teasp	Powdered mustard	5 ml
¼ pint	Chicken stock	150 ml
8 oz	Can of tomatoes	227 g

Wipe the chicken and cut into 8 portions. Peel and finely slice the onion. Heat the oil in a flameproof casserole and fry the onion till transparent.

Add the chicken portions and fry for about 10 minutes, turning frequently. Season.

Meanwhile, peel and dice the potatoes. Add to the pan with the derinded bacon, vinegar, cloves, bay leaf, nutmeg and seasoning. Stir the mustard into the stock (made with cubes if necessary) and pour into pan with the canned tomatoes and juice. Mix well, pressing tomatoes to break them up, and bring to the boil. Reduce the heat and simmer for about 30 minutes till the chicken and potatoes are tender.

Adjust the seasoning and discard bay leaf before serving.

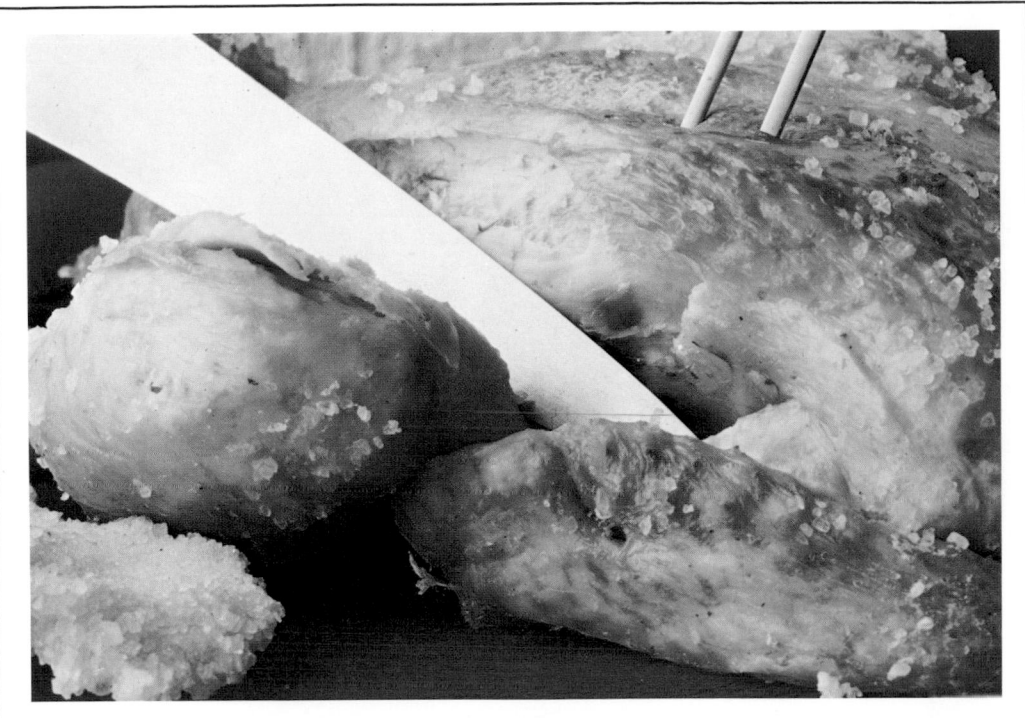

Chicken baked in salt

Overall timing 1¾ hours

Freezing Not suitable

To serve 4–6

3½ lb	Ovenready chicken	1.6 kg
1	Sprig of fresh tarragon	1
	Black pepper	
6 lb	Coarse sea-salt	2.6 kg

Preheat the oven to 450°F (230°C) Gas 8.

Wipe the chicken, put the tarragon inside and sprinkle inside and out with pepper. Truss with string.

Line a casserole with a large sheet of foil and spread with one-third of the salt. Place chicken breast-bone down on salt. Cover completely with remaining salt. Fold the foil over the top of the chicken and join together at top, sealing well. Bake, covered, near the top of the oven for 1½ hours.

Take the chicken out of the oven, unwrap and remove the crust of salt. Brush off any salt that clings, then carve the chicken in the usual way.

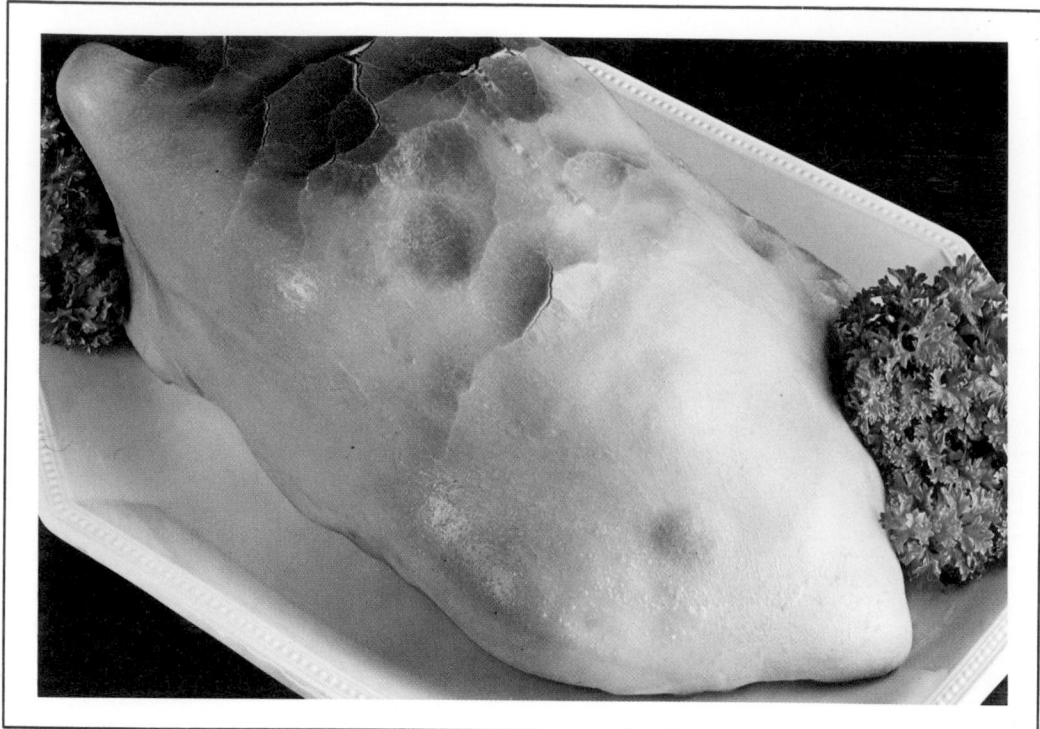

Pastry-wrapped stuffed chicken

Overall timing 2¼ hours

Freezing Not suitable

To serve 4

3 lb	Ovenready chicken	1.4 kg
	Salt	
1 oz	Butter	25 g
12 oz	Shortcrust pastry	350 g
1	Egg	1
Stuffing		
8 oz	Mushrooms	225 g
1 oz	Butter	25 g
2 tbsp	Sherry	2 x 15 ml
	Salt and pepper	
6 oz	Chicken livers	175 g
1	Small onion	1
2 oz	Dried breadcrumbs	50 g

First make stuffing. Slice mushrooms. Melt butter in a pan and fry mushrooms for 3 minutes. Add sherry and cook for 3 minutes. Season with salt and pepper.

Finely chop chicken livers. Peel and finely chop onion. Add both to pan with breadcrumbs and mix well. Heat gently for 5 minutes.

Season chicken inside and out with salt. Stuff with liver mixture and close the opening. Melt butter in a roasting tin and brown chicken on all sides for 20 minutes.

Preheat the oven to 400°F (200°C) Gas 6.

Roll out dough on a lightly floured surface till about ¼ inch (6 mm) thick and large enough to wrap round chicken. Remove chicken from roasting tin. Drain and allow to cool slightly, then place, breast side down, on dough. Moisten edges and wrap dough round chicken. Press edges together well.

Place chicken on greased baking tray with seam underneath. Use dough trimmings to decorate top. Brush with beaten egg and bake for 1½–1¾ hours. If pastry shows signs of overbrowning, cover with foil.

Chicken in soured cream

Overall timing 1 hour

Freezing Not suitable

To serve 4

3 lb	Chicken portions	1.4 kg
2 tbsp	Plain flour	2x15 ml
4 oz	Button mushrooms	125 g
1	Onion	1
2 oz	Butter	50 g
2 tbsp	Oil	2x15 ml
	Salt and pepper	
2 tbsp	Brandy	2x15 ml
¼ pint	Carton of soured cream	150 ml

Wash chicken portions and dry on kitchen paper. Coat lightly with the flour. Wipe and slice mushrooms. Peel and slice onion.

Heat butter and oil in a frying pan and fry onion till golden. Add floured chicken portions and brown on all sides. Season with salt and pepper. Cover and cook for 40 minutes.

Pour brandy over the chicken and heat for a few minutes, then set alight. When the flames have died down, add the sliced mushrooms and cook over a gentle heat for 5 minutes.

Add soured cream to pan. Heat through, stirring, for 2 minutes. Do not allow to boil. Serve at once with noodles and a mixed salad.

Poached chicken

Overall timing 2 hours

Freezing Not suitable

To serve 4

8	Chicken legs and wings	8
12 oz	Carrots	350 g
8 oz	Button onions	225 g
2	Stalks of celery	2
	Salt	
1 lb	Potatoes	450 g

Put chicken joints in a large saucepan and cover with cold water. Peel and chop carrots; peel onions; chop celery. Add a few pieces of carrot, four onions, all the celery and salt to chicken. Bring slowly to the boil, then reduce the heat until just simmering, cover and cook for about 1½ hours.

Meanwhile, cook remaining carrots and onions in boiling salted water for 5 minutes. Peel and chop potatoes and add to pan. Simmer for a further 20 minutes. Drain and keep hot.

Drain chicken (keep the cooking liquor and vegetables for soup) and serve on a warmed plate with the separately cooked carrots, onions and potatoes.

Chicken Kiev

Overall timing 1½ hours

Freezing Suitable: egg, crumb and fry after thawing

To serve 4

4 oz	Softened butter	125 g
2 tbsp	Lemon juice	2x15 ml
1	Garlic clove	1
1 tbsp	Chopped parsley	15 ml
	Salt and pepper	
4	Boneless chicken breasts	4
	Oil for frying	
3 tbsp	Plain flour	3x15 ml
1	Egg	1
3 tbsp	Fresh white breadcrumbs	3x15 ml

Work together the butter and lemon juice until smooth. Peel and crush the garlic and add to the butter with the parsley and seasoning. Mix well. Shape into a cylinder, wrap in foil and place in freezer for 1 hour to firm.

Place the chicken breasts between two sheets of dampened greaseproof paper on a flat surface and beat flat with a heavy knife or wooden mallet until thin.

Heat the oil in a deep-fryer to 350°F (170°C).

Place a piece of butter on each chicken breast. Roll chicken round butter and secure with a cocktail stick. Coat each piece of chicken all over with the flour, then dip in the beaten egg to cover and finally in the breadcrumbs, pressing them on well. Fry for 12–15 minutes until golden brown. Drain on kitchen paper, remove cocktail sticks and serve immediately with lemon wedges and a green salad.

Soufflé-topped chicken

Overall timing 1¼ hours

Freezing Not suitable

To serve 4–6

2 tbsp	Oil	2x15 ml
3 lb	Chicken portions	1.4 kg
	Salt and pepper	
1 lb	Can of sweetcorn kernels	450 g
2 tbsp	Fresh breadcrumbs	2x15 ml
Sauce		
3 oz	Butter	75 g
2 oz	Plain flour	50 g
¼ pint	Milk	150 ml
2	Eggs	2
¼ pint	Carton of single cream	150 ml
	Salt and pepper	
	Grated nutmeg	

Preheat the oven to 400°F (200°C) Gas 6.

Heat oil in flameproof casserole. Add chicken and cook for about 10 minutes until pieces are browned on all sides. Season with salt and pepper.

Drain corn and add to the casserole with 4 tbsp (4x15 ml) of the liquid.

To make the sauce, melt 2 oz (50 g) of the butter in a saucepan, sprinkle with the flour and cook till browned, stirring all the time. Gradually add milk and cook, stirring, for 5 minutes. Remove from heat.

Separate eggs. Mix cream, egg yolks, salt, pepper and a pinch of nutmeg in a bowl. Stir into the sauce and heat through but do not boil. Remove from heat and set aside.

Beat egg whites in a bowl until they hold stiff peaks. Fold into sauce with a metal spoon and pour over corn and chicken mixture. Sprinkle with breadcrumbs, dot with remaining butter and bake in the centre of the oven for 45 minutes. Serve with broccoli garnished with chopped hard-boiled eggs.

Crisp lemon chicken

Overall timing 30 minutes plus marination

Freezing Not suitable

To serve 4

8	Chicken portions	8
3 tbsp	Lemon juice	3x15 ml
2 tbsp	Oil	2x15 ml
2 oz	Plain flour	50 g
	Salt and pepper	
½ teasp	Paprika	2.5 ml
	Lemon wedges	

Wash and dry chicken portions. Mix together lemon juice and oil and rub into the chicken. Cover and leave to marinate for 2–3 hours.

Preheat the grill. Mix together the flour, seasoning and paprika.

Arrange chicken portions skin-side down on grill rack. Sift half the seasoned flour over the chicken and grill for 7–10 minutes.

Turn chicken portions over. Sprinkle with remaining sifted flour and grill for a further 7–10 minutes until crisp and golden, and juices run clear when a skewer is inserted. Arrange on a warmed serving dish and garnish with lemon wedges. Serve with a bean, cucumber and tomato salad.

Chicken Maryland

Overall timing 1¾ hours

Freezing Not suitable

To serve 8

8	Boned chicken breasts	8
	Salt	
	Cayenne pepper	
2oz	Plain flour	50g
2	Eggs	2
4oz	Fresh breadcrumbs	125g
	Oil for frying	
4	Bananas	4
12	Bacon rashers	12
Corn fritters		
4oz	Plain flour	125g
1	Whole egg	1
¼ pint	Milk	150ml
11½oz	Sweetcorn kernels	325g
1	Egg white	1

To make the fritter batter, sift flour and pinch of salt into a bowl and make a well in the centre. Add the whole egg and gradually beat in the milk. Drain corn and add. Leave batter to stand.

Cut each chicken breast in half. Season with salt and cayenne pepper. Dip into the flour, then into beaten eggs, then into breadcrumbs.

Heat the oil in a deep-fryer until hot enough to brown a cube of bread in 30 seconds. Fry the chicken pieces a few at a time for about 10–15 minutes, depending on thickness. Remove from pan, drain on kitchen paper and keep hot. Skim surface of oil.

Peel bananas and cut into three, then halve each piece lengthways. Derind and stretch bacon rashers and cut in half. Wrap a piece of bacon round each piece of banana and secure with a wooden cocktail stick. Fry in hot oil, then drain and keep hot.

Whisk egg white till stiff and fold into fritter batter. Drop in spoonfuls into hot oil and fry till puffed and golden brown. Drain. Arrange fritters, chicken and bacon-wrapped bananas on plate and serve.

Tunisian chicken

Overall timing 2¼ hours

Freezing Not suitable

To serve 4

3 lb	Ovenready chicken with giblets	1.4 kg
	Salt and pepper	
5 oz	Sweetcorn kernels	150 g
3	Carrots	3
3	Medium potatoes	3
4	Tomatoes	4
4 oz	Cheddar cheese	125 g
1	Egg	1
2 tbsp	Breadcrumbs	2x15 ml
1	Hard-boiled egg	1
1	Stalk of celery	1
1	Sprig of parsley	1
2 oz	Butter	50 g
4 tbsp	Oil	4x15 ml

Season chicken inside and out. Chop heart, liver and gizzard. Drain sweetcorn. Peel carrots and potatoes. Blanch, peel and quarter tomatoes.

Dice the cheese and mix with the sweetcorn, giblets, egg and breadcrumbs. Mash the hard-boiled egg with a fork and add to the mixture with seasoning. Mix well. Stuff the chicken with the mixture, then close opening.

Put carrots, potatoes and tomatoes into a flameproof casserole with celery and parsley. Cover with 2½ pints (1.5 litres) water and bring to the boil. Lower heat and add chicken with half the butter. Cover and simmer for 1½ hours.

Remove chicken and drain on kitchen paper. Strain cooking liquor and return to casserole. Purée vegetables and add to casserole. Heat soup through.

Heat remaining butter and oil in a frying pan. Put in whole chicken and brown evenly, turning it over with two spoons. Bring chicken and soup to table in separate dishes.

Chicken pineapple salad

Overall timing 30 minutes plus chilling

Freezing Not suitable

To serve 4–6

4 oz	Long grain rice	125 g
	Salt and pepper	
4 oz	Frozen sweetcorn kernels	125 g
1	Celery heart	1
1	Cold roast chicken	1
8 oz	Can of pineapple rings	227 g
4	Small firm tomatoes	4
2 oz	Black olives	50 g
3 tbsp	Salad oil	3x15 ml
1 tbsp	Lemon juice	15 ml
1 tbsp	Chopped chives	15 ml
1	Round lettuce	1
1	Hard-boiled egg	1

Cook the rice in boiling salted water till tender, adding the sweetcorn for the last 5 minutes of cooking. Drain and rinse under cold water, then drain thoroughly.

Trim celery heart and cut into 2 inch (5 cm) lengths. Put into a large bowl with the celery leaves. Cut the chicken into bite-size pieces, discarding the skin and bones. Add to the bowl.

Drain the pineapple; chop three of the rings. Quarter the tomatoes and add to the bowl with the chopped pineapple, olives, rice and sweetcorn.

Mix together the oil, lemon juice, chives and seasoning. Pour over the salad and toss lightly. Chill for 30 minutes.

Wash and dry the lettuce and use to line a salad bowl. Pile the salad into the centre and garnish with the remaining pineapple rings and the hard-boiled egg quartered lengthways. Serve with crusty bread.

Chicken croquettes

Overall timing 30 minutes

Freezing Suitable: reheat in 375°F (190°C) Gas 5 oven for 20 minutes

To serve 4–6

12 oz	Cooked boneless chicken	350 g
3 oz	Butter	75 g
3½ oz	Plain flour	90 g
½ pint	Milk	300 ml
	Salt and pepper	
	Grated nutmeg	
2	Egg yolks	2
1 tbsp	Grated cheese	15 ml
1 tbsp	Chopped parsley	15 ml
	Oil for frying	
1	Egg	1
4 oz	Dried breadcrumbs	125 g
	Sprigs of parsley	
	Lemon wedges	

Finely chop or mince chicken.

To make sauce, melt the butter in a saucepan over a low heat and stir in 2 tbsp (2x15 ml) of the flour. When the mixture begins to froth, add the cold milk, salt, pepper and a pinch of grated nutmeg. Whisk until the sauce thickens.

Remove from heat and stir in egg yolks and cheese. Turn into a bowl and mix in chicken and chopped parsley. Cool.

Heat oil for frying to 340°F (170°C) or till bread cube browns in 1 minute.

Using your hands, shape chicken mixture into small cylindrical croquettes. Roll them in the remaining flour, then in the lightly beaten egg to coat them completely and finally in the breadcrumbs, pressing them on well with a palette knife or spatula.

Fry the croquettes, four or five at a time, in the hot oil until golden brown. Drain on kitchen paper and serve hot, garnished with parsley and lemon.

Welsh chicken and mace pie

Overall timing 1 hour

Freezing Not suitable

To serve 6

1½ lb	Cooked chicken	700 g
4 oz	Cooked tongue	125 g
1	Onion	1
4	Leeks	4
3	Stalks of celery	3
2 oz	Butter	50 g
1 teasp	Ground mace	5 ml
1 tbsp	Chopped parsley	15 ml
½ pint	Chicken stock	300 ml
	Salt and pepper	
12 oz	Shortcrust pastry	350 g
1	Egg	1

Preheat oven to 400°F (200°C) Gas 6.

Chop chicken into medium-size pieces. Cut the tongue into strips. Peel and thinly slice onion. Trim leeks, then cut into thin slices. Trim and finely chop the celery. Melt butter.

Put chicken, tongue and prepared vegetables in a bowl with mace, parsley and butter and mix well. Place in a large pie dish and add stock and seasoning.

Roll out dough and place on dish. Press edge to dish to seal. Lightly beat the egg and brush over the dough. Bake for 40 minutes, or until the pastry is golden. Serve immediately with mashed potatoes.

Chicken pieces with nutty sauce

Overall timing 1 hour plus marination

Freezing Not suitable

To serve 4

5	Onions	5
1	Garlic clove	1
2 oz	Walnuts	50 g
	Salt	
3 tbsp	Lemon juice	3x15 ml
4	Boned chicken breasts	4
2 tbsp	Groundnut oil	2x15 ml
	Pinch of chilli powder	
2 oz	Roasted peanuts	50 g
2 teasp	Soy sauce	2x5 ml
½ pint	Water	300 ml

Peel and finely chop two onions. Peel and crush garlic. Place both in a mortar or blender with walnuts and salt. Crush or blend to a paste, gradually adding 2 tbsp (2x15 ml) lemon juice to give a creamy mixture. Cut chicken into bite-size pieces. Place in a shallow dish and pour walnut mixture over. Leave to marinate for 1 hour, turning occasionally.

Meanwhile, peel and finely chop two onions. Heat half oil in a frying pan and fry onions till crisp and golden. Remove from pan and drain. Preheat the grill.

Peel and finely chop remaining onion and purée in mortar or blender with chilli powder, salt and peanuts till smooth. Heat remaining oil in pan and fry peanut mixture for 3 minutes, stirring constantly. Stir in soy sauce, water and remaining lemon juice. Cook over low heat for 5 minutes.

Thread chicken pieces on to four oiled skewers. Grill for 10 minutes, turning frequently and brushing with walnut mixture. Add any remaining walnut mixture and fried onions to peanut sauce and heat through.

Poule-au-pot

Overall timing 4 hours

Freezing Not suitable

To serve 6

2 oz	Streaky bacon	50 g
4 oz	Pork sausagemeat	125 g
2 oz	Fresh breadcrumbs	50 g
2 tbsp	Chopped parsley	2x15 ml
	Salt and pepper	
2	Eggs	2
3½ lb	Boiling chicken	1.6 kg
4	Medium-size onions	4
4	Small turnips	4
6	Large carrots	6
2	Leeks	2
4	Stalks of celery	4
2 oz	Dripping	50 g
	Bouquet garni	
12 oz	Long grain rice	350 g

Derind bacon, reserving rinds, and chop finely. Mix sausagemeat, bacon, breadcrumbs, parsley and seasoning and bind with eggs. Spoon into chicken and truss.

Peel onions, turnips and carrots. Trim leeks and celery. Heat dripping in a large pan and brown chicken all over. Add one of the onions, turnips, leeks and celery stalks and two carrots and fry for 3 minutes. Pour off excess fat.

Add bouquet garni, bacon rinds, giblets and cold water to cover the chicken and bring to the boil. Skim off any scum. Cover and simmer for about 2¼ hours.

Discard vegetables, bacon rinds and bouquet garni. Add remaining vegetables and seasoning. Cover and simmer for a further 45 minutes. Remove from heat. Strain 2¼ pints (1.3 litres) of stock into another saucepan. Keep chicken hot.

Add rice to stock with salt and cover tightly. Bring to boil and simmer for 15–20 minutes till rice is tender.

Fluff rice and arrange on a serving dish. Place chicken on rice and discard trussing strings. Arrange vegetables around chicken and serve.

Chicken supreme

Overall timing 2 hours

Freezing Not suitable

To serve 4

2	Carrots	2
2	Onions	2
2	Leeks	2
1	Stalk of celery	1
	Salt	
2½ pints	Water or stock	1.5 litres
3 lb	Ovenready chicken	1.4 kg
½	Lemon	½
8 oz	Rice	225 g
Sauce		
2 oz	Butter	50 g
1 tbsp	Plain flour	15 ml
2	Egg yolks	2
2 tbsp	Single cream	2x15 ml
	Salt and pepper	

Peel carrots and onions. Chop leeks and celery. Bring salted water or stock to the boil in a flameproof casserole, add prepared vegetables and cook for 15 minutes.

Rub chicken with the lemon. Add to casserole, cover and simmer gently for 1 hour. (If you prefer, chicken joints can be used instead of a whole chicken – they need only to be cooked for 45 minutes.)

Measure out 1 pint (560 ml) stock from casserole and place in a saucepan. Continue cooking chicken for a further 15 minutes. Bring stock in saucepan to the boil, add rice and cook for 15 minutes.

Meanwhile, prepare sauce. Melt butter in a saucepan and stir in flour. Measure out another 1 pint (560 ml) stock from casserole and gradually stir into pan. Cook, stirring till thickened. Remove from heat and stir in egg yolks and then cream. Season.

Drain rice and place on warmed serving dish. Remove chicken from casserole, cut into portions and arrange on top of rice. Pour sauce over and serve.

Chicken with aubergine and tomatoes

Overall timing 50 minutes

Freezing Not suitable

To serve 4

1	Aubergine	1
	Salt and pepper	
1	Green pepper	1
2	Large onions	2
6 tbsp	Oil	6x15 ml
4	Chicken joints	4
¾ pint	Tomato juice	400 ml
12 oz	Ripe tomatoes	350 g

Slice the aubergine. Sprinkle with salt and leave for 15 minutes. Meanwhile, deseed and slice the pepper. Peel and slice the onions.

Heat the oil in a flameproof casserole, add the chicken and fry over a moderate heat, turning frequently, till browned all over. Remove from the pan and reserve.

Add the onions and pepper and fry for 5 minutes. Return the chicken to the casserole, add the tomato juice and seasoning and bring to the boil.

Rinse the aubergine and pat dry on kitchen paper. Add to the chicken, cover and simmer for 25 minutes.

Blanch, peel and quarter the tomatoes. Add to the chicken and cook for a further 5 minutes. Serve with plain boiled rice and a green salad.

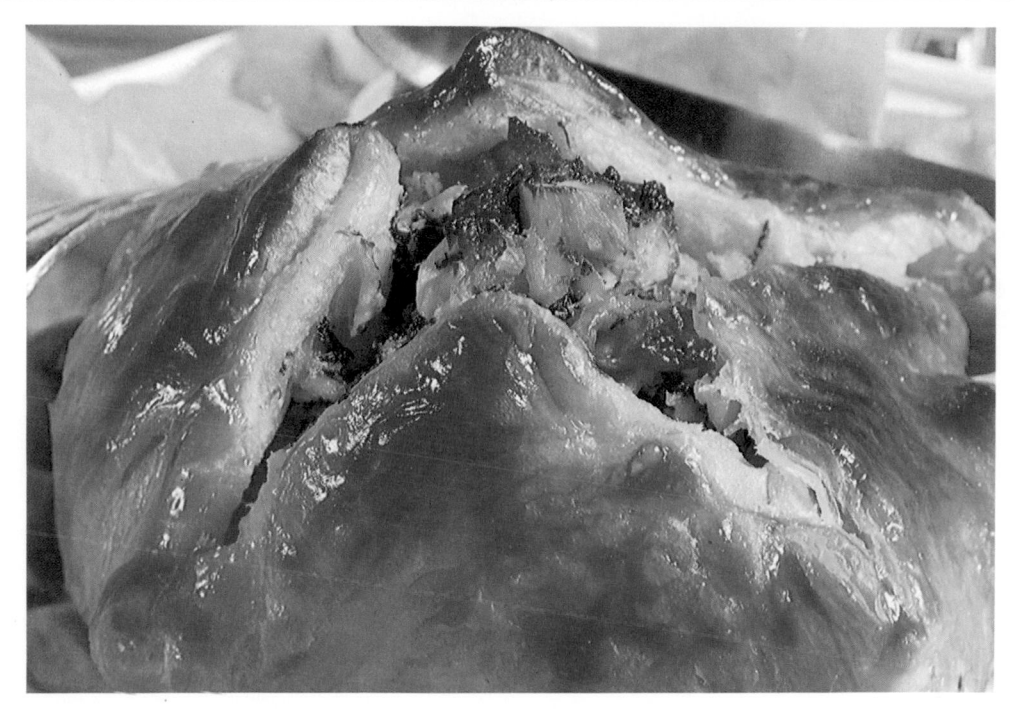

Chicken parcels

Overall timing 45 minutes

Freezing Suitable: bake from frozen, allowing 35–45 minutes

To serve 6

13 oz	Frozen puff pastry	375 g
1	Medium-size onion	1
1 oz	Butter	25 g
10 oz	Cooked boneless chicken	275 g
3 tbsp	Chopped parsley	3x15 ml
4 tbsp	Double cream	4x15 ml
	Salt and pepper	
3	Slices of cooked ham	3
1	Egg yolk	1
6	Lettuce leaves	6

Thaw pastry. Preheat oven to 400°F (200°C) Gas 6.

Peel and chop onion and fry in the butter till transparent.

Set aside six fairly large pieces of chicken and finely chop the rest. Put chopped chicken into a bowl with the parsley and fried onion. Lightly beat the cream, then stir into the chicken with seasoning.

Roll out the dough on a lightly floured surface. Cut out six 5 inch (12.5 cm) squares. Cut ham slices in half and place one piece in centre of each dough square. Top with a piece of chicken, then cover with chopped chicken mixture. Dampen dough edges with cold water. Fold corners to centre to cover the filling, pinching the edges together, but leaving a small hole in the top. Place parcels on a greased baking tray.

Beat the egg yolk with a pinch of salt and brush over parcels. Bake for 25 minutes or until well risen and golden brown. Serve the parcels on lettuce leaves.

Chicken in a basket

Overall timing 40 minutes

Freezing Not suitable

To serve 2

2x1 lb	Ovenready poussins	2x450 g
2 tbsp	Oil	2x15 ml
	Salt and pepper	
1 lb	Potatoes	450 g
	Oil for frying	
	Fresh parsley	
1	Small onion	1

Preheat the oven to 400°F (200°C) Gas 6.

Place the poussins in roasting tin. Brush with oil and season well. Roast for 30 minutes, or until juices from the legs run clear when pierced with a skewer.

Meanwhile, peel potatoes and cut into thin, matchstick chips. Heat oil in a deep-fryer to 340°F (170°C). Fry chips for 3–5 minutes till golden. Drain well.

Arrange napkins in two small baskets. Place chips in folds of cloth. Place poussins in baskets. Garnish with parsley sprigs and onion rings. Eat with your fingers or a knife and fork if preferred.

Variation

To make barbecue-style poussins, mix together 2 tbsp (2x15 ml) tomato purée, 1 tbsp (15 ml) Worcestershire sauce, 1 tbsp (15 ml) oil, 1 peeled and crushed garlic clove and seasoning. Spread over poussins, cover with foil and roast for 40 minutes. Serve as above.

Chicken with lentils

Overall timing 1¼ hours

Freezing Not suitable

To serve 6

12 oz	Continental lentils	350 g
1	Onion	1
1	Carrot	1
	Bouquet garni	
	Salt and pepper	
1 lb	Boned chicken	450 g
1 tbsp	Oil	15 ml
3 oz	Butter	75 g
1 tbsp	Chopped parsley	15 ml

Wash and pick over lentils. Place in a saucepan and add enough cold water just to cover. Peel and finely chop onion. Peel and halve carrot. Add to lentils with bouquet garni and seasoning. Bring to boil, cover and simmer for 35 minutes.

Meanwhile, cut chicken into neat pieces. Heat oil and half the butter in a frying pan, add chicken pieces and fry for 5 minutes, turning once. Add chicken to lentils, cover and simmer for a further 30 minutes.

Discard bouquet garni and carrot. Stir the remaining butter into lentils. Taste and adjust seasoning. Arrange chicken and lentils on a warmed serving dish and sprinkle with parsley. Serve immediately with a mixed salad.

Chicken with pineapple

Overall timing 45 minutes

Freezing Not suitable

To serve 2

1½ lb	Chicken joints	675 g
2 teasp	Potato flour or cornflour	2x5 ml
3 tbsp	Oil	3x15 ml
1 tbsp	Soy sauce	15 ml
1½ teasp	Dry sherry	7.5 ml
	Salt and pepper	
4 oz	Canned pineapple rings or chunks	125 g

Remove meat from chicken joints and cut it into chunky pieces.

Mix together potato flour or cornflour, half the oil, the soy sauce, sherry and seasoning in a bowl. Add the chicken pieces and coat well. Leave to marinate for 15 minutes.

Heat the rest of the oil in a heavy-based saucepan. Drain the chicken, saving the marinade, and add to the pan. Cook over a fairly high heat for 5 minutes, stirring constantly.

Drain the pineapple, reserving 4 tbsp (4x15 ml) of the syrup. Cut the rings into sections or halve the chunks. Add the reserved marinade from the chicken and the pineapple pieces to the pan and cook for a further 12 minutes, continually turning the chicken over.

When the chicken is golden brown, add the reserved pineapple syrup, adjust seasoning and cook for a further 5 minutes. Serve with saffron rice.

Chicken in foil

Overall timing 1 hour

Freezing Not suitable

To serve 2

2	Boned chicken or turkey breasts	2
	Salt and pepper	
1 tbsp	Plain flour	15 ml
2 oz	Butter	50 g
2	Sage leaves	2
1 tbsp	Brandy	15 ml
4 fl oz	Chicken stock	120 ml
4 oz	Chicken livers	125 g
2 oz	Mushrooms	50 g
1 oz	Cooked ham	25 g

Coat chicken or turkey breasts with seasoned flour. Melt half butter in a frying pan and fry chicken or turkey breasts on each side till golden. Add sage, brandy and stock and bring to boil. Cover and simmer for 15 minutes.

Preheat the oven to 400°F (200°C) Gas 6.

Finely chop chicken livers, mushrooms and ham. Melt remaining butter in another frying pan and stir-fry liver, mushrooms and ham for 5 minutes. Remove from heat.

Cut two large foil rectangles and put a chicken or turkey breast in centre of each. Spread liver mixture on top and spoon over pan juices. Wrap foil round to make secure parcels, then place in roasting tin. Bake for 20 minutes.

Stuffed turkey rolls

Overall timing 1¼ hours

Freezing Not suitable

To serve 2

1	Small onion	1
1	Garlic clove	1
2 oz	Butter	50 g
1	Large tomato	1
	Salt and pepper	
1 oz	Fresh breadcrumbs	25 g
1½ teasp	Chopped parsley	7.5 ml
½	Egg	½
2x6 oz	Turkey escalopes	2x175 g
2	Bacon rashers	2
5 tbsp	Dry white wine	5x15 ml
1 teasp	Lemon juice	5 ml

Peel and finely chop onion and garlic. Melt half butter in a saucepan and fry onion till golden.

Blanch, peel and chop tomato and add to pan with garlic and seasoning. Simmer till thick. Remove from heat; add crumbs, parsley and egg.

Season escalopes. Divide stuffing between them and roll up. Wrap a bacon rasher round each roll and secure with wooden cocktail sticks.

Melt remaining butter in frying pan and fry rolls till browned all over. Add wine and lemon juice, cover and simmer for 20 minutes.

Turkey fries

Overall timing 40 minutes plus marination

Freezing Not suitable

To serve 8

4 tbsp	Oil	4x15 ml
3 tbsp	Lemon juice	3x15 ml
	Salt	
8x4 oz	Slices of turkey breast	8x125 g
4 teasp	Dijon mustard	4x5 ml
2	Eggs	2
8 oz	Fresh breadcrumbs	225 g
2 oz	Butter	50 g
	Chopped parsley	
	Lemon wedges	

Mix 2 tbsp (2x15 ml) of the oil with the lemon juice and a pinch of salt in a shallow dish. Add the turkey, mix well and leave to marinate for 1 hour.

Drain the turkey and pat dry on kitchen paper. Spread thinly with the mustard. Beat the eggs lightly on a plate and use to coat turkey. Dip turkey slices into the breadcrumbs, pressing them on gently.

Melt the butter and remaining oil in a frying pan and gently fry the turkey for about 10 minutes on each side, till tender and golden.

Drain on kitchen paper and arrange on a warmed dish. Garnish with chopped parsley and lemon wedges and serve immediately with a tomato and onion salad dressed with vinaigrette.

Turkey with lemon sauce

Overall timing 30 minutes

Freezing Not suitable

To serve 6

6	Slices of turkey breast	6
	Salt and pepper	
2 tbsp	Plain flour	2x15 ml
2	Thick rashers of back bacon	2
3 oz	Butter	75 g
¼ pint	Chicken stock	150 ml
2 tbsp	Lemon juice	2x15 ml
2 tbsp	Chopped parsley	2x15 ml
	Lemon slices	
	Sprigs of parsley	

Place each slice of turkey between two sheets of damp greaseproof paper and flatten with a rolling pin. Season the flour and use to coat the turkey. Derind bacon and cut into strips.

Melt the butter in a frying pan and cook the bacon for 5 minutes. Add turkey pieces and fry for 3–5 minutes on each side. Remove turkey and bacon from pan and arrange on a warmed serving plate. Keep hot.

Add any remaining seasoned flour to pan and stir well with a wooden spoon, scraping the sediment from the bottom of the pan. Gradually add the stock (made with a cube if necessary) and bring to the boil. Simmer gently for 5 minutes.

Remove pan from heat and stir in the lemon juice and chopped parsley. Taste and adjust seasoning. Pour over the turkey breasts and garnish with lemon slices and parsley sprigs. Serve immediately with a mixed salad.

Oven-fried rabbit

Overall timing 1¼ hours

Freezing Not suitable

To serve 4–6

2 lb	Young rabbit	900 g
	Salt and pepper	
3 tbsp	Plain flour	3x15 ml
½ teasp	Paprika	2.5 ml
2	Eggs	2
2 tbsp	Milk	2x15 ml
2 oz	Dried breadcrumbs	50 g
1 oz	Butter	25 g
4 tbsp	Oil	4x15 ml
4 tbsp	Thick mayonnaise	4x15 ml
2 tbsp	Horseradish sauce	2x15 ml
2 tbsp	Single cream	2x15 ml
1 teasp	Lemon juice	5 ml

Preheat the oven to 350°F (180°C) Gas 4.

Cut rabbit into small pieces, removing small bones. Season flour, add paprika and coat rabbit pieces.

Beat eggs with milk. Dip rabbit into egg mixture then into breadcrumbs.

Heat butter and oil in a frying pan and brown rabbit pieces on both sides. Place on baking tray and bake for about 40 minutes till tender.

Meanwhile, mix mayonnaise, horseradish sauce, cream, lemon juice and seasoning. Serve with rabbit.

Stuffed drumsticks

Overall timing 2 hours

Freezing Not suitable

To serve 4

2x1 lb	Turkey drumsticks	2x450 g
	Salt and pepper	
4 oz	Smoked back bacon	125 g
	Rosemary leaves	
2 oz	Butter	50 g
2 teasp	Plain flour	2x5 ml
¼ pint	Chicken stock	150 ml
4 tbsp	Dry vermouth	4x15 ml

Preheat the oven to 375°F (190°C) Gas 5.

Remove bone from drumsticks. Return drumsticks to their original shape, then season. Derind and chop bacon and stuff into cavities in the drumsticks. Close openings with skewers. Pierce the skin in several places and insert the rosemary leaves. Rub butter over drumsticks and place in a flameproof casserole. Cover and bake for about 1¼ hours.

Lift out the drumsticks and remove the skewers. Cut into thick slices, arrange on a serving dish and keep hot.

Add the flour to the casserole and stir over a low heat for 1 minute. Gradually add the stock and vermouth and bring to the boil, stirring. Simmer for 2 minutes then adjust the seasoning to taste.

Pour sauce over the turkey.

Rabbit carbonnade

Overall timing 2½ hours

Freezing Not suitable

To serve 4–6

2½ lb	Ovenready rabbit	1.1 kg
3 tbsp	Plain flour	3x15 ml
2	Carrots	2
1	Onion	1
4 oz	Streaky bacon rashers	125 g
2 oz	Butter	50 g
	Bouquet garni	
1	Garlic clove	1
	Salt and pepper	
1 pint	Pale ale	560 ml

Preheat the oven to 350°F (180°C) Gas 4.

Cut the rabbit into neat pieces. Toss in the flour till lightly coated.

Peel and thinly slice the carrots. Peel and chop the onion. Derind the bacon and cut into strips. Melt the butter in a flameproof casserole and fry the carrots, onion and bacon for 5 minutes. Add the rabbit pieces and fry till browned.

Add the bouquet garni, peeled and crushed garlic and seasoning. Pour the ale over, cover tightly and cook in the oven for 1¾–2 hours till the rabbit is tender. Serve with boiled potatoes.

Roast pigeons with mushrooms

Overall timing 50 minutes

Freezing Not suitable

To serve 2

4 oz	Small onions	125 g
2	Small ovenready pigeons	2
2	Sprigs of rosemary	2
4	Sage leaves	4
3 oz	Streaky bacon rashers	75 g
3 oz	Butter	75 g
4 oz	Mushrooms	125 g
5 tbsp	Dry white wine	5x15 ml
	Salt and pepper	

Preheat the oven to 450°F (230°C) Gas 8.

Blanch the onions in boiling water for 5 minutes, then peel. Wipe the pigeons and put a sprig of rosemary, two sage leaves and a rasher of bacon into each. Put into a roasting tin and spread half the butter over. Roast for about 15 minutes till browned.

Meanwhile, derind and chop the remaining bacon. Melt the remaining butter in a flameproof casserole and fry the onions and bacon till just golden. Thickly slice the mushrooms. Add to onions and bacon and fry for 2 minutes.

Remove the pigeons from the oven and reduce the temperature to 400°F (200°C) Gas 6. Put the pigeons into the casserole on top of the vegetables, pour the wine over and season.

Cover the casserole, place in the oven and cook for a further 15–20 minutes till the pigeons are tender. Adjust the seasoning before serving.

Pigeons with saffron

Overall timing 1 hour

Freezing Not suitable

To serve 6

3	Ovenready pigeons	3
	Salt and pepper	
1 tbsp	Plain flour	15 ml
1 tbsp	Oil	15 ml
2 oz	Butter	50 g
6	Saffron strands	6
3 tbsp	Lemon juice	3x15 ml
1	Small onion	1
2 tbsp	Chopped parsley	2x15 ml

Quarter the pigeons. Lightly coat with seasoned flour. Heat the oil and butter in a saucepan, add the pigeon pieces and fry for about 10 minutes till lightly browned on all sides.

Meanwhile, pound the saffron in a small bowl. Add 2 tbsp (2x15 ml) warm water and leave to soak for 10 minutes.

Add saffron, soaking liquid and lemon juice to the pan. Cover and cook over a low heat for 20 minutes till meat is tender. Remove pigeon pieces from the pan, place on a warmed serving dish and keep hot.

Peel and finely chop the onion. Add to the liquid in the pan with parsley and seasoning. Cook for 3 minutes, then spoon over the pigeon quarters and serve immediately with boiled rice.

Duck with oranges

Overall timing 2 hours

Freezing Not suitable

To serve 4

4 lb	Ovenready duck	1.8 kg
	Salt and pepper	
½ pint	Hot chicken stock	300 ml
2 teasp	Caster sugar	2x5 ml
2 tbsp	White wine vinegar	2x15 ml
4	Oranges	4

Preheat the oven to 400°F (200°C) Gas 6.

Prick duck all over with a fork. Season well and place on rack in roasting tin. Roast for 45 minutes till brown and crisp.

Remove all but 1 tbsp (15 ml) of the fat from the tin. Pour hot stock over duck. Cover and roast for a further 30 minutes till cooked.

Heat sugar gently in a pan until it caramelizes, then remove from heat and add vinegar. Remove duck and strain juices from roasting tin into sugar mixture. Replace duck in tin and keep warm.

Cut the rind from one orange into thin matchsticks. Squeeze the juice from two oranges and add to the pan with the rind. Cook gently for 5 minutes till the rind has softened.

Remove duck from oven and cut into portions. Arrange on warmed serving dish and spoon over a little of the orange sauce. Peel and segment remaining oranges and use to garnish duck. Serve with sautéed potatoes and peas, and with the rest of the sauce served in a sauce or gravy boat.

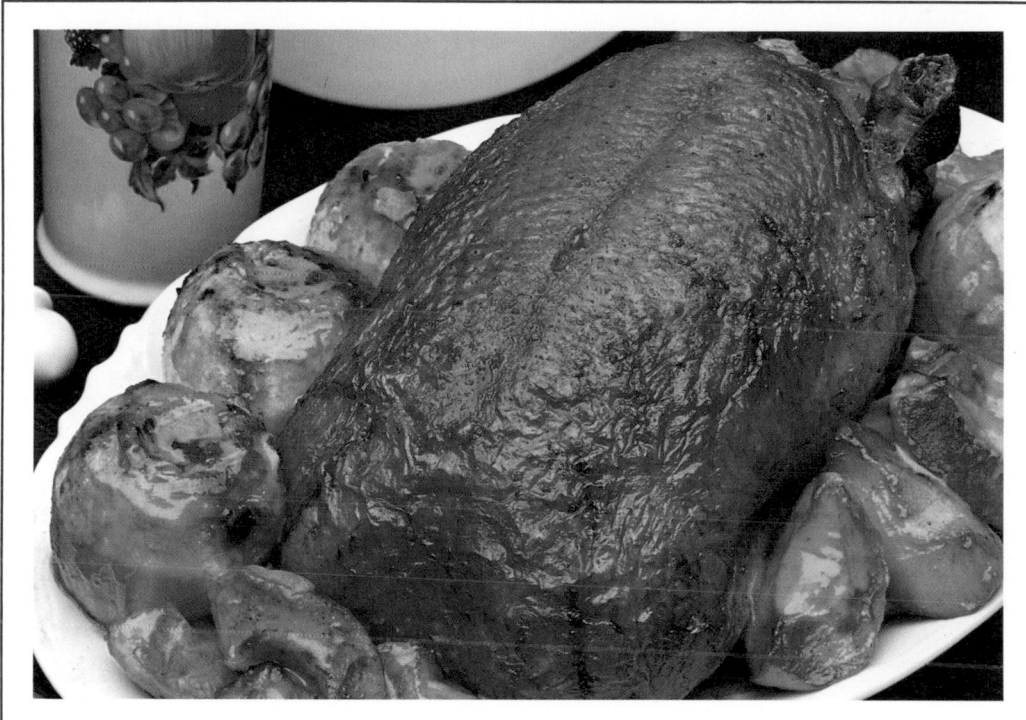

Duck with apples and cream

Overall timing 1 hour 20 minutes

Freezing Not suitable

To serve 4

3½ lb	Ovenready duck	1.6 kg
	Salt and pepper	
6	Granny Smith apples	6
1 oz	Butter	25 g
½ pint	Carton of single cream	284 ml

Preheat the oven to 400°F (200°C) Gas 6.

Sprinkle duck inside and out with salt and pepper. Prick all over with a fork and place on wire rack in roasting tin. Roast for 20 minutes, then reduce heat to 350°F (180°C) Gas 4.

Peel and core the apples. Cut two of them into quarters and leave the rest whole. Arrange around the duck, dot with butter and continue roasting for 1 hour or till tender.

Remove duck and apples from the tin. Place duck on serving plate. Keep hot. Pour off excess fat from pan juices, then stir in the cream. Replace apples in tin and baste thoroughly with the sauce. Cook for a further 5 minutes.

Arrange apples round duck. Spoon some sauce over. Serve rest separately.

Chicken liver brochettes

Overall timing 25 minutes

Freezing Not suitable

To serve 4

8 oz	Carton of chicken livers	225 g
2 oz	Piece of smoked streaky bacon	50 g
4 oz	Mushrooms	125 g
	Salt and pepper	
2 oz	Butter	50 g

Wash the chicken livers and dry on kitchen paper. Chop bacon into bite-size pieces. Wipe mushrooms.

Thread livers, bacon and mushrooms alternately on to skewers. Season with salt and pepper.

Melt the butter in a frying pan and cook brochettes for about 8 minutes, turning them from time to time. Alternatively, brush brochettes with oil and cook under a hot grill.

Serve hot with tomato sauce, rice and a mixed salad for lunch, or with crusty bread and butter for supper.

Chicken liver pancakes

Overall timing 45 minutes

Freezing Suitable: add cream and cheese and bake from frozen, covered, allowing 30–40 minutes

To serve 4

4 oz	Chicken livers	125 g
8 oz	Button mushrooms	225 g
1	Small onion	1
2 oz	Butter	50 g
	Salt and pepper	
6	Slices of cooked ham	6
3 tbsp	Single cream	3x15 ml
	Grated nutmeg	
2 oz	Cheddar cheese	50 g
Pancakes		
5 oz	Plain flour	150 g
¼ teasp	Salt	1.25 ml
2	Eggs	2
½ pint	Beer	300 ml
	Oil for frying	

Chop chicken livers. Chop mushrooms. Peel and finely chop onion. Melt butter in a saucepan and gently fry mushrooms and onion for 5 minutes. Add chopped livers and fry for 3–4 minutes. Season with salt and pepper.

To make pancakes, sift flour and salt into a bowl and make a well in the centre. Add eggs and beer and beat to a smooth batter. Heat a little oil in an 8 inch (20 cm) pancake or frying pan and make 12 pancakes.

Preheat oven to 400°F (200°C) Gas 6.

Cut slices of ham in half. Place one half on each pancake. Divide liver mixture between pancakes, then roll them up. Place side by side in greased baking dish. Pour cream over and sprinkle with nutmeg and grated cheese.

Bake for 15–20 minutes, or grill for 5 minutes. Serve hot.

Giblet fricassee

Overall timing 1½ hours

Freezing Not suitable

To serve 4

1¼ lb	Poultry giblets	600 g
1	Onion	1
3 tbsp	Oil	3x15 ml
¾ pint	Chicken stock	400 ml
1 teasp	Ground cumin	5 ml
	Salt and pepper	
1 tbsp	Plain flour	15 ml
2	Egg yolks	2
2 tbsp	Lemon juice	2x15 ml

Chop giblets. Peel and chop onion. Heat the oil in a saucepan and fry onion till transparent. Add giblets and brown on all sides. Pour in the stock and add cumin and seasoning. Bring to the boil, cover and simmer for about 1 hour or until giblets are tender.

Blend the flour with the egg yolks and mix in the lemon juice. Stir into fricassee and cook for a further 5 minutes, stirring. Serve with creamed potatoes and a mixed salad.

Savoury flans, pies and pizzas

Rich leek flan

Overall timing 1 hour

Freezing Suitable: reheat from frozen, covered, in 375°F (190°C) Gas 5 oven for 35 minutes

To serve 6–8

13 oz	Frozen puff pastry	375 g
2 lb	Leeks	900 g
2 oz	Butter	50 g
1 tbsp	Plain flour	15 ml
½ pint	Light stock	300 ml
	Salt and pepper	
1	Egg	1
1	Egg yolk	1
½ pint	Carton of single cream	284 ml

Thaw pastry. Preheat the oven to 425°F (220°C) Gas 7.

Trim leeks. Cut into 1 inch (2.5 cm) lengths. Blanch in boiling water for 5 minutes, then drain thoroughly.

Melt butter in a frying pan and fry the leeks for 5 minutes. Sprinkle with flour and cook until lightly browned. Gradually stir in the stock and bring to the boil. Season and cook gently for 10 minutes.

Meanwhile, roll out dough and use to line a 9 inch (23 cm) flan dish. Prick bottom several times with a fork.

Beat the whole egg, yolk and cream together in a bowl. Remove leeks from heat and add cream mixture. Pour into flan dish and spread evenly. Bake for 30 minutes till lightly set and golden. Serve hot.

Quiche lorraine

Overall timing 1½ hours

Freezing Suitable: reheat in hot oven

To serve 4–6

8 oz	Plain flour	225 g
	Salt and pepper	
5 oz	Butter	150 g
2 tbsp	Water	2x15 ml
2	Throughcut bacon rashers	2
3 oz	Cheddar cheese	75 g
2	Eggs	2
½ pint	Milk or single cream	300 ml

Sift the flour, salt and pepper into a bowl. Rub in 4 oz (125 g) of the butter till mixture resembles breadcrumbs. Gradually add the water and knead to a dough. Roll out and use to line a greased 8 inch (20 cm) pie plate or flan dish. Leave to stand for 30 minutes.

Preheat the oven to 400°F (200°C) Gas 6.

Derind and dice the bacon. Fry lightly in the remaining butter. Grate or thinly slice the cheese. Sprinkle bacon and cheese over the bottom of the flan case. Beat together the eggs, milk or cream and seasoning in a bowl. Pour mixture into flan. Do not overfill.

Bake for 15 minutes, then reduce heat to 325°F (170°C) Gas 3 and bake for further 25–30 minutes. Serve hot or cold with salad and potatoes.

Onion quiche

Overall timing 1½ hours

Freezing Suitable: reheat from frozen, covered, in 350°F (180°C) Gas 4 oven for 20 minutes

To serve 4

1 lb	Medium-size onions	450 g
2 oz	Lard	50 g
4 oz	Smoked streaky bacon	125 g
6 oz	Rich shortcrust pastry	175 g
3	Eggs	3
¼ pint	Milk	150 ml
¼ pint	Carton of single cream	150 ml
	Salt and pepper	

Preheat the oven to 400°F (200°C) Gas 6.

Peel and thinly slice the onions. Melt the lard in a frying pan and fry the onions over a moderate heat till pale golden.

Derind and dice the bacon and add to the pan. Fry for a further 4–5 minutes till the onions and bacon are golden brown.

Roll out the dough and use to line an 8½ inch (22 cm) flan dish. Prick the bottom and bake blind for 15 minutes.

Remove foil and baking beans and spread the onion and bacon mixture over the pastry base. Mix the eggs with the milk and cream and season to taste. Pour over the onions.

Bake for a further 25 minutes till lightly set and golden. Serve hot with mixed salads.

Bacon and corn flan

Overall timing 1 hour

Freezing Suitable: reheat in 425°F (220°C) Gas 7 oven for 10–15 minutes

To serve 6–8

4 oz	Streaky bacon rashers	125 g
8 oz	Shortcrust pastry	225 g
2	Eggs	2
¼ pint	Milk	150 ml
	Salt and pepper	
¼ teasp	Grated nutmeg	1.25 ml
	Cayenne pepper	
15 oz	Can of cream-style sweetcorn	425 g
4 oz	Strong Cheddar cheese	125 g

Preheat the oven to 450°F (230°C) Gas 8.

Derind and finely chop bacon. Put into a small ovenproof dish in the oven to draw off the fat.

Roll out the dough and use to line a 9 inch (23 cm) flan tin or pie plate.

Beat the eggs and milk together in a bowl and add salt, pepper, nutmeg and a pinch of cayenne pepper. Blend in the corn. Grate the cheese and mix three quarters of it into the egg and corn mixture.

Remove bacon from oven and brush a little of fat on the inside of the pastry case. Drain the bacon pieces and add half of them to the egg and corn mixture. Pour mixture into the pastry case. Sprinkle the rest of the cheese and remaining bacon on the top and bake in the centre of the oven for 20 minutes. Reduce the temperature to 350°F (180°C) Gas 4 and bake for a further 25 minutes. Serve hot or cool.

Welsh parsley flan

Overall timing 1 hour

Freezing Suitable: reheat from frozen in 350°F (180°C) Gas 4 oven for 25 minutes

To serve 4–6

8 oz	Shortcrust pastry	225 g
4 oz	Streaky bacon	125 g
1 oz	Butter	25 g
3	Eggs	3
½ pint	Milk	300 ml
3 tbsp	Chopped parsley	3x15 ml
	Salt and pepper	

Preheat the oven to 400°F (200°C) Gas 6.

Roll out the dough and use to line a 9 inch (23 cm) flan tin. Prick the bottom with a fork and bake blind for 15 minutes.

Meanwhile, derind and chop the bacon. Melt the butter in a frying pan and fry the bacon till golden. Arrange the bacon in the flan case. Reduce oven temperature to 350°F (180°C) Gas 4.

Beat the eggs, milk and parsley together, season to taste and pour over the bacon. Bake for a further 20–25 minutes till set. Serve hot or cold.

Tomato flan

Overall timing 1 hour plus chilling

Freezing Suitable: reheat in 350°F (180°C) Gas 4 oven for 25–30 minutes

To serve 6

9 oz	Plain flour	250 g
	Salt	
4 tbsp	Soured cream	4x15 ml
5 oz	Butter	150 g
Filling		
5	Tomatoes	5
6 oz	Cheese	175 g
8	Thin slices of French bread	8
¼ pint	Carton of double cream	150 ml
¼ pint	Carton of soured cream	141 g
4	Eggs	4
	Salt	
	Grated nutmeg	
½ teasp	Paprika	2.5 ml
1 oz	Butter	25 g

Sift flour and salt into bowl. Add soured cream, dot with butter pieces and knead lightly until smooth. Chill for 30 minutes.

Thinly slice tomatoes. Slice cheese and cut crusts off bread.

Preheat oven to 400°F (200°C) Gas 6.

Roll out dough and use to line 12 inch (30 cm) flan tin. Cover with layer of sliced tomatoes, then cheese and bread.

Beat double cream with soured cream, eggs, a pinch each of salt and nutmeg, and paprika. Pour into flan tin and dot top with butter. Bake for 30–40 minutes until firm and golden. Serve hot.

Onion flan

Overall timing 2¼ hours

Freezing Suitable: reheat from frozen in 350°F (180°C) Gas 4 oven for 20 minutes

To serve 4–6

1 teasp	Dried yeast	5 ml
	Pinch of sugar	
4 fl oz	Lukewarm water	120 ml
8 oz	Plain flour	225 g
1 teasp	Salt	5 ml
1	Egg	1
Filling		
5 oz	Bacon rashers	150 g
6 oz	Onions	175 g
1 oz	Butter	25 g
5 oz	Cheddar cheese	150 g

Mix yeast and sugar with most of the water and leave in a warm place for 15 minutes till frothy.

Sift flour and salt into bowl, make a well in the centre and add yeast mixture, any remaining water and egg. Mix well to a dough, then turn on to floured surface and knead for 5 minutes until smooth and elastic. Place dough in a clean bowl, cover with a damp cloth and leave to rise in a warm place for 45 minutes–1 hour, until doubled in size.

Preheat oven to 400°F (200°C) Gas 6.

Roll out dough on a floured surface and use to line a greased 10 inch (25 cm) loose-bottomed flan tin. Prove for 15 minutes.

Derind and chop bacon. Peel onions and cut into rings. Melt butter in a pan and fry onions for 5 minutes till golden. Slice the cheese.

Cover flan base with onions and bacon and arrange cheese slices on top. Bake for 30–35 minutes. Remove from tin and serve hot.

Asparagus quiche

Overall timing 1¼ hours

Freezing Suitable: thaw and refresh in hot oven for 10 minutes

To serve 4

8 oz	Shortcrust pastry	225 g
2 tbsp	Butter	2x15 ml
4 tbsp	Plain flour	4x15 ml
¾ pint	Milk	400 ml
	Salt and pepper	
	Pinch of grated nutmeg	
2	Eggs	2
4 oz	Mature cheese	125 g
12 oz	Can of asparagus	340 g

Preheat the oven to 425°F (220°C) Gas 7.

Roll out the dough to ¼ inch (6 mm) thick and use to line greased 10 inch (25 cm) flan ring or dish. Prick with fork. Bake blind for 5 minutes.

Melt the butter in a small saucepan. Stir in flour. Gradually stir in ½ pint (300 ml) of the milk. Season with salt, pepper and nutmeg. Bring to the boil, stirring constantly. Cook for 2 minutes. Remove pan from heat. Separate the eggs and stir one yolk into sauce. Grate the cheese and add to the sauce.

Pour the sauce into the flan case. Return to the oven and bake for 15 minutes.

Remove quiche from oven. Reduce heat to 375°F (190°C) Gas 5. Drain asparagus, cut into small lengths and arrange evenly over surface. Mix together the rest of the milk, the remaining egg yolk and 2 egg whites and pour this over top. Bake for 30 minutes more.

Tomato marjoram pizza

Overall timing 1½ hours

Freezing Suitable: cook in 450°F (230°C) Gas 8 oven for 35 minutes

To serve 4

Topping

1½ lb	Ripe tomatoes	700 g
1	Large onion	1
2	Garlic cloves	2
4 tbsp	Oil	4x15 ml
2 teasp	Dried marjoram	2x5 ml
1 teasp	Sugar	5 ml
	Salt and pepper	

Base

10 oz	Packet of bread mix	283 g
4 oz	Cheddar cheese	125 g
¼ teasp	Powdered mustard	1.25 ml

Blanch, peel and roughly chop the tomatoes. Peel and finely chop the onion. Peel and crush the garlic. Heat 3 tbsp (3x15 ml) of the oil in a saucepan and fry the onion till transparent. Add the tomatoes, garlic, 1 teasp (5 ml) of the marjoram, the sugar and seasoning. Bring to the boil, stirring. Cover and simmer for 15 minutes.

Empty the bread mix into a large bowl. Grate the cheese. Stir into mix with powdered mustard. Add hot water (according to packet instructions) and mix to a soft, but not sticky dough. Knead for 5 minutes, then roll out on a floured surface to a round 10 inches (25 cm) in diameter. Place in a greased 10 inch (25 cm) pizza pan or flan tin. Pinch up the edges to make a slight lip.

Spread the tomato mixture over the pizza base and sprinkle with the remaining marjoram. Put pizza in a warm place to rise for about 30 minutes till base has almost doubled its size.

Preheat the oven to 425°F (220°C) Gas 7.

Sprinkle the remaining oil over the pizza and bake for 25 minutes.

Storecupboard pizza

Overall timing 1 hour 10 minutes

Freezing Suitable: reheat from frozen in 400°F (200°C) Gas 6 oven for 40 minutes

To serve 4–6

14oz	Can of tomatoes	396g
2	Garlic cloves	2
1	Small onion	1
½ teasp	Dried basil	2.5ml
	Salt and pepper	
4oz	Can of sardines	125g
6oz	Cheddar cheese	175g
1	Can of anchovy fillets	1
12	Small black olives	12
2 tbsp	Grated Parmesan cheese	2x15ml
Base		
8oz	Self-raising flour	225g
	Pinch of salt	
3 tbsp	Oil	3x15ml

Preheat oven to 450°F (230°C) Gas 8.

Mix together mashed tomatoes and juice, crushed garlic, chopped onion, herbs, seasoning and drained and chopped sardines. Leave for 15 minutes.

Meanwhile, for the base, sift flour and salt into a bowl. Stir in oil and sufficient water to mix to a soft dough. Roll out dough to a large round and place on a greased baking tray. Pinch up edge to make a ridge. Brush with oil.

Spread tomato mixture over base. Cover with grated or sliced Cheddar and arrange anchovy fillets in a lattice shape on top. Garnish with olives and sprinkle with Parmesan.

Bake for 15 minutes. Reduce heat to 375°F (190°C) Gas 5 and bake for a further 20–25 minutes.

Olive and caper pizza

Overall timing 1¾ hours

Freezing Not suitable

To serve 2

6 oz	Potatoes	175 g
	Salt and pepper	
8 oz	Self-raising flour	225 g
2 oz	Butter	50 g
12 oz	Tomatoes	350 g
4	Anchovy fillets	4
1 tbsp	Capers	15 ml
4 oz	Black olives	125 g
4 tbsp	Milk	4x15 ml
2 teasp	Dried oregano	2x5 ml
1 tbsp	Olive oil	15 ml

Preheat the oven to 425°F (220°C) Gas 7.

Peel potatoes and cut into small chunks. Cook in boiling salted water till tender.

Meanwhile, sift the flour into a bowl and rub in the butter till the mixture resembles fine breadcrumbs. Blanch, peel and chop tomatoes. Chop anchovy fillets. Drain capers. Stone olives.

Drain potatoes and mash well. Stir into rubbed-in mixture. Add milk and mix to form a soft dough. Knead lightly till smooth. Roll out dough and use to line a greased 9 inch (23 cm) pizza pan or flan tin.

Arrange tomatoes, anchovies, capers and olives on top. Sprinkle with salt, pepper and oregano. Sprinkle olive oil over and bake for about 55 minutes till well risen and golden. Cut into wedges to serve.

Spring vegetable pie

Overall timing 2 hours

Freezing Not suitable

To serve 6

1 lb	Spring greens	450 g
2	Small globe artichokes	2
1½ lb	Fresh peas	700 g
	Salt and pepper	
1	Large onion	1
3 oz	Butter	75 g
8 oz	Shortcrust pastry	225 g
4	Eggs	4
4 tbsp	Grated Parmesan cheese	4x15 ml
1 tbsp	Chopped parsley	15 ml

Pick over the spring greens, discarding any damaged parts, and chop coarsely. Remove stems and tough outer leaves from artichokes and cut artichokes into quarters, discarding the hairy chokes. Shell peas. Bring a pan of lightly salted water to the boil, add the artichokes and peas and simmer for 10 minutes.

Peel and chop onion. Melt butter in large saucepan, add onion and fry till golden.

Drain artichokes and peas and add to the onion with the spring greens and seasoning. Mix well, cover tightly and simmer for 10 minutes, shaking the pan occasionally. Cool.

Preheat oven to 400°F (200°C) Gas 6.

Roll out two-thirds of dough and use to line an 8 inch (20cm) springform tin. Spread vegetables in tin. Beat three of the eggs lightly with cheese and parsley, then pour over vegetables. Roll out remaining dough and cover filling. Beat remaining egg and brush over pie. Place tin on a baking tray and bake for 30 minutes.

Remove sides of tin. Brush sides of pie with egg and bake for a further 10–15 minutes till golden.

Sicilian fish pie

Overall timing 2 hours

Freezing Not suitable

To serve 8

12 oz	Rich shortcrust pastry	350 g
2 tbsp	Caster sugar	2x15 ml
½ teasp	Grated lemon rind	2.5 ml
12 oz	White fish steaks	350 g
1	Large stalk of celery	1
3 oz	Stoned green olives	75 g
1	Large onion	1
3 tbsp	Olive oil	3x15 ml
1 tbsp	Drained capers	15 ml
2 tbsp	Tomato purée	2x15 ml
	Salt and pepper	
3	Courgettes	3
1	Egg	1
3 tbsp	Plain flour	3x15 ml
	Oil for deep frying	
1	Egg yolk	1

Make pastry, adding sugar and lemon rind with 3 egg yolks. Cube fish; chop celery; slice olives. Peel and thinly slice onion. Heat oil in a saucepan, add onion and fry till golden. Add celery, olives, capers, tomato purée, fish, ¼ pint (150 ml) water and seasoning. Simmer for 15 minutes.

Preheat oven to 350°F (180°C) Gas 4.

Cut courgettes into thin fingers. Beat egg; season flour. Dip courgettes into egg, then into flour. Deep fry till golden. Drain.

Divide dough into thirds. Roll out one and use to line a greased and floured 8 inch (20 cm) springform tin. Roll out remaining dough to two 8 inch (20 cm) rounds.

Layer fish mixture, courgettes and dough rounds in tin. Brush with beaten egg yolk and bake for 50 minutes. Remove from tin and serve hot.

Pork and apple pie

Overall timing 1½ hours

Freezing Not suitable

To serve 6

Pastry		
10 oz	Plain flour	275 g
2 teasp	Salt	2x5 ml
¼ teasp	Powdered mustard	1.25 ml
5 oz	Lard	150 g
Filling		
4 oz	Streaky bacon rashers	125 g
2	Medium-size onions	2
1½ lb	Lean minced pork	700 g
¼ teasp	Dried sage	1.25 ml
¼ pint	Chicken stock	150 ml
	Salt and pepper	
3	Dessert apples	3
4 tbsp	Demerara sugar	4x15 ml
¼ teasp	Grated nutmeg	1.25 ml

Preheat the oven to 400°F (200°C) Gas 6.

Sift the flour, salt and mustard into a bowl and rub in the lard. Add enough cold water to mix to a soft but not sticky dough and knead till smooth. Roll out two-thirds of the dough and use to line an 8½ inch (22 cm) round pie dish.

Derind and dice the bacon. Peel and finely chop the onions. Mix the pork with the bacon, onions, sage, stock and plenty of seasoning.

Peel, quarter, core and slice the apples. Put into a bowl with the sugar and nutmeg and toss gently till mixed.

Spread one-third of the pork in the pie dish and arrange half the apple mixture on top. Repeat the layers, finishing with the pork mixture.

Roll out the remaining dough to a round and use to cover the pie. Crimp the edges to seal. Place the pie on a baking tray. Bake just above the centre of the oven for 1 hour, covering the top of the pie lightly with foil after the first 30 minutes.

Ham, veal and pork pie

Overall timing 2½ hours plus overnight marination and chilling

Freezing Suitable

To serve 6–8

12 oz	Pie veal	350 g
2	Bay leaves	2
1 tbsp	Brandy	15 ml
	Salt and pepper	
8 oz	Cooked ham	225 g
12 oz	Belly of pork	350 g
4 oz	Streaky bacon	125 g
1 lb	Plain flour	450 g
5 oz	Butter	150 g
6 fl oz	Water	175 ml
2	Egg yolks	2

Cut veal into thin strips and place in a bowl with bay leaves, brandy and a pinch of salt.

Leave to marinate overnight. Cut ham into thin strips, add to veal and leave to marinate for another 2 hours.

Preheat the oven to 375°F (190°C) Gas 5.

Pass pork and bacon through a mincer twice. Mix with a little of the marinade and seasoning.

Sift flour and 1 teasp (5 ml) salt into a large bowl and make a well in the centre. Melt butter in water and bring to the boil. Pour quickly into the flour and mix well. Add one egg yolk and knead to a smooth dough.

Working quickly, roll out two-thirds of dough and use to line a greased 2 lb (900 g) loaf tin. Spread half the pork mixture on bottom, cover with ham and veal mixture and spread remaining pork mixture on top. Roll out remaining dough to fit pie. Seal edges. Put strips from leftover dough on sides of rectangle, moistening first to secure.

Lightly beat remaining egg yolk with a pinch of salt and brush over dough. Bake for 1 hour, then reduce heat to 170°F (325°C) Gas 3, cover with foil to prevent over-browning and bake for another hour.

Australian-style lamb pie

Overall timing 1¼ hours

Freezing Suitable: cover with pastry after thawing, then bake

To serve 4

1½ lb	Boned shoulder of lamb	700 g
	Salt and pepper	
2 tbsp	Plain flour	2x15 ml
1	Onion	1
8 oz	Carrots	225 g
4 oz	Mushrooms	125 g
1 oz	Butter	25 g
2 tbsp	Oil	2x15 ml
¾ pint	Stock	400 ml
2 tbsp	Chopped parsley	2x15 ml
6 oz	Shortcrust pastry	175 g
1	Egg	1

Wipe meat and cut into thin slices. Coat in seasoned flour. Peel and chop onion. Scrape and grate carrots. Wipe and slice mushrooms.

Heat butter and oil in frying pan and brown meat on all sides. Add onion, carrots and mushrooms and cook for 5 minutes. Stir in stock (made from cubes if necessary) and add seasoning. Cover and simmer gently for 10 minutes.

Preheat oven to 400°F (200°C) Gas 6.

Transfer meat mixture to pie dish and sprinkle with parsley. Roll out pastry and cover pie dish. Brush surface with lightly beaten egg and bake for 40–45 minutes until golden brown. Serve hot with jacket potatoes and minted peas.

Suet and bacon tart

Overall timing 45 minutes plus resting

Freezing Not suitable

To serve 8

8 oz	Streaky bacon rashers	225 g
4 oz	Cracklings from rendered suet	125 g
12 oz	Self-raising flour	350 g
2 oz	Chopped suet	50 g
2	Eggs	2
1 tbsp	Tomato purée	15 ml
¼ teasp	Chilli sauce	1.25 ml
	Salt and pepper	

Derind the bacon, then grill till crisp. Allow to cool, then break into pieces and mix with the suet cracklings.

Grease an 8 inch (20 cm) loose-bottomed cake tin.

Sift flour into bowl and add half the crackling mixture, the suet, eggs, tomato purée, chilli sauce, salt and pepper. Mix to a soft but not sticky dough. Knead lightly, then press into cake tin. Leave to rest for 20 minutes.

Preheat oven to 400°F (200°C) Gas 6.

Sprinkle rest of crackling mixture over dough and press in lightly. Bake for about 30 minutes till well risen and golden.

Cottage pie

Overall timing 1¼ hours

Freezing: Suitable: reheat in 425°F (220°C) Gas 7 oven for 1 hour

To serve 6

2 lb	Floury potatoes	900 g
	Salt and pepper	
2	Large onions	2
1 oz	Beef dripping	25 g
2 lb	Minced beef	900 g
2 tbsp	Plain flour	2x15 ml
½ pint	Strong beef stock	300 ml
14 oz	Can of tomatoes	397 g
8 oz	Frozen vegetables	225 g
¼ pint	Milk	150 ml
2 oz	Butter	50 g

Peel and quarter the potatoes; cook in boiling salted water till tender.

Preheat the oven to 375°F (190°C) Gas 5.

Peel and thinly slice onions. Heat dripping in a flameproof casserole and fry onions till transparent. Add beef and fry till browned.

Sprinkle in the flour and cook, stirring for 1 minute. Gradually add stock and bring to the boil, stirring. Add tomatoes and juice, seasoning and frozen vegetables and simmer for 5 minutes.

Drain potatoes. Add milk and butter and mash well. Spread potato over beef mixture. Bake for 30 minutes.

Savoury strudel

Overall timing 1½ hours

Freezing Suitable: bake from frozen, allowing extra 10–15 minutes

To serve 4–6

13 oz	Frozen puff pastry	370 g
1	Onion	1
2	Tomatoes	2
1	Green pepper	1
3 tbsp	Oil	3x15 ml
1 lb	Minced beef	450 g
3 tbsp	Tomato ketchup	3x15 ml
½ teasp	Worcestershire sauce	2.5 ml
	Salt and pepper	
4 oz	Mature Cheddar cheese	125 g
1	Egg yolk	1

Thaw pastry. Preheat oven to 425°F (220°C) Gas 7. Grease baking tray.

Peel and finely chop onion and tomatoes. Deseed and finely chop pepper. Heat oil in a frying pan. Cook onion till golden, then add beef and pepper. Cook for 5 minutes, then add tomatoes. Cook for 5 more minutes. Cool, then stir in tomato ketchup, Worcestershire sauce and seasoning.

Roll out dough thinly to a rectangle about 12x8 inches (30x45 cm). Spread beef mixture over dough, leaving border clear. Grate cheese over beef mixture, then fold borders on short sides over filling. Roll up from a long side and seal join.

Place strudel on baking tray. Decorate with trimmings, then brush with beaten egg yolk. Bake for 20 minutes. Reduce heat to 350°F (180°C) Gas 4 and cook for a further 20 minutes. Cut into slices to serve.

Cottage spinach roll

Overall timing 1¾ hours

Freezing Not suitable

To serve 4-6

8 oz	Plain flour	225 g
	Salt and pepper	
2	Eggs	2
2 lb	Spinach	900 g
3 oz	Butter	75 g
8 oz	Cottage cheese	225 g
¼ teasp	Grated nutmeg	1.25 ml
6 tbsp	Grated Parmesan cheese	6x15 ml

Sift the flour and ½ teasp (2.5 ml) salt into a bowl. Beat the eggs lightly in a bowl, pour half into the flour and mix with a palette knife. Add enough of the remaining egg to make a stiff dough. Knead till smooth, then chill for 30 minutes.

Meanwhile, wash and pick over the spinach. Put into a saucepan with only the water that clings to it. Cover and cook gently for 5 minutes. Drain thoroughly, then shred.

Melt 1 oz (25 g) of the butter in a frying pan, add the spinach and cook for 5 minutes, stirring occasionally. Pour into a bowl and add the cottage cheese, nutmeg, half the Parmesan and seasoning. Mix well. Leave to cool.

Roll out the dough on a floured surface to a rectangle about 15x12 inches (38x30 cm). With a long side nearest you, spread the filling over the dough, leaving a 1 inch (2.5 cm) border. Fold the bottom border over the filling and roll up. Pinch the ends together to seal.

Wrap the roll in a double thickness of muslin, tying the ends with string. Place in a large pan of boiling salted water, cover and simmer for 25 minutes.

Drain and unwrap the roll and place on a warmed serving dish. Melt the remaining butter. Cut the roll into thick slices, pour the butter over and sprinkle with the remaining Parmesan. Serve immediately.

Brazilian meat pasties

Overall timing 50 minutes

Freezing Suitable: omit hard-boiled eggs and bake from frozen in 425°F (220°C) Gas 7 oven for 30 minutes

To serve 4

13 oz	Frozen puff pastry	375 g
1	Onion	1
4 oz	Belly pork rashers	125 g
1 oz	Butter	25 g
8 oz	Minced beef	225 g
3 tbsp	Seedless raisins	3x15 ml
	Pinch of ground cloves	
	Salt and pepper	
$\frac{1}{4}$ teasp	Paprika	1.25 ml
2	Hard-boiled eggs	2
8	Stoned green olives	8
1	Egg	1

Thaw the pastry. Roll out to a rectangle 8x16 inches (20x40 cm). Cut into eight 4 inch (10 cm) squares.

Preheat oven to 400°F (200°C) Gas 6.

Peel and finely chop the onion. Derind and mince the belly pork rashers. Melt the butter in a frying pan and fry the onion and pork till golden. Add the minced beef and fry briskly, stirring frequently, till brown.

Remove from heat and add the raisins, cloves, salt, pepper and paprika. Mix well. Shell and coarsely chop the hard-boiled eggs. Chop the olives, add to the pan with the eggs and mix well.

Place one eighth of the meat mixture on half of each dough square. Brush the edges with a little of the beaten egg and fold dough over. Crimp edges to seal.

Arrange on a dampened baking tray and brush tops with beaten egg. Bake for about 25 minutes till well risen and golden.

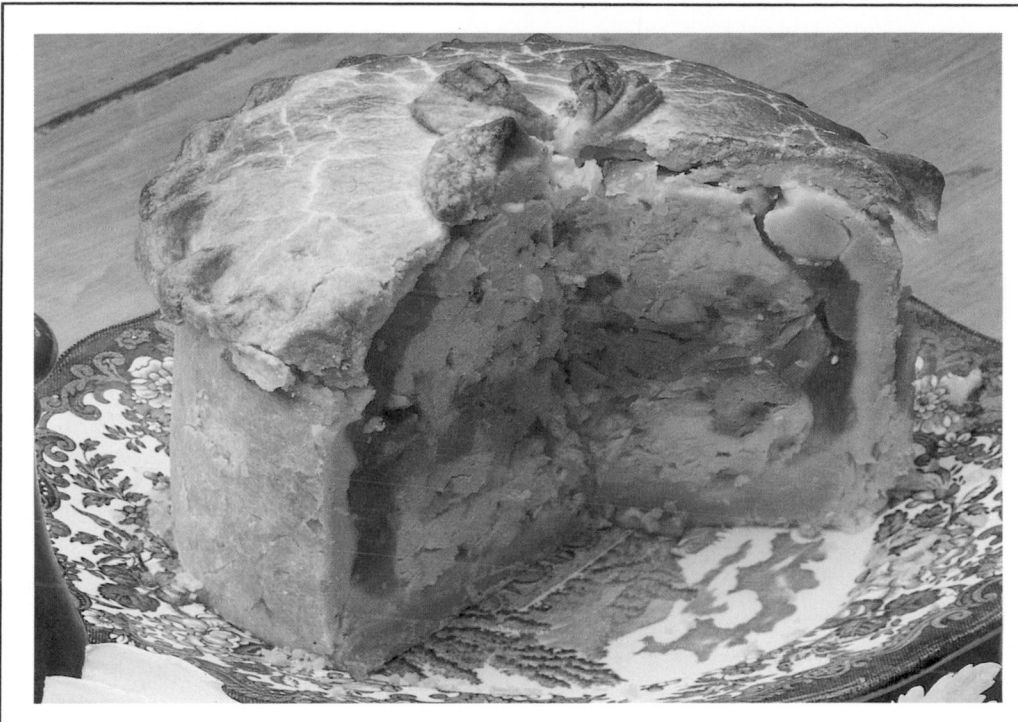

Raised chicken and ham pie

Overall timing 2¾ hours plus cooling

Freezing Suitable

To serve 6

12 oz	Hot water crust pastry	350 g
1½ lb	Boneless chicken	700 g
	Salt and pepper	
1 teasp	Grated lemon rind	5 ml
¼ teasp	Dried sage	1.25 ml
4 oz	Sliced cooked ham	125 g
1 teasp	Powdered gelatine	5 ml
6 tbsp	Chicken stock	6x15 ml
1	Egg	1

Roll out two-thirds of dough and use to line greased 6 inch (15 cm) loose-bottomed cake tin. Keep remaining dough for lid warm.

Preheat oven to 375°F (190°C) Gas 5.

Finely dice chicken, keeping breast and dark meat separate. Season both well and add lemon rind and sage. Dice ham. Cover dough bottom with half breast meat, then with half dark meat. Spread all ham on top, then repeat layering of dark and breast meats.

Moisten dough edges and place lid in position. Press down firmly to seal. Make a hole in centre and decorate top. Glaze with lightly beaten egg.

Bake for 1 hour, then reduce oven temperature to 350°F (180°C) Gas 4 and bake for a further 1–1¼ hours. Remove pie from oven, cool for 30 minutes then remove from tin and leave until cold.

Meanwhile, soften gelatine in cold stock in a small pan for 5 minutes. Then heat gently till gelatine dissolves; do not boil. Leave to cool.

When the jelly mixture begins to set, put a funnel or cone of foil or greaseproof paper into the centre hole in the pie. Pour in jelly and chill in refrigerator till set. Serve cold with salad.

Sausage in brioche

Overall timing 2½ hours plus rising

Freezing Not suitable

To serve 6–8

1 lb	Piece of fresh continental sausage	450 g
	Bouquet garni	
1	Onion	1
8 oz	Strong flour	225 g
¼ teasp	Salt	1.25 ml
1½ teasp	Dried yeast	7.5 ml
2 tbsp	Lukewarm water	2x15 ml
1 tbsp	Caster sugar	15 ml
2	Eggs	2
2 oz	Butter	50 g
1	Egg yolk	1

Put sausage into a saucepan with bouquet garni and peeled onion and cover with cold water. Bring to the boil and simmer very gently for 1¾ hours.

Meanwhile, sift flour and salt into a bowl. Sprinkle yeast on to the water, add a pinch of the sugar and mix well. Leave in a warm place till frothy, then add to flour with remaining sugar. Add eggs and melted butter to flour and mix to a soft dough. Knead till glossy, wrap in oiled polythene and leave in a warm place to rise.

Drain sausage, discarding flavourings, and allow to cool slightly. Remove the skin.

Preheat the oven to 425°F (220°C) Gas 7.

Roll out dough to a rectangle large enough to enclose the sausage. Place sausage in centre and fold dough round it, pinching edges to seal. Place, join down, on a baking tray. Leave to prove for 15 minutes.

Brush with beaten egg yolk and bake for about 25 minutes till crisp and golden. Serve hot, cut into thick slices.

Leek pie

Overall timing 1 hour

Freezing Suitable: reheat in 350°F (180°C) Gas 4 oven for 30 minutes

To serve 4

1½ lb	Leeks	700 g
2	Onions	2
2 oz	Butter	50 g
	Salt and pepper	
8 oz	Streaky bacon rashers	225 g
12 oz	Shortcrust pastry	350 g
1 tbsp	Cornflour	15 ml
¼ pint	Carton of single cream	150 ml
1	Egg	1

Preheat the oven to 400°F (200°C) Gas 6.

Wash, trim and slice leeks. Peel and slice onions. Melt butter in a frying pan and fry onions till golden. Add sliced leeks, salt and pepper and cook gently for 5 minutes.

Meanwhile, derind and lightly fry bacon rashers in another pan.

Roll out two-thirds of the dough and use to line a shallow pie dish. Cover with leek mixture and arrange bacon rashers on top. Mix cornflour with the cream and pour over.

Roll out remaining dough and cover filling. Seal and crimp edges, using any trimmings to decorate top. Glaze with beaten egg. Bake for 45 minutes until golden brown.

Ham pie

Overall timing 1 hour

Freezing Not suitable

To serve 4

8 oz	Shortcrust pastry	225 g
1 lb	Can of ham	453 g
1	Egg	1

Preheat the oven to 425°F (220°C) Gas 7.

Roll out the dough to $\frac{1}{4}$ inch (6 mm) thickness. Place ham in centre. Dampen the dough edges and fold around the ham. Seal well. Place in ovenproof dish and decorate with trimmings, if liked.

Lightly beat the egg and brush all over the dough. Bake for 40 minutes till golden.

Ham and vegetable bake

Overall timing 1 hour 10 minutes

Freezing Suitable: top with egg after reheating in 350°F (180°C) Gas 4 oven for 1¼ hours

To serve 4

8 oz	Frozen spinach	225 g
1 lb	Celeriac	450 g
2 lb	Potatoes	900 g
	Salt and pepper	
2½ oz	Butter	65 g
3 tbsp	Single cream	3x15 ml
3 fl oz	Hot milk	90 ml
1	Small stalk of celery	1
8 oz	Sliced ham	225 g
4 oz	Cheddar cheese	125 g
2	Eggs	2

Place spinach in a sieve to thaw. Peel celeriac and potatoes and cut into small chunks. Put prepared vegetable chunks into a saucepan of cold salted water and bring to the boil. Cook for 20 minutes till tender. Drain well and mash or purée with 2 oz (50 g) of the butter, the cream and enough milk to give a creamy purée. Season to taste.

Preheat oven to 400°F (200°C) Gas 6.

Wash and top and tail celery. Blanch in boiling water for 5 minutes. Drain well and cut into pieces.

Grease ovenproof dish with remaining butter. Spread the well-drained spinach over, arrange the chopped celery on top and cover with ham slices. Grate the cheese. Sprinkle over half the cheese and cover with the celeriac and potato purée. Bake on centre shelf of oven for 15 minutes.

In a bowl, lightly beat the eggs with salt and pepper. Pour over the purée, top with remaining cheese and return to oven. Bake for another 15 minutes till golden. Serve immediately.

Club sandwiches

Overall timing 30 minutes

Freezing Not suitable

To serve 4

12	Slices of bread	12
	Mayonnaise	
4	Slices of cooked chicken or turkey	4
4	Lettuce leaves	4
4–8	Back bacon rashers	4–8
5	Tomatoes	5

Preheat the grill.

Grill the bacon until crisp. Toast four slices of bread on both sides, but toast the remaining slices of bread on one side only. Slice the tomatoes.

To assemble the sandwiches, spread the untoasted sides of bread with mayonnaise. Place four pieces, toasted side down, on a board and top with the chicken or turkey slices. Cover with the completely toasted bread. Add the lettuce, bacon, tomato slices (reserving some for the garnish) and remaining bread, mayonnaise side down. Press lightly together, then halve the sandwiches diagonally. Garnish with the reserved tomato slices.

Country-style liver pâté

Overall timing 3 hours plus maturing

Freezing Suitable

To serve 12

1½ lb	Pig's liver	700 g
1 lb	Back bacon	450 g
8 oz	Lard	225 g
1	Egg	1
1 tbsp	Plain flour	15 ml
	Salt and pepper	
½ teasp	Ground allspice	2.5 ml
1	Pig's caul (optional)	1

Preheat the oven to 350°F (180°C) Gas 4.

Chop the liver. Derind and dice bacon. Put liver and bacon through a fine mincer. Melt the lard in a saucepan and gradually beat into minced liver and bacon in bowl. Beat egg and add with flour, seasoning and allspice. Mix well.

Line greased ovenproof dish with caul, if using, leaving edges hanging over sides. Add liver mixture and smooth top. Wrap caul edges over. Cover dish with lid or foil and place in a roasting tin containing 1 inch (2.5 cm) water. Bake for 1¾ hours.

Allow to cool, then leave in the refrigerator for 2–3 days to mature. Serve with crusty bread.

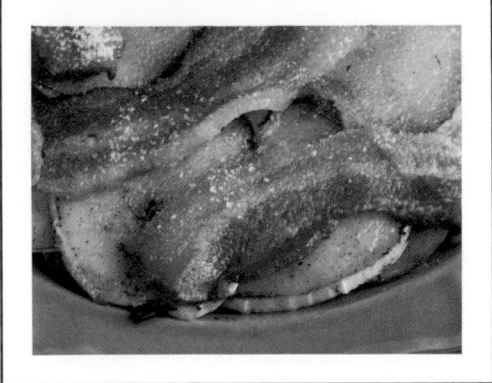

Bacon and apple rings

Overall timing 40 minutes

Freezing Not suitable

To serve 4

8 oz	Thin streaky bacon rashers	225 g
1 oz	Butter	25 g
2	Yellow Golden Delicious apples	2
2 tbsp	Caster sugar	2x15 ml

Derind the bacon. Melt the butter in a frying pan, add the bacon and fry till crisp. Drain on kitchen paper, place on a warmed serving plate and keep hot.

Wash, dry and core apples, but don't peel them. Cut into thin rings and cook in the frying pan till tender, turning them over with a spatula. Drain on kitchen paper, then arrange on the serving plate with the bacon.

Sprinkle with sugar and serve immediately with hot toast and butter.

Spanish kebabs

Overall timing 25 minutes plus marination

Freezing Not suitable

To serve 4

1 lb	Thick white fish fillets	450 g
2 tbsp	Oil	2x15 ml
2 tbsp	Lemon juice	2x15 ml
	Salt and pepper	
8 oz	Garlic sausage	225 g
8	Smoked streaky bacon rashers	8
16	Bay leaves	16
3 oz	Butter	75 g

Cut the fish into 16 neat cubes and put into a bowl with the oil, half the lemon juice and salt and pepper. Marinate for 1 hour, turning occasionally.

Preheat the grill and line the pan with foil. Cut the sausage into $\frac{1}{2}$ inch (12.5 mm) slices. Derind and stretch the bacon rashers and cut each in half. Thread the fish cubes, sausage, bay leaves and folded bacon on to greased skewers.

Place on the grill pan and brush the marinade over. Grill for about 10 minutes, turning and basting frequently, till the fish is tender.

Melt the butter in a saucepan and add the remaining lemon juice and seasoning. Serve this sauce with the kebabs.

Black pudding with apples

Overall timing 25 minutes

Freezing Not suitable

To serve 2

8 oz	Black pudding	225 g
2 oz	Butter	50 g
1	Onion	1
2	Dessert apples	2
	Fresh parsley	

Thickly slice the black pudding. Melt the butter in a frying pan and add the black pudding. Cook till crispy – if you cook them gently the slices will stay intact, instead of breaking away from the skin. Lift out with draining spoon and keep hot.

Peel onion and slice into rings. Fry gently in the butter till brown and just tender.

Core and slice the apples. Add to pan and cook for 5 minutes, turning slices over halfway. Add the pudding and cook the mixture for 2 minutes more.

Place black pudding, onion and apples on two warmed plates. Garnish with parsley sprigs and serve hot.

Crusty mushroom bread

Overall timing 1 hour

Freezing Suitable: cook after thawing

To serve 6–8

1	Round loaf of bread	1
4 oz	Butter	125 g
1 lb	Mushrooms	450 g
	Salt and pepper	
3 tbsp	Lemon juice	3 x 15 ml
½ pint	White sauce	300 ml
2	Eggs	2

Preheat the oven to 350°F (180°C) Gas 4.

Slice the top off the bread and scoop out most of the crumbs, leaving a ½ inch (12.5 mm) thick shell. Spread the inside with half the butter, place on a baking tray and bake for 10 minutes.

Meanwhile, finely chop the mushrooms. Melt the remaining butter in a saucepan and fry the mushrooms for 5 minutes, stirring frequently. Add salt, pepper and lemon juice. Stir the mushrooms into the white sauce.

Separate the eggs and beat the egg yolks, one at a time, into the sauce. Return to the heat and heat through gently. Whisk the egg whites till stiff but not dry. Gently fold into the mushroom mixture.

Pour the mixture into the bread shell and sprinkle the top with a few of the scooped out breadcrumbs, grated. Bake for 30 minutes till well risen and crisp. Serve hot.

Broccoli toasts

Overall timing 40 minutes

Freezing Not suitable

To serve 4

1 lb	Calabrese broccoli	450 g
½ pint	Beef stock	300 ml
8	Slices of bread	8
½ pint	Thick white sauce	300 ml
	Salt and pepper	
	Grated nutmeg	
½ teasp	Mixed herbs	2.5 ml
2	Hard-boiled eggs	2
1	Tomato	1
	Sprigs of parsley	
½	Red pepper	½

Trim broccoli and chop into large pieces. Bring stock to boil, add broccoli and cook for 7–10 minutes.

Toast bread and place on baking tray. Drain broccoli well, then divide it between toast.

Preheat oven to 375°F (190°C) Gas 5.

Heat sauce, then add seasoning, pinch of nutmeg and herbs. Finely chop one of the hard-boiled eggs and add to the sauce. Pour sauce over broccoli. Bake for 15 minutes.

Serve hot, garnished with remaining egg, sliced tomato, parsley and strips of pepper.

Pirozski

Overall timing 1 hour

Freezing Suitable: refresh in 350°F (180°C) Gas 4 oven for 10 minutes

To serve 6

7½ oz	Frozen puff pastry	212 g
8 oz	Liver pâté	225 g
1	Egg	1

Thaw pastry. Preheat the oven to 400°F (200°C) Gas 6.

Roll out dough very thinly on a floured surface and cut into 3 inch (7.5 cm) squares. Cut in half diagonally to make triangles. Put about 1 teasp (5 ml) liver pâté on half of the triangles. Moisten dough edges and cover with remaining triangles. Press edges together to seal.

Arrange triangles on greased baking tray and brush with beaten egg. Bake for 10–15 minutes till well risen and golden. Serve hot.

Provençal sandwiches

Overall timing 15 minutes

Freezing Not suitable

To serve 4

4	Crusty rolls	4
1	Garlic clove	1
4	Large lettuce leaves	4
2	Large tomatoes	2
2	Hard-boiled eggs	2
	Pickled vegetables or gherkins	
	Black olives	
	Cooked green beans	
	Anchovy fillets	
	Green or red pepper	
	Olive oil	
	Vinegar	

Halve the rolls and the garlic clove. Rub the cut surfaces of the rolls with the garlic. Place the lettuce leaves on the bottom halves of the rolls.

Slice the tomatoes. Shell and slice the eggs. Place the tomatoes and eggs on the lettuce, then add pickled vegetables or gherkins, olives, beans, anchovies and pepper strips, according to taste. Sprinkle with oil and vinegar, then place the tops of the rolls on the filling. Press gently together and serve.

Hot frankfurter salad

Overall timing 45 minutes

Freezing Not suitable

To serve 4

1 lb	Waxy potatoes	450 g
	Salt and pepper	
4	Frankfurters	4
2	Onions	2
4	Anchovy fillets	4
2 oz	Chopped gherkins	50 g
2 tbsp	Oil	2x15 ml
2 tbsp	White wine vinegar	2x15 ml

Peel and slice potatoes, then cook in boiling salted water for about 7 minutes till tender.

Heat frankfurters in boiling water for 5 minutes, then drain and slice. Peel and slice onions into rings. Finely chop anchovies and gherkins. Drain potatoes and mix with frankfurters and onions.

Beat together oil and vinegar, season and pour over the warm salad. Mix well and leave for 10 minutes. Add anchovies and gherkins and serve.

Tuna rolls

Overall timing 15 minutes

Freezing Not suitable

To serve 4

4	Long rolls	4
	Butter	
	Mayonnaise	
1x7 oz	Can of tuna fish	1x200 g
	Chopped parsley	
2	Hard-boiled eggs	2
	Radish roses	

Halve the rolls, not cutting all the way through, and butter the cut surfaces. Spread a thick layer of mayonnaise over the bottom cut surface.

Drain the tuna and flake it. Divide between the rolls and sprinkle with parsley. Arrange the sandwiches on a serving plate.

Shell and slice the eggs and use to garnish the sandwiches with radish roses.

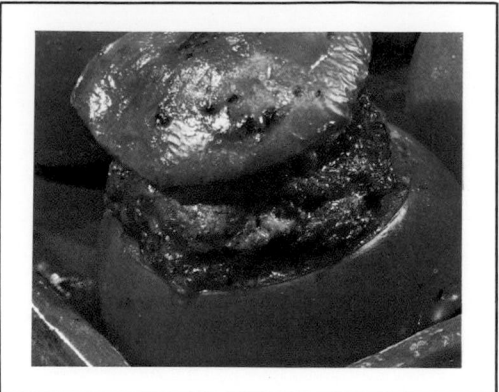

Beefy tomatoes

Overall timing 45 minutes

Freezing Not suitable

To serve 6

6	Large tomatoes	6
1	Large onion	1
8 oz	Corned beef	225 g
8 oz	Sausagemeat	225 g
2 tbsp	Chopped parsley	2x15 ml
1	Egg	1
$\frac{1}{4}$ teasp	Ground allspice	1.25 ml
	Salt and pepper	
	Oil	

Preheat the oven to 425°F (220°C) Gas 7.

Cut tops off tomatoes and reserve. Scoop out most of the flesh and place it in a bowl. Peel and finely chop onion. Add to bowl with the corned beef, sausagemeat and chopped parsley. Mash well. Beat in the egg, allspice and seasoning and mix well.

Stuff tomatoes with beef mixture and put the reserved "lids" on top. Place on a baking tray and sprinkle with oil. Bake for 20 minutes. Serve with crusty bread.

Nutty beefburgers

Overall timing 45 minutes

Freezing Not suitable

To serve 4

4 oz	Hazelnuts	125 g
1 oz	Butter	25 g
1	Large onion	1
1 lb	Lean minced beef	450 g
2 tbsp	Capers	2x15 ml
	Grated rind of 1 lemon	
$\frac{1}{4}$ teasp	Paprika	1.25 ml
$\frac{1}{2}$ teasp	Powdered mustard	2.5 ml
	Salt and pepper	
4	Egg yolks	4

Preheat the oven to 375°F (190°C) Gas 5.

Chop nuts. Melt butter in a frying pan and cook nuts till golden. Peel onion. Cut four equal rings and reserve. Finely chop remainder and mix with nuts, beef, half the capers, the lemon rind, paprika, mustard and seasoning.

Divide mixture into four portions. Shape into balls, place on a baking tray and flatten slightly making a well in centre of each. Bake for 25 minutes.

Place each burger on a lettuce leaf on serving plate. Press an onion ring into each well, then carefully place a raw egg yolk in each ring and garnish with remaining capers. If liked, bake for a further 10 minutes to cook egg yolk.

Ham and potato cake

Overall timing 1¼ hours

Freezing Not suitable

To serve 4

1½ lb	Medium-size potatoes	700 g
	Salt and pepper	
8 oz	Sliced cooked ham	225 g
8 oz	Cheese	225 g
3 oz	Butter	75 g
3 tbsp	Fresh breadcrumbs	3x15 ml
¼ pint	Milk	150 ml

Cook potatoes in boiling salted water for 20 minutes.

Meanwhile, chop the ham and grate cheese. Grease a 7 inch (18 cm) springform tin with a little of the butter and sprinkle breadcrumbs over the bottom and sides, shaking off any excess. Preheat oven to 350°F (180°C) Gas 4.

Drain and peel the potatoes, then cut into ¼ inch (6 mm) thick slices. Arrange a few of the slices, slightly overlapping, in the bottom of the tin. Melt the remaining butter and brush a little over the potatoes. Scatter some of the ham, then some of the cheese over and season. Continue layering, reserving a little of the butter, and finishing with a layer of potato topped with cheese. Pour the milk over and brush with remaining butter.

Bake for about 30 minutes till potatoes are tender and cheese has melted. Turn cake out of tin to serve.

Roast veal salad

Overall timing 20 minutes

Freezing Not suitable

To serve 2

½	Round lettuce	½
¼	Cucumber	¼
2	Large firm tomatoes	2
4	Radishes	4
2	Hard-boiled eggs	2
6 oz	Cold roast veal	175 g
2 tbsp	Oil	2x15 ml
2 teasp	White wine vinegar	2x5 ml
½ teasp	Powdered mustard	2.5 ml
	Salt and pepper	
	Sprigs of parsley	

Wash and dry lettuce. Use outside leaves to line a serving dish. Shred rest and put in bowl. Cut cucumber into matchsticks and add to shredded lettuce.

Cut tomatoes into wedges. Slice radishes. Add half of each to lettuce and cucumber.

Shell and halve hard-boiled eggs. Cut veal into neat cubes.

Put oil, vinegar, mustard and seasoning into a screw-top jar, cover and shake to mix. Add to shredded lettuce mixture and toss lightly. Place in lettuce-lined dish. Arrange eggs, veal and remaining tomatoes and radishes on top. Garnish with parsley.

Frankfurter kebabs

Overall timing 20 minutes

Freezing Suitable: cook from frozen

To serve 2

4	Frankfurters	4
12	Button onions	12
3 tbsp	Oil	3x15 ml
2 teasp	Coarse-grain mustard	2x5 ml

Preheat the grill.

Cut each frankfurter into three pieces. Blanch onions in boiling water for 5 minutes, then drain and peel. Thread onions and frankfurters alternately on to greased skewers.

Mix oil and mustard together. Brush over kebabs and grill for about 10 minutes, turning and brushing with mustard mixture frequently. Serve with mashed potatoes and pour any cooking juices over.

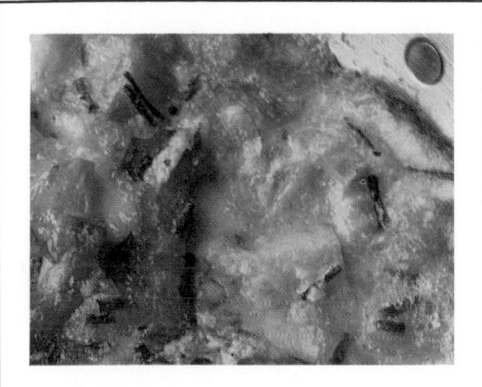

Welsh sausages

Overall timing 25 minutes

Freezing Suitable: reheat in 350°F (180°C) Gas 4 oven for 20–25 minutes

Makes 18–20

1	Small onion	1
5 oz	Hard cheese	150 g
9 oz	Fresh white breadcrumbs	250 g
1 tbsp	Chopped parsley or fresh fines herbes	15 ml
1 teasp	Powdered mustard	5 ml
	Salt and pepper	
2	Eggs	2
	Flour for coating	
2 oz	Dried breadcrumbs	50 g
	Oil for frying	

Peel and finely chop onion. Grate cheese. Place in bowl with fresh breadcrumbs, herbs, mustard and generous seasoning. Add 1 whole egg and 1 yolk and mix into ingredients with wooden spoon till well combined. Form mixture into small sausage shapes.

Lightly coat shapes in flour, then in lightly beaten egg white, then coat in dried breadcrumbs.

Heat ½ inch (12.5 mm) oil in a frying pan and when hot cook a few sausages at a time till crisp and golden all over. Drain on kitchen paper and serve hot or cold.

Peasant omelette

Overall timing 25 minutes

Freezing Not suitable

To serve 4

2	Waxy potatoes	2
1	Carrot	1
	Salt and pepper	
3 oz	Smoked streaky bacon rashers	75 g
3 oz	Butter	75 g
6	Eggs	6
1 tbsp	Chopped chives	15 ml
4	Thin slices of cheese	4

Peel and dice the potatoes; scrape and dice the carrot. Put into a pan, cover with cold salted water and bring to the boil. Simmer for 4 minutes, then drain.

Derind bacon and cut into strips. Preheat the grill.

Melt the butter in a frying pan and fry the bacon till transparent. Add the potatoes and carrots and fry over a moderate heat for 5 minutes, stirring frequently, till golden and tender.

Lightly beat the eggs in a bowl with salt, pepper and chives. Pour over the bacon and vegetables and cook till lightly set. Top with the slices of cheese and grill till melted. Serve immediately, cut into wedges.

Pilau rice

Overall timing 45 minutes plus soaking

Freezing Not suitable

To serve 4–6

1 lb	Patna rice	450 g
1	Large onion	1
1	Garlic clove	1
6	Whole allspice	6
8	Cardamom pods	8
4 oz	Butter or ghee	125 g
2 inch	Cinnamon stick	5 cm
8	Cloves	8
1 teasp	Ground turmeric	5 ml
	Salt	
2 oz	Flaked almonds	50 g
4 oz	Sultanas	125 g

Soak rice in cold water for 1 hour, then drain thoroughly.

Peel and finely chop the onion. Peel and crush garlic. Lightly crush allspice and cardamom pods. Melt 3 oz (75 g) of the fat in a saucepan. Add onion, garlic and spices and fry till onion is transparent but not browned.

Add rice and cook over a low heat, stirring, for 3–4 minutes. Add salt to taste and enough boiling water to come 1 inch (2.5 cm) above the rice. Cover pan tightly and simmer over a very low heat for about 20 minutes till water is absorbed and rice is tender.

Melt remaining fat in frying pan and fry almonds and sultanas for 3–5 minutes. Mix lightly into rice and serve immediately.

Curried cockles with rice

Overall timing 30 minutes

Freezing Not suitable

To serve 2

4 oz	Long grain rice	125 g
	Salt	
1 lb	Cockles	450 g
Curry sauce		
1	Small onion	1
1	Garlic clove	1
1 oz	Butter	25 g
1 tbsp	Curry powder	15 ml
	Ground cinnamon	
	Ground ginger	
	Sugar	
4 tbsp	Boiling water	4x15 ml
	Salt and pepper	

Cook the rice in boiling salted water till tender.

Meanwhile, scrub the cockles well under cold running water. Place them in a saucepan of salted water. Bring to the boil, cover and cook gently till the shells open. Discard any that do not open. Remove cockles from their shells and set aside. Strain the cooking liquor through a muslin-lined sieve into bowl.

Peel and finely chop onion and garlic. Melt butter in a frying pan and fry the onion and garlic till transparent. Add the curry powder and cook for a further 2 minutes. Add a large pinch each of cinnamon, ginger and sugar and the boiling water. Add 5 tbsp (5x15 ml) of the cooking liquor from the cockles. Taste, and season if necessary.

Stir the cockles into the sauce and heat through quickly. Put the drained rice on a warmed serving dish and pour the cockles and sauce over. Serve hot.

Prawn pilaf

Overall timing 1 hour

Freezing Not suitable

To serve 4

2	Large onions	2
2	Fresh green chillies	2
2	Garlic cloves	2
8 oz	Streaky bacon rashers	225 g
1 tbsp	Oil	15 ml
8 oz	Long-grain rice	225 g
14 oz	Can of tomatoes	397 g
	Salt	
$\frac{3}{4}$ pint	Chicken stock	400 ml
1 lb	Shelled prawns	450 g
2 tbsp	Chopped parsley	2x15 ml
2 tbsp	Grated Parmesan cheese	2x15 ml

Peel and slice onions. Deseed and slice chillies. Peel and crush garlic. Derind and chop bacon.

Heat the oil in a flameproof casserole. Add bacon and fry until well browned. Add the onions, chillies and garlic to the casserole. Cook until onions are soft and transparent but not brown, stirring occasionally.

Add the rice and stir for 2–3 minutes until grains are coated with oil. Add the tomatoes with their juice, salt and chicken stock. Bring rapidly to the boil, then reduce heat, cover and simmer for 15 minutes on a very low heat.

Stir and add the prawns. Cover and cook for a further 5 minutes.

Turn mixture into warmed serving dish. Sprinkle with parsley and cheese and serve immediately.

Fish paella

Overall timing 45 minutes

Freezing Not suitable

To serve 6

1	Large onion	1
2	Garlic cloves	2
4 tbsp	Oil	4x15 ml
1 lb	Long grain rice	450 g
14 oz	Can of tomatoes	397 g
4	Saffron strands	4
3½ pints	Chicken stock or water	2 litres
	Salt and pepper	
1½ lb	White fish fillets	700 g
1	Red pepper	1
14 oz	Can of artichoke hearts	397 g
14 oz	Can of broad beans	397 g
8 oz	Frozen peas	225 g

Peel and chop the onion. Peel and crush the garlic. Heat the oil in a flameproof casserole, add the onion and fry till transparent. Add the rice and garlic and fry, stirring, for 2 minutes.

Add the tomatoes and juice, the saffron, stock or water and seasoning and bring to the boil. Reduce the heat and simmer for 10 minutes.

Meanwhile, cut the fish into chunks. Halve and deseed the pepper and cut into 1 inch (2.5 cm) pieces. Drain the artichoke hearts and cut in half lengthways. Drain the beans.

Add all these ingredients to the pan with the peas and mix lightly. Cover and cook for a further 10 minutes till the rice is tender and the liquid is absorbed. Fluff the mixture with a fork. Taste and adjust seasoning. Serve immediately.

Lentil risotto

Overall timing 1 hour

Freezing Not suitable

To serve 6

8 oz	Continental lentils	225 g
1	Onion	1
4 oz	Butter	125 g
	Salt and pepper	
12 oz	Long grain rice	350 g
2 pints	Stock	1.1 litres
2 oz	Grated Parmesan cheese	50 g

Wash and pick over lentils. Peel and finely chop the onion. Melt the butter in a large saucepan, add the onion and cook till transparent. Add the lentils and enough water to cover. Season and bring to the boil. Reduce heat, cover and simmer for 1 hour.

Add the rice and stock. Bring back to the boil, reduce heat, cover and simmer for a further 15–18 minutes or until rice is just tender.

Stir in the Parmesan, and taste and adjust seasoning. Serve hot.

Arabian pilaf

Overall timing 30 minutes

Freezing Not suitable

To serve 4

1 oz	Butter	25 g
2 oz	Capelli d'angelo (angels' hair pasta)	50 g
1¼ pints	Chicken stock	700 ml
8 oz	Long grain rice	225 g
2 tbsp	Grated Parmesan cheese	2x15 ml
	Salt and pepper	

Melt the butter in a saucepan. Break up the pasta, add to the pan and fry, stirring, over a moderate heat till golden. Remove from pan and reserve.

Add the stock to the pan and bring to the boil. Stir in the rice, bring back to the boil and simmer gently for 15 minutes till the rice is just tender.

Stir in the fried pasta and cook for 2–3 minutes till pasta and rice are tender and all the liquid has been absorbed. Stir in Parmesan and seasoning with a fork. Transfer to a warmed serving dish and serve immediately.

Cannelloni with tuna fish

Overall timing 1½ hours

Freezing Suitable: reheat in 350°F (180°C) Gas 4 oven for 1 hour

To serve 4

12	Sheets of lasagne	12
	Salt and pepper	
2	Onions	2
2	Garlic cloves	2
2 oz	Capers	50 g
7 oz	Can of tuna fish	198 g
2 oz	Fresh breadcrumbs	50 g
1 tbsp	Lemon juice	15 ml
1	Egg	1
2 tbsp	Chopped parsley	2x15 ml
14 oz	Can of tomatoes	397 g
2 tbsp	Grated Parmesan cheese	2x15 ml

Place lasagne in saucepan of boiling, salted water and cook for 10–15 minutes or until tender. Drain in a colander, rinse with boiling water and spread out on a damp tea-towel to cool for a few minutes.

Peel and chop onions. Peel and crush garlic. Drain capers. Drain tuna fish oil into a frying pan, heat, add onions and fry until golden. Add garlic, tuna fish and capers and cook over low heat for 5 minutes, stirring. Remove from heat.

Preheat oven to 400°F (200°C) Gas 6. Grease ovenproof dish.

Add breadcrumbs (reserving 2 tbsp/2x15 ml) to fish mixture with lemon juice, egg, parsley and seasoning. Mix well. Place some of the fish mixture in centre of each lasagne sheet and roll around filling. Arrange rolls, joins down, in ovenproof dish.

Press tomatoes in their juice through a sieve, season and spread over cannelloni. Sprinkle with reserved breadcrumbs and then with Parmesan. Cook in centre of the oven for 30 minutes.

Aubergine and pasta casserole

Overall timing 1 hour

Freezing Not suitable

To serve 4–6

1	Large aubergine	1
	Salt and pepper	
1	Onion	1
1	Garlic clove	1
3 oz	Butter	75 g
1 lb	Tomatoes	450 g
2 teasp	Chopped fresh basil	2x5 ml
3 fl oz	Oil	90 ml
12 oz	Rigatoni	350 g
3 oz	Mozzarella cheese	75 g

Preheat oven to 400°F (200°C) Gas 6.

Cut aubergine into thin slices lengthways. Arrange slices on a plate, sprinkle with salt and leave for 30 minutes.

Meanwhile, peel and chop onion. Peel and crush garlic. Melt 2 oz (50 g) of the butter in a saucepan, add onion and garlic and fry till transparent.

Blanch, peel and finely chop tomatoes. Add to onion with seasoning. Simmer gently for 15 minutes. Remove from heat and stir in basil.

Rinse aubergine slices under running cold water and pat dry with kitchen paper. Heat oil in frying pan, add slices and cook for 4–5 minutes each side. Drain on kitchen paper.

Cook rigatoni in boiling salted water till tender. Drain and mix with tomato sauce. Season to taste. Put half the rigatoni mixture into greased ovenproof dish and arrange aubergine slices on top. Add remaining rigatoni mixture. Thinly slice cheese and arrange on top. Dot with remaining butter and bake for 15 minutes. Serve hot.

Seafood spaghetti

Overall timing 20 minutes

Freezing Not suitable

To serve 4

12 oz	Spaghetti	350 g
	Salt and pepper	
1	Garlic clove	1
3 tbsp	Oil	3x15 ml
8 oz	Large shelled prawns	225 g
10 oz	Can of baby clams or mussels	280 g
8 oz	Can of tomatoes	227 g
1 tbsp	Chopped parsley	15 ml

Cook spaghetti in boiling salted water till tender.

Meanwhile, peel and crush garlic. Heat oil in a large saucepan, add garlic and fry for 1 minute. Add prawns and fry, stirring, for 2–3 minutes.

Drain clams or mussels and add to pan with tomatoes and their juice and seasoning. Cook for about 3 minutes, stirring to break up tomatoes.

Drain spaghetti thoroughly. Add to seafood sauce with parsley and toss lightly over a low heat till well coated. Serve immediately.

Spaghetti with goat's cheese

Overall timing 35 minutes

Freezing Not suitable

To serve 2

1	Garlic clove	1
2	Anchovy fillets	2
2 tbsp	Olive oil	2x15 ml
1 tbsp	Chopped parsley	15 ml
	Salt and pepper	
8 oz	Spaghetti	225 g
4 oz	Firm goat's cheese	125 g
1 oz	Butter	25 g

Peel and crush the garlic into a bowl. Add the anchovy fillets and pound to a paste with a wooden spoon. Beat in the oil, parsley and seasoning. Leave to stand for 15 minutes.

Meanwhile, cook the spaghetti in boiling salted water till tender. Derind the cheese and cut into small cubes.

Drain the spaghetti in a colander. Melt the butter in the spaghetti pan and add the cheese. Cook, stirring, over a low heat for 2 minutes.

Return spaghetti to the pan and toss lightly till coated with butter. Arrange in a warmed serving dish, pour the anchovy dressing over and toss lightly before serving with crusty bread.

Crisp-topped macaroni with tuna

Overall timing 35 minutes

Freezing Not suitable

To serve 4

1	Onion	1
3 oz	Butter	75 g
¼ pint	Chicken stock	150 ml
	Salt and pepper	
1	Medium cauliflower	1
8 oz	Short-cut macaroni	225 g
6	Anchovy fillets	6
1 oz	Fresh breadcrumbs	25 g
7 oz	Can of tuna	198 g
4 tbsp	Grated Parmesan cheese	4x15 ml

Peel and chop the onion. Melt 1 oz (25 g) of the butter in a large saucepan and fry the onion till golden. Add the chicken stock and seasoning. Bring to the boil and simmer for 5 minutes.

Divide cauliflower into florets and cook in boiling salted water for 4 minutes. Remove with a draining spoon and reserve. Add macaroni to boiling water and cook till tender.

Meanwhile, melt remaining butter in a frying pan and fry cauliflower till golden. Roughly chop anchovies and add to pan with breadcrumbs. Fry till crisp. Remove from heat.

Preheat the grill.

Drain the macaroni and add to the stock mixture. Drain and flake tuna and stir carefully into the macaroni with half the Parmesan. Taste and adjust seasoning and heat through gently.

Pour the macaroni mixture into a flameproof dish and scatter cauliflower and breadcrumb mixture over it. Sprinkle with remaining cheese, then grill for 5 minutes till golden.

Lasagne alla bolognese

Overall timing 2 hours

Freezing Suitable: reheat in 350°F (180°C) Gas 4 oven for 1 hour

To serve 6

1	Onion	1
1	Carrot	1
1	Stalk of celery	1
4 oz	Streaky bacon	125 g
4 oz	Chuck steak	125 g
4 oz	Belly of pork	125 g
3 oz	Butter	75 g
1 tbsp	Tomato purée	15 ml
¼ pint	Hot stock	150 ml
3 tbsp	Dry white wine	3x15 ml
¼ pint	Milk	150 ml
1 lb	Fresh spinach	450 g
	Salt and pepper	
12 oz	Green lasagne	350 g
1 pint	White sauce	560 ml
3 oz	Grated Parmesan cheese	75 g

Peel and chop onion and carrot. Chop celery. Derind and chop bacon. Mince meats. Melt 1 oz (25 g) of butter in a saucepan, add bacon and meats and brown. Add vegetables, tomato purée, stock, wine and milk. Simmer gently for 45 minutes, stirring occasionally.

Meanwhile, wash spinach and remove coarse stalks. Place in a saucepan with 1 oz (25 g) of the butter and seasoning. Cook gently for 5–10 minutes. Chop finely and add to meat mixture.

Preheat oven to 375°F (190°C) Gas 5.

Cook lasagne in boiling, salted water till tender. Drain on damp tea-towel.

Cover bottom of greased ovenproof dish with a quarter of the lasagne. Spread half the meat mixture on top, then another quarter of the lasagne, half the white sauce and Parmesan. Repeat layers, finishing with white sauce and Parmesan. Dot with remaining butter. Bake for 20 minutes.

Spaghetti alla carbonara

Overall timing 20 minutes

Freezing Not suitable

To serve 4

12 oz	Spaghetti	350 g
	Salt and pepper	
2	Eggs	2
2 tbsp	Top of the milk	2x15 ml
4 oz	Streaky bacon rashers	125 g
1 tbsp	Oil	15 ml
2 oz	Grated Parmesan cheese	50 g

Cook the spaghetti in boiling salted water till tender.

Meanwhile, beat eggs, milk and pepper in a bowl. Derind and dice the bacon. Heat the oil in large frying pan, add the bacon and fry till crisp.

Drain the spaghetti and add to the bacon. Pour in the egg mixture, stirring, and toss over a gentle heat till the eggs just begin to set. Serve immediately, sprinkled with grated Parmesan.

Spaghetti with chicken sauce

Overall timing 1 hour

Freezing Suitable: cook spaghetti and almonds after reheating sauce

To serve 4

2	Thick rashers of streaky bacon	2
12 oz	Boned chicken breasts	350 g
2 oz	Butter	50 g
2 tbsp	Oil	2x15 ml
1 lb	Ripe tomatoes	450 g
1	Garlic clove	1
2 tbsp	Tomato purée	2x15 ml
½ teasp	Sugar	2.5 ml
	Salt and pepper	
¼ pint	Dry white wine	150 ml
12 oz	Spaghetti	350 g
1 oz	Chopped almonds	25 g

Derind and dice the bacon. Wipe and trim the chicken, discarding skin. Cut the meat into strips. Heat half the butter and the oil in a flameproof casserole, add the bacon and chicken and fry for 5 minutes till browned all over.

Blanch, peel and chop the tomatoes. Add to the pan with the peeled and crushed garlic, tomato purée, sugar and salt and pepper. Add the wine and bring to the boil, stirring. Reduce the heat, cover the pan tightly and simmer for 20 minutes.

Meanwhile, cook the spaghetti in boiling salted water till just tender. Drain in a colander.

Melt remaining butter in the saucepan, add the almonds and fry over a high heat till golden. Return the spaghetti to the pan with half the tomato chicken sauce, toss lightly and adjust seasoning to taste. Place in a warmed serving dish.

Season remaining sauce, pour into a warmed sauceboat and serve separately.

Turkey noodle bake

Overall timing 1½ hours

Freezing Not suitable

To serve 4

4 oz	Button mushrooms	125 g
8 oz	Noodles	225 g
	Salt and pepper	
3 tbsp	Plain flour	3x15 ml
1	Chicken stock cube	1
¼ teasp	Paprika	1.25 ml
5 tbsp	Single cream	5x15 ml
8 oz	Cooked turkey meat	225 g
2 oz	Cheddar cheese	50 g
1 oz	Fresh breadcrumbs	25 g
½ oz	Butter	15 g

Wipe and slice the mushrooms. Cook the noodles in boiling salted water for about 5 minutes till tender. Drain the noodles thoroughly, reserving 1 pint (560 ml) of the cooking water.

Blend the flour in a small bowl with a little of the measured cooking water. Put rest of water into a saucepan, stir in blended flour, crumbled stock cube, salt, pepper and paprika. Bring to the boil, stirring. Reduce the heat and add the mushrooms. Simmer for 10 minutes.

Preheat the oven to 350°F (180°C) Gas 4. Grease an 8 inch (20 cm) soufflé dish.

Remove pan from heat and stir in cream. Spread half the drained noodles over the bottom of the soufflé dish. Dice the turkey and arrange half over the noodles. Cover with half the sauce. Repeat the layers, finishing with sauce. Grate cheese and scatter over top. Sprinkle with breadcrumbs and dot with butter. Bake for 30 minutes.

Corsican spaghetti

Overall timing 1 hour

Freezing Suitable (sauce only): add olives after reheating

To serve 2

1	Onion	1
2 oz	Butter	50 g
8 oz	Ripe tomatoes	225 g
1	Garlic clove	1
8 oz	Minced beef	225 g
½	Small dried chilli	½
	Salt and pepper	
8 oz	Spaghetti	225 g
6	Stoned green olives	6
1 oz	Cheese	25 g

Peel and finely chop onion. Melt half the butter in a saucepan and fry the onion till lightly browned.

Blanch, peel and chop the tomatoes. Peel and crush the garlic and add to onions with the minced beef, tomatoes, the dried chilli and salt. Simmer for 45 minutes.

Cook the spaghetti in boiling salted water till tender. Drain thoroughly in a colander, then add remaining butter and leave to melt.

Remove chilli from sauce. Slice the green olives and add to the sauce. Taste and adjust seasoning.

Pile spaghetti in a warmed serving dish and pour meat sauce over. Serve the grated cheese separately.

Cheesy macaroni

Overall timing 30 minutes

Freezing Not suitable

To serve 4

8 oz	Long macaroni	225 g
	Salt and pepper	
2	Eggs	2
4 oz	Cooked ham	125 g
6 oz	Cheddar cheese	175 g
3 oz	Butter	75 g
	Cayenne pepper	

Preheat the oven to 425°F (220°C) Gas 7. Grease an 8 inch (20 cm) soufflé dish.

Place macaroni in saucepan of boiling salted water and cook till tender.

Meanwhile, lightly beat the eggs. Coarsely chop the ham. Grate the cheese. Drain macaroni and place in soufflé dish. Add 2 oz (50 g) of the butter, 5 oz (150 g) of the cheese, the eggs and ham to the dish. Add a pinch of cayenne and season to taste. Mix well. Sprinkle with remaining cheese and dot with the rest of the butter.

Bake on top shelf of oven for 10 minutes or till golden and lightly set. Serve immediately with a tomato salad.

Cheesy noodles with ham

Overall timing 1 hour

Freezing Not suitable

To serve 4

8 oz	Tagliatelle	225 g
	Salt and pepper	
4 oz	Cheese	125 g
3	Eggs	3
¾ pint	White sauce	400 ml
4 oz	Sliced cooked ham	125 g

Preheat the oven to 400°F (200°C) Gas 6.

Cook the noodles in boiling salted water for about 10 minutes till tender.

Grate cheese. Separate eggs. Stir yolks, 3 oz (75 g) of the cheese and seasoning into sauce.

Cut ham into strips and stir into the sauce. Drain noodles thoroughly and fold into sauce. Season to taste. Whisk the egg whites in a bowl till stiff but not dry and fold into the mixture with metal spoon.

Pour the mixture into a greased ovenproof dish. Sprinkle remaining grated cheese over and bake for about 30 minutes till set and golden. Serve immediately with whole green beans mixed with flaked almonds and butter.

Spinach and veal ravioli

Overall timing 1 hour 35 minutes

Freezing Suitable: cook after thawing

To serve 2

2 oz	Spinach	50 g
6 oz	Veal	175 g
1 oz	Lean cooked ham	25 g
1 oz	Butter	25 g
2 tbsp	Fresh breadcrumbs	2x15 ml
1 tbsp	Milk	15 ml
1	Egg	1
2 oz	Grated Parmesan cheese	50 g
$\frac{1}{4}$ teasp	Dried marjoram	1.25 ml
	Pinch of grated nutmeg	
	Salt and pepper	
12 oz	Ravioli cases	350 g
$\frac{1}{4}$ pint	Tomato sauce	150 ml

Wash spinach and chop roughly. Blanch in boiling water for 5 minutes. Drain.

Chop the veal and ham into small pieces. Melt butter in frying pan and fry veal and ham till brown. Drain and cool. Soak breadcrumbs in milk till milk is absorbed.

Put meats and spinach through a mincer, then mix to a paste. Add egg, soaked breadcrumbs, 2 tbsp (2x15 ml) of the Parmesan, the marjoram, nutmeg and seasoning. Mix together well.

Use mixture to stuff ready-made ravioli cases, which can easily be obtained from delicatessens and supermarkets, then close them up. Cook ravioli in boiling, salted water for about 10 minutes. Drain, place in warmed serving dishes and cover with hot tomato sauce. Sprinkle the ravioli with remaining Parmesan. Serve with a crisp green salad.

Spaghetti omelette

Overall timing 30 minutes

Freezing Not suitable

To serve 4–6

12 oz	Spaghetti	350 g
	Salt and pepper	
1 oz	Cheddar cheese	25 g
1	Garlic clove	1
1 oz	Grated Parmesan cheese	25 g
4	Eggs	4
1 tbsp	Chopped parsley	15 ml
6	Basil leaves	6
2 oz	Butter	50 g

Cook the spaghetti in boiling salted water till tender.

Meanwhile, grate the Cheddar cheese. Peel and crush the garlic. Mix together the garlic, cheeses, eggs, parsley, chopped basil and seasoning.

Drain the spaghetti and put into a large bowl. Pour the egg and cheese mixture over and mix well. Melt 1 oz (25 g) butter in frying pan. Add spaghetti mixture and press down well with the back of a spoon to form a cake. Fry over a low heat for about 5 minutes, pressing down to keep the cake flat.

Run a knife round the edge of the omelette to loosen it, then turn it out on to a board. Add remaining butter to the pan and, when melted, slide the omelette back into the pan. Fry for 3–5 minutes till firmly set. Place on a warmed serving dish and serve immediately, cut into wedges.

Lasagne col pesto

Overall timing 1 hour

Freezing Suitable: reheat, covered with foil, in 350°F (180°C) Gas 4 oven for 1 hour

To serve 4

12 oz	Lasagne	350 g
	Salt	
4 tbsp	Grated Parmesan cheese	4x15 ml
2 oz	Butter	50 g
Pesto		
2	Garlic cloves	2
4 tbsp	Chopped fresh basil	4x15 ml
4 tbsp	Olive oil	4x15 ml
1 oz	Grated Parmesan cheese	25 g
	Pinch of salt	

Cook the lasagne in boiling salted water for 15–20 minutes till tender. Drain thoroughly and spread out on a damp cloth to cool.

Preheat oven to 350°F (180°C) Gas 4.

To make the pesto, peel and chop garlic and put in mortar with basil. Pound with pestle, gradually adding oil, Parmesan and salt.

Spread one-third of the lasagne over the bottom of a greased ovenproof dish. Spread with one-third of the pesto and sprinkle over 1 tbsp (15 ml) Parmesan. Repeat layers twice, adding extra Parmesan to the top. Dot with butter and bake for 20 minutes till heated through.

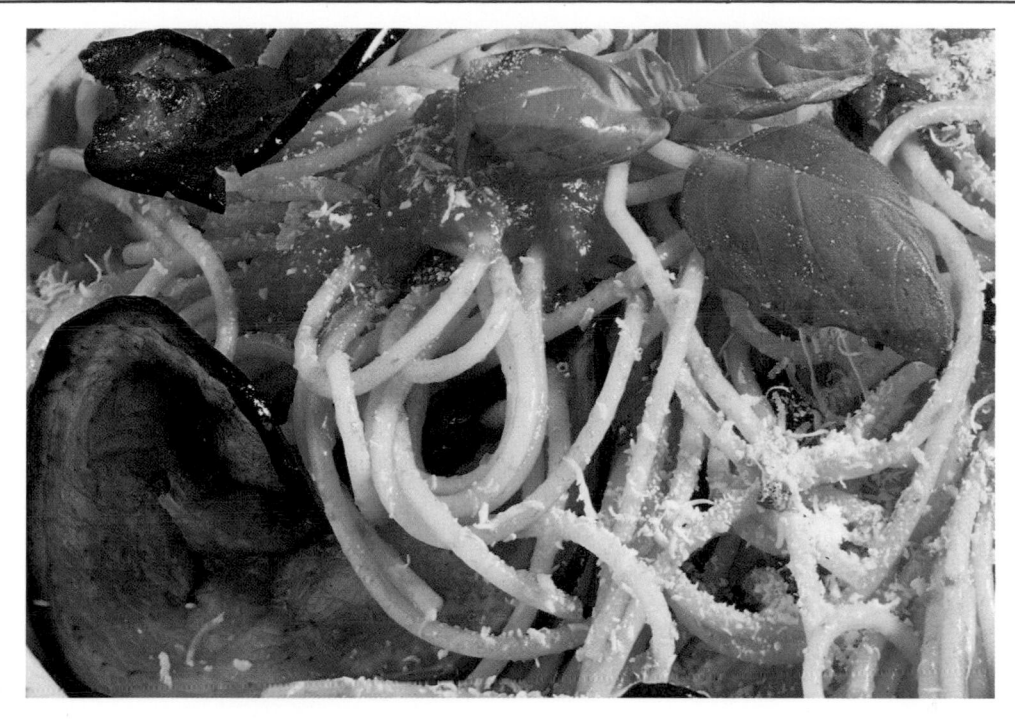

Spaghetti with aubergines

Overall timing 45 minutes plus draining

Freezing Not suitable

To serve 4

1	Large aubergine	1
	Salt and pepper	
1 lb	Ripe tomatoes	450 g
1	Garlic clove	1
	Oil	
2 teasp	Chopped fresh basil	2x5 ml
12 oz	Spaghetti	350 g
2 oz	Grated Parmesan cheese	50 g
	Sprig of basil	

Wash and thinly slice the aubergine. Put into a colander and sprinkle with salt. Leave to drain for 1 hour.

Blanch, peel and chop the tomatoes. Peel and crush garlic. Heat 3 tbsp (3x15 ml) oil in a saucepan, add garlic and fry for 1 minute. Add tomatoes, basil and seasoning, stir well and cook over a low heat for 15 minutes.

Cook spaghetti in boiling salted water till tender.

Meanwhile, rinse aubergine slices under running water and gently squeeze dry. Heat $\frac{1}{2}$ inch (12.5 mm) oil in a frying pan and fry aubergine slices, a few at a time, till crisp on both sides. Drain on kitchen paper and keep hot.

Drain spaghetti thoroughly. Put into a warmed serving dish and pour tomato sauce over. Add aubergine slices, sprinkle with cheese, garnish with sprig of basil and serve.

Macaroni niçoise

Overall timing 30 minutes

Freezing Not suitable

To serve 4

3	Anchovy fillets	3
12 oz	Tomatoes	350 g
1	Garlic clove	1
12 oz	Rigatoni	350 g
	Salt	
2 oz	Butter	50 g
2 oz	Grated Parmesan cheese	50 g
1 tbsp	Chopped fresh basil	15 ml

Chop the anchovies. Blanch, peel and cut tomatoes into thin slices. Place in a serving bowl with the anchovies and peeled and crushed garlic.

Cook the rigatoni in a large saucepan of boiling salted water till just tender. When cooked, drain in colander.

Melt butter in the saucepan and when frothy, add rigatoni and toss well. Add to the tomatoes and garlic, toss, then sprinkle with Parmesan and basil and serve immediately.

Spaghetti with bacon sauce

Overall timing 45 minutes

Freezing Not suitable

To serve 4

12 oz	Piece of smoked streaky bacon	350 g
1 tbsp	Oil	15 ml
1	Small red pepper	1
14 oz	Can of tomatoes	397 g
	Salt and pepper	
12 oz	Spaghetti	350 g
6 tbsp	Grated Parmesan cheese	6x15 ml

Remove the rind and any bones from the bacon. Cut into ¼ inch (6 mm) thick slices, then cut across into strips. Heat the oil in a saucepan, add the bacon and fry till golden all over.

Deseed and finely chop the pepper. Add to the pan and fry for 1 minute. Press the tomatoes and juice through a sieve into the pan and bring to the boil, stirring. Add seasoning, cover and simmer for 15 minutes.

Meanwhile, cook the spaghetti in boiling salted water till tender. Drain thoroughly and return to the pan. Add the sauce and all but 1 tbsp (15 ml) of the cheese. Toss lightly over a low heat for 2 minutes. Adjust the seasoning to taste.

Place spaghetti in a warmed serving dish and sprinkle with the remaining cheese. Serve immediately with fresh crusty bread.

Boer-style noodle supper

Overall timing 20 minutes

Freezing Not suitable

To serve 2

1 pint	Milk	560 ml
	Blade of mace	
6 oz	Noodles	175 g
1 oz	Butter	25 g
2	Eggs	2
¼ teasp	Ground cinnamon	1.25 ml
	Salt and pepper	

Put the milk in a saucepan with the mace and bring to the boil. Add the noodles and cook for about 5 minutes till tender. Drain, reserving the milk. Divide noodles between individual soup bowls and add half butter to each. Keep hot.

Separate the eggs. Beat the egg yolks in a bowl with the cinnamon and seasoning. Gradually strain the reserved milk on to the yolks, stirring constantly. Return to the pan.

Whisk the egg whites till stiff and fold into the yolk mixture. Cook over a low heat for 2–5 minutes without stirring till mixture begins to thicken. Do not allow to boil.

Pour egg mixture over the noodles and serve immediately with bread and a mixed salad.

Spaghetti with piquant sauce

Overall timing 50 minutes

Freezing Not suitable

To serve 4

1	Can of anchovy fillets	1
4 tbsp	Milk	4x15 ml
1 lb	Ripe tomatoes	450 g
1	Garlic clove	1
1	Dried red chilli	1
3 fl oz	Olive oil	90 ml
1 tbsp	Tomato purée	15 ml
2 tbsp	Capers	2x15 ml
12 oz	Spaghetti	350 g
	Salt and pepper	
4 oz	Stoned black olives	125 g

Drain the anchovies and put into a small bowl with the milk. Soak for 10 minutes. Blanch, peel and chop the tomatoes. Peel and crush the garlic; deseed and finely chop the chilli.

Heat the oil in a saucepan, add the garlic and cook for 2 minutes. Drain the anchovies, discarding the milk. Chop and add to the pan with the chilli. Fry for 3 minutes, pressing the anchovies with the back of a wooden spoon to break them up.

Add the tomatoes, tomato purée and capers. Bring to the boil, then cover and simmer for 15 minutes.

Meanwhile, cook the spaghetti in boiling salted water till tender. Drain thoroughly. Return to the pan and add the tomato and anchovy sauce and the black olives. Stir over a low heat for 3 minutes. Adjust seasoning to taste and serve hot.

Mushroom ravioli

Overall timing 45 minutes

Freezing Suitable: cook from frozen

To serve 4

12 oz	Strong flour	350 g
	Salt and pepper	
3	Eggs	3
1 lb	Mushrooms	450 g
1	Onion	1
2 oz	Butter	50 g

Sift flour and 1 teasp (5 ml) salt into a bowl. Add eggs and mix to a smooth, glossy dough.

Chop the mushrooms. Peel and finely chop onion. Melt half the butter in a frying pan and fry the onion for 5 minutes till transparent. Add mushrooms and seasoning and stir-fry over a high heat for about 5 minutes to evaporate any liquid. Reduce heat and cook gently for a further 5 minutes. Remove from heat and leave to cool.

Roll out the dough on a lightly floured surface and cut into 3 inch (7.5 cm) squares with a pastry wheel. Divide the mushroom mixture between the squares, then fold them over, pressing the edges together well to seal.

Put plenty of lightly salted water in a large saucepan and bring to the boil. Add the ravioli and cook for 10–15 minutes, then drain and place in a warmed serving dish. Melt the remaining butter, pour over the ravioli and toss well.

Neapolitan cannelloni

Overall timing 1½ hours

Freezing Suitable: reheat from frozen in 350°F (180°C) Gas 4 oven for 1 hour

To serve 4

12	Sheets of lasagne	12
8 oz	Mozzarella cheese	225 g
2 oz	Cooked ham	50 g
8 oz	Cream cheese	225 g
2	Eggs	2
	Salt and pepper	
1½ oz	Grated Parmesan cheese	40 g
Tomato sauce		
1	Onion	1
1	Garlic clove	1
1 tbsp	Oil	15 ml
14 oz	Can of tomatoes	397 g
1 tbsp	Chopped fresh basil	15 ml

Cook lasagne in boiling salted water for 10–15 minutes till tender. Drain and spread on a damp cloth to cool.

Thinly slice the Mozzarella. Dice ham. Place in a bowl with the cream cheese, eggs and seasoning. Mix well.

For the sauce, peel and finely chop onion. Peel and crush garlic. Heat oil in a saucepan, add onion and garlic and fry until golden. Add tomatoes in their juice, basil, salt and pepper. Cook for 10 minutes, stirring occasionally.

Preheat oven to 425°F (220°C) Gas 7.

Divide cheese mixture between lasagne sheets. Roll lasagne around filling and arrange, joins down, in greased ovenproof dish. Pour over the tomato sauce. Sprinkle half the Parmesan on top and bake for 15 minutes or until golden. Sprinkle with the rest of the Parmesan and serve immediately.

Spaghetti with sardine dressing

Overall timing 20 minutes

Freezing Not suitable

To serve 4

12 oz	Spaghetti	350 g
	Salt and pepper	
11½ oz	Can of sardines	326 g
2	Garlic cloves	2
3 oz	Butter	75 g

Cook the spaghetti in boiling salted water till tender.

Drain the sardines and put into a mortar. Peel and crush garlic and add to sardines. Pound to a paste with a pestle. Add the butter and mix well. Season to taste.

Drain the spaghetti and return to the pan. Add the sardine paste and toss lightly over a low heat till the spaghetti is coated. Place in a warmed serving dish and serve immediately with wedges of lemon.

Spaghetti with tomato sauce

Overall timing 30 minutes

Freezing Not suitable

To serve 4

1	Onion	1
2 lb	Cherry or plum tomatoes	900 g
	Bouquet garni	
	Pinch of sugar	
	Cayenne pepper or Tabasco sauce	
	Salt and pepper	
1 tbsp	Chopped fresh basil or parsley	15 ml
12 oz	Spaghetti	350 g

Peel and chop the onion. Halve the tomatoes. Put the onion and tomatoes in a saucepan with the bouquet garni and simmer gently until mushy.

Discard the bouquet garni, then rub the tomato sauce through a sieve, or purée in a blender. Return to the pan and add the sugar, a little cayenne or Tabasco sauce and seasoning. Stir in the herbs and reheat gently.

Meanwhile, cook the spaghetti in boiling salted water till just tender. Drain well and turn into a warmed serving dish. Pile the tomato sauce on top and serve.

Neapolitan rigatoni

Overall timing 50 minutes

Freezing Not suitable

To serve 2

2	Streaky bacon rashers	2
1	Onion	1
1	Garlic clove	1
1 oz	Lard	25 g
6 oz	Minced beef	175 g
5 tbsp	Beef stock	5x15 ml
5 tbsp	Red wine	5x15 ml
1 tbsp	Tomato purée	15 ml
1 teasp	Chopped fresh basil	5 ml
	Salt and pepper	
8 oz	Rigatoni	225 g

Derind and finely chop bacon. Peel and chop onion. Peel and crush garlic. Melt the lard in a saucepan, add bacon, onion and garlic and fry for 10 minutes till golden.

Add the minced beef and fry, stirring, till brown. Gradually stir in the stock, wine, tomato purée, basil and seasoning. Cover and simmer for 30 minutes.

Meanwhile, cook rigatoni in boiling salted water till tender. Drain thoroughly and pile on to a warmed serving dish. Keep hot.

Taste the sauce and adjust seasoning. Purée in a blender or press through a sieve, then reheat and spoon over rigatoni. Serve immediately with a mixed salad and grated Parmesan cheese.

Macaroni with mushrooms

Overall timing 30 minutes

Freezing Not suitable

To serve 4

4 oz	Button mushrooms	125 g
4 oz	Butter	125 g
8 fl oz	Carton of single cream	227 ml
12 oz	Short-cut macaroni	350 g
	Salt and pepper	
4 oz	Cooked ham	125 g
2 oz	Grated Parmesan cheese	50 g
½ pint	White sauce	300 ml

Finely chop the mushrooms. Place in a small saucepan with 2 oz (50 g) of the butter and cook gently for 5 minutes. Remove from heat and stir in cream.

Cook macaroni in boiling salted water till tender. Drain.

Cut the ham into pieces and add to the macaroni with 1 oz (25 g) of cheese, 1 oz (25 g) of butter and seasoning. Place macaroni in a flameproof dish with mushroom mixture and stir well. Cook gently for 10 minutes.

Preheat grill.

Pour white sauce over macaroni, sprinkle with remaining cheese and dot with remaining butter. Grill for 5 minutes.

Noodle tortilla

Overall timing 45 minutes

Freezing Not suitable

To serve 4

12 oz	Noodles	350 g
	Salt	
3 oz	Butter	75 g
4 oz	Cottage cheese	125 g
3	Eggs	3
¼ teasp	Ground allspice	1.25 ml
2 tbsp	Chopped parsley	2x15 ml

Cook the noodles in boiling salted water for about 5 minutes till tender. Drain thoroughly and put into a warm bowl. Stir in 2 oz (50 g) of the butter and the sieved cottage cheese. Lightly beat the eggs and stir into the noodles with salt, allspice and chopped parsley.

Preheat the grill. Melt the remaining butter in a frying pan. Add the noodle mixture and smooth the top. Cook over a moderate heat for 5 minutes till lightly set. Put the pan under the grill to brown the top.

Turn omelette on to a warmed serving plate and serve immediately.

Pasta with lamb and tomato sauce

Overall timing 1¼ hours

Freezing Not suitable

To serve 2

2	Bacon rashers	2
8 oz	Tomatoes	225 g
1	Onion	1
1	Garlic clove	1
2 tbsp	Oil	2x15 ml
6 oz	Minced lamb	175 g
¼ pint	Red wine	150 ml
	Salt and pepper	
8 oz	Pasta shapes	225 g

Derind and chop bacon. Blanch, peel and chop tomatoes. Peel and chop onion and garlic. Heat the oil in a saucepan, add the bacon and fry for 5 minutes. Add onion and garlic and fry gently till transparent. Add the minced lamb and fry for about 15 minutes till browned.

Stir in the red wine, tomatoes and seasoning. Cover and simmer for 40 minutes.

Meanwhile, cook pasta in boiling salted water till tender. Drain and place in warmed serving dish.

Spoon meat sauce over pasta and serve hot with a green salad.

Spaghetti with tuna

Overall timing 30 minutes

Freezing Not suitable

To serve 4

1	Onion	1
2	Garlic cloves	2
7 oz	Can of tuna	198 g
1 tbsp	Olive oil	15 ml
12 oz	Spaghetti	350 g
	Salt and pepper	
4	Anchovy fillets	4
2 tbsp	Tomato purée	2x15 ml
½ teasp	Sugar	2.5 ml
6 tbsp	Water	6x15 ml
1 tbsp	Chopped parsley	15 ml
2 teasp	Chopped fresh basil	2x5 ml

Peel and finely chop the onion; peel and crush the garlic. Drain the oil from the tuna into a saucepan. Add the olive oil and heat. Add the onion and garlic and fry till just golden.

Put the spaghetti into a saucepan of boiling salted water and cook gently till just tender.

Meanwhile, chop the anchovies and add to the onion with the tomato puree, sugar and water. Bring to the boil.

Flake the tuna fish and add to the pan with seasoning. Cover and simmer for 5 minutes.

Drain the spaghetti and add to the pan with the herbs. Toss lightly over a low heat for 2–3 minutes. Adjust seasoning to taste and serve immediately.

Striped vermicelli

Overall timing 45 minutes

Freezing Not suitable

To serve 4

1	Can of anchovies	1
6 tbsp	Milk	6x15 ml
1	Large onion	1
1	Garlic clove	1
2 tbsp	Oil	2x15 ml
14 oz	Can of tomatoes	397 g
	Salt and pepper	
	Chilli powder	
1 tbsp	Chopped parsley	15 ml
12 oz	Vermicelli	350 g
¼ pint	Carton of double cream	150 ml

Drain the anchovies and soak in the milk for 10 minutes.

Meanwhile, peel and finely chop the onion; peel and crush the garlic. Heat the oil in a small saucepan, add onion and garlic and fry till transparent. Add tomatoes and juice, salt, a pinch of chilli powder and parsley. Simmer for 20 minutes, stirring frequently.

Drain the anchovies and add to the tomato mixture. Purée in a blender or rub through a sieve. Season and reheat gently.

Cook the vermicelli in boiling salted water for 3 minutes till tender. Drain thoroughly and arrange on a warmed flat serving dish. Smooth the top and keep hot.

Warm the cream, then spread it in a wide band across the centre of the vermicelli. Spread the tomato sauce in a wide band on either side of the cream. Serve with hot garlic bread.

Tagliatelli with ham

Overall timing 25 minutes

Freezing Not suitable

To serve 4

12 oz	Tagliatelli	350 g
	Salt and pepper	
1	Large onion	1
2 oz	Butter	50 g
2 tbsp	Oil	2x15 ml
1	Garlic clove	1
4 oz	Lean cooked ham	125 g
2 teasp	Dried marjoram	2x5 ml
14 oz	Can of tomatoes	397 g
6 tbsp	Grated Parmesan cheese	6x15 ml

Cook the tagliatelli in boiling salted water till tender.

Meanwhile, peel and finely chop the onion. Heat the butter and oil in a large saucepan and fry the onion till transparent. Peel and crush the garlic and add to the pan. Chop the ham very finely and add to the pan with the marjoram and tomatoes with their juice. Season and cook for 10 minutes, stirring to break up the tomatoes.

Drain the tagliatelli and place in a warmed bowl. Add the sauce and Parmesan and toss well, adding seasoning to taste. Serve immediately with a watercress, cucumber and lettuce salad.

Spinach ravioli

Overall timing 1¼ hours

Freezing Suitable: cook ravioli from frozen, then add to tomato sauce

To serve 4–6

12oz	Strong flour	350g
	Salt and pepper	
3	Eggs	3
2	Bacon rashers	2
1	Large onion	1
1	Garlic clove	1
1 tbsp	Oil	15ml
4oz	Minced veal	125g
4oz	Sausagemeat	125g
¼ teasp	Grated nutmeg	1.25ml
6 tbsp	Dry white wine	6x15ml
1lb	Spinach	450g
14oz	Can of tomatoes	397g
2oz	Butter	50g

Sift flour and 1 teasp (5ml) salt into a bowl. Add eggs and mix to smooth, glossy dough.

Derind and dice bacon. Peel and finely chop onion; peel and crush garlic. Heat oil in a saucepan, add bacon, onion and garlic and fry for 5 minutes. Add the veal, sausagemeat and nutmeg and fry for 5 minutes. Stir in wine and seasoning and bring to the boil. Cover and simmer for 15 minutes.

Shred spinach and add to meat. Cover and simmer for a further 5 minutes.

Roll out dough to a large rectangle. Cut out rounds. Dot spoonfuls of spinach mixture on rounds. Fold in half and pinch edges to seal. Roll each half-moon round your forefinger and pinch ends together.

Cook ravioli in boiling salted water till tender. Drain. Press tomatoes through a sieve. Melt butter in pan, stir in tomatoes and seasoning and heat. Return ravioli to pan and toss lightly till coated.

Spaghetti with lamb sauce

Overall timing 1¾ hours

Freezing Not suitable

To serve 4

1½ lb	Boned shoulder of lamb	700 g
	Salt and pepper	
3 tbsp	Plain flour	3x15 ml
1	Large onion	1
3 tbsp	Olive oil	3x15 ml
2 teasp	Paprika	2x5 ml
¾ pint	Chicken stock	400 ml
2 tbsp	Tomato purée	2x15 ml
12 oz	Spaghetti	350 g

Cut the lamb into bite-size pieces. Season the flour and toss the meat in it till evenly coated. Peel and thinly slice the onion. Heat the oil in a saucepan, add the onion and fry till transparent. Add the meat and fry till browned all over. Sprinkle in any remaining flour and the paprika and cook for 1 minute, stirring.

Gradually add the stock and bring to the boil, stirring constantly. Add the tomato purée and seasoning, cover and simmer gently for about 1 hour till tender.

Break the spaghetti into 4 inch (10 cm) lengths. Add 1 pint (560 ml) water to the lamb and bring to the boil. Add the spaghetti and simmer till tender, stirring frequently.

Taste and adjust seasoning. Divide between warmed individual serving dishes, arranging the meat on top. Serve immediately.

Crusty noodle shapes

Overall timing 55 minutes

Freezing Not suitable

To serve 4

12 oz	Egg noodles	350 g
	Salt	
1 oz	Cheese	25 g
¾ pint	White sauce	400 ml
¼ teasp	Grated nutmeg	1.25 ml
2	Eggs	2
1 oz	Dried breadcrumbs	25 g
6 tbsp	Oil	6x15 ml
4 oz	Sliced cooked ham	125 g
4 oz	Mozzarella cheese	125 g
	Sprigs of parsley	
	Lemon	

Cook the noodles in boiling salted water for about 5 minutes till tender. Drain the noodles thoroughly and put into a bowl.

Grate the cheese and mix into the white sauce with nutmeg. Pour the sauce over the noodles and mix well. Press into a roasting tin to 1 inch (2.5 cm) thickness and leave to cool.

Preheat the oven to 450°F (230°C) Gas 8.

Beat the eggs in a bowl with salt. Spread the breadcrumbs on a sheet of greaseproof paper.

Cut the noodle mixture into diamond shapes or rounds with a biscuit cutter. Dip the shapes into the egg, then the breadcrumbs, pressing the crumbs on to the shapes to make them stick. Heat the oil in a frying pan and fry the shapes until golden on both sides. Drain on kitchen paper. Using a sharp knife, slice each one through the centre.

Halve each slice of ham and put a piece on the bottom half of each shape; top with a thin slice of Mozzarella. Replace the top half of each shape and arrange on a baking tray. Bake for about 10 minutes. Serve hot, garnished with parsley sprigs and lemon.

Ratatouille

Overall timing 1½ hours

Freezing Suitable

To serve 8

2	Large aubergines	2
1 lb	Courgettes	450 g
	Salt and pepper	
3	Large onions	3
2–3	Garlic cloves	2–3
2	Green peppers	2
1 lb	Ripe tomatoes	450 g
5 tbsp	Olive oil	5 x 15 ml
1 teasp	Sugar	5 ml

Cut the aubergines into 1 inch (2.5 cm) chunks. Cut courgettes into quarters lengthways, then into 1 inch (2.5 cm) lengths. Put the vegetables into a colander, sprinkle with salt and leave to drain for 30 minutes.

Meanwhile, peel and slice the onions. Peel and crush the garlic. Deseed and thinly slice the peppers. Blanch, peel and halve the tomatoes.

Heat the oil in a flameproof casserole, add the onions and garlic and fry gently till transparent. Dry the aubergines and courgettes on kitchen paper and add to the pan with the peppers, tomatoes, sugar and plenty of pepper. Cook for about 45 minutes till the vegetables are tender but not mushy. Adjust the seasoning and serve hot, or cool and chill before serving.

Aubergine cheese bake

Overall timing 2¼ hours

Freezing Suitable: bake from frozen in 350°F (180°C) Gas 4 oven for 45 minutes

To serve 4

1¼ lb	Aubergines	600 g
	Salt and pepper	
2 tbsp	Plain flour	2x15 ml
	Oil	
1	Small onion	1
14 oz	Can of tomatoes	397 g
½ teasp	Dried basil	2.5 ml
8 oz	Mozzarella cheese	225 g
3 oz	Grated Parmesan cheese	75 g

Remove stalks from aubergines and cut lengthways into ½ inch (12.5 mm) thick slices. Sprinkle with salt. Leave for 1 hour, then rinse and pat dry. Coat with flour.

Preheat the oven to 350°F (180°C) Gas 4.

Heat oil in a large frying pan and fry aubergine slices on both sides till golden. Drain on kitchen paper and keep warm.

Peel and finely chop onion. Fry till transparent, adding more oil to pan if necessary. Mash tomatoes and juice and add to pan with seasoning. Cook for 10 minutes. Stir in basil and simmer for a further 5 minutes.

Place a layer of aubergines in oiled ovenproof dish. Cover with slices of Mozzarella and spoon on a little tomato sauce. Sprinkle with Parmesan and a pinch of salt. Repeat layering, ending with Parmesan. Sprinkle a little oil over surface and bake for 15 minutes or until top begins to brown.

Aubergine boxes

Overall timing 1½ hours

Freezing Not suitable

To serve 4

1 lb	Aubergines	450 g
	Salt and pepper	
3	Anchovy fillets	3
2 oz	Mozzarella cheese	50 g
1 teasp	Dried basil	2x5 ml
2 teasp	Capers	2x5 ml
1	Large onion	1
2	Garlic cloves	2
2 tbsp	Oil	2x15 ml
14 oz	Can of tomatoes	397 g
1 tbsp	Worcestershire sauce	15 ml
4–5	Fresh tomatoes (optional)	4–5

Cook aubergines in boiling salted water for 5 minutes. Drain and leave to cool, then cut off stalks and make a lengthways cut through the aubergines leaving the halves still attached at one side. Ease open and remove most of the flesh with a teaspoon. Finely chop or mash the flesh and put into a bowl.

Drain and chop anchovies. Dice Mozzarella. Mix together aubergine flesh, anchovies, basil, Mozzarella, capers and seasoning. Stuff the hollowed-out aubergine shells with mixture.

Preheat the oven to 350°F (180°C) Gas 4.

Peel and chop onion. Peel and crush garlic. Heat oil in flameproof casserole and fry onion till brown. Stir in garlic, tomatoes, Worcestershire sauce and seasoning. Simmer gently for about 10 minutes or until the sauce has become quite "mushy".

Arrange the stuffed aubergines on top of sauce and bake for 45 minutes. You can add 4–5 fresh tomatoes about 15 minutes before the end of the cooking time – they add attractive colour as well as taste.

Cabbage parcels

Overall timing 1¼ hours

Freezing Not suitable

To serve 4

1	White cabbage	1
3 oz	Long grain rice	75 g
1	Small onion	1
6 tbsp	Oil	6x15 ml
8 oz	Minced beef	225 g
	Salt and pepper	
¼ teasp	Grated nutmeg	1.25 ml
1 teasp	Dried oregano	5 ml
8 fl oz	Stock	220 ml
1 oz	Butter	25 g
1 tbsp	Plain flour	15 ml
1	Egg	1
2	Egg yolks	2
6 tbsp	Lemon juice	6x15 ml
¾ pint	White sauce	400 ml

Remove core from cabbage and cook in boiling water for 5 minutes. Drain and cool, then peel away 16–20 leaves. Add rice to same pan of boiling water and cook till tender. Drain.

Peel and chop onion. Heat 4 tbsp (4x15 ml) oil in a frying pan and cook onion till transparent. Add mince, salt, pepper, nutmeg and oregano. Cook for 5–8 minutes. Cool, then mix in rice.

Place a little stuffing on each cabbage leaf. Fold in sides and roll into tight parcels. Heat rest of oil in flameproof casserole. Pack cabbage rolls tightly in casserole and pour in stock. Cut leftover cabbage heart in two and place on top. Cover and simmer gently for 40 minutes.

Transfer cabbage rolls to warmed serving dish. Pour cooking liquor into a measuring jug and make up to 8 fl oz (220 ml) with water if necessary.

Melt butter in saucepan, then stir in flour and cooking liquor and simmer until thickened. Beat egg and egg yolks with lemon juice till foamy. Add to pan off heat. Return to a gentle heat. Don't allow sauce to boil. Stir in white sauce and heat. Pour sauce over rolls

Braised lettuce

Overall timing 40 minutes

Freezing Not suitable

To serve 4

4	Small round lettuces	4
	Salt and pepper	
2	Onions	2
2	Carrots	2
4 oz	Streaky bacon rashers	125 g
1 oz	Butter	25 g
½ pint	Chicken stock	300 ml

Trim lettuces. Blanch in boiling salted water for 2 minutes, then drain thoroughly.

Peel and slice onions and carrots. Derind and thinly slice bacon. Melt butter in saucepan, add onions, carrots and bacon and fry gently for 10 minutes, stirring occasionally.

Pour in stock and add blanched lettuces and seasoning. Cover and simmer for 20 minutes.

Transfer bacon and vegetables to warmed serving dish and keep hot. Boil cooking liquor rapidly to reduce by half. Taste and adjust seasoning. Pour over lettuce and serve immediately with roast meats.

Casseroled lettuce rolls

Overall timing 1 hour

Freezing Not suitable

To serve 4

8 oz	Streaky bacon	225 g
10	Large lettuce leaves	10
2	Onions	2
2	Carrots	2
	Salt and pepper	
¼ pint	Stock	150 ml
2 tbsp	Lemon juice	2x15 ml
Stuffing		
1	Onion	1
2 tbsp	Oil	2x15 ml
8 oz	Chicken livers	225 g
2 oz	Long grain rice	50 g
½ pint	Chicken stock	300 ml
	Bouquet garni	
	Salt and pepper	

To make the stuffing, peel and chop onion. Heat oil in pan and fry onion till golden. Chop chicken livers. Add to pan and brown on all sides.

Add rice, stock, bouquet garni and seasoning. Bring to the boil. Cover and simmer for 15 minutes, shaking pan frequently.

Meanwhile, derind and halve bacon rashers, then use them to line bottom and sides of an ovenproof dish. Wash and dry lettuce leaves. Peel and slice onions into rings. Peel and thinly slice carrots. Blanch lettuce, onions and carrots in boiling salted water for 3 minutes. Drain thoroughly.

Preheat the oven to 350°F (180°C) Gas 4.

Spread out lettuce leaves. Taste stuffing and adjust seasoning. Divide between lettuce leaves. Fold in sides of leaves, then roll up tightly round stuffing. Arrange, join side down, in ovenproof dish. Add blanched onions and carrots. Mix stock, lemon juice and seasoning. Pour over lettuce. Cover tightly and bake for 25–30 minutes.

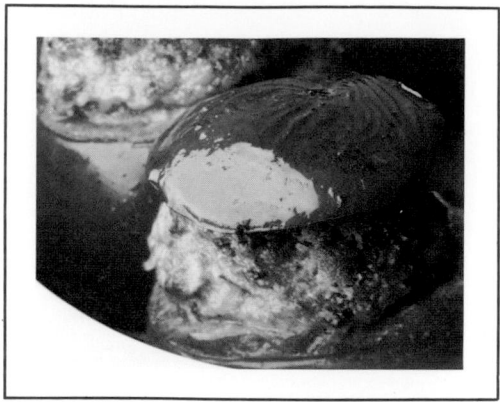

Sausagemeat tomatoes

Overall timing 45 minutes

Freezing Not suitable

To serve 4

8	Tomatoes	8
1	Large onion	1
4 tbsp	Oil	4x15 ml
12 oz	Pork sausagemeat	350 g
2 oz	Fresh breadcrumbs	50 g
1 tbsp	Chopped parsley	15 ml
	Salt and pepper	
1	Egg	1

Preheat the oven to 350°F (180°C) Gas 4.

Cut lids off the tomatoes and scoop out the flesh. Discard the seeds and chop the flesh. Peel and chop onion. Heat half the oil in a frying pan and fry onion till transparent. Add sausagemeat and fry until browned.

Remove from heat and stir in tomato flesh, breadcrumbs, parsley and seasoning. Bind with egg. Press mixture into tomato shells and replace lids.

Arrange tomatoes in ovenproof dish and brush with remaining oil. Bake for 30 minutes. Serve hot.

Lamb-stuffed onions

Overall timing 1¼ hours

Freezing Not suitable

To serve 6

6	Large onions	6
	Salt and pepper	
2 tbsp	Oil	2x15 ml
1½ teasp	Mixed spice	7.5 ml
1 lb	Minced lamb	450 g
1 oz	Fresh breadcrumbs	25 g
4 oz	Cottage cheese	125 g
1 oz	Butter	25 g
2 tbsp	Plain flour	2x15 ml
3 tbsp	Tomato purée	3x15 ml
½ pint	Light stock	300 ml

Peel onions and cook in boiling salted water for 15 minutes. Drain and cool. Remove slice from bottom of each onion. Cut slice from top and scoop out centres, leaving a ½ inch (12.5mm) shell. Put shells in flameproof casserole. Chop onion centres.

Heat oil and fry chopped onion with spice for 3 minutes. Add lamb and fry for 5 minutes. Stir in breadcrumbs, cheese and seasoning. Press into onion shells.

Melt butter, add flour and stir in tomato purée, stock and seasoning. Bring to the boil and pour over onions. Cover and simmer for 45 minutes till onions are tender.

Tomatoes stuffed with vegetables

Overall timing 30 minutes

Freezing Not suitable

To serve 4

3	Large waxy potatoes	3
3	Large carrots	3
4 oz	Green beans	125 g
2	Stalks of celery	2
	Salt and pepper	
4 oz	Frozen peas	125 g
6 tbsp	Mayonnaise	6 x 15 ml
	Lemon juice	
4	Large tomatoes	4
	Basil leaves	

Peel the potatoes. Scrape the carrots. Top and tail the beans. Wash and trim the celery. Dice all the vegetables. Cook in boiling salted water for 5 minutes. Add the peas and cook for a further 5 minutes or until tender. Drain well and cool.

Add the mayonnaise to the vegetables with a few drops of lemon juice and seasoning and mix well.

Halve the tomatoes and scoop out the seeds and centres. Fill with the vegetable mixture and arrange on a serving plate. Serve garnished with basil leaves.

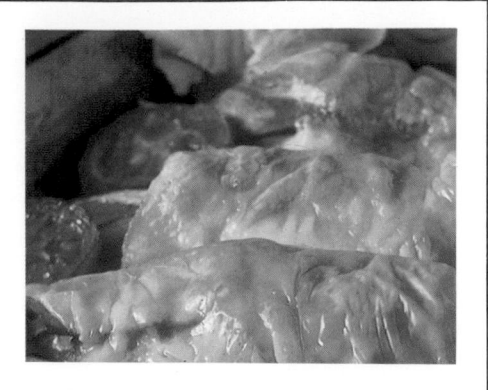

Chicory bake

Overall timing 45 minutes

Freezing Not suitable

To serve 2

2	Heads of chicory	2
	Salt and pepper	
½ teasp	Sugar	2.5 ml
1 oz	Butter	25 g
½ teasp	Lemon juice	2.5 ml
2	Slices of Gruyère cheese	2
2	Tomatoes	2
	Lettuce leaves	

Place chicory in saucepan of boiling water. Add pinch of salt, sugar, a knob of butter and lemon juice. Cook for 30 minutes.

Preheat the oven to 425°F (220°C) Gas 7.

Drain chicory. Wrap each head in slice of cheese. Place seam-side down in greased ovenproof dish and surround with halved tomatoes. Season well, dot with the rest of the butter and bake for 15 minutes. Garnish with lettuce leaves and serve hot.

Corn prawn salad

Overall timing 15 minutes plus 1 hour chilling

Freezing Not suitable

To serve 2

11½ oz	Can of sweetcorn kernels	326 g
3	Tomatoes	3
8 oz	Shelled prawns	225 g
Dressing		
1	Onion	1
2 tbsp	Herb vinegar	2x15 ml
3 tbsp	Oil	3x15 ml
	Salt and pepper	
1 tbsp	Chopped fresh sage	15 ml
1 tbsp	Chopped parsley	15 ml
1 tbsp	Chopped chives	15 ml

Drain sweetcorn. Blanch and peel tomatoes and cut into strips. Put sweetcorn, tomatoes and prawns in a serving dish.

To make the dressing, peel and finely chop onion. Mix together vinegar, oil and seasoning, then add the onion, sage, parsley and chives.

Pour dressing over salad, mix in well, cover and chill for 1 hour before serving.

Chicory rolls in cheese sauce

Overall timing 1¼ hours

Freezing Suitable: bake from frozen in cold oven set to 350°F (180°C) Gas 4 for 1 hour; increase to 450°F (230°C) Gas 8 for extra 10 minutes

To serve 4–6

4 oz	Butter	125 g
8	Large heads of chicory	8
2 tbsp	Lemon juice	2x15 ml
1 teasp	Sugar	5 ml
	Salt and pepper	
1 oz	Plain flour	25 g
½ pint	Milk	300 ml
	Grated nutmeg	
2	Egg yolks	2
2 oz	Grated Parmesan cheese	50 g
8	Thin slices of cooked ham	8

Melt half butter in a saucepan and add chicory, lemon juice, sugar and seasoning. Cover and cook gently for about 30 minutes, turning the chicory occasionally.

Meanwhile, make the sauce. Melt 1 oz (25 g) of remaining butter in another saucepan and stir in the flour. Remove from heat and gradually add milk. Return to heat and bring to the boil, stirring until thickened. Remove from heat and stir in a pinch of nutmeg, egg yolks, cheese and seasoning.

Preheat the grill.

Lift out chicory with draining spoon. Reserve cooking liquor. Wrap each chicory head in a slice of ham and arrange in a greased ovenproof dish. Add reserved liquor to sauce, beat well, then pour over chicory. Dot with the rest of the butter and grill for 5–10 minutes till golden on top. Serve immediately.

Asparagus milanese

Overall timing 30 minutes

Freezing Not suitable

To serve 4

1 lb	Asparagus	450 g
	Salt	
2 oz	Grated Parmesan cheese	50 g
2 oz	Butter	50 g

Cook asparagus in boiling salted water for 15–20 minutes till tender. Drain carefully on a tea-towel or kitchen paper, then place on a warmed serving dish and cool slightly. Sprinkle Parmesan over the asparagus tips.

Melt the butter in a small saucepan over a low heat. When golden brown, pour over the Parmesan. Serve immediately.

Alsace salad

Overall timing 15 minutes

Freezing Not suitable

To serve 6

2	Dessert apples	2
3	Boiled potatoes	3
1	Small cooked beetroot	1
2	Frankfurters	2
1	Onion	1
1	Hard-boiled egg	1
2 teasp	Chopped parsley	2x5 ml
	Sprigs of parsley	
8	Walnuts	8
3 tbsp	Olive oil	3x15 ml
1 tbsp	Wine vinegar	15 ml
1 teasp	Powdered mustard	5 ml
	Salt and pepper	

Peel, core and chop apples. Peel and dice potatoes and beetroot. Slice frankfurters. Peel onion and cut into rings. Shell egg and cut into 6 wedges.

Arrange prepared ingredients in rows in a serving dish and sprinkle with parsley. Garnish with parsley sprigs and walnuts.

To make dressing, mix oil with vinegar, mustard and seasoning. Pour dressing over salad and serve immediately.

Chive and mushroom pancakes

Overall timing 1¼ hours

Freezing Suitable: bake filled pancakes with sauce in 350°F (180°C) Gas 4 oven for 20 minutes

To serve 4–6

1 lb	Button mushrooms	450 g
1 oz	Butter	25 g
½ pint	Milk	300 ml
	Salt and pepper	
¼ teasp	Grated nutmeg	1.25 ml
1½ tbsp	Lemon juice	22.5 ml
½ pint	White sauce	300 ml
Pancakes		
5 oz	Plain flour	150 g
¼ teasp	Salt	1.25 ml
2	Eggs	2
2 tbsp	Chopped chives	2x15 ml
	Oil for frying	

Finely chop mushrooms. Melt butter in a saucepan and fry mushrooms for 3 minutes. Add milk, seasoning, nutmeg and lemon juice. Bring to the boil and simmer for 10 minutes. Strain, reserving the milk for the pancakes.

Make the pancakes as left, using the reserved milk instead of beer and adding the chives to the batter. Fry 12 pancakes.

Preheat the oven to 350°F (180°C) Gas 4.

Divide the mushroom filling between the pancakes and roll them to enclose the filling. Arrange in a greased ovenproof dish and pour the white sauce over. Bake for about 20 minutes. Serve immediately, garnished with extra fluted mushrooms, if liked.

Cottage baked potatoes

Overall timing 2 hours

Freezing Not suitable

To serve 6

6x8 oz	Potatoes	6x225 g
3 oz	Melted butter	75 g
	Salt and pepper	
3 oz	Cottage or cream cheese	75 g
5 tbsp	Milk	5x15 ml
2 teasp	Paprika	2x5 ml

Preheat the oven to 400°F (200°C) Gas 6.

Scrub and dry the potatoes and push a metal skewer lengthways through each one. Brush potatoes with a little melted butter and place on a baking tray. Bake for 1–1¼ hours till tender.

Take the potatoes out of the oven, remove skewers and cut a cross in the top of each. Lift the centre of each cross and scoop out some of the flesh. Put the flesh into a bowl and mash with a fork. Add half the remaining melted butter and mix thoroughly. Season well.

Mix the cheese, milk and rest of the butter in a bowl and beat till creamy. Spoon into the potatoes and cover with the mashed potato mixture. Sprinkle with paprika and salt.

Replace the potatoes on the baking tray and bake for about 15 minutes till the topping is golden. Arrange on a serving dish and serve immediately.

Carrots in batter

Overall timing 1 hour

Freezing Not suitable

To serve 4

1 lb	Carrots	450 g
1 oz	Butter	25 g
½ pint	Water	300 ml
¼ teasp	Salt	1.25 ml
	Oil for frying	
	Flour for coating	
Batter		
4 oz	Plain flour	125 g
6 tbsp	Milk	6x15 ml
2	Eggs	2
¼ teasp	Salt	1.25 ml
	Sprigs of parsley	

Scrape carrots and halve crossways. Melt butter in water in a saucepan. When boiling, add carrots and salt, cover and cook for 20 minutes.

To make the batter, sift flour into a large bowl and mix in the milk, eggs and salt until well combined and smooth.

Heat oil in deep fryer to 360°F (180°C).

Drain carrots and dry well on kitchen paper. Dip carrot pieces first in flour, then coat in batter. Use a skewer to lower carrots (four or five at a time) into the oil. Cook for 3 minutes till golden. Remove with a draining spoon, drain on kitchen paper and serve hot, garnished with parsley.

Country-style peas

Overall timing 45 minutes

Freezing Not suitable

To serve 6

4 oz	Button onions	125 g
2 lb	Fresh peas	900 g
3	Carrots	3
8 oz	New potatoes	225 g
1	Round lettuce	1
1	Thick streaky bacon rasher	1
2 oz	Butter	50 g
	Sprig of thyme	
	Sprig of tarragon	
	Bay leaf	
	Salt and pepper	

Blanch and peel onions. Shell peas; scrape and dice carrots. Scrub potatoes. Tear lettuce into pieces. Derind bacon and cut into strips.

Melt butter in a flameproof casserole and fry bacon and onions till bacon fat begins to run. Add remaining vegetables, herbs tied together, seasoning and ¼ pint (150 ml) water. Cover and simmer for 25 minutes till vegetables are tender. Remove herbs before serving.

Cheese and potato bake

Overall timing 1¼ hours

Freezing Not suitable

To serve 6

2 lb	New potatoes	900 g
3	Onions	3
2 tbsp	Oil	2x15 ml
1	Red pepper	1
8 oz	Sliced cooked ham	225 g
14 oz	Can of tomatoes	397 g
5	Small gherkins	5
12 oz	Red Leicester cheese	350 g
¼ pint	Soured cream	150 ml
2	Egg yolks	2
	Salt and pepper	
¼ teasp	Grated nutmeg	1.25 ml
2 oz	Butter	50 g

Preheat the oven to 400°F (200°C) Gas 6.

Scrub potatoes. Cook in boiling water for 30 minutes.

Peel and thinly slice onions. Fry in oil for 5 minutes. Deseed and slice red pepper, add to onion and fry for 5 minutes. Shred ham; add to pan with tomatoes, sliced gherkins and seasoning.

Drain potatoes and cool. Slice thickly. Slice cheese. Layer potatoes, cheese and tomato mixture in greased ovenproof dish. Mix soured cream, egg yolks, seasoning and nutmeg and pour over top. Dot with butter. Bake for 20 minutes.

Swiss style potatoes

Overall timing 1 hour

Freezing Not suitable

To serve 4

2 lb	Potatoes	900 g
3 tbsp	Caraway seeds	3x15 ml
1 tbsp	Sea-salt	15 ml
2 oz	Butter	50 g
8 oz	Curd cheese	225 g
4 fl oz	Milk	120 ml
1	Onion	1
2 tbsp	Chopped parsley	2x15 ml
2 tbsp	Chopped mustard and cress	2x15 ml
	Salt and pepper	
Garnish		
	Parsley sprigs	
	Mustard and cress	

Preheat the oven to 350°F (180°C) Gas 4.

Halve potatoes. Mix caraway seeds and sea-salt together in a bowl. Dip the cut sides of potatoes into mixture. Place potatoes in greased ovenproof dish with the caraway seeds facing up.

Melt the butter and pour a little over each potato half. Bake for 45 minutes.

Mix cheese with milk in a bowl. Peel and finely chop onion and add to bowl with parsley, mustard and cress and seasoning.

Divide cheese mixture between warmed serving plates and place the potatoes on top. Garnish with parsley and cress.

Tomatoes stuffed with buckling

Overall timing 40 minutes plus setting

Freezing Not suitable

To serve 2

1	Buckling	1
1½ tbsp	Thick mayonnaise	22.5 ml
2 teasp	Lemon juice	2x5 ml
	Salt	
1	Hard-boiled egg	1
1 teasp	Chopped parsley	5 ml
1 teasp	Chopped chives	5 ml
4 tbsp	Water	4x15 ml
	Pinch of sugar	
½ teasp	Vinegar	2.5 ml
2	Large tomatoes	2
2	Slices of Pumpernickel bread	2
	Butter	
	Lettuce leaves	
	Parsley	

Skin and bone the buckling. Chop flesh finely and place in a bowl. Add mayonnaise, lemon juice and salt. Shell and dice the hard-boiled egg and add with herbs to buckling mixture. Mix well.

Put water, sugar, pinch of salt and vinegar into a saucepan and heat till warm. Leave to cool, then add to buckling mixture.

Cut tops off tomatoes and remove the inside (this can be mixed into buckling mixture, if you like). Fill tomatoes with the buckling mixture and replace tops. Chill for 30 minutes.

Just before serving, put each tomato on to a slice of buttered Pumpernickel which should be slightly bigger than the base of the tomato. Serve on a bed of lettuce and garnish with parsley.

Courgettes with mozzarella

Overall timing 30 minutes plus chilling

Freezing Suitable: reheat from frozen in 350°F (180°C) Gas 4 oven for 45 minutes

To serve 2

1	Onion	1
1	Garlic clove	1
1 oz	Butter	25 g
3 tbsp	Oil	3x15 ml
8 oz	Can of tomatoes	226 g
¼ teasp	Dried basil	1.25 ml
4	Courgettes	4
2 tbsp	Plain flour	2x15 ml
	Salt and pepper	
4 oz	Mozzarella cheese	125 g

Peel and finely chop onion. Peel and crush garlic. Heat butter and 1 tbsp (15 ml) oil in a frying pan and fry onion and garlic till transparent.

Drain tomatoes. Add to pan with basil and cook over a low heat for 20 minutes. Purée mixture in a blender or push through a sieve.

Trim and slice courgettes. Coat slices with flour. Heat remaining oil in another frying pan and fry courgettes till lightly golden and tender. Drain on kitchen paper and season with salt and pepper.

Thinly slice Mozzarella. Layer courgettes, Mozzarella and tomato sauce in serving dish. Chill for 2–3 hours. Serve with hot garlic bread or toast and butter curls.

Deep-fried chicory

Overall timing 40 minutes

Freezing Not suitable

To serve 4

4	Heads of chicory	4
	Salt and pepper	
2 tbsp	Lemon juice	2x15 ml
	Oil for deep frying	
1	Egg	1
1 tbsp	Milk (optional)	15 ml
2 oz	Dried breadcrumbs	50 g

Blanch chicory in boiling salted water, with the lemon juice, for 10 minutes. Drain and leave on a wire rack until cool enough to handle, then pat dry with kitchen paper.

Heat oil in deep-fryer to 350°F (180°C).

Lightly beat egg in a large bowl with a pinch each of salt and pepper. If chicory heads are very large, add milk to the egg mixture to ensure there is sufficient coating mixture. Dip the chicory heads in the egg, then coat completely in the breadcrumbs.

Deep-fry coated chicory, two at a time, in the hot oil for 2–3 minutes or until golden brown. Drain on kitchen paper and keep warm while frying remaining chicory heads. Serve with any hot or cold meat and accompanied by sea-salt and butter to be added as you would with jacket potatoes – make a cross cut, add a knob of butter and freshly-ground sea-salt.

Deep-fried courgettes

Overall timing $2\frac{1}{4}$ hours

Freezing Not suitable

To serve 4

$1\frac{1}{4}$ lb	Courgettes	600 g
	Salt	
3 tbsp	Plain flour	3 x 15 ml
	Oil for frying	

Trim courgettes and cut into thin strips. Sprinkle with salt and leave for $1\frac{1}{2}$ hours.

Dry courgettes well on kitchen paper and coat in flour. Shake in a sieve to remove excess flour.

Heat oil in a deep-fryer.

Fry courgettes till lightly golden, then drain well on kitchen paper. Serve hot with tartare sauce.

Variations

Season the flour with a little paprika or ground coriander before coating courgettes.

Braised fennel

Overall timing 1 hour

Freezing Suitable

To serve 6

5	Bulbs of fennel	5
	Salt and pepper	
4 oz	Streaky bacon	125 g
1	Onion	1
2 oz	Butter	50 g
½ pint	Chicken stock	300 ml
	Bouquet garni	
	Sprigs of parsley	

Trim fennel. Cut each bulb in half and blanch in boiling salted water for 10 minutes. Drain.

Derind and finely chop bacon. Peel and chop onion. Melt butter in flameproof casserole and fry bacon for 5 minutes.

Arrange onion and fennel pieces on top of bacon. Cover with stock and add bouquet garni and seasoning. Cover and simmer for about 45 minutes till tender.

Remove bouquet garni. If liked, sprinkle fennel with grated Parmesan cheese. Garnish with parsley and serve with chicken or a bacon joint.

Tunisian stuffed courgettes

Overall timing 1¼ hours

Freezing Suitable: bake from frozen, covered, in 350°F (180°C) Gas 4 oven for about 45 minutes

To serve 4

1 lb	Courgettes	450 g
1	Onion	1
8 oz	Minced lamb	225 g
1 tbsp	Chopped parsley	15 ml
2	Eggs	2
	Cayenne	
	Salt and pepper	
4 tbsp	Plain flour	4x15 ml
4 tbsp	Oil	4x15 ml
8 oz	Can of tomatoes	227 g
	Parsley	

Trim courgettes. Using a long thin knife or melon-baller, scoop out centre of each whole courgette, working from both ends if necessary and trying to keep the sides an even thickness. Reserve cut-out flesh.

Peel and finely chop onion and mix with chopped courgette flesh, minced lamb, parsley, 1 egg, a pinch of cayenne and seasoning.

Fill courgettes with prepared mixture. Roll any leftover mixture into little meat balls. Beat remaining egg in a bowl and dip stuffed courgettes and meat balls in it. Coat lightly with flour.

Heat oil in a large frying pan. Add courgettes and meat balls and cook for about 20 minutes, turning to brown all sides. Remove from pan and drain on kitchen paper.

Sieve tomatoes and their juice. Add to pan juices with seasoning and cook over a moderate heat for about 15 minutes.

Return courgettes and meat balls to pan and cook for a further 15 minutes. Serve hot, sprinkled with chopped parsley.

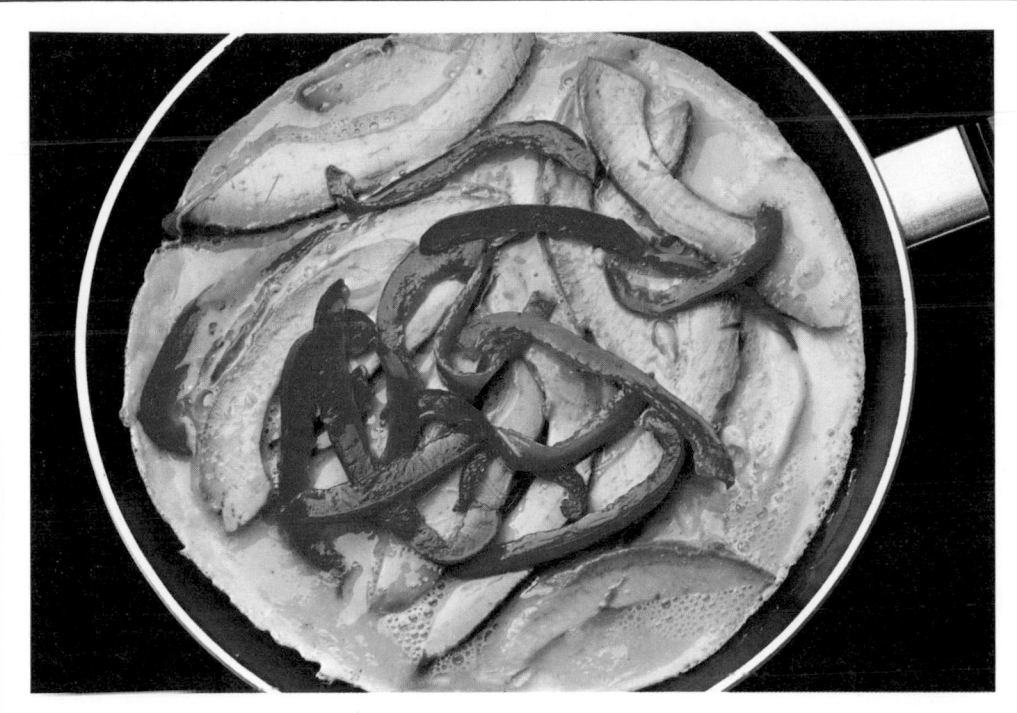

Avocado and pepper omelette

Overall timing 15 minutes

Freezing Not suitable

To serve 4

1	Red pepper	1
3 oz	Butter	75 g
2	Ripe avocados	2
1 tbsp	Lemon juice	15 ml
8	Eggs	8
1 tbsp	Water	15 ml
	Salt and pepper	

Deseed pepper and cut into long strips. Melt 1 oz (25 g) of the butter in an omelette or frying pan and fry pepper till just tender. Remove from pan and set aside.

Cut avocados in half lengthways and lift out stones. Peel, then cut avocado flesh into thick strips. Sprinkle with lemon juice to prevent discoloration.

Lightly beat together eggs, water and seasoning in a jug. Divide remaining butter into four pieces. Melt one piece in omelette pan.

Pour one-quarter of egg mixture into pan and cook till omelette starts to set. Run a spatula round the edge to loosen it and tilt the pan to let the uncooked egg run underneath. Continue to cook till the omelette is just soft and creamy.

Spread one-quarter of the pepper and avocado strips on top. Cook for 1 further minute, then fold over the omelette and slide it on to a warm serving plate. Serve immediately or keep it warm while you cook three more omelettes in the same way.

Avocado soufflé

Overall timing 45 minutes

Freezing Not suitable

To serve 2

1 oz	Butter	25 g
1 oz	Plain flour	25 g
¼ pint	Milk	150 ml
2	Ripe avocados	2
1 teasp	Lemon juice	5 ml
	Pinch of grated nutmeg	
	Salt and pepper	
	Pinch of ground cinnamon *or*	
1 teasp	Grated lemon rind (optional)	5 ml
3	Eggs	3

Preheat the oven to 400°F (200°C) Gas 6.

Melt the butter in a saucepan, stir in the flour and cook for 1 minute. Gradually stir in the milk. Bring to the boil, stirring till thickened. Remove from the heat.

Cut the avocados in half lengthways and lift out the stones. Cut out four very thin slices, sprinkle with lemon juice and reserve for the garnish. Remove remaining flesh with a teaspoon, place it in a bowl and mash well. Add to the sauce and beat vigorously until well blended. Add nutmeg, seasoning and cinnamon or lemon rind, if used.

Separate the eggs. Add the yolks one by one to the saucepan, beating well after each addition. Whisk egg whites with a pinch of salt till very stiff, then gently fold into the sauce.

Pour mixture into a greased 2 pint (1.1 litre) soufflé dish. Place on a baking tray and bake for about 30 minutes till well risen. Garnish with reserved avocado slices and serve immediately.

Endive ring

Overall timing 1 hour

Freezing Not suitable

To serve 4

2 lb	Curly endive	900 g
	Salt and pepper	
2 oz	Butter	50 g
2 oz	Plain flour	50 g
¾ pint	Milk	400 ml
	Grated nutmeg	
3	Eggs	3

Trim the endive and blanch in boiling salted water for 5 minutes. Plunge pan into cold water to cool quickly, then drain endive well and chop.

Preheat the oven to 325°F (170°C) Gas 3.

Melt butter in a saucepan, stir in flour and cook for 1 minute. Gradually stir in the milk. Bring to the boil, stirring, and simmer till thickened. Season with salt, pepper and nutmeg.

Remove pan from heat and stir in endive. Allow to cool slightly, then beat eggs into mixture. Turn into greased ring mould. Place mould in roasting tin with 1 inch (2.5 cm) water. Bake for 30 minutes. Invert on to a warmed serving dish and serve hot.

French stuffed lettuce

Overall timing 40 minutes

Freezing Not suitable

To serve 4

4	Round lettuces	4
1 pint	Chicken stock	560 ml
2 oz	Butter	50 g
1 oz	Plain flour	25 g
½ pint	Milk	300 ml
	Salt	
	Grated nutmeg	
4 oz	Cooked ham	125 g
3 oz	Mozzarella cheese	75 g
2	Egg yolks	2

Preheat the oven to 350°F (180°C) Gas 4.

Trim lettuces, discarding outer leaves if necessary. Bring stock to the boil in a large saucepan. Add lettuces, cover and cook for 5 minutes. Drain thoroughly, reserving cooking liquor. Allow lettuces to cool.

Melt 1 oz (25 g) of the butter in another saucepan. Add flour and cook, stirring, for 2 minutes. Gradually stir in milk. Bring to the boil, stirring, and cook for 3 minutes. Season with salt and a pinch of grated nutmeg.

Dice ham and Mozzarella and stir into sauce with egg yolks. Cook over a low heat for 2 minutes. Remove from heat and taste and adjust seasoning.

Cut cooled lettuces in half lengthways. Arrange four lettuce halves in a greased ovenproof dish, cut sides uppermost. Spoon sauce into each half and top with remaining lettuce halves. Add ¼ pint (150 ml) of the reserved cooking liquor and dot with remaining butter.

Cover with foil and bake for 15 minutes. Serve hot with French bread.

Baked sweet potatoes

Overall timing 1 hour

Freezing Not suitable

To serve 4

4x8 oz	Sweet potatoes	4x225 g
	Salt and pepper	
2 oz	Butter	50 g

Preheat the oven to 400°F (200°C) Gas 6,

Wash the sweet potatoes gently to avoid breaking the skins. Arrange on a greased baking tray and bake in the centre of the oven for about 45 minutes till tender when pierced with a skewer.

Arrange the sweet potatoes on a warmed serving dish and cut open along the top. Sprinkle a little salt and pepper into each and top with a knob of butter. Serve immediately.

Cauliflower ring

Overall timing 1¼ hours

Freezing Not suitable

To serve 4–6

1	Large cauliflower	1
	Salt and pepper	
4 oz	Butter	125 g
2 oz	Plain flour	50 g
¾ pint	Milk	400 ml
¼ teasp	Grated nutmeg	1.25 ml
4 oz	Gruyère or Cheddar cheese	125 g
3	Eggs	3
1 tbsp	Dried breadcrumbs	15 ml
	Sprigs of parsley	

Preheat oven to 375°F (190°C) Gas 5.

Trim cauliflower and divide into florets. Cook for 7–10 minutes in boiling salted water. Drain, chop and put in bowl.

To make sauce, melt 2 oz (50 g) of the butter in a pan, stir in flour and cook for 1 minute. Gradually stir in milk. Bring to the boil, stirring, and cook for 1 minute. Add seasoning and nutmeg. Grate cheese and stir 3 oz (75 g) into sauce.

Remove pan from heat. Pour about two-thirds of the sauce into a bowl and set aside. Stir eggs into sauce left in pan. Mix sauce thoroughly into cauliflower.

Grease a 9½ inch (24 cm) ring mould with half remaining butter. Sprinkle breadcrumbs on bottom. Fill with cauliflower mixture, pressing down well, and bake for 30–35 minutes.

Remove from oven and immerse mould up to rim in cold water. Turn up oven to 450°F (230°C) Gas 8. Run a knife blade around the sides of the mould, then carefully turn out on to ovenproof dish (if any of the mixture sticks to mould, quickly smooth it back into position with a knife and a little of remaining sauce).

Spread reserved sauce over cauliflower ring and sprinkle with remaining cheese. Melt remaining 1 oz (25 g) butter and pour over. Return to oven and bake for about 15 minutes until golden brown. Serve hot.

Cauliflower bake

Overall timing 1½ hours

Freezing Not suitable

To serve 4

1	Cauliflower	1
	Salt and pepper	
	Grated nutmeg	
1	Soft bread roll	1
1 pint	Milk	560 ml
1	Onion	1
4	Tomatoes	4
8 oz	Minced beef	225 g
5	Eggs	5
½ teasp	Paprika	2.5 ml
2 oz	Butter	50 g

Remove any leaves and trim cauliflower stalk. Put whole cauliflower into a pan containing 1½ inches (4 cm) of boiling, salted water. Add a pinch of grated nutmeg, cover and cook for 10 minutes.

Crumble the bread roll into a little of the milk in a large bowl. Peel and chop the onion. Chop three of the tomatoes. Add the mince, onion, chopped tomatoes and 1 egg to the bowl. Season with salt and pepper and mix well.

Preheat oven to 400°F (200°C) Gas 6.

Drain cauliflower; place in greased oven-proof dish. Spoon meat mixture round. Mix remaining eggs with the rest of the milk. Season with salt, pepper, a pinch of nutmeg and paprika. Pour over cauliflower and meat.

Cut the butter into pieces and put on top. Cut remaining tomato into quarters and place round cauliflower. Bake in oven for 1 hour.

Broccoli vinaigrette

Overall timing 20 minutes plus 20 minutes marination

Freezing Not suitable

To serve 6

1 lb	Broccoli	450 g
	Salt and pepper	
10 tbsp	Oil	10x15 ml
1 teasp	Powdered mustard	5 ml
4 tbsp	White wine vinegar	4x15 ml
1 teasp	Brown sugar	5 ml
1	Onion	1
2 tbsp	Chopped chives	2x15 ml
2 tbsp	Chopped parsley	2x15 ml
1 tbsp	Chopped fresh tarragon	15 ml
5	Small gherkins	5
2	Hard-boiled eggs	2
2	Tomatoes	2
5	Radishes	5

Trim broccoli leaves and coarse stems, then cook in boiling salted water for about 10 minutes. Drain well, then chop and divide pieces between six serving dishes or place in salad bowl.

Beat together oil, mustard, vinegar, sugar and seasoning. Peel and finely chop the onion and add to dressing with herbs. Finely chop gherkins and eggs and stir into dressing.

Blanch, peel and finely chop tomatoes. Chop radishes and stir both into dressing. Pour over broccoli and mix well. Leave for 20 minutes until completely cold. Serve with buttered toast.

Celery in yogurt sauce

Overall timing 45 minutes

Freezing Not suitable

To serve 4–6

2 lb	Green celery	900 g
	Salt and pepper	
1	Onion	1
1 oz	Bacon fat or pork dripping	25 g
2 oz	Butter	50 g
1 pint	Chicken stock	560 ml
Sauce		
½ oz	Butter	15 g
½ oz	Plain flour	15 g
¼ pint	Soured cream	150 ml
¼ pint	Plain yogurt	150 ml
	Grated nutmeg	
	Salt and pepper	

Trim celery and cut into short lengths. Blanch in boiling salted water for 5 minutes, then drain well.

Peel and chop onion. Heat bacon fat or dripping and butter in large frying pan and fry onion till transparent. Add the celery and sprinkle with pepper. Add the stock, cover and cook over a low heat for 20–30 minutes.

Remove from heat and drain liquid into a measuring jug. There should be ½ pint (300 ml) – make up to this amount with a little extra stock if necessary. Keep celery warm in a serving dish.

To make sauce, melt butter in a saucepan. Stir in flour and cook for 1 minute. Gradually stir in reserved stock. Bring to the boil stirring. Add soured cream, yogurt, a pinch of nutmeg and seasoning. Stir till smooth and creamy. Pour sauce over celery and serve hot.

Turkish potato fritters

Overall timing 50 minutes plus proving

Freezing Not suitable

To serve 4–6

8 oz	Floury potatoes	225 g
	Salt	
1 teasp	Bicarbonate of soda	5 ml
	Grated rind of ½ lemon	
10 oz	Packet of white bread mix	283 g
	Oil for deep frying	
Syrup		
14 oz	Sugar	400 g
2 tbsp	Lemon juice	2x15 ml
1 tbsp	Rose-water or liqueur	15 ml

Peel and quarter potatoes. Cook in boiling salted water for 20 minutes till tender. Drain and mash. Beat in soda and lemon rind.

Put bread mix into a bowl and mix in mashed potatoes. Gradually add sufficient warm water to make a thick, smooth dough. Turn on to a floured board and knead till little bubbles appear on the surface. Place in a bowl, cover with oiled polythene and leave to rise in a warm place for about 1 hour till doubled in size.

Meanwhile, to make the syrup, place sugar in a saucepan with ¾ pint (400 ml) water, lemon juice and rose-water or liqueur and heat till sugar dissolves. Bring to the boil and boil gently for 15 minutes till syrupy. Remove from heat and keep warm.

Heat oil in a deep-fryer to 360°F (180°C).

Break off lumps of dough with a spoon and lower into oil on a draining spoon. Fry for 3–5 minutes, turning once, till golden all over. Remove and drain on kitchen paper. Keep hot while you fry the rest. Put in a deep dish and pour warm syrup over.

Stuffed tomatoes au gratin

Overall timing 50 minutes

Freezing Not suitable

To serve 4

4	Large tomatoes	4
1½ lb	Fresh peas	700 g
1	Onion	1
2 tbsp	Oil	2x15 ml
	Salt and pepper	
2 oz	Butter	50 g
3 tbsp	Plain flour	3x15 ml
½ pint	Milk	300 ml
4 oz	Cheese	125 g
1 tbsp	Fresh breadcrumbs	15 ml

Preheat the oven to 400°F (200°C) Gas 6.

Halve the tomatoes and scoop out the flesh. Discard the seeds and chop the flesh. Shell the peas. Peel and finely chop the onion.

Heat the oil in a frying pan and fry the onion till transparent. Add the peas, cover and cook for 5 minutes. Stir in the chopped tomato flesh, season and continue cooking, covered, for 10 minutes.

Meanwhile, melt the butter in a saucepan. Stir in the flour and cook for 1 minute. Gradually stir in the milk and bring to the boil, stirring until thickened.

Grate the cheese. Mix three-quarters into the sauce with the pea mixture. Use to fill the tomato halves and arrange in an ovenproof dish. Mix the remaining cheese with the breadcrumbs and sprinkle over the tomatoes. Bake for 20 minutes and serve hot.

Vegetable croquettes

Overall timing 1¼ hours plus chilling

Freezing Suitable: deep fry after thawing

To serve 4

1½ lb	Floury potatoes	700 g
1	Large parsnip	1
	Salt and pepper	
2	Large leeks	2
1	Stalk of celery	1
2	Large carrots	2
2 oz	Butter	50 g
2 tbsp	Chopped parsley	2x15 ml
¼ teasp	Grated nutmeg	1.25 ml
2	Eggs	2
	Oil for deep frying	
4 tbsp	Plain flour	4x15 ml
	Sprigs of parsley	

Peel and chop the potatoes and parsnip. Cook in boiling salted water for 15–20 minutes till tender.

Meanwhile, trim and finely shred leeks and celery. Peel and grate carrots. Melt butter in a frying pan, add leeks and celery and fry till golden.

Drain potatoes and parsnip, return to pan and shake over a low heat to dry throughly. Remove from heat and mash to a smooth purée. Stir in fried vegetables and any pan juices. Add carrots, parsley, nutmeg and seasoning. Beat in eggs. Spread the mixture on a plate, cool, then chill for 2–3 hours till firm.

Heat oil in a deep-fryer to 340°F (170°C). Shape vegetable mixture into 20 balls with floured hands. Fry, a few at a time, for 5–6 minutes, till crisp and golden. Drain on kitchen paper. Serve hot, garnished with parsley.

Endive soufflé

Overall timing 50 minutes

Freezing Not suitable

To serve 4

4 oz	Butter	125 g
2 tbsp	Finely chopped onion	2x15 ml
2 tbsp	Finely chopped bacon	2x15 ml
4 tbsp	Diced cooked potato	4x15 ml
2 tbsp	Plain flour	2x15 ml
½ pint	Milk	300 ml
6	Eggs	6
	Salt and pepper	
6 tbsp	Chopped endive	6x15 ml

Preheat the oven to 375°F (190°C) Gas 5.

Melt 2 oz (50 g) of the butter in a frying pan. Add onion and bacon and fry till onion is transparent. Drain mixture in a sieve. Add the diced potato and set aside.

Melt the remaining butter in the frying pan, stir in the flour and cook for 1 minute. Gradually stir in the milk and bring to the boil, stirring. Simmer for 3 minutes, then remove from heat and cool slightly.

Separate the eggs. Beat yolks into the sauce, then fold in the potato and bacon mixture and seasoning. Whisk the egg whites in a bowl till stiff. Stir 1 tbsp (15 ml) of the whites into the sauce to lighten it. Stir in the endive, then carefully fold in the remaining egg whites.

Turn the mixture into a greased 6 inch (15 cm) soufflé dish and bake for 25–30 minutes till the soufflé is well risen and golden in colour. Serve immediately.

Cauliflower polonaise

Overall timing 35 minutes

Freezing Not suitable

To serve 4

1	Small cauliflower	1
	Salt	
4	Hard-boiled eggs	4
4 oz	Butter	125 g
2 tbsp	Dried breadcrumbs	2x15 ml
1 teasp	Paprika	5 ml

Trim cauliflower and cook whole in boiling salted water for about 20 minutes till just tender.

Meanwhile, shell and finely chop eggs.

Drain cauliflower. Place in a warmed serving dish and sprinkle with the eggs. Keep warm.

Melt butter in frying pan. Add breadcrumbs and paprika and stir-fry until crisp. Sprinkle over cauliflower and serve.

Cauliflower fritters

Overall timing 25 minutes

Freezing Not suitable

To serve 4

1	Large cauliflower	1
	Salt	
1	Egg	1
1	Egg white	1
2 oz	Plain flour	50 g
4 oz	Dried breadcrumbs	125 g
	Oil for frying	
	Grated Parmesan cheese	
	Chopped parsley	

Trim cauliflower and divide into 25–30 florets. Cook in boiling salted water for 7–10 minutes or till just tender. Drain and allow to cool.

In a bowl, beat together egg, egg white and a pinch of salt till frothy. Dip each floret into flour, then into egg mixture, then roll in breadcrumbs till well coated.

Heat oil to 320°F (160°C). Deep fry cauliflower till golden brown and crisp. Remove cauliflower from pan with a draining spoon and drain on kitchen paper. Serve hot, sprinkled with salt and a little grated Parmesan and chopped parsley mixed together.

Brussels sprouts with chestnuts

Overall timing 1 hour

Freezing Not suitable

To serve 4-6

12 oz	Chestnuts	350 g
¾ pint	Hot beef stock	400 ml
1½ lb	Brussels sprouts	700 g
	Salt	
	Grated nutmeg	
2 oz	Butter	50 g

Make a cut in each chestnut with a sharp knife, then place them in a saucepan. Cover with cold water, bring to the boil and cook for 10 minutes.

Drain chestnuts and peel off both outer and inner skins. Add to the stock and simmer gently for about 20 minutes till tender.

Meanwhile, trim the sprouts and cut a cross in the base of each one. Cook in boiling salted water for 10–12 minutes till tender. Drain and season with nutmeg.

Melt the butter in a pan, then add the drained chestnuts and sprouts. Gently shake the pan to coat the vegetables with butter. Turn into a warmed serving dish and serve.

Potato and onion bake √

Overall timing 1 hour

Freezing Not suitable

To serve 4

1½ lb	Potatoes	700 g
12 oz	Onions	350 g
3 oz	Butter	75 g
	Salt and pepper	

Preheat the oven to 400°F (200°C) Gas 6.

Peel the potatoes and slice very thinly (use a mandolin for best results). Put into a bowl of cold water to prevent discoloration. Peel and thinly slice the onions.

Drain the potatoes and dry with kitchen paper. Butter an ovenproof dish and cover the bottom with a layer of potato. Dot with butter, season and cover with a layer of onion. Dot with butter, season and repeat the layers till all the ingredients have been used, finishing with potato. Dot the top with the remaining butter.

Bake for about 40 minutes till the potatoes are tender and golden. Serve immediately.

Potato cake

Overall timing 50 minutes

Freezing Not suitable

To serve 4

2 lb	Potatoes	900 g
6 oz	Cheese	175 g
3	Eggs	3
½ pint	Milk	300 ml
	Salt and pepper	

Preheat the oven to 375°F (190°C) Gas 5.

Peel potatoes and grate into bowl. Grate cheese and add to potatoes. Beat in eggs, milk and seasoning. Pour into an ovenproof dish and bake for 40 minutes till top is golden. Serve hot.

Potato omelette

Overall timing 30 minutes

Freezing Not suitable

To serve 4

4x6 oz	Waxy potatoes	4x175 g
	Salt and pepper	
8 oz	Butter	225 g
2	Sage leaves	2
12	Eggs	12

Peel and dice the potatoes. Cook in boiling salted water for 4 minutes. Drain and pat dry.

Melt 2 oz (50 g) of the butter in a frying pan, add the potatoes and sage and fry over a moderate heat for 5–10 minutes till the potatoes are tender and golden. Discard sage leaves, remove potatoes and keep hot.

Lightly beat three of the eggs in a bowl with salt and pepper. Heat omelette pan and add one-quarter of the remaining butter. Pour eggs into pan and cook omelette. When almost set, put one-quarter of the potatoes along the centre and fold the sides in to cover them. Turn on to a warm plate with the join down and keep hot while you cook the remaining three omelettes.

Just before serving, cut along the tops of the omelettes to expose the filling. Serve immediately with a mixed salad.

Vegetable moussaka

Overall timing 2 hours

Freezing Not suitable

To serve 4–6

2	Large onions	2
1	Garlic clove	1
1	Large aubergine	1
	Salt and pepper	
2 oz	Butter	50 g
4 oz	Continental lentils	125 g
2 tbsp	Tomato purée	2x15 ml
1 pint	Light stock	560 ml
4	Small globe artichokes	4
1 tbsp	Lemon juice	15 ml
	Bouquet garni	
4 tbsp	Oil	4x15 ml
	Sprigs of parsley	

Peel and finely chop onions; peel and crush garlic. Slice aubergine, sprinkle with salt and leave to drain for 15 minutes.

Melt the butter in a saucepan, add onion and garlic and fry till golden. Add lentils, tomato purée and stock and simmer for about 1 hour till a thick purée.

Meanwhile, remove stem and coarse outer leaves from artichokes. Bring a pan of water to the boil, add lemon juice, bouquet garni and artichokes and simmer for 20–30 minutes till tender.

Rinse aubergines and dry on kitchen paper. Heat oil in a frying pan, add aubergines and fry till crisp and golden.

Preheat oven to 350°F (180°C) Gas 4.

Drain artichokes thoroughly, cut in half and remove chokes. Arrange cut sides up in greased ovenproof dish. Pour half lentil mixture over artichokes, then cover with half fried aubergine slices. Repeat the layers of lentil and aubergine and press down lightly. Bake for 30 minutes. Turn out and serve hot, garnished with parsley.

Venetian green beans

Overall timing 1¼ hours

Freezing Suitable

To serve 4–6

1¼ lb	Runner or French beans	600 g
1 lb	Fresh tomatoes *or*	450 g
14 oz	Can of tomatoes	397 g
1	Medium onion	1
1	Garlic clove	1
2 oz	Butter *or*	50 g
2 tbsp	Oil	2x15 ml
	Bouquet garni	
¼ teasp	Dried oregano or marjoram	1.25 ml
	Salt and pepper	

Top and tail beans and remove strings, if necessary. If using fresh tomatoes, blanch, peel and chop them; drain and chop canned tomatoes. Peel and chop the onion. Peel and crush garlic.

Heat the butter or oil in a saucepan and fry the onion till browned. Add beans, tomatoes, garlic, bouquet garni, oregano or marjoram and seasoning. Cover and simmer over a very low heat for 1 hour. If necessary add a little boiling water during cooking to prevent sticking. Serve hot.

Potato gnocchi

Overall timing 1½ hours plus chilling

Freezing Not suitable

To serve 6

2 lb	Floury potatoes	900 g
	Salt and pepper	
8 oz	Plain flour	225 g
1 teasp	Baking powder	5 ml
2	Eggs	2
6 oz	Slices of cheese	175 g
2 oz	Butter	50 g
3 tbsp	Grated Parmesan cheese	3x15 ml

Scrub the potatoes and cook in boiling salted water for about 30 minutes till tender. Drain, peel and press through a sieve into a large bowl.

Sift the flour and baking powder together, add to the potatoes and mix in with a wooden spoon. Beat in the eggs and seasoning. Spread out on a plate and chill for 2–3 hours till firm.

Preheat oven to 425°F (220°C) Gas 7.

Bring a large pan of salted water to the boil, then reduce heat till simmering. Put teaspoonfuls of the potato mixture into the water and cook for about 4 minutes or till they rise to the surface. Remove with a draining spoon and keep hot while you cook the rest.

Layer cooked dumplings in an ovenproof dish with slices of cheese and butter and sprinkle Parmesan on top. Brown in the oven for 5–10 minutes.

Fried ham and spinach

Overall timing 30 minutes

Freezing Not suitable

To serve 4

2 lb	Spinach	900g
	Salt and pepper	
6 oz	Slice of cooked ham	175 g
1	Garlic clove	1
3 tbsp	Oil	3x15 ml
2	Hard-boiled eggs	2
2 tbsp	Pine nuts (optional)	2x15 ml

Wash and pick over the spinach, discarding any withered leaves or coarse stalks. Drain thoroughly and blanch in lightly salted boiling water for 1 minute. Remove from heat, rinse under cold water and drain thoroughly. Chop coarsely.

Dice the ham and peel the garlic. Heat the oil in a large frying pan, add ham and garlic and fry for 2–3 minutes. Stir in the spinach, add plenty of pepper and fry gently for 5 minutes, stirring occasionally.

Meanwhile, shell and finely chop the eggs. Add to the pan with the pine nuts, if used, and cook for 2 minutes.

Discard garlic clove. Adjust seasoning to taste and arrange on a warmed serving dish. Serve immediately with thick slices of crusty bread.

Carrot soufflé

Overall timing 1 hour

Freezing Not suitable

To serve 4

1 lb	Carrots	450 g
2 oz	Butter	50 g
	Salt and pepper	
Sauce base		
2 oz	Butter	50 g
2 oz	Plain flour	50 g
1 pint	Milk	560 ml
	Salt and pepper	
3	Eggs	3

Peel and thinly slice the carrots, then cook in boiling water for 15 minutes. Drain and plunge into cold water to cool carrots quickly.

Melt butter in another pan, add drained carrots and cook for 5 minutes. Season with salt and pepper.

Preheat oven to 375°F (190°C) Gas 5.

For the sauce base, melt butter in a saucepan and stir in flour. Gradually add milk and bring to the boil, stirring until thickened. Season with salt and pepper and cool.

Separate the eggs. Mix the egg yolks and carrots into the sauce. Whisk the whites in a bowl until very stiff, then carefully fold into the carrot mixture. Pour into a greased 3 pint (1.7 litre) soufflé dish. Bake for about 30 minutes until the soufflé is golden and well risen. Serve immediately.

Bubble and squeak

Overall timing 15 minutes

Freezing Not suitable

To serve 4–6

1 lb	Mashed potatoes	450 g
1 lb	Cooked shredded cabbage	450 g
	Salt and pepper	
1 lb	Leftover cooked meat	450 g
2 oz	Butter	50 g

Beat together mashed potatoes and cabbage with a wooden spoon, adding plenty of seasoning. Dice meat.

Melt the butter in a heavy frying pan and add the potato and cabbage mixture, spreading it over the bottom of the pan. Mix in meat. Fry, turning the mixture occasionally, until crisp and golden brown. Serve immediately.

Boxty on the griddle

Overall timing 40 minutes

Freezing Suitable: reheat from frozen in 400°F (200°C) Gas 6 oven for 10 minutes

To serve 4

8 oz	Waxy potatoes	225 g
4 oz	Cooked mashed potatoes	125 g
4 oz	Plain flour	125 g
½ teasp	Bicarbonate of soda	2.5 ml
¾ pint	Milk	400 ml
	Salt and pepper	
	Oil for frying	

Peel the potatoes and grate into a large bowl. Add the mashed potatoes, sifted flour and bicarbonate of soda and mix together well. Make a well in the centre and gradually stir in enough milk to make a stiff batter. Season well.

Heat a lightly oiled griddle or heavy-based frying pan. Drop the batter in large spoonfuls on to the griddle or pan and cook over a moderate heat for 4 minutes on each side till crisp and golden.

Serve hot with fried black pudding, bacon and eggs.

Potato pancakes

Overall timing 45 minutes

Freezing Not suitable

To serve 4

1¼ lb	Waxy potatoes	600 g
2	Eggs	2
1 tbsp	Plain flour	15 ml
	Salt and pepper	
4 tbsp	Oil	4x15 ml

Peel the potatoes and grate coarsely into a bowl of cold water. Drain and squeeze dry in a cloth, then put into a dry bowl. Add the eggs, flour and seasoning and mix well.

Heat a little of the oil in a frying pan and add one-quarter of the potato mixture. Flatten into a pancake with the back of a fish slice and fry over a moderate heat for about 5 minutes till the edges are golden. Turn carefully and brown the other side. Remove from the pan and keep hot while rest of mixture is cooked.

Serve hot with roast or grilled meats and a green vegetable.

Rumanian vegetable casserole

Overall timing 1¼ hours

Freezing Not suitable

To serve 6–8

2	Waxy potatoes	2
2	Turnips	2
2	Medium-size onions	2
2	Garlic cloves	2
2	Carrots	2
1	Medium-size aubergine	1
2	Courgettes	2
2	Small leeks	2
4 oz	French beans	125 g
3	Large tomatoes	3
1 oz	Butter	25 g
2 tbsp	Oil	2x15 ml
4 oz	Shelled fresh peas	125 g
2 tbsp	Tomato purée	2x15 ml
	Bouquet garni	
	Salt and pepper	

Peel the potatoes, turnips, onions, garlic and carrots. Cut the potatoes, turnips, carrots, aubergine and courgettes into ¾ inch (2 cm) chunks. Cut the leeks and beans into 1 inch (2.5 cm) lengths. Quarter the tomatoes; slice the onions.

Heat the butter and oil in a flameproof casserole and fry the onions, leeks and garlic till golden. Add the remaining vegetables, tomato purée, bouquet garni and 1 pint (560 ml) water and mix well. Season and bring to the boil. Simmer gently for about 45 minutes till the vegetables are tender.

Bashed neeps

Overall timing 35 minutes

Freezing Not suitable

To serve 4–6

2 lb	Swedes	900 g
	Salt and pepper	
3 oz	Butter	75 g

Peel the swedes thickly, wash and cut into 1 inch (2.5 cm) chunks. Put into a saucepan of lightly salted cold water and bring to the boil. Reduce the heat, cover and simmer for 15–20 minutes till tender.

Drain thoroughly, then mash well till smooth with two-thirds of the butter. Season to taste.

Arrange in a warmed serving dish, top with the remaining butter and grind a little pepper over. Serve immediately.

Variations
"Clapshot" is a traditional mixed swede and potato dish from the Orkney Islands, off the north coast of Scotland. Cook equal quantities of swedes and floury potatoes in separate pans till tender. Drain well, then mash together with butter and seasoning and 1 small finely chopped onion or 2 tbsp (2x15 ml) chopped chives. Any leftovers can be fried in butter.

To turn Clapshot into a tasty lunch or supper dish, spread the mashed swede, potato and onion mixture in a shallow oven-proof dish. Make 4 hollows with the back of a spoon and break an egg into each one. Season and dot with butter, then bake in the centre of the oven, preheated to 425°F (220°C) Gas 7, for 8–10 minutes till the eggs are lightly set. Serve immediately with rashers of crispy fried bacon.

German broad beans

Overall timing 45 minutes

Freezing Suitable

To serve 4

2 lb	Unshelled broad beans	900 g
	Salt and pepper	
1	Chicken stock cube	1
2 oz	Streaky bacon	50 g
2	Onions	2
3 tbsp	Plain flour	3x15 ml
	Pinch of grated nutmeg	
½ pint	Carton of single cream	284 ml
1 tbsp	Chopped parsley	15 ml

Shell beans. Place in boiling, salted water and cook for 20 minutes or until tender. Drain cooking liquid into measuring jug and top up to ½ pint (300 ml) with water. Crumble in stock cube. Set beans and liquid in jug aside for the moment.

Derind and dice bacon; peel and chop onions. Put bacon and onions into a saucepan and fry gently for about 10 minutes. Remove pan from heat and stir in the flour. Gradually stir in the stock from the jug. Return pan to heat and cook gently for about 5 minutes, stirring constantly until sauce thickens. Remove from heat and season to taste with salt, pepper and nutmeg.

Stir in beans and cream and heat gently for a further 5 minutes, stirring. Transfer to warmed serving dish, garnish with parsley and serve.

Italian cauliflower omelette

Overall timing 20 minutes

Freezing Not suitable

To serve 2

12 oz	Cauliflower	350 g
	Salt and pepper	
1	Onion	1
2 oz	Butter	50 g
6	Eggs	6
2 tbsp	Grated Parmesan cheese	2x15 ml
½ teasp	Grated nutmeg	2.5 ml

Preheat the grill.

Cut cauliflower into tiny florets and cook in boiling salted water for 3–5 minutes till just tender.

Meanwhile, peel and finely chop onion. Melt butter in a frying pan and fry onion till golden. Add the drained cauliflower and seasoning and cook for 2 minutes, spreading evenly in the pan.

Beat the eggs in a bowl with the Parmesan and nutmeg. Pour evenly over the cauliflower and cook over a moderate heat till the omelette is nearly set.

Put the frying pan under the grill and cook till the top of the omelette is golden. Slide omelette on to a warmed serving plate and cut in two to serve.

Stuffed baked potatoes

Overall timing 1½ hours

Freezing Not suitable

To serve 8

8x8oz	Waxy potatoes	8x225g
1	Large onion	1
3oz	Butter	75g
8oz	Cooked ham	225g
6 tbsp	Dry white wine or cider	6x15ml
2oz	Fresh breadcrumbs	50g
2 tbsp	Chopped parsley	2x15ml
	Salt and pepper	
¼ pint	Chicken stock	150ml

Preheat the oven to 400°F (200°C) Gas 6.

Peel the potatoes. Cut a slice from one end of each so they stand upright. Cut a slice from the other end of each and hollow out the centres with a sharp knife, leaving a thick shell. Finely chop the scooped out pieces and slices cut from the tops of the potatoes.

Peel and finely chop the onion. Melt 1oz (25g) of the butter in a saucepan and fry the onion till transparent. Dice the ham and add to the pan with the wine or cider, chopped potatoes and breadcrumbs. Cover and cook for 5 minutes, then stir in the parsley and seasoning.

Spoon the mixture into the potatoes, pressing it down firmly. Stand potatoes upright in a greased ovenproof dish. Melt remaining butter with the stock and pour into the dish.

Bake for 50 minutes to 1 hour, basting frequently, till the potatoes are tender. Serve hot with a green salad.

Stuffed cabbage

Overall timing 2 hours 10 minutes

Freezing Not suitable

To serve 6

8 oz	Streaky bacon	225 g
2	Onions	2
2 tbsp	Oil	2×15 ml
1	Green cabbage	1
2	Tomatoes	2
1	Garlic clove	1
1¾ lb	Sausagemeat	750 g
4 oz	Rice	125 g
4 oz	Frozen peas	125 g
	Salt and pepper	
1¾ pints	Hot beef stock	1 litre

Derind and chop bacon. Peel and finely chop onions. Heat oil in frying pan. Add bacon and cook till crisp. Add onions and cook gently for 10 minutes.

Remove all large outer leaves of cabbage. On a large piece of muslin make two layers of leaves in a circular shape. Finely chop remaining cabbage.

Finely chop tomatoes. Peel and crush garlic. Add tomatoes and garlic to chopped cabbage with sausagemeat, rice, peas, bacon and onion and seasoning. Mix well and form into a ball. Place in centre of cabbage leaves, then remake cabbage shape so leaves cover stuffing. Lift corners of muslin and tie at top. Place cabbage in stock, cover and simmer for 1½ hours.

Breton beans

Overall timing 1½ hours

Freezing Suitable

To serve 4–6

8 oz	Dried butter beans	225 g
2	Onions	2
2	Cloves	2
1	Carrot	1
1	Garlic clove	1
¼ teasp	Dried mixed herbs	1.25 ml
2	Bay leaves	2
	Salt and pepper	
1 lb	Tomatoes	450 g
2 oz	Butter	50 g

Place beans in a saucepan, cover with water and simmer for 15 minutes.

Peel one onion and spike with cloves; peel and slice carrot. Peel and crush garlic. Drain beans and return to pan. Add onion, carrot, garlic and herbs. Cover with water and bring to the boil. Cover and cook for 50 minutes; add salt and cook for another 20.

Meanwhile, peel and chop remaining onions. Blanch, peel and quarter tomatoes. Melt butter in a saucepan and add onions, tomatoes and seasoning. Simmer for 20 minutes.

Drain beans and mix into tomato sauce.

Italian fried vegetables

Overall timing 1 hour

Freezing Not suitable

To serve 6

1	Large aubergine	1
	Salt and pepper	
8 oz	Courgettes	225 g
½	Cauliflower	½
8 oz	Large flat mushrooms	225 g
2	Large dessert apples	2
4	Eggs	4
6 oz	Fine breadcrumbs	175 g
3 oz	Plain flour	75 g
	Oil for deep frying	
	Sprigs of parsley	

Cut aubergine into ¼ inch (6 mm) thick slices. Sprinkle with salt and leave for 15 minutes.

Meanwhile, halve courgettes lengthways, then cut into 2 inch (5 cm) lengths. Divide cauliflower into florets. Blanch in boiling salted water for 3 minutes, then drain and rinse under cold water.

Quarter mushrooms. Peel and core apples and cut into thick rings. Rinse aubergines and pat dry with kitchen paper.

Beat eggs in shallow dish and spread breadcrumbs on a board. Coat vegetables in seasoned flour, then dip into egg and breadcrumbs.

Heat oil in a deep-fryer to 340°F (170°C). Fry aubergine slices for about 4 minutes, turning occasionally, till crisp and golden. Drain on kitchen paper and keep hot.

Fry courgettes and cauliflower florets for 5–6 minutes, and mushrooms and apples for 3–4 minutes. Drain on kitchen paper and keep hot.

Arrange all the fried vegetables on a warmed serving dish and garnish with parsley. Serve immediately with Tartare sauce and a green salad.

Stuffed cucumbers

Overall timing 1 hour

Freezing Suitable

To serve 6

3	Large cucumbers	3
2 oz	Cooked ham	50 g
4 oz	Minced beef	125 g
2 tbsp	Fresh breadcrumbs	2x15 ml
1 tbsp	Chopped parsley	15 ml
3 tbsp	Milk	3x15 ml
1	Egg	1
	Salt and pepper	
Sauce		
1	Onion	1
1	Leek	1
2 oz	Butter	50 g
1 oz	Plain flour	25 g
½ pint	Stock	300 ml
1 tbsp	Chopped parsley	15 ml
	Paprika	
	Salt	
1 tbsp	Vinegar	15 ml
4 fl oz	Top of milk	120 ml

Peel cucumbers. Halve them lengthways and scoop out seeds. Finely chop ham and mix with beef, breadcrumbs, parsley, milk, egg and seasoning. Stuff cucumbers with mixture.

To make sauce, peel and finely chop onion. Trim and finely chop leek. Melt butter in a saucepan and fry onion and leek till golden. Sprinkle flour into pan and cook for 1 minute, stirring. Gradually stir in stock, then add parsley, a pinch each of paprika and salt and the vinegar. Bring to the boil, stirring.

Arrange cucumbers on top of sauce and surround with any leftover stuffing. Cover and cook gently for 30 minutes. Turn cucumbers over halfway through cooking time.

Stir milk into sauce and heat through uncovered for 2 minutes.

Stuffed celeriac

Overall timing 1½ hours

Freezing Not suitable

To serve 4

4	Bulbs of celeriac	4
	Salt and pepper	
1 tbsp	Lemon juice	15 ml
2 oz	Streaky bacon	50 g
1	Large onion	1
8 oz	Minced beef	225 g
1 oz	Fresh breadcrumbs	25 g
1 oz	Grated Parmesan cheese	25 g

Cook celeriac in boiling salted water with lemon juice for 20 minutes. Drain and allow to cool slightly, then cut off tops and reserve. Scoop out insides and reserve.

Preheat the oven to 400°F (200°C) Gas 6.

Derind and dice bacon, then cook for 3 minutes in frying pan. Peel and finely chop onion, cutting a few large pieces for the garnish. Fry onions till golden. Remove large pieces and set aside.

Add mince to pan and cook for 5 minutes. Chop inside of two celeriac bulbs and add to pan with breadcrumbs, Parmesan and seasoning.

Fill celeriac with meat mixture. Replace tops, then place in greased ovenproof dish. Bake for 40 minutes, basting with pan juices halfway through. Serve garnished with reserved onion pieces.

Spanish stuffed peppers

Overall timing 1 hour

Freezing Suitable: bake for 1 hour

To serve 4

1 lb	Tomatoes	450 g
1	Onion	1
1	Garlic clove	1
¼ pint	Olive oil	150 ml
1 tbsp	Caster sugar	15 ml
	Pinch of cayenne	
½ teasp	Dried oregano	2.5 ml
	Salt and pepper	
8	Firm green peppers	8
14 oz	Smoked bacon	400 g
4 oz	Fresh breadcrumbs	125 g

Blanch, peel and chop tomatoes. Peel and chop onion. Peel and crush garlic. Heat 2 tbsp (2x15 ml) oil in saucepan, add tomatoes, onion, garlic, sugar, cayenne, oregano and seasoning. Simmer till reduced by half.

Cut off stalk end of each pepper, then deseed. Blanch in boiling salted water for 5 minutes, then drain.

Preheat the oven to 400°F (200°C) Gas 6.

To make stuffing, derind and mince bacon. Mix with crumbs and pepper to taste.

Pour 1 teasp (5 ml) oil into each pepper, then fill with stuffing. Pour remaining oil into ovenproof dish. Place peppers in dish with tomato sauce between them. Cover with foil and bake for 45 minutes.

Romanian peppers

Overall timing 1¼ hours

Freezing Not suitable

To serve 6

1 lb	Lean pork	450 g
2	Onions	2
2 oz	Butter	50 g
4 oz	Button mushrooms	125 g
8 oz	Tomatoes	225 g
½ pint	Water	300 ml
	Salt and pepper	
½ teasp	Paprika	2.5 ml
6	Green peppers	6
2 teasp	Cornflour	2x5 ml
4 tbsp	Top of milk	4x15 ml
	Tabasco sauce	

Dice the pork. Peel and finely chop onions. Melt butter in saucepan. Fry onions and pork for 10 minutes.

Slice mushrooms. Blanch, peel and chop tomatoes. Add mushrooms and tomatoes to the saucepan. Pour in water and cook for 40 minutes over a low heat. Season with salt, pepper and paprika.

Cut tops off peppers. Remove seeds. Place peppers and their tops in a saucepan of boiling water and cook for 5 minutes or until just soft. Lift out and drain. Keep warm.

Blend cornflour with top of milk. Stir into pork mixture, then bring just to the boil to thicken. Season with a few drops of Tabasco sauce. Mix well, then use mixture to fill peppers. Place tops on peppers to serve.

Leeks with mustard sauce

Overall timing 30 minutes

Freezing Not suitable

To serve 4–6

2 lb	Leeks	900 g
	Salt and pepper	
4 oz	Cheese	125 g
1	Small onion	1
1	Garlic clove	1
2 oz	Butter	50 g
2 tbsp	Plain flour	2x15 ml
¾ pint	Milk	400 ml
1 tbsp	Made mustard	15 ml

Trim leeks. Cook in boiling salted water for 15–20 minutes till tender. Drain, saving ¼ pint (150 ml) cooking liquor. Arrange leeks in warmed serving dish. Keep hot.

Grate cheese. Peel and chop onion and garlic. Melt the butter in a saucepan and fry the onion and garlic till golden. Stir in the flour and cook for 1 minute. Gradually add reserved cooking liquor and milk. Bring to the boil, stirring, and cook for 3 minutes. Stir in mustard, cheese and seasoning and heat through gently without boiling. Pour over leeks and serve immediately.

Leek and cheese soufflé

Overall timing 1 hour

Freezing Not suitable

To serve 4

2 oz	Butter	50 g
2 oz	Plain flour	50 g
$\frac{1}{4}$ pint	Warm milk	300 ml
2 oz	Red Leicester cheese	50 g
8 oz	Leeks	225 g
	Salt and pepper	
3	Large eggs	3

Melt the butter in a pan, stir in the flour and cook for 1 minute. Gradually add warm milk and bring to the boil, stirring. Simmer for 2 minutes. Remove from heat and leave to cool.

Grate the cheese. Trim and finely chop leeks. Blanch in boiling water for 5 minutes and drain thoroughly. Stir the grated cheese and leeks into sauce and season. Separate eggs. Beat the yolks into the sauce.

Whisk egg whites in a bowl till stiff but not dry. Stir 1 tbsp (15 ml) whisked whites into sauce to lighten it, then carefully fold in the rest. Turn mixture into greased 2 pint (1.1 litre) soufflé dish, place on baking tray and bake for 30–35 minutes till well risen and golden. Serve immediately.

Irish cabbage

Overall timing 40 minutes

Freezing Not suitable

To serve 4–6

14 oz	Potatoes	400 g
2	Small leeks	2
	Milk	
1 lb	Green cabbage	450 g
	Salt and pepper	
	Pinch of mace	
4 oz	Butter	125 g
	Sprigs of parsley	

Cook unpeeled potatoes in lightly salted water till just tender. Meanwhile, trim the leeks, then roughly chop both white and green parts. Just cover with milk and cook gently till soft.

Roughly chop cabbage and cook in boiling, lightly salted water for 7 minutes. Drain and cut into smaller pieces. Keep cabbage warm.

Drain potatoes; peel and put through a food mill or mash well. Mash in the leeks/milk mixture and season well with salt, pepper and mace. Place bowl over a pan of boiling water and gradually beat in the cabbage till light and fluffy.

Melt butter. Place vegetable mixture in warmed serving dish, make a well in the centre and pour in the hot butter. Garnish with parsley sprigs and serve immediately.

Stuffed mushrooms

Overall timing 1 hour

Freezing Suitable: reheat in 375°F (190°C) Gas 5 oven for 10 minutes

To serve 4

8	Cup mushrooms	8
2 oz	Fresh breadcrumbs	50 g
¼ pint	Warm milk	150 ml
1	Garlic clove	1
	Salt and pepper	
1	Egg	1
1	Egg yolk	1
4 oz	Grated Parmesan cheese	125 g
2 teasp	Chopped fresh marjoram	2x5 ml
8 teasp	Oil	8x5 ml
	Fresh parsley	

Preheat the oven to 350°F (180°C) Gas 4.

Carefully detach mushroom caps from stalks. Wipe caps and reserve. Chop stalks.

Soak breadcrumbs in warm milk, then squeeze out well, reserving milk. Peel garlic and place in mortar or blender with mushroom stalks, a little of the reserved milk and seasoning. Pound or blend till well combined. Put mixture into a bowl and add egg, egg yolk, grated Parmesan, marjoram and 2 teasp (2x5 ml) of oil. Mix well until creamy, then add salt.

Spread stuffing into hollow of each mushroom cap using a dampened knife. Arrange the stuffed mushrooms in an oiled baking dish. Sprinkle the top with the remaining oil and pepper and bake for about 30 minutes. Garnish with parsley and serve hot.

Sweet-sour beans

Overall timing 2½ hours plus 2 hours soaking

Freezing Not suitable

To serve 4

8 oz	Dried haricot beans	225 g
1 teasp	Salt	5 ml
1	Carrot	1
1	Onion	1
8	Green olives	8
Dressing		
6 tbsp	Oil	6x15 ml
2 tbsp	Wine vinegar	2x15 ml
1 teasp	Soft brown sugar	5 ml
½ teasp	Ground cinnamon	2.5 ml
	Salt and pepper	
1	Garlic clove	1
1 teasp	Dried savory	5 ml

Put the beans in a saucepan, cover with boiling water and leave to soak for 2 hours.

Add the salt, bring to the boil, cover and simmer for 2–2½ hours or till tender. Drain beans and cool.

Peel and slice carrot. Peel and chop onion. Place in bowl and add beans and olives.

To make dressing, mix all ingredients together. Pour over beans and toss.

Sweetcorn fritters

Overall timing 30 minutes

Freezing Not suitable

To serve 4

1 lb	Can of sweetcorn kernels	450 g
1	Egg	1
2 oz	Plain flour	50 g
	Salt	
1 tbsp	Oil	15 ml
	Grated rind of ½ lemon	
	Oil for deep frying	
	Grated Parmesan cheese	

Drain sweetcorn. Separate egg. Sift flour and pinch of salt into a mixing bowl. Make a well in centre, then put in egg yolk, oil and grated lemon rind. Stir until a smooth batter forms.

In another bowl, whisk egg white till stiff. Fold into batter with sweetcorn.

Heat oil in deep-fryer to 340°F (170°C).

Drop spoonfuls of batter into the hot oil – be careful because corn can burst – a few at a time, and fry for 5 minutes on each side or until golden. Remove with a fish slice and drain on kitchen paper. Keep warm while frying the rest.

Sprinkle grated Parmesan over and serve hot.

Lemon-braised leeks

Overall timing 1 hour

Freezing Not suitable

To serve 4

2 lb	Leeks	900 g
	Salt and pepper	
2	Carrots	2
1	Onion	1
3 oz	Butter	75 g
¼ pint	Stock	150 ml
2 tbsp	Plain flour	2x15 ml
½	Lemon	½

Preheat the oven to 350°F (180°C) Gas 4.

Trim leeks and blanch in boiling salted water for 5 minutes. Drain.

Peel and chop carrots. Peel and slice onion. Melt 1 oz (25 g) of the butter in a flameproof casserole and fry the carrots and onion till golden. Arrange leeks on top and add stock and seasoning.

Cream remaining butter with the flour to make a paste. Squeeze juice from lemon and work into the mixture with a fork. Spread over the leeks. Cover and cook in oven for 30–35 minutes. Serve with side dish of grated cheese and chunks of brown bread.

Cheesy vegetables

Overall timing 10 minutes

Freezing Not suitable

To serve 6

8 oz	Cream cheese	225 g
¼ pint	Carton of single cream	150 ml
2 lb	Hot cooked mixed vegetables (including beans, cauliflower, peas, carrots and mushrooms)	900 g
2 tbsp	Grated Parmesan cheese	2x15 ml
	Salt and pepper	

Beat the cream cheese and cream together in a bowl. Place the bowl over a pan of simmering water and heat through gently, stirring occasionally. Do not boil.

Arrange the vegetables in a warmed serving dish. Keep hot.

Beat the Parmesan into the cream cheese mixture and season to taste. Pour the hot sauce over the vegetables and serve immediately with roast or grilled meat, or as vegetarian lunch.

Greek pumpkin

Overall timing 1 hour

Freezing Not suitable

To serve 4–6

2 lb	Pumpkin	900 g
2	Medium onions	2
3 tbsp	Olive oil	3x15 ml
14 oz	Can of tomatoes	397 g
¼ teasp	Ground cumin	1.25 ml
2	Sprigs of flat-leafed parsley	2
	Salt and pepper	
½ pint	Water	300 ml

Scrape the seeds and fibrous centre out of the pumpkin. Cut into chunks, leaving the skin on. Peel the onions and cut through the root into eight wedges.

Heat the oil in a saucepan, add onions and fry till transparent. Add the tomatoes and juice, cumin and pumpkin. Chop the parsley and add with seasoning and the water. Bring to the boil, then cover and simmer for 25–35 minutes till the pumpkin is tender.

Adjust the seasoning and pour into a warmed serving dish. Serve hot with roast or grilled meat.

Lentils with bacon

Overall timing 1½ hours

Freezing Suitable

To serve 4

8 oz	Continental lentils	225 g
1	Large onion	1
8 oz	Smoked streaky bacon	225 g
3 tbsp	Oil	3 x 15 ml
1 teasp	Salt	5 ml
3 tbsp	Tomato purée	3 x 15 ml
1½ pints	Stock	850 ml

Wash and pick over the lentils. Peel and finely chop the onion. Derind and dice the bacon. Heat oil in a saucepan and fry onion and bacon till golden. Add the lentils and salt and cook for 10 minutes, stirring frequently.

Stir in the tomato purée and the stock and simmer for about 1 hour until the lentils are tender. Taste and adjust seasoning. Serve on slices of fried bread with a mixed salad.

Lentils with courgettes and potatoes

Overall timing 1½ hours

Freezing Not suitable

To serve 6

8 oz	Continental lentils	225 g
	Salt and pepper	
2	Bay leaves	2
1	Onion	1
2 tbsp	Oil	2x15 ml
12 oz	Courgettes	350 g
1	Garlic clove	1
2 tbsp	Lemon juice	2x15 ml
5	Fennel leaves	5
	Basil leaves	
	Sprig of rosemary	
1 teasp	Cumin seed	5 ml
8 oz	Potatoes	225 g
1 oz	Butter	25 g
	Chopped parsley	

Put lentils in a large saucepan. Add 2 pints (1.1 litres) water, seasoning and bay leaves. Bring to the boil and simmer for 5 minutes, then drain, reserving the liquid.

Peel and finely chop onion. Heat oil in a large saucepan and fry onion till transparent. Trim and thickly slice courgettes. Add to pan and stir-fry for 5 minutes. Peel and crush garlic and add to pan with lentils and lemon juice.

Finely chop fennel leaves and add to pan with a few basil leaves, a sprig of rosemary, the cumin and reserved lentil liquor. Simmer for 45 minutes.

Meanwhile, peel potatoes and cut into large chunks. Add to pan and simmer for a further 20 minutes or till the lentils are cooked.

Add the butter, and taste and adjust seasoning. Sprinkle with chopped parsley and serve hot with grated cheese or slices of boiled bacon.

Russian potatoes with cream V

Overall timing 1¼ hours

Freezing Not suitable

To serve 4

1½ lb	Waxy potatoes	700 g
	Salt and pepper	
2 oz	Button mushrooms	50 g
1	Small onion	1
2 oz	Butter	50 g
¼ pint	Soured cream	150 ml
2 tbsp	Chopped parsley	2x15 ml

Cook the potatoes in boiling salted water for about 30 minutes till tender. Drain and peel the potatoes, then cut into ¼ inch (6 mm) thick slices. Slice the mushrooms. Peel and thinly slice the onion.

Melt the butter in a frying pan and fry the onion till transparent. Add the mushrooms and fry for 2–3 minutes, stirring. Add the sliced potatoes and fry for 5 minutes, turning once.

Pour the cream over and season well. Turn potatoes gently till coated and continue cooking over a low heat for about 10 minutes till the potatoes have absorbed most of the cream.

Stir in the parsley, adjust the seasoning and serve hot.

Lettuce and ham supper

Overall timing 40 minutes

Freezing Not suitable

To serve 4

4	Round lettuces	4
1	Onion	1
1 oz	Butter	25 g
½ pint	Chicken stock	300 ml
	Salt and pepper	
4	Thick slices of cooked ham	4
1 teasp	Cornflour	5 ml
2 tbsp	Water	2x15 ml
¼ pint	Sherry	150 ml

Trim and wash lettuces. Drain well and cut in half lengthways. Peel and chop the onion.

Melt the butter in a saucepan and fry onions till golden. Add lettuces and fry for 3 minutes. Add stock, salt and pepper. Tightly cover pan and simmer gently for 15–20 minutes.

Cut ham slices in half and add to pan. Heat through gently for 3 minutes.

Carefully lift out the lettuce halves and ham, draining thoroughly. Arrange on a warmed serving dish and keep hot.

Blend cornflour with water, then stir into cooking liquor. Bring to the boil, stirring continuously. Remove from heat and stir in sherry. Taste and adjust seasoning. Pour over lettuce and ham and serve immediately with mashed potatoes and wholemeal bread.

Savoury pumpkin

Overall timing 1¼ hours plus 30 minutes standing

Freezing Not suitable

To serve 4–6

2 lb	Pumpkin	900 g
	Salt and pepper	
8 oz	Cheese	225 g
¼ teasp	Ground cumin	1.25 ml
3	Eggs	3
2 oz	Fresh breadcrumbs	50 g
2 tbsp	Chopped parsley	2x15 ml
1 oz	Butter	25 g

Scrape the seeds and fibrous centre out of the pumpkin. Remove the skin and grate the flesh into a bowl. Sprinkle with salt, mix well and leave to stand for 30 minutes.

Preheat the oven to 350°F (180°C) Gas 4.

Press the pumpkin with the back of a spoon to squeeze out as much liquid as possible. Grate the cheese and add to the pumpkin with cumin, eggs, breadcrumbs, parsley and seasoning and beat the mixture till smooth.

Pour into a greased ovenproof dish and smooth the top. Dot with butter and bake for about 45 minutes till set. Serve immediately with a tomato salad and fresh crusty bread and butter.

Macaroni with artichokes

Overall timing 35 minutes

Freezing Not suitable

To serve 2

2	Small globe artichokes	2
1 teasp	Lemon juice	5 ml
1	Garlic clove	1
2 tbsp	Olive oil	2x15 ml
1 tbsp	Chopped parsley	15 ml
8 oz	Penne macaroni	225 g
	Salt and pepper	

Cut off stems, tough outer leaves and pointed tops of artichokes and snip off the tips of outside leaves. Cut artichokes into quarters, remove chokes and place in bowl with lemon juice. Cover with water and leave to soak for 10 minutes.

Peel and crush garlic. Heat the oil in saucepan. Drain artichokes and add to pan with garlic. Cook gently over low heat for about 10 minutes till tender, turning them several times. Add parsley and cook for a further 5 minutes, stirring occasionally.

Meanwhile, cook macaroni in boiling salted water till tender. Drain thoroughly and add to artichokes. Mix well to coat pasta with oil and parsley, adding lots of seasoning, then turn into warmed serving dish. Serve hot with grated Parmesan cheese.

Lyonnaise beans

Overall timing 1 hour plus soaking

Freezing Not suitable

To serve 6

12 oz	Dried butter beans	350 g
	Salt and pepper	
2	Medium onions	2
2 oz	Butter	50 g
1 tbsp	Chopped parsley	15 ml

Soak beans in water to cover overnight. Drain.

Place beans in saucepan and add 1¾ pints (1 litre) fresh water. Cover and cook for about 1 hour till tender. Add a little salt towards the end of cooking time.

Peel and finely chop onions. Melt the butter in a saucepan and add the onions, parsley and seasoning. Cook gently till onions are transparent.

Drain beans well, then toss them in the onion and parsley mixture. Transfer to a warmed serving dish and serve.

Sicilian broad beans

Overall timing 1 hour 20 minutes plus optional cooking

Freezing Not suitable

To serve 4

12 oz	Fresh broad beans	350 g
12 oz	Fresh peas	350 g
1	Small onion	1
2 tbsp	Oil	2x15 ml
4 tbsp	Water or stock	4x15 ml
	Pinch of grated nutmeg	
	Salt and pepper	
4	Canned artichoke hearts	4
6	Leaves of fresh mint	6
½ teasp	Sugar	2.5 ml
2 teasp	Vinegar	2x5 ml

Shell beans and peas. Peel and chop onion. Heat oil in a saucepan and fry onion till transparent. Add beans, peas, water or stock, nutmeg and seasoning. Cover the pan and simmer gently for 30 minutes.

Drain artichokes and cut into eighths. Add to pan and continue cooking for 10 minutes. Stir in mint (some whole leaves, some chopped) and cook for 5 minutes more. Leave to cool slightly before serving.

If you wish to serve this dish cold, add sugar and vinegar with the mint. Stir well, then transfer to a serving dish and leave till cold. Chill for 15 minutes before serving.

Scalloped Chinese leaves

Overall timing 45 minutes

Freezing Not suitable

To serve 4

2 lb	Chinese leaves	900 g
1	Onion	1
1 pint	Milk	560 ml
	Salt and pepper	
1	Egg	1
2 tbsp	Chopped parsley	2x15 ml
1 oz	Butter	25 g
4 oz	Cheese	125 g

Preheat the oven to 375°F (190°C) Gas 5.

Trim stalk end of Chinese leaves. Remove any damaged outer leaves, then separate remaining leaves. Rinse and drain.

Peel and slice the onion and put into a large saucepan with the milk and a little salt. Bring just to boil, then add the Chinese leaves. Cover and simmer for 5 minutes.

Lift the Chinese leaves out of the milk with a draining spoon and arrange in a shallow ovenproof dish. Beat the egg in a bowl with the parsley and gradually add the milk, beating constantly. Add pepper and the butter and stir till melted. Pour over the Chinese leaves. Grate the cheese and sprinkle over the top. Bake for about 30 minutes till golden. Serve immediately with brown bread rolls.

Spicy stuffed peppers

Overall timing 1¼ hours

Freezing Not suitable

To serve 4

8	Green or red peppers	8
	Salt and pepper	
1	Onion	1
2 tbsp	Oil	2x15 ml
1 lb	Minced beef	450 g
1 pint	Beef stock	560 ml
6 oz	Long grain rice	175 g
1 teasp	Grated nutmeg	5 ml
1 tbsp	Brown sugar	15 ml
2 oz	Cheese	50 g

Cut stalk ends off peppers and remove seeds and membrane. Blanch in boiling salted water for 5 minutes, then drain. Arrange in a greased ovenproof dish.

Peel and chop onion and pepper lids. Heat oil in a saucepan and fry onion and pepper lids till just golden. Add beef and brown well. Stir in stock and bring to the boil. Add rice, nutmeg, sugar and seasoning and simmer for 15–20 minutes till rice is tender and has absorbed the stock.

Remove from heat. Grate cheese and stir into stuffing. Use to fill the peppers. Cover the dish with foil and bake for 20 minutes. Remove foil and bake for a further 10 minutes till golden.

Stuffed baked turnips

Overall timing 1¼ hours

Freezing Not suitable

To serve 4

4x8 oz	Turnips	4x225 g
	Salt and pepper	
1	Onion	1
1 oz	Butter	25 g
2 oz	Fresh breadcrumbs	50 g
8 oz	Sliced cooked ham	225 g
1	Egg yolk	1
¼ pint	Chicken stock	150 ml
3 oz	Cheese	75 g

Preheat the oven to 375°F (190°C) Gas 5.

Peel turnips. Cut off top third of each to make a lid. Scoop flesh out of base, leaving a thick shell, and chop flesh. Cook shells and lids in boiling salted water for 5 minutes, then drain.

Peel and chop onion. Melt butter in a saucepan, add onion and chopped turnip and fry till golden. Stir in breadcrumbs. Reserve four slices of ham, chop rest and add to stuffing with seasoning and egg yolk.

Press stuffing into turnips. Place a slice of ham on each and cover with lids. Put in ovenproof dish. Pour stock over, cover and bake for 20 minutes.

Grate cheese. Uncover turnips, sprinkle over cheese and bake for a further 10–15 minutes.

Marrow ratatouille

Overall timing 40 minutes

Freezing Suitable: add olives and Parmesan after reheating

To serve 2

1 lb	Marrow	450 g
	Salt and pepper	
1	Onion	1
1	Garlic clove	1
2	Tomatoes	2
1 oz	Butter	25 g
1 tbsp	Oil	15 ml
1 tbsp	Tomato purée	15 ml
5 tbsp	Stock	5x15 ml
1 teasp	Chopped fresh marjoram	5 ml
1 teasp	Chopped fresh basil	5 ml
½ teasp	Chopped fresh thyme	2.5 ml
6	Black olives	6
2 tbsp	Grated Parmesan cheese	2x15 ml

Peel the marrow, cut in half lengthways and scoop out seeds. Cut flesh into 2 inch (5 cm) slices. Blanch in boiling salted water for 5 minutes. Drain well.

Peel and slice the onion. Peel and crush the garlic. Blanch, peel and chop the tomatoes.

Heat butter and oil in a frying pan, add onion and garlic and cook for 5 minutes till transparent. Add marrow, tomatoes, tomato purée, stock, herbs and seasoning. Simmer for 10–15 minutes till the marrow is just tender.

Add the olives and sprinkle with grated Parmesan cheese. Serve hot with chunks of crusty fresh bread, or as an accompaniment to grilled meats.

Spinach dumplings

Overall timing 40 minutes plus setting

Freezing Suitable: cook from frozen for 12–15 minutes, then add melted butter and cheese.

To serve 6

2 lb	Spinach	900 g
$\frac{1}{2}$	Chicken stock cube	$\frac{1}{2}$
5 tbsp	Warm milk	5x15 ml
12 oz	Plain flour	350 g
3	Eggs	3
	Salt and pepper	
4 oz	Butter	125 g
8 oz	Fresh breadcrumbs	225 g
$\frac{1}{4}$ teasp	Grated nutmeg	1.25 ml
1 tbsp	Chopped parsley	15 ml
1 tbsp	Chopped chives	15 ml
4 oz	Emmenthal cheese	125 g

Wash spinach and put into a saucepan with only water that clings to it. Cover and cook for 5 minutes.

Dissolve stock cube in milk. Sift flour into a bowl, add eggs, milk and seasoning and mix to a soft dough.

Drain spinach thoroughly and chop finely. Melt half the butter in a frying pan, add breadcrumbs and fry till crisp and golden. Add to dough with nutmeg, parsley and chives. Add spinach and mix to a stiff dough.

Roll dough between floured hands into long sausage-shapes about $\frac{1}{2}$ inch (12.5 mm) in diameter. Leave to set.

Cut across dough into 1 inch (2.5 cm) lengths. Cook in boiling salted water for about 10 minutes till they float to the surface.

Lift out dumplings with a draining spoon, drain thoroughly and arrange in a warmed serving dish. Melt remaining butter, pour over dumplings and sprinkle with grated cheese. Toss lightly before serving with casseroles.

Spinach omelette

Overall timing 15 minutes

Freezing Not suitable

To serve 2

6 oz	Spinach	175 g
2 oz	Butter	50 g
	Salt and pepper	
6	Eggs	6
2 tbsp	Single cream	2x15 ml

Cut away blemishes and stalks from spinach. Wash, then shred coarsely. Melt 1½ oz (40 g) of the butter in a saucepan, add spinach and seasoning, cover and cook over a low heat for about 5 minutes till a purée.

Lightly beat the eggs in a bowl with seasoning. Melt the remaining butter in an omelette pan, add the egg mixture and cook gently till the omelette is lightly set.

Spread the spinach purée over half the omelette and spoon the cream over. Slide omelette out of the pan on to a warmed serving dish, tilting the pan so the omelette folds in half. Serve immediately with chips and a salad.

Marseilles marrow

Overall timing 45 minutes

Freezing Not suitable

To serve 6

1½ lb	Marrow	700 g
	Salt and pepper	
12 oz	Ripe tomatoes	350 g
2	Large onions	2
3 tbsp	Olive oil	3x15 ml
4 oz	Long grain rice	125 g
1 pint	Water	560 ml
1 tbsp	Chopped parsley	15 ml

Blanch marrow in boiling salted water for 10 minutes. Drain thoroughly. Cut in half lengthways, then cut across each half into 1 inch (2.5 cm) thick slices, removing the seeds.

Blanch, peel and halve the tomatoes. Peel and slice the onions. Heat the oil in a flameproof casserole and fry onions till pale golden.

Add the rice to the casserole and fry, stirring, for 2 minutes till the oil is absorbed. Add the water, tomatoes, marrow and seasoning. Bring to the boil, then cover and simmer gently for 15–20 minutes till rice is tender and most of the water has been absorbed.

Taste and adjust the seasoning, sprinkle with parsley and serve hot.

Sweet potato soufflé

Overall timing 1¼ hours

Freezing Not suitable

To serve 2

8 oz	Yam or sweet potatoes	225 g
¼ pint	Milk	150 ml
	Salt	
1 oz	Butter	25 g
1½ teasp	Plain flour	7.5 ml
2	Eggs	2
	Pinch of cayenne	
2 oz	Cheese	50 g

Preheat the oven to 375°F (190°C) Gas 5.

Peel the yam or sweet potato and cut into ½ inch (12.5 mm) cubes. Put into a saucepan with the milk and a little salt and bring to the boil. Cover and simmer for about 20 minutes till tender. Drain the yam or sweet potato, reserving the cooking liquor, then return it to the pan and mash over a low heat to make a dry, fluffy purée.

Melt the butter in a saucepan, add the flour and cook for 1 minute. Make the reserved cooking liquor up to ¼ pint (150 ml) with extra milk if necessary and gradually add to the roux. Bring to the boil, stirring constantly, and simmer for 2 minutes. Remove from the heat and allow to cool slightly.

Separate the eggs and beat the yolks into the sauce with the cayenne, grated cheese, a little salt and the yam or potato purée. Whisk the egg whites till stiff and fold into the sauce with a metal spoon.

Pour the mixture into a greased soufflé dish and bake for 30–35 minutes till well risen and golden. Serve immediately.

Mixed vegetables in milk

Overall timing 35 minutes

Freezing Not suitable

To serve 4

1	Large potato	1
1	Bulb of celeriac	1
2	Carrots	2
1	Turnip	1
1	Small cauliflower	1
8 oz	Green beans	225 g
¾ pint	Milk	400 ml
2 oz	Butter	50 g
	Salt and pepper	
2 tbsp	Plain flour	2x15 ml
4 tbsp	Single cream	4x15 ml

Peel and dice potato, celeriac, carrots and turnip. Divide cauliflower into small florets. Top and tail beans, remove strings and chop.

Heat milk with half the butter and salt. Add potato, celeriac, carrots and turnip and cook for 10 minutes. Add cauliflower and beans and cook for a further 5 minutes. Drain vegetables, reserving milk.

Melt remaining butter in pan, stir in flour and cook for 1 minute. Gradually stir in reserved milk and simmer till thickened. Add cooked vegetables and heat through. Remove from heat and stir in cream and seasoning to taste.

Peas bonne femme

Overall timing 45 minutes

Freezing Not suitable

To serve 4

2 lb	Fresh peas	900 g
6	Small onions	6
1	Round lettuce	1
1	Thick streaky bacon rasher	1
3 oz	Butter	75 g
1 tbsp	Chopped parsley	15 ml
½ teasp	Sugar	2.5 ml
¼ pint	Water	150 ml
	Salt and pepper	
1 teasp	Plain flour	5 ml

Shell peas. Blanch onions in boiling water for 5 minutes, then peel. Shred lettuce. Derind and chop bacon.

Melt 2 oz (50 g) butter in a saucepan and fry peas, onions, lettuce, parsley and bacon for 3 minutes, stirring. Add sugar, water and seasoning. Bring to the boil, cover and simmer for 15–20 minutes till peas and onions are tender.

Mix flour with remaining butter to a paste and add in small pieces to the vegetable mixture, stirring constantly. Cook for 3 minutes. Taste and adjust the seasoning and serve hot.

Stir-fried celery v

Overall timing 15 minutes

Freezing Not suitable

To serve 4

1	Large bunch of celery	1
2 teasp	Salt	2x5 ml
3 tbsp	Oil	3x15 ml
2 tbsp	Soy sauce	2x15 ml
½ teasp	Sugar	2.5 ml

Cut off leaves from celery, then chop into 2 inch (5 cm) pieces. Sprinkle with salt.

Heat oil in frying pan. When oil is very hot, add the celery and stir-fry for 5 minutes. Add soy sauce and sugar, mix well and serve immediately.

Mushrooms in batter

Overall timing 30 minutes

Freezing Not suitable

To serve 2–4

12 oz	Large open mushrooms	350 g
4½ oz	Plain flour	140 g
1 teasp	Salt	5 ml
1	Egg	1
1 tbsp	Oil	15 ml
¼ pint	Milk or water	150 ml
2	Egg whites	2
	Oil for frying	
	Sprigs of parsley	

Trim the mushrooms, then toss in ½ oz (15 g) of the flour.

Sift the remaining flour and salt into a bowl and make a well in the centre. Add the egg and oil and begin to mix with a wooden spoon, drawing the flour into the liquid. Gradually stir in the milk or water to make a thick smooth batter. Whisk the egg whites in a bowl till stiff but not dry and fold gently into the batter.

Heat oil in a deep-fryer to 340°F (170°C).

Spear a mushroom on a long skewer and dip into the batter. Using a second skewer, carefully push the mushroom off the skewer into the oil. Fry the mushrooms, a few at a time, for 3–4 minutes till crisp and golden. Remove from the pan with a draining spoon and drain on kitchen paper. Pile on to a warmed serving plate and garnish with sprigs of parsley.

Mushroom casserole

Overall timing 2½ hours

Freezing Not suitable

To serve 4

2 lb	Flat mushrooms	900 g
1 oz	Butter	25 g
1	Onion	1
1	Garlic clove	1
8 oz	Cooked ham	225 g
8 oz	Lean pork	225 g
4 oz	Streaky bacon	125 g
4	Sprigs of parsley	4
2	Eggs	2
1 tbsp	Fresh breadcrumbs	15 ml
	Salt and pepper	
½ oz	Dripping	15 g
1 tbsp	Oil	15 ml
1 teasp	Wine or cider vinegar	5 ml

Preheat the oven to 325°F (170°C) Gas 3.

Separate mushroom stalks from the caps. Halve or quarter caps if large and reserve. Chop the stalks. Melt the butter in a saucepan, add the chopped mushroom stalks and fry over a high heat until all the liquid has evaporated. Remove pan from heat.

Peel and finely chop the onion and garlic. Mince the ham, pork, derinded bacon and parsley. Add all these ingredients to the saucepan with the eggs, breadcrumbs and generous seasoning. Mix well.

Heat the dripping and oil in flameproof casserole. When hot, remove from heat and put in a layer of the mince mixture (don't pack tightly), followed by a layer of mushroom caps. Repeat until all the ingredients have been used up. Cover and bake for about 2 hours. Sprinkle with vinegar just before serving with a mixed salad.

Sweet-sour red cabbage

Overall timing 1 hour 20 minutes

Freezing Suitable

To serve 4

2 lb	Red cabbage	about 1 kg
2 oz	Streaky bacon	50 g
1	Onion	1
1	Cooking apple	1
6	Whole allspice	6
½ teasp	Salt	2.5 ml
2 teasp	Honey	2 x 5 ml
3 fl oz	Red wine or wine vinegar	90 ml

Discard any damaged outer leaves from the cabbage. Quarter, cut away core and thick ribs and shred leaves.

Derind and chop bacon. Peel and chop onion. Cook bacon in flameproof casserole over a low heat until fat starts to run. Add onion and cook for 5 minutes, stirring.

Peel, core and chop apple and add to casserole with cabbage. Crush allspice and add to casserole with salt, honey and wine or vinegar. Mix well, then cover and simmer for 1 hour.

If there's too much liquid at the end of cooking time, remove the lid and continue simmering. Serve hot.

Neapolitan beans

Overall timing 1½ hours plus soaking

Freezing Not suitable

To serve 4

4 oz	Dried haricot beans	125 g
1	Stalk of celery	1
1	Carrot	1
1	Garlic clove	1
2 tbsp	Oil	2x15 ml
2 tbsp	Chopped parsley	2x15 ml
14 oz	Can of tomatoes	397 g
1 tbsp	Chopped fresh savory	15 ml
	Salt and pepper	
1 pint	Strong chicken stock	560 ml
8 oz	Short macaroni	225 g

Put beans in a large pan and cover with plenty of cold water. Bring to the boil and boil for 2 minutes. Remove from heat, cover and leave to soak for 2 hours.

Drain beans well, then cover with boiling water and cook for 1 hour.

Chop celery. Peel and chop carrot. Peel and crush garlic. Heat oil in a saucepan, add celery, carrot, garlic and parsley and fry for 5 minutes.

Sieve tomatoes and juice and add to vegetables with savory and seasoning. Drain beans and purée two-thirds of them in a vegetable mill or press through a sieve. Add bean purée, whole beans and stock to vegetables. Bring to the boil.

Add the macaroni and stir well. Cook for 15–20 minutes, stirring occasionally. Taste and adjust seasoning before serving.

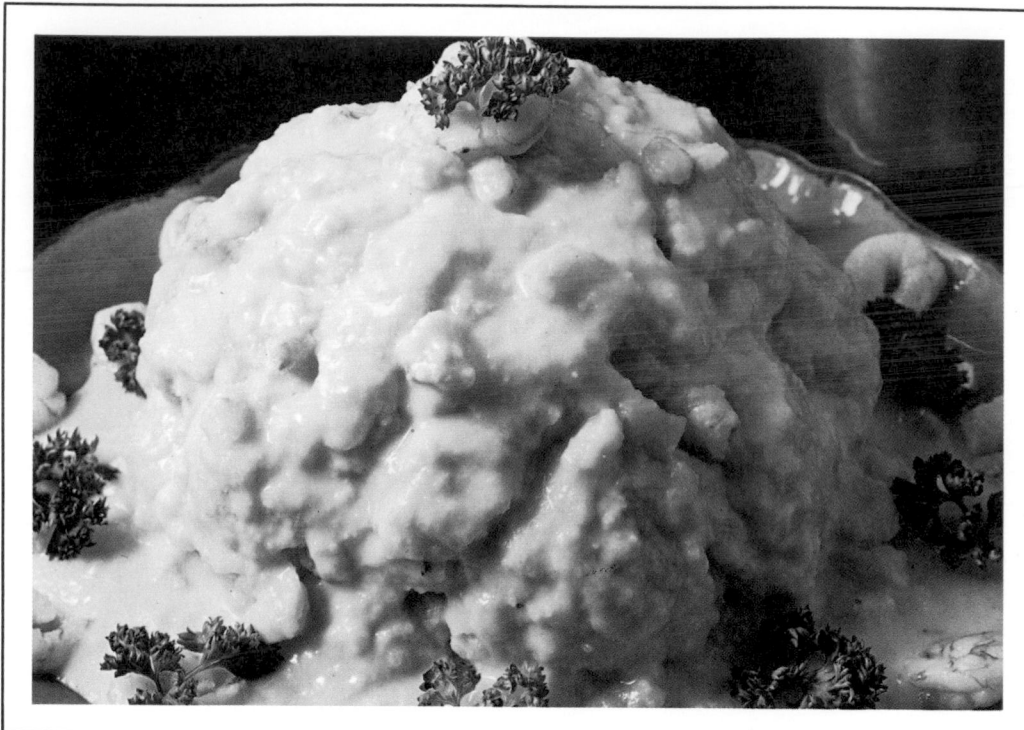

Norwegian cauliflower

Overall timing 25 minutes

Freezing Not suitable

To serve 4

1	Cauliflower	1
	Salt and pepper	
1 oz	Butter	25 g
2 oz	Fresh white breadcrumbs	50 g
½ pint	Milk	300 ml
	Pinch of sugar	
4 oz	Shelled prawns	125 g
1 tbsp	Brandy (optional)	15 ml
3 tbsp	Single cream	3x15 ml
	Sprigs of parsley	

Remove any leaves from the cauliflower and trim the stalk. Put cauliflower into a saucepan containing 1½ inches (4 cm) of boiling salted water, cover and cook for 20 minutes.

Meanwhile, melt the butter in another pan, add breadcrumbs and milk and cook for a few minutes, stirring. Add salt, pepper and sugar. Set aside a few shelled prawns for the garnish and add the rest to the pan. Cook for 5 minutes more, stirring.

Remove pan from heat and add brandy, if used, and cream. Return to a gentle heat for 1 minute.

Drain cauliflower, place on a warmed serving dish and pour over sauce. Garnish with reserved prawns and parsley.

Mushroom loaf

Overall timing 1 hour

Freezing Not suitable

To serve 4

1½ lb	Button mushrooms	700 g
1½ oz	Butter	40 g
½ pint	White sauce	300 ml
	Salt and pepper	
	Grated nutmeg	
3	Eggs	3

Preheat the oven to 350°F (180°C) Gas 4.

Trim the mushrooms. Reserve four for decoration and finely chop the rest. Melt 1 oz (25 g) butter in a saucepan and cook the chopped mushrooms for 5 minutes. Stir in the white sauce, then season with salt, pepper and a little grated nutmeg to taste.

Remove pan from heat and allow to cool slightly, then beat in the eggs one at a time. Pour the mixture into a greased 6 inch (15 cm) soufflé dish and bake for about 45 minutes till set.

Meanwhile, flute one of the reserved mushrooms and thinly slice the other three. Melt remaining butter in a saucepan and fry mushrooms till golden.

Turn out mushroom loaf and serve hot, garnished with fried mushrooms, on a bed of lettuce leaves.

Moravian mushrooms

Overall timing 30 minutes

Freezing Not suitable

To serve 6

1¼ lb	Button mushrooms	600 g
1 oz	Butter	25 g
½ teasp	Salt	2.5 ml
1 teasp	Cumin seeds	5 ml
1 tbsp	Finely chopped parsley	15 ml
1 tbsp	Plain flour	15 ml
1 teasp	Vinegar or lemon juice	5 ml
4 fl oz	Milk	120 ml
2 tbsp	Double cream	2x15 ml

Trim and slice the mushrooms.

Melt the butter in a saucepan and add the mushrooms, salt, cumin seeds and chopped parsley. Stir-fry over a high heat for 5 minutes, then stir in flour.

Gradually add vinegar or lemon juice and milk, stirring constantly. Lower the heat and simmer for 10 minutes, stirring frequently. Stir in cream and serve.

Bean cake

Overall timing 1¼–1½ hours

Freezing Suitable: reheat after thawing in 300°F (150°C) Gas 2 oven for 30 minutes

To serve 4

1 lb	Green beans	450 g
	Salt and pepper	
1	Celery stalk	1
3 oz	Butter	75 g
2 tbsp	Oil	2x15 ml
1 tbsp	Chopped onion	15 ml
1 tbsp	Chopped parsley	15 ml
1 oz	Plain flour	25 g
9 fl oz	Milk	250 ml
4 oz	Mature cheese	125 g
2 tbsp	Crisp breadcrumbs	2x15 ml
3	Eggs	3

Preheat the oven to 425°F (220°C) Gas 7.

String beans. Blanch for 5 minutes in boiling salted water. Drain.

Chop celery. Melt 2 oz (50 g) of the butter with the oil in a frying pan and brown the onion, celery and chopped parsley. Add beans, cover and cook very gently for 10 minutes.

Meanwhile, melt the remaining butter in a saucepan. Stir in flour and cook for 2 minutes, then gradually stir in milk. Simmer until thick. Grate cheese and add to sauce with seasoning.

Grease ovenproof dish and coat bottom and sides with breadcrumbs. Drain bean mixture and mix it into sauce until well combined, then mix in lightly beaten eggs. Spoon mixture into dish. Place dish in roasting tin of water and bake for 25 minutes. Reduce heat to 400°F (200°C) Gas 6 and bake for 10 more minutes.

Remove dish from oven, leave to stand for 5 minutes, then invert on to serving plate. Serve hot or cold.

Bean gratin

Overall timing 40 minutes

Freezing Not suitable

To serve 6

2 oz	Bread	50 g
	Milk	
1	Garlic clove	1
1 tbsp	Chopped parsley	15 ml
8 oz	Leftover cooked lamb or beef	225 g
	Salt and pepper	
2x14 oz	Cans of green beans *or*	2x397 g
1 lb	Frozen beans *or*	450 g
1¼ lb	Fresh cooked beans	600 g
1 oz	Butter	25 g
1 oz	Plain flour	25 g
¾ pint	Milk	400 ml
3 oz	Cheese	75 g
1	Egg	1

Preheat oven to 450°F (230°C) Gas 8.

Soak the bread in a little milk. Squeeze out, then put through a mincer with the peeled garlic, parsley and meat. Season with salt and pepper.

If using canned beans, drain them. Fill a well-greased gratin dish with alternate layers of beans and meat mixture, finishing with a bean layer.

Melt butter in a saucepan. Stir in flour and cook for 1 minute, then gradually add milk. Bring to the boil, stirring until thickened. Grate cheese and add to sauce. Cool slightly, then mix in beaten egg and seasoning.

Cover bean mixture in gratin dish with the sauce. Bake for about 10 minutes until the sauce is lightly browned.

Beans with egg sauce

Overall timing 25 minutes

Freezing Not suitable

To serve 6

1½ lb	French beans *or*	700 g
2x14 oz	Cans of whole or cut green beans	2x397 g
	Salt	
2 oz	Butter	50 g
4 tbsp	Fresh breadcrumbs	4x15 ml
1 oz	Margarine	25 g
1 oz	Plain flour	25 g
	Nutmeg	
1 teasp	Lemon juice	5 ml
¼ teasp	Dried mixed herbs	1.25 ml
3 tbsp	White wine or cider	3x15 ml
2	Hard-boiled eggs	2
1 teasp	Chopped chives	5 ml

If using fresh beans wash, top and tail them and remove strings. Break or cut into short lengths. Cook for 10–15 minutes in boiling, salted water until tender. Drain, saving 9 fl oz (250 ml) of the cooking liquor, and put beans into a warmed serving dish. Heat canned beans in their liquid and use this, made up to required amount with water, for sauce.

Melt the butter in a saucepan, add the breadcrumbs and lightly brown. Sprinkle over beans and keep warm.

To make the sauce, melt the margarine in the saucepan then stir in the flour. Remove pan from heat and blend in the reserved cooking liquor. Stir sauce over a medium heat until it comes to the boil and thickens, then add pinches of salt and nutmeg, lemon juice and mixed herbs.

Remove pan from heat and stir in wine or cider, chopped hard-boiled eggs and chives. Pour sauce over beans. Serve with lamb steaks and potato croquettes.

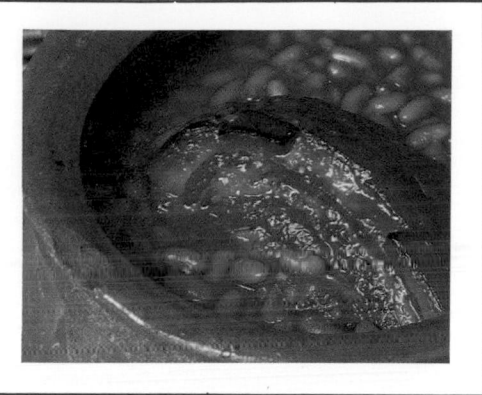

Boston baked beans

Overall timing 8 hours

Freezing Not suitable

To serve 6

1 lb	Dried haricot beans	450 g
2 tbsp	Black treacle	2x15 ml
2 oz	Brown sugar	50 g
2 teasp	French mustard	2x5 ml
½ teasp	White pepper	2.5 ml
1 lb	Piece of fat bacon with rind	450 g

Soak the beans for 2 hours.

Preheat oven to 350°F (180°C) Gas 4.

Drain the beans and cover them with fresh cold water. Bring to the boil and simmer for about 1½ hours. Drain and reserve ½ pint (300 ml) of the cooking liquor.

Add the treacle, sugar, mustard, pepper and reserved cooking liquor to the beans.

Derind bacon and score the skin in several places. Cut 2 or 3 slices from the bacon, and place these in the bottom of a heavy-based casserole. Pour in the bean mixture and top with the rest of the bacon and also the rind. Cover tightly and bake for 4½–5 hours or till the beans are tender and deep brown.

Use two forks, one in each hand, to shred the bacon rind and mix it in with the beans. Serve hot.

Baked stuffed onions

Overall timing 1½ hours

Freezing Not suitable

To serve 6

6	Large white onions	6
3 oz	Long grain rice	75 g
	Salt and pepper	
3 tbsp	Chopped parsley	3x15 ml
1 oz	Butter	25 g

Peel the onions, then blanch in boiling water for 10 minutes. Drain and cool.

Meanwhile, cook the rice in boiling salted water for 20 minutes or until tender. Drain if necessary, then mix with the parsley, butter and seasoning.

Cut a thin slice from the tops of the onions, then hollow out the centres with a spoon. Fill with the rice mixture.

Arrange the onions around a roasting joint for the last 30–45 minutes of the cooking time, till tender.

Celeriac with onions

Overall timing 50 minutes

Freezing Not suitable

To serve 4–6

1½ lb	Celeriac	700 g
	Salt and pepper	
1 tbsp	Lemon juice	15 ml
2	Medium onions	2
2 oz	Butter	50 g
1 oz	Pork dripping *or*	25 g
2 tbsp	Oil	2x15 ml
2 tbsp	Plain flour	2x15 ml
¾ pint	Chicken stock	400 ml

Peel celeriac and cut into ⅛ inch (3 mm) slices. Blanch in boiling salted water with the lemon juice for 5 minutes, then drain.

Peel and finely chop onions. Heat half the butter and all the dripping or oil in a large frying pan. Add onions and celeriac and cook till onions are transparent, turning the celeriac over once with tongs – take care not to break up the fragile slices.

Tilt the pan, sprinkle the flour over the fat and stir. Add the stock and seasoning. Move the pan to distribute the liquids evenly, then cover and cook over a very low heat for 30 minutes.

Transfer celeriac to a warmed serving dish. Strain the cooking juices, stir in remaining butter and seasoning to taste and pour over the celeriac.

Sunshine salad

Overall timing 15 minutes plus chilling

Freezing Not suitable

To serve 2

8 oz	Poached smoked haddock	225 g
1	Orange	1
1	Grapefruit	1
1	Green pepper	1
1	Onion	1
1 tbsp	Chopped parsley	15 ml
3 tbsp	Olive oil	3x15 ml
1 tbsp	Lemon juice	15 ml
	Salt and pepper	
2 oz	Black olives	50 g

Cut the haddock into small strips. Peel orange and grapefruit and slice or chop the flesh. Deseed and slice pepper. Peel onion and cut into thin rings.

Put prepared ingredients into salad bowl with the parsley. Add oil, lemon juice and seasoning. Toss salad well and chill. Garnish with stoned olives just before serving.

Sweet and sour corn salad

Overall timing 45 minutes including chilling

Freezing Not suitable

To serve 6

8 oz	Can of sweetcorn kernels	225 g
2 tbsp	Wine vinegar	2x15 ml
3 tbsp	Oil	3x15 ml
	Salt and pepper	
1 lb	Cold boiled potatoes	450 g
8 oz	Tomatoes	225 g
8 oz	Can of pineapple chunks	247 g
2	Bananas	2
5 tbsp	Lemon juice	5x15 ml
1	Small lettuce	1
Dressing		
1 tbsp	French mustard	15 ml
¼ pint	Soured cream or plain yogurt	150 ml
2 tbsp	Milk	2x15 ml
	Salt and pepper	
1 teasp	Paprika	5 ml

Drain sweetcorn and place in a bowl. Mix together vinegar, oil and seasoning and add to bowl. Mix well. Cover and chill.

Peel and dice potatoes. Slice tomatoes. Drain pineapple, reserving 2 tbsp (2x15 ml) of the juice. Peel and slice bananas. Put all these in a bowl and pour lemon juice over.

Mix together dressing ingredients with reserved pineapple juice. Add to potato mixture. Chill for 30 minutes.

Line serving dish with lettuce leaves and spoon potato mixture in a ring round the edge. Pile sweetcorn in the middle and serve.

Bacon and potato salad

Overall timing 55 minutes

Freezing Not suitable

To serve 6–8

2 lb	Medium-size waxy potatoes	900 g
	Salt and pepper	
8 oz	Streaky bacon rashers	225 g
1	Large onion	1
4 tbsp	White wine vinegar	4x15 ml
4 tbsp	Water	4x15 ml
1 teasp	Powdered mustard	5 ml
1 tbsp	Chopped chives	15 ml

Scrub the potatoes, cover with cold salted water and bring to the boil. Cook for about 30 minutes till tender.

Meanwhile, derind and dice the bacon and fry over a moderate heat till crisp and brown. Lift out of the pan with a draining spoon and put into a warmed serving dish. Cover with foil to keep hot.

Drain the potatoes and cut into $\frac{1}{2}$ inch (12.5 mm) thick slices. Add to the bacon and cover again.

Peel and roughly chop the onion, add to the bacon fat in the pan and fry over a moderate heat till golden. Add the vinegar, water, salt, pepper and mustard and bring to the boil.

Pour over the potatoes and bacon, turning them carefully till coated. Sprinkle with chives and serve immediately with fresh crusty bread.

Swiss salad

Overall timing 35 minutes

Freezing Not suitable

To serve 4

12 oz	Boiled new potatoes	350 g
1	Dessert apple	1
2 tbsp	White wine vinegar	2x15 ml
1 teasp	Made mustard	5 ml
4 tbsp	Oil	4x15 ml
	Salt and pepper	
½	Round lettuce	½
6 oz	Gruyère cheese	175 g
4	Hard-boiled eggs	4
2 teasp	Chopped chives	2x5 ml
1 teasp	Paprika	5 ml

Peel and slice the potatoes into a bowl. Peel, core and slice the apple and toss in the vinegar. Add to the potatoes.

Mix the mustard, oil and seasoning together in a bowl and pour over the potatoes and apple. Toss lightly.

Wash and dry the lettuce leaves and use to line salad bowl. Arrange the potato mixture on the lettuce.

Cut the cheese into matchsticks. Scatter the cheese round the edge and in the centre of the salad. Shell and slice the eggs and arrange on the salad. Sprinkle with the chives and paprika and serve immediately with crusty or wholemeal bread or rolls and butter.

Tropical salad

Overall timing 25 minutes plus cooling

Freezing Not suitable

To serve 2

Salad		
3½ oz	Packet of frozen prawns	100 g
4 oz	Long grain rice	125 g
1	Leek	1
8 oz	Cooked chicken	225 g
1	Small onion	1
Dressing		
2 tbsp	Mango chutney	2x15 ml
2 tbsp	Oil	2x15 ml
2 tbsp	Lemon juice	2x15 ml
1 teasp	Vinegar	5 ml
½ teasp	Worcestershire sauce	2.5 ml
½ teasp	Curry powder	2.5 ml
	Salt and pepper	
Garnish		
	Lettuce leaves	
1	Banana	1

Thaw prawns. Put rice in a pan of boiling salted water and cook for 10 minutes.

Wash, trim and finely slice the leek. Add to the pan and cook for a further 5 minutes or until rice is cooked. Drain and leave to cool.

Slice cooked chicken into thin strips. Peel and finely slice the onion. Add both to the rice with the prawns and mix.

To make the dressing, finely chop the mango chutney and put into a bowl with the oil, lemon juice, vinegar, Worcestershire sauce, curry powder and salt and pepper. Mix well.

Arrange rice mixture on top of lettuce leaves in a serving dish. Garnish with slices of banana and pour dressing over.

Tuna salad

Overall timing 15 minutes

Freezing Not suitable

To serve 4

1	Bulb of fennel	1
	Salt and pepper	
4	Tomatoes	4
6½ oz	Can of tuna	184g
3 tbsp	Oil	3x15 ml
1 tbsp	Wine vinegar	15 ml
	Chopped parsley	
1 oz	Black olives	25 g

Trim and slice the fennel. Blanch in boiling salted water for 5 minutes. Drain. Slice tomatoes. Drain tuna.

Place tuna in centre of serving dish and arrange fennel and tomato slices around it.

In a bowl, mix together oil, vinegar and seasoning. Pour dressing over salad and sprinkle with chopped parsley. Garnish with black olives and fennel leaves, if available.

Apple *and salami salad*

Overall timing 40 minutes

Freezing Not suitable

To serve 4

3	Small onions	3
3	Apples	3
8 oz	Salami	225 g
2	Large gherkins	2
1 tbsp	Vinegar	15 ml
1 tbsp	Lemon juice	15 ml
3 tbsp	Oil	3x15 ml
	Salt and pepper	
	Pinch of caster sugar	
$\frac{1}{4}$ teasp	Celery or mustard seeds	1.25 ml

Peel onions and cut into thin rings. Peel, core and chop apples. Dice salami and gherkins. Put them all in a salad bowl and mix well together.

Combine all remaining ingredients to make the dressing and pour over salad, mixing it in well. Leave for 20 minutes to blend the flavours before serving, with crusty bread and butter.

Spinach and avocado salad

Overall timing 20 minutes plus cooling

Freezing Not suitable

To serve 6

8 oz	Spinach	225 g
½	Lettuce	½
1	Avocado	1
1 tbsp	Oil	15 ml
1 tbsp	Lemon juice	15 ml
	Salt and pepper	
4 tbsp	Thick mayonnaise	4x15 ml
1	Hard-boiled egg	1

Trim spinach and wash thoroughly. Put into a pan with no extra water, cover and cook for 8–10 minutes till tender. Turn into a colander and press with wooden spoon to remove excess liquid. Leave to cool.

Wash, trim and dry lettuce. Reserve six medium-size leaves and finely shred the rest. Cut avocado in half and remove stone. Scoop out flesh and chop finely. Place in bowl with cooled spinach, shredded lettuce, oil and lemon juice. Mix together well and season to taste.

Arrange reserved lettuce leaves on serving plate and divide spinach mixture between them. Pipe or spoon mayonnaise on top. Cut hard-boiled egg into wedges and use to garnish.

Avocado and pine nut salad

Overall timing 15 minutes plus chilling

Freezing Not suitable

To serve 2

1	Large ripe avocado	1
1½ teasp	Lemon juice	7.5 ml
2	Gherkins	2
1 tbsp	Pine nuts	15 ml
1½ tbsp	Olive oil	22.5 ml
	Salt and pepper	
1	Garlic clove	1
4	Fresh mint leaves	4
2 tbsp	Plain yogurt	2x15 ml

Cut the avocado in half and remove the stone. Peel away the skin, dice the flesh and put into a bowl. Sprinkle with lemon juice and toss lightly till the avocado is coated.

Slice the gherkins thinly and add to the avocado with the pine nuts. Sprinkle with oil, season and toss.

Peel and crush the garlic into a small bowl. Wash the mint leaves and shred finely. Add to the garlic with the yogurt and mix well. Pour over the avocado and toss lightly. Chill for 1 hour.

Divide salad between two individual dishes and serve immediately with crusty rolls.

Asparagus and potato salad

Overall timing 25 minutes plus chilling

Freezing Not suitable

To serve 4

1 lb	New potatoes	450 g
	Salt and pepper	
1	Small onion	1
1 tbsp	Lemon juice	15 ml
¼ pint	Thick mayonnaise	150 ml
12 oz	Can of asparagus spears or tips	340 g
1	Hard-boiled egg	1
4	Anchovy fillets	4
2 teasp	Drained capers	2x5 ml

Scrape the potatoes and cut into even-sized chunks. Cook in boiling salted water for about 5 minutes till tender. Drain and place in a large bowl.

Peel the onion and chop finely. Stir gently into the potatoes with the lemon juice and plenty of seasoning. Add the mayonnaise and mix well.

Drain the asparagus (if using spears, cut into 2 inch/5 cm lengths), and fold gently into the salad. Arrange in a serving dish.

Shell the hard-boiled egg and cut into quarters lengthways. Arrange round the dish. Arrange anchovy fillets in a cross on the salad. Garnish with capers and chill for 30 minutes before serving with wholemeal or black bread.

Esau's salad

Overall timing 1 hour plus cooling

Freezing Not suitable

To serve 6

1 lb	Continental lentils	450 g
2 oz	Smoked bacon	50 g
4 tbsp	Oil	4x15 ml
2	Frankfurters	2
1 tbsp	Vinegar	15 ml
1 teasp	Made mustard	5 ml
	Salt and pepper	
1	Onion	1
1	Green pepper	1
2	Tomatoes	2
2	Hard-boiled eggs	2
1 tbsp	Chopped parsley or chives	15 ml

Put lentils in a saucepan and add enough water just to cover. Bring to the boil, cover and simmer for about 1 hour till tender. Drain and leave to cool.

Derind bacon and cut into strips. Heat 1 tbsp (15 ml) of the oil in a frying pan, add bacon and cook until golden. Remove from pan and allow to cool.

Put frankfurters in a pan, cover with water and bring to the boil. Drain and leave to cool.

Meanwhile, beat together the rest of the oil, the vinegar, mustard and seasoning in a serving dish.

Peel and slice onion. Deseed and slice pepper. Put cooled lentils, bacon, onion and pepper into the dish with the dressing and mix well.

Cut tomatoes into wedges. Shell eggs and cut into wedges. Slice frankfurters. Arrange on top of lentil salad and sprinkle with parsley or chives. Serve with black bread.

Fennel and tomato salad

Overall timing 30 minutes

Freezing Not suitable

To serve 4

1	Large bulb of fennel	1
	Salt and pepper	
1	Onion	1
4	Tomatoes	4
3 tbsp	Oil	3x15 ml
1 tbsp	Wine vinegar or lemon juice	15 ml

Trim fennel. Cut into thin slices and blanch in boiling salted water for 5 minutes. Drain.

Peel onion and cut into rings. Slice tomatoes. Arrange fennel, onion and tomatoes in layers in salad bowl.

In another bowl, mix together oil, vinegar or lemon juice and seasoning. Pour over salad. Chill for 15 minutes before serving.

Fish and potato salad

Overall timing 25 minutes

Freezing Not suitable

To serve 4

1	Onion	1
1	Carrot	1
1	Stalk of celery	1
2 pints	Cold water	1.1 litres
1	Slice of lemon	1
1 lb	Boneless white fish	450 g
1½ lb	Waxy potatoes	700 g
1 tbsp	Wine vinegar	15 ml
½ teasp	Powdered mustard	2.5 ml
4 tbsp	Oil	4x15 ml
2 tbsp	Chopped parsley	2x15 ml
	Salt and pepper	

Peel and halve the onion; scrape and halve the carrot. Wash, trim and halve the celery. Put into a saucepan with the water and slice of lemon and bring slowly to the boil.

Meanwhile, cut the fish into 2 inch (5 cm) pieces. Peel the potatoes and cut into ¼ inch (6 mm) thick slices. Add the fish and potatoes to the boiling court bouillon, and bring almost back to boiling point. Skim off any scum, reduce the heat, cover and poach for 8–10 minutes till the potatoes and fish are tender.

Drain the fish and potatoes carefully in a colander, discarding the other vegetables and lemon.

Put the wine vinegar, mustard and oil into a serving dish with the parsley and mix well. Add the fish and potatoes and toss lightly till coated. Taste and add seasoning if necessary. Serve while still warm with a crisp green salad.

Florida salad

Overall timing 20 minutes plus chilling

Freezing Not suitable

To serve 4

1	Fresh red chilli	1
3 tbsp	Olive oil	3x15 ml
2 teasp	Vinegar	2x5 ml
	Salt and pepper	
4	Slices of fresh pineapple *or*	4
8 oz	Can of pineapple slices in natural juice	227 g
1	Red pepper	1
1	Yellow or green pepper	1
3	Medium bananas	3
1	Large avocado	1

Deseed and finely chop the chilli. Put into a bowl with the oil, vinegar and seasoning and mix well with a fork.

Peel and chop the fresh pineapple, or drain and chop the canned pineapple, and add to the bowl. Deseed and chop the peppers and add to the bowl. Peel and slice the bananas. Halve the avocado, discard the stone, peel and cut into chunks. Add to the bowl with the bananas.

Toss the salad lightly and put into a serving dish. Chill for 30 minutes before serving with chicken or seafood.

Vegetable and herb salad

Overall timing 30 minutes

Freezing Not suitable

To serve 6

1 lb	Potatoes	450 g
	Salt and pepper	
8 oz	Cauliflower	225 g
4 oz	Green beans	125 g
4 oz	Frozen peas	125 g
4 tbsp	Oil	4x15 ml
2 tbsp	Vinegar	2x15 ml
2 tbsp	Chopped fresh mixed herbs	2x15 ml

Scrub the potatoes and cut into small chunks. Place in a saucepan, cover with water, add salt and bring to the boil. Boil gently for 2 minutes.

Divide cauliflower into florets. Add to the pan. Bring back to the boil. Cut beans into 1 inch (2.5 cm) lengths and add to pan with the peas. Simmer gently for 5 minutes or until the potatoes are tender.

Meanwhile, whisk together the oil, vinegar, herbs and seasoning.

Drain the vegetables well and place in salad bowl. While still hot, pour dressing over the vegetables and toss well. Allow to cool before serving.

Egg and parsley mayonnaise

Overall timing 15 minutes plus chilling

Freezing Not suitable

To serve 4

8	Hard-boiled eggs	8
2	Spring onions	2
3 tbsp	Chopped parsley	3x15 ml
¼ pint	Thick mayonnaise	150 ml
¼ pint	Carton of soured cream	150 ml
	Salt and pepper	

Shell and slice the hard-boiled eggs. Trim the spring onions and slice thinly. Arrange half the eggs in a shallow dish and sprinkle the spring onions and 2 tbsp (2x15 ml) of the parsley over.

Mix together the mayonnaise and soured cream and add seasoning to taste. Spoon three-quarters of the mayonnaise mixture over the eggs. Arrange the remaining egg slices decoratively on top and spoon the rest of the mayonnaise between them.

Chill for 1 hour before serving. Sprinkle with the reserved parsley and serve with slices of crusty brown bread.

Walnut cabbage salad

Overall timing 30 minutes plus maceration

Freezing Not suitable

To serve 4

½	Red cabbage	½
4 tbsp	Walnut or olive oil	4x15 ml
2 tbsp	Lemon juice	2x15 ml
2	Large oranges	2
1	Large dessert apple	1
1	Banana	1
2 oz	Walnut halves	50 g
1 oz	Seedless raisins	25 g

Shred the cabbage and toss with the oil and lemon juice. Leave to macerate in the refrigerator for 1 hour.

Peel the oranges and separate into segments. Peel, core and chop the apple. Peel and thickly slice the banana. Add the fruit to the cabbage with the walnuts and raisins. Toss together well, then serve.

Asparagus and ham salad

Overall timing 20 minutes plus chilling

Freezing Not suitable

To serve 4

12 oz	Can of asparagus spears	340 g
4 oz	Cooked ham	125 g
4	Pineapple rings	4
	Lettuce leaves	
8 tbsp	Mayonnaise	8x15 ml
½ teasp	Brandy (optional)	2.5 ml
2 tbsp	Lemon juice	2x15 ml
	Pinch of cayenne	
Garnish		
2	Tomatoes	2
2	Hard-boiled eggs	2
	Chopped parsley	

Drain and chop asparagus and place in a mixing bowl. Dice ham. Chop the pineapple rings. Add both to asparagus and mix together well.

Place lettuce in the bottom of individual glasses. Divide asparagus mixture evenly between them.

Mix mayonnaise with brandy, if using, lemon juice and cayenne. Divide dressing equally between glasses. Garnish with chopped tomato, sliced hard-boiled egg and chopped parsley. Chill for 10 minutes before serving.

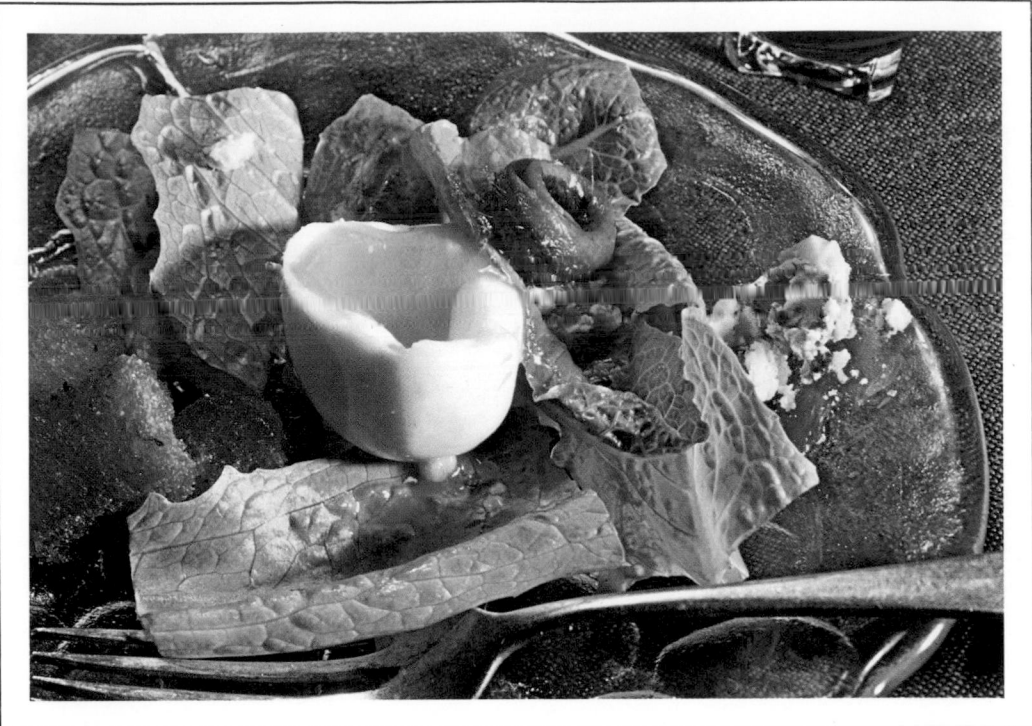

Caesar salad

Overall timing 15 minutes plus chilling

Freezing Not suitable

To serve 4

6 tbsp	Oil	6x15 ml
2 tbsp	Vinegar	2x15 ml
2	Garlic cloves	2
	Salt and pepper	
$\frac{1}{2}$	Cos lettuce	$\frac{1}{2}$
4	Eggs	4
2	Slices of bread	2
2 oz	Roquefort or Parmesan cheese	50g
4	Anchovy fillets	4

Beat together 4 tbsp (4x15 ml) of the oil, the vinegar, 1 peeled and crushed garlic clove and seasoning in a bowl. Cover and chill for 30 minutes.

Wash and dry lettuce. Tear leaves into pieces, put in a bowl and leave in the refrigerator to crisp.

Put eggs in a pan of cold water, bring to the boil and cook for 4–5 minutes. Drain and place in a bowl of cold water. Shell.

Rub bread slices all over with remaining halved garlic clove, then cut into 1 inch (2.5 cm) cubes. Fry in rest of oil till golden. Drain croûtons on kitchen paper.

Divide lettuce and croûtons between serving plates. Arrange eggs on top of lettuce, sprinkle over crumbled or grated cheese, then spoon dressing over. Garnish with rolled anchovy fillets and serve with crusty bread.

Carrot and cabbage slaw

Overall timing 15 minutes plus chilling

Freezing Not suitable

To serve 4

8 oz	Carrots	225 g
8 oz	White cabbage	225 g
4 tbsp	Wine vinegar	4x15 ml
5 tbsp	Oil	5x15 ml
½ teasp	Caraway seeds	2.5 ml
¼ teasp	Sugar	1.25 ml
	Salt and pepper	
2 oz	Streaky bacon	50 g
1	Large onion	1

Peel and grate carrots. Shred cabbage. In a salad bowl, mix together vinegar, 4 tbsp (4x15 ml) of the oil, caraway seeds, sugar and seasoning. Add carrots and cabbage and mix well. Cover the bowl and chill for 30 minutes.

Derind and chop the bacon. Heat remaining 1 tbsp (15ml) oil in frying pan and fry bacon for 3 minutes till crisp. Peel and finely chop onion, saving a few rings for garnish. Add chopped onion to pan and fry for a few minutes.

Remove salad from refrigerator. Put the hot bacon and onion mixture on top and garnish with onion rings. Serve with roasts or cold meat.

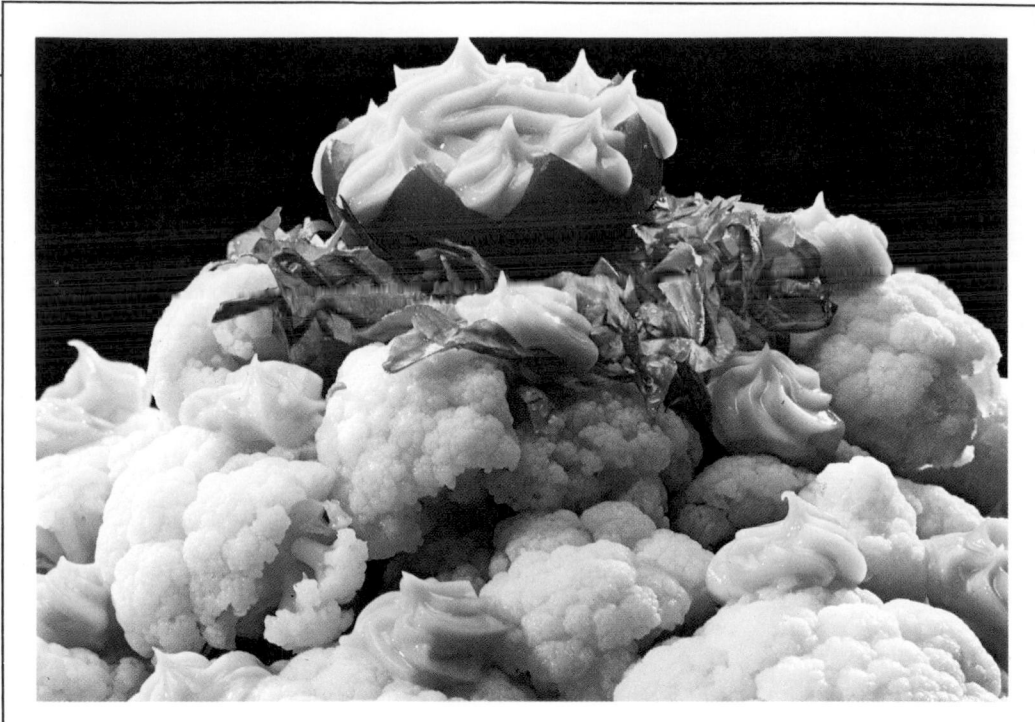

Cauliflower mayonnaise

Overall timing 30 minutes plus chilling

Freezing Not suitable

To serve 4

1	Large cauliflower	1
	Salt and pepper	
6 tbsp	Oil	6x15 ml
2 tbsp	Lemon juice	2x15 ml
3	Tomatoes	3
8	Lettuce leaves	8
¼ pint	Thick mayonnaise	150 ml

Divide cauliflower into large florets. Cook in boiling salted water for 5–10 minutes till just tender.

Meanwhile, put the oil, lemon juice and seasoning into a bowl and mix together with a fork.

Drain the cauliflower thoroughly and add to the dressing while still hot. Toss lightly, then chill for 1 hour.

Meanwhile, slice two of the tomatoes; cut the other in half in a zigzag pattern.

Arrange six lettuce leaves on a serving dish and pile the cauliflower on top. Shred the remaining lettuce and scatter over the cauliflower. Put a tomato half on top and arrange the tomato slices round the edge.

Pipe or spoon the mayonnaise into the tomato half and between the florets. Serve immediately with cold meats or smoked fish.

Chef's salad

Overall timing 20 minutes

Freezing Not suitable

To serve 4–6

1	Round lettuce	1
2	Heads of radicchio *or*	2
$\frac{1}{4}$	Red cabbage	$\frac{1}{4}$
4 oz	Cooked ham	125 g
3 oz	Gruyère or Emmenthal cheese	75 g
1	Small onion	1
2	Tomatoes	2
Dressing		
2 tbsp	Oil	2x15 ml
1 tbsp	Wine vinegar	15 ml
1 teasp	Dijon mustard or made English mustard	5 ml
	Salt and pepper	

Wash and dry lettuce. Line salad bowl with crisp whole leaves. Tear the rest into bite-size pieces and arrange on top.

Wash and dry radicchio and tear into pieces, or shred cabbage. Cut ham into $\frac{1}{2}$ inch (12.5 mm) dice. Slice cheese, then cut into small strips. Peel and slice onion and separate into individual rings. Cut tomatoes into wedges. Arrange all the prepared ingredients on top of the lettuce.

Mix together the dressing ingredients and pour over the salad. Toss thoroughly but gently. Garnish with garlic croûtons (see page 74), if liked.

Tunisian tuna salad

Overall timing 25 minutes plus chilling

Freezing Not suitable

To serve 6

2	Green peppers	2
1	Small onion	1
2x7 oz	Cans of tuna in oil	2x198 g
	Olive oil	
2 teasp	Red wine vinegar	2x5 ml
1 teasp	Lemon juice	5 ml
	Salt and pepper	
1	Garlic clove	1
4 oz	Gruyere or Cheddar cheese	125 g
4 oz	Stoned green olives	125 g
1 lb	Large firm tomatoes	450 g

Deseed the peppers and cut into thin strips. Peel the onion and slice thinly into rings.

Drain the oil from the tuna and put into a small bowl with enough olive oil to make it up to 4 tbsp (4x15 ml). Add the vinegar, lemon juice, seasoning and peeled and crushed garlic.

Flake the tuna; slice the cheese thickly, then cut into thin strips. Put into a large bowl with the onion, pepper and olives. Pour the dressing over and toss lightly till ingredients are evenly coated.

Wash and thinly slice the tomatoes and use to line the salad bowl. Arrange the tuna mixture on top, cover and chill for 30 minutes before serving.

Waldorf salad

Overall timing 15 minutes plus 1 hour refrigeration

Freezing Not suitable

To serve 4

4	Stalks of celery	4
8 oz	Dessert apples	225 g
1 tbsp	Lemon juice	15 ml
	Salt and pepper	
6 tbsp	Thick mayonnaise	6x15 ml
2 oz	Nuts	50 g

Chop celery. Peel, core and dice apples. Place in salad bowl with celery, lemon juice and a little salt. Chill for about 1 hour.

Remove from refrigerator and stir in mayonnaise, chopped nuts and seasoning to taste.

If serving this salad on a special occasion, divide mixture between hollowed-out apples that have been sprinkled with lemon juice. For a simpler, yet still effective presentation, serve on lettuce (shredded or leaves) in individual glass dishes and garnish with fine lemon slices.

Bean and herring salad

Overall timing 1½ hours

Freezing Not suitable

To serve 2

6 oz	Green beans	175 g
	Salt and pepper	
½ oz	Butter	15 g
2	Matjes herring fillets	2
2	Cooked potatoes	2
1	Onion	1
2 tbsp	Mayonnaise	2x15 ml
2 tbsp	Plain yogurt	2x15 ml
1 teasp	Lemon juice	5 ml
	Sugar	
	Chopped parsley	

Top and tail the beans and remove strings. Cut into short lengths. Put the beans into a saucepan of boiling salted water, add butter and cook for 10 minutes till just tender. Drain and leave to cool.

Slice the herrings and potatoes. Peel and finely chop the onion. Place in salad bowl and add herrings and potatoes. Lightly mix in beans.

Make the dressing by combining mayonnaise, yogurt, lemon juice and pepper and sugar to taste. Pour over the salad and chill for 1 hour. Serve garnished with chopped parsley.

Beetroot and apple salad

Overall timing 1 hour 40 minutes plus cooking

Freezing Not suitable

To serve 4–6

1¾ lb	Beetroot	750 g
	Salt	
4 tbsp	Oil	4x15 ml
2 tbsp	Wine vinegar or lemon juice	2x15 ml
1 teasp	Sugar	5 ml
8 oz	Dessert apples	225 g
1	Onion	1

Wash beetroot, then cut off tops. Take care not to pierce the skin when you are preparing beetroot or the colour will boil out, leaving them a rather washed out pink. Place prepared beetroot in saucepan and cover with water. Add a little salt, cover and simmer for 1¼ hours over a low heat. Leave to cool.

Drain beetroot, cut off root and pull off skin. Slice with a mandolin or fluted grater. Dry slices and put them in layers in a salad bowl.

Mix together oil, wine vinegar or lemon juice and sugar and pour over beetroot. Chill for 2 hours.

Peel, core and chop apples. Peel and finely chop onion. Mix into beetroot and serve before the beetroot has time to colour the apple and onion.

Buckling and potato salad

Overall timing 30 minutes

Freezing Not suitable

To serve 4-6

3	Buckling	3
8 oz	Cold boiled potatoes	225 g
8 oz	Red apples	225 g
2	Tomatoes	2
2	Hard-boiled eggs	2
	Sprig of dill or fennel	
Dressing		
4 tbsp	Olive oil	4x15 ml
3 tbsp	Lemon juice	3x15 ml
	Salt and pepper	

Slice buckling along backbone. Skin and fillet, then blanch in boiling water for 3 minutes. Break fish into large pieces and place in serving bowl.

Cut the potatoes into cubes and add to bowl. Core and dice apples. Add to fish and potatoes.

Mix the olive oil, lemon juice and seasoning together to make a dressing. Pour over the fish mixture. Toss carefully and leave for 15 minutes for the flavours to develop.

Wash tomatoes and cut into eighths. Shell and slice eggs and arrange with the tomatoes and herbs around the salad. Serve with hot, crusty bread.

Salade Béatrice

Overall timing 10 minutes plus chilling

Freezing Not suitable

To serve 4

1 lb	Cooked green beans	450 g
	Salt and pepper	
3 tbsp	Oil	3 x 15 ml
1 tbsp	White wine vinegar	15 ml
2	Tomatoes	2
1	Bunch of watercress	1
1	Hard-boiled egg yolk	1

Break or cut the beans into short lengths and put into a salad bowl. Season, add oil and vinegar and mix together well. Chill for 15 minutes.

Cut tomatoes into quarters and arrange around the edge of the salad bowl with the watercress.

Just before serving, garnish with sieved or finely chopped egg yolk. Toss salad at the table.

Salade niçoise

Overall timing 25 minutes

Freezing Not suitable

To serve 4

1 lb	Waxy potatoes	450 g
	Salt and pepper	
8 oz	Green beans	225 g
4 oz	Large black olives	125 g
2 tbsp	Drained capers	2x15 ml
1	Garlic clove	1
4 tbsp	Olive oil	4x15 ml
1 tbsp	Tarragon vinegar	15 ml
1 teasp	Lemon juice	5 ml
1 tbsp	Chopped parsley	15 ml
1	Large firm tomato	1
6	Anchovy fillets	6

Peel and dice the potatoes. Cook in boiling salted water for about 5 minutes till just tender. Top, tail and string the beans and cut into 1 inch (2.5 cm) lengths. Cook in another pan of boiling salted water for 5 minutes till tender.

Drain the vegetables and rinse under cold water. Drain thoroughly and put into a salad bowl. Add half the olives and the capers.

Peel and crush the garlic clove into a bowl. Add the oil, vinegar, lemon juice, parsley and pepper to taste and mix well, then pour over vegetables. Toss lightly till evenly coated.

Cut the tomato into thin wedges. Arrange on the salad with the remaining olives. Cut the anchovies into strips and arrange in a lattice on top of the salad. Serve immediately with French bread.

Raw mushroom salad

Overall timing 20 minutes plus chilling

Freezing Not suitable

To serve 4

12 oz	Button mushrooms	350 g
1 teasp	Lemon juice	5 ml
1 teasp	Made mustard	5 ml
2 tbsp	Single cream	2x15 ml
2 tbsp	Oil	2x15 ml
1½ teasp	White wine vinegar	7.5 ml
	Salt and pepper	
	Chopped parsley	

Thinly slice the mushrooms. Put into a salad bowl and sprinkle with the lemon juice.

Mix together the mustard, cream, oil, vinegar and seasoning. Pour this dressing over the mushrooms and toss carefully. Sprinkle chopped parsley on top. Chill for 30 minutes before serving.

Spanish salad

Overall timing 45 minutes plus 1 hour refrigeration

Freezing Not suitable

To serve 4

½	Cucumber	½
	Salt and pepper	
12 oz	Potatoes	350 g
12 oz	Can of asparagus spears	340 g
8 fl oz	Mayonnaise	220 ml
1 tbsp	French mustard	15 ml
½ teasp	Dried tarragon	2.5 ml
½	Red pepper	½

Peel and slice cucumber. Sprinkle with salt and chill for 1 hour.

Peel and dice potatoes, then cook in boiling salted water for 10 minutes. Drain and leave to cool.

Drain asparagus and dry spears on kitchen paper.

Mix together potatoes, mayonnaise, mustard, tarragon and seasoning and put into a shallow dish. Arrange asparagus on top like the spokes of a wheel. Drain cucumber slices and place one between each asparagus spear and one in the centre. Deseed and dice pepper and place on top of cucumber to add colour.

Sausage and potato salad v

Overall timing 25 minutes

Freezing Not suitable

To serve 2

12 oz	Medium-size new potatoes	350 g
	Salt and pepper	
1 tbsp	Dry white wine	15 ml
4–6 oz	German spicy sausage	125–175 g
1½ teasp	Chopped parsley	7.5 ml
½ teasp	Made mustard	2.5 ml
2 tbsp	Oil	2 x 15 ml
1½ teasp	Vinegar	7.5 ml
	Sprigs of parsley	

Scrub the potatoes, put into a saucepan, cover with cold salted water and bring to the boil. Simmer for about 15 minutes till tender. Drain and peel, then slice thickly and put into a serving dish. Sprinkle with the white wine.

Remove outer covering from the sausage and slice thickly. Add to the potatoes with the chopped parsley.

Mix the mustard, oil, pepper and vinegar together and pour over the salad. Toss gently. Garnish with sprigs of parsley and serve warm or cold.

Rice salad with anchovy dressing

Overall timing 40 minutes plus chilling

Freezing Not suitable

To serve 4

8 oz	Long grain rice	225 g
	Salt and pepper	
1	Can of anchovy fillets	1
2	Large hard-boiled eggs	2
1 teasp	Powdered mustard	5 ml
5 tbsp	Olive oil	5x15 ml
1	Carrot	1
1	Small onion	1
1	Green chilli	1
1	Red pepper	1
1	Small bulb of fennel	1
2 oz	Stoned black olives	50 g
1 teasp	Chopped chives	5 ml

Cook rice in boiling salted water for 15 minutes till tender. Drain and rinse under cold water to cool.

Drain anchovies and reserve half for garnish. Put the rest into a mortar and pound to a paste with the pestle. Shell and finely chop eggs. Add to mortar with mustard and pound together, gradually adding oil a few drops at a time. Season.

Peel carrot and cut shallow grooves at intervals along its length. Slice thinly and place in large bowl with rice.

Peel and finely chop onion; thinly slice chilli: deseed and slice pepper. Add these to the rice. Thinly slice fennel; chop fennel tops and add to salad. Toss lightly. Chill salad and dressing for 30 minutes.

Put salad into a serving dish and arrange reserved anchovies on top with olives and chives. Serve with dressing.

Greek salad

Overall timing 40 minutes including chilling

Freezing Not suitable

To serve 2

2	Large tomatoes	2
$\frac{1}{4}$	Cucumber	$\frac{1}{4}$
1	Small onion	1
2 oz	Black olives	50 g
8	Anchovy fillets	8
4 oz	Fetta or Wensleydale cheese	125 g
Dressing		
3 tbsp	Olive oil	3x15 ml
1 tbsp	Lemon juice	15 ml
	Salt and pepper	
	Pinch of dried marjoram	

Quarter tomatoes. Slice cucumber. Peel onion and cut into rings. Stone olives (optional). Roll up anchovy fillets. Cut cheese into chunks. Place all these ingredients in a serving bowl or divide them between two serving dishes.

To make the dressing, mix the oil and lemon juice with pinch of salt, pepper to taste and marjoram. Pour over salad, mix well and chill for 30 minutes before serving.

Another good alternative to Fetta is white Stilton – the important thing is to use a crumbly white cheese with a slightly sour taste. As in the authentic Greek version, it will absorb all the flavour of the oil dressing.

Kipper salad

Overall timing 20 minutes

Freezing Not suitable

To serve 4

4	Kipper fillets	4
4	Cold boiled potatoes	4
1	Cooked beetroot	1
1 tbsp	Chopped onion	15 ml
8 tbsp	Mayonnaise	8x15 ml
	Sprigs of parsley	

Place kippers upright in a jug, fill with boiling water and leave for 5 minutes. Drain, pat dry with kitchen paper, then chop into pieces. Cube potatoes and beetroot.

Put kippers, potatoes, beetroot and onion in salad bowl. Mix well. Spoon mayonnaise over and garnish with parsley sprigs.

Israeli sweet-sour salad

Overall timing 20 minutes plus chilling

Freezing Not suitable

To serve 4

2 tbsp	Sultanas	2x15 ml
1 lb	Carrots	450 g
4	Oranges	4
2	Avocados	4
2 tbsp	Lemon juice	2x15 ml
3 tbsp	Oil	3x15 ml
1 tbsp	Wine or cider vinegar	15 ml
	Salt and pepper	
	Ground ginger	

Put the sultanas into a bowl, cover with warm water and leave to soak.

Peel carrots and grate into serving dish. Add the juice of two of the oranges and mix well. Peel remaining oranges and separate into segments.

Peel avocados and remove stones. Cut flesh into chunks and sprinkle with lemon juice.

Drain sultanas and add to serving dish with oranges and avocados.

In a small bowl, beat the oil and vinegar with a pinch each of salt, pepper and ground ginger. Pour over salad and toss. Chill for 15 minutes before serving.

Fruity celeriac salad

Overall timing 45 minutes

Freezing Not suitable

To serve 4

8 oz	Celeriac	225 g
2	Apples	2
1	Orange	1
2 tbsp	Lemon juice	2x15 ml
2 oz	Cooked tongue	50 g
Dressing		
3 tbsp	Single cream	3x15 ml
5 tbsp	Plain yogurt	5x15 ml
$\frac{1}{2}$ teasp	Strong made mustard	2.5 ml
	Pinch of sugar	
	Salt and pepper	

Peel celeriac. Peel and core apples. Peel orange and roughly chop flesh. Grate celeriac and apples into a bowl, add orange and sprinkle with lemon juice. Cut tongue into thin strips and add to salad.

To make the dressing, mix together the cream, yogurt, mustard, sugar and seasoning. Add to salad, toss well and chill for 30 minutes before serving.

Tangy avocado salad

Overall timing 15 minutes plus chilling

Freezing Not suitable

To serve 4–6

2	Avocados	2
2	Dill pickles	2
2 oz	Pine nuts	50 g
1	Small onion	1
2 tbsp	Oil	2x15 ml
1 tbsp	Lemon juice	15 ml
	Salt and pepper	
2	Garlic cloves	2
1 tbsp	Chopped fresh mint	15 ml
$\frac{1}{2}$ pint	Plain yogurt	300 ml

Halve avocados and remove stones. Scoop out flesh and dice. Grate or chop pickles. Roughly chop pine nuts. Peel and finely chop onion.

Put prepared ingredients into serving dish and stir in oil, lemon juice and seasoning.

Peel and crush garlic and put into a bowl with mint and yogurt. Beat lightly with a fork. Pour over salad and mix in well. Chill for 1 hour.

Russian salad √

Overall timing 30 minutes

Freezing Not suitable

To serve 4

3	Medium potatoes	3
2	Carrots	2
4 oz	Green beans	125 g
2	Stalks of celery	2
	Salt and pepper	
4 oz	Frozen peas	125 g
2 tbsp	Capers	2x15 ml
	Juice of ½ lemon	
8 fl oz	Carton of double cream	227 ml
2	Hard-boiled eggs	2

Peel and dice potatoes and carrots. Top and tail beans and remove strings. Cut beans into small pieces. Trim and finely dice celery.

Place potatoes in boiling salted water and cook for 5 minutes. Remove with draining spoon, place in colander and rinse under cold water. Add carrots to pan and cook for 5 minutes. Remove and rinse. Add beans, peas and celery to pan and cook for 4 minutes. Remove and rinse.

Drain cooled vegetables and place in bowl with capers. Add lemon juice and salt and pepper. Pour cream over and mix carefully. Pile salad on to a serving plate.

Shell and quarter eggs and arrange round the edge of the plate.

Tunisian mixed salad

Overall timing 25 minutes plus chilling

Freezing Not suitable

To serve 4

1½ lb	Cooked waxy potatoes	700 g
8 oz	Cooked carrots	225 g
3	Canned artichoke hearts	3
6 oz	Cooked peas	175 g
2 tbsp	Drained capers	2x15 ml
12	Stoned black olives	12
12	Stoned green olives	12
4 tbsp	Olive oil	4x15 ml
2 tbsp	Lemon juice	2x15 ml
1 tbsp	Chopped parsley	15 ml
¼ teasp	Ground coriander	1.25 ml
	Salt and pepper	

Dice the potatoes and carrots. Drain the artichokes and cut into quarters. Put all the vegetables into a serving dish with the capers and olives.

Whisk the oil and lemon juice together with the parsley, coriander and plenty of seasoning. Pour the dressing over the salad and toss lightly. Chill for 30 minutes before serving with crusty bread.

Goat's cheese salad

Overall timing 1.5 minutes plus 1 hour chilling

Freezing Not suitable

To serve 4

12 oz	Goat's cheese	350 g
	Salt and pepper	
4 tbsp	Olive oil	4x15 ml
2 tbsp	Wine vinegar	2x15 ml
4	Stalks of celery	4
2 oz	Walnuts	50 g
	Fennel seed (optional)	

Slice cheese and put into serving bowl. Grind black pepper over it. Beat 2 tbsp (2x15 ml) oil and 1 tbsp (15 ml) vinegar together and pour over cheese.

Chop celery. Add celery and nuts to bowl. Toss lightly.

Beat together the rest of the oil and vinegar and pour over. Sprinkle with salt and crushed fennel seed, if used, and chill for 1 hour. Serve with crusty French bread.

Gouda salad

Overall timing 15 minutes

Freezing Not suitable

To serve 4–6

Salad		
1	Webb's lettuce	1
2 oz	Corn salad or watercress	50 g
1	Head of white chicory	1
4	Tomatoes	4
1	Hard-boiled egg	1
1	Onion	1
2 oz	Black olives	50 g
4 oz	Gouda cheese	125 g
Dressing		
2 tbsp	Oil	2x15 ml
1 tbsp	Wine vinegar	15 ml
1 tbsp	Chopped fresh fines herbes or	15 ml
1 teasp	Dried fines herbes	5 ml
	Salt and pepper	

Trim and wash lettuce and corn salad or watercress. Dry thoroughly. Trim, wash and shred chicory. Arrange lettuce leaves in salad bowl, scatter the chicory over and arrange corn salad or watercress in the centre.

Wipe and slice tomatoes. Shell and quarter hard-boiled egg. Peel and finely slice onion. Arrange on top of lettuce with the olives.

Cut cheese into thin matchstick strips. Sprinkle over top of salad.

To make dressing, put the oil, vinegar, herbs, salt and pepper into a bowl and mix well together. Pour over salad just before serving and toss.

Mimosa salad

Overall timing 15 minutes

Freezing Not suitable

To serve 4

3 tbsp	Single cream	3x15 ml
1 tbsp	Lemon juice	15 ml
	Salt and pepper	
1	Lettuce	1
1	Orange	1
4 oz	Black and white grapes	125 g
1	Banana	1
1	Hard-boiled egg yolk	1

In a salad bowl, mix together the cream, lemon juice and seasoning.

Wash and dry lettuce leaves. Peel the orange and cut into thin slices. Wash grapes. Peel and slice banana. Place the lettuce, orange, grapes and banana in salad bowl on top of dressing. Toss just before serving and garnish with sieved egg yolk.

Normandy salad

Overall timing 10 minutes plus chilling

Freezing Not suitable

To serve 4

1	Round lettuce	1
2	Dessert apples	2
$\frac{1}{2}$	Lemon	$\frac{1}{2}$
3 tbsp	Single cream	3x15 ml
1 tbsp	Cider vinegar	15 ml
	Grated nutmeg	
	Salt and pepper	
2 oz	Walnut halves	50 g

Wash and dry lettuce. Peel and core apples. Cut into thin rings. Rub cut surface of the lemon half over both sides of the apple rings to prevent browning. Place lettuce leaves and apple in a salad bowl and chill for 15 minutes.

Mix together the cream, cider vinegar, a pinch of grated nutmeg and seasoning in a small bowl. Just before serving, pour dressing over salad and toss. Garnish with walnut halves.

Pepper salad

Overall timing 30 minutes including cooling

Freezing Not suitable

To serve 4

4	Large red and yellow peppers	4
8 tbsp	Olive oil	8x15 ml
1 oz	Parmesan or strong Cheddar cheese	25 g
1 tbsp	Dried breadcrumbs	15 ml
2 tbsp	Capers	2x15 ml
	Pinch of dried marjoram or mint	
	Sea-salt	
1 tbsp	Vinegar	15 ml

Preheat the grill.

Halve peppers and place, rounded side up, under grill. Cook for a few minutes till skins are charred, then peel. Cut in half again and deseed.

Heat oil in frying pan and fry peppers gently for 7 minutes on each side. Arrange peppers in serving dish, alternating colours to achieve a spoked effect.

Grate cheese. Sprinkle over peppers with breadcrumbs, capers, marjoram or mint and sea-salt. Leave to cool slightly, then pour vinegar over. Serve straight away or cool and serve chilled.

Prawn and chicory salad

Overall timing 30 minutes plus chilling

Freezing Not suitable

To serve 4

2	Small heads of chicory	2
3 tbsp	Lemon juice	3x15 ml
4	Tomatoes	4
1	Fresh green chilli	1
8 oz	Shelled prawns	225 g
1 tbsp	White wine vinegar	15 ml
	Salt and pepper	
4 oz	Cream cheese	125 g
3 tbsp	Plain yogurt	3x15 ml
1	Garlic clove	1
$\frac{1}{4}$ teasp	Powdered mustard	1.25 ml
2 tbsp	Oil	2x15 ml

Remove any wilted outside leaves from the chicory, cut off the bases and scoop out the cores. Cut across into $\frac{1}{2}$ inch (12.5 mm) thick slices. Put into a bowl, add 2 tbsp (2x15 ml) of the lemon juice and toss.

Blanch, peel and quarter the tomatoes. Deseed and thinly slice the chilli. Put into a salad bowl with the tomatoes, prawns, vinegar and seasoning. Add the chicory and toss together lightly.

Put the cheese and yogurt into a bowl and beat till smooth. Add the peeled and crushed garlic, mustard, oil and remaining lemon juice. Season to taste and trickle over the salad. Chill for 15 minutes.

Just before serving, toss salad lightly till ingredients are evenly coated.

Prawn and egg salad

Overall timing 35 minutes

Freezing Not suitable

To serve 4–6

1	Lemon	1
12 oz	Shelled prawns	350 g
¼ teasp	Tabasco sauce	1.25 ml
	Salt and pepper	
4–6	Hard-boiled eggs	4–6
¼ pint	Thick mayonnaise	150 ml
1 teasp	Tomato purée	5 ml
½ teasp	Anchovy essence	2.5 ml
	Lettuce leaves	
2 oz	Black olives	50 g
4 oz	Unshelled prawns	125 g

Cut lemon in half across the segments; reserve one half. Finely grate rind of the other and reserve. Squeeze juice into a bowl.

Add shelled prawns to lemon juice with Tabasco sauce and seasoning. Leave to marinate for 15 minutes.

Meanwhile, shell eggs and cut in half lengthways. Divide the mayonnaise between two bowls. Add tomato purée and anchovy essence to one and grated lemon rind to the other.

Put the yellow mayonnaise mixture into a piping bag fitted with a star nozzle and pipe on to half the eggs. Pipe the pink mixture on to the remaining eggs.

Line a serving dish with lettuce leaves. Arrange the marinated prawns in a circle in the centre. Place eggs around the edge, alternating the colours, and garnish with the black olives.

Cut remaining lemon half into a basket shape and place in centre of the dish. Hang the whole unshelled prawns on the lemon and serve immediately.

Chicory and anchovy salad

Overall timing 15 minutes

Freezing Not suitable

To serve 4

4	Heads of chicory	4
4	Anchovy fillets	4
2 tbsp	Lemon juice	2x15 ml
½ teasp	Salt	2.5 ml
2 tbsp	Chopped parsley	2x15 ml
2	Hard-boiled egg yolks	2
Dressing		
1 tbsp	Wine or cider vinegar	15 ml
1 teasp	French mustard	5 ml
	Salt and pepper	
3 tbsp	Oil	3x15 ml

Trim and chop chicory. Drain and chop anchovy fillets. Place both in salad bowl. Add lemon juice and salt.

To make the dressing, mix together vinegar, mustard and seasoning in a small bowl. Gradually beat in oil until the dressing thickens.

Pour dressing over salad and toss. Sprinkle with chopped parsley and sieved or crumbled egg yolks.

Cockle salad

Overall timing 1 hour 20 minutes

Freezing Not suitable

To serve 4

2 lb	Fresh cockles	900 g
	Coarse salt	
1	Small onion	1
¼ pint	Dry white wine	150 ml
1	Lettuce	1
1 tbsp	Strong made mustard	15 ml
3 tbsp	Oil	3x15 ml
1 tbsp	Vinegar	15 ml
1 tbsp	Chopped parsley or chives	15 ml
	Salt and pepper	

Scrub cockles well under running cold water. Add as much coarse salt to a bowl of water as will dissolve and place the cockles in the water so that they open and release any sand or grit.

Remove cockles from bowl, then rinse under cold running water and drain.

Peel and chop onion. Put into saucepan with wine and boil till wine begins to evaporate. Add cockles and cook, stirring, for about 3 minutes till the shells open. Discard any that do not open. Strain the juice and reserve.

Line salad bowl with lettuce leaves. Remove cockles from shells and pile them on the lettuce. Mix together the reserved strained juice, mustard, oil, vinegar, parsley or chives and seasoning. Pour over cockles just before serving.

Crispy lettuce and cheese salad

Overall timing 15 minutes plus chilling

Freezing Not suitable

To serve 4–6

1	Large bulb of fennel	1
	Salt and pepper	
1	Cos lettuce	1
1	Onion	1
4 tbsp	Oil	4x15 ml
1 tbsp	Lemon juice	15 ml
3 oz	Grated Parmesan cheese	75 g
1 tbsp	Chopped parsley	15 ml

Trim fennel. Cut into small pieces and blanch in boiling salted water for 2 minutes. Drain.

Wash and dry lettuce. Shred finely. Peel and thinly slice onion. Put into a salad bowl with blanched fennel and lettuce and mix well together. Chill for 15 minutes to crisp.

Meanwhile, beat the oil and lemon juice together in a small bowl. Add salt and lots of freshly-ground black pepper.

Add Parmesan and chopped parsley to salad bowl and pour dressing over. Toss and serve immediately.

This salad makes a good accompaniment to many Italian-style dishes incorporating pasta and tomato sauce.

Cucumber and cider salad

Overall timing 10 minutes plus 1 hour chilling

Freezing Not suitable

To serve 4

2	Cucumbers	2
¼ pint	Dry cider	150 ml
3 tbsp	Chopped parsley	3x15 ml
1 teasp	Sugar	5 ml
	Salt and pepper	

Peel cucumbers. Cut them in half lengthways and scoop out the seeds with a spoon. Thinly slice cucumbers and put into a bowl.

Mix together the cider, parsley, sugar and seasoning. Pour over the cucumber and chill for at least 1 hour. Toss gently before serving.

Cucumber and fruit salad

Overall timing 15 minutes

Freezing Not suitable

To serve 2

$\frac{1}{2}$	Cucumber	$\frac{1}{2}$
1	Orange	1
$\frac{1}{4}$	Honeydew melon	$\frac{1}{4}$
2 oz	Black grapes	50 g
	Sprigs of dill	
Dressing		
3 tbsp	Soured cream	3x15 ml
$1\frac{1}{2}$ teasp	Lemon juice	7.5 ml
1 tbsp	Caster sugar	15 ml
1 tbsp	Chopped fresh dill	15 ml
	Salt and pepper	

Thinly slice cucumber. Put into a bowl. Peel orange, remove pips and cut flesh into pieces. Peel melon, remove seeds and cut flesh into thin slices. Add orange and melon to cucumber with grapes. Chill for 20 minutes.

To make the dressing, beat soured cream, lemon juice, sugar, dill and seasoning in a bowl.

Divide salad between two serving glasses and spoon a little of the dressing over each. Garnish with dill sprigs and keep in refrigerator till ready to serve.

Pears in chocolate sauce

Overall timing 40 minutes plus chilling

Freezing Not suitable

To serve 6

6	Firm pears	6
¾ pint	Water	400 ml
1 tbsp	Lemon juice	15 ml
4 oz	Caster sugar	125 g
1	Vanilla pod	1
3½ oz	Plain dessert chocolate	100 g
½ oz	Butter	15 g
	Vanilla ice cream	
	Crystallized violets (optional)	

Peel the pears and remove the stalks. Put the water, lemon juice, sugar and vanilla pod into a saucepan and heat gently till the sugar dissolves. Bring the syrup to the boil, add the pears and simmer for about 15 minutes till just tender. Leave pears to cool in the syrup, then lift them out with a draining spoon and chill for several hours. Reserve the syrup.

Break the chocolate into small pieces and put into a heatproof bowl with the butter. Stand the bowl over a pan of simmering water and stir till melted. Remove from the heat and beat in 2 tbsp (2x15 ml) of the pear syrup.

Arrange the pears in a serving dish and place scoops of ice cream between them. Decorate with crystallized violets, if liked. Spoon the chocolate sauce over the pears and serve.

Spicy fruit purée

Overall timing 1½ hours plus overnight maceration and cooling

Freezing Suitable

To serve 2

8 oz	Mixed dried fruit (figs, apricots, peaches, pears, prunes)	225 g
1 pint	Water	560 ml
3 oz	Granulated sugar	75 g
1	Apple	1
1 teasp	Ground cinnamon	5 ml
1 tbsp	Cornflour	15 ml

Put the dried fruit in a large bowl with three-quarters of the water and the sugar and leave to soak overnight.

Stone the prunes. Transfer fruit to a sauce-pan, add remaining water and bring to the boil. Cook over a low heat for about 15 minutes.

Peel, core and slice the apple and add with cinnamon to the pan. Cook for a further 45 minutes.

Drain fruit and return liquid to the pan. Push fruit through a sieve or blend to a purée, then return to the pan.

Mix cornflour with 1 tbsp (15 ml) cold water in a bowl, then stir into fruit mixture. Bring to the boil and boil for 5 minutes, stirring, until thick. Remove from heat and allow to cool. Pour into two serving glasses and chill for 2 hours before serving.

Spicy pumpkin dessert

Overall timing 45 minutes plus chilling

Freezing Not suitable

To serve 6

14 oz	Can of pumpkin purée	398 ml
2 oz	Butter	50 g
½ pint	Milk	300 ml
5 tbsp	Sugar	5 x 15 ml
3	Eggs	3
½ teasp	Ground cinnamon	2.5 ml
¼ teasp	Ground ginger	1.25 ml
¼ teasp	Grated nutmeg	1.25 ml
	Salt	
¼ pint	Carton of whipping cream	150 ml
	Glacé cherries	
	Candied angelica	

Preheat the oven to 350°F (180°C) Gas 4.

Put the pumpkin purée into a bowl and beat in the melted butter, milk, sugar, eggs, spices and a pinch of salt. In a separate bowl, whip the cream till it forms soft peaks, and fold into the mixture.

Pour the mixture into a greased 2 pint (1.1. litre) brioche mould and bake for about 30 minutes. Remove from the oven and leave to cool completely, then chill for 3–4 hours till firm.

Turn out the dessert on to a serving dish and decorate with glacé cherries and angelica. Serve with pouring cream.

Singapore coconut pudding

Overall timing 45 minutes plus 30 minutes soaking

Freezing Not suitable

To serve 4

3 oz	Desiccated coconut	75 g
4 fl oz	Boiling water	120 ml
8 oz	Caster sugar	225 g
3	Eggs	3
	Pinch of salt	
4 tbsp	Grated fresh coconut	4x15 ml

Put desiccated coconut in a bowl and pour over boiling water. Soak for 30 minutes, then pour through muslin or a fine sieve into a jug. Squeeze out liquid from coconut. Discard coconut.

Preheat the oven to 350°F (180°C) Gas 4.

Beat the sugar, eggs and salt till thick and foamy. Gradually add reserved coconut liquid.

Turn the mixture into a lightly greased 1 pint (560 ml) mould or four ovenproof dishes and place in roasting tin half-filled with hot water. Bake for 30 minutes.

Allow to cool, then invert over a serving plate to turn out. Chill until ready to serve, sprinkled with grated fresh coconut.

Upside-down cheesecake

Overall timing 1¼ hours plus chilling

Freezing Suitable

To serve 8

8 oz	Nice biscuits	225 g
4 oz	Butter	125 g
3 tbsp	Light soft brown sugar	3x15 ml
1 teasp	Ground cinnamon	5 ml
Filling		
12	Petits suisses	12
4 tbsp	Single cream	4x15 ml
4 teasp	Plain flour	4x5 ml
3 oz	Caster sugar	75 g
1 teasp	Vanilla essence	5 ml
1	Lemon	1
4	Eggs	4

Preheat the oven to 350°F (180°C) Gas 4.

Crush biscuits. Put butter, sugar and cinnamon into a saucepan and heat gently till sugar dissolves. Remove from heat and stir in biscuit crumbs. Press all but 4 tbsp (4x15 ml) over bottom and sides of greased 9 inch (23 cm) loose-bottomed flan tin.

Beat cheese with cream, flour, sugar, vanilla essence, grated rind of the lemon and 1 tbsp (15 ml) of the juice. Separate eggs. Beat yolks into the cheese mixture. Whisk whites till stiff and fold into cheese mixture. Pour into crumb case and smooth the top. Sprinkle remaining crumbs on top and press down lightly.

Bake for 45 minutes till set. Switch off the oven, open the door slightly and leave cheesecake in oven till cold. Chill for 2–3 hours, then invert on to a serving dish.

Raspberries jubilee

Overall timing 10 minutes plus 2 hours maceration

Freezing Not suitable

To serve 6

12 oz	Fresh or frozen raspberries	350 g
2–4 oz	Caster sugar	50–125 g
3 tbsp	Lemon juice	3x15 ml
1½ pints	Vanilla ice cream	850 ml
3 tbsp	Kirsch or brandy	3x15 ml

Put raspberries, sugar (add according to taste) and lemon juice in a bowl and macerate for 2 hours in the refrigerator. Chill serving plate.

Transfer raspberries and soaking juices to a saucepan and heat through gently.

Remove ice cream from freezer and place on serving plate. Spoon raspberries and syrup over. Warm Kirsch or brandy in ladle. Set alight and pour over ice cream. Serve immediately.

Marbled ice cream with chocolate sauce

Overall timing 20 minutes

Freezing Not suitable

To serve 4–6

2 teasp	Cornflour	2x5 ml
½ pint	Cold milk	300 ml
2 oz	Plain dessert chocolate or chocolate dots	50 g
2 tbsp	Granulated sugar	2x15 ml
½ teasp	Vanilla essence	2.5 ml
	Chocolate and vanilla ice cream	
4–6	Sponge fingers	4–6

Blend the cornflour in a bowl with a little milk. Put rest of milk in saucepan with the broken up chocolate or chocolate dots. Heat slowly until the chocolate melts, then stir in cornflour. Cook, stirring constantly, until the sauce comes to the boil and thickens. Stir in sugar and vanilla essence and cook, stirring, for 3 minutes more.

Turn ice cream out on to chilled serving plate and press sponge fingers into the top. Pour some of the sauce over. Serve immediately with the remaining sauce.

Rum and almond pastry cake

Overall timing $2\frac{1}{4}$ hours

Freezing Suitable: refresh from frozen in 350°F (180°C) Gas 4 oven for 30 minutes

Serves 6–8

13 oz	Frozen puff pastry	375 g
3 oz	Butter	75 g
3 oz	Caster sugar	75 g
2	Eggs	2
4 oz	Ground almonds	125 g
2 tbsp	Rum	2x15 ml
1 tbsp	Icing sugar	15 ml

Thaw pastry. To make filling, cream butter with sugar till light and fluffy. Beat in one whole egg and one egg yolk, reserving white. Fold in the ground almonds and rum. Cover and chill for 40 minutes.

Roll out dough to $\frac{1}{4}$ inch (6 mm) thickness. Cut out two rounds, one 8 inch (20 cm) and the other 9 inch (23 cm). Place smaller one on a dampened baking tray. Place almond filling in a ball in centre of dough round, leaving at least a 2 inch (5 cm) border all round. Brush edges with water.

Place second dough round on top and press edges together to seal. Using a knife, trim, then knock up edges and crimp. Chill for 15 minutes.

Preheat the oven to 450°F (230°C) Gas 8.

Brush pie with reserved beaten egg white. Leave for 1 minute, then brush again. Using the tip of a sharp knife, score top of pie to make a swirl pattern. Bake for 20 minutes, then reduce temperature to 400°F (200°C) Gas 6 and bake for a further 25 minutes, or until well risen and golden brown.

Remove from oven and increase heat to 475°F (240°C) Gas 9. Sift icing sugar over pie and return to oven to bake for 4–5 minutes to glaze. Remove from baking tray with palette knife and place on serving plate.

Strawberries and cream

Overall timing 15 minutes plus chilling

Freezing Not suitable

To serve 4

1 lb	Strawberries	450 g
Crème Chantilly		
8 fl oz	Carton of double cream	227 ml
¼ teasp	Vanilla essence	1.25 ml
	Icing sugar	

Hull and wipe the strawberries. Divide between individual serving dishes and chill for 1 hour.

Whip the cream till stiff peaks form, then fold in the vanilla essence and sugar to taste. Pipe the cream on top of the strawberries and serve immediately

Variation

Sprinkle the strawberries with fresh orange juice, or an orange liqueur such as Cointreau, before chilling.

Honey and lemon cheesecake

Overall timing 1¼ hours plus cooling

Freezing Suitable

To serve 12

6 oz	Rich shortcrust pastry	175 g
2	Eggs	2
1 lb	Curd cheese	450 g
6 tbsp	Thick honey	6x15 ml
2	Lemons	2
4 oz	Sultanas	125 g

Preheat the oven to 400°F (200°C) Gas 6.

Roll out dough and use to line 8½ inch (22 cm) loose-bottomed flan tin, reserving any trimmings. Prick bottom. Bake blind for 10 minutes, then remove from oven and reduce temperature to 350°F (180°C) Gas 4.

Separate the eggs. Put the yolks into a bowl with the cheese, honey and the grated rind of one of the lemons. Squeeze juice from both lemons and add to the bowl with the sultanas. Mix well.

In another bowl, whisk the egg whites to soft peaks and fold into the cheese mixture with a metal spoon. Pour into flan case and smooth the surface.

Roll out dough trimmings and cut into thin strips with a pastry wheel. Arrange in a lattice pattern over the filling. Bake for 50–55 minutes till set. Cool in tin, then turn out and serve cold.

Strawberries melba

Overall timing 15 minutes plus maceration

Freezing Not suitable

To serve 4–6

1 lb	Strawberries	450 g
4 oz	Raspberries	125 g
4 tbsp	Caster sugar	4x15 ml
2 teasp	Lemon juice	2x5 ml
1 oz	Slivered almonds	25 g

Hull the strawberries and pile in a serving dish.

Sieve the raspberries, then stir in the sugar and lemon juice until the sugar has dissolved. Pour over the strawberries and toss gently to coat. Leave to macerate for 1 hour.

Scatter the almonds over the top and serve.

Peach sundae

Overall timing 40 minutes plus maceration

Freezing Not suitable

To serve 2

2	Large ripe peaches	2
1 tbsp	Maraschino or peach brandy	15 ml
1½ oz	Caster sugar	40 g
1 tbsp	Apricot jam	15 ml
	Peach or vanilla ice cream	

Peel, halve and stone one of the peaches. Roughly chop the flesh and put into a bowl with the Maraschino or peach brandy and sugar. Macerate in the refrigerator for 30 minutes.

In a saucepan, melt the apricot jam with 1 tbsp (15 ml) of macerating liquid. Peel, halve and stone remaining peach. Divide chopped fruit and juices between two serving dishes and top each with cubes of ice cream and a peach half. Spoon the warmed jam over and serve immediately.

Pineapple jelly cream

Overall timing 20 minutes plus chilling

Freezing Suitable

To serve 2

½	Pineapple jelly tablet	½
¼ pint	Cold water	150 ml
7 oz	Canned crushed pineapple	200 g
6 tbsp	Whipping cream	6×15 ml
1	Egg white	1

Break up the jelly tablet and put into a small saucepan with half the water. Heat gently, stirring, till the jelly melts, then remove from heat.

Add the crushed pineapple and remaining water, mix well and pour into a large bowl. Chill till beginning to set.

Whip the cream till soft peaks form. Whisk the egg white till stiff but not dry. Fold the cream into the pineapple jelly mixture with a metal spoon, then carefully fold in the egg white.

Pour into two small dishes, smooth the top and chill till lightly set.

Clementines niçoise

Overall timing 15 minutes plus 2 hours maceration

Freezing Not suitable

To serve 8

8	Large clementines	8
1	Peach	1
4 oz	Cherries	125 g
8 oz	Can of pineapple rings	227 g
2 oz	Caster sugar	50 g
2 tbsp	Cointreau	2x15 ml
	Vanilla ice cream	

Slice the top off each clementine with a sharp knife and reserve. Scoop out the flesh with a teaspoon, taking care not to break the shell. Cover the empty shells and the tops and chill.

Cut the flesh into neat pieces, discarding the pips and pith. Peel the peach, cut in half and discard the stone. Cut into cubes. Stone the cherries, then chop flesh. Drain the pineapple and cut into pieces.

Put all the fruit into a bowl with the sugar and liqueur and leave to macerate for 2 hours.

Remove clementine shells and tops from the refrigerator. Divide the fruit and juices between the shells, add a scoop of ice cream and place the lids on top. Serve immediately in individual glass dishes.

Clementine rice mould

Overall timing 1¼ hours plus cooling

Freezing Not suitable

To serve 4–6

4 oz	Pudding rice	125 g
5	Clementines	5
¾ pint	Milk	400 ml
1 teasp	Vanilla essence	5 ml
	Salt	
4 oz	Caster sugar	125 g
1	Egg	1
1 oz	Butter	25 g
	Candied angelica	
Syrup		
¼ pint	Water	150 ml
3 oz	Sugar	75 g

Put the rice in a large saucepan of water, bring to the boil and boil for 5 minutes. Drain well.

Finely chop the peel and flesh of one clementine. Put into a saucepan with milk and bring almost to the boil. Remove from the heat, cover and leave to infuse for 10 minutes. Strain milk and return to pan. Add vanilla essence, a pinch of salt and rice. Cook gently, stirring occasionally, for 25–30 minutes till all milk has been absorbed. Add sugar and cook for a further 5 minutes.

Lightly beat egg. Remove cooked rice from heat and mix in egg and butter. Pour into a greased 2 pint (1.1 litre) soufflé dish. Cool, then chill for 2–3 hours.

To make syrup, put water and sugar into a saucepan and heat gently, stirring, till sugar has dissolved. Cut remaining clementines into wedges and add to syrup. Boil gently for 25 minutes till tender and syrup has caramelized.

Turn out rice mould onto serving plate. Arrange clementine wedges and angelica on top and around sides. Spoon over any remaining caramel, if liked, and serve with cream.

Coconut milk jelly

Overall timing 1 hour plus overnight chilling

Freezing Not suitable

To serve 6–8

1	Fresh coconut	1
	Milk	
	Pinch of salt	
7 oz	Caster sugar	200 g
½ teasp	Vanilla essence	2.5 ml
5 teasp	Powdered gelatine	5x5 ml

Use clean nail and hammer to pierce black "eyes" of coconut. Drain any milk inside into a measuring jug. Remove white flesh, but not inner rind, with grapefruit knife and grate.

Add sufficient milk to the coconut milk to make up to 1¾ pints (1 litre). Put milk in a saucepan with the salt, sugar and grated coconut and bring to the boil. Remove pan from heat, stir in vanilla essence and leave to cool.

Meanwhile, dissolve the gelatine in 3 tbsp (3x15 ml) cold water in a small bowl.

Stir gelatine into coconut mixture. Pour into a dampened 2 pint (1.1 litre) decorative jelly mould. Chill overnight.

To turn out, dip mould bottom into hot water for a few seconds, then invert jelly on to serving plate, tapping mould sharply so jelly slides out intact. Serve with coconut macaroons or biscuits.

Coffee water ice

Overall timing 2 hours

Freezing See method

To serve 6–8

9 oz	Granulated sugar	250 g
1 tbsp	Vanilla sugar	15 ml
1 pint	Water	560 ml
8 teasp	Instant coffee granules	8x5 ml
½ pint	Carton of whipping cream	300 ml
	Peppermint essence (optional)	

Put granulated and vanilla sugar and water in a saucepan. Stir until sugar has completely dissolved, then bring to the boil and boil for 5 minutes. Skim if necessary. Stir in the coffee granules and remove pan from heat. Allow mixture to cool completely.

Pour coffee mixture through a fine sieve or muslin-lined sieve into a freezer tray. Place in freezer or freezing compartment of refrigerator and leave for about 1 hour or until the mixture forms a granular mass. Do not stir.

In a bowl whip cream till just holding soft peaks, then add a few drops of peppermint essence, if using, to taste. Scrape out contents of freezer tray with a fork and divide ice between chilled serving glasses. Top each glass with peppermint-flavoured cream and serve with biscuits.

Rum and apricot pudding cake

Overall timing 55 minutes

Freezing Not suitable

To serve 6

1 pint	Milk	560 ml
½ teasp	Vanilla essence	2.5 ml
4	Eggs	4
4 tbsp	Caster sugar	4x15 ml
4 oz	Sponge cake	125 g
2 tbsp	Rum	2x15 ml
4 oz	Chopped glacé fruits	125 g
1 oz	Butter	25 g
8 oz	Apricot jam	225 g

Preheat the oven to 375°F (190°C) Gas 5.

Put the milk and vanilla essence into a saucepan and bring to the boil. Meanwhile, separate the eggs. Add the sugar to the yolks and beat together with a fork. Pour the hot milk over the yolks, stirring constantly.

Crumble the sponge cake into a bowl. Strain the custard over the cake and mix in half the rum, the glacé fruits and butter. Leave to cool.

Whisk the egg whites till stiff. Fold into the crumb mixture with a metal spoon. Pour the mixture into a greased and lined 2 pint (1.1 litre) soufflé dish and smooth the top. Bake for about 35–40 minutes till well risen and golden.

Put the apricot jam into a saucepan with remaining rum and heat gently till melted.

Serve the cake hot from the dish, with the apricot sauce separately in a sauceboat. Or, leave the cake to cool completely and turn out on to a serving dish. Pour the hot apricot sauce on top and serve immediately.

Sherry trifle

Overall timing 1½ hours including chilling time

Freezing Not suitable

To serve 6–8

1 pint	Milk	560 ml
3 tbsp	Custard powder	3x15 ml
2 tbsp	Sugar	2x15 ml
6 oz	Leftover sponge cake	175 g
2 tbsp	Raspberry jam	2x15 ml
1 lb 13 oz	Can of sliced peaches	822 g
6 tbsp	Sherry	6x15 ml
¼ pint	Carton of double or whipping cream	150 ml
1 oz	Toasted split almonds	25 g

Blend 6 tbsp (6x15 ml) of the milk with the custard powder and sugar. Bring remaining milk to the boil, then pour on to powder and stir well. Return to pan and bring back to the boil, stirring continuously until thickened. Put to one side to cool, covering surface with wet greaseproof to prevent a skin forming.

Cut sponge into small pieces and spread with jam. Arrange around the bottom and sides of serving dish.

Drain peaches. Mix 3 tbsp (3x15 ml) of syrup from can with the sherry and sprinkle over the sponge. Reserve a few peaches for decoration and arrange the rest on top of sponge.

Remove greaseproof paper and beat cooled custard well. Pour over fruit and chill for 1 hour.

Whip cream until stiff, then pipe on to trifle. Decorate with reserved peaches and sprinkle with toasted almonds.

Lemon sherbet

Overall timing 20 minutes plus freezing

Freezing See method

To serve 6

8 oz	Caster sugar	225 g
1 pint	Water	560 ml
¼ pint	Fresh lemon juice	150 ml
1	Egg white	1

Put the sugar and water in a pan and heat slowly, stirring until sugar dissolves. Bring to the boil and simmer for 10 minutes without stirring – do not let the syrup colour. Remove from heat and leave to cool.

Add lemon juice to syrup, then strain into freezer tray and freeze until mushy.

Remove mixture from freezer, turn into a bowl and beat well to break down crystals. Whisk egg white till soft peaks form. Fold into frozen mixture. Return to freezer tray and freeze till firm.

Plum crumb pudding

Overall timing 1½ hours plus chilling

Freezing Not suitable

To serve 8

4 oz	Sponge cake	125 g
3	Eggs	3
2 oz	Caster sugar	50 g
1 pint	Milk	560 ml
1 oz	Butter	25 g
	Grated rind of 1 lemon	
½ teasp	Ground cinnamon	2.5 ml
1 lb	Red plums	450 g

Preheat oven to 350°F (180°C) Gas 4. Grease and base-line a 9 inch (23 cm) springform tin.

Crumble the cake into a bowl. Separate two of the eggs, putting the yolks and remaining whole egg into a bowl with the sugar. Put the milk and butter into a saucepan and bring almost to the boil.

Beat the yolks and sugar together and pour the milk on to them, stirring constantly. Strain over the cake crumbs. Add the lemon rind and cinnamon, mix well and leave to stand for 15 minutes.

Meanwhile, wash and halve the plums, discarding the stones. Dry thoroughly on kitchen paper.

Whisk the 2 egg whites in a large bowl till stiff but not dry and fold into the crumb mixture with a metal spoon. Pour the mixture into the tin.

Arrange the plums cut sides down on the mixture and bake in the centre of the oven for about 50 minutes till set.

Remove from the oven and leave to cool in the tin, then chill for 3–4 hours. Remove pudding from tin and place on a serving dish. Serve cut into slices, with pouring cream.

Loganberry jelly ring

Overall timing 25 minutes plus chilling

Freezing Suitable

To serve 6

14½ oz	Can of loganberries	411 g
1	Raspberry jelly tablet	1
¼ pint	Carton of whipping cream	150 ml
	Langue de chat biscuits	

Drain loganberries, reserving syrup, and press through a sieve. Make up jelly, using loganberry syrup as part of the required amount of liquid. Stir in sieved fruit and leave to cool and set slightly.

Whip cream and fold into berry mixture, then pour into dampened 1½ pint (850 ml) ring mould. Chill till firm (2–4 hours). Chill serving plate at the same time.

Dip the mould in hot water to loosen, turn out on to chilled serving plate and arrange biscuits in centre of ring just before serving.

Chocolate mousse

Overall timing 15 minutes plus 3 hours chilling

Freezing Not suitable

To serve 4

1	Orange	1
3½ oz	Plain chocolate	100 g
1 oz	Butter	25 g
4	Eggs	4
	Pinch of salt	

Grate the orange rind finely, being careful not to remove any pith. Break the chocolate into pieces and melt in the top half of a double saucepan, or in a heatproof bowl over gently boiling water. Immediately the chocolate has melted pour into a heavy-based pan and add the butter and orange rind.

Separate the eggs. Add the yolks to the chocolate, stirring vigorously with a wooden spoon to prevent the mixture from boiling. Remove from heat. Cool.

Add pinch of salt to egg whites and whisk till stiff peaks form. Fold one or two spoonfuls into the chocolate mixture, to make it more liquid, then gently fold in the rest of the whites with a spatula or metal spoon. Take care not to let the mixture become flat and heavy.

Pour into a serving bowl and chill for 3 hours before serving.

Blackcurrant sorbet

Overall timing 4½ hours including refrigeration

Freezing See method

To serve 8

2 lb	Blackcurrants	900 g
	Blackcurrant cordial or liqueur	
9 oz	Caster sugar	250 g
2	Egg whites	2

Reserve a handful of blackcurrants, and put the rest through a food mill or sieve to make a purée. Measure the purée – you should have about 1 pint (560 ml). Top up with blackcurrant cordial or liqueur and/or water if necessary.

Add the sugar to the purée and mix well to dissolve sugar. Pour into a freezer tray and freeze for about 2 hours till mushy.

Beat the egg whites till stiff. Turn blackcurrant mixture into a bowl, mash lightly with a fork, then fold in the whisked egg whites, stirring to distribute evenly through purée. Turn into lightly oiled or dampened 1½ pint (850 ml) shallow container or 1¾ pint (1 litre) mould. Freeze for 2 hours till firmly set.

Immerse mould in hot water up to the rim, then quickly turn sorbet out on to a serving dish. Decorate sorbet with remaining blackcurrants, and allow to soften at room temperature for 20 minutes before serving.

Glacé fruit bombe

Overall timing 15 minutes plus maceration and freezing

Freezing See method

To serve 6–8

4 oz	Chopped glacé fruit	125 g
4 tbsp	Apricot brandy or sweet sherry	4x15 ml
1¾ pints	Non-dairy vanilla ice cream	1 litre
8 oz	Apricot jam	225 g

Put a 2 lb (900 g) loaf tin in the freezer or freezing compartment of the refrigerator. Place fruit in a bowl, add apricot brandy or sherry and leave to macerate for 30 minutes.

Put ice cream into a bowl, add fruit and liqueur and quickly mix well with a wooden spoon.

Remove tin from freezer and coat bottom and sides with a thick layer of the ice cream mixture. Spoon jam into the centre of the tin, then cover with remaining ice cream. Smooth surface with a dampened knife.

Freeze for at least 2 hours. Turn out of tin and cut into slices to serve.

Coffee charlotte

Overall timing 50 minutes plus chilling

Freezing Suitable

To serve 8

2 tbsp	Brandy	2x15 ml
30	Sponge fingers	30
5 oz	Caster sugar	150 g
$\frac{1}{4}$ pint	Strong black coffee	150 ml
2 teasp	Powdered gelatine	2x5 ml
4	Egg yolks	4
2 tbsp	Vanilla sugar	2x15 ml
$\frac{1}{2}$ pint	Carton of double cream	300 ml
15	Sugar coffee beans	15

Mix brandy with $\frac{1}{4}$ pint (150 ml) water in a shallow dish. Dip sponge fingers quickly in mixture to moisten them, then use to line sides of greased 10 inch (25 cm) springform tin. Place biscuits upright, sugared sides against tin, and trim ends to height of tin. Press lightly into place.

Put caster sugar and 3 tbsp (3x15 ml) water in heavy-based saucepan. Stir to dissolve sugar, then heat until golden brown. Stir in coffee and simmer for 2 minutes till caramel dissolves. Cool.

Dissolve gelatine in 2 tbsp (2x15 ml) cold water.

Put egg yolks and vanilla sugar in a bowl over a pan of hot water and whisk together till light and foamy. Stir coffee caramel into egg mixture and whisk till it starts to thicken. Stir in gelatine, then leave to cool until just on the point of setting.

Whip two-thirds of the cream until it holds soft peaks. Using a metal spoon, fold lightly into coffee mixture. Pour into centre of sponge finger-lined tin and chill till set.

Unclip tin and carefully transfer charlotte to a serving plate. Whip remaining cream until it holds stiff peaks. Pipe 15 rosettes round edge of charlotte. Place a coffee bean on top of each one. Pipe smaller rosettes round base.

Strawberry vacherin

Overall timing 2¼ hours plus cooling

Freezing Not suitable

To serve 8

6	Egg whites	6
12 oz	Caster sugar	350 g
1 lb	Strawberries	450 g
Crème Chantilly		
½ pint	Carton of double cream	284 ml
1 tbsp	Cold milk	15 ml
1	Ice cube	1
1 tbsp	Caster sugar	15 ml
¼ teasp	Vanilla essence	1.25 ml

Preheat the oven to 300°F (150°C) Gas 2.

Line two baking trays with non-stick paper. Draw a 10 inch (25 cm) square on one, and a 6 inch (15 cm) square on the other.

Whisk egg whites till stiff and dry. Sprinkle over 2 tbsp (2x15 ml) of the sugar and whisk in, then gradually whisk in remaining sugar to make a stiff, glossy meringue.

Using the marked squares as a guide, put large spoonfuls of meringue on to paper to make two squares with scalloped edges. Swirl into peaks. Place large square in centre of oven with small square below. Bake for about 1¼ hours till slightly browned and crisp. Cool.

Meanwhile, hull strawberries. To make the Crème Chantilly, whip cream with milk, ice cube, sugar and vanilla essence till it forms soft peaks. Chill till required.

Just before serving, carefully peel the paper from the meringue squares and place the large one on a flat board or serving dish. Spread or pipe two-thirds of the Crème Chantilly over and arrange two-thirds of the strawberries on top. Place the small meringue square on top and spread with the remaining crème. Decorate with remaining strawberries and serve immediately.

Champagne sorbet

Overall timing 20 minutes plus freezing

Freezing See method

To serve 6

8 oz	Caster sugar	225 g
1 pint	Water	560 ml
¼ pint	Champagne or dry cider	150 ml
1 tbsp	Lemon juice	15 ml
2	Egg whites	2

Put the sugar and water in a pan and heat gently, stirring until sugar dissolves. Bring to the boil and simmer for 10 minutes without stirring. Do not let the mixture colour. Remove from the heat and cool.

Add the Champagne or cider and lemon juice to the syrup, then pour into a 2 pint (1.1 litre) freezer tray. Freeze till mushy.

Remove mixture from freezer, turn into a bowl and beat well to break down any ice crystals. Whisk the egg whites until stiff and fold into the mixture. Return to the freezer tray and freeze till firm.

Strawberry milk ring

Overall timing 30 minutes plus setting

Freezing Not suitable

To serve 6

1	Lemon	1
5 teasp	Powdered gelatine	5x5ml
5 tbsp	Caster sugar	5x15ml
1	Large can of evaporated milk	1
½ pint	Buttermilk	300ml
	Pink food colouring	
1	Egg white	1
¼ pint	Carton of double cream	150ml
1lb	Fresh strawberries	450g

Grate the rind from the lemon and reserve. Squeeze out the juice and place in a small bowl. Sprinkle the gelatine over and dissolve. Stir in the sugar. Allow to cool slightly.

Pour the well-chilled evaporated milk into a large bowl and whisk till very thick and foamy. Whisk in the buttermilk, gelatine mixture, reserved lemon rind and a few drops of food colouring. Pour into a dampened 2 pint (1.1 litre) ring mould and chill for 3–4 hours till set.

Dip the mould up to the rim in hot water for a few seconds and turn out on to a serving plate.

Whisk the egg white till stiff. Whip the cream till stiff and fold into the whisked egg white. Hull the strawberries and pile half in the centre of the ring. Pipe the cream mixture on top and around the base of the ring. Decorate with the remaining strawberries and serve immediately.

Crème caramel

Overall timing 45 minutes

Freezing Not suitable

To serve 6

1 pint	Milk	560 ml
½	Vanilla pod	½
1	Piece lemon rind	1
4	Eggs	4
4 oz	Caster sugar	125 g

Preheat the oven to 350°F (180°C) Gas 4.

Put the milk, vanilla pod and lemon rind in a saucepan and bring to the boil. Remove from heat and lift out the vanilla pod and lemon rind.

In a bowl, beat eggs with half sugar and gradually pour in the hot milk, stirring constantly.

Melt the remaining sugar in a saucepan over a moderate heat till golden brown. Divide between six small moulds and turn them so the caramel coats the bottoms and sides.

Strain the custard mixture into the moulds and place them in a roasting tin half-filled with hot water. Bake for 45 minutes till set. Allow to cool in moulds and chill before turning out.

Blackberry special

Overall timing 4 hours including chilling but not cooling

Freezing Not suitable

To serve 6-8

6 oz	Plain flour	150 g
2	Egg yolks	2
3 oz	Caster sugar	75 g
3 oz	Butter	75 g
¼ teasp	Salt	1.25 ml
Filling		
1 lb	Blackberries	450 g
2 oz	Chopped mixed peel	50 g
3	Egg whites	3
6 oz	Caster sugar	175 g
6 oz	Ground almonds	175 g
1 teasp	Grated lemon rind	5 ml
¼ teasp	Ground cinnamon	1.25 ml
2 oz	Flaked almonds	25 g

Sift flour into a mixing bowl. Add egg yolks, sugar, small flakes of butter and salt. Mix to a pliable dough. Chill for 2 hours.

Preheat the oven to 375°F (190°C) Gas 5.

Roll out dough and use to line 9 inch (23 cm) flan ring on a baking tray. Bake blind for 15 minutes.

Remove flan case from oven and reduce heat to 300°F (150°C) Gas 2. Remove foil and beans. Add blackberries to flan and sprinkle with peel.

Whisk egg whites until very stiff. Fold in sugar followed by ground almonds, lemon rind and cinnamon. Put 3 tbsp (3x15 ml) of the mixture in a piping bag fitted with a large rose nozzle. Spread the remainder over blackberries. Sprinkle edges of flan with flaked almonds and decorate the top with swirls of piped egg white mixture.

Bake for 1 hour 10 minutes. Remove from oven and cut flan into wedges before it cools. When cold, remove flan ring and serve.

Caramel cornmeal mould

Overall timing 1 hour

Freezing Not suitable

To serve 6–8

¾ pint	Milk	400 ml
	Pinch of salt	
4 oz	Sugar	125 g
1	Bay leaf	1
18	Sugar lumps	18
9 tbsp	Warm water	9x15 ml
1 tbsp	Lemon juice	15 ml
5	Eggs	5
3 oz	Fine maizemeal	75 g

Preheat the oven to 400°F (200°C) Gas 6.

Put the milk in a saucepan with the salt, sugar and bay leaf. Bring to the boil. Remove from the heat, cover and leave to infuse for 10 minutes.

Put the sugar lumps, water and lemon juice into a small saucepan and heat gently, stirring till sugar dissolves. Bring to the boil and boil without stirring till a deep golden caramel colour. Watch pan carefully to see that caramel does not burn. Pour into an 8 inch (20 cm) round deep cake tin, turning it so that the bottom and sides are coated with the caramel.

Separate the eggs. Put the egg yolks and maizemeal into a bowl and mix together with a wooden spoon. Remove bay leaf from the milk. Gradually pour the hot milk on to the egg yolks, stirring continuously. Whisk the egg whites till stiff and fold into the mixture.

Pour the mixture into the prepared tin and place in a roasting tin containing 1 inch (2.5 cm) hot water. Bake for 35–40 minutes. While still warm, run knife round edge of mould and invert on to serving plate. Serve warm or cold, with pouring cream.

Cider and grape ring

Overall timing 15 minutes plus setting

Freezing Not suitable

To serve 4-6

1 pint	Medium sweet cider	600 ml
1 tbsp	Powdered gelatine	15 ml
1 tbsp	Lemon juice	15 ml
8 oz	White grapes	225 g
8 oz	Black grapes	225 g
2 tbsp	Caster sugar	2x15 ml

Put 6 tbsp (6x15 ml) of the cider in a heatproof bowl, sprinkle over the gelatine and leave until spongy – about 5 minutes.

Dissolve gelatine over a pan of hot water, then stir in the remaining cider and lemon juice. Remove bowl from the heat. Spoon enough of the cider jelly into a dampened 1½ pint (850 ml) ring mould just to cover it. Leave it to set in the refrigerator.

Reserve half of each kind of grape. Wash and cut remainder in half and remove pips. Arrange halves over the set jelly, then cover with more liquid jelly and leave to set. Continue layers, ending with jelly, then chill in refrigerator till set. Wash remaining grapes and remove most of moisture. Toss in caster sugar.

Dip the mould quickly in and out of hot water and invert over a serving plate so jelly slides out. Fill centre with sugared grapes. Serve with whipped cream and ginger biscuits.

Fruit salad with prunes

Overall timing 15 minutes plus maceration and chilling

Freezing Not suitable

To serve 6

8 oz	Plump prunes	225 g
¾ pint	Hot strong tea	400 ml
3	Oranges	3
1	Grapefruit	1
2	Bananas	2
1 tbsp	Lemon juice	15 ml
8 oz	Can of pineapple slices	227 g
2 tbsp	Brandy or sherry	2x15 ml

Put stoned prunes in a bowl and cover with strained tea. Soak for 30 minutes.

Cut the rind and pith away from the oranges and grapefruit with a serrated knife. Cut into slices across the segments, cutting large slices in halves or quarters. Place in glass serving bowl.

Peel and cut the bananas into thick slices and sprinkle with lemon juice to prevent discoloration. Add to bowl with drained prunes, lemon juice and pineapple slices with their syrup. Stir in the brandy or sherry and chill for at least 1 hour before serving.

Rum trifle

Overall timing 35 minutes plus chilling

Freezing Not suitable

To serve 4–6

2 tbsp	Cocoa powder	2x15 ml
4 oz	Caster sugar	125 g
1¼ pints	Milk	700 ml
4	Egg yolks	4
2 oz	Plain flour	50 g
4 tbsp	Rum	4x15 ml
4 tbsp	Water	4x15 ml
8	Trifle sponges	8

Mix the cocoa with 1 oz (25 g) of the sugar. Heat the milk in a saucepan and add ¼ pint (150 ml) of it to the cocoa mixture. Stir till well blended.

In another bowl, beat the egg yolks with remaining sugar and flour. Gradually add the remaining hot milk. Return to the saucepan and bring to the boil, stirring. Cook for 2 minutes till custard thickens. Pour half of the custard back into bowl and stir in cocoa mixture.

Line a glass bowl with greaseproof paper. Put rum and water on a plate. Split the sponges in half, then halve each half. Dip sponges in rum mixture just to moisten. Line bottom and sides of bowl with half the sponges.

Pour in the plain custard and cover with a layer of sponges. Pour the chocolate custard into the mould and cover with remaining sponges. Cover with foil or cling film and chill for at least 3 hours but preferably overnight.

Turn trifle out on to a plate, carefully remove greaseproof paper and decorate with whipped cream, if liked.

Cherry bread pudding

Overall timing 1 hour

Freezing Not suitable

To serve 4–6

7	Slices of bread	7
15 oz	Can of cherries	425 g
4	Eggs	4
4 oz	Caster sugar	125 g
¾ pint	Milk	400 ml
	Grated rind of ½ lemon	
1 tbsp	Icing sugar	15 ml

Preheat the oven to 350°F (180°C) Gas 4.

Cut the slices of bread into quarters diagonally. Arrange eight of the bread triangles over the bottom of an ovenproof dish.

Drain the cherries; halve and remove stones. Spread half the cherries over bread and cover with eight more triangles. Sprinkle over the remaining cherries and cover with the remaining bread, arranged in overlapping rows.

Beat the eggs with the sugar and add the milk. Sprinkle lemon rind over the bread and strain the egg mixture over. Sprinkle the surface with icing sugar and bake for 35 minutes. Serve hot.

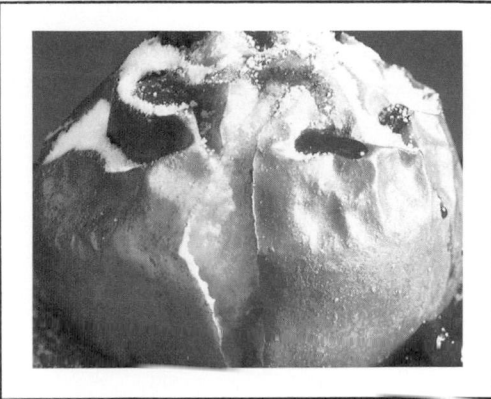

Baked apples

Overall timing 35 minutes

Freezing Not suitable

To serve 4

4	Large apples	4
8 tbsp	Jam	8x15 ml
1 oz	Butter	25 g
4 tbsp	Water	4x15 ml
4 tbsp	Caster sugar	4x15 ml

Preheat oven to 375°F (190°C) Gas 5.

Wash, dry and core apples. Place in a greased ovenproof dish and fill each apple with jam. Add small knob of butter to each.

Put water in bottom of dish, then bake for 25 minutes. Serve sprinkled with sugar.

Caramelized grapefruit

Overall timing 20 minutes

Freezing Not suitable

To serve 4

2	Grapefruit	2
1 teasp	Ground cinnamon	5 ml
4 tbsp	Caster sugar	4x15 ml

.Preheat the grill.

Cut grapefruit in half. Remove flesh with grapefruit knife, separate segments and discard membranes. Put segments into a bowl. Mix cinnamon with half the sugar and sprinkle over fruit.

Fill grapefruit shells with segments and sprinkle with remaining sugar. Grill for a few minutes till golden brown. Serve hot.

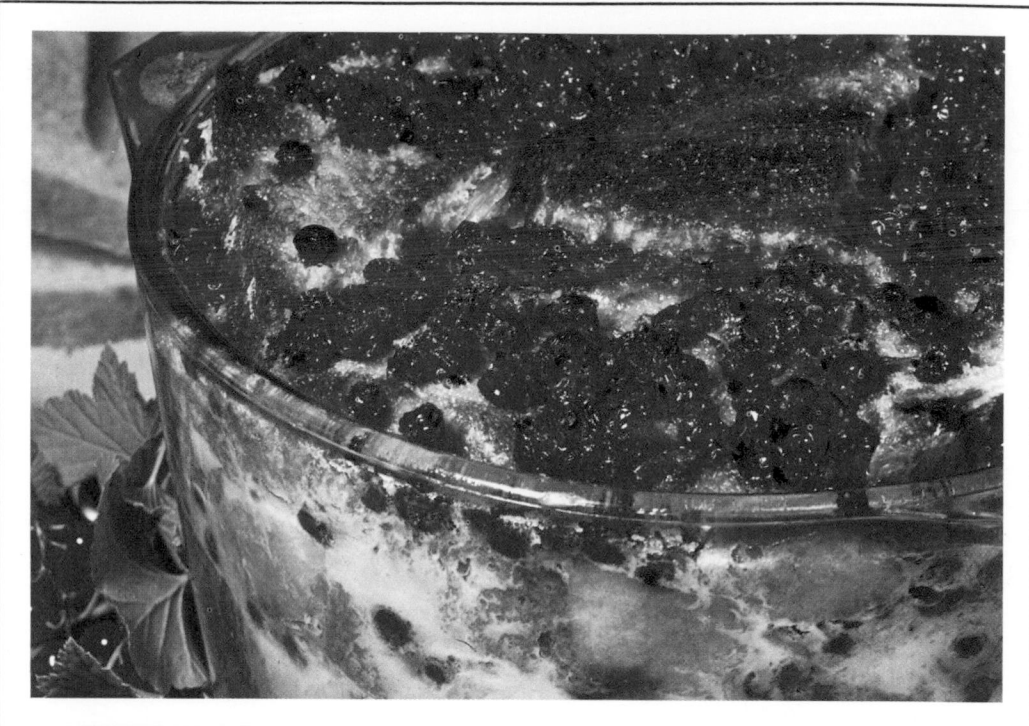

Redcurrant pudding

Overall timing 1½ hours

Freezing Suitable: reheat from frozen in 350°F (180°C) Gas 4 oven for 1 hour

To serve 6–8

12 oz	Redcurrants	350 g
12	Slices of stale bread	12
2 oz	Butter	50 g
1 pint	Milk	560 ml
1	Vanilla pod	1
2	Eggs	2
6 tbsp	Caster sugar	6x15 ml

Wash and drain the redcurrants. Remove the stalks. Remove the crusts from the bread. Spread with butter and cut into triangles.

Sprinkle a few redcurrants over the bottom of a well-greased 3 pint (1.7 litre) ovenproof dish and arrange some of the bread on top. Cover with redcurrants, then a layer of bread. Repeat the layers.

Put the milk and vanilla pod into a saucepan and bring to the boil. Remove from the heat and lift out the vanilla pod. Whisk the eggs with 5 tbsp (5x15 ml) of the sugar till frothy, then pour in the hot milk, whisking continuously. Strain the custard over the redcurrants and bread. Leave to soak for 20 minutes.

Preheat the oven to 375°F (190°C) Gas 5.

Sprinkle the remaining sugar over the pudding and bake for about 40 minutes till golden. Serve immediately.

Russian pudding

Overall timing 30 minutes

Freezing Not suitable

To serve 4–6

1½ pints	Milk	850 ml
	Pinch of salt	
	Grated rind of ½ lemon	
4 oz	Granulated sugar	125 g
3 oz	Semolina or ground rice	75 g
1	Egg	1
1 lb	Can of cherries	453 g
2 tbsp	Redcurrant jelly	2x15 ml

In a saucepan, heat the milk, salt, lemon rind and 2 oz (50 g) of the sugar. Stir in the semolina or ground rice. Remove from the heat.

Separate the egg and add the beaten yolk to the saucepan.

In a bowl, beat the egg white till stiff and carefully fold into the semolina or ground rice mixture.

Drain cherries. Place cherries and 2 tbsp (2x15 ml) of the juice in a pan. Stir in the redcurrant jelly and cook for 5 minutes.

Preheat the grill. Grease a flameproof serving dish. Pour in half the semolina or rice mixture, then all the cherry mixture and finally the rest of the semolina or rice. Sprinkle with the remaining sugar and place under the grill. Cook till the sugar caramelizes and turns golden but not brown – it should take about 3 minutes. Serve immediately.

Spotted Dick

Overall timing 2¼ hours

Freezing Suitable: boil for a further 2 hours

To serve 8

5 oz	Self-raising flour	150 g
½ teasp	Salt	2.5 ml
5 oz	Fresh breadcrumbs	150 g
5 oz	Shredded suet	150 g
3 oz	Caster sugar	75 g
8 oz	Currants	225 g
¼ pint	Milk	150 ml

Mix together the flour, salt, breadcrumbs, suet, sugar and currants in a large bowl. Make a well in the centre. Gradually add enough milk to make a soft but not sticky dough, using a knife to mix the dry ingredients into the liquid.

Form the dough into a roll on a floured surface. Wrap in greased greaseproof paper with a pleat in the top to allow room for the dough to rise. Wrap the roll loosely in foil, allowing room for expansion, and seal the joins tightly to keep water out.

Place in a large pan of boiling water, cover and simmer for 2 hours.

Remove from the heat, unwrap carefully and roll the pudding off the paper on to a warmed serving plate. Serve hot in slices with pouring custard.

Apricot dumplings

Overall timing 1¼ hours including refrigeration

Freezing Not suitable

Makes 16

2 oz	Butter	50 g
8 oz	Cottage cheese	225 g
	Pinch of salt	
2	Eggs	2
5 oz	Plain flour	150 g
16	Small apricots	16
16	Sugar lumps	16
To finish		
6 oz	Butter	175 g
2 tbsp	Caster sugar	2x15 ml
8 tbsp	Dried breadcrumbs	8x15 ml
1 teasp	Ground cinnamon	5 ml
	Icing sugar	

Beat together butter, sieved cheese, salt, eggs and flour. Chill 30 minutes.

Make a small slit in each apricot. Remove stone and replace with a sugar lump.

Roll out dough on a floured board. Cut into 16x2 inch (5 cm) squares. Put an apricot on to each square and draw dough around to form a dumpling. Drop dumplings into simmering water, cover and cook for 10 minutes. Turn over halfway through cooking.

Melt butter in a saucepan. Stir in sugar, breadcrumbs and cinnamon. Drain dumplings and toss in butter mixture. Dredge with icing sugar and serve hot.

Blackcurrant pancake tower

Overall timing 45 minutes

Freezing Suitable: assemble tower and make sauce after reheating pancakes

To serve 4–6

1½ lb	**Blackcurrants**	700 g
5 oz	Caster sugar	150 g
Pancakes		
6	**Eggs**	6
	Pinch of salt	
4 tbsp	Milk	4x15 ml
4 oz	Plain flour	125 g
2 tbsp	Caster sugar	2x15 ml
6 tbsp	Oil	6x15 ml

Put blackcurrants into a bowl and sprinkle with sugar.

To make pancakes, separate eggs. Beat yolks with salt and milk, then gradually beat in flour.

In another bowl, whisk egg whites till frothy. Add sugar and whisk until stiff. Fold whites into yolk mixture.

Heat 1 tbsp (15 ml) of oil in 8 inch (20 cm) frying pan. Add one-sixth of the batter and cook till pancake is golden brown underneath. Turn and cook other side. Place on serving dish and top with some of the fruit. Cook five more pancakes in the same way, placing each one on the "tower" as it is cooked with a layer of fruit.

Serve hot with custard.

Almond apricot desserts

Overall timing 1¼ hours

Freezing Not suitable

To serve 6

1 oz	Butter	25 g
1 oz	Caster sugar	25 g
8 oz	Apricot jam	225 g
3 tbsp	Lemon juice	3x15 ml
3	Eggs	3
2 oz	Ground almonds	50 g

Preheat the oven to 300°F (150°C) Gas 2.

Melt the butter in a saucepan and use to grease six small ovenproof dishes. Coat the inside of each dish with sugar.

Put the apricot jam and lemon juice into a saucepan and heat gently, stirring. Put pan into water to cool mixture quickly.

Separate the eggs. Stir the yolks and almonds into the jam mixture. Beat the egg whites in a mixing bowl until very stiff. Gently fold into the jam mixture.

Fill each dish to the top with the mixture. Place on a baking tray and bake for about 45 minutes.

Serve in the dishes or turn desserts out on to serving plates. Serve hot with custard, whipped cream or ice cream.

Sultana and macaroon pudding

Overall timing 1 hour 20 minutes

Freezing Suitable: serve cold

To serve 6

1 pint	Milk	560 ml
4 oz	Fresh breadcrumbs	125 g
3 oz	Butter	75 g
3	Eggs	3
2 oz	Caster sugar	50 g
8 oz	Sultanas	225 g
8 oz	Macaroons	225 g
Rum cream		
4	Eggs	4
3 oz	Caster sugar	75 g
4 tbsp	Rum	4x15 ml
	Juice of ½ lemon	

Preheat the oven to 400°F (200°C) Gas 6.

Put the milk into a saucepan and bring to the boil. Add the breadcrumbs and cook gently – just simmering – for 10 minutes.

Meanwhile, cream butter in a bowl till softened. Separate the eggs. Whisk the yolks with the sugar till light and fluffy, then gradually beat into the butter. Add the milk and breadcrumbs and the sultanas and mix well. Whisk the egg whites till stiff and fold into the mixture.

Arrange the sultana mixture and the macaroons in layers in a greased 8 inch (20 cm) brioche or kugelhopf mould, beginning and ending with the sultana mixture. Bake for 1 hour.

To make the rum cream, mix the eggs, sugar, rum, lemon juice and 3 fl oz (90 ml) water in a bowl. Place the bowl over a pan of simmering water and cook, stirring constantly, till the mixture is thick enough to coat the back of the spoon. Strain into a warmed sauceboat or serving dish.

Turn the pudding on to a warmed serving plate and serve hot, cut into thick wedges, with the rum cream.

Grapefruit soufflés

Overall timing 45 minutes

Freezing Not suitable

To serve 6

6	Grapefruit	6
3 oz	Butter	75 g
2 oz	Plain flour	50 g
	Finely grated rind of 1 orange	
1–2 oz	Caster sugar	25–50 g
3	Eggs	3

Preheat the oven to 375°F (190°C) Gas 5.

Slice tops off grapefruit and squeeze juice out of flesh very gently – measure out ½ pint (300 ml). Remove flesh and membranes with grapefruit knife and discard. Retain shells.

Melt the butter in a saucepan, stir in the flour and cook for 2 minutes. Gradually stir in the grapefruit juice. Bring to the boil and cook, stirring, for 2 minutes or until the sauce thickens. Add orange rind and sugar and stir until sugar dissolves. Remove from heat and leave to cool slightly.

Separate the eggs and beat the yolks into the sauce. Whisk the egg whites in a bowl till stiff, then carefully fold into the sauce mixture.

Place empty grapefruit shells in a foil-lined bun tin and fill with the mixture. Bake for 15–20 minutes till well risen and golden. Serve immediately.

Sussex pond pudding

Overall timing 4 hours

Freezing Not suitable

To serve 6–8

8 oz	Self-raising flour	225 g
4 oz	Shredded suet	125 g
¼ pint	Milk	150 ml
4 oz	Butter	125 g
4 oz	Soft brown sugar	125 g
1	Large thin-skinned lemon	1

Mix the flour and suet in a large bowl. Add the milk a little at a time to give a soft, but not sticky, dough. Knead the dough lightly. Roll out three-quarters of the dough and use to line a well-greased 2½ pint (1.5 litre) pudding basin.

Cream the butter and sugar together until fluffy and spread half the mixture over the bottom and sides of the pastry.

Pierce the lemon all over with a fine skewer (to help the juices run out during cooking). Stand the lemon upright in centre of the basin, then add the remaining creamed mixture.

Roll out remaining dough and cover the filling, sealing pastry edges well. Cover the basin with a piece of greased greaseproof paper which has a large pleat to allow for expansion. Cover with pleated foil and tie with string, making a handle to aid removal from saucepan.

Place basin in saucepan containing 3 inches (7.5 cm) boiling water. Cover and leave to boil for 3½ hours, topping up with extra boiling water as it evaporates.

Lift basin from saucepan. Remove foil and paper and run a knife round the sides of the basin to release the pudding. Invert on to a warmed serving plate and serve hot with pouring custard or cream.

Tapioca and caramel mould

Overall timing 1¼ hours

Freezing Not suitable

To serve 6

4 oz	Seed pearl tapioca	125 g
1½ pints	Milk	850 ml
4 tbsp	Caster sugar	4x15 ml
	Grated rind of 1 lemon	
4 oz	Granulated sugar	125 g
1 oz	Butter	25 g
3	Eggs	3

Preheat the oven to 400°F (200°C) Gas 6.

Put the tapioca, milk, caster sugar and lemon rind into a saucepan and bring to the boil, stirring. Simmer for 15 minutes, stirring occasionally with a wooden spoon to prevent the mixture sticking to the pan.

Meanwhile, put the granulated sugar into a saucepan with 2 tbsp (2x15 ml) water and stir over a low heat till the sugar dissolves. Stop stirring and boil steadily till golden brown. Pour into a 7 inch (18 cm) round cake tin, turning so the bottom and sides are coated.

Remove the tapioca from the heat and beat in the butter. Separate the eggs, putting the whites into a large bowl. Beat the yolks into the tapioca, then leave to cool, stirring occasionally.

Whisk the egg whites till stiff but not dry and fold gently into the tapioca with a metal spoon. Pour the mixture into the caramel-lined tin and bake for about 35 minutes till well risen and golden.

Run a knife round the edge of the mould and turn out on to a serving dish. Serve hot or cold with pouring cream.

Viennese sweet semolina

Overall timing 50 minutes

Freezing Not suitable

To serve 4–6

2 oz	Sultanas	50 g
1 pint	Milk	560 ml
1½ oz	Butter	40 g
3 oz	Semolina	75 g
4 tbsp	Caster sugar	4x15 ml

Preheat the oven to 350°F (180°C) Gas 4.

Soak the sultanas in warm water. Put the milk into a saucepan with butter. Heat till warm, then pour in the semolina and bring to the boil, stirring constantly. Simmer for 5 minutes, then stir in all but 1 tbsp (15 ml) of the sugar.

Drain sultanas and mix into semolina. Turn into a greased ovenproof dish and smooth top. Bake for 30 minutes.

Remove dish from oven and increase heat to 400°F (200°C) Gas 6. Mix the semolina with a fork to break it up. Return dish to oven for 5 minutes till mixture is dry and crisp. Turn on to a warmed serving dish, sprinkle with the reserved sugar and serve hot.

Coconut and cherry surprise

Overall timing 1 hour

Freezing Suitable: reheat in 375°F (190°C) Gas 5 oven for 10 minutes

To serve 8–10

8 oz	Shortcrust pastry	225 g
2½ oz	Ground almonds	65 g
14 oz	Can of cherry pie filling	379 g
1 oz	Desiccated coconut	25 g
Filling		
3 oz	Butter	75 g
3 oz	Caster sugar	75 g
2	Eggs	2
¼ teasp	Almond essence	1.25 ml
2 tbsp	Milk	2x15 ml
2 oz	Self-raising flour	50 g
2 oz	Desiccated coconut	50 g
1½ oz	Ground almonds	40 g

Topping		
3 tbsp	Desiccated coconut	3x15 ml
1	Egg yolk	1
1 teasp	Milk	5 ml

Roll out dough and use to line greased 10 inch (25 cm) springform tin. Sprinkle ground almonds over. Spread pie filling to within 1 inch (2.5 cm) of edge, then cover with coconut.

Preheat the oven to 400°F (200°C) Gas 6.

Make filling by creaming butter with sugar till pale and fluffy. Add eggs, essence and 1 tbsp (15 ml) milk and beat well. Fold in flour, followed by remaining milk, coconut and almonds.

Place mixture in blobs over pie filling and smooth evenly so no fruit is visible. Sprinkle with coconut and bake for 30 minutes.

Mix egg yolk and milk together. Brush over tart and bake for a further 10 minutes. Serve hot.

Flamed fruit salad

Overall timing 30 minutes

Freezing Not suitable

To serve 4

	Selection of any firm fresh fruit: apple, banana, cherries, orange, clementine, pear, peach, straw- berries and grapes	
1	Lemon	1
1 oz	Butter	25 g
3 tbsp	Caster sugar	3x15 ml
2 oz	Flaked almonds	50 g
3 tbsp	Rum	3x15 ml

Prepare the fruit and chop it into pieces. Mix these together in a bowl. Grate lemon and squeeze out juice. Add juice to fruit.

Put the butter and caster sugar into a saucepan. Heat without stirring, until the sugar caramelizes and becomes light brown. This will take about 5 minutes. Add the grated lemon rind and almonds. Cook for about 5 minutes, stirring occasionally, until the caramel and nuts are golden brown.

Remove pan from the heat. Add juices from mixed fruits and stir until caramel becomes a smooth syrup. Add the fruit and heat through for about 5 minutes, turning the mixture over frequently to distribute the syrup. Remove from heat.

Warm rum in a metal ladle, then set it alight and pour over fruit. Serve immediately with whipped cream or ice cream.

Fruit brochettes

Overall timing 20 minutes

Freezing Not suitable

To serve 6

3	Bananas	3
2	Oranges	2
1	Lemon	1
8 oz	Can of pineapple chunks	227 g
2 tbsp	Rum	2x15 ml
4 oz	Caster sugar	125 g
1 oz	Butter	25 g
3	Thick slices of bread	3

Peel the fruit. Cut bananas into 1 inch (2.5 cm) pieces; divide oranges and lemon into segments; drain pineapple chunks. Place fruit in a bowl, pour rum over and sprinkle with 2 tbsp (2x15 ml) of the sugar.

Preheat grill.

Butter the bread on both sides, cut into small cubes and roll in sugar to coat. Thread fruit and bread cubes on to skewers.

Cook under the grill (or on a barbecue) for 10 minutes, turning brochettes over from time to time and sprinkling them with any remaining sugar. Serve immediately with whipped cream or vanilla ice cream.

Apricot pancakes

Overall timing 45 minutes

Freezing Suitable: fill pancakes after thawing and reheating

To serve 4

2	Eggs	2
¼ pint	Milk	150 ml
2 fl oz	Water	60 ml
3 oz	Plain flour	75 g
1 oz	Caster sugar	25 g
	Vanilla essence	
	Pinch of salt	
3½ oz	Butter or lard	100 g
8 tbsp	Apricot jam	8x15 ml
	Icing sugar	
1 oz	Ground hazelnuts	25 g

Put eggs, milk and water into a bowl. Add the flour, caster sugar, a few drops of vanilla essence and salt. Whisk or beat well together until creamy and smooth.

Melt a knob of butter or lard in a small frying pan. Pour in a little of the batter and spread in a thin layer over the pan, using a spatula. When underside is cooked, flip the pancake over to brown the other side.

As soon as each pancake is ready, spread with apricot jam and roll up. Put on to a dish and keep warm in the oven while you cook the other pancakes, adding more butter or lard to the pan as necessary.

Before serving, dredge with icing sugar and sprinkle with ground hazelnuts or chopped nuts of your choice.

Blackberry pancakes

Overall timing 30 minutes

Freezing Not suitable

To serve 2

1½ oz	Plain flour	40 g
2 teasp	Caster sugar	2x5 ml
	Pinch of salt	
1	Egg	1
3 fl oz	Milk	90 ml
	Oil for frying	
Topping		
4 oz	Canned blackberries	125 g
3 tbsp	Honey	3x15 ml
1½ tbsp	Brandy	22.5 ml
	Vanilla ice cream	
1 oz	Walnuts	25 g

Sift flour, sugar and salt into a bowl. Make a well in the centre and add egg and milk. Whisk till smooth. Pour into jug and leave to stand for 5 minutes.

Lightly oil an 8 inch (20 cm) pancake pan and heat. Make four thin pancakes. Fold into quarters, arrange on a warmed serving plate and keep hot.

Place drained blackberries in a sieve and rinse under running water. Turn on to kitchen paper to drain.

Gently heat honey with brandy in a saucepan. Remove from heat before it boils.

To assemble pancakes, put a cube of ice cream on top of each and scatter with blackberries. Pour over hot honey mixture and sprinkle with chopped walnuts. Serve immediately.

Baked bananas

Overall timing 15 minutes

Freezing Not suitable

To serve 4

4	Large ripe bananas	4
2 oz	Butter	50 g
2 teasp	Caster sugar	2x5 ml
2 tbsp	Water	2x15 ml
	Ground cinnamon	

Preheat oven to 425°F (220°C) Gas 7.

Peel the bananas three-quarters of the way down. Fold back the skin to give a petal effect. Place in a greased ovenproof dish and dot each banana with butter. Sprinkle with sugar, water and a little ground cinnamon.

Bake for 10 minutes. Serve immediately with custard or vanilla ice cream.

Baked noodle pudding

Overall timing 1 hour

Freezing Not suitable

To serve 4

½ pint	Milk	300 ml
1 pint	Water	560 ml
8 oz	Noodles	225 g
2 oz	Butter	50 g
2	Eggs	2
2	Large dessert apples	2
2 oz	Walnut pieces	50 g
3 oz	Caster sugar	75 g
2 teasp	Poppy seeds	2x5 ml

Preheat the oven to 325°F (170°C) Gas 3.

Put the milk and water into a saucepan and bring to the boil. Add the noodles, bring back to the boil and simmer till tender. Drain noodles and put into a large bowl. Stir in the melted butter and beaten eggs till lightly coated.

Spread one-third of the noodles over the bottom of a greased ovenproof dish. Core and thinly slice the apples. Arrange half the slices over the noodles with half the walnuts. Sprinkle with one-third of the sugar and poppy seeds.

Repeat the layers, finishing with a layer of noodles arranged in a lattice pattern. Sprinkle with the remaining sugar and poppy seeds.

Bake for about 35 minutes till the apples are tender. Remove from the oven and cool completely before serving.

Bananas flambé

Overall timing 15 minutes

Freezing Not suitable

To serve 4

$\frac{1}{4}$ pint	Water	150 ml
3 oz	Caster sugar	75 g
8	Bananas	8
5 tbsp	Rum	5x15 ml
1	Small block of vanilla ice cream	1
2 oz	Flaked almonds	50 g

Put the water and sugar into a saucepan and cook until it starts to turn golden.

Peel the bananas. Leave whole or cut in half crossways. Add to the pan. Cook, uncovered, for 7 minutes, spooning syrup over occasionally. Remove from heat, stir in 4 tbsp (4x15 ml) of the rum and keep warm.

Place scoops of ice cream on a chilled serving dish. Cover with the bananas and spoon the syrup over.

Warm the remaining rum in a metal spoon or ladle. Set alight and pour over the bananas. Decorate with flaked almonds and serve immediately, while flaming.

Plum pudding

Overall timing 5½ hours plus maceration

Freezing Suitable: boil from frozen for about 2 hours

To serve 8–10

1 lb	Mixed sultanas, raisins and currants	450 g
12 oz	Prunes	350 g
5 oz	Chopped mixed peel	150 g
4 tbsp	Rum	4x15 ml
¼ pint	Light ale or lager	150 ml
3	Eggs	3
8 oz	Flaked almonds	225 g
1	Apple	1
2 teasp	Mixed spice	2x5 ml
2 teasp	Salt	2x5 ml
12 oz	Brown sugar	350 g
2	Oranges	2
2	Lemons	2
8 oz	Shredded suet	225 g
6 oz	Plain flour	175 g
5 oz	Fresh breadcrumbs	150 g

Put dried fruits and candied peel in a large bowl, add 3 tbsp (3x15 ml) rum and ale or lager and leave to macerate overnight.

Drain fruit, reserving liquid. Stone prunes, then add eggs, almonds, grated apple, mixed spice, salt, sugar and the juice and grated rind of oranges and lemons. Mix well.

Put suet in a bowl and work in flour and breadcrumbs. Mix in any liquid from macerated fruit and add a little more beer if mixture is too dry. Knead to a dough and mix in all remaining ingredients. Tip mixture on to a clean, floured tea-towel and tie the corners together. Suspend from a long wooden spoon in a large saucepan half filled with boiling water. Boil for 5 hours.

Drain pudding for 5 minutes before removing tea-towel. Warm remaining rum, set alight and pour over pudding. Serve hot with custard.

Fruity pancakes

Overall timing 1 hour

Freezing Not suitable

To serve 2

1½ oz	Plain flour	40 g
2 teasp	Caster sugar	2x5 ml
	Pinch of salt	
1	Egg	1
4 tbsp	Milk	4x15 ml
2 tbsp	Cider or white wine	2x15 ml
	Grated rind of ½ orange	
	Vanilla essence	
3	Sugar lumps	3
1	Orange	1
½ teasp	Ground cinnamon	2.5 ml
2	Dessert apples	2
	Oil for frying	

Sift flour, sugar and salt into a bowl. Make a well in the centre and add egg, milk, cider or wine, orange rind and a few drops of vanilla essence. Whisk till smooth. Pour batter into a jug.

Rub sugar lumps over surface of orange to absorb zest. Crush them and add cinnamon.

Peel orange, then chop flesh roughly. Place in a bowl. Peel, core and cube apples, then mix well with orange.

Preheat the grill.

Lightly oil an 8 inch (20 cm) pancake pan and heat. Pour in one-quarter of the batter and cook for 1–2 minutes till base bubbles and is firm. Spoon over one-quarter of the fruit and crushed sugar and cinnamon mixtures. Place under grill and cook for a few minutes till bubbling. Fold pancake and lift out on to a warmed serving dish. Cover and keep hot while you cook three other pancakes in the same way.

Serve whipped cream flavoured with orange juice separately, or serve with vanilla ice cream.

Honey-baked bananas

Overall timing 40 minutes

Freezing Not suitable

To serve 4

4	Bananas	4
4 tbsp	Lemon juice	4x15 ml
3 tbsp	Honey	3x15 ml
2 oz	Blanched almonds	50 g
3 tbsp	Fresh breadcrumbs	3x15 ml
2 oz	Butter	50 g
¼ pint	Soured cream	150 ml
3 tbsp	Orange juice	3x15 ml

Preheat the oven to 400°F (200°C) Gas 4.

Peel bananas. Arrange side by side in a greased ovenproof dish. Pour over lemon juice and honey. Mix the chopped almonds with the breadcrumbs and sprinkle over bananas. Cut butter into small pieces and scatter over bananas.

Bake for 30 minutes. Serve with soured cream mixed with orange juice.

Plum soufflé

Overall timing 1 hour

Freezing Not suitable

To serve 6

1½ lb	Ripe plums	700 g
2–4 oz	Sugar	50–125 g
6 tbsp	Water	6x15 ml
2½ oz	Butter	65 g
1 tbsp	Dried breadcrumbs	15 ml
2 oz	Plain flour	50 g
½ pint	Warm milk	300 ml
3	Large eggs	3
	Grated rind of 1 orange	

Preheat oven to 375°F (190°C) Gas 5.

Stone the plums and cut into quarters. Put into a saucepan with the sugar and water. Bring to the boil, cover and simmer for 10 minutes.

Grease a 3 pint (1.7 litre) soufflé dish with ½ oz (15 g) butter and coat with the breadcrumbs. Put two thirds of the plums in the dish with any juice.

Melt the remaining butter in a large saucepan, stir in the flour and cook for 1 minute. Gradually add the warm milk and bring to the boil, stirring constantly. Simmer for 2 minutes, then remove from the heat. Cool slightly.

Separate the eggs. Beat the yolks into the sauce with the orange rind and remaining plums. Whisk the egg whites till stiff but not dry. Stir one spoonful into sauce and fold in remainder. Pour mixture over the plums in the dish.

Stand dish in a roasting tin containing 1 inch (2.5 cm) hot water. Bake for 30–35 minutes till well risen and golden. Serve immediately.

Baked apricots

Overall timing 1 hour

Freezing Suitable: reheat from frozen in 400°F (200°C) Gas 6 oven for 15 minutes, then add syrup

To serve 6–8

12	Large apricots	12
½ pint	Milk	300 ml
2 tbsp	Custard powder	2x15 ml
1 tbsp	Caster sugar	15 ml
4 oz	Blanched almonds	125 g
5 oz	Macaroons	150 g
1½ oz	Candied orange peel	40 g
	Pinch of ground cinnamon	
6 tbsp	Redcurrant jelly	6x15 ml
4 tbsp	Water	4x15 ml

Preheat the oven to 400°F (200°C) Gas 6.

Halve apricots and remove stones. Arrange, cut sides up, in a greased ovenproof dish.

Prepare the custard according to packet instructions, using the milk, custard powder and sugar. Cool quickly by standing the pan in cold water. Stir the custard frequently to prevent a skin forming.

Chop almonds, macaroons and candied peel finely and stir into the custard with the cinnamon. Fill apricot halves with custard mixture. Bake for 30 minutes.

Meanwhile, mix together the redcurrant jelly and water in a small pan over a low heat. Spoon syrup carefully over the apricots and bake for a further 10 minutes.

Serve hot with whipped cream, or leave to cool, then chill and serve with ice cream or whipped cream.

Apple and marmalade charlotte

Overall timing 1 hour

Freezing Suitable: reheat in 400°F (200°C) Gas 6 oven for 10 minutes

To serve 8

2½ lb	Cooking apples	1.1 kg
4 tbsp	Water	4x15 ml
1 oz	Sugar	25 g
4 oz	Marmalade	125 g
1½ lb	Stale sliced bread	700 g
3 oz	Butter	75 g

Preheat oven to 400°F (200°C) Gas 6.

To make the filling, peel apples, core and slice into a large saucepan. Add water, cover and bring to the boil. Cook over medium heat for 12 minutes without removing the lid at all during cooking. Remove from heat and beat in sugar and marmalade with a wooden spoon.

Remove crusts and butter bread. Cut a third of slices into triangles, and the rest into wide fingers.

Grease a 3 pint (1.7 litre) charlotte mould and line the bottom with some of the bread triangles, buttered-side out. Overlap the slices as the bread tends to shrink during cooking. Line sides of mould with overlapping bread fingers, butter-side out.

Pour in apple mixture and top with remaining bread triangles, butter-side up. Cook on centre shelf of the oven for 30–40 minutes till golden brown.

Remove from oven. Leave to cool slightly in the mould. Run a knife around the edge and turn out on to a warmed serving plate. Serve hot with custard or cream.

Fruity rice pudding

Overall timing 1¼ hours

Freezing Suitable: reheat in 300°F (150°C) Gas 2 oven for 30 minutes

To serve 6–8

1¼ pints	Milk	700 ml
	Salt	
4	Strips of lemon rind	4
5 oz	Round grain rice	150 g
1½ lb	Apples	700 g
2	Bananas	2
1 oz	Butter	25 g
4 oz	Caster sugar	125 g
1 teasp	Ground cinnamon	5 ml
4 oz	Bottle of sweet cherries	125 g
2 oz	Shelled walnuts	50 g
3	Eggs	3

Preheat oven to 350°F (180°C) Gas 4.

Put the milk, pinch of salt and strips of lemon rind into a saucepan and bring to the boil. Add the rice. Cover and cook for 40 minutes on a low heat, stirring occasionally.

Meanwhile, peel and slice the apples and bananas. Melt the butter and 2 oz (50 g) of the sugar in a saucepan until golden brown. Add the apples and cook for 5 minutes, then add the bananas and cook for 2–3 minutes more. Sprinkle on the cinnamon, then stir in drained cherries and chopped walnuts.

Remove from heat, put mixture into a greased ovenproof dish and smooth over. Work quickly to prevent caramel setting.

Separate the eggs. Cream together the yolks and 1 oz (25 g) sugar in one bowl. In another, beat the whites and remaining sugar together until mixture is very stiff. Fold both mixtures into the cooked rice (take out the lemon peel first) then pour over the fruit. Bake for 30 minutes. Serve hot with cream.

Jam omelettes

Overall timing 10 minutes

Freezing Not suitable

To serve 2

3	Eggs	3
	Pinch of salt	
1 oz	Butter	25 g
3 tbsp	Jam	3x15 ml
1 tbsp	Caster sugar	15 ml

Beat eggs with salt in a bowl. Melt half butter in omelette pan. Add half the egg mixture and cook until set. Slip omelette out of pan on to plate, cooked side down.

Repeat with remaining egg mixture to make another omelette. Spoon jam into the middle of each omelette. Roll them up like pancakes and sprinkle with caster sugar.

To make the caramelized stripes, heat a skewer or toasting fork over a naked flame, then press lightly on top of the omelettes at intervals. Serve at once.

Nutty apple pudding

Overall timing 50 minutes

Freezing Not suitable

To serve 4–6

1½ lb	Cooking apples	700 g
¼ pint	Water	150 ml
2 oz	Flaked almonds	50 g
2 oz	Sultanas	50 g
7 oz	Wholemeal bread	200 g
4 oz	Demerara sugar	125 g
2 oz	Butter	50 g

Preheat the oven to 425°F (220°C) Gas 7.

Peel and core apples and slice into a saucepan. Add water, almonds and sultanas. Cover and cook over a gentle heat for 10 minutes. Remove from heat.

Crumble the bread into a bowl and mix in half the sugar. Grease an ovenproof dish with some of the butter and spread half the bread mixture over the bottom. Cover with apple mixture, then top with remaining bread. Sprinkle on rest of sugar and dot with remaining butter. Bake for about 20 minutes.

Peach meringue pudding

Overall timing 50 minutes

Freezing Not suitable

To serve 6

1 pint	Milk	560 ml
4 tbsp	Semolina	4x15 ml
2	Eggs	2
3 oz	Caster sugar	75 g
4	Ripe peaches	4
3 tbsp	Peach or raspberry jam	3x15 ml
1 oz	Toasted flaked almonds	25 g

Preheat the oven to 350°F (180°C) Gas 4.

Heat the milk in a saucepan and sprinkle in the semolina, stirring constantly. Bring to the boil and cook, stirring, for 3 minutes till thickened. Remove from the heat.

Separate the eggs. Beat the yolks into the semolina with 1 oz (25 g) of the sugar. Pour mixture into a 7 inch (18 cm) soufflé dish and smooth surface.

Peel and halve the peaches. Remove stones. Place a little jam in each peach half. Arrange in soufflé dish, some with the cut sides pressing against the sides of the dish and the rest jam-side down on the semolina.

Whisk the egg whites till stiff, then whisk in half the remaining sugar. Fold in the finely chopped almonds and the rest of the sugar. Pipe or spoon the meringue over the peaches.

Bake for 20 minutes till the meringue is lightly browned. Serve hot or leave to cool completely and chill before serving.

Pear brown betty

Overall timing 1 hour

Freezing Not suitable

To serve 6–8

2 lb	Ripe pears	900 g
8 oz	Stale breadcrumbs	225 g
4 oz	Caster sugar	125 g
2 oz	Butter	50 g

Preheat the oven to 375°F (190°C) Gas 5.

Peel and halve the pears. Remove the cores and cut flesh into ¼ inch (6 mm) slices.

Cover the bottom of a greased 8 inch (20 cm) springform tin with a quarter of the breadcrumbs. Arrange one-third of the pears on top and sprinkle with a little sugar. Repeat the layers till all the ingredients have been used.

Dot with the butter and bake for about 45 minutes till the pears are tender and the top is crisp and golden. Remove from the tin and serve hot or cold with pouring cream or custard.

Pear dumplings

Overall timing 1¼ hours plus chilling

Freezing Not suitable

To serve 4

12 oz	Plain flour	350 g
¼ teasp	Salt	1.25 ml
6 oz	Butter	175 g
	Grated rind of 1 orange	
2 tbsp	Caster sugar	2x15 ml
1	Egg yolk	1
Filling		
4	Ripe pears	4
2 oz	Butter	50 g
2 tbsp	Soft brown sugar	2x15 ml
½ teasp	Ground cinnamon	2.5 ml

Sift flour and salt into a bowl and rub in butter. Stir in the grated orange rind and caster sugar and add enough water to bind to a dough. Knead till smooth. Chill for 30 minutes.

Preheat the oven to 400°F (200°C) Gas 6.

Roll out dough and cut into four 8 inch (20 cm) squares.

Peel and halve pears and remove cores. Cream butter with soft brown sugar and cinnamon till pale and fluffy. Use to fill centres of pears. Press halves together and place one on each dough square.

Brush edges of dough squares with water. Bring the four corners of each square together at top of pears, sealing edges well. Roll out dough trimmings and cut into leaves. Lightly beat egg yolk with 1 tbsp (15 ml) water and brush over dough. Dip leaves in egg and press in place on top.

Place on a greased baking tray and bake for about 30 minutes till crisp and golden. Serve hot with whipped cream or vanilla ice cream.

Pineapple fritters

Overall timing 25 minutes

Freezing Not suitable

To serve 6

15½ oz	Can of pineapple rings	439 g
4 oz	Plain flour	125 g
1½ teasp	Caster sugar	7.5 ml
1	Whole egg	1
1 tbsp	Oil	15 ml
4 fl oz	Milk or water	120 ml
2	Egg whites	2
	Oil for frying	
3 tbsp	Icing sugar	3x15 ml

Drain the pineapple rings and dry on kitchen paper.

Sift flour and sugar into bowl. Beat in egg, oil and liquid till smooth. Whisk egg whites till stiff and fold into batter.

Heat oil in a deep-fryer to 340°F (170°C). Spear the pineapple rings on a fork, dip into the batter and carefully lower into the oil. Fry three at a time for 2–3 minutes till crisp and golden. Remove from the pan, drain on kitchen paper and keep hot while remaining fritters are cooked.

Arrange on a warmed serving plate, sift the icing sugar over and serve immediately with whipped cream.

French toast

Overall timing 25 minutes

Freezing Not suitable

To serve 4–6

10	Thin slices of bread	10
½–¾ pint	Milk	300–400 ml
2–3	Eggs	2–3
2 oz	Butter	50 g
2 oz	Caster sugar	50 g
1 teasp	Ground cinnamon (optional)	5 ml

Place bread on a baking tray or Swiss roll tin and pour over the milk. The more stale the bread, the more milk you will need to make the bread spongy. Soak for 10 minutes.

Whisk the eggs in a shallow dish till creamy. Lightly press bread with a fork to remove excess milk.

Melt butter in frying pan (reserve some if you cannot cook all slices at once). Dip bread in egg to coat, add to pan and fry for 3–4 minutes on each side. Sprinkle with caster sugar and cinnamon, if used, and serve immediately, with jam or golden or maple syrup.

Apple strudel

Overall timing 1¾ hours

Freezing Not suitable

To serve 8

10 oz	Strong plain flour	275 g
1	Large egg	1
4 oz	Butter	125 g
	Pinch of salt	
2½ lb	Bramley apples	1.1 kg
3 oz	Caster sugar	75 g
2 teasp	Ground cinnamon	2x5 ml
4 oz	Seedless raisins	125 g
1 tbsp	Grated lemon rind	15 ml
4 oz	Ground almonds	125 g
2 oz	Fresh breadcrumbs	50 g

Sift flour on to a work surface. Add egg. Melt half butter in a pan, then add 3 tbsp (3x15 ml) water and salt. Add mixture to flour and mix to a soft, sticky dough. Knead till smooth.

Leave in a warm place for 20 minutes.

Meanwhile, peel and core apples, then slice half very thinly. Coarsely grate rest into a bowl and mix in sugar, cinnamon, raisins, lemon rind, almonds and half breadcrumbs.

Place a large patterned tea-towel on a flat surface and sprinkle it with flour. Roll out dough on top till it is same shape as towel. Slide your hands between dough and tea-towel. Lift and stretch dough till thin enough to see pattern of tea-towel through. The rectangle should eventually measure about 20x16 inches (50x40 cm).

Preheat the oven to 400°F (200°C) Gas 6.

Brush dough with half remaining melted butter. Sprinkle with remaining breadcrumbs, leaving a 1 inch (2.5 cm) border all round. Spread almond mixture evenly over dough. Arrange apple slices on top. Fold border over filling, then roll up. Place on greased baking tray, curving to fit.

Brush with remaining butter and bake for 10 minutes. Reduce heat to 375°F (190°C) Gas 5 and bake for a further 30 minutes. Sprinkle with icing sugar and serve warm.

Apple soufflé omelette

Overall timing 50 minutes

Freezing Not suitable

To serve 2

2	Eggs	2
2 tbsp	Caster sugar	2x15 ml
4 tbsp	Milk	4x15 ml
¼ teasp	Vanilla essence	1.25 ml
1 oz	Butter	25 g
	Icing sugar	
2 tbsp	Brandy	2x15 ml
Filling		
12 oz	Cooking apple	350 g
1 tbsp	Water	15 ml
½ oz	Butter	15 g
3 tbsp	Granulated sugar	3x15 ml
	Vanilla essence	

To make the filling, peel, core and roughly chop apple. Place in saucepan with water and butter, cover and cook for 15 minutes. Remove from heat and add sugar and few drops of vanilla essence. Mix well, then cool.

To make omelette, separate one egg. Put the yolk in a bowl with the whole egg and the caster sugar and beat till light and frothy. Stir in milk and vanilla essence.

In another bowl, beat the egg white till very stiff. Stir 1 tbsp (15 ml) into yolk mixture to lighten it, then carefully fold in the rest with a metal spoon.

Preheat the grill.

Melt the butter in an omelette pan. When it begins to turn a light brown, pour in the egg mixture. Cook over a low heat for 5–7 minutes. Place under the grill until the top has set. Spread over the filling and fold over in half. Slide onto a warmed serving dish. Dredge with icing sugar. Warm the brandy, pour over the omelette and set alight. Serve flaming.

Individual coconut soufflés

Overall timing 45 minutes

Freezing Not suitable

To serve 8

½ pint	Milk	300 ml
5 tbsp	Caster sugar	5x15 ml
2 tbsp	Plain flour	2x15 ml
2 oz	Butter	50 g
4	Eggs	4
4 oz	Desiccated coconut	125 g
1 tbsp	Icing sugar	15 ml

Whisk 4 tbsp (4x15 ml) of the milk with 3 tbsp (3x15 ml) of the caster sugar and the flour. Bring the remaining milk to the boil in a saucepan. Add 2 tbsp (2x15 ml) of the boiling milk to the sugar mixture and whisk in well, then add to the milk in the pan, whisking vigorously all the time. Simmer gently till thickened, then cover, remove from heat and leave to cool for 15 minutes.

Preheat the oven to 375°F (190°C) Gas 5. Grease eight ovenproof moulds or ramekins with the butter and sprinkle with 1 tbsp (15 ml) of the sugar.

Separate the eggs. Add the yolks to the sauce with the coconut, whisking all the time. In a large bowl, whisk the egg whites till they hold stiff peaks, gradually adding the remaining sugar. Fold into the egg yolk mixture.

Three-quarters fill the moulds or ramekins with the mixture and sprinkle with icing sugar. Place on baking tray and bake for 20 minutes. Serve hot.

Banana pudding with rum sauce

Overall timing 1¼ hours

Freezing Suitable: reheat in 350°F (180°C) Gas 4 oven

To serve 6

2 lb	Bananas	900 g
3½ oz	Caster sugar	100 g
2 oz	Softened butter	50 g
2 oz	Plain flour	50 g
	Grated nutmeg	
2	Eggs	2
2 tbsp	Icing sugar	2x15 ml
1 tbsp	Rum or rum flavouring	15 ml
¼ pint	Carton of single cream	150 ml

Preheat the oven to 350°F (180°C) Gas 4.

Reserve half a large or 1 medium-sized banana for decoration. Peel the rest. Mash them with a fork in a bowl with sugar, butter, flour and a pinch of nutmeg.

Separate the eggs. Add yolks to banana mixture and beat well with a wooden spoon until smooth and creamy. Beat the egg whites till very stiff, then gently fold into the banana mixture.

Lightly grease and flour a pudding basin. Fill with the banana mixture and bake for 1 hour.

Remove from oven. Leave to cool slightly then turn out on to a warmed serving plate. Sprinkle with icing sugar and decorate with the reserved banana, sliced. Mix rum or rum flavouring into single cream and serve separately.

Banana soufflés

Overall timing 25 minutes

Freezing Not suitable

To serve 2

4	Ripe bananas	4
1 oz	Butter	25 g
3 oz	Caster sugar	75 g
	Vanilla essence	
2 tbsp	Rum	2x15 ml
2	Large eggs	2
2 tbsp	Icing sugar	2x15 ml

Preheat the oven to 425°F (220°C) Gas 7.

Make two lengthways slits with a sharp knife near to the top of each banana, leaving the skin joined at the stalk end. Roll back skin. Remove banana pulp with a teaspoon and place in a bowl. Mash well to a purée.

Put the banana purée into a saucepan with the butter, caster sugar, a few drops of vanilla essence and the rum. Cook for about 3 minutes over a low heat, stirring constantly. Remove from heat.

Separate eggs. Stir yolks into the banana mixture. Place pan in cold water to cool mixture quickly. Beat egg whites till firm, then lightly fold into cold banana mixture with a metal spoon.

Fill banana skins with mixture. Place on a baking tray and bake for about 10 minutes. Sprinkle with icing sugar and serve immediately with pouring cream.

Blackberry and pear meringue

Overall timing 50 minutes

Freezing Not suitable

To serve 6–8

12 oz	Ripe blackberries	350 g
2 oz	Caster sugar	50 g
3 tbsp	Ground almonds	3x15 ml
4	Large ripe pears	4
3	Egg whites	3
7 oz	Icing sugar	200 g

Preheat the oven to 350°F (180°C) Gas 4.

Hull the berries and arrange over the bottom of a shallow ovenproof dish. Mix the caster sugar and 2 tbsp (2x15 ml) of the almonds together and sprinkle over the berries.

Peel and halve the pears lengthways. Remove the cores. Arrange cut sides down in a single layer on the berries. Bake on the centre shelf of the oven for 20 minutes.

Put the egg whites and sifted icing sugar into a large heatproof bowl over a pan of simmering water. Whisk till the meringue is stiff and glossy. Spoon or pipe the meringue over the pears and sprinkle with the reserved almonds.

Return to the oven and bake for a further 10 minutes till lightly browned. Serve immediately.

Baked apple toasts

Overall timing 40 minutes

Freezing Not suitable

To serve 4

3 oz	Butter	75 g
4	Thick slices of crusty bread	4
4	Dessert apples	4
6 tbsp	Demerara sugar	6x15 ml

Preheat the oven to 425°F (220°C) Gas 7.

Butter the bread thickly on one side and arrange on a baking tray, buttered side up.

Peel, core and thinly slice the apples. Arrange half the slices on the bread so they overlap slightly and cover the bread. Sprinkle with a little of the sugar and place remaining apples on top.

Sprinkle apples with remaining sugar and bake for about 25 minutes till the sugar melts and caramelizes. Serve hot.

Berry-stuffed apples

Overall timing 30 minutes

Freezing Suitable: reheat from frozen in 375°F (190°C) Gas 5 oven for 20 minutes

To serve 4

14½ oz	Can of loganberries	411 g
4	Large apples	4
2 oz	Butter	50 g
4 tbsp	Brown sugar	4x15 ml

Preheat the oven to 375°F (190°C) Gas 5.

Drain loganberries, reserving syrup. Core apples. Place in a greased ovenproof dish and fill centres with loganberries. Surround with remaining berries and reserved syrup. Place a knob of butter on each apple and sprinkle with 1 tbsp (15 ml) sugar.

Bake for 25 minutes, basting occasionally with the juices in the dish, till tender. Serve apples hot with pouring cream.

Cherry pudding with jam sauce

Overall timing 1¾ hours

Freezing Not suitable

To serve 4–6

4 oz	Butter	125 g
4 oz	Caster sugar	125 g
2	Eggs	2
6 oz	Self-raising flour	175 g
4 oz	Glacé cherries	125 g
3 tbsp	Milk	3x15 ml
½ teasp	Almond essence	2.5 ml
Sauce		
4 tbsp	Red jam	4x15 ml
¼ pint	Water	150 ml
1 teasp	Arrowroot	5 ml
1 tbsp	Lemon juice	15 ml

Cream butter with sugar till pale and fluffy. Gradually beat in the eggs one at a time. Fold in the sifted flour and cherries, adding milk and almond essence to give a soft dropping consistency. Place in greased basin and cover with greased foil.

Put basin into a pan and fill up to rim of basin with boiling water. Cover and steam for 1½ hours.

To make the sauce, melt the jam with the water in a small pan, then sieve. Blend arrow-root with lemon juice and stir into sauce. Bring to the boil, stirring.

Turn pudding out of mould and serve immediately with the hot jam sauce.

Irish lemon pudding

Overall timing 1 hour

Freezing Not suitable

To serve 4–6

4 oz	Butter	125 g
6 oz	Caster sugar	175 g
4	Eggs	4
1	Lemon	1
3 tbsp	Plain flour	3x15 ml
½ pint	Milk	300 ml
1 tbsp	Icing sugar	15 ml

Preheat the oven to 400°F (200°C) Gas 6.

Cream the butter and caster sugar in a bowl till light and fluffy. Separate the eggs and add the yolks to the creamed mixture. Beat well. Grate rind from lemon and squeeze out juice. Beat into the creamed mixture. Gradually stir in the flour, then the milk.

Beat egg whites till stiff, then carefully fold into mixture. Turn into a greased 7 inch (18 cm) soufflé dish and sift icing sugar over. Place dish in roasting tin containing 1 inch (2.5 cm) hot water. Bake for 40–50 minutes till the pudding has risen and the top is golden. Serve hot or cold.

Caribbean pancakes

Overall timing 40 minutes

Freezing Not suitable

To serve 6

2½ oz	Plain flour	65 g
	Pinch of salt	
¼ teasp	Ground ginger	1.25 ml
1	Egg	1
¼ pint	Milk	150 ml
2 oz	Butter	50 g
Filling		
15½ oz	Can of pineapple rings	439 g
15½ oz	Can of creamed rice	439 g
4 tbsp	Rum	4x15 ml
6	Glacé cherries	6

Sift the flour, salt and ginger into a bowl. Add the egg and milk and beat till smooth. Melt butter and add one-quarter to batter.

Brush a little butter over an 8 inch (20 cm) pan and heat. Pour one-sixth of the batter into the pan, tilting it so that the bottom is covered. Cook till pancake is golden brown underneath, then flip over and cook other side. Make five more pancakes in this way.

Preheat the oven to 375°F (190°C) Gas 5.

Drain the pineapple rings, and reserve three. Finely chop the rest and put into a bowl. Add creamed rice and mix well. Divide the mixture between the pancakes. Roll up the pancakes loosely and arrange in an ovenproof dish. Heat through in the oven for 10 minutes.

Meanwhile, cut the reserved pineapple rings in half. Warm the rum in a small saucepan. Remove pancakes from oven and decorate with the halved pineapple rings and cherries. Pour the warm rum over, set alight and serve flaming, with scoops of vanilla ice cream.

Walnut pear pie

Overall timing 1 hour plus chilling

Freezing Suitable: decorate with cream after thawing

To serve 6–8

6 oz	Plain flour	175 g
4 oz	Butter	125 g
2 oz	Caster sugar	50 g
2 oz	Walnuts	50 g
2 teasp	Ground cinnamon	2x5 ml
1	Egg	1
Filling		
4	Ripe dessert pears	4
1½ oz	Caster sugar	40 g
¼ pint	Whipping cream	150 ml

Sift flour into a large bowl and rub in butter. Stir in sugar, finely chopped walnuts and cinnamon. Add egg with enough water to bind to a firm dough. Chill for 1 hour.

Preheat the oven to 375°F (190°C) Gas 5.

Roll out two-thirds of dough and use to line an 8 inch (20 cm) fluted flan dish. Peel, core and quarter pears. Arrange over pastry in a circle, core-side downwards and with the stem ends pointing towards the centre but not joining up. Sprinkle with 1 oz (25 g) caster sugar.

Roll out remaining dough and place over pears. Trim edges and pinch together to seal. Using a 3 inch (7.5 cm) pastry cutter, cut a circle out of the centre of the pastry lid. Brush pastry with egg white (from egg shell) and dredge with remaining caster sugar. Bake for 15 minutes, then reduce oven temperature to 350°F (180°C) Gas 4 and bake for a further 25 minutes. Cool in tin.

Whip cream and spoon or pipe into centre of pie before serving.

Traditional apple pie

Overall timing 1 hour

Freezing Not suitable

To serve 4–6

8 oz	Plain flour	225 g
	Pinch of salt	
4 oz	Butter	125 g
1½ lb	Cooking apples	700 g
4 tbsp	Brown sugar	4x15 ml
½ teasp	Ground cinnamon	2.5 ml
¼ teasp	Grated nutmeg	1.25 ml
¼ teasp	Ground cloves	1.25 ml
2 oz	Sultanas	50 g
	Milk	
1 tbsp	Caster sugar	15 ml

Preheat oven to 400°F (200°C) Gas 6.

Sift flour and salt together into a bowl and rub in butter. Add enough water to mix to a firm dough.

Peel, core and slice apples into a bowl. Add brown sugar, spices and sultanas. Put mixture in buttered 2 pint (1.1 litre) pie dish. Sprinkle over 2 tbsp (2x15 ml) of water.

Roll out dough and cover pie. Decorate with dough trimmings. Brush with milk and sprinkle with caster sugar.

Bake for 20 minutes. Reduce heat to 350°F (180°C) Gas 4 and bake for a further 20 minutes.

West Indian peanut pie

Overall timing 1¼ hours

Freezing Not suitable

To serve 6–8

Pastry		
4 oz	Self-raising flour	125 g
½ teasp	Salt	2.5 ml
2 tbsp	Caster sugar	2x15 ml
2 oz	Softened butter	50 g
1	Egg yolk	1
2 tbsp	Milk	2x15 ml
Filling		
4 oz	Roasted unsalted peanuts	125 g
1	Egg	1
3 oz	Sugar	75 g
4 oz	Golden syrup	125 g
½ teasp	Vanilla essence	2.5 ml

Preheat the oven to 350°F (180°C) Gas 4.

To make pastry, sift flour, salt and sugar into a bowl. Rub in the butter. Add egg yolk and gradually mix in enough milk to bind to a soft dough. Roll out dough and use to line an 8 inch (20 cm) fluted flan ring.

To make filling, preheat the grill. Remove the shells from the peanuts. Place nuts on a baking tray and grill them for 2 minutes, shaking the tray so they brown lightly all over. Remove and allow to cool.

Whisk the egg and sugar in a bowl till light and frothy. Add syrup and continue to beat till thick. Stir in the peanuts and vanilla essence.

Pour the peanut mixture into the flan ring and bake for 30 minutes. Cover with foil and bake for a further 5–10 minutes. Lift off the foil, leave the pie till almost cool, then remove from tin.

Apple and mincemeat tart

Overall timing 1 hour

Freezing Suitable: reheat in 350°F (180°C) Gas 4 oven for 40 minutes

To serve 6

8 oz	Shortcrust pastry	225 g
14½ oz	Jar of mincemeat	411 g
1 lb	Bramley apples	450 g
3 oz	Caster sugar	75 g
½ teasp	Ground allspice	2.5 ml
2 oz	Butter	50 g
1 tbsp	Plain flour	15 ml

Preheat the oven to 425°F (220°C) Gas 7. Roll out the dough and line a 9½ inch (24 cm) fluted loose-bottomed flan tin. Spread mincemeat evenly over pastry.

Peel, core and finely slice the apples. Mix with 2 oz (50 g) of sugar and the allspice. Arrange in circles on mincemeat.

In a bowl, cut and fold the butter with remaining 1 oz (25 g) sugar and flour until the mixture resembles fine breadcrumbs. Sprinkle evenly over the apples. Place flan on a baking tray.

Bake in oven for 15 minutes, then reduce to 375°F (190°C) Gas 5 and bake for a further 30 minutes. Remove from oven and allow to cool.

Lift tart from flan tin and place on serving plate. Spoon any topping from baking tray on to tart. Serve warm or cold, with whipped cream or vanilla ice cream.

Blackcurrant boats

Overall timing 1 hour 20 minutes

Freezing Not suitable

Makes 8

3 oz	Plain flour	75 g
1½ oz	Caster sugar	40 g
1	Egg	1
	Vanilla essence	
1½ oz	Butter	40 g
Filling		
11 oz	Can of blackcurrants	300 g
2 oz	Caster sugar	50 g
1 oz	Flaked almonds	25 g
¼ pint	Carton of double cream	150 ml
1 tbsp	Icing sugar	15 ml

Preheat the oven to 425°F (220°C) Gas 7.

Sift flour into a bowl, make a well in the centre and add sugar, egg and a few drops of vanilla essence. Add the butter, cut into pieces, and knead to a dough. Chill for 30 minutes.

Roll out dough to ¼ inch (6 mm) thick and use to line eight barquette tins. Prick and bake blind for 15–20 minutes till cooked and golden brown. Cool.

Drain blackcurrants and place in bowl. Sprinkle over the caster sugar and leave for 1 hour.

Preheat the grill. Spread flaked almonds on grill pan and toast. Whip cream till stiff with icing sugar. Spoon into piping bag.

Drain blackcurrants and divide between pastry boats. Pipe on cream and decorate with toasted almonds.

Canadian cherry pie

Overall timing 1¼ hours

Freezing Not suitable

To serve 6

8 oz	Shortcrust pastry	225 g
2 lb	Fresh cherries *or*	900 g
2x15 oz	Cans of cherries	2x425 g
1 oz	Ground rice	25 g
2 oz	Caster sugar	50 g
1	Lemon	1
1	Egg white	1
	Caster sugar	

Preheat the oven to 450°F (230°C) Gas 8.

Roll out two-thirds of dough and use to line 7½ inch (19 cm) fluted loose-bottomed flan tin.

Stone cherries (drain first if canned) and put into saucepan with rice and sugar. Grate rind from lemon and squeeze out juice. Add both to pan and bring to the boil, stirring. Simmer for 2 minutes. Cool.

Spread cherry mixture in pastry case. Roll out remaining dough and lay over filling. Moisten edges and press together to seal. Brush with lightly beaten egg white and dredge with caster sugar.

Bake for 10 minutes, then reduce heat to 350°F (180°C) Gas 4. Bake for a further 40–45 minutes till top is golden.

Custard tart

Overall timing 1½ hours plus cooling

Freezing Not suitable

To serve 4–6

8 oz	Plain flour	225 g
2 oz	Lard	50 g
2 oz	Butter	50 g
2–3 tbsp	Water	2–3x 15 ml
Filling		
1 pint	Milk	560 ml
1	Vanilla pod	1
	Strip of lemon rind	
4	Eggs	4
2 oz	Caster sugar	50 g
	Grated nutmeg	

Preheat the oven to 400°F (200°C) Gas 6.

Put the flour into a bowl and rub in the fat till the mixture resembles fine breadcrumbs. Gradually add the water and mix to a smooth dough.

Roll out the dough on a lightly floured surface and use to line a 9 inch (23 cm) flan tin or ring. Bake blind for 10 minutes. Remove from oven and reduce temperature to 350°F (180°C) Gas 4.

Put milk, vanilla pod and lemon rind into a pan and bring almost to the boil. Remove from heat and leave to infuse for 10 minutes. Remove vanilla pod and lemon rind.

Beat eggs and sugar in bowl. Pour in milk, stirring. Strain into flan case and sprinkle with nutmeg. Bake for 35 minutes or till just set. Cool.

Marmalade and ginger tart

Overall timing 1¼ hours

Freezing Not suitable

To serve 6–8

8 oz	Plain flour	225 g
1 teasp	Ground ginger	5 ml
4 oz	Butter	125 g
2 tbsp	Caster sugar	2x15 ml
1	Egg yolk	1
8 tbsp	Marmalade	8x15 ml

Sift flour and ginger into a bowl. Rub in the butter till the mixture resembles breadcrumbs. Add sugar and mix to a dough with the egg yolk and a little water. Knead lightly till smooth, then chill for 30 minutes.

Preheat the oven to 375°F (190°C) Gas 5.

Roll out about three-quarters of the dough on a floured surface and use to line a 9 inch (23 cm) pie plate or flan tin. Crimp the edges and prick base.

Spread a thick layer of marmalade over the tart base. Roll out the remaining dough and cut into strips with a pastry wheel. Make a lattice over the marmalade filling, pressing the joins to seal. Bake for about 40 minutes, till golden. Remove from tin and serve hot or cold with custard or ice cream.

Nectarine almond tart

Overall timing 50 minutes plus chilling

Freezing Suitable

To serve 4

8 oz	Plain flour	225 g
	Pinch of salt	
4 oz	Butter	125 g
2 oz	Caster sugar	50 g
1	Egg	1
Filling		
1 tbsp	Semolina	15 ml
1 tbsp	Ground almonds	15 ml
4 oz	Caster sugar	125 g
1¾ lb	Nectarines	800 g
½ oz	Split almonds	15 g

Sift the flour and salt into a bowl. Add butter, cut into flakes, sugar and egg and work into a dough. Chill for 30 minutes.

Preheat the oven to 425°F (220°C) Gas 7.

Roll out dough on a floured surface and use to line 9 inch (23 cm) loose-bottomed flan tin. Mix together the semolina, ground almonds and half the caster sugar. Sprinkle over the pastry.

Halve the nectarines and remove the stones. Arrange the fruit in the pastry case, cut sides down, and sprinkle with the remaining sugar and split almonds. Bake for 35–40 minutes.

Allow to cool slightly, then remove from tin and serve warm or cold with pouring cream.

Orange lasagne flan

Overall timing 1½ hours

Freezing Suitable: reheat in 350°F (180°C) Gas 4 oven for 30 minutes

To serve 8

4 oz	Lasagne	125 g
7½ oz	Frozen puff pastry	212 g
3	Thin-skinned oranges	3
2 tbsp	Rum (optional)	2x15 ml
5 tbsp	Thin-cut marmalade	5x15 ml
1 tbsp	Chopped walnuts	15 ml
Confectioners' custard		
1 pint	Milk	560 ml
	Pinch of salt	
1	Vanilla pod	1
	Strip of lemon rind	
4 oz	Caster sugar	125 g
4	Medium eggs	4
1 oz	Plain flour	25 g

Cook lasagne in boiling salted water till tender. Drain and cool.

Meanwhile, thaw pastry and make confectioners' custard. Put milk, salt, vanilla and rind into pan and bring to the boil. Remove from heat and infuse for 10 minutes. Beat sugar, eggs and flour till smooth. Strain in milk, stirring. Return to pan and cook gently, stirring, till thick. Grate rind of one orange and stir into custard with rum, if used.

Preheat the oven to 375°F (190°C) Gas 5.

Roll out dough and use to line 9 inch (23 cm) flan dish. Spread with 2 tbsp (2x15 ml) marmalade. Cover with half custard, then the lasagne and remaining custard.

Peel and thinly slice remaining oranges. Arrange slices over flan to cover completely. Bake for 45 minutes.

Melt remaining marmalade and spoon over oranges to glaze. Sprinkle with walnuts and serve warm with pouring cream.

Iced strawberry tartlets

Overall timing 40 minutes

Freezing Not suitable

Makes 4

6 oz	Rich shortcrust pastry	175 g
4 oz	Gooseberry jam	125 g
2 tbsp	Sherry	2x15 ml
12 oz	Strawberries	350 g
1 pint	Vanilla ice cream or lemon sorbet	560 ml

Preheat the oven to 375°F (190°C) Gas 5. Put baking tray in oven to heat.

Divide dough into four. Put one-quarter into each of four 3 inch (7.5 cm) tartlet dishes and press into shape. Prick bottoms with a fork and place on heated baking tray. Bake for about 25 minutes till crisp and golden. Remove from the oven and leave to cool completely.

Meanwhile, put the jam and sherry into a saucepan and heat gently till melted. Sieve into a sauceboat and leave to cool.

Hull the strawberries. Cut a quarter of them in half lengthways and put the rest into a serving dish.

Arrange the tartlets on a serving dish. Put a scoop of ice cream or sorbet into each and decorate with halved strawberries. Serve immediately with remaining strawberries and gooseberry sauce.

Lime tart

Overall timing 50 minutes plus chilling

Freezing Suitable

To serve 8

6 oz	Shortcrust pastry	175 g
4 teasp	Powdered gelatine	4x5 ml
4 tbsp	Water	4x15 ml
4	Eggs	4
4 oz	Caster sugar	125 g
3	Limes	3
¼ pint	Carton of double cream	150 ml

Preheat the oven to 400°F (200°C) Gas 6.

Roll out dough on a lightly floured surface and use to line an 8 inch (20 cm) flan tin. Bake blind for 10 minutes, then remove beans and foil and bake for a further 10 minutes till golden. Allow to cool, then carefully remove from the tin.

To make the filling, dissolve the gelatine in the water. Separate eggs. Whisk the yolks and sugar together till pale and creamy. Grate rind from limes and squeeze out the juice. Stir two-thirds of the rind and all the juice into the egg mixture. Stir in the gelatine.

Whip cream till stiff. In another bowl, whisk the egg whites till stiff peaks form. Carefully fold cream, then whisked whites into lime mixture. Spoon into pastry case and fluff up the surface.

Sprinkle with the remaining grated lime rind and chill for at least 3 hours or overnight before serving.

Hot apple flan

Overall timing 1 hour

Freezing Not suitable

To serve 6

7 oz	Plain flour	200 g
	Pinch of salt	
1 tbsp	Icing sugar	15 ml
3½ oz	Butter	100 g
Filling		
1½ lb	Cooking apples	700 g
2 oz	Butter	50 g
4½ oz	Icing sugar	140 g
3 tbsp	Calvados or brandy	3x15 ml

Preheat the oven to 400°F (200°C) Gas 6.

To make pastry, sift flour, salt and sugar into a bowl. Add butter and rub in until mixture resembles fine breadcrumbs. Add enough water to mix to a firm dough. Knead lightly. Roll out dough and use to line an 8 inch (20 cm) flan dish. Bake blind for 20–25 minutes.

Meanwhile, make filling. Peel and core apples. Cut into quarters or eighths, depending on size. Melt butter in a saucepan, add apples and cook over a high heat for a few minutes till light brown. Add 4 oz (125 g) icing sugar and 1 tbsp (15 ml) Calvados or brandy. Cover and cook gently till apples are just tender.

Spoon apples and a little of the juice into the warm flan case. Sift over remaining icing sugar. Keep in a warm oven until needed.

Warm remaining Calvados or brandy in a ladle, then pour over apples. Light immediately and take flan to table while still flaming.

French cherry tart

Overall timing 1 hour plus chilling

Freezing Not suitable

To serve 8

8 oz	Plain flour	225 g
	Pinch of salt	
3½ oz	Icing sugar	100 g
4 oz	Butter	125 g
1	Lemon	1
1	Egg	1
Filling		
4 teasp	Dried breadcrumbs	4x5 ml
13½ oz	Jar of cherry pie filling	382 g
3	Eggs	3
3 oz	Caster sugar	75 g
1 tbsp	Cornflour	15 ml
	Ground cinnamon	
1 oz	Cream cheese	25 g

Put the flour, salt and icing sugar into a bowl. Rub in butter. Grate rind and squeeze juice from lemon. Add rind to bowl with egg and mix to a dough. Chill for 30 minutes.

Preheat the oven to 425°F (220°C) Gas 7.

Roll out dough and use to line 10 inch (25 cm) flan ring placed on baking tray. Bake blind for about 15 minutes.

Remove flan case from oven and reduce heat to 375°F (190°C) Gas 5. Sprinkle breadcrumbs over bottom of flan case. Spread cherry pie filling on top.

Separate eggs. Whisk egg yolks with 2 tbsp (2x15 ml) lemon juice, the caster sugar and cornflour until creamy. Beat in cinnamon and cream cheese until smooth.

Beat egg whites until soft peaks form. Fold into yolk mixture. Pour over cherries. Bake for 30–40 minutes. Carefully remove tart from ring and place on a serving dish. Dredge with more icing sugar and serve warm with cream or ice cream.

Linzertorte

Overall timing 50 minutes

Freezing Suitable

To serve 12

8 oz	Plain flour	225 g
½ teasp	Ground cinnamon	2.5 ml
5 oz	Butter	150 g
3 oz	Ground almonds	75 g
3 oz	Caster sugar	75 g
½	Lemon	½
2	Egg yolks	2
8 oz	Raspberry jam	225 g

Sift flour and cinnamon into a large bowl. Rub in butter. Stir in almonds and caster sugar. Grate rind from lemon and squeeze out juice. Add both to bowl with egg yolks and mix to a soft dough. Knead lightly, then chill for 1 hour.

Preheat the oven to 375°F (190°C) Gas 5.

Roll out two-thirds of the dough on a floured surface and use to line an 8 inch (20 cm) flan tin. Don't trim away excess dough.

Spread jam over the pastry case. Roll out remaining dough and cut into strips. Arrange in a lattice pattern across the jam. Fold dough edges in, crimping to make a decorative border.

Bake for 30–35 minutes. Leave to cool in tin. Serve with pouring cream.

Rhubarb and apple pie

Overall timing 2¼ hours plus cooling

Freezing Suitable

To serve 8

12 oz	Plain flour	350 g
½ teasp	Salt	2.5 ml
4 tbsp	Caster sugar	4x15 ml
4 oz	Butter	125 g
¼ pint	Water	150 ml
1	Egg	1
Filling		
2 lb	Rhubarb	900 g
1 lb	Cooking apples	450 g
8 oz	Granulated sugar	225 g
1 teasp	Ground ginger	5 ml
6 tbsp	Water	6x15 ml

Preheat the oven to 375°F (190°C) Gas 5.

Cut rhubarb into 1 inch (2.5 cm) lengths. Peel, core and slice apples. Put fruit into a saucepan with sugar, ginger and water and bring to the boil. Cover and simmer for 15 minutes till pulpy. Purée in a blender or rub through a sieve and leave to cool.

Sift flour and salt into a bowl and stir in sugar. Put butter and water into a pan and heat gently till butter melts. Bring to the boil, then pour into flour mixture and mix to a soft dough.

Quickly roll out two-thirds of dough and use to line a 7 inch (18 cm) springform cake tin. Pour fruit purée into pastry case. Roll out remaining dough and use to cover pie. Seal edges and crimp. Make a neat hole in centre. Decorate top with dough trimmings. Beat egg and brush over pie.

Bake for 1 hour till pastry is golden. Cool in the tin. Serve with pouring cream or ice cream.

Spicy rhubarb pie

Overall timing 1¾ hours

Freezing Not suitable

To serve 6–8

9 oz	Plain flour	250 g
	Pinch of salt	
¼ teasp	Mixed spice	1.25 ml
½ teasp	Ground cinnamon	2.5 ml
5 oz	Butter	150 g
2 tbsp	Caster sugar	2x15 ml
2 lb	Rhubarb	900 g
6 oz	Granulated sugar	175 g
1	Egg yolk	1

Sift flour, pinch of salt and spices into a bowl. Rub in the butter till the mixture resembles fine breadcrumbs. Stir in the caster sugar and enough water to make a soft but not sticky dough. Knead lightly till smooth, then chill for 30 minutes.

Meanwhile, trim the rhubarb and cut into 1 inch (2.5 cm) lengths. Put into a bowl with all but 1 tbsp (15 ml) of the granulated sugar and mix well.

Preheat the oven to 400°F (200°C) Gas 6. Place a baking tray on the shelf just above the centre to heat up.

Roll out half the dough on a floured surface and use to line a 9 inch (23 cm) pie plate. Brush the edge with water. Pile the rhubarb into the pie in a dome shape. Roll out remaining dough and cover the pie, sealing and crimping the edges.

Beat the egg yolk and brush over top of pie. Place pie on hot baking tray and bake for 20 minutes. Reduce the temperature to 350°F (180°C) Gas 4 and bake for a further 25 minutes till crisp and golden.

Remove from the oven, sprinkle remaining sugar over and serve immediately with cream or pouring custard.

Banana tart

Overall timing 1 hour 50 minutes

Freezing Not suitable

To serve 8

7 oz	Plain flour	200 g
½ teasp	Baking powder	2.5 ml
½ teasp	Salt	2.5 ml
3 tbsp	Caster sugar	3x15 ml
3½ oz	Butter	100 g
1	Medium egg	1
Filling		
3 oz	Seedless raisins *or*	75 g
2 oz	Stoned dates	50 g
2 tbsp	Rum	2x15 ml
4	Ripe bananas	4
2	Eggs	2
3 oz	Caster sugar	75 g
4 fl oz	Double cream	113 ml
2 oz	Split almonds	50 g

Sift flour, baking powder, salt and sugar into a bowl. Rub in butter. Add egg with a little water if necessary to bind to a dough. Chill for 1 hour.

Put raisins, or chopped dates, to steep in rum.

Preheat the oven to 400°F (200°C) Gas 6.

Roll out dough and use to line 9 inch (23 cm) fluted flan ring. Prick and bake blind for 10 minutes. Remove beans and paper, and bake for a further 5 minutes. Remove from oven.

Drain dried fruit, reserving rum. Peel bananas and cut in diagonal slices. Cover bottom of pastry case with the bananas and most of the dried fruit.

Whisk eggs and sugar together till pale and thick. Whip cream with reserved rum. Blend both mixtures together and pour over the fruit in pastry case. Scatter over almonds and reserved dried fruit.

Bake for 25 minutes until puffed, golden brown and set. Serve hot with single cream.

Sunburst peach tart

Overall timing 1 hour

Freezing Not suitable

To serve 6

3 oz	Butter	75 g
4 oz	Caster sugar	125 g
3	Eggs	3
5 oz	Plain flour	150 g
	Grated rind of 1 lemon	
14 oz	Can of sliced peaches	397 g
2 oz	Hazelnuts	50 g

Preheat the oven to 350°F (180°C) Gas 4.

Cream the butter and sugar together till pale and fluffy. Beat in the eggs one at a time, beating well between each addition. Fold in the sifted flour and lemon rind with a metal spoon. Pour the mixture into a greased and lined 8 inch (20 cm) springform tin and smooth the surface.

Drain the peaches thoroughly and arrange the slices in circles on the cake mixture. Sprinkle the chopped hazelnuts over. Bake for about 45 minutes.

Remove from the tin, place on a warmed serving dish and serve immediately with pouring custard or cream.

Plum tart

Overall timing 1¾ hours

Freezing Not suitable

To serve 6–8

12 oz	Self-raising flour	350 g
8 oz	Butter	225 g
3 tbsp	Caster sugar	3x15 ml
1	Egg	1
3–4 tbsp	Milk to mix	3–4x 15 ml
Filling		
1 pint	Milk	560 ml
1 teasp	Vanilla essence	5 ml
1½ lb	Ripe yellow plums	700 g
4	Egg yolks	4
6 oz	Caster sugar	175 g
3 oz	Plain flour	75 g

To make filling, put milk and vanilla essence into saucepan and bring to the boil. Remove from heat, cover and leave to infuse for 10 minutes.

Meanwhile halve and stone plums. Beat egg yolks with sugar till pale and thick. Beat in sifted flour, then gradually stir in milk. Pour back into saucepan and cook gently, stirring, till thick. Leave to cool.

Preheat the oven to 400°F (200°C) Gas 6.

Sift flour into a bowl and rub in 6 oz (175 g) butter. Stir in sugar, and add egg and enough milk to give a soft dough. Roll out and use to line greased 8 inch (20 cm) square deep cake tin, moulding it into the corners. Rest in refrigerator for 15 minutes.

Pour filling into pastry-lined tin and arrange plums on top, pressing them in lightly. Bake for 30 minutes.

Meanwhile, melt remaining butter in a saucepan. Remove tart from tin and place on a baking tray. Brush sides and top edge of pastry with butter and bake for a further 10 minutes till pastry is crisp and golden. Serve hot or cold.

Tarte Tatin

Overall timing 1¼ hours

Freezing Not suitable

To serve 8–10

7 oz	Frozen puff pastry	212 g
3 oz	Unsalted butter	75 g
3 oz	Caster sugar	75 g
7	Large dessert apples	7

Thaw the pastry. Preheat the oven to 425°F (220°C) Gas 7.

Cut the butter into pieces and put into a 9 inch (23 cm) round cake tin with the sugar. Peel and core the apples; cut six of them in half. Arrange the apple halves on end around the side of the tin and place the whole apple in the centre.

Place the tin over a low heat and heat till the butter melts. Increase the heat and cook, shaking the tin occasionally, till the sugar caramelizes and is golden. Remove from the heat. Brush a little water round the edge of the tin.

Roll out the dough on a floured surface to a 9 inch (23 cm) round and place over the apples. Press down lightly.

Bake for 25–30 minutes till the pastry is well risen and golden brown. Leave to cool in the tin for 5 minutes.

Run a knife round the edge of the tart and turn out on to a serving dish so that the caramelized apples are on top. Serve hot or cold with whipped cream or scoops of vanilla ice cream.

Almond marmalade tart

Overall timing 1¼ hours

Freezing Suitable

To serve 6–8

3½ oz	Butter	100 g
3½ oz	Caster sugar	100 g
1	Egg	1
4 oz	Ground almonds	125 g
5 oz	Self-raising flour	150 g
¼ teasp	Salt	1.25 ml
Filling		
12 oz	Cooking apples	350 g
	Juice of ½ lemon	
2 tbsp	Sugar	2x15 ml
6 tbsp	Fine-cut marmalade	6x15 ml
1 tbsp	Dried breadcrumbs	15 ml

Put butter, sugar and egg into a bowl and beat until light and fluffy. Add almonds, sifted flour and salt and mix to a soft, but not sticky dough. Chill for 30 minutes.

Meanwhile, peel and core apples. Slice thinly into a bowl and sprinkle with lemon juice. Stir in the sugar and marmalade and leave to stand till pastry is ready.

Preheat the oven to 400°F (200°C) Gas 6.

Put half the dough into a greased 8 inch (20 cm) sandwich tin and spread out to cover the bottom. Prick and sprinkle breadcrumbs over. Spread the apple mixture over and cover with small spoonfuls of remaining pastry.

Bake for about 35 minutes till golden. Remove from tin and serve hot or cold, cut into slices, with cream or custard.

Wholemeal bread

Overall timing 3 hours minimum

Freezing Suitable

Makes 2–4 loaves

1 tbsp	Brown sugar	15 ml
1½ pints	Lukewarm water	850 ml
1 oz	Dried yeast	25 g
3 lb	Wholemeal flour	1.4 kg
1 tbsp	Salt	15 ml
1 oz	Lard	25 g

Dissolve 1 teasp (5 ml) of the sugar in 9 fl oz (250 ml) of the warm water in a bowl. Sprinkle the dried yeast on top. Leave for about 10 minutes till frothy.

Mix flour, salt and the remaining sugar in a bowl. Rub in the lard, then add the yeast liquid and the rest of the water. Mix to scone-like dough. Knead the dough thoroughly till it feels firm and elastic and no longer sticky. This should take 5–10 minutes. Shape the dough into a ball and place in an oiled polythene bag. Leave to rise till doubled in size.

Turn the dough on to a board and knead again till firm. Divide into two or four and flatten each piece firmly with the knuckles to knock out air. Shape and place in loaf tins.

Brush the tops with a little salted water and put each tin into an oiled polythene bag. Leave to rise till the dough comes to just over the top of the tin and springs back when pressed with a floured finger – about 1 hour at room temperature.

Preheat the oven to 450°F (230°C) Gas 8. Bake the loaves for 30–40 minutes. Turn out to cool on a wire rack.

Brioche

Overall timing 1¼ hours plus proving

Freezing Suitable: shape dough and bake after thawing

Makes 1 large or 12 small

2 teasp	Caster sugar	2x5 ml
2 tbsp	Lukewarm water	2x15 ml
2 teasp	Dried yeast	2x5 ml
8 oz	Strong plain flour	225 g
	Salt	
2 oz	Butter	50 g
2	Eggs	2
	Milk for glazing	

Dissolve ½ teasp (2.5 ml) sugar in water and sprinkle yeast on top. Leave till frothy.

Sift flour, a pinch of salt and remaining sugar into a large bowl. Add yeast mixture, melted butter and eggs and mix to a soft dough. Knead till smooth and glossy. Leave to rise in a warm place till doubled in size.

Knock back dough and knead for 3–4 minutes till smooth. To make one large brioche, cut off one-quarter of the dough and shape both pieces into balls. Place large one in lightly greased 8 inch (20 cm) brioche tin and push a finger down through centre to base. Place smaller ball in indentation and press down lightly.

To make 12 small brioches, divide dough into 12 pieces and remove one-quarter from each. Shape all pieces into balls. Place each large ball in a 3 inch (7.5 cm) brioche tin, push a finger down through centre, then top with small balls, pressing down lightly. Leave to rise till doubled in size.

Preheat the oven to 450°F (230°C) Gas 8. Brush each brioche with milk and bake for 8–10 minutes (small) or 15–20 minutes (large) till well risen and golden. Serve warm.

Italian fruit bread

Overall timing 1½ hours plus proving

Freezing Suitable: reheat in 350°F (180°C) Gas 4 oven for 10 minutes

To serve 5

12 oz	Strong plain flour	350 g
4 teasp	Dried yeast	4x5 ml
2 oz	Caster sugar	50 g
¼ pint	Lukewarm milk	150 ml
¼ teasp	Salt	1.25 ml
2 oz	Pine nuts	50 g
2 oz	Candied peel	50 g
2 oz	Seedless raisins	50 g
2 oz	Butter	50 g
1	Egg	1
1 tbsp	Marsala	15 ml

Mix together 4oz (125 g) flour, the yeast, 1 teasp (5 ml) sugar and the milk to a smooth batter. Leave till frothy.

Sift remaining flour and the salt into a large bowl. Add remaining sugar, the pine nuts, candied peel and raisins. Stir melted butter, beaten egg and Marsala into frothy batter, then add to fruit mixture. Mix to a soft dough. Turn out on to a lightly floured surface and knead till smooth and glossy. Cover with oiled polythene and leave to rise till doubled in size.

Knock back dough and knead till smooth. Shape into a smooth ball and place on greased baking tray. Leave to prove till doubled in size.

Preheat the oven to 400°F (200°C) Gas 6. Score a cross on top of the ball and bake for 10 minutes. Reduce the heat to 350°F (180°C) Gas 4 and bake for a further 25 minutes. Cool on a wire rack.

Caraway seed bread

Overall timing 1½ hours plus proving

Freezing Suitable: refresh in hot oven for 10 minutes

Makes 2 small or 1 large loaf

1 lb	Strong plain flour	450 g
1½ oz	Caster sugar	40 g
2 teasp	Dried yeast	2x5 ml
5 tbsp	Lukewarm water	5x15 ml
4 fl oz	Lukewarm milk	120 ml
1 teasp	Salt	5 ml
2 tbsp	Caraway seeds	2x15 ml
4 oz	Softened butter	125 g
2	Eggs	2
1 tbsp	Milk	15 ml

Mix together 4 oz (125 g) flour, 1 teasp (5 ml) sugar, the yeast, water and milk in a large bowl. Cover and leave in a warm place for about 20 minutes till frothy.

Mix remaining flour with salt, remaining sugar and caraway seeds. Add to yeast mixture with butter and beaten eggs. Mix well to a soft dough. Turn on to a lightly floured surface and knead till smooth and elastic. Cover and leave to rise until doubled in size.

Turn dough on to a lightly floured surface and knead till dough is firm again. Shape into two rolls about 6 inches (15 cm) long. Place on greased and floured baking tray. Make three cuts across top of each loaf. Brush with milk. Cover with polythene bag and leave to rise until loaves double in size.

Preheat the oven to 400°F (200°C) Gas 6. Bake the loaves for 30–35 minutes. Cool on a wire rack.

Milk buns

Overall timing About 3 hours

Freezing Suitable

Makes about 15

2 teasp	Dried yeast	2x5 ml
¼ pint	Lukewarm milk	150 ml
9 oz	Plain flour	250 g
4 teasp	Caster sugar	4x5 ml
½ teasp	Salt	2.5 ml
3½ oz	Butter	100 g

Mix yeast, all but 2 tbsp (2x15 ml) milk, 2 oz (50 g) flour and 3 teasp (3x5 ml) sugar to make a batter. Leave till frothy.

Add rest of flour and salt to batter. Mix by hand to soft dough that leaves bowl clean. Knead till smooth and no longer sticky. Leave to rise for 1 hour in warm place.

Cut butter into small pieces. Make a hollow in dough and drop in a few pieces of butter. Knead or squeeze into dough. Continue adding butter in this way till dough becomes silky and smooth. Divide into egg-size pieces and shape into rolls. Place on greased baking tray. Lightly mark a cross on each. Leave to rise till doubled in size.

Preheat the oven to 375°F (190°C) Gas 5.

Heat remaining milk and sugar and brush over rolls. Bake for 30 minutes till golden brown. Cool on wire rack.

Fruit and nut bread

Overall timing 35 minutes plus rising

Freezing Suitable

Makes 1 loaf

7 fl oz	Lukewarm milk	200 ml
4 teasp	Dried yeast	4x5 ml
2½ oz	Caster sugar	65 g
1 lb	Strong plain flour	450 g
1 teasp	Salt	5 ml
4 oz	Butter	125 g
2 oz	Stoned prunes	50 g
2 oz	Dried figs	50 g
2 oz	Sultanas	50 g
4 oz	Mixed nuts	125 g
1	Egg	1
1 tbsp	Icing sugar	15 ml

Mix ¼ pint (150 ml) milk with yeast and 1 teasp (5 ml) sugar. Leave till frothy.

Sift flour and salt into a large bowl. Add yeast mixture, melted butter, remaining sugar, chopped fruit and nuts and remaining milk. Mix to a soft dough. Leave to rise till doubled in size.

Knead until smooth. Shape into a rectangle and place in 2 lb (900 g) loaf tin. Leave to prove until doubled in size.

Preheat the oven to 425°F (225°C) Gas 7. Brush top of loaf with lightly beaten egg and bake for 15 minutes. Cover top with greaseproof paper and reduce heat to 400°F (200°C) Gas 6. Bake for further 20–30 minutes. Dredge with icing sugar and serve warm.

Sesame bread

Overall timing 2 hours plus proving

Freezing Suitable

Makes 2 loaves

6	Saffron strands	6
¼ pint	Lukewarm milk	150 ml
4 fl oz	Lukewarm water	120 ml
1 tbsp	Dried yeast	15 ml
4 teasp	Caster sugar	4x5 ml
1 lb	Strong plain flour	450 g
2 oz	Butter	50 g
2	Eggs	2
½ teasp	Salt	2.5 ml
2 tbsp	Sesame seeds	2x15 ml

Mix together saffron, all but 2 tbsp (2x15 ml) milk, the water, yeast, 1 teasp (5 ml) sugar and 2 tbsp (2x15 ml) flour. Leave in a warm place till frothy.

Melt butter and cool, then beat into batter with one egg and the remaining milk and sugar. Sift remaining flour and the salt over batter and mix to a soft dough. Knead till smooth. Leave to rise till doubled in size.

Knock back the dough. Knead till smooth and divide into six pieces. Roll into sausages about 9 inches (23 cm) long. Moisten ends of sausages with beaten egg. Plait three together, pinching together at both ends to seal. Repeat with remaining three sausages and arrange on greased baking tray. Leave to rise till doubled in size.

Preheat the oven to 375°F (190°C) Gas 5. Brush plaits carefully with beaten egg, then sprinkle with sesame seeds. Bake for about 35 minutes. Cool on wire rack.

Quick cottage loaf

Overall timing 1½ hours

Freezing Suitable

Makes 1 loaf

1 oz	Fresh yeast	25 g
12 fl oz	Lukewarm water	350 ml
1 tablet	Vitamin C	25 mg
1¼ lb	Strong plain flour	600 g
2 teasp	Salt	2x5 ml
1 teasp	Sugar	5 ml
½ oz	Lard	15 g

Blend the fresh yeast with the warm water. Crush vitamin tablet and add to the yeast liquid.

Sift the flour, salt and sugar into a bowl and rub in lard. Add the yeast liquid and mix to a dough that leaves the bowl clean. Turn the dough on to a lightly floured surface and knead till smooth and elastic.

To shape dough into a cottage loaf, divide it into two pieces with one about a third bigger than the other. Shape both into rounds and place smaller one on top. Press handle of wooden spoon through centre of both pieces. Place on baking tray and cover with oiled polythene. Leave to rise for 40–50 minutes.

Preheat the oven to 450°F (230°C) Gas 8. Dust loaf with flour and bake for 30–35 minutes.

Soda bread

Overall timing 1 hour

Freezing Suitable: bake after thawing

Makes 1 loaf

1 lb	Strong white or white and wholemeal flour	450 g
1 teasp	Salt	5 ml
2 teasp	Bicarbonate of soda	2x5 ml
4 teasp	Cream of tartar	4x5 ml
1 oz	Fat	25 g
9 fl oz	Milk	250 ml

Preheat the oven to 425°F (220°C) Gas 7.

Sift the flour, salt, soda and cream of tartar into a bowl. Rub in the fat and add enough milk to make a soft dough. Knead for 1 minute, then shape into a ball and place on a greased baking tray. Mark with a cross, cutting almost to the base of the dough.

Bake for 40–50 minutes till well risen, lightly browned and firm underneath.

Spicy fruit bread

Overall timing 1½ hours plus proving

Freezing Suitable: reheat in 350°F (180°C) Gas 4 oven for 20 minutes

To serve 8

3 oz	Light soft brown sugar	75 g
¼ pint	Milk	150 ml
4 teasp	Dried yeast	4x5 ml
12 oz	Strong plain flour	350 g
½ teasp	Salt	2.5 ml
1 teasp	Ground cinnamon	5 ml
	Ground cloves	
3 oz	Softened butter	75 g
1	Egg	1
6 oz	Sultanas	175 g
2 oz	Currants	50 g

Dissolve ½ teasp (2.5 ml) sugar in all but 2 tbsp (2x15 ml) of the milk and sprinkle yeast on top. Leave in warm place till frothy.

Sift the flour, salt, cinnamon and a pinch of cloves into a large bowl. Add the yeast mixture, butter, egg, remaining sugar, the sultanas and currants. Mix to a soft dough. Knead the dough on a floured surface till glossy. Wrap in oiled polythene and leave to rise till doubled in size.

Turn the dough out on to a floured surface and knead till smooth. Shape into a thick sausage and place on a greased baking tray. Cover with oiled polythene and leave to prove till doubled in size.

Preheat the oven to 400°F (200°C) Gas 6. Brush the dough with the reserved milk and bake for about 40 minutes. Cool on a wire rack.

Cheese yeast cake

Overall timing 2½ hours

Freezing Suitable: reheat in 350°F (180°C) Gas 4 oven for 15–20 minutes, then add jam and almonds

To serve 16

8 oz	Plain flour	225 g
2 oz	Caster sugar	50 g
3 teasp	Dried yeast	3x5 ml
6 tbsp	Lukewarm milk	6x15 ml
1 oz	Softened butter	25 g
1	Egg	1
	Pinch of salt	
Topping		
2 oz	Butter	50 g
8 oz	Curd cheese	225 g
4 tbsp	Cold custard	4x15 ml
	Grated rind of 1 lemon	
1	Egg	1
4 oz	Caster sugar	125 g
1½ lb	Dessert apples	700 g
4 tbsp	Apricot jam	4x15 ml
2 oz	Flaked almonds	50 g

Mix together 2 oz (50 g) flour, 1 teasp (5 ml) sugar, yeast and milk. Leave till frothy.

Add remaining flour and sugar, the softened butter, egg and salt. Mix well to form a soft dough. Knead till smooth, then leave to rise for 30 minutes in a warm place.

Roll out dough and line bottom of greased 7x11 inch (18x28 cm) roasting tin.

Preheat oven to 400°F (200°C) Gas 6.

To make topping, melt butter and brush half over dough. Beat cheese with custard, lemon rind, egg and sugar. Spread evenly over dough. Peel, core and slice apples. Arrange on top of creamed mixture. Brush with remaining melted butter and bake for 45 minutes.

Remove cake from tin. Heat jam and spread over apples. Sprinkle with almonds and serve warm.

Danish pastries

Overall timing 2 hours including chilling

Freezing Suitable

Makes 15

1½ oz	Caster sugar	40 g
3 fl oz	Lukewarm milk	90 ml
1 teasp	Dried yeast	5 ml
9 oz	Plain flour	250 g
½ teasp	Salt	2.5 ml
6 oz	Butter	175 g
	Almond paste	
1	Egg	1
4 oz	Icing sugar	125 g

Dissolve 1 teasp (5 ml) sugar in milk and sprinkle yeast on top. Leave till frothy. Sift flour and salt into bowl, rub in ½ oz (15 g) butter and add rest of sugar and yeast mixture. Mix to a dough. Shape remaining butter into an oblong. Roll out dough into an oblong twice size of butter. Place butter in centre and wrap dough round.

Turn dough so folds are at sides. Roll into an oblong three times longer than it is wide. Fold bottom third up, top third down. Chill for 10 minutes. Repeat turning, rolling and chilling twice.

Roll out dough into oblong, 15x9 inches (38x23 cm), cut into 15 squares and shape as below:

Cockscombs: Put almond paste in centre of each and fold in half, sealing with beaten egg. Make cuts in folded edge, almost to cut edges; spread out in a fan shape. Envelopes: Put almond paste in centre of each and fold opposite corners to centre, securing tips with beaten egg. Windmills: Make diagonal cuts from each corner almost to centre. Place almond paste in centre and fold one corner of each triangle to it. Press firmly to secure. Arrange shapes on baking trays and prove for 20 minutes.

Preheat the oven to 425°F (220°C) Gas 7. Brush with beaten egg and bake for 18 minutes. Mix icing sugar with 2 tbsp (2x15 ml) water and trickle over hot pastries.

Bagels

Overall timing 1¼ hours plus proving and cooling

Freezing Suitable: refresh from frozen in 400°F (200°C) Gas 6 oven for 10 minutes

Makes 10

1 teasp	Caster sugar	5 ml
6 tbsp	Lukewarm water	6x15 ml
1 teasp	Dried yeast	5 ml
9 oz	Strong plain flour	250 g
1 teasp	Salt	5 ml
1	Egg	1
1 tbsp	Oil	15 ml
1	Egg yolk	1
1 teasp	Caraway seeds	5 ml
1 teasp	Poppy seeds	5 ml
1 teasp	Coarse salt	5 ml

Dissolve sugar in water and sprinkle yeast on top. Leave till frothy.

Sift flour and salt into a large bowl. Add egg, oil and yeast mixture. Mix to a soft dough. Knead till smooth and glossy. Leave to rise till doubled in size.

Knock back dough and knead till smooth. Divide into 10 equal portions and roll into sausage shapes about 7 inches (18 cm) long. Wrap sausage shapes round to make rings and pinch ends together to seal. Smooth joins by rocking dough on a floured surface. Arrange on a baking tray, cover with oiled polythene and leave to rise till almost doubled in bulk.

Preheat oven to 425°F (220°C) Gas 7.

Poach bagels, in batches, in boiling water for 2 minutes, turning them once. Remove from the pan with a draining spoon and arrange on a floured baking tray.

When all the bagels are ready, brush them with egg yolk. Sprinkle some with caraway seeds, some with poppy seeds and some with coarse salt. Bake for about 15 minutes till crisp and golden brown. Cool on a wire rack.

Chelsea buns

Overall timing 1 hour plus proving

Freezing Suitable

Makes 6

1 lb	Strong plain flour	450 g
7 tbsp	Caster sugar	7x15 ml
8 fl oz	Lukewarm milk	225 ml
4 teasp	Dried yeast	4x5 ml
4 oz	Butter	125 g
1	Egg	1
4 oz	Mixed dried fruit	125 g
1 teasp	Mixed spice	5 ml

Mix 4 oz (125 g) flour with 1 teasp (5 ml) sugar, 7 fl oz (200 ml) milk and the yeast to a smooth batter. Leave till frothy.

Sift remaining flour and 4 teasp (4x5 ml) sugar into a bowl and rub in 3 oz (75 g) butter. Add egg and yeast mixture and mix to a soft dough. Knead till smooth and glossy. Leave to rise till doubled in size.

Knock back dough and knead till smooth. Roll out to a 9 inch (23 cm) square. Brush remaining butter, melted, over dough. Mix all but 1 tbsp (15 ml) of remaining sugar with fruit and spice and sprinkle over dough. Roll up, then cut across into six thick slices. Arrange, cut sides up, in greased 9x6 inch (23x15 cm) roasting tin, leaving equal space between. Prove till slices join together.

Preheat oven to 375°F (190°C) Gas 5. Brush buns with remaining milk and sprinkle with remaining sugar. Bake for about 35 minutes till golden. Cool on wire rack.

Pretzels

Overall timing 1 hour plus proving

Freezing Suitable: reheat in 375°F (190°C) Gas 5 oven for 5–10 minutes

Makes about 30

$\frac{1}{2}$ teasp	Caster sugar	2.5 ml
7 fl oz	Lukewarm water	200 ml
2 teasp	Dried yeast	2x5 ml
10 oz	Strong plain flour	275 g
1 teasp	Salt	5 ml
1 teasp	Poppy seeds	5 ml
1 oz	Butter	25 g
2	Eggs	2
2 tbsp	Coarse salt	2x15 ml

Dissolve sugar in water and sprinkle yeast on top. Leave in warm place till frothy.

Sift flour and salt into a bowl and stir in poppy seeds, yeast mixture, melted butter and one egg. Mix to soft dough. Leave to rise till doubled in size.

Knead till smooth. Break off small pieces and tie into loose knots, tucking ends in. Arrange pretzels on greased baking trays. Leave to prove till doubled in size.

Preheat the oven to 400°F (200°C) Gas 6. Beat remaining egg and brush over pretzels. Sprinkle with coarse salt and bake for about 10 minutes till crisp and golden. Cool on wire rack.

Currant buns

Overall timing 2¼ hours

Freezing Suitable

Makes 12

1 lb	Strong plain flour	450 g
3 oz	Caster sugar	75 g
1 tbsp	Dried yeast	15 ml
11 fl oz	Lukewarm milk	325 ml
½ teasp	Salt	2.5 ml
1 teasp	Mixed spice	5 ml
4 oz	Currants	125 g
2 oz	Butter	50 g
1	Egg	1

Mix together 2 oz (50 g) flour, 1 teasp (5 ml) sugar, the yeast and ½ pint (300 ml) milk to a batter. Leave till frothy.

Sift remaining flour, salt and spice into a mixing bowl. Add currants, 2 oz (50 g) sugar, the yeast mixture, melted butter and egg. Mix to a soft dough. Knead till smooth and elastic. Leave to rise till doubled in size.

Knock back dough, then divide into 12 pieces. Knead each piece into a smooth bun. Place on baking trays, cover and leave to prove till doubled in size.

Preheat the oven to 375°F (190°C) Gas 5.

To make glaze, dissolve remaining sugar in rest of milk and brush lightly over the buns. Bake for 15–20 minutes. While still hot, brush with remaining glaze.

Jam doughnuts

Overall timing 3–3½ hours including rising

Freezing Suitable: reheat from frozen in 400°F (200°C) Gas 6 oven for 8 minutes

Makes 12

8 oz	Strong plain flour	225 g
2 teasp	Dried yeast	2x5 ml
5 tbsp	Caster sugar	5x15 ml
6 tbsp	Lukewarm milk	6x15 ml
¼ teasp	Salt	1.25 ml
1½ oz	Butter	40 g
1	Egg	1
	Oil for frying	
	Jam	

Mix together 2 oz (50 g) flour, the yeast, 2 teasp (2x5 ml) sugar and the milk to a batter. Leave till frothy.

Sift remaining flour and salt into bowl. Add yeast mixture, melted butter and beaten egg and mix to a soft dough. Knead till smooth and elastic. Leave to rise till doubled in size.

Knock back dough, divide into 12 and shape into balls. Leave to prove.

Heat the oil in a deep-fryer to 360°F (180°C). Press a deep hole in each dough ball and fill with about 1 teasp (5 ml) jam. Seal jam in well by pinching dough together. Deep fry for about 10 minutes. Drain on kitchen paper and roll in remaining sugar while still hot.

Lemon buns

Overall timing 1 hour plus cooling

Freezing Suitable: refresh in 400°F (200°C) Gas 6 oven for 10 minutes

Makes 12

2 oz	Caster sugar	50 g
5 tbsp	Lukewarm milk	5x15 ml
2 teasp	Dried yeast	2x5 ml
8 oz	Strong plain flour	225 g
	Salt	
	Grated rind of 2 lemons	
1	Egg	1
1	Egg yolk	1
2 oz	Butter	50 g

Dissolve ½ teasp (2.5 ml) of the sugar in the milk and sprinkle the yeast on top. Leave in a warm place for 15 minutes till frothy.

Sift the flour and a pinch of salt into a bowl and stir in the remaining sugar and lemon rind. Add the yeast mixture, beaten egg and yolk and melted butter and mix to a stiff dough. Divide between greased 12-hole bun tray. Cover with oiled polythene and leave to rise in a warm place till doubled in size.

Preheat the oven to 375°F (190°C) Gas 5. Bake the buns for about 25 minutes till well risen. Cool on a wire rack.

Cherry and lemon loaf

Overall timing 1½ hours

Freezing Suitable

To serve 16

8 oz	Self-raising flour	225 g
	Pinch of salt	
4 oz	Butter	125 g
4 oz	Caster sugar	125 g
	Grated rind of 1 lemon	
1	Egg	1
4 fl oz	Milk	120 ml
4 oz	Glacé cherries	125 g

Preheat the oven to 350°F (180°C) Gas 4.

Sift all but 1 tbsp (15 ml) of flour and the salt into a bowl. Rub in butter until mixture resembles fine breadcrumbs. Stir in sugar and lemon rind. Make a well in centre and break in egg. Mix together, adding enough milk to give a soft consistency that won't drop unless flicked from the spoon. Coat cherries in reserved flour and fold into mixture.

Pour into greased and lined 2 lb (900 g) loaf tin and smooth surface. Bake for 45 minutes. Cover with greaseproof and bake for further 30 minutes. Cool on a wire rack.

Coffee ring cake

Overall timing 1½ hours

Freezing Suitable

To serve 16

5 oz	Butter	150g
5 oz	Caster sugar	150g
	Salt	
2	Large eggs	2
1	Orange	1
3 teasp	Instant coffee powder	3x5 ml
5 oz	Self-raising flour	150g
¼ teasp	Ground cinnamon	1.25 ml
2 oz	Plain chocolate	50g
Icing		
6 oz	Icing sugar	175 g
2 teasp	Instant coffee powder	2x5 ml
1 teasp	Cocoa	5 ml
2 tbsp	Hot water	2x15 ml
	Vanilla essence	

Preheat the oven to 325°F (170°C) Gas 3.

Cream butter with sugar and a pinch of salt till light and fluffy. Add eggs one at a time and beat well. Grate orange and add rind to bowl. Squeeze orange and mix 3 tbsp (3x15 ml) juice with the instant coffee. Sift flour and cinnamon and mix into the creamed mixture alternately with the orange/coffee mixture. Grate chocolate and fold in.

Spoon mixture into greased 8½ inch (22 cm) ring mould. Bake for 40–50 minutes. Cool on a wire rack.

To make the icing, sift icing sugar into bowl. Dissolve coffee and cocoa in hot water, then add to icing sugar with a few drops of vanilla essence and mix well. Pour over cooled cake and smooth surface with a knife.

Fatless sponge cake

Overall timing 1½ hours

Freezing Not suitable

To serve 8–10

4	Eggs	4
5 oz	Caster sugar	150 g
½ teasp	Vanilla essence	2.5 ml
2 oz	Plain flour	50 g
2 oz	Potato flour	50 g
1	Egg white	1

Preheat the oven to 350°F (180°C) Gas 4.

Separate eggs. Whisk the yolks with the sugar and vanilla essence in a bowl over a pan of hot water till mixture leaves a trail lasting 20 seconds when the beaters are lifted. Remove from the heat. Add the sifted flours and fold in with a wooden spatula or metal spoon.

Whisk egg whites till stiff. Add about one-quarter of the whites to the yolk mixture and stir in, then fold mixture into the remaining egg white with a metal spoon.

Turn mixture into greased and floured 9 inch (23 cm) fluted tin. Bake for 50 minutes to 1 hour or until top springs back when lightly pressed.

Tunisian fruit and nut cake

Overall timing 1¾ hours

Freezing Suitable

To serve 8

1 oz	Toasted hazelnuts	25 g
2 oz	Toasted pistachios	50 g
1	Orange	1
5	Eggs	5
8 oz	Caster sugar	225 g
4 oz	Dried breadcrumbs	125 g
2 oz	Plain flour	50 g
1 teasp	Baking powder	5 ml
½ teasp	Bicarbonate of soda	2.5 ml
½ teasp	Ground cinnamon	2.5 ml
4 oz	Sultanas	125 g

Preheat the oven to 350°F (180°C) Gas 4.

Chop the nuts finely. Finely grate rind from orange. Separate the eggs. Whisk the yolks with the sugar in a bowl over a pan of hot water till pale and thick.

Remove from the heat. Add orange rind, breadcrumbs, sifted flour, baking powder, bicarbonate of soda, cinnamon and nuts, and fold in with a metal spoon. Squeeze the orange and add 2 tbsp (2x15 ml) of the juice to the mixture with the sultanas. Whisk the egg whites till stiff but not dry and fold in carefully.

Pour mixture into greased and lined 9 inch (23 cm) springform tin. Bake for about 1 hour till firm and springy to the touch. Cool on a wire rack.

Whisky cake

Overall timing 2 hours plus cooling

Freezing Suitable

To serve 12

4 oz	Seedless raisins	125 g
4 tbsp	Whisky	4x15 ml
4 oz	Candied orange peel	125 g
	Grated rind of 1 orange	
6 oz	Butter	175 g
6 oz	Caster sugar	175 g
3	Eggs	3
4 oz	Plain flour	125 g
4 oz	Self-raising flour	125 g
¼ teasp	Ground cinnamon	1.25 ml

Preheat the oven to 350°F (180°C) Gas 4.

Soak the raisins in the whisky. Chop the candied peel and add to the raisins with the orange rind. Mix well and leave to soak for 10 minutes.

Cream the butter with the sugar till pale and fluffy. Beat the eggs and add, a little at a time, to the creamed mixture, beating well between each addition. Sift the flours and cinnamon over, add the fruit and soaking liquid and fold into the mixture with a metal spoon.

Spread the mixture in a greased and lined 8 inch (20 cm) round cake tin, smooth the surface and make a slight hollow in the centre. Bake for 1¼–1½ hours till a skewer inserted in the cake comes out clean. Allow to cool slightly in the tin, then transfer to a wire rack and leave to cool completely.

Moist date and ginger cake

Overall timing 1¼ hours

Freezing Suitable

To serve 12

8 oz	Stoned dates	225 g
1 teasp	Bicarbonate of soda	5 ml
¼ pint	Boiling water	150 ml
4 oz	Butter	125 g
4 oz	Soft dark brown sugar	125 g
2 tbsp	Black treacle	2x15 ml
1 tbsp	Golden syrup	15 ml
2	Eggs	2
8 oz	Self-raising flour	225 g
2 teasp	Ground ginger	2x5 ml
2 tbsp	Icing sugar	2x15 ml

Preheat the oven to 350°F (180°C) Gas 4.

Chop the dates and place in a small bowl. Sprinkle with bicarbonate of soda, then pour on the boiling water. Leave to cool.

Cream the butter with the sugar till light and fluffy. Beat in the black treacle and syrup, then the eggs, one at a time, beating well. Sift in the flour and ginger, and add the dates and soaking liquid. Stir till well blended.

Pour into a greased and lined 9 inch (23 cm) round cake tin. Bake for 50–60 minutes till the centre of the cake springs back when lightly pressed. Cool on a wire rack. Dredge with icing sugar before serving.

Sultana loaf cake

Overall timing 1½ hours

Freezing Suitable

To serve 16

8 oz	Self-raising flour	225 g
	Salt	
1 teasp	Ground ginger	5 ml
4 oz	Butter	125 g
2 oz	Caster sugar	50 g
6 oz	Sultanas	175 g
2 tbsp	Clear honey	2x15 ml
1	Egg	1
7 tbsp	Milk	7x15 ml

Preheat the oven to 350°F (180°C) Gas 4.

Sift the flour, a pinch of salt and the ginger into a large bowl. Rub in butter till the mixture resembles fine breadcrumbs. Stir in the sugar and sultanas. Make a well in the centre and add the honey, egg and half the milk. Mix together, adding the remaining milk if necessary to give a soft dropping consistency.

Spread the mixture in a greased and lined 2 lb (900 g) loaf tin and smooth the surface. Bake for 45 minutes. Cover the top lightly with foil and bake for a further 30 minutes till the loaf is springy when lightly pressed. Cool on a wire rack.

Marble ring cake

Overall timing 1½ hours

Freezing Suitable

To serve 10

4 oz	Butter	125 g
5 oz	Caster sugar	150 g
3	Eggs	3
7 oz	Self-raising flour	200 g
5 tbsp	Milk	5x15 ml
1 oz	Cocoa powder	25 g

Preheat the oven to 350°F (180°C) Gas 4.

Cream the butter with the sugar till mixture is pale and fluffy. Beat in the eggs, one at a time. Divide the mixture into two. Sift 4 oz (125 g) of the flour into one-half and fold in with 3 tbsp (3x15 ml) of the milk.

Sift the rest of the flour and the cocoa into the other half of the mixture and fold in with the remaining milk.

Spread a little of the plain mixture over the bottom and sides of a greased and floured 7½ inch (19 cm) ring mould. Carefully spread a thin layer of the chocolate mixture over the plain layer. Repeat the careful layering until both mixtures are used up.

Bake for 1 hour till well risen and firm to the touch. Cool cake slightly in the mould before turning out on to a wire rack to cool completely.

Swiss roll

Overall timing 30 minutes plus cooling

Freezing Suitable: fill after thawing

Makes 2

3	Large eggs	3
3 oz	Caster sugar	75 g
¼ teasp	Vanilla essence	1.25 ml
3 oz	Plain flour	75 g
	Pinch of salt	
1 tbsp	Warm water	15 ml
4 tbsp	Jam	4x15 ml

Preheat the oven to 400°F (200°C) Gas 6.

Separate the eggs. Whisk yolks with the sugar and vanilla in a bowl over a pan of hot water till mixture forms trails when beaters are lifted. Remove from heat. Sift flour and fold into mixture.

Whisk the whites with salt till mixture forms soft peaks that curl downwards. Fold into yolk mixture with a metal spoon, then fold in warm water. Place mixture in greased and lined Swiss roll tin, spreading to sides. Bake for 12–15 minutes till sides of sponge shrink a little.

Turn out sponge on to sheet of greaseproof paper sprinkled with caster sugar. Carefully peel away paper from sponge. Trim edges of sponge with a sharp knife.

Working quickly, spread jam over sponge. With the help of the greaseproof, roll up sponge away from you. Place seam-side down on wire rack to cool.

Caramel ring cake

Overall timing 1¼ hours

Freezing Suitable: ice cake after thawing

To serve 12

4 oz	Butter	125 g
6 oz	Soft brown sugar	175 g
1 tbsp	Golden syrup	15 ml
2	Eggs	2
6 oz	Self-raising flour	175 g
1 teasp	Ground cinnamon	5 ml
	Pinch of salt	
¼ teasp	Bicarbonate of soda	1.25 ml
3 fl oz	Milk	90 ml
	Vanilla essence	
Icing		
1 oz	Butter	25 g
2 tbsp	Golden syrup	2x15 ml
1 tbsp	Milk	15 ml
1 teasp	Vanilla essence	5 ml
8 oz	Icing sugar	225 g
1 tbsp	Ground cinnamon	15 ml

Preheat oven to 350°F (180°C) Gas 4.

Cream butter with sugar; beat in eggs and syrup. Sift in flour, cinnamon and salt and beat well. Mix soda with milk and a few drops of vanilla essence and add to mixture. Place in a greased and floured 9½ inch (24 cm) ring tin and bake for 45–50 minutes. Cool on wire rack.

For the icing, heat butter and golden syrup in saucepan. Stir in milk and essence and remove from heat. Sift half of icing sugar and the cinnamon into saucepan and stir well. Stir in rest of sifted sugar.

Pour icing over cake and smooth with spatula dipped in hot water.

Chocolate ring cake

Overall timing 1½ hours plus cooling

Freezing Suitable: ice and decorate after thawing

To serve 15–20

4 oz	Butter	125 g
5 oz	Caster sugar	150 g
	Pinch of salt	
	Grated rind of 1 lemon	
4	Eggs	4
1 tbsp	Rum	15 ml
5 oz	Plain flour	150 g
2 oz	Cornflour	50 g
1 teasp	Baking powder	5 ml
Chocolate filling		
6 oz	Unsalted butter	175 g
2 oz	Icing sugar	50 g
2 tbsp	Cocoa powder	2x15 ml

Icing and decoration

8 oz	Cooking chocolate	225 g
½ oz	Butter	15 g
1 oz	Nuts	25 g
15–20	Glacé cherries	15–20

Preheat the oven to 350°F (180°C) Gas 4.

Cream butter with sugar, then beat in salt, grated rind, eggs and rum. Sift flour, cornflour and baking powder together and fold into creamed mixture. Spoon into greased 9 inch (23 cm) ring mould and bake for 55 minutes. Cool on a wire rack.

To make the filling, cream butter with sugar and cocoa powder. Cut cake into three or four thin layers and sandwich together with filling, saving some to decorate the top.

Melt chocolate and spread over cake. Melt butter and cook chopped nuts till golden. Sprinkle round the bottom edge of the chocolate. Pipe remaining chocolate filling in swirls on cake. Add cherry to each.

Cocoa Madeira cake

Overall timing 1 hour 20 minutes

Freezing Suitable

To serve 10

6 oz	Butter	175 g
6 oz	Caster sugar	175 g
3	Eggs	3
4 oz	Self-raising flour	125 g
2 oz	Cocoa powder	50 g
	Pinch of salt	
3 tbsp	Madeira	3x15 ml
2 tbsp	Milk	2x15 ml
2 oz	Walnuts	50 g

Preheat the oven to 350°F (180°C) Gas 4.

Cream the butter with the sugar till light and fluffy. Beat the eggs and add to creamed mixture a little at a time, beating well after each addition. Sift together the flour, cocoa and salt. Add to creamed mixture a little at a time, alternating with the Madeira and milk. When the mixture is smooth and will flick easily from the spoon, fold in half the chopped walnuts.

Put mixture into greased and lined 7 inch (18 cm) round cake tin and smooth top. Bake for 45 minutes. Sprinkle with remaining walnuts and bake for further 15–20 minutes till skewer inserted into cake comes out clean. Cool on a wire rack.

Honey spice loaf

Overall timing 1 hour 20 minutes

Freezing Suitable

To serve 16

4 oz	Caster sugar	125 g
5 tbsp	Water	5x15 ml
8 oz	Honey	225 g
8 oz	Rye flour	225 g
	Salt	
1½ teasp	Bicarbonate of soda	7.5 ml
¼ teasp	Ground cloves	1.25 ml
½ teasp	Ground cinnamon	2.5 ml
¼ teasp	Ground mace	1.25 ml
2 teasp	Ground aniseed	2x5 ml
4 tbsp	Ground almonds	4x15 ml
½ teasp	Almond essence	2.5 ml
4 oz	Glacé fruits	125 g

Preheat the oven to 325°F (170°C) Gas 3.

Put the sugar and water into a saucepan and heat gently till sugar is dissolved. Pour into a large bowl, add the honey and beat for 2 minutes. Sift the flour, a pinch of salt, the bicarbonate of soda and spices into the mixture. Add the almonds and essence and beat for 4–5 minutes.

Cut the glacé fruits into pieces and stir into the mixture. Spread in a greased and lined 2 lb (900 g) loaf tin and smooth the top. Bake for about 55 minutes till a skewer inserted in the centre comes out clean. Cool in the tin for 10 minutes, then turn out on to a wire rack and leave to cool completely. Cut into slices to serve.

Lemon and cardamom cake

Overall timing 1¼–1½ hours

Freezing Suitable

To serve 8

8 oz	Self-raising flour	225 g
1 teasp	Ground cardamom	5 ml
4 oz	Butter	125 g
4 oz	Caster sugar	125 g
1	Lemon	1
1	Egg	1
2 tbsp	Milk	2x15 ml
1 oz	Flaked almonds	25 g
½ teasp	Ground cinnamon	2.5 ml

Preheat the oven to 350°F (180°C) Gas 4.

Sift flour and cardamom into a large bowl. Rub in the butter till mixture resembles fine breadcrumbs. Stir in all but 1 teasp (5 ml) of the sugar. Grate the lemon rind and squeeze out the juice. Add both to bowl with the egg. Gradually mix ingredients, adding enough milk to give a soft consistency that won't drop unless flicked from the spoon.

Put mixture into greased and lined 7 inch (18 cm) round cake tin and smooth the surface. Mix together the almonds, cinnamon and reserved sugar and sprinkle over cake. Bake for 1–1¼ hours till cake comes away from the sides. Cool in tin for a few minutes, then turn out on to a wire rack and cool completely.

Lemon shortcake

Overall timing 1 hour

Freezing Suitable

To serve 8

1	Lemon	1
8 oz	Plain flour	225 g
	Salt	
3 oz	Caster sugar	75 g
3 oz	Butter	75 g
1	Egg	1

Preheat the oven to 375°F (190°C) Gas 5.

Grate the rind of the lemon and squeeze out the juice. Sift the flour and a pinch of salt into a mixing bowl and stir in the sugar. Add the melted butter, egg, grated lemon rind and 2 tbsp (2x15 ml) lemon juice. Mix well and knead lightly until the mixture is smooth.

Roll out on a floured surface to fit a greased 8 inch (20 cm) sandwich tin or flan ring. Bake for 20 minutes till golden. Cool in the tin.

Yogurt cake

Overall timing 2 hours

Freezing Suitable

To serve 10

5 oz	Carton of natural yogurt	141 g
10 oz	Caster sugar	275 g
10 oz	Plain flour	275 g
1 tbsp	Baking powder	15 ml
	Salt	
2	Eggs	2
5 tbsp	Corn oil	5x15 ml
2 tbsp	Rum	2x15 ml
1 tbsp	Icing sugar	15 ml

Preheat the oven to 350°F (180°C) Gas 4.

Pour the yogurt into a large bowl and beat in the sugar. Sift the flour and baking powder with a pinch of salt. Beat together the eggs, oil and rum and add to the yogurt alternately with the flour mixture, beating till smooth.

Pour the mixture into a greased and lined 7 inch (18 cm) round cake tin. Bake for $1\frac{3}{4}$ hours, covering the top lightly with foil after 45 minutes, till a skewer inserted in the centre comes out clean. Cool on a wire rack.

Sift the icing sugar over the cake and mark the top into 10 slices. Serve with cherry jam.

Gingerbread

Overall timing 1¼ hours

Freezing Suitable

Makes 9

8 oz	Plain flour	225 g
1 teasp	Bicarbonate of soda	5 ml
1½ teasp	Ground ginger	7.5 ml
2 oz	Black treacle	50 g
4 oz	Golden syrup	125 g
3 oz	Butter	75 g
2 oz	Soft brown sugar	50 g
2	Eggs	2
2 tbsp	Milk	2x15 ml

Preheat the oven to 325°F (170°C) Gas 3.

Sift flour, soda and ginger into a bowl. Place treacle and golden syrup in a saucepan with butter and brown sugar. Heat till melted.

Beat eggs and milk. Add with melted ingredients to dry ingredients. Mix to a thick batter. Pour into a greased and lined 7 inch (18 cm) square tin. Bake for 1 hour.

Golden fruit cake

Overall timing 2 hours

Freezing Suitable

To serve 8–10

4 oz	Butter	125 g
4 oz	Caster sugar	125 g
2	Eggs	2
8 oz	Self-raising flour	225 g
	Pinch of salt	
2 oz	Glacé cherries	50 g
3 oz	Sultanas	75 g
2 oz	Candied peel	50 g
1–2 tbsp	Water	1–2 x 15 ml

Preheat the oven to 400°F (200°C) Gas 6.

Cream butter with sugar till light and fluffy. Add the eggs, one at a time, beating between each addition. Stir in the flour, salt, fruit and peel. Mix well, then add enough water to make a soft, but not sticky, dough.

Pour mixture into greased and lined 1 lb (450 g) loaf tin. Bake for 30 minutes, then lower oven temperature to 350°F (180°C) Gas 4 and bake for a further 1 hour. Cover with a piece of foil if the top begins to turn brown too quickly. Cool on a wire rack.

Hazelnut and honey cake

Overall timing 1¼ hours

Freezing Suitable

To serve 8

6 oz	Butter	175 g
4 oz	Light brown sugar	125 g
4 tbsp	Clear honey	4x15 ml
2	Whole eggs	2
2	Egg yolks	2
8 oz	Wholemeal self-raising flour	225 g
	Pinch of salt	
4 oz	Toasted hazelnuts	125 g
4 tbsp	Milk	4x15 ml

Preheat the oven to 350°F (180°C) Gas 4.

Cream the butter with the sugar and honey, then beat in the whole eggs and yolks. Fold in sifted flour, salt and chopped hazelnuts alternately with the milk.

Put mixture into a greased and lined 7 inch (18 cm) round cake tin. Bake for 1 hour until springy to the touch. Cool on wire rack. Coat with a fudgy icing if a more elaborate cake is desired.

Nutty honey cake

Overall timing 1 hour

Freezing Not suitable

To serve 8–10

6 oz	Butter	175 g
3 oz	Clear honey	75 g
5 oz	Plain flour	150 g
5 oz	Wholemeal flour	150 g
Filling		
4 oz	Mixed nuts	125 g
2 oz	Sultanas	50 g
1 teasp	Ground cinnamon	5 ml
	Clear honey	

Preheat the oven to 350°F (180°C) Gas 4.

Cream butter with honey till light and fluffy. Mix in sifted flours to make a dough. Roll out half dough on a floured surface and press into greased and lined 7 inch (18 cm) round tin.

Chop nuts and mix with sultanas and cinnamon. Bind with honey. Spread filling over dough in tin.

Roll out remaining dough and cover filling. Press edges to seal. Bake for 30–40 minutes till golden. Cool in the tin.

Orange and almond sponge

Overall timing 1 hour plus cooling

Freezing Suitable: ice after thawing

To serve 10

1	Large orange	1
5	Eggs	5
5 oz	Caster sugar	150 g
3½ oz	Self-raising flour	100 g
	Pinch of salt	
¼ teasp	Ground ginger	1.25 ml
½ teasp	Ground cinnamon	2.5 ml
5 oz	Ground almonds	150 g
	Almond essence	
5 oz	Icing sugar	150 g
1 tbsp	Curaçao	15 ml

Preheat the oven to 400°F (200°C) Gas 6.

Grate the rind from the orange and squeeze out the juice. Separate the eggs. Whisk egg yolks with the sugar till the mixture is pale and thick. Sift the flour, salt and spices over the mixture and add the ground almonds, three drops of essence, orange rind and 3 tbsp (3x15 ml) of the orange juice. Fold in gently.

Whisk the egg whites till stiff and fold into the mixture with a metal spoon. Carefully pour mixture into a greased and lined 9 inch (23 cm) cake tin and smooth the surface. Bake for about 35 minutes till springy to the touch. Cool on a wire rack.

Sift the icing sugar into a bowl and add the Curaçao and 1 tbsp (15 ml) of the remaining orange juice to make an icing that will coat the back of the spoon. Pour the icing on to the top of the cake. Lift the wire rack and tap it several times on the working surface so that the icing flows over the cake and trickles down the sides. Leave to set.

Praline-topped lemon cake

Overall timing 1½ hours

Freezing Suitable

To serve 8

4 oz	Butter	125 g
5 oz	Caster sugar	150 g
4	Eggs	4
5 oz	Plain flour	150 g
3 oz	Cornflour	75 g
2 teasp	Baking powder	2x5 ml
2 tbsp	Grated lemon rind	2x15 ml
2 oz	Almonds	50 g
Buttercream		
5 oz	Butter	150 g
5 oz	Icing sugar	150 g
1	Egg yolk	1
2 tbsp	Lemon juice	2x15 ml

Preheat the oven to 350°F (180°C) Gas 4.

Cream butter with 4 oz (125 g) sugar till light and fluffy. Separate eggs and beat egg yolks into creamed mixture. Sift flour, cornflour and baking powder together and fold into creamed mixture with lemon rind. Whisk egg whites till stiff and fold in.

Pour into greased and lined 8 inch (20 cm) cake tin and smooth surface. Bake for 50–60 minutes till top springs back when lightly pressed. Cool on wire rack.

Melt remaining sugar with 1 teasp (5 ml) water in a heavy-based saucepan. Boil until caramelized to a pale golden colour. Add chopped almonds and mix well. Spread on to a greased baking tray. Allow to cool and set hard, then break praline into tiny pieces with a rolling-pin.

To make buttercream, cream butter with sifted icing sugar till soft, then beat in egg yolk and lemon juice.

Cut cake into three layers and sandwich together with most of buttercream. Spread remainder on top and lightly press in praline.

Fresh cherry cake

Overall timing 1½ hours

Freezing Suitable

To serve 8

6	Digestive biscuits	6
1¾ lb	Fresh cherries	750 g
3 oz	Ground almonds	75 g
9 oz	Caster sugar	250 g
½ teasp	Ground cinnamon	2.5 ml
5	Eggs	5
2 tbsp	Kirsch	2x15 ml
1	Lemon	1
4 oz	Plain flour	125 g

Preheat the oven to 350°F (180°C) Gas 4.

Crush the biscuits and sprinkle over the bottom and sides of an oiled 10 inch (25 cm) cake tin.

Stone cherries. Arrange over the bottom of the coated cake tin.

Mix together the almonds, 2 oz (50 g) of the sugar and the cinnamon. Separate the eggs. Beat together the egg yolks, remaining sugar, Kirsch and grated rind and juice of the lemon. Stir in the almond mixture, then fold in the flour lightly. Whisk the egg whites till stiff and fold into the cake mixture using a metal spoon.

Spread the cake mixture over the cherries. Bake for 1 hour 10 minutes. Cool on a wire rack. Dredge with icing sugar before serving.

Spicy slab cake

Overall timing 1¼ hours

Freezing Suitable

To serve 12

10 oz	Butter	275 g
10 oz	Caster sugar	275 g
5	Eggs	5
10 oz	Self-raising flour	275 g
1 teasp	Ground ginger	5 ml
1 teasp	Ground cinnamon	5 ml
1 teasp	Grated nutmeg	5 ml
¼ teasp	Ground cloves	1.25 ml
8 oz	Stoned dates	225 g
4 oz	Walnuts	125 g
3 tbsp	Milk	3x15 ml

Preheat the oven to 350°F (180°C) Gas 4.

Cream the butter with the sugar till pale and fluffy. Beat the eggs lightly with a fork, then gradually beat into the creamed mixture. Sift the flour and spices into the bowl, add the chopped dates and walnuts and fold in with a metal spoon, adding the milk to give a soft dropping consistency.

Spread the mixture in a greased and lined 12x9 inch (30x23 cm) tin and smooth the top. Bake for about 45 minutes till firm and a skewer inserted in centre comes out clean. Cool on a wire rack. Cut into squares to serve.

Queen of Sheba cake

Overall timing 2 hours plus cooling

Freezing Suitable

To serve 8

10 oz	Plain chocolate	275 g
6	Eggs	6
9 oz	Butter	250 g
9 oz	Honey	250 g
5 oz	Plain flour	150 g
1 tbsp	Oil	15 ml
4 oz	Hazelnuts	125 g
4 oz	Split almonds	125 g
1 tbsp	Chocolate vermicelli	15 ml
3 tbsp	Icing sugar	3x15 ml

Preheat the oven to 350°F (180°C) Gas 4.

Gently melt 9 oz (250 g) of the chocolate. Separate the eggs. Cream the butter with the honey, then beat in the chocolate and egg yolks. Add sifted flour, oil and chopped nuts and beat well. Whisk the egg whites till stiff and fold into the mixture.

Turn into a greased and lined 9 inch (23 cm) cake tin. Bake for 1½ hours.

Meanwhile, make curls from remaining chocolate: melt chocolate in saucepan and pour on to oiled marble slab or Formica surface. When chocolate has almost set but is not hard, scrape off thin slivers or curls with a knife. Chill.

Cool cake on a wire rack.

Sprinkle chocolate vermicelli over cake, then sift icing sugar around edge. Arrange the chocolate curls in the centre.

Sachertorte

Overall timing 1½ hours plus cooling

Freezing Not suitable

To serve 8

4 oz	Plain chocolate	125 g
4 oz	Unsalted butter	125 g
6 oz	Caster sugar	175 g
5	Eggs	5
3 oz	Ground almonds	75 g
4 tbsp	Self-raising flour	4x15 ml
½ pint	Carton of double or whipping cream	268 ml
	Hazelnuts	
Icing		
8 oz	Plain chocolate	225 g
4 oz	Butter	125 g

Preheat the oven to 400°F (200°C) Gas 6.

Melt chocolate with butter till smooth. Beat in the sugar. Separate eggs and gradually add yolks to chocolate mixture, beating well. Whisk egg whites till stiff. Gently fold whites into chocolate mixture, followed by ground almonds and flour. Divide mixture between two greased 8 inch (20 cm) sandwich tins and smooth top. Bake for 20–25 minutes. Cool on a wire rack.

Whip half cream till thick and use to sandwich together the cooled cakes.

To make icing, melt chocolate with butter in a bowl placed over a pan of hot water. Leave to cool for 20–30 minutes until of a coating consistency, then spread over top and sides of cake. Whip remaining cream and pipe large swirls around the edge of the cake. Decorate each swirl with a hazelnut.

Special honey sponge

Overall timing 35 minutes plus cooling

Freezing Suitable: fill and decorate after thawing

To serve 8

7 oz	Self-raising flour	200 g
1 oz	Cornflour	25 g
½ teasp	Baking powder	2.5 ml
3 oz	Icing sugar	75 g
4 oz	Butter	125 g
4 oz	Caster sugar	125 g
1 tbsp	Clear honey	15 ml
2	Large eggs	2
4 fl oz	Milk	120 ml
3 oz	Nuts	75 g
Filling and decoration		
2 oz	Butter	50 g
4 oz	Icing sugar	125 g
1 tbsp	Clear honey	15 ml
1 tbsp	Warm water	15 ml
2 oz	Blanched almonds and walnuts	50 g
4 fl oz	Carton of double cream	113 ml

Preheat the oven to 350°F (180°C) Gas 4.

Sift flour, cornflour, baking powder and icing sugar together. Cream butter with caster sugar and honey. Beat in eggs, then fold in flour mixture alternately with milk. Stir in chopped nuts. Divide between two greased 7 inch (18 cm) sandwich tins. Bake for 20 minutes. Cool on wire rack.

To make the filling, cream butter with icing sugar, honey and water. Spread on one cake, sprinkle with most of the chopped nuts, then place second cake on top. Whip cream until stiff. Spoon into piping bag fitted with large star nozzle and pipe decorative swirls around top of cake. Decorate with rest of nuts.

Italian nut and honey cake

Overall timing 1 hour

Freezing Not suitable

To serve 10

6 oz	Almonds	175 g
4 oz	Walnuts	125 g
8 oz	Chopped mixed peel	225 g
$\frac{1}{4}$ teasp	Ground allspice	1.25 ml
$\frac{1}{2}$ teasp	Ground cinnamon	2.5 ml
1 teasp	Ground coriander	5 ml
5 oz	Plain flour	150 g
4 oz	Icing sugar	125 g
1 tbsp	Water	15 ml
5 oz	Clear honey	150 g

Preheat the oven to 425°F (220°C) Gas 7.

Spread the nuts on a baking tray and toast in the oven till golden. Remove from oven and roughly chop. Reduce oven temperature to 375°F (190°C) Gas 5.

Add chopped mixed peel, spices and flour to nuts and mix well together.

Reserve 1 tbsp (15 ml) of the icing sugar and put the rest in a heavy-based pan with the water and honey. Stir constantly over a low heat until bubbles appear on the surface. Remove from heat immediately. Gradually stir nut and fruit mixture into the syrup.

Turn into 8 inch (20 cm) loose-bottomed flan tin lined with rice paper and smooth surface with a wet knife blade. Sprinkle with reserved icing sugar. Bake for about 30 minutes. Mark into 10 portions and leave to cool in tin before cutting.

Mocha gâteau

Overall timing 1¼ hours

Freezing Suitable

To serve 12

2 teasp	Instant coffee	2x5 ml
4	Large eggs	4
4 oz	Caster sugar	125 g
4 oz	Plain flour	125 g
2 oz	Butter	50 g
2 oz	Milk chocolate flake	50 g
Filling and topping		
1 tbsp	Cornflour	15 ml
¼ pint	Milk	150 ml
3 tbsp	Caster sugar	3x15 ml
1 tbsp	Instant coffee	15 ml
1	Egg yolk	1
6 oz	Butter	175 g
3 oz	Icing sugar	75 g

Preheat the oven to 375°F (190°C) Gas 5.

Dissolve coffee in 1 tbsp (15 ml) water in large bowl over pan of hot water. Add eggs, sugar and pinch of salt and whisk till very thick. Remove bowl from pan. Sift flour and fold in alternately with melted butter. Pour into greased and lined 8 inch (20 cm) cake tin. Bake for 40 minutes. Cool on a wire rack.

To make filling, place cornflour in small saucepan and blend in milk. Add sugar and coffee and bring to the boil, stirring. Simmer for 2–3 minutes, stirring constantly. Remove from heat and cool slightly, then add egg yolk and beat well. Cook over gentle heat for 2 minutes, then remove from heat and leave to cool.

Beat butter with sifted icing sugar. Add cooled custard and beat to a smooth creamy consistency.

Cut sponge into two layers and sandwich back together with one-third of filling. Coat cake with remainder and decorate with crumbled flake.

Pear refrigerator cake

Overall timing 45 minutes plus 4 hours chilling

Freezing Not suitable

To serve 6

1 pint	Water	560 ml
2 tbsp	Lemon juice	2x15 ml
3 oz	Granulated sugar	75 g
1	Vanilla pod	1
4	Large firm pears	4
4 oz	Softened butter	125 g
3 oz	Icing sugar	75 g
2 oz	Ground almonds	50 g
7 oz	Nice biscuits	200 g
2 tbsp	Kirsch	2x15 ml
2 oz	Chocolate cake covering	50 g
2 tbsp	Single cream	2x15 ml

Put water, lemon juice, granulated sugar and vanilla pod into a saucepan and heat gently, stirring till sugar dissolves. Bring to the boil. Peel, core and quarter pears and add to the syrup. Simmer gently for 10 minutes till transparent. Remove from the heat and leave to cool in the syrup.

Cream butter with sifted icing sugar and ground almonds. Crush biscuits and add to mixture with the Kirsch.

Lift pears out of syrup and drain on kitchen paper. Reserve syrup. Thinly slice pears and fold into creamed mixture. Spoon into a 2 lb (900 g) loaf tin lined with foil. Smooth top, fold foil in over cake and put a weight on top. Chill for at least 4 hours.

Melt chocolate in a bowl over a pan of hot water. Remove from the heat and stir in 2 tbsp (2x15 ml) pear syrup and the cream.

Remove cake from tin and place on a serving dish. Spread warm chocolate icing over and leave to set.

Refrigerator coffee cake

Overall timing 1½ hours

Freezing Suitable

To serve 12

6 oz	Butter	175 g
6 oz	Caster sugar	175 g
1 teasp	Vanilla essence	5 ml
3	Eggs	3
8 oz	Self-raising flour	225 g
	Pinch of salt	
4 tbsp	Milk	4x15 ml
12	Sugar coffee beans	12
1 oz	Flaked almonds	25 g
Coffee cream		
4	Eggs	4
10 oz	Granulated sugar	275 g
14 oz	Butter	400 g
2 tbsp	Coffee essence	2x15 ml

Preheat the oven to 350°F (180°C) Gas 4.

Cream butter with sugar till light and fluffy. Beat in vanilla essence and eggs. Sift flour and salt and add to mixture alternately with milk. Pour into greased and lined 2 lb (900 g) loaf tin. Bake for 35 minutes. Cool on a wire rack.

Lightly beat eggs in a saucepan. Add sugar and heat very gently till sugar has dissolved. Remove from heat and allow to cool, stirring occasionally. Cream butter, then gradually beat in cold egg mixture and coffee essence.

Cut the sponge cake into three layers and sandwich back together with some of the cream. Place cake on a piece of foil on a plate and coat top and sides with cream, saving a little for decoration. Chill for at least 1 hour till cream is firm.

Slide cake off foil onto plate. Mark with ridges, using a fork. Decorate with remaining cream, coffee beans and almonds.

Battenberg cake

Overall timing 1½ hours plus cooling

Freezing Suitable: add almond paste after thawing

To serve 10

8 oz	Butter	225 g
8 oz	Caster sugar	225 g
4	Eggs	4
8 oz	Self-raising flour	225 g
4 tbsp	Milk	4x15 ml
	Red food colouring	
3 tbsp	Apricot jam	3x15 ml
8 oz	Almond paste	225 g

Preheat the oven to 375°F (190°C) Gas 5. Grease and line Swiss roll tin, making pleat in paper down centre to divide in half lengthways.

Cream butter with sugar. Beat in eggs. Sift flour and fold into creamed mixture with milk. Spread half mixture into one side of tin. Add a few drops of food colouring to remaining mixture and spread into other half of tin. Bake for about 45 minutes.

Cut each cake in half lengthways. Warm jam and use to stick cake pieces together in chequerboard pattern. Spread jam over cake. Sprinkle caster sugar over working surface, roll out almond paste and wrap round cake. Crimp edges and make diamond pattern on top using a sharp knife.

Coffee cream torte

Overall timing 1½ hours plus chilling

Freezing Suitable: add cream after thawing

To serve 12

2 teasp	Instant coffee powder	2x5 ml
4	Large eggs	4
5 oz	Caster sugar	150 g
	Pinch of salt	
4 oz	Plain flour	125 g
2 oz	Butter	50 g
¼ pint	Strong black coffee	150 ml
2 tbsp	Rum or Tia Maria	2x15 ml
½ pint	Double cream	284 ml
1 oz	Icing sugar	25 g
12	Chocolate truffles	12

Preheat the oven to 375°F (190°C) Gas 5.

Dissolve coffee in 1 tbsp (15 ml) water in a bowl placed over a pan of hot water. Add eggs, 4 oz (125 g) sugar and salt and whisk till thick. Remove bowl from pan. Sift flour and fold in alternately with melted butter. Pour into greased and lined 8 inch (20 cm) cake tin and bake for 40 minutes.

Dissolve remaining sugar in black coffee and stir in rum or Tia Maria. Spoon over cake, then cool and chill.

Whip cream with icing sugar till stiff. Turn out cake on to serving plate. Spread over half cream. Decorate with remaining cream and truffles.

Banana and walnut gâteau

Overall timing 1 hour plus cooling

Freezing Not suitable

To serve 8–10

4	Large eggs	4
6 oz	Caster sugar	175 g
2 tbsp	Warm water	2x15 ml
4 oz	Plain flour	125 g
1 teasp	Baking powder	5 ml
2 tbsp	Milk	2x15 ml
2 oz	Butter	50 g
½ pint	Carton of double cream	284 ml
5	Large bananas	5
	Chopped walnuts	
	Walnut halves	

Preheat the oven to 375°F (190°C) Gas 5.

Separate eggs. Beat yolks with sugar and water till light and fluffy. Sift flour with baking powder and add to yolk mixture alternately with milk. Melt butter and add.

Whisk egg whites till stiff and fold into mixture. Spoon into a greased and lined 8 inch (20 cm) round deep cake tin. Bake for 30–35 minutes. Cool on a wire rack.

Whip the cream till thick. Peel and slice the bananas.

Cut the cake into three layers. Sandwich back together with most of the cream and banana slices and the chopped walnuts. Decorate the top with the rest of the cream and bananas and walnut halves. Serve immediately.

Chocolate log

Overall timing 40 minutes plus chilling

Freezing Not suitable

To serve 10–12

2	Eggs	2
1½ oz	Caster sugar	40 g
1 oz	Plain flour	25 g
1 oz	Cornflour	25 g
1 oz	Chopped pistachio nuts or angelica	25 g
Filling and icing		
3½ oz	Softened butter	100 g
7 oz	Icing sugar	200 g
7 oz	Plain chocolate cake covering	200 g
2 tbsp	Rum or brandy (optional)	2x15 ml

Preheat the oven to 400°F (200°C) Gas 6.

Separate eggs. Beat whites in a bowl with sugar till stiff peaks form. Beat yolks till pale, then fold into whites. Sift flour and cornflour into mixture and fold in gently. Spread mixture evenly in greased and lined 13½x9½ inch (34x24 cm) Swiss roll tin and bake for 10 minutes till lightly golden. Turn cake out on to tea-towel. Carefully peel off paper and roll up cake enclosing towel. Cool.

Cream butter with sugar. Melt chocolate and beat into creamed mixture with rum or brandy, if using.

Unroll cake and spread with half chocolate mixture. Roll up and place on a serving plate, seam underneath. Cover cake with remaining chocolate mixture. Make marks in chocolate icing with a fork so that it looks like bark. Sprinkle log with chopped pistachio nuts or angelica and chill before serving.

Christening cake

Overall timing 3 hours plus overnight chilling

Freezing Suitable: fill and ice after thawing

To serve 30

12	Eggs	12
12 oz	Caster sugar	350 g
14 oz	Plain flour	400 g
2 oz	Butter	50 g
4 oz	Ground almonds	125 g
1 lb	Sugared almonds	450 g
	Silver balls	
Filling		
5	Egg yolks	5
9 oz	Granulated sugar	250 g
5 tbsp	Water	5x15 ml
12 oz	Unsalted butter	350 g
Icing		
1 lb	Icing sugar	450 g
2	Egg whites	2

Preheat the oven to 375°F (190°C) Gas 5.

Make cake mixture in two batches. Beat half eggs and sugar till thick and pale. Sift half flour and fold into egg mixture with half melted butter and almonds. Pour into greased and lined sandwich tins, one 6 inch (15 cm) and one 10 inch (25 cm). Bake for 15–20 minutes for small cake and 30 minutes for large cake. Cool on a wire rack. Make second batch and bake in 7 inch (18 cm) tin and 9 inch (22 cm) tin, allowing 30–35 minutes.

To make filling, put egg yolks into a bowl and whisk well. Dissolve sugar in water in a saucepan. Boil for 2–3 minutes, without allowing it to colour. Pour hot syrup on to egg yolks, beating continuously. Cool, then gradually work in softened butter. Use to sandwich cake layers together and to secure cakes on top of each other, largest on bottom. Chill overnight.

To make icing, sift icing sugar into a large bowl, add egg whites and beat well. Add 1–2 tbsp (1–2x15 ml) hot water to give a coating consistency. Coat the entire cake with icing. Place on a serving dish. Decorate with sugared almonds and silver balls.

Christmas cake

Overall timing Cake: 2–2½ hours. Icing: 30 minutes plus 24 hours standing

Freezing Not suitable

1¼ lb	Mixed dried fruit	600 g
2 oz	Candied peel	50 g
6 oz	Dark brown sugar	175 g
3 tbsp	Golden syrup	3x15 ml
4 oz	Butter	125 g
6 oz	Self-raising flour	175 g
6 oz	Plain flour	175 g
2 teasp	Bicarbonate of soda	2x5 ml
2 teasp	Mixed spice	2x5 ml
2	Large eggs	2
3 tbsp	Apricot jam	3x15 ml
12 oz	Almond paste	350 g
2	Egg whites	2
1 lb	Icing sugar	450 g
2 teasp	Lemon juice	2x5 ml
1 teasp	Glycerine	5 ml

Put fruit in saucepan with peel, sugar, syrup, butter and 8 fl oz (220 ml) water. Bring to the boil, then simmer for 3 minutes. Turn into a bowl and cool.

Preheat the oven to 325°F (170°C) Gas 3.

Sift flours, soda and spice three times, then add to fruit mixture. Beat in eggs. Place in greased and lined 8 inch (20 cm) cake tin, making a slight depression in centre. Bake for about 1½–2 hours or till skewer inserted in centre comes out clean. Cool in tin.

To decorate cake, brush top and sides with warmed apricot jam. Roll out almond paste and use to cover top and sides. Smooth all seams.

Whisk egg whites to a fairly stiff foam. Gradually beat in sifted icing sugar and lemon juice. When icing forms little peaks when lifted up with a knife blade, mix in glycerine. Cover bowl and leave for 24 hours.

Beat icing gently. Spread over cake, flicking up into peaks with a knife blade. Leave to set for a week before cutting.

Frosted walnut cake

Overall timing 1¼ hours plus cooling

Freezing Suitable: fill and ice after thawing

To serve 10

6 oz	White vegetable fat	175 g
12 oz	Caster sugar	350 g
½ teasp	Vanilla essence	2.5 ml
9 oz	Plain flour	250 g
1 tbsp	Baking powder	15 ml
7 fl oz	Milk	200 ml
4	Egg whites	4
Frosting		
1 lb	Cube sugar	450 g
¼ teasp	Cream of tartar	1.25 ml
2	Egg whites	2
½ teasp	Vanilla essence	2.5 ml
2 oz	Chopped walnuts	50 g
10	Walnut halves	10

Preheat the oven to 350°F (180°C) Gas 4.

Cream fat with sugar and vanilla essence till fluffy. Sift flour, baking powder and a pinch of salt together and fold into creamed mixture alternately with milk. Whisk egg whites till stiff and fold in. Divide between three greased and lined 8 inch (20 cm) sandwich tins. Bake for 30–35 minutes. Cool on a wire rack.

To make frosting, put sugar, cream of tartar and 6 fl oz (170 ml) water in a saucepan and stir over a low heat till sugar dissolves. Stop stirring and bring to the boil. Boil to a temperature of 240°F (116°C).

Meanwhile, whisk egg whites till stiff. Pour syrup in a thin stream on to whites, whisking constantly till frosting stands in soft peaks. Whisk in vanilla essence. Fold chopped walnuts into one-quarter of frosting and use to sandwich cakes together. Spread remaining frosting over cake and decorate with walnut halves.

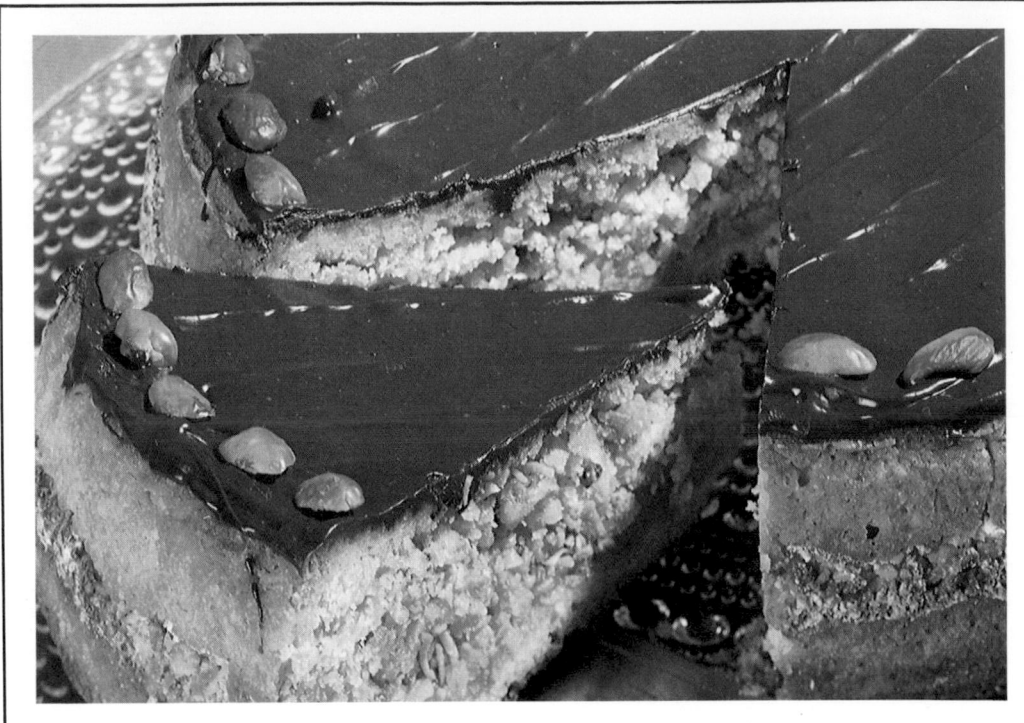

Chocolate pistachio gâteau

Overall timing 1 hour plus chilling

Freezing Not suitable

To serve 10

12 oz	Plain flour	350 g
	Pinch of salt	
9 oz	Butter	250 g
5 oz	Sugar	150 g
2	Egg yolks	2
Filling		
4 oz	Shelled pistachios	125 g
4	Egg whites	4
7 oz	Caster sugar	200 g
4 oz	Ground almonds	125 g
	Grated rind of $\frac{1}{2}$ lemon	
1 tbsp	Rum	15 ml
2 oz	Milk chocolate	50 g

Sift the flour and salt into a bowl and rub in the fat till the mixture resembles fine breadcrumbs. Stir in the sugar and egg yolks and mix to a soft dough. Chill for 30 minutes.

Preheat the oven to 400°F (200°C) Gas 6.

Divide the dough in half. Roll out and use to line two 9 inch (23 cm) sponge tins. Prick bottoms and bake blind for 15 minutes. Cool on a wire rack.

Reserve a few pistachios for decoration; finely chop the rest. Whisk the egg whites till soft peaks form. Gradually whisk in the sugar till the mixture is stiff and glossy. Fold the chopped nuts into the meringue with the ground almonds, grated lemon rind and rum. Spoon into the pastry cases. Place one pastry cake on a baking tray and invert the other on top. Return to the oven and bake for a further 15 minutes. Cool on a wire rack.

Melt the chocolate in a bowl over a pan of hot water. Spread over the top of the cake with a palette knife. Cut the reserved pistachios in half and arrange in a circle around the edge of the cake.

Small cakes and biscuits

Brownies

Overall timing 45 minutes plus cooling

Freezing Suitable

Makes 30

4 oz	Plain dessert chocolate	125 g
4 oz	Unsalted butter	125 g
1 teasp	Vanilla essence	5 ml
4	Eggs	4
½ teasp	Salt	2.5 ml
14 oz	Caster sugar	400 g
4 oz	Plain flour	125 g
4 oz	Walnuts	125 g

Preheat the oven to 350°F (180°C) Gas 4.

Put chocolate into a bowl with the butter and vanilla essence and place over a pan of simmering water. Stir till melted, then remove bowl from pan and cool.

Whisk eggs and salt till pale and fluffy. Sprinkle the sugar on top and continue whisking till evenly mixed. Fold in the chocolate mixture with a metal spoon, then fold in the sifted flour and coarsely chopped nuts.

Pour into a greased and lined 9x13 inch (23x33 cm) tin and smooth the top. Bake for about 25 minutes till firm. Cool in the tin, then cut into squares. If serving as a dessert top the brownies with whipped cream.

Iced marzipan biscuits

Overall timing 1½ hours plus cooling

Freezing Not suitable

Makes 30

14 oz	Plain flour	400 g
7 oz	Caster sugar	200 g
	Pinch of salt	
1	Large egg	1
7 oz	Butter	200 g
Filling and icing		
8 oz	Marzipan	225 g
5½ oz	Icing sugar	165 g
1 tbsp	Rum	15 ml
	Lemon or almond essence	
4 oz	Apricot jam	125 g
2 tbsp	Water	2x15 ml

Sift flour, sugar and salt into a bowl. Add egg and butter, cut into small pieces. Quickly knead together to form a smooth dough. Chill for 30 minutes.

Preheat the oven to 350°F (180°C) Gas 4.

Roll out dough to ¼ inch (6 mm) thickness. Cut out small shapes with a pastry cutter and place on a greased baking tray. Bake for 15 minutes.

Meanwhile, knead marzipan, 2 oz (50 g) icing sugar, rum and a few drops of essence together. Roll out to ⅛ inch (3 mm) thickness on a board dusted with icing sugar. Cut out shapes using the same cutter as for the pastry.

Remove pastry shapes from oven and immediately spread thickly with jam. Sandwich a piece of marzipan between two hot biscuits. Work quickly – the hot biscuits and jam need to adhere to the marzipan. Lift off baking trays and place on wire rack.

To make icing, mix together remaining icing sugar, a little almond essence and water and use to coat the warm biscuits. Leave to dry and cool.

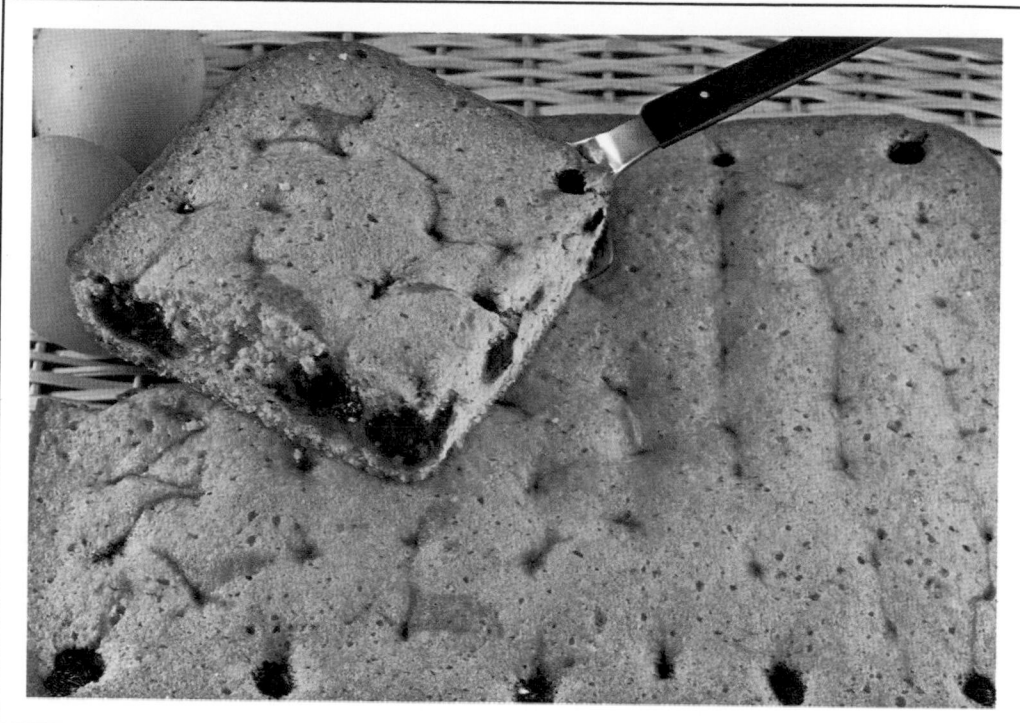

Date squares

Overall timing 1 hour

Freezing Suitable

Makes 12

1 lb	Stoned dates	450 g
3 tbsp	Water	3x15 ml
1 tbsp	Lemon juice	15 ml
7 oz	Self-raising flour	200 g
1 oz	Bran	25 g
4 oz	Butter	125 g
3 oz	Caster sugar	75 g
1	Egg	1
1 tbsp	Milk	15 ml

Preheat the oven to 350°F (180°C) Gas 4.

Chop dates and place in saucepan with water and lemon juice. Cook, stirring, till mixture is like a paste – about 5 minutes. Leave to cool.

Place flour and bran in mixing bowl. Rub in butter till mixture resembles breadcrumbs. Add 2 oz (50 g) of the sugar. Separate egg. Add yolk and milk to dough and knead till smooth.

Divide dough in half. Press one half over bottom of greased 9 inch (23 cm) square cake tin. Spread with date mixture. Roll out rest of dough and place on dates.

Lightly whisk egg white with a fork. Brush over top and sprinkle with remaining caster sugar. Bake for 30–35 minutes. Cut into squares while hot and leave in tin to cool before serving.

Duchesses

Overall timing 2 hours

Freezing Not suitable

Makes 12

2	Egg whites	2
4 oz	Caster sugar	125 g
2 oz	Ground hazelnuts	50 g
1 oz	Toasted hazelnuts	25 g
2 oz	Plain chocolate	50 g

Preheat the oven to 250°F (130°C) Gas $\frac{1}{2}$.

Whisk the egg whites with half the sugar till stiff. Carefully fold in the ground nuts, then the remaining sugar. Spoon the mixture into a piping bag fitted with a plain wide nozzle. Pipe 1 inch (2.5 cm) wide fingers about 3 inches (7.5 cm) long on to a baking tray lined with rice paper. Sprinkle with chopped toasted hazelnuts and bake for $1\frac{1}{2}$ hours.

Cut paper round fingers with a sharp knife, then remove from tray.

Melt the chocolate. Spread rice-papered sides of half the fingers with chocolate and join to remaining fingers. Leave to set.

Honey galettes

Overall timing 40 minutes plus chilling

Freezing Suitable: refresh in 375°F (190°C) Gas 5 oven for 5 minutes

Makes 8

6 oz	Self-raising flour	175 g
3½ oz	Butter	100 g
2 oz	Thick honey	50 g
1 tbsp	Caster sugar	15 ml
1	Lemon	1
1	Egg	1
	Granulated sugar	

Preheat the oven to 375°F (190°C) Gas 5.

Sift the flour into a mixing bowl. Make a well in the centre and add the softened butter, honey and caster sugar. Grate the rind from the lemon and add to the bowl with 1 tbsp (15 ml) of the juice. Separate the egg and add the yolk to the bowl. Mix well together with a wooden spoon until the mixture forms a ball and leaves the sides of the bowl clean. Chill for 30 minutes.

Divide mixture into eight and roll out each piece on a lightly floured surface to a round about ½ inch (12.5 mm) thick. Place on baking trays.

Whisk egg white lightly and brush over biscuits. Sprinkle each biscuit with 1–2 tbsp (1–2x15 ml) granulated sugar. Bake for about 15 minutes, then remove from trays and cool on wire rack.

Crunchy nut biscuits

Overall timing 1¼ hours

Freezing Suitable

Makes about 24

8 oz	Shelled hazelnuts	225 g
6 oz	Caster sugar	175 g
¼ teasp	Ground cinnamon	1.25 ml
4	Egg whites	4
	Pinch of cream of tartar	
¼ teasp	Vanilla essence	1.25 ml

Preheat oven to 300°F (150°C) Gas 2. Grease and flour baking trays.

Spread shelled nuts on grill pan and toast on all sides till golden brown. Roughly chop nuts and put in a bowl with sugar and cinnamon.

In another bowl, whisk egg whites with cream of tartar and vanilla essence till very stiff. Gently fold in nut mixture. Scrape the egg/nut mixture into a greased heavy-based frying pan and cook over a very low heat for about 15 minutes, turning mixture constantly with a wooden spoon, until it is pale brown.

Put spoonfuls of the mixture on prepared baking trays, about 1 inch (2.5 cm) apart. Bake for about 30 minutes, then reduce temperature to 250°F (130°C) Gas ½ and bake for a further 10 minutes until the biscuits are crisp.

Coconut macaroons

Overall timing 1¼ hours

Freezing Not suitable

Makes 15

4 oz	Desiccated coconut	125 g
1 teasp	Vanilla essence	5 ml
	Salt	
¼	Can of condensed milk	¼
2	Egg whites	2
½ teasp	Cream of tartar	2.5 ml

Preheat the oven to 300°F (150°C) Gas 2.

Place coconut, vanilla and a good pinch of salt in mixing bowl. Add condensed milk and mix to firm paste. Whisk egg whites and cream of tartar till stiff, then fold into paste.

Heap small spoonfuls of mixture on to baking tray lined with rice paper, leaving spreading space. Bake for 45 minutes. Turn off oven and leave inside for 15 minutes.

Choc-topped cookies

Overall timing 1 hour

Freezing Not suitable

Makes 55–60

2 oz	Stoned dates	50 g
2 oz	Seedless raisins	50 g
5 oz	Ground hazelnuts	150 g
3 oz	Milk chocolate	75 g
3 oz	Cornflour	75 g
3	Egg whites	3
	Salt	
8 oz	Caster sugar	225 g
4 oz	Plain chocolate cake covering	125 g

Preheat the oven to 350°F (180°C) Gas 4.

Coarsely chop dates and mix with raisins, hazelnuts, grated milk chocolate and cornflour. Beat egg whites with pinch of salt till stiff, then gradually beat in sugar. Fold in chocolate mixture.

With a teaspoon, place small portions on baking trays lined with rice paper, leaving spreading space. Bake for 35 minutes. Cool, then cut paper around biscuits.

Melt plain chocolate and brush over top and sides of biscuits. Leave to set before serving.

Lemon refrigerator cookies

Overall timing 20 minutes plus overnight chilling

Freezing Suitable: bake after thawing

Makes 48

8 oz	Plain flour	225 g
1 teasp	Baking powder	5 ml
4 oz	Butter	125 g
3 oz	Caster sugar	75 g
	Grated rind of 2 lemons	
½ teasp	Ground cinnamon	2.5 ml
1	Egg	1

Sift flour and baking powder into a bowl. Rub in butter till mixture resembles fine breadcrumbs. Add sugar, lemon rind and cinnamon, then beat the egg and mix well into the dough.

Shape the mixture into one or two sausage shapes about 1½ inches (4 cm) in diameter. Wrap in foil, twisting the ends to seal. Chill overnight.

Preheat the oven to 375°F (190°C) Gas 5.

Remove dough from foil wrapper and thinly slice. Place slices on greased baking trays. Bake for 10–12 minutes, till golden. Cool on wire rack.

Lemon spice squares

Overall timing 1½ hours

Freezing Suitable

Makes 9

4 oz	Butter	125 g
4 oz	Caster sugar	125 g
	Grated rind of 1 lemon	
2	Eggs	2
2 oz	Chopped candied lemon peel	50 g
4 oz	Plain flour	125 g
2 oz	Ground almonds	50 g
½ teasp	Ground cinnamon	2.5 ml
½ teasp	Ground cloves	2.5 ml
1½ teasp	Baking powder	7.5 ml
2 tbsp	Lemon juice	2x15 ml

Preheat the oven to 325°F (170°C) Gas 3.

Cream butter with sugar till light and fluffy. Add lemon rind and beat in the eggs. Stir in the candied lemon peel. Sift together the flour, spices and baking powder and fold into mixture, followed by the almonds and lemon juice.

Turn the mixture into a greased and lined 7 inch (18 cm) square cake tin and smooth the surface. Bake for 1 hour till top springs back when lightly pressed. Cool on a wire rack. Cut into squares to serve.

Shortbread fingers

Overall timing 1½ hours plus cooling

Freezing Not suitable

Makes 6

12 oz	Butter	350 g
4 oz	Caster sugar	125 g
8 oz	Plain flour	225 g
8 oz	Self-raising flour	225 g
¼ teasp	Salt	1.25 ml

Preheat the oven to 275°F (140°C) Gas 1.

Cream the butter with the sugar till pale and fluffy. Sift the two flours and salt together and work into the creamed mixture to make a dough.

Turn dough on to a floured surface and press out to a thick rectangle. Make decorative notches down the long sides by pinching with the fingers. Place on a baking tray and prick all over with a fork. Mark lines for the fingers.

Bake for 1 hour. Cool, then break into fingers on the marked lines. Dredge with extra caster sugar.

Scones

Overall timing 20 minutes

Freezing Not suitable

Makes 8

8 oz	Plain flour	225 g
3 teasp	Baking powder	3x5 ml
	Pinch of salt	
2 oz	Butter	50 g
2 tbsp	Caster sugar	2x15 ml
¼ pint	Milk	150 ml
	Milk or egg for glazing	

Preheat the oven to 450°F (230°C) Gas 8.

Sift flour, baking powder and salt into a mixing bowl. Rub in butter. Add sugar and milk and mix to a soft dough.

Roll out quickly to ½ inch (12.5 mm) thickness on a lightly floured board. Lightly flour scone cutter and cut out scones. Place on lightly floured baking tray and glaze tops with top of the milk or lightly beaten egg. Bake for 10 minutes. Wrap in tea-towel till ready to serve.

Variation

Peel, core and grate 1 dessert apple and scatter over rolled-out dough. Fold in half and press firmly together. Cut and bake as above.

Madeleines with cinnamon

Overall timing 50 minutes plus chilling

Freezing Suitable: bake after thawing

Makes 16

6 oz	Plain flour	175 g
3 oz	Butter	75 g
1 tbsp	Caster sugar	15 ml
1	Egg yolk	1
Filling		
4 oz	Butter	125 g
4 oz	Caster sugar	125 g
2	Eggs	2
2 oz	Ground almonds	50 g
¼ teasp	Almond essence	1.25 ml
4 oz	Self-raising flour	125 g
1 teasp	Ground cinnamon	5 ml
	Milk to mix	
	Apricot jam	
1 tbsp	Icing sugar	15 ml

Sift flour into a bowl and rub in fat. Stir in sugar, egg yolk and enough water to bind to a soft dough. Roll out to ¼ inch (6 mm) thickness and use to line two madeleine sheets. Trim the edges and chill for 30 minutes.

Preheat the oven to 375°F (190°C) Gas 5.

To make filling, cream butter with all but 1 tbsp (15 ml) caster sugar. Gradually beat in eggs, then mix in almonds and almond essence. Sift in flour and cinnamon and fold in with enough milk to give a soft dropping consistency.

Put ½ teasp (2.5 ml) jam into each pastry case, then spoon filling into each case. Bake for 15–20 minutes till the filling is golden and springs back when lightly pressed. Cool on a wire rack.

Mix icing sugar and remaining caster sugar together and sift over tartlets before serving.

Sponge fingers

Overall timing 30 minutes

Freezing Suitable

Makes 16

4	Eggs	4
4 oz	Caster sugar	125 g
1 oz	Cornflour	25 g
3 oz	Plain flour	75 g
	Icing sugar	

Preheat the oven to 375°F (190°C) Gas 5.

Separate the eggs. Whisk whites in a bowl with 2 tbsp (2x15 ml) of the caster sugar till soft peaks form. In another bowl, beat egg yolks with remaining caster sugar. Fold yolks into whites carefully, then gradually fold in the sifted flours.

Put mixture into a piping bag fitted with a plain wide nozzle and pipe fingers 3–4 inches (7.5–10 cm) long on to greased and floured baking trays, spacing them well apart. Dust lightly with sifted icing sugar and bake for 12 minutes. Cool on wire rack.

Spicy raisin biscuits

Overall timing 1 hour plus chilling

Freezing Not suitable

Makes 40

8 oz	Butter	225 g
8 oz	Caster sugar	225 g
1	Egg	1
2 tbsp	Rum	2x15 ml
8 oz	Seedless raisins	225 g
12 oz	Self-raising flour	350 g
	Salt	
$\frac{1}{2}$ teasp	Ground cloves	2.5 ml
1 teasp	Ground ginger	5 ml
1	Egg white	1

Cream butter with all but 1 tbsp (15 ml) sugar till pale and fluffy. Gradually beat in egg and rum. Stir in raisins. Sift flour, pinch of salt and spices into mixture and mix to a soft dough. Chill for 30 minutes.

Preheat the oven to 350°F (180°C) Gas 4.

Roll out dough on a floured surface till $\frac{1}{4}$ inch (6 mm) thick. Stamp out rounds with pastry cutter. Arrange on greased baking trays.

Beat egg white and remaining sugar together till frothy and brush over biscuits. Bake for about 15 minutes till pale golden. Cool on the trays for 3–4 minutes till firm, then transfer to a wire rack and leave to cool completely.

Spicy sweet fritters

Overall timing 45 minutes

Freezing Not suitable

Makes 20

9 oz	Plain flour	250 g
½ teasp	Ground ginger	2.5 ml
½ teasp	Ground allspice	2.5 ml
½ teasp	Ground mace	2.5 ml
	Salt	
4 oz	Icing sugar	125 g
3	Egg yolks	3
1 tbsp	Orange-flower water	15 ml
3½ oz	Butter	100 g
	Grated rind of 1 lemon	
	Oil for deep frying	

Sift flour, spices, pinch of salt and 3 oz (75 g) icing sugar into a bowl. Mix egg yolks and flower water with 2 tbsp (2x15 ml) cold water. Add to bowl with butter and rind. Mix to a soft dough.

Roll out dough till ¼ inch (6 mm) thick. Cut out fancy shapes with pastry cutters.

Heat oil in a deep-fryer to 340°F (170°C). Fry biscuits, a few at a time, for about 5 minutes till golden. Drain on kitchen paper. Sift the remaining icing sugar over.

Golden arcs

Overall timing 30 minutes

Freezing Not suitable

Makes 30

8 oz	Fine cornmeal	225 g
6 oz	Plain flour	175 g
2 teasp	Ground cardamom	2x5 ml
½ teasp	Ground coriander	2.5 ml
4 oz	Caster sugar	125 g
¼ teasp	Vanilla essence	1.25 ml
8 oz	Butter	225 g
4	Egg yolks	4

Preheat the oven to 400°F (200°C) Gas 6.

Sift the cornmeal, flour and spices into a bowl and stir in the sugar. Add the vanilla, butter and egg yolks and mix to a soft dough.

Put the mixture into a piping bag fitted with a star nozzle and pipe in 3 inch (7.5 cm) lengths on to a greased and floured baking tray. Bake for about 15 minutes till golden. Remove from the oven and allow to cool for 5 minutes. Transfer to a wire rack and leave to cool completely.

Orange liqueur biscuits

Overall timing 45 minutes plus chilling

Freezing Suitable: cut out and bake after thawing

Makes 36

2	Hard-boiled egg yolks	2
8 oz	Plain flour	225 g
4 oz	Caster sugar	125 g
	Salt	
	Ground cinnamon	
4 oz	Butter	125 g
2 tbsp	Orange liqueur	2 x 15 ml

Push egg yolks through a sieve into a mixing bowl. Sift in the flour and mix well. Make a well in centre and add sugar and a pinch each of salt and cinnamon.

Cut the butter into pieces and work into the mixture, a little at a time. Work in the liqueur and roll paste into a ball. Lightly dust with flour and leave in a cool place (not the refrigerator) for at least 1 hour.

Preheat the oven to 375°F (190°C) Gas 5.

Roll out the paste thinly and stamp out shapes with fancy pastry cutters. Place biscuits on a greased and lined baking tray and bake for 10–15 minutes, till light golden. Remove biscuits carefully from paper and cool on a wire rack.

Rhine biscuits

Overall timing 45 minutes plus chilling

Freezing Not suitable

Makes 30

9 oz	Plain flour	250 g
1 teasp	Ground cinnamon	5 ml
½ teasp	Ground cloves	2.5 ml
6 oz	Butter	175 g
4 oz	Caster sugar	125 g
	Grated rind of 1 lemon	
1	Egg	1
5 tbsp	Milk	5 x 15 ml

Sift the flour and spices into a bowl. Add the butter and rub in till the mixture resembles fine breadcrumbs. Stir in the sugar and lemon rind. Add the egg and enough milk to make a stiff dough. Knead lightly and chill for 1 hour.

Preheat the oven to 350°F (180°C) Gas 4.

Roll out the dough on a floured board till ¼ inch (6 mm) thick, then cut out shapes with a pastry cutter. Arrange on a greased and floured baking tray. Bake for 15–20 minutes till golden. Remove from the oven and leave to cool for 3 minutes. Transfer to a wire rack and leave to cool completely.

Almond crescents

Overall timing 30 minutes plus cooling

Freezing Suitable: bake from frozen, allowing 20–25 minutes

Makes 20

5 oz	Blanched almonds	150 g
2 oz	Caster sugar	50 g
	A few drops of vanilla essence	
1	Egg white	1
1 oz	Plain flour	25 g
1	Egg	1
1 oz	Flaked almonds	25 g
2 tbsp	Milk sweetened with icing sugar	2x15 ml

Preheat the oven to 400°F (200°C) Gas 6.

Mix chopped almonds with caster sugar and vanilla essence. Moisten with egg white until evenly combined. Add flour and gather mixture together with fingertips. Divide into "nut-sized" pieces. With lightly floured hands, roll into small cigar shapes with pointed ends. Brush each one with beaten egg and sprinkle with flaked almonds. Bend into a crescent shape.

Place on a greased baking tray and brush lightly with any remaining egg. Bake for about 10–15 minutes till evenly coloured. Remove from oven and brush immediately with sweetened milk. Using a palette knife or egg slice, carefully loosen crescents and transfer to wire rack to cool.

Macaroons

Overall timing 2½ hours

Freezing Not suitable

Makes 55

4	Egg whites	4
12 oz	Caster sugar	350 g
11 oz	Ground almonds	300 g
	Grated rind of 1 orange	
	Grated rind of 1 lemon	
	Pinch of salt	
1 teasp	Ground cinnamon	5 ml
½ teasp	Ground cardamom	2.5 ml

Preheat the oven to 275°F (140°C) Gas 1.

Whisk the egg whites till stiff. Gradually whisk in the caster sugar, a spoonful at a time. Fold in the almonds, orange and lemon rind, salt and spices.

Place heaped teaspoonfuls of mixture on baking trays lined with rice paper. Put on the middle and lower shelves of the oven and leave to dry for 1½–2 hours. Halfway through, swap trays round.

Cool on baking trays. Break paper from around each macaroon.

Pastry horns

Overall timing 4½ hours

Freezing Suitable· shape and bake after thawing

Makes 6

9 oz	Plain flour	250 g
	Pinch of salt	
8 oz	Butter	225 g
4 fl oz	Cold water	120 ml
1	Egg	1
	Caster sugar	
	Whipped cream	
	Jam	

Sift flour and salt into a bowl. Rub in half the butter, then add water and mix to a dough. Chill for 1 hour. Chill remaining butter.

Place chilled butter between two sheets of greaseproof paper and roll out to a 5x3 inch (13x8 cm) rectangle.

Roll out dough on floured surface to 10x8 inch (25x20 cm) rectangle. Put butter in centre. Fold down top third over butter, then fold up bottom third. Turn so that folds are to the side. Roll out to 5x14 inch (13x36 cm) rectangle and fold again as before. Chill for 15 minutes.

Repeat the rolling, turning and folding four more times, chilling between each process.

Preheat the oven to 425°F (220°C) Gas 7.

Roll out dough to ⅛ inch (3 mm) thick. Trim to a 15x6 inch (38x15 cm) rectangle, then cut into six 1 inch (2.5 cm) strips. Glaze the strips with beaten egg, then wrap them, glazed side out, round six pastry horn moulds, starting at the point and overlapping the dough slightly.

Place on a baking tray and dredge with caster sugar. Bake for 10 minutes till crisp and golden. Slide off the moulds and cool.

Fill the horns with cream and jam.

Soured cream pastries

Overall timing 10 minutes plus chilling

Freezing Not suitable

Makes 20

12 oz	Plain flour	350 g
6 oz	Butter	175 g
1	Egg yolk	1
¼ pint	Carton of soured cream	150 ml
Filling		
8 oz	Cream cheese	225 g
2 oz	Caster sugar	50 g
2 oz	Sultanas	50 g

Sift flour into a bowl and rub in the butter till the mixture resembles fine breadcrumbs. Add the egg yolk and soured cream and mix with a palette knife to make a soft dough. Chill for 1 hour.

Mix together the cream cheese, sugar and sultanas.

Preheat the oven to 400°F (200°C) Gas 6.

Roll out the dough and cut out 40 rounds with a fluted 2 inch (5 cm) cutter. Put a spoonful of the filling on to half the rounds, then cover with the remaining rounds and press the edges together to seal. Arrange on a baking sheet and bake for 25 minutes till golden brown.

Mille feuilles

Overall timing 40 minutes plus cooling

Freezing Not suitable.

Makes 6

7½ oz	Frozen puff pastry	212 g
1 pint	Milk	560 ml
	Pinch of salt	
1	Vanilla pod	1
	Strip of lemon rind	
4 oz	Caster sugar	125 g
4	Medium eggs	4
1 oz	Plain flour	25 g
2 tbsp	Rum	2x15 ml
	Icing sugar	

Thaw pastry. Preheat the oven to 425°F (220°C) Gas 7.

Put the milk, salt, vanilla pod and lemon rind into a saucepan and bring to the boil. Remove from the heat and infuse for 10 minutes.

Beat together the sugar, eggs and flour in a bowl till smooth. Gradually strain the milk into the bowl, stirring, then pour the mixture back into the saucepan. Bring to the boil, stirring, and simmer till thick. Stir in the rum. Remove from the heat. Cover with damp greaseproof paper and cool.

Halve dough and roll out into two rectangles, 12x4 inches (30x10 cm). Trim edges and knock up. Place on dampened baking trays. Mark one rectangle into six 2 inch (5 cm) slices with a sharp, pointed knife. Bake for about 10 minutes till well risen and golden. Allow to cool.

Place unmarked pastry rectangle on a board and spread with custard. Place marked pastry rectangle on top and dredge well with icing sugar. Cut into slices along marked lines. Eat same day.

Baklava

Overall timing 1½ hours

Freezing Suitable

Makes 8

4 oz	Unsalted butter	125 g
1 lb	Ready-made phyllo pastry	450 g
8 oz	Walnuts, almonds or pistachios	225 g
2 tbsp	Caster sugar	2x15 ml
½ teasp	Ground cinnamon	2.5 ml
Syrup		
4 oz	Clear honey	125 g
¼ pint	Water	150 ml
2 tbsp	Lemon juice	2x15 ml

Preheat the oven to 425°F (220°C) Gas 7.

Melt the butter in a small saucepan and brush a little over the bottom and sides of a 10x8 inch (25x20 cm) roasting tin.

Layer half the pastry sheets in the tin, brushing liberally with butter between each sheet, and folding in the edges so that sheets fit the tin. Keep rest of the pastry covered to prevent it drying out.

Mix together the chopped nuts, sugar and cinnamon and spread over pastry. Cover with remaining pastry layers, brushing each with butter. Brush the top layer well with any remaining butter.

Cut through the top two layers of pastry with a sharp knife to divide into four widthways, then cut each quarter in half diagonally so you have eight triangles. Bake for 15 minutes, then reduce heat to 350°F (180°C) Gas 4 and bake for a further 25–30 minutes till well risen and golden.

Meanwhile, make the syrup. Melt the honey in the water and add the lemon juice. Allow to cool.

Remove baklava from oven, pour cold syrup over and leave to cool in tin. Cut along the marked lines to serve.

Irish apple turnovers

Overall timing 2 hours including refrigeration

Freezing Suitable: refresh in 350°F (180°C) Gas 4 oven for 10–15 minutes

Makes 20 small or 12 large

9 oz	Plain flour	250 g
2 teasp	Baking powder	2x5 ml
5 oz	Caster sugar	150 g
5 oz	Butter	150 g
2 tbsp	Cold water	2x15 ml
1 lb	Cox's Orange Pippins	450 g
1 tbsp	Apricot jam	15 ml
2 tbsp	Mixed dried fruit	2x15 ml
	Icing sugar	

Sift flour, baking powder and sugar into a bowl and make a well in the centre. Cut the softened butter into small pieces and put round the edge. Add water and knead to make a smooth dough. Chill for 1 hour.

Preheat the oven to 350°F (180°C) Gas 4.

Core apples. Place them on a baking tray and bake for 20 minutes till tender. Peel them, then mash and mix with the apricot jam and dried fruit.

Increase the oven temperature to 400°F (200°C) Gas 6.

Roll out dough on a lightly floured board to ⅛ inch (3 mm) thickness. Cut out rounds or squares. Spoon a little apple mixture into the centre of each dough shape. Moisten edges with water, fold the dough over to form a half moon, triangle or rectangle, and press edges well together. Place on a greased baking tray.

Bake for 15–20 minutes. Dredge with icing sugar and serve warm with whipped cream or vanilla ice cream.

Jam puffs

Overall timing 20 minutes plus thawing

Freezing Not suitable

Makes 12

7½ oz	Frozen puff pastry	212g
1	Egg	1
5 tbsp	Jam	5x15 ml

Thaw pastry. Preheat the oven to 425°F (220°C) Gas 7.

Roll out dough to ¼ inch (6mm) thickness. Cut into 2 inch (5 cm) rounds with a pastry cutter. Mark the centres with a small cutter or a bottle lid. Do not cut through.

Place on a dampened baking tray and brush with beaten egg. Bake for about 10 minutes till well risen and golden. Cool on a wire rack.

Remove centres and put a heaped teaspoon of jam in each. Use centres of pastry as lids, if liked. Serve warm.

Palmiers

Overall timing 1½ hours plus chilling

Freezing Suitable: shape and bake after thawing

Makes 12–16

8 oz	Plain flour	225 g
½ teasp	Salt	2.5 ml
6 oz	Butter	175 g
2 teasp	Lemon juice	2x5 ml
¼ pint	Cold water	150 ml
	Caster sugar	

Sift flour and salt into a bowl and rub in 1½ oz (40 g) butter. Mix in lemon juice and enough water to make a soft but not sticky dough. Knead till smooth.

Roll out dough on floured surface to 15x5 inch (38x13 cm) rectangle. Divide remaining butter into three and cut into small pieces. Dot one-third of butter over top two-thirds of dough. Fold up bottom third, then fold top third over it. Press edges to seal and turn dough so folds are to the side.

Repeat rolling out, adding another third of fat and folding, then chill for 15 minutes. Repeat process again, using rest of butter, and chill for 15 minutes.

Preheat the oven to 425°F (220°C) Gas 7.

Roll out dough to ¼ inch (6 mm) thick. Sprinkle with caster sugar. Fold the long sides in to meet at the centre and sprinkle again with sugar. Fold the long sides in again to make four layers. Cut across folds to make ½ inch (12.5 mm) slices.

Arrange slices on dampened baking tray and flatten slightly. Bake for 6 minutes on each side. Serve warm.

Almond tartlets

Overall timing 1 hour plus cooling

Freezing Suitable: ice and decorate after thawing

Makes 12

14 oz	Shortcrust pastry	400 g
4	Eggs	4
3½ oz	Caster sugar	100 g
4 oz	Ground almonds	125 g
Decoration		
5 oz	Icing sugar	150 g
1 tbsp	Milk	15 ml
1 tbsp	Lemon juice	15 ml
12	Glacé cherries	12
	Angelica leaves	

Preheat the oven to 400°F (200°C) Gas 6.

Roll out the dough and use to line 12 tartlet tins. Bake blind for 10 minutes, then remove from oven.

Separate the eggs. Add sugar to yolks and whisk together till pale and thick. Fold in ground almonds. In another bowl, whisk egg whites till stiff, then fold into almond mixture.

Fill pastry cases with almond mixture. Place on a baking tray and bake for 15–20 minutes till centre is firm and springy. Leave to cool.

Sift the icing sugar into a bowl and beat in milk and lemon juice till smooth. Spread over tartlets. Decorate with whole glacé cherries and angelica leaves and leave till set.

Mince pies

Overall timing 30 minutes

Freezing Suitable: bake from frozen in 425°F (220°C) Gas 7 oven for 20–30 minutes

Makes 15–20

8 oz	Shortcrust pastry	225 g
8 oz	Mincemeat	225 g
3 tbsp	Brandy	3x15 ml
6 tbsp	Milk	6x15 ml
2 tbsp	Caster sugar	2x15 ml

Preheat the oven to 400°F (200°C) Gas 6.

Roll out the dough on a floured surface. Stamp out 20 rounds with a 2½ inch (6.5 cm) cutter, then 20 rounds with a 2 inch (5 cm) cutter. Press the larger rounds into a greased 20-hole bun tray.

Mix the mincemeat and brandy in a small bowl and divide between the pastry cases. Dip small dough rounds in the milk, then place one on each pie. Using a fork, press the edges together firmly to seal.

Sprinkle the caster sugar over the top. Bake for about 20 minutes till golden. Serve hot or cold.

Eclairs

Overall timing 1½ hours

Freezing Suitable: bake from frozen

Makes 16

4 oz	Choux paste	125 g
½ pint	Whipping cream	300 ml
2 tbsp	Caster sugar	2x15 ml
4 oz	Icing sugar	125 g
2 teasp	Drinking chocolate	2x5 ml
1–2 tbsp	Hot water	1–2x 15 ml

Preheat the oven to 425°F (220°C) Gas 7.

Spoon paste into piping bag fitted with ½ inch (12.5 mm) plain nozzle and pipe fingers, about 3 inches (7.5 cm) long, on greased baking trays. Leave plenty of space between fingers so they have room to expand during baking. Bake for about 30 minutes till golden and crisp. Transfer to a wire rack. Make a slit down side of each éclair to allow steam to escape and leave to cool.

Whip cream with sugar until just thick and holding soft peaks. Spoon cream into cooled éclairs and return to wire rack placed over greaseproof paper.

Mix icing sugar with drinking chocolate and hot water. The glacé icing should be thick enough to coat the back of a spoon. If too thick, add a little more water; if too runny, add more icing sugar. Dip top of one éclair at a time into icing. Leave on wire rack till icing is set. Eat the same day.

Index

THE EUROPEAN FOOTBALL YEARBOOK 20 13 14

THE EUROPEAN FOOTBALL YEARBOOK

20 13 14

General Editor
Mike Hammond

The only authoritative annual on the European game

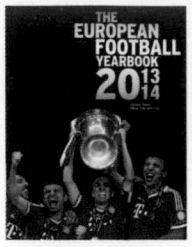

Further copies of The European Football Yearbook
2013/14 are available from:
www.carltonbooks.co.uk
hotline number +44 (0) 141 306 3100

The European Football Yearbook 2013/14

First published by Carlton Books Ltd, England in 2013

Printed by m press (sales) Ltd, England

ISBN 978-1-78097-374-6

UEFA – the Union of European Football Associations – is the governing body of football on the continent of Europe. UEFA's core mission is to promote, protect and develop European football at every level of the game, to promote the principles of unity and solidarity, and to deal with all questions relating to European football.

UEFA is an association of associations based on representative democracy, and is the governing body of European football.

UEFA
Route de Genève 46
Case postale
CH-1260 Nyon 2
Switzerland

Tel: +41 (0) 848 00 2727
Fax: +41 (0) 848 01 2727
Web: UEFA.com

Media Desk
Tel: +41 (0) 848 04 2727

All views expressed in the European Football Yearbook do not necessarily reflect those of UEFA. Every effort has been made to ensure the accuracy of the data in the European Football Yearbook, official and unofficial.

Front cover image: FC Bayern München captain Philipp Lahm lifts the UEFA Champions League trophy flanked by (l to r) Franck Ribéry, Thomas Müller and Mario Mandžukić

The European Football Yearbook 2011/12 and
The European Football Yearbook 2012/13
are available from:
www.calmproductions.com
orders@calmproductions.com
UK hotline 0845 408 2606

THE EUROPEAN FOOTBALL YEARBOOK 20 13 14

General Editor
Mike Hammond

Assistant Editor
Jesper Krogshede Sørensen

Nation-by-nation

Correspondents and Researchers

Nikolai Belov (Russia), José Del Olmo (Spain), Sean DeLoughry (Republic of Ireland), Tamás Dénes (Hungary), Arno Funck (Luxembourg), Stoyan Georgiev (Bulgaria), Marshall Gillespie (Northern Ireland), Clas Glenning (Sweden), Miron Goihman (Moldova), Marcel Haisma (Netherlands), Michael Hansen (Denmark), Romeo Ionescu (Romania), Michel Jambonet (France), Valery Karpushkin (Latvia), Mikael Kirakosyan (Armenia), Jesper Krogshede Sørensen (Faroe Islands, Italy), Fuad & Feda Krvavac (Bosnia & Herzegovina), Zdeněk Kučera (Czech Republic), Ambrosius Kutschera (Austria), Almantas Laužadis (Lithuania), Tarmo Lohioto (Estonia), Dag Lindholm (Norway), Ewan Macdonald (Scotland), Mica Madžarović (Montenegro), Erlan Manashev (Kazakhstan), Goran Mancevski (Former Yugoslav Republic of Macedonia), Rasim Mövsümov (Azerbaijan), Giovanni Nappi (Albania), Kazimerz Oleszek (Poland), Olexandr Pauk (Belarus, Ukraine), Humberto Pereira Silva (Portugal), Ivan Reić (Croatia), Mike Ritter & Silvia Schäfer (Germany), Grega Sever (Slovenia), Revaz Shengelia (Georgia), Vídir Sigurdsson (Iceland), Erdinç Sivritepe (Turkey), Dušan Stamenković (Serbia), Edouard Stutz (Switzerland), Matej Széher (Slovakia), Mel Thomas (Wales), Vesa Tikander (Finland), Serge Van Hoof (Belgium), Victor Vassallo (Malta), Georgios J Vassalos (Greece), Jacob Zelazo (Cyprus, Israel); additional assistance Gabriel Mantz

Photography

Getty Images, Sportsfile, Getty Images/AFP, Getty Images/ Bongarts, Action Images; additional assistance Apollon Limassol FC, Domenic Aquilina, Gábor Baricsa, Ekipa/www.ekipa.mk, Jussi Eskola/www.palloliitto.fi, Estonian FA, Football Association of Wales, Sander Ilvest, Badri Ketiladze, Boris Kharchenko, Roman Koksharov, Legia Warszawa, LSA, Ljubo Vukelič/Delo, Silvia Casals, NK Maribor/Taka, Marko Djurić, Fedja Krvavac, Pressball, Reuters, Enrique Serrano, SITA/Milo Fabian, Jakub Syrůček, Rokas Tenys, The New Saints FC, Vijesti

UEFA

Project management
David Farrelly

Editorial
Contributors: Sam Adams, Kevin Ashby, John Atkin, Paul Bryan, Chris Burke, Michael Harrold, Andrew Haslam, Trevor Haylett, Mark Pettit, Paul Saffer, James Wirth, Paul Woloszyn

Data
Andy Lockwood, Dmitri Mamykin, Dominique Maurer

Production

Print
m press (sales) ltd, England; Cliff Moulder

Distribution
Carlton Books Ltd; Martin Corteel

Design
m press (sales) ltd, Stephen Mines (UEFA)

Artwork/Layout
Keith Jackson

Graphics
Mikhail Sipovich

Data extraction
Delta3 (Davide Giulietti, Antonio Bellissimo, Paolo Calva, Roberto Tealdi, Carlo Bruno, Monica Gemmellaro)

Foreword
Jupp Heynckes

National three-letter codes

There are many instances throughout the European Football Yearbook where country names are abbreviated using three-letter codes. These codes are shown below, listed alphabetically by nation and divided into Europe and the Rest of the World.

Europe

ALB	Alb	Albania
AND	And	Andorra
ARM	Arm	Armenia
AUT	Aut	Austria
AZE	Aze	Azerbaijan
BLR	Blr	Belarus
BEL	Bel	Belgium
BIH	Bih	Bosnia & Herzegovina
BUL	Bul	Bulgaria
CRO	Cro	Croatia
CYP	Cyp	Cyprus
CZE	Cze	Czech Republic
DEN	Den	Denmark
ENG	Eng	England
EST	Est	Estonia
FRO	Fro	Faroe Islands
FIN	Fin	Finland
FRA	Fra	France
GEO	Geo	Georgia
GER	Ger	Germany
GRE	Gre	Greece
HUN	Hun	Hungary
ISL	Isl	Iceland
ISR	Isr	Israel
ITA	Ita	Italy
KAZ	Kaz	Kazakhstan
LVA	Lva	Latvia
LIE	Lie	Liechtenstein
LTU	Ltu	Lithuania
LUX	Lux	Luxembourg
MKD	Mkd	Former Yugoslav Republic of Macedonia (FYROM)
MLT	Mlt	Malta
MDA	Mda	Moldova
MNE	Mne	Montenegro
NED	Ned	Netherlands
NIR	Nir	Northern Ireland
NOR	Nor	Norway
POL	Pol	Poland
POR	Por	Portugal
IRL	Irl	Republic of Ireland
ROU	Rou	Romania
RUS	Rus	Russia
SMR	Smr	San Marino
SCO	Sco	Scotland
SRB	Srb	Serbia
SVK	Svk	Slovakia
SVN	Svn	Slovenia
ESP	Esp	Spain
SWE	Swe	Sweden
SUI	Sui	Switzerland
TUR	Tur	Turkey
UKR	Ukr	Ukraine
WAL	Wal	Wales

Rest of the World

AFG	Afg	Afghanistan
ALG	Alg	Algeria
ANG	Ang	Angola
ATG	Atg	Antigua & Barbuda
ARG	Arg	Argentina
AUS	Aus	Australia
BAH	Bah	Bahamas
BHR	Bhr	Bahrain
BAN	Ban	Bangladesh
BRB	Brb	Barbados
BEN	Ben	Benin
BER	Ber	Bermuda
BOL	Bol	Bolivia
BOT	Bot	Botswana
BRA	Bra	Brazil
BFA	Bfa	Burkina Faso
BDI	Bdi	Burundi
CMR	Cmr	Cameroon
CAN	Can	Canada
CPV	Cpv	Cape Verde Islands
CAY	Cay	Cayman Islands
CTA	Cta	Central African Republic
CHA	Cha	Chad
CHI	Chi	Chile
CHN	Chn	China
COL	Col	Colombia
COM	Com	Comoros
CGO	Cgo	Congo
COD	Cod	Congo DR
CRC	Crc	Costa Rica
CUB	Cub	Cuba
DJI	Dji	Djibouti
DOM	Dom	Dominican Republic
ECU	Ecu	Ecuador
EGY	Egy	Egypt
SLV	Slv	El Salvador
EQG	Eqg	Equatorial Guinea
ETH	Eth	Ethiopia
FIJ	Fij	Fiji
GAB	Gab	Gabon
GAM	Gam	Gambia
GHA	Gha	Ghana
GRN	Grn	Gronada
GUA	Gua	Guatemala
GUI	Gui	Guinea
GNB	Gnb	Guinea-Bissau
HAI	Hai	Haiti
HON	Hon	Honduras
HKG	Hkg	Hong Kong
IND	Ind	India
IDN	Idn	Indonesia
IRN	Irn	Iran
IRQ	Irq	Iraq
CIV	Civ	Ivory Coast
JAM	Jam	Jamaica
JPN	Jpn	Japan
JOR	Jor	Jordan
KEN	Ken	Kenya
KUW	Kuw	Kuwait

KGZ	Kgz	Kyrgyzstan
LIB	Lib	Lebanon
LBR	Lbr	Liberia
LBY	Lby	Libya
MAD	Mad	Madagascar
MWI	Mwi	Malawi
MAS	Mas	Malaysia
MLI	Mli	Mali
MTN	Mtn	Mauritania
MEX	Mex	Mexico
MAR	Mar	Morocco
MOZ	Moz	Mozambique
NAM	Nam	Namibia
ANT	Ant	Netherlands Antilles
NCL	Ncl	New Caledonia
NZL	Nzl	New Zealand
NIG	Nig	Niger
NGA	Nga	Nigeria
PRK	Prk	North Korea
OMA	Oma	Oman
PAK	Pak	Pakistan
PLE	Ple	Palestine
PAN	Pan	Panama
PAR	Par	Paraguay
PER	Per	Peru
PHI	Phi	Philippines
PUR	Pur	Puerto Rico
QAT	Qat	Qatar
RWA	Rwa	Rwanda
KSA	Ksa	Saudi Arabia
SEN	Sen	Senegal
SLE	Sle	Sierra Leone
SIN	Sin	Singapore
SOL	Sol	Solomon Islands
SOM	Som	Somalia
RSA	Rsa	South Africa
KOR	Kor	South Korea
SKN	Skn	St Kitts & Nevis
VIN	Vin	St Vincent & Grenadines
SDN	Sdn	Sudan
SUR	Sur	Surinam
SYR	Syr	Syria
TAH	Tah	Tahiti
TJK	Tjk	Tajikistan
TAN	Tan	Tanzania
THA	Tha	Thailand
TOG	Tog	Togo
TRI	Tri	Trinidad & Tobago
TUN	Tun	Tunisia
TKM	Tkm	Turkmenistan
UGA	Uga	Uganda
UAE	Uae	United Arab Emirates
USA	Usa	United States
URU	Uru	Uruguay
UZB	Uzb	Uzbekistan
VEN	Ven	Venezuela
VIE	Vie	Vietnam
ZAM	Zam	Zambia
ZIM	Zim	Zimbabwe

Contents

THE EUROPEAN FOOTBALL YEARBOOK 20¹³14

Foreword

It gives me great pleasure to be asked to write the foreword for the European Football Yearbook – a traditional honour, I know, that is reserved for the head coach of the previous season's UEFA Champions League winners.

Although I am no longer active in that role at FC Bayern München, I could not have wished for a more glorious season with which to end my time at this great club. Our ambition at the start of the 2012/13 campaign was to erase the unhappy memories of the previous one, in which we finished runners-up in all of the three major competitions we entered. We not only did that, but achieved our mission in grand style, making a dream come true for the club and all of its magnificent supporters.

The Bundesliga was won in record-breaking fashion, the DFB-Pokal was captured against our south German rivals VfB Stuttgart in Berlin and of course, above all, we made up for the 2012 UEFA Champions League final defeat on penalties against Chelsea FC in our own stadium by going to London and beating our main domestic rivals Borussia Dortmund 2-1 at the iconic Wembley Stadium to be crowned champions of Europe for the fifth time.

Furthermore, we broke new ground by becoming the first German club to achieve that fabulous treble.

The praise that was heaped on my players from far and wide was fully deserved. The success was only possible thanks to the hard work and application that they put in to every game. The spirit and resolve of everyone involved was truly remarkable. It just goes to show what is possible when the collective desire is so strong. Of course, to win so much also requires a great deal of natural ability and skill, and the Bayern class of 2012/13 had those qualities in abundance. It was truly a privilege and a joy to work with the team and be part of such a historic success story.

The European Football Yearbook is a first-class publication that is widely respected and admired across the continent. Its comprehensive coverage of every aspect of the European game makes it a goldmine of information. I am delighted to see Bayern players parading the UEFA Champions League trophy on this year's front cover, and I wish the Yearbook every success – both this year and in the future.

Jupp Heynckes
Head coach
FC Bayern München
UEFA Champions League winners
2012/13

Introduction

From the General Editor

Welcome to the new-look European Football Yearbook.

As regular readers of the publication will have noticed, this 2013/14 edition looks rather different from those of recent years.

Following last year's 25th anniversary, we have decided to go back to the future and restyle the Yearbook in the mould of the inaugural edition, from 1988/89, which means an increase in the format size, fewer pages and – most strikingly of all – full colour throughout.

With the publication now firmly under the UEFA.com umbrella – this is the seventh year that it has enjoyed the backing of the official website of European football's governing body – the desire to standardise output has been at the source of the changes, not just in terms of design but also in the style of the narrative and the configuration and presentation of the data.

This more contemporary, user-friendly approach has been adopted throughout the book, and we hope that its visual appeal will be appreciated by a broader and more varied readership.

Long-standing aficionados of the Yearbook can rest assured, however, that, despite the makeover, all of the publication's key features and reference points are still very much in place.

There are comprehensive reports – statistical and narrative – on all the UEFA competitions, headed by the UEFA Champions League and UEFA Europa League and with particular attention also given to the UEFA European Under-21 Championship in Israel and the UEFA Women's EURO in Sweden.

The European qualifying zone for the 2014 FIFA World Cup is afforded similarly in-depth coverage, with match details included for every game, and we have also previewed the final tournament in Brazil with a full match schedule and venue map.

A significant chunk of the book is reserved, as ever, for our popular Top 100 Players section, which profiles with photos, facts and figures all of the 2012/13 season's outstanding individual performers. And yes, Lionel Messi did make it in again – for the eighth year in a row – along with a rather large contingent from FC Bayern München.

The nation-by-nation section remains the Yearbook's principal focal point. An unrivalled source of reference, it has been strengthened and expanded this year by the inclusion in each UEFA member association's chapter of the country maps and European club competition lineups.

We have broken down the season's editorial review into distinct sections – domestic league, domestic cup, Europe and national team – and added a handy 'At a Glance' panel, in which the season's main outcomes are summarised. This includes new features in which the Player and Newcomer of the Season are profiled and the domestic league's Team of the Season is illustrated in graphic form.

The larger page size has enabled us to make the domestic league club-by-club data, including the ever-essential results/scorers and appearances/goals, more appealing on the eye by presenting it – in most cases – in a one-club-per-column format.

The flesh may look a bit different, but the bones of the Yearbook are still firmly intact!

The publication's aim, as it has been for over a quarter of a century, is to provide a unique and comprehensive annual source of reference on European football that is also attractive to look at and enjoyable to read.

I hope you agree that we have fulfilled that objective with this redesigned, all-colour 2013/14 edition. I look forward to receiving your comments and suggestions, positive or otherwise, at mike.hammond@uefa.ch.

A full list of acknowledgements can be found on page 5, and every one of those people deserve credit and recognition for their co-operation, but I would like to use this opportunity to extend special personal thanks to Jesper Krogshede Sørensen, Keith Jackson and Andy Lockwood.

With so many elements and contributions to monitor and control, especially during the busy months of May, June and July, getting the production process to run smoothly and to schedule is no straightforward task. However, with that trio of trusty lieutenants to assist me, this edition has been one of the least taxing that I have worked on.

Diligence and reliability are qualities that seem to me, alas, to be in increasingly short supply as the years advance, but Jesper, Keith and Andy have them in abundance. It is a privilege and a pleasure to work with them.

The final word of gratitude, as ever, goes to my wife and children, to whom I owe so much for their boundless love and support. Sue, Rebecca and Charlie – this one, like all the others, is for you.

Mike Hammond
1 August, 2013

UEFA competitions 2012/13

An all-German UEFA Champions League final might not have been what English fans wanted when UEFA decided to mark the Football Association's 150th anniversary by staging the game at Wembley, but FC Bayern München's 2-1 victory against Bundesliga rivals Borussia Dortmund was a splendid conclusion to the season, and a fixture that marked a shift in the power dynamic of European football.

In 2011/12, Spanish sides collected no fewer than six UEFA trophies, with the nation's brand of short-passing possession football seemingly set as the gold standard. When FC Barcelona and Real Madrid CF were kept apart in the UEFA Champions League semi-final draw, it raised the enticing possibility of the eternal Liga rivals meeting at Wembley.

That sense of Spanish invincibility crumbled dramatically over two nights in April. First of all Jupp Heynckes' powerful, pacy Bayern shredded Barça 4-0 in Munich; the following evening Jürgen Klopp's effervescent Dortmund overwhelmed Madrid 4-1. José Mourinho's side almost turned that result around, winning the second leg 2-0, but Barcelona were denied any such consolation, losing 3-0 in the return fixture at the Camp Nou.

Arjen Robben's late winner for Bayern at Wembley – coupled with European debutantes VfL Wolfsburg's victory against holders Olympique Lyonnais in the UEFA Women's Champions League final at Stamford Bridge two days earlier – meant that for the first time teams representing the same nation won the top trophies in both men's and women's club football in the same calendar year. Germany then completed a unique national treble in late July by winning UEFA Women's EURO 2013, beating Norway 1-0 in the final in Sweden to take the trophy for the sixth time in a row.

Chelsea FC, meanwhile, achieved an intriguing first. For the nine days between their UEFA Europa League final victory against SL Benfica in Amsterdam and Bayern's success at Wembley, the west London club held both of the biggest prizes in European club football simultaneously. Led by interim coach Rafael Benítez, the Blues made up for becoming the first UEFA Champions League holders to be eliminated from the competition in the group stage by romping to the final in Amsterdam, and becoming the first English club to have won all three major UEFA club trophies – the UEFA Cup Winners' Cup, UEFA Champions League and UEFA Europa League.

It was not, however, a vintage year for English sides. No Premier League club reached the UEFA Champions League quarter-finals – the first time that had happened for 17 years – while Stuart Pearce's national team lost all three of their games at the UEFA European Under-21 Championship in Israel. Spain, by contrast, purred through to the final, where they ran out 4-2 winners against Italy – a reminder perhaps that for all the northern European successes in the club competitions, the golden age of "tiki-taka" may not quite be over.

Signs of things to come could also be read from the outcomes of UEFA's less celebrated tournaments. FC Barcelona were relieved of the UEFA Futsal Cup by Kazakhstan's Kairat Almaty; Poland, led by the mercurial Ewa Pajor, took their first female trophy, the UEFA European Women's Under-17 Championship; Russia prevailed on penalties in the UEFA European Under-17 Championship in Slovakia; and, to round off an enthralling 2012/13 season, Serbia claimed a first victory in the UEFA European Under-19 Championship, staged in Lithuania.

Europe's footballing centre of balance may indeed be shifting, but, for all of Germany's successes in 2012/13, it could be as much towards the east as to the north.

Wembley delight for Bayern

For the third time in four years, FC Bayern München reached the UEFA Champions League final. However, unlike in 2010 and 2012, Germany's most decorated club came good when it mattered to be crowned European champions for the fifth time.

With defeats against FC Internazionale Milano and, most painfully, Chelsea FC – on penalties in their own stadium – still fresh in the memory, Bayern were in determined mood from the season's outset. After topping Group F, Jupp Heynckes' side eliminated Arsenal FC and Juventus before reaffirming their quality in stunning fashion with a 7-0 aggregate demolition of FC Barcelona – the largest margin of victory in a UEFA Champions League semi-final.

Waiting for Bayern at Wembley Stadium, granted its second final in three years in honour of the Football Association's 150th birthday, were domestic rivals Borussia Dortmund. It was the fourth UEFA Champions League final between clubs from the same country – but the first monopolised by the Bundesliga.

Eliminated at the group stage in 2011/12, Jürgen Klopp's young team were handed another tough draw, alongside the champions of Spain, England and the Netherlands. On this occasion, though, they not only survived but thrived, finishing ahead of Real Madrid CF as Manchester City FC propped up the table without a win. After FC Shakhtar Donetsk had been overcome in the round of 16, it looked as

Bayern's Jupp Heynckes (left) and Dortmund's Jürgen Klopp – opposing coaches in the UEFA Champions League final

if debutants Málaga CF would end the Dortmund journey, only for two added-time goals to turn the tie and sensationally propel them into the last four. There they faced a reunion with Madrid, and after Robert Lewandowski had become the first player to score four times in a European Cup semi-final match, Klopp's charges survived a second-leg fightback to book their place in north London.

Dortmund started positively in their second UEFA Champions League final – the first having brought victory in 1997 – yet were behind on the hour as Mario Mandžukić tapped in Arjen Robben's cross. İlkay

Gündoğan's penalty swiftly levelled matters – the first goal Heynckes' team had conceded in the competition for over seven hours – but it was Bayern who finished the stronger, grabbing a dramatic winner in the 80th minute as Robben, who like his penalty miss in the previous season's final, became the hero as he wriggled through the Dortmund defence to score.

That was the culmination of a season full of drama and intrigue. Paris Saint-Germain FC collected the most points in the group stage (15) and went on to reach the last eight for the first time since 1994/95, while Chelsea FC became the first holders to fall at the initial group stage, finishing behind Juventus and Shakhtar in Group E. Málaga marked their induction with three straight wins and finished ahead of AC Milan in Group C, Galatasaray AŞ recovered from a false start to finish runners-up to Manchester United FC in Group H, while FC Schalke 04's feat of becoming the first foreign side to win at Arsenal FC in almost a decade helped them eclipse their English rivals to finish top of Group B.

Real Madrid won an epic tie against United – thus helping to end Premier League participation in the round of 16 – while Barça recovered from a 2-0 first-leg defeat at Milan to win 4-0 at the Camp Nou. However, both Spanish heavyweights would fall – for the second season running – in the semi-finals as the 2012/13 UEFA Champions League turned into a tale of German domination – and, ultimately, of redemption and jubilation for Bayern.

Man of the match Arjen Robben raises the UEFA Champions League trophy after Bayern's 2-1 win against Borussia Dortmund at Wembley

UEFA Champions League

Qualifying rounds

The first goal of the 2012/13 UEFA Champions League season was scored on 3 July, 25 minutes into F91 Dudelange's 7-0 home win against SP Tre Penne when Frenchman Bryan Melisse opened the scoring for the Luxembourg champions. The first qualifying round also bore witness to the first hat-trick of the campaign, from Valletta FC's Michael Mifsud. Both Dudelange and Valletta reached the second qualifying round, as did Linfield FC, who ousted B36 Tórshavn on penalties in the first of many dramatic denouements over the course of the campaign.

The first major surprise came in the next round, with Dudelange beating FC Salzburg 1-0 at home in the first leg and then surviving the ambitious Austrian club's late second-leg fightback to progress on away goals. There were big second qualifying round victories for HJK Helsinki, FK Partizan and FC Basel 1893 in particular, although of that trio only the Swiss side would still be involved by the time the third qualifying round concluded.

Partizan were unexpectedly eliminated by AEL Limassol FC, losing each leg 1-0, but there were few other upsets. The heavyweight contests between FC Dynamo Kyiv and Feyenoord, and FC København and Club Brugge KV, went the way of the Ukrainian and Danish clubs respectively, while recent group stage participants FC BATE Borisov, GNK Dinamo Zagreb, CFR 1907 Cluj and Fenerbahçe SK all enjoyed comfortable wins and RSC Anderlecht put 11 goals without reply past Lithuania's FK Ekranas.

Play-offs

BATE, Dinamo and CFR Cluj confirmed their places in the group stage by coming through their play-off ties at the expense of Hapoel Ironi Kiryat Shmona FC, Basel and NK Maribor respectively. Anderlecht and Celtic FC both qualified for the competition proper for the first time in several years and, in the 'league section' of the play-off round, København and Fenerbahçe failed to make the cut, losing out narrowly to LOSC Lille and FC Spartak Moskva. Dynamo did come through, a 3-1 first-leg win at VfL Borussia Mönchengladbach effectively booking their place, while SC Braga won on penalties at Udinese Calcio and Málaga CF's remarkable journey began with victory over Panathinaikos FC.

Group stage

The newcomers from Spain's Costa del Sol faced Milan, FC Zenit St Petersburg and Anderlecht in **Group C** and, boasting the invaluable experience of coach Manuel Pellegrini, they thrived. A 3-0 opening home win against Zenit gave them the ideal start, and when they repeated that result in Brussels a fortnight later, Málaga were well placed to emulate Pellegrini's 2005/06 Villarreal CF side and reach the knockout rounds on their UEFA Champions League debut. A 1-0 home win against Milan, secured by Joaquín's second-half goal, all but confirmed it, and draws in their last three fixtures ensured Málaga won the section by four points.

That left Milan, Zenit and Anderlecht to scrap for second place, although the Rossoneri always held the edge having won 3-2 in St Petersburg on matchday two. Zenit revived their own hopes with a 1-0 home win against Anderlecht next time out – while Milan were losing at La Rosaleda – but defeat by the same scoreline in Belgium left Luciano Spalletti's team with too much to do. Despite rallying from 2-0 down to draw at home to Málaga in their penultimate fixture, Zenit's hopes were extinguished by Milan's 3-1 win at Anderlecht – featuring a spectacular overhead goal from Philippe Mexès – the same night. A 1-0 closing win at San Siro was enough only for the Russian side to finish third and qualify for the UEFA Europa League, leaving Anderlecht out of Europe at the foot of the table.

Chelsea's long quest to be crowned champions of Europe had ended in glorious fashion in Munich in May 2012, but the English side were to experience the shortest trophy defence in the UEFA Champions League era. It started so promisingly for Roberto Di Matteo's side as two goals from new Brazilian recruit Oscar put them in command against Italian champions Juventus at Stamford Bridge on matchday one of **Group E**. Arturo Vidal and Fabio Quagliarella responded for Juve, however, stretching the Bianconeri's run of consecutive European draws to seven. That became eight two weeks later as FC Shakhtar Donetsk – 2-0 home winners against Danish debutants FC Nordsjælland on the opening night – snatched a 1-1 draw in the first European game at the new Juventus Stadium.

Chelsea won 4-0 in Denmark in their second game, but the first sign of trouble came in the Donbass Arena on matchday three, a goal early in each half from Brazilian duo Alex Teixeira and Fernandinho helping Shakhtar to a 2-1 win. The holders' campaign looked to be back on track – just – as a Victor Moses header deep into added time settled a pulsating return fixture against the Ukrainian side 3-2 in Chelsea's favour. Juve, however, had stayed in touch despite being held in Denmark, concluding the sequence of draws at nine with a 4-0 victory over Nordsjælland in Turin.

Málaga winger Joaquín enjoys his winning goal against Milan

KEY FACT

6

Zlatan Ibrahimović's matchday one goal against FC Dynamo Kyiv made him the first player to score for six different sides in the UEFA Champions League – AFC Ajax, Juventus, FC Internazionale Milano, FC Barcelona, AC Milan and Paris Saint-Germain FC.

While Shakhtar cantered to a 5-2 win in Copenhagen in their penultimate fixture – Luiz Adriano scoring a hat-trick and Willian two – Chelsea's grip on the trophy was loosened in Turin. Quagliarella, Vidal and Sebastian Giovinco gave Juve a sumptuous 3-0 win that signalled the end of Di Matteo's reign as Chelsea manager six months after his success in Munich and left the holders' fate out of their hands. Under the interim stewardship of Rafael Benítez, the Blues thrashed Nordsjælland 6-1 at Stamford Bridge, but it counted for little as Juve won in Donetsk thanks to Olexandr Kucher's own goal, thereby overhauling their hosts to qualify as group winners. Chelsea, despite scoring more goals (16) in the group stage than any of the other 31 participants, therefore lost out on the head to head rule to Shakhtar (with away goals coming into play) and became the first UEFA Champions League holders to be eliminated in the group stage. Instead they transferred over to the UEFA Europa League – where a considerable consolation prize would await them in Amsterdam.

When the group stage draw was made at the end of August, the most eye-catching section was unquestionably **Group D** – the only one containing four national champions – and right from the start it lived up to its billing. Dortmund's run to the final started with a 1-0 home win against AFC Ajax – Robert Lewandowski scoring the first of his ten goals of the campaign in the 87th minute – but there was even more late drama in Spain, where all five goals came in the final quarter. Manchester City FC twice took the lead and twice lost it before Cristiano Ronaldo's 90th-minute winner gave Real Madrid the points.

There was no let up in the weeks that followed. Mario Balotelli's late penalty rescued a 1-1 draw for City at home to a dominant Dortmund while Ronaldo's stellar start to the tournament continued with a hat-trick as Madrid eased to victory in Amsterdam. Ajax bounced back with an unexpected 3-1 home win against City on matchday three and although they surrendered a two-goal lead in the reverse fixture, the 2-2 draw in Manchester left City's hopes hanging by a thread.

It was a different story for Dortmund, impressive 2-1 home victors against Madrid and only denied a repeat win in Spain by Mesut Özil's 89th-minute equaliser. The 4-1 win in Amsterdam that followed gave Jürgen Klopp's exuberant side first place as Madrid – whose coach José Mourinho became only the fourth coach, after Sir Alex Ferguson, Arsène Wenger and Carlo Ancelotti, to take charge of 100 UEFA Champions League matches – were held 1-1 by City, who dropped out of Europe altogether following their closing defeat in Dortmund. Ajax finished third despite their sixth successive defeat by Madrid, 4-1 at the Santiago Bernabéu, the Dutch club having conceded 20 goals during that run.

PSG's Zlatan Ibrahimović shields the ball from Dinamo Zagreb's Domagoj Vida

KEY FACT

10

Chelsea FC and CFR 1907 Cluj both finished with ten points, joining a small cluster of clubs who have failed to advance from a group stage on that total. FC Dynamo Kyiv (1999/2000, second group stage, and 2004/05), Borussia Dortmund (2002/03, second group stage), PSV Eindhoven (2003/04), Olympiacos FC (2004/05), SV Werder Bremen (2006/07) and Manchester City FC (2011/12) all missed out despite their double-figure points tallies.

Group A was a more straightforward prospect for Paris Saint-German FC and FC Porto, who both eased through. The tone was set from matchday one as PSG – in the group stage for the first time in eight seasons – ran out 4-1 winners at home to Dynamo Kyiv while Dinamo Zagreb lost 2-0 at home to Porto – the Croatian champions' seventh successive group stage defeat after their ill-starred 2011/12 campaign.

Although Dynamo briefly revived their own hopes at the expense of Dinamo on matchday two – when Porto were inflicting what would prove to be PSG's sole defeat of the competition, winning 1-0 at the Estádio do

Dragão – one point from two games against the Portuguese champions effectively ended the Ukrainian side's challenge. PSG continued to make comfortable progress with two wins against Dinamo – Zlatan Ibrahimović notching up all four goals of the Paris duo, and a 2-0 victory in Kyiv, as the 2-1 home win against Porto in the sixth and final round of games took the French side through as group winners. Dynamo were assured of third place and a UEFA Europa League spot by the time they travelled to Zagreb, but there was some consolation for Dinamo amid heavy snow as Ivan Krstanović's penalty deep into added time salvaged a 1-1 draw that prevented them from equalling Anderlecht's unenviable UEFA Champions League record of 12 successive defeats. It was also Dinamo's first goal of the 2012/13 group stage – after a wait of 567 minutes, added time included.

There was a minor surprise in **Group B** as FC Schalke 04 came out on top ahead of Arsenal FC, thanks chiefly to a 2-0 win in north London on matchday three – the first time a non-English club had won in Arsenal's new stadium, and the Gunners' first home defeat by overseas opposition in nine years. The defeat might have been even costlier for Wenger's side had they not already recorded wins at debutants Montpellier Hérault SC and at home to Olympiacos FC, although Schalke's win in London enabled them to leapfrog the English club to the top of the standings with seven points from their opening three matches.

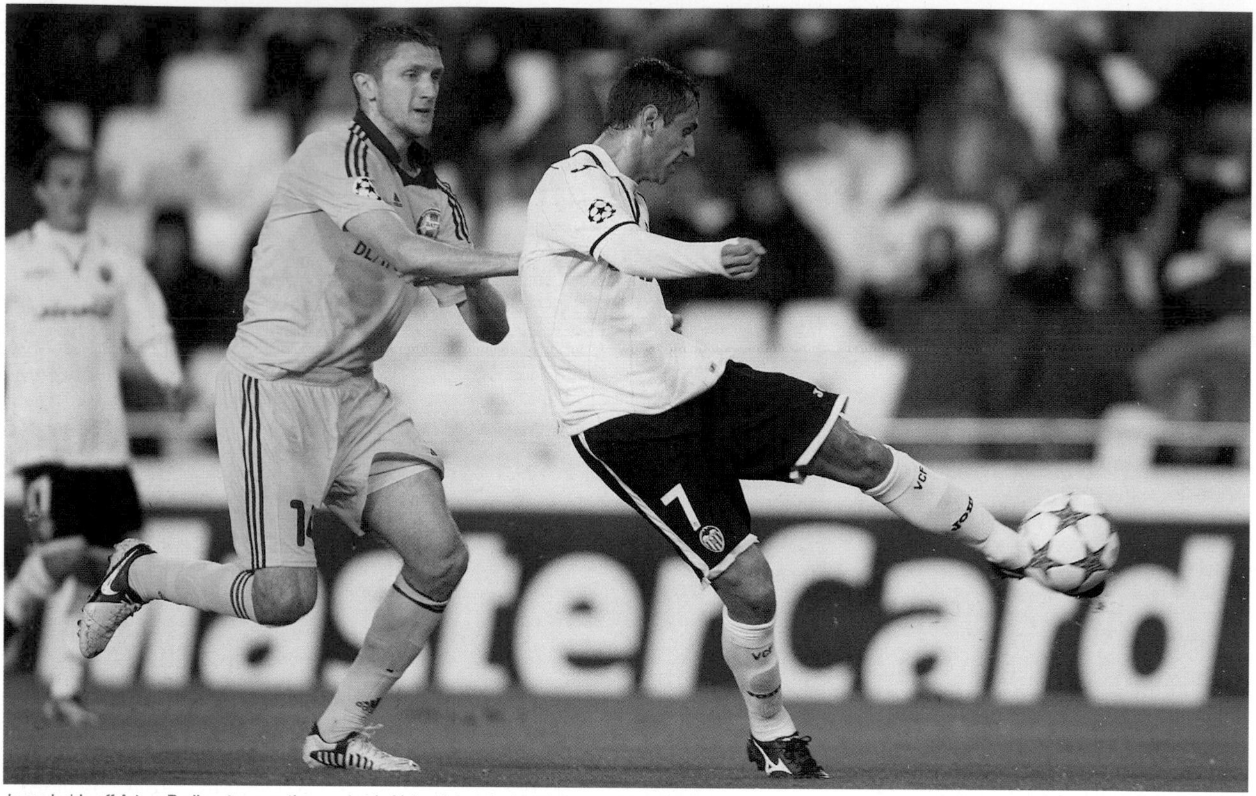

Jonas holds off Artem Radkov to open the scoring in Valencia's 4-2 win at home to BATE Borisov

Schalke kept their noses in front with a rousing comeback from two goals down to draw with the Gunners in Gelsenkirchen as Olympiacos posted a second successive victory against Montpellier to remain in contention. Hope did not last long, however, for the Greek champions. While they were losing 1-0 at Schalke in their penultimate fixture, Arsenal beat Montpellier 2-0 at home to ensure they would join the German club in the round of 16 – albeit as runners-up following defeat in Piraeus next time out.

Bayern set out on their **Group F** campaign with a point to prove and began with a 2-1 home win against Valencia CF. Their next opponents, FC BATE Borisov, started even better, recording their first group stage win at the 13th time of asking with a 3-1 triumph over LOSC Lille in northern France. To widespread astonishment the Belarusian champions staged an encore on matchday two, defeating Bayern by the same scoreline in Minsk.

Valencia kick-started their own campaign with a 2-0 home win against LOSC thanks to a pair of Jonas goals, and they were to bring BATE down to earth with back-to-back wins on matchdays three and four. Roberto Soldado's hat-trick gave the Spanish side a 3-0 away win, and he was also on target in the 4-2 home success. Bayern also accumulated six points over the same stretch, defeating LOSC 1-0 in France and 6-1 in Munich. The 1-1 matchday five draw at Mestalla meant visitors Bayern joined Valencia in the last 16, with LOSC left in fourth place behind BATE on head-to-head record despite a 2-0 away win against their Belarusian rivals. The top two reinforced their superiority in the final round of matches, Valencia winning 1-0 in Lille and Bayern putting four past BATE in Munich.

Group G was expected to be dominated by FC Barcelona and so it proved, although the Spanish giants did not have it all their own way despite wins against Spartak Moskva (3-2) and SL Benfica (2-0) in their opening two encounters. Celtic opened with a disappointing home draw against Benfica (0-0), and that looked set to prove costly given their woeful record in the competition outside Glasgow; instead, a 3-2 victory at Spartak brought them their first UEFA Champions League away win at the 21st attempt, leaving them well placed to progress.

KEY FACT

1

Chelsea FC became the first holders to have their trophy defence ended in the group stage. The London club had progressed to the knockout phase in all ten of their previous UEFA Champions League campaigns.

Neil Lennon's side produced another impressive away performance on matchday three, in Catalonia, but were cruelly denied a draw by Jordi Alba's winner four minutes into added time. In the rematch at Celtic Park, however, the tables were turned on Barcelona in memorable fashion, goals from Victor Wanyama and 18-year-old substitute Tony Watt giving Celtic a famous win and significantly bolstering their qualifying credentials. Benfica's hopes had suffered a blow with defeat in Moscow in their third game and, although they recovered to beat Spartak (2-0) and Celtic (2-1) at the Estádio do Sport Lisboa e Benfica – the venue for the 2013/14 UEFA Champions League final – they could only manage a goalless draw at Barcelona on matchday six, allowing Celtic to claim second place behind Barça thanks to a 2-1 home win over Spartak secured by a late Kris Commons penalty. Benfica had to settle for third place – although, like Chelsea, their European season would still have a long way to run.

Manchester United FC enjoyed a relatively stress-free group stage – which came as some relief after their premature elimination in 2011/12. Sir Alex Ferguson's side won their first four **Group H** outings, although they had

17

Real Madrid CF reached the UEFA Champions League knockout phase for the 17th time, and the 16th season in succession. The Spanish giants were last absent in 1996/97, when they did not feature in the competition. FC Barcelona finished as group winners for the 14th time – one more than Manchester United FC – and for the sixth season in succession.

to come from behind at both CFR Cluj and Braga, and rallied from 2-0 down to beat the Portuguese side at Old Trafford. Despite subsequent defeats at Galatasaray AŞ and at home to CFR – who thus became the first Romanian team to beat United – the three-time champions had already done enough to win the group, which featured only four home wins – as opposed to seven away – in its 12 fixtures.

The battle for second place appeared initially to be a straight fight between CFR – 2-0 winners in Portugal on matchday one – and Braga, who had moved to beat Galatasaray in Istanbul. Indeed, the Turkish team took only one point from their first three matches but, galvanised by Burak Yılmaz's six goals, including a hat-trick at CFR on matchday four, they recovered strongly, their matchday five win against United setting up a final-day showdown in Braga. Although the home side struck first, Burak levelled just before the hour and Aydın Yılmaz's 78th-minute strike – Galatasaray's first goal of the campaign not attributed to their prolific striker – transported Fatih Terim's team into the last 16 for the first time since 2001/02.

Round of 16

The draw for the round of 16 delivered some intriguing ties, but the attention naturally gravitated to the two heavyweight contests, between Manchester United and Real Madrid and Barcelona and Milan.

The first was rich in sub-plots, not least the reunion between Cristiano Ronaldo and the club he had left in 2009. That theme dominated the build-up to the first leg at the Santiago Bernabéu, but it was the Portuguese forward's former employers who struck first, Danny Welbeck heading United into a 20th-minute lead. The advantage lasted just ten minutes, and inevitably it was Ronaldo, with a towering header, who brought Madrid level. Both sides might have

scored again, with Fábio Coentrão and Robin van Persie each hitting the woodwork, but the tie remained level heading to Manchester.

There again it was United, with Wayne Rooney dropped to the bench, who struck first, a Sergio Ramos own goal giving them a deserved 48th-minute lead with the UEFA Champions League's 6,000th goal. United appeared to be in complete control, but the tie turned dramatically on 54 minutes when Nani was shown a red card for a raised foot – a decision that stunned the locals but which Madrid coach Mourinho exploited by introducing Luka Modrić to increase the pressure on the United defence. It was the Croatian midfielder, right on cue, who brought Madrid level with a brilliant curling shot in the 66th minute. With United now reeling, the stage was set for Ronaldo's second goal of the tie three minutes later – a close-range far-post strike that, despite United's late rally, would prove decisive, ensuring defeat for Sir Alex Ferguson in what was to be his final European game – and for Ryan Giggs on his 1,000th senior appearance.

The Milan-Barcelona tie was equally engrossing. Second-half goals from Kevin-Prince Boateng and Sulley Muntari gave Milan a 2-0 first-leg victory at San Siro, and as no team in the competition's modern incarnation had come back from a two-goal deficit without an away goal, the post-match celebrations of the Rossoneri following were understandable. However, Barcelona were to turn things around

in scintillating fashion in Catalonia. It took Lionel Messi just five minutes to halve Milan's advantage with a brilliant strike, and the Argentinian's second goal five minutes before half-time – seconds after Milan had squandered a gilt-edged chance at the other end – brought the aggregate score level. David Villa fired Barcelona in front early in the second period, and although the tie remained in the balance, the coup de grace was delivered two minutes into added time when Jordi Alba strode forward to complete a brilliant – and historic – 4-0 victory.

In contrast, it looked as if Bayern would make smooth progress to the quarter-finals as they eased to a first-leg victory at Arsenal. Toni Kroos crashed in the opening goal after just seven minutes, and when Thomas Müller doubled the advantage midway through the first half, Bayern were cruising. Their former striker Lukas Podolski briefly revived Arsenal

202

Sir Alex Ferguson retired in May 2013, and of his 1,500 games in charge of Manchester United FC a record 202 were in the UEFA Champions League, including qualifiers.

Luka Modrić had a major impact after coming on as a substitute in Real Madrid's 2-1 win over Manchester United at Old Trafford

hopes, but Mario Mandžukić restored Bayern's two-goal cushion with 13 minutes left. Olivier Giroud struck three minutes into the Munich return, however, and Bayern, lacking the drive and desire of the first leg, were suddenly in peril when Laurent Koscielny headed Arsenal's second four minutes from time. Heynckes' charges held on, though, to squeeze through on the away goals rule and leave England without a quarter-final representative for the first time since 1995/96.

PSG also recorded an away first-leg win, 2-1 at Valencia, before they too endured a scare on home soil. First-half goals at Mestalla from Ezequiel Lavezzi and Javier Pastore put Carlo Ancelotti's team in command and, despite Adil Rami's 90th-minute strike and Ibrahimović's subsequent red card, they still looked well placed to reach a second quarter-final. Valencia had other ideas, Jonas bringing them right back into contention after 55 minutes in a nervy second leg at the Parc des Princes. One more away goal would have ended PSG's campaign, but instead it was Lavezzi who equalised to take the Parisians through.

Juventus enjoyed a comfortable victory against Celtic – both away in the first leg and overall. They and their opponents had been absent from the round of 16 for several years – Juve since 2008/09, Celtic for a year longer – but it was the Italian side who made light of their lack of knockout experience, winning 3-0 in Glasgow and 5-0 on aggregate to reach the quarter-finals for the first time since 2006.

Dortmund also laid the groundwork for their progress away from home, coming from behind twice to draw 2-2 at Shakhtar before polishing off the Ukrainian champions with a 3-0 home win that took Klopp's team into the last eight for the first time since 1997/98, when they were the defending champions.

Knockout phase regulars Porto looked set for another quarter-final appearance when João Moutinho scored the only goal of a tight first leg against Málaga to inflict on the Spanish side a first UEFA Champions League defeat. Pellegrini's team responded perfectly, however, in the return, keeping a ninth clean sheet in their 12th European home game and reversing the outcome with goals from Isco and Roque Santa Cruz.

The Galatasaray-Schalke tie was also settled by a fine away performance – in this case in the second leg. A 1-1 draw in Istanbul seemed to have tipped the scales Schalke's way but that was merely the prelude for a pulsating game in Gelsenkirchen. Roman Neustädter put Schalke in front, Hamit Altıntop equalised with a stunning long-range strike before the ever-reliable Burak made it 2-1 to the visitors just before half-time. That left Schalke needing two more goals to

Umut Bulut scores to seal Galatasaray's passage to the quarter-finals at the end of a thrilling game against Schalke in Gelsenkirchen

stay in the competition. Winter recruit Michel Bastos supplied one of them, but with the German side throwing everything forward Umut Bulut broke away in the final seconds to win the game and the tie. It was Galatasaray's third successive away victory and sealed their place in the quarter-finals for the first time in 12 years.

KEY FACT

8

Burak Yılmaz found the net eight times for Galatasaray AŞ – more in a single UEFA Champions League season than any other Turkish player. Before his prolific streak, which constituted Galatasaray's first six goals of the campaign, Burak had not registered in 16 previous matches in the competition, qualifying games included.

Quarter-finals

Galatasaray's impressive away run was abruptly halted when they visited Real Madrid in the first leg of the quarter-final, a repeat of the clubs' 2000/01 meeting. On that occasion the Turkish team had lost 3-0 at the Santiago Bernabéu, and history was repeated as Cristiano Ronaldo and Karim Benzema scored in the first half-hour before Gonzalo Higuaín added a post-interval third.

Ronaldo was on target again seven minutes into the Istanbul return, seemingly ending Galatasaray hopes, but Emmanuel Eboué's spectacular effort made it 1-1 just before the hour, and when the club's two marquee signings of the January transfer window, Didier Drogba and Wesley Sneijder, each found the net in rapid succession with stylish finishes, Galatasaray suddenly sensed a miracle. They were unable to find the fourth goal that would have increased the pressure, however, and instead Ronaldo broke away to score in added time.

The most dramatic denouement came in Dortmund. After a goalless first leg at Málaga dominated by the visitors, the Spanish side travelled to Germany against the only unbeaten team left in the competition without the suspended Weligton and Manuel Iturra. Bidding to become the first debutants since Pellegrini's Villarreal side seven seasons previously to reach the semi-finals, Málaga initially made light of their absences as Joaquín shot them into a 25th-minute lead.

Lewandowski levelled five minutes before half-time, but Málaga exploited Dortmund's attacking approach again with eight minutes left, Eliseu tapping in to seemingly end the home side's challenge. Klopp's charges remained fully committed, however, and poured forward. Marco Reus made it 2-2 a minute into added time, and with seconds remaining, incredibly, Felipe Santana bundled in from close range to spark wild celebrations – not least from the Dortmund coaching staff. "I cannot explain what happened inside me after that goal," said Klopp. "I think I need to see a doctor. It feels like we've won the trophy."

Barcelona were also made to sweat as they looked to set a new European Cup record with a sixth successive semi-final appearance. Messi struck the first blow in their first leg at

12

For the first time since 2007/08, Lionel Messi did not finish as the competition's top goalscorer. Instead, it was Cristiano Ronaldo – the last player to deny Messi the prize – who took the honours with 12 goals, four more than he had managed five years previously.

PSG – although it would prove the Argentinian's final UEFA Champions League goal of the season as a hamstring injury restricted him to cameo roles thereafter – but that was cancelled out by Ibrahimović's riposte against his former club 11 minutes from time.

Xavi put Barça back in front from the penalty spot in the 89th minute, but four minutes into added time Ibrahimović knocked down for Blaise Matuidi to score with the last kick of the game and ensure the teams would reconvene at the Camp Nou with the scores level. There – with Messi on the bench – PSG went in front for the first time in the tie just

after half-time as Javier Pastore rounded off an incisive breakaway. Almost immediately, Messi was brought on and he played a key role in setting up Pedro for the decisive equaliser. Inspired and transformed by their half-fit talisman, Barça duly squeezed through on away goals.

In arguably the highest-profile quarter-final, Juventus travelled to Munich for the first leg against Bayern unbeaten in 18 European matches. That record was under threat within 25 seconds as David Alaba, with the seventh fastest goal in UEFA Champions League history, put Bayern in front from long range. It was the first goal Gianluigi Buffon had conceded in the competition for 490 minutes; a second followed just past the hour as Müller tapped in his fifth goal of the campaign.

Bastian Schweinsteiger believed Bayern had scored "one goal too few" in Munich, but his team had won 4-1 in Turin on matchday six of the 2009/10 competition and they produced another consummate away performance in Juve's new home. Mandžukić effectively ended the Serie A champions' hopes with a 64th-minute opener, and Pizarro wrapped up a second successive 2-0 victory with another a minute into added time, leaving two German clubs to join the two Spanish heavyweights in the last four.

Pedro wheels away in celebration after scoring the deciding goal in the Barcelona-PSG quarter-final

Robert Lewandowski smashes in his fourth goal of the evening as Dortmund defeat Real Madrid 4-1 in the first leg of the semi-final

Semi-finals

The draw for the semi-finals – in a break from tradition delayed until after the quarter-finals had been completed – set up two classic confrontations between Germany and Spain, with Bayern taking on Barcelona and Dortmund reacquainting themselves with group stage opponents Real Madrid.

If Bayern had proved their credentials with their two wins against Juventus, their semi-final displays would carry them to another level altogether. Beaten 4-0 at Barcelona in the 2008/09 quarter-finals, Heynckes' side turned the tables in spectacular fashion in the first leg in Munich. Müller opened the scoring in the 25th minute and Bayern – who mustered 13 attempts to the visitors' four – never looked back. Further goals from Mario Gomez (49) and Arjen Robben (73) rewarded their enterprise against a Barça side for whom Messi was evidently a long way short of full fitness, and Müller's second of the night with eight minutes left completed Barcelona's heaviest European away defeat. "We have been playing extraordinary football," said Heynckes. "Today's game was a perfect example."

Another exceptional night for Bayern followed eight days later at the Camp Nou, where, with Messi on the bench throughout, Barça were

again embarrassed, second-half goals from Robben and Müller either side of a Gerard Piqué own goal completing the biggest aggregate win in a UEFA Champions League semi-final and earning a third final appearance in four years for the German club. It was also Barcelona's heaviest aggregate defeat in UEFA competition, and the first time the Catalan club had lost both legs of a European tie since March 1987.

The second semi-final also kicked off in Germany as Dortmund welcomed Madrid – and again, the Bundesliga club scored four times. Lewandowski was the dominant figure, scoring all of his team's goals in a 4-1 win. Although his eighth-minute opener was

KEY FACT

50

Cristiano Ronaldo became the fifth player to hit 50 UEFA Champions League goals with his strike in the first leg of Madrid's semi-final against Dortmund. Raúl González, Lionel Messi, Ruud van Nistelrooy and Thierry Henry are the others.

cancelled out by Ronaldo's 50th UEFA Champions League strike, the Pole would not be denied the spotlight in the second half, adding further goals in the 50th and 55th minutes, the latter with a piece of individual brilliance, before completing a record-breaking four-goal haul from the penalty spot.

Despite the 4-1 scoreline Mourinho remained optimistic that Madrid could recover, although he acknowledged it would take "a crazy night when every chance is a goal and everyone performs at a high level". Madrid duly attacked from the off, with Higuaín, Ronaldo and Özil all passing up early openings, while at the other end Lewandowski and Gündoğan missed opportunities to settle Dortmund's nerves. The visitors were in control until Benzema broke the deadlock with seven minutes left. Now the home side's pressure intensified and when Sergio Ramos smashed in a second from close range, the Bernabéu believed again – only for Dortmund to survive the late onslaught and Madrid to run out of time. "It was a long 90 minutes tonight," said Klopp after consigning Madrid to a third straight semi-final exit. "We always make things exciting, one way or another."

Final

There had been widespread anticipation that Wembley Stadium, the venue for the 2012/13 UEFA Champions League final, would be staging El Clásico. Instead the famous north London venue was to play host to Der Klassiker – between FC Bayern München and Borussia Dortmund.

The all-German showdown was the fourth UEFA Champions League final between clubs from the same country. Bayern started with four players – Arjen Robben, captain Philipp Lahm, Bastian Schweinsteiger and Thomas Müller – who had endured the final defeats of 2010 and 2012, and seven who had begun the previous season's final against Chelsea. However, in a rousing atmosphere, it was Dortmund's final novices – lacking injured Bayern-bound playmaker Mario Götze – who settled more quickly. Manuel Neuer was the first goalkeeper called into action, tipping over a curling Robert Lewandowski shot, then reacting smartly to keep out Jakub Błaszczykowski's low first-time effort after the Dortmund midfielder had met a Marco Reus cross at the near post.

Reus himself was next to test the Bayern No1, who was equal to both that and a curling Sven Bender effort, but then, out of the blue, Bayern came close to snatching the lead. Mario Mandžukić rose above Bender to connect with Franck Ribéry's perfect left-wing centre and Roman Weidenfeller acrobatically tipped the header over. From the corner there was another Bayern opening, which Javi Martínez nodded onto the roof of the net.

The game had started at breakneck speed and there was no let-up as play swung from end to end, with the goalmouth action coming thick and fast. Around the half-hour mark both sides created a one-on-one opportunity, yet neither could capitalise as the two keepers expertly narrowed the angle. First Weidenfeller advanced to repel Robben, before Lewandowski was again thwarted by Neuer's legs. With half-time fast approaching, the ball fell between Mats Hummels and Robben and broke kindly for the Bayern man; again Weidenfeller was well positioned to make the save at close range, albeit with his face.

The half-time interval did not break the rhythm of the match, which picked up in exactly the same breathless manner following the resumption. Chances proved rarer, however, until Bayern broke the deadlock on the hour. Robben and Ribéry were the architects, swapping passes down the left before the Dutchman's low cut-back presented the unmarked Mandžukić with a simple tap-in.

For a moment Dortmund were reeling, but they regrouped and within eight minutes had found an equaliser. It came from the penalty spot, Dante having felled Reus in the area. İlkay Gündoğan held his nerve to send Neuer the wrong way. It was the first European goal Bayern had conceded in 432 minutes. Dortmund now poured forward for the winner, but they so nearly paid the price on the counterattack as Müller rounded Weidenfeller

FC Bayern München's victory was Germany's seventh in Europe's elite club competition, taking the country clear in fourth place in the all-time list of successes. Five of those wins belong to Bayern, who now trail only Real Madrid CF (9) and AC Milan (7) in the European Cup's all-time rankings, level in third place with Liverpool FC.

and slid the ball across goal. With Robben racing in to apply the decisive touch, Neven Subotić dived in to clear spectacularly off the line. Mandžukić then shot into the side netting after Müller had sprung the Dortmund offside trap once more, and Weidenfeller kept out another effort from Schweinsteiger.

Bayern, however, would not be denied. With 89 minutes on the clock, and extra time looming, Ribéry controlled a long, high ball into the box and flicked it into Robben's path. The No10 skilfully evaded two defenders before steadying himself to direct his shot past Weidenfeller and look on in joy as the ball trickled its way into the net.

Victory belonged to Bayern – champions of Europe for the fifth time.

"What we've achieved this season has been outstanding," said Heynckes, only the fourth coach to win the competition with two clubs. "There's never been a Bundesliga team that's consistently played at such a high level, winning the championship by 25 points, breaking almost all records. From the outset of the season we've been changing, improving, adapting; we have a team spirit and an ability to work together that I've never experienced. We lost the final last year but didn't resign ourselves to our fate. We upped the ante and worked harder, and this is the result. It's quite possible that a new era in Europe, under Bayern, might have begun."

Fifteen years elapsed between Jupp Heynckes' two UEFA Champions League successes – his first was at Real Madrid CF in 1998 – which is the longest any coach has gone between two European Cup wins; he is only the fourth to lift the trophy with two different clubs.

Mario Mandžukić (No9) puts Bayern 1-0 up against Dortmund at Wembley

First qualifying round

03/07/12, Jos Nosbaum, Dudelange
F91 Dudelange 7-0 SP Tre Penne
10/07/12, Stadio Olimpico, Serravalle
SP Tre Penne 0-4 F91 Dudelange
Aggregate: 0-11; F91 Dudelange qualify.

03/07/12, Hibernians Ground, Corradino
Valletta FC 8-0 FC Lusitans
10/07/12, Estadi Comunal, Andorra la Vella
FC Lusitans 0-1 Valletta FC
Aggregate: 0-9; Valletta FC qualify.

03/07/12, Windsor Park, Belfast
Linfield FC 0-0 B36 Tórshavn
10/07/12, Gundadalur, Torshavn
B36 Tórshavn 0-0 Linfield FC *(aet)*
Aggregate: 0-0; Linfield FC qualify 4-3 on penalties.

Second qualifying round

17/07/12, Jos Nosbaum, Dudelange
F91 Dudelange 1-0 FC Salzburg
24/07/12, Stadion Salzburg, Salzburg
FC Salzburg 4-3 F91 Dudelange
Aggregate: 4-4; F91 Dudelange qualify on away goals.

17/07/12, Lilleküla Stadium, Tallinn
FC Flora Tallinn 0-2 FC Basel 1893
24/07/12, St. Jakob-Park, Basel
FC Basel 1893 3-0 FC Flora Tallinn
Aggregate: 5-0; FC Basel 1893 qualify.

17/07/12, Töölö Football Stadium, Helsinki
HJK Helsinki 7-0 KR Reykjavík
24/07/12, KR-völlur, Reykjavik
KR Reykjavík 1-2 HJK Helsinki
Aggregate: 1-9; HJK Helsinki qualify.

17/07/12, U Nisy, Liberec
FC Slovan Liberec 1-0 FC Shakhter Karagandy
24/07/12, Shakhter, Karagandy
FC Shakhter Karagandy 1-1 FC Slovan Liberec
Aggregate: 1-2; FC Slovan Liberec qualify after extra time.

17/07/12, Yerevan Republican Stadium Vazgen Sargsyan, Yerevan
Ulisses FC 0-1 FC Sheriff
24/07/12, Stadionul Sheriff, Tiraspol
FC Sheriff 1-0 Ulisses FC
Aggregate: 2-0; FC Sheriff qualify.

17/07/12, Park Hall, Oswestry
The New Saints FC 0-0 Helsingborgs IF
25/07/12, Olympia, Helsingborg
Helsingborgs IF 3-0 The New Saints FC
Aggregate: 3-0; Helsingborgs IF qualify.

17/07/12, Štadión pod Dubňom, Zilina
MŠK Žilina 1-0 Hapoel Kiryat Shmona FC
24/07/12, Itztadion Kiryat Eliezer, Haifa
Hapoel Kiryat Shmona FC 2-0 MŠK Žilina
Aggregate: 2-1; Hapoel Kiryat Shmona FC qualify.

17/07/12, Tallaght Stadium, Dublin
Shamrock Rovers FC 0-0 FK Ekranas
24/07/12, Aukštaitija, Panevezys
FK Ekranas 2-1 Shamrock Rovers FC
Aggregate: 2-1; FK Ekranas qualify.

17/07/12, Skënderbeu, Korca
KS Skënderbeu 1-0 Debreceni VSC
24/07/12, Sóstói út, Nyiregyhaza
Debreceni VSC 3-0 KS Skënderbeu
Aggregate: 3-1; Debreceni VSC qualify.

17/07/12, Hibernians Ground, Corradino
Valletta FC 1-4 FK Partizan
24/07/12, FK Partizan, Belgrade
FK Partizan 3-1 Valletta FC
Aggregate: 7-2; FK Partizan qualify.

17/07/12, Dalga Stadium, Baku
Neftçi PFK 3-0 FC Zestafoni
24/07/12, David Abashidze, Zestaponi
FC Zestafoni 2-2 Neftçi PFK
Aggregate: 2-5; Neftçi PFK qualify.

18/07/12, Gorodskoi Stadion, Borisov
FC BATE Borisov 3-2 FK Vardar
25/07/12, National Arena Filip II, Skopje
FK Vardar 0-0 FC BATE Borisov
Aggregate: 2-3; FC BATE Borisov qualify.

18/07/12, Stadion Ljudski vrt, Maribor
NK Maribor 4-1 FK Željezničar
24/07/12, Asim Ferhatović Hase Stadion, Sarajevo
FK Željezničar 1-2 NK Maribor
Aggregate: 2-6; NK Maribor qualify.

18/07/12, Tsirion Stadium, Limassol
AEL Limassol FC 3-0 Linfield FC
25/07/12, Windsor Park, Belfast
Linfield FC 0-0 AEL Limassol FC
Aggregate: 0-3; AEL Limassol FC qualify.

18/07/12, Molde Stadion, Molde
Molde FK 3-0 FK Ventspils
24/07/12, Ventspils Olimpiskais Centrs, Ventspils
FK Ventspils 1-1 Molde FK
Aggregate: 1-4; Molde FK qualify.

18/07/12, Stadion Podgorica, Podgorica
FK Budućnost Podgorica 0-2 WKS Śląsk Wrocław
25/07/12, Municipal Stadium Wroclaw, Wroclaw
WKS Śląsk Wrocław 0-1 FK Budućnost Podgorica
Aggregate: 2-1; WKS Śląsk Wrocław qualify.

18/07/12, Ludogorets Arena, Razgrad
PFC Ludogorets Razgrad 1-1 GNK Dinamo Zagreb
25/07/12, Stadion Maksimir, Zagreb
GNK Dinamo Zagreb 3-2 PFC Ludogorets Razgrad
Aggregate: 4-3; GNK Dinamo Zagreb qualify.

Third qualifying round

31/07/12, Fir Park, Motherwell
Motherwell FC 0-2 Panathinaikos FC
08/08/12, OAKA Spiros Louis, Athens
Panathinaikos FC 3-0 Motherwell FC
Aggregate: 5-0; Panathinaikos FC qualify.

31/07/12, NSK Olimpiyskyi, Kyiv
FC Dynamo Kyiv 2-1 Feyenoord
07/08/12, Feyenoord Stadion, Rotterdam
Feyenoord 0-1 FC Dynamo Kyiv
Aggregate: 1-3; FC Dynamo Kyiv qualify.

01/08/12, Gorodskoi Stadion, Borisov
FC BATE Borisov 1-1 Debreceni VSC
07/08/12, Sóstói út, Nyiregyhaza
Debreceni VSC 0-2 FC BATE Borisov
Aggregate: 1-3; FC BATE Borisov qualify.

01/08/12, Molde Stadion, Molde
Molde FK 0-1 FC Basel 1893
08/08/12, St Jakob-Park, Basel
FC Basel 1893 1-1 Molde FK
Aggregate: 2-1; FC Basel 1893 qualify.

01/08/12, Itztadion Kiryat Eliezer, Haifa
Hapoel Kiryat Shmona FC 4-0 Neftçi PFK
08/08/12, Dalga Stadium, Baku
Neftçi PFK 2-2 Hapoel Kiryat Shmona FC
Aggregate: 2-6; Hapoel Kiryat Shmona FC qualify.

01/08/12, Celtic Park, Glasgow
Celtic FC 2-1 HJK Helsinki
08/08/12, Töölö Football Stadium, Helsinki
HJK Helsinki 0-2 Celtic FC
Aggregate: 1-4; Celtic FC qualify.

01/08/12, Stadion Ljudski vrt, Maribor
NK Maribor 4-1 F91 Dudelange
08/08/12, Jos Nosbaum, Dudelange
F91 Dudelange 0-1 NK Maribor
Aggregate: 1-5; NK Maribor qualify.

01/08/12, Constant Vanden Stock Stadium, Brussels
RSC Anderlecht 5-0 FK Ekranas
08/08/12, Vetra, Vilnius
FK Ekranas 0-6 RSC Anderlecht
Aggregate: 0-11; RSC Anderlecht qualify.

01/08/12, Stadionul Sheriff, Tiraspol
FC Sheriff 0-1 GNK Dinamo Zagreb
08/08/12, Stadion Maksimir, Zagreb
GNK Dinamo Zagreb 4-0 FC Sheriff
Aggregate: 5-0; GNK Dinamo Zagreb qualify.

01/08/12, Parken, Copenhagen
FC København 0-0 Club Brugge KV
08/08/12, Jan Breydelstadion, Bruges
Club Brugge KV 2-3 FC København
Aggregate: 2-3; FC København qualify.

Tom De Sutter (right) is congratulated by team-mates after scoring the first of Anderlecht's 11 goals against Ekranas in the third qualifying round

01/08/12, Municipal Stadium Wroclaw, Wroclaw
WKS Śląsk Wrocław 0-3 Helsingborgs IF
08/08/12, Olympia, Helsingborg
Helsingborgs IF 3-1 WKS Śląsk Wrocław
Aggregate: 6-1; Helsingborgs IF qualify.

01/08/12, Antonis Papadopoulos, Larnaca
AEL Limassol FC 1-0 FK Partizan
08/08/12, FK Partizan, Belgrade
FK Partizan 0-1 AEL Limassol FC
Aggregate: 0-2; AEL Limassol FC qualify.

01/08/12, Stadionul Dr. Constantin Rădulescu, Cluj-Napoca
CFR 1907 Cluj 1-0 FC Slovan Liberec
08/08/12, U Nisy, Liberec
FC Slovan Liberec 1-2 CFR 1907 Cluj
Aggregate: 1-3; CFR 1907 Cluj qualify.

01/08/12, Şükrü Saracoğlu, Istanbul
Fenerbahçe SK 1-1 FC Vaslui
08/08/12, Stadionul Ceahlăul, Piatra Neamt
FC Vaslui 1-4 Fenerbahçe SK
Aggregate: 2-5; Fenerbahçe SK qualify.

Play offs

21/08/12, Stadion Luzhniki, Moscow
FC Spartak Moskva 2-1 Fenerbahçe SK
Goals: 1-0 Emenike 59, 1-1 Kuyt 65, 2-1 D Kombarov 69
29/08/12, Şükrü Saracoğlu, Istanbul
Fenerbahçe SK 1-1 FC Spartak Moskva
Goals: 0-1 Ari 6, 1-1 Sow 69
Aggregate: 2-3; FC Spartak Moskva qualify.

21/08/12, St Jakob-Park, Basel
FC Basel 1893 1-2 CFR 1907 Cluj
Goals: 1-0 Streller 44, 1-1 Modou Sougou 66, 1-2 Modou Sougou 71
29/08/12, Stadionul Dr. Constantin Rădulescu, Cluj-Napoca
CFR 1907 Cluj 1-0 FC Basel 1893
Goal: 1-0 Kapetanos 20
Aggregate: 3-1; CFR 1907 Cluj qualify.

21/08/12, Olympia, Helsingborg
Helsingborgs IF 0-2 Celtic FC
Goals: 0-1 Commons 2, 0-2 Samaras 75
29/08/12, Celtic Park, Glasgow
Celtic FC 2-0 Helsingborgs IF
Goals: 1-0 Hooper 30, 2-0 Wanyama 88
Aggregate: 4-0; Celtic FC qualify.

21/08/12, Borussia-Park, Mönchengladbach
VfL Borussia Mönchengladbach 1-3 FC Dynamo Kyiv
Goals: 1-0 Ring 13, 1-1 Mikhalik 20, 1-2 Yarmolenko 36, 1-3 De Jong 81(og)
29/08/12, NSK Olimpiyskyi, Kyiv
FC Dynamo Kyiv 1-2 VfL Borussia Mönchengladbach
Goals: 0-1 Khacheridi 70(og), 0-2 Arango 78, 1-2 Ideye 88
Aggregate: 4-3; FC Dynamo Kyiv qualify.

21/08/12, Parken, Copenhagen
FC København 1-0 LOSC Lille
Goal: 1-0 César Santin 38
29/08/12, Grand Stade Lille Métropole, Villeneuve d'Ascq
LOSC Lille 2-0 FC København (aet)
Goals: 1-0 Digne 43, 2-0 Túlio de Melo 105
Aggregate: 2-1; LOSC Lille qualify after extra time.

22/08/12, Estádio Municipal de Braga, Braga
SC Braga 1-1 Udinese Calcio
Goals: 0-1 Basta 23, 1-1 Ismaily 68
28/08/12, Stadio Friuli, Udine
Udinese Calcio 1-1 SC Braga (aet)
Goals: 1-0 Armero 25, 1-1 Rúben Micael 72
Aggregate: 2-2; SC Braga qualify 5-4 on penalties.

22/08/12, Stadion Maksimir, Zagreb
GNK Dinamo Zagreb 2-1 NK Maribor
Goals: 1-0 Čop 10, 1-1 Badelj 39(og), 2-1 Badelj 74
28/08/12, Stadion Ljudski vrt, Maribor
NK Maribor 0-1 GNK Dinamo Zagreb
Goal: 0-1 Topol 13
Aggregate: 1-3; GNK Dinamo Zagreb qualify.

22/08/12, La Rosaleda, Malaga
Málaga CF 2-0 Panathinaikos FC
Goals: 1-0 Demichelis 17, 2-0 Eliseu 34
28/08/12, OAKA Spiros Louis, Athens
Panathinaikos FC 0-0 Málaga CF
Aggregate: 0-2; Málaga CF qualify.

22/08/12, Dinamo Stadion, Minsk
FC BATE Borisov 2-0 Hapoel Kiryat Shmona FC
Goals: 1-0 Rodionov 29, 2-0 Rodionov 78
28/08/12, Itztadion Ramat Gan, Ramat Gan
Hapoel Kiryat Shmona FC 1-1 FC BATE Borisov
Goals: 1-0 Lencse 67, 1-1 Pavlov 90+4
Aggregate: 1-3; FC BATE Borisov qualify.

22/08/12, GSP Stadium, Nicosia
AEL Limassol FC 2-1 RSC Anderlecht
Goals: 1-0 Dosa Júnior 34, 1-1 Mbokani 62, 2-1 Rui Miguel 72
28/08/12, Constant Vanden Stock Stadium, Brussels
RSC Anderlecht 2-0 AEL Limassol FC
Goals: 1-0 Mbokani 81, 2-0 Yakovenko 89
Aggregate: 3-2; RSC Anderlecht qualify.

Group stage

Group A

18/09/12, Stadion Maksimir, Zagreb (att: 4,683)
GNK Dinamo Zagreb 0-2 FC Porto
Goals: 0-1 Lucho González 41, 0-2 Defour 90+2
Referee: Orsato (ITA)

18/09/12, Parc des Princes, Paris (att: 42,536)
Paris Saint-Germain FC 4-1 FC Dynamo Kyiv
Goals: 1-0 Ibrahimović 19(p), 2-0 Thiago Silva 29, 3-0 Alex 32,
3-1 Miguel Veloso 87, 4-1 Pastore 90+1
Referee: Kuipers (NED)

03/10/12, Estádio do Dragão, Porto (att: 36,509)
FC Porto 1-0 Paris Saint-Germain FC
Goal: 1-0 Rodríguez 83
Referee: Webb (ENG)

03/10/12, NSK Olimpiyskyi, Kyiv (att: 47,804)
FC Dynamo Kyiv 2-0 GNK Dinamo Zagreb
Goals: 1-0 Gusev 3, 2-0 Pivarić 33(og)
Referee: Atkinson (ENG)

24/10/12, Estádio do Dragão, Porto (att: 29,317)
FC Porto 3-2 FC Dynamo Kyiv
Goals: 1-0 Varela 15, 1-1 Gusev 21, 2-1 Martínez 36, 2-2 Ideye 72,
3-2 Martínez 78
Referee: Kralovec (CZE)

24/10/12, Stadion Maksimir, Zagreb (att: 9,326)
GNK Dinamo Zagreb 0-2 Paris Saint-Germain FC
Goals: 0-1 Ibrahimović 33, 0-2 Ménez 43
Referee: Aydınus (TUR)

06/11/12, Parc des Princes, Paris (att: 41,060)
Paris Saint-Germain FC 4-0 GNK Dinamo Zagreb
Goals: 1-0 Alex 16, 2-0 Matuidi 61, 3-0 Ménez 65, 4-0 Hoarau 80
Referee: Gil (POL)

06/11/12, NSK Olimpiyskyi, Kyiv (att: 40,370)
FC Dynamo Kyiv 0-0 FC Porto
Referee: Undiano Mallenco (ESP)

21/11/12, Estádio do Dragão, Porto (att: 27,603)
FC Porto 3-0 GNK Dinamo Zagreb
Goals: 1-0 Lucho González 20, 2-0 João Moutinho 67,
3-0 Varela 85
Referee: Tagliavento (ITA)

21/11/12, NSK Olimpiyskyi, Kyiv (att: 36,712)
FC Dynamo Kyiv 0-2 Paris Saint-Germain FC
Goals: 0-1 Lavezzi 45, 0-2 Lavezzi 52
Referee: Stark (GER)

04/12/12, Stadion Maksimir, Zagreb (att: 3,663)
GNK Dinamo Zagreb 1-1 FC Dynamo Kyiv
Goals: 0-1 Yarmolenko 45+1, 1-1 Krstanović 90+5(p)
Referee: Todorov (BUL)

04/12/12, Parc des Princes, Paris (att: 45,512)
Paris Saint-Germain FC 2-1 FC Porto
Goals: 1-0 Thiago Silva 29, 1-1 Martínez 33, 2-1 Lavezzi 61
Referee: Thomson (SCO)

		Home					Away					Total				
	Pld	W	D	L	F	A	W	D	L	F	A	W	D	L	F	A	Pts
1 Paris Saint-Germain FC	6	3	0	0	10	2	2	0	1	4	1	5	0	1	14	3	15
2 FC Porto	6	3	0	0	7	2	1	1	1	3	2	4	1	1	10	4	13
3 FC Dynamo Kyiv	6	1	1	1	2	2	0	1	2	4	8	1	2	3	6	10	5
4 GNK Dinamo Zagreb	6	0	1	2	1	5	0	0	3	0	9	0	1	5	1	14	1

Group B

18/09/12, La Mosson, Montpellier (att: 27,522)
Montpellier Hérault SC 1-2 Arsenal FC
Goals: 1-0 Belhanda 9(p), 1-1 Podolski 16, 1-2 Gervinho 18
Referee: Velasco Carballo (ESP)

18/09/12, Georgios Karaiskakis Stadium, Piraeus (att: 30,363)
Olympiacos FC 1-2 FC Schalke 04
Goals: 0-1 Höwedes 41, 1-1 Abdoun 58, 1-2 Huntelaar 59
Referee: Fernández Borbalán (ESP)

03/10/12, Arsenal Stadium, London (att: 60,034)
Arsenal FC 3-1 Olympiacos FC
Goals: 1-0 Gervinho 42, 1-1 Mitroglou 45+1, 2-1 Podolski 56,
3-1 Ramsey 90+4
Referee: Moen (NOR)

03/10/12, Stadion Gelsenkirchen, Gelsenkirchen (att: 50,004)
FC Schalke 04 2-2 Montpellier Hérault SC
Goals: 0-1 Aït-Fana 13, 1-1 Draxler 26, 2-1 Huntelaar 53(p),
2-2 Camara 90
Referee: Karasev (RUS)

24/10/12, Arsenal Stadium, London (att: 60,049)
Arsenal FC 0-2 FC Schalke 04
Goals: 0-1 Huntelaar 76, 0-2 Afellay 86
Referee: Eriksson (SWE)

Klaas-Jan Huntelaar fires in Schalke's winner against Olympiacos in Piraeus

24/10/12, La Mosson, Montpellier (att: 22,843)
Montpellier Hérault SC 1-2 Olympiacos FC
Goals: 1-0 Charbonnier 49, 1-1 Torosidis 73, 1-2 Mitroglou 90+1
Referee: Orsato (ITA)

06/11/12, Stadion Gelsenkirchen, Gelsenkirchen (att: 54,142)
FC Schalke 04 2-2 Arsenal FC
Goals: 0-1 Walcott 18, 0-2 Giroud 26, 1-2 Huntelaar 45+2,
2-2 Farfán 67
Referee: Rizzoli (ITA)

06/11/12, Georgios Karaiskakis Stadium, Piraeus (att: 28,217)
Olympiacos FC 3-1 Montpellier Hérault SC
Goals: 1-0 Paulo Machado 4, 1-1 Belhanda 66(p), 2-1 Greco 80,
3-1 Mitroglou 82
Referee: Strahonja (CRO)

21/11/12, Arsenal Stadium, London (att: 59,760)
Arsenal FC 2-0 Montpellier Hérault SC
Goals: 1-0 Wilshere 49, 2-0 Podolski 63
Referee: Aydınus (TUR)

21/11/12, Stadion Gelsenkirchen, Gelsenkirchen (att: 52,254)
FC Schalke 04 1-0 Olympiacos FC
Goal: 1-0 Fuchs 77
Referee: Kuipers (NED)

04/12/12, La Mosson, Montpellier (att: 23,142)
Montpellier Hérault SC 1-1 FC Schalke 04
Goals: 0-1 Höwedes 56, 1-1 Herrera 59
Referee: Mateu Lahoz (ESP)

04/12/12, Georgios Karaiskakis Stadium, Piraeus (att: 20,120)
Olympiacos FC 2-1 Arsenal FC
Goals: 0-1 Rosický 38, 1-1 Maniatis 64, 2-1 Mitroglou 73
Referee: Undiano Mallenco (ESP)

		Pld	Home W	D	L	F	A	Away W	D	L	F	A	Total W	D	L	F	A	Pts
1	FC Schalke 04	6	1	2	0	5	4	2	1	0	5	2	3	3	0	10	6	12
2	Arsenal FC	6	2	0	1	5	3	1	1	1	5	5	3	1	2	10	8	10
3	Olympiacos FC	6	2	0	1	6	4	1	0	2	3	5	3	0	3	9	9	9
4	Montpellier Hérault SC	6	0	1	2	3	5	0	1	2	3	7	0	2	4	6	12	2

Group C

18/09/12, La Rosaleda, Malaga (att: 23,670)
Málaga CF 3-0 FC Zenit St Petersburg
Goals: 1-0 Isco 3, 2-0 Saviola 13, 3-0 Isco 76
Referee: Clattenburg (ENG)

18/09/12, Stadio Giuseppe Meazza, Milan (att: 27,593)
AC Milan 0-0 RSC Anderlecht
Referee: Collum (SCO)

03/10/12, Stadion Petrovski, St Petersburg (att: 21,570)
FC Zenit St Petersburg 2-3 AC Milan
Goals: 0-1 Emanuelson 13, 0-2 El Shaarawy 16, 1-2 Hulk 45+2, 2-2
Shirokov 49, 2-3 Hubočan 75(og)
Referee: Brych (GER)

03/10/12, Constant Vanden Stock Stadium, Brussels (att: 15,711)
RSC Anderlecht 0-3 Málaga CF
Goals: 0-1 Eliseu 45+1, 0-2 Joaquín 57(p), 0-3 Eliseu 64
Referee: Kassai (HUN)

24/10/12, Stadion Petrovski, St Petersburg (att: 19,500)
FC Zenit St Petersburg 1-0 RSC Anderlecht
Goal: 1-0 Kerzhakov 72(p)
Referee: Bebek (CRO)

24/10/12, La Rosaleda, Malaga (att: 27,683)
Málaga CF 1-0 AC Milan
Goal: 1-0 Joaquín 64
Referee: Proença (POR)

00/11/12, Constant Vanden Stock Stadium, Brussels (att: 16,437)
RSC Anderlecht 1-0 FC Zenit St Petersburg
Goal: 1-0 Mbokani 17
Referee: Gautier (FRA)

06/11/12, Stadio Giuseppe Meazza, Milan (att: 30,891)
AC Milan 1-1 Málaga CF
Goals: 0-1 Eliseu 40, 1-1 Pato 73
Referee: Webb (ENG)

21/11/12, Constant Vanden Stock Stadium, Brussels (att: 19,803)
RSC Anderlecht 1-3 AC Milan
Goals: 0-1 El Shaarawy 47, 0-2 Mexès 71, 1-2 De Sutter 78,
1-3 Pato 90+1
Referee: Skomina (SVN)

21/11/12, Stadion Petrovski, St Petersburg (att: 18,347)
FC Zenit St Petersburg 2-2 Málaga CF
Goals: 0-1 Buonanotte 8, 0-2 Seba Fernández 9, 1-2 Danny 49,
2-2 Fayzulin 87
Referee: Olegário Benquerença (POR)

04/12/12, La Rosaleda, Malaga (att: 21,769)
Málaga CF 2-2 RSC Anderlecht
Goals: 1-0 Duda 45, 1-1 Jovanović 50, 2-1 Duda 61,
2-2 Mbokani 89
Referee: Aytekin (GER)

04/12/12, Stadio Giuseppe Meazza, Milan (att: 29,508)
AC Milan 0-1 FC Zenit St Petersburg
Goal: 0-1 Danny 35
Referee: Chapron (FRA)

		Pld	Home W	D	L	F	A	Away W	D	L	F	A	Total W	D	L	F	A	Pts
1	Málaga CF	6	2	1	0	6	2	1	2	0	6	3	3	3	0	12	5	12
2	AC Milan	6	0	2	1	1	2	2	0	1	6	4	2	2	2	7	6	8
3	FC Zenit St Petersburg	6	1	1	1	5	5	1	0	2	1	4	2	1	3	6	9	7
4	RSC Anderlecht	6	1	0	2	2	6	0	2	1	2	3	1	2	3	4	9	5

Group D

18/09/12, BVB Stadion Dortmund, Dortmund (att: 65,829)
Borussia Dortmund 1-0 AFC Ajax
Goal: 1-0 Lewandowski 87
Referee: Tagliavento (ITA)

18/09/12, Estadio Santiago Bernabéu, Madrid (att: 70,381)
Real Madrid CF 3-2 Manchester City FC
Goals: 0-1 Džeko 68, 1-1 Marcelo 76, 1-2 Kolarov 85, 2-2 Benzema
87, 3-2 Cristiano Ronaldo 90
Referee: Skomina (SVN)

03/10/12, City of Manchester Stadium, Manchester (att: 43,657)
Manchester City FC 1-1 Borussia Dortmund
Goals: 0-1 Reus 61, 1-1 Balotelli 90(p)
Referee: Kralovec (CZE)

03/10/12, Amsterdam ArenA, Amsterdam (att: 49,491)
AFC Ajax 1-4 Real Madrid CF
Goals: 0-1 Cristiano Ronaldo 42, 0-2 Benzema 48, 1-2 Moisander 56, 1-3 Cristiano Ronaldo 79, 1-4 Cristiano Ronaldo 81
Referee: Eriksson (SWE)

24/10/12, Amsterdam ArenA, Amsterdam (att: 45,743)
AFC Ajax 3-1 Manchester City FC
Goals: 0-1 Nasri 22, 1-1 De Jong 45, 2-1 Moisander 57, 3-1 Eriksen 68
Referee: Moen (NOR)

24/10/12, BVB Stadion Dortmund, Dortmund (att: 65,829)
Borussia Dortmund 2-1 Real Madrid CF
Goals: 1-0 Lewandowski 36, 1-1 Cristiano Ronaldo 38, 2-1 Schmelzer 64
Referee: Kassai (HUN)

06/11/12, City of Manchester Stadium, Manchester (att: 40,222)
Manchester City FC 2-2 AFC Ajax
Goals: 0-1 De Jong 10, 0-2 De Jong 17, 1-2 Y Touré 22, 2-2 Agüero 74
Referee: Rasmussen (DEN)

06/11/12, Estadio Santiago Bernabéu, Madrid (att: 74,932)
Real Madrid CF 2-2 Borussia Dortmund
Goals: 0-1 Reus 28, 1-1 Pepe 34, 1-2 Arbeloa 45(og), 2-2 Özil 89
Referee: Çakır (TUR)

21/11/12, City of Manchester Stadium, Manchester (att: 45,740)
Manchester City FC 1-1 Real Madrid CF
Goals: 0-1 Benzema 10, 1-1 Agüero 73(p)
Referee: Rocchi (ITA)

21/11/12, Amsterdam ArenA, Amsterdam (att: 47,500)
AFC Ajax 1-4 Borussia Dortmund
Goals: 0-1 Reus 8, 0-2 Götze 36, 0-3 Lewandowski 41, 0-4 Lewandowski 67, 1-4 Hoesen 87
Referee: Proença (POR)

04/12/12, BVB Stadion Dortmund, Dortmund (att: 65,829)
Borussia Dortmund 1-0 Manchester City FC
Goal: 1-0 Schieber 57
Referee: Mažić (SRB)

04/12/12, Estadio Santiago Bernabéu, Madrid (att: 57,245)
Real Madrid CF 4-1 AFC Ajax
Goals: 1-0 Cristiano Ronaldo 13, 2-0 Callejón 28, 3-0 Kaká 49, 3-1 Boerrigter 59, 4-1 Callejón 88
Referee: Kralovec (CZE)

		Pld	|	Home W	D	L	F	A	|	Away W	D	L	F	A	|	Total W	D	L	F	A	Pts
1	Borussia Dortmund	6		3	0	0	4	1		1	2	0	7	4		4	2	0	11	5	14
2	Real Madrid CF	6		2	1	0	9	5		1	1	1	6	4		3	2	1	15	9	11
3	AFC Ajax	6		1	0	2	5	9		0	1	2	3	7		1	1	4	8	16	4
4	Manchester City FC	6		0	3	0	4	4		0	0	3	3	7		0	3	3	7	11	3

Group E

19/09/12, Stamford Bridge, London (att: 40,918)
Chelsea FC 2-2 Juventus
Goals: 1-0 Oscar 31, 2-0 Oscar 33, 2-1 Vidal 38, 2-2 Quagliarella 80
Referee: Proença (POR)

19/09/12, Donbass Arena, Donetsk (att: 45,816)
FC Shakhtar Donetsk 2-0 FC Nordsjælland
Goals: 1-0 Mkhitaryan 44, 2-0 Mkhitaryan 76
Referee: Gil (POL)

02/10/12, Juventus Stadium, Turin (att: 25,599)
Juventus 1-1 FC Shakhtar Donetsk
Goals: 0-1 Alex Teixeira 23, 1-1 Bonucci 25
Referee: Nijhuis (NED)

02/10/12, Parken, Copenhagen (att: 25,120)
FC Nordsjælland 0-4 Chelsea FC
Goals: 0-1 Mata 33, 0-2 David Luiz 79, 0-3 Mata 82, 0-4 Ramires 89
Referee: Strahonja (CRO)

23/10/12, Parken, Copenhagen (att: 22,404)
FC Nordsjælland 1-1 Juventus
Goals: 1-0 Beckmann 50, 1-1 Vučinić 81
Referee: Aytekin (GER)

23/10/12, Donbass Arena, Donetsk (att: 51,435)
FC Shakhtar Donetsk 2-1 Chelsea FC
Goals: 1-0 Alex Teixeira 3, 2-0 Fernandinho 52, 2-1 Oscar 88
Referee: Skomina (SVN)

07/11/12, Stamford Bridge, London (att: 41,067)
Chelsea FC 3-2 FC Shakhtar Donetsk
Goals: 1-0 Fernando Torres 6, 1-1 Willian 9, 2-1 Oscar 40, 2-2 Willian 47, 3-2 Moses 90+4
Referee: Velasco Carballo (ESP)

07/11/12, Juventus Stadium, Turin (att: 31,366)
Juventus 4-0 FC Nordsjælland
Goals: 1-0 Marchisio 6, 2-0 Vidal 23, 3-0 Giovinco 37, 4-0 Quagliarella 75
Referee: Stavrev (MKD)

20/11/12, Parken, Copenhagen (att: 17,054)
FC Nordsjælland 2-5 FC Shakhtar Donetsk
Goals: 1-0 Nordstrand 24, 1-1 Luiz Adriano 26, 2-1 Lorentzen 29, 2-2 Willian 44, 2-3 Willian 50, 2-4 Luiz Adriano 53, 2-5 Luiz Adriano 81
Referee: Gautier (FRA)

20/11/12, Juventus Stadium, Turin (att: 39,670)
Juventus 3-0 Chelsea FC
Goals: 1-0 Quagliarella 38, 2-0 Vidal 61, 3-0 Giovinco 90+1
Referee: Çakır (TUR)

05/12/12, Stamford Bridge, London (att: 40,048)
Chelsea FC 6-1 FC Nordsjælland
Goals: 1-0 David Luiz 38(p), 2-0 Fernando Torres 45+2, 2-1 John 46, 3-1 Cahill 51, 4-1 Fernando Torres 56, 5-1 Mata 63, 6-1 Oscar 71
Referee: Nijhuis (NED)

05/12/12, Donbass Arena, Donetsk (att: 50,104)
FC Shakhtar Donetsk 0-1 Juventus
Goal: 0-1 Kucher 56(og)
Referee: Eriksson (SWE)

		Pld	|	Home W	D	L	F	A	|	Away W	D	L	F	A	|	Total W	D	L	F	A	Pts
1	Juventus	6		2	1	0	8	1		1	2	0	4	3		3	3	0	12	4	12
2	FC Shakhtar Donetsk	6		2	0	1	4	2		1	1	1	8	6		3	1	2	12	8	10
3	Chelsea FC	6		2	1	0	11	5		1	0	2	5	5		3	1	2	16	10	10
4	FC Nordsjælland	6		0	1	2	3	10		0	0	3	1	12		0	1	5	4	22	1

Group F

19/09/12, Grand Stade Lille Métropole, Villeneuve d'Ascq (att: 38,122)
LOSC Lille 1-3 FC BATE Borisov
Goals: 0-1 Volodko 6, 0-2 Rodionov 20, 0-3 Olekhnovich 43, 1-3 Chedjou 60
Referee: Borski (POL)

Claudio Pizarro celebrates the first of his three goals for Bayern against LOSC

10/09/12, Fußball Arena München, Munich (att: 68,000)
FC Bayern München 2-1 Valencia CF
Goals: 1-0 Schweinsteiger 66, 2-0 Kroos 78, 2-1 Valdez 90+1
Referee: Aydinus (TUR)

02/10/12, Estadi de Mestalla, Valencia (att: 28,517)
Valencia CF 2-0 LOSC Lille
Goals: 1-0 Jonas 38, 2-0 Jonas 75
Referee: Rocchi (ITA)

02/10/12, Dinamo Stadion, Minsk (att: 24,636)
FC BATE Borisov 3-1 FC Bayern München
Goals: 1-0 Pavlov 23, 2-0 Rodionov 78, 2-1 Ribéry 90+1,
3-1 Renan Bressan 90+4
Referee: Stavrev (MKD)

23/10/12, Grand Stade Lille Métropole, Villeneuve d'Ascq
(att: 45,259)
LOSC Lille 0-1 FC Bayern München
Goal: 0-1 Müller 20(p)
Referee: Atkinson (ENG)

23/10/12, Dinamo Stadion, Minsk (att: 29,180)
FC BATE Borisov 0-3 Valencia CF
Goals: 0-1 Soldado 45+1(p), 0-2 Soldado 55, 0-3 Soldado 69
Referee: Thomson (SCO)

07/11/12, Estadi de Mestalla, Valencia (att: 22,795)
Valencia CF 4-2 FC BATE Borisov
Goals: 1-0 Jonas 26, 2-0 Soldado 29(p), 3-0 Feghouli 51, 3-1
Renan Bressan 53, 3-2 Mozolevski 83, 4-2 Feghouli 86
Referee: Hagen (NOR)

07/11/12, Fußball Arena München, Munich (att: 68,000)
FC Bayern München 6-1 LOSC Lille
Goals: 1-0 Schweinsteiger 5, 2-0 Pizarro 18, 3-0 Robben 23,
4-0 Pizarro 28, 5-0 Pizarro 33, 5-1 Kalou 57, 6-1 Kroos 66
Referee: Hategan (ROU)

20/11/12, Dinamo Stadion, Minsk (att: 22,800)
FC BATE Borisov 0-2 LOSC Lille
Goals: 0-1 Sidibé 14, 0-2 Bruno 31
Referee: Strahonja (CRO)

20/11/12, Estadi de Mestalla, Valencia (att: 35,407)
Valencia CF 1-1 FC Bayern München
Goals: 1-0 Feghouli 77, 1-1 Müller 82
Referee: Webb (ENG)

05/12/12, Grand Stade Lille Métropole, Villeneuve d'Ascq
(att: 40,036)
LOSC Lille 0-1 Valencia CF
Goal: 0-1 Jonas 36(p)
Referee: Stavrev (MKD)

05/12/12, Fußball Arena München, Munich (att: 68,000)
FC Bayern München 4-1 FC BATE Borisov
Goals: 1-0 Gomez 22, 2-0 Müller 54, 3-0 Shaqiri 65, 4-0 Alaba 83,
4-1 Filipenko 89
Referee: Collum (SCO)

			Home				Away				Total					
		Pld	W	D	L	F	A	W	D	L	F	A	W	D	L	F A	Pts
1	FC Bayern München	6	3	0	0	12	3	1	1	1	3	4	4	1	1	15 7	13
2	Valencia CF	6	2	1	0	7	3	2	0	1	5	2	4	1	1	12 5	13
3	FC BATE Borisov	6	1	0	2	3	6	1	0	2	6	9	2	0	4	9 15	6
4	LOSC Lille	6	0	0	3	1	5	1	0	2	3	8	1	0	5	4 13	3

Group G

19/09/12, Celtic Park, Glasgow (att: 57,759)
Celtic FC 0-0 SL Benfica
Referee: Rizzoli (ITA)

19/09/12, Camp Nou, Barcelona (att: 73,580)
FC Barcelona 3-2 FC Spartak Moskva
Goals: 1-0 Tello 14, 1-1 Dani Alves 29(og), 1-2 Rômulo 59,
2-2 Messi 72, 3-2 Messi 80
Referee: Mažić (SRB)

02/10/12, Estádio do Sport Lisboa e Benfica, Lisbon (att: 63,847)
SL Benfica 0-2 FC Barcelona
Goals: 0-1 Alexis Sánchez 6, 0-2 Fàbregas 55
Referee: Çakır (TUR)

02/10/12, Stadion Luzhniki, Moscow (att: 43,351)
FC Spartak Moskva 2-3 Celtic FC
Goals: 0-1 Hooper 12, 1-1 Emenike 41, 2-1 Emenike 48,
2-2 D Kombarov 71(og), 2-3 Samaras 90
Referee: Chapron (FRA)

23/10/12, Stadion Luzhniki, Moscow (att: 41,237)
FC Spartak Moskva 2-1 SL Benfica
Goals: 1-0 Rafael Carioca 3, 1-1 Lima 33, 2-1 Jardel 43(og)
Referee: Clattenburg (ENG)

23/10/12, Camp Nou, Barcelona (att: 77,781)
FC Barcelona 2-1 Celtic FC
Goals: 0-1 Samaras 18, 1-1 Iniesta 45, 2-1 Jordi Alba 90+4
Referee: Rocchi (ITA)

07/11/12, Estádio do Sport Lisboa e Benfica, Lisbon (att: 36,468)
SL Benfica 2-0 FC Spartak Moskva
Goals: 1-0 Cardozo 55, 2-0 Cardozo 69
Referee: Meyer (GER)

07/11/12, Celtic Park, Glasgow (att: 58,841)
Celtic FC 2-1 FC Barcelona
Goals: 1-0 Wanyama 21, 2-0 Watt 83, 2-1 Messi 90+1
Referee: Kuipers (NED)

20/11/12, Estádio do Sport Lisboa e Benfica, Lisbon (att: 47,065)
SL Benfica 2-1 Celtic FC
Goals: 1-0 John 7, 1-1 Samaras 32, 2-1 Garay 71
Referee: Kassai (HUN)

20/11/12, Stadion Luzhniki, Moscow (att: 67,325)
FC Spartak Moskva 0-3 FC Barcelona
Goals: 0-1 Dani Alves 16, 0-2 Messi 27, 0-3 Messi 39
Referee: Bebek (CRO)

05/12/12, Celtic Park, Glasgow (att: 59,168)
Celtic FC 2-1 FC Spartak Moskva
Goals: 1-0 Hooper 21, 1-1 Ari 39, 2-1 Commons 81(p)
Referee: Brych (GER)

05/12/12, Camp Nou, Barcelona (att: 50,659)
FC Barcelona 0-0 SL Benfica
Referee: Moen (NOR)

Lionel Messi (right) scores one his four goals in Barcelona's two games against Spartak Moskva

			Home				Away				Total					
		Pld	W	D	L	F	A	W	D	L	F	A	W	D	L	F	A	Pts
1	FC Barcelona	6	2 1 0 5 3	2 0 1 6 2	4 1 1 11 5	13
2	Celtic FC	6	2 1 0 4 2	1 0 2 5 6	3 1 2 9 8	10
3	SL Benfica	6	2 0 1 4 3	0 2 1 1 2	2 2 2 5 5	8
4	FC Spartak Moskva	6	1 0 2 4 7	0 0 3 3 7	1 0 5 7 14	3

Group H

19/09/12, Old Trafford, Manchester (att: 74,653)
Manchester United FC 1-0 Galatasaray AŞ
Goal: 1-0 Carrick 7
Referee: Stark (GER)

19/09/12, Estádio Municipal de Braga, Braga (att: 10,922)
SC Braga 0-2 CFR 1907 Cluj
Goals: 0-1 Rafael Bastos 19, 0-2 Rafael Bastos 34
Referee: Rasmussen (DEN)

02/10/12, Stadionul Dr. Constantin Rădulescu, Cluj-Napoca (att: 16,259)
CFR 1907 Cluj 1-2 Manchester United FC
Goals: 1-0 Kapetanos 14, 1-1 Van Persie 29, 1-2 Van Persie 49
Referee: Undiano Mallenco (ESP)

02/10/12, Ali Sami Yen Spor Kompleksi, Istanbul (att: 46,987)
Galatasaray AŞ 0-2 SC Braga
Goals: 0-1 Rúben Micael 27, 0-2 Alan 90+4
Referee: Hagen (NOR)

23/10/12, Old Trafford, Manchester (att: 73,195)
Manchester United FC 3-2 SC Braga
Goals: 0-1 Alan 2, 0-2 Alan 20, 1-2 Hernández 25, 2-2 Evans 62, 3-2 Hernández 75
Referee: Mažić (SRB)

23/10/12, Ali Sami Yen Spor Kompleksi, Istanbul (att: 39,013)
Galatasaray AŞ 1-1 CFR 1907 Cluj
Goals: 0-1 Nounkeu 19(og), 1-1 Burak Yılmaz 77
Referee: Tagliavento (ITA)

07/11/12, Estádio Municipal de Braga, Braga (att: 15,388)
SC Braga 1-3 Manchester United FC
Goals: 1-0 Alan 49(p), 1-1 Van Persie 80, 1-2 Rooney 84(p), 1-3 Hernández 90+2
Referee: Brych (GER)

07/11/12, Stadionul Dr. Constantin Rădulescu, Cluj-Napoca (att: 16,232)
CFR 1907 Cluj 1-3 Galatasaray AŞ
Goals: 0-1 Burak Yılmaz 18, 1-1 Modou Sougou 53, 1-2 Burak Yılmaz 61, 1-3 Burak Yılmaz 74
Referee: Collum (SCO)

20/11/12, Ali Sami Yen Spor Kompleksi, Istanbul (att: 50,278)
Galatasaray AŞ 1-0 Manchester United FC
Goal: 1-0 Burak Yılmaz 53
Referee: Velasco Carballo (ESP)

20/11/12, Stadionul Dr. Constantin Rădulescu, Cluj-Napoca (att: 14,635)
CFR 1907 Cluj 3-1 SC Braga
Goals: 1-0 Rui Pedro 7, 2-0 Rui Pedro 15, 2-1 Alan 17, 3-1 Rui Pedro 33
Referee: Karasev (RUS)

05/12/12, Old Trafford, Manchester (att: 71,521)
Manchester United FC 0-1 CFR 1907 Cluj
Goal: 0-1 Luís Alberto 56
Referee: Orsato (ITA)

05/12/12, Estádio Municipal de Braga, Braga (att: 8,964)
SC Braga 1-2 Galatasaray AŞ
Goals: 1-0 Mossoró 32, 1-1 Burak Yılmaz 58, 1-2 Aydın Yılmaz 78
Referee: Rizzoli (ITA)

			Home				Away				Total					
		Pld	W	D	L	F	A	W	D	L	F	A	W	D	L	F	A	Pts
1	Manchester United FC	6	2 0 1 4 3	2 0 1 5 3	4 0 2 9 6	12
2	Galatasaray AŞ	6	1 1 1 2 3	2 0 1 5 3	3 1 2 7 6	10
3	CFR 1907 Cluj	6	1 0 2 5 6	2 1 0 4 1	3 1 2 9 7	10
4	SC Braga	6	0 0 3 2 7	1 0 2 5 6	1 0 5 7 13	3

Round of 16

12/02/13, Celtic Park, Glasgow (att: 57,917)
Celtic FC 0-3 Juventus
Goals: 0-1 Matri 3, 0-2 Marchisio 77,
0-3 Vučinić 83
Referee: Undiano Mallenco (ESP)
06/03/13, Juventus Stadium, Turin (att: 39,011)
Juventus 2-0 Celtic FC
Goals: 1-0 Matri 24, 2-0 Quagliarella 65
Referee: Aydınus (TUR)
Aggregate: 5-0; Juventus qualify.

12/02/13, Estadi de Mestalla, Valencia (att: 36,000)
Valencia CF 1-2 Paris Saint-Germain FC
Goals: 0-1 Lavezzi 10, 0-2 Pastore 43,
1-2 Rami 90
Referee: Tagliavento (ITA)
06/03/13, Parc des Princes, Paris (att: 44,867)
Paris Saint-Germain FC 1-1 Valencia CF
Goals: 0-1 Jonas 55, 1-1 Lavezzi 66
Referee: Mažić (SRB)
Aggregate: 3-2; Paris Saint-Germain FC qualify.

13/02/13, Estadio Santiago Bernabéu, Madrid (att: 79,429)
Real Madrid CF 1-1 Manchester United FC
Goals: 0-1 Welbeck 20, 1-1 Cristiano Ronaldo 30
Referee: Brych (GER)
05/03/13, Old Trafford, Manchester (att: 74,959)
Manchester United FC 1-2 Real Madrid CF
Goals: 1-0 Sergio Ramos 48(og),
1-1 Modrić 66, 1-2 Cristiano Ronaldo 69
Referee: Çakır (TUR)
Aggregate: 2-3; Real Madrid CF qualify.

13/02/13, Donbass Arena, Donetsk (att: 49,050)
FC Shakhtar Donetsk 2-2 Borussia Dortmund
Goals: 1-0 Srna 31, 1-1 Lewandowski 41,
2-1 Douglas Costa 68, 2-2 Hummels 87
Referee: Webb (ENG)
05/03/13, BVB Stadion Dortmund, Dortmund (att: 65,413)
Borussia Dortmund 3-0 FC Shakhtar Donetsk
Goals: 1-0 Felipe Santana 31, 2-0 Götze 37,
3-0 Błaszczykowski 59
Referee: Skomina (SVN)
Aggregate: 5-2; Borussia Dortmund qualify.

19/02/13, Estádio do Dragão, Porto (att: 42,209)
FC Porto 1-0 Málaga CF
Goal: 1-0 João Moutinho 56
Referee: Clattenburg (ENG)

13/03/13, La Rosaleda, Malaga (att: 27,451)
Málaga CF 2-0 FC Porto
Goals: 1-0 Isco 43, 2-0 Santa Cruz 77
Referee: Rizzoli (ITA)
Aggregate: 2-1; Málaga CF qualify.

19/02/13, Arsenal Stadium, London (att: 59,974)
Arsenal FC 1-3 FC Bayern München
Goals: 0-1 Kroos 7, 0-2 Müller 21, 1-2
Podolski 55, 1-3 Mandžukić 77
Referee: Moen (NOR)
13/03/13, Fußball Arena München, Munich (att: 68,000)
FC Bayern München 0-2 Arsenal FC
Goals: 0-1 Giroud 3, 0-2 Koscielny 86
Referee: Kralovec (CZE)
Aggregate: 3-3; FC Bayern München qualify on away goals.

20/02/13, Stadio Giuseppe Meazza, Milan (att: 75,932)
AC Milan 2-0 FC Barcelona
Goals: 1-0 Boateng 57, 2-0 Muntari 81
Referee: Thomson (SCO)
12/03/13, Camp Nou, Barcelona (att: 94,944)
FC Barcelona 4-0 AC Milan
Goals: 1-0 Messi 5, 2-0 Messi 40, 3-0 David
Villa 55, 4-0 Jordi Alba 90+2
Referee: Kassai (HUN)
Aggregate: 4-2; FC Barcelona qualify.

20/02/13, Ali Sami Yen Spor Kompleksi, Istanbul (att: 50,734)
Galatasaray AŞ 1-1 FC Schalke 04
Goals: 1-0 Burak Yılmaz 12, 1-1 Jones 45
Referee: Collum (SCO)
12/03/13, Stadion Gelsenkirchen, Gelsenkirchen (att: 54,142)
FC Schalke 04 2-3 Galatasaray AŞ
Goals: 1-0 Neustädter 17, 1-1 Hamit
Altıntop 37, 1-2 Burak Yılmaz 42, 2-2 Michel
Bastos 63, 2-3 Umut Bulut 90+5
Referee: Eriksson (SWE)
Aggregate: 3-4; Galatasaray AŞ qualify.

Quarter-finals

02/04/13, Parc des Princes, Paris (att: 45,336)
Paris Saint-Germain FC 2-2 FC Barcelona
Goals: 0-1 Messi 38, 1-1 Ibrahimović 79,
1-2 Xavi 89(p), 2-2 Matuidi 90+4
Referee: Stark (GER)
10/04/13, Camp Nou, Barcelona (att: 96,022)
FC Barcelona 1-1 Paris Saint-Germain FC
Goals: 0-1 Pastore 50, 1-1 Pedro 71
Referee: Kuipers (NED)
Aggregate: 3-3; FC Barcelona qualify on away goals.

02/04/13, Fußball Arena München, Munich (att: 68,000)
FC Bayern München 2-0 Juventus
Goals: 1-0 Alaba 1, 2-0 Müller 63
Referee: Clattenburg (ENG)

10/04/13, Juventus Stadium, Turin (att: 40,823)
Juventus 0-2 FC Bayern München
Goals: 0-1 Mandžukić 64, 0-2 Pizarro 90+1
Referee: Velasco Carballo (ESP)
Aggregate: 0-4; FC Bayern München qualify.

03/04/13, La Rosaleda, Malaga (att: 28,548)
Málaga CF 0-0 Borussia Dortmund
Referee: Eriksson (SWE)
09/04/13, BVB Stadion Dortmund, Dortmund (att: 65,829)
Borussia Dortmund 3-2 Málaga CF
Goals: 0-1 Joaquín 25, 1-1 Lewandowski
40, 1-2 Eliseu 82, 2-2 Reus 90+1, 3-2 Felipe
Santana 90+3
Referee: Thomson (SCO)
Aggregate: 3-2; Borussia Dortmund qualify.

03/04/13, Estadio Santiago Bernabéu, Madrid (att: 76,462)
Real Madrid CF 3-0 Galatasaray AŞ
Goals: 1-0 Cristiano Ronaldo 9,
2-0 Benzema 29, 3-0 Higuaín 73
Referee: Moen (NOR)
09/04/13, Ali Sami Yen Spor Kompleksi, Istanbul (att: 49,975)
Galatasaray AŞ 3-2 Real Madrid CF
Goals: 0-1 Cristiano Ronaldo 7, 1-1 Eboué
57, 2-1 Sneijder 70, 3-1 Drogba 72,
3-2 Cristiano Ronaldo 90+2
Referee: Lannoy (FRA)
Aggregate: 3-5; Real Madrid CF qualify.

Semi-finals

23/04/13, Fußball Arena München, Munich (att: 68,000)
FC Bayern München 4-0 FC Barcelona
Goals: 1-0 Müller 25, 2-0 Gomez 49,
3-0 Robben 73, 4-0 Müller 82
Referee: Kassai (HUN)
01/05/13, Camp Nou, Barcelona (att: 95,877)
FC Barcelona 0-3 FC Bayern München
Goals: 0-1 Robben 49, 0-2 Piqué 72(og),
0-3 Müller 76
Referee: Skomina (SVN)
Aggregate: 0-7; FC Bayern München qualify.

24/04/13, BVB Stadion Dortmund, Dortmund (att: 65,829)
Borussia Dortmund 4-1 Real Madrid CF
Goals: 1-0 Lewandowski 8, 1-1 Cristiano
Ronaldo 43, 2-1 Lewandowski 50, 3-1
Lewandowski 55, 4-1 Lewandowski 66(p)
Referee: Kuipers (NED)
30/04/13, Estadio Santiago Bernabéu, Madrid (att: 79,429)
Real Madrid CF 2-0 Borussia Dortmund
Goals: 1-0 Benzema 83, 2-0 Sergio Ramos 88
Referee: Webb (ENG)
Aggregate: 3-4; Borussia Dortmund qualify

Final

25/05/13, Wembley Stadium, London (att: 86,298)

Borussia Dortmund 1-2 FC Bayern München
Goals: 0-1 Mandžukić 60, 1-1 Gündoğan 68(p), 1-2 Robben 89
Referee: Rizzoli (ITA)
Dortmund: Weidenfeller, Subotić, Bender (Nuri Şahin 90+2), Gündoğan, Lewandowski, Reus, Hummels, Błaszczykowski (Schieber 90), Grosskreutz, Piszczek, Schmelzer. Coach: Jürgen Klopp (GER)
Bayern: Neuer, Dante, Ribéry (Luiz Gustavo 90+1), Javi Martínez, Mandžukić (Gomez 90+4), Robben, Boateng, Lahm, Müller, Alaba, Schweinsteiger. Coach: Jupp Heynckes (GER)
Yellow cards: Dante 29 (Bayern), Grosskreutz 73 (Dortmund), Ribéry 73 (Bayern)

Arjen Robben celebrates after scoring Bayern's late winner in the UEFA Champions League final

Top goalscorers

12	Cristiano Ronaldo (Real Madrid)
10	Robert Lewandowski (Dortmund)
8	Burak Yılmaz (Galatasaray)
	Lionel Messi (Barcelona)
	Thomas Müller (Bayern)
5	Alan (Braga)
	Karim Benzema (Real Madrid)
	Jonas (Valencia)
	Ezequiel Lavezzi (PSG)
	Oscar (Chelsea)

Young stars

İlkay Gündoğan, 22
Borussia Dortmund
midfielder

Isco, 21
Málaga CF
attacking midfielder

Marco Verratti, 20
Paris Saint-Germain FC
midfielder

Raphaël Varane, 20
Real Madrid CF
defender

David Alaba, 20
FC Bayern München
defender

Kyriakos Papadopoulos, 21
FC Schalke 04
defender

Stephan El Shaarawy, 20
AC Milan
forward

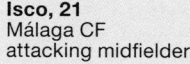

NB Ages as of 25 May 2013

Squads/Appearances/Goals

AFC AJAX

No	Name	Nat	DoB	Aps	(s)	Gls
Goalkeepers						
1	Kenneth Vermeer		10/01/86	6		
Defenders						
3	Toby Alderweireld	BEL	02/03/89	6		
17	Daley Blind		09/03/90	6		
4	Niklas Moisander	FIN	29/09/85	6		2
40	Fabian Sporkslede		03/08/93		(1)	
24	Ricardo van Rhijn		13/06/91	6		
Midfielders						
5	Christian Poulsen	DEN	28/02/80	6		
6	Eyong Enoh	CMR	23/03/86	1	(3)	
8	Christian Eriksen	DEN	14/02/92	6		1
10	Siem de Jong		28/01/89	6		3
20	Lasse Schøne	DEN	27/05/86	2	(3)	
7	Miralem Sulejmani	SRB	05/12/88		(1)	
Forwards						
49	Ryan Babel		19/12/86	4		
21	Derk Boerrigter		16/10/86	5	(1)	1
39	Viktor Fischer	DEN	09/06/94	1	(2)	
23	Daniel Hoesen		15/01/91	1	(2)	1
27	Jody Lukoki		15/11/92	1	(1)	
19	Tobias Sana	SWE	11/07/89	3	(2)	

RSC ANDERLECHT

No	Name	Nat	DoB	Aps	(s)	Gls
Goalkeepers						
1	Silvio Proto		23/05/83	6		
Defenders						
3	Olivier Deschacht		16/02/81	5		
30	Guillaume Gillet		09/03/84	6		
23	Roland Juhász	HUN	01/07/83		(1)	
16	Cheikhou Kouyaté	SEN	21/12/89	6		
14	Bram Nuytinck	NED	04/05/90	5		
20	Behrang Safari	SWE	09/02/85	2		
27	Marcin Wasilewski	POL	09/06/80	3		
Midfielders						
5	Lucas Biglia	ARG	30/01/86	6		
45	Massimo Bruno		17/09/93	5		
55	Fernando Canesin	BRA	27/02/92		(1)	
19	Sacha Kljestan	USA	09/09/85	4	(1)	
7	Guillermo Molins	SWE	26/09/88		(1)	
26	Dennis Praet		14/05/94	4	(1)	
70	Ronald Vargas	VEN	02/12/86		(1)	
Forwards						
21	Tom De Sutter		03/07/85	1	(2)	1
11	Milan Jovanović	SRB	18/04/81	5		1
10	Kanu	BRA	23/09/87	3	(1)	
25	Dieumerci Mbokani	COD	22/11/85	5		2
17	Olexandr Yakovenko	UKR	23/06/87		(5)	

ARSENAL FC

No	Name	Nat	DoB	Aps	(s)	Gls
Goalkeepers						
21	Łukasz Fabiański	POL	18/04/85	1		
24	Vito Mannone	ITA	02/03/88	4		
1	Wojciech Szczęsny	POL	18/04/90	3		
Defenders						
11	André Santos	BRA	08/03/83	1	(1)	
38	Martin Angha	SUI	22/01/94		(1)	
20	Kieran Gibbs		26/09/89	3		
25	Carl Jenkinson		08/02/92	5		
6	Laurent Koscielny	FRA	10/09/85	5		1
4	Per Mertesacker	GER	29/09/84	6		
3	Bacary Sagna	FRA	14/02/83	3		
18	Sébastien Squillaci	FRA	11/08/80	1		
5	Thomas Vermaelen	BEL	14/11/85	7		
Midfielders						
8	Mikel Arteta	ESP	26/03/82	7		
22	Francis Coquelin	FRA	13/05/91	3	(3)	
2	Abou Diaby	FRA	11/05/86	1		
47	Serge Gnabry	GER	14/07/95		(1)	
53	Jernade Meade		25/10/92	1		
15	Alex Oxlade-Chamberlain		15/08/93	3	(1)	
16	Aaron Ramsey	WAL	26/12/90	4	(3)	1
7	Tomáš Rosický	CZE	04/10/80	2	(1)	1
19	Santi Cazorla	ESP	13/12/84	7		
17	Theo Walcott		16/03/89	3	(2)	1
10	Jack Wilshere		01/01/92	3		1
Forwards						
23	Andrey Arshavin	RUS	29/05/81		(2)	
29	Marouane Chamakh	MAR	10/01/84	1		§
27	Gervinho	CIV	27/05/87	4	(2)	2
12	Olivier Giroud	FRA	30/09/86	4	(3)	2
9	Lukas Podolski	GER	04/06/85	6		4

FC BATE BORISOV

No	Name	Nat	DoB	Aps	(s)	Gls
Goalkeepers						
35	Andrei Gorbunov		29/05/83	6		
Defenders						
18	Maksim Bordachev		18/06/86	6		
21	Yegor Filipenko		10/04/88	5		1
33	Denis Polyakov		17/04/91	6		
14	Artem Radkov		26/08/85	4		
22	Marko Simić	SRB	16/06/87	3		
5	Aleksandr Yurevich		08/08/79		(1)	
Midfielders						
25	Dmitri Baga		04/01/90	3		
15	Aleksandr Hleb		01/05/81	6		
7	Artem Kontsevoi		20/05/83	1	(2)	
2	Dmitri Likhtarovich		01/03/78	4		
23	Edgar Olekhnovich		17/05/87	5		1
17	Aleksandr Pavlov		18/08/84	3		1
10	Renan Bressan		03/11/88	2	(4)	2
32	Mikhail Sivakov		16/01/88		(5)	
8	Aleksandr Volodko		18/06/86	6		1
Forwards						
13	Dmitri Mozolevski		30/04/85		(4)	1
20	Vitali Rodionov		11/12/83	6		2
78	Roman Vasilyuk		23/11/78		(2)	

SL BENFICA

No	Name	Nat	DoB	Aps	(s)	Gls
Goalkeepers						
1	Artur	BRA	25/01/81	6		
Defenders						
34	André Almeida		10/09/90	3	(1)	
24	Ezequiel Garay	ARG	10/10/86	6		1
33	Jardel	BRA	29/03/86	4	(1)	
4	Luisão	BRA	13/02/81	2		
25	Lorenzo Melgarejo	PAR	10/00/90	6		
14	Maxi Pereira	URU	08/06/84	4	(1)	
Midfielders						
10	Pablo Aimar	ARG	03/11/79	1	(1)	
89	André Gomes		30/07/93	1	(1)	
8	Bruno César	BRA	03/11/88	2	(3)	
17	Carlos Martins		29/04/82		(1)	
20	Nicolás Gaitán	ARG	23/02/88	2	(2)	
21	Nemanja Matić	SRB	01/08/88	5		
9	Nolito	ESP	15/10/86	1	(2)	
35	Enzo Pérez	ARG	22/02/86	5		
Forwards						
7	Óscar Cardozo	PAR	20/05/83	1	(4)	2
15	Ola John	NED	19/05/92	3	(1)	1
11	Lima	BRA	11/08/83	5		1
19	Rodrigo	ESP	06/03/91	4		
18	Eduardo Salvio	ARG	13/07/90	5		

FC BARCELONA

No	Name	Nat	DoB	Aps	(s)	Gls
Goalkeepers						
13	José Manuel Pinto		08/11/75	1		
1	Víctor Valdés		14/01/82	11		
Defenders						
21	Adriano	BRA	26/10/84	5	(1)	
15	Marc Bartra		15/01/91	4	(2)	
2	Dani Alves	BRA	06/05/83	10		1
18	Jordi Alba		21/03/89	9		2
14	Javier Mascherano	ARG	08/06/84	7	(1)	
19	Martín Montoya		14/04/91	1	(2)	
3	Gerard Piqué		02/02/87	8	(2)	
29	Carles Planas		04/03/91	1		
5	Carles Puyol		13/04/78	3	(1)	
Midfielders						
16	Sergio Busquets		16/07/88	8		
4	Cesc Fàbregas		04/05/87	6	(2)	1
8	Andrés Iniesta		11/05/84	9	(1)	1
30	Rafinha		12/02/93	1		
28	Sergi Roberto		07/02/92	1		
25	Alex Song	CMR	09/09/87	4	(4)	
11	Thiago Alcántara		11/04/91	1	(1)	
6	Xavi Hernández		25/01/80	11		1
Forwards						
9	Alexis Sánchez	CHI	19/12/88	5	(4)	1
7	David Villa		03/12/81	5	(5)	1
27	Gerard Deulofeu		13/03/94		(2)	
10	Lionel Messi	ARG	24/06/87	9	(2)	8
17	Pedro Rodríguez		28/07/87	10		1
37	Cristian Tello		11/08/91	2	(2)	

FC BAYERN MÜNCHEN

No	Name	Nat	DoB	Aps	(s)	Gls
Goalkeepers						
1	Manuel Neuer		27/03/86	13		
Defenders						
27	David Alaba	AUT	24/06/92	9	(2)	2
28	Holger Badstuber		13/03/89	4		
17	Jérôme Boateng		03/09/88	8	(1)	
26	Diego Contento		01/05/90	1		
4	Dante	BRA	18/10/83	11	(1)	
21	Philipp Lahm		11/11/83	12		
13	Rafinha	BRA	07/09/85	1	(1)	
5	Daniel Van Buyten	BEL	07/02/78	6		
Midfielders						
8	Javi Martínez	ESP	02/09/88	11		
39	Toni Kroos		04/01/90	8	(1)	3
30	Luiz Gustavo	BRA	23/07/87	3	(7)	
7	Franck Ribéry	FRA	07/04/83	11	(1)	1
10	Arjen Robben	NED	23/01/84	7	(2)	4
31	Bastian Schweinsteiger		01/08/84	11	(1)	2
11	Xherdan Shaqiri	SUI	10/10/91	1	(6)	1
25	Thomas Müller		13/09/89	12	(1)	8
44	Anatoliy Tymoshchuk	UKR	30/03/79	1	(3)	
Forwards						
33	Mario Gomez		10/07/85	2	(5)	2
9	Mario Mandžukić	CRO	21/05/86	8	(2)	3
14	Claudio Pizarro	PER	03/10/78	3	(3)	4

BORUSSIA DORTMUND

No	Name	Nat	DoB	Aps	(s)	Gls
Goalkeepers						
1	Roman Weidenfeller		06/08/80	13		
Defenders						
27	Felipe Santana	BRA	17/03/86	5	(2)	2
15	Mats Hummels		16/12/88	10	(1)	1
21	Oliver Kirch		21/08/82	1	(1)	
26	Łukasz Piszczek	POL	03/06/85	12		
29	Marcel Schmelzer		22/01/88	13		1
4	Neven Subotić	SRB	10/12/88	11		
Midfielders						
6	Sven Bender		27/04/89	9	(2)	
32	Leonardo Bittencourt		19/12/93		(1)	
16	Jakub Błaszczykowski	POL	14/12/85	8	(2)	1
10	Mario Götze		03/06/92	11		2
19	Kevin Grosskreutz		19/07/88	6	(4)	
8	İlkay Gündoğan		24/10/90	11	(1)	1
5	Sebastian Kehl		13/02/80	5	(4)	
7	Moritz Leitner		08/12/92	1	(3)	
18	Nuri Şahin	TUR	05/09/88		(3)	
44	Ivan Perišić	CRO	02/02/89	1	(4)	
11	Marco Reus		31/05/89	13		4
Forwards						
9	Robert Lewandowski	POL	21/08/88	12	(1)	10
23	Julian Schieber		13/02/89	1	(8)	

SC BRAGA

No	Name	Nat	DoB	Aps	(s)	Gls
Goalkeepers						
33	Beto		01/05/82	5		
1	Quim		13/11/75	1		
Defenders						
44	Douglão	BRA	15/08/86	3		
20	Elderson	NGA	20/01/88	3		
21	Ismaily	BRA	11/01/90	4		
25	Leandro Salino	BRA	22/04/85	6		
4	Nuno André Coelho		07/01/86	5	(1)	
26	Paulo Vinícius	BRA	12/08/84	4		
Midfielders						
30	Alan	BRA	19/09/79	6		5
27	Custódio		24/05/83	6		
45	Hugo Viana		15/01/83	5	(1)	
22	Djamal Mahamat	LBY	26/04/83		(1)	
8	Mossoró	BRA	04/07/83	2	(3)	1
5	Rúben Amorim		27/01/85	5		
14	Rúben Micael		19/08/86	5		1
Forwards						
83	Carlão	BRA	01/08/86		(1)	
17	Éder		22/12/87	6		
10	Hélder Barbosa		25/05/87		(5)	
9	Paulo César	BRA	05/01/80		(1)	
29	Zé Luis	CPV	24/01/91		(4)	

CFR 1907 CLUJ

No	Name	Nat	DoB	Aps	(s)	Gls
Goalkeepers						
1	Mário Felgueiras	POR	12/12/86	6		
Defenders						
20	Cadú	POR	21/12/81	6		
3	Ivo Pinto	POR	07/01/90	6		
12	Vasile Maftei		01/01/81		(1)	
13	Felice Piccolo	ITA	27/08/83	4		
24	Ionuț Rada		06/07/82	4	(1)	
8	Laszlo Sepsi		07/06/87	4		
Midfielders						
31	Matías Aguirregaray	URU	01/04/89	2	(3)	
45	Camora	POR	10/11/86	6		
10	Diogo Valente	POR	23/09/84		(1)	
23	Nicolas Godemèche	FRA	22/06/84	2	(2)	
25	Luís Alberto	BRA	17/11/83	5	(1)	1
6	Gabriel Mureșan		13/02/82	5	(1)	
16	Rafael Bastos	BRA	01/01/85	5	(1)	2
30	Rui Pedro	POR	02/07/88	2	(1)	3
Forwards						
19	Saša Bjelanović	CRO	11/06/79		(2)	
9	Pantelis Kapetanos	GRE	08/06/83	4	(2)	1
11	Viorel Nicoară		27/09/87		(2)	
99	Modou Sougou	SEN	18/12/84	5		1

GNK DINAMO ZAGREB

No	Name	Nat	DoB	Aps	(s)	Gls
Goalkeepers						
30	Ivan Kelava		20/02/88	6		
Defenders						
19	Josip Pivarić		30/01/89	5	(1)	
2	Ante Puljić		05/11/87	2	(1)	
4	Josip Šimunić		18/02/78	6		
13	Tonel	POR	13/04/80	2		
24	Domagoj Vida		29/04/89	6		
14	Šime Vrsaljko		10/01/92	4		
Midfielders						
6	Arijan Ademi		29/05/91	5		
77	Marcelo Brozović		16/11/92	6		
5	Adrián Calello	ARG	14/05/87	2	(2)	
17	Bryan Carrasco	CHI	31/01/91		(2)	
28	Alen Halilović		18/06/96		(3)	
3	Luis Ibáñez	ARG	15/07/88	2		
8	Mateo Kovačić		06/05/94	5	(1)	
10	Sammir		23/04/87	6		
Forwards						
21	Fatos Bećiraj	MNE	05/05/88	3	(1)	
90	Duje Čop		01/02/90	4	(2)	
99	Ivan Krstanović		05/01/83		(2)	1
55	Ante Rukavina		18/06/86	2	(2)	

CELTIC FC

No	Name	Nat	DoB	Aps	(s)	Gls
Goalkeepers						
1	Fraser Forster	ENG	17/03/88	8		
Defenders						
4	Efe Ambrose	NGA	18/10/88	6	(1)	
3	Emilio Izaguirre	HON	10/05/86	6		
23	Mikael Lustig	SWE	13/12/86	7		
2	Adam Matthews	WAL	13/01/92	4	(2)	
25	Thomas Rogne	NOR	29/06/90		(1)	
6	Kelvin Wilson	ENG	03/09/85	8		
Midfielders						
8	Scott Brown		25/06/85	6		
15	Kris Commons		30/08/83	6	(2)	1
33	Beram Kayal	ISR	02/05/88	2	(4)	
16	Joe Ledley	WAL	23/01/87	4	(2)	
21	Charlie Mulgrew		06/03/86	8		
67	Victor Wanyama	KEN	25/06/91	7		1
Forwards						
49	James Forrest		07/07/91	2	(3)	
88	Gary Hooper	ENG	26/01/88	6	(1)	2
7	Miku	VEN	19/08/85	2		
11	Lassad Nouioui	TUN	08/03/86		(2)	
9	Georgios Samaras	GRE	21/02/85	6		3
32	Tony Watt		29/12/93		(3)	1

CHELSEA FC

No	Name	Nat	DoB	Aps	(s)	Gls
Goalkeepers						
1	Petr Čech	CZE	20/05/82	6		
Defenders						
28	César Azpilicueta	ESP	28/08/89	1		
34	Ryan Bertrand		05/08/89	1	(2)	
24	Gary Cahill		19/12/85	4		1
3	Ashley Cole		20/12/80	5		
4	David Luiz	BRA	22/04/87	6		2
2	Branislav Ivanović	SRB	22/02/84	6		
19	Paulo Ferreira	POR	18/01/79		(1)	
26	John Terry		07/12/80	2		
Midfielders						
17	Eden Hazard	BEL	07/01/91	4	(2)	
8	Frank Lampard		20/06/78	3		
10	Juan Mata	ESP	28/04/88	5	(1)	3
12	John Obi Mikel	NGA	22/04/87	4	(1)	
11	Oscar	BRA	09/09/91	5	(1)	5
7	Ramires	BRA	24/03/87	6		1
6	Oriol Romeu	ESP	24/09/91	1		
Forwards						
9	Fernando Torres	ESP	20/03/84	5	(1)	3
13	Victor Moses	NGA	12/12/90	2	(2)	1
23	Daniel Sturridge		01/09/89		(2)	

FC DYNAMO KYIV

No	Name	Nat	DoB	Aps	(s)	Gls
Goalkeepers						
35	Maxym Koval		09/12/92	4		
1	Olexandr Shovkovskiy		02/01/75	2		
Defenders						
3	Betão	BRA	11/11/83	4	(1)	
2	Danilo Silva	BRA	24/11/86	3		
34	Yevhen Khacheridi		28/07/87	5		
17	Taras Mikhalik		28/10/83	5		
33	Taye Taiwo	NGA	16/04/85	6		
Midfielders						
23	Andriy Bogdanov		21/01/90		(2)	
99	Dudu	BRA	07/01/92	2		
19	Denys Garmash		19/04/90	4	(1)	
20	Oleh Gusev		25/04/83	4	(1)	2
25	Lukman Haruna	NGA	04/12/90	2	(1)	
21	Niko Kranjčar	CRO	13/08/84	2	(2)	
4	Miguel Veloso	POR	11/05/86	6		1
5	Ognjen Vukojević	CRO	20/12/83	4	(1)	
9	Andriy Yarmolenko		23/10/89	5	(1)	1
Forwards						
11	Ideye Brown	NGA	10/10/88	5	(1)	1
15	Marco Ruben	ARG	26/10/86	1	(1)	
13	Admir Mehmedi	SUI	16/03/91		(2)	
10	Artem Milevskiy		12/01/85	1	(1)	
85	Raffael	BRA	28/03/85	1	(1)	

GALATASARAY AŞ

No	Name	Nat	DoB	Aps	(s)	Gls
Goalkeepers						
25	Fernando Muslera	URU	16/06/86	10		
Defenders						
3	Cris	BRA	03/06/77	1		
27	Emmanuel Eboué	CIV	04/06/83	9	(1)	1
5	Gökhan Zan		07/09/81	1	(2)	
22	Hakan Balta		23/03/83	1		
13	Dany Nounkeu	CMR	11/04/86	9		
55	Sabri Sarıoğlu		26/07/84	1	(3)	
26	Semih Kaya		24/02/91	9	(1)	
Midfielders						
53	Nordin Amrabat	MAR	31/03/87	4	(6)	
7	Aydın Yılmaz		29/01/88		(3)	1
52	Emre Çolak		20/05/91	3	(3)	
50	Engin Baytar		11/07/83		(1)	
10	Felipe Melo	BRA	26/06/83	9		
4	Hamit Altıntop		08/12/82	9		1
11	Albert Riera	ESP	15/04/82	9		
8	Selçuk İnan		10/02/85	10		
14	Wesley Sneijder	NED	09/06/84	4		1
35	Yekta Kurtuluş		11/12/85	1	(1)	
Forwards						
17	Burak Yılmaz		15/07/85	8	(1)	8
12	Didier Drogba	CIV	11/03/78	4		1
9	Johan Elmander	SWE	27/05/81	3	(3)	
19	Umut Bulut		15/03/83	5	(5)	1

LOSC LILLE

No	Name	Nat	DoB	Aps	(s)	Gls
Goalkeepers						
16	Steeve Elana		11/07/80	2		
1	Mickaël Landreau		14/05/79	4		
Defenders						
25	Marko Baša	MNE	29/12/82	5		
18	Franck Béria		23/05/83	4		
21	Laurent Bonnart		25/12/79		(1)	
22	Aurélien Chedjou	CMR	20/06/85	5		1
2	Mathieu Debuchy		28/07/85	3		
3	Lucas Digne		20/07/93	4	(1)	
14	David Rozehnal	CZE	05/07/80	2	(1)	
15	Djibril Sidibé		29/07/92	2	(1)	1
Midfielders						
4	Florent Balmont		02/02/80	5		
5	Idrissa Gueye	SEN	26/09/89	3		
10	Marvin Martin		10/01/88	3	(2)	
24	Rio Mavuba		08/03/84	2	(1)	
7	Dimitri Payet		29/03/87	3	(3)	
17	Benoît Pedretti		12/11/80	4		
Forwards						
19	Gianni Bruno	BEL	19/08/91	2		1
8	Salomon Kalou	CIV	05/08/85	5		1
20	Ronny Rodelin		18/11/89	2	(1)	
26	Nolan Roux		01/03/88	3	(3)	
11	Ryan Mendes	CPV	08/01/90	1	(2)	
9	Túlio de Melo	BRA	31/01/85	2	(2)	

MANCHESTER CITY FC

No	Name	Nat	DoB	Aps	(s)	Gls
Goalkeepers						
1	Joe Hart		19/04/87	6		
Defenders						
22	Gaël Clichy	FRA	26/07/85	4		
13	Aleksandar Kolarov	SRB	10/11/85	1	(4)	1
4	Vincent Kompany	BEL	10/04/86	6		
6	Joleon Lescott		16/08/82	2		
3	Maicon	BRA	26/07/81	3		
33	Matija Nastasić	SRB	28/03/93	5		
2	Micah Richards		24/06/88	1		
5	Pablo Zabaleta	ARG	16/01/85	3	(2)	
Midfielders						
18	Gareth Barry		23/02/81	4		
14	Javi García	ESP	08/02/87	4	(1)	
7	James Milner		04/01/86	1	(1)	
8	Samir Nasri	FRA	26/06/87	6		
17	Jack Rodwell		11/03/91		(1)	
21	David Silva	ESP	08/01/86	3		
42	Yaya Touré	CIV	13/05/83	5		1
Forwards						
16	Sergio Agüero	ARG	02/06/88	4	(1)	2
45	Mario Balotelli	ITA	12/08/90		(4)	1
10	Edin Džeko	BIH	17/03/86	4	(2)	1
11	Scott Sinclair		26/03/89	1		
32	Carlos Tévez	ARG	05/02/84	3	(2)	

JUVENTUS

No	Name	Nat	DoB	Aps	(s)	Gls
Goalkeepers						
1	Gianluigi Buffon		28/01/78	10		
Defenders						
15	Andrea Barzagli		08/05/81	9		
19	Leonardo Bonucci		01/05/87	10		1
4	Martín Cáceres	URU	07/04/87	1	(1)	
3	Giorgio Chiellini		14/08/84	8		
11	Paolo De Ceglie		17/09/86	1		
26	Stephan Lichtsteiner	SUI	16/01/84	6		
2	Lúcio	BRA	08/05/78	1	(1)	
13	Federico Peluso		20/01/84	3		
Midfielders						
22	Kwadwo Asamoah	GHA	09/12/88	6	(1)	
24	Emanuele Giaccherini		05/05/85		(4)	
33	Mauricio Isla	CHI	12/06/88	2	(3)	
8	Claudio Marchisio		19/01/86	8		2
39	Luca Marrone		28/03/90	1		
20	Simone Padoin		18/03/84	2	(1)	
21	Andrea Pirlo		19/05/79	10		
6	Paul Pogba	FRA	15/03/93	3	(5)	
23	Arturo Vidal	CHI	22/05/87	9		3
Forwards						
18	Nicolas Anelka	FRA	14/03/79		(1)	
17	Nicklas Bendtner	DEN	16/01/88		(1)	
12	Sebastian Giovinco		26/01/87	4	(3)	2
32	Alessandro Matri		19/08/84	6	(3)	2
27	Fabio Quagliarella		31/01/83	4	(3)	4
9	Mirko Vučinić	MNE	01/10/83	6	(2)	2

MÁLAGA CF

No	Name	Nat	DoB	Aps	(s)	Gls
Goalkeepers						
13	Willy Caballero	ARG	28/09/81	9		
1	Carlos Kameni	CMR	18/02/84	1		
Defenders						
25	Antuñes	POR	01/04/87	4		
5	Martín Demichelis	ARG	20/12/80	9		
2	Jesús Gámez		10/04/85	7	(1)	
15	Nacho Monreal		26/02/86	2		
23	Oguchi Onyewu	USA	13/05/82	2	(1)	
21	Sergio Sánchez		03/04/86	5		
3	Weligton	BRA	26/08/79	8	(1)	
Midfielders						
20	Diego Buonanotte	ARG	19/04/88	2		1
6	Ignacio Camacho		04/05/90	6	(3)	
17	Duda	POR	27/06/80	3	(4)	2
18	Eliseu	POR	01/10/83	6	(1)	4
22	Isco		21/04/92	8		3
16	Manuel Iturra	CHI	23/06/84	7	(1)	
7	Joaquín		21/07/81	8		3
35	Lucas Piazón	BRA	20/01/94		(2)	
27	Francisco Portillo		13/06/90	2	(5)	
8	Jérémy Toulalan	FRA	10/09/83	6	(1)	
Forwards						
26	Juanmi		20/05/93		(1)	
10	Júlio Baptista	BRA	01/10/81	4		
24	Roque Santa Cruz	PAR	16/08/81	3	(7)	1
9	Javier Saviola	ARG	11/12/81	6		1
11	Seba Fernández	URU	23/05/85	2	(2)	1

MANCHESTER UNITED FC

No	Name	Nat	DoB	Aps	(s)	Gls
Goalkeepers						
1	David De Gea	ESP	07/11/90	7		
19	Anders Lindegaard	DEN	13/04/84	1		
Defenders						
28	Alexander Büttner	NED	11/02/89	3		
3	Patrice Evra	FRA	15/05/81	5		
6	Jonny Evans	NIR	03/01/88	5		1
5	Rio Ferdinand		07/11/78	4	(1)	
4	Phil Jones		21/02/92	3		
2	Rafael	BRA	09/07/90	6	(1)	
12	Chris Smalling		22/11/89	2		
15	Nemanja Vidić	SRB	21/10/81	2		
31	Scott Wootton		12/09/91	1	(1)	
Midfielders						
8	Anderson	BRA	13/04/88	3	(1)	
16	Michael Carrick		28/07/81	5		1
23	Tom Cleverley		12/08/89	5		
24	Darren Fletcher	SCO	01/02/84	3	(2)	
11	Ryan Giggs	WAL	29/11/73	3	(2)	
26	Shinji Kagawa	JPN	17/03/89	3		
17	Nani	POR	17/11/86	3	(1)	
25	Nick Powell		23/03/94	2		
22	Paul Scholes		16/11/74	1	(1)	
7	Luis Antonio Valencia	ECU	04/08/85	2	(2)	
18	Ashley Young		09/07/85		(2)	
Forwards						
14	Javier Hernández	MEX	01/06/88	5	(1)	3
41	Joshua King	NOR	15/01/92		(1)	
27	Federico Macheda	ITA	22/08/91	2		
10	Wayne Rooney		24/10/85	5	(1)	1
20	Robin van Persie	NED	06/08/83	5	(1)	3
19	Danny Welbeck		26/11/90	5	(2)	1

AC MILAN

No	Name	Nat	DoB	Aps	(s)	Gls
Goalkeepers						
32	Christian Abbiati		08/07/77	7		
1	Marco Amelia		02/04/82	1		
Defenders						
20	Ignazio Abate		12/11/86	4		
13	Francesco Acerbi		10/02/88	2		
77	Luca Antonini		04/08/82	2		
25	Daniele Bonera		31/05/81	4		
21	Kévin Constant	GUI	15/05/87	5	(1)	
2	Mattia De Sciglio		20/10/92	4	(1)	
15	Djamel Mesbah	ALG	09/10/84	1		
5	Philippe Mexès	FRA	30/03/82	6		1
76	Mario Yepes	COL	13/01/76	1	(2)	
17	Cristián Zapata	COL	30/09/86	4	(1)	
Midfielders						
23	Massimo Ambrosini		29/05/77	4		
10	Kevin-Prince Boateng	GHA	06/03/87	6	(1)	1
28	Urby Emanuelson	NED	16/06/86	5	(1)	1
16	Mathieu Flamini	FRA	07/03/84	3		
18	Riccardo Montolivo		18/01/85	6		
4	Sulley Ali Muntari	GHA	27/08/84	1	(1)	1
34	Nigel de Jong	NED	30/11/84	4		
8	Antonio Nocerino		09/04/85	2	(1)	
12	Bakaye Traoré	MLI	06/03/85		(1)	
Forwards						
22	Bojan Krkić	ESP	28/08/90	4	(2)	
92	Stephan El Shaarawy		27/10/92	6	(2)	2
19	M'Baye Niang	FRA	19/12/94	1	(1)	
9	Pato	BRA	02/09/89	1	(2)	2
11	Giampaolo Pazzini		02/08/84	4	(1)	
37	Andrea Petagna		30/06/95		(1)	
7	Robinho	BRA	25/01/84		(3)	

FC NORDSJÆLLAND

No	Name	Nat	DoB	Aps	(s)	Gls
Goalkeepers						
1	Jesper Hansen		31/03/85	6		
Defenders						
19	Mark Gundelach		07/01/92	1		
4	Henrik Kildentoft		18/03/85		(1)	
8	Patrick Mtiliga		28/01/81	6		
2	Jores Okore		11/08/92	5		
18	Michael Parkhurst	USA	24/01/84	6		
21	Ivan Runje	CRO	09/10/90	6		
Midfielders						
6	Enoch Adu	GHA	14/09/90	6		
17	Søren Christensen		29/06/86	2	(3)	
24	Kamal Issah	GHA	30/08/92		(1)	
20	Kasper Lorentzen		19/11/85	6		1
7	Nicolai Stokholm		01/04/76	6		
23	Mario Tičinović	CRO	20/08/91	1	(2)	
Forwards						
13	Oguzhan Aynaoglu		22/03/92		(1)	
10	Mikkel Beckmann		24/10/83	4	(1)	1
5	Anders Christiansen		08/06/90	1	(4)	
15	Joshua John	NED	01/10/88	6		1
22	Andreas Laudrup		10/11/90	2	(2)	
11	Morten Nordstrand		08/06/83	2	(3)	1

PARIS SAINT-GERMAIN FC

No	Name	Nat	DoB	Aps	(s)	Gls
Goalkeepers						
30	Salvatore Sirigu	ITA	12/01/87	10		
Defenders						
13	Alex	BRA	17/06/82	9		2
22	Sylvain Armand		01/08/80		(2)	
6	Zoumana Camara		03/04/79		(2)	
26	Christophe Jallet		31/10/83	7	(2)	
17	Maxwell	BRA	27/08/81	10		
3	Mamadou Sakho		13/02/90	2	(1)	
2	Thiago Silva	BRA	22/09/84	9		2
23	Gregory van der Wiel	NED	03/02/88	3	(2)	
Midfielders						
32	David Beckham	ENG	02/05/75	1	(1)	
12	Mathieu Bodmer		22/11/82	1		
20	Clément Chantôme		11/09/87	4	(2)	
29	Lucas Moura	BRA	13/08/92	4		
14	Blaise Matuidi		09/04/87	9		2
7	Jérémy Ménez		07/05/87	5	(2)	2
10	Nenê	BRA	19/07/81	2	(2)	
27	Javier Pastore	ARG	20/06/89	7	(3)	3
25	Adrien Rabiot		03/04/95	1		
4	Mohamed Sissoko	MLI	22/01/85	2	(1)	
28	Thiago Motta	ITA	28/08/82	2		
24	Marco Verratti	ITA	05/11/92	6	(3)	
Forwards						
19	Kevin Gameiro		09/05/87		(3)	
9	Guillaume Hoarau		05/03/84		(2)	1
18	Zlatan Ibrahimović	SWE	03/10/81	9		3
11	Ezequiel Lavezzi	ARG	03/05/85	7	(2)	5

MONTPELLIER HÉRAULT SC

No	Name	Nat	DoB	Aps	(s)	Gls
Goalkeepers						
16	Geoffrey Jourdren		04/02/86	4		
30	Jonathan Ligali		28/05/91	1		
1	Laurent Pionnier		24/05/82	1		
Defenders						
5	Henri Bedimo	CMR	04/06/84	5		
2	Garry Bocaly		19/04/88	3		
12	Daniel Congré		05/04/85	2	(2)	
21	Mathieu Deplagne		01/10/91	1		
21	Abdelhamid El Kaoutari		17/03/90	1		
4	Hilton	BRA	13/09/77	5		
22	Benjamin Stambouli		13/08/90	3	(1)	
3	Mapou Yanga-Mbiwa		15/05/89	6		
Midfielders						
10	Younes Belhanda	MAR	25/02/90	5	(1)	2
20	Rémy Cabella		08/03/90	6		
13	Marco Estrada	CHI	28/05/83	4	(1)	
28	Jonas Martin		09/04/90		(1)	
6	Joris Marveaux		15/08/82	1	(3)	
14	Romain Pitau		08/08/77		(1)	
23	Jamel Saihi	TUN	27/01/87	4		
15	Jonathan Tinhan		01/06/89		(2)	
Forwards						
18	Karim Aït-Fana	MAR	25/02/89	1	(1)	1
19	Souleymane Camara	SEN	22/12/82	4	(1)	1
9	Gaëtan Charbonnier		27/12/88	2	(1)	1
11	Emanuel Herrera	ARG	13/04/87	1	(2)	1
8	Anthony Mounier		27/09/87	5		
7	John Utaka	NGA	08/01/82	1	(1)	

OLYMPIACOS FC

No	Name	Nat	DoB	Aps	(s)	Gls
Goalkeepers						
1	Roy Carroll	NIR	30/09/77	4		
42	Balázs Megyeri	HUN	31/03/90	2		
Defenders						
15	Pablo Contreras	CHI	11/09/78	4		
20	José Holebas		27/06/84	5		
25	Charalambos Lykogiannis		22/10/93		(2)	
2	Ioannis Maniatis		12/10/86	6		1
24	Kostas Manolas		14/06/91	6		
3	François Modesto	FRA	19/08/78	4		
35	Vassilis Torosidis		10/06/85	5		1
Midfielders						
93	Djamel Abdoun	ALG	14/02/86	4	(2)	1
19	David Fuster	ESP	03/02/82	3	(3)	
26	Drissa Diakité	MLI	18/02/82	4		
8	Ljubomir Fejsa	SRB	14/08/88	1	(1)	
27	Leandro Greco	ITA	19/07/86	5	(1)	1
7	Ariel Ibagaza	ARG	27/10/76		(4)	
5	Paulo Machado	POR	31/03/86	6		1
23	Dimitrios Siovas		16/09/88	3		
Forwards						
10	Rafik Djebbour	ALG	08/03/84	3	(1)	
11	Kostas Mitroglou		12/03/88	3	(3)	4
9	Marko Pantelić	SRB	15/09/78		(1)	

FC PORTO

No	Name	Nat	DoB	Aps	(s)	Gls
Goalkeepers						
1	Helton	BRA	18/05/78	8		
Defenders						
26	Alex Sandro	BRA	26/01/91	5	(1)	
23	Abdoulaye Ba	SEN	01/01/91	2	(1)	
2	Danilo	BRA	15/07/91	7		
4	Maicon	BRA	14/09/88	3	(1)	
22	Eliaquim Mangala	FRA	13/02/91	6	(2)	
13	Miguel Lopes		19/12/86	1	(1)	
30	Nicolás Otamendi	ARG	12/02/88	8		
Midfielders						
6	André Castro		02/04/88		(2)	
35	Steven Defour	BEL	15/04/88	4	(3)	1
25	Fernando	BRA	25/07/87	5	(1)	
15	Marat Izmailov	RUS	21/09/82	1		
8	João Moutinho		08/09/86	8		2
3	Lucho González	ARG	19/01/81	8		2
Forwards						
27	Christian Atsu	GHA	10/01/92		(8)	
11	Kléber	BRA	02/05/90		(2)	
9	Jackson Martínez	COL	03/10/86	8		3
10	James Rodríguez	COL	12/07/91	6	(2)	1
17	Silvestre Varela		02/02/85	8		2

REAL MADRID CF

No	Name	Nat	DoB	Aps	(s)	Gls
Goalkeepers						
13	Antonio Adán		13/05/87	1		
1	Iker Casillas		20/05/81	5		
41	Diego López		03/11/81	6		
Defenders						
18	Raúl Albiol		04/09/85		(2)	
17	Álvaro Arbeloa		17/01/83	6	(1)	
5	Fábio Coentrão	POR	11/03/88	8		
12	Marcelo	BRA	12/05/88	2		1
24	Nacho		18/01/90	1		
3	Pepe	POR	26/02/83	7	(4)	1
11	Ricardo Carvalho	POR	18/05/78	1		
4	Sergio Ramos		30/03/86	9		1
2	Raphaël Varane	FRA	25/04/93	10	(1)	
Midfielders						
21	José Callejón		11/02/87	2	(2)	2
22	Ángel Di María	ARG	14/02/88	9	(2)	
15	Michael Essien	GHA	03/12/82	6	(1)	
34	José Rodríguez		16/12/94		(1)	
8	Kaká	BRA	22/04/82	2	(4)	1
6	Sami Khedira	GER	04/04/87	9	(2)	
19	Luka Modrić	CRO	09/09/85	6	(5)	1
10	Mesut Özil	GER	15/10/88	8	(2)	1
14	Xabi Alonso		25/11/81	10		
Forwards						
9	Karim Benzema	FRA	19/12/87	6	(4)	5
7	Cristiano Ronaldo	POR	05/02/85	12		12
20	Gonzalo Higuaín	ARG	10/12/87	6	(3)	1
29	Álvaro Morata		23/10/92		(1)	

FC SHAKHTAR DONETSK

No	Name	Nat	DoB	Aps	(s)	Gls
Goalkeepers						
30	Andriy Pyatov		28/06/84	8		
Defenders						
27	Dmytro Chygrynskiy		07/11/86	1		
5	Olexandr Kucher		22/10/82	7		
44	Yaroslav Rakitskiy		03/08/89	8		
26	Răzvan Raţ	ROU	26/05/81	8		
33	Darijo Srna	CRO	01/05/82	8		1
Midfielders						
29	Alex Teixeira	BRA	06/01/90	7	(1)	2
20	Douglas Costa	BRA	14/09/90		(5)	1
7	Fernandinho	BRA	04/05/85	8		1
3	Tomáš Hübschman	CZE	04/09/81	6		
77	Ilsinho	BRA	12/10/85	1	(5)	
6	Taras Stepanenko		08/08/89	2	(1)	
10	Willian	BRA	09/08/88	6		4
Forwards						
18	Marko Dević		27/10/83		(2)	
11	Eduardo	CRO	25/02/83	1	(2)	
9	Luiz Adriano	BRA	12/04/87	7		3
22	Henrikh Mkhitaryan	ARM	21/01/89	8		2
28	Taison	BRA	13/01/88	2		

VALENCIA CF

No	Name	Nat	DoB	Aps	(s)	Gls
Goalkeepers						
1	Diego Alves	BRA	24/06/85	2		
13	Vicente Guaita		18/02/87	6		
Defenders						
14	Antonio Barragán		12/06/87	3	(2)	
3	Aly Cissokho	FRA	15/09/87	7		
30	Carlos Delgado		22/04/90	1		
12	João Pereira	POR	25/02/84	4	(1)	
22	Jérémy Mathieu	FRA	29/10/83	1		
4	Adil Rami	FRA	27/12/85	6		1
20	Ricardo Costa	POR	16/05/81	6		
18	Víctor Ruiz		25/01/89	3		
Midfielders						
6	David Albelda		01/09/77	3	(2)	
23	Sergio Canales		16/02/91		(1)	
10	Éver Banega	ARG	29/06/88	2	(3)	
8	Sofiane Feghouli	ALG	26/12/89	8		3
5	Fernando Gago	ARG	10/04/86	3	(1)	
17	Andrés Guardado	MEX	20/09/86	7		
15	Jonathan Viera		21/10/89		(3)	
21	Daniel Parejo		16/04/89	4	(1)	
24	Tino Costa	ARG	09/01/85	8		
Forwards						
7	Jonas	BRA	01/04/84	6	(2)	5
11	Pablo Piatti	ARG	31/03/89		(2)	
9	Roberto Soldado		27/05/85	7		4
16	Nelson Valdez	PAR	28/11/83	1	(6)	1

FC SCHALKE 04

No	Name	Nat	DoB	Aps	(s)	Gls
Goalkeepers						
34	Timo Hildebrand		05/04/79	3		
36	Lars Unnerstall		20/07/90	5		
Defenders						
23	Christian Fuchs	AUT	07/04/86	5	(1)	1
4	Benedikt Höwedes		29/02/88	8		2
14	Kyriakos Papadopoulos	GRE	23/02/92	3	(1)	
35	Sead Kolašinac		20/06/93	3		
32	Joël Matip	CMR	08/08/91	6		
21	Christoph Metzelder		05/11/80	1		
22	Atsuto Uchida	JPN	27/03/88	5		
Midfielders						
11	Ibrahim Afellay	NED	02/04/86	2	(2)	1
27	Tranquillo Barnetta	SUI	22/05/85	2	(5)	
9	Michel Bastos	FRA	02/08/83	2		1
31	Julian Draxler		20/09/93	5	(1)	1
12	Marco Höger		16/09/89	4	(2)	
10	Lewis Holtby		18/09/90		(1)	
13	Jermaine Jones	USA	03/11/81	4	(2)	1
29	Max Meyer		18/09/95		(1)	
33	Roman Neustädter		18/02/88	8		1
Forwards						
17	Jefferson Farfán	PER	26/10/84	6	(1)	1
25	Klaas-Jan Huntelaar	NED	12/08/83	9		4
8	Ciprian Marica	ROU	02/10/85	1	(2)	
19	Chinedu Obasi	NGA	01/06/86		(2)	
20	Teemu Pukki	FIN	29/03/90	3	(2)	

FC SPARTAK MOSKVA

No	Name	Nat	DoB	Aps	(s)	Gls
Goalkeepers						
31	Andriy Dykan	UKR	16/07/77	2		
30	Sergei Pesyakov		16/12/88	2		
32	Artem Rebrov		04/03/84	2		
Defenders						
3	Sergei Bryzgalov		15/11/92		(3)	
2	Juan Insaurralde	ARG	03/10/84	5		
23	Dmitri Kombarov		22/01/87	6		
7	Kirill Kombarov		22/01/87	4	(1)	
34	Evgeni Makeev		24/07/89	4	(1)	
5	Nicolás Pareja	ARG	19/01/84	3		
17	Marek Suchý	CZE	29/03/88	4	(1)	
Midfielders						
49	Jano Ananidze	GEO	10/10/92	1	(2)	
25	Diniyar Bilyaletdinov		27/02/85	2		
20	Demy de Zeeuw	NED	26/05/83	1		
19	José Manuel Jurado	ESP	29/06/86	4	(1)	
21	Kim Källström	SWE	24/08/82	6		
8	Aiden McGeady	IRL	04/04/86	2	(1)	
6	Rafael Carioca	BRA	18/06/89	6		1
37	Rômulo	BRA	19/09/90	1		1
Forwards						
9	Ari	BRA	11/12/85	6		1
10	Artem Dzyuba		22/08/88	1	(3)	
29	Emmanuel Emenike	NGA	10/05/87	4		2
22	Aleksandr Kozlov		19/03/93		(1)	
11	Welliton	BRA	22/10/86		(2)	

FC ZENIT ST PETERSBURG

No	Name	Nat	DoB	Aps	(s)	Gls
Goalkeepers						
16	Vyacheslav Malafeev		04/03/79	6		
Defenders						
2	Aleksandr Anyukov		28/09/82	6		
3	Bruno Alves	POR	27/11/81	3	(2)	
4	Domenico Criscito	ITA	30/12/86	3		
14	Tomáš Hubočan	SVK	17/09/85	5		
6	Nicolas Lombaerts	BEL	20/03/85	6		
24	Aleksandar Luković	SRB	23/10/82	1		
82	Michael Lumb	DEN	09/01/88		(2)	
Midfielders						
34	Vladimir Bystrov		31/01/84	2	(3)	
27	Igor Denisov		17/05/84	4		
20	Viktor Fayzulin		22/04/86	3	(1)	1
25	Sergei Semak		27/02/76	3		
15	Roman Shirokov		06/07/81	6		1
28	Axel Witsel	BEL	12/01/89	5		
18	Konstantin Zyryanov		05/10/77	1	(3)	
Forwards						
9	Aleksandr Bukharov		12/03/85		(1)	
10	Danny	POR	07/08/83	2	(1)	2
77	Luka Djordjević	MNE	09/07/94		(1)	
29	Hulk	BRA	25/07/86	5		1
99	Maksim Kanunnikov		14/07/91		(3)	
11	Aleksandr Kerzhakov		27/11/82	5		1

Second UEFA trophy in two years for London club

Late Ivanović header stuns Benfica in Amsterdam

Fenerbahçe and Basel reach first European semi-finals

Chelsea complete unique double

Chelsea FC released Iberia's stranglehold on the UEFA Europa League, edging out SL Benfica in an absorbing final as they became the first team to hold the continent's two major club competition trophies simultaneously.

The three previous winners since the UEFA Cup was rebranded – and five of the six finalists – hailed from Portugal or Spain, but the balance of power shifted in the very last minute of the 317th and final day of the fourth edition. When Branislav Ivanović rose imperiously to send a towering header into the far corner the centre-back sealed a victory few could have have foreseen when Rafael Benítez was installed as interim Chelsea coach in November.

Then, the Blues were fighting for their UEFA Champions League survival, not yet part of a UEFA Europa League in which viewers came to expect the unexpected. Chelsea's triumph was an extension of the theme. BSC Young Boys bowed out despite picking up as many points as their group winners, Taison hit the "goal of the century" and Club Atlético de Madrid's 16-game winning run was ended by a side without a European victory in 44 years.

Worse was to follow for Atlético as their title defence was ended by FC Rubin Kazan in the round of 32, when history was made with the UEFA Europa League's first penalty shoot-out. FC Steaua Bucureşti prevailed to quickly end AFC Ajax's hopes of a final on home turf. Two of the other seven sides transferring from the

UEFA Champions League ahead of the knockout stage would be there instead.

Benfica and Chelsea are established heavyweights of European football, but 2012/13 was notable for the emergence of a few new names. KRC Genk extended their European campaign beyond Christmas for the first time, while FC Anji Makhachkala, FC Viktoria Plzeň, Rubin and Levante UD – in their first season of UEFA club competition – all reached the round of 16.

Fenerbahçe SK and FC Basel 1893 set new landmarks of their own in advancing to the semi-finals of UEFA club competition for the first time. Indeed, Basel became the first Swiss side to reach the last four in 35 years. Benfica and Chelsea then restored order, though the Portuguese team were pushed hard by Fenerbahçe.

The final was between teams whose histories largely read in reverse – old powerhouses Benfica against young turks Chelsea. They were united by flagging legs after marathon seasons, by a sense of belief and by a desire to win a first UEFA Europa League title. Benfica dominated the first hour, before Fernando Torres broke the deadlock with a goal borne of power, poise and purpose.

Óscar Cardozo quickly equalised from the spot but Ivanović completed a triumph over adversity for Chelsea, both on the night and in the season as a whole. Benítez was appointed knowing he would only be in

position until the end of the season. The former Liverpool FC boss came through some tough moments at Stamford Bridge, but his short reign finished successfully in Amsterdam as the London club celebrated a second major European triumph in as many years.

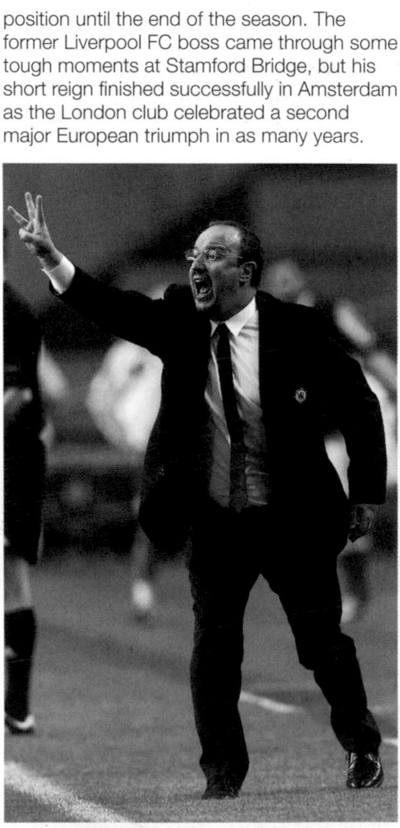

Rafael Benítez – the triumphant interim manager of UEFA Europa League winners Chelsea

UEFA Europa League final goalscorers Fernando Torres (left) and Branislav Ivanović pose with the trophy after Chelsea's 2-1 victory against Benfica in Amsterdam

Group stage

Nothing could be taken for granted in a group stage competitive to the last, where the record books were rewritten, predictions counted for nothing and occasionally even logic was defied. Liverpool FC made three times more passes than Udinese Calcio at Anfield on matchday two and lost. Holders Atlético's record run of 16 straight wins in UEFA competition was ended with a 2-0 defeat by an A. Académica de Coimbra team that had hitherto been without a European victory since 1969.

By then Atlético were already on the brink of the knockout stage after winning their opening three games with minimum fuss. Plzeň were not too far behind in a two-tiered **Group B**, with the evergreen Pavel Horváth, 37, pulling the strings in midfield. A 1-0 victory over Atlético on matchday six took them through as section winners – a marked improvement on the heavy hint of an electric drill coach Pavel Vrba expected from his wife on what was his 49th birthday.

Plzeň's Czech rivals AC Sparta Praha also progressed, in the process helping end a miserable campaign by 2012 runners-up Athletic Club: world-beaters 12 months earlier, a solitary victory was all they could muster in six outings this time round. That was four fewer than **Group I** winners and late goal specialists Olympique Lyonnais, contributing to a haul of 16 points unsurpassed by any of the other 47 group stage hopefuls.

Lyon were one of six sides to reach the round of 32 unbeaten, along with Genk, Tottenham Hotspur FC, S.S. Lazio, Hannover 96 and Rubin. The Russian club advanced alongside FC Internazionale Milano from **Group H**, a section effectively done and dusted with two games to spare – the gap between second and third by the end was eight points. Not so in **Group A,** where Young Boys made unfortunate, wholly unwanted history.

On paper this was perhaps the toughest group, pitting together Liverpool, Young Boys, Udinese and a big-spending Anji side who had shown their mettle with a resounding 6-0 play-off victory over AZ Alkmaar. It lived up to that billing. An eight-goal thriller in Switzerland set the tone as Liverpool came from 3-2

down to triumph 5-3 on the opening day, the Reds indebted to two late strikes from youngster Jonjo Shelvey.

No other game in the competition would conjure so many goals, but plenty could lay claim to parity in the excitement stakes. There were a few to choose from in Group A alone, including Udinese's clinical smash-and-grab at Anfield when they mustered 241 passes to Liverpool's 757 but still won 3-2. The excitement and drama went down to the last, when Liverpool, Anji and Young Boys all finished on ten points.

YB missed out on head-to-head record, the first time in UEFA Cup/UEFA Europa League history that a team had matched the points of the group winners and been eliminated. The Swiss side's haul of ten points was two more than VfB Stuttgart managed as Bruno Labbadia's team made light of terrible home form to advance. They did the damage on their travels, and became only the second team to register four first-half goals in the UEFA Europa League when they won 5-1 at **Group E** winners Steaua.

Stuttgart were one of four Bundesliga clubs in the group stage and all qualified for the knockout phase – for a while the UEFA Europa League, like the UEFA Champions League, had a noticeable German accent. Hannover, in **Group L**, were the only one of the quartet to top their section, a battling 2-2 draw away to a Levante team excelling in their maiden European campaign keeping their opponents second; at the foot of the group the challenge of FC Twente, survivors from the first qualifying round, ended.

VfL Borussia Mönchengladbach and Bayer 04 Leverkusen had to be content with runners-up berths in tough sections. Struggling to make an impression in domestic competition, Gladbach's problems were replicated in Europe as they managed only a point from their opening two games in **Group C**, a draw at AEL Limassol FC preceding a 4-2 home defeat by Fenerbahçe SK, the first of three away wins for the Turkish team. Back-to-back games against Olympique de Marseille looked daunting but four points revived the Foals' fortunes; they joined Fenerbahçe in the last 32.

It was much more straightforward for Leverkusen in **Group K**. Riding high in the Bundesliga – at Christmas they were second, ahead of Borussia Dortmund – four successive clean sheets helped seal progress with two games to spare. That they finished only second underlined the brilliance of FC Metalist Kharkiv. The Ukrainian outfit thrilled as they, too, secured an extension to their European adventure with two matches remaining.

Expansive football and late strikes were their stock in trade but it was an early goal from the tightest of angles that earned headlines worldwide against Rosenborg BK on matchday four (see sidebar). Metalist beat a much-changed Leverkusen team to seal top

Taison's knockout blow

Woe betide latecomers at the Metalist Stadium on 8 November. They would have seen on the scoreboard that the hosts, FC Metalist Kharkiv, already led Rosenborg BK – but why did the rest of the 34,235 crowd have an expression of utter wonderment?

The answer was Taison. The Brazilian had just treated them to a memorable goal, dispatching Fininho's hopeful, apparently harmless, long ball from the left into the top corner with an incredible first-time volley from the acutest of angles. He could not believe what he had done, clutching his head and shrugging his shoulders. Many in the stadium did the same.

"It was the goal of the year," said Bořek Dočkal, whose Rosenborg side lost 3-1. "Goal of the century, I don't know. It was so amazing!" The sentiment was shared in the Netherlands where the Telegraaf conceded that Marco van Basten's famous goal in the 1988 UEFA European Championship final may have at last been equalled.

FC Shakhtar Donetsk had seen enough: two months later they triggered the €15m buyout clause in Taison's contract to make him theirs.

spot but their own second string were preyed upon in their final outing as they slipped to a 1-0 defeat against an SK Rapid Wien side down to ten men for over half the match. That ended the Austrian outfit's run of eight successive UEFA Europa League losses, a joint-competition record.

Rapid's Harald Pichler was one of 45 players shown red cards during the competition – six came in **Group G** alone. Sporting Clube de Portugal were responsible for half, the cause and effect of a campaign that could not have been any more different from 2011/12 when the Lions roared into the knockout stages in unprecedented quick time after a mere three games. Here they exited with a whimper, a last-day victory not enough to avoid the wooden spoon.

At the other end of Group G, Genk reigned supreme, Mario Been's young team securing European football in the spring for the first time. They sealed progress with a game to spare and in the process ended the ten-match unbeaten European run at home of Videoton FC, who had stunned Trabzonspor AŞ on penalties in the play-offs to reach this stage. The loss effectively spoiled the Hungarian side's round of 32 ambitions, Basel coming good at the right time having picked up just two points from their opening three fixtures.

FC Dnipro Dnipropetrovsk managed nine in the same period in **Group F** under the tutelage of Juande Ramos, a two-time UEFA Cup winner with Sevilla FC. They ended up with five wins in an impressive campaign, the only blot on their copy book a thrilling 4-2 defeat at SSC Napoli on matchday four. The

visitors led 2-1 after 70 minutes but three late goals from Edinson Cavani turned the match on its head – and added to his early opener.

The Uruguay forward was at it again next time out, a last-gasp penalty earning a 2-1 win at AIK that rendered a potential head-to-head showdown against PSV Eindhoven on matchday six meaningless. Lazio made it a hat-trick of Italian teams through on the same night in a tight **Group J**, the Rome outfit managing the section's solitary away win at NK Maribor on matchday six.

Lazio advanced unbeaten, as did Tottenham, although the English side's status was still in the balance until two late goals at home to Panathinaikos FC in their final outing. There was also just one away victory in **Group D**, for section winners FC Girondins de Bordeaux, as they made light of a 3-0 defeat at Newcastle United FC to join the English team in the last 32.

KEY FACT

4

Edinson Cavani scored all four goals in SSC Napoli's 4-2 home win against FC Dnipro Dnipropetrovsk on matchday four – an exploit achieved just once before in the UEFA Europa League, by Radamel Falcao for FC Porto against Villarreal CF in the 2010/11 semi-finals. It was one of six last tricks in the 2012/13 competition,

---

Round of 32

Chelsea and Benfica were among three former European champions that entered the fray for the knockout stage, transferring from the UEFA Champions League after finishing third in their group. The trio was completed by Ajax, offered the unexpected opportunity to lift the trophy on home soil, but the Amsterdammers would suffer a unique, unwanted fate, becoming the first team to lose a UEFA Europa League penalty shoot-out.

It was all going to plan after the home leg against Steaua yielded a 2-0 victory. Iasmin Latovlevici sparked the comeback by halving the deficit 38 minutes into the Bucharest return and, following Vlad Chiricheş' stunning second-half strike, a scoreless period of extra time and missed penalties from Lasse Schøne and Niklas Moisander, it was Latovlevici who stepped up to complete a 4-2 spot-kick triumph.

"Bring on Chelsea!" was the cry from the Steaua dressing room. It was so very nearly 'Bring on Sparta!'. In a tie with special resonance for Petr Čech, the Czech keeper summed it up perfectly when he pointed out that his 100th appearance in UEFA club competition "did not go according to the script". Only a stunning 92nd-minute strike from Eden Hazard avoided the spectre of extra time after Sparta had cancelled out Chelsea's 1-0 away win.

Zenit, too, were given a real scare. Steaua became only the second side to recover a two-goal first-leg deficit in this competition's four-year history. Against the Russian champions, Liverpool so very nearly made it

Edinson Cavani (right) scores the third of his four goals for Napoli in their Group F win against Dnipro

two on one night. Like Ajax, Zenit travelled with a 2-0 first-leg lead, though crucially Hulk extended theirs early on. Roared on by the Kop, the red tide kept coming and by the hour mark it was 3-3.

Zenit held on, though, advancing on away goals to join Anji and Rubin in the last 16 on what was a perfect night for Russia's representatives. Anji's 4-2 aggregate victory over Hannover was no surprise, but Rubin's stunning triumph against Atlético was. Yet another 2-0 first-leg win – though this time away – set up victory, and even UEFA Europa League specialist Radamel Falcao's 30th goal in 31 appearances in this competition was not enough to revive the holders.

Levante were therefore Spain's last hope, their 4-0 aggregate triumph over Olympiacos FC bettered only by 5-0 wins for Inter against CFR 1907 Cluj, and, remarkably, Plzeň against Napoli – a stunning 3-0 victory in Naples setting up a triumph few foresaw. Basel also upset the odds against Dnipro, edging a tie that hung in the balance until late in an absorbing second leg.

Fenerbahçe won 1-0 against FC BATE Borisov, whose arrival in the competition

KEY FACT

2

After three seasons without one, the UEFA Europa League had its first penalty shoot-out as FC Steaua Bucureşti became just the second team to recover a two-goal first-leg deficit to advance in the competition. AFC Ajax were their round of 32 victims, going down 4-2 on spot kicks. There was soon a second shoot-out as FC Basel 1893 prevailed 4-1 against Tottenham Hotspur FC in the quarter-finals.

meant that for the first time 26 nations participated in a UEFA Europa League campaign (there had been 25 in each of the previous three editions). Newcastle, Stuttgart, Lazio, Bordeaux and Tottenham also advanced, while Benfica successfully negotiated a potentially thorny fixture against Bundesliga high-fliers Leverkusen, an Ola John wonder goal helping book their last-16 place against the run of play.

Round of 16

The tension was ratcheted further for the round of 16, and nowhere were hearts so firmly lodged in mouths as at San Siro. Tottenham's pairing with Inter evoked memories of their exhilarating 2010/11 UEFA Champions League group stage meetings when Gareth Bale made hay, scoring a hat-trick in Milan as ten-man Spurs came from 4-0 down to make it 4-3 and then inspiring the English side to a 3-1 home win against the then holders.

Bale came into this tie in scintillating form and the first leg in London was six minutes old when the Welshman opened the scoring. Further goals from Gylfi Sigurdsson and Jan Vertonghen earned a 3-0 victory but, crucially, Bale picked up a yellow card that ruled him out of the return. Inter stormed back at San Siro, strikes from Antonio Cassano and Rodrigo Palacio and a William Gallas own goal forcing extra time.

It had taken a monumental effort, and when Emmanuel Adebayor struck for the visitors six minutes into the additional 30 minutes the game was up – even if Ricardo Álvarez's 110th-minute header left Spurs holding on for an away-goals win. There was also extra time in the Rubin v Levante tie following 180 goalless minutes; José Rondón and Vladimir Dyadyun scored either side of the break to seal a first European quarter-final for the Russian side.

Tense, taut ties were the order of the day. The eight first legs produced just ten goals, three of them for Tottenham, and the only other team that could go into the second legs with any comfort were Lazio, 2-0 victors at Stuttgart. With Libor Kozák in their ranks that assurance was well-placed: the Czech forward struck twice in the opening eight minutes in Rome, completing his hat-trick and a 5-1 aggregate triumph late on. He ended as the competition's eight-goal top scorer.

Basel also went into the second instalment with a 2-0 lead, but their advantage looked precarious against Russian champions Zenit. Indeed, Axel Witsel halved the deficit and the writing was on the wall for the Swiss side when Marcelo Díaz was sent off before half-time. Yet they held on valiantly, Yann Sommer providing their last line of defence by saving Roman Shirokov's 86th-minute penalty.

Anji also ended their second leg with ten men, Mehdi Carcela-González seeing red with 35 minutes to go, and Newcastle eventually made them pay. There were 93 minutes on the clock and the crossbar was still rattling at the other end from Mbark Boussoufa's free-kick when perennial latecomer Papiss Cissé rose, unmarked, to head in the only goal of the tie.

If success for Basel and Newcastle caused shockwaves, Steaua almost produced a

Gareth Bale (left) in round of 16 action for Tottenham against Internazionale

Eduardo Salvio wraps up Benfica's qualification for the semi-finals with a late equaliser against Newcastle at St James' Park

record-equalling 31st UEFA Europa League appearance – he ended the season on 34.

André Villas-Boas is another who needs no introduction to this competition, but his Tottenham side were 2-0 down against Basel inside 34 minutes at White Hart Lane after goals from Valentin Stocker and Fabian Frei. An Adebayor strike and Sigurdsson's deflected effort made it 2-2 on the night and that is how it ended again the following week, a scintillating match bookended by goals from Clint Dempsey.

Basel could not profit from Jan Vertonghen's 91st-minute red card, but were superb in the shoot-out that followed extra time. Sommer denied Tom Huddlestone before Adebayor missed, allowing Díaz to bury the decisive penalty. Basel had reached the semi-finals of UEFA competition for the first time.

An hour earlier Fenerbahçe had broken their duck after a hard-fought 1-1 draw at Lazio sealed a 3-1 aggregate triumph. Aykut Kocaman's charges had done the damage in the home leg following Ogenyi Onazi's second booking of the night at the start of the second half. The hosts hit the post for a second time before Pierre Webó's 78th-minute penalty edged them ahead and Dirk Kuyt's added-time effort provided a killer blow.

minor earthquake as they pushed Chelsea to the wire. Leading 1-0 from the first leg, Vlad Chiricheş' goal on half-time at Stamford Bridge to cancel out Juan Mata's opener on the night made it 2-1 on aggregate, and left the European champions needing to score twice. They duly did, through John Terry and Fernando Torres.

Plzeň fell just short of a similar comeback as Fenerbahçe refused to buckle after Vladimír Darida had halved a 2-0 aggregate deficit with 29 minutes of the second leg in Istanbul remaining, the Turkish team ultimately indebted to a goal from 19-year-old Salih Uçan. Amid so much drama Benfica cruised on against Bordeaux, going through 4-2 on aggregate.

KEY FACT

8

Czech striker Libor Kozák scored eight times in S.S. Lazio's run to the quarter-finals to finish as the tournament's leading marksman. Remarkably, he did not find the net once in Serie A all season.

Torres was at it again in Moscow a week later, getting the Blues off to a perfect start with a sublime lob. After Iván Marcano's equaliser, Moses' second-half strike put the visitors back on track to a seemingly comfortable win. Goals from Gökdeniz Karadeniz and Natcho kept things interesting, but four unanswered goals was too big a mountain to climb.

Newcastle and Tottenham found the going somewhat tougher. Newcastle were up against it after being drawn with Benfica, and for a while Jorge Jesus' prediction of "an even tie" seemed prescient as Cissé gave the visitors a shock lead in Lisbon before Rodrigo quickly equalised. However, two goals in six second-half minutes – from substitute Lima and an Óscar Cardozo penalty – sealed a 3-1 triumph.

Cissé's header midway through the second half of the return set up a frenetic finale but the Eagles' class told and they earned a 1-1 draw after a late goal from Eduardo Salvio, making a

Quarter-finals

For the third successive season three teams from the same country reached the last eight, but England's aspirations of following the example of Portugal and Spain and converting that into the two finalists soon looked unlikely.

Chelsea did their bit, making light of a heavy workload as a 3-1 home win against Rubin brought a crushing end to the visitors' five-match unbeaten run on their travels in this competition. Returning to his best, Fernando Torres scored twice, the second a glorious header, either side of efforts from Victor Moses and a Bebras Natcho penalty.

Semi-finals

The Yellow Canaries were flying high, and so nearly landed in Amsterdam. Three times the home side stuck the woodwork against Benfica in the semi-final first leg, most profligately when Cristian directed a penalty against the upright. The Brazilian called for the half-time interval in tears but started the second period determined to make amends, and it was from his corner that Egemen Korkmaz headed in the only goal on 72 minutes – via the post, of course.

The hard-fought lead was quickly wiped out in Lisbon by Nicolás Gaitán a week later, but Kuyt's spot kick left Benfica needing to score

Egemen Korkmaz rises high to head in Fenerbahçe's winner at home to Benfica

David Luiz takes aim to score a spectacular goal for Chelsea at home to Basel – his second of the tie

twice more. They were not to be denied. Cardozo slid a neat finish past Volkan Demirel before the interval and secured a 3-2 aggregate victory with an instinctive strike just after the hour.

Basel's reward for ousting Tottenham was a semi-final against another London club, Chelsea. Murat Yakin's side welcomed the European champions to St Jakob-Park for the first leg hoping to maintain the impressive home form that had yielded four wins and two draws in the competition. However, they fell behind early on when Moses deflected in a Lampard corner from close range.

The hosts fought back and restored parity through Fabian Schär's penalty, only to be caught cold when David Luiz struck a free-kick beyond Sommer at the death. "This goal is a slap in the face," the keeper rued. The Swiss side dug deep when the teams reconvened at Stamford Bridge, and drew level on aggregate when Mohamed Salah swept past Čech just before the interval.

KEY FACT

4

Victory in the Netherlands made Chelsea the fourth side to win all three UEFA club competitions following their past successes in the European Cup Winners' Cup (1971, 1998) and UEFA Champions League (2012). They joined Juventus, FC Bayern München and Ajax, who had all previously collected the three trophies.

Chelsea simply moved up a gear, as Torres and Moses – with his fourth goal in as many games – scored in quick succession to put them ahead on the night before Luiz sealed a trip to Amsterdam, curling an impeccable left-footed strike from distance into the top corner.

Final

The final pitted together "the best two teams in the competition" according to Benfica coach Jorge Jesus, and it did not disappoint. An absorbing encounter kept viewers captivated from start to finish, when Branislav Ivanović's towering header in the last minute of added time earned Chelsea a dramatic victory.

Benfica dominated the first hour, their fluid, offensive-minded side hypnotising the Chelsea back line almost to submission. They attacked with verve, a flurry of balletic turns and intricate interplays. The script was only missing the final act as all too often they overcomplicated things, attempting one pass too many or fluffing their lines.

Then came the sucker punch when Čech's long throw was flicked on to Fernando Torres by Juan Mata. The striker turned his marker and held off Luisão before rounding Artur and

KEY FACT

34

Benfica forward Eduardo Salvio has played in more UEFA Europa League matches than any other player (34), but missed out on becoming the first player to win the competition three times, having triumphed twice before with Club Atlético de Madrid. Seven other players have also won it twice, though only one with different clubs – Radamel Falcao (Porto and Atlético).

clipping in. Benfica battled back and Óscar Cardozo's penalty after a César Azpilicueta handball had them level within eight minutes. The game then opened up, the pendulum swinging this way and that.

Cardozo had a stunning half-volley tipped over by Čech, and with two minutes left Lampard rattled the crossbar with a sumptuous strike. Extra time loomed, but Ivanović had other ideas, peeling away at the back post to direct an imperious looping header past Artur from Mata's deep corner. The trophy belonged to Chelsea.

Branislav Ivanović heads in Chelsea's last-gasp winner to defeat Benfica in Amsterdam

First qualifying round

03/07/12, Gundadalur, Torshavn
Víkingur 0-6 FC Gomel
12/07/12, Tsentralny, Gomel
FC Gomel 4-0 Víkingur
Aggregate: 10-0; FC Gomel qualify.

03/07/12, Bashkimi Stadium, Kumanovo
FK Shkëndija 79 0-0 Portadown FC
10/07/12, Shamrock Park, Portadown
Portadown FC 2-1 FK Shkëndija 79
Aggregate: 2-1; Portadown FC qualify.

05/07/12, Bashkimi Stadium, Kumanovo
FK Renova 4-0 AC Libertas
12/07/12, Stadio Olimpico, Serravalle
AC Libertas 0-4 FK Renova
Aggregate: 0-8; FK Renova qualify.

05/07/12, Gradski, Jagodina
FK Jagodina 0-1 FC Ordabasy Shymkent
12/07/12, Tsentralniy, Almaty
FC Ordabasy Shymkent 0-0 FK Jagodina
Aggregate: 1-0; FC Ordabasy Shymkent qualify.

05/07/12, Borås Arena, Boras
IF Elfsborg 8-0 Floriana FC
10/07/12, Hibernians Ground, Corradino
Floriana FC 0-4 IF Elfsborg
Aggregate: 0-12; IF Elfsborg qualify.

05/07/12, Gradski, Niksic
FK Rudar Pljevlja 0-1 FC Shirak
12/07/12, Gyumri City, Gyumri
FC Shirak 1-1 FK Rudar Pljevlja
Aggregate: 2-1; FC Shirak qualify.

05/07/12, Rakvere, Rakvere
JK Trans Narva 0-5 Inter Baku PIK
12/07/12, Dalga Stadium, Baku
İnter Baku PIK 2-0 JK Trans Narva
Aggregate: 7-0; İnter Baku PIK qualify.

05/07/12, La Frontière, Esch-sur-Alzette
FC Differdange 03 3-0 NSÍ Runavík
12/07/12, Gundadalur, Torshavn
NSÍ Runavík 0-3 FC Differdange 03
Aggregate: 0-6; FC Differdange 03 qualify.

05/07/12, Kuopion Keskuskenttä, Kuopio
KuPS Kuopio 2-1 Llanelli AFC
12/07/12, Stebonheath Park, Llanelli
Llanelli AFC 1-1 KuPS Kuopio
Aggregate: 2-3; KuPS Kuopio qualify.

05/07/12, Kadriorg, Tallinn
FC Levadia Tallinn 1-0 FC Šiauliai
12/07/12, Šiauliai central stadium, Šiauliai
FC Šiauliai 2-1 FC Levadia Tallinn
Aggregate: 2-2; FC Levadia Tallinn qualify on away goal.

05/07/12, Stadiumi Kombëtar Qemal Stafa, Tirana
KF Tirana 2-0 CS Grevenmacher
10/07/12, Jos Nosbaum, Dudelange
CS Grevenmacher 0-0 KF Tirana
Aggregate: 0-2; KF Tirana qualify.

05/07/12, Gundadalur, Torshavn
EB/Streymur 3-1 FC Gandzasar
12/07/12, Yerevan Republican Stadium Vazgen Sargsyan, Yerevan
FC Gandzasar 2-0 EB/Streymur
Aggregate: 3-3; FC Gandzasar qualify on away goal.

05/07/12, Hibernians Ground, Corradino
Birkirkara FC 2-2 FK Metalurg Skopje
12/07/12, Bashkimi Stadium, Kumanovo
FK Metalurg Skopje 0-0 Birkirkara FC
Aggregate: 2-2; FK Metalurg Skopje qualify on away goals.

05/07/12, Harjun Stadion, Jyvaskyla
JJK Jyväskylä 2-0 Stabæk Fotball
12/07/12, Nadderud, Bekkestua
Stabæk Fotball 3-2 JJK Jyväskylä
Aggregate: 3-4; JJK Jyväskylä qualify.

05/07/12, Kaplakrikavöllur, Hafnarfjördur
FH Hafnarfjördur 2-1 FC USV Eschen/Mauren
12/07/12, Sportpark Eschen-Mauren, Eschen
FC USV Eschen/Mauren 0-1 FH Hafnarfjördur
Aggregate: 1-3; FH Hafnarfjördur qualify.

05/07/12, Asim Ferhatović Hase Stadion, Sarajevo
FK Sarajevo 5-2 Hibernians FC
12/07/12, Hibernians Ground, Corradino
Hibernians FC 4-4 FK Sarajevo
Aggregate: 6-9; FK Sarajevo qualify.

11/07/12, Stadium of Marijampolė, Marijampolė
FK Sūduva 0-1 FC Daugava Daugavpils
12/07/12, Daugava, Daugavpils
FC Daugava Daugavpils 2-3 FK Sūduva
Aggregate: 3-3; FK Sūduva qualify on away goals.

05/07/12, The Racecourse Ground, Wrexham
Cefn Druids AFC 0-0 Myllykosken Pallo-47
12/07/12, Lahti Stadium, Lahti
Myllykosken Pallo-47 5-0 Cefn Druids AFC
Aggregate: 5-0; Myllykosken Pallo-47 qualify.

05/07/12, Estadi Comunal, Andorra la Vella
FC Santa Coloma 0-1 NK Osijek
12/07/12, Gradski vrt, Osijek
NK Osijek 3-1 FC Santa Coloma
Aggregate: 4-1; NK Osijek qualify.

05/07/12, Zimbru, Chisinau
FC Dacia Chisinau 1-0 NK Celje
12/07/12, Arena Petrol, Celje
NK Celje 0-1 FC Dacia Chisinau
Aggregate: 0-2; FC Dacia Chisinau qualify.

05/07/12, FC Twente Stadion, Enschede
FC Twente 6-0 UE Santa Coloma
12/07/12, Estadi Comunal, Andorra la Vella
UE Santa Coloma 0-3 FC Twente
Aggregate: 0-9; FC Twente qualify.

05/07/12, Solitude, Belfast
Cliftonville FC 1-0 Kalmar FF
12/07/12, Kalmar Arena, Kalmar
Kalmar FF 4-0 Cliftonville FC
Aggregate: 4-1; Kalmar FF qualify.

05/07/12, Dalymount Park, Dublin
Bohemian FC 0-0 Thór Akureyri
12/07/12, Thorsvöllur, Akureyri
Thór Akureyri 5-1 Bohemian FC
Aggregate: 5-1; Thór Akureyri qualify.

05/07/12, Richmond Park, Dublin
Saint Patrick's Athletic FC 1-0 ÍBV Vestmannaeyjar
12/07/12, Hasteinsvöllur, Vestmannaeyjar
ÍBV Vestmannaeyjar 2-1 Saint Patrick's Athletic FC
Aggregate: 2-2; Saint Patrick's Athletic FC qualify on away goal.

Elfsborg players celebrate one of their eight goals at home to Floriana

05/07/12, Nantporth, Bangor
Bangor City FC 0-0 FC Zimbru Chisinau
12/07/12, Zimbru, Chisinau
FC Zimbru Chisinau 2-1 Bangor City FC
Aggregate: 2-1; FC Zimbru Chisinau qualify.

05/07/12, Seaview, Belfast
Crusaders FC 0-3 Rosenborg BK
12/07/12, Lerkendal Stadion, Trondheim
Rosenborg BK 1-0 Crusaders FC
Aggregate: 4-0; Rosenborg BK qualify.

05/07/12, Municipal Stadium Poznan, Poznan
KKS Lech Poznań 2-0 FC Zhetysu Taldykorgan
12/07/12, Zhetysu, Taldykorgan
FC Zhetysu Taldykorgan 1-1 KKS Lech Poznań
Aggregate: 1-3; KKS Lech Poznań qualify.

05/07/12, Şähär stadionu, Lankaran
Xäzär Länkäran FK 2-2 JK Nõmme Kalju
10/07/12, Kadriorg, Tallinn
JK Nõmme Kalju 0-2 Xäzär Länkäran FK
Aggregate: 2-4; Xäzär Länkäran FK qualify.

05/07/12, Yerevan Republican Stadium Vazgen Sargsyan, Yerevan
FC Pyunik 0-3 FK Zeta
12/07/12, Stadion Podgorica, Podgorica
FK Zeta 1-2 FC Pyunik
Aggregate: 4-2; FK Zeta qualify.

05/07/12, ŠRC Stožice, Ljubljana
NK Olimpija Ljubljana 3-0 AS Jeunesse Esch
12/07/12, La Frontière, Esch-sur-Alzette
AS Jeunesse Esch 0-3 NK Olimpija Ljubljana
Aggregate: 0-6; NK Olimpija Ljubljana qualify.

05/07/12, Hidegkúti Nándor, Budapest
MTK Budapest 1-1 FK Senica
12/07/12, FK Senica, Senica
FK Senica 2-1 MTK Budapest
Aggregate: 3-2; FK Senica qualify.

05/07/12, Flamurtari, Vlora
KS Flamurtari 0-1 Budapest Honvéd FC
12/07/12, József Bozsik, Budapest
Budapest Honvéd FC 2-0 KS Flamurtari
Aggregate: 3-0; Budapest Honvéd FC qualify.

05/07/12, Stadio Olimpico, Serravalle
SP La Fiorita 0-2 SK Liepājas Metalurgs
12/07/12, Daugava, Liepaja
SK Liepājas Metalurgs 4-0 SP La Fiorita
Aggregate: 6-0; SK Liepājas Metalurgs qualify.

05/07/12, Niko Dovana, Durres
KS Teuta 0-3 FC Metalurgi Rustavi
12/07/12, Mikheil Meskhi, Tbilisi
FC Metalurgi Rustavi 6-1 KS Teuta
Aggregate: 9-1; FC Metalurgi Rustavi qualify.

05/07/12, Dalga Stadium, Baku
Bakı FK 0-0 ND Mura 05
12/07/12, Športni park, Lendava
ND Mura 05 2-0 Bakı FK
Aggregate: 2-0; ND Mura 05 qualify.

05/07/12, Tsentraluri, Kutaisi
FC Torpedo Kutaisi 1-1 FC Aktobe
12/07/12, Tsentralniy, Aktobe
FC Aktobe 1-0 FC Torpedo Kutaisi
Aggregate: 2-1; FC Aktobe qualify.

05/07/12, Gradski Stadium Banja Luka, Banjaluka
FK Borac Banja Luka 2-2 FK Čelik Nikšić
12/07/12, Gradski, Niksic
FK Čelik Nikšić 1-1 FK Borac Banja Luka
Aggregate: 3-3; FK Čelik Nikšić qualify on away goal.

Second qualifying round

19/07/12, Bashkimi Stadium, Kumanovo
FK Renova 0-2 FC Gomel
26/07/12, Tsentralny, Gomel
FC Gomel 0-1 FK Renova
Aggregate: 2-1; FC Gomel qualify.

19/07/12, Vitebsk Central sport complex, Vitebsk
FC Naftan Novopolotsk 3-4 FK Crvena zvezda
26/07/12, Stadion FK Crvena zvezda, Belgrade
FK Crvena zvezda 3-3 FC Naftan Novopolotsk
Aggregate: 7-6; FK Crvena zvezda qualify.

19/07/12, District Sport Complex, Orhei
FC Milsami Orhei 4-2 FC Aktobe
26/07/12, Tsentralniy, Aktobe
FC Aktobe 3-0 FC Milsami Orhei
Aggregate: 5-4; FC Aktobe qualify.

19/07/12, Daugava, Liepaja
SK Liepājas Metalurgs 2-2 Legia Warszawa
26/07/12, Stadion Wojska Polskiego im., Warsaw
Legia Warszawa 5-1 SK Liepājas Metalurgs
Aggregate: 7-3; Legia Warszawa qualify.

19/07/12, ŠRC Stožice, Ljubljana
NK Olimpija Ljubljana 0-0 Tromsø IL
26/07/12, Alfheim, Tromso
Tromsø IL 1-0 NK Olimpija Ljubljana *(aet)*
Aggregate: 1-0; Tromsø IL qualify after extra time.

19/07/12, Lovech Stadion, Lovech
PFC Lokomotiv Plovdiv 1936 4-4 Vitesse
26/07/12, Gelredome, Arnhem
Vitesse 3-1 PFC Lokomotiv Plovdiv 1936
Aggregate: 7-5; Vitesse qualify.

19/07/12, La Frontière, Esch-sur-Alzette
FC Differdange 03 0-1 KAA Gent
26/07/12, Jules Ottenstadion, Gent
KAA Gent 3-2 FC Differdange 03
Aggregate: 4-2; KAA Gent qualify.

Anji striker Samuel Eto'o – a double goalscorer in his team's 4-0 win at Honvéd

19/07/12, Kadriorg, Tallinn
FC Levadia Tallinn 1-3 Anorthosis Famagusta FC
26/07/12, Antonis Papadopoulos, Larnaca
Anorthosis Famagusta FC 3-0 FC Levadia Tallinn
Aggregate: 6-1; Anorthosis Famagusta FC qualify.

19/07/12, Råsundastadion, Solna
AIK 1-1 FH Hafnarfjördur
26/07/12, Kaplakrikavöllur, Hafnarfjördur
FH Hafnarfjördur 0-1 AIK
Aggregate: 1-2; AIK qualify.

19/07/12, Harjun Stadion, Jyvaskyla
JJK Jyväskylä 3-2 FK Zeta
26/07/12, Stadion Podgorica, Podgorica
FK Zeta 1-0 JJK Jyväskylä
Aggregate: 3-3; FK Zeta qualify on away goals.

19/07/12, Stadiumi Kombëtar Qemal Stafa, Tirana
KF Tirana 1-1 Aalesunds FK
26/07/12, Aalesund Stadion, Aalesund
Aalesunds FK 5-0 KF Tirana
Aggregate: 6-1; Aalesunds FK qualify.

19/07/12, Mestský, Mlada Boleslav
FK Mladá Boleslav 3-0 Thór Akureyri
26/07/12, Thorsvöllur, Akureyri
Thór Akureyri 0-1 FK Mladá Boleslav
Aggregate: 0-4; FK Mladá Boleslav qualify.

19/07/12, Gradski stadion Koprivnica, Koprivnica
NK Slaven Koprivnica 6-0 Portadown FC
26/07/12, Shamrock Park, Portadown
Portadown FC 2-4 NK Slaven Koprivnica
Aggregate: 2-10; NK Slaven Koprivnica qualify.

19/07/12, Saturn, Ramenskoye
FC Anji Makhachkala 1-0 Budapest Honvéd FC
26/07/12, József Bozsik, Budapest
Budapest Honvéd FC 0-4 FC Anji Makhachkala
Aggregate: 0-5; FC Anji Makhachkala qualify.

19/07/12, Lerkendal Stadion, Trondheim
Rosenborg BK 2-2 FC Ordabasy Shymkent
26/07/12, Tsentralniy, Almaty
FC Ordabasy Shymkent 1-2 Rosenborg BK
Aggregate: 3-4; Rosenborg BK qualify.

19/07/12, Antona Malatinského, Trnava
FC Spartak Trnava 3-1 Sligo Rovers FC
26/07/12, The Showgrounds, Sligo
Sligo Rovers FC 1-1 FC Spartak Trnava
Aggregate: 2-4; FC Spartak Trnava qualify.

19/07/12, Ruch, Chorzow
Ruch Chorzów 3-1 FK Metalurg Skopje
26/07/12, Bashkimi Stadium, Kumanovo
FK Metalurg Skopje 0-3 Ruch Chorzów
Aggregate: 1-6; Ruch Chorzów qualify.

19/07/12, Aarhus Stadion, Aarhus
AGF Aarhus 1-2 FC Dila Gori
26/07/12, Mikheil Meskhi, Tbilisi
FC Dila Gori 3-1 AGF Aarhus
Aggregate: 5-2; FC Dila Gori qualify.

19/07/12, Stade de Suisse, Berne
BSC Young Boys 1-0 FC Zimbru Chisinau
26/07/12, Zimbru, Chisinau
FC Zimbru Chisinau 1-0 BSC Young Boys
(aet)
Aggregate: 1-1; BSC Young Boys qualify
4-1 on penalties.

19/07/12, Stružni, Dolyorono
FC Shakhtyor Soligorsk 1-1 SV Ried
26/07/12, Keine Sorgen Arena, Ried im Innkreis
SV Ried 0-0 FC Chakhtyor Soligorsk
Aggregate: 1-1; SV Ried qualify on away goal

19/07/12, Stade de Genève, Geneva
Servette FC 2-0 FC Gandzasar
26/07/12, Yerevan Republican Stadium Vazgen Sargsyan, Yerevan
FC Gandzasar 1-3 Servette FC
Aggregate: 1-5; Servette FC qualify.

19/07/12, FC Twente Stadion, Enschede
FC Twente 1-1 FC Inter Turku
26/07/12, Turku Stadium, Turku
FC Inter Turku 0-5 FC Twente
Aggregate: 1-6; FC Twente qualify.

19/07/12, Şähär stadionu, Lankaran
Xäzär Länkäran FK 1-1 KKS Lech Poznań
26/07/12, Municipal Stadium Poznań, Poznan
KKS Lech Poznań 1-0 Xäzär Länkäran FK
Aggregate: 2-1; KKS Lech Poznań qualify.

19/07/12, Atatürk, Eskisehir
Eskişehirspor 2-0 Saint Johnstone FC
26/07/12, McDiarmid Park, Perth
Saint Johnstone FC 1-1 Eskişehirspor
Aggregate: 1-3; Eskişehirspor qualify.

19/07/12, Metalurh, Donetsk
FC Metalurh Donetsk 7-0 FK Čelik Nikšić
26/07/12, Gradski, Niksic
FK Čelik Nikšić 2-4 FC Metalurh Donetsk
Aggregate: 2-11; FC Metalurh Donetsk qualify.

19/07/12, Gradski vrt, Osijek
NK Osijek 1-3 Kalmar FF
26/07/12, Kalmar Arena, Kalmar
Kalmar FF 3-0 NK Osijek
Aggregate: 6-1; Kalmar FF qualify.

19/07/12, Mikheil Meskhi, Tbilisi
FC Metalurgi Rustavi 1-3 FC Viktoria Plzeň
26/07/12, Stadion města Plzně, Plzen
FC Viktoria Plzeň 2-0 FC Metalurgi Rustavi
Aggregate: 5-1; FC Viktoria Plzeň qualify.

19/07/12, Športni park, Lendava
ND Mura 05 0-0 PFC CSKA Sofia
26/07/12, Natsionalen Stadion Vasil Levski, Sofia
PFC CSKA Sofia 1-1 ND Mura 05
Aggregate: 1-1; ND Mura 05 qualify on away goal.

19/07/12, Georgi Asparuhov Stadion, Sofia
PFC Levski Sofia 1-0 FK Sarajevo
26/07/12, Asim Ferhatović Hase Stadion, Sarajevo
FK Sarajevo 3-1 PFC Levski Sofia
Aggregate: 3-2; FK Sarajevo qualify.

19/07/12, Itztadion Ramat Gan, Ramat Gan
Bnei Yehuda Tel-Aviv FC 2-0 FC Shirak
26/07/12, Gyumri City, Gyumri
FC Shirak 0-1 Bnei Yehuda Tel-Aviv FC
Aggregate: 0-3; Bnei Yehuda Tel-Aviv FC qualify.

19/07/12, GSP Stadium, Nicosia
APOEL FC 2-0 FK Senica
26/07/12, FK Senica, Senica
FK Senica 0-1 APOEL FC
Aggregate: 0-3; APOEL FC qualify.

19/07/12, Štadión Pasienky, Bratislava
ŠK Slovan Bratislava 1-1 Videoton FC
26/07/12, Sóstói, Szekesfehervar
Videoton FC 0-0 ŠK Slovan Bratislava
Aggregate: 1-1; Videoton FC qualify on away goal.

19/07/12, Zimbru, Chisinau
FC Dacia Chisinau 0-1 IF Elfsborg
26/07/12, Borås Arena, Boras
IF Elfsborg 2-0 FC Dacia Chisinau
Aggregate: 2-1; IF Elfsborg qualify.

19/07/12, Stadion Poljud, Split
HNK Hajduk Split 2-0 Skonto FC
26/07/12, Skonto Stadions, Riga
Skonto FC 1-0 HNK Hajduk Split
Aggregate: 1-2; HNK Hajduk Split qualify.

19/07/12, Karadjordje, Novi Sad
FK Vojvodina 1-1 FK Sūduva
26/07/12, Stadium of Marijampole, Marijampole
FK Sūduva 0-4 FK Vojvodina
Aggregate: 1-5; FK Vojvodina qualify.

19/07/12, Vetra, Vilnius
VMFD Žalgiris 1-1 FC Admira Wacker Mödling
26/07/12, Bundesstadion Südstadt, Maria Enzersdorf
FC Admira Wacker Mödling 5-1 VMFD Žalgiris
Aggregate: 6-2; FC Admira Wacker Mödling qualify.

19/07/12, Giuleşti - Valentin Stănescu, Bucharest
FC Rapid Bucureşti 3-1 Myllykosken Pallo-47
26/07/12, Saviniemi Football Stadium, Myllykoski
Myllykosken Pallo-47 0-2 FC Rapid Bucureşti
Aggregate: 1-5; FC Rapid Bucureşti qualify.

19/07/12, HaMoshava, Petach-Tikva
Maccabi Netanya FC 1-2 KuPS Kuopio
26/07/12, Kuopion Keskuskenttä, Kuopio
KuPS Kuopio 0-1 Maccabi Netanya FC
Aggregate: 2-2; KuPS Kuopio qualify on away goals.

19/07/12, Dalga Stadium, Baku
İnter Bakı PİK 1-1 Asteras Tripolis FC
26/07/12, Asteras Tripolis, Tripoli Arkadia
Asteras Tripolis FC 1-1 İnter Bakı PİK *(aet)*
Aggregate: 2-2; Asteras Tripolis FC qualify 4-2 on penalties.

19/07/12, Pecara, Siroki Brijeg
NK Široki Brijeg 1-1 Saint Patrick's Athletic FC
26/07/12, Richmond Park, Dublin
Saint Patrick's Athletic FC 2-1 NK Široki Brijeg *(aet)*
Aggregate: 3-2; Saint Patrick's Athletic FC qualify after extra time.

Third qualifying round

02/08/12, Kuopion Keskuskenttä, Kuopio
KuPS Kuopio 1-0 Bursaspor
09/08/12, Bursa Atatürk, Bursa
Bursaspor 6-0 KuPS Kuopio
Aggregate: 6-1; Bursaspor qualify.

02/08/12, Råsundastadion, Solna
AIK 3-0 KKS Lech Poznań
09/08/12, Municipal Stadium Poznań, Poznan
KKS Lech Poznań 1-0 AIK
Aggregate: 1-3; AIK qualify.

02/08/12, Kalmar Arena, Kalmar
Kalmar FF 1-0 BSC Young Boys
09/08/12, Stade de Suisse, Berne
BSC Young Boys 3-0 Kalmar FF
Aggregate: 3-1; BSC Young Boys qualify.

02/08/12, Stadion Dinamo im. Valeriy Lobanovskyi, Kyiv
FC Arsenal Kyiv 0-3(f) ND Mura 05
09/08/12, Stadion Ljudski vrt, Maribor
ND Mura 05 0-2 FC Arsenal Kyiv
Aggregate: 3-2; ND Mura 05 qualify.

02/08/12, Keine Sorgen Arena, Ried im Innkreis
SV Ried 2-1 Legia Warszawa
09/08/12, Stadion Wojska Polskiego im., Warsaw
Legia Warszawa 3-1 SV Ried
Aggregate: 4-3; Legia Warszawa qualify.

02/08/12, Saturn, Ramenskoye
FC Anji Makhachkala 2-0 Vitesse
09/08/12, Gelredome, Arnhem
Vitesse 0-2 FC Anji Makhachkala
Aggregate: 0-4; FC Anji Makhachkala qualify.

02/08/12, Ruch, Chorzow
Ruch Chorzów 0-2 FC Viktoria Plzeň
09/08/12, Stadion města Plzně, Plzen
FC Viktoria Plzeň 5-0 Ruch Chorzów
Aggregate: 7-0; FC Viktoria Plzeň qualify.

02/08/12, Alfheim, Tromso
Tromsø IL 1-1 FC Metalurh Donetsk
09/08/12, Metalurh, Donetsk
FC Metalurh Donetsk 0-1 Tromsø IL
Aggregate: 1-2; Tromsø IL qualify.

02/08/12, Abe Lenstra, Heerenveen
sc Heerenveen 4-0 FC Rapid Bucureşti
09/08/12, National Arena, Bucharest
FC Rapid Bucureşti 1-0 sc Heerenveen
Aggregate: 1-4; sc Heerenveen qualify.

02/08/12, Tannadice Park, Dundee
Dundee United FC 2-2 FC Dinamo Moskva
09/08/12, Arena Khimki, Moscow
FC Dinamo Moskva 5-0 Dundee United FC
Aggregate: 7-2; FC Dinamo Moskva qualify.

02/08/12, Tallaght Stadium, Dublin
Saint Patrick's Athletic FC 0-3 Hannover 96
09/08/12, Hannover Arena, Hannover
Hannover 96 2-0 Saint Patrick's Athletic FC
Aggregate: 5-0; Hannover 96 qualify.

02/08/12, Stade de Genève, Geneva
Servette FC 1-1 Rosenborg BK
09/08/12, Lerkendal Stadion, Trondheim
Rosenborg BK 0-0 Servette FC
Aggregate: 1-1; Rosenborg BK qualify on away goal.

02/08/12, FC Twente Stadion, Enschede
FC Twente 2-0 FK Mladá Boleslav
09/08/12, Mestský, Mlada Boleslav
FK Mladá Boleslav 0-2 FC Twente
Aggregate: 0-4; FC Twente qualify.

02/08/12, GSP Stadium, Nicosia
APOEL FC 2-1 Aalesunds FK
09/08/12, Aalesund Stadion, Aalesund
Aalesunds FK 0-1 APOEL FC
Aggregate: 1-3; APOEL FC qualify.

02/08/12, KRC Genk Arena, Genk
KRC Genk 2-1 FC Aktobe
09/08/12, Tsentralniy, Aktobe
FC Aktobe 1-2 KRC Genk
Aggregate: 2-4; KRC Genk qualify.

02/08/12, Itztadion Ramat Gan, Ramat Gan
Bnei Yehuda Tel-Aviv FC 0-2 PAOK FC
09/08/12, Stadio Toumba, Salonika
PAOK FC 4-1 Bnei Yehuda Tel-Aviv FC
Aggregate: 6-1; PAOK FC qualify.

02/08/12, Mikheil Meskhi, Tbilisi
FC Dila Gori 0-1 Anorthosis Famagusta FC
09/08/12, Antonis Papadopoulos, Larnaca
Anorthosis Famagusta FC 0-3 FC Dila Gori (w/o; match abandoned)
Aggregate: 1-3; FC Dila Gori qualify.

02/08/12, Horsens Idrætspark, Horsens
AC Horsens 1-1 IF Elfsborg
09/08/12, Borås Arena, Boras
IF Elfsborg 2-3 AC Horsens
Aggregate: 3-4; AC Horsens qualify.

02/08/12, Sóstói, Szekesfehervar
Videoton FC 1-0 KAA Gent
09/08/12, Jules Ottenstadion, Gent
KAA Gent 0-3 Videoton FC
Aggregate: 0-4; Videoton FC qualify.

02/08/12, Stadion FK Crvena zvezda, Belgrade
FK Crvena zvezda 0-0 AC Omonia
09/08/12, GSP Stadium, Nicosia
AC Omonia 0-0 FK Crvena zvezda (aet)
Aggregate: 0-0; FK Crvena zvezda qualify 6-5 on penalties.

02/08/12, National Arena, Bucharest
FC Steaua Bucureşti 0-1 FC Spartak Trnava
09/08/12, Antona Malatinského, Trnava
FC Spartak Trnava 0-3 FC Steaua Bucureşti
Aggregate: 1-3; FC Steaua Bucureşti qualify.

02/08/12, Hajduk, Split
HNK Hajduk Split 0-3 FC Internazionale Milano
09/08/12, Stadio Giuseppe Meazza, Milan
FC Internazionale Milano 0-2 HNK Hajduk Split
Aggregate: 3-2; FC Internazionale Milano qualify.

02/08/12, Asim Ferhatović Hase Stadion, Sarajevo
FK Sarajevo 2-1 FK Zeta
09/08/12, Stadion Podgorica, Podgorica
FK Zeta 1-0 FK Sarajevo
Aggregate: 2-2; FK Zeta qualify on away goal.

02/08/12, Tsentralny, Gomel
FC Gomel 0-1 Liverpool FC
09/08/12, Anfield, Liverpool
Liverpool FC 3-0 FC Gomel
Aggregate: 4-0; Liverpool FC qualify.

02/08/12, Estadio de San Mamés, Bilbao
Athletic Club 3-1 NK Slaven Koprivnica
09/08/12, Gradski stadion Koprivnica, Koprivnica
NK Slaven Koprivnica 2-1 Athletic Club
Aggregate: 3-4; Athletic Club qualify.

02/08/12, Asteras Tripolis, Tripoli Arkadia
Asteras Tripolis FC 1-1 CS Marítimo
09/08/12, Dos Barreiros, Funchal
CS Marítimo 0-0 Asteras Tripolis FC
Aggregate: 1-1; CS Marítimo qualify on away goal.

02/08/12, Karadjordje, Novi Sad
FK Vojvodina 2-1 SK Rapid Wien
09/08/12, Gerhard-Hanappi-Stadion, Vienna
SK Rapid Wien 2-0 FK Vojvodina
Aggregate: 3-2; SK Rapid Wien qualify.

02/08/12, Bundesstadion Südstadt, Maria Enzersdorf
FC Admira Wacker Mödling 0-2 AC Sparta Praha
09/08/12, Stadion Letná, Prague
AC Sparta Praha 2-2 FC Admira Wacker Mödling
Aggregate: 4-2; AC Sparta Praha qualify.

02/08/12, Atatürk, Eskisehir
Eskişehirspor 1-1 Olympique de Marseille
09/08/12, Parsemain, Istres
Olympique de Marseille 3-0 Eskişehirspor
Aggregate: 4-1; Olympique de Marseille qualify.

Play-offs

22/08/12, VfB Arena, Stuttgart
VfB Stuttgart 2-0 FC Dinamo Moskva
28/08/12, Arena Khimki, Moscow
FC Dinamo Moskva 1-1 VfB Stuttgart
Aggregate: 1-3; VfB Stuttgart qualify.

23/08/12, Alfheim, Tromso
Tromsø IL 3-2 FK Partizan
30/08/12, FK Partizan, Belgrade
FK Partizan 1-0 Tromsø IL
Aggregate: 3-3; FK Partizan qualify on away goals.

23/08/12, Molde Stadion, Molde
Molde FK 2-0 sc Heerenveen
30/08/12, Abe Lenstra, Heerenveen
sc Heerenveen 1-2 Molde FK
Aggregate: 1-4; Molde FK qualify.

23/08/12, Råsundastadion, Solna
AIK 0-1 PFC CSKA Moskva
30/08/12, Arena Khimki, Moscow
PFC CSKA Moskva 0-2 AIK
Aggregate: 1-2; AIK qualify.

23/08/12, Stadion Wojska Polskiego im., Warsaw
Legia Warszawa 1-1 Rosenborg BK
30/08/12, Lerkendal Stadion, Trondheim
Rosenborg BK 2-1 Legia Warszawa
Aggregate: 3-2; Rosenborg BK qualify.

23/08/12, U Nisy, Liberec
FC Slovan Liberec 2-2 FC Dnipro Dnipropetrovsk
30/08/12, Dnipro Arena, Dnipropetrovsk
FC Dnipro Dnipropetrovsk 4-2 FC Slovan Liberec
Aggregate: 6-4; FC Dnipro Dnipropetrovsk qualify.

23/08/12, Swissporarena, Lucerne
FC Luzern 2-1 KRC Genk
30/08/12, KRC Genk Arena, Genk
KRC Genk 2-0 FC Luzern
Aggregate: 3-2; KRC Genk qualify.

Vedad Ibišević opens the scoring for Stuttgart at home to Dinamo Moskva

23/08/12, Tynecastle, Edinburgh
Heart of Midlothian FC 0-1 Liverpool FC
30/08/12, Anfield, Liverpool
Liverpool FC 1-1 Heart of Midlothian FC
Aggregate: 2-1; Liverpool FC qualify.

23/08/12, Fir Park, Motherwell
Motherwell FC 0-2 Levante UD
30/08/12, Estadi Ciutat de València, Valencia
Levante UD 1-0 Motherwell FC
Aggregate: 3-0; Levante UD qualify.

23/08/12, Vetra, Vilnius
FK Ekranas 0 ■ FC Steaua Bucureşti
30/08/12, Stadionul Steaua, Bucharest
FC Steaua Bucureşti 3-0 FK Ekranas
Aggregate: 6-0; FC Steaua Bucureşti
qualify

23/08/12, Stadion Lokomotiv, Moscow
FC Anji Makhachkala 1-0 AZ Alkmaar
30/08/12, AZ Stadion, Alkmaar
AZ Alkmaar 0-5 FC Anji Makhachkala
Aggregate: 0-6; FC Anji Makhachkala
qualify.

23/08/12, Peristeri, Athens
Atromitos FC 1-1 Newcastle United FC
30/08/12, St James' Park, Newcastle
Newcastle United FC 1-0 Atromitos FC
Aggregate: 2-1; Newcastle United FC
qualify.

23/08/12, Dos Barreiros, Funchal
CS Marítimo 1-0 FC Dila Gori
30/08/12, Mikheil Meskhi, Tbilisi
FC Dila Gori 0-2 CS Marítimo
Aggregate: 0-3; CS Marítimo qualify.

23/08/12, Stadionul Sheriff, Tiraspol
FC Sheriff 1-2 Olympique de Marseille
30/08/12, Stade Vélodrome, Marseille
Olympique de Marseille 0-0 FC Sheriff
Aggregate: 2-1; Olympique de Marseille qualify.

23/08/12, Stade Municipal de Differdange, Differdange
F91 Dudelange 1-3 Hapoel Tel-Aviv FC
30/08/12, Itztadion Bloomfield, Tel-Aviv
Hapoel Tel-Aviv FC 4-0 F91 Dudelange
Aggregate: 7-1; Hapoel Tel-Aviv FC qualify.

23/08/12, Feijenoord Stadion, Rotterdam
Feyenoord 2-2 AC Sparta Praha
30/08/12, Stadion Letná, Prague
AC Sparta Praha 2-0 Feyenoord
Aggregate: 4-2; AC Sparta Praha qualify.

23/08/12, Herning Stadion, Herning
FC Midtjylland 0-0 BSC Young Boys
30/08/12, Stade de Suisse, Berne
BSC Young Boys 0-2 FC Midtjylland
Aggregate: 3-2; BSC Young Boys qualify.

23/08/12, Sóstói út, Nyíregyháza
Debreceni VSC 0-3 Club Brugge KV
30/08/12, Jan Breydelstadion, Bruges
Club Brugge KV 4-1 Debreceni VSC
Aggregate: 7-1; Club Brugge KV qualify.

23/08/12, National Arena, Bucharest
FC Dinamo Bucureşti 0-2 FC Metalist Kharkiv
30/08/12, Metalist Stadium, Kharkiv
FC Metalist Kharkiv 2-1 FC Dinamo Bucureşti
Aggregate: 4-1; FC Metalist Kharkiv qualify.

23/08/12, Roi Baudouin, Brussels
KSC Lokeren OV 2-1 FC Viktoria Plzeň
30/08/12, Stadion města Plzně, Plzen
FC Viktoria Plzeň 1-0 KSC Lokeren OV
Aggregate: 2-2; FC Viktoria Plzeň qualify
on away goal.

23/08/12, Bursa Atatürk, Bursa
Bursaspor 3-1 FC Twente
30/08/12, FC Twente Stadion, Enschede
FC Twente 4-1 Bursaspor (aet)
Aggregate: 5-4; FC Twente qualify after
extra time.

23/08/12, Municipal Stadium Wroclaw, Wroclaw
WKS Śląsk Wrocław 3-5 Hannover 96
30/08/12, Hannover Arena, Hannover
Hannover 96 5-1 WKS Śląsk Wrocław
Aggregate: 10-4; Hannover 96 qualify.

23/08/12, Dalga Stadium, Baku
Neftçi PFK 1-1 APOEL FC
30/08/12, GSP Stadium, Nicosia
APOEL FC 1-3 Neftçi PFK
Aggregate: 2-4; Neftçi PFK qualify.

23/08/12, Estadio de San Mamés, Bilbao
Athletic Club 6-0 HJK Helsinki
30/08/12, Finnair Stadium, Helsinki
HJK Helsinki 3-3 Athletic Club
Aggregate: 3-9; Athletic Club qualify.

23/08/12, Hüseyin Avni Aker Stadyumu, Trabzon
Trabzonspor AŞ 0-0 Videoton FC
30/08/12, Sóstói, Szekesfehervar
Videoton FC 0-0 Trabzonspor AŞ (aet)
Aggregate: 0-0; Videoton FC qualify 4-2 on
penalties.

23/08/12, Horsens Idrætspark, Horsens
AC Horsens 1-1 Sporting Clube de Portugal
30/08/12, José Alvalade, Lisbon
Sporting Clube de Portugal 5-0 AC Horsens
Aggregate: 6-1; Sporting Clube de Portugal
qualify.

23/08/12, Stadion FK Crvena zvezda, Belgrade
FK Crvena zvezda 0-0 FC Girondins de Bordeaux
30/08/12, Stade Chaban-Delmas, Bordeaux
FC Girondins de Bordeaux 3-2 FK Crvena zvezda
Aggregate: 3-2; FC Girondins de Bordeaux
qualify.

23/08/12, Stadion Ljudski vrt, Maribor
ND Mura 05 0-2 S.S. Lazio
30/08/12, Stadio Olimpico, Rome
S.S. Lazio 3-1 ND Mura 05
Aggregate: 5-1; S.S. Lazio qualify.

23/08/12, Stadion Podgorica, Podgorica
FK Zeta 0-5 PSV Eindhoven
30/08/12, PSV Stadion, Eindhoven
PSV Eindhoven 9-0 FK Zeta
Aggregate: 14-0; PSV Eindhoven qualify.

23/08/12, Stadio Toumba, Salonika
PAOK FC 2-1 SK Rapid Wien
30/08/12, Gerhard-Hanappi-Stadion, Vienna
SK Rapid Wien 3-0 PAOK FC
Aggregate: 4-2; SK Rapid Wien qualify.

23/08/12, Stadionul Ceahlăul, Piatra Neamt
FC Vaslui 0-2 FC Internazionale Milano
30/08/12, Stadio Giuseppe Meazza, Milan
FC Internazionale Milano 2-2 FC Vaslui
Aggregate: 4-2; FC Internazionale Milano
qualify.

Group A

20/09/12, Stade de Suisse, Berne
BSC Young Boys 3-5 Liverpool FC
Goals: 0-1 Ojala 4(og), 1-1 Nuzzolo 38, 1-2 Wisdom 40, 2-2 Ojala 53, 3-2 Zárate 63, 3-3 Coates 67, 3-4 Shelvey 76, 3-5 Shelvey 88

20/09/12, Stadio Friuli, Udine
Udinese Calcio 1-1 FC Anji Makhachkala
Goals: 0-1 Padelli 45(og), 1-1 Di Natale 90+2

04/10/12, Stadion Lokomotiv, Moscow
FC Anji Makhachkala 2-0 BSC Young Boys
Goals: 1-0 Eto'o 62(p), 2-0 Eto'o 90

04/10/12, Anfield, Liverpool
Liverpool FC 2-3 Udinese Calcio
Goals: 1-0 Shelvey 23, 1-1 Di Natale 46, 1-2 Coates 70(og), 1-3 Pasquale 72, 2-3 Suárez 75

25/10/12, Anfield, Liverpool
Liverpool FC 1-0 FC Anji Makhachkala
Goal: 1-0 Downing 53

25/10/12, Stade de Suisse, Berne
BSC Young Boys 3-1 Udinese Calcio
Goals: 1-0 Bobadilla 4, 2-0 Bobadilla 71, 2-1 Coda 74, 3-1 Bobadilla 81(p)

08/11/12, Stadio Friuli, Udine
Udinese Calcio 2-3 BSC Young Boys
Goals: 0-1 Bobadilla 27, 1-1 Di Natale 47, 1-2 Farnerud 65, 1-3 Nuzzolo 73, 2-3 Fabbrini 83

08/11/12, Stadion Lokomotiv, Moscow
FC Anji Makhachkala 1-0 Liverpool FC
Goal: 1-0 Traoré 45+1

22/11/12, Anfield, Liverpool
Liverpool FC 2-2 BSC Young Boys
Goals: 1-0 Shelvey 33, 1-1 Bobadilla 52, 2-1 Cole 72, 2-2 Zverotić 88

22/11/12, Stadion Lokomotiv, Moscow
FC Anji Makhachkala 2-0 Udinese Calcio
Goals: 1-0 Samba 72, 2-0 Eto'o 75

06/12/12, Stade de Suisse, Berne
BSC Young Boys 3-1 FC Anji Makhachkala
Goals: 1-0 Zárate 38, 1-1 Ahmedov 45+2, 2-1 Costanzo 52, 3-1 González 90

06/12/12, Stadio Friuli, Udine
Udinese Calcio 0-1 Liverpool FC
Goal: 0-1 Henderson 23

		Pld	Home W D L F A	Away W D L F A	Total W D L F A	Pts
1	Liverpool FC	6	1 1 1 5 5	2 0 1 6 4	3 1 2 11 9	10
2	FC Anji Makhachkala	6	3 0 0 5 0	0 1 2 2 5	3 1 2 7 5	10
3	BSC Young Boys	6	2 0 1 9 7	1 1 1 5 6	3 1 2 14 13	10
4	Udinese Calcio	6	0 1 2 3 5	1 0 2 4 7	1 1 4 7 12	4

Group B

20/09/12, Stadion města Plzně, Plzen
FC Viktoria Plzeň 3-1 A. Académica de Coimbra
Goals: 0-1 Wilson Eduardo 19, 1-1 Horváth 46, 2-1 Ďuriš 58, 3-1 Rajtoral 80

20/09/12, Itztadion Bloomfield, Tel-Aviv
Hapoel Tel-Aviv FC 0-3 Club Atlético de Madrid
Goals: 0-1 Rodríguez 37, 0-2 Diego Costa 40, 0-3 Raúl García 63

04/10/12, Cidade de Coimbra, Coimbra
A. Académica de Coimbra 1-1 Hapoel Tel-Aviv FC
Goals: 1-0 Cissé 47, 1-1 Damari 90+2

04/10/12, Estadio Vicente Calderón, Madrid
Club Atlético de Madrid 1-0 FC Viktoria Plzeň
Goal: 1-0 Rodríguez 90+3

25/10/12, Estadio Vicente Calderón, Madrid
Club Atlético de Madrid 2-1 A. Académica de Coimbra
Goals: 1-0 Diego Costa 48, 2-0 Emre Belözoğlu 67, 2-1 Cissé 85

25/10/12, Itztadion Bloomfield, Tel-Aviv
Hapoel Tel-Aviv FC 1-2 FC Viktoria Plzeň
Goals: 1-0 Maman 19, 1-1 Horváth 45+1, 1-2 Rajtoral 55

08/11/12, Cidade de Coimbra, Coimbra
A. Académica de Coimbra 2-0 Club Atlético de Madrid
Goals: 1-0 Wilson Eduardo 28, 2-0 Wilson Eduardo 70(p)

08/11/12, Stadion města Plzně, Plzen
FC Viktoria Plzeň 4-0 Hapoel Tel-Aviv FC
Goals: 1-0 Kolář 23, 2-0 Štípek 39, 3-0 Kolář 76, 4-0 Bakoš 84

22/11/12, Cidade de Coimbra, Coimbra
A. Académica de Coimbra 1-1 FC Viktoria Plzeň
Goals: 0-1 Horváth 57(p), 1-1 Edinho 88(p)

22/11/12, Estadio Vicente Calderón, Madrid
Club Atlético de Madrid 1-0 Hapoel Tel-Aviv FC
Goal: 1-0 Raúl García 7

06/12/12, Stadion města Plzně, Plzen
FC Viktoria Plzeň 1-0 Club Atlético de Madrid
Goal: 1-0 Procházka 26

06/12/12, Itztadion Bloomfield, Tel-Aviv
Hapoel Tel-Aviv FC 2-0 A. Académica de Coimbra
Goals: 1-0 Mare 56, 2-0 Maman 80

		Pld	Home W D L F A	Away W D L F A	Total W D L F A	Pts
1	FC Viktoria Plzeň	6	3 0 0 8 1	1 1 1 3 3	4 1 1 11 4	13
2	Club Atlético de Madrid	6	3 0 0 4 1	1 0 2 3 3	4 0 2 7 4	12
3	A. Académica de Coimbra	6	1 2 0 4 2	0 0 3 2 7	1 2 3 6 9	5
4	Hapoel Tel-Aviv FC	6	1 0 2 3 5	0 1 2 1 6	1 1 4 4 11	4

Group C

20/09/12, GSP Stadium, Nicosia
AEL Limassol FC 0-0 VfL Borussia Mönchengladbach

20/09/12, Şükrü Saracoğlu, Istanbul
Fenerbahçe SK 2-2 Olympique de Marseille
Goals: 1-0 Caner Erkin 28, 2-0 Alex 57, 2-1 Valbuena 83, 2-2 A Ayew 90+4

04/10/12, Stade Vélodrome, Marseille
Olympique de Marseille 5-1 AEL Limassol FC
Goals: 0-1 Ouon 22, 1-1 Fanni 42, 2-1 Lucas Mendes 61, 3-1 Rémy 76, 4-1 Gignac 90, 5-1 Rémy 90+3

04/10/12, Borussia-Park, Monchengladbach
VfL Borussia Mönchengladbach 2-4 Fenerbahçe SK
Goals: 1-0 De Jong 18, 1-1 Cristian 25, 1-2 Raul Meireles 40, 1-3 Kuyt 71, 2-3 De Camargo 74, 2-4 Cristian 87

25/10/12, Borussia-Park, Monchengladbach
VfL Borussia Mönchengladbach 2-0 Olympique de Marseille
Goals: 1-0 Daems 33(p), 2-0 Mlapa 67

25/10/12, GSP Stadium, Nicosia
AEL Limassol FC 0-1 Fenerbahçe SK
Goal: 0-1 Egemen Korkmaz 72

08/11/12, Stade Vélodrome, Marseille
Olympique de Marseille 2-2 VfL Borussia Mönchengladbach
Goals: 0-1 Hanke 20, 1-1 Barton 54, 2-1 J Ayew 67, 2-2 Arango 90+3

08/11/12, Şükrü Saracoğlu, Istanbul
Fenerbahçe SK 2-0 AEL Limassol FC
Goals: 1-0 Kuyt 11, 2-0 Sow 41

22/11/12, Borussia-Park, Monchengladbach
VfL Borussia Mönchengladbach 2-0 AEL Limassol FC
Goals: 1-0 De Camargo 79, 2-0 De Camargo 90+1

22/11/12, Stade Vélodrome, Marseille
Olympique de Marseille 0-1 Fenerbahçe SK
Goal: 0-1 Bekir İrtegün 39

06/12/12, GSP Stadium, Nicosia
AEL Limassol FC 0-3 Olympique de Marseille
Goals: 1-0 Orlando Sá 41, 2-0 Edmar 79, 3-0 Dickson 82

06/12/12, Şükrü Saracoğlu, Istanbul
Fenerbahçe SK 0-3 VfL Borussia Mönchengladbach
Goals: 0-1 Ciğerci 23, 0-2 Hanke 28(p), 0-3 De Jong 79

			Home					Away					Total					
		Pld	W	D	L	F	A	W	D	L	F	A	W	D	L	F	A	Pts
1	Fenerbahçe SK	6	1	1	1	4	5	3	0	0	6	2	4	1	1	10	7	13
2	VfL Borussia Mönchengladbach	6	2	0	1	6	4	1	2	0	5	2	3	2	1	11	6	11
3	Olympique de Marseille	6	1	1	1	7	4	0	1	2	2	7	1	2	3	9	11	5
4	AEL Limassol FC	6	1	1	1	3	1	0	0	3	1	9	1	1	4	4	10	4

Group D

20/09/12, Dos Barreiros, Funchal
CS Marítimo 0-0 Newcastle United FC

20/09/12, Stade Chaban-Delmas, Bordeaux
FC Girondins de Bordeaux 4-0 Club Brugge KV
Goals: 1-0 Sané 13, 2-0 Gouffran 27, 3-0 Engels 47(og), 4-0 Jussiê 66

04/10/12, St James' Park, Newcastle
Newcastle United FC 3-0 FC Girondins de Bordeaux
Goals: 1-0 Shola Ameobi 16, 2-0 Henrique 40(og), 3-0 Cissé 49

04/10/12, Jan Breydelstadion, Bruges
Club Brugge KV 2-0 CS Marítimo
Goals: 1-0 Bacca 57, 2-0 Vleminckx 71

25/10/12, St James' Park, Newcastle
Newcastle United FC 1-0 Club Brugge KV
Goal: 1-0 Obertan 48

25/10/12, Dos Barreiros, Funchal
CS Marítimo 1-1 FC Girondins de Bordeaux
Goals: 0-1 Gouffran 30, 1-1 Roberge 36

08/11/12, Jan Breydelstadion, Bruges
Club Brugge KV 2-2 Newcastle United FC
Goals: 1-0 Trickovski 14, 2-0 Jørgensen 19, 2-1 Anita 41, 2-2 Shola Ameobi 43

08/11/12, Stade Chaban-Delmas, Bordeaux
FC Girondins de Bordeaux 1-0 CS Marítimo
Goal: 1-0 Bellion 16

22/11/12, St James' Park, Newcastle
Newcastle United FC 1-1 CS Marítimo
Goals: 1-0 Marveaux 23, 1-1 Fidélis 79

22/11/12, Jan Breydelstadion, Bruges
Club Brugge KV 1-2 FC Girondins de Bordeaux
Goals: 0-1 Jussiê 3, 0-2 Jussiê 40, 1-2 Lestienne 86

06/12/12, Dos Barreiros, Funchal
CS Marítimo 2-1 Club Brugge KV
Goals: 1-0 Gonçalo Abreu 18, 1-1 Refaelov 85(p), 2-1 Héldon 87

06/12/12, Stade Chaban-Delmas, Bordeaux
FC Girondins de Bordeaux 2-0 Newcastle United FC
Goals: 1-0 Diabaté 29, 2-0 Diabaté 73

			Home					Away					Total					
		Pld	W	D	L	F	A	W	D	L	F	A	W	D	L	F	A	Pts
1	FC Girondins de Bordeaux	6	3	0	0	7	0	1	1	1	3	5	4	1	1	10	5	13
2	Newcastle United FC	6	2	1	0	5	1	0	2	1	2	4	2	3	1	7	5	9
3	CS Marítimo	6	1	2	0	3	2	0	1	2	1	4	1	3	2	4	6	6
4	Club Brugge KV	6	1	1	1	5	4	0	0	3	1	7	1	1	4	6	11	4

Marseille's Rafidina Abdullah (left) contests an aerial challenge with AEL's Paulo Sérgio

UEFA Europa League

Group E

20/09/12, VfB Arena, Stuttgart
VfB Stuttgart 2-2 FC Steaua Bucureşti
Goals: 1-0 Ibišević 5, 1-1 Chipciu 6, 1-2 Rusescu 80(p),
2-2 Niedermeier 85

20/09/12, Parken, Copenhagen
FC København 2-1 Molde FK
Goals: 1-0 Claudemir 20, 1-1 Diouf 45+1, 2-1 Cornelius 74

04/10/12, Molde Stadion, Molde
Molde FK 2-0 VfB Stuttgart
Goals: 1-0 Berget 58, 2-0 Chima 88

04/10/12, National Arena, Bucharest
FC Steaua Bucureşti 1-0 FC København
Goal: 1-0 Sigurdsson 83(og)

25/10/12, VfB Arena, Stuttgart
VfB Stuttgart 0-0 FC København

25/10/12, National Arena, Bucharest
FC Steaua Bucureşti 2-0 Molde FK
Goals: 1-0 Chiricheş 30, 2-0 Rusescu 32

08/11/12, Molde Stadion, Molde
Molde FK 1-2 FC Steaua Bucureşti
Goals: 0-1 Chipciu 21, 0-2 Latovlevici 37, 1-2 Chima 56

08/11/12, Parken, Copenhagen
FC København 0-2 VfB Stuttgart
Goals: 0-1 Ibišević 76, 0-2 Harnik 90+2

22/11/12, Molde Stadion, Molde
Molde FK 1-2 FC København
Goals: 0-1 César Santin 21(p), 1-1 Chima 62, 1-2 Gíslason 76

22/11/12, National Arena, Bucharest
FC Steaua Bucureşti 1-5 VfB Stuttgart
Goals: 0-1 Taşçı 5, 0-2 Harnik 18, 0-3 Sakai 23, 0-4 Okazaki 31,
0-5 Okazaki 55, 1-5 M Costea 83

06/12/12, VfB Arena, Stuttgart
VfB Stuttgart 0-1 Molde FK
Goal: 0-1 Angan 45+1

06/12/12, Parken, Copenhagen
FC København 1-1 FC Steaua Bucureşti
Goals: 0-1 Rusescu 72, 1-1 Vetokele 87

		Pld	Home W D L F A	Away W D L F A	Total W D L F A	Pts
1	FC Steaua Bucureşti	6	2 0 1 4 5	1 2 0 5 4	3 2 1 9 9	11
2	VfB Stuttgart	6	0 2 1 2 3	2 0 1 7 3	2 2 2 9 6	8
3	FC København	6	1 1 1 3 4	1 1 1 2 2	2 2 2 5 6	8
4	Molde FK	6	1 0 2 4 4	1 0 2 2 4	2 0 4 6 8	6

Group F

20/09/12, Stadio San Paolo, Naples
SSC Napoli 4-0 AIK
Goals: 1-0 Vargas 6, 2-0 Vargas 46, 3-0 Vargas 69,
4-0 Dzemaili 90+1

20/09/12, Dnipro Arena, Dnipropetrovsk
FC Dnipro Dnipropetrovsk 2-0 PSV Eindhoven
Goals: 1-0 Matheus 50, 2-0 Hutchinson 58(og)

04/10/12, Råsundastadion, Solna
AIK 2-3 FC Dnipro Dnipropetrovsk
Goals: 1-0 Danielsson 5, 1-1 Kalinić 41, 2-1 Goitom 45+1,
2-2 Mandzyuk 74, 2-3 Seleznyov 83

04/10/12, PSV Stadion, Eindhoven
PSV Eindhoven 3-0 SSC Napoli
Goals: 1-0 Lens 19, 2-0 Mertens 41, 3-0 Marcelo 52

25/10/12, PSV Stadion, Eindhoven
PSV Eindhoven 1-1 AIK
Goals: 0-1 Karikari 61, 1-1 Lens 80

25/10/12, Dnipro Arena, Dnipropetrovsk
FC Dnipro Dnipropetrovsk 3-1 SSC Napoli
Goals: 1-0 Fedetskiy 2, 2-0 Matheus 42, 3-0 Giuliano 64,
3-1 Cavani 75(p)

08/11/12, Råsundastadion, Solna
AIK 1-0 PSV Eindhoven
Goal: 1-0 Bangura 12

08/11/12, Stadio San Paolo, Naples
SSC Napoli 4-2 FC Dnipro Dnipropetrovsk
Goals: 1-0 Cavani 7, 1-1 Fedetskiy 34, 1-2 Zozulya 52,
2-2 Cavani 77, 3-2 Cavani 88, 4-2 Cavani 90+3

22/11/12, PSV Stadion, Eindhoven
PSV Eindhoven 1-2 FC Dnipro Dnipropetrovsk
Goals: 1-0 Wijnaldum 18, 1-1 Seleznyov 24, 1-2 Konoplyanka 74

22/11/12, Råsundastadion, Solna
AIK 1-2 SSC Napoli
Goals: 0-1 Dzemaili 20, 1-1 Daníelsson 35, 1-2 Cavani 90+3(p)

06/12/12, Stadio San Paolo, Naples
SSC Napoli 1-3 PSV Eindhoven
Goals: 1-0 Cavani 18, 1-1 Matavž 30, 1-2 Matavž 41, 1-3 Matavž 60

Dries Mertens puts PSV 2-0 up against Napoli in Eindhoven

06/12/12, Dnipro Arena, Dnipropetrovsk
FC Dnipro Dnipropetrovsk 4-0 AIK
Goals: 1-0 Kalinić 20(p), 2-0 Zozulya 39, 3-0 Zozulya 52,
4-0 Kravchenko 86

		Pld	| Home W D L F A	Away W D L F A	Total W D L F A	Pts
1	FC Dnipro Dnipropetrovsk	6	3 0 0 9 1	2 0 1 7 7	5 0 1 16 8	15
2	SSC Napoli	6	2 0 1 9 5	1 0 2 3 7	3 0 3 12 12	9
3	PSV Eindhoven	6	1 1 1 5 3	1 0 2 3 4	2 1 3 8 7	7
4	AIK	6	1 0 2 4 5	0 1 2 1 9	1 1 4 5 14	4

Group G

20/09/12, José Alvalade, Lisbon
Sporting Clube de Portugal 0-0 FC Basel 1893

20/09/12, KRC Genk Arena, Genk
KRC Genk 3-0 Videoton FC
Goals: 1-0 Vossen 22, 2-0 Buffel 78, 3-0 De Ceulaer 90+2

04/10/12, St Jakob-Park, Basel
FC Basel 1893 2-2 KRC Genk
Goals: 0-1 De Ceulaer 10, 0-2 Vossen 38, 1-2 Streller 70(p), 2-2 Streller 85

04/10/12, Sóstói, Szekesfehervar
Videoton FC 3-0 Sporting Clube de Portugal
Goals: 1-0 Paulo Vinícius 15, 2-0 Filipe Oliveira 21, 3-0 N Nikolić 35

25/10/12, Sóstói, Szekesfehervar
Videoton FC 2-1 FC Basel 1893
Goals: 1-0 Schär 2(og), 2-0 Marco Caneira 33, 2-1 Schär 90+1

25/10/12, KRC Genk Arena, Genk
KRC Genk 2-1 Sporting Clube de Portugal
Goals: 0-1 Hamalainen 7(og), 1-1 De Ceulaer 25, 2-1 Barda 88

08/11/12, José Alvalade, Lisbon
Sporting Clube de Portugal 1-1 KRC Genk
Goals: 1-0 Van Woltswinkel 64, 1-1 Plet 90+1

08/11/12, St Jakob-Park, Basel
FC Basel 1893 1-0 Videoton FC
Goal: 1-0 Streller 80

22/11/12, Sóstói, Szekesfehervar
Videoton FC 0-1 KRC Genk
Goal: 0-1 Barda 19

22/11/12, St Jakob-Park, Basel
FC Basel 1893 3-0 Sporting Clube de Portugal
Goals: 1-0 Schär 23, 2-0 Stocker 66, 3-0 D Degen 71

06/12/12, KRC Genk Arena, Genk
KRC Genk 0-0 FC Basel 1893

07/12/12, José Alvalade, Lisbon
Sporting Clube de Portugal 2-1 Videoton FC
Goals: 1-0 Labyad 65, 1-1 Sándor 80(p), 2-1 Viola 82

		Pld	| Home W D L F A	Away W D L F A	Total W D L F A	Pts
1	KRC Genk	6	2 1 0 5 1	1 2 0 4 3	3 3 0 9 4	12
2	FC Basel 1893	6	2 1 0 6 2	0 2 1 1 2	2 3 1 7 4	9
3	Videoton FC	6	2 0 1 5 2	0 0 3 1 6	2 0 4 6 8	6
4	Sporting Clube de Portugal	6	1 2 0 3 2	0 0 3 1 8	1 2 3 4 10	5

Group H

20/09/12, Stadio Giuseppe Meazza, Milan
FC Internazionale Milano 2-2 FC Rubin Kazan
Goals: 0-1 Ryazantsev 17, 1-1 Livaja 39, 1-2 Rondón 84, 2-2 Nagatomo 90+2

20/09/12, FK Partizan, Belgrade
FK Partizan 0-0 Neftçi PFK

04/10/12, Centralniy Stadion, Kazan
FC Rubin Kazan 2-0 FK Partizan
Goals: 1-0 Gökdeniz Karadeniz 45, 2-0 Ryazantsev 48

04/10/12, Tofiq Bähramov Republican stadium, Baku
Neftçi PFK 1-3 FC Internazionale Milano
Goals: 0-1 Coutinho 10, 0-2 Obi 30, 0-3 Livaja 42, 1-3 Canales 53

25/10/12, Stadio Giuseppe Meazza, Milan
FC Internazionale Milano 1-0 FK Partizan
Goal: 1-0 Palacio 88

25/10/12, Centralniy Stadion, Kazan
FC Rubin Kazan 1-0 Neftçi PFK
Goal: 1-0 Kasaev 16

08/11/12, Tofiq Bähramov Republican stadium, Baku
Neftçi PFK 0-1 FC Rubin Kazan
Goal: 0-1 Dyadyun 16

08/11/12, FK Partizan, Belgrade
FK Partizan 1-3 FC Internazionale Milano
Goals: 0-1 Palacio 51, 0-2 Palacio 75, 0-3 Guarín 87, 1-3 Tomić 90+1

22/11/12, Centralniy Stadion, Kazan
FC Rubin Kazan 3-0 FC Internazionale Milano
Goals: 1-0 Gökdeniz Karadeniz 1, 2-0 Rondón 65, 3-0 Rondón 90+2

22/11/12, Tofiq Bähramov Republican stadium, Baku
Neftçi PFK 1-1 FK Partizan
Goals: 1-0 Flavinho 10, 1-1 Mitrović 67

06/12/12, Stadio Giuseppe Meazza, Milan
FC Internazionale Milano 2-2 Neftçi PFK
Goals: 1-0 Livaja 9, 1-1 Sadiqov 52, 2-1 Livaja 54, 2-2 Canales 89

06/12/12, FK Partizan, Belgrade
FK Partizan 1-1 FC Rubin Kazan
Goals: 1-0 S Marković 53, 1-1 Rondón 59

		Pld	| Home W D L F A	Away W D L F A	Total W D L F A	Pts
1	FC Rubin Kazan	6	3 0 0 6 0	1 2 0 4 3	4 2 0 10 3	14
2	FC Internazionale Milano	6	1 2 0 5 4	2 0 1 6 5	3 2 1 11 9	11
3	FK Partizan	6	0 2 1 2 4	0 1 2 1 4	0 3 3 3 8	3
4	Neftçi PFK	6	0 1 2 2 5	0 2 1 2 3	0 3 3 4 8	3

Group I

20/09/12, Stade de Gerland, Lyon
Olympique Lyonnais 2-1 AC Sparta Praha
Goals: 1-0 Gomis 59, 2-0 Lisandro 62, 2-1 Krejčí 77

20/09/12, Estadio de San Mamés, Bilbao
Athletic Club 1-1 Hapoel Kiryat Shmona FC
Goals: 0-1 Rochet 14, 1-1 Susaeta 40

04/10/12, Itztadion Kiryat Eliezer, Haifa
Hapoel Kiryat Shmona FC 3-4 Olympique Lyonnais
Goals: 1-0 Abuhazira 7, 1-1 Fofana 17, 1-2 Monzón 22,
1-3 Réveillère 31, 2-3 Levi 51, 3-3 Abuhazira 66(p), 3-4 Fofana 90+2

04/10/12, Stadion Letná, Prague
AC Sparta Praha 3-1 Athletic Club
Goals: 1-0 Zápotočný 25, 2-0 Balaj 40, 3-0 Hušbauer 56(p),
3-1 De Marcos 73

25/10/12, Stadion Letná, Prague
AC Sparta Praha 3-1 Hapoel Kiryat Shmona FC
Goals: 1-0 Krejčí 7, 2-0 Kadlec 10, 3-0 Švejdík 44, 3-1 Abuhazira 76

25/10/12, Stade de Gerland, Lyon
Olympique Lyonnais 2-1 Athletic Club
Goals: 1-0 Lisandro 54, 1-1 Ibai Gómez 79, 2-1 Briand 86

08/11/12, Estadio de San Mamés, Bilbao
Athletic Club 2-3 Olympique Lyonnais
Goals: 0-1 Gomis 22, 0-2 Gourcuff 45+1, 1-2 Ander Herrera 48,
2-2 Aduriz 55(p), 2-3 Lacazette 63

08/11/12, Itztadion Kiryat Eliezer, Haifa
Hapoel Kiryat Shmona FC 1-1 AC Sparta Praha
Goals: 1-0 Tasevski 3, 1-1 Kweuke 24

22/11/12, Stadion Letná, Prague
AC Sparta Praha 1-1 Olympique Lyonnais
Goals: 0-1 Benzia 46, 1-1 Hušbauer 53

28/11/12, Itztadion Kiryat Eliezer, Haifa
Hapoel Kiryat Shmona FC 0-2 Athletic Club
Goals: 0-1 Llorente 34, 0-2 Toquero 76

06/12/12, Stade de Gerland, Lyon
Olympique Lyonnais 2-0 Hapoel Kiryat Shmona FC
Goals: 1-0 Sarr 15, 2-0 Benzia 58

06/12/12, Estadio de San Mamés, Bilbao
Athletic Club 0-0 AC Sparta Praha

			Home					Away					Total				
		Pld	W	D	L	F	A	W	D	L	F	A	W	D	L	F	A	Pts
1	Olympique Lyonnais	6	3	0	0	6	2	2	1	0	8	6	5	1	0	14	8	16
2	AC Sparta Praha	6	2	1	0	7	3	0	2	1	2	3	2	3	1	9	6	9
3	Athletic Club	6	0	2	1	3	4	1	0	2	4	5	1	2	3	7	9	5
4	Hapoel Kiryat Shmona FC	6	0	1	2	4	7	0	1	2	2	6	0	2	4	6	13	2

Group J

20/09/12, White Hart Lane, London
Tottenham Hotspur FC 0-0 S.S. Lazio

20/09/12, Stadion Ljudski vrt, Maribor
NK Maribor 3-0 Panathinaikos FC
Goals: 1-0 Berič 25, 2-0 Ibraimi 62, 3-0 Marcos Tavares 88(p)

04/10/12, Stadio Olimpico, Rome
S.S. Lazio 1-0 NK Maribor
Goal: 1-0 Ederson 62

04/10/12, OAKA Spiros Louis, Athens
Panathinaikos FC 1-1 Tottenham Hotspur FC
Goals: 0-1 Dawson 35, 1-1 Toché 77

25/10/12, Stadion Ljudski vrt, Maribor
NK Maribor 1-1 Tottenham Hotspur FC
Goals: 1-0 Berič 42, 1-1 Sigurdsson 58

25/10/12, OAKA Spiros Louis, Athens
Panathinaikos FC 1-1 S.S. Lazio
Goals: 0-1 Seitaridis 25(og), 1-1 Toché 90+1

08/11/12, White Hart Lane, London
Tottenham Hotspur FC 3-1 NK Maribor
Goals: 1-0 Defoe 22, 1-1 Berič 40, 2-1 Defoe 49, 3-1 Defoe 77

08/11/12, Stadio Olimpico, Rome
S.S. Lazio 3-0 Panathinaikos FC
Goals: 1-0 Kozák 23, 2-0 Kozák 40, 3-0 Floccari 59

22/11/12, Stadio Olimpico, Rome
S.S. Lazio 0-0 Tottenham Hotspur FC

22/11/12, OAKA Spiros Louis, Athens
Panathinaikos FC 1-0 NK Maribor
Goal: 1-0 Vitolo 67(p)

06/12/12, White Hart Lane, London
Tottenham Hotspur FC 3-1 Panathinaikos FC
Goals: 1-0 Adebayor 28, 1-1 Zeca 54, 2-1 Karnezis 76(og),
3-1 Defoe 82

06/12/12, Stadion Ljudski vrt, Maribor
NK Maribor 1-4 S.S. Lazio
Goals: 0-1 Kozák 16, 0-2 Radu 32, 0-3 Floccari 38, 0-4 Floccari 51,
1-4 Marcos Tavares 84

			Home					Away					Total				
		Pld	W	D	L	F	A	W	D	L	F	A	W	D	L	F	A	Pts
1	S.S. Lazio	6	2	1	0	4	0	1	2	0	5	2	3	3	0	9	2	12
2	Tottenham Hotspur FC	6	2	1	0	6	2	0	3	0	2	2	2	4	0	8	4	10
3	Panathinaikos FC	6	1	2	0	3	2	0	0	3	1	9	1	2	3	4	11	5
4	NK Maribor	6	1	1	1	5	5	0	0	3	1	5	1	1	4	6	10	4

Group K

20/09/12, Ernst-Happel-Stadion, Vienna
SK Rapid Wien 1-2 Rosenborg BK
Goals: 0-1 Elyounoussi 18, 0-2 Dorsin 60, 1-2 Katzer 66

20/09/12, BayArena, Leverkusen
Bayer 04 Leverkusen 0-0 FC Metalist Kharkiv

04/10/12, Lerkendal Stadion, Trondheim
Rosenborg BK 0-1 Bayer 04 Leverkusen
Goal: 0-1 Kiessling 76

04/10/12, Metalist Stadium, Kharkiv
FC Metalist Kharkiv 2-0 SK Rapid Wien
Goals: 1-0 Edmar 66, 2-0 Cleiton Xavier 80

25/10/12, Lerkendal Stadion, Trondheim
Rosenborg BK 1-2 FC Metalist Kharkiv
Goals: 1-0 Elyounoussi 46, 1-1 Marlos 81, 1-2 Cleiton Xavier 89

25/10/12, Ernst-Happel-Stadion, Vienna
SK Rapid Wien 0-4 Bayer 04 Leverkusen
Goals: 0-1 Wollscheid 37, 0-2 Castro 56, 0-3 Bellarabi 59,
0-4 Castro 90+2

08/11/12, BayArena, Leverkusen
Bayer 04 Leverkusen 3-0 SK Rapid Wien
Goals: 1-0 Hegeler 4, 2-0 Schürrle 53, 3-0 Friedrich 66

08/11/12, Metalist Stadium, Kharkiv
FC Metalist Kharkiv 3-1 Rosenborg BK
Goals: 1-0 Taison 4, 1-1 Dočkal 42, 2-1 Cleiton Xavier 70,
3-1 Torres 90+3

Cleiton Xavier savours scoring for Metalist at home to Rosenborg

22/11/12, Lerkendal Stadion, Trondheim
Rosenborg BK 3-2 SK Rapid Wien
Goals: 1-0 Chibuike 28, 1-1 Drahannuel 73, 1-2 Eyjólfsson 75, 2-2 Eljyburhoussi 70, 3-2 Prica 79

22/11/12, Metalist Stadium, Kharkiv
FC Metalist Kharkiv 2-0 Bayer 04 Leverkusen
Goals: 1-0 Cristaldo 46, 2-0 Cleiton Xavier 85

06/12/12, Ernst-Happel-Stadion, Vienna
SK Rapid Wien 1-0 FC Metalist Kharkiv
Goal: 1-0 Alar 13

06/12/12, BayArena, Leverkusen
Bayer 04 Leverkusen 1-0 Rosenborg BK
Goal: 1-0 Riedel 65

			Home					Away					Total					
		Pld	W	D	L	F	A	W	D	L	F	A	W	D	L	F	A	Pts
1	FC Metalist Kharkiv	6	3	0	0	7	1	1	1	1	2	2	4	1	1	9	3	13
2	Bayer 04 Leverkusen	6	2	1	0	4	0	2	0	1	5	2	4	1	1	9	2	13
3	Rosenborg BK	6	1	0	2	4	5	1	0	2	3	5	2	0	4	7	10	6
4	SK Rapid Wien	6	1	0	2	2	6	0	0	3	2	8	1	0	5	4	14	3

Group L

20/09/12, Estadi Ciutat de València, Valencia
Levante UD 1-0 Helsingborgs IF
Goal: 1-0 Juanfran 40

20/09/12, FC Twente Stadion, Enschede
FC Twente 2-2 Hannover 96
Goals: 1-0 Janssen 7, 2-0 Chadli 54, 2-1 Sobiech 67, 2-2 Wisgerhof 73(og)

04/10/12, Hannover Arena, Hannover
Hannover 96 2-1 Levante UD
Goals: 0-1 Míchel 10(p), 1-1 Huszti 21(p), 2-1 Ya Konan 49

04/10/12, Olympia, Helsingborg
Helsingborgs IF 2-2 FC Twente
Goals: 1-0 Djurdjić 7, 2-0 Djurdjić 43, 2-1 Bengtsson 74, 2-2 Douglas 88

25/10/12, Olympia, Helsingborg
Helsingborgs IF 1-2 Hannover 96
Goals: 0-1 Diouf 12, 1-1 Álvaro 90+1, 1-2 Ya Konan 90+3

25/10/12, Estadi Ciutat de València, Valencia
Levante UD 3-0 FC Twente
Goals: 1-0 Míchel 59(p), 2-0 Pedro Ríos 78, 3-0 Pedro Ríos 88

08/11/12, Hannover Arena, Hannover
Hannover 96 3-2 Helsingborgs IF
Goals: 1-0 Diouf 3, 2-0 Diouf 50, 2-1 Djurdjić 59, 2-2 Bedoya 67, 3-2 Huszti 90+1(p)

08/11/12, FC Twente Stadion, Enschede
FC Twente 0-0 Levante UD

22/11/12, Olympia, Helsingborg
Helsingborgs IF 1-3 Levante UD
Goals: 0-1 Ángel 8, 0-2 Diop 37, 0-3 Iborra 81, 1-3 Sørum 89

22/11/12, Hannover Arena, Hannover
Hannover 96 0-0 FC Twente

06/12/12, Estadi Ciutat de València, Valencia
Levante UD 2-2 Hannover 96
Goals: 0-1 Stindl 18, 0-2 Ya Konan 26, 1-2 Ángel 49, 2-2 Iborra 90+4

06/12/12, FC Twente Stadion, Enschede
FC Twente 1-3 Helsingborgs IF
Goals: 0-1 Djurdjić 6, 0-2 Bedoya 21, 0-3 Sørum 67, 1-3 Tadić 74

			Home					Away					Total					
		Pld	W	D	L	F	A	W	D	L	F	A	W	D	L	F	A	Pts
1	Hannover 96	6	2	1	0	5	3	1	2	0	6	5	3	3	0	11	8	12
2	Levante UD	6	2	1	0	6	2	1	1	1	4	3	3	2	1	10	5	11
3	Helsingborgs IF	6	0	1	2	4	7	1	0	2	5	5	1	1	4	9	12	4
4	FC Twente	6	0	2	1	3	5	0	2	1	2	5	0	4	2	5	10	4

Round of 32

14/02/13, Estadi Ciutat de València, Valencia (att: 12,850)
Levante UD 3-0 Olympiacos FC
Goals: 1-0 Pedro Ríos 10, 2-0 Barkero 40(p), 3-0 Martins 56
Referee: Gräfe (GER)
21/02/13, Georgios Karaiskakis Stadium, Piraeus (att: 29,174)
Olympiacos FC 0-1 Levante UD
Goal: 0-1 Martins 9
Referee: Jug (SVN)
Aggregate: 0-4; Levante UD qualify.

14/02/13, BayArena, Leverkusen (att: 25,375)
Bayer 04 Leverkusen 0-1 SL Benfica
Goal: 0-1 Cardozo 61
Referee: Mateu Lahoz (ESP)
21/02/13, Estádio do Sport Lisboa e Benfica, Lisbon (att: 37,357)
SL Benfica 2-1 Bayer 04 Leverkusen
Goals: 1-0 John 60, 1-1 Schürrle 75, 2-1 Matić 77
Referee: Kralovec (CZE)
Aggregate: 3-1; SL Benfica qualify.

UEFA Europa League

14/02/13, Amsterdam ArenA, Amsterdam (att: 51,493)
AFC Ajax 2-0 FC Steaua Bucureşti
Goals: 1-0 Alderweireld 28, 2-0 Van Rhijn 48
Referee: Todorov (BUL)
21/02/13, National Arena, Bucharest (att: 35,423)
FC Steaua Bucureşti 2-0 AFC Ajax (aet)
Goals: 1-0 Latovlevici 38, 2-0 Chiricheş 76
Referee: Tagliavento (ITA)
Aggregate: 2-2; FC Steaua Bucureşti qualify 4-2 on penalties.

14/02/13, Stadion Letná, Prague (att: 18,952)
AC Sparta Praha 0-1 Chelsea FC
Goal: 0-1 Oscar 82
Referee: Orsato (ITA)
21/02/13, Stamford Bridge, London (att: 38,642)
Chelsea FC 1-1 AC Sparta Praha
Goals: 0-1 Lafata 17, 1-1 Hazard 90+2
Referee: Stavrev (MKD)
Aggregate: 2-1; Chelsea FC qualify.

14/02/13, Stadio San Paolo, Naples (att: 13,606)
SSC Napoli 0-3 FC Viktoria Plzeň
Goals: 0-1 Darida 28, 0-2 Rajtoral 79, 0-3 Tecl 90
Referee: Van Boekel (NED)
21/02/13, Stadion města Plzně, Plzen (att: 11,607)
FC Viktoria Plzeň 2-0 SSC Napoli
Goals: 1-0 Kovařík 51, 2-0 Tecl 74
Referee: Kassai (HUN)
Aggregate: 5-0; FC Viktoria Plzeň qualify.

14/02/13, NSK Olimpiyskyi, Kyiv (att: 24,953)
FC Dynamo Kyiv 1-1 FC Girondins de Bordeaux
Goals: 1-0 Haruna 20, 1-1 Obraniak 23
Referee: Tudor (ROU)
21/02/13, Stade Chaban-Delmas, Bordeaux (att: 11,889)
FC Girondins de Bordeaux 1-0 FC Dynamo Kyiv
Goal: 1-0 Diabaté 41
Referee: Bebek (CRO)
Aggregate: 2-1; FC Girondins de Bordeaux qualify.

14/02/13, St James' Park, Newcastle (att: 30,157)
Newcastle United FC 0-0 FC Metalist Kharkiv
Referee: Hagen (NOR)
21/02/13, Metalist Stadium, Kharkiv (att: 39,973)
FC Metalist Kharkiv 0-1 Newcastle United FC
Goal: 0-1 Shola Ameobi 64(p)
Referee: Gumienny (BEL)
Aggregate: 0-1; Newcastle United FC qualify.

14/02/13, White Hart Lane, London (att: 31,762)
Tottenham Hotspur FC 2-1 Olympique Lyonnais
Goals: 1-0 Bale 45, 1-1 Umtiti 55, 2-1 Bale 90+3
Referee: Proença (POR)

Rodrigo Palacio registered a double for Inter at home to CFR Cluj

21/02/13, Stade de Gerland, Lyon (att: 38,761)
Olympique Lyonnais 1-1 Tottenham Hotspur FC
Goals: 1-0 Gonalons 17, 1-1 Dembélé 90
Referee: Stark (GER)
Aggregate: 2-3; Tottenham Hotspur FC qualify.

14/02/13, Neman, Grodno (att: 8,021)
FC BATE Borisov 0-0 Fenerbahçe SK
Referee: Kelly (IRL)
21/02/13, Şükrü Saracoğlu, Istanbul (att: 150)
Fenerbahçe SK 1-0 FC BATE Borisov
Goal: 1-0 Cristian 45+1(p)
Referee: Gautier (FRA)
Aggregate: 1-0; Fenerbahçe SK qualify.

14/02/13, Stadion Petrovski, St Petersburg (att: 19,748)
FC Zenit St Petersburg 2-0 Liverpool FC
Goals: 1-0 Hulk 69, 2-0 Semak 72
Referee: Velasco Carballo (ESP)
21/02/13, Anfield, Liverpool (att: 42,735)
Liverpool FC 3-1 FC Zenit St Petersburg
Goals: 0-1 Hulk 19, 1-1 Suárez 28, 2-1 Allen 43, 3-1 Suárez 59
Referee: Kuipers (NED)
Aggregate: 3-3; FC Zenit St Petersburg qualify on away goal.

14/02/13, Stadion Luzhniki, Moscow (att: 6,676)
FC Anji Makhachkala 3-1 Hannover 96
Goals: 0-1 Huszti 22, 1-1 Eto'o 34, 2-1 Ahmedov 48, 3-1 Boussoufa 64
Referee: Strahonja (CRO)
21/02/13, Hannover Arena, Hannover (att: 27,500)
Hannover 96 1-1 FC Anji Makhachkala
Goals: 1-0 Pinto 70, 1-1 Traoré 90+9
Referee: Eriksson (SWE)
Aggregate: 2-4; FC Anji Makhachkala qualify.

14/02/13, Stadio Giuseppe Meazza, Milan (att: 14,790)
FC Internazionale Milano 2-0 CFR 1907 Cluj
Goals: 1-0 Palacio 20, 2-0 Palacio 87
Referee: Koukoulakis (GRE)
21/02/13, Stadionul Dr. Constantin Rădulescu, Cluj-Napoca (att: 11,027)
CFR 1907 Cluj 0-3 FC Internazionale Milano
Goals: 0-1 Guarín 22, 0-2 Guarín 45+2, 0-3 Benassi 89
Referee: Gil (POL)
Aggregate: 0-5; FC Internazionale Milano qualify.

14/02/13, VfB Arena, Stuttgart (att: 15,200)
VfB Stuttgart 1-1 KRC Genk
Goals: 1-0 Gentner 42, 1-1 Plet 90+1
Referee: Neves Moreira De Sousa (POR)
21/02/13, KRC Genk Arena, Genk (att: 16,796)
KRC Genk 0-2 VfB Stuttgart
Goals: 0-1 Boka 45, 0-2 Gentner 59
Referee: Yefet (ISR)
Aggregate: 1-3; VfB Stuttgart qualify.

14/02/13, Estadio Vicente Calderón, Madrid (att: 21,334)
Club Atlético de Madrid 0-2 FC Rubin Kazan
Goals: 0-1 Gökdeniz Karadeniz 6, 0-2 Orbaiz 90+5
Referee: Vad (HUN)
21/02/13, Stadion Luzhniki, Moscow (att: 2,593)
FC Rubin Kazan 0-1 Club Atlético de Madrid
Goal: 0-1 Falcao 84
Referee: Hategan (ROU)
Aggregate: 2-1; FC Rubin Kazan qualify.

14/02/13, St Jakob-Park, Basel (att: 8,314)
FC Basel 1893 2-0 FC Dnipro Dnipropetrovsk
Goals: 1-0 Stocker 23, 2-0 Streller 67
Referee: Moen (NOR)
21/02/13, Dnipro Arena, Dnipropetrovsk (att: 26,501)
FC Dnipro Dnipropetrovsk 1-1 FC Basel 1893
Goals: 1-0 Seleznyov 76(p), 1-1 Schär 81(p)
Referee: Aytekin (GER)
Aggregate: 1-3; FC Basel 1893 quality.

14/02/13, Borussia-Park, Monchengladbach (att: 45,479)
VfL Borussia Mönchengladbach 3-3 S.S. Lazio
Goals: 1-0 Stranzl 17(p), 1-1 Floccari 57, 1-2 Kozák 64, 2-2 Marx 84(p), 3-2 Arango 88, 3-3 Kozák 90+4
Referee: Karasev (RUS)
21/02/13, Stadio Olimpico, Rome (att: 27,174)
S.S. Lazio 2-0 VfL Borussia Mönchengladbach
Goals: 1-0 Candreva 10, 2-0 González 33
Referee: Göçek (TUR)
Aggregate: 5-3; S.S. Lazio qualify.

Round of 16

07/03/13, Stadion města Plzně, Plzen (att: 11,701)
FÇ Viktoria Plzeň 0-1 Fenerbahçe SK
Goals: 0-1 Webó 81
Referee: Damato (ITA)
14/03/13, Şukru Saracoglu, Istanbul (att: 320)
Fenerbahçe SK 1-1 FC Viktoria Plzeň
Goals: 1-0 Galih Uçan 44, 1-1 Darida 61
Referee: Gräfe (GER)
Aggregate: 2-1; Fenerbahçe SK qualify.

07/03/13, VfB Arena, Stuttgart (att: 28,750)
VfB Stuttgart 0-2 S.S. Lazio
Goals: 0-1 Ederson 21, 0-2 Onazi 56
Referee: Tudor (ROU)
14/03/13, Stadio Olimpico, Rome (att: 120)
S.S. Lazio 3-1 VfB Stuttgart
Goals: 1-0 Kozák 6, 2-0 Kozák 8, 2-1 Hajnal 62, 3-1 Kozák 87
Referee: Hagen (NOR)
Aggregate: 5-1; S.S. Lazio qualify.

07/03/13, National Arena, Bucharest (att: 50,016)
FC Steaua Bucureşti 1-0 Chelsea FC
Goal: 1-0 Rusescu 34(p)
Referee: Karasev (RUS)
14/03/13, Stamford Bridge, London (att: 28,817)
Chelsea FC 3-1 FC Steaua Bucureşti
Goals: 1-0 Mata 34, 1-1 Chiricheş 45+1, 2-1 Terry 58, 3-1 Fernando Torres 71
Referee: Lannoy (FRA)
Aggregate: 3-2; Chelsea FC qualify.

07/03/13, Estádio do Sport Lisboa e Benfica, Lisbon (att: 33,248)
SL Benfica 1-0 FC Girondins de Bordeaux
Goal: 1-0 Carrasso 21(og)
Referee: Yefet (ISR)

14/03/13, Stade Chaban-Delmas, Bordeaux (att: 26,609)
FC Girondins de Bordeaux 2-3 SL Benfica
Goals: 0-1 Jardel 30, 1-1 Diabaté 74, 1-2 Cardozo 75, 2-2 Jardel 90+1(og), 2-3 Cardozo 90+2
Referee: Hategan (ROU)
Aggregate: 2-4; SL Benfica qualify.

07/03/13, White Hart Lane, London (att: 34,353)
Tottenham Hotspur FC 3-0 FC Internazionale Milano
Goals: 1-0 Bale 6, 2-0 Sigurdsson 18, 3-0 Vertonghen 53
Referee: Mateu Lahoz (ESP)
14/03/13, Stadio Giuseppe Meazza, Milan (att: 18,241)
FC Internazionale Milano 4-1 Tottenham Hotspur FC (aet)
Goals: 1-0 Cassano 20, 2-0 Palacio 52, 3-0 Gallas 75(og), 3-1 Adebayor 96, 4-1 Álvarez 110
Referee: Bebek (CRO)
Aggregate: 4-4; Tottenham Hotspur FC qualify on away goal.

07/03/13, Stadion Luzhniki, Moscow (att: 9,948)
FC Anji Makhachkala 0-0 Newcastle United FC
Referee: Vad (HUN)
14/03/13, St James' Park, Newcastle (att: 45,487)
Newcastle United FC 1-0 FC Anji Makhachkala
Goal: 1-0 Cissé 90+3
Referee: Mažić (SRB)
Aggregate: 1-0; Newcastle United FC qualify.

07/03/13, Estadi Ciutat de València, Valencia (att: 12,829)
Levante UD 0-0 FC Rubin Kazan
Referee: Gautier (FRA)
14/03/13, Stadion Luzhniki, Moscow (att: 1,889)
FC Rubin Kazan 2-0 Levante UD (aet)
Goals: 1-0 Rondón 100, 2-0 Dyadyun 112
Referee: Stavrev (MKD)
Aggregate: 2-0; FC Rubin Kazan qualify after extra time.

07/03/13, St Jakob-Park, Basel (att: 15,008)
FC Basel 1893 2-0 FC Zenit St Petersburg
Goals: 1-0 Díaz 83, 2-0 A Frei 90+4(p)
Referee: Orsato (ITA)
14/03/13, Stadion Petrovski, St Petersburg (att: 16,751)
FC Zenit St Petersburg 1-0 FC Basel 1893
Goal: 1-0 Witsel 30
Referee: Gil (POL)
Aggregate: 1-2; FC Basel 1893 qualify.

Quarter-finals

04/04/13, Stamford Bridge, London (att: 32,994)
Chelsea FC 3-1 FC Rubin Kazan
Goals: 1-0 Fernando Torres 16, 2-0 Moses 32, 2-1 Natcho 41(p), 3-1 Fernando Torres 70
Referee: Rocchi (ITA)

11/04/13, Stadion Luzhniki, Moscow (att: 18,410)
FC Rubin Kazan 3-2 Chelsea FC
Goals: 0-1 Fernando Torres 5, 1-1 Marcano 51, 1-2 Moses 55, 2-2 Gökdeniz Karadeniz 62, 3-2 Natcho 75(p)
Referee: Aydinus (TUR)
Aggregate: 4-5; Chelsea FC qualify.

04/04/13, White Hart Lane, London (att: 32,361)
Tottenham Hotspur FC 2-2 FC Basel 1893
Goals: 0-1 Stocker 30, 0-2 F Frei 34, 1-2 Adebayor 40, 2-2 Sigurdsson 58
Referee: Mažić (SRB)
11/04/13, St Jakob-Park, Basel (att: 36,500)
FC Basel 1893 2-2 Tottenham Hotspur FC (aet)
Goals: 0-1 Dempsey 23, 1-1 Salah 27, 2-1 Dragovic 49, 2-2 Dempsey 83
Referee: Olegário Benquerença (POR)
Aggregate: 4-4; FC Basel 1893 qualify 4-1 on penalties.

04/04/13, Estádio do Sport Lisboa e Benfica, Lisbon (att: 44,133)
SL Benfica 3-1 Newcastle United FC
Goals: 0-1 Cissé 12, 1-1 Rodrigo 25, 2-1 Lima 65, 3-1 Cardozo 71(p)
Referee: Gautier (FRA)
11/04/13, St James' Park, Newcastle (att: 52,157)
Newcastle United FC 1-1 SL Benfica
Goals: 1-0 Cissé 71, 1-1 Salvio 90+2
Referee: Bebek (CRO)
Aggregate: 2-4; SL Benfica qualify.

04/04/13, Şükrü Saracoğlu, Istanbul (att: 15,620)
Fenerbahçe SK 2-0 S.S. Lazio
Goals: 1-0 Webó 70(p), 2-0 Kuyt 90+1
Referee: Collum (SCO)
11/04/13, Stadio Olimpico, Rome (att: 490)
S.S. Lazio 1-1 Fenerbahçe SK
Goals: 1-0 Lulić 60, 1-1 Caner Erkin 73
Referee: Královec (CZE)
Aggregate: 1-3; Fenerbahçe SK qualify.

Marcelo Díaz strokes home the winning penalty for Basel in the quarter-final shoot-out against Tottenham

UEFA Europa League

Semi-finals

25/04/13, St Jakob-Park, Basel (att: 36,000)
FC Basel 1893 1-2 Chelsea FC
Goals: 0-1 Moses 12, 1-1 Schär 87(p), 1-2 David Luiz 90+4
Referee: Královec (CZE)
02/05/13, Stamford Bridge, London (att: 39,403)
Chelsea FC 3-1 FC Basel 1893
Goals: 0-1 Salah 45+1, 1-1 Fernando Torres 50, 2-1 Moses 52, 3-1 David Luiz 59
Referee: Eriksson (SWE)
Aggregate: 5-2; Chelsea FC qualify.

25/04/13, Şükrü Saracoğlu, Istanbul (att: 43,936)
Fenerbahçe SK 1-0 SL Benfica
Goal: 1-0 Egemen Korkmaz 72
Referee: Mažić (SRB)
02/05/13, Estádio do Sport Lisboa e Benfica, Lisbon (att: 55,402)
SL Benfica 3-1 Fenerbahçe SK
Goals: 1-0 Gaitán 9, 1-1 Kuyt 23(p), 2-1 Cardozo 35, 3-1 Cardozo 66
Referee: Lannoy (FRA)
Aggregate: 3-2; SL Benfica qualify.

Final

15/05/13, Amsterdam ArenA, Amsterdam (att: 46,163)
SL Benfica 1-2 Chelsea FC
Goals: 0-1 Fernando Torres 60, 1-1 Cardozo 68(p), 1-2 Ivanović 90+3
Referee: Kuipers (NED)
Benfica: Artur, Luisão, Cardozo, Salvio, Rodrigo (Lima 66), Gaitán, Matić, Garay (Jardel 78), Melgarejo (John 66), André Almeida, Pérez. Coach: Jorge Jesus (POR)
Chelsea: Čech, Ivanović, Cole, David Luiz, Ramires, Lampard, Fernando Torres, Mata, Oscar, Cahill, Azpilicueta. Coach: Rafael Benítez (ESP)
Yellow cards: Oscar 14 (Chelsea), Garay 45+1 (Benfica), Luisão 61 (Benfica)

Fernando Torres prepares to put Chelsea 1-0 up in the Amsterdam ArenA after sidestepping Benfica goalkeeper Artur

Top goalscorers

8	Libor Kozák (Lazio)
7	Óscar Cardozo (Benfica) Edinson Cavani (Napoli)
6	Fernando Torres (Chelsea) Rodrigo Palacio (Internazionale)
5	José Salomón Rondón (Rubin) Raúl Bobadilla (Young Boys)

Libor Kozák

Young stars

Aleksandar Dragovic, 22
FC Basel 1893
defender

Yevhen Konoplyanka, 23
FC Dnipro Dnipropetrovsk
midfielder

Salih Uçan, 19
Fenerbahçe SK
midfielder

Mohamed Salah, 20
FC Basel 1893
midfielder

Eduardo Salvio, 22
SL Benfica
forward

Victor Moses, 22
Chelsea FC
forward

Jelle Vossen, 24
KRC Genk
forward

NB Ages as of 15 May 2013

Squads/Appearances/Goals

CHELSEA FC

No	Name	Nat	DoB	Aps	(s)	Gls
Goalkeepers						
1	Petr Čech	CZE	20/05/82	9		
Defenders						
57	Nathan Aké	NED	18/02/95	1	(1)	
28	César Azpilicueta	ESP	28/08/89	8		
34	Ryan Bertrand		05/08/89	5		
24	Gary Cahill		19/12/85	4		
3	Ashley Cole		20/12/80	3		
4	David Luiz	BRA	22/04/87	7		2
2	Branislav Ivanović	SRB	22/02/84	5	(1)	1
19	Paulo Ferreira	POR	18/01/79	1		
26	John Terry		07/12/80	6		1
Midfielders						
30	Yossi Benayoun	ISR	05/05/80	3	(2)	
17	Eden Hazard	BEL	07/01/91	5	(2)	1
8	Frank Lampard		20/06/78	7		
21	Marko Marin	GER	13/03/89	1	(2)	
10	Juan Mata	ESP	28/04/88	5	(3)	1
12	John Obi Mikel	NGA	22/04/87	3	(1)	
11	Oscar	BRA	09/09/91	4	(5)	1
7	Ramires	BRA	24/03/87	8		
Forwards						
9	Fernando Torres	ESP	20/03/84	9		6
13	Victor Moses	NGA	12/12/90	5	(1)	4

SL BENFICA

No	Name	Nat	DoB	Aps	(s)	Gls
Goalkeepers						
1	Artur	BRA	25/1/81	9		
Defenders						
34	André Almeida		10/9/90	8		
24	Ezequiel Garay	ARG	10/10/86	8		
33	Jardel	BRA	29/3/86	2	(3)	1
4	Luisão	BRA	13/2/81	7		
14	Maxi Pereira	URU	8/6/84	2	(2)	
25	Lorenzo Melgarejo	PAR	10/8/90	8		
3	Roderick		30/3/91	2	(1)	
Midfielders						
10	Pablo Aimar	ARG	3/11/79	1		
89	André Gomes		30/7/93	3		
17	Carlos Martins		29/4/82	2	(2)	
20	Nicolás Gaitán	ARG	23/2/88	8	(1)	1
21	Nemanja Matić	SRB	1/8/88	8		1
35	Enzo Pérez	ARG	22/2/86	5	(3)	
23	Urreta	URU	19/3/90	1	(1)	
Forwards						
7	Óscar Cardozo	PAR	20/5/83	7	(2)	7
15	Ola John	NED	19/5/92	7	(1)	1
11	Lima	BRA	11/8/83	2	(5)	1
19	Rodrigo	ESP	6/3/91	4	(2)	1
18	Eduardo Salvio	ARG	13/7/90	5	(3)	1

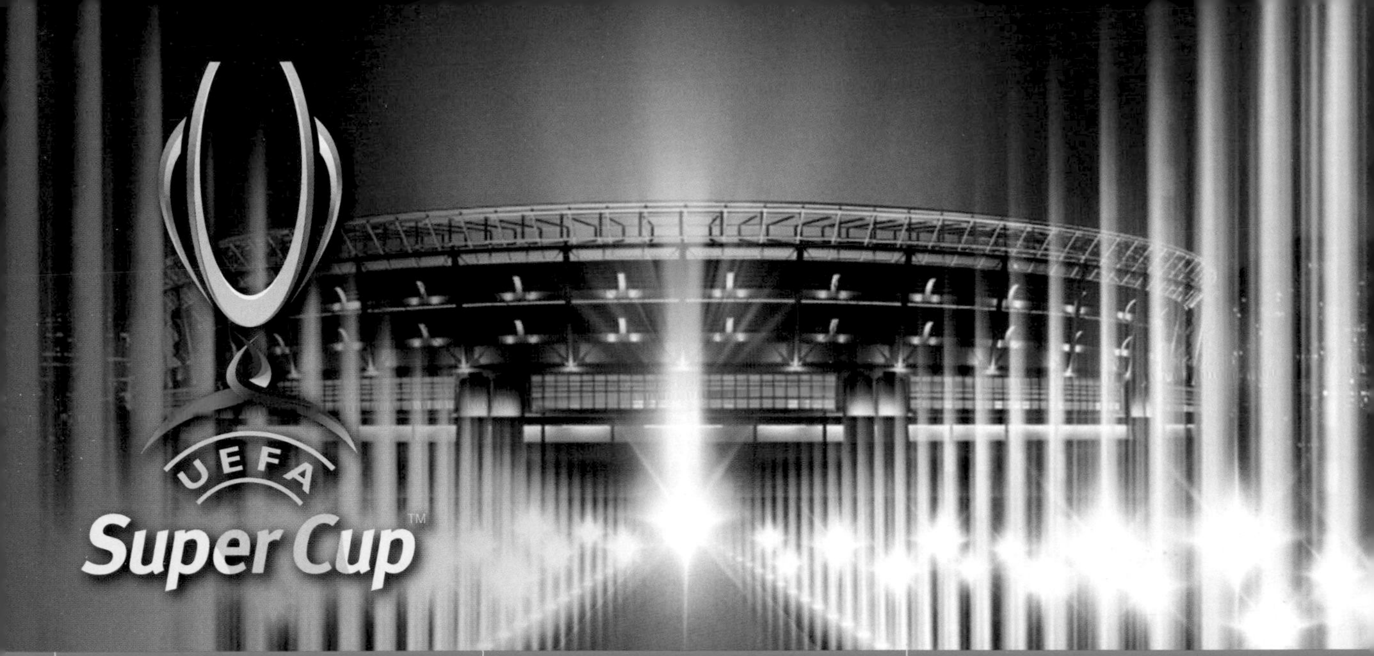

First-half hat-trick for classy Colombian

Chelsea overcome 4-1 at Stade Louis II

Competition bids farewell to Monaco

Fantastic Falcao steals the show

Radamel Falcao's second hat-trick in five days capped a wonderful performance from Club Atlético de Madrid as they defeated Chelsea FC in Monaco to claim their second UEFA Super Cup in three years.

"Extraordinary" was how Diego Simeone had described the Colombian's display against Athletic Club earlier in the week, and the Atlético coach was forced to seek new superlatives to sum up the striker's blistering treble as Falcao followed up immaculate finishes in the sixth and 19th minutes with another before half-time.

Chelsea's faint hope of a comeback was extinguished on the hour when defender João Miranda clipped the Spanish side's fourth goal over Petr Čech. Gary Cahill poked in the final UEFA Super Cup goal to be scored at Stade Louis II – 15 years after the Blues became the first club to lift the trophy there – but it was scant consolation for Roberto Di Matteo's UEFA Champions League winners.

The legion of red-and-white-clad fans did not have to wait long for the opener as the Atlético No9, star of the previous season's UEFA Europa League final, gave Adrián López's astute pass a deserving finish, curling the ball from the corner of the area over Čech's outstretched arm and in off a post.

The Chelsea keeper repelled a Gabi effort and then watched an Arda Turan header fizz wide before being beaten again. Having combined neatly with Adrián, Koke deceived David Luiz to slip in Falcao, who momentarily looked up, paused and flighted the ball into the top corner.

For the third goal, just before the interval, Arda charged down the right as he waited for Falcao to do likewise on the opposite flank. The Turkish international then cut inside and found his team-mate, who took out Ramires with his first touch and slotted the ball under Čech with his second.

The second half lacked similar thrills, but it did feature another fine goal from Miranda. It was Falcao's night, though, the Colombian's attacking master class providing Atlético with their fourth European trophy in just over two years.

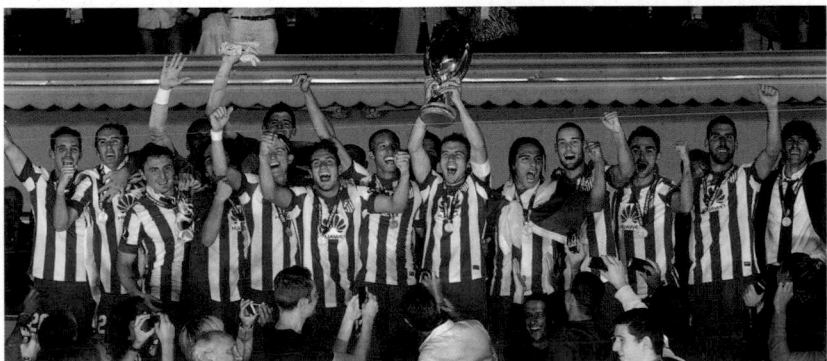

Atlético Madrid captain Gabi lifts the UEFA Super Cup in Monaco

Result

31/08/12, Stade Louis II, Monaco (att: 14,312)
Chelsea FC 1-4 Club Atlético de Madrid
Goals: 0-1 Falcao 6, 0-2 Falcao 19, 0-3 Falcao 45, 0-4 Miranda 60, 1-4 Cahill 75
Referee: Skomina (SVN)
Chelsea: Čech, Ivanović, Cole (Bertrand 90), David Luiz, Ramires (Oscar 46), Lampard, Fernando Torres, Mata (Sturridge 81), Mikel, Hazard, Cahill. Coach: Roberto Di Matteo (ITA)
Atlético: Courtois, Godín, Filipe Luís, Mario Suárez, Koke (Raúl García 81), Adrián López (Rodríguez 56), Falcao (Emre 87), Arda, Gabi, Juanfran, Miranda. Coach: Diego Simeone (ARG)
Yellow card: Ivanović 29 (Chelsea)

Manaus **6**

Fortaleza **5**

Natal **7**

Recife **9**

Salvador **11**

Brasília

Cuiabá **3**

2

Belo Horizonte **1**

São Paulo

Rio de Janeiro **10**

12

4

Curitiba

| 0 | 500 | 1000 km |
| 0 | 500 miles | |

8

Porto Alegre

1 Estádio Mineirão, Belo Horizonte
Capacity: 62,547
Matches: 6

2 Estádio Nacional, Brasília
Capacity: 70,064
Matches: 7

3 Arena Pantanal, Cuiaba
Capacity: 42,968
Matches: 4

4 Arena da Baixada, Curitiba
Capacity: 41,456
Matches: 4

5 Estádio Castelão, Fortaleza
Capacity: 64,846
Matches: 6

6 Arena Amazônia, Manaus
Capacity: 42,374
Matches: 4

BRAZIL

Match schedule

Group A

Date	Venue	Teams			Time	Match no.
12/06/14	Sao Paulo	Brazil	–	A2	17:00	1
13/06/14	Natal	A3	–	A4	13:00	2
17/06/14	Fortaleza	Brazi	–	A3	16:00	17
18/06/14	Manaus	A4	–	A2	16:00	18
23/06/14	Brasilia	A4	–	Brazil	17:00	33
23/06/14	Recife	A2	–	A3	17:00	34

Group B

Date	Venue	Teams			Time	Match no.
13/06/14	Salvador	B1	–	B2	16:00	3
13/06/14	Cuiaba	B3	–	B4	19:00	4
18/06/14	Rio de Janeiro	B1	–	B3	19:00	19
18/06/14	Porto Alegre	B4	–	B2	13:00	20
23/06/14	Curitiba	B4	–	B1	13:00	35
23/06/14	Sao Paulo	B2	–	B3	13:00	36

Group C

Date	Venue	Teams			Time	Match no.
14/06/14	Belo Horizonte	C1	–	C2	13:00	5
14/06/14	Recife	C3	–	C4	19:00	6
19/06/14	Brasilia	C1	–	C3	13:00	21
19/06/14	Natal	C4	–	C2	19:00	22
24/06/14	Cuiaba	C4	–	C1	17:00	37
24/06/14	Fortaleza	C2	–	C3	17:00	38

Group D

Date	Venue	Teams			Time	Match no.
14/06/14	Fortaleza	D1	–	D2	19:00	7
14/06/14	Manaus	D3	–	D4	22:00	8
19/06/14	Sao Paulo	D1	–	D3	16:00	23
20/06/14	Recife	D4	–	D2	13:00	24
24/06/14	Natal	D4	–	D1	13:00	39
24/06/14	Belo Horizonte	D2	–	D3	13:00	40

Group E

Date	Venue	Teams			Time	Match no.
15/06/14	Brasilia	E1	–	E2	13:00	9
15/06/14	Porto Alegre	E3	–	E4	16:00	10
20/06/14	Salvador	E1	–	E3	16:00	25
20/06/14	Curitiba	E4	–	E2	19:00	26
25/06/14	Manaus	E4	–	E1	17:00	41
25/06/14	Rio de Janeiro	E2	–	E3	17:00	42

Group F

Date	Venue	Teams			Time	Match no.
15/06/14	Rio de Janeiro	F1	–	F2	19:00	11
16/06/14	Curitiba	F3	–	F4	16:00	12
21/06/14	Belo Horizonte	F1	–	F3	13:00	27
21/06/14	Cuiaba	F4	–	F2	19:00	28
25/06/14	Porto Alegre	F4	–	F1	13:00	43
25/06/14	Salvador	F2	–	F3	13:00	44

Group G

Date	Venue	Teams			Time	Match no.
16/06/14	Salvador	G1	–	G2	13:00	13
16/06/14	Natal	G3	–	G4	19:00	14
21/06/14	Fortaleza	G1	–	G3	16:00	29
22/06/14	Manaus	G4	–	G2	16:00	30
26/06/14	Recife	G4	–	G1	13:00	45
26/06/14	Brasilia	G2	–	G3	13:00	46

Group H

Date	Venue	Teams			Time	Match no.
17/06/14	Belo Horizonte	H1	–	H2	13:00	15
17/06/14	Cuiaba	H3	–	H4	19:00	16
22/06/14	Rio de Janeiro	H1	–	H3	19:00	31
22/06/14	Porto Alegre	H4	–	H2	13:00	32
26/06/14	Sao Paulo	H4	–	H1	17:00	47
26/06/14	Curitiba	H2	–	H3	17:00	48

Round of 16

Date	Venue	Teams			Time	Match no.
28/06/14	Belo Horizonte	Winner Group A	–	Runner-up Group B	13:00	49
28/06/14	Rio de Janeiro	Winner Group C	–	Runner-up Group D	17:00	50
29/06/14	Fortaleza	Winner Group B	–	Runner-up Group A	13:00	51
29/06/14	Recife	Winner Group D	–	Runner-up Group C	17:00	52
30/06/14	Brasilia	Winner Group E	–	Runner-up Group F	13:00	53
30/06/14	Porto Alegre	Winner Group G	–	Runner-up Group H	17:00	54
01/07/14	Sao Paulo	Winner Group F	–	Runner-up Group E	13:00	55
01/07/14	Salvador	Winner Group H	–	Runner-up Group G	17:00	56

Quarter-finals

Date	Venue	Teams			Time	Match no.
04/07/14	Fortaleza	Winner 49	–	Winner 50	17:00	57
04/07/14	Rio de Janeiro	Winner 53	–	Winner 54	13:00	58
05/07/14	Salvador	Winner 51	–	Winner 52	17:00	59
05/07/14	Brasilia	Winner 55	–	Winner 56	13:00	60

Semi-finals

Date	Venue	Teams			Time	Match no.
08/07/14	Belo Horizonte	Winner 57	–	Winner 58	17:00	61
09/07/14	Sao Paulo	Winner 59	–	Winner 60	17:00	62

Third place play-off

Date	Venue	Teams			Time	Match no.
12/07/14	Brasilia	Loser 61	–	Loser 62	17:00	63

Final

Date	Venue	Teams			Time	Match no.
13/07/14	Rio de Janeiro	Winner 61	–	Winner 62	16:00	64

NB: All kick-offs are Brasilia local time.

7 Estádio das Dunas, Natal
Capacity: 42,086
Matches: 4

8 Estádio Beira-Rio, Porto Alegre
Capacity: 48.849
Matches: 5

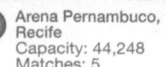

9 Arena Pernambuco, Recife
Capacity: 44,248
Matches: 5

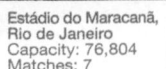

10 Estádio do Maracanã, Rio de Janeiro
Capacity: 76,804
Matches: 7

11 Arena Fonte Nova, Salvador
Capacity: 48,747
Matches: 6

12 Arena de São Paulo, Sao Paulo
Capacity: 65.807
Matches: 6

Brazil beckons Europe's elite

With almost two thirds of the European qualifying competition for the 2014 FIFA World Cup completed, there was still everything to play for in the nine groups as the national teams of the 53 UEFA member associations chased down 13 precious places at the final tournament in Brazil – nine automatic berths for the group winners plus another four to be decided in the play-offs from eight of the nine runners-up.

Holders Spain en route for finals after 1-0 win in France	**Germany, Italy and Netherlands in command of their groups**	**Belgium and Bosnia & Herzegovina well set for qualification**

Of the nine group seeds, only five went into the summer break on top of their respective sections. While World Cup mainstays Italy (Group B), Germany (Group C) and the Netherlands (Group D) all held sizeable leads, holders Spain appeared to have regained control of Group I , though Portugal remained under considerable threat from Russia in Group F.

Croatia trailed a multi-talented Belgium in Group A, while Greece were also three points adrift in Group G as goal-hungry Bosnia & Herzgovina charged towards a first appearance in a major tournament. England, though unbeaten, had their work cut out in Group H, where another Balkan side, Montenegro, held sway. Worse off still were Norway, down in fourth place in Group E, six points behind table-toppers Switzerland.

Group A

At the outset Group A had looked the most hotly contested of the nine sections. There were no makeweights and no clear favourites. However, it did not take long before two teams broke clear of the pack, Belgium and Croatia surprisingly turning the contest into a two-horse race as they left Serbia, the Former Yugoslav Republic of Macedonia, Wales and Scotland trailing in their wake.

Croatia, under new coach Igor Štimac, appeared to have the upper hand when they followed up an opening – if unconvincing – 1-0 win at home to FYROM with a 1-1 draw in Brussels. Former Belgian Pro League star Ivan Perišić slotted the visitors into a sixth-minute lead, but Guillaume Gillet smashed in a superb equaliser on the stroke of half time and the hosts held on to that precious point thanks to a gilt-edged chance spurned by Domagoj Vida in the closing seconds.

From then on both Belgium and Croatia matched each other victory for victory, each of them taking maximum points from their next four matches, in October and March, until, out of the blue, Štimac's side came a cropper in June at home to Scotland, losing 1-0 in Zagreb to a team that had taken just two points from their opening six games and were already eliminated. Robert Snodgrass was the man who provided Scotland's new boss Gordon Strachan with his first competitive victory – after earlier defeats by Wales (1-2 at home) and Serbia (0-2 away) – and, more significantly, put Belgium firmly in the driving seat at the top of the group.

While Croatia were losing, Belgium were posting their fifth successive victory, headed goals from Kevin De Bruyne and Marouane Fellaini giving them a 2-1 win at home to Serbia. With top-quality players in every position – from Thibaut Courtois in goal and Vincent Kompany in defence to Eden Hazard in midfield and Christian Benteke up front – there was enormous pressure on Belgium to make up for a decade of qualifying failure and take the direct route to Brazil. With a three-point lead, a superior goal difference and three games remaining – albeit one of them in Croatia – they were firmly on course to carry out that mission.

Belgium No10 Eden Hazard evades a tackle from Croatia's Domagoj Vida during the 1-1 draw in Brussels

Group B

With 14 points from 18, a four-point lead and three of their final four fixtures at home, Italy's qualification for Brazil – and a 15th successive appearance at the World Cup finals – seemed assured.

Cesare Prandelli's team, runners-up to Spain at UEFA EURO 2012, ended the season with an unbeaten record thanks to a defiant 0-0 draw in Prague against the Czech Republic. They were also held away to Bulgaria – 2-2 in their opening game – but the other four games yielded victories, including a 3-1 success against Denmark in Milan in which they had to play the entire second period a man short following the dismissal of striker Pablo Osvaldo, the scorer of both goals in Bulgaria and another in a 3-1 win away to Armenia four days earlier.

Italy were assisted in their bid for automatic qualification by the lack of a sustained challenge from any of the other teams in the group. The Czech Republic and Denmark, UEFA EURO 2012 participants both, proved erratic in the extreme, and while Bulgaria, the fourth-seeded team in the section, went into the summer recess in second spot and undefeated, only two of their six games were won – at home to Armenia (1-0) and Malta (6-0).

Bulgaria and Denmark shared two 1-1 draws, but if Morten Olsen's side appeared to have seized the initiative in the race for second place with a thumping 2-0 win over the Czechs in Olomouc, they ended it catastrophically on 11 June when they lost 4-1 at home to an Armenia side that four days earlier had suffered an equally sensational home defeat, 1-0 to Malta.

Malta's shock win – their first away from home in a competitive international for 20 years – was sealed by an early goal from record marksman Michael Mifsud, providing the striker with ample consolation for the penalty he had missed in Malta's previous qualifier, at home to Italy, a match decided by a double from Azzurri striker Mario Balotelli.

Group C

Despite the concession of two points at home to Sweden in a remarkable 4-4 draw, Germany's 100% success rate of qualifying for the World Cup never looked in danger as they carved out a five-point lead at the summit of the Group C table with six of their ten matches completed. The battle to finish as runners-up to the three-time winners looked set to go right down to the wire as Austria, Sweden and the Republic of Ireland headed towards the decisive autumn fixtures separated only by goal difference.

Rasmus Elm scores Sweden's dramatic late equaliser in the 4-4 draw against Germany in Berlin

Joachim Löw's side showed ominous form as they thrashed Ireland 6-1 in Dublin on their third outing – following opening wins against the Faroe Islands (3-0 at home) and Austria (2-1 away). It was Ireland's heaviest home defeat of all time, and it looked as if Sweden would be on the receiving end of something similar four days later in Berlin when Germany raced into a 4-0 lead. Incredibly, though, Erik Hamrén's team came storming back into the game, goals in the last 28 minutes from Zlatan Ibrahimović, Mikael Lustig, Johan Elmander and – in added time – Rasmus Elm stunning the home crowd and providing one of the greatest comebacks in the competition's history.

Germany posted convincing back-to-back wins over Kazakhstan in the spring to reassert their supremacy, but Sweden were unable to build on their Olympiastadion exploit, drawing 0-0 in the new Friends Arena against Ireland and losing 2-1 to Marcel Koller's ever-improving Austria in Vienna. An earlier 6-0 home win over the Faroe Islands helped Austria claim second place on goal difference, but it was the victory over Sweden – sealed by a spectacular diving header from Marc Janko – and, before that, a crucial 2-2 draw in Dublin – thanks to David Alaba's last-gasp equaliser – that really lifted the nation's hopes of a first World Cup appearance for 16 years.

Ireland and Sweden both joined Austria on 11 points with routine home wins over the Faroe Islands, Robbie Keane scoring all three goals for the former in a 3-0 win to take his all-time international haul to 59 – on his record 126th appearance – and Ibrahimović striking both of Sweden's in a 2-0 win to lift his tally to 41.

Group D

The only perfect record in the nine European qualifying groups at the end of the 2012/13 season belonged to the Netherlands as Louis van Gaal's side posted six wins out of six, scoring 20 goals and conceding just two. It was a magnificent return to the fold for the esteemed ex-AFC Ajax and FC Barcelona coach, who had failed to qualify the team for the 2002 World Cup in his previous spell as Oranje boss.

Van Gaal made several changes to the side that had lost all three games under previous incumbent Bert van Marwijk at UEFA EURO 2012 and was rewarded immediately with a 2-0 home win over Turkey and a 4-1 success against Hungary in Budapest. When Romania were also put to the sword in Bucharest with another 4-1 win, it was obvious that the other teams in Group D would have to settle for trying to finish second. Two further wins in Amsterdam in the spring – 3-0 against Estonia, 4-0 against Romania – reinforced the Netherlands' stranglehold on the section as newcomers such as Kenneth Vermeer, Bruno Martins Indi and Jeremain Lens continued to blend harmoniously with stalwarts like Robin van Persie, Arjen Robben and Rafael van der Vaart.

Hungary, so long in the international wilderness, stepped up as the best of the rest with three wins in their first four games, the most impressive of them at home to Turkey in which they came from a goal down to win 3-1. They were close to another crucial home

win, against Romania, five months later but in a match played behind closed doors they conceded an added-time equaliser to shed two precious points in a 2-2 draw. A more satisfactory share of the points came four days later when they held Turkey 1-1 in Istanbul, leaving their hosts with just seven points from six games and a mountain to climb to get back into play-off contention.

Romania, despite feeling the force of the group leaders home and away, were considerably better placed, with three of their remaining four games at home – including pivotal encounters against Hungary and Turkey in September – and the other in Andorra.

Group E

The only one of the nine sections without a UEFA EURO 2012 participant, Group E enabled each of its six teams to raise their ambitions and dream of World Cup qualification. In the event, it was Switzerland, finalists in both 2006 and 2010, who looked poised to take the automatic berth on offer, their return of four wins and two draws giving them a four-point cushion at the top of the standings. Second place belonged, somewhat surprisingly, to Albania, with Iceland in close pursuit and Norway and Slovenia also still in contention for a possible play-off spot.

In accruing their tally of 14 points, Ottmar Hitzfeld's side scored just eight times, but against that their own goal was breached just once – by a thumping header from Norway skipper Brede Hangeland in a 1-1 draw in Berne. Goalkeeper Diego Benaglio was magnificent in that game and he kept clean sheets on each of his other four appearances, all of which resulted in victory, including a

brace of 2-0 wins in Slovenia and Iceland and a last-gasp 1-0 success at home to Cyprus that sent the team into the summer shutdown in a position of some strength.

Had it not been for youngster Haris Seferovic's 90th-minute winner in Geneva and a late headed equaliser in Tirana the previous evening by Norway defender Tom Høgli, Albania would have been level on points with Switzerland. Having won 1-0 in Oslo in their previous qualifier, Gianni De Biasi's unheralded side were seeking a double over the group seeds, but static defending at a corner cost them dear after midfielder Valdet Rama had opened the scoring on his first competitive international start.

Iceland had even greater cause to regret the concession of a lead that night as they lost 4-2 at home to Slovenia – a team they had beaten 2-1 away. It was their third defeat to go with three victories, and only the second win for their opponents, tournament finalists in 2010. If Slovenia still faced an improbable task to finish second, Norway, with three of their last four fixtures at home, were far from out of it.

Group F

Portugal defeated Russia 1-0 in Lisbon on 7 June to leapfrog their opponents into top spot in Group F, but while the victory was all-important for Cristiano Ronaldo and co, their position was somewhat false. Although they held a two-point lead over Russia, their closest rivals had two games in hand on them having completed only half of their ten-match programme. Third-placed Israel also remained in contention, three points behind the leaders having played a game fewer, but as they still had to face both Russia and Portugal away, their hopes of topping the group seemed slim.

Russia, led by new coach Fabio Capello, made a bold statement of intent in the opening month of competition when they followed up a 2-0 home win over Northern Ireland with an emphatic 4-0 victory in Israel. Aleksandr Kerzhakov scored twice in Ramat Gan, and the FC Zenit St Petersburg striker struck again, after just six minutes, as Russia overcame Portugal 1-0 in Moscow the following month, with goalkeeper Igor Akinfeev and his defenders having to work overtime to preserve that early advantage. Another 1-0 win in the Luzhniki – against Azerbaijan – kept up the winning run, but Russia would have to wait eight months for their next qualifier as their scheduled March encounter away to Northern Ireland was postponed until August because of snow.

While Russia remained inactive, Portugal kept their hopes alive by coming from 3-1 down in Israel to salvage a point with a 93rd-minute equaliser from Fábio Coentrão, the ball rebounding in off his outstretched foot from close range as a nervous Israeli defence failed to clear. The two sides both won 2-0 away the following week – Portugal in Azerbaijan, Israel in Northern Ireland – to move within a point of Russia before Hélder Postiga, with his fifth goal of the competition, lifted the UEFA EURO 2012 semi-finalists to the group summit in June.

Group G

Defeated in the qualifying play-offs for both the 2010 World Cup and UEFA EURO 2012, Bosnia & Herzegovina were well placed to claim automatic qualification for the 2014 World Cup – and a first ever appearance at a major tournament – after registering 16 points from their opening six matches. Safet Sušić's side claimed a quarter of that total from Greece, their only challengers, but with the UEFA EURO 2012 quarter-finalists harvesting maximum points from their other four matches, including potentially hazardous trips to Latvia, Slovakia and Lithuania, all was not yet lost for Fernando Santos's team.

Bosnia & Herzegovina set the tone for their campaign with an opening 8-1 victory in Liechtenstein that featured hat-tricks from each of their vaunted strikers, Manchester City FC's Edin Džeko and VfB Stuttgart's Vedad Ibišević, following an opening brace from skipper Zvjezdan Misimović. This threesome would prove to be an unstoppable force over the course of the next nine months, scaling an important peak in March when they helped the team to a 3-1 win over Greece in Zenica, Džeko heading in two Misimović free-kicks and Ibišević bundling in the other goal – albeit after Misimović had seen his penalty saved.

Aleksandr Kerzhakov – the scorer of Russia's winning goal at home to Portugal

Yevhen Konoplyanka (10) strikes from distance for Ukraine against England in the 1-1 draw at Wembley

Having already drawn 0-0 in Piraeus, Sušić's side were now in pole position to win the group, and in June, while Greece won 1-0 in Lithuania, they reinforced their credentials with a thumping 5-0 win in Latvia, all the goals coming in the second half. The last of them came from Džeko, his eighth of the competition, which not only confirmed him as the European zone's highest individual marksman – two ahead of compatriot Ibišević and Israel's Tomer Hemed – but also enabled Bosnia & Herzegovina to move ahead of Germany as the competition's highest-scoring team, with 23 goals.

On the same day Slovakia, who reached the last 16 of the 2010 World Cup, missed the opportunity to exert some pressure on the top two when they could only draw 1-1 in Liechtenstein. Coming on the back of defeat by Greece and a 1-1 draw with Lithuania, both at home, it was a result that ended the tenure of their joint-coaching team of Stanislav Griga and Michal Hipp.

Group H

Heading into the decisive autumn qualifying phase there was little to choose between the top three teams in Group H. Indeed, while Montenegro, England and Ukraine all harboured ambitions of qualifying for Brazil directly as section winners, they also ran the risk of missing out on the play-offs.

England, unbeaten and with three home games out of four remaining, were entitled to

fancy their chances of finishing first, but as the only victories recorded in their first six outings had come at the expense of San Marino (twice) and Moldova, it was clear that Roy Hodgson's side would have to up their game considerably to fulfil their objective.

England's biggest faux pas was a 1-1 draw at Wembley against Ukraine, but given that they trailed for most of the game, to a magnificent long-range strike from Yevhen Konoplyanka, there was some relief at the final outcome, Frank Lampard's 87th-minute penalty having spared their blushes against the team they had beaten 1-0 at UEFA EURO 2012. While Moldova and San Marino were swept aside with ease – to the aggregate tune of 18 goals for, none against – the group seeds could only draw 1-1 in both Poland and Montenegro, surrendering a lead given to them by a Wayne Rooney header on each occasion.

Montenegro, who finished second to England in UEFA EURO 2012 qualification, were also held at home, 2-2 by Poland in their opening game, but after three wins out of three on their travels, they were poised to take a five-point lead at the top of the standings when in June they played host to Ukraine, a team they had already defeated 1-0 in Kyiv. But under new head coach Mykhailo Fomenko the visitors gained their revenge in some style, rifling in four second-half goals to stun the Podgorica crowd and put themselves right back into the qualifying mix. It was Ukraine's third successive victory, the first of them a lively 3-1 win in Warsaw against Poland that effectively scuppered the chances

of their UEFA EURO 2012 co-hosts, who suffered further agony when they could only draw 1-1 in Moldova.

Group I

Spain, the World Cup holders, and France, the 1998 winners and 2006 finalists, were paired together in the competition's only five-team section. It was not a group that either would have chosen for themselves, but it was worse still for the other three participants, Belarus, Finland and Georgia, all of whom knew from the outset that their ambitions would in all likelihood be restricted to finishing third.

Finland, to their enormous credit, set the cat among the pigeons in March by snatching a memorable 1-1 draw against the world and double European champions in Gijón, Teemu Pukki's 79th-minute strike cancelling out Sergio Ramos's opener and prompting a dramatic denouement in which Spain laid siege on Finland's goal but almost conceded a second on the breakaway.

With France defeating Georgia 3-1 on the same evening in Paris, Les Bleus now not only led the group by two points but had the opportunity to extend it to five – and effectively clinch their place in Brazil – when they hosted Spain at the Stade de France four days later. It was the second meeting of the two heavyweights, the first, in Madrid, having ended 1-1 when Olivier Giroud headed in Franck Ribéry's cross with the last touch of the game four minutes into added time. Having now surrendered four points at home, Spain knew that victory in Paris was crucial. As so often in the recent past, they delivered the goods on the big occasion, winning 1-0 with a scrambled 58th-minute goal from Pedro and a superb performance from stand-in goalkeeper Víctor Valdés, whose brilliant reaction save from a late Patrice Evra header cemented La Roja's return to the top of the standings.

It was Spain's third win out of three on the road, an 86th-minute Roberto Soldado strike proving enough to defeat gallant Georgia in Tbilisi before Belarus were crushed 4-0 with a vintage display in Minsk, Pedro proving to be the star of a sumptuous show with a hat-trick. France also opened their campaign with an away win, 1-0 in Helsinki, which they followed with a 3-1 victory at home to Belarus.

With Finland four points behind them in third place by the summer, Didier Deschamps' men looked certain of landing a play-off place, but after that crucial defeat to Vicente Del Bosque's side in Paris it seemed as if their only realistic hope of reclaiming top spot lay in winning all of their final three matches and hoping for another favour from the Finns when Spain visited Helsinki in September.

2014 FIFA World Cup

Group stage

Group A

07/09/12, Stadion Maksimir, Zagreb
Croatia 1-0 FYROM
Goal: 1-0 Jelavić 69
Referee: Yefet (ISR)
Croatia: Pletikosa, Strinić, Šimunić, Ćorluka (Vida 81), Rakitić (Kranjčar 46), Vukojević, Modrić, Srna, Mandžukić, Perišić, Eduardo (Jelavić 63). Coach: Igor Štimac (CRO)
FYROM: Bogatinov, Georgievski, Popov, Noveski, Sikov, Trickovski (Georgiev 73), Ristic (M Ivanovski 80), Pandev, Gligorov (Tasevski 82), Demiri, Ibraimi. Coach: Cedomir Janevski (MKD)
Yellow cards: Šimunić 40 (Croatia), Vukojević 58 (Croatia), Demiri 60 (FYROM), Georgievski 89 (FYROM), Jelavić 90+3 (Croatia)

07/09/12, Cardiff City Stadium, Cardiff
Wales 0-2 Belgium
Goals: 0-1 Kompany 41, 0-2 Vertonghen 83
Referee: Johannesson (SWE)
Wales: Myhill, Gunter, Matthews, Blake, Collins, A Williams, Edwards (King 80), Church (Robson-Kanu 72), Morison (Vokes 72), Ramsey, Bale. Coach: Chris Coleman (WAL)
Belgium: Courtois, Gillet, Vermaelen, Kompany, Vertonghen, Witsel, Dembélé (De Bruyne 64), Fellaini, Mirallas (Lukaku 46), E Hazard, Mertens. Coach: Marc Wilmots (BEL)
Red card: Collins 26 (Wales)
Yellow cards: Gillet 79 (Belgium), A Williams 83 (Wales), Vokes 85 (Wales), Vertonghen 89 (Belgium)

08/09/12, Hampden Park, Glasgow
Scotland 0-0 Serbia
Referee: Eriksson (SWE)
Scotland: McGregor, Hutton, Dixon, Berra, Caldwell, Adam, Morrison (Mackie 81), Webster, Miller (Rhodes 81), Snodgrass (Forrest 69), Naismith. Coach: Craig Levein (SCO)
Serbia: Stojković, Biševac, Nastasić, Ivanović, Tošić, Kolarov, Mijailović (Fejsa 46), Ignjovski, Ninković, Djuričić (Lekić 84), Lazović (Tadić 58). Coach: Siniša Mihajlović (SRB)
Yellow cards: Nastasić 30 (Serbia), Snodgrass 47 (Scotland), Ninković 80 (Serbia)

11/09/12, Roi Baudouin, Brussels
Belgium 1-1 Croatia
Goals: 0-1 Perišić 6, 1-1 Gillet 45+2
Referee: Undiano Mallenco (ESP)
Belgium: Courtois, Gillet, Vermaelen, Kompany, Vertonghen, Defour (Fellaini 67), Dembélé (De Bruyne 72), Witsel, Benteke, E Hazard, Mertens (Mirallas 81). Coach: Marc Wilmots (BEL)
Croatia: Pletikosa, Strinić, Šimunić, Radošević (Vukojević 78), Jelavić (Olić 59), Modrić, Srna, Schildenfeld, Mandžukić (Kalinić 88), Perišić, Vida. Coach: Igor Štimac (CRO)
Yellow cards: Srna 10 (Croatia), Schildenfeld 49 (Croatia), Dembélé 65 (Belgium), Gillet 67 (Belgium)

11/09/12, Hampden Park, Glasgow
Scotland 1-1 FYROM
Goals: 0-1 Noveski 11, 1-1 Miller 43
Referee: Karasev (RUS)
Scotland: McGregor, Hutton, Dixon, Berra, Caldwell, Morrison (Rhodes 66), Webster, Miller (Adam 58), Mackie (Naismith 77), Maloney, Forrest. Coach: Craig Levein (SCO)
FYROM: Bogatinov, Georgievski, Popov, Noveski, Sikov, Trickovski (Hasani 38), Pandev, Gligorov (Sumulikoski 70), Demiri, Ibraimi (Tasevski 89), M Ivanovski. Coach: Cedomir Janevski (MKD)
Yellow cards: Ibraimi 23 (FYROM), Hasani 40 (FYROM), Gligorov 52 (FYROM), Pandev 53 (FYROM), Adam 60 (Scotland), Sumulikoski 78 (FYROM)

11/09/12, Karadjordje, Novi Sad
Serbia 6-1 Wales
Goals: 1-0 Kolarov 16, 2-0 Tošić 24, 2-1 Bale 31, 3-1 Djuričić 39, 4-1 Tadić 55, 5-1 Ivanović 80, 6-1 Sulejmani 90
Referee: Duarte Gomes (POR)
Serbia: Stojković, Fejsa, Biševac, Nastasić, Ivanović, Tošić (Sulejmani 70), Tadić, Kolarov, Ignjovski (Mijailović 85), Djuričić (Lekić 81), Marković. Coach: Siniša Mihajlović (SRB)
Wales: Myhill, Gunter, Matthews (Ricketts 46), Edwards (Vaughan 46), Blake, A Williams, Allen (King 71), Church, Morison, Ramsey, Bale. Coach: Chris Coleman (WAL)
Yellow cards: Blake 62 (Wales), Ramsey 78 (Wales)

Christian Benteke rises high to head Belgium in front at home to Scotland

12/10/12, National Arena Filip II, Skopje
FYROM 1-2 Croatia
Goals: 1-0 Ibraimi 16, 1-1 Ćorluka 33, 1-2 Rakitić 60
Referee: Rasmussen (DEN)
FYROM: Bogatinov, Georgievski, Popov (Hasani 82), Noveski, Sikov (Grncarov 75), Trickovski, Sumulikoski (Gligorov 54), Ristic, Pandev, Demiri, Ibraimi. Coach: Cedomir Janevski (MKD)
Croatia: Pletikosa, Strinić, Šimunić, Ćorluka, Rakitić, Vukojević, Jelavić (Sammir 64), Modrić (Badelj 84), Srna, Mandžukić (Kalinić 72), Perišić. Coach: Igor Štimac (CRO)
Yellow cards: Ristic 8 (FYROM), Ćorluka 63 (Croatia), Vukojević 70 (Croatia), Modrić 74 (Croatia), Pandev 90 (FYROM)

12/10/12, Stadion FK Crvena zvezda, Belgrade
Serbia 0-3 Belgium
Goals: 0-1 Benteke 34, 0-2 De Bruyne 68, 0-3 Mirallas 90+1
Referee: Kralovec (CZE)
Serbia: Brkić, Biševac, Nastasić, Ivanović, Tošić (Stevanović 67), Tadić (Lekić 81), Kolarov, Mijailović, Ignjovski, Djuričić (Šćepović 56), Marković. Coach: Siniša Mihajlović (SRB)
Belgium: Courtois, Alderweireld, Vermaelen, Kompany, Vertonghen, Witsel, De Bruyne (Mirallas 87), Dembélé, Benteke, E Hazard (Mertens 55), Chadli. Coach: Marc Wilmots (BEL)
Yellow cards: Benteke 35 (Belgium), Kolarov 48 (Serbia), Witsel 53 (Belgium)

12/10/12, Cardiff City Stadium, Cardiff
Wales 2-1 Scotland
Goals: 0-1 Morrison 28, 1-1 Bale 81(p), 2-1 Bale 90
Referee: Meyer (GER)
Wales: Price, Gunter, B Davies, Vaughan, Blake, A Williams, Allen, Ledley (Robson-Kanu 72), Morison (C Davies 66), Ramsey, Bale. Coach: Chris Coleman (WAL)
Scotland: McGregor, Hutton, Berra, Caldwell, Maloney, D Fletcher, Brown (Adam 46), S Fletcher, Morrison (Miller 87), Commons (Mackie 87), Fox. Coach: Craig Levein (SCO)
Yellow cards: Caldwell 36 (Scotland), Bale 53 (Wales), Ramsey 63 (Wales), Allen 74 (Wales)

16/10/12, Roi Baudouin, Brussels
Belgium 2-0 Scotland
Goals: 1-0 Benteke 69, 2-0 Kompany 71
Referee: Hagen (NOR)
Belgium: Courtois, Alderweireld, Vermaelen, Kompany, Vertonghen, Witsel, De Bruyne, Dembélé (E Hazard 46), Benteke (Mboyo 87), Chadli, Mertens (Mirallas 56). Coach: Marc Wilmots (BEL)
Scotland: McGregor, Hutton, Berra, Caldwell, Maloney, D Fletcher, S Fletcher (Miller 76), Morrison (Phillips 80), McArthur, Commons (Mackie 46), Fox. Coach: Craig Levein (SCO)
Yellow cards: McGregor 61 (Scotland), Chadli 81 (Belgium)

16/10/12, Gradski vrt, Osijek
Croatia 2-0 Wales
Goals: 1-0 Mandžukić 27, 2-0 Eduardo 57
Referee: Tudor (ROU)
Croatia: Pletikosa, Strinić, Šimunić, Lovren (Schildenfeld 46), Rakitić, Modrić, Srna, Badelj, Mandžukić, Perišić (Vida 85), Eduardo (Kranjčar 77). Coach: Igor Štimac (CRO)
Wales: Price, Gunter, B Davies, Vaughan, Blake, A Williams, Allen, Ledley (Robson-Kanu 82), Morison (Church 61), King (Vokes 72), Bale. Coach: Chris Coleman (WAL)
Yellow cards: Lovren 25 (Croatia), Gunter 52 (Wales), Strinić 81 (Croatia)

16/10/12, National Arena Filip II, Skopje
FYROM 1-0 Serbia
Goal: 1-0 Ibraimi 59(p)
Referee: Nijhuis (NED)
FYROM: Pacovski, Georgievski, Noveski, Grncarov, Hasani, Demiri (Sumulikoski 86), Gligorov, Tasevski (Trickovski 73), Lazevski, Ibraimi, M Ivanovski (Ristovski 90+1). Coach: Cedomir Janevski (MKD)
Serbia: Brkić, Tomović, Kolarov, Biševac, Nastasić, Tošić, Tadić (Ivanović 68), Fejsa, Ignjovski, Djuričić (Lekić 61), Marković (Sulejmani 74). Coach: Siniša Mihajlović (SRB)
Red card: Tomović 59 (Serbia)
Yellow cards: Gligorov 20 (FYROM), Biševac 26 (Serbia), Noveski 29 (FYROM), Marković 43 (Serbia), Georgievski 44 (FYROM), Grncarov 70 (FYROM)

22/03/13, Stadion Maksimir, Zagreb
Croatia 2-0 Serbia
Goals: 1-0 Mandžukić 23, 2-0 Olić 37
Referee: Çakır (TUR)
Croatia: Pletikosa, Strinić (Lovren 82), Šimunić, Kovačić, Ćorluka, Rakitić, Modrić, Srna, Mandžukić, Olić (Vukojević 83), Kranjčar (Vida 63). Coach: Igor Štimac (CRO)
Serbia: Brkić, Stevanović (Tadić 57), Nastasić, Ivanović, Tošić, Šćepović (Djordjević 9), Kolarov, Radovanović, Ignjovski (Petrović 75), Djuričić, Marković. Coach: Siniša Mihajlović (SRB)
Yellow cards: Kolarov 39 (Serbia), Subotić 80 (Serbia), Fejsa 89+1 (Serbia)

22/03/13, National Arena Filip II, Skopje
FYROM 0-2 Belgium
Goals: 0-1 De Bruyne 26, 0-2 E Hazard 61(p)
Referee: Aytekin (GER)
FYROM: Pacovski, Todorovski, Noveski, Grncarov, Trickovski (Trajkovski 82), Jahovic (M Ivanovski 58), Pandev, Hasani (Tasevski 82), Demiri, Lazevski, Ibraimi. Coach: Cedomir Janevski (MKD)
Belgium: Courtois, Alderweireld, Vermaelen, Vertonghen, Witsel, De Bruyne, Dembélé, Benteke (Chadli 85), E Hazard, Fellaini, Van Buyten. Coach: Marc Wilmots (BEL)
Yellow cards: Vermaelen 36 (Belgium), Demiri 40 (FYROM), Lazevski 62 (FYROM), Grncarov 68 (FYROM), M Ivanovski 76 (FYROM)

22/03/13, Hampden Park, Glasgow
Scotland 1-2 Wales
Goals: 1-0 Hanley 45+2, 1-1 Ramsey 72(p), 1-2 Robson-Kanu 74
Referee: Gautier (FRA)
Scotland: McGregor, Hutton, Mulgrew, Hanley, Caldwell, Dorrans (Adam 64), Snodgrass, McArthur, S Fletcher (Miller 5), Maloney, Burke (Rhodes 86). Coach: Gordon Strachan (SCO)
Wales: Myhill, Gunter, B Davies, Ledley (Church 89), Ricketts, A Williams, Collison (King 58), Bellamy, Robson-Kanu, Ramsey, Bale (J Williams 46). Coach: Chris Coleman (WAL)
Red cards: Snodgrass 71 (Scotland), Ramsey 90+5 (Wales)
Yellow cards: Snodgrass 11 (Scotland), Robson-Kanu 31 (Wales), Ramsey 45+3 (Wales), Miller 52 (Scotland), Hanley 68 (Scotland), Snodgrass 71 (Scotland)

26/03/13, Roi Baudouin, Brussels
Belgium 1-0 FYROM
Goal: 1-0 E Hazard 62
Referee: Olegário Benquerença (POR)
Belgium: Courtois, Alderweireld, Vermaelen, Kompany, Vertonghen, Witsel, De Bruyne, Dembélé (Chadli 56), Benteke, E Hazard (Fellaini 90+2), Mertens (Mirallas 46). Coach: Marc Wilmots (BEL)
FYROM: Pacovski, Georgievski, Noveski, Sikov, Trickovski (Trajkovski 65), Pandev, Ristovski (Todorovski 70), Gligorov, Ibraimi, M Ivanovski, Tasevski (Hasani 46). Coach: Cedomir Janevski (MKD)
Yellow cards: Mirallas 50 (Belgium), Hasani 58 (FYROM)

26/03/13, Karadjordje, Novi Sad
Serbia 2-0 Scotland
Goals: 1-0 Djuričić 60, 2-0 Djuričić 65
Referee: Vad (HUN)
Serbia: Stojković, Nastasić, Ivanović, Tošić (Stevanović 90+3), Tadić (Djordjević 69), Fejsa (Petrović 85), Milivojević, Tomović, Basta, Djuričić, Subotić. Coach: Siniša Mihajlović (SRB)
Scotland: Marshall, Hutton, Hanley, Caldwell, Naismith, McArthur (Adam 46), Rhodes (Miller 80), Maloney (Burke 80), Whittaker, Boyd, Bridcutt. Coach: Gordon Strachan (SCO)
Yellow cards: Tošić 26 (Serbia), Adam 54 (Scotland), Rhodes 56 (Scotland), Nastasić 63 (Serbia), Boyd 77 (Scotland), Stojković 87 (Serbia)

26/03/13, Liberty Stadium, Swansea
Wales 1-2 Croatia
Goals: 1-0 Bale 21(p), 1-1 Lovren 77, 1-2 Eduardo 87
Referee: Banti (ITA)
Wales: Myhill, Gunter, B Davies, Ledley, Collins, A Williams, J Williams (Church 84), Bellamy, Robson-Kanu (Richards 64), King, Bale. Coach: Chris Coleman (WAL)
Croatia: Pletikosa, Strinić (Olić 73), Ćorluka, Lovren, Rakitić, Modrić, Srna, Sammir (Kovačić 61), Badelj (Schildenfeld 46), Mandžukić, Eduardo. Coach: Igor Štimac (CRO)
Yellow cards: Ćorluka 7 (Croatia), Lovren 21 (Croatia), Robson-Kanu 42 (Wales), Modrić 66 (Croatia), Kovačić 70 (Croatia)

07/06/13, Roi Baudouin, Brussels
Belgium 2-1 Serbia
Goals: 1-0 De Bruyne 13, 2-0 Fellaini 60, 2-1 Kolarov 87
Referee: Lannoy (FRA)
Belgium: Courtois, Alderweireld, Van Buyten, Kompany, Vertonghen, Witsel, De Bruyne (Lukaku 82), Fellaini (Dembélé 71), Benteke, Mirallas (E Hazard 64), Chadli. Coach: Marc Wilmots (BEL)
Serbia: Stojković, Biševac, Ivanović, Mitrović (Šćepović 69), Tadić, Kolarov, Fejsa, Marković, Basta, Milivojević (Petrović 69), Subotić. Coach: Siniša Mihajlović (SRB)
Yellow cards: Mitrović 33 (Serbia), Biševac 90+1 (Serbia)

07/06/13, Stadion Maksimir, Zagreb
Croatia 0-1 Scotland
Goal: 0-1 Snodgrass 26
Referee: Fernández Borbalán (ESP)
Croatia: Pletikosa, Strinić (Kalinić 70), Šimunić, Perišić (Eduardo 56), Rakitić, Kovačić, Srna, Schildenfeld, Sammir Mandžukić (Kranjčar 88), Olić. Coach: Igor Štimac (CRO)
Scotland: McGregor, Hutton, Whittaker, Hanley, Mulgrew, Maloney (Conway 75), Morrison, McArthur, Griffiths (Rhodes 64), Snodgrass, Bannan (Naismith 63). Coach: Gordon Strachan (SCO)
Yellow cards: McGregor 45+3 (Scotland), Rakitić 77 (Croatia), McArthur 78 (Scotland), Whittaker 90+2 (Scotland)

		Home					Away					Total					
		Pld	W	D	L	F	A	W	D	L	F	A	W	D	L	F	A	Pts
1	Belgium	7	3	1	0	6	2	3	0	0	7	0	6	1	0	13	2	19
2	Croatia	7	3	0	1	5	1	2	1	0	5	3	5	1	1	10	4	16
3	Serbia	7	2	0	1	8	4	0	1	3	1	5	2	1	4	9	9	7
4	Wales	6	1	0	2	3	5	1	0	2	3	9	2	0	4	6	14	6
5	Scotland	7	0	2	1	2	3	1	0	3	2	6	1	2	4	4	9	5
6	FYROM	6	1	0	2	2	4	0	1	2	1	3	1	1	4	3	7	4

REMAINING FIXTURES

06/09/13	*10/09/13*	*11/10/13*	*15/10/13*
FYROM - Wales	FYROM - Scotland	Croatia - Belgium	Belgium - Wales
Scotland - Belgium	Wales - Serbia	Wales - FYROM	Scotland - Croatia
Serbia - Croatia			Serbia - FYROM

Group B

07/09/12, Natsionalen Stadion Vasil Levski, Sofia
Bulgaria 2-2 Italy
Goals: 1-0 Manolev 30, 1-1 Osvaldo 36, 1-2 Osvaldo 40, 2-2 G Milanov 66
Referee: Atkinson (ENG)
Bulgaria: Mihaylov, Manolev, Bodurov, Y Minev, Popov (Tonev 82), V Minev, I Ivanov, G Milanov, Gadzhev (Sarmov 80), Dyakov, Gargorov (Mitsanski 62). Coach: Luboslav Penev (BUL)
Italy: Buffon, Maggio, Ogbonna (Peluso 69), Marchisio, Osvaldo, Giovinco (Destro 74), Giaccherini (Diamanti 64), Barzagli, De Rossi, Bonucci, Pirlo. Coach: Cesare Prandelli (ITA)
Yellow cards: Gadzhev 16 (Bulgaria), De Rossi 24 (Italy), Ogbonna 64 (Italy), Diamanti 85 (Italy), Dyakov 88 (Bulgaria)

2014 FIFA World Cup

08/09/12, Parken, Copenhagen
Denmark 0-0 Czech Republic
Referee: Stark (GER)
Denmark: Andersen, Kristensen (Andreasen 58), Kjær, Agger, Wass, Jacobsen, Kvist, Eriksen, Krohn-Dehli, Rommedahl (Mikkelsen 80), Jørgensen (Cornelius 71). Coach: Morten Olsen (DEN)
Czech Republic: Čech, Gebre Selassie, M Kadlec, Suchý, Sivok, Rezek (Hušbauer 89), Plašil (Darida 75), Hübschman, Vydra (Rajtoral 73), Jiráček, Pekhart. Coach: Michal Bílek (CZE)
Yellow cards: Kvist 44 (Denmark), Mikkelsen 89 (Denmark), Cornelius 90 (Denmark)

07/09/12, Ta' Qali National Stadium, Ta' Qali
Malta 0-1 Armenia
Goal: 0-1 Sarkisov 70
Referee: Eisner (AUT)
Malta: Hogg, A Muscat, Sciberras, Agius, Dimech, Bogdanovic, Briffa (Bajada 85), Mifsud, Cohen (R Fenech 74), Schembri, Borg. Coach: Pietro Ghedin (ITA)
Armenia: Kasparov, Hovsepyan, Arzumanyan (Aleksanyan 79), Mkrtchyan, Pizzelli (Sarkisov 64), Movsisyan, Mkoyan, Artak Yedigaryan (Manoyan 52), Mkhitaryan, Hayrapetyan, Özbiliz. Coach: Vardan Minasyan (ARM)
Yellow cards: Sciberras 39 (Malta), Mkoyan 44 (Armenia), Dimech 71 (Malta), Hovsepyan 82 (Armenia)

11/09/12, Natsionalen Stadion Vasil Levski, Sofia
Bulgaria 1-0 Armenia
Goal: 1-0 Manolev 43
Referee: Studer (SUI)
Bulgaria: Mihaylov, Manolev, Bodurov, Y Minev, Popov (Gargorov 79), V Minev, I Ivanov, G Milanov, Gadzhev (Sarmov 60), Mitsanski (Rangelov 66), Dyakov. Coach: Luboslav Penev (BUL)
Armenia: Berezovski, Hovsepyan, Arzumanyan, Mkrtchyan, Artur Yedigaryan (Sarkisov 76), Ghazaryan, Movsisyan, Mkoyan, Mkhitaryan, Hayrapetyan (Artak Yedigaryan 43), Özbiliz (Pizzelli 54). Coach: Vardan Minasyan (ARM)
Red cards: Dyakov 73 (Bulgaria), Pizzelli 73 (Armenia), Ghazaryan 77 (Armenia)
Yellow cards: G Milanov 33 (Bulgaria), Dyakov 42 (Bulgaria), Artak Yedigaryan 56 (Armenia), Mkrtchyan 58 (Armenia), Artur Yedigaryan 61 (Armenia), Ghazaryan 68 (Armenia), Dyakov 73 (Bulgaria), Mihaylov 73 (Bulgaria), Hovsepyan 74 (Armenia), Gargorov 90+1 (Bulgaria

11/09/12, Alberto Braglia, Modena
Italy 2-0 Malta
Goals: 1-0 Destro 5, 2-0 Peluso 90+2
Referee: Munukka (FIN)
Italy: Buffon, Peluso, Cassani, Marchisio, Osvaldo (Pazzini 69), Barzagli, Bonucci, Destro (Giovinco 82), Pirlo, Diamanti (Insigne 46), Nocerino. Coach: Cesare Prandelli (ITA)
Malta: Hogg, A Muscat (Camilleri 86), Sciberras, Agius, Dimech, Bogdanovic (Cohen 69), Briffa, Mifsud, Schembri, Herrera, Borg. Coach: Pietro Ghedin (ITA)
Yellow cards: A Muscat 51 (Malta), Schembri 71 (Malta), Cohen 75 (Malta), Hogg 90+1 (Malta)

12/10/12, Hrazdan Central Stadium, Yerevan
Armenia 1-3 Italy
Goals: 0-1 Pirlo 11(p), 1-1 Mkhitaryan 27, 1-2 De Rossi 64, 1-3 Osvaldo 81
Referee: Strahonja (CRO)
Armenia: Berezovski, Arzumanyan, Mkrtchyan, Artur Yedigaryan (Manucharyan 65), Movsisyan, Mkoyan, Aleksanyan, Artak Yedigaryan, Mkhitaryan, Manoyan (Sarkisov 77), Özbiliz. Coach: Vardan Minasyan (ARM)
Italy: Buffon, Maggio, Criscito, Marchisio, Giovinco (El Shaarawy 60), Barzagli, De Rossi, Osvaldo, Montolivo (Candreva 88), Bonucci, Pirlo (Giaccherini 74). Coach: Cesare Prandelli (ITA)
Yellow cards: Mkoyan 10 (Armenia), Bonucci 14 (Italy), Giovinco 45+1 (Italy), Artur Yedigaryan 57 (Armenia), Mkrtchyan 60 (Armenia), Manucharyan 76 (Armenia), Aleksanyan 81 (Armenia)

12/10/12, Natsionalen Stadion Vasil Levski, Sofia
Bulgaria 1-1 Denmark
Goals: 1-0 Rangelov 7, 1-1 Bendtner 40
Referee: Chapron (FRA)
Bulgaria: Mihaylov, Manolev, Bodurov, Y Minev, Rangelov (Tonev 61), Popov (Bozhinov 85), Bandalovski, I Ivanov, G Milanov, Gadzhev, G Iliev (I Milanov 35). Coach: Luboslav Penev (BUL)

Denmark: Andersen, Kristensen (Cornelius 36), Kjær, Agger, Wass (Mtiliga 54), Jacobsen, Kvist, Eriksen (J Poulsen 90+2), Krohn-Dehli, Rommedahl, Bendtner. Coach: Morten Olsen (DEN)
Red card: Bandalovski 26 (Bulgaria)
Yellow cards: Mtiliga 69 (Denmark), Cornelius 84 (Denmark)

12/10/12, Stadion města Plzně, Plzen
Czech Republic 3-1 Malta
Goals: 1-0 Gebre Selassie 34, 1-1 Briffa 38, 2-1 Pekhart 52, 3-1 Rezek 67
Referee: Salmanov (AZE)
Czech Republic: Čech, Gebre Selassie, M Kadlec, Sivok, Limberský, Rezek, Rajtoral (Petržela 61), Plašil, Hübschman, Jiráček (Darida 73), Pekhart (Lafata 82). Coach: Michal Bílek (CZE)
Malta: Hogg, A Muscat, Sciberras, Agius, Dimech, Herrera, Briffa, Mifsud, Schembri (P Fenech 87), Borg, Bajada (Azzopardi 89). Coach: Pietro Ghedin (ITA)

16/10/12, Stadion Letná, Prague
Czech Republic 0-0 Bulgaria
Referee: Bezborodov (RUS)
Czech Republic: Čech, Gebre Selassie, M Kadlec, Sivok, Limberský, Rezek (Lafata 80), Rajtoral (Darida 58), Plašil, Hübschman, Jiráček, Pekhart (Vydra 58). Coach: Michal Bílek (CZE)
Bulgaria: Mihaylov, Manolev, Zanev (I Milanov 42), Bodurov, Y Minev, Popov (Tonev 75), I Ivanov, G Milanov, Gadzhev (Bozhinov 61), Dyakov, G Iliev. Coach: Luboslav Penev (BUL)
Yellow cards: Dyakov 17 (Bulgaria), G Iliev 26 (Bulgaria), I Ivanov 70 (Bulgaria), Y Minev 77 (Bulgaria), Gebre Selassie 83 (Czech Republic)

16/10/12, Stadio Giuseppe Meazza, Milan
Italy 3-1 Denmark
Goals: 1-0 Montolivo 33, 2-0 De Rossi 37, 2-1 Kvist 45+1, 3-1 Balotelli 54
Referee: Skomina (SVN)
Italy: De Sanctis, Chiellini, Balzaretti, Abate, Marchisio (Candreva 74), Balotelli (Destro 89), Barzagli, De Rossi, Osvaldo, Montolivo (Giaccherini 85), Pirlo. Coach: Cesare Prandelli (ITA)
Denmark: Andersen, Stokholm, Kjær, Agger, Jacobsen, Kvist (Kahlenberg 60), Eriksen, Krohn-Dehli (J Poulsen 83), Rommedahl, Bendtner, Silberbauer (Lorentzen 72). Coach: Morten Olsen (DEN)
Red card: Osvaldo 46 (Italy)
Yellow cards: De Rossi 39 (Italy), Kvist 52 (Denmark), Stokholm 76 (Denmark), Bendtner 79 (Denmark), De Sanctis 90 (Italy)

22/03/13, Natsionalen Stadion Vasil Levski, Sofia
Bulgaria 6-0 Malta
Goals: 1-0 Tonev 6, 2-0 Tonev 38, 3-0 Popov 47, 4-0 Gargorov 55, 5-0 Tonev 68, 6-0 I Ivanov 78
Referee: Shemeulevitch (ISR)
Bulgaria: Mihaylov, Bodurov, Y Minev (Dimitrov 63), Popov, V Minev, I Ivanov, G Milanov, Gadzhev (Sarmov 70), Tonev, G Iliev, Gargorov (Bozhinov 56). Coach: Luboslav Penev (BUL)
Malta: Hogg, Caruana, Agius (Camilleri 56), Dimech, Briffa, Mifsud, Failla, Schembri, P Fenech (R Muscat 70), Herrera, Fenech. Coach: Pietro Ghedin (ITA)
Yellow card: Y Minev 63 (Bulgaria)

22/03/13, Andruv Stadión, Olomouc
Czech Republic 0-3 Denmark
Goals: 0-1 Cornelius 57, 0-2 Kjær 67, 0-3 Zimling 82
Referee: Neves Moreira De Sousa (POR)
Czech Republic: Čech, Gebre Selassie, M Kadlec, Sivok, Krejčí (Dočkal 64), Limberský, Vydra, Plašil (Kozák 74), Jiráček (Rosický 61), Lafata, Darida. Coach: Michal Bílek (CZE)
Denmark: Andersen, Zimling, Kjær, Agger, S Poulsen, Jacobsen, Stokholm, Eriksen, Krohn-Dehli, Jørgensen (Rommedahl 66), Cornelius (Makienok 85). Coach: Morten Olsen (DEN)
Yellow cards: Jørgensen 18 (Denmark), Darida 22 (Czech Republic), Zimling 54 (Denmark), Sivok 79 (Czech Republic), Kozák 80 (Czech Republic)

26/03/13, Yerevan Republican Stadium Vazgen Sargsyan, Yerevan
Armenia 0-3 Czech Republic
Goals: 0-1 Vydra 47, 0-2 Vydra 81, 0-3 Kolář 90+4
Referee: Balaj (ROU)
Armenia: Berezovski, Arzumanyan, Voskanyan, Pizzelli, Ghazaryan (Sarkisov 60), Hovhannisyan, Movsisyan, Aleksanyan, Mkhitaryan, Muradyan (Manoyan 78), Manucharyan (Özbiliz 50). Coach: Vardan Minasyan (ARM)
Czech Republic: Čech, Gebre Selassie, M Kadlec, Sivok (Suchý 43), Limberský, Vydra, Rosický, Plašil, Hübschman, Lafata (Kolář 74), Darida (Jiráček 85). Coach: Michal Bílek (CZE)
Yellow cards: Ghazaryan 9 (Armenia), Movsisyan 43 (Armenia)

26/03/13, Parken, Copenhagen
Denmark 1-1 Bulgaria
Goals: 0-1 Manolev 51, 1-1 Agger 63(p)
Referee: Aydınus (TUR)
Denmark: Andersen, Zimling (Makienok 85), Kjær, Agger, S Poulsen, Jacobsen, Stokholm, Eriksen, Krohn-Dehli (Schøne 69), Rommedahl (Jørgensen 54), Cornelius. Coach: Morten Olsen (DEN)
Bulgaria: Mihaylov, Manolev (Gargorov 87), Bodurov (Dimitrov 23), Popov (G Iliev 70), V Minev, I Ivanov, I Milanov, G Milanov, Gadzhev, Tonev, Dyakov. Coach: Luboslav Penev (BUL)
Yellow cards: Jørgensen 71 (Denmark), Dimitrov 80 (Bulgaria), G Milanov 90 (Bulgaria)

26/03/13, Ta' Qali National Stadium, Ta' Qali
Malta 0-2 Italy
Goals: 0-1 Balotelli 8(p), 0-2 Balotelli 45
Referee: Gözübüyük (NED)
Malta: Haber, Caruana, A Muscat, Sciberras, Dimech, Failla (Cohen 82), Briffa, Mifsud (Vella 88), Schembri, Herrera, Camilleri. Coach: Pietro Ghedin (ITA)
Italy: Buffon, De Sciglio, Abate, Marchisio, Balotelli (Gilardino 86), El Shaarawy (Cerci 76), Barzagli, Montolivo, Bonucci, Pirlo, Giaccherini (Candreva 61). Coach: Cesare Prandelli (ITA)
Yellow card: Buffon 16 (Italy)

07/06/13, Yerevan Republican Stadium Vazgen Sargsyan, Yerevan
Armenia 0-1 Malta
Goal: 0-1 Mifsud 8
Referee: Hunter (NIR)
Armenia: Berezovski, Voskanyan, Arzumanyan, Mkrtchyan, Pizzelli, Hovhannisyan, Aleksanyan, Mkhitaryan, Manoyan (Sarkisov 66), Manucharyan (Movsisyan 46), Özbiliz. Coach: Vardan Minasyan (ARM)
Malta: Haber, Caruana, Sciberras (P Fenech 57), Camilleri, Dimech, Failla, Briffa (R Muscat 85), Mifsud (Vella 90+3), Herrera, Schembri, Muscat. Coach: Pietro Ghedin (ITA)
Yellow cards: Briffa 15 (Malta), Muscat 45+2 (Malta), Caruana 59 (Malta), Dimech 83 (Malta)

07/06/13, Stadion Letná, Prague
Czech Republic 0-0 Italy
Referee: Moen (NOR)
Czech Republic: Čech, Gebre Selassie, M Kadlec, Sivok, Limberský (Suchý 20), Kozák, Rosický, Plašil, Hübschman, Jiráček (Kolář 00), Darida (V Kadlec 76). Coach: Michal Bílek (CZE)
Italy: Buffon, Chiellini, Marchisio, Balotelli, El Shaarawy (Giovinco 46), Barzagli, De Rossi, Montolivo, Bonucci, Abate, Pirlo (Aquilani 77). Coach: Cesare Prandelli (ITA)
Red card: Balotelli 72 (Italy)
Yellow cards: Darida 66 (Czech Republic), Balotelli 69 (Italy), Balotelli 72 (Italy), Montolivo 90+2 (Italy)

Mario Balotelli seals Italy's 3-1 win at home to Denmark with the third goal in Milan

11/06/13, Parken, Copenhagen
Denmark 0-4 Armenia
Goals: 0-1 Movsisyan 1, 0-2 Özbiliz 19, 0-3 Movsisyan 59, 0-4 Mkhitaryan 82
Referee: Nikolaev (RUS)
Denmark: Andersen, Zimling (Pedersen 28) (Makienok 53), Kjær, Bjelland (Okore 46), S Poulsen, Jacobsen, Kvist, Eriksen, Krohn-Dehli, Rommedahl, Cornelius. Coach: Morten Olsen (DEN)
Armenia: Berezovski, Haroyan, Arzumanyan, Mkrtchyan, Artur Yedigaryan (Pizzelli 86), Ghazaryan, Hovhannisyan, Movsisyan (Sarkisov 84), Aleksanyan, Mkhitaryan, Özbiliz (Aslanyan 90+1). Coach: Vardan Minasyan (ARM)
Yellow cards: Krohn-Dehli 5 (Denmark), Haroyan 36 (Armenia), Arzumanyan 42 (Armenia)

		Pld	Home W D L F A	Away W D L F A	Total W D L F A	Pts
1	Italy	6	2 0 0 5 1	2 2 0 7 3	4 2 0 12 4	14
2	Bulgaria	6	2 2 0 10 3	0 2 0 1 1	2 4 0 11 4	10
3	Czech Republic	6	1 2 1 3 4	1 1 0 3 0	2 3 1 6 4	9
4	Armenia	6	0 0 3 1 7	2 0 1 5 1	2 0 4 6 8	6
5	Denmark	6	0 2 1 1 5	1 1 1 5 4	1 3 2 6 9	6
6	Malta	6	0 0 2 0 3	1 0 3 2 11	1 0 5 2 14	3

REMAINING FIXTURES

06/09/13	*10/09/13*	*11/10/13*	*15/10/13*
Czech Republic - Armenia	Armenia - Denmark	Armenia - Bulgaria	Bulgaria - Czech Republic
Italy - Bulgaria	Italy - Czech Republic	Denmark - Italy	Denmark - Malta
Malta - Denmark	Malta - Bulgaria	Malta - Czech Republic	Italy - Armenia

Group C

07/09/12, Hannover Arena, Hannover
Germany 3-0 Faroe Islands
Goals: 1-0 Götze 28, 2-0 Özil 54, 3-0 Özil 71
Referee: Madden (SCO)
Germany: Neuer, Hummels, Khedira, Özil, Klose (Podolski 75), T Müller (Schürrle 66), Badstuber, Lahm, Mertesacker, Götze (Draxler 88), Reus. Coach: Joachim Löw (GER)
Faroe Islands: Nielsen, Næs, P Justinussen, Baldvinsson, Føroya, Davur (S Olsen 46), Benjaminsen, Hansson, S Samuelsen (Elttør 64), Holst, Edmundsson (K Olsen 85). Coach: Lars Olsen (DEN)
Yellow cards: Baldvinsson 4 (Faroe Islands), Lahm 42 (Germany)

07/09/12, Astana Arena, Astana
Kazakhstan 1-2 Republic of Ireland
Goals: 1-0 Nurdauletov 37, 1-1 Keane 89(p), 1-2 Doyle 90
Referee: Avram (ROU)
Kazakhstan: Sidelnikov, Kirov, Kislitsyn, Mukhtarov, Nurdauletov, Konysbayev (Gridin 85), Bogdanov, Ostapenko, Schmidtgal, Nuserbayev (Dzolchiev 69), Rozhkov. Coach: Miroslav Beránek (CZE)
Republic of Ireland: Westwood, Ward, O'Shea, St Ledger, Whelan, McGeady, McCarthy, Keane (Long 70), Cox (Doyle 58), Walters, O'Dea. Coach: Giovanni Trapattoni (ITA)
Yellow card: Nuserbayev 31 (Kazakhstan)

11/09/12, Ernst-Happel-Stadion, Vienna
Austria 1-2 Germany
Goals: 0-1 Reus 44, 0-2 Özil 52(p), 1-2 Junuzovic 57
Referee: Kuipers (NED)
Austria: Almer, Garics, Pogatetz, Fuchs, Ivanschitz (Jantscher 75), Arnautovic, Junuzovic, Harnik (Burgstaller 55), Baumgartlinger (Janko 85), Prödl, Kavlak. Coach: Marcel Koller (SUI)
Germany: Neuer, Schmelzer, Hummels, Khedira, Özil, Klose (Podolski 75), T Müller, Badstuber, Lahm, Kroos, Reus (Götze 46). Coach: Joachim Löw (GER)
Yellow cards: Prödl 18 (Austria), Fuchs 60 (Austria), Lahm 71 (Germany), Baumgartlinger 81 (Austria)

11/09/12, Malmö New Stadium, Malmo
Sweden 2-0 Kazakhstan
Goals: 1-0 Elm 37, 2-0 Berg 90+4
Referee: Boiko (UKR)
Sweden: Isaksson, Lustig, J Olsson, Granqvist, Elm (Svensson 64), Larsson, Ibrahimović, Elmander (Berg 85), Wernbloom, Safari, Toivonen (Bajrami 56). Coach: Erik Hamrén (SWE)
Kazakhstan: Sidelnikov, Kirov, Kislitsyn, Nurdauletov, Bogdanov, Ostapenko (Shakhmetov 46), Schmidtgal, Shabalin (Islamkhan 84), Nuserbayev (Gridin 68), Dmitrenko, Rozhkov. Coach: Miroslav Beránek (CZE)
Yellow cards: Elmander 27 (Sweden), Shakhmetov 65 (Kazakhstan), Ibrahimović 75 (Sweden)

2014 FIFA World Cup

12/10/12, Tórsvøllur, Torshavn
Faroe Islands 1-2 Sweden
Goals: 1-0 Baldvinsson 57, 1-1 Kacaniklic 65, 1-2 Ibrahimović 75
Referee: Sidiropoulos (GRE)
Faroe Islands: Nielsen, Næs, P Justinussen, Færø, Baldvinsson, Hansson (S Olsen 83), Benjaminsen, S Samuelsen, Udsen (Elttør 85), Holst (Hansen 71), Edmundsson. Coach: Lars Olsen (DEN)
Sweden: Isaksson, Lustig, J Olsson, Granqvist, M Olsson, Larsson, Källström (Svensson 62), Ibrahimović, Wernbloom, Wilhelmsson (Kacaniklic 62), Ranégie (Berg 77). Coach: Erik Hamrén (SWE)
Yellow cards: Benjaminsen 17 (Faroe Islands), Udsen 22 (Faroe Islands), Wernbloom 45+2 (Sweden), Hansson 79 (Faroe Islands)

12/10/12, Astana Arena, Astana
Kazakhstan 0-0 Austria
Referee: Bognar (HUN)
Kazakhstan: Sidelnikov, Kirov, Nurdauletov, Konysbayev (Gridin 90+4), Bogdanov, Ostapenko, Khairullin (Mukhtarov 90+1), Nuserbayev (Nurgaliyev 87), Dmitrenko, Rozhkov, Korobkin. Coach: Miroslav Beránek (CZE)
Austria: Almer, Garics, Pogatetz, Fuchs, Ivanschitz (Jantscher 73), Arnautovic, Junuzovic, Harnik (Weimann 86), Baumgartlinger (Janko 63), Prödl, Kavlak. Coach: Marcel Koller (SUI)
Yellow cards: Nuserbayev 82 (Kazakhstan), Ostapenko 90 (Kazakhstan), Janko 90+1 (Austria), Rozhkov 90+3 (Kazakhstan)

12/10/12, Dublin Arena, Dublin
Republic of Ireland 1-6 Germany
Goals: 0-1 Reus 32, 0-2 Reus 40, 0-3 Özil 54(p), 0-4 Klose 58, 0-5 Kroos 61, 0-6 Kroos 83, 1-6 A Keogh 90+2
Referee: Rizzoli (ITA)
Republic of Ireland: Westwood, Coleman, Ward, O'Shea, O'Dea, McCarthy, McGeady (A Keogh 68), Andrews, Cox (Brady 83), Fahey (Long 51), Walters. Coach: Giovanni Trapattoni (ITA)
Germany: Neuer, Schmelzer, Khedira (Kroos 46), Schweinsteiger, Özil, Klose (Schürrle 72), T Müller, Badstuber, Mertesacker, Boateng, Reus (Podolski 66). Coach: Joachim Löw (GER)
Yellow cards: Reus 30 (Germany), O'Dea 47 (Republic of Ireland), Long 77 (Republic of Ireland), Badstuber 86 (Germany)

16/10/12, Ernst-Happel-Stadion, Vienna
Austria 4-0 Kazakhstan
Goals: 1-0 Janko 24, 2-0 Janko 63, 3-0 Alaba 71, 4-0 Harnik 90+3
Referee: Kehlet (DEN)
Austria: Almer, Pogatetz, Fuchs, Arnautovic, Alaba (Leitgeb 81), Junuzovic, Harnik, Prödl (Dragovic 59), Klein, Kavlak, Janko (Jantscher 81). Coach: Marcel Koller (SUI)
Kazakhstan: Sidelnikov, Kirov, Mukhtarov, Nurdauletov, Konysbayev, Bogdanov, Gridin, Nurgaliyev (Khairullin 83), Dmitrenko (Gurman 74), Shakhmetov (Islamkhan 70), Korobkin. Coach: Miroslav Beránek (CZE)
Yellow cards: Bogdanov 56 (Kazakhstan), Nurgaliyev 80 (Kazakhstan), Harnik 82 (Austria), Kavlak 87 (Austria)

16/10/12, Tórsvøllur, Torshavn
Faroe Islands 1-4 Republic of Ireland
Goals: 0-1 Wilson 46, 0-2 Walters 53, 1-2 Hansen 68, 1-3 P Justinussen 73(og), 1-4 O'Dea 88
Referee: Jemini (ALB)
Faroe Islands: Nielsen, Næs, P Justinussen, Færø (E Jacobsen 61), Baldvinsson, Hansson, Benjaminsen, S Samuelsen, Udsen (Hansen 61), Holst, Edmundsson (Elttør 80). Coach: Lars Olsen (DEN)
Republic of Ireland: Westwood, Coleman, O'Shea, O'Dea, McCarthy, McGeady, Andrews (Meyler 90+1), Keane (Long 80), Walters, Wilson, Brady (Cox 46). Coach: Giovanni Trapattoni (ITA)
Yellow card: Hansen 69 (Faroe Islands)

16/10/12, Olympiastadion, Berlin
Germany 4-4 Sweden
Goals: 1-0 Klose 8, 2-0 Klose 15, 3-0 Mertesacker 39, 4-0 Özil 56, 4-1 Ibrahimović 62, 4-2 Lustig 64, 4-3 Elmander 76, 4-4 Elm 90+3
Referee: Proença (POR)
Germany: Neuer, Schweinsteiger, Özil, Klose, T Müller (Götze 67), Badstuber, Lahm, Mertesacker, Kroos, Boateng, Reus (Podolski 88). Coach: Joachim Löw (GER)
Sweden: Isaksson, Lustig, J Olsson, Granqvist, Elm, Larsson (Sana 78), Ibrahimović, Elmander, Wernbloom (Källström 46), Safari, Holmén (Kacaniklic 46)
Yellow cards: Isaksson 39 (Sweden), Reus 84 (Germany), Lahm 89 (Germany), Schweinsteiger 90+2 (Germany)

22/03/13, Ernst-Happel-Stadion, Vienna
Austria 6-0 Faroe Islands
Goals: 1-0 Hosiner 8, 2-0 Hosiner 20, 3-0 Ivanschitz 28, 4-0 Junuzovic 77, 5-0 Alaba 78, 6-0 Garics 82
Referee: Derdo (UKR)
Austria: Lindner, Garics, Dragovic, Pogatetz, Fuchs (Suttner 72), Ivanschitz (Weimann 63), Arnautovic, Alaba, Junuzovic, Kavlak (Leitgeb 56), Hosiner. Coach: Marcel Koller (SUI)
Faroe Islands: Nielsen, Næs, P Justinussen, Færø, Baldvinsson, Hansson, Benjaminsen, S Samuelsen (P Jacobsen 72), Elttør (Gregersen 87), Holst, Edmundsson (Hansen 78). Coach: Lars Olsen (DEN)
Yellow cards: Hosiner 13 (Austria), Hansson 40 (Faroe Islands), Næs 47 (Faroe Islands), Benjaminsen 55 (Faroe Islands)

22/03/13, Astana Arena, Astana
Kazakhstan 0-3 Germany
Goals: 0-1 T Müller 20, 0-2 Götze 22, 0-3 T Müller 74
Referee: Kakos (GRE)
Kazakhstan: Sidelnikov, Kirov, Logvinenko, Gurman, Nurdauletov, Dmitrenko, Ostapenko (Geteriev 82), Khairullin (Konysbaev 65), M Bayzhanov (Korobkin 36), Schmidtgal, Dzolchiev. Coach: Miroslav Beránek (CZE)
Germany: Neuer, Schmelzer, Höwedes, Khedira (Gündoğan 82), Schweinsteiger, Özil, Draxler (Podolski 19), T Müller (Schürrle 82), Lahm, Mertesacker, Götze. Coach: Joachim Löw (GER)
Yellow cards: Logvinenko 11 (Kazakhstan), Korobkin 56 (Kazakhstan), Dmitrenko 65 (Kazakhstan), Schweinsteiger 70 (Germany), Höwedes 89 (Germany)

22/03/13, Friends Arena, Solna
Sweden 0-0 Republic of Ireland
Referee: Undiano Mallenco (ESP)
Sweden: Isaksson, Lustig (Antonsson 46), J Olsson, Granqvist, Safari, Elm, Larsson (Durmaz 87), Källström, Ibrahimović, Hysén (Toivonen 73), Kacaniklic. Coach: Erik Hamrén (SWE)
Republic of Ireland: Forde, Coleman, O'Shea, McCarthy, Long (Sammon 87), Keane (Hoolahan 77), McClean (A Keogh 83), Walters, Wilson, Clark, Green. Coach: Giovanni Trapattoni (ITA)
Yellow cards: Green 40 (Republic of Ireland), McCarthy 75 (Republic of Ireland), Coleman 77 (Republic of Ireland)

26/03/13, Frankenstadion, Nuremberg
Germany 4-1 Kazakhstan
Goals: 1-0 Reus 23, 2-0 Götze 27, 3-0 Gündoğan 31, 3-1 Schmidtgal 46, 4-1 Reus 90
Referee: Özkahya (TUR)
Germany: Neuer, Schmelzer, Khedira, Özil, T Müller, Gündoğan, Lahm, Mertesacker, Götze, Boateng, Reus (Jansen 90). Coach: Joachim Löw (GER)
Kazakhstan: Sidelnikov, Kirov, Mukhtarov, Gurman, Nurdauletov (Dzolchiev 46), Konysbayev (Shomko 78), Dmitrenko, Ostapenko (Kukeyev 64), Schmidtgal, Engel, Korobkin. Coach: Miroslav Beránek (CZE)

26/03/13, Dublin Arena, Dublin
Republic of Ireland 2-2 Austria
Goals: 0-1 Harnik 11, 1-1 Walters 25(p), 2-1 Walters 45+1, 2-2 Alaba 90+2
Referee: Strahonja (CRO)
Republic of Ireland: Forde, Coleman, O'Shea, Whelan, McCarthy, Long (Green 83), McClean, Walters, Wilson, Clark (St Ledger 72), Sammon. Coach: Giovanni Trapattoni (ITA)
Austria: Lindner, Garics, Dragovic, Pogatetz, Fuchs, Arnautovic, Alaba, Junuzovic (Baumgartlinger 27), Harnik, Kavlak (Weimann 69), Hosiner (Janko 62). Coach: Marcel Koller (SUI)
Yellow cards: McCarthy 21 (Republic of Ireland), O'Shea 35 (Republic of Ireland), Kavlak 43 (Austria), Long 81 (Republic of Ireland)

07/06/13, Ernst-Happel-Stadion, Vienna
Austria 2-1 Sweden
Goals: 1-0 Alaba 26(p), 2-0 Janko 32, 2-1 Elmander 82
Referee: Rocchi (ITA)
Austria: Almer, Garics, Dragovic, Pogatetz (Prödl 46), Fuchs, Arnautovic, Alaba, Junuzovic (Schiemer 75), Harnik, Baumgartlinger, Janko (Weimann 46). Coach: Marcel Koller (SUI)
Sweden: Isaksson, Lustig, J Olsson, Granqvist, Elm (Svensson 60), Larsson, Källström (Toivonen 70), Ibrahimović, Elmander (Durmaz 84), Wendt, Kacaniklic. Coach: Erik Hamrén (SWE)
Yellow cards: Isaksson 26 (Sweden), Baumgartlinger 45 (Austria), Dragovic 60 (Austria), Elmander 62 (Sweden)

Toni Kroos (18) strikes the fifth of Germany's six goals against Ireland in Dublin

07/06/13, Dublin Arena, Dublin
Republic of Ireland 3-0 Faroe Islands
Goals: 1-0 Keane 5, 2-0 Keane 56, 3-0 Keane 81
Referee: Gestranius (FIN)
Republic of Ireland: Forde, Coleman, Wilson (Kelly 82), O'Shea, St Ledger, Whelan, McGeady (McClean 77), Hoolahan, Walters (Sammon 73), Keane, Cox. Coach: Giovanni Trapattoni (ITA)
Faroe Islands: Nielsen, Baldvinsson, Gregersen, Vatnsdal, S Samuelsen, Holst (H Samuelsen 84), P Justinussen, S Olsen, Frederiksberg, Jónsson, Klettskard (Edmundsson 64). Coach: Lars Olsen (DEN)
Yellow cards: Vatnsdal 44 (Faroe Islands), P Justinussen 70 (Faroe Islands), Hoolahan 73 (Republic of Ireland), Baldvinsson 86 (Faroe Islands)

11/06/13, Friends Arena, Solna
Sweden 2-0 Faroe Islands
Goals: 1-0 Ibrahimović 35, 2-0 Ibrahimović 82(p)
Referee: Yordanov (BUL)
Sweden: Hansson, Lustig, Granqvist, Bengtsson, Larsson (Durmaz 63), Källström (Svensson 58), Ibrahimović, Nilsson, Ekdal, Kacaniklic, Toivonen (J Olsson 83). Coach: Erik Hamrén (SWE)
Faroe Islands: Nielsen, Næs, V Davidsen, Gregersen, Hansson (Klettskard 81), Benjaminsen, Holst (S Samuelsen 79), Edmundsson, J Davidsen, P Justinussen, S Olsen (Vatnsdal 41). Coach: Lars Olsen (DEN)
Red card: Granqvist 79 (Sweden)
Yellow cards: P Justinussen 70 (Faroe Islands), S Samuelsen 78 (Faroe Islands), Benjaminsen 70 (Faroe Islands)

		Home					Away					Total					
	Pld	W	D	L	F	A	W	D	L	F	A	W	D	L	F	A	Pts
1 Germany	6	2	1	0	11	5	3	0	0	11	2	5	1	0	22	7	16
2 Austria	6	3	0	1	13	3	0	2	0	2	2	3	2	1	15	5	11
3 Sweden	6	2	1	0	4	0	1	1	1	7	7	3	2	1	11	7	11
4 Republic of Ireland	6	1	1	1	6	8	2	1	0	6	2	3	2	1	12	10	11
5 Kazakhstan	6	0	1	2	1	5	0	0	3	1	10	0	1	5	2	15	1
6 Faroe Islands	6	0	0	2	2	6	0	0	4	0	14	0	0	6	2	20	0

REMAINING FIXTURES

06/09/13	*10/09/13*	*11/10/13*	*15/10/13*
Germany - Austria	Austria - Republic of Ireland	Faroe Islands - Kazakhstan	Faroe Islands - Austria
Kazakhstan - Faroe Islands	Faroe Islands - Germany	Germany - Republic of Ireland	Republic of Ireland - Kazakhstan
Republic of Ireland - Sweden	Kazakhstan - Sweden	Sweden - Austria	Sweden - Germany

Group D
07/09/12, Estadi Comunal, Andorra la Vella
Andorra 0-5 Hungary
Goals: 0-1 Juhász 12, 0-2 Gera 32(p), 0-3 Szalai 54, 0-4 Priskin 68, 0-5 Koman 82
Referee: Aleckovic (BIH)
Andorra: Gómes, Vales, E García, Lima, Pujol, Vieira, Silva, Clemente (Lorenzo 72), M García (Maneiro 80), Moreno (Gómez 69), Rodrigues. Coach: Koldo (AND)
Hungary: Bogdán, Lipták, Vanczák, Juhász, Dzsudzsák, Szalai (Németh 82), Gera (Priskin 46), Koman, Laczkó, Hajnal (Elek 75), Korcsmár. Coach: Sándor Egervári (HUN)
Red card: Vales 67 (Andorra)
Yellow cards: Clemente 20 (Andorra), Koman 20 (Hungary), M García 32 (Andorra), Moreno 45+2 (Andorra), Vales 55 (Andorra), Vales 67 (Andorra), Pujol 73 (Andorra)

07/09/12, Lilleküla Stadium, Tallinn
Estonia 0-2 Romania
Goals: 0-1 Torje 55, 0-2 Marica 75
Referee: Mažić (SRB)
Estonia: Pareiko, Morozov, Dmitrijev, S Puri (Kink 76), Oper, Ojamaa (Lindpere 46), Vunk (Voskoboinikov 61), Vassiljev, Klavan, Jääger, Teniste. Coach: Tarmo Rüütli (EST)
Romania: Lobonţ, Mǎţel, Raţ, Bourceanu, Chiricheş, Grozav, Lazǎr (Pintilii 66), Marica (Niculae 85), Tǎnase, Torje, Goian (Gǎman 90+2). Coach: Victor Piţurcǎ (ROU)
Yellow cards: Grozav 45+1 (Romania), Dmitrijev 78 (Estonia), Marica 79 (Romania)

07/09/12, Amsterdam ArenA, Amsterdam
Netherlands 2-0 Turkey
Goals: 1-0 Van Persie 17, 2-0 Narsingh 90+3
Referee: Velasco Carballo (ESP)
Netherlands: Krul, Janmaat (Van Rhijn 46), Heitinga (Vlaar 86), Martins Indi, Willems, Clasie (Fer 50), Narsingh, Strootman, Van Persie, Sneijder, Robben. Coach: Louis van Gaal (NED)
Turkey: Tolga Zengin, Hasan Ali Kaldırım, Semih Kaya, Emre Belözoğlu (Nuri Şahin 60), Hamit Altıntop, Umut Bulut, Tunay Torun (Mevlüt Erdinç 81), Arda Turan, Mehmet Topal, Ömer Toprak, Sercan Sararer (Burak Yılmaz 70). Coach: Abdullah Avcı (TUR)
Yellow cards: Hasan Ali Kaldırım 42 (Turkey), Tunay Torun 66 (Turkey), Hamit Altıntop 83 (Turkey), Willems 88 (Netherlands)

11/09/12, Ferenc Puskás, Budapest
Hungary 1-4 Netherlands
Goals: 0-1 Lens 3, 1-1 Dzsudzsák 7(p), 1-2 Martins Indi 19, 1-3 Lens 53, 1-4 Huntelaar 74
Referee: Proença (POR)
Hungary: Bogdán, Lipták, Vanczák, Juhász, Priskin, Elek (Gyurcsó 61), Dzsudzsák, Varga, Gera (Németh 80), Koman (Hajnal 46), Korcsmár. Coach: Sándor Egervári (HUN)
Netherlands: Stekelenburg, Van Rhijn, Vlaar, Martins Indi (Mathijsen 64), Willems, Clasie, Narsingh, Strootman (Maher 78), Van Persie (Huntelaar 46), Sneijder, Lens. Coach: Louis van Gaal (NED)
Yellow cards: Clasie 7 (Netherlands), Korcsmár 10 (Hungary), Juhász 29 (Hungary), Dzsudzsák 37 (Hungary), Maher 49 (Netherlands)

11/09/12, National Arena, Bucharest
Romania 4-0 Andorra
Goals: 1-0 Torje 29, 2-0 Lazǎr 44, 3-0 Gǎman 90+1, 4-0 Maxim 90+5
Referee: Radovanović (MNE)
Romania: Lobonţ (Tǎtǎruşanu 46), Mǎţel, Raţ, Bourceanu, Chiricheş, Grozav, Lazǎr, Marica (Rusescu 54), Tǎnase (Maxim 80), Torje, Gǎman. Coach: Victor Piţurcǎ (ROU)
Andorra: Gómes, E García, Lima, Pujol (Peppe 79), Vieira, Clemente (Moreno 86), Ayala, Gómez (Silva 69), Lorenzo, M García, Rodrigues. Coach: Koldo (AND)
Yellow card: Lima 51 (Andorra)

11/09/12, Şükrü Saracoğlu, Istanbul
Turkey 3-0 Estonia
Goals: 1-0 Emre Belözoğlu 44, 2-0 Umut Bulut 60, 3-0 Selçuk İnan 75
Referee: Borski (POL)
Turkey: Tolga Zengin, Hasan Ali Kaldırım, Semih Kaya, Emre Belözoğlu (Nuri Şahin 82), Gökhan Gönül, Umut Bulut (Selçuk İnan 68), Arda Turan, Mehmet Topal, Burak Yılmaz, Ömer Toprak, Sercan Sararer (Tunay Torun 68). Coach: Abdullah Avcı (TUR)
Estonia: Pareiko, Rähn, Kruglov, Oper (Purje 56), Kink (Saag 77), Lindpere (S Puri 56), Vunk, Vassiljev, Klavan, Jääger, Teniste. Coach: Tarmo Rüütli (EST)
Red card: Jääger 19 (Estonia)
Yellow card: Purje 69 (Estonia)

12/10/12, Lilleküla Stadium, Tallinn
Estonia 0-1 Hungary
Goal: 0-1 Hajnal 47
Referee: Liany (ISR)
Estonia: Pareiko, Šišov, Rähn, Morozov, Kruglov, S Puri (Mošnikov 69), Oper, Kink (Vunk 87), Lindpere, Ojamaa (Purje 53), Vassiljev. Coach: Tarmo Rüütli (EST)
Hungary: Bogdán, Kádár, Dzsudzsák, Varga, Szalai, Gera (Szabics 80), Mészáros, Koltai (Gyurcsó 84), Hajnal, Korcsmár (Elek 61), Juhász. Coach: Sándor Egervári (HUN)
Yellow cards: Rähn 7 (Estonia), Vassiljev 33 (Estonia), Dzsudzsák 33 (Hungary), Szalai 37 (Hungary), Juhász 65 (Hungary)

2014 FIFA World Cup

12/10/12, Feyenoord Stadion, Rotterdam
Netherlands 3-0 Andorra
Goals: 1-0 Van der Vaart 7, 2-0 Huntelaar 15, 3-0 Schaken 50
Referee: Kulbakov (BLR)
Netherlands: Stekelenburg, Janmaat, Heitinga, Vlaar, Martins Indi, N de Jong, Schaken, Strootman (Emanuelson 75), Huntelaar, Van der Vaart (Afellay 71), Lens (Kuyt 71). Coach: Louis van Gaal (NED)
Andorra: Gómes, Lima, Pujol, Vieira, Vales, Moreira (Bernaus 82), Ayala, Gómez (Moreno 74), Lorenzo, M García, Rodrigues (San Nicolás 52). Coach: Koldo (AND)
Yellow cards: Moreira 40 (Andorra), Janmaat 42 (Netherlands)

12/10/12, Şükrü Saracoğlu, Istanbul
Turkey 0-1 Romania
Goal: 0-1 Grozav 45+1
Referee: Webb (ENG)
Turkey: Volkan Demirel, Hasan Ali Kaldırım, Semih Kaya, Emre Belözoğlu (Nuri Şahin 81), Hamit Altıntop (Mevlüt Erdinç 61), Gökhan Gönül, Umut Bulut, Arda Turan, Mehmet Topal, Ömer Toprak, Sercan Sararer (Emre Çolak 69). Coach: Abdullah Avcı (TUR)
Romania: Tătăruşanu, Raţ, Tamaş, Bourceanu, Chericheş, Marica (Chipciu 79), Torje, Grozav (Cociş 50), Goian, Pintilii, Stancu (Mutu 82). Coach: Victor Piţurcă (ROU)
Yellow card: Goian 49 (Romania)

16/10/12, Estadi Comunal, Andorra la Vella
Andorra 0-1 Estonia
Goal: 0-1 Oper 57
Referee: Meckarovski (MKD)
Andorra: Gómes, Lima, Pujol, Vieira, Silva (E Garcia 80), Vales, San Nicolás, Moreira (Clemente 69), Ayala (Riera 77), Lorenzo, M García. Coach: Koldo (AND)
Estonia: Pareiko, Šišov, Rähn, Kruglov, Oper, Kink (Ojamaa 83), Lindpere (S Puri 70), Vassiljev, Klavan, Purje, Neemelo (Vunk 46). Coach: Tarmo Rüütli (EST)
Yellow cards: Silva 31 (Andorra), Ayala 60 (Andorra), Oper 65 (Estonia)

16/10/12, Ferenc Puskás, Budapest
Hungary 3-1 Turkey
Goals: 0-1 Mevlüt Erdinç 22, 1-1 Koman 31, 2-1 Szalai 50, 3-1 Gera 58(p)
Referee: Orsato (ITA)
Hungary: Bogdán, Vanczák, Kádár, Elek (Pátkai 45+3), Varga, Szalai, Gera, Koman (Koltai 73), Mészáros, Hajnal (Pintér 77), Korcsmár. Coach: Sándor Egervári (HUN)
Turkey: Volkan Demirel, Egemen Korkmaz, Hasan Ali Kaldırım, Emre Belözoğlu, Hamit Altıntop, Ekici (Sercan Sararer 64), Nuri Şahin, Tunay Torun (Aydın Yılmaz 45+3), Mevlüt Erdinç, Caner Erkin (Umut Bulut 75), Ömer Toprak. Coach: Abdullah Avcı (TUR)
Yellow cards: Elek 17 (Hungary), Varga 52 (Hungary), Hamit Altıntop 57 (Turkey), Gera 86 (Hungary)

16/10/12, National Arena, Bucharest
Romania 1-4 Netherlands
Goals: 0-1 Lens 9, 0-2 Martins Indi 29, 1-2 Marica 40, 1-3 Van der Vaart 45+2(p), 1-4 Van Persie 86
Referee: Thomson (SCO)
Romania: Tătăruşanu, Raţ, Tamaş, Bourceanu (Lazăr 61), Chericheş, Marica, Torje (Popa 66), Grozav (Mutu 75), Goian, Pintilii, Stancu. Coach: Victor Piţurcă (ROU)
Netherlands: Stekelenburg, Van Rhijn, Heitinga, Vlaar, Martins Indi, N de Jong, Narsingh, Strootman, Van Persie, Van der Vaart (Afellay 76), Lens (Elia 89). Coach: Louis van Gaal (NED)
Yellow cards: Bourceanu 16 (Romania), Tamaş 45+2 (Romania), Strootman 53 (Netherlands), Raţ 82 (Romania), Lens 83 (Netherlands)

22/03/13, Estadi Comunal, Andorra la Vella
Andorra 0-2 Turkey
Goals: 0-1 Selçuk İnan 30, 0-2 Burak Yılmaz 45+2
Referee: Dunauskas (LTU)
Andorra: Gómes, Lima, C Martínez (Clemente 70), Vieira, Vales, Peppe (E Garcia 82), San Nicolás, Moreira, Ayala (Andorrá 78), Gómez, M García. Coach: Koldo (AND)
Turkey: Onur Kıvrak, Bekir İrtegün, Hasan Ali Kaldırım, Semih Kaya, Gökhan Gönül, Selçuk İnan, Umut Bulut (Olcay Şahan 82), Nuri Şahin (Kerim Frei 90+1), Arda Turan, Burak Yılmaz, Sercan Sararer (Alper Potuk 58). Coach: Abdullah Avcı (TUR)
Yellow cards: Peppe 70 (Andorra), Selçuk İnan 90+4 (Turkey)

22/03/13, Ferenc Puskás, Budapest
Hungary 2-2 Romania
Goals: 1-0 Vanczák 16, 1-1 Mutu 68(p), 2-1 Dzsudzsák 71(p), 2-2 Chipciu 90+2
Referee: Stark (GER)
Hungary: Király, Vanczák, Kádár, Dzsudzsák (Halmosi 90), Szalai, Koman, Pintér, Mészáros, Szabics (Varga 58), Hajnal (Kovács 80), Korcsmár. Coach: Sándor Egervári (HUN)
Romania: Tătăruşanu, Tamaş, Bourceanu, Chericheş, Grozav (Rusescu 71), Stancu, Mutu, Torje (Maxim 66), Goian, Radu, Pintilii (Chipciu 86). Coach: Victor Piţurcă (ROU)
Yellow cards: Goian 73 (Romania), Mutu 74 (Romania), Chericheş 87 (Romania)

22/03/13, Amsterdam ArenA, Amsterdam
Netherlands 3-0 Estonia
Goals: 1-0 Van der Vaart 47, 2-0 Van Persie 72, 3-0 Schaken 84
Referee: Meshkov (RUS)
Netherlands: Vermeer, Janmaat, De Vrij, Martins Indi, Blind, De Guzmán (Clasie 86), Lens (Schaken 73), Strootman, Van Persie, Sneijder (Van der Vaart 36), Robben. Coach: Louis van Gaal (NED)
Estonia: Pareiko, Morozov, Kruglov (Kink 62), S Puri, Oper (Zenjov 46), Ojamaa (Lindpere 77), Vunk, Vassiljev, Klavan, Jääger, Teniste. Coach: Tarmo Rüütli (EST)
Yellow card: Robben 42 (Netherlands)

26/03/13, Lilleküla Stadium, Tallinn
Estonia 2-0 Andorra
Goals: 1-0 Henri Anier 45+1, 2-0 Lindpere 61
Referee: Valášek (SVK)
Estonia: Pareiko, Morozov, Piiroja, Kink, Vassiljev, Mošnikov, Jääger, Purje (Zenjov 76), Ahjupera (Oper 55), Anier (Lindpere 55), Teniste. Coach: Tarmo Rüütli (EST)
Andorra: Gómes, Lima, C Martínez, Vieira, Vales, Peppe (E Garcia 66), San Nicolás, Moreira (Bernaus 79), Ayala, Gómez (Silva 85), M García. Coach: Koldo (AND)
Yellow card: Moreira 72 (Andorra)

26/03/13, Amsterdam ArenA, Amsterdam
Netherlands 4-0 Romania
Goals: 1-0 Van der Vaart 12, 2-0 Van Persie 56, 3-0 Van Persie 65(p), 4-0 Lens 90+1
Referee: Clattenburg (ENG)
Netherlands: Vermeer, Janmaat, De Vrij, Martins Indi, Blind, De Guzmán (Maher 73), Lens, Strootman, Van Persie (S De Jong 86), Van der Vaart (Clasie 79), Robben. Coach: Louis van Gaal (NED)
Romania: Pantilimon, Raţ, Tamaş, Bourceanu, Chericheş, Stancu, Grozav (Mutu 68), Popa (Torje 63), Gardoş, Pintilii, Tănase (Chipciu 60). Coach: Victor Piţurcă (ROU)
Yellow cards: Martins Indi 47 (Netherlands), Blind 61 (Netherlands), Chipciu 89 (Romania)

Robin van Persie scores from the penalty spot in the Netherlands' 4-0 win against Romania in Amsterdam

26/03/13, Şükrü Saracoğlu, Istanbul
Turkey 1-1 Hungary
Goals: 1-0 Burak Yılmaz 63, 1-1 Böde 71
Referee: Mažić (SRB)
Turkey: Onur Kıvrak, Bekir İrtegün, Hasan Ali Kaldırım, Semih Kaya, Alper Potuk (Hamit Altıntop 70), Gökhan Gönül, Selçuk İnan, Umut Bulut (Mevlüt Erdinç 80), Nuri Şahin (Kerim Frei 90), Arda Turan, Burak Yılmaz. Coach: Abdullah Avcı (TUR)
Hungary: Király, Vanczák, Kádár, Dzsudzsák, Varga, Szalai (Elek 78), Koman, Pintér, Mészáros, Hajnal (Böde 68), Korcsmár (Guzmics 46). Coach: Sándor Egervári (HUN)
Yellow cards: Varga 48 (Hungary), Dzsudzsák 58 (Hungary), Bekir İrtegün 59 (Turkey), Böde 76 (Hungary), Burak Yılmaz 87 (Turkey), Király 90+3 (Hungary)

		Pld	W	D	L	F	A	W	D	L	F	A	W	D	L	F	A	Pts
			Home					**Away**					**Total**					
1	Netherlands	6	4	0	0	12	0	2	0	0	8	2	6	0	0	20	2	18
2	Hungary	6	1	1	1	6	7	2	1	0	7	1	3	2	1	13	8	11
3	Romania	6	1	0	1	5	4	2	1	1	5	6	3	1	2	10	10	10
4	Turkey	6	1	1	1	4	2	1	0	2	3	5	2	1	3	7	7	7
5	Estonia	6	1	0	2	2	3	1	0	2	1	6	2	0	4	3	9	6
6	Andorra	6	0	0	3	0	8	0	0	3	0	9	0	0	6	0	17	0

REMAINING FIXTURES

06/09/13	*10/09/13*	*11/10/13*	*15/10/13*
Estonia - Netherlands	Andorra - Netherlands	Andorra - Romania	Hungary - Andorra
Romania - Hungary	Hungary - Estonia	Estonia - Turkey	Romania - Estonia
Turkey - Andorra	Romania - Turkey	Netherlands - Hungary	Turkey - Netherlands

Group E

07/09/12, Stadiumi Kombëtar Qemal Stafa, Tirana
Albania 3-1 Cyprus
Goals: 1-0 Sadiku 36, 1-1 Laban 45+5, 2-1 Çani 84, 3-1 Bogdani 87
Referee: Kuchin (KAZ)
Albania: Ujkani, Lila, Dallku, Cana, Sadiku (Hyka 58), Bulku, Vila (Bogdani 72), Mavraj, Sahiti (Çani 81), Meha, Kukeli. Coach: Gianni De Biasi (ITA)
Cyprus: Georgallides (Makridis 66), Dosa Júnior, I Charalambous, Merkis, Aloneftis, Charalambides (Christofi 56), Konstantinou (Avraam 76), Makrides, Demetriou, Laban, Nikolaou. Coach: Nikos Nioplias (GRE)
Yellow cards: Cana 11 (Albania), Laban 45+4 (Cyprus), Meha 45+4 (Albania), Sadiku 56 (Albania), Bogdani 88 (Albania), Makridis 90+3 (Cyprus)

07/09/12, Laugardalsvöllur, Reykjavik
Iceland 2-0 Norway
Goals: 1-0 Árnason 21, 2-0 Finnbogason 81
Referee: Gautier (FRA)
Iceland: Halldórsson, Steinsson, Bjarnason, G Sigurdsson, Gíslason (Finnbogason 73), Eiríksson, Árnason (Ottesen 50), Daníelsson, R Sigurdsson, Gunnarsson, Hallfredsson (E Jónsson 90+1). Coach: Lars Lagerbäck (SWE)
Norway: Pettersen, Wæhler, Hangeland, J A Riise, Nordtveit, Abdellaoue (King 67), Elyounoussi, B H Riise (Henriksen 90), Ruud, Eikrem, Braaten (Søderlund 67). Coach: Egil Olsen (NOR)
Yellow cards: Gunnarsson 29 (Iceland), B H Riise 67 (Norway)

07/09/12, ŠRC Stožice, Ljubljana
Slovenia 0-2 Switzerland
Goals: 0-1 Xhaka 20, 0-2 Inler 51
Referee: Tagliavento (ITA)
Slovenia: J Handanovič, Brečko, Šuler, Cesar, Birsa (Iličič 61), Jokič, Dedič (Ljubijankič 55), Kirm, Radosavljevič (Kurtič 80), Bačinovič, Matavž. Coach: Slaviša Stojanovič (SVN)
Switzerland: Benaglio, Lichtsteiner, Von Bergen, Barnetta, Inler, Derdiyok, Xhaka (Fernandes 85), Behrami, Rodriguez, Djourou, Shaqiri (Dzemaili 74). Coach: Ottmar Hitzfeld (GER)
Red card: Barnetta 75 (Switzerland)
Yellow cards: Barnetta 23 (Switzerland), Kirm 59 (Slovenia), Barnetta 75 (Switzerland), Iličič 83 (Slovenia), Rodriguez 90+1 (Switzerland)

11/09/12, Antonis Papadopoulos, Larnaca
Cyprus 1-0 Iceland
Goal: 1-0 Makridis 57
Referee: Delferiere (BEL)
Cyprus: Kissas, Dosa Júnior, I Charalambous, Merkis, Solomou, Christofi, Konstantinou (Aloneftis 66), Makrides (Demetriou 90+2), Dobrašinović (Sielis 77), Laban, Nikolaou. Coach: Nikos Nioplias (GRE)

Iceland: Halldórsson, Sævarsson, Ottesen, Bjarnason, G Sigurdsson, Gíslason, Eiríksson (A Skúlason 63), Daníelsson (Gudmundsson 77), R Sigurdsson, Gunnarsson, Hallfredsson (Finnbogason 46). Coach: Lars Lagerbäck (SWE)
Red card: Ottesen 87 (Iceland)
Yellow cards: Gíslason 73 (Iceland), Kissas 80 (Cyprus), Sielis 82 (Cyprus), Gudmundsson 83 (Iceland), Laban 89 (Cyprus)

11/09/12, Ullevaal Stadion, Oslo
Norway 2-1 Slovenia
Goals: 0-1 Šuler 17, 1-1 Henriksen 26, 2-1 J A Riise 90+4(p)
Referee: Aydınus (TUR)
Norway: Jarstein, Wæhler, Hangeland, J A Riise, Henriksen, Nordtveit (B H Riise 53), Abdellaoue (King 46), Elyounoussi (Søderlund 89), Ruud, Jenssen, Braaten. Coach: Egil Olsen (NOR)
Slovenia: Oblak, Brečko, Šuler, Cesar, Kurtič, Ljubijankič (Kelhar 90+1), Birsa (Pečnik 71), Jokič, Iličič, Bačinovič (Matič 60), Matavž. Coach: Slaviša Stojanovič (SVN)
Yellow cards: Nordtveit 6 (Norway), Jokič 20 (Slovenia), Ruud 54 (Norway), Cesar 78 (Slovenia), Kelhar 90+4 (Slovenia)

11/09/12, Swissporarena, Lucerne
Switzerland 2-0 Albania
Goals: 1-0 Shaqiri 22, 2-0 Inler 68(p)
Referee: Hategan (ROU)
Switzerland: Benaglio, Lichtsteiner, Von Bergen, Inler, Derdiyok, Xhaka (Drmic 90+1), Behrami (Dzemaili 73), Rodriguez, Stocker (Mehmedi 79), Djourou, Shaqiri. Coach: Ottmar Hitzfeld (GER)
Albania: Ujkani, Lila, Dallku, Cana, Agolli, Bulku, Vila (Roshi 55), Mavraj, Meha, Kukeli (Hyka 73), Bogdani (Çani 55). Coach: Gianni De Biasi (ITA)
Yellow cards: Behrami 31 (Switzerland), Dallku 48 (Albania), Stocker 75 (Switzerland), Inler 88 (Switzerland)

12/10/12, Stadiumi Kombëtar Qemal Stafa, Tirana
Albania 1-2 Iceland
Goals: 0-1 Bjarnason 19, 1-1 Çani 29, 1-2 G Sigurdsson 81
Referee: Asumaa (FIN)
Albania: Ujkani, Lila, Dallku, Cana, Bulku, Çani (Bogdani 85), Mavraj, Sadiku, Lika (Sahiti 75), Meha (Roshi 46), Kukeli. Coach: Gianni De Biasi (ITA)
Iceland: Halldórsson, Steinsson, Bjarnason (Gudmundsson 85), G Sigurdsson, Gíslason (Sævarsson 68), Arnason, R Sigurdsson, Gunnarsson, Finnbogason (L Jónsson 90+2), Hallfredsson, A Skúlason. Coach: Lars Lagerbäck (SWE)
Yellow cards: Árnason 51 (Iceland), Gunnarsson 56 (Iceland), Kukeli 58 (Albania), Cana 61 (Albania), Çani 73 (Albania), Steinsson 76 (Iceland)

12/10/12, Stadion Ljudski vrt, Maribor
Slovenia 2-1 Cyprus
Goals: 1-0 Matavž 38, 2-0 Matavž 61, 2-1 Aloneftis 83
Referee: Kružliak (SVK)
Slovenia: Handanovič, Brečko, Šuler, Cesar, Kurtič, Jokič, Dedič (Kampl 68), Kirm, Radosavljevič (Maroh 90+1), Iličič (Cvijanovič 84), Matavž. Coach: Slaviša Stojanovič (SVN)
Cyprus: Kissas, I Charalambous, Christou, A Charalambous, Christofi, Charalambides (Aloneftis 79), Konstantinou (Efrem 64), Marangos (Artymatas 46), Demetriou, Sielis, Dobrašinović. Coach: Nikos Nioplias (GRE)
Red card: Cesar 89 (Slovenia)
Yellow cards: Cesar 9 (Slovenia), Sielis 33 (Cyprus), Marangos 43 (Cyprus), Kurtič 56 (Slovenia), Cesar 89 (Slovenia)

12/10/12, Stade de Suisse, Berne
Switzerland 1-1 Norway
Goals: 1-0 Gavranovic 79, 1-1 Hangeland 81
Referee: Fernández Borbalán (ESP)
Switzerland: Benaglio, Lichtsteiner, Von Bergen, Barnetta (Gavranovic 71), Inler, Derdiyok, Xhaka, Behrami (Dzemaili 90+2), Rodriguez, Djourou, Shaqiri. Coach: Ottmar Hitzfeld (GER)
Norway: Jarstein, Hangeland, J A Riise, Henriksen, Nordtveit, Elyounoussi (Parr 90+2), Ruud, Jenssen (Eikrem 80), Søderlund (King 64), Braaten, Forren. Coach: Egil Olsen (NOR)
Yellow cards: Nordtveit 11 (Norway), Forren 30 (Norway), Derdiyok 39 (Switzerland), Lichtsteiner 43 (Switzerland), Jenssen 73 (Norway), Braaten 89 (Norway)

2014 FIFA World Cup

16/10/12, Stadiumi Kombëtar Qemal Stafa, Tirana
Albania 1-0 Slovenia
Goal: 1-0 Roshi 36
Referee: Hansson (SWE)
Albania: Berisha, Lila, Cana, Agolli, Bulku, Çani (Curri 75), Vila (Dallku 84), Mavraj, Sadiku (Salihi 46), Kukeli, Roshi. Coach: Gianni De Biasi (ITA)
Slovenia: Handanovič, Brečko, Šuler, Jokič, Dedič (Čavušević 59), Maroh, Kirm, Radosavljević (Kampl 77), Iličič (Šišič 73), Mertelj, Matavž. Coach: Slaviša Stojanovič (SVN)
Yellow cards: Mertelj 21 (Slovenia), Roshi 37 (Albania), Iličič 38 (Slovenia), Vila 44 (Albania), Kirm 58 (Slovenia), Lila 63 (Albania), Šuler 79 (Slovenia)

16/10/12, Antonis Papadopoulos, Larnaca
Cyprus 1-3 Norway
Goals: 1-0 Aloneftis 42, 1-1 Hangeland 44, 1-2 Elyounoussi 81(p), 1-3 King 83
Referee: Gil (POL)
Cyprus: Kissas (Georgallides 55), Dosa Júnior, I Charalambous, A Charalambous (Demetriou 46), Aloneftis (Mytidis 88), Solomou, Christofi, Efrem, Dobrašinović, Laban, Nikolaou. Coach: Nikos Nioplias (GRE)
Norway: Jarstein, Hangeland, J A Riise, Henriksen, Elyounoussi, Ruud, Eikrem (Gashi 90+2), Jenssen (Berisha 75), Søderlund (King 46), Braaten, Forren. Coach: Egil Olsen (NOR)
Yellow cards: Demetriou 49 (Cyprus), Dobrašinović 56 (Cyprus), Ruud 64 (Norway), Aloneftis 71 (Cyprus), Braaten 82 (Norway), J A Riise 88 (Norway)

16/10/12, Laugardalsvöllur, Reykjavik
Iceland 0-2 Switzerland
Goals: 0-1 Barnetta 66, 0-2 Gavranovic 79
Referee: Kelly (IRL)
Iceland: Halldórsson, E Jónsson (Baldvinsson 81), Steinsson, Bjarnason, G Sigurdsson, Gíslason (Gudmundsson 70), Árnason, R Sigurdsson, Finnbogason, Hallfredsson, A Skúlason. Coach: Lars Lagerbäck (SWE)
Switzerland: Benaglio, Lichtsteiner, Von Bergen, Barnetta (Klose 90+1), Inler, Xhaka, Behrami, Rodriguez, Gavranovic (Mehmedi 83), Djourou, Shaqiri (Dzemaili 80). Coach: Ottmar Hitzfeld (GER)
Yellow cards: E Jónsson 20 (Iceland), Gíslason 31 (Iceland), Steinsson 64 (Iceland), Benaglio 81 (Switzerland), Árnason 82 (Iceland), Hallfredsson 85 (Iceland)

22/03/13, Ullevaal Stadion, Oslo
Norway 0-1 Albania
Goal: 0-1 Salihi 67
Referee: Blom (NED)
Norway: Jarstein, Høgli, Hangeland, J A Riise, Henriksen, Nordtveit, Abdellaoue, Elyounoussi (King 62), Jenssen, Søderlund (Berisha 75), Forren. Coach: Egil Olsen (NOR)
Albania: Berisha, Lila, Dallku (Hysaj 80), Cana, Agolli, Bulku, Çani (Bogdani 75), Basha, Mavraj, Salihi (Curri 90), Roshi. Coach: Gianni De Biasi (ITA)
Red card: Lila 89 (Albania)
Yellow cards: Roshi 43 (Albania), Forren 52 (Norway), Cana 78 (Albania), Lila 85 (Albania), Lila 89 (Albania), Agolli 90+3 (Albania)

22/03/13, ŠRC Stožice, Ljubljana
Slovenia 1-2 Iceland
Goals: 1-0 Novakovič 34, 1-1 G Sigurdsson 55, 1-2 G Sigurdsson 78
Referee: Tritsonis (GRE)
Slovenia: Handanovič, Brečko, Cesar, Ilič, Krhin (Dedič 79), Kurtič, Ljubijankič (Matavž 65), Birsa (Lazarević 52), Novakovič, Jokič, Radosavljević. Coach: Srečko Katanec (SVN)
Iceland: Halldórsson, Sævarsson, Ottesen, Bjarnason, Sigthórsson (Daníelsson 90+2), G Sigurdsson, Finnbogason (Gudmundsson 46), R Sigurdsson, Gunnarsson, Hallfredsson (Gudjohnsen 76), A Skúlason. Coach: Lars Lagerbäck (SWE)
Yellow cards: Novakovič 29 (Slovenia), Ottesen 57 (Iceland), Gudmundsson 69 (Iceland), G Sigurdsson 90+3 (Iceland)

23/03/13, GSP Stadium, Nicosia
Cyprus 0-0 Switzerland
Referee: Gräfe (GER)
Cyprus: Georgallides, Dosa Júnior, I Charalambous, Solomou (Efrem 54), Christofi (Sotiriou 90+5), Charalambides (Alexandrou 75), Makrides, Dobrašinović, Theofilou, Laban, Nikolaou. Coach: Nikos Nioplias (GRE)
Switzerland: Sommer, Lichtsteiner, Von Bergen, Inler, Behrami (Derdiyok 76), Rodriguez, Stocker, Emeghara (Xhaka 46), Seferovic, Djourou (Senderos 52), Shaqiri. Coach: Ottmar Hitzfeld (GER)
Yellow cards: Solomou 7 (Cyprus), Seferovic 34 (Switzerland), Von Bergen 46 (Switzerland), Theofilou 80 (Cyprus), Senderos 89 (Switzerland)

07/06/13, Stadiumi Kombëtar Qemal Stafa, Tirana
Albania 1-1 Norway
Goals: 1-0 Rama 41, 1-1 Høgli 87
Referee: Collum (SCO)
Albania: Berisha, Teli, Dallku, Agolli, Bulku (Hysaj 90+1), Çani, Vila (Kaçe 84), Basha, Mavraj, Salihi (Osmani 77), Rama. Coach: Gianni De Biasi (ITA)
Norway: Jarstein, Høgli, Reginiussen, Hangeland, Henriksen, Nordtveit, Elyounoussi (Berisha 46), Ruud, King (Søderlund 70), Jenssen (Skjelbred 86), Braaten. Coach: Egil Olsen (NOR)
Yellow cards: Ruud 1 (Norway), Dallku 72 (Albania), Basha 83 (Albania)

07/06/13, Laugardalsvöllur, Reykjavik
Iceland 2-4 Slovenia
Goals: 0-1 Kirm 11, 1-1 Bjarnason 22, 2-1 Finnbogason 26(p), 2-2 Birsa 31(p), 2-3 Cesar 61, 2-4 Krhin 85
Referee: Zwayer (GER)
Iceland: Halldórsson, Sævarsson (Thorvaldsson 84), Bjarnason, Sigthórsson, Finnbogason, Árnason, Daníelsson, R. Sigurdsson, Gunnarsson (Gudjohnsen 52), Hallfredsson (Gíslason 63), A Skúlason. Coach: Lars Lagerbäck (SWE)
Slovenia: Handanovič, Brečko, Krhin, Cesar, Ilič, Kurtič, Birsa (Struna 90), Novakovič (Matavž 87), Jokič, Kirm, Kampl (Radosavljević 73). Coach: Srečko Katanec (SVN)
Yellow cards: Ilič 25 (Slovenia), Cesar 43 (Slovenia), Sævarsson 45+1 (Iceland), Sigthórsson 72 (Iceland), Kirm 86 (Slovenia)

08/06/13, Stade de Genève, Geneva
Switzerland 1-0 Cyprus
Goal: 1-0 Seferovic 90
Referee: Mazzoleni (ITA)
Switzerland: Benaglio, Lichtsteiner, Von Bergen, Inler, Behrami (Dzemaili 67), Rodriguez, Stocker (Barnetta 77), Gavranovic, Drmic (Seferovic 74), Djourou, Shaqiri. Coach: Ottmar Hitzfeld (GER)
Cyprus: Georgallides, I Charalambous, Merkis, A Charalambous, Aloneftis (Kyriakou 62), Sotiriou, Alexandrou, Makrides, Theofilou (Dobrašinović 90+4), Laban, Nikolaou. Coach: Nikos Nioplias (GRE)
Yellow cards: A Charalambous 13 (Cyprus), Sotiriou 20 (Cyprus), Makrides 33 (Cyprus), Inler 45 (Switzerland), I Charalambous 67 (Cyprus), Djourou 86 (Switzerland)

			Home					Away					Total					
		Pld	W	D	L	F	A	W	D	L	F	A	W	D	L	F	A	Pts
1	Switzerland	6	2	1	0	4	1	2	1	0	4	0	4	2	0	8	1	14
2	Albania	6	2	1	1	6	4	1	0	1	1	2	3	1	2	7	6	10
3	Iceland	6	1	0	2	4	6	2	0	1	4	3	3	0	3	8	9	9
4	Norway	6	1	0	1	2	2	1	2	1	5	5	2	2	2	7	7	8
5	Slovenia	6	1	0	2	3	5	1	0	2	5	5	2	0	4	8	10	6
6	Cyprus	6	1	1	1	2	3	0	0	3	2	6	1	1	4	4	9	4

REMAINING FIXTURES

06/09/13	*10/09/13*	*11/10/13*	*15/10/13*
Norway - Cyprus	Cyprus - Slovenia	Albania - Switzerland	Cyprus - Albania
Slovenia - Albania	Iceland - Albania	Iceland - Cyprus	Norway - Iceland
Switzerland - Iceland	Norway - Switzerland	Slovenia - Norway	Switzerland - Slovenia

Albania's Emiljano Vila (right) tussles for possession with Norway's Ruben Yttergård Jenssen

Group F

07/09/12, Tofiq Bähramov Republican stadium, Baku
Azerbaijan 1-1 Israel
Goals: 0-1 Natcho 50, 1-1 Abışov 65
Referee: Jug (SVN)
Azerbaijan: K Ağayev, Gökdemir (İsmayilov 59), Şükürov, Allahverdiyev, Cavadov, Chertoganov (Ämirquliyev 76), Subašić, Äliyev (Özkara 58), Räşad F Sadıqov, Abışov, Medvedev. Coach: Berti Vogts (GER)
Israel: Awat, Shpungin, Melikson (Ezra 71), Natcho, Alberman, Hemed (Damari 67), Shechter (Benayoun 74), Ziv, Mori, Vermouth, Tibi. Coach: Eli Gutman (ISR)
Yellow cards: Hemed 16 (Israel), Mori 81 (Israel), Ezra 84 (Israel)

07/09/12, Josy Barthel, Luxembourg
Luxembourg 1-2 Portugal
Goals: 1-0 Da Mota 14, 1-1 Cristiano Ronaldo 27, 1-2 Hélder Postiga 54
Referee: Tohver (EST)
Luxembourg: Joubert, Blaise, Schnell, Bettmer, Da Mota (Deville 79), Payal, Joachim, Bukvic, Mutsch, Jänisch, Gerson. Coach: Luc Holtz (LUX)
Portugal: Rui Patrício, Bruno Alves, Pepe, Miguel Veloso (Varela 46), Fábio Coentrão, Cristiano Ronaldo, João Moutinho, Raul Meireles (Custódio 67), Nani (Rúben Micael 81), João Pereira, Hélder Postiga. Coach: Paulo Bento (POR)
Yellow cards: Bruno Alves 78 (Portugal), Varela 86 (Portugal)

07/09/12, Stadion Lokomotiv, Moscow
Russia 2-0 Northern Ireland
Goals: 1-0 Fayzulin 30, 2-0 Shirokov 78(p)
Referee: Mateu Lahoz (ESP)
Russia: Akinfeev, Anyukov, Ignashevich, Denisov, Kerzhakov, V Berezutski, Shirokov, Dzagoev (Kokorin 58), Bystrov, Fayzulin (Glushakov 85), Kombarov. Coach: Fabio Capello (ITA)
Northern Ireland: Carroll, McAuley, J Evans, Baird, Davis, Ward (Little 76), K Lafferty, Brunt, C Evans (Shiels 84), Hughes, Cathcart. Coach: Michael O'Neill (NIR)
Yellow cards: Baird 43 (Northern Ireland), Anyukov 65 (Russia), Cathcart 77 (Northern Ireland), McAuley 86 (Northern Ireland)

11/09/12, Itztadion Ramat Gan, Ramat Gan
Israel 0-4 Russia
Goals: 0-1 Kerzhakov 7, 0-2 Kokorin 18, 0-3 Kerzhakov 64, 0-4 Fayzulin 77
Referee: Clattenburg (ENG)
Israel: Awat, Shpungin, Ben Haim, Natcho, Cohen (Ben Basat 46), Shechter (Sahar 46), Ziv, Benayoun (Vermouth 74), Ezra, Radi, Tibi. Coach: Eli Gutman (ISR)
Russia: Akinfeev, Anyukov (Eschenko 50), Ignashevich, Denisov, Glushakov, Kokorin (Fayzulin 34), Kerzhakov, V Berezutski, Shirokov, Bystrov (Samedov 23), Kombarov. Coach: Fabio Capello (ITA)
Yellow cards: Tibi 43 (Israel), Ziv 61 (Israel), Glushakov 59 (Russia), Ignashevich 90 (Russia)

11/09/12, Windsor Park, Belfast
Northern Ireland 1-1 Luxembourg
Goals: 1-0 Shiels 14, 1-1 Da Mota 87
Referee: Gladjović (???)
Northern Ireland: Carroll, McGivern, McAuley, J Evans, Baird, Davis, K Lafferty, Brunt, Hughes, Shiels (Norwood 83), Ferguson (Ward 74). Coach: Michael O'Neill (NIR)
Luxembourg: Joubert, Blaise, Schnell, Bettmer (Hoffmann 90+3), Da Mota, Payal, Joachim (Deville 46), Bukvic, Mutsch, Jänisch, Gerson (Philipps 50). Coach: Luc Holtz (LUX)
Yellow cards: McAuley 29 (Northern Ireland), K Lafferty 38 (Northern Ireland), Bettmer 45+2 (Luxembourg), Brunt 59 (Northern Ireland)

11/09/12, Estádio Municipal de Braga, Braga
Portugal 3-0 Azerbaijan
Goals: 1-0 Varela 64, 2-0 Hélder Postiga 85, 3-0 Bruno Alves 88
Referee: Marciniak (POL)
Portugal: Rui Patrício, Bruno Alves, Pepe, Miguel Veloso (Varela 63), Fábio Coentrão, Cristiano Ronaldo, João Moutinho, Raul Meireles, Nani (Rúben Amorim 76), João Pereira, Hélder Postiga (Éder 87). Coach: Paulo Bento (POR)
Azerbaijan: K Ağayev, Gökdemir (Chertoganov 89), Şükürov, Allahverdiyev, Özkara (Subašić 72), Räşad F Sadıqov, Abışov, C Hüseynov (İsmayilov 59), Medvedev, Ämirquliyev, Levin. Coach: Berti Vogts (GER)
Yellow cards: K Ağayev 45+1 (Azerbaijan), Cristiano Ronaldo 90+3 (Portugal)

12/10/12, Josy Barthel, Luxembourg
Luxembourg 0-6 Israel
Goals: 0-1 Radi 4, 0-2 Ben Basat 12, 0-3 Hemed 27, 0-4 Melikson 60, 0-5 Hemed 73, 0-6 Hemed 90+1
Referee: Trattou (CYP)
Luxembourg: Joubert, Schnell (Leweck 18), Bettmer, Da Mota, Payal (Hoffmann 78), Joachim (Deville 61), Bukvic, Philipps, Mutsch, Jänisch, Gerson. Coach: Luc Holtz (LUX)
Israel: Awat, Shpungin, Shish (Ziv 57), Melikson, Natcho (Biton 77), Alberman, Ben Basat, Hemed, Mori, Radi, Tibi (Keinan 55). Coach: Eli Gutman (ISR)
Yellow card: Jänisch 51 (Luxembourg)

12/10/12, Stadion Luzhniki, Moscow
Russia 1-0 Portugal
Goal: 1-0 Kerzhakov 6
Referee: Kassai (HUN)
Russia: Akinfeev, Anyukov, Ignashevich, Denisov, Kokorin, Kerzhakov (Eschenko 65), V Berezutski, Shirokov, Bystrov (Samedov 83), Fayzulin (Glushakov 46), Kombarov. Coach: Fabio Capello (ITA)
Portugal: Rui Patrício, Bruno Alves, Pepe, Miguel Veloso, Fábio Coentrão (Miguel Lopes 20), Cristiano Ronaldo, João Moutinho, Rúben Micael (Varela 67), Nani, João Pereira, Hélder Postiga (Éder 75). Coach: Paulo Bento (POR)
Yellow cards: Miguel Veloso 43 (Portugal), Shirokov 89 (Russia), Kokorin 90+3 (Russia)

16/10/12, Itztadion Ramat Gan, Ramat Gan
Israel 3-0 Luxembourg
Goals: 1-0 Hemed 14, 2-0 Ben Basat 36, 3-0 Hemed 48
Referee: Lechner (AUT)
Israel: Awat, Melikson (Abuhazira 81), Natcho, Alberman, Ben Basat, Hemed, Keinan, Mori, Gabai, Ziv, Radi (Vermouth 57; Ezra 71). Coach: Eli Gutman (ISR)
Luxembourg: Joubert, Blaise, Hoffmann, Peters (Philipps 81), Leweck, Bettmer, Da Mota (Laterza 86), Payal, Joachim (Deville 46), Mutsch, Jans. Coach: Luc Holtz (LUX)
Yellow cards: Ben Basat 8 (Israel), Mutsch 55 (Luxembourg), Payal 58 (Luxembourg), Hoffmann 72 (Luxembourg)

16/10/12, Estádio do Dragão, Porto
Portugal 1-1 Northern Ireland
Goals: 0-1 McGinn 30, 1-1 Hélder Postiga 79
Referee: Kinhöfer (GER)
Portugal: Rui Patrício, Bruno Alves, Pepe, Miguel Veloso, Cristiano Ronaldo, João Moutinho, Rúben Micael (Varela 61), Nani, Miguel Lopes (Rúben Amorim 46), João Pereira (Éder 74), Hélder Postiga. Coach: Paulo Bento (POR)
Northern Ireland: Carroll, McGivern, Cathcart, J Evans, Baird, Davis, K Lafferty, C Evans, McGinn, Norwood, Hughes. Coach: Michael O'Neill (NIR)
Yellow card: Pepe 80 (Portugal)

16/10/12, Stadion Luzhniki, Moscow
Russia 1-0 Azerbaijan
Goal: 1-0 Shirokov 84(p)
Referee: Stavrev (MKD)
Russia: Akinfeev, Ignashevich, Denisov, Kokorin, Kerzhakov (Dzagoev 79), V Berezutski, Shirokov, Samedov (Bystrov 62), Fayzulin (Glushakov 46), Eschenko, Kombarov. Coach: Fabio Capello (ITA)
Azerbaijan: K Ağayev, Şükürov, Cavadov, Chertoganov (Äliyev 84), Özkara, Subašić (Ämirquliyev 63), Gökdemir, Abışov, Nadirov (C Hüseynov 46), Medvedev, Levin. Coach: Berti Vogts (GER)
Yellow cards: Medvedev 14 (Azerbaijan), Cavadov 32 (Azerbaijan), Nadirov 38 (Azerbaijan), K Ağayev 43 (Azerbaijan), V Berezutski 57 (Russia)

14/11/12, Windsor Park, Belfast
Northern Ireland 1-1 Azerbaijan
Goals: 0-1 Äliyev 5, 1-1 Healy 90+6
Referee: Shvetsov (UKR)
Northern Ireland: Carroll, D Lafferty, McAuley, Cathcart (Healy 82), Baird, Shiels (McCourt 55), Davis, K Lafferty, McGinn (Brunt 67), Ferguson, Hughes. Coach: Michael O'Neill (NIR)
Azerbaijan: S Ağayev, Ramaldanov (Näziri 71), Özkara (Cavadov 79), Äliyev, Gökdemir (B Hüseynov 63), Abışov, C Hüseynov, Nadirov, Medvedev, Ämirquliyev, Levin. Coach: Berti Vogts (GER)
Yellow cards: Shiels 42 (Northern Ireland), Levin 49 (Azerbaijan), K Lafferty 57 (Northern Ireland), Äliyev 65 (Azerbaijan), Baird 79 (Northern Ireland), D Lafferty 90+1 (Northern Ireland), C Hüseynov 90+2 (Azerbaijan), Healy 90+2 (Northern Ireland), S Ağayev 90+4 (Azerbaijan)

2014 FIFA World Cup

22/03/13, Itztadion Ramat Gan, Ramat Gan
Israel 3-3 Portugal
Goals: 0-1 Bruno Alves 2, 1-1 Hemed 24, 2-1 Ben Basat 40, 3-1 Gershon 70, 3-2 Hélder Postiga 72, 3-3 Fábio Coentrão 90+3
Referee: Lannoy (FRA)
Israel: Awat, Shpungin, Ben Haim, Melikson (Refaelov 73), Natcho, Kayal, Ben Basat (Benayoun 81), Hemed (Atar 63), Yeiny, Gershon, Tibi. Coach: Eli Gutman (ISR)
Portugal: Rui Patrício, Bruno Alves (Hugo Almeida 74), Pepe, Miguel Veloso (Carlos Martins 60), Fábio Coentrão, Cristiano Ronaldo, João Moutinho, Raul Meireles, Varela (Vieirinha 60), João Pereira, Hélder Postiga. Coach: Paulo Bento (POR)
Yellow cards: Kayal 28 (Israel), Hemed 44 (Israel), Melikson 58 (Israel), Fábio Coentrão 58 (Portugal), Carlos Martins 66 (Portugal), Cristiano Ronaldo 72 (Portugal)

22/03/13, Josy Barthel, Luxembourg
Luxembourg 0-0 Azerbaijan
Referee: Sutton (IRL)
Luxembourg: Joubert, Hoffmann, Schnell, Da Mota (Laterza 67), Joachim (Deville 90+3), Philipps, Mutsch (Bettmer 90+4), Jans, Jänisch, Gerson, Bensi. Coach: Luc Holtz (LUX)
Azerbaijan: K Ağayev, Ramaldanov, Şükürov, Räşad Ä Sadıqov (C Hüseynov 87), Cavadov (Nadirov 59), Fardjad-Azad (Özkara 71), Äliyev, Räşad F Sadıqov, Abışov, Medvedev, İsmayilov. Coach: Berti Vogts (GER)
Yellow cards: Fardjad-Azad 15 (Azerbaijan), Joachim 19 (Luxembourg), Jänisch 33 (Luxembourg)

26/03/13, Tofiq Bähramov Republican stadium, Baku
Azerbaijan 0-2 Portugal
Goals: 0-1 Bruno Alves 63, 0-2 Hugo Almeida 79
Referee: Marriner (ENG)
Azerbaijan: K Ağayev, Ramaldanov, Şükürov, Mämmädov (Fardjad-Azad 69), Äliyev, Räşad F Sadıqov, Abışov, C Hüseynov, Nadirov (Levin 62), Medvedev, İsmayilov. Coach: Berti Vogts (GER)
Portugal: Rui Patrício, Bruno Alves, Pepe, Miguel Veloso, Fábio Coentrão, Vieirinha, João Moutinho, Danny (Varela 73), Raul Meireles (Hugo Almeida 58), João Pereira, Hélder Postiga (Custódio 82). Coach: Paulo Bento (POR)
Red card: Äliyev 55 (Azerbaijan)
Yellow cards: Pepe 33 (Portugal), Räşad F Sadıqov 39 (Azerbaijan), Şükürov 48 (Azerbaijan), Nadirov 51 (Azerbaijan), Äliyev 51 (Azerbaijan), Äliyev 55 (Azerbaijan)

26/03/13, Windsor Park, Belfast
Northern Ireland 0-2 Israel
Goals: 0-1 Refaelov 78, 0-2 Ben Basat 85
Referee: Kaasik (EST)
Northern Ireland: Carroll, D Lafferty, McAuley, J Evans, Clingan (McCourt 78), Davis, Paterson (Healy 84), Brunt, McGinn, Ferguson (Magennis 73), Hughes. Coach: Michael O'Neill (NIR)
Israel: Awat, Shpungin, Ben Haim, Melikson (Refaelov 69), Natcho, Ben Basat, Shechter (Benayoun 86), Yeiny, Gershon, Radi (Zahavi 60), Tibi. Coach: Eli Gutman (ISR)
Yellow cards: J Evans 36 (Northern Ireland), Brunt 90+4 (Northern Ireland)

Hélder Postiga (centre) awaits the adulation of his Portugal team-mates after scoring the only goal of the game at home to Russia

07/06/13, Bakcell Arena, Baku
Azerbaijan 1-1 Luxembourg
Goals: 1-0 Abışov 71, 1-1 Bensi 79
Referee: Fabian (HUN)
Azerbaijan: K Ağayev, Ramaldanov, Şükürov, Allahverdiyev, Räşad Ä Sadıqov, Cavadov, Räşad F Sadıqov, Abışov, Abdullayev (Mämmädov 84), Ämirquliyev (Subašić 62), Dadaşov. Coach: Berti Vogts (GER)
Luxembourg: Joubert, Hoffmann, Chanot, Martino, Bensi, Joachim, Philipps (Payal 46), Mutsch, Jans, Deville (Laterza 27; Da Mota 78), Gerson. Coach: Luc Holtz (LUX)
Red card: Subašić 85 (Azerbaijan)
Yellow cards: Mutsch 44 (Luxembourg), Bensi 61 (Luxembourg), Cavadov 73 (Azerbaijan), Räşad Ä Sadıqov 74 (Azerbaijan), Hoffmann 75 (Luxembourg), Laterza 76 (Luxembourg)

07/06/13, Estádio do Sport Lisboa e Benfica, Lisbon
Portugal 1-0 Russia
Goal: 1-0 Hélder Postiga 9
Referee: Skomina (SVN)
Portugal: Rui Patrício, Bruno Alves, Miguel Veloso, Fábio Coentrão, Cristiano Ronaldo, João Moutinho, Vieirinha (Custódio 90+2), Luís Neto, Raul Meireles (Rúben Amorim 73), João Pereira, Hélder Postiga (Nani 66). Coach: Paulo Bento (POR)
Russia: Akinfeev, Anyukov (Kozlov 31), Ignashevich, Zhirkov, Denisov, Kerzhakov (Smolov 68), V Berezutski, Shirokov, Bystrov, Fayzulin (Glushakov 21), Kombarov. Coach: Fabio Capello (ITA)
Yellow card: Luís Neto 88 (Portugal)

			Home					Away					Total					
		Pld	W	D	L	F	A	W	D	L	F	A	W	D	L	F	A	Pts
1	Portugal	7	2	1	0	5	1	2	1	1	7	5	4	2	1	12	6	14
2	Russia	5	3	0	0	4	0	1	0	1	4	1	4	0	1	8	1	12
3	Israel	6	1	1	1	6	7	2	1	0	9	1	3	2	1	15	8	11
4	Azerbaijan	7	0	2	1	2	4	0	2	2	1	5	0	4	3	3	9	4
5	Northern Ireland	5	0	2	1	2	4	0	1	1	1	3	0	3	2	3	7	3
6	Luxembourg	6	0	1	2	1	8	0	2	1	2	5	0	3	3	3	13	3

REMAINING FIXTURES

14/08/13	06/09/13	10/09/13	11/10/13	15/10/13
Northern Ireland - Russia	Israel - Azerbaijan Northern Ireland - Portugal Russia - Luxembourg	Luxembourg - Northern Ireland Russia - Israel	Azerbaijan - Northern Ireland Luxembourg - Russia Portugal - Israel	Azerbaijan - Russia Israel - Northern Ireland Portugal - Luxembourg

Group G

07/09/12, Skonto Stadions, Riga
Latvia 1-2 Greece
Goals: 1-0 Cauņa 42(p), 1-1 Spyropoulos 57, 1-2 Gekas 69
Referee: Bebek (CRO)
Latvia: Vaņins, Kļava, Krjauklis, Laizāns (Gauračs 80), Ivanovs, Cauņa, Višņakovs (Verpakovskis 75), Lukjanovs, Gorkšs, Rudņevs, Fertovs (Rugins 75). Coach: Aleksandrs Starkovs (LVA)
Greece: Karnezis, Maniatis, Spyropoulos, K Papadopoulos, Tziolis, Mitroglou (Samaras 46; Ninis 68), Torosidis, Gekas, Papastathopoulos, Katsouranis, Fortounis (Holebas 80). Coach: Fernando Santos (POR)
Yellow cards: Maniatis 23 (Greece), Tziolis 58 (Greece), Gorkšs 78 (Latvia), Lukjanovs 81 (Latvia), Kļava 90+2 (Latvia)

07/09/12, Rheinpark, Vaduz
Liechtenstein 1-8 Bosnia & Herzegovina
Goals: 0-1 Misimović 26, 0-2 Misimović 31, 0-3 Ibišević 33, 0-4 Ibišević 40, 0-5 Džeko 46, 1-5 Christen 61, 1-6 Džeko 64, 1-7 Džeko 81, 1-8 Ibišević 83
Referee: Borg (MLT)
Liechtenstein: Jehle, Oehri, Kaufmann, Quintans, Stocklasa, D Hasler, Burgmeier, Flatz (M Christen 46), Erne (Beck 71), N Hasler (F Eberle 89), Polverino. Coach: Hans-Peter Zaugg (SUI)
Bosnia & Herzegovina: Begović, Spahić, Šunjić, Vršajević, Pjanić (Vrančić 79), Ibišević, Misimović (Svraka 79), Džeko, Zahirović (Ibričić 78), Salihović, Vranješ. Coach: Safet Sušić (BIH)
Yellow cards: M Christen 73 (Liechtenstein), Beck 76 (Liechtenstein)

07/09/12, LFF, Vilnius
Lithuania 1-1 Slovakia
Goals: 1-0 Žaliukas 18, 1-1 Sapara 41
Referee: Gomez (ESP)
Lithuania: Karčemarskas, Šembkas, Radavičius, Andriuškevičius, Žaliukas, E Česnauskis (Novikovas 58), Šernas, Mikoliūnas (Labukas 75), Vičius (D Česnauskis 67), Klimavičius, Borovskij. Coach: Csaba László (HUN)

Slovakia: Mucha, Pekarík, Škrtel, Zabavník, Stoch (Breznaník 61), Sapara, Bakoš (Jakubko 79), Hubočan, Hamšík (Kucka 86), Pečovský, Ďuriš. Coach: Stanislav Griga & Michal Hipp (SVK)
Red cards: Pečovský 55 (Slovakia), Labukas 90+6 (Lithuania)
Yellow cards: Škrtel 52 (Slovakia), Vičius 60 (Lithuania), Bakoš 62 (Slovakia), Labukas 83 (Lithuania), Labukas 90+6 (Lithuania)

11/09/12, Bilino Polje, Zenica
Bosnia & Herzegovina 4-1 Latvia
Goals: 0-1 Gorkšs 5, 1-1 Misimović 12(p), 2-1 Pjanić 44, 3-1 Misimović 54, 4-1 Džeko 90+2
Referee: Aytekin (GER)
Bosnia & Herzegovina: Begović, Spahić, Pjanić, Ibišević (Medunjanin 87), Misimović, Džeko, Mujdža, Zahirović, Salihović (Šunjić 90+1), Lulić (Vršajević 30), Vranješ. Coach: Safet Sušić (BIH)
Latvia: Vaņins, Kļava, Krjauklis, Laizāns, Ivanovs, Cauņa, Višņakovs (Kamešs 61), Lukjanovs (Zjuzins 80), Gorkšs, Rugins, Rudņevs (Verpakovskis 61). Coach: Aleksandrs Starkovs (LVA)
Yellow cards: Krjauklis 18 (Latvia), Rudņevs 28 (Latvia)

11/09/12, Georgios Karaiskakis Stadium, Piraeus
Greece 2-0 Lithuania
Goals: 1-0 Ninis 55, 2-0 Mitroglou 72
Referee: Courtney (NIR)
Greece: Karnezis, Maniatis (Mitroglou 46), Spyropoulos, K Papadopoulos, Tziolis, Torosidis, Gekas (Mavrias 80), Ninis, Papastathopoulos, Katsouranis, Fortounis (Holebas 69). Coach: Fernando Santos (POR)
Lithuania: Karčemarskas, Šemberas, Žaliukas, E Česnauskis, Šernas (Rimkevičius 56), Mikoliūnas, Vičius, Klimavičius, Velička (Novikovas 76), Vaitkūnas, Borovskij (D Česnauskis 46). Coach: Csaba László (HUN)
Yellow cards: E Česnauskis 21 (Lithuania), Vičius 27 (Lithuania), Šernas 43 (Lithuania), Rimkevičius 59 (Lithuania), K Papadopoulos 62 (Greece), Mikoliūnas 84 (Lithuania)

11/09/12, Štadión Pasienky, Bratislava
Slovakia 2-0 Liechtenstein
Goals: 1-0 Sapara 36, 2-0 Jakubko 78
Referee: Evans (WAL)
Slovakia: Kuciak, Pekarík, Škrtel, Zabavník, Weiss (Breznaník 63), Stoch, Sapara, Bakoš (Jakubko 60), Saláta, Hamšík (Kucka 82), Guldan. Coach: Stanislav Griga & Michal Hipp (SVK)
Liechtenstein: Jehle, Oehri, Kaufmann, Stocklasa, D Hasler, Beck (F Eberle 70), Burgmeier, Erne, N Hasler, M Christen (Flatz 84), Polverino. Coach: Hans-Peter Zaugg (SUI)
Yellow cards: Polverino 29 (Liechtenstein), Burgmeier 39 (Liechtenstein), Zabavník 45+? (Slovakia), M Christen 49 (Liechtenstein), Weiss 60 (Slovakia), Jakubko 66 (Slovakia), D Hasler 71 (Liechtenstein)

12/10/12, Rheinpark, Vaduz
Liechtenstein 0-2 Lithuania
Goals: 0-1 E Česnauskis 51, 0-2 E Česnauskis 75
Referee: Vinčić (SVN)
Liechtenstein: B Büchel, Oehri, Kaufmann, Quintans, Stocklasa, Beck, Burgmeier, Erne (Ospelt 87), N Hasler (Kieber 74), Wieser (L Eberle 84), Polverino. Coach: Hans-Peter Zaugg (SUI)
Lithuania: Karčemarskas, Šemberas, Radavičius (Stankevičius 90+1), Kijanskas, Žaliukas, D Česnauskis (Šernas 58), E Česnauskis, Danilevičius (Rimkevičius 87), Mikoliūnas, Klimavičius, Novikovas. Coach: Csaba László (HUN)
Yellow cards: Šemberas 32 (Lithuania), Mikoliūnas 45 (Lithuania), Klimavičius 56 (Lithuania), E Česnauskis 56 (Lithuania), Beck 60 (Liechtenstein), Erne 62 (Liechtenstein), Quintans 64 (Liechtenstein), Stankevičius 90+4 (Lithuania)

12/10/12, Georgios Karaiskakis Stadium, Piraeus
Greece 0-0 Bosnia & Herzegovina
Referee: Damato (ITA)
Greece: Karnezis, Maniatis (Mitroglou 80), Spyropoulos, Tziolis, Samaras, Malezas (Karagounis 67), Torosidis, Gekas (Salpingidis 57), Papastathopoulos, Katsouranis. Coach: Fernando Santos (POR)
Bosnia & Herzegovina: Begović, Spahić, Ibišević, Misimović, Džeko, Mujdža, Zahirović, Salihović, Lulić (Stevanović 75), Medunjanin (Ibričić 75), Vranješ. Coach: Safet Sušić (BIH)
Yellow cards: Samaras 17 (Greece), Džeko 22 (Bosnia & Herzegovina), Vranješ 74 (Bosnia & Herzegovina), Fortounis 81 (Greece)

12/10/12, Štadión Pasienky, Bratislava
Slovakia 2-1 Latvia
Goals: 1-0 Hamšík 6(p), 2-0 Sapara 10, 2-1 Verpakovskis 84(p)
Referee: Makkelie (NED)
Slovakia: Kuciak, Pekarík, Škrtel (Ďurica 90), Breznaník, Weiss (Ďuriš 44), Stoch, Sapara, Bakoš (Hološko 61), Saláta, Hamšík, Pečovský. Coach: Stanislav Griga & Michal Hipp (SVK)
Latvia: Vaņins, Kļava, Krjauklis, Laizāns (Rugins 70), Ivanovs, Cauņa (Verpakovskis 77), Višņakovs, Lukjanovs (Gauračs 53), Gorkšs, Rudņevs, Fertovs. Coach: Jurijs Ševlakovs (LVA)
Yellow cards: Vaņins 6 (Latvia), Kļava 8 (Latvia), Breznaník 57 (Slovakia), Stoch 65 (Slovakia), Krjauklis 86 (Latvia), Gauračs 90+4 (Latvia)

16/10/12, Bilino Polje, Zenica
Bosnia & Herzegovina 3-0 Lithuania
Goals: 1-0 Ibišević 28, 2-0 Džeko 35, 3-0 Pjanić 41
Referee: Zelinka (CZE)
Bosnia & Herzegovina: Begović, Spahić, Pjanić (Stevanović 66), Ibišević, Misimović, Džeko, Mujdža (Vršajević 59), Zahirović, Salihović, Lulić (Zukanović 74), Vranješ. Coach: Safet Sušić (BIH)
Lithuania: Karčemarskas, Šemberas, Radavičius (Šernas 46), Kijanskas, Žaliukas, Labukas (Rimkevičius 66), Klimavičius, Panka (Pilibaitis 85), Novikovas, Borovskij, Stankevičius. Coach: Csaba László (HUN)
Yellow cards: Stevanović 80 (Bosnia & Herzegovina), Klimavičius 80 (Lithuania), Žaliukas 90+2 (Lithuania), Borovskij 90+2 (Lithuania)

16/10/12, Skonto Stadions, Riga
Latvia 2-0 Liechtenstein
Goals: 1-0 Kamešs 29, 2-0 Gauračs 77
Referee: Kovács (ROU)
Latvia: Vaņins, Laizāns (Gauračs 65), Ivanovs, Kamešs (Višņakovs 74), Cauņa, Verpakovskis (Zjuzins 85), Gorkšs, Rugins, Rudņevs, Fertovs, Bulvītis. Coach: Aleksandrs Starkovs (LVA)
Liechtenstein: Biçer, Oehri, Kaufmann, Quintans, Stocklasa, Burgmeier, Erne (Kieber 80), N Hasler (L Eberle 85), M Christen, Wieser, Polverino. Coach: Hans-Peter Zaugg (SUI)
Red card: Kaufmann 60 (Liechtenstein)
Yellow cards: Rugins 21 (Latvia), Ivanovs 54 (Latvia), Kaufmann 58 (Liechtenstein), Kaufmann 60 (Liechtenstein), Wieser 68 (Liechtenstein), Stocklasa 86 (Liechtenstein)

16/10/12, Štadión Pasienky, Bratislava
Slovakia 0-1 Greece
Goal: 0-1 Salpingidis 63
Referee: Collum (SCO)
Slovakia: Kuciak, Škrtel, Zabavník, Breznaník, Stoch (Weiss 69), Sapara, Saláta, Hamšík, Pečovský, Kucka (Gueye 82), Ďuriš (Hološko 72). Coach: Stanislav Griga & Michal Hipp (SVK)
Greece: Karnezis, Spyropoulos, Siovas, Maniatis 75, Tziolis, Samaras, Salpingidis, Torosidis, Gekas (Mitroglou 56), Ninis (Karagounis 86), Papastathopoulos, Katsouranis. Coach: Fernando Santos (POR)
Yellow cards: Sapara 13 (Slovakia), Karnezis 90+2 (Greece), Salpingidis 90+3 (Greece), Hološko 90+3 (Slovakia), Breznaník 90+5 (Slovakia)

22/03/13, Bilino Polje, Zenica
Bosnia & Herzegovina 3-1 Greece
Goals: 1-0 Džeko 30, 2-0 Ibišević 36, 3-0 Džeko 54, 3-1 Gekas 90+3
Referee: Kuipers (NED)
Bosnia & Herzegovina: Begović, Spahić, Ibišević (Stevanović 84), Misimović, Džeko, Mujdža (Vršajević 84), Zahirović, Lulić, Medunjanin (Rahimić 79), Vranješ, Zukanović. Coach: Safet Sušić (BIH)
Greece: Karnezis, Tzavelas (Gekas 46), Tziolis (Maniatis 58), Samaras, A Papadopoulos, Karagounis, Salpingidis (Christodoulopoulos 73), Torosidis, Papastathopoulos, Holebas, Katsouranis. Coach: Fernando Santos (POR)
Yellow cards: Tzavelas 35 (Greece), Katsouranis 48 (Greece), Lulić 64 (Bosnia & Herzegovina)

22/03/13, Rheinpark, Vaduz
Liechtenstein 1-1 Latvia
Goals: 1-0 Polverino 17, 1-1 Cauņa 30
Referee: Clancy (SCO)
Liechtenstein: Jehle, Oehri (Quintans 46), Stocklasa, D Hasler, Frick, Burgmeier, Erne (Gür 90+3), N Hasler, M Christen (Beck 72), Wieser, Polverino. Coach: René Pauritsch (AUT)
Latvia: Vaņins, Kļava, Laizāns (Višņakovs 46), Ivanovs, Kamešs (Žigajevs 56), Cauņa, Verpakovskis (Gauračs 66), Lazdiņš, Gorkšs, Rugins, Rudņevs. Coach: Aleksandrs Starkovs (LVA)
Yellow cards: Rugins 19 (Latvia), Stocklasa 22 (Liechtenstein), Burgmeier 37 (Liechtenstein), Lazdiņš 54 (Latvia), Polverino 61 (Liechtenstein), N Hasler 68 (Liechtenstein)

2014 FIFA World Cup

22/03/13, Štadión pod Dubňom, Zilina
Slovakia 1-1 Lithuania
Goals: 0-1 Šernas 19, 1-1 Jakubko 40
Referee: Oliver (ENG)
Slovakia: Kuciak, Škrtel, Ďurica, Pečovský (Bakoš 70), Sapara, Jakubko, Hubočan, Hamšík, Švento, Kucka, Mak (Ďuriš 64). Coach: Stanislav Griga & Michal Hipp (SVK)
Lithuania: Karčemarskas (Arlauskis 46), Šemberas, Kijanskas, Mikuckis, E Česnauskis, Matulevičius, Šernas (Lukša 90), Mikoliūnas, Ivaškevičius, Kalonas (Novikovas 69), Panka. Coach: Csaba László (HUN)
Yellow cards: Panka 14 (Lithuania), Šemberas 18 (Lithuania), Škrtel 38 (Slovakia), Šernas 40 (Lithuania), Kijanskas 54 (Lithuania), Jakubko 84 (Slovakia)

07/06/13, Skonto Stadions, Riga
Latvia 0-5 Bosnia & Herzegovina
Goals: 0-1 Lulić 48, 0-2 Ibišević 53, 0-3 Medunjanin 63, 0-4 Pjanić 80, 0-5 Džeko 82
Referee: Dean (ENG)
Latvia: Vaņins, Mihadjuks, Kļava, Bulvītis, Ivanovs, Kamešs (Gabovs 59), Verpakovskis (Lazdiņš 15), Gorkšs, Gauračs (Šabala 64), Fertovs, Siņeļņikovs. Coach: Aleksandrs Starkovs (LVA)
Bosnia & Herzegovina: Begović, Spahić, Rahimić (Višća 69), Pjanić, Ibišević, Džeko, Mujdža, Salihović (Ibričić 79), Lulić, Medunjanin (Stevanović 70), Zukanović. Coach: Safet Sušić (BIH)
Red card: Fertovs 11 (Latvia)
Yellow cards: Siņeļņikovs 84 (Latvia), Šabala 90 (Latvia)

07/06/13, Rheinpark, Vaduz
Liechtenstein 1-1 Slovakia
Goals: 1-0 M Büchel 13, 1-1 Ďurica 73
Referee: Strömbergsson (SWE)
Liechtenstein: Jehle, Oehri, Kaufmann, Quintans, D Hasler, Frick (Vogt 24), M Büchel, A Christen, N Hasler, M Christen (Beck 90), Wieser (Gubser 90+5). Coach: René Pauritsch (AUT)
Slovakia: Kuciak, Ďurica, Lásik (Ďubek 24), Čišovský, Stoch, Sapara, Hološko (Bakoš 70), Hubočan (Pauschek 46), Hamšík, Švento, Mak. Coach: Stanislav Griga & Michal Hipp (SVK)
Yellow cards: A Christen 16 (Liechtenstein), Pauschek 82 (Slovakia), N Hasler 85 (Liechtenstein)

07/06/13, LFF, Vilnius
Lithuania 0-1 Greece
Goal: 0-1 Christodoulopoulos 20
Referee: Olegário Benquerença (POR)
Lithuania: Zubas, Kijanskas, Mikuckis, E Česnauskis (D Česnauskis 86), Matulevičius, Kalonas, Mikoliūnas (Žulpa 73), Ivaškevičius (Eliošius 86), Panka, Borovskij, Stankevičius. Coach: Csaba László (HUN)
Greece: Karnezis, Maniatis, Manolas, Samaras, Karagounis, Torosidis, Christodoulopoulos, Gekas (Salpingidis 65), Papastathopoulos, Holebas (Tzavelas 46), Katsouranis (Tziolis 85). Coach: Fernando Santos (POR)
Yellow cards: Karagounis 36 (Greece), Samaras 55 (Greece), E Česnauskis 58 (Lithuania), Salpingidis 78 (Greece)

		Pld	Home W	D	L	F	A	Away W	D	L	F	A	Total W	D	L	F	A	Pts
1	Bosnia & Herzegovina	6	3	0	0	10	2	2	1	0	13	1	5	1	0	23	3	16
2	Greece	6	1	1	0	2	0	3	0	1	5	4	4	1	1	7	4	13
3	Slovakia	6	2	1	1	5	3	0	2	0	2	2	2	3	1	7	5	9
4	Lithuania	6	0	1	1	1	2	1	1	2	3	6	1	2	3	4	8	5
5	Latvia	6	1	0	2	3	7	0	1	2	3	7	1	1	4	6	14	4
6	Liechtenstein	6	0	2	2	3	12	0	0	2	0	4	0	2	4	3	16	2

REMAINING FIXTURES

_06/09/13_	_10/09/13_	_11/10/13_	_15/10/13_
Bosnia & Herzegovina - Slovakia	Greece - Latvia	Bosnia & Herzegovina - Liechtenstein	Greece - Liechtenstein
Latvia - Lithuania	Lithuania - Liechtenstein	Greece - Slovakia	Latvia - Slovakia
Liechtenstein - Greece	Slovakia - Bosnia & Herzegovina	Lithuania - Latvia	Lithuania - Bosnia & Herzegovina

Group H

07/09/12, Zimbru, Chisinau
Moldova 0-5 England
Goals: 0-1 Lampard 4(p), 0-2 Lampard 29, 0-3 Defoe 32, 0-4 Milner 74, 0-5 Baines 83
Referee: Van Boekel (NED)
Moldova: Namasco, Armas, Golovatenco, Onica, Epureanu, Covalciuc, Gatcan, Picusciac (Sidorenco 76) (Ovseannicov 85), Bulgaru, Suvorov (Dedov 46), Patras. Coach: Ion Caras (MDA)
England: Hart, Johnson, Baines, Gerrard (Carrick 46), Lescott, Terry, Milner, Lampard, Defoe (Welbeck 68), Cleverley, Oxlade-Chamberlain (Walcott 58). Coach: Roy Hodgson (ENG)
Yellow cards: Bulgaru 3 (Moldova), Johnson 5 (England)

07/09/12, Stadion Podgorica, Podgorica
Montenegro 2-2 Poland
Goals: 0-1 Błaszczykowski 6(p), 1-1 Drinčić 27, 2-1 Vučinić 45+3, 2-2 Mierzejewski 55
Referee: Jakobsson (ISL)
Montenegro: M Božović, Pavićević, Baša, Jovanović (Kasalica 65), Volkov, Vukčević (Peković 71), Jovetić, Vučinić, Zverotić, Drinčić (Džudović 84), Savić. Coach: Branko Brnović (MNE)
Poland: Tytoń, Glik, Borysiuk (Murawski 69), Polanski, Lewandowski (Saganowski 90+2), Obraniak, Wawrzyniak, Błaszczykowski, Grosicki (Mierzejewski 46), Piszczek, Wasilewski. Coach: Waldemar Fornalik (POL)
Red cards: Pavićević 69 (Montenegro), Obraniak 73 (Poland)
Yellow cards: Vučinić 16 (Montenegro), Pavićević 68 (Montenegro), Polanski 83 (Poland), Džudović 89 (Montenegro)

11/09/12, Wembley Stadium, London
England 1-1 Ukraine
Goals: 0-1 Konoplyanka 38, 1-1 Lampard 87(p)
Referee: Çakır (TUR)
England: Hart, Johnson, Baines (Bertrand 73), Gerrard, Lescott, Jagielka, Milner, Lampard, Defoe, Cleverley (Welbeck 62), Oxlade-Chamberlain (Sturridge 69). Coach: Roy Hodgson (ENG)
Ukraine: Pyatov, Selin (Shevchuk 75), Khacheridi, Tymoshchuk, Garmash, Zozulya (Devič 89), Gusev, Konoplyanka, Yarmolenko, Rotan (Nazarenko 90+2), Rakitskiy. Coach: Oleh Blokhin (UKR)
Red card: Gerrard 88 (England)
Yellow cards: Defoe 47 (England), Gerrard 54 (England), Selin 56 (Ukraine), Lescott 70 (England), Milner 74 (England), Garmash 80 (Ukraine), Khacheridi 86 (Ukraine), Gerrard 88 (England), Johnson 90+3 (England)

11/09/12, Municipal Stadium Wroclaw, Wroclaw
Poland 2-0 Moldova
Goals: 1-0 Błaszczykowski 33(p), 2-0 Wawrzyniak 81
Referee: Spathas (GRE)
Poland: Tytoń, Glik, Borysiuk (Krychowiak 75), Polanski, Lewandowski, Wawrzyniak, Błaszczykowski, Mierzejewski (Sobiech 71), Saganowski (Sobota 46), Piszczek, Wasilewski. Coach: Waldemar Fornalik (POL)
Moldova: Namasco, Armas, Golovatenco, Racu, Epureanu, Covalciuc, Gatcan, Picusciac, Suvorov (Alexeev 81), Patras (Ovseannicov 46), Ivanov (Onica 73). Coach: Ion Caras (MDA)
Yellow cards: Gatcan 6 (Moldova), Wasilewski 55 (Poland)

11/09/12, Stadio Olimpico, Serravalle
San Marino 0-6 Montenegro
Goals: 0-1 Djordjević 24, 0-2 Bećiraj 26, 0-3 Bećiraj 51, 0-4 Zverotić 69, 0-5 Delibašić 78, 0-6 Delibašić 82
Referee: Doyle (IRL)
San Marino: A Simoncini, Brolli (Vannucci 84), F Vitaioli, Cervellini, D Simoncini, Alessandro Della Valle, Gasperoni, Coppini, D Rinaldi, Marani (Cibelli 64), M Vitaioli (Mazza 80). Coach: Giampaolo Mazza (ITA)
Montenegro: M Božović, Baša, Volkov, Vukčević (Zverotić 66), Jovetić, Bećiraj (Kasalica 75), Damjanović, Peković (Džudović 66), Savić, Djordjević (Delibašić 66). Coach: Branko Brnović (MNE)
Yellow cards: F Vitaioli 19 (San Marino), Djordjević 24 (Montenegro), D Simoncini 40 (San Marino), Cervellini 81 (San Marino)

12/10/12, Wembley Stadium, London
England 5-0 San Marino
Goals: 1-0 Rooney 35(p), 2-0 Welbeck 37, 3-0 Rooney 70, 4-0 Welbeck 72, 5-0 Oxlade-Chamberlain 77
Referee: Mažeika (LTU)
England: Hart, Walker, Baines, Carrick (Shelvey 66), Jagielka, Cahill, Walcott (Lennon 10), Cleverley, Welbeck, Rooney (Carroll 73), Oxlade-Chamberlain. Coach: Roy Hodgson (ENG)

Wayne Rooney rises above the Montenegro defence to give England a 1-0 lead in Podgorica

San Marino: A Simoncini, F Vitaioli (Bacciocchi 84), Palazzi, Brolli, D Simoncini, Alessandro Della Valle, Cibelli, Coppini (Buscarini 76), Cervellini, D Rinaldi (Selva 79), Gasperoni. Coach: Giampaolo Mazza (ITA)
Yellow cards: A Simoncini 34 (San Marino), D Rinaldi 65 (San Marino)

12/10/12, Zimbru, Chisinau
Moldova 0-0 Ukraine
Referee: Turpin (FRA)
Moldova: Namasco, Golovatenco, Onica, Racu, Epureanu, Covalciuc (A Pascenco 61), Gatcan, Picusciac (Doros 84), Bulgaru, Suvorov (Ovseannicov 79), Dedov. Coach: Ion Caras (MDA)
Ukraine: Pyatov, Selin, Khacheridi, Tymoshchuk, Garmash (Seleznyov 60), Zozulya (Milevskiy 74), Gusev (Dević 79), Yarmolenko, Rotan, Mikhalik, Butko. Coach: Andriy Bal (UKR)
Yellow cards: Rotan 54 (Ukraine), Onica 63 (Moldova), Khacheridi 70 (Ukraine)

16/10/12, Olimpico, Serravalle
San Marino 0-2 Moldova
Goals: 0-1 Dadu 72(p), 0-2 Epureanu 78
Referee: Panayi (CYP)
San Marino: A Simoncini, F Vitaioli, Palazzi (Vannucci 46), G Bollini, D Simoncini, Alessandro Della Valle, Buscarini, Mazza (Cibelli 61), Cervellini, Marani (Selva 67), M Vitaioli. Coach: Giampaolo Mazza (ITA)
Moldova: Namasco, Golovatenco, Onica, Epureanu, Gatcan, Picusciac (Cebotari 82), Bulgaru, Bordian, Suvorov (Patras 59), Dedov (Dadu 71), Alexeev. Coach: Ion Caras (MDA)
Yellow cards: M Vitaioli 51 (San Marino), Bordian 55 (Moldova), D Simoncini 56 (San Marino), F Vitaioli 63 (San Marino), Buscarini 72 (San Marino)

16/10/12, NSK Olimpiyskyi, Kyiv
Ukraine 0-1 Montenegro
Goal: 0-1 Damjanović 45
Referee: Koukoulakis (GRE)
Ukraine: Pyatov, Selin, Tymoshchuk, Kucher, Gusev, Konoplyanka, Rotan, Seleznyov (Nazarenko 82), Mikhalik, Butko (Yarmolenko 62), Dević (Zozulya 52). Coach: Andriy Bal (UKR)
Montenegro: M Božović, Baša, Jovanović, Volkov, Jovetić (Vučinić 86), Damjanović (Vučević 72), Peković, Zverotić (Novaković 88), Drinčić, Džudović, Savić. Coach: Branko Brnović (MNE)
Yellow cards: Peković 17 (Montenegro), Zverotić 44 (Montenegro), Drinčić 45+3 (Montenegro), Kucher 45+4 (Ukraine), Božović 45+4 (Montenegro), Gusev 74 (Ukraine), Savić 76 (Montenegro), Selin 78 (Ukraine), Vučinić 88 (Montenegro)

17/10/12, National Stadium Warsaw, Warsaw
Poland 1-1 England
Goals: 0-1 Rooney 31, 1-1 Glik 70
Referee: Rocchi (ITA)
Poland: Tytoń, Glik, Polanski, Krychowiak, Lewandowski, Obranlak (Borysiuk 90), Wszołek (Mierzejewski 63), Wawrzyniak, Grosicki (Milik 83), Piszczek, Wasilewski. Coach: Waldemar Fornalik (POL)
England: Hart, Johnson, Cole, Gerrard, Jagielka, Lescott, Milner, Carrick, Defoe (Welbeck 67), Rooney (Oxlade-Chamberlain 73), Cleverley. Coach: Roy Hodgson (ENG)
Yellow cards: Polanski 11 (Poland), Cole 38 (England), Glik 64 (Poland)

14/11/12, Stadion Podgorica, Podgorica
Montenegro 3-0 San Marino
Goals: 1-0 Delibašić 14, 2-0 Delibašić 31, 3-0 Zverotić 68
Referee: Szabo (HUN)
Montenegro: M Božović, Pavićević, Baša (Kecojević 71), Volkov, Vukčević, Delibašić, Bećiraj, Novaković, Zverotić, Savić (Djordjević 46), Kasalica (Igumanović 77). Coach: Branko Brnović (MNE)
San Marino: A Simoncini, Palazzi, Vannucci, Benedettini (Alex Della Valle 83), Alessandro Della Valle, G Bollini, Cibelli (Gasperoni 89), Coppini, Cervellini, D Rinaldi, M Vitaioli (Buscarini 74). Coach: Giampaolo Mazza (ITA)
Yellow cards: Novakarnis 26 (Montenegro), G Bollini 39 (San Marino), Benedettini 47 (San Marino), Alessandro Della Valle 54 (San Marino)

22/03/13, Zimbru, Chisinau
Moldova 0-1 Montenegro
Goal: 0-1 Vučinić 78
Referee: Orsato (ITA)
Moldova: S Pascenco, Golovatenco, Gatcan, Dedov, Bulgaru, Bordian, Epureanu, Ionita, Gheorghiev (Josan 77), A Pascenco, Sidorenco. Coach: Ion Caras (MDA)
Montenegro: M Božović, Pavićević, Baša, Volkov, Jovetić, Vučinić (Novaković 80), Peković, Zverotić, Kasalica (Damjanović 45), V Božović (Vukčević 64), Savić. Coach: Branko Brnović (MNE)
Red cards: Peković 61 (Montenegro), Gatcan 90 (Moldova)
Yellow cards: Peković 9 (Montenegro), Pavićević 46 (Montenegro), Peković 61 (Montenegro), Gheorghiev 69 (Moldova), Gatcan 90 (Moldova), Gatcan 90+1 (Moldova)

22/03/13, National Stadium Warsaw, Warsaw
Poland 1-3 Ukraine
Goals: 0-1 Yarmolenko 2, 0-2 Gusev 7, 1-2 Piszczek 18, 1-3 Zozulya 45
Referee: Kralovec (CZE)
Poland: Boruc, Bocnisch, Krychowiak, Lewandowski, Glik, Błaszczykowski, Majewski (Teodorczyk 76), Rybus (Kosecki 46), Łukasik (Obranlak 60), Piszczek, Wasilewski. Coach: Waldemar Fornalik (POL)
Ukraine: Pyatov, Khacheridi, Kucher, Stepanenko (Tymoshchuk 60), Yarmolenko, Zozulya, Gusev (Morozyuk 90+3), Shevchuk, Rotan, Fedetskiy, Garmash (Bezus 90+2). Coach: Mykhailo Fomenko (UKR)
Yellow cards: Rotan 17 (Ukraine), Garmash 33 (Ukraine), Łukasik 44 (Poland), Stepanenko 45+1 (Ukraine), Tymoshchuk 87 (Ukraine), Morozyuk 90+4 (Ukraine)

22/03/13, Stadio Olimpico, Serravalle
San Marino 0-8 England
Goals: 0-1 Alessandro Della Valle 12(og), 0-2 Oxlade-Chamberlain 29, 0-3 Defoe 35, 0-4 Young 39, 0-5 Lampard 42, 0-6 Rooney 54, 0-7 Sturridge 70, 0-8 Defoe 77
Referee: Bieri (SUI)
San Marino: A Simoncini, F Vitaioli, Palazzi, Gasperoni, Alessandro Della Valle, D Simoncini, M Vitaioli, F Bollini (Valentini 81), Cervellini, Selva (D Rinaldi 75), Cibelli (Buscarini 67). Coach: Giampaolo Mazza (ITA)
England: Hart, Walker, Baines, Cleverley (Osman 56), Lescott, Smalling, Oxlade-Chamberlain, Lampard (Parker 66), Defoe, Rooney (Sturridge 56), Young. Coach: Roy Hodgson (ENG)
Yellow cards: D Simoncini 53 (San Marino), Cervellini 59 (San Marino)

26/03/13, Stadion Podgorica, Podgorica
Montenegro 1-1 England
Goals: 0-1 Rooney 6, 1-1 Damjanović 76
Referee: Eriksson (SWE)
Montenegro: M Božović, Baša, Volkov, Vukčević (Krkotić 63), Jovetić, Vučinić, Novaković (Damjanović 46), Zverotić, V Božović (Delibašić 75), Džudović, Savić. Coach: Branko Brnović (MNE)
England: Hart, Johnson, Cole, Gerrard, Lescott, Smalling, Milner, Carrick, Welbeck, Rooney, Cleverley (Young 77). Coach: Roy Hodgson (ENG)
Yellow cards: Novaković 27 (Montenegro), Johnson 30 (England), Welbeck 42 (England), Volkov 64 (Montenegro), Krkotić 90+3 (Montenegro)

2014 FIFA World Cup

26/03/13, National Stadium Warsaw, Warsaw
Poland 5-0 San Marino
Goals: 1-0 Lewandowski 21(p), 2-0 Piszczek 28, 3-0 Lewandowski 50(p),
4-0 Teodorczyk 61, 5-0 Kosecki 90+2
Referee: Johnsen (NOR)
Poland: Boruc, Salamon (Wasilewski 87), Polanski, Krychowiak,
Lewandowski, Wawrzyniak, Glik (Kosecki 46), Mierzejewski, Grosicki,
Milik (Teodorczyk 59), Piszczek. Coach: Waldemar Fornalik (POL)
San Marino: A Simoncini, Alex Della Valle (Buscarini 80), Palazzi, F
Vitaioli, Alessandro Della Valle, G Bollini (Bacciocchi 57), M Vitaioli, F
Bollini, Coppini, Selva (D Rinaldi 51), Gasperoni. Coach: Giampaolo
Mazza (ITA)
Yellow cards: Alessandro Della Valle 21 (San Marino), Polanski 43
(Poland), Krychowiak 47 (Poland), Milik 54 (Poland), Alex Della Valle 55
(San Marino), F Bollini 68 (San Marino), Gasperoni 85 (San Marino)

26/03/13, Chornomorets, Odessa
Ukraine 2-1 Moldova
Goals: 1-0 Yarmolenko 61, 2-0 Khacheridi 70, 2-1 Suvorov 80
Referee: Hansen (DEN)
Ukraine: Pyatov, Khacheridi, Tymoshchuk, Kucher, Stepanenko,
Yarmolenko, Zozulya, Gusev (Grechishkin 90), Seleznyov (Bezus 62),
Shevchuk, Fedetskiy. Coach: Mykhailo Fomenko (UKR)
Moldova: Namasco, Golovatenco, Dedov (Suvorov 78), Bulgaru, Bordian,
Epureanu, Ionita, Gheorghiev, Pascenco (Onica 67), Bugaiov (Doros 69),
Sidorenco. Coach: Ion Caras (MDA)
Red card: Stepanenko 90+2 (Ukraine)
Yellow cards: Seleznyov 59 (Ukraine), Gheorghiev 60 (Moldova)

07/06/13, Zimbru, Chisinau
Moldova 1-1 Poland
Goals: 0-1 Błaszczykowski 7, 1-1 Sidorenco 37
Referee: Teixeira (ESP)
Moldova: Namasco, Armas, Golovatenco, Ionita, Gatcan, A Antoniuc
(Ovseannicov 82), Dedov, Bordian (Cebotari 71), Epureanu, Suvorov (A
Pascenco 74), Sidorenco. Coach: Ion Caras (MDA)
Poland: Boruc, Jędrzejczyk, Komorowski, Rybus (Kosecki 64), Polanski
(Sobiech 79), Krychowiak, Lewandowski, Wawrzyniak, Błaszczykowski,
Salamon, Mierzejewski (Zieliński 62). Coach: Waldemar Fornalik (POL)
Yellow cards: A Antoniuc 53 (Moldova), Gatcan 65 (Moldova)

07/06/13, Stadion Podgorica, Podgorica
Montenegro 0-4 Ukraine
Goals: 0-1 Garmash 52, 0-2 Konoplyanka 77, 0-3 Fedetskiy 85,
0-4 Bezus 90+3
Referee: Gräfe (GER)
Montenegro: M Božović, Pavićević, Baša, Volkov, Kecojević, Jovetić
(Damjanović 43), Vučinić, Peković, Zverotić, V Božović (Delibašić 63),
Kasalica (Bećiraj 75). Coach: Branko Brnović (MNE)
Ukraine: Pyatov, Tymoshchuk, Yarmolenko (Kovpak 90+2), Zozulya,
Gusev, Konoplyanka, Rotan (Bezus 90+1), Fedetskiy, Garmash
(Kravchenko 69), Rakitskiy, Edmar. Coach: Mykhailo Fomenko (UKR)
Red cards: Zozulya 45+1 (Ukraine), Volkov 66 (Montenegro), Pavićević
81 (Montenegro)
Yellow cards: Volkov 6 (Montenegro), Rotan 19 (Ukraine), V Božović
45+3 (Montenegro), Fedetskiy 45+3 (Ukraine), Pavićević 39 (Montenegro),
Damjanović 52 (Montenegro), Volkov 66 (Montenegro), Pavićević 79
(Montenegro)

			Home				Away				Total				
		Pld	W	D	L	F A	W	D	L	F A	W	D	L	F A	Pts
1	Montenegro	7	1 2 1	6 7		3 0 0	8 0		4 2 1	14 7		14
2	England	6	1 1 0	6 1		2 2 0	15 2		3 3 0	21 3		12
3	Ukraine	6	1 0 1	2 2		2 2 0	8 2		3 2 1	10 4		11
4	Poland	6	2 1 1	9 4		0 2 0	3 3		2 3 1	12 7		9
5	Moldova	7	0 2 2	1 7		1 0 2	3 4		1 2 4	4 11		5
6	San Marino	6	0 0 3	0 16		0 0 3	0 13		0 0 6	0 29		0

REMAINING FIXTURES

06/09/13	*10/09/13*	*11/10/13*	*15/10/13*
England - Moldova	San Marino - Poland	England - Poland	England - Poland
Poland - Montenegro	Ukraine - England	Montenegro -	Montenegro -
Ukraine - San Marino		Moldova - San Marino	Moldova
		Ukraine - Poland	San Marino - Ukraine

Pedro (left) bundles in Spain's winning goal off France goalkeeper Hugo Lloris in Paris

Group I

07/09/12, Olympic Stadium, Helsinki
Finland 0-1 France
Goal: 0-1 Diaby 20
Referee: Thomson (SCO)
Finland: Hradecky, Moisander, Toivio, R Eremenko, Hetemaj (A Eremenko
65), Pukki, Arkivuo, Sparv, Halsti, Ring, Hämäläinen (Kuqi 78). Coach:
Mixu Paatelainen (FIN)
France: Lloris, Yanga-Mbiwa, Evra, Sakho, Cabaye (Matuidi 73), Ribéry
(Gomis 89), Benzema, Mavuba, Réveillère, Ménez (Valbuena 63), Diaby.
Coach: Didier Deschamps (FRA)
Yellow cards: Cabaye 15 (France), Halsti 26 (Finland), Sparv 55 (Finland),
Yanga-Mbiwa 64 (France), Matuidi 73 (France), Moisander 83 (Finland)

07/09/12, Boris Paichadze National Stadium, Tbilisi
Georgia 1-0 Belarus
Goal: 1-0 Okriashvili 51
Referee: Todorov (BUL)
Georgia: Loria, Okriashvili (Sirbiladze 83), Grigalava, Kashia, Amisulashvili,
Khizanishvili, Kankava, Daushvili, Targamadze, Ananidze (Gorgiashvili 75),
Mchedlidze (Kvirkvelia 56). Coach: Temur Ketsbaia (GEO)
Belarus: Veremko, Kulchy, Martynovich, Kornilenko, Renan Bressan,
Nekhaichik (Bordachev 30), Putilo, Zhavnerchik (Balanovich 34), Polyakov,
Tigorev (Dragun 62), Verkhovtsov. Coach: Georgi Kondratiev (BLR)
Yellow cards: Kankava 30 (Georgia), Martynovich 54 (Belarus),
Loria 86 (Georgia)

11/09/12, Stade de France, Paris
France 3-1 Belarus
Goals: 1-0 Capoue 49, 2-0 Jallet 68, 2-1 Putilo 72, 3-1 Ribéry 80
Referee: Göçek (TUR)
France: Lloris, Yanga-Mbiwa, Evra, Sakho, Cabaye (Matuidi 75), Ribéry
(Ménez 90), Giroud (Valbuena 61), Benzema, Mavuba, Jallet, Capoue.
Coach: Didier Deschamps (FRA)
Belarus: Veremko, Martynovich, Radkov, Renan Bressan (Kulchy 46),
Kislyak, Putilo, Polyakov, Verkhovtsov (Balanovich 70), Bordachev,
Rodionov (Kornilenko 62), Dragun. Coach: Georgi Kondratiev (BLR)
Yellow cards: Verkhovtsov 31 (Belarus), Yanga-Mbiwa 72 (France)

11/09/12, Boris Paichadze National Stadium, Tbilisi
Georgia 0-1 Spain
Goal: 0-1 Soldado 86
Referee: Moen (NOR)
Georgia: Loria (Kvaskhvadze 73), Lobzhanidze, Kvirkvelia, Kashia,
Amisulashvili, Khizanishvili, Kankava, Daushvili, Targamadze (Dzalamidze
64), Okriashvili, Mchedlidze (Sirbiladze 79). Coach: Temur Ketsbaia (GEO)
Spain: Casillas, Piqué, Iniesta, Xavi, Xabi Alonso, Sergio Ramos,
Busquets (Pedro 57), Arbeloa (Fàbregas 80), Jordi Alba, Soldado, Silva
(Santi Cazorla 64). Coach: Vicente del Bosque (ESP)

12/10/12, Dinamo Stadion, Minsk
Belarus 0-4 Spain
Goals: 0-1 Jordi Alba 12, 0-2 Pedro 21, 0-3 Pedro 69, 0-4 Pedro 72
Referee: Gumienny (BEL)
Belarus: Veremko, Dragun (Chukhlei 79), Martynovich, Shitov, Plaskonny,
Volodko (Kislyak 46), Hleb, Tigorev, Bordachev, Rodionov (Renan Bressan
65), Filipenko. Coach: Georgi Kondratiev (BLR)

Spain: Casillas, Xavi (Villa 76), Fàbregas, Pedro, Xabi Alonso, Sergio Ramos (Albiol 70), Busquets, Arbeloa, Jordi Alba, Santi Cazorla, Silva (Iniesta 56). Coach: Vicente del Bosque (ESP)
Yellow cards: Silva 31 (Spain), Dragun 39 (Belarus), Shitov 59 (Belarus)

12/10/12, Olympic Stadium, Helsinki
Finland 1-1 Georgia
Goals: 0-1 Kashia 56, 1-1 Hämäläinen 63
Referee: Aranovskiy (UKR)
Finland: Mäenpää, Moisander, Ojala, R Eremenko, Pukki (Hetemaj 62), Sparv, Uronen, Ring, A Eremenko, Hämäläinen, Raitala. Coach: Mixu Paatelainen (FIN)
Georgia: Revishvili, Kobakhidze, Grigalava, Kashia, Amisulashvili, Khizanishvili, Kankava, Daushvili, Targamadze (Kenia 81), Okriashvili (Ananidze 67), Mchedlidze (Devdariani 59). Coach: Temur Ketsbaia (GEO)
Red card: A Eremenko 59 (Finland)
Yellow cards: A Eremenko 14 (Finland), Okriashvili 41 (Georgia), A Eremenko 59 (Finland), Hetemaj 88 (Finland)

16/10/12, Dinamo Stadion, Minsk
Belarus 2-0 Georgia
Goals: 1-0 Renan Bressan 6, 2-0 Dragun 28
Referee: Schörgenhofer (AUT)
Belarus: Veremko, Dragun, Hleb, Renan Bressan (Volodko 85), Pavlov (Kislyak 83), Polyakov, Tigorev, Verkhovtsov, Bordachev, Rodionov (Chukhlei 90+1). Coach: Georgi Kondratiev (BLR)
Georgia: Revishvili, Devdariani (Mchedlidze 46), Grigalava, Kashia, Amisulashvili, Khizanishvili, Kankava, Daushvili, Targamadze (Kenia 75), Okriashvili (Ananidze 49), Kobakhidze. Coach: Temur Ketsbaia (GEO)
Yellow cards: Targamadze 35 (Georgia), Tigorev 43 (Belarus), Polyakov 45+2 (Belarus), Khizanishvili 51 (Georgia), Kankava 68 (Georgia), Bordachev 73 (Belarus), Hleb 90 (Belarus), Mchedlidze 90 (Georgia), Grigalava 90 (Georgia)

16/10/12, Estadio Vicente Calderón, Madrid
Spain 1-1 France
Goals: 1-0 Sergio Ramos 25, 1-1 Giroud 90+4
Referee: Brych (GER)
Spain: Casillas, Iniesta (Fernando Torres 75), Xavi, Fàbregas, Pedro, Xabi Alonso, Sergio Ramos, Arbeloa (Juanfran 50), Jordi Alba, Silva (Santi Cazorla 13). Coach: Vicente del Bosque (ESP)
France: Lloris, Debuchy, Evra, Sakho, Cabaye, Ribéry, Benzema (Giroud 88), Matuidi, Ménez (Sissoko 68), Gonalons (Valbuena 57), Koscielny. Coach: Didier Deschamps (FRA)
Yellow cards: Koscielny 42 (France), Gonalons 45+1 (France), Juanfran 90+2 (Spain)

22/03/13, Stade de France, Paris
France 3-1 Georgia
Goals: 1-0 Giroud 45+1, 2-0 Valbuena 47, 3-0 Ribéry 61, 3-1 Kobakhidze 71
Referee: Dobek (CRO)
France: Lloris, Varane, Sakho, Ribéry (Ménez 79), Valbuena (Rémy 66), Giroud, Benzema, Matuidi (Sissoko 81), Jallet, Pogba, Clichy. Coach: Didier Deschamps (FRA)
Georgia: Loria, Kashia, Amisulashvili, Khizanishvili, Kobakhidze, Daushvili, Targamadze (Gelashvili 84), Ananidze (Kenia 46), Vatsadze (Dvalishvili 74), Kvirkvelia, Lobzhanidze. Coach: Temur Ketsbaia (GEO)
Yellow card: Amisulashvili 79 (Georgia)

22/03/13, El Molinón, Gijon
Spain 1-1 Finland
Goals: 1-0 Sergio Ramos 49, 1-1 Pukki 79
Referee: Hategan (ROU)
Spain: Víctor Valdés, Piqué, Iniesta, Villa (Negredo 65), Fàbregas (Mata 76), Sergio Ramos, Busquets, Arbeloa, Jordi Alba, Santi Cazorla (Pedro 46), Silva. Coach: Vicente del Bosque (ESP)
Finland: Mäenpää, Moisander, Toivio, R Eremenko, Hetemaj, Pukki (Halsti 90+4), Arkivuo, Tainio (Sparv 69), Ring, Hämäläinen, Raitala. Coach: Mixu Paatelainen (FIN)
Yellow cards: Mäenpää 85 (Finland), Moisander 90+1 (Finland), Silva 90+1 (Spain)

26/03/13, Stade de France, Paris
France 0-1 Spain
Goal: 0-1 Pedro 58
Referee: Kassai (HUN)
France: Lloris, Evra, Varane, Cabaye (Ménez 70), Ribéry, Valbuena, Benzema (Sissoko 82), Matuidi, Jallet (Giroud 90+2), Pogba, Koscielny. Coach: Didier Deschamps (FRA)

Spain: Víctor Valdés, Piqué, Iniesta (Mata 90+3), David Villa (Jesús Navas 61), Xavi, Pedro (Fàbregas 76), Xabi Alonso, Sergio Ramos, Busquets, Arbeloa, Monreal. Coach: Vicente del Bosque (ESP)
Red card: Pogba 78 (France)
Yellow cards: Xavi 32 (Spain), Cabaye 54 (France), Matuidi 68 (France), Pogba 77 (France), Pogba 78 (France), Fàbregas 78 (Spain), Arbeloa 86 (Spain)

07/06/13, Olympic Stadium, Helsinki
Finland 1-0 Belarus
Goal: 1-0 Shitov 57(og)
Referee: Hacmon (ISR)
Finland: Mäenpää, Pasanen, R Eremenko, Hetemaj, Pukki (Forssell 77), Arkivuo (Hurme 53), Halsti, Tainio (Sparv 68), Ring, Hämäläinen, Raitala. Coach: Mixu Paatelainen (FIN)
Belarus: Veremko, Dragun (Pavlov 66), Martynovich, Shitov (Kalachev 79), Hleb, Putilo, Kislyak, Balanovich (Nekhaichik 17), Bordachev, Rodionov, Filipenko. Coach: Georgi Kondratiev (BLR)
Red card: Nekhaichik 90+1 (Belarus)
Yellow cards: Halsti 5 (Finland), Nekhaichik 77 (Belarus), Pasanen 82 (Finland), Nekhaichik 90+1 (Belarus)

11/06/13, Tsentralny, Gomel
Belarus 1-1 Finland
Goals: 0-1 Pukki 24, 1-1 Verkhovtsov 85
Referee: Kovařík (CZE)
Belarus: Veremko, Dragun, Martynovich (Sitko 80), Trubilo, Veretilo (Kislyak 46), Olekhnovich, Hleb, Putilo (Renan Bressan 64), Verkhovtsov, Rodionov, Kalachev. Coach: Georgi Kondratiev (BLR)
Finland: Mäenpää, Pasanen, Moisander, Hurme, R Eremenko, Hetemaj, Pukki (Furuholm 76), Sparv, Ring, Hämäläinen (Arajuuri 83), Raitala. Coach: Mixu Paatelainen (FIN)
Yellow cards: Hetemaj 5 (Finland), R Eremenko 9 (Finland), Veretilo 33 (Belarus), Kislyak 50 (Belarus), Hurme 71 (Finland), Arajuuri 84 (Finland)

			Home				Away				Total				
		Pld	W	D	L	F	A	W	D	L	F	A	W D L F A		Pts
1	Spain	5	0	2	0	2	2	3	0	0	6	0	3 2 0 8 2		11
2	France	5	2	0	1	6	3	1	1	0	2	1	3 1 1 8 4		10
3	Finland	5	1	1	1	2	2	0	2	0	2	2	1 3 1 4 4		6
4	Georgia	5	1	0	1	1	1	0	1	2	2	6	1 1 3 3 7		4
5	Belarus	5	1	1	1	0	0	0	0	1	3		1 1 4 4 10		4

REMAINING FIXTURES

06/09/13	*10/09/13*	*11/10/13*	*15/10/13*
Finland - Spain	Belarus - France	Spain - Belarus	France - Finland
Georgia - France	Georgia - Finland		Spain - Georgia

Top goalscorers (all groups)

8 Edin Džeko (Bosnia & Herzegovina)

6 Vedad Ibišević (Bosnia & Herzegovina)
Tomer Hemed (Israel)

5 Wayne Rooney (England)
Marco Reus (Germany)
Mesut Özil (Germany)
Robin van Persie (Netherlands)
Hélder Postiga (Portugal)

4 David Alaba (Austria)
Zvjezdan Misimović (Bosnia & Herzegovina)
Frank Lampard (England)
Eden Ben Basat (Israel)
Andrija Delibašić (Montenegro)
Jeremain Lens (Netherlands)
Rafael van der Vaart (Netherlands)
Robbie Keane (Republic of Ireland)
Pedro (Spain)
Zlatan Ibrahimović (Sweden)
Gareth Bale (Wales)

UEFA UNDER21™ CHAMPIONSHIP

Stylish Spain retain their title

Spain arrived in Israel for the 2013 UEFA European Under-21 Championship as defending champions and favourites. Expectations of a repeat success were high, and Julen Lopetegui's brilliant young team managed to exceed them by winning all five games, their fluid football proving too much even for a resolute and talented Italy side in the Jerusalem final.

Captain Thiago Alcántara stole the show in that game, scoring three goals before half-time, but it was a triumph for cohesion and teamwork as Spain reproduced the telepathic style that has helped the nation dominate the senior international scene in recent times.

Qualifying was, as usual, highly competitive. With just seven places available alongside hosts Israel, high-profile casualties were inevitable. Indeed, only two of the teams that contested the 2011 finals in Denmark – England and Spain – returned in 2013, with Portugal and France among those who fell by the wayside. The latter were undone in the play-offs by a gifted Norway side, and Tor Ole Skullerud's men would cause another stir in the summer.

It was business as usual for Spain as they cruised through qualifying, with Rodrigo's haul of 11 goals topping the scoring charts. Álvaro Morata then took over the mantle in Israel, coming off the bench in the first two games to earn victories against Russia and Germany. The latter were involved in the game of the finals as the tournament opened with a classic, Rainer Adrion's side fighting back from 2-0 down against the Netherlands only to concede in added time as a Leroy Fer header brought the Jong Oranje a memorable victory.

A late goal also scuppered Israel on matchday one, against Norway, while Italy ended England's run of 889 minutes without conceding to defeat Stuart Pearce's side at Bloomfield. The Azzurrini went on to punish a ten-man Israel outfit, winning 4-0, as the Dutch continued to score freely, putting five past Russia to confirm their semi-final place with a Group B game to spare.

In Group A, Norway stunned England, and a draw between Norway and Italy ended home hopes despite Israel's farewell 1-0 win against England, who became the fourth team to finish on zero points at an eight-team finals. They were soon joined in that unenviable club by Russia as Germany bowed out with victory.

Having relied on late goals in their first two games, Spain finally found their scoring boots and hit three past Norway to storm into the final. By contrast, the Dutch were running out of steam and could not break down an obdurate Italy, who squeezed through thanks to Fabio Borini's late strike. However, Devis Mangia's men could do nothing to stifle Thiago, Isco and co in the Jerusalem decider as Spain retained their crown in thrilling style with a sumptuous 4-2 victory.

Spain captain Thiago Alcántara lifts the trophy in Jerusalem

Álvaro Morata heads in Spain's winning goal against Russia

Final Tournament

Excitement was high in Israel ahead of the biggest football tournament the country had ever staged. The hosts were not just hoping to put on a good show but also to savour some success of their own, and they nearly got off to the ideal start. However, after leading ten-man Norway 2-1 in the tournament's opening game, they spurned the chance to open up with three points when Harmeet Singh scored an added time equaliser in Netanya.

That late drama continued as the group stage progressed. Italian midfielder Lorenzo Insigne's 75th-minute free-kick ended England's nine-game winning run in the other Group A encounter before Leroy Fer got in on the act the next day, firing the Netherlands to a dramatic 3-2 victory against Germany.

Spain also had to wait until the 82nd minute to open up Russia as the defending champions kicked off with a win thanks to substitute Morata. The Real Madrid CF forward repeated the trick against Germany, his winner coming later still as La Rojita reached the semi-finals with a game to spare. Italy punctured home ambitions with a 4-0 success in Tel-Aviv to signal their intent, while Pearce's England, lacking several of their best players for a variety of reasons, bowed out early after being taught a lesson in finishing by a Norway side that continued to impress.

No team, though, posed a greater threat than the Netherlands in the early throes of the competition. They put five goals past Russia, with coach Cor Pot enjoying the luxury of

fielding a first XI that boasted 56 senior caps between them. The two qualifiers from Group B were settled ahead of matchday three, but the order in which they finished had yet to be decided. A second-string Netherlands outfit never stood a chance as Lopetegui's side ran out 3-0 victors to claim top spot, with Morata yet again opening the scoring.

The Israeli public were rewarded for their loyalty when the biggest crowd for a match at Jerusalem's Teddy Stadium (the attendance record would be broken again in the final saw them earn a 1-0 off victory against England in Group A, Ofir Kriaf grabbing the only goal amidst much local jubilation. More late goals at Bloomfield meant Italy topped Group A after Andrea Bertolacci's strike with virtually the last kick of the game earned a point against Norway, leaving Skullerud's team with the daunting task of facing the holders in the last four.

Spain's first-half performance against Norway at Netanya featured some of the most fluent,

Ofir Kriaf – Israel's match-winner against England

attractive football of the tournament. They had to overcome an inspired opponent, however, in goalkeeper Ørjan Håskjold Nyland, who repelled a succession of Spanish efforts before Rodrigo finally ended his resistance on the stroke of half-time. Two late goals, including another from Morata, duly confirmed Spain's progress. The other semi-final was far tighter as Italy pressed and harried a Netherlands side that dominated possession but could not find a way through. The key intervention would come at the other end 11 minutes from time as Liverpool FC's Fabio Borini pounced to put his team in the Jerusalem final.

The 29,320 spectators who attended the final could have been forgiven for thinking that the two most successful sides in the competition's history would produce a low-scoring affair, the two sides having conceded just one goal between them to that point. In the event, two were scored in the first ten minutes, and although Italy got the second of them to raise the possibility of an upset with a terrific strike from Ciro Immobile, it soon became the Thiago show.

The FC Barcelona midfielder had scored a spectacular goal in the 2011 final, and he surpassed that exploit at the Teddy with a first-half hat-trick as Spain saved some of their best football for last. Italy, however, remained committed to the final whistle, and although, as at UEFA EURO 2012 a year earlier, they ended up second best to their Mediterranean rivals, they contributed to the outstanding quality of the football on view. Like the new European U21 champions, they departed the competition with their heads held high and – perhaps more importantly – considerable promise for the future.

Qualifying round

Group 1

2011/12 Results
Cyprus 6-0 San Marino
San Marino 0-3 Bosnia & Herzegovina
Germany 4-1 Cyprus
Greece 2-3 Belarus
Germany 7-0 San Marino
Belarus 1-1 Bosnia & Herzegovina
Cyprus 0-2 Greece
Belarus 0-1 Germany
Greece 2-0 San Marino
Germany 3-0 Bosnia & Herzegovina
Cyprus 1-3 Belarus
San Marino 0-8 Germany
Bosnia & Herzegovina 5-1 Cyprus
Belarus 1-3 Greece
Greece 4-5 Germany
San Marino 0-2 Belarus
Cyprus 2-1 Bosnia & Herzegovina
Greece 0-1 Bosnia & Herzegovina
Cyprus 0-3 Germany
Germany 1-0 Greece
San Marino 1-2 Cyprus
Bosnia & Herzegovina 3-0 Belarus
San Marino 0-0 Greece
Bosnia & Herzegovina 3-1 San Marino

2012/13 Results
15/08/12, Dinamo-Juni, Minsk
Belarus 0-3 Cyprus
Goals: 0-1 Englezou 13, 0-2 Mytidis 50, 0-3 Anyukevich 73(og)

07/09/12, Asim Ferhatović Hase Stadion, Sarajevo
Bosnia & Herzegovina 4-0 Greece
Goals: 1-0 Bilbija 8, 2-0 Bilbija 11, 3-0 Bešić 15, 4-0 Djurić 16

07/09/12, Ostseestadion, Rostock
Germany 3-0 Belarus
Goals: 1-0 Beister 57, 2-0 Leitner 64(p), 3-0 Polter 75

10/09/12, Asim Ferhatović Hase Stadion, Sarajevo
Bosnia & Herzegovina 4-4 Germany
Goals: 1-0 Djurić 11, 1-1 Kirchhoff 21, 2-1 Djurić 23, 3-1 Djurić 38, 3-2 Polter 59, 3-3 Leitner 65, 4-3 Grahovac 74, 4-4 Polter 87

10/09/12, Gorodskoi Stadion, Borisov
Belarus 1-0 San Marino
Goal: 1-0 Anyukevich 79

10/09/12, Peristeri, Athens
Greece 1-0 Cyprus
Goal: 1-0 Potouridis 64

		Pld	W	D	L	F	A	Pts
1	Germany	10	9	1	0	39	9	28
2	Bosnia & Herzegovina	10	6	2	2	25	12	20
3	Greece	10	4	1	5	14	15	13
4	Belarus	10	4	1	5	11	17	13
5	Cyprus	10	4	0	6	16	20	12
6	San Marino	10	0	1	9	2	34	1

Group 2

2011/12 Results
Lithuania 0-1 Slovenia
Finland 0-0 Malta
Lithuania 1-2 Malta
Finland 1-0 Slovenia
Lithuania 0-1 Sweden
Malta 1-4 Slovenia
Sweden 4-0 Lithuania
Malta 1-2 Finland
Slovenia 2-0 Ukraine
Sweden 1-1 Slovenia
Malta 2-2 Ukraine
Finland 0-1 Sweden
Malta 0-2 Lithuania
Slovenia 2-0 Lithuania
Ukraine 1-1 Finland
Ukraine 2-0 Lithuania
Malta 0-1 Sweden
Ukraine 6-0 Sweden
Slovenia 2-1 Malta
Lithuania 1-0 Ukraine
Slovenia 1-1 Finland
Sweden 4-0 Malta
Finland 1-2 Ukraine
Sweden 3-0 Finland

2012/13 Results
15/08/12, Turku Stadium, Turku
Finland 3-4 Lithuania
Goals: 1-0 Kymantas 4(og), 1-1 Nakrošius 19, 2-1 Dalla Valle 23, 3-1 Sumusalo 39, 3-2 Novikovas 64, 3-3 Vilkaitis 67, 3-4 Paulius 90+2

15/08/12, Obolon
Ukraine 2-0 Slovenia
Goals: 1-0 Korkishko 16, 2-0 Rybalka 42(p)

06/09/12, Obolon
Ukraine 5-1 Malta
Goals: 0-1 Vella 21, 1-1 Rybalka 26, 2-1 Rybalka 47, 3-1 Korkishko 55, 4-1 Rybalka 59, 5-1 Grechishkin 87

06/09/12, Stadion Ljudski vrt, Maribor
Slovenia 2-1 Sweden
Goals: 1-0 Berić 44, 1-1 J Johansson 61, 2-1 Lazarevič 82(p)

10/09/12, Kalmar Arena, Kalmar
Sweden 2-1 Ukraine
Goals: 1-0 Ajdarević 5, 2-0 Ishak 7, 2-1 Bogdanov 82

10/09/12, Stadium of Marijampole football club, Marijampole
Lithuania 1-3 Finland
Goals: 1-0 Vilkaitis 13, 1-1 Väyrynen 48, 1-2 Mäntylä 63, 1-3 Forsell 76

		Pld	W	D	L	F	A	Pts
1	Sweden	10	7	1	2	18	10	22
2	Slovenia	10	6	2	2	15	8	20
3	Ukraine	10	5	2	3	21	10	17
4	Finland	10	3	3	4	12	14	12
5	Lithuania	10	3	0	7	9	18	9
6	Malta	10	1	2	7	8	23	5

Group 3

2011/12 Results
Andorra 0-1 Wales
Andorra 0-5 Montenegro
Armenia 4-1 Montenegro
Czech Republic 8-0 Andorra
Andorra 0-1 Armenia
Czech Republic 1-1 Armenia
Montenegro 3-1 Wales
Wales 1-0 Montenegro
Wales 0-1 Czech Republic
Montenegro 4-0 Andorra
Armenia 0-2 Czech Republic
Armenia 0-0 Wales
Wales 4-0 Andorra
Czech Republic 2-1 Montenegro
Andorra 1-5 Czech Republic
Armenia 4-1 Andorra

2012/13 Results
15/08/12, The Racecourse Ground, Wrexham
Wales 0-1 Armenia
Goal: 0-1 Hambardzumyan 7(p)

07/09/12, Gradski, Niksic
Montenegro 0-0 Czech Republic

10/09/12, Chance Arena, Jablonec nad Nisou
Czech Republic 5-0 Wales
Goals: 1-0 Novák 17, 2-0 Wágner 60, 3-0 Vaněk 68, 4-0 Tecl 73(p), 5-0 Tecl 79

10/09/12, Stadion Podgorica, Podgorica
Montenegro 0-0 Armenia

		Pld	W	D	L	F	A	Pts
1	Czech Republic	8	6	2	0	24	3	20
2	Armenia	8	4	3	1	11	5	15
3	Montenegro	8	3	2	3	14	8	11
4	Wales	8	3	1	4	7	10	10
5	Andorra	8	0	0	8	2	32	0

The Czech Republic's Stanislav Tecl scored twice in his team's 5-0 win over Wales

Group 4

2011/12 Results
Faroe Islands 0-0 Northern Ireland
Northern Ireland 4-0 Faroe Islands
Serbia 1-0 Northern Ireland
Northern Ireland 0-3 Denmark
Serbia 5-1 Faroe Islands
FYROM 1-1 Serbia
Denmark 4-0 Faroe Islands
Serbia 0-0 Denmark
FYROM 1-0 Faroe Islands
FYROM 1-1 Denmark
Northern Ireland 0-2 Serbia
FYROM 1-0 Northern Ireland
Faroe Islands 1-1 FYROM
Denmark 6-5 FYROM
Faroe Islands 0-2 Serbia

2012/13 Results
15/08/12, Gundadalur, Torshavn
Faroe Islands 1-1 Denmark
Goals: 0-1 Makienok 42, 1-1 R Jacobsen 87

07/09/12, Aalborg Stadion, Aalborg
Denmark 1-1 Serbia
Goals: 1-0 Makienok 36, 1-1 Ninković 84

07/09/12, The Oval, Belfast
Northern Ireland 1-3 FYROM
Goals: 1-0 Magennis 10, 1-1 Spirovski 48,
1-2 Timov 72, 1-3 Aleksandar Stankov 90+2

10/09/12, Mladost, Krusevac
Serbia 5-1 FYROM
Goals: 1-0 Mudrinski 10, 2-0 Milunović 39,
3-0 Jojić 67, 4-0 Jojić 70, 4-1 Fazli 77, 5-1
Malbašić 81

10/09/12, Aalborg Stadion, Aalborg
Denmark 3-0 Northern Ireland
Goals: 1-0 E Larsen 8, 2-0 Albæk 28(p), 3-0
Laudrup 45+1

		Pld	W	D	L	F	A	Pts
1	Serbia	8	5	3	0	17	1	10
2	Denmark	8	4	4	0	19	8	16
3	FYROM	8	3	3	2	14	15	12
4	Northern Ireland	0	1	1	0	3	13	4
5	Faroe Islands	8	0	3	5	3	18	3

Group 5

2011/12 Results
Croatia 0-1 Georgia
Estonia 0-0 Switzerland
Georgia 2-7 Spain
Switzerland 4-0 Croatia
Spain 2-0 Georgia
Croatia 0-2 Spain
Georgia 0-1 Switzerland
Estonia 0-1 Croatia
Switzerland 5-0 Georgia
Spain 6-0 Estonia
Croatia 4-0 Estonia
Spain 3-0 Switzerland
Estonia 0-1 Spain
Croatia 1-2 Switzerland
Estonia 1-2 Georgia

2012/13 Results
15/08/12, Mikheil Meskhi, Tbilisi
Georgia 1-1 Croatia
Goals: 1-0 Skhirtladze 20, 1-1 Kramarić 37

06/09/12, Mikheil Meskhi, Tbilisi
Georgia 2-1 Estonia
Goals: 1-0 Dzalamidze 28, 1-1 Taar 35,
2-1 Parunashvili 83

06/09/12, Tourbillon, Sion
Switzerland 0-0 Spain

10/09/12, Rico Perez, Alicante
Spain 6-0 Croatia
Goals: 1-0 Sarabia 3, 2-0 Gerard 10, 3-0
Álvaro Vázquez 17, 4-0 Isco 34,
5-0 Montoya 38, 6-0 Álvaro Vázquez 81

10/09/12, Arena Thun, Thun
Switzerland 3-0 Estonia
Goals: 1-0 Schär 15, 2-0 St Zuber 51(p),
3-0 Seferovic 88

		Pld	W	D	L	F	A	Pts
1	Spain	8	7	1	0	27	2	22
2	Switzerland	8	5	2	1	15	4	17
3	Georgia	8	3	1	4	8	18	10
4	Croatia	8	2	1	5	7	16	7
5	Estonia	8	0	1	7	2	19	1

Group 6

2011/12 Results
Moldova 0-2 Portugal
Albania 0-3 Poland
Poland 0-2 Russia
Albania 4-3 Moldova
Portugal 1-1 Poland
Moldova 0-6 Russia
Poland 4-3 Albania
Russia 2-1 Portugal
Albania 0-1 Russia
Portugal 5-0 Moldova
Poland 0-1 Moldova
Albania 2-2 Portugal
Moldova 2-4 Poland
Portugal 1-0 Russia
Portugal 0-1 Albania
Russia 0 Albania

2012/13 Results
06/09/12, Sheriff small Arena, Tiraspol
Moldova 3-1 Albania
Goals: 1-0 Khachaturov 8, 2-0 Leuca 87,
2-1 Prençi 90+2

06/09/12, Centralni, Yekaterinburg
Russia 4-1 Poland
Goals: 0-1 Sobiech 7, 1-1 Bibilov 22,
2-1 Cheryshev 74, 3-1 Smolov 88,
4-1 Cheryshev 90+3

*10/09/12, Gdynski Osrodek Sportu i Rekre,
Gdynia*
Poland 0-0 Portugal

10/09/12, Centralni, Yekaterinburg
Russia 2-2 Moldova
Goals: 0-1 Cheptine 43, 1-1 Grigoryev 74,
2-1 Smolov 81, 2-2 Jardan 90+2

		Pld	W	D	L	F	A	Pts
1	Russia	8	5	2	1	17	5	17
2	Portugal	8	4	3	1	15	6	15
3	Poland	8	3	2	3	13	13	11
4	Moldova	8	2	1	5	10	24	7
5	Albania	8	1	2	5	11	18	5

Spain's Álvaro Vázquez grabbed a double against Croatia

Group 7

2011/12 Results
Turkey 6-1 Liechtenstein
Republic of Ireland 2-1 Hungary
Liechtenstein 0-3 Turkey
Hungary 0-3 Italy
Turkey 1-0 Republic of Ireland
Liechtenstein 2-7 Italy
Turkey 2-1 Hungary
Italy 2-0 Turkey
Liechtenstein 1-4 Republic of Ireland
Turkey 0-2 Italy
Republic of Ireland 2-0 Liechtenstein
Italy 2-0 Hungary
Hungary 1-0 Turkey
Republic of Ireland 2-2 Italy
Liechtenstein 0-4 Hungary

2012/13 Results
14/08/12, The Showgrounds, Sligo
Republic of Ireland 0-1 Turkey
Goal: 0-1 Gouzihan 84

06/09/12, Giuseppe Capozza, Casarano
Italy 7-0 Liechtenstein
Goals: 1-0 De Luca 8, 2-0 Immobile 28,
3-0 De Luca 39, 4-0 El Shaarawy 44,
5-0 Viviani 46+1, 6-0 El Shaarawy 54,
7-0 Sala 80(p)

06/09/12, Széktöi, Kecskemet
Hungary 2-1 Republic of Ireland
Goals: 1-0 Futács 15, 2-0 Kovács 28,
2-1 Brady 40(p)

10/09/12, Giuseppe Capozza, Casarano
Italy 2-4 Republic of Ireland
Goals: 0-1 Murray 23, 1-1 Caldirola 35,
1-2 Doran 57, 1-3 Henderson 59,
1-4 Doran 76, 2-4 El Shaarawy 89

10/09/12, Széktöi, Kecskemet
Hungary 2-0 Liechtenstein
Goals: 1-0 Fiola 39, 2-0 Balogh 90

		Pld	W	D	L	F	A	Pts
1	Italy	8	6	1	1	27	8	19
2	Turkey	8	5	0	3	13	7	15
3	Republic of Ireland	8	4	1	3	15	10	13
4	Hungary	8	4	0	4	11	10	12
5	Liechtenstein	8	0	0	8	4	35	0

Group 8

2011/12 Results
Iceland 2-1 Belgium
England 6-0 Azerbaijan
Iceland 0-2 Norway
Belgium 4-1 Azerbaijan
Azerbaijan 0-2 Norway
Iceland 0-3 England
Azerbaijan 2-2 Belgium
Norway 1-2 England
Norway 2-2 Belgium
England 5-0 Iceland
Belgium 2-1 England
England 4-0 Belgium
Azerbaijan 1-0 Iceland
Norway 1-0 Azerbaijan
Iceland 1-2 Azerbaijan
Norway 2-1 Iceland

2012/13 Results
06/09/12, Freethiel, Beveren
Belgium 1-3 Norway
Goals: 0-1 Singh 12(p), 0-2 Berget 60,
1-2 Batshuayi 70, 1-3 Bakenga 90+2

06/09/12, Dalga Stadium, Baku
Azerbaijan 0-2 England
Goals: 0-1 Caulker 28, 0-2 Shelvey 83

10/09/12, B2net Stadium, Chesterfield
England 1-0 Norway
Goal: 1-0 Wickham 43

10/09/12, Freethiel, Beveren
Belgium 5-0 Iceland
Goals: 1-0 Vetokele 25, 2-0 Van Tricht 69,
3-0 Batshuayi 74, 4-0 Vetokele 89,
5-0 Batshuayi 90+3

		Pld	W	D	L	F	A	Pts
1	England	8	7	0	1	24	3	21
2	Norway	8	5	1	2	13	7	16
3	Belgium	8	3	2	3	17	15	11
4	Azerbaijan	8	2	1	5	6	18	7
5	Iceland	8	1	0	7	4	21	3

Group 9

2011/12 Results
Romania 0-0 Kazakhstan
Slovakia 2-0 Latvia
Latvia 0-3 France
Kazakhstan 1-1 Romania
Romania 2-0 Latvia
Kazakhstan 0-1 Slovakia
France 2-0 Kazakhstan
Latvia 0-6 Slovakia
Romania 0-2 France
France 3-0 Romania
France 2-0 Slovakia
Slovakia 0-2 Romania
France 3-0 Latvia
Romania 2-0 Slovakia
Kazakhstan 0-3 France
Kazakhstan 0-0 Latvia

2012/13 Results
*06/09/12, Zemgales Olympic Centre,
Jelgava*
Latvia 1-1 Kazakhstan
Goals: 0-1 Kuantayev 57, 1-1 Rakeļs 75

07/09/12, National Training Centre, Senec
Slovakia 2-1 France
Goals: 0-1 Varane 4, 1-1 Žilák 21,
2-1 Oršula 67

10/09/12, National Training Centre, Senec
Slovakia 6-0 Kazakhstan
Goals: 1-0 Mak 13(p), 2-0 Štetina 35,
3-0 Mak 45+2, 4-0 Oršula 68,
5-0 Kolčák 88, 6-0 Lalkovič 90

10/09/12, Skonto Stadions, Riga
Latvia 0-4 Romania
Goals: 0-1 Alexe 11, 0-2 Matei 52,
0-3 Răduţ 72, 0-4 Răduţ 81

		Pld	W	D	L	F	A	Pts
1	France	8	7	0	1	19	2	21
2	Slovakia	8	5	0	3	17	7	15
3	Romania	8	4	2	2	11	6	14
4	Kazakhstan	8	0	4	4	2	14	4
5	Latvia	8	0	2	6	1	21	2

Group 10

2011/12 Results
Luxembourg 1-4 Austria
Bulgaria 0-1 Netherlands
Scotland 0-0 Bulgaria
Netherlands 4-0 Luxembourg
Austria 0-1 Netherlands
Luxembourg 1-5 Scotland
Scotland 2-2 Austria
Bulgaria 3-2 Luxembourg
Austria 0-2 Bulgaria
Netherlands 1-2 Scotland
Bulgaria 1-1 Austria
Scotland 0-0 Netherlands
Bulgaria 2-2 Scotland
Luxembourg 0-5 Netherlands
Austria 4-1 Luxembourg
Netherlands 5-0 Bulgaria

2012/13 Results
06/09/12, Saint Mirren Park, Paisley
Scotland 3-0 Luxembourg
Goals: 1-0 Armstrong 63, 2-0 Griffiths 68,
3-0 Watt 83(p)

07/09/12, Willem II, Tilburg
Netherlands 4-1 Austria
Goals: 1-0 Nuytinck 8, 2-0 Zeefuik 28, 3-0
Wijnaldum 38, 3-1 Sabitzer 56, 4-1 Ten
Voorde 66

10/09/12, Cashpoint-Arena, Altach
Austria 3-2 Scotland
Goals: 1-0 Gregoritsch 8, 1-1 Watt 54,
1-2 Russell 75, 2-2 Weimann 76, 3-2
Holzhauser 90+1

10/09/12, Deich, Ettelbruck
Luxembourg 1-3 Bulgaria
Goals: 1-0 Goncalo Almeida 2, 1-1
Chochev 12, 1-2 Kirilov 48, 1-3 Kirilov 69

		Pld	W	D	L	F	A	Pts
1	Netherlands	8	6	1	1	21	3	19
2	Scotland	8	3	4	1	16	9	13
3	Bulgaria	8	3	3	2	11	12	12
4	Austria	8	3	2	3	15	14	11
5	Luxembourg	8	0	0	8	6	31	0

England's Connor Wickham (left) vies for possession with Norway's Thomas Rogne during the Group 8 encounter in Chesterfield

Play-offs

11/10/12, National Training Centre, Senec (att: 3,260)
Slovakia 0-2 Netherlands
Goals: 0-1 Van Ginkel 55, 0-2 Van Ginkel 82
Referee: Gautier (FRA)
Slovakia: Šulla, Pauschek (Holúbek 58), Gyömber, Kiss (Oršula 76), Greguš, Štetina, Mak, Mikovič (Vojtuš 87), Kolčák, Čonka, Lásik. Coach: Ivan Galád (SVK)
Netherlands: Zoet, Leerdam, Bruma, Nuytinck (Dijks 85), Blind, Clasie, Van Ginkel, Maher, L de Jong, Wijnaldum, Wildschut (Cabral 74). Coach: Cor Pot (NED)

15/10/12, Sparta Stadium, Rotterdam (att: 8,850)
Netherlands 2-0 Slovakia
Goals: 1-0 Wijnaldum 56, 2-0 L de Jong 68(p)
Referee: Hansen (DEN)
Netherlands: Zoet, Leerdam, Bruma, Nuytinck, Blind, Van Haaren (Wildschut 46), Van Ginkel (Bacuna 84), Maher, L de Jong (Zeefuik 84), Wijnaldum, Cabral. Coach: Cor Pot (NED)
Slovakia: Šulla, Pauschek, Gyömber, Kiss (Greguš 46), Mak, Mikovič (Škvarka 76), Holúbek, Kolčák, Oršula (Vojtuš 69), Čonka, Považanec. Coach: Ivan Galád (SVK)
Aggregate: 4-0; Netherlands qualify.

11/10/12, Municipal El Plantío, Burgos (att: 12,161)
Spain 5-0 Denmark
Goals: 1-0 Rodrigo 16, 2-0 Rodrigo 18, 3-0 Rodrigo 21, 4-0 Rodrigo 66, 5-0 Isco 79(p)
Referee: Madden (SCO)
Spain: De Gea, Montoya, Planas, Barba, Iñigo Martínez, Romeu, Muniain (Deulofeu 84), Illarramendi, Rodrigo (Álvaro Vázquez 75), Isco, Tello (Sarabia 62). Coach: Julen Lopetegui (ESP)
Denmark: Rønnow, Fenger, Jørgensen, Vestergaard, Kirkeskov, Delaney, E Larsen, Albæk (Høegh 83), Helenius, Christiansen (Braithwaite 63), Kusk (Laudrup 67). Coach: Morten Wieghorst (DEN)

16/10/12, Aalborg Stadion, Aalborg (att: 5,282)
Denmark 1-3 Spain
Goals: 0-1 Muniain 24, 0-2 Álvaro Vázquez 62, 1-2 Christiansen 90+1, 1-3 Álvaro Vázquez 90+2
Referee: Marciniak (POL)
Denmark: Rønnow, Fenger, Jørgensen, Høegh, Kirkeskov, Delaney, Fischer (Kusk 74), Albæk, Braithwaite (Helenius 63), Christiansen, Laudrup (Gundelach 81). Coach: Morten Wieghorst (DEN)
Spain: De Gea, Montoya, Planas, Amat, Iñigo Martínez, Romeu (Camacho 46), Muniain (Sarabia 57), Illarramendi (Sergi Roberto 65), Álvaro Vázquez, Isco, Tello. Coach: Julen Lopetegui (ESP)
Aggregate: 1-8; Spain qualify.

Fedor Smolov scored three goals in Russia's play-off victory against the Czech Republic

12/10/12, Chance Arena, Jablonec nad Nisou (att: 2,116)
Czech Republic 0-2 Russia
Goals: 0-1 Smolov 33, 0-2 Smolov 74(p)
Referee: Hategan (ROU)
Czech Republic: Koubek, Lecjaks, Hejda, Čmovš, Nitrianský, Hanousek (Vaněk 4), Kopic (Wágner 62), Daníček, Kadlec, Tecl, Pospíšil (Vůch 87). Coach: Jakub Dovalil (CZE)
Russia: Zabolotni, Tsallagov, Logashov, Belyaev, Burlak, Kirillov (Bibilov 69), Petrov, Shatov, Yakovlev (Kanunnikov 81), Smolov, Cheryshev. Coach: Nikolai Pisarev (RUS)

16/10/12, Centralni, Yekaterinburg (att: 20,000)
Russia 2-2 Czech Republic
Goals: 1-0 Smolov 6(p), 1-1 Wágner 12, 1-2 Wágner 64, 2-2 Kirillov 83
Referee: Munukka (FIN)
Russia: Zabolotni, Tsallagov, Schennikov, Belyaev, Burlak, Kirillov (Zotov 90), Petrov, Shatov, Kanunnikov (Bibilov 90), Smolov, Cheryshev. Coach: Dmitri Ulyanov (RUS)
Czech Republic: Koubek, Lecjaks, Čmovš, Kalas, Vaněk (Tecl 66), Wágner, Krejčí (Vůch 78), Kadlec, Mareček, Pospíšil (Daníček 86), Holeš. Coach: Jakub Dovalil (CZE)
Red cards: Kalas 75 (Czech Republic), Kadlec 87 (Czech Republic)
Aggregate: 4-2; Russia qualify.

12/10/12, BayArena, Leverkusen (att: 7,382)
Germany 1-1 Switzerland
Goals: 1-0 Rudy 82(p), 1-1 Drmic 87
Referee: Mateu Lahoz (ESP)
Germany: Leno, Jantschke, Sobiech, Kirchhoff, Rudy, Holtby, Mlapa (Polter 73), Leitner (Volland 80), Esswein (Bellarabi 46), Jung, Beister. Coach: Rainer Adrion (GER)
Switzerland: Bürki, Widmer, Daprelà, Schär, Affolter, Abrashi, Kasami, Wiss (Buff 75), Seferovic (Drmic 72), Toko (Koch 84), Zuber. Coach: Pierluigi Tami (SUI)
Red card: Schär 81 (Switzerland)

16/10/12, Swissporarena, Lucerne (att: 10,277)
Switzerland 1-3 Germany
Goals: 0-1 Holtby 8, 0-2 Sobiech 20, 0-3 Polter 45, 1-3 Drmic 75
Referee: Jug (SVN)
Switzerland: Bürki, Widmer, Daprelà, Koch, Affolter, Abrashi, Kasami (Buff 46), Wiss (Seferovic 68), Drmic, Toko (Hajrovic 46), Zuber. Coach: Pierluigi Tami (SUI)
Germany: Leno, Jantschke, Thesker, Sobiech, Rudy, Holtby, Polter (Funk 90), Jung, Moritz, Bellarabi (Esswein 65), Beister (Mlapa 78). Coach: Rainer Adrion (GER)
Aggregate: 2-4; Germany qualify.

12/10/12, Carrow Road, Norwich (att: 17,266)
England 1-0 Serbia
Goal: 1-0 Dawson 65(p)
Referee: Aytekin (GER)
England: Butland, Smith, Rose, Rodwell (Lowe 46), Caulker, Dawson, Zaha, Henderson, Sordell (Wickham 78), Ince, Sterling (Townsend 66). Coach: Stuart Pearce (ENG)
Serbia: Aleksić, Medojević, Gudelj, Lazović (Kojić 79), Despotović, Marković (Čaušić 46), Mladenović, Pantić, Milunović, Milivojević, Malbašić (Jojić 60). Coach: Aleksandar Janković (SRB)

16/10/12, Mladost, Krusevac (att: 9,500)
Serbia 0-1 England
Goal: 0-1 Wickham 90+4
Referee: Göçek (TUR)
Serbia: Aleksić, Kosanović, Medojević, Gudelj, Rodić, Mudrinski, Lazović (Malbašić 59), Čaušić, Kolić (Despotović 59), Milivojević, Pinkovic (Marković 70), Leoni, Aleksandar Janković (SRB)
England: Butland, Smith, Rose, Lowe, Caulker, Dawson, Zaha (Sterling 76), Henderson, Sordell (Lees 82), Ince, Delfouneso (Wickham 89). Coach: Stuart Pearce (ENG)
Red cards: Medojević 90+5 (Serbia), Rose 90+5 (England)
Aggregate: 0-2; England qualify.

12/10/12, Océane Stadium, Le Havre (att: 6,720)
France 1-0 Norway
Goal: 1-0 Varane 22
Referee: Tohver (EST)
France: Ahamada, Corchia, Mavinga, Varane, Mangala, M'Vila, Cabella (Griezmann 77), Pajot, Ben Yedder (Lacazette 69), Grenier (Guilavogui 66), Knockaert. Coach: Erick Mombaerts (FRA)
Norway: Østbø, Hedenstad, Rogne, Strandberg, Elabdellaoui, Konradssen, Singh (De Lanlay 67), Berget (Svensson 83), Johansen, Pedersen, Nielsen. Coach: Per Joar Hansen (NOR)

16/10/12, Marienlyst, Drammen (att: 2,150)
Norway 5-3 France
Goals: 1-0 Singh 13(p), 2-0 Nielsen 19, 3-0 Rogne 27, 3-1 Guilavogui 28, 4-1 Konradssen 57, 5-1 Berget 66, 5-2 Lacazette 84, 5-3 Griezmann 87
Referee: Valeri (ITA)
Norway: Nyland, Hedenstad, Rogne, Strandberg, Elabdellaoui, Konradssen (Semb Berge 90+2), Singh (Johansen 90), Berget, Pedersen, Nielsen, Nordtveit. Coach: Per Joar Hansen (NOR)
France: Ahamada, Corchia, Mavinga, Varane, Mangala, M'Vila, Cabella, Guilavogui (Griezmann 64), Lacazette, Pajot (Saivet 59), Knockaert (Niang 58). Coach: Erick Mombaerts (FRA)
Red card: Lacazette 86 (France)

Aggregate: 5-4; Norway qualify.

12/10/12, Adriatico, Pescara (att: 11,102)
Italy 1-0 Sweden
Goal: 1-0 Immobile 17
Referee: Artur Soares (POR)
Italy: Bardi, De Sciglio, Frascatore, Capuano, Marrone, Caldirola, Saponara (Rossi 59), Florenzi (Viviani 82), Immobile (Gabbiadini 76), Insigne, De Luca. Coach: Devis Mangia (ITA)
Sweden: Johnsson, M Johansson, Jansson, Pettersson, Demir, Hamad, Hiljemark, J Johansson, Claesson, Ishak, Armenteros (Jönsson 70). Coach: Håkan Ericson (SWE)

16/10/12, Kalmar Arena, Kalmar (att: 6,453)
Sweden 2-3 Italy
Goals: 0-1 Insigne 68, 0-2 Florenzi 71, 1-2 Ishak 72, 2-2 Hiljemark 77, 2-3 Immobile 86
Referee: Oliver (ENG)
Sweden: Johnsson, M Johansson, Jansson, Pettersson, Demir (Claesson 77), Hamad, Hiljemark, J Johansson (Jönsson 74), Albornoz, Ishak, Celik (Armenteros 70). Coach: Håkan Ericson (SWE)
Italy: Bardi, De Sciglio, Frascatore, Capuano, Marrone, Caldirola, Florenzi (Crimi 82), Rossi, Immobile (Saponara 90), Insigne, De Luca (Gabbiadini 59). Coach: Devis Mangia (ITA)

Aggregate: 2-4; Italy qualify.

Top goalscorers (qualifying/play-offs)

11	Rodrigo (Spain)
9	Jan Chramosta (Czech Republic)
8	Peniel Mlapa (Germany)
	Genero Zeefuik (Netherlands)
	Jordan Rhodes (Scotland)
7	Fedor Smolov (Russia)
6	Armando Sadiku (Albania)
	Nemanja Bilbija (Bosnia & Herzegovina)
	Milan Djurić (Bosnia & Herzegovina)
	Manolo Gabbiadini (Italy)
	Isco (Spain)
	Mikael Ishak (Sweden)

Final tournament

Group A

05/06/13, Netanya Municipal Stadium, Netanya (att: 10,850)
Israel 2-2 Norway
Goals: 1-0 Biton 16(p), 1-1 Pedersen 24, 2-1 Turgeman 71, 2-2 Singh 90+1
Referee: Gil (POL)
Israel: Kleyman, Dasa, Kabha (Kriaf 38), Biton (Zaguri 75), Kalebat, Golasa, Dabbur, Gotlib, Tawatha, Barouch (Turgeman 57), Ben Harush. Coach: Guy Luzon (ISR)
Norway: Nyland, Strandberg, Hedenstad, Elabdellaoui, Berget (Nielsen 76), Pedersen, Semb Berge, De Lanlay (Linnes 46), Konradssen (Singh 76), Eikrem, Johansen. Coach: Tor Ole Skullerud (NOR)
Red card: Hedenstad 44 (Norway)
Yellow cards: Konradssen 38 (Norway), Kalebat 44 (Israel), Barouch 45+2 (Israel), Golasa 46 (Israel)

05/06/13, Bloomfield, Tel-Aviv (att: 10,675)
England 0-1 Italy
Goal: 0-1 Insigne 79
Referee: Gautier (FRA)
England: Butland, Clyne, Caulker, Dawson, Henderson, Robinson, Lowe, Shelvey (McEachran 75), Redmond, Sordell (Chalobah 65), Wickham (Delfouneso 82). Coach: Stuart Pearce (ENG)
Italy: Bardi, Donati, Biraghi, Verratti, Caldirola, Florenzi, Marrone (Rossi 87), Immobile (Gabbiadini 60), Insigne, Bianchetti, Borini (Destro 78). Coach: Devis Mangia (ITA)
Yellow cards: Lowe 66 (England), Clyne 77 (England), Bianchetti 88 (Italy), Insigne 90+4 (Italy)

08/06/13, Ha Moshava, Petach-Tikva (att: 6,150)
England 1-3 Norway
Goals: 0-1 Semb Berge 15, 0-2 Berget 34, 0-3 Eikrem 52, 1-3 Dawson 57(p)
Referee: Boiko (UKR)
England: Butland, Smith, Caulker, Dawson (Wisdom 85), Henderson, Lowe (Wickham 46), Rose, Chalobah, Zaha, Ince, Redmond (Shelvey 67). Coach: Stuart Pearce (ENG)
Norway: Nyland, Rogne (Nordtveit 83), Strandberg, Elabdellaoui, Singh, Berget, Pedersen, Nielsen, Semb Berge (Linnes 57), Eikrem (Ibrahim 68), Johansen. Coach: Tor Ole Skullerud (NOR)
Yellow cards: Semb Berge 57 (Norway), Henderson 82 (England), Chalobah 90+1 (England)

08/06/13, Bloomfield, Tel-Aviv (att: 13,750)
Italy 4-0 Israel
Goals: 1-0 Saponara 18, 2-0 Gabbiadini 42, 3-0 Gabbiadini 53, 4-0 Florenzi 71
Referee: Haţegan (ROU)
Italy: Bardi, Donati, Biraghi, Verratti (Sansone 70), Caldirola, Florenzi, Immobile, Insigne (Rossi 40), Gabbiadini (Destro 57), Bianchetti, Saponara. Coach: Devis Mangia (ITA)

Israel: Kleyman, Dasa (Werta 46), Wahaba, Zaguri, Biton, Kalebat (Azam 83), Golasa, Tawatha, Turgeman (Barouch 67), Ben Harush, Kriaf. Coach: Guy Luzon (ISR)
Red card: Golasa 37 (Israel)
Yellow card: Verratti 60 (Italy)

11/06/13, Teddy Stadium, Jerusalem (att: 22,183)
Israel 1-0 England
Goal: 1-0 Kriaf 80
Referee: Boiko (UKR)
Israel: Kleyman, Davidaze, Wahaba, Zaguri, Biton, Dabbur (Altman 55), Turgeman (Barouch 63), Werta, Sallalich (Azam 87), Ben Harush, Kriaf. Coach: Guy Luzon (ISR)
England: Steele, Clyne, Wisdom, Lees, Rose, Chalobah (Sordell 78), McEachran (Redmond 71), Zaha, Ince (Henderson 46), Shelvey, Wickham. Coach: Stuart Pearce (ENG)

11/06/13, Bloomfield, Tel-Aviv (att: 7,130)
Norway 1-1 Italy
Goals: 1-0 Strandberg 90(p), 1-1 Bertolacci 90+4
Referee: Bebek (CRO)
Norway: Østbø, Linnes, Rogne (Strandberg 54), Hedenstad, Berisha, Nielsen (Kastrati 60), Henriksen, Nordtveit, De Lanlay, Konradssen, King (Ibrahim 74). Coach: Tor Ole Skullerud (NOR)
Italy: Bardi, Donati, Capuano, Caldirola, Destro (Gabbiadini 72), Sansone, Paloschi (Bertolacci 46), Saponara (Bertolacci 46), Regini, Rossi (Florenzi 61), Crimi. Coach: Devis Mangia (ITA)
Yellow cards: Rogne 45+1 (Norway), Ibrahim 79 (Norway), Caldirola 87 (Italy), Donati 90+1 (Italy)

		Pld	W	D	L	F	A	Pts
1	Italy	3	2	1	0	6	1	7
2	Norway	3	1	2	0	6	4	5
3	Israel	3	1	1	1	3	6	4
4	England	3	0	0	3	1	5	0

Manolo Gabbiadini (No11) takes on Israel's Omri Ben Harush

Group B

06/06/13, Teddy Stadium, Jerusalem (att: 8,127)
Spain 1-0 Russia
Goal: 1-0 Morata 82
Referee: Jug (SVN)
Spain: De Gea, Montoya, Illarramendi, Bartra, Iñigo Martínez, Rodrigo (Canales 78), Thiago Alcántara, Tello (Koke 85), Moreno, Muniain (Morata 63), Isco. Coach: Julen Lopetegui (ESP)
Russia: Zabolotni, Tsallagov (Kirillov 80), Schennikov, Chicherin, Burlak, Petrov, Shatov, Yakovlev, Belyaev, Cheryshev (Kanunnikov 58), Bibilov (Grigoryev 46). Coach: Nikolai Pisarev (RUS)
Yellow cards: Schennikov 23 (Russia), Grigoryev 73 (Russia), Shatov 86 (Russia)

06/06/13, Ha Moshava, Petach-Tikva (att: 7,664)
Netherlands 3-2 Germany
Goals: 1-0 Maher 24, 2-0 Wijnaldum 38, 2-1 Rudy 47(p), 2-2 Holtby 81, 3-2 Fer 90
Referee: Bebek (CRO)
Netherlands: Zoet, Van Rhijn, De Vrij, Martins Indi, Blind, Strootman, De Jong, Maher (Fer 82), John (Depay 82), Wijnaldum (Jozefzoon 68), Van Ginkel. Coach: Cor Pot (NED)
Germany: Leno, Jantschke, Thesker, Rudy, Rode (Polter 80), Holtby, Mlapa (Volland 39), Ginter, Sorg, Herrmann, Lasogga (Clemens 61). Coach: Rainer Adrion (GER)
Yellow cards: Thesker 42 (Germany), Zoet 46 (Netherlands), Lasogga 52 (Germany)

09/06/13, Teddy Stadium, Jerusalem (att: 4,589)
Netherlands 5-1 Russia
Goals: 1-0 Wijnaldum 39, 2-0 De Jong 61, 2-1 Cheryshev 65, 3-1 John 69, 4-1 Hoesen 83, 5-1 Fer 90+2
Referee: Gautier (FRA)
Netherlands: Zoet, Van Rhijn, De Vrij, Martins Indi, Blind, Strootman (Clasie 77), De Jong (Hoesen 81), Maher (Fer 73), John, Wijnaldum, Van Ginkel. Coach: Cor Pot (NED)
Russia: Zabolotni, Tsallagov, Schennikov, Chicherin, Burlak, Petrov, Shatov (Bibilov 77), Smolov (Panyukov 73), Yakovlev (Cheryshev 54), Belyaev, Dzagoev. Coach: Nikolai Pisarev (RUS)
Red card: Chicherin 50 (Russia)
Yellow cards: Burlak 51 (Russia), Dzagoev 88 (Russia), Tsallagov 90+1 (Russia), Cheryshev 90+4 (Russia)

09/06/13, Netanya Municipal Stadium, Netanya (att: 11,750)
Germany 0-1 Spain
Goal: 0-1 Morata 86
Referee: Gil (POL)
Germany: Leno, Jantschke, Thesker, Rudy (Rüdiger 82), Rode (Can 70), Volland, Holtby, Ginter, Sorg, Herrmann (Lasogga 64), Clemens. Coach: Rainer Adrion (GER)
Spain: De Gea, Montoya, Illarramendi, Bartra, Iñigo Martínez, Koke, Rodrigo (Morata 73), Thiago Alcántara, Tello (Muniain 85), Moreno, Isco (Camacho 89). Coach: Julen Lopetegui (ESP)
Yellow cards: Rode 45 (Germany), Herrmann 60 (Germany), Lasogga 75 (Germany), Moreno 77 (Spain), Koke 83 (Spain), Can 88 (Germany)

The Netherlands' Georginio Wijnaldum is shadowed by Russia's Pavel Yakovlev

12/06/13, Ha Moshava, Petach-Tikva (att: 10,024)
Spain 3-0 Netherlands
Goals: 1-0 Morata 26, 2-0 Isco 32, 3-0 Álvaro Vázquez 90+1
Referee: Haţegan (ROU)
Spain: De Gea, Nacho, Iñigo Martínez, Thiago Alcántara (Marc Muniesa 79), Morata, Camacho (Illarramendi 52), Álvaro, Sarabia, Muniain, Carvajal, Isco (Álvaro Vázquez 62). Coach: Julen Lopetegui (ESP)
Netherlands: Bizot, Clasie, Jozefzoon, Leerdam, Van Der Hoorn, Nuytinck, Fer, Trindade de Vilhena (Maher 71), Van Aanholt, Hoesen, Depay. Coach: Cor Pot (NED)
Yellow cards: Illarramendi 56 (Spain), Hoesen 85 (Netherlands), Fer 90 (Netherlands), Morata 90+2 (Spain)

12/06/13, Netanya Municipal Stadium, Netanya (att: 8,134)
Russia 1-2 Germany
Goals: 1-0 Dzagoev 22, 1-1 Herrmann 34, 1-2 Rudy 60(p)
Referee: Jug (SVN)
Russia: Filtsov, Tsallagov, Schennikov, Burlak, Petrov, Belyaev, Cheryshev (Smolov 77), Emelyanov (Shatov 43), Grigoryev (Yakovlev 49), Bibilov, Dzagoev. Coach: Nikolai Pisarev (RUS)
Germany: Baumann, Jantschke, Thesker, Sobiech, Mustafi, Rode (Funk 70), Volland, Holtby (Rudy 46), Ginter, Herrmann, Clemens (Polter 46). Coach: Rainer Adrion (GER)
Red card: Schennikov 39 (Russia)
Yellow cards: Cheryshev 10 (Russia), Emelyanov 17 (Russia), Herrmann 32 (Germany), Dzagoev 39 (Russia), Bibilov 68 (Russia), Belyaev 87 (Russia)

		Pld	W	D	L	F	A	Pts
1	Spain	3	3	0	0	5	0	9
2	Netherlands	3	2	0	1	8	6	6
3	Germany	3	1	0	2	4	5	3
4	Russia	3	0	0	3	2	8	0

Semi-finals

15/06/13, Netanya Municipal Stadium, Netanya (att: 12,074)
Spain 3-0 Norway
Goals: 1-0 Rodrigo 45+1, 2-0 Isco 87, 3-0 Morata 90+3
Referee: Boiko (UKR)
Spain: De Gea, Montoya, Illarramendi, Bartra, Iñigo Martínez, Koke, Rodrigo (Morata 59), Thiago Alcántara, Tello (Muniain 74), Moreno, Isco (Sarabia 89). Coach: Julen Lopetegui (ESP)
Norway: Nyland, Strandberg, Hedenstad, Elabdellaoui, Berget, Pedersen, Henriksen, Semb Berge, Eikrem (Nordtveit 75), Johansen (Berisha 80), King (Nielsen 16). Coach: Tor Ole Skullerud (NOR)
Yellow cards: Bartra 25 (Spain), Eikrem 49 (Norway), Illarramendi 83 (Spain)

15/06/13, Ha Moshava, Petach-Tikva (att: 10,123)
Italy 1-0 Netherlands
Goal: 1-0 Borini 79
Referee: Haţegan (ROU)
Italy: Bardi, Donati, Verratti, Caldirola, Florenzi, Immobile (Gabbiadini 63), Insigne (Sansone 85), Bianchetti, Regini, Borini, Rossi (Crimi 90+2). Coach: Devis Mangia (ITA)
Netherlands: Zoet, Van Rhijn, De Vrij (Van Der Hoorn 75), Martins Indi, Blind (Fer 84), Strootman, De Jong, Maher, John (Depay 69), Wijnaldum, Van Ginkel. Coach: Cor Pot (NED)
Yellow cards: Borini 5 (Italy), Verratti 16 (Italy), Blind 83 (Netherlands), Gabbiadini 83 (Italy), Donati 90 (Italy), Martins Indi 90 (Netherlands), Sansone 90+5 (Italy)

Final

18/06/13, Teddy Stadium, Jerusalem (att: 29,320)
Italy 2-4 Spain
Goals: 0-1 Thiago Alcántara 6, 1-1 Immobile 10, 1-2 Thiago Alcántara 31, 1-3 Thiago Alcántara 38(p), 1-4 Isco 66(p), 2-4 Borini 90
Referee: Jug (SVN)
Italy: Bardi, Donati, Verratti (Crimi 76), Caldirola, Florenzi (Saponara 58), Immobile (Gabbiadini 58), Insigne, Bianchetti, Regini, Borini, Rossi. Coach: Devis Mangia (ITA)
Spain: De Gea, Montoya, Illarramendi, Bartra, Iñigo Martínez, Koke (Camacho 86), Thiago Alcántara, Tello (Muniain 71), Morata (Rodrigo 80), Moreno, Isco. Coach: Julen Lopetegui (ESP)
Yellow cards: Koke 12 (Spain), Verratti 18 (Italy), Tello 27 (Spain), Iñigo Martínez 47 (Spain), Regini 65 (Italy), Caldirola 71 (Italy), Crimi 78 (Italy)

Top goalscorers (final tournament)

4	Álvaro Morata (Spain)
3	Isco (Spain)
	Thiago Alcántara (Spain)
2	Sebastian Rudy (Germany)
	Fabio Borini (Italy)
	Manolo Gabbiadini (Italy)
	Leroy Fer (Netherlands)
	Georginio Wijnaldum (Netherlands)

Squads/Appearances/Goals

ENGLAND

No	Name	DoB	Aps	(s)	Gls	Club
Goalkeepers						
1	Jack Butland	10/03/93	2			Birmingham *
13	Jason Steele	18/08/90	1			Middlesbrough
23	Declan Rudd	16/01/91				Preston *
Defenders						
4	Steven Caulker	29/12/91	2			Tottenham
2	Nathaniel Clyne	05/04/91	2			Southampton
6	Craig Dawson	06/05/90	2		1	West Brom
7	Tom Lees	18/11/90	1			Leeds
9	Jack Robinson	01/09/93	1			Liverpool
11	Danny Rose	02/07/90	2			Sunderland *
3	Adam Smith	29/04/91	1			Millwall *
5	Andre Wisdom	09/05/93	1	(1)		Liverpool
Midfielders						
12	Nathaniel Chalobah	12/12/94	2	(1)		Watford *
8	Jordan Henderson	17/06/90	2	(1)		Liverpool
16	Thomas Ince	30/01/92	2			Blackpool
17	Henri Lansbury	12/10/90				Nottingham Forest
10	Jason Lowe	02/09/91	2			Blackburn
14	Josh McEachran	01/03/93	1	(1)		Middlesbrough *
19	Nathan Redmond	06/03/94	2	(1)		Birmingham
18	Jonjo Shelvey	27/02/92	2	(1)		Liverpool
21	Marvin Sordell	17/02/91	1	(1)		Bolton
Forwards						
20	Nathan Delfouneso	02/02/91		(1)		Blackpool *
22	Connor Wickham	31/03/93	2	(1)		Sunderland
15	Wilfried Zaha	10/11/92	2			Crystal Palace *

ISRAEL

No	Name	DoB	Aps	(s)	Gls	Club
Goalkeepers						
18	Barak Levi	07/01/93				M. Tel-Aviv
1	Boris Kleyman	26/10/90	3			H. Tel-Aviv
23	Arik Yanko	21/12/91				Hakoah Ramat Gan
Defenders						
20	Omri Ben Harush	07/03/90	3			M. Netanya
2	Eli Dasa	03/12/92	2			Beitar Jerusalem
3	Ofir Davidaze	05/05/91	1			H. Beer Sheva
12	Edi Gotlib	16/08/92	1			H. Akko
4	Ido Levi	31/07/90				M. Netanya
13	Taleb Tawatha	21/06/92	2			M. Haifa
5	Ben Wahaba	27/03/92	2			H. Beer Sheva
16	Ofer Werta	23/05/90	1	(1)		Ashdod
Midfielders						
21	Omri Altman	23/03/94		(1)		Fulham (ENG)
19	Ahad Azam	14/01/92		(2)		H. Haifa
8	Nir Biton	30/10/91	3		1	Ashdod
10	Eyal Golasa	07/10/91	2			M. Haifa
6	Marwan Kabha	23/02/91	1			M. Petach-Tikva
22	Ofir Kriaf	17/03/91	2	(1)	1	Beitar Jerusalem
17	Sintayehu Sallalich	20/06/91	1			H. Kiryat Shmona
7	Israel Zaguri	29/01/90	2	(1)		H. Ramat Gan
Forwards						
14	Orr Barouch	29/11/91	1	(2)		Bnei Yehuda
11	Munas Dabbur	14/05/92	2			M. Tel-Aviv
9	Mohamed Kalebat	15/06/90	2			Bnei Sakhnin
15	Alon Turgeman	09/06/91	2	(1)	1	M. Haifa

GERMANY

No	Name	DoB	Aps	(s)	Gls	Club
Goalkeepers						
12	Oliver Baumann	02/06/90	1			Freiburg
23	Timo Horn	12/05/93				Köln
1	Bernd Leno	04/03/92	2			Leverkusen
Defenders						
13	Matthias Ginter	19/01/94	3			Freiburg
2	Tony Jantschke	07/04/90	3			Mönchengladbach
15	Sead Kolasinac	20/06/93				Schalke
5	Shkodran Mustafi	17/04/92	1			Sampdoria (ITA)
17	Antonio Rüdiger	03/03/93		(1)		Stuttgart
4	Lasse Sobiech	18/01/91	1			Greuther Fürth
16	Oliver Sorg	29/05/90	2			Freiburg
3	Stefan Thesker	11/04/91	3			Hoffenhelm
Midfielders						
22	Emre Can	12/01/94		(1)		Bayern
19	Christian Clemens	04/08/91	2	(1)		Köln
7	Patrick Funk	11/02/90		(1)		St Pauli *
18	Patrick Herrmann	12/02/91	3		1	Mönchengladbach
10	Lewis Holtby	18/09/90	3		1	Tottenham (ENG)
20	Christoph Moritz	27/01/90				Schalke
8	Sebastian Rode	11/10/90	3			Eintracht Frankfurt
6	Sebastian Rudy	28/02/90	2	(1)	2	Hoffenheim
Forwards						
21	Pierre-Michel Lasogga	15/12/91	1	(1)		Hertha
11	Peniel Mlapa	20/02/91	1			Mönchengladbach
14	Sebastian Polter	01/04/91		(2)		Nürnberg
9	Kevin Volland	30/07/92	2	(1)		Hoffenheim

ITALY

No	Name	DoB	Aps	(s)	Gls	Club
Goalkeepers						
1	Francesco Bardi	18/01/92	5			Novara *
12	Simone Colombi	01/07/91				Modena *
22	Nicola Leali	17/02/93				Virtus *
Defenders						
13	Matteo Bianchetti	17/03/93	4			Verona *
3	Cristiano Biraghi	01/09/92	2			Cittadella *
6	Luca Caldirola	01/02/91	5			Brescia *
5	Marco Capuano	14/10/91	1			Pescara
2	Giulio Donati	05/02/90	5			Grosseto *
19	Vasco Regini	09/09/90	3			Empoli
Midfielders						
16	Andrea Bertolacci	11/01/91		(1)	1	Genoa
23	Marco Crimi	17/03/90	1	(2)		Grosseto
7	Alessandro Florenzi	11/03/91	4	(1)	1	Roma
10	Lorenzo Insigne	04/06/91	4		1	Napoli
8	Luca Marrone	28/03/90	1			Juventus
21	Fausto Rossi	03/12/90	3	(2)		Brescia *
15	Nicola Sansone	10/09/91	1	(2)		Parma
18	Riccardo Saponara	21/12/91	2	(1)	1	Empoli *
4	Marco Verratti	05/11/92	4			PSG (FRA)
Forwards						
20	Fabio Borini	29/03/91	3		2	Liverpool (ENG)
14	Mattia Destro	20/03/91	1	(2)		Roma
11	Manolo Gabbiadini	26/11/91	1	(4)	2	Bologna *
9	Ciro Immobile	20/02/90	4		1	Genoa
17	Alberto Paloschi	04/01/90	1			Chievo

NETHERLANDS

No	Name	DoB	Aps	(s)	Gls	Club
Goalkeepers						
16	Marco Bizot	10/03/91	1			Groningen
23	Nick Marsman	01/10/90				Go Ahead Eagles
1	Jeroen Zoet	06/01/91	3			RKC
Defenders						
5	Daley Blind	09/03/90	3			Ajax
3	Stefan de Vrij	05/02/92	3			Feyenoord
4	Bruno Martins Indi	08/02/92	3			Feyenoord
14	Bram Nuytinck	04/05/90	1			Anderlecht (BEL)
20	Patrick van Aanholt	29/08/90	1			Vitesse *
13	Mike van der Hoorn	15/10/92	1	(1)		Utrecht
2	Ricardo van Rhijn	13/06/91	3			Ajax
Midfielders						
6	Jordy Clasie	27/06/91	1	(1)		Feyenoord
17	Leroy Fer	05/01/90	1	(3)	2	Twente
11	Ola John	19/05/92	3		1	Benfica (POR)
12	Kelvin Leerdam	24/06/90	1			Feyenoord
10	Adam Maher	20/07/93	3	(1)	1	AZ
8	Kevin Strootman	13/02/90	3			PSV
19	Tonny Trindade de Vilhena	03/01/95	1			Feyenoord
18	Marco van Ginkel	01/12/92	3			Vitesse
15	Georginio Wijnaldum	11/11/90	3		2	PSV
Forwards						
22	Memphis Depay	13/02/94	1	(2)		PSV
21	Danny Hoesen	15/01/91	1	(1)	1	Ajax
7	Florian Jozefzoon	09/02/91	1	(1)		RKC
9	Luuk de Jong	27/08/90	3		1	Mönchengladbach (GER)

RUSSIA

No	Name	DoB	Aps	(s)	Gls	Club
Goalkeepers						
16	Aleksandr Filtsov	02/01/90	1			Krasnodar
12	Stanislav Kritsuk	01/12/90				Braga (POR)
1	Nikolai Zabolotni	16/04/90	2			Rostov
Defenders						
15	Maksim Belyaev	30/09/91	3			Rostov *
13	Sergei Bryzgalov	15/11/92				Spartak Moskva
5	Taras Burlak	22/02/90	3			Lokomotiv Moskva
4	Nikita Chicherin	18/08/90	2			Dinamo Moskva
23	Aleksei Nikitin	27/01/92				Yenisey
3	Georgi Schennikov	27/04/91	3			CSKA Moskva
Midfielders						
20	Shota Bibilov	06/08/90	2	(1)		Volga
22	Alan Dzagoev	17/06/90	2		1	CSKA Moskva
18	Roman Emelyanov	08/05/92	1			Illychivets (UKR) *
19	Maksim Grigoryev	06/07/90	1	(1)		Lokomotiv Moskva
6	Yuri Kirillov	19/01/90		(1)		Dinamo Moskva
7	Sergei Petrov	02/01/91	3			Krasnodar
8	Oleg Shatov	29/07/90	2	(1)		Anji
2	Ibragim Tsallagov	12/12/90	3			Krylya Sovetov
14	Pavel Yakovlev	07/04/91	2	(1)		Spartak Moskva
21	Aleksandr Zotov	27/08/90				Tom *
Forwards						
17	Denis Cheryshev	26/12/90	2	(1)	1	Real Madrid (ESP)
11	Maksim Kanunnikov	14/07/91		(1)		Amkar
9	Andrei Panyukov	25/09/94		(1)		Khimki *
10	Fedor Smolov	09/02/90	1	(1)		Anji

NORWAY

No	Name	DoB	Aps	(s)	Gls	Club
Goalkeepers						
23	Gudmund Kongshavn	23/01/91				Vålerenga
12	Ørjan Håskjold Nyland	10/09/90	3			Molde
1	Arild Østbø	19/04/91	1			Strømmen *
Defenders						
6	Omar Elabdellaoui	05/12/91	3			Braunschweig (GER) *
5	Vegar Eggen Hedenstad	26/06/91	3			Freiburg (GER)
2	Martin Linnes	20/09/91	1	(2)		Molde
3	Thomas Rogne	29/06/90	2			Celtic (SCO)
14	Fredrik Semb Berge	06/02/90	3		1	Odd
4	Stefan Strandberg	25/07/90	3	(1)	1	Rosenborg
Midfielders						
9	Valon Berisha	07/02/93	1	(1)		Salzburg (AUT)
16	Yann-Erik de Lanlay	14/05/92	2			Viking
18	Magnus Wolff Eikrem	08/08/90	3		1	Molde
13	Markus Henriksen	25/07/92	2			AZ (NED)
22	Abdisalam Ibrahim	01/05/91		(2)		Strømsgodset *
20	Stefan Johansen	08/01/91	3			Strømsgodset
17	Anders Konradssen	18/07/90	2			Rennes (FRA)
15	Håvard Nordtveit	21/06/90	1	(2)		Mönchengladbach (GER)
7	Harmeet Singh	12/11/90	1	(1)	1	Feyenoord (NED)
Forwards						
8	Jo Inge Berget	11/09/90	3		1	Molde
19	Flamur Kastrati	14/11/91		(1)		Erzgebirge (GER)
21	Joshua King	15/01/92	2			Blackburn (ENG)
11	Håvard Nielsen	15/07/93	2	(2)		Salzburg (AUT)
10	Marcus Pedersen	08/06/90	3		1	OB (DEN) *

SPAIN

No	Name	DoB	Aps	(s)	Gls	Club
Goalkeepers						
1	David de Gea	07/11/90	5			Man. United (ENG)
23	Joel	17/06/90				Wigan (ENG) *
13	Diego Mariño	09/05/90				Villarreal
Defenders						
16	Álvaro González	08/01/90	1			Zaragoza
5	Marc Bartra	15/01/91	4			Barcelona
20	Daniel Carvajal	11/01/92	1			Leverkusen (GER)
6	Iñigo Martínez	17/05/91	5			Real Sociedad
15	Marc Muniesa	27/03/92		(1)		Barcelona
2	Martín Montoya	14/04/91	4			Barcelona
18	Alberto Moreno	05/07/92	4			Sevilla
4	Nacho	18/01/90	1			Real Madrid
Midfielders						
14	Ignacio Camacho	04/05/90	1	(2)		Málaga
7	Sergio Canales	16/02/91		(1)		Valencia
3	Asier Illarramendi	08/03/90	4	(1)		Real Sociedad
22	Isco	21/04/92	5		3	Málaga
8	Koke	08/01/92	3	(1)		Atlético
17	Pablo Sarabia	11/05/92	1	(1)		Getafe
10	Thiago Alcántara	11/04/91	5		3	Barcelona
Forwards						
21	Álvaro Vázquez	27/04/91		(1)	1	Getafe
12	Álvaro Morata	23/10/92	2	(3)	4	Real Madrid
19	Iker Muniain	19/12/92	2	(3)		Athletic
9	Rodrigo	06/03/91	3	(1)	1	Benfica (POR)
11	Cristian Tello	11/08/91	4			Barcelona

NB Clubs indicated are those with which the players concluded the 2012/13 season. Loan clubs are indicated with a *

The European Football Yearbook 2013/14 89

| Drulović's side capture nation's first U19 title | France defeated 1-0 in closely-contested final | No hat-trick triumph for semi-final fallers Spain |

Serbia triumph in Lithuania

A new name was added to the UEFA European Under-19 Championship roll of honour in 2013 as Serbia claimed the trophy for the first time with a memorable triumph in Lithuania.

Serbia had lost all four of their previous U19 semi-finals, but with ex-FC Porto striker Ljubinko Drulović in charge they ended that jinx by overcoming Portugal on penalties before edging a tight final against France in Marijampole. Andrija Luković scored the only goal 12 minutes after half-time, the midfielder slotting in coolly after typically incisive work from FK Partizan striker Aleksandar Mitrović – already a senior international and the tournament's stand-out individual.

There were several surprises in the elite round, not least from Georgia, who knocked out England and Belgium to reach the finals for the first time. The tournament therefore featured two debutants, with the hosts also making their inaugural appearance. Paired with the Netherlands, Spain and Portugal in Group A, Lithuania could hardly have been handed a tougher draw.

Not unexpectedly, Antanas Vingilys's team struggled to provide cheer for the home fans. They fell 2-0 behind within 30 minutes of their opening fixture against the Netherlands, and although they recovered well to level at 2-2, Rai Vloet's added-time winner gave the Dutch the points. Lithuania also lost to Spain (0-1) and Portugal (2-4), although Gratas

Sirgedas provided some consolation by finishing as the competition's joint top scorer. His three goals placed him level with Portugal's Alexandre Guedes and Dutch forward Anass Achahbar, whose team also bowed out early, a 4-1 defeat in their second fixture against Portugal proving fatal. Spain had beaten their Iberian neighbours 1-0 in their opening fixture, the first of three victories for the holders en route to a fourth successive semi-final.

Serbia celebrate their UEFA European Under-19 Championship win

Serbia controlled Group B from the outset, reaching a third semi-final in five years with a game to spare thanks to wins against Turkey (2-1) and Georgia (1-0). France joined them in the last four despite a frustrating opening draw against Georgia, their subsequent 2-1 victory over Turkey, which eliminated their opponents, proving crucial. A 1-1 draw in their third fixture against a much-changed Serbia meant that France went through as runners-up behind their opponents. Meanwhile, Turkey overtook Georgia to claim third place with a closing 4-2 win.

Portugal, in the last four for the first time since 2003, looked set for the final when Guedes put them 2-1 up against Serbia in Alytus with 11 minutes remaining, but Mijat Gačinović responded with an equaliser, and in the ensuing penalty shoot-out goalkeeper Predrag Rajković saved twice before Mitrović settled the contest. The second semi-final proved no less eventful, Spain's José Rodríguez and France's Yassine Benzia swapping first-half goals before Antoine Conte, who had conceded the penalty with which the holders opened the scoring, found redemption with an extra-time winner for Francis Smerecki's side.

Having ousted the 2011 and 2012 winners, France went into the final as favourites, but it was Serbia, gutsy and disciplined to the last, who emerged as worthy tournament winners, the final whistle bringing wild and prolonged celebrations from Drulović and his jubilant players.

Qualifying round

Group 1

02-07/11/12 Tatabanya, Telki

Austria 9-0 Andorra, Hungary 1-1 Bulgaria, Austria 2-1 Bulgaria, Andorra 0-3 Hungary, Hungary 1-2 Austria, Bulgaria 7-0 Andorra

		Pld	W	D	L	F	A	Pts
1	Austria	3	3	0	0	13	2	9
2	Bulgaria	3	1	1	1	9	3	4
3	Hungary	3	1	1	1	5	3	4
4	Andorra	3	0	0	3	0	19	0

Group 2

21-26/11/12 Paphos

Finland 2-0 Montenegro, Denmark 3-1 Cyprus, Finland 0-1 Cyprus, Montenegro 2-3 Denmark, Denmark 3-0 Finland, Cyprus 1-1 Montenegro

		Pld	W	D	L	F	A	Pts
1	Denmark	3	3	0	0	9	3	9
2	Cyprus	3	1	1	1	3	4	4
3	Finland	3	1	0	2	2	4	3
4	Montenegro	3	0	1	2	3	6	1

Group 3

09-14/10/12 Plewiska, Międzychód, Szamotuly, Wronki, Swarzedz

Poland 2-0 San Marino, Netherlands 5-0 Malta, San Marino 0-4 Netherlands, Poland 5-0 Malta, Netherlands 3-1 Poland, Malta 4-0 San Marino

		Pld	W	D	L	F	A	Pts
1	Netherlands	3	3	0	0	12	1	9
2	Poland	3	2	0	1	8	3	6
3	Malta	3	1	0	2	4	10	3
4	San Marino	3	0	0	3	0	10	0

Group 4

10-18/10/12 Lurgan, Banbridge, Portadown, Ballymena

Greece 0-0 Moldova, Czech Republic 1-1 Northern Ireland, Czech Republic 2-0 Moldova, Northern Ireland 0-2 Greece, Greece 1-0 Czech Republic, Moldova 1-8 Northern Ireland

		Pld	W	D	L	F	A	Pts
1	Czech Republic	3	2	1	0	5	2	7
2	Greece	3	1	1	1	3	2	4
3	Northern Ireland	3	1	1	1	9	4	4
4	Moldova	3	0	1	2	1	10	1

Group 5

11-16/10/12 Bascharage, Hesperange, Grevenmacher

Germany 5-0 FYROM, Republic of Ireland 5-2 Luxembourg, Germany 5-0 Luxembourg, FYROM 0-1 Republic of Ireland, Republic of Ireland 2-2 Germany, Luxembourg 0-1 FYROM

		Pld	W	D	L	F	A	Pts
1	Germany	3	2	1	0	12	2	7
2	Republic of Ireland	3	2	1	0	8	4	7
3	FYROM	3	1	0	2	1	6	3
4	Luxembourg	3	0	0	3	2	11	0

Group 6

11-16/10/12 Oliveira do Bairro, Luso, Mealhada, Agueda, Coimbra

France 2-1 Israel, Portugal 2-0 Latvia, France 6-0 Latvia, Israel 0-5 Portugal, Portugal 2-2 France, Latvia 3-5 Israel

		Pld	W	D	L	F	A	Pts
1	France	3	2	1	0	10	3	7
2	Portugal	3	2	1	0	9	2	7
3	Israel	3	1	0	2	6	10	3
4	Latvia	3	0	0	3	3	13	0

Group 7

12-17/10/12 Fier, Vlora

Belgium 1-0 Belarus, Italy 3-0 Albania, Belarus 1-1 Italy, Belgium 1-3 Albania, Italy 1-2 Belgium, Albania 0-2 Belarus

		Pld	W	D	L	F	A	Pts
1	Belgium	3	2	0	1	4	4	6
2	Italy	3	1	1	1	5	3	4
3	Belarus	3	1	1	1	3	2	4
4	Albania	3	1	0	2	3	6	3

Group 8

11-16/10/12 Sarajevo

Slovakia 5-0 Kazakhstan, Norway 3-1 Bosnia & Herzegovina, Slovakia 0-4 Bosnia & Herzegovina, Kazakhstan 2-6 Norway, Norway 1-2 Slovakia, Bosnia & Herzegovina 4-2 Kazakhstan

		Pld	W	D	L	F	A	Pts
1	Bosnia & Herzegovina	3	2	0	1	9	5	6
2	Norway	3	2	0	1	10	5	6
3	Slovakia	3	2	0	1	7	5	6
4	Kazakhstan	3	0	0	3	4	15	0

Group 9

09-14/10/12 Hamilton, Falkirk

Scotland 4-0 Armenia, Switzerland 1-1 Romania, Scotland 1-0 Romania, Armenia 0-4 Switzerland, Switzerland 3-4 Scotland, Romania 1-0 Armenia

		Pld	W	D	L	F	A	Pts
1	Scotland	3	3	0	0	9	3	9
2	Switzerland	3	1	1	1	8	5	4
3	Romania	3	1	1	1	2	2	4
4	Armenia	3	0	0	3	0	9	0

Group 10

10-15/10/12 Bakovci, Bistrica

Wales 1-3 Sweden, Russia 0-0 Slovenia, Wales 2-1 Slovenia, Sweden 1-3 Russia, Russia 2-1 Wales, Slovenia 1-1 Sweden

		Pld	W	D	L	F	A	Pts
1	Russia	3	2	1	0	5	2	7
2	Sweden	3	1	1	1	5	5	4
3	Wales	3	1	0	2	4	6	3
4	Slovenia	3	0	2	1	2	3	2

Group 11

26-31/10/12 Zagreb, Zapresic, Sesvete

Croatia 2-0 Georgia, Azerbaijan 1-2 Iceland, Croatia 2-2 Iceland, Georgia 1-1 Azerbaijan, Azerbaijan 1-7 Croatia, Iceland 0-2 Georgia

		Pld	W	D	L	F	A	Pts
1	Croatia	3	2	1	0	11	3	7
2	Georgia	3	1	1	1	3	3	4
3	Iceland	3	1	1	1	4	5	4
4	Azerbaijan	3	0	1	2	3	10	1

Group 12

26/09-01/10/12 Tallinn

Ukraine 6-0 Faroe Islands, England 3-0 Estonia, Faroe Islands 0-6 England, Ukraine 2-0 Estonia, England 1-1 Ukraine, Estonia 2-1 Faroe Islands

		Pld	W	D	L	F	A	Pts
1	England	3	2	1	0	10	1	7
2	Ukraine	3	2	1	0	9	1	7
3	Estonia	3	1	0	2	2	6	3
4	Faroe Islands	3	0	0	3	1	14	0

Elite round

Group 1

05/06/13, Lindabrunn, Lindabrunn
France 3-0 Sweden
05/06/13, Sport- und Freizeitzentrum Traiskirchen, Traiskirchen
Austria 6-0 Bosnia & Herzegovina
07/06/13, Lindabrunn, Lindabrunn
Bosnia & Herzegovina 0-1 France
07/06/13, Sport- und Freizeitzentrum Traiskirchen, Traiskirchen
Austria 3-0 Sweden
10/06/13, Sport- und Freizeitzentrum Traiskirchen, Traiskirchen
France 1-0 Austria
10/06/13, Lindabrunn, Lindabrunn
Sweden 3-2 Bosnia & Herzegovina

		Pld	W	D	L	F	A	Pts
1	France	3	3	0	0	5	0	9
2	Austria	3	2	0	1	9	1	6
3	Sweden	3	1	0	2	3	8	3
4	Bosnia & Herzegovina	3	0	0	3	2	10	0

Group 2

06/06/13, FK Srem, Jakovo
Serbia 4-0 Slovakia
06/06/13, FK Obilić, Belgrade
Republic of Ireland 2-2 Switzerland
08/06/13, FK Obilić, Belgrade
Serbia 0-1 Switzerland
08/06/13, FK Srem, Jakovo
Slovakia 3-2 Republic of Ireland
11/06/13, FK Srem, Jakovo
Republic of Ireland 0-0 Serbia
11/06/13, FK Obilić, Belgrade
Switzerland 0-0 Slovakia

		Pld	W	D	L	F	A	Pts
1	Serbia	3	1	1	1	4	1	4
2	Switzerland	3	1	1	1	3	4	4
3	Slovakia	3	1	1	1	4	6	4
4	Republic of Ireland	3	0	3	0	4	4	3

Group 3

04/06/13, Sports Center CF Fão, Fao
Denmark 5-0 Czech Republic
04/06/13, Estádio do Mar, Matosinhos
Portugal 7-0 Bulgaria
06/06/13, Póvoa do Varzim Municipal Stadium, Povoa do Varzim
Denmark 5-0 Bulgaria
06/06/13, Cidade de Barcelos, Barcelos
Czech Republic 1-4 Portugal
09/06/13, Cidade de Barcelos, Barcelos
Portugal 1-0 Denmark
09/06/13, Póvoa do Varzim Municipal Stadium, Povoa do Varzim
Bulgaria 1-2 Czech Republic

		Pld	W	D	L	F	A	Pts
1	Portugal	3	3	0	0	12	1	9
2	Denmark	3	2	0	1	10	1	6
3	Czech Republic	3	1	0	2	3	10	3
4	Bulgaria	3	0	0	3	1	14	0

Group 4

05/06/13, Gdynski Osrodek Sportu i Rekre, Gdynia
Croatia 1-1 Greece
05/06/13, Gdynski Osrodek Sportu i Rekre, Gdynia
Spain 1-0 Poland
07/06/13, Stadion Miejski im. Kazimierza Deyny, Starogard Gdanski
Spain 2-0 Greece
07/06/13, Stadion Miejski im. Kazimierza Deyny, Starogard Gdanski
Poland 0-2 Croatia
10/06/13, Stadion Miejski im. Kazimierza Deyny, Starogard Gdanski
Croatia 1-1 Spain
10/06/13, Lechia, Gdansk
Greece 1-1 Poland

		Pld	W	D	L	F	A	Pts
1	Spain	3	2	1	0	4	1	7
2	Croatia	3	1	2	0	4	2	5
3	Greece	3	0	2	1	2	4	2
4	Poland	3	0	1	2	1	4	1

Group 5

05/06/13, Nedre Eiker, Mjondalen
Germany 3-1 Cyprus
05/06/13, Nedre Eiker, Mjondalen
Netherlands 2-1 Norway
07/06/13, Idrettsparken, Notodden
Netherlands 0-1 Cyprus
07/06/13, Idrettsparken, Notodden
Norway 3-1 Germany
10/06/13, Idrettsparken, Notodden
Germany 0-1 Netherlands
10/06/13, Nedre Eiker, Mjondalen
Cyprus 0-3 Norway

		Pld	W	D	L	F	A	Pts
1	Netherlands	3	2	0	1	3	2	6
2	Norway	3	2	0	1	7	3	6
3	Germany	3	1	0	2	4	5	3
4	Cyprus	3	1	0	2	2	6	3

Group 6

24/05/13, De Leunen, Geel
Scotland 2-2 Belgium
24/05/13, KSV Bornem Stadion, Bornem
England 1-1 Georgia
26/05/13, KFC Oosterzonen Stadion, Westerlo
Scotland 1-3 Georgia
26/05/13, De Leunen, Geel
Belgium 1-1 England
29/05/13, KFC Oosterzonen Stadion, Westerlo
England 3-0 Scotland
29/05/13, KSV Bornem Stadion, Bornem
Georgia 2-0 Belgium

		Pld	W	D	L	F	A	Pts
1	Georgia	3	2	1	0	6	2	7
2	England	3	1	2	0	5	2	5
3	Belgium	3	0	2	1	3	5	2
4	Scotland	3	0	1	2	3	8	1

Group 7

22/05/13, FC Krasnodar Academy Stadium, Krasnodar
Ukraine 0-1 Italy
22/05/13, FC Krasnodar Academy Stadium, Krasnodar
Turkey 2-1 Russia

24/05/13, FC Krasnodar Academy Stadium, Krasnodar
Turkey 5-1 Italy
24/05/13, FC Krasnodar Academy Stadium, Krasnodar
Russia 1-2 Ukraine
27/05/13, FC Krasnodar Academy Stadium, Krasnodar
Ukraine 0-2 Turkey
27/05/13, Kuban, Krasnodar
Italy 3-3 Russia

		Pld	W	D	L	F	A	Pts
1	Turkey	3	3	0	0	9	2	9
2	Italy	3	1	1	1	5	8	4
3	Ukraine	3	1	0	2	2	4	3
4	Russia	3	0	1	2	5	7	1

Top goalscorers (qualifying)

7 Tomislav Kiš (Croatia)
Bruma (Portugal)

6 Anass Achahbar (Netherlands)

5 Kristian Lindberg (Denmark)
Yussuf Poulsen (Denmark)
Armin Hodžić (Bosnia & Herzegovina)

Final tournament

Group A

20/07/13, Dariaus ir Giréno stadionas, Kaunas
Lithuania 2-3 Netherlands
Goals: 0-1 Achahbar 10, 0-2 Achahbar 29, 1-2 Artimavičius 38, 2-2 Sirgedas 83, 2-3 Vloet 90+5
Referee: Strömbergsson (SWE)

20/07/13, Marijampolé, Marijampole
Spain 1-0 Portugal
Goal: 1-0 Ramírez 19
Referee: Zwayer (GER)

23/07/13, SRC Alytus, Alytus
Netherlands 1-4 Portugal
Goals: 0-1 Alexandre Guedes 32, 0-2 Leandro Silva 73, 0-3 Ricardo Horta 87, 0-4 Alexandre Guedes 89, 1-4 Vloet 90+1
Referee: Oliver (ENG)

23/07/13, Dariaus ir Giréno stadionas, Kaunas
Lithuania 0-2 Spain
Goals: 0-1 Hernández 6, 0-2 Hernández 74
Referee: Kulbakov (BLR)

26/07/13, Dariaus ir Giréno stadionas, Kaunas
Portugal 4-2 Lithuania
Goals: 1-0 Marcos Lopes 8, 2-0 Petrauskas 45(og), 3-0 Tobias Figueiredo 51(p), 3-1 Sirgedas 53, 4-1 Carlos Mané 65, 4-2 Sirgedas 90+2
Referee: Grinfeld (ISR)

26/07/13, SRC Alytus, Alytus
Netherlands 2-3 Spain
Goals: 1-0 Leemans 36, 1-1 Ramírez 68, 1-2 Vadillo 81, 1-3 Vico 83, 2-3 Achahbar 90+1(p)
Referee: Kulbakov (BLR)

		Pld	W	D	L	F	A	Pts
1	Spain	3	3	0	0	6	2	9
2	Portugal	3	2	0	1	8	4	6
3	Netherlands	3	1	0	2	6	9	3
4	Lithuania	3	0	0	3	4	9	0

Group B

20/07/13, Marijampolé, Marijampole
Serbia 2-1 Turkey
Goals: 1-0 Luković 17, 2-0 Mitrović 54, 2-1 Recep Niyaz 88
Referee: Oliver (ENG)

20/07/13, SRC Alytus, Alytus
Georgia 0-0 France
Referee: Alecković (BIH)

23/07/13, Marijampolé, Marijampole
Serbia 1-0 Georgia
Goal: 1-0 Meleg 74
Referee: Grinfeld (ISR)

23/07/13, SRC Alytus, Alytus
Turkey 1-2 France
Goals: 0-1 Hunou 6, 0-2 Benzia 64, 1-2 İbrahim Yılmaz 87(p)
Referee: Strömbergsson (SWE)

26/07/13, Dariaus ir Giréno stadionas, Kaunas
France 1-1 Serbia
Goals: 1-0 Hunou 30, 1-1 Pavlovski 77
Referee: Zwayer (GER)

26/07/13, Marijampolé, Marijampole
Turkey 4-2 Georgia
Goals: 1-0 Endeladze 3, 1-1 Okan Deniz 16, 2-1 Okan Deniz 18, 2-2 Katcharava 50, 3-2 Recep Niyaz 58, 4-2 Cenk Şahin 80
Referee: Mažeika (LTU)

		Pld	W	D	L	F	A	Pts
1	Serbia	3	2	1	0	4	2	7
2	France	3	1	2	0	3	2	5
3	Turkey	3	1	0	2	6	6	3
4	Georgia	3	0	1	2	2	5	1

Semi-finals

29/07/13, SRC Alytus, Alytus
Serbia 2-2 Portugal *(aet; 3-2 on pens)*
Goals: 1-0 Djurdjević 6, 1-1 Bernardo Silva 55, 1-2 Alexandre Guedes 79, 2-2 Gačinović 85
Referee: Oliver (ENG)

29/07/13, Dariaus ir Giréno stadionas, Kaunas
Spain 1-2 France (aet)
Goals: 1-0 Rodríguez 27(p), 1-1 Benzia 29, 1-2 Conte 105
Referee: Grinfeld (ISR)

Final

01/08/13, Marijampolé, Marijampole (att: 6,211)
France 0-1 Serbia
Goal: 0-1 Luković 57
Referee: Kulbakov (BLR)
France: Beunardeau, Ikoko, Conte, Azouni, Hunou (Gbamin 76), Benzia, Rabiot, Moreira, Laporte, Martial (Rodrigues 56), Jean (Nangis 66). Coach: Francis Smerecki (FRA)
Serbia: Rajković, Golubović, Milinković-Savić, Antić, Filipović, Djurdjević (Ožegović 88), Pavlovski (Urošević 90+3), Luković (Meleg 68), Mitrović, Veljković, Maksimović. Coach: Ljubinko Drulović (SRB)
Yellow cards: Azouni 43 (France), Veljković 50 (Serbia), Benzia 63 (France), Rabiot 81 (France), Rajković 90 (Serbia)

Top goalscorers (final tournament)

3 Gratas Sirgedas (Lithuania)
Anass Achahbar (Netherlands)
Alexandre Guedes (Portugal)

2 Okan Deniz (Turkey)
Iker Hernández (Spain)
Rai Vloet (Netherlands)
Recep Niyaz (Turkey)
Sandro Ramírez (Spain)
Andrija Luković (Serbia)
Yassine Benzia (France)
Adrien Hunou (France)

Squads/Appearances/Goals

FRANCE

No	Name	DoB	Aps	(s)	Gls	Club
Goalkeepers						
1	Quentin Beunardeau	27/02/94	5			Le Mans
16	Mouez Hassen	05/03/95				Nice
Defenders						
4	Antoine Conte	29/01/94	5		1	PSG
2	Jordan Ikoko	03/02/94	5			PSG
13	Aymeric Laporte	27/05/94	5			Athletic (ESP)
3	Benjamin Mendy	17/07/94	2			Marseille
12	Steven Moreira	13/08/94	3	(1)		Rennes
5	Lucas Rougeaux	10/03/94		(1)		Nice
Midfielders						
6	Larry Azouni	23/03/94	4			Marseille
15	Jean-Philippe Gbamin	25/09/95		(3)		Lens
8	Adrien Hunou	19/01/94	5		2	Rennes
11	Adrien Rabiot	03/04/95	5			PSG
7	Kévin Rodrigues	05/03/94	2	(3)		Toulouse
Forwards						
9	Yassine Benzia	08/09/94	5		2	Lyon
17	Corentin Jean	15/07/95	3			Troyes
14	Anthony Martial	05/12/95	4	(1)		Monaco
10	Lenny Nangis	24/03/94	2	(2)		Caen
18	Opa Nguette	08/07/94		(2)		Valenciennes

LITHUANIA

No	Name	DoB	Aps	(s)	Gls	Club
Goalkeepers						
12	Edvinas Gertmonas	01/06/96				Tauras
1	Tomas Švedkauskas	22/06/94	3			Roma (ITA)
Defenders						
3	Julius Aleksandravičius	13/01/95	3			Lietava
4	Lukas Artimavičius	12/08/94	2		1	Atlantas
6	Rolandas Baravykas	23/08/95	2	(1)		Atlantas
5	Lukas Čerkauskas	12/03/94	1	(1)		Ekranas
15	Justinas Januševskis	26/03/94	1	(1)		Trakai
2	Džiugas Petrauskas	21/03/94	3			Baltija
Midfielders						
20	Klaidas Jaškus	22/04/94	2			Atletas
19	Gabrielius Judickas	04/07/95				Novara (ITA)
9	Lukas Narbutas	10/05/94	3			Ekranas
7	Deimantas Petravičius	02/09/95	1			Nottingham Forest (ENG)
17	Gratas Sirgedas	17/12/94	1	(2)	3	Ekranas
14	Vykintas Slivka	29/04/95	2			Ekranas
10	Simonas Stankevičius	03/10/95	3			Leicester (ENG)
Forwards						
11	Donatas Kazlauskas	31/03/94	3			Atlantas
13	Lukas Spalvis	27/07/94	3			AaB (DEN)
8	Klaudijus Upstas	30/10/94				Tauras

GEORGIA

No	Name	DoB	Aps	(s)	Gls	Club
Goalkeepers						
12	Bačho Mikava	12/01/94	1			Torpedo Kutaisi
1	Gabriel Tebluadze	10/11/94	2			Metalurgi Rustavi
Defenders						
3	Lasha Dvali	14/05/95	3			Skonto (LVA)
5	Levan Gegechkori	05/06/94				Merani
16	Aleksandre Gureshidze	23/04/95				Dinamo Tbilisi
2	Davit Mtivlishvili	26/10/94	3			Torpedo Kutaisi
4	Nika Sandokhadze	20/02/94	3			Torpedo Kutaisi
13	Nika Tchanturia	19/01/95	3			Torpedo Kutaisi
Midfielders						
8	Avto Endeladze	17/09/94	3		1	Zestafoni
9	Teimuraz Markozashvili	09/08/94	3			Torpedo Kutaisi
7	Guram Samushia	05/09/94	1	(1)		Zestafoni
15	Dachi Tsnobiladze	28/01/94	2	(1)		Metalurgi Rustavi
6	Daviti Ubilava	27/01/94	1	(1)		Torpedo Kutaisi
Forwards						
10	Bachana Arabuli	05/01/94	2			Dila
11	Nika Katcharava	13/01/94	1	(2)	1	Rubin (GEO)
14	Giorgi Pantsulaia	06/01/94	3			Torpedo Kutaisi
18	Luka Zarandia	17/02/96		(2)		Torpedo Kutaisi
17	Budu Zivzivadze	10/03/94	2	(1)		Dinamo Tbilisi

NETHERLANDS

No	Name	DoB	Aps	(s)	Gls	Club
Goalkeepers						
16	Nick Olij	01/08/95				AZ
1	Mickey van der Hart	13/06/94	3			Ajax
Defenders						
13	Wesley Iloedt	06/03/94				AZ
4	Terence Kongolo	14/02/94	3			Feyenoord
15	Clint Leemans	15/09/95	1		1	PSV
2	Kenny Tete	09/10/95	3			Ajax
3	Sven van Beek	28/07/94	2			Feyenoord
5	Lucas Woudenberg	25/04/94	3			Feyenoord
Midfielders						
8	Yassine Ayoub	06/03/94	3			Utrecht
6	Michael Chacon	11/04/94	2	(1)		Heerenveen
14	Huseyin Dogan	22/01/94		(2)		Sparta
10	Mimoun Mahi	13/03/94	3			Sparta
17	Rai Vloet	08/05/95	2	(1)	2	PSV
Forwards						
9	Anass Achahbar	13/01/94	3		3	Feyenoord
7	Bilal Basacikoglu	26/03/95	3			Heerenveen
11	Brahim Darri	14/09/94	1	(1)		Vitesse
12	Danzell Gravenberch	13/02/94	1	(2)		Ajax
18	Roy Talsma	31/08/94				Vitesse

PORTUGAL

No	Name	DoB	Aps	(s)	Gls	Club
Goalkeepers						
1	Bruno Varela	04/11/94	4			Benfica
12	Rui Silva	07/02/94				Nacional
Defenders						
13	Edgar Ié	01/05/94	4			Barcelona (ESP)
14	Fábio Cardoso	19/04/94		(1)		Benfica
2	João Cancelo	27/05/94	4			Benfica
5	Luís Rafael	09/05/95	4			Porto
15	Rebocho	23/01/95		(1)		Benfica
4	Rudinilson Silva	20/08/94	1			Benfica
3	Tobias Figueiredo	02/02/94	4		1	Sporting
Midfielders						
10	Bernardo Silva	10/08/94	4		1	Benfica
11	Hélder Costa	12/01/94	2	(1)		Benfica
6	João Teixeira	06/02/94		(3)		Benfica
8	Leandro Silva	04/05/94	3		1	Porto
17	Marcos Lopes	28/12/95	4		1	Man City (ENG)
16	Tomás Podstawski	30/01/95	4			Porto
Forwards						
18	Alexandre Guedes	11/02/94	4		3	Sporting
7	Carlos Mané	11/03/94	2	(2)	1	Sporting
9	Ricardo Horta	15/09/94		(4)	1	Setúbal

SPAIN

No	Name	DoB	Aps	(s)	Gls	Club
Goalkeepers						
13	Rubén Blanco	25/07/95	4			Celta
1	Alfonso Herrero	21/04/94				Real Madrid
Defenders						
2	Héctor Bellerín	19/03/95	2			Arsenal (ENG)
15	Julio Cesar	07/12/95	2			Sporting Gijón
16	Rubén Duarte	18/10/95	2			Espanyol
3	José Gaya	25/05/95	3			Valencia
5	Borja López	02/02/94	4			Sporting Gijón
18	Jaime Sánchez	11/03/95	4			Real Madrid
Midfielders						
4	Pablo Iñiguez	20/01/94	3			Villarreal
11	Moi Gómez	23/06/94	4			Villarreal
6	José Rodríguez	16/12/94	4		1	Real Madrid
14	Lucas Torro	19/07/94	1	(2)		Real Madrid
17	Adama Traoré	25/01/96		(4)		Barcelona
7	Álvaro Vadillo	12/09/94	4		1	Betis
10	Fede Vico	04/07/94	3	(1)	1	Anderlecht (BEL)
Forwards						
9	Iker Hernández	08/04/94	2	(1)	2	Real Sociedad
12	Sandro Ramírez	09/07/95	2	(2)	2	Barcelona
8	Alex Serrano	06/02/95		(2)		Sporting Gijón

SERBIA

No	Name	DoB	Aps	(s)	Gls	Club
Goalkeepers						
12	Stefan Čupić	07/05/94	1			OFK Beograd
1	Predrag Rajković	31/10/95	4			Jagodina
Defenders						
5	Nikola Antić	04/01/94	5			Rad
6	Aleksandar Filipović	20/12/94	5			OFK Beograd
2	Petar Golubović	13/07/94	4			OFK Beograd
3	Slobodan Urošević	15/04/94	1	(3)		Rad
15	Miloš Veljković	26/09/95	5			Tottenham (ENG)
Midfielders						
13	Mijat Gaćinović	08/02/95		(2)	1	Vojvodina
11	Andrija Luković	24/10/94	4		2	Rad
18	Nemanja Maksimović	26/01/95	4			unattached
8	Dejan Meleg	01/10/94	1	(4)	1	Ajax (NED)
4	Sergej Milinković-Savić	27/02/95	4			Vojvodina
10	Marko Pavlovski	07/02/94	5		1	OFK Beograd
16	Milan Vojvodić	20/01/94	1	(1)		Spartak
Forwards						
17	Aleksandar Čavrić	18/05/94	1			OFK Beograd
9	Uroš Djurdjević	02/03/94	5		1	Rad
14	Aleksandar Mitrović	16/09/94	4		1	Partizan
7	Ognjen Ožegović	09/06/94	1	(2)		Crvena zvezda

TURKEY

No	Name	DoB	Aps	(s)	Gls	Club
Goalkeepers						
12	Cantuğ Temel	10/06/94				Ordusupor
1	Onurcan Piri	28/09/94	3			Giresunspor
Defenders						
5	Ahmet Çalık	26/02/94	3			Gençlerbirliği
4	Hakan Çinemre	13/02/94	2			Fenerbahçe
3	İlkay Durmuş	01/05/94	2			Gençlerbirliği
15	Ozan Tufan	23/03/95	3			Bursaspor
2	Serdar Yazıcı	25/04/94	2			Eskişehirspor
Midfielders						
7	Cenk Şahin	22/09/94	3		1	İstanbul BB
17	Ibrahim Coşkun	03/03/95	1	(1)		Auxerre (FRA)
13	İsmail Güven	16/04/94		(2)		Konyaspor
8	Okay Yokuşlu	09/03/94	2			Kayserispor
10	Recep Niyaz	01/01/95	2	(1)	2	Fenerbahçe
6	Salih Uçan	06/01/94	3			Fenerbahçe
14	Süheyl Çetin	22/06/95	1			Bursaspor
Forwards						
9	İbrahim Yılmaz	06/02/94	2		1	İstanbul BB
11	Okan Aydın	08/05/94	2	(1)		Leverkusen (GER)
16	Okan Deniz	20/05/94	1	(2)	2	Bursaspor
18	Sinan Bakış	22/04/94	1	(1)		Leverkusen (GER)

Russia rely on penalty prowess

Russia's deadly accuracy from the penalty spot eventually came to define the 2013 UEFA European Under-17 Championship finals in Slovakia as Dmitri Khomukha's side won shoot-outs in both the semi-final and final to lift the trophy for the second time.

Their only previous success in the competition, in 2006, had also come with a final victory on penalties, and the class of 2013 provided an encore following two goalless knockout encounters. After they had stifled an impressive Italy in the final, goalkeeper and captain Anton Mitryushkin saved from Davide Di Molfetta, Giacomo Sciacca and Andrea Palazzi to allow Sergei Makarov to step up and smash in the penalty that secured the trophy.

Slovakia and Sweden qualified from Group A on their final tournament bow. Backed by impressive support, the hosts made the ideal start, an added-time winner from substitute Martin Slaninka giving them victory against Austria. The same player then completed his team's comeback from 2-0 down to draw with Switzerland, and the point they required to progress came in a mutually satisfactory goalless draw with Sweden.

Gustav Engvall's strike enabled Roland Larsson's Sweden team to surprise Switzerland 1-0 on their finals debut, and three days later they withstood a fearsome second-half onslaught from Austria to earn a point and edge themselves closer to the semi-finals. With their form improving game

on game, Austria secured third place in the section – and qualification for the FIFA U-17 World Cup – with a 2-1 victory over Switzerland.

Russia unveiled their potential early, opening Group B with a 3-0 win against Ukraine, while Italy managed to keep a skilful Croatia side goalless. The Azzurrini were then 1-0 down to Ukraine with five minutes remaining before Mario Pugliese completed the turnaround to make it 2-1 in added time. Croatia again drew 0-0 in their second game, against Russia, which meant that a 1-1 draw between the two eventual finalists was enough to take both sides through. Croatia's 2-1 win against Ukraine put them level on points with the top two but out of the tournament on the three-way head-to-head rule. They did, however, claim the consolation prize of a first World Cup qualification.

With momentum growing, Italy hit top speed in the semi-final, ending home hopes with a 2-0 win over Slovakia as Pugliese and Elio Capradossi each scored their second goals of the tournament. Things were much tighter in the other game. After a 0-0 draw against a Sweden side reduced to ten men, the outcome was finally settled at the end of an epic penalty shoot-out, with Ramil Sheydaev scoring the decisive kick to win it 10-9 for Russia. Another goalless stalemate – the fifth in 15 matches – and another shoot-out win for Russia would conclude the competition in somewhat predictable style three days later.

Russia celebrate their UEFA European Under-17 Championship triumph

UEFA European Under-17 Championship

Valmir Berisha – Sweden's top scorer in qualifying with five goals

Qualifying round

Group 1

25-30/09/12 Indjija, Jakovo

Belarus 1-0 Moldova, Serbia 5-0 Armenia, Belarus 5-0 Armenia, Moldova 0-4 Serbia, Serbia 7-0 Belarus, Armenia 0-3 Moldova

		Pld	W	D	L	F	A	Pts
1	Serbia	3	3	0	0	16	0	9
2	Belarus	3	2	0	1	6	7	6
3	Moldova	3	1	0	2	3	5	3
4	Armenia	3	0	0	3	0	13	0

Group 2

03-08/10/12 Myllykoski

Germany 5-0 San Marino, Finland 3-0 Andorra, Andorra 1-10 Germany, Finland 5-0 San Marino, Germany 8-1 Finland, San Marino 1-1 Andorra

		Pld	W	D	L	F	A	Pts
1	Germany	3	3	0	0	23	2	9
2	Finland	3	2	0	1	9	8	6
3	San Marino	3	0	1	2	1	11	1
4	Andorra	3	0	1	2	2	14	1

Group 3

23-28/10/12 St Nicolas, Oudenaarde, Eeklo

Netherlands 2-1 Latvia, Belgium 2-0 Lithuania, Lithuania 0-0 Netherlands, Belgium 5-0 Latvia, Netherlands 2-1 Belgium, Latvia 1-0 Lithuania

		Pld	W	D	L	F	A	Pts
1	Netherlands	3	2	1	0	4	2	7
2	Belgium	3	2	0	1	8	2	6
3	Latvia	3	1	0	2	2	7	3
4	Lithuania	3	0	1	2	0	3	1

Group 4

19-24/10/12 Sliven, Stara Zagora

Poland 2-1 Bulgaria, Spain 2-0 Azerbaijan, Azerbaijan 0-1 Poland, Spain 0-1 Bulgaria, Poland 0-1 Spain, Bulgaria 4-1 Azerbaijan

		Pld	W	D	L	F	A	Pts
1	Bulgaria	3	2	0	1	6	3	6
2	Poland	3	2	0	1	3	2	6
3	Spain	3	2	0	1	3	1	6
4	Azerbaijan	3	0	0	3	1	7	0

Group 5

24-29/09/12 Sarajevo

Greece 0-0 Slovenia, France 3-1 Bosnia & Herzegovina, Greece 1-2 Bosnia & Herzegovina, Slovenia 1-0 France, France 2-2 Greece, Bosnia & Herzegovina 0-1 Slovenia

		Pld	W	D	L	F	A	Pts
1	Slovenia	3	2	1	0	2	0	7
2	France	3	1	1	1	5	4	4
3	Bosnia & Herzegovina	3	1	0	2	3	5	3
4	Greece	3	0	2	1	3	4	2

Group 6

10-15/10/12 Hall in Tirol, Schwaz

Switzerland 3-0 Faroe Islands, Austria 0-0 Cyprus, Cyprus 1-5 Switzerland, Austria 6-0 Faroe Islands, Switzerland 1-1 Austria, Faroe Islands 1-1 Cyprus

		Pld	W	D	L	F	A	Pts
1	Switzerland	3	2	1	0	9	2	7
2	Austria	3	1	2	0	7	1	5
3	Cyprus	3	0	2	1	2	6	2
4	Faroe Islands	3	0	1	2	1	10	1

Group 7

21/10-14/11/12 Tallinn

Northern Ireland 4-0 Wales, England 2-0 Estonia, England 1-0 Wales, Estonia 1-1 Northern Ireland, Northern Ireland 2-3 England, Wales 1-3 Estonia

		Pld	W	D	L	F	A	Pts
1	England	3	3	0	0	6	2	9
2	Northern Ireland	3	1	1	1	7	4	4
3	Estonia	3	1	1	1	4	4	4
4	Wales	3	0	0	3	1	8	0

Group 8

18-23/10/12 Tatabanya, Telki

Italy 1-0 Albania, Hungary 5-0 Liechtenstein, Italy 4-0 Liechtenstein, Albania 0-1 Hungary, Hungary 3-2 Italy, Liechtenstein 0-6 Albania

		Pld	W	D	L	F	A	Pts
1	Hungary	3	3	0	0	9	2	9
2	Italy	3	2	0	1	7	3	6
3	Albania	3	1	0	2	6	2	3
4	Liechtenstein	3	0	0	3	0	15	0

Group 9

29/09-04/10/12 Ta' Qali

Norway 2-1 Malta, Portugal 4-2 Iceland, Norway 2-0 Iceland, Malta 1-2 Portugal, Portugal 0-1 Norway, Iceland 2-0 Malta

		Pld	W	D	L	F	A	Pts
1	Norway	3	3	0	0	5	1	9
2	Portugal	3	2	0	1	6	4	6
3	Iceland	3	1	0	2	4	6	3
4	Malta	3	0	0	3	2	6	0

Group 10

29/09-04/10/12 Kumanovo, Skopje

Republic of Ireland 1-1 Sweden, Romania 1-1 FYROM, Republic of Ireland 4-1 FYROM, Sweden 2-1 Romania, Romania 0-2 Republic of Ireland, FYROM 0-4 Sweden

		Pld	W	D	L	F	A	Pts
1	Republic of Ireland	3	2	1	0	7	2	7
1	Sweden	3	2	1	0	7	2	7
3	Romania	3	0	1	2	2	5	1
4	FYROM	3	0	1	2	2	9	1

Group 11

25-30/09/12 Kyjov, Mikulov, Lanzhot

Czech Republic 3-0 Russia, Denmark 3-0 Montenegro, Montenegro 0-2 Czech Republic, Denmark 1-2 Russia, Czech Republic 3-0 Denmark, Russia 3-0 Montenegro

		Pld	W	D	L	F	A	Pts
1	Czech Republic	3	3	0	0	8	0	9
2	Russia	3	2	0	1	5	4	6
3	Denmark	3	1	0	2	4	5	3
4	Montenegro	3	0	0	3	0	8	0

Group 12

14-19/10/12 Solin, Sinj, Split, Dugopolje, Imotski

Turkey 3-0 Kazakhstan, Croatia 4-2 Israel, Turkey 2-4 Israel, Kazakhstan 0-2 Croatia, Croatia 4-3 Turkey, Israel 6-2 Kazakhstan

		Pld	W	D	L	F	A	Pts
1	Croatia	3	3	0	0	10	5	9
2	Israel	3	2	0	1	12	8	6
3	Turkey	3	1	0	2	8	8	3
4	Kazakhstan	3	0	0	3	2	11	0

Group 13

30/10-04/11/12 Tbilisi

Scotland 5-2 Luxembourg, Georgia 1-3 Ukraine, Scotland 0-0 Ukraine, Luxembourg 1-3 Georgia, Georgia 3-0 Scotland, Ukraine 6-0 Luxembourg

		Pld	W	D	L	F	A	Pts
1	Ukraine	3	2	1	0	9	1	7
2	Georgia	3	2	0	1	7	4	6
3	Scotland	3	1	1	1	5	5	4
4	Luxembourg	3	0	0	3	3	14	0

Elite round

Group 1

21/03/13, Gradski stadion, Sinj
Croatia 3-2 Spain
21/03/13, SC Hrvatskih vitezova, Dugopolje
Belgium 1-4 France
23/03/13, SC Hrvatskih vitezova, Dugopolje
Croatia 1-0 France
23/03/13, Gradski stadion, Sinj
Spain 2-1 Belgium
26/03/13, Gradski stadion, Sinj
Belgium 1-1 Croatia
26/03/13, SC Hrvatskih vitezova, Dugopolje
France 3-2 Spain

		Pld	W	D	L	F	A	Pts
1	Croatia	3	2	1	0	5	3	7
2	France	3	2	0	1	7	4	6
3	Spain	3	1	0	2	6	7	3
4	Belgium	3	0	1	2	3	7	1

Group 2

25/03/13, WFV Hirschstetten, Vienna
Serbia 2-0 Georgia
25/03/13, Sportzentrum Schwechat-Ranners, Schwechat-Rannersdorf
Republic of Ireland 1-0 Austria
27/03/13, WFV Hirschstetten, Vienna
Georgia 3-0 Republic of Ireland
27/03/13, Sportzentrum Schwechat-Ranners, Schwechat-Rannersdorf
Serbia 0-1 Austria
30/03/13, WFV Hirschstetten, Vienna
Republic of Ireland 1-1 Serbia
30/03/13, FAC Team Für Wien, Vienna
Austria 2-1 Georgia

		Pld	W	D	L	F	A	Pts
1	Austria	3	2	0	1	3	2	6
2	Serbia	3	1	1	1	3	2	4
3	Republic of Ireland	3	1	1	1	2	4	4
4	Georgia	3	1	0	2	4	4	3

Group 3

26/03/13, Globall Football Park, Telki
Hungary 3-2 Finland
26/03/13, Globall Football Park, Telki
Sweden 4-1 Belarus
28/03/13, Globall Football Park, Telki
Hungary 3-0 Belarus
28/03/13, Globall Football Park, Telki
Finland 0-5 Sweden
31/03/13, Globall Football Park, Telki
Sweden 1-1 Hungary
31/03/13, Grosics Gyula, Tatabanya
Belarus-Finland (cancelled)

		Pld	W	D	L	F	A	Pts
1	Sweden	3	2	1	0	10	2	7
2	Hungary	3	2	1	0	7	3	7
3	Finland	2	0	0	2	2	8	0
4	Belarus	2	0	0	2	1	7	0

Group 4

26/03/13, Tönnies Arena, Rheda-Wiedenbrück
Ukraine 5-1 Estonia
26/03/13, Tönnies Arena, Rheda-Wiedenbrück
Germany 5-2 Bulgaria
28/03/13, Hembergstadion, Iserlohn
Germany 6-0 Estonia
28/03/13, Montanhydraulik-Stadion, Holzwickede
Bulgaria 0-0 Ukraine
31/03/13, Weserstadion, Ahlen
Ukraine 1-0 Germany
31/03/13, Hembergstadion, Iserlohn
Estonia 1-4 Bulgaria

		Pld	W	D	L	F	A	Pts
1	Ukraine	3	2	1	0	6	1	7
2	Germany	3	2	0	1	11	3	6
3	Bulgaria	3	1	1	1	6	6	4
4	Estonia	3	0	0	3	2	15	0

Group 5

22/03/13, Kleinholz, Olten
Czech Republic 1-1 Israel
22/03/13, Brühl, Grenchen
Switzerland 0-0 Poland
24/03/13, Kleinholz, Olten
Israel 1-2 Switzerland
24/03/13, Brühl, Grenchen
Czech Republic 1-1 Poland
27/03/13, Stadion FC Solothurn, Solothurn
Switzerland 1-0 Czech Republic
27/03/13, Kleinholz, Olten
Poland 2-1 Israel

		Pld	W	D	L	F	A	Pts
1	Switzerland	3	2	1	0	3	1	7
2	Poland	3	1	2	0	3	2	5
3	Czech Republic	3	0	2	1	2	3	2
4	Israel	3	0	1	2	3	5	1

Group 6

23/03/13, St George's Park Main Stadium, Burton-on-Trent
Slovenia 1-2 Russia
23/03/13, St George's Park Main Stadium, Burton-on-Trent
England 1-0 Portugal
25/03/13, St George's Park Main Stadium, Burton-on-Trent
Portugal 3-1 Slovenia
25/03/13, Pirelli Stadium, Burton-on-Trent
England 1-2 Russia
28/03/13, Pirelli Stadium, Burton-on-Trent
Slovenia 1-2 England
28/03/13, St George's Park Main Stadium, Burton-on-Trent
Russia 0-1 Portugal

		Pld	W	D	L	F	A	Pts
1	Russia	3	2	0	1	4	3	6
2	England	3	2	0	1	4	3	6
3	Portugal	3	2	0	1	4	2	6
4	Slovenia	3	0	0	3	3	7	0

Group 7

21/03/13, Sportpark "In de Bandert", Echt
Norway 0-1 Italy
21/03/13, Sportpark Parkzicht, Uden
Netherlands 2-2 Northern Ireland
23/03/13, Sportpark Parkzicht, Uden
Norway 2-1 Northern Ireland
23/03/13, Sportpark "In de Bandert", Echt
Italy 1-0 Netherlands
26/03/13, Sportpark Parkzicht, Uden
Netherlands 1-1 Norway
26/03/13, Sportpark "In de Bandert", Echt
Northern Ireland 0-0 Italy

		Pld	W	D	L	F	A	Pts
1	Italy	3	2	1	0	2	0	7
2	Norway	3	1	1	1	3	3	4
3=	Netherlands	3	0	2	1	3	4	2
3=	Northern Ireland	3	0	2	1	3	4	2

Timo Werner's 13 goals in the qualifying competition were not enough to take Germany through to the final tournament in Slovakia

Top goalscorers (qualifying)

13	Timo Werner (Germany)
6	Donis Avdijaj (Germany)
5	Valmir Berisha (Sweden)
	Nemanja Radonjić (Serbia)
	Maurice Multhaup (Germany)
	Andriy Boryachuk (Ukraine)
	Luka Belić (Serbia)
	Shon Zalman Weissman (Israel)
	Kiril Despodov (Bulgaria)
	Luka Zarandia (Georgia)
	Donát Zsótér (Hungary)

UEFA European Under-17 Championship

Final tournament

Group A

05/05/13, Štadión MFK Dubnica, Dubnica nad Vahom
Slovakia 1-0 Austria
Goal: 1-0 Slaninka 80+2
Referee: Gözübüyük (NED)

05/05/13, Štadión MŠK Žilina, Zilina
Switzerland 0-1 Sweden
Goal: 0-1 Engvall 38
Referee: Sidiropoulos (GRE)

08/05/13, Štadión MFK Dubnica, Dubnica nad Vahom
Austria 1-1 Sweden
Goals: 0-1 Suljic 44, 1-1 Zivotic 49
Referee: Doyle (IRL)

08/05/13, Štadión MŠK Žilina, Zilina
Slovakia 2-2 Switzerland
Goals: 0-1 Trachsel 22, 0-2 Kamber 29, 1-2 Varga 39, 2-2 Slaninka 69
Referee: Stoyanov (BUL)

11/05/13, Štadión MŠK Žilina, Zilina
Sweden 0-0 Slovakia
Referee: Vinčić (SVN)

11/05/13, Štadión MFK Dubnica, Dubnica nad Vahom
Austria 2-1 Switzerland
Goals: 1-0 Baumgartner 11, 2-0 Ripic 35, 2-1 Kamber 57
Referee: Dunauskas (LTU)

		Pld	W	D	L	F	A	Pts
1	Slovakia	3	1	2	0	3	2	5
2	Sweden	3	1	2	0	2	1	5
3	Austria	3	1	1	1	3	3	4
4	Switzerland	3	0	1	2	3	5	1

Group B

05/05/13, Štadión FC ViOn, Zlate Moravce
Russia 3-0 Ukraine
Goal(s): 1-0 Khodzhaniyazov 47, 2-0 Mayrovich 62, 3-0 Zhemaletdinov 79
Referee: Stoyanov (BUL)

Italy duo Elio Capradossi (left) and Mario Pugliese were among the final tournament's top scorers with two goals apiece

05/05/13, Štadión FC Nitra, Nitra
Croatia 0-0 Italy
Referee: Doyle (IRL)

08/05/13, Štadión FC ViOn, Zlate Moravce
Russia 0-0 Croatia
Referee: Dunauskas (LTU)

08/05/13, Štadión FC Nitra, Nitra
Ukraine 1-2 Italy
Goals: 1-0 Vachiberadze 61, 1-1 Parigini 75, 1-2 Pugliese 80+3
Referee: Vinčić (SVN)

11/05/13, Štadión FC Nitra, Nitra
Italy 1-1 Russia
Goals: 0-1 Gasilin 12, 1-1 Capradossi 43
Referee: Gözübüyük (NED)

11/05/13, Štadión FC ViOn, Zlate Moravce
Ukraine 1-2 Croatia
Goals: 1-0 Tsygankov 17, 1-1 Halilović 40(p), 1-2 Murić 72
Referee: Sidiropoulos (GRE)

		Pld	W	D	L	F	A	Pts
1	Russia	3	1	2	0	4	1	5
2	Italy	3	1	2	0	3	2	5
3	Croatia	3	1	2	0	2	1	5
4	Ukraine	3	0	0	3	2	7	0

Semi-finals

14/05/13, Štadión MŠK Žilina, Zilina
Slovakia 0-2 Italy
Goals: 0-1 Pugliese 3, 0-2 Capradossi 64
Referee: Dunauskas (LTU)

14/05/13, Štadión MŠK Žilina, Zilina
Russia 0-0 Sweden *(10-9 on pens)*
Referee: Vinčić (SVN)

Final

17/05/13, Štadión MŠK Žilina, Zilina
(att: 3,412)
Italy 0-0 Russia *(4-5 on pens)*
Referee: Sidiropoulos (GRE)
Italy: Scuffet, Calabria, Dimarco, Pugliese, Capradossi, Sciacca, Tutino (Di Molfetta 67), Palazzi, Cerri, Steffè (Parigini 80+1), Vido (Bonazzoli 63). Coach: Daniele Zoratto (ITA)
Russia: Mitryushkin, Parshikov, Likhachev, Khodzhaniyazov, Yakuba, S. Makarov, Golovin (Buranov 62), Zuev (Gasilin 49), Barinov, Zhemaletdinov (A. Makarov 41), Sheydaev. Coach: Dmitri Khomukha (RUS)
Yellow cards: Parshikov 22 (Russia), Zhemaletdinov 36 (Russia), Vido 53 (Italy)

Top goalscorers (final tournament)

2	Elio Capradossi (Italy)
	Mario Pugliese (Italy)
	Martin Slaninka (Slovakia)
	Robin Kamber (Switzerland)

Squads/Appearances/Goals

AUSTRIA

No	Name	DoB	Aps	(s)	Gls
Goalkeepers					
1	Marcel Hartl	22/07/96			
21	Alexander Schlager	01/02/96	3		
Defenders					
19	Dominik Baumgartner	20/07/96	3		1
11	Petar Gluhakovic	25/03/96	3		
15	Manuel Haas	07/05/96			
5	Michael Lercher	04/01/96	3		
3	Stefan Peric	13/02/97	3		
14	Marcel Probst	21/07/96		(1)	
Midfielders					
8	Sascha Horvath	22/08/96	3		
10	Valentino Lazaro	24/03/96	3		
6	Raphael Mathis	25/01/96		(1)	
12	Thomas Steiner	06/02/96		(1)	
4	Lukas Tursch	29/03/96	3		
Forwards					
7	Adrian Grbic	04/08/96	3		
13	Luca Mayr	06/04/96		(2)	
9	Tobias Pellegrini	03/04/96	1	(2)	
2	Daniel Ripic	14/03/96	2	(1)	1
17	Nikola Zivotic	26/01/96	3		1

CROATIA

No	Name	DoB	Aps	(s)	Gls
Goalkeepers					
12	Ivo Grbić	18/01/96			
1	Marko Marić	03/01/96	3		
Defenders					
5	Duje Ćaleta-Car	17/09/96	3		
15	Lukas Ćuljak	05/03/96			
13	Hrvoje Džijan	26/06/96			
14	Anton Krešić	29/01/96			
3	Petar Mamić	06/03/96	3		
6	Franjo Prce	07/01/96	3		
2	Marko Stolnik	08/07/96	2	(1)	
Midfielders					
7	Josip Bašić	02/03/96	3		
9	Fran Brodić	08/01/97	3		
16	Ivan Fiolić	29/04/96		(1)	
17	Karlo Lulić	10/05/96		(1)	
8	Ante Roguljić	11/03/96	3		
4	Ivan Šunjić	09/10/96	3		
11	Frane Vojković	20/12/96	3		
Forwards					
10	Alen Halilović	18/06/96	3		1
18	Robert Murić	12/03/96	1	(2)	1

ITALY

No	Name	DoB	Aps	(s)	Gls
Goalkeepers					
12	Emil Audero	18/01/97			
1	Simone Scuffet	31/05/96	5		
Defenders					
16	Arturo Calabresi	17/03/96			
2	Davide Calabria	06/12/96	5		
5	Elio Capradossi	11/03/96	5		2
3	Federico Dimarco	10/11/97	5		
13	Matteo Lomolino	11/03/96			
6	Giacomo Sciacca	19/04/96	5		
Midfielders					
8	Andrea Palazzi	24/02/96	5		
10	Vittorio Parigini	25/03/96		(4)	1
17	Alessandro Piu	30/07/96	1	(1)	
4	Mario Pugliese	26/03/96	5		2
15	Demetrio Steffè	30/07/96	2	(1)	
14	Alberto Tibolla	31/01/96	3	(1)	
7	Gennaro Tutino	20/08/96	4	(1)	
Forwards					
11	Federico Bonazzoli	21/05/97	3	(2)	
9	Alberto Cerri	16/04/96	4		
19	Davide Di Molfetta	23/06/96		(1)	
18	Luca Vido	03/02/97	3	(1)	

SLOVAKIA

No	Name	DoB	Aps	(s)	Gls
Goalkeepers					
1	Martin Junas	09/03/96	4		
12	Juraj Semanko	02/01/96			
Defenders					
2	Andrej Kadlec	02/02/96	3		
15	Šimon Kupec	11/02/96	3		
14	Erik Otrísal	28/06/96	1		
4	Martin Slaninka	26/03/96		(4)	2
18	Atila Varga	11/04/96	4		1
3	Denis Vavro	10/04/96	3		
5	Michal Vodecký	22/08/96	2	(1)	
Midfielders					
8	Jakub Grič	05/07/96	4		
17	Lukáš Haraslín	26/05/96	4		
7	Miroslav Káčer	02/02/96	3	(1)	
11	Filip Lesniak	14/05/96	4		
16	Tomáš Zázrivec	16/06/96		(1)	
Forwards					
13	Lukáš Čmelík	13/04/96	1	(3)	
10	Nikolas Špalek	12/02/97	4		
9	Tomáš Vestenický	06/04/96	4		
6	Martin Vlček	05/02/96		(1)	

SWITZERLAND

No	Name	DoB	Aps	(s)	Gls
Goalkeepers					
1	Fabian Fellmann	23/07/96	3		
12	Mateo Matic	07/01/96			
Defenders					
4	Marko Drakul	06/08/96	3		
5	Nico Elvedi	30/09/96	3		
3	Olivier Kleiner	03/02/96	2		
2	Nicolas Stettler	28/04/96	3		
16	Nils Von Niederhäusern	10/01/96	2		
Midfielders					
8	Eric Briner	01/02/96	3		
10	Anto Grgic	28/11/96	1	(1)	
6	Deni Kadoic	03/04/96	3		
14	Robin Kamber	15/02/96	2	(1)	2
13	Phi Nguyen	03/07/96		(1)	
15	Marsel Stevic	22/02/96			
Forwards					
7	Jolan Forestal	06/03/96	1	(1)	
9	Nicolas Hunziker	23/02/96	2	(1)	
17	Joao De Oliveira	06/01/96	2	(1)	
18	Kilian Pagliuca	02/09/96	1	(2)	
11	Marco Trachsel	02/08/96	2		1

RUSSIA

No	Name	DoB	Aps	(s)	Gls
Goalkeepers					
12	Aleksei Kuznetsov	20/08/96			
1	Anton Mitryushkin	08/02/96	5		
Defenders					
4	Dzhamaldin Khodzhaniyazov	18/07/96	5		1
3	Aleksandr Likhachev	22/07/96	5		
14	Anatoli Nikolaesh	17/04/96			
2	Vladislav Parshikov	19/02/96	5		
5	Denis Yakuba	26/05/96	5		
Midfielders					
15	Dmitri Barinov	11/09/96	3	(1)	
8	Danila Buranov	11/02/96	2	(2)	
16	Aleksandr Dovbnya	14/02/96			
10	Aleksandr Golovin	30/05/96	5		
6	Sergei Makarov	03/10/96	5		
13	Egor Rudkovski	04/03/96		(3)	
18	Rifat Zhemaletdinov	20/09/96	1	(4)	1
Forwards					
7	Aleksandr Makarov	24/04/96	4	(1)	
9	Aleksei Gasilin	01/03/96	2	(2)	1
14	Maksim Mayrovich	06/02/96	1	(1)	1
19	Ramil Sheydaev	15/03/96	2		
11	Aleksandr Zuev	26/06/96	5		

SWEDEN

No	Name	DoB	Aps	(s)	Gls
Goalkeepers					
1	Sixten Mohlin	17/01/96	1		
12	Hampus Strömgren	08/07/96			
Defenders					
2	Jakob Bergman	02/01/96		(1)	
5	Johan Ramhorn	03/05/96	1	(1)	
4	Sebastian Ramhorn	03/05/96	4		
6	Noah Sonko Sundberg	06/06/96	3		
3	Ali Suljic	18/09/97	4		1
7	Linus Wahlqvist	11/11/96	4		
Midfielders					
8	Elias Andersson	31/01/96	3		
9	Valmir Berisha	06/06/96	2	(1)	
11	Anton Jönsson Salétros	12/04/96	3	(1)	
13	Viktor Nordin	18/01/96		(2)	
10	Erdal Rakip	13/02/96	3	(1)	
14	Isak Ssewankambo	27/02/96	4		
Forwards					
15	Gentrit Citaku	25/02/96	2		
16	Gustav Engvall	29/04/96	3		1
17	Mirza Halvadzic	15/02/96	3	(1)	
18	Christer Lipovac	07/03/96	1	(3)	

UKRAINE

No	Name	DoB	Aps	(s)	Gls
Goalkeepers					
12	Dmytro Bezruk	30/03/96			
1	Vadym Soldatenko	28/05/96	3		
Defenders					
6	Ihor Kyryukhantsev	29/01/96	1		
16	Pavlo Lukyanchuk	19/05/96	3		
13	Olexandr Osman	18/04/96	2		
14	Stanislav Shtanenko	05/02/96	2		
19	Ihor Yarovoy	08/04/96		(1)	
17	Olexandr Zinchenko	15/12/96	3		
Midfielders					
15	Danylo Knysh	03/03/96	1	(2)	
4	Bogdan Kuksenko	11/02/96	3		
3	Valeriy Luchkevych	11/01/96	3		
5	Pavlo Makohon	25/09/96	2		
8	Pavlo Orikhovskiy	13/05/96		(1)	
20	Maxym Tretyakov	06/03/96	2	(1)	
11	Viktor Tsygankov	15/11/97	3		1
10	Beka Vachiberadze	05/03/96	3		1
Forwards					
7	Nutsu Ardelyan	18/06/96		(1)	
9	Andriy Boryachuk	23/04/96	2	(1)	

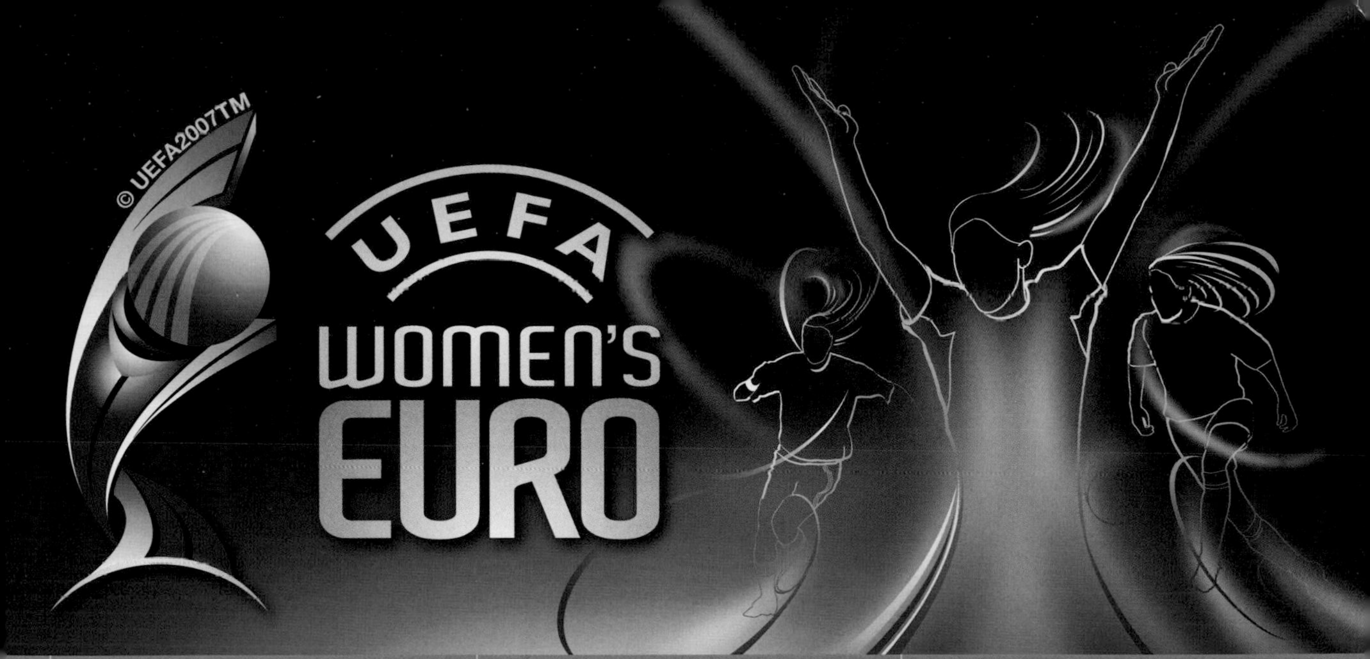

UEFA WOMEN'S EURO

Germany's long reign continues

Germany won the UEFA European Women's Championship. Again. It was their sixth successive victory and eighth in all following previous wins in 2009, 2005, 2001, 1997, 1995, 1991 and 1989. Of all those successes, however, their 2013 triumph in Sweden was probably the least convincing.

Their 12-year run of victories in all UEFA Women's EURO games was ended with a dramatic comeback by Spain to draw 2-2 in qualifying. Then, in their first match in Sweden, Silvia Neid's side were held to a 0-0 draw by the Netherlands, having not dropped a point at the final tournament since 1997. Furthermore, an unbeaten record stretching back a year longer was ended in their last pool game by Norway.

Yet 11 days later, Norway were beaten 1-0 and Germany were champions once again.

With stalwarts such as Birgit Prinz, Ariane Hingst and Kerstin Garefrekes retired from the team, and Kim Kulig and Babett Peter among six key injury casualties, the consensus was that 2013 would be the year that Germany would finally be dethroned. But it was not to be.

Sweden were the side many identified to knock them off their perch. There was unprecedented backing for the hosts, resulting in total ticket sales of 216,888 – over 75,000 more than any previous UEFA Women's EURO. With Pia Sundhage having taken over the coaching reins in autumn 2012

Sweden's Lotta Schelin, the tournament's top scorer with five goals

and Lotta Schelin powering the side up front, expectations were high. Schelin had a penalty saved in the opening game against Denmark but then hit form, her five goals comfortably winning her the tournament's Golden Boot. However, when they met Germany in the semi-finals, Schelin and Sweden drew a blank and lost 1-0. The squad would still be feted during a half-time walkabout at the final, however, in front of a tournament record crowd of 41,301.

Others felt France, after finishing fourth at the 2011 FIFA Women's World Cup and 2012

Olympics, were in with a shout of a first European triumph. They boasted the only perfect record in qualifying, and they would also be the sole side to win all of their group games in Sweden, including a 3-0 victory that eliminated 2009 runners-up England. Hot favourites to beat Denmark in the quarter-finals, France were held 1-1 and then beaten 4-2 on penalties, with goalkeeper Stina Petersen, who had saved two spot kicks against Sweden, again proving the heroine.

Denmark's run was then ended, also 4-2 on penalties, by Norway. Although they had topped their group by beating Germany, Norway were not among the pre-tournament favourites. Indeed their qualifying form had been so shaky that the team changed their coach, with Even Pellerud returning to the position in which he had achieved such success between 1989 and 1996. Nevertheless, the combination of experience – Ingvild Stensland, Trine Rønning and Solveig Gulbrandsen – and youth – Caroline Graham Hansen and Ada Hegerberg – helped them top a section that also included Iceland and the Netherlands before they ousted Spain and Denmark in the knockout rounds.

But for two missed penalties in the Solna final, the European crown would have been Norway's. But the holders' third 1-0 win in succession, courtesy of substitute Anja Mittag's 49th-minute goal, meant that once again it was Germany who went home with the trophy.

Germany goalkeeper Nadine Angerer, a star performer in the final against Norway, lifts the 2013 UEFA Women's EURO trophy

Norway goalkeeper Ingrid Hjelmseth makes a save during the semi-final penalty shoot-out victory over Denmark

Group stage

UEFA Women's EURO 2013 began with four consecutive draws, and three of them were upsets. In Group A, Denmark held hosts Sweden 1-1 on their big day, with Stina Petersen saving penalties from Lotta Schelin and Kosovare Asllani, while in Group B, Iceland secured a first-ever point as they drew 1-1 against Norway and the Netherlands ended a winning run for Germany that stretched all the way back to 1997, holding Silvia Neid's side 0-0.

Group C, on the other hand, immediately produced positive results, with France overcoming Russia 3-1 and Spain beating England 3-2 thanks to a last-gasp goal. That set the tone for the section. England needed a late Toni Duggan equaliser to hold Russia 1-1, and France beat Spain 1-0 to win the group. France then eliminated England with a handsome 3-0 win, while Spain made sure of second place with a 1-1 draw against Russia.

In Group B, Germany bounced back to overcome Iceland 4-0 as Norway pipped the Netherlands 1-0. By the time Germany and Norway were both through, but it was still a surprise that the holders' 17-year unbeaten run in the competition was ended 1-0 by Even Pellerud's team. Meanwhile, Iceland's first ever finals win, 1-0 against the Netherlands, earned them a quarter-final place as the best third-placed team.

Sweden recovered from their opening draw to hit top gear in Group A, equalling the finals record with a 5-0 victory against Finland and

then beating Italy 3-1, the Azzurre having previously overcome Denmark 2-1 to claim the runners-up spot. Denmark then conceded a late goal to draw 1-1 with Finland and finish third. As they, like Russia, had two points, a drawing of lots was required to determine the second best third-placed team. The luck was with Denmark.

Quarter-finals

Sweden's free-scoring form continued against Iceland in Halmstad. Marie Hammarström and Josefine Öqvist struck early, then it became the Schelin show as she added her fourth and fifth goals of the finals. It was closer in Vaxjo, with Simone Laudehr's goal proving sufficient to give Germany a second successive quarter-final win against Italy.

A day later in Kalmar, Norway saw off Spain 3-1, but there was a shock in Linkoping as Denmark knocked out France. Although Louisa Necib's penalty salvaged a 1-1 draw for Les Bleues in regular play, her team were beaten 4-2 on spot kicks, Danish goalkeeper Petersen this time saving from Necib to add to her two penalty stops in the opening group game against Sweden.

Semi-finals

Sweden against Germany would have been many observers' idea of a dream final, but instead it was in the last four, in Gothenburg, that the hosts and holders came face to face. Between them they put on a show to match the occasion. Sweden generally had the

better of the game, but they could not force their way through the tight German defence, and it was Dzsenifer Marozsán, in for injured forward Célia Okoyino da Mbabi, whose 33rd-minute goal settled matters, jabbing the ball past keeper Kristin Hammarström and watching on as it slowly trickled its way just inside the post.

A day later in Norrkoping, Denmark were involved in another penalty shoot-out, having equalised late through Johanna Rasmussen after falling behind to Marit Fiane Christensen's third-minute opener. This time, however, Denmark's luck ran out, Ingrid Hjelmseth saving their first two kicks from Line Røddik Hansen and Theresa Nielsen before evergreen Trine Rønning stepped up to strike the decisive blow for Norway.

Final

For the fourth time since 1989, Germany and Norway contested a UEFA Women's EURO final. On the half-hour Norway were awarded a penalty, but German goalkeeper Nadine Angerer, aiming for a fifth winner's medal, saved brilliantly from Rønning. Not for the first time in the tournament, Germany were struggling to impose their game, so coach Silvia Neid sent on Anja Mittag at the break, and the veteran of the 2005 final win against Norway duly scored within four minutes of her introduction after a delightful passing move and run from the restored Okoyino da Mbabi. When Angerer saved a second penalty, from Solveig Gulbrandsen, Germany's victory was sealed.

Qualifying group stage

Group 1

2011/12 Results

Bosnia & Herzegovina 0-1 Italy
Poland 0-3(f) Russia
FYROM 0-9 Italy
Russia 4-1 Bosnia & Herzegovina
Poland 2-0 Greece
FYROM 1-1 Greece
Italy 2-0 Russia
Poland 4-0 Bosnia & Herzegovina
FYROM 2-6 Bosnia & Herzegovina
Greece 0-4 Russia
Poland 0-5 Italy
FYROM 0-3 Poland
Italy 2-0 Greece
Greece 2-3 Bosnia & Herzegovina
Russia 8-0 FYROM
Italy 4-0 Bosnia & Herzegovina
Greece 1-1 Poland
Russia 0-2 Italy
Greece 2-2 FYROM
Italy 9-0 FYROM
Bosnia & Herzegovina 0-2 Poland
Russia 4-0 Greece
Poland 4-0 FYROM
Bosnia & Herzegovina 0-1 Russia

2012/13 Results

15/09/12, Goce Delcev, Prilep
FYROM 0-6 Russia

15/09/12, Asim Ferhatović Hase Stadion, Sarajevo
Bosnia & Herzegovina 1-1 Greece

16/09/12, Stadio Comunale Riviera delle Palme, San Benedetto del Tronto
Italy 1-0 Poland

19/09/12, Panionios, Athens
Greece 0-0 Italy

19/09/12, Asim Ferhatović Hase Stadion, Sarajevo
Bosnia & Herzegovina 1-0 FYROM

19/09/12, Moskva, Moscow
Russia 1-1 Poland

		Pld	W	D	L	F	A	Pts
1	Italy	10	9	1	0	35	0	28
2	Russia	10	7	1	2	21	6	22
3	Poland	10	5	2	3	17	11	17
4	Bosnia & Herzegovina	10	3	1	6	12	21	10
5	Greece	10	0	5	5	7	20	5
6	FYROM	10	0	2	8	5	49	2

Group 2

2011/12 Results

Germany 4-1 Switzerland
Kazakhstan 0-3 Romania
Turkey 1-10 Spain
Switzerland 4-1 Romania
Kazakhstan 2-0 Turkey
Turkey 0-0 Kazakhstan
Romania 0-3 Germany
Spain 3-2 Switzerland
Kazakhstan 0-4 Spain
Romania 7-1 Turkey
Germany 17-0 Kazakhstan
Romania 0-4 Spain
Turkey 1-2 Romania
Switzerland 8-1 Kazakhstan
Spain 2-2 Germany
Turkey 0-5 Germany
Romania 3-0 Kazakhstan
Germany 5-0 Spain
Switzerland 5-0 Turkey
Spain 13-0 Kazakhstan
Switzerland 0-6 Germany
Germany 5-0 Romania
Switzerland 4-3 Spain
Spain 4-0 Turkey
Romania 4-2 Switzerland

2012/13 Results

15/09/12, Atatürk Olimpiyat Stadium, Istanbul
Turkey 1-3 Switzerland

15/09/12, Shakhter, Karagandy
Kazakhstan 0-7 Germany

19/09/12, Shakhter, Karagandy
Kazakhstan 1-0 Switzerland

19/09/12, MSV Arena, Duisburg
Germany 10-0 Turkey

19/09/12, Pabellón de la Ciudad del Fútbol 1, Madrid
Spain 0-0 Romania

		Pld	W	D	L	F	A	Pts
1	Germany	10	9	1	0	64	3	28
2	Spain	10	6	2	2	43	14	20
3	Romania	10	5	1	4	20	20	16
4	Switzerland	10	5	0	5	29	24	15
5	Kazakhstan	10	2	1	7	4	55	7
6	Turkey	10	0	1	9	4	48	1

Group 3

2011/12 Results

Iceland 6-0 Bulgaria
Iceland 3-1 Norway
Belgium 2-1 Hungary
Norway 6-0 Hungary
Iceland 0-0 Belgium
Hungary 0-1 Iceland
Bulgaria 0-1 Northern Ireland
Northern Ireland 0-2 Iceland
Belgium 0-1 Norway
Bulgaria 0-4 Hungary
Belgium 5-0 Bulgaria
Northern Ireland 3-1 Norway
Hungary 2-2 Northern Ireland
Bulgaria 0-1 Belgium
Belgium 2-2 Northern Ireland
Bulgaria 0-3 Norway
Hungary 0-5 Norway
Belgium 1-0 Iceland
Northern Ireland 0-1 Hungary
Northern Ireland 4-1 Bulgaria
Norway 11-0 Bulgaria
Iceland 3-0 Hungary
Hungary 1-3 Belgium
Norway 2-0 Northern Ireland
Bulgaria 0-10 Iceland

2012/13 Results

15/09/12, Ullevaal Stadion, Oslo
Norway 3-2 Belgium

15/09/12, Laugardalsvöllur, Reykjavik
Iceland 2-0 Northern Ireland

19/09/12, City stadium, Sopron
Hungary 9-0 Bulgaria

19/09/12, Windsor Park, Belfast
Northern Ireland 0-2 Belgium

19/09/12, Ullevaal Stadion, Oslo
Norway 2-1 Iceland

		Pld	W	D	L	F	A	Pts
1	Norway	10	8	0	2	35	9	24
2	Iceland	10	7	1	2	28	4	22
3	Belgium	10	6	2	2	18	8	20
4	Northern Ireland	10	3	2	5	12	15	11
5	Hungary	10	3	1	6	18	22	10
6	Bulgaria	10	0	0	10	1	54	0

Group 4

2011/12 Results

Israel 0-5 France
Wales 0-2 Republic of Ireland
Republic of Ireland 1-3 France
Israel 1-6 Scotland
Republic of Ireland 2-0 Israel
Wales 1-4 France
France 5-0 Israel
Scotland 2-2 Wales
Israel 0-2 Wales
France 2-0 Scotland
France 4-0 Wales
Scotland 2-1 Republic of Ireland
Scotland 8-0 Israel
Republic of Ireland 0-1 Wales
Wales 5-0 Israel
Republic of Ireland 0-1 Scotland

2012/13 Results

15/09/12, Parc Y Scarlets, Llanelli
Wales 1-2 Scotland

15/09/12, Roudourou, Guingamp
France 4-0 Republic of Ireland

19/09/12, Itztadion Ramat Gan, Ramat Gan
Israel 0-2 Republic of Ireland

19/09/12, Tynecastle, Edinburgh
Scotland 0-0 France

		Pld	W	D	L	F	A	Pts
1	France	8	8	0	0	32	2	24
2	Scotland	8	5	1	2	21	12	16
3	Wales	8	3	1	4	12	14	10
4	Republic of Ireland	8	3	0	5	8	11	9
5	Israel	8	0	0	8	1	35	0

Group 5

2011/12 Results

Belarus 2-1 Estonia
Estonia 1-4 Ukraine
Ukraine 0-0 Slovakia
Finland 6-0 Estonia
Slovakia 3-1 Estonia
Belarus 2-2 Finland
Slovakia 3-0 Belarus
Ukraine 0-1 Belarus
Slovakia 0-1 Finland
Ukraine 5-0 Estonia
Finland 2-0 Slovakia
Estonia 2-4 Belarus
Ukraine 1-2 Finland
Finland 4-0 Belarus
Slovakia 0-2 Ukraine

2012/13 Results

25/08/12, Haapsalu, Haapsalu
Estonia 0-2 Slovakia

15/09/12, Lilleküla Stadium, Tallinn
Estonia 0-5 Finland

15/09/12, Spartak Stadion, Mogilev
Belarus 0-5 Ukraine

19/09/12, Finnair Stadium, Helsinki
Finland 0-1 Ukraine

19/09/12, Spartak Stadion, Mogilev
Belarus 1-0 Slovakia

		Pld	W	D	L	F	A	Pts
1	Finland	8	6	1	1	22	4	19
2	Ukraine	8	5	1	2	18	4	16
3	Belarus	8	4	1	3	10	17	13
4	Slovakia	8	3	1	4	8	7	10
5	Estonia	8	0	0	8	5	31	0

Group 6

2011/12 Results

Serbia 2-2 England
Netherlands 6-0 Serbia
England 4-0 Slovenia
Croatia 0-3 Netherlands
Slovenia 1-2 Serbia
Croatia 3-3 Slovenia
Netherlands 0-0 England
Serbia 4-2 Croatia
Slovenia 0-2 Netherlands
England 2-0 Serbia
Netherlands 2-0 Croatia
Croatia 0-6 England
Netherlands 3-1 Slovenia
Croatia 1-4 Serbia
England 1-0 Netherlands
Serbia 0-4 Netherlands
Slovenia 0-4 England

2012/13 Results

15/09/12, Športni park, Lendava
Slovenia 1-0 Croatia

19/09/12, Gradski Stadion, Indjija
Serbia 3-0 Slovenia

19/09/12, Bescot, Walsall
England 3-0 Croatia

		Pld	W	D	L	F	A	Pts
1	England	8	6	2	0	22	2	20
2	Netherlands	8	6	1	1	20	2	19
3	Serbia	8	4	1	3	15	18	13
4	Slovenia	8	1	1	6	6	21	4
5	Croatia	8	0	1	7	6	26	1

Group 7

2011/12 Results

Austria 1-1 Czech Republic
Armenia 0-8 Portugal
Armenia 0-5 Denmark
Czech Republic 1-0 Portugal
Denmark 3-0 Austria
Portugal 0-3 Denmark
Austria 3-0 Armenia
Portugal 0-1 Austria
Czech Republic 5-0 Armenia
Denmark 11-0 Armenia

Célia Okoyino da Mbabi struck 17 goals for Germany in qualifying

Portugal 6-0 Armenia
Portugal 2-5 Czech Republic
Armenia 2-4 Austria
Czech Republic 0-2 Denmark
Austria 1-0 Portugal
Czech Republic 2-3 Austria
Denmark 1-0 Czech Republic

2012/13 Results

15/09/12, NV Arena, St Polten
Austria 3-1 Denmark

19/09/12, Yerevan Republican Stadium after Vazgen Sargsyan, Yerevan
Armenia 0-2 Czech Republic

19/09/12, Jokri Park, Vejle
Denmark 2-0 Portugal

		Pld	W	D	L	F	A	Pts
1	Denmark	8	7	0	1	28	3	21
2	Austria	8	6	1	1	16	9	19
3	Czech Republic	8	4	1	3	16	9	13
4	Portugal	8	2	0	6	16	13	6
5	Armenia	8	0	0	8	2	44	0

Play-offs

20/10/12, Hampden Park, Glasgow
Scotland 1-1 Spain
24/10/12, Pabellón de la Ciudad del Fútbol 1, Madrid
Spain 3-2 Scotland *(aet)*
Aggregate: 4-3; Spain qualify after extra time.

20/10/12, Sport Complex, Sevastopol
Ukraine 2-3 Iceland
25/10/12, Laugardalsvöllur, Reykjavik
Iceland 3-2 Ukraine
Aggregate: 6-4; Iceland qualify.

21/10/12, NV Arena, St Polten
Austria 0-2 Russia
25/10/12, Olimp 2, Rostov-na-Donu
Russia 1-1 Austria
Aggregate: 3-1; Russia qualify.

Top goalscorers (qualifying/play-offs)

17	Célia Okoyino da Mbabi (Germany)
11	Ramona Bachmann (Switzerland)
	Verónica Boquete (Spain)
	Margrét Lára Vidarsdóttir (Iceland)
10	María Paz (Spain)
9	Patrizia Panico (Italy)
	Isabell Herlovsen (Norway)
	Pernille Harder (Denmark)
8	Alexandra Popp (Germany)
	Manon Melis (Netherlands)
	Anna Żelazko (Poland)
	Adriana (Spain)
	Daryna Apanaschenko (Ukraine)
	Kim Little (Scotland)

Final tournament

Group A

10/07/13, Örjans vall, Halmstad (att: 3,011)
Italy 0-0 Finland
Referee: Albon (ROU)
Italy: Marchitelli, D'Adda, Tuttino, Gabbiadini, Panico, Parisi, Camporese (Iannella 70), Bartoli, Stracchi, Manieri, Salvai. Coach: Antonio Cabrini (ITA)
Finland: Korpela, Hyyrynen, Lehtinen, Kivistö, Kukkonen, Tolvanen (Kuikka 73), Alanen, Heroum, Talonen, Westerlund, Sjölund (Lyytikäinen 61). Coach: Andrée Jeglertz (SWE)
Yellow cards: Camporese 24 (Italy), Alanen 45+1 (Finland), Westerlund 47 (Finland), Lyytikäinen 62 (Finland)

10/07/13, Gamla Ullevi, Gothenburg (att: 16,128)
Sweden 1-1 Denmark
Goals: 0-1 Knudsen 26, 1-1 Fischer 35
Referee: Steinhaus (GER)
Sweden: K Hammarström, Rohlin, Fischer, Thunebro, Schelin, Asllani, Göransson (Dahlkvist 63), Öqvist (Jakobsson 79), Seger, Samuelsson, M Hammarström. Coach: Pia Sundhage (SWE)
Denmark: S Petersen, Røddik, Søndergaard Pedersen, Ørntoft, Knudsen, Harder, Veje (Rydahl 62), Rasmussen (L Jensen 89), S Pedersen (Nadim 46), Nielsen, Brogaard. Coach: Kenneth Heiner-Møller (DEN)
Yellow cards: Ørntoft 66 (Denmark), Nielsen 84 (Denmark)

13/07/13, Örjans vall, Halmstad (att: 2,190)
Italy 2-1 Denmark
Goals: 1-0 Gabbiadini 55, 2-0 Mauro 60, 2-1 Brogaard 66
Referee: Staubli (SUI)
Italy: Marchitelli, D'Adda, Tuttino, Gabbiadini, Panico (Rosucci 72), Parisi (Mauro 58), Iannella (Domenichetti 85), Bartoli, Stracchi, Manieri, Salvai. Coach: Antonio Cabrini (ITA)
Denmark: S Petersen, Røddik, Søndergaard Pedersen, Ørntoft, Knudsen, Harder, Veje (Rydahl 65), Rasmussen, S Pedersen (Nadim 46), Nielsen (Madsen 86), Brogaard. Coach: Kenneth Heiner-Møller (DEN)
Yellow cards: Bartoli 45+1 (Italy), Tuttino 84 (Italy), Manieri 88 (Italy)

13/07/13, Gamla Ullevi, Gothenburg (att: 16,414)
Finland 0-5 Sweden
Goals: 0-1 Fischer 15, 0-2 Fischer 36, 0-3 Asllani 38, 0-4 Schelin 60, 0-5 Schelin 87
Referee: Dorcioman (ROU)
Finland: Korpela, Hyyrynen, Lehtinen, Kivistö, Kukkonen, Tolvanen (Saario 31), Alanen, Heroum, Talonen (Vanhanen 69), Westerlund, Lyytikäinen (Kuikka 87). Coach: Andrée Jeglertz (SWE)
Sweden: K Hammarström, Rohlin, Fischer, Thunebro, Schelin, Asllani (Hjohlman 72), Jakobsson, Öqvist (Göransson 67), L Nilsson, Seger, M Hammarström (Dahlkvist 57). Coach: Pia Sundhage (SWE)

16/07/13, Örjans vall, Halmstad (att: 7,288)
Sweden 3-1 Italy
Goals: 1-0 Manieri 47(og), 2-0 Schelin 49, 3-0 Öqvist 57, 3-1 Gabbiadini 78
Referee: Kulcsár (HUN)
Sweden: K Hammarström, Rohlin, Fischer, Thunebro (Schough 79), Dahlkvist, Schelin, Asllani (Sjögran 46), Öqvist, Seger (L Nilsson 64), Samuelsson, M Hammarström. Coach: Pia Sundhage (SWE)
Italy: Marchitelli, Gama, D'Adda, Girelli (Domenichetti 52), Parisi, Iannella, Mauro (Panico 63), Rosucci, Brumana (Gabbiadini 63), Manieri, Motta. Coach: Antonio Cabrini (ITA)
Yellow cards: Motta 35 (Italy), Rosucci 60 (Italy), Fischer 90+1 (Sweden)

16/07/13, Gamla Ullevi, Gothenburg (att: 8,360)
Denmark 1-1 Finland
Goals: 1-0 Brogaard 29, 1-1 Sjölund 87
Referee: Monzul (UKR)
Denmark: S Petersen, Røddik, Søndergaard Pedersen, Ørntoft, Knudsen, Rydahl (Rasmussen 64), Harder (Smidt Nielsen 85), Nadim (Christiansen 64), Nielsen, Brogaard, Sandvej. Coach: Kenneth Heiner-Møller (DEN)
Finland: Meriluoto, Hyyrynen, Lehtinen (Kuikka 46), Saario, Kivistö (Kivelä 79), Kukkonen, Nokso-Koivisto, Alanen, Heroum (Talonen 69), Westerlund, Sjölund. Coach: Andrée Jeglertz (SWE)
Yellow cards: Saario 64 (Finland), Kukkonen 90 (Finland)

		Pld	W	D	L	F	A	Pts
1	Sweden	3	2	1	0	9	2	7
2	Italy	3	1	1	1	3	4	4
3	Denmark	3	0	2	1	3	4	2
4	Finland	3	0	2	1	1	6	2

Group B

11/07/13, Kalmar Arena, Kalmar (att: 3,867)
Norway 1-1 Iceland
Goals: 1-0 Hegland 26, 1-1 M Vidarsdóttir 87(p)
Referee: Kulcsár (HUN)
Norway: Hjelmseth, Christensen, Stensland (Mykjåland 75), Akerhaugen, Mjelde, Rønning, Gulbrandsen, Hansen (Kaurin 84), Hegland, Isaksen, Hegerberg (Thorsnes 75). Coach: Even Pellerud (NOR)
Iceland: G Gunnarsdóttir, Atladóttir (Viggósdóttir 63), Gísladóttir, Magnúsdóttir, S B Gunnarsdóttir, K Jónsdóttir, M Vidarsdóttir, Lárusdóttir, Brynjarsdóttir (Ómarsdóttir 83), Fridriksdóttir (Thorsteinsdóttir 63), Hönnudóttir. Coach: Sigurdur Eyjolfsson (ISL)
Yellow cards: Magnúsdóttir 34 (Iceland), Christensen 86 (Norway)

11/07/13, Växjö Arena, Vaxjo (att: 8,861)
Germany 0-0 Netherlands
Referee: Spinelli (ITA)
Germany: Angerer, Bartusiak, Maier, Krahn, Kessler (Laudehr 46), Lotzen (Leupolz 73), Marozsán, Mittag, Okoyino da Mbabi, Cramer, Goessling. Coach: Silvia Neid (GER)
Netherlands: Geurts, Bito, Koster, Van den Heiligenberg, Hoogendijk, Van den Ven, Spitse, Melis, Van de Donk, Martens, Slegers. Coach: Roger Reijners (NED)
Yellow cards: Maier 15 (Germany), Kessler 36 (Germany), Cramer 73 (Germany), Bito 87 (Netherlands)

14/07/13, Kalmar Arena, Kalmar (att: 4,256)
Norway 1-0 Netherlands
Goal: 1-0 Gulbrandsen 54
Referee: Albon (ROU)
Norway: Hjelmseth, Christensen, Stensland, Akerhaugen, Mjelde, Rønning, Gulbrandsen (Dekkerhus 72), Hansen (Thorsnes 79), Hegland, Isaksen, Hegerberg (Bjånesøy 72). Coach: Even Pellerud (NOR)
Netherlands: Geurts, Bito, Koster, Van den Heiligenberg (Worm 60), Hoogendijk, Van de Ven, Spitse (Dekker 86), Melis, Van de Donk (Versteegt 77), Martens, Slegers. Coach: Roger Reijners (NED)

14/07/13, Växjö Arena, Vaxjo (att: 4,620)
Iceland 0-3 Germany
Goals: 0-1 Lotzen 24, 0-2 Okoyino da Mbabi 55, 0-3 Okoyino da Mbabi 84
Referee: Heikkinen (FIN)
Iceland: G Gunnarsdóttir, Viggósdóttir, Gísladóttir, Magnúsdóttir, S B Gunnarsdóttir (Ó Vidarsdóttir 60), K Jónsdóttir, M Vidarsdóttir, Lárusdóttir (Omarsdottir 46; Odinsdottir 70), Thorsteinsdóttir, Hönnudóttir. Coach: Sigurdur Eyjolfsson (ISL)
Germany: Angerer, Bartusiak, Maier, Krahn, Kessler, Lotzen (Bajramaj 64), Marozsán (Mittag 74), Okoyino da Mbabi, Cramer, Leupolz, Goessling (Laudehr 70). Coach: Silvia Neid (GER)
Yellow cards: Cramer 53 (Germany), K Jónsdóttir 78 (Iceland)

13/07/13, Kalmar Arena, Kalmar (att: 11,340)
Germany 0-1 Norway
Goal: 0-1 Isaksen 45+1
Referee: Staubli (SUI)
Germany: Angerer, Bartusiak, Maier, Krahn, Laudehr (Behringer 66), Kessler, Lotzen (Däbritz 79), Marozsán, Okoyino da Mbabi, Leupolz (Mittag 66), Wensing. Coach: Silvia Neid (GER)
Norway: Hjelmseth, Lund, Akerhaugen, Mjelde, Thorsnes (Hansen 58), Tofte Ims (Gulbrandsen 58), Holstad Berge, Isaksen, Haavi (Stensland 72), Hegerberg, Dekkerhus. Coach: Even Pellerud (NOR)
Yellow card: Tofte Ims 31 (Norway)

17/07/13, Växjö Arena, Vaxjo (att: 3,406)
Netherlands 0-1 Iceland
Goal: 0-1 Brynjarsdóttir 30
Referee: Dorcioman (ROU)
Netherlands: Geurts, Bito, Koster, Van den Heiligenberg, Hoogendijk, Van de Ven (Smit 77), Spitse, Melis, Van de Donk, Martens, Slegers (Dekker 46). Coach: Roger Reijners (NED)
Iceland: G Gunnarsdóttir, Atladóttir, Gísladóttir, Magnúsdóttir, S B Gunnarsdóttir, K Jónsdóttir, M Vidarsdóttir (Thorsteinsdóttir 62), Lárusdóttir, Brynjarsdóttir, Fridriksdóttir

(Ó Vidarsdóttir 86), Hönnudóttir. Coach: Sigurdur Eyjolfsson (ISL)
Yellow cards: Koster 16 (Netherlands), Slegers 28 (Netherlands), Magnúsdóttir 90+2 (Iceland)

		Pld	W	D	L	F	A	Pts
1	Norway	3	2	1	0	3	1	7
2	Germany	3	1	1	1	3	1	4
3	Iceland	3	1	1	1	2	4	4
4	Netherlands	3	0	1	2	0	2	1

Group C

12/07/13, Norrköpings Idrottsparken, Norrkoping (att: 2,980)
France 3-1 Russia
Goals: 1-0 Delie 21, 2-0 Delie 32, 3-0 Le Sommer 67, 3-1 Morozova 84
Referee: Palmqvist (SWE)
France: Bouhaddi, Renard, Boulleau, Georges, Soubeyrand (Catala 76), Franco, Bussaglia, Le Sommer, Thiney (Necib 66), Delie (Thomis 61), Abily. Coach: Bruno Bini (FRA)
Russia: Todua, Petrova, Savchenkova (Pozdeeva 35; Skotnikova 68), Terekhova, Sochneva, Sidorovskaya, Kostyukova, Medved (Gordeeva 35), Tsybutovich, Korovkina, Morozova. Coach: Sergei Lavrentyev (RUS)
Yellow cards: Kostyukova 23 (Russia), Skotnikova 90 (Russia)

12/07/13, Linköping Arena, Linkoping (att: 5,190)
England 2-3 Spain
Goals: 0-1 Verónica Boquete 5, 1-1 Aluko 8, 1-2 Hermoso 86, 2-2 Bassett 89, 2-3 Putellas 90+3
Referee: Monzul (UKR)
England: Bardsley, A Scott, Houghton, J Scott, Stoney, Aluko (Carney 72), Asante, White, F Williams, Yankey (Clarke 90+1), Bassett. Coach: Hope Powell (ENG)
Spain: Tirapu, Ruth García, Sonia (Putellas 73), Verónica Boquete, Adriana, Silvia Meseguer, Laibarri (Vicky 61), Ibarra, Marta Torrejón, Paredes, Hermoso. Coach: Ignacio Quereda (ESP)
Yellow cards: Calderón 36 (Spain), Paredes 75 (Spain), Bassett 77 (England)

Marie-Laure Delie scores for France against Russia

15/07/13, Linköping Arena, Linkoping (att: 3,629)
England 1-1 Russia
Goals: 0-1 Korovkina 38, 1-1 Duggan 90+2
Referee: Steinhaus (GER)
England: Bardsley, A Scott, Houghton (Duggan 64), J Scott, Stoney, Aluko (K Smith 78), Asante, White, F Williams, Yankey (Carney 17), Bassett. Coach: Hope Powell (ENG)
Russia: Todua, Petrova, Savchenkova (Dyachkova 84), Terekhova (Kurochkina 90+3), Sochneva, Sidorovskaya, Kostyukova, Medved, Tsybutovich, Korovkina (Shlyapina 90), Morozova. Coach: Sergei Lavrentyev (RUS)
Yellow cards: F Williams 55 (England), K Smith 90+3 (England)

15/07/13, Norrköpings Idrottsparken, Norrkoping (att: 5,068)
Spain 0-1 France
Goal: 0-1 Renard 5
Referee: Vitulano (ITA)
Spain: Tirapu, Diéguez, Sonia (Vicky 78), Verónica Boquete, Adriana (Putellas 78), Sandra (Erika Vázquez 85), Silvia Meseguer, Ibarra, Marta Torrejón, Paredes, Hermoso. Coach: Ignacio Quereda (ESP)
France: Bouhaddi, Renard, Boulleau, Georges, Soubeyrand (Thomis 46), Franco, Bussaglia, Necib (Le Sommer 63), Thiney, Delie, Abily. Coach: Bruno Bini (FRA)

18/07/13, Linköping Arena, Linkoping (att: 7,332)
France 3-0 England
Goals: 1-0 Le Sommer 9, 2-0 Necib 62, 3-0 Renard 64
Referee: Heikkinen (FIN)
France: Deville, Renard, Soubeyrand (Bussaglia 46), Franco, Le Sommer, Henry (Catala 60), Thomis, Necib, Houara (Abily 46), Delannoy. Coach: Bruno Bini (FRA)
England: Bardsley, A Scott, Houghton, Bradley, Stoney, Aluko (K Smith 60), Asante (J Scott 46), White, F Williams, Carney (Clarke 73), Duggan. Coach: Hope Powell (ENG)
Yellow card: F Williams 76 (England)

18/07/13, Norrköpings Idrottsparken, Norrkoping (att: 2,157)
Russia 1-1 Spain
Goal: 0-1 Verónica Boquete 14, 1-1 Terekhova 44
Referee: Palmqvist (SWE)
Russia: Todua, Petrova, Savchenkova, Terekhova, Sochneva (Bessolova 58), Sidorovskaya, Kostyukova (Makarenko 34), Medved, Tsybutovich, Korovkina, Morozova. Coach: Sergei Lavrentyev (RUS)
Spain: Tirapu, Ruth García, Verónica Boquete, Adriana (Erika Vázquez 84), Putellas (Sonia 68), Vicky (Calderón 64), Silvia Meseguer, Marta Torrejón, Paredes, Hermoso. Coach: Ignacio Quereda (ESP)
Yellow cards: Medved 58 (Russia), Korovkina 83 (Russia)

		Pld	W	D	L	F	A	Pts
1	France	3	3	0	0	7	1	9
2	Spain	3	1	1	1	4	4	4
3	Russia	3	0	2	1	3	5	2
4	England	3	0	1	2	3	7	1

Quarter-finals

21/07/13, Örjans vall, Halmstad (att: 7,468)
Sweden 4-0 Iceland
Goals: 1-0 M Hammarström 3, 2-0 Öqvist 14, 3-0 Schelin 19, 4-0 Schelin 59
Referee: Heikkinen (FIN)
Sweden: K Hammarström, Rohlin, Fischer, Thunebro, Schelin (Konradsson 67), Asllani, Jakobsson, Öqvist (Göransson 46), Seger, Samuelsson, M Hammarström (Dahlkvist 63). Coach: Pia Sundhage (SWE)
Iceland: G Gunnarsdóttir, Atladóttir, Ó Vidarsdóttir, Gísladóttir, S B Gunnarsdóttir, K Jónsdóttir (Viggósdóttir 81), M Vidarsdóttir (Jensen 79), Lárusdóttir, Brynjarsdóttir, Fridriksdóttir (Thorsteinsdóttir 65), Hönnudóttir. Coach: Sigurdur Eyjolfsson (ISL)
Yellow card: Fridriksdóttir 50 (Iceland)

21/07/13, Växjö Arena, Vaxjo (att: 9,265)
Italy 0-1 Germany
Goal: 0-1 Laudehr 26
Referee: Kulcsár (HUN)
Italy: Marchitelli, D'Adda, Tuttino, Gabbiadini, Panico, Parisi (Mauro 75), Camporese (Iannella 46), Bartoli, Stracchi, Manieri, Salvai (Di Criscio 69). Coach: Antonio Cabrini (ITA)
Germany: Angerer, Bartusiak, Maier, Krahn, Laudehr, Kessler, Lotzen, Mittag (Marozsán 52), Okoyino Da Mbabi (Däbritz 68), Cramer, Goessling. Coach: Silvia Neid (GER)
Yellow cards: Tuttino 27 (Italy), Parisi 39 (Italy), Salvai 63 (Italy), Stracchi 87 (Italy), Di Criscio 90 (Italy)

22/07/13, Kalmar Arena, Kalmar (att: 10,435)
Norway 3-1 Spain
Goals: 1-0 Gulbrandsen 24, 2-0 Paredes 43(og), 3-0 Hegerberg 64, 3-1 Hermoso 90+2
Referee: Steinhaus (GER)
Norway: Hjelmseth, Christensen, Stensland, Akerhaugen, Mjelde, Rønning, Gulbrandsen, Hansen (Ryland 81), Hegland, Isaksen (Dekkerhus 76), Hegerberg (Thorsnes 71). Coach: Even Pellerud (NOR)
Spain: Tirapu, Ruth García (Erika Vázquez 62), Verónica Boquete, Adriana (Borja 77), Putellas, Silvia Meseguer, Calderón, Ibarra (Landa 70), Marta Torrejón, Paredes, Hermoso. Coach: Ignacio Quereda (ESP)
Yellow card: Landa 83 (Spain)

22/07/13, Linköping Arena, Linkoping (att: 7,448)
France 1-1 Denmark *(aet; 2-4 on pens)*
Goals: 0-1 Rasmussen 28, 1-1 Necib 71(p)
Referee: Vitulano (ITA)
France: Bouhaddi, Renard, Boulleau, Georges (Delannoy 57), Soubeyrand (Thomis 46), Franco, Bussaglia, Le Sommer, Necib, Thiney, Abily. Coach: Bruno Bini (FRA)
Denmark: S Petersen, Røddik, Søndergaard Pedersen, Ørntoft, Arnth, Knudsen, Harder, Veje (Nadim 67), Rasmussen (Rydahl 61), Nielsen, Brogaard (L Jensen 74). Coach: Kenneth Heiner-Møller (DEN)
Yellow cards: Arnth 47 (Denmark), Renard 114 (France)

Denmark forward Johanna Rasmussen (centre) is congratulated by team-mates after scoring against France

Semi-finals

24/07/13, Gamla Ullevi, Gothenburg (att: 16,608)
Sweden 0-1 Germany
Goal: 0-1 Marozsán 33
Referee: Staubli (SUI)
Sweden: K. Hammarström, Rohlin, Fischer, Thunebro, Schelin, Asllani, Göransson (Sjögran 65), Öqvist (Jakobsson 74), Seger, Samuelsson (Dahlkvist 82), M. Hammarström. Coach: Pia Sundhage (SWE)
Germany: Angerer, Bartusiak, Maier, Krahn, Laudehr, Kessler, Lotzen (Leupolz 78), Marozsán (Schmidt 89), Mittag, Cramer, Goessling. Coach: Silvia Neid (GER)
Yellow cards: Fischer 5 (Sweden), Laudehr 43 (Germany)

25/07/13, Norrköpings Idrottsparken, Norrkoping (att: 9,260)
Norway 1-1 Denmark *(aet; 4-2 on pens)*
Goals: 1-0 Christensen 3, 1-1 Knudsen 87
Referee: Monzul (UKR)
Norway: Hjelmseth, Christensen, Stensland, Akerhaugen, Mjelde, Rønning, Gulbrandsen, Hansen (Thorsnes 58), Hegland, Isaksen (Dekkerhus 63), Hegerberg (Haavi 80). Coach: Even Pellerud (NOR)
Denmark: S. Petersen, Røddik, Søndergaard Pedersen, Ørntoft (Madsen 82), Arnth (Nadim 67), Knudsen, Rydahl (Rasmussen 68), Harder, Veje, Nielsen, Brogaard. Coach: Kenneth Heiner-Møller (DEN)
Yellow cards: Stensland 76 (Norway), Hjelmseth 84 (Norway)

Final

28/07/13, Friends Arena, Solna (att: 41,301)
Germany 1-0 Norway
Goals: 1-0 Mittag 49
Referee: Dorcioman (ROU)
Germany: Angerer, Bartusiak, Maier, Krahn, Laudehr (Schmidt 77), Kessler, Lotzen (Mittag 46), Marozsán, Okoyino Da Mbabi, Cramer, Goessling. Coach: Silvia Neid (GER)
Norway: Hjelmseth, Christensen (Kaurin 85), Stensland (Isaksen 76), Akerhaugen, Mjelde, Rønning, Gulbrandsen (Thorsnes 68), Hansen, Hegland, Hegerberg, Dekkerhus. Coach: Even Pellerud (NOR)
Yellow card: Krahn 70 (Germany)

Top goalscorers *(final tournament)*

5	Lotta Schelin (Sweden)
3	Nilla Fischer (Sweden)
2	Marie-Laure Delie (France)
	Louisa Necib (France)
	Melania Gabbiadini (Italy)
	Eugénie Le Sommer (France)
	Josefine Öqvist (Sweden)
	Verónica Boquete (Spain)
	Jennifer Hermoso (Spain)
	Wendie Renard (France)
	Célia Okoyino da Mbabi (Germany)
	Mia Brogaard (Denmark)
	Solveig Gulbrandsen (Norway)
	Mariann Knudsen (Denmark)

DENMARK

No	Name	DoB	Aps	(s)	Gls	Club
Goalkeepers						
22	Katrine Abel	28/06/90				Taastrup
1	Stina Petersen	09/02/86	5			Brøndby
16	Cecilie Sørensen	25/03/87				Skjold
Defenders						
5	Janni Arnth	15/10/86	2			Fortuna
19	Mia Brogaard	15/10/81	5		2	Brøndby
12	Line Jensen	23/08/91		(2)		Fortuna
18	Theresa Nielsen	20/07/86	5			Brøndby
14	Malene Olsen	02/02/83				Brøndby
4	Christina Ørntoft	02/07/85	5			Brøndby
2	Line Røddik	31/01/88	5			Tyresö (SWE)
21	Cecilie Sandvej	13/06/90	1			Brøndby
Midfielders						
9	Nanna Christiansen	17/06/89		(1)		Brøndby
20	Sine Hovesen	19/08/87				Brøndby
6	Mariann Knudsen	16/11/84	5		2	Linköping (SWE)
8	Julie Rydahl	09/01/82	2	(3)		Brøndby
15	Sofie Pedersen	24/04/92	2			Fortuna
23	Karoline Smidt Nielsen	12/05/94		(1)		Fortuna
3	Katrine Søndergaard Pedersen	13/04/77	5			Stabæk (NOR)
Forwards						
10	Pernille Harder	15/11/92	5			Linköping (SWE)
7	Emma Madsen	18/11/88		(2)		Brøndby
17	Nadia Nadim	02/01/88	1	(4)		Fortuna
13	Johanna Rasmussen	02/07/83	3	(2)	1	Kristianstads (SWE)
11	Katrine Veje	19/06/91	4			Malmö (SWE)

FINLAND

No	Name	DoB	Aps	(s)	Gls	Club
Goalkeepers						
23	Tinja-Riikka Korpela	05/05/86	2			Lillestrøm (NOR)
1	Minna Meriluoto	04/10/85	1			Mölndal (SWE)
12	Siiri Välimaa	14/04/90				NiceFutis
Defenders						
3	Tuija Hyyrynen	10/03/88	3			Umeå (SWE)
6	Laura Kivistö	26/06/81	3			PK-35
4	Susanna Lehtinen	08/05/83	3			Örebro (SWE)
22	Pirjo Leppikangas	12/09/87				PK-35
16	Anna Westerlund	09/04/89	3			Piteå (SWE)
Midfielders						
11	Nora Heroum	20/07/94	3			Honka
13	Heidi Kivelä	06/11/88		(1)		PK-35
18	Natalia Kuikka	01/12/95		(3)		Merilappi United
7	Annika Kukkonen	12/04/90	3			Sunnanå (SWE)
2	Nea-Stina Liljedahl	16/01/93				Honka
17	Jaana Lyytikäinen	22/10/82	1	(1)		Åland
19	Henni Malinen	17/11/88				Honka
8	Katri Nokso-Koivisto	22/11/82	1			Lillestrøm (NOR)
5	Tiina Saario	15/01/82	1	(1)		Åland
Forwards						
10	Emmi Alanen	30/04/91	3			Kokkola F10
15	Leena Puranen	16/10/86				Mölndal (SWE)
20	Annica Sjölund	31/03/85	2		1	Mölndal (SWE)
14	Sanna Talonen	15/06/84	2	(1)		Örebro (SWE)
9	Marianna Tolvanen	27/12/92	2			Honka
21	Ella Vanhanen	15/09/93		(1)		Pallokissat

ENGLAND

No	Name	DoB	Aps	(s)	Gls	Club
Goalkeepers						
1	Karen Bardsley	14/10/84	2			Lincoln
13	Rachel Brown	02/07/80				Everton
23	Siobhan Chamberlain	15/08/83				Bristol
Defenders						
2	Alex Scott	14/10/84	3			Arsenal
15	Laura Bassett	02/08/83	2		1	Birmingham
19	Gemma Bonner	13/07/91				Liverpool
5	Sophie Bradley	20/10/89	1			Lincoln
21	Lucia Bronze	28/10/91				Liverpool
3	Stephanie Houghton	23/04/88	3			Arsenal
6	Casey Stoney	13/05/82	3			Lincoln
Midfielders						
8	Anita Asante	27/04/85	3			Göteborg (SWE)
14	Karen Carney	01/08/87	1	(2)		Birmingham
10	Fara Williams	25/01/84	3			Liverpool
4	Jill Scott	02/02/87	2	(1)		Everton
22	Kelly Smith	29/10/78		(2)		Arsenal
20	Jade Moore	22/10/90				Birmingham
16	Jordan Nobbs	08/12/92				Arsenal
Forwards						
7	Eniola Aluko	21/02/87	3		1	Chelsea
12	Jessica Clarke	05/05/89		(2)		Lincoln
17	Toni Duggan	25/07/91	1	(1)	1	Everton
18	Dunia Susi	10/08/87				Chelsea
9	Ellen White	09/05/89	3			Arsenal
11	Rachel Yankey	01/11/79	2			Arsenal

FRANCE

No	Name	DoB	Aps	(s)	Gls	Club
Goalkeepers						
21	Karima Benameur	13/04/88				PSG
16	Sarah Bouhaddi	17/10/86	3			Lyon
1	Céline Deville	24/01/02	1			Lyon
Defenders						
3	Laure Boulleau	22/10/86	3			PSG
22	Sabrina Delannoy	18/05/86	1	(1)		PSG
7	Corine Franco	05/10/83	4			Lyon
4	Laura Georges	20/08/84	3			Lyon
5	Ophélie Meilleroux	18/01/84				Montpellier
2	Wendie Renard	20/07/90	4		2	Lyon
11	Julie Soyer	30/06/85				Juvisy
Midfielders						
23	Camille Abily	05/12/84	3	(1)		Lyon
8	Élise Bussaglia	24/09/85	3	(1)		Lyon
10	Amandine Henry	28/09/89	1			Lyon
15	Jessica Houara	29/09/87	1			PSG
9	Eugénie Le Sommer	18/05/89	3	(1)	2	Lyon
14	Louisa Necib	23/01/87	3	(1)	2	Lyon
6	Sandrine Soubeyrand	16/08/73	4			Juvisy
17	Gaëtane Thiney	28/10/85	4			Juvisy
Forwards						
20	Viviane Asseyi	20/11/93				Montpellier
19	Sandrine Brétigny	02/07/84				Frankfurt (GER)
13	Camille Catala	06/05/91		(2)		Juvisy
18	Marie-Laure Delie	29/01/88	2		2	Montpellier
12	Élodie Thomis	13/08/86	1	(3)		Lyon

GERMANY

No	Name	DoB	Aps	(s)	Gls	Club
Goalkeepers						
1	Nadine Angerer	10/11/78	6			Frankfurt
21	Laura Benkarth	14/10/92				Freiburg
12	Almuth Schult	09/02/91				Wolfsburg
Defenders						
3	Saskia Bartusiak	09/09/82	6			Frankfurt
15	Jennifer Cramer	24/02/93	5			Potsdam
17	Josephine Henning	08/09/89				Wolfsburg
5	Annike Krahn	01/07/85	6			PSG (FRA)
4	Leonie Maier	29/09/92	6			Bayern
2	Bianca Schmidt	23/01/90		(2)		Frankfurt
22	Luisa Wensing	08/02/93	1			Wolfsburg
Midfielders						
7	Melanie Behringer	18/11/85		(1)		Frankfurt
20	Lena Goessling	08/03/86	5			Wolfsburg
8	Nadine Kessler	04/04/88	6			Wolfsburg
6	Simone Laudehr	12/07/86	4	(2)	1	Frankfurt
16	Melanie Leupolz	14/04/94	2	(2)		Freiburg
9	Lena Lotzen	11/09/93	6		1	Bayern
10	Dzsenifer Marozsán	18/04/92	5	(1)	1	Frankfurt
Forwards						
19	Fatmire Bajramaj	01/04/88		(1)		Frankfurt
23	Sara Däbritz	15/02/95		(2)		Freiburg
18	Svenja Huth	25/01/91				Frankfurt
14	Isabelle Linden	15/01/91				Leverkusen
11	Anja Mittag	16/05/85	3	(3)	1	Malmö (SWE)
13	Célia Okoyino da Mbabi	27/06/88	5		2	Frankfurt

ITALY

No	Name	DoB	Aps	(s)	Gls	Club
Goalkeepers						
12	Chiara Marchitelli	04/05/85	4			Tavagnacco
1	Sara Penzo	16/12/89				Brescia
22	Katia Schroffenegger	28/04/91				Jena (GER)
Defenders						
16	Elisa Bartoli	07/05/91	3			Torres Terra Sarda
3	Roberta D'Adda	05/10/81	4			Brescia
5	Federica Di Criscio	12/05/93		(1)		Verona
2	Sara Gama	27/03/89	1			Brescia
20	Raffaella Manieri	21/11/86	4			Torres Terra Sarda
21	Giorgia Motta	18/03/84	1			Torres Terra Sarda
6	Laura Neboli	14/03/88				Duisburg (GER)
23	Cecilia Salvai	02/12/93	3			Rapid Lugano (SUI)
Midfielders						
13	Elisa Camporese	16/03/84	2			Tavagnacco
7	Giulia Domenichetti	29/04/84		(2)		Torres Terra Sarda
10	Cristiana Girelli	23/04/90	1			Verona
14	Sandy Iannella	06/04/87	2	(2)		Torres Terra Sarda
11	Alice Parisi	11/12/90	4			Tavagnacco
17	Martina Rosucci	09/05/92	1	(1)		Brescia
18	Daniela Stracchi	02/09/83	3			Torres Terra Sarda
4	Alessia Tuttino	15/03/83	3			Tavagnacco
Forwards						
19	Paola Brumana	26/11/82	1			Tavagnacco
8	Melania Gabbiadini	28/08/83	3	(1)	2	Verona
15	Ilaria Mauro	22/05/88	1	(2)	1	Tavagnacco
9	Patrizia Panico	08/02/75	3	(1)		Torres Terra Sarda

ICELAND

No	Name	DoB	Aps	(s)	Gls	Club
Goalkeepers						
13	Gudbjörg Gunnarsdóttir	18/05/85	4			Avaldsnes IL (NOR)
1	Thóra Helgadóttir	05/05/81				Malmö (SWE)
12	Sandra Sigurdardóttir	02/10/86				Stjarnan
Defenders						
15	Anna Bjork Kristjansdóttir	14/10/89				Stjarnan
2	Sif Atladóttir	15/07/85	3			Kristianstads (SWE)
17	Elisa Vidarsdóttir	26/05/91				ÍBV
5	Hallbera Gísladóttir	14/09/86	4			Piteå (SWE)
8	Katrín Jónsdóttir	31/05/77	4			Umeå (SWE)
10	Dóra Maria Lárusdóttir	24/07/85	4			Valur
3	Ólína Vidarsdóttir	16/11/82	1	(2)		Chelsea (ENG)
21	Soffia Gunnarsdóttir	22/10/87				Stjarnan
4	Glódís Viggósdóttir	27/06/95	1	(2)		Stjarnan
Midfielders						
14	Dagný Brynjarsdóttir	10/08/91	4		1	Valur
19	Fanndís Fridriksdóttir	09/05/90	3			Kolbotn (NOR)
6	Hólmfrídur Magnúsdóttir	20/09/84	3			Avaldsnes IL (NOR)
18	Gudný Björk Ódinsdóttir	27/09/88		(1)		Kristianstads (SWE)
11	Katrín Ómarsdóttir	27/06/87		(2)		Liverpool (ENG)
7	Sara Bjork Gunnarsdóttir	29/09/90	4			Malmö (SWE)
20	Thórunn Jónsdóttir	17/12/84				Avaldsnes IL (NOR)
Forwards						
22	Rakel Hönnudóttir	30/12/88	4			Breidablik
23	Elín Jensen	01/03/95		(1)		Valur
9	Margrét Lára Vidarsdóttir	25/07/86	4		1	Kristianstads (SWE)
16	Harpa Thorsteinsdóttir	27/06/86	1	(3)		Stjarnan

NETHERLANDS

No	Name	DoB	Aps	(s)	Gls	Club
Goalkeepers						
23	Angela Christ	06/03/89				PSV/FC Eindhoven
1	Loes Geurts	12/01/86	3			Vittsjö GIK (SWE)
16	Sari van Veenendaal	03/04/90				Twente
Defenders						
2	Dyanne Bito	10/08/81	3			Telstar
6	Anouk Hoogendijk	06/05/85	3			Ajax
3	Daphne Koster	13/03/81	3			Ajax
22	Mirte Roelvink	23/11/85				PSV/FC Eindhoven
15	Leonne Stentler	23/04/86				Ajax
5	Claudia van den Heiligenberg	25/03/85	3			Ajax
Midfielders						
12	Maayke Heuver	26/07/90				Twente
14	Renée Slegers	05/02/89	3			Linköping (SWE)
8	Sherida Spitse	29/05/90	3			Twente
10	Danielle van de Donk	05/08/91	3			PSV/FC Eindhoven
4	Merel van Dongen	11/02/93				Alabama Crimson Tide (USA)
20	Desiree van Lunteren	30/12/92				Ajax
Forwards						
21	Chantal de Ridder	19/01/89				Ajax
18	Anouk Dekker	15/11/86		(2)		Twente
11	Lieke Martens	16/12/92	3			Duisburg (GER)
9	Manon Melis	31/08/86	3			Malmö (SWE)
13	Sylvia Smit	04/07/86		(1)		PEC Zwolle
7	Kirsten van de Ven	11/05/85	3			Tyresö (SWE)
19	Mandy Versteegt	23/02/90		(1)		Ajax
17	Siri Worm	20/04/92		(1)		Twente

NORWAY

No	Name	DoB	Aps	(s)	Gls	Club
Goalkeepers						
23	Nora Gjøen	20/02/92				Kolbotn
1	Ingrid Hjelmseth	10/04/80	6			Stabæk
12	Silje Vesterbekkmo	22/06/83				Røa
Defenders						
5	Toril Akerhaugen	05/03/82	6			Stabæk
3	Marit Christensen	11/12/80	5		1	Amazon Grimstad
15	Nora Holstad Berge	26/03/87	1			Arna-Bjørnar
2	Marita Lund	29/01/89	1			Lillestrøm
6	Maren Mjelde	06/11/89	6			Potsdam (GER)
7	Trine Rønning	14/06/82	5			Stabæk
18	Ingrid Ryland	29/05/89		(1)		Arna-Bjørnar
Midfielders						
22	Cathrine Dekkerhus	17/09/92	2	(3)		Stabæk
8	Solveig Gulbrandsen	12/01/81	5	(1)	2	Vålerenga FB
19	Ingvild Isaksen	10/02/89	5	(1)	1	Kolbotn
17	Lene Mykjåland	20/02/87		(1)		Lillestrøm
4	Ingvild Stensland	03/08/81	5	(1)		Stabæk
14	Gry Tofte Ims	02/03/86	1			Klepp
Forwards						
13	Melissa Bjånesøy	18/04/92		(1)		IL Sandviken
20	Emilie Haavi	16/06/92	1	(1)		Lillestrøm
10	Caroline Hansen	18/02/95	5	(1)		Stabæk
21	Ada Hegerberg	10/07/95	6			Potsdam (GER)
16	Kristine Hegland	08/08/92	5		1	Arna-Bjørnar
11	Leni Kaurin	21/03/81		(2)		Stabæk
9	Elise Thorsnes	14/08/88	1	(5)		Stabæk

SPAIN

No	Name	DoB	Aps	(s)	Gls	Club
Goalkeepers						
13	Dolores Gallardo	10/06/93				Atlético
23	María José Pons	08/08/84				Espanyol
1	Ainhoa Tirapu	04/09/84	4			Athletic
Defenders						
6	Miriam Diéguez	04/05/86	1			Barcelona
17	Elisabeth Ibarra	29/06/81	4			Athletic
3	Leire Landa	19/12/86		(1)		Athletic
18	Marta Torrejón	27/02/90	4			Espanyol
4	Melisa	20/06/84				Barcelona
20	Irene Paredes	04/07/91	4			Athletic
5	Ruth García	26/03/87	3			Levante
Midfielders						
7	Priscila Borja	28/04/85		(1)		Atlético
16	Nagore Calderón	02/06/93	2	(1)		Atlético Madrid
21	Jennifer Hermoso	09/05/90	4		2	Tyresö (SWE)
22	Amanda Sampedro	26/06/93				Atlético
11	Sandra	01/01/81	1			Espanyol
15	Silvia Meseguer	12/03/89	4			Espanyol
2	Virginia Torrecilla	04/09/94				Barcelona
14	Vicky Losada	05/03/91	1	(2)		Barcelona
Forwards						
10	Adriana	07/11/86	4			New York Flash (USA)
19	Erika Vázquez	16/02/83		(3)		Athletic
12	Alexia Putellas	04/02/94	2	(2)	1	Barcelona
8	Sonia	15/11/84	2	(1)		Barcelona
9	Verónica Boquete	09/04/87	4		2	Tyresö (SWE)

RUSSIA

No	Name	DoB	Aps	(s)	Gls	Club
Goalkeepers						
12	Yulia Grichenko	10/03/90				Kubanochka
21	Margarita Shirokova	14/01/92				Rossiyanka
1	Elvira Todua	31/01/86	3			Rossiyanka
Defenders						
6	Yulia Bessolova	23/08/92		(1)		Izmailovo
4	Maria Dyachkova	26/05/82		(1)		Zvezda 2005 Perm
2	Yulia Gordeeva	05/01/88		(1)		Izmailovo
15	Anastasia Kostyukova	15/05/85	3			Zorkiy
22	Daria Makarenko	07/03/92		(1)		Russia
18	Elena Medved	23/01/85	3			Zorkiy
16	Natalia Pertseva	04/06/84				Rossiyanka
5	Olga Petrova	09/07/86	3			Rossiyanka
13	Alla Sidorovskaya	27/07/83	3			Izmailovo
19	Ksenia Tsybutovich	26/06/87	3			Ryazan-VDV
Midfielders						
9	Anastasia Pozdeeva	12/06/93		(1)		Zvezda 2005 Perm
8	Valentina Savchenkova	29/04/83	3			Ryazan-VDV
14	Tatiana Skotnikova	27/11/78		(1)		Rossiyanka
3	Ekaterina Stepanenko	21/05/83				Izmailovo
10	Elena Terekhova	05/07/87	3		1	Ryazan-VDV
Forwards						
20	Nelli Korovkina	01/11/89	3		1	Izmailovo
7	Olesya Kurochkina	06/09/83		(1)		Izmailovo
23	Elena Morozova	15/03/87	3		1	Zorkiy
17	Natalia Shlyapina	13/07/83		(1)		Rossiyanka
11	Ekaterina Sochneva	12/08/85	3			Zorkiy

SWEDEN

No	Name	DoB	Aps	(s)	Gls	Club
Goalkeepers						
1	Kristin Hammarström	29/03/82	5			Göteborg
12	Hedvig Lindahl	29/04/83				Kristianstads
21	Sofia Lundgren	20/09/82				Sweden
Defenders						
5	Nilla Fischer	02/08/84	5		3	Linköping
16	Lina Nilsson	17/06/87	1	(1)		Malmö
2	Charlotte Rohlin	02/12/80	5			Linköping
18	Jessica Samuelsson	30/01/92	4			Linköping
3	Stina Segerström	17/06/82				Göteborg
6	Sara Thunebro	26/04/79	5			Tyresö
Midfielders						
7	Lisa Dahlkvist	06/02/87	1	(4)		Tyresö
11	Antonia Göransson	16/09/90	2	(2)		Potsdam (GER)
4	Amanda Ilestedt	17/01/93				Malmö
10	Sofia Jakobsson	23/04/90	2	(2)		Chelsea (ENG)
13	Emmelie Konradsson	09/04/89		(1)		Umeå
20	Marie Hammarström	29/03/82	5		1	Göteborg
19	Elin Magnusson	02/06/82				Örebro
14	Josefine Öqvist	23/07/83	5		2	Kristianstads
17	Caroline Seger	19/03/85	5			Tyresö
15	Therese Sjögran	08/04/77		(2)		Malmö
Forwards						
9	Kosovare Asllani	29/07/89	5		1	PSG (FRA)
23	Jenny Hjohlman	13/02/90		(1)		Umeå
8	Lotta Schelin	27/02/84	5		5	Lyon (FRA)
22	Olivia Schough	11/03/91		(1)		Göteborg

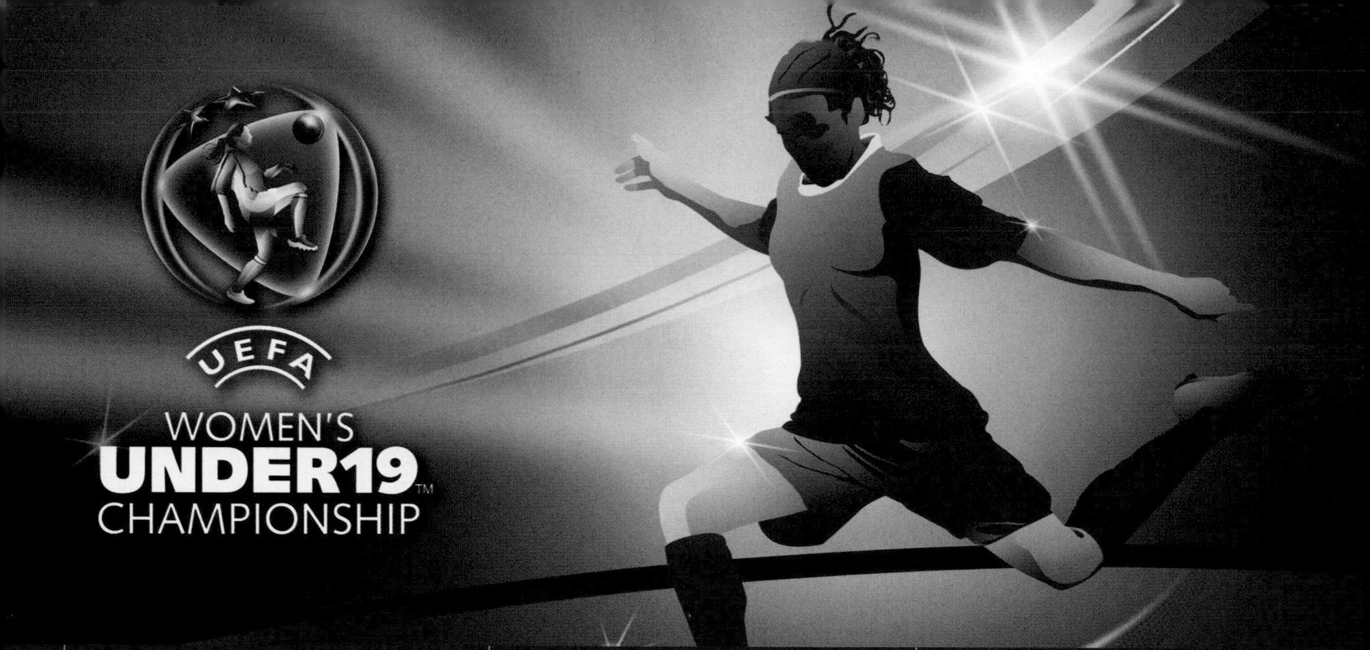

Recent winners all qualify for final tournament

Holders Sweden lead way to Wales

Scandinavian quartet completed by best runners-up Norway

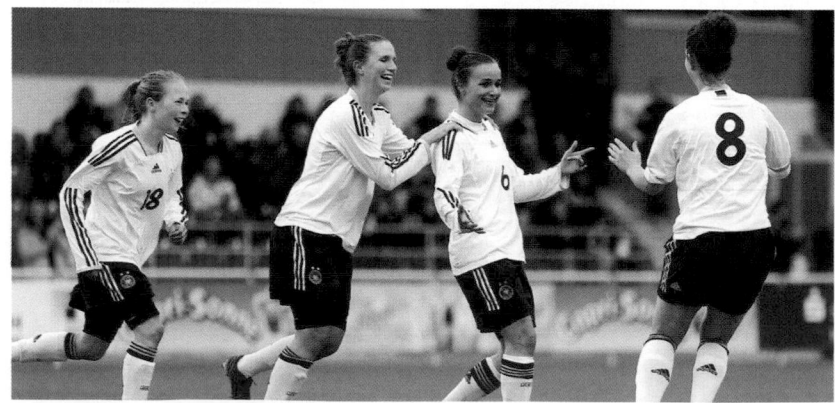

Headline acts return to form

The presence of four first-time qualifiers at the 2012 UEFA Women's Under-19 Championship finals in Turkey hinted at a power shift at this level of the women's game. However, the race to qualify for the 2013 tournament brought a return to normality as the traditional powerhouses all rediscovered their form, with France, England, Germany and holders Sweden, the previous four winners of the competition, all coming through to qualify for the August gathering in Wales.

Germany's progress through the second qualifying round – they, France and England were given a bye through the first stage – was seamless, with Maren Meinert's side winning three games out of three. No other team scored more goals (16) or conceded fewer (one) in the second qualifying round.

France also made light work of a difficult section. A team largely hewn from the side that won the FIFA U-17 Women's World Cup in October 2012 negotiated an impressive route past Belgium, Russia and Switzerland, claiming maximum points, while Sweden, too, profited from rich youthful pickings as 17-year-old Marija Banusic contributed ten goals in their six qualifiers. Four wins and two draws ensured the team's right to defend the title they had captured with a 1-0 extra-time win over Spain in the 2012 final.

It was not so simple for England. Their bid looked to be over before it had begun when Serbia stunned them 5-4, Jovana Damnjanović adding two goals to her competition-record tally of 14 in qualifying. Mo Marley's team then saw off Hungary 3-0, and another win by the same scoreline in their last outing, against hosts Norway, ensured their progress, Nikita Parris capping a superb performance with a fine individual goal.

Although defeated, Norway claimed the sole qualifying place reserved for the best runner-up – against considerable odds. Jarl Torske's team were assured of second place in their group following a 5-2 victory over Serbia in their second game, but with only the results against the teams placed first and third in the section taken into account to draw up the 'runners-up table', they needed Hungary, whom they had thrashed 7-0 in their opening game, to take third place. At one stage Hungary trailed Serbia 3-1, but they then scored three goals in eight minutes to turn that game on its head and put Norway through – on goal difference at the expense of Group 3 runners-up Scotland.

Neighbours Denmark, who topped Scotland's group, made more serene progress, their tally of six wins overall matched only by Finland, who claimed the scalps of Spain and Portugal, 2012 runners-up and semi-finalists respectively, en route to their first finals since 2005. It ensured the presence of four Scandinavian teams among the eight finalists and also added extra spice to the occasion for Jarmo Matikainen, the Finnish coach of host nation Wales.

Lina Magull (No6) takes the acclaim after opening the scoring for Germany against the Czech Republic

First qualifying round

Group 1

20-25/10/12 Indjija, Jakovo

Republic of Ireland 3-0 Cyprus, Serbia 15-0 Latvia, Republic of Ireland 11-0 Latvia, Cyprus 0-10 Serbia, Serbia 2-3 Republic of Ireland, Latvia 0-1 Cyprus

	Pld	W	D	L	F	A	Pts
1 Republic of Ireland	3	3	0	0	17	2	9
2 Serbia	3	2	0	1	27	3	6
3 Cyprus	3	1	0	2	1	13	3
4 Latvia	3	0	0	3	0	27	0

Group 2

20-25/10/12 Lindabrunn, Gloggnitz

Italy 6-0 Kazakhstan, Austria 2-1 Greece, Greece 1-1 Italy, Austria 5-0 Kazakhstan, Italy 3-0 Austria, Kazakhstan 0-3 Greece

	Pld	W	D	L	F	A	Pts
1 Italy	3	2	1	0	10	1	7
2 Austria	3	2	0	1	7	4	6
3 Greece	3	1	1	1	5	3	4
4 Kazakhstan	3	0	0	3	0	14	0

Group 3

20-25/10/12 Sesvete, Zagreb, Velika Gorica

Ukraine 10-0 Faroe Islands, Belgium 1-0 Croatia, Ukraine 2-1 Croatia, Faroe Islands 0-4 Belgium, Belgium 0-0 Ukraine, Croatia 4-1 Faroe Islands

	Pld	W	D	L	F	A	Pts
1 Ukraine	3	2	1	0	12	1	7
2 Belgium	3	2	1	0	5	0	7
3 Croatia	3	1	0	2	5	4	3
4 Faroe Islands	3	0	0	3	1	18	0

Group 4

20-25/10/12 Szombathely, Buk

Hungary 3-0 Lithuania, Poland 0-2 Northern Ireland, Hungary 2-3 Northern Ireland, Lithuania 0-9 Poland, Poland 2-3 Hungary, Northern Ireland 4-0 Lithuania

	Pld	W	D	L	F	A	Pts
1 Northern Ireland	3	3	0	0	9	2	9
2 Hungary	3	2	0	1	8	5	6
3 Poland	3	1	0	2	11	5	3
4 Lithuania	3	0	0	3	0	16	0

Group 5

20-25/10/12 Antalya

Scotland 8-0 Belarus, Norway 2-0 Turkey, Norway 2-1 Belarus, Turkey 0-2 Scotland, Scotland 0-1 Norway, Belarus 0-2 Turkey

	Pld	W	D	L	F	A	Pts
1 Norway	3	3	0	0	5	1	9
2 Scotland	3	2	0	1	10	1	6
3 Turkey	3	1	0	2	2	4	3
4 Belarus	3	0	0	3	1	12	0

Group 6

20-25/10/12 Esbjerg, Varde

Iceland 4-0 Slovakia, Denmark 11-0 Moldova, Denmark 5-0 Slovakia, Moldova 0-5 Iceland, Iceland 1-3 Denmark, Slovakia 1-1 Moldova

	Pld	W	D	L	F	A	Pts
1 Denmark	3	3	0	0	19	1	9
2 Iceland	3	2	0	1	10	3	6
3 Slovakia	3	0	1	2	1	10	1
4 Moldova	3	0	1	2	1	17	1

Group 7

20-25/10/12 Albena, Kavarna

Spain 16-0 Estonia, Finland 6-0 Bulgaria, Spain 7-0 Bulgaria, Estonia 0-11 Finland, Finland 2-1 Spain, Bulgaria 3-1 Estonia

	Pld	W	D	L	F	A	Pts
1 Finland	3	3	0	0	19	1	9
2 Spain	3	2	0	1	24	2	6
3 Bulgaria	3	1	0	2	3	14	3
4 Estonia	3	0	0	3	1	30	0

Group 8

20-25/10/12 Sarajevo

Czech Republic 6-1 Bosnia & Herzegovina, Portugal 2-1 FYROM, Czech Republic 9-0 FYROM, Bosnia & Herzegovina 0-1 Portugal, Portugal 2-2 Czech Republic, FYROM 0-2 Bosnia & Herzegovina

	Pld	W	D	L	F	A	Pts
1 Czech Republic	3	2	1	0	17	3	7
2 Portugal	3	2	1	0	5	3	7
3 Bosnia & Herzegovina	3	1	0	2	3	7	3
4 FYROM	3	0	0	3	1	13	0

Group 9

20-25/10/12 Krymsk

Sweden 6-0 Slovenia, Russia 5-0 Azerbaijan, Sweden 10-0 Azerbaijan, Slovenia 1-1 Russia, Russia 0-0 Sweden, Azerbaijan 0-6 Slovenia

	Pld	W	D	L	F	A	Pts
1 Sweden	3	2	1	0	16	0	7
2 Russia	3	1	2	0	6	1	5
3 Slovenia	3	1	1	1	7	7	4
4 Azerbaijan	3	0	0	3	0	21	0

Group 10

20-25/10/12 Eizmos, Kriens, Weggis

Switzerland 5-0 Israel, Netherlands 4-1 Romania, Netherlands 2-0 Israel, Romania 0-1 Switzerland, Switzerland 5-2 Netherlands, Israel 0-2 Romania

	Pld	W	D	L	F	A	Pts
1 Switzerland	3	3	0	0	11	2	9
2 Netherlands	3	2	0	1	8	6	6
3 Romania	3	1	0	2	3	5	3
4 Israel	3	0	0	3	0	9	0

Second qualifying round

Group 1

04-09/04/13 Delft, 's-Gravenzande

Republic of Ireland 1-0 Italy, Sweden 1-0 Netherlands, Italy 2-5 Sweden, Republic of Ireland 2-1 Netherlands, Sweden 2-0 Republic of Ireland, Netherlands 2-0 Italy

	Pld	W	D	L	F	A	Pts
1 Sweden	3	2	1	0	5	2	7
2 Republic of Ireland	3	2	0	1	3	3	6
3 Netherlands	3	1	0	2	3	3	3
4 Italy	3	0	1	2	2	5	1

Group 2

04-09/04/13 La Louvière

Switzerland 4-0 Russia, France 2-0 Belgium, Belgium 2-0 Switzerland, France 6-1 Russia, Switzerland 0-3 France, Russia 0-1 Belgium

	Pld	W	D	L	F	A	Pts
1 France	3	3	0	0	11	1	9
2 Belgium	3	2	0	1	3	2	6
3 Switzerland	3	1	0	2	4	5	3
4 Russia	3	0	0	3	1	11	0

Group 3

04-09/04/13 Livingston, Falkirk, Hamilton

Denmark 1-0 Scotland, Ukraine 0-0 Austria, Denmark 2-1 Austria, Scotland 4-2 Ukraine, Ukraine 0-3 Denmark, Austria 0-4 Scotland

	Pld	W	D	L	F	A	Pts
1 Denmark	3	3	0	0	6	1	9
2 Scotland	3	2	0	1	8	3	6
3 Ukraine	3	0	1	2	2	7	1
4 Austria	3	0	1	2	1	6	1

Group 4

04-09/04/13 Jessheim, Kongsvinger

England 4-5 Serbia, Norway 7-0 Hungary, Serbia 2-5 Norway, England 3-0 Hungary, Norway 0-3 England, Hungary 4-3 Serbia

	Pld	W	D	L	F	A	Pts
1 England	3	2	0	1	10	5	6
2 Norway	3	2	0	1	12	5	6
3 Hungary	3	1	0	2	4	13	3
4 Serbia	3	1	0	2	10	13	3

Group 5

04-09/04/13 Mealhada, Coimbra, Tocha

Finland 2-1 Portugal, Northern Ireland 1-1 Iceland, Finland 1-0 Iceland, Portugal 2-0 Northern Ireland, Northern Ireland 0-5 Finland, Iceland 1-0 Portugal

	Pld	W	D	L	F	A	Pts
1 Finland	3	3	0	0	8	1	9
2 Iceland	3	1	1	1	2	2	4
3 Portugal	3	1	0	2	3	3	3
4 Northern Ireland	3	0	1	2	1	8	1

Group 6

04-09/04/13 Viernheim, Heidelberg, Walldorf

Germany 2-1 Spain, Czech Republic 2-0 Greece, Germany 9-0 Greece, Spain 2-1 Czech Republic, Czech Republic 0-5 Germany, Greece 3-2 Spain

	Pld	W	D	L	F	A	Pts
1 Germany	3	3	0	0	16	1	9
2 Czech Republic	3	1	0	2	3	7	3
3 Spain	3	1	0	2	5	6	3
4 Greece	3	1	0	2	3	13	3

Top goalscorers (qualifying rounds)

14	Jovana Damnjanović (Serbia)
10	Marija Banusic (Sweden)
8	Camilla Andersen (Denmark)
7	Adelina Engman (Finland)
	Simone Magill (Northern Ireland)
	Alexia Putellas (Spain)
6	Mima Stanković (Serbia)
	Laura Ortiz (Spain)

Final tournament (Wales)

Group A	Group B
Wales	Sweden
Denmark	Finland
England	Germany
France	Norway

First-time qualifiers claim surprise victory

Sweden edged out by single goal in final

Last four-team tournament to be staged at UEFA HQ

Poland prevail in Nyon

The last four-team UEFA European Women's Under-17 Championship final tournament included three debutants, one of which, Poland, went on to collect the trophy.

Sweden and Belgium were also making their first appearances, with the lineup completed by Spain, who were bidding for a third title to match the achievement of 2012 winners Germany.

The Germans were absent from the finals for the first time in the competition's six-year history, finishing third in a second qualifying round group topped by Belgium. Meanwhile, three-time runners-up and FIFA U-17 Women's World Cup holders France were edged out in qualifying by Spain. Also missing were the Netherlands, for whom Anna Miedema scored a record tally of 18 goals in the first qualifying round.

While there were newcomers among the qualifiers, it was also a watershed moment for the tournament itself – the last to be staged in Nyon after six seasons as its home. It was also the last four-team competition, the next one to be expanded to eight participants and scheduled for late 2013 in England.

First into action at Colovray Stadium were Belgium and Poland, and it was the latter who struck first through Katarzyna Konat. Belgium levelled through Tine De Caigny but Poland came back to seal a 3-1 win with goals from

Paulina Dudek and the outstanding Ewa Pajor. Known in her homeland as the female Lionel Messi, Pajor teased Belgium with her skill and ability to carve out goalscoring opportunities.

The second semi-final was a game of contrasting styles as Spain's swift passing and movement was countered by Sweden's more physical and direct approach. Nothing could separate the sides at half-time, Nahikari García's opener having been cancelled out by Sweden's Stina Blackstenius, and when the sides scored another goal apiece in the second period – with Jennifer Karlsson (Sweden) and Maddi Torre (Spain) on target

– the match had to be decided by penalties. Sweden goalkeeper Emma Holmgren proved to be the sudden-death match winner, stepping forward to score the decisive kick in a 5-4 success.

The final would be a tight hard-fought affair, and it was Poland who emerged victorious as Ewelina Kamczyk's shot on the turn after 15 minutes turned out to be the only goal, earning the country its first female international title. Meanwhile, Spain ended the tournament on a high by claiming third place with a comprehensive 4-0 win against Belgium, with García's goal in that game enough for her to top the goalscorers list with two.

Poland raise the trophy after their victory over Sweden in Nyon

First qualifying round

Group 1

19-24/10/12 Orhei, Vadul lui Voda, Ternovca
Switzerland 11-0 Bulgaria, Belgium 8-0 Moldova, Bulgaria 0-9 Belgium, Switzerland 8-0 Moldova, Belgium 1-2 Switzerland, Moldova 0-1 Bulgaria

	Pld	W	D	L	F	A	Pts
1 Switzerland	3	3	0	0	21	1	9
2 Belgium	3	2	0	1	18	2	6
3 Bulgaria	3	1	0	2	1	20	3
4 Moldova	3	0	0	3	0	17	0

Group 2

10-15/09/12 Belfast, Castledawson, Ballymena, Coleraine
Italy 5-0 Israel, England 0-0 Northern Ireland, England 5-0 Israel, Northern Ireland 1-0 Italy, Italy 4-1 England, Israel 1-4 Northern Ireland

	Pld	W	D	L	F	A	Pts
1 Northern Ireland	3	2	1	0	5	1	7
2 Italy	3	2	0	1	9	2	6
3 England	3	1	1	1	6	4	4
4 Israel	3	0	0	3	1	14	0

Group 3

01-06/10/12 Marijampole, Alytus
France 5-0 Bosnia & Herzegovina, Hungary 9-0 Lithuania, Bosnia & Herzegovina 3-3 Hungary, France 12-0 Lithuania, Hungary 0-5 France, Lithuania 0-5 Bosnia & Herzegovina

	Pld	W	D	L	F	A	Pts
1 France	3	3	0	0	22	0	9
2 Hungary	3	1	1	1	12	8	4
3 Bosnia & Herzegovina	3	1	1	1	8	8	4
4 Lithuania	3	0	0	3	0	26	0

Group 4

06-11/09/12 Beltinci, Odranci
Czech Republic 3-0 Estonia, Iceland 3-0 Slovenia, Czech Republic 4-0 Slovenia, Estonia 1-5 Iceland, Slovenia 3-0 Estonia, Iceland 0-0 Czech Republic

	Pld	W	D	L	F	A	Pts
1 Czech Republic	3	3	0	0	9	0	9
2 Iceland	3	2	0	1	8	3	6
3 Slovenia	3	1	0	2	3	7	3
4 Estonia	3	0	0	3	1	11	0

Group 5

29/09-04/10/12 Strumica
Denmark 4-0 FYROM, Scotland 2-3 Serbia, Denmark 6-0 Serbia, FYROM 0-7 Scotland, Scotland 0-2 Denmark, Serbia 4-0 FYROM

	Pld	W	D	L	F	A	Pts
1 Denmark	3	3	0	0	12	0	9
2 Serbia	3	2	0	1	7	8	6
3 Scotland	3	1	0	2	9	5	3
4 FYROM	3	0	0	3	0	15	0

Group 6

30/10-03/11/12 Lindabrunn, Purbach am See
Sweden 9-0 Croatia, Austria 4-1 Azerbaijan, Sweden 7-1 Azerbaijan, Croatia 0-10 Austria, Azerbaijan 6-0 Croatia, Austria 2-2 Sweden

	Pld	W	D	L	F	A	Pts
1 Sweden	3	2	1	0	18	3	7
2 Austria	3	2	1	0	16	3	7
3 Azerbaijan	3	1	0	2	8	11	3
4 Croatia	3	0	0	3	0	25	0

Group 7

29/10-03/11/12 Salonika
Russia 6-1 Romania, Germany 1-1 Greece, Germany 5-0 Romania, Greece 1-2 Russia, Russia 1-7 Germany, Romania 0-1 Greece

	Pld	W	D	L	F	A	Pts
1 Germany	3	2	1	0	13	2	7
2 Russia	3	2	0	1	9	9	6
3 Greece	3	1	1	1	3	3	4
4 Romania	3	0	0	3	1	12	0

Group 8

20-25/10/12 Meppel, Oosterwolde
Netherlands 15-0 Montenegro, Ukraine 6-0 Kazakhstan, Montenegro 1-0 Ukraine, Netherlands 11-0 Kazakhstan, Ukraine 0-16 Netherlands, Kazakhstan 1-4 Montenegro

	Pld	W	D	L	F	A	Pts
1 Netherlands	3	3	0	0	42	0	9
2 Montenegro	3	2	0	1	5	16	6
3 Ukraine	3	1	0	2	6	17	3
4 Kazakhstan	3	0	0	3	1	21	0

Group 9

01-06/10/12 Molodechno, Minsk
Republic of Ireland 3-0 Belarus, Finland 11-0 Georgia, Republic of Ireland 7-0 Georgia, Belarus 0-3 Finland, Finland 1-2 Republic of Ireland, Georgia 1-4 Belarus

	Pld	W	D	L	F	A	Pts
1 Republic of Ireland	3	3	0	0	12	1	9
2 Finland	3	2	0	1	15	2	6
3 Belarus	3	1	0	2	4	7	3
4 Georgia	3	0	0	3	1	22	0

Group 10

28/08-02/09/12 Riga, Ogre
Wales 0-2 Turkey, Norway 8-0 Latvia, Norway 5-1 Turkey, Latvia 0-4 Wales, Wales 0-5 Norway, Turkey 1-0 Latvia

	Pld	W	D	L	F	A	Pts
1 Norway	3	3	0	0	18	1	9
2 Turkey	3	2	0	1	4	5	6
3 Wales	3	1	0	2	4	7	3
4 Latvia	3	0	0	3	0	13	0

Group 11

03-08/09/12 Banska Bystrica, Brezno, Dolna Zdana, Kremnicka
Spain 8-0 Faroe Islands, Poland 4-0 Slovakia, Spain 4-0 Slovakia, Faroe Islands 0-3 Poland, Poland 0-3 Spain, Slovakia 4-1 Faroe Islands

	Pld	W	D	L	F	A	Pts
1 Spain	3	3	0	0	15	0	9
2 Poland	3	2	0	1	7	3	6
3 Slovakia	3	1	0	2	4	9	3
4 Faroe Islands	3	0	0	3	1	15	0

Second qualifying round

Group 1

07/03-03/04/13 Tessenderlo, Beringen, Tongeren
Denmark 1-1 Belgium, Netherlands 1-5 Germany, Germany 1-2 Denmark, Netherlands 0-3 Belgium, Denmark 2-2 Netherlands, Belgium 0-0 Germany

	Pld	W	D	L	F	A	Pts
1 Belgium	3	1	2	0	4	1	5
2 Denmark	3	1	2	0	5	4	5
3 Germany	3	1	1	1	6	3	4
4 Netherlands	3	0	1	2	3	10	1

Group 2

27/03-14/04/13 St Polten, Neulengbach, Lindabrunn
Republic of Ireland 1-2 Poland, Norway 2-0 Austria, Norway 0-3 Poland, Austria 4-1 Republic of Ireland, Republic of Ireland 0-0 Norway, Poland 1-1 Austria

	Pld	W	D	L	F	A	Pts
1 Poland	3	2	1	0	6	2	7
2 Norway	3	1	1	1	2	3	4
3 Austria	3	1	1	1	5	4	4
4 Republic of Ireland	3	0	1	2	2	6	1

Group 3

24-29/03/13 Oullins, Decines
France 3-1 Northern Ireland, Spain 3-0 Finland, France 2-0 Finland, Northern Ireland 0-2 Spain, Spain 1-1 France, Finland 0-1 Northern Ireland

	Pld	W	D	L	F	A	Pts
1 Spain	3	2	1	0	6	1	7
2 France	3	2	1	0	6	2	7
3 Northern Ireland	3	1	0	2	2	5	3
4 Finland	3	0	0	3	0	6	0

Group 4

09-14/04/13 Slany, Roudnice, Prague
Switzerland 0-1 Sweden, Czech Republic 2-2 Italy, Sweden 2-1 Czech Republic, Switzerland 2-1 Italy, Czech Republic 2-0 Switzerland, Italy 1-0 Sweden

	Pld	W	D	L	F	A	Pts
1 Sweden	3	2	0	1	3	2	6
2 Czech Republic	3	1	1	1	5	4	4
3 Italy	3	1	1	1	4	4	4
4 Switzerland	3	1	0	2	4	3	3

Semi-finals

25/06/13, Colovray, Nyon
Belgium 1-3 Poland
Goals: 0-1 Konat 25, 1-1 De Caigny 29, 1-2 Dudek 43, 1-3 Pajor 67

25/06/13, Colovray, Nyon
Spain 2-2 Sweden (4-0 on pens)
Goals: 1-0 García 20, 1-1 Blackstenius 27, 1-2 Karlsson 62, 2-2 Torre 75

Third place play-off

28/06/13, Colovray, Nyon
Belgium 0-4 Spain
Goals: 0-1 Baetens 21(og), 0-2 García 31, 0-3 Caldentey 40+2, 0-4 Guijarro 57

Final

28/06/13, Colovray, Nyon (att: 500)
Poland 1-0 Sweden
Goal: 1-0 Kamczyk 15
Referee: Budimir (CRO)
Poland: Okulewicz, Matysik, Dudek (Zapała 78), Redzia, Kamczyk, Konat, Dereń, Michalczyk, Grzywińska, Wasil, Pajor. Coach: Zbigniew Witkowski (POL)
Sweden: Holmgren, Ohlsson, Gibson, Strömberg (Ekholm 58), Andersson, Angeldal, Blackstenius, Grabus (Karlsson 41), Oskarsson, Björn, Östervall (Johnsson Haahr 69). Coach: Yvonne Ekroth (SWE)
Yellow cards: Dereń 13 (Poland), Gibson 67 (Sweden)

Lyon denied hat-trick of titles at Stamford Bridge

Second-half penalty proves enough for German debutants

Conny Pohlers lifts trophy with third different club

Shock win for Wolfsburg

On the face of it there was nothing unusual about Germany's seventh UEFA Women's Champions League triumph in 12 attempts. That it came at the expense of Olympique Lyonnais, however, constituted an enormous surprise – not least because the French club's conquerors, just-crowned domestic double winners VfL Wolfsburg, were European debutants at the start of the campaign.

Lyon went into the final at Stamford Bridge strongly favoured to secure an unprecedented third straight European title. They had not lost a 90-minute match for the entirety of Patrice Lair's three-year reign as coach – a run comprising over 100 matches – and at the

turn of the year had added United States winger Megan Rapinoe to an all-star squad containing most of the France national team plus Sweden forward Lotta Schelin. They reached the final at a canter, scoring 40 goals and conceding just one in their eight fixtures.

Moreover, Lyon had beaten German opposition in the previous two finals, overcoming 1. FFC Turbine Potsdam 2-0 at Fulham in 2011 and 1. FFC Frankfurt by the same score in Munich 12 months later. Wolfsburg, in the German second tier as recently as 2005/06, were making their European debut, but they had impressed in dismissing Arsenal Ladies FC in the semi-finals and, with both domestic trophies already in the bag, were not short on confidence.

Wolfsburg went into the final without several key players through suspension, illness and injury, but although Lyon dominated the first half they failed to score. With 17 minutes to go, Laura Georges handled in the Lyon box and Martina Müller, a Wolfsburg player since their relegation season of 2004/05, smashed the penalty past Sarah Bouhaddi, who, like Lara Dickenmann, Wendie Renard, Amandine Henry and Louisa Necib, was appearing in her fourth straight final.

Up until a fortnight earlier Wolfsburg had never won a major trophy, but at the final whistle in west London they were celebrating a remarkable treble – due reward for an ambitious recruitment drive that had peaked in 2011 with the signing of experienced striker Conny Pohlers.

With the fourth of her six goals during the triumphant campaign Pohlers became the first player to reach 40 in UEFA women's club competition, ending Hanna Ljungberg's near decade-long stint at the top of the all-time rankings. Having previously triumphed with Potsdam in 2005 and Frankfurt three years later, Pohlers became the first player to win the trophy with three different clubs. Wolfsburg themselves emulated Frankfurt (2002), Potsdam (2005) and FCR 2001 Duisburg (2009) in winning the trophy at the first attempt, a feat no non-German club has managed.

Captain Nadine Kessler lifts the trophy surrounded by jubilant Wolfsburg team-mates

Qualifying round

Group 1

11-16/08/12 Beltinci, Lendava
FC Zürich 2-0 ŽNK Pomurje Beltinci,
FK Gintra Universitetas 2-3 Ataşehir
Belediyespor, FC Zürich 4-0 Ataşehir
Belediyespor, ŽNK Pomurje Beltinci
9-1 FK Gintra Universitetas, FK Gintra
Universitetas 0-8 FC Zürich, Ataşehir
Belediyespor 2-4 ŽNK Pomurje Beltinci

	Pld	W	D	L	F	A	Pts
1 FC Zürich	3	3	0	0	14	0	9
2 ŽNK Pomurje Beltinci	3	2	0	1	13	5	6
3 Ataşehir Belediyespor	3	1	0	2	5	10	3
4 FK Gintra Universitetas	3	0	0	3	3	20	0

Group 2

11-16/08/12 Subotica, Novi Sad
BIIK Shymkent 3-0 Pärnu JK, FC NSA Sofia
0-7 ZFK Spartak Subotica, FC NSA Sofia
2-0 Pärnu JK, ZFK Spartak Subotica 0-2
BIIK Shymkent, BIIK Shymkent 4-0 FC NSA
Sofia, Pärnu JK 0-1 ZFK Spartak Subotica

	Pld	W	D	L	F	A	Pts
1 BIIK Shymkent	3	3	0	0	9	0	9
2 ZFK Spartak Subotica	3	2	0	1	8	2	6
3 FC NSA Sofia	3	1	0	2	2	11	3
4 Pärnu JK	3	0	0	3	0	6	0

Group 3

11-16/08/12 Ta' Qali
SU 1° Dezembro 4-0 Glentoran, CFF Olimpia
Cluj 8-0 Birkirkara FC, SU 1° Dezembro 1-0
Birkirkara FC, Glentoran 2-4 CFF Olimpia
Cluj, CFF Olimpia Cluj 1-1 SU 1° Dezembro,
Birkirkara FC 1-3 Glentoran

	Pld	W	D	L	F	A	Pts
1 CFF Olimpia Cluj	3	3	0	0	10	3	9
2 SU 1° Dezembro	3	2	0	1	6	4	6
3 Glentoran	3	1	0	2	5	9	3
4 Birkirkara FC	3	0	0	3	1	12	0

Group 4

11-16/08/12 Bratislava, Senec
RTP Unia Racibórz 5-0 ŠK Slovan
Bratislava, FC Bobruichanka 5-1
Ekonomist, RTP Unia Racibórz 7-1
Ekonomist, ŠK Slovan Bratislava 3-2 FC
Bobruichanka, FC Bobruichanka 0-5 RTP
Unia Racibórz, Ekonomist 0-8 ŠK Slovan
Bratislava

	Pld	W	D	L	F	A	Pts
1 RTP Unia Racibórz	3	3	0	0	17	1	9
2 ŠK Slovan Bratislava	3	2	0	1	11	7	6
3 FC Bobruichanka	3	1	0	2	7	9	3
4 Ekonomist	3	0	0	3	2	20	0

Group 5

11-16/08/12 Sarajevoa
WFC SFK 2000 Sarajevo 4-0 Peamount
United, ASA Tel-Aviv FC 5-0 UWIC LFC,
Peamount United 5-0 ASA Tel-Aviv FC,
WFC SFK 2000 Sarajevo 1-0 UWIC LFC,
ASA Tel-Aviv FC 1-1 WFC SFK 2000
Sarajevo, UWIC LFC 0-4 Peamount United

	Pld	W	D	L	F	A	Pts
1 WFC SFK 2000 Sarajevo	3	2	1	0	6	1	7
2 Peamount United	3	2	0	1	9	4	6
3 ASA Tel-Aviv FC	3	1	1	1	6	6	4
4 UWIC LFC	3	0	0	3	0	10	0

Group 6

11-16/08/12 Larnaca, Limassol
Apollon Limassol LFC 7-0 KÍ Klaksvík,
WFC Kharkiv 14-1 KS Ada Velipoje,
KÍ Klaksvík 1-2 WFC Kharkiv, Apollon
Limassol LFC 21-0 KS Ada Velipoje, WFC
Kharkiv 0-3 Apollon Limassol LFC, KS Ada
Velipoje 1-11 KÍ Klaksvík

	Pld	W	D	L	F	A	Pts
1 Apollon Limassol LFC	3	3	0	0	31	0	9
2 WFC Kharkiv	3	2	0	1	16	5	6
3 KÍ Klaksvík	3	1	0	2	12	10	3
4 KS Ada Velipoje	3	0	0	3	2	46	0

Group 7

11-16/08/12 Strumica
FC PAOK Thessaloniki 1-0 ZFK Nase
Taksi-SNT 2010, MTK Hungária FC 5-0
Skonto FK, FC PAOK Thessaloniki 8-0
Skonto FK, ZFK Nase Taksi-SNT 2010 0-7
MTK Hungária FC, MTK Hungária FC 2-0
FC PAOK Thessaloniki, Skonto FK 2-5 ZFK
Nase Taksi-SNT 2010

	Pld	W	D	L	F	A	Pts
1 MTK Hungária FC	3	3	0	0	14	0	9
2 FC PAOK Thessaloniki	3	2	0	1	9	2	6
3 ZFK Nase Taksi-SNT 2010	3	1	0	2	5	10	3
4 Skonto FK	3	0	0	3	2	18	0

Group 8

11-16/08/12 Vantaa
PK-35 Vantaa 6-0 FC Noroc Nimoreni,
Glasgow City LFC 3-2 WFC Osijek,
Glasgow City LFC 11-0 FC Noroc
Nimoreni, WFC Osijek 1-3 PK-35 Vantaa,
PK-35 Vantaa 1-1 Glasgow City LFC, FC
Noroc Nimoreni 1-11 WFC Osijek

	Pld	W	D	L	F	A	Pts
1 Glasgow City LFC	3	2	1	0	15	3	7
2 PK-35 Vantaa	3	2	1	0	10	2	7
3 WFC Osijek	3	1	0	2	14	7	3
4 FC Noroc Nimoreni	3	0	0	3	1	28	0

Round of 32

25/09/12, Stadion Letzigrund, Zurich
FC Zürich 1-1 FCF Juvisy Essonne
*04/10/12, Stade Léo Lagrange,
Sainte-Genevieve des Bois*
FCF Juvisy Essonne 1-0 FC Zürich
Aggregate: 2-1; FCF Juvisy Essonne qualify.

26/09/12, DCS Stadium, Stratford-upon-Avon
**Birmingham City LFC 2-0 ASD CF
Bardolino Verona**
03/10/12, Marc'Antonio Bentegodi, Verona
**ASD CF Bardolino Verona 3-0 Birmingham
City LFC** *(aet)*
Aggregate: 3-2; ASD CF Bardolino Verona
qualify after extra time.

26/09/12, Gradski, Subotica
ZFK Spartak Subotica 0-1 Göteborg FC
03/10/12, Valhalla, Gothenburg
Göteborg FC 3-0 ZFK Spartak Subotica
Aggregate: 4-0; Göteborg FC qualify.

26/09/12, Tsirion Stadium, Limassol
Apollon Limassol LFC 2-3 ASD Torres CF
03/10/12, Vanni Sanna, Sassari
ASD Torres CF 3-1 Apollon Limassol LFC
Aggregate: 6-3; ASD Torres CF qualify.

26/09/12, Myyrmäki Urheilupuisto, Vantaa
PK-35 Vantaa 0-7 Olympique Lyonnais
03/10/12, Stade de Gerland, Lyon
Olympique Lyonnais 5-0 PK-35 Vantaa
Aggregate: 12-0; Olympique Lyonnais qualify.

26/09/12, Cluj Arena, Cluj-Napoca
CFF Olimpia Cluj 1-1 SV Neulengbach
03/10/12, Wienerwaldstadion, Neulengbach
SV Neulengbach 2-2 CFF Olimpia Cluj
Aggregate: 3-3; CFF Olimpia Cluj qualify on
away goals.

26/09/12, BIIK Stadium, Shymkent
BIIK Shymkent 0-4 Røa IL
04/10/12, Røa Stadium, Oslo
Røa IL 4-0 BIIK Shymkent
Aggregate: 8-0; Røa IL qualify.

26/09/12, Petershill Park, Glasgow
Glasgow City LFC 1-2 Fortuna Hjørring
03/10/12, Hjørring Stadion, Hjørring
Fortuna Hjørring 0-0 Glasgow City LFC
Aggregate: 2-1; Fortuna Hjørring qualify.

26/09/12, Nadderud, Oslo
Stabæk FK 2-0 Brøndby IF
03/10/12, Brøndby, Brøndby
Brøndby IF 3-3 Stabæk FK
Aggregate: 3-5; Stabæk FK qualify.

26/09/12, Stade Maurice Dufrasne, Liege
**Standard Femina de Liège 1-3 1. FFC
Turbine Potsdam**
03/10/12, Karl Liebknecht, Potsdam
**1. FFC Turbine Potsdam 5-0 Standard
Femina de Liège**
Aggregate: 8-1; 1. FFC Turbine Potsdam
qualify.

26/09/12, Mini Estadi, Barcelona
FC Barcelona 0-3 Arsenal Ladies FC
04/10/12, Meadow Park, Borehamwood
Arsenal Ladies FC 4-0 FC Barcelona
Aggregate: 7-0; Arsenal Ladies FC qualify.

26/09/12, Stjörnuvöllur, Gardabaer
Stjarnan 0-0 FK Zorkiy Krasnogorsk
04/10/12, Saturn, Ramenskoye
FK Zorkiy Krasnogorsk 3-1 Stjarnan
Aggregate: 3-1; FK Zorkiy Krasnogorsk qualify.

27/09/12, OSiR, Racibórz
RTP Unia Racibórz 1-5 VfL Wolfsburg
04/10/12, VfL-Stadion, Wolfsburg
VfL Wolfsburg 6-1 RTP Unia Racibórz
Aggregate: 11-2; VfL Wolfsburg qualify.

27/09/12, Asim Ferhatović, Sarajevo
WFC SFK 2000 Sarajevo 0-3 AC Sparta Praha
11/10/12, FK Viktoria Žižkov, Prague
AC Sparta Praha 3-0 WFC SFK 2000 Sarajevo
Aggregate: 6-0; AC Sparta Praha qualify.

27/09/12, Hidegkúti Nándor, Budapest
MTK Hungária FC 0-4 FC Malmö
03/10/12, Malmö Idrottsplats, Malmo
FC Malmö 6-1 MTK Hungária FC
Aggregate: 10-1; FC Malmö qualify.

27/09/12, Kyocera Stadion, Den Haag
ADO Den Haag 1-4 FC Rossiyanka
04/10/12, Krasnoarmeysk, Krasnoarmeysk
FC Rossiyanka 1-2 ADO Den Haag
Aggregate: 5-3; FC Rossiyanka qualify.

Round of 16

31/10/12, Rodina, Moscow
FK Zorkiy Krasnogorsk 0-9 Olympique Lyonnais
07/11/12, Stade de Gerland, Lyon
Olympique Lyonnais 2-0 FK Zorkiy Krasnogorsk
Aggregate: 11-0; Olympique Lyonnais qualify.

31/10/12, Nadderud, Oslo
Stabæk FK 0-0 FCF Juvisy Essonne
08/11/12, Leo Lagrange, Bonneuil-sur-Marne
FCF Juvisy Essonne 2-1 Stabæk FK
Aggregate: 2-1; FCF Juvisy Essonne qualify.

31/10/12, Hjørring Stadion, Hjorring
Fortuna Hjørring 1-1 Göteborg FC
07/11/12, Valhalla, Gothenburg
Göteborg FC 3-2 Fortuna Hjørring
Aggregate: 4-3; Göteborg FC qualify.

31/10/12, Malmö Idrottsplats, Malmo
FC Malmö 1-0 ASD CF Bardolino Verona
07/11/12, Marc'Antonio Bentegodi, Verona
ASD CF Bardolino Verona 0-2 FC Malmö
Aggregate: 0-3; FC Malmö qualify.

31/10/12, Vanni Sanna, Sassari
ASD Torres CF 4-1 CFF Olimpia Cluj
08/11/12, Cluj Arena, Cluj-Napoca
CFF Olimpia Cluj 0-3 ASD Torres CF
Aggregate: 1-7; ASD Torres CF qualify.

01/11/12, Bohemians Praha, Prague
AC Sparta Praha 0-1 FC Rossiyanka
08/11/12, Rodina, Moscow
FC Rossiyanka 2-2 AC Sparta Praha
Aggregate: 3-2; FC Rossiyanka qualify.

Conny Pohlers of Wolfsburg – the competition's joint top scorer with eight goals

01/11/12, Meadow Park, Borehamwood
Arsenal Ladies FC 2-1 1. FFC Turbine Potsdam
07/11/12, Karl Liebknecht, Potsdam
1. FFC Turbine Potsdam 3-4 Arsenal Ladies FC
Aggregate: 4-6; Arsenal Ladies FC qualify.

01/11/12, VfL-Stadion, Wolfsburg
VfL Wolfsburg 4-1 Røa IL
07/11/12, Nedre Eiker, Mjondalen
Røa IL 1-1 VfL Wolfsburg
Aggregate: 2-5; VfL Wolfsburg qualify.

Quarter-finals

20/03/13, Meadow Park, Borehamwood
Arsenal Ladies FC 3-1 ASD Torres CF
Goals: 1-0 K. Smith 23, 2-0 Nobbs 49, 3-0 Little 63, 3-1 Maendly 71
Referee: Steinhaus (GER)
27/03/13, Vanni Sanna, Sassari
ASD Torres CF 0-1 Arsenal Ladies FC
Goal: 0-1 Fahey 4
Referee: Albon (ROU)
Aggregate: 1-4; Arsenal Ladies FC qualify.

20/03/13, Stade de Gerland, Lyon
Olympique Lyonnais 5-0 FC Malmö
Goals: 1-0 Thomis 18, 2-0 Schelin 24, 3-0 Schelin 62, 4-0 Abily 71, 5-0 Necib 89
Referee: Staubli (SUI)
28/03/13, Malmö Idrottsplats, Malmo
FC Malmö 0-3 Olympique Lyonnais
Goals: 0-1 Schelin 15, 0-2 Rapinoe 53, 0-3 Renard 89
Referee: Monzul (UKR)
Aggregate: 0-8; Olympique Lyonnais qualify.

20/03/13, VfL Wolfsburg Arena, Wolfsburg
VfL Wolfsburg 2-1 FC Rossiyanka
Goals: 1-0 Popp 5, 2-0 Müller 32, 2-1 Henning 46(og)
Referee: Dorcioman (ROU)
28/03/13, Stadion Luzhniki, Moscow
FC Rossiyanka 0-2 VfL Wolfsburg
Goals: 0-1 Pohlers 71, 0-2 Goessling 88
Referee: Heikkinen (FIN)
Aggregate: 1-4; VfL Wolfsburg qualify.

20/03/13, Leo Lagrange, Bonneuil-sur-Marne
FCF Juvisy Essonne 1-0 Göteborg FC
Goal: 1-0 Machart 17
Referee: Baitinger (GER)
27/03/13, Valhalla, Gothenburg
Göteborg FC 1-3 FCF Juvisy Essonne
Goals: 1-0 Averbuch 65, 1-1 Catala 77, 1-2 Catala 86, 1-3 Cayman 90+1
Referee: Spinelli (ITA)
Aggregate: 1-4; FCF Juvisy Essonne qualify.

Semi-finals

13/04/13, Stade de Gerland, Lyon
Olympique Lyonnais 3-0 FCF Juvisy Essonne
Goals: 1-0 Schelin 18, 2-0 Renard 63, 3-0 Schelin 90+3
Referee: Mitsi (GRE)
21/04/13, Robert Bobin, Evry
FCF Juvisy Essonne 1-6 Olympique Lyonnais
Goals: 0-1 Rapinoe 6, 0-2 Schelin 19, 0-3 Schelin 51, 0-4 Abily 63, 0-5 Tonazzi 71, 0-6 Tonazzi 78, 1-6 Diani 84
Referee: Kulcsár (HUN)
Aggregate: 1-9; Olympique Lyonnais qualify.

14/04/13, Meadow Park, Borehamwood
Arsenal Ladies FC 0-2 VfL Wolfsburg
Goals: 0-1 Pohlers 29, 0-2 Müller 85
Referee: Monzul (UKR)
21/04/13, VfL Wolfsburg Arena, Wolfsburg
VfL Wolfsburg 2-1 Arsenal Ladies FC
Goals: 1-0 Wagner 14, 1-1 Little 54, 2-1 Kessler 61
Referee: Spinelli (ITA)
Aggregate: 4-1; VfL Wolfsburg qualify.

Final

23/05/13, Stamford Bridge, London (att: 19,258)
VfL Wolfsburg 1-0 Olympique Lyonnais
Goal: 1-0 Müller 73(p)
Referee: Albon (ROU)
Wolfsburg: A Vetterlein, Wensing, Jakabfi (Magull 78), Blässe, Popp, Kessler, Hartmann, Müller, Pohlers (Omilade 82), Henning, Goessling. Coach: Ralf Kellermann (GER)
Lyon: Bouhaddi, Renard, Georges, Henry, Rapinoe (Dickenmann 46; Majri 89), Schelin, Necib, Thomis, Franco, Bompastor, Abily (Le Sommer 67). Coach: Patrice Lair (FRA)
Yellow cards: Renard 89 (Lyon), Magull 90 (Wolfsburg)

Top goalscorers

8	Patrizia Panico (Torres)
	Conny Pohlers (Wolfsburg)
7	Lotta Schelin (Lyon)
6	Laëtitia Tonazzi (Lyon)
5	Natasa Andonova (Potsdam)
	Camille Abily (Lyon)
	Louisa Necib (Lyon)
	Martina Müller (Wolfsburg)

| First triumph after four semi-final defeats | Dinamo seen off in thrilling final | Defending champions Barcelona take third place |

Kairat the pride of Kazakhstan

Kairat Almaty took the European futsal title to Kazakhstan, becoming the country's first ever UEFA champions at any level, and they did so in memorable fashion at the UEFA Futsal Cup final tournament in the Georgian capital of Tbilisi.

No side from Kazakhstan had ever previously played in a UEFA final of any description. But having lost four previous UEFA Futsal Cup semi-finals, Kairat overcame holders FC Barcelona 5-4 before holding off 2007 winners MFK Dinamo 4-3 in the decider.

Never before had Georgia hosted a UEFA final tournament, but Iberia Star Tbilisi, the only club to have entered every edition of the competition, were awarded the honour having made the final four for the first time at the 12th attempt. The host club had changed their coach and much of their squad in the weeks leading up to the tournament, and the disruption was evident as Dinamo knocked them out with a comfortable 5-2 win in front of a noisy 7,200 crowd at the Tbilisi Palace of Sport.

It was the second semi-final, however, that provided the main drama of the opening night. Deploying goalkeeper Higuita as a virtual outfield player, former Kairat player Cacau – who had become coach only in February – outfoxed Barcelona tactically, with a Fumasa hat-trick helping to inflict the holders' first ever European defeat. Cacu described that win as "historic" but there was more to come two days later. Twelve months on from losing to Barcelona in Lleida, Dinamo were in a joint-record fifth final, and started as narrow favourites. They were fortunate to go in level at half-time after a late equaliser had made it 1-1, but they seemed out for the count as Leo Santana, Fumasa and – with a long-range punt – Higuita put Kairat 4-1 up.

Conversely, the action was only just hotting up. A Higuita clearance rebounded in off Cirilo and then Talù made it 4-3 with four minutes left. Dinamo surged forward, hitting the post twice in the last few seconds, but Kairat somehow held on to their precious lead to take the match and the title.

"We have faced the best teams in the world," Cacau said. "If we had had a little more composure, the final score could have been better. But I think the dramatic ending makes it more beautiful still."

Barcelona took third place with a 4-1 defeat of Iberia Star, but already their thoughts had turned to trying to return to Europe in 2013/14. Despite the two disappointing defeats, Iberia Star made history for Georgia, hosting a tournament in which new nations established themselves among futsal's elite.

WINNERS
UEFA Futsal Cup Finals 2013

Kairat Almaty players pose with the trophy after their 2013 UEFA Futsal Cup success

UEFA Futsal Cup

Preliminary round

Group A

08-10/08/12 Trebinje

KMF Leotar Trebinje 9-1 Balzan Youths FC, Balzan Youths FC 0-3 Lexmax Chisinau, Lexmax Chisinau 1-4 KMF Leotar Trebinje

	Pld	W	D	L	F	A	Pts
1 KMF Leotar Trebinje	2	2	0	0	13	2	6
2 Lexmax Chisinau	2	1	0	1	4	4	3
3 Balzan Youths FC	2	0	0	2	1	12	0

Group B

08-11/08/12 Birkerod

Helvécia Futsal London 2-1 Edro Vlorë, København 1-6 Lidselmash Lida, Lidselmash Lida 2-1 Helvécia Futsal London, København 6-3 Edro Vlorë, Edro Vlorë 2-5 Lidselmash Lida, Helvécia Futsal London 2-7 København

	Pld	W	D	L	F	A	Pts
1 Lidselmash Lida	3	3	0	0	13	4	9
2 København	3	2	0	1	14	11	6
3 Helvécia Futsal London	3	1	0	2	5	10	3
4 Edro Vlorë	3	0	0	3	6	13	0

Group C

08-11/08/12 Wiener Neustadt

Eden College Futsal 3-2 TUFAD Ankara S., 1. FC Allstars Wiener Neustadt 9-4 Futsal Minerva, Futsal Minerva 9-6 Eden College Futsal, 1. FC Allstars Wiener Neustadt 3-2 TUFAD Ankara S., TUFAD Ankara S. 6-5 Futsal Minerva, Eden College Futsal 5-2 1. FC Allstars Wiener Neustadt

	Pld	W	D	L	F	A	Pts
1 Eden College Futsal	3	2	0	1	14	13	6
2 1. FC Allstars Wiener Neustadt	3	1	1	1	14	12	4
3 TUFAD Ankara S.	3	1	1	1	11	11	4
4 Futsal Minerva	3	1	0	2	18	21	3

Group D

08-11/08/12 Paris

Futsal Topsport Antwerpen 18-0 FC Santos, Paris Sporting Club 6-3 Hamburg Panthers, Hamburg Panthers 8-6 Futsal Topsport Antwerpen, Paris Sporting Club 18-2 FC Santos, FC Santos 5-5 Hamburg Panthers, Futsal Topsport Antwerpen 4-4 Paris Sporting Club

	Pld	W	D	L	F	A	Pts
1 Paris Sporting Club	3	2	1	0	28	9	7
2 Hamburg Panthers	3	1	1	1	16	17	4
3 Futsal Topsport Antwerpen	3	1	1	1	28	12	4
4 FC Santos	3	0	1	2	7	41	1

Sergio Lozano – Barcelona's top marksman at the final tournament

Group E

08-11/08/12 Andorra la Vella

Maccabi Nahalat Itzhak 3-3 Shahumyan, FC Encamp 2-4 Vegakameratene, Vegakameratene 0-0 Maccabi Nahalat Itzhak, FC Encamp 6-2 Shahumyan, Shahumyan 1-4 Vegakameratene, Maccabi Nahalat Itzhak 7-4 FC Encamp

	Pld	W	D	L	F	A	Pts
1 Vegakameratene	3	2	1	0	8	3	7
2 Maccabi Nahalat Itzhak	3	1	2	0	10	7	5
3 FC Encamp	3	1	0	2	12	13	3
4 Shahumyan	3	0	1	2	6	13	1

Group F

08-11/08/12 Varna

FS Ilves Tampere 3-0 Cardiff City FC, FC Grand Pro Varna 7-2 Ibra Göteborg, Ibra Göteborg 3-5 FS Ilves Tampere, FC Grand Pro Varna 4-1 Cardiff City FC, Cardiff City FC 0-8 Ibra Göteborg, FS Ilves Tampere 0-0 FC Grand Pro Varna

	Pld	W	D	L	F	A	Pts
1 FC Grand Pro Varna	3	2	1	0	11	3	7
2 FS Ilves Tampere	3	2	1	0	8	3	7
3 Ibra Göteborg	3	1	0	2	13	12	3
4 Cardiff City FC	3	0	0	3	11	5	0

Group G

09-12/08/12 Skopje

KF Jedinstvo Bijelo Polje 7-6 FC Anzhi Tallinn, KMF Zelezarec Skopje 3-1 Bekentas Vilnius, Bekentas Vilnius 2-7 KF Jedinstvo Bijelo Polje, KMF Zelezarec Skopje 2-2 FC Anzhi Tallinn, FC Anzhi Tallinn 3-2 Bekentas Vilnius, KF Jedinstvo Bijelo Polje 2-5 KMF Zelezarec Skopje

	Pld	W	D	L	F	A	Pts
1 KMF Zelezarec Skopje	3	2	1	0	10	5	7
2 KF Jedinstvo Bijelo Polje	3	2	0	1	16	13	6
3 FC Anzhi Tallinn	3	1	1	1	11	11	4
4 Bekentas Vilnius	3	0	0	3	5	13	0

Main round

Group 1

06-09/09/12 Nicosia

AC Omonia 3-3 Slov-Matic Bratislava, Luparense C/5 2-0 FC Grand Pro Varna, AC Omonia 5-3 FC Grand Pro Varna, Slov-Matic Bratislava 0-0 Luparense C/5, FC Grand Pro Varna 2-7 Slov-Matic Bratislava, Luparense C/5 5-1 AC Omonia

	Pld	W	D	L	F	A	Pts
1 Luparense C/5	3	2	1	0	7	1	7
2 Slov-Matic Bratislava	3	1	2	0	10	5	5
3 AC Omonia	3	1	1	1	9	11	4
4 FC Grand Pro Varna	3	0	0	3	5	14	0

Group 2

05-08/09/12 Riga

KMF Ekonomac Kragujevac 6-2 Vegakameratene, FK Nikars Riga 6-1 KMF Zelezarec Skopje, KMF Zelezarec Skopje 1-8 KMF Ekonomac Kragujevac, FK Nikars Riga 2-1 Vegakameratene, Vegakameratene 4-2 KMF Zelezarec Skopje, KMF Ekonomac Kragujevac 4-3 FK Nikars Riga

	Pld	W	D	L	F	A	Pts
1 KMF Ekonomac Kragujevac	3	3	0	0	18	6	9
2 FK Nikars Riga	3	2	0	1	11	6	6
3 Vegakameratene	3	1	0	2	7	10	3
4 KMF Zelezarec Skopje	3	0	0	3	4	18	0

Group 3

04-07/09/12 Chrudim

City'US Târgu Mureş 3-1 KMF Leotar Trebinje, FK EP Chrudim 3-2 Energy Lviv, Energy Lviv 6-3 City'US Târgu Mureş, FK EP Chrudim 4-0 KMF Leotar Trebinje, KMF Leotar Trebinje 2-6 Energy Lviv, City'US Târgu Mureş 5-4 FK EP Chrudim

	Pld	W	D	L	F	A	Pts
1 Energy Lviv	3	2	0	1	14	8	6
2 FK EP Chrudim	3	2	0	1	11	7	6
3 City'US Târgu Mureş	3	2	0	1	11	11	6
4 KMF Leotar Trebinje	3	0	0	3	3	13	0

Group 4

05-08/09/12 Litija

Iberia Star Tbilisi 3-2 Paris Sporting Club, FC Litija 7-2 Athina '90 Athens, Athina '90 Athens 1-3 Iberia Star Tbilisi, FC Litija 3-3 Paris Sporting Club, Paris Sporting Club 7-1 Athina '90 Athens, Iberia Star Tbilisi 1-2 FC Litija

	Pld	W	D	L	F	A	Pts
1 FC Litija	3	2	1	0	12	6	7
2 Iberia Star Tbilisi	3	2	0	1	7	5	6
3 Paris Sporting Club	3	1	1	1	12	7	4
4 Athina '90 Athens	3	0	0	3	4	17	0

Group 5

05-08/09/12 Split

MNK Split 5-0 Akademia FC Pniewy, MNK Split 1-0 Lidselmash Lida, Akademia FC Pniewy 0-5 MFK Dinamo, Lidselmash Lida 1-5 MFK Dinamo, Lidselmash Lida 5-0 Akademia FC Pniewy, MNK Split 1-11 MFK Dinamo

	Pld	W	D	L	F	A	Pts
1 MFK Dinamo	3	3	0	0	21	2	9
2 MNK Split	3	2	0	1	7	11	6
3 Lidselmash Lida	3	1	0	2	6	6	3
4 Akademia FC Pniewy	3	0	0	3	0	15	0

Group 6

05-08/09/12 Gyor

Araz Naxçivan 0-5 Eden College Futsal, Győri ETO FC 3-0 Club Futsal Eindhoven, Club Futsal Eindhoven 3-4 Araz Naxçivan, Győri ETO FC 6-2 Eden College Futsal, Eden College Futsal 3-6 Club Futsal Eindhoven, Araz Naxçivan 5-5 Győri ETO FC

	Pld	W	D	L	F	A	Pts
1 Győri ETO FC	3	2	1	0	14	7	7
2 Araz Naxçivan	3	1	1	1	9	13	4
3 Club Futsal Eindhoven	3	1	0	2	9	10	3
4 Eden College Futsal	3	1	0	2	10	12	3

Elite round

Group A

10-13/10/12 Lasko

FC Barcelona 18-0 MNK Split, FC Litija 5-3 Araz Naxçivan, Araz Naxçivan 1-7 FC Barcelona, FC Litija 10-1 MNK Split, MNK Split 1-3 Araz Naxçivan, FC Barcelona 3-0 FC Litija

	Pld	W	D	L	F	A	Pts
1 FC Barcelona	3	3	0	0	28	1	9
2 FC Litija	3	2	0	1	15	7	6
3 Araz Naxçivan	3	1	0	2	9	13	3
4 MNK Split	3	0	0	3	2	33	0

Group B

10-13/10/12 Kragujevac

KMF Ekonomac Kragujevac 4-1 FK EP Chrudim, Kairat Almaty 5-1 Slov-Matic Bratislava, KMF Ekonomac Kragujevac 3-3 Slov-Matic Bratislava, FK EP Chrudim 5-6 Kairat Almaty, Slov-Matic Bratislava 1-4 FK EP Chrudim, Kairat Almaty 5-0 KMF Ekonomac Kragujevac

	Pld	W	D	L	F	A	Pts
1 Kairat Almaty	3	3	0	0	16	6	9
2 KMF Ekonomac Kragujevac	3	1	1	1	7	9	4
3 FK EP Chrudim	3	1	0	2	10	11	3
4 Slov-Matic Bratislava	3	0	1	2	5	12	1

Group C

10-13/10/12 Murcia

MFK Dinamo 7-2 FK Nikars Riga, Murcia FS 8-3 Energy Lviv, Energy Lviv 0-5 MFK Dinamo, Murcia FS 6-1 FK Nikars Riga, FK Nikars Riga 1-3 Energy Lviv, MFK Dinamo 4-2 Murcia FS

	Pld	W	D	L	F	A	Pts
1 MFK Dinamo	3	3	0	0	16	4	9
2 Murcia FS	3	2	0	1	16	8	6
3 Energy Lviv	3	1	0	2	6	14	3
4 FK Nikars Riga	3	0	0	3	4	16	0

Group D

11-14/10/12 Tbilisi

SL Benfica 3-3 Győri ETO FC, Iberia Star Tbilisi 6-1 Luparense C/5, Luparense C/5 2-3 SL Benfica, Iberia Star Tbilisi 2-2 Győri ETO FC, Győri ETO FC 3-2 Luparense C/5, SL Benfica 4-7 Iberia Star Tbilisi

	Pld	W	D	L	F	A	Pts
1 Iberia Star Tbilisi	3	2	1	0	15	7	7
2 Győri ETO FC	3	1	2	0	8	7	5
3 SL Benfica	3	1	1	1	10	12	4
4 Luparense C/5	3	0	0	3	5	12	0

Semi-finals

26/04/13, Sportis Sasakhle, Tbilisi
Iberia Star Tbilisi 2-5 MFK Dinamo
Goals: 0-1 Pula 11, 0-2 Dieguinho 11, 0-3 Pula 22, 1-3 Augusto 27, 1-4 Dieguinho 33, 1-5 Fukin 35, 2-5 Fabinho 39

26/04/13, Sportis Sasakhle, Tbilisi
Kairat Almaty 5-4 FC Barcelona
Goals: 1-0 Fumasa 2, 2-0 Fumasa 7, 2-1 Lin 7, 2-2 Torras 15, 2-3 Wilde 20, 3-3 Alexandre Moraes 24, 4-3 Lin 36, 5-3 Fumasa 38, 5-4 Fernandez 39

Third place play-off

28/04/13, Sportis Sasakhle, Tbilisi
Iberia Star Tbilisi 1-4 FC Barcelona
Goals: 0-1 Lozano 1, 0-2 Aicardo 6, 1-2 Fabinho 12, 1-3 Augusto 20(og), 1-4 Lozano 28

Final

28/04/13, Sportis Sasakhle, Tbilisi (att: 5,120)
MFK Dinamo 3-4 Kairat Almaty
Goals: 0-1 Popov 10(og), 1-1 Sergeev 18, 1-2 Leo Santana 22, 1-3 Fumasa 28, 1-4 Higuita 32, 2-4 Cirilo 35, 3-4 Tatù 36
Referees: Francesco Massini (ITA)/ Eduardo Fernandes Coelho (POR)
MFK Dinamo: Popov, Gustavo, Romulo, Tatù, Fukin, Pula, Nando, Sergeev, Cirilo, Dieguinho, Suchilin, Fernandinho. Coach: Faustino Pérez (ESP)
Kairat: Khalyavin, Higuita, Leo Santana, Fumasa, Leo, Joan, Pengrin, Suleimenov, Henrique Elgart, Alexandre Moraes, Euler, Betão. Coach: Cacau (BRA)
Yellow cards: Nando 38 (MFK Dinamo), Euler 38 (Kairat)

Top goalscorers (final tournament)

4	Fumasa (Kairat Almaty)
2	Sergio Lozano (FC Barcelona)
	Pula (MFK Dinamo)
	Fabinho (Iberia Star Tbilisi)
	Dieguinho (MFK Dinamo)

Fumasa of Kairat Almaty celebrates after scoring his side's third goal during the final

UEFA FUTSAL EURO

| Seven group winners qualify with perfect records | Holders Spain lead the way with goal spree | September play-offs to decide final four places |

Big guns headed for Belgium

Eight of the 12 places at UEFA Futsal EURO 2014 in Antwerp were filled after the main round of the competition, with holders Spain, former winners Italy and Russia, 2010 runners-up Portugal, Azerbaijan, the Czech Republic and Slovenia all confirming their places alongside hosts Belgium with 100% records.

Not one of those nations was involved when the qualifying process began in January with the preliminary round. Four countries were making their competition debuts – Denmark, Sweden, Wales and, in their first ever UEFA tournament, Gibraltar. The latter, playing their first futsal internationals, lost to Montenegro and France before beating San Marino 7-5, while Denmark were victorious twice. However, it was Sweden who stood out among the newcomers, beating Israel, Andorra and Estonia to progress to the next stage along with fellow group winners Montenegro, Georgia, Greece, Norway and first-time qualifiers England.

Two months later, in the main round, where 28 nations chased seven automatic qualifying places and eight berths in the September play-offs, all six of those preliminary round group winners were eliminated. Surprises were at a premium and the established names quickly found form, none more so than Spain, seeking a fifth straight European title having lost their second successive FIFA Futsal World Cup final to Brazil the previous autumn.

Indeed, Spain had the best main round record, overcoming the Former Yugoslav Republic of Macedonia 5-1, Sweden 13-0 and

Croatia, who had made the 2012 semi-finals as hosts, by a 10-0 scoreline. Russia, Italy, Portugal, Azerbaijan, the Czech Republic and Slovenia also topped their sections with three wins out of three, but it was not plain sailing for all of them.

Slovenia were grouped with two other sides who had also played in the 2012 finals – Ukraine and hosts Turkey. In their opener Slovenia edged past Turkey 5-3 having trailed early in the second half, but they then hit form to dismiss two-time runners-up Ukraine 8-3 and England 5-2. Slovakia, meanwhile, looked

set to make their first finals as they were leading Azerbaijan late in the game before two goals in a minute from Biro Jade and Namig Mammadkarimo turned the game in Bratislava.

Slovakia did end with the best record of the third-placed sides so they found consolation with a place in the play-offs alongside group runners-up Ukraine, the Netherlands, Hungary, Romania, Croatia, Serbia and potential first-time finalists Bosnia & Herzegovina. The two-legged ties were set for 17 and 24 September, with the 12-team finals running from 28 January to 8 February 2014.

Spain's Raúl Campos in main round action as the holders defeat Sweden 13-0

Preliminary round

Group A
23-26/01/13 Nico

Montenegro 10-2 Gibraltar, France 12-0 San Marino, San Marino 0-11 Montenegro, France 6-2 Gibraltar, Gibraltar 7-5 San Marino, Montenegro 1-1 France

	Pld	W	D	L	F	A	Pts
1 Montenegro	3	2	1	0	22	3	7
2 France	3	2	1	0	19	3	7
3 Gibraltar	3	1	0	2	11	21	3
4 San Marino	3	0	0	3	5	30	0

Group B
23-26/01/13 Paola

Malta 0-9 Georgia, Georgia 5-5 Moldova, Moldova 4-1 Malta

	Pld	W	D	L	F	A	Pts
1 Georgia	2	1	1	0	14	5	4
2 Moldova	2	1	1	0	9	6	4
3 Malta	2	0	0	2	1	13	0

Group C
25-27/01/13 Kaunas

Lithuania 3-4 England, England 2-1 Cyprus, Cyprus 0-1 Lithuania

	Pld	W	D	L	F	A	Pts
1 England	2	2	0	0	6	4	6
2 Lithuania	2	1	0	1	4	4	3
3 Cyprus	2	0	0	2	1	3	0

Group D
23-26/01/13 Blagoevgrad

Greece 4-1 Wales, Bulgaria 0-0 Armenia, Armenia 0-5 Greece, Bulgaria 2-1 Wales, Wales 2-4 Armenia, Greece 5-1 Bulgaria

	Pld	W	D	L	F	A	Pts
1 Greece	3	3	0	0	14	2	9
2 Armenia	3	1	1	1	4	7	4
3 Bulgaria	3	1	1	1	3	6	4
4 Wales	3	0	0	3	4	10	0

Group E
23-26/01/13 Andorra la Vella

Israel 2-4 Sweden, Andorra 4-3 Estonia, Estonia 2-5 Israel, Andorra 2-4 Sweden, Sweden 2-0 Estonia, Israel 2-2 Andorra

	Pld	W	D	L	F	A	Pts
1 Sweden	3	3	0	0	10	4	9
2 Israel	3	1	1	1	9	8	4
3 Andorra	3	1	1	1	8	9	4
4 Estonia	3	0	0	3	5	11	0

Group F
23-26/01/13 Yverdon

Albania 2-4 Denmark, Switzerland 0-5 Norway, Norway 5-2 Albania, Switzerland 2-3 Denmark, Denmark 1-3 Norway, Albania 2-8 Switzerland

	Pld	W	D	L	F	A	Pts
1 Norway	3	3	0	0	13	3	9
2 Denmark	3	2	0	1	8	7	6
3 Switzerland	3	1	0	2	10	10	3
4 Albania	3	0	0	3	6	17	0

Fábio Lima of Group 5 winners Portugal

Main round

Group 1
27-30/03/13 Bari, Andria

Hungary 4-3 Montenegro, Italy 5-1 Finland, Finland 2-5 Hungary, Italy 6-0 Montenegro, Montenegro 1-3 Finland, Hungary 1-9 Italy

	Pld	W	D	L	F	A	Pts
1 Italy	3	3	0	0	20	2	9
2 Hungary	3	2	0	1	10	14	6
3 Finland	3	1	0	2	6	11	3
4 Montenegro	3	0	0	3	4	13	0

Group 2
27-30/03/13 Bratislava

Azerbaijan 6-0 Norway, Slovakia 1-1 Bosnia & Herzegovina, Bosnia & Herzegovina 2-3 Azerbaijan, Slovakia 4-3 Norway, Norway 0-4 Bosnia & Herzegovina, Azerbaijan 2-1 Slovakia

	Pld	W	D	L	F	A	Pts
1 Azerbaijan	3	3	0	0	11	3	9
2 Bosnia & Herzegovina	3	1	1	1	10	7	4
3 Slovakia	3	1	1	1	9	9	4
4 Norway	3	0	0	3	3	14	0

Group 3
27-30/03/13 Jelgava

Russia 5-1 Kazakhstan, Latvia 2-6 Romania, Romania 1-2 Russia, Latvia 0-2 Kazakhstan, Kazakhstan 1-1 Romania, Russia 6-0 Latvia

	Pld	W	D	L	F	A	Pts
1 Russia	3	3	0	0	13	2	9
2 Romania	3	1	1	1	8	5	4
3 Kazakhstan	3	1	1	1	4	6	4
4 Latvia	3	0	0	3	2	14	0

Group 4
27-30/03/13 Águilas

Croatia 7-0 Sweden, Spain 5-1 FYROM, FYROM 2-3 Croatia, Spain 13-0 Sweden, Sweden 2-4 FYROM, Croatia 0-10 Spain

	Pld	W	D	L	F	A	Pts
1 Spain	3	3	0	0	28	1	9
2 Croatia	3	2	0	1	10	12	6
3 FYROM	3	1	0	2	7	10	3
4 Sweden	3	0	0	3	2	24	0

Group 5
27-30/03/13 Zrenjanin

Portugal 6-1 Greece, Serbia 2-0 Poland, Poland 2-5 Portugal, Serbia 5-0 Greece, Greece 4-3 Poland, Portugal 2-1 Serbia

	Pld	W	D	L	F	A	Pts
1 Portugal	3	3	0	0	13	4	9
2 Serbia	3	2	0	1	8	2	6
3 Greece	3	1	0	2	5	14	3
4 Poland	3	0	0	3	5	11	0

Group 6
27-30/03/13 Rotterdam

Czech Republic 4-1 Georgia, Netherlands 2-1 Belarus, Belarus 3-4 Czech Republic, Netherlands 7-3 Georgia, Georgia 5-4 Belarus, Czech Republic 5-1 Netherlands

	Pld	W	D	L	F	A	Pts
1 Czech Republic	3	3	0	0	13	5	9
2 Netherlands	3	2	0	1	10	9	6
3 Georgia	3	1	0	2	9	15	3
4 Belarus	3	0	0	3	8	11	0

Group 7
27-30/03/13 Erzurum

Turkey 3-5 Slovenia, Ukraine 7-0 England, Turkey 4-3 England, Slovenia 8-3 Ukraine, England 2-5 Slovenia, Ukraine 4-2 Turkey

	Pld	W	D	L	F	A	Pts
1 Slovenia	3	3	0	0	18	8	9
2 Ukraine	3	2	0	1	14	10	6
3 Turkey	3	1	0	2	9	12	3
4 England	3	0	0	3	5	16	0

Play-off draw

17 & 24/09/13

**Ukraine v Hungary
Romania v Serbia
Bosnia & Herzegovina v Netherlands
Slovakia v Croatia**

THE EUROPEAN FOOTBALL YEARBOOK 20¹³/₁₄

TOP 100 PLAYERS

Welcome to the Top 100 Players chapter.

This popular and much talked-about feature of the European Football Yearbook contains profiles of the 100 footballers who, in the considered opinion of the Yearbook's editorial think tank, particularly distinguished themselves with their achievements in 2012/13.

Some of the inclusions are obvious, others less so, but we feel that the representation is broad and fair. Should you agree or disagree with our selection, by all means send an email to the address below and let us have your thoughts.

On the facing page is an alphabetical list of all the chosen players together with their club(s) and country. The 100 profiles – from Akinfeev to Zabaleta – run through to page 156, each of them containing a photograph and a brief narrative, plus essential career details and the vital statistics from 2012/13.

Please note that all data is up to date as of 1 August 2013.

Enjoy.

Mike Hammond
General Editor
mike.hammond@uefa.ch

Igor Akinfeev (PFC CSKA Moskva, Russia)
David Alaba (FC Bayern München, Austria)
Jozy Altidore (AZ Alkmaar, United States)
Pierre-Emerick Aubameyang (AS Saint-Étienne, Gabon)
Carlos Bacca (Club Brugge KV, Colombia)
Leighton Baines (Everton FC, England)
Gareth Bale (Tottenham Hotspur FC, Wales)
Andrea Barzagli (Juventus, Italy)
Christian Benteke (Aston Villa FC, Belgium)
Lucas Biglia (RSC Anderlecht, Argentina)
Jakub Błaszczykowski (Borussia Dortmund, Poland)
Leonardo Bonucci (Juventus, Italy)
Wilfried Bony (Vitesse, Ivory Coast)
Borja Valero (ACF Fiorentina, Spain)
Alexandru Bourceanu (FC Steaua Bucureşti, Romania)
Gianluigi Buffon (Juventus, Italy)
Burak Yılmaz (Galatasaray AŞ, Turkey)
Óscar Cardozo (SL Benfica, Paraguay)
Michael Carrick (Manchester United FC, England)
Edinson Cavani (SSC Napoli, Uruguay)
Cleiton Xavier (FC Metalist Kharkiv, Brazil)
Andreas Cornelius (FC Kobenhavn, Denmark)
Thibaut Courtois (Club Atlético de Madrid, Belgium)
Cristiano Ronaldo (Real Madrid CF, Portugal)
Dante (FC Bayern München, Brazil)
David de Gea (Manchester United FC, Spain)
Siem de Jong (AFC Ajax, Netherlands)
Antonio Di Natale (Udinese Calcio, Italy)
Rafik Djebbour (Olympiacos FC, Greece)
Julian Draxler (FC Schalke 04, Germany)
Stephan El Shaarawy (AC Milan, Italy)
Christian Eriksen (AFC Ajax, Denmark)
Radamel Falcao (Club Atlético de Madrid, Colombia)
Rio Ferdinand (Manchester United FC, England)
Fernandinho (FC Shakhtar Donetsk, Brazil)
Nicolás Gaitán (SL Benfica, Argentina)
Mario Götze (Borussia Dortmund, Germany)
İlkay Gündoğan (Borussia Dortmund, Germany)
Marek Hamšík (SSC Napoli, Slovakia)
Samir Handanovič (FC Internazionale Milano, Slovenia)
Eden Hazard (Chelsea FC, Belgium)
Pavel Horváth (FC Viktoria Plzeň, Czech Republic)
Philipp Hosiner (FC Admira Wacker Mödling/FK Austria Wien, Austria)
Mats Hummels (Borussia Dortmund, Germany)
Zlatan Ibrahimović (Paris Saint-Germain FC, Sweden)
Sergei Ignashevich (PFC CSKA Moskva, Russia)
Saša Ilić (FK Partizan, Serbia)
Andrés Iniesta (FC Barcelona, Spain)
Isco (Málaga CF, Spain)
Javi Martínez (FC Bayern München, Spain)
João Moutinho (FC Porto, Portugal)
Jordi Alba (FC Barcelona, Spain)
Stevan Jovetić (ACF Fiorentina, Montenegro)
Stefan Kiessling (Bayer 04 Leverkusen, Germany)
Yevhen Konoplyanka (FC Dnipro Dnipropetrovsk, Ukraine)
Philipp Lahm (FC Bayern München, Germany)

Erik Lamela (AS Roma, Argentina)
Frank Lampard (Chelsea FC, England)
Robert Lewandowski (Borussia Dortmund, Poland)
Mario Mandžukić (FC Bayern München, Croatia)
Eliaquim Mangala (FC Porto, France)
Federico Marchetti (S.S. Lazio, Italy)
Jackson Martínez (FC Porto, Colombia)
Juan Mata (Chelsea FC, Spain)
Blaise Matuidi (Paris Saint-Germain FC, France)
Lionel Messi (FC Barcelona, Argentina)
Michu (Swansea City AFC, Spain)
Henrikh Mkhitaryan (FC Shakhtar Donetsk, Armenia)
Thomas Müller (FC Bayern München, Germany)
Fernando Muslera (Galatasaray AŞ, Uruguay)
Álvaro Negredo (Sevilla FC, Spain)
Manuel Neuer (FC Bayern München, Germany)
Mesut Özil (Real Madrid CF, Germany)
Graziano Pellè (Feyenoord, Italy)
Andrea Pirlo (Juventus, Italy)
Marco Reus (Borussia Dortmund, Germany)
Franck Ribéry (FC Bayern München, France)
Arjen Robben (FC Bayern München, Netherlands)
Raul Rusescu (FC Steaua Bucureşti, Romania)
Sammir (GNK Dinamo Zagreb, Croatia)
Santi Cazorla (Arsenal FC, Spain)
Bastian Schweinsteiger (FC Bayern München, Germany)
Selçuk İnan (Galatasaray AŞ, Turkey)
Sergio Ramos (Real Madrid CF, Spain)
Roberto Soldado (Valencia CF, Spain)
Valentin Stocker (FC Basel 1893, Switzerland)
Marco Streller (FC Basel 1893, Switzerland)
Luis Suárez (Liverpool FC, Uruguay)
Neven Subotić (Borussia Dortmund, Serbia)
Thiago Silva (Paris Saint-Germain FC, Brazil)
Mathieu Valbuena (Olympique de Marseille, France)
Robin van Persie (Manchester United FC, Netherlands)
Raphaël Varane (Real Madrid CF, France)
Kenneth Vermeer (AFC Ajax, Netherlands)
Jan Vertonghen (Tottenham Hotspur FC, Belgium)
Arturo Vidal (Juventus, Chile)
Roman Weidenfeller (Borussia Dortmund, Germany)
Pontus Wernbloom (PFC CSKA Moskva, Sweden)
Willian (FC Shakhtar Donetsk/FC Anji Makhachkala, Brazil)
Pablo Zabaleta (Manchester City FC, Argentina)

NB Clubs indicated are those the players belonged to in the 2012/13 season.

Key to competitions: WCF = FIFA World Cup final tournament; WCQ = FIFA World Cup qualifying round; ECF = UEFA EURO final tournament; ECQ = UEFA EURO qualifying round; CC = FIFA Confederations Cup; CA = Copa América; ANF = Africa Cup of Nations final tournament; ANQ = Africa Cup of Nations qualifying round; CGC = CONCACAF Gold Cup

Igor Akinfeev
Goalkeeper

Height 184cm
Born 08/04/86, Vidnoye, Russia

One of Europe's most consistent goalkeepers since he emerged as a teenager in PFC CSKA Moskva's 2005 UEFA Cup triumph, Akinfeev enjoyed arguably his finest season yet in 2012/13. A defiant last line of defence in CSKA's Russian double-winning side, he was beaten only 28 times in 29 league outings – a feat that earned him the Premier Liga's player of the season prize – and proved equally difficult to score against in the Russian Cup. Restored to the national side by new Russia coach Fabio Capello after sitting out UEFA EURO 2012, he conceded just once in five FIFA World Cup qualifiers.

International career

RUSSIA
Debut 28/04/04 v Norway (a, Oslo, friendly), lost 2-3
Caps 59 **Goals** 0
Major tournaments UEFA EURO 2004; UEFA EURO 2008; UEFA EURO 2012

Club career

Major honours UEFA Cup (2005); Russian Championship (2003, 2005, 2006, 2013); Russian Cup (2005, 2006, 2008, 2009, 2011, 2013)
Clubs 03- PFC CSKA Moskva

2012/13 appearances/goals

Domestic league Russian Premier-Liga 29/-
European UEFA Europa League play-offs 2/-
National team FIFA World Cup 2014 qualifying 5/-; Friendlies 2/-

David Alaba

Left-back/midfielder

Height 180cm
Born 24/06/92, Vienna, Austria

Voted Austrian footballer of the year for the second year running at the end of 2012, Alaba repeatedly proved his worth in the 2014 FIFA World Cup qualifying campaign, scoring in four consecutive matches, including a potentially crucial last-minute equaliser against the Republic of Ireland in Dublin. Deployed in midfield by Austria boss Marcel Koller, he was the left-back of choice in Jupp Heynckes' FC Bayern München side, playing a decisive role in the club's phenomenally successful campaign. Suspended for the 2012 UEFA Champions League final, he played the full 90 minutes in the Wembley victory against Borussia Dortmund.

International career

AUSTRIA
Debut 14/10/09 v France (a, Paris, WCQ), lost 1-3
First goal 16/10/12 v Kazakhstan (h, Vienna, WCQ), won 4-0
Caps 25 **Goals** 4

Club career

Major honours UEFA Champions League (2013); German Championship (2010, 2013); German Cup (2010, 2013)
Clubs 09- FC Bayern München (GER)

2012/13 appearances/goals

Domestic league German Bundesliga 22(1)/3
European UEFA Champions League 9(2)/2
National team FIFA World Cup 2014 qualifying 4/4; Friendlies 2/-

Jozy Altidore

Striker

Height 185cm
Born 06/11/89, Livingston, New Jersey, USA

With 31 domestic goals for AZ Alkmaar in 2012/13, Altidore scored more in one season for a top-flight European club than any other American player in history. The pacy, muscular forward struck 23 times in the Eredivisie to save his club from a potential relegation battle. His tally included three hat-tricks, the third of them, in a 6-0 win against FC Utrecht, taking him just nine minutes. He was the top scorer in the Dutch Cup with eight, completing his haul with the winner in the final against PSV Eindhoven. A man in demand, the 23-year-old joined Sunderland AFC on a four-year contract in July.

International career

UNITED STATES
Debut 17/11/07 v South Africa (a, Johannesburg, friendly), won 1-0
First goal 06/02/08 v Mexico (h, Houston, friendly), drew 2-2
Caps 60 **Goals** 17
Major tournaments FIFA Confederations Cup 2009, FIFA World Cup 2010

Club career

Major honours Dutch Cup (2013)
Clubs 06-08 New York Red Bulls; 08-11 Villarreal CF (ESP); 09 Xerez CD (ESP) (loan); 09-10 Hull City AFC (ENG) (loan); 11 Bursaspor (TUR) (loan); 11-13 AZ Alkmaar (NED); 13- Sunderland AFC (ENG)

2012/13 appearances/goals

Domestic league Dutch Eredivisie 33/23
European UEFA Europa League play-offs 2/-
National team FIFA World Cup 2014 qualifying 7(1)/3; Friendlies 3/1

Pierre-Emerick Aubameyang

Striker

Height 187cm
Born 18/06/89, Laval, France

An effervescent, all-action striker, Aubameyang was voted the best African player in Ligue 1 at the end of a 2012/13 campaign in which he scored 19 league goals for AS Saint-Étienne, including the winner away to Paris Saint-Germain FC, and helped Les Verts to their first major silverware in 32 years – in the French League Cup. The Gabon international was a talismanic figure in Christophe Galtier's side, but his second season at the Stade Geoffroy-Guichard turned out to be his last as the 24-year-old left in the summer to join German Bundesliga heavyweights Borussia Dortmund on a five-year contract.

International career

GABON
Debut 28/03/09 v Morocco (a, Casablanca, WCQ), won 2-1
First goal 28/03/09 v Morocco (a, Casablanca, WCQ), won 2-1
Caps 33 **Goals** 12
Major tournaments Africa Cup of Nations 2010; Africa Cup of Nations 2012

Club career

Major honours French League Cup (2013)
Clubs 08-11 AC Milan (ITA); 08-09 Dijon FCO (FRA) (loan); 09-10 LOSC Lille (FRA) (loan); 10-11 AS Monaco FC (FRA) (loan); 11-13 AS Saint-Étienne (FRA); 13- Borussia Dortmund (GER)

2012/13 appearances/goals

Domestic league French Ligue 1 36(1)/19
National team FIFA World Cup 2014 qualifying 3/3; Africa Cup of Nations 2013 qualifying 2/-

Carlos Bacca

Striker

Height 181cm
Born 08/09/86, Barranquilla, Colombia

RSC Anderlecht won the 2012/13 Belgian league title, but it was third-placed Club Brugge KV who supplied the official player of the season in Bacca, a Colombian striker who also topped the goal charts with 25 goals. Underused the previous season following his January arrival from Atletico Junior, he proved especially prolific at the start of the campaign, during Georgos Leekens' short spell as coach, finding the target in eight successive matches and reaching double figures before the end of October. His consistent marksmanship inevitably drew interest from elsewhere, and in July he left Belgium for southern Spain, joining Sevilla FC.

International career

COLOMBIA
Debut 11/08/10 v Bolivia (a, La Paz, friendly), drew 1-1
First goal 11/08/10 v Bolivia (a, La Paz, friendly), drew 1-1
Caps 4 **Goals** 2

Club career

Clubs 07-12 Atlético Junior; 07 & 08 Barranquilla FC (loan); 07-08 AC Minervén FC; 12-13 Club Brugge KV (BEL); 13- Sevilla FC (ESP)

2012/13 appearances/goals

Domestic league Belgian Pro League (inc play-offs) 33(2)/25
European UEFA Europa League 5/1; UEFA Europa League play-offs 1(1)/2
National team FIFA World Cup 2014 qualifying (1)/-; Friendlies 1(1)/1

Leighton Baines

Left-back

Height 170cm
Born 11/12/84, Kirkby, England

The only outfield player in the Premier League to start and finish all 38 games in 2012/13, Baines was also voted into the division's official team of the season for the second year in a row. The mop-haired 28-year-old earned the recognition above all for his attacking prowess, his pinpoint crosses from the left as potent a weapon for Everton FC as his immaculate free-kicks. Although his international career has been stymied by the presence of Ashley Cole, Baines managed nine outings in 2012/13 and also scored his first England goal – albeit with a heavy deflection – in the opening FIFA World Cup qualifier away to Moldova.

International career

ENGLAND
Debut 03/03/10 v Egypt (h, London, friendly), won 3-1
First goal 07/09/12 v Moldova (a, Chisinau, WCQ), won 5-0
Caps 17 **Goals** 1
Major tournaments UEFA EURO 2012

Club career

Clubs 02-07 Wigan Athletic FC; 07- Everton FC

2012/13 appearances/goals

Domestic league English Premier League 38/5
National team FIFA World Cup 2014 qualifying 4/1; Friendlies 3(2)/-

Gareth Bale

Attacking midfielder

Height 183cm
Born 16/07/89, Cardiff, Wales

Voted the best player in England both by his fellow professionals and the media, Bale's form for Tottenham Hotspur FC and Wales was so relentlessly brilliant that he was repeatedly mentioned in the same breath as Lionel Messi and Cristiano Ronaldo. The young jet-heeled left-footer enjoyed the more advanced attacking role granted to him at Spurs by André Villas-Boas and he responded with a career-best haul of 21 Premier League goals. Many ranked as goal-of-the-season candidates – as did his stunning last-minute strike that brought Wales a 2-1 win against Scotland in Cardiff, one of five international goals he scored in 2012/13.

International career

WALES
Debut 27/05/06 v Trinidad & Tobago (n, Graz, friendly), won 2-1
First goal 07/10/06 v Slovakia (h, Cardiff, ECQ), lost 1-5
Caps 41 **Goals** 11

Club career

Clubs 06-07 Southampton FC (ENG); 07- Tottenham Hotspur FC (ENG)

2012/13 appearances/goals

Domestic league English Premier League 33/21
European UEFA Europa League 7/3
National team FIFA World Cup 2014 qualifying 6/4; Friendlies 2/1

Andrea Barzagli
Centre-back

Height 186cm
Born 08/05/81, Fiesole, Italy

At 32, Barzagli is now an established figure in central defence for both Juventus and Italy. A peripheral member of the Azzurri's 2006 FIFA World Cup-winning squad, he is set to travel to the 2014 tournament as a stalwart of Cesare Prandelli's side, having played every minute of the team's first six qualifiers and also started their three most important games at the FIFA Confederations Cup. It was a busy season too at club level for the powerful Tuscan, who racked up 45 appearances for Juve, helping the Bianconeri to a successful Serie A title defence and a quarter-final place in the UEFA Champions League.

International career

ITALY
Major honours FIFA World Cup (2006)
Debut 17/11/04 v Finland (h, Messina, friendly), won 1-0
Caps 45 **Goals** 0
Major tournaments FIFA World Cup 2006; UEFA EURO 2008; UEFA EURO 2012; FIFA Confederations Cup 2013

Club career

Major honours German Championship (2009); Italian Championship (2012, 2013)
Clubs 98-01 Rondinella Calcio; 00 AC Pistoiese (loan); 01-03 Piacenza Calcio; 01-03 Ascoli Calcio (loan); 03-04 AC Chievo Verona; 04-08 US Città di Palermo; 08-11 VfL Wolfsburg (GER); 11- Juventus

2012/13 appearances/goals

Domestic league Italian Serie A 34/-
European UEFA Champions League 9/-
National team FIFA World Cup 2014 qualifying 6/-; FIFA Confederations Cup 2013 3/-; Friendlies 3/-

Christian Benteke
Striker

Height 190cm
Born 03/12/90, Kinshasha, DR Congo

Aston Villa FC would almost certainly have been relegated from the Premier League had it not been for the excellence up front of their new recruit from KRC Genk. Benteke was preferred to England international Darren Bent as the team's sole central striker in manager Paul Lambert's youthful side, and he repaid that faith by scoring 19 league goals, including a superb hat-trick in a crucial 6-1 home win over fellow strugglers Sunderland AFC at the end of April. The abrasive, powerful 22-year-old also established himself as the first-choice centre-forward for Belgium, scoring six international goals in 2012/13.

International career

BELGIUM
Debut 19/05/10 v Bulgaria (h, Brussels, friendly), won 2-1
First goal 15/08/12 v Netherlands (h, Brussels, friendly), won 4-2
Caps 14 **Goals** 6

Club career

Major honours Belgian Championship (2009)
Clubs 07-09 KRC Genk; 09-11 R. Standard de Liège; 09-10 KV Kortrijk (loan); 10-11 KV Mechelen (loan); 11-12 KRC Genk; 12- Aston Villa FC (ENG)

2012/13 appearances/goals

Domestic league English Premier League 32(2)/19
National team FIFA World Cup 2014 qualifying 6/2; Friendlies 3(1)/4

Lucas Biglia
Midfielder

Height 178cm
Born 30/01/86, Mercedes, Argentina

There were several prominent individual contributions to RSC Anderlecht's 2012/13 Belgian championship success. Goalkeeper Silvio Proto and top scorer Dieumerci Mbokani both had a major impact, but it was the team's long-serving Argentinian playmaker who arguably did most to ensure a successful title defence. Biglia missed only three of the 40 matches and scored the all-important equaliser in the last-day decider against SV Zulte Waregem, after which he was afforded a special lap of honour by the Anderlecht fans. It had already been announced that his seven-year spell in Brussels would end with that game, and in July he signed for S.S. Lazio.

International career

ARGENTINA
Debut 09/02/11 v Portugal (n, Geneva, friendly), won 2-1
Caps 10 **Goals** 0
Major tournaments Copa América 2011

Club career

Major honours Belgian Championship (2007, 2010, 2012, 2013)
Clubs 04-05 Argentinos Juniors; 05-06 CA Independiente; 06-13 RSC Anderlecht (BEL); 13- S.S. Lazio (ITA)

2012/13 appearances/goals

Domestic league Belgian Pro League 37/5
European UEFA Champions League 6/-; UEFA Champions League qualifying/play-offs 4/-
National team FIFA World Cup 2014 qualifying 1(2)/-; Friendlies 1/-

Jakub Błaszczykowski

Midfielder

Height 175cm
Born 14/12/85, Truskolasy, Poland

Although Borussia Dortmund won no trophies in 2012/13, having to bow to the supremacy of FC Bayern München in every competition they entered, the season was a success on an individual level for right-sided midfielder Błaszczykowski, who was rewarded with a new five-year contract in the summer. Despite injury problems he scored 14 goals in all competitions – twice as many as in the 2011/12 double-winning campaign and just one fewer than he had amassed in all of his previous five seasons at the club put together. The captain of Poland, he also struck three times in FIFA World Cup qualifying.

International career

POLAND
Debut 28/3/06 v Saudi Arabia (a, Riyadh, friendly), won 2-1
First goal 22/8/07 v Russia (a, Moscow, friendly), drew 2-2
Caps 61 **Goals** 13
Major tournaments UEFA EURO 2012

Club career

Major honours Polish Championship (2005); German Championship (2011, 2012); German Cup (2012)
Clubs 03-04 KS Częstochowa; 05-07 Wisła Kraków; 07- Borussia Dortmund (GER)

2012/13 appearances/goals

Domestic league German Bundesliga 23(4)/11
European UEFA Champions League 8(2)/1
National team FIFA World Cup 2014 qualifying 4/3; Friendlies 2(1)/-

Leonardo Bonucci

Centre-back

Height 190cm
Born 01/05/87, Viterbo, Italy

The fall guy for Italy at the 2013 FIFA Confederations Cup when he missed the decisive penalty in the semi-final shoot-out against Spain, Bonucci would clearly have wished for a happier conclusion to a season in which he continued to further his reputation as one of the classiest defenders in Europe. His third season with Juventus brought him a second successive Serie A winner's medal, and he also enjoyed an excellent debut campaign in the UEFA Champions League, starting all ten of Juve's matches and scoring an important goal on his home debut in the competition against FC Shakhtar Donetsk.

International career

ITALY
Debut 03/03/10 v Cameroon (n, Monaco, friendly), drew 0-0
First goal 03/06/10 v Mexico (n, Brussels, friendly), lost 1-2
Caps 31 **Goals** 2
Major tournaments FIFA World Cup 2010; UEFA EURO 2012; FIFA Confederations Cup 2013

Club career

Major honours Italian Championship (2006, 2012, 2013)
Clubs 05-07 FC Internazionale Milano; 07-09 FC Treviso; 09 AC Pisa (loan); 09-10 AS Bari; 10- Juventus

2012/13 appearances/goals

Domestic league Italian Serie A 33/-
European UEFA Champions League 10/1
National team FIFA World Cup 2014 qualifying 5/-; FIFA Confederations Cup 2013 2(1)/-; Friendlies 2(1)/-

Wilfried Bony

Striker

Height 182cm
Born 10/12/88, Bingerville, Ivory Coast

The goals flowed like never before for the Ivorian striker in 2012/13 as he scooped the Dutch Eredivisie top scorer crown with 31 strikes for Vitesse. Bony found the net consistently all season, scoring 16 times before the winter break and 15 after his return from the Africa Cup of Nations in South Africa. Autumn highlights included a double in the Arnhem club's 2-0 victory at AFC Ajax and the winner at PSV Eindhoven. In the spring, following his return from international duty, he registered in nine successive matches. Relentlessly pursued by several clubs, he joined Swansea City AFC for a club record fee in July.

International career

IVORY COAST
Debut 09/10/10 v Burundi (a, Bujumbura, ANQ), won 1-0
First goal 05/06/11 v Benin (a, Cotonou, ANQ), won 6-2
Caps 20 **Goals** 8
Major tournaments Africa Cup of Nations 2012; Africa Cup of Nations 2013

Club career

Major honours Czech Championship (2010); Ivory Coast Cup (2006)
Clubs 06-08 Issia Wazi FC; 07-08 AC Sparta Praha B (CZE) (loan); 08-11 AC Sparta Praha (CZE); 11-13 Vitesse (NED); 13- Swansea City AFC (WAL)

2012/13 appearances/goals

Domestic league Dutch Eredivisie 30/31
European UEFA Europa League qualifying 4/2
National team FIFA World Cup 2014 qualifying 2(1)/3; Africa Cup of Nations 2013 1(1)/1; Friendlies 1/-

Borja Valero
Midfielder

Height 175cm
Born 12/01/85, Madrid, Spain

ACF Fiorentina came within a whisker of qualifying for the 2013/14 UEFA Champions League play-offs. Instead they had to settle for a place in the equivalent round of the UEFA Europa League after finishing fourth in Serie A. That was a significant improvement on the previous season, and pivotal to the club's resurgence was the outstanding form throughout the campaign of midfield fulcrum Valero. Newly signed from Villarreal CF after their shock relegation, the Spanish pass master took no time at all to endear himself to the Viola fans, quickly establishing himself as a key man in Vincenzo Montella's progressive, entertaining side.

International career
SPAIN
Debut 04/06/11 v United States (a, Boston, friendly), won 4-0
Caps 1 **Goals** 0

Club career
Clubs 05-07 Real Madrid CF B; 07-08 RCD Mallorca; 08-11 West Bromwich Albion FC (ENG); 09-10 RCD Mallorca (loan); 10-11 Villarreal CF (loan); 11-12 Villarreal CF; 12- ACF Fiorentina (ITA)

2012/13 appearances/goals
Domestic league Italian Serie A 37/1

Alexandru Bourceanu
Midfielder

Height 176cm
Born 24/04/85, Galati, Romania

FC Steaua București's captain enjoyed an outstanding campaign on all fronts in 2012/13. Leading the club to their first Romanian championship title for seven years was the obvious highlight, but Bourceanu also made a name for himself internationally – both with Steaua in the UEFA Europa League, where they went from the third qualifying round all the way to the last 16, and with Romania in the 2014 FIFA World Cup qualifying competition, in which he started all six matches. A defensive midfielder with a natural authority, the 28-year-old appears to have the class and composure to succeed in any company.

International career
ROMANIA
Debut 11/02/09 v Croatia (h, Bucharest, friendly), lost 1-2
Caps 20 **Goals** 0

Club career
Major honours Romanian Championship (2013)
Clubs 04-08 FCM Dunărea Galați; 08-09 FC Oțelul Galați; 09-11 FC Politehnica Timișoara; 11- FC Steaua București

2012/13 appearances/goals
Domestic league Romanian Seria I 32/3
European UEFA Europa League 9/-; UEFA Europa League qualifying/play-offs 3/-
National team FIFA World Cup 2014 qualifying 6/-; Friendlies 1(2)/-

Gianluigi Buffon
Goalkeeper

Height 191cm
Born 28/01/78 Carrara, Italy

Buffon's 12th season at Juventus ended with his fourth Scudetto, his first as club captain. He was just as imperious as in the undefeated 2011/12 campaign, conceding 19 goals in 32 outings. The Italian national side, like Juve, are just as indebted to the 35-year-old's enduring talent, as he demonstrated in a vintage display against the Czech Republic in a FIFA World Cup qualifier. With five appearances at the 2013 FIFA Confederations Cup, he lifted his international cap tally to 133 – three behind Italy's record-holder Fabio Cannavaro. Assuming he makes it back to Brazil next summer, the 2014 World Cup will be his tenth international tournament.

International career
ITALY
Major honours FIFA World Cup (2006)
Debut 29/10/97 v Russia (a, Moscow, WCQ), drew 1-1
Caps 133 **Goals** 0
Major tournaments FIFA World Cup 1998; FIFA World Cup 2002; UEFA EURO 2004; FIFA World Cup 2006; UEFA EURO 2008; FIFA Confederations Cup 2009; FIFA World Cup 2010; UEFA EURO 2012; FIFA Confederations Cup 2013

Club career
Major honours UEFA Cup (1999); Italian Championship (2002, 2003, 2012, 2013); Italian Cup (1999)
Clubs 95-01 Parma FC; 01- Juventus

2012/13 appearances/goals
Domestic league Italian Serie A 32/-
European UEFA Champions League 10/-
National team FIFA World Cup 2014 qualifying 5/-; FIFA Confederations Cup 2013 5/-; Friendlies 3/-

Burak Yılmaz

Striker

Height 186cm
Born 15/07/85, Antalya, Turkey

During his first season at Galatasaray AŞ, Burak proved his goalscoring pedigree at European as well as domestic level. Previous visits to the UEFA Champions League with Beşiktaş JK, Fenerbahçe SK and Trabzonspor AŞ had yielded a meagre return, but for his new club he scored eight goals – six in the group stage, including a perfect hat-trick against CFR 1907 Cluj, plus two against FC Schalke 04 in the round of 16. The Turkish international also kept the home fires burning, fuelling Cimbom's Süper Lig triumph with 24 goals and thus retaining the golden boot he had won with 33 for Trabzonspor in 2011/12.

International career

TURKEY
Debut 12/04/06 v Azerbaijan (a, Baku, friendly), drew 1-1
First goal 03/06/11 v Belgium (a, Brussels, ECQ), drew 1-1
Caps 26 **Goals** 8

Club career

Major honours Turkish Championship (2013); Turkish Cup (2007, 2010)
Clubs 02-06 Antalyaspor; 06-08 Beşiktaş JK; 08 Manisaspor; 08-10 Fenerbahçe SK; 09-10 Eskişehirspor (loan); 10-12 Trabzonspor AŞ; 12- Galatasaray AŞ

2012/13 appearances/goals

Domestic league Turkish Süper Lig 27(3)/24
European UEFA Champions League 8(1)/8
National team FIFA World Cup 2014 qualifying 3(1)/2; Friendlies 2(2)/-

Óscar Cardozo

Striker

Height 194cm
Born 20/05/83, Juan Eulogio Estigarribia, Paraguay

SL Benfica challenged strongly for three major trophies in 2012/13 yet ended up empty-handed. The dismay of Cardozo, the club's long-serving centre-forward, was especially heartfelt in the UEFA Europa League after he had scored seven goals in the competition, including the double that eliminated Fenerbahçe SK in the semi-finals and the equaliser in the final against Chelsea FC. The towering left-footer was also on target 16 times in the Portuguese Liga and six in the Portuguese Cup, his second-half substitution in the final defeat by Vitória SC engendering much debate as Benfica had been 1-0 up when he was taken off.

International career

PARAGUAY
Debut 07/10/06 v Australia (a, Brisbane, friendly), drew 1-1
First goal 05/06/07 v Mexico (a, Mexico City, friendly), won 1-0
Caps 47 **Goals** 9
Major tournaments Copa América 2007; FIFA World Cup 2010

Club career

Major honours Portuguese Championship (2010)
Clubs 05 3 de Febrero; 05-06 Club Nacional; 06-07 Newell's Old Boys (ARG); 07- SL Benfica (POR)

2012/13 appearances/goals

Domestic league Portuguese Liga 20(7)/16
European UEFA Champions League 1(4)/2, UEFA Europa League 7(2)/7
National team FIFA World Cup 2014 qualifying 3(1)/-; Friendlies 1/1

Michael Carrick

Midfielder

Height 188cm
Born 28/07/81, Wallsend, England

Carrick's fifth Premier League winner's medal was accompanied by widespread acclaim of the kind the doughty midfielder had never previously experienced during his seven seasons at Manchester United FC. Nominated on the PFA six-man player of the year shortlist and voted by his Old Trafford peers as United's player of the season, he warranted the recognition for his outstanding contribution to the club's record-extending 20th English title. The team's go-to man in central midfield, his accurate and probing passes were a feature of United's play throughout the campaign, and he was also called up regularly for international duty with England.

International career

ENGLAND
Debut 25/05/01 v Mexico (h, Derby, friendly), won 4-0
Caps 29 **Goals** 0
Major tournaments FIFA World Cup 2006; FIFA World Cup 2010

Club career

Major honours UEFA Champions League (2008); FIFA Club World Cup (2008); English Premier League (2007, 2008, 2009, 2011, 2013); English League Cup (2010)
Clubs 98-04 West Ham United FC; 99 Swindon Town FC (loan); 00 Birmingham City FC (loan); 04-06 Tottenham Hotspur FC; 06- Manchester United FC

2012/13 appearances/goals

Domestic league English Premier League 34(2)/1
European UEFA Champions League 5/1
National team FIFA World Cup 2014 qualifying 3(1)/-; Friendlies 3/-

Edinson Cavani
Striker

Height 188cm
Born 14/02/87, Salto, Uruguay

Another goal-laden season at SSC Napoli, with 29 in Serie A, two in the Coppa Italia and seven in Europe, lifted Cavani's cumulative tally for the club past the hundred mark – 104 in 138 matches, to be precise – and confirmed the 26-year-old Uruguayan as one of the world's foremost strikers. Hat-tricks against S.S. Lazio, AS Roma and FC Internazionale Milano helped him to top the Serie A capocannonieri charts, and he also broke new ground with four goals in a UEFA Europa League match against FC Dnipro Dnipropetrovsk. A French record fee was paid by Paris Saint-Germain FC in the summer to acquire his services.

International career

URUGUAY
Major honours *Copa América (2011)*
Debut 06/02/08 v Colombia (h, Montevideo, friendly), drew 2-2
First goal 06/02/08 v Colombia (h, Montevideo, friendly), drew 2-2
Caps 54 **Goals** 17
Major tournaments FIFA World Cup 2010; Copa América 2011; FIFA Confederations Cup 2013

Club career

Major honours *Uruguayan Championship (2006 apertura); Italian Cup (2012)*
Clubs 06-07 Danubio FC; 07-10 US Città di Palermo (ITA); 10-13 SSC Napoli (ITA); 13- Paris Saint-Germain FC (FRA)

2012/13 appearances/goals

Domestic league Italian Serie A 33(1)/29
European UEFA Europa League 4(3)/7
National team FIFA World Cup 2014 qualifying 5(2)/2; FIFA Confederations Cup 2013 4/3; Friendlies 3/1

Cleiton Xavier
Attacking midfielder

Height 178cm
Born 23/03/83, Sao Jose de Tapera, Brazil

FC Metalist Kharkiv ended a run of six successive third-place finishes in the Ukrainian Premier League by claiming the runners-up spot in 2012/13 and thus qualifying for a first shot at the UEFA Champions League. Central to Metalist's successful campaign were the 15 goals – plus the subtle passing, skilful dribbling and set-piece expertise – of their top-scoring Brazilian. Still uncapped by his country at the end of the season, the 30-year-old must have felt he could do no more to warrant a first international call-up. He also sparkled in the UEFA Europa League, scoring in four successive group games – all victories – for Myron Markevych's side.

International career

BRAZIL
Uncapped

Club career

Clubs 01-02 CS Alagoano; 02-08 SC Internacional; 05 Sport Recife (loan); 05 Brasiliense FC (loan); 06 SE Gama (loan); 06 Marília FC (loan); 07-08 Figueirense FC (loan); 09-10 SE Palmeiras; 10- FC Metalist Kharkiv (UKR)

2012/13 appearances/goals

Domestic league Ukrainian Premier League 28(1)/15
European UEFA Europa League 7/4; UEFA Europa League play-offs 2/1

Andreas Cornelius
Striker

Height 193cm
Born 16/03/93, Copenhagen, Denmark

Largely unknown in the summer of 2012, Cornelius could not have foreseen in his wildest dreams the progress he would make during his first full campaign as a professional. By the end of it he was not only a Danish champion with FC København but also the Superliga's leading scorer, on 18 goals, and – with Nicklas Bendtner injured – the attacking focal point of the Danish national side. Robust, resourceful, strong in the air and two-footed, the 20-year-old ticks all the boxes for a traditional centre-forward. English Premier League newcomers Cardiff City FC certainly saw it that way as they snapped him up for a club-record fee in June.

International career

DENMARK
Debut 08/09/12 v Czech Republic (h, Copenhagen, WCQ), drew 0-0
First goal 22/03/13 v Czech Republic (a, Olomouc, WCQ), won 3-0
Caps 7 **Goals** 1

Club career

Major honours *Danish Superliga (2013)*
Clubs 12-13 FC København; 13- Cardiff City FC (WAL)

2012/13 appearances/goals

Domestic league Danish Superliga 29(3)/18
European UEFA Champions League qualifying/play-offs 1(3)/-; UEFA Europa League 5(1)/1
National team FIFA World Cup 2014 qualifying 3(2)/1; Friendlies 2/-

Thibaut Courtois

Goalkeeper

Height 198cm
Born 11/05/92, Bree, Belgium

Courtois's second season on loan at Club Atlético de Madrid from Chelsea FC was every bit as impressive as his first. It began with a 4-1 victory over his parent club in the UEFA Super Cup and ended with a man-of-the-match display against Real Madrid CF in the final of the Copa del Rey which Atlético won 2-1 to defeat their city rivals for the first time since 1999. In between, the giant keeper excelled in the Spanish Liga, winning the prestigious Zamora trophy with 20 goals conceded in 37 outings. The 21-year-old was even more resilient for Belgium, beaten only twice in seven FIFA World Cup qualifiers.

International career

BELGIUM
Debut 15/11/11 v France (a, Paris, friendly), drew 0-0
Caps 10 **Goals** 0

Club career

Major honours UEFA Europa League (2012); UEFA Super Cup (2012); Belgian Championship (2011); Spanish Cup (2013)
Clubs 09-11 KRC Genk; 11- Chelsea FC (ENG); 11- Club Atlético de Madrid (ESP) (loan)

2012/13 appearances/goals

Domestic league Spanish Liga 37/-
National team FIFA World Cup 2014 qualifying 7/-; Friendlies 1/-

Cristiano Ronaldo

Striker

Height 184cm
Born 05/02/85, Funchal, Madeira, Portugal

The only trophy Cristiano Ronaldo won with Real Madrid CF in 2012/13 was the Spanish Super Cup, but it was another season of phenomenal personal achievement for the Portuguese superstar. He became the fastest player ever to reach 200 goals for Madrid, doing so on just his 197th appearance, and ended the season with 34 strikes in the Liga – as in 2011/12, second only to FC Barcelona's Lionel Messi – plus a competition-best 12 in the UEFA Champions League, including one in each leg of the round of 16 tie against former club Manchester United FC. He also won his 100th cap for Portugal, at just 27 years of age.

International career

PORTUGAL
Debut 20/08/03 v Kazakhstan (h, Chaves, friendly), won 1-0
First goal 12/06/04 v Greece (h, Porto, ECF), lost 1-2
Caps 104 **Goals** 39
Major tournaments UEFA EURO 2004; FIFA World Cup 2006; UEFA EURO 2008; FIFA World Cup 2010; UEFA EURO 2012

Club career

Major honours UEFA Champions League (2008); FIFA Club World Cup (2008); English Premier League (2007, 2008, 2009); Spanish Championship (2012); English FA Cup (2004); Spanish Cup (2011); English League Cup (2006, 2009); Clubs 95-03 Sporting Clube de Portugal 02-03 Manchester United FC (ENG); 09- Real Madrid CF (ESP)

2012/13 appearances/goals

Domestic league Spanish Liga 30(4)/34
European UEFA Champions League 12/12
National team FIFA World Cup 2014 qualifying 6/1; Friendlies 3/3

Dante

Centre-back

Height 188cm
Born 18/10/83, Salvador, Brazil

Almost a decade after starting out in European football with French club LOSC Lille, Brazilian centre-back Dante finally made it into the big time, his first season at FC Bayern München ending with an unprecedented treble of Bundesliga, DFB-Pokal and UEFA Champions League. The big-haired left-footer was not at his best against Borussia Dortmund at Wembley, conceding the penalty that put Bayern's opponents back in the game, but over the campaign as a whole there were few more consistent performers in Jupp Heynckes' all-conquering team. He was rewarded with his first cap for Brazil, aged 29, and appeared at the 2013 FIFA Confederations Cup.

International career

BRAZIL
Major honours FIFA Confederations Cup (2013)
Debut 06/02/13 v England (a, London, friendly), lost 1-2
First goal 22/06/13 v Italy (h, Salvador, CC), won 4-2
Caps 5 **Goals** 1
Major tournaments FIFA Confederations Cup 2013

Club career

Major honours UEFA Champions League (2013); Belgian Championship (2008); German Championship (2013); German Cup (2013)
Clubs 02-04 EC Juventude; 04-06 LOSC Lille (FRA); 06-07 R. Charleroi SC (BEL); 07-09 R. Standard de Liège (BEL); 09-12 VfL Borussia Mönchengladbach (GER); 12- FC Bayern München (GER)

2012/13 appearances/goals

Domestic league German Bundesliga 29/1
European UEFA Champions League 11(1)/-
National team FIFA Confederations Cup 2013 (2)/1; Friendlies 3/-

David de Gea
Goalkeeper

Height 190cm
Born 07/11/90, Madrid, Spain

There was widespread concern during his first season as a Manchester United FC player that De Gea might not be up to the task of replacing Edwin van der Sar, but the young Spanish goalkeeper came on in leaps and bounds during his second campaign at Old Trafford, his acrobatic saves thwarting United's opponents time and again as Sir Alex Ferguson's team regained the Premier League title. Voted into the league's team of the year by his fellow professionals, the 22-year-old carried his fine club form into the UEFA European Under-21 Championship finals in Israel, where he won the title for the second time with Spain.

International career

SPAIN
Uncapped

Club career

Major honours *UEFA Europa League (2010); UEFA Super Cup (2010); English Premier League (2013)*
Clubs 09-11 Club Atlético de Madrid; 11- Manchester United FC (ENG)

2012/13 appearances/goals

Domestic league English Premier League 28/-
European UEFA Champions League 7/-

Siem de Jong
Attacking midfielder

Height 185cm
Born 28/01/89, Aigle, Switzerland

As his younger brother Luuk left FC Twente for German club VfL Borussia Mönchengladbach, De Jong remained in the Netherlands, at AFC Ajax, and was rewarded for his loyalty with promotion to the position of club captain. It proved a wise move by coach Frank de Boer as the 24-year-old attacking midfielder went on to enjoy another outstanding campaign, starting all 34 Eredivisie matches and finishing as the club's top scorer for the second season running as they completed a hat-trick of Dutch titles. There was more joy to come post-season when he scored his first two goals for the Netherlands in a friendly against Indonesia.

International career

NETHERLANDS
Debut 11/08/10 v Ukraine (a, Donetsk, friendly), drew 1-1
First goal 07/06/13 v Indonesia (a, Jakarta, friendly), won 3-0
Caps 4 **Goals** 2

Club career

Major honours *Dutch Championship (2011, 2012, 2013); Dutch Cup (2010)*
Clubs 07- AFC Ajax

2012/13 appearances/goals

Domestic league Dutch Eredivisie 34/12
European UEFA Champions League 6/3; UEFA Europa League 2/-
National team FIFA World Cup 2014 qualifying (1)/-; Friendlies 1(1)/2

Antonio Di Natale
Striker

Height 177cm
Born 13/10/77, Naples, Italy

For the fourth Serie A campaign in a row Di Natale racked up more than 20 league goals for Udinese Calcio as he moved past the 150-mark for the club. Although his international career ended at UEFA EURO 2012, there was no sign of wear and tear from the 35-year-old at club level. On the contrary, the goals continued to gush forth from the Udinese skipper, and he was at his sharpest in the final weeks when he struck eight in as many games – all victories – to lead the club into fifth place. His final tally of 23 was six fewer than that of Serie A's top marksman Edinson Cavani but seven more than anyone else could manage.

International career

ITALY
Debut 20/11/02 v Turkey (h, Pescara, friendly), drew 1-1
First goal 18/02/04 v Czech Republic (h, Palermo, friendly), drew 2-2
Caps 42 **Goals** 11
Major tournaments UEFA EURO 2008; FIFA World Cup 2010; UEFA EURO 2012

Club career

Clubs 96-04 Empoli FC; 97-98 Iperzola Ponteroncariale (loan); 98 AS Varese 1910 (loan); 98-99 FCE Viareggio (loan); 04- Udinese Calcio

2012/13 appearances/goals

Domestic league Italian Serie A 31(2)/23
European UEFA Champions League play-offs 2/-; UEFA Europa League 3(3)/3

Rafik Djebbour

Striker

Height 185cm
Born 08/03/84, Grenoble, France

Djebbour's eighth season in Greek football turned out to be his best by a distance, particularly in front of goal. With his Algerian international team-mate Djamel Abdoun serving as a more than able accomplice, the 29-year-old striker powered Olympiacos FC to their 40th championship title, registering 20 goals to top the Superleague scoring charts. He reached that total by early March, having moved into double figures in December with a brace in a 2-2 draw against arch-rivals Panathinaikos FC. He also scored twice in the Greek Cup, including the extra time winner in the final against Asteras Tripolis FC that completed Olympiacos's double.

International career

ALGERIA
Debut 15/08/06 v Gabon (n, Aix-en-Provence, friendly), lost 0-2
First goal 06/06/08 v Liberia (h, Blida, WCQ), won 3-0
Caps 32 **Goals** 5
Major tournaments FIFA World Cup 2010

Club career

Major honours Greek Championship (2011, 2012, 2013); Greek Cup (2012, 2013)
Clubs 03-04 AJ Auxerre (FRA); 04-05 RAA La Louvière (BEL); 05 Ethikos Asteras FC (GRE); 06 Atromitos FC (GRE); 07-08 Panionios GSS (GRE); 08-11 AEK Athens FC (GRE); 11- Olympiacos FC (GRE)

2012/13 appearances/goals

Domestic league Greek Superleague 23(2)/20
European UEFA Champions League 3(1)/-; UEFA Europa League 2/-
National team FIFA World Cup 2014 qualifying 2(1)/-; Africa Cup of Nations 2013 qualifying (1)/-; Friendlies 1/-

Julian Draxler

Attacking midfielder

Height 187cm
Born 20/09/93, Gladbeck, Germany

The German national team is not short of young talent as the 2014 FIFA World Cup looms, but Draxler could turn out to be the joker in Joachim Löw's pack as the Nationalmannschaft journey to Brazil in search of their fourth global title. The 19-year-old's special talent was no secret to Bundesliga watchers before the 2012/13 season, but by the end of it, in which he scored ten league goals plus a first at both UEFA Champions League and senior international level, there was no doubt as to his potential. Local rivals Borussia Dortmund were keen to sign him, but he chose to renew his contract with Schalke until 2018.

International career

GERMANY
Debut 28/05/12 v Switzerland (a, Basel, friendly), lost 3-5
First goal 02/06/13 v United States (a, Washington, friendly), lost 3-4
Caps 6 **Goals** 1

Club career

Major honours German Cup (2011)
Clubs 11- FC Schalke 04

2012/13 appearances/goals

Domestic league German Bundesliga 24(6)/10
European UEFA Champions League 5(1)/1
National team FIFA World Cup 2014 qualifying 1(1)/-; Friendlies 2(1)/1

Stephan El Shaarawy

Striker

Height 178cm
Born 27/10/92, Savona, Italy

But for El Shaarawy's glut of goals in the first half of the season, AC Milan's ambitions of finishing in the top three of Serie A would almost certainly have sunk without trace. The mid-season signing of fellow Italian international Mario Balotelli eased the burden of the 20-year-old winger-cum-striker, and he was far less prolific after Christmas, adding just two more goals to the 14 struck during the autumn – when he was the division's leading marksman – but he had already left a lasting impression on the Rossoneri faithful. With his pace and trickery, not to mention his extravagant hairstyle, cult-hero status at San Siro seems assured.

International career

ITALY
Debut 15/08/12 v England (n, Berne, friendly), lost 1-2
First goal 14/11/12 v France (h, Parma, friendly), lost 1-2
Caps 10 **Goals** 1
Major tournaments FIFA Confederations Cup 2013

Club career

Clubs 08-11 Genoa CFC; 10-11 Calcio Padova (loan); 11- AC Milan

2012/13 appearances/goals

Domestic league Italian Serie A 34(3)/16
European UEFA Champions League 6(2)/2
National team FIFA World Cup 2014 qualifying 2(1)/-; FIFA Confederations Cup 2013 1(1)/-; Friendlies 3(2)/1

Christian Eriksen
Midfielder

Height 180cm
Born 14/02/92, Middelfart, Denmark

A disappointing UEFA EURO 2012 with Denmark left no scars on Eriksen as he won a third successive Dutch title with AFC Ajax. His influence in central midfield was just as profound as it had been in the previous two campaigns, but he improved his goal output in 2012/13, scoring ten times in the Eredivisie and opening his UEFA Champions League account in the 3-1 home win over Manchester City FC. The 21-year-old started all ten matches for Denmark, although a return trip to the FIFA World Cup, where he was the youngest competitor in 2010, looked unlikely after a 4-0 home defeat by Armenia.

International career
DENMARK
Debut 03/03/10 v Austria (a, Vienna, friendly), lost 1-2
First goal 04/06/11 v Iceland (a, Reykjavik, ECQ), won 2-0
Caps 36 **Goals** 3
Major tournaments FIFA World Cup 2010; UEFA EURO 2012

Club career
Major honours *Dutch Championship (2011, 2012, 2013); Dutch Cup (2010)*
Clubs 10- AFC Ajax (NED)

2012/13 appearances/goals
Domestic league Dutch Eredivisie 33/10
European UEFA Champions League 6/1; UEFA Europa League 2/-
National team FIFA World Cup 2014 qualifying 6/-; Friendlies 4/1

Radamel Falcao
Striker

Height 175cm
Born 10/02/86, Magdalena, Colombia

The 2012/13 season began with a bang for the Colombian international striker as he scored two hat-tricks in a week for Club Atlético de Madrid, the second of them in the UEFA Super Cup against Chelsea FC, which the Spanish club won 4-1. Another trophy came his way at the end of the season when Real Madrid CF were defeated 2-1 in the final of the Copa del Rey, while in the league his 28 goals helped Atlético finish third to qualify for the UEFA Champions League. He would not be taking part, though, as he left in the summer to join ambitious French Ligue 1 newcomers AS Monaco FC.

International career
COLOMBIA
Debut 07/02/07 v Uruguay (h, Cucuta, friendly), lost 1-3
First goal 03/06/07 v Montenegro (n, Matsumoto, Kirin Cup), won 1-0
Caps 46 **Goals** 17
Major tournaments Copa América 2011

Club career
Major honours *UEFA Europa League (2011, 2012); UEFA Super Cup (2012); Argentinian Championship (clausura 2008); Portuguese Championship (2011); Portuguese Cup (2010, 2011); Spanish Cup (2013)*
Clubs 05-09 CA River Plate (ARG); 09-11 FC Porto (POR); 11-13 Club Atlético de Madrid (ESP); 13- AS Monaco FC (FRA)

2012/13 appearances/goals
Domestic league Spanish Liga 34/28
European UEFA Europa League 2/1
National team FIFA World Cup 2014 qualifying 7/6; Friendlies 1/-

Rio Ferdinand
Centre-Back

Height 187 cm
Born 07/11/78, London, England

Manchester United FC's 2012/13 Premier League title triumph was the sixth with Ferdinand at the heart of their defence, and the 34-year-old centre-back was every bit as impressive as he had been in his first title win a decade earlier. Fittingly, his first goal for the club in five seasons came in Sir Alex Ferguson's last home game, against Swansea City AFC, ensuring that the manager departed Old Trafford with a win. The Londoner's fine form triggered a surprise recall to the England side, almost two years since his previous appearance, but he withdrew from Roy Hodgson's squad and subsequently announced his international retirement.

International career
ENGLAND
Debut 15/01/97 v Cameroon (h, London, friendly), won 2-0
First goal 15/06/02 v Denmark (n, Niigata, WCF), won 3-0
Caps 81 **Goals** 3
Major tournaments FIFA World Cup 1998; FIFA World Cup 2002; FIFA World Cup 2006

Club career
Major honours *UEFA Champions League (2008); FIFA Club World Cup (2008); English Premier League (2003, 2007, 2008, 2009, 2011, 2013); English League Cup (2006, 2009)*
Clubs 95-00 West Ham United FC; 96 AFC Bournemouth (loan); 00-02 Leeds United AFC; 02- Manchester United FC

2012/13 appearances/goals
Domestic league English Premier League 26(2)/1
European UEFA Champions League 3(1)/-

Fernandinho
Midfielder

Height 176cm
Born 04/05/85, Londrina, Brazil

No fewer than 11 Brazilians contributed to FC
Shakhtar Donetsk's third successive Ukrainian
league and cup double, and the pick of the
crop was Fernandinho. The club's long-
serving defensive midfielder concluded a
glorious season - his eighth at the club - by
scoring the opening goal in the Ukrainian Cup
final against FC Chornomorets Odesa. He
had found the net earlier in the season in a
UEFA Champions League win over holders
Chelsea FC, his superb all round performance
that evening perhaps sowing the seed for his
summer transfer to the London club's
domestic rivals Manchester City FC.

International career
BRAZIL
Debut 10/08/11 v Germany (a, Stuttgart, friendly),
lost 2-3
Caps 5 Goals 0

Club career
Major honours UEFA Cup (2009); Ukrainian
Championship (2006, 2008, 2010, 2011, 2012,
2013); Ukrainian Cup (2008, 2011, 2012, 2013)
Clubs 02-05 Atlético Paranaense; 05-13 FC
Shakhtar Donetsk (UKR); 13- Manchester City FC
(ENG)

2012/13 appearances/goals
Domestic league Ukrainian Premier League
23(1)/2
European UEFA Champions League 8/1

Nicolás Gaitán
Attacking midfielder

Height 173cm
Born 23/02/88, San Martin, Argentina

One of the most skilful attacking midfielders
operating in European football, Gaitán was
not always handed a starting berth in the SL
Benfica team by coach Jorge Jesus during
the 2012/13 season, but when he did play,
he invariably had an impact. Setting up
goals for strikers Lima and Óscar Cardozo
was his speciality and he was credited with
ten assists in the Liga. The 25-year-old
Argentinian was particularly prominent in
helping Benfica reach the final of the UEFA
Europa League, his sweet finish with the
outside of the left foot in the semi-final
second leg against Fenerbahçe SK an
obvious highlight.

International career
ARGENTINA
Debut 30/09/09 v Ghana (h, Cordoba, friendly),
won 2-0
Caps 6 Goals 0

Club career
Clubs 08-10 CA Boca Juniors; 10- SL Benfica (POR)

2012/13 appearances/goals
Domestic league Portuguese Liga 11(12)/3
European UEFA Champions League 2(2)/-; UEFA
Europa League 8(1)/1

Mario Götze
Midfielder

Height 176cm
Born 03/06/92, Memmingen, Germany

The announcement in April that Götze was
leaving Borussia Dortmund at the end of the
season to join FC Bayern München caused a
major shockwave in German football. While
Bayern fans were delighted that their club had
triggered the release clause in the young
German international's contract to sign him
for a Bundesliga record fee, there was
understandable despair at Dortmund.
Although the 2012/13 season ended without
a trophy for Jürgen Klopp's side, Götze was
in dazzling form throughout. There was heavy
irony in the fact that he was injured for the
UEFA Champions League final and therefore
unavailable to play against his impending
employers.

International career
GERMANY
Debut 17/11/10 v Sweden (a, Gothenburg,
friendly), drew 0-0
First goal 10/08/11 v Brazil (h, Stuttgart, friendly),
won 3-2
Caps 22 Goals 5

Club career
Major honours German Championship (2011,
2012); German Cup (2012)
Clubs 09-13 Borussia Dortmund; 13- FC Bayern
München

2012/13 appearances/goals
Domestic league German Bundesliga 23(5)/10
European UEFA Champions League 11/2
National team FIFA World Cup 2014 qualifying
3(2)/3; Friendlies 1(1)/-

İlkay Gündoğan
Midfielder

Height 180cm
Born 24/10/90, Gelsenkirchen, Germany

Borussia Dortmund's journey to the UEFA Champions League final brought international recognition for several of their players. Among the most prominent was Gündoğan, who distinguished himself repeatedly with his calm but busy authority in central midfield. His ability to win the ball, hold on to it then see and execute the right pass was one of the staples of Dortmund's play, and he also had the nerve to step up and score the equaliser in the Wembley final against FC Bayern München, coolly sending Manuel Neuer the wrong way from the penalty spot. His excellent club form earned him a regular berth in the German national side.

International career

GERMANY
Debut 11/10/11 v Belgium (h, Dusseldorf, ECQ), won 3-1
First goal 26/03/13 v Kazakhstan (h, Nuremberg, WCQ), won 4-1
Caps 7 Goals 1
Major tournaments UEFA EURO 2012

Club career

Major honours German Championship (2012); German Cup (2012)
Clubs 08-09 VfL Bochum 1848; 09-11 1. FC Nürnberg; 11- Borussia Dortmund

2012/13 appearances/goals

Domestic league German Bundesliga 26(2)/3
European UEFA Champions League 11(1)/1
National team FIFA World Cup 2014 qualifying 1(1)/1; Friendlies 2(1)/-

Marek Hamšík
Attacking midfielder

Height 180cm
Born 27/07/87, Banska Bystrica, Slovakia

While his SSC Napoli team-mate Edinson Cavani topped the Serie A scoring charts in 2012/13, Hamšík was officially credited with the largest number of assists, his tally of ten placing him at the head of the rankings above AS Roma's Francesco Totti (eight). The Slovakian schemer also scored 11 goals, taking his total in all competitions over six seasons with the club to 70. A midfielder of craft and invention with strength in both feet, he was the only Napoli player to feature in all 38 Serie A games – 37 in the starting XI – as they qualified for the UEFA Champions League by finishing runners-up to Juventus.

International career

SLOVAKIA
Debut 07/02/07 v Poland (n, Jerez, friendly), drew 2-2
First goal 13/10/07 v San Marino (h, Dubnica, ECQ), won 7-0
Caps 64 Goals 10
Major tournaments FIFA World Cup 2010

Club career

Major honours Italian Cup (2012)
Clubs 04 ŠK Slovan Bratislava; 04-07 Brescia Calcio (ITA); 07- SSC Napoli (ITA)

2012/13 appearances/goals

Domestic league Italian Serie A 37(1)/11
European UEFA Europa League (4)/-
National team FIFA World Cup 2014 qualifying 6/1; Friendlies 4/1

Samir Handanovič
Goalkeeper

Height 193cm
Born 14/07/84, Ljubljana, Slovenia

FC Internazionale Milano had a poor season in 2012/13, finishing ninth in Serie A and failing to qualify for Europe, but it would have been a lot worse without the excellence of their newly signed Slovenian international goalkeeper. Handanovič, who replaced Brazilian Júlio César, conceded 53 goals in 35 league appearances – 18 more than in his final season at Udinese Calcio, when he was an ever-present – but that statistic did not take into account the number of spectacular saves he was required to make. He was also on top form in the UEFA Europa League, conceding just ten goals in as many games.

International career

SLOVENIA
Debut 17/11/04 v Slovakia (a, Trnava, friendly), drew 0-0
Caps 63 Goals 0
Major tournaments FIFA World Cup 2010

Club career

Clubs 03-04 NK Domžale; 03-04 NK Zagorje (loan); 04-12 Udinese Calcio (ITA); 05-06 Treviso FBC (ITA) (loan); 06 S.S. Lazio (ITA) (loan); 06-07 Rimini Calcio (ITA) (loan); 12- FC Internazionale Milano (ITA)

2012/13 appearances/goals

Domestic league Italian Serie A 35/-
European UEFA Europa League 8/-; UEFA Europa League qualifying 2/-
National team FIFA World Cup 2014 qualifying 4/-; Friendlies 2/-

Eden Hazard
Attacking midfielder

Height 170cm
Born 07/01/91, La Louviere, Belgium

Recruited at some cost by Chelsea FC from LOSC Lille, with whom he won back-to-back Ligue 1 player of the year crowns, Hazard proved that the money was well spent with a scintillating debut season in the Premier League. A constant threat to opposition defences with his deft footwork, vision and, above all, explosive change of pace, the 22-year-old Belgian racked up 62 appearances in all competitions, embellishing them with 13 goals and no fewer than 26 assists. It was a memorable season also for the youngster at international level as he helped steer Belgium to the top of their FIFA World Cup qualifying group.

International career

BELGIUM
Debut 19/11/08 v Luxembourg (a, Luxembourg, friendly), drew 1-1
First goal 07/10/11 v Kazakhstan (h, Brussels, ECQ), won 4-1
Caps 37 **Goals** 5

Club career

Major honours UEFA Europa League (2013); French Championship (2011); French Cup (2011)
Clubs 07-12 LOSC Lille (FRA); 12- Chelsea FC (ENG)

2012/13 appearances/goals

Domestic league English Premier League 31(3)/9
European UEFA Champions League 4(2)/-; UEFA Europa League 5(2)/1
National team FIFA World Cup 2014 qualifying 5(2)/2; Friendlies 2/1

Pavel Horváth
Midfielder

Height 178cm
Born 22/04/75, Prague, Czech Republic

At the age of 38 Horváth celebrated the third Czech championship title of his career and the second in three seasons as captain of FC Viktoria Plzeň. The veteran schemer was hugely influential as Pavel Vrba's side held off the challenge of AC Sparta Praha to cap a superb campaign in which the club also prospered once again in Europe, travelling from the second qualifying round of the UEFA Europa League all the way to the round of 16. He became the competition proper's oldest goalscorer three times over, setting the final mark at 37 years and 214 days with his penalty in the matchday five 1-1 draw at A. Académica de Coimbra.

International career

CZECH REPUBLIC
Debut 09/02/99 v Belgium (a, Brussels, friendly), won 1-0
Caps 19 **Goals** 0
Major tournaments UEFA EURO 2000

Club career

Major honours Czech Championship (2007, 2011, 2013); Portuguese Championship (2002); Czech Cup (1997, 1999, 2003, 2007, 2008, 2010); Portuguese Cup (2002)
Clubs 93 SK Slavia Praha; 94-96 FK Jablonec; 96-2000 SK Slavia Praha; 2000-02 Sporting Clube de Portugal (POR); 02 Galatasaray AŞ (TUR); 02-04 FK Teplice; 04-06 Vissel Kobe (JPN); 06-08 AC Sparta Praha; 08- FC Viktoria Plzeň

2012/13 appearances/goals

Domestic league Czech 1. Liga 27/4
European UEFA Europa League 9/3; UEFA Europa League qualifying/play-offs 6/2

Philipp Hosiner
Striker

Height 179cm
Born 15/09/89, Eisenstadt, Austria

The 2012/13 season began well enough for Hosiner at FC Admira Wacker Mödling, but it got much better after he joined FK Austria Wien on the last day of August. He went on to plunder 27 Bundesliga goals as the Violetten stormed to the Austrian title. With five goals already for Admira, his final tally put him clear on top of the Bundesliga scoring ladder and incorporated the rare feat of successive hat-tricks, the first of them coming back at Admira in a 6-4 victory. Recalled to the Austrian national team, the 23-year-old scored twice within the first 20 minutes of his return, in a FIFA World Cup qualifier against the Faroe Islands.

International career

AUSTRIA
Debut 07/10/11 v Azerbaijan (a, Baku, ECQ), won 4-1
First goal 22/03/13 v Faroe Islands (h, Vienna, WCQ), won 6-0
Caps 3 **Goals** 2

Club career

Major honours Austrian Championship (2013)
Clubs 08-09 TSV 1860 München II (GER); 09-10 SV Sandhausen (GER); 10-11 First Vienna FC; 11-12 FC Admira Wacker Mödling; 12- FK Austria Wien

2012/13 appearances/goals

Domestic league Austrian Bundesliga 34(2)/32
European UEFA Europa League qualifying 1(3)/2
National team FIFA World Cup 2014 qualifying 2/2

Mats Hummels
Centre-back

Height 192cm
Born 16/12/88, Bergisch Gladbach, Germany

Rewarded for his part in Borussia Dortmund's back-to-back German title triumphs with a new long-term contract, Hummels enjoyed another regal season in the heart of the Ruhr club's rearguard. Although the Schwarzgelben won no trophies in 2012/13, the 24-year-old centre-back continued to further his reputation as one of Europe's most elegant young defenders. A couple of high-profile errors might have dented it to a degree, but he was a key man in Dortmund's journey to the UEFA Champions League final, not least with his late equaliser at FC Shakhtar Donetsk and an inspirational appearance as a late subsititue in the extraordinary quarter-final fightback against Málaga CF.

International career

GERMANY
Debut 13/05/10 v Malta (h, Aachen, friendly), won 3-0
First goal 26/05/12 v Switzerland (a, Basel, friendly), lost 3-5
Caps 24 **Goals** 1
Major tournaments UEFA EURO 2012

Club career

Major honours German Championship (2011, 2012); German Cup (2012)
Clubs 07-09 FC Bayern München; 08-09 Borussia Dortmund (loan); 09- Borussia Dortmund

2012/13 appearances/goals

Domestic league German Bundesliga 28/1
European UEFA Champions League 10(1)/1
National team FIFA World Cup 2014 qualifying 2/-; Friendlies 3/-

Zlatan Ibrahimović
Striker

Height 192cm
Born 03/10/81, Malmo, Sweden

Ibrahimović strengthened his status as one of the finest footballers of the modern era with a magnificent debut campaign in France for Paris Saint-Germain FC. The tall, graceful Swedish striker spearheaded PSG's drive to the Ligue 1 title with a personal-best tally of 30 goals, tacking the French championship on to those he had previously conquered in the Netherlands, Italy and Spain. In addition to being the top scorer, he was also officially recognised as the Ligue 1 player of the year. The highlight of his international season was a sensational four-goal haul in a friendly against England that marked the opening of Sweden's new national stadium.

International career

SWEDEN
Debut 31/01/01 v Faroe Islands (h, Vaxjo, friendly), drew 0-0
First goal 07/10/01 v Azerbaijan (h, Solna, WCQ), won 3-0
Caps 90 **Goals** 41
Major tournaments FIFA World Cup 2002; UEFA EURO 2004; FIFA World Cup 2006; UEFA EURO 2008; UEFA EURO 2012

Club career

Major honours UEFA Super Cup (2009); FIFA Club World Cup (2009); Dutch Championship (2002, 2004); Italian Championship (2007, 2008, 2009, 2011); Spanish Championship (2010); French Championship (2013); Dutch Cup (2002)
Clubs 99-01 Malmö FF; 01-04 AFC Ajax (NED); 04-06 Juventus (ITA); 06-09 FC Internazionale Milano (ITA); 09-11 FC Barcelona (ESP); 10-11 AC Milan (ITA) (loan); 11-12 AC Milan (ITA); 12- Paris Saint-Germain FC (FRA)

2012/13 appearances/goals

Domestic league French Ligue 1 33(1)/30
European UEFA Champions League 9/3
National team FIFA World Cup 2014 qualifying 6/4; Friendlies 4/4

Sergei Ignashevich
Centre-back

Height 186cm
Born 14/07/79, Moscow, Russia

A rigorous defence was the key to PFC CSKA Moskva's league and cup double in 2012/13, and experienced Russian international Ignashevich was at the heart of it, his partnership with Vasili Berezutski providing a formidable barrier in front of goalkeeper Igor Akinfeev. The no-nonsense Muscovite missed only two league matches all season as he captured the fourth Premier-Liga winner's medal of his career. He also enjoyed a seventh success in the Russian Cup, although he was suspended for the final against FC Anji Makhachkala. He was on the field, however, for every minute of the nine matches that made up Fabio Capello's first season in charge of Russia.

International career

RUSSIA
Debut 21/08/02 v Sweden (h, Moscow, friendly), drew 1-1
First goal 07/06/03 v Switzerland (a, Basel, ECQ), drew 2-2
Caps 87 **Goals** 5
Major tournaments UEFA EURO 2008; UEFA EURO 2012

Club career

Major honours UEFA Cup (2005); Russian Premier-Liga (2002, 2005, 2006, 2013); Russian Cup (2001, 2005, 2006, 2008, 2009, 2011, 2013)
Clubs 98-99 FC Spartak Orekhevo; 99-00 PFC Krylya Sovetov Samara; 01-03 FC Lokomotiv Moskva; 04- PFC CSKA Moskva

2012/13 appearances/goals

Domestic league Russian Premier-Liga 28/-
European UEFA Europa League play-offs 2/-
National team FIFA World Cup 2014 qualifying 5/-; Friendlies 4/-

Saša Ilić

Attacking midfielder

Height 178cm
Born 30/12/77, Pozarevac, Serbia

A living club legend, Ilić captured his ninth domestic title with FK Partizan in 2012/13. The first of those triumphs, in 1996/97, featured just one appearance from the then 19-year-old, but all of the others were stamped with his classy orchestrating skills and sweetly timed passes. At 35, he was as influential as ever, marshalling the Belgrade club to an unprecedented sixth successive title and revelling in the adulation of the Partizan fans. Despite a heavy workload in Europe – 12 matches in total – his performance level remained high through to the end of the Serbian Superliga campaign as Partizan withstood a spring surge from FK Crvena zvezda.

International career

YUGOSLAVIA/SERBIA & MONTENEGRO/ SERBIA
Debut 16/08/00 v Northern Ireland (a, Belfast, friendly), won 2-1
First goal 17/04/02 v Lithuania (h, Smederevo, friendly), won 4-1
Caps 37 **Goals** 4
Major tournaments FIFA World Cup 2006

Club career

Major honours Yugoslav Championship (1997, 1999, 2002); Serbian & Montenegrin Championship (2003, 2005); Turkish Championship (2006); Serbian Championship (2010, 2011, 2012, 2013); Yugoslav Cup (1998, 2001); Serbian Cup (2011)
Clubs 96-05 FK Partizan; 04 RC Celta de Vigo (ESP) (loan); 05-07 Galatasaray AŞ (TUR); 07-10 FC Salzburg (AUT); 09 Larissa FC (GRE) (loan); 10- FK Partizan

2012/13 appearances/goals

Domestic league Serbian Superliga 24(1)/5
European UEFA Champions League qualifying 3(1)/-; UEFA Europa League 6/-; UEFA Europa League play-offs 1(1)/-

Andrés Iniesta

Attacking midfielder

Height 170cm
Born 11/05/84, Fuentealbilla, Spain

The player of the tournament at UEFA EURO 2012 – and winner of the UEFA Best Player in Europe award two months later – did his best to help Spain complete a trophy treble at the 2013 FIFA Confederations Cup, but despite another excellent showing in Brazil, Iniesta was as helpless as his team-mates as the hosts thrashed them 3-0 in the final. It was another draining season for the FC Barcelona midfield maestro, the highlight of which was his club's Spanish title triumph. While Lionel Messi hogged the headlines with his phenomenal goalscoring, it was the Barça No8 who kept feeding him with those sharp, intricate passes that have become his trademark.

International career

SPAIN
Major honours FIFA World Cup (2010); UEFA European Championship (2008, 2012)
Debut 27/05/06 v Russia (h, Albacete, friendly), drew 0-0
First goal 07/02/07 v England (a, Manchester, friendly), won 1-0
Caps 87 **Goals** 10
Major tournaments FIFA World Cup 2006; UEFA EURO 2008; FIFA World Cup 2010; UEFA EURO 2012; FIFA Confederations Cup 2013

Club career

Major honours UEFA Champions League (2006, 2009, 2011); UEFA Super Cup (2009, 2011); FIFA Club World Cup (2009, 2011); Spanish Championship (2005, 2006, 2009, 2010, 2011, 2013); Spanish Cup (2009, 2012)
Clubs 00- FC Barcelona

2012/13 appearances/goals

Domestic league Spanish Liga 24(7)/3
European UEFA Champions League 9(1)/1
National team FIFA World Cup 2014 qualifying 4(1)/-; FIFA Confederations Cup 2013 4(1)/-; Friendlies 4(2)/-

Isco

Attacking midfielder

Height 176cm
Born 21/04/92, Benalmadena, Spain

Málaga CF's thrilling run to the quarter-finals of the UEFA Champions League offered the perfect showcase for Isco's sparkling talent. Two goals on his group stage debut, in a 3-0 win against FC Zenit St Petersburg, got him and the team off to the perfect start, and by the time of his team's heartbreaking exit against Borussia Dortmund, the 21-year-old had become a star. Capped by Spain for the first time in a February friendly against Uruguay, he was a key contributor to his country's summer triumph at the UEFA European Under-21 Championship. On his return from Israel he signed a five-year contract with Real Madrid CF.

International career

SPAIN
Debut 06/02/13 v Uruguay (n, Doha, friendly), won 3-1
Caps 1 **Goals** 0

Club career

Clubs 10-11 Valencia CF; 11-13 Málaga CF; 13-Real Madrid CF

2012/13 appearances/goals

Domestic league Spanish Liga 36(1)/9
European UEFA Champions League 8/3; UEFA Champions League play-offs 2/-
National team Friendlies (1)/-

Javi Martínez
Midfielder

Height 190cm
Born 02/09/88, Estella, Spain

A Bundesliga-record signing from Athletic Club, Javi Martínez took a while to find his feel at FC Bayern München, but soon became a central cog in Jupp Heynckes's side, his discipline as a holding midfielder serving as a platform for other players to carry the attack to the opposition. His season peaked in Bayern's 7-0 aggregate defeat of FC Barcelona in the semi-finals of the UEFA Champions League, with observers in Germany and Spain uniting in praise for the way he disrupted and ultimately destroyed the Catalans' touch-and-move passing game. He joined forces with some of those Barça players in June at the FIFA Confederations Cup.

International career

SPAIN
Major honours FIFA World Cup (2010); UEFA European Championship (2012)
Debut 29/05/10 v Saudi Arabia (n, Innsbruck, friendly), won 3-2
Caps 13 **Goals** 0
Major tournaments FIFA World Cup 2010; UEFA EURO 2012; FIFA Confederations Cup 2013

Club career

Clubs 05-06 CA Osasuna B; 06-12 Athletic Club; 12- FC Bayern München (GER)

2012/13 appearances/goals

Domestic league German Bundesliga 19(8)/3
European UEFA Champions League 11/-
National team FIFA Confederations Cup 2013 1(2)/-; Friendlies 2/-

João Moutinho
Midfielder

Height 170cm
Born 08/09/86, Portimao, Portugal

A third season at FC Porto brought a third successive league title for João Moutinho. There would not be a fourth, however, as the Portuguese international midfielder decided to move abroad for the first time in his career and join the nouveaux riches of AS Monaco FC. He will be badly missed at the Estádio do Dragão, where his tackling, passing and leadership qualities drove Porto on to their second undefeated title triumph in three seasons, pipping SL Benfica at the post. Rarely absent from the Porto starting XI, he was the only player to feature from the first whistle in all 11 of Portugal's internationals in 2012/13.

International career

PORTUGAL
Debut 17/08/05 v Egypt (h, Ponta Delgada, friendly), won 2-0
First goal 31/05/08 v Georgia (h, Viseu, friendly), won 2-0
Caps 59 **Goals** 2
Major tournaments UEFA EURO 2008; UEFA EURO 2012

Club career

Major honours UEFA Europa League (2011); Portuguese Championship (2011, 2012, 2013); Portuguese Cup (2007, 2008, 2011)
Clubs 04-10 Sporting Clube de Portugal; 10-13 FC Porto; 13- AS Monaco FC (FRA)

2012/13 appearances/goals

Domestic league Portuguese Liga 27/1
European UEFA Champions League 8/2
National team FIFA World Cup 2014 qualifying 7/-; Friendlies 4/-

Jordi Alba
Left-back

Height 170cm
Born 21/03/89, L'Hospitalet, Spain

FC Barcelona's major new recruit during the summer of 2012 enjoyed an excellent title-winning debut season at the Camp Nou. Following on from an outstanding UEFA EURO 2012 with Spain, the effervescent left-back slotted comfortably into Tito Vilanova's first XI, claiming as his own a position the club had struggled adequately to fill in the past. He scored a couple of valuable late UEFA Champions League goals against Celtic FC and AC Milan and also found the net three times for Spain as he cemented his place in Vicente del Bosque's side – one in a FIFA World Cup qualifier against Belarus and two against Nigeria at the FIFA Confederations Cup.

International career

SPAIN
Major honours UEFA European Championship (2012)
Debut 11/10/11 v Scotland (h, Alicante, friendly), won 3-1
First goal 01/07/12 v Italy (n, Kyiv, ECF), won 4-0
Caps 22 **Goals** 4
Major tournaments UEFA EURO 2012; FIFA Confederations Cup 2013

Club career

Clubs 07-08 Valencia CF B; 08-12 Valencia CF; 08-09 Gimnàstic de Tarragona (loan); 12- FC Barcelona

2012/13 appearances/goals

Domestic league Spanish Liga 27(2)/2
European UEFA Champions League 9/2
National team FIFA World Cup 2014 qualifying 4/1; FIFA Confederations Cup 2013 4/2; Friendlies 3/-

Stevan Jovetić
Striker

Height 184cm
Born 02/11/89, Podgorica, Montenegro

A flexible forward who can operate as a central striker, on the wing or in the fashionable 'false No9' position, Jovetić confirmed the potential he had shown for ACF Fiorentina in the 2011/12 season with another impressive Serie A campaign, scoring 13 goals to help the Viola finish fourth. After five years in Florence, the 23-year-old sought pastures new in the summer and joined Manchester City FC, where he will return to the UEFA Champions League, a competition he graced on his last appearance in 2009/10. He scored his tenth international goal for Montenegro in an August friendly against Latvia but fired blanks in the season's FIFA World Cup qualifiers.

International career

MONTENEGRO
Debut 24/03/07 v Hungary (h, Podgorica, friendly), won 2-1
First goal 20/08/08 v Hungary (a, Budapest, friendly), drew 3-3
Caps 27 **Goals** 10

Club career

Major honours Serbian Championship (2008); Serbian Cup (2008)
Clubs 06-08 FK Partizan (SRB); 08-13 ACF Fiorentina (ITA); 13- Manchester City FC (ENG)

2012/13 appearances/goals

Domestic league Italian Serie A 31/13
National team FIFA World Cup 2014 qualifying 6/-; Friendlies 1/1

Stefan Kiessling
Striker

Height 191cm
Born 25/01/84, Lichtenfels, Germany

FC Bayern München won all the team prizes going in 2012/13, but the individual award for the Bundesliga's top scorer was claimed by Bayer 04 Leverkusen's Kiessling. The 29-year-old started all 34 games and scored 25 goals, one more than Borussia Dortmund's Robert Lewandowski. The blond striker's tally eclipsed not only his own previous personal best of 21 but also Ulf Kirsten's club record of 22. No fewer than 11 of his strikes opened the scoring, which was also a new high for the Rhineland club. The consistency of his performances led to calls for his reintroduction to the German national team, but Joachim Löw remained unmoved.

International career

GERMANY
Debut 28/03/07 v Denmark (h, Duisburg, friendly), lost 0-1
Caps 6 **Goals** 0
Major tournaments FIFA World Cup 2010

Club career

Clubs 01-06 1. FC Nürnberg; 06- Bayer 04 Leverkusen

2012/13 appearances/goals

Domestic league German Bundesliga 34/25
European UEFA Europa League 4(2)/1

Yevhen Konoplyanka
Winger

Height 176cm
Born 29/09/89, Kirovohrad, Ukraine

Many footballers dream of scoring a goal at Wembley, but few have done so in such style as Konoplyanka, whose majestic long-range strike against England in Ukraine's opening 2014 FIFA World Cup qualifier will remain embedded in the memories of those who witnessed it. That goal confirmed at a stroke the quality the young winger had demonstrated on home soil at UEFA EURO 2012, and there would be more to come from the 23-year-old at club level with FC Dnipro Dnipropetrovsk as Juande Ramos's side cruised through the UEFA Europa League group stage with a tournament-high tally of 15 points.

International career

UKRAINE
Debut 25/05/10 v Lithuania (h, Kharkiv, friendly), won 4-0
First goal 29/05/10 v Romania (h, Lviv, friendly), won 3-2
Caps 28 **Goals** 7
Major tournaments UEFA EURO 2012

Club career

Clubs 07- FC Dnipro Dnipropetrovsk

2012/13 appearances/goals

Domestic league Ukrainian Premier League 15(5)/2
European UEFA Europa League 6(1)/1; UEFA Europa League play-offs 2/2
National team FIFA World Cup 2014 qualifying 3/2; Friendlies 2(1)/-

Philipp Lahm
Full-back

Height 170cm
Born 11/11/83, Munich, Germany

There have been many famous captains of FC Bayern München, but none of them, not even the great Franz Beckenbauer, ever experienced the joy of lifting the Bundesliga shield, the DFB-Pokal and the European Cup in the same season. That unique thrill was reserved for Lahm, the full-back with the small stature and the big heart who skippered Bayern to glory on all three fronts in 2012/13. The UEFA Champions League trophy was the one the 29-year-old wanted the most – the first major international prize of his career after several major tournament near-misses with Germany and the pain of defeat by Chelsea FC on home soil 12 months earlier.

International career
GERMANY
Debut 18/02/04 v Croatia (a, Split, friendly), won 2-1
First goal 28/04/04 v Romania (a, Bucharest, friendly), lost 1-5
Caps 98 **Goals** 5
Major tournaments UEFA EURO 2004; FIFA World Cup 2006; UEFA EURO 2008; FIFA World Cup 2010; UEFA EURO 2012

Club career
Major honours UEFA Champions League (2013); German Championship (2006, 2008, 2010, 2013); German Cup (2006, 2008, 2010, 2013)
Clubs 03- FC Bayern München; 03-05 VfB Stuttgart (loan)

2012/13 appearances/goals
Domestic league German Bundesliga 28(1)/-
European UEFA Champions League 12/-
National team FIFA World Cup 2014 qualifying 5/-; Friendlies 2/-

Erik Lamela
Winger/Striker

Height 183cm
Born 04/03/92, Buenos Aires, Argentina

After a modest debut season at AS Roma following a high-profile transfer from CA River Plate, Lamela exploded into life in 2012/13. A devastating burst of form in mid-autumn, when he scored seven goals in six Serie A games, alerted everyone to the left-footer's talent, and he went into the festive break with ten goals to his name after bagging a brace against AC Milan. Although he only added a further five goals, the 21-year-old's reputation was made, with Roma skipper Francesco Totti leading the chorus of approval. His season, however, ended in disappointment as Roma lost the Italian Cup final to arch-rivals S.S. Lazio.

International career
ARGENTINA
Debut 25/05/11 v Paraguay (h, Resistencia, friendly), won 4-2
Caps 2 **Goals** 0

Club career
Clubs 08-11 CA River Plate; 11- AS Roma (ITA)

2012/13 appearances/goals
Domestic league Italian Serie A 30(3)/15
National team Friendlies (1)/-

Frank Lampard
Midfielder

Height 183cm
Born 20/06/78, Romford, England

Two hot topics simmered around Chelsea FC's long-serving midfielder throughout the season. The first concerned his bid to become the club's all-time top goalscorer; the second was whether he would have his contract renewed. The month of May brought happiness for Lampard on both fronts, with Bobby Tambling's record of 202 goals being equalled and overtaken in the same match, against Aston Villa FC, and a new one-year contract extension being signed five days later. In between, he skippered the Blues to victory in the UEFA Europa League final. To his 15 Premier League goals in 2012/13 the midfielder added six for England, including the winner against Brazil at Wembley.

International career
ENGLAND
Debut 10/10/99 v Belgium (h, Sunderland, friendly), won 2-1
First goal 20/08/03 v Croatia (h, Ipswich, friendly), won 3-1
Caps 97 **Goals** 29
Major tournaments UEFA EURO 2004; FIFA World Cup 2006; FIFA World Cup 2010

Club career
Major honours UEFA Champions League (2012); UEFA Europa League (2013); English Premier League (2005, 2006, 2010); English FA Cup (2007, 2009, 2010, 2012); English League Cup (2005, 2007)
Clubs 95-01 West Ham United FC; 96 Swansea City AFC (WAL) (loan); 01- Chelsea FC

2012/13 appearances/goals
Domestic league English Premier League 21(8)/15
European UEFA Champions League 3/-; UEFA Europa League 7/-
National team FIFA World Cup 2014 qualifying 3/4; Friendlies 3(1)/2

Robert Lewandowski
Striker

Height 184cm
Born 21/08/88, Warsaw, Poland

With 24 goals in the Bundesliga and ten in the UEFA Champions League, Lewandowski enjoyed the finest season of his career, establishing himself beyond doubt as one of Europe's deadliest centre-forwards. He was especially sharp in the second half of the season, scoring in 12 consecutive Bundesliga matches – a club record – and making history by registering all four goals in Dortmund's 4-1 win over Real Madrid CF in the first leg of the UEFA Champions League semi-final. It was a dazzling display of finishing from the Pole, but he could not find the net in the final against FC Bayern München as his team went down 2-1 at Wembley.

International career

POLAND
Debut 10/09/08 v San Marino (a, Serravalle, WCQ), won 2-0
First goal 10/09/08 v San Marino (a, Serravalle, WCQ), won 2-0
Caps 54 **Goals** 17
Major tournaments UEFA EURO 2012

Club career

Major honours Polish Championship (2010); German Championship (2011, 2012); Polish Cup (2009); German Cup (2012)
Clubs 06-08 Znicz Pruszków; 08-10 KKS Lech Poznań; 10- Borussia Dortmund (GER)

2012/13 appearances/goals

Domestic league German Bundesliga 29(2)/24
European UEFA Champions League 12(1)/10
National team FIFA World Cup 2014 qualifying 6/2; Friendlies 3/-

Mario Mandžukić
Striker

Height 186cm
Born 21/05/86, Slavonski Brod, Croatia

Snapped up by FC Bayern München from VfL Wolfsburg, Mandžukić was fortunate in that his arrival in Munich coincided with a long term injury to resident central striker Mario Gomez. It enabled the Croatian star of UEFA EURO 2012 to hit the ground running, and he made the most of his opportunity, scoring eight Bundesliga goals before the end of October. His integration into Jupp Heynckes' side was so seamless that Gomez struggled to get his place back when fit. For the UEFA Champions League final it was the new man who got the nod, and he seized the moment by scoring the opening goal in Bayern's 2-1 victory.

International career

CROATIA
Debut 17/11/07 v FYROM (a, Skopje, ECQ), lost 0-2
First goal 10/09/08 v England (h, Zagreb, WCQ), lost 1-4
Caps 41 **Goals** 11
Major tournaments UEFA EURO 2012

Club career

Major honours UEFA Champions League (2013); Croatian Championship (2008, 2009, 2010); German Championship (2013); Croatian Cup (2008, 2009); German Cup (2013)
Clubs 04-05 NK Marsonia; 05-07 NK Zagreb; 07-10 GNK Dinamo Zagreb; 10-12 VfL Wolfsburg (GER); 12- FC Bayern München (GER)

2012/13 appearances/goals

Domestic league German Bundesliga 22(2)/15
European UEFA Champions League 8(2)/3
National team FIFA World Cup 2014 qualifying 7/2; Friendlies 2/1

Eliaquim Mangala
Centre-back

Height 187cm
Born 13/02/91, Colombes, France

Mangala spent his first season at FC Porto on the outside looking in, but there was no more champing at the bit for the tall, imposing central defender in 2012/13. On the contrary, he played so well so often that by the end of the season, with the club celebrating a hat-trick of Portuguese titles, he was not only being talked of as a transfer target for several of Europe's leading clubs but had also been rewarded with his first senior international cap for France. A long-serving member of his country's Under-21 side, he made his full debut for Les Bleus in a June friendly against Uruguay in Montevideo.

International career

FRANCE
Debut 05/06/13 v Uruguay (a, Montevideo, friendly), lost 0-1
Caps 1 **Goals** 0

Club career

Major honours Belgian Championship (2009); Portuguese Championship (2012, 2013); Belgian Cup (2011)
Clubs 08-11 R. Standard de Liège (BEL); 11- FC Porto (POR)

2012/13 appearances/goals

Domestic league Portuguese Liga 22(1)/4
European UEFA Champions League 6(2)/-
National team Friendlies 1/-

Federico Marchetti
Goalkeeper

Height 188cm
Born 07/02/83, Bassano del Grappa, Italy

A recall to the Italian national side – and a place in Italy's 2013 FIFA Confederations Cup squad – was due reward for Marchetti after a hugely impressive campaign in goal for S.S. Lazio that ended with victory in the Coppa Italia. The 30-year-old keeper was outstanding in the final against city rivals AS Roma as Lazio triumphed 1-0 in the Stadio Olimpico. It was the first major honour of his career and a perfect conclusion to a season in which he was widely lauded as the most consistent goalkeeper in Serie A. He also played a prominent role in helping Lazio become Italy's first UEFA Europa League quarter-finalists.

International career
ITALY
Debut 10/06/09 v Northern Ireland (n, Atteridgeville, friendly), won 4-3
Caps 9 **Goals** 0
Major tournaments FIFA World Cup 2010; FIFA Confederations Cup 2013

Club career
Major honours Italian Cup (2013)
Clubs 02-05 Torino FC; 02-03 US Pro Vercelli (loan); 03 FC Crotone (loan); 04 Treviso FBC (loan); 05 US Pro Vercelli (loan); 05 US AlbinoLeffe; 05-06 AS Biellese; 06-09 US AlbinoLeffe; 08-09 Cagliari Calcio (loan); 09-11 Cagliari Calcio; 11- S.S. Lazio

2012/13 appearances/goals
Domestic league Italian Serie A 33/-
European UEFA Europa League 9/-; UEFA Europa League play-offs 1/-
National team Friendlies (1)/-

Jackson Martínez
Striker

Height 185cm
Born 03/10/86, Quibdo, Colombia

FC Porto have a proud tradition of recruiting little known but highly talented footballers from Latin America, and they certainly hit the jackpot when they bought Martinez from Mexican club Chiapas FC. The Colombian striker enjoyed a dream debut campaign in Europe, powering Porto to the Portuguese league title with 26 goals and another three in the group stage of the UEFA Champions League. For most of the Liga campaign he averaged a goal a game. Indeed, he found the target at least once in 17 of his first 20 league outings, including one majestic back-heeled strike against Sporting Clube de Portugal.

International career
COLOMBIA
Debut 05/09/09 v Ecuador (h, Medellin, WCQ), won 2-0
First goal 05/09/09 v Ecuador (h, Medellin, WCQ), won 2-0
Caps 20 **Goals** 8
Major tournaments Copa América 2011

Club career
Major honours Colombian Championship (finalización 2009); Portuguese Championship (2013)
Clubs 06-10 Independiente Medellin; 10-12 Chiapas FC (MEX); 12- FC Porto (POR)

2012/13 appearances/goals
Domestic league Portuguese Liga 30/26
European UEFA Champions League 8/3
National team FIFA World Cup 2014 qualifying 1/-; Friendlies 3/3

Juan Mata
Attacking midfielder

Height 175cm
Born 28/04/88, Burgos, Spain

A creator and goalscorer in one, Mata was voted Chelsea FC's player of the year for the second successive season. If anything, the young Spanish left-footer was even more impressive in 2012/13 than in his debut campaign. He amassed 64 appearances for the Blues in all competitions – ten more than the previous season – and registered 20 goals and 35 assists. The quality of his play never dropped below the highest standard, his effort and application matched by sublime technique, vision and awareness. The one trophy he won was the UEFA Europa League, Branislav Ivanović's last-gasp winning goal set up by his perfectly-flighted corner.

International career
SPAIN
Major honours FIFA World Cup (2010); UEFA European Championship (2012)
Debut 28/03/09 v Turkey (h, Madrid, WCQ), won 1-0
First goal 09/09/09 v Estonia (h, Merida, WCQ), won 3-0
Caps 29 **Goals** 8
Major tournaments FIFA Confederations Cup 2009; FIFA World Cup 2010; UEFA EURO 2012; FIFA Confederations Cup 2013

Club career
Major honours UEFA Champions League (2012); UEFA Europa League (2013); Spanish Cup (2008); English FA Cup (2012)
Clubs 06-07 Real Madrid Castilla; 07-11 Valencia CF; 11- Chelsea FC (ENG)

2012/13 appearances/goals
Domestic league English Premier League 31(4)/12
European UEFA Champions League 5(1)/3; UEFA Europa League 5(3)/1
National team FIFA World Cup 2014 qualifying (2)/-; FIFA Confederations Cup 2013 2(2)/1; Friendlies 3(1)/1

Blaise Matuidi

Midfielder

Height 175cm
Born 09/04/87, Toulouse, France

A graduate of France's national academy at Clairefontaine, Matuidi finally made it into the big time in 2012/13, earning widespread praise for his gritty, all-purpose midfield play in Paris Saint-Germain's Ligue 1 title-winning side and securing a regular berth in the French national team. At the start of the season he was not an automatic choice for PSG, let alone Les Bleus, but Carlo Ancelotti, the coach at the Parc des Princes, gradually shaped his midfield around the 26-year-old and was amply rewarded – not just domestically but also in the UEFA Champions League, where he scored two goals, including a late equaliser at home to FC Barcelona in the quarter-finals.

International career

FRANCE
Debut 07/09/10 v Bosnia & Herzegovina (a, Sarajevo, ECQ), won 2-0
Caps 14 **Goals** 0
Major tournaments UEFA EURO 2012

Club career

Major honours French Championship (2013)
Clubs 04-07 ES Troyes AC; 07-11 AS Saint-Étienne; 11- Paris Saint-Germain FC

2012/13 appearances/goals

Domestic league French Ligue 1 35(2)/5
European UEFA Champions League 9/2
National team FIFA World Cup 2014 qualifying 3(2)/-; Friendlies 5/-

---

Lionel Messi

Striker

Height 170cm
Born 24/06/87, Rosario, Argentina

Those who regard him as the greatest footballer of all time were given yet more evidence to strengthen their case in 2012/13 as Messi continued to defy logic and reason with his incredible goalscoring feats. The wondrously gifted left-footer has yet to win a trophy with Argentina, but it can safely be said that FC Barcelona, for all the world-class players that have graced their ranks, have never possessed anyone who has contributed so much so often and for so long. Another 60 goals in 2012/13 lifted the four-time FIFA Ballon d'Or winner's all-time tally for the club to 313 – just one of a cascade of scoring records that he has set, and will doubtless continue to bolster in the years to come.

International career

ARGENTINA
Debut 17/08/05 v Hungary (a, Budapest, friendly), won 2-1
First goal 01/03/06 v Croatia (n, Basel, friendly), lost 2-3
Caps 82 **Goals** 35
Major tournaments FIFA World Cup 2006; Copa América 2007; FIFA World Cup 2010; Copa América 2011

Club career

Major honours UEFA Champions League (2006, 2009, 2011); UEFA Super Cup (2009, 2011); FIFA Club World Cup (2009, 2011); Spanish Championship (2005, 2006, 2009, 2010, 2011, 2013); Spanish Cup (2009, 2012)
Clubs 04- FC Barcelona (ESP)

2012/13 appearances/goals

Domestic league Spanish Liga 28(4)/46
European UEFA Champions League 9(2)/8
National team FIFA World Cup 2014 qualifying 6(2)/5; Friendlies 4/4

Michu

Striker

Height 185cm
Born 21/03/86, Oviedo, Spain

Miguel Pérez Cuesta, aka Michu, was an unfamiliar name to English football followers when he joined Swansea City AFC in July 2012 from Rayo Vallecano de Madrid. The club's new manager, Michael Laudrup, knew all about him, though, and after just a handful of appearances, so did everyone else. The skilful Spanish striker scored four goals in his first three games, including two on his debut, and went on to become one of the revelations of the season. His final tally of 18 Premier League goals was the fifth highest in the division, and he also helped Swansea win the the League Cup, their first major trophy, scoring in both the semi-final and the final.

International career

SPAIN
Uncapped

Club career

Major honours English League Cup (2013)
Clubs 03-07 Real Oviedo; 07-11 RC Celta de Vigo; 11-12 Rayo Vallecano de Madrid; 12- Swansea City AFC (WAL)

2012/13 appearances/goals

Domestic league English Premier League 35/18

Henrikh Mkhitaryan
Attacking midfielder

Height 178cm
Born 21/01/89, Yerevan, Armenia

FC Shakhtar Donetsk's extraordinary run of 15 straight victories at the start of the Ukrainian Premier League season was fuelled by an equally remarkable scoring sequence from their Armenian attacking midfielder. Mkhitaryan scored ten league goals in the whole of the previous season, but he equalled that mark after just six games of the 2012/13 campaign. By the winter break he had 18 goals to his name and by the end of the season a league-high tally of 25. In three seasons at Shakhtar he won three league and cup doubles, but there would be no fourth as he joined Borussia Dortmund in July on a four-year contract.

International career

ARMENIA
Debut 14/01/07 v Panama (n. Los Angeles, friendly), drew 1-1
First goal 28/03/09 v Estonia (h, Yerevan, WCQ), drew 2-2
Caps 39 **Goals** 11

Club career

Major honours Armenian Championship (2006, 2007, 2008, 2009); Ukrainian Championship (2011, 2012, 2013); Armenian Cup (2009); Ukrainian Cup (2011, 2012, 2013)
Clubs 06-09 FC Pyunik; 09-10 FC Metalurh Donetsk (UKR); 10-13 FC Shakhtar Donetsk (UKR); 13- Borussia Dortmund (GER)

2012/13 appearances/goals

Domestic league Ukrainian Premier League 27(2)/25
European UEFA Champions League 8/2
National team FIFA World Cup 2014 qualifying 6/2; Friendlies 3/1

Thomas Müller
Attacking midfielder

Height 186cm
Born 13/09/89, Weilheim, Germany

After a below-par campaign in 2011/12, Müller was back to his very best as FC Bayern München swept all before them in 2012/13. It was his highest-scoring campaign to date, with 23 goals in total including eight in the UEFA Champions League, making him Bayern's top scorer in that competition with twice as many as anyone else. He was particularly prominent in the semi-final annihilation of FC Barcelona, scoring three of Bayern's seven goals. The ever-willing 23-year-old's outstanding club form was combined with a productive season for Germany as he helped to propel the Nationalmannschaft towards the 2014 FIFA World Cup finals.

International career

GERMANY
Debut 03/03/10 v Argentina (h, Munich, friendly), lost 0-1
First goal 13/06/10 v Australia (n, Durban, WCF), won 4-0
Caps 41 **Goals** 13
Major tournaments FIFA World Cup 2010; UEFA EURO 2012

Club career

Major honours UEFA Champions League (2013); German Championship (2010, 2013); German Cup (2010, 2013)
Clubs 08- FC Bayern München

2012/13 appearances/goals

Domestic league German Bundesliga 25(3)/13
European UEFA Champions League 12(1)/8
National team FIFA World Cup 2014 qualifying 6/2; Friendlies 3/1

Fernando Muslera
Goalkeeper

Height 190cm
Born 16/06/86, Buenos Aires, Argentina

Galatasaray AŞ were well served in goal as they retained the Turkish title and reached the quarter-finals of the UEFA Champions League. Muslera's second season in Istanbul was every bit as impressive as his first. He missed just one game of the club's Süper Lig triumph and was an ever-present in the first UEFA Champions League campaign of his career, saving a penalty from Manchester United FC winger Nani on his debut at Old Trafford. A busy season continued into the summer as he helped Uruguay to a fourth-place finish at the FIFA Confederations Cup in Brazil, winning his 50th cap in the process.

International career

URUGUAY
Major honours Copa América 2011
Debut 10/10/09 v Ecuador (a, Quito, WCQ), won 2-1
Caps 50 **Goals** 0
Major tournaments Copa América 2007; FIFA World Cup 2010; Copa América 2011; FIFA Confederations Cup 2013

Club career

Major honours Turkish Championship (2012, 2013); Italian Cup (2009)
Clubs 04-06 Montevideo Wanderers FC; 06-07 Club Nacional (loan); 07-11 S.S. Lazio (ITA); 11- Galatasaray AŞ (TUR)

2012/13 appearances/goals

Domestic league Turkish Süper Lig 33/-
European UEFA Champions League 10/-
National team FIFA World Cup 2014 qualifying 7/-; FIFA Confederations Cup 2013 4/-; Friendlies 4/-

Álvaro Negredo
Striker

Height 186cm
Born 20/08/85, Madrid, Spain

Negredo ended a four-year association with Sevilla FC by joining Manchester City FC in the summer. His farewell appearance could not have gone much better as he struck all four goals in a 4-3 home win over Valencia CF. His exploit not only put the Andalusians into the UEFA Europa League but also lifted his all-time tally of Liga goals past the century mark. English football should suit the brawny 28-year-old, whose physical prowess is accompanied by a refined technique and an explosive left-foot shot. 2012/13 was the most prolific season of his career, with 25 goals in the Liga – the most by a Spaniard – and another six in the Copa del Rey.

International career
SPAIN
Major honours UEFA European Championship (2012)
Debut 10/10/09 v Armenia (a, Yerevan, WCQ), won 2-1
First goal 14/10/09 v Bosnia & Herzegovina (a, Zenica, WCQ), won 5-2
Caps 14 **Goals** 6
Major tournaments UEFA EURO 2012

Club career
Major honours Spanish Cup (2010)
Clubs 04-05 Rayo Vallecano de Madrid; 05-07 Real Madrid CF B; 07-09 UD Almería; 09-13 Sevilla FC; 13- Manchester City FC (ENG)

2012/13 appearances/goals
Domestic league Spanish Liga 34(2)/25
National team FIFA World Cup 2014 qualifying (1)/-; Friendlies (1)/-

Manuel Neuer
Goalkeeper

Height 193cm
Born 27/03/86, Gelsenkirchen, Germany

Neuer's standing as one of the world's best goalkeepers was reinforced in the 2013 UEFA Champions League final as he made save after save to thwart Borussia Dortmund. A first season at FC Bayern München without silverware was followed by a clean sweep of trophies in his second, the highlight coming at Wembley with that epic 2-1 win over his former club FC Schalke 04's arch-rivals. The only Bayern player to start all 13 matches in the competition, he went into the final with four successive clean sheets, two apiece against Juventus and FC Barcelona, and was equally tough to beat in both the Bundesliga and the German Cup.

International career
GERMANY
Debut 02/06/09 v United Arab Emirates (a, Dubai, friendly), won 7-2
Caps 38 **Goals** 0
Major tournaments FIFA World Cup 2010; UEFA EURO 2012

Club career
Major honours UEFA Champions League (2013); German Championship (2013); German Cup (2011, 2013)
Clubs 05-11 FC Schalke 04; 11- FC Bayern München

2012/13 appearances/goals
Domestic league German Bundesliga 31/-
European UEFA Champions League 13/-
National team FIFA World Cup 2014 qualifying 6/-; Friendlies 1/-

Mesut Özil
Attacking midfielder

Height 182cm
Born 15/10/88, Gelsenkirchen, Germany

The signing of Luka Modrić from Tottenham Hotspur FC threatened Özil's position as Real Madrid CF's first choice in the 'hole' behind the central striker, but the 24-year-old German international responded positively to the challenge with a catalogue of top-notch performances and was invariably selected by José Mourinho for all of the big games. By the end of the season he was credited with 29 assists to go with his ten goals. For Germany he was equally productive, finding the net five times in the team's opening four 2014 FIFA World Cup qualifying ties. The busy left-footed schemer will undoubtedly be one to watch in Brazil next summer.

International career
GERMANY
Debut 11/02/09 v Norway (h, Dusseldorf, friendly), lost 0-1
First goal 05/09/09 v South Africa (h, Leverkusen, friendly), won 2-0
Caps 46 **Goals** 14
Major tournaments FIFA World Cup 2010; UEFA EURO 2012

Club career
Major honours Spanish Championship (2012); German Cup (2009); Spanish Cup (2011)
Clubs 06-08 FC Schalke 04; 08-10 SV Werder Bremen; 10- Real Madrid CF (ESP)

2012/13 appearances/goals
Domestic league Spanish Liga 23(9)/9
European UEFA Champions League 8(2)/1
National team FIFA World Cup 2014 qualifying 6/5; Friendlies 2/-

Graziano Pellè
Striker

Height 193cm
Born 15/07/85, San Cesario di Lecce, Italy

There was no great burden of expectation on Pellè's broad shoulders when he joined Feyenoord on loan from Parma FC in late August 2012. In four previous seasons of Eredivisie football with AZ Alkmaar the Italian centre-forward had cobbled together just 14 goals. In Rotterdam, however, it would be a very different story. With coach Ronald Koeman shaping the Feyenoord attack around him and playing to his strengths, the big striker became a goalscoring machine – and a huge fans' favourite. He found the net 14 times before Christmas and – after penning a permanent deal with the club – 13 times in the new year to finish up as the Eredivisie's second highest scorer.

International career

ITALY
Uncapped

Club career

Major honours *Dutch Championship (2009)*
Clubs 04-07 US Lecce; 05 Calcio Catania (loan); 06 FC Crotone; 06-07 AC Cesena (loan); 07-11 AZ Alkmaar (NED); 11-13 Parma FC; 12 UC Sampdoria (loan); 12 Feyenoord (NED) (loan); 13- Feyenoord (NED)

2012/13 appearances/goals

Domestic league Dutch Eredivisie 29/27

Andrea Pirlo
Midfielder

Height 177cm
Born 19/05/79, Flero, Italy

It was asking a lot for Pirlo to repeat his heroics of the 2011/12 season, when he masterminded Juventus's invincible Scudetto triumph and rolled back the years for Italy at UEFA EURO 2012, but he certainly gave it his best shot. The Serie A title was successfully defended by the Bianconeri, again in relative comfort and with his stamp very much in evidence, and the bearded midfield maestro continued to figure prominently for the Azzurri, celebrating his 100th cap with a trademark free-kick to open the scoring against Mexico in Italy's first match of the 2013 FIFA Confederations Cup. At 34, he clearly has much still to give.

International career

ITALY
Major honours FIFA World Cup (2006)
Debut 07/09/02 v Azerbaijan (a, Baku, ECQ), won 2-0
First goal 30/05/04 v Tunisia (a, Tunis, friendly), won 4-0
Caps 102 **Goals** 13
Major tournaments UEFA EURO 2004; FIFA World Cup 2006; UEFA EURO 2008; FIFA Confederations Cup 2009; FIFA World Cup 2010; UEFA EURO 2012; FIFA Confederations Cup 2013

Club career

Major honours UEFA Champions League (2003, 2007); UEFA Super Cup (2003, 2007); FIFA World Club Cup (2007); Italian Championship (2004, 2011, 2012, 2013); Italian Cup (2003)
Clubs 95-98 Brescia Calcio; 98-01 FC Internazionale Milano; 99-00 Reggina Calcio (loan); 01 Brescia Calcio (loan); 01-11 AC Milan; 11- Juventus

2012/13 appearances/goals

Domestic league Italian Serie A 32/5
European UEFA Champions League 10/-
National team FIFA World Cup 2014 qualifying 6/1; FIFA Confederations Cup 2013 3/1; Friendlies 3(1)/1

Marco Reus
Attacking midfielder

Height 180cm
Born 31/05/89, Dortmund, Germany

Back at his hometown club after a three-year spell with VfL Borussia Mönchengladbach, Reus revelled in the familiar surroundings, bringing speed, creativity and finishing power to a Borussia Dortmund side that failed to complete a hat-trick of Bundesliga titles yet played thrilling football all season in the UEFA Champions League. Having scored an excellent goal on his first away game in the competition, against Manchester City FC, the German international struck three more times en route to the final. He also found the net on 14 occasions in the Bundesliga and cemented his place in Joachim Löw's Nationalmannschaft with five FIFA World Cup qualifying goals.

International career

GERMANY
Debut 07/10/11 v Turkey (a, Istanbul, ECQ), won 3-1
First goal 26/05/12 v Switzerland (a, Basel, friendly), lost 3-5
Caps 15 **Goals** 7
Major tournaments UEFA EURO 2012

Club career

Clubs 07-09 Rot Weiss Ahlen; 09-12 VfL Borussia Mönchengladbach; 12- Borussia Dortmund

2012/13 appearances/goals

Domestic league German Bundesliga 27(5)/14
European UEFA Champions League 13/4
National team FIFA World Cup 2014 qualifying 5/5; Friendlies 2/-

Franck Ribéry

Attacking midfielder/Winger

Height 170cm
Born 01/04/83, Boulogne-sur-Mer, France

The image of Ribéry driving down the left touchline, sizing up the full-back and darting past him towards the penalty area was burned into the minds of FC Bayern München fans at the end of the club's unforgettable 2012/13 season. The maverick French winger celebrated turning 30 by producing the most consistently dazzling form of his career, and it earned him a third German double plus the ultimate glory of victory in the UEFA Champions League. His contribution to all three trophies was immense, and it was his deft touch that set up Arjen Robben for the late winning goal at Wembley against Borussia Dortmund.

International career

FRANCE
Debut 27/05/06 v Mexico (h, Paris, friendly), won 1-0
First goal 27/06/06 v Spain (n, Hanover, WCF), won 3-1
Caps 73 **Goals** 12
Major tournaments FIFA World Cup 2006; UEFA EURO 2008; FIFA World Cup 2010; UEFA EURO 2012

Club career

Major honours UEFA Champions League (2013); German Championship (2008, 2010, 2013); Turkish Cup (2005); German Cup (2008, 2010, 2013)
Clubs 01-02 US Boulogne; 02-03 Olympique Alès; 03-04 Stade Brestois 29; 04-05 FC Metz; 05 Galatasaray AŞ (TUR); 05-07 Olympique de Marseille; 07- FC Bayern München (GER)

2012/13 appearances/goals

Domestic league German Bundesliga 24(3)/10
European UEFA Champions League 11(1)/1
National team FIFA World Cup 2014 qualifying 5/2; Friendlies 3(1)/-

Arjen Robben

Winger

Height 180cm
Born 23/01/84, Bedum, Netherlands

Robben spent much of the 2012/13 season in the treatment room, but he found fitness and form at the business end of the campaign and enjoyed the greatest moment of his career when he clipped the ball past Borussia Dortmund goalkeeper Roman Weidenfeller to score the winning goal for FC Bayern München in the UEFA Champions League final. It was a moment of deliverance that made up for all the big-match heartbreak the dazzling Dutch winger had endured in the past. Also responsible for Bayern's first goal in the 2-1 win, with the perfect pass for Mario Mandžukić's tap-in, he was officially named man of the match at Wembley.

International career

NETHERLANDS
Debut 30/04/03 v Portugal (h, Eindhoven, friendly), drew 1-1
First goal 11/10/03 v Moldova (h, Eindhoven, ECQ), won 5-0
Caps 68 **Goals** 18
Major tournaments UEFA EURO 2004; FIFA World Cup 2006; UEFA EURO 2008; FIFA World Cup 2010; UEFA EURO 2012

Club career

Major honours UEFA Champions League (2013); Dutch Championship (2003); English Premier League (2005, 2006); Spanish Championship (2008); German Championship (2010, 2013); English FA Cup (2007); German Cup (2010, 2013); English League Cup (2005, 2007)
Clubs 00-02 FC Groningen; 02-04 PSV Eindhoven; 04-07 Chelsea FC (ENG); 07-09 Real Madrid CF (ESP); 09- FC Bayern München (GER)

2012/13 appearances/goals

Domestic league German Bundesliga 11(5)/5
European UEFA Champions League 7(2)/4
National team FIFA World Cup 2014 qualifying 3/-; Friendlies 3(1)/1

Raul Rusescu

Striker

Height 181cm
Born 09/07/88, Ramnicu Valcea, Romania

FC Steaua Bucureşti's top marksman in the 2011/12 Liga I with 13 goals, Rusescu upped his tally to 21 in 2012/13 and finished five clear at the top of the division's scoring charts. The tricky, technically gifted striker was the focal point of Steaua's first Romanian title win for seven years, and he also scored some memorable goals in the UEFA Europa League, including a vital long-range strike against FC København and a coolly converted penalty against Chelsea FC. Although largely overlooked by Romania head coach Victor Piţurcă, he caught the eye of a number of foreign clubs and signed a five-year contract with Sevilla FC in June.

International career

ROMANIA
Debut 11/09/12 v Andorra (h, Bucharest, WCQ), won 4-0
Caps 2 **Goals** 0

Club career

Major honours Romanian Championship (2009, 2013)
Clubs 05-11 FC Unirea Urziceni; 06-07 FC Dunărea Giurgiu (loan); 07-08 CS Otopeni (loan); 11-13 FC Steaua Bucureşti; 13- Sevilla FC (ESP)

2012/13 appearances/goals

Domestic league Romanian Liga I 29(5)/21
European UEFA Europa League 7(2)/4; UEFA Europa League qualifying/play-offs 3(1)/1
National team FIFA World Cup 2014 qualifying (2)/-

Sammir
Midfielder

Height 178cm
Born 23/04/87, Itabuna, Brazil

Starring in the Croatian Prva Liga is different from standing out in the UEFA Champions League – as GNK Dinamo Zagreb discovered for the second season running in another fraught campaign – but the club's crafty Brazilian-born playmaker managed to do both during a season in which he followed the lead of former Dinamo striker Eduardo by opting to play international football for Croatia. The 26-year-old schemer was Dinamo's top scorer, with 13 goals, in the club's eighth successive domestic title triumph – the seventh in which he had been involved. He was also an ever-present in the UEFA Champions League group stage.

International career

CROATIA
Debut 12/10/12 v FYROM (a, Skopje, WCQ), won 2-1
Caps 4 **Goals** 0

Club career

Major honours Croatian Championship (2007, 2008, 2009, 2010, 2011, 2012, 2013); Croatian Cup (2007, 2008, 2009, 2011, 2012)
Clubs 05-06 Atlético Paranaense (BRA); 05-06 Paulista FC (BRA) (loan); 06-07 Venda Nova FC (BRA); 06 AD São Caetano (BRA) (loan); 07 GNK Dinamo Zagreb (loan); 07- GNK Dinamo Zagreb

2012/13 appearances/goals

Domestic league Croatian 1. HNL 25(3)/13
European UEFA Champions League 6/-; UEFA Champions League qualifying/play-offs 5/-
National team FIFA World Cup 2014 qualifying 2(1)/-; Friendlies (1)/-

Santi Cazorla
Attacking midfielder

Height 169cm
Born 13/12/84, Llanera, Spain

Arsenal FC made three major signings in the summer of 2012, but while Olivier Giroud and Lukas Podolski both took time to adapt to English football, Santi Cazorla was on fire from the start. Those positive early impressions were sustained as the Spaniard appeared in every Premier League game and ended the campaign with 12 goals. He was not short of assists, either, setting up all four goals in the Gunners' crucial 4-1 win at home to Wigan Athletic FC in May. With so many top-class Spanish midfielders available for selection, the 28-year-old will probably need an even stronger showing in 2013/14 to earn a FIFA World Cup starting berth in Brazil.

International career

SPAIN
Major honours UEFA European Championship (2008, 2012)
Debut 31/05/08 v Peru (h, Huelva, friendly), won 2-1
First goal 19/11/08 v Chile (h, Villarreal, friendly), won 3-0
Caps 56 **Goals** 9
Major tournaments UEFA EURO 2008; FIFA Confederations Cup 2009; UEFA EURO 2012; FIFA Confederations Cup 2013

Club career

Clubs 03-06 Villarreal CF; 06-07 RC Recreativo de Huelva; 07-11 Villarreal CF; 11-12 Málaga CF; 12- Arsenal FC (ENG)

2012/13 appearances/goals

Domestic league English Premier League 37(1)/12
European UEFA Champions League 7/-
National team FIFA World Cup 2014 qualifying 2(2)/-; FIFA Confederations Cup 2013 1(1)/-; Friendlies 4(1)/3

Bastian Schweinsteiger
Midfielder

Height 183cm
Born 01/08/84, Kolbermoor, Germany

Back to his imperious best after an injury-marred 2011/12 campaign that ended in penalty shoot-out despair against Chelsea FC, Schweinsteiger was the midfield heartbeat of FC Bayern München's treble-winning side. Consistently effective on all fronts, he scored the first goal of the club's successful UEFA Champions League campaign – against Valencia CF – and also the one that clinched the Bundesliga title – at Eintracht Frankfurt – with six games still to play. He appeared only three times for Germany, which meant that his 100th appearance was delayed until 2013/14, at the end of which, all things being equal, he will appear at his third FIFA World Cup.

International career

GERMANY
Debut 06/06/04 v Hungary (h, Kaiserslautern, friendly), lost 0-2
First goal 08/06/05 v Russia (h, Monchengladbach, friendly), drew 2-2
Caps 98 **Goals** 23
Major tournaments UEFA EURO 2004; FIFA Confederations Cup 2005; FIFA World Cup 2006; UEFA EURO 2008; FIFA World Cup 2010; UEFA EURO 2012

Club career

Major honours UEFA Champions League (2013); German Championship (2003, 2005, 2006, 2008, 2010, 2013); German Cup (2003, 2005, 2006, 2008, 2010, 2013)
Clubs 02- FC Bayern München

2012/13 appearances/goals

Domestic league German Bundesliga 27(1)/7
European UEFA Champions League 11(1)/2
National team FIFA World Cup 2014 qualifying 3/-

Selçuk İnan
Midfielder

Height 182cm
Born 10/02/85, Hatay, Turkey

A pivotal member of Galatasaray AŞ's Turkish Süper Lig-winning side for the second successive season, Selçuk excelled also in Europe, his accurate passing and set-piece expertise helping the Istanbul side into the quarter-finals of the UEFA Champions League, where they lost to Real Madrid CF. His consistently high level of performance persuaded Cimbom coach Fatih Terim to appoint him as club captain midway through the season, and the 20-year old midfield general revelled in the extra responsibility. He also played well for Turkey, scoring three goals during the season, but a place at the 2014 FIFA World Cup looked a long shot as the qualifying competition entered its final phase.

International career
TURKEY
Debut 13/10/07 v Moldova (a, Chisinau, ECQ), drew 1-1
First goal 24/05/12 v Georgia (n, Salzburg, friendly), won 3-1
Caps 28 **Goals** 4

Club career
Major honours Turkish Championship (2012, 2013); Turkish Cup (2010)
Clubs 02-05 Dardanelspor; 05-08 Manisaspor; 08-11 Trabzonspor; 11- Galatasaray AŞ

2012/13 appearances/goals
Domestic league Turkish Süper Lig 31/6
European UEFA Champions League 10/-
National team FIFA World Cup 2014 qualifying 2(1)/2; Friendlies 4(1)/1

Sergio Ramos
Centre-back

Height 183cm
Born 30/03/86, Seville, Spain

Four days before his 27th birthday, in a FIFA World Cup qualifier against Finland, Sergio Ramos became the youngest European footballer to win a 100th senior international cap. The Real Madrid CF defender featured in all 16 matches played by Spain in 2012/13, eventually overtaking club colleague Xabi Alonso to become his country's fourth most-capped player. It was a long and tiring season for the rugged Andalusian centre-back, but he was seldom found wanting. The bigger the game, the better he seemed to play, and he also chipped in with important goals – for Spain against France and Finland, for Madrid against FC Barcelona and Borussia Dortmund.

International career
SPAIN
Major honours FIFA World Cup (2010); UEFA European Championship (2008, 2012)
Debut 26/03/05 v China (h, Salamanca, friendly), won 3-0
First goal 13/10/05 v San Marino (a, Serravalle, WCQ), won 6-0
Caps 108 **Goals** 9
Major tournaments FIFA World Cup 2006; UEFA EURO 2008; FIFA Confederations Cup 2009; FIFA World Cup 2010; UEFA EURO 2012; FIFA Confederations Cup 2013

Club career
Major honours Spanish Championship (2007, 2008, 2012); Spanish Cup (2011)
Clubs 02-05 Sevilla FC; 05- Real Madrid CF

2012/13 appearances/goals
Domestic league Spanish Liga 26/1
European UEFA Champions League 9/1
National team FIFA World Cup 2014 qualifying 5/2; FIFA Confederations Cup 2013 5/-; Friendlies 3(3)/1

Roberto Soldado
Striker

Height 179cm
Born 27/05/85, Valencia, Spain

A guarantee of goals since he joined hometown club Valencia CF from Getafe CF in 2010, Soldado was on target a personal-best 30 times in his third season at the club. He stretched his final Liga total to 24 with a double on the final day at Sevilla FC, but Valencia's 4-3 defeat denied the club a return to the UEFA Champions League – a competition in which the striker had scored four goals in two games against FC BATE Borisov the previous autumn. Although often overlooked by Spain, the 28-year-old strengthened his case for regular inclusion in Vicente del Bosque's side with important winning goals against Georgia and Uruguay. He left Valencia for Tottenham Hotspur FC in the summer.

International career
SPAIN
Debut 02/06/07 v Latvia (a, Riga, ECQ), won 2-0
First goal 29/02/12 v Venezuela (h, Malaga, friendly), won 5-0
Caps 11 **Goals** 6
Major tournaments FIFA Confederations Cup 2013

Club career
Major honours Spanish Championship (2008)
Clubs 02-08 Real Madrid CF; 06-07 CA Osasuna (loan); 08-10 Getafe CF; 10-13 Valencia CF; 13- Tottenham Hotspur FC (ENG)

2012/13 appearances/goals
Domestic league Spanish Liga 33(2)/24
European UEFA Champions League 7/4
National team FIFA World Cup 2014 qualifying 1/1; FIFA Confederations Cup 2013 2/1; Friendlies (3)/1

Valentin Stocker
Midfielder

Height 178cm
Born 12/04/89, Lucerne, Switzerland

A rising star of the Swiss game since he scored on his international debut as a 19-year-old, Stocker enjoyed his most productive campaign yet, not only playing a dominant role in FC Basel 1893's fourth successive Swiss Super League title triumph – and the fifth of his career – but also winning new admirers abroad with his classy offerings in the UEFA Europa League. He scored the opening goal of the knockout ties against both FC Dnipro Dnipropetrovsk and Tottenham Hotspur FC as Basel advanced against the odds to a first ever European semi-final. A vote of confidence from Swiss national coach Ottmar Hitzfeld was due reward for a splendid season.

International career
SWITZERLAND
Debut 20/08/08 v Cyprus (h, Geneva, friendly), won 4-1
First goal 20/08/08 v Cyprus (h, Geneva, friendly), won 4-1
Caps 17 **Goals** 3

Club career
Major honours Swiss Championship (2008, 2010, 2011, 2012, 2013); Swiss Cup (2008, 2010, 2012)
Clubs 07- FC Basel 1893

2012/13 appearances/goals
Domestic league Swiss Super League 29(2)/6
European UEFA Champions League qualifying/play-offs 3(1)/-; UEFA Europa League 13/3
National team FIFA World Cup 2014 qualifying 3/-; Friendlies (2)/-

Marco Streller
Striker

Height 195cm
Born 18/06/81, Basel, Switzerland

2012/13 was a season of hyperactivity for FC Basel 1893, whose extended participation in Europe entailed a total of 62 competitive matches. Streller, the club captain, played in 52 of them, the majority up front on his own rather than alongside long-standing strike partner Alex Frei in new coach Murat Yakin's preferred 4-2-3-1 formation. The tall left-footer maintained his form throughout, scoring 14 goals in the Super League to win the sixth championship title of his career and adding another five in Europe – a spectacular strike against CFR 1907 Cluj in the UEFA Champions League play-offs plus four in the team's historic run to the UEFA Europa League semi-finals.

International career
SWITZERLAND
Debut 11/10/03 v Republic of Ireland (h, Basel, ECQ), won 2-0
First goal 16/11/05 v Turkey (a, Istanbul, WCQ), lost 2-4
Caps 37 **Goals** 12
Major tournaments FIFA World Cup 2006; UEFA EURO 2008

Club career
Major honours Swiss Championship (2004, 2008, 2010, 2011, 2012, 2013); German Championship (2007); Swiss Cup (2008, 2010, 2012)
Clubs 00-04 FC Basel 1893; 01-02 FC Concordia Basel (loan); 02-03 FC Thun (loan); 04-07 VfB Stuttgart (GER); 06 1. FC Köln (GER) (loan); 07- FC Basel 1893

2012/13 appearances/goals
Domestic league Swiss Super League 30(2)/14
European UEFA Champions League qualifying/play-offs 6/1; UEFA Europa League 11/4

Luis Suárez
Striker

Height 181cm
Born 24/01/87, Salto, Uruguay

A magnificent season for Liverpool FC ended in bizarre fashion for the Uruguayan international when he was banned for ten games for biting the arm of Chelsea FC defender Branislav Ivanović during a Premier League match at Anfield. Suárez's Jekyll and Hyde reputation was epitomised by the last-minute equaliser he scored in that game. It was one of 23 league goals he struck for the Merseysiders during a season in which he was rarely out of the news. The quality of his football was sensational, earning him a place in the PFA team of the year alongside Manchester United FC's Robin van Persie – the only player who outscored him.

International career
URUGUAY
Major honours Copa América (2011)
Debut 07/02/07 v Colombia (a, Cucuta, friendly), won 3-1
First goal 13/10/07 v Bolivia (h, Montevideo, WCQ), won 5-0
Caps 69 **Goals** 34
Major tournaments FIFA World Cup 2010; Copa América 2011; FIFA Confederations Cup 2013

Club career
Major honours Uruguayan Championship (2006); Dutch Championship (2011); Dutch Cup (2010); English League Cup (2012)
Clubs 05-06 Club Nacional; 06-07 FC Groningen (NED); 07-11 AFC Ajax (NED); 11- Liverpool FC (ENG)

2012/13 appearances/goals
Domestic league English Premier League 33/23
European UEFA Europa League 4(2)/3; UEFA Europa League qualifying/play-offs 2/1
National team FIFA World Cup 2014 qualifying 5/2; FIFA Confederations Cup 2013 4(1)/3; Friendlies 2(1)/2

Neven Subotić

Centre-back

Height 192cm
Born 10/12/88, Rrnjavor, Bosnia & Herzegovina

A tower of strength in the Borussia Dortmund defence throughout the season, Subotić's most striking performances were reserved for the UEFA Champions League. The Serbian international with the American accent started 11 games in Europe and was rock-solid in the majority of them, helping the club to remain undefeated all the way through to the second leg of the semi-final. They also lost the final, 2-1 to FC Bayern München, but the 24-year-old will forever be remembered for one incredible goal-line clearance he made to intercept Thomas Müller's cross and prevent a simple tap-in for Arjen Robben with the score at 1-1.

International career

SERBIA
Debut 28/03/09 v Romania (a, Constanta, WCQ), won 3-2
First goal 10/06/09 v Faroe Islands (a, Torshavn, WCQ), won 2-0
Caps 34 **Goals** 2
Major tournaments FIFA World Cup 2010

Club career

Major honours German Championship (2011, 2012); German Cup (2012)
Clubs 07-08 1. FSV Mainz 05 (GER); 08- Borussia Dortmund (GER)

2012/13 appearances/goals

Domestic league German Bundesliga 25/3
European UEFA Champions League 11/-
National team FIFA World Cup 2014 qualifying 3/-

Thiago Silva

Centre-Back

Height 183cm
Born 22/09/84, Rio de Janeiro, Brazil

Sold by AC Milan to Paris Saint-Germain FC in tandem with Zlatan Ibrahimović, Thiago Silva did not have quite the same impact in the City of Light as the mercurial Swede – largely because of the number of matches he missed through injury – but he still did enough to challenge him for the Ligue 1 player of the year award. Widely regarded as the world's most accomplished central defender, the 28-year-old had two brilliant games against FC Barcelona in the UEFA Champions League and was immense also for Brazil at the FIFA Confederations Cup, skippering the team to victory on home soil. What price an encore at the 2014 FIFA World Cup?

International career

BRAZIL
Major honours FIFA Confederations Cup (2013)
Debut 12/10/08 v Venezuela (a, San Cristobal, WCQ), won 4-0
First goal 30/05/12 v United States (a, Landover, friendly), won 4-1
Caps 39 **Goals** 1
Major tournaments FIFA World Cup 2010; Copa América 2011; FIFA Confederations Cup 2013

Club career

Major honours Italian Championship (2011); French Championship (2013); Brazilian Cup (2007)
Clubs 01-03 RS Futebol Clube; 04 EC Juventude; 04 FC Porto (POR); 05 FC Dínamo Moskva (RUS); 06-09 Fluminense FC; 09-12 AC Milan (ITA); 12- Paris Saint-Germain FC (FRA)

2012/13 appearances/goals

Domestic league French Ligue 1 22/-
European UEFA Champions League 9/2
National team FIFA Confederations Cup 2013 5/-; Friendlies 7/-

Mathieu Valbuena

Attacking midfielder

Height 171cm
Born 28/09/84, Bruges, France

Under new coach Élie Baup, Olympique de Marseille rose eight places up the table from the previous season to finish second in Ligue 1 and qualify for the UEFA Champions League. Central to their climb was Valbuena, whose seventh season at the Stade Vélodrome was considered by many to be his best. The diminutive wide midfielder missed just one league fixture and played with unwavering consistency, providing 12 assists – the joint highest number in the division with LOSC Lille's Dimitri Payet. He also starred under his former Marseille boss Didier Deschamps for France, scoring in successive internationals against Italy, Germany and Georgia.

International career

FRANCE
Debut 26/05/10 v Costa Rica (h, Lens, friendly), won 2-1
First goal 26/05/10 v Costa Rica (h, Lens, friendly), won 2-1
Caps 23 **Goals** 5
Major tournaments FIFA World Cup 2010; UEFA EURO 2012

Club career

Major honours French Championship (2010); French League Cup (2010, 2011, 2012)
Clubs 04-06 FC Libourne-Saint-Seurin; 06- Olympique de Marseille

2012/13 appearances/goals

Domestic league French Ligue 1 37/3
European UEFA Europa League 2(2)/1; UEFA Europa League qualifying/play-offs 3(1)/-
National team FIFA World Cup 2014 qualifying 2(3)/1; Friendlies 5(1)/2

Robin van Persie
Striker

Height 188cm
Born 06/08/83, Rotterdam, Netherlands

The acquisition of Van Persie from Arsenal FC provided Manchester United FC with the firepower they needed to regain the Premier League trophy. The Dutchman scored a league-best tally of 26 goals, many of them at crucial times as United were frequently forced to come from behind. Fittingly it was his sublime hat-trick at home to Aston Villa FC that wrapped up the title, bringing him the first domestic championship triumph of his career after seven barren seasons at Arsenal. Life was also good at international level. He scored five goals as the Netherlands cruised towards the 2014 FIFA World Cup and in June was appointed as the new Oranje captain.

International career

NETHERLANDS
Debut 04/06/05 v Romania (h, Rotterdam, WCQ), won 2-0
First goal 08/06/05 v Finland (a, Helsinki, WCQ), won 4-0
Caps 76 **Goals** 35
Major tournaments FIFA World Cup 2006; UEFA EURO 2008; FIFA World Cup 2010; UEFA EURO 2012

Club career

Major honours *UEFA Cup (2002); English Premier League (2013); English FA Cup (2005)*
Clubs 01-04 Feyenoord; 04-12 Arsenal FC (ENG); 12- Manchester United FC (ENG)

2012/13 appearances/goals

Domestic league English Premier League 35(3)/26
European UEFA Champions League 5(1)/3
National team FIFA World Cup 2014 qualifying 5/5; Friendlies 3/1

Raphaël Varane
Centre-back

Height 191cm
Born 25/04/93, Lille, France

A star was born at Real Madrid CF in 2012/13 as Varane emerged from nowhere to cement a regular place in central defence with a succession of eye-catching performances. The young Frenchman started all six of Madrid's knockout fixtures in the UEFA Champions League and was still only 19 when he gave two exceptional displays of athleticism and composure against Manchester United FC in the round of 16. He also demonstrated his big-match temperament as Madrid knocked FC Barcelona out of the Spanish Cup, scoring in both legs of the semi-final. A few weeks later he was handed his first two senior international caps for France.

International career

FRANCE
Debut 22/03/13 v Georgia (h, Paris, WCQ), won 3-1
Caps 2 **Goals** 0

Club career

Major honours *Spanish Championship (2012)*
Clubs 10-11 RC Lens; 11- Real Madrid CF (ESP)

2012/13 appearances/goals

Domestic league Spanish Liga 12(3)/-
European UEFA Champions League 10(1)/-
National team FIFA World Cup 2014 qualifying 2/-

Kenneth Vermeer
Goalkeeper

Height 182cm
Born 10/01/86, Amsterdam, Netherlands

Uncapped at senior level prior to the 2012/13 season, Vermeer put forward a strong case to be the Netherlands' No1 goalkeeper at the 2014 FIFA World Cup by keeping clean sheets in each of his first four internationals – against Germany, Estonia, Romania and (as a half-time substitute) Indonesia. His selection by Oranje boss Louis van Gaal was the logical consequence of an exceptional campaign between the posts for AFC Ajax. For the second season running the native Amsterdammer helped his club to the Eredivisie title with a string of authoritative displays, earning himself a reputation as a penalty-saving specialist into the bargain.

International career

NETHERLANDS
Debut 14/11/12 v Germany (h, Amsterdam, friendly), drew 0-0
Caps 4 **Goals** 0

Club career

Major honours *Dutch Championship (2011, 2012, 2013); Dutch Cup (2006, 2007, 2010)*
Clubs 05- AFC Ajax; 07-08 Willem II (loan)

2012/13 appearances/goals

Domestic league Dutch Eredivisie 30/-
European UEFA Champions League 6/-; UEFA Europa League 2/-
National team FIFA World Cup 2014 qualifying 2/-; Friendlies 1(1)/-

Jan Vertonghen

Centre-back/Left-back

Height 189cm
Born 24/04/87, Sint-Niklaas, Belgium

A place in the PFA Premier League team of the year was Vertonghen's reward for an exceptional debut campaign with Tottenham Hotspur FC. The new recruit from AFC Ajax was a model of consistency all season for the London club, his versatility as a defender supplemented by an ability to pose danger in the attacking third with his aerial strength and powerful left-foot shot. He scored seven goals in all for Spurs, including one against FC Internazionale Milano in the UEFA Europa League, and was also on target twice for the Belgian national side, for whom he played the full 90 minutes in all 11 internationals.

International career

BELGIUM
Debut 02/06/07 v Portugal (h, Brussels, ECQ), lost 1-2
First goal 12/08/09 v Czech Republic (a, Teplice, friendly), lost 1-3
Caps 49 **Goals** 4

Club career

Major honours Dutch Championship (2011, 2012); Dutch Cup (2010)
Clubs 06-12 AFC Ajax (NED); 06-07 RKC Waalwijk (NED) (loan); 12- Tottenham Hotspur FC (ENG)

2012/13 appearances/goals

Domestic league English Premier League 34/4
European UEFA Europa League 12/1
National team FIFA World Cup 2014 qualifying 7/1; Friendlies 4/1

Arturo Vidal

Midfielder

Height 181cm
Born 22/05/87, Santiago, Chile

Vidal's second season at Juventus ended with a second Serie A winner's medal. Nobody deserved it more. The Chilean international was outstanding from first kick to last, his energy and will to win driving the team on from midfield and his eye for a goal proving decisive on several occasions. He was Juve's joint top scorer in the league, five of his ten goals coming in four games during the title run-in. He also struck three goals in the UEFA Champions League, two of them against holders Chelsea FC. A couple of FIFA World Cup qualifying strikes for Chile in June – in vital wins against Paraguay and Bolivia – rounded off a memorable season.

International career

CHILE
Debut 07/02/07 v Venezuela (a, Maracaibo, friendly), won 1-0
First goal 05/09/09 v Venezuela (h, Santiago, WCQ), drew 2-2
Caps 47 **Goals** 6
Major tournaments FIFA World Cup 2010; Copa América 2011

Club career

Major honours Chilean Championship (apertura 2006; clausura 2006; apertura 2007); Italian Championship (2012, 2013)
Clubs 05-07 Colo-Colo; 07-11 Bayer 04 Leverkusen (GER); 11- Juventus (ITA)

2012/13 appearances/goals

Domestic league Italian Serie A 20(2)/10
European UEFA Champions League 9/3
National team FIFA World Cup 2014 qualifying 4/2; Friendlies 2/-

Roman Weidenfeller

Goalkeeper

Height 188cm
Born 06/08/80, Diez, Germany

Weidenfeller's 11th season at Borussia Dortmund yielded no silverware but it did bring him wider recognition on a scale he had never previously experienced. The captain of Dortmund on their fabulous UEFA Champions League run, he was a heroic figure on several occasions but never more so than in the final, when he denied FC Bayern München with a string of defiant saves – only to be cruelly beaten at the finish by Arjen Robben's 89th-minute winning strike. At 33 it would appear that international football has passed him by, but there will be plenty more active service for Dortmund, his contract having been extended until 2016.

International career

GERMANY
Uncapped

Club career

Major honours German Championship (2010, 2011); German Cup (2011)
Clubs 99-02 1. FC Kaiserslautern; 02- Borussia Dortmund

2012/13 appearances/goals

Domestic league German Bundesliga 31/-
European UEFA Champions League 13/-

Pontus Wernbloom
Midfielder

Height 187cm
Born 25/06/86, Kungalv, Sweden

PFC CSKA Moskva's 2012/13 season ended in triumph with a Russian league and cup double. Pivotal to the club's success was their all-Swedish midfield, in which Wernbloom was re-united with his former partner at AZ Alkmaar, Rasmus Elm. The pair's telepathic understanding guaranteed solidity and flair in equal measure, with the ex-IFK Göteborg star standing out in particular for his non-stop energy and commitment to attack. He blotted his copybook by receiving a red card in the cup final against FC Anji Makhachkala, but it was his crucial goal against FC Terek Grozny a few weeks earlier – his fourth of the season – that paved the way for the Premier-Liga triumph.

International career

SWEDEN
Debut 18/01/07 v Ecuador (a, Cuenca, friendly), lost 1-2
First goal 03/09/10 v Hungary (h, Solna, ECQ), won 2-0
Caps 32 **Goals** 2
Major tournaments UEFA EURO 2012

Club career

Major honours Swedish Championship (2007); Russian Championship (2013); Swedish Cup (2008); Russian Cup (2013)
Clubs 05-09 IFK Göteborg; 09-12 AZ Alkmaar (NED); 12- PFC CSKA Moskva (RUS)

2012/13 appearances/goals

Domestic league Russian Premier-Liga 23(3)/4
European UEFA Europa League play-offs (2)/-
National team FIFA World Cup 2014 qualifying 3/-; Friendlies 2(3)/-

Willian
Winger

Height 174cm
Born 09/08/88, Ribeirao Pires, Brazil

With four goals in the UEFA Champions League group stage, Willian was one of the principal architects of FC Shakhtar Donetsk's passage into the knockout phase. Indeed, his two away goals against Chelsea FC effectively knocked the holders out of the competition. However, by the time the round of 16 took place, the nifty Brazilian winger was no longer at the club, having been enticed across the border by the ambitious Russians of FC Anji Makhachkala. Things did not work out quite so well at his new club, largely because of injury, but the range of his talent suggests that, at 25, he is a sound investment.

International career

BRAZIL
Debut 10/11/11 v Gabon (a, Libreville, friendly), won 2-0
Caps 2 **Goals** 0

Club career

Major honours UEFA Cup (2009); Ukrainian Championship (2008, 2010, 2011, 2012, 2013); Ukrainian Cup (2008, 2011, 2012, 2013)
Clubs 06-07 SC Corinthians; 07-13 FC Shakhtar Donetsk (UKR); 13- FC Anji Makhachkala (RUS)

2012/13 appearances/goals

Domestic league Ukrainian Premier League 9(5)/2; Russian Premier-Liga 6(1)/1
European UEFA Champions League 6/4; UEFA Europa League 3/-

Pablo Zabaleta
Right-back

Height 176cm
Born 16/01/85, Buenos Aires, Argentina

Many of the Manchester City FC players who won the Premier League title in 2011/12 struggled to rediscover the same form in the season that followed, but an exception to that rule was Zabaleta, who actually played better in 2012/13. The Argentinian right-back was the only City player to appear in the PFA Premier League team of the year, a fitting reward for nine months of effort and application during which his level of consistency seldom dipped. It was ironic, therefore, that City's most dependable performer should be sent off in the FA Cup final, his 84th-minute dismissal being followed soon afterwards by Wigan Athletic FC's winning goal.

International career

ARGENTINA
Debut 17/08/05 v Hungary (a, Budapest, friendly), won 2-1
Caps 31 **Goals** 0
Major tournaments Copa América 2011

Club career

Major honours Copa Sudamericana (2002); English Premier League (2012); Spanish Cup (2006); English FA Cup (2011)
Clubs 02-05 CA San Lorenzo; 05-08 RCD Espanyol (ESP); 08- Manchester City FC (ENG)

2012/13 appearances/goals

Domestic league English Premier League 29(1)/2
European UEFA Champions League 3(2)/-
National team FIFA World Cup 2014 qualifying 4/-; Friendlies 3/-

UEFA

Route de Genève 46

Case postale

CH-1260 Nyon 2

Switzerland

Tel: +41 (0) 848 00 2727

Fax: +41 (0) 848 01 2727

Web: UEFA.com

Media Desk

Tel: +41 (0) 848 04 2727

Founded: 15 June 1954

Affiliated national associations: 54

Number of clubs: 178,224

Number of players: 17,688,690

Number of female players: 1,996,618

Number of referees: 267,592

(all figures are approximate)

UEFA Executive Committee

President

Michel Platini (France)

Vice-Presidents

Şenes Erzik (Turkey)

Ángel María Villar Llona (Spain)

Marios N Lefkaritis (Cyprus)

Giancarlo Abete (Italy)

Grigoriy Surkis (Ukraine)

Members

Karen Espelund (Norway)

Sergei Fursenko (Russia)

David Gill (England)

Peter Gilliéron (Switzerland)

Allan Hansen (Denmark)

František Laurinec (Slovakia)

Avraham Luzon (Israel)

Borislav Mihaylov (Bulgaria)

Wolfgang Niersbach (Germany)

Mircea Sandu (Romania)

Michael van Praag (Netherlands)

Advisor

Fernando Gomes (Portugal)

Honorary President

Lennart Johansson (Sweden)

General Secretary

Gianni Infantino

UEFA EVENTS CALENDAR 2013/14

National team	Club

2014 FIFA World Cup

06/09/2013	Qualifying round matches
10/09/2013	Qualifying round matches
11/10/2013	Qualifying round matches
15/10/2013	Qualifying round matches
15/11/2013	Play-off matches, first leg
19/11/2013	Play-off matches, second leg
06/12/2013	Final tournament draw (Bahia, Brazil)
12/06-13/07/2014	Final tournament (Brazil)

 ## UEFA EURO 2016

23/02/2014	Qualifying draw (Nice, France)
10/06-10/07/2016	Final tournament (France)

 ## 2015 UEFA European Under-21 Championship

05-06/09/2013	Qualifying round matches
09-10/09/2013	Qualifying round matches
10-11/10/2013	Qualifying round matches
14-15/10/2013	Qualifying round matches
14-15/11/2013	Qualifying round matches
18-19/11/2013	Qualifying round matches
04-05/03/2014	Qualifying round matches
23-28/05/2014	Qualifying round matches
01-08/06/2014	Qualifying round matches

 ## 2013/14 UEFA Champions League

29/08/2013	Group stage draw (Monaco)
17-18/09/2013	Group stage, Matchday 1
01-02/10/2013	Group stage, Matchday 2
22-23/10/2013	Group stage, Matchday 3
05-06/11/2013	Group stage, Matchday 4
26-27/11/2013	Group stage, Matchday 5
10-11/12/2013	Group stage, Matchday 6
13/12/2013	Round of 16 draw (Nyon, Switzerland)
18-19/02/2014	Round of 16, first leg
25-26/02/2014	Round of 16, first leg
11-12/03/2014	Round of 16, second leg
18-19/03/2014	Round of 16, second leg
21/03/2014	Quarter-final draw (Nyon, Switzerland)
01-02/04/2014	Quarter-finals, first leg
08-09/04/2014	Quarter-finals, second leg
11/04/2014	Semi-final and Final draw (Nyon, Switzerland)
22-23/04/2014	Semi-final, first leg
29-30/04/2014	Semi-final, second leg
24/05/2014	Final (Lisbon, Portugal)

Youth & Amateur

2013/14 UEFA Europa League

30/08/2013	Group stage draw (Monaco)
19/09/2013	Group stage, Matchday 1
03/10/2013	Group stage, Matchday 2
24/10/2013	Group stage, Matchday 3
07/11/2013	Group stage, Matchday 4
28/11/2013	Group stage, Matchday 5
12/12/2013	Group stage, Matchday 6
13/12/2013	Round of 32 and Round of 16 draw (Nyon, Switzerland)
20/02/2014	Round of 32, first leg
27/02/2014	Round of 32, second leg
13/03/2014	Round of 16, first leg
20/03/2014	Round of 16, second leg
21/03/2014	Quarter-final draw (Nyon, Switzerland)
03/04/2014	Quarter-finals, first leg
10/04/2014	Quarter-finals, second leg
11/04/2014	Semi-final draw (Nyon, Switzerland)
24/04/2014	Semi-final, first leg
01/05/2014	Semi-final, second leg
14/05/2014	Final (Turin, Italy)

2013 UEFA Super Cup

30/08/2013	Final (Prague, Czech Republic)

2013 FIFA Club World Cup

11-21/12/2013	Final tournament (Morocco)

2013/14 UEFA European Under-19 Championship

06/09-19/11/2013	Qualifying round matches
28/11/2013	Elite round draw (Nyon, Switzerland)
01/04-08/06/2014	Elite round matches
17/06/2014	Final tournament draw (Hungary, exact venue tbd)
19-31/07/2014	Final tournament (Hungary)

2014/15 UEFA European Under-19 Championship

28/11/2013	Qualifying round draw (Nyon, Switzerland)

2013/14 UEFA European Under-17 Championship

21/09-19/11/2013	Qualifying round matches
28/11/2013	Elite round draw (Nyon, Switzerland)
01-31/03/2014	Elite round matches
04/04/2014	Final tournament draw (Malta, Exact venue tbd)
09-21/05/2014	Final tournament (Malta)

2014/15 UEFA European Under-17 Championship

28/11/2013	Qualifying round draw (Nyon, Switzerland)

Women's

2013/14 UEFA Women's Champions League

09-10/10/2013	Round of 32, first leg
16-17/10/2013	Round of 32, second leg
09-10/11/2013	Round of 16, first leg
13-14/11/2013	Round of 16, second leg
21/11/2013	Quarter-finals, Semi-finals and Final draw (Nyon, Switzerland)
22-23/03/2014	Quarter-finals, first leg
29-30/03/2014	Quarter-finals, second leg
19-20/04/2014	Semi-finals, first leg
26-27/04/2014	Semi-finals, second leg
22/05/2014	Final (Lisbon, Portugal)

2013/14 UEFA European Women's Under-19 Championship

21-26/09/2013	First qualifying round matches
20/11/2013	Second qualifying round draw (Nyon, Switzerland)
05-10/04/2014	Second qualifying round matches
22/04/2014	Final tournament draw (Norway, exact venue tbd)
15-27/07/2014	Final tournament (Norway)

2014/15 UEFA European Women's Under-19 Championship

12/11/2013	First qualifying round draw (Nyon, Switzerland)

2013/14 UEFA European Women's Under-17 Championship

30/09-21/10/2013	Second qualifying round matches
26/11-08/12/2013	Final tournament (England)

2014/15 UEFA European Women's Under-17 Championship

12/11/2013	First qualifying round draw (Nyon, Switzerland)

Futsal

2014 UEFA European Futsal Championship

15-18/09/2013	Play-off matches, first leg
22-25/09/2013	Play-off matches, second leg
31/10/2013	Final tournament draw (Antwerp, Belgium)
28/01-08/02/2014	UEFA Futsal EURO 2014 (Belgium)

2012/13 UEFA Futsal Cup

27/08-01/09/2013	Preliminary round matches
01-06/10/2013	Main round matches
18/10/2013	Elite round draw
19-24/11/2013	Elite round matches
23/03/2014	Final tournament draw
24-27/04/2014	UEFA Futsal Cup Finals (venue tbd)

UEFA

UEFA Executive Committee meetings

19-20/09/2013	Dubrovnik, Croatia
12-13/12/2013	Bilbao, Spain
23-24/01/2014	Nyon, Switzerland
26/03/2014	Astana, Kazakhstan
13/05/2014	Turin, Italy

RESPECT

Nation-by-nation

Welcome to the Nation-by-nation section of the European Football Yearbook.

Here you will find separate chapters, alphabetically arranged, on each of the UEFA member associations (new member Gibraltar excepted) containing the following information.

Association directory

The member association's official logo, name, address, contact details and senior officials as of 31 July 2013.

Map/club index

A map of the country illustrating the locations of the top-division clubs, which are listed in alphabetical order, plus any clubs promoted to the top division at the end of the 2012/13 (2012) season. Teams qualified for the 2013/14 UEFA Champions League and UEFA Europa League are indicated as such with colour coding and club logos.

Note that locations are those where the club played all or the majority of their home matches during the 2012/13 (2012) season.

Review

A narrative review of the season, headed by an appropriate photo, is divided into four sections – Domestic league, Domestic cup, Europe and National team.

Domestic league final table

The final standings of the member association's top division including home, away and total records. The champions are indicated in bold type.

Key: Pld = matches played, W = matches won, D = matches drawn, L = matches lost, F = goals for (scored), A = goals against (conceded), Pts = points

················· = play-off line

‒ ‒ ‒ ‒ ‒ ‒ ‒ ‒ = relegation line

Any peculiarities, such as the deduction of points, clubs withdrawn or relegation issues, are indicated as NB at the foot of the table.

Season at a glance

EUROPEAN QUALIFICATION
The clubs qualified for the 2013/14 UEFA Champions League and UEFA Europa League are indicated with (in brackets) the round for which they have qualified. Champions and Cup winners are highlighted.

The league's top scorer(s), promoted club(s), relegated club(s) and the result of the domestic cup final(s) are also listed.

PLAYER OF THE SEASON, NEWCOMER OF THE SEASON, TEAM OF THE SEASON These are either official selections or personal choices of the correspondents.

National team

Home and away kits, international honours and major international tournament appearances head this section. Also included are the member association's top five international cap-holders and goalscorers. Players active in 2012/13 are highlighted in bold.

Results 2012/13

Details on all senior international matches played between August 2012 and June 2013 with date, opponent, venue, result, scorer(s) and goal time(s).

Key: H = home, A = away, N = neutral, og = own goal, p = penalty, (aet) = after extra time, (WCQ) = 2014 FIFA World Cup qualification round match, (CC) = FIFA Confederations Cup

Appearances 2012/13

Details on all participants in the aforementioned matches (coaches and players), including name, date of birth and, for each player, club(s), match-by-match appearances and all-time international caps and goals scored.

Opponents are ranged across the top and abbreviated with the appropriate three-letter country codes – capital letters identify a competitive match (i.e. FIFA World Cup qualifier or FIFA Confederations Cup).

Changes of national team coach are indicated with the appropriate appointment dates; temporary coaches are indicated in brackets.

Non-native coaches and clubs are indicated with the appropriate three-letter country code.

Key: G = goalkeeper, D = defender, M = midfielder, A = attacker, s = substitute, * = sending-off.

The number appearing after the letter indicates the minute in which a substitution took place. The number preceding an asterisk indicates the minute in which a sending-off occurred.

European club competitions

Details including opponent, result, scorers, goal times, lineups and red cards of all matches played by the member association's clubs in the 2012/13 UEFA Champions League and UEFA Europa League, including qualifying rounds and play-offs. Each team's entry is headed by home and away kits (those used in 2012/13) and the club logo. The home kit is on the left.

Domestic league club-by-club

Information on each top-division club, displayed in alphabetical order, is provided in five parts:

1) Club name followed by the coach(es)/ manager(s) used during the season and, in the case of new appointments, the dates on which they took place. Non-native coaches/managers are indicated with the appropriate three-letter country code.

2) The year the club was founded, the club's home stadium(s) (with capacity) and, where applicable, the official club website.

3) Major honours, including European, international and domestic competitions. National 'super cups', secondary leagues and minor or age-restricted knockout competitions are not included.

4) League fixtures chronologically listed, including dates, opponents, results and goalscorers.

Key: h = home, a = away, og = own goal, (p) = penalty, (w/o) = walkover/forfeit

5) A list of all players used in the league campaign, including name, nationality (where non-native), date of birth, playing position, appearances and goals. Where applicable, and known, squad numbers are also included.

Key: No = squad (jersey) number, Name = first name and family name, or, in some instances, 'football' name, Nat = nationality (native unless listed with three-letter country code), DoB = date of birth, Pos = playing position, Aps = number of appearances in the starting lineup, (s) = number of appearances as a substitute, Gls = number of goals scored, G = goalkeeper, D = defender, M = midfielder; A = attacker.

Top goalscorers

A list of the top ten (and equal) goalscorers in the member association's top division. League goals only are shown.

Promoted clubs

Information on each promoted club is provided in three parts:

1) Club name followed by the coach(es)/ manager(s) used during the season and, in the case of new appointments,

the dates on which they took place. Non-native coaches/managers are indicated with the appropriate three-letter country code.

2) The year the club was founded, the club's home stadium(s) (with capacity) and, where applicable, the official club website.

3) Major honours, including European, international and domestic competitions. National 'super cups', secondary leagues and minor or age-restricted knockout competitions are not included.

Second level final table

The final classification of the member association's second level (i.e. feeder league to the top division) table(s). Play-off details, where applicable, are also indicated.

Key: Pld = matches played, W = matches won, D = matches drawn, L = matches lost, F = goals for (scored), A = goals against (conceded), Pts = points.

- - - - - - - - - = promotion line (at the top)

················ = play-off line

- - - - - - - - - = relegation line (at the bottom)

Any peculiarities, such as the deduction of points, clubs withdrawn or promotion issues, are indicated as NB at the foot of the final league table.

Domestic cups

Results from the member association's main domestic knockout competition, beginning at the round in which the top-division clubs (or some of them) enter.

Goalscorers and times of goals are indicated from the quarter-final stage, with complete lineups, referees and sendings-off added for the final. Details of the latter stages of significant secondary knockout competitions are also included for some member associations.

Key: (aet) = after extra time, (w/o) = walkover/forfeit

NB A complete key to all three-letter country codes can be found on page 6.

ALBANIA
Federata Shqiptarë e Futbollit (FShF)

Address	Rruga e Elbasanit AL-1000 Tiranë	**President**	Armand Duka
Tel	+355 42 346 605	**General secretary**	Ilir Shulku
Fax	+355 42 346 609	**Media officer**	Tritan Kokona
E-mail	fshf@fshf.org.al	**Year of formation**	1930
Website	fshf.org	**National stadium**	Qemal Stafa, Tirana (16,230)

KATEGORIA SUPERIORE CLUBS

1. KF Apolonia
2. KS Besa
3. KS Bylis
4. KS Flamurtari
5. KS Kastrioti
6. FK Kukësi
7. KF Laçi
8. KS Luftëtari
9. KS Shkumbini
10. KS Skënderbeu
11. KS Teuta
12. KF Tirana
13. FK Tomori
14. KF Vllaznia

PROMOTED CLUBS

15. KS Lushnja
16. FK Partizani

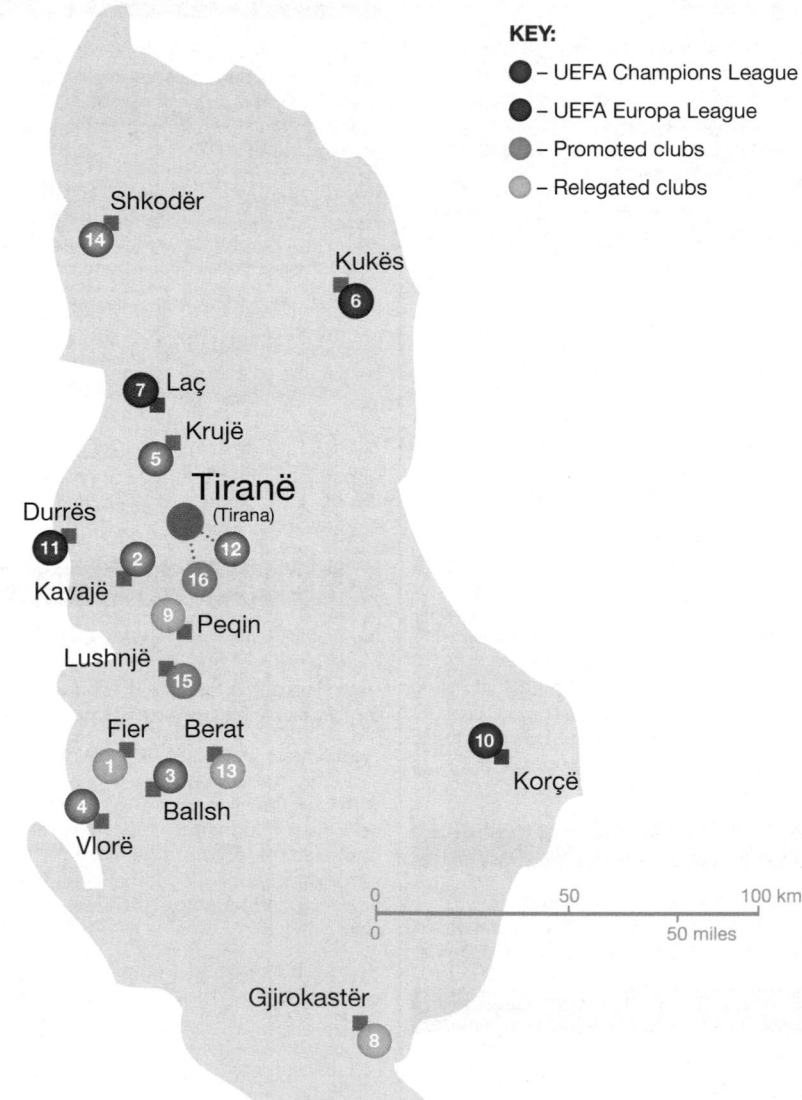

KEY:
- – UEFA Champions League
- – UEFA Europa League
- – Promoted clubs
- – Relegated clubs

Shkodër
Kukës
Laç
Krujë
Tiranë (Tirana)
Durrës
Kavajë
Peqin
Lushnjë
Fier   Berat
Ballsh
Vlorë
Korçë
Gjirokastër

Skënderbeu scoop title hat-trick

KS Skënderbeu confirmed their status as Albanian football's team of the moment by capturing the Kategoria Superiore crown for the third season in succession. The hat-trick was completed under the direction of a new coach, Mirel Josa steering the Korce club to glory with two matches to spare.

The 2012/13 season was otherwise notable for its surprises, with top-flight debutants FK Kukësi taking the league runners-up spot, KF Laçi winning the Albanian Cup and the national team exceeding all hopes and expectations to keep alive the seemingly impossible dream of 2014 FIFA World Cup qualification.

Unbeaten autumn run sets up title defence

Laç beat Bylis to win first Albanian Cup

World Cup dream alive and kicking

Domestic league

Skënderbeu had gone 78 years without an Albanian championship win when they took the title in 2010/11. Both that and the following triumph in 2011/12 were achieved with a coach who did not begin the season at the club – Shpëtim Duro and Stanislav Lový, respectively. Josa, however, was in charge throughout. He got off to the perfect start in force, masterminding a majestic run in the first half of the season that brought the defending champions ten wins and three draws, putting them ten points clear at the winter break. Leading from the front was Croatian striker Pero Pejić with ten goals.

Although Skënderbeu were defeated on the resumption 1-0 at home by KF Vllaznia – one of Josa's former clubs – they won the next four games and were able to afford another couple of defeats in the closing stretch before securing the title with a 2-0 win at home to KS Kastrioti. To that point Skënderbeu had conceded a miserly ten goals. Their final game was untypical of what had gone before as they went down 4-3 at Kukës, the Kategoria Superiore newcomers clinching second place – and preserving their unbeaten home record – in some style as rivals KS Teuta fell to a shock 4-1 defeat at relegated FK Tomori.

With a double against Skënderbeu, Kukës's Serbian striker Lazar Popović took his tally of goals to 16 – three behind the league's hot shot striker, Migen Memelli of KS Flamurtari, who finished fourth.

Record champions KF Tirana ended out of the European places, in fifth, but there was good news elsewhere in the capital as former giants FK Partizoni won a second successive promotion to join their erstwhile rivals in the 2013/14 top division, which was to be reduced back to 12 teams.

Domestic cup

The semi-finals of the Albanian Cup produced a couple of shocks as Skënderbeu and Kukës were both eliminated, the former having won all six of their group stage fixtures.

KS Bylis, their conquerors, were unable however to claim their first major trophy, that distinction falling instead to Laç, who eventually profited from the early dismissal in the final of Bylis's Besmir Arifaj when midfielder Emiljano Çela pounced to score a dramatic 118th-minute winner. It was the second successive final to be decided by a single goal scored in extra time.

Europe

There was collective disappointment for Albanian clubs on the European front, notably for Skënderbeu, who fired 2011/12 title-winning coach Lový after failing to defend a 1-0 first-leg lead against Debreceni VSC. Tirana were the only one of the four teams to win a tie, against opposition from Luxembourg.

National team

Little was expected of the Albanian national side, under new Italian head coach Gianni de Biasi, ahead of the 2014 World Cup qualifying campaign – particularly with the experienced triumvirate of Altin Lala, Klodian Duro and Ervin Skela all overlooked for selection – but despite a damaging home defeat by Iceland in their third fixture, the team stormed back into contention for the play-offs by taking seven points from their next three matches.

Indeed, it was so nearly nine as only a late equaliser conceded at home to Norway prevented a double over the Scandinavians following a memorable 1-0 win in Oslo secured by a tenth international goal from star striker Hamdi Salihi, who had travelled there all the way from China.

Domestic league: Kategoria Superiore 2012/13 final table

		Pld	Home					Away					Total					Pts
			W	D	L	F	A	W	D	L	F	A	W	D	L	F	A	
1	**KS Skënderbeu**	26	11	1	1	26	4	7	3	3	17	10	18	4	4	43	14	58
2	FK Kukësi	26	10	3	0	31	10	5	4	4	18	15	15	7	4	49	25	52
3	KS Teuta	26	10	2	1	21	7	4	4	5	11	17	14	6	6	32	24	48
4	KS Flamurtari	26	8	4	1	26	8	5	3	5	23	25	13	7	6	49	33	46
5	KF Tirana	26	8	3	2	20	13	4	4	5	10	10	12	7	7	30	23	43
6	KF Vllaznia	26	8	2	3	18	10	3	3	7	12	16	11	5	10	30	26	38
7	KF Laçi	26	8	3	2	21	11	3	2	8	11	20	11	5	10	32	31	38
8	KS Kastrioti	26	9	0	4	20	14	1	4	8	5	21	10	4	12	25	35	34
9	KS Besa	26	6	4	3	16	11	2	4	7	7	15	8	8	10	23	26	32
10	KS Bylis	26	7	4	2	23	7	2	2	9	9	22	9	6	11	32	29	30
11	KS Shkumbini	26	6	4	3	12	11	1	4	8	6	22	7	8	11	18	33	29
12	FK Tomori	26	4	5	4	14	14	0	2	11	16	36	4	7	15	30	50	19
13	KS Luftëtari	26	4	2	7	18	22	1	2	10	6	22	5	4	17	24	44	19
14	KF Apolonia	26	1	7	5	9	16	0	3	10	7	24	1	10	15	16	40	13

NB KS Bylis – 3 pts deducted.

SEASON AT A GLANCE

EUROPEAN QUALIFICATION 2013/14

Champion: KS Skënderbeu (second qualifying round)

Cup winner: KF Laçi (first qualifying round)
FK Kukësi (first qualifying round)
KS Teuta (first qualifying round)

Top scorer — Migen Memelli (Flamurtari), 19 goals
Relegated clubs — KF Apolonia, KS Luftëtari, FK Tomori, KS Shkumbini
Promoted clubs — KS Lushnja, FK Partizani
Cup final — KF Laçi 1-0 KS Bylis

**KATEGORIA SUPERIORE TEAM
OF THE SEASON**
(4-4-2)
Coach: Josa *(Skënderbeu)*

**PLAYER OF
THE SEASON
Gilman Lika**
(KF Tirana)

Tirana finished the season down in fifth place, but the leadership skills of the club's new captain proved to be invaluable during a turbulent season that featured an overhaul of the coaching staff and board at its halfway point. Lika led on the field by example, starting all 26 matches and scoring nine goals

**NEWCOMER OF
THE SEASON
Gledi Mici**
(KS Flamurtari)

KF Tirana's attacking midfielder Mario Morina and dynamic KS Besa winger Idriz Batha both enjoyed breakthrough seasons, but it was Mici who shone brightest. The 22-year-old left-back featured in 23 league games and was highly praised by Flamurtari coach Ernest Gjoka, among others, for his mixture of craft and graft.

Shehi *(Skënderbeu)*

Smajli *(Vllaznia)* — Bici *(Skënderbeu)* — Osmani *(Vllaznia/Teuta)* — Arapi *(Skënderbeu)*

Muzaka *(Flamurtari)* — Allmuça *(Kukës)* — Lilaj *(Skënderbeu)* — G Lika *(Tirana)*

Popović *(Kukës)* — Plaku *(Skënderbeu)*

NATIONAL TEAM

Home Kit   Away Kit

TOP FIVE ALL-TIME CAPS
Altin Lala (78); Klodian Duro (76);
Erjon Bogdani & Ervin Skela (75);
Foto Strakosha (73)

TOP FIVE ALL-TIME GOALS
Erjon Bogdani (18); Alban Bushi (14);
Ervin Skela (13); Altin Rraklli (11);
Sokol Kushta, **Hamdi Salihi** & Igli Tare (10)

Results 2012/13

Date	Opponent		Venue	Score	Scorers
15/08/12	Moldova	H	Tirana	0-0	
07/09/12	Cyprus (WCQ)	H	Tirana	3-1	Sadiku (36), Çani (84), Bogdani (87)
11/09/12	Switzerland (WCQ)	A	Lucerne	0-2	
12/10/12	Iceland (WCQ)	H	Tirana	1-2	Çani (29)
16/10/12	Slovenia (WCQ)	H	Tirana	1-0	Roshi (36)
14/11/12	Cameroon	N	Geneva (SUI)	0-0	
06/02/13	Georgia	H	Tirana	1-2	Bogdani (25)
22/03/13	Norway (WCQ)	A	Oslo	1-0	Salihi (67)
26/03/13	Lithuania	H	Tirana	4-1	Meha (32), Çani (37), Basha (44), Palionis (59og)
07/06/13	Norway (WCQ)	H	Tirana	1-1	Rama (41)

Appearances 2012/13

Coach: Gianni De Biasi (ITA) 16/06/56

Player	DOB	Club	Mda	CYP	SUI	ISL	SVN	Cmr	Geo	NOR	Ltu	NOR	Caps	Goals
Samir Ujkani	05/07/88	Palermo (ITA) /Chievo (ITA)	G46	G	G	G			s46		s23		20	-
Armend Dallku	16/06/83	Vorskla (UKR)	D	D	D	D	s84	s59		D80		D	62	1
Lorik Cana	27/07/83	Lazio (ITA)	D	D	D	D	D	D	D	D	s70		67	1
Mërgim Mavraj	09/06/86	Greuther Fürth (GER)	D	D	D	D	D	D		D	D	D	11	-
Andi Lila	12/02/86	Giannina (GRE)	D	D	D	D	D	D	D	D89*	D78		37	-
Ervin Bulku	03/03/81	Sepahan (IRN)	M	M	M	M	M	M59	M88	M		M91	51	1
Elis Bakaj	25/06/87	Chornomorets Odesa (UKR)	M52					s59	M56				27	1
Emiljano Vila	12/03/88	Giannina (GRE)	M73	M72	M55		M84	M59	M62		s81	M84	22	2
Ledian Memushaj	07/12/86	Lecce (Ita)	M46										3	-
Hamdi Salihi	19/01/84	DC United (USA) /Jiangsu Sainty (CHN)	A61	A81		s75	s46			A90		A77	43	10
Edgar Çani	08/07/90	Polonia Warszawa (POL) /Catania (ITA)	A46	s81	s55	A85	A75	A78		A75	A64	A	12	4
Etrit Berisha	10/03/89	Kalmar (SWE)	s40				G	G	G40	G	G20	G	0	
Erjon Bogdani	14/04/77	Siena (ITA)	s46	s72	A55	s85			A65	s75	A70		75	10
Odhise Roshi	22/05/91	FSV Frankfurt (GER)	s16		s55	s16	M	M79	M74	M			13	1
Jahmir Hyka	08/03/88	Luzern (SUI)	s52	s58	s73						s76		35	2
Hajr Zeqiri	11/10/88	Rizespor (TUR)	s61										4	-
Ansi Agolli	11/10/82	Qarabağ (AZE)	s73		M		D		M73	M	D84	D	41	2
Burim Kukeli	16/01/84	Zürich (SUI)		M	M73	M	M						4	-
Alban Meha	26/04/86	Paderborn (GER)		M	M	M46					M76		4	1
Armando Sadiku	27/05/91	Lugano (SUI)		A58		A	A46	A70	s56		s64		9	1
Gilman Lika	13/01/87	Tirana					M75		s74				20	-
Debatik Curri	28/12/83	Gençlerbirliği (TUR)					s75	s46	D	s90			41	1
Renato Arapi	28/08/86	Skënderbeu						D	s73				3	-
Sabien Lilaj	10/02/89	Skënderbeu						M46			M81		7	-
Armando Vajushi	03/12/91	Litex (BUL)						s70	s46		s64		4	-
Bekim Balaj	11/01/91	Sparta Praha (CZE)						s78	s65				2	-
Kristi Vangjeli	05/09/85	Chornomorets Odesa (UKR)						s78					35	-
Tefik Osmani	08/06/85	Teuta							D46	D		s77	12	-
Elseid Hysaj	20/02/94	Empoli (ITA)							s62	s80	s78	s91	4	-
Gjergji Muzaka	26/09/84	Flamurtari							s88				23	1
Migjen Basha	05/01/87	Torino (ITA)								M	M	M	3	1
Valdet Rama	20/11/87	Valladolid (ESP)									M64	M	2	-
Franc Veliu	11/11/88	Flamurtari									s84		7	-
Admir Teli	02/06/81	Qarabağ (AZE)										D	16	-
Ergys Kaçe	08/07/93	PAOK (GRE)										s84	1	-

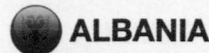

European club competitions 2012/13

KS SKËNDERBEU

Second qualifying round - Debreceni VSC (HUN)
H 1-0 *Plaku (65)*
Shehi, Arapi, Fagu, Orelesi, Plaku (Bici 90+3), Allmuça, Muzaka, Xhafa (Kuli 83), Vucaj, Radaš, Gvozdenović. Coach: Stanislav Levý (CZE)
A 0-3
Shehi, Arapi, Fagu (Kuli 85), Orelesi, Plaku, Allmuça (Kërçiku 66), Muzaka, Xhafa, Vucaj (Bici 89), Radaš, Gvozdenović. Coach: Stanislav Levý (CZE)

KF TIRANA

First qualifying round - CS Grevenmacher (LUX)
H 2-0 *Muçollari (40), Ferraj (45+2)*
I Lika, Kalari, Pisha, Bala (Morina 89), Duro (Çota 66), Ferraj (Tusha 65), Pashaj, G Lika, Ahmataj, Taku, Muçollari. Coach: Julián Rubio Sánchez (ESP)
A 0-0
I Lika, Kalari, Pisha, Bala, Ferraj (Tusha 15; Çota 70), Karabeci, Pashaj, G Lika, Ahmataj (Dabulla 90+3), Taku, Muçollari. Coach: Julián Rubio Sánchez (ESP)
Red card: Pisha 89

Second qualifying round - Aalesunds FK (NOR)
H 1-1 *Çota (38)*
I Lika, Sina, Dushku, Ferraj (Morina 76), Karabeci, Pashaj, G Lika, Çota, Ahmataj, Taku, Muçollari (Tusha 76). Coach: Julián Rubio Sánchez (ESP)
A 0-5
I Lika, Sina (Morina 53), Pisha, Dushku, Ferraj (Peposhi 58), Karabeci (Muçollari 69), Pashaj, G Lika, Çota, Ahmataj, Taku. Coach: Julián Rubio Sánchez (ESP)

KS TEUTA

First qualifying round - FC Metalurgi Rustavi (GEO)
H 0-3
Rizvani, Sheta, Buiu, Nika, Dosti (Eminhazeri 72), A Hoxha, Osmani (Bakiasi 70), Jakupi, Mançaku (Pajaziti 63), Deliallisi, Veliaj. Coach: Hasan Lika (ALB)
A 1-6 *Deliallisi (65)*
Rizvani, Sheta, Buiu, R Hoxha, Nika (Pajaziti 46), Dosti (Devolli 57), Osmani, Jakupi, Mançaku, Deliallisi, Veliaj (A Hoxha 38). Coach: Hasan Lika (ALB)

KS FLAMURTARI

First qualifying round - Budapest Honvéd FC (HUN)
H 0-1
Koliqi, Mici, Pezo, Brahja, Progni (Memelli 61), Sosa (Kuqi 61), Lena, Veliu, Arbëri, Telushi, Pejić. Coach: Shkëlqim Muça (ALB)
A 0-2
Koliqi, Mici, Pezo, Sosa (Pepa 70), Lena, Veliu, Arbëri, Telushi (Çela 73), Rajović, Pejić (Kuqi 84), Memelli. Coach: Shkëlqim Muça (ALB)

KF APOLONIA

Coach: Ernest Gjoka; (28/10/12) (Elidon Demiri)
1925 • Loni Papuçiu (7,000) •
kfapoloniafier.wordpress.com
Major honours
Albanian Cup (1) 1998

2012

Date	Opponent		Score	Scorers
25/08	Kastrioti	h	1-1	Ribaj
31/08	Skënderbeu	a	0-2	
15/09	Kukës	h	0-0	
23/09	Vllaznia	a	1-1	Ribaj
29/09	Luftëtari	h	0-3	
06/10	Bylis	h	0-1	
21/10	Laç	a	0-1	
27/10	Tomori	h	2-2	Rama 2
03/11	Shkumbini	a	0-0	
10/11	Teuta	h	1-2	Ndoni
18/11	Tirana	a	0-2	
25/11	Besa	a	2-1	Ribaj (p), Papa
02/12	Flamurtari	a	1-3	Ribaj

2013

Date	Opponent		Score	Scorers
10/02	Kastrioti	a	1-4	Ribaj
17/02	Skënderbeu	h	0-1	
23/02	Kukës	a	0-1	
03/03	Vllaznia	h	1-3	Ribaj (p)
09/03	Luftëtari	a	2-3	Dushku, Ndoni
17/03	Bylis	a	0-3	
30/03	Laç	h	1-1	Ribaj
07/04	Tomori	a	0-1	
13/04	Shkumbini	h	1-1	Dushku
21/04	Teuta	a	1-2	Ribaj (p)
27/04	Tirana	h	0-0	
04/05	Besa	a	1-1	Dushku
11/05	Flamurtari	h	0-0	

No	Name	Nat	DoB	Pos	Aps	(s)	Gls
18	Sulaimon Bolaji Adekunle	NGA	26/10/90	D	22		
4	Sodiq Ololade Atanda	NGA	26/08/93	A	12		
18	Florent Azizaj	GER	15/01/93	M	4	(6)	
12	Entri Çako		20/03/92	G	2	(1)	
12	Vilson Čaković	SRB	22/02/91	G	11		
3	Emiljano Çela		21/07/85	D	6		
15	Gazmend Çimili		17/04/87	M	23	(1)	
13	Thomas Culver	USA	19/10/86	M		(1)	
14	Endri Dautaj		12/03/91	M	6	(2)	
16	Igli Dekavelli		25/04/92	D	6		
9	Rigers Dushku		08/03/91	A	20	(3)	3
19	Realdo Fili		14/05/96	D		(1)	
22	Evangjelos Jakupi		08/11/90	D	12	(1)	
13	Hermes Lamaj		03/01/92	D	1	(3)	
4	Albi Llënga		11/06/89	D	7		
1	Eduart Miço		01/12/83	G	13		
17	Ledio Muçaj		04/09/92	M	18	(2)	
26	Renato Naçi		26/11/83	D	5	(5)	
6	Rudin Nako		20/05/87	D	13		
16	Kostadin Ndoni		31/03/89	D	22		2
20	Enriko Papa		12/03/93	M	6	(10)	1
28	Dušan Popović	SRB	20/04/81	M	6	(1)	
22	Albi Prifti		05/08/93	D	7	(3)	
24	Andi Prifti		01/08/88	M	11		
27	Edison Qafa		16/11/89	A		(2)	
7	Renaldo Rama		27/01/90	A	12		2
8	Besmir Ramaj		25/08/94	M		(2)	
10	Andi Ribaj		21/11/89	A	26		8
8	Ermal Sako		08/05/89	M	1	(11)	
19	Aladin Sallaku		14/09/95	M		(2)	
19	Guido Tepshi		08/04/90	A		(7)	
2	Anayo Morrise Thankgod	NGA	15/12/88	M	14	(5)	
26	Ervis Troka		11/01/95	M		(1)	

KS BESA

Coach: Ilir Daja
1925 • Besa (7,000) • no website
Major honours
Albanian Cup (2) 2007, 2010

2012

Date	Opp	H/A	Score	Scorers
25/08	Laç	a	1-1	Kaja
03/09	Tomori	h	3-0	Mihani, Sefa, Berisha
16/09	Shkumbini	a	0-1	
21/09	Teuta	h	1-0	Berisha
29/09	Tirana	a	1-1	Sefa
07/10	Luftëtari	a	2-0	Počuča, Dita
20/10	Flamurtari	h	1-0	Malinić
28/10	Kastrioti	a	0-2	
03/11	Skënderbeu	h	1-1	Mihani
11/11	Kukës	a	0-3	
18/11	Vllaznia	h	0-0	
25/11	Apolonia	a	1-2	Sefa
02/12	Bylis	h	1-3	Sefa

2013

Date	Opp	H/A	Score	Scorers
09/02	Laç	h	1-2	Sefa
16/02	Tomori	a	0-1	
24/02	Shkumbini	h	1-1	Bajaziti
02/03	Teuta	a	0-1	
10/03	Tirana	h	2-1	Çikalleshi (p), Batha
17/03	Luftëtari	h	2-0	Sefa, Dita
30/03	Flamurtari	a	0-0	
06/04	Kastrioti	h	2-0	Çikalleshi 2 (1p)
13/04	Skënderbeu	a	0-2	
21/04	Kukës	a	0-2	
27/04	Vllaznia	a	1-0	Berisha
04/05	Apolonia	h	1-1	Malinić
11/05	Bylis	a	1-1	Poçi

No	Name	Nat	DoB	Pos	Aps	(s)	Gls
33	Abraham Alechenwu	NGA	26/03/86	D	20		
19	Florent Aziri	GER	03/09/88	M	6	(3)	
30	Darlien Bajaziti		07/07/94	A	2	(4)	1
22	Idriz Batha		28/03/92	A	20		1
1	Ibrahim Beite		05/09/89	G	3		
10	Bernard Berisha		24/10/91	M	21		3
14	Dorian Bubeqi		26/10/78	A		(4)	
16	Sajmir Çalhaha		21/11/90	M	1		
7	Sokol Çikalleshi		27/07/90	A	3		3
4	Bruno Dita		18/02/93	D	15	(9)	2
33	Didmar Duro		10/00/00	D	2		
9	Isa Eminihazeri		09/09/87	A	1	(8)	
18	Arbnor Fejzullahu		08/04/93	D	18	(2)	
16	Mateo Hasa		23/05/93	D	3	(6)	
12	Alban Hoxha		23/11/87	G	23		
15	Erand Hoxha		25/04/85	D	7	(2)	
6	Ervis Kaja		29/07/87	D	21		1
14	Blerim Krasniqi		05/07/96			(1)	
5	Gëzim Krasniqi		05/01/90	D	22		
3	Besmir Kulolli		04/05/94	D		(1)	
20	Bojan Malinić	SRB	08/09/91	A	4	(7)	2
6	Haxhi Matera		17/05/94	M		(1)	
23	Meglid Mihani		01/08/83	M	13	(5)	2
34	Argjend Mustafa		30/08/92	M	11	(7)	
2	Skerdian Perja		03/03/91	M	4	(1)	
13	Artion Poçi		23/07/77	M	8	(5)	1
11	Predrag Počuča	CRO	24/01/86	A	16	(1)	1
7	Daniel Roshi		24/04/88	M	10	(3)	
29	Fatjon Sefa		23/07/84	A	23	(1)	6
7	Parid Xhihani		18/07/83	A	8	(2)	

KS BYLIS

Coach: Agim Canaj; (20/11/12) Naci Şenşoy (TUR)
1972 • Adush Muça (5,000) • no website

2012

Date	Opp	H/A	Score	Scorers
26/08	Flamurtari	h	1-1	Adebayo
01/09	Kastrioti	a	1-2	Mohammed
15/09	Skënderbeu	h	1-1	Arbëri
23/09	Kukës	a	0-1	
29/09	Vllaznia	h	0-1	
06/10	Apolonia	a	1-0	Gega
20/10	Luftëtari	h	2-0	Izuchukwuka, Meto
28/10	Laç	h	4-0	Izuchukwuka 3 (1p), Sefa
04/11	Tomori	a	0-0	
10/11	Shkumbini	h	2-0	Izuchukwuka, Idrizi
17/11	Teuta	a	0-3	
24/11	Tirana	h	1-0	Bakiu
02/12	Besa	a	3-1	Shoshi, Meto, Bakiu

2012

Date	Opp	H/A	Score	Scorers
13/02	Flamurtari	a	0-3	
17/02	Kastrioti	h	0-0	
24/02	Skënderbeu	a	0-3	(w/o; original result 2-2 Izuchukwuka 2)
02/03	Kukës	h	3-0	Izuchukwuka 2, Xhafa
10/03	Vllaznia	a	0-1	
17/03	Apolonia	h	3-0	Adebayo, Izuchukwuka, Xhafa
30/03	Luftëtari	a	1-1	Gërxho
07/04	Laç	a	1-3	Bakiu
12/04	Tomori	h	4-1	Arbëri, Bakiu 2, Prifti
20/04	Shkumbini	a	1-2	Bakiu
27/04	Teuta	h	1-2	Bakiu
04/05	Tirana	a	1-2	Sefa
11/05	Besa	h	1-1	Izuchukwuka

No	Name	Nat	DoB	Pos	Aps	(s)	Gls
5	Adigun Adebayo Junior	NGA	15/11/90	D	13		2
23	Klodian Arbëri		10/09/79	A	23	(2)	2
26	Besmir Arifaj		06/02/85	M	10	(6)	
19	Endri Bakiu		06/01/87	A	17	(7)	7
2	Olalekan Alindo Bola	NGA	10/02/93	D	12	(1)	
13	Orgest Buzi		20/09/94	D		(2)	
8	Denis Silva	BHA	03/09/86	D	8	(1)	
77	Stivi Frashëri		29/08/90	G	18		
21	Armand Gega		21/01/87	D	1	(4)	1
20	Julian Gërxho		21/01/85	A	6	(3)	1
1	Egland Haxho		10/11/88	G	8		
21	John Huan Aodongu	NGA	14/03/90	M	4	(3)	
13	Hektor Idrizi		15/04/89	D	25		1
14	Michael Ebere Ikpe	NGA	25/12/94	A	2	(1)	
7	Solomonson Izuchukwuka	NGA	23/12/88	A	17	(1)	11
16	Adeniyi Segun James	NGA	20/12/92	M	1	(6)	
22	Shkëlzen Këlmendi		14/01/85	D	9	(5)	
21	Erald Kolgega		09/08/94	M		(3)	
17	Agim Meto		02/02/86	M	18	(1)	2
14	Adewale Mohammed	NGA	18/10/93	M	3		1
9	Peter Oladeji Olayinka	NGA	18/11/95	A	6	(8)	
17	Romario Prifti		14/02/96	A		(3)	1
2	Kire Ristevski		22/10/90	D	24		
15	Irdi Rrapaj		15/09/93	A		(1)	
8	Jetmir Sefa		30/01/87	M	21	(1)	2
5	Marenglen Shoshi		29/01/87	D	12		1
16	Xhulio Tahiraj		27/12/96	M	1		
4	Olsi Teqja		27/07/88	M	18	(1)	
10	Fjodor Xhafa		08/03/77	A	8	(13)	2

KS FLAMURTARI

Coach: Shkëlqim Muça;
(3/9/12) Julián Rubio Sánchez (ESP);
(21/12/12) Ernest Gjoka
1923 • Flamurtari (9,000) • skflamurtari.com
Major honours
Albanian League (1) 1991;
Albanian Cup (3) 1985, 1988, 2009

2012

Date	Opp	H/A	Score	Scorers
26/08	Bylis	a	1-1	Memelli
31/08	Laç	h	0-1	
16/09	Tomori	a	2-0	Pepa, Lena
22/09	Shkumbini	h	1-1	Memelli (p)
30/09	Teuta	a	1-2	Memelli
06/10	Tirana	h	1-1	Bratić
20/10	Besa	a	0-1	
27/10	Luftëtari	a	3-2	Memelli 3
03/11	Kastrioti	h	3-0	Veliu, Muzaka, Memelli
17/11	Kukës	a	2-0	Bratić, Memelli (p)
21/11	Skënderbeu	a	1-3	Muzaka
24/11	Vllaznia	a	3-3	og (Osmani), Muzaka, Pepa
02/12	Apolonia	h	3-1	Muzaka, Memelli (p), Lena

2013

Date	Opp	H/A	Score	Scorers
13/02	Bylis	h	3-0	Memelli 3
17/02	Laç	a	2-1	Sosa, og (Çela)
23/02	Tomori	h	5-2	Zeqiri, Memelli 2, Muzaka 2 (1p)
02/03	Shkumbini	a	3-0	Muzaka 2, Memelli
10/03	Teuta	h	1-1	Muzaka
16/03	Tirana	a	6-3	Muzaka 2, Pepa 2, Lena, Memelli (p)
30/03	Besa	h	0-0	
07/04	Luftëtari	h	3-0	Memelli 2 (1p), Pepa
13/04	Kastrioti	a	0-3	
21/04	Skënderbeu	h	1-0	Memelli
27/04	Kukës	a	1-6	Muzaka
04/05	Vllaznia	h	3-1	Idrizi, Nelaj, Lena
11/05	Apolonia	a	0-0	

No	Name	Nat	DoB	Pos	Aps	(s)	Gls
16	Polizoi Arbëri		09/09/88	D	10		
6	Alvaro Bishaj		02/10/91	D	4	(2)	
20	Davor Bratić	CRO	01/05/87	M	21	(1)	2
19	Dejvi Bregu		24/10/95	M	2		
2	Andi Hasani		29/08/94	D	2		
5	Ardit Hoxha		20/07/94	M		(1)	
21	Urnils Idrizi		23/02/91	A	1	(5)	1
77	Enea Koliqi		13/02/86	G	20		
20	Taulant Kuqi		11/11/85	M	13	(6)	
22	Vlade Lazarevski	MKD	09/06/83	D	2	(2)	
10	Njazi Lena	MKD	25/06/86	M	17	(3)	4
19	Ledio Liçaj		19/01/87	M	2	(3)	
17	Migen Memelli		25/04/80	A	22		19
7	Lorenco Metaj		16/09/94	D		(1)	
3	Gledian Mici		06/02/91	D	22	(1)	
14	Gjergji Muzaka		26/08/84	M	23	(1)	12
24	Rofrenc Nelaj		03/02/93	A	2	(3)	1
15	Brunild Pepa		22/11/90	A	11	(11)	5
8	Toni Pezo	CRO	14/02/91	M	16	(3)	
22	Edison Plepi		20/01/87	A		(1)	
18	Blažo Rajović	MNE	26/03/86	D	24		
9	Rafael Sosa	ARG	07/05/88	A	7	(7)	1
19	Bruno Telushi		14/11/90	A	13	(10)	
11	Franc Veliu		11/11/88	D	24		1
7	Petar Vukčević	MNE	15/08/87	M	6	(9)	
89	Klodian Xhelili		23/11/88	G	6	(1)	
88	Hajr Zeqiri		11/10/88	M	7	(3)	1

KS KASTRIOTI

Coach: Artan Mërgjyshi; (01/10/12) (Shaban Dollaku)
1946 • Kastrioti (5,500) • no website

2012

25/08	Apolonia	a	1-1	Çela
01/09	Bylis	h	2-1	Sekseri, Gocaj
17/09	Laç	a	0-3	
23/09	Tomori	h	1-0	Fataki
30/09	Shkumbini	h	1-1	Gocaj
07/10	Teuta	h	0-1	
21/10	Tirana	a	0-0	
28/10	Besa	h	2-0	Çela, Gocaj
03/11	Flamurtari	a	0-3	
10/11	Luftëtari	a	0-2	
18/11	Skënderbeu	h	1-2	Sykaj
24/11	Kukës	a	1-3	Daja
01/12	Vllaznia	h	3-2	Fataki, Turdiu

2013

10/02	Apolonia	h	4-1	Shehaj, Çela, Hysa, Moçka (p)
17/02	Bylis	a	0-0	
23/02	Laç	h	2-1	Shehaj, Turdiu (p)
03/03	Tomori	a	2-1	Fataki, Tanushaj
09/03	Shkumbini	h	1-0	Kalari
16/03	Teuta	a	0-1	
31/03	Tirana	h	0-3	
06/04	Besa	a	0-2	
13/04	Flamurtari	h	3-0	Hysa, Karapici, Shaba
21/04	Luftëtari	h	1-0	Kalari
26/04	Skënderbeu	a	0-2	
04/05	Kukës	h	0-3	
11/05	Vllaznia	a	0-2	

No	Name	Nat	DoB	Pos	Aps	(s)	Gls
19	Nikola Asćerić	SRB	19/04/91	A		(1)	
11	Ervin Beqiri		06/09/90	A		(1)	
17	Arbër Bitinçka		26/11/91	D		(1)	
23	Petar Borovicanin	SRB	06/09/85	D	3	(1)	
2	Fatmir Caca		28/05/85	D	23		
9	Semirjan Çela		01/01/89	M	19		3
4	Asjon Daja		14/03/90	M	14	(1)	1
13	Albert Fataki	COD	25/05/89	A	16	(3)	3
21	Olsi Gocaj		30/09/88	A	23		3
3	Leudan Goga		15/04/94	M	1		
1	Eldorado Hasani		15/10/94	G	1		
5	Rigers Hoxha		03/09/85	D	12	(5)	
10	Vilfor Hysa		09/09/89	A	10	(1)	2
8	Renaldo Kalari		25/06/84	M	9	(2)	2
7	Artan Karapici		19/04/80	D	18	(3)	1
13	Alban Koleci		08/06/89	M	1		
15	Fejzi Kuka		04/06/94	M		(1)	
22	Nemanja Lazić	SRB	10/04/90	A	5	(2)	
12	Shpëtim Moçka		20/10/89	G	19		1
12	Alfred Osmani		20/02/83	G	6		
18	Redi Pengili		06/04/91	D	2	(2)	
10	Vasilije Prodanović	SRB	24/11/85	M	4	(4)	
4	Andi Rexhepi		05/05/94	D		(1)	
8	Isidor Sekseri		19/11/86	M	10	(1)	1
17	Stivi Shaba		19/09/92	M	5	(14)	1
19	Ardit Shehaj		23/09/90	A	8	(11)	2
15	Arsen Sykaj		16/04/90	D	22		1
3	Eduart Tanushaj		20/06/83	A	3	(6)	1
11	Erald Turdiu		15/07/84	M	23		3
17	Daniel Xhafa		26/08/96	D	1		
16	Erjon Gani Xhafa		31/05/82	D	21	(1)	
16	Erjon Haki Xhafa		29/06/86	D	7	(6)	

FK KUKËSI

Coach: Armando Cungu
1930 • Zeqir Ymeri (4,500) • no website

2012

26/08	Luftëtari	h	0-0	
01/09	Vllaznia	h	0-0	
15/09	Apolonia	a	0-0	
23/09	Bylis	h	1-0	Popović
30/09	Laç	a	1-1	Malindi
06/10	Tomori	a	3-1	Progri, Popović 2
20/10	Shkumbini	a	1-1	Progri
28/10	Teuta	h	1-1	Allmuça (p)
04/11	Tirana	a	2-1	Allmuça (p), Hoxha
14/11	Besa	h	3-0	Biskup, Popović, Progri
17/11	Flamurtari	a	0-2	
24/11	Kastrioti	h	3-1	Progri, Popović, Allmuça
01/12	Skënderbeu	a	0-2	

2013

10/02	Luftëtari	a	3-1	Alikaj, Malota, Popović
16/02	Vllaznia	a	0-1	
23/02	Apolonia	h	1-0	Popović
02/03	Bylis	a	0-3	
09/03	Laç	h	2-1	Popović, Brahja
17/03	Tomori	a	5-2	Allmuça 2 (1p), Progri, Biskup, Inzaghi
30/03	Shkumbini	h	5-1	Popović 3, Manuka, Malindi
07/04	Teuta	a	1-1	Malota
13/04	Tirana	h	2-1	Brahja, Popović
21/04	Besa	a	2-0	Progri, Allmuça (p)
27/04	Flamurtari	h	6-1	Allmuça 2 (1p), Hoxha 2, Progri, Popović
04/05	Kastrioti	a	3-0	Malacarne, Mziu, Popović
11/05	Skënderbeu	h	4-3	Alikaj, Popović 2, Allmuça (p)

No	Name	Nat	DoB	Pos	Aps	(s)	Gls
25	Serxhio Abdurrahmani		17/07/92	A		(3)	
19	Enkeleid Alikaj		27/12/81	M	18	(6)	2
14	Igli Allmuça		25/10/80	M	25		9
6	Luko Biskup	CRO	14/06/81	M	15	(5)	2
5	Julian Brahja		06/12/80	D	21		2
1	Argjend Halili		16/11/92	G	25		
13	Rraman Hallaçi		12/11/83	D	25		
20	Ylli Hoxha		26/12/87	M	18	(2)	3
29	Inzaghi	GNB	25/04/85	A		(1)	1
21	Miloš Jevdjević	SRB	11/01/81	A		(6)	
12	Ervis Koçi		13/11/84	G	1		
4	Vilson Lila		06/10/89	D		(4)	
17	Lucas Malacarne	ARG	25/11/89	D	13	(1)	1
18	Enzo Malindi		15/01/88	M	10	(13)	2
18	Julian Malo		02/02/85	A	1	(5)	
24	Renato Malota		24/06/89	D	20	(3)	2
8	Gentian Manuka		02/08/91	A	5	(6)	1
23	Besar Musolli		28/02/89	D	16	(5)	
11	Sokol Mziu		07/08/85	M	1	(10)	1
22	Roland Peqini		25/11/90	D	24		
9	Lazar Popović	SRB	10/01/83	A	23		16
32	Matteo Prandelli	ITA	22/11/88	A		(2)	
7	Gerard Progri		06/11/86	M	25		7

KF LAÇI

Coach: Përparim Daiu; (28/8/12) Stavri Nica;
(26/9/12) (Ylber Zani); (22/10/12) Ramadan Shehu;
(01/01/13) Stavri Nica
1960 • Laç (3,500) • no website
Major honours
Albanian Cup (1) 2013

2012

25/08	Besa	h	1-1	Vucaj (p)
31/08	Flamurtari	a	1-0	Emurlahu
17/09	Kastrioti	h	3-0	Marashi, Vucaj, Emurlahu
24/09	Skënderbeu	a	0-3	
30/09	Kukës	h	1-1	Buljan (p)
07/10	Vllaznia	a	0-1	
21/10	Apolonia	h	1-0	Emurlahu
28/10	Bylis	a	0-4	
03/11	Luftëtari	h	3-0	Vucaj, Buljan, Nimani
14/11	Tomori	h	4-3	Sefgjini, Shazivari, Vucaj, Hoti
18/11	Shkumbini	h	1-1	Bilibashi
25/11	Teuta	h	1-0	Nimani
02/12	Tirana	a	1-2	Nimani

2013

09/02	Besa	a	2-1	Çela, Zefi (p)
17/02	Flamurtari	h	1-2	Nimani
23/02	Kastrioti	a	1-2	Nimani
01/03	Skënderbeu	h	0-2	
09/03	Kukës	h	1-2	og (Hoxha)
17/03	Vllaznia	h	2-1	Emurlahu, Shazivari
30/03	Apolonia	a	1-1	Buljan
07/04	Bylis	h	3-1	Blloku, Vucaj 2
13/04	Luftëtari	a	3-0	Vucaj 2 (1p), Zefi
20/04	Tomori	a	0-2	
27/04	Shkumbini	h	1-0	Ndreka
03/05	Teuta	a	0-1	
10/05	Tirana	h	0-0	

No	Name	Nat	DoB	Pos	Aps	(s)	Gls
14	Orjand Abazaj		17/01/85	A	5	(1)	
31	Edvan Bakaj		09/10/87	G	15	(1)	
18	Mishel Bilibashi		08/03/89	M	20	(2)	1
14	Albion Blloku		29/06/83	D	9	(3)	1
4	Stipe Buljan	CRO	21/09/83	D	24	(1)	3
13	Roland Bushi		26/02/91	A		(2)	
21	Emiljano Çela		21/07/85	M	11		1
33	Sadush Danaj		06/11/88	D	8	(3)	
2	Elton Doku		01/10/86	D	12	(3)	
20	Burhan Emurlahu	MKD	11/03/82	A	18	(1)	4
22	Salvador Gjonaj		26/09/92	A	1		
13	Arbër Haliti		25/01/92	M	1	(4)	
9	Erjon Hoti		08/05/83	M	5	(5)	1
17	Enis Imami		19/12/92	M	1	(2)	
24	Daniel Jubani		07/12/93	D	1	(2)	
6	Sajmir Kastrati		07/03/87	D	16	(1)	
9	Bledar Marashi		03/10/90	M	3	(9)	1
33	Antonio Marku		24/03/92	M	3	(3)	
3	Borko Milenković	SRB	10/07/84	D	20	(4)	
5	Henri Ndreka		27/03/83	D	17		1
19	Valdano Nimani		05/03/87	A	21		5
11	Taulant Sefgjini		21/07/86	M	16	(2)	1
11	Elio Shazivari		14/04/85	M	10	(11)	2
1	Edvin Ujka		10/04/95	G	1		
1	Bledar Vashaku		08/11/81	G	10	(1)	
10	Erjon Vucaj		25/12/90	M	24		8
23	Edison Xhixha		16/09/92	M	1	(3)	
22	Alfred Zefi		20/08/91	M	14	(3)	2

KS LUFTËTARI

Coach: Ilorli Dede; (28/10/12) Edi Martini; (01/04/13) Arjan Bellaj
1929 • Gjirokastra (7,000) • no website

2012

Date	Opponent	H/A	Score	Scorers
26/08	Kukës	a	0-0	
02/09	Teuta	h	4-1	Nikolić, Liçaj, Rraboshta, Shenaj
16/09	Vllaznia	a	0-3	
22/09	Tirana	h	0-1	
29/09	Apolonia	a	3-0	Çaço, Rraboshta, Nikolić
07/10	Besa	h	0-2	
20/10	Bylis	a	0-2	
27/10	Flamurtari	h	2-3	Shenaj, Liçaj
03/11	Laç	a	0-3	
10/11	Kastrioti	h	2-0	Liçaj, Çaço
17/11	Tomori	a	1-1	Boçi
25/11	Skënderbeu	h	0-1	
01/12	Shkumbini	a	1-2	Mersini

2013

Date	Opponent	H/A	Score	Scorers
10/02	Kukës	h	1-3	Çaço
16/02	Teuta	a	0-2	
23/02	Vllaznia	h	2-1	Cate Fonseca, Boçi
02/03	Tirana	a	1-2	Hoxha
09/03	Apolonia	h	3-2	Cate Fonseca, Beqiri, Lluka
17/03	Besa	a	0-2	
30/03	Bylis	h	1-1	Cate Fonseca
07/04	Flamurtari	a	0-3	
13/04	Laç	h	0-3	
21/04	Kastrioti	a	0-1	
27/04	Tomori	h	2-2	Cate Fonseca (p), Lluka
04/05	Skënderbeu	a	0-1	
11/05	Shkumbini	h	1-2	Nora

No	Name	Nat	DoB	Pos	Aps	(s)	Gls
11	Andi Bakiasi		02/10/88	M	2	(1)	
17	Eldor Batha		04/01/94	D	2	(3)	
20	Orjand Beqiri		21/02/85	D	22		1
14	Romario Biraçaj		11/06/94	M	1	(5)	
4	Alis Boçi		08/02/91	D	14		2
9	Shefqet Boni		31/01/96	M		(1)	
6	Mikol Brahimaj		25/01/87	M	5		
7	Elvis Çaço		26/04/89	M	17	(4)	3
11	Culu Fonseca	BRA	00/03/78	A	10		4
11	Ardit Çunaj		05/10/92	D	2	(3)	
8	Stève Fanka	CMR	28/02/88	D		(2)	
20	Nazmi Gaba		25/09/95	M	1	(1)	
18	Lundro Gjini		02/08/94	M	1		
5	Rustem Hoxha		04/07/91	D	3	(3)	1
18	Marjol Kazma		10/01/95	A	1	(1)	
15	Ledio Liçaj		19/01/87	M	10	(1)	3
14	Julian Lluka		14/02/91	M	11	(11)	2
8	Ergys Mersini		30/09/88	M	18	(5)	1
11	Aleksandar Milić	SRB	10/03/88	A	2	(4)	
12	Marko Milivojević	SRB	08/02/88	G	7		
22	Milan Nikolić	SRB	30/03/83	D	18	(4)	2
2	Jetmir Nina		21/05/86	D	13		
18	Arlind Nora		14/06/95	A	14	(5)	1
3	Jamie Phoenix	ENG	15/01/84	A		(1)	
16	Behar Ramadani		06/04/90	D	7		
9	Jasmin Rraboshta		30/04/90	A	15	(3)	2
1	Erind Selimaj		22/05/89	G	12		
3	Bledar Shalari		26/12/85	D		(2)	
13	Ylli Shameti		17/06/84	D	11		
17	Fejzo Shenaj		24/11/84	M	13	(1)	2
37	Erinato Shurdhi		26/05/87	M	4	(1)	
5	Besmir Sinani		23/05/85	D	20	(1)	
15	Nertil Stoja		11/10/86	D	10	(5)	
3	Luka Teodorović	MNE	21/01/86	M	11		
12	Mihal Thano		29/04/93	G	7		
26	Spiro Thimjo		10/03/92	A	1		
7	Elton Zholi		27/05/86	M		(8)	
37	Apostol Zoica		08/04/94	D		(1)	

KS SHKUMBINI

Coach: Gugash Magani; (12/11/12) Kristaq Mile
1924 • Fusha Sportive (6,000) • ksshkumbini.com

2012

Date	Opponent	H/A	Score	Scorers
26/08	Teuta	h	0-1	
02/09	Tirana	a	0-3	
16/09	Besa	h	1-0	E Magani
22/09	Flamurtari	a	1-1	Gjata
30/09	Kastrioti	a	1-1	Dervishi
06/10	Skënderbeu	a	0-2	
20/10	Kukës	h	1-1	Mustafaj
28/10	Vllaznia	h	0-1	
03/11	Apolonia	a	0-0	
10/11	Bylis	h	0-2	
18/11	Laç	h	1-1	Mustafaj
25/11	Tomori	a	0-0	
01/12	Luftëtari	h	2-1	Lluca, Duka

2013

Date	Opponent	H/A	Score	Scorers
10/02	Teuta	a	0-3	
17/02	Tirana	h	1-0	Mustafaj (p)
24/02	Besa	a	1-1	Lluca (p)
02/03	Flamurtari	h	0-3	
09/03	Kastrioti	a	1-1	
17/03	Skënderbeu	h	0-1	
30/03	Kukës	a	1-5	Gjata
07/04	Vllaznia	h	1-0	Isaj
13/04	Apolonia	a	1-1	Sekseri
20/04	Bylis	h	2-1	Dervishi, Lluca
27/04	Laç	a	0-1	
04/05	Tomori	h	2-1	Mile 2 (1p)
11/05	Luftëtari	a	2-1	Lluca, Mile (p)

No	Name	Nat	DoB	Pos	Aps	(s)	Gls
12	Selami Ajazi		19/03/91	G	9	(1)	
16	Klejdis Branica		10/05/92	D	2	(8)	
22	Roland Dervishi		16/02/82	A	13	(3)	2
14	Bledar Devolli		14/01/78	M	10	(1)	
25	Mikel Duka		09/01/91	D	8	(9)	1
23	Orgest Gava		29/03/90	M	6	(2)	
19	Arvist Gjata		23/06/87	A	18		2
6	Albano Isaj		19/01/91	M	10	(4)	1
4	Ganiol Karaili		22/09/90	M	7	(1)	
18	Ervis Katazi		19/02/90	A	2	(9)	
1	Livia Koloni		30/09/79	G	17		
21	Emiljano Lluca		27/09/88	M	15	(5)	4
3	Emiljan Lundraxhiu		09/05/94	M	3		
22	Artur Magani		08/07/94	A	1	(7)	
8	Endrien Magani		06/06/91	D	24	(1)	1
9	Vangjell Mile		01/07/86	A	9	(1)	3
21	Emiljano Musta		31/01/92	M	13		
10	Erjon Mustafaj		29/01/89	M	12	(5)	3
3	Jurgen Nexha		30/08/93	D		(3)	
7	Lorenc Pasha		24/01/78	D	22		
5	Daniel Ramazani		14/01/87	D	19	(2)	
2	Alfred Salliu		10/02/81	D	11	(1)	
25	Isidor Sekseri		19/11/86	M	13		1
9	Enea Sulka		17/11/93	D	7	(9)	
13	Jurgen Vogli		12/06/93	M	20		
15	Klajdi Xhyra		20/09/96	D	15	(2)	

KS SKËNDERBEU

Coach: Mirel Josa
1923 • Skënderbeu (7,000) • ksskenderbeu.com
Major honours
Albanian League (4) 1933, 2011, 2012, 2013

2012

Date	Opponent	H/A	Score	Scorers
24/08	Vllaznia	a	3-1	Pejić 3
31/08	Apolonia	h	2-0	Plaku (p), Orelesi
15/09	Bylis	a	1-1	Pejić
24/09	Laç	h	3-0	Bici, Plaku, Pejić
30/09	Tomori	a	0-0	
06/10	Shkumbini	h	2-0	Arapi, Lilaj
21/10	Teuta	h	2-0	Pejić, Tomić
27/10	Tirana	h	2-0	Pejić 2
03/11	Besa	a	1-1	Plaku
18/11	Kastrioti	a	2-0	Tomić, Plaku
21/11	Flamurtari	h	3-1	Pejić 2, Plaku
25/11	Luftëtari	a	1-0	Plaku
01/12	Kukës	h	2-0	Orelesi, Dimo

2013

Date	Opponent	H/A	Score	Scorers
08/02	Vllaznia	h	0-1	
17/02	Apolonia	a	1-0	Bici
24/02	Bylis	h	3-0	(w/o; original result 2-2 Pejić, Bici)
01/03	Laç	a	2-0	Plaku, Bici
09/03	Tomori	h	4-2	Lilaj, Çaushaj, Plaku 2
17/03	Shkumbini	a	1-0	Çaushaj
30/03	Teuta	h	0-0	
07/04	Tirana	a	0-1	
13/04	Besa	h	2-0	Ademir, Fagu
21/04	Flamurtari	a	0-1	
26/04	Kastrioti	h	2-0	Bici, Lilaj
04/05	Luftëtari	h	1-0	Plaku
11/05	Kukës	a	3-4	Pejić, Lilaj, Shkëmbi

No	Name	Nat	DoB	Pos	Aps	(s)	Gls
20	Ademir	BRA	20/09/85	D	18	(1)	1
3	Renato Arapi		28/08/86	D	14	(1)	1
15	Ditmar Bici		26/02/89	D	24		5
17	Ilirjan Çaushaj		18/03/87	M	7	(10)	2
5	Jurgo Çipi		03/01/87	G	0		
2	Amarildo Dimo		28/09/92	M	0	(9)	1
7	Erbim Fagu		15/04/87	A	2	(4)	1
30	Fernando	BRA	19/02/00	A		(3)	
78	Ivan Gvozdenović	SRB	19/08/78	D	25		
18	Dorian Kërçiku		30/08/93	M	9	(7)	
31	Bekim Kull		19/09/82	M	3	(11)	
88	Sabien Lilaj		19/02/90	M	13	(1)	4
12	Erjon Llapanji		10/05/84	G		(1)	
19	Bakary Nimaga	MLI	06/12/94	A	1	(4)	
8	Nurudeen Orelesi	NGA	10/04/89	M	25		2
22	Pero Pejić	CRO	28/11/82	A	21	(2)	12
9	Sebino Plaku		20/05/85	A	25		10
33	Marko Radaš	CRO	26/10/83	D	12	(2)	
1	Orges Shehi		25/09/77	G	26		
10	Bledi Shkëmbi		13/08/79	M	19	(1)	1
24	Artnard Tahirllari		12/02/92	A	1	(3)	
23	Željko Tomić	CRO	21/12/85	M	10	(3)	2
4	Endrit Vrapi		23/05/82	D	17	(4)	

 **ALBANIA**

KS TEUTA

Coach: Hasan Lika; (03/09/12) Gentian Begeja;
(12/01/13) Gugash Magani
1925 • Niko Dovana (8,000) • kfteuta.com
Major honours
Albanian League (1) 1994;
Albanian Cup (3) 1995, 2000, 2005

2012

26/08	Shkumbini	a	1-0	Nika
02/09	Luftëtari	a	1-4	Mançaku (p)
14/09	Tirana	h	1-1	Deliallisi
21/09	Besa	a	0-1	
30/09	Flamurtari	h	2-1	Sheta, Dosti
07/10	Kastrioti	a	1-0	Jakupi
21/10	Skënderbeu	h	0-2	
28/10	Kukës	a	1-1	Nika
04/11	Vllaznia	h	1-0	Mançaku
10/11	Apolonia	a	2-1	Xhafa 2
17/11	Bylis	h	3-0	Sakaj, Nika, Xhafa
25/11	Laç	a	0-1	
01/12	Tomori	h	3-1	Pajaziti, Tahiri 2

2013

10/02	Shkumbini	h	3-0	Xhafa 2, Osmani
16/02	Luftëtari	h	2-0	Xhafa 2
23/02	Tirana	a	1-1	Hyshmeri
02/03	Besa	h	1-0	Mançaku
10/03	Flamurtari	a	1-1	Xhafa
16/03	Kastrioti	h	1-0	Jakupi
30/03	Skënderbeu	h	0-0	
07/04	Kukës	h	1-1	Jakupi
14/04	Vllaznia	a	0-2	
21/04	Apolonia	h	2-1	Mançaku (p), Xhafa
27/04	Bylis	a	2-1	Jakupi, Hodo
03/05	Laç	h	1-0	Osmani
09/05	Tomori	a	1-4	Xhafa

No	Name	Nat	DoB	Pos	Aps	(s)	Gls
4	Buiu	BRA	14/01/86	D	14		
18	Arbër Çyrbia		18/09/93	D	1	(3)	
23	Alfred Deliallisi		28/03/93	M	7	(14)	1
8	Albi Dosti		13/09/91	A	7	(8)	1
9	Isa Eminhazeri		09/09/87	A	3	(7)	
13	Bledar Hodo		21/06/85	D	10	(2)	1
14	Altin Hoxha		21/10/90	D	3	(12)	
5	Rustem Hoxha		04/07/91	D	3		
12	Sulejman Hoxha		13/02/90	G	2		
29	Renato Hyshmeri		04/03/89	M	18	(3)	1
3	Akil Jakupi		01/08/82	D	23		4
21	Bledar Mançaku		05/01/82	M	17	(5)	4
3	Kristi Marku		13/04/95	D	7	(2)	
6	Rexhep Memini		04/10/94	D	4		
25	Vedat Muriqi		24/04/94	A	2	(4)	
7	Ansi Nika		22/08/90	A	21	(3)	3
19	Tefik Osmani		08/06/85	D	12		2
13	Leutrim Pajaziti		19/07/92	A		(5)	1
9	Ermir Rezi		12/05/94	A		(1)	
1	Bledian Rizvani		02/01/85	G	24		
27	Artan Sakaj		08/12/80	D	24		1
2	Arjan Sheta		13/02/81	D	21		1
26	Shaqir Stafa		27/01/86	D	1		
10	Flamur Tahiri	MKD	24/11/90	M	21	(1)	2
19	Guido Tepshi		08/04/91	M	1	(2)	
28	Emiljano Veljaj		09/02/85	M	17	(4)	
22	Daniel Xhafa		01/05/77	A	23		10

KF TIRANA

Coach: Julián Rubio Sánchez (ESP);
(29/08/12) (Alban Tafaj); (16/09/12) Artur Lekbello;
(28/10/12) Alban Tafaj; (18/02/13) Nevil Dede
1920 • Selman Stërmasi (8,000) & Qemal Stafa (16,230)
• sktirana.com
Major honours
Albanian League (25) 1930, 1931, 1932, 1933, 1934, 1936,
1937, 1965, 1966, 1968, 1970, 1982, 1985, 1988, 1989, 1995,
1996, 1997, 1999, 2000, 2003, 2004, 2005, 2007, 2009;
Albanian Cup (15) 1939, 1963, 1976, 1977, 1983, 1984, 1986,
1994, 1996, 1999, 2001, 2002, 2006, 2011, 2012

2012

25/08	Tomori	a	1-0	Duro (p)
02/09	Shkumbini	h	3-0	Morina 2, Çota
14/09	Teuta	a	1-1	Ahmataj
22/09	Luftëtari	a	1-0	Çota
29/09	Besa	h	1-1	Pisha
06/10	Flamurtari	a	1-1	Morina
21/10	Kastrioti	h	0-0	
27/10	Skënderbeu	a	0-2	
04/11	Kukës	h	1-2	G Lika
10/11	Vllaznia	h	1-0	Duro (p)
18/11	Apolonia	h	2-0	G Lika, Çota
24/11	Bylis	a	0-1	
02/12	Laç	h	2-1	Duro, G Lika

2013

10/02	Tomori	h	1-0	Limani
17/02	Shkumbini	a	0-1	
23/02	Teuta	h	1-1	Abilaliaj
02/03	Luftëtari	a	2-1	Morina 2
10/03	Besa	a	1-2	G Lika
16/03	Flamurtari	h	3-6	Morina, Taku, G Lika
31/03	Kastrioti	a	3-0	Abilaliaj, G Lika, Çota
07/04	Skënderbeu	h	1-0	G Lika
13/04	Kukës	a	1-2	Çota
20/04	Vllaznia	h	1-0	G Lika (p)
27/04	Apolonia	a	0-0	
04/05	Bylis	h	2-1	G Lika, Limani
10/05	Laç	a	0-0	

No	Name	Nat	DoB	Pos	Aps	(s)	Gls
9	Arbër Abilaliaj		06/06/86	A	4	(9)	2
23	Julian Ahmataj		24/05/79	M	20	(1)	1
12	Marsel Çaka		31/03/95	G	5		
20	Mirel Çota		14/05/88	A	16	(6)	5
2	Klodian Duro		21/12/77	M	12	(1)	3
6	Erjon Dushku		25/02/85	D	14	(2)	
11	Nertil Ferraj		11/09/87	D	2	(7)	
14	Herby Fortunat	HAI	28/06/82	A	1	(2)	
22	Fabio Hoxha		07/05/93	A		(2)	
19	Erjon Hoxhallari		15/10/95	D	5		
7	Fatmir Hysenbelliu		04/04/92	M	9	(1)	
19	Renaldo Kalari		25/06/84	A	2		
13	Erindo Karabeci		28/04/87	M	13	(6)	
17	Gilman Lika		13/01/87	M	26		9
1	Ilion Lika		17/05/80	G	19		
24	Mensur Limani		04/12/84	M	8	(11)	2
27	Mario Morina		16/10/92	A	23	(1)	6
4	Gentian Muça		13/05/87	D	10	(2)	
28	Elton Muçollari		14/09/80	M	7	(6)	
21	Entonio Pashaj		10/11/84	M	15		
21	Eleandro Pema		09/02/85	M	3		
25	Ardit Peposhi		14/03/93	M	8	(6)	
3	Francesco Pigoni	ITA	29/03/86	D	7		
5	Arjan Pisha		18/01/77	D	18		1
33	Xhino Sejdo		30/04/91	G	2	(1)	
10	Eugen Shima		31/10/92	M	1	(2)	
2	Elvis Sina		14/11/78	D	11	(5)	
26	Afrim Taku		04/08/89	M	25		1
24	Gerti Tushe		02/05/91	M		(1)	
77	Miodrag Zec	MNE	04/10/82	M		(1)	

FK TOMORI

Coach: Kristaq Mile; (08/11/12) Mardit Muzhaj
1923 • Tomori (12,500) • no website

2012

25/08	Tirana	h	0-1	
03/09	Besa	a	0-3	
16/09	Flamurtari	h	0-2	
23/09	Kastrioti	a	0-1	
30/09	Skënderbeu	h	0-0	
06/10	Kukës	a	1-3	Mile
21/10	Vllaznia	h	2-2	Owoeye, Hysko
27/10	Apolonia	a	2-2	Hysko, Frashëri
04/11	Bylis	h	0-1	
11/11	Laç	a	3-4	Mile, G Arbëri (p), Muzhaj
17/11	Luftëtari	h	1-1	Ofoyen
24/11	Shkumbini	h	0-0	
01/12	Teuta	a	1-3	Mile

2013

10/02	Tirana	a	0-1	
16/02	Besa	h	1-0	Muzhaj
23/02	Flamurtari	a	2-5	Mitraj, Muzhaj
03/03	Kastrioti	h	1-2	James
09/03	Skënderbeu	a	2-4	Elmazi, Mitraj
17/03	Kukës	a	2-5	James, Muzhaj
31/03	Vllaznia	h	1-2	Mitraj
07/04	Apolonia	a	1-0	Mitraj
13/04	Bylis	h	1-4	Mitraj
20/04	Laç	h	2-0	Muzhaj, Sulejmani
27/04	Luftëtari	a	2-2	Muzhaj, og (Cate Fonseca)
04/05	Shkumbini	a	1-2	Avdo
09/05	Teuta	h	4-1	Mitraj, Owoeye, Karamani, James

No	Name	Nat	DoB	Pos	Aps	(s)	Gls
17	Gersi Arbëri		01/08/84	D	18	(2)	1
17	Xhoni Arbëri		17/04/93	M		(1)	
24	Aleksander Arza		12/06/95	D	1		
11	Algert Avdo		13/01/86	D		(6)	1
25	Andi Bakiasi		02/10/88	D		(3)	
2	Laert Bejko		22/07/83	D	3	(3)	
27	Reni Berberi		10/07/95	M	1	(1)	
26	Enea Bitri		26/08/96	D	1		
18	Spartak Elmazi		03/12/87	M	22	(1)	1
10	Erlis Frashëri		13/05/88	A	4	(5)	1
11	Klevis Gjoni		26/02/87	M	4	(2)	
11	Viktor Gjyla		11/05/82	D	8		
13	Bledar Hodo		21/06/85	M	12		
22	Rigers Hysko		09/07/86	D	10		2
22	Enea Isufi		31/10/91	M	8	(7)	
7	Adeniyi James	NGA	20/12/92	M	12		3
19	Pllumb Jusufi	MKD	10/02/88	D	4	(1)	
34	Fatjon Karamani		06/07/84	D	13	(2)	1
34	Marenglen Kule		12/03/83	M	2	(1)	
1	Ervin Llani		20/04/83	G	20		
9	Vangjëll Mile		01/07/86	A	12		4
9	Aldo Mitraj		12/01/87	D	12		6
44	Mario Muzhaj		24/11/94	M	11	(4)	6
16	Berion Myzyri		25/11/95	A	1	(4)	
23	Eni Naço		23/08/90	G	2		
2	Charles Ofoyen	NGA	26/07/85	D	23		1
16	Sunday Oluwatosin	NGA	10/08/95	A	8	(1)	
15	Kehinde Owoeye	NGA	31/07/94	A	19	(3)	2
7	Donald Paja		30/12/91	A	3	(5)	
4	Ervin Rexha		01/11/91	M	22		
26	Erdet Shinko		05/05/87	A		(4)	
31	Josel Shtrepi		13/05/93	G	4	(1)	
22	Shaqir Stafa		27/01/86	D	2	(2)	
10	Ervin Sulejmani		26/04/86	D	12		1
8	Enri Tafaj		22/05/89	D	11	(2)	
30	Jurica Vručina	CRO	31/10/89	A	1	(3)	

KF VLLAZNIA

Coach: Ohpëtim Duro; (20/12/12) Artan Bushati
1919 • Loro Boriçi (16,000) • fkvllaznia.net
Major honours
Albanian League (9) 1945, 1946, 1972, 1974, 1978,
1983, 1992, 1998, 2001;
Albanian Cup (6) 1965, 1972, 1979, 1981, 1987, 2008

2012
24/08	Skënderbeu	h	1-3	Smajli
01/09	Kukës	a	0-0	
16/09	Luftëtari	h	3-0	Smajli 2 (1p), Drägoi
23/09	Apolonia	h	1-1	Drägoi
29/09	Bylis	a	1-0	Delić
07/10	Laç	h	1-0	Drägoi
21/10	Tomori	a	2-2	Hysa, Smajli (p)
28/10	Shkumbini	h	1-0	Osmani
04/11	Teuta	a	0-1	
10/11	Tirana	h	0-1	
18/11	Besa	h	0-0	
24/11	Flamurtari	h	3-3	Rexha 2, Delić
01/12	Kastrioti	a	2-3	Rexha, Drägoi

2013
08/02	Skënderbeu	a	1-0	Hajdari
16/02	Kukës	h	1-0	Rexha
23/02	Luftëtari	a	1-2	Gjini
03/03	Apolonia	a	3-1	Hajdari, Smajli (p), Rexha
10/03	Bylis	h	1-0	Drägoi
17/03	Laç	a	1-2	Gjini
31/03	Tomori	h	2-1	Hajdari 2
07/04	Shkumbini	a	0-1	
14/04	Teuta	h	2-0	Smajli 2 (2p)
20/04	Tirana	a	0-1	
27/04	Besa	h	0-1	
04/05	Flamurtari	a	1-3	Shtupina
11/05	Kastrioti	h	2-0	Guri, Vecaj

No	Name	Nat	DoB	Pos	Aps	(s)	Gls
3	Izmir Bala		04/02/94	D	2		
17	Florind Bardhulla		19/11/92	M	11	(2)	
3	Halim Begaj		29/11/85	D	11	(5)	
8	Amarildo Belisha		11/07/81	M	22	(1)	
10	Elvin Duqhi		27/09/80	D	20	(2)	
17	Ergi Durshi		09/08/95	M	3		
22	Ivan Delić	MNE	15/02/86	M	13	(5)	2
6	Bokim Doma		30/09/93	D	6	(3)	
12	Enis Djokovic	MNE	27/02/87	G	2		
14	Christian Drägoi	ROU	17/04/82	M	19		6
26	Jurgen Gjini		21/03/93	M	4	(8)	2
25	Sidrit Guri		28/10/93	A	2	(2)	1
11	Arsen Hajdari		25/07/89	A	24		4
31	Ervin Hallunaj		14/04/90	G	2		
20	Samet Hepaj		19/02/94	A		(1)	
10	Vilfor Hysa		09/09/89	A	4	(6)	1
14	Arlind Kalaja		27/12/95	D		(1)	
8	Noris Kozmaj		16/10/95	M		(1)	
4	Ervis Kraja		26/06/83	D	2	(3)	
17	Arsid Kruja		08/06/93	M	5	(1)	
16	Paolo Markolaj		31/10/93	A	1	(1)	
33	Antonio Marku		24/03/92	M	7	(2)	
20	Ilir Nallbani		11/07/82	M	12	(5)	
5	Teulant Nikshiqi		21/05/94	D		(1)	
19	Tefik Osmani		17/04/84	D	13		1
18	Denis Pjeshka		28/05/95	D		(1)	
24	Kastriot Rexha		27/09/88	A	15	(5)	5
2	Samit Ruqi		10/05/95	M	2		
44	Klodian Semina		19/01/89	D	13	(2)	
10	Ardit Shijaku		14/01/91	M	2		
7	Ndriçim Shtupina		18/03/87	M	9	(8)	1
2	Dritan Smajli		12/02/85	D	22		7
5	Alsid Tafili		20/08/87	A	16	(4)	
18	Stivi Vecaj		29/01/94	M		(1)	1
21	Miroslav Vujadinović	MNE	22/04/79	G	22		

Top goalscorers
19	Migen Memelli (Flamurtari)
10	Lazar Popovic (Kukës)
12	Gjergji Muzaka (Flamurtari)
	Pero Pejić (Skënderbeu)
11	Solomonson Izuchukwuka (Bylis)
10	Sebino Plaku (Skënderbeu)
	Daniel Xhafa (Teuta)
9	Igli Allmuça (Kukës)
	Gilman Lika (Tirana)
8	Andi Ribaj (Apolonia)
	Erjon Vucaj (Laç)

Promoted clubs

KS LUSHNJA
Coach: Artan Bano
1927 • Abdurrahman "Roza" Haxhiu • kslushnja.webs.com

FK PARTIZANI
Coach: Nikolin Çoçlli; (25/11/12) Shpëtim Duro;
(04/03/13) Hasan Lika
1946 • Selman Stërmasi (8,000); Qemal Stafa (16,230);
Olimpik (1,000) • partizani.net
Major honours
Albanian League (15) 1947, 1948, 1949, 1954, 1957, 1958,
1959, 1961, 1963, 1964, 1971, 1979, 1981, 1987, 1993;
Albanian Cup (15) 1948, 1949, 1957, 1958, 1961, 1964,
1966, 1968, 1970, 1973, 1980, 1991, 1993, 1997, 2004

SECOND LEVEL FINAL TABLE 2012/13
		Pld	W	D	L	F	A	Pts
1	KS Lushnja	30	20	6	4	48	22	66
2	FK Partizani	30	16	8	6	39	33	56
3	KS Tërbuni	30	11	10	9	40	30	43
4	KF Mamurrasi	30	12	7	11	48	45	43
5	KS Pogradeci	30	13	3	14	49	44	42
6	KF Himara	30	11	9	10	32	29	42
7	KS Burreli	30	12	6	12	32	31	42
8	KS Ada	30	11	8	11	34	31	41
9	KS Kamza	30	11	8	11	00	47	41
10	KS Butrinti	30	10	10	10	20	00	40
11	FK Dinamo Tirana	30	11	7	12	40	37	40
12	KF Lusasani	30	12	4	14	42	40	40
13	KS Besëlidhja	30	10	8	12	28	30	38
14	KS Iliria	30	10	7	13	35	37	37
15	KF Gramshi	30	8	7	15	18	41	31
16	KF Noftëtari	30	4	8	18	22	47	20

Domestic Cup: Kupa e Shqipërisë 2012/13

FIRST ROUND
(26/09/12 & 03/10/12)
Ada 2-1, 0-1 Tomori *(2-2; Tomori on away goal)*
Besëlidhja 2-4, 2-1 Kukës *(4-5)*
Burreli 1-4, 1-6 Besa *(2-10)*
Butrinti 2-0, 0-3 Shkumbini *(2-3)*
Dinamo 0-1, 0-1 Kamza *(0-2)*
Elbasan 0-0, 0-1 Apolonia *(0-1)*
Gramozi 0-4, 0-3 (w/o) Teuta *(0-7)*
Gramshi 1-0, 0-5 Luftëtari *(1-5)*
Himara 0-2, 1-2 Kastrioti *(1-4)*
Iliria 0-2, 1-2 Vllaznia *(1-4)*
Lushnja 5-0, 2-0 Pogradec *(7-0)*
Mamurrasi 0-3; 0-1 Laç *(0-3)*
Naftëtari 0-1, 1-4 Flamurtari *(1-5)*
Olimpiku 2-2, 2-7 Skënderbeu *(4-9)*
Partizani 1-2, 0-1 Tirana *(1-3)*
Tërbuni 0-2, 0-1 Bylis *(0-3)*

SECOND ROUND
(24/10/12 & 07/11/12)
Apolonia 1-2, 0-0 Kastrioti *(1-2)*
Besa 0 1, 1-1 Flamurtari *(1-2)*
Kamza 0-1, 0-3 Skënderbeu *(0-4)*
Kukës 4-0, 2-3 Tirana *(6-3)*
Luftëtari 2-1, 1-3 Bylis *(3-4)*
Lushnja 0-0, 2-4 Teuta *(2-4)*
Shkumbini 1-0, 1-2 Vllaznia *(2-2; Shkumbini on away goal)*
Tomori 0-0, 1-3 Laç *(1-3)*

GROUP STAGE
Group A
(08/12/12)	*(03/02/13)*
Shkumbini 1-4 Skënderbeu	Shkumbini 0-2 Kukës
(09/12/12)	*(04/02/13)*
Kukës 1-0 Kastrioti	Skënderbeu 5-1 Kastrioti
(15/12/12)	*(20/02/13)*
Kastrioti 4-2 Shkumbini	Kastrioti 0-3 Kukës
Skënderbeu 4-2 Kukës	Skënderbeu 3-1 Shkumbini
(19/12/12)	*(06/03/13)*
Kastrioti 1-2 Skënderbeu	Kukës 2-3 Skënderbeu
Kukës 2-0 Shkumbini	Shkumbini 0-2 Kastrioti

Final standings
1 Skënderbeu 18 pts; 2 Kukës 12 pts *(qualified)*;
3 Kastrioti 6 pts; 4 Shkumbini 0 pt *(eliminated)*

Group B
(09/12/12)	*(04/02/13)*
Flamurtari 0-1 Bylis	Teuta 2-3 Bylis
Laç 4-0 Teuta	*(20/02/13)*
(16/12/12)	Bylis 2-3 Flamurtari
Bylis 2-1 Laç	Teuta 1-2 Laç
Teuta 2-3 Flamurtari	*(06/03/13)*
(19/12/12)	Flamurtari 3-0 Teuta
Bylis 5-0 Teuta	Laç 3-2 Bylis
Flamurtari 2-1 Laç	
(02/02/13)	
Laç 1-0 Flamurtari	

Final standings
1 Bylis 12 pts; 2 Laç 12 pts *(qualified)*;
3 Flamurtari 12 pts, 4 Teuta 0 pt *(eliminated)*

SEMI-FINALS
(03/04/13 & 17/04/13)
Kukës 0-0 Laç
Laç 2-1 Kukës *(Nimani 33, Çela 79; Peqlnl 65)*
(Laç 2-1)
Skënderbeu 1-1 Bylis *(Lilaj 88; Olayinka 81)*
Bylis 1-0 Skënderbeu *(Gërxho 53)*
(Bylis 2-1)

FINAL
(17/05/13)
Qemal Stafa, Tirana
KF LAÇI 1 *(Çela 118)*
KS BYLIS 0
(aet)
Referee: Pashaj
LAÇ: Bakaj, Kastrati, Buljan, Ndreka, Doku
(Bilibashi 91), Çela, Zefi, Vucaj, Shazivari (Sefgjini
70), Nimani, Emurlahu
BYLIS: Frashëri, Idrizi, Adebayo, Ristevski, Bola,
Izuchukwuka (Ikpe 97), Sefa, Gërxho, Arifaj, Xhafa
(Meto 57), Olayinka (Këlmendi 117)
Sent off: Arifaj (20)

ANDORRA
Federació Andorrana de Fútbol (FAF)

Address	c/ Batlle Tomàs	**President**	Antoni Giribet Fiter
	4 Baixos	**General secretary**	Tomás Gea
	AD-700 Escaldes-	**Media officer**	Andrea Vidal
	Engordany	**Year of formation**	1934
Tel	+376 805 830	**National stadium**	Comunal, Andorra la
Fax	+376 862 006		Vella (1,249)
E-mail	info@faf.ad		
Website	faf.ad		

PRIMERA DIVISIÓ CLUBS

1. FC Encamp
2. UE Engordany
3. Inter Club d'Escaldes
 4. FC Lusitans
5. CE Principat
6. UE Sant Julià
 7. FC Santa Coloma
 8. UE Santa Coloma

PROMOTED CLUB

9. FC Ordino

Ordino
Encamp
Escaldes-Engordany
Andorra la Vella
Sant Julià de Lória

0   10   20 km
0   10 miles

KEY:

● – UEFA Champions League
● – UEFA Europa League
● – Promoted club
● – Relegated club

Lusitans lead the way

The same four clubs that had challenged for Andorra's two main domestic prizes in 2011/12 were at it again in 2012/13, but while FC Lusitans retained the Primera Divisió title with room to spare, there was a new name on the Copa Constitució as UE Santa Coloma prevailed in the final against bogey side UE Sant Julià.

A 16-match unbeaten run proved decisive for Lusitans in the league, while the highlight of UE Santa Coloma's cup campaign was a 6-0 aggregate defeat of holders and local rivals FC Santa Coloma in the semi-final.

Successful title defence for high-scoring champions	First cup win for UE Santa Coloma	Barren run continues for national team

Domestic league

Defeated 2-1 at UE Santa Coloma in their second league fixture, Lusitans won each of their next six games – including 3-0 at home to FC Santa Coloma and 4-1 at Sant Julià – to take command of the Primera Divisió title race. A mid-season change of coach, with Carlos Sánchez replacing Salvador Estruch, did not interrupt the team's flow. Indeed, the new man's second game in charge brought an 11-0 win over FC Encamp, and by the time of the league split Lusitans held a three-point lead.

The gap between the four teams that broke away into the championship group was just four points, but evidence of the difference in class between that quartet and the rest was the 17-point gap that separated fourth-placed FC Santa Coloma from fifth-placed CE Principat.

Lusitans won their opening two play-off matches, and their next victory, 4-2 at Sant Julià, secured the title with two games to spare.

The unbeaten run ended as it had begun, with a 2-1 defeat at UE Santa Coloma, but despite that and a last-day draw the team with the Portuguese roots still ended up with a five-point winning

margin. They scored more than twice as many goals as runners-up FC Santa Coloma – 65 to 31 – and provided the league's top two marksmen in 17-goal Bruninho and 12-goal Luís Miguel.

Domestic cup

With the league season concluded, the spotlight fell on the cup, in which, predictably enough, each of the four teams in the championship play-offs made it through to the semi-finals, Sant Julià in fanfare style with a 10-0 aggregate win over just-relegated UE Engordany.

The semi-finals did not, however, run to form, with Sant Julià edging champions Lusitans 2-1 while UE Santa Coloma cruised past FC Santa Coloma with a pair of 3-0 victories. The final – a repeat of the 2010 and 2011 editions, both of which Sant Julià had won – looked to be heading to the same conclusion until a minute from time when Jordi Rubio, with his second goal of the game, made it 2-2.

The winner, four minutes into extra time, was fit to win any final as UE Santa Coloma substitute Luís Miguel scored with an audacious volley from the halfway line.

Europe

As usual, there was no joy for any of Andorra's European entrants. Only three of them took part in 2012/13 – as opposed to four in each of the previous two campaigns – but the collective outcome was the same, with not so much as a consolation draw between them. Lusitans' 8-0 defeat away to Valletta FC in the first qualifying round of the UEFA Champions League was especially painful.

National team

Andorra's sorry sequence of competitive defeats stretched to 40 matches as the makeweights of 2014 FIFA World Cup qualifying Group D lost all of their opening six fixtures without scoring. On the positive side, the first four of them brought progressively better defending, with five goals conceded in the first game, at home to Hungary, four in Romania, three in the Netherlands and just one at home to Estonia. But the hopeless task of head coach Koldo, the team's former goalkeeper, was thrown into sharper focus by the fact that after three and a half years – and 24 matches – in charge he had experienced nothing other than defeat, his team conceding 57 goals during that run and scoring just twice.

Domestic league: Primera Divisió 2012/13 final tables

PLAY-OFFS

Championship group	Pld	Home W	D	L	F	A	Away W	D	L	F	A	Total W	D	L	F	A	Pts
1 FC Lusitans	20	7	3	0	30	7	6	2	2	35	10	13	5	2	65	17	44
2 FC Santa Coloma	20	5	5	0	14	7	5	4	1	17	9	10	9	1	31	16	39
3 UE Santa Coloma	20	6	1	3	22	12	5	3	2	25	13	11	4	5	47	25	37
4 UE Sant Julià	20	4	2	4	16	11	6	2	2	22	7	10	4	6	38	18	34

Relegation group	Pld	Home W	D	L	F	A	Away W	D	L	F	A	Total W	D	L	F	A	Pts
5 CE Principat	20	4	1	5	11	15	2	2	6	12	20	6	3	11	23	35	21
6 Inter Club d'Escaldes	20	3	0	7	11	24	3	0	7	11	18	6	0	14	22	42	18
7 FC Encamp	20	3	1	6	11	36	2	1	7	7	19	5	2	13	18	55	17
8 UE Engordany	20	3	2	5	12	25	1	1	8	8	31	4	3	13	20	56	15

FIRST PHASE

	Pld	Home W	D	L	F	A	Away W	D	L	F	A	Total W	D	L	F	A	Pts
1 FC Lusitans	14	5	2	0	25	5	5	1	1	30	6	10	3	1	55	11	33
2 UE Santa Coloma	14	5	1	1	18	5	4	2	1	21	9	9	3	2	39	14	30
3 UE Sant Julià	14	4	1	2	14	6	5	2	0	18	3	9	3	2	32	9	30
4 FC Santa Coloma	14	4	3	0	11	5	4	2	1	14	7	8	5	1	25	12	29
5 CE Principat	14	2	1	4	8	13	1	2	4	9	17	3	3	8	17	30	12
6 FC Encamp	14	1	1	5	8	33	2	0	5	6	16	3	1	10	14	49	10
7 UE Engordany	14	1	1	5	8	23	1	1	5	6	24	2	2	10	14	47	8
8 Inter Club d'Escaldes	14	0	0	7	5	23	2	0	5	9	15	2	0	12	14	38	6

NB League splits into two groups of four after 14 matches.

SEASON AT A GLANCE

EUROPEAN QUALIFICATION 2013/14

 Champion: FC Lusitans (first qualifying round)

 Cup winner: UE Santa Coloma (first qualifying round)
FC Santa Coloma (first qualifying round)

Top scorer	Bruninho (Lusitans), 17 goals
Relegated club	UE Engordany
Promoted club	FC Ordino
Cup final	UE Santa Coloma 3-2 UE Sant Julià *(aet)*

PLAYER OF THE SEASON
Bruninho
(FC Lusitans)

An attacking midfielder with the ability to unbalance any opponent, Bruninho struck 17 goals – the best total in the Primera Divisió - as Lusitans enjoyed league success for the second consecutive season. One of a number of Portuguese nationals in the team, his consistent form ensured that Lusitans never took their eye off the prize.

NEWCOMER OF THE SEASON
Marc Rebés
(FC Santa Coloma)

The 18-year-old midfielder emerged as one of the revelations of the campaign, his reputation growing throughout the season with each assured display as FC Santa Coloma finished second in the league. Already an Andorran Under-21 international, Rebès can anticipate senior recognition from his country for many years to come.

PRIMERA DIVISIÓ TEAM OF THE SEASON
(4-5-1)
Coach: Sánchez *(Lusitans)*

Casals *(FC Santa Coloma)*
Ribolleda *(FC Santa Coloma)* — Sonejee *(Lusitans)* — Rafael Santos *(Lusitans)* — Rubio *(UE Santa Coloma)*
Peppe *(Sant Julià)* — Bruninho *(Lusitans)* — Rodríguez *(Encamp)*
Atabu *(Lusitans)* — Peppe *(Sant Julià)*
Kiko *(UE Sant Julià)*

Home Kit　　　　Away Kit

NATIONAL TEAM

TOP FIVE ALL-TIME CAPS
Óscar Sonejee (92); Ildefons Lima (80); Manolo Jiménez & Koldo (78); Txema (72)

TOP FIVE ALL-TIME GOALS
Ildefons Lima (7); Jesús Julián Lucendo (3); Emiliano González, **Marc Pujol**, Justo Ruiz, Juli Sánchez, **Óscar Sonejee** & **Fernando Silva** (2)

Results 2012/13

Date	Opponent		Venue	Score
14/08/12	Liechtenstein	A	Vaduz	0-1
07/09/12	Hungary (WCQ)	H	Andorra la Vella	0-5
11/09/12	Romania (WCQ)	A	Bucharest	0-4
12/10/12	Netherlands (WCQ)	A	Rotterdam	0-3
16/10/12	Estonia (WCQ)	H	Andorra la Vella	0-1
14/11/12	Iceland	H	Sant Julia de Loria	0-2
22/03/13	Turkey (WCQ)	H	Andorra la Vella	0-2
26/03/13	Estonia (WCQ)	A	Tallinn	0-2

Appearances 2012/13

Coach: Koldo 04/09/70			Lie	HUN	ROU	NED	EST	Isl	TUR	EST	Caps	Goals
José Antonio Gómes	03/12/86	Carabanchel (ESP) /Fortuna (ESP)	G66	G	G	G	G		G	G	31	-
Adrián Rodrigues	14/08/88	Lermeño (ESP)	D57	D	D	D52		D			7	-
Ildefons Lima	10/12/79	FC Andorra	D	D	D	D	D		D	D	80	7
Emili García	11/01/89	FC Andorra	D46	D	D		s80		s82	s66	17	-
David Maneiro	16/02/89	FC Andorra	D	s80							5	-
Marc Vales	04/04/90	Real Madrid C (ESP)	M	M 67*			D	D	D	D	27	-
Márcio Vieira	10/10/84	Atlético Monzon (ESP)	M46	M	M	M	M	M55	M	M	49	-
Ludovic Clemente	09/05/86	FC Andorra	M71	M72	M86		s68	s70	s70		7	-
Marc Pujol	21/08/82	FC Andorra	M46	M	M79	M	M	M71			57	2
Sergi Moreno	25/11/87	Bakú Hellín (ESP)	M	M69	s86	s74		M66			45	-
Fernando Silva	10/03/77	Guadiana (ESP)	A66	A	s69		A80			s85	51	2
Óscar Sonejee	26/03/76	Lusitans	s46					D			92	2
Edu Puppo	28/01/83	Sant Julia	s46		s79			s55	M82	M66	9	-
Josep Manuel Ayala	00/04/80	FC Andorra	s46		M	M	M77	M	M78	M	68	1
Àlexandre Martínez	04/03/87	UE Santa Coloma	s57								7	-
Ferran Pol	28/02/83	FC Andorra	s66					G			4	-
Juan Carlos Toscano	14/08/84	FC Andorra	s66								20	-
Marc García	21/03/88	Vic (ESP)	s71	D80	D	D	D	D55	D	D	12	-
Sebastià Gómez	01/11/83	FC Andorra		s69	A69	A74		s66	A	A85	20	-
Iván Lorenzo	15/04/86	Barbastro (ESP)		s72	M	M	M	M70			12	-
Víctor Hugo Moreira	05/10/82	Lusitans				M82	M68		M	M79	10	-
Moisés San Nicolás	17/09/93	FC Andorra			s52	D	D		D	D	5	-
Marc Bernaus	02/02/77	unattached				s82				s79	32	1
Gabriel Riera	05/06/85	UE Santa Coloma					s77	A66			17	1
Jordi Rubio	01/11/87	UE Santa Coloma						s55			16	-
Samir Bousenine	07/02/91	FC Santa Coloma						s55			5	-
Cristopher Pousa	29/06/92	FC Santa Coloma						s74			2	-
Cristian Martínez	16/10/89	FC Andorra							M70	M	18	1
Xavier Andorrà	07/06/85	UE Santa Coloma								s78	26	-

European club competitions 2012/13

FC LUSITANS

First qualifying round - Valletta FC (MLT)
A 0-8
Benítez, Hugo Veloso (Fernando Gonçalves 52), Yael, Bertran, Luís Pinto, Pedro Reis, Bruninho, Atabu, Rafael Brito, Franklim Soares (Luís Miguel 23), Leonel Maciel (Meza 85). Coach: Vicenç Marquès (AND)
H 0-1
Ricardo Fernández, Zarioh, Yael, Luís Pinto (Atabu 72), Luís Miguel (Pedro Reis 65), Fernando Gonçalves, Bruno da Silva (Franklim Soares 90), Bruninho, Moreira, Rafael Brito, Leonel Maciel. Coach: Vicenç Marquès (AND)
Red card: Luís Pinto 90+5

FC SANTA COLOMA

First qualifying round - NK Osijek (CRO)
H 0-1
Casals, Fité, Sonejee, Rebes, Pousa, Renato Mota (Mercadé 60), Urbani, Juli Sánchez, Ribolleda, Javi Sánchez (Jiménez 70), Romero (Genís García 63). Coach: Luis Blanco (ESP)
A 1-3 *Bousenine (81)*
Casals, Fité, Rebes (Genís García 44), Pousa, Urbani (Renato Mota 70), Ribolleda, Mercadé, Bousenine, G Sánchez, Javi Sánchez, Romero (Abdian 80). Coach: Luis Blanco (ESP)

UE SANTA COLOMA

First qualifying round - FC Twente (NED)
A 0-6
Periánez, Orosa, Martínez, Salvat, Sirvan, Codina (Crespo 77), Soria, Bernat, Lopez (Pedescoll 90+4), Riera (Vall 69), Rubio. Coach: Lluis Miguel Aloy (AND)
Red card: Salvat 84
H 0-3
Rivas, Pedescoll, Orosa, Martínez, Sirvan, Codina, Soria, Vall (Blázquez 46), Bernat (Pereira 64), Riera (Jimenez 69), Rubio. Coach: Lluis Miguel Aloy (AND)

Domestic cup: Copa Constitució 2012/13

SECOND ROUND

(24/02/13)
Encamp B 0-4 Encamp
Ordino 2-0 Inter Escaldes
Rànger's 0-7 Principat
UE Santa Coloma B 0-6 Engordany

Byes – Lusitans, FC Santa Coloma, UE Santa Coloma, Sant Julià

QUARTER-FINALS

(28/04/13 & 05/05/13)
Encamp 1-0 FC Santa Coloma *(Rodríguez 52)*
FC Santa Coloma 3-0 Encamp *(Rebés 14, Barreiro 49, Lino 73)*
(FC Santa Coloma 3-1)
Engordany 0-7 Sant Julià *(Riera 18, Vila 39, Serra 51, 70, F Girau 53p, 71, Acosta 80)*
Sant Julià 12-0 Engordany *(F Girau 17, 57, 75, Vila 26, 33, 38, 65, Peppe 51, Riera 52, 59, Muñoz 77, L Girau 88)*
(Sant Julià 19-0)

Principat 0-1 UE Santa Coloma *(Rubio 65)*
UE Santa Coloma 7-1 Principat *(Salvat 19, Vall 45+1, 58, 72, 90, Luís Miguel 83, 84; Palomo 56)*
(UE Santa Coloma 8-1)

(28/04/13 & 06/05/13)
Ordino 0-2 Lusitans *(Veloso 15, Bruninho 90+3)*
Lusitans 3-1 Ordino *(Bertran 47, Zarioh 62, Sánchez 79p; Gomes 85p)*
(Lusitans 5-1)

SEMI-FINALS

(12/05/13 & 19/05/13)
Sant Julià 0-0 Lusitans
Lusitans 1-2 Sant Julià *(Bruninho 32; Riera 39, Ruiz 42)*
(Sant Julià 2-1)

UE Santa Coloma 3-0 FC Santa Coloma *(Rubio 62p, Bernat 85, 90+1)*
FC Santa Coloma 0-3 UE Santa Coloma *(Rubio 6p, Anton 69, Bernat 90p)*
(UE Santa Coloma 6-0)

FINAL

(26/05/13)
Estadi Comunal, Andorra la Vella
UE SANTA COLOMA 3 *(Rubio 24, 89, Luís Miguel 94)*
UE SANT JULIÀ 2 *(Serra 6, Riera 26)*
(aet)
Referee: Rui Maciel
UE SANTA COLOMA: Periánez, López (Luís Miguel 78), Martínez, Blazquez (Pedescoll 45), Rubio, Bousenine, Riera, Sirvan, Codina (Salvat 61), Vall, Bernat
SANT JULIÀ: Hugo Fernandes, Muñoz (Martínez 105), Varela, Ruiz, Yael, F Girau (Wagner 81), Peppe, Serra, Acosta, Vila, Riera

Top goalscorers

17	Bruninho (Lusitans)
12	Luís Miguel (Lusitans)
10	Francisco Girau (Sant Julià)
9	Pedro Reis (Lusitans)
	Alejandro Izquierdo (Principat)
	Josep Vall (UE Santa Coloma)
8	Alejandro Romero (FC Santa Coloma)
	Victor Bernat (UE Santa Coloma)
7	Diego Marinho (Inter Escaldes)
6	Atabu (Lusitans)
	Fabio Serra (Sant Julià)
	Manuel Veiga Riera (Sant Julià)
	Jordi Rubio (UE Santa Coloma)

Second level

SECOND LEVEL FINAL TABLE 2012/13

		Pld	W	D	L	F	A	Pts
1	FC Ordino	22	22	0	0	119	10	66
2	FC Lusitans B	22	14	2	6	60	32	44
3	FC Santa Coloma B	22	13	2	7	48	39	41
4	Atlètic Club d'Escaldes	22	11	5	6	53	40	38
5	CE Principat B	22	10	4	8	55	56	34
6	FC Casa del Benfica	22	11	0	11	43	42	33
7	UE Santa Coloma B	22	10	1	11	41	48	31
8	UE Extremenya	22	9	2	11	41	33	29
9	Rànger's FC	22	9	1	12	57	72	28
10	FC Encamp B	22	5	2	15	38	60	17
11	Penya Encarnada	22	5	0	17	30	103	15
12	La Massana	22	3	1	18	16	66	7

NB FC Lusitans B & FC Santa Coloma B ineligible for promotion - Atlètic Club d'Escaldes therefore enter play-offs; La Massana – 3 pts deducted.

PROMOTION/RELEGATION PLAY-OFFS

(19/05/13 & 26/05/13)
Encamp 3-0 Atlètic Escaldes
Atlètic Escaldes 1-5 Encamp
(Encamp 8-1)

ARMENIA
Hayastani Futboli Federacia (HFF)

Address	Khanjyan Street 27 AM-0010 Yerevan	**President**	Ruben Hayrapetyan
Tel	+374 10 568883	**Vice-president**	Armen Minasyan
Fax	+374 10 547173	**Media officer**	Tigran Israelyan
E-mail	media@ffa.am	**Year of formation**	1992
Website	ffa.am	**National stadium**	Hanrapetakan, Yerevan (14,400)

PREMIER LEAGUE CLUBS

1. FC Ararat
2. FC Banants
3. FC Gandzasar
4. Impuls FC
5. FC Mika
6. FC Pyunik
7. FC Shirak
8. Ulisses FC

PROMOTED CLUB

9. FC Alashkert

Gyumri

7

5

Yerevan Abovyan

6

9 0

Ararat

4

0   50   100 km
0   50 miles

Kapan

3

KEY:

● – UEFA Champions League
● – UEFA Europa League
● – Promoted club
● – Relegated club

Shirak show staying power

In switching from its traditional calendar-year season to a more mainstream autumn-to-spring schedule, the Armenian Premier League obliged its eight participants to play each other six times in a marathon transitional campaign that began in the early spring of 2012 and came to its conclusion, 42 games later, in mid-May 2013.

The long ride was enjoyed by FC Shirak Gyumri, who rose six places from the previous campaign, in 2011, to become Armenian champions for the fourth time. They were denied a domestic double, however, by a youthful FC Pyunik, who defeated them 1-0 in the cup final.

First league title in 14 years for Gyumri club

Eight teams compete in long transitional campaign

Pyunik deny champions in Armenian Cup final

Domestic league

It took plenty of stamina to win the 2012/13 league title, and Shirak provided it to end a 14-year wait for the country's top prize, coach Vardan Bichakhchyan steering the team home with two matches in hand as a 1-0 win at Pyunik coincided with a defeat for their lone challengers FC Mika at FC Banants, who would finish bottom of the table and be relegated for the first time.

Shirak ended up with a nine-point winning margin, their lead at the end of 2012 having stood at just three points. Their most consistently productive period came the previous summer, when they stitched together eight successive victories – thanks largely to their all-African attack of Yoro Lamien Ly (Senegal) and Ismaël Fofana (Ivory Coast). That pair contributed 32 of Shirak's 70 goals between them, with the long-serving Andranik Barikyan adding another dozen. The team's most assiduous performer was goalkeeper Artur Harutyunyan, who started 41 matches – the same number as the league's top scorer, 22-goal Norayr Gyozalyan of FC Impuls.

Mika, who finished 12 points clear in second place, were practically an all-Armenian team, with Brazilian defender Alex their only prominent import, although they were coached by a foreigner, Slovakian Zsolt Hornyák. Mika led the standings on more than one occasion but lacked the same staying power as Shirak and were therefore unable to add a first league title to their six Armenian Cup wins.

Domestic cup

Having defeated Pyunik four days before the cup final to take the league title, Shirak were widely expected to stage a repeat performance at the Hrazdan stadium in Yerevan. Bichakhchyan's team had won the trophy in April 2012, beating Impuls 1-0 in the final, but although the holders dominated their opponents for large chunks of the game, their double ambitions were undone by a 39th-minute strike from 20-year-old defender Taron Voskanyan that secured the trophy for Pyunik for the sixth time. A single-goal victory was in keeping with a low-scoring competition that yielded just 16 goals in its 15 matches.

Europe

2011 Armenian champions Ulisses FC finished a lowly sixth in 2012/13 and they failed to make an impression in Europe, losing home and away to FC Sheriff.

Shirak, however, did win a European tie for the first time as they edged past Montenegrin side FK Rudar Pljevlja. None of the four Armenian sides, however, made it past the second qualifying round.

National team

Hopes of a 2014 FIFA World Cup qualifying campaign to match that of UEFA EURO 2012, when Armenia came close to reaching the play-offs, were scuppered by three successive home defeats, the last of them a humiliating 1-0 loss to Malta. But if that result was a huge surprise, so too was the one four days later as Vardan Minasyan's side staged an extraordinary recovery, destroying Denmark 4-0 in Copenhagen.

There was too much ground for Armenia to make up in their final four fixtures, but as a way of halting a four-match losing run it was quite a statement of intent. Yura Movsisyan, who had just completed a fine season in Russia, struck the first two goals, and the scoring was completed by Henrikh Mkhitaryan, the main man in FC Shakhtar Donetsk's Ukrainian double-winning campaign, whose 82nd-minute strike placed him level with Artur Petrosyan as Armenia's all-time top scorer.

Domestic league: Premier League 2012/13 final table

		Pld	Home					Away					Total					Pts
			W	D	L	F	A	W	D	L	F	A	W	D	L	F	A	
1	**FC Shirak**	42	16	3	2	43	18	10	7	4	27	20	26	10	6	70	38	88
2	FC Mika	42	16	3	2	35	15	8	4	9	22	25	24	7	11	57	40	79
3	FC Gandzasar	42	11	5	5	27	14	7	8	6	21	23	18	13	11	48	37	67
4	FC Pyunik	42	12	2	7	42	22	7	4	10	25	29	19	6	17	67	51	63
5	Impuls FC	42	10	4	7	32	23	8	2	11	34	42	18	6	18	66	65	60
6	Ulisses FC	42	6	10	5	24	17	5	2	14	17	33	11	12	19	41	50	45
7	FC Ararat	42	7	2	12	19	30	2	4	15	9	39	9	6	27	28	69	33
8	FC Banants	42	4	9	8	24	29	1	7	13	13	35	5	16	21	37	64	31

SEASON AT A GLANCE

EUROPEAN QUALIFICATION 2013/14

Champion: FC Shirak (first qualifying round)

Cup winner: FC Pyunik (first qualifying round)

FC Mika (first qualifying round)
FC Gandzasar (first qualifying round)

Top scorer   Norayr Gyozalyan (Impuls), 22 goals
Relegated club   Impuls FC (withdrew)
Promoted club   FC Alashkort
Cup final   FC Pyunik 1-0 FC Shirak

PREMIER LEAGUE TEAM OF THE SEASON
(4-2-3-1)
Coach: Dichakhchyan (Shirak)

PLAYER OF THE SEASON
Andranik Barikyan
(FC Shirak)

A loyal one-club man, Barikyan was actually on Shirak's books when they landed the title in 1999. At the age of 32 he produced the best form of his career, proving to be as much of a menace without the ball as he was with it. He scored 12 goals, set up eight more and spent the rest of his time keeping opposition defences on their toes.

NEWCOMER OF THE SEASON
Taron Voskanyan
(FC Pyunik)

Pyunik have a reputation for nurturing talented academy products, and Voskanyan looks set to be another success story. The 20-year-old defender's career gathered pace in 2012/13. He scored four league goals as well as the cup final winner and made his senior international debut in a 4-2 friendly win against Lithuania in November.

A Boyrayan
(Gandzasar)

K Hovhannisyan   Voskanyan   Alex   Aleksanyan
(Pyunik)   (Pyunik)   (Mika)   (Beitar)

K Muradyan   A Mkrtchyan
(Shirak)   (Mika)

Pachajyan   Azatyan
(Shirak)   (Mika)
N Davtyan
(Impuls)

Barikyan
(Shirak)

ARMENIA

NATIONAL TEAM

Home Kit   Away Kit

TOP FIVE ALL-TIME CAPS
Sargis Hovsepyan (131); **Roman Berezovski** (79); Artur Petrosyan (69); Harutyun Vardanyan (63); **Robert Arzumanyan** (60)

TOP FIVE ALL-TIME GOALS
Henrikh Mkhitaryan & Artur Petrosyan (11); **Gevorg Ghazaryan** & **Edgar Manucharyan** (8); Ara Hakobyan, **Yura Movsisyan** & **Marcos Pizzelli** (7)

Results 2012/13

15/08/12	Belarus	H	Yerevan	1-2	*Verkhovtsov (73og)*
07/09/12	Malta (WCQ)	A	Ta' Qali	1-0	*Sarkisov (70)*
11/09/12	Bulgaria (WCQ)	A	Sofia	0-1	
12/10/12	Italy (WCQ)	H	Yerevan	1-3	*Mkhitaryan (27)*
14/11/12	Lithuania	H	Yerevan	4-2	*Manucharyan (7), Mkrtchyan (49), Mkhitaryan (55), Özbiliz (72)*
05/02/13	Luxembourg	N	Valence (FRA)	1-1	*Manucharyan (44)*
26/03/13	Czech Republic (WCQ)	H	Yerevan	0-3	
07/06/13	Malta (WCQ)	H	Yerevan	0-1	
11/06/13	Denmark (WCQ)	A	Copenhagen	4-0	*Movsisyan (1, 59), Özbiliz (19), Mkhitaryan (82)*

Appearances 2012/13

Coach: Vardan Minasyan	05/01/74		Blr	MLT	BUL	ITA	Ltu	Lux	CZE	MLT	DEN	Caps	Goals
Roman Berezovski	05/08/74	Dinamo Moskva (RUS)	G		G	G	G	G	G	G	G	79	-
Sargis Hovsepyan	02/11/72	Pyunik	D	D	D		D5					131	2
Hrayr Mkoyan	02/09/86	Shirak /České Budějovice (CZE)	D	D	D	D		s80				22	-
Valeri Aleksanyan	04/09/84	Sanat Naft (IRN)	D	s79		D	D		D	D	D	26	-
Artak Yedigaryan	18/03/90	Metalurh Donetsk (UKR) /Pyunik	D60	D52	s43	D	s5 /64	s46				16	-
Artur Yedigaryan	26/06/87	Pyunik /Hoverla (UKR)	M46		M76	M65	s83				M86	30	-
Gevorg Ghazaryan	05/04/88	Metalurh Donetsk (UKR)	M81		M 77*		M	M64	M60		M	31	8
Henrikh Mkhitaryan	21/01/89	Shakhtar Donetsk (UKR)	M	M	M	M	M73	M	M	M	M	39	11
Marcos Pizzelli	03/10/84	Kuban (RUS)	M90	M64	s54 73*		M	M	M	M	s86	29	7
Aras Özbiliz	09/03/90	Kuban (RUS)	M	M	M54	M	M75	M	s50	M	M91	10	3
Yura Movsisyan	02/08/87	Krasnodar (RUS) /Spartak Moskva (RUS)	A	A	A	A			A	s46	A84	21	7
David Manoyan	05/07/90	Pyunik	s46	s52		M77	s16		s78	M66		15	-
Levon Hayrapetyan	17/04/89	Lechia Gdańsk (POL)	s60	M	D43							14	-
Artur Sarkisov	19/01/87	Volga (RUS)	s81	s64	s76	s77		s72	s60	s66	s84	17	3
Kamo Hovhannisyan	05/10/92	Pyunik	s90				D	D	D	D	D	9	-
Gevorg Kasparov	25/07/80	Mika		G								20	-
Robert Arzumanyan	24/07/85	SKA-Energia (RUS) /Aktobe (KAZ)	D79	D	D	D29		D87	D	D	D	60	4
Karlen Mkrtchyan	25/11/88	Metalurh Donetsk (UKR)	M	M	M	M83	s78			M	M	29	1
Edgar Manucharyan	19/01/87	Ural (RUS)				s65	A16	A72	A50	A46		40	8
Taron Voskanyan	22/02/93	Pyunik					s29	s87	D	D		4	-
Hovhannes Hambartsumyan	04/10/90	Banants					s64	D46				5	-
Masis Voskanyan	11/07/90	Roeselare (BEL)					s73					2	-
Edgar Malakyan	22/09/90	Plzeň (CZE)					s75					13	-
Artem Khachaturov	18/06/92	Sheriff (MDA)						D80				1	-
Karen Muradyan	01/11/92	Shirak							M78	M78		2	-
Norayr Aslanyan	25/03/91	Emmen (NED)						s64			s91	2	-
Varazdat Haroyan	24/08/92	Pyunik									D	3	-

European club competitions 2012/13

ULISSES FC

Second qualifying round - FC Sheriff (MDA)
H 0-1
Hovhannisyan, N Grigoryan, Sahakyan, D Grigoryan, Balabekyan (Adamyan 66; Hakhnazaryan 78), Aragoney (Bareghamyan 66), Ugrekhelidze, Simonyan, Jikia, A Grigoryan, Ngavouka-Tseke. Coach: Sevada Arzumanyan (ARM)
A 0-1
Hovhannisyan, N Grigoryan, Sahakyan, D Grigoryan (Balabekyan 63), Aragoney (Machkalyan 85), Bareghamyan, Ugrekhelidze, Simonyan (Hakhnazaryan 81), Jikia, A Grigoryan, Ngavouka-Tseke. Coach: Sevada Arzumanyan (ARM)

FC SHIRAK

First qualifying round - FK Rudar Pljevlja (MNE)
A 1-0 *Ly (71)*
Artur Harutyunyan, H Grigoryan, Kadio, Ly, Mkoyan, T Davtyan, Fofana (Hakobyan 88), Barikyan, Muradyan (Tigranyan 71), Hovhannisyan, Diop (Mkrtchyan 80). Coach: Vardan Bichakhchyan (ARM)
H 1-1 *Diop (14)*
Artur Harutyunyan, H Grigoryan, Kadio, Ly (Mkrtchyan 90+1), Mkoyan, T Davtyan, Fofana (Hakobyan 82), Barikyan (Tigranyan 63), Muradyan, Hovhannisyan, Diop. Coach: Vardan Bichakhchyan (ARM)

Second qualifying round - Bnei Yehuda Tel-Aviv FC (ISR)
A 0-2
Artur Harutyunyan, Kadio, Ly, Tigranyan (T Davtyan 71), Mkoyan, Fofana (Mkrtchyan 83), Hakobyan (Barikyan 60), Muradyan, Paltajyan, Hovhannisyan, Diop. Coach: Vardan Bichakhchyan (ARM)
Red card: Barikyan 76
H 0 1
Artur Harutyunyan, Kadio, Ly, Tigranyan, Mkoyan, T Davtyan (Nalbandyan 57), Fotana, Mkrtchyan (Hakobyan 65), Muradyan, Hovhannisyan (Davoyan 67), Diop. Coach: Vardan Bichakhchyan (ARM)

FC PYUNIK

First qualifying round - FK Zeta (MNE)
H 0-3
Ohanyan, A Hovhannisyan, Hovsepyan, K Hovhannisyan, Ghukas Poghosyan (D Minasyan 57), Yusbashyan, G Hovhannisyan, Ayvazyan, Voskanyan, Bakalyan (H Hovhannisyan 53), Gagik Poghosyan (G Malakyan 75). Coach: Suren Chakhalyan (ARM)

A 2-1 *Tatoyan (19), Gagik Poghosyan (88)*
Ohanyan, A Hovhannisyan, Hovsepyan, K Hovhannisyan, H Hovhannisyan (Ayvazyan 58), Yusbashyan, G Hovhannisyan, Voskanyan, Tatoyan (Grigoryan 46), Bakalyan (Melkonyan 84), Gagik Poghosyan. Coach: Suren Chakhalyan (ARM)

FC GANDZASAR

First qualifying round - EB/Streymur (FRO)
A 1-3 *Gustavo Correia (72)*
Armen Khachatryan, Keita (Nasibyan 75), Diego Lomba, Tatintsyan, Vukomanović (Seedorf 54), Krasovski, Doumbia (Sargsyan 62), Gustavo Correia, A Avagyan, Obradović, Kasule. Coach: Samvel Sargsyan (ARM)
H 2-0 *H Avagyan (67), Diego Lomba (72)*
A Beglaryan, Keita, Manucharyan (Seedorf 51), Diego Lomba, Tatintsyan, Vukomanović (Sargsyan 65), Gustavo Correia, A Avagyan, Nasibyan (H Avagyan 61), Obradović, Kasule. Coach: Samvel Sargsyan (ARM)

Second qualifying round - Servette FC (SUI)
A 0 2
A Beglaryan, Keita (Seedorf 58), Diego Lomba, Tatintsyan, Vukomanović, Krasovski (Manucharyan 53), Gustavo Correia, A Avagyan, Nasibyan (Grigoryan 64), Obradović, Kasule. Coach: Samvel Sargsyan (ARM)
H 1-3 *H Avagyan (90+1)*
A Beglaryan, Keita (Nasibyan 73), Seedorf, Manucharyan, Diego Lomba, Tatintsyan (Doumbia 55), Vukomanović, Gustavo Correia (H Avagyan 63), A Avagyan, Obradović, Kasule. Coach: Samvel Sargsyan (ARM)

ARMENIA

FC ARARAT

Coach: Albert Safaryan;
(25/05/12) Abraham Khashmanyan
1935 • Kotaik, Abovyan (5,000) • fcararat.com
Major honours
USSR League (1) 1973;
Armenian League (1) 1993;
USSR Cup (2) 1973, 1975;
Armenian Cup (5) 1993, 1994, 1995, 1997, 2008

2012

01/04	Shirak	h	1-2	Hakobyan	
07/04	Mika	a	0-3		
14/04	Impuls	a	1-4	A Minasyan	
22/04	Ulisses	h	2-1	Gharabaghtsyan, Voskanyan (p)	
28/04	Banants	a	0-2		
05/05	Pyunik	h	2-3	K Khachatryan 2	
13/05	Gandzasar	h	0-1		
16/05	Gandzasar	a	0-1		
20/05	Shirak	a	0-4		
27/05	Mika	h	0-3		
02/06	Impuls	h	0-2		
10/06	Ulisses	a	1-3	Kirakosyan	
16/06	Banants	h	1-3	V Mkrtchyan	
24/06	Pyunik	a	0-6		
01/07	Gandzasar	a	0-0		
29/07	Shirak	h	0-2		
05/08	Mika	a	0-1		
12/08	Impuls	a	2-1	Veranyan, Sargsyan	
18/08	Ulisses	h	1-2	Nranyan	
25/08	Banants	a	1-1	Navoyan	
01/09	Pyunik	h	0-2		
15/09	Gandzasar	h	3-1	Voskanyan 3 (1p)	
22/09	Shirak	a	2-3	og (Paltajyan), Voskanyan (p)	
30/09	Mika	h	1-0	Safaryan	
07/10	Impuls	h	1-0	D Grigoryan	
27/10	Banants	h	1-0	Kirakosyan	
03/11	Pyunik	a	0-1		
07/11	Ulisses	a	0-0		
11/11	Gandzasar	a	0-2		
17/11	Shirak	h	0-1		
25/11	Mika	a	0-1		
01/12	Impuls	a	1-0	Nranyan	

2013

10/03	Ulisses	a	0-1		
16/03	Banants	a	0-0		
30/03	Pyunik	h	1-3	Sargsyan (p)	
07/04	Gandzasar	h	2-1	Veranyan, Nranyan	
13/04	Shirak	h	1-3	Veranyan	
21/04	Mika	h	1-0	Sargsyan (p)	
27/04	Impuls	h	1-2	Dorunts	
03/05	Ulisses	h	0-0		
12/05	Banants	h	1-1	Nranyan	
18/05	Pyunik	a	0-2		

No	Name	Nat	DoB	Pos	Aps	(s)	Gls
8	Karen Avoyan		22/08/86	A	1	(1)	
1	Mayis Azizyan		01/05/78	G	14		
2	Armen Dorunts		01/11/90	D	5	(2)	1
13	Vaghinak Eloyan		19/02/93	A		(3)	
4	Vardges Gebeshyan		11/06/94	D		(1)	
14	Tigran Gharabaghtsyan		06/06/84	A	27	(5)	1
3	Davit G Grigoryan		12/09/87	D	16	(4)	1
4	Hovhannes Grigoryan		09/03/85	D	5	(1)	
7	Mkhitar Grigoryan		20/02/86	M		(1)	
6	Norayr Grigoryan		07/06/83	M	9		
15	Ara Hakobyan		04/11/80	A	3	(6)	1
4	Rafik Harutyunyan		08/06/92	D		(2)	
99	Arman Hovhannisyan		07/07/92	G	9	(1)	
15	Razmik Hovhannisyan		12/02/91	M	1	(2)	
3	Eduard Ismailov	UKR	06/03/90	D		(1)	
19	Vachagan Karapetyan		12/03/83	D	23	(1)	
33	Yamadou Keita	MLI	16/10/89	A	5	(3)	
16	Gorik Khachatryan		16/06/88	M	34	(4)	

10	Karen N Khachatryan	10/06/85	A	7	(4)	2
21	Avetik Kirakosyan	21/06/83	M	37	(3)	2
2	Vahe Martirosyan	15/01/88	A	34	(1)	
4	Artur Mesropyan	15/01/85	D	8	(1)	
3	Virab Meytikhanyan	25/09/81	D	4	(1)	
7	Hrant Mikayelyan	01/05/94	M		(1)	
12	Artur H Minasyan	04/06/77	M	29	(3)	1
20	Hayk Minasyan	16/10/88	M		(1)	
8	Harutyun Mirzoyan	28/05/94	M	1	(6)	
17	Arayik Mkrtchyan	08/07/93	A		(1)	
10	Hayk Mkrtchyan	05/11/89	A	1	(2)	
16	Varuzhan Mkrtchyan	23/09/93	M	5	(6)	1
1	Martik Mkrtumyan	04/03/85	G	6		
13	Karen Navoyan	10/08/79	M	24	(7)	1
9	Gevorg Nranyan	08/03/86	A	17	(4)	4
13	Gevorg Ohanyan	29/01/92	M		(3)	
12	Armen Papyan	29/05/89	M	3	(2)	
23	Alexander Petrosyan	28/05/86	A	22	(4)	
12	Arsen Petrosyan	27/09/91	G	13		
5	Artur Petrosyan	15/06/83	M	11	(13)	
19	Galust Petrosyan	05/09/81	A	4	(2)	
17	Narek Petrosyan	25/11/90	M		(8)	
4	Rafayel Safaryan	30/01/86	D	16	(2)	1
8	Andranik Sargsyan	07/03/85	M	17	(6)	3
18	Khoren Veranyan	24/09/86	M	21	(6)	3
11	Tigran Voskanyan	21/01/89	M	30	(7)	5

FC BANANTS

Coach: Rafayel Nazaryan;
(16/01/13) Volodymyr Pyatenko (UKR)
1992 • Banants (3,500) • fcbanants.am
Major honours
Armenian Cup (2) 1992, 2007

2012

31/03	Pyunik	h	1-1	Dashyan	
07/04	Gandzasar	a	0-3		
16/04	Shirak	h	3-0	Hambartsumyan, Santos du Bala, Shahnazaryan	
22/04	Mika	a	1-2	G Karapetyan	
28/04	Ararat	h	2-0	G Karapetyan, Hambartsumyan (p)	
05/05	Ulisses	a	0-0		
12/05	Impuls	a	1-1	Hambartsumyan	
16/05	Impuls	h	1-2	Santos du Bala (p)	
20/05	Pyunik	a	0-4		
26/05	Gandzasar	h	0-1		
03/06	Shirak	a	1-2	Gyozalyan	
16/06	Ararat	a	3-1	Hambartsumyan, V Poghosyan, G Karapetyan	
20/06	Mika	h	0-1		
24/06	Ulisses	h	2-3	Dashyan, Santos du Bala	
30/06	Impuls	h	2-5	Sujyan, Hovhannisyan	
29/07	Pyunik	h	0-3		
04/08	Gandzasar	a	1-1	Ananyan	
19/08	Mika	a	0-0		
25/08	Ararat	h	1-1	Sujyan	
01/09	Ulisses	a	2-2	Ananyan, Dashyan	
15/09	Impuls	a	2-2	G Karapetyan, Ararat Arakelyan	
22/09	Pyunik	a	0-1		
29/09	Gandzasar	h	0-0		
05/10	Shirak	a	1-2	Kocharyan	
27/10	Ararat	a	0-1		
04/11	Ulisses	h	1-1	Dashyan	
07/11	Shirak	h	1-1	Dashyan	
10/11	Impuls	h	2-3	Harutyunyan, Dashyan (p)	
18/11	Pyunik	h	2-0	G Karapetyan, Ararat Arakelyan	
21/11	Mika	h	1-1	Dashyan	
24/11	Gandzasar	a	0-2		
03/12	Shirak	h	2-2	Hambartsumyan, Ararat Arakelyan	

2013

10/03	Mika	a	0-2	
16/03	Ararat	h	0-0	
30/03	Ulisses	a	0-0	
06/04	Impuls	a	0-1	

13/04	Pyunik	a	0-4		
20/04	Gandzasar	h	1-1	Minasyan	
27/04	Shirak	a	0-2		
03/05	Mika	h	2-1	S Karapetyan, Minasyan	
12/05	Ararat	a	1-1	Hambartsumyan	
18/05	Ulisses	h	0-2		

No	Name	Nat	DoB	Pos	Aps	(s)	Gls
17	Levon Ananyan		15/09/94	M	6	(2)	2
6	Ararat Arakelyan		01/02/84	M	24		3
2	Artashes Arakelyan		10/06/89	D	27	(2)	
17	Davit Asatryan		10/01/95	D	1	(3)	
10	Andrey Atanasov	BUL	09/04/87	M	3	(1)	
13	Eduard Avagyan		21/03/96	M	4	(8)	
12	Khachatur Avetisyan		06/05/93	A	1	(4)	
6	Armen Barseghyan		01/01/93	M		(3)	
19	Gagik Daghbashyan		19/10/90	D	40		
5	Artak Dashyan		20/11/89	M	22	(5)	7
4	Sipan Davtyan		20/04/95	M		(4)	
11	Roman Debelko	UKR	08/08/93	M	6	(4)	
22	Stepan Ghazaryan		11/01/85	G	19		
9	Pavlo Grishchenko	UKR	06/07/90	M	10		
14	Narek Gyozalyan		10/07/92	D	30	(1)	1
5	Artur Hakobyan		13/09/88	D		(1)	
19	Hovhannes Hambartsumyan		04/10/90	D	36		6
11	Karen Harutyunyan		05/08/86	M	12	(6)	1
20	Benik Hovhannisyan		12/10/90	M	2	(3)	1
9	Gevorg Karapetyan		10/06/90	A	24	(12)	5
17	Sargis Karapetyan		24/04/90	M	37	(2)	1
15	Grisha Khachatryan		01/03/92	D	10		
19	Andranik Kocharyan		29/01/94	M	12	(13)	1
14	Nairi Minasyan		26/08/95	M	18	(9)	2
15	Argishti Petrosyan		16/10/93	D	2	(5)	
18	Ararat Poghosyan		11/09/93	D	12	(11)	
16	Valter Poghosyan		16/05/92	M	24	(8)	1
19	Aramayis Qyosayan		13/01/95	A		(3)	
9	Santos du Bala	BRA	02/02/81	A	8	(2)	3
6	Hovhannes Sarafyan		03/01/94	M	1	(4)	
23	Aram Sargsyan		13/05/96	M		(3)	
1	Nikolay Sargsyan		02/05/81	G	1		
4	Aram Shahnazaryan		21/04/94	D	25	(2)	1
26	Davit Sujyan		03/01/92	M	17	(17)	2
1	Artur Toroyan		01/02/92	G	22		
16	Ararat Yeganyan		13/02/94	A	6	(7)	

FC GANDZASAR

Coach: Abraham Khashmanyan;
(20/05/12) Samvel Sargsyan;
(17/09/12) Sevada Arzumanyan
2004 • Lernagorts (3,500) • no website

2012

01/04	Ulisses	a	0-0		
07/04	Banants	h	3-0	Gustavo Correia, Vukomanović, Ara Khachatryan (p)	
14/04	Pyunik	a	1-0	Obradović	
21/04	Impuls	h	0-1		
05/05	Mika	a	2-0	Vukomanović, H Avagyan	
09/05	Shirak	h	1-2	Keita	
13/05	Ararat	a	1-0	Vukomanović (p)	
16/05	Ararat	h	1-0	Cuico	
20/05	Ulisses	h	0-1		
26/05	Banants	a	1-0	og (Khachatryan)	
09/06	Impuls	a	1-1	Diego Lomba	
17/06	Shirak	a	1-2	Keita	
23/06	Mika	a	2-3	Vukomanović, A Avagyan	
01/07	Ararat	h	0-0		
29/07	Ulisses	a	2-0	A Zakaryan, Seedorf	
04/08	Banants	h	1-1	Seedorf	
09/08	Pyunik	a	2-4	Diego Lomba, Seedorf	
18/08	Impuls	h	3-0	Manucharyan, Keita, Doumbia	
26/08	Shirak	h	1-0	Diego Lomba	
02/09	Mika	a	0-0		
15/09	Ararat	a	1-3	Diego Lomba	
19/09	Ulisses	h	0-1		
29/09	Banants	a	0-0		

05/10	Pyunik	h	2-0	*Diego Lomba 2*
28/10	Shirak	a	0-2	
04/11	Mika	h	3-2	*Doumbia, og (Alex), Seedorf*
07/11	Pyunik	h	1-0	*Keita*
11/11	Ararat	h	2-0	*Seedorf, Diego Lomba*
17/11	Ulisses	a	0-0	
21/11	Impuls	a	0-3	
24/11	Banants	h	2-0	*Diego Lomba 2*
02/12	Pyunik	a	1-1	*Doumbia*
2013				
09/03	Impuls	h	2-1	*N Beglaryan, William*
17/03	Shirak	h	0-0	
30/03	Mika	a	2-1	*Petrosyan, N Beglaryan*
07/04	Ararat	a	1-2	*William*
13/04	Ulisses	h	1-0	*H Avagyan*
20/04	Banants	a	1-1	*Dashyan*
27/04	Pyunik	h	1-1	*N Beglaryan*
03/05	Impuls	a	2-1	*Dashyan, Doumbia*
12/05	Shirak	a	2-2	*Melkonyan, N Beglaryan*
18/05	Mika	h	1-0	*N Beglaryan*

No	Name	Nat	DoB	Pos	Aps	(s)	Gls
4	Sergey Avagimyan	RUS	05/07/89	D		(1)	
21	Artur Avagyan		04/07/87	D	36	(1)	1
18	Hayrapet Avagyan		08/05/89	A	6	(21)	2
1	Arsen Beglaryan		18/02/93	G	25		
22	Narek Beglaryan		01/09/85	A	10		5
10	Sergiu Cuico	MDA	02/02/83	A		(4)	1
7	Artak Dashyan		20/11/89	M	10		2
10	Diego Lomba	BRA	02/02/88	M	38		9
8	Diakaridia Doumbia	MLI	16/11/83	M	20	(3)	4
27	Vruyr Grigoryan		06/07/92	D	9	(11)	
11	Gustavo Correia	BRA	11/08/86	A	9	(2)	1
17	Alen Hambartsumyan		01/03/92	A	1	(5)	
22	Aghvan Hayrapetyan		19/01/87	D		(6)	
17	Tigran Ivanyan		02/09/94	A		(1)	
19	Alen Karapetyan		09/03/96	M		(1)	
30	Noah Kasule	UGA	05/05/85	M	39		
7	Yamadou Keita	MLI	16/10/89	A	24	(4)	4
22	Ara Khachatryan		21/10/81	M	24	(2)	1
9	Armen Khachatryan		25/09/84	G	1		
[illegible]	Léo	BRA	07/01/86	D		(1)	
6	Hovhannes Machkalyan		29/05/95	M		(4)	
9	Beniamin Manucharyan		02/01/81	M	15	(6)	1
8	Samvel Melkonyan		15/08/84	A	5	(3)	1
19	Sargis Nasibyan		07/07/90	A	7	(15)	
2	Goran Obradović	SRB	25/12/86	D	39		1
15	Alexander Petrosyan		28/05/86	D	7		1
89	Gevorg Prazyan		24/07/89	G	16		
8	Santos du Bala	BRA	02/02/81	A	1	(6)	
6	Andranik Sargsyan		07/03/85	M	8	(5)	
10	Regilio Seedorf	NED	13/12/88	M	15	(1)	5
15	Aleksei Skvartsov	RUS	13/01/92	M	1		
18	Norayr Tamrazyan		18/01/89	M		(1)	
13	Armen Tatintsyan		04/10/81	D	22	(2)	
14	Dejan Vukomanović	BIH	31/12/90	M	31	(5)	4
19	William	BRA	22/12/93	A	7		2
10	Hirac Yagan		03/01/89	M	11	(1)	
3	Artashes Zakaryan		29/11/87	D	15	(6)	1
16	Karen Zakaryan		28/01/78	D	10	(3)	

IMPULS FC

Coach: Armen Gyulbudaghyants

2009 • Ayg, Ararat (2,000); Arnar, Ijevan (3,000) • no website

2012				
31/03	Mika	h	1-2	*Gyozalyan*
07/04	Pyunik	a	3-1	*Timov 2, N Davtyan*
14/04	Ararat	h	4-1	*og (Alexander Petrosyan), Gyozalyan, N Davtyan, Hakobyan*
21/04	Gandzasar	a	1-0	*Gyozalyan*
05/05	Shirak	a	1-3	*Ayvazyan*
08/05	Ulisses	h	1-0	*Gyozalyan (p)*
12/05	Banants	h	1-1	*Ishkhanyan*
16/05	Banants	a	2-1	*Timov, Gyozalyan*
20/05	Mika	a	2-4	*Timov 2*
24/05	Pyunik	h	3-0	*Gyozalyan, Ayvazyan 2*
02/06	Ararat	a	2-0	*Barseghyan, N Davtyan*
09/06	Gandzasar	h	1-1	*Timov*
16/06	Ulisses	a	0-4	
23/06	Shirak	h	0-2	
30/06	Banants	a	5-2	*Hovsepyan, Gyozalyan 2, Ayvazyan 2*
28/07	Mika	h	2-1	*Ayvazyan, Gyozalyan*
04/08	Pyunik	a	2-1	*Gyozalyan, Hovsepyan*
12/08	Ararat	h	1-2	*Gyozalyan*
18/08	Gandzasar	a	0-3	
25/08	Ulisses	h	2-0	*N Davtyan, Veranyan*
02/09	Shirak	a	1-1	*Barseghyan*
15/09	Banants	h	2-2	*Gyozalyan 2*
19/09	Mika	a	2-2	*N Davtyan, Betancourt*
29/09	Pyunik	h	2-4	*Gyozalyan (p), Timov*
07/10	Ararat	a	0-1	
27/10	Ulisses	a	1-2	*Gyozalyan*
03/11	Shirak	h	3-1	*Gyozalyan 2, Hovsepyan*
10/11	Banants	a	3-2	*Betancourt, Gyozalyan (p), Vardanyan*
18/11	Mika	h	1-1	*Hovsepyan*
21/11	Gandzasar	h	3-0	*Gyozalyan, N Davtyan, Barseghyan*
25/11	Pyunik	a	2-3	*Khachatryan, Gyozalyan (p)*
01/12	Ararat	h	0-1	
2013				
09/03	Gandzasar	a	1-2	*Barseghyan*
16/03	Ulisses	h	2-0	*Hovsepyan, Timov*
30/03	Shirak	a	3-4	*Hovsepyan, Barseghyan, Ayvazyan*
06/04	Banants	h	1-0	*Gyozalyan*
13/04	Mika	a	0-1	
20/04	Pyunik	h	1-0	*Gyozalyan*
27/04	Ararat	a	2-1	*N Davtyan 2*
03/05	Gandzasar	h	1-2	*Betancourt*
12/05	Ulisses	a	1-4	*Yeghiazaryan*
18/05	Shirak	h	0-2	

No	Name	Nat	DoB	Pos	Aps	(s)	Gls
8	Vahagn Ayvazyan		[illegible]	[illegible]	[illegible]	[illegible]	[illegible]
28	Artur Barseghyan		16/11/86	A	37	(3)	5
23	Diego Betancourt	COL	19/05/91	A	12	(11)	3
22	Narek Davtyan		24/08/88	M	34	(2)	8
12	Tigran V Davtyan		30/03/92	G	10		
10	Armen Dilanyan		17/11/90	M	1	(15)	
21	Gor Elazyan		01/06/91	G	29		
5	Juliano Gimenez	BRA	04/12/84	D	9		
15	Norayr Gyozalyan		15/03/90	A	41		22
13	Samvel Hakobyan		11/09/93	A	2	(12)	1
3	Aghvan Hayrapetyan		19/01/87	M	4	(1)	
14	Artak S Hovhannisyan		08/09/88	M		(2)	
31	Rumyan Hovsepyan		13/11/91	M	36	(4)	6
2	Hayk Ishkhanyan		24/06/89	D	22	(2)	1
15	Edvard Kakosyan		04/06/86	D	16		
14	Artak Khachatryan		08/12/90	M	22	(5)	1
17	Aram Loretsyan		07/03/93	M	3	(20)	
8	Constantin Mandricenco	MDA	19/02/91	M	21		
9	Vahe Mirakyan		06/01/93	M	1	(15)	
5	Maksim Puzanov	RUS	17/03/93	M	10	(3)	
15	Mher Sahakyan		01/01/93	M		(10)	
10	Alhassan Shilla	GHA	26/10/82	D	39		
20	Filip Timov	MKD	22/05/92	M	35	(3)	8
3	Yeghishe Vardanyan		19/08/92	M	16	(9)	1
4	Hovhannes Veranyan		08/03/95	M	1	(9)	1
8	Hayk Voskanyan		23/06/96	M		(2)	
26	Vachik Yeghiazaryan		08/11/92	D	34		1

FC MIKA

Coach: Zsolt Hornyák (SVK)

1997 • Mika stadium (7,000) • fomika.am

Major honours

Armenian Cup (6) 2000, 2001, 2003, 2005, 2006, 2011

2012				
31/03	Impuls	a	2-1	*Alex, Gevorg Poghosyan*
07/04	Ararat	h	3-0	*og (A Minasyan), A Mkrtchyan, og (Artur Petrosyan)*
15/04	Ulisses	a	2-1	*A Mkrtchyan 2 (2p)*
22/04	Banants	h	2-1	*Alex, Muradyan*
28/04	Pyunik	a	0-0	
05/05	Gandzasar	h	0-2	
13/05	Shirak	h	2-1	*Muradyan 2*
16/05	Shirak	a	1-1	*Demel*
20/05	Impuls	h	4-2	*Ghazaryan, Gevorg Poghosyan 2, Muradyan*
27/05	Ararat	a	3-0	*Adamyan, Ghazaryan, Armen Petrosyan*
02/06	Ulisses	h	3-1	*Gevorg Poghosyan, Ghazaryan, Muradyan*
17/06	Pyunik	h	3-2	*Azatyan, Demel 2*
20/06	Banants	a	1-0	*Azatyan*
23/06	Gandzasar	a	3-2	*Azatyan, A Mkrtchyan, Muradyan*
30/06	Shirak	a	0-2	
28/07	Impuls	a	1-2	*Azatyan*
05/08	Ararat	h	1-0	*Muradyan*
10/08	Ulisses	a	2-1	*Alex, Azatyan*
19/08	Banants	h	1-0	*Muradyan*
26/08	Pyunik	a	1-0	*A Mkrtchyan (p)*
02/09	Gandzasar	h	0-0	
15/09	Shirak	h	3-1	*Azatyan, Beglaryan, Muradyan*
19/09	Impuls	h	2-2	*Muradyan, Voskanyan*
30/09	Ararat	a	0-1	
07/10	Ulisses	h	1-0	*Alex*
28/10	Pyunik	h	2-1	*Beglaryan, Satumyan*
04/11	Gandzasar	a	2-3	*Beglaryan, Harutyunyan*
11/11	Shirak	a	0-3	
18/11	Impuls	a	1-1	*Beglaryan*
21/11	Banants	a	1-1	*Satumyan*
25/11	Ararat	h	1-0	*Muradyan*
01/12	Ulisses	a	1-0	*Satumyan*
2013				
10/03	Banants	h	2-0	*Muradyan 2*
17/03	Pyunik	a	0-2	
30/03	Gandzasar	h	1-2	*Muradyan*
07/04	Shirak	h	0-0	
13/04	Impuls	h	1-0	*Muradyan*
21/04	Ararat	a	0-1	
27/04	Ulisses	h	2-0	*Muradyan 2*
03/05	Banants	a	1-2	*Muradyan (p)*
12/05	Pyunik	h	1-0	*Voskanyan*
18/05	Gandzasar	a	0-1	

No	Name	Nat	DoB	Pos	Aps	(s)	Gls
6	Artur Adamyan		22/04/92	M	30	(6)	1
22	Alex	BRA	06/01/82	D	38		4
21	Alik Arakelyan		21/05/96	M	1	(11)	
15	Davit Arshakyan		16/08/94	A		(3)	
14	Areg Azatyan		23/06/90	A	29	(4)	6
10	Narek Beglaryan		01/09/85	A	11	(3)	4
9	Boti Demel	CIV	03/03/89	A	4	(4)	3
32	Armen Fishyan		02/04/86	G	11		
23	Rafayel Ghazaryan		17/05/90	M	37	(5)	3
23	Arman Hakobyan		14/03/91	M	1	(1)	
11	Henrik Harutyunyan		16/12/91	A	1	(16)	1
20	Ashot Karapetyan		12/05/93	D	8	(8)	
1	Gevorg Kasparov		25/07/80	G	24		
	Armen Khachatryan		25/09/84	G	7		
17	Aghvan Mkrtchyan		27/02/81	D	39	(1)	5
10	Edgar Mkrtchyan		14/07/94	A	1	(5)	
21	Vardan Movsisyan		18/08/91	D	35	(2)	
23	Semyon Muradyan		21/03/88	M	5	(34)	18
2	Armen S Petrosyan		26/09/85	M	37		1
19	Artur T Petrosyan		02/05/94	D		(1)	
13	Gevorg Poghosyan		26/08/86	D	40		4
4	Gor Poghosyan		11/06/88	D	9	(15)	
24	Norik Sargsyan		27/02/95	D		(4)	

25	Vardges Satumyan		07/02/90	M	38	(4)	3
28	Sargis Shahinyan		10/09/95	M	15	(25)	
18	Alexander Tadevosyan		09/08/90	D	2	(5)	
6	Ignat Tyan	RUS	17/03/86	M		(1)	
22	Vladimir Ulikhanyan		19/09/95	M		(2)	
26	Andranik Voskanyan		11/04/90	M	39		2

FC PYUNIK

Coach: Suren Chakhalyan;
(16/01/13) Rafayel Nazaryann
1992 • Hanrapetakan (14,400); Pyunik Artificial (2,000);
Armenia Football Academy (1,000) • fcpyunik.am
Major honours
Armenian League (13) 1992 (shared), 1996, 1997, 2001,
2002, 2003, 2004, 2005, 2006, 2007, 2008, 2009, 2010;
Armenian Cup (6) 1996, 2002, 2004, 2009, 2010, 2013

2012

31/03	Banants	a	1-1	*H Hovhannisyan*
07/04	Impuls	h	1-3	*Ghukas Poghosyan*
14/04	Gandzasar	h	0-1	
21/04	Shirak	a	1-0	*K Hovhannisyan*
28/04	Mika	h	0-0	
05/05	Ararat	a	3-2	*H Hovhannisyan, Yusbashyan, Ayvazyan*
12/05	Ulisses	a	1-1	*Ayvazyan*
16/05	Ulisses	h	4-2	*K Hovhannisyan 2, H Hovhannisyan, Artak Yedigaryan*
20/05	Banants	h	4-0	*Hovsepyan (p), Bakalyan, Ayvazyan 2*
24/05	Impuls	a	0-3	
17/06	Mika	a	2-3	*D Minasyan, Voskanyan*
20/06	Shirak	h	1-3	*Ayvazyan*
24/06	Ararat	h	6-0	*Hovsepyan, Gagik Poghosyan, G Malakyan 2, K Hovhannisyan, Ghukas Poghosyan*
30/06	Ulisses	h	3-1	*Ayvazyan 2, K Hovhannisyan*
29/07	Banants	a	3-0	*Artur Yedigaryan, K Hovhannisyan 2*
04/08	Impuls	h	1-2	*Ayvazyan (p)*
09/08	Gandzasar	h	4-2	*Hovsepyan (p), Gagik Poghosyan, K Hovhannisyan, Ayvazyan*
19/08	Shirak	a	1-2	*G Malakyan*
26/08	Mika	h	0-1	
01/09	Ararat	a	2-0	*Ayvazyan, D Minasyan*
15/09	Ulisses	a	0-3	
22/09	Banants	h	1-0	*Manoyan*
29/09	Impuls	h	4-2	*Manoyan, og (Shilla), D Minasyan 2*
05/10	Gandzasar	a	0-2	
28/10	Mika	h	1-2	*Manoyan*
03/11	Ararat	h	1-0	*Haroyan*
07/11	Gandzasar	a	0-2	
11/11	Ulisses	h	3-1	*Gagik Poghosyan, Voskanyan, Manukyan*
18/11	Banants	a	0-2	
21/11	Shirak	h	1-2	*D Minasyan*
25/11	Impuls	h	3-2	*K Hovhannisyan, Ayvazyan, Manoyan*
02/12	Gandzasar	h	1-1	*Manoyan (p)*

2013

09/03	Shirak	a	1-0	*Yusbashyan*
17/03	Mika	h	2-0	*og (Alex), Bakalyan*
30/03	Ararat	a	3-1	*Gagik Poghosyan 2, K Hovhannisyan*
06/04	Ulisses	a	1-1	*Baloyan*
13/04	Banants	h	4-0	*Voskanyan 2, Baloyan, Ayvazyan*
20/04	Impuls	a	0-1	
27/04	Gandzasar	a	1-1	*Baloyan*
03/05	Shirak	h	0-1	
12/05	Mika	a	0-1	
18/05	Ararat	h	2-0	*Haroyan, Baloyan*

No	Name	Nat	DoB	Pos	Aps	(s)	Gls
16	Narek Aslanyan		01/01/96	M		(6)	
22	Viulen Ayvazyan		01/01/95	A	8	(23)	12

24	Vardan Bakalyan		04/04/95	A	22	(11)	2
20	Sargis Baloyan	RUS	24/08/92	A	8	(1)	4
10	Artur Grigoryan		10/07/93	M	13	(2)	
3	Varazdat Haroyan		24/08/92	D	27	(1)	2
91	Edgar Harutyunyan		09/02/95	A		(4)	
32	Gevorg Harutyunyan		14/08/94	G	1		
11	Arman Hovhannisyan		07/07/93	D	27	(4)	
20	Grigor Hovhannisyan		08/12/93	D	16	(9)	
32	Hovhannes Hovhannisyan		15/10/93	A	19	(9)	3
29	Kamo Hovhannisyan		05/10/92	M	41	(1)	10
4	Sargis Hovsepyan		02/11/72	D	20		3
25	Tigran Kandikyan		11/03/93	G	3		
15	Davit Levonyan		22/01/94	D	1	(2)	
9	Edgar Malakyan		22/09/90	M	4	(3)	
13	Gor Malakyan		12/06/94	M	16	(12)	3
11	Davit Manoyan		05/07/90	M	26		5
1	Gor Manukyan		27/09/93	G	16		1
77	Arman Melkonyan	RUS	13/02/94	M	11	(7)	
16	Davit Minasyan		09/03/93	M	15	(12)	5
5	Vaspurak Minasyan		29/06/94	M	15	(7)	
1	Albert Ohanyan		14/05/93	G	19		
1	Arsen Petrosyan		27/09/91	G	3		
30	Arsen Piloyan		01/01/94	A		(3)	
28	Gagik Poghosyan		04/05/93	M	23	(9)	5
7	Ghukas Poghosyan		06/02/94	M	15	(12)	2
8	Ashot Sardaryan		23/03/92	M	8	(1)	
50	Eduard Tatoyan		09/08/93	D	1	(2)	
24	Gegham Tumbaryan		01/01/93	D		(1)	
18	Taron Voskanyan		22/02/93	D	38		4
17	Artak Yedigaryan		18/03/90	D	8	(2)	1
6	Artur Yedigaryan		26/06/87	M	3		1
15	Artur Yusbashyan		07/09/79	M	33	(2)	2
21	Davit Zakaryan		19/04/94	D	2	(5)	
36	Albert Zohrabyan		01/10/94	M		(2)	

FC SHIRAK

Coach: Vardan Bichakhchyan
1958 • Gyumri City (4,500); Arnar, Ijevan (3,000) •
no website
Major honours
Armenian League (4) 1992 (shared), 1994, 1999, 2013;
Armenian Cup (1) 2012

2012

01/04	Ararat	a	2-1	*Hovhannisyan, Fofana*
07/04	Ulisses	h	1-0	*Barikyan (p)*
16/04	Banants	a	0-3	
21/04	Pyunik	h	0-1	
05/05	Impuls	h	3-1	*Hakobyan, Mkrtchyan, Ly*
09/05	Gandzasar	a	2-1	*og (Sargsyan), Ly*
13/05	Mika	a	1-2	*Barikyan*
16/05	Mika	h	1-1	*Barikyan*
20/05	Ararat	h	4-0	*Barikyan 3 (1p), Nalbandyan*
27/05	Ulisses	a	1-1	*Kadio*
03/06	Banants	h	2-1	*Nalbandyan, Fofana*
17/06	Gandzasar	h	2-1	*Fofana, Ly*
20/06	Pyunik	a	3-1	*Mkrtchyan, Fofana, Barikyan*
23/06	Impuls	a	2-0	*Fofana, Ly*
30/06	Mika	a	2-0	*Fofana, Ly*
29/07	Ararat	a	2-0	*Fofana, Ly*
05/08	Ulisses	h	2-1	*Ly 2*
19/08	Pyunik	a	2-1	*Fofana, Ly*
26/08	Gandzasar	a	1-1	*Kadio*
02/09	Impuls	h	1-1	*Mkoyan*
15/09	Mika	a	1-3	*Mkrtchyan*
22/09	Ararat	h	3-2	*Fofana, Barikyan, Mkrtchyan*
30/09	Ulisses	a	1-2	*Hakobyan 2*
05/10	Banants	a	2-1	*Fofana 2*
28/10	Gandzasar	h	2-0	*Barikyan (p), Fofana*
03/11	Impuls	a	1-3	*Barikyan*
07/11	Banants	a	2-1	*Barikyan (p)*
11/11	Mika	h	3-0	*Pachajyan, Ly, Barikyan*
17/11	Ararat	a	1-0	*Ly*
21/11	Pyunik	a	2-1	*Pachajyan, Fofana*

25/11	Ulisses	h	2-0	*Hakobyan, Nalbandyan*
03/12	Banants	a	2-2	*Fofana, Ly*

2013

09/03	Pyunik	h	0-1	
17/03	Gandzasar	a	0-0	
30/03	Impuls	h	4-3	*Diop, Odhiambo, K Muradyan, Ly*
07/04	Mika	a	0-0	
13/04	Ararat	h	3-1	*Ly 2, Diop*
21/04	Ulisses	a	0-0	
27/04	Banants	h	2-0	*Hakobyan, Ly (p)*
03/05	Pyunik	a	1-0	*Ly*
12/05	Gandzasar	h	2-2	*Diop, Ly (p)*
18/05	Impuls	a	2-0	*Diop, Pachajyan*

No	Name	Nat	DoB	Pos	Aps	(s)	Gls
	Norayr Abrahamyan		30/10/85	G	1		
8	Karen Aleksanyan		17/06/80	M	32	(2)	
12	Andranik Barikyan		11/09/80	A	27	(8)	12
24	Aghvan Davoyan		21/03/90	M	11	(7)	
25	Artur Davtyan		13/05/90	M	2	(4)	
5	Tigran L Davtyan		10/06/78	M	34	(2)	
29	Dame Diop	SEN	15/02/93	M	15	(4)	4
9	Ismaël Fofana	CIV	08/09/88	A	29	(1)	14
14	Hovhannes Grigoryan		09/03/85	D	12	(1)	
13	Davit Hakobyan		21/03/93	M	26	(11)	5
15	Ararat Harutyunyan		24/08/75	M	3	(3)	
22	Artur Harutyunyan		02/08/85	G	41		
21	Gevorg Hovhannisyan		16/06/83	D	32	(4)	1
4	Didier Kadio	CIV	05/04/90	D	39		2
13	Samuel Kyere	GHA	06/08/92	D	7		
35	Yoro Lamien Ly	SEN	27/08/88	M	33	(6)	18
17	Davit Marikyan		08/05/93	D	3		
	Artyom Mikaelyan		12/07/91	D	1		
7	Hrayr Mkoyan		02/09/86	D	18	(4)	1
18	Ara Mkrtchyan		03/11/84	A	19	(16)	4
	Aram Muradyan		01/01/96	A		(1)	
25	Karen Muradyan		01/11/92	M	37	(4)	1
16	Mkrtich Nalbandyan		05/02/89	A		(20)	3
9	George Odhiambo	KEN	31/12/92	A	6	(4)	1
11	Levon Pachajyan		20/09/83	M	14	(9)	3
20	Rafayel Paltajyan		02/02/84	M	5		
23	Armen Tigranyan		27/11/85	M	15	(9)	
31	Aram Tosunyan		29/05/93	M		(5)	

ULISSES FC

Coach: Sevada Arzumanyan;
(17/09/12) Karen Barseghyan
2006 • Hanrapetakan (14,400); Kotaik, Abovyan (5,000)
• no website
Major honours
Armenian League (1) 2011

2012

01/04	Gandzasar	h	0-0	
07/04	Shirak	a	0-1	
15/04	Mika	h	1-2	*D Grigoryan*
22/04	Ararat	a	1-2	*Jikia*
05/05	Banants	h	0-0	
08/05	Impuls	a	0-1	
12/05	Pyunik	h	1-1	*Balabekyan*
16/05	Pyunik	a	2-4	*Ugrekhelidze, Bareghamyan*
20/05	Gandzasar	a	1-0	*og (Obradović)*
27/05	Shirak	h	1-1	*D Grigoryan*
02/06	Mika	a	1-3	*N Grigoryan*
10/06	Ararat	h	3-1	*Adamyan, Jikia 2*
16/06	Impuls	h	4-0	*Jikia, Ngavouka-Tseke, D Grigoryan, Balabekyan*
24/06	Banants	a	3-2	*Ngavouka-Tseke, Balabekyan 2*
30/06	Pyunik	a	1-3	*Jikia*
29/07	Gandzasar	a	0-2	
05/08	Shirak	a	1-2	*Balabekyan*
10/08	Mika	h	1-2	*Aragoney*
18/08	Ararat	a	2-1	*Aragoney, Jikia*
25/08	Impuls	a	0-2	

01/09	Banants	h	2-2	D Grigoryan, Ngavouka-Tseke	
15/09	Pyunik	h	3-0	S Melkonyan, D Grigoryan, Sahakyan	
19/09	Gandzasar	a	1-0	Balabekyan	
30/09	Shirak	h	0-2		
07/10	Mika	a	0-1		
27/10	Impuls	h	2-1	A Grigoryan, Balabekyan	
04/11	Banants	a	1-1	Balabekyan	
07/11	Ararat	a	0-1		
11/11	Pyunik	a	1-3	Balabekyan (p)	
17/11	Gandzasar	h	0-0		
25/11	Shirak	a	0-2		
01/12	Mika	h	0-1		
2013					
10/03	Ararat	h	1-0	Balabekyan	
16/03	Impuls	a	0-0		
30/03	Banants	h	0-0		
06/04	Pyunik	h	1-1	Andrikyan	
13/04	Gandzasar	a	0-1		
21/04	Shirak	h	0-0		
27/04	Mika	a	0-2		
03/05	Ararat	a	0-0		
12/05	Impuls	h	4-1	Jikia, Nalbandyan 2, Sahakyan	
18/05	Banants	a	2-0	Nalbandyan, Balabekyan	

No	Name	Nat	DoB	Pos	Aps	(s)	Gls
10	Artyom M Adamyan		02/09/80	A	13	(9)	1
88	Manvel Afrikyan		08/08/85	G	12	(1)	
4	Artak Andrikyan		24/01/88	D	18	(2)	1
13	Aragoney	BRA	07/03/87	M	10	(8)	2
11	Arsen Balabekyan		24/11/86	A	24	(16)	11
5	Aram Bareghamyan		01/06/88	M	27	(8)	1
15	Artavazd Boyajyan		19/12/90	M	8	(5)	
4	Juliano Gimenez	BRA	04/12/84	D	1	(1)	
33	Artak G Grigoryan		19/10/87	A	35	(1)	1
8	David Z Grigoryan		28/12/82	M	35	(4)	5
2	Hovhannes Grigoryan		09/03/85	D	11	(2)	
5	Norayr Grigoryan		07/06/83	M	18	(2)	1
3	Tigran Hakhnazaryan		18/04/87	D	27	(2)	
20	Orbeli Hambardsumyan		20/09/90	A	1	(0)	
14	Geylam Hamlynyan		23/06/90	M	10	(0)	
99	Eduard Hovhannisyan		28/02/90	G	28		
30	Shota Jikia	GEO	30/12/84	A	29	(9)	7
10	Artur Kocharyan		11/07/74	A	3	(0)	
77	Giorgi Krasovski	GEO	20/12/79	M	3	(2)	
7	Hovhannes Machkalyan		29/05/95	M	1	(14)	
11	Samvel Melkonyan		15/03/84	A	7	(4)	1
80	Vardan Melkonyan		08/06/93	M		(1)	
18	Sergey Mkrtchyan		09/02/83	M		(1)	
14	Mkrtich Nalbandyan		05/02/89	A	5	(2)	3
91	Lie Pato Ngavouka-Tseke	CGO	15/01/91	M	24	(8)	3
22	Gevorg Nranyan		09/03/86	A	3	(1)	
26	Argishti Petrosyan		16/10/92	D	7	(1)	
9	Galust Petrosyan		05/09/81	A	2	(6)	
87	Norayr Sahakyan		09/07/87	M	32	(6)	2
77	Erik Sargsyan		21/08/92	D		(2)	
14	Andranik Shahgeldyan		10/11/94	M		(1)	
8	Mikheil Simonyan		29/07/87	D	29	(2)	
24	Albert Tadevosyan		13/09/90	A	2	(4)	
23	Virab Tokhyan		01/01/93	M		(1)	
17	Tengiz Ugrekhelidze	GEO	29/07/81	D	29	(1)	1
16	Revik Yeghiazaryan		01/06/91	M	6	(2)	
12	Artur Yeranosyan		28/03/87	G	2		

Top goalscorers

22	Norayr Gyozalyan (Impuls)
18	Semyon Muradyan (Mika)
	Yoro Lamien Ly (Shirak)
14	Ismaël Fofana (Shirak)
12	Viulen Ayvazyan (Pyunik)
	Andranik Barikyan (Shirak)
11	Arsen Balabekyan (Ulisses)
10	Kamo Hovhannisyan (Pyunik)
9	Artak Dashyan (Banants/Gandzasar)
	Diego Lomba (Gandzasar)
	Narek Beglaryan (Mika/Gandzasar)

Domestic cup: Armenian Independence Cup 2012/13

PRELIMINARY ROUND

(14/11/12 & 28/11/12)
Banants 0-0, 0-0 Alashkert *(0-0 aet; 4-5 on pens)*

QUARTER-FINALS

(02/03/13 & 12/03/13)
Alashkert 0-0 Gandzasar
Gandzasar 1-0 Alashkert *(N Beglaryan 65)*
(Gandzasar 1-0)

Pyunik 2-2 Impuls *(Zakaryan 56, 62; Hovsepyan 20, Betancourt 80)*
Impuls 0-3 Pyunik *(Gagik Poghosyan 5, Bakalyan 82, K Hovhannisyan 90)*
(Pyunik 5-2)

Celebration time for Armenian Cup winners Pyunik

(03/03/13 & 13/03/13)
Shirak 1-0 Ararat *(Diop 3)*
Ararat 0-0 Shirak
(Shirak 1-0)

Ulisses 0-0 Mika
Mika 2-0 Ulisses *(A Mkrtchyan 56, 82)*
(Mika 2-0)

SEMI-FINALS

(02/04/13 & 17/04/13)
Gandzasar 0-1 Pyunik *(Zakaryan 27)*
Pyunik 1-1 Gandzasar *(Gagik Poghosyan 25; William 43)*
(Pyunik 2-1)

(03/04/13 & 16/04/13)
Mika 0-1 Shirak *(Diop 75)*
Shirak 0-0 Mika
(Shirak 1-0)

FINAL

(07/05/13)
Hrazdan stadium, Yerevan
FC PYUNIK 1 *(Voskanyan 39)*
FC SHIRAK 0
Referee: *Arsenyan*
PYUNIK: *Manukyan, K Hovhannisyan, G Hovhannisyan (Aslanyan 80), Voskanyan, Artak Yedigaryan (A Hovhannisyan 41), Manoyan, V Minasyan (D Minasyan 53), Ghukas Poghosyan, Sardaryan (Ayvazyan 60), Yusbashyan, Bakalyan*
SHIRAK: *Artur Harutyunyan, Hovhannisyan, Kadio, Kyere, Tigranyan (T Davtyan 46), Aleksanyan, Diop (Ly 60) Hakobyan (Odhiambo 69), K Muradyan, Pachajyan, Barikyan*

Promoted club

FC ALASHKERT

Coach: Armen Sanamyan
2012 • Nairi (3,500) • no website

SECOND LEVEL FINAL TABLE 2012/13

		Pld	W	D	L	F	A	Pts
1	FC Alashkert	36	24	6	6	80	31	78
2	FC Mika-2	36	18	7	11	60	51	61
3	FC Pyunik-2	36	18	7	11	69	53	61
4	FC Gandzasar-2	36	18	6	12	76	59	60
5	FC Ararat-2	36	16	9	11	60	51	57
6	FC Banants-2	36	17	3	16	57	47	54
7	FC Shengavit	36	14	4	18	46	57	46
8	FC Shirak-2	36	11	8	17	49	54	41
9	FC King Deluxe	36	10	3	23	44	79	33
10	Impuls FC-2	36	5	5	26	46	105	20

AUSTRIA
Österreichischer Fussball-Bund (ÖFB)

Address   Ernst-Happel-Stadion
Sektor A/F
Meiereistrasse 7
AT-1020 Wien

Tel   +43 1 727 180
Fax   +43 1 728 1632
E-mail   office@oefb.at
Website   oefb.at

President   Leo Windtner
General secretary   Alfred Ludwig
Media officer   Christoph Walter
Year of formation   1904
National stadium   Ernst-Happel-
Stadion, Vienna
(50,000)

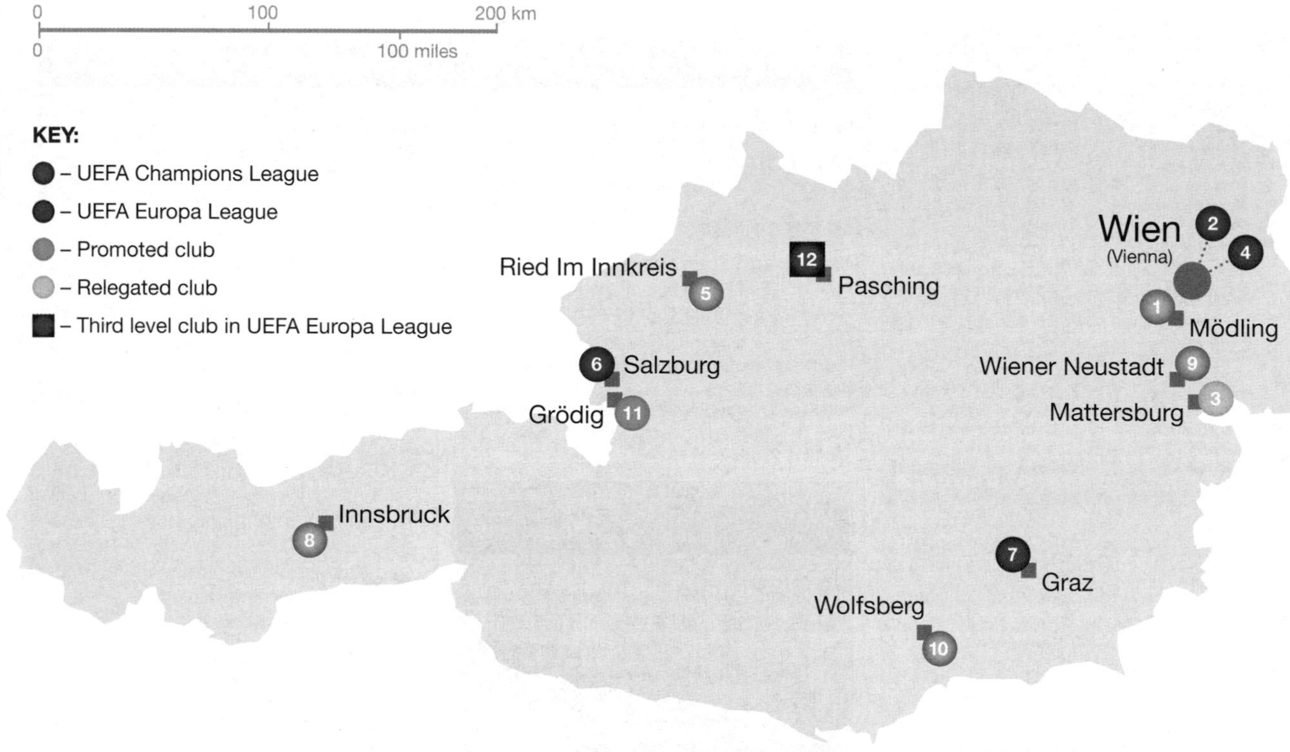

KEY:

● – UEFA Champions League
● – UEFA Europa League
● – Promoted club
● – Relegated club
■ – Third level club in UEFA Europa League

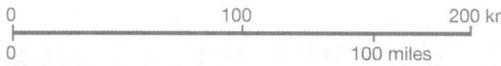

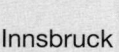

Ried Im Innkreis
Pasching
Wien (Vienna)
Mödling
Salzburg
Wiener Neustadt
Grödig
Mattersburg
Innsbruck
Wolfsberg
Graz

BUNDESLIGA CLUBS

1. FC Admira Wacker Mödling
2. FK Austria Wien
3. SV Mattersburg
4. SK Rapid Wien
5. SV Ried
6. FC Salzburg
7. SK Sturm Graz
8. FC Wacker Innsbruck
9. SC Wiener Neustadt
10. Wolfsberger AC

PROMOTED CLUB

11. SV Grödig

OTHER CLUB

12. FC Pasching

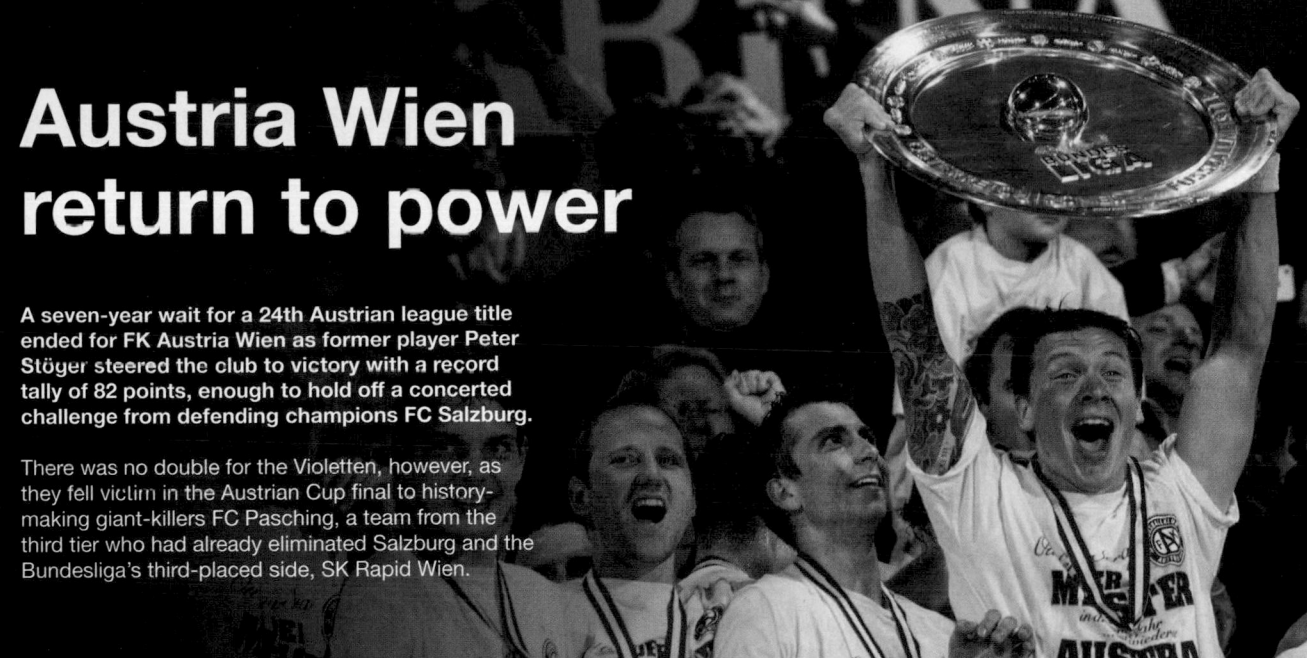

Austria Wien return to power

A seven-year wait for a 24th Austrian league title ended for FK Austria Wien as former player Peter Stöger steered the club to victory with a record tally of 82 points, enough to hold off a concerted challenge from defending champions FC Salzburg.

There was no double for the Violetten, however, as they fell victim in the Austrian Cup final to history-making giant-killers FC Pasching, a team from the third tier who had already eliminated Salzburg and the Bundesliga's third-placed side, SK Rapid Wien.

| Violetten win Bundesliga with record points tally | Third-tier Pasching claim sensational cup win | World Cup recovery opens up play-off place |

Domestic league

Out of Europe after finishing fourth in 2011/12, Austria Wien brought back Stöger from SC Wiener Neustadt for a second spell in charge (after a brief stint in 2005) and he was to add a fourth Bundesliga title to the three he had won as a player with the club in the early 1990s. Another significant new arrival was striker Philipp Hosiner, who joined in mid-August from FC Admira Wacker Mödling and went on to score at a rate of virtually a goal per game to top the Bundesliga scoring charts.

Right from the outset Stöger's men proved to be organised, defensively solid and tough to beat. But so did Salzburg, who also entered the campaign under a new coach - little known German, Roger Schmidt, who replaced double-winning Dutchman Ricardo Moniz. Rapid were also involved in the early jousting at the top before they fell away, but they did win both pre-Christmas games against Salzburg, and as a consequence Austria Wien, who beat Rapid twice, held a seven-point lead at the winter break.

That advantage stretched to 13 points in the early spring as Salzburg became bogged down by draws. Schmidt's men would finish powerfully but although they had the upper hand on Austria in the direct duels, they had too much ground to make up. The Violetten duly sealed the title in the penultimate round with a 4-0 win over SV Mattersburg, whose ten-year top-flight residence ended four days later after a 1-0 defeat by relegation rivals Admira.

Domestic cup

An 11th domestic double beckoned for Austria Wien, but Pasching's sensational run to the Austrian Cup final was to have a fitting end as Daniel Sobkova's 47th-minute strike enabled his team to become the first third-division club to win the trophy. Having beaten Rapid 1-0 in Vienna in the quarter-final and Salzburg 2-1 away in the semis, Gerald Baumgartner's side gave as good as they got against the champions, and a first major trophy more than made up for the disappointment of missing out on promotion from the Regionalliga Mitte.

Europe

The country's European campaign was defined by Salzburg's staggering defeat to Luxembourg's F91 Dudelange in the second qualifying round of the UEFA Champions League. Only Rapid made it through to the UEFA Europa League group stage (where there had been three Austrian teams in 2011/12), but Peter Schöttel's side found the going tough, their only points coming from a last-day win against FC Metalist Kharkiv.

National team

The Austrian national team headed optimistically into the 2014 FIFA World Cup qualifying campaign under a new coach, former Swiss international Marcel Koller, but their opening two results were identical to those in the UEFA EURO 2012 qualifiers – an unfortunate 2-1 home defeat by Germany and a drab goalless stalemate in Kazakhstan.

The team recovered quickly by beating Kazakhstan 4-0 at home, and after another big home win against the Faroe Islands (6-0), the goals they scored in those two games increased appreciably in value when they held the Republic of Ireland 2-2 in Dublin and defeated Sweden 2-1 in Vienna, enabling them to enter the summer break second on goal difference. Although three of their final four fixtures were away, there was genuine hope that a team including German-based stars such as Martin Harnik, Marko Arnautovic and UEFA Champions League winner David Alaba – who scored in four successive qualifiers – could press hard for a place in the play-offs.

Domestic league: Bundesliga 2012/13 final table

		Pld	Home					Away					Total					
			W	D	L	F	A	W	D	L	F	A	W	D	L	F	A	Pts
1	**FK Austria Wien**	36	12	3	3	42	15	13	4	1	42	16	25	7	4	84	31	82
2	FC Salzburg	36	12	5	1	51	19	10	6	2	40	20	22	11	3	91	39	77
3	SK Rapid Wien	36	8	6	4	30	19	8	3	7	27	20	16	9	11	57	39	57
4	SK Sturm Graz	36	8	5	5	32	27	5	4	9	17	29	13	9	14	49	56	48
5	Wolfsberger AC	36	5	6	7	27	28	7	5	6	26	28	12	11	13	53	56	47
6	SV Ried	36	8	4	6	33	23	5	3	10	27	36	13	7	16	60	59	46
7	SC Wiener Neustadt	36	6	6	6	16	21	3	3	12	16	39	9	9	18	32	60	36
8	FC Wacker Innsbruck	36	7	1	10	21	31	4	2	12	20	44	11	3	22	41	75	36
9	FC Admira Wacker Mödling	36	6	3	9	33	33	3	5	10	14	35	9	8	19	47	68	35
10	SV Mattersburg	36	8	2	8	24	25	1	6	11	12	42	9	8	19	36	67	35

SEASON AT A GLANCE

EUROPEAN QUALIFICATION 2013/14

Champion: FK Austria Wien (third qualifying round)
FC Salzburg (third qualifying round)

Cup winner: FC Pasching (play-offs)
SK Rapid Wien (third qualifying round)
SK Sturm Graz (second qualifying round)

Top scorer	Philipp Hosiner (Admira/Austria Wien), 32 goals
Relegated club	SV Mattersburg
Promoted club	SV Grödig
Cup final	FC Pasching 1-0 FK Austria Wien

BUNDESLIGA TEAM OF THE SEASON
(4-5-1)
Coach: Stöger (Austria Wien)

PLAYER OF THE SEASON
Philipp Hosiner
(FK Austria Wien)

Signed in late August from FC Admira Wacker Mödling, for whom he had already scored five goals, Hosiner went on to add 27 more for Austria Wien, including three hat-tricks and seven doubles, to make a major contribution to his new team's title triumph. He also bagged a brace for the Austrian national team on only his second appearance.

NEWCOMER OF THE SEASON
Valon Berisha
(FC Salzburg)

The versatile Norwegian midfielder joined Salzburg from Viking FK aged 19 and made a tremendous impact, scoring six times and providing 13 assists. Whether offering cover to the defence or providing the ammunition for the forwards, notably Spanish hot shot Jonathan Soriano, the Norwegian international proved to be an invaluable buy.

Lindner (Austria Wien)
Trimmel (Rapid) — Vujadinović (Sturm) — Ortlechner (Austria Wien) — Suttner (Austria Wien)
Liendl (Wolfsberg) — Berisha (Salzburg) — Jun (Austria Wien)
Gorgon (Austria Wien) — Mané (Salzburg)
Hosiner (Austria Wien)

AUSTRIA

NATIONAL TEAM

Home Kit   **Away Kit**

INTERNATIONAL TOURNAMENT APPEARANCES
FIFA World Cup Finals (7) 1934 (4th), 1954 (3rd), 1958, 1978 (2nd phase), 1982 (2nd phase), 1990, 1998
UEFA European Championship (1) 2008

TOP FIVE ALL-TIME CAPS
Andreas Herzog (103); Anton Polster (95); Gerhard Hanappi (93); Karl Koller (86); Friedl Koncilia & Bruno Pezzey (84)

TOP FIVE ALL-TIME GOALS
Anton Polster (44); Hans Krankl (34); Johann Horvath (29); Erich Hof (28); Anton Schall (27)

Results 2012/13

15/08/12	Turkey	H	Vienna	2-0	Kavlak (2), Ivanschitz (6p)
11/09/12	Germany (WCQ)	H	Vienna	1-2	Junuzovic (57)
12/10/12	Kazakhstan (WCQ)	A	Astana	0-0	
16/10/12	Kazakhstan (WCQ)	H	Vienna	4-0	Janko (24, 63), Alaba (71), Harnik (90+3)
14/11/12	Ivory Coast	H	Linz	0-3	
06/02/13	Wales	A	Swansea	1-2	Janko (75)
22/03/13	Faroe Islands (WCQ)	H	Vienna	6-0	Hosiner (8, 20), Ivanschitz (28), Junuzovic (77), Alaba (78), Garics (82)
26/03/13	Republic of Ireland (WCQ)	A	Dublin	2-2	Harnik (11), Alaba (90+2)
07/06/13	Sweden (WCQ)	H	Vienna	2-1	Alaba (26p), Janko (32)

Appearances 2012/13

Coach: Marcel Koller (SUI)	11/11/60		Tur	GER	KAZ	KAZ	Civ	Wal	FRO	IRL	SWE	Caps	Goals
Robert Almer	20/03/84	Düsseldorf (GER)	G	G	G	G		G			G	8	-
György Garics	08/03/84	Bologna (ITA)	D	D	D		D46		D	D	D	33	2
Emanuel Pogatetz	16/01/83	Wolfsburg (GER) /West Ham (ENG)	D	D	D	D	D46	D	D	D	D46	56	2
Sebastian Prödl	21/06/87	Bremen (GER)	D	D	D	D59	s46	D			s46	40	3
Markus Suttner	16/04/87	Austria Wien	D				D	D88	s72			7	-
Christian Fuchs	07/04/86	Schalke (GER)	M84	D	D	D			D72	D	D	54	1
Veli Kavlak	03/11/88	Beşiktaş (TUN)	M	M	M	M	s58	M76	M56	M69		25	1
Julian Baumgartlinger	02/01/88	Mainz (GER)	M90	M85	M63		s46			s27	M	27	-
Andreas Ivanschitz	15/10/83	Mainz (GER)	M62	M75	M73		M64	M62	M63			61	11
Zlatko Junuzovic	26/09/07	Bremen (GER)	M72	M	M	M	s62	M	M72	M73	27	4
Martin Harnik	10/06/07	Stuttgart (GER)	A72	A55	A86	M	s76			M	M	36	9
Jakob Jantscher	08/01/89	Salzburg /Dinamo Moskva (RUS)	s62	s75	s73	s81	M76	s62				15	1
Christoph Leitgeb	14/04/85	Salzburg	s72			s81	M46	s76	s56			32	-
Rubin Okotie	06/06/87	Sturm	s72									5	-
Guido Burgstaller	29/04/89	Rapid Wien	s84	s55								5	-
Yasin Pehlivan	05/01/89	Gaziantepspor (TUR)	s90									17	-
Marko Arnautovic	19/04/89	Bremen (GER)		M	M	M	M	M	M	M	M	27	7
Marc Janko	25/06/83	Trabzonspor (TUR)		s85	s63	A81	A	A		s62	A46	34	15
Andreas Weimann	05/08/91	Aston Villa (ENG)			s86		s64	M62	s63	s69	s46	6	-
Florian Klein	17/11/86	Salzburg				D	s46	D				14	-
David Alaba	24/06/92	Bayern (GER)				M81	M58	M	M	M	M	25	4
Aleksandar Dragovic	06/03/91	Basel (SUI)				s59	D		D	D	D	21	-
Heinz Lindner	17/07/90	Austria Wien					G		G	G		4	-
Franz Schiemer	21/03/86	Salzburg						s88			s75	25	4
Philipp Hosiner	15/05/89	Austria Wien							A	A62		3	2

AUSTRIA

FC SALZBURG

CHAMPIONS LEAGUE

Second qualifying round - F91 Dudelange (LUX)
A 0-1
Walke, Mendes da Silva, Schwegler, Maierhofer, Cristiano (Lindgren 74), Zárate (Jonathan Soriano 53), Ulmer, Švento (Klein 6), Sekagya, Leitgeb, Hinteregger. Coach: Roger Schmidt (GER)
Red card: Jonathan Soriano 90
H 4-3 *Jantscher (28), Hinteregger (37), Cristiano (81p), Zárate (82)*
Walke, Mendes da Silva, Schwegler (Klein 74), Jantscher, Maierhofer (Cristiano 46), Ilsanker, Ulmer, Hierländer, Leitgeb (Zárate 59), Hinteregger, Teigl. Coach: Roger Schmidt (GER)

SK RAPID WIEN

EUROPA LEAGUE

Third qualifying round - FK Vojvodina (SRB)
A 1-2 *Alar (90+6)*
Königshofer , Sonnleitner, Kulovits, Heikkinen, Boyd, Hofmann, Katzer, Drazan (Trimmel 68), Pichler, Burgstaller (Alar 78), Schimpelsberger. Coach: Peter Schöttel (AUT)
H 2-0 *Alar (90+1p), Boyd (90+8)*
Königshofer , Sonnleitner, Heikkinen, Boyd, Hofmann, Katzer, Drazan, Prager (Alar 71), Trimmel, Burgstaller (Kulovits 90+4), Gerson. Coach: Peter Schöttel (AUT)

Play-offs - PAOK FC (GRE)
A 1-2 *Alar (25)*
Königshofer , Sonnleitner, Heikkinen, Hofmann (Kulovits 77), Katzer, Ildiz, Grozurek (Schrammel 65), Burgstaller, Alar (Boyd 82), Gerson, Schimpelsberger. Coach: Peter Schöttel (AUT)
H 3-0 *Alar (31), Boyd (48), Hofmann (90+3)*
Königshofer , Sonnleitner, Heikkinen (Prager 69), Boyd, Hofmann, Katzer, Ildiz, Trimmel (Schrammel 84), Burgstaller, Alar, Gerson. Coach: Peter Schöttel (AUT)

Group K
Match 1 - Rosenborg BK (NOR)
H 1-2 *Katzer (66)*
Königshofer , Sonnleitner, Heikkinen, Boyd, Hofmann, Katzer, Ildiz (Prager 70), Trimmel, Burgstaller (Grozurek 85), Alar, Gerson. Coach: Peter Schöttel (AUT)
Match 2 - FC Metalist Kharkiv (UKR)
A 0-2
Königshofer , Sonnleitner, Heikkinen, Hofmann (Kulovits 87), Katzer, Ildiz, Prager, Trimmel, Burgstaller, Alar (Grozurek 76), Gerson. Coach: Peter Schöttel (AUT)
Red card: Burgstaller 90+3
Match 3 - Bayer 04 Leverkusen (GER)
H 0-4
Königshofer , Sonnleitner, Kulovits, Heikkinen (Boyd 46), Katzer, Drazan, Ildiz (Schimpelsberger 63), Prager, Trimmel, Alar (Schrammel 78), Gerson. Coach: Peter Schöttel (AUT)
Match 4 - Bayer 04 Leverkusen (GER)
A 0-3
Königshofer , Schrammel, Sonnleitner, Kulovits, Boyd (Prokopic 86), Wydra, Grozurek, Pichler, Trimmel, Gerson, Schimpelsberger. Coach: Peter Schöttel (AUT)
Match 5 - Rosenborg BK (NOR)
A 2-3 *Schrammel (53), Boyd (66)*
Novota, Schrammel, Sonnleitner, Heikkinen, Boyd, Pichler (Wydra 83), Trimmel, Burgstaller, Alar (Drazan 51), Gerson, Schimpelsberger (Grozurek 86). Coach: Peter Schöttel (AUT)
Match 6 - FC Metalist Kharkiv (UKR)
H 1-0 *Alar (13)*
Königshofer , Schrammel, Sonnleitner, Heikkinen, Wydra (Kulovits 46), Pichler, Trimmel (Drazan 63), Burgstaller, Alar (Boyd 76), Gerson, Schimpelsberger. Coach: Peter Schöttel (AUT)
Red card: Pichler 44

FC ADMIRA WACKER MÖDLING

EUROPA LEAGUE

Second qualifying round - VMFD Žalgiris (LTU)
A 1-1 *Hosiner (12)*
Tischler, Windbichler, Palla (Schrott 84), Plassnegger, Drescher, Ježek, Mevoungou, Hosiner (Ouédraogo 65), Schwab (Thürauer 81), Sabitzer, Toth. Coach: Dietmar Kühbauer (AUT)

H 5-1 *Schwab (4), Ježek (14p, 52), Ouédraogo (31), Hosiner (70)*
Tischler, Windbichler, Plassnegger, Drescher, Ježek (Schick 62), Ouédraogo, Mevoungou, Schwab (Hosiner 56), Sabitzer (Seebacher 82), Toth, Weber. Coach: Dietmar Kühbauer (AUT)

Third qualifying round - AC Sparta Praha (CZE)
H 0-2
Tischler, Windbichler, Plassnegger (Schick 77), Drescher, Ježek (Seebacher 71), Schachner, Ouédraogo (Hosiner 60), Mevoungou, Schwab, Sabitzer, Weber. Coach: Dietmar Kühbauer (AUT)
A 2-2 *Thürauer (19), Sulimani (69)*
Tischler, Plassnegger, Pöllhuber, Thürauer, Schrott, Mevoungou (Schachner 62), Sulimani (Schicker 80), Schwab (Hosiner 64), Seebacher, Sabitzer, Weber. Coach: Dietmar Kühbauer (AUT)

SV RIED

EUROPA LEAGUE

Second qualifying round - FC Shakhtyor Soligorsk (BLR)
A 1-1 *Hadžić (70p)*
Gebauer, Ziegl (Zulj 80), Schicker, Gartler (Guillem Martí 90), Nacho (Walch 86), Riegler, Meilinger, Hinum, Hadžić, Reiter, Reifeltshammer. Coach: Heinz Fuchsbichler (AUT)
H 0-0
Gebauer, Schicker, Guillem Martí (Iván Carril 59), Nacho, Riegler, Meilinger (Schreiner 88), Hinum, Hadžić, Zulj (Ziegl 46), Reiter, Reifeltshammer. Coach: Heinz Fuchsbichler (AUT)

Third qualifying round - Legia Warszawa (POL)
H 2-1 *Gartler (52), Hadžić (62p)*
Gebauer, Ziegl, Schicker, Gartler (Zulj 71), Grössinger (Nacho 60), Riegler, Meilinger (Guillem Martí 79), Hinum, Hadžić, Reiter, Reifeltshammer. Coach: Heinz Fuchsbichler (AUT)
A 1-3 *Žulj (76)*
Gebauer, Ziegl (Iván Carril 58), Schicker, Gartler, Nacho (Grössinger 56), Riegler, Meilinger, Hinum, Hadžić (Zulj 73), Reiter, Reifeltshammer. Coach: Heinz Fuchsbichler (AUT)

Domestic league club-by-club

FC ADMIRA WACKER MÖDLING
Coach: Dietmar Kühbauer
1905 • Trenkwalder Arena (12,000) • admirawacker.at
Major honours
Austrian League (8) 1927, 1928, 1932, 1934, 1936, 1937, 1939, 1966;
Austrian Cup (5) 1928, 1932, 1934, 1964, 1966

2012
22/07	Ried	h	0-2	
29/07	Wacker	a	2-1	Hosiner 2
05/08	Wiener Neustadt	h	4-0	Ouédraogo 2, Hosiner, Sabitzer
12/08	Austria Wien	a	0-1	
18/08	Salzburg	h	4-2	Hosiner 2, Sabitzer, Schicker
25/08	Sturm	a	2-3	Thürauer, Sabitzer
01/09	Wolfsberg	h	1-1	Schicker
15/09	Rapid	a	0-0	
22/09	Mattersburg	h	5-1	Schrott, Ouédraogo, Thürauer, Schick, Schicker
29/09	Ried	a	1-1	Schwab (p)
06/10	Wacker	h	4-1	Schick, Ouédraogo, Schwab, Sabitzer
20/10	Wiener Neustadt	a	1-2	Schick
27/10	Austria Wien	h	4-6	Schick, Schachner, Thürauer, Schwab (p)
03/11	Salzburg	a	0-5	
10/11	Sturm	h	1-2	Sulimani
17/11	Wolfsberg	a	1-1	Sulimani
25/11	Rapid	h	0-2	
01/12	Mattersburg	a	0-3	
08/12	Ried	h	0-3	
15/12	Wacker	a	1-3	Sax

2013
16/02	Wiener Neustadt	h	1-2	Ouédraogo
23/02	Austria Wien	a	0-4	
02/03	Sturm	a	2-1	og (Focker), Schwab
09/03	Wolfsberg	h	0-1	
13/03	Salzburg	h	1-1	Tito
16/03	Rapid	a	1-1	Ouédraogo
30/03	Mattersburg	h	1-0	Schwab
06/04	Ried	a	1-4	Schwab (p)
13/04	Wacker	h	4-3	Schösswendtner, Daniel Lucas 2, Windbichler
20/04	Wiener Neustadt	a	0-3	
28/04	Austria Wien	h	0-2	
04/05	Salzburg	a	1-2	Toth
11/05	Sturm	h	3-0	Schick, Ježek, Schwab
18/05	Wolfsberg	a	0-0	
22/05	Rapid	h	0-2	
26/05	Mattersburg	a	1-2	Daniel Lucas

No	Name	Nat	DoB	Pos	Aps	(s)	Gls
13	Stephan Auer		11/01/91	D	13	(3)	
14	Daniel Lucas	ESP	23/05/85	A	10	(5)	3
5	Daniel Drescher		07/10/89	D	9	(5)	
27	Thomas Ebner		22/02/92	D	16		
19	Bernhard Fucik		26/09/90	A		(2)	
24	Daniel Gremsl		02/08/92	A		(2)	
16	Philipp Hosiner		15/05/89	A	6		5
7	Patrik Ježek	CZE	28/12/76	M	16	(6)	1
35	Markus Lackner		05/04/91	D	1	(2)	
30	Andreas Leitner		25/03/94	G	1	(1)	
77	Jürgen Macho		24/08/77	G	12		
15	Patrick Mevoungou	CMR	15/02/86	M	7	(6)	
10	Matúš Mikuš	SVK	08/07/91	A		(2)	
9	Issiaka Ouédraogo	BFA	19/08/88	A	24	(1)	6
3	Stefan Palla		15/05/92	D	26		
4	Gernot Plassnegger		23/03/78	D	25		
6	Peter Pöllhuber		30/04/85	D	12		
19	Oliver Pranjic		28/09/94	M	1	(2)	
33	Markus Rusek		26/12/93	M	1		
24	Marcel Sabitzer		17/03/94	M	17		4
34	Maximilian Sax		22/11/92	A	4	(8)	1
8	Bernhard Schachner		10/01/86	M	22	(2)	1
28	Thorsten Schick		19/05/90	M	19	(4)	5
18	Rene Schicker		28/09/84	M		(9)	3
21	Christoph Schösswendtner		16/07/88	D	14		1
14	Andreas Schrott		24/08/81	D	14	(1)	1
22	Stefan Schwab		27/09/90	M	24	(9)	7
23	Rene Seebacher		24/07/88	D	7	(3)	
7	Patrick Seeger		25/08/86	A	4	(3)	
20	Benjamin Sulimani		26/09/88	A	6	(7)	2
13	Lukas Thürauer		21/12/87	M	25	(1)	3
1	Patrick Tischler		09/07/87	G	23	(2)	
16	Tito	ESP	02/07/88	M	9		1
26	Daniel Toth		10/06/87	M	6	(8)	1
31	Thomas Weber		29/04/93	D	7	(2)	
2	Richard Windbichler		02/04/91	D	16	(6)	1

FK AUSTRIA WIEN
Coach: Peter Stöger
1911 • Generali-Arena (13,400) • fk-austria.at
Major honours
Austrian League (24) 1924, 1926, 1949, 1950, 1953, 1961, 1962, 1963, 1969, 1970, 1976, 1978, 1979, 1980, 1981, 1984, 1985, 1986, 1991, 1992, 1993, 2003, 2006, 2013; Austrian Cup (27) 1921, 1924, 1925, 1926, 1933, 1935, 1936, 1948, 1949, 1960, 1962, 1963, 1967, 1971, 1974, 1977, 1980, 1982, 1986, 1990, 1992, 1994, 2003, 2005, 2006, 2007, 2009

2012
25/07	Wolfsberg	a	1-0	Jun
28/07	Sturm	h	0-1	
05/08	Rapid	a	3-0	Kienast 2, Simkovic
12/08	Admira	h	1-0	Stankovic
19/08	Ried	a	1-0	Grünwald
25/08	Wacker	a	2-0	og (Švejnoha), Jun
01/09	Wiener Neustadt	a	2-0	Suttner, Simkovic
16/09	Mattersburg	a	4-2	Hosiner 2, Rogulj, Gorgon
22/09	Salzburg	h	0-1	
29/09	Wolfsberg	h	1-1	Jun
07/10	Sturm	a	1-1	Hosiner
21/10	Rapid	h	2-0	Gorgon 2
27/10	Admira	a	6-4	Hosiner 3, Simkovic, Rogulj, Gorgon
04/11	Ried	h	6-1	Hosiner 3, Jun, Stankovic, Linz
10/11	Wacker	a	3-0	Mader, Jun, Hosiner
17/11	Wiener Neustadt	h	3-0	Ortlechner, Kienast, Grünwald
24/11	Mattersburg	h	3-1	Hosiner 2, Gorgon
02/12	Salzburg	a	0-0	
08/12	Wolfsberg	a	6-3	Hosiner 3, Koch, Gorgon, Dilaver
16/12	Sturm	h	3-1	Hosiner, Suttner, Stankovic

2013
17/02	Rapid	a	2-1	Hosiner 2
23/02	Admira	h	4-0	Gorgon, Dilaver, Kienast 2 (1p)
27/02	Ried	a	3-1	Grünwald, Jun, Kienast
02/03	Wacker	h	4-0	Koch, og (Kofler), Hosiner 2
09/03	Wiener Neustadt	a	0-0	
17/03	Mattersburg	a	4-0	Gorgon, Grünwald, Hosiner 2
31/03	Salzburg	h	1-1	Grünwald (p)
06/04	Wolfsberg	h	0-4	
14/04	Sturm	a	1-1	Grünwald (p)
21/04	Rapid	h	2-2	Jun 2
28/04	Admira	a	2-0	Mader, Ortlechner
04/05	Ried	h	3-1	Hosiner 2, Jun
11/05	Wacker	a	3-0	Hosiner 2, Barazite
18/05	Wiener Neustadt	h	3-1	Hosiner, Grünwald (p), Kienast
22/05	Mattersburg	h	4-0	Gorgon 2, Suttner, Jun
26/05	Salzburg	a	0-3	

No	Name	Nat	DoB	Pos	Aps	(s)	Gls
9	Nacer Barazite	NED	27/05/90	A	1	(4)	1
27	Emir Dilaver		07/05/91	M	19	(7)	2
20	Alexander Gorgon		28/10/88	M	29	(2)	10
10	Alexander Grünwald		01/05/89	M	16	(10)	7
25	James Holland	AUS	15/05/89	M	34		
16	Philipp Hosiner		15/05/89	A	28	(2)	27
11	Tomáš Jun	CZE	17/01/83	A	32	(1)	10
42	Roman Kienast		29/03/84	A	4	(25)	7
30	Fabian Koch		24/06/89	D	19	(2)	2
22	Marin Leovac	CRO	07/08/88	D	2		
13	Heinz Lindner		17/07/90	G	36		
9	Roland Linz		09/08/81	A	3	(4)	1
17	Florian Mader		14/09/82	M	26	(4)	2
3	Georg Margreitter		07/11/88	D	3		
18	Thomas Murg		14/11/94	M		(7)	
14	Manuel Ortlechner		04/03/80	D	36		2
4	Kaja Rogulj	CRO	15/06/86	D	29		2
5	Lukas Rotpuller		31/03/91	D	4	(5)	
8	Tomas Simkovic		16/04/87	M	16	(12)	3
23	Srdjan Spiridinovic		13/10/93	M		(2)	
19	Marko Stankovic		17/02/86	A	12	(14)	3
29	Markus Suttner		16/04/87	D	35		3
7	Dare Vršič	SVN	26/09/84	M	12	(5)	

SV MATTERSBURG
Coach: Franz Lederer
1922 • Pappelstadion (15,700) • svm.at

2012
21/07	Wiener Neustadt	h	2-0	Mörz, Röcher
28/07	Salzburg	a	2-3	Bürger, Höller
04/08	Sturm	h	3-1	Naumoski 2, Lovin
11/08	Wacker	a	1-2	Seidl
18/08	Wolfsberg	a	1-0	Seidl
25/08	Ried	h	2-1	Potzmann, Bürger
02/09	Rapid	a	0-3	
16/09	Austria Wien	h	2-4	Potzmann, Naumoski
22/09	Admira	a	1-5	Potzmann
29/09	Wiener Neustadt	a	0-0	
06/10	Salzburg	h	1-3	Höller
20/10	Sturm	a	0-0	
27/10	Wacker	h	1-2	Röcher
03/11	Wolfsberg	h	1-1	Bürger
10/11	Ried	a	1-6	Rodler
17/11	Rapid	h	0-3	
24/11	Austria Wien	a	1-3	Rodler
01/12	Admira	h	3-0	Naumoski (p), Bürger 2
08/12	Wiener Neustadt	h	1-0	Höller
15/12	Salzburg	a	0-7	

2013
16/02	Sturm	h	0-0	
23/02	Wacker	a	0-2	
02/03	Ried	h	1-0	Seidl
09/03	Rapid	a	2-2	Bürger, Gartner
13/03	Wolfsberg	a	0-1	
17/03	Austria Wien	h	0-4	
30/03	Admira	a	0-1	
06/04	Wiener Neustadt	a	0-0	
13/04	Salzburg	h	1-2	Höller
20/04	Sturm	a	2-2	Pöllhuber, Bürger
27/04	Wacker	h	1-2	Bürger
04/05	Wolfsberg	h	3-1	Lovin, Klemen 2
11/05	Ried	a	1-1	Höller
18/05	Rapid	h	2-0	Bürger, Klemen
22/05	Austria Wien	a	0-4	
26/05	Admira	h	0-1	

No	Name	Nat	DoB	Pos	Aps	(s)	Gls
22	Markus Bocskor		01/10/82	G	1		
1	Thomas Borenitsch		15/12/80	G	35		
33	Patrick Bürger		27/06/87	A	00		0
11	Wilfried Domoraud	FRA	18/09/88	M	2	(8)	
17	Patrick Farkas		09/09/92	D	34	(1)	
15	Christian Gartner		03/04/94	M	8	(9)	1
8	Alois Höller		15/03/89	D	28	(5)	5
9	Ingo Klemen		29/07/86	A	6	(8)	3
20	Florin Lovin	ROU	11/02/82	M	21	(11)	2
30	Ivica Majstorović	CRO	20/09/81	D	16		
4	Nedeljko Malić	BIH	09/11/89	M			
5	Michael Mörz		02/04/80	M	11	(10)	1
7	Adnan Mravac	BIH	10/04/82	D	30		
24	Ilco Naumoski	MKD	29/07/83	A	24	(4)	4
25	Michael Novak		30/12/90	D	8		
2	Alexander Pöllhuber		30/04/85	D	11	(3)	1
16	Marvin Potzmann		07/12/93	M	9	(5)	3
19	Manuel Prietl		03/08/91	M	31	(2)	
18	Lukas Rath		18/01/92	D	14	(1)	
13	Christian Ressler		13/07/91	A		(5)	
27	Thorsten Röcher		11/06/91	A	23	(11)	2
26	Martin Rodler		24/02/89	D	16	(5)	2
12	Manuel Seidl		26/10/88	M	19	(3)	3
28	Ronald Spuller		22/06/81	M		(3)	
23	Philipp Steiner		20/12/86	M	7	(4)	

AUSTRIA

SK RAPID WIEN

Coach: Peter Schöttel; (21/04/13) Zoran Barisic
1899 • Gerhard Hanappi Stadion (17,500) • skrapid.at
Major honours
*Austrian League (32) 1912, 1913, 1916, 1917, 1919, 1920,
1921, 1923, 1929, 1930, 1935, 1938, 1940, 1941, 1946,
1948, 1951, 1952, 1954, 1956, 1957, 1960, 1964, 1967,
1968, 1982, 1983, 1987, 1988, 1996, 2005, 2008;
German League (1) 1941;
Austrian Cup (14) 1919, 1920, 1927, 1946, 1961, 1968,
1969, 1972, 1976, 1983, 1984, 1985, 1987, 1995;
German Cup (1) 1938*

2012

21/07	Wacker	h	4-0	Boyd 2, Kulovits, Drazan
28/07	Wiener Neustadt	a	1-0	Sonnleitner
05/08	Austria Wien	h	0-3	
12/08	Salzburg	a	2-0	Alar, Grozurek
18/08	Sturm	h	3-0	Burgstaller, Alar, S Hofmann
26/08	Wolfsberg	a	0-1	
02/09	Mattersburg	a	2-0	Boyd 2, Trimmel
15/09	Admira	h	0-0	
23/09	Ried	a	2-0	Burgstaller, Trimmel
29/09	Wacker	a	2-0	Katzer, Grozurek
07/10	Wiener Neustadt	h	1-1	Boyd
21/10	Austria Wien	a	0-2	
28/10	Salzburg	h	2-0	S Hofmann, Boyd
03/11	Sturm	a	1-2	Burgstaller
11/11	Wolfsberg	h	0-2	
17/11	Mattersburg	a	3-0	Alar 2, Boyd
25/11	Admira	a	2-0	Alar (p), Burgstaller
01/12	Ried	h	4-3	Boyd, Alar 3 (1p)
09/12	Wacker	h	2-1	Alar, Boyd
15/12	Wiener Neustadt	a	0-1	

2013

17/02	Austria Wien	h	1-2	Trimmel
24/02	Salzburg	a	3-3	Boyd, Burgstaller, Sabitzer
27/02	Sturm	h	1-1	Bošković
03/03	Wolfsberg	a	1-2	Burgstaller
09/03	Mattersburg	h	2-2	Boyd, Alar
16/03	Admira	h	1-1	Pichler
30/03	Ried	a	2-3	Alar 2
06/04	Wacker	h	1-1	Boyd
13/04	Wiener Neustadt	h	2-0	Katzer, Alar
21/04	Austria Wien	a	2-2	Alar, Sabitzer
27/04	Salzburg	h	1-3	Alar
05/05	Sturm	a	3-1	Sabitzer, Sonnleitner, Starkl
11/05	Wolfsberg	h	0-0	
18/05	Mattersburg	a	0-2	
22/05	Admira	h	2-0	Trimmel, Wydra
26/05	Ried	h	3-0	Schaub 2, Boyd

No	Name	Nat	DoB	Pos	Aps	(s)	Gls
33	Deni Alar		18/01/90	A	25	(6)	15
39	Eldis Bajrami	MKD	12/12/92	M		(1)	
32	Branko Bošković	MNE	21/06/80	M	7	(3)	1
9	Terrence Boyd	USA	16/02/91	A	25	(5)	13
30	Guido Burgstaller		29/04/89	A	29	(3)	6
37	Lukas Denner		19/06/91	D		(1)	
17	Kristijan Dobras		09/10/92	M		(1)	
19	Christopher Drazan		02/10/90	A	5	(4)	1
35	Gerson	BRA	07/01/92	D	26		
26	Lukas Grozurek		22/12/91	A	8	(16)	2
8	Markus Heikkinen	FIN	13/10/78	M	17	(9)	
38	Maximilian Hofmann		07/08/93	D		(1)	
11	Steffen Hofmann	GER	09/09/80	M	20		2
20	Muhammed Ildiz		14/05/91	M	12	(3)	
14	Markus Katzer		11/12/79	D	21	(2)	2
31	Lukas Königshofer		16/03/89	G	26		
7	Stefan Kulovits		19/04/83	M	14	(9)	1
1	Ján Novota	SVK	29/11/83	G	10		
27	Harald Pichler		18/06/87	D	18	(4)	1
23	Thomas Prager		13/09/85	M	6	(4)	
16	Boris Prokopic		29/03/88	M	1	(1)	
24	Marcel Sabitzer		17/03/94	M	10	(6)	3
21	Louis Schaub		29/12/94	M	6	(10)	2
36	Michael Schimpelsberger		12/02/91	D	16		
4	Thomas Schrammel		05/09/87	D	16	(2)	
6	Mario Sonnleitner		08/10/86	D	34		2
34	Dominik Starkl		06/11/93	A	2	(6)	1
28	Christopher Trimmel		24/02/87	M	29	(2)	4
25	Dominik Wydra		21/03/94	M	13	(4)	1

SV RIED

**Coach: Heinz Fuchsbichler;
(10/11/12) Gerhard Schweitzer;
(16/02/13) Michael Angerschmid**
1912 • Keine Sorgen Arena (7,680) • svried.at
Major honours
Austrian Cup (2) 1998, 2011

2012

22/07	Admira	a	2-0	Gartler 2
29/07	Wolfsberg	h	0-2	
05/08	Wacker	h	2-0	Hadžić, Guillem Martí
12/08	Wiener Neustadt	a	3-2	Zulj, Gartler, Reiter
19/08	Austria Wien	h	0-1	
25/08	Mattersburg	a	1-2	Hadžić
01/09	Sturm	h	0-1	
15/09	Salzburg	a	1-1	Ziegl
23/09	Rapid	h	0-2	
29/09	Admira	h	1-1	Zulj
06/10	Wolfsberg	a	5-2	Meilinger, Gartler 2, Walch, Hammerer
20/10	Wacker	a	0-1	
27/10	Wiener Neustadt	h	3-1	Zulj, Hadžić, Nacho
04/11	Austria Wien	a	1-6	Zulj
10/11	Mattersburg	h	6-1	Gartler 3, Walch 2, Zulj
17/11	Sturm	a	1-3	Gartler
24/11	Salzburg	h	3-1	Walch, Hammerer, Hadžić (p)
01/12	Rapid	a	3-4	Gartler, Hadžić (p), Grössinger
08/12	Admira	a	3-0	Meilinger, Zulj, Gartler

2013

16/02	Wacker	h	3-0	Riegler 2, Walch
20/02	Wolfsberg	h	1-1	Zulj
23/02	Wiener Neustadt	a	0-0	
27/02	Austria Wien	h	1-3	Reifeltshammer
02/03	Mattersburg	a	0-1	
09/03	Sturm	h	1-2	Vastic
16/03	Salzburg	a	2-2	Meilinger 2
30/03	Rapid	h	3-2	Gartler, Meilinger, Nacho
06/04	Admira	h	4-1	Meilinger, og (Tito), Zulj 2
13/04	Wolfsberg	a	3-1	Zulj, Hadžić (p), Grössinger
20/04	Wacker	a	0-2	
27/04	Wiener Neustadt	h	2-1	Gartler (p), Vastic
04/05	Austria Wien	a	1-3	Gartler
11/05	Mattersburg	h	1-1	og (Mravac)
19/05	Sturm	h	1-3	Gartler
22/05	Salzburg	h	2-2	Reifeltshammer, Zulj
26/05	Rapid	a	0-3	

No	Name	Nat	DoB	Pos	Aps	(s)	Gls
7	Rene Gartler		21/10/85	A	28	(1)	15
1	Thomas Gebauer	GER	30/06/82	G	35		
13	Markus Grössinger		01/08/89	M	5	(15)	2
9	Guillem Martí	ESP	05/09/85	A	1	(2)	1
20	Anel Hadžić	BIH	16/08/89	D	29	1	6
21	Markus Hammerer		31/08/89	A	4	(16)	2
18	Thomas Hinum		24/07/87	M	30	(2)	
29	Edin Ibrahimović	BIH	16/08/91	M		(2)	
10	Iván Carril	ESP	13/02/85	M	2	(7)	
26	Maximilian Karner		03/01/90	D	5	(1)	
16	Marco Meilinger		03/08/91	M	33	(2)	6
25	Patrick Möschl		06/03/93	M		(3)	
11	Nacho	ESP	06/11/82	A	14	(15)	2
28	Thomas Reifeltshammer		03/07/88	D	34		2
23	Mario Reiter		23/10/86	M	13	(4)	1
14	Jan Marc Riegler		18/04/88	D	26	(1)	2
6	Andreas Schicker		06/07/86	D	27	(2)	
35	Wolfgang Schober		06/07/89	G	1		
19	Emanuel Schreiner		02/02/89	D	12	(6)	
8	Gernot Trauner		25/03/92	M	10	(5)	
17	Toni Vastic		17/01/93	M	3	(12)	2
33	Clemens Walch		10/07/87	A	22	(5)	5
4	Marcel Ziegl		20/12/92	M	30	(1)	1
22	Robert Zulj		05/12/92	A	32	(2)	11

FC SALZBURG

Coach: Roger Schmidt (GER)
1933 • Bullen Arena Wals-Siezenheim (30,900) •
redbulls.com/soccer/salzburg
Major honours
*Austrian League (7) 1994, 1995, 1997, 2007, 2009, 2010, 2012;
Austrian Cup (1) 2012*

2012

21/07	Sturm	a	2-0	Jonathan Soriano 2
28/07	Mattersburg	h	3-2	Schiemer, Jonathan Soriano, Zárate
04/08	Wolfsberg	a	2-0	Jonathan Soriano 2
12/08	Rapid	h	0-2	
18/08	Admira	a	4-4	Nielsen 3, Maierhofer
25/08	Wiener Neustadt	h	1-1	Berisha
01/09	Wacker	a	4-0	Jantscher, Berisha, Schiemer, Jonathan Soriano
15/09	Ried	h	1-1	Jonathan Soriano
22/09	Austria Wien	a	1-0	Berisha
30/09	Sturm	h	3-2	Berisha, Mané 2
06/10	Mattersburg	a	3-1	Jonathan Soriano 2 (2p), Vorsah
20/10	Wolfsberg	h	4-1	Mané, Leitgeb, og (Thonhofer), Teigl
28/10	Rapid	a	0-2	
03/11	Admira	h	5-0	Leitgeb 2, Jonathan Soriano 2, og (Windbichler)
11/11	Wiener Neustadt	a	3-0	Schiemer, Jonathan Soriano 2
18/11	Wacker	h	2-0	Mané, Teigl
24/11	Ried	a	1-3	Teigl
02/12	Austria Wien	h	1-1	Mané
08/12	Sturm	a	1-1	Mané
15/12	Mattersburg	h	7-0	Mané 3, Teigl, Berisha, Hierländer, Jonathan Soriano (p)

2013

24/02	Rapid	h	3-3	Kampl, Jonathan Soriano (p), Hinteregger
02/03	Wiener Neustadt	h	3-1	Jonathan Soriano 2, Alan
06/03	Wolfsberg	a	1-1	Schiemer
10/03	Wacker	a	3-2	Teigl, Jonathan Soriano (p), Mané
13/03	Admira	a	1-1	Leitgeb
16/03	Ried	h	2-2	Jonathan Soriano, Hinteregger
31/03	Austria Wien	a	1-1	Kampl
07/04	Sturm	h	3-0	Jonathan Soriano 2, Mané
13/04	Mattersburg	a	2-1	Mané, Jonathan Soriano
20/04	Wolfsberg	h	6-2	Alan 3 (1p), Jonathan Soriano 3
27/04	Rapid	a	3-1	Alan 2 (1p), Švento
04/05	Admira	a	2-1	Alan, Mané
12/05	Wiener Neustadt	a	6-0	Jonathan Soriano, Alan 2, Kampl, Berisha, og (Martschinko)
18/05	Wacker	h	3-1	Kampl, Alan, Mané
22/05	Ried	a	2-2	Alan, Mané
26/05	Austria Wien	h	3-0	Mané 2, Sekagya

No	Name	Nat	DoB	Pos	Aps	(s)	Gls
27	Alan	BRA	10/07/89	A	8	(6)	11
14	Valon Berisha	NOR	07/02/93	M	29	(1)	6
20	Thomas Dähne	GER	04/01/94	G	1		
5	Christopher Dibon		02/11/90	D	3		
3	Douglas	BRA	07/03/84	D	1	(1)	
31	Bright Edomwonyi	NGA	24/07/94	A		(1)	
1	Eddie Gustafsson	SWE	31/01/77	G	5		
22	Stefan Hierländer		03/02/91	M	17	(3)	1
26	Martin Hinteregger		07/09/92	D	16	(8)	2
13	Stefan Ilsanker		18/05/89	M	18	(8)	
7	Jakob Jantscher		08/01/89	M	5	(2)	1
26	Jonathan Soriano	ESP	24/09/85	A	32	(1)	26
44	Kevin Kampl	SVN	09/10/90	M	23		4
8	Florian Klein		17/11/86	D	18	(2)	
27	Valentino Lazaro		24/03/96	M	2	(3)	
24	Christoph Leitgeb		14/04/85	M	19	(3)	4
9	Stefan Maierhofer		16/08/82	A	1	(9)	1
4	Sadio Mané	SEN	10/04/92	A	25	(1)	16
4	Davide Mendes da Silva	NED	04/08/82	M	4	(2)	
16	Håvard Nielsen	NOR	15/07/93	A	10	(14)	3
34	Yusuf Otubanjo	NGA	12/09/92	A		(1)	
29	Rodnei	BRA	11/09/85	D	13	(2)	
15	Franz Schiemer		21/03/86	D	27		4
6	Christian Schwegler	SUI	06/06/84	D	17		
23	Ibrahim Sekagya	UGA	19/12/80	D	12	(5)	1
18	Dušan Švento	SVK	01/08/85	M	11		1
39	Georg Teigl		09/02/91	A	8	(25)	5
17	Andreas Ulmer		30/10/85	D	26		
45	Isaac Vorsah	GHA	21/06/88	D	14	(1)	1
33	Alexander Walke	GER	06/06/83	G	30		
11	Gonzalo Zárate	ARG	06/08/84	M	1	(4)	1

SK STURM GRAZ

Coach: Peter Hyballa (GER);
(27/04/13) Markus Schopp
1909 • UPC-Arena (15,400) • sksturm.at
Major honours
Austrian League (3) 1998, 1999, 2011;
Austrian Cup (4) 1996, 1997, 1999, 2010

2012

21/07	Salzburg	h	0-2	
28/07	Austria Wien	a	1-0	Okotie
04/08	Mattersburg	a	1-3	Sukuta-Pasu
11/08	Wolfsberg	h	4-1	Szabics, Okotie 2, Sukuta-Pasu
18/08	Rapid	a	0-3	
25/08	Admira	h	3-2	Sukuta-Pasu 2, Vujadinović
01/09	Ried	a	1-0	og (Reifeltshammer)
15/09	Wacker	h	3-0	Vujadinović 2, Szabics
22/09	Wiener Neustadt	a	1-1	Weber
30/09	Salzburg	a	2-3	Okotie, F Kainz
07/10	Austria Wien	h	1-1	F Kainz (p)
20/10	Mattersburg	h	0-0	
03/11	Rapid	h	2-1	Sukuta-Pasu, F Kainz
10/11	Admira	a	2-1	Vujadinović, Okotie
17/11	Ried	h	3-1	Okotie 2, Szabics
24/11	Wacker	a	3-0	(w/o; original result 1-0 Sukuta-Pasu)
27/11	Wolfsberg	a	1-1	Szabics
01/12	Wiener Neustadt	h	3-1	Sukuta-Pasu 2, Dudić
08/12	Salzburg	h	1-1	Sukuta-Pasu
16/12	Austria Wien	a	1-3	Okotie

2013

16/02	Mattersburg	a	0-0	
23/02	Wolfsberg	h	1-3	Vujadinović
27/02	Rapid	a	1-1	Vujadinović
02/03	Admira	h	1-2	Schloffer
09/03	Ried	a	2-1	Schloffer, Sukuta-Pasu
16/03	Wacker	h	3-2	Säumel 2, Szabics
30/03	Wiener Neustadt	a	0-1	
07/04	Salzburg	a	0-3	
14/04	Austria Wien	h	1-1	Sukuta-Pasu
20/04	Mattersburg	h	2-2	Madl, Sukuta-Pasu
27/04	Wolfsberg	a	0-3	
05/05	Rapid	h	1-3	Hölzl
11/05	Admira	a	0-0	
18/05	Ried	h	0-1	og (Grössinger) Vujadinović, Ciftci
22/05	Wacker	a	1-2	Okotie
26/05	Wiener Neustadt	h	0-3	

No	Name	Nat	DoB	Pos	Aps	(s)	Gls
37	Željko Balen	CRO	11/10/90	D	1		
39	Ervin Bevab		09/04/91	D		(1)	
10	Darko Bodul	CRO	11/01/89	M	5	(6)	
9	Haris Bukva		15/03/88	M	14	(8)	
34	Serkan Ciftci		03/08/89	A		(8)	1
12	Milan Dudić	SRB	01/11/79	D	23		1
17	Martin Ehrenreich		10/05/83	D	17	(3)	
5	Ferdinand Feldhofer		23/10/79	D	3	(3)	
22	Johannes Focher	GER	20/01/90	G	22		
1	Christian Gratzei		19/09/81	G	14		
7	Mario Haas		16/09/74	A		(1)	
8	Andreas Hölzl		16/03/85	M	13	(5)	1
29	Philipp Hütter		17/08/90	D	3	(1)	
14	Florian Kainz		24/10/92	M	22	(4)	3
26	Tobias Kainz		31/07/92	M	15	(3)	
21	Leonhard Kaufmann		12/01/89	M	13	(4)	
27	Christian Klem		21/04/91	D	34		
20	Matthias Koch		01/04/88	M	7	(9)	
35	Anel Kocijan		19/11/92	A		(1)	
30	Christoph Kröpfl		04/05/90	M	12	(7)	
15	Michael Madl		21/03/88	D	33		1
25	Rubin Okotie		06/06/87	A	25	(5)	9
2	Reinhold Ranftl		24/01/92	M	3	(1)	
28	Jürgen Säumel		08/09/84	M	11	(1)	2
18	David Schloffer		28/04/92	M	9	(15)	2
19	Richard Sukuta-Pasu	GER	24/06/90	A	29	(2)	12
11	Imre Szabics	HUN	22/03/81	A	17	(5)	6
13	Nikola Vujadinović	MNE	31/07/86	D	33		7
6	Manuel Weber		28/08/85	M	18	(6)	1

FC WACKER INNSBRUCK

Coach: Walter Kogler; (20/10/12) Roland Kirchler
1915 • Tivoli (17,400) • fc-wacker-innsbruck.at
Major honours
Austrian League (10) 1971, 1972, 1973, 1975, 1977,
1989, 1990, 2000, 2001, 2002; Austrian Cup (7) 1970,
1973, 1975, 1978, 1979, 1989, 1993

2012

21/07	Rapid	a	0-4	
29/07	Admira	h	1-2	Schreter
05/08	Ried	a	0-2	
11/08	Mattersburg	h	2-1	Marcelo Fernandes, Wernitznig
18/08	Wiener Neustadt	h	2-3	Wernitznig, Perstaller
25/08	Austria Wien	a	0-2	
01/09	Salzburg	h	0-4	
15/09	Sturm	a	0-3	
22/09	Wolfsberg	h	0-1	
29/09	Rapid	h	0-2	
06/10	Admira	a	1-4	Schütz
20/10	Ried	h	1-0	Schreter
27/10	Mattersburg	a	2-1	Abrahám, og (Bürger)
03/11	Wiener Neustadt	a	1-0	Wallner
10/11	Austria Wien	h	0-3	
18/11	Salzburg	a	0-2	
24/11	Sturm	h	0-3	(w/o; original result 0-1)
01/12	Wolfsberg	a	2-2	Perstaller, Schilling
09/12	Rapid	a	1-2	og (Sonnleitner)
15/12	Admira	h	3-1	Wallner 2 (1p), Bergmann

2013

16/02	Ried	a	0-3	
23/02	Mattersburg	h	2-0	og (Novak), Wernitznig
27/02	Wiener Neustadt	h	1-0	Schütz
02/03	Austria Wien	a	0-4	
10/03	Salzburg	a	2-3	Wallner, Schütz
16/03	Sturm	a	2-3	Wallner, Schilling
30/03	Wolfsberg	h	2-3	Wernitznig, Abrahám
06/04	Rapid	h	1-1	Perstaller
13/04	Admira	a	3-4	Hinterseer, Schütz, Perstaller
20/04	Ried	h	2-0	Hinterseer, Wernitznig
27/04	Mattersburg	a	2-1	og (Majstorović), Wernitznig
04/05	Wiener Neustadt	a	2-2	Piesinger, Hauser
11/05	Austria Wien	h	1-1	Wallner
18/05	Salzburg	h	1-3	Wallner
22/05	Sturm	h	2-1	Hinterseer, Wernitznig
26/05	Wolfsberg	a	3-2	Perstaller 2, Schilling

No	Name	Nat	DoB	Pos	Aps	(s)	Gls
3	Tomáš Abrahám	CZE	18/04/79	M	26	(1)	2
14	Thomas Bergmann		20/09/89	M	26	(3)	1
11	Carlos Merino	ESP	15/03/80	M	21	(4)	
5	Dario Djakovic		20/04/87	D	22		
20	Markus Egger		15/01/90	G	1	(1)	
19	Alexander Fröschl		15/07/92	A	2	(2)	
28	Fabian Hafner		17/07/93	D		(1)	
7	Alexander Hauser		23/06/84	D	27	(4)	1
16	Lukas Hinterseer		28/03/91	A	8	(5)	3
4	Marco Kofler		08/05/89	D	24	(4)	
15	Marco Köfler		14/11/90	D	1		
17	Andreas Kuen		24/03/95	M		(2)	
25	Thomas Löffler		01/05/89	M	4	(3)	
9	Marcelo Fernandes	BRA	01/01/91	A	4	(4)	1
22	Julius Perstaller		08/04/89	A	10	(18)	6
6	Simon Piesinger		13/05/92	M	14	(15)	1
1	Szabolcs Sáfár	HUN	20/08/74	G	35		
23	Christoph Saurer		22/01/86	M	26	(8)	
29	Christian Schilling		06/01/92	D	17	(1)	3
13	Marcel Schreter		29/09/81	A	17	(9)	2
26	Daniel Schütz		19/06/91	M	22	(6)	4
28	Sebastian Siller		18/05/89	D	7	(1)	
8	Martin Švejnoha	CZE	25/11/77	M	33		
10	Roman Wallner		04/02/82	A	25	(1)	6
24	Christopher Wernitznig		24/02/90	M	23	(10)	7
18	Sascha Wörgetter		22/10/93	M	1	(2)	

SC WIENER NEUSTADT

Coach: Heimo Pfeifenberger
2008 • Stadion Wiener Neustadt (7,500) • scwn.at

2012

21/07	Mattersburg	a	0-2	
28/07	Rapid	h	0-1	
05/08	Admira	a	0-4	
12/08	Ried	h	2-3	Tadic, Friesenbichler
18/08	Wacker	a	3-2	Friesenbichler 3
25/08	Salzburg	a	1-1	Hlinka
01/09	Austria Wien	h	0-2	
15/09	Wolfsberg	a	0-6	
22/09	Sturm	h	1-1	Hlinka
29/09	Mattersburg	h	0-0	
07/10	Rapid	a	1-1	Rakowitz
20/10	Admira	h	2-1	Wallner, Rakowitz
27/10	Ried	a	1-3	Fröschl
03/11	Wacker	h	0-1	
11/11	Salzburg	h	0-3	
17/11	Austria Wien	a	0-3	
24/11	Wolfsberg	h	2-1	Offenbacher (p), Tadic
01/12	Sturm	a	1-3	Tadic
08/12	Mattersburg	a	0-1	
15/12	Rapid	h	1-0	Tadic

2013

16/02	Admira	a	2-1	Hlinka (p), Tadic
23/02	Ried	h	0-0	
27/02	Wacker	a	0-1	
02/03	Salzburg	a	1-3	Terzić
09/03	Austria Wien	h	0-0	
16/03	Wolfsberg	a	1-1	Ramsebner
30/03	Sturm	h	1-0	Offenbacher
06/04	Mattersburg	h	0-0	
13/04	Rapid	a	0-2	
20/04	Admira	h	3-0	Ramsebner, Mimm 2
27/04	Ried	a	1-2	Rakowitz
04/05	Wacker	h	2-2	Fröschl 2
12/05	Salzburg	a	0-6	
18/05	Austria Wien	a	1-3	Tadic
22/05	Wolfsberg	h	2-0	Tadic, Hlinka
26/05	Sturm	a	3-0	Pollhammer, Offenbacher, Rauter

No	Name	Nat	DoB	Pos	Aps	(s)	Gls
10	Michael Berger		01/12/90	D	10	(1)	
30	Bernd Besenhierr		24/11/00	M		(?)	
23	Christoph Freitag		21/01/90	M	5	(9)	
9	Günter Friesenbichler		04/09/79	A	11	(12)	4
33	Thomas Fröschl		20/09/88	A	11	(10)	0
5	Peter Hlinka	SVK	05/12/70	M	31	(1)	4
8	Dominik Hofbauer		19/09/90	M	18	(5)	
3	Thomas Kral		08/01/90	D	4		
19	Jiří Leňko	CZE	29/04/85	D	13	(3)	
31	Matthias Maak		25/05/92	D	15	(2)	
22	Christoph Martschinko		13/02/94	D	24	(2)	
6	Dennis Mimm		18/03/83	D	28	(3)	2
10	Daniel Offenbacher		18/02/92	M	28	(6)	3
17	Osman Bozkurt	TUR	10/08/84	A	1	(8)	
37	Thomas Piermayr		02/08/89	D	20	(1)	
26	Mario Pollhammer		20/06/89	M	20	(9)	1
37	Luka Radulovic		17/04/90	D		(1)	
12	Stefan Rakowitz		03/04/90	M	21	(9)	3
25	Christian Ramsebner		26/03/89	D	19		2
20	Herbert Rauter		27/01/82	A	15		1
16	Manfred Rottensteiner		09/01/93	M	1		
27	Jörg Siebenhandl		18/01/90	G	28		
11	Dario Tadic		11/05/90	A	20	(7)	7
14	Arvedin Terzić	BIH	02/04/89	M	4	(2)	1
1	Thomas Vollnhofer		02/09/84	G	8		
15	Manuel Wallner		25/10/88	D	29		1
7	Daniel Wolf		04/05/85	M	10	(10)	

WOLFSBERGER AC

Coach: Nenad Bjelica (CRO)
1931 • Lavanttal Arena (7,300) • rzpelletswac.at

2012

25/07	Austria Wien	h	0-1	
29/07	Ried	a	2-0	Solano, Liendl
04/08	Salzburg	h	0-2	
11/08	Sturm	a	1-4	Jacobo
18/08	Mattersburg	h	0-1	
26/08	Rapid	h	1-0	Baldauf
01/09	Admira	a	1-1	Jacobo
15/09	Wiener Neustadt	h	6-0	Falk 3, Topčagić, Liendl 2
22/09	Wacker	a	1-0	Falk
29/09	Austria Wien	a	1-1	Topčagić
06/10	Ried	h	2-5	Rubén Rivera, Liendl
20/10	Salzburg	a	1-4	Falk
03/11	Mattersburg	a	1-1	Falk
11/11	Rapid	a	2-0	Falk 2
17/11	Admira	h	1-1	Liendl
24/11	Wiener Neustadt	a	1-2	Liendl (p)
27/11	Sturm	h	1-1	Solano
01/12	Wacker	h	2-2	Falk, Liendl
08/12	Austria Wien	h	3-6	Falk, De Paula, Jacobo

2013

20/02	Ried	a	1-1	Topčagić
23/02	Sturm	a	3-1	Topčagić, Liendl, Kerhe
03/03	Rapid	h	2-1	Topčagić, Thonhofer
06/03	Salzburg	h	1-1	Rubén Rivera
09/03	Admira	a	1-0	Rubén Rivera
13/03	Mattersburg	h	1-0	Baldauf
16/03	Wiener Neustadt	h	1-1	Jacobo
30/03	Wacker	a	3-2	Topčagić 2, Jacobo
06/04	Austria Wien	a	4-0	Jacobo 2, Kerhe, Topčagić
13/04	Ried	h	1-3	Jacobo
20/04	Salzburg	a	2-6	De Paula, Putsche
27/04	Sturm	h	3-0	Topčagić, Liendl (p), Jacobo
04/05	Mattersburg	a	1-3	Topčagić
11/05	Rapid	a	0-0	
18/05	Admira	h	0-0	
22/05	Wiener Neustadt	a	0-2	
26/05	Wacker	h	2-3	og (Kofler), Stückler

No	Name	Nat	DoB	Pos	Aps	(s)	Gls
7	Dario Baldauf		27/03/85	D	33		2
20	David De Paula	ESP	03/05/84	M	28	(4)	2
1	Christian Dobnik		10/07/86	G	35		
6	Christian Falk		01/04/87	A	12	(5)	10
21	Max Friesacher		16/07/90	G	1		
16	Boris Hüttenbrenner		23/09/85	M	7	(6)	
11	Jacobo	ESP	04/02/84	M	31	(1)	9
17	Nenad Jovanovic		09/11/79	D	28		
3	Manuel Kerhe		30/06/87	M	29	(5)	2
18	Mario Kröpfl		21/12/89	M	3	(9)	
10	Michael Liendl		25/10/85	M	35	(1)	9
8	Gernot Messner		10/10/80	M	1	(3)	
27	Michele Polverino	LIE	26/09/84	M	27	(3)	
19	Roland Putsche		22/03/91	M	13	(7)	1
12	Maximilian Ritscher		11/01/94	D		(1)	
9	Rubén Rivera	ESP	03/05/85	A	11	(19)	3
28	José Solano	ESP	04/02/85	D	11	(2)	2
26	Michael Sollbauer		15/05/90	D	34		
22	Stephan Stückler		31/10/85	A	6	(14)	1
4	Gernot Suppan		18/11/85	D	6		
5	Christian Thonhofer		26/05/85	D	24	(1)	1
29	Mihret Topčagić	BIH	21/06/88	A	18	(13)	10
23	Sandro Zakany		23/09/87	M	3	(11)	

Top goalscorers

32	Philipp Hosiner (Admira/Austria Wien)
26	Jonathan Soriano (Salzburg)
16	Sadio Mané (Salzburg)
15	Deni Alar (Rapid)
	Rene Gartler (Ried)
13	Terrence Boyd (Rapid)
12	Richard Sukuta-Pasu (Sturm)
11	Rubert Zulj (Ried)
	Alan (Salzburg)
10	Alexander Gorgon (Austria Wien)
	Tomáš Jun (Austria Wien)
	Christian Falk (Wolfsberg)
	Mihret Topčagić (Wolfsberg)

Promoted club

SV GRÖDIG

Coach: Adolf Hütter
1948 • Untersberg-Arena (2,955) • sv-groedig.at

SECOND LEVEL FINAL TABLE 2012/13

		Pld	W	D	L	F	A	Pts
1	SV Grödig	36	23	6	7	71	30	75
2	SCR Altach	36	19	8	9	57	39	65
3	SC Austria Lustenau	36	18	7	11	60	39	61
4	SKN St Pölten	36	14	12	10	65	60	54
5	Kapfenberger SV	36	14	11	11	56	50	53
6	SV Horn	36	13	7	16	50	55	46
7	First Vienna FC	36	13	7	16	48	64	46
8	TSV Hartberg	36	8	9	19	35	54	33
9	FC Blau-Weiss Linz	36	5	11	20	38	67	26
10	FC Lustenau 07	36	10	8	18	44	66	38

NB FC Lustenau 07 excluded at end of season and placed last.

Domestic cup: ÖFB-Cup 2012/13

FIRST ROUND

(12/07/12)
Floridsdorfer AC 0-1 Altach

(13/07/12)
Amstetten 0-1 Schwechat
Austria Klagenfurt 3-2 Horn
Deutschlandsberg 1-2 Hartberg
Gratkorn 0-0 Wacker Innsbruck *(aet; 4-5 on pens)*
Grazer AK 3-2 Vienna *(aet)*
Hard 1-0 Schwaz
Kalsdorf 3-1 Wallern
Parndorf 0-3 Admira
Pasching 2-1 Austria Salzburg
Saalfelden 0-4 Grödig
Salzburger AK 0-5 Allerheiligen
St Florian 2-1 Blau-Weiss Linz
Villacher SV 4-2 Rohrendorf
Vöcklamarkt 3-4 Lustenau 07
Wattens 0-1 Sturm Graz
Wiener Sportklub 0-2 Salzburg

(14/07/12)
Ardagger 2-3 Dornbirn *(aet)*
Bad Vöslau 1-0 St Pölten
Bregenz 1-2 Kapfenberg
DSV Leoben 1-3 Mattersburg
Gaflenz 1-2 Sollenau
Kufstein 1-4 Ried
LASK 7-0 Spittal/Drau
Micheldorf 0-1 Viktoria Wien
Oberwart 1-3 Austria Wien
Ostbahn XI 1-8 Wolfsberg
Retz 1-7 Austria Lustenau
SAK Klagenfurt 1-2 St Johann
Stegersbach 3-2 Reutte *(aet)*

(15/07/12)
Heiligenkreuz 0-5 Rapid Wien
Wolfurt 2-4 Wiener Neustadt *(aet)*

SECOND ROUND

(24/09/12)
Kalsdorf 3-0 Hartberg

(25/09/12)
Austria Klagenfurt 2-0 Admira *(aet)*
Dornbirn 2-3 Austria Wien
Hard 0-3 Altach
LASK 2-0 Grödig
Pasching 3-2 Austria Lustenau *(aet)*
Schwechat 0-5 Sturm Graz
Sollenau 1-5 Wacker Innsbruck *(aet)*
St Johann 0-3 Lustenau 07
Stegersbach 1-3 Salzburg
Viktoria Wien 3-3 Kapfenberg *(aet; 4-1 on pens)*
Villacher SV 3-1 Wiener Neustadt

(26/09/12)
Allerheiligen 1-4 Rapid Wien
Bad Vöslau 2-3 Mattersburg
Grazer AK 0-6 Wolfsberg
St Florian 1-1 Ried *(aet; 4-5 on pens)*

THIRD ROUND

(30/10/12)
LASK 2-2 Mattersburg *(aet; 7-6 on pens)*
Lustenau 07 1-2 Wolfsberg
Pasching 2-1 Austria Klagenfurt
Sturm Graz 1-2 Wacker Innsbruck
Viktoria Wien 0-1 Ried

(31/10/12)
Kalsdorf 1-3 Salzburg
Rapid Wien 4-2 Altach *(aet)*
Villacher SV 0-4 Austria Wien

QUARTER-FINALS

(16/04/13)
Rapid 0-1 Pasching *(Nacho Casanova 61)*
Wacker Innsbruck 0-3 Salzburg *(Jonathan Soriano 44, 89, Švejnoha 53og)*

(17/04/13)
Ried 2-1 LASK *(Zulj 41, Meilinger 106; Vujanovic 90+4) (aet)*
Wolfsberg 1-2 Austria Wien *(Rubén Rivera 83; Hosiner 20, Grünwald 67)*

SEMI-FINALS

(07/05/13)
Salzburg 1-2 Pasching *(Nielsen 48; Kovacec 69, Kerschbaumer 79)*

(08/05/13)
Ried 1-3 Austria Wien *(Gartler 76; Hosiner 52, Jun 85, Gorgon 90+2)*

FINAL

(30/05/13)
Ernst-Happel-Stadion, Vienna
FC PASCHING 1 *(Sobkova 47)*
FK AUSTRIA WIEN 0
Referee: *Eisner*
PASCHING: Berger, Kerschbaumer, Grasegger, Kablar, Prettenthaler, Perchtold, Krammer (Mössner 82), Schobesberger (Hamdemir 70), Sobkova (Petrovic 80), Kovacec, Nacho Casanova
AUSTRIA WIEN: Lindner, Dilaver, Rogulj, Ortlechner, Koch (Stankovic 78), Mader (Simkovic 54), Holland, Grünwald (Kienast 65), Gorgon, Hosiner, Jun

AZERBAIJAN

Azärbaycan Futbol Federasiyaları Assosiasiyası (AFFA)

Address	Nobel Prospekti 2208
	AZ-1025 Bakı
Tel	+994 12 404 27 77
Fax	+994 12 404 27 72
E-mail	info@affa.az
Website	affa.az

President	Rövnaq Abdullayev
General secretary	Elkhan Mämmädov
Media officer	Mikayıl Narimanoğlu
Year of formation	1992
National stadium	Tofiq Bähramov
	adına Respublika,
	Baku (32,200)

Zaqatala
(9)

0 ———————— 100 ———————— 200 km
0 ———————— 100 miles

Qäbälä
(7)

(11)
Tovuz

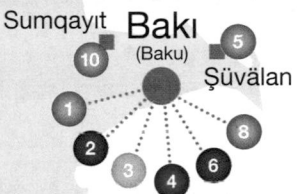

Sumqayıt   **Bakı**
(10)   (Baku)   (5)
                      Şüvälan
(1)
(2)   (8)
      (3)   (4) (6)

Länkäran
(12)

PREMYER LIQA CLUBS

(1) **Bakı FK**

(2) **İnter Bakı PİK**

(3) **Käpäz PFK**

(4) **Neftçi PFK**

(5) **Olimpik-Şüvälan PFK**

(6) **Qarabağ FK**

(7) **Qäbälä FK**

(8) **Rävan Bakı FK**

(9) **Simurq PFK**

(10) **Sumqayıt FK**

(11) **Turan Tovuz PFK**

 (12) **Xäzär Länkäran FK**

KEY:

● – UEFA Champions League

● – UEFA Europa League

● – Relegated clubs

Neftçi nail the double

The 2012/13 season in Azerbaijan was dominated by one team. Neftçi PFK not only secured their third successive Premyer Liqa title and a first domestic cup win for nine years but also made history by becoming the country's first participant in the group stage of a UEFA club competition.

Böyükağa Hacıyev's side were powered by a strong foreign contingent, with new Chilean striker Nicolás Canales in particular having a major impact. Qarabağ FK and İnter Bakı PFK both pressed Neftçi hard in the league, while Xäzär Länkäran FK took the runners-up berth in the cup.

Record champions claim title hat-trick	Penalty shoot-out triumph seals cup win	Hacıyev's team also make waves in Europe

Domestic league

Neftçi had never previously won three league crowns in succession. Having twice fallen one short previously, in 1998 and 2006, there was a great deal of satisfaction in making it third time lucky in 2013. It was not an easy ride to victory. They lost a quarter of their matches and conceded at an average of a goal per game. But in Canales they possessed a goalscorer who invariably found the net when it mattered most, most crucially in the game that effectively decided the title – a 2-1 away win over Qarabağ on 4 May.

Neftçi had lost all of their previous three encounters with Qurban Qurbanov's team. Another defeat against a side that went into the fixture on the back of five successive wins would have enabled Qarabağ, seeking a first title for 20 years, to move to the top of the table on the head-to-head rule. Instead, Neftçi prevailed with a Canales double to move six points clear with three games to play. Ten days later, following draws against Simurq PFK and Qäbälä FK, the title was theirs.

İnter, coached by ex-Georgian international defender Kakhaber Tskhadadze, would probably have taken the title had they found any form in the big games against Neftçi and Qarabağ. Instead they failed to beat either of them, scraping together just four points out of a possible 24, which nullified their fine defensive record and left them in third place five points adrift of the champions.

Olimpik-Şüvälan PFK ended up with the same number of points as İnter but four places behind them – as the top team in the 'relegation pool', in which, with Brazilian striker Nildo on fire, they won nine of their ten fixtures and drew the other. Käpäz PFK finished bottom of that group but, as in 2011/12, following a decision by the Association of Football Federations of Azerbaijan (AFFA), no clubs were relegated or promoted.

Domestic cup

Xäzär Länkäran, runners-up in the league to Neftçi in both 2010/11 and 2011/12, finished a lowly ninth in 2012/13 but managed to reach the final of the cup, where Welshman John Toshack led them out against Neftçi.

They had chances to claim the trophy for the fourth time in seven years but were eventually defeated on penalties after a goalless draw, with Neftçi skipper Räşad Sadiqov converting the winning kick.

Europe

Neftçi's presence in the group stage of the UEFA Europa League – following a play-off win over APOEL FC of Cyprus, UEFA Champions League quarter-finalists the previous season – was a major boon to the standing of Azeri football. They did not win any of their six games, but two points taken from Serbian champions FK Partizan and a 2-2 draw away to FC Internazionale Milano made it a worthwhile exercise.

National team

There were no victories either for the Azerbaijan national team in their first seven 2014 FIFA World Cup qualifying games. Draws at home to Israel and away to Northern Ireland plus a resilient display against Russia in Moscow – where only a late penalty denied them another point – gave cause for optimism, but better was expected in the two games against Luxembourg than another couple of draws. The team's most prominent performer was 25-year-old Ruslan Abışov, who left Xäzär Länkäran for leading Russian club FC Rubin Kazan in the winter.

Domestic league: Premyer Liqa 2012/13 final table

SECOND PHASE Championship Pool	Pld	Home					Away					Total					Pts
		W	D	L	F	A	W	D	L	F	A	W	D	L	F	A	
1 Neftçi PFK	32	11	2	3	36	14	8	3	5	23	18	19	5	8	59	32	62
2 Qarabağ FK	32	9	5	2	23	11	7	6	3	20	15	16	11	5	43	26	59
3 İnter Bakı PİK	32	10	5	1	22	6	6	4	6	16	16	16	9	7	38	22	57
4 Simurq PFK	32	8	5	3	18	9	4	7	5	14	17	12	12	8	32	26	48
5 Bakı FK	32	5	7	4	17	13	4	7	5	16	14	9	14	9	33	27	41
6 Qäbälä FK	32	5	5	6	17	17	5	3	8	15	23	10	8	14	32	40	38

Relegation Pool	Pld	Home					Away					Total					Pts
		W	D	L	F	A	W	D	L	F	A	W	D	L	F	A	
7 Olimpik-Şüvälan PFK	32	10	4	2	35	13	6	5	5	22	19	16	9	7	57	32	57
8 Rävan Bakı FK	32	7	2	7	24	22	5	2	9	22	32	12	4	16	46	54	40
9 Xäzär Länkäran FK	32	7	5	4	27	17	3	5	8	13	20	10	10	12	40	37	40
10 Sumqayıt FK	32	7	3	6	20	19	2	5	9	11	30	9	8	15	31	49	35
11 Turan Tovuz PFK	32	4	3	9	24	35	4	3	9	10	24	8	6	18	34	59	30
12 Käpäz PFK	32	3	4	9	9	20	2	0	14	14	44	5	4	23	23	64	19

NB League splits into top and bottom halves after 22 games, after which the clubs play exclusively against teams in their group.

SEASON AT A GLANCE

EUROPEAN QUALIFICATION 2013/14

Champion/Cup winner: Neftçi PFK (second qualifying round)

Qarabağ FK (first qualifying round)
İnter Bakı PFK (first qualifying round)
Xäzär Länkäran FK (first qualifying round)

Top scorers   Nicolás Canales (Neftçi), 26 goals
Relegated clubs   Käpäz PFK, Turan Tovuz PFK
Promoted clubs   None
Cup final   Neftçi PFK 0-0 Xäzär Länkäran FK *(aet; 5-3 on pens)*

PREMYER LIQA TEAM OF THE SEASON
(4-4-2)
Coach: Haciyev (Neftçi)

Pietrzkiewicz (Simurq)

Medvedev (Qarabağ)   Ramaldanov (Simurq)   Teli (Qarabağ)   Bruno Bertucci (Neftçi)

Wobay (Neftçi)   Georgievski (Inter)   Ramos (Neftçi)   Piţ (Xäzär Länkäran)

Canales (Neftçi)   Nildo (Olimpik-Şüvälan)

PLAYER OF THE SEASON
Nicolás Canales
(Neftçi PFK)

A newcomer to the Premyer Liqa, the Chilean forward could hardly have enjoyed a finer debut campaign, topping the scoring charts with 26 league goals and winning the double. The 27-year-old's predatory instincts often proved the difference in delicately balanced games and he also scored in both European games against FC Internazionale Milano.

NEWCOMER OF THE SEASON
Cavid Tağıyev
(Olimpik-Şüvälan PFK)

With new regulations requiring each Premyer Liqa club to field at least one player under the age of 21, an opportunity arose for a whole raft of promising youngsters. Tağıyev was arguably the best of the bunch, maturing rapidly at Olimpik-Şüvälan while drawing widespread acclaim for the variety and splendour of some of his goals.

AZERBAIJAN

Home Kit 10   10 Away Kit

NATIONAL TEAM

TOP FIVE ALL-TIME CAPS
Räşad F Sadıqov (82); Aslan Kärimov (79);
Tärlan Ähmädov (73); Mahmud Qurbanov
(72); Qurban Qurbanov (68)

TOP FIVE ALL-TIME GOALS
Qurban Qurbanov (12); **Vaqif Cavadov** (8);
Elvin Mämmädov & Branimir Subašić (7);
Zaur Tağızadä (6)

Results 2012/13

15/08/12	Bahrain	H	Baku	3-0	Subašić (35), Özkara (59), C Hüseynov (79)
07/09/12	Israel (WCQ)	H	Baku	1-1	Abışov (65)
11/09/12	Portugal (WCQ)	A	Braga	0-3	
16/10/12	Russia (WCQ)	A	Moscow	0-1	
14/11/12	Northern Ireland (WCQ)	A	Belfast	1-1	Äliyev (5)
06/02/13	Liechtenstein	N	Dubai (UAE)	1-0	Cavadov (75p)
22/03/13	Luxembourg (WCQ)	A	Luxembourg	0-0	
26/03/13	Portugal (WCQ)	H	Baku	0-2	
29/05/13	Qatar	A	Doha	1-1	Dadaşov (89)
07/06/13	Luxembourg (WCQ)	H	Baku	1-1	Abışov (71)

Appearances 2012/13

Coach: Berti Vogts (GER)	30/12/46		Bhr	ISR	POR	RUS	NIR	Lie	LUX	POR	Qat	LUX	Caps	Goals
Kamran Ağayev	09/02/86	Xäzär Länkäran /Bakı	G	G	G	G			G	G	G	G	40	-
Ali Gökdemir	17/09/91	Hannover (GER)	D	M59	M89	M	M63				M57		8	-
Räşad F Sadıqov	16/06/82	Qarabağ	D	D	D				D	D	s57	D	82	4
Elnur Allahverdiyev	02/11/83	Xäzär Länkäran	D73	D	D						D		28	-
Maksim Medvedev	29/09/89	Qarabağ	D	D	D	D	D	D	D	D	D46		21	-
Vüqar Nadirov	15/06/87	Qarabağ	M73			M46	M	M72	s59	M62			50	4
Ruslan Abışov	10/10/87	Xäzär Länkäran /Rubin (RUS)	M76	M	M	D	D		M	M	M	M	34	4
Cavid Hüseynov	09/03/88	Adana Demirspor (TUR) /Bakı	M		M59	s46	M		s72	s87	M	s69	33	1
Rahid Ämirquliyev	01/09/89	Xäzär Länkäran	M46	s76	M	s63	M	s46				M62	29	-
Branimir Subašić	07/04/82	Xäzär Länkäran /Qarabağ	A82	A	s72	A63					A46	s62 85*	39	7
Rauf Äliyev	12/02/89	Qarabağ /Bakı	A46	A58		s84	A		A	A	A 55*		28	5
Ufuk Budak	26/05/90	Eskişehirspor (TUR)	s46										9	-
Cihan Özkara	14/07/91	Kayseri Erciyesspor (TUR) /Sivasspor (TUR)	s46	s58	A72	A	M79	M64	s71				9	1
Volodimir Levin	23/01/84	İnter Bakı	s73		D	D	D			s62	D		26	-
Rizvan Umarov	05/04/93	Elche (ESP)	s73										3	-
Aleksandr Chertoganov	08/02/80	Qäbälä	s76	M76	s89	M84							53	-
Vaqif Cavadov	25/05/89	Qarabağ	s82	M		M	s79	s64	M59		s46	M	48	8
Mahir Şükürov	12/12/82	Neftçi		D	D	D			D	D		D	65	3
Äfran İsmayilov	08/10/88	Qarabağ		s59	s59				M	M	M69		15	1
Sälahät Ağayev	04/01/91	Sumqayıt					G	G46					3	-
Rasim Ramaldanov	24/01/86	Simurq				D71	D	D	D	D	D	D	6	-
Bädavi Hüseynov	11/07/91	Qarabağ				s63	D				s46		4	-
Elhad Näziri	29/12/92	Milsami (MDA)				s71							1	-
Räşad Ä Sadıqov	08/10/83	Neftçi					D	M87				M	21	-
Vurğun Hüseynov	25/04/88	Qäbälä					M46						14	-
Elvin Mämmädov	18/07/88	Bakı					M90		M69	s46	s84		31	7
Rüfät Dadaşov	29/09/91	Kaiserslautern (GER)					A46			A	A		3	1
Anar Näzirov	08/09/85	Qäbälä					s46						1	-
Pardis Fardjad-Azad	12/04/88	Sumqayıt					s46	M71	s69				3	-
Qara Qarayev	12/10/92	Qarabağ					s90			D			2	-
Arif İsayev	28/07/85	Denizlispor (TUR)									M46		5	-
Araz Abdullayev	18/04/92	Neftçi										M84	4	-

European club competitions 2012/13

NEFTÇI PFK

CHAMPIONS
LEAGUE

Second qualifying round - FC Zestafoni (GEO)
H 3-0 *İmamverdiyev (22), Wobay (24), Canales (63)*
R Mehdiyev, Mälikov, Mitreski, Sadiqov,
Flavinho (A Abdullayev 62), Wobay, Canales,
Ramos, Bruno Bertucci, İmamverdiyev
(Seyidov 77), Yunuszadä (Yunisoğlu 70).
Coach: Tärlan Ähmädov (AZE)
A 2-2 *Wobay (22), Sadiqov (52p)*
R Mehdiyev, Mälikov, Mitreski, Sadiqov
(E Mehdiyev 82), Flavinho, Wobay (A
Abdullayev 75), Canales, Ramos, Bruno
Bertucci, İmamverdiyev (Seyidov 69),
Yunuszadä. Coach: Tärlan Ähmädov (AZE)

**Third qualifying round - Hapoel Kiryat
Shmona FC (ISR)**
A 0-4
R Mehdiyev, Mälikov, Mitreski, Sadiqov, Flavinho
(A Abdullayev 80), Wobay, Canales, Ramos,
Bruno Bertucci, İmamverdiyev (Seyidov 59),
Yunuszadä Coach: Tärlan Ähmädov (AZE)
H 2-2 *Wobay (31), İmamverdiyev (76)*
Stamenković, Yunisoğlu, Sadiqov, Flavinho,
Wobay, Canales, Ramos, Bruno Bertucci,
Seyidov (İmamverdiyev 63), E Mehdiyev (A
Abdullayev 79), Yunuszadä. Coach: Tärlan
Ähmädov (AZE)

EUROPA
LEAGUE

Play-offs - APOEL FC (CYP)
H 1-1 *Şükürov (82p)*
Stamenković, Mitreski, Sadiqov, Flavinho,
Wobay (Abdullayev 76), Canales, Ramos,
Bruno Bertucci, Şükürov, İmamverdiyev
(Seyidov 65), Yunuszadä. Coach: Böyükağa
Hacıyev (AZE)
A 3-1 *İmamverdiyev (22), Wobay (30),
Flavinho (60)*
Stamenković, Mitreski, Sadiqov, Flavinho,
Wobay (Abdullayev 76), Canales (Quliyev
86), Ramos, Bruno Bertucci, Şükürov,
İmamverdiyev (Seyidov 72), Yunuszadä.
Coach: Böyükağa Hacıyev (AZE)
Red card: Yunuszadä 83

Group H
Match 1 - FK Partizan (SRB)
A 0-0
Stamenković, Quliyev, Mitreski, Sadiqov,
Flavinho (A Abdullayev 78), Wobay
(E Mehdiyev 87), Canales, Ramos, Bruno
Bertucci, Şükürov, İmamverdiyev (Seyidov
58). Coach: Böyükağa Hacıyev (AZE)
Match 2 - FC Internazionale Milano (ITA)
H 1-3 *Canales (53)*
Stamenković, Mitreski, Sadiqov, Flavinho,
Wobay, Canales, Ramos, Bruno Bertucci,
Nurähmädov (Seyidov 46), Şükürov,
Yunuszadä. Coach: Böyükağa Hacıyev (AZE)
Match 3 - FC Rubin Kazan (RUS)
A 0-1
Stamenković, Quliyev, Mitreski, Sadiqov,
Flavinho, Wobay, Canales, Ramos, Bruno
Bertucci, Seyidov (A Abdullayev 50),
Şükürov. Coach: Böyükağa Hacıyev (AZE)
Match 4 - FC Rubin Kazan (RUS)
H 0-1
Stamenković, Quliyev, Mitreski, Sadiqov
(Seyidov 57), Flavinho, Wobay, Canales,
Ramos, Bruno Bertucci, Şükürov
(Yunuszadä 88), Mehdiyev (Abdullayev 53).
Coach: Böyükağa Hacıyev (AZE)
Match 5 - FK Partizan (SRB)
H 1-1 *Flavinho (10)*
Stamenković, Quliyev, Mitreski, Sadiqov,
Flavinho, Wobay, Canales, Bruno Bertucci,
İmamverdiyev (A Abdullayev 61), E
Mehdiyev, Yunuszadä. Coach: Böyükağa
Hacıyev (AZE)
Match 6 - FC Internazionale Milano (ITA)
A 2-2 *Sadiqov (52), Canales (89)*
Stamenković, Quliyev, Mitreski, Sadiqov
(Seyidov 77), Flavinho, Wobay, Canales,
Ramos, Bruno Bertucci, Şükürov (Mehdiyev
46), İmamverdiyev (A Abdullayev 90+3).
Coach: Böyükağa Hacıyev (AZE)

BAKI FK

EUROPA
LEAGUE

First qualifying round - ND Mura 05 (SVN)
H 0-0
A Mämmädov, Rodríguez, Ivanovs, Kargbo,
Česnauskis, Juninho, Horvat (E Mämmädov
61), Mähärrämov, Verpakovskis (Parks
69), Kovačević, Šolić (Hacıyev 55). Coach:
Novruz Äzimov (AZE)
A 0-2
A Mämmädov, Rodríguez, Ivanovs, Kargbo,
Česnauskis, Juninho (Novruzov 79),
E Mämmädov (Verpakovskis 72), Kovačević,
Popkhadze, Parks, Hacıyev (Šolić 29).
Coach: Novruz Äzimov (AZE)

XÄZÄR LÄNKÄRAN FK

EUROPA
LEAGUE

First qualifying round - JK Nõmme Kalju (EST)
H 2-2 *Subašić (7), Scarlatache (30)*
Ağayev, Allahverdiyev, Alviž, Sadio (Ricardo
Vilana 71), Éder Bonfim, Subašić, Brenes,
Ämirquliyev, Abışov, Piţ, Scarlatache.
Coach: Yunis Hüseynov (AZE)
A 2-0 *Abışov (41), Subašić (85)*
Ağayev, Allahverdiyev, Alviž, Sadio (Brenes
84), Éder Bonfim, Subašić (Ricardo Vilana
88), Ämirquliyev, Abışov, Piţ (Abdullayev
90+2), Todorov, Scarlatache. Coach: Yunis
Hüseynov (AZE)

**Second qualifying round - KKS Lech
Poznań (POL)**
H 1-1 *Subašić (4)*
Ağayev, Allahverdiyev, Alviž (Brenes 46),
Sadio, Éder Bonfim, Subašić, Ämirquliyev,
Abışov, Piţ (Ricardo Vilana 80), Todorov,
Scarlatache. Coach: Yunis Hüseynov (AZE)
A 0-1
Ağayev, Allahverdiyev, Alviž, Sadio (Brenes
65), Éder Bonfim, Subašić, Ämirquliyev,
Abışov, Piţ, Todorov (Ricardo Vilana 80),
Scarlatache. Coach: Yunis Hüseynov (AZE)
Red card: Ämirquliyev 90+1

İNTER BAKI PİK

EUROPA
LEAGUE

First qualifying round - JK Trans Narva (EST)
A 5-0 *Tskhadadze (11, 35), Mämmädov (62), Adamia (70), Hacıyev (76p)*
Lomaia, Abramidze, Georgievski, Adamia (Genov 82), Mämmädov (Hacıyev 67), Levin, Kandelaki, Abdoulaye, Daşdämirov, Niasse, Tskhadadze (Schutz 73). Coach: Kakhaber Tskhadadze (GEO)
H 2-0 *Georgievski (21), Hacıyev (86)*
Tevdoradze, Abramidze, Georgievski, Adamia (Hacıyev 77), Mämmädov (Genov 86), Levin, Abdoulaye, Daşdämirov, Niasse, Tskhadadze (Schutz 60), Ämircanov. Coach: Kakhaber Tskhadadze (GEO)

Second qualifying round - Asteras Tripolis FC (GRE)
H 1-1 *Schutz (46)*
Lomaia, Abramidze, Georgievski, Adamia (Genov 89), Mämmädov (Hacıyev 46), Levin, Kandelaki, Abdoulaye, Schutz, Niasse (Zlatinov 71), Ämircanov. Coach: Kakhaber Tskhadadze (GEO)
A 1-1 *Schutz (88) (aet; 2-4 on pens)*
Lomaia, Georgievski, Hacıyev (Mämmädov 67), Adamia (Genov 61), Zlatinov, Levin (Tskhadadze 71), Kandelaki, Abdoulaye, Daşdämirov, Schutz, Barmettler. Coach: Kakhaber Tskhadadze (GEO)

BAKI FK

Coach: Božidar Bandović (SRB)
1997 • Bakı FK training center (2,000) • fcbaku.com
Major honours
Azerbaijan League (2) 2006, 2009;
Azerbaijan Cup (3) 2005, 2010, 2012

2012

10/08	Simurq	h	0-0		
18/08	Rävan	a	1-1	*Parks*	
26/08	Käpäz	h	3-1	*Novruzov, Mantzios 2*	
14/09	Turan	h	1-1	*Kargbo*	
30/09	Sumqayıt	a	0-1		
04/10	Qäbälä	h	1-1	*Šolić*	
20/10	Qarabağ	a	1-1	*Rodríguez*	
26/10	İnter	h	0-0		
30/10	Olimpik-Şüvalan	a	1-2	*Horvat*	
03/11	Käpäz	a	0-0		
18/11	Xäzär Länkäran	h	2-0	*Juninho, Rodríguez*	
25/11	Neftçi	h	1-2	*E Mämmädov*	
02/12	Qäbälä	a	2-0	*Juninho, Novruzov*	
06/12	Xäzär Länkäran	a	1-1	*Šolić*	
15/12	Qarabağ	h	0-0		
18/12	Neftçi	a	1-1	*Quliyev*	
22/12	İnter	a	0-1		

2013

10/02	Sumqayıt	h	1-1	*Pena*	
13/02	Turan	a	4-0	*Pena, E Mämmädov, Šolić, Novruzov*	
16/02	Olimpik-Şüvalan	h	2-0	*og (Juanfran), Horvat*	
22/02	Simurq	a	0-0		
03/03	Rävan	h	2-1	*Pena 2*	
12/03	Neftçi	h	1-1	*Pena*	
30/03	Simurq	a	1-0	*Pena*	
06/04	İnter	h	1-2	*Näbiyev*	
13/04	Qäbälä	a	1-1	*R Äliyev (p)*	
21/04	Qarabağ	h	0-1		
28/04	Simurq	h	2-1	*Hüseynov, R Äliyev*	
05/05	İnter	a	1-2	*Hüseynov*	
09/05	Qäbälä	h	0-1		
14/05	Qarabağ	a	1-3	*Mario*	
19/05	Neftçi	a	1-0	*Horvat*	

No	Name	Nat	DoB	Pos	Aps	(s)	Gls
17	Ramazan Abbasov		22/09/83	M	6	(1)	
18	Vadim Abdullayev		17/12/94	M		(1)	
1	Kamran Ağayev		09/02/86	G	7		
38	Namiq Äläsgärov		03/02/95	M	3		
14	Elvin Äliyev		21/08/84	D	5	(2)	
11	Rauf Äliyev		12/02/89	A	8	(3)	2
25	Şähriyar Äliyev		25/12/92	D	30		
26	Leandro Becerra	ARG	26/01/84	M	2	(2)	
7	Deividas Česnauskis	LTU	30/06/81	M	13	(4)	
28	Ferdi Elmas	TUR	13/02/85	M	3	(4)	
99	Rähman Hacıyev		25/07/93	M	11	(1)	
10	Lucas Horvat	ARG	13/10/85	M	21	(4)	3
18	Cavid Hüseynov		09/03/88	M	9	(3)	2
3	Deniss Ivanovs	LVA	11/01/84	D	13	(5)	
8	Juninho	BRA	15/03/84	M	21	(4)	2
6	Ibrahim Kargbo	SLE	10/04/82	M	18	(5)	1
24	Nenad Kovačević	SRB	11/11/80	M	11		
22	Evangelos Mantzios	GRE	22/04/83	A	7	(1)	2
17	Mario	ESP	25/03/85	M	3	(2)	1
15	Cämşid Mähärrämov		03/10/83	D	8		
16	Aqil Mämmädov		01/05/89	G	1	(1)	
11	Elvin Mämmädov		18/07/88	M	21	(7)	2
21	Novruz Mämmädov		20/03/90	D	2	(2)	
5	Aqil Näbiyev		16/06/82	D	8		1
19	Nurlan Novruzov		03/03/93	A	7	(8)	3
82	Edin Nuredinoski	MKD	21/04/82	G	24		
36	Winston Parks	CRC	12/10/81	A	1	(4)	1
24	Marius Pena	ROU	02/05/85	A	12	(3)	6
27	Giorgi Popkhadze	GEO	25/09/86	D	17	(2)	
29	Äziz Quliyev		02/05/87	D	15	(3)	1
18	Tural Qürbätov		01/03/93	A	1	(2)	
26	Risto Ristović	SRB	05/05/88	M	5	(4)	
2	Edemir Rodríguez	BOL	21/10/84	D	16	(1)	2
77	Aleksandar Šolić	CRO	29/01/83	M	19	(10)	3
23	Māris Verpakovskis	LVA	15/10/79	A	4	(4)	

İNTER BAKI PİK

Coach: Kakhaber Tskhadadze (GEO)
2004 • AZAL Arena (3,000); Şäfa (6,500) • inter.az
Major honours
Azerbaijan League (2) 2008, 2010

2012

05/08	Qarabağ	h	1-1	*og (Teli)*	
10/08	Qäbälä	a	0-1		
19/08	Xäzär Länkäran	h	0-0		
25/08	Turan	a	3-2	*Adamia, Levin, Georgievski*	
15/09	Sumqayıt	h	1-0	*Djako*	
23/09	Olimpik-Şüvalan	a	0-0		
04/10	Rävan	a	2-0	*Hacıyev, Tskhadadze*	
20/10	Simurq	h	1-0	*Tskhadadze*	
26/10	Bakı	a	0-0		
30/10	Käpäz	h	3-1	*Niasse 2, Tskhadadze*	
04/11	Sumqayıt	a	0-0		
18/11	Turan	h	2-0	*Zärgärov, Tskhadadze*	
24/11	Simurq	a	0-1		
02/12	Rävan	h	2-0	*Tskhadadze (p), Zärgärov*	
09/12	Olimpik-Şüvalan	h	0-0		
15/12	Käpäz	a	2-0	*Levin, Hacıyev*	
17/12	Neftçi	h	1-1	*Niasse*	
22/12	Bakı	h	1-0	*Tskhadadze (p)*	

2013

11/02	Xäzär Länkäran	a	3-2	*Mämmädov, Tskhadadze, Zärgärov*	
17/02	Qäbälä	h	2-1	*Daşdämirov, Zärgärov*	
23/02	Neftçi	a	0-2		
03/03	Qarabağ	a	0-0		
13/03	Qäbälä	a	2-1	*Mämmädov, Fomenko*	
30/03	Neftçi	h	0-1		
06/04	Bakı	h	2-1	*Mämmädov, Fomenko*	
13/04	Qarabağ	a	2-3	*Fomenko, Bayramov*	
20/04	Simurq	h	5-0	*Fomenko 2, Genov 2, Mansurov*	
28/04	Neftçi	a	0-2		
04/05	Bakı	h	2-1	*Tskhadadze, Léo Rocha*	
09/05	Qarabağ	h	0-0		
14/05	Simurq	a	0-1		
19/05	Qäbälä	h	1-0	*Mansurov*	

No	Name	Nat	DoB	Pos	Aps	(s)	Gls
47	Abdulla Abatsiyev		16/08/93	M	16	(2)	
20	Bruce Abdoulaye	CGO	15/04/82	D	27	(2)	
44	Valeri Abramidze	GEO	17/01/80	D	9	(6)	
10	Giorgi Adamia	GEO	10/03/81	A	4	(1)	1
87	İlqar Äläkbärov		06/10/93	D	4	(3)	
77	Ruslan Ämircanov		01/02/85	D	21	(3)	
87	Heinz Barmettler	DOM	21/07/87	D	2		
24	Fuad Bayramov		30/11/94	M	12	(4)	1
29	Ruslan Cäfärov		26/01/93	D	1	(2)	
21	Arif Daşdämirov		10/02/87	D	18	(7)	1
13	Coşqun Diniyev		13/09/95	M		(2)	
30	Arafat Djako	TOG	10/11/88	A	3	(1)	1
30	Yuriy Fomenko	UKR	31/12/86	A	11	(2)	5
9	Daniel Genov	BUL	19/05/89	A	4	(15)	2
5	Slavco Georgievski	MKD	30/03/80	M	30		
8	Nizami Hacıyev		18/02/88	M	10	(10)	2
18	Ilia Kandelaki	GEO	26/12/81	D	25		
91	Léo Rocha	BRA	07/03/85	M	3	(6)	1
15	Volodimir Levin		23/01/84	D	28		2
1	Giorgi Lomaia	GEO	08/08/79	G	25		
7	Ramil Mansurov		30/09/93	A	1	(4)	2
11	Asif Mämmädov		05/08/86	M	23	(8)	1
25	Ibrahima Niasse	SEN	18/04/88	M	26	(1)	3
96	Elşän Poladov		30/11/79	G	1		
17	Robertinho	BRA	13/06/88	A		(1)	
23	Tales Schutz	POL	22/08/81	A	4	(6)	
74	Revaz Tevdoradze	GEO	14/04/88	G	6		
28	Bachana Tskhadadze	GEO	23/10/87	A	28	(1)	8
6	Samir Zärgärov		29/08/86	M	10	(9)	4

KÄPÄZ PFK

Coach: Fuad İsmayılov;
(19/08/12) Mahmud Qurbanov
1959 • Gäncä şähär stadionu (25,000);
Dalğa Arena (6,700) • pfckapaz.com
Major honours
Azerbaijan League (3) 1995, 1998, 1999;
Azerbaijan Cup (4) 1994, 1997, 1998, 2000

2012

04/08	Turan	h	1-2	İ Beraia
10/08	Xäzär Länkäran	a	0-4	
18/08	Olimpik-Şüvalan	h	0-2	
26/08	Bakı	a	1-3	Fomenko
15/09	Qäbälä	h	1-0	B Soltanov
24/09	Simurq	a	1-2	Ş Kärimov
30/09	Rävan	a	2-1	Fomenko, B Soltanov
04/10	Qarabağ	h	0-0	
19/10	Neftçi	a	1-4	Äliyev
26/10	Sumqayıt	h	0-0	
30/10	İnter	a	1-3	Äzizov
03/11	Bakı	h	0-0	
19/11	Qäbälä	a	0-2	
24/11	Xäzär Länkäran	h	0-1	
02/12	Turan	a	1-5	og (Krutskevich)
07/12	Qarabağ	a	1-3	Fomenko
15/12	İnter	h	0-2	
20/12	Sumqayıt	h	1-2	İmamäliyev

2013

09/02	Neftçi	h	0-3	
16/02	Rävan	h	0-0	
23/02	Olimpik-Şüvalan	a	0-3	
03/03	Simurq	h	1-1	Ş Kärimov
13/03	Olimpik-Şüvalan	h	1-3	Quliyev
30/03	Sumqayıt	a	0-1	
06/04	Xäzär Länkäran	h	1-1	Häsänäliyev
12/04	Rävan	a	0-3	
19/04	Turan	h	0-1	
27/04	Sumqayıt	h	1-0	Paşayev
03/05	Xäzär Länkäran	a	0-1	
08/05	Rävan	h	3-1	Asani, Serebriakov 2
13/05	Turan	a	5-3	Paşayev 3 (1p), Asani, Serehriakov
20/05	Olimpik-Şüvalan	a	0-4	

No	Name	Nat	DoB	Pos	Aps	(s)	Gls
22	Tural Abbaszadä		26/10/92	G	6		
19	Atin Abdullayev		28/05/89	A	2	(2)	
88	Bujanım... ri	MKD	10/08/88	M	25		?
17	Cuyhun Ähmädov		22/09/00	M	2	(5)	
20	Emin Äliyev		09/10/90	M	13	(5)	1
10	Zaur Äsädov		14/07/82	M	2	(5)	
14	Elxan Äzizov		30/09/89	A	11	(9)	1
4/	Kamrul Balıyev		08/01/91	M		(3)	
10	Dobimberdy Ballayew	MM	16/06/88	A	3		
66	Ljubo Baranin	SRB	25/08/86	D	8		
11	Goga Beraia	RUS	26/01/84	M	1	(2)	
9	Irakli Beraia	RUS	26/01/84	M	3		1
10	Guy Feutchine	CMR	18/11/76	M	17		
30	Yuriy Fomenko	UKR	31/12/86	A	17	(1)	3
8	Elvin Häsänäliyev		07/08/93	M	13	(8)	1
24	Färid Häşimzadä		15/04/88	D	2		
2	Samir Hüseynli		20/07/92	D	2		
3	Täbriz Hüseynli		24/10/91	D	4	(1)	
6	Mähärräm Hüseynov		05/07/92	M	23	(3)	
23	Vüqar İbrahimov		20/10/92	D	2	(1)	
2	Vüsal İbrahimov		23/08/91	M		(1)	
13	Emin İmamäliyev		07/08/80	M	10		1
2	Äli İsmayılov		19/12/81	D	3		
18	Elgiz Kärämli		28/02/92	M	11	(1)	
1	Ramil Kärimov		13/05/90	G	5		
15	Şahin Kärimov		12/01/85	D	28	(2)	2
15	Cämşid Mähärrämov		03/10/83	D	9		
4	Azär Mämmädov		07/02/76	D	13	(1)	
5	Mätläb Mämmädov		14/08/81	D		(3)	
2	Nicat Mämmädov		01/05/89	D	9	(2)	
11	Ziyabil Mämmädov		19/12/91	A		(4)	
23	Ravil Müslümov		05/05/92	A	1	(5)	
4	Mähärräm Müslümzadä		12/08/91	D	7	(1)	
7	Pärvin Paşayev		29/08/88	M	11	(7)	4
5	Färid Quliyev		01/01/86	A	11	(1)	1
2	Ivan Radoš	CRO	21/02/84	G	10	(1)	
17	Pirkuly Saparov	TKM	16/10/87	D	2		
29	Giorgi Sepiashvili	GEO	29/09/90	D	14	(3)	
30	Vladislav Serebriakov	RUS	02/01/93	A	6	(4)	3
9	Alan Soltanov	RUS	12/06/91	D	9	(3)	
9	Bäxtiyar Soltanov		21/06/89	A	9	(2)	2
17	Renat Sultanov		18/08/83	D	1		
18	Nikolai Svezhintsev	RUS	07/07/83	M	21	(2)	
16	Xäyal Zeynalov		13/05/82	G	11	(1)	

NEFTÇİ PFK

Coach: Böyükağa Hacıyev
1937 • İsmät Qayıbov adına Bakıxanov qäsäbä stadionu
(4,500), Bakcell Arena (11,000) • neftchipfk.com
Major honours
Azerbaijan League (8) 1992, 1996, 1997, 2004, 2005,
2011, 2012, 2013;
Azerbaijan Cup (6) 1995, 1996, 1999, 2002, 2004, 2013

2012

11/08	Qarabağ	a	0-1	
18/08	Qäbälä	h	3-0	İmamverdiyev 2, Wobay
15/09	Xäzär Länkäran	a	2-1	Canales, Flavinho
24/09	Sumqayıt	a	2-3	og (Mustafayev), Canales
08/10	Turan	h	2-1	Sadiqov (p), Ramos
19/10	Käpäz	h	4-1	Wobay, Canales 2, A Abdullayev
28/10	Rävan	a	0-2	
31/10	Simurq	h	2-1	Canales 2 (1p)
03/11	Qäbälä	a	1-2	Canales
17/11	Sumqayıt	h	8-1	Canales 4, Wobay 2, İmamverdiyev, Bruno Bertucci
25/11	Bakı	a	2-1	Canales (p), Flavinho
02/12	Qarabağ	h	0-1	
10/12	Rävan	h	2-0	Seyidov, Canales
14/12	Xäzär Länkäran	a	1-2	Canales
18/12	Bakı	h	1-1	Sadiqov
22/12	Olimpik-Şüvalan	h	4-2	Flavinho, Wobay, Sadiqov, İmamverdiyev
25/12	İnter	h	1-1	Canales

2013

09/02	Käpäz	a	3-0	Flavinho, Canales, A Abdullayev
13/02	Olimpik-Şüvalan	a	2-1	Canales 2
17/02	Simurq	a	2-0	Canales, Sadiqov
23/02	İnter	a	2-0	Canales, og (Abramidze)
03/03	Turan	a	3-2	Flavinho, A Abdullayev, İmamverdiyev
12/03	Bakı	a	1-1	A Abdullayev
30/03	İnter	h	1-0	Wobay
06/04	Qarabağ	h	1-2	Canales
13/04	Simurq	a	1-0	Wobay
20/04	Qäbälä	h	2-1	Dênis Silva, Canales
28/04	İnter	h	2-1	Canales 2 (1p)
04/05	Qarabağ	a	2-1	Canales 2
09/05	Simurq	h	1-1	Wobay
14/05	Qäbälä	a	1-1	Sadiqov
19/05	Bakı	h	0-1	

No	Name	Nat	DoB	Pos	Aps	(s)	Gls
17	Araz Abdullayev		18/04/92	M	18	(9)	4
8	Elşän Abdullayev		05/02/94	A		(3)	
12	Emil Balayev		17/04/94	G	2		
16	Bruno Bertucci	BRA	27/05/90	D	20	(4)	1
2	José Cabión	CHI	14/11/83	D		(1)	
11	Nicolás Canales	CHI	27/06/85	A	31		26
3	Dênis Silva	BRA	28/12/85	D	13	(1)	1
9	Flavinho	BRA	27/07/83	M	28		5
25	Cavid İmamverdiyev		01/08/90	M	10	(13)	5
28	Emin Mehdiyev		22/09/92	A	10	(9)	
5	Igor Mitreski	MKD	19/02/79	D	27		
14	Bakhodir Nasimov	UZB	02/05/87	A	1	(7)	
21	Kamil Nurähmädov		10/06/91	A		(3)	
20	Eşqin Quliyev		11/12/90	M		(3)	
4	Tärlan Quliyev		10/08/92	M		(3)	
15	Éric Ramos	PAR	12/06/87	M	31		1
7	Rodriguinho	BRA	05/02/82	M	1	(1)	
6	Räşad Ä Sadiqov		08/10/83	M	26	(2)	5
19	Mirhüseyn Seyidov		10/08/92	M	10	(9)	1
30	Saša Stamenković	SRB	05/01/85	G	30		
22	Mahir Şükürov		12/12/82	D	26	(2)	
10	Julius Wobay	SLE	19/05/84	M	28	(4)	8
3	Saša Yunisoğlu		18/12/85	D	1		
32	Elvin Yunuszadä		22/08/92	D	21	(3)	

OLİMPİK-ŞÜVÄLAN PFK

Coach: Vaqif Sadıqov
1996 • AZAL Arena (3,000); Mehdi Hüseynzadä adına
Sumqayıt şähär stadionu (15,000) • azalpfc.az

2012

04/08	Sumqayıt	a	2-2	Tağıyev, Benouahi
11/08	Rävan	h	3-1	Nildo, Benouahi 2
18/08	Käpäz	a	2-0	Nildo 2
16/09	Qarabağ	h	6-2	Arsenijević, Nildo 4, Benouahi (p)
23/09	İnter	h	0-0	
29/09	Qäbälä	a	0-0	
03/10	Xäzär Länkäran	h	0-2	
20/10	Turan	a	0-1	
26/10	Simurq	a	1-1	Tağızadä
30/10	Bakı	h	2-1	İgbekoyi, Nildo
04/11	Qarabağ	a	0-2	
18/11	Rävan	a	0-1	
25/11	Sumqayıt	h	1-1	Benouahi (p)
02/12	Xäzär Länkäran	a	2-1	Tağızadä, Benouahi
09/12	İnter	a	0-0	
15/12	Turan	h	0-0	
22/12	Neftçi	a	2-4	Benouahi, Nildo (p)

2013

09/02	Simurq	h	1-1	Nildo
13/02	Neftçi	h	1-2	Nildo
16/02	Bakı	h	0-2	
23/02	Käpäz	h	3-0	Tağıyev, Säfiyaroğlu, İgbekoyi
03/03	Qäbälä	h	6-1	İgbekoyi, Tağıyev 2, Arsenijević, Benouahi, John
13/03	Käpäz	a	3-1	Nildo 2 (1p), İgbekoyi
30/03	Xäzär Länkäran	a	1-1	Kļava
07/04	Turan	h	2-0	Nildo, John
14/04	Sumqayıt	a	2-0	Tağızadä, Nildo
19/04	Rävan	h	3-2	Nildo, John 2
28/04	Xäzär Länkäran	h	2-0	İgbekoyi, Tağıyev
03/05	Turan	a	2-0	Nildo 2
08/05	Sumqayıt	h	1-0	Nildo
14/05	Rävan	a	5-3	Tağızadä, İgbekuyi, Novruzov, Nildo 2 (1p)
20/05	Käpäz	h	4-0	İgbekoyi 2, Tağızadä, Kļava

No	Name	Nat	DoB	Pos	Aps	(s)	Gls
25	Elgün Abbaslı		11/04/92	M		(1)	
1	Amil Ağacanov		24/07/83	G	8		
4	Ailton	BRA	23/07/87	D	27		
16	Branislav Arandjlović	BRB	02/08/82	M	30	(1)	2
11	Zoumi Benouahi	MAR	07/03/87	M	24	(1)	9
32	Vladimir Bogdanović	SRB	05/10/86	M	7	(7)	
99	Orxan Häsänov		18/12/91	A	7	(8)	
12	Cahangir Häsänzadä		04/08/79	G	19		
17	Viktor İgbekoyi	NGA	01/09/86	M	28	(1)	8
77	Arif İsayev		28/07/85	M		(4)	
28	Will John	USA	13/06/85	M	3	(3)	4
2	Juanfran	ESP	10/01/86	D	29		
25	Oskars Kļava	LVA	08/08/83	M	20	(5)	2
27	Ruslan Mäcidov		22/04/85	G	5	(1)	
8	Elşän Mämmädov		04/05/80	A		(4)	
5	Aqil Näbiyev		16/06/82	D	1	(1)	
23	Tural Närimanov		27/10/89	D	6	(5)	
3	Usim Nduka		23/03/85	D	25	(2)	
16	Nildo	BRA	07/12/83	A	30	(2)	21
1	Taqim Novruzov		21/11/88	M	28	(1)	1
14	Habil Nurähmädov		24/06/92	M		(2)	
28	Artur Patras	MDA	10/01/88	M	5	(2)	
4	Orxan Säfiyaroğlu		22/02/90	M	7	(3)	1
26	Etibar Şahmärdanov		18/10/92	M	2		
8	Elman Tagayev	TKM	02/06/89	M	8		
7	Cavid Tağıyev		22/07/92	M	17	(9)	5
22	Ruslan Tağızadä		09/12/93	D	15	(10)	5
37	Andrius Velička	LTU	05/04/79	A	3	(13)	
10	Tärlan Xälilov		27/08/84	M		(2)	
77	Saşa Yunisoğlu		18/12/85	D		(1)	

AZERBAIJAN

QARABAĞ FK

Coach: Qurban Qurbanov

1987 • Dalğa Arena (6,700); Tofiq Bähramov adına
Respublika stadionu (32,200) • qarabagh.com
Major honours
Azerbaijan League (1) 1993;
Azerbaijan Cup (3) 1993, 2006, 2009

2012

05/08	İnter	a	1-1	*Muarem*
11/08	Neftçi	h	1-0	*Qarayev*
19/08	Sumqayıt	a	6-1	*Richard, Sadıqov (p), Nadirov, Muarem, Qurbanov, Yusifov*
24/08	Rävan	h	0-0	
16/09	Olimpik-Şüvalan	a	2-6	*Richard 2*
23/09	Turan	a	1-0	*Sadıqov (p)*
29/09	Simurq	a	0-0	
04/10	Käpäz	a	0-0	
20/10	Bakı	h	1-1	*Richard (p)*
27/10	Xäzär Länkäran	a	0-2	
31/10	Qäbälä	h	1-2	*Muarem*
04/11	Olimpik-Şüvalan	h	2-0	*Muarem, Cavadov*
18/11	Simurq	a	2-1	*Richard, og (Süleymanov)*
24/11	Turan	h	1-1	*og (Rähimov)*
02/12	Neftçi	a	1-0	*Nadirov*
07/12	Käpäz	h	3-1	*Richard, Cavadov, İsmayılov*
15/12	Bakı	a	0-0	
20/12	Xäzär Länkäran	h	1-0	*Nadirov*

2013

10/02	Qäbälä	a	1-1	*Richard (p)*
16/02	Sumqayıt	h	3-0	*Cavadov, Teli, Sadıqov*
22/02	Rävan	a	3-2	*Richard, Agolli, Teli*
03/03	İnter	h	0-0	
12/03	Simurq	a	0-1	
30/03	Qäbälä	h	1-0	*Richard*
06/04	Neftçi	a	2-1	*Richard 2 (1p)*
13/04	İnter	h	3-2	*Medvedev, Nadirov, Opara*
21/04	Bakı	a	1-0	*Richard (p)*
28/04	Qäbälä	a	2-0	*Reynaldo 2*
04/05	Neftçi	h	1-2	*Richard (p)*
09/05	İnter	a	0-0	
14/05	Bakı	h	3-1	*Muarem, Nadirov, og (Ivanovs)*
19/05	Simurq	h	0-0	

No	Name	Nat	DoB	Pos	Aps	(s)	Gls
16	Elnur Abdulov		18/09/92	A	2	(4)	
33	Mostafa Afroto	EGY	17/03/89	M		(4)	
25	Ansi Agolli	ALB	11/10/82	D	27		1
6	Hacı Ähmädov		23/11/93	D	4	(4)	
11	Rauf Äliyev		12/02/89	A	10	(8)	
15	Toğrul Bilallı		08/08/92	M	2		
70	Vaqif Cavadov		25/05/89	A	16	(8)	3
55	Bädavi Hüseynov		11/07/91	D	11	(6)	
3	Kamil Hüseynov		04/02/92	D		(1)	
9	Tural İsgändärov		12/04/92	A		(3)	
22	Äfran İsmayılov		08/10/88	M	12	(10)	1
5	Maksim Medvedev		29/09/89	D	23	(1)	1
10	Muarem Muarem	MKD	22/10/88	M	23	(6)	5
27	Elvin Musazadä		25/11/89	M	1		
88	Emin Mustafayev		01/01/90	M		(1)	
17	Vüqar Nadirov		15/06/87	A	19	(9)	5
28	Emeka Opara	NGA	02/12/84	A	6	(4)	1
2	Qara Qarayev		12/10/92	D	27	(1)	1
18	İlqar Qurbanov		25/04/86	M	14	(8)	1
21	Reynaldo	BRA	24/08/89	A	8	(1)	2
20	Richard	BRA	20/03/89	M	29	(1)	13
14	Räşad F Sadıqov		16/06/82	D	24	(1)	3
11	Branimir Subašić		07/04/82	A	2	(5)	
24	Admir Teli	ALB	02/06/81	D	29	(1)	2
88	Cristián Torres	ARG	18/06/85	M	6		
89	Miro Varvodić	CRO	15/05/89	G	15		
1	Färhad Väliyev		01/11/80	G	17		
44	Eltun Yaqublu		19/08/91	D	1		
7	Namiq Yusifov		14/08/86	M	24	(6)	1

QÄBÄLÄ FK

Coach: Fatih Kavlak (TUR);
(25/09/12) Ramiz Mämmädov;
(02/04/13) (Luis Aragón Bayona) (ESP)
2005 • Qäbälä şähär stadionu (2,500); Qäbälä rayon
Böyük Ämili känd stadionu (1,000) • gabalafc.az

2012

04/08	Simurq	a	1-1	*Kelhar*
10/08	İnter	h	1-0	*Lourival Assis*
18/08	Neftçi	a	0-3	
26/08	Sumqayıt	h	4-1	*Bruno Barbosa, Kalabane 2, Abdullayev*
15/09	Käpäz	a	0-1	
24/09	Rävan	h	1-3	*Chertoganov*
29/09	Olimpik-Şüvalan	h	0-0	
04/10	Bakı	a	1-0	*Mendy*
21/10	Xäzär Länkäran	a	1-0	*Kamanan*
27/10	Turan	h	0-1	
31/10	Qarabağ	a	2-1	*Abdullayev, Dodô*
03/11	Neftçi	h	2-1	*Lourival Assis, Dodô*
19/11	Käpäz	h	2-0	*Mendy, Abdullayev (p)*
25/11	Rävan	a	3-1	*Mendy, Abdullayev, Lourival Assis (p)*
02/12	Bakı	h	0-2	
08/12	Sumqayıt	a	1-0	*Mendy*
16/12	Simurq	h	0-1	
15/12	Turan	a	2-0	*Abdullayev (p), Dodô*

2013

10/02	Qarabağ	h	1-1	*Žinko*
17/02	İnter	a	1-2	*Kamanan*
23/02	Xäzär Länkäran	h	2-0	*Kamanan 2*
03/03	Olimpik-Şüvalan	a	1-6	*Dabo*
13/03	İnter	h	1-2	*Mendy*
30/03	Qarabağ	a	0-1	
05/04	Simurq	h	1-1	*Lourival Assis*
13/04	Bakı	a	1-1	*Mendy*
21/04	Neftçi	a	1-2	*Lourival Assis*
28/04	Qarabağ	h	0-2	
03/05	Simurq	a	0-2	
09/05	Bakı	a	1-0	*Lourival Assis*
14/05	Neftçi	h	1-1	*Kamanan*
19/05	İnter	a	0-1	

No	Name	Nat	DoB	Pos	Aps	(s)	Gls
34	Ürfan Abbasov		14/10/92	D	25	(3)	
27	Räşad Abdullayev		01/10/81	M	25		5
7	Yaşar Abuzärov		09/09/77	M		(10)	
19	Rövşän Ämiraslanov		18/03/86	M	4	(4)	
20	Räşid Ämiraslanov		04/05/92	M		(1)	
21	Elmar Baxşıyev		03/08/80	M	15	(4)	
8	Bruno Barbosa	BRA	15/02/88	M	13	(4)	1
24	Tärzin Cahangirov		17/01/92	M	6	(1)	
18	Aleksandr Chertoganov		08/02/80	M	19	(2)	1
14	Moustapha Dabo	SEN	27/02/86	A	6	(1)	1
26	Daniel Cruz	BRA	01/06/82	D	12	(1)	
25	Diego	BRA	11/05/79	G	16		
77	Dodô	BRA	16/10/87	M	28	(2)	3
16	Ifeanyi Emeghara	NGA	24/03/84	D	2	(2)	
3	Vurğun Hüseynov		25/04/88	D	3	(4)	
15	Oumar Kalabane	GUI	08/04/81	D	27		2
11	Yannick Kamanan	FRA	05/10/81	A	23	(7)	5
84	Dejan Kelhar	SVN	05/04/84	D	28		1
22	Lourival Assis	BRA	03/02/84	M	20	(7)	6
88	Nodar Mämmädov		03/06/88	D	6	(3)	
9	Victor Mendy	SEN	22/12/81	A	15	(9)	6
37	Kamal Mirzäyev		14/09/94	M	5		
5	Muammer Erdoğdu	TUR	07/07/87	D		(1)	
45	Murad Musayev		13/06/94	D	1		
30	Anar Näzirov		08/03/85	G	16		
8	Cristian Pulhac	ROU	17/08/84	D	9	(1)	
39	Sadiq Quliyev		09/03/95	D	1		
4	Amit Quluzadä		20/11/92	M	7		
90	Ceyhun Sultanov		12/06/79	M		(3)	
28	Müşviq Teymurov		15/01/93	D	1	(2)	
6	Nikola Valentić	SRB	06/09/83	M	9	(1)	
23	Şähriyar Xälilov		21/08/91	D	7	(8)	
99	Amil Yunanov		06/01/93	A		(5)	
5	Luka Žinko	SVN	23/03/83	M	3	(5)	1

RÄVAN BAKI FK

Coach: Cevat Güler (TUR);
(25/08/12) (Bähmän Häsänov);
(23/09/12) Kemal Alispahić (BIH);
(21/12/12) Ramil Äliyev
2009 • Dalğa Arena (6,700); Bayıl Arena (3,000) •
revanfc.az

2012

05/08	Xäzär Länkäran	h	1-1	*Bundu*
11/08	Olimpik-Şüvalan	a	1-3	*Varea*
18/08	Bakı	h	1-1	*Mikayılov*
24/08	Qarabağ	a	0-0	
15/09	Simurq	h	0-2	
24/09	Qäbälä	a	3-1	*Varea, Torres, Qurbanov*
30/09	Käpäz	h	1-2	*Varea*
04/10	İnter	h	0-2	
21/10	Sumqayıt	h	1-0	*Varea*
28/10	Neftçi	h	2-0	*Orlovschi, Varea (p)*
31/10	Turan	a	2-2	*Vidaković 2*
04/11	Xäzär Länkäran	a	0-4	
18/11	Olimpik-Şüvalan	h	1-0	*Qurbanov*
25/11	Qäbälä	h	1-3	*Mikayılov*
02/12	İnter	a	0-2	
10/12	Neftçi	a	0-2	
16/12	Sumqayıt	h	2-3	*Orlovschi, Varea*
20/12	Simurq	a	0-3	*(w/o; original result 0-1)*

2013

09/02	Turan	h	2-0	*Adamović, Kalonas*
16/02	Käpäz	a	2-0	*Kalonas, Abbasov*
22/02	Qarabağ	h	2-3	*Varea, Kalonas*
03/03	Bakı	a	1-2	*Rähimov*
13/03	Xäzär Länkäran	h	1-0	*Varea (p)*
30/03	Turan	a	6-2	*Kalonas 2, Varea 3 (1p), Adamović*
07/04	Sumqayıt	h	3-0	*Kalonas, Adamović, Barlay*
12/04	Käpäz	h	3-0	*Varea 2, Mikayılov*
19/04	Olimpik-Şüvalan	a	2-3	*Abbasov, Kalonas*
27/04	Turan	h	1-0	*Mehdiyev*
04/05	Sumqayıt	a	1-4	*Varea*
08/05	Käpäz	a	1-3	*Qarayev*
14/05	Olimpik-Şüvalan	h	3-5	*Orlovschi, Adamović, Abbasov*
20/05	Xäzär Länkäran	a	2-1	*Adamović, Kalonas*

No	Name	Nat	DoB	Pos	Aps	(s)	Gls
17	Ramazan Abbasov		22/09/83	M	10	(4)	3
20	Miloš Adamović	SRB	19/06/88	A	12		5
19	Hüseyn Axundov		30/04/88	M	5	(7)	
8	Tural Axundov		01/08/88	D	23	(1)	
25	Äli Äliyev		02/02/94	M		(4)	
18	Samuel Barlay	SLE	15/09/86	M	27	(1)	1
26	Francis Bossman	GHA	24/06/84	M	11	(4)	
23	Sallieu Bundu	SLE	03/07/84	A	3		1
17	Rüfät Cälilov		13/04/92	D		(2)	
15	Tural Cälilov		28/11/86	M	9	(3)	
6	Anar Häsänov		18/10/97	M		(2)	
7	Ramil Häşimzadä		26/03/91	M	2	(5)	
4	Ekrem Hodžić	BIH	07/08/79	D	9	(1)	
11	Anar Hüseynov		05/12/93	M		(2)	
17	Emin İbrahimov		03/01/93	M	1	(1)	
10	Mindaugas Kalonas	LTU	28/02/84	A	12	(1)	8
12	Davud Kärimi		08/10/94	G	13	(1)	
16	Orxan Lalayev		12/10/91	D	12	(2)	
15	Nodar Mämmädov		03/06/88	D	12	(2)	
25	Ayaz Mehdiyev		22/02/93	M	9	(2)	1
22	Tofiq Mikayılov		11/04/86	M	19	(12)	3
7	Elvin Musazadä		25/11/89	M	2	(2)	
28	Emin Mustafayev		01/01/90	M	2		
5	Nicolai Orlovschi	MDA	01/04/85	D	19	(1)	3
6	Vüsal Qarayev		08/07/86	M	1	(4)	1
28	Amit Quluzadä		20/11/92	M	4	(7)	
27	Nuran Qurbanov		10/03/93	M	16	(1)	2
12	Sadiq Ramazanov		02/01/93	G	1		
3	Cämil Rähimli		04/04/94	M	1		
13	Şähriyar Rähimov		04/04/89	M	25	(2)	1
11	Łukasz Sapela	POL	21/09/82	G	18		
11	Sheriff Suma	SLE	12/10/86	D	5	(5)	
20	Cristián Torres	ARG	18/06/85	M	15	(2)	1
14	Juan Varea	ARG	23/04/86	A	31		14
10	Nemanja Vidaković	SRB	29/09/85	A	3	(10)	2
3	Miloš Zečević	SRB	17/05/83	D	20		

SİMURQ PFK

Coach: Giorgi Chikhradze (GEO)
2005 • Zaqatala şähär stadionu (3,500) • simurqpfk.az

2012

04/08	Qäbälä	h	1-1	Qırtımov
10/08	Bakı	a	0-0	
18/08	Turan	h	3-0	Popović 2, Božić
15/09	Rävan	a	2-0	Rožić, Burkhardt
20/09	Xäzär Länkäran	a	2-0	Burkhardt, Poljak
24/09	Käpäz	a	2-1	Poljak, Burkhardt
29/09	Qarabağ	h	0-0	
04/10	Sumqayıt	h	1-0	Božić
20/10	İnter	a	0-1	
26/10	Olimpik-Şüvalan	h	1-1	Sättarlı
31/10	Neftçi	a	1-2	Poladov
04/11	Turan	a	1-0	Poljak
18/11	Qarabağ	a	1-2	Božić (p)
24/11	İnter	h	1-0	Popović
02/12	Sumqayıt	a	1-0	Poljak
10/12	Xäzär Länkäran	h	2-2	Sättarlı, Burkhardt
16/12	Qäbälä	a	1-0	Božić
20/12	Rävan	h	3-0	(w/o; original result 1-0 Popović)

2013

09/02	Olimpik-Şüvalan	a	1-1	Popović
17/02	Neftçi	h	0-2	
22/02	Bakı	h	0-0	
03/03	Käpäz	a	1-1	Božić
12/03	Qarabağ	h	1-0	Eyyubov
30/03	Bakı	h	0-1	
05/04	Qäbälä	a	1-1	Bušić
13/04	Neftçi	a	0-1	
20/04	İnter	a	0-5	
28/04	Bakı	a	1-2	Burkhardt
03/05	Qäbälä	a	2-0	Qurbanov 2
09/05	Neftçi	h	1-1	Eyyubov
14/05	İnter	h	1-0	Popović (p)
19/05	Qarabağ	a	0-2	

No	Name	Nat	DoB	Pos	Aps	(s)	Gls
28	Rüstäm Abasov		07/08/91	D	1		
6	Anderson de Q	BRA	14/12/80	M	21	(6)	
25	Mario Božić	BIH	25/05/83	M	24	(1)	6
27	Marcin Burkhardt	POL	25/09/83	M	17	(7)	5
12	Tomislav Bušić	CRO	02/02/86	A	2	(7)	1
20	Räşad Eyyubov		03/12/92	D	9	(6)	2
0	Qärib Ibrahimov		11/09/00	M	16	(6)	
62	Çavad Kazımov		08/08/94	D		(1)	
28	Nenad Kišö	BIH	30/04/88	M	10	(1)	
72	Dmitri Kramarenko		12/09/74	G	4		
24	Mehman Mämmädov		29/10/92	D		(1)	
17	Rüstäm Mämmädov		04/08/84	D	2	(3)	
14	Asif Mirili		10/12/91	M	8	(5)	
22	Dawid Pietrzkiewicz	POL	09/02/88	G	28		
7	Ruslan Poladov		30/11/79	D	19	(7)	1
15	Stjepan Poljak	CRO	17/11/83	M	24	(5)	4
10	Zdravko Popović	CRO	02/01/83	A	23	(5)	6
2	İlkin Qırtımov		04/11/90	D	28		1
19	Nicat Qurbanov		17/02/92	D	7	(11)	2
3	Rasim Ramaldanov		24/01/86	D	24		
21	Murad Sättarlı		09/05/92	A	19	(11)	2
27	Bäxtiyar Soltanov		21/06/89	A	2	(1)	
79	Nenad Stojanović	SRB	22/10/79	A	7	(6)	
34	Elçin Süleymanov		29/01/91	D	1		
13	Aleksandr Şemonayev		01/04/85	D	29		
4	Dilaver Zrnanović	BIH	17/11/84	D	27	(1)	

SUMQAYIT FK

Coach: Bernhard Raab (GER)
2010 • Mehdi Hüseynzadä adına Sumqayıt şähär stadionu (15,000); Bayıl Arena (3,000) • sumqayitpfc.az

2012

04/08	Olimpik-Şüvalan	h	2-2	Äliyev, Fardjad-Azad
11/08	Turan	a	1-0	Qurbanov (p)
19/08	Qarabağ	h	1-6	Allahquliyev
26/08	Qäbälä	a	1-4	Qurbanov
15/09	İnter	a	0-1	
24/09	Neftçi	h	3-2	Äliyev, Fardjad-Azad, M Ağayev
30/09	Bakı	h	1-0	Fardjad-Azad
04/10	Simurq	a	0-1	
21/10	Poladov	h	0-1	
26/10	Käpäz	a	0-0	
31/10	Xäzär Länkäran	h	1-1	Hacıyev
04/11	İnter	h	0-0	
17/11	Neftçi	a	1-8	Cäfärquliyev
25/11	Olimpik-Şüvalan	a	1-1	Fardjad-Azad
02/12	Simurq	h	0-1	
08/12	Qäbälä	a	0-1	
16/12	Rävan	a	3-2	Fardjad-Azad, Pamuk, Sultanov (p)
20/12	Käpäz	h	2-1	Allahquliyev, Mirzabekov

2013

10/02	Bakı	a	1-1	Äliyev
16/02	Qarabağ	a	0-3	
24/02	Turan	h	0-1	
03/03	Xäzär Länkäran	a	2-2	Hüseynpur, Äliyev
11/03	Turan	h	4-0	Fardjad-Azad 4
30/03	Käpäz	h	1-0	Doymuş (p)
07/04	Rävan	a	0-3	
14/04	Olimpik-Şüvalan	h	0-2	
21/04	Xäzär Länkäran	a	0-1	
27/04	Käpäz	a	0-1	
04/05	Rävan	h	4-1	Taner, Qurbanov 2, Can
08/05	Olimpik-Şüvalan	a	0-1	
13/05	Xäzär Länkäran	h	1-0	Qurbanov
20/05	Turan	a	1-2	Qurbanov (p)

No	Name	Nat	DoB	Pos	Aps	(s)	Gls
4	Qumar Abasov		01/02/78	D	28		
95	Murad Ağayev		09/02/93	M	20	(2)	1
1	Sälahät Ağayev		04/01/91	G	23		
11	Sabir Allahquliyev		12/05/88	A	11	(14)	2
2	Slavik Alxasov		06/02/93	D	29		
19	Orxan Äliyev		21/12/06	A	15	(2)	4
78	Can Alıgün	TUR	02/10/00	M	7	(0)	1
70	Jamil Camaläddinov		12/01/95	M	1		
86	Eldar Cankişiyev		26/07/94	M		(1)	
17	Emin Cäfärquliyev		17/06/90	D	10	(13)	1
22	Erdal Çelik	GER	01/01/88	D	2		
3	Murat Doymuş	GER	19/11/85	D	25	(1)	1
7	Pardis Fardjad-Azad		12/04/88	M	21	(2)	9
5	Aftandil Hacıyev		13/08/81	D	15	(2)	1
92	Bäxtiyar Häsänalızadä		29/12/92	D	12	(1)	
27	Ramil Häşimzadä		26/03/91	M	6	(4)	
50	Murad Hüseynov		25/01/89	A		(5)	
77	Mirzağa Hüseynpur		11/03/90	M	12	(2)	1
90	Anar Mähärrämov		12/02/92	G	2		
21	Magomed Mirzabekov	RUS	16/11/90	M	22	(6)	1
2	Muhammed Ali Atam	TUR	21/05/88	D	1	(1)	
22	Xäyal Mustafayev		27/12/80	D	10	(3)	
8	Aqşin Muxtaroğlu		16/06/92	M	6	(7)	
50	Ruslan Näsirli		12/01/95	A	2	(3)	
76	Uğur Pamuk		26/06/89	A	14		1
91	Ruslan Qurbanov		12/09/91	A	19	(5)	6
12	Elçin Sadıqov		14/06/89	G	7		
10	Ceyhun Sultanov		12/06/79	M	14		1
6	Taner Taktak	TUR	26/01/90	M	13	(7)	1

TURAN TOVUZ PFK

Coach: Äsgär Abdullayev; (11/10/12) Äfqan Talıbov
1992 • Tovuz şähär stadionu (6,350); Dalğa Arena (6,700); İsmät Qayıbov adına Bakıxanov qäsäbä stadionu (4,500) • turanpfc.com
Major honours
Azerbaijan League (1) 1994

2012

04/08	Käpäz	a	2-1	Pipia, A Mämmädov
11/08	Sumqayıt	h	0-1	
18/08	Simurq	a	0-3	
25/08	İnter	h	2-3	Ballo, A Mämmädov
14/09	Bakı	a	1-1	Günlü
23/09	Qarabağ	h	0-1	
29/09	Xäzär Länkäran	h	2-1	Ballo 2
08/10	Neftçi	a	1-2	Pipia
20/10	Olimpik-Şüvalan	h	1-0	Günlü
27/10	Qäbälä	a	1-0	Rukavina
31/10	Rävan	h	2-2	Ağakişiyev, Krutskevich
04/11	Simurq	h	1-1	Quliyev
18/11	İnter	a	0-2	
24/11	Qarabağ	a	1-1	Ballo
02/12	Käpäz	h	5-1	Ballo 3, Quliyev, Günlü
15/12	Olimpik-Şüvalan	h	0-0	
20/12	Qäbälä	h	0-2	

2013

09/02	Rävan	a	0-2	
13/02	Bakı	h	0-4	
17/02	Xäzär Länkäran	a	2-4	Ballo, Günlü
24/02	Sumqayıt	a	1-0	Ballo
03/03	Neftçi	h	2-3	Beraia, Günlü
11/03	Sumqayıt	h	0-4	
30/03	Rävan	h	2-6	A Mämmädov, F Äliyev
07/04	Olimpik-Şüvalan	h	0-2	
13/04	Xäzär Länkäran	a	2-2	Rukavina, Günlü
19/04	Käpäz	a	1-0	Ballo
27/04	Bakı	a	0-1	
03/05	Olimpik-Şüvalan	a	0-2	
08/05	Xäzär Länkäran	a	0-1	
13/05	Käpäz	h	3-5	Qädiri (p), Ballo 2
20/05	Sumqayıt	h	2-1	Günlü (p), Janelidze

No	Name	Nat	DoB	Pos	Aps	(s)	Gls
16	Abülfät Abbasov		03/01/93	M	3	(1)	
9	Murad Ağakişiyev		13/06/85	M	18	(5)	1
2	Färmayıl Äliyev		29/03/90	D	13	(8)	1
10	Hafiz Äliyev		17/02/83	M	13	(2)	
99	Salif Ballo	MLI	22/08/88	M	21	(7)	12
85	Kamal Bayramov		15/00/08	G	8		
4	Vügar Baybalayev		03/06/90	M	5	(4)	
23	Irakli Beraia	RUS	26/01/84	M	8	(10)	1
5	Sergey Çernışev		27/04/90	M		(1)	
1	Levan Chkhetiani	GEO	17/08/87	M	3	(1)	
1	Ivan Crnhovac	CRO	12/07/83	G	5		
14	Aleksandr Gogoberishvili	GEO	17/02/77	M	2		
14	Ender Günlü	FRA	09/05/84	M	27		7
23	Räşad Häcizadä		21/03/92	M	1		
2	Hüseyn İsgändärov		07/12/84	D	1	(1)	
24	Orxan İsmayılov		21/04/89	D	1		
20	David Janelidze	GEO	01/09/89	A	7	(8)	1
13	Marius Kazlauskas	LTU	05/04/84	D	11		
13	Bayram Kärimov		21/03/89	D	1	(1)	
26	Olexandr Krutskevich	UKR	13/11/80	D	26		1
25	Nugzar Kvirtia	GEO	16/09/84	M	4	(4)	
13	Nikoloz Maisuradze	GEO	29/05/85	D	8		
20	Elşad Manafov		08/03/92	D	4	(6)	
7	Azär Mämmädov		18/06/90	M	19	(7)	3
16	Elmixan Mämmädov		09/01/94	D	2		
8	Budaq Näsirov		15/07/96	M	11	(3)	
11	Gogi Pipia	GEO	04/02/85	A	4	(6)	2
15	Räşad Piriyev		01/10/91	A		(1)	
28	Andriy Popoviç		14/03/92	G	14	(1)	
2	Dmytro Pospelov	UKR	16/10/91	M	13	(1)	
19	Asäf Qädiri		17/08/84	M	9	(5)	1
5	Färid Quliyev		06/01/86	A	10	(3)	2
6	Mikayıl Rähimov		11/05/87	M	26		
21	Antonio Rukavina	CRO	06/05/85	M	25	(1)	2
5	Vasif Rzayev		15/03/93	M	2	(1)	
27	Natiq Sährätov		10/10/90	G	2	(1)	
3	Anatoli Stukalov	KAZ	03/04/90	M	1	(1)	
25	Yaroslav Sukhanov	UKR	08/04/93	D	1		
18	Seymur Tağıyev		07/04/92	M		(2)	
28	Mikayıl Yusifov		24/04/82	D	2		
24	Ruslan Zubkov	UKR	24/11/91	D	10		
3	Ante Zurak	CRO	13/08/84	D	2		

 AZERBAIJAN

XÄZÄR LÄNKÄRAN FK

Coach: Yunis Hüseynov; (01/11/12) (Emin Quliyev);
(14/11/12) Carles Martorell Baqués (ESP);
(26/02/13) (Emin Quliyev);
(17/03/13) John Toshack (WAL)
2004 • Länkäran şähär märkäzi stadionu (15,000);
Mehdi Hüseynzadä adına Sumqayıt şähär stadionu
(15,000) • lankaranfc.com
Major honours
Azerbaijan League (1) 2007;
Azerbaijan Cup (3) 2007, 2008, 2011

2012
05/08	Rävan	a	1-1	Subašić
10/08	Käpäz	h	4-0	Scarlatache, Abışov, Pіţ, Alviž
19/08	İnter	a	0-0	
15/09	Neftçi	a	1-2	Sadio
20/09	Simurq	h	0-2	
29/09	Turan	a	1-2	Sadio
03/10	Olimpik-Şüvalan	a	2-0	Scarlatache 2
21/10	Qäbälä	h	1-1	Alviž (p)
27/10	Qarabağ	h	2-0	Sialmas 2
31/10	Sumqayıt	a	1-1	Kazımlı
04/11	Rävan	h	4-0	Pіţ, Sialmas 2, Sadio
18/11	Bakı	a	0-2	
24/11	Käpäz	a	1-0	Subašić (p)
02/12	Olimpik-Şüvalan	h	1-2	Subašić
06/12	Bakı	h	1-1	Ämirquliyev
10/12	Simurq	a	2-2	Abdullayev, og (Şemonayev)
14/12	Neftçi	h	2-1	Sialmas, Pіţ
20/12	Qarabağ	a	0-1	

2013
11/02	İnter	h	2-3	Pamuk, Ramazanov
17/02	Turan	h	4-2	Scarlatache 2, Gökhan, Sadio
23/02	Qäbälä	a	0-2	
03/03	Sumqayıt	h	2-2	Alviž 2 (2p)
12/03	Rävan	a	0-1	
30/03	Olimpik-Şüvalan	h	1-1	Álvaro Silva
06/04	Käpäz	a	2-1	Sialmas, Pіţ
13/04	Turan	a	2-2	Abdullayev, Alviž (p)
21/04	Sumqayıt	h	0-0	
28/04	Olimpik-Şüvalan	a	0-2	
03/05	Käpäz	h	1-0	Sadio
08/05	Turan	h	1-0	Kazımlı
13/05	Sumqayıt	a	0-1	
20/05	Rävan	h	1-2	Gökhan

No	Name	Nat	DoB	Pos	Aps	(s)	Gls
10	Elnur Abdullayev		16/02/86	M	18	(8)	2
42	Kamran Abdullazadä		20/03/95	M	1	(4)	
15	Ruslan Abışov		10/10/87	M	17		1
2	Elnur Allahverdiyev		02/11/83	D	21		
4	Álvaro Silva	ESP	30/03/84	D	11		1
6	Robert Alviž	CRO	06/09/84	M	22	(1)	5
14	Rahid Ämirquliyev		01/09/89	D	29	(1)	1
85	Kamal Bayramov		15/08/85	G	1		
99	Beto	BRA	25/10/81	A	2	(3)	
97	Elnur Cäfärov		28/03/97	A	1	(1)	
30	Toni Doblas	ESP	06/08/80	G	6	(1)	
8	Éder Bonfim	BRA	03/04/81	D	16	(1)	
24	Gökhan Güleç	TUR	25/09/85	A	6	(5)	2
17	Kazım Kazımlı		05/09/93	M	3	(9)	2
35	Luciano Olguín	ARG	09/03/82	A	3	(2)	
99	Marin Oršulić	CRO	25/08/87	M	10	(3)	
9	Uğur Pamuk		26/06/89	A	6	(4)	1
16	Adrian Pіţ	ROU	16/07/83	M	28		4
55	Ağabala Ramazanov		20/01/93	M	7	(12)	1
15	Tounkara Sadio	MLI	27/04/92	M	21	(7)	5
25	Orxan Sadıqlı		19/03/93	G	25		
27	Adrian Scarlatache	ROU	05/12/86	D	27		5
11	Dimitris Sialmas	GRE	19/06/86	A	14	(7)	6
9	Branimir Subašić		07/04/82	A	16		3
4	Akif Tağıyev		24/04/93	M		(3)	
21	Radomir Todorov	BUL	11/08/80	D	26		
3	Vanderson	BRA	27/09/84	D	15	(3)	

Top goalscorers

26	Nicolás Canales (Neftçi)
21	Nildo (Olimpik-Şüvälan)
14	Juan Varea (Rävan)
13	Richard (Qarabağ)
12	Salif Ballo (Turan)
9	Pardis Fardjad-Azad (Sumqayıt)
8	Bachana Tskhadadze (İnter)
	Yuriy Fomenko (Käpäz/İnter)
	Julius Wobay (Neftçi)
	Zouhir Benouahi (Olimpik-Şüvälan)
	Viktor Igbekoyi (Olimpik-Şüvälan)
	Mindaugas Kalonas (Rävan)

Second level

SECOND LEVEL FINAL TABLE 2012/13

		Pld	W	D	L	F	A	Pts
1	Ağsu FK	24	20	3	1	65	18	63
2	Qaradağ Lökbatan PFK	24	20	3	1	61	8	63
3	Neftçala FK	24	17	3	4	51	18	54
4	Şahdağ Qusar FK	24	12	6	6	40	30	42
5	MOİK Bakı PFK	24	11	6	7	39	28	39
6	Täräqqi Gäncä FK	24	12	1	11	24	24	37
7	Bakılı Bakı PFK	24	7	7	10	30	38	28
8	Lokomotiv-Bіläcäri FK	24	7	3	14	28	38	24
9	Şuşa PFK	24	7	2	15	29	40	23
10	Energetik Mingäçevir PFK	24	5	4	15	26	52	19
11	Qala FK	24	5	3	16	21	49	18
12	Göyäzän Qazax PFK	24	4	5	15	23	61	17
13	Şämkir FK	24	3	6	15	23	56	15

NB No promotion.

Domestic cup: Azärbaycan kuboku 2012/13

FIRST ROUND

(22/10/12)
Qala 2-4 Käpäz

(24/10/12)
MOİK 0-0 Bakılı Bakı *(aet; 3-1 on pens)*
Qaradağ Lökbatan 7-0 Lokomotiv
Şuşa 0-1 Neftçala
Täräqqi 3-1 Ağsu

1/8 FINALS

(28/11/12)
Bakı 3-1 Sumqayıt
Käpäz 0-2 Qarabağ *(aet)*
Qäbälä 2-0 Qaradağ Lökbatan
MOİK 0-3 İnter
Olimpik-Şüvalan 0-1 Simurq
Rävan 2-1 Neftçala
Täräqqi 0-5 Neftçi
Turan 1-1 Xäzär Länkäran *(aet; 3-5 on pens)*

QUARTER-FINALS

(27/02/13 & 07/03/13)
Bakı 1-1 İnter *(Näbiyev 90+2; Kandelaki 80)*
İnter 2-2 Bakı *(Tskhadadze 42, 60; Šolić 32, Ş Äliyev 68)*
(3-3; Bakı on away goals)
Qäbälä 1-1 Qarabağ *(Dodô 33; Nadirov 56)*
Qarabağ 0-0 Qäbälä
(1-1; Qarabağ on away goal)

Rävan 1-2 Xäzär Länkäran *(Zečević 6; Ämirquliyev 74, Pamuk 80)*
Xäzär Länkäran 4-1 Rävan *(Ramazanov 8, 81p, 90+2, Olguín 28; Adamović 69)*
(Xäzär Länkäran 6-2)

Simurq 0-0 Neftçi
Neftçi 1-0 Simurq *(Flavinho 120) (aet)*
(Neftçi 1-0)

SEMI-FINALS

(17/04/13 & 24/04/13)
Bakı 1-0 Xäzär Länkäran *(Pena 82p)*
Xäzär Länkäran 2-0 Bakı *(Ramazanov 45+1, Ämirquliyev 82)*
(Xäzär Länkäran 2-1)

Neftçi 2-1 Qarabağ *(A Abdullayev 62p, Nasimov 90; Nadirov 55)*
Qarabağ 2-2 Neftçi *(Richard 41p, Opara 86; Yunuszadä 42, Canales 77)*
(Neftçi 4-3)

FINAL

(28/05/13)
Tofiq Bähramov adına Respublika stadionu, Baku
NEFTÇİ PFK 0
XÄZÄR LÄNKÄRAN FK 0
(aet; 5-3 on pens)
Referee: Ağayev
NEFTÇİ: Stamenković, Şükürov, Yunuszadä, Dênis Silva, Bruno Bertucci, Sadiqov, Flavinho, Wobay, Ramos, A Abdullayev (Mehdiyev 98), Canales
XÄZÄR LÄNKÄRAN: Doblas, Vanderson (Pamuk 71), Álvaro Silva, Allahverdiyev, Éder Bonfim (Sadio 46), Abdullayev, Ämirquliyev, Todorov, Scarlatache, Ramazanov, Oršulić (Sialmas 51)

BELARUS

Belorusskaja Federacija Futbola (BFF)

Address	Prospekt Pobediteli 20/3	**President**	Sergei Roumas
	BY-220020 Minsk	**General secretary**	Sergei Safaryan
Tel	+375 172 545 600	**Media officer**	Aleksandr Aleinik
Fax	+375 172 544 478	**Year of formation**	1989
E-mail	info@bff.by	**National stadium**	Dinamo, Minsk
Website	bff.by		(40,000)

PREMIER LEAGUE CLUBS

 ① **FC BATE Borisov**

② **FC Belshina Bobruisk**

③ **FC Brest**
NB Renamed FC Dinamo Brest for 2013 season.

 ④ **FC Dinamo Minsk**

⑤ **FC Gomel**

 ⑥ **FC Minsk**

⑦ **FC Naftan Novopolotsk**

⑧ **FC Neman Grodno**

⑨ **FC Shakhtyor Soligorsk**

⑩ **FC Slavia Mozyr**

⑪ **FC Torpedo Zhodino**

PROMOTED CLUB

⑫ **FC Dnepr Mogilev**

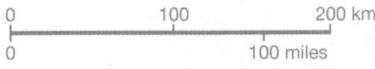

0 — 100 — 200 km
0 — 100 miles

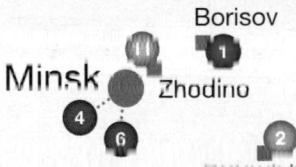

Novopolotsk ⑦

Borisov ①   Mogilev ⑫

Minsk   Zhodino
④   ⑥

Grodno ⑧   ② Bobruisk

⑨
Soligorsk

⑤ Gomel

Brest ③   Mozyr ⑩

KEY:

● – UEFA Champions League

● – UEFA Europa League

● – Promoted club

BATE in seventh heaven

FC BATE Borisov maintained their vice-like grip on the Belarusian Premier League in 2012, winning it for the seventh year in a row. It was the club's ninth title in all – a national record - and the fifth under their dynamic young coach Viktor Goncharenko.

Furthermore, BATE reached the UEFA Champions League group stage for the third time in five years and registered their first two wins - the second of them, remarkably, against eventual winners FC Bayern München.

Borisov outfit claim seventh successive domestic title

Goncharenko's team defeat Bayern 3-1 in Europe

FC Minsk overcome capital rivals Dinamo in cup final

Domestic league

In a Premier League reduced from 12 to 11 teams – and therefore from 33 to 30 matches – BATE increased their points tally from 66 to 68, which brought them a seven-point victory margin over FC Shakhtyor Soligorsk, who finished runners-up on 61 points for the second season running.

The title was secured two rounds from the end with a 5-1 home win over FC Minsk. The same opponents had defeated BATE 1-0 on the opening day, and as the perennial champions had also lost 2-0 to FC Gomel in the Super Cup, a sense of anticipation grew that the men from Borisov might be vulnerable. That notion was swiftly dismissed as Goncharenko's team reeled off 11 successive victories.

BATE were inspired once again by their Brazilian-born midfielder Renan Bressan, although he was unable to top the league's scoring charts for the third season running, finishing three goals adrift of Shakhtyor's Dmitri Osipenko. Another Shakhtyor striker, Dmitri Komarovski, ended up joint second, his 11 goals including a record-breaking five-minute hat-trick in an early-season 7-0 rout of FC Minsk.

FC Dinamo Minsk swapped positions with Gomel from 2011 to finish third, the mid-season appointment of ex-USSR striker Oleh Protasov proving pivotal as the team won eight and drew three of their last 13 games.

Domestic cup

Protasov also led Dinamo into the final of the Belarusian Cup, where they met local rivals FC Minsk. Vadim Skripchenko's side had lost the 2012 final on penalties to FC Naftan Novopolotsk but this time they prevailed by the same method after a 1-1 draw in Zhodino to take the trophy for the first time. Minsk were accustomed to late drama, having required added-time winners to defeat both Gomel and FC Torpedo Zhodino in the previous two rounds. Torpedo had earlier eliminated BATE – although at the time, in October, their opponents' focus was evidently elsewhere.

Europe

BATE reached a European group stage for the fifth successive season, returning to the UEFA Champions League proper for the third time after going unbeaten through six qualifying and play-off ties.

Goncharenko's men had failed to win a group game in the competition in 12 previous attempts, but they rectified that immediately by defeating LOSC Lille 3-1 away and then, even more sensationally, downing Bayern by the same scoreline a fortnight later in Minsk. Alas, they peaked too soon and lost their next four games to drop into the UEFA Europa League, where they were immediately eliminated by Fenerbahçe SK.

National team

The 2012/13 season began for national team coach Georgi Kondratiev at the London Olympics, where his side exited in the first round after defeats by Brazil and Egypt. Pitched into a desperately difficult 2014 FIFA World Cup qualifying section, the senior team, liberally sprinkled with Russian Premier-Liga players, lost their opening three games.

However, they responded well to being given the runaround by Spain in Minsk when, four days later, they gained their first points, goals from Stanislav Dragun and Bressan delivering a 2-0 win against Georgia. Just one point from two games against Finland in June ended the international season on a disappointing note.

Domestic league: Premier League 2012 final table

		Pld	Home					Away					Total					Pts
			W	D	L	F	A	W	D	L	F	A	W	D	L	F	A	
1	**FC BATE Borisov**	30	11	2	2	31	10	10	3	2	20	6	21	5	4	51	16	68
2	FC Shakhtyor Soligorsk	30	8	4	3	31	13	10	3	2	28	11	18	7	5	59	24	61
3	FC Dinamo Minsk	30	9	3	3	21	12	7	5	3	16	7	16	8	6	37	19	56
4	FC Gomel	30	7	5	3	22	9	7	3	5	17	15	14	8	8	39	24	50
5	FC Neman Grodno	30	6	5	4	23	15	4	6	5	20	21	10	11	9	43	36	41
6	FC Minsk	30	6	5	4	22	18	5	1	9	14	28	11	6	13	36	46	39
7	FC Belshina Bobruisk	30	6	5	4	17	13	1	4	10	9	27	7	9	14	26	40	30
8	FC Brest	30	6	2	7	18	15	2	3	10	9	23	8	5	17	27	38	29
9	FC Naftan Novopolotsk	30	5	3	7	13	18	2	5	8	10	22	7	8	15	23	40	29
10	FC Slavia Mozyr	30	6	3	6	13	17	1	3	11	9	41	7	6	17	22	58	27
11	FC Torpedo Zhodino	30	4	4	7	10	19	1	5	9	7	20	5	9	16	17	39	24

SEASON AT A GLANCE

EUROPEAN QUALIFICATION 2013/14

 Champion: FC BATE Borisov (second qualifying round)

 Cup winner: FC Minsk (second qualifying round)
FC Shakhtyor Soligorsk (second qualifying round)
FC Dinamo Minsk (first qualifying round)

Top scorer Dmitri Osipenko (Shakhtyor), 14 goals
Relegated clubs None
Promoted club FC Dnepr Mogilev
Cup final FC Minsk 1-1 FC Dinamo Minsk (aet; 4-1 on pens)

PLAYER OF THE SEASON
Stanislav Dragun
(FC Dinamo Minsk)

A commanding figure throughout the season, the Dinamo skipper was equally influential in attack and defence. The club's leading scorer with seven league goals, he came further to the fore with Belarus at the London Olympics and in FIFA World Cup qualifying. He joined Russian club PFC Krylya Sovetov Samara in early 2013.

NEWCOMER OF THE SEASON
Denis Polyakov
(FC BATE Borisov)

The young right-back lived up to expectations after joining the perennial champions from FC Shakhtyor Soligorsk. Quick-thinking and dependable, he swiftly established himself in the BATE starting XI at the age of 21 and was an ever-present in the UEFA Champions League. He also made his mark in the Belarus national side.

PREMIER LEAGUE TEAM OF THE SEASON
(4-4-2)
Coach: Goncharenko (BATE)

Gorbunov (BATE)

Polyakov (BATE) — Kashevski (Gomel) — Simić (BATE) — Bordachev (BATE)

Denisevich (Neman) — Dragun (Dinamo Minsk) — Renan Bressan (BATE) — Pavlov (BATE)

Rodionov (BATE) — Osipenko (Shakhtyor)

BELARUS

NATIONAL TEAM

Home Kit   Away Kit

TOP FIVE ALL-TIME CAPS
Aleksandr Kulchy (102); Sergei Gurenko (80); Sergei Omelyanchuk (74); Sergei Shtanyuk (71); Maksim Romashchenko (64)

TOP FIVE ALL-TIME GOALS
Maksim Romashchenko (20); Vitali Kutuzov (13); Vyacheslav Hleb & **Sergei Kornilenko** (12); Valentin Belkevich & Roman Vasilyuk (10)

Results 2012/13

Date	Opponent		Venue	Score	Scorers
15/08/12	Armenia	A	Yerevan	2-1	Renan Bressan (44, 66)
07/09/12	Georgia (WCQ)	A	Tbilisi	0-1	
11/09/12	France (WCQ)	A	Paris	1-3	Putilo (72)
12/10/12	Spain (WCQ)	H	Minsk	0-4	
16/10/12	Georgia (WCQ)	H	Minsk	2-0	Renan Bressan (6), Dragun (28)
14/11/12	Israel	A	Jerusalem	2-1	Kislyak (45+1), Balanovich (46)
06/02/13	Hungary	N	Belek (TUR)	1-1	Volodko (58)
21/03/13	Jordan	A	Amman	0-1	
25/03/13	Canada	N	Doha (QAT)	2-0	Rodionov (29), Khvashchinski (87)
03/06/13	Estonia	A	Tallinn	2-0	Putilo (32), Rodionov (80)
07/06/13	Finland (WCQ)	A	Helsinki	0-1	
11/06/13	Finland (WCQ)	H	Gomel	1-1	Verkhovtsov (85)

Appearances 2012/13

Coach: **Georgi Kondratiev**   07/01/60

Player	DOB	Club	Arm	GEO	FRA	ESP	GEO	Isr	Hun	Jor	Can	Est	FIN	FIN	Caps	Goals
Sergei Veremko	16/10/82	Krylya Sovetov (RUS)	G46	G	G	G	G	G	G	G			G	G	21	-
Maksim Zhavnerchik	09/02/85	Kuban (RUS)	D	D34				D							6	-
Aleksandr Martynovich	26/08/87	Krasnodar (RUS)	D	D	D	D		D	D			D46	D	D80	31	2
Dmitri Verkhovtsov	10/10/86	Krylya Sovetov (RUS)	D	D	D70		D	s46	D	D	D	D		D	35	3
Maksim Bordachev	18/06/86	BATE	D60	s30	D	D	D	s73	D			D	D	D	25	2
Yan Tigorev	10/03/84	Lokomotiv Moskva (RUS)	M	M62		M	M	M46		M46					28	-
Sergei Kislyak	06/08/87	Krasnodar (RUS) /Rubin (RUS)	M46		M	s46	s83	M	M78	s46	s51	M	M	s46	36	4
Renan Bressan	03/11/88	BATE /Alania (RUS)	M71	M	M46	s65	M85	s46	M	M	M46	M46		s64	13	3
Pavel Nekhaichik	15/07/88	Dinamo Moskva (RUS) /BATE	M	M30								M72	s17 91*		8	-
Anton Putilo	10/06/87	Freiburg (GER) /Volga (RUS)	M97	M	M		M84	M			M89	M72	M	M64	35	6
Sergei Kornilenko	14/06/83	Krylya Sovetov (RUS)	A46	A	s62			A65							56	12
Yuri Zhevnov	17/04/81	Zenit (RUS)	s46												53	-
Dmitri Komarovski	10/10/86	Shakhtyor Soligorsk	s46												3	-
Stanislav Dragun	04/06/88	Dinamo Minsk /Krylya Sovetov (RUS)	s46	s62	M	M79	M	M	M53	M46	M51		M66	M	16	3
Oleg Veretilo	10/07/88	Dinamo Minsk	s60							s46	D		D46		6	-
Andrei Khachaturyan	02/09/87	Shakhtyor Soligorsk	s71						s78						2	-
Sergei Balanovich	29/08/87	Shakhtyor Soligorsk	s97	s34	s70			M89	s46	M63	M79	s62	M17		10	1
Denis Polyakov	17/04/91	BATE			D	D	D								4	-
Aleksandr Kulchy	01/11/73	Sibir (RUS)		M	s46										102	5
Artem Radkov	26/08/85	BATE			D					D					11	-
Vitali Rodionov	11/12/83	BATE			A62	A65	A91		A80	A68	A81	s72	A	A	37	8
Igor Shitov	24/10/86	Mordovia (RUS)			D					D	D	D	D79		37	1
Pavel Plaskonny	29/01/85	Dinamo Minsk			D										16	1
Yegor Filipenko	10/04/88	BATE			D	D	D46		D			s46	D		25	-
Aleksandr Volodko	18/06/86	BATE				M46	s85	s84	s53						4	1
Aleksandr Hleb	01/05/81	BATE				M	M					s72	M	M	60	6
Andrei Chukhlei	02/10/87	Ural (RUS)				s79	s91			M46	s89				6	-
Aleksandr Pavlov	18/08/84	BATE					M83			s46	s46	s46	s66		13	-
Vitali Trubilo	07/01/85	Dinamo Minsk							D73	M46	D46			D	12	-
Ilya Aleksiyevich	10/02/91	Gomel /BATE						s65							3	-
Vladimir Khvashchinski	10/05/90	Brest /Dinamo Minsk						s89	s80	s68	s81				4	1
Edgar Olekhnovich	17/05/87	BATE							s46	M	M46		M		4	-
Aleksandr Gutor	18/04/89	Dinamo Minsk								G	G				2	-
Maksim Skavysh	13/11/89	Baltika (RUS)										A62			1	-
Pavel Sitko	17/12/85	Shakhtyor Soligorsk										s46	s80		13	1
Timofei Kalachev	01/05/81	Rostov (RUS)											s79	M	55	7

European club competitions 2012/13

FC BATE BORISOV

CHAMPIONS
LEAGUE

Second qualifying round - FK Vardar (MKD)
H 3-2 *Mozolevski (41), Rodionov (90+2, 90+4)*
Gorbunov, Likhtarovich (Rudik 69), Volodko, Mozolevski, Radkov, Pavlov (Kontsevoi 69), Bordachev, Rodionov, Simić, Olekhnovich, Polyakov. Coach: Viktor Goncharenko (BLR)
A 0-0
Gorbunov, Likhtarovich (Rudik 73), Yurevich, Kontsevoi, Volodko, Mozolevski (Pavlov 79), Radkov, Bordachev, Rodionov, Simić, Olekhnovich. Coach: Viktor Goncharenko (BLR)

Third qualifying round - Debreceni VSC (HUN)
H 1-1 *Sidibe (90+3og)*
Gorbunov, Likhtarovich (Rudik 56), Yurevich, Kontsevoi (Pavlov 56), Volodko, Mozolevski, Radkov, Hleb (Vasilyuk 74), Bordachev, Rodionov, Simić. Coach: Viktor Goncharenko (BLR)
A 2-0 *Mozolevski (26), Volodko (59)*
Gorbunov, Volodko (Rudik 84), Mozolevski, Rudik, Hleb, Bordachev, Rodionov (Pavlov 84), Simić, Olekhnovich, Baga (Yurevich 16), Polyakov. Coach: Viktor Goncharenko (BLR)

Play-offs - Hapoel Kiryat Shmona FC (ISR)
H 2-0 *Rodionov (29, 78)*
Gorbunov, Likhtarovich (Pavlov 62), Volodko, Renan Bressan (Sivakov 83), Mozolevski (Vasilyuk 62), Radkov, Hleb, Bordachev, Rodionov, Simić, Polyakov. Coach: Viktor Goncharenko (BLR)
A 1-1 *Pavlov (90+4)*
Gorbunov, Likhtarovich (Yurevich 60), Volodko, Mozolevski, Radkov, Hleb (Pavlov 63), Bordachev, Rodionov, Simić, Sivakov (Olekhnovich 83), Polyakov. Coach: Viktor Goncharenko (BLR)

Group F
Match 1 - LOSC Lille (FRA)
A 3-1 *Volodko (6), Rodionov (20), Olekhnovich (43)*
Gorbunov, Likhtarovich (Sivakov 66), Volodko, Radkov, Hleb, Pavlov (Renan Bressan 80), Bordachev, Rodionov (Mozolevski 89), Simić, Olekhnovich, Polyakov. Coach: Viktor Goncharenko (BLR)

Match 2 - FC Bayern München (GER)
H 3-1 *Pavlov (23), Rodionov (78), Renan Bressan (90+4)*
Gorbunov, Likhtarovich (Sivakov 66), Volodko, Hleb, Pavlov (Renan Bressan 84), Bordachev, Rodionov (Mozolevski 87), Filipenko, Simić, Olekhnovich, Polyakov. Coach: Viktor Goncharenko (BLR)
Match 3 - Valencia CF (ESP)
H 0-3
Gorbunov, Likhtarovich (Sivakov 53), Volodko (Renan Bressan 75), Hleb, Pavlov (Mozolevski 66), Bordachev, Rodionov, Filipenko, Simić, Olekhnovich, Polyakov. Coach: Viktor Goncharenko (BLR)
Match 4 - Valencia CF (ESP)
A 2-4 *Renan Bressan (53), Mozolevski (83)*
Gorbunov, Likhtarovich (Sivakov 55), Volodko, Renan Bressan (Kontsevoi 88), Radkov, Hleb (Mozolevski 77), Bordachev, Rodionov, Filipenko, Baga, Polyakov. Coach: Viktor Goncharenko (BLR)
Match 5 - LOSC Lille (FRA)
H 0-2
Gorbunov, Volodko (Kontsevoi 46), Renan Bressan, Radkov, Hleb (Sivakov 77), Bordachev, Rodionov, Filipenko, Olekhnovich (Vasilyuk 83), Baga, Polyakov. Coach: Viktor Goncharenko (BLR)
Match 6 - FC Bayern München (GER)
A 1-4 *Filipenko (89)*
Gorbunov, Kontsevoi (Renan Bressan 58), Volodko, Radkov, Hleb, Bordachev (Yurevich 84), Rodionov (Vasilyuk 66), Filipenko, Olekhnovich, Baga, Polyakov. Coach: Viktor Goncharenko (BLR)
Red card: Polyakov 69

EUROPA
LEAGUE

Round of 32 - Fenerbahçe SK (TUR)
H 0-0
Gorbunov, Yurevich, Volodko, Radkov, Hleb (Kurlovich 79), Bordachev, Rodionov, Filipenko, Olekhnovich, Baga (Mozolevski 64), Rudik (Pavlov 46). Coach: Viktor Goncharenko (BLR)
A 0-1
Gorbunov, Yurevich (Aleksiyevich 75), Volodko (Pavlov 64), Hleb, Bordachev (Mozolevski 84), Rodionov, Filipenko, Olekhnovich, Baga, Gaiduchik, Rudik. Coach: Viktor Goncharenko (BLR)
Red card: Baga 20

FC NAFTAN NOVOPOLOTSK

EUROPA
LEAGUE

Second qualifying round - FK Crvena zvezda (SRB)
H 3-4 *Gavryushko (47p, 67), Zhukovski (76)*
Dovgyallo, Kobets (Zhukovski 73), Berezovskiy, Gorbachev, Trukhov, Bukatkin, Černych, Naumov, Kovalenko (Gavryushko 46), Zyulev (Obrazov 27), Sorokin. Coach: Igor Kovalevich (BLR)
A 3-3 *Sorokin (21), Naumov (58), Kovalenko (82)*
Dovgyallo, Kobets (Zhukovski 82), Berezovskiy, Gorbachev, Trukhov, Bukatkin, Černych, Naumov, Gavryushko (Kovalenko 59), Sorokin (Zyulev 63), Obrazov. Coach: Vasili Zaitsev (BLR)
Red card: Bukatkin 68

FC SHAKHTYOR SOLIGORSK

EUROPA
LEAGUE

Second qualifying round - SV Ried (AUT)
H 1-1 *Osipenko (44)*
Tsygalko, Balanovich (Tsevan 84), Kolomyts, Postnikov, Yanushkevich, Grenkov, Komarovski, Sitko (Rios 80), Khachaturyan, Rozhkov, Osipenko (Leonchik 88). Coach: Vladimir Zhuravel (BLR)
A 0-0
Tsygalko, Balanovich, Kolomyts, Postnikov, Yanushkevich, Grenkov, Komarovski (Leonchik 79), Sitko (Rios 80), Khachaturyan, Rozhkov, Osipenko. Coach: Vladimir Zhuravel (BLR)

FC GOMEL

First qualifying round - Víkingur (FRO)
A 6-0 Hleb (53, 55), Voronkov (57), Aleksiyevich (58), Kashevski (69), Levitski (80)
Ostojić, Voronkov, Matveichik (Timoshenko 68), Kirilchik, Kashevski, Aleksiyevich, Hleb, Klimovich, Kuzmenok, Nowak (Levitski 46), Demidovich (Platonov 59). Coach: Oleg Kubarev (BLR)
H 4-0 Demidovich (49, 56), Kashevski (71), Timoshenko (88)
Sakovich, Lutsevich, Kirilchik, Kashevski, Kozeka, Yevseyenko (Matveichik 46), Timoshenko, Levitski, Nowak (Hleb 46; Yakhno 64), Platonov, Demidovich. Coach: Oleg Kubarev (BLR)

Second qualifying round - FK Renova (MKD)
A 2-0 Demidovich (20), Nowak (39)
Ostojić, Voronkov (Yevseyenko 70), Matveichik, Kirilchik, Kashevski, Kozeka, Klimovich, Levitski, Nowak (Timoshenko 68), Platonov, Demidovich (Yakhno 84). Coach: Oleg Kubarev (BLR)
H 0-1
Bushma, Voronkov, Matveichik (Yevseyenko 90+2), Kirilchik, Kashevski, Kozeka, Klimovich, Levitski, Nowak , Platonov, Demidovich (Timoshenko 77). Coach: Oleg Kubarev (BLR)

Third qualifying round - Liverpool FC (ENG)
H 0-1
Bushma, Voronkov, Matveichik, Kirilchik, Kashevski, Kozeka (Timoshenko 90), Alumona, Klimovich, Levitski (Demidovich 84), Nowak (Lipatkin 74), Platonov. Coach: Oleg Kubarev (BLR)
A 0-3
Bushma, Voronkov, Matveichik, Kashevski, Kozeka (Kirilchik 75), Aleksiyevich, Alumona, Klimovich (Yevseyenko 86), Kuzmenok, Nowak (Lipatkin 63), Platonov. Coach: Oleg Kubarev (BLR)

FC BATE BORISOV
Coach: Viktor Goncharenko
1996 • City Stadium (5,392) • fcbate.by
Major honours
Belarusian League (9) 1999, 2002, 2006, 2007, 2008, 2009 2010, 2011, 2012;
Belarusian Cup (2) 2006, 2010

2012

Date	Opponent		Score	Scorers
24/03	Minsk	a	0-1	
31/03	Belshina	h	3-1	Mozolevski 2, Renan Bressan
06/04	Brest	a	2-0	Kontsevoi, Rodionov
14/04	Neman	h	2-0	Mozolevski 2
21/04	Dinamo Minsk	a	2-0	Baga 2
28/04	Shakhtyor	h	1-0	Mozolevski
03/05	Torpedo	a	2-0	Renan Bressan, Mozolevski
07/05	Naftan	h	3-0	Mozolevski, Baga, Kontsevoi
12/05	Gomel	a	1-0	Baga
18/05	Slavia	h	2-1	Rodionov, Renan Bressan
24/05	Minsk	h	2-0	Rodionov 2
11/06	Belshina	a	1-0	Rudik
15/06	Brest	h	0-1	
27/06	Neman	a	2-1	Kontsevoi, Baga
01/07	Dinamo Minsk	h	1-3	Renan Bressan
07/07	Shakhtyor	a	1-1	Olekhnovich
13/07	Torpedo	h	0-0	
12/08	Naftan	a	4-0	Simić, Renan Bressan, Pavlov, Vasilyuk
17/08	Gomel	h	0-0	
02/09	Gomel	a	2-1	Vasilyuk, Renan Bressan
15/09	Torpedo	h	2-0	Pavlov, Simić
23/09	Dinamo Minsk	a	0-0	
28/09	Neman	h	5-1	Renan Bressan 2 (1p), Pavlov, Rodionov 2
07/10	Belshina	a	1-0	Rudik
18/10	Slavia	a	2-1	Kurlovich, Mozolevski
28/10	Brest	h	3-1	Olekhnovich, Mozolevski, Renan Bressan
03/11	Naftan	a	0-1	
11/11	Minsk	h	5-1	Renan Bressan 2 (1p), og (Rakhmanov), Rodionov 2
17/11	Slavia	a	0-0	
25/11	Shakhtyor	h	2-1	Olekhnovich, Kontsevoi

No	Name	Nat	DoB	Pos	Aps	(s)	Gls
25	Dmitri Baga		04/01/90	M	17	(3)	5
11	Zaven Bodoyan	ARM	22/10/89	M	2	(4)	
18	Maksim Bordachev		18/06/86	D	18	(2)	
21	Yegor Filipenko		10/04/88	D	18	(1)	
35	Andrei Gorbunov		29/05/83	G	27		
30	Aleksandr Gutor		18/04/89	G	3		
15	Aleksandr Hleb		01/05/81	M	5	(1)	
7	Artem Kontsevoi		20/05/83	M	14	(5)	4
24	Yevgeni Kuntsevich		16/08/88	D	1	(1)	
27	Vadim Kurlovich		30/10/92	M	1	(3)	1
2	Dmitri Likhtarovich		01/03/78	M	10	(9)	
9	Maycon	BRA	06/06/86	M			
13	Dmitri Mozolevski		30/04/85	A	17	(5)	9
23	Edgar Olekhnovich		17/05/87	M	13	(7)	3
17	Aleksandr Pavlov		18/08/84	M	15	(6)	3
33	Denis Polyakov		17/04/91	D	22	(2)	
14	Artem Radkov		26/08/85	D	27		
10	Renan Bressan		03/11/88	M	21	(5)	11
20	Vitali Rodionov		11/12/83	A	19	(11)	8
77	Filipp Rudik		22/03/87	M	13	(5)	2
22	Marko Simić	SRB	16/06/87	D	22		2
32	Mikhail Sivakov		16/01/88	M	7		
78	Roman Vasilyuk		23/11/78	A	6	(3)	2
8	Aleksandr Volodko		18/06/86	M	14	(11)	
5	Aleksandr Yurevich		08/08/79	D	18	(4)	

FC BELSHINA BOBRUISK
Coach: Sergei Yaromko; (20/07/12) Vitali Pavlov; (23/07/12) Aleksandr Sednev
1976 • Spartak (3,700); Lokomotiv, Zhlobin (2,380) • fcbelshina.by
Major honours
Belarusian League (1) 2001;
Belarusian Cup (3) 1997, 1999, 2001

2012

Date	Opponent		Score	Scorers
24/03	Brest	h	3-1	Bliznyuk 2, Skavysh
31/03	BATE	a	1-3	Maltsev
06/04	Neman	h	0-0	
10/04	Dinamo Minsk	a	0-1	
14/04	Shakhtyor	h	0-4	
21/04	Torpedo	a	1-0	Gordeichuk
29/04	Naftan	h	0-0	
03/05	Gomel	a	0-1	
07/05	Slavia	h	3-0	Gordeichuk, Bliznyuk, Kabanov
12/05	Minsk	a	0-3	
11/06	BATE	h	0-1	
15/06	Neman	a	0-1	
19/06	Brest	a	1-1	Skavysh
23/06	Dinamo Minsk	a	1-0	Bliznyuk
27/06	Shakhtyor	a	1-2	Gordeichuk
01/07	Torpedo	h	0-0	
07/07	Naftan	a	0-3	
11/08	Slavia	a	0-1	
19/08	Minsk	h	3-0	Branfilov, Skavysh, Kovb
01/09	Torpedo	a	2-2	Bulyga, Kovb
15/09	Dinamo Minsk	h	0-2	
22/09	Neman	a	0-0	
07/10	BATE	h	0-1	
14/10	Gomel	h	1-1	Bliznyuk
20/10	Brest	a	0-4	
27/10	Naftan	h	3-2	Yatsenko, Khaletski, Mrinski
03/11	Minsk	a	2-2	Tolkanitsa, Bulyga
10/11	Slavia	h	0-0	
17/11	Shakhtyor	a	1-3	Kovb
25/11	Gomel	h	3-1	Bulyga 2, Skavysh

No	Name	Nat	DoB	Pos	Aps	(s)	Gls
9	Gennadi Bliznyuk		30/07/80	A	24	(1)	5
7	Nikolai Branfilov		16/12/77	D	24		1
8	Vitali Bulyga		12/01/80	D	11		4
3	Aleksandr Bylina		26/03/81	D	23	(1)	
22	Dominykas Galkevičius	LTU	16/10/86	M	4	(3)	
26	Mikhail Gordeichuk		23/10/89	M	16	(6)	3
77	Taras Kabanov	UKR	23/01/83	A	7	(5)	1
4	Aleksei Khaletski		19/06/84	D	8	(1)	1
1	Ruslan Kopantsov		12/05/81	G	13		
5	Mikhail Kostin	RUS	10/03/85	A	10	(1)	
39	Dmitri Kovb		20/01/87	A	6	(6)	3
17	Igor Lisitsa		10/04/88	M	14	(8)	
11	Yevgeni Loshankov		02/01/79	M	7	(1)	
14	Igor Maltsev		11/03/86	M	8	(6)	1
10	Viktor Melnyk	UKR	11/08/80	M	11		
21	Aleksandr Mrinski		09/08/90	A		(5)	1
19	Aleksandr Perepechko		07/04/89	M	10	(4)	
2	Aleksandr Shagoiko		27/07/80	D	26	(1)	
15	Maksim Skavysh		13/11/89	A	18	(12)	4
22	Denys Skepskiy	UKR	05/07/87	M	14	(2)	
30	Simas Skinderis	LTU	17/02/81	G	17		
11	Aleksei Timoshenko		09/12/86	M	8		
23	Aleksandr Tolkanitsa		09/05/89	M	10	(11)	1
8	Olexiy Tupchiy	UKR	22/08/86	M	8		
14	Dmitri Turlin		08/09/85	M	6	(11)	
44	Olexandr Yatsenko	UKR	24/02/85	D	27	(1)	1
55	Eduard Zhevnerov		01/11/87	D		(2)	

FC BREST

Coach: Sergei Kovalchuk;
(09/07/12) Vladimir Kurnev
1960 • GOSK Brestskiy (10,080) • dynamo.brest.by
Major honours
Belarusian Cup (1) 2007

2012

24/03	Belshina	a	1-3	Matyukhevich
06/04	BATE	h	0-2	
10/04	Neman	a	1-1	Premudrov
14/04	Dinamo Minsk	h	1-2	Khvashchinski
21/04	Shakhtyor	a	1-0	Khvashchinski
29/04	Torpedo	h	1-0	Khvashchinski
03/05	Naftan	a	0-1	
07/05	Gomel	h	0-1	
12/05	Slavia	a	1-2	Gogoladze
16/05	Minsk	h	0-1	
15/06	BATE	a	1-0	Zabara
19/06	Belshina	h	1-1	Burko
23/06	Neman	a	1-1	Khvashchinski
27/06	Dinamo Minsk	a	0-1	
01/07	Shakhtyor	h	1-2	Burko
07/07	Torpedo	a	0-1	
13/07	Naftan	h	2-1	Sokol, Gogoladze
19/08	Slavia	h	1-2	Kutsenko (p)
26/08	Minsk	a	1-2	Gogoladze
02/09	Shakhtyor	a	2-4	Gogoladze, Khvashchinski
15/09	Gomel	h	2-1	Sokol (p), Goncearov
22/09	Torpedo	a	0-0	
30/09	Dinamo Minsk	h	2-0	Papush, Khvashchinski
07/10	Neman	a	0-3	
20/10	Belshina	h	4-0	Gogoladze, Khvashchinski 2, Kutsenko
27/10	BATE	a	1-3	Khvashchinski
01/11	Naftan	a	0-2	
10/11	Naftan	a	1-1	
17/11	Minsk	a	0-0	
25/11	Slavia	h	2-0	Kutsenko, Klopotski

No	Name	Nat	DoB	Pos	Aps	(s)	Gls
5	Kirill Aleksiyuk			M	8		
6	Igor Burko		09/09/08	D			
87	Yuriy Druchyk	UKR	02/02/87	D	10	(1)	
23	Valeri Fomichev		23/03/88	G	21		
24	Vitali Gaiduchik		12/07/89	D	28		
25	Ucha Gogoladze	GEO	02/05/90	A	17	(10)	5
19	Aleksei Goncearov	MDA	21/02/84	D	10	(5)	1
10	Vladimir Khvashchinski		10/05/90	A	28		9
1	Andrei Klimovich		27/08/88	G	9		
4	Yevgeni Klopotski		12/08/93	D	17	(2)	1
28	Valeriy Kutsenko	UKR	02/11/86	D	11	(1)	3
7	Dmitri Makar		01/10/81	M	1	(2)	
15	Aleksandr Matyukhevich		02/04/90	A	8	(8)	1
88	Simon Ogar Veron	NGA	24/04/87	M	28		
14	Olexandr Papush	UKR	14/01/85	M	18	(7)	1
9	Gedeminas Paulauskas	LTU	27/10/82	D	4	(2)	
16	Kirill Premudrov		11/06/92	M	18	(3)	1
27	Serhiy Semenyuk	UKR	27/01/91	D	18	(4)	
30	Andrei Shemruk		27/04/94	A	10	(7)	
9	Kirill Shreitor		06/08/86	A	9	(3)	
20	Nikolai Signevich		20/02/92	A	2	(6)	
31	Viktor Sokol		09/05/81	M	10	(12)	2
22	Andrei Solovei		13/12/94	M		(6)	
11	Sergei Vabishchevich		15/03/93	M	2	(3)	
5	Olexandr Zabara	UKR	05/07/84	M	12	(3)	1

FC DINAMO MINSK

Coach: Aleksandr Sednev;
(09/07/12) Oleh Protasov (UKR)
1927 • Dinamo-Yuni (4,500); Dinamo (40,000) •
dinamo-minsk.by
Major honours
USSR League (1) 1982;
*Belarusian League (7) 1992, 1993, 1994, 1995 (spring),
1995 (autumn), 1997, 2004;*
Belarusian Cup (3) 1992, 1994, 2003

2012

25/03	Gomel	a	0-0	
01/04	Slavia	h	3-1	Dragun, Politevich, Plaskonny
06/04	Minsk	a	0-0	
10/04	Belshina	h	1-0	Afanasiyev
14/04	Brest	a	2-1	Damjanović 2
21/04	BATE	h	0-2	
29/04	Neman	a	0-0	
07/05	Shakhtyor	h	1-2	Simović
12/05	Torpedo	h	0-0	
16/05	Naftan	h	4-2	Damjanović 3, Kibuk
11/06	Slavia	a	2-0	Pankovets, og (Kovalevski)
15/06	Minsk	h	1-0	Plaskonny
19/06	Gomel	h	0-1	
23/06	Belshina	a	0-1	
27/06	Brest	h	1-0	Zita
01/07	BATE	a	3-1	Afanasiyev, og (Polyakov), Figueredo
08/08	Neman	h	1-1	Stasevich
12/08	Shakhtyor	a	0-0	
18/08	Torpedo	h	2-0	Politevich, Damjanović
26/08	Naftan	a	2-0	Figueredo, Dragun
02/09	Neman	h	1-0	Dragun
15/09	Belshina	h	2-0	Dragun, Figueredo
23/09	BATE	h	0-0	
30/09	Brest	a	0-2	
07/10	Naftan	h	1-1	Dragun
20/10	Minsk	a	2-0	Cócaro, Dragun
27/10	Slavia	a	4-1	Stasevich 2, Figueredo
04/11	Shakhtyor	a	1-1	Danilov
10/11	Gomel	h	1-0	Figueredo
17/11	Torpedo	a	2-0	Dragun, Figueredo (p)

No	Name	Nat	DoB	Pos	Aps	(s)	Gls
8	Mikhail Afanasiyev		04/11/86	M	14	(12)	2
7	Aleksandr Bychenok		30/05/85	M	8	(4)	
24	Artem Bykov		19/10/92	M	1	(3)	
23	Danilo Cócaro	URU	22/08/91	A	7	(5)	2
11	Jovan Damjanović	SRB	04/10/82	A	21	(4)	6
99	Aleksandr Danilov		10/09/80	M	26		1
2	Stanislav Dragun		04/06/88	M	29		7
21	Hernán Figueredo	URU	15/05/85	M	14	(2)	6
32	Dmitri Gushchenko		12/05/88	G	2		
14	Vitali Kibuk		07/01/89	A	1	(15)	1
17	Aleksandr Kondratyev		02/02/90	D		(2)	
18	Nikita Korzun		06/03/95	M		(1)	
15	Pavel Kruk		03/02/92	D	2		
80	Leonardo	BRA	09/06/92	A		(5)	
5	Maxym Lisovyi	UKR	21/05/85	M	6	(5)	
33	Dmitri Molosh		10/12/81	D	2		
4	Aleksei Pankovets		18/04/81	D	13	(2)	1
3	Pavel Plaskonny		29/01/85	D	26		2
6	Sergei Politevich		09/04/90	D	27		2
10	Gleb Rossadkin		05/04/95	A		(5)	
44	Slobodan Simović	SRB	25/05/89	M	25	(3)	1
22	Igor Stasevich		21/10/85	M	28	(1)	3
1	Aleksandr Sulima		01/08/79	G	28		
9	Dmytro Tereshchenko	UKR	04/04/87	M	4	(2)	
85	Vitali Trubilo		07/01/85	D	7	(3)	
20	Oleg Veretilo		10/07/88	D	26		
25	Yaroslav Yampol	UKR	21/04/90	M	1	(7)	
13	Bruno Mbanangoyé Zita	GAB	15/07/80	M	12	(5)	1

FC GOMEL

Coach: Oleg Kubarev
1995 • Traktor (17,600) • fcgomel.by
Major honours
Belarusian League (1) 2003;
Belarusian Cup (2) 2002, 2011

2012

25/03	Dinamo Minsk	h	0-0	
31/03	Shakhtyor	a	2-1	Hleb, Sheryakov
06/04	Torpedo	h	2-0	Kashevski, Kozeka
10/04	Naftan	h	0-0	
21/04	Slavia	h	3-0	Platonov, Nowak, Demidovich
29/04	Minsk	a	2-1	Platonov, Kashevski
03/05	Belshina	h	1-0	Platonov
07/05	Brest	a	1-0	Aleksiyevich
12/05	BATE	h	0-1	
18/05	Neman	a	3-0	Sheryakov 2, Kashevski
19/06	Dinamo Minsk	a	1-0	Nowak
11/06	Shakhtyor	h	1-1	Hleb
15/06	Torpedo	a	0-1	
23/06	Naftan	a	1-0	Demidovich
08/07	Minsk	h	2-2	Kashevski, Platonov
17/08	BATE	a	0-1	
26/08	Neman	h	1-1	Kashevski
02/09	BATE	h	1-2	Aleksiyevich
08/09	Slavia	a	2-0	Tigirlas, Platonov
15/09	Brest	a	1-2	Tigirlas
22/09	Naftan	h	2-0	Aleksiyevich, Kashevski
29/09	Minsk	a	1-1	Kashevski (p)
07/10	Slavia	h	4-1	Tigirlas, Sheryakov, Alumona, Voronkov
14/10	Belshina	a	1-1	Nowak
20/10	Shakhtyor	a	1-4	Platonov
01/11	Brest	h	2-0	Platonov, Tigirlas
04/11	Torpedo	h	3-0	Kozeka, Sheryakov 2 (1p)
10/11	Dinamo Minsk	a	0-1	
17/11	Neman	h	0-1	
25/11	Belshina	a	1-3	Platonov

No	Name	Nat	DoB	Pos	Aps	(s)	Gls
8	Ilya Aleksiyevich			M	25	(2)	3
9	Aleksandr Alumona	RUS	18/12/83	A		(6)	1
1	Vladimir Bushma		24/11/83	G	24		
23	Grigori Chetverik	RUS	19/03/88	M		(1)	
17	Vadim Demidovich		20/09/85	A	4	(9)	2
17	Vladimir Demidovich	EGY	18/02/82	M	4	(1)	
9	Vyacheslav Hleb		12/02/83	M	10	(2)	2
6	Nikolai Kashevski		05/10/80	D	27	(1)	7
5	Pavel Kirilchik		04/01/81	M	13	(8)	
13	Dmitri Klimovich		09/01/84	D	28		
7	Sergei Kozeka		17/09/86	D	25	(4)	2
20	Sergei Kubarev		17/06/92	M	1		
25	Igor Kuzmenok		06/07/90	D	28		
21	Artur Levitski		17/03/85	M	6	(8)	
19	Nikolai Lipatkin	RUS	23/05/86	A	2	(5)	
3	Sergei Matveichik		05/06/88	M	21	(1)	
17	Vitali Novik		01/01/94	M		(1)	
26	Tomasz Nowak	POL	30/10/85	M	16	(8)	3
33	Srdjan Ostojić	SRB	10/01/83	G	5		
92	Ezequiel Palomeque	COL	07/10/92	D	2		
32	Dmitri Platonov		07/02/86	A	21	(7)	8
16	Andrei Sakovich		15/04/92	G	1		
11	Andriy Sheryakov	UKR	10/11/82	A	12	(8)	6
27	Igor Tigirlas	MDA	24/02/84	M	11	(4)	4
18	Aleksei Timoshenko		09/12/86	M		(3)	
18	Olexiy Tupchiy	UKR	22/08/86	M	3	(5)	
2	Ihor Voronkov	UKR	24/04/81	M	28	(2)	1
10	Pavel Yevseyenko		30/10/80	M	5	(1)	

FC MINSK

Coach: Vadim Skripchenko
1995 • Dinamo (40,000); Torpedo (5,200) • fcminsk.by
Major honours
Belarusian Cup (1) 2013

2012

24/03	BATE	h	1-0	Razin	
31/03	Neman	a	1-0	Pavlyuchek	
06/04	Dinamo Minsk	h	0-0		
10/04	Shakhtyor	a	0-7		
14/04	Torpedo	h	1-2	Razin (p)	
20/04	Naftan	a	3-1	Razin (p), Kovel, Vasilyuk	
29/04	Gomel	h	1-2	Sachivko	
03/05	Slavia	a	0-1		
12/05	Belshina	h	3-0	Vasilyuk 2, Kovel	
16/05	Brest	h	1-0	Kovel	
24/05	BATE	a	0-2		
11/06	Neman	h	4-4	Kovel, Sachivko, Mayevski, Razin	
15/06	Dinamo Minsk	a	0-1		
23/06	Shakhtyor	h	0-2		
27/06	Torpedo	a	1-2	Kovel	
01/07	Naftan	h	1-0	Kovel	
08/07	Gomel	a	2-2	Vasilyuk, Gigevich	
14/07	Slavia	h	3-2	Vasilyuk, Gigevich, Sachivko	
19/08	Belshina	a	0-3		
26/08	Brest	h	2-1	Kovel, Wojciechowski	
15/09	Slavia	h	3-0	Razin, Wojciechowski, Gigevich	
22/09	Shakhtyor	a	2-0	Wojciechowski, Levitski	
29/09	Gomel	h	1-1	Kovel	
07/10	Torpedo	a	0-1		
20/10	Dinamo Minsk	h	0-2		
27/10	Neman	a	1-2	Razin	
03/11	Belshina	h	2-2	Wojciechowski, Gigevich	
11/11	BATE	a	1-5	Wojciechowski	
17/11	Brest	h	0-0		
25/11	Naftan	a	2-1	Rozhok 2	

No	Name	Nat	DoB	Pos	Aps	(s)	Gls
2	Roman Begunov		22/03/93	D	15	(4)	
4	Jean Claude Bozga	ROU	01/06/84	D	16	(1)	
25	Aboubacar Camara	GUI	03/11/88	M	6	(4)	
13	Marius Činikas	LTU	17/05/86	D	7	(3)	
8	Sergei Gigevich		26/01/87	M	29		4
7	Samson Godwin	NGA	11/11/83	M	14	(3)	
25	Artem Gurenko		01/06/94	D		(1)	
20	Oleh Karamushka	UKR	03/04/84	M	5	(1)	
10	Sergei Koshel		14/03/86	D		(7)	
99	Dmitri Kovb		20/01/87	A	2	(5)	
30	Leonid Kovel		29/07/86	A	17	(5)	8
1	Artur Lesko		25/05/84	G	19	(1)	
17	Artur Levitski		17/03/85	M	8	(1)	1
24	Igor Logvinov		23/08/83	G	11	(1)	
3	Maksim Lukashevich		28/03/92	M		(2)	
2	Aleksandr Makas		08/10/91	A	5	(9)	
20	Ivan Mayevski		05/05/88	M	19	(4)	1
5	Yuri Ostroukh		21/01/88	D	22	(2)	
16	Kirill Pavlyuchek		27/06/84	D	6	(3)	1
9	Sergei Pushnyakov		08/02/93	M	5	(8)	
21	Artem Rakhmanov		10/07/90	D	10	(3)	
6	Andrei Razin		12/08/79	M	23	(2)	6
29	Serhiy Rozhok	UKR	25/04/85	M	25	(1)	2
99	Sergei Rusak		03/09/93	M		(1)	
11	Aleksandr Sachivko		05/01/86	M	26		3
15	Sergei Shchegrikovich		19/12/90	M	1	(6)	
14	Aleksandr Sverchinski		16/09/91	D	10	(1)	
7	Nerijus Valskis	LTU	04/08/87	M	6	(4)	
10	Roman Vasilyuk		23/11/78	A	12	(2)	5
28	Paweł Wojciechowski	POL	24/04/90	D	11	(1)	5

FC NAFTAN NOVOPOLOTSK

Coach: Igor Kovalevich; (23/05/12) Igor Gasyuto; (31/05/12) Igor Kovalevich
1995 • Atlant (5,300); Central Sportkomplex (CSK), Vitebsk (8,300) • fcnaftan.com
Major honours
Belarusian Cup (2) 2009, 2012

2012

25/03	Shakhtyor	h	1-2	Shkabara	
31/03	Torpedo	a	1-0	Zhukovski	
10/04	Gomel	a	0-0		
14/04	Slavia	a	1-2	Zhukovski	
20/04	Minsk	h	1-3	Zhukovski	
29/04	Belshina	a	0-0		
02/05	Brest	h	1-0	Černych	
07/05	BATE	a	0-3		
12/05	Neman	h	2-1	Bukatkin 2	
16/05	Dinamo Minsk	a	2-4	Gorbachev, Gavryushko	
24/05	Shakhtyor	a	0-0		
11/06	Torpedo	h	0-0		
23/06	Gomel	h	0-1		
27/06	Slavia	h	0-0		
01/07	Minsk	a	0-1		
07/07	Belshina	h	3-0	Bukatkin, Trukhov, Černych	
13/07	Brest	a	1-2	Kovalenko	
12/08	BATE	h	0-4		
18/08	Neman	a	0-3		
26/08	Dinamo Minsk	h	0-2		
01/09	Slavia	a	1-1	Černych	
15/09	Shakhtyor	h	1-2	Teplov	
22/09	Gomel	a	0-2		
30/09	Torpedo	h	1-1	Bukatkin	
07/10	Dinamo Minsk	a	1-1	Zhukovski (p)	
20/10	Neman	h	1-0	Černych	
27/10	Belshina	a	2-3	Zubovich, Teplov	
03/11	BATE	h	1-0	Zyulev	
10/11	Brest	a	1-0	Černych	
25/11	Minsk	h	1-2	Yakimov	

No	Name	Nat	DoB	Pos	Aps	(s)	Gls
3	Vitaliy Berezovskiy	UKR	11/04/84	D	18	(1)	
8	Nikita Bukatkin		07/03/88	M	27		4
13	Fedor Černych	LTU	21/05/91	A	29	(1)	5
16	Igor Dovgyallo		17/07/85	G	15		
6	Aleksei Gavrilovich		05/01/90	D	25		
22	Aleksandr Gavryushko		23/01/86	A	9	(12)	1
4	Mikhail Gorbachev		29/07/83	D	30		1
2	Aleksandr Kobets		11/06/81	M	22	(5)	
29	Serhiy Kovalenko	UKR	10/05/84	A	5	(13)	1
15	Nikita Naumov		15/11/89	D	18	(2)	
44	Denis Obrazov		24/06/88	D	16		
1	Nikolai Romanyuk		02/06/84	G	14		
1	Nikolai Rudenok		15/12/90	G	1		
10	Oleg Shkabara		15/02/83	M	11		1
37	Roman Sorokin	RUS	17/05/85	M	16	(5)	
20	Artem Teplov		14/10/92	D	2	(8)	2
7	Igor Trukhov		19/08/76	M	16	(7)	1
17	Andrei Yakimov		17/11/89	M	1	(4)	1
25	Mikhail Yeremchuk		14/11/80	M	1	(4)	
	Nikolai Yezerski		17/06/84	D		(1)	
5	Valeri Zhukovski		21/05/84	M	9	(18)	4
9	Yegor Zubovich		01/06/89	A	21	(6)	1
33	Igor Zyulev		05/01/84	M	24	(2)	1

FC NEMAN GRODNO

Coach: Sergei Solodovnikov
1964 • Central Sportkomplex Neman (9,000) • fcneman.by
Major honours
Belarusian Cup (1) 1993

2012

24/03	Slavia	a	3-1	Savitski, Kryvobok 2	
31/03	Minsk	h	0-1		
06/04	Belshina	a	0-0		
10/04	Brest	h	1-1	Denisevich	
14/04	BATE	a	0-2		
29/04	Dinamo Minsk	h	0-0		
03/05	Shakhtyor	a	1-1	Voronkov	
07/05	Torpedo	h	1-1	Kovalenok	
12/05	Naftan	a	1-2	Pecha	
18/05	Gomel	h	0-3		
24/05	Slavia	h	8-0	Kryvobok 3, Denisevich 2, Vitus, Savitski 2	
15/06	Belshina	h	1-0	Savitski	
27/06	BATE	h	1-2	Lyasyuk	
11/06	Minsk	a	4-4	Savitski, Denisevich (p), Levitski, Voronkov	
23/06	Brest	a	1-1	Kovalenok	
08/07	Dinamo Minsk	a	1-1	Kovalenok	
13/07	Shakhtyor	h	1-1	Kryvobok	
12/08	Torpedo	a	5-1	Levitski, Lyasyuk, Denisevich 2 (1p), Veselinov	
18/08	Naftan	h	3-0	Lyasyuk, Denisevich, Jablan	
26/08	Gomel	a	1-1	Savostyanov	
02/09	Dinamo Minsk	a	0-1		
22/09	Belshina	h	0-0		
28/09	BATE	a	1-5	Denisevich	
07/10	Brest	h	3-0	Denisevich 2 (1p), Vitus	
20/10	Naftan	a	0-1		
27/10	Minsk	h	2-1	Savitski, Lyasyuk	
03/11	Slavia	a	1-0	Lyasyuk	
11/11	Shakhtyor	h	0-4		
17/11	Gomel	a	1-0	Lyasyuk	
25/11	Torpedo	h	2-1	Lyasyuk 2	

No	Name	Nat	DoB	Pos	Aps	(s)	Gls
14	Aleksandr Anyukevich		10/04/92	D	11	(4)	
29	Artur Bombel		14/12/92	A		(7)	
16	Sergei Chernik		20/07/88	G	29		
9	Ivan Denisevich		09/11/84	A	26		10
19	Aleksandr Dmitrijev	EST	18/02/82	M	9		
15	Milan Jablan	SRB	30/01/85	D	11		1
10	Dmitri Kovalenok		03/11/77	A	7	(16)	3
77	Ihor Kryvobok	UKR	28/07/78	A	11	(13)	6
8	Sergei Levitski		17/03/90	M	17	(5)	2
32	Andrei Lyasyuk		14/04/83	A	13	(10)	8
30	Boris Pankratov		30/12/82	G	1		
38	Ivan Pecha	SVK	23/01/86	D	19		1
5	Dmitri Rovneiko		13/05/80	D	15	(3)	
18	Pavel Rybak		11/09/83	D	28		
88	Pavel Savitski		12/07/94	A	25	(5)	6
3	Yevgeni Savostyanov		30/01/88	M	25		1
33	Aleksandr Semenov	RUS	11/06/82	A		(6)	
26	Dmitri Shmatko		26/07/89	D	1	(1)	
7	Aleksei Suchkov		10/06/81	M	16	(2)	
13	Vladimir Veselinov	SRB	25/05/84	M	18	(2)	1
23	Maksim Vitus		11/02/89	D	18	(5)	2
80	Andrei Voronkov		08/02/89	A	7	(5)	2
25	Igor Yasinski		04/07/90	M	23	(2)	
77	Aleksandr Yedeshko		28/01/93	M		(3)	

FC SHAKHTYOR SOLIGORSK

Coach: Vladimir Zhuravel
1963 • Stroitel (4,200) • fcshakhtor.by
Major honours
Belarusian League (1) 2005;
Belarusian Cup (1) 2004

2012

25/03	Naftan	a	2-1	Osipenko, Sitko
31/03	Gomel	h	1-2	Osipenko
06/04	Slavia	a	2-0	Komarovski, Osipenko
10/04	Minsk	h	7-0	Balanovich 2, Komarovski 4, Rios
14/04	Belshina	a	4-0	Kolomyts, Khachaturyan, Osipenko, Alumona
21/04	Brest	h	0-1	
28/04	BATE	a	0-1	
03/05	Neman	h	1-1	Balanovich
07/05	Dinamo Minsk	a	2-1	Yanush 2
18/05	Torpedo	h	1-0	Yanush
24/05	Naftan	h	0-0	
11/06	Gomel	a	1-1	Khachaturyan
16/06	Slavia	h	5-0	Yanush 2, Kolomyts, Sitko, Rios
23/06	Minsk	a	2-0	Yanush, Osipenko
27/06	Belshina	h	2-1	Osipenko, Rios
01/07	Brest	a	2-1	Postnikov, Osipenko
07/07	BATE	h	1-1	Osipenko
13/07	Neman	a	1-1	Khachaturyan
12/08	Dinamo Minsk	h	1-0	Rios
26/08	Torpedo	a	3-2	Yanushkevich, Osipenko 2
02/09	Brest	h	4-2	Osipenko, Rios, Komarovski, Khachaturyan
15/09	Naftan	a	2-1	Komarovski 2
09/09	Minsk	h	0-2	
30/09	Slavia	h	0-0	
20/10	Gomel	h	4-1	Rios, Kolomyts 2, Khachaturyan
28/10	Torpedo	a	2-0	Rios, Yanush
04/11	Dinamo Minsk	h	1-1	Sitko
11/11	Neman	a	4-0	og (Suchkov), Yanush, Komarovski, Osipenko
17/11	Belshina	h	3-1	Osipenko 2, Komarovski
25/11	BATE	a	1-2	Komarovski

No	Name	Nat	DoB	Pos	Aps	(s)	Gls
11	Aleksandr Alumona	RUS	18/12/83	A		(10)	1
2	Sergei Balanovich		29/08/87	D	21	(8)	3
9	Aleksandr Grenkov		20/01/78	M	18	(7)	
35	Andrei Khachaturyan		02/09/87	M	24		5
3	Yuri Kolomyts	RUS	30/04/79	D	30		4
15	Dmitri Komarovski		10/10/86	A	30		11
14	Jevgenijs Kosmačovs	LVA	18/02/88	A		(5)	
22	Eduardas Kurskis	LTU	17/10/76	G	2		
7	Andrei Leonchik		02/01/77	M	20	(4)	
77	Dmitri Osipenko		12/12/82	A	28	(2)	14
4	Yevgeni Postnikov	RUS	16/04/86	D	30		1
17	Aleksei Rios		14/05/87	M	16	(11)	7
35	Igor Rozhkov		24/06/81	M	21	(1)	
24	Pavel Sitko		17/12/85	M	12	(13)	3
13	Andrei Tsevan		15/03/86	M	7	(7)	
70	Yuri Tsygalko		27/05/83	G	28		
23	Kirill Vergeichik		23/08/91	A		(3)	
10	Nikolai Yanush		09/09/84	A	14	(8)	8
5	Aleksei Yanushkevich		15/01/86	D	29		1

FC SLAVIA MOZYR

Coach: Yuri Maleyev
1987 • Yunost (5,300); City, Khoiniki (1,512) • slaviya.by
Major honours
Belarusian League (2) 1996, 2000;
Belarusian Cup (2) 1996, 2000

2012

24/03	Neman	h	1-3	Volkov
01/04	Dinamo Minsk	a	1-3	Strakhanovich
06/04	Shakhtyor	h	0-2	
10/04	Torpedo	a	0-0	
14/04	Naftan	h	2-1	Zuyev, Chelyadko
21/04	Gomel	a	0-3	
03/05	Minsk	h	1-0	Volkov
07/05	Belshina	a	0-3	
12/05	Brest	h	2-1	Strakhanovich, Navikas
18/05	BATE	a	1-2	Strakhanovich
24/05	Neman	a	0-8	
11/06	Dinamo Minsk	h	0-2	
16/06	Shakhtyor	a	0-5	
23/06	Torpedo	h	1-0	Volkov (p)
27/06	Naftan	a	0-2	
14/07	Minsk	a	2-3	Volkov 2 (1p)
11/08	Belshina	h	1-0	Volkov
19/08	Brest	a	2-1	Volkov (p), og (Aloksiyan)
01/09	Naftan	h	1-1	Khilkevich
08/09	Gomel	h	0-2	
15/09	Minsk	a	0-3	
30/09	Shakhtyor	a	0-0	
07/10	Gomel	a	1-4	Volkov
18/10	BATE	h	1-2	Irkha
23/10	Torpedo	h	3-2	Volkov 2 (1p), Laptev
27/10	Dinamo Minsk	a	2-4	Yudenkov, Volkov
03/11	Neman	h	0-1	
10/11	Belshina	a	0-2	
17/11	BATE	a	0-0	
25/11	Brest	a	0-2	

No	Name	Nat	DoB	Pos	Aps	(s)	Gls
6	Mihajlo Čakić	SRB	07/05/90	M	7	(1)	
22	Pavel Chelyadko		03/03/93	D	27	(3)	1
5	Sergei Dubovenko		27/06/00	M	4	(16)	
1	Vladimir Gayev		28/10/77	G	30		
4	Vyacheslav Golik	RUS	01/05/89	D	2	(6)	
36	Sergei Irkha		25/03/94	M	21	(5)	1
11	Yakov Kazak		01/08/95	M	9	(3)	
7	Yuri Kendysh		10/06/90	M	9	(2)	
2	Sergei Khaletski		14/04/84	D	26	(1)	
17	Vladimir Khilkevich		31/10/87	M	26	(4)	1
20	Andrei Klimenko		28/03/83	A		(1)	
18	Sergei Kovalchuk		12/12/80	D	18		
27	Denis Kovalevski		02/05/92	D	22		
15	Denis Laptev		01/08/91	M	1	(4)	1
12	Andrei Mamatyuk	RUS	13/04/91	M	1	(6)	
8	Mikhail Martinovich		14/09/79	M	5	(1)	
25	Donatas Navikas	LTU	30/06/83	M	10	(5)	1
13	Yevgeni Novak		06/12/83	D	2		
29	Yevgeni Pankov	RUS	24/11/83	M	5	(1)	
4	Sergei Rayevski		19/06/88	M	3	(5)	
28	Anatoli Savinski		23/01/86	G	1		
13	Aleksei Skvernyuk		18/04/90	M	9	(1)	
88	Anton Smirnov	RUS	07/08/83	M	7		
3	Aleksandr Stashchenyuk		23/02/83	D	1	(1)	
21	Oleg Strakhanovich		13/10/79	M	23	(1)	3
77	Yaroslav Svorak	UKR	07/02/89	M	2	(1)	
30	Rodion Syamuk	UKR	11/03/89	G	1		
23	Dmitri Usachev		20/02/88	D	8	(2)	
19	Roman Volkov		08/01/87	A	23	(5)	11
14	Ruslan Yudenkov		28/04/87	M	24	(5)	1
9	Yevgeni Zuyev		02/03/83	A	5	(6)	1

FC TORPEDO ZHODINO

Coach – Sergei Gurenko; (04/05/12) Vadim Brazovski; (02/11/12) (Aleksandr Marteshkin); (07/11/12) Igor Kriushenko
1961 • Torpedo (3,020) • torpedo-belaz.by

2012

31/03	Naftan	h	0-1	
06/04	Gomel	a	0-2	
10/04	Slavia	h	0-0	
14/04	Minsk	a	2-1	Solovei 2
21/04	Belshina	h	0-1	
29/04	Brest	a	0-1	
03/05	BATE	h	0-2	
07/05	Neman	a	1-1	Chelyadinski
12/05	Dinamo Minsk	h	0-0	
18/05	Shakhtyor	a	0-1	
11/06	Naftan	a	0-0	
15/06	Gomel	h	1-0	Vaskov
23/06	Slavia	a	0-1	
27/06	Minsk	h	2-1	Solovei, Vaskov
01/07	Belshina	a	0-0	
07/07	Brest	h	1-0	Yatskevich
13/07	BATE	a	0-1	
12/08	Neman	h	1-5	Vergeichik
18/08	Dinamo Minsk	a	0-2	
26/08	Shakhtyor	h	2-3	Vergeichik, Chelyadinski
01/09	Belshina	h	2-2	Karshakevich, Yaroslavski
15/09	BATE	a	0-0	
22/09	Brest	h	0-0	
30/09	Naftan	h	1-1	Chelyadinski
07/10	Minsk	h	1-0	Vaskov
23/10	Slavia	a	2-3	Mendy (p), Ryzhko
28/10	Shakhtyor	h	0-2	
04/11	Gomel	a	0-3	
17/11	Dinamo Minsk	h	0-2	
27/11	Neman	a	1-2	Khlebosolov

No	Name	Nat	DoB	Pos	Aps	(s)	Gls
20	Dmitri Aliseiko		28/08/92	A		(1)	
2	Artem Chelyadinski		29/12/77	M	29		3
1	Pavel Chesnovski		01/01/86	G	20	(1)	
10	Vadim Demidovich		20/03/88	M	14	(2)	
27	Maksim Karpovich		27/02/86	M	14	(2)	
21	Valeri Karshakevich		15/02/88	D	14	(2)	1
7	Yuri Kendysh		10/06/90	M	11		
70	Dmitri Khlebosolov		07/10/90	A	3	(6)	1
28	Denis Kishkurno		11/09/90	M		(1)	
5	Yuri Korolyuk		10/01/90	M	4	(3)	
17	Aleksei Kozlov		11/01/83	M	27		
5	Vitali Lanko		04/04/77	A	21	(3)	
99	Yevgeni Loshankov		02/01/79	M	6	(3)	
18	Pascal Mendy	SEN	11/01/79	A	25	(1)	1
16	Dmitri Parechin		17/11/79	G	4		
14	Dmitri Rekish		14/09/88	M	8	(7)	
26	Anton Ryabtsev		19/02/84	D	12	(4)	
13	Yuri Ryzhko		10/10/89	D	12	(1)	1
92	Aleksandr Selyava		17/05/92	M	2	(4)	
11	Dmitri Shchegrikovich		07/12/83	M	23	(2)	
23	Dmitri Sholudko		17/08/89	M	1	(4)	
15	Artem Solovei		01/11/90	M	22	(4)	3
25	Sergei Tikhonovski		26/06/90	M	6	(8)	
19	Artem Vaskov		21/10/88	D	14	(8)	3
9	Kirill Vergeichik		23/08/91	A	5	(6)	2
3	Vyacheslav Yaroslavski		14/05/85	M	25		1
8	Aleksandr Yatskevich		04/01/85	A	12	(9)	1
10	Vladimir Yurchenko		26/01/89	A		(5)	

BELARUS

Top goalscorers

14 Dmitri Osipenko (Shakhtyor)

11 Renan Bressan (BATE)
Dmitri Komarovski (Shakhtyor)
Roman Volkov (Slavia)

10 Ivan Denisevich (Neman)

9 Dmitri Mozolevski (BATE)
Vladimir Khvashchinski (Brest)

8 Vitali Rodionov (BATE)
Dmitri Platonov (Gomel)
Leonid Kovel (Minsk)
Andrei Lyasyuk (Neman)
Nikolai Yanush (Shakhtyor)

Promoted club

FC DNEPR MOGILEV

Coach: Vyacheslav Gerashchenko
1960 • Spartak (7,300) • fcdnepr.by
Major honours
Belarusian League (1) 1998

SECOND LEVEL FINAL TABLE 2012

		Pld	W	D	L	F	A	Pts
1	FC Dnepr Mogilev	28	20	3	5	75	22	63
2	FC Gorodeya	28	18	6	4	49	21	60
3	FC Vitebsk	28	19	2	7	57	30	59
4	FC SKVICH Minsk	28	16	7	5	61	19	55
5	FC Slutsk	28	15	7	6	59	27	52
6	FC Granit Mikashevichi	28	14	8	6	41	23	50
7	FC Vedrich-97 Rechitsa	28	9	12	7	40	24	39
8	FC Volna Pinsk	28	8	10	10	24	45	34
9	FC Bereza-2010	28	9	6	13	41	48	33
10	FC Smorgon	28	7	10	11	23	32	31
11	FC Lida	28	8	6	14	32	49	30
12	FC Polotsk	28	7	5	16	24	55	26
13	FC Khimik Svetlogorsk	28	5	9	14	29	52	24
14	FC DSK Gomel	28	1	5	22	9	62	8
15	FC Rudensk	28	4	4	20	15	70	7

NB FC Rudensk – 9 pts deducted.

PROMOTION/RELEGATION PLAY-OFFS
(29/11/12 & 02/12/12)
Gorodeya 1-0 Torpedo
Torpedo 4-0 Gorodeya
(Torpedo 4-1)

Domestic cup: Kubok Belarusii 2012/13

SECOND ROUND

(19/07/12)
Beltransgaz Slonim 4-1 Granit
Smorgon 1-3 Neman

(21/07/12)
DSK Gomel 0-2 Bereza-2010
Isloch Minsk 0-3 FC Minsk
Khimik Svetlogorsk 0-2 Gorodeya
Lida 0-2 Slavia
Neman Mosty 1-7 Brest
Slutsk 1-2 Dnepr
Vitebsk 1-2 Torpedo Zhodino
Zhlobin 0-2 Belshina
Zvezda-BGU Minsk 0-2 SKVICH Minsk

(22/07/12)
Polotsk 1-1 Gomel *(aet; 6-7 on pens)*

(22/08/12)
Vedrich-97 0-1 Dinamo Minsk

(06/09/12)
Volna 0-0 Naftan *(aet; 3-2 on pens)*

(08/09/12)
Gomelzheldortrans Gomel 0-1 Shakhtyor Soligorsk

(09/09/12)
Rudensk 0-4 BATE

THIRD ROUND

(26/09/12)
Belshina 1-0 Bereza-2010
Dinamo Minsk 5-0 Volna
Dnepr 1-2 SKVICH Minsk
Shakhtyor Soligorsk 3-0 Beltransgaz Slonim
Slavia 1-5 Brest

(11/10/12)
Gorodeya 0-2 FC Minsk

(13/10/12)
BATE 0-1 Torpedo Zhodino

(21/11/12)
Neman 1-1 Gomel *(aet; 4-5 on pens)*

QUARTER-FINALS

(16/03/13)
Belshina 1-4 Torpedo Zhodino *(Gordeichuk 68; Chelyadinski 45, D Platonov 56, 58, Levitski 77)*

Dinamo Minsk 0-0 Shakhtyor Soligorsk *(aet; 4-2 on pens)*

(17/03/13)
FC Minsk 3-2 Gomel *(Vasilyuk 72p, Wojciechowski 77, Rozhok 90+4; Matveyenko 31, 66)*

SKVICH Minsk 1-0 Brest *(Margolenko 94) (aet)*

SEMI-FINALS

(03/04/13)
FC Minsk 1-0 Torpedo Zhodino *(Razin 90+3)*

Dinamo Minsk 5-0 SKVICH Minsk *(Curelea 28, Figueredo 32, 72, Sychev 79, Bykov 82)*

FINAL

(26/05/13)
Torpedo Stadium, Zhodino
FC MINSK 1 *(Sosnovski 33)*
FC DINAMO MINSK 1 *(Figueredo 36p)*
(aet; 4-1 on pens)
Referee: *Kruk*
FC MINSK: *Bushma, Begunov, Rnić, Sosnovski, Razin (Kibuk 54), Kozeka, Pushnyakov (Rozhok 94), Bukatkin, Sachivko, Vasilyuk, Volkov (Gigevich 69)*
DINAMO MINSK: *Gutor, Veretilo, Plaskonny, Trubilo, Politevich, Simović, Bykov, Danilov (Bychenok 82), Figueredo, Stasevich, Curelea (Cócaro 97)*

FC Minsk enjoy their final triumph against Dinamo

BELGIUM

Union Royale Belgo des Sociétés de Football Association (URBSFA) /
Koninklijke Belgische Voetbalbond (KBVB)

Address	145 Avenue Houba de Strooper BE-1020 Bruxelles	**President**	François De Keersmaecker
Tel	+32 2 477 1211	**General secretary**	Steven Martens
Fax	+32 2 478 2391	**Media officer**	Stefan Van Loock
E-mail	urbsfa.kbvb@footbel.com	**Year of formation**	1895
Website	footbel.com	**National stadium**	Roi Baudouin, Brussels (50,024)

PRO LEGUE CLUBS

1. **RSC Anderlecht**
2. **K. Beerschot AC**
3. **Cercle Brugge KSV**
4. **R. Charleroi SC**

5. **Club Brugge KV**
6. **KRC Genk**
7. **KAA Gent**
8. **KV Kortrijk**
9. **K. Lierse SK**
10. **KSC Lokeren OV**
11. **KV Mechelen**
12. **RAEC Mons**
13. **Oud-Heverlee Leuven**
14. **R. Standard de Liège**
15. **Waasland-Beveren**
16. **SV Zulte Waregem**

PROMOTED CLUB

17. **KV Oostende**

KEY:

● – UEFA Champions League
● – UEFA Europa League
● – Promoted club
● – Relegated club

Anderlecht taken to the wire

A season in which Belgian football returned to prominence on the international stage with a strong showing from the Red Devils in the 2014 FIFA World Cup qualifying campaign also delivered an intriguing battle for domestic honours, with RSC Anderlecht surviving an unlikely challenge from SV Zulte Waregem to retain the league title and KRC Genk lifting the Belgian Cup.

Anderlecht's 32nd championship win was not sealed until the conclusion of their 40th and final fixture, a 1-1 draw at home to Zulte Waregem ensuring that coach John van den Brom's first season in charge ended in triumph.

Brussels giants claim 32nd league crown

Zulte Waregem edged out in last-day duel

Star-studded national team on the rise

Domestic league

The extended format of Belgium's Pro League, with its layered play-off system and long fixture schedule, is not to everyone's taste, but with the exception of its inaugural season, in 2009/10, it has delivered on its promise to ensure an exciting denouement to the title race. For much of the 2012/13 campaign it seemed as if Anderlecht might have things all their own way, but while the expected challenge from Club Brugge KV, Genk and R. Standard de Liège never materialised, Zulte Waregem refused to budge from the defending champions' shadow.

At the end of the regular season Anderlecht held a four-point lead, which, by the competition's idiosyncratic rules of engagement, was promptly halved prior to the championship play-offs. Likewise, the teams placed 3-6 after 30 matches were able to close what appeared to be a considerable gap between themselves and the top two, and when Anderlecht and Zulte Waregem both made a hash of their opening few play-off games, the table began to condense still further.

However, the two front-runners recovered their form just in time to set up a classic winner-takes-all final-day fixture in Brussels. In fact, Anderlecht, with a two-point lead, needed only a draw to retain the title, and that is what they got, skipper Lucas Biglia's deflected 59th-minute free-kick providing a suitably rapid response to Jens Naessens' opener three minutes earlier and ensuring that Anderlecht did not suffer a third consecutive defeat to Francky Dury's provincial upstarts.

Biglia was an inspired figure throughout the campaign, running the Anderlecht midfield. The club's 85 goals were shared around, with Dieumerci Mbokani once again finishing as the leading marksman, on 19 – four more than in 2011/12. At the other end goalkeeper Silvio Proto was equally influential, coming to his team's rescue on several occasions, while there were also highly encouraging contributions from young guns Massimo Bruno and Dennis Praet.

While Anderlecht's title win ensured participation in the 2013/14 UEFA Champions League group stage, Zulte Waregem's consolation prize was a place in the third qualifying round of the same competition.

Club Brugge, who sacked new boss Georges Leekens early in the campaign following a string of defeats, finished strongly under Spaniard Juan Carlos Garrido (ex-Villarreal CF), outperforming the other five teams in the play-offs and ending up just three points shy of Anderlecht. Deeply indebted to the 25 goals of Colombian striker Carlos Bacca, Club Brugge were joined in UEFA Europa League qualification by Standard, although not before the Liège side had negotiated an additional play-off, the second leg of which brought a resounding 7-0 win over KAA Gent.

Domestic cup

Genk's return to Europe was secured by victory in the Belgian Cup, Mario Been's team finding two late goals to see off a stubborn Cercle Brugge KSV side in the final. The latter's more important battle perhaps was to survive the relegation play-offs – which they achieved – but a first major honour in 28 years would not have been unwelcome for a team led into battle at the Roi Baudouin stadium by Lorenzo Staelens, a former stalwart of city rivals Club Brugge. It was not to be, however, as Genk edged home with two goals in the last seven minutes from Bennard Yao Kumordzi and Jelle Vossen.

Continued on page 221

Domestic league: Pro League 2012/13 final tables

CHAMPIONSHIP PLAY-OFFS	Pld	Home W	D	L	F	A	Away W	D	L	F	A	Total W	D	L	F	A	Pts
1 **RSC Anderlecht**	10	2	2	1	8	4	2	1	2	8	7	4	3	3	16	11	49
2 SV Zulte Waregem	10	2	1	2	11	12	2	2	1	9	8	4	3	3	20	20	47
3 Club Brugge KV	10	3	0	2	8	8	3	1	1	13	9	6	1	3	21	17	46
4 R. Standard de Liège	10	3	1	1	10	7	2	1	2	8	10	5	2	3	18	17	42
5 KRC Genk	10	1	2	2	5	7	2	1	2	6	5	3	3	4	11	12	40
6 KSC Lokeren OV	10	1	1	3	9	12	0	1	4	6	12	1	2	7	15	24	31

PRO LEAGUE	Pld	Home W	D	L	F	A	Away W	D	L	F	A	Total W	D	L	F	A	Pts
1 RSC Anderlecht	30	12	2	1	35	10	8	5	2	34	17	20	7	3	69	27	67
2 SV Zulte Waregem	30	8	3	4	27	19	11	3	1	22	10	19	6	5	49	29	63
3 KRC Genk	30	10	3	2	36	18	5	7	3	27	22	15	10	5	63	40	55
4 Club Brugge KV	30	8	5	2	29	13	7	4	4	37	30	15	9	6	66	43	54
5 KSC Lokeren OV	30	5	7	3	24	20	9	2	4	29	18	14	9	7	53	38	51
6 R. Standard de Liège	30	9	1	5	28	15	6	4	5	26	18	15	5	10	54	33	50
7 RAEC Mons	30	6	2	7	25	30	7	3	5	23	23	13	5	12	48	53	44
8 KV Mechelen	30	7	1	7	24	23	5	4	6	20	19	12	5	13	44	42	41
9 KV Kortrijk	30	7	4	4	24	15	4	2	9	7	15	11	6	13	31	30	39
10 Oud-Heverlee Leuven	30	5	6	4	26	27	3	6	6	20	24	8	12	10	46	51	36
11 R. Charleroi SC	30	6	2	7	17	21	4	2	9	13	28	10	4	16	30	49	34
12 KAA Gent	30	5	4	6	16	16	3	6	6	17	24	8	10	12	33	40	34
13 Waasland-Beveren	30	4	6	5	15	20	3	3	9	13	29	7	9	14	28	49	30
14 K. Lierse SK	30	3	7	5	13	20	2	4	9	15	33	5	11	14	28	53	26
15 K. Beerschot AC	30	4	3	8	20	34	2	2	11	11	27	6	5	19	31	61	23
16 Cercle Brugge KSV	30	3	3	9	16	27	0	2	13	14	38	3	5	22	30	65	14

NB After 30 rounds the top six clubs enter a championship play-off, carrying forward half of their points total (half points rounded upwards); clubs placed 7-14 enter two play-off groups; clubs placed 15 &16 enter relegation play-off group.

SEASON AT A GLANCE

EUROPEAN QUALIFICATION 2013/14

 Champion: RSC Anderlecht (group stage)
SV Zulte Waregem (third qualifying round)

 Cup winner: KRC Genk (play-offs)
Club Brugge KV (third qualifying round)
R. Standard de Liège (second qualifying round)

Top scorer   Carlos Bacca (Club Brugge), 25 goals
Relegated club   K. Beerschot AC
Promoted club   KV Oostende
Cup final   KRC Genk 2-0 Cercle Brugge KSV

PLAYER OF THE SEASON
Carlos Bacca
(Club Brugge KV)

In his first full season at Club Brugge the explosive, technically proficient Colombian striker found the net 25 times to help the team finish third and clinch a UEFA Europa League spot. Having topped the scoring charts, the former Atlético Junior star was duly voted Belgium's player of the season by his fellow professionals.

NEWCOMER OF THE SEASON
Dennis Praet
(RSC Anderlecht)

The 19-year-old midfielder caught the eye with his delightful range of passing, tight ball control and artistry. Praet gained invaluable European experience, featuring in five of Anderlecht's UEFA Champions League group games, and provided enough evidence to suggest that full international honours would soon be coming his way.

PRO LEAGUE TEAM OF THE SEASON
(3-4-3)
Coach: Dury *(Zulte Waregem)*

Proto *(Anderlecht)*

De Fauw *(Zulte Waregem)* — Kouyaté *(Anderlecht)* — Nuytinck *(Anderlecht)*

Lestienne *(Club Brugge)* — Biglia *(Anderlecht)* — Vainqueur *(Standard)* — Hazard *(Zulte Waregem)*

Vossen *(Genk)* — Bacca *(Club Brugge)* — Mbokani *(Anderlecht)*

BELGIUM

NATIONAL TEAM

Home Kit 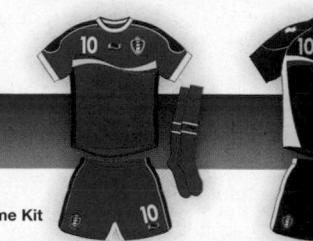  Away Kit

INTERNATIONAL TOURNAMENT APPEARANCES

FIFA World Cup (11) 1930, 1934, 1938, 1954, 1970, 1982 (2nd phase), 1986 (4th), 1990 (2nd round), 1994 (2nd round), 1998, 2002 (2nd round). UEFA European Championship (3) 1972 (3rd), 1980 (runners-up), 2000.

TOP FIVE ALL-TIME CAPS

Jan Ceulemans (96); **Timmy Simons** (93); Eric Gerets & Franky Van Der Elst (86); Vincenzo Scifo (84)

TOP FIVE ALL-TIME GOALS

Paul Van Himst & Bernard Voorhoof (30); Marc Wilmots (28); Jef Mermans (27); Raymond Braine & Robert De Veen (26)

Results 2012/13

15/08/12	Netherlands	H	Brussels	4-2	Benteke (20), Mertens (75), Lukaku (77), Vertonghen (80)
07/09/12	Wales (WCQ)	A	Cardiff	2-0	Kompany (41), Vertonghen (83)
11/09/12	Croatia (WCQ)	H	Brussels	1-1	Gillet (45+2)
12/10/12	Serbia (WCQ)	A	Belgrade	3-0	Benteke (34), De Bruyne (68), Mirallas (90+1)
16/10/12	Scotland (WCQ)	H	Brussels	2-0	Benteke (69), Kompany (71)
14/11/12	Romania	A	Bucharest	1-2	Benteke (23)
06/02/13	Slovakia	H	Bruges	2-1	E Hazard (10p), Mertens (90)
22/03/13	FYROM (WCQ)	A	Skopje	2-0	De Bruyne (26), E Hazard (62p)
26/03/13	FYROM (WCQ)	H	Brussels	1-0	E Hazard (62)
29/05/13	United States	A	Cleveland	4-2	Mirallas (6), Benteke (56, 71), Fellaini (64)
07/06/13	Serbia (WCQ)	H	Brussels	2-1	De Bruyne (13), Fellaini (60)

Appearances 2012/13

Coach: Marc Wilmots	22/02/69		Ned	WAL	CRO	SRB	SCO	Rou	Svk	MKD	MKD	Usa	SRB	Caps	Goals
Thibaut Courtois	11/05/92	Atlético (ESP)	G	G	G	G	G			G	G		G	10	-
Guillaume Gillet	09/03/84	Anderlecht	D	D	D			D				s72		20	1
Daniel Van Buyten	07/02/78	Bayern (GER)	D46				D	D	D				D	71	10
Thomas Vermaelen	14/11/85	Arsenal (ENG)	D	D	D	D	D			D	D	D36		43	1
Jan Vertonghen	24/04/87	Tottenham (ENG)	D	D	D	D	D	D	D	D	D	D	D	49	4
Steven Defour	15/04/88	Porto (POR)	M		M67		M58					M77		38	1
Axel Witsel	12/01/89	Benfica (POR) /Zenit (RUS)	M	M	M	M	M	M	M86	M	M		M	39	5
Eden Hazard	07/01/91	Chelsea (ENG)	M58	M	M	M55	s46		M	M	M92		s64	37	5
Nacer Chadli	02/08/89	Twente (NED)	M67			M	M			s85	s56		M	14	2
Kevin Mirallas	05/10/87	Olympiacos (GRE) /Everton (ENG)	M56	A46	s81	s87	s56		M46		s46	M	M64	36	7
Christian Benteke	03/12/90	Genk /Aston Villa (ENG)	A63	A	A	A87	A58	A46	A85	A	s41	A		14	6
Toby Alderweireld	02/03/89	Ajax (NED)	s46		D	D		D	D	D	D	D		25	-
Kevin De Bruyne	28/06/91	Bremen (GER)	s56	s64	s72	M87	M	M	M62	M	M	M68	M82	13	3
Moussa Dembélé	16/07/87	Fulham (ENG) /Tottenham (ENG)	s58	M64	M72	M	M46		M	M	M56	M41	s71	49	5
Romelu Lukaku	13/05/93	West Brom (ENG)	s63	s46			s58	s46				A83	s82	21	3
Dries Mertens	06/05/87	PSV (NED)	s67	M	M81	s55	M56	M60	s62		M46	s68		19	2
Vincent Kompany	10/04/86	Man. City (ENG)	D	D	D	D	D				D	D72	D	55	4
Marouane Fellaini	22/11/87	Everton (ENG)	M	s67			M		M		s92	M	M71	42	7
Ilombe Mboyo	27/04/87	Gent				s87	s60							2	-
Simon Mignolet	06/08/88	Sunderland (ENG)					G					G		12	-
Jelle Vossen	22/03/89	Genk					s58							11	2
Jean-François Gillet	31/05/79	Torino (ITA)						G						9	-
Nicolas Lombaerts	20/03/85	Zenit (RUS)						D62						21	2
Radja Nainggolan	04/05/88	Cagliari (ITA)						s46 /78						4	-
Jelle Van Damme	10/10/83	Standard Liège						s62						30	-
Thomas Buffel	19/02/81	Genk						s78						35	6
Timmy Simons	11/12/76	Nürnberg (GER)						s86				s77		93	6
Sébastien Pocognoli	01/08/87	Hannover (GER)										s36		8	-
Thorgan Hazard	29/03/93	Zulte Waregem										s83		1	-

Europe

Genk were Belgium's last team standing in 2012/13 European competition, reaching the last 32 of the UEFA Europa League as group winners before succumbing to VfB Stuttgart with their first defeat in eight matches, a 2-0 loss at home coming after a promising 1-1 draw in Germany.

No other Pro League side made it beyond Christmas, with Club Brugge bowing out at the group stage of the same competition and Anderlecht qualifying for the UEFA Champions League proper but winning only one game in their group – 1-0 at home to FC Zenit St Petersburg – and finishing bottom.

National team

Belgium's bid to end a decade in the international wilderness appeared to be firmly on track as Marc Wilmots' team of many talents plundered 19 points from a possible 21 in a World Cup qualifying group that provided them with no easy games. Croatia were the only other team that stayed with them, but their shock home defeat to Scotland in June coupled with Belgium's 2-1 home win against Serbia enabled the Red Devils to take a three-point lead into their last three matches, one of which was away to their sole challengers for top spot.

The two teams had shared a 1-1 draw in Brussels at the start of the campaign, but while that was a setback to Belgian

hopes, a run of five successive victories – to add to their opening 2-0 win in Wales – proved that they were a team of substance as well as style, the array of gifted individuals at Wilmots' disposal collectively bonding to obtain the desired results.

The 2012/13 season also turned out to be a memorable one at club level for many of Belgium's star turns, especially in England, where newcomers Eden Hazard (Chelsea FC), Jan Vertonghen (Tottenham Hotspur FC) and Christian Benteke (Aston Villa FC) all took the Premier League by storm. Trophies were garlanded across Europe by several of Belgium's finest, although disappointingly Hazard and FC Bayern München's Daniel Van Buyten played no part in either of their clubs' victorious European finals.

European club competitions 2012/13

RSC ANDERLECHT

Third qualifying round - FK Ekranas (LTU)
H 5-0 De Sutter (2), Kanu (21), Mbokani (41, 52), Jovanović (87)
Proto, Deschacht, Biglia, Odoi, Kanu (Kljestan 62), Jovanović, Safari, De Sutter (Yakovenko 80), Mbokani, Wasilewski, Gillet (Fernando Canesin 69). Coach: John van den Brom (NED)
A 6-0 Kljestan (9), Praet (31), Yakovenko (45+3), De Sutter (47), Molins (62), Fernando Canesin (87)
Proto, Deschacht, Biglia (Mareček 46), Mbenza, Odoi, Yakovenko, Kljestan, Safari, De Sutter (Fernando Canesin 59), Praet, Gillet (Molins 46). Coach: John van den Brom (NED)

Play-offs - AEL Limassol FC (CYP)
A 1-2 Mbokani (62)
Proto, Biglia, Odoi, Kanu, Jovanović (Yakovenko 74), Kouyaté, Kljestan, Safari, Mbokani, Wasilewski, Gillet. Coach: John van den Brom (NED)
Red card: Jovanović 75
H 2-0 Mbokani (81), Yakovenko (89)
Proto, Deschacht, Biglia, Odoi (Juhász 80), Kanu, Kouyaté, Kljestan, De Sutter (Yakovenko 65), Mbokani, Wasilewski, Gillet (Bruno 74). Coach: John van den Brom (NED)

Group C
Match 1 - AC Milan (ITA)
A 0-0
Proto, Deschacht, Biglia, Kanu (Yakovenko 89), Nuytinck, Kouyaté (Praet 79), Kljestan, Mbokani, Wasilewski, Gillet, Bruno (Juhász 79). Coach: John van den Brom (NED)
Match 2 - Málaga CF (ESP)
H 0-3
Proto, Deschacht, Biglia, Kanu, Jovanović (Yakovenko 59), Nuytinck, Kouyaté, Mbokani, Wasilewski, Gillet, Bruno (Kljestan 46). Coach: John van den Brom (NED)
Match 3 - FC Zenit St Petersburg (RUS)
A 0-1
Proto, Deschacht, Biglia, Kanu, Jovanović, Nuytinck, Kouyaté, De Sutter, Praet (Yakovenko 73), Wasilewski (Molins 83), Gillet. Coach: John van den Brom (NED)
Match 4 - FC Zenit St Petersburg (RUS)
H 1-0 Mbokani (17)
Proto, Biglia, Jovanović, Nuytinck, Kouyaté, Kljestan, Safari, Mbokani, Praet (Kanu 79), Gillet, Bruno (Yakovenko 72). Coach: John van den Brom (NED)
Match 5 - AC Milan (ITA)
H 1-3 De Sutter (78)
Proto, Deschacht, Biglia, Jovanović (Fernando Canesin 77), Nuytinck, Kouyaté, Kljestan, Mbokani, Praet (De Sutter 75), Gillet, Bruno (Yakovenko 66). Coach: John van den Brom (NED)
Red card: Nuytinck 70
Match 6 - Málaga CF (ESP)
A 2-2 Jovanović (50), Mbokani (89)
Proto, Deschacht, Biglia, Jovanović (Vargas 85), Kouyaté, Kljestan, Safari, Mbokani, Praet (De Sutter 71), Gillet, Bruno. Coach: John van den Brom (NED)

CLUB BRUGGE KV

Third qualifying round - FC København (DEN)
A 0-0
Kujović, Hoefkens, Zimling (Van Acker 68), Tchité (Akpala 74), Refaelov, Blondel, Larsen, Donk, Meunier, Jordi, Odjidja-Ofoe. Coach: Georges Leekens (BEL)
H 2-3 Jordi (24), Odjidja-Ofoe (66)
Kujović, Hoefkens (Akpala 81), Zimling (Víctor Vázquez 84), Tchité, Refaelov (Lestienne 90), Blondel, Larsen, Donk, Meunier, Jordi, Odjidja-Ofoe. Coach: Georges Leekens (BEL)

Play-offs - Debreceni VSC (HUN)
A 3-0 Blondel (58), Refaelov (77), Bacca (90+1)
Jorgačević, Hoefkens, Zimling (Víctor Vázquez 85), Tchité (Bacca 67), Refaelov, Blondel, Larsen, Donk, Meunier, Jordi, Odjidja-Ofoe (Jørgensen 90). Coach: Georges Leekens (BEL)
H 4-1 Larsen (25), Víctor Vázquez (48), Tchité (50), Bacca (66)
Jorgačević, Hoefkens, Tchité, Refaelov, Blondel (Van Acker 61), Víctor Vázquez, Larsen (Almebäck 54), Donk, Meunier (Jørgensen 46), Jordi, Bacca. Coach: Georges Leekens (BEL)

Group D
Match 1 - FC Girondins de Bordeaux (FRA)
A 0-4
Jorgačević, Høgli (Lestienne 73), Almebäck, Hoefkens, Tchité, Jørgensen, Blondel (Odjidja-Ofoe 74), Víctor Vázquez, Van Acker (Engels 46), Jordi, Bacca. Coach: Georges Leekens (BEL)
Match 2 - CS Marítimo (POR)
H 2-0 *Bacca (57), Vleminckx (71)*
Jorgačević, Almebäck, Hoefkens, Vleminckx, Blondel, Víctor Vázquez, Lestienne (Trickovski 89), Buysse, Jordi, Odjidja-Ofoe, Bacca. Coach: Georges Leekens (BEL)
Match 3 - Newcastle United FC (ENG)
A 0-1
Jorgačević, Høgli, Hoefkens, Refaelov (Trickovski 55), Jørgensen, Blondel (Van Acker 84), Lestienne, Buysse, Jordi, Odjidja-Ofoe, Bacca. Coach: Georges Leekens (BEL)
Match 4 - Newcastle United FC (ENG)
H 2-2 *Trickovski (14), Jørgensen (19)*
Jorgačević, Høgli, Almebäck, Hoefkens, Jørgensen, Lestienne, Trickovski (Tchité 46), Donk, Jordi, Odjidja-Ofoe (Lagrou 81), Bacca. Coach: Philippe Clement (BEL)
Match 5 - FC Girondins de Bordeaux (FRA)
H 1-2 *Lestienne (86)*
Kujović, Almebäck (Blondel 46), Hoefkens, Refaelov (Vleminckx 46), Jørgensen, Lestienne, Donk, Buysse, Jordi, Odjidja-Ofoe, Bacca (Meunier 60). Coach: Juan Carlos Garrido (ESP)
Match 6 - CS Marítimo (POR)
A 1-2 *Refaelov (85p)*
Jorgačević, Høgli, Almebäck, Tchité (Donk 74), Refaelov, Vleminckx, Blondel (Odjidja-Ofoe 71), Meunier, Van Acker (Lestienne 74), Jordi, Verstraete. Coach: Juan Carlos Garrido (ESP)

KSC LOKEREN OV

Play-offs - FC Viktoria Plzeň (CZE)
H 2-1 *Harbaoui (10), Mijat Maric (90+4p)*
Barry, Taravel, Mijat Maric, Overmeire, Persoons, Harbaoui, Leko (Miloš Marić 86), De Ceulaer (De Pauw 80), Galitsios, Patosi (Mokulu 75), De Bock. Coach: Peter Maes (BEL)
A 0-1
Barry, Taravel, Mijat Maric, Overmeire, Persoons, Harbaoui, Leko (Miloš Marić 73), De Ceulaer (De Pauw 80), Galitsios, Patosi (Mokulu 80), De Bock. Coach: Peter Maes (BEL)

KRC GENK

Third qualifying round - FC Aktobe (KAZ)
H 2-1 *Vossen (18p), Joseph-Monrose (44)*
Köteles, Tshimanga, Hyland, Joseph-Monrose, Vossen (Barda 76), Gorius, Ngcongca, Buffel (Limbombe 46), Nadson, Dani Fernández (Nwanganga 84), Benteke. Coach: Mario Been (NED)
A 2-1 *Benteke (36), Buffel (51)*
Köteles, Tshimanga, Hyland, Vossen (Camus 88), Gorius, Ngcongca, Barda (Joseph-Monrose 41), Buffel (Nwanganga 83), Nadson, Dani Fernández, Benteke. Coach: Mario Been (NED)
Play-offs - FC Luzern (SUI)
A 1-2 *Vossen (12)*
Köteles, Tshimanga, Hyland, Joseph-Monrose (Limbombe 84), Vossen, Gorius (Koulibaly 46), Ngcongca, Buffel (Nwanganga 84), Nadson, Dani Fernández, Benteke. Coach: Mario Been (NED)
H 2-0 *Dani Fernández (56), Masika (88)*
Köteles, Koulibaly, Hyland, Joseph-Monrose, Vossen (Hubert 90+5), Gorius, Ngcongca (Croux 84), Buffel, Nadson, Dani Fernández, Nwanganga (Masika 86). Coach: Mario Been (NED)

Group G
Match 1 - Videoton FC (HUN)
H 3-0 *Vossen (22), Buffel (78), De Ceulaer (90+2)*
Van Hout, Koulibaly, Hyland, Joseph-Monrose (Plet 81), Vossen (Yao Kumordzi 86), Gorius, Hamalainen, Simaeys, Buffel, Dani Fernández (Nadson 83), De Ceulaer. Coach: Mario Been (NED)
Match 2 - FC Basel 1893 (SUI)
A 2-2 *De Ceulaer (10), Vossen (38)*
Van Hout, Tshimanga, Koulibaly, Vossen, Gorius, Ngcongca, Buffel (Nwanganga 67), Nadson, Dani Fernández, De Ceulaer (Hamalainen 77), Yao Kumordzi (Plet 86). Coach: Mario Been (NED)
Match 3 - Sporting Clube de Portugal (POR)
H 2-1 *De Ceulaer (25), Barda (88)*
Van Hout, Koulibaly, Joseph-Monrose (Barda 83), Vossen (Yao Kumordzi 90+3), Gorius, Hamalainen, Ngcongca, Buffel, Nadson, Dani Fernández, De Ceulaer (Plet 62). Coach: Mario Been (NED)
Match 4 - Sporting Clube de Portugal (POR)
A 1-1 *Plet (90+1)*
Van Hout, Tshimanga, Koulibaly, Hyland (Plet 67), Joseph-Monrose (Masika 77), Vossen, Gorius, Ngcongca, Buffel, Nadson, Dani Fernández. Coach: Mario Been (NED)

Match 5 - Videoton FC (HUN)
A 1-0 *Barda (19)*
Van Hout, Tshimanga, Hyland, Joseph-Monrose (Masika 76), Vossen (Yao Kumordzi 90), Gorius, Ngcongca, Barda (Plet 70), Buffel, Nadson, Dani Fernández. Coach: Mario Been (NED)
Match 6 - FC Basel 1893 (SUI)
H 0-0
Köteles, Koulibaly, Hubert, Hyland, Hamalainen, Plet, Ngcongca, Barda (Joseph-Monrose 69), Dani Fernández, De Ceulaer (Masika 58), Limbombe (Schrijvers 89). Coach: Mario Been (NED)

Round of 32 - VfB Stuttgart (GER)
A 1-1 *Plet (90+1)*
Köteles, Tshimanga, Koulibaly, Hyland, Vossen (Plet 68), Ngcongca, Simaeys, Barda, Buffel, De Ceulaer (Joseph-Monrose 83), Yao Kumordzi (Gorius 74). Coach: Mario Been (NED)
H 0-2
Köteles, Tshimanga, Koulibaly, Hyland, Gorius, Plet, Ngcongca, Simaeys, Buffel (Ojo 77), De Ceulaer (Joseph-Monrose 71), Yao Kumordzi (Barda 61). Coach: Mario Been (NED)

KAA GENT

KAA GENT

Second qualifying round - FC Differdange 03 (LUX)
A 1-0 *César Arzo (27)*
Padt, Corstjens, Melli, Brüls, Barić, César Arzo, Kola (Arbeitman 71), Van der Bruggen, Messoudi (Foket 79), Conté, Maréval. Coach: Trond Sollied (NOR)
H 3-2 *Melli (41), Conté (63), Kola (73)*
Boeckx, Corstjens, Melli, Brüls, Barić, César Arzo (N'Diaye 74), Kola, Van der Bruggen (Raman 80), Messoudi (Arbeitman 85), Wallace, Conté. Coach: Trond Sollied (NOR)

Third qualifying round - Videoton FC (HUN)
A 0-1
Padt, Melli, Brüls (Soumahoro 82), Arbeitman, N'Diaye, César Arzo, Van der Bruggen, Rafinha, Messoudi (Remacle 72), Conté, Maréval. Coach: Trond Sollied (NOR)
H 0-3
Padt, Gecov (Messoudi 60), Melli, Brüls, Arbeitman, Remacle, N'Diaye, Barić (Kola 60), César Arzo, Conté, Maréval (Wallace 69). Coach: Trond Sollied (NOR)
Red cards: Brüls 64, Messoudi 85

Domestic league club-by-club

RSC ANDERLECHT

Coach: John van den Brom (NED)
1908 • Constant Vanden Stock (28,063) • rsca.be
Major honours
UEFA Cup Winners' Cup (2) 1976, 1978; UEFA Cup (1)
1983; UEFA Super Cup (2) 1976, 1978;
Belgian League (32) 1947, 1949, 1950, 1951, 1954,
1955, 1956, 1959, 1962, 1964, 1965, 1966, 1967, 1968,
1972, 1974, 1981, 1985, 1986, 1987, 1991, 1993, 1994,
1995, 2000, 2001, 2004, 2006, 2007, 2010, 2012, 2013;
Belgian Cup (9) 1965, 1972, 1973, 1975, 1976, 1988,
1989, 1994, 2008

2012

28/07	Kortrijk	a	1-1	Deschacht
04/08	Beerschot	h	1-0	Kanu
12/08	Cercle Brugge	a	3-0	Mbokani 3
18/08	Mons	h	2-1	Jovanović, Yakovenko
25/08	Leuven	a	1-1	Yakovenko
02/09	Genk	h	2-2	Jovanović, Bruno
15/09	Lierse	a	1-1	Kanu
22/09	Zulte Waregem	a	3-2	Mbokani, Yakovenko, De Sutter
29/09	Lokeren	h	3-0	Mbokani 2, Deschacht
07/10	Standard	a	1-2	Jovanović
19/10	Waasland-Beveren	h	2-0	Biglia, Jovanović
27/10	Charleroi	a	0-2	
30/10	Gent	h	5-0	De Sutter 2, Praet, Bruno, Yakovenko
03/11	Mechelen	a	4-1	Kouyaté, De Sutter 3
11/11	Club Brugge	h	6-1	Bruno, Mbokani, Jovanović (p), Kljestan, Biglia (p), Praet
18/11	Kortrijk	h	1-0	Mbokani
24/11	Beerschot	a	4-1	Bruno, Mbokani, Gillet (p), Yakovenko
01/12	Cercle Brugge	h	2-1	Biglia (p), Vargas
08/12	Mons	a	5-0	Mbokani 3, Kanu, Gillet (p)
16/12	Lierse	h	2-1	Mbokani 2 (1p)
23/12	Genk	h	4-0	Gillet, Kanu, Suárez 2, Yakovenko
27/12	Lierse	a	4-1	Mbokani, Jovanović, De Sutter, Vargas

2013

09/01	Lokeren	a	2-0	De Sutter, Yakovenko
09/02	Standard	h	2-2	Biglia, Gillet
10/02	Waasland-Beveren	a	2-1	Mbokani, Kanu
15/02	Charleroi	h	2-0	Mbokani, Bruno
24/02	Club Brugge	a	2-2	Bruno, Armenteros
27/02	Zulte Waregem	h	0-1	
09/03	Mechelen	h	1-0	De Sutter
16/03	Gent	a	1-1	Jovanović
01/04	Genk	h	1-2	Nuytinck
06/04	Standard	a	0-0	
14/04	Club Brugge	h	1-1	Mbokani
17/04	Lokeren	h	3-0	Jovanović, De Sutter, Kljestan
21/04	Zulte Waregem	a	1-2	Mbokani
28/04	Club Brugge	a	1-2	Bruno
05/05	Standard	h	2-0	Gillet 2 (1p)
12/05	Genk	a	2-1	Suárez, og (Hyland)
16/05	Lokeren	a	4-2	Kljestan, Suárez 2, De Zeeuw
19/05	Zulte Waregem	h	1-1	Biglia

No	Name	Nat	DoB	Pos	Aps	(s)	Gls
7	Samuel Armenteros	SWE	27/05/90	A		(3)	1
5	Lucas Biglia	ARG	30/01/86	M	37		5
45	Massimo Bruno		17/09/93	M	26	(7)	7
15	Cyriac Gohi Bi	CIV	05/08/90	A		(2)	
21	Tom De Sutter		03/07/85	A	21	(10)	12
6	Demy de Zeeuw	NED	26/05/83	M	3	(9)	1
3	Olivier Deschacht		16/02/81	D	25	(2)	2

55	Fernando Canesin	BRA	27/02/92	M	1	(3)	
30	Guillaume Gillet		09/03/84	D	32		6
4	Osama Hawsawi	KSA	31/03/84	D	1		
11	Milan Jovanović	SRB	18/04/81	A	31	(2)	8
23	Roland Juhász	HUN	01/07/83	D	1	(2)	
13	Thomas Kaminski		23/10/92	G	1		
10	Kanu	BRA	23/09/87	A	14	(7)	4
19	Sacha Kljestan	USA	09/09/85	M	31	(4)	3
16	Cheikhou Kouyaté	SEN	21/12/89	M	32	(1)	1
6	Bedi Mbenza	COD	11/09/84	M		(1)	
25	Dieumerci Mbokani	COD	22/11/85	A	27		19
7	Guillermo Molins	SWE	26/09/88	D	1	(2)	
14	Bram Nuytinck	NED	04/05/90	D	33		1
8	Denis Odoi		27/05/88	D	10	(4)	
26	Dennis Praet		14/05/94	M	22	(5)	2
1	Silvio Proto		23/05/83	G	39		
77	Reynaldo	BRA	24/08/89	M	1		
20	Behrang Safari	SWE	09/02/85	D	18	(2)	
9	Matías Suárez	ARG	09/05/88	A	8	(3)	3
39	Anthony Vanden Borre		24/10/87	D		(1)	
70	Ronald Vargas	VEN	02/12/86	M	5	(6)	2
27	Marcin Wasilewski	POL	09/06/80	D	13	(9)	
17	Olexandr Yakovenko	UKR	23/06/87	M	7	(18)	7

K. BEERSCHOT AC

Coach: Adrie Koster (NED);
(29/11/12) Wim De Corte;
(23/01/13) Jacky Mathijssen
1999 • Olympisch Stadion (12,400) • beerschot.be
Major honours
Belgian Cup (2) 1997, 2005

2012

28/07	Lokeren	h	2-4	Alpaslan, og (Mijat Maric)
04/08	Anderlecht	a	0-1	
11/08	Zulte Waregem	h	1-1	De Corte Ari
18/08	Club Brugge	a	1-3	S Wuytens
25/08	Charleroi	h	2-0	Losada, S Wuytens
01/09	Mechelen	a	2-0	Ojo, Losada
16/09	Standard	h	3-2	Coulibaly 2, Mununga
22/09	Kortrijk	h	2-1	Brillant, Losada (p)
29/09	Mons	a	0-1	
05/10	Gent	h	2-2	Coulibaly, og (César Arzo)
20/10	Genk	a	0-3	
27/10	Leuven	h	1-3	Losada
31/10	Cercle Brugge	a	1-3	Mununga
03/11	Waasland-Beveren	h	1-2	Veselinović
10/11	Lierse	a	3-1	Veselinović 2, François
18/11	Lokeren	a	0-1	
24/11	Anderlecht	h	1-4	Laerenbergh
01/12	Zulte Waregem	a	0-0	
09/12	Club Brugge	h	1-7	Dayan
15/12	Charleroi	a	0-1	
22/12	Mechelen	h	0-1	
27/12	Standard	a	0-3	

2013

19/01	Kortrijk	a	0-4	
26/01	Mons	h	0-0	
02/02	Gent	a	1-2	Ogunjimi
09/02	Genk	h	0-2	
16/02	Leuven	a	1-1	Raman
23/02	Lierse	h	1-3	Raman
09/03	Waasland-Beveren	a	2-3	Raman, Losada
16/03	Cercle Brugge	h	3-1	Bodor, Dayan 2 (1p)
30/03	Cercle Brugge	h	1-0	Raman
06/04	Cercle Brugge	a	0-1	
13/04	Cercle Brugge	h	1-2	Lépicier
20/04	Cercle Brugge	a	1-2	Raman

No	Name	Nat	DoB	Pos	Aps	(s)	Gls
21	Alpaslan Öztürk	TUR	10/07/93	A	25	(1)	1
27	Boldizsár Bodor	HUN	27/04/82	D	6	(4)	1
4	Frédéric Brillant	FRA	26/06/85	D	31		1
22	Maxime Chanot	LUX	21/11/89	D	9		
14	Elimane Coulibaly		15/03/80	A	11		3
29	Roei Dayan	ISR	19/09/84	A	6	(6)	3
6	Wim De Decker		06/04/82	M	28		1
24	Giel Deferm		30/06/88	D	9	(1)	
30	Stefan Deloose		14/01/90	G	6		
24	Guillaume François		03/06/90	A	10	(8)	1
7	Goran Galešić	BIH	11/03/89	M	6	(6)	
28	Connor Laerenbergh		18/03/93	A	1	(1)	1
5	Maël Lépicier	COD	14/01/86	M	8		1
17	Hernán Losada	ARG	09/05/82	M	25		5
31	Dor Malul	ISR	30/04/89	D	4	(4)	
2	Stefano Marzo		22/03/91	D	15	(4)	
25	Tomislav Mikulić	CRO	30/06/82	D	21		
10	Joachim Mununga		30/06/88	A	17	(7)	2
27	Kennedy Nwanganga	NGA	15/08/90	A	5	(2)	
11	Vusumuzi Nyoni	ZIM	21/04/84	M	22		
31	Marvin Ogunjimi		12/10/87	A	7	(3)	1
23	Funso Ojo		28/08/91	M	19	(5)	1
27	Benito Raman		07/11/94	A	6	(5)	5
30	Raúl Bravo	ESP	14/04/81	D	8	(3)	
30	Stijn Stijnen		07/04/81	G	20		
11	Joey Suk	IDN	08/07/89	A	7	(4)	
20	Thibaut Van Acker		21/11/91	M	11		
20	Koen Van Langendonck		09/06/89	G	8	(2)	
9	Dalibor Veselinović	SRB	12/09/87	A	5	(4)	3
28	Wamberto		07/10/94	A	2	(4)	
3	Dries Wuytens		18/03/91	D	1		
15	Stijn Wuytens		08/10/89	M	15	(1)	2
29	Georgiy Zhukov		19/11/94	M		(3)	

CERCLE BRUGGE KSV

Coach: Bob Peeters; (27/10/12) (Lorenzo Staelens);
(05/11/12) Foeke Booy (NED);
(02/04/13) Lorenzo Staelens
1899 • Jan Breydelstadion (29,042) • cerclebrugge.be
Major honours
Belgian League (3) 1911, 1927, 1930;
Belgian Cup (2) 1927, 1985

2012

29/07	Genk	a	3-3	Van Eenoo 2, Vetokele
04/08	Kortrijk	h	1-2	Portier
12/08	Anderlecht	h	0-3	
18/08	Leuven	a	2-3	Yashchuk (p), Rudy
25/08	Lierse	h	0-2	
01/09	Waasland-Beveren	a	0-2	
15/09	Lokeren	h	0-1	
23/09	Club Brugge	a	0-4	
29/09	Charleroi	h	2-2	Rudy
06/10	Zulte Waregem	a	1-3	Gudjohnsen (p)
20/10	Mechelen	h	1-2	Gudjohnsen
26/10	Standard	a	1-2	Gudjohnsen
31/10	Beerschot	h	3-1	Bakenga, Gudjohnsen (p), Evens
03/11	Mons	a	2-3	Bakenga 2
10/11	Gent	h	2-2	Rudy, Bakenga
17/11	Genk	h	3-1	Evens, Gudjohnsen, Uchebo
24/11	Kortrijk	a	1-3	Bakenga
01/12	Anderlecht	a	1-2	Bakenga
08/12	Leuven	h	1-2	Gudjohnsen (p)
15/12	Lierse	a	1-1	Van Eenoo
22/12	Waasland-Beveren	h	2-2	Smolders 2
26/12	Lokeren	a	0-3	

2013

02/02	Zulte Waregem	h	1-2	Uchebo
09/02	Mechelen	a	0-2	
16/02	Standard	h	0-1	
20/02	Charleroi	a	1-2	Mertens
23/02	Gent	a	0-2	
28/02	Club Brugge	h	0-3	
09/03	Mons	h	1-3	Boghossian
16/03	Beerschot	a	1-3	Buyl
30/03	Beerschot	a	0-1	
06/04	Beerschot	h	1-0	William Carvalho
13/04	Beerschot	a	2-1	Mertens, Boi
20/04	Beerschot	h	2-1	William Carvalho, Bakenga

No	Name	Nat	DoB	Pos	Aps	(s)	Gls
25	Mushenga Bakenga	NOR	08/08/92	A	18	(9)	7
15	Joaquín Boghossian	URU	19/06/87	A	1	(5)	1
24	Frederik Boi		25/10/81	D	12		1
40	Stephen Buyl		02/09/92	A	1	(3)	1
39	Jo Coppens		21/12/90	G	9	(1)	
8	Hans Cornelis		23/10/82	D	25		
30	Kristof D'Haene		06/06/90	D	14	(14)	
19	Francis Dickoh	GHA	13/12/82	D	7		
4	Bernt Evens		09/11/78	D	32		2
22	Joey Godee	NED	02/03/89	A	7	(1)	
22	Eidur Smári Gudjohnsen	ISL	15/09/78	A	12	(1)	6
18	Kevin Janssens		29/05/86	A		(8)	
5	Gregory Mertens		02/02/91	M	15		2
37	Niels Mestdagh		03/01/93	D	2	(1)	
34	Arne Naudts		27/11/93	A		(3)	
3	Anthony Portier		01/06/82	D	13		1
14	Rudy	POR	05/01/89	A	16	(12)	3
7	Tim Smolders		26/08/80	M	18	(6)	2
10	Michael Uchebo	NGA	27/09/90	A	20	(12)	2
24	Lukas Van Eenoo		06/02/91	M	29	(1)	3
28	Karel Van Roose		01/04/90	M	11	(4)	
25	Bram Verbist		05/03/83	G	25		
7	Igor Vetokele		23/03/92	A	4	(1)	
6	Arnar Thór Vidarsson	ISL	15/03/78	M	32		
21	William Carvalho	POR	07/04/92	M	18	(5)	2
26	Stef Wils		02/08/92	D	22	(1)	
9	Oleh Yashchuk	UKR	26/10/77	A	11	(1)	1

R. CHARLEROI SC

Coach: Yannick Ferrera; (14/02/13) Luka Peruzović (CRO); (18/03/13) Mario Notaro (ITA)
1904 • Pays de Charleroi (22,000) • sporting-charleroi.be

2012

28/07	Mechelen	a	2-4	Kaya, Milicevic
04/08	Club Brugge	h	0-1	
11/08	Kortrijk	a	1-0	Kudemor
19/08	Standard	h	2-6	Gnohéré, Bojovic
25/08	Beerschot	a	0-2	
01/09	Gent	h	1-1	Bojović
15/09	Mons	a	3-2	Kage, Gnohéré, Badibanga
23/09	Genk	h	1-2	Badibanga
29/09	Cercle Brugge	a	0-1	
06/10	Leuven	h	0-4	
20/10	Lierse	a	1-0	Rossini
27/10	Anderlecht	h	2-0	Rossini, og (Wasilewski)
31/10	Zulte Waregem	a	1-4	Badibanga
03/11	Lokeren	h	0-2	
10/11	Waasland-Beveren	a	0-0	
17/11	Mechelen	h	1-1	Rossini
25/11	Club Brugge	a	0-1	
01/12	Kortrijk	h	2-0	Milicevic, Aoulad
07/12	Standard	a	1-6	Rossini
15/12	Beerschot	h	1-0	Kudemor
23/12	Gent	a	2-1	Aoulad, Bopp
26/12	Mons	h	1-2	Rossini

2013

02/02	Zulte Waregem	h	1-2	Uchebo
09/02	Mechelen	a	0-2	
16/02	Standard	h	0-1	
20/02	Charleroi	a	1-2	Mertens
23/02	Gent	a	0-2	
28/02	Club Brugge	h	0-3	
09/03	Mons	h	1-3	Boghossian
16/03	Beerschot	a	1-3	Buyl
30/03	Beerschot	a	0-1	
06/04	Beerschot	h	1-0	William Carvalho
13/04	Beerschot	a	2-1	Mertens, Boi
20/04	Beerschot	h	2-1	William Carvalho, Bakenga

No	Name	Nat	DoB	Pos	Aps	(s)	Gls
20	Mohammed Aoulad		29/08/91	M	6	(4)	2
9	Vicente Arze	BOL	22/11/85	M		(4)	
29	Ziguy Badibanga		26/11/91	A	14	(9)	3
23	Cyprien Baguette		12/05/89	G	1		
21	Mijuško Bojović	MNE	09/08/88	D	25		2
28	Viktor Bopp	GER	31/10/89	M	6	(7)	1
6	Dorian Dessoleil		07/08/92	D	5		
13	Christophe Diandy	SEN	25/11/90	M	28	(1)	
3	Elvedin Džinić	SVN	25/08/85	D	13	(8)	1
27	Ederson	BRA	14/01/86	M	21	(4)	
99	Mynor Escoe	CRC	06/04/91	A	4	(8)	
14	Samuel Fabris		30/01/91	M	6	(5)	
22	Guillaume François		03/06/90	A	5	(4)	
31	Harlem Gnohéré	CIV	21/02/88	A	8	(8)	2
80	Kenneth Houdret		09/08/83	M	1	(8)	
4	Omar Jarun	PLE	10/12/93	D	1	(1)	
10	Hervé Kage		10/04/89	M	13	(3)	1
24	Onur Kaya		20/04/86	M	30	(4)	4
25	Abraham Kudemor	GHA	25/02/85	M	20	(5)	2
26	Grégory Lazitch		26/05/92	D		(1)	
30	Leandro	BRA	31/03/85	M	1		
35	Parfait Mandanda	COD	10/10/89	G	25		
8	Martos	ESP	04/01/84	M	29		
77	Danijel Milicevic	SUI	05/01/86	M	21	(5)	3
19	Francis N'Ganga	CGO	16/06/85	D	29	(2)	
17	Matan Ohayon	ISR	25/02/86	D	17		
16	Pedro	ESP	10/03/84	M		(1)	
10	David Pollet		12/08/88	A	14		6
86	Giuseppe Rossini		23/08/86	A	18	(4)	6
5	Mourad Satli	ALG	29/01/90	D	22	(5)	
1	Mihail Sifakis	GRE	09/09/84	G	10		
33	Jamal Thiaré	SEN	31/03/93	A	2	(2)	1
93	Jean-Christophe Vergerolle	FRA	12/07/85	D	1		

CLUB BRUGGE KV

Coach: Georges Leekens; (04/11/12) (Philippe Clement); (15/11/12) Juan Carlos Garrido (ESP)
1891 • Jan Breydelstadion (29,042) • clubbrugge.be
Major honours
Belgian League (13) 1920, 1973, 1976, 1977, 1978, 1980, 1988, 1990, 1992, 1996, 1998, 2003, 2005; Belgian Cup (10) 1968, 1970, 1977, 1986, 1991, 1995, 1996, 2002, 2004, 2007

2012

28/07	Waasland-Beveren	h	3-1	Refaelov 2 (1p), Meunier
04/08	Charleroi	a	1-0	Meunier
11/08	Mechelen	a	3-3	Refaelov 2 (1p), Meunier
18/08	Beerschot	h	3-1	Bacca, Blondel, Meunier
26/08	Mons	a	3-1	Tchité, Víctor Vázquez, Bacca
02/09	Standard	h	4-2	Bacca 2, Refaelov (p), Tchité
14/09	Kortrijk	a	1-1	Bacca
23/09	Cercle Brugge	h	4-0	Lestienne 3, Bacca
30/09	Gent	a	2-2	Bacca (p), Lestienne
07/10	Genk	h	1-1	Bacca
20/10	Leuven	a	1-4	Bacca
28/10	Lokeren	h	2-3	Tchité 2
31/10	Lierse	a	2-3	Bacca 2
04/11	Zulte Waregem	h	0-1	
11/11	Anderlecht	a	1-6	Lestienne
17/11	Waasland-Beveren	a	6-2	Bacca 2, Refaelov 2, Lestienne, Vleminckx
25/11	Charleroi	h	1-0	Vleminckx
01/12	Mechelen	h	1-1	Vleminckx
09/12	Beerschot	a	7-1	Donk, Bacca 2, Lestienne, Tchité, Zimling, Refaelov
15/12	Mons	h	2-0	Bacca, Lestienne
23/12	Standard	a	3-1	Lestienne 2, Bacca
26/12	Kortrijk	h	0-0	

2013

27/01	Gent	h	0-0	
03/02	Genk	a	1-4	Bacca
09/02	Leuven	h	3-1	Lestienne, Refaelov, Trickovski
17/02	Lokeren	a	1-1	Víctor Vázquez
24/02	Anderlecht	h	2-2	Odjidja-Ofoe, Bacca
28/02	Cercle Brugge	a	3-0	Duarte, Gudjohnsen, Odjidja-Ofoe
09/03	Zulte Waregem	a	2-1	Bacca, Gudjohnsen
16/03	Lierse	h	3-0	Lestienne, Bacca 2
01/04	Standard	h	0-2	
05/04	Lokeren	a	4-1	Lestienne, Duarte, Odjidja-Ofoe 2 (1p)
14/04	Anderlecht	a	1-1	og (Odoi)
18/04	Zulte Waregem	h	3-4	Donk, Jørgensen, Odjidja-Ofoe
21/04	Genk	a	2-0	Bacca, Gudjohnsen
28/04	Anderlecht	h	2-1	Lestienne 2
05/05	Lokeren	a	2-1	Lestienne, Refaelov
12/05	Standard	a	4-2	Lestienne, Duarte, Bacca, Víctor Vázquez
16/05	Zulte Waregem	a	2-5	Donk 2
19/05	Genk	h	1-0	Bacca

No	Name	Nat	DoB	Pos	Aps	(s)	Gls
6	Enoch Adu	GHA	14/09/90	M	8	(3)	
15	Joseph Akpala	NGA	24/08/90	A	2	(1)	
3	Michael Almebäck	SWE	04/04/88	D	12	(1)	
7	Carlos Bacca	COL	08/09/86	A	33	(2)	25
11	Jonathan Blondel		03/04/84	M	14	(1)	1
21	Bart Buysse		16/10/86	D	14		
28	Laurens De Bock		07/11/92	D	7	(4)	
18	Ryan Donk	NED	30/03/86	D	31	(1)	4
31	Óscar Duarte	CRC	03/06/89	D	17		3
22	Eidur Smári Gudjohnsen	ISL	15/09/78	A	6	(12)	3
4	Carl Hoefkens		06/10/78	D	23	(1)	
2	Tom Høgli	NOR	24/02/84	D	20	(4)	
22	Jordi	ESP	16/05/87	D	15		
39	Bojan Jorgačević	SRB	12/02/82	G	12		
10	Jesper Jørgensen	DEN	05/05/84	M	18	(7)	1
33	Vladan Kujović	SRB	23/08/78	G	28	(1)	
14	Jim Larsen	DEN	06/11/85	D	13		
16	Maxime Lestienne		17/06/92	A	31	(7)	17
45	Brandon Mechele		28/01/93	M		(3)	
19	Thomas Meunier		12/09/91	M	15	(6)	4
32	Vadis Odjidja-Ofoe		21/02/89	M	28	(3)	5
8	Lior Refaelov	ISR	26/04/86	M	22	(6)	10
5	Frederik Stenman	SWE	02/06/83	D	13	(4)	
10	Mohammed Tchité	COD	31/01/84	A	14	(7)	5
17	Ivan Trickovski	MKD	18/04/87	A	4	(14)	1
20	Thibaut Van Acker		21/11/91	M	4	(4)	
41	Birger Verstraete		16/04/94	M	4		
13	Víctor Vázquez	ESP	20/01/87	M	24	(4)	3
9	Björn Vleminckx		01/12/85	A	3	(7)	3
6	Niki Zimling	DEN	19/04/85	M	5	(2)	1

KRC GENK

Coach: Mario Been (NED)
1988 • Cristal Arena (25,010) • krcgenk.be
Major honours
Belgian League (3) 1999, 2002, 2011;
Belgian Cup (4) 1998, 2000, 2009, 2013

2012

29/07	Cercle Brugge	h	3-3	Benteke 2, Vossen
05/08	Leuven	a	2-2	Benteke, Buffel
12/08	Lokeren	h	1-0	Buffel
18/08	Lierse	a	1-1	Joseph-Monrose
26/08	Zulte Waregem	h	2-0	Gorius, Vossen
02/09	Anderlecht	a	2-2	De Ceulaer, Joseph-Monrose
15/09	Waasland-Beveren	h	1-1	Vossen
23/09	Charleroi	a	2-1	Vossen, Gorius
29/09	Mechelen	h	2-1	Vossen, De Ceulaer
07/10	Club Brugge	a	1-1	De Ceulaer
20/10	Beerschot	h	3-0	Vossen, Joseph-Monrose, Plet
28/10	Kortrijk	a	1-1	Vossen
31/10	Standard	h	0-2	
03/11	Gent	a	2-1	Barda, Plet
11/11	Mons	h	5-1	Vossen 2, Gorius, Plet 2
17/11	Cercle Brugge	a	1-3	og (Portier)
25/11	Leuven	h	1-1	Plet
02/12	Lokeren	a	4-3	Vossen 3 (1p), Joseph-Monrose
09/12	Lierse	h	4-1	Gorius, Barda 2 (1p), Plet
16/12	Zulte Waregem	a	2-3	og (Godeau), Hyland
23/12	Anderlecht	h	2-4	Koulibaly, Plet
26/12	Waasland-Beveren	a	1-1	Vossen

2013

19/01	Charleroi	h	3-1	Barda (p), Vossen, Plet
26/01	Mechelen	a	1-2	Buffel
03/02	Club Brugge	h	4-1	Hyland 2 (1p), Barda, Limbombe
09/02	Beerschot	a	2-0	Vossen 2
17/02	Kortrijk	h	2-0	Simaeys, Plet
24/02	Standard	a	0-0	
09/03	Gent	h	3-2	Buffel, Yao Kumordzi, Gorius
16/03	Mons	a	5-1	Gorius (p), Yao Kumordzi, Ojo, De Ceulaer 2
01/04	Anderlecht	a	2-1	Kara, Vossen
07/04	Zulte Waregem	h	1-1	Ngcongca
13/04	Lokeren	h	2-1	Plet, Ngcongca
16/04	Standard	a	0-3	
21/04	Club Brugge	h	0-2	
28/04	Lokeren	a	0-0	
03/05	Zulte Waregem	a	4-0	og (Godeau), Joseph-Monrose, De Ceulaer, Barda
12/05	Anderlecht	h	1-2	Kara
16/05	Standard	h	1-1	Gorius
19/05	Club Brugge	a	0-1	

No	Name	Nat	DoB	Pos	Aps	(s)	Gls
18	Elyaniv Barda	ISR	15/12/81	A	9	(14)	6
9	Christian Benteke		03/12/90	A	5		3
19	Thomas Buffel		19/02/81	M	38	(1)	4
15	Fabien Camus	TUN	28/02/85	M		(3)	
37	Jordy Croux		15/01/94	M	3	(3)	
21	Dani Fernández	ESP	20/01/83	D	25	(1)	
23	Benjamin De Ceulaer		19/12/83	A	23	(3)	6
10	Julien Gorius	FRA	17/03/85	M	36	(2)	7
11	Brian Hamalainen	DEN	29/05/89	D	12	(2)	
6	David Hubert		12/02/88	D	1	(2)	
7	Khaleem Hyland	TRI	05/06/89	M	32	(1)	3
8	Steven Joseph-Monrose	FRA	20/07/90	A	31	(6)	5
2	Sérigne Modou Kara	SEN	11/11/89	D	9	(1)	
26	László Köteles	HUN	01/09/84	G	23		
5	Kalidou Koulibaly	FRA	20/06/91	D	31		1
35	Anthony Limbombe		15/07/94	M	2	(7)	1
36	Ayub Masika	KEN	10/09/92	M	3	(8)	
20	Nadson	BRA	18/10/84	D	15	(3)	
16	Anele Ngcongca	RSA	20/10/87	D	29		2
27	Kennedy Nwaganga	NGA	15/08/90	A		(4)	
6	Kim Ojo	NGA	02/12/88	A	1	(9)	1
14	Glynor Plet	NED	30/01/87	A	8	(19)	10
38	Siebe Schrijvers		18/07/96	M		(1)	
17	Jeroen Simaeys		12/05/85	D	16		1
15	Derrick Tshimanga		06/11/88	D	28		
1	Kristof Van Hout		09/02/87	G	17		
9	Jelle Vossen		22/03/89	A	31	(1)	17
40	Sandy Walsh	NED	14/03/95	D		(1)	
45	Bennard Yao Kumordzi	GHA	21/03/85	M	12	(13)	2

KAA GENT

Coach: Trond Sollied (NOR);
(23/10/12) (Manu Ferrera); (01/11/12) Bob Peeters;
(09/01/13) Víctor Fernández (ESP)
1898 • Jules Ottenstadion (12,919) • kaagent.be
Major honours
Belgian Cup (3) 1964, 1984, 2010

2012

29/07	Lierse	h	2-0	Arbeitman 2
05/08	Zulte Waregem	a	1-3	Remacle (p)
12/08	Leuven	h	1-1	Wallace
18/08	Waasland-Beveren	a	2-0	Van der Bruggen, Brüls
26/08	Lokeren	h	2-1	Thijs (p), Brüls
01/09	Charleroi	a	1-1	Conté
15/09	Mechelen	h	0-2	
21/09	Standard	a	2-1	og (Van Damme), César Arzo
30/09	Club Brugge	h	0-0	Mboyo, Remacle (p)
05/10	Beerschot	a	2-2	N'Diaye, César Arzo
20/10	Kortrijk	h	0-1	
27/10	Mons	h	2-0	Mboyo 2
30/10	Anderlecht	a	0-5	
03/11	Genk	h	1-2	Soumahoro
10/11	Cercle Brugge	a	2-2	Mboyo 2 (1p)
17/11	Lierse	a	0-2	
24/11	Zulte Waregem	a	0-1	
01/12	Leuven	a	1-1	N'Diaye
08/12	Waasland-Beveren	h	0-2	
15/12	Lokeren	a	2-2	Mboyo 2
22/12	Charleroi	h	1-2	Mboyo
26/12	Mechelen	a	0-1	

2013

19/01	Standard	h	0-0	
27/01	Club Brugge	a	0-0	
02/02	Beerschot	h	2-1	Mboyo 2 (1p)
09/02	Kortrijk	a	0-1	
16/02	Mons	a	2-0	Mboyo, Kage
23/02	Cercle Brugge	h	2-0	Soumahoro, Mboyo
09/03	Genk	a	2-3	Kola, Mboyo
16/03	Anderlecht	h	1-1	Kola
30/03	Mons	h	2-1	Mboyo 2 (1p)
06/04	Kortrijk	a	0-0	
13/04	Lierse	a	2-1	Mboyo (p), Kage
20/04	Lierse	h	3-0	Mboyo, Nahayo, Coulibaly
27/04	Kortrijk	h	1-0	Mboyo
04/05	Mons	a	1-1	Lepoint
11/05	Leuven	a	4-1	Soumahoro, Kage, Van der Bruggen, Mboyo (p)
18/05	Leuven	h	4-1	Jorge López 2, Brüls, Coulibaly
23/05	Standard	h	1-0	Mboyo
26/05	Standard	a	0-7	

No	Name	Nat	DoB	Pos	Aps	(s)	Gls
23	Shlomi Arbeitman	ISR	14/05/85	A	3	(7)	2
1	Frank Boeckx		27/09/86	G	17		
23	Christian Brüls		30/09/88	M	27	(6)	3
28	César Arzo	ESP	21/01/86	D	31		2
28	Ibrahima Conté	GUI	03/04/91	M	13	(3)	1
16	Elimane Coulibaly	SEN	15/03/80	A	1	(7)	2
23	Stijn De Smet		27/03/85	A	4	(3)	
30	Magnus Eriksson	SWE	08/04/90	A	2	(2)	
32	Thomas Foket		25/09/84	M	4	(2)	
3	Marcel Gecov	CZE	01/01/88	M	5	(2)	
3	David Hubert		12/02/88	M	17		
30	Jorge López	ESP	19/09/78	A	8	(7)	2
11	Hervé Kage		10/04/89	M	14	(1)	3
16	Rodgers Kola	ZAM	04/07/89	A	7	(4)	2
26	Christophe Lepoint		24/10/84	M	6	(6)	1
31	Rémi Maréval	FRA	24/02/83	D	28	(1)	
9	Ilombe Mboyo	COD	27/04/87	A	33	(1)	20
6	Juan Alberto Melli	ESP	06/06/84	D	21	(1)	
20	Mohamed Messoudi		07/01/84	M	4	(14)	
13	Mamoutou N'Diaye	MLI	15/03/90	M	18	(1)	2
5	Valery Nahayo	BDI	15/04/84	D	15	(3)	1
33	Sergio Padt	NED	06/06/90	G	23		
2	Pau Condrós	ESP	01/04/87	D	21	(1)	
19	Rafinha	BRA	29/06/82	D	23	(1)	
27	Benito Raman		07/11/94	A	1	(3)	
7	Jordan Remacle		14/02/87	M	13	(5)	2
10	Renato Neto	BRA	27/09/91	M	16	(1)	
6	Milan Savić	SRB	04/04/94	M	1		
22	Matija Škarabot	SVN	04/02/88	D	2	(1)	
24	Yaya Soumahoro	CIV	28/09/89	A	14	(17)	3
8	Bernd Thijs		28/06/78	M	2		1
17	Hannes Van der Bruggen		01/04/93	M	23	(9)	2
25	Wallace	BRA	29/10/86	D	8	(3)	1
23	Ervin Zukanović	BIH	11/02/87	D	15		

KV KORTRIJK

Coach: Hein Vanhaezebrouck
1971 • Guldensporenstadion (9,500) • kvk.be

2012

28/07	Anderlecht	h	1-1	Zukanović
04/08	Cercle Brugge	a	1-1	N'Tam Matton
11/08	Charleroi	h	0-1	
18/08	Zulte Waregem	a	0-2	
25/08	Waasland-Beveren	h	2-1	Mitrović, Pavlović
02/09	Lokeren	a	1-0	Zukanović
14/09	Club Brugge	h	1-1	Zukanović
22/09	Beerschot	a	1-2	Dejaegere
30/09	Standard	h	2-1	Zukanović, Chavarría
06/10	Mechelen	a	2-0	Chavarría, N'For
20/10	Gent	a	1-0	Oussalah
28/10	Genk	h	1-1	Chavarría
31/10	Mons	a	0-1	
03/11	Lierse	h	4-1	Dejaegere, Zukanović (p), Chavarría, Capon
10/11	Leuven	a	0-0	
18/11	Anderlecht	a	0-1	
24/11	Cercle Brugge	h	3-1	Chavarría 2, Mulemo
01/12	Charleroi	a	0-1	
08/12	Zulte Waregem	h	1-2	Mitrović
15/12	Waasland-Beveren	a	0-1	
21/12	Lokeren	h	2-3	N'For, Oussalah
26/12	Club Brugge	h	0-0	

2013

19/01	Beerschot	h	4-0	Oussalah 2, Pavlović, De Mets
25/01	Standard	a	0-2	
02/02	Mechelen	h	2-1	Mitrović, Chavarría
09/02	Gent	h	1-0	Dejaegere
17/02	Genk	a	0-2	

23/02	Mons	h	0-1	
09/03	Lierse	a	0-1	
16/03	Leuven	h	0-0	
30/03	Lierse	a	0-0	
06/04	Gent	h	0-0	
13/04	Mons	h	3-0	*Carević, N'For, De Mets*
20/04	Mons	a	1-2	*Oussalah*
27/04	Gent	a	0-1	
04/05	Lierse	h	0-3	

No	Name	Nat	DoB	Pos	Aps	(s)	Gls
21	Brecht Capon		22/04/88	D	24	(4)	1
18	Mario Carević	CRO	29/03/82	M	11	(3)	1
18	Pablo Chavarría	ARG	02/01/88	A	28		7
17	Gertjan De Mets		02/04/87	D	30		2
19	Brecht Dejaegere		29/05/91	M	27	(6)	3
9	Kévin Dupuis	FRA	14/01/87	A	4	(11)	
22	Jimmy Kamghain	FRA	03/07/92	A	4	(9)	
16	Darren Keet	RSA	05/08/89	G	34	(1)	
24	Blandel Koussalouha	FRA	25/10/91	M		(5)	
12	Gregory Mahau		09/05/94	M	1	(1)	
15	Baptiste Martin	FRA	14/05/85	D	30	(1)	
20	Thomas Matton		24/10/85	M	8	(4)	1
25	Stefan Mitrović	SRB	29/03/88	D	16	(6)	3
14	Landry Mulemo	COD	17/09/86	D	17	(5)	1
4	Ismaïla N'Diaye	SEN	22/01/88	M	9	(10)	
10	Ernest N'For	CMR	28/04/86	A	28	(3)	4
11	Mustapha Oussalah	MAR	19/02/82	M	29	(2)	5
8	Nebojša Pavlović	SRB	09/04/81	M	28	(1)	2
1	Rémi Pillot	FRA	27/07/90	G	1		
15	Dylan Ragolle		05/11/94	D	1	(1)	
29	Romain Reynaud	FRA	02/03/83	D	24		
5	Alassane També	FRA	26/01/92	D	10	(8)	
23	Baptiste Ulens		24/07/87	M	5	(4)	
1	Kristof Van Hout		09/02/87	G	1		
24	Olivier Verstraete		14/01/95	M	1	(2)	
9	David Wijns		09/01/87	D	4	(10)	
23	Ervin Zukanović	BIH	11/02/87	D	21		5

K. LIERSE SK
Coach: Chris Janssens;
(12/11/12) Hany Ramzy (EGY); (14/03/13) Eric Van Meir
1906• Herman Vanderpoortenstadion (14,538) •
lierse.com
Major honours
Belgian League (4) 1932, 1942, 1960, 1997;
Belgian Cup (2) 1969, 1999

2012

29/07	Gent	a	0-2	
03/08	Standard	h	0-0	
11/08	Mons	a	1-1	*Hazurov*
18/08	Genk	h	1-1	*Adesanya*
25/08	Cercle Brugge	a	3-0	*Bouarabia 2, Menga*
01/09	Leuven	h	1-1	*Hazurov*
15/09	Anderlecht	h	1-1	*Menga*
22/09	Waasland-Beveren	a	1-1	*A Said (p)*
29/09	Zulte Waregem	h	1-4	*Bidaoui*
06/10	Lokeren	a	2-2	*Hazurov, og (Gueye)*
20/10	Charleroi	h	0-1	
27/10	Mechelen	a	0-3	
31/10	Club Brugge	h	3-2	*Bouarabia 2, A Said*
03/11	Kortrijk	a	1-4	*El Gabbas*
10/11	Beerschot	h	1-3	*Hazurov*
17/11	Gent	h	2-0	*Hazurov 2*
23/11	Standard	a	0-3	
01/12	Mons	h	0-1	
09/12	Genk	a	1-4	*Hazurov*
15/12	Cercle Brugge	h	1-1	*Bouarabia*
23/12	Leuven	a	2-2	*Hazurov, El Gabbas (p)*
27/12	Anderlecht	a	1-4	*El Gabbas*

2013

19/01	Waasland-Beveren	h	0-0	
26/01	Zulte Waregem	a	0-2	
02/02	Lokeren	h	1-1	*Hazurov*
09/02	Charleroi	a	0-1	
16/02	Mechelen	h	0-2	
23/02	Beerschot	a	3-1	*Swinkels, Abou Moslem, Bouarabia*
09/03	Kortrijk	h	1-0	*Bouarabia*
16/03	Club Brugge	a	0-3	
30/03	Kortrijk	h	0-0	
06/04	Mons	a	1-2	*El Gabbas*
13/04	Gent	h	1-2	*El Gabbas*
20/04	Gent	a	0-3	
27/04	Mons	h	0-1	
04/05	Kortrijk	a	3-0	*S Said, og (Martin), Vercauteren*

No	Name	Nat	DoB	Pos	Aps	(s)	Gls
20	Ahmed Abou Moslem	EGY	26/02/92	D	7	(2)	1
19	Jason Adesanya		26/05/93	A	4	(16)	1
33	Lens Annab		20/07/88	M	5	(2)	
17	Ibrahim Ayew	GHA	16/04/88	M	17		
35	Cofie Bekoe	GHA	16/03/88	M	4	(8)	
8	Soufiane Bidaoui		20/04/90	M	13	(7)	1
25	Rachid Bouarabia	FRA	22/03/85	M	35	(1)	7
14	Daylon Claasen	RSA	28/01/90	M	6	(1)	
27	Glenn Claes		08/03/94	M	1	(1)	
16	Miguel Dachelet		16/01/88	D	19	(1)	
7	Mohamed El Gabbas	EGY	21/10/87	A	15	(12)	5
8	Ashour El Takky	EGY	28/11/80	M	4		
23	Ahmed Farag	EGY	10/03/81	D	9	(1)	
15	Frédéric Frans		03/01/89	D	8	(1)	
12	Nathan Goris		30/03/90	G	4		
9	Geoffry Hairemans		21/08/91	A	4	(6)	
24	Kostadin Hazurov	BUL	05/08/85	A	30	(2)	9
5	Jonas Heymans		06/02/93	D	10	(1)	
19	Benjamin Lambot		02/05/87	M	25	(2)	
22	Essam Mahmoud	EGY	20/06/77	G	2		
33	Dolly Menga		02/05/93	A	18	(2)	2
13	Richard Ofori	GHA	24/04/93	D	6	(2)	
9	Christian Pouga	CMR	19/06/86	A	3	(4)	
13	Ahmed Said	EGY	13/03/84	D	27	(1)	2
29	Saladin Said	ETH	29/10/88	A	1	(4)	1
23	Karim Saïdi	TUN	24/03/83	D	17		
22	Matz Sels		26/02/92	G	30		
9	Mostafa Shebeita	EGY	10/05/86	A	6	(1)	
2	Jasper Sols		30/06/95	A		(1)	
4	Arjan Swinkels	NED	15/10/84	D	16		1
16	Nick Van de walle		20/06/96	M		(1)	
17	Jasper Van der Heyden		03/07/95	A	1	(2)	
6	Julien Vercauteren		12/01/93	M	2	(6)	1
18	Thomas Wils		24/04/90	M	34		
13	Hussain Yasser	QAT	09/01/84	M	13	(3)	

KSC LOKEREN OV
Coach: Peter Maes
1970 • Daknamstadion (9,271) • sporting.be
Major honours
Belgian Cup (1) 2012

2012

28/07	Beerschot	a	4-2	*Patosi, De Ceulaer, Miloš Marić, Mijat Maric (p)*
04/08	Mons	h	2-2	*De Ceulaer 2*
12/08	Genk	a	0-1	
18/08	Mechelen	h	2-1	*Miloš Marić, Harbaoui*
26/08	Gent	a	1-2	*Taravel*
02/09	Kortrijk	h	0-1	
15/09	Cercle Brugge	a	1-0	*Persoons*

22/09	Leuven	h	2-2	*Mokulu, Miloš Marić*
29/09	Anderlecht	a	0-3	
06/10	Lierse	a	2-2	*De Pauw, Patosi*
20/10	Zulte Waregem	a	3-0	*Mijat Maric (p), Taravel, Harbaoui*
28/10	Club Brugge	a	3-2	*Harbaoui, De Pauw, Patosi*
31/10	Waasland-Beveren	h	2-0	*Patosi, Miloš Marić*
03/11	Charleroi	a	2-0	*Patosi, Miloš Marić*
09/11	Standard	h	2-1	*Harbaoui, Patosi*
18/11	Beerschot	h	1-0	*Mokulu*
24/11	Mons	a	2-1	*Persoons, Gueye*
02/12	Genk	h	3-4	*Leko, Mokulu, Persoons*
08/12	Mechelen	a	1-2	*Miloš Marić*
15/12	Gent	h	2-2	*Leko, Harbaoui*
21/12	Kortrijk	a	3-2	*Mijat Maric 2 (1p), Harbaoui*
26/12	Cercle Brugge	h	3-0	*Mijat Maric, Harbaoui, De Pauw*

2013

19/01	Leuven	a	6-2	*Mokulu 3, Leko, Persoons, Patosi*
26/01	Anderlecht	h	0-2	
02/02	Lierse	a	1-1	*Persoons*
09/02	Zulte Waregem	h	1-1	*Walter Fernández*
17/02	Club Brugge	h	1-1	*Miloš Marić*
23/02	Waasland-Beveren	a	0-0	
09/03	Charleroi	h	1-1	*Persoons*
16/03	Standard	a	2-0	*De Pauw, Harbaoui*
30/03	Zulte Waregem	a	1-1	*Taravel*
05/04	Club Brugge	h	1-4	*Mokulu*
13/04	Genk	a	1-2	*Mokulu*
17/04	Anderlecht	a	0-3	
20/04	Standard	h	4-1	*Mokulu, De Pauw, Harbaoui 2*
27/04	Genk	h	0-0	
05/05	Club Brugge	a	1-2	*Harbaoui*
11/05	Zulte Waregem	h	2-3	*Mijat Maric (p), Harbaoui*
16/05	Anderlecht	h	2-4	*og (Nuytinck), Taravel*
19/05	R Standard	a	3-4	*Mijat Maric, Júnior Dutra 2*

No	Name	Nat	DoB	Pos	Aps	(s)	Gls
1	Boubacar "Copa" Barry	CIV	30/12/79	G	27		
17	Alexandre Corryn		03/01/94	M	6	(3)	
28	Laurens De Bock		07/11/92	D	21		
11	Benjamin De Ceulaer		19/12/83	A	5		3
28	Preben De Man		27/09/95	M		(1)	
29	Nill De Pauw		06/01/90	A	23	(5)	5
3	Hassan El Mouataz	MAR	21/09/81	D	12	(1)	
19	Baye Djiby Fall	SEN	20/04/85	A		(2)	
13	Georgios Galitsios	GRE	06/07/86	D	37		
22	Paolo Grbac	CRO	09/07/90	M		(2)	
23	Ibrahima Gueye	SEN	19/02/78	D	5	(3)	1
9	Hamdi Harbaoui	TUN	05/01/85	A	36	(1)	12
19	Júnior Dutra	BRA	25/04/88	A	8	(7)	2
12	Jugoslav Lazić	SRB	12/12/79	G	13	(1)	
10	Ivan Leko	CRO	07/02/78	M	25	(6)	2
5	Mijat Maric	SUI	30/04/84	D	40		7
18	Miloš Marić	SRB	05/03/82	M	12	(22)	6
36	Cédric Mitu	COD	14/01/95	A		(1)	
14	Benjamin Mokulu		11/10/89	A	21	(10)	9
7	Killian Overmeire		06/12/85	M	39		
24	Ayanda Patosi	RSA	31/08/92	M	19	(3)	7
8	Koen Persoons		12/07/83	M	35		6
20	Enes Sağlik		08/07/91	A	9	(22)	
2	Alexander Scholz	DEN	24/10/92	D	11		
4	Jérémy Taravel	FRA	17/04/87	D	26		4
16	Jore Trompet		30/07/92	M	3	(11)	
6	Tsholola Tshinyama "Tiko"	COD	12/12/80	M	2	(2)	
11	Walter Fernández	ESP	14/08/89	M	5	(6)	1

KV MECHELEN

Coach: Harm van Veldhoven (NED)
1904 • Veolia Stadion (13,123) • kvmechelen.be
Major honours
UEFA Cup Winners' Cup (1) 1988;
UEFA Super Cup (1) 1989;
Belgian League (4) 1943, 1946, 1948, 1989;
Belgian Cup (1) 1987

2012

28/07	Charleroi	h	4-2	Henkens 2, De Petter 2
04/08	Waasland-Beveren	a	0-0	
11/08	Club Brugge	h	3-3	Enevoldsen, Van Tricht, De Petter
18/08	Lokeren	a	1-2	Destorme
26/08	Standard	a	2-3	Junker, Enevoldsen
01/09	Beerschot	h	0-2	
15/09	Gent	a	2-0	Destorme, Cordaro
22/09	Mons	h	3-0	Diabang 2, Henkens
29/09	Genk	a	1-2	De Witte
06/10	Kortrijk	h	0-2	
20/10	Cercle Brugge	a	2-1	Iddi, Pedersen
27/10	Lierse	h	3-0	Enevoldsen 2, Pedersen
31/10	Leuven	a	1-3	Destorme
03/11	Anderlecht	h	1-4	Pedersen
10/11	Zulte Waregem	a	1-1	Pedersen
17/11	Charleroi	a	1-1	Pedersen
24/11	Waasland-Beveren	h	0-1	
01/12	Club Brugge	a	1-1	Pedersen
08/12	Lokeren	h	2-1	Iddi, Henkens
15/12	Standard	h	0-2	
22/12	Beerschot	a	2-0	Destorme, Iddi
26/12	Gent	h	1-0	Ondoam

2013

19/01	Mons	a	3-2	Pedersen 2, Iddi
26/01	Genk	h	2-1	Pedersen, Iddi
02/02	Kortrijk	a	1-2	Junker
09/02	Cercle Brugge	h	2-0	De Witte, Junker
16/02	Lierse	a	2-0	Junker, De Petter
23/02	Leuven	h	1-2	De Witte
09/03	Anderlecht	a	0-1	
16/03	Zulte Waregem	h	2-3	Diabang, Enevoldsen
30/03	Charleroi	h	0-0	
06/04	Waasland-Beveren	a	0-1	
13/04	Leuven	a	3-0	Van Damme, Pedersen, Diabang
20/04	Leuven	h	1-5	De Witte
27/04	Waasland-Beveren	h	2-0	Bateau 2
04/05	Charleroi	a	2-1	Pedersen, Biset

No	Name	Nat	DoB	Pos	Aps	(s)	Gls
6	Sheldon Bateau	TRI	29/01/91	D	18	(4)	2
20	Wouter Biebauw		21/05/84	G	8		
19	Maxime Biset		26/03/86	M	31		1
8	Xavier Chen		05/10/83	D	16		
29	Alessandro Cordaro		02/05/86	M	34		1
3	Steven De Petter		22/11/85	M	21	(1)	4
4	Seth De Witte		18/10/87	D	25	(1)	4
18	David Destorme		30/08/79	M	28	(3)	4
7	Boubacar Diabang	BIH	13/07/88	A	9	(13)	4
20	Thomas Enevoldsen	DEN	27/07/87	M	15	(16)	5
26	Antonio Ghomsi	CMR	22/04/86	D	26	(3)	
22	Robin Henkens		12/09/88	M	19	(7)	4
10	Abdul-Yakinu Iddi	GHA	25/05/86	M	19	(6)	5
9	Mads Junker	DEN	21/04/81	A	14	(16)	4
32	Senad Karahmet	BIH	25/02/92	D	1	(3)	
1	Tomislav Pacovski	MKD	28/06/82	G	22		
3	Boris Pandža	BIH	15/12/86	D	4		
17	Nicklas Pedersen	DEN	10/10/87	A	21	(4)	12
23	Olivier Renard		24/05/79	G	6		
11	Mats Rits		18/07/93	M	6	(6)	
12	Jaime Ruiz	COL	03/01/84	A		(4)	
8	Jerry Van Dam	FRA	08/12/88	D	5	(1)	
24	Joachim Van Damme		23/07/91	D	9	(5)	1
5	Kenny Van Hoevelen		24/06/83	D	13		
21	Anthony Van Loo		05/10/88	D	19	(2)	
31	Wannes Van Tricht		13/11/93	M	7	(7)	1
11	Kevin Vandenbergh		16/05/83	A		(1)	
28	Jordi Vanlerberghe		27/03/96	M		(1)	

RAEC MONS

Coach: Enzo Scifo
1910 • Charles Tondreau (10,150) • raec-mons.be

2012

28/07	Leuven	h	5-2	Matumona, Timmermans, Franquart, Jarju, Nong
04/08	Lokeren	a	2-2	Nicaise, Jarju
11/08	KLierse	h	1-1	Sapina
18/08	Anderlecht	a	1-2	Jarju
26/08	Club Brugge	a	1-3	Jarju (p)
01/09	Zulte Waregem	a	4-2	Monteyne, Nong 2, Matthys
15/09	Charleroi	h	2-3	Van Imschoot, Jarju
22/09	Mechelen	a	0-3	
29/09	Beerschot	h	1-0	Perbet
06/10	Waasland-Beveren	a	2-2	Nong, Perbet
21/10	Standard	h	3-1	Jarju, Nong 2
27/10	Gent	a	0-2	
31/10	Kortrijk	h	1-0	Perbet (p)
03/11	Cercle Brugge	h	0-2	Perbet, Van Imschoot, Lépicier
11/11	Genk	a	1-5	Perbet
17/11	Leuven	a	3-1	Perbet 3
24/11	Lokeren	h	1-2	Perbet
01/12	Genk	h	3-0	Perbet 2, Angeli
08/12	Anderlecht	h	0-5	
15/12	Club Brugge	h	0-2	
22/12	Zulte Waregem	h	1-1	Jarju
26/12	Charleroi	a	2-1	Nong, Matumona

2013

19/01	Mechelen	h	2-3	Jarju, Perbet
26/01	Beerschot	a	0-0	
02/02	Waasland-Beveren	h	3-0	Lorenzi (p), Chatelle, Angeli
10/02	Standard	a	1-0	Arbeitman
16/02	Gent	h	0-2	
23/02	Kortrijk	a	1-0	Arbeitman
09/03	Cercle Brugge	a	3-1	og (Mertens), Jarju, Nong
16/03	Genk	h	1-5	Arbeitman (p)
30/03	Gent	a	1-2	Sapina
06/04	Lierse	h	2-1	Sapina, Nong
13/04	Kortrijk	a	0-3	
20/04	Kortrijk	h	2-1	Jarju 2
27/04	Lierse	a	1-0	Jarju
04/05	Gent	h	1-1	Matthys

No	Name	Nat	DoB	Pos	Aps	(s)	Gls
27	Arnor Angeli		25/02/91	M	12	(13)	2
23	Shlomi Arbeitman	ISR	14/05/85	A	10		3
1	Cédric Berthelin	FRA	25/12/76	G	14		
25	Arnaud Bratour		12/12/89	A		(3)	
12	Thomas Chatelle		31/03/81	M	11	(3)	1
18	Dylan De Belder		03/04/92	A	3	(18)	
6	Matthieu Debisschop	FRA	29/02/84	M	13	(3)	
4	Peter Franquart	FRA	04/01/85	D	12	(2)	1
22	Mustapha Jarju	GAM	18/07/86	A	35	(1)	12
16	Bahattin Köse	GER	26/08/90	A		(13)	
23	Flavien Le Postollec	FRA	19/02/84	M	24		
5	Maël Lépicier	FRA	14/01/86	D	10	(4)	1
20	Grégory Lorenzi	FRA	17/12/83	D	10		1
7	Tim Matthys		23/12/83	M	13	(2)	2
10	Zola Matumona	COD	26/11/83	M	20	(1)	2
45	Pieterjan Monteyne		01/01/83	D	35		1
20	Benjamin Nicaise	FRA	28/09/80	M	9	(7)	1
13	Aloys Nong	CMR	16/10/83	A	29	(4)	9
39	Brice Ntambwe		29/04/93	M	4	(2)	
11	Vusumuzi Nyoni	ZIM	21/04/84	M	13	(1)	
19	Jérémy Perbet	FRA	12/12/84	A	15	(6)	12
30	Jérémy Sapina	FRA	01/02/85	D	23	(2)	3
24	Adrien Saussez		25/08/91	G	2		
29	Nicolas Timmermans		04/11/82	D	25	(4)	1
15	Daan Van Gijseghem		02/03/88	D	20	(1)	
8	Tom Van Imschoot		04/09/81	M	14	(9)	2
26	Olivier Werner		16/04/85	G	20	(1)	

OUD-HEVERLEE LEUVEN

Coach: Ronny Van Geneugden
2002 • Den Dreef (8,700) • ohl.be

2012

28/07	Mons	a	2-5	Geraerts, Sawaneh
05/08	Genk	h	2-2	Gíslason, Sawaneh (p)
12/08	Gent	a	1-1	Sawaneh
18/08	Cercle Brugge	h	0-2	Ngolok, Sawaneh (p), Geraerts
25/08	Anderlecht	h	1-1	Sawaneh
01/09	Lierse	a	1-1	Pouga
15/09	Zulte Waregem	h	0-1	
22/09	Lokeren	a	2-2	Raymaekers, Geraerts
29/09	Waasland-Beveren	h	5-2	Pouga 2, Gíslason, Sawaneh 2
06/10	Charleroi	a	4-0	Chuka 3, Sawaneh
20/10	Club Brugge	h	4-1	Sawaneh 3 (1p), Karuru
27/10	Beerschot	a	3-1	Van Goethem, Geraerts, Gíslason
31/10	Mechelen	h	3-1	Pouga, Chuka, Sawaneh (p)
04/11	Standard	a	0-2	
10/11	Kortrijk	h	0-0	
17/11	Mons	h	1-3	Pouga
25/11	Genk	a	1-1	Sawaneh (p)
01/12	Gent	h	1-1	Geraerts
08/12	Cercle Brugge	a	1-1	Sawaneh (p)
16/12	Anderlecht	a	1-2	Sawaneh
22/12	Lierse	h	2-2	Sawaneh (p), Geraerts
26/12	Zulte Waregem	a	1-2	Chuka

2013

19/01	Lokeren	h	2-6	Azevedo, Geraerts
26/01	Waasland-Beveren	a	0-2	
02/02	Charleroi	h	1-0	Chuka
09/02	Club Brugge	h	1-3	Geraerts
16/02	Beerschot	h	1-1	Sawaneh
23/02	Mechelen	a	2-1	Weuts, Chuka
09/03	Standard	h	0-4	
16/03	Kortrijk	a	0-0	
30/03	Waasland-Beveren	h	3-1	Cerigioni, Chuka, Dehond
06/04	Charleroi	a	0-3	
13/04	Mechelen	h	0-3	
20/04	Mechelen	a	5-1	Mikulić, Sawaneh 2 (1p), Robson, Cerigioni
27/04	Charleroi	h	0-0	
04/05	Waasland-Beveren	a	1-0	Ruytinx
11/05	Gent	h	1-4	Ruytinx
18/05	Gent	a	1-4	Ngolok

No	Name	Nat	DoB	Pos	Aps	(s)	Gls
29	Mazin Al-Huthayfi	KSA	02/02/85	M		(2)	
14	Thomas Azevedo		31/08/91	A	6	(22)	1
26	Logan Bailly		27/12/85	G	38		
15	Wout Bastiaens		30/04/94	D	1		
2	Frederik Boi		25/10/81	D	2		
19	Loris Brogno		18/09/92	M	2	(5)	
6	Ludovic Buyssens		13/03/86	D	11	(6)	
11	Alessandro Cerigioni		30/09/92	A	8	(1)	2
23	Derick Ogbu Chuka	NGA	19/03/90	A	31	(6)	8
18	Jonas De Roeck		20/12/79	D	12	(3)	
29	Joren Dehond		08/08/95	A		(5)	1
20	Karel Geraerts		05/01/82	M	32		8
27	Stefán Gíslason	ISL	15/03/80	D	28	(1)	3
7	Ovidy Karuru	ZIM	23/01/89	M	13	(8)	1
1	Yves Lenaerts		27/02/83	G		(1)	
25	Tomislav Mikulić	CRO	04/01/82	D	13		1
28	Evariste Ngolok		15/11/88	M	22	(6)	2
9	Christian Pouga	CMR	19/06/86	A	9	(10)	5
4	Wim Raymaekers		04/04/85	D	13		1
3	Robson	BRA	10/07/83	M	27	(1)	1
13	Bjorn Ruytinx		18/08/80	A	3	(11)	2
12	Ebrahima Ibou Sawaneh	GAM	07/09/86	A	35	(1)	19
4	Kenny Thompson		26/04/85	D	20	(2)	
6	Kenneth Van Goethem		13/02/84	M	31		1
32	Gunther Vanaudenaerde		23/01/84	D	31	(1)	
25	Christopher Verbist		08/10/91	A	1		
17	Koen Weuts		18/09/90	M	23	(2)	
31	Ben Yagan		09/02/95	M	6	(6)	

R. STANDARD DE LIÈGE

Coach: Ron Jans; (22/10/12) (Peter Balette);
(27/10/12) Mircea Rednic (ROU)
1898 • Maurice Dufrasne (27,500) • standard.be
Major honours
Belgian League (10) 1958, 1961, 1963, 1969, 1970,
1971, 1982, 1983, 2008, 2009;
Belgian Cup (6) 1954, 1966, 1967, 1981, 1993, 2011

2012

29/07	Zulte Waregem	h	0-1	
03/08	Lierse	a	0-0	
10/08	Waasland-Beveren	h	3-1	Seijas, og (Sibum), Nacho González (p)
19/08	Charleroi	a	6-2	Ezekiel 2, Ajdarevic, Seijas, Buyens 2
26/08	Mechelen	h	3-2	Buyens, Ezekiel, Nacho González
02/09	Club Brugge	a	2-4	Nacho González (p), Biton
15/09	Beerschot	a	2-3	Ezekiel, Nacho González (p)
21/09	Gent	h	1-2	Buyens
30/09	Kortrijk	a	1-2	Nacho González (p)
07/10	Anderlecht	h	2-1	Bulot 2
21/10	Mons	a	1-3	Cissé
26/10	Cercle Brugge	h	2-1	Ezekiel, Nacho González
31/10	Genk	a	2-0	Batshuayi, Seijas
03/11	Leuven	h	2-0	Vainqueur, Batshuayi
09/11	Lokeren	a	1-2	Van Damme
18/11	Zulte Waregem	a	0-0	
23/11	Lierse	h	3-0	Ezekiel 2, M'Poku
02/12	Waasland-Beveren	a	2-0	Ezekiel, Vainqueur
07/12	Charleroi	h	6-1	Buyens, Vainqueur, Buzaglo, Goreux, og (Milicevic), Ezekiel
15/12	Mechelen	a	2-0	Ezekiel, Batshuayi
23/12	Club Brugge	h	1-3	Ezekiel
27/12	Beerschot	h	3-0	Van Damme, Batshuayi, Ezekiel

2013

19/01	Gent	a	0-0	
25/01	Kortrijk	h	2-0	Batshuayi, Van Damme
03/02	Anderlecht	a	2-2	Batshuayi, Buyens
10/02	Mons	h	0-1	
16/02	Cercle Brugge	a	1-0	Ezekiel
24/02	Genk	h	0-0	
09/03	Leuven	a	4-0	Ezekiel, Batshuayi, Ciman, Bulot
16/03	Lokeren	h	0-2	
01/04	Club Brugge	a	2-0	Batshuayi, Buyens
06/04	Anderlecht	h	0-0	
12/04	Zulte Waregem	a	4-3	Vainqueur, M'Poku, Kanu, Ezekiel
16/04	Genk	h	3-0	Buyens, M'Poku, Batshuayi
20/04	Lokeren	a	1-4	M'Poku
28/04	Zulte Waregem	a	1-0	M'Poku (p)
05/05	Anderlecht	a	0-2	
12/05	Club Brugge	h	2-4	og (Duarte), M'Poku (p)
16/05	Genk	a	1-1	Ezekiel
19/05	Lokeren	h	4-3	Ghoochannejhad, Arslanagic, Batshuayi 2
23/05	Gent	a	0-1	
26/05	Gent	h	7-0	Batshuayi, Bulot, M'Poku 3 (2p), Ghoochannejhad 2

No	Name	Nat	DoB	Pos	Aps	(s)	Gls
8	Astrit Ajdarevic	SWE	17/04/90	M	7	(13)	1
89	Anıl Koç	TUR	29/01/95	M	2	(3)	
36	Dino Arslanagic		24/04/93	D	11		1
23	Michy Batshuayi		02/10/93	A	26	(8)	12
9	Dudu Biton	ISR	01/03/88	A	1	(9)	1
11	Frédéric Bulot	FRA	27/09/90	A	33	(3)	4
17	Yoni Buyens		10/03/88	M	40	(1)	8
8	Maor Bar Buzaglo	ISR	14/01/88	M	8	(12)	1
6	Laurent Ciman		05/08/85	D	37		1
44	Ibrahima Cissé		28/02/94	D	10	(8)	1
10	Adrian Cristea	ROU	30/11/83	M	3	(5)	
24	Zié Diabaté	CIV	02/03/89	D	7	(3)	
39	Imoh Ezekiel	NGA	24/10/93	A	29	(4)	16
7	Ezekiel Fryers	ENG	09/09/92	D	6	(1)	
25	Rami Gershon	ISR	12/08/88	D	1		
7	Reza Ghoochannejhad	IRN	20/09/87	A	4	(5)	3
2	Réginal Goreux	HAI	31/12/87	D	19		1
25	Kanu	BRA	05/03/84	D	27	(1)	1
1	Eiji Kawashima	JPN	20/03/83	G	40		
28	Luiz Phellype	BRA	27/09/93	A		(3)	
45	François Marquet		17/04/95	A	1		
18	Anthony Moris		29/04/90	G	2		
40	Paul-José M'Poku		19/04/92	M	24	(5)	9
89	Geoffrey Mujangi Bia		12/08/89	M	1		
14	Nacho González	URU	14/05/82	M	10	(2)	6
13	Kensuke Nagai	JPN	05/03/89	A	4	(7)	
2	Loïc Nego	FRA	15/01/91	D	1	(1)	
31	Marvin Ogunjimi		12/10/87	A	3	(2)	
14	Yuji Ono	JPN	22/12/92	A	3	(6)	
4	Daniel Opare	GHA	18/10/90	D	12	(1)	
20	Luis Manuel Seijas	VEN	23/06/86	M	8	(10)	3
9	George Ţucudean	ROU	30/04/91	A	1	(10)	
21	William Vainqueur	FRA	19/11/88	A	37	(4)	4
37	Jelle Van Damme		10/10/83	M	35		3
3	Yohan Tavares	POR	02/03/88	D	2	(1)	

WAASLAND-BEVEREN

Coach: Dirk Geeraerd; (19/11/12) Glen De Boeck
2010 • Freethiel (12,930) • waasland-beveren.be

2012

28/07	Club Brugge	a	1-3	Augusto da Silva
04/08	Mechelen	h	0-0	
10/08	Standard	a	1-3	Ndabashinze
18/08	Gent	h	0-2	
25/08	Kortrijk	a	1-2	Augusto da Silva
01/09	Cercle Brugge	h	2-0	Badash, Ladriere
15/09	Genk	a	1-1	Shish
22/09	Lierse	h	1-1	Badash
29/09	Leuven	a	2-5	Lepoint, Badash (p)
06/10	Mons	h	2-2	Seoudi, Badash (p)
19/10	Anderlecht	a	0-2	
27/10	Zulte Waregem	a	0-2	
31/10	Lokeren	a	0-2	
03/11	Beerschot	a	2-1	Cavens, Lepoint
10/11	Charleroi	h	0-0	
17/11	Club Brugge	h	2-6	Ladriere, Sonck (p)
24/11	Mechelen	a	1-0	Lepoint
02/12	Standard	h	0-2	
08/12	Gent	a	2-0	Lepoint, Rowell (p)
15/12	Kortrijk	h	1-0	Badash
22/12	Cercle Brugge	a	2-2	Doumbia, Lepoint
26/12	Genk	h	1-1	Badash

2013

19/01	Lierse	a	0-0	
26/01	Leuven	h	2-0	Badash, De Smet
02/02	Mons	a	0-3	
10/02	Anderlecht	h	1-2	Remacle
16/02	Zulte Waregem	a	0-2	
23/02	Lokeren	h	0-0	
09/03	Beerschot	h	3-2	Badash (p), Remacle, De Smet
16/03	Charleroi	a	0-3	
30/03	Leuven	a	1-3	De Smet
06/04	Mechelen	h	1-0	Sonck
13/04	Charleroi	a	1-1	De Smet
20/04	Charleroi	h	0-0	
28/04	Mechelen	a	0-2	
04/05	Leuven	a	0-1	

No	Name	Nat	DoB	Pos	Aps	(s)	Gls
4	Mohammed Aoulad		29/08/91	M		(1)	
11	Augusto da Silva	BRA	17/11/83	M	8	(12)	2
9	Barak Badash	ISR	30/08/82	A	19	(6)	8
6	Karim Belhocine	FRA	02/04/78	M	30		
22	Siebe Blondelle		20/04/86	D	27	(1)	
7	Jurgen Cavens		19/08/78	A	10	(10)	1
1	Michael Clepkens		30/01/86	G	12		
26	Colin Coosemans		03/08/92	G	24		
16	Daniel Cruz	COL	09/05/81	M	6	(4)	
19	Cédric D'Ulivo	FRA	29/09/89	D	26		
17	Stijn De Smet		27/03/85	A	13		4
5	Kassim Doumbia	MLI	18/06/90	D	8	(5)	1
8	Rachid Farssi		15/01/85	D	20	(6)	
39	Mohammad Ghdir	ISR	21/01/91	A	2	(3)	
21	Jonas Ivens		14/10/84	D	14		
23	Benoît Ladriere		27/04/87	M	10	(13)	2
3	Kristof Lardenoit		08/07/83	D	17	(1)	
30	Christophe Lepoint		24/10/84	M	15	(1)	5
17	Alain Mendy	SEN	17/11/89	M	2	(2)	
21	Dugary Ndabashinze	BDI	08/10/89	M	5	(3)	1
25	Vito Plut	SVN	08/07/88	A	10	(10)	
10	Jordan Remacle		14/02/87	A	14		2
15	Jonny Rowell	ENG	10/09/89	M	13	(3)	1
10	Mickaël Seoudi	FRA	13/10/86	A	6	(6)	1
12	Gal Shish	ISR	28/01/89	D	23	(2)	1
13	Bas Sibum	NED	26/12/82	M	35		

14	Kristof Snelders		05/09/82	A		(3)	
14	Wesley Sonck		09/08/78	A	19	(4)	2
24	René Sterckx		18/01/91	M	1	(3)	
24	Roel Van Hemert	NED	21/11/84	D	3		
20	Franco Zennaro		01/04/93	M	4	(1)	

SV ZULTE WAREGEM

Coach: Francky Dury
2001 • Regenboogstadion (8,500) • essevee.be
Major honours
Belgian Cup (1) 2006

2012

29/07	Standard	a	1-0	*Berrier*
05/08	Gent	h	3-1	*Trajkovski, Berrier 2*
11/08	Beerschot	a	1-1	*Berrier*
18/08	Kortrijk	h	2-0	*Naessens, Lendrić*
26/08	Genk	a	0-2	
01/09	Mons	h	2-4	*Leye (p), Hinostroza*
14/09	Leuven	a	1-0	*Naessens*
22/09	Anderlecht	a	2-3	*Trajkovski, Naessens*
29/09	Lierse	a	4-1	*Habibou 3, Berrier*
06/10	Cercle Brugge	h	3-1	*Berrier 2, Habibou*
20/10	Lokeren	h	0-3	
27/10	Waasland-Beveren	a	2-0	*Berrier 2*
31/10	Charleroi	h	4-1	*Berrier (p), Hazard, Verboom, Leye*
04/11	Club Brugge	a	1-0	*Hazard*
10/11	Mechelen	h	1-1	*Leye*
18/11	Standard	h	0-0	
24/11	Gent	a	1-0	*Lendrić*
01/12	Beerschot	h	0-0	
08/12	Kortrijk	a	2-1	*Naessens, Leye (p)*
16/12	Genk	h	3-2	*Malanda-Adje, Leye (p), Berrier*
22/12	Mons	a	1-1	*Leye*
26/12	Leuven	h	2-1	*Habibou 2*

2013

26/01	Lierse	h	2-0	*D'Haene, Berrier*
02/02	Cercle Brugge	a	2-1	*Leye, Delaplace*
09/02	Lokeren	a	1-1	*Hazard*
16/02	Waasland-Beveren	h	2-0	*Leye, Delaplace*
27/02	Anderlecht	a	1-0	*Berrier*
03/03	Charleroi	a	1-0	*Leye*
09/03	Club Brugge	h	1-2	*Skúlason*
16/03	Mechelen	a	3-2	*Naessens, Trajkovski, Conté*
30/03	Lokeren	h	1-1	*Leye*
07/04	Genk	a	1-1	*De Fauw*
12/04	Standard	h	3-4	*Leye, og (Van Damme), Godeau*
18/04	Club Brugge	a	4-3	*Leye 3, Berrier*
21/04	Anderlecht	h	2-1	*Leye (p), Malanda-Adje*
28/04	Standard	a	0-1	
03/05	Genk	h	0-4	
11/05	Lokeren	a	3-2	*De Fauw 2, Malanda-Adje*
16/05	Club Brugge	h	5-2	*Hazard (p), Leye 2, De Fauw, og (Almebäck)*
19/05	Anderlecht	a	1-1	*Naessens*

No	Name	Nat	DoB	Pos	Aps	(s)	Gls
33	Franck Berrier	FRA	02/02/84	M	37	(2)	14
1	Sammy Bossut		11/08/85	G	34		
22	Sébastien Bruzzese		01/03/89	G	6		
3	Steve Colpaert		13/09/86	D	33		
17	Ibrahima Conté	GUI	03/04/91	M	8	(6)	1
24	Karel D'Haene		05/09/80	D	40		1
4	Davy De Fauw		08/07/81	D	40		4
27	Jimmy De Jonghe		13/02/92	M	4	(2)	
31	Klaas De Rock		26/09/93	M		(1)	
28	Jonathan Delaplace	FRA	20/03/86	M	37	(2)	2
21	Bruno Godeau		10/05/92	D	18	(2)	1
7	Mouhamadou Habib Habibou	FRA	16/04/87	A	7	(7)	6
8	Brian Hamalainen	DEN	29/05/89	D	5		
8	Thorgan Hazard		29/03/93	M	33	(1)	4
18	Hernán Hinostroza	PER	21/12/93	M	5	(6)	1
11	Ivan Lendrić	CRO	08/08/91	A	2	(18)	2
14	Mbaye Leye	SEN	01/12/82	A	34	(2)	17
28	Bernard Malanda-Adje		28/08/94	D	31	(4)	3
26	Jens Naessens		01/04/91	A	22	(12)	6
4	Pietro Perdichizzi		16/12/92	D	1		
29	Jérémy Serwy		04/06/91	M	1		
16	Ólafur Ingi Skúlason	ISL	01/04/83	M	11	(16)	1
10	Aleksandar Trajkovski	MKD	05/09/92	A	12	(12)	3
17	David Vandenbroeck		12/07/85	D		(1)	
15	Niels Vandenbroucke		15/03/91	D	2	(1)	
19	Pepijn Vangansbeke		27/06/93	A		(1)	
26	Bryan Verboom		30/01/92	D	17	(3)	1

Mid-table/relegation play-offs 2012/13

PLAY-OFF 2A FINAL TABLE

		Pld	Home					Away					Total					Pts
			W	D	L	F	A	W	D	L	F	A	W	D	L	F	A	
1	KAA Gent	6	3	0	0	6	1	1	2	0	3	2	4	2	0	9	3	14
2	RAEC Mons	6	2	1	0	5	3	1	0	2	2	5	3	1	2	7	8	10
3	K. Lierse SK	6	0	1	2	1	3	1	0	2	4	5	1	1	4	5	8	4
4	KV Kortrijk	6	1	1	1	3	3	0	1	2	1	3	1	2	3	4	6	2

NB KV Kortrijk – 3 pts deducted.

PLAY-OFF 2B FINAL TABLE

		Pld	Home					Away					Total					Pts
			W	D	L	F	A	W	D	L	F	A	W	D	L	F	A	
1	Oud-Heverlee Leuven	6	1	1	1	3	4	2	0	1	6	4	3	1	2	9	8	10
2	KV Mechelen	6	1	1	1	3	5	2	0	1	5	2	3	1	2	8	7	10
3	R. Charleroi SC	6																
4	Waasland-Beveren	6	1	1	1	1	1	0	1	2	2	6	1	2	3	3	7	5

UEFA EUROPA LEAGUE QUALIFICATION PLAY-OFFS

FIRST ROUND	SECOND ROUND
(11/05/13 & 18/05/13)	*(23/05/13 & 26/05/13)*
Leuven 1-4 Gent	Gent 1-0 Standard
Gent 4-1 Leuven	Standard 7-0 Gent
(Gent 8-2)	*(Standard 7-1)*

PLAY-OFF 3 FINAL TABLE

		Pld	Home					Away					Total					Pts
			W	D	L	F	A	W	D	L	F	A	W	D	L	F	A	
1	Cercle Brugge KSV	4	2	0	0	3	1	1	0	1	2	2	3	0	1	5	3	9
2	K. Beerschot AC	4	1	0	1	2	2	0	0	2	1	3	1	0	3	3	5	6

NB K. Beerschot AC carried 3 pts forward from regular season; Cercle Brugge KSV subsequently entered promotion/relegation play-offs.

BELGIUM

Top goalscorers

25	Carlos Bacca (Club Brugge)
20	Ilombe Mboyo (Gent)
19	Dieumerci Mbokani (Anderlecht)
	Ebrahima Ibou Sawaneh (Leuven)
17	Maxime Lestienne (Club Brugge)
	Jelle Vossen (Genk)
	Mbaye Leye (Zulte Waregem)
16	Imoh Ezekiel (Standard)
14	Franck Berrier (Zulte Waregem)
12	Tom De Sutter (Anderlecht)
	Hamdi Harbaoui (Lokeren)
	Nicklas Pedersen (Mechelen)
	Mustapha Jarju (Mons)
	Jérémy Perbet (Mons)
	Michy Batshuayi (Standard)

Promoted club

KV OOSTENDE

Coach: Frederik Vanderbiest
1981 • Albertparkstadion (8,125) • kvo.be

SECOND LEVEL FINAL TABLE 2012/13

		Pld	W	D	L	F	A	Pts
1	KV Oostende (*2, *3)	34	24	5	5	64	25	77
2	Royal Mouscron-Péruwelz	34	20	7	7	58	29	67
3	KVC Westerlo	34	17	12	5	54	29	63
4	K. Sint-Truidense VV	34	17	6	11	54	36	57
5	R. Boussu Dour Borinage	34	15	10	9	44	34	55
6	Lommel United	34	14	8	12	50	48	50
7	White Star Woluwe FC (*1)	34	14	7	13	41	49	49
8	KAS Eupen	34	13	10	11	44	37	49
9	AFC Tubize	34	12	10	12	43	42	46
10	R. Antwerp FC	34	12	9	13	42	44	45
11	KSV Roeselare	34	10	12	12	44	47	42
12	KFC Dessel Sport	34	11	8	15	35	42	41
13	SC Eendracht Aalst	34	10	11	13	38	52	41
14	FC Molenbeek Brussels	34	9	6	19	34	49	33
15	CS Visé	34	8	9	17	47	57	33
16	KSK Heist	34	8	6	20	39	57	30
17	KSV Oudenaarde	34	8	9	17	36	60	30
18	Sint-Niklaas	34	7	9	18	34	64	30

NB (*) period champions;
KSV Oudenaarde – 3 pts deducted.

PROMOTION/RELEGATION PLAY-OFFS

		Pld	W	D	L	F	A	Pts
1	Cercle Brugge KSV	6	4	0	2	13	8	12
2	Royal Mouscron-Péruwelz	6	4	0	2	9	9	12
3	KVC Westerlo	6	3	1	2	11	4	10
4	White Star Woluwe FC	6	0	1	5	4	16	1

Domestic cup: Coupe de Belgique/ Beker van België 2012/13

SIXTH ROUND

(25/09/12)
Mouscron-Péruwelz 2-3 Standard *(aet)*

(26/09/12)
Anderlecht 2-0 Boussu Dour Borinage
Brussels 1-3 Waasland-Beveren *(aet)*
Club Brugge 3-0 Woluwe-Zaventem
Deinze 2-4 Charleroi *(aet)*
Gent 8-0 Bocholt
Hoogstraten 1-3 Cercle Brugge
KV Mechelen 6-0 Entente Bertrigeoise
Lokeren 3-0 Dessel
Mons 3-0 Ciney
Oostende 2-1 Leuven
Sint-Truiden 1-1 Beerschot *(aet; 4-2 on pens)*
Union Saint-Gilloise 0-6 Genk
Westerlo 2-0 Lierse
White Star Woluwe 1-2 Kortrijk *(aet)*
Zulte Waregem 1-0 Koksijde

SEVENTH ROUND

(27/11/12)
Anderlecht 2-0 KV Mechelen *(aet)*

(28/11/12)
Club Brugge 0-1 Cercle Brugge
Gent 0-0 Lokeren *(aet; 4-2 on pens)*
Kortrijk 1-0 Mons
Waasland-Beveren 0-3 Oostende
Westerlo 5-5 Sint-Truiden *(aet; 2-4 on pens)*
Zulte Waregem 2-2 Charleroi *(aet; 4-2 on pens)*

(29/11/12)
Genk 1-0 Standard

QUARTER-FINALS

(11/12/12 & 16/01/13)
Gent 1-1 Anderlecht *(Mboyo 14; Jovanović 10)*
Anderlecht 1-0 Gent *(De Sutter 17)*
(Anderlecht 2-1)

(12/12/12 & 16/01/13)
Cercle Brugge 2-1 Oostende *(Bakenga 24, Mertens 79p; De Schutter 89)*
Oostende 1-2 Cercle Brugge *(Schmisser 72; Van Eenoo 49, Mertens 90+1p)*
(Cercle Brugge 4-2)

Sint-Truiden 0-0 Kortrijk
Kortrijk 1-0 Sint-Truiden *(Dejaegere 79)*
(Kortrijk 1-0)

(13/12/12 & 16/01/13)
Zulte Waregem 0-5 Genk *(Barda 8, Gorius 15, De Ceulaer 36, 59, Buffel 51)*
Genk 0-1 Zulte Waregem *(Leye 68p)*
(Genk 5-1)

SEMI-FINALS

(30/01/13 & 02/03/13)
Anderlecht 1-0 Genk *(Jovanović 30)*
Genk 1-0 Anderlecht *(Vossen 62) (aet)*
(1-1; Genk 7-6 on pens)

(03/03/13 & 27/03/13)
Kortrijk 1-2 Cercle Brugge *(Chavarría 4; D'Haene 26, Bakenga 62)*
Cercle Brugge 2-2 KV Kortrijk *(Uchebo 73, 120; Pavlović 29, N'For 52) (aet)*
(Cercle Brugge 4-3)

FINAL

(09/05/13)
King Baudouin, Brussels
KRC GENK 2 *(Kumordzi 83, Vossen 88)*
CERCLE BRUGGE KSV 0
Referee: *Verbist*
GENK: *Köteles, Ngcongca, Koulibaly, Simaeys, Tshimanga, Buffel, Hyland, Yao Kumordzi, Joseph-Monrose (Plet 81), De Ceulaer (Barda 72), Vossen (Gorius 90+3)*
CERCLE: *Verbist, Cornelis, Wils, D'Haene (Boghossian 87), Boi (Bakenga 65), Mertens, Vidarsson, William Carvalho, Smolders, Uchebo, Rudy (Buyl 86)*

Khaleem Hyland (left) and Bennard Yao Kumordzi show off the Belgian Cup after their team's 2-0 victory over Cercle Brugge

BOSNIA & HERZEGOVINA

Nogometni / Fudbalski savez Bosne i Hercegovine (NFSBiH)

Address	Ulica Ferhadija 30	**President**	Elvedin Begić
	BA-71000 Sarajevo	**General secretary**	Jasmin Baković
Tel	+387 33 276 660	**Media officer**	Slavica Pecikoza
Fax	+387 33 444 332	**Year of formation**	1992
E-mail	nsbih@bih.net.ba	**National stadium**	Bilinjo Pole, Zenica
Website	nfsbih.ba		(13,000)

PREMIER LEAGUE CLUBS

1. FK Borac Banja Luka
2. NK Čelik Zenica
3. NK GOŠK Gabela
4. NK Gradina
5. FK Leotar
6. FK Olimpik Sarajevo
7. FK Radnik Bijeljina
8. FK Rudar Prijedor
9. FK Sarajevo
10. NK Široki Brijeg
11. FK Slavija Sarajevo
12. NK Travnik
13. FK Velež
14. FK Željezničar
15. HŠK Zrinjski
16. NK Zvijezda

PROMOTED CLUBS

17. NK Vitez
18. FK Mladost Velika Obarska

KEY:
- – UEFA Champions League
- – UEFA Europa League
- – Promoted clubs
- – Relegated clubs

Osim's Željezničar on top again

The Premijer Liga was of secondary importance to most football followers in Bosnia & Herzegovina in 2012/13 as Safet Sušić's national side captured the attention by dominating their 2014 FIFA World Cup qualifying group, but it was a memorable campaign nonetheless for FK Željezničar, who retained their title after seeing off the challenge of city rivals FK Sarajevo.

Amar Osim's side could not complete a second straight double, however, as despite stretching their unbeaten run in the domestic cup to 36 matches, they lost the two-legged final on penalties to NK Široki Brijeg after a pair of 1-1 draws.

Successful title defence for Sarajevo Blues	Široki Brijeg gain cup revenge with shoot-out win	National team close in on World Cup place

Domestic league

A third league title in four seasons confirmed Željezničar as the country's premier force and Osim as not just the best but the most durable coach in the land. In a league where coaches seldom last one season, the Sarajevo-born 46-year-old completed his fourth in charge at the Grbavica, adorning it with a fifth major trophy as Željo eased home with two matches to spare, finishing six points ahead of Sarajevo.

Both clubs from the capital were unbeaten at home, but it was Željezničar's ability to win away – never an easy task in the Premijer Liga – that proved decisive, their nine wins on the road contrasting with Sarajevo's four. Osim's men managed four in succession in the spring to take charge of the title race. Their rivals' only hope was to complete the double over Željezničar in early May – they had beaten them 1-0 at home in the autumn – but a goalless draw left the defending champions nine points clear with three games remaining, effectively ending the contest.

Sarajevo striker Emir Hadžić scored five goals on the final day to deny Željo's Eldin Adilović a second successive golden boot. The champions actually scored 20

goals fewer than in 2011/12, but Adilović and midfield general Muamer Svraka were once again the team's stars – along with Croatian goalkeeper Marjan Antolović. FK Borac Banja Luka finished third in the Premijer Liga but were not permitted to take up their European place as a result of licensing issues. It was the same for several other clubs, which allowed HŠK Zrinjski, the division's ninth-placed team, to claim a UEFA Europa League spot.

Domestic cup

Široki Brijeg, sixth in the league, also made it into Europe by reaching the cup final, where, for the second successive season, they faced Željezničar. A single goal had settled the 2012 final in the Sarajevo club's favour, and once again there was little to choose between the two sides, 1-1 draws in each leg preceding a penalty shoot-out at the Pecara Stadium, which the home side won when Svraka's effort was saved by Luka Bilobrk. It was Široki Brijeg's second cup win, and first for six years.

Europe

Premijer Liga clubs struggled once again in Europe, but as three of the four clubs fell at the first hurdle Sarajevo defended

the nation's honour by getting through two of the UEFA Europa League's three qualifying rounds, their highlight a 3-1 home win against PFC Levski Sofia.

National team

Play-off losers to Portugal in two successive qualifying campaigns, Bosnia & Herzegovina's burning desire to qualify for a first major tournament by the direct route was plain to see as Safet Sušić's side did all that was asked of them in their opening six 2014 World Cup qualifiers. They amassed 16 points, four of them off main rivals Greece, to sit proudly atop the Group G table with a three-point cushion and a huge goal difference.

The team were empowered by the magic triangle of skipper Zvjezdan Misimović and strike duo Edin Džeko and Vedad Ibišević, whose collective attacking verve and proficiency was showcased in the opening 8-1 defeat of Liechtenstein and several times thereafter. After defeating Greece 3-1 in Zenica in March, hopes of reaching Brazil naturally turned to expectation. Despite a couple of tricky ties against Slovakia to come, qualification was very much in Bosnia & Herzegovina's hands, with eternal fame beckoning Sušić and his players if they could see the job through.

Domestic league: Premijer Liga 2012/13 final table

		Pld	Home					Away					Total					Pts
			W	D	L	F	A	W	D	L	F	A	W	D	L	F	A	
1	**FK Željezničar**	30	11	4	0	24	4	9	2	4	24	16	20	6	4	48	20	66
2	FK Sarajevo	30	13	2	0	34	5	4	7	4	18	14	17	9	4	52	19	60
3	FK Borac Banja Luka	30	11	3	1	31	7	3	6	6	12	18	14	9	7	43	25	51
4	NK Čelik Zenica	30	10	4	1	31	16	4	5	6	13	14	14	9	7	44	30	51
5	FK Olimpik Sarajevo	30	8	4	3	16	11	5	6	4	18	15	13	10	7	34	26	49
6	NK Široki Brijeg	30	11	3	1	33	6	2	3	10	15	25	13	6	11	48	31	45
7	FK Slavija Sarajevo	30	8	3	4	17	11	4	4	7	12	17	12	7	11	29	28	43
8	FK Leotar	30	8	2	5	20	18	2	7	6	8	22	10	9	11	28	40	39
9	HŠK Zrinjski	30	8	5	2	18	19	3	4	8	8	23	11	6	13	26	42	39
10	FK Rudar Prijedor	30	7	3	5	26	18	3	3	9	11	24	10	6	14	37	42	36
11	NK Zvijezda	30	8	4	3	26	17	2	2	11	12	27	10	6	14	38	44	36
12	FK Radnik Bijeljina	30	7	7	1	19	10	1	4	10	8	25	8	11	11	27	35	35
13	FK Velež	30	5	7	3	19	13	3	3	9	12	21	8	10	12	31	34	34
14	NK Travnik	30	6	5	4	16	13	3	2	10	13	32	9	7	14	29	45	34
15	NK GOŠK Gabela	30	5	5	5	15	15	2	4	9	14	27	7	9	14	29	42	30
16	NK Gradina	30	1	5	9	10	22	0	1	14	7	35	1	6	23	17	57	9

SEASON AT A GLANCE

EUROPEAN QUALIFICATION 2013/14

Champion: FK Željezničar (second qualifying round)

Cup winner: NK Široki Brijeg (second qualifying round)
FK Sarajevo (first qualifying round)
HŠK Zrinjski (first qualifying round)

Top scorers	Emir Hadžić (Sarajevo), 20 goals
Relegated clubs	NK Gradina, NK GOŠK Gabela
Promoted clubs	NK Vitez, FK Mladost Velika Obarska
Cup final	NK Široki Brijeg 1-1; 1-1 FK Željezničar *(agg 2-2; 5-4 on pens)*

PREMIJER LIGA TEAM OF THE SEASON
(4-4-2)
Coach: Osim *(Željezničar)*

PLAYER OF THE SEASON
Muamer Svraka
(FK Željezničar)

The ace in Amar Osim's pack, Svraka weighed in with eight goals from midfield and supplemented his excellent league efforts with a string of sparkling displays in the cup. The 25-year-old inevitably caught the eye of national team coach Safet Sušić and scored twice from the substitutes' bench in friendly wins against Algeria and Slovenia.

NEWCOMER OF THE SEASON
Armin Hodžić
(FK Željezničar)

The highly-rated teenage striker joined Liverpool FC in May 2011 but was returned to Željezničar for the 2012/13 campaign. Although his outings were restricted, he proved his value with four crucial goals in the spring. He also made a mark at international level with a cluster of goals for the Bosnia & Herzegovina Under-19 side.

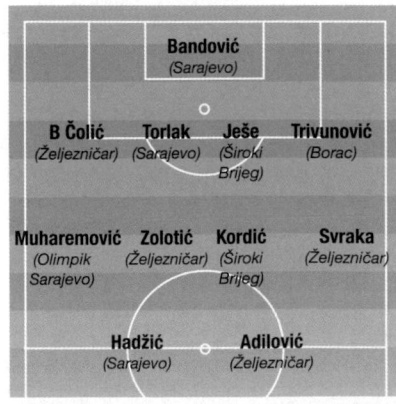

Bandović *(Sarajevo)*
B Čolić *(Željezničar)* — Torlak *(Sarajevo)* — Ješe *(Široki Brijeg)* — Trivunović *(Borac)*
Muharemović *(Olimpik Sarajevo)* — Zolotić *(Željezničar)* — Kordić *(Široki Brijeg)* — Svraka *(Željezničar)*
Hadžić *(Sarajevo)* — Adilović *(Željezničar)*

BOSNIA & HERZEGOVINA

NATIONAL TEAM

Home Kit   Away Kit

TOP FIVE ALL-TIME CAPS
Zvjezdan Misimović (73); Emir Spahić (65), Edin Džeko (53); Elvir Bolić (51); Sergej Barbarez (47)

TOP FIVE ALL-TIME GOALS
Edin Džeko (29); Zvjezdan Misimović (24); Elvir Bolić (22); Sergej Barbarez & Vedad Ibišević (17)

Results 2012/13

Date	Opponent		Venue	Score	Scorers
15/08/12	Wales	A	Llanelli	2-0	Ibišević (21), Stevanović (53)
07/09/12	Liechtenstein (WCQ)	A	Vaduz	8-1	Misimović (26, 31), Ibišević (33, 40, 83), Džeko (46, 64, 81)
11/09/12	Latvia (WCQ)	H	Zenica	4-1	Misimović (12p, 54), Pjanić (44), Džeko (90+2)
12/10/12	Greece (WCQ)	A	Piraeus	0-0	
16/10/12	Lithuania (WCQ)	H	Zenica	3-0	Ibišević (28), Džeko (35), Pjanić (41)
14/11/12	Algeria	A	Algiers	1-0	Svraka (90+1)
06/02/13	Slovenia	A	Ljubljana	3-0	Ibišević (36), Pjanić (41), Svraka (80)
22/03/13	Greece (WCQ)	H	Zenica	3-1	Džeko (30, 54), Ibišević (36)
07/06/13	Latvia (WCQ)	A	Riga	5-0	Lulić (48), Ibišević (53), Medunjanin (53), Pjanić (80), Džeko (82)

Appearances 2012/13

Coach: Safet Sušić	13/04/55		Wal	LIE	LVA	GRE	LTU	Alg	Svn	GRE	LVA	Caps	Goals
Asmir Begović	20/06/87	Stoke (ENG)	G	G	G	G	G	G	G82	G	G	21	-
Mensur Mujdža	28/03/84	Freiburg (GER)	D87		D	D	D59			D84	D	20	-
Emir Spahić	18/08/80	Sevilla (ESP)/Anji (RUS)	D	D	D	D	D	D	D60	D	D	65	3
Boris Pandža	15/12/86	Mechelen (BEL)	D71									21	-
Sejad Salihović	08/10/84	Hoffenheim (GER)	D	D	D91	D	D	D			D79	34	4
Miralem Pjanić	02/04/90	Roma (ITA)	M82	M79	M		M66	M72	M		M	40	8
Adnan Zahirović	23/03/90	Spartak Nalchik (RUS)/Dinamo Minsk (BLR)	M87	M78	M	M	M		M	M		17	-
Miroslav Stevanović	29/07/90	Vojvodina (SRB)/Sevilla (ESP)	M		s75	s66	M		M70	s84	s70	8	1
Senad Lulić	18/01/86	Lazio (ITA)	M62		M30	M75	M74	M72	D	M	M	25	1
Edin Džeko	17/03/86	Man. City (ENG)	A	A	A	A	A	A63	A	A	A	53	29
Vedad Ibišević	06/08/84	Stuttgart (GER)	A74	A	A87	A	A	A63	A70	A84	A	46	17
Muhamed Bešić	10/09/92	Hamburg (GER)/Ferencváros (HUN)	s62						s72			7	-
Toni Šunjić	15/12/88	Zorya (UKR)	s71	D	s91							3	-
Muamer Svraka	14/02/88	Željezničar	s74	s79				s72	s63			5	2
Ivan Sesar	29/08/89	Sarajevo	s82						s72			2	-
Damir Vrančić	04/10/85	Braunschweig (GER)	s87	s79								4	-
Ognjen Vranješ	24/10/89	Krasnodar (RUS)/Alania (RUS)	s87	D	D	D	D	D72		D	D	10	-
Avdija Vršajević	06/03/86	Hajduk Split (CRO)		M	s30		s59	s63	s60	s84		6	-
Zvjezdan Misimović	05/06/82	Dinamo Moskva (RUS)/Guizhou Renhe (CHN)		M79	M	M	M	M63		M		73	24
Senijad Ibričić	26/09/85	Gaziantepspor (TUR)/Kasımpaşa (TUR)		s78		s75		s63	s70		s79	42	4
Haris Medunjanin	08/03/85	Gaziantepspor (TUR)			s87	M75		s63	M63	M79	M70	27	5
Ervin Zukanović	11/02/87	Kortrijk (BEL)/Gent (BEL)					s74	D	D	D	D	5	-
Edin Višća	17/02/90	İstanbul BB (TUR)							s70		s69	3	-
Asmir Avdukić	13/05/81	Borac Banja Luka							s82			3	-
Elvir Rahimić	04/04/76	CSKA Moskva (RUS)								s79	M69	39	-

European club competitions 2012/13

Domestic league club-by-club

FK ŽELJEZNIČAR

Second qualifying round - NK Maribor (SVN)
A 1-4 *Adilović (15)*
Antolović, Kvesić, Kerla, Bogičević, Zolotić, Adilović, Zeba, Selimović (Bešlija 71), B Čolić, Svraka, Jamak (Stanić 81). Coach: Amar Osim (BIH)
H 1-2 *Kvesić (59)*
Antolović, Kvesić, Kerla, Bogičević, Zolotić, Adilović, Zeba (Bekrić 46), B Čolić, Bešlija (Stanić 56), Svraka, Jamak (Vasilić 65). Coach: Amar Osim (BIH)
Red card: B Čolić 53, Stanić 61, Svraka 64

NK ŠIROKI BRIJEG

Second qualifying round - Saint Patrick's Athletic FC (IRL)
H 1-1 *Wagner (90+3)*
Bilobrk, D Džidić, Bertoša, Ješe, Jurčević, Wagner, Ćorić, Ocvirk, Ž-Išić (I Džidić 46), Roskam (Kordić 55), Zlomislić (Ricardo Balano 67). Coach: Marijan Bloudek (BIH)
Red card: Jurčević 43
A 1-2 *I Džidić (65)*
Bilobrk, I Džidić (D Džidić 85), Bertoša, Ješe, Ricardo Baiano (Ivanković 85), Šilić, Kordić, Wagner, Ćorić, Zlomislić, Bloudek (Roskam 63). Coach: Marijan Bloudek (BIH)

FK BORAC BANJA LUKA

First qualifying round - FK Čelik Nikšić (MNE)
H 2-2 *Stokić (39), Dugić (42)*
Avdukić, Marković, Stupar (Žižović 30),

Dugić, Grahovac, Stokić (O Radulović 64), Milić, Žlvković (Siniša Dujaković 78), Kantar, Žarić, Krunić. Coach: Slaviša Božičić (SRB)
Red cards: Kantar 85, Siniša Dujaković 90+3
A 1-1 *Grahovac (58)*
Avdukić, A Radulović (Kunić 81), Marković, Žižović (O Radulović 56), Dugić (Stefan Dujaković 36), Grahovac, Stokić, Milić, Živković, Žarić, Krunić. Coach: Slaviša Božičić (SRB)
Red card: Živković 50

FK SARAJEVO

First qualifying round - Hibernians FC (MLT)
H 5-2 *Suljić (2), Torlak (45+1), Karamatić (54p), Hadžić (79), Tatomirović (90)*
Adilović, Sesar, Torlak, Husejinović (Šunjevarić 82), Tatomirović, Gujić, Haskić, Tadejević (Karamatić 46), Zlatković, Čomor (Hadžić 68), Suljić. Coach: Dragan Jović (BIH)
A 4-4 *Hadžić (13, 27), Suljić (23), Šunjevarić (90)*
Adilović, Sesar, Torlak, Husejinović (Šunjevarić 67), Hadžić (Haskić 82), Tatomirović, Gujić, Belošević (Karamatić 46), Zlatković, Čomor, Suljić. Coach: Dragan Jović (BIH)

Second qualifying round - PFC Levski Sofia (BUL)
A 0-1
Adilović, Sesar, Torlak, Husejinović (Karamatić 90), Hadžić, Tatomirović, Belošević (Tadejević 76), Dupovac, Zlatković, Čomor (Šunjevarić 76), Suljić. Coach: Dragan Jović (BIH)
H 3-1 *Husejinović (12, 62), Suljić (14)*
Adilović, Sesar, Torlak, Husejinović (Čomor 69), Hadžić, Tatomirović, Šunjevarić, Belošević, Dupovac, Zlatković (Tadejević 30), Suljić (Karamatić 78). Coach: Dragan Jović (BIH)

Third qualifying round - FK Zeta (MNE)
H 2-1 *Suljić (17), Belošević (43)*
Bandović, Sesar (Haskić 85), Torlak, Husejinović, Hadžić, Tatomirović, Šunjevarić (Čomor 75), Belošević, Dupovac, Zlatković, Suljić (Karamatić 64). Coach: Dragan Jović (BIH)
A 0-1
Bandović, Sesar, Torlak, Husejinović, Hadžić, Tatomirović, Šunjevarić (Čomor 58), Belošević (Karamatić 58), Dupovac, Zlatković, Suljić. Coach: Dragan Jović (BIH)

FK BORAC BANJA LUKA

Coach: Slaviša Božičić (SRB); (13/07/12) Slobodan Starčević; (04/05/13) (Oliver Jandrić); (20/05/13) (Branislav Krunić)
1926 • Gradski (10,000) • fkborac.net
Major honours
Bosnian-Herzegovinian League (1) 2011;
Yugoslav Cup (1) 1988;
Bosnian-Herzegovinian Cup (1) 2010

2012

04/08	Zvijezda	h	3-0	Stokić 2, Krunić
12/08	Željezničar	a	0-1	
18/08	Slavija	h	1 2	Stokić
26/08	Zrinjski	a	0-1	
01/09	Radnik	h	1-0	Grahovac
15/09	Čelik	a	1-0	Teinović
23/09	Prijedor	h	4-0	Stokić 2 (1p), Kantar, Kunić
29/09	Gradina	a	3-1	Trivunović, Krunić, Kunić
06/10	Olimpik	h	2-1	Raspudić, Stokić
20/10	Sarajevo	a	0-2	
28/10	Velež	h	1-0	Kantar
03/11	Leotar	a	0-2	
10/11	Široki Brijeg	h	0-0	
17/11	Travnik	a	1-1	Kantar
24/11	Gabela	h	1-0	Krunić

2013

02/03	Zvijezda	a	1-1	Stokić
09/03	Željezničar	h	2-0	Stokić, Trivunović
16/03	Slavija	a	2-1	Stokić, Maletić
30/03	Zrinjski	h	5-1	Bilbija 4, Kantar
06/04	Radnik	a	0-0	
10/04	Čelik	h	2-0	Stokić, Maletić (p)
13/04	Prijedor	a	1-1	Trivunović
20/04	Gradina	h	1-0	Bilbija
24/04	Olimpik	a	1-1	Bilbija
27/04	Sarajevo	h	1-1	Raščić
04/05	Velež	a	0-1	
08/05	Leotar	h	5-0	Bilbija, Raščić, Zeljković, Stokić, Subić
11/05	Široki Brijeg	a	0-4	
18/05	Travnik	h	2-2	Bilbija 2
26/05	Gabela	a	2-0	Grahovac, Raščić

No	Name	Nat	DoB	Pos	Aps	(s)	Gls
1	Asmir Avdukić		13/06/81	G	24		
5	Alen Bašlić		20/09/80	M	11		
10	Nemanja Bilbija		02/11/90	A	12		8
9	Slaviša Dugić		17/01/85	A	5	(4)	
13	Siniša Dujaković		22/11/91	M	2	(2)	
16	Stefan Dujaković		04/08/92	M	1	(6)	
11	Srdjan Grahovac		19/10/92	M	26	(3)	2
23	Vladan Grujić		17/05/81	M	7	(4)	
20	Vedran Kantar		31/03/85	M	20	(4)	4
79	Branislav Krunić		28/01/79	M	16		3
17	Petar Kunić		15/07/93	A	2	(8)	2
33	Darko Maletić		20/10/80	M	13		2
30	Siniša Marčetić		13/07/79	G	6	(1)	
5	Bojan Marković		12/11/85	D	1		
10	Fedor Predragović		08/04/95	M		(1)	
4	Aleksandar Radulović		09/02/87	M	7	(7)	
19	Ognjen Radulović		27/01/91	M	4		
15	Boris Raspudić		11/10/82	M	29		1
9	Admir Raščić		16/09/81	A	3	(11)	3
12	Nebojša Runić		18/09/92	D	6		
14	Joco Stokić		07/04/87	M	26		12
6	Milan Stupar	SRB	09/01/80	D	5	(2)	
18	Aleksandar Subić		27/09/93	D	5	(16)	1
7	Dalibor Teinović		22/03/77	M	19	(2)	1
26	Vule Trivunović		13/03/83	D	21	(1)	3
3	Nikola Vasiljević		19/12/83	D	21	(1)	
22	Draško Žarić		09/10/78	D	13	(4)	
5	Mladen Zeljković	SRB	18/11/87	D	14		1
8	Mladen Žižović		27/12/80	M	11	(10)	

NK ČELIK ZENICA

Coach: Vlado Jagodić
1945 • Bilino Polje (13,000) • nkcelik.ba
Major honours
Bosnian-Herzegovinian League (3) 1994, 1996, 1997;
Bosnian-Herzegovinian Cup (2) 1995, 1996

2012

05/08	Sarajevo	a	0-0	
11/08	Velež	h	2-0	*Mešanović, Barać*
18/08	Leotar	a	0-1	
26/08	Široki Brijeg	h	2-1	*Mešanović 2*
01/09	Travnik	a	1-2	*Barać (p)*
15/09	Borac	h	1-2	*Kajkut*
22/09	Zvijezda	a	0-1	
29/09	Željezničar	h	1-2	*Čović*
06/10	Slavija	a	1-2	*Travančić*
20/10	Zrinjski	h	2-0	*Kajkut, Nestorović*
27/10	Radnik	a	2-2	*Kajkut, Maletić*
04/11	Gabela	a	0-0	
10/11	Prijedor	h	2-1	*Kajkut, Smriko*
17/11	Gradina	a	1-0	*Mešanović*
24/11	Olimpik	h	1-1	*Barać*

2013

02/03	Sarajevo	h	3-2	*Kajkut 3*
09/03	Velež	a	1-2	*Dedić*
16/03	Leotar	h	1-1	*Dedić*
30/03	Široki Brijeg	h	1-0	*Dedić*
06/04	Travnik	a	2-1	*Kajkut, og (Grabus)*
10/04	Borac	a	0-2	
13/04	Zvijezda	h	4-1	*Stajić 2, Horić, Popović*
21/04	Željezničar	a	1-1	*Mešanović*
24/04	Slavija	h	4-1	*Mešanović, Barać, Bajraktarević, Kajkut*
28/04	Zrinjski	a	2-0	*Mešanović, Kajkut*
05/05	Radnik	h	2-2	*Mešanović, Kajkut*
08/05	Gabela	h	2-1	*Kajkut, Dedić*
11/05	Prijedor	a	1-1	*Barać*
18/05	Gradina	h	2-1	*Travančić, Mešanović*
26/05	Olimpik	a	2-0	*Dedić, Mešanović*

No	Name	Nat	DoB	Pos	Aps	(s)	Gls
25	Adi Adilović		20/02/83	G	14	(1)	
8	Semir Bajraktarević		14/10/87	M	22	(4)	1
19	Stipe Barać	CRO	18/05/85	M	27		5
20	Dejan Božičić		28/10/83	A	4	(4)	
14	Zoran Brković		02/05/84	D	12	(2)	
16	Dženan Bureković		29/05/95	M	2	(2)	
22	Meksud Čolić		14/04/92	A		(7)	
4	Mehmedalija Čović		16/03/86	D	15		1
18	Alen Dedić		11/05/85	M	13	(5)	5
7	Armin Duvnjak		15/02/90	M		(3)	
12	Salih Hinović		09/02/90	G	1		
6	Kenan Horić		02/05/90	M	27		1
24	Vedad Jaganjac		02/05/94	D		(1)	
13	Emir Jusić		13/06/86	D	27		
11	Saša Kajkut		07/07/84	A	23		12
7	Elmir Kuduzović		28/02/85	D	5	(1)	
22	Slobodan Lakičević	MNE	12/01/88	D	14	(1)	
5	Stefan Maletić	SRB	09/04/87	D	17	(2)	1
3	Vladimir Marković		26/08/85	M	6	(3)	
10	Jasmin Mešanović		21/06/92	A	27	(1)	10
4	Darko Mišić	CRO	27/07/91	D	12	(1)	
21	Marko Nestorović	SRB	15/07/84	M	14	(7)	1
1	Adis Nurković		28/04/86	G	15		
15	Milan Popović		18/08/94	M	2	(10)	1
11	Jasmin Smriko		20/01/91	A	1	(2)	1
27	Duško Stajić		11/07/82	A	10	(3)	2
17	Anid Travančić		07/09/93	M	15	(8)	2

NK GOŠK GABELA

Coach: Slaven Musa; (13/08/12) Dario Zadro;
(31/08/12) Ivan Katalinić (CRO);
(31/01/13) Davor Mladina (CRO)
1919 • Podavala (2,000) • no website

2012

04/08	Gradina	a	1-1	*Jusufbašić*
12/08	Zvijezda	h	1-0	*Jusufbašić*
18/08	Olimpik	a	0-1	
26/08	Željezničar	h	2-3	*Jusufbašić 2*
02/09	Sarajevo	a	0-4	
16/09	Slavija	h	0-0	
22/09	Velež	a	3-1	*Jusufbašić, Ramović 2*
30/09	Zrinjski	a	0-0	
06/10	Leotar	a	2-4	*Hrkač, Bekić*
21/10	Radnik	h	0-0	
28/10	Široki Brijeg	a	0-5	
04/11	Čelik	h	0-0	
10/11	Travnik	h	0-0	
18/11	Prijedor	h	1-1	*Jusufbašić*
24/11	Borac	a	0-1	

2013

03/03	Gradina	h	1-0	*Bošnjak*
09/03	Zvijezda	a	1-2	*Biševic*
17/03	Olimpik	h	1-1	*Kojić*
30/03	Željezničar	a	0-2	
06/04	Sarajevo	h	0-2	
10/04	Slavija	a	1-2	*Jordan*
14/04	Velež	h	0-0	
21/04	Zrinjski	a	3-0	*Bekić, Ivičić 2*
24/04	Leotar	h	3-1	*Ivičić, Bekić, Jusufbašić*
27/04	Radnik	a	1-1	*Perić*
04/05	Široki Brijeg	h	3-2	*Bekić, Ivičić 2*
08/05	Čelik	a	1-2	*Ivičić*
11/05	Travnik	h	3-1	*Bekić, Ramović, Jusufbašić*
18/05	Prijedor	a	1-1	*Helvida*
26/05	Borac	h	0-2	

No	Name	Nat	DoB	Pos	Aps	(s)	Gls
23	Ricardo Alcalá	MEX	20/07/86	M		(2)	
1	Boris Bačak		17/04/87	G	5		
19	Stjepan Badrov		01/12/87	M	1		
21	Almir Bekić		01/06/89	M	21		5
11	Elvis Bibić		04/03/92	A	10	(4)	
22	Ramazan Biševič	MNE	11/02/92	M	13	(1)	1
6	Josip Bonacin	CRO	02/07/84	D	11		
6	Miljenko Bošnjak	CRO	11/04/87	M	24		1
16	Marin Božić		22/07/93	D	3		
13	Stipe Dodig	CRO	15/01/93	D	8	(8)	
10	Marko Grgić		30/06/87	M	8	(3)	
10	Armin Helvida		20/02/86	D	21	(1)	1
8	Ante Hrkač	CRO	11/03/92	M	9	(1)	1
8	Tomislav Ivičić	CRO	27/10/87	A	9	(5)	6
21	Tihomir Jelavić		17/08/91	D	18	(3)	
2	Marko Jordan	CRO	27/10/90	A	6		1
14	Perica Jurić		10/04/93	M		(3)	
18	Sabahudin Jusufbašić		13/01/90	A	24	(2)	8
22	Matej Karačić		04/08/93	M	3	(4)	
4	Zlatko Kojić		17/04/90	D	19	(1)	1
17	Ivan Kukavica		17/05/93	D	3	(1)	
6	Ivan Kvesić		25/11/93	M	3	(3)	
7	Ajdin Maksumić		24/07/85	M	6		
18	Danijel Marić		01/08/92	M	1	(1)	
20	Andrija Milinković	CRO	27/06/90	A	10	(2)	
17	Mate Paponja	CRO	17/02/91	D	7	(5)	
17	Ivan Perić	CRO	20/08/93	D	15	(5)	1
7	Ilija Rajič	CRO	18/01/88	M	1	(10)	
7	Sinan Ramović		13/10/92	M	20	(6)	3
1	Antonio Soldo		23/10/88	G	17		
1	Marko Sušac		23/10/88	G	8	(1)	
17	Vedad Šabanović		22/10/89	D	8	(2)	
9	Mario Vasilj	CRO	25/01/95	M	5	(2)	
2	Filip Žderić	CRO	11/12/91	D	13		

NK GRADINA

Coach: Samir Adanalić; (27/08/12) Denis Sadiković;
(20/09/12) Boris Gavran; (24/09/12) Nedžad Bajrović;
(11/10/12) Fuad Grbešić; (31/12/12) Nedžad Bajrović
1963 • Gradski (3,000); Banja Ilidža, Gradačac (3,500)
• ofkgradina.ba

2012

04/08	Gabela	h	1-1	*Zoletić*
11/08	Olimpik	h	1-1	*Džafić*
18/08	Sarajevo	a	1-3	*Džafić*
25/08	Velež	h	1-3	*Turbić*
01/09	Leotar	a	0-3	
15/09	Široki Brijeg	h	2-2	*Huseinbašić, Turbić*
22/09	Travnik	a	0-2	
29/09	Borac	h	1-3	*Popara*
06/10	Zvijezda	a	1-5	*Huseinbašić*
20/10	Željezničar	h	1-2	*Zeljković*
28/10	Slavija	a	1-2	*Katanec*
03/11	Zrinjski	h	1-2	*Turbić*
10/11	Radnik	a	0-1	
17/11	Čelik	h	0-1	
24/11	Prijedor	a	0-4	

2013

03/03	Gabela	a	0-1	
09/03	Olimpik	a	1-2	*Likić (p)*
16/03	Sarajevo	h	0-0	
30/03	Velež	a	1-2	*Turbić*
06/04	Leotar	h	0-1	
10/04	Široki Brijeg	a	0-2	
13/04	Travnik	h	0-1	
21/04	Borac	a	0-1	
24/04	Zvijezda	h	1-3	*Delić*
27/04	Željezničar	a	0-4	
04/05	Slavija	h	0-0	
08/05	Zrinjski	a	1-2	*Brčkalić*
11/05	Radnik	h	1-0	*Šehrić*
18/05	Čelik	a	1-2	*Udovičić*
26/05	Prijedor	h	0-2	

No	Name	Nat	DoB	Pos	Aps	(s)	Gls
10	Elvedin Aletić		01/03/95	M	2	(10)	
8	Emir Alić		21/06/91	D	5		
88	Dino Andrić		08/04/94	M	2	(4)	
13	Enes Brčkalić		24/09/89	M	13	(2)	1
18	Armin Delić		19/05/83	M	13		1
7	Hamdija Džaferović		01/07/94	A	2	(1)	
10	Adin Džafić		12/11/89	A	3		2
20	Amir Hamzić		05/01/75	M	10	(1)	
19	Osman Hodžić		04/02/88	D	18	(1)	
77	Ermin Huseinbašić		11/07/93	A	13	(1)	2
6	Haris Ibrić		11/08/92	A		(3)	
18	Kristijan Ivešić		06/11/87	M	6	(1)	
5	Adin Jahić		05/03/95	D	14	(1)	
88	Amer Jugo		02/12/82	M	2	(1)	
33	Matija Katanec	CRO	04/05/90	D	13		1
18	Adnan Likić		09/08/86	D	10	(1)	1
6	Nail Mašić		01/02/94	M		(2)	
22	Salih Muminović		06/10/91	M	17	(2)	
14	Damir Muratović		03/02/92	M	2	(1)	
14	Nenad Novaković	CRO	23/03/86	D	1		
44	Amer Ordagić		05/05/93	M	13	(1)	
	Edis Osmanović		30/06/88	A	1		
2	Kenan Pirić		07/07/94	G	16		
99	Almir Popara		13/02/92	A	10	(8)	1
55	Anel Salibašić		28/01/89	M	16	(5)	
13	Dražen Savić		17/05/88	D	3	(3)	
13	Emir Selimović		03/03/93	M	15	(9)	
14	Irfan Selimović		16/08/95	M	1	(2)	
7	Damir Smajlović		27/03/83	A	18	(3)	
10	Malik Smajlović		07/07/88	M	1	(2)	
7	Sanel Šehrić		12/11/90	M	12	(1)	1
1	Ibrahim Škahić		25/10/93	D	12		
9	Damir Tosunović		05/11/85	A	6	(1)	
8	Alen Turbić		18/01/82	A	17	(7)	4
2	Emil Tursunović		15/05/94	M	2	(1)	
15	Stefan Udovičić		20/09/91	D	7	(3)	1
20	Mahir Vejzović		06/11/94	M	3	(2)	
17	Faris Zahirović		09/08/93	D	1	(2)	1
6	Muamer Zoletić		20/01/83	M	9		1
3	Adnan Zukić		29/08/91	D	7		
1	Damir Zukić		02/03/85	G	14		

FK LEOTAR

Coach: Vladimir Gačinović (SRB)
1925 • Police (9,000) • fkleotar.com
Major honours
Bosnian-Herzegovinian League (1) 2003

2012

04/08	Zrinjski	h	1-0	*Šaraba*
11/08	Radnik	a	0-0	
18/08	Čelik	h	1-0	*Filipović*
25/08	Prijedor	a	1-3	*Filipović*
01/09	Gradina	h	3-0	*Janković, G Cimirot, Radivojević*
15/09	Olimpik	a	0-1	
22/09	Sarajevo	h	0-3	
30/09	Velež	a	1-1	*Janković*
06/10	Gabela	h	4-2	*Janković, Vasiljević, Sušić, Filipović*
20/10	Široki Brijeg	h	1-3	*Radivojević (p)*
27/10	Travnik	a	1-1	*Šaraba*
03/11	Borac	h	2-0	*Novaković, Filipović*
10/11	Zvijezda	a	1-0	*Radivojević*
17/11	Željezničar	h	0-2	
25/11	Slavija	a	0-0	

2013

03/03	Zrinjski	a	0-2	
09/03	Radnik	h	1-2	*Janković (p)*
16/03	Čelik	a	1-1	*Filipović*
30/03	Prijedor	h	2-1	*Janković, Grubješić*
06/04	Gradina	a	1-0	*Novaković*
10/04	Olimpik	h	1-0	*Stojčev*
14/04	Sarajevo	a	0-0	
21/04	Velež	h	0-0	
24/04	Gabela	a	1-3	*G Cimirot*
27/04	Široki Brijeg	h	1-1	*Stojčev*
04/05	Travnik	a	1-3	*Stojčev*
08/05	Borac	h	0-5	
11/05	Zvijezda	h	1-1	*Stojčev*
18/05	Željezničar	a	0-4	
26/05	Slavija	h	2-1	*Milović, Grubješić*

No	Name	Nat	DoB	Pos	Aps	(s)	Gls
21	Nemanja Andjušić		17/10/96	M	2	(6)	
4	Srdjan Andrić		10/00/85	M	25		
20	Gojko Cimirot		27/07/90	A	26		2
2	Milorad Cimirot		27/07/90	A	12	(5)	
10	Litston Churchill		11/03/90	M		(1)	
15	Dušan Danilović	SRB	17/10/87	M	2	(4)	
13	Boban Djerić		20/08/93	D	1	(13)	
19	Borivoje Filipović	SRB	28/08/82	A	27	5	5
10	Njegoš Goločevac	SRB	21/08/83	M	8	(5)	
8	Nikola Grubješić	SRB	29/06/84	A	10	(2)	2
11	Dejan Janković	SRB	06/01/86	M	25		5
12	Mladen Kukrika		11/01/81	G	5		
22	Ivan Marinković	SRB	31/10/87	M	18	(5)	
11	Marko Miholjević		21/04/96	M	5	(6)	
1	Boško Milenković	SRB	22/06/78	G	14		
5	Djoko Milović		16/09/92	M	15	(6)	1
18	Borko Novaković	SRB	24/04/81	M	25		2
3	Mile Pjaca		27/06/96	A	1	(4)	
21	Dejan Ponjević	SRB	10/02/89	M	9	(4)	
5	Dejan Popović		17/02/95	D	9	(2)	
3	Nikola Prebiračević	SRB	23/01/87	A	9		
8	Jovan Radivojević	SRB	29/10/82	M	12	(2)	3
1	Nenad Rajić		28/12/82	G	11		
10	Miloš Stojčev	MNE	19/01/87	M	13		4
8	Marko Simović		13/07/96	A		(1)	
13	Pavle Sušić	SRB	15/04/88	M	8	(1)	1
5	Zdravko Šaraba		15/05/89	D	24		2
16	Nedjo Tasovac		21/02/95	M	1	(2)	
7	Vladimir Todorović		08/12/86	D		(2)	
14	Aleksandar Vasiljević	SRB	19/06/82	D	13		1

FK OLIMPIK SARAJEVO

Coach: Nedim Jusufbegović;
(19/09/12) Husref Musemić;
(10/02/13) Denis Sadiković;
(10/04/13) Nedim Jusufbegović
1993 • Otoka (3,500) • olimpic.ba

2012

05/08	Prijedor	h	1-1	*Regoje*
11/08	Gradina	a	1-1	*Muharemović*
18/08	Gabela	h	1-0	*Bućan (p)*
25/08	Sarajevo	h	0-1	
01/09	Velež	a	1-1	*Vidović*
15/09	Leotar	h	1-0	*Djelmić*
23/09	Široki Brijeg	a	0-0	
29/09	Travnik	h	2-0	*Smajić 2*
06/10	Borac	a	1-2	*Karić*
20/10	Zvijezda	h	2-1	*Karić 2*
27/10	Željezničar	a	0-1	
03/11	Slavija	h	1-0	*Djurić*
11/11	Zrinjski	a	4-1	*Kapić, Muharemović, Djelmić, Vidović*
17/11	Radnik	h	1-0	*Muharemović*
24/11	Čelik	a	1-1	*Vidović*

2013

02/03	Prijedor	a	2-1	*Djelmić, Regoje*
09/03	Gradina	h	2-1	*Smajić, Mišić*
17/03	Gabela	a	1-1	*Kapić*
30/03	Sarajevo	a	1-3	*Kapić*
06/04	Velež	h	1-1	*Duljević*
10/04	Leotar	a	0-1	
13/04	Široki Brijeg	h	2-1	*Vidović, Muharemović*
21/04	Travnik	a	3-2	*Muharemović 2, Smajić*
24/04	Borac	h	1-1	*Karić*
27/04	Zvijezda	a	2-0	*Islamagić, Karić*
04/05	Željezničar	h	1-2	*Karić*
08/05	Slavija	a	1-0	*Muharemović*
11/05	Zrinjski	h	0-0	
18/05	Radnik	a	0-0	
26/05	Čelik	h	0-2	

No	Name	Nat	DoB	Pos	Aps	(s)	Gls
28	Alen Bašić		20/09/80	D	12		
15	Zead Bućan		08/03/81	M	6	(2)	1
14	Ognjen Djelmić		17/08/88	M	24	(5)	3
7	Miloš Djordjević	SRB	16/02/94	M		(1)	
30	Slobodan Ćima		02/01/93	M	7	(6)	1
19	Eldin Dučić		06/00/90	M		(1)	
13	Haris Duljević		16/11/93	M	25	1	1
10	Dženan Durak		04/02/91	M	10	(10)	
1	Irfan Fejzić		01/07/86	G	15	(1)	
3	Haris Hajradinović		18/02/94	D	4	(1)	
12	Dino Hamzić		22/01/88	G	15		
24	Vernes Islamagić		27/07/94	D	4	(1)	1
13	Perica Ivetić		28/11/86	M	25		
25	Ervin Jusufović		07/05/95	M		(1)	
17	Semir Kapić		28/06/86	A	17	(3)	3
19	Mahir Karić		14/12/86	M	24	(3)	6
81	Dejan Limić		09/07/85	M		(1)	
15	Toni Markić		25/10/90	D	4	(2)	
5	Adi Mehremić		26/04/92	D	1	(2)	
18	Marko Mišić		07/09/92	M	3	(6)	1
8	Veldin Muharemović		05/12/84	M	25		7
23	Almir Pliska		12/08/87	A	1	(1)	
11	Rijad Pljevljak		31/05/91	A	1	(3)	
6	Bojan Regoje		02/12/82	D	24		2
7	Bratislav Ristić	SRB	21/01/80	M		(3)	
3	Mirza Rizvanović		27/09/86	D	9	(2)	
16	Fenan Salčinović		28/06/87	M	2	(5)	
9	Irhan Smajić		08/09/90	A	15	(12)	4
4	Nihad Suljević		05/11/80	D	4	(2)	
5	Asim Škaljić		09/08/81	D	14		
16	Alen Škoro		30/03/81	A	3	(3)	
24	Miloš Vidović	SRB	03/10/89	M	27		4
99	Muamer Vila		11/11/85	M	4	(7)	
18	Amir Zolj		24/11/89	M	5	(2)	

FK RADNIK BIJELJINA

Coach: Darko Nestorović; (27/08/12) (Jovica Lukić);
(02/09/12) Srdjan Bajić
1945 • Gradski (4,000) • no website

2012

04/08	Velež	a	0-3	
11/08	Leotar	h	0-0	
18/08	Široki Brijeg	a	0-2	
25/08	Travnik	h	2-2	*Ostojić, Ćulum*
01/09	Borac	a	0-1	
15/09	Zvijezda	h	0-0	
23/09	Željezničar	a	1-1	*Basara*
29/09	Slavija	a	0-0	*Nikić, Basara*
06/10	Zrinjski	a	1-2	*Basara*
21/10	Gabela	a	0-0	
27/10	Čelik	h	2-2	*Zeljković, Basara*
03/11	Prijedor	a	0-2	
10/11	Gradina	h	1-0	*Kapetan*
17/11	Olimpik	a	0-1	
24/11	Sarajevo	h	2-1	*Basara, Nikić*

2013

02/03	Velež	h	2-1	*Nikić, Ristić*
09/03	Leotar	a	2-1	*Katanec, Basara*
17/03	Široki Brijeg	h	4-0	*Basara, Jevtić, Ristić, Obradović*
30/03	Travnik	a	1-2	*Nikić*
06/04	Borac	h	0-0	
10/04	Zvijezda	a	1-1	*Basara (p)*
13/04	Željezničar	h	0-3	
21/04	Slavija	a	0-1	
24/04	Zrinjski	h	2-0	*Basara, Obradović*
27/04	Gabela	h	1-1	*Obradović*
04/05	Čelik	a	2-2	*Kapetan, Ristić*
08/05	Prijedor	h	1-0	*Katanec*
11/05	Gradina	a	0-0	
18/05	Olimpik	h	0-0	
26/05	Sarajevo	a	0-5	

No	Name	Nat	DoB	Pos	Aps	(s)	Gls
7	Marko Basara	MNE	20/07/84	M	28	(1)	8
18	Miodoudou Ousovic		19/10/92	M	11	(3)	
10	Danijel Ćulum		19/08/80	M	13	(7)	1
12	Dragan Djordjic		29/04/89	G	1		
4	Marko Jevtić	SRB	21/05/82	D	26		1
7	Stevan Javanovic	MNE	07/00/00	A	1	1	
8	Armin Kapetan		11/03/86	A	25	(1)	2
18	Željko Karamatić	SRB	08/06/88	A	10	(2)	
8	Matija Katanec	CRO	04/05/90	D	13		2
5	Jovo Kojić		08/04/88	D	29		
13	Vladanko Komlenović	SRB	15/12/88	M	4	(9)	
17	Željko Krsmanović		11/12/90	D	9	(4)	
14	Nenad Kutlačić		04/03/81	D	1	(2)	
1	Mladen Lučić		06/07/85	G	29		
13	Dušan Milošević		28/06/95	M		(1)	
6	Igor Mirković		30/11/85	M	23	(5)	
11	Zoran Nikić		05/01/90	A	19	(5)	4
14	Radoslav Novaković		14/09/94	A		(1)	
16	Marko Obradović	MNE	30/06/91	A	6	(7)	3
3	Stanko Ostojić	SRB	15/01/85	M	26		1
2	Miloš Petrušić		02/03/89	D	1	(1)	
9	Miroslav Rikanović		20/01/83	M	1	(4)	
9	Dragan Ristić		27/02/82	A	24		3
4	Boško Takovac	SRB	16/01/86	D	9		
9	Filip Vujić		06/07/88	A		(6)	
2	Mladen Zeljković	SRB	18/11/87	D	13		1

FK RUDAR PRIJEDOR

Coach: Velimir Stojnić; (21/03/13) Vlado Čapljić
1928 • Gradski (5,000) • rudarprijedor.com

2012

05/08	Olimpik	a	1-1	Ramić	
12/08	Sarajevo	h	1-3	Mikić	
18/08	Velež	a	1-0	Mikić	
25/08	Leotar	h	3-1	Acevedo, Handžić, Rastoka	
02/09	Široki Brijeg	a	1-2	Lamondzhava	
15/09	Travnik	h	1-0	Mikić	
23/09	Borac	a	0-4		
29/09	Zvijezda	h	2-0	og (Savić), Vuković	
06/10	Željezničar	a	0-1		
20/10	Slavija	h	0-1		
03/11	Radnik	h	2-0	Kokanović, Mikić	
10/11	Čelik	a	1-2	Kokanović	
15/11	Zrinjski	a	0-0		
18/11	Gabela	h	1-1	Handžić	
24/11	Gradina	h	4-0	Handžić 2, Savić, Srndović	

2013

02/03	Olimpik	h	1-2	Srndović	
09/03	Sarajevo	a	0-3		
16/03	Velež	h	2-3	Mikić, Pejić	
30/03	Leotar	a	1-2	Mikić (p)	
06/04	Široki Brijeg	h	2-1	Handžić 2	
10/04	Travnik	a	1-0	Mišan	
13/04	Borac	h	1-1	Mišan	
20/04	Zvijezda	a	1-4	Srndović	
24/04	Željezničar	h	1-3	Ramić	
28/04	Slavija	a	1-3	Mikić (p)	
04/05	Zrinjski	h	4-1	Handžić, Milutinović, Mikić, Rastoka	
08/05	Radnik	a	0-1		
11/05	Čelik	h	1-1	Savić	
18/05	Gabela	h	1-1	Mišan	
26/05	Gradina	a	2-0	Radulović, Vuković	

No	Name	Nat	DoB	Pos	Aps	(s)	Gls
2	Eduardo Acevedo	DOM	10/12/85	D	23	(1)	1
19	Denis Bajalica	CRO	31/01/91	D	15		
1	Boriša Bodiroga		13/12/88	G	25		
4	Miodrag Gigović		06/08/84	D	27		
11	Haris Handžić		20/06/90	A	24	(2)	7
20	Nermin Hodžić		13/07/94	M	1		
13	Emilko Janković		27/03/84	D	11	(1)	
18	Aleksandar Jovičić		18/01/95	M	2	(1)	
15	Vladimir Karalić		22/03/84	A		(3)	
21	Nemanja Kokanović		28/11/84	M	12	(3)	2
3	Goran Kotaran		11/01/79	M	16	(2)	
8	Apollon Lamondzhava	GEO	02/03/91	M	3	(6)	1
20	Borislav Mikić		20/12/75	M	25		8
12	Danijel Milanović	SRB	10/07/91	G	5		
13	Zoran Milutinović		01/03/88	M	11		1
7	Zoran Miodragović		02/05/93	M		(1)	
7	Igor Mišan		05/05/90	M	13		3
17	Nebojša Pejić		05/01/88	M	14		1
16	Tomislav Puljić		05/11/92	D	4	(3)	
10	Ognjen Radulović		27/01/91	M	6	(4)	1
6	Anel Ramić	MNE	15/04/87	M	25	(3)	2
9	Marinko Rastoka	SRB	10/06/91	D	14	(8)	2
18	Rastko Rokvić		05/10/94	A		(2)	
11	Damir Rovčanin		12/03/88	A	2	(6)	
18	Duško Sakan		03/03/89	M	2	(6)	
5	Boris Savić		18/01/88	M	24		2
14	Miloš Srndović		01/04/92	A	6	(11)	3
7	Nebojša Šodić		15/07/85	D	2		
10	Borislav Topić		22/05/84	M	6		
22	Veljko Vuković	SRB	14/07/89	M	12	(8)	2

FK SARAJEVO

Coach: Dragan Jović; (16/03/13) Husref Musemić; (08/05/13) (Abdulah Oruč)
1946 • Olimpijski Asim Ferhatović Hase (34,600) • fksinfo.com

Major honours
Yugoslav League (2) 1967, 1985;
Bosnian-Herzegovinian League (1) 2007;
Bosnian-Herzegovinian Cup (4) 1997, 1998, 2002, 2005

2012

05/08	Čelik	h	0-0		
12/08	Prijedor	a	3-1	Belošević 2, Husejinović	
18/08	Gradina	h	3-1	Torlak, Hadžić, Belošević (p)	
25/08	Olimpik	a	1-0	Belošević (p)	
02/09	Gabela	h	4-0	Hadžić 3, Belošević	
15/09	Velež	h	4-1	Belošević 2 (1p), Hadžić, Čomor	
22/09	Leotar	a	3-0	Hadžić 2, Suljić	
30/09	Široki Brijeg	h	2-1	Husejinović, Torlak	
06/10	Travnik	a	0-0		
20/10	Borac	h	2-0	Torlak, Tadejević	
27/10	Zvijezda	a	2-2	Belošević (p), Husejinović	
03/11	Željezničar	h	1-0	Nuhanović	
11/11	Slavija	a	0-0		
18/11	Zrinjski	h	1-0	Dupovac	
24/11	Radnik	a	1-2	Hadžić	

2013

02/03	Čelik	a	2-3	Melunović, Hadžić	
09/03	Prijedor	h	3-0	Hadžić 2, Melunović	
16/03	Gradina	a	0-0		
30/03	Olimpik	h	3-1	Hadžić 2, Todorović	
06/04	Gabela	a	2-0	Hadžić, Džakmić	
10/04	Velež	a	0-0		
14/04	Leotar	a	0-0		
21/04	Široki Brijeg	a	1-2	Suljić	
24/04	Travnik	h	1-0	Torlak	
28/04	Borac	a	1-1	Melunović	
04/05	Zvijezda	h	4-1	Suljić, Hadžić, Tatomirović, Haurdić	
08/05	Željezničar	a	0-0		
11/05	Slavija	h	1-0	Džakmić	
18/05	Zrinjski	a	2-2	Haurdić, Todorović	
26/05	Radnik	h	5-0	Hadžić 5	

No	Name	Nat	DoB	Pos	Aps	(s)	Gls
12	Almin Abdihožić		28/11/90	G	2		
18	Edin Ademović	SRB	10/02/87	M	1	(3)	
27	Almir Aganspahić		12/09/96	A		(1)	
19	Dejan Bandović		11/06/83	D	28		
23	Zoran Belošević	SRB	20/06/83	D	13		8
89	Denis Čomor		03/01/90	M	6	(7)	1
25	Secouba Diatta	SEN	22/12/92	M		(1)	
29	Amer Dupovac		30/11/90	D	26		1
17	Muhamed Džakmić		23/08/85	M	13		2
17	Boris Gujić		09/07/86	D	3	(6)	
10	Emir Hadžić		19/07/84	A	27		20
10	Faris Handžić		27/05/95	M		(5)	
8	Anes Haurdić		01/03/90	M	12		2
8	Adnan Hrelja		10/10/90	M	1	(3)	
7	Ermin Huseinbašić		11/07/93	A		(2)	
7	Said Husejinović		13/05/88	M	14	(1)	3
21	Žarko Karamatić	SRB	08/06/88	M	4	(4)	
9	Sulejman Krpić		01/01/91	A		(5)	
9	Alen Melunović	SRB	26/01/90	A	11		3
4	Nemanja Mijušković	MNE	04/03/92	D	1	(1)	
8	Samir Nuhanović	SVN	05/11/87	M	4	(7)	1
22	Amer Osmanagić		07/05/89	M	6	(4)	
88	Samir Radovac		25/01/96	M	7	(1)	
5	Ivan Sesar		29/08/89	M	11		
99	Asmir Suljić		11/09/91	A	22	(4)	3
16	Radan Šušnjavarić	SRB	10/02/83	M	17	(6)	
28	Mario Tadejević	CRO	28/03/89	D	19	(6)	1
14	Ivan Tatomirović	SRB	11/09/89	D	29		1
13	Ognjen Todorović		24/03/89	M	12	(2)	2
6	Sedin Torlak		12/01/85	D	24	(1)	4
77	Nemanja Zlatković	SRB	21/08/88	M	17	(2)	

NK ŠIROKI BRIJEG

Coach: Marijan Bloudek; (06/08/12) Slaven Musa
1948 • Pecara (7,000) • nk-sirokibrijeg.com

Major honours
Bosnian-Herzegovinian League (2) 2004, 2006;
Bosnian-Herzegovinian Cup (2) 2007, 2013

2012

05/08	Slavija	h	0-0		
12/08	Zrinjski	a	0-1		
18/08	Radnik	h	2-0	Kordić, Wagner	
26/08	Čelik	a	1-2	Wagner	
02/09	Prijedor	h	2-1	Roskam, Ricardo Baiano	
15/09	Gradina	a	2-2	Kordić, Roskam	
23/09	Olimpik	h	0-0		
30/09	Sarajevo	a	1-2	Ricardo Baiano	
06/10	Velež	h	2-1	Šilić (p), Barišić	
20/10	Leotar	a	3-1	Wagner, Šilić, Ješe (p)	
28/10	Gabela	h	5-0	Barišić, Wagner 2, Zlomislić, Roskam	
03/11	Travnik	h	5-0	Barišić, Ćorić, D Džidić, M Marić	
10/11	Borac	a	0-0		
17/11	Zvijezda	h	1-0	Roskam	
25/11	Željezničar	a	1-2	Šilić	

2013

03/03	Slavija	a	1-0	I Džidić	
10/03	Zrinjski	h	3-0	Kordić, D Džidić, Roskam	
17/03	Radnik	a	0-4		
30/03	Čelik	h	0-1		
06/04	Prijedor	a	1-2	Ljubić	
10/04	Gradina	h	2-0	Wagner, I Džidić	
13/04	Olimpik	a	1-2	Wagner	
21/04	Sarajevo	h	2-1	Kordić 2	
24/04	Velež	a	0-0		
27/04	Leotar	h	1-1	I Džidić	
04/05	Gabela	a	2-3	Ješe (p), Barišić	
08/05	Travnik	a	1-2	M Marić	
11/05	Borac	h	4-0	Kordić 4 (2p)	
18/05	Zvijezda	a	1-2	Kordić	
26/05	Željezničar	h	4-1	Ivanković, Serdarušić, Kordić 2	

No	Name	Nat	DoB	Pos	Aps	(s)	Gls
23	Ivan Barišić		13/07/93	A	10	(11)	5
6	Mateo Bertoša	CRO	10/08/88	D	13	(1)	
12	Luka Bilobrk		08/12/85	G	27		
22	Sandro Bloudek	CRO	16/02/86	M		(3)	
5	Slavko Brekalo		25/02/90	D	7		
16	Dino Ćorić		30/06/90	D	21	(1)	1
2	Damir Džidić		15/02/87	D	12	(1)	2
3	Ivica Džidić		08/02/84	D	17	(1)	3
18	Jure Ivanković		15/11/85	M	18	(5)	1
8	Vedran Ješe	CRO	03/02/81	D	25	(1)	2
11	Krešimir Kordić		03/09/81	A	16	(9)	12
4	Danijel Kožul		01/08/88	M	7	(6)	
20	Zvonimir Kožulj		15/11/93	M	6	(1)	
14	Davor Landeka		18/09/84	M	9	(3)	
7	Mario Ljubić		05/03/85	M	11	(3)	1
20	Mirko Marić		16/05/95	M	7	(6)	2
1	Nikola Marić		29/08/79	G	3	(1)	
25	Stipo Marković		03/12/93	D	17	(5)	
9	Ricardo Baiano		10/09/80	A	4	(5)	2
19	Mateo Roskam	CRO	03/04/93	A	18	(8)	5
17	Ante Serdarušić		24/01/83	M	18	(4)	1
10	Dalibor Šilić		23/01/79	M	16	(4)	3
15	Wagner	BRA	01/01/78	M	25		7
21	Damir Zlomislić		20/07/91	M	23	(1)	1

FK SLAVIJA SARAJEVO

Coach: Vlado Čapljić; (04/01/13) Milomir Šešlija
1908 • SC Slavija (4,500) • fkslavija.com
Major honours
Bosnian-Herzegovinian Cup (1) 2009

2012

05/08	Široki Brijeg	a	0-0	
12/08	Travnik	h	1-0	Kokot
18/08	Borac	a	2-1	Mamić, Rašević
26/08	Zvijezda	h	1-0	Vidić (p)
01/09	Željezničar	a	0-2	
16/09	Gabela	a	0-0	
23/09	Zrinjski	h	1-1	Rašević
29/09	Radnik	a	0-2	
06/10	Čelik	h	2-1	Papaz, Dudo
20/10	Prijedor	a	1-0	Aleksić
28/10	Gradina	a	2-1	Benović, Vidić (p)
03/11	Olimpik	a	0-1	
11/11	Sarajevo	h	0-0	
17/11	Velež	a	3-0	Rašević, Perišić, Aleksić
27/11	Leotar	h	0-0	

2013

03/03	Široki Brijeg	h	0-1	
09/03	Travnik	a	2-1	Kokot, Dudić
16/03	Borac	h	1-2	Kokot
31/03	Zvijezda	a	1-1	Dudić
07/04	Željezničar	h	1-2	Kokot
10/04	Gabela	h	2-1	Kokot, Dudić
14/04	Zrinjski	a	1-2	Aleksić
21/04	Radnik	h	1-0	Dudić (p)
24/04	Čelik	a	1-4	Lemez
28/04	Prijedor	h	3-1	Dudić (p), Rašević, Perišić
05/05	Gradina	a	0-0	
08/05	Olimpik	h	0-1	
11/05	Sarajevo	a	0-1	
20/05	Velež	h	2-0	I Radovanović, Dudić
26/05	Leotar	a	1-2	Kokot

No	Name	Nat	DoB	Pos	Aps	(s)	Gls
26	Radoslav Aleksić	SRB	06/03/86	A	27		3
20	Vukašin Benović		31/07/86	D	25	(1)	1
25	Ljubiša Berjan		11/08/94	M		(7)	
21	Haris Bešlija		27/09/96	M		(10)	
27	Miloš Djordjević		10/02/01	D		(0)	
10	Feuja Dudić		01/02/00	A	13	(3)	0
8	Edin Dudo		30/01/81	M	27		1
1	Ratko Dujković		16/03/73	G	22		
25	Faris Fazlagiić		05/04/87	M	14		
4	Nemanja Gigović		01/10/94	M	1	(5)	
22	Dragan Ikonić		27/03/94	M		(2)	
17	Marko Jovanović	SRB	07/02/89	M	1	(3)	
10	Zoran Kokot		09/12/85	A	27		6
24	Mladen Lemez		25/04/90	A	6		1
21	Ivan Mamić		15/09/90	A	23	(6)	1
22	Marko Mirosavjević	CRO	22/05/90	M		(3)	
3	Branko Ojdanić		21/06/90	D	2	(1)	
5	Predrag Papaz		20/01/87	D	15		1
16	Marko Perišić		25/01/91	M	24	(5)	2
6	Goran Popović		28/04/89	D	12	(3)	
19	Nemanja Pušara		21/08/91	A	1	(14)	
9	Igor Radovanović		02/08/85	A	4	(6)	1
24	Saša Radovanović		10/07/91	D	13		
7	Dejan Rašević		25/11/83	A	24	(2)	4
4	Jovan Svitlica		03/07/91	D	19		
23	Stefan Tomović		15/01/91	G	8	(1)	
4	Srdjan Urošević	SRB	30/04/84	M	1	(1)	
9	Lazar Vidić	SRB	10/07/89	A	13		2

NK TRAVNIK

Coach: Nermin Bašić; (17/01/13) Elvedin Beganović;
(21/04/13) Nermin Bašić
1922 • Pirota (3,000) • no website

2012

04/08	Željezničar	h	0-0	
12/08	Slavija	a	0-1	
18/08	Zrinjski	h	0-1	
25/08	Radnik	a	2-1	Lihovac, Zatagić
01/09	Čelik	h	2-1	Mišić, Popović
15/09	Prijedor	a	0-1	
22/09	Gradina	h	2-0	Zatagić, Ribić
29/09	Olimpik	a	0-1	
06/10	Sarajevo	h	1-0	Popović
20/10	Velež	a	0-6	
27/10	Leotar	h	1-1	Ribić
03/11	Široki Brijeg	a	0-5	
10/11	Gabela	h	0-0	
17/11	Borac	h	1-1	Popović
24/11	Zvijezda	a	1-3	N Varupa

2013

02/03	Željezničar	a	0-2	
09/03	Slavija	h	1-2	Isaković
24/03	Zrinjski	a	2-1	Turković, Simeunović
31/03	Radnik	h	2-1	E Varupa (p), Popović
07/04	Čelik	a	1-2	Simeunović
10/04	Prijedor	h	0-1	
14/04	Gradina	a	1-0	E Varupa
20/04	Olimpik	h	2-3	Anel Ćurić, Simeunović
24/04	Sarajevo	a	0-1	
28/04	Velež	h	0-0	
04/05	Leotar	a	3-1	Zatagić, Popović 2
08/05	Široki Brijeg	h	2-1	Turković, E Varupa (p)
11/05	Gabela	a	1-3	Isaković
18/05	Borac	a	2-2	Turković 2
26/05	Zvijezda	h	2-1	Kovačević, Turković

No	Name	Nat	DoB	Pos	Aps	(s)	Gls
11	Armel Ćiro		22/02/91	M	2	(8)	
10	Anel Ćurić		28/07/88	M	13		1
1	Alen Delić		25/03/83	G	1	(1)	
24	Dženan Duraković		20/06/90	M	3	(4)	
22	Amar El Dasti	JOR	07/10/90	M		(2)	
15	Niljuz Fazlić		06/06/00	D	2	(0)	
12	Nevres Fejzić		04/11/90	G	20		
4	Suvad Grabus		14/12/81	D	8	(4)	
21	Haris Hećo		29/05/87	M	14		
16	Ibrahim Hrvat		19/11/92	M		(1)	
8	Aladin Isaković		23/07/85	A	2	(6)	2
8	Alem Karalić		24/12/93	M	1	(2)	
25	Mahir Karić		05/03/92	M	1	(5)	
6	Adnan Kovačević		09/09/93	D	21	(5)	1
18	Neven Laštro		01/10/88	M	27		
7	Adin Lihovac		22/08/87	D	9	(2)	1
4	Darko Mišić	CRO	27/07/91	D	14		1
21	Jure Pejić		25/11/91	M	6	(2)	
1	Amel Pjanić		07/09/85	G	2		
11	Rijad Pljevljak		31/05/91	A		(2)	
9	Nebojša Popović	CRO	04/04/92	A	25		6
13	Haris Redžepi		20/07/88	M	10	(2)	
5	Nihad Ribić		10/11/81	D	23		2
12	Alija Salešević		04/12/94	G	1	(1)	
17	Deni Simeunović	CRO	12/02/92	M	21	(5)	3
22	Adnan Smajić		31/03/92	A	1	(6)	
7	Nail Šehović		18/01/90	M			
20	Senad Tabaković		26/09/91	D	18	(2)	
2	Sinbad Terzić		22/02/81	D	28		
24	Eldar Torlak		15/10/93	M	1	(2)	
15	Nedo Turković		23/10/89	A	11	(3)	5
3	Elvedin Varupa		16/11/75	M	13	(1)	3
14	Nermin Varupa		18/04/91	M	15	(3)	1
11	Haris Zatagić		15/03/85	D	11	(11)	3

FK VELEŽ

Coach: Asmir Džafić; (23/09/12) (Dženan Zaimović);
(03/10/12) Ibro Rahimić
1922 • Vrapčići (2,500) • fkvelez.ba
Major honours
Yugoslav Cup (2) 1981, 1986

2012

04/08	Radnik	h	3-0	Ćemalović 2, Hebibović
11/08	Čelik	h	0-2	
18/08	Prijedor	h	0-1	
25/08	Gradina	a	3-1	Hebibović 2, Ćurić
01/09	Olimpik	h	1-1	Okić
15/09	Sarajevo	a	1-4	Hebibović
22/09	Gabela	h	1-3	Serdarević
30/09	Leotar	h	1-1	Ćemalović
06/10	Široki Brijeg	a	1-2	Okić
20/10	Travnik	h	6-0	Okić, Ćemalović 3, Ćurić, Demić
28/10	Borac	a	0-1	
03/11	Zvijezda	h	2-1	Ćemalović, Zvonić
11/11	Željezničar	a	0-1	
17/11	Slavija	h	0-3	
25/11	Zrinjski	a	1-2	Hajdarević

2013

02/03	Radnik	a	1-2	Šišić
09/03	Čelik	h	2-1	Ćemalović, Okić
16/03	Prijedor	a	3-2	Okić 2, Majkić
30/03	Gradina	h	1-1	Merzić
06/04	Olimpik	a	1-1	Majkić
10/04	Sarajevo	h	0-0	
14/04	Gabela	a	1-0	og (Paponja)
21/04	Leotar	a	0-0	
24/04	Široki Brijeg	h	0-0	
28/04	Travnik	a	0-0	
04/05	Borac	h	1-0	Okić
08/05	Zvijezda	a	0-1	
11/05	Željezničar	h	0-1	
18/05	Slavija	a	0-2	
26/05	Zrinjski	h	1-1	Majkić

No	Name	Nat	DoB	Pos	Aps	(s)	Gls
12	Adnan Bobić		04/02/87	G	17		
22	Mirza Ćemalović		06/07/93	M	17	(3)	8
23	Anel Ćurić		28/07/88	M	8	(2)	2
11	Adin Dino Hajdarević		10/10/90	A	9	(0)	1
13	Anel Hebibović		07/07/90	M	21	(5)	4
19	Maid Jaganjac		11/06/92	A	4	(1)	
15	Amer Jazvin		11/10/90	D		(1)	
3	Admir Kajtaz		30/03/78	D	5	(1)	
6	Zlatko Kazazić		10/02/89	M	20	(1)	
25	Milan Knežević		01/01/88	D		(4)	
7	Mustafa Kodro		29/08/81	M	21	(1)	
	Željko Kuzmić	SRB	02/11/94	G		(1)	
20	Bojan Letić		21/12/92	M	14	(1)	
23	Marsel Mace		24/12/91	A	2	(4)	
2	Amer Mahimić		02/06/90	D	11	(2)	
6	Danijel Majkić		16/12/87	M	13		3
15	Fadil Marić		12/08/93	M	1		
16	Adi Mehremić		26/04/92	D	10	(2)	
16	Samir Merzić		29/06/84	D	21		1
21	Ajdin Nuhić		01/11/91	M	13	(3)	
20	Šefko Okić		26/07/88	A	27		7
4	Senedin Oštraković		13/04/92	G	13		
19	Matijas Pejić		18/03/88	D	2	(2)	
23	Almir Pliska		12/08/87	A	5	(7)	
8	Nedžad Serdarević		20/09/84	M	7	(8)	1
15	Aldin Šišić		29/09/90	M	6	(5)	1
9	Arnel Škaljić		09/08/81	M	6	(2)	
22	Lazar Vidić	SRB	10/07/89	A	6	(6)	
10	Admir Vladavić		29/06/82	M	15		
19	Amir Zolj		24/11/89	D	8	(4)	
4	Denis Zvonić		08/02/92	D	21	(5)	1

FK ŽELJEZNIČAR

Coach: Amar Osim
1921 • Grbavica (14,000) • fkzeljeznicar.ba
Major honours
Yugoslav League (1) 1972;
Bosnian-Herzegovinian League (6) 1998, 2001, 2002,
2010, 2012, 2013;
Bosnian-Herzegovinian Cup (5) 2000, 2001, 2003,
2011, 2012

2012

Date	Opponent		Score	Scorers
04/08	Travnik	a	0-0	
12/08	Borac	h	1-0	Svraka
18/08	Zvijezda	a	4-1	Selimović, Adilović, Svraka 2
26/08	Gabela	a	3-2	Zeba, Selimović, Adilović
01/09	Slavija	h	2-0	Kerla, Bešlija
15/09	Zrinjski	a	0-1	
23/09	Radnik	h	1-1	Jamak
29/09	Čelik	a	2-1	Adilović, Brković
06/10	Prijedor	h	1-0	Zeba
20/10	Gradina	a	2-1	Bogičević, Bekrić
27/10	Olimpik	h	1-0	Adilović
03/11	Sarajevo	a	0-1	
11/11	Velež	h	1-0	Adilović
17/11	Leotar	a	2-0	Adilović, Bekrić
25/11	Široki Brijeg	h	2-1	Svraka, Bekrić (p)
2013				
02/03	Travnik	h	2-0	og (Laštro), Bogičević
09/03	Borac	a	0-2	
17/03	Zvijezda	h	2-1	Adilović 2
30/03	Gabela	h	2-0	Selimović, Svraka
06/04	Slavija	a	2-0	Hodžić, Adilović
10/04	Zrinjski	h	0-0	
13/04	Radnik	a	3-0	Hodžić, E Čolić, Adilović
20/04	Čelik	h	1-1	Tomić
24/04	Prijedor	a	3-1	Svraka 2, Adilović
27/04	Gradina	h	4-0	Svraka, Adilović 2 (1p), Hodžić
04/05	Olimpik	a	2-1	Hodžić, Adilović (p)
08/05	Sarajevo	h	0-0	
11/05	Velež	a	0-0	
18/05	Leotar	h	4-0	Adilović 3, Bogičević
26/05	Široki Brijeg	a	1-4	Adilović

No	Name	Nat	DoB	Pos	Aps	(s)	Gls
9	Eldin Adilović		08/02/86	A	29	(1)	18
1	Marjan Antolović	CRO	07/05/89	G	30		
90	Samir Bekrić		21/06/84	M	15	(3)	3
20	Mirsad Bešlija		06/07/79	M	1	(9)	1
6	Jadranko Bogičević		11/03/83	D	25		3
4	Danijel Brković		03/06/91	M	1	(8)	1
17	Benjamin Čolić		23/07/91	D	26	(1)	
2	Elvir Čolić		17/07/86	A	8	(8)	1
18	Josip Ćutuk		04/05/85	D	4		
44	Eldar Hasanović		12/01/90	M	7	(3)	
15	Armin Hodžić		17/11/94	A	7	(8)	4
24	Nermin Jamak		25/08/86	M	16	(6)	1
15	Semir Kerla		26/09/87	D	12	(1)	1
3	Josip Kvesić		21/09/90	D	15		
29	Šaban Pehilj		23/09/92	A		(6)	
14	Damir Sadiković		07/04/95	M		(2)	
16	Vernes Selimović		08/05/83	M	22	(4)	3
27	Sulejman Smajić		13/08/84	M	2	(4)	
11	Srdjan Stanić		06/07/89	A	20	(2)	
23	Muamer Svraka		14/02/88	M	24	(1)	8
25	Tomislav Tomić		16/11/90	M	9	(4)	1
85	Yani Urdinov	MKD	28/03/91	D	9		
19	Velibor Vasilić		19/10/80	D	19	(2)	
10	Zajko Zeba		22/05/83	M	11	(2)	2
8	Nermin Zolotić		07/07/93	M	18	(1)	

HŠK ZRINJSKI

Coach: Dragan Perić; (07/04/13) Branko Karačić
1912 • Bijeli Brijeg (15,000) • hskzrinjski.ba
Major honours
Bosnian-Herzegovinian League (2) 2005, 2009;
Bosnian-Herzegovinian Cup (1) 2008

2012

Date	Opponent		Score	Scorers
05/08	Leotar	a	0-1	
12/08	Široki Brijeg	h	1-0	Marjanović
18/08	Travnik	a	1-0	Pehar
26/08	Borac	h	1-0	Stojkić
02/09	Zvijezda	a	0-2	
15/09	Željezničar	h	1-0	Stojkić
23/09	Slavija	a	1-1	Stojkić
30/09	Gabela	a	1-0	Bubalo
06/10	Radnik	h	2-1	I Aničić, Radeljić
20/10	Čelik	a	0-2	
03/11	Gradina	a	2-1	Arežina 2
11/11	Olimpik	h	1-4	M Aničić
15/11	Prijedor	h	0-0	
18/11	Sarajevo	a	0-0	
25/11	Velež	h	2-1	Arežina, I Aničić
2013				
03/03	Leotar	h	2-0	Radeljić 2
10/03	Široki Brijeg	a	0-3	
17/03	Travnik	h	1-2	Radeljić
30/03	Borac	a	1-5	Marković
06/04	Zvijezda	h	1-2	Stojkić (p)
10/04	Željezničar	a	0-0	
14/04	Slavija	h	2-1	Bekić, Stojkić
21/04	Gabela	h	0-3	
24/04	Radnik	a	0-2	
28/04	Čelik	h	0-2	
04/05	Prijedor	a	1-4	Crnov
08/05	Gradina	h	2-1	Radeljić, Pehar
11/05	Olimpik	a	0-0	
18/05	Sarajevo	h	2-2	Poredski, Muminović
26/05	Velež	a	1-1	Bekić

No	Name	Nat	DoB	Pos	Aps	(s)	Gls
10	Igor Aničić	SRB	07/01/89	A	8	(4)	2
27	Marin Aničić		17/08/89	M	22	(1)	1
18	Filip Arežina		08/11/92	M	15	(9)	3
15	Hrvoje Barišić	CRO	03/02/91	M	3	(1)	
9	Amer Bekić		05/08/92	A	9	(8)	2
7	Luka Brlenić	CRO	07/02/92	M	10	(3)	
21	Ivan Bubalo	CRO	22/05/90	A	5	(3)	1
10	Ivan Crnov	CRO	01/02/90	M	11	(1)	1
17	Ante Ćilić		08/09/93	M	6	(7)	
2	Velibor Djurić		05/05/82	M	6	(3)	
19	Ivan Ferenc		11/06/91	A	1	(1)	
14	Gligor Gligorov	MKD	15/03/87	M	3		
2	Daniel Graovac		08/07/93	D	14		
23	Robert Grbavac		17/09/90	M	1		
1	Adnan Hadžić		15/01/88	G	8		
14	Dario Krišto	CRO	05/03/89	M	6	(3)	
2	Josip Lisica	CRO	19/03/93	M	2		
8	Lazar Marjanović	SRB	08/09/89	M	14	(4)	1
5	Toni Markić		25/10/90	M	8	(5)	
4	Goran Marković	MNE	09/02/86	D	16		1
26	Davor Martinović		06/11/93	M		(1)	
12	Igor Melher		01/11/79	G	12		
15	Hrvoje Miličević	CRO	20/04/93	M	24		
23	Milan Muminović		02/10/83	M	15	(9)	1
26	Marko Odak		29/03/95	D	2	(3)	
11	Mile Pehar		01/02/91	D	15	(7)	2
24	Matija Poredski	CRO	09/11/88	A	7	(4)	1
6	Anto Radeljić		31/12/90	D	24		5
6	Josip Sesar		16/10/92	D	9	(1)	
16	Pero Stojkić		09/12/86	D	19	(3)	5
13	Vučina Ščepanović	SRB	17/11/82	M	15	(2)	
22	Nikola Vasilj		16/10/92	G	10		
20	Igor Žuržinov	SRB	30/05/81	D	10	(1)	

NK ZVIJEZDA

Coach: Zoran Kuntić (SRB);
(19/12/12) Milomir Odović
1922 • Banja Ilidža (3,500) • nkzvijezda.ba

2012

Date	Opponent		Score	Scorers
04/08	Borac	a	0-3	
12/08	Gabela	a	0-1	
18/08	Željezničar	h	1-4	E Halilović
26/08	Slavija	a	0-1	
02/09	Zrinjski	h	2-0	Savić, og (Markić)
16/09	Radnik	a	0-0	
22/09	Čelik	h	1-0	A Halilović
29/09	Prijedor	a	0-2	
06/10	Gradina	h	5-1	Pandža 2, Bogdanović, Savić, Kojić
20/10	Olimpik	a	1-2	Vehabović
27/10	Sarajevo	h	2-2	M Džafić, A Halilović
03/11	Velež	a	1-2	Pandža
10/11	Leotar	h	0-1	
17/11	Široki Brijeg	a	0-1	
24/11	Travnik	h	3-1	Pandža, Savić, M Džafić
2013				
03/03	Borac	h	1-1	Stanceski
09/03	Gabela	h	2-1	Diatta, M Džafić
17/03	Željezničar	a	1-2	Savić
30/03	Slavija	h	1-1	Sušić
04/04	Zrinjski	a	2-1	Bogdanović, Diatta
10/04	Radnik	h	1-1	M Džafić (p)
13/04	Čelik	a	1-4	Savić
20/04	Prijedor	h	4-1	M Džafić (p), Diatta, Ordagić, S Husić
24/04	Gradina	a	3-1	Mus, Ordagić, S Husić
27/04	Olimpik	h	0-2	
04/05	Sarajevo	a	1-4	M Džafić
08/05	Velež	h	1-0	Diatta
11/05	Leotar	a	1-1	M Džafić
18/05	Široki Brijeg	h	2-1	A Halilović, M Džafić
26/05	Travnik	a	1-2	A Džafić

No	Name	Nat	DoB	Pos	Aps	(s)	Gls
5	André Luiz	BRA	22/12/91	M	13	(2)	
22	Jasmin Bogdanović		10/05/90	D	24	(1)	2
25	Secouba Diatta	SEN	22/12/92	M	12		4
26	Fahrudin Djurdjevic	MKD	17/02/92	A	6	(3)	
23	Ahmed Džafić		28/02/93	A	1		1
13	Mirza Džafić		30/03/81	A	17	(5)	8
19	Almir Halilović		30/01/85	M	13	(8)	3
23	Emir Halilović		04/11/89	M	1	(1)	1
20	Edin Husić		10/11/85	M	4		
10	Senad Husić		12/04/90	A	9	(3)	2
9	Samir Isanović		23/07/95	M		(1)	
11	Omer Jahić		12/04/93	M	14	(6)	
6	Ivan Jakovljević	SRB	26/05/89	D	14		
15	Rusmir Jusić		20/10/80	D	6	(2)	
7	Dejan Kojić		31/05/86	A	6	(6)	1
1	Nikola Kovačević	SRB	02/11/90	G	3		
25	Armin Kurbašić		24/07/94	G	2		
12	Ivan Mandušić		05/04/93	G		(1)	
7	Eldin Mašić		02/01/87	M	14		
8	Slobodan Milanović		27/08/92	A	5	(8)	
32	Nikola Mirković	SRB	26/07/91	G	24		
3	Jasmin Moranjkić		11/10/83	M	19	(1)	
4	Saša Mus	CRO	19/07/86	D	13		1
18	Amer Ordagić		05/05/93	M	10	(3)	2
9	Dalibor Pandža		23/03/91	A	13	(2)	4
11	Eldar Pilavdžić		23/07/93	M		(3)	
21	Dejan Ponjević	SRB	24/03/90	M	12	(1)	
14	Mirsad Ramić		06/12/92	A	1	(5)	
9	Ilija Ristanić		11/02/86	M	8	(4)	
21	Srdjan Savić		27/09/85	A	24	(2)	5
12	Raif Smajić		14/06/85	G	1		
6	Perica Stanceski	MKD	29/01/85	M	12		1
7	Pavle Sušić	SRB	15/04/88	M	13	(1)	1
14	Nebojša Šodić		15/07/85	D	10		
17	Ermin Vehabović		22/11/87	A	6	(3)	1

Top goalscorers

20	Emir Hadžić (Sarajevo)
18	Eldin Adilović (Željezničar)
12	Joco Stokić (Borac)
	Saša Kajkut (Čelik)
	Krešimir Kordić (Široki Brijeg)
10	Jasmin Mešanović (Čelik)
9	Marko Basara (Radnik)
8	Nemanja Bilbija (Borac)
	Sabahudin Jusufbašić (Gabela)
	Borislav Mikić (Prijedor)
	Zoran Belošević (Sarajevo)
	Mirza Ćemalović (Velež)
	Muamer Svraka (Željezničar)
	Mirza Džafić (Zvijezda)

Promoted clubs

NK VITEZ
Coach: Valentin Plavčić
1947 • Gradski (2,000) • no website

FK MLADOST VELIKA OBARSKA
Coach: Miroslav Milovanović
1948 • Velika Obarska (1,500) • no website

SECOND LEVEL FINAL TABLES 2012/13

PRVA LIGA FBIH		Pld	W	D	L	F	A	Pts
1	NK Vitez	28	16	7	5	54	24	55
2	FK Radnički Lukavac	28	12	9	7	40	29	45
3	HNK Branitelj Mostar	28	13	5	10	43	41	44
4	FK Rudar Kakanj	28	12	6	10	32	25	42
5	NK Bratstvo Gračanica	28	12	6	10	34	28	42
6	FK Sloboda Tuzla	28	13	2	13	40	27	41
7	NK Jedinstvo Bihać	28	12	5	11	45	33	41
8	HNK Čapljina	28	12	5	11	36	45	41
9	NK Iskra Bugojno	28	10	7	11	32	33	37
10	NK Podgrmeč Sanski Most	28	10	6	12	29	43	36
11	NK Budućnost Banovići	28	10	6	12	36	35	36
12	NK Troglav Livno	28	9	7	12	30	37	34
13	NK Bosna Visoko	28	9	6	13	28	37	33
14	FK Goražde	28	9	5	14	35	46	32
15	FK Krajina Cazin	28	8	4	16	25	56	28

NB NK Krajišnik Velika Kladuša withdrew after round 15 – their matches were annulled.

PRVA LIGA RS		Pld	W	D	L	F	A	Pts
1	FK Mladost Velika Obarska	26	15	5	6	51	31	50
2	FK Sloboda Mrkonjić Grad	26	12	7	7	35	22	42
3	FK Kozara Gradiška	26	13	4	9	42	39	43
4	FK Sloga Doboj	26	12	6	8	46	29	42
5	FK Podrinje Janja	26	12	5	9	44	26	41
6	FK Drina Višegrad	26	11	4	11	29	31	37
7	FK Modriča	26	11	3	12	39	39	36
8	FK Sloboda Bosanski Novi	26	11	3	12	32	35	36
9	FK Mladost Gacko	26	10	6	10	33	41	36
10	FK Drina Zvornik	26	9	8	9	39	38	35
11	FK Sutjeska Foča	26	8	7	11	26	21	31
12	FK Rudar Ugljevik	26	9	3	14	30	45	30
13	FK Borac Bosanski Šamac	26	7	7	12	28	45	28
14	FK Ljubić Prnjavor	26	5	6	15	27	59	21

Domestic cup: Kup Bosne i Hercegovine 2012/13

1/16 FINALS

(18/09/12)
Sarajevo 1-0 Gradina

(19/09/12)
Branitelj Mostar 0-2 Široki Brijeg
Čapljina 1-1 Borac Banja Luka 1 (4-2 on pens)
Čelik 2-1 Podgrmeč Sanski Most
Leotar 0-1 Slavija Sarajevo
Modriča 0-1 Orašje
Olimpik Sarajevo 0-0 Vitez *(3-0 on pens)*
Rudar Prijedor 0-1 Zrinjski
Radnik Bijeljina 6-0 Rudar Zenica
Rijeka Vitez 2-1 Drina Višegrad
Sloboda Mrkonjić Grad 0-3 Željezničar
Sloga Doboj 4-0 Tomislav Tomislavgrad
Sutjeska Foča 1-0 Famos-SAŠK Napredak Sarajevo
Travnik 1-3 Gabela
Velež 3-0 Mladost Donji Svilaj
Zvijezda 5-0 Rudar Ugljevik

1/8 FINALS

(03/10/12 & 23/10/12)
Slavija Sarajevo 1-3, 0-3 Željezničar *(1-6)*

(03/10/12 & 24/10/12)
Čelik 2-0, 1-0 Rijeka Vitez *(3-0)*
Gabela 1-0, 0-0 Radnik Bijeljina *(1-0)*
Olimpik Sarajevo 0-0, 0-0 Čapljina *(0-0; 4-1 on pens)*
Orašje 0-6, 0-1 Široki Brijeg *(0-7)*
Sutjeska Foča 1-1, 1-2 Sloga Doboj *(2-3)*
Zrinjski 3-1, 1-2 Sarajevo *(4-3)*
Zvijezda 1-2, 3-0 Velež *(4-2)*

QUARTER-FINALS

(06/11/12 & 21/11/12)
Zvijezda 3-2 Zrinjski *(Savić 38p, Vehabović 45, Pandža 55; Marjanović 24, Radeljić 69)*
Zrinjski 7-0 Zvijezda *(J. Anišić 1, 20, Marinović 65)*
(Zrinjski 9-5)

(07/11/12 & 21/11/12)
Gabela 1-2 Sloga Doboj *(Jusufbašić 2; Kršić 45, Djorić 48)*
Sloga Doboj 1-1 Gabela *(D Panić 35; Jusufbašić 69p)*
(Sloga Doboj 3-2)

Olimpik Sarajevo 0-1 Željezničar *(Bekrić 87)*
Željezničar 3-0 Olimpik Sarajevo *(Jamak 47, 60, Adilović 87)*
(Željezničar 4-0)

Široki Brijeg 1-1 Čelik *(Wagner 11; Kajkut 83)*
Čelik 1-1 Široki Brijeg *(Barać 59; Ćorić 80)*
(2-2; Široki Brijeg 5-4 on pens)

SEMI-FINALS

(13/03/13 & 03/04/13)
Sloga Doboj 2-4 Široki Brijeg *(Djorić 20, Dujković 80p; Wagner 43, 52, Roskam 60, Kordić 67)*
Široki Brijeg 4-0 Sloga Doboj *(Kordić 16, Barišić 39, I Džidić 60, M Marić 73)*
(Široki Brijeg 8-2)

Željezničar 0-0 Zrinjski
Zrinjski 0-2 Željezničar *(Adilović 45+2, Stanić 57)*
(Željezničar 2-0)

FINAL

(30/04/13)
Stadion Grbavica, Sarajevo
FK ŽELJEZNIČAR 1 *(E Čolić 18)*
NK ŠIROKI BRIJEG 1 *(Kordić 6)*
Referee: Čuić
ŽELJEZNIČAR: Antolović, Kerla, B Čolić, Vasilić, Urdinov, Selimović (Bekrić 83), Svraka, Jamak (Hodžić 67), Tomić, E Čolić, Adilović
ŠIROKI BRIJEG: Bilobrk, I Džidić, Bertoša, Ješe, Ćorić, Wagner, Ivanković (Kožulj 88), M Marić (Landeka 55), Zlomislić, Roskam, Kordić (Barišić 90)

(14/05/13)
Stadion Pecara, Široki Brijeg
NK ŠIROKI BRIJEG 1 *(Wagner 63)*
FK ŽELJEZNIČAR 1 *(Pehilj 90)*
Referee: Jakupović
ŠIROKI BRIJEG: Bilobrk, I Džidić, Bertoša, Ješe, Ćorić (Serdarušić 82), Wagner, Ljubić, Ivanković (Šilić 90), Zlomislić, Roskam (Landeka 55), Kordić
ŽELJEZNIČAR: Antolović, Bogićević, B Čolić, Vasilić, Tomić (Pehilj 83), Selimović (Smajić 68), Jamak (Hasanović 83), Svraka, Stanić, E Čolić, Adilović

(agg 2-2; ŠIROKI BRIJEG 5-4 on pens)

BULGARIA

Bulgarski Futbolen Soyuz (BFS)

Address	26 Tzar Ivan Assen II Street	**President**	Borislav Mihaylov
	BG-1124 Sofia	**General secretary**	Borislav Popov
Tel	+359 2 942 6202	**Media officer**	Pavel Kolev
Fax	+359 2 942 6201	**Year of formation**	1923
E-mail	bfu@bfunion.bg	**National stadium**	Vasil Levski, Sofia
Website	bfunion.bg		(43,230)

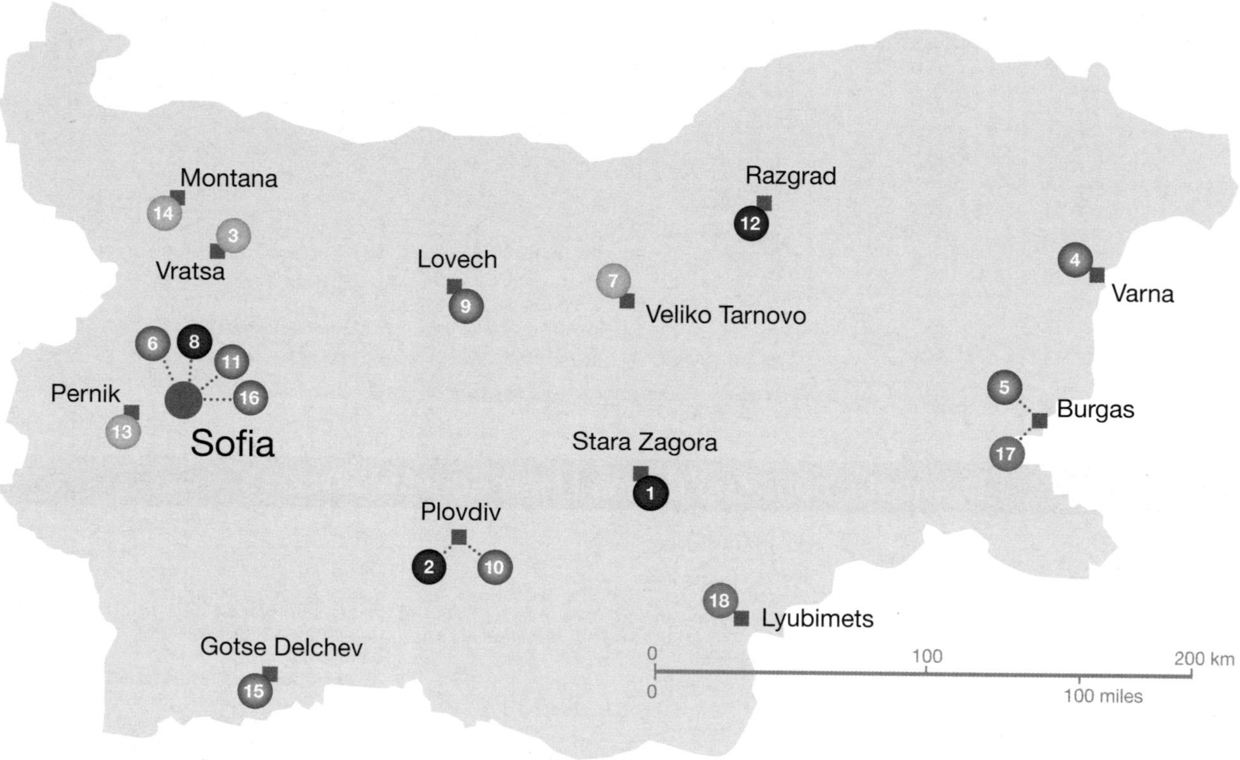

PREMIER LEAGUE CLUBS

1. PFC Beroe Stara Zagora
2. PFC Botev Plovdiv
3. OFC Botev Vratsa
4. PFC Cherno More Varna
5. PSFC Chernomorets Burgas
6. PFC CSKA Sofia
7. FC Etar Veliko Tarnovo
8. PFC Levski Sofia
9. PFC Litex Lovech
10. PFC Lokomotiv Plovdiv 1936
11. PFC Lokomotiv Sofia
12. PFC Ludogorets Razgrad
13. PFC Minior Pernik
14. PFC Montana 1921
15. PFC Pirin Gotse Delchev
16. PFC Slavia Sofia

PROMOTED CLUBS

17. FC Neftochimic 1962 Burgas
18. FC Lyubimets 2007

KEY:
- ⬤ – UEFA Champions League
- ⬤ – UEFA Europa League
- ⬤ – Promoted clubs
- ⬤ – Relegated clubs

Own goal gifts Ludogorets the title

For the second season running PFC Ludogorets Razgrad won the Bulgarian A PFG title on the final day. The championship crown was effectively handed to them on a plate by rivals PFC Levski Sofia, who conceded a late own goal to drop two vital points and let the defending champions leapfrog them to the top of the final standings.

Ten days earlier Levski had suffered similar heartbreak when they lost the final of the Bulgarian Cup on penalties to PFC Beroe Stara Zagora. Even worse news was to befall Levski's traditional rivals PFC CSKA Sofia, who were declared bankrupt at the end of the season.

| Successful title defence secured in thrilling climax | Levski let championship slip from their grasp | Further agony for Sofia Blues as Beroe win the cup |

Domestic league

Ludogorets had overcome direct rivals CSKA to win their first title on the final day the previous season, but when they conceded an added-time winner to Levski in a match billed as the title decider on 18 May, two rounds from the finish, it looked as if the club from the capital, now on a run of seven straight victories and with a one-point advantage, would go on to claim their 27th title. Indeed, they had just one more game to play because their penultimate fixture was a 3-0 walkover against FC Etar Veliko Tarnovo, who had withdrawn from the league earlier that month.

But in the big game on the final day, at home to PFC Slavia Sofia, a team in mid-table with nothing to play for, Levski fluffed their lines, defender Dimitar Vezalov turning the ball into his own net 16 minutes from time to equalise an earlier effort from Levski's star striker Basile de Carvalho – the league's top scorer – and throw away the two points that would have secured the title.

As Levski's nerves got to them, Ludogorets remained cool, a straightforward 3-0 win at relegated PFC Montana 1921 giving the unfashionable, unheralded provincial club back-to-back titles.

The man in charge of both was coach Ivaylo Petev, and once again he worked wonders with the resources at his disposal. Up until that last-gasp defeat at Levski the team had lost just once, and although they scored 20 goals fewer than in 2011/12, with not one player reaching double figures, they conceded a miserly 13, keeping 18 clean sheets despite the use of three goalkeepers.

Their standout performers were Bulgarian internationals Yordan Minev and Svetoslav Dyakov, although the star of the championship overall was 21-year-old Georgi Milanov of PFC Litex Lovech, who, despite having the legendary Hristo Stoichkov at the controls, finished in a disappointing fifth place. Stoichkov subsequently left for CSKA, only to run into a financial firestorm that prevented the club from taking their place in the UEFA Europa League. That went instead to fourth-placed PFC Botev Plovdiv.

Domestic cup

Beroe's Bulgarian Cup triumph – their second in four seasons – was secured on penalties at the end of a final of unremitting drama. Levski went down to ten men just before half-time but came back from a 3-1 deficit with 11 minutes remaining to send the game into extra time. In the shoot-out five of the first six penalties were missed, but Ivo Ivanov, Borislav Stoychev and Elias all converted to reduce Levski's valiant efforts to nought.

Europe

A woeful season for Bulgaria in Europe resulted in immediate elimination for all four teams, the only victory in eight matches being claimed by Levski, whose 1-0 home win over FK Sarajevo was overturned by a 3-1 second-leg defeat.

National team

Luboslav Penev missed the 1994 FIFA World Cup, in which Bulgaria finished fourth, through illness, but his ambition to return to the game's greatest stage as his country's head coach 20 years later was kept alive as Bulgaria avoided defeat in their first six qualifiers.

Granted, only two of those matches produced victories – at home to Armenia and Malta – but draws away to the Czech Republic and Denmark, neither of whom could match Bulgaria's consistency, enabled Penev's side to end the season second in the group behind Italy and with realistic hopes of reaching the play-offs.

Domestic league: A PFG 2012/13 final table

		Pld	Home					Away					Total					Pts
			W	D	L	F	A	W	D	L	F	A	W	D	L	F	A	
1	**PFC Ludogorets Razgrad**	30	13	2	0	33	6	9	4	2	25	7	22	6	2	58	13	72
2	PFC Levski Sofia	30	13	2	0	33	8	9	3	3	26	12	22	5	3	59	20	71
3	PFC CSKA Sofia	30	11	3	1	25	7	8	3	4	29	13	19	6	5	54	20	63
4	PFC Botev Plovdiv	30	11	2	2	33	6	7	4	4	18	15	18	6	6	51	21	60
5	PFC Litex Lovech	30	8	2	5	34	14	7	3	5	22	10	15	5	10	56	24	50
6	PSFC Chernomorets Burgas	30	8	4	3	20	13	6	1	8	12	16	14	5	11	32	29	47
7	PFC Beroe Stara Zagora	30	7	3	5	19	14	6	3	6	17	24	13	6	11	36	38	45
8	PFC Slavia Sofia	30	9	3	3	27	12	3	3	9	13	23	12	6	12	40	35	42
9	PFC Lokomotiv Plovdiv 1936	30	8	2	5	25	15	2	7	6	12	19	10	9	11	37	34	39
10	PFC Cherno More Varna	30	7	6	2	20	10	2	2	11	13	29	9	8	13	33	39	35
11	PFC Pirin Gotse Delchev	30	6	3	6	18	24	4	1	10	9	33	10	4	16	27	57	34
12	PFC Lokomotiv Sofia	30	5	5	5	15	14	2	5	8	12	24	7	10	13	27	38	31
13	OFC Botev Vratsa	30	5	5	5	14	18	3	2	10	9	33	8	7	15	23	51	31
14	PFC Minior Pernik	30	4	2	9	14	24	1	3	11	6	25	5	5	20	20	49	20
15	PFC Montana 1921	30	4	1	10	17	26	0	3	12	10	31	4	4	22	27	57	16
16	FC Etar Veliko Tarnovo	30	2	3	10	9	33	2	1	12	11	42	4	4	22	20	75	13

NB FC Etar Veliko Tarnovo - 3 pts deducted and excluded after round 26; their remaining matches were awarded as 0-3 defeats.

SEASON AT A GLANCE

EUROPEAN QUALIFICATION 2013/14

Champion: PFC Ludogorets Razgrad (second qualifying round)

Cup winner: PFC Beroe Stara Zagora (second qualifying round)

PFC Levski Sofia (first qualifying round)
PFC Botev Plovdiv (first qualifying round)

Top scorer	Basile de Carvalho (Levski), 19 goals
Relegated clubs	FC Etar Veliko Tarnovo (excluded), PFC Montana 1921, PFC Minior Pernik, OFC Botev Vratsa
Promoted clubs	FC Neftochimic 1962 Burgas, FC Lyubimets 2007
Cup final	PFC Beroe Stara Zagora 3-3 PFC Levski Sofia (aet; 3-1 on pens)

A PFG TEAM OF THE SEASON
(4-4-2)
Coach: Stoichkov (Litex)

PLAYER OF THE SEASON
Georgi Milanov
(PFC Litex Lovech)

In December 2012 the then 20-year-old Bulgarian international midfielder became the youngest man to scoop his country's player of the year award, and he maintained his impressive performance level in the new year, striking 16 goals in 27 league games – the same number of appearances made for Litex by his twin brother Iliya.

NEWCOMER OF THE SEASON
Todor Nedelev
(PFC Botev Plovidv)

Botev's star turn on their first season back in the top flight was a 19-year-old. Nedelev pulled the strings in midfield and ended the season with nine league goals – second only at the club to 17-goal Ivan Tsvetkov, 14 years his senior. Blessed with great skill and vision, the youngster helped the Plovdiv club to an unexpected fourth place.

V Stoyanov *(Ludogorets)*
Mulder *(Levski)* — Guldan *(Ludogorets)* — Bodurov *(Litex)* — Minev *(Ludogorets)*
Lucas Sasha *(CSKA)*
Nedelev *(Botev Plolvdiv)* — G Milanov *(Litex)* — Mendes Rodrigues *(Levski)*
Carvalho *(Levski)* — Tsvetkov *(Botev Plovdiv)*

NATIONAL TEAM

Home Kit   Away Kit

INTERNATIONAL TOURNAMENT APPEARANCES

FIFA World Cup (7) 1962, 1966, 1970, 1974, 1986 (2nd round), 1994 (4th), 1998
UEFA European Championship (2) 1996, 2004

TOP FIVE ALL-TIME CAPS

Stiliyan Petrov (106); Borislav Mihaylov (102); Hristo Bonev (96); Krasimir Balakov (92); Martin Petrov (91)

TOP FIVE ALL-TIME GOALS

Dimitar Berbatov (48); Hristo Bonev (47); Hristo Stoichkov (37); Emil Kostadinov (26); Lyubomir Angelov, Ivan Kolev & Petar Zhekov (25)

Results 2012/13

Date	Opponent		Venue	Score	Scorers
15/08/12	Cyprus	H	Sofia	1-0	Mitsanski (66)
07/09/12	Italy (WCQ)	H	Sofia	2-2	Manolev (30), G Milanov (66)
11/09/12	Armenia (WCQ)	H	Sofia	1-0	Manolev (43)
12/10/12	Denmark (WCQ)	H	Sofia	1-1	Rangelov (7)
16/10/12	Czech Republic (WCQ)	A	Prague	0-0	
14/11/12	Ukraine	H	Sofia	0-1	
22/03/13	Malta (WCQ)	H	Sofia	6-0	Tonev (6, 38, 68), Popov (47), Gargorov (55), I Ivanov (78)
26/03/13	Denmark (WCQ)	A	Copenhagen	1-1	Manolev (51)
30/05/13	Japan	A	Toyota	2-0	Manolev (3), Hasebe (70og)
04/06/13	Kazakhstan	A	Almaty	2-1	G Iliev (55), I Ivanov (60)

Appearances 2012/13

Coach: Luboslav Penev	31/08/66		Cyp	ITA	ARM	DEN	CZE	Ukr	MLT	DEN	Jpn	Kaz	Caps	Goals
Nikolay Mihaylov	28/06/88	Twente (NED)	G62	G	G	G	G		G	G			27	-
Yordan Minev	14/10/80	Ludogorets	D	D	D	D	D	D	D63		D	D	11	-
Nikolay Bodurov	30/05/86	Litex	D	D	D	D	D	D	D	D23			19	-
Ivan Ivanov	25/02/88	Partizan (SRB)	D	D	D	D	D	D	D	D	D	D	35	3
Veselin Minev	14/10/80	Antalyaspor (TUR)/Botev Plovdiv	D90	D	D			s46		D	D	D	17	-
Stanislav Manolev	16/12/85	PSV (NED)/Fulham (ENG)	M67	M	M	M	M	M		M87	M79	M71	32	4
Georgi Milanov	19/02/92	Litex	M	M	M	M	M	M46	M	M	s65		12	1
Vladimir Gadzhev	18/07/87	Levski	M67	M80	M60	M	M61		M70	M	M56	M	17	-
Svetoslav Dyakov	31/05/84	Ludogorets	M	M	M73*		M	s46		M	M	M	11	-
Ivelin Popov	26/10/87	Gaziantepspor (TUR)/Kuban (RUS)	A57	A82	A79	A85	A75	A77	M	M70	M65	M	42	9
Emil Gargorov	16/02/81	Ludogorets	A80	A62	s79				A56	s87			17	2
Ilian Mitsanski	20/12/85	Kaiserslautern (GER)/Ingolstadt (GER)	s57	s62	A66						A	s78	0	1
Vladislav Stoyanov	08/06/87	Sheriff (MDA)/Ludogorets	s02								G		6	-
Georgi Sarmov	07/08/85	Kasımpaşa (TUR)	s67	s80	s60			M46	s70				12	-
Alexander Tonev	03/02/90	Lech (POL)	s67	s82		s61	s75	s77	M	A			11	3
Ivan Stoyanov	24/07/83	Ludogorets	s80										12	-
Ivan Bandalovski	23/11/86	CSKA Sofia	s90			D26*							12	-
Dimitar Rangelov	09/02/83	Luzern (SUI)		s66	A61		s61						27	3
Georgi Iliev	05/09/81	Cherno More				M35	M	M64	M	s70	M69	M75	19	2
Iliya Milanov	19/02/92	Litex				s35	s42			D	D40		4	-
Valeri Bozhinov	15/02/86	Verona (ITA)/Vicenza (ITA)				s85	s61	A61		s56		A55	42	6
Petar Zanev	18/10/85	Volyn (UKR)					D42	D46					22	-
Stoyan Kolev	03/02/76	Chernomorets Burgas						G					16	-
Marquinhos	30/04/82	Changchun Yatai (CHN)						s46					4	-
Ivan Tsvetkov	31/08/79	Botev Plovdiv						s64					1	-
Radoslav Dimitrov	12/08/88	Slavia Sofia							s63	s23	D		3	-
Spas Delev	22/09/89	CSKA Sofia									A60	s71	7	-
Alexander D Alexandrov	13/04/86	Cherno More									s40	D	2	-
Hristo Zlatinski	22/01/85	Lokomotiv Plovdiv									s56	s75	6	-
Stefan Velev	02/05/89	Levski									s69		1	-
Yordan Hristov	12/02/84	Botev Plovdiv									s79		1	-
Plamen Iliev	30/11/91	Levski										G55	2	-
Mihail Ivanov	07/08/89	Levski										s55	1	-

European club competitions 2012/13

PFC LUDOGORETS RAZGRAD

Second qualifying round - GNK Dinamo Zagreb (CRO)
H 1-1 *Marcelinho (67)*
Golubović, Barthe, Genchev, Dyakov (Moţi 83), Ivanov (Alexandrov 86), Gargorov, Minev, Guldan, I Stoyanov (Guela 90+1), Júnior Caiçara, Marcelinho. Coach: Ivaylo Petev (BUL)
A 2-3 *Gargorov (12), Marcelinho (36)*
Golubović, Barthe, Genchev, Dyakov, Ivanov (Moţi 88), Gargorov (Bakalov 76), Minev, Guldan, I Stoyanov (Guela 74), Júnior Caiçara, Marcelinho. Coach: Ivaylo Petev (BUL)
Red cards: Marcelinho 57, Ivanov 90+8

PFC CSKA SOFIA

Second qualifying round - ND Mura 05 (SVN)
A 0-0
Černý, Yanchev, Yanev (Yovchev 84), Sheridan, Bandalovski, Nílson António, Anicet, Popov, Yanev (Lucas Sasha 80), Krachunov, Priso (Karachanakov 71). Coach: Stoicho Mladenov (BUL)
Red card: Sheridan 69
H 1-1 *Popov (18)*
Černý, Yanchev, Yanev, Lucas Sasha, Nílson António, Anicet, Popov, Yanev (Yovchev 88), Krachunov, Karachanakov (Granchov 78), Priso. Coach: Stoicho Mladenov (BUL)

PFC LEVSKI SOFIA

Second qualifying round - FK Sarajevo (BIH)
H 1-0 *Raykov (72)*
Iliev, Mulder, Élie, Angelov, Ivanov, Starokin (Procházka 71), Yovov (Raykov 60), Cristovão, Carvalho, Marcinho (João Silva 82), Gadzhev. Coach: Ilian Iliev (BUL)
A 1-3 *Carvalho (34p)*
Iliev, Mulder, Angelov, Ivanov, Starokin, Procházka, Raykov, Opoku (João Silva 71), Carvalho, Marcinho (Tonev 82), Gadzhev. Coach: Ilian Iliev (BUL)

PFC LOKOMOTIV PLOVDIV 1936

Second qualifying round - Vitesse (NED)
H 4-4 *Todorov (24), Lazarov (49, 64), Tássio (90+2)*
Gospodinov, Rodrigues, V Georgiev (Tássio 57), Venkov, Bengelloun, Todorov, Serginho (Eli Marques 72), Zlatinski (Kiriakidis 85), D Georgiev, Salamastrakis, Lazarov. Coach: Emil Velev (BUL)
A 1-3 *Zlatinski (80p)*
Kunchev, V Georgiev, Venkov, Todorov, Tássio (Malamov 58), Zlatinski, D Georgiev (Yordanov 56), Eli Marques (Timonov 72), Salamastrakis, Kiriakidis, Lazarov. Coach: Emil Velev (BUL)

Domestic league club-by-club

PFC BEROE STARA ZAGORA

Coach: Ivko Ganchev; (18/10/12) Petar Hubchev
1916 • Beroe (15,000) • beroe.bg
Major honours
Bulgarian League (1) 1986;
Bulgarian Cup (2) 2010, 2013

2012

Date	Opponent		Score	Scorers
11/08	Botev Vratsa	h	4-0	Andonov 3, Élio
19/08	Ludogorets	a	1-3	Élio
26/08	Etar	h	1-0	og (Gadzhalov)
01/09	Slavia	a	1-6	Pedro Eugénio
16/09	Levski	h	1-2	David Caiado (p)
22/09	Botev Plovdiv	a	2-1	Elias, Andonov
30/09	Montana	h	2-2	Andonov (p), Elias
05/10	Cherno More	a	1-2	og (Simeonov)
17/10	Chernomorets	h	0-1	
27/10	Pirin	h	2-3	Pedro Eugénio 2
04/11	Lokomotiv Sofia	a	2-2	Andonov, T Hristov
10/11	Litex	h	1-0	David Caiado
18/11	CSKA	a	0-2	
28/11	Lokomotiv Plovdiv	h	1-2	Andonov (p)
09/12	Minior	a	0-3	

2013

Date	Opponent		Score	Scorers
02/03	Botev Vratsa	a	0-0	
10/03	Ludogorets	h	0-0	
16/03	Etar	a	2-0	Krumov, V Hristov
30/03	Slavia	h	2-1	Andonov, V Hristov
07/04	Levski	a	0-2	
10/04	Botev Plovdiv	h	2-1	V Hristov, Andonov
14/04	Montana	a	3-1	Sayoud, Atanasov, David Caiado
21/04	Cherno More	h	1-0	Andonov
28/04	Chernomorets	a	1-0	Andonov
02/05	Pirin	a	0-0	
07/05	Lokomotiv Sofia	h	1-1	David Caiado
11/05	Litex	a	2-1	Sayoud (p), Atanasov
19/05	CSKA	h	0-1	
22/05	Lokomotiv Plovdiv	a	2-1	Sitoe, Andonov
25/05	Minior	h	1-0	Zafirov

No	Name	Nat	DoB	Pos	Aps	(s)	Gls
12	Kiril Akalski		17/10/85	G	13		
9	Alberto Louzeiro	POR	22/11/82	M	22	(1)	
7	Georgi Andonov		28/06/83	A	20	(3)	12
80	Emil Angelov		17/07/80	A	2	(1)	
22	Isus Angelov		30/03/94	M		(1)	
11	Doncho Atanasov		02/04/83	A	13	(1)	2
88	David Caiado	POR	02/05/87	M	19	(4)	4
15	Georgi Dinkov		20/05/91	D	7	(6)	
14	Ignat Dishliev		08/06/87	D	3	(1)	
27	Igor Djoman	FRA	01/05/86	M	6	(5)	
21	Elias	BRA	04/09/81	M	23	(1)	2
29	Élio	POR	26/03/85	A	13	(6)	2
25	Miroslav Enchev		08/09/91	D	1	(1)	
10	Fernando Livramento	POR	03/03/82	M	9	(5)	
9	Ivan Goranov		10/06/92	M	3	(8)	
23	Todor Hristov		25/09/87	M	9	(1)	1
10	Ventsislav Hristov		09/11/88	A	7	(2)	3
2	Zdravko Iliev		19/10/84	D	10	(2)	
9	Ivo Ivanov		11/03/85	D	16	(2)	
22	João Sales	BRA	19/10/84	A	3	(6)	
73	Ivan Karadzhov		12/07/89	G	15		
17	Plamen Krumov		04/11/85	D	11		1
18	Dieudonné Owona	CMR	28/02/86	D	1		
77	Pedro Eugénio	POR	26/06/90	D	20	(1)	3
19	Veselin Penev		11/08/82	D	21		
19	Martin Raynov		25/04/92	M	3	(7)	
11	Rodolfo	BRA	13/03/89	A	2	(7)	
71	Amir Sayoud	ALG	31/08/90	M	7	(4)	2
70	Jerry Sitoe	MOZ	23/11/90	A	3	(4)	1
33	Teodor Skorchev		04/09/86	G	2		
5	Borislav Stoychev		26/11/86	D	11		
23	Plamen Tenev		13/06/95	M			
16	Stefan Velev		02/05/89	M	9	(4)	
3	Vladimir Zafirov		21/03/83	D	26	(1)	1
18	Atanas Zehirov		13/02/89	M		(2)	

PFC BOTEV PLOVDIV

Coach: Ferario Spasov; (11/12/12) Stanimir Stoilov
1912 • Hristo Botev (22,000) • botevplovdiv.bg
Major honours
Bulgarian League (2) 1929, 1967;
Bulgarian Cup (2) 1962, 1981

2012

11/08	Slavia	h	3-0	Tsvetkov 3
19/08	Levski	a	1-3	Arthur Henrique
26/08	Chernomorets	h	2-0	Vander, Tsvetkov
01/09	Montana	h	3-1	Vander, Tsvetkov, Ognyanov (p)
15/09	Cherno More	a	0-0	
22/09	Beroe	h	1-2	Tsvetkov
29/09	Pirin	a	1-0	Grncarov
06/10	Lokomotiv Sofia	h	2-0	Nedelev 2
21/10	Litex	a	1-0	Vander
27/10	CSKA	h	1-1	Tsvetkov (p)
04/11	Lokomotiv Plovdiv	a	2-2	Nedelev 2
10/11	Minior	h	2-0	Tsvetkov 2
17/11	Botev Vratsa	h	0-0	
28/11	Ludogorets	h	0-1	
08/12	Etar	a	2-1	Kostov, Nedelev

2013

01/03	Slavia	a	2-2	Vander, Ognyanov
09/03	Levski	h	2-0	Grncarov, Tsvetkov
15/03	Chernomorets	a	2-1	Vander, Tsvetkov
31/03	Montana	a	2-0	Nedelev, Ognyanov
06/04	Cherno More	h	3-1	Nedelev, Ognyanov, Luís Pedro
10/04	Beroe	a	1-2	Vander
13/04	Pirin	h	5-0	Luís Pedro 2, Nedelev 2, Ognyanov
20/04	Lokomotiv Sofia	a	2-1	Kostov, Tsvetkov
28/04	Litex	h	1-0	Tsvetkov
04/05	CSKA	a	0-1	
08/05	Lokomotiv Plovdiv	h	0-0	
13/05	Minior	a	2-0	Tsvetkov 2
18/05	Botev Vratsa	h	5-0	Tsvetkov 2 (1p), Ognyanov, Galchev, Kostov
22/05	Ludogorets	a	0-2	
25/05	Etar	h	3-0	(w/o)

No	Name	Nat	DoB	Pos	Aps	(s)	Gls
26	Arthur Henrique	BRA	14/01/87	D	22	(?)	1
60	Hamza Abdallah		17/10/00	A	0	(11)	
00	Habib Bamogo	BFA	08/06/82	D		(3)	
6	Kostadin Dyakov		30/07/88	M	3	(15)	
71	Boris Galchev		31/10/83	M	13		1
3	Boban Grncarov	MKD	12/08/82	D	26		2
11	Yordan Hristov		12/02/84	M	23	(3)	
1	Hristo Ivanov		06/04/82	G	4		
16	Tomáš Jirsák	CZE	29/06/84	M	24	(1)	
3	Asen Karaslavov		08/06/90	D	9	(1)	
18	Stanislav Kostov		02/10/91	M	9	(13)	3
9	Luís Pedro	NED	27/04/90	A	8	(3)	3
14	Veselin Minev		14/10/80	D	7	(1)	
8	Todor Nedelev		02/07/93	M	23	(6)	9
7	Mariyan Ognyanov		30/07/88	M	22	(6)	6
13	Nikolay Pavlov		12/11/87	A		(8)	
14	Marlon Pereira	NED	26/03/87	M	9		
14	Angel Rahov		01/06/86	D	9	(1)	
10	Rubén Palazuelos	ESP	04/11/83	M	14		
23	Ernestas Šetkus	LTU	25/05/85	G	11		
83	Civard Sprockel	NED	10/05/83	D	12		
1	Adam Stachowiak	POL	18/12/86	G	14		
89	Stefan Stanchev		26/04/89	D	7	(1)	
19	Ivan Tsvetkov		31/08/79	A	29		17
10	Vander	BRA	10/03/88	M	19	(4)	6
2	Serkan Yusein		31/03/96	M		(2)	

OFC BOTEV VRATSA

Coach: Giuliano Sonzogni (ITA);
(19/09/12) Antoni Zdravkov
1921 • Hristo Botev (7,000) • botevvratsa.com

2012

11/08	Beroe	a	0-4	
18/08	Pirin	h	1-2	Iliev
26/08	Lokomotiv Sofia	a	0-3	
31/08	Litex	h	0-4	
15/09	CSKA	a	0-3	
22/09	Lokomotiv Plovdiv	h	1-0	Ammendola
30/09	Minior	a	1-0	Atanasov
05/10	Chernomorets	a	1-2	og (Terziev)
21/10	Ludogorets	h	1-1	Atanasov
27/10	Etar	a	0-1	
04/11	Slavia	h	1-0	Yakimov
10/11	Levski	a	0-2	
17/11	Botev Plovdiv	h	0-0	
28/11	Montana	a	0-0	
09/12	Cherno More	h	1-0	Iliev

2013

02/03	Beroe	h	0-0	
10/03	Pirin	a	1-2	Yakimov
16/03	Lokomotiv Sofia	h	0-0	
30/03	Litex	a	1-5	Atanasov
06/04	CSKA	h	3-4	Atanasov (p), P Petrov, Iliev (p)
10/04	Lokomotiv Plovdiv	a	1-0	Kokonov
14/04	Minior	h	0-0	
20/04	Chernomorets	h	0-2	
27/04	Ludogorets	a	1-4	Tonev
03/05	Etar	h	2-1	Atanasov (p), Iliev (p)
07/05	Slavia	a	2-1	Yakimov, Rangelov
10/05	Levski	h	1-3	Atanasov
18/05	Botev Plovdiv	a	0-5	
22/05	Montana	h	3-1	Iliev 2, Marchetti
25/05	Cherno More	a	1-1	Iliev

No	Name	Nat	DoB	Pos	Aps	(s)	Gls
10	Massimiliano Ammendola	ITA	15/05/90	M	6	(4)	1
18	Sasha Aneff	URU	26/06/91	A		(5)	
18	Tsvetomir Angelov		22/03/93	M		(2)	
17	Andrei Atanasov		09/04/87	A	19	(2)	6
2	Augusto	BRA	29/04/91	D	1	(1)	
4	Pablo Caballero	URU	21/01/87	M	1	(1)	
8	Nicolás Celeste	URU	02/01/90	M	7	(1)	
21	Zdravko Chavdarov		24/01/81	G	7	(1)	
20	Roberto Floriano	ITA	14/08/86	A	2	(1)	
6	Asen Georgiev		09/07/93	D	11	(4)	
14	Nainan Georgiev		21/04/95	M		(1)	
2	Radoslav Georgiev		14/01/92	D	1	(1)	
19	Nikolay Hristov		07/08/89	M	24	(2)	
7	Iliya Iliev		20/12/74	M	29		7
12	Dimitar Ivanov		31/12/91	G	1		
26	Kiril Ivanov		13/08/94	M	1	(2)	
21	Mihail Ivanov		07/08/89	G	11		
3	Jairo	BRA	31/12/92	D	20	(1)	
5	Kassio	BRA	14/09/92	D	3	(1)	
17	Ivan Kokonov		17/08/91	A	8	(6)	1
22	Ruslan Kuang		25/10/85	D	19		
9	Ignacio Lores	URU	26/04/91	M	7	(1)	
2	Alessandro Marchetti	ITA	13/05/88	D	7	(1)	1
13	Nikolay Marinov		13/08/86	M	18	(3)	
17	Krasi Milev		17/04/96	M		(1)	
9	Georgi Mirchev		19/11/84	M	2	(2)	
16	Niokola Mishev		26/12/94	M		(1)	
1	Hristo Mitov		24/01/85	G	11		
6	Tihomir Naydenov		25/03/86	D	4	(5)	
14	Nikolay Nikolov		21/05/85	M	7	(6)	
18	Pavel Petkov		26/01/90	M		(1)	
8	Lyuboslav Petrov		24/03/92	M	1		
19	Petar Petrov		15/05/87	D	8	(2)	1
2	Giuseppe Pira	ITA	01/01/92	D	3		
9	Rumen Rangelov		30/11/85	A	2	(8)	1
8	Vladislav Romanov		07/02/88	M	10		
4	Darko Savić	SRB	19/01/79	D	20		
10	Boris Tonchev		07/04/94	M	2		
16	Tsvetelin Tonev		03/01/92	M	4	(5)	1
8	Svetoslav Valeriev		03/03/88	D		(5)	
3	Martin Vasilev		02/01/92	D	4	(5)	
23	Vasil Velev		15/01/84	M	11		
15	Vicente	BRA	18/02/89	M	19	(3)	
11	Alexander Yakimov		27/04/89	M	23	(5)	3

PFC CHERNO MORE VARNA

Coach: Stefan Genov; (24/09/12) Adalbert Zafirov;
(17/12/12) Georgi Ivanov
1945 • Ticha (8,000) • chernomorepfc.bg

2012

11/08	Ludogorets	h	0-3	
18/08	Etar	a	1-0	Edenilson
25/08	Slavia	h	0-0	
31/08	Levski	a	0-4	
15/09	Botev Plovdiv	h	0-0	
23/09	Montana	a	1-3	G Iliev
30/09	Chernomorets	h	1-1	G Iliev
05/10	Beroe	h	2-1	Bozhilov, D Atanasov
21/10	Pirin	a	2-3	Manolov, R Kolev
27/10	Lokomotiv Sofia	h	2-0	Palomino 2
04/11	Litex	a	1-4	G Iliev
10/11	CSKA	h	0-0	
17/11	Lokomotiv Plovdiv	a	0-1	
28/11	Minior	h	2-0	D Atanasov, Edenilson
09/12	Botev Vratsa	a	0-1	

2013

03/03	Ludogorets	a	0-2	
09/03	Etar	h	0-1	
16/03	Slavia	a	0-1	
30/03	Levski	h	1-1	Bozhilov
06/04	Botev Plovdiv	a	1-3	Raykov
10/04	Montana	h	2-1	Edenilson, G Iliev
14/04	Chernomorets	a	3-3	R Kolev, Hidalgo, Bozhilov
21/04	Beroe	a	0-1	
28/04	Pirin	h	5-1	Bozhilov, G Iliev, Inkango, Raykov, Kapitanov
02/05	Lokomotiv Sofia	a	0-0	
08/05	Litex	h	2-0	G Iliev
11/05	CSKA	a	2-3	Inkango, og (Bandalovski)
18/05	Lokomotiv Plovdiv	h	3-0	Edenilson, Inkango, G Iliev
22/05	Minior	a	2-0	Edenilson, Inkango
25/05	Botev Vratsa	h	1-1	Bozhilov

No	Name	Nat	DoB	Pos	Aps	(s)	Gls
15	Alexander Dragomirov Alexandrov		13/04/86	D	30		
25	Alexander Emilov Alexandrov		20/07/94	D	14		
20	Stanion Angelov		01/00/91	M		(6)	
11	Doncho Atanasov		02/04/83	M	9	(3)	2
91	Zhivko Atanasov		03/02/91	D	12	(6)	
14	Georgi Bozhilov		12/02/87	A	23	(4)	5
5	Samuel Camazzola	BRA	30/08/82	M	16	(3)	
27	Martin Dechev		12/04/90	D	8		
4	Detelin Dimitrov		17/01/83	D	13		
6	Edenilson	BRA	13/09/87	M	23	(1)	5
86	Marlon Fernández	VEN	16/01/86	M		(1)	
83	Cristian Hidalgo	ESP	21/09/83	M	12	(2)	1
99	Atanas Iliev		09/10/94	A		(4)	
21	Georgi Iliev		05/09/81	M	29		7
19	Bruce Inkango	FRA	18/05/84	A	6	(4)	4
30	Iiyan Kapitanov		25/01/92	A	6	(10)	1
33	Georgi Kitanov		06/03/95	G	28		
22	Plamen Kolev		09/02/88	G	1		
55	Rosen Kolev		04/07/90	D	25		2
13	Todor Kolev		22/09/89	M	2	(3)	
18	Sebastjan Komel	SVN	18/02/86	D	10	(1)	
10	Miroslav Manolov		20/05/85	A	21	(4)	1
33	Emil Mihaylov		01/05/88	M	1		
9	Hermes Palomino	VEN	04/08/88	A	6	(12)	2
19	Hristiyan Popov		25/01/92	M	2	(5)	
11	Simeon Raykov		11/11/89	M	13	(1)	2
23	Simeon Simeonov		13/07/83	M	5	(10)	
16	Slavi Stalev		28/02/94	D	1	(1)	
18	Ivelin Yanev		23/11/81	D	2	(1)	

BULGARIA

PSFC CHERNOMORETS BURGAS

Coach: Dimitar Dimitrov
2005 • Lazur (18,000) • chernomoretz.bg

2012

11/08	Levski	a	0-1	
19/08	CSKA	h	1-1	Boli
26/08	Botev Plovdiv	a	0-2	
01/09	Lokomotiv Plovdiv	h	1-1	Boli
15/09	Montana	a	0-1	
23/09	Minior	h	2-0	og (Bournelaha), N'Lundulu
30/09	Cherno More	a	1-1	Nikolov (p)
05/10	Botev Vratsa	h	2-1	Hristov, Ouattara
17/10	Beroe	a	1-0	Palankov
27/10	Ludogorets	h	1-0	Palankov
04/11	Pirin	a	1-0	Ouattara
10/11	Etar	h	2-1	Hristov 2
17/11	Lokomotiv Sofia	a	3-0	Hristov 2, Ouattara
28/11	Slavia	h	2-0	Ouattara, Baltanov
08/12	Litex	a	0-1	

2013

03/03	Levski	h	0-2	
10/03	CSKA	a	0-2	
15/03	Botev Plovdiv	h	1-2	Angelov
31/03	Lokomotiv Plovdiv	a	0-2	
06/04	Montana	h	1-0	Pehlivanov
10/04	Minior	a	1-0	Arnaud
14/04	Cherno More	h	3-3	Baltanov 2 (1p), Arnaud
20/04	Botev Vratsa	a	2-0	Yordanov, N'Lundulu
28/04	Beroe	h	0-1	
03/05	Ludogorets	a	0-3	
07/05	Pirin	h	1-0	og (Petrov)
13/05	Etar	a	3-0	(w/o)
18/05	Lokomotiv Sofia	h	3-1	Yordanov, Tsonkov, Filipov
22/05	Slavia	a	0-3	
25/05	Litex	h	0-0	

No	Name	Nat	DoB	Pos	Aps	(s)	Gls
14	Milcho Angelov		02/01/95	A	3	(5)	1
78	Loris Arnaud	FRA	16/04/87	M	4	(2)	2
7	Borislav Baldhiyski		12/10/90	M	6	(2)	
30	Luchezar Baltanov		11/07/88	M	9	(7)	3
20	Alexander Bashliev		16/11/89	D	3	(4)	
94	Yannick Boli	CIV	13/01/88	A	8	(1)	2
1	Nik Dashev		13/10/81	G	4		
14	Plamen Dimov		29/10/90	D	13	(1)	
19	Stanislav Dryanov		04/02/95	A	4	(8)	
2	Trayan Dyankov		21/06/76	D	20		
37	Jérémy Faug-Porret	FRA	04/02/87	D	15		
15	Venelin Filipov		20/08/90	M	26	(3)	1
43	Yanko Georgiev		22/10/88	G	1		
11	Ventsislav Hristov		09/11/88	A	11	(3)	5
12	Stoyan Kolev		03/02/76	G	24		
17	Daniel Mladenov		25/05/87	M	3	(3)	
92	Gaël N'Lundulu	FRA	29/04/92	M	19	(2)	2
18	Aurélien Ngeyitala	COD	20/05/94	M	3	(4)	
5	Nikolay Nikolov		26/01/81	D	4	(1)	1
32	Issouf Ouattara	BFA	10/07/88	M	22		4
6	Todor Palankov		13/01/84	M	25	(1)	2
20	Yani Pehlivanov		28/03/88	D	9	(5)	1
18	Krum Stoyanov		19/11/92	D	10	(2)	
55	Georgi Terziev		18/04/92	D	26		
17	Vanco Trajanov	MKD	08/09/78	M	12		
8	Rumen Trifonov		22/02/85	M		(3)	
5	Tihomir Trifonov		25/11/86	D	1		
22	Tsvetomir Tsonkov		25/06/81	M	22	(2)	1
9	Preslav Yordanov		21/09/89	A	8	(17)	2
39	Yanis Youcef	FRA	02/10/89	M	4	(2)	

PFC CSKA SOFIA

Coach: Stoicho Mladenov; (07/01/13) Miodrag Ješić (SRB); (12/03/13) Milen Radukanov
1948 • Bulgarska Armia (22,000) • cska.bg

Major honours
Bulgarian League (31) 1948, 1951, 1952, 1954, 1955, 1956, 1957, 1958, 1959, 1960, 1961, 1962, 1966, 1969, 1971, 1972, 1973, 1975, 1976, 1980, 1981, 1982, 1983, 1987, 1989, 1990, 1992, 1997, 2003, 2005, 2008; Bulgarian Cup (20) 1951, 1954, 1955, 1961, 1965, 1969, 1972, 1973, 1974 (as Soviet Army Cup), 1981, 1983, 1985, 1987, 1988, 1989, 1993, 1997, 1999, 2006, 2011

2012

11/08	Litex	a	0-1	
19/08	Chernomorets	a	1-1	og (Dyankov)
25/08	Lokomotiv Plovdiv	h	0-0	
31/08	Minior	a	4-1	Karachanakov 2, Yovchev 2
15/09	Botev Vratsa	h	3-0	Anicet 2 (1p), Karachanakov
22/09	Ludogorets	a	0-1	
30/09	Etar	h	3-1	Serginho, Tássio, Anicet (p)
06/10	Slavia	a	2-0	Lucas Sasha, Venkov
20/10	Levski	h	1-0	Nyuiadzi
27/10	Botev Plovdiv	a	1-0	Tássio
04/11	Montana	h	1-0	Tássio (p)
10/11	Cherno More	a	0-0	
18/11	Beroe	h	2-0	Michel 2 (1p)
28/11	Pirin	h	5-0	Michel 3, Tássio, Anicet
09/12	Lokomotiv Sofia	a	1-0	Serginho

2013

02/03	Litex	h	0-2	
10/03	Chernomorets	h	2-0	Serginho 2
16/03	Lokomotiv Plovdiv	a	2-0	Bandalovski, og (Gospodinov)
31/03	Minior	h	3-0	Kamburov, Lores, Bandalovski
06/04	Botev Vratsa	a	4-3	Marcinho, Michel 2, Lucas Sasha
11/04	Ludogorets	h	0-0	
14/04	Etar	a	4-0	Venkov, Anicet, Kamburov (p), Delev
21/04	Slavia	a	2-1	Anicet, Delev
27/04	Levski	a	1-2	Marcinho
04/05	Botev Plovdiv	h	1-0	Marcinho
07/05	Montana	a	1-0	Delev 2, Kamburov
11/05	Cherno More	h	3-2	Vasilev, og (Alexander D Alexandrov), Serginho
19/05	Beroe	a	1-0	Krachunov
22/05	Pirin	h	3-0	Michel (p), og (Drenovichki), Delev
25/05	Lokomotiv Sofia	a	1-2	Dolapchiev

No	Name	Nat	DoB	Pos	Aps	(s)	Gls
19	Anicet	MAD	16/03/90	M	26		6
11	Ivan Bandalovski		23/11/86	D	23		2
18	Tomáš Černý	CZE	04/10/85	G	29		
18	Ivaylo Chochev		18/02/93	M	6	(4)	
48	Borislav Chorbadzhiyski		08/08/95	D		(1)	
7	Spas Delev		22/09/89	A	12	(2)	5
45	Grigor Dolapchiev		23/02/94	M		(4)	1
25	Angel Granchov		16/10/92	D	8	(3)	
20	Bogomil Hristov		06/01/94	M	1	(3)	
6	Milen Ivanov		10/05/93	M	1		
22	Marin Kamburov		13/10/80	A	6	(5)	3
71	Anton Karachanakov		17/01/92	M	9		3
55	Ilias Kiriakidis	GRE	08/05/85	M		(4)	
66	Plamen Krachunov		11/01/89	D	21		1
9	Ignacio Lores	URU	26/04/91	M	9	(4)	1
8	Lucas Sasha	BRA	03/01/90	M	28	(1)	2
9	Marcinho	BRA	08/08/84	A	6	(1)	3
9	Michel	BRA	08/09/83	A	14	(2)	8
43	Yulian Nenov		01/01/94	A		(1)	
16	Nílson António	CPV	08/05/87	D	5		
14	Serge Nyuiadzi	FRA	17/09/91	A	5	(3)	1
14	Alexandru Păcurar	ROU	20/01/82	D	3	(2)	
16	Apostol Popov		22/12/82	D	26		
30	Vasil Popov		13/11/95	D	1	(1)	
99	Njongo Priso	CMR	24/12/88	M	19	(3)	
2	Jérémie Rodrigues	FRA	01/11/80	D	1		
9	Sebastián Sciorilli	ARG	08/04/89	A	2	(2)	
10	Serginho	POR	16/06/85	M	12	(7)	5
9	Cillian Sheridan	IRL	23/02/89	A	3		
46	Stoyan Stoichkov		15/05/95	A		(1)	
5	Kostadin Stoyanov		02/05/86	D	7	(1)	
31	Valdermar Stoyanov		30/12/94	M		(1)	
85	Bozhidar Stoychev		01/05/91	G	1		
29	Tássio	BRA	08/10/84	A	2	(9)	4
22	Tengarrinha	POR	17/02/89	M	1	(4)	
21	Ventsislav Vasilev		08/07/88	D	8	(3)	1
4	Mihail Venkov		28/07/83	D	18		2
5	Todor Yanchev		19/05/76	M	15		
15	Stanko Yovchev		15/04/88	A	2	(3)	2

FC ETAR VELIKO TARNOVO

Coach: Tsanko Tsvetanov; (08/10/12) (Kaloyan Chakarov); (22/10/12) Serdar Dayat (TUR); (28/04/13) (Grigor Petkov)
2002 • Ivaylo (20,000); Hadzi Dimitar (15,000) • etar1924.com

2012

12/08	Montana	a	3-2	Luiz Eduardo 2, Sadula
18/08	Cherno More	h	0-1	
26/08	Beroe	a	0-1	
01/09	Pirin	h	0-1	
16/09	Lokomotiv Sofia	a	0-3	
23/09	Litex	h	0-4	
30/09	CSKA	a	1-3	Hikmet
06/10	Lokomotiv Plovdiv	h	1-1	Saidhodzha
21/10	Minior	a	0-1	
27/10	Botev Vratsa	h	1-0	K Trifonov
04/11	Ludogorets	a	0-4	
10/11	Chernomorets	h	1-2	Petrov
17/11	Slavia	h	1-1	Saidhodzha
28/11	Levski	a	1-7	Nerylon
08/12	Botev Plovdiv	h	1-2	og (Arthur Henrique)

2013

02/03	Montana	h	2-1	Saidhodzha, Cienciała
09/03	Cherno More	h	1-0	Mehmet
16/03	Beroe	h	0-2	
30/03	Pirin	a	2-2	Risholt, Karlsson
08/04	Lokomotiv Sofia	h	2-2	Lyubenov, Saidhodzha
10/04	Litex	a	1-6	Castellana
14/04	CSKA	h	0-4	
20/04	Lokomotiv Plovdiv	a	0-3	
28/04	Minior	h	0-3	
03/05	Botev Vratsa	a	1-2	Shayesteh
07/05	Ludogorets	h	1-5	Cienciała
13/05	Chernomorets	h	0-3	(w/o)
18/05	Slavia	a	0-3	(w/o)
22/05	Levski	a	0-3	(w/o)
25/05	Botev Plovdiv	a	0-3	(w/o)

No	Name	Nat	DoB	Pos	Aps	(s)	Gls
7	Radoslav Anev		01/02/85	M	9		
28	Atanas Atanasov		14/07/85	D	11		
32	Mateusz Bąk	POL	26/02/83	G	2	(1)	
20	Dimitar Baydakov		15/02/93	A	1	(3)	
10	Beto	BRA	25/11/86	M	2	(2)	
18	Kasali Casal	ENG	21/10/87	D	2		
5	Laurent Castellana	BEL	17/01/87	D	10		1
21	Sławomir Cienciała	POL	30/11/86	D	6	(2)	2
88	Ventsislav Dimitrov		27/03/88	G	7		
30	Eli Marques	BRA	14/03/82	D	8		
8	Fatih Yılmaz	TUR	05/03/89	M	8		
10	Jacques Fey	FRA	20/06/89	M	10	(1)	1
1	Nenad Filipović	SRB	24/04/87	G	9		
13	Kostadin Gadzhalov		20/07/89	D	7	(2)	
16	Georgi Gaidarov		10/12/84	D	1		
23	Grégory Gendrey	FRA	10/07/86	M	2	(2)	
22	Paul Grischok	GER	26/02/86	M		(2)	1
10	Ahmet Hikmet		05/10/84	M	7	(2)	1
4	Krzysztof Hrymowicz	POL	29/12/83	D	4	(4)	
92	Bircent Karageren		06/12/92	M		(2)	
22	Sonny Karlsson	SWE	14/06/88	A	3	(4)	1
9	Luiz Eduardo	BRA	24/05/85	A	7	(1)	2
11	Lyubomir Lyubenov		25/08/80	A	9	(2)	1
2	Azrack-Yassine Mahamat	CHA	24/03/88	M	12	(4)	
3	Milcho Makendzhiev		31/10/89	D	11	(3)	
14	Mehmet Mehmet	SWE	23/12/85	M	2	(3)	1
4	Nerylon	BRA	15/01/88	D	2	(7)	1
17	Nikolay Nikolaev		01/10/92	D	4	(5)	
33	Ivaylo Petkov		15/07/95	G	1		
8	Nikolay Petrov		30/09/88	M	15		1
23	Yoan Pivaty	FRA	29/01/90	A	5	(4)	
12	Michał Protasewicz	POL	26/09/85	D	7		
2	Patrik Rikama-Hinnenberg	FIN	08/02/83	D	7		
3	Kai Risholt	NOR	10/04/79	D	8	(3)	1
15	Ivaylo Rusev		19/04/87	D	5		
29	Chetin Sadula		16/06/87	A	14		1
	Dormushali Saidhodzha		16/05/86	A	17	(2)	4
17	Sulaiman Sesay-Fullah	SLE	16/09/91	A	1	(2)	
7	Faysal Shayesteh	AFG	21/06/91	M	8	(2)	1
7	Martin Stankev		29/07/89	M	5	(4)	
11	Jasar Takak	NED	03/04/82	M	4		
21	Germain Tiko	CMR	29/04/90	M	5		
12	Krasen Trifonov		05/12/82	M	12	(2)	1
6	Tihomir Trifonov		25/11/86	D	2		
21	Tsvetomir Tsankov		06/06/84	G	4		
1	Pavle Velimirović	MNE	11/04/90	G	4		
16	Valentin Veselinov		15/06/92	M		(2)	

PFC LEVSKI SOFIA

Coach: Ilian Iliev; (12/04/13) (Nikolay Mitov)
1914 • Georgi Asparuhov (29,000) • levski.bg
Major honours
Bulgarian League (26) 1933, 1937, 1942, 1946, 1947,
1949, 1950, 1953, 1965, 1968, 1970, 1974, 1977, 1979,
1984, 1985, 1988, 1993, 1994, 1995, 2000, 2001, 2002,
2006, 2007, 2009;
Bulgarian Cup (26) 1942 (as Tsar's Cup), 1946, 1947,
1949, 1950, 1956, 1957, 1959, 1967, 1970, 1971, 1976,
1977, 1979 (as Soviet Army Cup), 1982, 1984, 1986,
1991, 1992, 1994, 1998, 2000, 2002, 2003, 2005, 2007

2012
11/08	Chernomorets	h	1-0	*Carvalho*
19/08	Botev Plovdiv	h	3-1	*Raykov 2, Angelov*
25/08	Montana	a	2-0	*Carvalho, Mulder*
31/08	Cherno More	h	4-0	*Cristóvão, Carvalho 2, Marcinho*
16/09	Beroe	a	2-1	*Marcinho, Carvalho*
22/09	Pirin	a	2-0	*Carvalho (p), Yordanov*
29/09	Lokomotiv Sofia	a	1-1	*Carvalho*
05/10	Litex	h	2-1	*Carvalho, Raykov*
20/10	CSKA	a	0-1	
27/10	Lokomotiv Plovdiv	a	2-1	*Élie, João Silva*
04/11	Minior	a	4-0	*og (Boumelaha), Carvalho, Gadzhev, Cristóvão*
10/11	Botev Vratsa	h	2-0	*Marcinho, Mulder*
18/11	Ludogorets	a	1-2	*Yordanov*
28/11	Etar	h	7-1	*Carvalho 4 (1p), Vutov, og (Rusev), Yordanov*
08/12	Slavia	a	3-1	*D Dimov, João Silva 2*
2013				
03/03	Chernomorets	a	2-0	*Carvalho 2*
09/03	Botev Plovdiv	a	0-2	
17/03	Montana	h	0-0	
30/03	Cherno More	a	1-1	*Mihelič*
07/04	Beroe	h	2-0	*Yordanov, Carvalho*
10/04	Pirin	a	1-1	*Élie*
13/04	Lokomotiv Sofia	a	2-1	*Carvalho (p), João Silva*
20/04	Litex	a	2-1	*Mendes Rodrigues, Yovov*
27/04	CSKA	h	2-1	*Yovov, João Silva*
02/05	Lokomotiv Plovdiv	a	1-0	*Cristóvao*
06/05	Minior	h	2-1	*João Silva, Mendes Rodrigues*
10/05	Botev Vratsa	a	3-1	*Carvalho, Mendes Rodrigues (p), João Silva*
18/05	Ludogorets	h	1-0	*Angelov*
22/05	Etar	a	1-0	
25/05	Slavia	h	1-1	*Carvalho*

No	Name	Nat	DoB	Pos	Aps	(s)	Gls
4	Stanislav Angelov		12/04/78	M	21	(2)	2
20	Alexander Bashliev		16/11/89	D	2	(1)	
19	Basile de Carvalho	GNB	31/10/81	A	24	(1)	19
16	Cristóvão	POR	25/03/83	M	21	(3)	3
7	Daniel Dimov		21/01/89	M	15	(4)	1
21	Plamen Dimov		29/10/90	D	1		
3	Romain Élie	FRA	03/06/85	D	23	(1)	2
45	Vladimir Gadzhev		18/07/87	M	18	(4)	1
23	Plamen Ivanov Iliev		30/11/91	G	26		
14	Plamen Tonev Iliev		04/02/94	M	1		
89	Mihail Ivanov		08/07/92	G	2		
9	João Silva	POR	21/05/90	A	7	(18)	7
31	Marcinho	BRA	25/03/81	M	10	(2)	3
11	Garry Mendes Rodrigues	NED	27/11/90	M	13	(1)	3
29	Rene Mihelič	SVN	05/07/88	M	7	(2)	1
55	Yordan Miliev		05/10/87	D	5	(1)	
9	Dustley Mulder	NED	27/01/85	D	26		2
28	Nuno Pinto	POR	06/08/86	D	16	(2)	
8	Agyemang Opoku	GHA	06/07/89	A		(1)	
8	Roman Procházka	SVK	14/03/89	M	16	(5)	
11	Simeon Raykov		11/11/89	M	8	(2)	3
6	Orlin Starokin		08/01/87	D	11	(5)	
71	Borislav Tsonev		29/04/95	M		(2)	
1	Ivaylo Vasilev		15/01/91	G	1		
4	Milen Vasilev		30/01/89	M	2	(1)	
77	Stefan Velev		02/05/89	M	10	(3)	
13	Dimitar Vezalov		13/04/87	D	10	(1)	
30	Antonio Vutov		06/06/96	M		(4)	1
11	Iliyan Yordanov		03/04/89	A	13	(10)	4
10	Hristo Yovov		04/11/77	M	10	(10)	2

PFC LITEX LOVECH

Coach: Hristo Stoichkov
1921 • Gradski (7,000) • pfclitex.com
Major honours
Bulgarian League (4) 1998, 1999, 2010, 2011;
Bulgarian Cup (4) 2001, 2004, 2008, 2009

2012
11/08	CSKA	h	1-0	*Zakov*
19/08	Lokomotiv Plovdiv	a	1-1	*G Milanov*
25/08	Minior	h	0-0	
31/08	Botev Vratsa	a	4-0	*Zakov 2, Tsvetkov, G Milanov*
16/09	Ludogorets	h	0-2	
23/09	Etar	a	4-0	*Tsvetkov, Isa, Zakov, Vajushi*
29/09	Slavia	h	5-0	*G Milanov (p), Vajushi 2, Tsvetkov, Isa*
05/10	Levski	a	1-2	*G Milanov*
21/10	Botev Plovdiv	h	0-1	
27/10	Montana	a	3-1	*G Milanov 3 (1p)*
04/11	Cherno More	a	4-1	*Isa 3, Slavchev*
10/11	Beroe	a	0-1	
18/11	Pirin	h	5-0	*Vajushi, Isa 2, Ivanov, Zakov*
28/11	Lokomotiv Sofia	a	2-0	*Vajushi, Kostadinov*
08/12	Chernomorets	h	1-0	*G Milanov*
2013				
02/03	CSKA	a	2-0	*Vajushi 2*
09/03	Lokomotiv Plovdiv	h	2-2	*Isa, G Milanov*
17/03	Minior	a	2-1	*G Milanov 2*
30/03	Botev Vratsa	h	5-1	*G Milanov, Vajushi 2, Isa, Vanger*
07/04	Ludogorets	a	0-0	
10/04	Etar	h	6-1	*Grozev, Stênio Júnior, Vanger, G Milanov 2, Kostadinov*
14/04	Slavia	a	1-2	*Isa*
20/04	Levski	h	1-2	*I Milanov*
28/04	Botev Plovdiv	a	0-1	
05/05	Montana	h	2-0	*og (Pashov), Vanger*
08/05	Cherno More	a	0-1	
11/05	Beroe	h	1-2	*Isa (p)*
19/05	Pirin	a	2-0	*Grozev, G Milanov*
22/05	Lokomotiv Sofia	h	1-2	*G Milanov (p)*
25/05	Chernomorets	a	0-0	

No	Name	Nat	DoB	Pos	Aps	(s)	Gls
3	Ivelin Aladzhov		29/04/94	D	1		
30	Evgeni Alexandrov		14/06/88	G	1		
20	Kostadin Bashov		26/11/82	A		(6)	
33	Nikolay Bodurov		30/05/86	D	18		
2	Vasil Bozhikov		02/06/88	D	26	(1)	
13	Papis Dembo Coly	SEN	19/07/90	A		(2)	
11	Reyan Daskalov		10/02/95	A		(1)	
20	Kiril Despodov		11/11/96	A	1	(1)	
2	Kiril Dinchev		08/05/89	D	1	(4)	
5	Emil Grozev		15/03/91	D	5	(3)	2
24	Edon Hasani	ALB	01/09/92	M	5	(4)	
9	Ismail Isa		26/06/89	A	22	(2)	11
77	Galin Ivanov		15/04/88	M	8	(3)	1
23	Nebojša Jelenković	SRB	26/05/78	M	13		
8	Nikola Kolev		06/06/95	M	1	(3)	
15	Tomi Kostadinov		30/08/90	M	4	(12)	2
17	Georgi Milanov		19/02/92	M	27		16
18	Iliya Milanov		19/02/92	D	27		1
3	Anton Nedyalkov		30/04/93	M	14	(3)	
1	Ilko Pirgov		23/05/86	G	29		
16	Strahil Popov		30/08/90	M	27		
6	Rumen Rumenov		07/06/93	M		(1)	
6	Simeon Slavchev		25/09/93	M	13	(4)	1
20	Krasimir Stanoev		14/09/94	M		1	
10	Stênio Júnior	BRA	10/06/91	A	6	(9)	1
27	Momchil Tsvetanov		03/12/90	M	9	(7)	
21	Alexander Tsvetkov		31/08/90	M	23	(1)	3
14	Armando Vajushi	ALB	03/12/91	A	28	(2)	9
7	Vanger	BRA	27/01/87	A	12	(2)	3
10	Gerasim Zakov		07/09/84	A	9	(6)	5

PFC LOKOMOTIV PLOVDIV 1936

Coach: Emil Velev; (08/10/12) Stefan Genov
1936 • Lokomotiv (13,000) • lokomotivpd.com
Major honours
Bulgarian League (1) 2004

2012
12/08	Lokomotiv Sofia	a	1-1	*Zlatinski (p)*
19/08	Litex	h	1-1	*Petrov*
25/08	CSKA	a	0-0	
01/09	Chernomorets	a	1-1	*Abushev*
16/09	Minior	h	5-1	*Stefanov, Zlatinski, D Georgiev, V Georgiev, Kovachev*
22/09	Botev Vratsa	a	1-1	
29/09	Ludogorets	h	2-5	*Kotev, Abushev*
06/10	Etar	a	1-1	*Kavdanski*
21/10	Slavia	h	1-0	*Abushev*
27/10	Levski	h	1-2	*og (Nuno Pinto)*
04/11	Botev Plovdiv	a	2-2	*Abushev 2*
10/11	Montana	a	2-1	*Kavdanski, D Atanasov*
17/11	Cherno More	a	1-0	*Stefanov*
28/11	Beroe	a	2-1	*Malamov, og (Zafirov)*
09/12	Pirin	h	1-0	*Abushev*
2013				
02/03	Lokomotiv Sofia	h	2-0	*Kavdanski, Stefanov*
09/03	Litex	a	2-2	*Abushev, Diego*
16/03	CSKA	h	0-2	
31/03	Chernomorets	a	2-0	*Malamov, Sadula*
06/04	Minior	a	1-1	*Yurukov*
10/04	Botev Vratsa	h	0-1	
15/04	Ludogorets	a	0-1	
20/04	Etar	h	3-0	*Diego, Kotev, V Mirchev*
28/04	Slavia	a	0-2	
02/05	Levski	h	0-1	
08/05	Botev Plovdiv	h	0-0	
13/05	Montana	a	4-0	*Zlatinski, V Georgiev, V Mirchev, D Georgiev*
18/05	Cherno More	a	0-3	
22/05	Beroe	h	1-2	*Zlatinski*
25/05	Pirin	a	1-2	*V Mirchev*

No	Name	Nat	DoB	Pos	Aps	(s)	Gls
4	Rangel Abushev		26/05/89	M	24	(4)	7
28	Atanas Atanasov		14/07/85	D	7		
33	Dimo Atanasov		24/10/85	M	7	(6)	1
21	Stoycho Bebelekov		01/04/95	D		(1)	
44	Hristo Dermendzhiev	CYP	10/01/90	D	2	(1)	
1	Petar Denchev		10/10/85	G	8		
7	Diego	BRA	11/05/90	M	22	(2)	2
71	Ivaylo Dimitrov		26/06/87	D	1		
26	Nikolay Dyulgerov		10/03/88	M	3	(6)	
23	Daniel Georgiev		06/11/82	M	25		2
3	Valeri Georgiev		28/07/84	D	27		2
22	Yordan Gospodinov		15/06/78	G	20		
55	Martin Kavdanski		13/02/87	D	19	(1)	3
20	Rosen Kolev		07/05/95	M	1	(1)	
6	Kiril Kotev		18/04/82	D	21	(1)	2
5	Pavel Kovachev		01/04/87	D	13	(1)	1
55	Kristiyan Kumbarov		24/01/94	D	1		
1	Stefano Kunchev		20/04/91	G	8		
39	Atanas Kurdov		28/10/88	A	7	(3)	
89	Stanislav Malamov		21/09/89	M	18	(7)	2
17	Kostadin Markov		19/02/79	D	23	(1)	
21	Georgi Mechechiev		27/04/78	D	1		
95	Serafim Mihaylov		25/04/95	A		(5)	
24	Konstantin Mirchev		24/07/78	M	1	(1)	
9	Vladislav Mirchev		23/01/87	A	7	(7)	3
14	Nikolay Nikolov		03/05/94	A	1	(2)	
19	Marin Petrov		07/08/77	M	3	(3)	1
99	Miroslav Radev		30/03/94	M		(1)	
19	Chetin Sadula		16/06/87	A	4	(8)	1
71	Hristo Spasov		13/06/88	A	2	(2)	
15	Hristo Stamov		02/01/94	D		(1)	
7	Nikolay Stankov		11/12/84	M	2	(2)	
88	Georgi Stefanov		13/07/88	M	21	(7)	3
10	Todor Timonov		03/09/86	M	4	(2)	
4	Iliyan Yordanov		03/04/89	M	1		
82	Yordan Yurukov		02/10/83	M	4	(1)	1
11	Zapryan Zapryanov		15/06/94	M	1	(6)	
16	Hristo Zlatinski		22/01/85	M	26		4

PFC LOKOMOTIV SOFIA
Coach: Anton Velkov; (19/11/12) Emil Velev
1929 • Slavia (15,000); Georgi Asparuhov (29,000);
Chavdar Tsvetkov (3,500) • no website
Major honours
Bulgarian League (4) 1940, 1945, 1964, 1978;
Bulgarian Cup (3) 1948, 1953 (as Soviet Army Cup), 1995

2012

12/08	Lokomotiv Plovdiv	h	1-1	Telkiyski
18/08	Minior	a	0-0	
26/08	Botev Vratsa	h	3-0	og (Jairo), Pavlov, Dobrev
31/08	Ludogorets	a	1-2	Hristov
16/09	Etar	h	3-0	Peev 2 (p), Hristov
23/09	Slavia	a	0-2	
29/09	Levski	h	1-1	Pavlov
06/10	Botev Plovdiv	a	0-2	
21/10	Montana	h	0-0	
27/10	Cherno More	a	0-2	
04/11	Beroe	h	2-2	Dafchev (p), Pavlov
10/11	Pirin	a	0-2	
17/11	Chernomorets	a	0-3	
28/11	Litex	h	0-2	
09/12	CSKA	a	1-1	Peev (p)

2013

02/03	Lokomotiv Plovdiv	a	0-2	
10/03	Minior	h	1-0	Pavlov
16/03	Botev Vratsa	a	0-0	
31/03	Ludogorets	h	0-1	
06/04	Etar	a	2-2	Peev, Dyulgerov
09/04	Slavia	h	1-0	Pavlov
13/04	Levski	a	1-2	Bibishkov
20/04	Botev Plovdiv	h	1-2	Bibishkov
28/04	Montana	a	3-2	Iliev, Pavlov, Bibishkov
02/05	Cherno More	h	0-0	
07/05	Beroe	a	1-1	Iliev
10/05	Pirin	h	0-1	
18/05	Chernomorets	a	1-3	Marquinhos
22/05	Litex	a	2-1	Peev, Iliev
25/05	CSKA	h	2-1	Pisarov, Iliev

No	Name	Nat	DoB	Pos	Aps	(s)	Gls
76	Krum Bibishkov		02/09/79	A	6	(6)	3
88	Atanas Bornosuzov		05/10/79	M	13	(4)	
6	Alexander Branekov		31/05/87	D	27		
10	Marcho Dafchev		12/05/78	M	7	(1)	1
16	Martin Dimitrov		17/07/87	M	21	(2)	
11	Kristiyan Dobrev		23/09/78	D	16	(1)	1
18	Alexander Dyulgerov		19/04/90	D	20	(2)	1
21	Daniel Gadzhev		21/06/85	M	7	(1)	
84	Valentin Galev		01/01/84	G	14		
5	Iliyan Garov		08/01/84	D	3	(1)	
23	Georgi Hristov		10/01/85	A	11	(2)	2
14	Dimitar Krasimirov Iliev		25/09/88	A	12	(14)	4
8	Dani Kiki		08/01/88	M	1	(1)	
90	Branimir Kostadinov		04/03/89	A	7	(2)	
8	Alexander Manolov		06/12/91	M	1	(11)	
28	Marquinhos		30/04/82	M	7	(1)	1
33	Emil Mihaylov		01/05/88	G	5		
1	Bozhidar Mitrev		31/03/ 87	G	11		
26	Nikolay Nikolov		26/01/81	D	7	(1)	
9	Antonio Pavlov		02/09/88	A	11	(12)	6
77	Daniel Peev		06/10/84	M	26	(3)	5
22	Pavel Petkov		26/01/90	M	2	(2)	
19	Svetoslav Petrov		20/08/88	M	12	(3)	
13	Iskren Pisarov		05/10/85	A	6	(4)	1
90	Mladen Stoev		26/01/84	M		(2)	
12	Dimitar Telkiyski		05/05/77	M	15		1
23	Tom	BRA	18/03/86	M	13		
21	Rumen Trifonov		22/02/85	M	15		
22	Antonio Tsankov		07/02/90	M		(5)	
3	Yordan Varbanov		15/02/80	D	11		
99	Georg Vasilev		29/10/95	M		(1)	
7	Vasil Velev		15/01/84	M	6	(3)	
2	Kostadin Velkov		26/03/89	D	15	(3)	
13	Wilker	BRA	16/06/87	A	1	(2)	
7	Ivelin Yanev		23/11/81	D	1		

PFC LUDOGORETS RAZGRAD
Coach: Ivaylo Petev
1947 • Ludogorets Arena (5,000) • ludogorets.com
Major honours
Bulgarian League (2) 2012, 2013;
Bulgarian Cup (1) 2012

2012

11/08	Cherno More	a	3-0	Barthe, Gargorov 2
19/08	Beroe	h	3-1	Barthe, I Stoyanov, og (Ivanov)
25/08	Pirin	a	2-0	Marcelinho 2
31/08	Lokomotiv Sofia	h	2-1	Ivanov, Gargorov
16/09	Litex	h	2-0	Gargorov, Burgzorg
22/09	CSKA	h	1-0	Marcelinho
29/09	Lokomotiv Plovdiv	a	5-2	Marcelinho, Guela, Gargorov 2, Burgzorg
05/10	Minior	h	3-0	Marcelinho, I Stoyanov, Ivanov (p)
21/10	Botev Vratsa	a	1-1	Genchev
27/10	Chernomorets	a	0-1	
04/11	Etar	h	4-0	Ivanov, Moți, Juninho Quixadá, Bakalov
10/11	Slavia	a	0-0	
18/11	Levski	h	2-1	Genchev 2
28/11	Botev Plovdiv	a	1-0	og (Grncarov)
08/12	Montana	h	3-0	Guldan, I Stoyanov (p), Alexandrov

2013

03/03	Cherno More	h	2-0	Marcelinho, Bakalov
10/03	Beroe	a	0-0	
16/03	Pirin	h	1-1	Barthe
31/03	Lokomotiv Sofia	a	1-0	Alexandrov
07/04	Litex	h	0-0	
11/04	CSKA	a	0-0	
15/04	Lokomotiv Plovdiv	h	1-0	Juninho Quixadá
21/04	Minior	a	2-1	Bakalov, Guldan
27/04	Botev Vratsa	h	4-1	Ivanov, Bakalov, Alexandrov, I Stoyanov
03/05	Chernomorets	h	3-0	Bezjak 2, I Stoyanov
07/05	Etar	a	5-1	Dyakov 2, I Stoyanov 2, Bezjak
11/05	Slavia	h	2-1	Bezjak 2
18/05	Levski	a	0-1	
22/05	Botev Plovdiv	h	2-0	I Stoyanov 2 (1p)
25/05	Montana	a	3-0	Dyakov, Alexandrov 2

No	Name	Nat	DoB	Pos	Aps	(s)	Gls
7	Mihail Alexandrov		11/06/89	M	7	(8)	5
19	Dimo Bakalov		19/12/88	M	4	(11)	4
5	Alexandre Barthe	FRA	05/03/86	D	14		3
9	Roman Bezjak	SVN	21/02/89	A	5	(9)	5
14	Michell Burgzorg	NED	25/07/88	M	2	(10)	2
20	Choko	BRA	18/01/90	D	5	(1)	
91	Ivan Čvorović		15/06/85	G	10		
18	Svetoslav Dyakov		31/05/84	M	28		3
23	Emil Gargorov		15/02/81	M	18	(4)	6
8	Stanislav Genchev		15/02/81	M	25	(3)	3
1	Uroš Golubović	SRB	19/08/76	G	6		
99	Franck Guela	CIV	19/06/86	A	5	(8)	1
33	Ľubomír Guldan	SVK	30/01/83	D	22		2
10	Sebastián Hernández	COL	02/10/86	A	3	(6)	
22	Miroslav Ivanov		11/09/81	M	25	(1)	4
11	Juninho Quixadá	BRA	12/12/85	A	8	(8)	2
80	Júnior Caiçara	BRA	27/04/89	D	28		
6	Georgi Kostadinov		07/09/90	M	2	(4)	
33	Tero Mäntylä	FIN	18/04/91	D	5		
84	Marcelinho	BRA	24/08/84	M	24	(1)	6
15	Nemanja Milisavljević	SRB	01/11/84	M	1	(5)	
25	Yordan Minev		14/10/80	D	23	(1)	
27	Cosmin Moți	ROU	12/03/84	D	19	(2)	1
73	Ivan Stoyanov		24/07/83	M	23	(5)	9
21	Vladislav Stoyanov		08/06/87	G	14		
77	Vitinha	POR	11/02/86	M	4		

PFC MINIOR PERNIK
Coach: Stoycho Stoev; (18/09/12) Nikolay Todorov
1945 • Minior (15,000) • minyor.com

2012

12/08	Pirin	a	1-2	Stoychev
18/08	Lokomotiv Sofia	h	0-0	
25/08	Litex	a	0-0	
31/08	CSKA	h	1-4	M Vasilev
16/09	Lokomotiv Plovdiv	a	1-5	Bibishkov
23/09	Chernomorets	a	0-2	
30/09	Botev Vratsa	h	0-1	
05/10	Ludogorets	a	0-3	
21/10	Etar	h	1-0	M Vasilev
27/10	Slavia	h	0-0	
04/11	Levski	h	0-4	
10/11	Botev Plovdiv	a	0-2	
18/11	Montana	h	2-1	Yurukov, Pisarov
28/11	Cherno More	a	0-2	
09/12	Beroe	h	3-0	Hadzhiev, V Vasilev, og (Elias)

2013

02/03	Pirin	h	2-0	Tsvetkov, Pavlov
10/03	Lokomotiv Sofia	a	0-1	
17/03	Litex	h	1-2	Madou
31/03	CSKA	a	0-3	
06/04	Lokomotiv Plovdiv	h	1-1	Okechukwu
10/04	Chernomorets	h	0-1	
14/04	Botev Vratsa	a	0-2	
21/04	Ludogorets	h	1-2	Alexandrov
28/04	Etar	a	3-0	Pavlov 2 (1p), Okechukwu
02/05	Slavia	h	2-4	Petrov, og (Dyakov)
06/05	Levski	a	1-2	Pavlov
13/05	Botev Plovdiv	h	0-2	
18/05	Montana	a	0-2	
22/05	Cherno More	h	0-2	
25/05	Beroe	a	0-1	

No	Name	Nat	DoB	Pos	Aps	(s)	Gls
7	Alexander Alexandrov		28/03/94	M	8		1
1	Nikolay Bankov		19/11/90	G	4		
39	Farid Benramdane	ALG	16/03/89	M	2		
76	Krum Bibishkov		02/09/79	A	9		1
99	Sabri Boumelaha	ALG	21/09/89	D	9	(2)	
42	Farès Brahimi	ALG	22/10/88	M	13	(2)	
11	Mario Dimitrov		25/10/94	A		(5)	
39	Kaloyan Evgeniev		19/01/94	M		(4)	
6	Kamen Hadzhiev		22/09/91	D	8		1
5	Ahmed Hikmet		05/10/84	M	8	(2)	
4	Nikolay Hristozov		06/03/82	D	4	(1)	
11	Ilian Iliev		06/11/88	M	10	(3)	
23	Ventsislav Ivanov		20/05/82	A	5	(2)	
9	Franck Madou	CIV	15/09/87	A	2	(3)	1
3	Ivan Mihov		08/06/91	D	8	(1)	
15	Salas Okechukwu	NGA	15/05/89	M	11	(7)	2
5	Adrian Olegov		01/05/85	D	12		
10	Tomislav Pavlov		28/06/91	M	13	(10)	4
19	Petar Petrov		19/04/84	M	15		1
22	Boyan Peykov		01/05/84	G	25		
8	Iskren Pisarov		05/10/85	M	6	(3)	1
2	Viktor Raychev		26/05/86	D	9	(3)	
31	Svetlin Slavchev		24/09/90	M	1		
17	Viktor Sofroniev		04/04/81	D	9	(3)	
25	Stefan Stanchev		26/04/89	D	14		
27	Stoyan Stefanov		28/07/83	A		(4)	
20	David Stoyanov		13/03/91	D	19	(2)	
13	Ivaylo Stoyanov		13/07/90	M	8	(6)	
5	Borislav Stoychev		26/11/86	D	10		1
33	Tom	BRA	18/03/86	M	14		
17	Vanco Trajanov	MKD	08/09/78	M	6		
14	Ivaylo Tsvetkov		28/08/79	M	23	(2)	1
7	Milen Vasilev		30/01/89	M	9	(1)	2
23	Ventsislav Vasilev		08/07/88	D	11		1
9	Nikolay Vladinov		01/04/87	M		(6)	
78	Jean-Baptiste Yakassongo	BEL	20/03/89	A	7	(4)	
24	Dimitar Yalamov		26/03/87	D		(2)	
8	Yordan Yordanov		14/04/92	M	10	(6)	
77	Yordan Yurukov		02/10/83	M	8	(3)	1

PFC MONTANA 1921

Coach: Atanas Dzhambazki; (12/03/13) (Stoycho Stoev); (18/03/13) (Georgi Stankov)
1921 • Ogosta (4,000) • no website

2012

12/08	Etar	h	2-3	Todorov, Michev
18/08	Slavia	a	1-2	Petrov
25/08	Levski	h	0-2	
01/09	Botev Plovdiv	a	1-3	Antonov
15/09	Chernomorets	h	1-0	Todorov
23/09	Cherno More	h	3-1	Kovachev, Vodenicharov, Hristov
30/09	Beroe	a	2-2	Antonov, Hristov
06/10	Pirin	h	3-0	Vodenicharov, Antonov, Hristov
21/10	Lokomotiv Sofia	a	0-0	
27/10	Litex	h	1-3	Pashov
04/11	CSKA	a	0-1	
10/11	Lokomotiv Plovdiv	h	1-2	Antonov (p)
18/11	Minior	h	1-2	Todorov
28/11	Botev Vratsa	h	0-0	
08/12	Ludogorets	a	0-3	

2013

02/03	Etar	a	1-2	Mihov
09/03	Slavia	h	0-1	
17/03	Levski	a	0-0	
31/03	Botev Plovdiv	h	0-2	
06/04	Chernomorets	a	0-1	
10/04	Cherno More	a	1-2	Mladenov
14/04	Beroe	h	1-3	Zlatinov
21/04	Pirin	a	2-4	V Ivanov, Todorov
28/04	Lokomotiv Sofia	a	2-3	V Ivanov, Brahimi
03/05	Litex	a	0-1	
07/05	CSKA	h	1-3	og (A Popov)
13/05	Lokomotiv Plovdiv	a	0-4	
18/05	Minior	h	2-0	V Ivanov, Michev
22/05	Botev Vratsa	a	1-3	Mladenov
25/05	Ludogorets	h	0-3	

No	Name	Nat	DoB	Pos	Aps	(s)	Gls
19	Miroslav Antonov		10/03/86	A	14		4
1	Atanas Arshinkov		08/04/87	G	1		
21	Samir Ayass		24/12/90	M		(3)	
21	Farès Brahimi	ALG	22/10/88	M	6	(7)	1
17	Ahmed Chobiyou		09/00/07	M	5	(10)	
25	Martin Dechev		12/04/90	D	10		
4	Victor Deniran	NGA		D	5	(1)	
4	Martin Dimov		01/03/86	M	1		
13	Boyan Gaytanov		02/12/89	A		2	
5	Spas Georgiev		21/06/92	M	2	(1)	
18	Deyan Hristov		29/08/83	A	5	(6)	3
8	Dimitar Vasilev Iliev		27/07/86	M	27	(1)	
11	Ilian Iliev		06/11/88	M	2		
1	Hristo Ivanov		06/04/82	G	11		
19	Ventsislav Ivanov		20/05/82	A	8	(5)	3
8	Anton Kostadinov		24/06/82	M	17	(2)	
20	Martin Kovachev		12/03/82	D	23	(1)	1
25	Milen Lahchev		01/04/87	D	14		
4	Anton Lichkov		05/08/80	D	26		
2	Georgi Mechechiev		27/04/78	D	14		
9	Kristiyan Ivanov Metodiev		05/11/93	A		(1)	
11	Vladimir Michev		20/11/85	M	12	(7)	2
3	Ivan Mihov		08/06/91	D	14		1
32	Cololo Minou	CGO	03/07/90	G	4	(1)	
11	Daniel Mladenov		25/05/87	M	13	(2)	2
17	Georgi Pashov		04/03/90	D	17	(1)	1
16	Dimitar Petkov		24/08/87	M	8	(4)	
20	Petar Petrov		19/04/84	M	3	(7)	1
6	Martin Sechkov		17/11/86	D	8	(1)	
18	Slavcho Shokolarov		20/08/89	M	6	(6)	
26	Petar Stanev		21/05/91	D			
27	Thiago Miracema	BRA	08/12/87	M	5	(5)	
7	Yordan Todorov		12/11/81	M	21	(3)	4
1	Veselin Tsvetkovski		08/03/89	G	12		
9	Dimitar Vodenicharov		26/12/87	M	4	(4)	2
23	Ivailo Yanachkov		24/08/87	G	2		
9	Vladislav Zlatinov		23/03/83	A	10	(2)	1

PFC PIRIN GOTSE DELCHEV

Coach: Yakov Paparkov; (16/08/12) Tencho Tenev
1925 • Gradski (5,000) • fcpirin.dir.bg

2012

12/08	Minior	h	2-1	Lapantov (p), Gutsev
18/08	Botev Vratsa	a	2-1	Kocev, Lapantov (p)
25/08	Ludogorets	h	0-2	
01/09	Etar	a	1-0	Hodza
15/09	Slavia	h	0-3	
22/09	Levski	h	0-3	
29/09	Botev Plovdiv	a	0-1	
06/10	Montana	a	0-3	
21/10	Cherno More	h	3-2	Hazurov (p), Pirgov 2
27/10	Beroe	a	3-2	Gutsev, Hazurov, Panayotov
04/11	Chernomorets	h	0-1	
10/11	Lokomotiv Sofia	h	2-0	V Marchev, Lazarov (p)
18/11	Litex	a	0-5	
28/11	CSKA	a	0-5	
09/12	Lokomotiv Plovdiv	a	0-1	

2013

02/03	Minior	a	0-2	
10/03	Botev Vratsa	h	2-1	Hodza, Hazurov
16/03	Ludogorets	a	1-1	Bliznakov
30/03	Etar	h	2-2	Hazurov, Hodza
06/04	Slavia	a	0-2	
10/04	Levski	h	1-1	Vitanov (p)
13/04	Botev Plovdiv	a	0-5	
21/04	Montana	h	4-2	Vitanov, Lazarov, V Marchev, Bliznakov
28/04	Cherno More	a	1-5	Petrov
02/05	Beroe	h	0-0	
07/05	Chernomorets	a	0-1	
10/05	Lokomotiv Sofia	a	1-0	V Marchev
19/05	Litex	h	0-2	
22/05	CSKA	h	0-7	
25/05	Lokomotiv Plovdiv	h	2-1	Hodza 2

No	Name	Nat	DoB	Pos	Aps	(s)	Gls
83	Abdi Abdikov		09/09/83	G	24		
77	Mario Bliznakov		09/08/82	A	13	(1)	2
14	Nikolay Demikov		06/09/84	M		(1)	
4	Atanas Drenovichki		05/04/90	D	27	(2)	
6	Atanas Fidanin		09/08/86	D	29		
5	Lyubomir Gutsev		18/03/90	D	30		2
9	Borislav Hazurov		10/04/85	A	21	(5)	4
7	Albin Hodza	FRA	07/02/88	A	15	(5)	5
22	Anton Kirov		02/07/90	D	1	(7)	
29	Dragi Kocev	MKD	25/02/87	M	14	(10)	1
5	Rumen Lapantov		11/04/84	M	17	(9)	2
8	Petar Lazarov		27/08/85	M	30		2
23	Ilian Marchev		09/09/92	D	1	(1)	
10	Veselin Marchev		07/02/90	M	29		3
17	Nikola Nikolov		01/01/89	M		(4)	
21	Vasil Panayotov		16/07/90	M	28	(1)	1
28	Georgi Petrov		06/07/91	A	1	(11)	1
3	Dimitar Pirgov		23/10/89	D	30		2
11	Viktor Shishkov		07/09/86	M	1	(11)	
16	Svilen Shterev		14/12/93	M		(6)	
30	Ivan Stoyanov		09/07/91	D		(5)	
14	Lyubomir Vitanov		11/05/81	M	13		2
88	Angel Yusev		23/07/88	G	6	(1)	

PFC SLAVIA SOFIA

Coach: Martin Kushev; (30/11/12) (Voin Voinov); (12/01/13) Velislav Vutsov
1913 • Slavia (15,000) • pfcslavia.com
Major honours
Bulgarian League (7) 1928, 1930, 1936, 1939, 1941, 1943, 1996;
Bulgarian Cup (7) 1952, 1963, 1964, 1966, 1975, 1980 (as Soviet Army Cup), 1996

2012

11/08	Botev Plovdiv	a	0-3	
18/08	Montana	h	2-1	José Júnior, Sandanski
25/08	Cherno More	a	0-3	
01/09	Beroe	h	6-1	José Júnior 2 (1p), Popara, Lazarov 2 (1p), P Dimitrov
15/09	Pirin	a	3-0	Zlatinov, Zhelev, Zlatkov
23/09	Lokomotiv Sofia	h	2-0	Zlatinov, R Dimitrov
29/09	Litex	a	0-5	
06/10	CSKA	h	0-0	
21/10	Lokomotiv Plovdiv	a	0-1	
27/10	Minior	h	0-0	
04/11	Botev Vratsa	a	0-1	
10/11	Ludogorets	h	0-0	
17/11	Etar	a	0-1	Zlatinov
28/11	Chernomorets	a	0-2	
08/12	Levski	h	1-3	Lazarov

2013

01/03	Botev Plovdiv	h	2-2	Ivanov, Fernando Livramento
09/03	Montana	a	1-0	Vasilev
16/03	Cherno More	h	1-0	Fernando Livramento
30/03	Beroe	a	1-2	Popara
06/04	Pirin	h	2-0	Zhelev, Fernando Livramento
09/04	Lokomotiv Sofia	a	0-1	
14/04	Litex	a	2-1	Lazarov, og (Bozhikov)
21/04	CSKA	a	1-2	Sandanski
28/04	Lokomotiv Plovdiv	a	2-0	Genev, Ivanov
02/05	Minior	a	4-2	Antonov, Ivanov 2, Yanchev
07/05	Botev Vratsa	h	1-2	Antonov
11/05	Ludogorets	a	1-2	Ivanov
18/05	Etar	h	3-0	(w/o)
22/05	Chernomorets	h	3-0	Ivanov, Dimitrov, Popara (p)
25/05	Levski	a	1-1	og (Vezalay)

No	Name	Nat	DoB	Pos	Aps	(s)	Gls
23	Taisuke Akiyoshi	JPN	18/04/89	M	7	(4)	
19	Miroslav Antonov		10/03/86	A	6	(2)	2
17	Dimo Atanasov		24/10/06	M			
25	Nikolay Chipev		20/02/89	M	2	(2)	
88	Petar Dimitrov		28/02/82	M	14	(9)	2
20	Radoslav Dimitrov		12/08/88	D	26		1
21	Bogomil Dyakov		12/04/84	D	9	(2)	
26	Nikolay Dyulgerov		10/03/88	M		(1)	
35	Fernando Livramento	POR	03/03/82	M	11	(2)	3
18	Filip Filipov		02/08/88	D	12		
15	Miklós Gaál	HUN	13/05/81	D	1	(1)	
22	Viktor Genev		27/10/88	D	18	(1)	1
5	Spas Georgiev		21/06/92	M		(1)	
71	Hugo López	ESP	15/05/88	M	1	(3)	
33	Galin Ivanov		15/04/88	M	11	(2)	6
44	José Júnior	BRA	18/07/85	A	4		3
29	Vasil Kaloyanov		11/10/88	A	2	(10)	
17	Ivan Kokonov		17/08/91	A	3	(5)	
9	Todor Kolev		08/02/80	A		(3)	
32	Stefano Kunchev		20/04/91	G	2		
77	Zdravko Lazarov		20/02/76	A	23	(4)	4
7	Daisuke Matsui	JPN	05/11/81	M	8	(3)	
1	Georgi Petkov		14/03/76	G	26		
12	Emil Petrov		22/07/83	G	1		
5	Petar Petrov		11/05/87	D	4	(1)	
10	Pavle Popara	SRB	20/05/87	M	17	(2)	3
14	Yanko Sandanski		23/11/78	M	18	(8)	2
24	Maksim Stoykov		13/01/91	A	1	(1)	
33	Tsvetomir Todorov		31/03/91	M		(1)	
11	Radoslav Vasilev		12/10/90	A	8	(4)	1
5	Todor Yanchev		19/05/76	M	12		1
8	Chavdar Yankov		29/03/84	M	9	(4)	
3	Zhivko Zhelev		23/07/79	D	24		2
9	Vladislav Zlatinov		23/03/83	A	9	(5)	3
6	Daniel Zlatkov		06/03/89	D	23	(1)	1

BULGARIA

19	Basile de Carvalho (Levski)
17	Ivan Tsvetkov (Botev Plovdiv)
16	Georgi Milanov (Litex)
12	Georgi Andonov (Beroe)
11	Ismail Isa (Litex)
9	Todor Nedelev (Botev Plovdiv)
	Armando Vajushi (Litex)
	Ivan Stoyanov (Ludogorets)
8	Ventsislav Hristov (Chernomorets/Beroe)
	Michel (CSKA)

Promoted clubs

FC NEFTOCHIMIC 1962 BURGAS

Coach: Dimcho Nenov; (09/04/13) Anton Spasov
1962 • Lazur (18,000); Nesebar (10,000) • neftochimic.com

FC LYUBIMETS 2007

Coach: Stamen Belchev; (11/09/12) (Veselin Velikov);
(28/09/12) Krasimir Mechev;
(09/01/13) Veselin Velikov
2007 • Gradski (5,000) • lubimetzfc.dir.bg

SECOND LEVEL FINAL TABLE 2012/13

		Pld	W	D	L	F	A	Pts
1	FC Neftochimic 1962 Burgas	26	16	6	4	49	22	54
2	FC Lyubimets 2007	26	16	3	7	44	28	51
3	FC Rakovski 2011	26	13	9	4	38	28	48
4	PFC Svetkavitsa Targovishte	26	13	8	5	34	20	47
5	FC Bansko 1951	26	13	7	6	48	26	46
6	PFC Spartak 1919 Pleven	26	11	9	6	33	25	42
7	PFC Spartak 1918 Varna	26	10	8	8	26	19	38
8	PFC Chavdar Etropole	26	11	4	11	31	32	37
9	PFC Kaliakra Kavarna	26	9	7	10	33	31	34
10	FC Pirin 2002 Razlog	26	8	9	9	33	28	33
11	PFC Vidima-Rakovski Sevlievo	26	8	5	13	33	31	29
12	PFC Shumen 2010	26	8	5	13	32	52	29
13	FC Septemvri Simitli	26	4	3	19	18	39	15
14	OFC Sliven 2000	26	0	1	25	4	75	-2

NB OFC Sliven 2000 - 3 pts deducted and withdrew after round 13; their remaining matches were awarded as 0-3 defeats.

Domestic cup: Kupa na Bulgariya 2012/13

SECOND ROUND

(30/10/12 & 24/11/12)
Bansko 6-1, 2-1 Vidima-Rakovski *(8-2)*
Evrokolezh 0-3, 1-6 Botev Plovdiv *(1-9)*
Spartak Varna 2-2, 2-2 Rakovski 2011 *(aet 4-4; 5-4 on pens)*

(31/10/12 & 23/11/12)
Lokomotiv Plovdiv 0-0, 0-2 Litex Lovech *(0-2)*
Lokomotiv Sofia 2-0, 1-3 Master Burgas *(3-3; Lokomotiv Sofia on away goal)*
Lyubimets 2-2, 0-3 Slavia Sofia *(2-5)*

(31/10/12 & 24/11/12)
Beroe Stara Zagora 1-0, 3-1 Akademik Svishtov *(4-1)*
Botev Vratsa 1-1, 0-1 Neftochimic Burgas *(1-2)*
Levski Sofia 3-0, 1-0 Pirin Razlog *(4-0)*
Lokomotiv Mezdra 4-0, 1-4 Kaliakra Kavarna *(aet 5-4; Lokomotiv Mezdra on away goal)*
Ludogorets Razgrad 1-2, 1-0 CSKA Sofia *(2-2; CSKA Sofia on away goal)*
Minior Pernik 2-1, 2-3 Etar Veliko Tarnovo *(4-4; Minior on away goal)*
Pirin Gotse Delchev 3-2, 0-0 Montana *(3-2)*
Silistra 2009 1-1, 1-3 Chavdar Etropole *(2-4)*
Strusmka Slava Simitli 0-0, 0-2 Cherno More Varna *(0-2)*

(01/11/12 & 23/11/12)
Spartak Plovdiv 0-4, 0-5 Chernomorets Burgas *(0-9)*

THIRD ROUND

(02/12/12 & 12/12/12)
Spartak Varna 0-1, 1-7 Litex Lovech *(1-8)*

(02/12/12 & 15/12/12)
Bansko 1-1, 1-2 Minior Pernik *(2-3)*
Beroe Stara Zagora 4-0, 4-1 Lokomotiv Mezdra *(8-1)*
Chavdar Etropole 0-2, 0-5 CSKA Sofia *(0-7)*
Levski Sofia 4-0, 0-1 Cherno More Varna *(4-1)*

(02/12/12 & 16/12/12)
Pirin Gotse Delchev 1-0, 1-1 Neftochimic Burgas *(2-1)*
Slavia Sofia 3-0, 1-0 Botev Plovdiv *(4-0)*

(03/12/12 & 15/12/12)
Lokomotiv Sofia 3-1, 0-1 Chernomorets Burgas *(3-2)*

QUARTER-FINALS

(13/03/13 & 03/04/13)
Beroe Stara Zagora 1-0 Pirin Gotse Delchev *(Élio 25)*
Pirin Gotse Delchev 1-3 Beroe Stara Zagora *(V Marchev 73; Elias 20, Andonov 45, Djoman 65)*
(Beroe Stara Zagora 4-1)

Levski Sofia 1-0 Litex Lovech *(Mendes Rodrigues 22)*
Litex Lovech 2-1 Levski Sofia *(G Milanov 49, Isa 75; Mulder 40)*
(2-2; Levski Sofia on away goal)

Lokomotiv Sofia 0-0 CSKA Sofia
CSKA Sofia 0-1 Lokomotiv Sofia *(Peev 85p)*
(Lokomotiv Sofia 1-0)

Minior Pernik 2-5 Slavia Sofia *(Petrov 66, Yalamov 72; P Dimitrov 10, 17, Zhelev 33, Fernando Livramento 48, Lazarov 61)*
Slavia Sofia 0-1 Minior Pernik *(Okechukwu 88)*
(Slavia Sofia 5-3)

SEMI-FINALS

(17/04/13 & 24/04/13)
Levski Sofia 3-1 Lokomotiv Sofia *(Mendes Rodrigues 64, 75, Velev 83; Iliev 81)*
Lokomotiv Sofia 0-0 Levski Sofia
(Levski Sofia 3-1)

(18/04/13 & 25/04/13)
Slavia Sofia 0-0 Beroe Stara Zagora
Beroe Stara Zagora 1-0 Slavia Sofia *(Andonov 87)*
(Beroe Stara Zagora 1-0)

FINAL

(15/05/13)
Gradski stadium, Lovech
PFC BEROE STARA ZAGORA 3 *(Élio 16, 28, Andonov 79)*
PFC LEVSKI SOFIA 3 *(Yordanov 24, João Silva 80, Mendes Rodrigues 87)*
(aet; 3-1 on pens)
Referee: Krustev
BEROE: Karadzhov, Krumov, Stoychev, Zafirov (Sayoud 93) Penev, Alberto Louzeiro, Elias, David Caiado, Djoman, Élio (Sitoe 64), Andonov (Ivanov 85)
LEVSKI: Plamen I Iliev, Mulder, Élie, D Dimov, Nuno Pinto, Gadzhev (Cristóvão 60), Yovov, Velev, Yordanov (João Silva 74), Mendes Rodrigues, Carvalho (Angelov 91)
Sent off: Yovov (44)

Bulgarian Cup winners Beroe savour their penalty shoot-out win over Levski

CROATIA
Hrvatski Nogometni Savez (HNS)

Address	Vukovarska 269A		**President**	Davor Šuker
	HR-1000 Zagreb		**General secretary**	Damir Vrbanović
Tel	+385 1 2361 555		**Media officer**	Tomislav Pacak
Fax	+385 1 2441 500		**Year of formation**	1912
E-mail	info@hns-cff.hr		**National stadium**	Maksimir, Zagreb
Website	hns-cff.hr			(37,168)

1. HNL CLUBS

1 HNK Cibalia
 2 GNK Dinamo Zagreb
 3 HNK Hajduk Split
4 NK Inter Zaprešić
5 NK Istra
 6 NK Lokomotiva Zagreb

7 NK Osijek
 8 HNK Rijeka
9 NK Slaven Koprivnica
10 RNK Split
11 NK Zadar
12 NK Zagreb

PROMOTED CLUB

13 NK Hrvatski dragovoljac

KEY:

⬤ – UEFA Champions League
⬤ – UEFA Europa League
⬤ – Promoted club
⬤ – Relegated clubs

Easy does it for dominant Dinamo

GNK Dinamo Zagreb's domination of Croatian football continued in 2012/13 with an eighth successive league title. The club from the capital were streets ahead of the opposition, wrapping up the silverware with five matches remaining and finishing with a 20-point winning margin.

At the head of the distant chasing pack were Dinamo's stadium-sharing rivals NK Lokomotiva Zagreb, whose best season in 99 years was complemented by an appearance in the cup final, which they narrowly lost to HNK Hajduk Split. Meanwhile, former Hajduk player Igor Štimac made a promising start as Croatia's national coach.

Eighth successive championship win for Zagreb club	Lokomotiva finish runners-up in league and cup	Hajduk lift Croatian Cup for sixth time

Domestic league

The 1. HNL was reduced from 16 clubs to 12, but while Dinamo were pushed slightly harder, losing four matches, they were still far too good for the opposition, streaking away early on and extending their advantage as the season progressed. Despite their superior class they felt obliged to use two coaches, Ante Čačić going the same way, in mid-season, as the man he had replaced at a similar juncture a year earlier, Krunoslav Jurčić, who would be restored to the position for a third spell - and would go on to capture his seventh title with the club (three as a coach, four as a player).

Under Jurčić, Dinamo lost just once – at NK Osijek in the first spring fixture. Thereafter they won all bar three matches and kept ten successive clean sheets, with goalkeeper Ivan Kelava setting a new league record of 950 minutes without conceding until Lokomotiva defender Ante Puljić ended it in the penultimate round.

Tomislav Ivković's Lokomotiva failed to win any of their last three league games but still took second place with a four-point cushion over HNK Rijeka. It was Lokomotiva's highest league finish and brought a first European qualification. Rijeka boasted the league's top scorer in Leon Benko, who struck 18 goals – three more than Lokomotiva's Andrej Kramarić and five more than Dinamo's star performer, Sammir.

Domestic cup

Hajduk finished fourth in the 1. HNL – after two successive runners-up spots – but found solace in the Croatian Cup. Mišo Krstičević led them through to the final, but he was sacked just before the first leg, with former Hajduk and Juventus centre-back Igor Tudor entrusted to inspire the team to victory over Lokomotiva. He succeeded, but Hajduk were forced to come from behind in both matches, winning 2-1 in Split and drawing 3-3 in a second-leg thriller at the Maksimir.

Europe

For the second season running Dinamo came through three preliminary rounds to reach the group stage of the UEFA Champions League. The champions of Bulgaria, Moldova and Slovenia were all clinically despatched during the summer, but once again Croatia's finest found the going too tough in the autumn. Grouped with FC Porto, Paris Saint-Germain FC and FC Dynamo Kyiv, they were headed for a second successive whitewash until the 95th minute of their final game, at home to Dynamo, when Ivan Krstanović's penalty delivered their first point and first goal.

National team

The promise shown by Croatia under Slaven Bilić at UEFA EURO 2012 was carried forward into the 2014 FIFA World Cup qualifiers under Štimac. In fact, everything was going perfectly to plan until the last fixture of the season, at home to Scotland, when Croatia fell to a shock 1-0 defeat. They had won five of their previous six fixtures and drawn the other away to Belgium, but that one setback left them with an uphill task to dislodge Marc Wilmots' side from the Group A summit with three games remaining, albeit one of them at home to their direct rivals.

A friendly against South Korea at Fulham FC's Craven Cottage in February, which Croatia won 4-0, proved to be a memorable occasion for three distinguished Croatian internationals as Darijo Srna, Stipe Pletikosa and Josip Šimunić all collected their 100th caps. Another stadium in London would be the venue for further Croatian joy three months later as Mario Mandžukić opened the scoring for FC Bayern München in their UEFA Champions League final victory at Wembley.

Domestic league: 1. HNL 2012/13 final table

			Home					Away					Total					
		Pld	W	D	L	F	A	W	D	L	F	A	W	D	L	F	A	Pts
1	**GNK Dinamo Zagreb**	33	14	3	0	45	8	10	2	4	23	12	24	5	4	68	20	77
2	NK Lokomotiva Zagreb	33	11	3	3	32	18	5	6	5	22	20	16	9	8	54	38	57
3	HNK Rijeka	33	9	5	3	24	16	6	3	7	22	26	15	8	10	46	42	53
4	HNK Hajduk Split	33	9	4	4	28	14	5	6	5	17	17	14	10	9	45	31	52
5	RNK Split	33	13	2	2	32	12	2	5	9	17	25	15	7	11	49	37	52
6	NK Istra	33	5	9	2	16	11	6	2	9	19	21	11	11	11	35	32	44
7	NK Osijek	33	7	5	4	15	15	2	7	8	10	18	9	12	12	25	33	39
8	NK Slaven Koprivnica	33	7	5	5	21	23	3	4	9	14	27	10	9	14	35	50	39
9	NK Zadar	33	6	5	5	26	26	3	4	10	13	35	9	9	15	39	61	36
10	NK Inter Zaprešić	33	4	5	7	13	17	4	6	7	23	24	8	11	14	36	41	35
11	HNK Cibalia	33	6	3	7	18	18	3	2	12	11	26	9	5	19	29	44	32
12	NK Zagreb	33	5	2	9	15	26	2	4	11	13	34	7	6	20	28	60	27

SEASON AT A GLANCE

EUROPEAN QUALIFICATION 2013/14

Champion: GNK Dinamo Zagreb (second qualifying round)

Cup winner: HNK Hajduk Split (second qualifying round)
NK Lokomotiva Zagreb (second qualifying round)
HNK Rijeka (second qualifying round)

Top scorer	Leon Benko (Rijeka), 18 goals
Relegated clubs	NK Zagreb, HNK Cibalia, NK Inter Zaprešić
Promoted club	NK Hrvatski dragovoljac
Cup final	HNK Hajduk Split 2-1; 3-3 NK Lokomotiva Zagreb (5-4)

1. HNL TEAM OF THE SEASON
(4-1-3-2)
Coach: Ivković (Lokomotiva)

PLAYER OF THE SEASON
Sammir
(GNK Dinamo Zagreb)

A Dinamo player since 2006, the gifted Brazilian-born playmaker broke new ground in 2012/13, not just with a personal-best tally of 13 goals that helped his club to yet another Croatian title, but also in making himself available to play international football for his adopted land. He made his debut against FYROM in October.

NEWCOMER OF THE SEASON
Alen Halilović
(GNK Dinamo Zagreb)

Dubbed the 'new Luka Modrić', Halilović produced a string of glittering displays for Dinamo, becoming, at 16, the youngest debutant and goalscorer in the history of the Croatian top flight. He also flourished in national colours at the UEFA European Under-17 Championship before making his senior debut eight days short of his 17th birthday.

Kelava (Dinamo)
Boras (Lokomotiva) Barbarić (Lokomotiva) Šimunić (Dinamo) Milić (Istra)
Ademi (Dinamo)
Andrijašević (Hajduk) Sammir (Dinamo) Antolić (Lokomotiva)
Rebić (Split) Benko (Rijeka)

CROATIA

NATIONAL TEAM

Home Kit   Away Kit

INTERNATIONAL TOURNAMENT APPEARANCES

FIFA World Cup (3) 1998 (3rd), 2002, 2006.
UEFA European Championship (4) 1996 (qtr-finals), 2004, 2008 (qtr-finals), 2012

TOP FIVE ALL-TIME CAPS
Darijo Srna (104); **Stipe Pletikosa** (103); **Josip Šimunić** (102); Dario Šimić (100); **Ivica Olić** (85)

TOP FIVE ALL-TIME GOALS
Davor Šuker (45); **Eduardo** (27); **Darijo Srna** (20); **Ivica Olić** (16); **Niko Kranjčar** & Goran Vlaović (15)

Results 2012/13

Date	Opponent		Venue	Score	Scorers
15/08/12	Switzerland	H	Split	2-4	Eduardo (20, 64)
07/09/12	FYROM (WCQ)	H	Zagreb	1-0	Jelavić (69)
11/09/12	Belgium (WCQ)	A	Brussels	1-1	Perišić (6)
12/10/12	FYROM (WCQ)	A	Skopje	2-1	Ćorluka (33), Rakitić (60)
16/10/12	Wales (WCQ)	H	Osijek	2-0	Mandžukić (27), Eduardo (57)
06/02/13	South Korea	N	London (ENG)	4-0	Mandžukić (32), Srna (40), Jelavić (57), Petrić (85)
22/03/13	Serbia (WCQ)	H	Zagreb	2-0	Mandžukić (23), Olić (37)
26/03/13	Wales (WCQ)	A	Swansea	2-1	Lovren (77), Eduardo (87)
07/06/13	Scotland (WCQ)	H	Zagreb	0-1	
10/06/13	Portugal	N	Geneva (SUI)	0-1	

Appearances 2012/13

Coach: Igor Štimac	06/09/67		Sui	MKD	BEL	MKD	WAL	Kor	SRB	WAL	SCO	Por	Caps	Goals
Stipe Pletikosa	08/01/79	Rostov (RUS)	G	G	G	G	G	G	G	G	G		103	-
Darijo Srna	01/05/82	Shakhtar Donetsk (UKR)	D	D	M	D	D	D	D	D	D	D	104	20
Vedran Ćorluka	05/02/86	Lokomotiv Moskva (RUS)	D46	D81	D			D	D	D		D87	64	4
Mario Maloča	04/05/89	Hajduk Split	D										1	-
Danijel Pranjić	02/12/81	Sporting (POR)	D										46	
Milan Badelj	25/02/89	Hamburg (GER)	M60			s84	M			M46			8	1
Niko Kranjčar	13/08/84	Dynamo Kyiv (UKR)	M46	s46			s77	M58	M63		s88		79	15
Ivan Rakitić	10/03/88	Sevilla (ESP)	M	M46		M	M	M	M	M	M	M59	53	9
Ivica Olić	14/09/79	Wolfsburg (GER)	A46		s59			A46	A83	s73	A	A66	85	16
Eduardo	25/02/83	Shakhtar Donetsk (UKR)	A67	A63			A77			A	s56		55	27
Mario Mandžukić	21/05/86	Bayern (GER)	A46	A	A88	A72	A	A46	A	A	A88		41	11
Domagoj Vida	29/04/89	Dinamo Zagreb /Dynamo Kyiv (UKR)	s46	s81	D		s85		s63			D	17	-
Ivan Strinić	17/07/87	Dnipro (UKR)	s46	D	D	D	D	D46	D82	D73	D70	D50	30	-
Ivan Perišić	02/02/89	Dortmund (GER) /Wolfsburg (GER)	s46	M	M	M	M85				M56	s73	20	1
Ante Vukušić	04/06/91	Hajduk Split	s46										1	-
Ognjen Vukojević	20/12/83	Dynamo Kyiv (UKR) /Spartak Moskva (RUS)	s60	M	s78	M	M65			s83		M66	49	4
Luka Modrić	09/09/85	Tottenham (ENG) /Real Madrid (ESP)	s67	M	M	M84	M	M71	M	M		M	66	8
Josip Šimunić	18/02/78	Dinamo Zagreb		D	D	D	D	D	D		D		102	3
Nikica Jelavić	27/08/85	Everton (ENG)		s63	A59	A64		s46					26	5
Gordon Schildenfeld	18/03/85	Dinamo Moskva (RUS) /PAOK (GRE)			D			s46			s46	D	19	-
Josip Radošević	03/04/94	Hajduk Split			M78								1	-
Nikola Kalinić	05/01/88	Dnipro (UKR)			s88	s72					s70	s66	17	5
Sammir	23/04/87	Dinamo Zagreb			s64		s58			M61	M		4	-
Dejan Lovren	05/07/89	Lyon (FRA)					D46	s46	s82	D			17	2
Mladen Petrić	01/01/81	Fulham (ENG)						s46					45	13
Franko Andrijašević	22/06/91	Hajduk Split						s65					1	-
Arijan Ademi	29/05/91	Dinamo Zagreb						s71				s59	2	-
Mateo Kovačić	06/05/94	Internazionale (ITA)							M	s61	M	s66	4	-
Danijel Subašić	27/10/84	Monaco (FRA)										G	5	-
Hrvoje Milić	10/05/89	Istra										M	1	-
Ivo Iličević	14/11/86	Hamburg (GER)										A73	7	1
Alen Halilović	18/06/96	Dinamo Zagreb										s50	1	-
Igor Bubnjić	17/07/92	Slaven Koprivnica										s87	1	-

European club competitions 2012/13

GNK DINAMO ZAGREB

CHAMPIONS LEAGUE

Second qualifying round - PFC Ludogorets Razgrad (BUL)
A 1-1 *Rukavina (90+2)*
Kelava, Ibáñez, Kovačić, Sammir, Tomečak (Rukavina 89), Tonel, Vrsaljko, Badelj, Pivarić (Bećiraj 56), Vida, Čop (Alispahić 75). Coach: Ante Čačić (CRO)
H 3-2 *Rukavina (33, 60), Vida (90+8)*
Kelava, Ibáñez (Alispahić 46), Calello (Čop 62), Kovačić, Sammir, Tonel, Vrsaljko, Badelj, Bećiraj (Peko 72), Vida, Rukavina. Coach: Ante Čačić (CRO)

Third qualifying round - FC Sheriff (MDA)
A 1-0 *Bećiraj (14)*
Kelava, Šimunić, Leko, Sammir (Calello 69), Tonel, Badelj, Pivarić, Bećiraj (Čop 61), Pokrivač, Vida, Rukavina (Alispahić 82). Coach: Ante Čačić (CRO)
H 4-0 *Vida (16), Bećiraj (34), Čop (78), Ibáñez (87)*
Kelava, Šimunić, Ademi, Leko, Tonel, Badelj, Pivarić, Alispahić (Peko 64), Bećiraj (Čop 77), Vida, Rukavina (Ibáñez 84). Coach: Ante Čačić (CRO)

Play-offs - NK Maribor (SVN)
H 2-1 *Čop (10), Badelj (74)*
Kelava, Šimunić, Ademi, Leko (Peko 46), Sammir (Vrsaljko 88), Tonel, Badelj, Pivarić, Vida, Rukavina (Bećiraj 57), Čop. Coach: Ante Čačić (CRO)
A 1-0 *Tonel (12)*
Kelava, Ibáñez, Šimunić, Ademi (Calello 46), Sammir (Krstanović 83), Tonel, Badelj, Pivarić, Bećiraj (Leko 46), Vida, Čop. Coach: Ante Čačić (CRO)

Group A
Match 1 - FC Porto (POR)
H 0-2
Kelava, Šimunić, Calello (Kovačić 80), Ademi (Bećiraj 58), Sammir, Tonel, Pivarić, Vida, Rukavina (Carrasco 67), Brozović, Čop. Coach: Ante Čačić (CRO)
Match 2 - FC Dynamo Kyiv (UKR)
A 0-2
Kelava, Šimunić, Calello (Čop 46), Ademi, Kovačić, Sammir (Carrasco 78), Tonel, Pivarić, Bećiraj (Rukavina 58), Vida, Brozović. Coach: Ante Čačić (CRO)
Match 3 - Paris Saint-Germain FC (FRA)
H 0-2
Kelava, Puljić, Ibáñez (Calello 46), Šimunić, Kovačić (Halilović 90+1), Sammir, Vrsaljko, Pivarić, Vida, Brozović, Čop (Rukavina 70). Coach: Ante Čačić (CRO)
Match 4 - Paris Saint-Germain FC (FRA)
A 0-4
Kelava, Puljić, Šimunić (Čop 62), Ademi, Kovačić (Halilović 86), Sammir, Vrsaljko, Pivarić, Vida, Rukavina (Calello 73), Brozović. Coach: Ante Čačić (CRO)

Match 5 - FC Porto (POR)
A 0-3
Kelava, Šimunić, Ademi, Kovačić, Sammir (Puljić 76), Vrsaljko, Pivarić, Bećiraj (Krstanović 86), Vida, Brozović, Čop (Halilović 84). Coach: Ante Čačić (CRO)
Match 6 - FC Dynamo Kyiv (UKR)
H 1-1 *Krstanović (90+5p)*
Kelava, Ibáñez, Šimunić, Ademi, Kovačić, Sammir, Vrsaljko, Bećiraj, Vida, Brozović (Pivarić 71), Čop (Krstanović 60). Coach: Krunoslav Jurčić (CRO)

HNK HAJDUK SPLIT

EUROPA LEAGUE

Second qualifying round - Skonto FC (LVA)
H 2-0 *Vukušić (34), Trebotić (58)*
Blažević, Vršajević, Andrijašević (Stojanović 88), Vukušić, Radošević, Jozinović, Caktaš, Maloča, Jonjić, Trebotić (Kukoč 78), Sušić (Ozobić 66). Coach: Mišo Krstičević (CRO)
A 0-1
Blažević, Stojanović, Milović, Vršajević, Oremuš (Tomaš 90+4), Vukušić, Radošević, Luštica, Caktaš (Vuković 77), Maloča, Maglica (Ozobić 61). Coach: Mišo Krstičević (CRO)

Third qualifying round - FC Internazionale Milano (ITA)
H 0-3
Blažević, Milović, Vršajević, Andrijašević (Milić 54), Oremuš (Tomaš 78), Vukušić, Radošević, Jozinović, Caktaš, Ozobić (Maglica 46), Maloča. Coach: Mišo Krstičević (CRO)
A 2-0 *Vukušić (23p), Vuković (58)*
Blažević, Milić, Milović, Vršajević, Andrijašević (Caktaš 59), Oremuš, Vukušić, Radošević, Jozinović, Maloča (Jonjić 10), Vuković (Luštica 83). Coach: Mišo Krstičević (CRO)

NK SLAVEN KOPRIVNICA

EUROPA LEAGUE

Second qualifying round - Portadown FC (NIR)
H 6-0 *Breen (1og), Bušić (13, 33), Rak (56, 71, 80)*
Rodić, Kokalović, Bubnjić (Pilipović 72), Bušić (Šaban 58), Brlek, Delić, Vugrinec (Grgić 64), Purić, Rak, Maras, Batarelo. Coach: Roy Ferenčina (CRO)

A 4-2 *Bubnjić (10), Brlek (14), Šaban (62, 64)*
Rodić, Takač, Grgić, Bubnjić (Kokalović 62), Šaban, Brlek, Delić (Bušić 68), Šestak, Kuprešak, Maras, Batarelo (Čanadjija 46). Coach: Roy Ferenčina (CRO)

Third qualifying round - Athletic Club (ESP)
A 1-3 *Delić (19)*
Rodić, Kokalović, Grgić, Bubnjić, Čanadjija, Bušić (Šaban 53), Delić (Glavica 59), Purić, Rak (Pilipović 81), Maras, Batarelo. Coach: Roy Ferenčina (CRO)
H 2-1 *Maras (28), Gregurina (68)*
Rodić, Kokalović, Bubnjić, Čanadjija (Grgić 74), Bušić, Glavica, Delić (Vugrinec 59), Purić, Rak, Maras, Batarelo (Gregurina 66). Coach: Roy Ferenčina (CRO)

NK OSIJEK

EUROPA LEAGUE

First qualifying round - FC Santa Coloma (AND)
A 1-0 *Miličević (77)*
Vargić, Vrgoč, Kurtović, Pušić, Perošević (Zulim 81), Lešković, Ibriks, Jugović, Petrović (Miličević 41), Kvržić (M Mišić 89), Smoje. Coach: Stanko Mršić (CRO)
H 3-1 *Kvržić (28), Perošević (56), Jugović (70)*
Vargić, Vrgoč, Kurtović (Zulim 75), Perošević, Lešković, Ibriks, Jugović, Petrović, Kvržić (J Mišić 47), Smoje, Miličević (Novaković 88). Coach: Stanko Mršić (CRO)

Second qualifying round - Kalmar FF (SWE)
H 1-3 *Miličević (5)*
Vargić, Vrgoč, Kurtović, Perošević, Lešković, Ibriks, Jugović, Petrović (J Mišić 72), Kvržić (Dugandžić 79), Smoje, Miličević (Aleksić 66). Coach: Stanko Mršić (CRO)
Red card: Lešković 63
A 0-3
Vargić, Vrgoč, Kurtović (J Mišić 67), Dugandžić (Pavić 83), Perošević, Ibriks, Jugović, Kvržić, Smoje, Miličević (Pongračić 58), Leko. Coach: Stanko Mršić (CRO)
Red card: Kvržić 88

Domestic league club-by-club

HNK CIBALIA

Coach: Samir Toplak; (30/07/12) Željko Kopić;
(11/12/12) Miroslav Bojko
1919 • HNK Cibalia (10,000) • hnk-cibalia.hr

2012

22/07	Slaven	h	0-3	
28/07	Dinamo	a	1-2	Bartolović
04/08	Inter	h	1-1	Puljić
11/08	Istra	h	0-1	
18/08	Split	a	1-3	Bartolović
25/08	Zadar	h	0-0	
31/08	Zagreb	a	1-0	Vitaić
15/09	Lokomotiva	h	3-2	Bartolović, Mazalović 2
22/09	Osijek	a	0-1	
29/09	Rijeka	h	4-1	og (Neretljak), Matoš 2 (1p), Terzić
05/10	Hajduk	a	0-4	
20/10	Slaven	a	1-2	Matoš (p)
27/10	Dinamo	h	0-1	
03/11	Inter	a	0-0	
10/11	Istra	a	0-3	
17/11	Split	h	2-1	Mazalović (p), Filipović
24/11	Zadar	a	1-4	og (Heister)
01/12	Zagreb	h	1-1	Mišić
07/12	Lokomotiva	a	0-1	

2013

16/02	Osijek	h	2-0	Mazalović 2 (2p)
23/02	Rijeka	a	0-0	
02/03	Hajduk	h	0-2	
09/03	Slaven	a	2-0	Mazalović (p), Mišić
16/03	Rijeka	h	0-1	
30/03	Split	a	0-1	
06/04	Lokomotiva	h	2-0	Mazalović (p), Filipović
13/04	Hajduk	a	1-2	Bartolović
20/04	Dinamo	h	0-1	
27/04	Istra	a	1-2	Bartolović
04/05	Zadar	h	2-3	Vitaić 2
10/05	Zagreb	a	2-0	Vitaić (p), Terzić
18/05	Inter	h	1-0	Vitaić (p)
26/05	Osijek	a	0-1	

No	Name	Nat	DoB	Pos	Aps	(s)	Gls
20	Mate Bajić		03/11/95	D	1		
11	Mladen Bartolović	BIH	10/04/77	A	23	(5)	5
18	Drago Ćorić		04/02/93	M	2	(5)	
25	Marko Čulić		10/02/87	M	12	(3)	
20	Marko Dabro		28/03/97	A	1	(3)	
19	Petar Filipović		14/09/90	M	19	(1)	2
2	Josip Gegić		05/01/90	D	2	(3)	
21	Tomislav Jonjić		19/05/83	M	1	(2)	
21	Tomislav Jurić		08/04/90	M	1	(4)	
9	Ivan Koledić		27/09/89	A	7	(12)	
30	Mario Lučić		25/06/80	D	5		
1	Mladen Matković		12/05/89	G	27		
4	Marin Matoš		26/01/89	M	20	(2)	3
28	Tomislav Mazalović		10/06/90	M	28		7
17	Mato Miloš		30/06/93	D	9	(2)	
3	Petar Mišić		10/11/93	M	23	(7)	2
15	Matej Mitrović		10/11/93	D	32	(1)	
13	Luka Muž-enjak		07/04/93	D	17	(5)	
19	Leopold Novak		03/12/90	M	2		
12	Michael Paradjiković		09/01/92	G	6	(1)	
10	Tomislav Pavličić		06/12/83	M	15	(4)	
8	Jakov Puljić		04/08/93	M	5	(15)	1
24	Dario Rugašević		29/01/91	D	30		
26	Marko Terzić		25/05/91	M	11	(11)	2
16	Niko Tokić		07/06/88	A	2	(9)	
22	Frane Vitaić		07/06/82	M	30	(1)	5
14	Matias Zubak		17/10/89	A		(1)	
13	Dario Župarić		03/05/92	D	32		

GNK DINAMO ZAGREB

Coach: Ante Čačić; (26/11/12) Krunoslav Jurčić
1945 • Maksimir (37,168) • gnkdinamo.hr
Major honours
Inter Cities Fairs Cup (1) 1967;
Yugoslav League (4) 1948, 1954, 1958, 1982;
Croatian League (15) 1993, 1996, 1997, 1998, 1999, 2000,
2003, 2006, 2007, 2008, 2009, 2010, 2011, 2012, 2013;
Yugoslav Cup (8) 1951, 1960, 1963, 1965, 1969,
1973, 1980, 1983;
Croatian Cup (12) 1994, 1996, 1997, 1998, 2001, 2002,
2004, 2007, 2008, 2009, 2011, 2012

2012

21/07	Inter	h	1-1	Sammir
28/07	Cibalia	h	2-1	Leko (p), Čop
04/08	Istra	a	1-0	Sammir (p)
12/08	Split	h	4-2	Badelj, Šimunić, Sammir (p), Čop
18/08	Zadar	a	3-1	Čop, Sammir 2 (1p)
25/08	Zagreb	h	6-0	Alispahić, Vida, Sammir 2 (1p), Bećiraj, Leko
01/09	Lokomotiva	a	3-1	Rukavina, Vida, Sammir (p)
14/09	Osijek	h	0-0	
22/09	Rijeka	a	0-3	
29/09	Hajduk	h	3-1	Sammir 2 (1p), Čop
07/10	Slaven	a	4-1	og (Gregurina), Ibáñez, Rukavina, Halilović
20/10	Inter	a	2-0	Puljić, Čop
27/10	Cibalia	a	1-0	Krstanović
02/11	Istra	h	3-1	Vida 2, Sammir
10/11	Split	a	0-1	
17/11	Zadar	h	5-0	Kovačić, Halilović, Bećiraj, Pivarić, Krstanović
25/11	Zagreb	a	1-0	
30/11	Lokomotiva	h	1-0	Čop

2013

10/02	Osijek	a	1-2	Ademi
17/02	Rijeka	h	4-1	Krstanović, Čop 3
27/02	Hajduk	a	2-1	Krstanović, Ibáñez
02/03	Slaven	h	3-0	Sammir, Ademi, Pivarić
10/03	Osijek	h	0-0	
16/03	Istra	a	0-0	
30/03	Zadar	h	5-0	Krstanović, Šimunović, Bećiraj, Pivarić, Ademi
05/04	Zagreb	a	3-0	Bećiraj, Krstanović 2
14/04	Inter	h	2-0	Husejinović, Brozović
20/04	Cibalia	a	1-0	Jedvaj
27/04	Slaven	h	1-0	og (Bubnjić)
05/05	Rijeka	a	0-0	
11/05	Split	h	2-0	Rukavina, Husejinović
18/05	Lokomotiva	a	2-1	Pamić, Sammir
26/05	Hajduk	h	3-1	Pamić, Rukavina, Brozović

No	Name	Nat	DoB	Pos	Aps	(s)	Gls
13	Lee Addy	GHA	07/07/90	D	8		
6	Arijan Ademi		29/05/91	M	19	(5)	3
20	Mehmed Alispahić	BIH	24/11/87	M	7	(6)	1
16	Milan Badelj		25/02/89	M	2		1
21	Fatos Bećiraj	MNE	05/05/88	A	20	(7)	4
26	Fran Brodić		08/01/97	A		(1)	
77	Marcelo Brozović		16/11/92	M	18	(5)	2
5	Adrián Calello	ARG	14/05/87	M	5	(1)	
15	Josip Ćalušić		11/10/93	D		(2)	
17	Bryan Carrasco	CHI	31/01/91	D	3		
90	Duje Čop		01/02/90	A	15	(4)	9
28	Alen Halilović		18/06/96	M	7	(11)	2
17	Said Husejinović	BIH	13/05/88	M	6	(4)	2
23	Luis Ibáñez	ARG	10/05/88	D	17	(3)	2
16	Tin Jedvaj		28/11/95	D	13		1
30	Ivan Kelava		20/02/88	G	33		
8	Mateo Kovačić		06/05/94	M	9	(2)	1
99	Ivan Krstanović		05/01/83	A	14	(8)	7
7	Jerko Leko		09/04/80	M	12	(2)	2
77	Zvonko Pamić		04/02/91	M	3	(6)	2
18	Ivan Peko		05/01/90	A	1	(6)	
12	Josip Pivarić		30/01/89	D	24	(4)	3
23	Nikola Pokrivač		26/11/85	M	2	(2)	
28	Ante Puljić		05/11/87	D	6	(4)	1
55	Ante Rukavina		18/06/86	A	16	(7)	4
10	Sammir		23/04/87	M	25	(3)	13
4	Josip Šimunić		18/02/78	D	25		1
5	Jozo Šimunović		04/08/94	D	2	(1)	1
26	Dino Špehar		08/02/94	A		(1)	
11	Ivan Tomečak		07/12/89	M	5	(3)	
13	Tonel	POR	13/04/80	D	6		
24	Domagoj Vida		29/04/89	D	15		4
14	Šime Vrsaljko		10/01/92	D	25		

HNK HAJDUK SPLIT

Coach: Mišo Krstičević; (29/04/13) Igor Tudor
1911 • Poljud (34,200) • hajduk.hr
Major honours
Yugoslav League (9) 1927, 1929, 1950, 1952, 1955,
1971, 1974, 1975, 1979;
Croatian League (6) 1992, 1994, 1995, 2001, 2004, 2005;
Yugoslav Cup (9) 1967, 1972, 1974, 1975, 1976, 1977,
1984, 1987, 1991;
Croatian Cup (6) 1993, 1995, 2000, 2003, 2010, 2013

2012

22/07	Istra	a	0-0	
29/07	Split	h	1-0	Andrijašević
05/08	Zadar	a	4-2	Vukušić, Caktaš, Andrijašević, Vuković
12/08	Zagreb	h	5-1	Vukušić 2, Caktaš 2, Maglica
19/08	Lokomotiva	a	0-2	
26/08	Osijek	h	1-1	Caktaš
01/09	Rijeka	a	0-1	
15/09	Inter	a	1-1	Milić
23/09	Slaven	h	3-1	Andrijašević 2, Vuković
29/09	Dinamo	a	1-3	Caktaš
05/10	Cibalia	h	4-0	Vuković 2 (2p), Caktaš, Milić
21/10	Istra	h	0-1	
28/10	Split	a	1-0	Vršajević
03/11	Zadar	h	3-0	Vuković, Bencun, Kiš
09/11	Zagreb	a	1-0	Andrijašević
17/11	Lokomotiva	h	0-0	
24/11	Osijek	a	0-1	
02/12	Rijeka	h	1-1	Maglica
07/12	Inter	h	1-0	Milić

2013

16/02	Slaven	a	2-0	Jonjić, Vuković
27/02	Dinamo	h	1-2	Jozinović
02/03	Cibalia	a	2-0	Maglica 2
09/03	Istra	a	1-2	Vuković (p)
17/03	Zadar	a	1-1	Caktaš
30/03	Zagreb	h	3-2	Maloča (p), Caktaš, Vuković
07/04	Inter	a	1-1	Andrijašević
13/04	Cibalia	h	2-1	Caktaš, Vuković
21/04	Slaven	h	1-2	Kouassi
28/04	Rijeka	h	1-2	Sušić
04/05	Split	a	1-2	Kouassi
12/05	Lokomotiva	h	0-0	
18/05	Osijek	h	1-0	Maglica
26/05	Dinamo	a	1-3	og (Pamić)

No	Name	Nat	DoB	Pos	Aps	(s)	Gls
7	Franko Andrijašević		22/06/91	M	22	(2)	6
30	Josip Bašić		02/03/96	M		(1)	
32	Marko Bencun		09/11/92	A	4	(7)	1
1	Goran Blažević		07/06/86	G	29		
18	Mijo Caktaš		08/05/92	M	29	(1)	9
16	Ivan Jakov Djoni		25/07/94	A		(2)	
19	Josip Elez		25/04/94	D		(2)	
13	Antonio Jakoliš		28/02/92	A	2	(5)	
27	Matej Jonjić		29/01/91	D	7	(4)	1
17	Goran Jozinović		27/08/90	D	18	(4)	1
12	Lovre Kalinić		03/04/90	G	4		
33	Tomislav Kiš		04/04/94	A		(11)	1
77	Jean Kouassi	CIV	25/09/94	A	10	(3)	2
21	Miro Kovačić		29/08/94	M		(2)	
17	Tonči Kukoč		25/09/90	M		(1)	
35	Luka Lučić		02/01/95	D	1		
16	Steven Luštica	AUS	12/04/91	M	1	(6)	
9	Anton Maglica		11/11/91	A	13	(4)	5
22	Mario Maloča		04/05/89	D	23		1
2	Dino Mikanović		07/05/94	D		(1)	
4	Antonio Milić		10/03/94	M	21	(5)	3
5	Goran Milović		29/01/89	D	22	(1)	
14	Tonči Mujan		19/07/95	A		(2)	
23	Zoran Nižić		11/10/89	D	5	(1)	
11	Mirko Oremuš		06/09/88	M	24	(2)	
20	Filip Ozobić		08/04/91	M	1	(5)	
32	Mario Pašalić		09/02/95	M		(2)	
15	Zoran Plazonić		01/02/89	M	4	(3)	
2	Josip Radošević		03/04/94	M	17		
28	Rúben Lima	POR	03/10/89	D	18	(4)	
3	Danijel Stojanović		18/08/84	D	18	(2)	
31	Tino-Sven Sušić	BEL	13/02/92	M	11	(6)	1
29	Ivo-Valentino Tomas		28/07/93	M	2	(2)	
10	Dinko Trebotić		30/07/90	M		(1)	
6	Avdija Vršajević	BIH	06/03/86	D	26		1
24	Ivan Vuković	MNE	09/02/87	A	26	(3)	9
13	Ante Vukušić		04/06/91	A	5		3

NK INTER ZAPREŠIĆ

Coach: Borimir Perković; (10/03/13) Rajko Magić
1929 • ŠRC Zaprešić (4,500) • inter.hr
Major honours
Croatian Cup (1) 1992

2012

21/07	Dinamo	a	1-1	Oršić	
27/07	Lokomotiva	h	0-1		
04/08	Cibalia	a	1-1	Šarić (p)	
10/08	Osijek	h	0-3		
18/08	Istra	a	1-3	Kramarić	
24/08	Rijeka	h	2-0	Šarić 2 (2p)	
01/09	Split	a	0-1		
15/09	Hajduk	h	1-1	Oršić	
22/09	Zadar	a	5-1	Budimir 3 (1p), Oršić, Jurić	
29/09	Slaven	h	2-2	Šarić, Budimir	
05/10	Zagreb	a	1-1	Šarić	
20/10	Dinamo	h	0-2		
26/10	Lokomotiva	a	3-2	Oršić, Kramarić 2	
03/11	Cibalia	h	0-0		
10/11	Osijek	a	1-1	Budimir	
16/11	Istra	h	2-0	Kramarić, Milardović	
24/11	Rijeka	a	1-2	Oršić	
30/11	Split	h	0-2		
07/12	Hajduk	a	0-1		

2013

15/02	Zadar	h	0-1		
23/02	Slaven	a	2-2	Oršić 2	
01/03	Zagreb	a	1-2	Budimir (p)	
09/03	Rijeka	a	1-2	Oršić	
15/03	Split	h	0-0		
28/03	Lokomotiva	a	2-2	Oršić 2	
07/04	Hajduk	h	1-1	Budimir (p)	
14/04	Dinamo	a	0-2		
19/04	Istra	a	0-2		
27/04	Zadar	a	2-1	Oršić, Budimir	
03/05	Zagreb	h	2-0	Mlinar, Budimir (p)	
11/05	Osijek	a	2-0	Budimir, Šarić (p)	
18/05	Cibalia	h	0-1		
26/05	Slaven	h	2-0	Mlinar, Oršić (p)	

No	Name	Nat	DoB	Pos	Aps	(s)	Gls
5	Matej Bagarić		16/01/89	D	25		
4	Luka Batur		28/11/89	D	13		
19	Ivan Blažević		25/07/92	M	1	(3)	
13	Tomislav Bosec		14/06/90	A	1	(4)	
8	Ante Budimir		22/07/91	A	31		10
7	Marko Buljat		10/01/90	D	18	(7)	
25	Marko Ćosić		02/03/94	M		(1)	
1	Matej Delač		20/08/92	G	14		
19	Uroš Djerić	SRB	27/05/92	A		(1)	
17	Josip Filipović		08/05/96	D	8	(3)	
27	Borko Gorgiev		13/02/95	M	2	(5)	
6	Bernard Gulić		09/04/92	D	4	(1)	
29	Irfan Hadjić	BIH	15/06/93	A	3		
31	Luka Hadjić		28/02/93	M	2	(1)	
21	Haris Hajradinović	BIH	18/02/94	D	2	(6)	
17	Tomislav Haramuštek		17/07/93	M		(2)	
15	Ivan Herceg		10/02/90	D	26	(2)	
22	Tomi Jurić	AUS	22/07/91	A	4	(8)	1
7	Mirko Kramarić		27/01/89	M	20	(7)	4
9	Matija Matko		20/09/82	A	5	(8)	
18	Josip Milardović		10/01/82	M	22	(3)	1
14	Frano Mlinar		30/03/92	M	30		2
20	Mislav Oršić		29/12/92	M	33		12
18	Hrvoje Plazanić		18/09/90	D	19	(4)	
28	Nikola Pokrivač		26/11/85	M	12		
2	Nikola Radojičić	SRB	19/01/92	D	3	(2)	
6	Milan Runudić	SRB	29/03/92	D	2	(1)	
32	Krševan Santini		11/04/87	G	19		
16	Tomislav Šarić		24/06/90	M	28	(3)	6
13	Filip Šćrbec		03/06/91	M	1	(6)	
19	Mario Šimić		28/08/92	M		(3)	
26	Stephan Vujcic	GER	03/01/86	M	15	(10)	

NK ISTRA

Coach: Igor Pamić
1948 • Aldo Drosina (8,923) • nkistra1961.hr

2012

22/07	Hajduk	h	0-0		
29/07	Slaven	a	1-3	Križman	
04/08	Dinamo	h	0-1		
11/08	Cibalia	a	1-0	Križman	
18/08	Inter	h	3-1	Križman, Havojić, Jugović	
25/08	Split	h	1-0	Ottochian	
01/09	Zadar	a	1-1	Pamić	
15/09	Zagreb	h	0-0		
21/09	Lokomotiva	a	0-1		
29/09	Osijek	h	1-3	Roce	
06/10	Rijeka	a	1-2	Bačelić-Grgić (p)	
21/10	Hajduk	a	1-0	Roce	
26/10	Slaven	h	0-0		
02/11	Dinamo	a	1-3	Roce	
10/11	Cibalia	h	3-0	Roce, Aganović 2	
16/11	Inter	a	0-2		
24/11	Split	a	1-2	Roce	
01/12	Zadar	h	1-1	Bačelić-Grgić (p)	
07/12	Zagreb	h	1-2	Roce	

2013

16/02	Lokomotiva	h	2-2	Bačelić-Grgić 2 (1p)	
23/02	Osijek	a	0-0		
03/03	Rijeka	h	1-1	Bačelić-Grgić (p)	
09/03	Hajduk	a	2-1	Milić, Budicin	
16/03	Dinamo	h	0-0		
29/03	Osijek	a	4-0	Roce 3, Aganović	
06/04	Zadar	a	2-3	Roce, Milić	
13/04	Zagreb	h	0-0		
19/04	Inter	a	2-0	Križman, Milić	
27/04	Cibalia	h	2-1	Milić, Križman	
05/05	Slaven	a	0-1		
10/05	Rijeka	a	1-0	Hadjić	
18/05	Split	a	1-0	Havojić	
26/05	Lokomotiva	h	1-1	Roce	

No	Name	Nat	DoB	Pos	Aps	(s)	Gls
21	Adnan Aganović		03/10/87	M	16	(2)	3
7	Mislav Andjelković		22/04/88	M	17	(1)	
8	Stipe Bačelić-Grgić		16/02/88	M	16	(10)	5
23	Slavko Blagojević		21/03/87	M	25	(4)	
6	Fausto Budicin		01/05/82	D	30		1
2	Igor Čagalj		08/10/82	D	20		
13	Chung Woon	KOR	30/06/89	D	10	(2)	
14	Luka Hadjić		28/02/93	M	5	(5)	1
30	Tomislav Havojić		17/06/84	M	11	(1)	2
27	Ivor Horvat		19/08/91	D	2	(3)	
4	Vedran Jerković		13/10/91	M	3	(3)	
1	Antonio Ježina		05/06/89	G	11		
28	Igor Jugović		23/01/89	M	8	(7)	1
10	Sandi Križman		17/08/89	A	28		5
30	Siniša Linić		23/08/82	M	2	(3)	
3	Hrvoje Milić		10/05/89	D	29	(2)	4
9	Jure Obšivač		28/05/90	M	11		
20	Andrea Ottochian		28/06/88	M	12	(8)	1
19	Alen Pamić		15/10/89	M	12	(2)	1
16	Nikola Prelčec		12/11/89	M	5	(11)	
26	Krešimir Prgomet		20/06/86	A	9	(6)	
12	Andrej Prskalo		01/05/87	M	19		
25	Božidar Radošević		04/04/89	G	3		
11	Goran Roce		12/04/86	A	23	(2)	11
9	Ahmad Sharbini		21/02/84	A	3	(3)	
4	Slobodan Stranatić		27/11/85	D	3		
5	Mateo Sušić	BIH	18/11/90	M	25	(2)	
17	Ivan Zgrablić		15/03/91	D	7	(8)	

NK LOKOMOTIVA ZAGREB

Coach: Tomislav Ivković
1914 • Maksimir (37,168) • nklokomotiva.hr

2012

20/07	Zagreb	a	2-0	Bručić, Boras	
27/07	Inter	a	1-0	Antolić (p)	
03/08	Osijek	h	0-0		
11/08	Rijeka	a	2-2	Brozović, Boras	
19/08	Hajduk	h	2-0	Kramarić, Boras	
24/08	Slaven	a	2-3	Kramarić, Boras	
01/09	Dinamo	h	1-3	Kramarić (p)	
15/09	Cibalia	a	2-3	Kramarić 2 (1p)	
21/09	Istra	h	1-0	Kramarić (p)	
30/09	Split	a	1-1	Martinac	
05/10	Zadar	h	2-1	Bručić, Kramarić	
19/10	Zagreb	h	1-1	Kramarić	
26/10	Inter	h	2-3	Barbarić, Kramarić	
04/11	Osijek	a	2-1	Mesarić, Kramarić	
11/11	Rijeka	h	2-1	Trebotić, Martinac	
17/11	Hajduk	h	0-0		
23/11	Slaven	h	3-1	Antolić, Barbarić, Kramarić (p)	
30/11	Dinamo	a	0-1		
07/12	Cibalia	h	1-0	Antolić	

2013

16/02	Istra	a	2-2	Boras, Kramarić (p)	
22/02	Split	h	3-2	Puljić, Antolić, Kramarić	
02/03	Zadar	a	0-1		
08/03	Zadar	h	4-1	Barbarić, Boras, Mesarić, Kramarić	
15/03	Zagreb	h	4-2	Pjaca, Antolić, Bručić, Barbarić	
28/03	Inter	h	2-2	Šitum, Chago	
06/04	Cibalia	a	0-2		
13/04	Slaven	h	5-1	og (Pranjić), Barbarić, Pjaca, Kramarić, Peko	
20/04	Rijeka	a	3-1	Antolić, Šitum, Peko	
26/04	Split	h	1-0	og (Galović)	
03/05	Osijek	h	1-0	Antolić	
12/05	Hajduk	h	0-0		
18/05	Dinamo	h	1-2	Puljić	
26/05	Istra	a	1-1	Chago	

No	Name	Nat	DoB	Pos	Aps	(s)	Gls
7	Domagoj Antolić		30/06/90	M	28	(1)	7
4	Tomislav Barbarić		29/03/89	D	27		5
14	Ivan Boras		31/10/91	M	28	(3)	6
23	Marcelo Brozović		16/11/92	M	6		1
11	Luka Ibrahim		17/04/92	D	30	(1)	3
15	Mathias Chago	CMR	13/03/88	M	4	(1)	2
20	Andrej Kramarić		19/06/91	A	31	(1)	16
21	Igor Lovrić		07/10/87	G	6	(1)	
24	Ivan Lovrić		10/04/90	M		(3)	
8	Mate Maleš		13/01/89	M	20	(1)	
10	Tomislav Martinac		27/06/83	M	1	(16)	2
5	Leonard Mesarić		10/08/83	D	32		2
2	Filip Mrzljak		16/04/93	D	12	(4)	
3	Mario Musa		06/07/90	D	16	(4)	
24	Darijan Pavičić		09/03/94	M	9	(3)	
25	Pejo Pejić		10/12/92	M		(5)	
17	Ivan Peko		05/01/90	A	3	(4)	2
1	Dominik Picak		12/02/92	G	22		
19	Marko Pjaca		06/05/95	M	11	(6)	2
6	Ante Puljić		05/11/87	D	8		2
30	Darijan Radelić Žarkov		21/07/92	G	5		
45	Lamin Samateh	GAM	26/06/92	D	14	(3)	
18	Mario Šitum		04/04/92	A	16	(10)	2
31	Filip Škvorc		22/07/91	A	3		
21	Marin Tomšić		17/10/93	M		(3)	
23	Dinko Trebotić		30/07/90	M	20	(2)	1
27	Goran Zakarić	BIH	07/11/92	M	12	(10)	

NK OSIJEK

Coach: Stanko Mršić; (13/05/13) (Miroslav Žitnjak)
1947 • Gradski vrt (19,500) • nk-osijek.hr
Major honours
Croatian Cup (1) 1999

2012

Date	Opp		Score	Scorers
22/07	Zadar	a	0-0	
29/07	Zagreb	h	1-0	Kvržić
03/08	Lokomotiva	a	0-0	
10/08	Inter	a	3-0	Perošević 2, J Mišić
18/08	Rijeka	h	1-1	Perošević (p)
26/08	Hajduk	a	1-1	Lešković
02/09	Slaven	h	1-2	Kvržić (p)
14/09	Dinamo	a	0-0	
22/09	Cibalia	h	1-0	Ibriks
29/09	Istra	a	3-1	Milićević 2, Lešković
06/10	Split	h	2-2	Lešković, Milićević
20/10	Zadar	a	2-0	Pušić, Pongračić
26/10	Zagreb	a	1-2	Kvržić
04/11	Lokomotiva	h	1-2	Zubak
10/11	Inter	h	1-1	Zubak
18/11	Rijeka	a	1-3	Zubak
24/11	Hajduk	h	0-0	
01/12	Slaven	a	0-2	
2013				
10/02	Dinamo	h	2-1	Vrgoč, Pušić
16/02	Cibalia	a	0-2	
23/02	Istra	h	0-0	
01/03	Split	a	0-0	
10/03	Dinamo	a	0-0	
15/03	Slaven	a	0-0	
29/03	Istra	h	0-4	
06/04	Rijeka	a	0-1	
13/04	Zadar	h	1-0	Kvržić
20/04	Split	a	1-4	Perošević
27/04	Zagreb	h	1-0	Lešković
03/05	Lokomotiva	a	0-1	
11/05	Inter	h	0-2	
18/05	Hajduk	a	0-1	
26/05	Cibalia	h	1-0	Perošević

No	Name	Nat	DoB	Pos	Aps	(s)	Gls
14	Ivan Aleksić		06/03/93	D	16	(2)	
11	Gavro Bagić		02/05/85	A	1	(5)	
9	Dragan Blatnjak	BIH	01/08/81	M	9		
9	Marko Dugandžić		07/04/94	A	1	(5)	
18	Marin Glavaš		17/03/92	M	5	(13)	
15	Ivan Ibriks		06/10/87	D	27	(1)	1
7	Ivan Jakovljević		03/10/90	A	2	(5)	
17	Vedran Jugović		10/09/89	M	11		
26	Bruno Krstanović		18/05/88	M	2	(3)	
4	Hrvoje Kurtović		06/10/83	M	25		
21	Zoran Kvržić	BIH	07/08/88	M	29	(1)	4
28	Mislav Leko		19/12/87	D	13	(2)	
13	Marko Lešković		27/04/91	D	27	(1)	4
6	Andrej Lukić		02/04/94	M	2	(10)	
9	Karlo Lulić		10/05/96	M		(1)	
25	Marko Malenica		08/02/94	G	1		
17	Nikola Mandić		19/03/95	A	1	(6)	
1	Zvonimir Mikulić		05/02/90	G	14		
26	Ivan Milićević		11/02/88	A	11	(1)	3
22	Benedikt Mioc		06/10/94	M		(1)	
27	Josip Mišić		28/06/94	M	5	(5)	1
8	Matija Mišić		30/01/92	M	6	(4)	
16	Saša Novaković		27/05/91	D	13	(4)	
3	Antonio Pavić		18/11/94	D	5	(3)	
10	Antonio Perošević		06/03/92	A	21	(1)	5
20	Nikša Petrović		27/01/92	A	1		
7	Mihael Pongračić		24/08/93	M	13	(13)	1
5	Domagoj Pušić		24/10/91	M	21	(1)	2
24	Ivo Smoje		21/11/78	D	27		
16	Andrej Šimunec		01/03/95	D	1		
22	Tomislav Šorša		11/05/89	M	1		
23	Josip Tomašević		26/09/93	D	1		
25	Ivan Vargić		15/03/87	G	18		
2	Branko Vrgoč		18/12/89	D	20		1
20	Matias Zubak		17/10/89	A	4	(4)	3
19	Marin Zulim		26/10/91	A	9	(6)	

HNK RIJEKA

Coach: Elvis Scoria; (27/02/13) Matjaž Kek (SVN)
1946 • Kantrida (11,000) • nk-rijeka.hr
Major honours
Yugoslav Cup (2) 1978, 1979;
Croatian Cup (2) 2005, 2006

2012

Date	Opp		Score	Scorers
20/07	Split	a	0-2	
27/07	Zadar	h	0-0	
03/08	Zagreb	a	1-0	Weitzer
11/08	Lokomotiva	h	2-2	Weitzer, Benko
18/08	Osijek	a	1-1	Mujanović
24/08	Inter	a	0-2	
01/09	Hajduk	h	1-0	Kreilach
16/09	Slaven	a	3-1	Cesarec, Benko, Močinić
22/09	Dinamo	h	3-0	Cesarec, Weitzer, Kreilach (p)
29/09	Cibalia	a	1-4	
06/10	Istra	h	2-1	Cesarec, Datković
20/10	Split	h	2-3	Benko, Datković
27/10	Zadar	a	4-2	Cesarec, Benko, Kreilach (p), Čulina
03/11	Zagreb	h	1-0	Benko
11/11	Lokomotiva	a	1-0	Neretljak
18/11	Osijek	h	3-1	Brezovec, Cesarec 2
24/11	Inter	h	2-1	Benko 2
02/12	Hajduk	a	1-1	Benko
08/12	Slaven	h	0-0	
2013				
17/02	Dinamo	a	1-4	Benko
23/02	Cibalia	h	0-0	
03/03	Istra	a	1-1	Kreilach (p)
09/03	Inter	h	2-1	Kreilach, Cesarec
16/03	Cibalia	a	1-0	Benko
29/03	Slaven	h	2-1	Benko 2
06/04	Osijek	h	1-0	Benko
12/04	Split	a	1-3	Benko
20/04	Lokomotiva	h	1-3	Benko
28/04	Hajduk	a	2-1	Mujanović, Benko
05/05	Dinamo	h	0-0	
10/05	Istra	a	0-1	
18/05	Zadar	h	2-3	Mujanović, Jogan
26/05	Zagreb	a	4-1	Benko 2, Jugović, Čulina

No	Name	Nat	DoB	Pos	Aps	(s)	Gls
11	Mehmed Alispahić	BIH	24/11/87	M	13	(1)	
19	Leon Benko		11/11/83	A	30		18
30	Josip Brezovec		12/03/86	M	30		2
3	Kristijan Čaval		11/10/78	D	14	(4)	
26	Danijel Cesarec		08/01/83	A	20	(2)	7
10	Antonini Čulina		27/01/92	M	13	(13)	2
6	Niko Datković		21/04/93	D	15	(1)	2
77	Drago Gabrić		27/09/86	M	6	(6)	
88	Kris Jogan	SVN	14/09/91	A	1	(4)	1
29	Vedran Jugović		31/07/89	M	11	(1)	1
5	Dario Knežević		20/04/82	D	31		
17	Damir Kreilach		16/04/89	M	30		5
12	Robert Lisjak		05/02/78	M	17	(1)	
1	Ivan Mance		04/02/83	M	15		
28	Luka Marić		25/04/87	M	16	(4)	
90	Andréa Mbuyi-Mutombo	BEL	10/06/90	A	7	(13)	
22	Łukasz Mierzejewski	POL	31/08/82	D	14	(3)	
7	Mato Miloš		30/06/93	D	2	(5)	
16	Ivan Močinić		30/04/93	M	9	(10)	1
8	Goran Mujanović		29/09/83	A	22	(7)	3
23	Mato Neretljak		03/06/79	D	23	(2)	1
4	Matija Škarabot	SVN	04/02/88	D	13		
12	Ivan Vargić		15/03/87	G	1		
11	Jurica Vranješ		31/01/80	M	2	(4)	
13	Ivor Weitzer		24/05/88	M	8	(13)	3

NK SLAVEN KOPRIVNICA

Coach: Roy Ferečina; (10/03/13) Roman Sović
1907 • Gradski (3,800) • nk-slaven-belupo.hr

2012

Date	Opp		Score	Scorers
22/07	Cibalia	a	3-0	Bubnjić, Rak 2
29/07	Istra	h	3-1	Delić 2, Glavica
05/08	Split	a	0-2	
12/08	Zadar	h	2-0	Maras, Vugrinec (p)
17/08	Zagreb	a	2-1	og (Oršulić), Grgić
24/08	Lokomotiva	h	3-2	Vugrinec, Batarelo, Gregurina
02/09	Osijek	a	2-1	Delić, Vugrinec
16/09	Rijeka	h	1-3	Vugrinec
23/09	Hajduk	a	1-3	Bušić
29/09	Inter	a	2-2	Vugrinec, Glavica
07/10	Dinamo	h	1-4	Delić
20/10	Cibalia	h	2-1	Vugrinec 2 (1p)
26/10	Istra	a	0-0	
03/11	Split	h	2-2	Vugrinec (p), Čanadjija
10/11	Zadar	a	0-1	
17/11	Zagreb	h	1-0	Čanadjija
23/11	Lokomotiva	a	1-3	Šaban
01/12	Osijek	h	2-0	Čanadjija, Glavica
08/12	Rijeka	a	0-0	
2013				
16/02	Hajduk	h	0-2	
23/02	Inter	h	2-2	Rak, Purić
02/03	Dinamo	a	0-3	
09/03	Cibalia	a	0-0	
15/03	Osijek	h	0-0	
29/03	Rijeka	a	1-2	Novinić
06/04	Split	h	0-0	
13/04	Lokomotiva	a	1-5	Barić
21/04	Hajduk	h	1-1	Delić
27/04	Dinamo	a	0-1	
04/05	Istra	h	1-0	Čanadjija
11/05	Zadar	a	1-1	Glavica
18/05	Zagreb	h	0-3	
26/05	Inter	a	0-2	

No	Name	Nat	DoB	Pos	Aps	(s)	Gls
13	Mario Barić		15/04/85	D	11	(4)	1
30	Ante Batarelo		21/11/84	M	15	(3)	1
10	Petar Brlek		29/01/94	M	8	(14)	
6	Igor Bubnjić		17/07/92	D	21	(4)	1
30	Tomislav Bušić		02/02/86	A	8	(9)	1
7	Dario Čanadjija		17/04/94	M	20	(3)	4
14	Mateas Delić		17/06/88	A	26	(4)	5
23	Stjepan Geng		02/03/93	D	11	(4)	
11	Dejan Glavica		20/08/91	M	25	(3)	4
20	Mario Gregurina		23/03/88	M	18	(2)	1
5	Mato Grgić		27/09/87	D	22	(2)	1
17	Matej Herent		22/02/93	M	2	(3)	
18	Mario Jelavić		20/08/93	A	3	(5)	
8	Igor Jugović		23/01/89	M	7	(1)	
4	Elvis Kokalović		17/07/88	D	26		
22	Pejo Kuprešak		24/10/92	M		(3)	
26	Alen Maras		27/02/82	D	24	(5)	1
22	Enes Novinić		18/07/85	A	3	(1)	1
1	Tomislav Pelin		26/03/81	G	6	(1)	
3	Borislav Pilipović	BIH	25/03/84	D	6	(5)	
24	Jurica Pranjić		16/02/87	D	8	(1)	
16	Vedran Purić		16/03/86	D	23	(1)	1
21	Nikola Rak		29/08/87	M	18	(3)	3
12	Silvio Rodić		25/07/87	G	27		
9	Martin Šaban		26/12/87	A	8	(13)	1
15	Davor Vugrinec		24/03/75	A	17	(2)	8

RNK SPLIT

Coach: Tonči Bašić; (15/10/12) Zoran Vulić;
(14/05/13) Goran Sablić
1912 • Park mladeži (8,000) • rnksplit.hr

2012

20/07	Rijeka	h	2-0	Vojnović, Baraban
29/07	Hajduk	a	0-1	
05/08	Slaven	h	2-0	Vitaić (p), Baraban
12/08	Dinamo	a	2-4	Belle, Bagarić
18/08	Cibalia	h	3-1	Vitaić 2, Pehar
25/08	Istra	a	0-1	
01/09	Inter	h	1-0	Pehar
15/09	Zadar	h	3-1	Erceg, Pehar, Vitaić
21/09	Zagreb	a	1-2	Vojnović
30/09	Lokomotiva	h	1-1	Kvesić
06/10	Osijek	a	2-2	Vitaić, Rebić
20/10	Rijeka	a	3-2	Rebić, Vitaić, Glumac
28/10	Hajduk	h	0-1	
03/11	Slaven	a	2-2	Vojnović, Rebić
10/11	Dinamo	h	1-0	Rebić
17/11	Cibalia	a	1-2	Baraban
24/11	Istra	h	2-0	Belle, Radeljić
30/11	Inter	a	2-0	Rebić, Belle
08/12	Zadar	a	0-1	

2013

15/02	Zagreb	h	3-2	Belle 2, Vojnović
22/02	Lokomotiva	a	2-3	Križanac 2
01/03	Osijek	h	0-0	
09/03	Zagreb	a	4-1	Rebić 2, Belle (p), Erceg
15/03	Inter	a	0-0	
30/03	Cibalia	h	1-0	Erceg
06/04	Slaven	a	0-0	
12/04	Rijeka	h	3-1	Rebić, Barišić, Erceg
20/04	Osijek	h	4-1	Rebić, Glumac, Baraban, Erceg
26/04	Lokomotiva	a	0-1	
04/05	Hajduk	h	2-1	Erceg 2
11/05	Dinamo	a	0-2	
18/05	Istra	h	0-1	
26/05	Zadar	a	2-2	Belle, Rebić

No	Name	Nat	DoB	Pos	Aps	(s)	Gls
32	Dražen Bagarić		12/11/92	A	6	(8)	1
0	Ivan Baraban		22/01/00	A	17	(10)	4
19	Josip Barišić		14/11/86	A		(7)	1
34	Henry Belle	CMR	25/01/89	A	28	(2)	7
29	Mario Brlečić		10/01/89	M	2		
10	Ante Erceg		12/12/89	M	13	(13)	7
16	Marin Galić		07/00/00	D	17	(1)	
3	Denis Glavina	03/03/86	M	10			
6	Tomislav Glumac	14/00/01	D	18	(8)	8
24	Josip Fuček		26/02/85	A	1	(1)	
33	Mirko Hrgović	BIH	05/02/79	D	25	(1)	
19	Dražen Jelić		09/07/82	A	1	(6)	
4	Ivica Križanac		13/04/79	D	12		2
15	Mario Kvesić	BIH	12/01/92	M	1	(10)	1
25	Filip Marčić		22/02/85	D	12	(5)	
21	Romano Obilinović		27/09/79	A		(3)	
23	Goran Paracki		21/01/87	M	27	(1)	
17	Mate Pehar		25/02/88	M	21	(1)	3
20	Ivan Radeljić	BIH	14/09/80	D	13	(5)	1
16	Tomislav Radotić		13/12/81	D	28		
13	Damir Rašić		05/10/88	D		(1)	
11	Ante Rebić		21/09/93	A	25	(4)	10
24	Ante Tokić		10/06/94	D	1	(1)	
5	Velimir Vidić	BIH	12/04/79	D	14	(1)	
8	Ante Vitaić		07/06/82	M	16	(2)	6
22	Aljoša Vojnović		24/10/85	A	24	(5)	4
1	Andrija Vuković		03/08/83	G	28		
12	Daniel Zagorac		07/02/87	G	5		
13	Zajko Zeba	BIH	22/05/83	M	3	(1)	

NK ZADAR

Coach: Dalibor Zebić; (24/09/12) Ferdo Milin
1945 • Stanovi (5,800) • nkzadar.hr

2012

22/07	Osijek	h	0-0	
27/07	Rijeka	h	0-0	
05/08	Hajduk	h	2-4	Jolić, Ćurjurić
12/08	Slaven	a	0-2	
18/08	Dinamo	h	1-3	Ivančić
25/08	Cibalia	a	0-0	
01/09	Istra	h	1-1	Mršić
15/09	Split	a	1-3	Begonja
22/09	Inter	h	1-5	Mršić
29/09	Zagreb	h	4-0	Mršić (p), Begonja, Ćurjurić 2
05/10	Lokomotiva	a	1-2	Ivančić
20/10	Osijek	a	0-2	
27/10	Rijeka	h	2-4	Banović, Jerbić
03/11	Hajduk	a	0-3	
10/11	Slaven	h	1-0	Mršić
17/11	Dinamo	a	0-5	
24/11	Cibalia	h	4-1	Mršić, Perica 2, Begonja
01/12	Istra	a	1-1	Perica
08/12	Split	h	1-0	Šimurina

2013

15/02	Inter	a	1-0	Perica
22/02	Zagreb	a	1-2	Heister
02/03	Lokomotiva	h	1-0	Gržan
08/03	Lokomotiva	a	1-4	Con
17/03	Hajduk	h	1-1	Banović
30/03	Dinamo	a	0-5	
06/04	Istra	h	3-2	Perica 2, Ivančić
13/04	Osijek	a	0-1	
19/04	Zagreb	a	1-1	Mršić
27/04	Inter	h	1-2	Ivančić
04/05	Cibalia	a	3-2	Ivančić, Muić, Banović
11/05	Slaven	h	1-1	Bilaver
18/05	Rijeka	a	3-2	Ivančić, Banović, Perica
26/05	Split	h	2-2	Buljat, Perica (p)

No	Name	Nat	DoB	Pos	Aps	(s)	Gls
17	Igor Banović		12/05/87	M	25	(2)	4
10	Luka Begonja		23/05/92	M	27	(3)	3
9	Josip Bilaver		14/08/84	M	20	(5)	1
18	Mario Bilen		23/01/85	D	9		
25	Tomislav Brnadić	BIH	09/10/81	D	1	(1)	
13	Jurica Buljat		19/09/86	D	9		1
14	Frane Ćirjak		23/06/95	M		(1)	
	Marin Con		08/02/85	D	4	(2)	1
14	Ivan Ćurjurić			M	7	(4)	4
19	Toni Đulić		26/07/93	G	28		
7	Šime Gržan		30/11/93	M	10	(11)	1
26	Marcel Heister	GER	29/07/92	M	15	(4)	1
25	Frane Ikić		19/06/94	D		(2)	
8	Josip Ivančić		29/03/91	A	21	(7)	6
15	Jure Jerbić		28/06/90	M	29		1
1	Antonio Ježina		05/06/89	G	5	(1)	
21	Ivan Jolić	BIH	18/05/80	A	5	(4)	1
21	Denis Ljubović		20/03/88	D	12		
22	Antonio Mršić		05/06/87	M	26	(1)	6
27	Domagoj Muić		05/09/93	M	2	(5)	1
18	Stipe Perica		07/07/95	A	14	(6)	8
19	Igor Prahić		15/04/87	D	29		
23	Marko Rašo		25/07/89	M		(1)	
4	Ante Sarić		17/06/92	D	22	(5)	
8	Jakov Surać		12/02/75	M	4	(15)	
5	Ivan Šimurina		08/01/81	A	9	(4)	1
5	Želimir Terkeš	BIH	08/01/81	A		(1)	
16	Ivan Tokić		06/06/92	D	8	(4)	
3	Ivan Anton Vasilj		05/04/91	D	17	(5)	
23	Roberto Viduka		18/01/95	D	1		
23	Dragan Župan		26/05/82	M	4	(1)	

NK ZAGREB

Coach: Dražen Besek; (03/09/12) Luka Bonačić;
(08/11/12) Miroslav Blazević
1903 • Kranjčevićeva (12,000) • nkzagreb.hr
Major honours
Croatian League (1) 2002

2012

20/07	Lokomotiva	h	0-2	
29/07	Osijek	a	0-1	
03/08	Rijeka	h	0-1	
12/08	Hajduk	a	1-5	Vojtuš
17/08	Slaven	h	1-2	Abdurahimi
25/08	Dinamo	a	0-6	
31/08	Cibalia	h	0-1	
15/09	Istra	a	0-1	
21/09	Split	h	2-1	Djengoue, Abdurahimi
29/09	Zadar	a	0-4	
05/10	Inter	h	1-1	Abdurahimi
19/10	Lokomotiva	a	1-1	Šovšić (p)
26/10	Osijek	h	2-1	Mitrović, Štrok
03/11	Rijeka	a	0-1	
09/11	Hajduk	h	0-1	
17/11	Slaven	a	0-1	
25/11	Dinamo	h	1-0	Abdurahimi
01/12	Cibalia	a	1-0	Medić
07/12	Istra	h	2-1	Vojtuš (p), Abdurahimi (p)

2013

15/02	Split	a	2-3	Medić, Šovšić (p)
22/02	Zadar	h	2-1	Medić, Abdurahimi
01/03	Inter	a	2-1	Abdurahimi, Mitrović
09/03	Split	h	1-4	Abdurahimi
15/03	Lokomotiva	a	2-4	Ćurjurić, Abdurahimi
30/03	Hajduk	a	2-3	Šovšić (p), Jurendić
05/04	Dinamo	h	0-3	
13/04	Istra	a	0-1	
19/04	Zadar	h	1-1	Medić
27/04	Osijek	a	0-1	
03/05	Inter	a	0-2	
10/05	Cibalia	h	0-2	
18/05	Slaven	a	3-0	Abdurahimi 2, Medić
26/05	Rijeka	h	1-4	Abdurahimi

No	Name	Nat	DoB	Pos	Aps	(s)	Gls
16	Besart Abdurahimi		31/07/90	M	29	(1)	12
17	Tomislav Barišić		06/03/93	D	9	(1)	
14	Dino Bevab	BIH	13/01/93	D	23	(3)	
31	Tibor Čiča		31/12/93	M		(3)	
24	Ivan Ćurjurić		29/09/89	M	4	(6)	1
8	Sven Dedić		15/04/91	M	2	(9)	
7	Nestor Djengoue	CMR	06/01/91	A	11	(1)	1
21	Ivica Džolan		11/10/88	D	1	(1)	
9	Nikola Frljužec		29/06/89	A	1	(1)	
99	Ivan Graf		17/06/87	D	13		
25	Kenan Hadjić	BIH	23/01/91	M	12	(3)	
15	Jakša Herceg		15/02/89	G		(1)	
23	Dražen Jelić		09/07/82	A		(1)	
7	Josip Jurendić		26/04/87	M	16	(4)	1
20	Denis Kolinger		14/01/94	D	11	(3)	
4	Dominik Kovačić		05/01/94	D	11	(1)	
8	Filip Krovinović		29/08/95	M		(3)	
1	Dominik Livaković		09/01/95	G	23		
10	Lovro Medić		23/10/90	A	28	(1)	5
11	Ante Mitrović		01/04/88	A	10	(10)	2
13	Safet Nadarević	BIH	19/02/80	D	20		
13	Marin Oršulić		28/06/87	D	9	(3)	
11	Mateo Pavlović		09/06/90	D	18		
5	Mladen Pelaić		20/08/83	D	15	(1)	
10	Damir Šovšić		05/02/90	M	31		3
22	Dino Štiglec		03/10/90	D	14	(4)	
26	Hrvoje Štrok		14/07/80	M	22	(5)	1
19	Krešimir Trepsić		12/08/92	A	1	(3)	
12	Igor Vidaković		20/08/83	G	10		
29	Jakub Vojtuš	SVK	22/10/93	A	8	(7)	2
30	Vlado Zadro	BIH	17/03/87	M	4	(3)	

 **CROATIA**

Top goalscorers

18	Leon Benko (Rijeka)
15	Andrej Kramarić (Lokomotiva)
13	Sammir (Dinamo)
12	Mislav Oršić (Inter)
	Besart Abdurahimi (Zagreb)
11	Goran Roce (Istra)
10	Ante Budimir (Inter)
	Ante Rebić (Split)
9	Duje Čop (Dinamo)
	Mijo Caktaš (Hajduk)
	Ivan Vuković (Hajduk)

Promoted club

NK HRVATSKI DRAGOVOLJAC

Coach: Krešimir Sunara; (24/03/13) Krešimir Ganjto
1975 • NSC Stjepan Spajić (5,000) •
hrvatski-dragovoljac.com

SECOND LEVEL FINAL TABLE 2012/13

		Pld	W	D	L	F	A	Pts
1	NK Hrvatski dragovoljac	30	16	5	9	39	25	53
2	NK Solin	30	14	9	7	43	39	51
3	NK Rudeš	30	14	8	8	47	30	50
4	HNK Šibenik	30	13	10	7	42	31	48
5	NK Vinogradar Jastrebarsko	30	14	6	10	43	39	48
6	NK Zelina	30	13	7	10	46	30	46
7	NK Pomorac Kostrena	30	13	7	10	51	39	46
8	NK Dugopolje	30	14	4	12	39	42	46
9	NK Lučko	30	12	9	9	31	28	45
10	HNK Gorica	30	10	10	10	40	35	40
11	NK Radnik Sesvete	30	12	4	14	42	43	40
12	NK Mosor Žrnovnica	30	9	11	10	31	40	38
13	NK Junak Sinj	30	10	6	14	34	43	36
14	NK Imotski	30	9	4	17	26	41	31
15	NK Primorac 1929	30	6	10	14	25	43	28
16	NK HAŠK Zagreb	30	3	6	21	24	55	15

NB HNK Šibenik – 1 pt deducted.

Domestic cup: Hrvatski Nogometni Kup 2012/13

FIRST ROUND

(28/8/12)
Vrsar 5-0 Tomislav Pan

(29/8/12)
Bjelovar 1-2 Vinodol
Gorica 4-0 Sloboda Slakovec
GOŠK Dubrovnik 3-0 Jedinstvo Omladinac *(w/o)*
Ivančica 2-2 Oriolik *(aet; 6-5 on pens)*
Koprivnica 0-0 Vuteks Sloga *(aet; 5-4 on pens)*
Krka 0-3 Nedelišće *(w/o)*
Libertas 2-1 Mladost Ždralovi
Lokomotiva 7-0 Slavija Pleternica
Mladost Repušnica 1-2 Zrinski
Novalja 3-1 Zagorec
Slunj 2-1 Zadrugar
Tekstilac Ravnice 1-1 Višnjevac *(aet; 5-6 on pens)*
Virovitica 1-4 Split
Zadar 5-1 Belišće
Zelina 9-0 Mladost M. Otok

SECOND ROUND

(25/9/12)
Gorica 3-0 Inter
Lokomotiva 4-2 Segesta
Vrsar 0-3 Dinamo Zagreb

(26/9/12)
GOŠK Dubrovnik 1-1 Šibenik *(aet; 3-2 on pens)*
Ivančica 1-2 Slaven Koprivnica
Libertas 3-0 Varaždin *(w/o)*
Koprivnica 2-1 Pomorac *(aet)*
Nedelišće 1-0 Rijeka *(aet)*
Novalja 0-1 Osijek
Slunj 0-4 Hajduk
Split 5-1 Zagora
Vinodol 0-2 Cibalia
Višnjevac 1-2 Istra
Zadar 2-0 Konavljanin
Zelina 3-0 Karlovac *(w/o)*
Zrinski 0-4 Zagreb

The Croatian Cup belongs to Hajduk Split for the sixth time

THIRD ROUND

(30/10/12)
Dinamo Zagreb 2-3 Zadar *(aet)*
Lokomotiva 3-2 Libertas
Osijek 3-2 Istra *(aet)*
Slaven Koprivnica 2-0 Koprivnica *(aet)*
Zagreb 1-2 Zelina

(31/10/12)
Cibalia 1-0 Gorica
GOŠK Dubrovnik 2-0 Nedelišće *(aet)*
Hajduk 2-1 Split

QUARTER-FINALS

(20/11/12 & 27/11/12)
GOŠK Dubrovnik 0-1 Lokomotiva *(Kramarić 68)*
Lokomotiva 0-0 GOŠK Dubrovnik
(Lokomotiva 1-0)

(20/11/12 & 28/11/12)
Zadar 1-0 Slaven Koprivnica *(Mršić 41p)*
Slaven Koprivnica 3-1 Zadar *(Vugrinec 4, Šaban 77, Bubnjić 90+2; Mršić 48)*
(Slaven Koprivnica 3-2)

(21/11/12 & 27/11/12)
Cibalia 1-1 Osijek *(Bartolović 63; Lešković 66)*
Osijek 1-3 Cibalia *(Lešković 51; Koledić 1, Puljić 53, Bartolović 90+3)*
(Cibalia 4-2)

(27/11/12 & 12/12/12)
Zelina 1-1 Hajduk *(Fuček 56; Vršajević 29)*
Hajduk 2-0 Zelina *(Milić 14, Andrijašević 76)*
(Hajduk 3-1)

SEMI-FINALS

(03/04/13 & 17/04/13)
Cibalia 1-1 Lokomotiva *(Mazalović 22; Kramarić 59)*
Lokomotiva 3-0 Cibalia *(Šitum 19, Antolić 43, Kramarić 89)*
(Lokomotiva 4-1)

(10/04/13 & 17/04/13)
Slaven Koprivnica 1-2 Hajduk *(Vugrinec 77; Sušić 56, Stojanović 90)*
Hajduk 1-1 Slaven Koprivnica *(Milić 72; Glavica 32)*
(Hajduk 3-2)

FINAL

(08/05/13)
Poljud, Split
HNK HAJDUK SPLIT 2 *(Maglica 66, Kouassi 69)*
NK LOKOMOTIVA ZAGREB 1 *(Antolić 53)*
Referee: Burilo
HAJDUK: Blažević, Maloča, Milović, Vršajević, Jozinović, Rúben Lima, Sušić, Andrijašević (Jakoliš 29), Caktaš, Kouassi (Stojanović 83), Vuković (Maglica 65)
LOKOMOTIVA: Picak, Mesarić, Barbarić, Boras, Bručić, Maleš, Trebotić (Chago 71), Pjaca (Peko 65), Antolić, Šitum, Kramarić (Musa 90)

(22/05/13)
Maksimir, Zagreb
NK LOKOMOTIVA ZAGREB 3 *(Šitum 8, Kramarić 70, Bručić 90+2)*
HNK HAJDUK SPLIT 3 *(Vuković 44, Sušić 50, Stojanović 72)*
Referee: Vučemilović
LOKOMOTIVA: Picak, Mrzljak (Peko 52), Barbarić, Puljić, Bručić, Boras, Antolić, Maleš (Chago 87), Pjaca (Musa 82), Šitum, Kramarić
HAJDUK: Kalinić, Maloča, Milović, Vršajević (Oremuš 65), Jozinović, Rúben Lima, Sušić, Caktaš, Kouassi, Vuković (Stojanović 51), Maglica (Jakoliš 82)

(HAJDUK 5-4)

CYPRUS

Kypriaki Omospondia Podosfairon (KOP)/ Cyprus Football Association (CFA)

Address	10 Achaion Street	**President**	Costakis
	2413 Engomi, PO Box 25071		Koutsokoumnis
	CY-1306 Nicosia	**General secretary**	Phivos Vakis
Tel	+357 22 352 341	**Media officer**	Kyriacos Giorgallis
Fax	+357 22 590 544	**Year of formation**	1934
E-mail	info@cfa.com.cy	**National stadium**	GSP, Nicosia (22,859)
Website	cfa.com.cy		

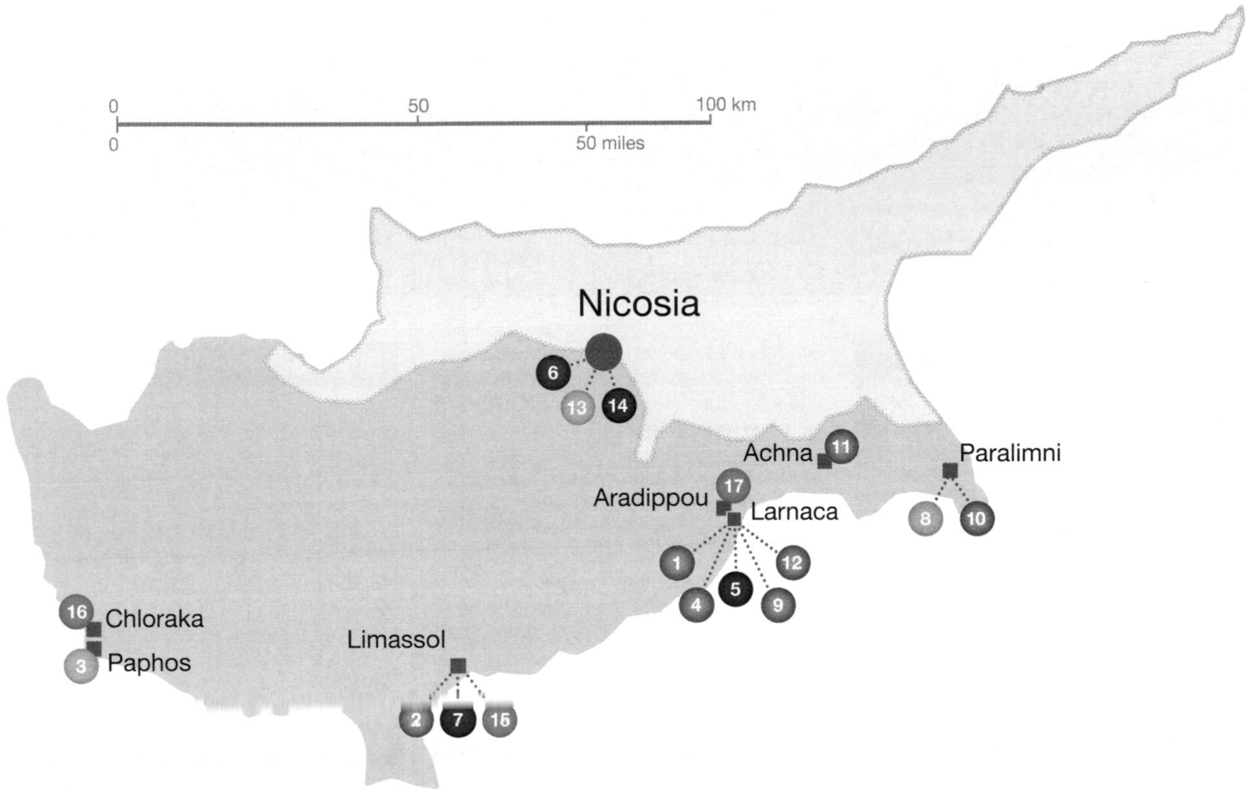

0   50   100 km
0   50 miles

Nicosia

6
13 14

Achna 11
Paralimni
Aradippou 17
Larnaca
1 12
8 10
4 5 9

16 Chloraka
3 Paphos

Limassol
2 7 15

A KATIGORIA CLUBS

1 AEK Larnaca FC

2 AEL Limassol FC

3 AEP Paphos FC

4 Alki Larnaca FC

5 Anorthosis Famagusta FC

6 APOEL FC

7 Apollon Limassol FC

8 Ayia Napa FC

9 Doxa Katokopia FC

10 Enosis Neon Paralimni FC

11 Ethnikos Achnas FC

12 Nea Salamis Famagusta FC

13 Olympiakos Nicosia FC

14 AC Omonia

PROMOTED CLUBS

15 Aris Limassol FC

16 AEK Kouklia FC

17 Ermis Aradippou FC

KEY:

● – UEFA Champions League

● – UEFA Europa League

● – Promoted clubs

● – Relegated clubs

Record 22nd title for APOEL

After stunning Europe with their run to the UEFA Champions League quarter-finals in 2011/2, APOEL FC were back to enjoying more familiar pleasures in 2012/13, the Nicosia club coming from behind to overtake Anorthosis Famagusta FC and capture a record-extending 22nd Cypriot championship crown.

APOEL were eliminated surprisingly early from Europe, with AEL Limassol FC, the surprise 2011/12 Cypriot champions, stealing their thunder in the UEFA Europa League. AEL lost a second successive domestic cup final, however, going down 2-1 to city rivals Apollon Limassol FC.

Coach Jovanović quits after fourth league triumph

Anorthosis fall away after brilliant start

Apollon win Limassol derby to take Cypriot Cup

Domestic league

Ivan Jovanović, the man who led APOEL on their European joyride, ended an outstanding second spell in charge of the club with a third A Katigoria title in five seasons. It was his fourth in total, the first having come during a brief stint in 2003/04. For much of the season it looked as if the Serbian coach would have to settle for a second successive runners-up spot, with his counterpart at Anorthosis, Israeli Roni Levy, overseeing a storming start that brought the club 17 wins and three draws in their opening 20 matches and opened up a six-point lead at the top of the table.

Remarkably, though, by the time of the play-off split, half a dozen matches later, that six-point advantage belonged not to Anorthosis but to APOEL, Jovanović's side having run up eight consecutive victories without conceding, the last of them 2-0 away to Anorthosis. The erstwhile leaders promptly dismissed Levy and replaced him with Pambos Christodoulou, AEL's title-winning coach, who had lost his job the previous October. The change, however, brought no improvement in results, and although APOEL also struggled for form in the play-offs, the other two participants, AC Omonia and AEK Larnaca FC, were too far adrift going into them to mount a challenge.

Omonia were the form team at this stage, and it was they who confirmed APOEL's title when they hammered Anorthosis 4-0 with two rounds to play.

APOEL thanked their Nicosia rivals by beating them 4-3 next time out, although the championship-winning celebrations were somewhat muted by the news that Jovanović would be leaving at the end of the season. As he headed off to the United Arab Emirates, his place was taken by Portuguese coach Paulo Sérgio.

Domestic cup

AEL had also opted to bring in a man from Portugal when they dismissed Christodoulou in the autumn, and it was Jorge Costa, the ex-FC Porto and Portugal defender, who steered the club into their second successive Cypriot Cup final, with the scalps of APOEL and 2012 winners Omonia captured en route.

But while AEL were the favourites, having taken ten points off their city rivals Apollon in the league, three of them just four days earlier, it was Christakis Christoforou's side who took the trophy for the seventh time, claiming a 2-1 extra-time victory after AEL's top scorer Vouho had missed a penalty.

Europe

AEL narrowly missed out on a UEFA Champions League place, edged out in the play-offs by RSC Anderlecht, but they competed in the UEFA Europa League group stage and signed off with a memorable 3-0 win over Olympique de Marseille. Omonia, Anorthosis and APOEL all failed to progress beyond the preliminary stages, the latter surprisingly coming a cropper in the play-offs against Neftçi PFK of Azerbaijan.

National team

The fortunes of the Cypriot national team have declined in recent years, and there was little sign of a reverse in that trend during the opening fixtures of the 2014 FIFA World Cup qualifying campaign, three of Cyprus's first four games ending in defeat.

The sole exception was a 1-0 home win against Iceland, and although further encouragement was gained from a 0-0 draw at home to group leaders Switzerland, the concession of a last-minute winner to the same opponents in the June re-match in Geneva ended the season on a frustrating low for Nikos Nioplias's side.

Domestic league: A Katigoria 2012/13 final table

		Pld	Home					Away					Total					Pts
			W	D	L	F	A	W	D	L	F	A	W	D	L	F	A	
1	**APOEL FC**	32	10	3	3	31	11	13	1	2	31	8	23	4	5	62	19	73
2	Anorthosis Famagusta FC	32	9	5	2	33	15	11	3	2	27	14	20	8	4	60	29	68
3	AC Omonia	32	13	1	2	40	9	7	5	4	26	18	20	6	6	66	27	66
4	AEK Larnaca FC	32	8	0	8	26	16	11	4	1	29	12	19	4	9	55	28	61
5	AEL Limassol FC	32	9	6	1	32	15	9	4	3	27	16	18	10	4	59	31	64
6	Apollon Limassol FC	32	8	4	4	24	15	5	5	6	16	16	13	9	10	40	31	48
7	Doxa Katakopia FC	32	4	7	5	14	22	6	2	8	19	25	10	9	13	33	47	39
8	Enosis Neon Paralimni FC	32	3	4	9	13	26	4	6	6	15	23	7	10	15	28	49	31
9	Ethnikos Achnas FC	32	4	8	4	21	19	3	4	9	20	31	7	12	13	41	50	33
10	Alki Larnaca FC	32	3	3	10	20	35	5	5	6	23	23	8	8	16	43	58	32
11	Nea Salamis Famagusta FC	32	5	3	8	15	19	3	4	9	12	25	8	7	17	27	44	31
12	Olympiakos Nicosia FC	32	6	4	6	27	28	2	6	8	19	28	8	10	14	46	56	31
13	Ayia Napa FC	26	1	2	10	6	26	1	0	12	9	33	2	2	22	15	59	8
14	AEP Paphos FC	26	2	1	10	7	27	2	2	9	10	37	4	3	19	17	64	6

NB After 26 matches the top 12 clubs split into three groups of four, after which they play exclusively against teams in their group; AEP Paphos FC – 9 pts deducted; Olympiakos Nicosia FC - 3 pts deducted.

SEASON AT A GLANCE

EUROPEAN QUALIFICATION 2013/14

Champion: APOEL FC (third qualifying round)

Cup winner: Apollon Limassol FC (play-offs)
Anorthosis Famagusta FC (second qualifying round)
AC Omonia (first qualifying round)

Top scorer	Bernardo Vasconcelos (Alki), 18 goals
Relegated clubs	AEP Paphos FC, Ayia Napa FC, Olympiakos Nicosia FC
Promoted clubs	Aris Limassol FC, AEK Kouklia FC, Ermis Aradippou FC
Cup final	Apollon Limassol FC 2-1 AEL Limassol FC (aet)

PLAYER OF THE SEASON
Dimitris Christofi
(AC Omonia)

Omonia endured a generally disappointing campaign but finished it in style, galvanised by the attacking efforts of Christofi. The 24-year-old Cypriot international weighed in with eight goals as Omonia put together an impressive sequence of results that included eye-catching wins over APOEL FC and Anorthosis Famagusta FC.

NEWCOMER OF THE SEASON
Alex Konstantinou
(Apollon Limassol FC)

New to Cypriot football in 2012/13 after starting his career in the lower reaches of English league football, the young winger drew attention to himself with an intoxicating blend of incisive dribbling and technical class. Konstantinou starred in Apollon's cup triumph before earning a first call-up to the Cyprus national team.

A KATIGORIA TEAM OF THE SEASON
(4-4-2)
Coach: Jovanović *(APOEL)*

Hogg *(Paralimni)*

Shpungin *(Omonia)* — Borda *(APOEL)* — Dosa Júnior *(AEL)* — Demetriou *(AEK)*

Efrem *(Omonia)* — Juliano Spadacio *(Anorthosis)* — Nuno Morais *(APOEL)* — Edmar *(AEL)*

Christofi *(Omonia)* — Bernardo Vasconcelos *(Alki)*

NATIONAL TEAM

Home Kit   Away Kit

TOP FIVE ALL-TIME CAPS
Ioannis Okkas (104); **Michalis Konstantinou** (87); Pambos Pittas (82); Nikos Panayiotou (75); **Kostas Charalambides** & Georgios Theodotou (70)

TOP FIVE ALL-TIME GOALS
Michalis Konstantinou (32); Ioannis Okkas (26); **Kostas Charalambides** (11); Marios Agathokleos & **Efstathios Aloneftis** (10)

Results 2012/13

15/08/12	Bulgaria	A	Sofia	0-1		
07/09/12	Albania (WCQ)	A	Tirana	1-3	*Laban (45+5)*	
11/09/12	Iceland (WCQ)	H	Larnaca	1-0	*Makrides (57)*	
12/10/12	Slovenia (WCQ)	A	Maribor	1-2	*Aloneftis (83)*	
16/10/12	Norway (WCQ)	H	Larnaca	1-3	*Aloneftis (42)*	
14/11/12	Finland	H	Nicosia	0-3		
06/02/13	Serbia	H	Nicosia	1-3	*Makrides (19)*	
23/03/13	Switzerland (WCQ)	H	Nicosia	0-0		
08/06/13	Switzerland (WCQ)	A	Geneva	0-1		

Appearances 2012/13

Coach: Nikos Nioplias (GRE)	17/01/65		Bul	ALB	ISL	SVN	NOR	Fin	Srb	SUI	SUI	Caps	Goals
Antonis Georgallides	30/01/82	Alki	G	G46		s55	G	G	G	G	G	49	-
Athos Solomou	30/11/85	APOEL	D85		D		D	D62	D	M54		13	-
Georgios Merkis	30/07/84	Apollon	D	D	D						D	21	-
Dosa Júnior	28/07/86	AEL	D	D	D		D	D	D	D		7	-
Ilias Charalambous	25/09/80	Vaslui (ROU)	D	D	D	D	D	D88	D	D	D	62	-
Vincent Laban	09/09/84	Anorthosis	M	M	M		M	M		M	M	7	1
Siniša Dobrašinović	17/02/77	Zhetysu (KAZ)/unattached	M71		M77	M	M	M	s57	D	s94	25	1
Konstantinos Makrides	13/01/82	Metalurh Donetsk (UKR)	M56	M	M92				M86	M	M	63	5
Kostas Charalambides	25/07/81	APOEL	M56	M56		M79			M65	M75		70	11
Nektarios Alexandrou	19/12/83	APOEL	M56							s75	M	21	-
Efstathios Aloneftis	29/03/83	APOEL	A73	M	s66	s79	M88	M46			M62	53	10
Dimitris Christofi	28/09/88	Omonia	s56	s56	M	M	A	A62	M60	A95		31	3
Marios Nikolaou	04/10/83	AEL	s56	M	M		M	M46	M57	M	M	44	1
Michalis Konstantinou	19/02/78	AEL	s56	A76	A66	A64						87	32
Jason Demetriou	18/11/87	AEK Larnaca	s71	D	s92	M	s46	s46				20	-
Georgios Vasiliou	12/08/84	Apollon	s73					s46	s86			5	-
Christos Marangos	09/05/83	AEK Larnaca	s85			M46			M			22	1
Christos Mastrou	30/01/88	Anorthosis		s46								2	-
Andreas Avraam	06/06/87	Omonia/Anorthosis		s76						s65		28	5
Anastasios Kissas	18/01/88	APOEL			G	G	G55					10	-
Valentinos Sielis	01/03/90	Anorthosis			s77	D		D	D			8	-
Paraskevas Christou	02/02/84	U Cluj (ROU)				D						31	-
Angelis Charalambous	31/05/89	Apollon				D	D46				D	4	-
Kostakis Artymatas	15/04/93	Paralimni				s46		s71				2	-
Georgios Efrem	05/07/89	Omonia				s64	M	M71	s60	s54		20	-
Nestoras Mytidis	01/06/91	AEK Larnaca					s88		s74			8	-
Stelios Parpas	25/07/85	AEL						s62				3	-
Pieros Sotiriou	13/01/93	Olympiakos Nicosia						s62	A74	s95	A	4	-
Marios Antoniades	14/05/90	APOEL						s88				1	-
Christos Theofilou	30/04/80	AEL								D	D94	12	-
Charalambos Kyriakou	15/10/89	Omonia									s62	1	-

European club competitions 2012/13

AEL LIMASSOL FC

Second qualifying round - Linfield FC (NIR)
H 3-0 *Vouho (16), Ouon (29), Dickson (54)*
Degra, Dosa Júnior, Monteiro (Paulo Sérgio 54), Luciano Bebê (Rui Miguel 59), Marcos Airosa, Carlitos, Ouon, Gilberto, Dédé (Nikolaou 75), Dickson, Vouho. Coach: Pambos Christodoulou (CYP)
A 0-0
Degra, Dosa Júnior, Maykon, Rui Miguel (Dédé 70), Edmar (Dickson 60), Nikolaou (Konstantinou 77), Paulo Sérgio, Luciano Bebê, Carlitos, Ouon, Vouho. Coach: Pambos Christodoulou (CYP)

Third qualifying round - FK Partizan (SRB)
H 1-0 *Vouho (13)*
Degra, Dosa Júnior, Monteiro (Edmar 67), Luciano Bebê (Rui Miguel 60), Marcos Airosa, Carlitos, Ouon, Gilberto, Dédé, Dickson, Vouho (Nikolaou 80). Coach: Pambos Christodoulou (CYP)
A 1-0 *Dosa Júnior (23)*
Degra, Dosa Júnior, Monteiro, Edmar (Paulo Sérgio 85), Nikolaou, Luciano Bebê (Gilberto 60), Marcos Airosa, Carlitos, Ouon, Dédé, Vouho (Dickson 72). Coach: Pambos Christodoulou (CYP)
Red card: Monteiro 28

Play-offs - RSC Anderlecht (BEL)
H 2-1 *Dosa Júnior (34), Rui Miguel (72)*
Degra, Dosa Júnior, Edmar (Gilberto 85), Nikolaou, Paulo Sérgio (Dickson 65), Luciano Bebê (Rui Miguel 50), Marcos Airosa, Carlitos, Ouon, Dédé, Vouho. Coach: Pambos Christodoulou (CYP)
A 0-2
Degra, Dosa Júnior, Monteiro (Gilberto 37), Rui Miguel (Maykon 79), Edmar (Dickson 62), Nikolaou, Marcos Airosa, Carlitos, Ouon, Dédé, Vouho. Coach: Pambos Christodoulou (CYP)

Group C
Match 1 - VfL Borussia Mönchengladbach (GER)
H 0-0
Degra, Dosa Júnior, Maykon (Luciano Bebê 75), Parpas, Rui Miguel, Edmar (Paulo Sérgio 70), Nikolaou, Marcos Airosa, Gilberto, Dédé, Vouho (Orlando Sá 57). Coach: Pambos Christodoulou (CYP)
Match 2 - Olympique de Marseille (FRA)
A 1-5 *Ouon (22)*
Degra, Dosa Júnior, Monteiro, Nikolaou (Konstantinou 76), Theofilou, Paulo Sérgio, Luciano Bebê (Parpas 76), Ouon, Dédé, Vouho (Orlando Sá 87). Coach: Lazaros Semos (GRE)
Match 3 - Fenerbahçe SK (TUR)
H 0-1
Degra, Dosa Júnior, Monteiro, Rui Miguel, Nikolaou (Luciano Bebê 78), Paulo Sérgio (Gilberto 70), Marcos Airosa, Carlitos, Ouon, Dédé, Vouho (Orlando Sá 73). Coach: Jorge Costa (POR)
Match 4 - Fenerbahçe SK (TUR)
A 0-2
Degra, Parpas, Monteiro (Edmar 60), Rui Miguel, Nikolaou, Paulo Sérgio (Dickson 60), Konstantinou (Vouho 73), Luciano Bebê, Carlitos, Ouon, Dédé. Coach: Jorge Costa (POR)
Red card: Ouon 70
Match 5 - VfL Borussia Mönchengladbach (GER)
A 0-2
Degra, Dosa Júnior, Parpas (Dickson 70), Orlando Sá, Rui Miguel (Konstantinou 85), Edmar, Nikolaou, Luciano Bebê, Marcos Airosa, Carlitos, Dédé. Coach: Jorge Costa (POR)
Red card: Luciano Bebê 76
Match 6 - Olympique de Marseille (FRA)
H 3-0 *Orlando Sá (41), Edmar (79), Dickson (82)*
Degra, Dosa Júnior (Kyriakou 90), Parpas (Theofilou 84), Orlando Sá (Vouho 72), Edmar, Nikolaou, Paulo Sérgio, Carlitos, Ouon, Dédé, Dickson. Coach: Jorge Costa (POR)

AC OMONIA

Third qualifying round - FK Crvena zvezda (SRB)
A 0-0
Leoni, Pavićević, Danielson, Scaramozzino, Nuno Assis (Bruno Aguiar 69), Shpungin, André Alves (João Alves 89), Renato Margaça (Freddy 78), Leandro, Marco Soares, Christofi. Coach: Neophytos Larkou (CYP)
H 0-0 *(aet; 5-6 on pens)*
Leoni, Pavićević, Freddy, Avraam (André Alves 83), Danielson, Scaramozzino, Nuno Assis (Bruno Aguiar 73), Shpungin, Leandro (Renato Margaça 95), Marco Soares, Christofi. Coach: Neophytos Larkou (CYP)

APOEL FC

Second qualifying round - FK Senica (SVK)
H 2-0 *Aílton (33), Alexandrou (40)*
Chiotis, Aílton, Charalambides (Aloneftis 77), Alexandrou, Benachour (Hélder Sousa 76), Manduca (Adorno 90), Hélio Pinto, Nuno Morais, Borda, Mário Sérgio, Zuela. Coach: Ivan Jovanović (SRB)
A 1-0 *Hélio Pinto (73)*
Chiotis, Aílton, Charalambides (Aloneftis 74), Alexandrou, Benachour (Hélder Sousa 63), Manduca, Hélio Pinto (Charalambous 88), Nuno Morais, Borda, Mário Sérgio, Zuela. Coach: Ivan Jovanović (SRB)

Third qualifying round - Aalesunds FK (NOR)
H 2-1 *Mário Sérgio (34), Aloneftis (80)*
Chiotis, Charalambides (Aloneftis 64), Alexandrou, Adorno (Budimir 56), Benachour (Hélder Sousa 83), Manduca, Hélio Pinto, Nuno Morais, Borda, Mário Sérgio, Zuela. Coach: Ivan Jovanović (SRB)

CYPRUS

A 1-0 *Adorno (36)*
Chiotis, Charalambides (Aloneftis 78), Alexandrou, Adorno (Budimir 83), Benachour (Hélder Sousa 89), Manduca, Hélio Pinto, Nuno Morais, Borda, Mário Sérgio, Zuela. Coach: Ivan Jovanović (SRB)

Play-offs - Neftçi PFK (AZE)
A 1-1 *Benachour (83)*
Chiotis, Budimir (Solomou 88), Charalambides (Adorno 58), Alexandrou, Hélio Pinto, Nuno Morais, Borda, Mário Sérgio, Zuela, Hélder Sousa (Benachour 46), Aloneftis. Coach: Ivan Jovanović (SRB)
H 1-3 *Benachour (44)*
Chiotis, Klukowski (Charalambides 63), Budimir, Alexandrou, Benachour (Hélder Sousa 72), Manduca (Adorno 80), Hélio Pinto, Nuno Morais, Borda, Mário Sérgio, Aloneftis. Coach: Ivan Jovanović (SRB)

ANORTHOSIS FAMAGUSTA FC

Second qualifying round - FC Levadia Tallinn (EST)
A 3-1 *Juliano Spadacio (45p), Laborde (55), Toni Calvo (62)*
Blažić, Paulo Jorge, Colin, Alexa, Toni Calvo, Juliano Spadacio, Okkas (Rezek 70), Laban (Ohayon 65), Laborde (Andić 80), Ilič, William Boaventura. Coach: Roni Levy (ISR)
H 3-0 *Toni Calvo (13), Okkas (41), Laborde (62)*
Blažić, Paulo Jorge, Colin, Alexa, Toni Calvo (Ohayon 56), Juliano Spadacio, Okkas (Rezek 56), Laban (Evandro Roncatto 74), Laborde, Ilič, William Boaventura. Coach: Roni Levy (ISR)

Third qualifying round - FC Dila Gori (GEO)
A 1-0 *Okkas (69)*
Blažić, Paulo Jorge, Colin, Alexa, Toni Calvo (Ohayon 78), Juliano Spadacio, Okkas (Rezek 75), Laban (Evandro Roncatto 65), Laborde, Ilič, William Boaventura. Coach: Roni Levy (ISR)
H 0-3 *(w/o; match abandoned after 83 mins at 0-3)*
Blažić, Paulo Jorge, Colin, Alexa, Juliano Spadacio, Okkas (Evandro Roncatto 75), Laban, Laborde, Ilič, William Boaventura, Ohayon (Rezek 57). Coach: Roni Levy (ISR)
Red card: Laban 79

Domestic league club-by-club

AEK LARNACA FC

Coach: Ran Ben Shimon (ISR)
1994 • Neo GSZ (12,000) • aek.com.cy
Major honours
Cypriot Cup (1) 2004

2012
02/09	Alki	a	1-0	Mytides
16/09	Apollon	h	2-0	Pintado 2
22/09	Omonia	a	1-0	Alexandre Afonso
29/09	Olympiakos	h	1-0	Demetriou
06/10	Nea Salamis	a	0-0	
20/10	Ayia Napa	h	3-0	Nakajima-Farran, Maachi, og (Ginho)
28/10	Ethnikos	a	1-0	Palić
03/11	AEP	a	3-0	Pintado 2, Daemen
11/11	AEL	h	1-2	og (Dosa Júnior)
18/11	APOEL	a	2-1	Serrán, Demetriou
24/11	Anorthosis	a	2-3	Maachi, Palić
01/12	Paralimni	a	2-1	Alexandre Afonso, Maachi
09/12	Doxa	h	1-2	Maachi
16/12	Alki	h	2-0	Alexandre Afonso, Pavlou
22/12	Apollon	a	2-1	Demetriou, David Català

2013
06/01	Omonia	h	2-1	Pintado 2
12/01	Olympiakos	a	2-0	Maachi, Chando
19/01	Nea Salamis	h	1-2	Chando
26/01	Ayia Napa	a	1-1	Chando
03/02	Ethnikos	h	2-1	Maachi, Chando
11/02	AEP	h	4-0	Palić, Van Dijk, Maachi, Chando
27/02	AEL	a	2-2	Maachi, Joan Tomàs
03/03	APOEL	h	0-1	
09/03	Anorthosis	a	1-1	Alexandre Afonso
16/03	Paralimni	h	5-0	Chando, Maachi, Joan Tomàs, Palić, Alexandre Afonso
31/03	Doxa	a	6-2	Chando 2, Maachi 2, Joan Tomàs, Bangura
06/04	Anorthosis	a	3-0	Alexandre Afonso, og (Paulo Jorge), Joan Tomàs
13/04	Omonia	h	0-2	
21/04	APOEL	h	0-1	
27/04	APOEL	a	1-0	Alexandre Afonso
12/05	Anorthosis	h	0-1	
18/05	Omonia	a	1-3	Linssen

No	Name	Nat	DoB	Pos	Aps	(s)	Gls
4	Alexandre Afonso	BRA	15/08/83	M	27	(4)	7
10	Mustapha Bangura	SLE	24/10/89	M		(5)	1
9	Chando	ESP	18/07/82	A	13	(3)	8
8	Tom Daemen	NED	17/06/85	M		(6)	1
6	David Català	ESP	01/12/89	M	28		1
18	Tim de Cler	NED	08/11/78	D	19	(1)	
20	Jason Demetriou		18/11/87	D	19		3
21	Igor Gabilondo	ESP	10/02/79	M	6		
12	Kenny Gillet	FRA	03/01/86	D	13	(3)	
37	Serginho Greene	NED	24/06/82	D	8	(2)	
55	Guy Haimov	ISR	09/03/86	G	29		
13	Joan Tomàs	ESP	17/05/85	M	12	(2)	4
26	Dimitris Kyprianou		02/02/93	M		(1)	
7	Edwin Linssen	NED	28/08/80	M	5	(6)	1
16	Nassir Maachi	NED	09/09/85	A	23	(3)	11
14	Christos Marangos		09/05/83	M	19	(2)	
88	Mércio	BRA	26/05/80	M	9	(4)	
2	Eleftherios Mertakas		16/03/85	D	7	(3)	
18	Ander Murillo	ESP	22/07/83	D	19	(4)	
40	Nestoras Mytidis		01/06/91	A	4		1
17	Issey Nakajima-Farran	CAN	16/05/84	M	4	(6)	1
25	Antun Palić	CRO	25/06/88	M	22	(7)	4
23	Kyriakos Pavlou		04/09/86	A	5	(20)	1
23	Gorka Pintado	ESP	24/03/78	A	14	(7)	6
1	Pulpo	ESP	28/10/87	G	3	(1)	
3	Albert Serrán	ESP	17/07/84	D	15	(4)	1
5	Gregoor van Dijk	NED	16/11/81	M	29		1

AEL LIMASSOL FC

Coach: Pambos Christodoulou; (23/10/12) Jorge Costa (POR)
1930 • Tsirion (13,000) • aelfc.com
Major honours
Cypriot League (6) 1941, 1953, 1955, 1956, 1968, 2012; Cypriot Cup (6) 1939, 1940, 1948, 1985, 1987, 1989

2012
03/09	Doxa	a	3-1	Parpas, Gilberto, Orlando Sá (p)
15/09	Alki	h	3-1	Konstantinou, Vouho, Nikolaou
24/09	Apollon	a	0-0	
29/09	Omonia	h	1-1	Luciano Bebê
08/10	Olympiakos	a	0-0	
20/10	Nea Salamis	h	2-1	Vouho 2 (1p)
29/10	Ayia Napa	a	4-0	Rui Miguel 2, Orlando Sá, Nikolaou
03/11	Ethnikos	h	1-1	Dosa Júnior
11/11	AEK	a	2-1	Monteiro, Konstantinou
17/11	AEP	a	3-1	Konstantinou 2, Paulo Sérgio
26/11	APOEL	h	1-3	Luciano Bebê
01/12	Anorthosis	a	1-1	Dédé
10/12	Paralimni	h	1-1	Vouho
16/12	Doxa	h	2-0	Dosa Júnior, Monteiro
22/12	Alki	a	3-2	Edmar, Paulo Sérgio, Vouho

2013
05/01	Apollon	h	3-2	Vouho 2, Luciano Bebê
13/01	Omonia	a	0-2	
20/01	Olympiakos	h	1-1	Paulo Sérgio
27/01	Nea Salamis	a	1-0	Monteiro
02/02	Ayia Napa	h	2-0	Vouho, Orlando Sá
10/02	Ethnikos	a	3-1	Vouho, Orlando Sá, Dosa Júnior (p)
27/02	AEK	h	2-2	Dosa Júnior, Orlando Sá
02/03	AEP	h	4-0	Monteiro, Vouho, Paulo Sérgio 2
09/03	APOEL	a	0-2	
16/03	Anorthosis	h	1-1	Maykon
30/03	Paralimni	a	2-1	Sachetti, Dosa Júnior (p)
06/04	Paralimni	h	1-2	Maykon
13/04	Apollon	h	2-1	Rui Miguel, Maykon
20/04	Doxa	a	1-1	Rui Miguel
27/04	Doxa	h	3-0	Paulo Sérgio, Eleftheriou, Edmar
11/05	Paralimni	h	3-0	Vouho, Luciano Bebê, Maykon
18/05	Apollon	a	3-1	Konstantinou 2 (1p), Theofilou

No	Name	Nat	DoB	Pos	Aps	(s)	Gls
8	Ebo Andoh	GHA	06/05/89	A	8	(12)	
23	Carlitos	CPV	23/04/85	M	15	(1)	
77	Dédé	ANG	04/07/81	M	17	(3)	1
32	Matías Degra	ARG	18/06/83	G	28		
84	Chris Dickson	GHA	28/12/84	A	2	(4)	
2	Dosa Júnior		28/07/86	D	27		5
11	Edmar	BRA	19/04/82	M	17	(6)	2
40	Georgios Eleftheriou		30/09/84	M	13	(3)	1
91	Embalo	GNB	03/05/93	M	3	(3)	
70	Gilberto	ANG	21/09/82	M	7	(1)	1
22	Isli Hidi	ALB	15/10/80	G	4	(1)	
37	Maksym Ilchysh	UKR	05/11/92	D		(1)	
19	Michalis Konstantinou		19/02/78	A	11	(8)	6
	Andreas Kyriakou		05/02/94	D	3		
20	Luciano Bebê	BRA	11/03/81	M	19	(2)	4
21	Marco Airosa	ANG	06/08/84	D	14		
3	Maykon	BRA	20/04/84	D	11	(4)	4
7	Monteiro	POR	15/08/88	M	19	(4)	4
12	Marios Nikolaou		04/10/83	M	20	(5)	2
29	Carlos Ohene	GHA	21/07/93	M	1	(1)	
9	Orlando Sá	POR	26/05/88	A	10	(10)	5
29	Edwin Ouon	RWA	26/01/81	D	19		
5	Stelios Parpas		25/07/85	D	8	(2)	1
17	Paulo Sérgio	POR	24/01/84	M	20	(7)	6
10	Rui Miguel	POR	15/11/83	M	14	(2)	4
55	Esteban Sachetti	ARG	21/11/85	M	12	(1)	1
15	Christos Theofilou		30/04/80	D	10	(1)	1
99	Vouho	CIV	25/06/87	A	20	(4)	11

AEP PAPHOS FC

Coach: Ioannis Topalidis (GRE);
(08/11/12) Horácio Gonçalves (POR);
(26/11/12) Saša Jovanović (SRB)
2000 • Pafiako (10,000) • aepfc.com

2012

01/09	Anorthosis	a	1-5	Silas
15/09	Nea Salamis	h	1-0	Tall
22/09	Paralimni	a	1-1	Garpozis (p)
30/09	Ayia Napa	h	3-0	Hugo Sousa, Melissas, Andrezinho
07/10	Doxa	a	0-1	
20/10	Ethnikos	h	0-0	
28/10	Alki	a	2-0	Aguinaldo 2
03/11	AEK	h	0-3	
10/11	Apollon	a	0-4	
17/11	AEL	h	1-3	Aguinaldo
24/11	Omonia	a	2-4	Silas 2
02/12	APOEL	a	0-2	
09/12	Olympiakos	a	1-3	Makris
15/12	Anorthosis	h	0-2	
23/12	Nea Salamis	a	1-1	Saúlo

2013

05/01	Paralimni	h	0-1	
12/01	Ayia Napa	a	2-1	Tall, Makris
19/01	Doxa	h	0-4	
26/01	Ethnikos	a	0-3	
02/02	Alki	h	1-4	Balú
11/02	AEK	a	0-4	
26/02	Apollon	h	0-1	
02/03	AEL	a	0-4	
09/03	Omonia	h	1-2	Garpozis (p)
17/03	APOEL	a	0-6	
30/03	Olympiakos	h	0-5	

No	Name	Nat	DoB	Pos	Aps	(s)	Gls
80	Demosthenis Agathokleous		31/03/95	G	1		
11	Aguinaldo	ANG	04/03/89	A	9	(3)	3
27	Andrezinho	BRA	15/02/85	A	6	(3)	1
23	Balú	BRA	22/02/85	D	11		1
72	Kostadin Bashov	BUL	26/11/82	A	5		
14	Dimitris Christofi		25/08/94	M	2	(3)	
44	Cris	POR	17/01/84	M	10	(5)	
60	Andreas Daniel		29/08/93	M	1		
7	Charalambos Demosthenous		16/04/90	M	8	(5)	
42	Edgar Marcelino	POR	10/06/81	M	7	(1)	
21	Angelos Efthymiou		18/01/84	M	3	(5)	
16	Dimitris Filippou		16/06/92	A	2	(2)	
16	Polis Filippou		16/06/92	A	6	(6)	
84	Lambros Fylaktou		20/01/93	D	9	(2)	
19	Alexandros Garpozis		05/09/80	D	20	(1)	2
39	Sofoklis Georgiou		02/11/93	M		(1)	
31	Vladan Grujić	BIH	17/05/81	M	3	(3)	
17	Hugo Sousa	POR	04/06/92	D	8	(4)	1
6	Dimitrios Ioannou	GRE	15/03/77	M	23		
46	Nikolas Ioannou		02/07/94	M	1	(1)	
81	Loizos Kakoyiannis		02/05/81	D	1		
9	Dimitrios Kiliaras	GRE	23/03/86	M	10		
45	Andreas Makris		27/11/95	M	9	(5)	2
33	Manolo Reina	ESP	01/04/85	G	15		
22	Pashalis Melissas	GRE	09/03/82	M	10		1
29	Dimitrios Petkakis	GRE	01/08/83	D	10		
15	Erind Priftis	ALB	27/05/91	G	7		
12	Saúlo	BRA	18/02/82	M	7	(4)	1
4	Ioannis Savva		18/08/91	D	21	(1)	
59	Marios Savva		31/03/95	M		(1)	
1	Zsolt Sebők	HUN	03/04/79	G	2		
50	Serjão	BRA	09/12/79	A	9	(7)	
48	Georgios Sielis		23/10/86	M	6		
10	Silas	POR	09/10/76	M	15	(1)	3
5	Gora Tall	SEN	20/05/85	D	22		2
28	Ioannis Varnavidis		09/08/92	M	5	(10)	
8	Stefanos Voskaridis		01/02/80	M	2	(4)	

ALKI LARNACA FC

Coach: Kostas Kaiafas;
(05/12/12) Neophytos Larkou;
(09/04/13) Kostas Kaiafas
1948 • Neo GSZ (12,000) • alkifc.com.cy

2012

02/09	AEK	h	0-1	
15/09	AEL	a	1-3	Cristian
22/09	APOEL	h	1-3	Bernardo Vasconcelos
29/09	Anorthosis	a	0-3	
06/10	Paralimni	h	1-1	Jonathan Aspas
21/10	Doxa	a	1-0	Kapiloto (p)
28/10	AEP	h	0-2	
04/11	Apollon	h	1-3	Arnal
11/11	Omonia	a	0-1	
17/11	Olympiakos	h	0-0	
25/11	Nea Salamis	a	1-1	Beckel
02/12	Ayia Napa	h	0-2	
09/12	Ethnikos	a	2-0	Arnal, Cafú
16/12	AEK	a	0-2	
22/12	AEL	h	2-3	Jonathan Aspas, Ohene

2013

06/01	APOEL	a	1-1	Cafú
14/01	Anorthosis	h	0-3	
20/01	Paralimni	a	1-1	Nakajima-Farran
28/01	Doxa	h	2-2	Bernardo Vasconcelos 2
02/02	AEP	a	4-1	Gligorov, Eduardo Pinceli, Cafú 2
10/02	Apollon	a	1-2	Sidnei
26/02	Omonia	h	2-4	Bernardo Vasconcelos 2
03/03	Olympiakos	a	2-2	Bernardo Vasconcelos, Eduardo Pinceli
09/03	Nea Salamis	h	1-0	Bernardo Vasconcelos (p)
16/03	Ayia Napa	a	3-0	Bernardo Vasconcelos 2, Marković
30/03	Ethnikos	h	6-5	Jonathan Aspas (p), Nakajima-Farran, Bernardo Vasconcelos 2 (1p), Beckel, Sidnei
07/04	Ethnikos	a	1-1	Bernardo Vasconcelos
14/04	Olympiakos	h	2-1	Bernardo Vasconcelos 2
21/04	Nea Salamis	a	3-1	Bernardo Vasconcelos 2 (1p), Beckel
28/04	Nea Salamis	h	1-2	Bernardo Vasconcelos
11/05	Ethnikos	h	1-3	Nakajima-Farran
19/05	Olympiakos	a	2-4	Konstantinou, Bernardo Vasconcelos (p)

No	Name	Nat	DoB	Pos	Aps	(s)	Gls
99	Andreas Anastasiou		13/06/95	M		(1)	
11	Arnal	ESP	21/11/80	A	8	(4)	2
4	Barge	POR	04/01/84	D	25		
10	Boei Beckel	IDN	07/10/87	M	23	(1)	3
9	Bernardo Vasconcelos	POR	10/06/79	A	19	(5)	18
83	Corrin Brooks-Meade	ENG	19/03/88	G	10	(1)	
60	Bruno Fernandes	GNB	06/11/78	D	13	(1)	
17	Cafú	CPV	07/11/77	A	19	(8)	4
96	Naby Camara	SEN	14/05/94	D	3	(1)	
2	Kostas Charalambous		12/08/95	M		(2)	
4	Bruno Cirillo	ITA	21/03/77	D	7		
21	Cristian	ESP	21/09/83	M	3	(7)	1
31	Eduardo Pinceli	BRA	23/04/83	M	10		2
20	Emiliano Fusco	ARG	02/03/86	D	24		
15	Gerasimos Fylaktou		24/07/91	M	6	(5)	
30	Antonis Georgallides		30/01/82	G	20		
16	Nikola Gligorov	MKD	15/08/83	M	18	(8)	1
7	James Dens	BRA	14/08/86	D	6		
8	Jonathan Aspas	ESP	28/02/82	M	16	(8)	3
55	Nisso Kapiloto	ISR	01/10/89	D	22	(1)	1
26	Noel Kaseke	ZIM	24/12/80	M	15		
97	Stavros Konstantinou		19/03/97	M	1	(2)	1
77	Leandros Lillis		13/09/96	A	3	(3)	
81	Marjan Marković	SRB	28/09/81	D	7	(2)	1
46	Louka Mihailovic		20/11/96	M	2		
84	Issey Nakajima-Farran	CAN	16/05/84	M	8	(7)	3
94	Carlos Ohene	GHA	21/07/93	M	3	(9)	1
95	Yusif Rahman	GHA	26/01/93	D	4	(4)	
5	Santamaria	POR	11/02/82	D	21	(1)	
27	Sidnei	BRA	02/11/86	M	26	(6)	2
40	Stélvio	ANG	24/01/89	M	8	(3)	
12	Dimitris Stylianou		05/07/84	G	2		

ANORTHOSIS FAMAGUSTA FC

Coach: Roni Levy (ISR);
(02/04/13) Pambos Christodoulou
1911 • Antonis Papadopoulos (9,782) • anorthosis.com
Major honours
Cypriot League (13) 1950, 1957, 1958, 1960, 1962,
1963, 1995, 1997, 1998, 1999, 2000, 2005, 2008;
Cypriot Cup (10) 1949, 1959, 1962, 1964, 1971, 1975,
1998, 2002, 2003, 2007

2012

01/09	AEP	h	5-1	Juliano Spadacio 2, Okkas, Toni Calvo, Rezek
15/09	Paralimni	h	1-1	William Boaventura
22/09	Doxa	a	2-0	Juliano Spadacio, Rezek
29/09	Alki	h	3-0	Juliano Spadacio 2, Rezek
07/10	Apollon	a	2-0	Laborde, Rezek
21/10	Omonia	h	2-0	Juliano Spadacio (p), Rezek
28/10	Olympiakos	a	3-1	Laborde, Rezek, Evandro Roncatto
04/11	Nea Salamis	h	1-0	Juliano Spadacio (p)
11/11	Ayia Napa	a	1-0	Okkas
19/11	Ethnikos	h	5-1	Okkas, Rezek, Juliano Spadacio 2 (1p), Itzhaki
24/11	AEK	a	3-2	Rezek, Ilić, Toni Calvo
01/12	AEL	h	1-1	Rezek
08/12	APOEL	a	1-0	Rezek
15/12	AEP	a	2-0	Okkas, Laborde
23/12	Paralimni	a	2-1	Laborde, Juliano Spadacio

2013

05/01	Doxa	h	3-0	Rezek, Itzhaki, Juliano Spadacio
14/01	Alki	a	3-0	Okkas 2, Juliano Spadacio (p)
20/01	Apollon	h	0-0	
26/01	Omonia	a	3-1	Itzhaki 2, Rezek
03/02	Olympiakos	h	4-3	Itzhaki 3, Okkas
10/02	Nea Salamis	a	1-2	Laborde
27/02	Ayia Napa	h	5-1	Juliano Spadacio 2 (2p), Itzhaki, Ohayon, Toni Calvo
02/03	Ethnikos	a	2-2	Itzhaki 2
09/03	AEK	h	1-1	Laborde
16/03	AEL	a	1-1	Itzhaki
31/03	APOEL	h	0-2	
06/04	AEK	h	0-3	
13/04	APOEL	a	0-0	
20/04	Omonia	h	0-0	
28/04	Omonia	a	0-1	
12/05	AEK	a	1-0	Evandro Roncatto
18/05	APOEL	h	2-1	Itzhaki 2 (1p)

No	Name	Nat	DoB	Pos	Aps	(s)	Gls
5	Dan Alexa	ROU	28/10/79	M	20	(2)	
2	Marko Andić	SRB	14/12/83	D	26	(2)	
42	Adamos Andreou		18/12/94	M		(1)	
30	Andreas Avraam		06/06/87	A	6	(2)	
4	Jurgen Colin	NED	20/01/81	D	21	(2)	
40	Dimitris Economou		10/11/82	D		(1)	
11	Evandro Roncatto	BRA	24/05/86	A	4	(14)	2
44	George Galamaz	ROU	05/04/81	D	6	(1)	
33	Branko Ilić	SVN	06/02/83	D	26		1
41	Panagiotis Loizides		28/02/95	D		(1)	
10	Barak Itzhaki	ISR	25/09/84	A	19	(4)	13
27	Emil Jula	ROU	03/01/80	A	2	(6)	
8	Juliano Spadacio	BRA	16/11/80	M	27	(1)	14
20	Vincent Laban		09/09/84	M	12	(9)	
21	Ricardo Laborde	COL	16/02/88	M	23	(2)	6
31	Christos Mastrou		30/01/88	G	12	(2)	
99	Moshe Ohayon	ISR	24/05/83	M	6	(14)	1
9	Ioannis Okkas		11/02/77	A	13	(16)	7
3	Paulo Jorge	POR	16/06/80	D	18	(1)	
17	Jan Rezek	CZE	05/05/82	A	26	(1)	12
80	Rui Duarte	POR	11/10/80	D	10	(1)	
23	Valentinos Sielis		01/03/90	D	9	(1)	
19	Giannis Skopelitis	GRE	02/05/78	M	26	(3)	
7	Toni Calvo	ESP	28/03/78	M	17	(4)	3
16	Matthieu Valverde	FRA	14/05/83	G	20		
88	William Boaventura	BRA	14/02/80	D	3		1

APOEL FC

Coach: Ivan Jovanović (SRB)
1926 • GSP (22,859) • apoelfc.com.cy
Major honours
Cypriot League (22) 1936, 1937, 1938, 1939, 1940,
1947, 1948, 1949, 1952, 1965, 1973, 1980, 1986,
1990, 1992, 1996, 2002, 2004, 2007, 2009, 2011, 2013;
Cypriot Cup (19) 1937, 1941, 1947, 1951, 1963, 1968,
1969, 1973, 1976, 1978, 1979, 1984, 1993, 1995, 1996,
1997, 1999, 2006, 2008

2012

03/09	Paralimni	a	5-0	Adorno 3, Manduca (p), Charalambides
16/09	Doxa	h	3-1	Adorno 2, Aloneftis
22/09	Alki	a	3-1	Budimir, Manduca, Adorno
30/09	Apollon	h	1-0	Adorno
07/10	Omonia	a	0-0	
22/10	Olympiakos	h	4-0	Nuno Morais 2, Adorno, Manduca (p)
27/10	Nea Salamis	a	3-0	Hélio Pinto 2, Aloneftis
05/11	Ayia Napa	h	4-1	Adorno 3, Manduca (p)
11/11	Ethnikos	a	1-0	Borda
18/11	AEK	h	1-2	Hélio Pinto
26/11	AEL	a	3-1	Hélio Pinto, Manduca (p), Charalambides
02/12	AEP	a	2-0	Manduca, Benachour
08/12	Anorthosis	h	0-1	
15/12	Paralimni	h	1-0	Adorno
22/12	Doxa	a	3-0	Manduca 2, Adorno

2013

06/01	Alki	h	1-1	Mário Sérgio
14/01	Apollon	a	2-1	Benachour, Hélio Pinto
19/01	Omonia	h	1-1	Hélio Pinto
27/01	Olympiakos	a	2-0	Manduca 2
02/02	Nea Salamis	h	2-0	Alexandrou, Biton
11/02	Ayia Napa	a	2-0	Borda, Biton
27/02	Ethnikos	h	1-0	Biton
03/03	AEK	h	1-0	Beckmann
09/03	AEL	h	2-0	Alexandrou, Nuno Morais
17/03	AEP	h	6-0	Mário Sérgio, Beckmann, Biton 2, Charalambides 2
31/03	Anorthosis	a	2-0	Biton, Nuno Morais
06/04	Omonia	a	0-3	
13/04	Anorthosis	h	0-0	
21/04	AEK	a	1-0	Mário Sérgio
27/04	AEK	h	0-1	
12/05	Omonia	h	4-3	Aloneftis, Budimir, Nuno Morais, Manduca (p)
18/05	Anorthosis	a	1-2	Manduca (p)

No	Name	Nat	DoB	Pos	Aps	(s)	Gls
12	Aldo Adorno	PAR	08/04/82	A	14	(3)	13
11	Nektarios Alexandrou		19/12/89	M	19	(5)	2
46	Efstathios Aloneftis		29/03/83	M	15	(8)	3
15	Marios Antoniades		14/05/90	D	4	(2)	
90	Mikkel Beckmann	DEN	24/10/83	M	7	(5)	2
8	Selim Benachour	TUN	08/09/81	M	10	(9)	2
9	Dudu Biton	ISR	01/03/88	A	7	(6)	6
27	Aritz Borda	ESP	03/01/85	D	24		2
7	Mario Budimir	CRO	13/02/86	A	12	(12)	2
10	Kostas Charalambides		25/07/81	M	17	(11)	4
22	Dionissis Chiotis		04/06/77	G	5		
19	Marios Elia		14/04/79	D	2		
31	Hélder Sousa	POR	13/10/77	M	1	(3)	
23	Hélio Pinto	POR	29/02/84	M	24	(5)	6
35	Christos Karipidis	GRE	02/12/82	D	17	(1)	
88	Anastasios Kissas		18/01/88	G		(1)	
5	Michael Klukowski	CAN	27/05/81	D	15	(1)	
21	Gustavo Manduca	BRA	08/06/80	A	32		12
6	Marcelo Oliveira	BRA	05/09/81	D	11	(1)	
28	Mário Sérgio	POR	28/07/81	D	24		3
26	Nuno Morais	POR	29/01/84	M	27		5
17	Marinos Satsias		24/05/78	M		(3)	
9	Esteban Solari	ARG	20/07/80	A		(3)	
77	Athos Solomou		30/11/85	M	10	(6)	
20	Alexandros Tziolis	GRE	13/02/85	M	24	(6)	
78	Urko Pardo	ESP	28/01/83	G	27		
30	Zuela	ANG	03/08/83	D	4	(2)	

APOLLON LIMASSOL FC

Coach: George Burley (SCO);
(20/09/12) Nikodimos Papavasiliou (GRE);
(12/03/13) Christakis Christoforou
1954 • Tsirion (13,000) • apollon.com.cy
Major honours
Cypriot League (3) 1991, 1994, 2006;
Cypriot Cup (7) 1966, 1967, 1986, 1992, 2001, 2010, 2013

2012

01/09	Ethnikos	h	2-0	Papoulis, Merkis
16/09	AEK	a	0-2	
24/09	AEL	a	0-2	
30/09	APOEL	a	0-1	
07/10	Anorthosis	h	0-2	
20/10	Paralimni	a	3-0	Souanis, Papoulis, Roberto
27/10	Doxa	h	1-0	Markovski
04/11	Alki	a	3-1	Parlov, Setti, Roberto
10/11	AEP	h	4-0	Papoulis 2, Hamdani, Dady
18/11	Omonia	a	2-1	Parlov, Theodoridis
25/11	Olympiakos	a	1-1	Roberto
01/12	Nea Salamis	h	3-1	Papoulis, Dady, Markovski
08/12	Ayia Napa	h	1-0	Papoulis
16/12	Ethnikos	a	1-1	Papoulis
22/12	AEK	h	1-2	Papoulis (p)

2013

05/01	AEL	a	2-3	Roberto 2
14/01	APOEL	h	1-2	Merkis
20/01	Anorthosis	a	0-0	
26/01	Paralimni	h	0-0	
02/02	Doxa	a	0-0	
10/02	Alki	h	2-1	Theodoridis, Charalambous
26/02	AEP	a	1-0	Roberto
02/03	Omonia	a	1-2	Solari
09/03	Olympiakos	h	1-1	og (Paulo Pina)
16/03	Nea Salamis	a	0-2	
31/03	Ayia Napa	h	2-1	Solari (p), Charalambous
06/04	Doxa	a	0-0	
13/04	AEL	a	1-2	Serra
20/04	Paralimni	h	4-1	Souanis, Solari 3 (1p)
27/04	Paralimni	a	1-0	Papoulis
12/05	Doxa	a	1-1	Solari
18/05	AEL	h	1-3	Solari (p)

No	Name	Nat	DoB	Pos	Aps	(s)	Gls
83	Bruno Vale	POR	08/04/83	G	28		
4	Horacio Cardozo	ARG	29/11/79	M	10	(1)	
27	Angelis Charalambous		31/05/89	D	21	(2)	2
30	Dady	CPV	13/08/81	A	7	(3)	2
31	Michalis Fani		04/02/81	G	4		
97	Andreas Fragkou		19/01/97	M	1		
77	Dimitrios Froxylias	GRE	28/06/93	M	5	(1)	
56	Rachid Hamdani	MAR	08/04/85	M	17	(1)	1
14	Iván Amaya	ESP	03/09/78	D		(1)	
11	Alex Konstantinou		11/04/92	A	11	(12)	
48	Charalambos Kyriacou		09/02/95	M	6	(5)	
5	Bojan Markovski	MKD	08/08/83	D	15	(2)	2
16	Georgios Merkis		30/07/84	D	13	(1)	2
81	Miguelito	POR	04/02/81	D	19		
17	Kyriakos Panagi		22/04/96	M	1	(2)	
26	Fotios Papoulis	GRE	22/01/85	M	25	(1)	9
4	Ivan Parlov	CRO	18/04/84	M	20	(3)	2
22	Paulinho	BRA	24/08/83	D	5	(7)	
29	Roberto	ESP	04/02/80	A	24	(4)	6
13	Emmanuel Serra	ARG	17/05/86	M	10	(3)	1
19	Sebastián Setti	ARG	09/02/84	M	11	(2)	1
32	Esteban Solari	ARG	20/07/80	A	8	(3)	7
9	Dimitrios Souanis	GRE	17/01/85	A	13	(14)	2
8	Andreas Stavrou		27/10/88	M	6	(7)	
28	Marios Stylianou		23/09/93	M	4		
42	Stylianos Stylianou		06/07/95	M		(1)	
20	Romeo Surdu	ROU	12/01/84	A		(1)	
10	Georgios Theodoridis	GRE	03/07/80	M	21	(3)	2
2	Toni	POR	23/07/79	D	28		
88	Georgios Vasiliou		12/08/84	M	11	(9)	

AYIA NAPA FC

Coach: Nikos Kolompourdas (GRE);
(25/02/13) Costas Loizou
1990 • Tasos Markou, Paralimni (8,000) • ayianapafc.com

2012

02/09	Omonia	a	0-5	
15/09	Olympiakos	h	1-1	og (Nicolaou)
23/09	Nea Salamis	a	0-1	
30/09	AEP	a	0-3	
06/10	Ethnikos	h	1-0	Riera (p)
20/10	AEK	a	0-3	
29/10	AEL	h	0-4	
05/11	APOEL	a	1-4	og (Klukowski)
11/11	Anorthosis	h	0-1	
17/11	Paralimni	a	0-1	
25/11	Doxa	h	0-2	
02/12	Alki	a	2-0	Kolokoudias (p), Barboudis
08/12	Apollon	a	0-1	
15/12	Omonia	h	0-3	
23/12	Olympiakos	a	2-3	Riera, Jackson

2013

05/01	Nea Salamis	h	1-2	Nikić
12/01	AEP	h	1-2	Pierettis
19/01	Ethnikos	a	1-2	Kolokoudias
26/01	AEK	h	1-1	Kolokoudias
02/02	AEL	a	0-2	
11/02	APOEL	h	0-2	
27/02	Anorthosis	a	1-5	Miguel Vargas
03/03	Paralimni	h	1-4	Miguel Vargas
09/03	Doxa	a	1-2	Fausto
16/03	Alki	h	0-3	
31/03	Apollon	a	1-2	Kolokoudias

No	Name	Nat	DoB	Pos	Aps	(s)	Gls
8	Nikos Barboudis	GRE	06/08/89	D	20		1
1	Savvas Channas		13/01/91	G	1		
31	Athos Chrysostomou		06/08/81	G	13		
4	Fabeta	POR	01/04/87	D	6	(1)	
21	Fausto	POR	12/01/85	D	12		1
14	Michael Felgate	ENG	01/04/91	D	10	(2)	
15	Christos Gerimos		24/05/93	G		(1)	
23	Ginho	POR	08/06/85	M	18		
16	Hugo Soares	POR	16/10/82	M	23		
12	Jackson	BRA	05/01/87	A	11	(2)	1
27	Konstantinos Kafkarkou		08/07/93	M		(1)	
32	Antonis Katsis		06/09/89	D	15	(7)	
19	Georgios Kolokoudias		03/05/89	A	17	(5)	4
34	Michalis Konstantinou		18/09/93	M	1	(1)	
9	Predrag Lazić	SRB	15/01/82	M	22	(1)	
26	Marquinhos	BRA	26/01/86	M	8	(5)	
25	Antonis Mertakkas		10/06/80	D	6	(5)	
55	Miguel Vargas	POR	18/11/78	M	4	(3)	2
7	Branislav Nikić	BIH	15/01/86	M	5	(6)	1
29	Kweku Seth Osei	GHA	17/09/93	D		(1)	
6	Paulo Sérgio	BRA	21/07/81	M	10	(1)	
13	Ori Peso	ISR	08/01/87	D	7		
3	Adamos Pierettis		27/11/82	D	11	(5)	1
17	Giorgos Pieroulli		02/01/93	M		(1)	
10	Ricardo Catchana	POR	10/08/83	A	7	(3)	
11	Riera	POR	15/09/86	A	10	(4)	2
15	Robson	BRA	03/11/86	M	4		
2	Martinos Solomou		11/07/80	A	5	(6)	
5	Petros Sotiriou		05/10/82	D	3	(1)	
24	Zacharias Theodorou		07/07/93	M	12	(4)	
20	Nektarios Tziortzis		09/11/90	M	3	(5)	
28	Vítor Afonso	POR	15/04/83	A	10	(6)	
22	Maciej Zając	POL	07/03/78	G	12		

DOXA KATOKOPIA FC

Coach: Marios Konstantinou;
(01/11/12) Loukas Hadjiloukas
1954 • Ammochostos, Larnaca (4,000) •
doxakatokopiasfc.com

2012

03/09	AEL	h	1-3	Fofana
16/09	APOEL	a	1-3	Ricardo Fernandes
22/09	Anorthosis	h	0-2	
29/09	Paralimni	a	0-1	
07/10	AEP	h	1-0	Fofana
21/10	Alki	h	0-1	
27/10	Apollon	a	0-1	
03/11	Omonia	h	1-1	Ricardo Fernandes
10/11	Olympiakos	a	2-1	Leandro Silva, Fofana
18/11	Nea Salamis	h	1-0	Toy
25/11	Ayia Napa	a	2-0	Ricardo Fernandes, Leandro Silva
02/12	Ethnikos	h	1-1	Fofana
09/12	AEK	a	2-1	Ricardo Fernandes, Fofana
16/12	AEL	a	0-2	
22/12	APOEL	h	0-3	

2013

05/01	Anorthosis	a	0-3	
12/01	Paralimni	h	1-1	Toy
19/01	AEP	a	4-0	Fofana, Jorge Troiteiro 2, Siontis
28/01	Alki	a	2-2	Ricardo Fernandes, Akinsola
02/02	Apollon	h	0-0	
10/02	Omonia	a	0-3	
27/02	Olympiakos	h	1-1	Carlos André
02/03	Nea Salamis	a	1-0	Ricardo Fernandes
09/03	Ayia Napa	h	2-1	Fofana (p), Jorge Troiteiro
16/03	Ethnikos	a	1-3	Pablo Suárez
31/03	AEK	h	2-6	João Leonardo, Jorge Troiteiro
06/04	Apollon	a	0-0	
13/04	Paralimni	h	1-0	Fofana (p)
20/04	AEL	h	1-1	og (Maykon)
27/04	AEL	a	0-3	
12/05	Apollon	h	1-1	Pablo Suárez
18/05	Paralimni	a	4-2	Pablo Suárez, Fofana 3

No	Name	Nat	DoB	Pos	Aps	(s)	Gls
11	Abel Pereira	POR	15/04/90	D	20	(2)	
77	Kabiru Akinsola	NGA	21/01/91	A	2	(6)	1
30	Alexandre Negri	BRA	27/03/81	G	28		
4	Adama Bamba	CIV	04/01/92	M		(2)	
7	Carlos André	POR	15/04/82	M	20	(6)	1
13	Carlos Marques	POR	06/02/83	D	11	(4)	
8	Castanheira	POR	07/09/77	M	19	(7)	
17	Andreas Chatzigeorgiou		12/06/93	M	1		
22	Konstantinos Christodoulou		22/03/96	A		(4)	
16	Amik Ciani	FRA	01/12/82	A	2	(7)	
26	Gaossou Fofana	CIV	17/04/84	M	29	(1)	11
18	Semir Hadžibulić	SRB	16/08/86	M	7	(5)	
25	João Leonardo	BRA	30/07/85	D	28		1
21	Jorge Troiteiro	ESP	09/04/84	M	20	(11)	4
34	Leandro Silva	BRA	11/01/89	D	24		2
12	Michalis Morfis		15/01/79	G	4		
44	Mohamed N'Dao	CIV	02/03/93	M	4	(3)	
3	Pablo Suárez	ESP	25/04/84	D	17	(6)	3
2	Juan Pedro Pina	ESP	29/06/85	D	14		
10	Ricardo Fernandes	POR	21/04/78	M	22	(3)	6
5	Esteban Sachetti	ARG	21/11/85	M	12		
6	Stefanos Siontis	GRE	04/09/87	D	27	(1)	1
19	Rafael Sofokleous		19/02/93	M	2	(2)	
21	Sozos Sozou		06/08/92	D	2	(4)	
4	Tiago Conceição	POR	17/04/89	D	7	(2)	
23	Toy	CPV	15/06/77	A	21	(4)	2
14	Michael Weir	ENG	18/02/91	M	9	(2)	

ENOSIS NEON PARALIMNI FC

Coach: Zouvanis Zouvani; (03/10/12) Ton Caanen (NED);
(13/04/13) Marios Karas
1936 •Tasos Markou (8,000) • enpfc.com

2012

03/09	APOEL	h	0-5	
15/09	Anorthosis	a	1-1	Leonardo
22/09	AEP	h	1-1	Leonardo
29/09	Doxa	h	1-0	Milhazes (p)
06/10	Alki	a	1-1	Leonardo
20/10	Apollon	h	0-3	
27/10	Omonia	a	0-2	
04/11	Olympiakos	h	1-2	Yakubu
10/11	Nea Salamis	a	2-0	Leonardo, Yakubu
17/11	Ayia Napa	h	1-0	Milhazes (p)
24/11	Ethnikos	a	0-0	
01/12	AEK	h	1-2	Leonardo (p)
10/12	AEL	a	1-1	Okoduwa
15/12	APOEL	a	0-1	
23/12	Anorthosis	h	1-2	Konstantinou

2013

05/01	AEP	a	1-0	Oravec
12/01	Doxa	a	1-1	Daemen (p)
20/01	Alki	h	1-1	Langlet
26/01	Apollon	a	0-0	
02/02	Omonia	h	0-1	
09/02	Olympiakos	h	3-2	Mrdaković 2, Stathakis
27/02	Nea Salamis	h	0-0	
03/03	Ayia Napa	a	4-1	Anderson, og (Fausto), Mrdaković 2
09/03	Ethnikos	h	1-1	Krivokapić
16/03	AEK	a	0-5	
30/03	AEL	h	1-2	Artymatas
06/04	AEL	a	2-1	Mrdaković 2 (1p)
13/04	Doxa	a	0-1	
20/04	Apollon	h	1-4	Artymatas
27/04	Apollon	a	0-1	
11/05	AEL	a	0-3	
18/05	Doxa	h	2-4	Mrdaković, Artymatas

No	Name	Nat	DoB	Pos	Aps	(s)	Gls
5	Anderson	BRA	10/01/83	D	17	(1)	1
4	Kostakis Artymatas		15/04/93	M	16	(2)	3
23	Bouna Coundoul	SEN	04/03/82	G	5		
28	Tom Daemen	NED	17/06/85	M	12	(1)	1
13	Aldo Duscher	ARG	29/03/79	M	8		
10	Filipe Gui	POR	28/09/84	M	7	(1)	
2	Aris Galanopoulos	GRE	29/09/81	D	12	(2)	
17	Demos Goumenos		25/12/78	D	12	(1)	
1	Andrew Hogg	MLT	02/03/85	G	24		
6	Hugo Faria	POR	15/02/83	M	21	(2)	
45	Michalis Karas		20/01/93	D	2		
16	Georgios Kolanis		04/11/80	M	15	(7)	
24	Andreas Konstantinou		12/10/80	D	14	(3)	1
32	Loizos Kosma		25/06/95	M	5	(4)	
22	Andreas Kittos		09/09/90	G	3		
	Simeon Kittos		11/05/96	D	1		
88	Radovan Krivokapić	MNE	14/08/78	M	9	(2)	1
7	Dejan Krljanović	SVN	12/07/89	A		(1)	
3	Yoann Langlet	MTN	25/12/82	M	13	(3)	1
42	Leonardo	BRA	18/02/92	M	11		5
39	Nicolas Liotatis		17/06/95	D		(1)	
55	Milhazes	POR	17/03/81	D	23		2
37	Antonis Moulazimis		14/09/96	A	1	(1)	
29	Dimitris Moulazimis		15/01/92	D	20	(4)	
9	Miljan Mrdaković	SRB	06/05/82	A	11	(4)	7
43	Dimitris Oikonomou		04/03/95	D		(1)	
30	Emmanuel Okoduwa	NGA	21/11/83	A	5	(5)	1
14	Tomáš Oravec	SVK	03/07/80	A	9	(10)	1
38	Konstantinos Pierettis		16/04/96	M		(2)	
33	Panayiotis Pittatzis		13/11/96	M	2	(2)	
11	Onisiforos Rousias		12/12/92	A	1	(7)	
19	Rui	EQG	28/05/85	D	29	(1)	
35	Konstantinos Skitsas		11/05/94	A		(1)	
40	Petros Spyrou		23/09/96	M		(1)	
36	Dimitris Tingou		15/01/95	M		(1)	
18	Stavros Stathakis	GRE	30/10/87	D	11	(8)	1
8	Georgios Tofas		17/06/89	A	5	(2)	
12	Shaibu Yakubu	GHA	02/11/86	A	19	(4)	2
30	Andreas Zouvanis		31/03/95	M	1		
15	Zé Vítor	POR	11/02/82	M	8	(1)	

ETHNIKOS ACHNAS FC

Coach: Nikos Papadopoulos (GRE);
(14/10/12) Nikos Andronikou;
(05/12/12) Stephen Constantine;
(25/02/13) Nikos Kolobourdas (GRE)
1968 • Dasaki (5,000) • fcachna.com.cy

2012

01/09	Apollon	a	0-2	
15/09	Omonia	h	1-1	Penta
23/09	Olympiakos	a	1-3	Oliveira
30/09	Nea Salamis	h	1-1	Vattis
06/10	Ayia Napa	a	0-1	
20/10	AEP	h	0-0	
28/10	AEK	h	0-1	
03/11	AEL	h	1-1	Marco Paixão
11/11	APOEL	h	0-1	
19/11	Anorthosis	a	1-5	Vattis
24/11	Paralimni	h	0-0	
02/12	Doxa	a	1-1	Marco Paixão
09/12	Alki	h	0-2	
16/12	Apollon	h	1-1	Vattis
22/12	Omonia	a	1-2	Oseni

2013

05/01	Olympiakos	h	1-1	Mashinya
13/01	Nea Salamis	a	1-0	Marco Aurélio
19/01	Ayia Napa	h	2-1	Arnal, Marco Aurélio
26/01	AEP	a	3-0	Skulić, Arnal, Silas
03/02	AEK	a	1-2	og (Mertakas)
10/02	AEL	a	1-3	Marco Paixão
27/02	APOEL	a	0-1	
02/03	Anorthosis	h	2-2	Skulić, Kenmogne
09/03	Paralimni	a	1-1	Marco Paixão
16/03	Doxa	h	3-1	Silas, Marco Paixão, Kenmogne
30/03	Alki	a	5-6	Marco Aurélio, Kenmogne 2, Marco Paixão 2 (1p)
07/04	Alki	h	1-1	Marco Paixão
14/04	Nea Salamis	a	2-1	Marco Paixão, Maghradze
21/04	Olympiakos	a	2-4	Pitsillidis, Marco Paixão
28/04	Olympiakos	h	3-1	Marco Aurélio, Kenmogne, Marco Paixão
11/05	Alki	a	3-1	Marco Paixão 2, Penta
19/05	Nea Salamis	h	2-2	Marco Paixão 2

No	Name	Nat	DoB	Pos	Aps	(s)	Gls
5	Allyson	BRA	28/01/82	D	8		
32	Nikos Arabatzis	GRE	10/03/84	D	12		
24	Arnal	ESP	21/11/80	A	10	(5)	2
88	Matthieu Bemba	FRA	04/03/88	M	5	(3)	
25	Vinko Buden	CRO	18/01/86	D	6	(1)	
26	Christoforos Christofi		23/03/91	M	4	(2)	
16	Elpidoforos Elia		05/08/85	M	21	(2)	
99	Emmanuel Kenmogne	CMR	02/09/80	A	13	(11)	5
4	Abdelkarim Kissi	MAR	05/05/80	A	8	(3)	
2	Levan Maghradze	GEO	05/12/77	D	23	(2)	1
1	Arkadiusz Malarz	POL	19/06/80	G	22		
5	Marco Aurélio	BRA	27/03/83	D	27	(2)	4
9	Marco Paixão	POR	19/09/84	A	30	(1)	15
28	Edward Mashinya	ZIM	22/02/84	A	8	(13)	1
14	Christodoulos Michael		05/12/95	M		(1)	
8	Oliveira	POR	01/05/84	M	11	(1)	1
4	Waheed Oseni	NGA	17/01/88	D	14		1
11	Marcelo Penta	ARG	26/08/85	M	11	(6)	2
6	Angelos Perikleous		05/01/90	M	1	(6)	
17	Nikos Pitsillidis		17/12/93	A		(5)	1
39	Andreas Pittaras		03/08/90	A		(3)	
10	Christos Poyiatzis		12/04/78	A	10	(13)	
33	Fredrik Risp	SWE	15/12/80	D	11	(2)	
44	Marko Šarlija	CRO	31/01/82	G	10		
20	Silas	POR	01/09/76	M	15	(1)	2
15	Dimitrios Simov		09/04/92	D	29		
53	Ernad Skulić	CRO	02/05/80	D	15		2
7	Elias Vattis		28/02/86	M	22	(8)	3
18	Vítor Lima	POR	10/08/81	M	6	(2)	

NEA SALAMIS FAMAGUSTA FC

Coach: Nikos Andreou; (21/11/12) Mirsad Jonuz (MKD)
1948 • Ammochostos (4,000) • neasalamis.com.cy
Major honours
Cypriot Cup (1) 1990

2012

01/09	Olympiakos	a	1-2	Gray
15/09	AEP	a	0-1	
23/09	Ayia Napa	h	1-0	Hélio Roque
30/09	Ethnikos	a	1-1	Pedro Moreira
06/10	AEK	h	0-0	
20/10	AEL	a	1-2	Hélio Roque
27/10	APOEL	h	0-3	
04/11	Anorthosis	a	0-1	
10/11	Paralimni	h	0-2	
18/11	Doxa	h	0-1	
25/11	Alki	h	1-1	og (Santamaria)
01/12	Apollon	a	1-3	Oper
08/12	Omonia	h	0-1	
15/12	Olympiakos	h	3-2	Gray, Lambropoulos, Oper
23/12	AEP	h	1-1	Oper

2013

05/01	Ayia Napa	a	2-1	og (Nikić), Oper
13/01	Ethnikos	h	0-1	
19/01	AEK	a	2-1	David Sousa, Oper
27/01	AEL	h	0-1	
02/02	APOEL	a	0-2	
10/02	Anorthosis	a	2-1	Alimi, Englezou
27/02	Paralimni	a	0-0	
02/03	Doxa	h	0-1	
09/03	Alki	a	0-1	
16/03	Apollon	h	2-0	Rujovič, Sotirović
30/03	Omonia	a	0-6	
07/04	Olympiakos	a	0-0	
14/04	Ethnikos	h	1-2	Lambropoulos
21/04	Alki	h	1-3	Englezou
28/04	Alki	a	2-1	Hélio Roque, Lambropoulos
11/05	Olympiakos	h	3-0	Hélio Roque (p), Lambropoulos, Gray
19/05	Ethnikos	a	2-2	Hélio Roque 2 (1p)

No	Name	Nat	DoB	Pos	Aps	(s)	Gls
20	Adamos Adamou		02/07/93	M	1	(1)	
17	Jerome Agbo	GHA	19/06/94	M	11	(6)	
16	Armend Alimi	ALB	11/12/87	M	17		1
1	Srdjan Blažić	MNE	26/11/82	G	15		
99	Evagoras Chatzifragkiskou		29/10/86	G	4		
8	Christos Chatzipantelidis	GRE	12/08/81	M	7	(8)	
10	David Sousa	ESP	03/02/80	M	14	(5)	1
2	Eduardo Pincelli	BRA	23/04/83	M	8	(4)	
33	Nikos Englezou		11/07/93	M	11	(9)	2
26	Károly Graszl	HUN	08/01/85	D	23	(3)	
11	Julian Gray	ENG	21/09/79	M	27	(4)	3
50	Solomon Grimes	LBR	24/07/87	D	21	(1)	
28	Hélio Roque	POR	20/07/85	M	29		6
13	Iván Benítez	ESP	31/05/88	D	23		
13	Zoltán Kovács	HUN	29/10/84	D	13		
5	Georgios Lambropoulos	GRE	26/10/84	M	28		4
3	Jimmy Modeste	CPV	08/07/81	D	28		
6	Christos Modestou		03/07/88	M	2	(4)	
21	Pericles Moustakas		23/06/83	D	7		
27	Andres Oper	EST	07/11/77	A	16	(12)	5
14	Timotheos Pavlou		08/09/94			(3)	
25	Pedro Moreira	CPV	16/01/83	M	2	(9)	1
4	Rodrigão Ribeiro	BRA	18/04/78	D	8		
77	Enes Rujovič	SVN	29/05/89	M	2	(4)	1
19	Saavedra	POR	01/02/81	M	14	(5)	
9	Semedo	CPV	26/12/79	A	8	(4)	
30	Modestos Sotiriou		03/07/93	A	1	(5)	
82	Vuk Sotirović	SRB	13/07/82	M	9	(2)	1
7	Prodromos Therapontos		25/03/89	M	3	(5)	

OLYMPIAKOS NICOSIA FC

Coach: Nikodimos Papavasiliou (GRE);
(25/09/12) Renos Demetriades;
(11/02/13) Marios Konstantinou
1931 • GSP (22,859) • olympiacos.com.cy
Major honours
Cypriot League (3) 1967, 1969, 1971;
Cypriot Cup (1) 1977

2012

01/09	Nea Salamis	h	2-1	Hélder Castro, Chidi
15/09	Ayia Napa	a	1-1	Henrique
23/09	Ethnikos	h	3-1	Henrique 2, Chidi
29/09	AEK	a	0-1	
08/10	AEL	a	0-0	
22/10	APOEL	a	0-4	
28/10	Anorthosis	h	1-3	Sotiriou
04/11	Paralimni	a	2-1	Henrique, Sotiriou
10/11	Doxa	h	1-2	Sotiriou
18/11	Alki	a	0-0	
25/11	Apollon	h	1-1	Henrique
03/12	Omonia	a	0-2	
09/12	AEP	h	3-1	Mércio, Panayiotou, Henrique
15/12	Nea Salamis	a	2-3	Henrique 2 (1p)
23/12	Ayia Napa	h	3-2	Paulo Pina, Hélder Castro 2

2013

05/01	Ethnikos	a	1-1	Hélder Castro
12/01	AEK	h	0-2	
20/01	AEL	a	1-1	Sotiriou
27/01	APOEL	h	0-2	
03/02	Anorthosis	a	3-4	Monachello 2, Michail
09/02	Paralimni	h	2-3	Monachello, Sotiriou
27/02	Doxa	a	1-1	Michail
03/03	Alki	h	2-2	Hélder Castro, Henrique
09/03	Apollon	a	1-1	Manolo Gaspar
16/03	Omonia	h	1-4	Henrique
30/03	AEP	a	5-0	Sotiriou, Monachello, Henrique, N'Dao, Pedro Duarte
07/04	Nea Salamis	h	0-0	
14/04	Alki	a	1-2	Monachello
21/04	Ethnikos	h	4-2	Henrique, Hélder Castro, Monachello, Michail
28/04	Ethnikos	a	1-3	Monachello
11/05	Nea Salamis	a	0-3	
19/05	Alki	h	4-2	Sotiriou 2, Michail, Henrique

No	Name	Nat	DoB	Pos	Aps	(s)	Gls
35	Jamiu Alimi	NGA	05/10/92	D	6		
12	Cesinha	BRA	11/07/81	M		(5)	
15	Philip Chidi	NGA	20/02/84	A	15	(2)	2
23	Mamadou Djikiné	MLI	16/05/87	M	13	(5)	
10	Hélder Castro	POR	24/01/86	M	25	(3)	6
9	Henrique	POR	31/03/80	A	26	(2)	13
78	Sani Kaita	NGA	02/05/86	M		(2)	
1	Paweł Kapsa	POL	24/07/82	G	31		
93	Georgios Karkotis		16/01/93	D		(2)	
96	Evangelos Kyriakou		03/02/92	M		(1)	
2	Manolo Gaspar	ESP	03/02/81	D	10		1
70	Mario	ESP	25/03/85	M	3	(5)	
19	Giannis Mavrou		19/07/94	A		(5)	
8	Mércio	BRA	26/05/80	M	14		1
73	Marcos Michail		13/06/91	A	4	(12)	4
73	Gaetano Monachello	ITA	09/02/93	M	13	(1)	7
24	Mohamed N'Dao	CIV	09/02/93	M	10		1
11	Nikos Nicolaou		10/05/79	D	17	(6)	
30	Giannis Pachipis		04/11/94	M	3	(3)	
94	Konstantinos Panagi		08/10/94	G	1		
45	Emilios Panayiotou		22/09/92	M	2	(13)	1
13	Paulo Pina	CPV	04/01/81	D	27		1
21	Pedro Duarte	POR	22/04/78	M	28		1
33	Georgios Pelagias		10/05/85	D	17	(5)	
6	Kyriakos Polykarpou		17/03/80	M	19	(5)	
4	Boris Rotenberg	FIN	19/05/86	D	10	(3)	
20	Pieros Sotiriou		13/01/93	A	28	(1)	8
7	Robert Stambolziev	AUS	26/10/90	M	13	(11)	
17	Tiago Costa	POR	22/04/85	D	17		
55	Esteban Sachetti	ARG	21/11/85	M	12	(1)	1
15	Christos Theofilou		30/04/80	M	10	(1)	
99	Vouho	CIV	25/06/87	A	20	(4)	11

AC OMONIA

Coach: Neophytos Larkou;
(26/09/12) Toni Savevski (MKD)
1948 • GSP (22,859) • omonia.com.cy
Major honours
Cypriot League (20) 1961, 1966, 1972, 1974, 1975,
1976, 1977, 1978, 1979, 1981, 1982, 1983, 1984, 1985,
1987, 1989, 1993, 2001, 2003, 2010;
Cypriot Cup (14) 1965, 1972, 1974, 1980, 1981, 1982,
1983, 1988, 1991, 1994, 2000, 2005, 2011, 2012

2012

01/09	Ayia Napa	h	5-0	og (Fabeta), Leandro, Christofi, Avraam, Freddy (p)
15/09	Ethnikos	a	1-1	Christofi
22/09	AEK	a	0-1	
29/09	AEL	a	1-1	Freddy
07/10	APOEL	h	0-0	
21/10	Anorthosis	a	0-2	
27/10	Paralimni	h	2-0	Leandro, Schembri
03/11	Doxa	a	1-1	André Alves (p)
11/11	Alki	h	1-0	Leandro
18/11	Apollon	a	1-2	Leandro
24/11	AEP	h	4-2	Freddy (p), Efrem, Renato Margaça, João Alves
03/12	Olympiakos	h	2-0	Freddy 2 (1p)
08/12	Nea Salamis	a	1-0	Marco Soares
15/12	Ayia Napa	a	3-0	Schembri, André Alves, Christofi
22/12	Ethnikos	h	2-1	Alabi, Schembri

2013

06/01	AEK	a	1-2	Danielson
13/01	AEL	h	2-0	Christofi, Freddy
19/01	APOEL	a	1-1	Alabi
26/01	Anorthosis	h	1-3	André Alves
02/02	Paralimni	a	1-0	André Alves
10/02	Doxa	h	3-0	Efrem 2, Leandro
26/02	Alki	a	4-2	João Paulo, André Alves, Christofi, Alabi
02/03	Apollon	h	2-1	Christofi, João Paulo
09/03	AEP	a	2-1	Schembri, Christofi
16/03	Olympiakos	a	4-1	André Alves 3, Efrem
30/03	Nea Salamis	h	6-0	Marco Soares 2, Nuno Assis, Efrem, André Alves 2
06/04	APOEL	h	3-0	Efrem 2, Leandro
13/04	AEK	a	3-0	Bruno Aguiar, André Alves
20/04	Anorthosis	a	0-0	
28/04	Anorthosis	h	4-0	André Alves 2, Schembri, Nuno Assis
12/05	APOEL	a	3-4	og (Karipidis), Christofi, André Alves
18/05	AEK	h	3-1	Schembri, André Alves 2 (1p)

No	Name	Nat	DoB	Pos	Aps	(s)	Gls
2	Rasheed Alabi	NGA	09/01/86	D	23	(1)	3
25	André Alves	BRA	10/10/83	A	22	(7)	16
11	Andreas Avraam		06/06/87	M	3	(1)	1
10	Bruno Aguiar	POR	24/02/81	M	3	(10)	1
18	Christoforos Charalambous		09/07/92	D	1	(2)	
77	Dimitris Christofi		28/09/88	A	31	(1)	8
14	Danielson	BRA	09/06/81	D	15	(7)	1
13	Marios Demetriou		25/12/92	M		(1)	
7	Georgios Efrem		05/07/89	M	18	(8)	7
9	Freddy	ANG	14/08/89	A	12	(14)	6
6	João Alves	POR	18/08/80	M	4	(10)	1
23	João Paulo	POR	06/06/81	M	18	(4)	2
31	José Moreira	POR	20/03/82	G	11		
40	Charalambos Kyriakou		15/10/89	M	8	(3)	
44	Leandro	HUN	19/03/82	D	29	(1)	
61	Johnny Leoni	SUI	30/06/84	G	3		
26	Ohad Levita	ISR	17/02/86	G	18		
60	Marco Soares	CPV	02/01/85	M	26		3
21	Nuno Assis	POR	25/11/77	M	27	(1)	2
1	Savo Pavićević	MNE	11/12/80	D	6		
28	Renato Margaça	POR	17/07/85	M	7	(10)	1
8	Onisiforos Rousias		12/12/92	A		(1)	
17	Anthony Scaramozzino	FRA	30/04/85	D	29		
30	André Schembri	MLT	27/05/86	M	14	(11)	6
24	Yuval Shpungin	ISR	03/04/87	D	24	(2)	

Top goalscorers

18	Bernardo Vasconcelos (Alki)
10	André Alves (Omonia)
15	Marco Paixão (Ethnikos)
14	Juliano Spadacio (Anorthosis)
13	Barak Itzhaki (Anorthosis)
	Aldo Adorno (APOEL)
	Henrique (Olympiakos)
12	Jan Rezek (Anorthosis)
	Gustavo Manduca (APOEL)
11	Nassir Maachi (AEK)
	Vouho (AEL)
	Gaossou Fofana (Doxa)

Promoted clubs

ARIS LIMASSOL FC
Coach: Dimitris Ioannou
1930 • Tsirion (14,000) • aris-fc.com

AEK KOUKLIA FC
Coach: Fangio Buyse (BEL)
1968 • Dimotiko, Chloraka (3,500) • aekkouklion.com

ERMIS ARADIPPOU FC
Coach: Nikos Andronikou;
(14/10/12) Nikos Panayiotou
1958 • Aradippou Municipal (4,500) • no website

SECOND LEVEL FINAL TABLE 2012/13

		Pld	W	D	L	F	A	Pts
1	Aris Limassol FC	32	19	8	5	75	29	65
2	AEK Kouklia FC	32	21	2	9	69	37	65
3	Ermis Aradippou FC	32	17	7	8	47	34	58
4	Anagennisis Derynia FC	32	13	8	11	31	29	47
5	APEP Kyperounda FC	26	12	6	8	35	25	42
6	Nikos & Sokratis Erimis FC	26	12	5	9	37	33	41
7	Omonia Aradippou FC	26	9	8	9	40	40	35
8	Othellos Athienou FC	26	9	7	10	28	35	34
9	PAEEK FC	26	9	6	11	35	37	33
10	AEZ Zakakiou FC	26	10	2	14	34	45	32
11	Onisilos Sotira FC	26	8	8	10	21	32	29
12	Chalkanoras Idaliou FC	26	5	13	34	42	15	
13	Akritas Chloraka FC	26	4	5	17	23	42	14
14	Ethnikos Assia FC	26	3	3	20	25	74	12

*NB After 26 rounds top four clubs enter play-off round;
Akritas Chloraka FC & Onisilos Sotira FC – 3 pts deducted.*

PROMOTION/RELEGATION PLAY-OFF

(23/05/13)
Nea Salamis 3-0 Anagennisis Derynia

Domestic cup: Cyprus Cup 2012/13

SECOND ROUND

(31/10/12)
AEK Kouklia 2-3 Ethnikos Achnas *(aet)*
AEZ 0-2 Olympiakos
Alki 6-0 Akritas
APOEL 8-1 Chalkanoras
Apollon 5-0 APEP
Doxa 0-1 Anagennisis Derynia
Ethnikos Assia 0-4 Paralimni
Omonia Aradippou 0-3 AEK Larnaca
Onisilos 0-2 Anorthosis
Othellos 1-2 Nea Salamis

(07/11/12)
Aris 1-3 AEP *(aet)*

(21/11/12)
Ayia Napa 2-0 Nikos & Sokratis

Byes – AEL, Ermis, Omonia, PAEEK

THIRD ROUND

(09/01/13 & 16/01/13)
AEP 2-2, 4-1 PAEEK *(6-3)*
Ayia Napa 0-1, 3-0 Anagennisis Derynia *(3-1)*
Ermis 0-1, 0-0 Paralimni *(0-1)*
Ethnikos Achnas 0-2, 0-2 Omonia *(0-4)*

(09/01/13 & 23/01/13)
AEL 0-2, 3-1 APOEL *(3-3; AEL on away goals)*
Anorthosis 1-1, 2-1 Alki *(aet; 3-2)*

(09/01/13 & 30/01/13)
AEK Larnaca 1-0, 3-3 Olympiakos *(4-3)*

(23/01/13 & 30/01/13)
Nea Salamis 0-1, 0-1 Apollon *(0-2)*

QUARTER-FINALS

(13/02/13 & 06/03/13)
Omonia 4-0 Anorthosis *(Efrem 39, Nuno Assis 62, Freddy 90, Schembri 90)*
Anorthosis 0-2 Omonia *(Schembri 59, Freddy 82)*
(Omonia 6-0)

(20/02/13 & 06/03/13)
Ayia Napa 0-2 Apollon *(Papoulis 19, Surdu 90)*
Apollon 1-1 Ayia Napa *(Charalambous 33, Hugo Soares 42)*
(Apollon 3-1)

(20/02/13 & 13/03/13)
AEP 1-4 AEL *(Sielis 45; Orlando Sá 7, Rui Miguel 40, Maykon 66, Monteiro 73)*
AEL 3-0 AEP *(Konstantinou 4, Paulo Sérgio 10, Dosa Júnior 41p)*
(AEL 7-1)

(06/03/13 & 13/03/13)
Paralimni 1-1 AEK Larnaca *(Mrdaković 90; Joan Tomàs 1)*
AEK Larnaca 2-0 Paralimni *(Alexandre Afonso 57p, Pintado 90)*
(AEK Larnaca 3-1)

SEMI-FINALS

(10/04/13 & 17/04/13)
Apollon 2-0 AEK Larnaca *(Papoulis 16, Konstantinou 75)*
AEK Larnaca 1-1 Apollon *(Alexandre Afonso 29; Surdu 64)*
(Apollon 3-1)

Omonia 0-0 AEL
AEL 1-0 Omonia *(Vouho 45)*
(AEL 1-0)

FINAL

(22/05/13)
Tsirion, Limassol
APOLLON LIMASSOL FC 2 *(Cardozo 95, Surdu 118p)*
AEL LIMASSOL FC 1 *(Vouho 120+15)*
(aet)
Referee: Skomina (SVN)
APOLLON: Bruno Vale, Toni, Merkis, Charalambous, Hamdani, Theodoridis (Paulinho 73; Cardozo 92), Vasiliou, Kyriacou (Konstantinou 86), Papoulis, Surdu, Roberto
AEL: Degra, Marco Airosa (Maykon 17), Ouon, Dosa Júnior, Dédé, Luciano Bebê, Sachetti, Monteiro, Carlitos (Konstantinou 98), Orlando Sá (Paulo Sérgio 91), Vouho

Romeo Surdu scores the decisive penalty for Apollon in a dramatic cup final against Limassol rivals AEL

CZECH REPUBLIC

Fotbalová asociace České republiky (FAČR)

Address	Diskařská 2431/4	**President**	Miroslav Pelta
	CZ-160 17 Praha	**General secretary**	Rudolf Řepka
Tel	+420 2 3302 9111	**Media officer**	Jaroslav Kolář
Fax	+420 2 3335 3107	**Year of formation**	1901
E-mail	facr@fotbal.cz		
Website	fotbal.cz		

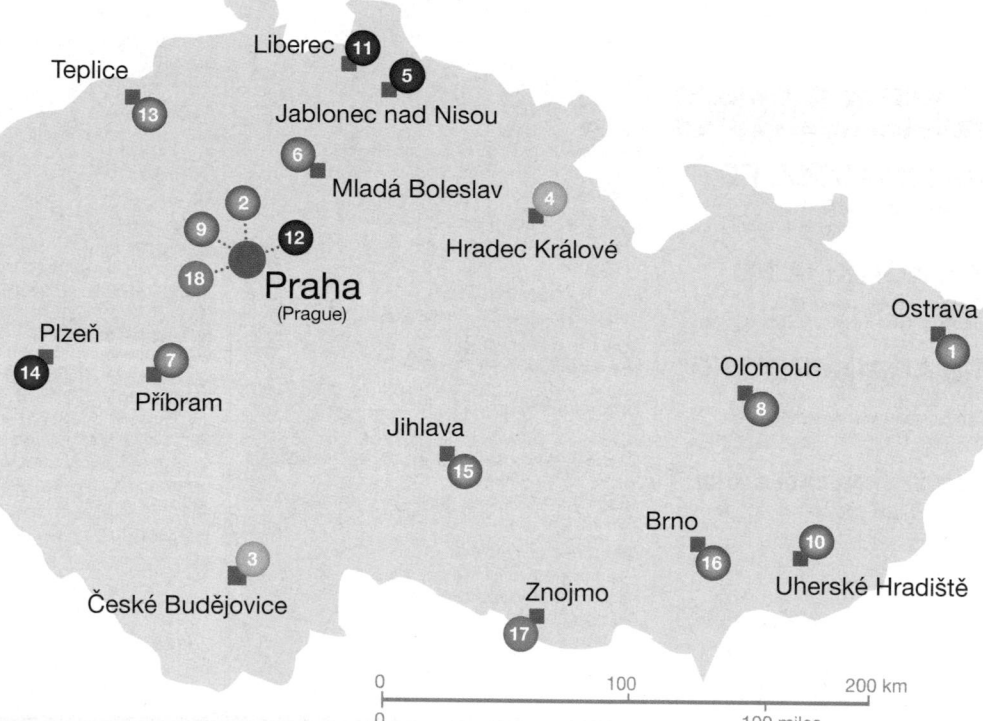

1. LIGA CLUBS

1. FC Baník Ostrava
2. FK Dukla Praha
3. SK Dynamo České Budějovice
4. FC Hradec Králové
5. FK Jablonec
6. FK Mladá Boleslav
7. 1. FK Příbram
8. SK Sigma Olomouc
9. SK Slavia Praha
10. 1. FC Slovácko
11. FC Slovan Liberec
12. AC Sparta Praha
13. FK Teplice
14. FC Viktoria Plzeň
15. FC Vysočina Jihlava
16. FC Zbrojovka Brno

PROMOTED CLUBS

17. 1. SC Znojmo
18. Bohemians 1905

KEY:

- – UEFA Champions League
- – UEFA Europa League
- – Promoted clubs
- – Relegated clubs

Viktoria Plzeň reclaim league crown

Dethroned as Czech champions by FC Slovan Liberec on the final day of the 2011/12 1. Liga campaign, FC Viktoria Plzeň recaptured the crown in a season that brought further recognition and success for the club in Europe.

Plzeň and AC Sparta Praha both reached the knockout phase of the UEFA Europa League, but it was Pavel Vrba's provincial side who edged out the record champions from the capital in a thrilling two-horse race for the title. FK Jablonec had also contended in the autumn before going into freefall, but they recovered to win the Czech Cup.

| **Last-day triumph for Vrba's away-day specialists** | **Third straight season without trophy for Sparta** | **Jablonec defeat Mladá Boleslav to win Czech Cup** |

Domestic league

Once again it took all 30 rounds of the 1. Liga before the identity of the Czech champions was revealed. Plzeň led the table at the winter break, holding a two-point lead over Jablonec, with Sparta a point further adrift. Before long, though, there were only two teams in it, with Plzeň and Sparta locked together with six games remaining, their head-to-head encounters having both resulted in 1-0 home wins.

With their European commitments over, it was down to which of the two teams could hold their nerve in the closing straight. Neither quite managed it. Fast-finishing defending champions FC Slovan Liberec defeated both clubs, the second of those victories coming in the penultimate round in Plzen, where the home side, requiring a win to seal the title, fluffed their lines once more against the team that had denied them the previous season.

This time, however, Vrba's side had a shot at redemption, away to just-relegated FC Hradec Králové on the final day, and they made no mistake, cruising to a 3-0 win that enabled them to finish two points ahead of Vítězslav Lavička's Sparta, who also ended their campaign with a 3-0 home win – against FK Dukla Praha.

It was the third successive season that Sparta, winners of 30 Czech and Czechoslovakian league titles, had finished the season empty-handed. But while they had been the form team at home, dropping just seven points at the Letná, it was Plzeň's ability to claim maximum points on the road that earned them a second title in three seasons.

Both clubs played enterprising attacking football, but Plzeň had just that little bit of extra quality and drive. The midfield combination of Pavel Horváth – 38 at the end of term – and 22-year-old Vladimír Darida provided the perfect blend of experience and youth, and there were excellent contributions also from fellow Czech internationals František Rajtoral and David Limberský.

Having lost a number of key players to foreign clubs since the team's 2010/11 title triumph, among them UEFA EURO 2012 stars Petr Jiráček and Václav Pilář, Vrba deserved special praise for filling in the holes and keeping Plzeň competitive.

Jaroslav Šilhavý's Liberec botched their title defence in the autumn, but after going into the winter break in ninth place they stormed up the table during the spring, those two victories over Sparta and Plzeň contributing to a nine-game winning streak that lifted them all the way to third place, securing European football once again for 2013/14.

Domestic cup

Jablonec's league campaign was a mirror image of Liberec's. The mid-season sale of their two best players - prolific marksman David Lafata to Sparta and midfield linchpin Jan Kovařík to Plzeň – hampered their title ambitions, but they held their form in the Czech Cup, ousting Plzeň in the quarter-finals and Liberec in the semis, the second leg of which came after four successive league defeats.

Coach Václav Kotal paid the price for that poor run and was replaced by Roman Skuhravý, who was on hand, less than a fortnight after his appointment, to lead Jablonec to victory in the final against 2011 winners FK Mladá Boleslav. Jan Chramosta, Mladá Boleslav's free-scoring Czech Under-21 international striker, had scored the winner away to Sparta in the semi-final and appeared to be on course for an encore in the final until six minutes

Continued on page 278

Domestic league: 1. Liga 2012/13 final table

		Pld	Home					Away					Total					Pts
			W	D	L	F	A	W	D	L	F	A	W	D	L	F	A	
1	FC Viktoria Plzeň	30	9	3	3	27	12	11	2	2	27	9	20	5	5	54	21	65
2	AC Sparta Praha	30	12	2	1	33	10	7	4	4	22	13	19	6	5	55	23	63
3	FC Slovan Liberec	30	10	4	1	26	12	6	2	7	20	22	16	6	8	46	34	54
4	FK Jablonec	30	7	5	3	25	18	6	5	4	24	23	13	10	7	49	41	49
5	SK Sigma Olomouc	30	8	3	4	24	14	5	5	5	14	15	13	8	9	38	29	47
6	FK Dukla Praha	30	9	5	1	31	13	2	8	5	17	24	11	13	6	48	37	46
7	SK Slavia Praha	30	9	4	2	30	11	2	5	8	11	22	11	9	10	41	33	42
8	FK Mladá Boleslav	30	8	2	5	19	17	2	6	7	15	26	10	8	12	34	43	38
9	1. FC Slovácko	30	6	3	6	18	16	4	4	7	19	25	10	7	13	37	41	37
10	FC Vysočina Jihlava	30	6	8	1	18	11	1	7	7	18	31	7	15	8	36	42	36
11	1. FK Příbram	30	5	7	3	18	17	2	4	9	9	22	7	11	12	27	39	32
12	FK Teplice	30	6	5	4	20	20	2	3	10	16	27	8	8	14	36	47	32
13	FC Zbrojovka Brno	30	7	2	6	25	25	2	3	10	9	28	9	5	16	34	53	32
14	FC Baník Ostrava	30	5	5	5	20	18	2	3	10	14	26	7	8	15	34	44	29
15	SK Dynamo České Budějovice	30	6	3	6	14	16	1	2	12	10	33	7	5	18	24	49	26
16	FC Hradec Králové	30	3	6	6	18	24	2	4	9	9	20	5	10	15	27	44	25

SEASON AT A GLANCE

EUROPEAN QUALIFICATION 2013/14

Champion: FC Viktoria Plzeň (second qualifying round)

Cup winner: FK Jablonec (third qualifying round)
AC Sparta Praha (second qualifying round)
FC Slovan Liberec (second qualifying round)

Top scorer David Lafata (Jablonec/Sparta), 20 goals
Relegated clubs FC Hradec Králové, SK Dynamo České Budějovice
Promoted clubs 1. SC Znojmo, Bohemians 1905
Cup final FK Jablonec 2-2 FK Mladá Boleslav (5-4 on pens)

1. LIGA TEAM OF THE SEASON
(4-4-2)
Coach: Lavička (Sparta)

| Vaclík (Sparta) |
| Holek (Sparta) · Procházka (Plzeň) · Trousil (Slovácko) · Limberský (Plzeň) |
| Štajner (Liberec) · Vácha (Liberec/Sparta) · Horváth (Plzeň) · Koloušek (Jihlava) |
| Kadlec (Sparta) · Lafata (Jablonec/Sparta) |

**PLAYER OF THE SEASON
Václav Kadlec**
(AC Sparta Praha)

The lively 21-year-old striker registered four goals in his final three league games to finish with 14 for the season – an impressive tally given that he suffered a fractured skull in November. That total placed him joint second in the 1. Liga to his new Sparta team-mate David Lafata. Kadlec's efforts also earned him a return to the Czech Republic squad.

**NEWCOMER OF THE SEASON
Vladimír Darida**
(FC Viktoria Plzeň)

After making his debut at UEFA EURO 2012, the gifted young midfielder became a regular in the Czech Republic side. He was at the heart of the champions' midfield alongside veteran skipper Pavel Horváth, adding value with his set pieces, clever passing and powerful shooting. A goal and an assist on the last day helped wrap up the title.

NATIONAL TEAM

CZECH REPUBLIC

Home Kit   Away Kit

Results 2012/13

15/08/12	Ukraine	A	Lviv	0-0	
08/09/12	Denmark (WCQ)	A	Copenhagen	0-0	
11/09/12	Finland	H	Teplice	0-1	
12/10/12	Malta (WCQ)	H	Plzeň	3-1	*Gebre Selassie (34), Pekhart (52), Rezek (67)*
16/10/12	Bulgaria (WCQ)	H	Prague	0-0	
14/11/12	Slovakia	H	Olomouc	3-0	*Lafata (3, 6), Dočkal (73)*
06/02/13	Turkey	A	Manisa	2-0	*Krejčí (4), Lafata (28)*
22/03/13	Denmark (WCQ)	H	Olomouc	0-3	
26/03/13	Armenia (WCQ)	A	Yerevan	3-0	*Vydra (47, 81), Kolář (90+4)*
07/06/13	Italy (WCQ)	H	Prague	0-0	

Appearances 2012/13

Coach: **Michal Bílek**	**13/04/65**		Ukr	DEN	Fin	MLT	BUL	Svk	Tur	DEN	ARM	ITA	Caps	Goals
Petr Čech	20/05/82	Chelsea (ENG)	G	G		G	G			G	G	G	101	-
Theodor Gebre Selassie	24/12/86	Bremen (GER)	D78	D		D	D	D	D	D	D	D	23	1
Tomáš Sivok	15/09/83	Beşiktaş (TUR)	D	D	D	D	D	D46	D	D	D43	D	40	3
Michal Kadlec	13/12/84	Leverkusen (GER)	D	D	D70	D	D		D	D	D	D	47	8
David Limberský	06/10/83	Plzeň	D			D	D	D74	D	D	D	D20	20	-
Tomáš Hübschman	04/09/81	Shakhtar Donetsk (UKR)	M	M	M83	M	M				M	M	54	-
Vladimír Darida	08/08/90	Plzeň	M87	s75	M	s73	s58	M79	M88	M	M85	M76	13	-
Petr Jiráček	02/03/86	Wolfsburg (GER) /Hamburg (GER)	M84		M	M	M73	M		s63	M61	s85	M86	21	3
Daniel Kolář	27/10/85	Plzeň	M46								s74	s86	16	2
Václav Pilař	13/10/88	Wolfsburg (GER)	M65										14	3
David Lafata	18/09/81	Jablonec /Sparta Praha	A57		s46	s82	s80	A67	A03	A	A74		27	6
Milan Petržela	19/06/83	Augsburg (GER)	s48		s40	s61							14	-
Tomáš Pekhart	26/05/89	Nürnberg (GER)	s57	A	A46	A82	A58						18	1
Jan Rezek	05/05/82	Anorthosis (CYP)	s65	M89	s83	A	M80						21	4
František Rajtoral	12/03/86	Plzeň	s78	s73	D	M61	M58						10	-
Josef Hušbauer	16/03/90	Sparta Praha	s84	s89									2	-
Marek Suchý	29/03/88	Spartak Moskva (RUS)	s87	D	D			D	s88		s43	s20	11	-
Jaroslav Plašil	05/01/82	Bordeaux (FRA)		M75	M46	M	M	M	M	M74	M	M	84	6
Matěj Vydra	01/05/92	Watford (ENG)		M73	s46		s58	s67	M56	M	M		7	2
Jan Laštůvka	07/07/82	Dnipro (UKR)			G				G				3	-
Václav Kadlec	20/05/92	Sparta Praha			A46						s76		3	1
Roman Hubník	06/06/84	Hertha (GER)			s70								24	2
Tomáš Vaclík	29/03/89	Sparta Praha						G					1	-
Bořek Dočkal	30/09/88	Rosenborg (NOR)						M	s56	s64			3	1
Michal Ordoš	27/01/83	Sigma						M82	s73				2	-
Ladislav Krejčí	05/07/92	Sparta Praha						M67	M63	M64			3	1
Martin Latka	28/09/84	Slavia Praha						s46					1	-
Libor Kozák	30/05/89	Lazio (ITA)						s67		s74		A	3	-
Tomáš Kalas	15/05/93	Vitesse (NED)						s74					1	-
Tomáš Hořava	29/05/88	Sigma						s79					1	-
Martin Pospíšil	26/06/91	Sigma						s82					1	-
Tomáš Rosický	04/10/80	Arsenal (ENG)							M73	s61	M	M	91	20
Stanislav Tecl	01/09/90	Plzeň							s63				1	-

from time, when Jablonec midfielder Jan Kopic equalised to make it 2-2. With no extra time, it was straight into a penalty shoot-out, which Jablonec won 5-4, Kopic again proving to be the hero with the decisive kick.

Europe

Not content with mounting a sustained challenge for the Czech title, Plzeň and Sparta both represented their country stylishly in the UEFA Europa League.

Vrba's men, drawing on the valuable experience of the 2011/12 UEFA Champions League, came through three qualifying rounds before topping a group containing holders Club Atlético de Madrid and then sensationally routing SSC Napoli 5-0 on aggregate in the round of 32.

They lost narrowly to Fenerbahçe SK in the next round, having entered it as the last remaining Czech team following Sparta's narrow defeat to eventual

winners Chelsea FC. Sparta's fate was sealed only in added time at Stamford Bridge after two gutsy performances in keeping with those that had eliminated, among others, Feyenoord and 2011/12 runners-up Athletic Club.

National team

The Czech Republic's frustrating habit of failing to build on UEFA European Championship promise in the FIFA World Cup resurfaced again in the qualifying campaign for the 2014 tournament. Quarter-finalists at UEFA EURO 2012, Michal Bílek's side fell short of what was expected of them in their opening six fixtures, failing to score in four of them and claiming just half of the 18 points available.

The low point was a 3-0 home defeat by Denmark, although that was swiftly followed by the high of a 3-0 win of their own in Armenia. Goalkeeper Petr Čech became only the second Czech footballer – after Karel Poborský – to reach 100 caps

Petr Čech reached a century of international caps in the Czech Republic's 3-0 win over Armenia

in that Yerevan victory but he hardly had a save to make when his team held Italy 0-0 at home in June. It was a result that kept the Czech Republic in contention for a play-off spot but effectively ended all hope of automatic qualification for Brazil.

European club competitions 2012/13

FC SLOVAN LIBEREC

Second qualifying round - FC Shakhter Karagandy (KAZ)

H 1-0 *Hadaščok (23)*
Bičík, Kelić, Vácha, Nezmar, Blažek (Šural 60), Bosančić, Kušnír, Hadaščok (Delarge 78), Janů, Štajner, Fleišman. Coach: Jaroslav Šilhavý (CZE)

A 1-1 *Blažek (120)*
Bičík, Kelić, Vácha, Nezmar, Breznaník, Kušnír, Hadaščok (Bosančić 63), Janů, Šural, Štajner (Blažek 85), Fleišman. Coach: Jaroslav Šilhavý (CZE)

Third qualifying round - CFR 1907 Cluj (ROU)

A 0-1
Bičík, Kelić, Vácha, Bosančić, Breznaník, Kušnír (Lyulka 46), Tóth, Hadaščok (Blažek 67), Šural, Štajner (Morozenko 89), Fleišman. Coach: Jaroslav Šilhavý (CZE)

H 1-2 *Šural (58)*
Bičík, Kelić, Karišik (Nezmar 76), Vácha, Lyulka, Blažek (Hadaščok 66), Bosančić, Breznaník, Janů (Morozenko 54), Šural, Fleišman. Coach: Jaroslav Šilhavý (CZE)

Play-offs - FC Dnipro Dnipropetrovsk (UKR)

H 2-2 *Breznaník (62), Vácha (90p)*
Bičík, Kelić, Vácha, Nezmar, Lyulka, Bosančić (Maicon 46), Breznaník, Kušnír (Hadaščok 60), Janů (Morozenko 83), Šural, Fleišman. Coach: Jaroslav Šilhavý (CZE)

A 2-4 *Breznaník (61), Kelić (72)*
Bičík, Kelić, Vácha, Nezmar, Lyulka, Bosančić (Karišik 27), Breznaník, Kušnír (Rabušic 79), Hadaščok (Blažek 61), Janů, Fleišman. Coach: Jaroslav Šilhavý (CZE)
Red card: Nezmar 25

AC SPARTA PRAHA

Third qualifying round - FC Admira Wacker Mödling (AUT)

A 2-0 *Mevoungou (29og), Kweuke (58)*
Vaclík, Pamić, Švejdík, Kweuke, Kerić (Kadlec 54), Kadeřábek (Přikryl 80), Hušbauer, Krejčí (Zápotočný 89), Vidlička, Holek, Jarošík. Coach: Vítězslav Lavička (CZE)

H 2-2 *Kweuke (36, 39)*
Vaclík, Pamić, Švejdík, Přikryl (Skalák 50), Kweuke, Kadlec (Kerić 89), Kadeřábek (Grajciar 81), Hušbauer, Vidlička, Holek, Jarošík. Coach: Vítězslav Lavička (CZE)

Play-offs - Feyenoord (NED)
A 2-2 Kadlec (23, 27)
Vaclík, Pamić, Švejdík, Matějovský (Holek 83), Kweuke, Kadlec (Pavelka 86), Kadeřábek (Přikryl 69), Skalák, Hušbauer, Vidlička, Jarošík. Coach: Vítězslav Lavička (CZE)
H 2-0 Kadlec (61p), Jarošík (70)
Vaclík, Pamić, Švejdík, Přikryl (Krejčí 67), Matějovský (Holek 77), Kweuke, Kadlec, Kadeřábek (Skalák 88), Hušbauer, Vidlička, Jarošík. Coach: Vítězslav Lavička (CZE)

Group I
Match 1 - Olympique Lyonnais (FRA)
A 1-2 Krejčí (77)
Vaclík, Pamić, Švejdík, Přikryl (Krejčí 71), Kweuke, Kadlec, Kadeřábek, Pavelka (Holek 58), Hušbauer (Balaj 85), Vidlička, Jarošík. Coach: Vítězslav Lavička (CZE)
Match 2 - Athletic Club (ESP)
H 3-1 Zápotočný (25), Balaj (40), Hušbauer (56p)
Vaclík, Pamić, Švejdík, Matějovský (Pavelka 79), Balaj, Kadlec (Přikryl 87), Zápotočný, Hušbauer, Krejčí (Skalák 72), Holek, Jarošík. Coach: Vítězslav Lavička (CZE)
Match 3 - Hapoel Kiryat Shmona FC (ISR)
H 3-1 Krejčí (7), Kadlec (10), Švejdík (44)
Vaclík, Pamić, Švejdík, Matějovský, Kweuke (Balaj 62), Kadlec (Přikryl 68), Zápotočný, Hušbauer, Krejčí (Kadeřábek 80), Holek, Jarošík. Coach: Vítězslav Lavička (CZE)
Match 4 - Hapoel Kiryat Shmona FC (ISR)
A 1-1 Kweuke (24)
Vaclík, Švejdík, Matějovský, Kweuke (Balaj 79), Kadeřábek (Skalák 74), Hybš, Zápotočný, Hušbauer, Krejčí (Přikryl 63), Holek, Jarošík. Coach: Vítězslav Lavička (CZE)
Match 5 - Olympique Lyonnais (FRA)
H 1-1 Hušbauer (53)
Vaclík, Pamić, Švejdík, Matějovský (Jirásek 90), Kweuke, Kadeřábek (Pamić 53), Zápotočný, Hušbauer, Krejčí (Skalák 90+2), Holek, Jarošík. Coach: Vítězslav Lavička (CZE)
Match 6 - Athletic Club (ESP)
A 0-0
M Čech, Švejdík, Matějovský (Jánoš 87), Kweuke (Balaj 82), Kadeřábek (Kadlec 69), Skalák, Hybš, Zápotočný, Hušbauer, Vidlička, Holek. Coach: Vítězslav Lavička (CZE)

Round of 32 - Chelsea FC (ENG)
H 0-1
Vaclík, Švejdík, Matějovský, Lafata (Kweuke 76), Kadlec, Hybš, Zápotočný, Hušbauer (Bednář 85), Krejčí (Pamić 81), Holek, Vácha. Coach: Vítězslav Lavička (CZE)
A 1-1 Lafata (17)
Vaclík, Švejdík, Přikryl, Matějovský, Lafata (Kweuke 82), Kadlec (Bednář 90+3), Hybš, Zápotočný, Krejčí, Holek, Vácha. Coach: Vítězslav Lavička (CZE)

FO VIKTORIA PLZEŇ

Second qualifying round - FC Metalurgi Rustavi (GEO)
A 3-1 Horváth (14, 59), Kolář (32)
Bolek, Limberský, Horváth, Fillo (Štípek 85), Ďuriš, Ševinský, Darida, Procházka, Malakyan (Zeman 65), Kolář (Hanousek 88), Rajtoral. Coach: Pavel Vrba (CZE)
H 2-0 Ďuriš (7), Darida (10)
Bolek, Limberský, Horváth, Fillo (Hora 63), Ďuriš, Ševinský, Darida, Procházka, Malakyan (Řezník 77), Kolář (Hanousek 83), Rajtoral. Coach: Pavel Vrba (CZE)

Third qualifying round - Ruch Chorzów (POL)
A 2-0 Štípek (79), Ďuriš (85)
Bolek, Limberský, Horváth, Fillo, Ďuriš (Hejda 90), Ševinský, Darida, Hora (Štípek 74), Procházka, Kolář (Hanousek 88), Rajtoral. Coach: Pavel Vrba (CZE)
H 5-0 Ďuriš (2, 12, 28), Bakoš (54), Hanousek (87)
Bolek, Limberský (Řezník 71), Horváth (Hanousek 76), Fillo (Štípek 60), Ďuriš, Ševinský, Darida, Procházka, Bakoš, Kolář, Rajtoral. Coach: Pavel Vrba (CZE)

Play-offs - KSC Lokeren OV (BEL)
A 1-2 Rakoš (29)
Kozáčik, Hanousek (Hejda 00), Limberský, Horváth, Fillo (Hora 55), Ďuriš (Řezník 85), Ševinský, Darida, Procházka, Bakoš, Rajtoral. Coach: Pavel Vrba (CZE)
Red card: Ševinský 90+3
H 1-0 Bakoš (37)
Kozáčik, Hanousek (Fillo 88), Limberský, Horváth, Ďuriš (Hora 77), Řezník, Darida, Procházka, Bakoš, Rajtoral (Malakyan 90+1), Čišovský. Coach: Pavel Vrba (CZE)

Group B
Match 1 - A Académica de Coimbra (POR)
H 3-1 Horváth (46), Ďuriš (58), Rajtoral (80)
Kozáčik, Hanousek, Limberský, Horváth, Ďuriš (Fillo 76), Řezník, Darida, Hora (Zeman 61), Procházka, Rajtoral (Malakyan 90+2), Čišovský. Coach: Pavel Vrba (CZE)
Match 2 - Club Atlético de Madrid (ESP)
A 0-1
Kozáčik, Hanousek, Limberský, Ďuriš, Řezník, Ševinský, Darida (Hejda 90+1), Procházka, Bakoš (Štípek 90+3), Rajtoral (Hora 89), Čišovský. Coach: Pavel Vrba (CZE)
Match 3 - Hapoel Tel-Aviv FC (ISR)
A 2-1 Horváth (45+1), Rajtoral (55)
Kozáčik, Limberský, Horváth, Ďuriš (Zeman 73), Řezník, Ševinský, Darida, Bakoš (Hejda 87), Kolář (Hora 81), Rajtoral, Čišovský. Coach: Pavel Vrba (CZE)
Match 4 - Hapoel Tel-Aviv FC (ISR)
H 4-0 Kolář (23, 76), Štípek (39), Bakoš (84)
Kozáčik, Limberský, Horváth (Zeman 80), Ďuriš, Řezník, Darida, Procházka, Bakoš (Malakyan 85), Kolář, Čišovský, Štípek (Hora 67). Coach: Pavel Vrba (CZE)
Match 5 - A Académica de Coimbra (POR)
A 1-1 Horváth (57p)
Kozáčik, Limberský, Horváth, Ďuriš (Malakyan 84), Řezník, Darida, Hora (Ševinský 89), Procházka, Bakoš, Čišovský, Štípek (Zeman 73). Coach: Pavel Vrba (CZE)
Match 6 - Club Atlético de Madrid (ESP)
H 1-0 Procházka (26)
Kozáčik, Limberský, Horváth (Ševinský 90+2), Ďuriš, Řezník, Darida, Procházka, Bakoš, Kolář (Štípek 89), Rajtoral (Zeman 74), Čišovský. Coach: Pavel Vrba (CZE)

Round of 32 - SSC Napoli (ITA)
A 3-0 Darida (28), Rajtoral (79), Tecl (90)
Kozáčik, Limberský, Horváth, Řezník, Darida, Kovařík, Procházka, Bakoš (Tecl 59), Kolář (Hejda 90), Rajtoral (Fillo 85), Čišovský. Coach: Pavel Vrba (CZE)
H 2-0 Kovařík (51), Tecl (74)
Kozáčik, Limberský, Horváth, Řezník, Darida, Kovařík, Procházka, Bakoš (Tecl 57), Kolář (Štípek 89), Rajtoral (Fillo 83), Čišovský. Coach: Pavel Vrba (CZE)

Round of 16 - Fenerbahçe SK (TUR)
H 0-1
Kozáčik, Horváth, Ďuriš (Fillo 69), Řezník, Darida, Kovařík, Procházka, Bakoš (Tecl 60), Kolář (Hejda 89), Rajtoral, Čišovský. Coach: Pavel Vrba (CZE)
A 1-1 Darida (61)
Kozáčik, Limberský, Horváth (Ďuriš 71), Řezník, Darida, Kovařík, Procházka, Bakoš (Tecl 64), Kolář, Rajtoral (Fillo 87), Čišovský. Coach: Pavel Vrba (CZE)

Domestic league club-by-club

FK MLADÁ BOLESLAV

Second qualifying round - Thór Akureyri (ISL)
H 3-0 *Magera (33, 43), Šćuk (80)*
Šeda, Rolko, Šírl, Mareš (Nešpor 79), Kúdela, Bořil, Šćuk, Magera, Chramosta, Sivrić (Ondřejka 66), Smejkal. Coach: Miroslav Koubek (CZE)
A 1-0 *Magera (31)*
Šeda, Rolko, Mareš, Kúdela, Bořil, Nešpor (Ondřejka 63), Šćuk, Magera, Kysela (Brunclík 46), Sivrić, Smejkal (Johana 80). Coach: Miroslav Koubek (CZE)

Third qualifying round - FC Twente (NED)
A 0-2
Šeda, Johana, Brunclík (Táborský 84), Mareš, Kúdela, Bořil, Nešpor (Ondřejka 69), Šćuk, Magera (Zbrožek 62), Kysela, Sivrić. Coach: Miroslav Koubek (CZE)
H 0-2
Šeda, Johana, Šírl, Brunclík (Opiela 79), Mareš (Nešpor 60), Kúdela, Zbrožek, Bořil, Magera (Ondřejka 22), Kysela, Sivrić. Coach: Miroslav Koubek (CZE)

FC BANÍK OSTRAVA

Coach: Radoslav Látal; (30/10/12) Martin Pulpit; (30/05/13) Tomáš Bernady
1922 • Stadion Bazaly (17,372) • fcb.cz
Major honours
Czechoslovakian/Czech League (4) 1976, 1980, 1981, 2004;
Czechoslovakian/Czech Cup (4) 1973, 1978, 1991, 2005

2012				
27/07	Jablonec	a	0-2	
04/08	Slavia	h	2-2	*Kukec, Milosavljev*
13/08	České Budějovice	a	2-1	*Mach, Kukec*
19/08	Plzeň	h	1-3	*Onuchukwu*
26/08	Hradec Králové	a	1-1	*Kukec*
01/09	Sigma	h	1-2	*Fantiš*
17/09	Jihlava	a	2-3	*Kraut, Fantiš*
21/09	Liberec	a	2-2	*Kraut, Fantiš*
29/09	Mladá Boleslav	h	2-2	*Majtán, Lukeš*
08/10	Sparta	a	0-2	
20/10	Brno	h	1-1	*Frydrych*
27/10	Příbram	a	1-2	*Kukec*
03/11	Teplice	h	3-2	*Majtán, Kukec, Lukeš*
09/11	Dukla	a	0-2	
17/11	Slovácko	a	2-1	*Majtán, Kraut*
23/11	Slavia	a	2-0	*Kaprálik, Zeher*
2013				
23/02	České Budějovice	h	0-0	
03/03	Plzeň	a	1-1	*Milosavljev*
09/03	Hradec Králové	h	3-0	*Baroš 3*
15/03	Sigma	a	0-1	
06/04	Liberec	h	0-1	
15/04	Mladá Boleslav	a	0-2	
20/04	Sparta	h	0-1	
23/04	Jihlava	h	1-0	*Fantiš*
29/04	Brno	a	1-2	*Stožický*
04/05	Příbram	h	2-0	*Baroš 2*
13/05	Teplice	a	2-3	*Frydrych 2*
22/05	Dukla	h	2-2	*og (Vorel), Fantiš*
26/05	Slovácko	a	0-2	
01/06	Jablonec	h	0-1	

No	Name	Nat	DoB	Pos	Aps	(s)	Gls
2	Jan Baránek		26/06/93	D	1	(1)	
27	Milan Baroš		28/10/81	A	10	(2)	5
30	Michal Bárta		23/12/89	G	18		
23	Antonín Buček		24/02/84	G	11		
6	Lukáš Droppa		22/04/89	M	25	(3)	
15	Antonín Fantiš		15/04/92	A	26	(1)	5
8	Milan Ferenčík	SVK	13/02/91	M		(1)	
20	Martin Foltýn		17/08/93	M	1		
19	Michal Frydrych		27/02/90	D	28		3
28	Ján Greguš	SVK	29/01/91	M	4	(2)	
7	Jan Hable		04/01/89	M	10		
21	Daniel Holzer		18/08/95	M		(3)	
3	Zdenko Kaprálik	SVK	28/08/85	D	25		1
9	Dominik Kraut		15/01/90	A	13	(14)	3
20	Davor Kukec	CRO	16/03/86	M	20	(6)	5
4	Martin Lukeš		17/11/78	M	19	(4)	2
5	Petr Mach		22/03/85	D	17	(1)	1
8	Tomáš Majtán		30/03/87	A	8	(1)	3
12	Vladan Milosavljev	SRB	01/02/87	M	15	(9)	2
18	Ebus Onuchukwu	NGA	09/04/84	A		(6)	1
1	Jiří Pavlenka		14/04/92	G	1		
22	Petr Soukup		13/05/87	A	7	(3)	
11	Jaroslav Starý		09/02/88	D	4		
10	Jan Staško		15/04/93	A	6	(5)	
18	Vlastimil Stožický		19/08/83	M	8	(4)	1
28	Patrizio Stronati		17/11/94	D	6		
25	Václav Svěrkoš		01/11/83	A	1	(3)	
17	Dalibor Vašenda		02/06/91	M	13	(4)	
14	Michal Velner		05/10/91	D	2	(2)	
26	Benjamin Vomáčka		27/06/78	D	18	(2)	
7	Tomáš Vrťo		06/09/88	M		(4)	
16	Jan Zawada		06/06/88	D	13		
10	Róbert Zeher	SVK	12/02/85	A		(3)	1

FK DUKLA PRAHA

Coach: Luboš Kozel
1959 • Stadium: Juliska (4,590) • fkdukla.cz

2012				
28/07	Sparta	h	1-1	*Hašek (p)*
04/08	Liberec	a	2-3	*Hašek, Malý*
10/08	Teplice	h	4-0	*Pázler, Přeučil, Berger, Kalouda*
17/08	Slovácko	h	2-2	*Hašek, Pázler*
25/08	Příbram	a	1-1	*Borek*
02/09	Plzeň	h	1-4	*og (Fillo)*
15/09	České Budějovice	a	1-1	*Vorel*
23/09	Slavia	h	0-0	
01/10	Jablonec	a	2-2	*Berger, Vrzal*
05/10	Hradec Králové	h	1-0	*Pospěch*
21/10	Sigma	a	1-2	*Malý*
26/10	Jihlava	h	2-2	*Berger, Pospěch (p)*
04/11	Brno	a	3-1	*Borek 2, Marek*
09/11	Baník	h	2-0	*Pospěch, Svatonský*
19/11	Mladá Boleslav	a	0-3	
23/11	Liberec	h	3-0	*Pospěch 2, Vorel*
2013				
22/02	Teplice	a	1-1	*Kalouda*
04/03	Slovácko	a	0-0	
08/03	Příbram	h	1-0	*Přeučil*
17/03	Plzeň	a	0-4	
29/03	České Budějovice	h	4-0	*Borek 2, Pospěch, Božić*
05/04	Slavia	a	0-0	
13/04	Jablonec	h	5-1	*Néstor Albiach 2, Pospěch 2, Malý (p)*
21/04	Hradec Králové	a	3-0	*Borek, Přeučil, Pospěch*
26/04	Sigma	h	0-0	
03/05	Jihlava	a	1-1	*Borek*
14/05	Brno	h	3-2	*Pospěch, Berger, Néstor Albiach*
22/05	Baník	a	2-2	*Ouedraogo, Vrzal*
24/05	Mladá Boleslav	h	2-1	*Néstor Albiach, Kalouda*
01/06	Sparta	a	0-3	

No	Name	Nat	DoB	Pos	Aps	(s)	Gls
13	Tomáš Berger		22/08/85	A	23	(2)	4
5	Tomáš Borek		04/04/86	M	28		7
22	Tomislav Božić	CRO	01/11/87	D	18	(5)	1
16	Vojtěch Engelman		04/07/89	A		(7)	
14	Patrik Gedeon		19/07/75	M	27		
4	Matěj Hanousek		02/06/93	D	1		
8	Pavel Hašek		27/06/83	M	16	(2)	3
26	Lukáš Kalouda		20/05/87	M	8	(8)	3
24	Petr Malý		01/06/84	M	19	(4)	3
20	Josef Marek		11/06/87	A	3	(11)	1
8	Néstor Albiach	ESP	18/08/92	A	9	(3)	4
3	Ismael Ouedraogo	BFA	10/03/91	M	1	(2)	1
8	Jan Pázler		10/01/91	A	7	(5)	2
10	Miroslav Podrazký		18/08/84	M	6	(6)	
17	Zbyněk Pospěch		24/10/82	A	21	(6)	10
4	Tomáš Pospíšil		30/01/91	D	1		
7	Vojtěch Přeučil		19/09/90	A	11	(14)	3
1	Filip Rada		05/09/84	G	30		
15	José Romera	ESP	08/09/87	D	21	(1)	
21	Jan Svatonský		12/05/84	A	7	(5)	1
19	Lukáš Štětina	SVK	28/07/91	D	16	(6)	
9	Jan Vorel		01/09/78	D	29		2
23	Ondřej Vrzal		01/03/87	D	28		2

SK DYNAMO ČESKÉ BUDĚJOVICE

Coach: František Cipro; (03/09/12) (Jiří Lerch);
(07/09/12) Miroslav Soukup;
(20/02/13) (Pavol Švantner)
1905 • Stadion Střelecký ostrov (6,746) • dynamocb.cz

2012

28/07	Sigma	h	1-0	Otepka (p)
05/08	Mladá Boleslav	a	2-3	Marković 2
13/08	Baník	h	1-2	Otepka (p)
19/08	Sparta	a	1-3	Marković
26/08	Liberec	h	0-2	
01/09	Brno	a	1-3	Sandro
15/09	Dukla	h	1-1	Řezníček
22/09	Příbram	a	1-1	Řepka
29/09	Teplice	h	3-2	Táborský, Klesa, Machovec
07/10	Jablonec	a	1-2	Řezníček
20/10	Slovácko	h	0-0	
29/10	Plzeň	a	0-1	
04/11	Hradec Králové	a	1-0	Řezníček (p)
09/11	Slavia	h	2-1	Machovec, Táborský
16/11	Jihlava	a	0-1	
24/11	Mladá Boleslav	h	0-1	

2013

23/02	Baník	a	0-0	
01/03	Sparta	h	0-2	
09/03	Liberec	a	1-3	Hora
15/03	Brno	h	1-1	Mkoyan
29/03	Dukla	a	0-4	
05/04	Příbram	h	0-1	
13/04	Teplice	a	0-4	
19/04	Jablonec	h	2-1	Táborský, Benát
27/04	Slovácko	a	0-2	
03/05	Plzeň	a	2-3	Linhart, Táborský
10/05	Hradec Králové	h	1-0	Hora
22/05	Slavia	a	0-3	
26/05	Jihlava	h	2-1	Wermke, Halama
01/06	Sigma	a	0-1	

No	Name	Nat	DoB	Pos	Aps	(s)	Gls
22	Petr Benát		20/05/80	M	15	(2)	1
20	Václav Čadek		30/03/93	M		(2)	
26	Jaroslav Černý		23/06/79	M	2	(3)	
29	Michal Daněk		06/07/83	G	27	(1)	
7	Aleš Dvořák		09/03/91	D		(1)	
7	Jiří Funda		21/06/95	D		1	
12	Ján Halama		11/07/83	D	10	(2)	1
16	Aleš Hanzlík		06/02/87	D	12	(5)	
18	Jakub Hora		23/02/91	A	12		2
13	Ivo Horák		27/01/95	M		(1)	
18	Hudson	BRA	18/07/86	M		(5)	
20	Petr Javorek		09/02/86	M	17	(5)	
21	Václav Ježdík		03/07/87	D	5	(1)	
10	Michal Klesa		13/05/83	M	18	(6)	1
30	Zdeněk Křížek		16/01/83	G	3		
6	Roman Lengyel		03/11/78	D	29		
4	Zdeněk Linhart		05/03/94	A	3	(10)	1
23	Jaroslav Machovec	SVK	05/09/86	M	22		2
14	Edgar Malakyan	ARM	22/09/90	M	2	(3)	
13	Miroslav Marković	SRB	04/11/89	A	11	(4)	3
22	Hrayr Mkoyan	ARM	02/09/86	D	7		1
21	František Němec		19/07/92	A		(4)	
5	Pavel Novák		30/11/89	D	18	(3)	
9	Rudolf Otepka		13/11/73	M	12	(2)	2
3	Michal Petráň		26/06/92	M		(1)	
9	David Radouch		06/01/93	M		(2)	
11	Michal Rakovan		15/04/89	M	4		
2	Tomáš Řepka		02/01/74	D	10		1
7	Jakub Řezníček		26/05/88	A	17	(6)	3
15	Jan Riegel		03/08/80	D	5	(1)	
19	Filip Rýdel		30/03/84	M	22	(3)	
25	Sandro	BRA	19/03/86	M	24	(1)	1
17	Ivo Táborský		10/05/85	A	20	(2)	4
2	Roman Wermke		23/07/94	M	2	(3)	1
17	Emir Zeba	BIH	10/06/89	M		(4)	

FC HRADEC KRÁLOVÉ

Coach: Jiří Plíšek; (21/04/13) Luboš Prokopec
1905 • Všesportovní stadion (7,100) • fchk.cz
Major honours
Czechoslovakian League (1) 1960; Czech Cup (1) 1995

2012

29/07	Plzeň	a	0-3	
03/08	Jablonec	h	2-2	Dvořák (p), Uškovič
12/08	Jihlava	h	1-1	Šisler
19/08	Sigma	a	1-1	Šisler
26/08	Baník	h	1-1	Holeš
02/09	Sparta	a	0-1	
16/09	Brno	h	2-0	Uškovič, Šisler
23/09	Mladá Boleslav	a	0-1	
30/09	Liberec	h	2-2	Dvořák, Harba
05/10	Dukla	a	0-1	
21/10	Teplice	h	2-0	Dvořák, Uškovič (p)
27/10	Slovácko	a	1-1	Hochmeister
04/11	České Budějovice	h	0-1	
10/11	Příbram	a	0-1	
18/11	Slavia	h	3-2	Uškovič 2, Halilović
24/11	Jablonec	a	2-3	Harba, Halilović

2013

22/02	Jihlava	a	0-0	
03/03	Sigma	h	0-2	
09/03	Baník	a	0-3	
17/03	Sparta	h	1-2	Štěpán
31/03	Brno	a	3-1	Šisler, Hochmeister, Uškovič
07/04	Mladá Boleslav	h	2-2	Šisler, Plašil
13/04	Liberec	a	0-1	
21/04	Dukla	h	0-3	
28/04	Teplice	a	2-0	Šisler, Schwarz
05/05	Slovácko	h	2-3	Pávek, Kulič
10/05	České Budějovice	a	0-1	
21/05	Příbram	h	0-0	
26/05	Slavia	a	0-1	
01/06	Plzeň	h	0-3	

No	Name	Nat	DoB	Pos	Aps	(s)	Gls
14	Pavel Dvořák		19/02/89	A	12		3
27	Milan Fukal		16/05/75	D	22		
22	Vojtěch Hadaščok		08/01/92	A	8	(4)	
18	Tomáš Hájek		01/12/92	D	5		
26	Emir Halilović	BIH	04/11/90	M	0	(9)	1
00	Haris Harba	BIH	12/01/94	M	27		2
5	Radek Hochmeister		06/09/82	D	26		2
4	Tomáš Holeš		31/03/93	M	24		1
15	Peter Jánošík	SVK	02/01/82	D	14	(2)	
13	Jiří Janoušek		17/11/89	M	1	(2)	
28	Filip Klapka		20/06/81	M	4	(5)	
14	Martin Kopáč		19/10/92	M		(1)	
1	Tomáš Koubek		26/08/92	G	20		
10	Marek Kulič		11/10/75	A	9	(3)	1
20	Jiří Lindr		07/08/86	G	10		
6	Tomáš Malinský		25/08/91	A	3	(2)	
23	Tomáš Mrázek		11/05/86	A		(1)	
24	Michal Pávek		13/02/85	D	5	(8)	1
25	Marek Plašil		19/12/85	D	12		1
16	Jiří Poděbradský		09/09/82	D	28		
22	Tomáš Rezek		05/05/84	M		(6)	
3	Petr Schwarz		12/11/91	M	8	(5)	1
2	Tomáš Strnad		08/12/80	M	14	(7)	
10/23	Jan Šisler		24/04/88	M	26		6
7	Vojtěch Štěpán		08/06/85	M	27		1
21	Dušan Uškovič	SVK	09/04/85	A	11	(10)	6
8	Radek Voltr		28/11/92	A	1	(4)	
18	Aleksei Yedunov	RUS	11/03/86	A		(1)	
9	Asim Zec	BIH	23/01/94	A		(5)	
11	Jaroslav Zelený		20/08/92	D	5	(9)	

FK JABLONEC

Coach: Václav Kotal; (05/05/13) Roman Skuhravý
1945 • Chance arena (6,108) • fkjablonec.cz
Major honours
Czech Cup (2) 1998, 2013

2012

27/07	Baník	h	2-0	Zoubele, Lafata
03/08	Hradec Králové	a	2-2	Lafata, Kopic
11/08	Liberec	h	1-0	og (Lyulka)
19/08	Brno	a	4-1	Eliáš, Vaněk, Lafata (p), Čížek
27/08	Sparta	h	1-2	Beneš
31/08	Teplice	a	4-0	Čížek 2, Lafata 2 (1p)
14/09	Příbram	h	2-2	Zoubele, Kovařík
22/09	Slovácko	a	1-0	Lafata
01/10	Dukla	a	2-1	Novák, Lafata
07/10	České Budějovice	h	2-1	Lafata 2 (1p)
21/10	Plzeň	a	1-1	Beneš
27/10	Slavia	h	0-0	
02/11	Jihlava	a	1-0	Kopic
10/11	Mladá Boleslav	h	2-3	Piták, Lafata
18/11	Sigma	a	1-0	Lafata
24/11	Hradec Králové	h	3-2	Lafata 2 (1p), Štochl

2013

23/02	Liberec	a	0-1	
03/03	Brno	h	2-0	Zoubele, Čížek
10/03	Sparta	a	2-2	Čížek 2
17/03	Teplice	h	0-0	
30/03	Příbram	a	3-3	Novák 2, Loučka
07/04	Slovácko	h	4-1	Vaněk, Kopic, og (Košút), Piták
13/04	Dukla	a	1-5	Loučka
19/04	České Budějovice	a	1-2	Pázler
27/04	Plzeň	h	1-3	Čížek
05/05	Slavia	a	1-5	Hubník
12/05	Jihlava	h	1-1	Hubník
22/05	Mladá Boleslav	a	1-1	Hubník
26/05	Sigma	h	2-1	Čížek, Kopic
01/06	Baník	a	1-0	Piták

No	Name	Nat	DoB	Pos	Aps	(s)	Gls
23	Vít Beneš		12/08/88	D	28	(1)	2
22	Tomáš Čížek		27/11/78	M	18	(6)	8
8	Daniel Rossi	BRA	04/01/81	M	10		
19	David Pilař		21/11/88	M	10	(6)	1
3	Aleš Hanzlík	BIH	01/00/90	M		(3)	
21	Michal Hubník		01/06/83	A	4	(6)	3
10	Tomáš Jablonský		21/06/87	M	17	(5)	
2	Radim Jurča		09/02/93	M		(1)	
11	Jan Kopic		04/06/90	M	27	(2)	4
16	Jan Kovařík		19/06/88	M	12	(2)	1
27	Vojtěch Kubista		19/03/93	D	1		
8	Marek Kysela		10/07/92	D	14		
21	David Lafata		18/09/81	A	16		13
15	Luboš Loučka		25/08/82	D	30		2
7	Filip Novák		26/06/90	D	28	(1)	3
16	Jan Pázler		10/01/91	A	3	(7)	1
12	Karel Piták		28/01/80	M	22	(4)	3
1	Michal Špit		09/04/75	G	13	(1)	
25	Jakub Štochl		02/02/87	D	6	(8)	1
26	Lukáš Třešňák		03/05/88	A	7	(16)	
29	Roman Valeš		06/03/90	G	17	(1)	
28	Ondřej Vaněk		05/07/90	D	18	(10)	2
19	Lukáš Zoubele		20/12/85	M	18	(7)	3

 **CZECH REPUBLIC**

FK MLADÁ BOLESLAV

Coach: Miroslav Koubek; (23/09/12) Ladislav Minář
1902 • Městský stadion (5,000 • fkmb.cz
Major honours
Czech Cup (1) 2011

2012

29/07	Teplice	a	0-1	
05/08	České Budějovice	h	3-2	Sivrić 2, Mareš
12/08	Příbram	a	1-1	Brunclík
18/08	Slavia	h	1-0	Kúdela
26/08	Plzeň	a	0-2	
02/09	Jihlava	h	1-3	Magera (p)
15/09	Slovácko	a	1-3	Nešpor
23/09	Hradec Králové	h	1-0	Nešpor
29/09	Baník	a	2-2	Sivrić, Nešpor
06/10	Sigma	h	0-1	
22/10	Liberec	a	0-2	
26/10	Brno	h	1-0	Štohanzl
03/11	Sparta	h	1-1	Mareš
10/11	Jablonec	a	3-2	Magera (p), Štohanzl, Nešpor
19/11	Dukla	h	3-0	Johana 2, Magera
24/11	České Budějovice	a	1-0	Johana

2013

24/02	Příbram	h	1-0	og (Hájovský)
03/03	Slavia	a	1-1	Štohanzl
10/03	Plzeň	h	0-2	
23/03	Jihlava	a	0-1	
29/03	Slovácko	h	2-0	Mareš, Ščuk
07/04	Hradec Králové	a	2-2	Magera, Ščuk
15/04	Baník	h	2-0	Magera, Ščuk
21/04	Sigma	a	2-2	Nešpor, Johana
28/04	Liberec	a	2-3	Nešpor, Sivrić
05/05	Brno	a	1-1	Magera (p)
12/05	Sparta	a	0-4	
22/05	Jablonec	h	1-1	Johana
26/05	Dukla	a	1-2	Johana
01/06	Teplice	h	0-4	

No	Name	Nat	DoB	Pos	Aps	(s)	Gls
8	Jan Bořil		11/01/91	D	29		
7	David Brunclík		17/04/85	M	9	(2)	1
33	Kerem Bulut	AUS	03/02/92	A		(4)	
19	Jan Chramosta		12/10/90	A	3	(6)	
29	Radek Dosoudil		20/06/83	D	15	(1)	
35	Martin Fillo		07/02/86	M	2	(5)	
5	Tomáš Janíček		07/09/82	D	9	(1)	
14	David Jarolím		17/05/79	M	10	(1)	
2	Petr Johana		01/11/76	D	26		6
11	Ondřej Kúdela		26/03/87	M	20	(4)	1
10	Marek Kulič		11/10/75	A	1	(4)	
20	Jan Kysela		17/12/85	D	19	(2)	
18	Lukáš Magera		17/01/83	A	15	(3)	6
9	Jakub Mareš		26/01/87	M	26	(2)	3
31	Mirzad Mehanovič	SVN	05/01/93	M		(1)	
27	Miroslav Miller		19/08/80	G	22		
16	Martin Nešpor		05/06/90	A	21	(3)	6
26	Václav Ondřejka		30/04/88	A	6	(7)	
33	Lukáš Opiela	SVK	13/01/86	M	5	(4)	
4	Adrian Rolko		14/09/78	D	1	(1)	
30	Filip Rozsíval		21/01/93	M	1	(1)	
24	Matej Sivrić	CRO	31/01/90	M	15	(7)	4
10	Roman Sloboda	SVK	14/01/87	M	3	(6)	
25	Michal Smejkal		18/06/91	D		(1)	
22	Jakub Synek		14/08/90	A	1	(4)	
17	Jasmin Ščuk	BIH	14/07/90	M	18	(4)	3
12	Jan Šeda		17/12/85	G	8		
3	František Ševinský		31/03/79	D	6	(3)	
6	Radek Šírl		20/03/81	D	12		
15	Jan Štohanzl		20/03/85	M	17	(7)	3
22	Ivo Táborský		10/05/85	M	1	(1)	
21	Ondřej Zahustěl		18/06/91	M	4	(1)	
13	Kristián Zbrožek		02/01/90	D	5	(1)	

1. FK PŘÍBRAM

Coach: David Vavruška; (30/08/12) Karol Marko;
(11/03/13) František Straka
1948 • Na Litavce (7,900) • fkpribram.cz

2012

28/07	Liberec	h	0-4	
05/08	Sparta	a	1-2	Trapp
12/08	Mladá Boleslav	h	1-1	Střihavka
19/08	Teplice	a	0-0	
25/08	Dukla	h	1-1	Dejmek
01/09	Slovácko	h	0-1	
14/09	Jablonec	a	2-2	Krbeček, Trapp
22/09	České Budějovice	h	1-1	Trapp
28/09	Jihlava	a	1-2	Trapp
07/10	Plzeň	h	1-0	Mareš
19/10	Slavia	a	1-2	Koukal
27/10	Baník	h	2-1	Kalivoda, Wágner
04/11	Sigma	a	1-6	Danoski
10/11	Hradec Králové	h	0-0	
18/11	Brno	a	0-1	
25/11	Sparta	h	0-1	

2013

24/02	Mladá Boleslav	a	0-1	
02/03	Teplice	h	3-1	Al-Mashaan 2, Valenta
08/03	Dukla	a	0-1	
16/03	Slovácko	a	1-0	Hájovský
30/03	Jablonec	h	3-3	Hájovský, Wágner, Střihavka
05/04	České Budějovice	a	1-0	T Pilík (p)
13/04	Jihlava	h	2-2	Trapp, Tarczal
19/04	Plzeň	a	0-2	
27/04	Slavia	h	2-0	Wágner 2
04/05	Baník	a	0-2	
11/05	Sigma	h	0-2	
21/05	Hradec Králové	a	0-0	
26/05	Brno	h	2-0	Wágner, Koukal
01/06	Liberec	a	1-1	Wágner

No	Name	Nat	DoB	Pos	Aps	(s)	Gls
26	Martin Abraham		20/09/78	M	2	(2)	
14	Aziz Al-Mashaan	KUW	19/10/88	M	12	(1)	2
26	Aleksandar Andrejević	SRB	28/03/92	M	1		
9	Antonín Barák		03/12/94	M		(1)	
20	Zoran Danoski	MKD	20/10/90	M	5	(7)	1
17	Radek Dejmek		02/02/88	D	15	(1)	1
24	Josef Divíšek		24/09/90	D	10	(3)	
4	Tomáš Hájovský	SVK	10/12/82	D	21		2
5	Marek Hanuš		11/10/93	M			
22	Aleš Hruška		23/11/85	G	29		
12	Daniel Huňa		25/06/79	A	1	(2)	
2	Jakub Jugas		05/05/92	D	22	(1)	
13	David Kalivoda		25/08/82	M	5	(5)	1
13	Zdeněk Koukal		14/03/84	M	17	(5)	2
10	Tomáš Krbeček		27/10/85	A	23	(4)	1
2	Jan Kvída		17/01/91	D	1		
18	Martin Macháček		01/05/89	D			
21	Jiří Mareš		16/02/92	M	12	(2)	1
3	Milan Mišůn		21/02/90	D	24		
14	Pavel Pilík		13/02/92	M	4	(4)	
25	Tomáš Pilík		20/12/88	M	19	(1)	1
7	Lukáš Pleško		21/05/77	D	22	(3)	
1	Jakub Rondzik	SVK	22/11/86	G	1		
17	Filip Řezáč		08/02/93	A		(1)	
8	Lukáš Stratil		29/01/94	M		(3)	
9	David Střihavka		04/03/83	A	22	(4)	2
11	Martin Šlapák		25/03/87	A	15	(9)	
6	Daniel Tarczal		22/03/85	M	13		1
16	Petr Trapp		06/12/85	M	16	(3)	5
19	Róbert Valenta	SVK	10/11/90	A	4	(2)	1
29	Tomáš Wágner		06/03/90	A	15	(11)	6

SK SIGMA OLOMOUC

Coach: Roman Pivarník; (06/05/13) Martin Kotůlek
1919 • Andrův stadion (12,566) • sigmafotbal.cz
Major honours
Czech Cup (1) 2012

2012

28/07	České Budějovice	a	0-1	
05/08	Slovácko	h	2-0	Škerle, Ordoš (p)
10/08	Slavia	a	1-1	Ordoš
19/08	Hradec Králové	h	1-1	Vepřek
24/08	Jihlava	a	1-1	Doležal
01/09	Baník	a	2-1	Ordoš 2
16/09	Liberec	h	3-0	Pospíšil, Ordoš, Doležal
24/09	Sparta	a	2-1	Ordoš 2
28/09	Brno	h	1-1	Dreksa
06/10	Mladá Boleslav	a	1-0	Ordoš (p)
21/10	Dukla	h	2-1	Ordoš, Navrátil
28/10	Teplice	a	1-1	Petr
04/11	Příbram	h	6-1	Ordoš 3, Petr 2, Klesnil
11/11	Plzeň	a	0-3	
18/11	Jablonec	h	0-1	
24/11	Slovácko	a	1-1	Doležal

2013

24/02	Slavia	h	2-1	Doležal, Ordoš
03/03	Hradec Králové	a	2-0	Navrátil 2
09/03	Jihlava	h	3-0	Ordoš, Schulmeister, Doležal
15/03	Baník	h	1-0	Doležal
29/03	Liberec	a	0-1	
06/04	Sparta	h	0-3	
12/04	Brno	a	0-2	
21/04	Mladá Boleslav	h	2-2	Doležal, Plšek
26/04	Dukla	a	0-0	
06/05	Teplice	h	0-2	
11/05	Příbram	a	2-0	Navrátil, Falta
22/05	Plzeň	h	0-1	
26/05	Jablonec	a	1-2	Navrátil
01/06	České Budějovice	h	1-0	Navrátil

No	Name	Nat	DoB	Pos	Aps	(s)	Gls
39	Martin Blaha		08/08/85	G	11		
11	Lukáš Chlebek		19/02/90	D		(1)	
8	Daniel Rossi	BRA	04/01/81	M	14		
26	Martin Doležal		03/05/90	A	19	(5)	7
3	Pavel Dreksa		17/09/89	D	22		1
20	Šimon Falta		23/04/93	D		(5)	1
29	Igor Golban	RUS	31/07/90	D	2		
4	Jakub Habusta		03/05/93	M		(1)	
20	Marek Heinz		04/08/77	M		(1)	
17	Tomáš Hořava		29/05/88	M	26	(1)	
18	Daniel Houska		29/06/93	M	3	(2)	
10	Michal Hubník		01/06/83	A	7	(6)	
23	Tomáš Janotka		04/03/82	D	12	(2)	
5	Jan Javůrek		16/05/89	M	5	(2)	
16	Zdeněk Klesnil		28/10/86	A	5	(4)	1
24	Václav Koutný		04/10/91	D	8	(1)	
25	Jan Navrátil		13/04/90	A	22	(6)	6
7	Michal Ordoš		27/01/83	A	23	(1)	14
22	Jakub Petr		10/04/90	A	14	(15)	3
6	Jakub Plšek		13/12/93	M	4	(5)	1
26	Martin Pospíšil		26/06/91	M	26	(2)	1
16	Jakub Rolinc		03/05/92	A	1	(2)	
11	Jan Schulmeister		11/03/86	A	20	(6)	1
8	Ondřej Sukup		08/12/88	D	2		
13	Martin Šindelář		22/01/91	M	15	(6)	
4	Aleš Škerle		14/06/82	D	22		1
1	Martin Šustr		03/10/90	G		(1)	
14	Adam Varadi		03/05/90	A		(9)	
21	Michal Vepřek		17/06/85	D	25	(2)	1
27	Zdeněk Zlámal		05/11/85	G	19		

SK SLAVIA PRAHA

Coach: Petr Rada; (30/04/13) Michal Petrouš
1892 • Synot Tip Aréna (20,800) • slavia.cz
Major honours
Czechoslovakian/Czech League (12) 1925, 1929, 1930,
1931, 1933, 1934, 1935, 1937, 1947, 1996, 2008, 2009;
Czech Cup (3) 1997, 1999, 2002

2012

30/07	Jihlava	h	3-3	*Vošahlík 2, Kisel*
04/08	Baník	a	2-2	*Kisel, Nitrianský*
10/08	Sigma	h	1-1	*Kisel*
18/08	Mladá Boleslav	a	0-1	
23/08	Brno	h	5-0	*Kisel 2, Škoda, Zmrhal, Latka*
02/09	Liberec	a	0-0	
19/09	Teplice	h	2-0	*Nitrianský, Petrák*
23/09	Dukla	a	0-0	
29/09	Sparta	h	1-0	*Latka*
05/10	Slovácko	a	0-3	
19/10	Příbram	h	2-1	*Nitrianský, Škoda*
27/10	Jablonec	a	0-0	
04/11	Plzeň	h	0-1	
09/11	České Budějovice	a	1-2	*Škoda*
18/11	Hradec Králové	a	2-3	*Nitrianský, Kisel*
23/11	Baník	h	0-2	

2013

24/02	Sigma	a	1-2	*Gecov*
03/03	Mladá Boleslav	h	1-1	*Mičola*
08/03	Brno	a	1-0	*Juhar*
16/03	Liberec	h	3-1	*Dobrotka, Škutka, Kisel*
31/03	Teplice	a	1-1	*Vošahlík*
05/04	Dukla	h	0-0	
13/04	Sparta	a	1-3	*Vošahlík*
22/04	Slovácko	h	1-0	*Kisel*
27/04	Příbram	a	0-2	
05/05	Jablonec	h	5-1	*Juhar 2, Mičola 2, Gecov*
11/05	Plzeň	h	1-0	*Škoda*
22/05	České Budějovice	h	3-0	*Mičola 3*
26/05	Hradec Králové	h	3-0	*Kisel, Čonka, Hurka*
01/06	Jihlava	a	1-3	*Hubáček*

No	Name	Nat	DoB	Pos	Aps	(s)	Gls
29	Martin Berkovec		12/02/89	G	2		
3	Milan Bortel	SVK	07/04/87	D	12		
13	Róbert Cicman	SVK	03/09/84	D	2	(6)	
2	Marek Červenka		17/12/92	A		(1)	
19	Matúš Čonka	SVK	11/01/90	D	10	(3)	1
34	Kamil Contofalský	SVK	03/06/78	G	27		
6	Martin Dobrotka	SVK	22/01/85	D	8	(1)	1
30	Martin Dostál		23/09/89	D	6	(3)	
10	Martin Fenin		16/04/87	A	4	(3)	
10	Tomáš Frejlach		24/11/85	M		(2)	
15	Marcel Gecov		01/01/88	M	10	(2)	2
4	David Hubáček		23/02/77	D	23		1
23	Martin Hurka		20/04/93	M		(3)	1
20	Lukáš Jarolím		29/07/76	M	7	(3)	
9	Martin Juhar	SVK	09/03/88	M	24	(2)	3
11	Karol Kisel	SVK	15/03/77	M	25	(1)	9
18	Štěpán Koreš		14/02/89	M	6	(9)	
28	Martin Latka		28/09/84	D	14		2
25	Tomáš Mičola		26/09/88	M	12	(8)	6
5	Milan Nitrianský		13/12/90	D	25		4
14	Ondřej Petrák		11/03/92	M	24	(2)	1
34	Matej Rakovan	SVK	14/03/90	G	1		
8	Rudolf Skácel		17/07/79	M	2	(3)	
13	Viktor Šimeček		14/07/93	M		(1)	
21	Milan Škoda		16/01/86	A	21	(7)	4
33	David Škutka	SVK	25/05/88	A	6	(6)	1
12	Luboš Tusjak		15/02/92	M	8	(3)	
7	Stanislav Vlček		26/02/76	M		(4)	
17	Jan Vošahlík		08/03/89	A	18	(2)	4
16	Jaromír Zmrhal		02/08/93	M	24	(4)	1

1. FC SLOVÁCKO

Coach: Miroslav Soukup; (15/08/12) (Jiří Dekař);
(25/08/12) Svatopluk Habanec
1894 • Městský fotbalový stadion Miroslava Valenty
(8,121) • fcslovacko.cz

2012

28/07	Brno	h	0-1	
05/08	Sigma	a	0-2	
12/08	Sparta	h	1-4	*Trousil*
17/08	Dukla	a	2-2	*Kovář, Volešák*
25/08	Teplice	h	2-1	*Volešák (p), Došek*
01/09	Příbram	a	1-0	*Lukáš*
15/09	Mladá Boleslav	h	3-1	*Došek, Hlúpik, Volešák*
22/09	Jablonec	h	0-1	
30/09	Plzeň	a	1-1	*Došek*
05/10	Slavia	h	3-0	*Hlúpik, Kovář, Volešák (p)*
20/10	České Budějovice	a	0-0	
27/10	Hradec Králové	h	1-1	*Trousil*
05/11	Liberec	a	2-3	*Trousil, Došek*
10/11	Jihlava	h	3-0	*Došek 2, Daníček*
17/11	Baník	h	1-2	*Košút*
24/11	Sigma	h	1-1	*Kerbr*

2013

24/02	Sparta	a	0-4	
04/03	Dukla	h	0-1	
10/03	Teplice	a	4-0	*Došek 2, Valenta, Trousil*
16/03	Příbram	h	0-1	
29/03	Mladá Boleslav	a	0-2	
07/04	Jablonec	a	1-4	*Košút*
14/04	Plzeň	h	0-2	
22/04	Slavia	a	0-1	
27/04	České Budějovice	h	2-0	*Došek, Haša*
05/05	Hradec Králové	a	3-2	*Valenta 2, Volešák*
11/05	Liberec	h	0-3	
22/05	Jihlava	a	1-1	*Došek*
26/05	Baník	h	2-0	*Došek 2*
01/06	Brno	a	3-1	*Kuncl, Kovář, Došek*

No	Name	Nat	DoB	Pos	Aps	(s)	Gls
2	Vlastimil Daníček		15/07/91	D	23	(1)	1
7	Libor Došek		24/04/78	A	25	(2)	13
16	Lukáš Fujerik		09/12/83	M		(3)	
28	Martin Hála		24/03/92	M		(5)	
15	Roman Haša		15/02/93	M	4	(3)	1
4	Marek Havlík		08/07/95	M		(1)	
1	Milan Heča		23/03/91	G	1		
8	Filip Hlúpik		30/04/91	M	22	(2)	2
10	Stanislav Hofmann		17/06/90	D	8	(3)	
21	Milan Kerbr		10/09/89	A	20	(6)	1
5	Michal Kordula		11/02/78	M	1		
22	Tomáš Košút	SVK	13/01/90	D	12	(5)	2
20	Marián Kovář		13/08/93	M	12	(12)	3
3	Lukáš Kubáň		22/06/87	D	14		
17	Martin Kuncl		01/04/84	D	24	(1)	1
15	Marek Kuzma		22/06/88	A	2	(3)	
9	Jan Lukáš		25/05/88	A	2	(11)	1
25	Jan Martykán		17/03/83	M	3	(1)	
1	Dušan Melichárek		29/11/83	G	29		
19	Radek Mezlík		20/05/82	D	21		
6	Petr Reinberk		23/05/89	D	20	(1)	
25	Jiří Skalák		12/03/92	A	3	(6)	
12	Velice Sumulikoski	MKD	24/04/81	M	4	(1)	
7	Zdeněk Šturma		09/07/87	M		(1)	
24	Michal Trávník		17/05/94	M	2	(9)	
26	Jan Trousil		09/04/76	D	27	(1)	4
11	Jiří Valenta		14/02/88	M	25		3
23	Ladislav Volešák		07/04/84	M	24	(3)	5

FC SLOVAN LIBEREC

Coach: Jaroslav Šilhavý
1958 • U Nisy (9,900) • fcslovanliberec.cz
Major honours
Czech League (3) 2002, 2006, 2012;
Czech Cup (1) 2000

2012

28/07	Příbram	a	4-0	*Štajner (p), og (Hájovský), Vácha, Fleišman*
04/08	Dukla	h	3-2	*Šural 3*
11/08	Jablonec	a	0 1	
19/08	Jihlava	h	1-1	*Šural*
26/08	České Budějovice	a	2-0	*Šural, Maicon*
02/09	Slavia	h	0-0	
16/09	Sigma	a	0-3	
21/09	Baník	h	2-2	*Blažek 2*
30/09	Hradec Králové	a	2-2	*Štajner 2 (1p)*
07/10	Brno	a	1-2	*Bosančić*
22/10	Mladá Boleslav	h	2-0	*Delarge, Vácha*
28/10	Sparta	a	1-2	*Blažek*
05/11	Slovácko	h	3-2	*Štajner, Šural, Hadaščok*
11/11	Teplice	a	0-3	
17/11	Plzeň	h	1-2	*Bosančić*
23/11	Dukla	a	0-3	

2013

23/02	Jablonec	h	1-0	*Štajner*
01/03	Jihlava	a	0-0	
09/03	České Budějovice	h	3-1	*Kušnír, Rybalka, Fleišman*
16/03	Slavia	a	1-3	*Štajner*
29/03	Sigma	h	1-0	*Delarge*
07/04	Baník	a	1-0	*Delarge*
13/04	Hradec Králové	h	1-0	*Rybalka*
20/04	Brno	h	2-0	*Rabušic 2*
28/04	Mladá Boleslav	a	3-2	*Rabušic 2, Štajner*
04/05	Sparta	h	2-0	*Rabušic, Štajner*
11/05	Slovácko	a	3-0	*Pavelka, Rabušic, Delarge*
21/05	Teplice	h	3-1	*Kelić, Pavelka, Rabušic*
26/05	Plzeň	a	2-1	*Rabušic, Hušek*
01/06	Příbram	h	1-1	*Šural*

No	Name	Nat	DoB	Pos	Aps	(s)	Gls
30	David Bičík		06/04/81	G	14		
9	Jan Blažek		20/03/88	A	8	(6)	3
30	Daniel Bojčuk		28/08/90	G		(1)	
10	Miloš Bosančić	SRB	22/05/88	M	8	(4)	2
11	Michal Breznaník	SVK	16/12/85	M	6		
5	Vladimír Coufal		22/08/92	D	3	(7)	
4	Erik Daniel		04/02/92	M	1	(1)	
28	John Delarge	CGO	24/06/90	A	14	(6)	4
25	Jiří Fleišman		02/10/84	D	23		2
11	Martin Frýdek		24/03/92	D	12	(2)	
15	Vojtěch Hadaščok		08/01/92	A	3	(7)	1
1	Zbyněk Hauzr		20/04/73	G	3		
7	Luboš Hušek		26/01/84	M	3	(1)	1
4	Michal Janec	SVK	28/04/92	D	1		
7	Tomáš Janů		17/09/73	D	14	(11)	
3	Miloš Karišik	SRB	07/10/88	D	11	(2)	
2	Renato Kelić	CRO	31/03/91	D	28		1
29	Tomáš Komenda		07/05/91	A		(1)	
15	Radoslav Kováč		27/11/79	D	13		
16	Přemysl Kovář		14/10/85	G	13		
13	Ondřej Kušnír		05/04/84	D	20	(1)	1
8	Serhiy Lyulka	UKR	22/02/90	D	12		
21	Maicon	BRA	28/07/89	M	4	(4)	1
20	Yevhen Morozenko	UKR	16/12/91	M	2	(2)	
22	Zbyněk Musiol		01/07/91	A		(4)	
18	Moustapha N'Diaye	SEN	24/08/94	A	1	(7)	
7	Jan Nezmar		05/07/77	D	5	(6)	
8	David Pavelka		18/05/91	M	11	(2)	2
19	Michael Rabušic		17/09/89	A	19	(5)	8
10	Serhiy Rybalka	UKR	01/04/90	M	14		2
12	Isaac Sackey	GHA	04/04/94	M	5	(3)	
24	Jiří Štajner		27/05/76	M	21	(1)	8
23	Josef Šural		30/05/90	A	22	(3)	7
14	Martin Tóth	SVK	13/10/86	D	3	(1)	
6	Lukáš Vácha		13/05/89	M	13		2

AC SPARTA PRAHA

Coach: Vítězslav Lavička
1893 • Generali Arena (18,872) • sparta.cz
Major honours
Czechoslovakian/Czech League (30) 1926, 1927, 1932,
1936, 1938, 1946, 1948, 1952, 1954, 1965, 1967, 1984,
1985, 1987, 1988, 1989, 1990, 1991, 1993, 1994, 1995,
1997, 1998, 1999, 2000, 2001, 2003, 2005, 2007, 2010;
Czechoslovakian/Czech Cup (13) 1964, 1972, 1976, 1980,
1984, 1988, 1989, 1992, 1996, 2004, 2006, 2007, 2008

2012

28/07	Dukla	a	1-1	Kweuke	
05/08	Příbram	h	2-1	Kadeřábek, Kweuke	
12/08	Slovácko	a	4-1	Pavelka, Balaj, Hušbauer, Kadlec (p)	
19/08	České Budějovice	h	3-1	Kadlec, Kweuke, Kadeřábek	
27/08	Jablonec	a	2-1	Jarošík, Přikryl	
02/09	Hradec Králové	h	1-0	Balaj	
15/09	Plzeň	a	0-1		
24/09	Sigma	h	1-2	Kadlec (p)	
29/09	Slavia	a	0-1		
08/10	Baník	h	2-0	Zápotočný, Kadlec	
21/10	Jihlava	a	1-1	Kadlec	
28/10	Liberec	h	2-1	Jarošík, Švejdík	
03/11	Mladá Boleslav	a	1-1	Hušbauer (p)	
11/11	Brno	h	2-0	Kweuke 2	
17/11	Teplice	h	1-0	Balaj	
25/11	Příbram	a	0-0		

2013

24/02	Slovácko	h	4-0	Kadlec 2, Zápotočný, Bednář	
01/03	České Budějovice	a	2-0	Lafata 2	
10/03	Jablonec	h	2-2	Přikryl, Zápotočný	
17/03	Hradec Králové	h	1-0	Krejčí 2	
30/03	Plzeň	h	1-0	Lafata	
06/04	Sigma	a	3-0	Kadlec 2, Krejčí	
13/04	Slavia	h	3-1	og (Hubáček), Kadlec, Krejčí	
20/04	Baník	a	1-0	Kweuke	
26/04	Jihlava	h	2-2	Lafata, Bednář	
04/05	Liberec	a	0-2		
12/05	Mladá Boleslav	h	4-0	Lafata 3, Jarošík	
22/05	Brno	a	2-3	Hušbauer, Kadlec	
26/05	Teplice	a	3-0	og (Krátký), Kadlec, Hušbauer	
01/06	Dukla	h	3-0	Vácha, Kadlec 2	

No	Name	Nat	DoB	Pos	Aps	(s)	Gls
9	Bekim Balaj	ALB	11/01/91	A	9	(3)	3
29	Roman Bednář		26/03/83	A	1	(10)	2
38	Aleš Čermák		01/10/94	M		(4)	
37	Peter Grajciar	SVK	17/09/83	M	2	(5)	
25	Mario Holek		28/10/86	M	16	(3)	
22	Josef Hušbauer		16/03/90	M	23	(3)	4
19	Matěj Hybš		03/01/93	D	11	(2)	
32	Adam Jánoš		20/07/92	D		(1)	
39	Jiří Jarošík		27/10/77	M	20	(1)	3
26	Milan Jirásek		14/05/92	M		(2)	
16	Pavel Kadeřábek		25/04/92	M	10	(9)	2
14	Václav Kadlec		20/05/92	A	25	(1)	14
15	Andrej Kerić	CRO	11/02/86	A		(2)	
12	Tiémoko Konaté	CIV	03/03/90	M		(1)	
23	Ladislav Krejčí		05/07/92	M	24	(1)	4
11	Léonard Kweuke	CMR	12/07/87	A	10	(11)	6
21	David Lafata		18/09/81	A	12		7
8	Marek Matějovský		20/12/81	M	22	(2)	
26	Pablo Gil	ESP	08/10/88	D	1	(1)	
3	Manuel Pamić	CRO	20/08/86	D	19		
18	David Pavelka		18/05/91	M	7		1
27	Roman Polom		11/01/92	D	3	(4)	
7	Tomáš Přikryl		04/07/92	A	10	(11)	2
17	Jiří Skalák		12/03/92	A	3	(4)	
4	Ondřej Švejdík		03/12/82	D	28	(1)	1
6	Lukáš Vácha		13/05/89	M	14		1
31	Tomáš Vaclík		29/03/89	G	30		
24	Vlastimil Vidlička		02/07/81	D	17	(2)	
20	Tomáš Zápotočný		13/09/80	D	13	(2)	3

FK TEPLICE

Coach: Lukáš Přerost; (02/10/12) Zdeněk Ščasný
1945 • Na Stínadlech (18,221) • fkteplice.cz
Major honours
Czech Cup (2) 2003, 2009

2012

29/07	Mladá Boleslav	h	1-0	Mahmutović	
05/08	Brno	a	1-1	og (Pašek)	
10/08	Dukla	a	0-4		
19/08	Příbram	h	0-0		
25/08	Slovácko	a	1-2	Vachoušek	
31/08	Jablonec	h	0-4		
19/09	Slavia	a	0-2		
23/09	Plzeň	h	1-1	Mahmutović	
29/09	České Budějovice	a	2-3	Jarolím, Vachoušek	
07/10	Jihlava	h	3-1	Vůch, Jarolím, Podaný	
21/10	Hradec Králové	a	0-2		
28/10	Sigma	h	1-0	Mahmutović	
03/11	Baník	a	2-3	Mahmutović 2 (1p)	
11/11	Liberec	h	3-0	Mahmutović, Lüftner, Jarolím	
17/11	Sparta	a	0-1		
25/11	Brno	h	2-0	Chovanec, Mahmutović	

2013

22/02	Dukla	h	1-1	Jarolím	
02/03	Příbram	a	1-3	Litsingi	
10/03	Slovácko	h	0-4		
17/03	Jablonec	a	0-0		
31/03	Slavia	h	1-1	Vondrášek	
07/04	Plzeň	a	1-2	Litsingi	
13/04	České Budějovice	h	4-0	Litsingi, Matula, Mahmutović (p), og (Novák)	
19/04	Jihlava	a	1-1	Mahmutović	
28/04	Hradec Králové	h	0-2		
06/05	Sigma	a	2-0	Mahmutović, Matula	
13/05	Baník	h	3-2	Rosa, Litsingi, Mahmutović	
21/05	Liberec	a	1-3	Podaný	
26/05	Sparta	h	0-3		
01/06	Mladá Boleslav	a	4-0	Jindráček 2, Mahmutović, Litsingi	

No	Name	Nat	DoB	Pos	Aps	(s)	Gls
14	Aldin Čajić	BIH	11/09/92	M	7	(3)	
24	Ján Chovanec	SVK	22/03/84	M	18	(3)	1
16	Petr Dolejš		01/04/86	M	1	(5)	
30	Tomáš Grigar		01/02/83	G	29		
18	David Jablonský		08/10/91	D	15	(3)	
10	Lukáš Janič		30/12/86	M		(3)	
10	Marek Jarolím		21/05/84	M	9	(2)	4
6	Václav Ježdík		03/07/87	D	11	(2)	
19	Martin Jindráček		29/11/89	A	13	(7)	2
2	Tomáš Jursa		09/03/89	M	4	(2)	
3	Josef Kaufman		27/03/84	D	13		
12	Andrej Kerić	CRO	11/02/86	A	5	(11)	
10	Karel Kodeš		13/03/91	A		(1)	
7	Marek Krátký		08/06/93	D	5	(1)	
28	Francis Litsingi	CGO	09/10/86	M	14		5
5	Admir Ljevaković	BIH	07/08/84	M	21		
4	Michael Lüftner		14/03/94	D	10	(3)	1
2	Petr Lukáš		24/04/78	D	13	(1)	
25	Aidin Mahmutović	BIH	06/04/86	A	27	(2)	12
20	Milan Matula		22/04/84	D	20		2
11	Alen Melunović	BIH	26/01/90	A		(12)	
26	Jakub Podaný		15/06/87	M	18	(2)	2
22	Antonín Rosa		12/11/86	D	20		1
1	Martin Slavík		21/09/79	G	1		
8	Štěpán Vachoušek		26/07/79	M	23	(5)	2
10	Richard Veverka		16/12/87	M		(2)	
17	Tomáš Vondrášek		26/10/87	D	19	(3)	1
27	Egon Vůch		01/02/91	A	14	(11)	1

FC VIKTORIA PLZEŇ

Coach: Pavel Vrba
1911 • Doosan Arena (11,753) • fcviktoria.cz
Major honours
Czech League (2) 2011, 2013;
Czech Cup (1) 2010

2012

29/07	Hradec Králové	h	3-0	Kolář, Bakoš, og (Poděbradský)	
05/08	Jihlava	a	1-1	Kolář	
12/08	Brno	h	2-3	Procházka, Rajtoral	
19/08	Baník	a	3-1	Ševinský, Horváth, Hanousek	
26/08	Mladá Boleslav	h	2-0	Hanousek, Procházka	
02/09	Dukla	a	4-1	Bakoš 2, Darida, Hanousek	
15/09	Sparta	h	1-0	Horváth (p)	
23/09	Teplice	a	1-1	Ďuriš	
30/09	Slovácko	h	1-1	Rajtoral	
07/10	Příbram	a	0-1		
20/10	Jablonec	h	1-1	Čišovský	
29/10	České Budějovice	a	1-0	Čišovský	
04/11	Slavia	a	1-0	og (Hubáček)	
11/11	Sigma	h	3-0	Kolář, Darida, Hora	
17/11	Liberec	a	2-1	Štípek, Darida	
26/11	Jihlava	h	1-0	Bakoš	

2013

25/02	Brno	a	3-1	Bakoš 2, Rajtoral	
03/03	Baník	h	1-1	Procházka	
10/03	Mladá Boleslav	a	2-0	Kolář, Horváth (p)	
17/03	Dukla	h	4-0	Bakoš, Čišovský, Kovařík, Adamov	
30/03	Sparta	a	0-1		
07/04	Teplice	h	2-1	Bakoš 2	
14/04	Slovácko	a	2-0	Kolář, Horváth (p)	
19/04	Příbram	h	2-0	Hejda, og (Střihavka)	
27/04	Jablonec	a	3-1	Kolář, Procházka, Bakoš	
03/05	České Budějovice	h	3-2	Darida 2, Řezník	
11/05	Slavia	h	0-1		
22/05	Sigma	a	1-0	Kolář	
26/05	Liberec	h	1-2	Štípek	
01/06	Hradec Králové	a	3-0	Darida, Procházka, Čišovský	

No	Name	Nat	DoB	Pos	Aps	(s)	Gls
20	Roman Adamov	RUS	21/06/82	A	1	(5)	1
23	Marek Bakoš	SVK	15/04/83	A	24	(4)	10
13	Petr Bolek		13/06/84	G	3		
20	Daniel Černý		19/07/94	A		(1)	
16	Marián Čišovský	SVK	02/11/79	D	23		4
16	Vladimír Darida		08/08/90	M	28	(1)	6
12	Michal Ďuriš	SVK	01/06/88	A	17	(9)	1
17	Martin Fillo		07/02/86	M	3	(11)	
5	Marek Hanousek		06/08/91	M	7	(3)	3
2	Lukáš Hejda		09/03/90	D	2	(13)	1
17	Jakub Hora		23/02/91	A	5	(7)	1
10	Pavel Horváth		22/04/75	M	27		4
26	Daniel Kolář		27/10/85	M	20	(1)	7
6	Matěj Končal		08/12/93	M		(2)	
19	Jan Kovařík		19/06/88	M	14		1
21	Matúš Kozáčik	SVK	27/12/83	G	27		
8	David Limberský		06/10/83	D	28		
22	Edgar Malakyan	ARM	22/09/90	M	2	(4)	
21	Václav Procházka		08/05/84	D	26	(1)	5
27	František Rajtoral		12/03/86	D	25	(3)	3
14	Radim Řezník		20/01/89	D	26		1
15	František Ševinský		31/03/79	D	10	(4)	1
29	David Štípek		31/05/92	M	4	(6)	2
9	Stanislav Tecl		01/09/90	A	6	(8)	
7	Martin Zeman		28/03/89	M	2	(4)	

FC VYSOČINA JIHLAVA

Coach: František Komňacký
1948 • Městský stadion (4,075) • fcvysocina.cz

2012

30/07	Slavia	a	3-3	Vaculík, Koloušek, Tecl (p)
05/08	Plzeň	h	1-1	Karlík
12/08	Hradec Králové	a	1-1	Tecl
19/08	Liberec	a	1-1	Jungr
24/08	Sigma	h	1-1	Tecl
02/09	Mladá Boleslav	a	3-1	Tecl 2 (1p), Koloušek
17/09	Baník	h	3-2	Tecl, Šourek, Koloušek
23/09	Brno	a	1-5	Tecl
28/09	Příbram	h	2-1	og (Koukal), Tecl (p)
07/10	Teplice	a	1-3	Tecl
21/10	Sparta	h	1-1	Tecl
26/10	Dukla	a	2-2	Karlík, Obert
02/11	Jablonec	h	0-1	
10/11	Slovácko	a	0-3	
16/11	České Budějovice	h	1-0	Kučera
26/11	Plzeň	a	0-1	

2013

22/02	Hradec Králové	h	0-0	
01/03	Liberec	h	0-0	
09/03	Sigma	a	0-3	
23/03	Mladá Boleslav	h	1-0	Rada
08/04	Brno	h	2-0	Šourek, Šimonek
13/04	Příbram	a	2-2	Karlík, Masopust
19/04	Teplice	h	1-1	Kliment
23/04	Baník	a	0-1	
26/04	Sparta	a	2-2	og (Jarošík), Vaculík
03/05	Dukla	h	1-1	Karlík
12/05	Jablonec	a	1-1	Jungr
22/05	Slovácko	h	1-1	Šimonek
26/05	České Budějovice	a	1-2	Jungr
01/06	Slavia	h	3-1	Vaculík, Koloušek, Marek

No	Name	Nat	DoB	Pos	Aps	(s)	Gls
29	Jaromír Blažek		29/12/72	G	28		
25	Peter Čvirik	SVK	13/06/79	D	7	(3)	
4	Petar Gavrić	CRO	21/10/86	D	1	(1)	
1	Jan Hanuš		28/04/88	G	2		
22	Tomáš Josl		12/11/84	M	22	(1)	
9	Marek Jungr		11/04/87	M	26	(1)	3
20	Karol Karlík	SVK	29/06/88	M	22	(1)	4
12	Jan Kliment		01/09/93	M	1	(8)	1
21	Václav Koloušek		13/04/76	M	16	(6)	4
18	Jan Kosak		03/02/92	M	6	(12)	
15	Lukáš Kryštůfek		15/08/92	D	2	(2)	
16	Tomáš Kučera		20/07/91	M	6	(12)	1
14	Tomáš Marek		20/04/81	D	11		1
26	Lukáš Masopust		12/02/93	M	27	(2)	1
10	Muris Mešanović	BIH	06/07/90	A	4	(8)	
8	Igor Obert	SVK	14/07/82	D	12		1
3	Tomáš Rada		15/02/83	D	23	(1)	1
28	Tomáš Sedláček		29/08/80	A	2	(12)	
19	Arnold Šimonek	SVK	19/09/90	A	11	(1)	2
6	Ondřej Šourek		26/04/83	D	28		2
7	Stanislav Tecl		01/09/90	A	11		10
17	Petr Tlustý		17/01/86	D	29	(1)	
24	Václav Tomeček		24/08/91	M	1	(4)	
11	Lukáš Vaculík		06/06/83	M	29		3
7	David Vaněček		09/03/91	A	3	(3)	
20	Václav Vašíček		10/02/91	A		(2)	

FC ZBROJOVKA BRNO

Coach: Petr Čuhel; (09/04/13) Ludevít Grmela
1913 • Městský stadion (10,785) • fczbrno.cz
Major honours
Czechoslovakian League (1) 1978;
Czechoslovakian Cup (1) 1960

2012

28/07	Slovácko	a	1-0	Pernica
05/08	Teplice	h	1-1	Halaška
12/08	Plzeň	a	3-2	Pernica, Mezlík, Halaška
19/08	Jablonec	h	1-4	Fall
23/08	Slavia	a	0-5	
01/09	České Budějovice	h	3-1	Švancara 2, Glaser
16/09	Hradec Králové	a	0-2	
23/09	Jihlava	h	5-1	Švancara 2, Škoda 2, Pernica
28/09	Sigma	a	1-1	Švancara
07/10	Liberec	h	2-1	Zavadil, Přerovský
20/10	Baník	a	1-1	Lutonský
26/10	Mladá Boleslav	a	0-1	
04/11	Dukla	h	1-3	og (Berger)
11/11	Sparta	a	0-2	
18/11	Příbram	h	1-0	Lutonský
25/11	Teplice	a	0-2	

2013

23/02	České Budějovice	h	0-0	
03/03	Plzeň	a	1-1	Milosavljev
09/03	Hradec Králové	h	3-0	Baroš 3
15/03	Sigma	h	0-1	
06/04	Liberec	h	0-1	
15/04	Mladá Boleslav	a	0-2	
20/04	Sparta	h	0-1	
23/04	Jihlava	h	1-0	Fantiš
29/04	Brno	a	1-2	Stožický
04/05	Příbram	h	2-0	Baroš 2
13/05	Teplice	a	2-3	Frydrych 2
22/05	Dukla	h	2-2	og (Vorel), Fantiš
26/05	Slovácko	a	0-2	
01/06	Jablonec	h	0-1	

No	Name	Nat	DoB	Pos	Aps	(s)	Gls
6	Muamer Avdić	BIH	07/01/93	D	1	(1)	
5	Jakub Brabec		06/08/92	D	16		
16	Petr Buchta		15/07/92	D	10	(4)	
1	Martin Doležal		03/09/90	M	19		
11	Lamine Fall	SEN	10/07/02	M	1		1
25	Tomáš Frejlach		24/11/85	M	6		2
8	Petr Glaser		30/07/88	M	7	(7)	2
14	Milan Halaška		08/01/88	A	5	(6)	2
17	Václav Hladký		14/11/90	G	1		
30	Martin Husár	SVK	01/02/85	D	25	(2)	
24	Alois Hyčka		22/07/90	D	10	(3)	
12	Milan Jurdík		08/11/91	A	5	(4)	
25	Josef Kaufman		27/03/84	D	9	(1)	
2	Miroslav Král		16/09/86	D	3		
29	Karel Kroupa		27/04/80	A	7	(2)	2
12	Tomáš Kunc		22/02/93	A		(3)	
6	Lukáš Křeček		18/09/86	M	1		
19	Milan Lutonský		10/08/93	M	26		2
26	Jan Malík		04/11/89	D		(1)	
12	Miroslav Markovič	SVK	04/11/89	A	6	(2)	
10	Pavel Mezlík		25/06/83	M	26		4
29	Petr Nekuda		27/04/90	A		(2)	
3	David Pašek		27/10/89	D	18	(1)	1
4	Luděk Pernica		16/06/90	D	28		3
20	Radek Petr		24/02/87	G	11		
21	Daniel Přerovský		05/03/92	M	3	(12)	1
18	Jindřich Stehlík		30/06/92	A		(2)	
13	Martin Sus		08/05/89	M	11	(9)	
2	Petr Šíma		25/02/83	M		(1)	
27	Michal Škoda		01/03/88	A	13	(5)	3
22	Josip Šoljić	CRO	18/06/87	D	16	(1)	
9	Petr Švancara		05/11/77	A	16	(3)	6
28	Mohamed Traoré	GUI	17/05/93	A	2	(9)	
7	Pavel Zavadil		30/04/78	M	29		4

20	David Lafata (Jablonec/Sparta)
14	Michal Ordoš (Sigma)
	Václav Kadlec (Sparta)
13	Libor Došek (Slovácko)
12	Aidin Mahmutović (Teplice)
10	Zbyněk Pospěch (Dukla)
	Marek Bakoš (Plzeň)
	Stanislav Tecl (Jihlava)
9	Karol Kisel (Slavia)
8	Tomáš Čížek (Jablonec)
	Michael Rabušic (Liberec)
	Jiří Štajner (Liberec)

Promoted clubs

1. SC ZNOJMO

Coach: Leoš Kalvoda
2001 • HOSTAN Arena (5,000) • 1scznojmo.cz

BOHEMIANS 1905

Coach: Jozef Weber
1905 • Ďolíček (6,000) • bohemians.cz
Major honours
Czechoslovakian League (1) 1983

SECOND LEVEL FINAL TABLE 2012/13

		Pld	W	D	L	F	A	Pts
1	1. SC Znojmo	30	17	7	6	45	24	58
2	Bohemians 1905	30	16	8	6	50	25	56
3	FK Baník Sokolov	30	14	8	8	36	26	50
4	1. HFK Olomouc	30	15	5	10	41	44	50
5	FK Varnsdorf	30	15	4	11	49	37	49
6	FC Zlín	30	14	6	10	49	37	48
7	FK Pardubice	30	14	4	12	47	31	46
8	FK Viktoria Žižkov	30	12	9	9	38	30	45
9	MFK OKD Karviná	30	11	9	10	43	43	42
10	FK Ústí nad Labem	30	11	6	13	32	42	39
11	FK Bohemians Praha	30	6	17	7	30	33	35
12	FC MAS Táborsko	30	8	10	12	35	42	34
13	FK Baník Most	30	8	7	15	33	48	31
14	FC Vlašim	30	8	7	15	37	58	31
15	FK Čáslav	30	6	7	17	24	43	25
16	SFC Opava	30	5	6	19	34	60	21

Domestic cup: Pohár České Pošty 2012/13

SECOND ROUND

(28/08/12)
Čáslav 1-1 Táborsko *(5-4 on pens)*
Králův Dvůr 2-1 Příbram

(29/08/12)
ARSENAL Česká Lípa 2-0 Varnsdorf
Brumov 3-5 Slovácko
Frýdek-Místek 0-1 Zlín
HS Kroměříž 2-0 Břeclav
Karlovy Vary 0-0 Viktoria Žižkov *(1-3 on pens)*
Karviná 1-2 Baník Ostrava
Kolín 0-1 Dukla Praha
Meteor Praha 3-1 Bohemians 1905
Prostějov 1-4 Sigma Olomouc
Slavoj Vyšehrad 2-0 Písek
Sokol Jablonec 3-1 Vilémov
Sokol Nové Strašecí 0-1 Chomutov
Sparta Kutná Hora 0-1 Slavia Praha
Strakonice 1-1 Bohemians Praha *(1-4 on pens)*
Svitavy 1-2 Vysočina Jihlava
Třebíč 0-0 Znojmo *(7-6 on pens)*
Uničov 3-3 Opava *(5-3 on pens)*
Ústí nad Labem 2-0 Baník Most
Vlašim 0-1 Pardubice
Zábřeh 1-1 HFK Olomouc *(8-9 on pens)*

(05/09/12)
Hlučín 1-1 Fotbal Třinec *(3-4 on pens)*
Horní Měcholupy 1-3 Teplice
Jiskra Domažlice 1-1 České Budějovice *(5-4 on pens)*
Loko Vltavín 0-3 Jablonec
Slovan Rosice 2-1 Zbrojovka Brno

(06/09/12)
Dvůr Králové 1-4 Hradec Králové

Byes - Mladá Boleslav, Slovan Liberec, Sparta
Praha, Viktoria Plzeň

THIRD ROUND

(26/09/12)
ARSENAL Česká Lípa 0-0 Slovan Liberec *(2-4 on pens)*
Bohemians Praha 0-1 Hradec Králové
Čáslav 1-1 Mladá Boleslav *(3-4 on pens)*
Fotbal Třinec 1-0 Baník Ostrava
HFK Olomouc 2-2 Dukla Praha *(3-4 on pens)*
HS Kroměříž 0-4 Slovácko
Chomutov 2-3 Viktoria Plzeň
Meteor Praha 0-6 Jablonec
Sokol Jablonec 2-2 Slovan Rosice *(1-3 on pens)*
Třebíč 2-2 Králův Dvůr *(3-1 on pens)*

(02/10/12)
Jiskra Domažlice 2-0 Pardubice
Ústí nad Labem 2-2 Slavia Praha *(5-4 on pens)*

(03/10/12)
Zlín 2-2 Vysočina Jihlava *(4-5 on pens)*

(10/10/12)
Vyšehrad 0-7 Teplice
Uničov 0-3 Sigma Olomouc

(31/10/12)
Viktoria Žižkov 1-1 Sparta Praha *(3-4 on pens)*

FOURTH ROUND

(17/10/12 & 31/10/12)
Slovan Rosice 1-4, 0-3 Slovan Liberec *(1-7)*

(31/10/12 & 28/11/12)
Dukla Praha 0-1, 2-2 Sigma Olomouc *(2-3)*
Třebíč 0-2, 0-2 Slovácko *(0-4)*

(06/11/12 & 27/11/12)
Ústí nad Labem 1-7, 0-5 Jablonec *(1-12)*

(06/11/12 & 28/11/12)
Fotbal Třinec 1-1, 0-3 Mladá Boleslav *(1-4)*

(07/11/12 & 28/11/12)
Jiskra Domažlice 0-2, 1-2 Teplice *(1-4)*

(29/11/12 & 05/03/13)
Vysočina Jihlava 1-1, 1-1 Sparta Praha *(2-2; 2-3 on pens)*

(29/11/12 & 23/03/13)
Hradec Králové 2-1, 0-1 Viktoria Plzeň *(2-2; Viktoria Plzeň on away goal)*

QUARTER-FINALS

(02/04/13 & 10/04/13)
Mladá Boleslav 3-1 Slovácko *(Šćuk 42, Johana 88, Dosoudil 90+2; Trousil 39)*
Slovácko 0-1 Mladá Boleslav *(Mareš 24)*
(Mladá Boleslav 4-1)

(03/04/13 & 10/04/13)
Jablonec 2-1 Viktoria Plzeň *(Piták 62, 76p; Čišovský 5)*
Viktoria Plzeň 3-4 Jablonec *(Daniel Rossi 72og, Darida 73, Zeman 87; Novák 4, Vaněk 6, 53, 70)*
(Jablonec 6-4)

(03/04/13 & 16/04/13)
Sigma Olomouc 2-4 Sparta Praha *(Navrátil 72, Varadi 87; Kadlec 60, 66, Kweuke 64, Hušbauer 79)*
Sparta Praha 4-2 Sigma Olomouc *(Kadeřábek 7, Kweuke 49, 70, Jánoš 88; Navrátil 48, Škerle 90)*
(Sparta Praha 8-4)

Slovan Liberec 2-0 Teplice *(Rabušic 24, Delarge 31)*
Teplice 2-2 Slovan Liberec *(Chovanec 5, Vůch 71; Delarge 38, Pavelka 79)*
(Slovan Liberec 4-2)

SEMI-FINALS

(24/04/13 & 08/05/13)
Slovan Liberec 4-3 Jablonec *(Štajner 37p, 38, 59, Delarge 63; Vaněk 11, 58, Třešňák 67)*
Jablonec 2-0 Slovan Liberec *(Hubník 52, Piták 63)*
(Jablonec 5-4)

(01/05/13 & 08/05/13)
Mladá Boleslav 1-1 Sparta Praha *(Chramosta 73; Krejčí 52)*
Sparta Praha 1-2 Mladá Boleslav *(Jarošík 2; Bořil 59, Chramosta 69)*
(Mladá Boleslav 3-2)

FINAL

(17/05/13)
Letní stadion, Chomutov
FK JABLONEC 2 *(Hubník 19, Kopic 84)*
FK MLADÁ BOLESLAV 2 *(Zahustěl 29, Chramosta 45)*
(5-4 on pens)
Referee: *Příhoda*
JABLONEC: *Špit, Kubista (Piták 46), Eliáš, Loučka, Vaněk, Beneš, Daniel Rossi, Novák, Čížek (Zoubele 77), Jablonský (Kopic 46), Hubník*
MLADÁ BOLESLAV: *Miller, Kúdela, Johana, Ševinský, Bořil, Mareš (Synek 85), Jarolím, Šćuk, Zahustěl (Kysela 71), Chramosta, Nešpor (Ondřejka 12)*

Jablonec defeated Mladá Boleslav on penalties to win the Czech Cup for the second time

DENMARK
Dansk Boldspil-Union (DBU)

Address House of Football,
DBU Allé 1
DK-2605 Brøndby
Tel +45 43 262 222
Fax +45 43 262 245
E-mail dbu@dbu.dk
Website dbu.dk

President Allan Hansen
General secretary Jim Stjerne Hansen
Media officer Lars Berendt
Year of formation 1889
National stadium Parken, Copenhagen
(38,065)

SUPERLIGA CLUBS

 1 **Aalborg BK**

2 **AGF Aarhus**

3 **Brøndby IF**

 4 **Esbjerg fB**

5 **AC Horsens**

 6 **FC København**

7 **FC Midtjylland**

 8 **FC Nordsjælland**

9 **Odense BK**

 10 **Randers FC**

11 **Silkeborg IF**

12 **SønderjyskE**

PROMOTED CLUBS

13 **Viborg FF**

14 **FC Vestsjælland**

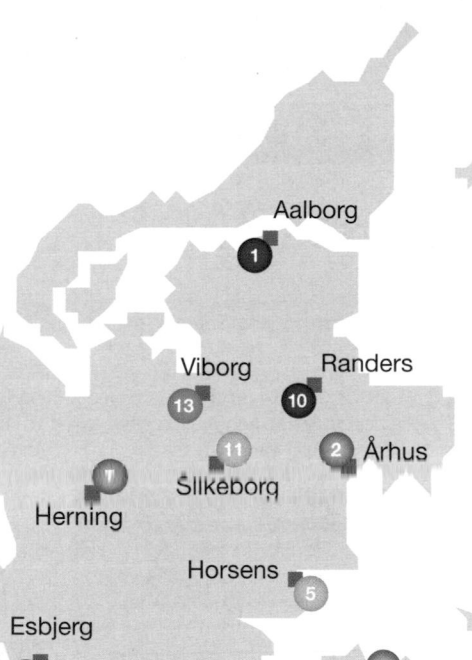

KEY:
● – UEFA Champions League
● – UEFA Europa League
● – Promoted clubs
● – Relegated clubs

0   100   200 km

0   100 miles

FC København return to the summit

Order was restored to the Danish Superliga in 2012/13 as serial champions FC København, under new Belgian coach Ariël Jacobs, recaptured the league title that they had surprisingly surrendered to FC Nordsjælland the previous season.

Twelve points clear at the winter break, FCK cruised home unchallenged to book a place in the group stage of the UEFA Champions League. Nordsjælland finished as worthy runners-up, while top-flight newcomers Randers FC and Esbjerg fB caused a surprise not just by filling the next two positions but also reaching the Danish Cup final.

New boss Jacobs leads capital club to tenth title

Esbjerg beat Randers 1-0 in cup final

Brøndby narrowly escape relegation

Domestic league

København's tenth Superliga crown – and ninth in the 21st century – was a foregone conclusion from early on. They moved into top spot after four matches and proceeded to stretch their lead as the weeks progressed. Jacobs, a 2011/12 Belgian title-winner with RSC Anderlecht, settled in quickly, and there was little the opposition could do to halt the FCK juggernaut during the autumn – particularly with towering young centre-forward Andreas Cornelius and new signing Nicolai Jørgensen scoring at will. Undefeated after 13 games, they were finally beaten in late October, 1-0 at AC Horsens, but responded with six successive victories to take them into the winter shutdown with a virtually unassailable lead.

That winning run was stretched to nine games at the restart, and it was simply a matter of time before the Superliga trophy was returned to the Copenhagen club's possession. With the pressure off, Jacobs' men decelerated towards victory. Indeed, they won only one of their last ten fixtures – curiously, away to closest challengers Nordsjælland – and it was with a 0-0 draw at traditional rivals Brøndby IF, before a crowd of 21,031 on the first Sunday in May, that the title was mathematically sealed.

Brøndby were grateful not just for that point but also the gate receipts. Ailing financially, the celebrated club from the Copenhagen suburbs were in serious danger of aggravating that situation with a first ever relegation. Bottom at Christmas, it was only on the final day, with a last-gasp win at Horsens (when a draw would have sufficed), that they secured their safety, sending down their hosts instead.

Domestic cup

Randers and Esbjerg had been relegated alongside each other in 2010/11 and promoted together in 2011/12, and the two clubs from opposite ends of the Jutland peninsula were to experience similar fortunes once again in 2012/13. Randers, under English coach Colin Todd, took third place in the Superliga, while Esbjerg finished fourth. The two clubs also met in the Danish Cup final, and it was Esbjerg who claimed the trophy – for the first time since 1976 – with a 55th-minute header from Youssef Toutouh. It was a fitting farewell for coach Jess Thorup, who left to take charge of the Danish Under-21 side.

Europe

Granted automatic entry to the UEFA Champions League, Nordsjælland were drawn in a tough group alongside Juventus, FC Shakhtar Donetsk and holders Chelsea FC. It was a predictably arduous campaign for Kasper Hjulmand and his players, but a 1-1 draw at home to Juve at least spared them a whitewash. FCK narrowly failed to provide a double Danish representation, losing after extra time to LOSC Lille in the play-offs. They resurfaced in the UEFA Europa League but failed to get beyond the group stage. A double over Molde FK salvaged a certain Scandinavian pride, but disappointing results at home against VfB Stuttgart and FC Steaua Bucureşti ended Danish interest in Europe before Christmas.

National team

Just six points from their opening six FIFA World Cup qualifiers suggested that Denmark would not be travelling to Brazil in the summer of 2014. Morten Olsen's team signed off the season with an alarming 4-0 thrashing by Armenia in Copenhagen – the country's heaviest home defeat in a competitive international. Coming after earlier draws at Parken against the Czech Republic and Bulgaria, it was an enormous setback, effectively obliterating the advantage Denmark might have had on those two rivals for the Group B runners-up spot following their splendid 3-0 victory away to the Czechs in March.

Domestic league: Superliga 2012/13 final table

			Home					Away					Total					
		Pld	W	D	L	F	A	W	D	L	F	A	W	D	L	F	A	Pts
1	**FC København**	33	12	4	1	38	12	6	7	3	24	20	18	11	4	62	32	65
2	FC Nordsjælland	33	11	5	1	41	15	6	4	6	19	22	17	9	7	60	37	60
3	Randers FC	33	10	2	4	20	13	5	5	7	16	29	15	7	11	36	42	52
4	Esbjerg fB	33	9	2	5	27	15	4	6	7	11	17	13	8	12	38	32	47
5	Aalborg BK	33	6	6	4	22	18	7	2	8	29	28	13	8	12	51	46	47
6	FC Midtjylland	33	7	7	3	29	22	5	1	7	22	25	12	11	10	51	47	47
7	AGF Aarhus	33	5	7	5	21	22	6	1	9	29	27	11	8	14	50	49	41
8	SønderjyskE	33	5	2	10	26	32	7	3	6	27	25	12	5	16	53	57	41
9	Brøndby IF	33	4	6	6	20	24	5	6	6	19	21	9	12	12	39	45	39
10	Odense BK	33	5	3	8	29	27	5	5	7	23	32	10	8	15	52	59	38
11	AC Horsens	33	5	5	7	18	27	3	5	8	13	22	8	10	15	31	49	34
12	Silkeborg IF	33	4	3	9	15	28	4	4	9	23	38	8	7	18	38	66	31

SEASON AT A GLANCE

EUROPEAN QUALIFICATION 2013/14

Champion: FC København (group stage)
FC Nordsjælland (third qualifying round)

Cup winner: Esbjerg fB (play-offs)
Randers FC (third qualifying round)
Aalborg BK (second qualifying round)

Top scorer	Andreas Cornelius (København), 18 goals
Relegated clubs	Silkeborg IF, AC Horsens
Promoted clubs	Viborg FF, FC Vestsjælland
Cup final	Esbjerg fB 1-0 Randers FC

**SUPERLIGA TEAM
OF THE SEASON**
(4-4-2)
Coach: Jacobs (København)

**PLAYER OF
THE SEASON
Andreas Cornelius**
(FC København)

A sensational debut season
for FCK turned out to be
his last at the club, with English Premier
League newcomers Cardiff City FC
paying a club record fee to take the beefy
young striker to south Wales. A teenager
for most of the campaign, he topped the
Superliga scoring charts with 18 goals for
the champions and also made his mark
in the Danish national team.

**NEWCOMER OF
THE SEASON
Martin Braithwaite**
(Esbjerg fB)

A winger/attacking
midfielder with pace and
skill, Braithwaite had already showcased
his potential in 2011/12 as he helped
Esbjerg gain promotion to the Superliga.
In 2012/13, under greater scrutiny from
opposition defences, the youngster
continued his rise with nine league
goals in an outstanding campaign that
concluded with a Danish Cup win.

Hradecky (Esbjerg)

Jacobsen (København) · Okore (Nordsjælland) · Sigurdsson (København) · Mtiliga (Nordsjælland)

Claudemir (København) · Keller (Randers) · Stokholm (Nordsjælland) · Braithwaite (Esbjerg)

Helenius (AaB) · Cornelius (København)

DENMARK

NATIONAL TEAM

Home Kit   Away Kit

INTERNATIONAL HONOURS
UEFA European Championship (1) 1992

INTERNATIONAL TOURNAMENT APPEARANCES
FIFA World Cup (4) 1986 (2nd round), 1998 (qtr-finals), 2002 (2nd round), 2010
UEFA European Championship (8) 1964 (4th), 1984 (semi-finals), 1988, 1992 (Winners), 1996, 2000, 2004 (qtr-finals), 2012.

TOP FIVE ALL-TIME CAPS
Peter Schmeichel (129); **Dennis Rommedahl** (126); Jon Dahl Tomasson (112); Thomas Helveg (109); Michael Laudrup (104)

TOP FIVE ALL-TIME GOALS
Poul "Tist" Nielsen & Jon Dahl Tomasson (52); Pauli Jørgensen (44); Ole Madsen (42); Preben Elkjær (38)

Results 2012/13

15/08/12	Slovakia	H	Odense	1-3	*Mikkelsen (22)*
08/09/12	Czech Republic (WCQ)	H	Copenhagen	0-0	
12/10/12	Bulgaria (WCQ)	A	Sofia	1-1	*Bendtner (40)*
16/10/12	Italy (WCQ)	A	Milan	1-3	*Kvist (45+1)*
14/11/12	Turkey	A	Istanbul	1-1	*Bendtner (65p)*
06/02/13	FYROM	A	Skopje	0-3	
22/03/13	Czech Republic (WCQ)	A	Olomouc	3-0	*Cornelius (57), Kjær (67), Zimling (82)*
26/03/13	Bulgaria (WCQ)	H	Copenhagen	1-1	*Agger (63p)*
05/06/13	Georgia	H	Aalborg	2-1	*Pedersen (76), Eriksen (88)*
11/06/13	Armenia (WCQ)	H	Copenhagen	0-4	

Appearances 2012/13

Coach: Morten Olsen	14/08/49		Svk	CZE	BUL	ITA	Tur	Mkd	CZE	BUL	Geo	ARM	Caps	Goals
Stephan Andersen	26/11/81	Évian (FRA)	G	G	G	G	G		G	G	G	G	22	-
Lars Jacobsen	20/09/79	København	D	D	D	D		D	D	D	D	D	62	1
Daniel Agger	12/12/84	Liverpool (ENG)	D75	D	D	D		D	D	D			56	7
Jores Okore	11/08/92	Nordsjælland	D				s53			D	s46		7	-
Jesper Juelsgård Kristensen	26/01/89	Midtjylland	D										1	-
William Kvist Jørgensen	24/02/85	Stuttgart (GER)	M61	M	M	M60		s32			s60	M	38	1
Niki Zimling	19/04/85	Club Brugge (BEL) /Mainz (GER)	M46					M80	M	M85	M12	M28	20	1
Christian Eriksen	14/02/92	Ajax (NED)	M46	M	M92	M	M	M53	M	M	M	M	36	3
Tobias Mikkelsen	18/09/86	Greuther Fürth (GER)	A75	s80									8	1
Nicklas Bendtner	16/01/88	Arsenal (ENG) /Juventus (ITA)	A46		A	A	A77						55	22
Michael Krohn-Dehli	06/06/83	Brøndby /Celta (ESP)	A	A	A	A83	A66	M82	A	A69	s46	A	34	6
Jakob Poulsen	07/07/83	Monaco (FRA)	s46		s92	s83	s46						28	1
Lasse Schøne	27/05/86	Ajax (NED)	s46					s82		s69	s12 /79		16	2
Nicklas Helenius Jensen	08/05/91	AaB	s46				s77						2	-
Nicolai Stokholm	01/04/76	Nordsjælland	s61			M	M		M	M	M60		8	-
Lasse Nielsen	08/01/88	AaB	s75										1	-
Kasper Lorentzen	19/11/85	Nordsjælland	s75			s72	A46						6	1
Simon Kjær	26/03/89	Wolfsburg (GER)		D	D	D	D	D53	D	D		D	35	1
Daniel Wass	31/05/89	Évian (FRA)		D	D54		D	D					10	-
Thomas Kristensen	17/04/83	København		M58	M36								7	-
Dennis Rommedahl	22/07/78	Brøndby		A80	A	A		A62	s66	A54	A46	A	126	21
Nicolai Jørgensen	15/01/91	København		A71				A32	A66	s54			6	-
Leon Andreasen	23/04/83	Hannover (GER)		s58									16	2
Andreas Cornelius	16/03/93	København		s71	s36			A	A85	A	A	A	7	1
Patrick Mtiliga	28/01/81	Nordsjælland			s54								6	-
Michael Silberbauer	07/07/81	OB				D72							25	1
Thomas Kahlenberg	20/03/83	Wolfsburg (GER)				s60							39	4
Kris Stadsgaard	01/08/85	København				D							3	-
Kevin Conboy	15/10/87	NEC (NED)				D							1	-
Casper Sloth	26/03/92	AGF				M46	s80						2	-

Appearances 2012/13 (contd.)

			Svk	CZE	BUL	ITA	Tur	Mkd	CZE	BUL	Geo	ARM	Caps	Goals
Emil Larsen	22/06/91	OB					s46						1	-
Viktor Fischer	09/06/94	Ajax (NED)					s66	s62					2	-
Kasper Schmeichel	05/11/86	Leicester (ENG)						G					1	-
Nicklas Pedersen	10/10/87	Mechelen (BEL)					s53				s60	s28 /53	11	1
Simon Busk Poulsen	07/10/84	Sampdoria (ITA)							D	D	D74	D	25	-
Simon Makienok Christoffersen	21/11/90	Brøndby							s85	s85	s74	s53	4	-
Andreas Bjelland	11/07/88	Twente (NED)									D	D46	8	1
Martin Braithwaite	05/06/91	Esbjerg									A60		1	-
Kasper Kusk	10/11/91	AaB									s79		1	-

European club competitions 2012/13

FC NORDSJÆLLAND

CHAMPIONS LEAGUE

Group E
Match 1 - FC Shakhtar Donetsk (UKR)
A 0-2
Hansen, Okore, Adu, Stokholm, Mtiliga, Beckmann, John (Laudrup 81), Christensen (Christiansen 62), Parkhurst, Lorentzen (Nordstrand 72), Runje. Coach: Kasper Hjulmand (DEN)
Match 2 - Chelsea FC (ENG)
H 0-4
Hansen, Okore, Adu, Stokholm, Mtiliga, Beckmann (Christensen 75), Nordstrand (Tičinović 65), John, Parkhurst, Lorentzen (Laudrup 85), Runje. Coach: Kasper Hjulmand (DEN)
Match 3 - Juventus (ITA)
H 1-1 *Beckmann (50)*
Hansen, Okore, Adu, Stokholm, Mtiliga, Beckmann (Nordstrand 67), John, Parkhurst, Lorentzen (Christiansen 88), Runje, Laudrup (Christensen 71). Coach: Kasper Hjulmand (DEN)
Match 4 - Juventus (ITA)
A 0-4
Hansen, Okore, Adu (Christensen 46), Stokholm, Mtiliga, Beckmann (Nordstrand 73), John, Parkhurst, Lorentzen, Runje, Laudrup (Christiansen 46). Coach: Kasper Hjulmand (DEN)
Match 5 - FC Shakhtar Donetsk (UKR)
H 2-5 *Nordstrand (24), Lorentzen (29)*
Hansen, Okore, Adu, Stokholm, Mtiliga, Nordstrand (Tičinović 75), John (Aynaoglu 82), Christensen (Christiansen 59), Parkhurst, Lorentzen, Runje. Coach: Kasper Hjulmand (DEN)

FC KØBENHAVN

CHAMPIONS LEAGUE

Match 6 - Chelsea FC (ENG)
A 1-6 *John (46)*
Hansen, Christiansen (Kildentoft 61), Adu, Stokholm, Mtiliga, John, Parkhurst, Gundelach, Lorentzen, Runje (Beckmann 9), Tičinović (Issah 65). Coach: Kasper Hjulmand (DEN)

Third qualifying round - Club Brugge KV (BEL)
H 0-0
Wiland, Jacobsen, Ottesen, Claudemir, César Santin, Kristensen, Sigurdsson, Jørgensen, Oviedo, Cornelius, Bolaños (Vingaard 70). Coach: Ariël Jacobs (BEL)
A 3-2 *Jørgensen (61), Bolaños (78), César Santin (90+5)*
Wiland, Jacobsen, Ottesen, Claudemir, César Santin, Kristensen, Sigurdsson, Jørgensen (Grindheim 85), Oviedo, Vingaard (Cornelius 71), Bolaños (Bengtsson 90). Coach: Ariël Jacobs (BEL)

Play-offs - LOSC Lille (FRA)
H 1-0 *César Santin (38)*
Wiland, Jacobsen, Bengtsson, Stadsgaard, Claudemir, César Santin (Cornelius 65), Kristensen, Sigurdsson, Jørgensen, Oviedo (Delaney 79), Bolaños (Vingaard 87). Coach: Ariël Jacobs (BEL)
A 0-2 *(aet)*
Wiland, Jacobsen, Bengtsson, Stadsgaard, Claudemir, César Santin (Cornelius 60), Kristensen, Sigurdsson, Jørgensen, Oviedo (Delaney 114), Bolaños (Vetokele 85). Coach: Ariël Jacobs (BEL)

EUROPA LEAGUE

Group E
Match 1 - Molde FK (NOR)
H 2-1 *Claudemir (20), Cornelius (74)*
Christensen, Jacobsen, Bengtsson, Stadsgaard, Claudemir, César Santin (Vetokele 65), Kristensen, Sigurdsson, Jørgensen (Vingaard 26), Cornelius, Bolaños (Delaney 82). Coach: Ariël Jacobs (BEL)
Match 2 - FC Steaua Bucureşti (ROU)
A 0-1
Wiland, Jacobsen, Bengtsson (César Santin 86), Stadsgaard, Claudemir, Kristensen, Sigurdsson, Jørgensen, Gíslason (Vingaard 73), Delaney, Cornelius. Coach: Ariël Jacobs (BEL)
Match 3 - VfB Stuttgart (GER)
A 0-0
Wiland, Jacobsen, Bengtsson, Stadsgaard, Claudemir, César Santin (Cornelius 84), Kristensen, Sigurdsson, Gíslason (Grindheim 80), Delaney, Bolaños. Coach: Ariël Jacobs (BEL)
Match 4 - VfB Stuttgart (GER)
H 0-2
Christensen, Jacobsen, Bengtsson, Stadsgaard, Claudemir, Grindheim (Jørgensen 58), César Santin, Kristensen (Bolaños 79), Sigurdsson, Delaney, Cornelius. Coach: Ariël Jacobs (BEL)
Match 5 - Molde FK (NOR)
A 2-1 *César Santin (21p), Gíslason (76)*
Christensen, Jacobsen, Bengtsson, Stadsgaard, Claudemir, César Santin (Amankwaa 87), Kristensen, Sigurdsson, Gíslason, Delaney, Cornelius (Bolaños 80). Coach: Ariël Jacobs (BEL)
Match 6 - FC Steaua Bucureşti (ROU)
H 1-1 *Vetokele (87)*
Christensen, Jacobsen, Bengtsson, Stadsgaard, Claudemir (Vetokele 65), Kristensen, Sigurdsson, Jørgensen, Gíslason (César Santin 73), Delaney, Cornelius. Coach: Ariël Jacobs (BEL)

FC MIDTJYLLAND

Play-offs - BSC Young Boys (SUI)
H 0-3
Lössl, Villafañe (Afriyie 77), Juelsgård, Olsen, Albæk, Sviatchenko, Bak Nielsen, Hassan, Nworuh (Rasmussen 59), Uzochukwu, Igboun. Coach: Glen Riddersholm (DEN)
Red card: Rasmussen 69
A 2-0 *Igboun (75p), Bak Nielsen (89)*
Lössl, Villafañe, Juelsgård, Andersson (Bak Nielsen 83), Albæk, Sviatchenko, Larsen (Nworuh 68), Ojuola, Hassan (Christensen 76), Uzochukwu, Igboun. Coach: Glen Riddersholm (DEN)

AC HORSENS

Third qualifying round - IF Elfsborg (SWE)
H 1-1 *Fagerberg (90+2p)*
Rønnow, Rasmussen, Andersen, Fagerberg, Kielstrup, Spelmann, Kortegaard, Jørgensen (Toft 67), Mehl (Kløve 62), Agesen, Drachmann. Coach: Johnny Mølby (DEN)
A 3-2 *Jørgensen (4), Kortegaard (13, 36)*
Rønnow, Rasmussen, Andersen, Fagerberg (Toft 82), Kielstrup, Spelmann, Kortegaard, Jørgensen, Agesen, Drachmann, Kløve (Nøhr 90). Coach: Johnny Mølby (DEN)

Play-offs - Sporting Clube de Portugal (POR)
H 1-1 *Spelmann (15)*
Rønnow, Nøhr, Rasmussen, Fagerberg (Hajdarević 75), Kielstrup, Spelmann, Kortegaard, Retov, Agesen, Drachmann, Kløve (Bjerregaard 86). Coach: Johnny Mølby (DEN)
A 0-5
Rønnow, Rasmussen, Aslam, Andersen, Fagerberg (Bjerregaard 46), Kielstrup, Spelmann (Hajdarević 62), Kortegaard, Retov (Nøhr 70), Drachmann, Kløve. Coach: Johnny Mølby (DEN)

AGF AARHUS

Second qualifying round - FC Dila Gori (GEO)
H 1-2 *Kure (3)*
Rasmussen, Håland, Eckersley, Petersen, Nørregaard, Jørgensen, Graulund (Devdariani 59), Akharraz (Berg 74), Sorin, Jóhannsson (Skhirtladze 74), Kure. Coach: Peter Sørensen (DEN)
A 1-3 *Skender (34og)*
Rasmussen, Håland, Eckersley, Nørregaard, Jørgensen, Akharraz (Petersen 64), Sorin, Jóhannsson (Graulund 43), Devdariani (Larsen 71), Kirkeskov, Sloth. Coach: Peter Sørensen (DEN)

Domestic league club-by-club

AALBORG BK

Coach: Kent Nielsen
1885 • Nordjyske Arena (13,800) • fodbold.aabsport.dk
Major honours
Danish League (3) 1995, 1999, 2008
Danish Cup (2) 1966, 1970

2012

13/07	AGF	a	1-1	Curth
22/07	Brøndby	h	2-1	Andersen, Helenius
28/07	København	a	0-3	
04/08	Nordsjælland	h	1-1	L Nielsen
12/08	Horsens	a	4-1	Kusk 2, Helenius, Wichmann
17/08	Midtjylland	h	3-0	Helenius, L Nielsen, Kusk
26/08	OB	a	4-0	Helenius (p), Augustinussen, Dalsgaard, Andersen
31/08	SønderjyskE	a	4-0	I. Nielsen, Curth 2, Kusk
16/09	Randers	h	4-0	Curth, Kusk 2, Kayke
24/09	Esbjerg	a	0-2	
30/09	Silkeborg	a	1-2	Petersen
07/10	Brøndby	a	3-1	Kusk, Helenius 2
20/10	SønderjyskE	h	2-1	Kristensen, Helenius
26/10	Nordsjælland	a	0-1	
05/11	Midtjylland	h	1-3	Kusk
11/11	København	a	0-4	
18/11	Horsens	h	2-0	Petersen, Toft
23/11	Randers	a	1-0	Helenius
03/12	AGF	h	0-3	

2013

01/03	Silkeborg	a	2-3	Pedersen, Kristensen
06/03	OB	h	2-2	Helenius 2
09/03	Esbjerg	a	0-0	
28/03	Horsens	a	2-2	Frederiksen, Helenius
01/04	Esbjerg	a	0-1	
04/04	Nordsjælland	h	0-1	
08/04	Silkeborg	h	1-0	Helenius
14/04	OB	a	4-3	Frederiksen 2, Helenius, Petersen
21/04	København	h	1-1	Helenius (p)
29/04	Midtjylland	a	3-2	Augustinussen, Dalsgaard, Wichmann
04/05	SønderjyskE	a	0-1	
12/05	Brøndby	h	1-1	Helenius
16/05	AGF	a	0-3	
20/05	Randers	h	?-?	Helenius, Thelander

No	Name	Nat	DoB	Pos	Aps	(s)	Gls
18	Lucas Andersen		13/09/94	M	7		2
9	Thomas Augustinussen		20/03/81	M	19	(6)	2
31	Jakob Blåberg		11/01/95	D	1		
10	Caspar Sloth		09/10/90	D	?	(2)	
10	Jeppe Curth		21/03/84	A	11	(10)	4
20	Henrik Dalsgaard		27/07/89	D	31		2
7	Anders Due		17/03/82	M	16	(10)	
19	Søren Frederiksen		08/07/89	A	10	(4)	3
21	Nicholas Gotfredsen		05/02/89	D	1		
28	Hallur Hansson	FRO	08/07/92	M	1	(2)	
11	Nicklas Helenius Jensen		08/05/91	A	33		16
30	Kayke	BRA	01/04/88	A	1	(5)	1
2	Patrick Kristensen		28/04/87	M	16	(12)	2
17	Kasper Kusk		10/11/91	M	32	(1)	8
1	Nicolai Larsen		09/03/91	G	33		
3	Jakob Ahlmann Nielsen		18/01/91	D	29		
4	Lasse Nielsen		08/01/88	D	28		3
32	Kasper Pedersen		13/01/93	D	3		1
5	Kenneth Emil Petersen		15/01/85	D	29		3
26	Rasmus Thelander		09/07/91	D	4	(7)	1
23	Nicolaj Thomsen		08/05/93	M	11	(10)	
29	Rolf Toft		04/08/92	M		(9)	1
14	Mathias Wichmann		06/08/91	M	17	(10)	2
8	Rasmus Würtz		18/09/83	M	28	(1)	

AGF AARHUS

Coach: Peter Sørensen
1880 • NRGi Park (19,433) • agf.dk
Major honours
Danish League (5) 1955, 1956, 1957, 1960, 1986;
Danish Cup (9) 1955, 1957, 1960, 1961, 1965, 1987, 1988, 1992, 1996

2012

13/07	AaB	h	1-1	Jørgensen (p)
23/07	Esbjerg	h	0-0	
29/07	Randers	a	1-2	Petersen
05/08	Brøndby	h	3-1	Devdariani, Jóhannsson, og (Stenderup)
12/08	København	a	0-3	
19/08	Nordsjælland	h	0-1	
27/08	Horsens	a	4-1	Jóhannsson 4 (1p)
01/09	Silkeborg	a	4-0	Jóhannsson 2, og (Mikkelsen), Graulund
17/09	Midtjylland	h	3-2	Jóhannsson 2, Devdariani
21/09	SønderjyskE	h	2-2	og (Stenlid), Jóhannsson
30/09	OB	a	2-1	Devdariani, Jóhannsson
06/10	SønderjyskE	a	3-0	Jóhannsson (p), Petersen, Eckersley
22/10	Randers	h	1-1	Skhirtladze
28/10	OB	a	4-2	Akharraz 2, Vatsadze, Sloth
04/11	København	h	0-2	
09/11	Horsens	h	0-2	
16/11	Nordsjælland	h	0-2	
26/11	Midtjylland	h	1-1	Povlsen
03/12	AaB	a	3-0	Petersen, Jóhannsson, Vatsadze
10/12	Silkeborg	h	3-3	Jóhannsson, Pasanen, Jönsson

2013

04/03	Esbjerg	a	1-2	Vatsadze
10/03	Brøndby	h	0-3	
17/03	OB	h	2-1	Kure, Akharraz
29/03	Nordsjælland	a	2-4	Petersen 2
01/04	Brøndby	a	2-3	Sorin 2
05/04	Esbjerg	h	0-1	
12/04	Silkeborg	a	1-3	og (Flinta)
20/04	Horsens	h	0-0	
28/04	København	a	0-0	
05/05	Randers	a	0-1	
11/05	SønderjyskE	h	2-1	Akharraz, Larsen
16/05	AaB	h	3-0	Larsen, Petersen, Devdariani
20/05	Midtjylland	a	2-0	Skhirtladze, Kure

No	Name	Nat	DoB	Pos	Aps	(s)	Gls
17	Osama Akharraz		26/11/90	A	29	(4)	4
9	Søren Berg		15/05/76	M	3	(4)	
30	David Devdariani	GEO	28/10/87	A	16	(10)	4
11	William Eckersley	ENG	07/09/85	D	24		1
32	Frôlafe Eqbedi	NGA	06/06/90	M	1	(1)	
11	Peter Graulund		20/09/70	A	1	(5)	1
4	Atle Roar Håland	NOR	26/07/77	D	3	(1)	
20	Aron Jóhannsson	ISL	10/11/90	A	15	(3)	14
16	Jens Jönsson		10/01/93	D	9	(6)	1
10	Martin Jørgensen		06/10/75	M	7	(7)	1
37	Mikkel Kirkeskov		05/09/91	D	31		
27	Anders Kure		12/09/85	D	17	(2)	2
14	Søren Larsen		06/09/81	A	4	(12)	2
15	Morten Moldskred	NOR	13/06/80	A		(1)	
8	Hjalte Bo Nørregaard		08/04/81	M	19	(6)	
23	Emil Ousager		19/07/87	G		(1)	
2	Petri Pasanen	FIN	24/09/80	D	23		1
7	Stephan Petersen		15/11/85	M	28	(1)	6
25	Kasper Povlsen		26/09/89	M	19	(2)	1
24	Frans Dhia Putros		14/07/93	D	1	(1)	
1	Steffen Rasmussen		30/09/82	G	33		
26	Emil Scheel		18/03/90	M	2	(15)	
22	David Skhirtladze	GEO	16/03/93	M	17	(3)	2
38	Casper Sloth		26/03/92	M	27	(2)	1
28	Marcus Solberg		17/02/95	A	1	(3)	
18	Arthur Sorin	FRA	01/11/85	D	24	(1)	2
21	Mate Vatsadze	GEO	17/12/88	A	9	(4)	3

BRØNDBY IF

Coach: Aurelijus Skarbalius (LTU)
1964 • Brøndby Stadion (29,000) • brondby.com
Major honours
Danish League (10) 1985, 1987, 1988, 1990, 1991, 1996, 1997, 1998, 2002, 2005;
Danish Cup (7) 1989, 1994, 1998, 2003, 2005, 2008

2012

15/07	OB	h	0-1	
22/07	AaB	a	1-2	Gehrt
30/07	Silkeborg	h	2-1	og (Jakobsen), Makienok
05/08	AGF	a	1-3	Makienok
12/08	SønderjyskE	h	0-1	
18/08	København	h	1-1	Goodson
26/08	Esbjerg	h	1-1	Dumic
02/09	Nordsjælland	a	0-0	
16/09	Horsens	h	2-2	Jensen (p), Larsen
23/09	Midtjylland	a	1-1	Jensen (p)
30/09	Randers	a	2-3	Thygesen, Makienok
07/10	AaB	h	1-3	Makienok
21/10	København	a	0-1	
28/10	Midtjylland	a	1-0	Antipas
04/11	OB	h	0-3	
11/11	Silkeborg	a	2-1	Makienok 2
18/11	Esbjerg	a	2-2	Makienok, Gehrt
25/11	Horsens	h	2-0	Rommedahl, Makienok
02/12	Nordsjælland	a	0-3	
07/12	SønderjyskE	a	2-2	Rommedahl, Antipas

2013

03/03	Randers	h	0-2	
10/03	AGF	a	3-0	Makienok 2, Larsen
17/03	Midtjylland	h	1-1	Antipas
29/03	Esbjerg	a	0-1	
01/04	AGF	h	3-2	Albrechtsen 2, Makienok
07/04	Randers	a	1-0	Makienok
14/04	SønderjyskE	a	0-3	
21/04	Silkeborg	a	2-2	Thygesen, Antipas
28/04	OB	a	2-1	Larsen (p), Antipas
05/05	København	h	0-0	
12/05	AaB	a	1-1	Goodson
16/05	Nordsjælland	h	4-0	Makienok 2, Rommedahl, Phiri
20/05	Horsens	a	1-0	Phiri

No	Name	Nat	DoB	Pos	Aps	(s)	Gls
18	Nicolaj Agger		23/10/88	A	2		
14	Oke Akpoveta	NGA	12/12/91	A	7	(12)	
3	Martin Albrechtsen		31/03/80	D	18	(3)	2
36	Kristian Andersen		01/09/94	M		(8)	
80	Quincy Antipas	ZIM	20/04/84	A	21		5
10	Martin Bernburg		26/12/85	A		(3)	
35	Patrick da Silva		23/10/94	D	12		
20	Dario Dumic		30/01/92	D	15	(6)	1
33,32	Riza Durmisi		08/01/94	D		(4)	
16	Simon Falkesgaard		03/01/91			(1)	
22	Mathias Gehrt		07/06/92	M	15	(12)	2
7	Clarence Goodson	USA	17/05/82	D	18	(1)	2
31	Frederik Holst		24/09/94	D	17	(7)	
26	Mike Jensen		19/02/88	M	19		2
27	Jan Kristiansen		04/08/81	M	17	(4)	
23	Michael Krohn-Dehli		06/06/83	M	5	(1)	
17	Jens Larsen		21/02/91	M	30		3
9	Simon Makienok Christoffersen		21/11/90	A	25	(6)	14
12	Brent McGrath	AUS	18/06/91	A		(10)	
19	Daniel Norouzi		30/01/92	D	6		
34	Lebogang Phiri	RSA	09/11/94	M	5		2
2	Anders Randrup		16/07/88	D	18	(2)	
11	Dennis Rommedahl		22/07/78	M	25	(3)	3
24	Franck Semou		25/08/92	M	10	(6)	
4	Daniel Stenderup		31/05/89	D	7		
15	Mikkel Thygesen		22/10/84	A	28	(1)	2
1	Michael Tørnes		08/01/86	G	26		

ESBJERG FB
Coach: Jess Thorup
1924 • Blue Water Arena (17,172) • efb.dk
Major honours
Danish League (5) 1961, 1962, 1963, 1965, 1979;
Danish Cup (3) 1964, 1976, 2013

2012

15/07	Silkeborg	h	2-3	*J Ankersen, Lange*
23/07	AGF	a	0-0	
28/07	SønderjyskE	h	1-2	*Smárason*
04/08	København	h	1-2	*J Ankersen*
13/08	Randers	a	0-1	
19/08	Horsens	h	0-0	
26/08	Brøndby	a	1-1	*Braithwaite*
02/09	Midtjylland	a	0-1	
14/09	OB	h	3-0	*Braithwaite 2, Lange*
24/09	AaB	a	2-0	*Braithwaite 2*
28/09	Nordsjælland	a	0-3	
07/10	København	h	2-2	*J Ankersen 2*
21/10	Horsens	a	0-0	
28/10	SønderjyskE	h	1-2	*J Ankersen*
02/11	Silkeborg	h	1-0	*Lange*
12/11	Midtjylland	a	0-0	
18/11	Brøndby	a	2-2	*Toutouh, Lekven*
25/11	Nordsjælland	h	1-0	*Ernemann*
01/12	OB	a	0-3	
08/12	Randers	a	1-2	*P Ankersen*

2013

04/03	AGF	h	2-1	*Andreasen, Lange*
09/03	AaB	a	0-0	
29/03	Brøndby	h	1-0	*J Ankersen*
01/04	AaB	a	1-0	*Andersen*
05/04	AGF	a	1-0	*Andreasen*
09/04	SønderjyskE	a	1-3	*Andreasen (p)*
14/04	Randers	h	4-0	*Toutouh, Smárason 2, Braithwaite*
22/04	Midtjylland	h	0-1	
26/04	Silkeborg	a	3-0	*Smárason*
05/05	Horsens	h	1-0	*Braithwaite*
12/05	København	a	2-0	*P Ankersen, Braithwaite*
16/05	OB	h	6-2	*J Ankersen, Braithwaite, Smárason 2, P Ankersen, Knudsen*
20/05	Nordsjælland	a	0-1	

No	Name	Nat	DoB	Pos	Aps	(s)	Gls
11	Mikkel Agger		01/11/92	A		(6)	
12	Sebastian Andersen		23/12/88	M	8	(20)	1
20	Hans Henrik Andreasen		10/01/79	M	11		3
19	Jakob Ankersen		22/09/90	M	31	(1)	7
3	Peter Ankersen		22/09/90	D	26		3
5	Martin Bergvold		20/02/84	M	3	(6)	
32	Martin Braithwaite		05/06/91	A	32	(1)	9
10	Njogu Demba-Nyrén	GAM	26/06/79	A	1	(11)	
4	Davidson Drobo-Ampem	GER	26/03/88	D	14		
7	Steffen Ernemann		26/04/82	M	15	(8)	1
8	Kenneth Fabricius		03/11/81	A	8	(7)	
2	Kian Hansen		03/03/89	D	29		
1	Lukas Hradecky	FIN	24/11/89	G	33		
24	Nicolai Høgh		09/11/83	D	23	(1)	
23	Jonas Knudsen		16/09/92	D	32		1
22	Jesper Lange		11/01/86	A	21	(9)	4
6	Magnus Lekven	NOR	13/01/88	M	23		1
21	Jerry Lucena	PHI	11/08/80	M	12	(5)	
10	Emil Lyng		03/08/89	A		(1)	
17	Casper Nielsen		29/04/94	M		(1)	
31	Søren Rieks		07/04/87	A	2		
9	Arnór Smárason	ISL	07/09/88	M	12	(6)	6
27	Steven Somers		09/09/91	M		(1)	
15	Youssef Toutouh		06/10/92	M	20	(3)	2
26	Mikkel Vendelbo		15/08/87	M	7		
25	Mikkel Vestergaard		22/11/92	A		(1)	

AC HORSENS
Coach: Johnny Mølby
1994 • Casa Arena (10,400) • achorsens.dk

2012

16/07	Nordsjælland	h	0-4	
20/07	Silkeborg	a	2-0	*Kløve, Toft*
27/07	Midtjylland	a	2-2	*Kortegaard, Fagerberg*
06/08	SønderjyskE	a	2-0	*Kløve, Spelmann (p)*
12/08	AaB	h	1-4	*Fagerberg*
19/08	Esbjerg	a	0-0	
27/08	AGF	h	1-4	*Hajdarević*
02/09	Randers	a	1-0	*Toft*
16/09	Brøndby	a	2-2	*Spelmann (p), Andersen*
23/09	OB	h	2-2	*Kortegaard, Andersen*
29/09	København	h	1-1	*Nworuh*
07/10	Silkeborg	a	1-1	*Bjerregaard*
21/10	Esbjerg	h	0-0	
29/10	København	h	1-0	*Kielstrup*
04/11	Randers	a	0-0	
09/11	AGF	h	2-0	*Andersen, Kryger*
18/11	AaB	a	0-2	
25/11	Brøndby	a	0-2	
30/11	SønderjyskE	h	1-3	*Toft*
09/12	Midtjylland	h	0-2	

2013

03/03	Nordsjælland	a	0-1	
10/03	OB	h	2-0	*Takyi, Nworuh*
15/03	København	a	1-2	*Takyi*
28/03	AaB	h	2-2	*Bjerregaard, Aslam*
31/03	OB	a	0-2	
07/04	Nordsjælland	h	0-2	
13/04	Midtjylland	a	2-5	*Kløve, Spelmann (p)*
20/04	AGF	a	0-0	
28/04	Randers	h	1-0	*Rasmussen*
05/05	Esbjerg	a	0-1	
13/05	Silkeborg	h	2-0	*og (Nielsen), Spelmann*
16/05	SønderjyskE	a	2-4	*og (Paulsen), Kløve*
20/05	Brøndby	h	0-1	

No	Name	Nat	DoB	Pos	Aps	(s)	Gls
19	Mads Agesen		17/03/83	D	20	(4)	
5	Alexander Juel Andersen		29/01/91	D	31		3
4	Nabil Aslam		03/08/84	D	11	(6)	1
29	André Bjerregaard		03/09/91	M	14	(14)	2
16	Mikkel Cramer		25/01/92	M	2	(1)	
20	Janus Drachmann		11/05/88	M	24	(3)	
8	Ken Fagerberg	SWE	09/01/89	A	12	(6)	2
25	Kenan Hajdarević	BIH	29/01/90	A		(4)	1
6	Søren Jensen		01/03/84	D	2	(2)	
9	Steffen Kielstrup		18/10/84	M	27	(1)	1
26	Troels Kløve		23/10/90	M	18	(9)	4
13	Thomas Kortegaard		02/07/84	D	21	(1)	2
15	Lasse Kryger		03/11/82	M	12	(9)	1
18	Jeppe Mehl		21/09/86	M	14	(2)	
11	Jude Nworuh	NGA	09/06/89	A	13	(8)	2
2	Anders Nøhr		03/09/81	D	10	(1)	
17	Esben Petersen		11/01/93	M		(3)	
3	Morten Rasmussen		26/03/85	D	28		1
14	Martin Retov		05/05/80	M	21	(1)	
30	Frederik Rønnow		04/08/92	G	33		
27	Henrik Smedegaard		06/06/85	D		(4)	
10	Martin Spelmann		21/03/87	M	30		4
7	Charles Takyi	GHA	12/11/84	A	10	(1)	2
12	Henrik Toft		15/04/81	A	10	(11)	3
31	Oguzhan Özcelik		26/04/94	M			

FC KØBENHAVN
Coach: Ariël Jacobs (BEL)
1992 • Parken (38,065) • fck.dk
Major honours
Danish League (10) 1993, 2001, 2003, 2004, 2006, 2007, 2009, 2010, 2011, 2013;
Danish Cup (5) 1995, 1997, 2004, 2009, 2012

2012

15/07	Midtjylland	h	4-2	*César Santin 2, Cornelius, Oviedo*
22/07	SønderjyskE	a	1-1	*Abdellaoue*
28/07	AaB	h	3-0	*Cornelius, César Santin, Abdellaoue*
04/08	Esbjerg	a	2-1	*Vingaard, Cornelius*
12/08	AGF	h	3-0	*César Santin 2 (1p), Cornelius*
18/08	Brøndby	h	1-1	*Jørgensen*
25/08	Randers	a	3-2	*Jørgensen, Cornelius, Ottesen*
02/09	OB	a	2-2	*Cornelius, Jørgensen*
15/09	Nordsjælland	h	2-1	*Vetokele, Cornelius*
23/09	Silkeborg	h	5-0	*Cornelius 2, Jørgensen 2, Vingaard*
29/09	Horsens	a	1-1	*Cornelius*
07/10	Esbjerg	h	2-2	*César Santin, Jørgensen*
21/10	Brøndby	h	1-0	*Stadsgaard*
29/10	Horsens	a	0-1	
04/11	AGF	a	2-0	*Bolaños, Stadsgaard*
11/11	AaB	h	4-0	*Jørgensen 2, og (Petersen), César Santin*
18/11	Midtjylland	a	2-1	*Sigurdsson, Jørgensen*
25/11	SønderjyskE	a	2-1	*Cornelius 2*
02/12	Randers	a	2-0	*Cornelius, Sigurdsson*
09/12	Nordsjælland	a	4-1	*Delaney, César Santin 2, Cornelius*

2013

03/03	OB	a	3-2	*og (Høegh), Jørgensen, Claudemir*
10/03	Silkeborg	h	3-1	*Jørgensen, Cornelius 2*
15/03	Horsens	h	2-1	*César Santin, Claudemir*
29/03	Midtjylland	a	2-2	*César Santin, Cornelius*
01/04	Silkeborg	a	0-1	
07/04	OB	h	1-1	*Bengtsson*
15/04	Nordsjælland	a	3-2	*Sigurdsson, Vetokele, Cornelius*
21/04	AaB	a	1-1	*Bolaños*
28/04	AGF	a	0-0	
05/05	Brøndby	a	0-0	
12/05	Esbjerg	h	0-2	
16/05	Randers	a	0-1	
20/05	SønderjyskE	a	1-1	*Vetokele*

No	Name	Nat	DoB	Pos	Aps	(s)	Gls
34	Mads Aaquist		31/12/94	D		(1)	
7	Mostafa Abdellaoue	NOR	01/08/88	A	3	(2)	2
32	Danny Amankwaa		30/01/94	A	1	(8)	
3	Pierre Bengtsson	SWE	12/04/88	D	26	(3)	1
7	Martin Bergvold		20/02/84	M	1	(1)	
30	Christian Bolaños	CRC	17/05/84	M	22	(1)	2
31	Jakob Busk		12/09/93	G	1		
11	César Santin	BRA	24/02/81	A	26	(6)	11
1	Kim Christensen		16/07/79	G	11	(1)	
6	Claudemir	BRA	27/03/88	M	29	(2)	2
29	Andreas Cornelius		16/03/93	A	29	(3)	18
27	Thomas Delaney		03/09/91	M	13	(8)	1
19	Rúrik Gíslason	ISL	25/02/88	M	7	(7)	
8	Christian Grindheim	NOR	17/07/83	M	2	(5)	
2	Lars Jacobsen		20/09/79	D	30		
15	Michael Jakobsen		02/01/86	D	5	(2)	
12	Daniel Jensen		25/06/79	M	5	(5)	
14	Nicolai Jørgensen		15/01/91	M	21	(6)	11
16	Thomas Kristensen		13/04/83	M	25	(2)	
5	Sölvi Geir Ottesen	ISL	18/02/84	D	5	(1)	1
19	Bryan Oviedo	CRC	18/02/90	D	4	(2)	1
25	Christoffer Remmer		16/01/93	D	3	(1)	
17	Ragnar Sigurdsson	ISL	19/06/86	D	31		3
4	Kris Stadsgaard		01/08/85	D	27		2
9	Igor Vetokele	BEL	23/03/92	A	4	(11)	3
20	Martin Vingaard		20/03/85	M	10	(9)	2
21	Johan Wiland	SWE	24/01/81	G	21		
35	Mikkel Wohlgemuth		04/06/95	M	1		

FC MIDTJYLLAND

Coach: Glen Riddersholm
1999 • MCH Arena (11,809) • fcm.dk

2012

15/07	København	a	2-4	Igboun, Janssen
21/07	Nordsjælland	h	3-1	Hassan, Janssen, Albæk
27/07	Horsens	a	2-2	og (Rasmussen), Hvilsom
08/08	Randers	h	2-1	Igboun, Albæk
10/08	OB	a	1-2	Igboun
17/08	AaB	a	0-3	
26/08	Silkeborg	h	1-1	og (Mikkelsen)
02/09	Esbjerg	a	1-0	Igboun
17/09	AGF	a	2-3	Olsen, Hassan
23/09	Brøndby	h	1-1	Albæk
01/10	SønderjyskE	h	1-3	Lauridsen
07/10	Randers	a	1-2	Albæk
21/10	OB	h	1-1	Ipša
28/10	Brøndby	h	1-1	Andersson
05/11	AaB	a	3-1	Andersson, Larsen, Bak Nielsen
12/11	Esbjerg	h	0-0	
18/11	København	a	1-2	Albæk
26/11	AGF	a	1-1	Albæk
02/12	Silkeborg	h	1-3	Rasmussen
09/12	Horsens	a	2-0	Janssen, Rasmussen

2013

02/03	SønderjyskE	h	1-0	Andersson
11/03	Nordsjælland	h	1-1	Albæk
17/03	Brøndby	a	1-1	Andersson
29/03	København	h	2-2	Andersson 2
01/04	Nordsjælland	a	1-3	Andersson
06/04	SønderjyskE	a	2-0	Igboun, Hassan
13/04	Horsens	h	5-2	Hassan, Rasmussen 2, Igboun, Olsen (p)
22/04	Esbjerg	a	1-0	Olsen
29/04	AaB	h	2-3	Rasmussen, Igboun
06/05	OB	a	1-0	Andersson
12/05	Randers	h	3-0	Sviatchenko, Olsen (p), Andersson
16/05	Silkeborg	a	1-1	Albæk
20/05	AGF	h	3-2	Andersson, Igboun, Sviatchenko

No	Name	Nat	DoB	Pos	Aps	(s)	Gls
3	Kolja Afriyie	GER	06/04/82	D	18		
17	Mads Albæk		14/01/90	M	31	(1)	9
8	Petter Andersson	SWE	20/02/85	M	24	(2)	9
32	Kristian Bak Nielsen		20/10/82	D	26	(1)	1
36	Rilwan Hassan	NGA	09/02/91	M	27	(4)	4
14	Jakob Haugaard		01/05/92	G	6		
22	Mads Hvilsom		23/08/92	A		(1)	1
44	Sylvester Igboun	NGA	08/09/90	A	21	(4)	8
20	Kristijan Ipša	CRO	04/04/86	D	14	(1)	1
11	Tim Janssen	NED	06/03/86	A	9	(13)	3
26	Patrick Jensen		04/04/94	D	3	(2)	
0	Jesper Juelsgård Kristiansen		26/01/89	D	29	(1)	
5	Benjamin Kibebe	SWE	13/08/81	D	5	(4)	
23	Frank Kristensen		10/03/77	A		(6)	
15	Marco Larsen		15/05/93	A	6	(7)	1
15	Jesper Lauridsen		27/03/91	D	7	(5)	1
1	Jonas Lössl		01/02/89	G	27		
39	Jude Nworuh	NGA	09/06/89	A		(6)	
29	Noah Ojuola	NGA	12/05/93	D	2	(1)	
11	Danny Olsen		11/06/85	M	26	(3)	4
33	Ebere Onuachu	NGA	28/05/94	A		(1)	
37	Mads Pedersen		17/01/93	M	1	(5)	
9	Morten "Duncan" Rasmussen		31/01/85	A	19	(8)	5
28	André Rømer		18/07/93	M	4	(3)	
27	Pione Sisto	SDN	04/02/95	M	1	(9)	
18	Erik Sviatchenko		04/10/91	D	26	(2)	2
43	Izunna Uzochukwu	NGA	11/04/90	M	24	(2)	
2	Santiago Villafañe	ARG	19/05/88	D	7	(4)	

FC NORDSJÆLLAND

Coach: Kasper Hjulmand
2003 • Farum Park (10,300) • fcn.dk
Major honours
Danish League (1) 2012;
Danish Cup (2) 2010, 2011

2012

16/07	Horsens	a	4-0	Lorentzen, Laudrup, Stokholm, Gytkjær
21/07	Midtjylland	a	1-3	Stokholm
29/07	OB	h	1-1	Christensen (p)
04/08	AaB	a	1-1	John
11/08	Silkeborg	h	6-1	John 4, Parkhurst, Lorentzen
19/08	Esbjerg	a	1-0	Parkhurst
24/08	SønderjyskE	h	4-1	John, Mtiliga, Christensen, Beckmann
02/09	Brøndby	h	0-0	
15/09	København	a	1-2	og (Christensen)
22/09	Randers	h	1-1	John
28/09	Esbjerg	h	3-0	John, Lorentzen, Stokholm
05/10	OB	a	0-3	
19/10	Silkeborg	h	3-0	Nordstrand, Okore, Laudrup
26/10	AaB	h	1-0	Okore
03/11	SønderjyskE	a	2-1	Nordstrand, Beckmann
10/11	Randers	a	2-2	Christensen, Stokholm (p)
16/11	AGF	h	2-0	John, Lorentzen
25/11	Esbjerg	a	0-1	
02/12	Brøndby	h	3-0	Christiansen, Beckmann, Tičinović
09/12	København	a	1-4	Beckmann (p)

2013

03/03	Horsens	h	1-0	Lindberg
11/03	Midtjylland	a	1-1	Bech
29/03	AGF	h	4-2	Christensen 2, John, Nordstrand
01/04	Midtjylland	h	3-1	Nordstrand, Bech, Okore
04/04	AaB	a	1-0	og (Augustinussen)
07/04	Horsens	a	2-0	Petry, Nordstrand
15/04	København	h	2-3	Mtiliga, Nordstrand
21/04	Randers	a	0-0	
27/04	SønderjyskE	h	2-2	Christensen, Nordstrand
03/05	Silkeborg	a	2-2	Tičinović, Okore
10/05	OB	h	4-1	Stokholm, Christiansen 2, Aynaoglu
16/05	Brøndby	a	0-4	
20/05	Esbjerg	h	1-0	O'Brien

No	Name	Nat	DoB	Pos	Aps	(s)	Gls
6	Enoch Adu	GHA	14/09/90	M	16	(2)	
13	Oguzhan Aynaoglu		22/03/92	A	2	(5)	1
18	Uffe Bech		13/01/93	A	5		2
10	Mikkel Beckmann		24/10/83	A	9	(6)	4
5	Francisco Calvo	CRC	08/07/92	D		(3)	
17	Søren Christensen		29/06/86	M	26		6
5	Anders Christiansen		08/06/90	M	14	(8)	3
33	Pascal Gregor		18/02/94	D	3	(2)	
19	Mark Gundelach		07/01/92	D	16	(9)	
24	Christian Gytkjær		06/05/90	A		(2)	1
34	Emiliano Hansen		09/03/95	M	1	(2)	
	Iljutjenko Fiorheilo		31/03/93	D	33		
24	Kamal Issah	GHA	30/08/93	M	1	(2)	
31	Mikkel Jensen		21/01/95	A		(1)	
39	Nicolai Johannesen		22/05/94	D	1	(2)	
15	Joshua John	NED	01/10/88	A	19	(3)	10
9	Henrik Kildentoft		18/03/85	D	3	(1)	
22	Andreas Laudrup		10/11/90	M	7	(9)	2
12	Rawez Lawan	SWE	04/10/87	A	3	(2)	
36	Kristian Lindberg		14/02/94	A	6	(8)	1
20	Kasper Lorentzen		19/11/85	M	17	(3)	4
35	Andreas Maxsø		18/03/94	D	1	(1)	
9	Tobias Mikkelsen		18/09/86	A	2		
8	Patrick Mtiliga		28/01/81	D	25	(1)	2
11	Morten Nordstrand		08/06/83	A	17	(5)	7
4	Conor O'Brien	USA	24/03/92	M	7	(3)	1
2	Jores Okore		11/08/92	D	29		4
18	Michael Parkhurst	USA	24/01/84	D	15	(1)	2
19	Lasse Petry		19/09/92	M	8	(8)	1
9	Ricardo Bueno	BRA	15/08/87	A	3	(7)	
21	Ivan Runje	CRO	09/10/90	D	28		
31	Ragnvald Soma	NOR	10/11/79	D	1		
7	Nicolai Stokholm		01/04/76	M	29	(1)	5
23	Mario Tičinović	CRO	20/08/91	A	16	(2)	2

ODENSE BK

Coach: Troels Bech
1887 • TRE-FOR Park (15,761) • ob.dk
Major honours
Danish League (3) 1977, 1982, 1989;
Danish Cup (5) 1983, 1991, 1993, 2002, 2007

2012

15/07	Brøndby	a	1-0	Schoop
22/07	Randers	h	0-1	
29/07	Nordsjælland	a	1-1	Traoré
03/08	Silkeborg	a	1-0	Skoubo
10/08	Midtjylland	h	2-1	E Larsen, Skoubo
20/08	SønderjyskE	a	2-1	Gíslason, E Larsen
26/08	AaB	h	0-4	
02/09	København	h	2-2	Johansson, Gíslason
14/09	Esbjerg	a	0-3	
23/09	Horsens	a	2-2	Vadócz, og (Kryger)
30/09	AGF	h	1-2	Pedersen
05/10	Nordsjælland	h	3-0	Vadócz 2, Kadrii
21/10	Midtjylland	a	1-1	Vadócz
28/10	AGF	h	2-4	Silberbauer, E Larsen
04/11	Brøndby	a	3-2	Jensen, E Larsen, Andreasen
11/11	SønderjyskE	h	5-0	Pedersen, Ruud (p), Kadrii 2, E Larsen
19/11	Randers	a	2-3	Skoubo, Pedersen
24/11	Silkeborg	h	2-0	Vadócz, Jensen
01/12	Esbjerg	a	3-0	Johansson, Pedersen 2

2013

03/03	København	h	2-3	E Larsen, Bodul
06/03	AaB	a	2-2	Bodul, N'Koum
10/03	Horsens	a	0-2	
17/03	AGF	a	1-2	E Larsen
28/03	Randers	h	0-0	
31/03	Horsens	h	2-0	Kadrii, Dodul
07/04	København	a	1-1	Ruud
14/04	AaB	h	3-4	E Larsen, Pedersen, Ruud (p)
21/04	SønderjyskE	a	1-4	Skoubo
28/04	Brøndby	h	1-2	Kadrii
06/05	Midtjylland	h	0-1	
10/05	Nordejælland	a	1-4	Pedersen
16/05	Esbjerg	a	2-6	Sørensen, Vadócz
20/05	Silkeborg	h	3-3	Bodul, og (Jónsson), Skoubo

No	Name	Nat	DoB	Pos	Aps	(s)	Gls
4	Hans Henrik Andreasen		10/01/79	M	6	(12)	1
14	Hannes Anier	EST	16/01/93	A		(3)	
10	Darko Bodul	CRO	11/01/89	A	12	(2)	4
5	Anders Møller Christensen		26/07/77	D	31		
1	Jesper Christiansen		24/04/78	G	22	(1)	
6	Mohammed Diarra	GUI	20/06/92	M	3	(4)	
21	Búrik Gíslason	ISL	25/02/88	M	7	(1)	2
26	Daniel Høegh		06/01/91	D	25		
9	Rasmus Falk Jensen		15/01/92	M	18	(1)	2
20	Timmi Johansen		08/05/87	D		(2)	
10	Andreas Johansson	SWE	05/07/78	M	14	(3)	2
24	Bashkim Kadrii		09/07/91	A	33		5
7	Emil Larsen		22/06/91	M	28		7
4	Kasper Larsen		25/01/93	D	17	(5)	
18	David Löfqvist	SWE	06/08/86	M		(10)	
23	Cedric N'Koum	CMR	24/11/89	A	4	(14)	1
19	Marcus Pedersen	NOR	08/06/90	A	19	(5)	7
8	Tore Reginiussen	NOR	10/04/86	D		(2)	
2	Espen Ruud	NOR	26/02/84	D	32		3
16	Jacob Schoop		23/12/88	M	20	(5)	1
8	Michael Silberbauer		07/07/81	M	23	(1)	1
11	Morten Skoubo		30/06/80	A	12	(13)	6
25	Christian Sørensen		06/08/92	M	1	(2)	1
17	Mads Toppel		30/01/82	G	11	(1)	
18	Kalilou Traoré	MLI	09/09/87	M	2	(3)	1
21	Krisztián Vadócz	HUN	30/05/85	M	23	(1)	7

DENMARK

RANDERS FC

Coach: Colin Todd (ENG)
1898 • AutoC Park (12,000) • randersfc.dk
Major honours
Danish Cup (4) 1967, 1968, 1973, 2006

2012
14/07	SønderjyskE	a	1-6	Kamper
22/07	OB	a	1-0	Rise
29/07	AGF	h	2-1	Rise, Schwartz
05/08	Midtjylland	a	1-2	Sane
13/08	Esbjerg	h	1-0	Kristensen
18/08	Silkeborg	a	1-0	Fischer
25/08	København	h	2-3	Schwartz 2 (1p)
02/09	Horsens	h	0-1	
16/09	AaB	a	0-4	
22/09	Nordsjælland	a	1-1	Schwartz
30/09	Brøndby	h	3-2	Kamper, Brock-Madsen, Fischer
07/10	Midtjylland	h	2-1	Kamper, Schwartz
22/10	AGF	a	1-1	Keller
27/10	Silkeborg	h	2-1	Schwartz, Boya
04/11	Horsens	h	0-0	
10/11	Nordsjælland	a	2-2	Fischer, Schwartz
19/11	OB	h	3-2	Brock-Madsen, Schwartz, Borring
23/11	AaB	h	0-1	
02/12	København	a	0-2	
08/12	Esbjerg	h	2-1	Schwartz 2

2013
03/03	Brøndby	a	2-0	Schwartz (p), Brock-Madsen
08/03	SønderjyskE	h	2-0	Brock-Madsen 2
17/03	Silkeborg	h	1-0	Schwartz
28/03	OB	a	0-0	
31/03	SønderjyskE	a	2-0	Borring 2
07/04	Brøndby	h	0-1	
14/04	Esbjerg	a	0-4	
21/04	Nordsjælland	h	0-0	
28/04	Horsens	a	0-1	
05/05	AGF	h	1-0	Schwartz
12/05	Midtjylland	a	0-3	
16/05	København	h	1-0	Boya
20/05	AaB	a	2-2	Schwartz, og (L Nielsen)

No	Name	Nat	DoB	Pos	Aps	(s)	Gls
7	Theódór Elmar Bjarnason	ISL	04/03/87	M	14	(3)	
29	Jonas Borring		04/01/85	M	10	(11)	3
10,20	Pierre Boya	CMR	16/01/84	A	7	(8)	2
44	Nicolai Brock-Madsen		09/01/93	A	18	(10)	5
8	Lorenzo Davids	NED	04/09/86	M	4	(1)	
8,10	Charlie Davies	USA	25/06/86	A	3	(20)	
5	Anders Egholm		15/05/83	D	2		
19	Oliver Feldballe		03/04/90	M	3	(6)	
13	Mads Fenger		10/09/90	D	32		
21	Alexander Fischer		16/09/86	M	27	(2)	3
18	Christopher Geertsen		24/01/93	M		(1)	
6	Rasmus Hansen		12/04/86	M		(3)	
25	Peter Friis Jensen		02/05/88	G	1		
17	Jonas Kamper		30/05/83	M	27	(3)	3
3	Christian Keller		17/08/80	M	27		1
20	Frank Kristensen		10/03/77	A	3	(3)	1
1	David Ousted		01/02/85	G	32		
38	Nicolai Poulsen		15/08/93	M	1	(5)	
9	Lasse Rise		09/06/86	M	5	(3)	2
14	Tidiane Sane	SEN	10/07/85	M	20		1
11	Ronnie Schwartz		29/08/89	A	30	(1)	14
15	Chris Sørensen		27/07/77	D	32		
33	Adama Tamboura	MLI	18/05/85	D	25	(5)	
4	Johnny Thomsen		26/02/82	M	33		
23	Remco van der Schaaf	NED	28/02/79	D	7	(2)	

SILKEBORG IF

Coach: Kels Bordinggaard;
(12/11/12) (Viggo Jensen)
1917 • Mascot Park (10,000) • silkeborgif.com
Major honours
Danish League (1) 1994;
Danish Cup (1) 2001

2012
15/07	Esbjerg	a	3-2	Pourié 2, Risgård
20/07	Horsens	h	0-2	
30/07	Brøndby	a	1-2	Pourié
03/08	OB	h	0-1	
11/08	Nordsjælland	a	1-6	Bech
18/08	Randers	h	0-1	
26/08	Midtjylland	a	1-1	Pourié
01/09	AGF	h	0-4	
15/09	SønderjyskE	a	2-0	Pourié, Vidarsson
23/09	København	a	0-5	
30/09	AaB	a	2-1	Kiilerich, Pourié
07/10	Horsens	h	1-1	Svensson
19/10	Nordsjælland	a	0-3	
27/10	Randers	a	1-2	Pourié
02/11	Esbjerg	a	0-1	
11/11	Brøndby	h	1-2	H Pedersen
17/11	SønderjyskE	h	3-2	Flinta, Hansen, Pourié
24/11	OB	h	0-1	
02/12	Midtjylland	a	3-1	Bech 2, Flinta
10/12	AGF	a	3-3	Mikkelsen 2 (1p), Pourié

2013
01/03	AaB	h	3-2	Bech, Risgård, Pourié
10/03	København	a	1-3	Mikkelsen
17/03	Randers	a	0-1	
28/03	SønderjyskE	h	0-5	
01/04	København	h	1-0	Pourié
08/04	AaB	a	0-1	
12/04	AGF	h	3-1	Pourié 2, Svensson
21/04	Brøndby	a	2-2	Risgård, Holst
26/04	Esbjerg	a	0-1	
03/05	Nordsjælland	h	2-2	Svensson, Risgård
13/05	Horsens	a	0-2	
16/05	Midtjylland	h	1-1	Flyger
20/05	OB	a	3-3	Pourié, og (Christensen), Holst

No	Name	Nat	DoB	Pos	Aps	(s)	Gls
10	Jesper Bech		25/05/82	A	26	(2)	4
14	Dennis Flinta		14/11/83	M	29	(1)	2
27	Daniel Flyger		05/02/86	A		(5)	1
20	Frank Hansen		23/02/83	M	31		1
1	Lasse Heinze		03/04/86	G	25		
7	Christian Lamhauge Holst	FRO	25/12/81	M	14	(8)	2
23	Jeppe Illum		25/03/92	M	9	(5)	
4	Simon Jakobsen		17/11/90	D	10	(3)	
28	Ari Mohr Jónsson	FRO	22/07/94	D	2	(1)	
13	Sune Kiilerich		18/12/90	D	20	(1)	1
24	Nicolaj Køhlert		21/01/93	M	3	(6)	
18	Emil La Cour		19/07/91	M	1	(3)	
2	Jesper Mikkelsen		26/07/80	D	30		3
15	Steven Morrissey	JAM	25/07/86	A		(1)	
1	Gunnar Nielsen	FRO	07/10/86	G	8		
15, 6	Daniel Pedersen		27/07/92	D	24	(5)	
19	Henrik "Tømrer" Pedersen		10/06/75	A	1	(7)	
5	Christopher Poulsen		11/00/81	D	20	(2)	
9	Marvin Pourié	GER	08/01/91	A	28	(1)	14
26	Thorbjørn Holst Rasmussen		21/03/87	D	9		
21	Kasper Risgård		04/01/83	M	24	(3)	4
25	Nicolaj Ritter		08/05/92	M	11	(9)	
11	Adeola Runsewe	NGA	01/12/89	M	13	(5)	
33	Robert Skov		20/05/96	M		(2)	
22	Martin Svensson		10/08/89	M	18	(4)	3
8	Bjarni Vidarsson	ISL	05/03/88	M	7	(5)	1

SØNDERJYSKE

Coach: Lars Søndergaard
2004 • Haderslev Fodboldstadion (10,000) •
soenderjyske.dk

2012
14/07	Randers	h	6-1	T Hansen, H Hansen, Antipas, O'Brien, Vibe, Storbæk (p)
22/07	København	h	1-1	Hédinsson
28/07	Esbjerg	a	2-1	Vibe, Paulsen
06/08	Horsens	h	0-2	
12/08	Brøndby	a	1-0	Vibe
20/08	OB	h	1-2	O'Brien
24/08	Nordsjælland	a	1-4	Antipas
31/08	AaB	h	0-4	
15/09	Silkeborg	h	0-2	
21/09	AGF	a	2-2	O'Brien, Bechmann
01/10	Midtjylland	a	3-1	Bechmann, Vibe, Hajdarević
06/10	AGF	h	0-3	
20/10	AaB	a	1-2	Lodberg
28/10	Esbjerg	a	2-1	Vibe, Hédinsson
03/11	Nordsjælland	h	1-2	Bechmann
11/11	OB	a	0-5	
17/11	Silkeborg	h	2-3	Bechmann, Hédinsson
25/11	København	a	1-2	Hédinsson
30/11	Horsens	a	3-1	Bechmann, Hédinsson, Paulsen
07/12	Brøndby	h	2-2	O'Brien, Hédinsson

2013
02/03	Midtjylland	a	0-1	
08/03	Randers	a	0-2	
28/03	Silkeborg	a	5-0	Vibe 3, Madsen, Paulsen
31/03	Randers	h	0-2	
06/04	Midtjylland	h	0-2	
09/04	Esbjerg	h	3-1	Vibe, Hart, og (P Ankersen)
14/04	Brøndby	a	3-0	Bechmann, Vibe, Oggesen
21/04	OB	h	4-1	Bechmann 2, H Hansen, Absalonsen
27/04	Nordsjælland	a	2-2	Absalonsen, Vibe
04/05	AaB	h	1-0	Vibe
11/05	AGF	a	1-2	Absalonsen
16/05	Horsens	h	4-2	H Hansen (p), Vibe, Absalonsen, og (Andersen)
20/05	København	a	1-1	Lodberg

No	Name	Nat	DoB	Pos	Aps	(s)	Gls
11	Johan Absalonsen		16/09/85	A	16	(5)	4
22	Rabiu Afolabi	NGA	18/04/80	D	4	(1)	
10	Quincy Antipas	ZIM	20/04/84	A	7		2
9	Tommy Bechmann		22/12/81	A	24	(8)	8
16	Henrik Bødker		06/06/83	M	18		
7	Daniel Christensen		19/09/88	M	25	(6)	
25	Kenan Hajdarević	BIH	29/01/90	A		(7)	1
8	Henrik Hansen		28/07/79	M	31		3
31	Morten Hansen		04/09/93	D		(1)	
16	Rasmus Hansen		12/04/86	M	4	(6)	
6	Thomas Hansen		18/01/83	D	13	(4)	1
19	Florian Hart	AUT	11/05/90	D	28	(3)	1
18	Eyjólfur Hédinsson	ISL	01/01/85	M	12	(3)	6
4	Hallgrímur Jónasson	ISL	04/05/86	D	17	(1)	
5	Niels Lodberg		14/10/80	D	26	(1)	2
10	Nicolaj Madsen		16/07/88	M	11		1
12	Søren Mussmann		29/06/93	D	2	(2)	
22	Conor O'Brien	USA	20/10/88	M	19	(1)	4
24	Andreas Oggesen		18/03/94	M	4	(7)	1
1	Håkon Opdal	NOR	11/06/82	G	13		
20	Bjørn Paulsen		02/07/91	A	19	(12)	3
15	Adigun Salami	NGA	06/05/88	M		(2)	
1	Marin Skender	CRO	12/08/79	G	13		
27	Kenneth Stenild		11/09/87	G	7	(1)	
23	Jarl André Storbæk	NOR	21/09/78	D	6		1
28	Gill Swerts	BEL	23/09/82	D	11	(3)	
14	Jacob Tjørnelund		31/12/91	D	2	(6)	
31	Mikael Uhre		30/09/94	A		(5)	
17	Lasse Vibe		22/02/87	M	31	(2)	13

Top goalscorers

18	Andreas Cornelius (København)
16	Nicklas Helenius Jensen (AaB)
14	Aron Jóhannsson (AGF)
	Simon Makienok Christoffersen (Brøndby)
	Ronnie Schwartz (Randers)
	Marvin Pourié (Silkeborg)
13	Lasse Vibe (SønderjyskE)
11	César Santin (København)
	Nicolai Jørgensen (København)
10	Joshua John (Nordsjælland)

Promoted clubs

VIBORG FF

Coach: Ove Christensen
1896 • Energi Viborg Arena (9,566) • vff.dk
Major honours
Danish Cup (1) 2000

FC VESTSJÆLLAND

Coach: Ove Pedersen
2008 • Slagelse Stadion (10,000) • fcvvikings.dk

SECOND LEVEL FINAL TABLE 2012/13

		Pld	W	D	L	F	A	Pts
1	Viborg FF	33	17	11	5	60	30	62
2	FC Vestsjælland	33	17	11	5	39	27	62
3	Vejle BK-Kolding	33	16	10	7	46	29	58
4	Lyngby BK	33	17	5	11	55	42	56
5	FC Fredericia	33	11	11	11	53	48	44
6	HB Køge	33	12	8	13	39	45	44
7	FC Hjørring	33	10	10	13	38	41	40
8	Brønshøj BK	33	12	9	12	41	36	39
9	Hobro IK	33	9	11	13	37	43	38
10	Akademisk BK	33	8	13	12	33	34	37
11	Skive IK	33	10	7	16	47	55	37
12	FC Fyn	33	2	8	23	26	84	11

NB FC Fyn withdrew after round 19 – their remaining matches were awarded as 0-3 defeats; Brønshøj BK – 6 pts deducted; FC Fyn – 3 pt deducted.

Domestic cup: Landspokalturneringen 2012/13

SECOND ROUND

(28/08/12)
Esbjerg IF 92 3-3 Lindholm *(aet; 4-2 on pens)*
Hobro 1-4 SønderjyskE
Ledøje-Smørum 0-1 Hvidovre
Marienlyst 2-3 Rishøj
Ringkøbing 1-2 Aarhus Fremad

(29/08/12)
Aalborg Freja 0-1 Randers
AB Tårnby 1-7 HB Køge
Avedøre 0-1 Næstved
Frederikssund 0-3 BSV
Helsingør 4-4 Vestsjælland *(aet; 7-8 on pens)*
Herlufsholm 0-3 Brønshøj
Kjellerup 1-7 Hjørring
NB Bornholm 0-1 OB
Nordvest 1-2 Brøndby
Sydalliancen 0-4 Lyngby
Sønderborg 1-2 Fredericia
Viborg 1-1 Esbjerg *(aet; 10-11 on pens)*
Viby 2-0 Skive

(04/09/12)
Svendborg 0-2 Silkeborg

(11/09/12)
Aarup 1-3 Vejle-Kolding
Lystrup 1-9 Blokhus
Morud 1-3 Otterup
Skjold 0-2 Svebølle

(12/09/12)
Egedal 0-1 Vanløse
Føroyar 0-4 HIK
Skovbakken 0-3 AaB

Vallensbæk 1-1 B93 *(aet; 5-6 on pens)*
Varde 1-4 AGF

Byes – Horsens, København, Midtjylland, Nordsjælland

THIRD ROUND

(25/09/12)
Aarhus Fremad 0-3 AGF
Næstved 1-2 Randers
Svebølle 1-3 Nordsjælland *(aet)*
Vanløse 1-0 BSV

(26/09/12)
B93 0-3 Brøndby
Blokhus 0-1 Silkeborg
Fredericia 0-3 København
Hvidovre 3-7 OB
Rishøj 0-1 Midtjylland
Vejle-Kolding 3-1 Vestsjælland
Viby 1-6 Lyngby

(03/10/12)
Brønshøj 1-3 AaB
Esbjerg IF 92 0-3 Esbjerg
HIK 3-2 HB Køge
Otterup 2-3 Horsens

(24/10/12)
Hjørring 0-4 SønderjyskE

THIRD ROUND

(31/10/12)
Lyngby 3-2 AGF
Nordsjælland 2-3 Midtjylland *(aet)*
Vanløse 0-3 OB
Vejle-Kolding 0-1 Randers

(01/11/12)
HIK 0-4 Horsens
SænderjyskE 0-3 København

(07/11/12)
Brøndby 3-0 Silkeborg

(08/11/12)
Esbjerg 0-0 AaB *(aet; 4-2 on pens)*

QUARTER-FINALS

(28/11/12)
Brøndby 1-0 København *(Jensen 91) (aet)*

Lyngby 1-2 Esbjerg *(Perdedaj 68; Andersen 35, Knudsen 47)*

(29/11/12)
Randers 2-1 Midtjylland *(Schwartz 48, Fischer 61; Andersson 43)*

(05/12/12)
OB 2-4 Horsens *(Johansson 12, Høegh 81; Bjerregaard 3, Spelmann 5p, 112, Kryger 98) (aet)*

SEMI-FINALS

(13/03/13 & 18/04/13)
Brøndby 1-1 Esbjerg *(Larsen 73p; Toutouh 33)*
Esbjerg 3-1 Brøndby *(Braithwaite 79, 103, Lange 117; Rommedahl 22) (aet)*
(Esbjerg 4-2)

(10/04/13 & 17/04/13)
Randers 1-0 Horsens *(Brock-Madsen 52)*
Horsens 2-3 Randers *(Takyi 26, Toft 30; Spelmann 29og, Schwartz 56, Boya 80)*
(Randers 4-2)

FINAL

(09/05/13)
Parken, Copenhagen
ESBJERG FB 1 *(Toutouh 55)*
RANDERS FC 0
Referee: Hansen
ESBJERG: Hradecky, P Ankersen, Hansen, Drobo-Ampem, Knudsen, J Ankersen, Lekven, Andreasen, Smárason (Høgh 90+3), Toutouh (Andersen 70), Braithwaite (Lyng 78)
RANDERS: Ousted, Thomsen, Fenger, Sørensen, Tamboura, Kamper, Keller, Bjarnason, Fischer (Borring 60), Schwartz, Brock-Madsen (Boya 72)

The FA

ENGLAND
The Football Association (FA)

Address	Wembley Stadium GB-London SW1P 9EQ	**Chairman**	Greg Dyke
Tel	+44 844 980 8200	**General secretary**	Alex Horne
Fax	+44 844 980 8201	**Media officer**	Scott Field
E-mail	info@thefa.com	**Year of formation**	1863
Website	thefa.com	**National stadium**	Wembley Stadium, London (90,000)

PREMIER LEAGUE CLUBS

1. Arsenal FC
2. Aston Villa FC
3. Chelsea FC
4. Everton FC
5. Fulham FC
6. Liverpool FC
7. Manchester City FC
8. Manchester United FC
9. Newcastle United FC
10. Norwich City FC
11. Queens Park Rangers FC
12. Reading FC
13. Southampton FC
14. Stoke City FC
15. Sunderland AFC
16. Swansea City AFC
17. Tottenham Hotspur FC
18. West Bromwich Albion FC
19. West Ham United FC
20. Wigan Athletic FC

PROMOTED CLUBS

21. Cardiff City FC
22. Hull City AFC
23. Crystal Palace FC

KEY:
- UEFA Champions League
- UEFA Europa League
- Promoted clubs
- Relegated clubs
- Relegated club in UEFA Europa League

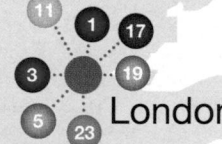

Newcastle 9 15
Sunderland
Kingston upon Hull 22
6 Wigan
4 20 Manchester
Liverpool 7 8
Stoke-on-Trent
14
West Bromwich 18
2 Birmingham
Norwich 10
11 1 17
Reading 3 19
12
5 23
London
Swansea
16 Cardiff
21
Southampton
13

0		100		200 km
0		100 miles		

Sir Alex leaves United on a high

After 1,500 matches in charge, Sir Alex Ferguson's reign as manager of Manchester United FC finally came to an end in May 2013. The 71-year-old Scot retired in style after leading the club to a record 20th English league title.

United regained the Premier League crown with ease, completing the job with four matches to spare as defending champions Manchester City FC and the usual contenders from London struggled to rise to the challenge. A poor season in Europe for English clubs was partially rescued by Chelsea FC's UEFA Europa League triumph, while the two domestic knockout competitions were won by unfancied Wigan Athletic FC and Swansea City AFC.

| Record 20th league title for Old Trafford club | Wigan and Swansea upset the odds in domestic cups | UEFA Europa League triumph for Chelsea |

Domestic league

Of the 13 Premier League titles won by Ferguson, the last was among the least stressful. The dramatic denouement of the previous season, when City snatched the title from United with virtually the last kick of the campaign, served as a source of motivation for the Old Trafford club and although they had company at the top of the table for much of the autumn, with early front-runners Chelsea and the defending champions both putting up a fight, a last-minute 3-2 win at City in early December enabled United to go six points clear and establish a platform from which to launch their traditional mid-season surge.

After falling to a shock 1-0 defeat at Norwich City FC in mid-November, United went 18 matches unbeaten, winning 16 of them. With ten games to play their lead over City had doubled to 12 points, and although Roberto Mancini's side defiantly won 2-1 at Old Trafford to raise the prospect of another incredible late-season turnaround, the truth was that their victory served only to delay the inevitable. A fortnight later – and a day after City had lost 3-1 at Tottenham Hotspur FC – that 20th title was secured as United defeated struggling Aston Villa FC 3-0 at Old

Trafford. Their match winner – as he had so often been during the course of the campaign – was Dutch striker Robin van Persie, who scored a hat-trick, the second of his goals a magnificent left-foot volley that placed an appropriately stylish seal on a comprehensive championship triumph.

It was not until a couple of weeks later that the news of Ferguson's retirement was announced. It was timed to enable him to bow out in fanfare style on the day that his team collected the Premiership trophy – the final home game of the season against Swansea, which United won 2-1 thanks to a late winning goal from Rio Ferdinand. The centre-back had been one of the champions' most consistent performers throughout the campaign, part of a solid central spine featuring goalkeeper David de Gea, midfield fulcrum Michael Carrick and the brilliant Van Persie, whose 26 goals enabled him to win the Premier League's golden boot for the second season running, having registered 30 for Arsenal FC the previous term.

The signing of the Dutch striker was considered by many, Ferguson among them, as the key factor in the title race. City manager Roberto Mancini had been keen to buy him before United swooped, but instead the club brought in a number

of players who struggled to add value to the championship-winning side, and with several of the previous season's stars not performing to the same lofty standard – notably goalkeeper Joe Hart, skipper Vincent Kompany, midfielder David Silva and striker Sergio Agüero – City were unable to put United under any sustained pressure. Second place was always in their possession, but the 11-point deficit in the final table told its own story, and after the club's failure to win anything other than the pre-season Community Shield (they defeated Chelsea 3-2 at Villa Park), Mancini was given the sack – less than 12 months after he had been handed a five-year contract. He was replaced in the summer by Málaga CF's Chilean coach Manuel Pellegrini.

Chelsea also appointed a new manager in the summer, re-hiring former boss José Mourinho, twice a Premier League winner in his previous spell from 2004-07. The west Londoners started the 2012/13 campaign with Roberto Di Matteo, but just six months after steering the club to UEFA Champions League-winning glory in Munich the Italian was jettisoned and replaced, on an interim basis, by ex-Liverpool FC manager Rafael Benítez. It was not a popular move with a large proportion of the Chelsea support, and when the Spaniard's first three league games failed

to produce a win, the Blues' meagre tally of four points from a possible 21 (including Di Matteo's last four games) meant they were no longer realistic contenders for the Premier League title.

Chelsea were involved in several competitions at the time of Benítez's arrival. The UEFA Europa League was not one of those, but it would prove to be a lifeline for both him and the club all the way to the team's victory over SL Benfica in the final. Although there was no way back in the Premier League, Chelsea did finish strongly, winning six and drawing two of their last eight games to hold off London rivals Arsenal FC and Tottenham and secure third place, enabling Mourinho to come in and take over a club with a guaranteed starting berth in the group stage of the 2013/14 UEFA Champions League.

Not for the first time, Arsenal and Spurs were engaged in a bitter contest for fourth spot, and as usual it was the Gunners who claimed it, Arsène Wenger's side receiving the consolation prize of a UEFA Champions League play-off place after yet another season without a trophy – their eighth in succession. Tottenham, under new coach André Villas-Boas, looked to have stolen a march on their north London rivals when they defeated them 2-1 at White Hart Lane in early March to establish a seven-point advantage, but despite the presence in their ranks of the brilliant Gareth Bale, who scored 21 goals, they allowed a resurgent Arsenal – eight wins and two draws in their last ten games – to come back and pip them by a point.

Like Tottenham, Liverpool possessed a player of individual brilliance in Luis Suárez, but the capricious Uruguayan striker's tally of 23 goals was insufficient to lift his team above seventh place, which was one position below Merseyside rivals Everton. David Moyes, who was handed the poisoned chalice of following in Ferguson's giant footsteps at Manchester United, was thus able to depart Goodison Park with a little local victory, but the six-year contract he was offered at Old Trafford suggested that his new employers were unconcerned by the Scot's failure to win any silverware of note during his 11 seasons at Everton.

Neither Liverpool nor Everton qualified for Europe, which was a disappointing outcome for both clubs. Newcastle

Wigan midfielder Ben Watson (left) looks on as his header flies past Manchester City keeper Joe Hart to win the FA Cup final

United FC, who finished fifth in 2011/12, plummeted 11 places and only just scrambled clear of relegation – as did their north-east neighbours Sunderland AFC, who replaced manager Martin O'Neill with the Italian Paolo Di Canio at the end of March. Aston Villa also endured a tortuous campaign at the wrong end of the table, but new manager Paul Lambert's risky policy of fielding youth rather than experience was ultimately justified by the 19 goals of 22-year-old Christian Benteke. The Belgian striker would probably have been considered the bargain buy of the season had it not been for Swansea's swashbuckling Spaniard Michu, whose 18 goals helped the Welsh side to an impressive ninth-place finish in their first season under Michael Laudrup.

Swansea were joined in the 2013/14 Premier League by another Welsh club as Cardiff City FC won the Championship (second division) ahead of Hull City AFC, with Crystal Palace FC making up the promoted trio after a play-off final victory against Watford FC. Cardiff thus returned to the English top flight after a 51-year absence – and at the end of a season in which their new Malaysian owners

switched the club's colours from traditional blue to 'lucky' red. Blue and white hoops certainly brought no favours to Queens Park Rangers FC or Reading FC, who were both relegated early – despite changing their manager in mid-stream – and the same colour combination proved unfortunate too as Wigan, so often the Premier League's great escape artists, filled the final place in the drop zone after a 4-1 defeat at Arsenal in the penultimate round.

Domestic cup

Wigan's relegation came just three days after the greatest day in the Lancashire club's history – a 1-0 win over Manchester City at Wembley in the FA Cup final. Rank outsiders at the start, Roberto Martínez's side ran the favourites ragged for much of the game, with young winger Callum McManaman in especially dazzling form, and they got the win their ambition and endeavour deserved when substitute Ben Watson headed home in the 90th minute. Wigan's best performance in the earlier rounds had come in the quarter-final, when they

destroyed Everton 3-0 at Goodison Park. No wonder the Merseysiders appointed Martínez as Moyes' replacement

There were even greater feats of giant-killing in the League Cup, where League 2 (fourth division) side Bradford City AFC caused a sensation by reaching the final after knocking out Wigan, Arsenal and Aston Villa. The minnows from Yorkshire were put in their place at Wembley, though, as Swansea, who had knocked out Chelsea in the semi-finals, ran out easy 5-0 winners, with Michu scoring once and Nathan Dyer and Jonathan De Guzmán twice each.

Like Wigan, it was Swansea's first ever major trophy in English football. It also booked the club a place in the third qualifying round of the 2013/14 UEFA Europa League. Wigan's win in the senior cup competition put them straight through to the group stage. Not only would they be competing in Europe for the first time, but as a second-tier club, having become the only team to win the FA Cup and suffer relegation from the top flight in the same season.

Europe

For the first time since 1995/96 there were no English teams in the quarter-finals of the UEFA Champions League. Having provided at least one finalist in seven of the eight previous seasons, it was a bitter pill for the Premier League to swallow. Manchester United and Arsenal both reached the knockout phase but came unstuck against Real Madrid CF and FC Bayern München, respectively, good away performances undone by defeats at home. Manchester City had a wretched time in their group, drawing all three matches at home and losing all three away, while Chelsea became the first UEFA Champions League holders to be knocked out in the group stage, Juventus and FC Shakhtar Donetsk combining to eliminate them despite their ten points and 16 goals.

Whereas City dropped out of Europe altogether, Chelsea resurfaced in the UEFA Europa League and would make the most of their second chance, Benítez leading the team past AC Sparta Praha, FC Steaua Bucureşti, FC Rubin Kazan and FC Basel 1893 before they overcame Benfica 2-1 in Amsterdam with a last-gasp headed goal from defender

Branislav Ivanović to sample a second European triumph in as many seasons.

Chelsea were one of three English quarter-finalists in the UEFA Europa League. Tottenham and Newcastle also reached that stage, Liverpool having fallen by the wayside in the round of 32 after an away-goals defeat by FC Zenit St Petersburg. Entertaining Spurs squeezed through captivating ties against Olympique Lyonnais and FC Internazionale Milano before losing on penalties to Basel, while Newcastle needed just one goal to see off both FC Metalist Kharkiv and FC Anji Makhachkala before falling to Benfica.

National team

England experienced mixed fortunes in Roy Hodgson's first full season as head coach. They beat UEFA EURO 2012 conquerors Italy, got the better of FIFA World Cup hosts Brazil, winning 2-1 at Wembley and drawing 2-2 in the Maracanã, and hammered 18 goals without reply in three of their World Cup qualifiers. Yet their presence in Brazil in the summer of 2014 was far from certain because of the three 1-1 draws they

registered in the qualifying campaign against their principal group rivals. Only a late Frank Lampard penalty salvaged a point at Wembley against Ukraine, and England were unable to protect first-half leads, provided by Wayne Rooney headers, away to both Poland and Montenegro. With four games left, three of them at home, Hodgson's side were still handily placed to top the group, but they could ill-afford any more slip-ups.

While Steven Gerrard and Ashley Cole, who both collected 100th caps in 2012/13, remain core figures in the side alongside Lampard and Rooney, there will be no trip to the World Cup finals for two other members of the old guard, centre-backs John Terry and Rio Ferdinand, who both withdrew their services during the season.

England possess a number of quality youngsters, such as the versatile Phil Jones, midfield dynamo Jack Wilshere and winger Alex Oxlade-Chamberlain, but all three of those players were absent from – though eligible for – the UEFA European Under-21 Championship finals in Israel, where Stuart Pearce's depleted team finished bottom of their group after losing all three matches.

Alex Oxlade-Chamberlain, one of England's promising youngsters, in World Cup qualifying action against Poland

 **ENGLAND**

Domestic league: Premier League 2012/13 final table

		Pld	Home					Away					Total					Pts
			W	D	L	F	A	W	D	L	F	A	W	D	L	F	A	
1	**Manchester United FC**	38	16	0	3	45	19	12	5	2	41	24	28	5	5	86	43	89
2	Manchester City FC	38	14	3	2	41	15	9	6	4	25	19	23	9	6	66	34	78
3	Chelsea FC	38	12	5	2	41	16	10	4	5	34	23	22	9	7	75	39	75
4	Arsenal FC	38	11	5	3	47	23	10	5	4	25	14	21	10	7	72	37	73
5	Tottenham Hotspur FC	38	11	5	3	29	18	10	4	5	37	28	21	9	8	66	46	72
6	Everton FC	38	12	6	1	33	17	4	9	6	22	23	16	15	7	55	40	63
7	Liverpool FC	38	9	6	4	33	16	7	7	5	38	27	16	13	9	71	43	61
8	West Bromwich Albion FC	38	9	4	6	32	25	5	3	11	21	32	14	7	17	53	57	49
9	Swansea City AFC	38	6	8	5	28	26	5	5	9	19	25	11	13	14	47	51	46
10	West Ham United FC	38	9	6	4	34	22	3	4	12	11	31	12	10	16	45	53	46
11	Norwich City FC	38	8	7	4	25	20	2	7	10	16	38	10	14	14	41	58	44
12	Fulham FC	38	7	3	9	28	30	4	7	8	22	30	11	10	17	50	60	43
13	Stoke City FC	38	7	7	5	21	22	2	8	9	13	23	9	15	14	34	45	42
14	Southampton FC	38	6	7	6	26	24	3	7	9	23	36	9	14	15	49	60	41
15	Aston Villa FC	38	5	5	9	23	28	5	6	8	24	41	10	11	17	47	69	41
16	Newcastle United FC	38	9	1	9	24	31	2	7	10	21	37	11	8	19	45	68	41
17	Sunderland AFC	38	5	8	6	20	19	4	4	11	21	35	9	12	17	41	54	39
18	Wigan Athletic FC	38	4	6	9	26	39	5	3	11	21	34	9	9	20	47	73	36
19	Reading FC	38	4	8	7	23	33	2	2	15	20	40	6	10	22	43	73	28
20	Queens Park Rangers FC	38	2	8	9	13	28	2	5	12	17	32	4	13	21	30	60	25

SEASON AT A GLANCE

EUROPEAN QUALIFICATION 2013/14

Champion: Manchester United FC (group stage)
Manchester City FC (group stage)
Chelsea FC (group stage)
Arsenal FC (play-offs)

FA Cup winner: Wigan Athletic FC (group stage)
League Cup winner: Swansea City AFC (third qualifying round)

Tottenham Hotspur FC (play-offs)

Top scorers	Robin van Persie (Man. United), 26 goals
Relegated clubs	Queens Park Rangers FC, Reading FC, Wigan Athletic FC
Promoted clubs	Cardiff City FC, Hull City AFC, Crystal Palace FC
FA Cup final	Wigan Athletic FC 1-0 Manchester City FC
League Cup final	Swansea City AFC 5-0 Bradford City AFC

PREMIER LEAGUE TEAM OF THE SEASON
(4-4-2)
Coach: Ferguson (Man. United)

PLAYER OF THE SEASON
Gareth Bale
(Tottenham Hotspur FC)

In world-class form throughout the season, Bale drew widespread gasps of admiration for his pace and skill and also conjured up 21 goals – the third highest tally in the Premier League. It was not just the quantity that caught the eye, but the quality too. He rifled in countless efforts from distance, many of them decisive and late in the game.

NEWCOMER OF THE SEASON
Callum McManaman
(Wigan Athletic FC)

Never more than a Premier League substitute until mid-March, the 22-year-old illuminated the last two months of the season with his willingness and ability to take on defenders. Man of the match in Wigan's FA Cup final win against Manchester City FC, he would have been present for England at the UEFA European Under-21 Championship but for injury.

De Gea (Man. United)

Zabaleta (Man. City) — Ferdinand (Man. United) — Vertonghen (Tottenham) — Baines (Everton)

Hazard (Chelsea) — Carrick (Man. United) — Mata (Chelsea) — Bale (Tottenham)

Suárez (Liverpool) — Van Persie (Man. United)

NATIONAL TEAM

Home Kit   Away Kit

INTERNATIONAL HONOURS
FIFA World Cup (1) 1966.

INTERNATIONAL TOURNAMENT APPEARANCES
FIFA World Cup (13) 1950, 1954 (qtr-finals), 1958, 1962 (qtr-finals), 1966 (Winners), 1970 (qtr-finals), 1982 (2nd phase), 1986 (qtr-finals), 1990 (4th), 1998 (2nd round), 2002 (qtr-finals), 2006 (qtr-finals), 2010 (2nd round)
UEFA European Championship (8) 1968 (3rd), 1980, 1988, 1992, 1996 (semi-finals), 2000, 2004 (qtr-finals), 2012 (qtr-finals)

TOP FIVE ALL-TIME CAPS
Peter Shilton (125); David Beckham (115); Bobby Moore (108); Bobby Charlton (106); Billy Wright (105)

TOP FIVE ALL-TIME GOALS
Bobby Charlton (49); Gary Lineker (48); Jimmy Greaves (44); Michael Owen (40); **Wayne Rooney** (36)

Results 2012/13

Date	Opponent	H/A/N	Venue	Score	Scorers
15/08/12	Italy	N	Berne (SUI)	2-1	Jagielka (27), Defoe (79)
07/09/12	Moldova (WCQ)	A	Chisinau	5-0	Lampard (4p, 29), Defoe (32), Milner (74), Baines (83)
11/09/12	Ukraine (WCQ)	H	London	1-1	Lampard (87p)
12/10/12	San Marino (WCQ)	H	London	5-0	Rooney (35p, 70), Welbeck (37, 72), Oxlade-Chamberlain (77)
17/10/12	Poland (WCQ)	A	Warsaw	1-1	Rooney (31)
14/11/12	Sweden	A	Solna	2-4	Welbeck (35), Caulker (38)
06/02/13	Brazil	H	London	2-1	Rooney (27), Lampard (60)
22/03/13	San Marino (WCQ)	A	Serravalle	8-0	Alessandro Della Valle (12og), Oxlade-Chamberlain (29), Defoe (35, 77), Young (39), Lampard (42), Rooney (54), Sturridge (70)
26/03/13	Montenegro (WCQ)	A	Podgorica	1-1	Rooney (6)
29/05/13	Republic of Ireland	H	London	1-1	Lampard (23)
02/06/13	Brazil	A	Rio de Janeiro	2-2	Oxlade-Chamberlain (67), Rooney (79)

Appearances 2012/13

Coach: Roy Hodgson — 09/08/47

Player	DOB	Club	Ita	MDA	UKR	SMR	POL	Swe	Bra	SMR	MNE	Irl	Bra	Caps	Goals
Jack Butland	10/03/93	Birmingham	G46											1	*
Kyle Walker	28/05/90	Tottenham	D			D			D					5	-
Gary Cahill	19/12/85	Chelsea	D		D		D	D				D	D	15	2
Phil Jagielka	17/08/82	Everton	D61		D	D	D					D	D	18	1
Leighton Baines	11/12/84	Everton	D78	D	D73	D		D	s46	D		s53	D31	17	1
Adam Johnson	14/07/87	Man. City	M											12	2
Frank Lampard	20/06/78	Chelsea	M	s46				s46	M66			M	M	97	20
Michael Carrick	28/07/81	Man. United	M	s46		M60	M				M	M	M	29	-
Tom Cleverley	12/08/89	Man. United	M	M	M62	M	M	M61	M46	M56	M77			9	-
Ashley Young	09/07/85	Man. United	M62					M61		M	s77			29	7
Andy Carroll	06/01/89	Liverpool /West Ham	A46			s73								9	2
John Ruddy	24/10/86	Norwich	s46											1	-
Jermain Defoe	07/10/82	Tottenham	s46	A68	A		A67		A			s33		54	19
Joleon Lescott	16/08/82	Man. City	s61	D	D		D			D	D			26	1
James Milner	04/01/86	Man. City	s62	M	M		M		s61		M	s87	M	38	1
Jake Livermore	14/11/89	Tottenham	s69											1	-
Ryan Bertrand	05/08/89	Chelsea	s78		s73									2	-
Joe Hart	19/04/87	Man. City	G	G	G	G	G	G	G	G	G	G46	G	32	-
Glen Johnson	23/08/84	Liverpool	D	D			D	D74	D		D	D46	D61	48	1
John Terry	07/12/80	Chelsea	D											78	6
Steven Gerrard	30/05/80	Liverpool	M46	M 88*			M	M74	M		M			102	19
Alex Oxlade-Chamberlain	15/08/93	Arsenal	M58	M69	M	s73				M		M87	s61	12	3
Theo Walcott	16/03/89	Arsenal	s58		M10			M76				M	M84	33	4
Danny Welbeck	26/11/90	Man. United	s68	s62	A	s67	A	A61		M				16	5
Daniel Sturridge	01/09/89	Chelsea /Liverpool			s69			s61			s56	A33		6	1
Wayne Rooney	24/10/85	Man. United			A73	A73	A	A56	A	A	A	A		83	36
Aaron Lennon	16/04/87	Tottenham			s10			s76						21	-
Jonjo Shelvey	27/02/92	Liverpool			s66									1	-
Ashley Cole	20/12/80	Chelsea					D		D46		D	D53	s31	103	-

Appearances 2012/13 (contd.)

			Ita	MDA	UKR	SMR	POL	Swe	Bra	SMR	MNE	Irl	Bra	Caps	Goals
Steven Caulker	29/12/91	Tottenham						D74						1	1
Leon Osman	17/05/81	Everton						M		s56				2	-
Raheem Sterling	08/12/94	Liverpool						M84						1	-
Jack Wilshere	01/01/92	Arsenal						s61	M					7	-
Carl Jenkinson	08/02/92	Arsenal						s74						1	-
Ryan Shawcross	04/10/87	Stoke						s74						1	-
Tom Huddlestone	28/12/86	Tottenham						s74						4	-
Wilfried Zaha	10/11/92	Crystal Palace						s84						1	-
Chris Smalling	22/11/89	Man. United							D	D	D			6	-
Scott Parker	13/10/80	Tottenham								s66				18	-
Ben Foster	03/04/83	West Brom										s46		6	-
Phil Jones	21/02/92	Man. United										s46	M	7	-
Jack Rodwell	11/03/91	Man. City											s84	3	-

European club competitions 2012/13

CHELSEA FC

Group E

Match 1 - Juventus (ITA)
H 2-2 *Oscar (31, 33)*
Čech, Ivanović, Cole, David Luiz, Ramires (Bertrand 69), Lampard, Fernando Torres, Oscar (Mata 75), Mikel, Hazard, Terry. Coach: Roberto Di Matteo (ITA)

Match 2 - FC Nordsjælland (DEN)
A 4-0 *Mata (33, 82), David Luiz (79), Ramires (89)*
Čech, Ivanović, Cole, David Luiz, Ramires, Lampard, Fernando Torres, Mata (Mikel 83), Oscar, Moses (Hazard 65), Cahill. Coach: Roberto Di Matteo (ITA)

Match 3 - FC Shakhtar Donetsk (UKR)
A 1-2 *Oscar (88)*
Čech, Ivanović, Cole, David Luiz, Ramires, Lampard (Hazard 18), Fernando Torres (Sturridge 70), Mata, Oscar, Mikel, Terry. Coach: Roberto Di Matteo (ITA)

Match 4 - FC Shakhtar Donetsk (UKR)
H 3-2 *Fernando Torres (6), Oscar (40), Moses (90+4)*
Čech, Ivanović, David Luiz, Ramires, Fernando Torres (Sturridge 90), Mata, Oscar (Moses 79), Mikel, Hazard, Cahill, Bertrand. Coach: Roberto Di Matteo (ITA)

Match 5 - Juventus (ITA)
A 0-3
Čech, Ivanović, Cole, David Luiz, Ramires, Mata, Oscar, Mikel (Fernando Torres 71), Hazard, Cahill, Azpilicueta (Moses 60). Coach: Roberto Di Matteo (ITA)

Match 6 - FC Nordsjælland (DEN)
H 6-1 *David Luiz (38p), Fernando Torres (45+2, 56), Cahill (51), Mata (63), Oscar (71)*
Čech, Ivanović, Cole (Bertrand 60), David Luiz, Romeu, Ramires (Oscar 65), Fernando Torres, Mata (Paulo Ferreira 74), Moses, Hazard, Cahill. Coach: Rafael Benítez (ESP)

Round of 32 - AC Sparta Praha (CZE)
A 1-0 *Oscar (82)*
Čech, Ivanović, Ramires, Lampard, Fernando Torres, Mata (Oscar 82), Hazard, Marin (Benayoun 68), Cahill, Azpilicueta, Bertrand. Coach: Rafael Benítez (ESP)
H 1-1 *Hazard (90+2)*
Čech, Ramires, Fernando Torres, Mata, Oscar (Hazard 68), Mikel, Moses, Cahill, Terry, Azpilicueta, Bertrand. Coach: Rafael Benítez (ESP)

Round of 16 - FC Steaua Bucureşti (ROU)
A 0-1
Čech, Ivanović, David Luiz, Lampard, Fernando Torres, Oscar, Mikel, Hazard (Marin 75), Terry, Benayoun (Mata 64), Bertrand. Coach: Rafael Benítez (ESP)
H 3-1 *Mata (34), Terry (58), Fernando Torres (71)*
Čech, Cole, David Luiz, Ramires, Fernando Torres, Mata (Moses 90), Oscar, Mikel, Hazard (Benayoun 90+3), Terry, Azpilicueta. Coach: Rafael Benítez (ESP)

Quarter-final - FC Rubin Kazan (RUS)
H 3-1 *Fernando Torres (16, 70), Moses (32)*
Čech, David Luiz, Ramires, Lampard, Fernando Torres, Mata (Oscar 78), Moses (Hazard 65), Terry, Azpilicueta, Benayoun (Marin 82), Bertrand. Coach: Rafael Benítez (ESP)
A 2-3 *Fernando Torres (5), Moses (55)*
Čech, David Luiz, Ramires (Mikel 60), Lampard (Ivanović 90+1), Fernando Torres, Moses, Ferreira, Terry, Azpilicueta, Benayoun (Oscar 77), Aké. Coach: Rafael Benítez (ESP)

Semi-final - FC Basel 1893 (SUI)
A 2-1 *Moses (12), David Luiz (90+4)*
Čech, Ivanović, Cole, David Luiz, Ramires, Lampard (Oscar 79), Fernando Torres, Moses, Hazard (Mata 70), Terry, Azpilicueta. Coach: Rafael Benítez (ESP)
H 3-1 *Fernando Torres (50), Moses (52), David Luiz (59)*
Čech, Ivanović, David Luiz (Aké 82), Ramires (Oscar 66), Lampard, Fernando Torres, Moses, Hazard (Mata 75), Cahill, Azpilicueta, Bertrand. Coach: Rafael Benítez (ESP)

Final - SL Benfica (POR)
N 2-1 *Fernando Torres (60), Ivanović (90+3)*
Čech, Ivanović, Cole, David Luiz, Ramires, Lampard, Fernando Torres, Mata, Oscar, Cahill, Azpilicueta. Coach: Rafael Benítez (ESP)

MANCHESTER CITY FC

Group D

Match 1 - Real Madrid CF (ESP)
A 2-3 *Džeko (68), Kolarov (85)*
Hart, Maicon (Zabaleta 74), Kompany, Nasri (Kolarov 37), Javi García, Barry, Silva (Džeko 63), Clichy, Tévez, Y Touré. Coach: Roberto Mancini (ITA)

Match 2 - Borussia Dortmund (GER)
H 1-1 *Balotelli (90p)*
Hart, Kompany, Zabaleta, Nasri (Kolarov 57), Džeko, Javi García (Rodwell 34), Agüero, Silva, Clichy (Balotelli 81), Nastasić, Y Touré. Coach: Roberto Mancini (ITA)

Match 3 - AFC Ajax (NED)
A 1-3 *Nasri (22)*
Hart, Richards, Kompany, Lescott (Kolarov 63), Milner (Balotelli 78), Nasri, Džeko, Agüero, Barry (Tévez 71), Clichy, Y Touré. Coach: Roberto Mancini (ITA)

Match 4 - AFC Ajax (NED)
H 2-2 *Y Touré (22), Agüero (74)*
Hart, Kompany, Zabaleta, Nasri, Javi García (Balotelli 46), Agüero, Barry (Kolarov 85), Clichy, Tévez (Džeko 66), Nastasić, Y Touré. Coach: Roberto Mancini (ITA)

Match 5 - Real Madrid CF (ESP)
H 1-1 *Agüero (73p)*
Hart, Maicon, Kompany, Zabaleta, Nasri (Tévez 60), Džeko, Kolarov (Javi García 46), Agüero (Milner 88), Silva, Nastasić, Y Touré. Coach: Roberto Mancini (ITA)

Match 6 - Borussia Dortmund (GER)
A 0-1
Hart, Maicon, Kompany, Lescott, Nasri (Zabaleta 69), Džeko (Balotelli 64), Sinclair (Agüero 57), Javi García, Barry, Tévez, Nastasić. Coach: Roberto Mancini (ITA)

MANCHESTER UNITED FC

CHAMPIONS LEAGUE

Group H

Match 1 - Galatasaray AŞ (TUR)
H 1-0 *Carrick (7)*
De Gea, Rafael, Evra, Evans, Valencia, Vidić, Carrick, Nani, Van Persie (Hernández 81), Scholes (Fletcher 79), Kagawa (Welbeck 84). Coach: Sir Alex Ferguson (SCO)

Match 2 - CFR 1907 Cluj (ROU)
A 2-1 *Van Persie (29, 49)*
De Gea, Rafael, Evra, Ferdinand, Evans (Wootton 79), Anderson, Rooney, Hernández (Welbeck 83), Van Persie, Cleverley, Fletcher. Coach: Sir Alex Ferguson (SCO)

Match 3 - SC Braga (POR)
H 3-2 *Hernández (25, 75), Evans (62)*
De Gea, Rafael, Evans, Rooney, Hernández (Giggs 79), Carrick, Van Persie, Cleverley, Fletcher, Kagawa (Nani 46), Büttner. Coach: Sir Alex Ferguson (SCO)

Match 4 - SC Braga (POR)
A 3-1 *Van Persie (80), Rooney (84p), Hernández (90+2)*
De Gea, Evra, Evans (Ferdinand 57), Valencia, Anderson, Rooney, Giggs, Smalling, Hernández, Nani (Rafael 73), Welbeck (Van Persie 64). Coach: Sir Alex Ferguson (SCO)

Match 5 - Galatasaray AŞ (TUR)
A 0-1
Lindegaard, Rafael, Jones, Anderson (Young 74), Hernández, Carrick, Welbeck (King 85), Cleverley, Fletcher, Powell (Macheda 74), Büttner. Coach: Sir Alex Ferguson (SCO)

Match 6 - CFR 1907 Cluj (ROU)
H 0-1
De Gea, Jones, Rooney, Giggs (Fletcher 86), Smalling, Hernández, Welbeck, Cleverley (Scholes 45), Powell (Macheda 73), Büttner, Wootton. Coach: Sir Alex Ferguson (SCO)

Round of 16 - Real Madrid CF (ESP)
A 1-1 *Welbeck (20)*
De Gea, Rafael, Evra, Jones, Ferdinand, Evans, Rooney (Anderson 84), Carrick, Welbeck (Valencia 73), Van Persie, Kagawa (Giggs 64). Coach: Sir Alex Ferguson (SCO)
H 1-2 *Sergio Ramos (48og)*
De Gea, Rafael (Valencia 87), Evra, Ferdinand, Giggs, Vidić, Carrick, Nani, Welbeck (Young 81), Van Persie, Cleverley (Rooney 73). Coach: Sir Alex Ferguson (SCO)
Red card: Nani 56

ARSENAL FC

CHAMPIONS LEAGUE

Group B

Match 1 - Montpellier Hérault SC (FRA)
A 2-1 *Podolski (16), Gervinho (18)*
Mannone, Diaby, Mertesacker, Vermaelen, Arteta, Podolski (Walcott 90), Giroud (Ramsey 76), Santi Cazorla (Coquelin 90), Jenkinson, Gervinho, Gibbs. Coach: Steve Bould (ENG)

Match 2 - Olympiacos FC (GRE)
H 3-1 *Gervinho (42), Podolski (56), Ramsey (90+4)*
Mannone, Vermaelen, Koscielny, Arteta, Podolski (Ramsey 80), Oxlade-Chamberlain (Walcott 71), Santi Cazorla, Coquelin, Jenkinson, Gervinho (Giroud 80), Gibbs. Coach: Steve Bould (ENG)

Match 3 - FC Schalke 04 (GER)
H 0-2
Mannone, Mertesacker, Vermaelen, Arteta, Podolski (Arshavin 83), André Santos, Ramsey, Santi Cazorla, Coquelin, Jenkinson (Gnabry 83), Gervinho (Giroud 76). Coach: Steve Bould (ENG)

Match 4 - FC Schalke 04 (GER)
A 2-2 *Walcott (18), Giroud (26)*
Mannone, Sagna, Mertesacker, Vermaelen, Koscielny, Arteta, Podolski (André Santos 90+1), Wilshere, Giroud, Walcott, Santi Cazorla (Coquelin 90+1). Coach: Arsène Wenger (FRA)

Match 5 - Montpellier Hérault SC (FRA)
H 2-0 *Wilshere (49), Podolski (63)*
Szczęsny, Sagna, Mertesacker, Vermaelen, Koscielny, Arteta, Podolski, Wilshere, Giroud (Gervinho 85), Oxlade-Chamberlain (Ramsey 70), Santi Cazorla (Coquelin 84). Coach: Arsène Wenger (FRA)

Match 6 - Olympiacos FC (GRE)
A 1-2 *Rosický (38)*
Szczęsny, Vermaelen, Rosický (Arshavin 46), Oxlade-Chamberlain, Ramsey, Squillaci, Coquelin, Jenkinson, Gervinho, Chamakh, Meade (Angha 83). Coach: Arsène Wenger (FRA)

Round of 16 - FC Bayern München (GER)
H 1-3 *Podolski (55)*
Szczęsny, Sagna, Mertesacker, Vermaelen, Koscielny, Arteta, Podolski (Giroud 72), Wilshere, Walcott, Ramsey (Rosický 71), Santi Cazorla. Coach: Arsène Wenger (FRA)
A 2-0 *Giroud (3), Koscielny (86)*
Fabiański, Mertesacker, Koscielny, Rosický, Arteta, Giroud, Walcott (Oxlade-Chamberlain 72), Ramsey (Gervinho 72), Santi Cazorla, Jenkinson, Gibbs. Coach: Arsène Wenger (FRA)

TOTTENHAM HOTSPUR FC

EUROPA LEAGUE

Group J

Match 1 - S.S. Lazio (ITA)
H 0-0
Lloris, Dempsey (Sigurdsson 76), Vertonghen, Lennon (Townsend 81), Bale, Naughton, Defoe, Dembélé (Mason 90+4), Walker, Sandro, Caulker. Coach: André Villas-Boas (POR)

Match 2 - Panathinaikos FC (GRE)
A 1-1 *Dawson (35)*
Lloris, Dempsey (Sigurdsson 67), Vertonghen, Huddlestone (Sandro 80), Lennon (Townsend 76), Bale, Defoe, Dembélé, Dawson, Walker, Caulker. Coach: André Villas-Boas (POR)

Match 3 - NK Maribor (SVN)
A 1-1 *Sigurdsson (58)*
Lloris, Vertonghen, Huddlestone, Lennon, Naughton, Defoe, Sigurdsson (Dempsey 75), Walker, Sandro (Livermore 84), Townsend (Falqué 46), Caulker. Coach: André Villas-Boas (POR)

Match 4 - NK Maribor (SVN)
H 3-1 *Defoe (22, 49, 77)*
Lloris, Vertonghen, Huddlestone, Lennon (Falqué 90+1), Adebayor, Bale (Mason 86), Naughton, Defoe (Dempsey 82), Dawson, Walker, Carroll. Coach: André Villas-Boas (POR)

Match 5 - S.S. Lazio (ITA)
A 0-0
Lloris, Dempsey (Defoe 64), Vertonghen, Adebayor, Bale, Naughton, Sigurdsson (Lennon 64), Walker, Sandro, Caulker, Carroll (Dembélé 77). Coach: André Villas-Boas (POR)

Match 6 - Panathinaikos FC (GRE)
H 3-1 *Adebayor (28), Karnezis (76og), Defoe (82)*
Friedel, Dempsey (Sigurdsson 80), Vertonghen, Lennon (Livermore 87), Adebayor, Naughton, Defoe, Walker, Sandro, Caulker, Carroll (Dembélé 75). Coach: André Villas-Boas (POR)

Round of 32 - Olympique Lyonnais (FRA)
H 2-1 *Bale (45, 90+3)*
Friedel, Dempsey (Holtby 67), Vertonghen, Lennon (Sigurdsson 79), Parker (Livermore 90+2), Adebayor, Bale, Gallas, Dembélé, Walker, Assou-Ekotto. Coach: André Villas-Boas (POR)
A 1-1 *Dembélé (90)*
Friedel, Vertonghen, Lennon (Dempsey 66), Parker (Livermore 85), Adebayor, Bale, Gallas, Holtby (Sigurdsson 74), Dembélé, Walker, Assou-Ekotto. Coach: André Villas-Boas (POR)

Round of 16 - FC Internazionale Milano (ITA)
H 3-0 *Bale (6), Sigurdsson (18), Vertonghen (53)*
Friedel, Vertonghen, Lennon (Naughton 82), Parker, Bale, Gallas, Defoe, Dembélé (Livermore 64), Sigurdsson (Holtby 70), Walker, Assou-Ekotto. Coach: André Villas-Boas (POR)
A 1-4 *Adebayor (96) (aet)*
Friedel, Vertonghen, Parker, Adebayor, Gallas, Naughton (Caulker 104), Defoe (Holtby 56), Dembélé, Sigurdsson, Walker, Livermore (Lennon 70). Coach: André Villas-Boas (POR)

Quarter-final - FC Basel 1893 (SUI)
H 2-2 *Adebayor (40), Sigurdsson (58)*
Friedel, Vertonghen, Lennon (Sigurdsson 24), Parker, Adebayor, Bale, Gallas, Holtby (Dempsey 63), Naughton, Dembélé, Assou-Ekotto (Dawson 57). Coach: André Villas-Boas (POR)

A 2-2 *Dempsey (23, 83) (aet; 1-4 on pens)*
Friedel, Dempsey, Vertonghen, Parker (Huddlestone 78), Adebayor, Holtby, Naughton (Assou-Ekotto 79), Dembélé (Carroll 59), Dawson, Sigurdsson, Walker. Coach: André Villas-Boas (POR)
Red card: Vertonghen 90+1

NEWCASTLE UNITED FC

Play-offs - Atromitos FC (GRE)
A 1-1 *R Taylor (45+1)*
Harper, Williamson, Anita, Cissé (Campbell 77), Perch, Gosling (Amalfitano 64), R Taylor, Bigirimana, Marveaux (Gutiérrez 71), Obertan, Tavernier. Coach: Alan Pardew (ENG)
H 1-0 *Vučkič (21)*
Krul, Coloccini, Simpson, Williamson, Perch (Tavernier 59), Gosling, R Taylor (Vučkič 11), Ba, Bigirimana, Marveaux (Amalfitano 90+2), Obertan. Coach: Alan Pardew (ENG)

Group D
Match 1 - CS Marítimo (POR)
A 0-0
Elliot, Santon, Williamson, Perch, Gosling, Amalfitano (Ferguson 76), Bigirimana, Shola Ameobi, Obertan (Marveaux 81), S Taylor, Vučkič (Sammy Ameobi 53). Coach: Alan Pardew (ENG)

Match 2 - FC Girondins de Bordeaux (FRA)
H 3-0 *Shola Ameobi (16), Henrique (40og), Cissé (49)*
Elliot (Harper 46), Cabaye (Bigirimana 61), Simpson, Williamson, Anita, Cissé, Perch, Shola Ameobi, Tioté (Gosling 71), Obertan, Ferguson. Coach: Alan Pardew (ENG)

Match 3 - Club Brugge KV (BEL)
H 1-0 *Obertan (48)*
Harper, Santon, Anita (Shola Ameobi 46), Cissé, Perch, Bigirimana, Tioté, Obertan, S Taylor, Sammy Ameobi (Coloccini 73), Ferguson (Cabaye 81). Coach: Alan Pardew (ENG)

Match 4 - Club Brugge KV (BEL)
A 2-2 *Anita (41), Shola Ameobi (43)*
Krul, Coloccini, Williamson (S Taylor 59), Anita, Bigirimana (Cabaye 72), Marveaux, Shola Ameobi, Tioté, Obertan, Sammy Ameobi (Amalfitano 83), Tavernier. Coach: Alan Pardew (ENG)

Match 5 - CS Marítimo (POR)
H 1-1 *Marveaux (23)*
Krul, Coloccini, Santon, Simpson, Anita, Cissé (Amalfitano 51), Ben Arfa (Ba 40), Bigirimana, Marveaux, S Taylor, Sammy Ameobi (Abeid 77). Coach: Alan Pardew (ENG)

Match 6 - FC Girondins de Bordeaux (FRA)
A 0-2
Elliot, Williamson (Coloccini 74), Perch, Bigirimana, Marveaux, Shola Ameobi (Cissé 81), Sammy Ameobi (Anita 46), Ranger, Ferguson, Tavernier, Abeid. Coach: Alan Pardew (ENG)

Round of 32 - FC Metalist Kharkiv (UKR)
H 0-0
Krul, Coloccini, Santon, Cabaye, Sissoko, Cissé, Yanga-Mbiwa, Gutiérrez, Tioté (Shola Ameobi 79), Obertan (Marveaux 62), S Taylor. Coach: Alan Pardew (ENG)
A 1-0 *Shola Ameobi (64p)*
Krul, Coloccini, Cabaye (Bigirimana 87), Simpson, Sissoko, Anita (Perch 76), Cissé (Gutiérrez 76), Yanga-Mbiwa, Marveaux, Shola Ameobi, Haïdara. Coach: Alan Pardew (ENG)

Round of 16 - FC Anji Makhachkala (RUS)
A 0-0
Elliot, Cabaye (Tioté 84), Simpson, Sissoko, Anita (S Taylor 76), Ben Arfa (Shola Ameobi 64), Yanga-Mbiwa, Perch, Marveaux, Obertan, Haïdara. Coach: Alan Pardew (ENG)
H 1-0 *Cissé (90+3)*
Elliot, Santon, Cabaye (Gutiérrez 37), Sissoko, Anita (Campbell 71), Cissé, Yanga-Mbiwa, Marveaux, Tioté, S Taylor, Haïdara. Coach: Alan Pardew (ENG)

Quarter-final - SL Benfica (POR)
A 1-3 *Cissé (12)*
Krul, Santon, Cabaye, Simpson (Gosling 83), Sissoko, Cissé, Yanga-Mbiwa, Perch (Anita 62), Gutiérrez, Marveaux (Shola Ameobi 81), S Taylor. Coach: Alan Pardew (ENG)
H 1-1 *Cissé (71)*
Krul, Cabaye, Simpson, Williamson, Sissoko, Anita (Ben Arfa 63), Cissé, Yanga-Mbiwa, Gutiérrez, Bigirimana (Shola Ameobi 46), Haïdara (Marveaux 67). Coach: Alan Pardew (ENG)

LIVERPOOL FC

Third qualifying round - FC Gomel (BLR)
A 1-0 *Downing (67)*
Jones, Johnson (Kelly 46), José Enrique, Gerrard, Cole (Sterling 23), Henderson (Lucas 65), Downing, Spearing , Carragher, Borini, Škrtel. Coach: Brendan Rodgers (NIR)
H 3-0 *Borini (21), Gerrard (41), Johnson (72)*
Reina, Johnson, José Enrique, Agger, Suárez, Gerrard, Downing, Lucas (Spearing 86), Borini, Shelvey (Adam 76), Škrtel (Carragher 77). Coach: Brendan Rodgers (NIR)

Play-offs - Heart of Midlothian FC (SCO)
A 1-0 *Webster (78og)*
Reina, Agger, Henderson, Spearing (Allen 67), Carragher, Adam, Borini (Morgan 90+2), Sterling, Shelvey, Kelly, Robinson (Downing 62). Coach: Brendan Rodgers (NIR)
H 1-1 *Suárez (88)*
Reina, Suárez, Gerrard, Henderson (Borini 76), Downing, Carragher, Allen, Shelvey, Kelly, Škrtel, Morgan (Sterling 62). Coach: Brendan Rodgers (NIR)

Group A
Match 1 - BSC Young Boys (SUI)
A 5-3 *Ojala (4og), Wisdom (40), Coates (67), Shelvey (76, 88)*
Jones, José Enrique, Nuri Şahin, Assaidi (Shelvey 67), Pacheco (Borini 62), Henderson, Coates, Downing (Sterling 77), Carragher, Suso, Wisdom. Coach: Brendan Rodgers (NIR)
Match 2 - Udinese Calcio (ITA)
H 2-3 *Shelvey (23), Suárez (75)*
Reina, Johnson, Assaidi (Suárez 65), Henderson (Gerrard 65), Coates, Downing, Carragher, Allen, Borini (Sterling 80), Shelvey, Robinson. Coach: Brendan Rodgers (NIR)
Match 3 - FC Anji Makhachkala (RUS)
H 1-0 *Downing (53)*
Jones, Johnson (Sterling 46), Nuri Şahin, Agger, Suárez, Gerrard, Assaidi, Downing, Shelvey (Allen 79), Škrtel, Wisdom. Coach: Brendan Rodgers (NIR)

Match 4 - FC Anji Makhachkala (RUS)
A 0-1
Jones, Cole (Assaidi 77), Henderson, Coates, Downing, Carragher, Shelvey, Coady (Suso 61), Flanagan, Wisdom, Morgan (Pacheco 61). Coach: Brendan Rodgers (NIR)
Match 5 - BSC Young Boys (SUI)
H 2-2 *Shelvey (33), Cole (72)*
Reina, Nuri Şahin, Cole (Sterling 75), Assaidi, Henderson, Downing, Carragher, Suso (Suárez 61), Shelvey, Škrtel, Wisdom (Gerrard 31). Coach: Brendan Rodgers (NIR)
Match 6 - Udinese Calcio (ITA)
A 1-0 *Henderson (23)*
Reina, Johnson, José Enrique, Nuri Şahin (Shelvey 12), Suárez, Henderson, Downing, Carragher, Allen, Suso (Sterling 71), Škrtel. Coach: Brendan Rodgers (NIR)

Round of 32 - FC Zenit St Petersburg (RUS)
A 0-2
Reina, Johnson, José Enrique, Suárez, Gerrard, Henderson, Downing, Carragher, Allen, Sterling (Lucas 78), Škrtel. Coach: Brendan Rodgers (NIR)
H 3-1 *Suárez (28, 59), Allen (43)*
Reina, Johnson, José Enrique, Agger, Suárez, Gerrard, Henderson (Assaidi 60), Downing (Sterling 84), Lucas, Carragher, Allen (Shelvey 59). Coach: Brendan Rodgers (NIR)

ARSENAL FC
Manager: Arsène Wenger (FRA)
1886 • Emirates Stadium (60,361) • arsenal.com
Major honours
UEFA Cup Winners' Cup (1) 1994;
Inter Cities Fairs Cup (1) 1970;
English League (13) 1931, 1933, 1934, 1935, 1938, 1948, 1953, 1971, 1989, 1991, 1998, 2002, 2004;
FA Cup (10) 1930, 1936, 1950, 1971, 1979, 1993, 1998, 2002, 2003, 2005;
League Cup (2) 1987, 1993

2012

18/08	Sunderland	h	0-0	
26/08	Stoke	a	0-0	
02/09	Liverpool	a	2-0	Podolski, Santi Cazorla
15/09	Southampton	h	6-1	og (Hooiveld), Podolski, Gervinho 2, og (Clyne), Walcott
23/09	Man. City	a	1-1	Koscielny
29/09	Chelsea	h	1-2	Gervinho
06/10	West Ham	a	3-1	Giroud, Walcott, Santi Cazorla
20/10	Norwich	a	0-1	
27/10	QPR	h	1-0	Arteta
03/11	Man. United	a	1-2	Santi Cazorla
10/11	Fulham	h	3-3	Giroud 2, Podolski
17/11	Tottenham	h	5-2	Mertesacker, Podolski, Giroud, Santi Cazorla, Walcott
24/11	Aston Villa	a	0-0	
28/11	Everton	a	1-1	Walcott
01/12	Swansea	h	0-2	
08/12	West Brom	h	2-0	Arteta 2 (2p)
17/12	Reading	h	5-2	Podolski, Santi Cazorla 3, Walcott
22/12	Wigan	a	1-0	Arteta (p)
29/12	Newcastle	h	7-3	Walcott 3, Oxlade-Chamberlain, Podolski, Giroud 2

2013

01/01	Southampton	a	1-1	og (Guly do Prado)
13/01	Man. City	h	0-2	
20/01	Chelsea	a	1-2	Walcott
23/01	West Ham	h	5-1	Podolski, Giroud 2, Santi Cazorla, Walcott
30/01	Liverpool	h	2-2	Giroud, Walcott
02/02	Stoke	h	1-0	Podolski
09/02	Sunderland	a	1-0	Santi Cazorla
23/02	Aston Villa	h	2-1	Santi Cazorla 2
03/03	Tottenham	a	1-2	Mertesacker
16/03	Swansea	a	2-0	Monreal, Gervinho
30/03	Reading	h	4-1	Gervinho, Santi Cazorla, Giroud, Arteta (p)
05/04	West Brom	a	2-1	Rosický 2
13/04	Norwich	h	3-1	Arteta (p), Giroud, Podolski
16/04	Everton	h	0-0	
20/04	Fulham	a	1-0	Mertesacker
28/04	Man. United	h	1-1	Walcott
04/05	QPR	a	1-0	Walcott
14/05	Wigan	h	4-1	Podolski 2, Walcott, Ramsey
19/05	Newcastle	a	1-0	Koscielny

No	Name	Nat	DoB	Pos	Aps	(s)	Gls
11	André Santos	BRA	08/03/83	D	3	(5)	
23	Andrey Arshavin	RUS	29/05/81	A		(7)	
8	Mikel Arteta	ESP	26/03/82	M	34		6
22	Francis Coquelin	FRA	13/05/91	M	3	(8)	
2	Abou Diaby	FRA	11/05/86	M	10	(1)	
21	Łukasz Fabiański	POL	18/04/85	G	4		
27	Gervinho	CIV	27/05/87	M	12	(6)	5
28	Kieran Gibbs		26/09/89	D	23	(4)	
12	Olivier Giroud	FRA	30/09/86	A	24	(10)	11
47	Serge Gnabry	GER	14/07/95	M		(1)	
25	Carl Jenkinson		08/02/92	D	14		
6	Laurent Koscielny	FRA	10/09/85	D	20	(5)	2
24	Vito Mannone	ITA	02/03/88	G	9		
4	Per Mertesacker	GER	29/09/84	D	33	(1)	3
54	Miquel	ESP	28/09/92	D		(1)	
17	Nacho Monreal	ESP	26/02/86	D	9	(1)	
15	Alex Oxlade-Chamberlain		15/08/93	M	11	(14)	1
9	Lukas Podolski	GER	04/06/85	A	25	(8)	11
16	Aaron Ramsey	WAL	26/12/90	M	21	(15)	1
7	Tomáš Rosický	CZE	04/10/80	M	7	(3)	2
3	Bacary Sagna	FRA	14/02/83	D	25		
19	Santi Cazorla	ESP	13/12/84	M	37	(1)	12
1	Wojciech Szczęsny	POL	18/04/90	G	25		
5	Thomas Vermaelen	BEL	14/11/85	D	25	(4)	
14	Theo Walcott		16/03/89	A	24	(8)	14
10	Jack Wilshere		01/01/92	M	20	(5)	

ASTON VILLA FC

Manager: Paul Lambert (SCO)
1874 • Villa Park (42,640) • avfc.co.uk
Major honours
European Champion Clubs' Cup (1) 1982;
UEFA Super Cup (1) 1982;
English League (7) 1894, 1896, 1897, 1899,
1900, 1910, 1981;
FA Cup (7) 1887, 1895, 1897, 1905, 1913, 1920, 1957;
League Cup (5) 1961, 1975, 1977, 1994, 1996

2012

18/08	West Ham	a	0-1	
25/08	Everton	h	1-3	El Ahmadi
02/09	Newcastle	a	1-1	Clark
15/09	Swansea	h	2-0	Lowton, Benteke
22/09	Southampton	a	1-4	Bent
30/09	West Brom	h	1-1	Bent
07/10	Tottenham	a	0-2	
20/10	Fulham	a	0-1	
27/10	Norwich	h	1-1	Benteke
03/11	Sunderland	a	1-0	Agbonlahor
10/11	Man. United	h	2-3	Weimann 2
17/11	Man. City	a	0-5	
24/11	Arsenal	h	0-0	
27/11	Reading	h	1-0	Benteke
01/12	QPR	a	1-1	Holman
08/12	Stoke	h	0-0	
15/12	Liverpool	a	3-1	Benteke 2, Weimann
23/12	Chelsea	a	0-8	
26/12	Tottenham	h	0-4	
29/12	Wigan	h	0-3	

2013

01/01	Swansea	a	2-2	Weimann, Benteke (p)
12/01	Southampton	h	0-1	
19/01	West Brom	a	2-2	Benteke, Agbonlahor
29/01	Newcastle	h	1-2	Benteke (p)
02/02	Everton	a	3-3	Benteke 2, Agbonlahor
10/02	West Ham	h	2-1	Benteke (p), N'Zogbia
23/02	Arsenal	a	1-2	Weimann
04/03	Man. City	a	0-1	
09/03	Reading	a	2-1	Benteke, Agbonlahor
16/03	QPR	h	3-2	Agbonlahor, Weimann, Benteke
31/03	Liverpool	h	1-2	Benteke
05/04	Stoke	a	3-1	Agbonlahor, Lowton, Benteke
13/04	Fulham	h	1-1	N'Zogbia
22/04	Man. United	a	0-3	
29/04	Sunderland	h	6-1	Vlaar, Weimann, Benteke 3, Agbonlahor
04/05	Norwich	a	2-1	Agbonlahor 2
11/05	Chelsea	h	1-2	Benteke
19/05	Wigan	a	2-2	Bent, Vlaar

No	Name	Nat	DoB	Pos	Aps	(s)	Gls
11	Gabriel Agbonlahor		13/10/86	A	24	(4)	9
12	Marc Albrighton		18/11/89	M	4	(5)	
32	Nathan Baker		23/04/91	D	25	(1)	
25	Barry Bannan	SCO	01/12/89	M	18	(6)	
27	Joe Bennett		28/03/90	D	21	(4)	
9	Darren Bent		06/02/84	A	8	(8)	3
20	Christian Benteke	BEL	03/12/90	A	32	(2)	19
21	Jordan Bowery		02/07/91	A	3	(7)	
6	Ciaran Clark	IRL	26/09/89	D	28	(1)	1
24	Simon Dawkins		01/12/87	A		(4)	
14	Nathan Delfouneso		02/02/91	A	1		
16	Fabian Delph		21/11/89	M	19	(5)	
8	Karim El Ahmadi	MAR	27/01/85	M	12	(8)	1
38	Gary Gardner		26/06/92	M		(2)	
1	Shay Given	IRL	20/04/76	G	2		
22	Brad Guzan	USA	09/09/84	G	36		
31	Chris Herd	AUS	04/04/89	M	9		
14	Brett Holman	AUS	27/03/84	M	16	(11)	1
7	Stephen Ireland	IRL	22/08/86	M	9	(4)	
30	Eric Lichaj	USA	17/11/88	D	9	(8)	
34	Matthew Lowton		09/06/89	D	37		2
10	Charles N'Zogbia	FRA	28/05/86	M	11	(10)	2
29	Enda Stevens	IRL	09/07/90	D	6	(1)	
18	Yacouba Sylla	FRA	29/11/90	M	7	(4)	
4	Ron Vlaar	NED	16/02/85	D	27		2
26	Andreas Weimann	AUT	05/08/91	A	26	(4)	7
15	Ashley Westwood		01/04/90	M	28	(2)	
37	Derrick Williams	IRL	17/01/93	D		(1)	

CHELSEA FC

Manager: Roberto Di Matteo (ITA);
(21/11/12) (Rafael Benítez (ESP))
1905 • Stamford Bridge (41,841) • chelseafc.com
Major honours
UEFA Champions League (1) 2012;
UEFA Cup Winners' Cup (2) 1971, 1998;
UEFA Europa League (1) 2013;
UEFA Super Cup (1) 1998;
English League (4) 1955, 2005, 2006, 2010;
FA Cup (7) 1970, 1997, 2000, 2007, 2009, 2010, 2012;
League Cup (4) 1965, 1998, 2005, 2007

2012

19/08	Wigan	a	2-0	Ivanović, Lampard (p)
22/08	Reading	h	4-2	Lampard (p), Cahill, Fernando Torres, Ivanović
25/08	Newcastle	h	2-0	Hazard (p), Fernando Torres
15/09	QPR	h	0-0	
22/09	Stoke	h	1-0	Cole
29/09	Arsenal	a	2-1	Fernando Torres, Mata
06/10	Norwich	h	4-1	Fernando Torres, Lampard, Hazard, Ivanović
20/10	Tottenham	a	4-2	Cahill, Mata 2, Sturridge
28/10	Man. United	h	2-3	Mata, Ramires
03/11	Swansea	a	1-1	Moses
11/11	Liverpool	h	1-1	Terry
17/11	West Brom	a	2-1	Hazard
25/11	Man. City	h	0-0	
28/11	Fulham	h	0-0	
01/12	West Ham	a	1-3	Mata
08/12	Sunderland	a	3-1	Fernando Torres 2 (1p), Mata
23/12	Aston Villa	h	8-0	Fernando Torres, David Luiz, Ivanović, Lampard, Ramires 2, Oscar (p), Hazard
26/12	Norwich	a	1-0	Mata
30/12	Everton	a	2-1	Lampard 2

2013

02/01	QPR	h	0-1	
12/01	Stoke	a	4-0	og 2 (Walters 2), Lampard (p), Hazard
16/01	Southampton	h	2-2	Ba, Hazard
20/01	Arsenal	h	2-1	Mata, Lampard (p)
30/01	Reading	a	2-2	Mata, Lampard
02/02	Newcastle	a	2-3	Lampard, Mata
09/02	Wigan	h	4-1	Ramires, Hazard, Lampard, Marin
24/02	Man. City	a	0-2	
02/03	West Brom	h	1-0	Ba
07/03	West Ham	h	2-0	Lampard, Hazard
30/03	Southampton	a	1-2	Terry
07/04	Sunderland	h	2-1	og (Kilgallon), Ivanović
17/04	Fulham	h	3-0	David Luiz, Terry 2
21/04	Liverpool	a	2-2	Oscar, Hazard (p)
28/04	Swansea	h	2-0	Oscar, Lampard (p)
05/05	Man. United	h	1-0	Mata
08/05	Tottenham	h	2-2	Oscar, Ramires
11/05	Aston Villa	a	2-1	Lampard 2
19/05	Everton	h	2-1	Mata, Fernando Torres

No	Name	Nat	DoB	Pos	Aps	(s)	Gls
57	Nathan Aké	NED	18/02/95	D	1	(2)	
28	César Azpilicueta	ESP	28/08/89	D	24	(3)	
29	Demba Ba	SEN	25/05/85	A	11	(3)	2
30	Yossi Benayoun	ISR	05/05/80	M		(6)	
34	Ryan Bertrand		05/08/89	D	14	(5)	
24	Gary Cahill		19/12/85	D	24	(2)	2
1	Petr Čech	CZE	20/05/82	G	36		
3	Ashley Cole		20/12/80	D	31		1
4	David Luiz	BRA	22/04/87	D	29	(1)	2
17	Fernando Torres	ESP	20/03/84	A	28	(8)	8
17	Eden Hazard	BEL	07/01/91	M	31	(3)	9
2	Branislav Ivanović	SRB	22/02/84	D	33	(1)	5
8	Frank Lampard		20/06/78	M	21	(8)	15
35	Lucas Piazón	BRA	20/01/94	A		(1)	
21	Marko Marin	GER	13/03/89	M	2	(4)	1
10	Juan Mata	ESP	28/04/88	M	31	(4)	12
12	John Obi Mikel	NGA	22/04/87	M	19	(3)	
11	Victor Moses	NGA	12/12/90	A	12	(11)	1
19	Oscar	BRA	09/09/91	M	24	(10)	4
19	Paulo Ferreira	POR	18/01/79	D		(2)	
7	Ramires	BRA	24/03/87	M	28	(7)	5
16	Raul Meireles	POR	17/03/83	M	1	(2)	
6	Oriol Romeu	ESP	24/09/91	M	4	(2)	
23	Daniel Sturridge		01/09/89	A	1	(6)	1
26	John Terry		07/12/80	D	11	(3)	4
22	Ross Turnbull		04/01/85	G	2	(1)	

EVERTON FC

Manager: David Moyes (SCO)
1878 • Goodison Park (40,157) • evertonfc.com
Major honours
UEFA Cup Winners' Cup (1) 1985;
English League (9) 1891, 1915, 1928, 1932, 1939,
1963, 1970, 1985, 1987;
FA Cup (5) 1906, 1933, 1966, 1984, 1995

2012

20/08	Man. United	h	1-0	Fellaini
25/08	Aston Villa	a	3-1	Pienaar, Fellaini, Jelavić
01/09	West Brom	a	0-2	
17/09	Newcastle	h	2-2	Baines, Anichebe
22/09	Swansea	a	3-0	Anichebe, Mirallas, Fellaini
29/09	Southampton	h	3-1	Osman, Jelavić 2
06/10	Wigan	a	2-2	Jelavić, Baines (p)
21/10	QPR	a	1-1	og (Júlio César)
28/10	Liverpool	h	2-2	Osman, Naismith
03/11	Fulham	a	2-2	Fellaini 2
10/11	Sunderland	h	2-1	Fellaini, Jelavić
17/11	Reading	h	1-2	Naismith
24/11	Norwich	h	1-1	Naismith
28/11	Arsenal	h	1-1	Fellaini
01/12	Man. City	h	1-1	Fellaini
09/12	Tottenham	h	2-1	Pienaar, Jelavić
15/12	Stoke	a	1-1	og (Shawcross)
22/12	West Ham	a	2-1	Anichebe, Pienaar
26/12	Wigan	h	2-1	Osman, Jagielka
30/12	Chelsea	h	1-2	Pienaar

2013

02/01	Newcastle	a	2-1	Baines, Anichebe
12/01	Swansea	h	0-0	
21/01	Southampton	h	0-0	
30/01	West Brom	a	2-1	Baines 2 (1p)
02/02	Aston Villa	h	3-3	Anichebe, Fellaini 2
10/02	Man. United	a	0-2	
23/02	Norwich	a	2-1	Osman
02/03	Reading	h	3-1	Fellaini, Pienaar, Mirallas
16/03	Man. City	h	2-0	Osman, Jelavić
30/03	Stoke	h	1-0	Mirallas
07/04	Tottenham	a	2-2	Jagielka, Mirallas
13/04	QPR	h	2-0	Gibson, Anichebe
16/04	Arsenal	a	0-0	
20/04	Sunderland	a	0-1	
27/04	Fulham	h	1-0	Pienaar
05/05	Liverpool	a	0-0	
12/05	West Ham	h	2-0	Mirallas 2
19/05	Chelsea	a	1-2	Naismith

No	Name	Nat	DoB	Pos	Aps	(s)	Gls
28	Victor Anichebe	NGA	23/04/88	A	19	(7)	6
3	Leighton Baines		11/12/84	D	38		5
20	Ross Barkley		05/12/93	M	2	(5)	
23	Séamus Coleman	IRL	11/10/88	D	24	(2)	
15	Sylvain Distin	FRA	16/12/77	D	31	(3)	
34	Shane Duffy	IRL	01/01/92	D		(1)	
25	Marouane Fellaini	BEL	22/11/87	M	31		11
4	Darron Gibson	IRL	25/10/87	M	22	(1)	1
19	Magaye Gueye	SEN	06/07/90	M		(2)	
5	John Heitinga	NED	15/11/83	D	17	(9)	
2	Tony Hibbert		20/02/81	D	4	(2)	
16	Thomas Hitzlsperger	GER	05/04/82	M	4	(3)	
24	Tim Howard	USA	06/03/79	G	36		
6	Phil Jagielka		17/08/82	D	36		2
7	Nikica Jelavić	CRO	27/08/85	A	26	(11)	7
11	Kevin Mirallas	BEL	05/10/87	M	23	(4)	6
1	Ján Mucha	SVK	05/12/82	G	2		
14	Steven Naismith	SCO	14/09/86	A	13	(18)	4
18	Phil Neville		21/01/77	D	18		
21	Leon Osman		17/05/81	M	36		5
8	Bryan Oviedo	CRC	02/02/90	M	1	(14)	
22	Steven Pienaar	RSA	17/03/82	M	35		6
27	Apostolos Vellios	GRE	08/01/92	A		(6)	

FULHAM FC

Manager: Martin Jol (NED)
1879 • Craven Cottage (25,478) • fulhamfc.com

2012

Date	Opponent	H/A	Score	Scorers
18/08	Norwich	h	5-0	Duff, Petrić 2, Kacaniklic, Sidwell (p)
25/08	Man. United	a	2-3	Duff, og (Vidić)
01/09	West Ham	a	0-3	
15/09	West Brom	h	3-0	Berbatov 2 (1p), Sidwell
22/09	Wigan	a	2-1	Rodallega, Duff
29/09	Man. City	h	1-2	Petrić (p)
07/10	Southampton	a	2-2	og (Hooiveld), Richardson
20/10	Aston Villa	h	1-0	Baird
27/10	Reading	a	3-3	Ruiz, Baird, Berbatov
03/11	Everton	h	2-2	Ruiz, Sidwell
10/11	Arsenal	a	3-3	Berbatov 2 (1p), Kacaniklic
18/11	Sunderland	h	1-3	Petrić
24/11	Stoke	a	0-1	
28/11	Chelsea	a	0-0	
01/12	Tottenham	h	0-3	
10/12	Newcastle	h	2-1	Sidwell, Rodallega
15/12	QPR	a	1-2	Petrić
22/12	Liverpool	a	0-4	
26/12	Southampton	h	1-1	Berbatov
29/12	Swansea	h	1-2	Ruiz

2013

Date	Opponent	H/A	Score	Scorers
01/01	West Brom	a	2-1	Berbatov, Kacaniklic
12/01	Wigan	h	1-1	Karagounis
19/01	Man. City	a	0-2	
30/01	West Ham	h	3-1	Berbatov, Rodallega, og (O'Brien)
02/02	Man. United	h	0-1	
09/02	Norwich	a	0-0	
23/02	Stoke	h	1-0	Berbatov
02/03	Sunderland	a	2-2	Berbatov (p), Riether
17/03	Tottenham	a	1-0	Berbatov
01/04	QPR	h	3-2	Berbatov 2 (1p), og (Hill)
07/04	Newcastle	a	0-1	
13/04	Aston Villa	a	1-1	og (Delph)
17/04	Chelsea	h	0-3	
20/04	Arsenal	h	0-1	
27/04	Everton	a	0-1	
04/05	Reading	h	2-4	Ruiz 2
12/05	Liverpool	h	1-3	Berbatov
19/05	Swansea	a	3-0	Kacaniklic, Berbatov, Emanuelson

No	Name	Nat	DoB	Pos	Aps	(s)	Gls
6	Chris Baird	NIR	25/02/82	D	14	(5)	2
9	Dimitar Berbatov	BUL	30/01/81	A	32	(1)	15
17	Matthew Briggs		19/03/91	D	3	(2)	
24	Ashkan Dejagah	IRN	05/07/86	A	13	(8)	
30	Moussa Dembélé	BEL	16/07/87	A	2		
19	Mahamadou Diarra	MLI		M	7	(1)	
16	Damien Duff	IRL	02/03/79	M	27	(4)	3
28	Urby Emanuelson	NED	16/06/86	M	5	(8)	1
33	Eyong Enoh	CMR	23/03/86	M	8	(1)	
12	Emmanuel Frimpong	GHA	10/01/92	M	2	(4)	
5	Brede Paulsen Hangeland	NOR	20/06/81	D	35		
18	Aaron Hughes	NIR	08/11/79	D	23	(1)	
31	Alex Kacaniklic	SWE	13/08/91	M	16	(4)	4
14	Georgios Karagounis	GRE	06/03/77	M	20	(5)	1
8	Pajtim Kasami	SUI	02/06/92	M		(2)	
2	Stephen Kelly	IRL	06/09/83	D		(2)	
21	Kerim Frei	TUR	19/11/93	M	2	(5)	
25	Stanislav Manolev	BUL		D	4	(1)	
10	Mladen Petrić	CRO	01/01/81	A	9	(14)	5
15	Kieran Richardson		21/10/84	M	12	(2)	1
27	Sascha Riether	GER	23/03/83	D	35		1
3	John Arne Riise	NOR	24/09/80	D	29	(2)	
20	Hugo Rodallega	COL	25/07/85	A	14	(15)	3
11	Bryan Ruiz	CRC	18/08/85	A	26	(3)	5
1	Mark Schwarzer	AUS	06/10/72	G	36		
4	Philippe Senderos	SUI	14/02/85	D	18	(3)	
7	Steve Sidwell		14/12/82	M	24	(4)	4
40	Alex Smith		31/10/91	D		(1)	
12	David Stockdale		20/09/85	G	2		

LIVERPOOL FC

Manager: Brendan Rodgers (NIR)
1892 • Anfield (45,362) • liverpoolfc.com
Major honours
European Champion Clubs' Cup/UEFA Champions
League (5) 1977, 1978, 1981, 1984, 2005;
UEFA Cup (3) 1973, 1976, 2001;
UEFA Super Cup (3) 1977, 2001, 2005;
English League (18) 1901, 1906, 1922, 1923, 1947,
1964, 1966, 1973, 1976, 1977, 1979, 1980, 1982, 1983,
1984, 1986, 1988, 1990;
FA Cup (7) 1965, 1974, 1986, 1989, 1992, 2001, 2006;
League Cup (8) 1981, 1982, 1983, 1984, 1995, 2001,
2003, 2012

2012

Date	Opponent	H/A	Score	Scorers
18/08	West Brom	a	0-3	
26/08	Man. City	h	2-2	Škrtel, Suárez
02/09	Arsenal	h	0-2	
15/09	Sunderland	a	1-1	Suárez
23/09	Man. United	h	1-2	Gerrard
29/09	Norwich	a	5-2	Suárez 3, Nuri, og (Barnett)
07/10	Stoke	h	0-0	
20/10	Reading	h	1-0	Sterling
28/10	Everton	a	2-2	og (Baines), Suárez
04/11	Newcastle	a	1-1	Suárez
11/11	Chelsea	a	1-1	Suárez
17/11	Wigan	h	3-0	Suárez 2, José Enrique
25/11	Swansea	a	0-0	
28/11	Tottenham	a	1-2	og (Bale)
01/12	Southampton	h	1-0	Agger
09/12	West Ham	h	3-2	Johnson, Cole, Shelvey
15/12	Aston Villa	h	1-3	Gerrard
22/12	Fulham	h	4-0	Škrtel, Gerrard, Downing, Suárez
26/12	Stoke	a	1-3	Gerrard (p)
30/12	QPR	a	3-0	Suárez 2, Agger

2013

Date	Opponent	H/A	Score	Scorers
02/01	Sunderland	h	3-0	Sterling, Suárez 2
13/01	Man. United	a	1-2	Sturridge
19/01	Norwich	h	5-0	Henderson, Suárez, Sturridge, Gerrard, og (R Bennett)
30/01	Arsenal	a	2-2	Suárez, Henderson
03/02	Man. City	a	2-2	Sturridge, Gerrard
11/02	West Brom	h	0-2	
17/02	Swansea	h	5-0	Gerrard (p), Coutinho, José Enrique, Suárez, Sturridge (p)
02/03	Wigan	a	4-0	Downing, Suárez 3
10/03	Tottenham	h	3-2	Suárez, Downing, Gerrard (p)
16/03	Southampton	a	1-3	Coutinho
31/03	Aston Villa	a	2-1	Henderson, Gerrard (p)
07/04	West Ham	h	0-0	
13/04	Reading	a	0-0	
21/04	Chelsea	h	2-2	Sturridge, Suárez
27/04	Newcastle	a	6-0	Agger, Henderson 2, Sturridge 2, Borini
05/05	Everton	h	0-0	
12/05	Fulham	a	3-1	Sturridge 3
19/05	QPR	h	1-0	Coutinho

No	Name	Nat	DoB	Pos	Aps	(s)	Gls
5	Daniel Agger	DEN	12/12/84	D	35		3
24	Joe Allen	WAL	14/03/90	M	21	(6)	
11	Oussama Assaidi	MAR	15/08/88	M		(4)	
29	Fabio Borini	ITA	29/03/91	A	5	(8)	1
23	Jamie Carragher		28/01/78	D	16	(8)	
9	Andy Carroll		06/01/89	A		(2)	
35	Conor Coady		25/02/93	D		(1)	
16	Sebastián Coates	URU	07/10/90	D	2	(3)	
10	Joe Cole		08/11/81	M		(6)	1
10	Philippe Coutinho	BRA	12/06/92	M	12	(1)	3
19	Stewart Downing		22/07/84	M	25	(4)	3
8	Steven Gerrard		30/05/80	M	36		9
14	Jordan Henderson		17/06/90	M	16	(14)	5
44	Jordan Ibe		08/12/95	M		(2)	
2	Glen Johnson		23/08/84	D	36		1
1	Brad Jones	AUS	19/03/82	G	7		
3	José Enrique	ESP	23/01/86	D	25	(4)	2
34	Martin Kelly		27/04/90	D	4		
21	Lucas	BRA	09/01/87	M	24	(2)	
4	Nuri Şahin	TUR	05/09/88	M	7		1
25	Pepe Reina	ESP	31/08/82	G	31		
33	Jonjo Shelvey		27/02/92	M	9	(10)	1
37	Martin Škrtel	SVK	15/12/84	D	23	(2)	2
31	Raheem Sterling		08/12/94	A	19	(5)	2
15	Daniel Sturridge		01/09/89	A	11	(3)	10
7	Luis Suárez	URU	24/01/87	A	33		23
30	Suso	ESP	19/11/93	M	8	(6)	
47	Andre Wisdom		09/05/93	D	12		

MANCHESTER CITY FC

Manager: Roberto Mancini (ITA);
(13/05/13) (Brian Kidd)
1894 • Etihad Stadium (47,715) • mcfc.co.uk
Major honours
UEFA Cup Winners' Cup (1) 1970;
English League (3) 1937, 1968, 2012;
FA Cup (5) 1904, 1934, 1956, 1969, 2011;
League Cup (2) 1970, 1976

2012

Date	Opponent	H/A	Score	Scorers
19/08	Southampton	h	3-2	Tévez, Džeko, Nasri
26/08	Liverpool	a	2-2	Y Touré, Tévez
01/09	QPR	h	3-1	Y Touré, Džeko, Tévez
15/09	Stoke	a	1-1	Javi García
23/09	Arsenal	h	1-1	Lescott
29/09	Fulham	a	2-1	Agüero, Džeko
06/10	Sunderland	h	3-0	Kolarov, Agüero, Milner
20/10	West Brom	a	2-1	Džeko 2
27/10	Swansea	h	1-0	Tévez
03/11	West Ham	h	0-0	
11/11	Tottenham	h	2-1	Agüero, Džeko
17/11	Aston Villa	h	5-0	Silva, Agüero 2 (1p), Tévez 2 (1p)
25/11	Chelsea	a	0-0	
28/11	Wigan	a	2-0	Balotelli, Milner
01/12	Everton	h	1-1	Tévez (p)
09/12	Man. United	h	2-3	Y Touré, Zabaleta
15/12	Newcastle	a	3-1	Agüero, Javi García, Y Touré
22/12	Reading	h	1-0	Barry
26/12	Sunderland	a	0-1	
29/12	Norwich	a	4-3	Džeko 2, Agüero, og (Bunn)

2013

Date	Opponent	H/A	Score	Scorers
01/01	Stoke	h	3-0	Zabaleta, Džeko, Agüero (p)
13/01	Arsenal	a	2-0	Milner, Džeko
19/01	Fulham	h	2-0	Silva 2
29/01	QPR	a	0-0	
03/02	Liverpool	h	2-2	Džeko, Agüero
09/02	Southampton	a	1-3	Džeko
24/02	Chelsea	h	2-0	Y Touré, Tévez
04/03	Aston Villa	a	1-0	Tévez
16/03	Everton	a	0-2	
30/03	Newcastle	a	4-0	Tévez, Silva, Kompany, Y Touré
08/04	Man. United	a	2-1	Milner, Agüero
17/04	Wigan	h	1-0	Tévez
21/04	Tottenham	a	1-3	Nasri
07/05	West Ham	h	2-1	Agüero, Y Touré
04/05	Swansea	a	0-0	
07/05	West Brom	h	1-0	Džeko
14/05	Reading	a	2-0	Agüero, Džeko
19/05	Norwich	h	2-3	Rodwell 2

No	Name	Nat	DoB	Pos	Aps	(s)	Gls
16	Sergio Agüero	ARG	02/06/88	A	22	(8)	12
45	Mario Balotelli	ITA	12/08/90	A	7	(1)	1
18	Gareth Barry		23/02/81	M	27	(4)	1
22	Gaël Clichy	FRA	26/07/85	D	26	(2)	
34	Nigel de Jong	NED	30/11/84	M	1		
10	Edin Džeko	BIH	17/03/86	A	16	(16)	14
1	Joe Hart		19/04/87	G	38		
14	Javi García	ESP	08/02/87	M	17	(7)	2
13	Aleksandar Kolarov	SRB	10/11/85	D	11	(9)	1
4	Vincent Kompany	BEL	10/04/86	D	26		1
6	Joleon Lescott		16/08/82	D	17	(9)	1
7	Maicon	BRA	26/07/81	D	4	(5)	
7	James Milner		04/01/86	M	19	(7)	4
8	Samir Nasri	FRA	26/06/87	M	22	(6)	2
33	Matija Nastasić	SRB	28/03/93	D	21		
62	Abdul Razak	CIV	11/11/92	M		(3)	
44	Karim Rekik	NED	02/12/94	D	1		
2	Micah Richards		24/06/88	D	7		
17	Jack Rodwell		11/03/91	M	6	(5)	2
21	David Silva	ESP	08/01/86	M	29	(3)	4
11	Scott Sinclair		26/03/89	M	2	(9)	
32	Carlos Tévez	ARG	05/02/84	A	28	(6)	11
28	Kolo Touré	CIV	19/03/81	D	10	(5)	
42	Yaya Touré	CIV	13/05/83	M	32		7
5	Pablo Zabaleta	ARG	16/01/85	D	29	(1)	2

MANCHESTER UNITED FC

Manager: Sir Alex Ferguson (SCO)
1878 • Old Trafford (76,212) • manutd.com
Major honours
European Champion Clubs' Cup/UEFA Champions League (3) 1968, 1999, 2008;
UEFA Cup Winners' Cup (1) 1991;
UEFA Super Cup (1) 1991;
European/South American Cup (1) 1999;
FIFA Club World Cup (1) 2008;
English League (20) 1908, 1911, 1952, 1956, 1957, 1965, 1967, 1993, 1994, 1996, 1997, 1999, 2000, 2001, 2003, 2007, 2008, 2009, 2011, 2013;
FA Cup (11) 1909, 1948, 1963, 1977, 1983, 1985, 1990, 1994, 1996, 1999, 2004;
League Cup (4) 1992, 2006, 2009, 2010

2012

20/08	Everton	a	0-1	
25/08	Fulham	h	3-2	Van Persie, Kagawa, Rafael
02/09	Southampton	a	3-2	Van Persie 3
15/09	Wigan	h	4-0	Scholes, Hernández, Büttner, Powell
23/09	Liverpool	a	2-1	Rafael, Van Persie (p)
29/09	Tottenham	h	2-3	Nani, Kagawa
07/10	Newcastle	h	3-0	Evans, Evra, Cleverley
20/10	Stoke	h	4-2	Rooney 2, Van Persie, Welbeck
28/10	Chelsea	a	3-2	og (David Luiz), Van Persie, Hernández
03/11	Arsenal	h	2-1	Van Persie, Evra
10/11	Aston Villa	a	3-2	Hernández 2, og (Vlaar)
17/11	Norwich	a	0-1	
24/11	QPR	h	3-1	Evans, Fletcher, Hernández
28/11	West Ham	h	1-0	Van Persie
01/12	Reading	a	4-3	Anderson, Rooney 2 (1p), Van Persie
09/12	Man. City	a	3-2	Rooney 2, Van Persie
15/12	Sunderland	h	3-1	Van Persie, Cleverley, Rooney
23/12	Swansea	a	1-1	Evra
26/12	Newcastle	h	4-3	Evans, Evra, Van Persie, Hernández
29/12	West Brom	h	2-0	og (McAuley), Van Persie
2013				
01/01	Wigan	a	4-0	Hernández 2, Van Persie 2
13/01	Liverpool	h	2-1	Van Persie, Vidić
20/01	Tottenham	a	1-1	Van Persie
30/01	Southampton	h	2-1	Rooney 2
02/02	Fulham	a	1-0	Rooney
10/02	Everton	h	2-0	Giggs, Van Persie
23/02	QPR	a	2-0	Rafael, Giggs
02/03	Norwich	h	4-0	Kagawa 3, Rooney
16/03	Reading	h	1-0	Rooney
30/03	Sunderland	a	1-0	og (Bramble)
08/04	Man. City	h	1-2	og (Kompany)
14/04	Stoke	a	2-0	Carrick, Van Persie (p)
17/04	West Ham	a	2-2	Valencia, Van Persie
22/04	Aston Villa	h	3-0	Van Persie 3
28/04	Arsenal	a	1-1	Van Persie (p)
05/05	Chelsea	h	0-1	
12/05	Swansea	h	2-1	Hernández, Ferdinand
19/05	West Brom	a	5-5	Kagawa, og (Olsson), Büttner, Van Persie, Hernández

No	Name	Nat	DoB	Pos	Aps	(s)	Gls
8	Anderson	BRA	13/04/88	M	9	(8)	1
28	Alexander Büttner	NED	11/02/89	D	4	(1)	2
16	Michael Carrick		28/07/81	M	34	(2)	1
23	Tom Cleverley		12/08/89	M	18	(4)	2
1	David De Gea	ESP	07/11/90	G	28		
6	Jonny Evans	NIR	03/01/88	D	21	(2)	3
3	Patrice Evra	FRA	15/05/81	D	34		4
5	Rio Ferdinand		07/11/78	D	26	(2)	1
24	Darren Fletcher	SCO	01/02/84	M	2	(1)	1
11	Ryan Giggs	WAL	29/11/73	M	12	(10)	2
14	Javier Hernández	MEX	01/06/88	A	9	(13)	10
4	Phil Jones		21/02/92	D	13	(4)	
26	Shinji Kagawa	JPN	17/03/89	M	17	(3)	6
13	Anders Lindegaard	DEN	13/04/84	G	10		
17	Nani	POR	17/11/86	M	7	(4)	1
25	Nick Powell		23/03/94	M		(2)	1
2	Rafael	BRA	09/07/90	D	27	(1)	3
10	Wayne Rooney		24/10/85	A	22	(5)	12
22	Paul Scholes		16/11/74	M	8	(8)	1
12	Chris Smalling		22/11/89	D	10	(5)	
7	Luis Antonio Valencia	ECU	04/08/85	M	24	(6)	1
20	Robin van Persie	NED	06/08/83	A	35	(3)	26
15	Nemanja Vidić	SRB	21/10/81	D	18	(1)	1
19	Danny Welbeck		26/11/90	A	13	(14)	1
18	Ashley Young		09/07/85	M	17	(2)	

NEWCASTLE UNITED FC

Manager: Alan Pardew
1881 • St James' Park (52,387) • nufc.co.uk
Major honours
Inter Cities Fairs Cup (1) 1969;
English League (4) 1905, 1907, 1909, 1927;
FA Cup (6) 1910, 1924, 1932, 1951, 1952, 1955

2012

18/08	Tottenham	h	2-1	Ba, Ben Arfa (p)
25/08	Chelsea	a	0-2	
02/09	Aston Villa	h	1-1	Ben Arfa
17/09	Everton	a	2-2	Ba 2
23/09	Norwich	h	1-0	Ba
29/09	Reading	a	2-2	Ba 2
07/10	Man. United	h	0-3	
21/10	Sunderland	a	1-1	Cabaye
28/10	West Brom	h	2-1	Ba, Cissé
04/11	Liverpool	a	1-1	Cabaye
11/11	West Ham	h	0-1	
17/11	Swansea	h	1-2	Ba
25/11	Southampton	a	0-2	
28/11	Stoke	a	1-2	Cissé
03/12	Wigan	h	3-0	Ba 2 (1p), Bigirimana
10/12	Fulham	a	1-2	Ben Arfa
15/12	Man. City	h	1-3	Ba
22/12	QPR	h	1-0	Shola Ameobi
26/12	Man. United	a	3-4	Perch, og (Evans), Cissé
29/12	Arsenal	a	3-7	Ba 2, Marveaux
2013				
02/01	Everton	h	1-2	Cissé
12/01	Norwich	a	0-0	
19/01	Reading	h	1-2	Cabaye
29/01	Aston Villa	a	2-1	Cissé, Cabaye
02/02	Chelsea	h	3-2	Gutiérrez, Sissoko 2
09/02	Tottenham	a	1-2	Gouffran
24/02	Southampton	h	4-2	Sissoko, Cissé, Cabaye (p), og (Hooiveld)
02/03	Swansea	a	0-1	
10/03	Stoke	h	2-1	Cabaye, Cissé
17/03	Wigan	a	1-2	Santon
30/03	Man. City	h	0-4	
07/04	Fulham	h	1-0	Cissé
14/04	Sunderland	h	0-3	
20/04	West Brom	a	1-1	Gouffran
27/04	Liverpool	h	0-6	
04/05	West Ham	a	0-0	
12/05	QPR	a	2-1	Ben Arfa (p), Gouffran
19/05	Arsenal	h	0-1	

No	Name	Nat	DoB	Pos	Aps	(s)	Gls
28	Sammy Ameobi		01/05/92	A	1	(7)	
23	Shola Ameobi	NGA	12/10/81	A	4	(19)	1
8	Vurnon Anita	NED	04/04/89	M	17	(8)	
19	Demba Ba	SEN	25/05/85	A	19	(1)	13
10	Hatem Ben Arfa	FRA	07/03/87	M	16	(3)	4
20	Gaël Bigirimana		22/10/93	M	3	(10)	1
4	Yohan Cabaye	FRA	14/01/86	M	25	(1)	6
41	Adam Campbell		01/01/95	A		(3)	
9	Papiss Cissé	SEN	03/06/85	A	35	(1)	8
2	Fabricio Coloccini	ARG	22/01/82	D	22		
26	Mathieu Debuchy	FRA	28/07/85	D	14		
21	Rob Elliot	IRL	30/04/86	G	9	(1)	
31	Shane Ferguson	NIR	12/07/91	M	4	(5)	
15	Dan Gosling		02/02/90	M		(3)	
11	Yoan Gouffran	FRA	25/05/86	A	14	(1)	
18	Jonás Gutiérrez	ARG	05/07/83	M	34		1
19	Massadio Haïdara	FRA	02/12/92	D	2	(2)	
37	Steve Harper		14/03/75	G	5	(1)	
1	Tim Krul	NED	03/04/88	G	24		
22	Sylvain Marveaux	FRA	15/04/86	M	10	(12)	1
25	Gabriel Obertan	FRA	26/02/89	A	4	(10)	
14	James Perch		28/09/85	D	19	(8)	1
30	Nile Ranger		11/04/91	A		(2)	
3	Davide Santon	ITA	02/01/91	D	31		1
5	Danny Simpson		04/01/87	D	18	(1)	
7	Moussa Sissoko	FRA	16/08/89	M	12		3
34	James Tavernier		31/10/91	D		(2)	
16	Ryan Taylor		19/08/84	M		(1)	
27	Steven Taylor		23/01/86	D	24	(1)	
24	Cheick Tioté	CIV	21/06/86	M	22	(2)	
6	Mike Williamson		08/11/83	D	19		
13	Mapou Yanga-Mbiwa	FRA	15/05/89	D	11	(3)	

NORWICH CITY FC

Manager: Chris Hughton (IRL)
1902 • Carrow Road (26,034) • canaries.co.uk
Major honours
League Cup (2) 1962, 1985

2012

18/08	Fulham	a	0-5	
25/08	QPR	h	1-1	Jackson
01/09	Tottenham	a	1-1	Snodgrass
15/09	West Ham	h	0-0	
23/09	Newcastle	a	0-1	
29/09	Liverpool	h	2-5	Morison, Holt
06/10	Chelsea	a	1-4	Holt
20/10	Arsenal	h	1-0	Holt
27/10	Aston Villa	a	1-1	Turner
03/11	Stoke	h	1-0	Johnson
10/11	Reading	a	0-0	
17/11	Man. United	h	1-0	Pilkington
24/11	Everton	a	1-1	Bassong
28/11	Southampton	a	1-1	Snodgrass
02/12	Sunderland	h	2-1	Bassong, Pilkington
08/12	Swansea	a	4-3	Whittaker, Bassong, Holt, Snodgrass
15/12	Wigan	h	2-1	Pilkington, Hoolahan
22/12	West Brom	h	1-2	Snodgrass
26/12	Chelsea	h	0-1	
29/12	Man. City	h	3-4	Pilkington, R Martin 2
2013				
01/01	West Ham	a	1-2	R Martin
12/01	Newcastle	h	0-0	
19/01	Liverpool	h	0-5	
30/01	Tottenham	h	1-1	Hoolahan
02/02	QPR	a	0-0	
09/02	Fulham	h	0-0	
23/02	Everton	h	2-1	Kamara, Holt
02/03	Man. United	a	0-4	
09/03	Southampton	h	0-0	
17/03	Sunderland	a	1-1	Hoolahan
30/03	Wigan	a	0-3	
06/04	Swansea	h	2-2	Snodgrass, Turner
13/04	Arsenal	a	1-3	Turner
20/04	Reading	h	2-1	R Bennett, E Bennett
27/04	Stoke	a	0-1	
04/05	Aston Villa	h	1-2	Holt (p)
12/05	West Brom	h	4-0	Snodgrass, Holt, og (McAuley), Howson
19/05	Man. City	a	3-2	Pilkington, Holt, Howson

No	Name	Nat	DoB	Pos	Aps	(s)	Gls
20	Leon Barnett		30/11/85	D	6	(2)	
	Sébastien Bassong	CMR	09/07/86	D	34		3
19	Luciano Becchio	ARG	28/12/83	A	2	(6)	
17	Elliott Bennett		18/12/88	M	9	(15)	1
24	Ryan Bennett		06/03/90	D	10	(5)	1
28	Mark Bunn		16/11/84	G	22	(1)	
42	Lee Camp	NIR	22/08/84	G	1	(2)	
15	David Fox		13/12/83	M		(2)	
18	Javier Garrido	ESP	15/03/85	D	34		
9	Grant Holt		12/04/81	A	28	(6)	8
14	Wes Hoolahan	IRL	20/05/82	M	28	(5)	3
8	Jonny Howson		21/05/88	M	22	(8)	2
10	Simeon Jackson	CAN	28/03/87	A	5	(8)	1
4	Bradley Johnson		28/04/87	M	37		1
16	Kei Kamara	SLE	01/09/84	A	7	(4)	1
37	Harry Kane		28/07/93	A	1	(2)	
25	Chris Martin		04/11/88	A		(1)	
2	Russell Martin	SCO	04/01/86	D	30	(1)	3
16	Steve Morison	WAL	29/08/83	A	4	(15)	1
12	Anthony Pilkington	IRL	06/06/88	M	25	(5)	5
	John Ruddy		24/10/86	G	15		
7	Robert Snodgrass	SCO	07/09/87	M	35	(2)	6
11	Andrew Surman		20/08/86	M	4		
17	Alexander Tettey	NOR	04/04/86	M	21	(6)	
23	Marc Tierney		23/08/85	D	1		
6	Michael Turner		09/11/83	D	25	(1)	3
3	Steven Whittaker	SCO	16/06/84	D	12	(1)	1

QUEENS PARK RANGERS FC

Manager: Mark Hughes (WAL);
(23/11/12) Harry Redknapp
1882 • Loftus Road (18,682) • qpr.co.uk
Major honours
League Cup (1) 1967

2012

18/08	Swansea	h	0-5	
25/08	Norwich	a	1-1	Zamora
01/09	Man. City	a	1-3	Zamora
15/09	Chelsea	h	0-0	
23/09	Tottenham	a	1-2	Zamora
01/10	West Ham	h	1-2	Taarabt
06/10	West Brom	a	2-3	Taarabt, Granero
21/10	Everton	h	1-1	og (Baines)
27/10	Arsenal	a	0-1	
04/11	Reading	h	1-1	Cissé
10/11	Stoke	a	0-1	
17/11	Southampton	h	1-3	Hoilett
24/11	Man. United	a	1-3	Mackie
27/11	Sunderland	a	0-0	
01/12	Aston Villa	h	1-1	Mackie
08/12	Wigan	a	2-2	Nelsen, Cissé
15/12	Fulham	h	2-1	Taarabt 2
22/12	Newcastle	a	0-1	
26/12	West Brom	h	1-2	Cissé
30/12	Liverpool	h	0-3	

2013

02/01	Chelsea	a	1-0	Wright-Phillips
12/01	Tottenham	h	0-0	
19/01	West Ham	a	1-1	Rémy
29/01	Man. City	h	0-0	
02/02	Norwich	h	0-0	
09/02	Swansea	a	1-4	Zamora
23/02	Man. United	a	0-2	
02/03	Southampton	a	2-1	Rémy, Bothroyd
09/03	Sunderland	h	3-1	Rémy, Townsend, Jenas
16/03	Aston Villa	a	2-3	Jenas, Townsend
01/04	Fulham	a	2-3	Taarabt, Rémy
07/04	Wigan	h	1-1	Rémy
13/04	Everton	a	0-2	
20/04	Stoke	h	0-2	
28/04	Reading	a	0-0	
04/05	Arsenal	h	0-1	
12/05	Newcastle	h	1-2	Rémy (p)
19/05	Liverpool	a	0-1	

No	Name	Nat	DoB	Pos	Aps	(s)	Gls
21	Tal Ben Haim	ISR	31/03/82	D	2	(1)	
19	José Bosingwa	POR	24/08/82	D	22	(1)	
37	Jay Bothroyd		05/05/82	A	2	(2)	1
9	Djibril Cissé	FRA	12/08/81	A	12	(6)	3
4	Shaun Derry		06/12/77	M	10	(8)	
42	Samba Diakité	MLI	24/01/89	D	11	(3)	
18	Kieron Dyer		29/12/78	M	1	(3)	
20	Fábio	BRA	09/07/90	D	13	(8)	
32	Alejandro Faurlín	ARG	09/08/86	M	10	(1)	
5	Anton Ferdinand		18/02/85	D	10	(3)	
8	Esteban Granero	ESP	02/07/87	M	19	(5)	1
1	Robert Green		18/01/80	G	14	(2)	
27	Michael Harriman	IRL	23/10/92	D	1		
6	Clint Hill		19/10/78	D	31		
23	David 'Junior' Hoilett	CAN	05/06/90	A	15	(11)	1
16	Jermaine Jenas		18/02/83	M	8	(4)	2
8	Andrew Johnson		10/02/81	A	2	(1)	
33	Júlio César	BRA	03/09/79	G	24		
12	Jamie Mackie	SCO	22/09/85	A	17	(12)	2
40	Stéphane Mbia	CMR	20/05/86	M	29		
17	Ryan Nelsen	NZL	18/10/77	D	21		1
15	Nedum Onuoha		12/11/86	D	15	(8)	
7	Park Ji-sung	KOR	25/02/81	M	15	(5)	
18	Loïc Rémy	FRA	02/01/87	A	13	(1)	6
5	Christopher Samba	CGO	23/08/84	D	10		
10	Adel Taarabt	MAR	24/05/89	M	25	(6)	5
29	Andros Townsend		16/07/91	M	12		2
3	Armand Traoré	SEN	10/08/89	D	24	(2)	
11	Shaun Wright-Phillips		25/10/81	M	14	(6)	1
25	Bobby Zamora		16/01/81	A	16	(5)	4

READING FC

Manager: Brian McDermott; (26/03/13) Nigel Adkins
1871 • Madejski Stadium (24,082) • readingfc.co.uk

2012

18/08	Stoke	h	1-1	Le Fondre (p)
22/08	Chelsea	a	2-4	Pogrebnyak, Guthrie
16/09	Tottenham	h	1-3	Robson-Kanu
22/09	West Brom	a	0-1	
29/09	Newcastle	h	2-2	Kébé, Hunt
06/10	Swansea	a	2-2	Pogrebnyak, Hunt
20/10	Liverpool	a	0-1	
27/10	Fulham	h	3-3	Leigertwood, McCleary, Robson-Kanu
04/11	QPR	a	1-1	Gorkšs
10/11	Norwich	h	0-0	
17/11	Everton	h	2-1	Le Fondre 2 (1p)
24/11	Wigan	a	2-3	Morrison, og (Al Habsi)
27/11	Aston Villa	a	0-1	
01/12	Man. United	h	3-4	Robson-Kanu, Le Fondre, Morrison
08/12	Southampton	a	0-1	
11/12	Sunderland	a	0-3	
17/12	Arsenal	h	2-5	Le Fondre, Kébé
22/12	Man. City	h	0-1	
26/12	Swansea	h	0-0	
29/12	West Ham	h	1-0	Pogrebnyak

2013

01/01	Tottenham	a	1-3	Pogrebnyak
12/01	West Brom	h	3-2	Kébé, Le Fondre (p), Pogrebnyak
19/01	Newcastle	a	2-1	Le Fondre 2
30/01	Chelsea	h	2-2	Le Fondre 2
02/02	Sunderland	h	2-1	Kébé 2
09/02	Stoke	a	1-2	Mariappa
23/02	Wigan	a	0-3	
02/03	Everton	a	1-3	Robson-Kanu
09/03	Aston Villa	h	1-2	og (Baker)
16/03	Man. United	a	0-1	
30/03	Arsenal	a	1-4	Robson-Kanu
06/04	Southampton	h	0-2	
13/04	Liverpool	h	0-0	
20/04	Norwich	h	1-2	McCleary
28/04	QPR	h	0-0	
04/05	Fulham	a	4-2	Robson-Kanu 2 (1p), Le Fondre, Karacan
14/05	Man. City	h	0-2	
19/05	West Ham	a	2-4	McCleary, Le Fondre

No	Name	Nat	DoB	Pos	Aps	(s)	Gls
28	Hope Akpan		14/08/91	M	6	(3)	
30	Nick Blackman		11/11/89	A	3	(8)	
24	Shaun Cummings		25/02/89	D	9		
29	Daniel Carriço	POR	04/08/88	D	1	(2)	
1	Adam Federici	AUS	31/01/85	G	21		
17	Kaspars Gorkšs	LVA	06/11/81	D	14		1
2	Chris Gunter	WAL	21/07/89	D	20		
20	Danny Guthrie		18/04/87	M	19	(2)	1
23	Ian Harte	IRL	31/08/77	D	15	(1)	
19	Noel Hunt	IRL	26/12/82	M	10	(14)	2
4	Jem Karacan	TUR	21/02/89	M	21		1
14	Jimmy Kébé	MLI	19/01/84	M	16	(2)	5
27	Stephen Kelly	IRL	06/09/83	D	16		
9	Adam Le Fondre		02/12/86	A	11	(23)	12
8	Mikele Leigertwood	ATG	12/11/82	M	29	(1)	1
6	Adrian Mariappa	JAM	03/10/86	D	29		1
11	Jobi McAnuff	JAM	09/11/81	M	38		
21	Alex McCarthy		03/12/89	G	13		
12	Garath McCleary	JAM	15/05/87	M	15	(16)	3
15	Sean Morrison		08/01/91	D	15	(1)	2
5	Alex Pearce	IRL	09/11/88	D	18	(1)	
7	Pavel Pogrebnyak	RUS	08/11/83	A	26	(3)	5
33	Jason Roberts	GRN	25/01/78	A	8	(3)	
19	Hal Robson-Kanu	WAL	21/05/89	A	13	(12)	7
44	Dominic Samuel		01/04/94	A		(1)	
3	Nicky Shorey		19/02/81	D	16	(1)	
16	Jay Tabb	IRL	21/02/84	M	12		
41	Stuart Taylor		28/11/80	G	4		

SOUTHAMPTON FC

Manager: Nigel Adkins;
(18/01/13) Mauricio Pochettino (ARG)
1885 • St Mary's Stadium (32,689) • saintsfc.co.uk
Major honours
FA Cup (1) 1976

2012

19/08	Man. City	a	2-3	Lambert, S Davis
25/08	Wigan	h	0-2	
02/09	Man. United	h	2-3	Lambert, Schneiderlin
15/09	Arsenal	a	1-6	Fox
22/09	Aston Villa	h	4-1	Lambert 2 (1p), Clyne, Puncheon
29/09	Everton	a	1-3	Ramírez
07/10	Fulham	h	2-2	José Fonte 2
20/10	West Ham	a	1-4	Lallana
28/10	Tottenham	h	1-2	Rodriguez
05/11	West Brom	a	0-2	
10/11	Swansea	h	1-1	Schneiderlin
17/11	QPR	a	3-1	Lambert, Puncheon, og (Ferdinand)
25/11	Newcastle	h	2-0	Lallana, Ramírez
28/11	Norwich	h	1-1	Lambert
01/12	Liverpool	a	0-1	
08/12	Reading	h	1-0	Puncheon
22/12	Sunderland	a	0-1	
26/12	Fulham	a	1-1	Lambert (p)
29/12	Stoke	a	3-3	Lambert, Rodriguez, og (Wilkinson)

2013

01/01	Arsenal	h	1-1	Ramírez
12/01	Aston Villa	a	1-0	Lambert (p)
16/01	Chelsea	a	2-2	Lambert, Puncheon
21/01	Everton	h	0-0	
30/01	Man. United	a	1-2	Rodriguez
02/02	Wigan	a	2-2	Lambert, Schneiderlin
09/02	Man. City	h	3-1	Puncheon, S Davis, og (Barry)
24/02	Newcastle	a	2-4	Schneiderlin, Lambert
02/03	QPR	h	1-2	Ramírez
09/03	Norwich	a	0-0	
16/03	Liverpool	h	3-1	Schneiderlin, Lambert, Rodriguez
30/03	Chelsea	h	2-1	Rodriguez, Lambert
06/04	Reading	a	2-0	Rodriguez, Lallana
13/04	West Ham	h	1-1	Ramírez
20/04	Swansea	a	0-0	
27/04	West Brom	h	0-3	
04/05	Tottenham	a	0-1	
12/05	Sunderland	a	1-1	Puncheon
19/05	Stoke	h	1-1	Lambert

No	Name	Nat	DoB	Pos	Aps	(s)	Gls
31	Artur Boruc	POL	20/02/80	G	20		
27	Richard Chaplow		02/02/85	M		(3)	
2	Nathaniel Clyne		05/04/91	D	34		1
18	Jack Cork		25/06/89	M	28		
1	Kelvin Davis		29/09/76	G	9	(1)	
8	Steven Davis	NIR	01/01/85	M	22	(10)	2
33	Steve De Ridder	BEL	25/02/87	M		(4)	
13	Danny Fox	SCO	29/05/86	D	14	(6)	1
12	Paulo Gazzaniga	ARG	02/01/92	G	9		
21	Guly do Prado	BRA	31/12/81	M	8	(10)	
5	Jos Hooiveld	NED	22/04/83	D	23	(2)	
6	José Fonte	POR	22/12/83	D	25	(2)	2
20	Adam Lallana		10/05/88	M	26	(4)	3
7	Rickie Lambert		16/02/82	A	35	(3)	15
24	Emmanuel Mayuka	ZAM	21/11/90	A	1	(10)	
42	Jason Puncheon		26/06/86	M	25	(7)	6
10	Gastón Ramírez	URU	02/12/90	M	20	(6)	5
29	Ben Reeves		19/11/91	D		(3)	
22	Frazer Richardson		29/10/82	D	2	(3)	
9	Jay Rodriguez		29/07/89	A	24	(11)	6
4	Morgan Schneiderlin	FRA	08/11/89	M	36		5
11	Billy Sharp		05/02/86	A		(2)	
23	Luke Shaw		12/07/95	D	22	(3)	
16	James Ward-Prowse		01/11/94	M	4	(11)	
3	Maya Yoshida	JPN	24/08/88	D	31	(1)	

STOKE CITY FC

Manager: Tony Pulis (WAL)
1868 • Britannia Stadium (28,218) • stokecityfc.com
Major honours
League Cup (1) 1972

2012

18/08	Reading	a	1-1	*Kightly*
26/08	Arsenal	h	0-0	
01/09	Wigan	a	2-2	*Walters (p), Crouch*
15/09	Man. City	h	1-1	*Crouch*
22/09	Chelsea	a	0-1	
29/09	Swansea	h	2-0	*Crouch 2*
07/10	Liverpool	a	0-0	
20/10	Man. United	a	2-4	*og (Rooney), Kightly*
27/10	Sunderland	h	0-0	
03/11	Norwich	a	0-1	
10/11	QPR	h	1-0	*Adam*
19/11	West Ham	a	1-1	*Walters*
24/11	Fulham	h	1-0	*Adam*
28/11	Newcastle	h	2-1	*Walters, Jerome*
01/12	West Brom	a	1-0	*Whitehead*
08/12	Aston Villa	a	0-0	
15/12	Everton	h	1-1	*Jones*
22/12	Tottenham	h	0-0	
26/12	Liverpool	h	3-1	*Walters 2, Jones*
29/12	Southampton	h	3-3	*Jones, Upson, Jerome*

2013

01/01	Man. City	a	0-3	
12/01	Chelsea	h	0-4	
19/01	Swansea	a	1-3	*Owen*
20/01	Wigan	h	2-2	*Shawcross, Crouch*
02/02	Arsenal	a	0-1	
09/02	Reading	h	2-1	*Huth, Jerome*
23/02	Fulham	a	0-1	
02/03	West Ham	h	0-1	
10/03	Newcastle	a	1-2	*Walters (p)*
16/03	West Brom	h	0-0	
30/03	Everton	a	0-1	
06/04	Aston Villa	h	1-3	*Kightly*
14/04	Man. United	h	0-2	
20/04	QPR	a	2-0	*Crouch, Walters (p)*
27/04	Norwich	h	1-0	*Adam*
05/05	Sunderland	a	1-1	*Walters*
12/05	Tottenham	h	1-2	*N'Zonzi*
19/05	Southampton	a	1-1	*Crouch*

No	Name	Nat	DoB	Pos	Aps	(s)	Gls
16	Charlie Adam	SCO	10/12/85	M	22	(5)	3
1	Asmir Begovic	BIH	20/06/87	G	38		
2	Geoff Cameron	USA	11/07/85	D	29	(6)	
25	Peter Crouch		30/01/81	A	28	(6)	7
24	Rory Delap	IRL	06/07/76	M		(1)	
13	Maurice Edu	USA	18/04/86	M		(1)	
26	Matthew Etherington		14/08/81	M	21	(10)	
4	Robert Huth	GER	18/08/84	D	35		1
33	Cameron Jerome		14/08/86	A	8	(18)	3
9	Kenwyne Jones	TRI	05/10/84	A	10	(16)	3
21	Michael Kightly		24/01/86	M	14	(8)	3
15	Steven N'Zonzi	FRA	15/12/88	M	35		1
10	Michael Owen		14/12/79	A		(8)	1
8	Wilson Palacios	HON	29/07/84	M		(4)	
7	Jermaine Pennant		15/01/83	M	1		
17	Ryan Shawcross		04/10/87	D	37		1
22	Brek Shea	USA	28/02/90	M		(2)	
30	Ryan Shotton		30/10/88	D	20	(3)	
20	Matthew Upson		18/04/79	D	1		1
19	Jonathan Walters	IRL	20/09/83	A	38		8
6	Glenn Whelan	IRL	13/01/84	M	31	(1)	
18	Dean Whitehead		12/01/82	M	12	(14)	1
28	Andy Wilkinson		06/08/84	D	19	(5)	
12	Marc Wilson	IRL	17/08/87	D	19		

SUNDERLAND AFC

Manager: Martin O'Neill (NIR);
(31/03/13) Paolo Di Canio (ITA)
1879 • Stadium of Light (49,000) • safc.com
Major honours
English League (6) 1892, 1893, 1895, 1902, 1913, 1936;
FA Cup (2) 1937, 1973

2012

18/08	Arsenal	a	0-0	
01/09	Swansea	a	2-2	*Fletcher 2*
15/09	Liverpool	h	1-1	*Fletcher*
22/09	West Ham	a	1-1	*Fletcher*
29/09	Wigan	h	1-0	*Fletcher*
06/10	Man. City	a	0-3	
21/10	Newcastle	h	1-1	*og (Ba)*
27/10	Stoke	a	0-0	
03/11	Aston Villa	h	0-1	
10/11	Everton	a	1-2	*Johnson*
17/11	Fulham	a	3-1	*Fletcher, Cuéllar, Sessegnon*
24/11	West Brom	h	2-4	*Gardner, Sessegnon*
27/11	QPR	h	0-0	
02/12	Norwich	a	1-2	*Gardner*
08/12	Chelsea	h	1-3	*Johnson*
11/12	Reading	h	3-0	*McClean, Fletcher, Sessegnon*
15/12	Man. United	a	1-3	*Campbell*
22/12	Southampton	a	1-0	*Fletcher*
26/12	Man. City	h	1-0	*Johnson*
29/12	Tottenham	h	1-2	*O'Shea*

2013

02/01	Liverpool	a	0-3	
12/01	West Ham	h	3-0	*Larsson, Johnson, McClean*
19/01	Wigan	a	3-2	*Gardner (p), Fletcher 2*
29/01	Swansea	h	0-0	
02/02	Reading	a	1-2	*Gardner (p)*
09/02	Arsenal	h	0-1	
23/02	West Brom	a	1-2	*Sessegnon*
02/03	Fulham	h	2-2	*Gardner (p), Sessegnon*
09/03	QPR	a	1-3	*Fletcher*
17/03	Norwich	h	1-1	*Gardner (p)*
30/03	Man. United	h	0-1	
07/04	Chelsea	a	1-2	*og (Azpilicueta)*
14/04	Newcastle	a	3-0	*Sessegnon, Johnson, Vaughan*
20/04	Everton	h	1-0	*Sessegnon*
29/04	Aston Villa	h	1-6	*Rose*
06/05	Stoke	h	1-1	*O'Shea*
12/05	Southampton	h	1-1	*Bardsley*
19/05	Tottenham	a	0-1	

No	Name	Nat	DoB	Pos	Aps	(s)	Gls
2	Phil Bardsley	SCO	28/06/85	D	11	(7)	1
19	Titus Bramble		21/07/81	D	12	(4)	
9	Fraizer Campbell		13/09/87	A	1	(11)	1
6	Lee Cattermole		21/03/88	M	10		
14	Jack Colback		24/10/89	M	30	(5)	
24	Carlos Cuéllar	ESP	23/08/81	D	26		1
27	Ahmed Elmohamady	EGY	09/09/87	M		(2)	
26	Steven Fletcher	SCO	26/03/87	A	28		11
8	Craig Gardner		25/11/86	M	32	(1)	6
9	Danny Graham		12/08/85	A	11	(2)	
21	Adam Johnson		14/07/87	M	35		5
12	Matthew Kilgallon		08/01/84	D	6		
34	Billy Knott		28/11/92	M		(1)	
7	Sebastian Larsson	SWE	06/06/85	M	36	(2)	1
30	Mikael Mandron	FRA	11/10/94	A		(2)	
18	Abdou Kader Mangane	SEN	23/03/83	D		(2)	
23	James McClean	IRL	22/04/89	M	24	(12)	2
11	James McFadden	SCO	14/04/83	A		(3)	
18	David Meyler	IRL	29/05/89	M		(3)	
22	Simon Mignolet	BEL	06/08/88	G	38		
37	Adam Mitchell	IRL	02/12/94	A		(1)	
4	Alfred N'Diaye	FRA	06/03/90	M	15	(1)	
16	John O'Shea	IRL	30/04/81	D	34		2
11	Kieran Richardson		21/10/84	M	1		
3	Danny Rose		02/06/90	D	25	(2)	1
25	Louis Saha	FRA	08/08/78	A		(11)	
28	Stéphane Sessegnon	BEN	01/06/84	M	34	(1)	7
15	David Vaughan	WAL	18/02/83	M	6	(18)	1
10	Connor Wickham		31/03/93	A	3	(9)	

SWANSEA CITY AFC

Manager: Michael Laudrup (DEN)
1912 • Liberty Stadium (20,520) • swanseacity.net
Major honours
League Cup (1) 2013;
Welsh Cup (10) 1913, 1932, 1950, 1961, 1966, 1981, 1982, 1983, 1989, 1991

2012

18/08	QPR	a	5-0	*Michu 2, Dyer 2, Sinclair*
25/08	West Ham	h	3-0	*Rangel, Michu, Graham*
01/09	Sunderland	h	2-2	*Routledge, Michu*
15/09	Aston Villa	a	0-2	
22/09	Everton	h	0-3	
29/09	Stoke	a	0-2	
06/10	Reading	a	2-2	*Michu, Routledge*
20/10	Wigan	h	2-1	*Pablo Hernández, Michu*
27/10	Man. City	a	0-1	
03/11	Chelsea	h	1-1	*Pablo Hernández*
10/11	Southampton	a	1-1	*Dyer*
17/11	Newcastle	a	2-1	*Michu, De Guzmán*
25/11	Liverpool	h	0-0	
28/11	West Brom	h	3-1	*Michu, Routledge 2*
01/12	Arsenal	a	2-0	*Michu 2*
08/12	Norwich	h	3-4	*Michu 2, De Guzmán*
16/12	Tottenham	a	0-1	
23/12	Man. United	h	1-1	*Michu*
26/12	Reading	h	0-0	
29/12	Fulham	a	2-1	*Graham, De Guzmán*

2013

01/01	Aston Villa	h	2-2	*Routledge, Graham*
12/01	Everton	a	0-0	
19/01	Stoke	h	3-1	*Davies, De Guzmán 2*
29/01	Sunderland	a	0-0	
02/02	West Ham	a	0-1	
09/02	QPR	h	4-1	*Michu 2, Rangel, Pablo Hernández*
17/02	Liverpool	a	0-5	
02/03	Newcastle	h	1-0	*Moore*
09/03	West Brom	a	1-2	*Moore*
16/03	Arsenal	h	0-2	
20/03	Tottenham	a	1-2	*Michu*
06/04	Norwich	a	2-2	*Michu, Moore*
20/04	Southampton	h	0-0	
28/04	Chelsea	a	0-2	
04/05	Man. City	h	0-0	
07/05	Wigan	a	3-2	*Rangel, Shechter, Tiendalli*
12/05	Man. United	h	1-2	*Michu*
19/05	Fulham	h	0-3	

No	Name	Nat	DoB	Pos	Aps	(s)	Gls
26	Kemy Agustien	NED	20/08/86	M	4	(14)	
2	Kyle Bartley		22/05/91	D	1	(1)	
4	Leon Britton		16/09/82	M	30	(3)	
4	Chico Flores	ESP	06/03/87	D	26		
33	Ben Davies	WAL	24/04/93	D	33	(4)	1
20	Jonathan de Guzmán	NED	13/09/87	M	33	(4)	5
12	Nathan Dyer		29/11/87	M	25	(12)	3
27	Mark Gower		05/10/78	M		(1)	
9	Danny Graham		12/08/85	A	10	(8)	3
24	Ki Sung-yong	KOR	24/01/89	M	20	(9)	
14	Roland Lamah	BEL	31/12/87	M	1	(4)	
9	Michu	ESP	21/03/86	A	35		18
16	Garry Monk		06/03/79	D	10	(1)	
19	Luke Moore		13/02/86	A	4	(13)	3
11	Pablo Hernández	ESP	11/04/85	M	27	(3)	3
22	Ángel Rangel	ESP	26/10/82	D	30	(3)	3
15	Wayne Routledge		07/01/85	M	30	(6)	5
11	Itay Shechter	ISR	22/02/87	A	7	(11)	1
11	Scott Sinclair		26/03/89	M		(1)	1
5	Alan Tate		02/09/82	D	2	(1)	
3	Neil Taylor	WAL	07/02/89	D	4	(2)	
21	Dwight Tiendalli	NED	21/10/85	D	11	(3)	1
25	Gerhard Tremmel	GER	16/11/78	G	12	(2)	
1	Michel Vorm	NED	20/10/83	G	26		
6	Ashley Williams	WAL	23/08/84	D	37		

TOTTENHAM HOTSPUR FC

Manager: André Villas-Boas (POR)
1882 • White Hart Lane (36,310) • tottenhamhotspur.com
Major honours
UEFA Cup Winners' Cup (1) 1963;
UEFA Cup (2) 1972, 1984;
English League (2) 1951, 1961;
FA Cup (8) 1901, 1921, 1961, 1962, 1967, 1981, 1982, 1991;
League Cup (4) 1971, 1973, 1999, 2008

2012

18/08	Newcastle	a	1-2	Defoe
25/08	West Brom	h	1-1	Assou-Ekotto
01/09	Norwich	h	1-1	Dembélé
16/09	Reading	a	3-1	Defoe 2, Bale
23/09	QPR	h	2-1	og (Faurlín), Defoe
29/09	Man. United	a	3-2	og (Evans), Bale, Dempsey
07/10	Aston Villa	h	2-0	Caulker, Lennon
20/10	Chelsea	h	2-4	Gallas, Defoe
28/10	Southampton	a	2-1	Bale, Dempsey
03/11	Wigan	h	0-1	
11/11	Man. City	a	1-2	Caulker
17/11	Arsenal	a	2-5	Adebayor, Bale
25/11	West Ham	h	3-1	Defoe 2, Bale
28/11	Liverpool	a	2-1	Lennon, Bale
01/12	Fulham	a	3-0	Sandro, Defoe 2
09/12	Everton	a	1-2	Dempsey
16/12	Swansea	h	1-0	Vertonghen
22/12	Stoke	h	0-0	
26/12	Aston Villa	a	4-0	Defoe, Bale 3
29/12	Sunderland	a	2-1	og (Cuéllar), Lennon

2013

01/01	Reading	h	3-1	Dawson, Adebayor, Dempsey
12/01	QPR	a	0-0	
20/01	Man. United	h	1-1	Dempsey
30/01	Norwich	a	1-1	Bale
03/02	West Brom	h	1-0	Bale
09/02	Newcastle	h	2-1	Bale 2
25/02	West Ham	a	3-2	Bale 2, Sigurdsson
03/03	Arsenal	h	2-1	Bale, Lennon
10/03	Liverpool	a	2-3	Vertonghen 2
17/03	Fulham	h	0-1	
30/03	Swansea	a	2-1	Vertonghen, Bale
07/04	Everton	h	2-2	Adebayor, Sigurdsson
21/04	Man. City	a	3-1	Dempsey, Defoe, Bale
27/04	Wigan	a	2-2	Bale, og (Boyce)
04/05	Southampton	h	1-0	Bale
08/05	Chelsea	a	2-2	Adebayor, Sigurdsson
12/05	Stoke	a	2-1	Dempsey, Adebayor
19/05	Sunderland	h	1-0	Bale

No	Name	Nat	DoB	Pos	Aps	(s)	Gls
10	Emmanuel Adebayor	TOG	26/02/84	A	18	(7)	5
32	Benoît Assou-Ekotto	CMR	24/03/84	D	12	(3)	1
11	Gareth Bale	WAL	16/07/89	M	33		21
46	Tom Carroll		28/05/92	M		(7)	
33	Steven Caulker		29/12/91	D	17	(1)	2
20	Michael Dawson		18/11/83	D	23	(4)	1
18	Jermain Defoe		07/10/82	A	27	(7)	11
19	Moussa Dembélé	BEL	16/07/87	M	26	(4)	1
2	Clint Dempsey	USA	09/03/83	M	22	(7)	7
27	Iago Falqué	ESP	04/01/90	M		(1)	
24	Brad Friedel	USA	18/05/71	G	11		
13	William Gallas	FRA	17/08/77	D	16	(3)	1
15	Lewis Holtby	GER	18/09/90	M	4	(7)	
6	Tom Huddlestone		28/12/86	M	11	(9)	
21	Jermaine Jenas		18/02/83	M		(1)	
4	Younes Kaboul	FRA	04/01/86	D	1		
37	Harry Kane		28/07/93	A		(1)	
7	Aaron Lennon		16/04/87	M	33	(1)	4
29	Jake Livermore		14/11/89	M	4	(7)	
25	Hugo Lloris	FRA	26/12/86	G	27		
18	Kyle Naughton		11/11/88	D	13	(1)	
8	Scott Parker		13/10/80	M	15	(6)	
30	Sandro	BRA	15/03/89	M	22		1
22	Gylfi Sigurdsson	ISL	08/09/89	M	12	(21)	3
32	Andros Townsend		16/07/91	M		(5)	
11	Rafael van der Vaart	NED	11/02/83	M	1	(1)	
5	Jan Vertonghen	BEL	24/04/87	D	34		4
28	Kyle Walker		28/05/90	D	36		

WEST BROMWICH ALBION FC

Manager: Steve Clarke (SCO)
1878 • The Hawthorns (27,877) • wba.co.uk
Major honours
English League (1) 1920;
FA Cup (5) 1888, 1892, 1931, 1954, 1968;
League Cup (1) 1966

2012

18/08	Liverpool	h	3-0	Gera, Odemwingie (p), Lukaku
25/08	Tottenham	a	1-1	Morrison
01/09	Everton	h	2-0	Long, McAuley
15/09	Fulham	a	0-3	
22/09	Reading	h	1-0	Lukaku
30/09	Aston Villa	a	1-1	Long
06/10	QPR	h	3-2	Morrison, Gera, Mulumbu
20/10	Man. City	h	1-2	Long
28/10	Newcastle	a	1-2	Lukaku
05/11	Southampton	h	2-0	Odemwingie 2
10/11	Wigan	a	2-1	Morrison, og (Caldwell)
17/11	Chelsea	h	2-1	Long, Odemwingie
24/11	Sunderland	a	4-2	Gera, Long, Lukaku (p), og (Gardner)
28/11	Swansea	a	1-3	Lukaku
01/12	Stoke	h	0-1	
08/12	Arsenal	a	0-2	
16/12	West Ham	h	0-0	
22/12	Norwich	a	2-1	Gera, Lukaku
26/12	QPR	a	2-1	Brunt, og (Green)
29/12	Man. United	h	0-2	

2013

01/01	Fulham	h	1-2	Lukaku
12/01	Reading	a	2-3	Lukaku 2
19/01	Aston Villa	h	2-2	Brunt, Odemwingie
30/01	Everton	a	1-2	Long
03/02	Tottenham	a	0-1	
11/02	Liverpool	h	2-0	McAuley, Lukaku
23/02	Sunderland	h	2-1	Lukaku 2 (1p)
02/03	Chelsea	a	0-1	
09/03	Swansea	h	2-1	Lukaku, og (De Guzmán)
16/03	Stoke	h	0-0	
30/03	West Ham	a	1-3	Dorrans (p)
06/04	Arsenal	h	1-2	Morrison (p)
20/04	Newcastle	h	1-1	Jones
27/04	Southampton	a	3-0	Fortuné, Lukaku, Long
04/05	Wigan	h	2-3	Long, McAuley
07/05	Man. City	a	1-0	Long
12/05	Norwich	a	0-4	
19/05	Man. United	h	5-5	Morrison, Lukaku 3, Mulumbu

No	Name	Nat	DoB	Pos	Aps	(s)	Gls
43	Isaiah Brown		07/01/97	M		(1)	
11	Chris Brunt	NIR	14/12/84	M	23	(8)	2
25	Craig Dawson		06/05/90	D	1		
17	Graham Dorrans	SCO	05/05/87	M	21	(5)	1
32	Marc-Antoine Fortuné	FRA	02/07/81	A	9	(12)	1
1	Ben Foster		03/04/83	G	30		
22	Zoltán Gera	HUN	22/04/79	M	14	(2)	4
18	Gonzalo Jara	CHI	29/08/85	D		(1)	
28	Billy Jones		24/03/87	D	24	(3)	1
9	Shane Long	IRL	22/01/87	A	25	(9)	8
20	Romelu Lukaku	BEL	13/05/93	A	20	(15)	17
23	Gareth McAuley	NIR	05/12/79	D	36		3
7	James Morrison	SCO	25/05/86	M	33	(2)	5
21	Youssuf Mulumbu	COD	25/01/87	M	28		2
13	Boaz Myhill	WAL	09/11/82	G	8		
24	Peter Odemwingie	NGA	15/07/81	A	13	(12)	5
3	Jonas Olsson	SWE	10/03/83	D	36		
4	Goran Popov	MKD	02/10/84	D	10	(2)	
12	Steven Reid	IRL	10/03/81	M	11		
6	Liam Ridgewell		21/07/84	D	28	(2)	
8	Markus Rosenberg	SWE	27/09/82	A	5	(19)	
30	Gabriel Tamaş	ROU	09/11/83	D	7	(4)	
14	Jerome Thomas		23/03/83	M	4	(6)	
15	George Thorne		04/01/93	M	3	(2)	
5	Claudio Yacob	ARG	18/07/87	M	29	(1)	

WEST HAM UNITED FC

Manager: Sam Allardyce
1895 • Upton Park (35,303) • whufc.com
Major honours
UEFA Cup Winners' Cup (1) 1965;
FA Cup (3) 1964, 1975, 1980

2012

18/08	Aston Villa	h	1-0	Nolan
25/08	Swansea	a	0-3	
01/09	Fulham	h	3-0	Nolan, Reid, Taylor
15/09	Norwich	a	0-0	
22/09	Sunderland	h	1-1	Nolan
01/10	QPR	a	2-1	Jarvis, Vaz Té
06/10	Arsenal	h	1-3	Diamé
20/10	Southampton	h	4-1	Noble 2 (1p), Nolan, Maïga
27/10	Wigan	a	1-2	Tomkins
03/11	Man. City	h	0-0	
11/11	Newcastle	h	1-0	Nolan
19/11	Stoke	h	1-1	O'Brien
25/11	Tottenham	a	1-3	Carroll
28/11	Man. United	a	0-1	
01/12	Chelsea	h	3-1	C Cole, Diamé, Maïga
09/12	Liverpool	a	2-3	Noble (p), og (Gerrard)
16/12	West Brom	a	0-0	
22/12	Everton	h	1-2	C Cole
29/12	Reading	a	0-1	

2013

01/01	Norwich	h	2-1	Noble (p), O'Brien
12/01	Sunderland	a	0-3	
19/01	QPR	h	1-1	J Cole
23/01	Arsenal	a	1-5	Collison
30/01	Fulham	a	1-3	Nolan
02/02	Swansea	h	1-0	Carroll
10/02	Aston Villa	a	1-2	og (Westwood)
25/02	Tottenham	h	2-3	Carroll (p), J Cole
02/03	Stoke	a	1-0	Collison
17/03	Chelsea	a	0-2	
30/03	West Brom	h	3-1	Carroll 2, O'Neil
07/04	Liverpool	a	0-0	
13/04	Southampton	a	1-1	Carroll
17/04	Man. United	h	2-2	Vaz Té, Diamé
20/04	Wigan	h	2-0	Jarvis, Nolan
27/04	Man. City	a	1-2	Carroll
04/05	Newcastle	h	0-0	
12/05	Everton	a	0-2	
19/05	Reading	h	4-2	Nolan 3, Vaz Té

No	Name	Nat	DoB	Pos	Aps	(s)	Gls
15	Yossi Benayoun	ISR	05/05/80	M	4	(7)	
8	Andy Carroll		06/01/89	A	22	(2)	7
29	Marouane Chamakh	MAR	10/01/84	A	2	(1)	
9	Carlton Cole		12/10/83	A	14	(13)	2
26	Joe Cole		08/11/81	M	7	(4)	2
19	James Collins	WAL	23/08/83	D	29		
10	Jack Collison	WAL	02/10/88	M	5	(12)	2
20	Guy Demel	CIV	13/06/81	D	28	(3)	
21	Mohamed Diamé	SEN	14/06/87	M	31	(2)	3
23	Alou Diarra	FRA	15/07/81	M	1	(2)	
46	Robert Hall		20/10/83	A		(1)	
22	Jussi Jääskeläinen	FIN	19/04/75	G	38		
7	Matt Jarvis		22/05/86	M	29	(3)	2
11	Modibo Maïga	MLI	03/09/86	M	2	(15)	2
3	George McCartney	NIR	29/04/81	D	9	(3)	
16	Mark Noble		08/05/87	M	25	(3)	4
4	Kevin Nolan		24/06/82	M	35		10
17	Joey O'Brien	IRL	17/02/86	D	32	(1)	2
32	Gary O'Neil		18/05/83	M	17	(7)	1
18	Emanuel Pogatetz	AUT	16/01/83	D	1	(5)	
33	Dan Potts		13/04/94	D	1	(1)	
2	Winston Reid	NZL	03/07/88	D	36		1
27	Jordan Spence		24/05/90	D		(4)	
14	Matthew Taylor		27/11/81	M	14	(14)	1
5	James Tomkins		29/03/89	D	18	(8)	1
12	Ricardo Vaz Té	POR	01/10/86	A	18	(6)	3

ENGLAND

WIGAN ATHLETIC FC

Manager: Roberto Martínez (ESP)
1932 • DW Stadium (25,138) • wiganlatics.co.uk
Major honours
FA Cup (1) 2013

2012

19/08	Chelsea	h	0-2	
25/08	Southampton	a	2-0	Di Santo, Koné
01/09	Stoke	h	2-2	Maloney (p), Di Santo
15/09	Man. United	a	0-4	
22/09	Fulham	h	1-2	Koné
29/09	Sunderland	a	0-1	
06/10	Everton	h	2-2	Koné, Di Santo
20/10	Swansea	a	1-2	Boyce
27/10	West Ham	h	2-1	Ramis, McArthur
03/11	Tottenham	a	1-0	Watson
10/11	West Brom	h	1-2	Koné
17/11	Liverpool	a	0-3	
24/11	Reading	h	3-2	Jordi Gómez 3
28/11	Man. City	a	0-2	
03/12	Newcastle	a	0-3	
08/12	QPR	h	2-2	McCarthy 2
15/12	Norwich	a	1-2	Maloney
22/12	Arsenal	h	0-1	
26/12	Everton	a	1-2	Koné
29/12	Aston Villa	a	3-0	Ramis, Boyce, Koné

2013

01/01	Man. United	h	0-4	
12/01	Fulham	a	1-1	Di Santo
19/01	Sunderland	h	2-3	og (Vaughan), Henríquez
29/01	Stoke	a	2-2	McArthur, Di Santo
02/02	Southampton	h	2-2	Caldwell, Maloney
09/02	Chelsea	a	1-4	Maloney
23/02	Reading	a	3-0	Koné 2, Figueroa
02/03	Liverpool	h	0-4	
17/03	Newcastle	h	2-1	Beausejour, Koné
30/03	Norwich	h	1-0	Koné
07/04	QPR	a	1-1	Maloney
17/04	Man. City	a	0-1	
20/04	West Ham	a	0-2	
27/04	Tottenham	h	2-2	Boyce, McManaman
04/05	West Brom	a	3-2	Koné, McArthur, McManaman
07/05	Swansea	h	2-3	Espinoza, McCarthy
14/05	Arsenal	a	1-4	Maloney
19/05	Aston Villa	h	2-2	Boyce, og (Baker)

No	Name	Nat	DoB	Pos	Aps	(s)	Gls
26	Ali Al Habsi	OMA	30/12/81	G	29		
3	Antolín Alcaraz	PAR	30/07/82	D	8	(2)	
22	Jean Beausejour	CHI	01/06/84	M	32	(2)	1
19	Mauro Boselli	ARG	22/05/85	A	1	(6)	
17	Emmerson Boyce	BRB	24/09/79	D	36		4
5	Gary Caldwell	SCO	12/04/82	D	25		1
44	Eduard Campabadal	ESP	26/01/93	D		(1)	
9	Franco Di Santo	ARG	07/04/89	A	24	(11)	5
18	Roger Espinoza	HON	25/10/86	M	6	(6)	1
31	Maynor Figueroa	HON	02/05/83	D	33		1
20	Fraser Fyvie	SCO	27/03/93	M		(1)	
25	Román Golobart	ESP	21/03/92	D	2	(1)	
11	Angelo Henríquez	CHI	13/04/94	A		(4)	1
1	Joel	ESP	17/06/90	G	9		
6	David Jones		04/11/84	M	8	(5)	
14	Jordi Gómez	ESP	24/05/85	M	17	(15)	3
2	Arouna Koné	CIV	11/11/83	A	32	(2)	11
10	Shaun Maloney	SCO	24/01/83	M	34	(2)	6
16	James McArthur	SCO	07/10/87	M	24	(10)	3
4	James McCarthy	IRL	12/11/90	M	38		3
15	Callum McManaman		25/04/91	A	8	(12)	2
32	Ryo Miyaichi	JPN	14/12/92	A		(4)	
11	Victor Moses	NGA	12/12/90	A	1		
24	Piscu	ESP	25/02/87	D	3	(2)	
21	Iván Ramis	ESP	25/10/84	D	16		2
33	Paul Scharner	AUT	11/03/80	M	14		
23	Ronnie Stam	NED	18/06/84	M	11	(6)	
8	Ben Watson		09/07/85	M	7	(5)	1

Top goalscorers

26	Robin van Persie (Man. United)
23	Luis Suárez (Liverpool)
21	Gareth Bale (Tottenham)
19	Christian Benteke (Aston Villa)
18	Michu (Swansea)
17	Romelu Lukaku (West Brom)
15	Frank Lampard (Chelsea)
	Dimitar Berbatov (Fulham)
	Demba Ba (Newcastle/Chelsea)
	Rickie Lambert (Southampton)

Promoted clubs

CARDIFF CITY FC

Manager: Malky Mackay (SCO)
1899 • Cardiff City Stadium (26,828) • cardiffcityfc.co.uk
Major honours
FA Cup (1) 1927;
Welsh Cup (22) 1912, 1920, 1922, 1923, 1927, 1928, 1930, 1956, 1959, 1964, 1965, 1967, 1968, 1969, 1970, 1971, 1973, 1974, 1976, 1988, 1992, 1993

HULL CITY AFC

Manager: Steve Bruce
1904 • KC Stadium (25,586) • hullcityafc.net

CRYSTAL PALACE FC

Manager: Dougie Freedman (SCO);
(23/10/12) (Lennie Lawrence & Curtis Fleming (IRL));
(04/11/12) Ian Holloway
1905 • Selhurst Park (26,225) • cpfc.co.uk

SECOND LEVEL FINAL TABLE 2012/13

		Pld	W	D	L	F	A	Pts
1	Cardiff City FC	46	25	12	9	72	45	87
2	Hull City AFC	46	24	7	15	61	52	79
3	Watford FC	46	23	8	15	85	58	77
4	Brighton & Hove Albion FC	46	19	18	9	69	43	75
5	Crystal Palace FC	46	19	15	12	73	62	72
6	Leicester City FC	46	19	11	16	71	48	68
7	Bolton Wanderers FC	46	18	14	14	69	61	68
8	Nottingham Forest FC	46	17	16	13	63	59	67
9	Charlton Athletic FC	46	17	14	15	65	59	65
10	Derby County FC	46	16	13	17	65	62	61
11	Burnley FC	46	16	13	17	62	60	61
12	Birmingham City FC	46	15	16	15	63	69	61
13	Leeds United AFC	46	17	10	19	57	66	61
14	Ipswich Town FC	46	16	12	18	48	61	60
15	Blackpool FC	46	14	17	15	62	63	59
16	Middlesbrough FC	46	18	5	23	61	70	59
17	Blackburn Rovers FC	46	14	16	16	55	62	58
18	Sheffield Wednesday FC	46	16	10	20	53	61	58
19	Huddersfield Town FC	46	15	13	18	53	73	58
20	Millwall FC	46	15	11	20	51	62	56
21	Barnsley FC	46	14	13	19	56	70	55
22	Peterborough United FC	46	15	9	22	66	75	54
23	Wolverhampton Wanderers FC	46	14	9	23	55	69	51
24	Bristol City FC	46	11	8	27	59	84	41

PROMOTION PLAY-OFFS

(09/05/13)
Leicester 1-0 Watford
(12/05/13)
Watford 3-1 Leicester
(Watford 3-2)

(10/05/13)
Crystal Palace 0-0 Brighton
(13/05/13)
Brighton 0-2 Crystal Palace
(Crystal Palace 2-0)

(27/05/13)
Crystal Palace 1-0 Watford *(aet)*

Domestic cup: FA Cup 2012/13

THIRD ROUND

(05/01/13)
Aldershot 3-1 Rotherham
Aston Villa 2-1 Ipswich
Barnsley 1-0 Burnley
Blackburn 2-0 Bristol City
Bolton 2-2 Sunderland
Brighton 2-0 Newcastle
Charlton 0-1 Huddersfield
Crawley 1-3 Reading
Crystal Palace 0-0 Stoke
Derby 5-0 Tranmere
Fulham 1-1 Blackpool
Hull 1-1 Leyton Orient
Leeds 1-1 Birmingham
Leicester 2-0 Burton
Luton 1-0 Wolves
Macclesfield 2-1 Cardiff
Man. City 3-0 Watford
Middlesbrough 4-1 Hastings
Millwall 1-0 Preston
Nottingham Forest 2-3 Oldham
Oxford 0-3 Sheffield United
Peterborough 0-3 Norwich
QPR 1-1 West Brom
Sheffield Wednesday 0-0 MK Dons
Southampton 1-5 Chelsea
Southend 2-2 Brentford
Tottenham 3-0 Coventry
West Ham 2-2 Man. United
Wigan 1-1 Bournemouth

(06/01/13)
Mansfield 1-2 Liverpool
Swansea 2-2 Arsenal

(07/01/13)
Cheltenham 1-5 Everton

Replays
(15/01/13)
Birmingham 1-2 Leeds
Blackpool 1-2 Fulham *(aet)*
Bournemouth 0-1 Wigan
Brentford 2-1 Southend
Leyton Orient 1-2 Hull *(aet)*
MK Dons 2-0 Sheffield Wednesday
Stoke 4-1 Crystal Palace *(aet)*
Sunderland 0-2 Bolton
West Brom 0-1 QPR

(16/01/13)
Arsenal 1-0 Swansea
Man. United 1-0 West Ham

FOURTH ROUND

(25/01/13)
Millwall 2-1 Aston Villa

(26/01/13)
Bolton 1-2 Everton
Brighton 2-3 Arsenal
Derby 0-3 Blackburn
Huddersfield 1-1 Leicester
Hull 0-1 Barnsley
Macclesfield 0-1 Wigan
Man. United 4-1 Fulham
Middlesbrough 2-1 Aldershot
Norwich 0-1 Luton
QPR 2-4 MK Dons
Reading 4-0 Sheffield United
Stoke 0-1 Man. City

(27/01/13)
Brentford 2-2 Chelsea
Leeds 2-1 Tottenham
Oldham 3-2 Liverpool

Replays
(12/02/13)
Leicester 1-2 Huddersfield

(17/02/13)
Chelsea 4-0 Brentford

FIFTH ROUND

(16/02/13)
Arsenal 0-1 Blackburn
Luton 0-3 Millwall
MK Dons 1-3 Barnsley
Oldham 2-2 Everton

(17/02/13)
Huddersfield 1-4 Wigan
Man. City 4-0 Leeds

(18/02/13)
Man. United 2-1 Reading

(27/02/13)
Middlesbrough 0-0 Chelsea

Replay
(26/02/13)
Everton 3-1 Oldham

QUARTER-FINALS

(09/03/13)
Everton 0-3 Wigan *(Figueroa 30, McManaman 31, Jordi Gómez 33)*
Man. City 5-0 Barnsley *(Tévez 11, 31, 50, Kolarov 27, Silva 65)*

(10/03/13)
Man. United 2-2 Chelsea *(Hernández 5, Rooney 11; Hazard 59, Ramires 68)*
Millwall 0-0 Blackburn

Replays
(13/03/13)
Blackburn 0-1 Millwall *(Shittu 42)*

(01/04/13)
Chelsea 1-0 Man. United *(Ba 49)*

SEMI-FINALS

(13/04/13)
Wigan 2-0 Millwall *(Maloney 25, McManaman 78)*
Manchester City 2-1 Chelsea *(Nasri 35, Agüero 47; Ba 66)*

FINAL

(11/05/13)
Wembley Stadium, London
WIGAN ATHLETIC FC 1 *(Watson 90)*
MANCHESTER CITY FC 0
Referee: *Marriner*
WIGAN: *Joel, Boyce, Alcaraz, Scharner, McArthur, McCarthy, Jordi Gómez (Watson 81), Espinoza, McManaman, Maloney, Koné*
MAN. CITY: *Hart, Zabaleta, Kompany, Nastasić, Clichy, Barry (Džeko 90), Y Touré, Silva, Agüero, Nasri (Milner 54), Tévez (Rodwell 69)*
Sent off: *Zabaleta (84)*

Domestic cup: League Cup 2012/13

QUARTER-FINALS

(11/12/12)
Bradford 1-1 Arsenal *(Thompson 16; Vermaelen 88) (aet; 3-2 on pens)*
Norwich 1-4 Aston Villa *(Morison 19; Holman 21, Weimann 79, 85, Benteke 90)*

(12/12/12)
Swansea 1-0 Middlesbrough *(Hines 81og)*

(19/12/12)
Leeds 1-5 Chelsea 5 *(Becchio 37; Mata 47, Ivanović 64, Moses 66, Hazard 81, Fernando Torres 83)*

SEMI-FINALS

(08/01/13 & 22/01/13)
Bradford 3-1 Aston Villa *(Wells 19, McArdle 77, McHugh 88; Weimann 82)*
Aston Villa 2-1 Bradford *(Benteke 24, Weimann 89; Hanson 55)*
(Bradford 4-3)

(09/01/13 & 23/01/13)
Chelsea 0-2 Swansea *(Michu 39, Graham 90)*
Swansea 0-0 Chelsea
(Swansea 2-0)

FINAL

(24/02/13)
Wembley Stadium, London
SWANSEA CITY AFC 5 *(Dyer 16, 48, Michu 40, De Guzmán 59p, 90+1)*
BRADFORD CITY AFC 0
Referee: *Friend*
SWANSEA: *Tremmel, Rangel, Williams, Ki (Monk 62), Davies (Tiendalli 84), Dyer (Lamah 78), Britton, De Guzmán, Routledge, Pablo Hernández, Michu*
BRADFORD: *Duke, Darby, McHugh, McArdle, Good (Davies 46), Atkinson, Jones, Doyle, Thompson (Hines 73), Wells (McLaughlin 57), Hanson*
Sent off: *Duke (56)*

ESTONIA

Eesti Jalgpalli Liit (EJL)

Address	A. Le Coq Arena, Asula 4c EE-11312 Tallinn	**President**	Aivar Pohlak
Tel	+372 627 9960	**General secretary**	Anne Rei
Fax	+372 627 9969	**Media officer**	Mihkel Uiboleht
E-mail	efa@jalgpall.ee	**Year of formation**	1921
Website	jalgpall.ee	**National stadium**	A. Le Coq Arena, Tallinn (9,692)

0   50   100 km

0   50 miles

Tallinn

Sillamäe

Narva

Paide

Kuressaare

Viljandi

Tartu

MEISTRILIIGA CLUBS

 1 FC Flora Tallinn

2 FC Kuressaare

 3 FC Levadia Tallinn

 4 JK Nõmme Kalju

5 Paide Linnameeskond

6 JK Sillamäe Kalev

7 JK Tallinna Kalev

8 JK Tammeka Tartu

 9 JK Trans Narva

10 FC Viljandi

PROMOTED CLUB

11 FC Infonet

KEY:

● – UEFA Champions League

● – UEFA Europa League

● – Promoted club

● – Club withdrawn from Meistriliiga

Nõmme Kalju – a new name on the trophy

JK Nõmme Kalju inscribed their name on the Meistriliiga trophy for the first time with a resounding title triumph that left regular challengers from the capital, FC Flora Tallinn and FC Levadia Tallinn, trailing helplessly in their wake.

Kalju were led to victory by Igor Prins, his experienced playing squad featuring several fellow former Estonian internationals and a number of foreign imports. Together they contributed 106 league goals in their 36 matches. The national team could have done with some of those as the UEFA EURO 2012 play-off participants struggled badly in their FIFA World Cup qualifying group.

Provincial club claim first Meitsriliiga crown

Igor Prins' title winners rack up over 100 goals

Flora beat champions to claim sixth Estonian Cup

Domestic league

Runners-up to Flora in 2011, Kalju made plain their intention right from the start as they followed an opening 0-0 draw against Levadia with eight successive wins. From that moment on they were the team to beat – a feat duly achieved by just one opponent, Flora, who overcame them 1-0 in Tallinn on two occasions, the second of which after Kalju had already bagged the silverware.

Fittingly the title was secured by a goal from Kristen Viikmäe – in a 1-0 win at FC Kuressaare – after which the 33-year-old stalwart announced his retirement. He was one of only 20 players used by the champions throughout the 36-match campaign.

Another Kalju thirtysomething, Tarmo Neemelo, enjoyed a fabulous season, striking 22 goals – one fewer than the league's top marksman, Russian import Vladislav Ivanov, who spread his tally between two clubs, JK Sillamäe Kalev and JK Trans Narva - and there were useful contributions also from the team's sizeable foreign legion, notably Japanese playmaker Hidetoshi Wakui, who scored ten goals and was the architect of many others.

By contrast, Flora and Levadia relied almost exclusively on local talent. Indeed, Levadia started the 2012 campaign with the accent very much on youth and development, and under the steady guiding hand of another celebrated ex-Estonian international, 143-cap Marko Kristal, they did well to finish second in the league as well as lift the 2011/12 Estonian Cup.

Domestic cup

Levadia's possession of that trophy was not four months old, however, when they had to surrender it following an epic 4-3 extra-time defeat to Kalju in the last 16 of the 2012/13 competition. Prins' men went on to reach the final the following spring with two five-goal wins, but they were denied simultaneous possession of the two major domestic trophies when Flora defeated them 3-1 to claim their sixth Estonian Cup – and third in four years – thanks to a double from midfielder Andre Frolov.

Marko Lelov was the winning coach, his tenure having begun on an interim basis seven months earlier when he replaced 2011 Meistriliiga-winning boss Martin Reim.

Europe

A third successive whitewash in European club competition was avoided as Levadia squeezed past Lithuanian side FC Šiauliai on away goals in the first qualifying round of the UEFA Europa League – before losing 6-1 on aggregate against Anorthosis Famagusta FC. Flora, Kalju and Trans were all first-fence fallers but, like Levadia, they would be back for another shot at European redemption in 2013/14.

National team

Having defied all odds to reach the qualifying play-offs of UEFA EURO 2012, Tarmo Rüütli's national team endured a sobering start to their 2014 World Cup campaign, losing without scoring against Romania (home), Turkey (away) and Hungary (home) before stopping the rot with an edgy 1-0 win in Andorra courtesy of long-serving striker Andres Oper's record-extending 38th international goal. Andorra were defeated again at home, 2-0, with promising Norway-based youngster Henri Anier opening the scoring, but that followed another goalless defeat, against the Netherlands in Amsterdam, in which a glaring miss from Martin Vunk summed up the team's enduring despair in front of goal.

Domestic league: Meistriliiga 2012 final table

		Pld	Home					Away					Total					
			W	D	L	F	A	W	D	L	F	A	W	D	L	F	A	Pts
1	**JK Nõmme Kalju**	**36**	**14**	**4**	**0**	**53**	**9**	**15**	**1**	**2**	**53**	**8**	**29**	**5**	**2**	**106**	**17**	**92**
2	FC Levadia Tallinn	36	11	4	3	41	14	14	4	0	44	8	25	8	3	85	22	83
3	FC Flora Tallinn	36	14	0	4	45	8	12	3	3	42	16	26	3	7	87	24	81
4	JK Trans Narva	36	7	4	7	27	23	9	3	6	25	21	16	7	13	52	44	55
5	JK Sillamäe Kalev	36	7	5	6	24	20	8	5	5	27	23	15	10	11	51	43	55
6	Paide Linnameeskond	36	5	4	9	18	33	6	5	7	16	19	11	9	16	34	52	42
7	FC Viljandi	36	4	2	12	18	47	2	6	10	15	41	6	8	22	33	88	26
8	FC Kuressaare	36	2	7	9	17	37	3	4	11	14	43	5	11	20	31	80	26
9	JK Tallinna Kalev	36	4	3	11	13	40	0	6	12	14	47	4	9	23	27	87	21
10	JK Tammeka Tartu	36	3	6	9	17	32	1	2	15	13	47	4	8	24	30	79	20

NB FC Viljandi withdrew from 2013 Meistriliiga; JK Tammeka Tartu therefore avoided relegation

SEASON AT A GLANCE

EUROPEAN QUALIFICATION 2013/14

 Champion: JK Nõmme Kalju (second qualifying round)

 Cup winner: FC Flora Tallinn (first qualifying round)
FC Levadia Tallinn (first qualifying round)
JK Trans Narva (first qualifying round)

Top scorer	Vladislav Ivanov (Sillamäe/Trans), 23 goals
Relegated club	FC Viljandi (withdrew)
Promoted club	FC Infonet
Cup final	FC Flora Tallinn 3-1 JK Nõmme Kalju

MEISTRILIIGA TEAM OF THE SEASON
(4-4-2)
Coach: Prins *(Kalju)*

PLAYER OF THE SEASON
Igor Morozov
(FC Levadia Tallinn)

At 23, the Estonian international defender was one of the oldest players in a youthful Levadia squad. The team captain was the club's top marksman in the Meistriliiga with 12 goals, his tally incorporating a hat-trick of penalties in a remarkable 5-4 win against rivals FC Flora Tallinn. He left for Poland in the winter to join KSP Polonia Warszawa.

NEWCOMER OF THE SEASON
Zakaria Beglarishvili
(FC Flora Tallinn)

A midfield general in the making, the Georgian Under-21 international enjoyed an exceptional third season with Flora. Technically proficient, particularly with his ball control and dribbling, the young left-footer's haul of 17 goals in 28 top-flight outings was bettered by only two players. It also earned him a transfer home, where he joined FC Sioni Bolnisi.

NATIONAL TEAM

Home Kit   Away Kit

TOP FIVE ALL-TIME CAPS
Martin Reim (157); Marko Kristal (143);
Andres Oper (133); Mart Poom (120);
Kristen Viikmäe (115)

TOP FIVE ALL-TIME GOALS
Andres Oper (38); Indrek Zelinski (27);
Eduard Ellmann-Eelma (21); Arnold Pihlak &
Konstantin Vassiljev (17)

Results 2012/13

Date	Opponent		Venue	Score	Scorers
15/08/12	Poland	H	Tallinn	1-0	*Vassiljev (90+2)*
07/09/12	Romania (WCQ)	H	Tallinn	0-2	
11/09/12	Turkey (WCQ)	A	Istanbul	0-3	
12/10/12	Hungary (WCQ)	H	Tallinn	0-1	
16/10/12	Andorra (WCQ)	A	Andorra la Vella	1-0	*Oper (57)*
08/11/12	Oman	A	Muscat	2-1	*Anier (85), Kams (88)*
14/11/12	United Arab Emirates	A	Abu Dhabi	1-2	*Ahjupera (45)*
06/02/13	Scotland	A	Aberdeen	0-1	
22/03/13	Netherlands (WCQ)	A	Amsterdam	0-3	
26/03/13	Andorra (WCQ)	H	Tallinn	2-0	*Anier (45+1), Lindpere (61)*
03/06/13	Belarus	H	Tallinn	0-2	
07/06/13	Trinidad & Tobago	H	Tallinn	1-0	*Anier (13)*
11/06/13	Kyrgyzstan	H	Tallinn	1-1	*S Puri (45+2)*

Appearances 2012/13

Coach: **Tarmo Rüütli** 11/08/54

Player	DOB	Club	Pol	ROU	TUR	HUN	AND	Omn	Uae	Sco	NED	AND	Blr	Tri	Tkm	Caps	Goals
Sergei Pareiko	31/01/77	Wisła Kraków (POL)	G	G	G	G	G		G	G	G	G		G		46	-
Tihhon Šišov	11/02/83	Kalju	D			D	D	D	D				s81		D	42	-
Alo Bärengrub	12/02/84	Kalju	D					D	D				s86		s57	42	-
Igor Morozov	27/05/89	Levadia /Polonia Warszawa (POL)	D	D		D		D	D59	D	D	D	D	D		22	-
Dmitri Kruglov	24/05/84	Rostov (RUS)	D57		M	D	D		D	M62			D	D	s63	85	1
Sander Puri	07/05/88	KuPS (FIN) /unattached /JOL Milton (000)	M	M76	s56	M69	s70			M59	M		M86	s57	M78	53	3
Aleksandr Dmitrijev	18/02/82	Gomel (BLR) /Levadia	M83	M									M59	M57	s57	80	-
Martin Vunk	21/08/84	Panachaiki (GRE) /Sillamäe	M57	M61	M	s87	s46	M82	s68		M		s59	M	s71	56	1
Joel Lindpere	05/10/81	NY Red Bulls (USA) /Chicago Fire (USA)	M57	s46	M56	M	M70			s74	s77	s55		s57	M	88	6
Andres Oper	07/11/77	Nea Salamis (CYP)	A46	A	A56	A	A		s46	A46	A46	s55				133	38
Henrik Ojamaa	20/05/91	Motherwell (SCO)	A46	A46		A53	s83			A73	A77					10	-
Kaimar Saag	05/08/88	Vejle-Kolding (DEN)	s46		s77											43	3
Vladimir Voskoboinikov	02/02/83	Dinamo Tbilisi (GEO) /Kalju	s46	s61									s59	s57	s71	36	4
Konstantin Vassiljev	16/08/84	Amkar (RUS)	s57	M	M	M	M		M	M	M	M	M			63	17
Taijo Teniste	31/01/88	Sogndal (NOR)	s57	D	D					D	D	D			D63	21	-
Tarmo Kink	06/10/85	Varese (ITA) /Győr (HUN)	s57	s76	M77	M87	M83		s46	M59	s62	M	M81		M71	75	5
Sergei Mošnikov	07/01/88	Pogoń (POL) /Górnik Zabrze (POL)	s83			s69		M64	M68		M		M	s57	M71	16	-
Enar Jääger	18/11/84	Aalesund (NOR) /unattached		D	D 19*					D	D	D	D81	D		96	-

Appearances 2012/13 (contd.)

Coach:			Pol	ROU	TUR	HUN	AND	Omn	Uae	Sco	NED	AND	Blr	Tri	Tkm	Caps	Goals
Ragnar Klavan	30/10/85	Augsburg (GER)	D	D			D			D	D					86	2
Taavi Rähn	16/05/81	Tianjin Songjiang (CHN) /Hunan Xiangtao (CHN)			D	D	D	s82	s59				D 65*		D	73	-
Ats Purje	03/08/85	KuPS (FIN)			s56	s53	M	A74	s46	s59		M76				44	4
Tarmo Neemelo	10/02/82	Kalju					A46									22	1
Artur Kotenko	20/08/81	Jaro (FIN) /Dnepr (BLR)						G76							G	28	-
Ken Kallaste	31/08/88	Kalju						D								1	-
Ilja Antonov	05/12/92	Levadia						M57								1	-
Karl Mööl	04/03/92	Flora						M46								1	-
Siim Luts	12/03/89	Flora /Norrköping (SWE)						M	M46	s59			M59	M57	s78	12	-
Gert Kams	25/05/85	Flora /SJK (FIN)						s46	M74	s73						26	2
Eino Puri	07/05/88	Kalju						s57								4	-
Henri Anier	17/12/90	Viking (NOR) /Fredrikstad (NOR)						s64	A46			A55	A59	A57		7	3
Andre Frolov	18/04/88	Flora						s74								1	-
Stanislav Pedõk	06/06/88	Flora						s76								1	-
Jarmo Ahjupera	13/04/84	Győr (HUN)							A46	s46		A55				20	1
Sergei Zenjov	20/04/89	Karpaty (UKR)								s46	s76		A57	A		25	5
Raio Piiroja	11/07/79	Chengdu Blades (CHN)											D	D		111	8
Pavel Londak	14/05/80	Bodø/Glimt (NOR)											G			24	-
Kristen Viikmäe	10/02/79	Haiba											A41			115	15
Rimo Hunt	05/11/85	Levadia											s41	A57		2	-
Andrei Sidorenkov	12/02/84	Gomel (BLR)											s59	s81		23	-
Mikk Reintam	22/05/90	JJK (FIN)													D57	3	-

European club competitions 2012/13

FC FLORA TALLINN

Second qualifying round - FC Basel 1893 (SUI)
H 0-2
Pedõk, Mets, Beglarishvili, Alliku (Mašitšev 71), Jürgenson, Baranov, Palatu, Frolov, Mööl (Luts 71), Minkenen, Luigend (Peitre 76). Coach: Martin Reim (EST)
A 0-3
Pedõk, Peitre, Mets, Alliku, Luts, Laabus (Beglarishvili 76), Baranov, Palatu, Frolov, Luigend (Minkenen 86), Prosa (Mööl 70). Coach: Ain Tammus (EST)

FC LEVADIA TALLINN

First qualifying round - FC Šiauliai (LTU)
H 1-0 *Juvenal (63og)*
Smishko, Artjunin, Morozov, Antonov, Subbotin, Podholjuzin, Taar, Kulinitš, Pebre (Toomet 84), Kaljumäe, Hunt. Coach: Marko Kristal (EST)
A 1-2 *Rättel (76)*
Smishko, Artjunin, Morozov, Antonov, Subbotin (Leitan 88), Podholjuzin, Taar, Kulinitš, Pebre (Toomet 59), Kaljumäe, Hunt (Rättel 54). Coach: Marko Kristal (EST)

Second qualifying round - Anorthosis Famagusta FC (CYP)
H 1-3 *Morozov (82)*
Smishko, Artjunin, Morozov, Antonov, Subbotin, Podholjuzin, Taar (Rättel 61), Kulinitš, Pebre (Toomet 57), Kaljumäe, Hunt (Teever 74). Coach: Marko Kristal (EST)
A 0-3
Smishko, Artjunin (Pikk 68), Morozov, Antonov, Rättel, Subbotin (Toomet 63), Podholjuzin, Taar (Hunt 80), Kulinitš, Pebre, Kaljumäe. Coach: Marko Kristal (EST)

Domestic league club-by-club

JK NÕMME KALJU

First qualifying round - Xäzär Länkäran FK (AZE)

A 2-2 *Wakui (5), Puri (70)*
Teleš, Bärengrub, Jorge Rodrigues, Puri, Ceesay, Quintieri (Jevdokimov 87), Konsa (Melts 85), Viikmäe, Kallaste, Wakui, Šišov. Coach: Igor Prins (EST)

H 0-2
Teleš, Bärengrub, Jorge Rodrigues, Puri, (Jevdokimov 80), Ceesay, Quintieri, Konsa, Viikmäe, Kallaste, Wakui, Šišov. Coach: Igor Prins (EST)

JK TRANS NARVA

First qualifying round - İnter Bakı PİK (AZE)

H 0-5
Malkov, Kazakov, Gussev (Škinjov 85), Medeckis, Gruznov (Kutuzov 61), Abramenko, Leontovitš (Borisovs 63), Grigorjev, Kitto, Alekseev, Kuplovs-Oginskis. Coach: Aleksei Yagudin (RUS)

A 0-2
Malkov, Kazakov, Gussev (Ovsjannikov 84), Medeckis, Gruznov (Borisovs 57), Abramenko, Leontovitš (Kutuzov 88), Grigorjev, Kitto, Alekseev, Kuplovs-Oginskis. Coach: Aleksei Yagudin (RUS)

FC FLORA TALLINN

Coach: Martin Reim; (14/10/12) (Marko Lelov)
1990 • A. Le Coq Arena (9,692); Sportland Arena (800)
• fcflora.ee
Major honours
Estonian League (9) 1994, 1995, 1998, 1998 (autumn), 2001, 2002, 2003, 2010, 2011;
Estonian Cup (6) 1995, 1998, 2008, 2009, 2011, 2013

2012

10/03	Sillamäe	a	2-0	Mööl, Luts
17/03	Viljandi	a	2-0	Mööl, Pukk
20/03	Levadia	a	1-1	Frolov
24/03	Tammeka	h	4-0	Mets, Frolov 2, Relov
31/03	Kuressaare	h	0-1	
07/04	Tallinna Kalev	a	3-0	Frolov, Minkenen 2 (1p)
10/04	Paide	h	1-0	Kams
14/04	Kalju	a	0-2	
21/04	Trans	h	2-1	Luigend, Prosa
28/04	Trans	a	2-1	Beglarishvili, Kams
05/05	Kalju	h	1-0	Alliku
12/05	Paide	a	5-0	Minkenen, Beglarishvili 3, Mööl
19/05	Tallinna Kalev	h	5-0	Beglarishvili 3, Alliku, Luigend
22/05	Kuressaare	a	3-1	Luigend, Jürgenson, Alliku
09/06	Levadia	h	0-1	
16/06	Tammeka	a	2-0	Beglarishvili, Laabus
26/06	Viljandi	h	5-0	Mööl 2, Frolov 2, Beglarishvili
30/06	Sillamäe	h	3-0	Kams 2, Minkenen (p)
21/07	Kalju	a	0-2	
30/07	Paide	h	3-0	Minkenen 2 (1p), Prosa
04/08	Tallinna Kalev	a	1-1	Mašitšev (p)
11/08	Kuressaare	h	2-0	Mööl, Beglarishvili
20/08	Levadia	a	4-5	Minkenen, Beglarishvili 2, Kams
25/08	Tammeka	h	5-1	Prosa, Beglarishvili 2, Palatu, Pukk
29/08	Viljandi	a	2-0	Jürgenson, Luigend
01/09	Sillamäe	a	2-1	Palatu 2
15/09	Sillamäe	h	4-0	Jürgenson 2, Alliku, Luts
18/09	Viljandi	h	5-0	Alliku 3, Mets, Minkenen
22/09	Tammeka	a	3-0	Frolov, Mets, Mašitšev
29/09	Levadia	h	1-2	Mašitšev
02/10	Kuressaare	a	2-0	Prosa, Beglarishvili (p)
06/10	Tallinna Kalev	h	3-1	Mets, Minkenen, Frolov
09/10	Trans	h	0-1	
20/10	Paide	a	6-0	Luts, Prosa 2, Beglarishvili 2, Frolov
27/10	Kalju	h	1-0	
03/11	Trans	a	2-2	Alliku, Frolov (p)

Name	Nat	DoB	Pos	Aps	(s)	Gls
Mihkel Aksalu		07/11/84	G	7		
Rauno Alliku		02/03/90	A	18	(8)	8
Nikita Baranov		19/08/92	D	21	(1)	
Zakaria Beglarishvili	GEO	30/04/90	M	21	(7)	17
Aleksei Belov		04/03/92	A	1	(3)	1
Andre Frolov		18/04/88	M	34	(1)	10
Aleksei Jahhimovitš		30/03/90	D	3	(3)	
Markus Jürgenson		09/09/87	D	33		4
Gert Kams		25/05/85	D	26	(1)	5
Reio Laabus		14/03/90	M	2	(11)	1
Karl-Eerik Luigend		15/01/93	M	23	(4)	4
Siim Luts		12/03/89	M	22	(4)	3
Nikolai Mašitšev		05/12/88	M	13	(10)	3
Karol Mets		16/05/93	D	31	(1)	4
Valeri Minkenen	FIN	09/04/89	M	28	(1)	9
Karl Mööl		04/03/92	M	19	(10)	6
Karl Palatu		05/12/82	D	33		3
Stanislav Pedõk		06/06/88	G	28		
Meelis Peitre		27/03/90	D	13	(7)	
Albert Prosa		01/10/90	A	17	(12)	7
Martti Pukk		20/02/77	A	1	(16)	2
Mait Toom		07/05/90	G	1	(1)	
Kaarel Torop		20/09/92	A	1	(1)	

FC KURESSAARE

Coach: Sergei Zamogilnoı
1997 • Kuressaare linnastaadion (2,000)
• fckuressaare.ee

2012

10/03	Paide	a	1-2	Luup
31/03	Flora	a	1-0	Pajunurm
10/04	Levadia	a	0-5	
14/04	Viljandi	a	1-3	Luup
21/04	Tallinna Kalev	h	3-3	Reinsalu, Pohlak 2
28/04	Tallinna Kalev	a	1-2	Ilves
05/05	Viljandi	h	0-0	
08/05	Tammeka	h	1-1	Könninge
12/05	Levadia	h	0-2	
19/05	Tammeka	a	0-0	
22/05	Flora	h	1-3	Ilves
09/06	Sillamäe	h	0-0	
16/06	Trans	h	0-0	
26/06	Kalju	a	0-2	
14/07	Tallinna Kalev	a	2-1	M Rajaver, Könninge
17/07	Sillamäe	h	2-2	Valmas, Pajunurm (p)
21/07	Viljandi	a	0-6	
30/07	Levadia	a	0-7	
04/08	Tammeka	h	3-2	Tikerberi, Luup, Ilves
11/08	Flora	a	0-2	
18/08	Sillamäe	h	1-2	U Rajaver
05/09	Trans	a	0-2	
28/08	Kalju	h	0-9	
01/09	Paide	a	1-1	Valmas
04/09	Trans	a	2-1	Valmas 2
08/09	Paide	h	0-1	
15/09	Paide	h	1-1	Pajunurm
18/09	Kalju	a	1-6	Ilves
22/09	Trans	h	0-3	
29/09	Sillamäe	a	1-2	Tikerberi
02/10	Flora	h	0-2	
06/10	Tammeka	a	2-2	Könninge, Ilves
09/10	Kalju	h	0-1	
20/10	Levadia	h	0-1	
27/10	Viljandi	h	3-3	Pajunurm (p), Viira, Tikerberi
03/11	Tallinna Kalev	a	3-0	Pajunurm (p), Tikerberi, Ilves (p)

Name	Nat	DoB	Pos	Aps	(s)	Gls
Rene Aljas		18/12/86	M	24	(7)	
Taavi Lehismann		20/04/80	D		(1)	
Vladimir Gerasimov		11/12/89	M	32	(2)	
Andre Ilves		19/12/90	A	21	(6)	6
Endrik Jäger		13/01/90	M	1	(3)	
Theodor Kaljo		16/01/95	D		(1)	
Thorwald-Eirik Kaljo		10/03/93	M		(1)	
Egon Kasuk		13/11/87	M		(1)	
Algis Kelder		15/07/92	D	3	(7)	
Sami-Sander Kivi		11/05/90	D	15	(1)	
Märt Kluge		08/03/84	D	11		
Jaanis Kriska		23/06/88	D		(1)	
Greger Könninge		23/01/91	M	31	(1)	3
Tauno Laja		16/04/91	M	7	(1)	
Mihhail Lavrentjev		22/02/90	D	31		
Amor Luup		18/02/92	M	25	(4)	3
Mikk Metsa		19/03/93	M	6	(2)	
Märten Pajunurm		29/04/93	M	29	(1)	5
Pelle Pohlak		31/12/88	D	17	(7)	2
Margus Rajaver		16/07/89	A	7	(13)	1
Urmas Rajaver		03/01/88	D	22	(3)	1
Rauno Reiman		13/09/92	D	18	(2)	
Riido Reiman		19/02/94	G	5	(1)	
Raido Reinsalu		20/09/90	A	9	(3)	1
Arli Saar		28/04/85	M		(4)	
Sander Seeman		12/09/92	M	5	(9)	
Mairo Tikerberi		30/03/93	A	8	(4)	4
Taavi Trasberg		17/07/93	M	9	(1)	
Elari Valmas		02/07/88	A	35		4
Sander Viira		29/08/89	D	25	(2)	1

ESTONIA

FC LEVADIA TALLINN
Coach: Marko Kristal
1998 • Maarjamäe (2,000); Maarjamäe artificial (1,000);
Kadriorg (5,500) • fclevadia.ee
Major honours
*Estonian League (7) 1999, 2000, 2004, 2006, 2007,
2008, 2009;
Estonian Cup (7) 1999, 2000, 2004, 2005, 2007,
2010, 2012*

2012

10/03	Kalju	a	0-0	
17/03	Trans	h	4-0	Morozov 2 (1p), Pebre, Subbotin
20/03	Flora	h	1-1	Leitan
24/03	Sillamäe	a	0-0	
31/03	Tammeka	h	1-0	Subbotin
07/04	Viljandi	a	3-0	Morozov, Hunt, Toomet
10/04	Kuressaare	h	5-0	Toomet 2, Leitan 3
14/04	Tallinna Kalev	a	2-1	Morozov (p), og (Mitsuyama)
21/04	Paide	h	1-0	Hunt
28/04	Paide	a	5-1	Rättel 3, Toomet 2
05/05	Tallinna Kalev	h	0-0	
12/05	Kuressaare	a	2-0	Hunt 2
19/05	Viljandi	h	2-0	Kulinitš, Toomet
22/05	Tammeka	h	1-0	Podholjuzin
09/06	Flora	a	1-0	Hunt
16/06	Sillamäe	h	1-1	Hunt
26/06	Trans	a	2-1	Morozov 2
30/06	Kalju	h	1-1	Subbotin
23/07	Tallinna Kalev	a	6-0	Toomet, Rättel 3, Kaljumäe, Teever
30/07	Kuressaare	h	7-0	Taar 3, Subbotin, Hunt, Rättel 2
04/08	Viljandi	a	5-0	Pikk, Hunt 2, Taar 2
07/08	Paide	h	4-0	Morozov (p), Antonov, Pikk, Raudsepp
11/08	Tammeka	a	3-0	Subbotin 2, Pebre
20/08	Flora	h	5-4	Teever, Morozov 3 (3p), Taar
25/08	Sillamäe	a	1-1	Morozov (p)
28/08	Trans	h	0-2	
01/09	Kalju	a	2-2	Taar, Subbotin
15/09	Kalju	h	0-1	
18/09	Trans	a	6-0	Subbotin, og (Abramenko), Teever, Hunt 2, Taar
22/09	Sillamäe	h	0-2	
29/09	Flora	a	2-1	Teever 2
02/10	Tammeka	h	3-0	Rättel 2, Teever
06/10	Viljandi	h	2-1	Morozov, Subbotin
20/10	Kuressaare	a	1-0	Teever
27/10	Tallinna Kalev	h	4-1	Pikk, Teever, Kaljumäe 2
03/11	Paide	a	2-1	Antonov 2

Name	Nat	DoB	Pos	Aps	(s)	Gls
Ilja Antonov		05/12/92	M	29	(4)	3
Artjom Artjunin		24/01/90	D	33		
Trevor Elhi		11/04/93	M	1	(4)	
Rimo Hunt		05/11/85	A	27	(8)	11
Kevin Ingermann		06/07/93	D			
Marek Kaljumäe		18/02/91	M	28	(3)	3
Aleksandr Kulinitš		24/05/92	D	31	(2)	1
Taavi Laurits		23/01/90	A	1	(7)	
Vitali Leitan		01/12/78	A	5	(6)	4
Igor Morozov		27/05/89	D	34		12
Andero Pebre		07/08/91	M	15	(5)	2
Artur Pikk		05/03/93	D	15	(1)	3
Priit Pikker		15/03/86	G	3		
Maksim Podholjuzin		13/11/92	D	30	(3)	1
Artur Rättel		08/02/93	A	19	(12)	10
Andreas Raudsepp		13/12/93	M	13	(8)	1
Roman Smishko	UKR	18/03/83	D			
Igor Subbotin		26/06/90	M	27	(6)	9
Albert Taar		15/01/90	M	17	(13)	8
Ingemar Teever		24/02/83	A	13	(2)	8
Janar Toomet		10/08/89	A	22	(4)	7

JK NÕMME KALJU
Coach: Igor Prins
1923 • Kadriorg (5,500); Sportland Arena (800)
• jkkalju.ee
Major honours
Estonian League (1) 2012

2012

10/03	Levadia	h	0-0	
24/03	Tallinna Kalev	h	3-1	Jevdokimov 2 (1p), Viikmäe
27/03	Paide	a	3-1	og (Nõmme), Puri, Quintieri
31/03	Viljandi	h	4-0	Koogas, Neemelo 2, Viikmäe
07/04	Trans	h	4-1	Neemelo 2, Konsa, Quintieri
10/04	Sillamäe	a	2-0	Quintieri, Konsa
14/04	Flora	h	2-0	Quintieri, Šišov
21/04	Tammeka	a	4-0	Jevdokimov (p), og (Lilleväli), Bärengrub 2
28/04	Tammeka	h	3-0	Viikmäe, Puri, Neemelo
05/05	Flora	a	0-1	
12/05	Sillamäe	h	5-0	Wakui, Melts, Neemelo 2, Viikmäe
19/05	Trans	a	2-1	Konsa, Wakui
22/05	Viljandi	a	3-0	Neemelo 2, Viikmäe
09/06	Paide	h	1-0	Wakui
16/06	Tallinna Kalev	a	5-0	Konsa, Wakui 2, og (A Savitski), Jevdokimov
26/06	Kuressaare	h	2-0	Wakui, Melts
30/06	Levadia	a	1-1	Ceesay
14/07	Tammeka	a	4-1	Terehhov, Wakui, Konsa, og (S Valtna)
21/07	Flora	h	2-0	Puri, Ceesay
28/07	Sillamäe	a	2-0	Wakui 2 (1p)
06/08	Trans	h	1-0	Terehhov
11/08	Viljandi	h	3-0	Ceesay, Jevdokimov, Kallaste
18/08	Paide	a	2-0	Ceesay, Jevdokimov
28/08	Kuressaare	a	9-0	Wakui, Quintieri, og (Kivi), Jevdokimov 2, Neemelo 3, Bärengrub
01/09	Levadia	h	2-2	Koogas, Viikmäe
04/09	Tallinna Kalev	h	7-0	Jevdokimov 2, Neemelo, Quintieri, Melts, Konsa, Šišov
15/09	Levadia	a	1-0	Terehhov
18/09	Kuressaare	h	6-1	Neemelo, Jevdokimov 2, Puri 2, Cole
22/09	Tallinna Kalev	a	3-1	Konsa, Bärengrub, Ceesay
29/09	Paide	h	1-1	Neemelo
02/10	Viljandi	a	9-1	Jevdokimov (p), Neemelo 5, Puri, Melts 2
06/10	Trans	a	2-0	Bärengrub, Neemelo
09/10	Kuressaare	a	1-0	Viikmäe
20/10	Sillamäe	h	2-2	Neemelo, Ceesay
27/10	Flora	a	0-1	
03/11	Tammeka	h	5-1	Konsa, Quintieri 3, Viikmäe

Name	Nat	DoB	Pos	Aps	(s)	Gls
Alo Bärengrub		12/02/84	D	32		5
Marco Bianchi	ITA	03/08/90	D	1	(1)	
Yankuba Ceesay	GAM	26/06/84	M	13	(6)	6
George Cole	GAM	18/11/89	M	1	(6)	1
Jüri Jevdokimov		03/06/88	A	23	(7)	13
Jorge Rodrigues	POR	19/03/82	D	14		
Ken Kallaste		31/08/88	D	36		1
Oliver Konsa		04/03/85	A	28	(4)	8
Andres Koogas		05/09/87	D	28	(1)	2
Tanel Melts		20/11/88	M	21	(9)	5
Tarmo Neemelo		10/02/82	A	22	(4)	22
Eino Puri		07/05/88	M	32		6
Damiano Quintieri	ITA	04/05/90	M	13	(11)	9
Tihhon Šišov		11/02/83	D	34		2
Hideaki Takeda	JPN	22/05/85	A	5	(8)	
Vitali Teleš		17/10/83	G	36		
Sergei Terehhov		18/04/75	M	7	(14)	3
Kristen Viikmäe		10/02/79	A	15	(15)	8
Denis Vnukov		01/11/91	M		(1)	
Hidetoshi Wakui	JPN	12/02/83	M	35		10

PAIDE LINNAMEESKOND
Coach: Meelis Rooba
1999 • Paide linnastaadion (400); Paide linnastaadion
artificial (500) • linnameeskond.com

2012

10/03	Kuressaare	h	2-1	Eteria, Rõivassepp
17/03	Tallinna Kalev	a	0-1	
24/03	Viljandi	a	0-1	
27/03	Kalju	h	1-3	Mägi
07/04	Sillamäe	h	1-1	Goldberg
10/04	Flora	a	0-1	
14/04	Tammeka	h	2-0	Goldberg, Mägi
21/04	Levadia	a	0-1	
28/04	Levadia	h	1-5	Kõll
05/05	Tammeka	a	2-1	Allas, Rõivassepp
12/05	Flora	h	0-5	
19/05	Sillamäe	a	1-1	Kõll
22/05	Trans	h	0-0	
09/06	Kalju	a	0-1	
16/06	Viljandi	h	2-0	Nõmme, Eteria
26/06	Tallinna Kalev	h	1-0	Goldberg
17/07	Trans	a	0-2	
21/07	Tammeka	h	4-1	Tikenberg (p), Varendi, Goldberg 2
30/07	Flora	a	0-3	
04/08	Sillamäe	h	2-0	Varendi, Tubarik
07/08	Levadia	a	0-4	
11/08	Trans	a	0-0	
18/08	Kalju	h	0-2	
25/08	Viljandi	h	0-2	
28/08	Tallinna Kalev	a	3-0	Tubarik, Tikenberg, Rõivassepp
01/09	Kuressaare	h	1-1	Reinsoo
08/09	Kuressaare	a	1-0	Mägi (p)
15/09	Kuressaare	a	1-1	Ištšuk
18/09	Tallinna Kalev	h	0-0	
22/09	Viljandi	a	2-0	Goldberg, Voolaid
29/09	Kalju	a	1-1	Veis
02/10	Trans	h	2-3	og (Prikhodko), Rooba
06/10	Sillamäe	a	2-1	Goldberg, Mägi (p)
20/10	Flora	h	0-6	
27/10	Tammeka	a	1-1	Tikenberg
03/11	Levadia	h	1-2	Rõivassepp

Name	Nat	DoB	Pos	Aps	(s)	Gls
Teet Allas		02/06/77	D	7	(2)	1
Tambet Anso		10/09/89	A		(1)	
Lauri Ellram		18/02/84	M		(4)	
Tengiz Eteria	GEO	11/12/89	A	26	(4)	2
Stanislav Goldberg		30/10/92	M	27	(4)	7
Mihhail Ištšuk		23/09/86	A	3	(6)	1
Martin Kaalma		14/04/77	G	6		
Rauno Kald		11/03/91	D	25	(6)	
Ervin Kõll		18/03/89	M	20	(3)	2
Rauno Kööp		18/08/89	A		(2)	
Richard Leht		15/04/93	A	2	(6)	
Ville Oskari Lehtonen	FIN	22/01/90	M	3	(4)	
Timo Lomp		26/07/88	D	26	(4)	
Andre Mägi		14/01/88	D	27	(2)	4
Mait Nõmme		01/07/83	D	17	(4)	1
Aiko Orgla		24/05/87	G	30		
Rene Puhke		16/08/94	M	1	(9)	
Eerik Reinsoo		12/05/88	M	30	(1)	1
Urmas Rooba		08/07/78	D	9	(2)	1
Sander Rõivassepp		23/08/90	M	27	(3)	4
Karel Seire		02/04/95	D		(1)	
Alen Stepanjan		23/07/91	M		(2)	
Tiit Tikenberg		28/01/83	A	20	(7)	3
Carl Tubarik		31/07/81	D	34		2
Martin Ustaal		06/02/93	M	8	(5)	
Tõnis Vanna		05/06/84	D	15		
Lauri Varendi		29/12/88	M	16	(10)	2
Andrei Veis		06/04/90	D	6	(2)	1
Karel Voolaid		04/07/77	A	11	(11)	1

JK SILLAMÄE KALEV

Coach: Valeri Bondarenko;
(06/08/12) (Algimantas Briaunys (LTU))
1951 • Sillamäe Kalevi (600);
Sillamäe Kalevi artificial (500) • fcsillamae.ee

2012

10/03	Flora	h	0-2	
17/03	Tammeka	a	0-0	
24/03	Levadia	h	0-0	
31/03	Tallinna Kalev	h	4-1	Ivanov 2, Vihrov, Malinin
07/04	Paide	a	1-1	Paponov
10/04	Kalju	h	0-2	
14/04	Trans	a	2-0	Ivanov 2
21/04	Viljandi	h	2-0	Paponov, Ivanov
28/04	Viljandi	a	3-0	Podelis, Ivanov, Paponov
05/05	Trans	a	0-1	
12/05	Kalju	a	0-5	
19/05	Paide	h	1-1	Ivanov
22/05	Tallinna Kalev	a	2-1	Paponov (p), Valaitis
09/06	Kuressaare	h	0-0	
16/06	Levadia	a	1-1	Tamberg
26/06	Tammeka	h	2-0	Ivanov 2 (1p)
30/06	Flora	a	0-3	
14/07	Viljandi	h	2-2	Ivanov, Volodin
17/07	Kuressaare	a	2-2	Bebikh, Gladiļins
21/07	Trans	a	1-0	Debikh
28/07	Kalju	h	0-2	
04/08	Paide	a	0-2	
11/08	Tallinna Kalev	h	3-0	Kabaev, Bebikh 2
18/08	Kuressaare	a	2-1	Sillaste, Kabaev
25/08	Levadia	h	1-1	Bebikh
28/08	Tammeka	a	3-0	Gnedojus, Volodin, Aidara
01/09	Flora	h	1-2	Kabaev
15/09	Flora	a	0-4	
18/09	Tammeka	h	3-1	Kabaev 2, Zahovaiko
22/09	Levadia	a	2-0	Gnedojus, Bebikh
29/09	Kuressaare	h	2-1	Bebikh, Aidara
02/10	Tallinna Kalev	a	3-0	Gnedojus, Kabaev, Bebikh
06/10	Paide	h	1-2	Gnedojus
20/10	Kalju	a	2-2	Kabaev 2
27/10	Trans	h	0-3	
03/11	Viljandi	a	5-0	Gnedojus, Zahovaiko 3, Volodin

Name	Nat	DoB	Pos	Aps	(s)	Gls
Kassım Aıdara	FRA	12/05/87	M	3	(7)	2
Pavel Aleksejev		24/02/91	D	8	(4)	
Aleksandr Bebikh	RUS	29/08/89	A	18		8
Igor Dudarev	RUS	12/08/93	D	22		
Romāns Gladiļins	LVA	28/10/88	M	21	(4)	1
Kazimieras Gnedojus	LTU	28/02/86	D	30	(1)	5
Vladislav Ivanov	RUS	24/01/86	A	16	(1)	10
Evgeni Kabaev	RUS	02/08/88	A	13		8
Sergei Korsunov	FIN	22/02/92	M	9	(11)	
Davit Lortkipanidze	GEO	07/03/91	M		(7)	
Ramūnas Macežiskas	LTU	11/10/88	A	2	(8)	
Vladimir Malinin	RUS	12/02/92	M	23	(6)	1
Edgaras Mastianica	LTU	26/10/88	M	17		
Aleksei Naumov	RUS	02/02/72	D	8	(2)	
Roman Nesterovski		09/06/89	M	29	(3)	
Kirill Novikov		08/12/89	M	5	(6)	
Maksim Paponov		11/06/90	M	13	(1)	4
Gintas Podelis	LTU	01/12/86	A	5	(3)	1
Ats Sillaste		08/04/88	M	17	(11)	1
Mihhail Starodubtsev		14/08/82	G	36		
Tanel Tamberg		06/06/92	D	15	(1)	1
Irakli Torinava	RUS	12/04/94	M		(1)	
Eimantas Valaitis	LTU	03/06/82	D	32		1
Andrei Veis		04/06/90	D	6	(5)	
Sergei Vihrov		02/03/86	M	15	(7)	1
Aleksandr Volkov		11/10/94	A	3	(10)	
Aleksandr Volodin		29/03/88	M	27	(1)	3
Vjatšeslav Zahovaiko		29/12/81	A	2	(4)	4

JK TALLINNA KALEV

Coach: Sergei Ratnikov
1911 • Kalevi (12,000); Kalevi artificial (1,360) • jkkalev.ee
Major honours
Estonian League (2) 1923, 1930

2012

10/03	Viljandi	h	2-1	Aidara, Tomson
17/03	Paide	h	1-0	Tomson
20/03	Trans	h	0-0	
24/03	Kalju	a	1-3	Aidara
31/03	Sillamäe	a	1-4	Kägo
07/04	Flora	h	0-3	
10/04	Tammeka	a	1-2	Ed Stüf
14/04	Levadia	h	1-2	Tomson
21/04	Kuressaare	a	3-3	Mitsuyama 2, Ed Stüf
28/04	Kuressaare	h	2-1	Mitsuyama, Kase
05/05	Levadia	a	0-0	
12/05	Tammeka	h	1-0	Mitsuyama (p)
19/05	Flora	a	0-5	
22/05	Sillamäe	h	1-2	Aidara
09/06	Trans	a	1-5	Kägo
16/06	Kalju	h	0-5	
26/06	Paide	a	0-1	
14/07	Kuressaare	h	1-2	Aidara
23/07	Levadia	a	0-6	
28/07	Tammeka	h	1-1	Mitsuyama (p)
04/08	Flora	h	1-1	Alijev
11/08	Sillamäe	a	0-3	
14/08	Viljandi	a	1-1	Alijev
20/08	Trans	h	0-1	
28/08	Paide	h	0-3	
01/09	Viljandi	h	2-2	Gunther, E Ratnikov
04/09	Kalju	a	0-7	
15/09	Viljandi	a	1-2	Alijev
18/09	Paide	a	0-0	
22/09	Kalju	a	1-3	Alijev
29/09	Trans	a	1-1	E Ratnikov
02/10	Sillamäe	h	0-3	
06/10	Flora	a	1-3	Kase
20/10	Tammeka	a	1-4	Kase
27/10	Levadia	a	1-4	E Ratnikov
03/11	Kuressaare	h	0-3	

Name	Nat	DoB	Pos	Aps	(s)	Gls
Kassim Aidara	FRA	12/05/87	M	19		4
Rejal Alijev		14/06/89	M	23	(5)	4
Ionel Armean	FIN	26/10/91	D	28		
Garreth Wayne Gunther	USA	09/01/89	A	18		1
Deniss Jõqiste		05/02/90	M	2	(7)	
Filippoo Kobushi	FIN	11/08/90	M	14	(3)	
Marek Kahr		09/12/81	D	4	(3)	
Mart Kaljuste		11/09/90	G	11	(1)	
Aleksandr Karpõtšev		16/08/82	D	1	(3)	
Martin Kase		02/09/93	A	30	(2)	3
Sergei Kobjakov		13/03/81	D		(5)	
Igor Koroljov		19/08/88	D	9	(4)	
Johannes Kukebal		19/07/93	M	24	(5)	
Aleksandr Kulikov		25/08/88	A	2	(2)	
Christian Körtsmik		07/02/91	M	1	(2)	
Risto Kägo		04/08/89	M	20	(5)	2
Juhan Lilleorg		26/01/94	A		(1)	
Kevin Lutsokert		21/04/92	M		(2)	
Rameš Mamedov		30/01/83	D	7	(1)	
Emmanuel Mbia Ekobena	CMR	27/01/87	D	2	(2)	
Hiroyuki Mitsuyama	JPN	23/07/84	D	29		5
Mart-Mattis Niinepuu		23/07/92	G	17		
Henry Niinlaub		15/10/92	A	2	(3)	
Daniil Ratnikov		10/02/88	A	4	(3)	
Eduard Ratnikov		13/09/83	M	3	(5)	3
Kristjan Rõivassepp		19/07/81	M		(3)	
Aleksei Savitski		03/10/85	D	24	(1)	
Daniil Savitski		04/05/89	G	1		
Daniil Savitski		04/05/89	D		(1)	
Alex Sander Sepp		08/04/95	M		(4)	
Alen Stepanjan		23/07/91	M	6	(5)	
Edwin Stüf		30/07/89	A	19	(9)	2
Ervin Stüf		03/12/90	M	2	(3)	
Kristjan Suurjärv		23/05/88	D	8		
Stanislav Tokarev		10/06/93	G	6		
Rasmus Tomson		20/05/90	A	20	(5)	3
Eric Ntambue Tshibangu	FRA	04/12/88	G	1		
Denis Vnukov		01/11/91	M	13		
Sean Tremaine Whalen	USA	16/02/81	M	26	(2)	

JK TAMMEKA TARTU

Coach: Kristjan Tiirik ;
(19/07/12) (Joti Stamatopoulos (GRE))
1989 • Tamme (1,500); Annelinna Gümnaasium
artificial (500) • jktammeka.ee

2012

17/03	Sillamäe	h	0-0	
24/03	Flora	a	0-4	
31/03	Levadia	a	0-1	
10/04	Tallinna Kalev	h	2-1	Tšernjavski, Saks
14/04	Paide	a	0-2	
21/04	Kalju	a	0-4	
28/04	Kalju	a	0-3	
05/05	Paide	h	1-2	Hurt
08/05	Kuressaare	a	1-1	S Valtna
12/05	Tallinna Kalev	a	0-1	
19/05	Kuressaare	h	0-1	
22/05	Levadia	a	0-1	
02/06	Trans	h	0-2	
09/06	Viljandi	h	1-1	Saks
16/06	Flora	h	0-2	
26/06	Sillamäe	a	0-2	
30/06	Trans	h	2-3	Kaldoja (p), Paabut
14/07	Kalju	h	1-4	M Valtna
17/07	Viljandi	a	2-3	Kaldoja 2 (1p)
21/07	Paide	a	1-4	Nimo
28/07	Tallinna Kalev	h	1-1	Perlin
04/08	Kuressaare	a	2-3	Perlin, Hurt
11/08	Levadia	a	0-3	
18/08	Viljandi	h	0-0	
25/08	Flora	a	1-5	Tiirik
28/08	Sillamäe	h	0-3	
01/09	Trans	a	0-2	
15/09	Trans	h	2-1	Tamm, Tutk
18/09	Sillamäe	a	1-3	og (Bebikh)
22/09	Flora	h	0-2	
29/09	Viljandi	h	4-0	Nimo, Barry, Kaldoja, Laas
02/10	Levadia	a	0-3	
06/10	Kuressaare	h	2-2	Nimo, Kaldoja
20/10	Tallinna Kalev	a	4-1	Barry 3, Hurt
27/10	Paide	h	1-1	Nimo
03/11	Kalju	a	1-5	Pakk

Name	Nat	DoB	Pos	Aps	(s)	Gls
Chris Anderson		05/10/92	D	13	(4)	
Ousmane Barry	GUI	27/09/91	A	5	(1)	4
Martin Haljak		16/06/90	D	6	(1)	
Ando Hausenberg		10/01/87	D	2		
Martin Hurt		27/06/84	D	23		5
Georgi Ivanov		19/06/92	A	6	(6)	
Tanel Joosep		08/08/90	D	4		
Kaspar Kaldoja		01/01/90	D	24	(1)	5
Michael Kaltenhauser	GER	27/05/90	G	10		
Karli Kütt		17/02/93	G	2		
Mikk Laas		30/09/90	M	28	(2)	1
Uku Lilleväli		22/05/93	D	6		
Jürgen Lorenz		11/05/93	M	8	(15)	
Andrus Lukjanov		21/11/89	G	24	(1)	
Preche Amour Florian Mboungou	CGO	14/10/92	M	14		
Meelis Meisalu		18/04/91	M	1	(3)	
Martin Naggel		22/05/90	D	19	(4)	
Alexander Frank Nimo	USA	21/03/90	M	29		4
Ander Paabut		28/09/90	A	8	(9)	1
Andre Paju		05/01/95	M		(1)	
Maido Pakk		23/11/89	A	15	(2)	1
Olari Perlin		28/02/90	A	6	(6)	2
Artur Pikk		05/03/93	D	10	(2)	
Kevin Rääbis		02/01/94	A		(1)	
Janno Saks		10/07/91	M	15		2
Heiko Tamm		18/03/87	M	27	(1)	1
Siim Tenno		04/08/90	M	16		
Simo Tenno		05/09/92	M	10	(3)	
Kristjan Tiirik		25/08/82	A	5	(6)	1
Hannes Tiru		12/10/93	A		(4)	
Marek Tšernjavski		15/05/92	A	4	(6)	1
Rauno Tutk		10/04/88	D	35		1
Mikk Valtna		18/11/85	A	5	(12)	1
Siim Valtna		31/07/87	D	16		1
Kristjan Vomm		30/07/90	M		(1)	

JK TRANS NARVA

Coach: Sergei Prikhodko (RUS);
(21/04/12) (Aleksei Yagudin (RUS))
1979 • Kreenholm (1,000) • fctrans.ee
Major honours
Estonian Cup (1) 2001

2012

Date	Opponent		Score	Scorers
17/03	Levadia	a	0-4	
20/03	Tallinna Kalev	a	0-0	
07/04	Kalju	a	1-4	Medeckis
14/04	Sillamäe	a	0-2	
21/04	Flora	a	1-2	Kazakov
28/04	Flora	h	1-2	Kuplovs-Oginskis
05/05	Sillamäe	h	1-0	Leontovitš
12/05	Viljandi	a	1-0	Leontovitš
19/05	Kalju	h	1-2	Gussev (p)
22/05	Paide	a	0-0	
02/06	Tammeka	h	2-0	Gruznov, Séhi
09/06	Tallinna Kalev	h	5-1	Alekseev 2, Medeckis, Kutuzov, Leontovitš
16/06	Kuressaare	a	0-0	
26/06	Levadia	a	1-2	Alekseev
30/06	Tammeka	a	3-2	Gussev 2, Alekseev
17/07	Paide	h	2-0	Grigorjev, Alekseev
21/07	Sillamäe	h	0-1	
28/07	Viljandi	h	1-1	Fjodorov
31/07	Viljandi	h	3-1	Leontovitš, Gussev, Medeckis
06/08	Kalju	a	0-1	
11/08	Paide	h	0-0	
20/08	Tallinna Kalev	a	1-0	Dubõkin
25/08	Kuressaare	h	2-0	Alekseev, Ivanov
28/08	Levadia	a	2-0	Alekseev, Medeckis
01/09	Tammeka	h	4-0	Alekseev 2, Ivanov, Dubõkin
04/09	Kuressaare	h	1-2	Zaicevs
15/09	Tammeka	a	1-2	Ivanov
18/09	Levadia	a	0-6	
22/09	Kuressaare	a	3-0	Ivanov 3
29/09	Tallinna Kalev	h	1-1	Dubõkin
02/10	Paide	a	3-2	Ivanov 2, Kutuzov
06/10	Kalju	h	0-2	
09/10	Flora	a	1-0	Ivanov
20/10	Viljandi	a	5-2	Bukatkin, Ivanov, Alekseev, Leontovitš, Gruznov
27/10	Sillamäe	a	3-0	Ivanov 2, Gussev
03/11	Flora	h	2-2	Ivanov, Dubõkin

Name	Nat	DoB	Pos	Aps	(s)	Gls
Aleksandrs Abramenko	LVA	09/01/85	D	29	(1)	
Aleksandr Alekseev	RUS	23/08/89	A	23	(5)	10
Dmitrijs Borisovs	LVA	20/12/87	M	8	(5)	
Maksim Bukatkin	RUS	16/07/85	M	12	(2)	1
Aleksandr Dubõkin		06/05/83	M	12	(3)	4
Vladislav Fjodorov		31/07/92	M	5	(9)	1
Erik Grigorjev		31/12/86	D	25		1
Maksim Gruznov		21/04/74	A	11	(19)	2
Vitali Gussev		16/03/83	A	33	(1)	5
Vladislav Ivanov	RUS	24/01/86	A	17		13
Sergei Kazakov		02/01/80	M	32	(1)	1
Jevgenijs Kazura	LVA	24/01/88	D	14		
Stanislav Kitto		30/11/72	D	29	(1)	
Aleksandr Kulik		23/07/81	D	13		
Aleksejs Kuplovs-Oginskis	LVA	21/01/88	M	25		1
Vitaly Kutuzov	RUS	29/06/90	A	1	(14)	2
Sergei Leontovitš		04/03/87	M	17	(5)	5
German-Guri Lvov		16/01/96	A		(1)	
Vladimir Malkov	RUS	15/01/80	G	16		
Emmanuel Mbia Ekobena	CMR	27/01/87	M		(1)	
Dmitrijs Medeckis	LVA	24/03/85	M	15	(12)	4
Igor Ovsjannikov		23/02/92	D	11	(2)	
Sergey Prikhodko	RUS	09/05/84	G	20		
Elysée Irié Bi Séhi	CIV	13/09/89	M	26	(5)	1
Artjom Škinjov		30/01/96	A		(2)	
Nikolajs Zaicevs	LVA	03/01/92	M	2	(6)	1

FC VILJANDI

Coach: Zaur Tshilingarashvili
2011 • Viljandi linnastaadion (1,000) • no website

2012

Date	Opponent		Score	Scorers
10/03	Tallinna Kalev	a	1-2	Sinilaid
17/03	Flora	h	0-2	
24/03	Paide	a	1-0	Ottis
31/03	Kalju	a	0-4	
07/04	Levadia	h	0-3	
14/04	Kuressaare	h	3-1	Mütt 2, Leimann
21/04	Sillamäe	a	0-2	
28/04	Sillamäe	h	0-3	
05/05	Kuressaare	a	0-0	
12/05	Trans	h	0-1	
19/05	Levadia	a	0-2	
22/05	Kalju	h	0-3	
09/06	Tammeka	a	1-1	Klemmer
16/06	Paide	h	0-2	
26/06	Flora	a	0-5	
14/07	Sillamäe	a	2-2	Tšegodajev, Laurits
17/07	Tammeka	h	3-2	Krillo 2, Tšegodajev
21/07	Kuressaare	h	6-0	Laurits 2, Mütt 2, Krillo (p), Indermitte
28/07	Trans	a	1-1	Indermitte
31/07	Trans	a	1-3	Lätt
04/08	Levadia	h	0-5	
11/08	Kalju	a	0-3	
14/08	Tallinna Kalev	h	1-1	Leimann
18/08	Tammeka	h	0-0	
25/08	Paide	a	2-0	Tšegodajev, Leimann
28/08	Flora	h	0-2	
01/09	Tallinna Kalev	a	2-2	Belov, og (Kukebal)
15/09	Tallinna Kalev	h	2-1	Krillo (p), Leimann
18/09	Flora	a	0-5	
22/09	Paide	h	0-2	
29/09	Tammeka	a	0-4	
02/10	Kalju	h	1-9	Sinilaid
06/10	Levadia	a	1-2	Leimann
20/10	Trans	h	2-5	Torop, Laht (p)
27/10	Kuressaare	a	3-3	Laht, Tšegodajev, Mütt
03/11	Sillamäe	h	0-5	

Name	Nat	DoB	Pos	Aps	(s)	Gls
Rasmus Armas		27/04/89	G	1		
Aleksei Belov		04/03/92	A	8	(6)	1
Elton Brauer		23/08/93	D	7	(5)	
Roman Dmitriev	RUS	26/09/93	G	6		
Joel Indermitte		27/12/92	D	32	(2)	2
Erkki Junolainen		05/01/92	A	3	(19)	
Kaarel Kaarlimäe		13/10/91	M	1	(3)	
Sander Karu		25/07/92	D	30	(5)	
Bert Klemmer		15/10/93	M	16	(3)	1
Eron Krillo		18/10/91	M	25	(4)	4
Sander Laht		26/09/91	M	13	(17)	2
Taavi Laurits		23/01/90	A	6	(5)	3
Jaan Leimann		08/10/89	A	29	(5)	5
Sander Lepik		14/02/93	A	2	(5)	
Elvis Liivamägi		21/01/92	D	27	(4)	
Silver Lätt		26/01/92	M	24	(2)	1
Mikk Metsa		19/03/93	M	3	(5)	
Rasmus Munskind		31/08/89	M	7	(4)	
Marten Mütt		25/05/92	D	26	(1)	5
Ott Ottis		14/06/89	M	31		1
Siim-Sten Palm		18/08/92	G	14		
Sander Sinilaid		07/10/90	M	34		2
Kaarel Torop		20/09/92	A	6	(3)	1
Martin Tšegodajev		30/11/90	D	30	(3)	4
Alan Ventsel		02/09/88	G	15		

Top goalscorers

23	Vladislav Ivanov (Sillamäe/Trans)
22	Tarmo Neemelo (Kalju)
17	Zakaria Beglarishvili (Flora)
13	Jüri Jevdokimov (Kalju)
12	Igor Morozov (Levadia)
11	Rimo Hunt (Levadia)
10	Andre Frolov (Flora)
	Artur Rättel (Levadia)
	Hidetoshi Wakui (Kalju)
	Aleksandr Alekseev (Trans)

Promoted club

FC INFONET

Coach: Aleksandr Puštov
2002 • Lasnamäe KJH (300) • fcinfonet.com

SECOND LEVEL FINAL TABLE 2012

		Pld	W	D	L	F	A	Pts
1	FC Infonet	36	26	5	5	94	33	83
2	FC Flora II Tallinn	36	20	9	7	66	32	69
3	JK Tarvas Rakvere	36	21	5	10	66	58	68
4	SK 10 Tartu	36	15	9	12	65	58	54
5	FC Levadia II Tallinn	36	15	8	13	77	56	53
6	SK Tamme Auto Kiviõli	36	12	8	16	78	83	44
7	FC Puuma Tallinn	36	12	7	17	55	61	43
8	JK Tammeka II Tartu	36	10	7	19	55	83	37
9	Pärnu Linnameeskond	36	9	9	18	43	72	36
10	FC Lootus Kohtla-Järve	36	6	1	29	40	103	15

NB FC Flora II Tallinn ineligible for promotion;
JK Tarvas Rakvere entered play-offs;
FC Lootus Kohtla-Järve – 4 pts deducted.

PROMOTION/RELEGATION PLAY-OFFS

(11/11/12 & 17/11/12)
Tarvas Rakvere 1-2 Tallinna Kalev
Tallinna Kalev 1-0 Tarvas Rakvere
(Tallinna Kalev 3-1)

Domestic cup: Eesti karikas 2012/13

FIRST ROUND

(05/06/12)
Haiba 4-3 Legion

(06/06/12)
Levadia 12-0 Toompea 1994
Levadia-3 0-3 Laagri

(10/06/12)
Kalev-Juunior 0-2 Olympic

(12/06/12)
Pokkeriprod 3-2 Soccernet

(19/06/12)
Ajax-2 2-5 Velldoris
Alko 1-2 Viljandi
Flora 12-0 Loo
Kalju 17-0 Eestimaa Kasakad
Rummu Dünamo 3-1 aaMeraaS
Tammeka 4-0 Lokomotiv

(20/06/12)
Ajax w/o Tääksi
Alexela 2-4 Maardu
Baltika Keskerakond 1-14 Infonet
EMÜ 1-3 Tulevik
Flora-2 8-1 Jalgpallihaigla
Helios 0-4 Ambla
Joker 0-9 Emmaste
Kalev-3 3-4 Maccabi
Kalju-3 2-1 Akhtamar *(aet)*
Kernu Kadakas 3-0 Rogul
Kose 3-2 Kaitseliit Kalev-2
Kärdla 3-0 Tabasalu
Noorus-96 3-1 Igiliikur
Otepää 2-1 Tallinna Ülikool
Piraaja 1-5 SK 10
Quattromed 9-0 Löök
SK 10-2 w/o Leisi
Sporting 3-1 Balteco
Suure-Jaani Utd 3-1 Infonet-2
Trummi 2-6 Visadus

(21/06/12)
Ararat 10-0 Aspen
Ganvix 3-2 Eesti koondis
Kristiine 2-3 Kalju-2
Tallinna Kalev 12-3 Kiiu
TÜ Fauna 0-3 Kaitseliit Kalev

(26/06/12)
Navi 1-0 Lihula
Reliikvia 0-8 Atli

(01/07/10)
Eston Villa 0-0 Lalla

(02/07/12)
Suema Cargobus 1-3 Võru

(04/07/12)
Dünamo 2-1 Sörve
Hell Hunt 1-4 Elva
Lootus 0-1 Puuma *(w/o; original result 4-1)*
Metropool 1-7 Tamme Auto
Pärnu 4-2 Luunja
Rada w/o Tammeka-2

(06/07/12)
Järva-Jaani 3-2 Imavere Forss

(11/07/12)
Twister 1-2 Kuressaare

SECOND ROUND

(11/07/12)
Eston Villa 0-6 Flora
Quattromed-2 0-8 Tarvas
Viljandi 6-1 Noorus-96

(13/07/12)
Ganvix 6-1 Ambla
Paide 10-0 Haiba
Suure-Jaani Utd 4-1 Koeru

(17/07/12)
Olympic 1-5 Quattromed

(18/07/12)
Lootos 3-1 Kumake
Nõmme Utd 1-2 Kose
Puuma 1-0 Warrior
Rummu Dünamo 1-2 Pärnu
Visadus 0-1 Infonet

(19/07/12)
Otepää 0-1 SK 10-2

(22/07/12)
Ajax 0-2 Emmaste
Kalju-3 0-2 Velldoris
Kernu Kadakas 1-2 Saaremaa
Maccabi 3-1 Taebla *(aet)*
Rada 3-2 Kaitseliit Kalev

(24/07/12)
Sillamäe 6-0 Keila
Võru 1-1 Pubi Trehv *(aet; 4-3 on pens)*

(25/07/12)
Dünamo 0-5 Tamme Auto
Elva 6-1 Welco Elekter
Maardu 5-0 Järva-Jaani

(30/07/12)
Sporting 3-4 Atli *(aet)*

(31/07/12)
Tallinna Kalev 0-4 Kalju
Tammeka 3-0 Tulevik

(07/08/12)
Ararat 3-2 Kuressaare

(08/08/12)
Flora-2 6-0 MRJK
Kärdla 0-1 Navi *(aet)*

(14/08/12)
Trans 6-0 Laagri

(15/08/12)
Pokkeriprod 0-18 Levadia
SK 10 3-3 Kalju-2 *(aet; 7-6 on pens)*

THIRD ROUND

(21/08/12)
SK 10-2 0-3 Kalju

(22/08/12)
Infonet 5-0 Ararat
Puuma 0-2 Sillamäe
Quattromed 9-2 Maccabi
Viljandi 2-0 Tarvas

(28/08/12)
Kose 3-6 Ganvix
Maardu 0-1 Võru

(04/09/12)
Levadia 17-1 Atli

(05/09/12)
Suure-Jaani Utd 1-2 Elva
Velldoris 3-2 Lootos

(09/09/12)
Trans w/o Saaremaa

(12/09/12)
Emmaste 0-4 Tammeka
Flora-2 0-0 Paide *(aet; 4-3 on pens)*
Pärnu 3-2 Navi
SK 10 1-9 Flora
Tamme Auto w/o Rada

1/8 FINALS

(25/09/12)
Kalju 4-3 Levadia *(aet)*

(10/10/12)
Ganvix 8-1 Velldoris
Infonet 1-1 Tammeka *(aet; 2-4 on pens)*
Pärnu 4-2 Võru
Tamme Auto 0-1 Sillamäe

(13/10/12)
Quattromed 1-7 Trans

(24/10/12)
Elva 0-2 Flora
Viljandi 3-1 Flora-2

QUARTER-FINALS

(16/04/13)
Trans 2-1 Sillamäe *(Shesterkov 20, Nesterovski 89; Tjapkin 35)*

(17/04/13)
Kalju 5-0 Ganvix *(Voskoboinikov 20p, 58, 79, Quintieri 31, Dupikov 46)*
Pärnu 0-6 Flora *(Adou 15, 82, Laabus 35, Gussev 48, 79, Prosa 68)*
Bye – Tammeka *(Viljandi were dissolved before quarter-finals)*

SEMI-FINALS

(30/04/13)
Kalju 5-1 Tammeka *(Bärengrub 4, Quintieri 13, 55, Puri 18, Neemelo 52; Puri 16og)*
Trans 0-3 Flora *(Jürgenson 28p, Prosa 52, Van de Streek 53)*

FINAL

(18/05/13)
A Le Coq Arena, Tallinn
FC FLORA TALLINN 3 *(Frolov 15, 48p, Jürgenson 60)*
JK NÕMME KALJU 1 *(Bärengrub 44)*
Referee: *Roos*
FLORA: *Meerits, Jürgenson, Mets, Palatu, Baranov, Van de Streek, Mööl (Sappinen 69), Frolov, Luigend (Logua 75), Post (Prosa 72), Alliku*
KALJU: *Teleš, Šišov, Koogas, Kallaste, Bärengrub, Puri, Wakui, Toomet (Quintieri 61), Kimbaloula (Terehhov 80), Neemelo, Voskoboinikov (Dupikov 71)*
Sent off: *Šišov (84)*

Flora raise the trophy

FAROE ISLANDS

Fótbóltssamband Føroya (FSF)

Address	Gundadalur, PO Box 3028
	FO-110 Tórshavn
Tel	+298 351979
Fax	+298 319079
E-mail	fsf@football.fo
Website	football.fo

President	Christian Andreasen
General secretary	Virgar Hvidbro
Media officer	Ísak Mikladal
Year of formation	1979
National stadium	Tórsvøllur, Torshavn
	(6,040)

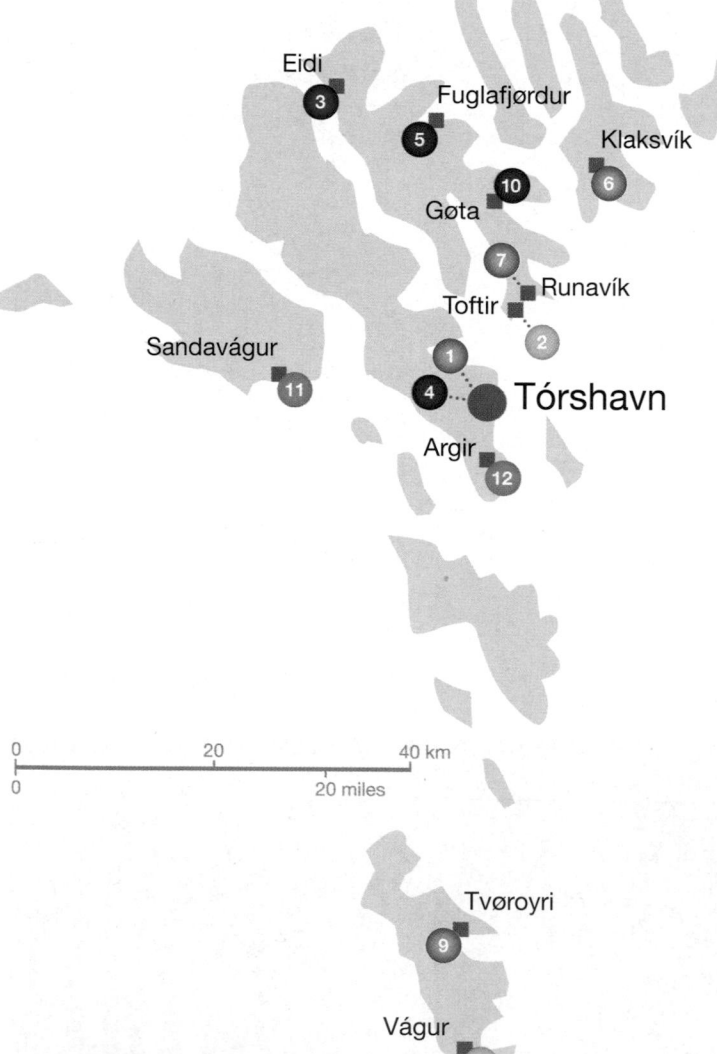

MEISTARADEILDIN CLUBS

1. B36 Tórshavn
2. B68 Toftir
3. EB/Streymur
4. HB Tórshavn
5. ÍF Fuglafjørdur
6. KÍ Klaksvík
7. NSÍ Runavík
8. FC Suduroy
9. TB Tvøroyri
10. Víkingur

PROMOTED CLUBS

11. 07 Vestur
12. AB Argir

KEY:

- – UEFA Champions League
- – UEFA Europa League
- – Promoted clubs
- – Relegated clubs

Happy ending for EB/Streymur

Cup specialists EB/Streymur were unable to win the domestic knockout competition for the fifth time in six years, losing a thrilling final on penalties to Víkingur, but Hedin Askham's team more than made up for that disappointment by winning the national title for only the second time, their triumph being sealed on the final day after a close tussle with ÍF Fuglafjordur.

It was a poor year for defending champions B36 Tórshavn, who finished sixth, and also a forgettable season internationally as the Faroe Islands, newly led by Lars Olsen of EURO '92 fame, lost every match.

Eidi club's cup despair compensated by title triumph	Víkingur take domestic cup after epic final	Only defeats for new national team boss Olsen

Domestic league

EB/Streymur, runners-up to B36 in 2011, did not get off to the best of starts in their bid for the Meistaradeildin title, taking just two points from their opening three games. Eight wins in their next nine outings put them back on track, but another stutter then followed, allowing KÍ Klaksvík to take over at the summit at the mid-point of the season. Eventually, though, as ÍF faded away, EB/Streymur found themselves locked in a direct duel for the title with Flemming Christensen's ÍF, a team without a league championship win since 1979.

Askham, EB/Streymur's coach since July 2009, when he replaced 2008 title-winning boss Sigrídur Clementsen, was to prove his mettle in the run-in, overseeing a late surge that brought eight wins and two draws in the last ten matches. Star striker Arnbjørn Theodor Hansen scored 11 times during that run, including twice in the title-clinching last-day 3-2 win over NSÍ Runavík.

In the event, with the equally in-form ÍF only drawing 0-0 at home to HB Tórshavn – a result that gave the club from the capital third place, and European football, on goal difference ahead of KÍ – EB/Streymur could have

lost against NSÍ and still been crowned champions, but had ÍF won, anything less than a victory would have been fatal for EB/Streymur as their rivals boasted a superior goal difference.

A major factor in that advantage was the 22-goal haul of ÍF's Brazilian import Clayton, which included three hat-tricks and five doubles – though, significantly, no goals in the three games against the eventual champions, from which his team took just one point.

Domestic cup

As is customary, the Faroese Cup final took place several weeks before the denouement of the championship, and the match between EB/Streymur and Víkingur, on 25 August, was regarded by many as one of the most exciting in the islands' history.

Seeking a fifth win on their sixth successive final appearance, EB/Streymur took the lead three times, but Víkingur pegged them back on each occasion, lastly in extra time after their opponents had been reduced to ten men. The fixture's first penalty shoot-out required 14 spot-kicks before, of all people, Arnbjørn Theodor Hansen

missed his effort to give Víkingur – and their coach, ex-Faroe Islands boss Jógvan Martin Olsen – the trophy.

Europe

There was no joy for the Faroe Islands' European representation as all four teams fell at the first hurdle. The only positive result was EB/Streymur's 3-1 home win against FO Qundzuour, but they lost the second leg 2-0 in Armenia to bow out on away goals

National team

The appointment of Denmark's EURO '92-winning captain Olsen was considered something of a coup, but the 52-year-old's first season in charge of the Faroe Islands yielded no dividends. The team played eight matches and lost the lot, including six FIFA World Cup qualifiers.

Admittedly, defeats were expected in those competitive encounters, but with just two goals scored – both at home – the hope was that things would improve in the autumn, when points – and goals - would be up for grabs in home and away encounters against fellow Group C strugglers Kazakhstan.

FAROE ISLANDS

Domestic league: Meistaradeildin 2012 final table

		Pld	Home					Away					Total					Pts
			W	D	L	F	A	W	D	L	F	A	W	D	L	F	A	
1	**EB/Streymur**	27	7	6	1	25	16	10	1	2	25	11	17	7	3	50	27	58
2	ÍF Fuglafjørdur	27	7	4	2	24	13	9	2	3	31	10	16	6	5	55	23	54
3	HB Tórshavn	27	8	2	3	34	13	5	4	5	22	21	13	6	8	56	34	45
4	KÍ Klaksvík	27	6	4	4	31	21	7	2	4	28	23	13	6	8	59	44	45
5	Víkingur	27	8	4	2	27	21	4	7	2	16	14	12	9	6	43	35	45
6	B36 Tórshavn	27	6	3	5	23	19	4	5	4	19	17	10	8	9	42	36	38
7	NSÍ Runavík	27	6	2	6	17	15	3	2	8	21	27	9	4	14	38	4	31
8	TB Tvøroyri	27	4	2	7	18	29	1	7	6	12	21	5	9	13	30	50	24
9	B68 Toftir	27	2	5	6	12	18	4	1	9	11	25	6	6	15	23	43	24
10	FC Suduroy	27	2	2	9	7	29	0	1	13	9	49	2	3	22	16	78	9

SEASON AT A GLANCE

EUROPEAN QUALIFICATION 2013/14

Champion: EB/Streymur (first qualifying round)

Cup winner: Víkingur (first qualifying round)
ÍF Fuglafjørdur (first qualifying round)
HB Tórshavn (first qualifying round)

Top scorers	Clayton (ÍF) & Páll Andrasson Klettskard (KÍ), 22 goals
Relegated clubs	FC Suduroy, B68 Toftir
Promoted clubs	07 Vestur, AB Argir
Cup final	Víkingur 3-3 EB/Streymur (aet; 5-4 on pens)

MEISTARADEILDIN TEAM OF THE SEASON
(4-4-2)
Coach: Christensen (ÍF)

PLAYER OF THE SEASON
Clayton
(ÍF Fuglafjørdur)

The 33-year-old Brazilian forward did not begin the season as a regular starter for ÍF, but he opened his scoring account in mid-May with a hat-trick in a 4-1 victory against HB Tórshavn and never looked back, blitzing a further 19 goals to finish joint top of the scorers' charts and help his club to their best final placing since their title triumph in 1979.

NEWCOMER OF THE SEASON
Hallur Hansson
(HB Tórshavn)

The 20-year-old was the fulcrum of HB's dynamic midfield and consequently earned a move to Danish Super League side Aalborg BK a month before the end of the season. Hansson made his senior debut for the Faroe Islands against Iceland in August and shone sufficiently to start against Germany in a FIFA World Cup qualifier a month later.

FAROE ISLANDS

NATIONAL TEAM

Home Kit • Away Kit

TOP FIVE ALL-TIME CAPS
Óli Johannesen (83); **Fródi Benjaminsen** (74); **Jákup Mikkelsen** (73); Jens Martin Knudsen (65); Julian Johnsson (62)

TOP FIVE ALL-TIME GOALS
Rógvi Jacobsen (10); Todi Jónsson (9); Uni Arge (8); John Petersen (6); **Fródi Benjaminsen** (5)

Results 2012/13

15/08/12	Iceland	A	Reykjavik	0-2	
07/09/12	Germany (WCQ)	A	Hannover	0-3	
12/10/12	Sweden (WCQ)	H	Torshavn	1-2	*Baldvinsson (57)*
16/10/12	Republic of Ireland (WCQ)	H	Torshavn	1-4	*Hansen (68)*
21/02/13	Thailand	A	Bangkok	0-2	
22/03/13	Austria (WCQ)	A	Vienna	0-6	
07/06/13	Republic of Ireland (WCQ)	A	Dublin	0-3	
11/06/13	Sweden (WCQ)	A	Solna	0-2	

Appearances 2012/13

Coach: Lars Olsen (DEN) 02/02/61

Player	DOB	Club	Isl	GER	SWE	IRL	Tha	AUT	IRL	SWE	Caps	Goals
Jákup Mikkelsen	14/08/70	ÍF	G46								73	-
Jónas Tór Næs	27/12/86	Valur (ISL)	D71	D	D	D	D	D		D	31	-
Rógvi Baldvinsson	06/12/89	Bristol R. (ENG) /Ålgård (NOR) /Bryne (NOR)	D	D	D	D	D	D	D		12	1
Ódmar Færø	01/11/89	B36 /Forfar (SCO)	D	D	D	D61	D46	D			6	-
Pól Jóhannus Justinussen	13/01/89	NSÍ	D	D	D	D	s46	D	M	M	13	-
Fródi Benjaminsen	14/12/77	HB	M	M	M	M		M		M	74	5
Hallur Hansson	08/07/92	HB /AaB (DEN)	M		M83	M		M		M87	6	-
Christian Lamhauge Holst	25/12/81	Silkeborg (DEN)	M	M	M71	M		M	M84	M59	37	3
Daniel Udsen	18/03/83	Helsingør (DEN)	M79	M46	M85	M61					11	-
Símun Samuelsen	21/05/85	HB	M65	M64	M	M	M	M72	M	s59	44	1
Jóan Símun Edmundsson	26/07/91	Viking (NOR) /Fredericia (DEN)	A65	A85	A	A80	A78	A78	s64	A	21	1
Gunnar Nielsen	07/10/86	Man. City (ENG) /unattached /Silkeborg (DEN)	s46	G	G	G	G	G	G	G	16	-
Finnur Justinussen	30/03/89	Jönköping (SWE)	s65								1	-
Petur Dam Jacobsen	05/12/82	EB/Streymur	s65				M88	s72			4	-
René S Joensen	08/02/93	Brøndby (DEN)	s71								1	-
Bogi Løkin	22/10/88	ÍF	s79								18	1
Súni Olsen	07/03/81	B36		s46	s83				M	M41	49	3
Hjalgrím Elttør	03/03/83	KÍ		s64	s85	s80		M87			27	-
Klæmint A Olsen	17/07/90	NSÍ		s85							1	-
Arnbjørn T Hansen	27/02/86	EB/Streymur			s71	s61	A56	s78			15	3
Erling D Jacobsen	13/02/90	Víkingur				s61	s88				4	-
Viljormur Davidsen	19/07/91	Jerv (NOR) /Fredericia (DEN)					D			D	2	-
Kaj Leo í Bartalsstovu	23/06/91	Víkingur					M75				1	-
Høgni Madsen	04/02/85	ÍF					M46				3	-
Karl Løkin	16/04/91	ÍF					s46				1	-
Andreas Lava Olsen	09/10/87	Frem (DEN)					s56				7	1
Gilli Sørensen	11/08/92	B36					s75				1	-
Páll A Klettskard	17/05/90	KÍ					s78		A64	s87	3	-
Atli Gregersen	15/06/82	Víkingur						s87	D	D	21	-
Jónhard Frederiksberg	27/08/80	NSÍ							D		14	-
Ári Mohr Jónsson	22/07/94	Silkeborg (DEN)							D		1	-
Heini Vatnsdal	18/10/91	HB							M	s41	2	-
Hans Pauli Samuelsen	18/10/84	EB/Streymur							s84		4	-
Jóhan Troest Davidsen	31/01/88	HB								D	25	-

European club competitions 2012/13

B36 TÓRSHAVN

First qualifying round - Linfield FC (NIR)
A 0-0
M Joensen, S Joensen, Rasmussen, Færø, S Olsen, A Danielsen, Borg (Sørensen 67), Jacobsen, Cieślewicz (Matras 90+2), B Olsen (Skorini 84), Eysturoy. Coach: Mikkjal Thomassen (FRO)
H 0-0 *(aet; 3-4 on pens)*
M Joensen, S Joensen, Rasmussen, Færø, S Olsen, A Danielsen, Borg (Sørensen 74; D Olsen 19), Jacobsen, Cieślewicz, B Olsen (Matras 100), Eysturoy. Coach: Mikkjal Thomassen (FRO)

VÍKINGUR

First qualifying round - FC Gomel (BLR)
H 0-6
Túri, H Jacobsen, A Gregersen, Lambanum, Vatnhamar, B Hansen, E Jacobsen (Blé 51), Djurhuus (Bassene 70), Bartalsstovu, Niclassen (Hedin Hansen 61), Hjartvard Hansen. Coach: Jógvan Martin Olsen (FRO)
A 0-4
Túri, H Jacobsen, A Gregersen, Blé, Vatnhamar, B Hansen, E Jacobsen, Djurhuus (Sørensen 81), Bartalsstovu, Niclassen (Lambanum 46), Hjartvard Hansen (Lervig 90+2). Coach: Jógvan Martin Olsen (FRO)

EB/STREYMUR

First qualifying round - FC Gandzasar (ARM)
H 3-1 *Hanssen (9p, 33p), Samuelsen (25)*
Tórgard, Á Olsen, G Hansen, Hanssen, A Dam (B Olsen 68), Samuelsen, Fredriksberg, P Hansen, Danielsen, A Hansen, Niclasen. Coach: Hedin Askham (FRO)
A 0-2
Tórgard, Á Olsen, G Hansen, Hanssen, A Dam (J Hansen 80), Anghel, Samuelsen, Fredriksberg, P Hansen, Danielsen (B Olsen 74), Niclasen (A Hansen 90). Coach: Hedin Askham (FRO)

NSÍ RUNAVÍK

First qualifying round - FC Differdange 03 (LUX)
A 0-3
K Joensen, M Jacobsen, J Joensen, Mortensen, K Olsen, Árni Fredriksberg, M Olsen (Líknargøtu 82) S Jacobsen, Andras Frederiksberg, Arge, P Joensen. Coach: Kári Reynheim (FRO)
H 0-3
K Joensen (Høj 35), M Jacobsen, J Joensen, Mortensen, K Olsen (Líknargøtu 66), Árni Fredriksberg, M Olsen, S Jacobsen, Andras Frederiksberg, Arge (Ellingsgaard 83), P Joensen. Coach: Kári Reynheim (FRO)

Domestic league club-by-club

B36 TÓRSHAVN
Coach: Mikkjal Thomassen
1936 • Gundadalur (5,000) • b36.fo
Major honours
Faroe Islands League (9) 1946, 1948, 1950, 1959, 1962, 1997, 2001, 2005, 2011;
Faroe Islands Cup (5) 1965, 1991, 2001, 2003, 2006

2012

Date	Opponent		Score	Scorers
24/03	Suduroy	h	1-0	Souaré
01/04	KÍ	a	2-0	Jacobsen, S Olsen
05/04	ÍF	h	1-1	D Olsen
15/04	TB	a	4-1	Cieślewicz 2 (1p), S Olsen, Borg
21/04	EB/Streymur	h	1-2	Rasmussen
29/04	B68	h	1-2	Jacobsen
05/05	HB	a	1-2	Jacobsen
13/05	Víkingur	h	3-0	Cieślewicz, S Joensen, Sørensen
20/05	NSÍ	a	1-3	og (K Olsen)
28/05	ÍF	a	1-1	B Olsen
10/06	B68	a	1-1	Cieślewicz
13/06	HB	h	1-0	D Olsen
16/06	KÍ	h	2-3	D Olsen, A Danielsen
24/06	TB	h	2-2	S Olsen, S Joensen
29/06	Víkingur	a	2-3	Borg (1p)
22/07	EB/Streymur	a	1-1	A Danielsen (p)
29/07	NSÍ	h	5-1	D Olsen 2, B Olsen, og (Justinussen), Zachariasen
05/08	Suduroy	a	2-0	A Danielsen (p), Cieślewicz
11/08	TB	a	0-0	
19/08	ÍF	h	0-0	
29/08	HB	a	0-2	
02/09	B68	h	1-0	Cieślewicz
12/09	EB/Streymur	h	1-4	Borg
15/09	Suduroy	h	3-1	Borg, K Danielsen, Cieślewicz
23/09	KÍ	a	4-3	Sørensen, S Olsen, A Danielsen (p), Cieślewicz
29/09	NSÍ	a	0-0	
06/10	Víkingur	h	1-1	A Danielsen (p)

No	Name	Nat	DoB	Pos	Aps	(s)	Gls
17	Hørdur Askham		22/09/94	M		(6)	
9	Jákup á Borg		26/10/79	A	17	(3)	5
17	Robert Hedin Brockie		21/12/92	M	2		
11	Łukasz Cieślewicz	POL	15/11/87	A	23	(3)	8
8	Atli Danielsen		15/08/83	M	25	(1)	5
22	Karl Martin Eivindsson Danielsen		20/04/95	D	2	(3)	1
20	Høgni Eysturoy		14/07/90	D	15	(1)	
5	Odmar Færø		01/11/89	D	6		
13	Símun Hansen		11/12/82	A	13	(9)	
18	Benjamin Heinesen		26/03/96	M		(1)	
1	Jákup Højgaard		06/02/94	G	1	(1)	
10	Róaldur Jacobsen		23/01/91	M	27		3
6	Jákup Toftum Joensen		24/05/92	A		(1)	
16	Meinhard Joensen		27/11/79	G	24		
3	Símun Joensen		12/07/83	D	24	(1)	2
17	Patrick Larsen		03/05/95	M		(6)	
5	Herbert í Lon		01/12/79	D		(2)	
22	Klæmint Matras		20/05/81	M	13	(1)	
5	Ámund Nolsøe		20/02/91	D		(1)	
19	Bárdur Olsen		05/12/85	M	22	(5)	2
21	Dánjal Rói Olsen		04/08/90	A	9	(6)	5
7	Súni Olsen		07/03/81	D	20	(1)	4
24	Magnus Emil Poulsen		16/04/80	G	2	(1)	
18	Sigurd Poulsen		17/11/95	M		(1)	
4	Jonas Flindt Rasmussen	DEN	07/11/88	D	23		1
14	Heini í Skorini		14/05/83	M	12	(4)	
5	Sékou Tidiane Souaré	CIV	09/04/83	D	3		1
23	Rasmus Dan Sørensen		27/05/95	M	7	(10)	2
6	Gunnar Zachariasen		22/01/92	M	7	(3)	1

B68 TOFTIR

Coach: Pauli Poulsen;
(14/09/12) Bill McLeod Jacobsen
1962 • Svangarskard (1,200) • b68.fo
Major honours
Faroe Islands League (3) 1984, 1985, 1992

2012

25/03	HB	a	0-4	
31/03	ÍF	h	0-2	
05/04	Víkingur	a	0-2	
15/04	NSÍ	h	3-2	Gueye, Petersen (p), J Hansen
21/04	Suduroy	a	1-0	Jacobsen
29/04	B36	a	2-1	og (Rasmussen), Jacobsen
05/05	KÍ	h	0-2	
12/05	TB	a	1-3	Andreasen
19/05	EB/Streymur	h	1-2	Jacobsen
28/05	Víkingur	h	1-1	Jónleif Højgaard
10/06	B36	h	1-1	Gueye
13/06	KÍ	a	0-3	
17/06	ÍF	a	0-2	
24/06	NSÍ	a	2-0	Jónleif Højgaard, Ó Olsen
30/06	TB	h	1-1	Gueye
22/07	Suduroy	h	2-0	Johannesen, Andreasen
27/07	EB/Streymur	a	0-0	
04/08	HB	h	1-2	og (Mortensen)
11/08	NSÍ	h	1-1	Jacobsen
18/08	Víkingur	a	0-2	
29/08	KÍ	h	1-3	A Olsen
02/09	B36	a	0-1	
12/09	Suduroy	a	1-2	Jónleif Højgaard
16/09	HB	a	0-4	
23/09	ÍF	h	0-0	
29/09	EB/Streymur	h	0-1	
06/10	TB	a	4-1	Petersen, E Hansen 2, H Højgaard

No	Name	Nat	DoB	Pos	Aps	(s)	Gls
14	Jon Volf Andersen	DEN	04/06/90	M	2	(6)	
8	Kristian Anthon Andreasen		30/08/85	A	10	(12)	2
19	Ibrahima Camara	SEN	30/07/89	A	2	(1)	
13	Uni Sigmundsson Djurhuus		01/09/92	A		(1)	
17	Hákun Edmundsson		21/03/96	D		(4)	
6	Ndende Adama Gueye	SEN	05/01/83	M	26		3
18	Einar Tróndargjógv Hansen		02/04/88	D	23		2
14	Jústinus Ragnhardson Hansen		14/05/85	M	15	(1)	1
7	Øssur Hansen		07/01/71	M	1	(2)	
9	Dánjal Pauli Højgaard		27/12/83	D	14	(3)	
16	Haraldur Reinert Højgaard		21/03/95	D	3	(6)	1
20	Jóhan Dávur Højgaard		11/06/82	D	25		
15	Jónleif Højgaard		26/10/88	A	16	(2)	3
5	Oddur Árnason Højgaard		12/09/89	D	14	(11)	
11	Christian Høgni Jacobsen		12/05/80	A	26		4
13	Henning Gledisheygg Joensen		19/12/89	M		(2)	
4	Niclas Frídrikur Joensen		20/05/86	D	14		
13	Bjarki Johannesen		31/05/92	M	15	(8)	1
1	Hans Jørgensen		13/08/90	G	27		
18	Ahmed Keita	SEN	12/05/87	A		(3)	
7	Remi Langgaard		16/12/91	M	19	(2)	
10	André Olsen		23/10/90	M	21	(3)	1
4	Óli Højgaard Olsen		24/11/85	A	6	(6)	1
11	Jann Ingi Petersen		07/01/84	M	16		2
14	Ingvard Emil Ronaldsson		22/06/88	M		(1)	
9	Emmanuel Ukpai	NGA	11/10/87	A	2	(3)	

EB/STREYMUR

Coach: Hedin Askham
1993 • Vid Margáir (1,000) • eb-streymur.fo
Major honours
Faroe Islands League (2) 2008, 2012;
Faroe Islands Cup (4) 2007, 2008, 2010, 2011

2012

25/03	KÍ	h	1-1	A Hansen
30/03	Víkingur	a	1-2	A Hansen
05/04	TB	h	1-1	Bø
15/04	Suduroy	h	3-0	Bø, Anghel, Samuelsen
21/04	B36	a	2-1	Niclasen 2
29/04	HB	h	2-2	Samuelsen, Hanssen
05/05	ÍF	a	2-1	Niclasen, A Hansen
13/05	NSÍ	h	1-0	Bø
19/05	B68	a	2-1	A Hansen, Niclasen
28/05	TB	a	3-0	Niclasen 3
10/06	HB	a	1-0	Samuelsen
13/06	ÍF	h	2-1	Hanssen, G Hansen
16/06	Víkingur	h	0-1	
23/06	Suduroy	a	2-0	A Hansen, Samuelsen
29/06	NSÍ	a	0-1	
22/07	B36	h	1-1	Hanssen
27/07	B68	h	0-0	
03/08	KÍ	a	3-1	G Hansen, og (Á Christiansen), Danielsen
11/08	Suduroy	h	4-2	G Hansen, A Hansen 2, Anghel
19/08	TB	h	3-2	Niclasen, A Hansen, Samuelsen
29/08	ÍF	a	1-1	Djurhuus
02/09	HB	h	3-2	G Hansen, Bø 2
12/09	B36	a	4-1	A Hansen 3, Samuelsen
16/09	KÍ	h	1-1	A Hansen
23/09	Víkingur	a	3-2	Hanssen, A Hansen 2
29/09	B68	a	1-0	Jacobsen
06/10	NSÍ	h	3-2	A Hansen 2, Jacobsen

No	Name	Nat	DoB	Pos	Aps	(s)	Gls
10	Sorin Vasile Anghel		16/07/79	A	24	(1)	2
8	Egil á Bø		02/04/74	D	16	(1)	5
9	Arnar Dam		19/10/91	A	7	(11)	
8	Ragnar Bogason Dam		17/09/94	D		(1)	
17	Niels Pauli Bjartalid Danielsen		18/01/89	A	20	(5)	1
12	Marni Djurhuus		06/09/85	D	25		1
14	Jónhard Frederiksberg		27/08/80	D	27		
22	Arnbjørn Theodor Hansen		27/02/86	A	19	(5)	16
4	Gert Åge Hansen		25/07/84	D	24	(1)	4
20	Jóhannes Hansen		31/12/95	M		(4)	
16	Pauli Gregersen Hansen		09/04/80	M	13	(5)	
7	Levi Hanssen		24/02/88	M	24		4
6	Pætur Dam Jacobsen		05/12/82	M	15	(1)	2
23	Leif Niclasen		01/10/86	D	23	(4)	8
3	Árni Grunnveit Olsen		13/09/93	M	8	(5)	
18	Brian Olsen		22/08/85	M		(9)	
5	Poul Grunnveit Olsen		30/09/91	D	1		
11	Hans Pauli Samuelsen		18/10/84	M	24	(1)	6
1	René Tórgard		03/08/79	G	27		

HB TÓRSHAVN

Coach: Sigfrídur Clementsen
1904 • Gundadalur (5,000) • hb.fo
Major honours
Faroe Islands League (21) 1955, 1960, 1963, 1964,
1965, 1971, 1973, 1974, 1975, 1978, 1981, 1982, 1988,
1990, 1998, 2002, 2003, 2004, 2006, 2009, 2010;
Faroe Islands Cup (26) 1955, 1957, 1959, 1962, 1963,
1964, 1968, 1969, 1971, 1972, 1973, 1975, 1976, 1978,
1979, 1980, 1981, 1982, 1984, 1987, 1988, 1989, 1992,
1995, 1998, 2004

2012

25/03	B68	h	4-0	C Mouritsen, Benjaminsen, Fløtum, Samuelsen
01/04	Suduroy	a	1-0	Hansson
05/04	KÍ	a	1-1	C Mouritsen
15/04	Víkingur	h	1-1	C Mouritsen (p)
21/04	NSÍ	a	4-2	Fløtum 2, Hansson 2
29/04	EB/Streymur	a	2-2	Samuelsen, Fløtum
04/05	B36	h	2-1	Fløtum, Slættalíd
12/05	ÍF	h	1-4	Hansson
19/05	TB	a	2-4	Slættalíd, Nolsøe
28/05	KÍ	h	5-0	Benjaminsen (p), Nolsøe, Holm, Samuelsen, C Mouritson
10/06	EB/Streymur	h	0-1	
13/06	B36	a	0-1	
17/06	Suduroy	h	6-0	Samuelsen 3, Jensen, Benjaminsen (p), Rubeksen
24/06	Víkingur	a	2-2	Benjaminsen (p), Fløtum
30/06	ÍF	a	0-2	
22/07	NSÍ	h	2-4	Jespersen, Mortensen
28/07	TB	h	4-1	C Mouritsen 2, Alex, Fløtum
04/08	B68	a	2-1	Samuelsen, C Mouritsen
10/08	Víkingur	h	0-0	
19/08	KÍ	a	2-1	Benjaminsen, og (Gángó)
29/08	B36	h	2-0	C Mouritsen, og (B Olsen)
02/09	EB/Streymur	a	2-3	Benjaminsen 2 (1p)
12/09	NSÍ	a	0-2	
16/09	B68	h	4-0	Poulsen, K Mouritsen 2, C Mouritsen
23/09	Suduroy	a	4-0	C Mouritsen, Benjaminsen, Haraldsen, Alex
29/09	TB	h	3-1	Samuelsen, C Mouritsen 2
06/10	ÍF	a	0-0	

No	Name	Nat	DoB	Pos	Aps	(s)	Gls
2	Alex	BRA	28/03/81	D	26		2
7	Fródi Benjaminsen		14/12/77	M	24		8
19	Jógvan Rói Davidsen		09/10/91	M	15	(5)	
5	Jóhan Troest Davidsen		31/01/88	D	11		
14	Magnus Egilsson		19/03/94	M		(1)	
10	Andrew av Fløtum		13/06/79	A	21	(3)	7
1	Teitur Matras Gestsson		18/08/92	G	25		
16	Símun Rógvi Hansen		10/04/87	G	2	(1)	
6	Hallur Hansson		08/07/92	M	20		4
13	Gunnar Højgaard Haraldsen		21/11/87	D		(11)	1
3	Rógvi Sjúrdarson Holm		24/01/90	D	24	(1)	1
24	Tróndur Jensen		06/02/93	M	11	(6)	1
17	Rókur av Fløtum Jespersen		16/03/85	M	12		1
13	Høgni Midjord		04/02/91	A	1	(3)	
20	Vagnur Mohr Mortensen		10/02/83	D	20		1
11	Christian Restorff Mouritsen		03/12/88	M	27		12
21	Kristin Restorff Mouritsen		23/04/91	M	8	(14)	2
22	Eli Falkvard Nielsen		23/09/92	M	2	(3)	
15	Jógvan Andrias Skeel Nolsøe		20/05/92	A	11	(9)	2
8	Rógvi Poulsen		31/10/89	M	6	(5)	1
12	Hendrik Rubeksen		01/11/83	A	2	(10)	1
9	Símun Samuelsen		21/05/85	A	27		8
4	Jákup Slættalíd		11/01/88	D	2	(6)	2

FAROE ISLANDS

ÍF FUGLAFJØRDUR

Coach: Flemming Christensen (DEN)
1946 • Fløtugerdi (3,000) • if.fo
Major honours
Faroe Islands League (1) 1979

2012

25/03	NSÍ	h	2-1	*Eliasen, Skibsted*
31/03	B68	a	2-0	*Skibsted, Johansen*
05/04	B36	a	1-1	*J Ellingsgaard*
15/04	KÍ	h	2-0	*Poulsen, J Ellingsgaard*
21/04	Víkingur	h	1-2	*Zachariassen*
29/04	TB	a	0-1	
05/05	EB/Streymur	h	1-2	*U Petersen*
12/05	HB	a	4-1	*Clayton 3, J Ellingsgaard*
20/05	Suduroy	a	6-0	*Madsen, Clayton 3, Skibsted 2*
28/05	B36	h	1-1	*Clayton*
10/06	TB	h	1-1	*Clayton*
13/06	EB/Streymur	a	1-2	*og (Hanssen)*
17/06	B68	h	2-0	*Lakjuni 2*
24/06	KÍ	a	0-1	
30/06	HB	h	2-0	*Clayton 2*
27/07	Suduroy	h	3-2	*K Løkin, J Ellingsgaard (p), Lakjuni*
01/08	Víkingur	a	4-1	*Clayton 2, Lakjuni, Asmussen*
05/08	NSÍ	a	2-1	*Asmussen, J Ellingsgaard*
11/08	KÍ	h	5-2	*og (Gángó), Clayton 2, Madsen, Eliasen*
19/08	B36	a	2-0	*Eliasen, Sarić*
29/08	EB/Streymur	h	1-1	*Lakjuni*
02/09	TB	a	2-1	*Clayton 2*
12/09	Víkingur	a	3-0	*Lakjuni, Clayton 2*
16/09	NSÍ	h	3-1	*Clayton 3*
23/09	B68	a	0-0	
29/09	Suduroy	a	4-1	*Clayton, J Ellingsgaard, Eliasen, A Ellingsgaard*
06/10	HB	h	0-0	

No	Name	Nat	DoB	Pos	Aps	(s)	Gls
8	Thomas Asmussen	DEN	21/06/90	M	23	(1)	2
18	Clayton	BRA	24/11/78	A	23	(4)	22
76	Bartal Eliasen		23/08/76	D	25		4
9	Ari Ólavsson Ellingsgaard		03/02/93	M		(7)	1
3	Jan Ólavsson Ellingsgaard		26/06/90	D	26		6
16	Hallgrím Gregersen Hansen		24/12/94	G	1		
15	Jákup Johansen		27/04/93	M	1	(19)	1
7	Aleksandar Jovević	SRB	10/04/78	M	1	(8)	
14	Dánjal á Lakjuni		22/09/90	M	20	(7)	6
10	Bogi Abrahamsson Løkin		22/10/88	M	10	(2)	
6	Karl Løkin		16/04/91	M	25		1
5	Høgni Madsen		04/02/85	M	21	(4)	2
1	Jákup Mikkelsen		16/08/70	G	23		
19	Heri Hansen Nesá		07/01/90	D		(4)	
2	Áki Petersen		01/12/84	D	6	(3)	
13	Uni Reinert Petersen		30/01/90	D	19		1
11	Frank Højbjerg Poulsen		03/11/88	M	15	(5)	1
4	Nenad Sarić	SRB	05/07/81	M	17	(6)	1
9	Simon Skibsted	DEN	25/11/91	M	12	(1)	4
25	Tórdur Thomsen		11/06/86	G	3		
17	Høgni Justinus Zachariassen		26/08/82	M	26		1

KÍ KLAKSVÍK

Coach: Páll Gudlaugsson
1904 • Djúpumýra (4,000) • ki.fo
Major honours
Faroe Islands League (17) 1942, 1945, 1952, 1953, 1954, 1956, 1957, 1958, 1961, 1966, 1967, 1968, 1969, 1970, 1972, 1991, 1999;
Faroe Islands Cup (5) 1966, 1967, 1990, 1994, 1999

2012

25/03	EB/Streymur	a	1-1	*Olsen*
01/04	B36	h	0-2	
05/04	HB	h	1-1	*Jakobsen*
15/04	ÍF	a	0-2	
21/04	TB	h	0-0	
28/04	NSÍ	h	3-2	*Djordjević, Klettskard 2*
05/05	B68	a	2-0	*Elttør, Klettskard*
13/05	Suduroy	h	5-1	*Klakstein, Isaksen 2, H Heinesen, Á Christiansen*
20/05	Víkingur	a	1-0	*Elttør*
28/05	HB	a	0-5	
09/06	NSÍ	a	2-0	*Klettskard 2*
13/06	B68	h	3-0	*Klettskard 2, Lakjuni*
16/06	B36	a	3-2	*Lakjuni, Á Christiansen, Jakobsen*
24/06	ÍF	h	1-0	*Klettskard*
30/06	Suduroy	a	4-1	*H Heinesen, Lakjuni, Klakstein, Klettskard (p)*
22/07	TB	a	6-1	*Klettskard, Klakstein, H Heinesen, Elttør, Olsen, Joensen*
27/07	Víkingur	h	3-3	*Hammer, Klettskard 2*
03/08	EB/Streymur	h	1-3	*Olsen*
11/08	ÍF	a	2-5	*H Heinesen, B Heinesen*
19/08	HB	h	1-2	*Klettskard*
29/08	B68	a	3-1	*Klettskard, Jakobsen, Joensen*
02/09	NSÍ	h	2-1	*Klettskard 2*
12/09	TB	h	1-1	*Jakobsen*
16/09	EB/Streymur	a	1-1	*Olsen*
23/09	B36	h	3-4	*Klettskard 2, Olsen*
29/09	Víkingur	a	3-4	*Olsen 2, Klettskard*
06/10	Suduroy	h	7-1	*Olsen 2, H Heinesen, Klettskard 3 (1p), Andreasen*

No	Name	Nat	DoB	Pos	Aps	(s)	Gls
15	Petur Andreasen		19/02/94	A		(5)	1
6	Álvur Fuglø Christiansen		29/05/89	M	23	(1)	2
14	Gunnar Christiansen		08/08/92	D	4	(1)	
8	Filip Djordjević	SRB	07/03/94	M	11	(2)	1
10	Hjalgrím Elttør		03/03/83	A	26		3
30	András Gángó	HUN	02/03/84	G	27		
20	John Hammer		17/02/89	M	14	(1)	1
11	Bárdur Johnson Heinesen		19/09/90	M	9	(7)	1
12	Henry Heinesen		01/06/88	M	20	(1)	5
5	Jógvan Isaksen		25/04/90	D	25		2
19	Johan Jacobsen		02/07/92	M	4	(10)	
13	Kristoffur Jakobsen		07/11/88	M	17	(7)	4
7	Ivan Joensen		20/02/92	D	8	(9)	2
4	Tórur Justesen		04/01/95	M	1	(1)	
4	Sørmundur Árni Kalsø		20/01/92	D	18	(4)	
21	Hedin Klakstein		30/04/92	M	4	(12)	3
9	Páll Andrasson Klettskard		17/05/90	A	24	(3)	22
18	Hedin á Lakjuni		19/02/78	A	24		3
4	Poul Nolsøe Mikkelsen		19/04/95	D		(1)	
27	Andy Ólavur Olsen		03/12/84	M	27		9
3	Ísak Simonsen		12/10/93	D	11	(8)	

NSÍ RUNAVÍK

Coach: Kári Reynheim
1957 • Vid Løkin (4,000) • nsi.fo
Major honours
Faroe Islands League (1) 2007;
Faroe Islands Cup (2) 1986, 2002

2012

25/03	ÍF	a	1-2	*Mortensen*
01/04	TB	h	2-0	*M Olsen, K Olsen*
05/04	Suduroy	h	0-0	
15/04	B68	a	2-3	*K Olsen 2*
21/04	HB	h	2-4	*Árni Frederiksberg, K Olsen*
28/04	KÍ	a	2-3	*Mortensen, K Olsen*
04/05	Víkingur	h	0-2	
13/05	EB/Streymur	a	0-1	
20/05	B36	h	3-1	*Árni Frederiksberg 2, K Olsen*
28/05	Suduroy	a	2-0	*K Olsen (p), Mortensen*
09/06	KÍ	h	0-2	
13/06	Víkingur	a	1-1	*Mortensen*
17/06	TB	a	3-1	*K Olsen 2, M Olsen*
24/06	B68	h	0-2	
29/06	EB/Streymur	h	1-0	*M Olsen*
22/07	HB	a	4-2	*K Olsen 2 (1p), Justinussen, Árni Frederiksberg*
29/07	B36	a	1-5	*Mortensen*
05/08	ÍF	h	1-2	*K Olsen (p)*
11/08	B68	a	1-1	*K Olsen*
19/08	Suduroy	h	5-1	*Árni Frederiksberg 2, Mortensen 2, M Olsen*
29/08	Víkingur	h	1-0	*Líknargøtu*
02/09	KÍ	a	1-2	*K Olsen*
12/09	HB	h	2-0	*Árni Frederiksberg, J Joensen*
16/09	ÍF	a	1-3	*Justinussen*
23/09	TB	h	0-1	
29/09	B36	h	0-0	
06/10	EB/Streymur	a	2-3	*D Danielsen, J Joensen*

No	Name	Nat	DoB	Pos	Aps	(s)	Gls
24	Óli Arge		24/03/91	M	9	(6)	
17	Bjarki Danielsen		29/10/84	M	1	(6)	
7	Debes Danielsen		12/08/86	M	7	(9)	1
76	Viljormur í Heidunum Davidsen		19/07/91	D	3		
8	Ari Ólavsson Ellingsgaard		03/02/93	M	10	(2)	
23	Andras Frederiksberg		02/12/92	M	21	(1)	
11	Árni Frederiksberg		13/06/92	M	26		7
15	Árni Gregersen		11/08/93	M		(1)	
20	Pætur Høj		02/09/94	G	1	(1)	
13	Rógvi Højgaard		24/10/89	M		(2)	
3	Monrad Holm Jacobsen		23/04/91	D	26	(1)	
21	Sjúrdur Jacobsen		29/08/76	D	24		
4	Jens Joensen		17/05/89	D	20	(4)	2
1	Kristian Joensen		21/12/92	G	26		
5	Pál Mohr Joensen		20/08/92	D	13	(11)	
12	Pól Jóhannus Justinussen		13/01/89	D	12		2
2	Per Langgaard		30/05/91	D		(1)	
16	Andrias Klein á Líknargøtu		09/05/90	M	6	(9)	1
9	Jann Martin Mortensen		18/07/89	A	23	(2)	7
10	Klæmint Andrasson Olsen		17/07/90	A	27		14
18	Magnus Hendriksson Olsen		26/10/86	A	24	(1)	4
6	Helgi Lamhauge Petersen		05/04/78	A	18	(2)	

FC SUDUROY

Coach: Pól Frídrikur Joensen;
(22/05/12) (Tórdur Holm); (31/05/12) Saša Kolman (SVN)
2010 • Vesturi á Eidinum (3,300) • fcsuduroy.com
Major honours
Faroe Islands League (1) 2000 (as VB Vágur);
Faroe Islands Cup (1) 1974 (as VB Vágur)

2012

Date	Opp		Score	Scorers
24/03	B36	a	0-1	
01/04	HB	h	0-1	
05/04	NSÍ	a	0-0	
15/04	EB/Streymur	a	0-3	
21/04	B68	h	0-1	
29/04	Víkingur	a	0-4	
05/05	TB	h	1-1	Jón Poulsen
13/05	KÍ	a	1-5	Jón Poulsen
20/05	ÍF	h	0-6	
28/05	NSÍ	h	0-2	
10/06	Víkingur	h	1-1	Augustinussen
13/06	TB	a	0-3	
17/06	HB	a	0-6	
23/06	EB/Streymur	h	0-2	
30/06	KÍ	h	1-4	Jón Poulsen
22/07	B68	a	0-2	
27/07	ÍF	a	2-3	John Poulsen 2
05/08	B36	h	0-2	
11/08	EB/Streymur	a	2-4	John Poulsen, Jón Poulsen
19/08	NSÍ	a	1-5	Asare
29/08	TB	h	1-0	John Poulsen
02/09	Víkingur	a	1-3	Vatnsdal
12/09	B68	h	2-1	John Poulsen (p), Djurhuus
15/09	B36	a	1-3	John Poulsen
23/09	HB	h	0-4	
29/09	ÍF	h	1-4	John Poulsen
06/10	KÍ	a	1-7	og (Justesen)

No	Name	Nat	DoB	Pos	Aps	(s)	Gls
17	David Asare	GHA	29/04/92	M	25	(1)	1
9	Jóan Pauli Augustinussen		16/12/80	M	27		1
3	Salmundur Bech		16/01/96	M		(2)	
18	Tóki Brattalíd		05/03/93	A		(6)	
14	Dan Djurhuus		15/08/78	M	10	(2)	1
2	Búi Egilsson		04/01/96	A		(2)	
14	Dánjal Godtfred		07/03/96	D	1	(1)	
13	Suni úr Hørg		24/12/82	D	22	(3)	
16	Jón Áki Jacobsen		02/11/95	D	23	(3)	
1	Kári Jacobsen		28/08/95	G		(3)	
11	Fridrik Andri Joensen		27/03/91	A	2	(13)	
12	Óli Andreas Juul Johannesen		07/04/92	D		(1)	
8	Heri Eydunsson Kjærbo		01/06/95	D	12	(5)	
14	Janus Mohr Kjærbo		17/09/77	D	1		
4	Saša Kolman	SVN	01/05/84	D	22		
32	Stanislav Kuzma	SVN	16/09/76	G	27		
2	Bjartur í Lágabø		21/06/87	D		(1)	
11	Eydstein í Lágabø		27/11/83	D	1		
19	Kári í Lágabø		12/06/83	D	18	(1)	
6	Bogi Lisberg		29/01/94	M		(1)	
18	Høgni Midjord		04/02/91	A	7	(1)	
10	Tóki Krosslá Mortensen		01/01/96	M		(1)	
15	Ingi Poulsen		19/11/93	M	18	(3)	
20	John Tordar Poulsen		17/09/85	A	22	(4)	7
10	Jón Krosslá Poulsen		17/02/88	M	16	(2)	4
7	Poul Narvi Poulsen		22/09/86	A	22	(1)	
6	Brandur Magnusarson Suduroy		04/07/94	M	1	(8)	
6	Teitur Tausen		27/03/91	D		(2)	
5	Heini Vatnsdal		18/10/91	M	20		1

TB TVØROYRI

Coach: Milan Kuljić (SRB)
1892 • Vesturi á Eidinum (3,300); Vid Stórá (3,000) • th fo
Major honours
Faroe Islands League (7) 1943, 1949, 1951, 1976, 1977, 1980, 1987;
Faroe Islands Cup (5) 1956, 1958, 1960, 1961, 1977

2012

Date	Opp		Score	Scorers
25/03	Víkingur	h	0-2	
01/04	NSÍ	a	0-2	
05/04	EB/Streymur	a	1-1	Timić (p)
15/04	B36	h	1-4	Timić (p)
21/04	KÍ	a	0-0	
29/04	ÍF	h	1-0	Janković
05/05	Suduroy	a	1-1	M Tausen
12/05	B68	h	3-1	Grkajac 2, Ingason
19/05	HB	h	4-2	Timić 2, og (Slættalíd), G Sørensen
28/05	EB/Streymur	h	0-3	
10/06	ÍF	a	1-1	Grkajac
13/06	Suduroy	h	3-0	Timić (p), Janković, Ingason
17/06	NSÍ	h	1-3	G Sørensen
24/06	B36	a	2-2	D Mortensen, Timić (p)
30/06	B68	a	1-1	G Sørensen
22/07	KÍ	h	1-6	og (Hammer)
28/07	HB	a	1-4	G Sørensen
05/08	Víkingur	a	0-1	
11/08	B36	h	0-0	
19/08	EB/Streymur	a	0-0	Timić, Janković
29/08	Suduroy	a	0-1	
02/09	ÍF	h	1-2	Ó Johannesen
12/09	KÍ	a	1-1	Ó Johannesen
16/09	Víkingur	h	2-2	G Sørensen 2
23/09	NSÍ	a	1-0	Kuljić
29/09	HB	h	1-3	Kuljić
06/10	B68	h	1-4	Janković

No	Name	Nat	DoB	Pos	Aps	(s)	Gls
10	Bárdur Anntinnur Dimon		09/07/83	M	14	(8)	
14	Eirikur Magnusarson Ellendersen		05/03/94	D	12	(2)	
20	Jón Magnusarson Ellendersen		28/08/90	M	2	(3)	
32	Igor Grkajac	SRB	26/04/87	A	9	(3)	3
17	Poul Kjartan Ingason		28/09/95	A	7	(18)	2
5	Dmitrije Janković	SRB	05/11/75	D	26		4
1	Henri Jensen		11/07/00	M	01	(1)	
13	Óli Johannesen		08/05/72	D	23	(2)	2
3	Patrik Johannesen		07/09/95	A		(3)	
11	Teitur Justinussen			M		(9)	
23	Milan Kuljić	SRB	24/12/75	M		(5)	2
18	Dan Mortensen		31/10/78	A	27		1
15	Hanus Mortensen		26/02/91	A	25	(1)	
12	Heini Mortensen		26/02/91	D	1		
2	Tórur Mortensen		08/09/77	A	6	(1)	
6	Gunleif Olsen		05/11/90	M	11	(6)	
3	Teitur Jespersen Olsen		10/05/95	D	1		
12	Benjamin Petersen		16/08/90	A		(2)	
4	Nenad Stanković	SRB	08/08/77	M	11		
1	Ivan Stojković	SRB	30/01/77	G	27		
4	Aron Stanković		22/12/88	D	2	(3)	
12	Gilli Sørensen		11/08/92	A	22	(2)	6
8	Martin Tausen		04/05/90	D	21	(4)	1
9	Ragnar Tausen		06/09/94	A	8	(2)	
21	Bojan Timić	SRB	12/02/83	A	21		7

VÍKINGUR

Coach: Jógvan Martin Olsen
2008 • Sarpugerdi (2,000) • vikingur.fo
Major honours
Faroe Islands League (6) 1983, 1986, 1993, 1994, 1995, 1998 (as GÍ Gøta),
Faroe Islands Cup (8) 1983, 1985, 1996, 1997, 2000, 2005 (as GÍ Gøta), 2009, 2012

2012

Date	Opp		Score	Scorers
25/03	TB	a	2-0	A Gregersen (p), B Hansen
30/03	EB/Streymur	h	2-1	og (Anghel), Blé
05/04	B68	h	2-0	Blé, Bartalsstovu
15/04	HB	a	1-1	Bartalsstovu
21/04	ÍF	a	2-1	Bassene, Hjartvard Hansen
29/04	Suduroy	h	4-0	og (John Poulsen), og (Hørg), Bassene, Hjartvard Hansen
04/05	NSÍ	a	2-0	Blé 2 (1p)
13/05	B36	a	0-3	
20/05	KÍ	h	0-1	
28/05	B68	a	1-1	Qvist
10/06	Suduroy	a	1-1	A Gregersen
13/06	NSÍ	h	1-1	Lambanum
16/06	EB/Streymur	h	1-0	B Hansen
24/06	HB	h	2-2	Bartalsstovu, Hjartvard Hansen
29/06	B36	h	3-2	Bartalsstovu, Hjartvard Hansen, B Hansen
27/07	KÍ	a	3-3	Vatnhamar, Bartalsstovu, Djordjević
01/08	ÍF	h	1-4	Hjartvard Hansen
05/08	TB	h	1-0	I I Jacobsen
10/08	HB	a	0-0	
18/08	B68	h	2-0	Djordjević, Hjartvard Hansen
29/08	NSÍ	a	0-1	
02/09	Suduroy	h	3-1	Hjartvard Hansen, Vatnhamar, Bartalsstovu
12/09	ÍF	h	0-3	
16/09	TB	a	2-2	Bartalsstovu, og (Ó Johannesen)
23/09	EB/Streymur	a	2-3	Bassene, Hjartvard Hansen
29/09	KÍ	h	4-3	Bartalsstovu 4 (1p)
06/10	B36	a	1-1	Blé

No	Name	Nat	DoB	Pos	Aps	(s)	Gls
21	Kaj Leo í Bartalsstovu		23/06/91	A	24		11
14	Joseph Youssoupa Bassene	SEN	14/11/88	M	8	(16)	7
7	Evraud Blé	CIV	02/01/82	M	24	(1)	5
2	Petur Gullstein Dalbø		15/03/91	D	2	(5)	
9	Filip Djordjević	SRB	07/03/94	M	10	(1)	2
16	Hans Jørgin Djurhuus		29/11/78	D	15	(2)	
4	Atli Gregersen		15/06/82	D	21		2
18	Per Gregersen		14/06/91	M		(5)	
12	Bárdur Jógvansson Hansen		13/03/92	D	24		3
17	Hedin Hansen		30/07/93	M	2	(8)	
25	Hjartvard Hansen		17/09/88	A	16	(8)	8
13	Erling Dávidsson Jacobsen		13/02/90	D	26		
3	Hanus Jacobsen		25/05/85	D	21	(1)	1
27	Magnus Jarnskor		14/12/95	M		(1)	
8	Fritleif í Lambanum		13/04/86	M	17	(9)	1
18	Dánjal Pauli Lervig		26/04/91	D	9	(3)	
23	Niclas Niclassen		26/07/79	M	23	(1)	
27	Martin Olsen		22/12/89	A		(2)	
19	Jan Poulsen		14/05/87	D		(1)	
11	Lasse Qvist	DEN	17/01/87	A	8		1
22	Ingi Sørensen		24/11/90	M	1	(6)	
1	Géza Tamas Túri	HUN	11/03/74	G	27		
10	Sølvi Vatnhamar		05/05/86	A	22		2

Top goalscorers

22	Clayton (ÍF)
	Páll Andrasson Klettskard (KÍ)
16	Arnbjørn Theodor Hansen (EB/Streymur)
14	Klæmint Andrasson Olsen (NSÍ)
12	Christian Restorff Mouritsen (HB)
11	Kaj Leo í Bartalsstovu (Víkingur)
9	Andy Ólavur Olsen (KÍ)
8	Łukasz Cieślewicz (B36)
	Leif Niclasen (EB/Streymur)
	Fródi Benjaminsen (HB)
	Símun Samuelsen (HB)
	Hjartvard Hansen (Víkingur)

Domestic cup: Løgmanssteypid 2012

SECOND ROUND

(09/04/12)
AB 5-2 Giza/Hoyvík
B68 2-1 07 Vestur
ÍF 2-4 EB/Streymur
KÍ 4-2 NSÍ
Suduroy 5-0 Skála
TB 1-3 HB
Undrid 5-5 B71 *(aet; 3-5 on pens)*
Víkingur 1-0 B36

QUARTER-FINALS

(25/04/12)
AB 1-3 EB/Streymur *(Midjord 83; Samuelsen 49, Niclasen 77, Anghel 80)*
B68 1-2 Víkingur *(N Joensen 99; A Gregersen 117, 119p) (aet)*
KÍ 3-5 HB *(H Heinesen 7, 34, Jacobsen 111; Benjaminsen 66, Isaksen 70og, Fløtum 93, Samuelsen 105, K Mouritsen 119) (aet)*
Suduroy 5-1 B71 *(John Poulsen 61, 69p, 78p, Augustinussen 64, Mýrini 84og; Rubeksen 25)*

SEMI-FINALS

(09/05/12 & 23/05/12)
EB/Streymur 4-1 HB *(Samuelsen 37p, Anghel 56, A Hansen 77, 90; Hansson 7)*
HB 5-2 EB/Streymur *(Anghel 16og, Samuelsen 33, Holm 59, Hansson 82, Benjaminsen 90; Anghel 63, Hanssen 69)*
(6-6; EB/Streymur on away goals)

Víkingur 1-0 Suduroy *(Blé 12p)*
Suduroy 2-1 Víkingur *(Jón Poulsen 48, Augustinussen 90; Qvist 59)*
(2-2; Víkingur on away goal)

FINAL

(25/08/12)
Tórsvøllur, Torshavn
VÍKINGUR 3 *(Djurhuus 55, A Gregersen 77p, Hj Hansen 111)*
EB/STREYMUR 3 *(Frederiksberg 31, Hanssen 70p, Niclasen 95)*
(aet; 5-4 on pens)
Referee: Forná
VÍKINGUR: Túri, A Gregersen, B Hansen, Djurhuus, E Jacobsen, Niclassen (Lambanum 81), H Jacobsen, Djordjević (Hj Hansen 78), Blé, Bartalsstovu, Vatnhamar (Bassene 101)
EB/STREYMUR: Tórgard, G Hansen, Anghel, Niclasen (A Dam 101), Frederiksberg, Djurhuus, Samuelsen, Hanssen, P Hansen (A Hansen 64), Jacobsen, Danielsen
Sent off: Jacobsen (103)

Promoted clubs

07 VESTUR

Coach: Piotr Krakowski (POL)
2007 • Á Dungasandi (1,000) • 07vestur.fo

AB ARGIR

Coach: Sámal Erik Hentze
1973 • Inni í Vika (2,000) • ab.fo

SECOND LEVEL FINAL TABLE 2012

		Pld	W	D	L	F	A	Pts
1	07 Vestur	27	22	2	3	68	19	68
2	AB Argir	27	20	1	6	82	25	61
3	Skála ÍF	27	16	6	5	58	29	54
4	HB Tórshavn II	27	14	5	8	53	34	47
5	KÍ Klaksvík II	27	12	2	13	57	58	38
6	Víkingur II	27	11	3	13	53	52	36
7	EB/Streymur II	27	8	6	13	36	59	30
8	B71 Sandoy	27	8	3	16	48	72	27
9	B68 Toftir II	27	4	2	21	29	80	14
10	NSÍ Runavik II	27	4	2	21	30	86	14

Víkingur players celebrate their penalty shoot-out win over EB/Streymur

FINLAND

Suomen Palloliitto – Finlands Bollförbund (SPL-FBF)

Address	Urheilukatu 5, PO Box 191	**President**	Pertti Alaja
	FI-00251 Helsinki	**General secretary**	Timo Huttunen
Tel	+358 9 742 151	**Media officer**	Sami Terävä
Fax	+358 9 742 15200	**Year of formation**	1907
E-mail	sami.terava@palloliitto.fi	**National stadium**	Olympic Stadium,
Website	palloliitto.fi		Helsinki (40,600)

VEIKKAUSLIIGA CLUBS

 ① HJK Helsinki

 ② FC Honka Espoo

 ③ FC Inter Turku

④ FF Jaro

 ⑤ JJK Jyväskylä

⑥ KuPS Kuopio

⑦ FC Lahti

 ⑧ IFK Mariehamn

⑨ Myllykosken Pallo-47

 ⑩ TPS Turku

⑪ Valkeakosken Haka

⑫ VPS Vaasa

PROMOTED CLUB

 ⑬ RoPS Rovaniemi

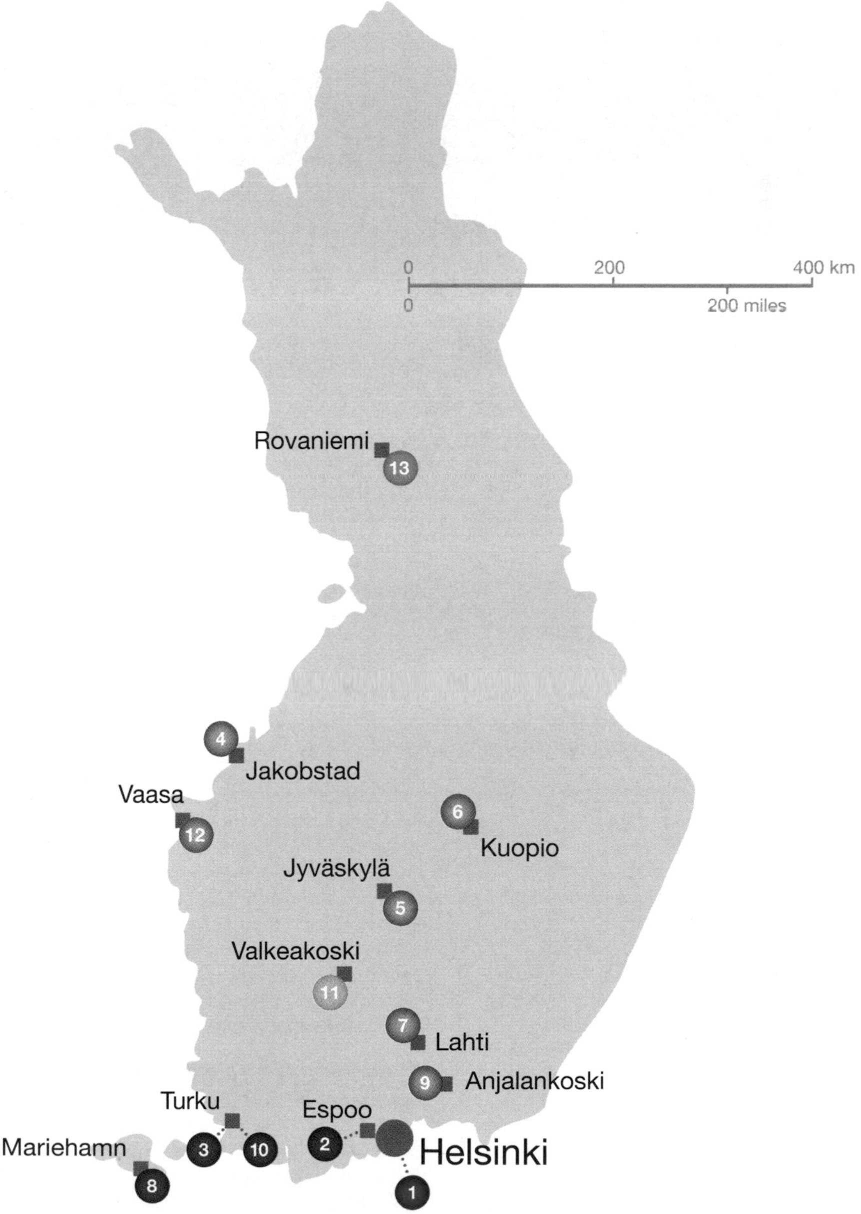

KEY:

● – UEFA Champions League

● – UEFA Europa League

● – Promoted club

● – Relegated club

Rovaniemi ⑬

Jakobstad ④

Vaasa ⑫

Kuopio ⑥

Jyväskylä ⑤

Valkeakoski ⑪

Lahti ⑦

Anjalankoski ⑨

Turku

Espoo

Mariehamn ③ ⑩ ② Helsinki

⑧ ①

0   200   400 km
0   200 miles

Muurinen's HJK make history

Although not as dominant as in the three previous seasons, HJK Helsinki duly retained their Veikkausliiga title to become champions of Finland for the 25th time. No club had ever won four successive championships, so it was a historic feat for the club and their coach, Antti Muurinen, the man in charge throughout the successful run.

A second straight double escaped the club from the capital, though, as FC Honka Espoo defeated them in the cup semi-finals and went on to collect their first major trophy with victory over KuPS Kuopio. The two clubs from Turku also qualified for Europe.

Unprecedented fourth straight title for Helsinki club

Turku rivals join HJK on the Veikkausliiga podium

First silverware for Finnish Cup winners Honka

Domestic league

HJK began the season as title favourites despite the loss of several key players to foreign clubs and defeat to TPS Turku in the final of the pre-season League Cup. It was TPS's city rivals FC Inter Turku, however, who made the best start to the Veikkausliiga campaign, winning their first four matches without conceding a goal.

HJK caught the 2011 runners-up by winning their first head-to-head battle in May, and thereafter the two clubs shadowed each other closely, Inter taking a slight lead before losing their way – as sadly has become their custom – during the run-in.

HJK, in contrast, won their last four matches, sealing the title on the final day with a 6-3 win away to JJK Jyväskylä. Indeed, Muurinen's men made it unbeaten through their last 12 games – following a worrying mid-season slump – and the key player in that late resurgence was national team stalwart Mika Väyrynen, a new arrival from Leeds United AFC in July.

Gambian import Demba Savage finished as HJK's top marksman, with 12 goals – one more than 17-year-old revelation Joel Pohjanpalo, who opened his account with a sensational hat-trick in the first game of the season.

Georgian Irakli Sirbiladze topped the league's scoring charts with 17 goals for Inter. The linchpin of the runners-up, once again, was Mika Ojala, who scored 12 goals and set up another 18. Inter effectively lost the title in the Turku derbies, taking just two points from nine – results that helped TPS to finish third.

Domestic cup

Mika Lehkosuo's Honka had a league campaign to forget, but they salvaged their season by winning the Finnish Cup. Honka surprised HJK in the semi-final on penalties, and after a four-month wait until the final, they beat KuPS 1–0 with midfielder Antti Mäkijärvi's first-half goal. KuPS did themselves no favours by having two men sent off. Indeed, Honka were their bogey team throughout the season as they also lost to them in all three league fixtures.

Europe

KuPS lasted three qualifying rounds of the UEFA Europa League in 2012/13, bettering the efforts of Finland's other three starters in that competition, but HJK's European ambitions were again left unfulfilled as they missed out on group stage participation.

That was the main reason why Muurinen's contract was not renewed after the season. The most successful club coach in Finnish football history, with seven titles, he was replaced by former HJK player Sixten Boström.

National team

Mixu Paatelainen's Finland made a poor start to 2014 FIFA World Cup qualification by losing 1-0 to France in Helsinki and dropping two further points at home to Georgia. However, they were to spring an enormous surprise in March when they held the mighty Spain to a 1-1 draw in Gijon, FC Schalke 04 striker Temmu Pukki scoring a late equaliser and the defence valiantly resisting a relentless late siege.

The team's ambition to finish third in the group and improve their coefficient for UEFA EURO 2016 qualification was refuelled in June when they took four points from back-to-back games with Belarus, Pukki scoring another important goal away from home to further enhance his international credentials.

Domestic league: Veikkausliiga 2012 final table

		Pld	Home					Away					Total					Pts
			W	D	L	F	A	W	D	L	F	A	W	D	L	F	A	
1	**HJK Helsinki**	33	12	5	0	36	10	7	2	7	27	23	19	7	7	63	33	64
2	FC Inter Turku	33	11	4	2	31	19	6	3	7	26	23	17	7	9	57	42	58
3	TPS Turku	33	11	1	5	38	17	5	5	6	17	16	16	6	11	55	33	54
4	IFK Mariehamn	33	8	8	0	23	11	5	4	8	27	32	13	12	8	50	43	51
5	FC Lahti	33	12	1	3	26	17	4	1	12	19	32	16	2	15	45	49	50
6	Myllykosken Pallo-47	33	9	5	2	23	12	4	5	8	16	21	13	10	10	39	33	49
7	FC Honka Espoo	33	9	4	4	26	18	3	3	10	11	20	12	7	14	37	38	43
8	VPS Vaasa	33	7	1	8	19	22	5	6	6	17	16	12	7	14	36	38	43
9	JJK Jyväskylä	33	7	2	8	31	36	5	2	9	23	29	12	4	17	54	65	40
10	KuPS Kuopio	33	6	3	8	20	29	4	3	9	19	24	10	6	17	39	53	36
11	FF Jaro	33	5	4	7	12	21	3	5	9	16	30	8	9	16	28	51	33
12	Valkeakosken Haka	33	6	3	7	18	20	3	2	12	14	37	9	5	19	32	57	32

SEASON AT A GLANCE

EUROPEAN QUALIFICATION 2013/14

Champion: HJK Helsinki (second qualifying round)

Cup winner: FC Honka Espoo (second qualifying round)
FC Inter Turku (first qualifying round)
TPS Turku (first qualifying round)
IFK Mariehamn (first qualifying round)

Top scorer	Irakli Sirbiladze (Inter), 17 goals
Relegated club	Valkeakosken Haka
Promoted club	RoPS Rovaniemi
Cup final	FC Honka Espoo 1-0 KuPS Kuopio

VEIKKAUSLIIGA TEAM OF THE SEASON
(4-4-2)
Ooaohi Korkoakunnas (MYPA)

PLAYER OF THE SEASON
Irakli Sirbiladze
(FC Inter Turku)

The powerful Georgian striker was voted players' player of the year as well as finishing as the Veikkausliiga's top goalscorer. Having come in for Fortuna Düsseldorf-bound Timo Furuholm at Inter Turku, he proved a more than worthy replacement, scoring 17 top-flight goals and setting up several others to help his new club finish runners-up to HJK Helsinki.

NEWCOMER OF THE SEASON
Joel Pohjanpalo
(HJK Helsinki)

Just 17 and with one league appearance as a substitute behind him, Pohjanpalo announced himself on the opening day of the season in remarkable fashion with a three-minute hat-trick against IFK Mariehamn. He went on to score 11 times in all for the champions, adding another three goals in Europe. He also ended 2012 with a first senior cap for Finland.

Wallén (HJK)

Sorsa (HJK) — Lyyski (Mariehamn) — Lindström (HJK) — Hurme (TPS)

Ojala (Inter) — Kolehmainen (TPS) — Gruborovics (JJK) — Savage (HJK)

Sirbiladze (Inter) — Sihvola (MYPA)

FINLAND

NATIONAL TEAM

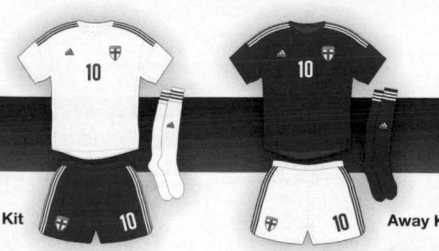

Home Kit   Away Kit

TOP FIVE ALL-TIME CAPS
Jari Litmanen (137); Sami Hyypiä & Jonatan Johansson (105); Ari Hjelm (100); Joonas Kolkka (98)

TOP FIVE ALL-TIME GOALS
Jari Litmanen (32); **Mikael Forssell** (29); Jonatan Johansson (22); Ari Hjelm (20); Mixu Paatelainen (18)

Results 2012/13

15/08/12	Northern Ireland	A	Belfast	3-3	*Sparv (22), Pukki (24), Hetemaj (78)*
07/09/12	France (WCQ)	H	Helsinki	0-1	
11/09/12	Czech Republic	A	Teplice	1-0	*Pukki (43)*
12/10/12	Georgia (WCQ)	H	Helsinki	1-1	*Hämäläinen (63)*
14/11/12	Cyprus	A	Nicosia	3-0	*Pukki (14), Hetemaj (27p), Kolehmainen (85)*
23/01/13	Thailand	A	Chiang Mai	3-1	*Sumusalo (5), Forssell (12, 87)*
26/01/13	Sweden	N	Chiang Mai (THA)	0-3	
06/02/13	Israel	A	Netanya	1-2	*Forsell (87)*
22/03/13	Spain (WCQ)	A	Gijon	1-1	*Pukki (79)*
26/03/13	Luxembourg	A	Luxembourg	3-0	*Ring (43), Forssell (49p), Toivio (90)*
07/06/13	Belarus (WCQ)	H	Helsinki	1-0	*Shitov (57og)*
11/06/13	Belarus (WCQ)	A	Gomel	1-1	*Pukki (24)*

Appearances 2012/13

Coach: Mixu Paatelainen	03/02/67		Nir	FRA	Cze	GEO	Cyp	Tha	Swe	Isr	ESP	Lux	BLR	BLR	Caps	Goals
Niki Mäenpää	23/01/85	VVV (NED)	G		G	G	G			G	G	G46	G	G	15	-
Kari Arkivuo	23/06/83	Häcken (SWE)	D	D	D		D70	D75	D	D	D	D71	D53		25	1
Joona Toivio	10/03/88	Djurgården (SWE) /Molde (NOR)	D	D	s45		D	D	D46		D	s71			20	2
Niklas Moisander	29/09/85	AZ (NED) /Ajax (NED)	D	D	D61	D				D	D	D		D	34	1
Jere Uronen	13/07/94	Helsingborg (SWE)	D			D	D								4	-
Tim Sparv	20/02/87	Groningen (NED)	M	M	s77	M	M			M	s69	M	s68	M	32	1
Roman Eremenko	19/03/87	Rubin (RUS)	M	M	M	M				M	M	M	M	M	52	2
Alexei Eremenko	24/03/83	Rubin (RUS)	M69	s65	M	M59*				s46					57	14
Kasper Hämäläinen	08/08/86	Djurgården (SWE) /Lech (POL)	M69	M78	M77	M	M83	M65			M	M76	M	M83	34	6
Teemu Pukki	29/03/90	Schalke (GER)	A46	A	A88	A62	A70			A	A94	A46	A77	A76	23	6
Njazi Kuqi	25/03/83	Atromitos (GRE)	A83	s78	s90		s83					s83			12	5
Riku Riski	16/08/89	Hønefoss (NOR)	s46				M46	M75	M			s76			11	1
Perparim Hetemaj	12/12/86	Chievo (ITA)	s69	M65	M	s62	M62				M		M	M	21	3
Toni Kolehmainen	20/07/88	TPS /Hønefoss (NOR)	s69		s88		s62			M					7	3
Daniel Sjölund	22/04/83	Djurgården (SWE)	s83		s46 /90		s78								37	2
Lukas Hradecky	24/11/89	Esbjerg (DEN)		G					G			s46			14	-
Markus Halsti	19/03/84	Malmö (SWE)		D			s70	D80	D77		s94	D	D		15	-
Alexander Ring	09/04/91	Mönchengladbach (GER)		M	M	M	M78				M	M83	M	M	17	1
Juhani Ojala	19/06/89	Young Boys (SUI)			D45	D	D			D					7	-
Jukka Raitala	15/09/88	Heerenveen (NED)			D	D				D95	D	D	D	D	21	-
Mika Väyrynen	28/12/81	HJK			M46			M	M32						59	5
Paulus Arajuuri	15/06/88	Kalmar (SWE)			s61			s80	s46				s83		6	-
Mika Ojala	21/06/88	Häcken (SWE)					s46	M69	M46						7	-
Joel Pohjanpalo	13/09/94	HJK					s70								1	-
Jesse Joronen	21/03/93	Fulham (ENG)						G							1	-
Mikko Sumusalo	12/03/90	HJK						D96	D						3	1
Teemu Tainio	27/11/79	HJK						M46	M		M69	M56	M68		57	6
Rasmus Schüller	18/06/91	HJK						M	M58			s56			3	-
Mikael Forssell	15/03/81	HJK						A	A	A73		s46	s77		86	29
Joni Kauko	12/07/90	Lahti						s46	s58						3	-
Sebastian Mannström	29/10/88	HJK						s65	s32						5	-
Jarkko Hurme	04/06/86	TPS						s75		s95		s53	D		6	-
Roni Porokara	12/12/83	unattached						s75							23	5
Tuomas Rannankari	21/05/91	Greuther Fürth (GER)						s96							2	-
Petteri Pennanen	19/09/90	TPS							s69						1	-
Lum Rexhepi	03/08/92	Honka							s77						1	-
Petteri Forsell	16/10/90	Bursaspor (TUR)								s73					1	1
Petri Pasanen	24/09/80	AGF (DEN)											D	D	72	1
Timo Furuholm	11/10/87	Halle (GER)												s76	9	2

European club competitions 2012/13

HJK HELSINKI

CHAMPIONS
LEAGUE

Second qualifying round - KR Reykjavík (ISL)
H 7-0 *Mäkelä (13, 78, 83), Väyrynen (20p), Pohjanpalo (48, 67), Schüller (57)*
Wallén, Hakanpää (Lindström 46), Lahti, Mannström, Väyrynen (Okkonen 62), Mäkelä, Pohjanpalo, Sumusalo, Savage, Sorsa, Schüller (Perovuo 75). Coach: Antti Muurinen (FIN)
A 2-1 *Sadik (60), Lindström (72)*
Wallén, Kansikas, Okkonen (Schüller 26; Lod 59), Lahti, Sadik, Lindström, Alho, Mäkelä, Sumusalo, Perovuo, Sorsa (Pelvas 70). Coach: Antti Muurinen (FIN)

Third qualifying round - Celtic FC (SCO)
A 1-2 *Schüller (48)*
Wallén, Lahti, Mannström, Lindström, Väyrynen (Okkonen 74), Mäkelä (Sadik 60), Sumusalo, Perovuo, Savage, Sorsa, Schüller (Pohjanpalo 84). Coach: Antti Muurinen (FIN)
H 0-2
Wallén, Lahti, Mannström (Zeneli 67), Lindström, Väyrynen, Pohjanpalo (Pelvas 78), Sumusalo, Perovuo (Sadik 70), Savage, Sorsa, Schüller. Coach: Antti Muurinen (FIN)

EUROPA
LEAGUE

Play-offs - Athletic Club (ESP)
A 0-6
Wallén, Lahti, Mannström, Sadik (Mäkelä 71), Lindström, Väyrynen (Zeneli 65), Sumusalo, Perovuo, Savage, Sorsa, Schüller (Mattila 46). Coach: Antti Muurinen (FIN)
H 3-3 *Schüller (25), Perovuo (62), Pohjanpalo (70)*
Wallén, Kansikas, Moren (Savage 76), Lahti, Mannström, Zeneli, Pelvas, Pohjanpalo, Perovuo, Sorsa (Okkonen 55), Schüller (Hakanpää 65). Coach: Antti Muurinen (FIN)
Red card: Pelvas 82

FC INTER TURKU

EUROPA
LEAGUE

Second qualifying round - FC Twente (NED)
A 1-1 *Bouwman (38)*
Reponen, Antúnez, Nyman, Bouwman (Asís 90+2), Sirbiladze, Aho, Paajanen (Kauppi 85), Ojala (Gnabouyou 81), Diallo, Kauko, Lehtonen. Coach: Job Dragtsma (NED)
H 0-5
Reponen, Antúnez, Nyman (Nikkari 46), Bouwman, Sirbiladze, Gnabouyou (Asís 46), Aho, Paajanen, Ojala (Duah 74), Diallo, Kauko. Coach: Job Dragtsma (NED)

JJK JYVÄSKYLÄ

EUROPA
LEAGUE

First qualifying round - Stabæk Fotball (NOR)
H 2-0 *Gruborovics (16), Wusu (66)*
Korhonen, Reintam, Van Gelderen, Pasoja, Innanen, Manninen (Hilska 90+1), Gruborovics, Markkula (Turpeenniemi 66), Wusu, Poutiainen, Virtanen (Tuomanen 55). Coach: Kari Martonen (FIN)
A 2-3 *Van Gelderen (45), Innanen (51)*
Korhonen, Reintam, Van Gelderen, Pasoja, Tuomanen, Innanen (Hilska 87), Gruborovics, Markkula, Wusu, Poutiainen, Virtanen (Turpeenniemi 63). Coach: Kari Martonen (FIN)

Second qualifying round - FK Zeta (MNE)
H 3-2 *Gruborovics (27p, 43, 47)*
Korhonen, Reintam, Van Gelderen, Pasoja, Tuomanen, Innanen (Turpeenniemi 86), Gruborovics, Markkula, Wusu (Markkanen 90+2), Poutiainen, Virtanen (Hilska 25). Coach: Kari Martonen (FIN)
A 0-1
Korhonen, Reintam, Van Gelderen, Pasoja, Tuomanen (Linjala 85), Innanen (Hilska 86), Gruborovics, Markkula, Wusu, Markkanen (Turpeenniemi 59), Poutiainen. Coach: Kari Martonen (FIN)

KUPS KUOPIO

EUROPA
LEAGUE

First qualifying round - Llanelli AFC (WAL)
H 2-1 *Joenmäki (5p), Purje (19)*
Hilander, Nissinen, Kärkkäinen, Hynynen, Joenmäki, James (Puri 46), Purje (Voutilainen 85), Ilo, Tabe, Obiefule, Berg (Venäläinen 62). Coach: Esa Pekonen (FIN)
A 1-1 *Paananen (59)*
Hilander, Nissinen, Kärkkäinen, Hynynen, Joenmäki, James (Paananen 46), Purje, Ilo, Tabe, Obiefule, Venäläinen. Coach: Esa Pekonen (FIN)

Second qualifying round - Maccabi Netanya FC (ISR)
A 2-1 *Paananen (36, 45)*
Hilander, Nissinen, Taipale, Kärkkäinen, Hynynen, Joenmäki, Purje (Zahovaiko 86), Paananen (James 76), Ilo (Puri 68), Tabe, Obiefule. Coach: Esa Pekonen (FIN)
H 0-1
Hilander, Nissinen, Taipale, Kärkkäinen, Hynynen (Puri 86), Joenmäki, Purje, Paananen (James 90), Ilo (Venäläinen 75), Tabe, Obiefule. Coach: Esa Pekonen (FIN)

Third qualifying round - Bursaspor (TUR)
H 1-0 *Puri (73)*
Hilander, Nissinen, Taipale, Kärkkäinen, Hynynen, Joenmäki, Paananen (James 90+1), Ilo (Venäläinen 81), Puri, Tabe, Obiefule. Coach: Esa Pekonen (FIN)
A 0-6
Hilander, Nissinen, Taipale (Hoivala 78), Kärkkäinen, Hynynen, Joenmäki (Puri 41), Purje, Paananen, Ilo (Venäläinen 46), Tabe, Obiefule. Coach: Esa Pekonen (FIN)

 **FINLAND**

MYLLYKOSKEN PALLO-47

EUROPA LEAGUE

First qualifying round - Cefn Druids AFC (WAL)
A 0-0
Kuismala, Vesala, Kukka (Sihvola 62), Gela, O'Neill, Ramadingaye, Oksanen, Koskinen, Aho (Vuorinen 37), A Lody, Saxman (O'Shaughnessy 78). Coach: Toni Korkeakunnas (FIN)
H 5-0 *A Lody (25), Saxman (37), Williams (44), O'Neill (47), Opoku (70)*
Kuismala, Sesay, Vesala, Kukka, Opoku, O'Neill (Selin 67), Ramadingaye (O'Shaughnessy 67), Koskinen, A Lody (Vuorinen 60), Saxman, Williams. Coach: Toni Korkeakunnas (FIN)

Second qualifying round - FC Rapid Bucureşti (ROU)
A 1-3 *Williams (26)*
Kuismala, Sesay (Kukka 66), Vesala, Gela (Selin 81), O'Neill, Oksanen, Koskinen, Aho, A Lody, Saxman (Ramadingaye 72), Williams. Coach: Toni Korkeakunnas (FIN)
H 0-2
Kuismala, Sesay, Vesala, Gela, Oksanen, Koskinen, Selin (Anttilainen 46), Aho, A Lody (Sihvola 46), Saxman, Williams (Kukka 67). Coach: Toni Korkeakunnas (FIN)

Domestic league club-by-club

HJK HELSINKI
Coach: Antti Muurinen
1907 • Sonera Stadium (10,800) • hjk.fi
Major honours
Finnish League (25) 1911, 1912, 1917, 1918, 1919, 1923, 1925, 1936, 1938, 1964, 1973, 1978, 1981, 1985, 1987, 1988, 1990, 1992, 1997, 2002, 2003, 2009, 2010, 2011, 2012;
Finnish Cup (11) 1966, 1981, 1984, 1993, 1996, 1998, 2000, 2003, 2006, 2008, 2011

2012

15/04	Mariehamn	h	3-1	*Pohjanpalo 3*
19/04	TPS	a	1-3	*Perovuo (p)*
23/04	Jaro	h	4-1	*Lindström, Pelvas, Savage, Sumusalo*
29/04	MYPA	a	0-1	
02/05	KuPS	a	3-0	*Mannström, Mäkelä 2*
06/05	Inter	h	2-1	*Mannström, Pohjanpalo*
12/05	KuPS	h	2-0	*Pohjanpalo, Savage*
16/05	Haka	a	1-0	*Savage*
21/05	Honka	h	3-0	*Mäkelä 2, Savage*
24/05	VPS	a	0-1	
27/05	Lahti	h	2-0	*Mannström, Pelvas*
16/06	JJK	a	3-0	*Pelvas 2, Mäkelä*
20/06	Mariehamn	a	0-2	
25/06	TPS	h	0-0	
28/06	Jaro	a	2-2	*Mäkelä, Savage*
02/07	MYPA	h	1-1	*Pohjanpalo*
07/07	Inter	a	0-2	
21/07	Haka	h	1-0	*Mäkelä*
28/07	Honka	a	0-1	
04/08	VPS	h	3-3	*Pelvas, Savage, Väyrynen*
12/08	Lahti	a	0-3	
18/08	JJK	h	2-0	*Mannström, Väyrynen (p)*
26/08	Mariehamn	h	5-1	*Savage 2, Zeneli, Sadik, Mäkelä*
02/09	TPS	a	2-1	*Väyrynen, Mäkelä*
14/09	Jaro	h	0-0	
17/09	MYPA	a	4-1	*Hakanpää, Savage, Pohjanpalo 2*
23/09	Inter	h	1-1	*Schüller*
26/09	KuPS	h	4-1	*Savage, Pelvas 3 (1p)*
01/10	Haka	a	2-2	*Mäkelä, Moren*
08/10	Honka	h	1-0	*Savage*
19/10	VPS	a	3-1	*Pohjanpalo, og (Abdulahi), Sadik*
22/10	Lahti	h	2-0	*Sadik (p), Savage*
27/10	JJK	a	6-3	*Mannström, Schüller, Pohjanpalo 2, Sadik 2*

No	Name	Nat	DoB	Pos	Aps	(s)	Gls
17	Nikolai Alho		12/03/93	A		(9)	
12	Sherif Ashraf	EGY	01/01/87	A	4	(4)	
5	Rami Hakanpää		09/10/78	D	21	(1)	1
2	Tuomas Kansikas		15/05/81	D	21	(1)	
6	Timi Lahti		28/06/90	D	24	(1)	
11	Mathias Lindström		14/01/81	D	18		1
31	Robin Lod		17/04/93	M	1	(6)	
18	Juho Mäkelä		23/06/83	A	19	(8)	10
7	Sebastian Mannström		29/10/88	M	21	(9)	5
25	Sakari Mattila		14/07/89	D	5	(6)	
3	Valtteri Moren		15/06/91	D	4	(3)	1
4	Antti Okkonen		06/06/82	M	20	(2)	
15	Akseli Pelvas		08/02/89	A	11	(11)	8
22	Joel Perovuo		11/08/85	M	14	(11)	1
20	Joel Pohjanpalo		13/09/94	A	23	(5)	11
9	Berat Sadik		14/09/86	A	8	(4)	5
35	Saku-Pekka Sahlgren		08/04/92	G	2	(1)	
26	Demba Savage	GAM	17/06/88	M	27	(3)	12
28	Rasmus Schüller		18/06/91	M	24	(1)	2
27	Sebastian Sorsa		15/01/84	M	20	(1)	
21	Mikko Sumusalo		12/03/90	D	18	(2)	1
16	Mika Väyrynen		28/12/81	M	9	(2)	3
1	Ville Wallén		26/06/76	G	31		
8	Erfan Zeneli		28/12/86	M	18	(6)	1

FC HONKA ESPOO
Coach: Mika Lehkosuo
1957 • Tapiolan urheilupuisto (5,000) • fchonka.fi
Major honours
Finnish Cup (1) 2012

2012

15/04	VPS	h	1-1	*Vasara*
18/04	Lahti	a	1-2	*Aalto*
22/04	JJK	h	0-2	
29/04	Mariehamn	a	0-0	
05/05	TPS	h	0-2	
12/05	Jaro	a	1-0	*Otaru*
16/05	MYPA	h	2-1	*Dudu, Aalto*
21/05	HJK	a	0-3	
24/05	KuPS	h	1-0	*Väyrynen*
27/05	Haka	a	1-2	*Yaghoubi*
16/06	Inter	h	2-1	*Mäkijärvi, Koskinen (p)*
20/06	VPS	a	0-2	
25/06	Lahti	h	3-2	*Vasara, Koskinen (p), Mäkijärvi*
28/06	JJK	a	1-0	*Väyrynen*
03/07	Mariehamn	h	2-2	*Väyrynen 2*
09/07	TPS	a	1-2	*Väyrynen*
15/07	Jaro	h	2-0	*Väyrynen, Heikkilä*
22/07	MYPA	a	0-0	
28/07	HJK	h	1-0	*Väyrynen*
05/08	KuPS	a	2-0	*Vasara, Aalto*
12/08	Haka	h	2-2	*Väyrynen, Vasara*
18/08	Inter	a	1-2	*Väyrynen*
27/08	VPS	h	1-2	*Vasara*
31/08	Lahti	a	2-3	*Väyrynen, Mäkijärvi*
15/09	JJK	h	3-0	*Vasara 2, Rexhepi*
18/09	Mariehamn	a	1-1	*Aalto*
22/09	TPS	h	0-1	
26/09	Jaro	a	0-1	
04/10	MYPA	h	1-1	*Mäkijärvi*
08/10	HJK	a	0-1	
19/10	KuPS	h	2-1	*Simpanen, Rahimi*
22/10	Haka	a	0-1	
27/10	Inter	h	3-0	*Vasara, Mäkijärvi, Äijälä*

No	Name	Nat	DoB	Pos	Aps	(s)	Gls
5	Henri Aalto		20/04/89	D	29	(1)	4
24	Patrick Aaltonen		18/03/94	D	15	(1)	
16	Santeri Ahola		10/01/92	M	2	(3)	
11	Ilari Äijälä		30/09/86	D	9	(5)	1
15	MacPherlin Dudu	NGA	18/07/85	A	11	(6)	1
26	Dani Hatakka		12/03/94	D	9	(3)	
4	Tapio Heikkilä		08/04/90	D	33		1
7	Jaakko Hietikko		13/01/94	A		(2)	
2	Sampo Koskinen		01/03/79	D	20	(2)	2
19	Mikael Lähde		13/01/93	A	4	(8)	
21	Antti Mäkijärvi		08/12/93	M	19	(9)	5
6	Kevin Mombilo		06/05/93	A	2	(8)	
20	Nicholas Otaru		15/07/86	M	27	(1)	1
1	Tuomas Peltonen		20/10/77	G	23		
9	Tomi Petrescu		24/07/86	M	13	(8)	
23	Youness Rahimi		13/02/95	A	1	(6)	1
13	Lum Rexhepi		03/08/92	D	17	(1)	1
8	Juuso Simpanen		08/06/91	A	21	(5)	1
6	Duarte Tammilehto		15/02/90	M	23	(3)	
14	Jussi Vasara		14/05/87	A	29	(2)	8
7	Tim Väyrynen		30/03/93	A	22	(6)	10
12	Walter Viitala		16/08/92	G	10		
3	Hermanni Vuorinen		27/01/85	A	3	(2)	
17	Moshtagh Yaghoubi		08/11/94	A	21	(6)	1

FC INTER TURKU

Coach: Job Dragtsma (NED)
1990 • Veritas Stadion (9,300) • fcinter.com
Major honours
Finnish League (1) 2008;
Finnish Cup (1) 2009

2012

19/04	VPS	a	2-0	Paajanen, Širbiladze
22/04	MYPA	h	2-0	Sirbiladze, Paajanen
29/04	Lahti	a	5-0	Lehtonen, Ojala, Kauppi, Sirbiladze, Kauko
02/05	Jaro	a	1-0	Bouwman
06/05	HJK	a	1-2	Kauko
12/05	JJK	a	2-1	Ojala, Paajanen
16/05	KuPS	h	2-1	Bouwman, Antúnez
21/05	Mariehamn	a	1-2	Sirbiladze
24/05	Haka	h	4-1	Ojala, Paajanen, og (Salonen), Gnabouyou
30/05	Lahti	h	2-0	Bouwman, Ojala
16/06	Honka	a	1-2	Ojala
19/06	Jaro	h	1-1	Sirbiladze
25/06	VPS	h	1-1	Ojala
28/06	MYPA	a	0-4	
02/07	Lahti	a	3-4	Ojala, Nikkari, Sirbiladze
07/07	HJK	h	2-0	Kauko, Ojala
15/07	JJK	h	3-2	Sirbiladze, Bouwman, Ojala (p)
22/07	KuPS	a	6-0	Kauko, Gnabouyou, Lehtonen, Sirbiladze, Antúnez, Asis
30/07	Mariehamn	h	0-3	
05/08	Haka	a	2-0	Sirbiladze, Duah
12/08	TPS	a	1-4	Gnabouyou
18/08	Honka	a	2-1	Sirbiladze, Bouwman
26/08	Jaro	h	3-1	Ojala (p), Sirbiladze, Asis
02/09	VPS	h	2-0	Sirbiladze 2
14/09	MYPA	a	0-0	
17/09	TPS	h	3-3	Sirbiladze 2, Gnabouyou
23/09	HJK	a	1-1	og (Mäkelä)
26/09	JJK	a	0-0	
03/10	KuPS	h	1-4	Sirbiladze
08/10	Mariehamn	h	1-0	Sirbiladze
19/10	Haka	a	2-1	Ojala 2 (1p)
22/10	TPS	h	0-0	
27/10	Honka	a	0-3	

No	Name	Nat	DoB	Pos	Aps	(s)	Gls
14	Joni Aho		12/04/86	D	32	(1)	
4	Daniel Antúnez	USA	10/02/86	D	24	(1)	2
9	Maximiliano Asis	ARG	27/05/87	A	3	(19)	2
1	Magnus Bahne		15/03/79	G	15		
8	Pim Bouwman	NED	30/01/91	M	30		5
19	Babacar Diallo	SEN	25/03/89	D	7		
33	Stef Doedee	NED	17/02/87	G	9		
21	Sulomon Duah		17/11/93	A	4	(11)	1
11	Guy Gnabouyou	FRA	01/12/89	A	13	(11)	4
24	Joni Kauko		12/07/90	M	23	(1)	4
16	Kalle Kauppi		06/05/92	M	17	(10)	1
27	Aleksi Laiho		17/06/93	M	1	(2)	
29	Henri Lehtonen		28/07/80	M	29	(1)	2
20	Matias Louanto		25/12/94	M		(1)	
30	Blend Miftari		03/12/95	A		(1)	
23	Ville Nikkari		05/11/88	D	27		1
7	Ari Nyman		07/02/84	M	25	(6)	
25	Friday Faith Obilor	NGA	05/03/91	D	7		
17	Mika Ojala		21/06/88	A	26	(2)	12
25	Severi Paajanen		23/10/86	M	29	(3)	4
13	Eemeli Reponen		06/06/90	G	9	(1)	
10	Irakli Sirbiladze	GEO	27/09/82	A	33		17
3	Toni Viljanen		23/05/95	M		(1)	

FF JARO

Coach: Alexei Eremenko Sr
1965 • Centralplan (5,000) • ffjaro.fi

2012

19/04	MYPA	a	0-2	
28/04	HJK	a	1-4	Vaganov
29/04	KuPS	h	1-0	Niang (p)
02/05	Inter	h	0-1	
05/05	Haka	a	1-4	Wargh
12/05	Honka	h	0-1	
16/05	VPS	h	1-1	Tahvanainen
21/05	Lahti	h	0-2	
24/05	JJK	a	1-1	og (Turpeenniemi)
27/05	Mariehamn	h	0-3	
16/06	TPS	a	3-2	Banner, Vasilyev, Wargh
19/06	Inter	a	1-1	Jonke
25/06	MYPA	h	1-0	Tahvanainen
28/06	HJK	h	2-2	Jonke, Wargh
02/07	KuPS	a	0-1	
07/07	Haka	h	1-0	Jonke
15/07	Honka	a	0-2	
21/07	VPS	h	0-0	
29/07	Lahti	a	2-0	Jonke, Aho (p)
05/08	JJK	h	0-3	
11/08	Mariehamn	a	0-2	
19/08	TPS	h	0-1	
26/08	Inter	a	1-3	Niang
02/09	MYPA	h	0-3	
14/09	HJK	a	0-1	
17/09	KuPS	h	1-1	Brunell
23/09	Haka	a	0-0	
26/09	Honka	h	1-0	Niang
01/10	VPS	a	1-2	Jonke
07/10	Lahti	h	2-1	Niang, Jonke
19/10	JJK	a	2-4	Emet, Ashraf
22/10	Mariehamn	h	3-3	Ashraf, Emet, Jonke
27/10	TPS	a	2-1	Kula, Ashraf

No	Name	Nat	DoB	Pos	Aps	(s)	Gls
10	Jussi Aalto		28/07/83	A	11	(9)	
6	Dickson Agyeman	BEL	14/09/85	M	20		
3	Heikki Aho		16/03/83	D	17		1
9	Sherif Ashraf	EGY	01/01/87	A	7		3
7	Mike Banner	USA	20/10/84	D	28		1
22	Johan Brunell		29/05/91	D	9	(2)	1
20	Akil DeFreitas	TRI	07/11/86	A	2	(9)	
25	Iidle Elmi	SOM	01/01/95	A		(2)	
16	Jonas Emet		13/02/88	M	9	(16)	2
2	Tillmann Grove	GER	07/03/88	D	6	(8)	
9	Tommi Haanpää		21/04/90	A		(7)	
23	Steven Irwin	ENG	29/09/90	M	9		
19	Frank Jonke	CAN	30/01/83	A	21		7
1	Artur Kotenko	EST	20/08/81	G	25		
15	Markus Kronholm		02/04/91	M	28	(3)	
18	Thomas Kula		24/05/91	M	8	(8)	1
30	Papa Niang	SEN	05/12/88	A	27	(4)	4
31	Jesse Öst		20/10/90	G	8		
17	Kevin Peth		26/04/93	D	1	(1)	
8	Jari Sara		25/04/89	D	22	(2)	
19	Simon Skrabb		19/01/95	M	18	(10)	
21	Timo Tahvanainen		26/06/86	A	19	(11)	2
27	Ilya Vaganov	RUS	15/01/89	D	25	(1)	1
4	Maksim Vasilyev	RUS	31/01/87	D	30		1
11	Mattias Wargh		15/10/82	A	13		3

JJK JYVÄSKYLÄ

Coach: Kari Martonen
1992 • Harjun stadion (4,600) • fcjjk.com

2012

15/04	KuPS	a	2-2	Liniala, Wusu
19/04	Haka	h	1-1	Gruborovics
22/04	Honka	a	2-0	Innanen, Gruborovics (p)
30/04	VPS	h	0-2	
05/05	Lahti	h	2-1	Van Gelderen, Gruborovics (p)
12/05	Inter	a	1-2	Pasoja
16/05	Mariehamn	h	5-2	Wusu, Gruborovics 2 (1p), Innanen 2
21/05	TPS	a	3-2	Van Gelderen, Wusu, Gruborovics
24/05	Jaro	h	1-1	Gruborovics
27/05	MYPA	a	1-0	Wusu
11/06	KuPS	h	1-5	Gruborovics (p)
16/06	HJK	h	0-3	
25/06	Haka	a	1-3	Wusu
28/06	Honka	h	0-1	
02/07	VPS	a	0-3	
08/07	Lahti	h	3-1	Nieminen, Gruborovics, Wusu
15/07	Inter	a	2-3	Gruborovics, Wusu
22/07	Mariehamn	a	3-3	Markkanen 3
29/07	TPS	h	2-1	Hilska, Wusu
05/08	Jaro	a	3-0	Innanen, Wusu 2
11/08	MYPA	h	0-3	
18/08	HJK	a	0-2	
26/08	KuPS	a	3-2	Gruborovics 2, Innanen
02/09	Haka	h	5-0	Saksela, Innanen 2, Korte, Hanslian
15/09	Honka	a	0-3	
18/09	VPS	h	1-2	og (Woodbine)
23/09	Lahti	a	1-2	Markkanen
26/09	Inter	h	0-0	
01/10	Mariehamn	h	3-2	Markkanen 2, Innanen
07/10	TPS	a	0-1	
19/10	Jaro	h	4-2	Innanen 2, Manninen, Markkanen
22/10	MYPA	a	1-2	Manninen
27/10	HJK	h	3-6	Hilska 2, Järvinen

No	Name	Nat	DoB	Pos	Aps	(s)	Gls
10	Tamás Gruborovics	HUN	03/07/84	M	32		12
19	Benno Hanslian		16/08/93	D		(2)	1
15	Antto Hilska		22/09/93	A	14	(13)	3
7	Mikko Innanen		08/09/82	A	30	(2)	10
11	Topi Järvinen		26/09/94	M		(4)	1
30	Janne Korhonen		28/11/79	G	32		
8	Eero Korte		20/09/87	M	10	(1)	1
13	Tuomas Latikka		20/09/85	M		(9)	
17	Lasse Linjala		13/08/87	A	1	(17)	1
9	Mikko Manninen		25/05/85	M	25	(2)	2
21	Eero Markkanen		03/07/91	A	7	(7)	7
16	Niko Markkula		27/06/90	D	18	(5)	
2	Samu Nieminen		14/01/92	D	20	(1)	1
5	Juha Pasoja		16/11/76	D	20		1
23	Patrick Poutiainen		14/06/91	M	12	(10)	
3	Mikk Reintam	EST	22/05/90	D	15	(2)	
22	Janne Saksela		14/03/93	D	8	(1)	1
12	Antto Tapaninen		16/06/89	D	16	(3)	
6	Jukka-Pekka Tuomanen		04/12/85	M	28		
18	Janne Turpeenniemi		17/05/89	D	19	(3)	
4	Jordi van Gelderen	NED	26/04/90	D	23		2
31	Ville Viljala		04/02/95	G	1		
26	Jani Virtanen		06/05/88	M	13	(7)	
20	Babatunde Wusu	NGA	18/04/84	A	19	(1)	10

KUPS KUOPIO

Coach: Esa Pekonen
1923 • Keskuskentän jalkapallostadion (3,700) • kups.fi
Major honours
Finnish League (5) 1956, 1958, 1966, 1974, 1976;
Finnish Cup (2) 1968, 1989

2012

15/04	JJK	h	2-2	*Venäläinen, Obiefule*
19/04	Mariehamn	a	1-1	*Zahovaiko*
22/04	TPS	h	1-1	*Paananen*
29/04	Jaro	a	0-1	
02/05	HJK	h	0-3	
05/05	MYPA	h	1-2	*James*
12/05	HJK	a	0-2	
16/05	Inter	a	1-2	*Hynynen*
21/05	Haka	h	3-0	*Voutilainen, Ilo, Purje*
24/05	Honka	a	0-1	
27/05	VPS	h	0-3	
11/06	JJK	a	5-1	*Purje 2, Obiefule, og (Turpeenniemi), Puri*
17/06	Lahti	h	1-2	*Purje*
25/06	Mariehamn	h	2-0	*Puri, James*
28/06	TPS	a	0-3	
02/07	Jaro	h	1-0	*Ilo*
08/07	MYPA	a	1-1	*Paananen*
22/07	Inter	h	0-6	
29/07	Haka	a	2-0	*Purje, Voutilainen*
05/08	Honka	h	0-2	
12/08	VPS	a	1-0	*Venäläinen*
18/08	Lahti	h	1-0	*Venäläinen*
26/08	JJK	h	2-3	*Hynynen, Tabe*
02/09	Mariehamn	a	0-2	
13/09	TPS	h	1-3	*Kärkkäinen*
17/09	Jaro	a	1-1	*Ilo*
23/09	MYPA	a	1-2	*Kärkkäinen, Dudu*
26/09	HJK	a	1-4	*Dudu*
03/10	Inter	a	4-1	*Purje, Holopainen, James 2*
07/10	Haka	h	1-1	*Holopainen*
19/10	Honka	a	1-2	*Ilo*
22/10	VPS	h	2-1	*Koljonen, Dudu*
27/10	Lahti	a	1-2	*Voutilainen*

No	Name	Nat	DoB	Pos	Aps	(s)	Gls
28	Jan Berg		22/05/85	D	2	(3)	
29	MacPherlin Dudu	NGA	18/07/85	A	11	(2)	3
1	Mika Hilander		17/08/83	G	21		
24	Atte Hoivala		10/02/92	D	9	(4)	
3	Pietari Holopainen		26/09/82	D	13	(1)	2
7	Antti Hynynen		30/05/84	M	23	(1)	2
20	Miikka Ilo		09/05/82	A	20	(6)	4
10	Chris James	NZL	04/07/87	M	15	(4)	4
9	Markus Joenmäki		11/02/88	D	19	(1)	
6	Pyry Kärkkäinen		10/11/86	D	29	(1)	2
18	Ali Koljonen		25/07/88	M	7	(3)	1
26	Aleksi Mäkinen		05/11/93	D		(1)	
2	Joni Nissinen		21/04/91	D	16		
25	Paul Obiefule	NGA	15/05/86	M	26	(1)	2
13	Aleksi Paananen		25/01/93	M	15	(8)	2
16	Joonas Pöntinen		19/03/90	G	12		
22	Sander Puri	EST	07/05/88	A	11	(8)	2
11	Ats Purje	EST	08/03/85	A	23	(4)	6
21	Sami Räsänen		17/10/92	D	6	(5)	
19	Johann Smith	USA	25/04/87	A	4		
17	Ebrima Sohna	GAM	14/12/88	M	12		
23	Etchu Tabe	USA	12/07/86	D	18	(4)	1
4	Tero Taipale		14/12/72	M	19	(3)	
27	Ilja Venäläinen		27/09/80	A	19	(11)	3
8	Jerry Voutilainen		29/03/95	M	7	(10)	3
14	Vjatšeslav Zahovaiko	EST	29/12/81	A	6		1

FC LAHTI

Coach: Tommi Kautonen
1996 • Lahden stadion (7,400) • fclahti.fi

2012

15/04	Haka	h	1-0	*Shala*
18/04	Honka	h	2-1	*Kari 2 (1p)*
22/04	VPS	a	1-2	*Tynkkynen*
29/04	Inter	h	0-5	
05/05	JJK	a	1-2	*Shala*
13/05	Mariehamn	a	0-2	
16/05	TPS	h	2-0	*Kari, Rafael*
21/05	Jaro	a	2-0	*Sinisalo, Kari (p)*
24/05	MYPA	h	0-0	
27/05	HJK	a	0-2	
30/05	Inter	a	0-2	
17/06	KuPS	a	2-1	*Bernhardt, Rafael (p)*
20/06	Haka	h	0-1	
25/06	Honka	a	2-3	*Hietanen 2*
28/06	VPS	h	1-0	*Bernhardt*
02/07	Inter	h	4-3	*Rafael, Klinga, Bäckman, Shala*
08/07	JJK	a	1-3	*Mero*
16/07	Mariehamn	h	2-0	*Länsitalo, Köse*
22/07	TPS	a	0-4	
29/07	Jaro	h	0-2	
04/08	MYPA	a	1-3	*Shala*
12/08	HJK	h	3-0	*Hietanen, Sinisalo, Bäckman*
18/08	KuPS	a	0-1	
25/08	Haka	a	3-0	*Mäkitalo (p), og (Kuusijärvi), Ngueukam*
31/08	Honka	h	3-2	*Ngueukam 2, Shala*
14/09	VPS	a	3-1	*Ngueukam 2, Rafael*
23/09	JJK	h	2-0	*Hauhia, Hietanen*
26/09	Mariehamn	a	2-2	*Hauhia, Ngueukam*
01/10	TPS	h	1-0	*Shala*
07/10	Jaro	a	1-2	*Shala*
19/10	MYPA	h	3-1	*Hietanen, Mero, Rafael*
22/10	HJK	a	0-2	
27/10	KuPS	h	2-1	*Alho, Ngueukam*

No	Name	Nat	DoB	Pos	Aps	(s)	Gls
93	Nikolai Alho		12/03/93	A	2	(6)	1
8	Jani Bäckman		20/03/88	A	23	(4)	2
27	Edgar Bernhardt	GER	30/03/86	M	10		2
6	Hendrik Grossöhmichen	GER	06/06/85	D	14	(2)	
3	Mikko Hauhia		03/09/84	D	32		2
18	Konsta Hietanen		20/07/84	M	30		5
15	Antti Hukka		09/09/87	D	2	(2)	
21	Tommi Kari		22/09/86	A	9		4
20	Jonne Kemppinen		25/08/81	A		(4)	
19	Matti Klinga		10/12/94	M	26	(6)	1
5	Ibrahim Köse		04/03/92	M	4	(18)	1
13	Jussi Länsitalo		30/06/90	A	22	(6)	1
11	Jaakko Lepola		14/03/90	M	8	(6)	
17	Mika Mäkitalo		12/06/85	M	22		1
2	Joel Mero		07/02/95	D	15	(4)	2
88	Ariel Ngueukam	CMR	15/11/88	A	9		7
9	Rafael	BRA	01/08/78	A	19	(8)	5
22	Robin Saastamoinen		22/06/93	A	1	(3)	
28	Drilon Shala		20/03/87	A	28	(2)	7
4	Jukka Sinisalo		21/05/82	D	29		2
12	Viktor Szentpéteri	HUN	01/11/79	G	25		
23	Ville Taulo		14/08/88	M	9		
1	Juha Tuomi		07/11/89	G	8		
16	Mikko Tuomi		21/06/94	M	1	(1)	
14	Olli Tynkkynen		04/02/94	M	6	(10)	1
7	Jukka Veltheim		18/06/84	M	9		

IFK MARIEHAMN

Coach: Pekka Lyyski
1919 • Wiklöf Holding Arena (4,000) •
ifkmariehamn.com/fotboll

2012

15/04	HJK	a	1-3	*Ekhalie*
19/04	KuPS	h	1-1	*Forsell*
22/04	Haka	a	2-0	*Kangaskolkka, Forsell*
29/04	Honka	h	0-0	
05/05	VPS	a	2-1	*Kojola, Forsell*
13/05	Lahti	h	2-0	*Forsell (p), Jagne*
16/05	JJK	a	2-5	*Kangaskolkka, Ekhalie*
21/05	Inter	h	2-1	*Jagne, Gadžo*
24/05	TPS	h	2-1	*Forsell (p), Wiklöf*
27/05	Jaro	a	3-0	*Forsell, Kangaskolkka 2*
17/06	MYPA	h	0-0	
20/06	HJK	h	2-0	*Jagne, Kangaskolkka*
25/06	KuPS	a	0-2	
28/06	Haka	h	1-0	*Ekhalie*
03/07	Honka	a	2-2	*Forsell 2*
07/07	VPS	h	0-0	
16/07	Lahti	a	0-2	
22/07	JJK	h	3-3	*Kangaskolkka 2, Forsell*
30/07	Inter	a	3-0	*Kangaskolkka 2, Wiklöf*
06/08	TPS	a	1-1	*Lyyski*
11/08	Jaro	a	1-1	*Ingves, Byskata*
20/08	MYPA	a	1-2	*Kangaskolkka*
26/08	HJK	a	1-5	*Kangaskolkka*
02/09	KuPS	h	2-0	*Gadžo 2*
14/09	Haka	a	1-1	*Wiklöf*
18/09	Honka	h	1-1	*Kangaskolkka*
23/09	VPS	a	3-1	*Wiklöf 2, Wirtanen*
26/09	Lahti	h	2-2	*Kangaskolkka, Gadžo*
01/10	JJK	a	2-3	*Östlind, Kangaskolkka*
08/10	Inter	a	0-1	
19/10	TPS	h	1-0	*Jagne*
22/10	Jaro	a	3-3	*Jagne, Kangaskolkka (p), Ekhalie*
27/10	MYPA	h	2-2	*Wiklöf, Kangaskolkka (p)*

No	Name	Nat	DoB	Pos	Aps	(s)	Gls
7	Rezgar Amani		01/06/92	A	7	(9)	
1	Ludwig Bergström	SWE	22/08/83	G	6		
90	Patrick Byskata		13/08/90	M	22	(7)	1
15	Amos Ekhalie	KEN	08/07/88	M	22	(8)	4
10	Petteri Forsell		16/10/90	M	18		9
30	Ermin Gadžo	BIH	19/05/90	M		(16)	4
9	Wilhelm Ingves		10/01/90	A	4	(13)	1
19	Saihou Jagne	SWE	10/10/86	A	16	(9)	5
33	Aleksei Kangaskolkka		29/10/88	A	28	(1)	16
2	Kristian Kojola		12/09/86	D	32		1
26	Erik Lundberg		20/03/94	D		(1)	
8	Jani Lyyski		16/03/83	D	27		1
11	Mika Niskala		28/03/81	M	24	(1)	
4	Johannes Nordström		23/01/93	D	1	(2)	
21	Simon Nurme	SWE	24/11/82	G	27		
6	Marcus Olofsson	SWE	04/08/82	M	22	(9)	
16	Robin Östlind	SWE	14/03/90	M	10	(2)	1
17	Mason Trafford	CAN	21/08/86	D	30		
18	Jarkko Värttö		24/02/89	D	33		
14	Mattias Wiklöf	SWE	24/05/79	A	24	(3)	6
5	Tommy Wirtanen		19/01/83	M	10	(2)	1

MYLLYKOSKEN PALLO-47

Coach: Toni Korkeakunnas
1947 • Saviniemen jalkapallostadion (4,100) • mypa.fi
Major honours
Finnish League (1) 2005;
Finnish Cup (3) 1992, 1995, 2004

2012

15/04	TPS	a	1-0	*Sihvola*
19/04	Jaro	h	2-0	*Kukka, Ramandingaye*
22/04	Inter	h	0-2	
29/04	HJK	h	1-0	*Sihvola*
05/05	KuPS	a	2-1	*O'Neill, Aho*
12/05	Haka	h	3-1	*Oksanen 2, Sihvola*
16/05	Honka	a	1-2	*Sesay*
21/05	VPS	h	1-0	*A Lody*
24/05	Lahti	a	0-0	
27/05	JJK	h	0-1	
17/06	Mariehamn	a	0-0	
20/06	TPS	a	0-1	
25/06	Jaro	a	0-1	
28/06	Inter	h	4-0	*Sihvola, Williams, O'Neill, Gela*
02/07	HJK	a	1-1	*Williams*
08/07	KuPS	h	1-1	*O'Neill*
15/07	Haka	a	1-3	*O'Neill*
22/07	Honka	h	0-0	
29/07	VPS	a	0-2	
04/08	Lahti	h	3-1	*Sihvola 2, og (Tynkkynen)*
11/08	JJK	a	3-0	*Sihvola 3*
20/08	Mariehamn	h	2-1	*Williams, Sihvola*
26/08	TPS	h	1-1	*Sihvola (p)*
02/09	Jaro	a	3-0	*Sihvola, Saxman, O'Neill*
14/09	Inter	h	0-0	
17/09	HJK	h	1-4	*Aho*
23/09	KuPS	a	0-2	
26/09	Haka	h	1-0	*Anttilainen*
04/10	Honka	a	1-1	*Saxman*
07/10	VPS	h	1-1	*Williams*
19/10	Lahti	a	1-3	*Williams*
22/10	JJK	h	2-1	*og (Tuomanen), Sihvola*
27/10	Mariehamn	a	2-2	*Sihvola, O'Neill*

No	Name	Nat	DoB	Pos	Aps	(s)	Gls
19	Nosh A Lody		17/07/89	D	26		1
18	Tuomas Aho		27/05/81	D	25		2
30	Sasha Anttilainen		10/12/86	A	11	(9)	1
8	Xhevdet Gela		14/11/89	M	29	(1)	1
28	Riku Heinonen		05/06/94	M	2	(1)	
21	Ville Iiskola		26/04/85	G	5		
13	Yusuf Jama		27/07/93	D		(1)	
20	Eetu Kaipio		29/03/89	M	5	(1)	
16	Antti Koskinen		19/07/88	D	20	(5)	
1	Antti Kuismala		20/01/76	G	28		
4	Niko Kukka		30/09/87	D	14	(4)	1
11	Riley O'Neill	CAN	09/09/85	A	26	(3)	6
5	Patrick O'Shaughnessy		29/01/93	D	9	(10)	
15	Ville Oksanen		25/02/87	M	14	(13)	2
7	David Opoku	GHA	31/01/92	A	7	(6)	
14	David Ramandingaye		14/09/89	M	20	(6)	1
24	Ville Saxman		15/11/89	M	11	(8)	2
17	Marko Selin		10/05/88	M	7	(8)	
2	Hassan Sesay	SLE	22/10/87	M	21	(4)	1
9	Pekka Sihvola		22/04/84	A	27	(1)	14
23	Pyry Soiri		22/09/94	M		(2)	
3	Tommi Vesala		12/01/86	D	26	(4)	
6	Joni Vuorinen		05/11/89	D	13	(5)	
27	Olajide Williams	NGA	20/07/88	A	17	(5)	5

TPS TURKU

Coach: Marko Rajamäki
1922 • Veritas Stadion (9,300) • fctps.fi
Major honours
Finnish League (8) 1928, 1939, 1941, 1949, 1968, 1971, 1972, 1975;
Finnish Cup (3) 1991, 1994, 2010

2012

15/04	MYPA	h	0-1	
19/04	HJK	h	3-1	*Ääritalo, Kolehmainen (p), Ristola*
22/04	KuPS	a	1-1	*Ristola*
29/04	Haka	h	2-0	*Ääritalo, Ristola*
05/05	Honka	a	2-0	*Ääritalo, Pennanen*
13/05	VPS	h	1-0	*Pennanen*
16/05	Lahti	a	0-2	
21/05	JJK	h	2-3	*Ääritalo, Pennanen*
24/05	Mariehamn	a	1-2	*Ääritalo*
16/06	Jaro	h	2-3	*Hyyrynen 2*
20/06	MYPA	h	1-0	*Lähde (p)*
25/06	HJK	h	0-0	
28/06	KuPS	h	3-0	*Lehtonen, Okaru, Eriba*
02/07	Haka	a	0-1	
09/07	Honka	h	2-1	*Ristola, Lähde*
14/07	VPS	a	3-1	*Okaru, Ristola, Ääritalo*
22/07	Lahti	h	4-0	*Ääritalo, Ristola, Lehtonen 2*
29/07	JJK	a	1-2	*Pennanen*
06/08	Mariehamn	h	1-1	*og (Lyysi)*
12/08	Inter	h	4-1	*Ristola, Pennanen, Hyyrynen 2*
19/08	Jaro	a	1-0	*Okaru*
22/08	Haka	h	9-2	*Okaru, Hyyrynen 2, Ristola 3, Nyberg, Pennanen, Lehtonen*
26/08	MYPA	a	1-1	*Okaru*
02/09	HJK	h	1-2	*S Mäkinen*
13/09	KuPS	a	3-1	*Ääritalo, Hyyrynen, Riski*
17/09	Inter	a	3-3	*Tanska, Ristola, Lähde*
22/09	Honka	a	1-0	*Okaru*
26/09	VPS	h	1-0	*Okaru*
01/10	Lahti	a	0-1	
07/10	JJK	h	1-0	*Okaru*
19/10	Mariehamn	a	0-1	
22/10	Inter	h	0-0	
27/10	Jaro	h	1-2	*Rasimus*

No	Name	Nat	DoB	Pos	Aps	(s)	Gls
11	Mika Ääritalo		25/07/85	A	13	(8)	8
66	Dickson Agyeman	BEL	14/09/85	M	6		
22	Kennedy Eriba	NGA	21/12/90	A	7	(16)	1
26	Matias Hilska		28/08/95	M		(1)	
32	Matej Hradecky		17/04/95	M		(2)	
18	Jarkko Hurme		04/06/86	D	27		
9	Mikko Hyyrynen		01/11/77	A	11	(16)	7
13	Toni Kolehmainen		20/07/88	M	22		1
5	Juho Lähde		11/02/91	M	21	(3)	3
21	Juho Lehtonen		03/08/92	A	5	(14)	4
12	Jukka Lehtovaara		15/03/88	G	6		
3	Kalle Mäkinen		01/02/89	D	8	(1)	
25	Santeri Mäkinen		09/04/92	M	21	(3)	1
28	Leroy Maluka	RSA	22/12/85	A		(1)	
1	Henrik Moisander		29/09/85	G	27	(2)	
6	Jaakko Nyberg		19/12/80	D	29	(1)	1
24	Dennis Okaru	NGA	05/12/90	A	21	(9)	8
10	Petteri Pennanen		19/09/90	M	25	(2)	6
7	Sami Rähmönen		19/04/87	D	32		
27	Konsta Rasimus		15/12/90	M	9		1
17	Roope Riski		16/08/91	A	2	(6)	1
19	Aleksi Ristola		06/11/89	A	29	(3)	11
4	Ville-Valtteri Starck		03/02/95	D		(1)	
2	Jani Tanska		29/07/88	D	32		1

VALKEAKOSKEN HAKA

Coach: Sami Ristilä; (23/08/12) Asko Jussila; (10/09/12) Juha Malinen
1934 • Tehtaan kenttä (3,500) • fchaka.fi
Major honours
Finnish League (9) 1960, 1962, 1965, 1977, 1995, 1998, 1999, 2000, 2004;
Finnish Cup (12) 1955, 1959, 1960, 1963, 1969, 1977, 1982, 1985, 1988, 1997, 2002, 2005

2012

15/04	Lahti	a	0-1	
19/04	JJK	h	4-1	*Kastrati 2, Metzger 2*
22/04	Mariehamn	h	0 2	
29/04	TPS	a	0-2	
05/05	Jaro	h	4-1	*Robinson, Dema 2 (1p), Puustinen*
12/05	MYPA	a	1-3	*Puustinen*
16/05	HJK	h	0-1	
21/05	KuPS	a	0-3	
24/05	Inter	a	1-4	*Pirinen*
27/05	Honka	h	2-1	*Luoto, Metzger*
16/06	VPS	h	0-1	
20/06	Lahti	a	1-0	*Robinson*
25/06	JJK	h	3-1	*Robinson 3 (1p)*
28/06	Mariehamn	a	0-1	
02/07	TPS	h	1-0	*Mattila*
07/07	Jaro	a	0-1	
15/07	MYPA	h	3-1	*Pirinen, Robinson 2*
21/07	HJK	a	0-1	
29/07	KuPS	h	0-2	
05/08	Inter	h	0-2	
12/08	Honka	a	2-2	*Bright, Hjelm*
19/08	VPS	a	1-2	*Hjelm*
22/08	TPS	a	2-9	*Bright, Hjelm*
25/08	Lahti	h	0-3	
02/09	JJK	a	0-5	
14/09	Mariehamn	h	1-1	*C Matrone*
23/09	Jaro	h	0-0	
26/09	MYPA	a	0-1	
01/10	HJK	h	2-2	*Robinson (p), Bright*
07/10	KuPS	a	1-1	*Hjelm*
19/10	Inter	h	1-2	*Dema*
22/10	Honka	h	1-0	*Pirinen*
27/10	VPS	a	1-0	*Dema*

No	Name	Nat	DoB	Pos	Aps	(s)	Gls
25	Nana Attakora	CAN	27/03/89	D	8		
23	Kris Bright	NZL	05/09/85	A	13		3
7	Dema	BRA	28/04/83	M	13	(2)	4
21	Jonne Hjelm		14/01/88	A	11	(1)	4
19	Topi Järvi		10/05/93	A	1	(16)	
2	Jusu Karvonen		17/01/93	M	1	(3)	
16	Kastriot Kastrati		02/10/93	A	10	(4)	2
12	Ville Kauppinen		10/01/93	G	11		
32	Kert Kütt	EST	09/10/80	G	13		
6	Pauli Kuusijärvi		21/03/86	D	19	(3)	
17	Lassi Luoto		22/07/86	M	9	(12)	1
11	Claudio Matrone		08/06/90	M	17	(8)	1
8	Marco Matrone		02/07/87	M	25	(3)	
22	Jarno Mattila		10/11/84	D	23	(1)	1
15	Shane McFaul	IRL	23/05/86	M	20	(2)	
16	Obi Metzger	SLE	19/09/87	A	16	(8)	3
20	Antti Ojanperä		06/04/83	D	29	(1)	
1	Saku Pesonen		30/11/85	G	6		
10	Juha Pirinen		22/10/91	M	17	(11)	3
14	Sasha Popovits		08/05/93	A	6	(3)	
21	Jami Puustinen		19/01/87	A	5	(4)	1
5	Shane Robinson	IRL	17/12/80	M	31		8
4	Juuso Salonen		28/07/91	D	21	(3)	
3	Sami Sanevuori		20/02/86	D	29		
16	Jordan Seabrook	USA	27/06/87	A	6	(5)	
31	Mihály Szeróvay	HUN	14/04/82	G	3		
24	Elias Tolvanen		03/02/95	M		(2)	

 **FINLAND**

VPS VAASA

Coach: Olli Huttunen
1924 • Hietalahden jalkapallostadion (4,600) • vepsu.fi
Major honours
Finnish League (2) 1945, 1948

2012

15/04	Honka	a	1-1	*Strandvall*	
19/04	Inter	h	0-2		
22/04	Lahti	h	2-1	*Parikka, Morrissey*	
30/04	JJK	a	2-0	*Morrissey, Strandvall*	
05/05	Mariehamn	h	1-2	*Parikka*	
13/05	TPS	a	0-1		
16/05	Jaro	h	1-1	*og (Vasilyev)*	
21/05	MYPA	a	0-1		
24/05	HJK	h	1-0	*Morrissey*	
27/05	KuPS	a	3-0	*Morrissey 3*	
16/06	Haka	a	1-0	*Parikka (p)*	
20/06	Honka	h	2-0	*Morrissey 2*	
25/06	Inter	a	1-1	*Morrissey*	
28/06	Lahti	a	0-1		
02/07	JJK	h	2-0	*Parikka, Luokkala*	
07/07	Mariehamn	a	0-0		
14/07	TPS	h	1-3	*O'Neil*	
21/07	Jaro	a	0-0		
29/07	MYPA	h	2-0	*Heini, Parikka (p)*	
04/08	HJK	a	3-3	*Parikka 2 (1p), Strandvall*	
12/08	KuPS	h	0-1		
19/08	Haka	h	2-1	*Morrissey 2*	
27/08	Honka	a	2-1	*og (Rexhepi), Lod*	
02/09	Inter	a	0-2		
14/09	Lahti	h	1-3	*Engström*	
18/09	JJK	a	2-1	*Morrissey, Koskimaa*	
23/09	Mariehamn	h	1-3	*Morrissey*	
26/09	TPS	a	0-1		
01/10	Jaro	h	2-1	*Morrissey, Lod*	
07/10	MYPA	a	1-1	*Björk*	
19/10	HJK	h	1-3	*Parikka (p)*	
22/10	KuPS	a	1-2	*Morrissey*	
27/10	Haka	h	0-1		

No	Name	Nat	DoB	Pos	Aps	(s)	Gls
14	Denis Abdulahi		22/05/90	M	24	(6)	
10	Tony Björk		25/10/83	M	10	(1)	1
11	Kim Böling		04/02/92	A	2	(19)	
12	Bouna Coundoul	SEN	04/03/82	G	19		
4	Jesper Engström		24/04/92	M	11	(13)	1
6	Cheyne Fowler	RSA	08/03/82	M	26	(3)	
7	Riku Heini		09/12/90	M	29	(2)	1
1	Janne Henriksson		05/08/81	G	9		
2	Augustine Jibrin	NGA	07/10/88	D	14	(3)	
12	Peter Kauppi		18/09/76	G	1		
24	Juuso Kevari		10/07/92	G	4		
23	Tero Koskela		13/10/76	M		(1)	
3	Ville Koskimaa		21/05/83	D	24		1
18	Robin Lod		17/04/93	M	9	(2)	2
20	Ville Luokkala		01/06/88	M	15	(4)	1
17	Mustafa Maki		17/09/88	M	6	(11)	
26	Steven Morrissey	JAM	25/07/86	A	26	(2)	15
23	Miika Niemi		04/03/94	A		(2)	
15	Liam O'Neil	WAL	31/07/93	D	18		1
9	Jarno Parikka		21/07/86	A	21	(5)	8
16	Jyrki Saranpää		30/08/83	A	15	(13)	
8	Sebastian Strandvall		16/09/86	M	20	(4)	3
5	Antti Uimaniemi		30/01/86	D	31		
19	O'Brian Woodbine	JAM	11/01/88	D	29		

Top goalscorers

17	Irakli Sirbiladze (Inter)
16	Aleksei Kangaskolkka (Mariehamn)
15	Steven Morrissey (VPS)
14	Pekka Sihvola (MYPA)
12	Demba Savage (HJK)
	Mika Ojala (Inter)
	Tamás Gruborovics (JJK)
11	Joel Pohjanpalo (HJK)
	Aleksi Ristola (TPS)
10	Juho Mäkelä (HJK)
	Tim Väyrynen (Honka)
	Mikko Innanen (JJK)
	Babatunde Wusu (JJK)

Promoted club

ROPS ROVANIEMI

Coach: Kari Virtanen
1950 • Keskuskenttä (2,400) • rops.fi
Major honours
Finnish Cup (1) 1986

SECOND LEVEL FINAL TABLE 2012

		Pld	W	D	L	F	A	Pts
1	RoPS Rovaniemi	27	18	5	4	53	20	59
2	SJK Seinäjoki	27	14	5	8	42	29	47
3	FC Viikingit	27	14	3	10	36	36	45
4	PK-35 Vantaa	27	13	4	10	54	31	43
5	OPS Oulu	27	10	8	9	34	35	38
6	AC Oulu	27	9	10	8	38	35	37
7	FC KooTeePee	27	10	5	12	30	33	35
8	JIPPO Joensuu	27	7	7	13	31	44	28
9	FC Hämeenlinna	27	5	7	15	18	48	22
10	HIFK Helsinki	27	5	6	16	29	54	21

Domestic cup: Suomen Cup 2012

FIFTH ROUND

(18/03/12)
FC Muurola 0-5 FC Hämeenlinna

(22/03/12)
KPV 0-5 JJK
VG-62 0-5 KooTeePee

(24/03/12)
FC Jazz 3-2 SJK *(aet)*
Gnistan 1-0 BK-46
NuPS 1-7 JIPPO
Reipas 0-4 LPS
TPV 0-3 AC Oulu

(25/03/12)
JPS 3-2 Pallo-Iirot *(aet)*
MaKu/Baltika 1-8 Lahti
MaPS 2-3 EIF
SC Riverball 1-0 Härmä

(27/03/12)
JäPS 2-1 FC Espoo
Klubi 04 1-2 Mariehamn *(aet)*
NoPS 1-7 Haka

(31/03/12)
FC Santa Claus 3-4 MP
PS Kemi 3-1 GBK *(aet)*
RiPS 1-3 Kuusysi

(01/04/12)
Futura 2-5 HIFK

(10/04/12)
Atlantis 3-0 Kiffen

SIXTH ROUND

(31/03/12)
SC Riverball 0-4 Haka

(01/04/12)
JPS 0-3 LPS

(05/04/12)
PS Kemi 2-2 Jaro *(aet; 4-5 on pens)*

(06/04/12)
MP 0-2 MYPA

(07/04/12)
JIPPO 1-0 Lahti *(aet)*

(10/04/12)
EIF 4-1 Kuusysi
FC Hämeenlinna 0-4 Honka
Mariehamn 4-1 JJK

(11/04/12)
KooTeePee 2-0 HIFK

(12/04/12)
JäPS 0-1 Gnistan

(13/04/12)
AC Oulu 0-2 KuPS

(15/04/12)
Atlantis 2-2 FC Jazz *(aet; 4-2 on pens)*

SEVENTH ROUND

(22/04/12)
EIF 0-2 JIPPO

(25/04/12)
Atlantis 0-3 Honka
Gnistan 1-4 Mariehamn
KooTeePee 2-1 Inter *(aet)*
KuPS 0-0 TPS *(aet; 8-7 on pens)*

(26/04/12)
Haka 1-2 MYPA *(aet)*
HJK 2-1 Jaro
LPS 0-2 VPS

QUARTER-FINALS

(08/05/12)
JIPPO 0-3 MYPA *(Sihvola 9, 70, O'Shaughnessy 84)*

(09/05/12)
HJK 3-0 KooTeePee *(Ashraf 33, Alho 35, Zeneli 90+2)*
Honka 2-0 VPS *(Äijälä 27p, Simpanen 57)*
KuPS 3-0 Mariehamn *(Venäläinen 41, Hynynen 68, Ilo 85)*

SEMI-FINALS

(31/05/12)
Honka 1-1 HJK *(Tammilehto 13; Zeneli 53) (aet; 5-4 on pens)*

(30/08/12)
KuPS 1-0 MYPA *(Puri 37)*

FINAL

(29/09/12)
Sonera Stadium, Helsinki
FC HONKA ESPOO 1 *(Mäkijärvi 24)*
KUPS KUOPIO 0
Referee: Gestranius
HONKA: *Peltonen, Koskinen, Rexhepi, Heikkilä, Aalto, Tammilehto, Yaghoubi, Otaru, Vasara (Petrescu 82), Mäkijärvi, Väyrynen*
KUPS: *Pöntinen, Hoivala (Venäläinen 57), Kärkkäinen, Tabe, Hynynen, Obiefule, Sohna, Puri, James, Ilo (Paananen 67), Purje (Smith 78)*
Sent off: Tabe (40), Puri (72)

FRANCE
Fédération Française de Football (FFF)

Address	87 boulevard de Grenelle FR-75738 Paris Cedex 15	**President**	Noël Le Graët
		Chief executive	Florence Hardouin
		Media officer	François Manardo
Tel	+33 1 4431 7300	**Year of formation**	1919
Fax	+33 1 4431 7373	**National stadium**	Stade de France,
E-mail	competitions. internationales@fff.fr		Saint-Denis (81,338)
Website	fff.fr		

LIGUE 1 CLUBS

1. AO Ajaccio
2. SC Bastia
3. FC Girondins de Bordeaux
4. Stade Brestois 29
5. Évian Thonon Gaillard FC
6. LOSC Lille
7. FC Lorient
8. Olympique Lyonnais
9. Olympique de Marseille
10. Montpellier Hérault OC
11. AS Nancy-Lorraine
12. OGC Nice
13. Paris Saint-Germain FC
14. Stade de Reims
15. Stade Rennais FC
16. AS Saint-Étienne
17. FC Sochaux-Montbéliard
18. Toulouse FC
19. ES Troyes AC
20. Valenciennes FC

PROMOTED CLUBS

21. AS Monaco FC
22. En Avant Guingamp
23. FC Nantes

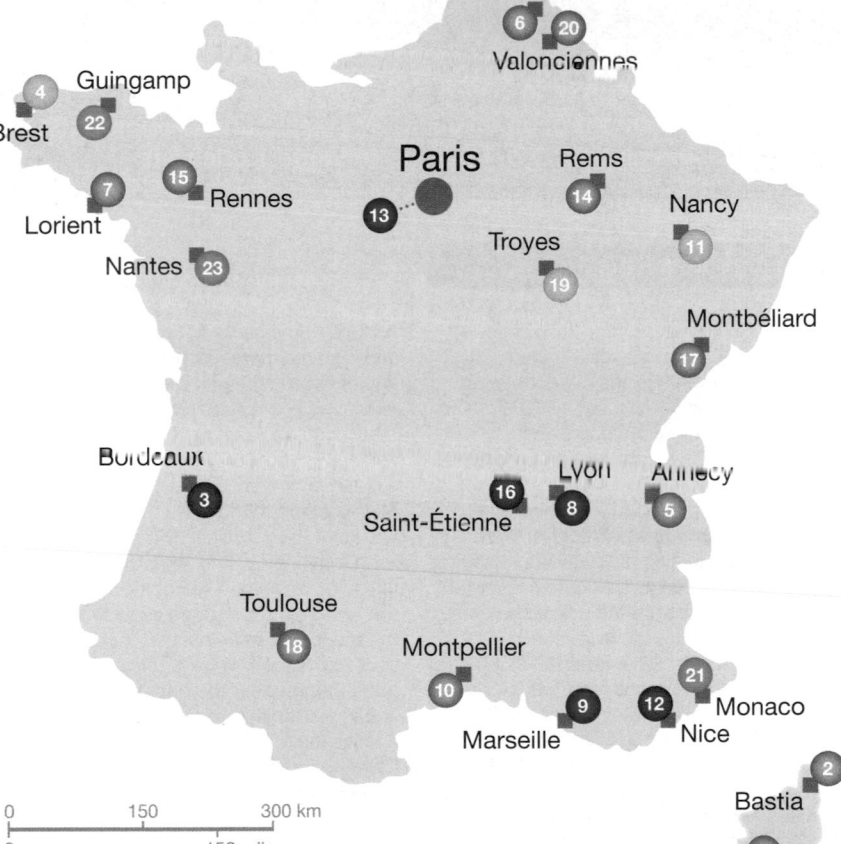

KEY:
- – UEFA Champions League
- – UEFA Europa League
- – Promoted clubs
- – Relegated clubs

PSG back in the big time

The French championship crown returned to the capital for the first time in 19 years as Paris Saint-Germain FC, bolstered by a plethora of big-name signings, foremost among them top-scoring Swedish striker Zlatan Ibrahimović, won the Ligue 1 title ahead of Olympique de Marseille and Olympique Lyonnais.

Domestic cup honours went to AS Saint-Étienne – in the League Cup – and FC Girondins de Bordeaux – in the Coupe de France – after PSG had suffered quarter-final elimination from both competitions on penalties. Carlo Ancelotti's team also reached the last eight of the UEFA Champions League.

Heavy investment pays off for Parisian club

Marseille and Lyon outlasted in Ligue 1 title race

Bordeaux and St-Étienne win domestic cups

Domestic league

PSG's ambitious transfer policy, made possible by the club's new Qatari owners, made them the overwhelming pre-season favourites for the 2012/13 Ligue 1 title. Ancelotti had been appointed midway through the previous season, when the Parisians disappointingly finished runners-up to surprise champions Montpellier Hérault SC. It was widely anticipated that his first full season at the helm would deliver that long-awaited league title, especially after the purchase of Ibrahimović and defender Thiago Silva from AC Milan plus winger Ezequiel Lavezzi from SSC Napoli, but for much of the campaign it was anything but plain sailing for the former Milan and Chelsea FC coach.

PSG drew their opening three matches, and although they hit the victory trail in September, winning all four games that month, those dropped points in August forced them to play catch-up, with Marseille, under new coach Élie Baup, setting the early pace thanks to wins in their opening six fixtures. Lyon, coached by Rémi Garde, would also come into the picture – notably after a stunning 4-1 victory at the Stade Vélodrome in late November – and by the halfway stage all three clubs were locked together on 38

points from 19 matches, with PSG occupying top spot on goal difference.

As Ibrahimović scored prolifically at one end – he reached 20 goals on the first day of February – and the defence displayed impressive resilience at the other, with goalkeeper Salvatore Sirigu setting a club record of 947 minutes without conceding, PSG consolidated their position at the summit in the early weeks of the new year. Marseille and Lyon remained within striking distance, however, and when Ancelotti's men took just one point from three away fixtures, the prospects of an exciting three-way fight to the finish were rekindled. It was then, though, that the depth of PSG's squad – supplemented by the January acquisition of 37-year-old Englishman David Beckham – showed its value, five successive victories, all without the concession of a goal, burning off their pursuers' challenge. The title was wrapped up with a 1-0 win at Lyon on 12 May and celebrated, in elaborate style, six days later at the Parc des Princes with a 3-1 win at home to bottom club Stade Brestois 29.

Ibrahimović ended the campaign with 30 league goals – the biggest golden-boot winning tally in France's top division since Marseille's Jean-Pierre Papin struck the same number in 1989/90. The

Swede's value to the PSG cause could hardly be overstated, but he was not the only member of Ancelotti's triumphant squad to excel. Blaise Matuidi enjoyed an outstanding campaign in midfield alongside the promising young Italian Marco Verratti, Maxwell was exceptional at left-back, while Thiago Silva and Sirigu were the chief contributors to the team's formidable defensive record – just 23 goals conceded in 38 games.

PSG also boasted Ligue 1's best attack, scoring 69 goals – 27 more than Marseille, who, thanks largely to their consistent ability to defend a one-goal lead, claimed second place, albeit with a 12-point deficit on the champions. Twelve of the club's 21 victories were by a 1-0 margin, and only three were with a differential of more than one goal. Midfielder Mathieu Valbuena was their star turn, and the season also witnessed the return to form of striker André-Pierre Gignac and the maturing talent of 23-year-old Cameroonian centre-back Nicolas N'Koulou, who, like goalkeeper Steve Mandanda, started every game. Although delighted to finish eight places higher than the previous season, Marseille's pleasure was tempered by the three defeats they suffered against arch-rivals PSG – one in the league and one apiece in the two cups, all by the same 2-0 scoreline, all at the Parc des Princes.

Lyon, having dropped outside the top three for the first time in 14 seasons in 2011/12, were relieved to return to the podium in 2012/13. They began the season by defeating Montpellier on penalties after a 2-2 draw to win the French Super Cup – in the United States – but that would be their only silverware of the campaign. Like Marseille, they struggled against PSG, losing both matches, but on their day they provided excellent entertainment, with the goals of strikers Bafétimbi Gomis and Lisandro López supplemented in the closing weeks of the season by some stunning strikes from up-and-coming midfielder Clément Grenier.

Fourth place was claimed, against the odds, by OGC Nice. The Cote d'Azur club got off to a miserable start, winning only one of their first ten matches, but, with former Lyon boss Claude Puel at the reins and ex-AFC Ajax striker Darío Cvitanich banging in the goals, they staged a dramatic recovery, a 2-0 win at AC Ajaccio on the final day enabling them to leapfrog St-Étienne and LOSC Lille, who shared a 1-1 draw in northern France, and secure a UEFA Europa League place.

LOSC, the 2010/11 double winners, thus missed out on European qualification. Without the inspirational talent of Eden Hazard, sold to Chelsea FC, Rudi Garcia's side were understandably underpowered, although new signings Salomon Kalou and Dimitri Payet did their best to plug the gap during the club's first season at their splendid new stadium, the Grand Stade Lille Métropole. One of the ten venues assigned to host matches at UEFA EURO 2016, it was the first of the four brand new stadiums for that tournament to be completed, with others in Bordeaux, Lyon and Nice set to follow.

Montpellier, not unexpectedly, were never in contention to defend their league title. With star striker Olivier Giroud sold to Arsenal FC, René Girard's side struggled from the start and eventually rolled home in ninth place. It was a season of disappointment too for ES Troyes AC, who followed promotion with immediate relegation, joining Brest and AS Nancy-Lorraine in the bottom three.

Up from Ligue 2 came two of French football's biggest names, AS Monaco FC and FC Nantes, with En Avant Guingamp

alongside. Monaco were led to the title by experienced Italian coach Claudio Ranieri, and with a new wealthy Russian owner, Dmitri Rybolovlev, splashing the cash during the close season on several top-class players, including João Moutinho and Radamel Falcao, the likelihood is that the 2004 UEFA Champions League runners-up will be ready to mount a sustained challenge to PSG and the rest of the Ligue 1 elite in 2013/14. The champions would be led into that battle not by Ranieri's compatriot Ancelotti, who left in the summer for Real Madrid CF, but by former Bordeaux and France boss Laurent Blanc.

Domestic cup

The first of the two domestic cup finals at the Stade de France brought together St-Étienne and Stade Rennais FC. Both clubs were bidding not only to win the League Cup for the first time but also to end a long drought without major silverware. Les Verts had won nothing of note since the end of the club's halcyon period, in 1981, when they captured their record tenth championship title, whereas Rennes's barren run stretched back a further ten years to the second of their two Coupe de France wins.

While Rennes won all four of their matches en route to the final in regulation play, St-Étienne needed penalty shoot-out wins in three of their ties, including the quarter-final against PSG and the semi-final against LOSC, both of which ended goalless. There would be another clean sheet for Christophe Galtier's side in Saint-Denis as they successfully protected an 18th-minute lead provided not by their prolific Ligue 1 top scorer Pierre-Emerick Aubameyang but by the man who had scored the extra-time winner for Marseille against Lyon in the previous season's final, Brazilian striker Brandão.

Lyon's hold of the Coupe de France lasted just one round as they were ousted on penalties by third-tier SAS Épinal. There was further spot-kick misery too for PSG as they fell in the quarter-final to Évian Thonon Gaillard FC. The Annecy-based side went on to thrash Lorient FC 4-0 at home to reach their first major final. Awaiting them at the Stade France were Bordeaux, who had come through five away ties, the last of them at Troyes, to reach the final of the competition for the first time since back-to-back wins in 1986 and 1987.

The Girondins' giant Mali international striker Cheik Diabaté had scored

Bordeaux striker Cheik Diabaté scores the opening goal of the French Cup final past Évian goalkeeper Bertrand Laquait

important goals in the quarter-final and semi-final, and he was to be the star of the show again, opening and closing the scoring – and missing a penalty – in a riveting contest that did credit to both teams. Although largely outplayed, Évian, passionately supported by their legion of pink-clad fans, twice came from behind to equalise – only to be dealt a cruel blow with a minute of normal time remaining when Diabaté latched on to a deft pass from Nicolas Maurice-Belay to score the winner. It was Bordeaux's fourth victory in the competition and the first major trophy for coach Francis Gillot. It also ensured the Girondins' return to European competition in 2013/14, where they would join St-Étienne in the UEFA Europa League.

Europe

Top dogs at home, PSG were also France's most impressive performers on the continental stage in 2012/13. As both Montpellier and LOSC finished bottom of their respective UEFA Champions League groups, totalling just five points in tandem, the club from the capital won five of their six games, posting more

points in the group stage than any other club. Ibrahimović became the first player in the competition to score for six different clubs, and the Swede also set up all four goals in the home win over GNK Dinamo Zagreb. He was outscored though by Lavezzi, who found the net five times in total, including one in each leg of the round of 16 tie against Valencia, which PSG edged 3-2 on aggregate to set up a mouth-watering quarter-final with FC Barcelona. Ancelotti's men would hold their own against the Catalans, extending their unbeaten home record in Europe to 24 matches with a last-minute equaliser at the Parc des Princes and even taking the lead in Camp Nou before finally succumbing on the away goals rule.

With a three-pronged task force of Marseille, Lyon and Bordeaux, there were high hopes that France could make an impact in the UEFA Europa League, but not one of that esteemed trio reached the quarter-finals. Marseille came a cropper in the group stage, and although Lyon and Bordeaux mastered that element of the competition, each topping their group, the early rounds of the knockout phase ensnared them both. Lyon

conceded late goals in both legs to come off second best in a captivating round of 32 tie against Tottenham Hotspur FC, while Bordeaux, having sneaked past FC Dynamo Kyiv, lost both legs in the round of 16 to another latecomer from the UEFA Champions League, SL Benfica.

National team

Didier Deschamps, France's triumphant captain at the 1998 FIFA World Cup and UEFA EURO 2000, experienced mixed fortunes in his first season as Les Bleus' head coach. A popular choice to replace Blanc, who stood down after UEFA EURO 2012, his 11 games in charge delivered a negative balance sheet of four wins, two draws and five defeats. However, three of those wins came in World Cup qualifiers – away to Finland (1-0) and at home to Belarus (3-1) and Georgia (3-1) – and four of the defeats were in friendlies.

The season's pivotal fixtures were the two qualifiers against Spain, and although France emerged from the first contest, in Madrid, with a precious 1-1 draw courtesy of a last-gasp Giroud header, they allowed their rivals to retake command of Group I when they lost the return 1-0 at the Stade de France. It was always going to be tough for Les Bleus to top the group ahead of the world and European champions, but having gone into that game with a two-point lead – following Spain's shock 1-1 draw at home to Finland – there was huge disappointment that they had not at least consolidated their position with a draw.

With three fixtures remaining, France's chances of direct qualification for Brazil were not entirely compromised, but a post-season tour to South America brought two further defeats – 1-0 to Uruguay in Montevideo and 3-0 to the World Cup hosts in Porto Alegre. Deschamps journeyed across the Atlantic without man of the moment Franck Ribéry, rested after his treble-winning heroics with FC Bayern München, but several new faces did make the trip, with promising colts such as the Lyon duo of Grenier and Alexandre Lacazette and FC Porto defender Eliquim Mangala adding to the potential shown in the spring qualifiers by another couple of 20-year-old stars-in-waiting, Real Madrid CF centre-back Raphaël Varane and Juventus midfielder Paul Pogba.

Ezequiel Lavezzi scores his second goal of the tie against Valencia to put PSG into the UEFA Champions League quarter-finals

Domestic league: Ligue 1 2012/13 final table

		Pld	Home					Away					Total					Pts
			W	D	L	F	A	W	D	L	F	A	W	D	L	F	A	
1	**Paris Saint-Germain FC**	38	13	4	2	34	10	12	4	3	35	13	25	8	5	69	23	83
2	Olympique de Marseille	38	12	4	3	25	18	9	4	6	17	18	21	8	9	42	36	71
3	Olympique Lyonnais	38	11	4	4	34	17	8	6	5	27	21	19	10	9	61	38	67
4	OGC Nice	38	11	5	3	35	17	7	5	7	22	29	18	10	10	57	46	64
5	AS Saint-Étienne	38	11	4	4	36	13	5	11	3	24	19	16	15	7	60	32	63
6	LOSC Lille	38	9	7	3	32	16	7	7	5	27	24	16	14	8	59	40	62
7	FC Girondins de Bordeaux	38	8	8	3	22	19	5	8	6	18	15	13	16	9	40	34	55
8	FC Lorient	38	10	6	3	38	25	4	5	10	19	33	14	11	13	57	58	53
9	Montpellier Hérault SC	38	11	3	3	33	14	4	2	13	21	37	15	7	16	54	51	52
10	Toulouse FC	38	7	7	5	30	26	6	5	8	19	21	13	12	14	49	47	51
11	Valenciennes FC	38	9	6	4	32	21	3	6	10	17	32	12	12	14	49	53	48
12	SC Bastia	38	9	3	7	30	26	4	5	10	20	40	13	8	17	50	66	47
13	Stade Rennais FC	38	6	5	8	23	27	7	2	10	25	32	13	7	18	48	59	46
14	Stade de Reims	38	8	7	4	20	13	2	6	11	13	29	10	13	15	33	42	43
15	FC Sochaux-Montbéliard	38	6	5	8	25	26	4	6	9	16	31	10	11	17	41	57	41
16	Évian Thonon Gaillard FC	38	6	7	6	31	25	4	3	12	15	28	10	10	18	46	53	40
17	AC Ajaccio	38	7	5	7	19	20	2	10	7	20	31	9	15	14	39	51	40
18	AS Nancy-Lorraine	38	5	5	9	17	26	4	6	9	21	32	9	11	18	38	58	38
19	ES Troyes AC	38	6	8	5	25	24	2	5	12	18	37	8	13	17	43	61	37
20	Stade Brestois 29	38	5	3	11	17	26	3	2	14	15	36	8	5	25	32	62	29

NB AC Ajaccio – 2 pts deducted.

SEASON AT A GLANCE

EUROPEAN QUALIFICATION 2013/14

Champion: Paris Saint-Germain FC (group stage)
Olympique de Marseille (group stage)
Olympique Lyonnais (third qualifying round)

Cup winner: FC Girondins de Bordeaux (group stage)
League Cup winner: AS Saint-Étienne (third qualifying round)
OGC Nice (play-offs)

Top scorer	Zlatan Ibrahimović (PSG), 30 goals
Relegated clubs	Stade Brestois 29, ES Troyes AC, AS Nancy-Lorraine
Promoted clubs	AS Monaco FC, En Avant Guingamp, FC Nantes
French Cup final	FC Girondins de Bordeaux 3-2 Évian Thonon Gaillard FC
League Cup final	AS Saint-Étienne 1-0 Stade Rennais FC

LIGUE 1 TEAM OF THE SEASON
(4-4-2)
Coach: Galtier *(St-Étienne)*

PLAYER OF THE SEASON
Zlatan Ibrahimović
(Paris Saint-Germain FC)

The 31-year-old Swedish striker enjoyed an outstanding debut season in Paris following his big-money transfer from AC Milan. He scored twice on his home league debut and finished 11 goals ahead of his closest competitor in the Ligue 1 scoring charts. A talismanic figure throughout the campaign, PSG lost only once when he scored.

NEWCOMER OF THE SEASON
Clément Grenier
(Olympique Lyonnais)

The gifted 22-year-old midfielder emerged from the shadows to help Lyon snatch third place in the league. He contributed seven goals in 28 games for Les Gones and ended the season with a couple of spectacular long-range free-kicks against OGC Nice and Stade Rennais FC, which helped to seal a call up for France's summer trip to South America.

Sirigu
(PSG)

Jallet *(PSG)* Thiago Silva *(PSG)* N'Koulou *(Marseille)* Maxwell *(PSG)*

Verratti *(PSG)* Matuidi *(PSG)*

Payet *(LOSC)* Valbuena *(Marseille)*

Aubameyang *(St-Étienne)* Ibrahimović *(PSG)*

FRANCE

NATIONAL TEAM

Home Kit Away Kit

Results 2012/13

Date	Opponent		Venue	Score	Scorers
15/08/12	Uruguay	H	Le Havre	0-0	
07/09/12	Finland (WCQ)	A	Helsinki	1-0	Diaby (20)
11/09/12	Belarus (WCQ)	H	Paris	3-1	Capoue (49), Jallet (68), Ribéry (80)
12/10/12	Japan	H	Paris	0-1	
16/10/12	Spain (WCQ)	A	Madrid	1-1	Giroud (90+4)
14/11/12	Italy	A	Parma	2-1	Valbuena (37), Gomis (67)
06/02/13	Germany	H	Paris	1-2	Valbuena (44)
22/03/13	Georgia (WCQ)	H	Paris	3-1	Giroud (45+1), Valbuena (47), Ribéry (61)
26/03/13	Spain (WCQ)	H	Paris	0-1	
05/06/13	Uruguay	A	Montevideo	0-1	
09/06/13	Brazil	A	Porto Alegre	0-3	

Appearances 2012/13

Coach: Didier Deschamps	15/10/68		Uru	FIN	BLR	Jpn	ESP	Ita	Ger	GEO	ESP	Uru	Bra	Caps	Goals
Hugo Lloris	26/12/86	Lyon /Tottenham (ENG)	G	G	G	G	G	G	G	G	G		G	47	-
Mathieu Debuchy	28/07/85	LOSC /Newcastle (ENG)	D28			D46	D	D46					D	14	1
Mapou Yanga-Mbiwa	15/05/89	Montpellier	D	D	D									3	-
Mamadou Sakho	13/02/90	PSG	D	D	D	D	D	D	D	D			D	14	-
Patrice Evra	15/05/81	Man. United (ENG)	D	D	D		D	D	D		D			49	-
Rio Mavuba	08/03/84	LOSC	M46	M	M									9	-
Maxime Gonalons	10/03/89	Lyon	M			s68	M57	s84						6	-
Franck Ribéry	07/04/83	Bayern (GER)	M	M89	M90	s68	M	M63	M	M78	M			73	12
Mathieu Valbuena	28/09/84	Marseille	M75	s63	s61	s46	s57	M73	M86	M66	M	M67	M70	23	5
Olivier Giroud	30/09/86	Arsenal (ENG)	A74		A61	A	s88	A63	s81	A	s92	A58	s70	19	3
Karim Benzema	19/12/87	Real Madrid (ESP)	A63	A	A	A46	A88		A	A	A82		A70	58	15
Christophe Jallet	31/10/83	PSG	s28		D	s46				D	D92			5	1
Étienne Capoue	11/07/88	Toulouse	s46		M	M68		M84	s46			M67		6	1
Marvin Martin	10/01/88	LOSC	s63											15	2
Bafétimbi Gomis	06/08/85	Lyon	s74	s89		s75		s63				s58	s82	12	3
Jimmy Briand	02/08/85	Lyon	s75											5	-
Anthony Réveillère	10/11/79	Lyon		D				s46						20	1
Abou Diaby	11/05/86	Arsenal (ENG)		M										16	1
Yohan Cabaye	14/01/86	Newcastle (ENG)		M73	M75		M		M		M70	s76	M82	23	1
Jérémy Ménez	07/05/87	PSG		M63	s90	M68	M68	s63	s86	s78	s70			24	2
Blaise Matuidi	09/04/87	PSG		s73	s75	M46	M	M	M46	M81	M	M76	M70	14	-
Laurent Koscielny	10/09/85	Arsenal (ENG)				D	D	D	D46		D	D		10	-
Gaël Clichy	26/07/85	Man. City (ENG)				D				D				17	-
Moussa Sissoko	16/08/89	Toulouse /Newcastle (ENG)				M	s68	M91	M81	s81	s82			9	-
Clément Chantôme	11/09/87	PSG				s46 /75								1	-
Yoann Gourcuff	11/07/86	Lyon					s73				M58			31	4
Benoît Trémoulinas	28/12/85	Bordeaux					s91				D			2	-
Bacary Sagna	14/02/83	Arsenal (ENG)							D		D			34	-
Adil Rami	27/12/85	Valencia (ESP)						s46				D		26	1

Appearances 2012/13 (contd.)

			Uru	FIN	BLR	Jpn	ESP	Ita	Ger	GEO	ESP	Uru	Bra	Caps	Goals
Raphaël Varane	25/04/93	Real Madrid (ESP)								D	D			2	-
Paul Pogba	15/03/93	Juventus (ITA)								M	M 78*			2	-
Loïc Rémy	02/01/87	QPR (ENG)								s66				18	4
Steve Mandanda	28/03/85	Marseille										G		16	-
Eliaquim Mangala	13/02/91	Porto (POR)										D		1	-
Dimitri Payet	29/03/87	LOSC										M	M	5	-
Alexandre Lacazette	28/05/91	Lyon										s58	s70	2	-
Clément Grenier	07/01/91	Lyon										s67	s70	2	-
Josuha Guilavogui	19/09/90	St-Étienne										s67	M	2	-
Jérémy Mathieu	29/10/83	Valencia (ESP)											D	2	-

European club competitions 2012/13

MONTPELLIER HÉRAULT SC

Group B

Match 1 - Arsenal FC (ENG)
H 1-2 *Belhanda (9p)*
Jourdren, Bocaly, Yanga-Mbiwa, Hilton, Bedimo, Mounier (Aït-Fana 68), Belhanda, Estrada (Herrera 78), Camara (Stambouli 78), Cabella, Saihi. Coach: René Girard (FRA)

Match 2 - FC Schalke 04 (GER)
A 2-2 *Aït-Fana (13), Camara (90)*
Jourdren, Bocaly, Yanga-Mbiwa, Hilton, Belhanda (Tinhan 68), Estrada (Marveaux 68), Aït-Fana (Congré 55), Camara, Cabella, Stambouli, Saihi. Coach: René Girard (FRA)
Red card: Bocaly 52

Match 3 - Olympiacos FC (GRE)
H 1-2 *Charbonnier (49)*
Pionnier, Yanga-Mbiwa, Hilton, Bedimo, Utaka, Mounier (Estrada 62), Charbonnier (Camara 68), Belhanda, Cabella, Stambouli, Saihi (Marveaux 85). Coach: Pascal Baills (FRA)

Match 4 - Olympiacos FC (GRE)
A 1-3 *Belhanda (66p)*
Jourdren, Bocaly, Yanga-Mbiwa, Hilton (Congré 79), Bedimo, Marveaux, Mounier (Tinhan 62), Belhanda, Camara, Cabella (Charbonnier 46), Saihi. Coach: René Girard (FRA)

Match 5 - Arsenal FC (ENG)
A 0-2
Jourdren, Yanga-Mbiwa, Bedimo, Mounier, Charbonnier (Martin 69), Belhanda, Congré, Estrada (Marveaux 80), Cabella (Herrera 69), El Kaoutari, Deplagne. Coach: René Girard (FRA)

Match 6 - FC Schalke 04 (GER)
H 1-1 *Herrera (59)*
Ligali, Yanga-Mbiwa, Hilton, Bedimo, Mounier (Belhanda 68), Herrera, Congré, Estrada, Camara (Utaka 67), Cabella, Stambouli (Pitau 46). Coach: René Girard (FRA)

PARIS SAINT-GERMAIN FC

Group A

Match 1 - FC Dynamo Kyiv (UKR)
H 4-1 *Ibrahimović (19p), Thiago Silva (29), Alex (32), Pastore (90+1)*
Sirigu, Thiago Silva (Camara 81), Ménez (Nenê 77), Alex, Matuidi, Maxwell, Ibrahimović (Lavezzi 73), Chantôme, Verratti, Jallet, Pastore. Coach: Carlo Ancelotti (ITA)

Match 2 - FC Porto (POR)
A 0-1
Sirigu, Thiago Silva, Sakho, Ménez (Lavezzi 73; Pastore 80), Nenê, Matuidi, Maxwell, Ibrahimović, Chantôme, Van der Wiel (Jallet 62), Verratti. Coach: Carlo Ancelotti (ITA)

Match 3 - GNK Dinamo Zagreb (CRO)
A 2-0 *Ibrahimović (33), Ménez (43)*
Sirigu, Thiago Silva, Ménez (Hoarau 77), Bodmer (Sissoko 60), Alex (Camara 46), Matuidi, Maxwell, Ibrahimović, Verratti, Jallet, Pastore. Coach: Carlo Ancelotti (ITA)

Match 4 - GNK Dinamo Zagreb (CRO)
H 4-0 *Alex (16), Matuidi (61), Ménez (65), Hoarau (80)*
Sirigu, Thiago Silva, Sissoko (Verratti 46), Ménez (Hoarau 76), Lavezzi (Pastore 68), Alex, Matuidi, Maxwell, Ibrahimović, Rabiot, Jallet. Coach: Carlo Ancelotti (ITA)

Match 5 - FC Dynamo Kyiv (UKR)
A 2-0 *Lavezzi (45, 52)*
Sirigu, Thiago Silva, Sissoko (Chantôme 68), Nenê (Pastore 87), Lavezzi, Alex, Matuidi, Maxwell, Ibrahimović, Van der Wiel, Verratti (Armand 78). Coach: Carlo Ancelotti (ITA)

Match 6 - FC Porto (POR)
H 2-1 *Thiago Silva (29), Lavezzi (61)*
Sirigu, Thiago Silva, Ménez (Jallet 86), Lavezzi (Verratti 70), Alex, Matuidi, Maxwell, Ibrahimović, Chantôme, Van der Wiel, Pastore (Nenê 88). Coach: Carlo Ancelotti (ITA)

Round of 16 - Valencia CF (ESP)
A 2-1 *Lavezzi (10), Pastore (43)*
Sirigu, Sakho, Lavezzi (Ménez 76), Alex, Matuidi, Maxwell, Ibrahimović, Verratti, Jallet, Pastore (Armand 88), Lucas (Chantôme 53). Coach: Carlo Ancelotti (ITA)
Red card: Ibrahimović 90+2
H 1-1 *Lavezzi (66)*
Sirigu, Thiago Silva, Lavezzi, Alex, Matuidi, Maxwell, Chantôme, Jallet (Van der Wiel 27), Pastore, Thiago Motta (Gameiro 58), Lucas (Sakho 83). Coach: Carlo Ancelotti (ITA)

Quarter-final - FC Barcelona (ESP)
H 2-2 *Ibrahimović (79), Matuidi (90+4)*
Sirigu, Thiago Silva, Lavezzi (Ménez 66), Alex, Matuidi, Maxwell, Ibrahimović, Jallet, Pastore (Gameiro 76), Lucas, Beckham (Verratti 70). Coach: Carlo Ancelotti (ITA)
A 1-1 *Pastore (50)*
Sirigu, Thiago Silva, Lavezzi (Gameiro 81), Alex, Maxwell, Ibrahimović, Verratti (Beckham 83), Jallet (Van der Wiel 88), Pastore, Thiago Motta, Lucas. Coach: Carlo Ancelotti (ITA)

LOSC LILLE

Play-offs - FC København (DEN)
A 0-1
Landreau, Digne, Balmont (Gueye 46), Payet (Roux 62), Kalou, Túlio de Melo, Martin (Pedretti 90+2), Rozehnal, Béria, Chedjou, Mavuba. Coach: Rudi Garcia (FRA)
H 2-0 *Digne (43), Túlio de Melo (105) (aet)*
Landreau, Digne, Balmont (Gueye 105), Payet (Roux 91), Kalou, Túlio de Melo, Martin (Pedretti 83), Béria, Chedjou, Mavuba, Baša. Coach: Rudi Garcia (FRA)

Group F
Match 1 - FC BATE Borisov (BLR)
H 1-3 *Chedjou (60)*
Landreau, Debuchy (Sidibé 85), Digne, Balmont, Payet, Kalou, Túlio de Melo (Ryan Mendes 46), Martin (Roux 46), Chedjou, Mavuba, Baša. Coach: Rudi Garcia (FRA)
Match 2 - Valencia CF (ESP)
A 0-2
Landreau, Debuchy, Balmont, Gueye, Payet, Ryan Mendes (Rodelin 73), Pedretti, Béria, Chedjou (Digne 82), Baša, Roux (Túlio de Melo 64). Coach: Rudi Garcia (FRA)
Red card: Debuchy 86
Match 3 - FC Bayern München (GER)
H 0-1
Landreau, Digne, Balmont, Kalou (Payet 56), Túlio de Melo, Martin, Sidibé, Pedretti (Rozehnal 90), Béria, Chedjou, Roux (Ryan Mendes 77). Coach: Rudi Garcia (FRA)
Match 4 - FC Bayern München (GER)
A 1-6 *Kalou (57)*
Landreau, Debuchy, Balmont, Payet (Túlio de Melo 46), Kalou (Martin 72), Rozehnal (Mavuba 46), Pedretti, Béria, Chedjou, Baša, Roux. Coach: Rudi Garcia (FRA)
Match 5 - FC BATE Borisov (BLR)
A 2-0 *Sidibé (14), Bruno (31)*
Elana, Digne, Gueye, Kalou (Payet 69), Martin (Bonnart 77), Rozehnal, Sidibé, Pedretti, Bruno (Roux 65), Rodelin, Baša. Coach: Rudi Garcia (FRA)
Red card: Sidibé 74
Match 6 - Valencia CF (ESP)
H 0-1
Elana, Digne, Balmont (Payet 70), Gueye, Kalou, Béria, Bruno (Roux 77), Rodelin, Chedjou, Mavuba (Martin 55), Baša. Coach: Rudi Garcia (FRA)

OLYMPIQUE LYONNAIS

Group I
Match 1 - AC Sparta Praha (CZE)
H 2-1 *Gomis (59), Lisandro (62)*
Vercoutre, B Koné, Grenier, Lisandro (Monzón 67), Lacazette, Réveillère, Dabo (Umtiti 43), Biševac, Malbranque (Fofana 83), Gomis, Gonalons. Coach: Rémi Garde (FRA)
Match 2 - Hapoel Kiryat Shmona FC (ISR)
A 4-3 *Fofana (17, 90+2), Monzón (22), Réveillère (31)*
Vercoutre, B Koné, Lovren, Fofana, Grenier (Benzia 54), Lisandro, Réveillère, Briand, Monzón, Gonalons, Ghezzal (Malbranque 63). Coach: Rémi Garde (FRA)
Match 3 - Athletic Club (ESP)
H 2-1 *Lisandro (54), Briand (86)*
Vercoutre, B Koné, Lovren, Fofana, Lisandro (Gomis 66), Réveillère, Malbranque (Lacazette 65), Briand, Monzón, Gonalons, Umtiti. Coach: Rémi Garde (FRA)

Match 4 - Athletic Club (ESP)
A 3-2 *Gomis (22), Gourcuff (45+1), Lacazette (63)*
Vercoutre, Lovren, Fofana, Gourcuff, Lacazette (Ferri 82), Réveillère, Biševac, Gomis (Lisandro 73), Monzón (Malbranque 69), Gonalons, Umtiti. Coach: Rémi Garde (FRA)
Match 5 - AC Sparta Praha (CZE)
A 1-1 *Benzia (46)*
Vercoutre, B Koné, Fofana, Grenier, Gourcuff (Pléa 69), Ferri, Réveillère, Monzón, Umtiti, Benzia (Novillo 71), Ghezzal. Coach: Rémi Garde (FRA)
Match 6 - Hapoel Kiryat Shmona FC (ISR)
H 2-0 *Sarr (15), Benzia (58)*
Lopes, Zeffane, B Koné, Fofana, Gourcuff (S Koné 46), Michel Bastos, Ferri, Monzón, Benzia (Martial 80), Pléa (Novillo 70), Sarr. Coach: Rémi Garde (FRA)

Round of 32 - Tottenham Hotspur FC (ENG)
A 1-2 *Umtiti (55)*
Vercoutre, Lovren, Fofana, Lisandro (Ghezzal 89), Lacazette, Réveillère, Biševac, Malbranque (Grenier 83), Gomis, Gonalons, Umtiti. Coach: Rémi Garde (FRA)
H 1-1 *Gonalons (17)*
Vercoutre, Lovren, Fofana, Grenier, Lisandro (Ghezzal 73), Lacazette (Malbranque 65), Réveillère, Biševac, Gomis (Briand 82), Gonalons, Umtiti. Coach: Rémi Garde (FRA)

FC GIRONDINS DE BORDEAUX

Play-offs - FK Crvena zvezda (SRB)
A 0-0
Carrasso, Ciani, Obraniak, Sané, Ben Khalfallah (Diabaté 53), Gouffran (N'Guémo 90+1), Maurice-Belay (Jussiê 82), Mariano, Sertic, Planus, Trémoulinas. Coach: Francis Gillot (FRA)
H 3-2 *Gouffran (53, 90+3p), Jussiê (71)*
Carrasso, Henrique (Plašil 70), Obraniak, Sané, Gouffran, Jussiê (Marange 73), Maurice-Belay, Mariano, Sertic, Planus (Saivet 71), Trémoulinas. Coach: Francis Gillot (FRA)
Red card: Maurice-Belay 64

Group D
Match 1 - Club Brugge KV (BEL)
H 4-0 *Sané (13), Gouffran (27), Engels (47og), Jussiê (66)*
Carrasso, Henrique, Sané, Gouffran (Sertic 62), Jussiê, Diabaté, Plašil, Saivet (Sacko 75), Mariano, Planus, Trémoulinas (Marange 67). Coach: Francis Gillot (FRA)
Match 2 - Newcastle United FC (ENG)
A 0-3
Carrasso, Henrique, Obraniak (Diabaté 46), Sané, Gouffran (Bellion 68), Jussiê, Plašil (N'Guémo 46), Saivet, Mariano, Planus, Trémoulinas. Coach: Francis Gillot (FRA)

Match 3 - CS Marítimo (POR)
A 1-1 *Gouffran (30)*
Olimpa, Henrique, Obraniak (Saivet 77), N'Guémo, Gouffran, Jussiê (Sertic 64), Plašil, Maurice-Belay (Sacko 80), Mariano, Planus, Trémoulinas. Coach: Francis Gillot (FRA)
Match 4 - CS Marítimo (POR)
H 1-0 *Bellion (16)*
Carrasso, Henrique, Sané, Ben Khalfallah (Marange 77), Bellion (Sacko 63), Diabaté (N'Guémo 63), Plašil, Maurice-Belay, Mariano, Sertic, Trémoulinas. Coach: Francis Gillot (FRA)
Match 5 - Club Brugge KV (BEL)
A 2-1 *Jussiê (3, 40)*
Carrasso, Henrique, Sané, N'Guémo, Jussiê (Bellion 74), Plašil (Ben Khalfallah 79), Maurice-Belay (Diabaté 46), Mariano, Sertic, Planus, Trémoulinas. Coach: Francis Gillot (FRA)
Match 6 - Newcastle United FC (ENG)
H 2-0 *Diabaté (29, 73)*
Olimpa, Ben Khalfallah, Bellion, Diabaté (Sacko 88), Poko, Saivet, Chalmé, Marange, Sertic, Planus, Poundje. Coach: Francis Gillot (FRA)

Round of 32 - FC Dynamo Kyiv (UKR)
A 1-1 *Obraniak (23)*
Carrasso, Henrique, Obraniak, Sané, Bellion (Saivet 61), Plašil (Poko 90+2), Maurice-Belay (Rolán 66), Faubert, Sertic, Planus, Trémoulinas. Coach: Francis Gillot (FRA)
H 1-0 *Diabaté (41)*
Carrasso, Obraniak (Plašil 84), Diabaté, Poko, Saivet, Faubert, Marange, Sertic, Planus, Trémoulinas (Maurice-Belay 85), Poundje. Coach: Francis Gillot (FRA)

Round of 16 - SL Benfica (POR)
A 0-1
Carrasso, Henrique, Obraniak, Sané, Rolán (Bellion 66), Plašil, Maurice-Belay (Ben Khalfallah 79), Faubert (Traoré 43), Mariano, Sertic, Trémoulinas. Coach: Francis Gillot (FRA)
H 2-3 *Diabaté (74), Jardel (90+1og)*
Carrasso, Henrique, Obraniak, Sané, Diabaté, Plašil, Maurice-Belay (Sacko 78), Saivet, Mariano (Ben Khalfallah 72), Sertic (Poko 68), Trémoulinas. Coach: Francis Gillot (FRA)

OLYMPIQUE DE MARSEILLE

Third qualifying round - Eskişehirspor (TUR)
A 1-1 *Gignac (49)*
Mandanda, N'Koulou, Cheyrou, Gignac (J Ayew 72), A Ayew, Morel, Mbia, Amalfitano, Kaboré, Fanni, Valbuena (Raspentino 87). Coach: Élie Baup (FRA)

Domestic league club-by-club

H 3-0 *A Ayew (7, 66), Gignac (36)*
Mandanda, N'Koulou, Cheyrou, Gignac (Abdullah 79), A Ayew, Morel, Mbia (Azpilicueta 82), Amalfitano, Kaboré, Fanni, Valbuena (J Ayew 73). Coach: Élie Baup (FRA)
Red card: Cheyrou 75

Play-offs - FC Sheriff (MDA)
A 2-1 *J Ayew (18, 53)*
Mandanda, N'Koulou, J Ayew (Omrani 88), Gignac (Rémy 74), Abdullah, Morel, Mbia, Amalfitano, Kaboré, Fanni, Valbuena (Raspentino 62). Coach: Élie Baup (FRA)
H 0-0
Mandanda, N'Koulou, Cheyrou, J Ayew, A Ayew, Rémy (Gignac 67), Abdullah, Morel, Amalfitano (Valbuena 79), Kaboré, Mango. Coach: Élie Baup (FRA)

Group C
Match 1 - Fenerbahçe SK (TUR)
A 2-2 *Valbuena (83), A Ayew (90+4)*
Mandanda, N'Koulou, N'Diaye (Cheyrou 42), Barton (J Ayew 71), A Ayew, Rémy (Gignac 63), Morel, Amalfitano, Kaboré, Fanni, Valbuena. Coach: Élie Baup (FRA)
Match 2 - AEL Limassol FC (CYP)
H 5-1 *Fanni (42), Lucas Mendes (61), Rémy (76, 90+3), Gignac (90)*
Mandanda, N'Koulou (M'Bow 83), Lucas Mendes, Barton, J Ayew, Rémy, Abdullah (Valbuena 52), Kaboré, Fanni, Raspentino (Gignac 69), Aloe. Coach: Élie Baup (FRA)
Match 3 - VfL Borussia Mönchengladbach (GER)
A 0-2
Mandanda, Abdallah (Cheyrou 83), N'Koulou, Lucas Mendes, Barton, J Ayew, Rémy (A Ayew 65), Amalfitano, Kaboré, Fanni, Valbuena (Raspentino 77). Coach: Élie Baup (FRA)
Match 4 - VfL Borussia Mönchengladbach (GER)
H 2-2 *Barton (54), J Ayew (67)*
Mandanda, Lucas Mendes, Barton, Cheyrou, J Ayew (Abdullah 86), A Ayew, Rémy, Morel, Amalfitano (Valbuena 68), Diawara (Kaboré 82), Fanni. Coach: Élie Baup (FRA)
Match 5 - Fenerbahçe SK (TUR)
H 0-1
Mandanda, Abdallah, Lucas Mendes, Barton (Jobello 85), J Ayew, A Ayew, Abdullah, Morel, Amalfitano, Fanni, Raspentino (Cheyrou 69). Coach: Élie Baup (FRA)
Match 6 - AEL Limassol FC (CYP)
A 0-3
Bracigliano, Abdallah (Azouni 74), Lucas Mendes, N'Diaye, Rémy, Abdullah, M'Bow, Jobello (Osei 78), Fanni, Omrani (Santiago 63), Raspentino. Coach: Élie Baup (FRA)

AC AJACCIO

Coach: Alex Dupont; (21/12/12) Albert Emon
1910 • François-Coty (10,800) • ac-ajaccio.com

2012

11/08	Nice	a	1-0	Eduardo
19/08	PSG	h	0-0	
25/08	Valenciennes	a	0-3	
01/09	Évian	h	2-0	Medjani, Cavalli
16/09	Lyon	a	0-2	
23/09	Bordeaux	a	2-2	Faty, Belghazouani
29/09	Brest	h	1-0	Mostefa
06/10	LOSC	a	0-2	
21/10	Bastia	h	0-0	
28/10	Lorient	a	4-4	Belghazouani, Mutu, Eduardo 2
04/11	Marseille	h	0-2	
10/11	Toulouse	a	4-2	Sammaritano, Belghazouani 2, Diarra
17/11	Sochaux	h	0-1	
24/11	Nancy	a	1-1	Mutu (p)
30/11	St-Étienne	h	0-0	
08/12	Montpellier	a	0-3	
12/12	Reims	h	2-0	Mutu, og (Tacalfred)
15/12	Troyes	a	2-3	Lasne, Cavalli

2013

11/01	PSG	a	0-0	
19/01	Valenciennes	h	1-1	Mutu
26/01	Évian	a	1-1	Oliech
03/02	Lyon	h	3-1	Belghazouani, Mutu 2 (1p)
09/02	Bordeaux	h	1-0	Faty
16/02	Brest	a	1-1	Oliech
23/02	LOSC	h	1-1	Belghazouani
02/03	Bastia	a	0-1	
09/03	Lorient	h	1-0	Zubar
15/03	Marseille	a	0-0	
30/03	Toulouse	h	2-3	og (Zebina), Mutu
06/04	Sochaux	a	0-0	
13/04	Nancy	h	1-1	Mostefa
24/04	St-Étienne	a	2-4	Mutu 2 (1p)
27/04	Montpellier	h	2-1	Delort (p), Oliech
04/05	Reims	a	1-1	Mutu
11/05	Troyes	h	0-1	
18/05	Rennes	a	1-1	Diawara
26/05	Nice	h	0-2	

No	Name	Nat	DoB	Pos	Aps	(s)	Gls
7	Benjamin André		03/08/90	M	19	(8)	
13	Fabrice Begeorgi		20/04/87	A	2	(7)	
10	Chahir Belghazouani	MAR	06/10/86	M	22	(7)	6
26	Samuel Bouhours		26/06/87	D	29		
18	Johan Cavalli		12/09/81	M	28	(4)	2
2	Matthieu Chalmé		07/10/80	D	12		
9	Andy Delort		09/10/91	A	1	(15)	1
27	Sigamary Diarra	MLI	10/01/84	M	21	(8)	1
22	Fousseiny Diawara	MLI	28/02/80	D	18	(3)	2
29	Eduardo	BRA	05/08/80	A	15		3
4	Ricardo Faty	SEN	11/09/83	D	22	(3)	2
28	Felipe Saad	BRA	11/09/83	D	10	(1)	
15	David Gigliotti		30/05/85	M		(1)	
5	Ammar Jemal	TUN	20/04/87	D		(1)	
19	Paul Lasne		16/01/89	M	17	(11)	1
20	Anthony Lippini		07/11/88	D	7	(1)	
23	Arnaud Maire		06/03/79	D	4	(2)	
6	Carl Medjani	ALG	15/05/85	D	19		1
14	Mehdi Mostefa	ALG	30/08/83	M	29	(4)	2
12	Adrian Mutu	ROU	08/01/79	A	26	(2)	11
30	David Oberhauser		29/11/89	G		(1)	
1	Guillermo Ochoa	MEX	13/07/85	G	38		
29	Dennis Oliech	KEN	02/02/85	A	9	(3)	3
8	Jean-Baptiste Pierazzi		17/08/85	M	10	(8)	
17	Yohann Poulard		01/07/76	D	36		
12	Frédéric Sammaritano		23/03/86	M	9	(13)	1
24	Damien Tiberi		23/08/85	D		(5)	
6	Ronald Zubar		20/09/85	D	15		1

SC BASTIA

Coach: Frédéric Hantz
1905 • Armand Cesari (16,460) • sc-bastia.net
Major honours
French Cup (1) 1981

2012

11/08	Sochaux	a	3-2	Modeste, Maoulida 2
18/08	Reims	h	2-1	Modeste (p), Ilan
25/08	Rennes	a	2-3	Marque, Marchal
01/09	St-Étienne	h	0-3	
15/09	Évian	a	0-3	
22/09	PSG	h	0-4	
29/09	Nice	a	2-2	Rothen, Modeste
06/10	Troyes	h	3-2	og (Rincón), Modeste, Maoulida
21/10	Ajaccio	a	0-0	
28/10	Bordeaux	h	3-1	Thauvin 2, Khazri
04/11	Lyon	a	2-5	Khazri, Rothen (p)
10/11	Valenciennes	h	2-3	Modeste (p), Palmieri
17/11	Brest	a	0-3	
24/11	Lorient	h	2-1	Modeste, Khazri
01/12	LOSC	a	0-0	
07/12	Toulouse	h	0-0	
12/12	Marseille	h	1-2	Modeste
13/12	Montpellier	a	0-4	
22/12	Nancy	h	4-2	Rothen, Modeste 2, Yatabaré

2013

13/01	Reims	a	2-1	Ilan, Thauvin
20/01	Rennes	h	0-2	
27/01	St-Étienne	a	0-3	
02/02	Évian	h	0-0	
08/02	PSG	a	1-3	Khazri
16/02	Nice	h	0-1	
23/02	Troyes	a	0-0	
02/03	Ajaccio	h	1-0	Maoulida
10/03	Bordeaux	a	0-1	
16/03	Lyon	h	4-1	Thauvin 2, Modeste, Khazri
30/03	Valenciennes	a	4-3	Maoulida 2, Thauvin 2 (1p)
06/04	Brest	h	4-0	Khazri, Thauvin 2, Modeste (p)
13/04	Lorient	a	1-4	Modeste
21/04	LOSC	h	1-2	Khazri
27/04	Toulouse	h	0-0	
04/05	Marseille	a	1-2	Thauvin
11/05	Montpellier	h	3-1	Beauvue, Modeste 2
18/05	Nancy	a	2-1	Ilan, Modeste
26/05	Sochaux	h	0-0	

No	Name	Nat	DoB	Pos	Aps	(s)	Gls
6	Gaël Angoula		18/07/82	D	15	(3)	
33	Joseph Barbato		11/08/94	A	1	(4)	
14	Claudio Beauvue		16/04/88	M	8	(7)	1
16	Landry Bonnefoi		28/09/83	G	7	(1)	
18	Yannick Cahuzac		18/01/85	M	18	(1)	
24	Jérémy Choplin		09/02/85	D	24	(3)	
29	Gilles Cioni		14/06/84	D	24	(4)	
9	Yassin El Azzouzi		13/01/83	A		(1)	
19	Jacques Faty	SEN	25/02/84	D	10	(2)	
21	Féthi Harek	ALG	21/10/82	D	31	(2)	
28	Ilan	BRA	18/09/80	A	10	(12)	3
2	Samuel Inkoom	GHA	01/06/89	D	2	(2)	
33	Abdoulaye Keita	MLI	05/01/94	M		(5)	
10	Wahbi Khazri	TUN	08/02/91	M	22	(7)	7
40	Michaël Landreau		14/05/79	G	19		
33	Mathias Llambrich		06/02/93	M		(1)	
1	Macedo Novaes	BRA	30/03/83	G	12		
8	Toifilou Maoulida		08/06/79	A	19	(12)	6
7	Sylvain Marchal		10/02/80	D	30		1
11	François Marque		31/07/83	D	5	(1)	1
19	Maka Mary		27/03/89	D	5	(2)	
27	Anthony Modeste		14/04/88	A	35	(1)	15
15	Julian Palmieri		17/12/86	D	30	(5)	1
25	Jérôme Rothen		31/03/78	M	27	(1)	3
4	Julien Sablé		11/09/80	M	14	(7)	
20	Matthieu Sans		16/06/88	D	2	(1)	
17	Florian Thauvin		26/01/93	M	25	(7)	10
23	Christophe Vincent		08/11/92	M		(2)	
22	Sambou Yatabaré	MLI	02/03/89	M	23	(5)	1

FC GIRONDINS DE BORDEAUX

Coach: Francis Gillot
1881 • Chaban-Delmas (34,263) • girondins.com

Major honours
French League (6) 1950, 1984, 1985, 1987, 1999, 2009;
French Cup (4) 1941, 1986, 1987, 2013;
League Cup (3) 2002, 2007, 2009

2012
11/08	Évian	a	3-2	Obraniak, Gouffran, Saivet
19/08	Rennes	h	1-0	Obraniak
26/08	PSG	a	0-0	
02/09	Nice	h	1-1	Saivet
15/09	Valenciennes	a	0-0	
23/09	Ajaccio	a	2-2	Henrique, Gouffran
30/09	Lyon	a	2-2	Trémoulinas, Diabaté
07/10	Brest	a	1-1	Diabaté
19/10	LOSC	h	1-1	Obraniak
28/10	Bastia	a	1-3	Gouffran
04/11	Toulouse	h	1-0	Gouffran
11/11	Lorient	a	4-0	Jussiè, Obraniak, Saivet, Gouffran
18/11	Marseille	h	1-0	Gouffran
25/11	Montpellier	a	0-1	
01/12	Sochaux	h	2-2	og (Roussillon), Gouffran
09/12	Reims	a	0-0	
13/12	St-Étienne	a	0-0	
16/12	Nancy	a	1-1	Saivet
22/12	Troyes	h	0-0	

2013
12/01	Rennes	a	2-0	Gouffran, Saivet
20/01	PSG	h	0-1	
27/01	Nice	a	1-0	Saivet
02/02	Valenciennes	h	2-0	Bellion, Obraniak
09/02	Ajaccio	a	0-1	
17/02	Lyon	h	0-4	
24/02	Brest	h	0-2	
03/03	LOSC	a	1-2	Plašil (p)
10/03	Bastia	h	1-0	Diabaté
17/03	Toulouse	a	0-0	
30/03	Lorient	h	1-1	Obraniak
05/04	Marseille	a	0-1	
13/04	Montpellier	h	4-2	Sané, Diabaté, Plašil, Saivet
21/04	Sochaux	a	2-2	Mariano, Diabaté
27/04	Reims	h	0-0	
03/05	St-Étienne	a	0-1	
11/05	Nancy	h	3-2	Biyogo Poko, Saivet, Diabaté
18/05	Troyes	a	0-1	
26/05	Évian	h	2-1	Diabaté 2 (1p)

No	Name	Nat	DoB	Pos	Aps	(s)	Gls
11	David Bellion		27/11/82	A	6	(7)	1
8	Fahid Ben Khalfallah	TUN	09/10/82	M	10	(16)	
17	André Biyogo Poko	GAB	01/01/93	M	7	(7)	1
16	Cédric Carrasso		30/12/81	G	38		
21	Matthieu Chalmé		07/10/80	D	1		
2	Michaël Ciani		06/04/84	D	3		
14	Cheick Diabaté	MLI	25/04/88	A	12	(11)	8
22	Julien Faubert		01/08/83	M	10	(3)	
9	Yoan Gouffran		25/05/86	A	20		8
3	Henrique	BRA	02/05/83	D	22	(2)	1
10	Jussiè	BRA	19/09/83	A	9	(6)	1
23	Florian Marange		03/03/86	D	15	(4)	
25	Mariano	BRA	23/06/86	D	32		1
19	Nicolas Maurice-Belay		19/04/85	A	22	(7)	
7	Landry N'Guémo	CMR	28/11/85	M	10	(1)	
4	Ludovic Obraniak	POL	10/11/84	M	28	(2)	6
27	Marc Planus		07/03/82	D	27	(1)	
18	Jaroslav Plašil	CZE	05/01/82	M	28	(5)	2
29	Maxime Poundje		16/08/92	D	6	(1)	
9	Diego Rolán	URU	24/03/93	A	5	(2)	
12	Hadi Sacko		24/03/94	A		(4)	
20	Henri Saivet		26/10/90	A	23	(11)	8
6	Ludovic Sané	SEN	03/03/87	D	33		1
26	Grégory Sertic		05/08/89	M	18	(8)	
24	Abdou Traoré	MLI	17/01/88	M	6	(3)	
28	Benoît Trémoulinas		28/12/85	D	27	(1)	1

STADE BRESTOIS 29

Coach: Landry Chauvin; (04/04/13) Corentin Martins
1950 • Francis-Le-Blé (16,000) • sb29.com

2012
10/08	Nancy	a	0-1	
18/08	Évian	h	1-0	Baysse
26/08	St-Étienne	a	0-4	
01/09	Troyes	h	2-1	Ben Basat, Dernis
15/09	Nice	a	2-4	Ayité (p), Baysse
22/09	Valenciennes	h	2-1	Ayité, Ben Basat (p)
29/09	Ajaccio	a	0-1	
07/10	Bordeaux	h	1-1	Ben Basat
21/10	Lyon	a	0-1	
27/10	Toulouse	a	1-3	Lesoimier
02/11	Lorient	h	2-0	Ben Basat, Benschop
10/11	LOSC	a	0-1	
17/11	Bastia	h	3-0	Touré 2, Ben Basat (p)
24/11	Reims	a	0-1	
02/12	Marseille	h	1-2	Benschop
08/12	Rennes	a	2-2	Lesoimier, Benschop
12/12	Montpellier	a	1-2	Ben Basat
15/12	Sochaux	a	2-1	Chafni, Ben Basat
21/12	PSG	h	0-3	

2013
12/01	Évian	a	2-0	Ben Basat (p), Grougi
19/01	St-Étienne	h	0-1	
26/01	Troyes	a	1-2	Ben Basat
02/02	Nice	h	0-2	
09/02	Valenciennes	a	1-2	Raspentino
16/02	Ajaccio	h	1-1	Raspentino
24/02	Bordeaux	a	2-0	og (Trémoulinas), Kantari (p)
03/03	Lyon	h	1-1	Chafni
09/03	Toulouse	h	0-1	
16/03	Lorient	a	0-4	
31/03	LOSC	h	1-2	Raspentino
06/04	Bastia	a	0-4	
13/04	Reims	h	0-2	
20/04	Marseille	a	0-1	
27/04	Rennes	h	0-2	
04/05	Montpellier	a	1-2	Raspentino
11/05	Sochaux	h	0-2	
18/05	PSG	a	1-3	Benschop
26/05	Nancy	h	1-2	Benschop

No	Name	Nat	DoB	Pos	Aps	(s)	Gls
33	André Auras	SEN	22/04/91	M	4	(4)	
7	Jonathan Ayité	TOG	21/07/85	A	9	(13)	2
17	Adama Ba	MTN	27/08/93	M	2	(5)	
12	Paul Baysse		18/05/88	D	18		2
9	Eden Ben Basat	ISR	08/09/86	A	17	(3)	9
23	Charlison Benschop	NED	21/08/89	A	14	(13)	5
16	Lionel Cappone		08/02/79	G		(1)	
5	Kamel Chafni	MAR	11/06/82	M	24	(7)	2
33	Brendan Chardonnet		22/12/84	D		(1)	
22	Ousmane Coulibaly	MLI	09/07/89	D	14		
2	Jhon Jairo Culma	COL	17/03/81	M	5		
6	Geoffrey Dernis		24/12/80	M	10	(12)	1
28	Timothée Dieng		09/04/92	M	2		
21	Brahim Ferradj	ALG	04/09/87	M	8	(1)	
8	Bruno Grougi		26/04/83	M	24	(6)	1
9	Magaye Gueye	SEN	06/07/90	A	5	(2)	
30	Joan Hartock		17/02/87	G	2		
33	Florian Julien		27/07/93	A	1		
34	Ahmed Kantari	MAR	28/06/85	D	29		1
13	Abel Khaled		09/11/92	M		(7)	
15	Florian Lejeune		20/05/91	D	8	(2)	
19	Benoît Lesoimier		21/02/83	M	21	(6)	2
27	Mario Lička	CZE	30/04/82	M	17	(7)	
29	Grégory Lorenzi		17/12/84	D	10		
4	Tripy Makonda		24/01/90	M	6	(1)	
4	Johan Martial		30/05/91	D	18	(1)	
5	Bernard Mendy		20/08/81	D	30	(1)	
19	Florian Raspentino		06/06/89	A	17	(2)	4
26	Abdoulwhaïd Sissoko		20/03/90	M	35	(2)	
11	Richard Soumah	GUI	06/10/86	M	5	(4)	
1	Alexis Thébaux		17/03/85	G	36		
10	Larsen Touré	GUI	20/07/84	A	13	(6)	2
8	Ismaël Traoré	CIV	18/08/86	D	14	(3)	

ÉVIAN THONON GAILLARD FC

Coach: Pablo Correa (URU);
(03/09/12) Pascal Dupraz
2009 • Parc des Sports d'Annecy (15,693) • etgfc.com

2012
11/08	Bordeaux	h	2-3	Wass, Khelifa
18/08	Brest	a	0-1	
24/08	Lyon	h	1-1	Barbosa
01/09	Ajaccio	a	0-2	
15/09	Bastia	h	3-0	Barbosa 2, Sagbo
23/09	Marseille	a	0-1	
29/09	Lorient	h	1-1	Khelifa
06/10	Montpellier	h	3-2	Khelifa 3
20/10	Toulouse	h	0-4	
03/11	LOSC	h	0-2	
07/11	Sochaux	a	1-2	Adnane
10/11	Reims	a	2-1	Bérigaud, Adnane
17/11	St-Étienne	h	2-2	Rabiu, Angoula
24/11	Rennes	a	1-0	Dhaouadi
01/12	Nancy	h	1-1	Dja Djédjé
08/12	PSG	a	0-4	
12/12	Troyes	h	2-0	Barbosa 2
15/12	Nice	a	2-3	Sagbo, Barbosa
23/12	Valenciennes	a	1-2	Khelifa

2013
12/01	Brest	h	0-2	
18/01	Lyon	a	0-0	
26/01	Ajaccio	h	1-1	Wass
02/02	Bastia	a	0-0	
10/02	Marseille	h	1-1	Sagbo (p)
16/02	Lorient	a	1-2	Betão
23/02	Montpellier	a	0-1	
02/03	Toulouse	a	0-0	
09/03	Sochaux	h	5-1	Barbosa 2, Khelifa 2 (1p), Bérigaud
16/03	LOSC	a	2-1	Khelifa, og (Kalou)
30/03	Reims	h	2-2	Sagbo, N'Sikulu
07/04	St-Étienne	a	0-1	
13/04	Rennes	h	4-2	og (Kana-Biyik), Bérigaud, Ninković, Sagbo
21/04	Nancy	a	1-3	Khelifa
28/04	PSG	h	0-1	
04/05	Troyes	a	0-1	
12/05	Nice	h	4-0	Bérigaud, Rabiu, Khelifa 2
18/05	Valenciennes	h	2-0	Khelifa, Ehret
26/05	Bordeaux	a	1-2	Sagbo (p)

No	Name	Nat	DoB	Pos	Aps	(s)	Gls
27	Youssouf Adnane		16/07/85	A	7	(11)	2
30	Stephan Andersen	DEN	26/11/81	G	8	(1)	
17	Aldo Angoula		04/05/81	D	18	(4)	1
34	Nadjib Baouia		25/02/92	D		(1)	
14	Cédric Barbosa		06/03/76	M	27	(3)	8
9	Kévin Bérigaud		09/05/88	A	30	(5)	4
3	Betão	BRA	11/11/83	D	16		1
22	Cédric Cambon		20/09/86	D	16	(4)	
12	Diogo Campos	BRA	31/12/90	A		(1)	
26	Brice Dja Djédjé	CIV	23/12/90	D	27		1
15	Zouhier Dhaouadi	TUN	01/01/88	M	1	(7)	1
1	Johann Durand		17/06/81	G	1	(1)	
28	Fabrice Ehret		28/09/79	D	9	(6)	1
8	Sidney Govou		27/07/79	A	5	(13)	
3	David Jarolím	CZE	17/05/79	M	4	(1)	
29	Saber Khelifa	TUN	14/10/86	A	21	(4)	13
8	Djakaridja Koné	BFA	22/07/86	M	15	(1)	
19	Guillaume Lacour		02/08/80	M	13	(6)	
16	Bertrand Laquait		13/04/77	G	29		
7	Ali M'Madi	COM	21/04/90	A	2		
11	Iheb Mbarki	TUN	14/02/92	D	6	(9)	
25	Jonathan Mensah	GHA	13/07/90	D	6		
21	Cédric Mongongu	COD	22/06/89	D	18		
33	Clarck N'Sikulu	COD	07/07/92	M		(6)	1
23	Miloš Ninković	SRB	25/12/84	M	15	(2)	1
2	Mohammed Rabiu	GHA	31/12/90	M	23	(5)	2
7	Yannick Sagbo	CIV	12/04/88	A	23	(12)	6
24	Olivier Sorlin		09/04/79	M	36		
4	Éric Tié Bi	CIV	20/07/90	M	8	(11)	
18	Daniel Wass	DEN	31/05/89	D	34		2

LOSC LILLE

Coach: Rudi Garcia
1944 • Grand Stade Lille Métropole (50,186) • losc.fr
Major honours
French League (3) 1946, 1954, 2011;
French Cup (6) 1946, 1947, 1948, 1953, 1955, 2011

2012

11/08	St-Étienne	a	2-1	Chedjou, Pedretti
17/08	Nancy	h	1-1	Kalou
25/08	Nice	a	2-2	Payet, Sidibé
02/09	PSG	h	1-2	Chedjou
15/09	Troyes	a	1-1	Payet
23/09	Lyon	h	1-1	Roux
28/09	Rennes	a	0-2	
06/10	Ajaccio	h	2-0	Roux, Ryan Mendes
19/10	Bordeaux	a	1-1	Baša
27/10	Valenciennes	h	2-1	og (Bong), Payet
03/11	Évian	a	2-0	Roux, Balmont
10/11	Brest	h	1-0	Kalou
16/11	Lorient	a	0-2	
25/11	Marseille	a	0-1	
01/12	Bastia	h	0-0	
08/12	Sochaux	a	1-1	Roux
11/12	Toulouse	h	2-0	Baša, Payet
15/12	Reims	a	1-1	Payet
22/12	Montpellier	h	4-1	Roux 2, Payet, Ryan Mendes

2013

12/01	Nancy	a	2-2	Roux, Payet
20/01	Nice	h	0-2	
27/01	PSG	a	0-1	
02/02	Troyes	h	1-1	Origi
10/02	Lyon	a	3-1	Chedjou, Balmont, Kalou (p)
15/02	Rennes	h	2-0	og (Mavinga), Payet
23/02	Ajaccio	a	3-1	og (Poulard), Payet 2
03/03	Bordeaux	h	2-1	Rodelin, Kalou
09/03	Valenciennes	a	3-1	Rodelin, Túlio de Melo, Pedretti
16/03	Évian	h	1-2	Kalou
31/03	Brest	a	2-1	Kalou, Roux
07/04	Lorient	h	5-0	Kalou 2, Payet, Digne (p), Rodelin
14/04	Marseille	h	0-0	
21/04	Bastia	a	2-1	Digne, Baša
26/04	Sochaux	h	3-3	Kalou 2, Baša
04/05	Toulouse	a	2-4	Baša, Kalou
10/05	Reims	h	3-0	Kalou 2, Payet
18/05	Montpellier	a	0-0	
26/05	St-Étienne	h	1-1	Kalou

No	Name	Nat	DoB	Pos	Aps	(s)	Gls
4	Florent Balmont		02/02/80	M	30	(4)	2
25	Marko Baša	MNE	29/12/82	D	34		5
18	Franck Béria		23/05/83	D	24		
21	Laurent Bonnart		25/12/79	D	4	(1)	
19	Gianni Bruno	BEL	19/08/91	A	3	(10)	
22	Aurélien Chedjou	CMR	20/06/85	D	34		3
2	Mathieu Debuchy		28/07/85	D	15		
10	Lucas Digne		20/07/93	D	31	(2)	2
16	Steeve Elana		11/07/80	G	20		
5	Idrissa Gueye	SEN	26/09/89	M	21	(8)	
8	Salomon Kalou	CIV	05/08/85	A	25	(3)	14
28	Viktor Klonaridis	BEL	28/07/92	A		(3)	
1	Mickaël Landreau		14/05/79	G	15		
10	Marvin Martin		10/01/88	M	29	(3)	
6	Rio Mavuba		08/03/84	M	17	(2)	
30	Barel Mouko	CGO	05/04/79	G	3		
33	Divock Origi	BEL	18/04/95	A		(10)	1
7	Dimitri Payet		29/03/87	M	37	(1)	12
17	Benoît Pedretti		12/11/80	M	14	(15)	2
20	Ronny Rodelin		18/11/89	A	20	(3)	3
14	Nolan Roux		01/03/88	A	22	(10)	8
14	David Rozehnal	CZE	05/07/80	D	6	(6)	
11	Ryan Mendes	CPV	08/01/90	A	3	(6)	2
15	Djibril Sidibé		29/07/92	D	7	(7)	1
9	Túlio de Melo	BRA	31/01/85	A	4	(19)	1

FC LORIENT

Coach: Christian Gourcuff
1926 • Le Moustoir-Yves-Allainmat (18,110) • fclweb.fr
Major honours
French Cup (1) 2002

2012

11/08	PSG	a	2-2	og (Maxwell), Aliadière
18/08	Montpellier	h	2-1	Traoré, Aliadière
25/08	Troyes	a	2-2	Barthelme, Mvuemba (p)
01/09	Nancy	h	3-0	Giuly, Koné, Traoré
16/09	Rennes	a	2-1	Traoré 2
22/09	Nice	h	1-1	Monnet-Paquet
29/09	Évian	a	1-1	Sunu
07/10	Lyon	h	1-1	Aliadière
20/10	Valenciennes	a	1-6	Corgnet
28/10	Ajaccio	h	4-4	Lautoa, Aliadière 2, Sunu
02/11	Brest	a	0-2	
11/11	Bordeaux	h	0-4	
16/11	LOSC	h	2-0	Bourillon, Corgnet
24/11	Bastia	a	1-2	Koné
02/12	Toulouse	h	1-0	Corgnet
09/12	Marseille	a	3-0	Aliadière (p), Corgnet, Monnet-Paquet
12/12	Sochaux	h	2-0	Traoré, Koné
16/12	St-Étienne	a	2-0	Aliadière, Traoré
22/12	Reims	h	2-2	Barthelme, Pedrinho

2013

12/01	Montpellier	h	0-2	
19/01	Troyes	h	3-2	Monnet-Paquet, Reale, Damien
26/01	Nancy	a	1-2	Aliadière
02/02	Rennes	h	2-2	Jouffre, Aliadière
09/02	Nice	a	1-1	Mareque
16/02	Évian	h	2-1	Aliadière (p), Monnet-Paquet
24/02	Lyon	a	1-3	Aliadière
02/03	Valenciennes	h	1-1	Monnet-Paquet
09/03	Ajaccio	a	0-1	
16/03	Brest	h	4-0	Quercia, Jouffre, Lautoa, Sunu
30/03	Bordeaux	a	1-1	Aliadière
07/04	LOSC	a	0-5	
13/04	Bastia	h	4-1	Jouffre, Corgnet, Aliadière 2
21/04	Toulouse	a	1-0	Aliadière
27/04	Marseille	a	0-1	
04/05	Sochaux	a	0-1	
12/05	St-Étienne	h	3-1	Monnet-Paquet, Robert, Jouffre
18/05	Reims	a	0-1	
26/05	PSG	h	1-3	Le Lan (p)

No	Name	Nat	DoB	Pos	Aps	(s)	Gls
31	Mohammed Abu	GHA	14/11/91	M	6	(1)	
11	Jérémie Aliadière		30/03/83	A	31		15
16	Fabien Audard		28/03/78	G	34		
23	Mathias Autret		01/03/91	M	4	(15)	
17	Maxime Baca		02/06/83	D	22	(4)	
28	Maxime Barthelme		08/09/88	M	31	(3)	2
6	Grégory Bourillon		01/07/84	D	23	(3)	2
7	Benjamin Corgnet		06/04/87	M	24	(2)	5
10	Mathieu Coutadeur		20/06/86	M	21	(1)	
5	Bruno Ecuélé Manga	GAB	16/07/88	D	17		
25	Innocent Emeghara	SUI	27/05/89	A		(1)	
25	Lamine Gassama	SEN	20/10/89	D	16		
19	Ludovic Giuly		10/07/76	M	4	(13)	1
8	Yann Jouffre		23/07/84	M	30	(2)	4
2	Lamine Koné		01/02/89	D	31	(1)	3
24	Wesley Lautoa		25/08/87	D	26	(1)	2
14	Arnaud Le Lan		22/03/78	D	11	(2)	1
1	Benjamin Lecomte		26/04/91	G	4	(1)	
13	Mario Lemina		01/09/93	M	5	(5)	
12	Lucas Mareque	ARG	12/01/83	D	9	(1)	1
22	Kévin Monnet-Paquet		19/08/88	A	28	(7)	6
26	Rémi Mulumba		02/11/92	M	1	(1)	
7	Arnold Mvuemba		28/01/85	M	4		1
9	Pedrinho	POR	06/03/85	M	7	(2)	1
20	Julien Quercia		17/08/86	A	3	(4)	1
27	Enzo Reale		07/10/91	M	10	(10)	1
15	Fabien Robert		06/01/91	A	1	(3)	1
4	Jacques Alaixys Romao	TOG	18/01/84	M	18		
18	Gilles Sunu		30/03/91	A	2	(15)	3
21	Alain Traoré	BFA	31/12/88	M	14		6

OLYMPIQUE LYONNAIS

Coach: Rémi Garde
1950 • Gerland (41,044) • olweb.fr
Major honours
French League (7) 2002, 2003, 2004, 2005, 2006, 2007, 2008;
French Cup (5) 1964, 1967, 1973, 2008, 2012;
League Cup (1) 2001

2012

11/08	Rennes	a	1-0	Gourcuff
18/08	Troyes	h	4-1	Gomis 2, Michel Bastos, Lisandro
24/08	Évian	a	1-1	Michel Bastos
01/09	Valenciennes	h	3-2	Michel Bastos, Gomis (p), Grenier
16/09	Ajaccio	h	2-0	Lovren, Lisandro
23/09	LOSC	a	1-1	Lisandro
30/09	Bordeaux	h	0-2	
07/10	Lorient	a	1-1	Gomis
21/10	Brest	h	1-0	Gomis
04/11	Bastia	h	5-2	Gonalons, Lacazette, Lisandro (p), Briand, Malbranque (p)
11/11	Sochaux	a	1-1	Gonalons
18/11	Reims	h	3-0	og (Weber), Gomis, Lisandro
25/11	Toulouse	a	0-3	
28/11	Marseille	a	4-1	Gomis 3 (1p), Malbranque
01/12	Montpellier	h	1-0	Gomis
09/12	St-Étienne	a	1-0	Michel Bastos
12/12	Nancy	h	1-1	Michel Bastos
16/12	PSG	a	0-1	
22/12	Nice	h	3-0	Lisandro, Réveillère, Gomis (p)

2013

12/01	Troyes	a	2-1	Gonalons, Umtiti
18/01	Évian	h	0-0	
25/01	Valenciennes	a	2-0	Fofana, Gomis
03/02	Ajaccio	a	1-3	Lacazette
10/02	LOSC	h	1-3	Lisandro
17/02	Bordeaux	a	4-0	Grenier 2 (1p), Fofana, Lacazette
24/02	Lorient	h	3-1	Lisandro, Ghezzal, Mvuemba
03/03	Brest	a	1-1	og (Makonda)
10/03	Marseille	h	0-0	
16/03	Bastia	a	1-4	Lisandro
31/03	Sochaux	h	1-2	Gomis (p)
07/04	Reims	a	0-1	
14/04	Toulouse	h	3-1	Grenier, Koné, Gomis
19/04	Montpellier	a	2-1	Lisandro, Grenier
28/04	St-Étienne	h	1-1	Gourcuff
05/05	Nancy	a	3-0	Gomis 2, Gourcuff
12/05	PSG	h	0-1	
19/05	Nice	a	1-1	Grenier
26/05	Rennes	h	2-0	Lisandro (p), Grenier

No	Name	Nat	DoB	Pos	Aps	(s)	Gls
33	Farès Bahlouli		08/04/95	M		(1)	
25	Yassine Benzia		08/09/94	A	3	(13)	
15	Milan Biševac	SRB	31/08/83	D	29	(1)	
19	Jimmy Briand		02/08/85	A	8	(7)	1
20	Aly Cissokho		15/09/87	D	2		
3	Cris	BRA	03/06/77	D	2		
14	Mouhamadou Dabo		28/11/86	D	29	(1)	
12	Jordan Ferri		12/03/92	M		(7)	
6	Gueïda Fofana		16/05/91	M	17	(10)	2
31	Rachid Ghezzal		09/05/92	M	10	(4)	1
18	Bafétimbi Gomis		06/08/85	A	29	(8)	16
21	Maxime Gonalons		10/03/89	M	35		3
8	Yoann Gourcuff		11/07/86	M	15	(3)	3
7	Clément Grenier		07/01/91	M	20	(8)	7
9	Bakary Koné	BFA	27/04/88	D	14		1
10	Alexandre Lacazette		28/05/91	A	27	(4)	3
9	Lisandro López	ARG	02/03/83	A	26	(5)	11
1	Hugo Lloris		26/12/86	G	2		
16	Clinton N'Jie	POR	01/10/90	G	5		
5	Dejan Lovren	CRO	05/07/89	D	18		1
17	Steed Malbranque		06/01/80	M	30	(1)	2
33	Anthony Martial		05/12/95	A		(3)	
11	Michel Bastos	BRA	02/08/83	M	7	(5)	5
20	Fabián Monzón	ARG	13/04/87	D	2	(3)	
28	Arnold Mvuemba		28/01/85	M	5	(12)	1
24	Clinton N'Jie	CMR	15/08/93	A		(4)	
24	Jérémy Pied		23/02/89	A		(1)	
27	Alassane Pléa		10/03/93	M		(1)	
13	Anthony Réveillère		10/11/79	D	27		1
23	Samuel Umtiti		14/11/93	D	25	(1)	1
1	Rémy Vercoutre		26/06/80	G	31		

OLYMPIQUE DE MARSEILLE

Coach: Élie Baup
1899 • Vélodrome (60,000) • om.net
Major honours
UEFA Champions League (1) 1993;
French League (9) 1937, 1948, 1971, 1972, 1989, 1990,
1991, 1992, 2010;
French Cup (10) 1924, 1926, 1927, 1935, 1938, 1943,
1969, 1972, 1976, 1989;
League Cup (3) 2010, 2011, 2012

2012
12/08	Reims	a	1-0	Cheyrou
19/08	Sochaux	h	2-0	Gignac, Fanni
26/08	Montpellier	a	1-0	Gignac
02/09	Rennes	h	3-1	Morel, Gignac, og (Danzé)
16/09	Nancy	a	1-0	J Ayew
23/09	Évian	h	1-0	Amalfitano
30/09	Valenciennes	a	1-4	J Ayew
07/10	PSG	h	2-2	Gignac 2
21/10	Troyes	a	0-1	
04/11	Ajaccio	a	2-0	A Ayew, J Ayew
11/11	Nice	a	2-2	A Ayew, Valbuena
18/11	Bordeaux	a	0-0	
25/11	LOSC	h	1-0	J Ayew
28/11	Lyon	h	1-4	Rémy
02/12	Brest	a	2-1	Diawara, A Ayew
09/12	Lorient	h	0-3	
12/12	Bastia	a	2-1	Valbuena, A Ayew (p)
15/12	Toulouse	a	1-0	Gignac
23/12	St-Étienne	h	1-0	A Ayew

2013
13/01	Sochaux	a	1-3	J Ayew
19/01	Montpellier	h	3-2	A Ayew, J Ayew, Gignac
26/01	Rennes	a	2-2	A Ayew, J Ayew
03/02	Nancy	h	0-1	
10/02	Évian	a	1-1	Gignac
16/02	Valenciennes	h	1-0	Fanni
24/02	PSG	a	0-2	
03/03	Troyes	h	2-1	N'Koulou, Gignac
10/03	Lyon	a	0-0	
15/03	Ajaccio	h	0-0	
31/03	Nice	a	1-0	Gignac
05/04	Bordeaux	h	1-0	Gignac
14/04	LOSC	a	0-0	
20/04	Brest	h	1-0	Cheyrou
27/04	Lorient	a	1-0	Valbuena
04/05	Bastia	h	2-1	Gignac 2
11/05	Toulouse	h	2-1	A Ayew 2
18/05	St-Étienne	a	0-2	
26/05	Reims	h	0-0	

No	Name	Nat	DoB	Pos	Aps	(s)	Gls
2	Kassim Abdallah	COM	09/04/87	D	11	(2)	
13	Rafidine Abdullah		15/01/94	M	3	(12)	
18	Morgan Amalfitano		20/03/85	M	20	(6)	1
33	Fabrice Apruzzese		08/05/85	A		(1)	
10	André Ayew	GHA	17/12/89	A	35		9
8	Jordan Ayew	GHA	11/09/91	A	19	(16)	7
2	César Azpilicueta	ESP	28/08/89	D	2		
6	Joey Barton	ENG	02/09/82	M	20	(5)	
7	Benoît Cheyrou		03/05/81	M	25		2
21	Souleymane Diawara	SEN	24/12/78	D	8	(3)	1
24	Rod Fanni		06/12/81	D	33		2
9	André-Pierre Gignac		05/12/85	A	28	(3)	13
19	Charles Kaboré	BFA	09/02/88	M	16	(1)	
14	Foued Kadir	ALG	05/12/83	M	5	(10)	
4	Lucas Mendes	BRA	03/07/90	D	22	(3)	
30	Steve Mandanda		28/03/85	G	38		
17	Stéphane Mbia	CMR	20/05/86	M	1		
27	Modou Sougou	SEN	18/12/84	A	4	(10)	
15	Jérémy Morel		02/04/84	D	36		1
3	Nicolas N'Koulou	CMR	27/03/90	D	38		1
25	Billel Omrani		02/06/93	A		(1)	
27	Florian Raspentino		06/06/89	A		(7)	
11	Loïc Rémy		02/01/87	A	2	(12)	1
4	Jacques-Alaixys Romao	TOG	18/01/84	M	15		
28	Mathieu Valbuena		28/09/84	M	37		3

MONTPELLIER HÉRAULT SC

Coach: René Girard
1974 • La Mosson (32,500) • mhscfoot.com
Major honours
French League (1) 2012;
French Cup (1) 1990

2012
10/08	Toulouse	h	1-1	Camara
18/08	Lorient	a	1-2	Herrera
26/08	Marseille	h	0-1	
01/09	Sochaux	a	3-1	Belhanda (p), Herrera, Cabella
14/09	Reims	a	1-3	Cabella
21/09	St-Étienne	h	1-1	Camara
29/09	Nancy	a	2-0	Belhanda, Camara
06/10	Évian	h	2-3	Estrada, Camara
20/10	Rennes	a	1-2	Belhanda (p)
27/10	Nice	h	3-1	Camara, Utaka, og (Civelli)
03/11	Troyes	a	1-1	Belhanda
11/11	PSG	h	1-1	Cabella
17/11	Valenciennes	a	1-1	Charbonnier
25/11	Bordeaux	h	1-0	Cabella
01/12	Lyon	a	0-1	
08/12	Ajaccio	h	3-0	Utaka, Cabella, Belhanda
12/12	Brest	a	2-1	og (Martial), Utaka
15/12	Bastia	h	4-0	Estrada, Herrera, Belhanda, Mounier
22/12	LOSC	a	1-4	Camara

2013
12/01	Lorient	h	2-0	Charbonnier 2
19/01	Marseille	a	2-3	Herrera, Utaka
26/01	Sochaux	h	2-0	Herrera, Utaka
03/02	Reims	h	3-1	Camara, Estrada, Belhanda
09/02	St-Étienne	a	1-4	Cabella
16/02	Nancy	h	1-0	Herrera
23/02	Évian	a	1-0	Belhanda
01/03	Rennes	h	2-0	Hilton, Camara
10/03	Nice	a	0-2	
16/03	Troyes	h	1-1	Charbonnier
29/03	PSG	a	0-1	
06/04	Valenciennes	h	3-1	Camara, Congré, Belhanda
13/04	Bordeaux	a	2-4	Cabella, Stambouli
19/04	Lyon	h	1-2	Belhanda
27/04	Ajaccio	a	1-2	Mounier
04/05	Brest	h	2-1	Estrada, Camara (p)
11/05	Bastia	a	1-0	Utaka
18/05	LOSC	h	0-0	
26/05	Toulouse	a	0-2	

No	Name	Nat	DoB	Pos	Aps	(s)	Gls
18	Karim Aït-Fana	MAR	25/02/89	M	3	(5)	
5	Henri Bedimo	CMR	04/06/84	D	29	(3)	
18	Younes Belhanda	MAR	25/02/90	M	29	(1)	10
2	Garry Bocaly		19/04/88	D	6	(1)	
20	Rémy Cabella		08/03/90	M	26	(5)	7
9	Souleymane Camara	SEN	22/12/82	A	28	(5)	10
9	Gaëtan Charbonnier		27/12/88	A	10	(16)	4
12	Daniel Congré		05/04/85	D	35	(1)	1
26	Bryan Dabo		18/02/92	M	8	(8)	
25	Mathieu Deplagne		01/10/91	D	2	(1)	
21	Abdelhamid El Kaoutari	MAR	17/03/90	D	23		
13	Marco Estrada	CHI	28/05/83	M	21	(3)	4
11	Emanuel Herrera	ARG	13/04/87	A	21	(11)	6
4	Hilton	BRA	13/09/77	D	30	(1)	1
27	Cyril Jeunechamp		18/12/75	D	6	(2)	
16	Geoffrey Jourdren		04/02/86	G	33		
30	Jonathan Ligali		28/05/91	G	1		
28	Jonas Martin		09/04/90	M	4	(12)	
31	Joris Marveaux		15/08/82	D	1	(6)	
31	Teddy Mezague		27/05/90	D	5		
8	Anthony Mounier		27/09/87	A	13	(13)	2
14	Laurent Pionnier		24/05/82	G	4	(1)	
14	Romain Pitau		08/07/77	M	10	(6)	
23	Jamel Saihi	TUN	27/01/87	M	10		
22	Benjamin Stambouli		13/08/90	D	18	(3)	1
15	Jonathan Tinhan		01/06/89	M		(1)	
7	John Utaka	NGA	08/01/82	A	26	(2)	6
3	Mapou Yanga-Mbiwa		15/05/89	D	16		

AS NANCY-LORRAINE

Coach: Jean Fernandez; (11/01/13) Patrick Gabriel
1967 • Marcel-Picot (20,085) • asnl.net
Major honours
French Cup (1) 1978;
League Cup (1) 2006

2012
11/08	Brest	h	1-0	Mollo
17/08	LOSC	a	1-1	Bakar
25/08	Toulouse	h	0-1	
01/09	Lorient	a	0-3	
16/09	Marseille	h	0-1	
22/09	Reims	a	0-2	
29/09	Montpellier	h	0-2	
05/10	St-Étienne	a	0-4	
20/10	Sochaux	h	1-1	Puygrenier
27/10	PSG	h	0-1	
03/11	Nice	a	1-2	Sané
09/11	Rennes	h	1-3	Zenke
17/11	Troyes	a	3-3	Puygrenier, Mollo, André Luiz
24/11	Ajaccio	h	1-1	Bakar
01/12	Évian	a	1-1	Mollo
08/12	Valenciennes	a	1-1	Lotiès
12/12	Lyon	h	1-1	Lotiès
16/12	Bordeaux	h	1-1	Bakar
22/12	Bastia	a	2-4	Moukandjo, André Luiz

2013
12/01	LOSC	h	2-2	Grange, Ayasse
19/01	Toulouse	a	1-2	Karaboué
26/01	Lorient	a	2-1	Alo'o Efoulou, Puygrenier
03/02	Marseille	a	1-0	Sané
09/02	Reims	h	1-2	Puygrenier
16/02	Montpellier	a	0-1	
23/02	St-Étienne	h	0-3	
02/03	Sochaux	a	2-1	Moukandjo (p), Zitte
09/03	PSG	a	1-2	Moukandjo
17/03	Nice	h	1-0	Bakar
30/03	Rennes	a	2-0	Ayasse, Bakar
06/04	Troyes	h	1-0	Grange
13/04	Ajaccio	a	1-1	Alo'o Efoulou
21/04	Évian	h	3-1	Alo'o Efoulou, Moukandjo 2
27/04	Valenciennes	a	0-0	
05/05	Lyon	h	0-3	
11/05	Bordeaux	a	2-3	Karaboué, Sané
18/05	Bastia	h	1-2	Puygrenier
26/05	Brest	a	2-1	Puygrenier 2

No	Name	Nat	DoB	Pos	Aps	(s)	Gls
14	Paul Alo'o Efoulou	CMR	12/11/83	A	13	(10)	3
34	Ibrahim Amadou		06/04/93	D		(1)	
5	André Luiz	BRA	27/01/80	D	18		2
27	Thomas Ayasse		17/02/87	M	14	(3)	2
11	Djamel Bakar		06/04/89	A	33	(2)	5
23	Jean-Landry Bassilekin	CMR	23/01/92	A		(1)	
33	Abdou Coulibaly		03/06/93	M	2	(7)	
29	Romain Grange		21/07/88	M	10	(10)	2
16	Damien Grégorini		02/03/79	G	23		
17	Massadio Haïdara		02/12/92	D	17		
7	Ziri Hammar	ALG	25/07/92	M	4	(4)	
2	Hélder	BRA	13/04/88	D	4		
21	Julien Jeanvier		31/03/92	D	4	(2)	
2	Yassine Jebbour	MAR	24/08/91	D	17		
12	Junior Joachim		13/05/92	A		(2)	
18	Lossémy Karaboué		18/03/88	M	35	(2)	2
4	Jordan Lotiès		05/08/84	M	21	(4)	2
25	Jeff Louis	HAI	08/08/90	M	2	(11)	
6	Thomas Mangani		29/04/87	D	26	(8)	
9	Yohan Mollo		18/07/89	M	16	(1)	3
9	Benjamin Moukandjo	CMR	12/11/88	M	25	(10)	5
26	Vincent Muratori		03/08/87	D	14	(1)	
1	Guy Roland N'Dy Assembé	CMR	28/02/86	G	15		
28	Sébastien Puygrenier		28/01/82	D	36		7
15	Fouad Rachid	COM	15/11/91	M	1	(1)	
3	Joël Sami	COD	13/11/84	D	25	(4)	
20	Salif Sané		25/08/90	D	34		3
22	Simon Zenke	NGA	24/12/88	A	5	(4)	1
35	Florent Zitte		17/05/93	A	4	(4)	1

OGC NICE

Coach: Claude Puel
1904 • Municipal du Ray (18,500) • ogcnice.com
Major honours
French League (4) 1951, 1952, 1956, 1959;
French Cup (3) 1952, 1954, 1997

2012

11/08	Ajaccio	h	0-1	
18/08	Valenciennes	a	0-0	
25/08	LOSC	h	2-2	Pejčinović, Bauthéac
02/09	Bordeaux	a	1-1	Traoré
15/09	Brest	h	4-2	Meriem, Pejčinović, Bauthéac, Eysseric
22/09	Lorient	a	1-1	Meriem
29/09	Bastia	h	2-2	Cvitanich, Civelli
06/10	Reims	a	1-3	Cvitanich
20/10	St-Étienne	h	1-1	Bauthéac
27/10	Montpellier	a	1-3	Cvitanich (p)
03/11	Nancy	h	2-1	Traoré, Bauthéac
11/11	Marseille	a	2-2	Cvitanich, Abriel
18/11	Toulouse	h	1-0	Cvitanich
24/11	Sochaux	h	1-0	Cvitanich (p)
01/12	PSG	h	2-1	Bauthéac, Eysseric
08/12	Troyes	a	1-0	Cvitanich
11/12	Rennes	h	1-0	Cvitanich (p)
15/12	Évian	h	3-2	Cvitanich 2, Maupay
22/12	Lyon	a	0-3	

2013

13/01	Valenciennes	h	5-0	Cvitanich 2, Civelli, Eysseric, Digard
20/01	LOSC	a	2-0	Civelli, Maupay
27/01	Bordeaux	h	0-1	
02/02	Brest	a	2-0	Pejčinović, Meriem
09/02	Lorient	h	1-1	Eysseric
16/02	Bastia	a	1-0	Maupay
22/02	Reims	h	2-0	Eysseric (p), Civelli
02/03	St-Étienne	a	0-4	
10/03	Montpellier	h	2-0	Bahoken 2
17/03	Nancy	a	0-1	
31/03	Marseille	h	0-1	
06/04	Toulouse	a	4-3	Bauthéac 2, Cvitanich, Anin
14/04	Sochaux	h	3-0	Traoré, Digard, Cvitanich
21/04	PSG	a	0-3	
28/04	Troyes	h	3-1	Civelli, Cvitanich, Bruins
05/05	Rennes	a	3-0	Cvitanich 2 (1p), Bauthéac
12/05	Évian	a	0-4	
19/05	Lyon	h	1-1	Cvitanich (p)
26/05	Ajaccio	a	2-0	Cvitanich, Bauthéac

No	Name	Nat	DoB	Pos	Aps	(s)	Gls
7	Fabrice Abriel		06/07/79	M	19	(9)	1
17	Kevin Anin		05/07/86	M	10	(3)	1
29	Jérémie Daliveau	OMN	20/05/92	A		(7)	
11	Eric Bauthéac		24/08/87	M	33	(2)	9
23	Alexy Bosetti		23/04/93	A	4	(23)	
20	Luigi Bruins	NED	09/03/87	M	5	(5)	1
2	Renato Civelli	ARG	14/10/83	D	34		5
15	Kafoumba Coulibaly	CIV	26/10/85	D	1		
12	Darío Cvitanich	ARG	16/05/84	A	29		19
28	Fabian Dao Castellana		28/07/93	M		(2)	
30	Joris Delle		29/03/90	G	12	(2)	
30	Kevin Diaz		18/08/88	M	5	(3)	
6	Didier Digard		12/07/86	M	36		2
13	Franck Dja Djedje	CIV	02/06/86	A	3		
13	Valentin Eysseric		25/03/92	D	21	(3)	5
26	Diacko Fofana		27/04/94	D		(4)	
25	Romain Genevois	HAI	28/10/87	D	22	(3)	
5	Kévin Gomis		20/01/89	D	12	(1)	
20	Abraham Gneki Guié	CIV	25/07/86	A	1	(2)	
3	Thimothée Kolodziejczak		01/10/91	D	37		
18	Neal Maupay		14/08/96	A	3	(12)	3
18	Camel Meriem		14/08/79	M	14	(10)	3
18	Luciano Monzón	ARG	13/04/87	D	1		
1	David Ospina	COL	31/08/88	G	26		
21	Lloyd Palun	GAB	28/11/88	M	10	(2)	
4	Nemanja Pejčinović	SRB	04/11/87	D	28	(1)	3
9	Xavier Pentecôte		13/08/86	A		(2)	
14	Jérémy Pied		23/02/89	A	18	(8)	
33	Grégoire Puel		20/02/92	M	8		
33	Albert Rafetraniaina	MAD	09/09/96	D		(1)	
34	Lucas Rougeaux		10/03/94	D		(1)	
8	Mahamane Traoré	MLI	31/08/88	M	23	(1)	3

PARIS SAINT-GERMAIN FC

Coach: Carlo Ancelotti (ITA)
1970 • Parc des Princes (47,428) • psg.fr
Major honours
UEFA Cup Winners' Cup (1) 1996;
French League (3) 1986, 1994, 2013;
French Cup (8) 1982, 1983, 1993, 1995, 1998, 2004, 2006, 2010;
League Cup (3) 1995, 1998, 2008

2012

11/08	Lorient	h	2-2	Ibrahimović 2 (1p)
19/08	Ajaccio	a	0-0	
26/08	Bordeaux	h	0-0	
02/09	LOSC	a	2-1	Ibrahimović 2
14/09	Toulouse	h	2-0	Pastore, Ibrahimović
22/09	Bastia	a	4-0	Ménez, Ibrahimović 2, Matuidi
29/09	Sochaux	h	2-0	Gameiro 2
07/10	Marseille	a	2-2	Ibrahimović 2
20/10	Reims	h	1-0	Gameiro
27/10	Nancy	a	2-1	Ibrahimović
03/11	St-Étienne	h	1-2	Hoarau
11/11	Montpellier	a	1-1	Maxwell
17/11	Rennes	h	1-2	Nenê
24/11	Troyes	h	4-0	Maxwell, Matuidi, Ibrahimović 2
01/12	Nice	a	1-2	Ibrahimović
08/12	Évian	h	4-0	Ibrahimović, Lavezzi, Thiago Motta, Gameiro
11/12	Valenciennes	a	4-0	Ibrahimović 3, Lavezzi
16/12	Lyon	h	1-0	Matuidi
21/12	Brest	a	3-0	Ibrahimović, Gameiro, og (Mendy)

2013

11/01	Ajaccio	h	0-0	
20/01	Bordeaux	a	1-0	Ibrahimović
27/01	LOSC	h	1-0	og (Chedjou)
01/02	Toulouse	a	4-0	Pastore, Ibrahimović, Sakho, Van der Wiel
08/02	Bastia	h	3-1	Ménez, Ibrahimović (p), Lavezzi
17/02	Sochaux	a	2-3	Alex, og (Roussillon)
24/02	Marseille	h	2-0	og (N'Koulou), Ibrahimović
02/03	Reims	a	0-1	
09/03	Nancy	h	2-1	Ibrahimović 2
17/03	St-Étienne	a	2-2	Pastore, Ibrahimović (p)
29/03	Montpellier	h	1-0	Gameiro
06/04	Rennes	a	2-0	Ménez, Ibrahimović
13/04	Troyes	h	1-0	Matuidi
21/04	Nice	h	3-0	Ménez, Ibrahimović (p), Chantôme
28/04	Évian	a	1-0	Pastore
05/05	Valenciennes	h	1-1	Alex
12/05	Lyon	a	1-0	Ménez
19/05	Brest	h	3-1	Ibrahimović 2, Matuidi
26/05	Lorient	a	3-1	Ibrahimović, Gameiro 2

No	Name	Nat	DoB	Pos	Aps	(s)	Gls
13	Alex	BRA	17/06/82	D	22	(2)	2
16	Alphonse Areola		27/02/93	G	1	(1)	
22	Sylvain Armand		01/08/80	D	11	(7)	
32	David Beckham	ENG	02/05/75	M	2	(8)	
12	Mathieu Bodmer		22/11/82	M	1	(3)	
6	Zoumana Camara		03/04/79	D	5	(1)	
20	Clément Chantôme		11/09/87	M	16	(12)	1
33	Kingsley Coman		13/06/96	M		(1)	
33	Antoine Conte		29/01/94	D		(1)	
1	Nicolas Douchez		22/04/80	G	4		
19	Kévin Gameiro		09/05/87	A	7	(18)	8
9	Guillaume Hoarau		05/03/84	A	1	(5)	1
18	Zlatan Ibrahimović	SWE	03/10/81	A	33	(1)	30
26	Christophe Jallet		31/10/83	D	20	(7)	
11	Ezequiel Lavezzi	ARG	03/05/85	A	25	(3)	3
40	Ronan Le Crom		13/07/74	G		(1)	
29	Lucas Moura	BRA	13/08/92	M	9	(1)	
14	Blaise Matuidi		09/04/87	M	35	(2)	5
17	Maxwell	BRA	27/08/81	D	33		2
7	Jérémy Ménez		07/05/87	M	24	(6)	5
10	Nenê	BRA	19/07/81	M	5	(4)	1
27	Javier Pastore	ARG	20/06/89	M	30	(4)	4
25	Adrien Rabiot		03/04/95	M	1	(5)	
3	Mamadou Sakho		13/02/90	D	24	(3)	1
30	Salvatore Sirigu	ITA	12/01/87	G	33		
4	Mohamed Sissoko	MLI	22/01/85	M	1	(2)	
28	Thiago Motta	ITA	28/08/82	M	11	(1)	1
2	Thiago Silva	BRA	22/09/84	D	22		
5	Siaka Tiéné	CIV	22/02/82	D	2		
23	Gregory van der Wiel	NED	03/02/88	D	17	(5)	1
24	Marco Verratti	ITA	05/11/92	M	23	(4)	

STADE DE REIMS

Coach: Hubert Fournier
1911 • Auguste-Delaune (21,684) • stade-de-reims.com
Major honours
French League (6) 1949, 1953, 1955, 1958, 1960, 1962;
French Cup (2) 1950, 1958

2012

12/08	Marseille	h	0-1	
18/08	Bastia	a	1-2	Fauvergue
25/08	Sochaux	h	1-0	og (Privat)
01/09	Toulouse	a	1-1	og (Abdennour)
14/09	Montpellier	h	3-1	Diego, Glombard, Courtet
22/09	Nancy	h	2-0	Courtet, Diego (p)
30/09	St-Étienne	a	0-0	
06/10	Nice	h	3-1	Diego, Courtet 2
20/10	PSG	a	0-1	
27/10	Troyes	h	1-1	Mandi
03/11	Rennes	a	0-0	
10/11	Évian	h	1-2	og (Cambon)
18/11	Lyon	a	0-3	
24/11	Brest	h	0-0	
01/12	Valenciennes	a	0-1	
09/12	Bordeaux	h	0-0	
12/12	Ajaccio	a	0-2	
15/12	LOSC	h	1-1	Weber
22/12	Lorient	a	2-2	Fortes, Courtet

2013

13/01	Bastia	h	1-2	Courtet
19/01	Sochaux	a	0-1	
26/01	Toulouse	h	1-1	Krychowiak
02/02	Montpellier	a	1-3	Courtet
09/02	Nancy	a	2-1	Ayité, Fortes
17/02	St-Étienne	h	1-1	Courtet
22/02	Nice	a	0-2	
02/03	PSG	h	1-0	Krychowiak
09/03	Troyes	a	2-4	De Préville, Fortes
16/03	Rennes	h	1-0	Fofana
30/03	Évian	a	2-2	Ayité, Courtet
07/04	Lyon	h	1-0	Krychowiak (p)
13/04	Brest	a	2-0	Fauvergue, Diego
21/04	Valenciennes	h	0-1	
27/04	Bordeaux	a	0-0	
04/05	Ajaccio	h	1-1	Mandi
10/05	LOSC	a	0-3	
18/05	Lorient	h	1-0	Krychowiak (p)
26/05	Marseille	a	0-0	

No	Name	Nat	DoB	Pos	Aps	(s)	Gls
16	Kossi Agassa	TOG	07/07/78	G	33		
10	Floyd Ayité	TOG	15/12/88	A	15	(8)	2
28	Yann Benedick		01/02/92	A			
21	Bocundji Ca	GNB	28/12/86	M	21	(12)	
18	Gaëtan Courtet		22/02/89	A	21	(9)	9
12	Nicolas De Préville		08/01/91	A	4	(6)	1
6	Antoine Devaux		21/02/85	M	30	(5)	
11	Diego	BRA	30/08/91	M	27	(2)	4
13	Nicolas Fauvergue		13/10/84	A	12	(11)	2
2	Mohamed Fofana	MLI	07/03/85	D	14	(1)	1
7	Odair Fortes	CPV	31/03/87	A	17	(6)	3
5	Kamel Ghilas	ALG	09/03/84	A	9	(14)	
24	Florent Ghisolfi		28/02/85	D	3	(6)	
27	Christopher Glombard		05/06/89	D	25	(2)	1
4	Grzegorz Krychowiak	POL	29/01/90	M	34	(1)	4
1	Johan Liébus		05/11/78	G	1	(1)	
23	Aïssa Mandi		22/10/91	D	27	(2)	2
33	Bilel Ouali	ALG	07/10/93	M		(2)	
19	Alexi Peuget		18/12/90	M		(1)	
40	Johnny Placide	HAI	29/01/88	G	4		
8	Johann Ramaré		05/06/84	M	19	(3)	
15	Khalid Sekkat	MAR	12/05/84	D	1		
3	Franck Signorino		19/09/81	D	20	(2)	
26	Pape Souaré	SEN	06/06/90	D	20	(1)	
22	Mickaël Tacalfred		23/04/81	D	26	(2)	
9	Julien Toudic		23/02/85	A	1	(10)	
25	Anthony Weber		11/06/87	D	34	(1)	1

FRANCE

Top goalscorers

30	Zlatan Ibrahimović (PSG)
19	Darío Cvitanich (Nice)
	Pierre-Emerick Aubameyang (St-Étienne)
16	Bafétimbi Gomis (Lyon)
15	Anthony Modeste (Bastia)
	Jérémie Aliadière (Lorient)
	Wissam Ben Yedder (Toulouse)
14	Salomon Kalou (LOSC)
13	Saber Khelifa (Évian)
	André-Pierre Gignac (Marseille)

Promoted clubs

AS MONACO FC

Coach: Claudio Ranieri (ITA)
1919 • Louis II (18,524) • asm-fc.com
Major honours
French League (7) 1961, 1963, 1978, 1982, 1988, 1997, 2000;
French Cup (5) 1960, 1963, 1980, 1985, 1991;
League Cup (1) 2003

EN AVANT GUINGAMP

Coach: Jocelyn Gourvennec
1912 • Roudourou (18,126) • eaguingamp.com
Major honours
French Cup (1) 2009

FC NANTES

Coach: Michel Der Zakarian
1943 • La Beaujoire (37,583) • fcnantes.com
Major honours
French League (8) 1965, 1966, 1973, 1977, 1980,
1983, 1995, 2001;
French Cup (3) 1979, 1999, 2000

SECOND LEVEL FINAL TABLE 2012/13

		Pld	W	D	L	F	A	Pts
1	AS Monaco FC	38	21	13	4	64	33	76
2	En Avant Guingamp	38	20	10	8	63	38	70
3	FC Nantes	38	19	12	7	54	29	69
4	SM Caen	38	17	12	9	48	28	63
5	Angers SCO	38	17	10	11	39	39	61
6	Le Havre AC	38	16	11	11	52	47	59
7	Dijon FCO	38	15	14	9	52	49	59
8	Nîmes Olympique	38	17	7	14	52	42	58
9	AJ Auxerre	38	13	10	15	51	53	49
10	Tours FC	38	12	13	13	40	49	49
11	AC Arles-Avignon	38	10	16	12	36	48	46
12	RC Lens	38	9	18	11	39	53	45
13	FC Istres	38	11	10	17	38	45	43
14	Clermont Foot Auvergne	38	9	16	13	33	47	43
15	Chamois Niortais FC	38	8	18	12	39	42	42
16	LB Châteauroux	38	8	18	12	43	47	42
17	Stade Lavallois MFC	38	10	12	16	47	54	42
18	Le Mans FC	38	11	7	20	39	62	40
19	CS Sedan Ardennes	38	6	13	19	41	58	31
20	GFC Ajaccio	38	6	10	22	34	54	25

NB GFC Ajaccio – 3 pts deducted.

Domestic cup: Coupe de France 2012/13

1/32 FINALS

(05/01/13)
Amiens 1-1 Évian *(aet; 3-5 on pens)*
Amnéville 1-2 Raon-l'Étape *(aet)*
Belfort 1-3 Le Havre
Boulogne 0-1 Toulouse
Chauray 1-5 Lorient
Consolat Marseille 1-1 Moulins *(aet; 4-5 on pens)*
Drouais 1-5 Nancy
Le Mans 1-2 Le Poiré-sur-Vie
LOSC 3-2 Nîmes
Montceau 0-1 Troyes
Plabennec 1-0 Reims
Rouen 1-1 AC Ajaccio *(aet; 3-2 on pens)*
St-Malo 1-1 Vertou *(aet; 2-4 on pens)*
Savigneux Montbrison 1-1 Vénissieux *(aet; 1-3 on pens)*
Stade Bordelais 1-0 Carquefou
Thaon 0-1 Sochaux

(06/01/13)
Arras 3- 4 PSG
CA Bastia 2-0 SC Bastia
Bourg-Péronnas 1-2 Montpellier
Caen 2-3 St-Étienne
Châteauroux 2-3 Bordeaux
Dieppe 2-3 Nantes
Épinal 3-3 Lyon *(aet; 4-2 on pens)*
Lens 2-1 Rennes
Lozère 2-0 Arles
Luçon 1-1 Brest *(aet; 2-4 on pens)*
Marseille 2-1 Guingamp *(aet)*
Meaux 1-0 Le Portel
Metz 2-3 Nice
Muret 0-2 Fontenay
Pontarlier 1-2 Sedan

(07/01/13)
Istres 3-3 Valenciennes *(aet; 4-3 on pens)*

1/16 FINALS

(22/01/13)
Épinal 1-1 Nantes *(aet; 4-3 on pens)*
Fontenay 0-5 Troyes
Lozère 0-3 Le Havre
Sedan 0-1 Lorient
Vertou 0-2 Évian

(23/01/13)
CA Bastia 1-3 Brest
Meaux 0-0 St-Étienne *(aet; 3-5 on pens)*
Montpellier 2-3 Sochaux *(aet)*
Moulins 1-2 Bordeaux
Nice 2-2 Nancy *(aet; 2-4 on pens)*
PSG 3-1 Toulouse
Raon-l'Étape 1-0 Istres
Stade Bordelais 0-3 Lens
Vénissieux 0-0 Le Poiré-sur-Vie *(aet; 4-3 on pens)*

(24/01/13)
Plabennec 1-3 LOSC

(30/01/13)
Rouen 1-2 Marseille

1/8 FINALS

(26/02/13)
Évian 3-1 Le Havre
St-Étienne 3-2 LOSC
Sochaux 1-2 Troyes

(27/02/13)
Lorient 3-0 Brest
PSG 2-0 Marseille
Raon-l'Étape 2-2 Bordeaux *(aet; 3-5 on pens)*
Vénissieux 0-2 Nancy *(aet)*

(28/02/13)
Lens 2-0 Épinal

QUARTER-FINALS

(16/04/13)
St-Étienne 1-2 Lorient *(Aubameyang 75; Barthelme 44, Aliadière 90)*
Troyes 3-0 Nancy *(Bréchet 52, Faussurier 75, Camus 81)*

(17/04/13)
Évian 1-1 PSG *(Khelifa 44; Pastore 9) (aet; 4-1 on pens)*
Lens 2-3 Bordeaux *(Carrasso 11og, Berodich 90; Sertic 59, Diabaté 81, 85)*

SEMI-FINALS

(08/05/13)
Évian 4-0 Lorient *(Ninković 10, Sagbo 20, Bérigaud 33, Baouia 80)*

(14/05/13)
Troyes 1-2 Bordeaux *(Bahebeck 7; Diabaté 41, Bréchet 63og)*

FINAL

(31/05/13)
Stade de France, Saint-Denis
FC GIRONDINS DE BORDEAUX 3 *(Diabaté 39, 89, Saivet 53)*
ÉVIAN THONON GAILLARD FC 2 *(Sagbo 51, Dja Djédjé 70)*
Referee: Fautrel
BORDEAUX: Carrasso, Mariano, Henrique, Sané, Trémoulinas, Plašil (Biyogo Poko 67), Sertic, Maurice-Belay, Obraniak, Siavet, Diabaté
ÉVIAN: Laquait, Dja Djédjé, Cambon, Betão, Wass, Rabiu (Tié Bi 82), Sorlin, Bérigaud, Ninković (Barbosa 59), Khelifa, Sagbo (Angoula 90)

Domestic cup: Coupe de la Ligue 2012/13

QUARTER-FINALS

(27/11/12)
St-Étienne 0-0 PSG *(aet; 5-3 on pens)*

(28/11/12)
Montpellier 3-2 Nice *(Cabella 26, Herrera 52, Tinhan 83; Bosetti 22, Bauthéac 66p)*
SC Bastia 0-3 LOSC *(Bruno 11, Rodelin 62, Sidibé 84)*
Rennes 2-1 Troyes *(Pitroipa 8, Alessandrini 88; Jean 22)*

SEMI-FINALS

(15/01/13)
St-Étienne 0-0 LOSC *(aet; 7-6 on pens)*

(16/01/13)
Rennes 2-0 Montpellier *(Féret 7, Mevlüt 51)*

FINAL

(20/04/13)
Stade de France, Saint-Denis
AS SAINT-ÉTIENNE 1 *(Brandão 18)*
STADE RENNAIS FC 0
Referee: Buquet
ST-ÉTIENNE: Ruffier, Clerc, Zouma, Brison, Perrin, Cohade, Lemoine, Guilavogui, Brandão, Aubameyang, Mollo (Hamouma 73)
RENNES: Costil, Danzé (Apam 57), Boye, Mavinga, Kana-Biyik, Makoun, Féret (Montaño 90+1), Diallo, Pajot, Pitroipa, Mevlüt (C Diarra 18)

GEORGIA
Georgian Football Federation (GFF)

Address	76a Chavchavadze Ave. GE-0162 Tbilisi	**President**	Domenti Sichinava
Tel	+995 32 912 680	**General secretary**	Revaz Arveladze
Fax	+995 32 915 995	**Media officer**	Otar Giorgadze
E-mail	gff@gff.ge	**Year of formation**	1990
Website	gff.ge	**National stadium**	Boris Paichadze, Tbilisi (53,279)

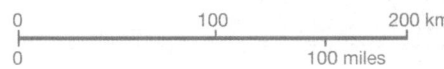

UMAGLESI LIGA CLUBS

 1 FC Chikhura Sachkhere

 2 FC Dila Gori

3 FC Dinamo Batumi

 4 FC Dinamo Tbilisi

5 FC Kolkheti Poti

6 FC Merani Martvili

7 FC Metalurgi Rustavi

8 FC Sioni Bolnisi

 9 FC Torpedo Kutaisi

10 FC WIT Georgia

11 FC Zestafoni

12 FC Zugdidi

PROMOTED CLUBS

13 FC Guria Lanchkhuti

14 FC Spartaki Tskhinvali

KEY:
● – UEFA Champions League
● – UEFA Europa League
● – Promoted clubs
● – Relegated clubs

Dinamo Tbilisi by a distance

Absent from Europe for the first time in 19 years, FC Dinamo Tbilisi returned to a position of domestic dominance, winning their first Georgian championship since 2007/08 and their first league and cup double in a decade.

They were led to victory by Czech coach Dušan Uhrin Jr, the namesake son of the man who had overseen the club's previous Umaglesi Liga triumph. FC Dila Gori, who posted a record-breaking 11 straight victories during the autumn, claimed the runners-up spot while the season's surprise package, FC Chikhura Sachkhere, finished fourth and reached the final of the Georgian Cup.

Domestic double for nation's most decorated club

Uhrin Jr repeats father's title-winning feat

Runners-up Dila benefit from record-breaking run

Domestic league

With Dinamo Tbilisi's focus exclusively on domestic concerns following their disappointing fourth-place finish in 2011/12, and Uhrin newly recruited to follow in the footsteps of his father, who coached the club successfully from 2006-08, expectations of a return to power were high. A bright start, with Spanish duo Xisco and Mikel Álvaro both prominent in attack alongside Jaba Dvali, a new signing from defending champions FC Zestafoni, gave Dinamo the early initiative, but they found company at the top of the table during the first phase of the championship in the shape of Dila.

The club from Gori, 100 km north-west of the capital, got off to a terrible start, losing their first three games, but experienced a complete reversal of fortune after appointing Giorgi Daraselia as coach. In his first game Dila defeated Dinamo 2-0 and then went on to beat all of the other ten teams in the Umaglesi Liga one after the other, conceding just one goal in the process. Dinamo halted that run with a 3-0 win but by the end of the first phase, with 22 matches played, Dila were just three points in arrears

The title race resumed in the six-team championship pool at the beginning of March, and it was now that Dinamo began to pull clear, their 14th post-independence title being wrapped up two rounds from the end with a 4-0 home win over third-placed FC Torpedo Kutaisi. With 26 points claimed from a maximum 30, Uhrin's men were a class apart during the spring and ended up ten points clear of runners-up Dila.

With 24 wins out of 32, and a huge tally of 88 goals, 24 of them to the league's top scorer Xisco, their victory was emphatic – as underlined in their final game when they thrashed Zestafoni 6-1. The champions of the previous two seasons ended 36 points adrift of Dinamo and failed to qualify for Europe.

Domestic cup

One trophy for Uhrin and his players became two as they completed the double with a 3-1 win in the Georgian Cup final against Chikhura. Three second-half goals – from Giorgi Merebashvili, Levan Khmaladze and Irakli Dzaria – ended the plucky resistance of Soso Pruidze's underdogs, who had lost heavily to the champions in their previous three league meetings. Having finished fourth in only their second Umaglesi Liga campaign, Chikhura were already assured of a first European qualification. For Dinamo, a tenth Georgian Cup triumph completed an eighth domestic double.

Europe

In the absence of Dinamo, it was Dila who put up the best performance of Georgia's four European entrants in 2012/13, getting past AGF Aarhus of Denmark and Anorthosis Famagusta FC of Cyprus (with a memorable 3-0 away win) before bowing out in the UEFA Europa League play-offs to Portugal's CS Marítimo.

National team

Temur Ketsbaia's national team opened their 2014 FIFA World Cup qualifying campaign with a trio of positive performances – a 1-0 home win over Belarus and a 1-1 draw in Finland sandwiching a wonderfully defiant display at home to holders Spain, in which goalkeeper Giorgi Loria excelled until he suffered a serious injury and missed the closing minutes, during which the visitors scored the only goal of the game. Subsequent defeats in Belarus and France left Georgia in danger of finishing bottom of Group I – a prospect not improved by a confidence-denting 4-0 friendly defeat against the Republic of Ireland in June.

Domestic league: Umaglesi Liga 2012/13 final table

SECOND PHASE
Championship Pool

		Pld	Home					Away					Total					Pts
			W	D	L	F	A	W	D	L	F	A	W	D	L	F	A	
1	**FC Dinamo Tbilisi**	32	15	1	0	59	12	9	5	2	29	11	24	6	2	88	23	78
2	FC Dila Gori	32	10	0	6	31	13	12	2	2	29	13	22	2	8	60	26	68
3	FC Torpedo Kutaisi	32	12	3	1	34	12	7	4	5	23	18	19	7	6	57	30	64
4	FC Chikhura Sachkhere	32	10	3	3	25	13	7	3	6	24	25	17	6	9	49	38	57
5	FC Zestafoni	32	7	3	6	14	15	5	3	8	21	23	12	6	14	35	38	42
6	FC Zugdidi	32	8	3	5	22	21	2	3	11	9	31	10	6	16	31	52	36

Relegation Pool

		Pld	Home					Away					Total					Pts
			W	D	L	F	A	W	D	L	F	A	W	D	L	F	A	
7	FC Metalurgi Rustavi	32	6	4	6	15	18	6	4	6	14	17	12	8	12	29	35	44
8	FC Merani Martvili	32	8	1	7	20	17	2	3	11	11	34	10	4	18	31	51	34
9	FC WIT Georgia	32	2	7	7	12	19	6	2	8	13	23	8	9	15	25	42	33
10	FC Sioni Bolnisi	32	3	6	7	16	27	5	3	8	15	24	8	9	15	31	51	33
11	FC Dinamo Batumi	32	4	3	9	22	25	4	4	8	17	30	8	7	17	39	55	31
12	FC Kolkheti Poti	32	2	5	9	12	23	1	3	12	10	33	3	8	21	22	56	17

NB League splits into top and bottom halves after 22 games, after which the clubs play exclusively against teams in their group.

SEASON AT A GLANCE

EUROPEAN QUALIFICATION 2013/14

Champion/Cup winner: FC Dinamo Tbilisi (second qualifying round)

FC Dila Gori (second qualifying round)
FC Torpedo Kutaisi (first qualifying round)
FC Chikhura Sachkhere (first qualifying round)

Top scorer	Xisco (Dinamo Tbilisi), 24 goals
Relegated clubs	FC Kolkheti Poti, FC Dinamo Batumi
Promoted clubs	FC Guria Lanchkhuti, FC Spartaki Tskhinvali
Cup final	FC Dinamo Tbilisi 3-1 FC Chikhura Sachkhere

UMAGLESI LIGA TEAM OF THE SEASON
(3-4-3)
Coach: Uhrin (Dinamo Tbilisi)

PLAYER OF THE SEASON
Xisco
(FC Dinamo Tbilisi)

The top ten of the Umaglesi Liga scoring charts featured four Dinamo players. On top of the pile, with 24 goals, was the team's experienced 32-year-old Spanish striker. A Spanish champion and UEFA Cup winner with Valencia CF in 2004, Xisco's second season in Georgia brought him not just individual recognition but winner's medals in both league and cup.

NEWCOMER OF THE SEASON
Giorgi Pantsulaia
(FC Torpedo Kutaisi)

The son of Mamuka Pantsulaia – joint-top scorer in Georgia's first post-independence championship – the 19-year-old emerged as a firm favourite at Torpedo, helping the club finish third in the league. He made 20 appearances from the bench, providing several assists, before starting the club's penultimate fixture and marking it with two goals.

Loria *(Dinamo Tbilisi)*

Oniani *(Dila/Torpedo)* — Kvaratskhelia *(Dinamo Tbilisi)* — Kvirkvelia *(Dila)*

Dolidze *(Torpedo)* — Mikel Álvaro *(Dinamo Tbilisi)* — Khmaladze *(Dinamo Tbilisi)* — Grajciar *(Dinamo Tbilisi)*

Dvali *(Dinamo Tbilisi)* — Xisco *(Dinamo Tbilisi)* — Merebashvili *(Dinamo Tbilisi)*

GEORGIA

NATIONAL TEAM

Home Kit   Away Kit

TOP FIVE ALL-TIME CAPS
Levan Kobiashvili (100); **Zurab Khizanishvili** (90); Kakha Kaladze (83); Giorgi Nemsadze (69); Aleksandre Iashvili (67)

TOP FIVE ALL-TIME GOALS
Shota Arveladze (26); Temur Ketsbaia (17); Aleksandre Iashvili (15); Giorgi Demetradze & Levan Kobiashvili (12)

Results 2012/13

15/08/12	Luxembourg	A	Obercorn	2-1	Mchedlidze (2), Amisulashvili (31)	
07/09/12	Belarus (WCQ)	H	Tbilisi	1-0	Okriashvili (51)	
11/09/12	Spain (WCQ)	H	Tbilisi	0-1		
12/10/12	Finland (WCQ)	A	Helsinki	1-1	Kashia (56)	
16/10/12	Belarus (WCQ)	A	Minsk	0-2		
14/11/12	Egypt	H	Tbilisi	0-0		
06/02/13	Albania	A	Tirana	2-1	Vatsadze (41), Lobjanidze (82)	
22/03/13	France (WCQ)	A	Paris	1-3	Kobakhidze (71)	
02/06/13	Republic of Ireland	A	Dublin	0-4		
05/06/13	Denmark	A	Aalborg	1-2	Dzaria (52)	

Appearances 2012/13

Coach: Temur Ketsbaia	18/03/68		Lux	BLR	ESP	FIN	BLR	Egy	Alb	FRA	Irl	Den	Caps	Goals
Giorgi Loria	27/01/86	Dinamo Tbilisi	G	G	G73			G			G 20*	G	20	-
Guram Kashia	04/07/87	Vitesse (NED)	D 14*	D	M	D	D	M	M	M	M	D	24	1
Akaki Khubutia	17/03/86	Gaz Metan (ROU) /Mordovia (RUS)	D								D	D	10	-
Aleksandre Amisulashvili	20/08/82	Krasnodar (RUS) /Krylya Sovetov (RUS)	D78	D	D	D	D	D		D			32	3
Gia Grigalava	05/08/89	Volga (RUS)	D	D		D	D	D	D46				11	-
Jaba Kankava	18/03/86	Kryvbas (UKR) /Dnipro (UKR)	M		M	M	M		s46		M	M	43	4
Aleksandre Kobakhidze	11/02/87	Arsenal Kyiv (UKR) /Dnipro (UKR)	M46			M	M	M56	M63	M	M90	M87	15	3
David Targamadze	22/08/89	Illychivets (UKR)	M46	M	M64	M81	M75	M46	M	M84	s46	s63	16	2
Jano Ananidze	10/10/92	Spartak Moskva (RUS)	M68	M75	s67	s49				M46	M20	M63	20	2
Tornike Okriashvili	12/02/92	Illychivets (UKR)	M90	M83	M	M67	M49		s46				8	1
Levan Mchedlidze	24/03/90	Empoli (ITA)	A46	A56	A79	A59	s46		A21				20	2
Ucha Lobjanidze	23/02/87	Kryvbas (UKR)	s46		D			D	D	D	D46	s63	29	1
Murtaz Daushvili	01/05/89	Karpaty (UKR)	s46	M	M	M	M			M	M54	M73	20	-
Irakli Sirbiladze	27/09/82	Inter Turku (FIN)	s46	s83	s79							s46	4	-
Aleksandre Guruli	09/11/85	Dila	s68					s56					6	1
Giorgi Popkhadze	25/09/86	Bakı (AZE)	s78								s69	D	11	-
Nikoloz Gelashvili	05/08/85	Bochum (GER)	s90						s61	s84	A61	s87	16	-
Zurab Khizanishvili	06/10/81	Kayserispor (TUR)		D	D	D	D		D	D	D	D	90	1
David Kvirkvelia	27/06/80	Dila		s56	D			D	s46	D	D69		54	-
Tornike Gorgiashvili	27/04/88	Zestafoni		s75				s76			s90		4	-
Nika Dzalamidze	06/01/92	Jagiellonia (POL)			s64				s46	M46			4	-
Roin Kvaskhvadze	31/05/89	Zestafoni			s73				G				2	-
Nukri Revishvili	02/03/87	Krasnodar (RUS)				G	G						21	-
David Devdariani	28/10/87	AGF (DEN)			s59	A46							6	-
Levan Kenia	18/10/90	Karpaty (UKR)			s81	s75			M61	s46			23	3
Irakli Dzaria	01/12/87	Dinamo Tbilisi						M76	s63		s54	M63	5	1

Appearances 2012/13 (contd.)

			Lux	BLR	ESP	FIN	BLR	Egy	Alb	FRA	Irl	Den	Caps	Goals
Shota Grigalashvili	21/06/86	Alania (RUS)						M69					10	-
Jaba Dvali	08/02/85	Dinamo Tbilisi						A46					1	-
Vladimer Dvalishvili	20/04/86	Polonia Warszawa (POL) /Legia (POL)						s46			s74	A46	25	4
Irakli Kobalia	13/03/92	Zugdidi						s69					1	-
Ilia Kandelaki	26/12/81	İnter Bakı (AZE)							D46				15	-
Mate Vatsadze	17/12/88	AGF (DEN)							s21 /76	A74			7	1
Gulverd Tomashvili	13/10/88	Dila							s76				1	-
Omar Migineishvili	02/06/84	Torpedo Kutaisi									s20		1	-
Irakli Maisuradze	22/08/88	Dila									s61		2	-
Merab Gigauri	05/06/93	Torpedo Kutaisi										s73	1	-

European club competitions 2012/13

FC ZESTAFONI

Second qualifying round - Neftçi PFK (AZE)
A 0-3
Kvaskhvadze, Gongadze, Sadjaia, Kobakhidze, Gorgiashvili, Dvali, Sharikadze, Menteshashvili, Eliava (Tornike Grigalashvili 77), Aptsiauri (Guguchia 66), Owonikoko (Mujiri 59). Coach: Gia Chiabrishvili (GEO)
H 2-2 *Mujiri (16), Dvali (19)*
Kvaskhvadze, Gongadze (Eliava 90), Tornike Grigalashvili, Kobakhidze, Tedore Grigalashvili, Gorgiashvili (Aptsiauri 63), Mujiri, Dvali, Sharikadze, Menteshashvili, Owonikoko (Benashvili 55). Coach: Gia Chiabrishvili (GEO)

FC DILA GORI

Second qualifying round - AGF Aarhus (DEN)
A 2-1 *Vatsadze (34), Aladashvili (84)*
Skender, Salukvadze, Arziani, Shashiashvili, Aladashvili, Vatsadze (Modebadze 82), Gogua, Kvirkvelia, Guruli, Bechvaia (Kashia 53), Tomashvili (Oniani 46). Coach: Teimuraz Shalamberidze (GEO)
H 3-1 *Vatsadze (62, 83), Shashlashvili (74)*
Skender, Salukvadze, Oniani, Shashiashvili, Aladashvili (Akhalkatsi 57), Vatsadze, Gogua (Modebadze 77), Grigalashvili, Kvirkvelia, Guruli, Kashia (Bechvaia 27). Coach: Teimuraz Shalamberidze (GEO)

Third qualifying round - Anorthosis Famagusta FC (CYP)
H 0-1
Skender, Salukvadze, Oniani, Shashiashvili, Vatsadze, Gogua, Grigalashvili (Aladashvili 46), Modebadze (Gvalia 62), Kvirkvelia, Guruli, Bechvaia (Katsitadze 77). Coach: Teimuraz Shalamberidze (GEO)
Red card: Gogua 57
A 3-0 *(w/o; match abandoned after 83 mins at 3-0 Vatsadze (54, 80), Salukvadze (78))*
Skender, Salukvadze, Oniani, Shashiashvili, Vatsadze, Grigalashvili, Kvirkvelia, Guruli, Bechvaia, Gvalia, Kakhelishvili (Akhalkatsi 46). Coach: Teimuraz Shalamberidze (GEO)

Play-offs - CS Marítimo (POR)
A 0-1
Skender, Salukvadze, Oniani, Shashiashvili, Gogua, Grigalashvili (Akhalkatsi 70), Kvirkvelia, Guruli (Iluridze 62), Klimiashvili (Kakhelishvili 56), Bechvaia, Gvalia. Coach: Teimuraz Shalamberidze (GEO)
H 0-2
Skender, Salukvadze (Tomashvili 17), Oniani, Iluridze (Akhalkatsi 46), Vatsadze, Gogua, Grigalashvili, Kvirkvelia, Guruli, Bechvaia, Kashia (Kakhelishvili 63). Coach: Teimuraz Shalamberidze (GEO)

FC METALURGI RUSTAVI

First qualifying round - KS Teuta (ALB)
A 3-0 *Tatanashvili (77), Kvaratskhelia (84, 90+2p)*
Bediashvili, Kakushadze (Tekturmanidze 46), Maisuradze, Sukhiashvili, Kvaratskhelia, Razmadze, Japaridze, Sikharulidze (Tatanashvili 75), Dobrovolski (Mikaberidze 60), Getsadze, Makhviladze. Coach: Koba Jorjikashvili (GEO)
H 6-1 *Tekturmanidze (14, 19), Tatanashvili (37, 69), Getsadze (59), Mikaberidze (73)*
Bediashvili, Maisuradze, Sukhiashvili (Dobrovolski 54), Kvaratskhelia (Gavashelishvili 46), Razmadze (Kavtaradze 46), Tekturmanidze, Japaridze, Getsadze, Makhviladze, Tatanashvili, Mikaberidze. Coach: Koba Jorjikashvili (GEO)

GEORGIA

Second qualifying round - FC Viktoria Plzeň (CZE)
H 1-3 *Tatanashvili (29)*
Bediashvili, Maisuradze, Sukhiashvili, Razmadze, Gavashelishvili, Japaridze, Kavtaradze (Dobrovolski 46), Getsadze, Makhviladze, Tatanashvili (Janelidze 67), Mikaberidze (Sikharulidze 67). Coach: Koba Jorjikashvili (GEO)
A 0-2
Bediashvili, Kakushadze (Lobjanidze 46), Maisuradze, Sukhiashvili, Japaridze, Dobrovolski, Getsadze (Kavtaradze 74), Makhviladze, Tatanashvili (Sikharulidze 61), Mikaberidze, Intskirveli. Coach: Koba Jorjikashvili (GEO)

FC TORPEDO KUTAISI

First qualifying round - FC Aktobe (KAZ)
H 1-1 *Sabanadze (62)*
Migineishvili, Gamezardashvili, Guruli, Sabanadze, Kukhianidze (Pantsulaia 81), Digmelashvili, Dolidze (Ioseliani 75), Datunaishvili, Gotsiridze (Bolkvadze 58), Rigvava, Kvakhadze. Coach: Gia Geguchadze (GEO)
A 0-2
Migineishvili, Gamezardashvili, Guruli, Sabanadze, Digmelashvili (Pirtskhalava 57), Dolidze (Grigalashvili 63), Datunaishvili, Gotsiridze (Tugushi 79), Rigvava, Kvakhadze, Bolkvadze. Coach: Gia Geguchadze (GEO)

Domestic league club-by-club

FC CHIKHURA SACHKHERE
Coach: Soso Pruidze
1938 • Central (700) • fcchikhura.ge

2012

10/08	Kolkheti	a	2-0	Sajaia, Kvaskhvadze
18/08	Dila	a	3-2	Gotsiridze 2, Dekanoidze
25/08	WIT Georgia	a	1-0	Odikadze (p)
02/09	Merani	a	0-1	
14/09	Sioni	h	2-1	Odikadze 2 (2p)
22/09	Zugdidi	a	2-4	Lomashvili, Kvaskhvadze
26/09	Dinamo Tbilisi	h	0-0	
30/09	Zestafoni	a	0-0	
07/10	Metalurgi	h	1-0	Digmelashvili
20/10	Torpedo	a	1-3	Chkhetiani
27/10	Dinamo Batumi	h	3-0	Odikadze (p), Kvaskhvadze, Chkhetiani
31/10	Kolkheti	h	2-1	Sharashenidze, Gusharashvili
04/11	Dila	h	0-2	
11/11	WIT Georgia	h	4-0	og (Kasradze), Odikadze (p), Sharashenidze, Dekanoidze
17/11	Merani	h	1-0	og (Karkuzashvili)
24/11	Sioni	a	3-0	Kirkitadze 2, Odikadze
28/11	Zugdidi	h	2-0	Odikadze (p), Kirkitadze
02/12	Dinamo Tbilisi	a	2-5	Chikvaidze, Kirkitadze
11/12	Zestafoni	h	3-1	Kvaskhvadze, Kirkitadze, Chkhetiani
15/12	Metalurgi	a	1-1	Berianidze
19/12	Torpedo	h	0-0	
23/12	Dinamo Batumi	a	2-0	Kirkitadze, Bakuradze (p)

2013

09/03	Torpedo	a	0-0	
17/03	Zugdidi	a	3-1	Dekanoidze 2, Kvaskhvadze
30/03	Zestafoni	h	1-0	Odikadze
06/04	Dinamo Tbilisi	a	0-3	
14/04	Dila	h	1-2	Dekanoidze
19/04	Torpedo	h	1-1	Kvaskhvadze
27/04	Zugdidi	h	2-1	Gotsiridze, Kirkitadze
04/05	Zestafoni	a	4-1	Chikvaidze, Rekhviashvili, Gotsiridze, Kvaskhvadze
12/05	Dinamo Tbilisi	h	2-4	Dekanoidze, Sajaia
18/05	Dila	a	0-4	

Name	Nat	DoB	Pos	Aps	(s)	Gls
Levan Bakuradze		18/01/86	M	2	(12)	1
Jaba Berianidze		22/08/81	M	9	(4)	1
David Bolkvadze		05/06/80	M	7	(2)	
Lasha Chelidze		13/03/85	D	15	(2)	
Lasha Chikvaidze		04/10/89	D	22	(1)	2
Gaga Chkhetiani		24/08/83	A	5	(16)	3
Besik Dekanoidze		03/01/90	M	31		6
Badri Demetrashvili		03/01/91	M		(2)	
David Digmelashvili		18/01/80	M	26		1
Zurab Dzamsashvili		13/10/81	D	6	(8)	
Revaz Gotsiridze		17/01/81	A	16	(3)	4
Nika Gusharashvili		25/07/83	D	14	(1)	1
Shota Kashia		22/10/84	D	8		
Giorgi Kimadze		10/02/92	M	7	(10)	
David Kirkitadze		03/09/92	M	27	(1)	7
Niko Kvaskhvadze		15/04/88	M	26	(1)	7
Vaja Lomashvili		04/09/85	D	28	(1)	1
Nikoloz Maisuradze		29/05/89	M	4	(7)	
Zurab Mtskerashvili		13/04/86	G	7	(1)	
Tornike Mumladze		23/07/92	A	1	(6)	
Giorgi Murvelashvili		23/08/88	D	3		
Temur Nadiradze		19/03/92	M		(2)	
Zaza Nadiradze		21/01/93	M		(1)	
David Odikadze		14/04/86	D	28		8
Giorgi Rekhviashvili		01/02/88	D	6	(1)	1
Edik Sajaia		16/02/81	D	19		2
Teimuraz Sharashenidze		21/12/92	M	8	(4)	2
Giorgi Somkhishvili		27/11/80	G	25		
Irakli Zabakhidze		11/04/84	M	2	(3)	

FC DILA GORI
Coach: Teimuraz Shalamberidze; (15/09/12) Giorgi Daraselia; (26/02/13) Valdas Ivanauskas (LTU)
1936 • Tengiz Burjanadze (4,843) • fcdila.ge
Major honours
Georgian Cup (1) 2012

2012

13/08	WIT Georgia	h	0-1	
18/08	Chikhura	h	2-3	Vatsadze 2
26/08	Sioni	h	2-3	Katsitadze, Akhalkatsi
03/09	Zugdidi	a	0-0	
15/09	Dinamo Tbilisi	h	2-0	Modebadze, Guruli (p)
22/09	Zestafoni	a	1-0	Kakhelishvili
26/09	Metalurgi	h	3-0	Kvirkvelia, Modebadze, Bechvaia
30/09	Torpedo	a	1-0	Akhalkatsi
07/10	Dinamo Batumi	h	2-0	Kakhelishvili, Guruli
20/10	Kolkheti	a	3-0	Gogua, Klimiashvili, Tomashvili
27/10	Merani	h	2-1	Nathan Júnior 2
31/10	WIT Georgia	a	2-0	Arziani, Klimiashvili
04/11	Chikhura	a	2-0	Tomashvili 2
11/11	Sioni	a	2-0	Modebadze (p), Oniani
18/11	Zugdidi	h	3-0	Gvalia, Kakhelishvili, Oniani
24/11	Dinamo Tbilisi	a	0-3	
28/11	Zestafoni	h	1-0	Oniani
02/12	Metalurgi	a	2-0	Gorelishvili, Aladashvili
08/12	Torpedo	h	0-1	
15/12	Dinamo Batumi	a	2-1	Kvirkvelia (p), Salukvadze
19/12	Kolkheti	h	1-0	og (Chaduneli)
23/12	Merani	a	3-2	Akhalkatsi 2, Modebadze (p)

2013

09/03	Zestafoni	h	2-1	Gvalia (p), Nathan Júnior
17/03	Dinamo Tbilisi	a	0-0	
30/03	Zugdidi	h	6-0	Modebadze 2, Iluridze, Arabuli 2, Gorelishvili
06/04	Torpedo	h	1-2	Modebadze
14/04	Chikhura	a	2-1	Modebadze 2 (1p)
19/04	Zestafoni	a	3-0	Modebadze, Nathan Júnior 2
27/04	Dinamo Tbilisi	h	0-1	
04/05	Zugdidi	a	2-1	Arabuli, Modebadze (p)
12/05	Torpedo	a	4-5	Gvalia, Aburjania, Arabuli 2
18/05	Chikhura	h	4-0	Nathan Júnior 2, Leonardo, Gogua

Name	Nat	DoB	Pos	Aps	(s)	Gls
Giorgi Aburjania		02/01/95	M	4	(1)	1
Roman Akhalkatsi		20/02/81	M	9	(7)	4
Kakhaber Aladashvili		11/08/83	D	11	(3)	1
Bachana Arabuli		05/01/94	A	1	(3)	5
Zurab Arziani	RUS	19/10/87	M	9	(8)	1
Giga Bechvaia		29/08/86	M	18	(5)	1
Roman Goginashvili		23/01/84	M	1	(1)	
Gogita Gogua		04/09/83	M	21	(1)	2
Mikheil Gorelishvili		29/05/93	M	8	(12)	2
Aleksandre Guruli		09/11/85	M	14	(1)	2
Lasha Gvalia		06/10/91	M	16	(1)	3
Giorgi Iluridze		20/02/92	M	5	(5)	1
Nikoloz Jishkariani		04/06/90	D	3	(3)	
Giorgi Kakhelishvili		22/05/87	M	19	(4)	3
Shota Kashia		22/10/84	D	4	(6)	
Valerian Katsitadze		17/01/85	M	3		1
Gocha Khojava		16/03/85	M	2	(3)	
Valter Khorguashvili		13/08/87	D	1		
Irakli Klimiashvili		30/05/88	M	12	(6)	2
Aleksandre Kvakhadze		17/08/84	D	9		
David Kvirkvelia		27/06/80	D	29		2
Leonardo	BRA	09/06/92	M	11	(3)	1
Ilia Lomidze		04/11/89	D	1		
Nestor Lomidze		25/09/93	M	1		
Irakli Maisuradze		22/08/88	M	7	(1)	
Zurab Mamaladze		10/02/82	G	1		
Giorgi Mamuchashvili		12/04/90	M		(1)	
Data Mikadze		01/08/93	M	1		
Nika Mnatobishvili		27/09/92	M	1		
Irakli Modebadze		04/10/84	A	15	(6)	11
Nathan Júnior	BRA	10/03/89	A	17	(4)	7
Giorgi Oniani		23/11/83	D	18	(2)	3
Lasha Salukvadze		21/12/81	D	10	(4)	1
Giorgi Shashiashvili		01/09/79	A	17		
Beka Shekriladze		28/11/83	G	10		
Marin Skender	CRO	12/08/79	G	21		
Gulverd Tomashvili		13/10/88	D	18	(1)	3
Lasha Totadze		24/08/88	D	4		
Mate Vatsadze		17/12/88	A	2		2

FC DINAMO BATUMI

Coach: Aleksandre Kantidze
1923 • Chele Arena, Kobuleti (3,800) • no website
Major honours
Georgian Cup (1) 1998

2012

10/08	Sioni	a	2-2	Gogitidze, Jorbenadze
18/08	Zugdidi	a	0-2	
25/08	Dinamo Tbilisi	h	0-3	
02/09	Zestafoni	h	0-0	
14/09	Metalurgi	h	0-2	
22/09	Torpedo	a	1-5	Jorbenadze
26/09	Merani	h	4-0	Jorbenadze 3, Mujiri
30/09	Kolkheti	h	3-1	Jorbenadze, Beridze, Tymchyshyn
07/10	Dila	a	0-2	
20/10	WIT Georgia	h	0-1	
27/10	Chikhura	a	0-3	
31/10	Sioni	h	0-1	
04/11	Zugdidi	h	0-4	
11/11	Dinamo Tbilisi	a	3-5	Beridze 2, Batsikadze
18/11	Zestafoni	a	3-3	Tsnobiladze 2, Batsikadze
24/11	Metalurgi	a	1-2	Diasamidze
28/11	Torpedo	h	0-2	
02/12	Merani	a	1-3	Diasamidze
08/12	Kolkheti	a	2-1	Diasamidze 2
15/12	Dila	h	1-2	Sichinava
19/12	WIT Georgia	a	1-1	Mujiri
23/12	Chikhura	h	0-2	

2013

09/03	Merani	a	1-0	Makariani
17/03	WIT Georgia	h	2-0	Chimakadze 2 (1p)
30/03	Sioni	a	1-0	Guruli
06/04	Kolkheti	a	1-1	Chimakadze
14/04	Metalurgi	h	0-1	
19/04	Merani	h	6-0	Koshkadze, Guruli, Chimakadze 2, Koridze, Mujiri
27/04	WIT Georgia	a	2-3	Guruli (p), Jvania
04/05	Sioni	h	1-1	Jvania
12/05	Kolkheti	h	2-2	Chimakadze 2
18/05	Metalurgi	a	1-0	Koridze

Name	Nat	DoB	Pos	Aps	(s)	Gls
Amiran Abuselidze		10/03/93	M	3	(4)	
Archil Bajelidze		07/04/86	M	6	(1)	
Paata Baladze		18/09/91	M	1	(3)	
Aleksandre Batsikadze		30/01/90	A	6	(8)	2
Tornike Beridze		11/09/90	M	13	(7)	3
Besik Chimakadze		24/06/88	A	10		7
Thierry Clovis	CIV	15/08/93	A	4	(2)	
Nika Diasamidze		02/09/94	M	9	(14)	4
Jemal Gabunia		09/11/89	D	7	(1)	
Gela Gogitidze		25/11/90	D	14	(1)	1
Aleksandre Guruli		09/11/85	M	8		3
Mikheil Jorbenadze		18/11/87	A	10	(2)	6
Giga Jvania		16/01/82	D	10		2
Nika Khukhia		31/08/88	D	18		
Nodar Kiknavelidze		25/04/93	M	5	(4)	
Erekle Kiladze		11/01/90	M	3		
Vaja Koridze		05/01/87	D	8	(4)	2
Aleksandre Koshkadze		04/12/81	M	8		1
Irakli Kvekveskiri		12/03/90	M	11		
Zviad Lobjanidze		27/02/87	D	31		
Karen Makariani		03/03/88	D	18	(2)	1
Boris Makharadze		08/11/90	M	21		
Shota Maminashvili		30/08/86	G	9		
Amiran Mujiri		02/02/74	A	20	(6)	3
Nika Nasuashvili		20/03/91	A	1		
Mirza Partenadze		16/05/90	M	14		
Ivan Pitsan	UKR	19/01/90	G	16		
Lasha Ramishvili		30/01/90	M	3		
Gizo Shengelia		17/08/83	M	5		
Data Sichinava		21/03/89	M	5	(10)	1
Roman Takidze		30/01/94	G	2		
Valerian Tevdoradze		11/10/93	M	13	(11)	
Kakhi Todadze		15/08/91	D	2		
Lasha Totadze		24/08/88	M	5	(1)	
Irakli Tsanava		28/10/85	M	9	(2)	
Irakli Tsnobiladze		05/01/90	A	5	(8)	2
Olexandr Tymchyshyn	UKR	29/02/87	M	11	(1)	1
Beka Varshanidze		01/11/93	M	6	(2)	
Giorgi Zoidze		23/05/91	M	2		

FC DINAMO TBILISI

Coach: Dušan Uhrin (CZE)
1925 • Boris Paichadze (53,279) • fcdinamo.ge
Major honours
UEFA Cup Winners Cup (1) 1981;
USSR League (2) 1964, 1978;
Georgian League (14) 1990, 1991, 1992, 1993, 1994,
1995, 1996, 1997, 1998, 1999, 2003, 2005, 2008, 2013;
USSR Cup (2) 1976, 1979;
Georgian Cup (10) 1992, 1993, 1994, 1995, 1996,
1997, 2003, 2004, 2009, 2013

2012

11/08	Metalurgi	a	1-0	Khmaladze
18/08	Torpedo	h	3-2	Xisco 2 (1p), Mikel Álvaro
25/08	Dinamo Batumi	a	3-0	Dvali, Mikel Álvaro, Robertinho
02/09	Kolkheti	h	5-0	Dvali 3, Mikel Álvaro, Xisco
15/09	Dila	a	0-2	
22/09	WIT Georgia	h	5-0	Xisco 2 (1p), Kvaratskhelia, Merebashvili 2
26/09	Chikhura	a	0-0	
30/09	Sioni	h	7-2	Dvali 2, Khmaladze, Voskoboinikov, Merebashvili 2, Mikel Álvaro
06/10	Zugdidi	a	1-1	Dvali
20/10	Merani	a	4-0	Xisco, Mikel Álvaro 2, Dvali
27/10	Zestafoni	h	2-1	Mikel Álvaro, Xisco
31/10	Metalurgi	a	3-0	Dvali, og (Intskirveli), Kvaratskhelia
04/11	Torpedo	a	2-2	Dvali, Mikel Álvaro
11/11	Dinamo Batumi	h	5-3	Khmaladze, Xisco 2, Dvali 2
18/11	Kolkheti	a	2-0	Mikel Álvaro, Xisco
24/11	Dila	h	3-0	Merebashvili, Tvildiani, Khmaladze
28/11	WIT Georgia	a	1-1	Xisco
02/12	Chikhura	h	5-2	Xisco 3, Mikel Álvaro, Dvali
08/12	Sioni	a	5-0	Kvaratskhelia, Dvali, Xisco 2 (1p), Khmaladze
15/12	Zugdidi	h	2-0	Xisco, Dvali
19/12	Merani	h	3-1	Xisco, Merebashvili, Dvali
23/12	Zestafoni	a	1-2	Mikel Álvaro

2013

09/03	Zugdidi	h	3-0	Xisco, Mikel Álvaro, Dvali
17/03	Dila	h	0-0	
30/03	Torpedo	a	1-1	Xisco
06/04	Chikhura	a	3-0	Xisco 2, Khmaladze
14/04	Zestafoni	a	1-0	Khmaladze
19/04	Zugdidi	a	2-0	Gvelesiani, Khmaladze
27/04	Dila	a	1-0	Mikel Álvaro
04/05	Torpedo	h	4-0	Dvali 2, Mikel Álvaro, Grajciar
12/05	Chikhura	a	4-2	Grajciar, Xisco (p), Merebashvili, Carles Coto
18/05	Zestafoni	h	6-1	Grajciar 2, Dvali, Ustaritz, Xisco 2

Name	Nat	DoB	Pos	Aps	(s)	Gls
Carles Coto	ESP	11/02/88	M	8	(9)	1
Jaba Dvali		08/02/85	A	23	(4)	20
Irakli Dzaria		01/12/87	M	23	(4)	
Darko Glisic	MKD	23/09/91	D	14	(11)	
Peter Grajciar	SVK	17/09/83	M	9	(1)	4
Giorgi Gvelesiani		05/05/91	D	5	(3)	1
Jambul Jigauri		08/07/92	M	1	(1)	
Levan Kakubava		15/10/90	D	1	(1)	
Otar Khizaneishvili		26/06/81	D	19	(1)	
Levan Khmaladze		06/04/83	M	30	(1)	9
David Khocholava		08/02/93	D	1	(2)	
Givi Kvaratskhelia		05/11/79	D	31		3
Nika Kvekveskiri		29/05/92	M	2	(6)	
Irakli Lekvtadze		30/08/91	M	1	(1)	
Giorgi Loria		27/01/86	G	24		
Emmanuel Mendy	SEN	30/03/90	D	1		
Giorgi Merebashvili		15/08/86	M	31	(1)	7
Mikel Álvaro	ESP	20/12/82	M	25	(5)	14
Patrick Milchraum	GER	26/05/84	D	4	(1)	
Giorgi Papava		16/02/93	M	2	(5)	
Lasha Parunashvili		14/02/93	M		(1)	
Giorgi Rekhviashvili		01/02/88	D	17		
Robertinho	BRA	13/06/88	M		(14)	1
Konstantine Sepiashvili		19/03/86	G	1		
Giorgi Seturidze		01/04/85	D	27		
Giorgi Shashiashvili		01/09/79	D	5		
Dimitri Tatanashvili		19/10/83	A		(6)	
Archil Tvildiani		31/01/93	D	3	(3)	1
Ustaritz	ESP	16/02/83	D	6	(1)	1
Vladimir Voskoboinikov	EST	02/02/83	A	4	(9)	1
Xisco	ESP	05/09/80	A	28		24
Albert Yagüe	ESP	27/02/85	A		(1)	
Tornike Zarkua		01/09/90	G	7		

FC KOLKHETI POTI

Coach: David Makharadze; (11/11/12) Soso Pilia
1913 • Phazisi (3,000) • no website

2012

10/08	Chikhura	h	0-2	
17/08	Sioni	a	0-0	
25/08	Zugdidi	h	1-1	Datunaishvili
02/09	Dinamo Tbilisi	a	0-5	
15/09	Zestafoni	h	0-2	
22/09	Metalurgi	a	1-2	Tskhvitaria
26/09	Torpedo	h	1-1	Tskhvitaria
30/09	Dinamo Batumi	a	1-3	Kvantaliani
06/10	Merani	h	0-1	
20/10	Dila	h	0-3	
27/10	WIT Georgia	a	0-2	
31/10	Chikhura	a	1-2	Datunaishvili
04/11	Sioni	h	0-1	
11/11	Zugdidi	a	0-1	
18/11	Dinamo Tbilisi	h	0-2	
24/11	Zestafoni	a	1-2	Pavliashvili
28/11	Metalurgi	h	2-3	og (Intskirveli), Datunaishvili
02/12	Torpedo	a	1-2	Gogonaia
08/12	Dinamo Batumi	h	1-2	Gabunia
15/12	Merani	a	0-4	
19/12	Dila	a	0-1	
23/12	WIT Georgia	h	1-1	Kvantaliani

2013

09/03	Metalurgi	a	0-1	
17/03	Sioni	h	2-1	Parulava, Kvantaliani
30/03	Merani	a	1-0	Janashia
06/04	Dinamo Batumi	h	1-1	Bukhaidze
14/04	WIT Georgia	a	0-0	
19/04	Metalurgi	a	0-0	
27/04	Sioni	a	2-6	Vítor Rossini, Bukhaidze
04/05	Merani	h	1-2	Gogonaia (p)
12/05	Dinamo Batumi	a	2-2	Kvantaliani 2
18/05	WIT Georgia	h	2-0	Korchilava, Sichinava

Name	Nat	DoB	Pos	Aps	(s)	Gls
Iakob Apkhazava		30/04/91	M	1	(1)	
Konstantine Baramidze		12/07/91	M	1	(3)	
Levan Bubuteishvili		14/06/83	G	8		
Giorgi Bukhaidze		09/12/91	A	9	(7)	2
Gia Chaduneli		15/05/95	D	11	(1)	
Lasha Chaladze		05/11/87	M	2	(1)	
Zviad Chedia		16/01/92	M		(1)	
Zviad Chkhetiani		17/10/83	D	8	(3)	
Pavle Datunaishvili		25/08/83	M	16	(3)	3
Jemal Gabunia		09/11/89	D	17	(1)	1
Omar Gogonaia		24/01/90	D	21	(6)	2
Vasil Guchashvili		25/01/85	A	1	(4)	
Bidzina Gujabidze		15/09/92	M		(1)	
Levan Gulua		06/05/91	M	3	(2)	
Zamir Janashia		26/02/88	M	10		1
Sulkhan Kakhidze		19/01/94	M		(2)	
Levan Kakulia		28/05/92	M	10		
Lasha Kebadze		27/08/83	M	16		
Mikheil Kharshiladze		07/02/88	G	13	(1)	
Luka Khomasuridze		13/04/88	M		(3)	
Beka Khoshtaria		30/08/92	M	3	(4)	
Giorgi Kilasonia		21/05/86	M	23	(1)	
Mikheil Koberidze		04/05/87	M	5	(5)	
Aleksandre Korchilava		11/09/91	M	11	(5)	1
Giorgi Krasovski		20/12/79	M	23	(2)	
Shalva Kvantaliani		26/03/91	A	22	(6)	5
Mamuka Loria		19/02/92	D	4	(2)	
David Megrelishvili		25/09/91	D	2	(1)	
Ardalion Mikaberidze		02/06/86	G	11		
Irakli Moistsrapishvili		11/05/91	M	4		
Tornike Mosiashvili		09/10/91	M	2	(8)	
Teimuraz Parulava		20/07/83	D	26		1
Ilia Pavliashvili		12/08/89	M	13	(3)	1
Mikheil Rusia		07/05/91	M	1		
Nika Sichinava		17/07/94	A		(4)	1
Giorgi Tkeshelashvili		24/08/85	D	8		
Amiran Tsabria		02/10/87	M	5	(5)	
Giorgi Tskhadaia		23/04/88	D	11	(2)	
Paata Tskhvitaria		17/09/89	D	20	(1)	2
Vítor Rossini	BRA	06/01/88	A	9		1

FC MERANI MARTVILI

Coach: Archil Chkhaberidze;
(09/03/13) Malkhaz Jvania
1936 • Central (2,000) • no website

2012

11/08	Zestafoni	a	1-3	Lomia
18/08	WIT Georgia	h	1-0	Ambroladze
25/08	Metalurgi	a	0-1	
02/09	Chikhura	h	1-0	Rekhviashvili
15/09	Torpedo	a	0-4	
22/09	Sioni	h	1-0	Nozadze
26/09	Dinamo Batumi	a	0-4	
30/09	Zugdidi	h	1-2	Lomia
06/10	Kolkheti	a	1-0	Lomia
20/10	Dinamo Tbilisi	h	0-4	
27/10	Dila	a	1-2	Didava (p)
31/10	Zestafoni	h	0-3	
04/11	WIT Georgia	a	0-0	
11/11	Metalurgi	h	0-0	
17/11	Chikhura	a	0-1	
24/11	Torpedo	h	3-0	Iobashvili, Lomia, Toronjadze
28/11	Sioni	a	1-2	Lomia
02/12	Dinamo Batumi	h	3-1	og (Gogitidze), Ambroladze, Lomia
08/12	Zugdidi	a	2-3	Lomia 2
15/12	Kolkheti	h	4-0	Nozadze, Lomia 3
19/12	Dinamo Tbilisi	a	1-3	Toronjadze
23/12	Dila	h	2-3	Lomia 2

2013

09/03	Dinamo Batumi	h	0-1	
17/03	Metalurgi	a	1-1	Kuchukhidze
30/03	Kolkheti	h	0-1	
06/04	WIT Georgia	h	2-0	Lomia 2
14/04	Sioni	a	1-3	Lomia (p)
19/04	Dinamo Batumi	a	0-6	
27/04	Metalurgi	h	1-0	Iobashvili
04/05	Kolkheti	a	2-1	Kuchukhidze, Poniava
12/05	WIT Georgia	a	0-0	
18/05	Sioni	h	1-2	Toronjadze

Name	Nat	DoB	Pos	Aps	(s)	Gls
Giga Ambroladze		28/12/90	A	12	(8)	2
Christel Baneba Ngamen	CMR	23/06/92	M	3	(5)	
Tsotne Bukia		03/01/90	M	21	(8)	
Beka Chkhetiani		15/07/89	M		(6)	
Nika Darjania		03/01/94	M		(1)	
Givi Didava		21/03/76	D	30		1
Giorgi Gabisonia		25/03/91	M		(1)	
Levan Gegechkori		05/06/94	D	19	(4)	
Giorgi Gegia		25/08/95	M	1	(1)	
Boris Gelacheishvili		30/01/88	D	2	(1)	
Lasha Gongadze		01/03/90	M	7	(1)	
Gaga Gugunashvili		25/01/88	M		(2)	
Valerian Iobashvili		03/12/88	D	26		2
Giga Jvania		16/01/82	D	14		
Givi Karkuzashvili		20/09/86	D	24	(3)	
Gela Khubua		25/01/84	D	8	(1)	
Roman Kikalishvili		18/03/90	M	1		
Lasha Kuchukhidze		14/03/92	M	23	(1)	2
Saba Lomia		07/07/90	A	26	(6)	16
Tevdore Lursmanashvili		20/05/92	D	1		
Giorgi Mchedlishvili		18/01/92	D	8	(2)	
Giorgi Megreladze		21/07/78	A	1		
Kichi Meliava		14/04/92	M	23	(7)	
Indiko Moniava		01/01/93	M		(2)	
Tsotne Moniava		15/02/94	M	1		
Mikheil Mujrishvili		30/04/84	G	1		
Nodar Nozadze		11/06/87	A	16	(6)	2
Papuna Poniava		10/03/94	M	29		1
Giorgi Rekhviashvili		15/04/86	A	12	1	1
Berdia Sharvadze		24/01/93	M		(5)	
Joni Sherozia		09/09/90	G	31		
Mamuka Toronjadze		13/05/86	M	11	(16)	3
Beka Zakradze		30/05/90	M	1	(2)	

FC METALURGI RUSTAVI

Coach: Koba Jorjikashvili; (07/10/12) Giorgi Kipiani
1948 • Poladi (4,656) • fcm.ge
Major honours
Georgian League (2) 2007, 2010

2012

11/08	Dinamo Tbilisi	h	0-1	
18/08	Zestafoni	a	1-0	Tatanashvili
25/08	Merani	h	1-0	Tatanashvili
02/09	Torpedo	h	0-4	
14/09	Dinamo Batumi	a	2-0	Mikaberidze, Tatanashvili
22/09	Kolkheti	h	2-0	Sikharulidze, Mikaberidze
26/09	Dila	a	0-3	
30/09	WIT Georgia	h	0-2	
07/10	Chikhura	a	0-2	
20/10	Sioni	h	1-0	Sikharulidze
27/10	Zugdidi	a	1-2	Sikharulidze
31/10	Dinamo Tbilisi	a	0-3	
04/11	Zestafoni	h	1-1	Sukhiashvili
11/11	Merani	a	0-0	
18/11	Torpedo	a	0-0	
24/11	Dinamo Batumi	h	2-1	Tatanashvili, Janelidze
28/11	Kolkheti	a	3-2	Sikharulidze 2, Tatanashvili
02/12	Dila	h	0-2	
08/12	WIT Georgia	a	1-0	Sikharulidze
15/12	Chikhura	h	1-0	Sikharulidze
19/12	Sioni	a	0-0	
23/12	Zugdidi	h	5-1	Getsadze, Tatanashvili 2, Dobrovolski, Kavtaradze

2013

09/03	Kolkheti	h	1-0	Pipia (p)
17/03	Merani	h	1-1	Lobjanidze
30/03	WIT Georgia	a	3-2	Sikharulidze, Akhalkatsi, Lobjanidze
06/04	Sioni	h	0-0	
14/04	Dinamo Batumi	h	1-0	Pipia
19/04	Kolkheti	a	0-0	
27/04	Merani	a	0-1	
04/05	WIT Georgia	h	0-0	
12/05	Sioni	a	2-2	Getsadze, Lobjanidze
18/05	Dinamo Batumi	h	0-1	

Name	Nat	DoB	Pos	Aps	(s)	Gls
Roman Akhalkatsi		20/02/81	M	5	(4)	1
Mikheil Alavidze		06/11/87	G	6		
Zurab Batiashvili		06/02/80	G	15		
Grigol Bediashvili		07/02/80	G	4		
Denis Dobrovolski		10/10/85	D	19	(5)	1
Giorgi Ganugrava		21/02/88	M	5	(2)	
Giorgi Gavashelishvili		31/10/89	D	16	(3)	
Revaz Getsadze		11/01/85	M	16	(4)	2
Giorgi Gureshidze		21/01/91	M		(2)	
Ivan Hosman	CRO	11/11/89	G	7		
Aleksandre Intskirveli		24/08/81	D	26	(1)	
David Janelidze		12/09/89	A		(6)	1
Lasha Japaridze		16/04/85	D	26		
Tornike Kakushadze		01/02/91	D		(1)	
Giorgi Kavtaradze		01/01/89	M	15	(12)	1
Ivane Khabelashvili		05/09/93	M	7	(9)	
Giorgi Khidesheli		21/12/85	M		(1)	
Levan Korgalidze		21/02/80	M		(1)	
Vakhtang Kvaratskhelia		30/03/84	A	4	(3)	
Zviad Lobjanidze		19/04/90	M	6	(4)	3
Irakli Maisuradze		22/08/88	M	21		
Mikheil Makhviladze		22/07/78	D	25		
Zurab Menteshashvili		30/01/80	M	2	(1)	
Giorgi Mikaberidze		17/02/88	M	11	(13)	2
Gogi Pipia		18/02/85	A	6	(1)	2
Luka Razmadze		30/12/83	M	24	(3)	
Dato Sajaia		23/08/93	M	7	(2)	
Irakli Sikharulidze		18/07/90	A	23	(1)	8
Anzor Sukhiashvili		27/10/88	D	29	(1)	1
Dimitri Tatanashvili		19/10/83	A	17	(5)	7
Giorgi Tekurmanidze		17/09/90	M	9	(6)	
Dachi Tsnobiladze		28/01/94	M	1		

FC SIONI BOLNISI

Coach: Khvicha Kasrashvili;
(26/08/12) (Joni Jagidisi); (02/09/12) Armaz Jeladze
1936 • Teimuraz Stepania (3,500) • no website
Major honours
Georgian League (1) 2006

2012

10/08	Dinamo Batumi	h	2-2	Jikia, Ugulava
18/08	Kolkheti	h	0-0	
26/08	Dila	a	3-2	Jikia 2, Kutsurua
02/09	WIT Georgia	h	1-1	Svanidze
14/09	Chikhura	a	1-2	Jikia (p)
22/09	Merani	a	0-1	
26/09	Zugdidi	h	0-0	
30/09	Dinamo Tbilisi	a	2-7	Jikia, Mantskava
07/10	Zestafoni	h	0-2	
20/10	Metalurgi	a	0-1	
27/10	Torpedo	h	0-2	
31/10	Dinamo Batumi	a	1-0	Peikrishvili
04/11	Kolkheti	a	1-0	Jikia
11/11	Dila	h	0-2	
17/11	WIT Georgia	a	0-0	
24/11	Chikhura	h	0-3	
28/11	Merani	h	2-1	Isiani, Chedia
02/12	Zugdidi	a	0-2	
08/12	Dinamo Tbilisi	h	0-5	
15/12	Zestafoni	a	0-1	
19/12	Metalurgi	h	0-0	
23/12	Torpedo	a	1-4	Chankotadze

2013

09/03	WIT Georgia	a	2-0	Hajduczek, Tskhadaia
17/03	Kolkheti	a	1-2	Mikuchadze (p)
30/03	Dinamo Batumi	h	0-1	
06/04	Metalurgi	h	0-0	
14/04	Merani	h	3-1	Mikuchadze 3 (2p)
19/04	WIT Georgia	h	0-3	
27/04	Kolkheti	h	6-2	Klimiashvili, Lekvtadze, Akhalaia, Svanidze, Ugrekhelidze 2
04/05	Dinamo Batumi	a	1-1	Mantskava
12/05	Metalurgi	h	2-2	Svanidze, Akhalaia
18/05	Merani	a	2-1	Svanidze, Akhalaia

Name	Nat	DoB	Pos	Aps	(s)	Gls
Lado Akhalaia		30/08/91	A	7	(1)	3
Giorgi Bibileishvili		29/05/89	M	1	(4)	
Mindia Bobgiashvili		02/08/93	G	25		
Giorgi Chankotadze		06/05/91	A	4	(8)	1
Giorgi Chedia		28/08/88	M	17		1
Tengiz Chikviladze		12/08/83	D	19		
Giorgi Chivadze		14/06/94	M	3		
Zaal Eliava		02/01/85	D	10		
Gogita Gogatishvili		02/02/90	A		(2)	
Giorgi Gordeziani		02/02/90	M		(1)	
Paweł Hajduczek	POL	17/05/82	M	9		1
Vili Isiani		22/03/91	M	6	(15)	1
Rezo Jikia		01/09/80	A	17	(1)	6
Vladimer Jojua		05/12/80	M	18	(5)	
Revaz Kemoklidze		18/03/79	D	20	(1)	
Lasha Kemukhtashvili		09/04/92	M		(1)	
Gela Khubua		25/01/84	M	3		
Zurab Khurtsidze		21/06/91	M		(2)	
Irakli Klimiashvili		30/05/88	M	6		1
Giorgi Kutsurua		09/07/86	M	13	(6)	1
Irakli Lekvtadze		30/08/91	M	7	(1)	1
Vakhtang Lobjanidze		18/11/89	G	3		
David Lomaia		18/05/85	D	3	(1)	
Nodar Machavariani		14/01/87	D	11	(1)	
Giorgi Mantskava		25/10/81	M	18	(6)	2
Mirza Merlani		05/10/80	G	4		
Akaki Mikuchadze		30/11/80	A	9	(1)	4
Vaja Nemsadze		07/11/90	M	6		
Giorgi Okropiridze		01/03/86	M	12	(3)	
Manuchar Okropiridze		19/02/90	M	1	(2)	
Sergo Orbeladze		01/05/82	D	21		
Giorgi Peikrishvili		28/02/83	M	8	(5)	1
Dachi Popkhadze		27/04/84	D	5		
Gal Sapir	ISR	10/06/90	M	2	(1)	
David Svanidze		14/10/79	D	27		4
Tornike Tarkhnishvili		30/06/90	M	14	(1)	
Giorgi Tskhadaia		23/04/88	M	5	(3)	1
Vladimer Ugrekhelidze		24/11/85	M	11	(7)	2
Jaba Ugulava		08/04/92	M	5	(6)	1

FC TORPEDO KUTAISI

Coach: Gia Geguchadze
1946 • Central (11,880) • fctorpedo.ge
Major honours
Georgian League (3) 2000, 2001, 2002;
Georgian Cup (2) 1999, 2001

2012

11/08	Zugdidi	h	1-0	Sabanadze	
18/08	Dinamo Tbilisi	a	2-3	Kvakhadze, Grigalashvili	
26/08	Zestafoni	h	1-0	Datunaishvili	
02/09	Metalurgi	a	4-0	Kukhianidze (p), Chelidze, Beriashvili, Bolkvadze	
15/09	Merani	h	4-0	Gigauri, Dolidze, Sabanadze, Kukhianidze	
22/09	Dinamo Batumi	h	5-1	Shergelashvili 2, Sabanadze, Kukhianidze, Pantsulaia	
26/09	Kolkheti	a	1-1	Datunaishvili	
30/09	Dila	h	0-1		
07/10	WIT Georgia	a	3-1	Beriashvili, Datunaishvili, Sabanadze	
20/10	Chikhura	h	3-1	Beriashvili, Sabanadze 2	
27/10	Sioni	a	2-0	Sabanadze, Dolidze	
31/10	Zugdidi	a	1-2	Pirtskhalava	
04/11	Dinamo Tbilisi	h	2-2	Grigalashvili 2	
11/11	Zestafoni	a	0-1		
18/11	Metalurgi	h	1-0	Kukhianidze	
24/11	Merani	a	0-3		
28/11	Dinamo Batumi	a	2-0	Datunaishvili, Tugushi	
02/12	Kolkheti	h	2-1	Grigalashvili, Sabanadze	
08/12	Dila	a	1-0	Sabanadze	
15/12	WIT Georgia	h	2-0	Beriashvili, Tugushi (p)	
19/12	Chikhura	a	0-0		
23/12	Sioni	h	4-1	Kukhianidze (p), Sabanadze, Grigalashvili, Beriashvili	

2013

09/03	Chikhura	h	0-0		
17/03	Zestafoni	a	0-0		
30/03	Dinamo Tbilisi	h	1-1	Beriashvili	
06/04	Dila	a	2-1	Beriashvili 2	
14/04	Zugdidi	h	2-0	Tugushi, Grigalashvili	
19/04	Chikhura	a	1-1	Beriashvili	
27/04	Zestafoni	h	1-0	Kukhianidze (p)	
04/05	Dinamo Tbilisi	a	0-4		
12/05	Dila	h	5-4	Kukhianidze (p), Pantsulaia 2, Dolidze 2	
18/05	Zugdidi	a	4-1	Tugushi, Pirtskhalava, Gavashelishvili, Dolidze	

Name	Nat	DoB	Pos	Aps	(s)	Gls
Giorgi Beriashvili		01/09/86	A	28	(1)	9
Valeri Bolkvadze		25/02/88	M	1	(15)	1
Zaza Chelidze		12/01/87	D	30		1
Giorgi Datunaishvili		09/02/85	M	26		4
Grigol Dolidze		25/10/82	M	27	(1)	5
Mamia Gavashelishvili		08/01/95	A		(1)	1
Merab Gigauri		05/06/93	M	18	(10)	1
Elguja Grigalashvili		30/12/89	M	26	(3)	6
Giorgi Guruli		31/07/88	D	32		
Beka Kakushadze		28/12/94	M		(3)	
Giorgi Kukhianidze		01/07/92	M	25	(6)	7
Aleksandre Kvakhadze		17/08/84	D	12		1
Vakhtang Kvaratskhelia		30/03/88	A		(1)	
Temur Markozashvili		09/08/94	M		(2)	
Omar Migineishvili		02/06/84	G	32		
Giorgi Oniani		23/11/83	D	4		
Giorgi Pantsulaia		06/01/94	A	1	(20)	3
Nikoloz Pirtskhalava		15/05/87	M	6	(15)	2
Data Rigvava		02/10/91	D	26		
Nika Sabanadze		02/05/91	A	21	(5)	10
Lasha Shergelashvili		17/01/92	M	9		2
Vaja Tabatadze		01/02/91	D	14	(1)	
Beka Tugushi		24/01/89	A	14	(10)	4

FC WIT GEORGIA

Coach: Merab Kochlashvili; (06/04/13) Zurab Beridze
1968 • Mtskheta Park, Mtskheta (2,000) • witgeorgia.ge
Major honours
Georgian League (2) 2004, 2009;
Georgian Cup (1) 2010

2012

13/08	Dila	a	1-0	Vasadze	
18/08	Merani	a	0-1		
25/08	Chikhura	h	0-1		
02/09	Sioni	a	1-1	Lobjanidze	
15/09	Zugdidi	h	0-0		
22/09	Dinamo Tbilisi	a	0-5		
26/09	Zestafoni	h	2-3	Chimakadze 2	
30/09	Metalurgi	a	2-0	Chimakadze, Gogiashvili	
07/10	Torpedo	h	1-3	Chimakadze (p)	
20/10	Dinamo Batumi	a	1-0	Gabrichidze	
27/10	Kolkheti	a	2-0	Chimakadze, Gureshidze	
31/10	Dila	h	0-2		
04/11	Merani	h	0-0		
11/11	Chikhura	a	0-4		
17/11	Sioni	h	0-0		
24/11	Zugdidi	a	0-2		
28/11	Dinamo Tbilisi	h	1-1	Gabrichidze	
02/12	Zestafoni	a	2-1	Lobjanidze, Koripadze	
08/12	Metalurgi	h	0-1		
15/12	Torpedo	a	0-2		
19/12	Dinamo Batumi	h	1-1	Gibradze	
23/12	Kolkheti	a	1-1	Adamadze	

2013

09/03	Sioni	h	0-2		
17/03	Dinamo Batumi	a	0-2		
30/03	Metalurgi	h	2-3	Janelidze, Lobjanidze	
06/04	Merani	a	0-2		
14/04	Kolkheti	h	0-0		
19/04	Sioni	a	3-0	Javashvili, Adamadze, Vasadze	
27/04	Dinamo Batumi	h	3-2	Kukhaleishvili, Janelidze (p), Lobjanidze	
04/05	Metalurgi	a	2-0	Kukhaleishvili, Gibradze	
12/05	Merani	h	0-0		
18/05	Kolkheti	a	0-0		

Name	Nat	DoB	Pos	Aps	(s)	Gls
Guram Adamadze		31/08/88	D	20		2
Beka Buachidze		06/09/94	M		(1)	
Giorgi Bunturi		31/03/96	M		(1)	
Besik Chimakadze		24/06/88	A	15	(1)	5
Nika Daushvili		16/10/89	G	32		
Shota Davlashelidze		25/03/93	M	17	(5)	
Lasha Gabrichidze		21/02/89	A	10	(8)	2
Giorgi Gagnidze		07/02/95	A	1		
Valiko Gakharia		23/01/94	M	1		
Revaz Ganiashvili		27/05/90	D	8	(1)	
Giorgi Getiashvili		07/03/90	D	21	(2)	
Irakli Gibradze		26/10/91	M	12	(11)	2
Jemal Gogiashvili		06/05/88	D	20	(8)	1
Guram Gureshidze		08/10/89	M	31		1
Nodar Iashvili		24/01/93	M	4		
Giorgi Janelidze		25/09/89	M	8		2
Otar Javashvili		17/08/93	M	21	(2)	1
Giga Jugeli		08/11/91	A	1	(7)	
Giorgi Kalandia		18/01/93	M		(1)	
Lasha Kasradze		26/07/89	D	27		
David Khurtsilava		09/03/88	D	25		
Giorgi Koripadze		03/10/89	M	21	(6)	1
Levan Kukhaleishvili		24/02/92	M	9	(5)	2
Elguja Lobjanidze		17/09/92	A	5	(17)	4
Giorgi Mchedlishvili		18/01/92	D	7		
Andro Sopromadze		25/03/93	M	1	(4)	
Badri Tetunashvili		09/02/90	D	2	(2)	
David Ubilava		27/01/94	M	5	(2)	
Giorgi Vasadze		14/06/89	M	27	(1)	2
Beka Zakradze		30/05/90	M	1	(6)	

FC ZESTAFONI

**Coach: Gia Chiabrishvili; (02/09/12) (Giorgi Kipiani);
(15/09/12) Zaza Zamtaradze;
(11/12/12) (Giorgi Mikadze);
(19/12/12) Kakha Kacharava**
1936 • David Abashidze (5,000) • fczestafoni.ge
Major honours
Georgian League (2) 2011, 2012;
Georgian Cup (1) 2008

2012

11/08	Merani	h	3-1	Gorgiashvili, Aptsiauri, Milchraum	
18/08	Metalurgi	h	0-1		
26/08	Torpedo	a	0-1		
02/09	Dinamo Batumi	h	0-0		
15/09	Kolkheti	a	2-0	Babunashvili, Kvernadze	
22/09	Dila	h	0-1		
26/09	WIT Georgia	a	3-2	Tsinamdzgvrishvili 2, Sharikadze	
30/09	Chikhura	h	0-0		
07/10	Sioni	a	2-0	Kachkachishvili, Tsinamdzgvrishvili	
20/10	Zugdidi	h	1-0	Sharikadze	
27/10	Dinamo Tbilisi	a	1-2	Babunashvili	
31/10	Merani	a	3-0	Sharikadze, Tornike Grigalashvili, Gorgiashvili	
04/11	Metalurgi	a	1-1	Tsinamdzgvrishvili	
11/11	Torpedo	h	1-0	Gorgiashvili	
18/11	Dinamo Batumi	a	3-3	Benashvili, Tornike Grigalashvili, Sharvadze	
24/11	Kolkheti	h	2-1	Benashvili, Sharikadze	
20/11	Dila	a	0-1		
02/12	WIT Georgia	h	1-2	Menteshashvili	
11/12	Chikhura	a	1-3	Sardalishvili	
15/12	Sioni	h	1-0	Jelić	
19/12	Zugdidi	a	3-0	Demel, Tedore Grigalashvili, Menteshashvili	
23/12	Dinamo Tbilisi	h	2-1	Babunashvili, Gongadze	

2013

09/03	Dila	a	1-2	Gorgiashvili	
17/03	Torpedo	h	0-0		
30/03	Chikhura	a	0-1		
06/04	Zugdidi	a	0-1		
14/04	Dinamo Tbilisi	h	0-3		
19/04	Dila	h	0-3		
27/04	Torpedo	a	0-1	Demel	
04/05	Chikhura	h	2-1		
12/05	Zugdidi	h	2-0	Gorgiashvili 2	
18/05	Dinamo Tbilisi	a	1-6	Demel	

Name	Nat	DoB	Pos	Aps	(s)	Gls
Tornike Aptsiauri		28/11/79	M	19	(3)	1
Shota Babunashvili		17/11/80	M	20	(5)	3
Aleksi Benashvili		20/03/89	M	10	(2)	2
Giorgi Chankotadze		06/05/91	A		(2)	
Vakhtang Chanturishvili		05/08/93	M	2	(3)	
Boti Demel	CIV	03/03/89	A	12	(5)	3
Zaal Eliava		02/01/85	D	6	(2)	
Avto Endeladze		17/09/94	M	5	(2)	
Nodar Gachechiladze		05/01/93	M		(1)	
Malkhaz Gagoshidze		20/02/93	M	4	(4)	
Teimuraz Gongadze		08/09/85	D	23		1
Tornike Gorgiashvili		27/04/88	M	12	(10)	6
Tedore Grigalashvili		12/05/93	M	26		1
Tornike Grigalashvili		28/01/93	D	24	(2)	2
Igor Jelić	SRB	28/12/89	M	17	(3)	1
Giorgi Kachkachishvili		08/08/90	D	19		1
Ilia Kerdzevadze		19/01/96	M		(1)	
Guguna Kiknadze		07/02/90	M		(1)	
Mamuka Kobakhidze		23/08/92	D	15	(1)	
Levan Kutalia		19/07/89	M	8	(1)	
Roin Kvaskhvadze		31/05/89	G	28		
Otar Kvernadze		10/09/93	A	5	(8)	1
Zurab Mamaladze		10/02/82	G	1		
Zurab Menteshavili		30/01/80	M	15		2
Kakhaber Meshveliani		14/04/92	G	3		
Patrick Milchraum	GER	26/05/84	D	16	(1)	1
David Mujiri		02/01/78	M	3	(3)	
Oriol	ESP	23/05/81	D	7		
Abayomi Owonikoko	NGA	13/09/92	A	2	(1)	
Dimitar Petkov	BUL	24/08/87	M	3	(1)	
David Rajamashvili		28/10/88	M	9	(5)	
Mohamed Rekrouk	ALG	20/01/93	M	1	(4)	
Mirian Robakidze		14/03/95	M		(1)	
Guram Samushia		05/09/94	M	3	(5)	
Mishiko Sardalishvili		19/09/92	A	3	(5)	1
Levan Sharikadze		16/07/89	M	18	(4)	4
Berdia Sharvadze		24/01/93	M	1	(2)	1
Rati Tsinamdzgvrishvili		22/03/88	A	12	(5)	4

FC ZUGDIDI

Coach: Elguja Kometiani
2005 • Central, Ganmukhuri (1,500) • no website

2012

11/08	Torpedo	a	0-1	
18/08	Dinamo Batumi	h	2-0	Kutalia 2 (1p)
25/08	Kolkheti	a	1-1	Gamezardashvili
03/09	Dila	h	0-0	
15/09	WIT Georgia	a	0-0	
22/09	Chikhura	h	4-2	Kobalia 2, Gabedava, Lomia
26/09	Sioni	a	0-0	
30/09	Merani	a	2-1	Lomia, Popkhadze
06/10	Dinamo Tbilisi	h	1-1	Kobalia
20/10	Zestafoni	a	0-1	
27/10	Metalurgi	h	2-1	Gamezardashvili (p), Kobalia
31/10	Torpedo	h	2-1	Gamezardashvili, Kobalia
04/11	Dinamo Batumi	a	4-0	Gabedava 2, Koshkadze, og (Kvekveskiri)
11/11	Kolkheti	h	1-0	Gabedava
18/11	Dila	a	0-3	
24/11	WIT Georgia	h	2-0	Oniani, Sikharulia
28/11	Chikhura	a	0-2	
02/12	Sioni	h	2-0	Kobalia, Lomia
08/12	Merani	h	3-2	Kobalia, Bolkvadze, Sikharulia
15/12	Dinamo Tbilisi	a	0-2	
19/12	Zestafoni	h	0-3	
23/12	Metalurgi	a	1-5	Lashkarava

2013

09/03	Dinamo Tbilisi	a	0-3	
17/03	Chikhura	h	1-3	Ekhvaia
30/03	Dila	a	0-6	
06/04	Zestafoni	h	0-0	
14/04	Torpedo	a	0-2	
19/04	Dinamo Tbilisi	h	0-2	
27/04	Chikhura	a	1-2	Gabedava
04/05	Dila	h	1-2	Sikharulia
12/05	Zestafoni	a	0-2	
18/05	Torpedo	h	1-4	Gabedava

Name	Nat	DoB	Pos	Aps	(s)	Gls
Levan Akobia		11/02/80	D	16		
Makar Akubardia		20/01/88	D	8	(1)	
Nikoloz Apakidze		04/04/92	D	17	(2)	
Giorgi Berishvili		17/04/93	M	1	(1)	
David Bolkvadze		05/06/80	M	16	(1)	1
Murtaz Changelia		26/06/92	A	1		
Lasha Dzagania		14/01/88	G	29		
Irakli Ekhvaia		09/01/89	M	8	(7)	1
Giorgi Gabedava		03/10/89	A	23	(3)	6
David Gamezardashvili		07/05/82	D	20		3
Luka Guguchia		10/12/92	M	6	(8)	
Romeo Kankia		27/05/92	M	9		
Levan Kantaria		05/07/91	M	1	(1)	
Giorgi Khubua		19/04/93	M	6	(4)	
Nika Khukhia		31/05/88	D	1	(1)	
Nika Kiria		04/01/94	M		(1)	
Irakli Kobalia		13/03/92	A	13	(4)	7
Luka Koberidze		09/09/94	M		(4)	
Koka Kometiani		10/03/94	D	1	(1)	
Aleksandre Koshkadze		04/12/81	M	15	(3)	1
Lasha Kukava		12/01/92	M	3	(9)	
Levan Kutalia		19/07/89	M	14	(3)	2
Giorgi Kvartskhava		01/09/92	D	7		
Zurab Kvartskhava		20/10/93	M	1		
Giorgi Lashkarava		21/03/93	A	1		1
Shota Lomia		13/02/84	M	16	(8)	3
Archil Makatsaria		19/03/92	G	3		
Zurab Malania		07/10/96	M		(4)	
Roin Oniani		14/06/75	M	19	(3)	1
Akaki Parjikia		25/09/93	M	2	(11)	
Lukhumi Pataraia		18/01/93	M		(1)	
Dachi Popkhadze		27/01/84	D	14		1
Nika Shonia		14/10/91	M	2		
Zviad Sikharulia		01/08/92	M	27	(4)	3
Valiko Tkemaladze		14/11/87	M	18	(1)	
Sevasti Todua		13/05/76	D	21		
Shakhi Toloraia		28/11/94	M		(1)	
Levan Tsurtsumia		28/01/89	M	13	(6)	

Top goalscorers

24	Xisco (Dinamo Tbilisi)
20	Jaba Dvali (Dinamo Tbilisi)
16	Saba Lomia (Merani)
14	Mikel Álvaro (Dinamo Tbilisi)
12	Besik Chimakadze (WIT Georgia/Dinamo Batumi)
11	Irakli Modebadze (Dila)
10	Nika Sabanadze (Torpedo)
9	Levan Khmaladze (Dinamo Tbilisi) Giorgi Beriashvili (Torpedo)
8	David Odikadze (Chikhura) Irakli Sikharulidze (Metalurgi)

Promoted clubs

FC GURIA LANCHKHUTI

Coach: Teimuraz Loria
1952 • Evgrapi Shevardnadze (4,500) • no website

FC SPARTAKI TSKHINVALI

Coach: Vladimer Khachidze
2007 • Bendela, Tbilisi (400) • fcspartak.ge

SECOND LEVEL FINAL TABLES 2012/13

GROUP A		Pld	W	D	L	F	A	Pts
1	FC Guria Lanchkhuti	33	27	4	2	86	20	85
2	FC Dinamo-2 Tbilisi	33	21	6	6	100	42	69
3	FC Sasko Tbilisi	33	20	4	9	84	38	64
4	FC Gagra	33	16	5	12	63	46	53
5	FC Meshakhte Tkibuli	33	13	6	14	42	66	45
6	FC Imereti Khoni	33	12	7	14	37	46	43
7	FC Chiatura	33	12	7	14	39	47	43
8	FC STU Tbilisi	33	12	3	18	63	75	39
9	FC Skuri Tsalenjikha	33	10	8	15	33	51	38
10	FC Betlemi Keda	33	10	5	18	40	76	35
11	FC Sulori Vani	33	7	4	22	30	72	25
12	FC Racha Ambrolauri	33	7	3	23	39	77	24

GROUP B		Pld	W	D	L	F	A	Pts
1	FC Spartaki Tskhinvali	30	25	2	3	82	15	77
2	FC Lokomotivi Tbilisi	30	19	6	5	70	29	63
3	FC Shukura Kobuleti	30	19	4	7	56	25	61
4	FC Kolkheti Khobi	30	18	3	9	43	28	57
5	FC Samtredia	30	17	4	9	53	37	55
6	FC Samgurali Tskhaltubo	30	13	7	10	59	48	46
7	FC Algeti Marneuli	30	10	3	17	39	55	33
8	FC Mertskhali Ozurgeti	30	5	10	15	37	52	25
9	FC Chkherimela Kharagauli	30	6	2	22	34	91	20
10	FC Liakhvi Achabeti	30	4	6	20	29	74	18
11	FC Adeli Batumi	30	4	3	23	27	75	15

NB FC Aeti Sokhumi withdrew after round 7 – their matches were annulled.

Domestic cup: Sakartvelos Tasi 2012/13

SECOND ROUND

(29/08/12 & 17/09/12)
Guria 2-0, 2-0 Skuri *(4-0)*

(29/08/12 & 18/09/12)
Aeti 1-3, 3-3 Sioni *(4-6)*
Chikhura 2-0, 2-0 Kolkheti Khobi *(4-0)*
Chkherimela 4-2, 0-3 Dinamo Batumi *(4-5)*
Dinamo Tbilisi 8-0, 6-1 STU *(14-1)*
Liakhvi 2-1, 1-5 Spartaki Tskhinvali *(3-6)*
Mertskhali 0-3, 0-2 Shukura *(0-5)*
Samgurali 0-2, 1-3 Kolkheti Poti *(1-5)*
Samtredia 0-0, 2-0 Merani Martvili *(2-0)*
WIT Georgia 0-1, 2-1 Lokomotivi Tbilisi *(2-2; WIT Georgia on away goals)*
Zugdidi 4-1, 3-2 Imereti *(7-3)*

(30/08/12 & 17/09/12)
Gagra 4-0, 2-0 Chiatura *(6-0)*

Byes – Dila, Metalurgi, Torpedo, Zestafoni

THIRD ROUND

(26/02/13 & 02/03/13)
Chikhura 8-0, 3-0 Shukura *(11-0)*
Dila 6-0, 3-0 Samtredia *(9-0)*
Dinamo Batumi 2-1, 0-1 Metalurgi *(2-2; Metalurgi on away goal)*
Guria 0-1, 3-2 Zestafoni *(3-3; Guria on away goals)*
Kolkheti Poti 0-1, 0-3 Dinamo Tbilisi *(0-4)*
Sioni 3-0, 1-1 Zugdidi *(4-1)*
Torpedo 1-1, 2-0 Gagra *(3-1)*
WIT Georgia 1-1, 1-1 Spartaki Tskhinvali *(2-2 aet; 0-3 on pens)*

QUARTER-FINALS

(13/03/13 & 10/04/13)
Chikhura 3-0 Dila *(Lomashvili 52, 57, Bolkvadze 64)*
Dila 1-2 Chikhura *(Kakhelishvili 90; Chelidze 25, Gotsiridze 73)*
(Chikhura 5-1)

Guria 0-0 Dinamo Tbilisi
Dinamo Tbilisi 3-2 Guria *(Merebashvili 3p, 7, Glisic 87; Kakaladze 10, Kverenchkhiladze 82)*
(Dinamo Tbilisi 3-2)

Metalurgi 1-0 Spartaki Tskhinvali *(Intskirveli 79)*
Spartaki Tskhinvali 1-1 Metalurgi *(Burdzenadze 23; Gavashelishvili 76)*
(Metalurgi 2-1)

Torpedo 3-1 Sioni *(Pantsulaia 8, Sabanadze 10, Dolidze 17; Mikuchadze 53)*
Sioni 2-0 Torpedo *(Bibileishvili 52, Ugulava 90+4)*
(3-3; Sioni on away goal)

SEMI-FINALS

(23/04/13 & 08/05/13)
Chikhura 2-0 Sioni *(Lomashvili 17p, Rekhviashvili 30)*
Sioni 1-0 Chikhura *(Mikuchadze 65p)*
(Chikhura 2-1)

Metalurgi 2-1 Dinamo Tbilisi *(Akhalkatsi 68, Sajaia 84; Dvali 28)*
Dinamo Tbilisi 5-0 Metalurgi *(Mikel Álvaro 21, 66, Xisco 57, Khmaladze 69, Merebashvili 87)*
(Dinamo Tbilisi 6-2)

FINAL

(22/05/13)
Mikheil Meskhi stadium, Tbilisi
FC DINAMO TBILISI 3 *(Merebashvili 58, Khmaladze 62, Dzaria 75)*
FC CHIKHURA SACHKHERE 1 *(Sajaia 90)*
Referee: Silagava
DINAMO TBILISI: Loria, Seturidze, Ustaritz, Kvaratskhelia, Glisic, Grajciar, Dzaria, Khmaladze, Merebashvili (Milchrum 88), Dvali (Carles Coto 90+3), Xisco (Papava 90+2)
Sent off: Ustaritz (78)
CHIKHURA: Somkhishvili, Kashia, Sajaia, Chikvaidze, Chelidze, Lomashvili, Digmelashvili (Kirkitadze 61), Bolkvadze (Kimadze 71), Dekanoidze, Kvaskhvadze, Gotsiridze

GERMANY
Deutscher Fussball-Bund (DFB)

Address	Otto-Fleck-Schneise 6
	Postfach 710265
	DE-60492 Frankfurt
	am Main
Tel	+49 69 67 880
Fax	+49 69 67 88266
E-mail	info@dfb.de
Website	dfb.de

President	Wolfgang Niersbach
General secretary	Helmut Sandrock
Media officer	Ralf Köttker
Year of formation	1900

BUNDESLIGA CLUBS

1. FC Augsburg
 2. Bayer 04 Leverkusen
 3. FC Bayern München
 4. Borussia Dortmund
5. VfL Borussia Mönchengladbach
 6. Eintracht Frankfurt
7. Fortuna Düsseldorf
 8. SC Freiburg
9. SpVgg Greuther Fürth
10. Hamburger SV
11. Hannover 96
12. TSG 1899 Hoffenheim
13. 1. FSV Mainz 05
14. 1. FC Nürnberg
 15. FC Schalke 04
 16. VfB Stuttgart
17. SV Werder Bremen
18. VfL Wolfsburg

PROMOTED CLUBS

19. Hertha BSC Berlin
20. Eintracht Braunschweig

KEY:
- ● – UEFA Champions League
- ● – UEFA Europa League
- ● – Promoted clubs
- ● – Relegated clubs

Brilliant Bayern break new ground

No follower of FC Bayern München will ever forget the 2012/13 season. Close to perfection, it delivered everything the club could have hoped for, and much more besides. Jupp Heynckes' all-conquering side won every competition they entered, becoming the first club to capture the treble of Bundesliga, DFB-Pokal and UEFA Champions League.

While Bayern stole the show on all fronts, there was excellence too from Borussia Dortmund, who joined their domestic rivals in the first all-German European Cup final, losing a classic game at Wembley only to a late Arjen Robben goal.

| Unprecedented treble for Heynckes' side | Bundesliga records tumble in runaway triumph | Dortmund defeated in Wembley showdown |

Domestic league

The 50th season of the Bundesliga was utterly dominated by the country's biggest and most successful club. Bayern, having surrendered the previous two championships to Dortmund and gone two years without the title for the first time since the mid-1990s, were fully committed from the outset to reasserting themselves as the best team in the land. They went into the new league campaign in a positive frame of mind thanks to a 2-1 win over Dortmund in the German Super Cup – a match played before a full house of 69,000 fans in Munich. Not even the staunchest of Bayern supporters, however, could have imagined how brilliantly they would begin their bid for a record 23rd title.

They not only won each of their opening eight fixtures – the first of 25 Bundesliga records they would set during the season – but did so in such a powerful, convincing manner that the title race appeared to be over before it was even two months old. Heynckes' team scored 26 goals in that run, conceding just two. Each victory was by two goals or more, and with newly-signed Croatian striker Mario Mandžukić finding his scoring touch straight away, the prospects for the other 17 teams were ominous.

Dortmund, for one, were already a dozen points in arrears.

Bayern's run was halted by a 2-1 home defeat to Heynckes' former club Bayer 04 Leverkusen. It was the first time the Rhinelanders had beaten Bayern in Munich for 23 years, but in the grand scheme of things its value was peripheral. The leaders would drop six more points in the run-up to Christmas – all in 1-1 draws – yet the nominal title of 'autumn champions' was theirs with three games to spare, and by the winter break they were sitting pretty at the top of the table with a nine-point lead. Most impressive of all was their away form, with seven wins and one draw in their eight fixtures and just one goal conceded.

If Bayern were a class apart in the first half of the season, they were even more dominant in the second – despite the announcement that Heynckes would be replaced in the summer by former FC Barcelona boss Pep Guardiola. Their 17 games yielded 16 wins and one draw – an away fixture at Dortmund in which they rested several key players ahead of the teams' more important encounter at Wembley three weeks later. It was a show of strength superior to anything the Bundesliga had ever witnessed. Records were smashed one after the other, the final table alone framing several of them, including most points (91), most wins (29),

biggest winning margin (25 points), biggest goal difference (+80), fewest goals conceded (18) and fewest defeats (one).

Although the team's final tally of 98 goals was not a new landmark – the 1971/72 Bayern side struck 101 in winning the title – it was a stunning feat all the same. The team's biggest win of the campaign was 9-2 at home to Hamburger SV and there were also three 6-1 victories (against VfB Stuttgart, SV Werder Bremen and Hannover 96). The goals were shared around the side, with 17 Bayern players getting in on the act – plus four from the opposition. Mandžukić finished up as the club's top marksman, on 15, with three other players also reaching double figures – Thomas Müller (13), Mario Gomez (11) and Franck Ribéry (ten). The Croatian's excellent debut season in Bavaria was matched by fellow newcomers Dante, formidable in defence, and Javi Martínez, who proved to be the perfect foil for Bastian Schweinsteiger in central midfield. Captain Philipp Lahm and goalkeeper Manuel Neuer were as dependable as ever, while Toni Kroos excelled in midfield until an injury cut short his season in early April. It was at that time, with a 1-0 win at Eintracht Frankfurt, that Bayern sealed the title with six matches still to play – another record.

Dortmund's bid to win a hat-trick of Bundesliga titles was shredded by Bayern, but Jürgen Klopp's side managed to claim the runners-up spot, finishing a point ahead of third-placed Leverkusen. A repeat of their 2011/12 title-winning tally would still have left them ten points adrift of Bayern, so they were always fighting a losing battle on that front. Four home defeats, however, constituted a disappointment – as did the 42 goals they conceded. On the positive side, new signing Marco Reus blended in superbly, forming a devastating attacking trident with Mario Götze and prolific central striker Robert Lewandowski, who scored 24 goals and found the net in 12 successive appearances.

Lewandowski's haul was up two on his 2011/12 output, but he was edged out of first place in the Bundesliga scoring charts by Leverkusen's Stefan Kiessling, who registered consistently throughout the season, a sustained burst in the final few games not just lifting his final tally to 25 but also securing his club's place alongside Bayern and Dortmund in the group stage of the 2013/14 UEFA Champions League. Leverkusen's

experiment of having two coaches on the bench worked well, although at the end of the season Sascha Lewandowski stepped aside to enable Sami Hyypiä, the former Liverpool FC and Finland defender, to assume the responsibility alone.

FC Schalke 04 changed their coach in mid-season, replacing Huub Stevens with youth team boss Jens Keller after a run of six games without a win dropped the team from second to seventh place. Keller steadied the ship in the spring, and with new signing Michel Bastos and hot prospect Julian Draxler both performing admirably, Schalke managed to claw their way back to fourth place, a last-day 2-1 win at SC Freiburg securing the final UEFA Champions League berth. Had Freiburg beaten Schalke, that prize would have been theirs. Christian Streich's youthful, unheralded side performed minor miracles all season and were fully deserving of their fifth-place finish. One place behind them – and also qualified for the UEFA Europa League – were another surprise package, newly promoted Frankfurt, who returned with a bang – five wins in their first six games – and, with Alexander Meier contributing 16 goals, never left the top

six all season. It was a tremendous feat by coach Armin Veh, the man who led VfB Stuttgart to the 2006/07 Bundesliga title.

Freiburg and Frankfurt's joy meant despair for some of the league's other, more ambitious, clubs. Hannover failed to re-qualify for Europe because of poor away form, whereas Hamburger SV were undone by seven defeats at home, where they managed only 18 goals. Stuttgart, another with a shabby home record, spent most of the season precariously close to the relegation zone, while VfL Borussia Mönchengladbach, fourth the previous season, dropped to eighth. Bremen were very nearly relegated, surviving only in the penultimate match, a 1-1 draw with Frankfurt, after which they fired Thomas Schaaf, the club's coach for the past 14 years. Big-budget VfL Wolfsburg were equally disappointing, taking 11th place after winning just three times in their own stadium.

Bottom-placed SpVgg Greuther Fürth did not win once at home. Their immediate return to the second division was confirmed long before the final day, on which Fortuna Düsseldorf, who had not been in the bottom two all season, joined them in automatic relegation when TSG 1899 Hoffenheim grabbed a dramatic win at Dortmund. Hoffenheim's fourth coach of the campaign, Markus Gisdol, then completed the club's great escape with a convincing play-off win over 1. FC Kaiserslautern. Hertha BSC Berlin, play-off losers in 2011/12, won the 2. Bundesliga in impressive style under Dutch coach Jos Luhukay to make a rapid return to the elite, and they were followed up by Eintracht Braunschweig, who thus ended a 28-year wait for Bundesliga football.

Domestic cup

Bayern claimed a record 16th victory in the German Cup with a 3-2 defeat of southern rivals Stuttgart in Berlin. The win completed their historic treble and brought them a seventh domestic double in the new millennium. Bayern appeared to be cruising with a little over an hour gone when a second goal of the evening from Gomez – who had scored a hat-trick in the 6-1 semi-final dismantling of Wolfsburg – put them 3-0 in front. But Stuttgart's Austrian forward Martin Harnik, the team's semi-final match-winner against Freiburg, responded by

Leverkusen striker Stefan Kiessling heads home against Hoffenheim – one of 25 goals he scored to become the Bundesliga's top marksman

scoring twice, in the 71st and 80th minutes, and there were a few more edgy moments for the Bayern fans to suffer before they could acclaim their all-conquering, history-making heroes – not least departing boss Heynckes – at the final whistle.

Europe

Without a victory in the UEFA Champions League for 12 years, Germany guaranteed an end to that barren spell by providing both finalists in 2012/13. There could only be one winner of course, but both Bayern and Dortmund arrived at Wembley as more than worthy European champions-in-waiting. Bayern had cut Barcelona down to size with a 7-0 aggregate demolition in the semi-final, while Dortmund took care of the other Liga heavyweights, overcoming Real Madrid CF after a magnificent 4-1 home win in which Lewandowski scored all four goals. Prior to that both teams had topped their group, with Bayern then seeing off Arsenal FC and Juventus, the latter 4-0 on aggregate, as Dortmund overcame FC Shakhtar Donetsk then – in unimaginable drama with two added-time goals – Málaga CF.

The stage was set for an epic final, and that is what the two teams produced. The match could have gone either way, but after İlkay Gündoğan had equalised Mandžukić's opener from the penalty spot, it was Robben, a penalty-missing villain in the previous season's final against Chelsea FC, who stepped up to become the hero with the winning goal a minute from the end of normal time.

As Bayern and Dortmund went all the way, Schalke dropped out of the competition in the round of 16 stage, eliminated by Galatasaray AŞ after they, too, had won their group. Mönchengladbach did not make it as far as the group stage, defeated in the play-offs by FC Dynamo Kyiv, but they did get through to the knockout phase of the UEFA Europa League, where S.S. Lazio ended their interest in the round of 32. There were three other Bundesliga sides through to that stage of the competition, but only one made further progress. Leverkusen and Hannover were knocked out by SL Benfica and FC Anji Makhachkala, respectively, before Stuttgart, who defeated KRC Genk, followed Gladbach's lead by going out to Lazio in the round of 16.

National team

With the country captivated by the continuing exploits of Bayern and Dortmund in Europe, the German national team were effectively relegated to second billing in 2012/13. Not that Joachim Löw's team, drawn heavily from those two clubs, disappointed. On the contrary, their place in the 2014 FIFA World Cup finals seemed all but guaranteed after they took 16 points from their first six qualifying matches. It should have been a maximum 18, but incredibly they squandered a 4-0 lead at home to Sweden, allowing the visitors to score four times in the second half and snatch a point. That setback came four days after Löw's men had trounced the Republic of Ireland 6-1 in Dublin with one of their finest performances in years.

Miroslav Klose scored once against Ireland and twice against Sweden to take his international goal tally to 67 – one shy of Gerd Müller's all-time scoring record for (West) Germany. Injury would deny the Lazio striker the opportunity to match or break it in the next two qualifiers, back-to-back ties against Kazakhstan that Germany won comfortably to strengthen their lead at the top of the Group C table. Klose did return in the final international fixture of the season, against Jürgen Klinsmann's United States in Washington DC, but he failed to score and was on the losing side in a 4-3 defeat. Four days earlier Löw's men had defeated Ecuador 4-2 in Florida, with Lukas Podolski's double including the fastest goal ever scored by the Nationalmannschaft – after just nine seconds.

None of Germany's Bayern contingent made that post-season trip to America. After what they had achieved for their club over the previous nine and a half months, it was hardly a surprise that they should be granted temporary leave of absence from international duty. It will be a different story, of course, in Brazil next summer, when a full-strength Germany will assuredly start as one of the favourites to lift the World Cup.

Miroslav Klose puts Germany 2-0 up against Sweden with his 67th international goal

Domestic league: Bundesliga 2012/13 final table

		Pld	Home					Away					Total					Pts
			W	D	L	F	A	W	D	L	F	A	W	D	L	F	A	
1	**FC Bayern München**	34	14	2	1	56	11	15	2	0	42	7	29	4	1	98	18	91
2	Borussia Dortmund	34	10	3	4	40	19	9	6	2	41	23	19	9	6	81	42	66
3	Bayer 04 Leverkusen	34	12	3	2	36	15	7	5	5	29	24	19	8	7	65	39	65
4	FC Schalke 04	34	10	3	4	35	22	6	4	7	23	28	16	7	11	58	50	55
5	SC Freiburg	34	8	4	5	25	18	6	5	6	20	22	14	9	11	45	40	51
6	Eintracht Frankfurt	34	9	4	4	32	23	5	5	7	17	23	14	9	11	49	46	51
7	Hamburger SV	34	8	2	7	18	18	6	4	7	24	35	14	6	14	42	53	48
8	VfL Borussia Mönchengladbach	34	8	5	4	27	20	4	6	7	18	29	12	11	11	45	49	47
9	Hannover 96	34	9	5	3	34	23	4	1	12	26	39	13	6	15	60	62	45
10	1. FC Nürnberg	34	7	6	4	24	19	4	5	8	15	28	11	11	12	39	47	44
11	VfL Wolfsburg	34	3	8	6	21	30	7	5	5	26	22	10	13	11	47	52	43
12	VfB Stuttgart	34	5	4	8	20	28	7	3	7	17	27	12	7	15	37	55	43
13	1. FSV Mainz 05	34	7	5	5	22	19	3	7	7	20	25	10	12	12	42	44	42
14	SV Werder Bremen	34	5	5	7	23	30	3	5	9	27	36	8	10	16	50	66	34
15	FC Augsburg	34	5	5	7	19	22	3	4	10	14	29	8	9	17	33	51	33
16	TSG 1899 Hoffenheim	34	5	4	8	21	30	3	3	11	21	37	8	7	19	42	67	31
17	Fortuna Düsseldorf	34	5	6	6	24	28	2	3	12	15	29	7	9	18	39	57	30
18	SpVgg Greuther Fürth	34	0	4	13	10	36	4	5	8	16	24	4	9	21	26	60	21

SEASON AT A GLANCE

EUROPEAN QUALIFICATION 2013/14

Champion/Cup winner: FC Bayern München (group stage)
Borussia Dortmund (group stage)
Bayer 04 Leverkusen (group stage)
FC Schalke 04 (play-offs)

SC Freiburg (group stage)
Eintracht Frankfurt (play-offs)
VfB Stuttgart (third qualifying round)

Top scorer	Stefan Kiessling (Leverkusen), 25 goals
Relegated clubs	SpVgg Greuther Fürth, Fortuna Düsseldorf
Promoted clubs	Hertha BSC Berlin, Eintracht Braunschweig
Cup final	FC Bayern München 3-2 VfB Stuttgart

PLAYER OF THE SEASON
Franck Ribéry
(FC Bayern München)

The 2012/13 season was by common consent the finest of the Frenchman's career. An incessant threat to opposition defences with his pace and trickery down Bayern's left flank, Ribéry added an extra dimension to his game with his defensive awareness. His classy Bundesliga displays were matched by sustained excellence in the UEFA Champions League.

NEWCOMER OF THE SEASON
Julian Draxler
(FC Schalke 04)

One of Germany's most gifted young footballers, the 19-year-old registered ten goals and four assists for Schalke in the 2012/13 Bundesliga and also opened his UEFA Champions League account. A memorable breakthrough season ended in fitting style when Draxler scored his first senior goal for Germany – in a 4-3 defeat against the United States.

BUNDESLIGA TEAM OF THE SEASON
(4-2-3-1)
Coach: Heynckes *(Bayern)*

Weidenfeller *(Dortmund)*
Lahm *(Bayern)* — Hummels *(Dortmund)* — Dante *(Bayern)* — Alaba *(Bayern)*
Javi Martínez *(Bayern)* — Schweinsteiger *(Bayern)*
Müller *(Bayern)* — Götze *(Dortmund)* — Ribéry *(Bayern)*
Lewandowski *(Dortmund)*

GERMANY

NATIONAL TEAM

Home Kit   Away Kit

INTERNATIONAL HONOURS*
FIFA World Cup (3) 1954, 1974, 1990
UEFA European Championship (3) 1972, 1980, 1996

INTERNATIONAL TOURNAMENT APPEARANCES*
FIFA World Cup (17) 1934 (3rd), 1938, 1954 (Winners), 1958 (4th), 1962 (qtr-finals), 1966 (runners-up), 1970 (3rd), 1974 (Winners), 1978 (2nd phase), 1982 (runners-up), 1986 (runners-up), 1990 (Winners), 1994 (qtr-finals), 1998 (qtr-finals), 2002 (runners-up), 2006 (3rd), 2010 (3rd)
UEFA European Championship (11) 1972 (Winners), 1976 (runners-up), 1980 (Winners), 1984, 1988 (semifinals), 1992 (runners-up), 1996 (Winners), 2000, 2004, 2008 (runners-up), 2012 (semi-finals)

TOP FIVE ALL-TIME CAPS
Lothar Matthäus (150); **Miroslav Klose** (127); **Lukas Podolski** (110); Jürgen Klinsmann (108); Jürgen Kohler (105)

TOP FIVE ALL-TIME GOALS
Gerd Müller (68); **Miroslav Klose** (67); Jürgen Klinsmann & Rudi Völler (47); **Lukas Podolski** (46)

(before 1992 as West Germany)*

Results 2012/13

15/08/12	Argentina	H	Frankfurt	1-3	Höwedes (83)
07/09/12	Faroe Islands (WCQ)	H	Hanover	3-0	Götze (28), Özil (54, 71)
11/09/12	Austria (WCQ)	A	Vienna	2-1	Reus (44), Özil (52p)
12/10/12	Republic of Ireland (WCQ)	A	Dublin	6-1	Reus (32, 40), Özil (54p), Klose (58), Kroos (61, 83)
16/10/12	Sweden (WCQ)	H	Berlin	4-4	Klose (8, 15), Mertesacker (39), Özil (56)
14/11/12	Netherlands	A	Amsterdam	0-0	
06/02/13	France	A	Paris	2-1	T Müller (51), Khedira (74)
22/03/13	Kazakhstan (WCQ)	A	Astana	3-0	T Müller (20, 74), Götze (22)
26/03/13	Kazakhstan (WCQ)	H	Nuremberg	4-1	Reus (23, 90), Götze (27), Gündoğan (31)
29/05/13	Ecuador	N	Boca Raton (USA)	4-2	Podolski (1, 17), L Bender (4, 24)
02/06/13	United States	A	Washington	3-4	Westermann (52), Kruse (79), Draxler (81)

Appearances 2012/13

Coach: Joachim Löw	03/02/60		Arg	FRO	AUT	IRL	SWE	Ned	Fra	KAZ	KAZ	Ecu	Usa	Caps	Goals
Ron-Robert Zieler	12/02/89	Hannover	G 30*											2	-
Jérôme Boateng	03/09/88	Bayern	D			D	D					D		29	-
Mats Hummels	16/12/88	Dortmund	D25	D	D			D	D					24	1
Holger Badstuber	13/03/89	Bayern	D	D	D	D	D							30	1
Marcel Schmelzer	22/01/88	Dortmund	D		D	D				D	D			11	-
Lars Bender	27/04/89	Leverkusen	M74					M82	s89			M90	D46	14	3
Sami Khedira	04/04/87	Real Madrid (ESP)	M69	M	M	M46			M	M82	M			39	3
Thomas Müller	13/09/89	Bayern	M30	M68	M	M	M67	M84	M89	M82	M			41	13
Mesut Özil	15/10/88	Real Madrid (ESP)	M69	M	M	M	M		M	M	M			46	14
Marco Reus	31/05/89	Dortmund	M	M	M46	M66	M88	M90			M90			15	7
Miroslav Klose	09/06/78	Lazio (ITA)	A62	A75	A75	A72	A						A79	127	67
Bendikt Höwedes	29/02/88	Schalke	s25					D	D	D		D	D	14	1
Marc-André ter Stegen	30/04/92	Mönchengladbach	s30									G		3	-
André Schürrle	06/11/90	Leverkusen	s62	s68		s72		s84	s68	s82		s69	M65	24	7
İlkay Gündoğan	24/10/90	Dortmund	s69					M	M	s82	M			7	1
Toni Kroos	04/01/90	Bayern	s69		M		s46	M		s57				35	4
Mario Götze	03/06/92	Dortmund	s74	M88	s46		s67	A72		A	A			22	5
Manuel Neuer	27/03/86	Bayern		G	G	G	G	G		G	G			38	-
Philipp Lahm	11/11/83	Bayern		D	D		D	D	D	D	D			98	5
Per Mertesacker	29/09/84	Arsenal (ENG)	D		D	D	D	D	D	D	D	D	D46	90	2
Lukas Podolski	04/06/85	Arsenal (ENG)	s75	s75	s66	s88	s72	M68	s19		M89	M		110	46
Julian Draxler	20/09/93	Schalke	s88				s90		M19		M57	M		6	1
Bastian Schweinsteiger	01/08/84	Bayern				M	M		M					98	23
Lewis Holtby	18/09/90	Schalke					M87							3	-

Appearances 2012/13 (contd.)

			Arg	FRO	AUT	IRL	SWE	Ned	Fra	KAZ	KAZ	Ecu	Usa	Caps	Goals
Sven Bender	27/04/89	Dortmund						s82					M46	4	-
Roman Neustädter	18/02/88	Schalke						s87				M66		2	-
René Adler	15/01/85	Hamburg							G			G		12	-
Mario Gomez	10/07/85	Bayern							A57					58	25
Marcell Jansen	04/11/85	Hamburg									s90	D	D46	39	3
Heiko Westermann	14/08/83	Hamburg										D	s46	26	4
Sidney Sam	31/01/88	Leverkusen										M69	s65	2	-
Max Kruse	19/03/88	Freiburg										A79	s46	2	1
Aaron Hunt	04/09/86	Bremen										s57		3	-
Stefan Reinartz	01/01/89	Leverkusen										s66	M	3	-
Dennis Aogo	14/01/87	Hamburg										s79	s46	12	-
Nicolai Müller	25/09/87	Mainz										s89	s79	2	-
Philipp Wollscheid	06/03/89	Leverkusen										s90	s46	2	-

European club competitions 2012/13

BORUSSIA DORTMUND

Group D
Match 1 - AFC Ajax (NED)
H 1-0 *Lewandowski (87)*
Weidenfeller, Subotić, Kehl, Gündoğan (Leitner 89), Lewandowski, Götze (Schieber 88), Reus, Hummels, Błaszczykowski (Perišić 73), Piszczek, Schmelzer. Coach: Jürgen Klopp (GER)

Match 2 - Manchester City FC (ENG)
A 1-1 *Reus (61)*
Weidenfeller, Subotić, Bender, Gündoğan (Grosskreutz 82), Lewandowski, Götze (Kehl 88), Reus, Hummels (Felipe Santana 74), Błaszczykowski, Piszczek, Schmelzer. Coach: Jürgen Klopp (GER)

Match 3 - Real Madrid CF (ESP)
H 2-1 *Lewandowski (36), Schmelzer (64)*
Weidenfeller, Subotić, Kehl, Bender (Gündoğan 67), Lewandowski, Götze (Schieber 87), Reus (Perišić 90+1), Hummels, Grosskreutz, Piszczek, Schmelzer. Coach: Jürgen Klopp (GER)

Match 4 - Real Madrid CF (ESP)
A 2-2 *Reus (28), Arbeloa (45og)*
Weidenfeller, Subotić, Kehl, Gündoğan (Perišić 80), Lewandowski, Götze (Leitner 90+1), Reus (Bender 74), Hummels, Grosskreutz, Piszczek, Schmelzer. Coach: Jürgen Klopp (GER)

Match 5 - AFC Ajax (NED)
A 4-1 *Reus (8), Götze (36), Lewandowski (41, 67)*
Weidenfeller, Subotić, Bender (Perišić 63), Gündoğan, Lewandowski, Götze (Błaszczykowski 70), Reus (Schieber 79), Hummels, Grosskreutz, Piszczek, Schmelzer. Coach: Jürgen Klopp (GER)

Match 6 - Manchester City FC (ENG)
H 1-0 *Schieber (57)*
Weidenfeller, Leitner, Gündoğan, Reus (Błaszczykowski 46), Hummels, Grosskreutz, Kirch (Bittencourt 88), Schieber (Lewandowski 77), Felipe Santana, Schmelzer, Perišić. Coach: Jürgen Klopp (GER)

Round of 16 - FC Shakhtar Donetsk (UKR)
A 2-2 *Lewandowski (41), Hummels (87)*
Weidenfeller, Kehl, Bender, Lewandowski, Götze, Reus (Schieber 90+1), Hummels, Błaszczykowski (Leitner 80), Piszczek, Felipe Santana, Schmelzer. Coach: Jürgen Klopp (GER)

H 3-0 *Felipe Santana (31), Götze (37), Błaszczykowski (59)*
Weidenfeller, Subotić, Bender (Kehl 46), Gündoğan (Nuri Şahin 82), Lewandowski, Götze, Reus, Błaszczykowski (Grosskreutz 70), Piszczek, Felipe Santana, Schmelzer. Coach: Jürgen Klopp (GER)

Quarter-final - Málaga CF (ESP)
A 0-0
Weidenfeller, Subotić, Kehl (Bender 80), Gündoğan, Lewandowski, Götze (Kirch 90+2), Reus (Schieber 69), Grosskreutz, Piszczek, Felipe Santana, Schmelzer. Coach: Jürgen Klopp (GER)

H 3-2 *Lewandowski (40), Reus (90+1), Felipe Santana (90+3)*
Weidenfeller, Subotić, Bender (Nuri Şahin 73), Gündoğan (Hummels 86), Lewandowski, Götze, Reus, Błaszczykowski (Schieber 72), Piszczek, Felipe Santana, Schmelzer. Coach: Jürgen Klopp (GER)

Semi-final - Real Madrid CF (ESP)
H 4-1 *Lewandowski (8, 50, 55, 66p)*
Weidenfeller, Subotić, Bender, Gündoğan (Schieber 90+1), Lewandowski, Götze, Reus, Hummels, Błaszczykowski (Kehl 82), Piszczek (Grosskreutz 83), Schmelzer. Coach: Jürgen Klopp (GER)

A 0-2
Weidenfeller, Subotić, Bender (Felipe Santana 90+1), Gündoğan, Lewandowski (Kehl 87), Götze (Grosskreutz 14), Reus, Hummels, Błaszczykowski, Piszczek, Schmelzer. Coach: Jürgen Klopp (GER)

Final - FC Bayern München (GER)
N 1-2 *Gündoğan (68p)*
Weidenfeller, Subotić, Bender (Nuri Şahin 90+2), Gündoğan, Lewandowski, Reus, Hummels, Błaszczykowski (Schieber 90), Grosskreutz, Piszczek, Schmelzer. Coach: Jürgen Klopp (GER)

FC BAYERN MÜNCHEN

CHAMPIONS
LEAGUE

Group F
Match 1 - Valencia CF (ESP)
H 2-1 *Schweinsteiger (38), Kroos (76)*
Neuer, Dante, Ribéry (Müller 46), Javi
Martínez (Luiz Gustavo 69), Robben, Pizarro
(Mandžukić 63), Boateng, Lahm, Badstuber,
Schweinsteiger, Kroos. Coach: Jupp
Heynckes (GER)
Match 2 - FC BATE Borisov (BLR)
A 1-3 *Ribéry (90+1)*
Neuer, Dante, Ribéry, Javi Martínez (Shaqiri 58),
Mandžukić (Pizarro 75), Boateng, Lahm, Müller,
Badstuber (Schweinsteiger 77), Luiz Gustavo,
Kroos. Coach: Jupp Heynckes (GER)
Match 3 - LOSC Lille (FRA)
A 1-0 *Müller (20p)*
Neuer, Dante, Ribéry (Shaqiri 46),
Javi Martínez, Mandžukić, Boateng,
Lahm, Müller (Alaba 84), Badstuber,
Schweinsteiger, Kroos (Luiz Gustavo 81).
Coach: Jupp Heynckes (GER)
Match 4 - LOSC Lille (FRA)
H 6-1 *Schweinsteiger (5), Pizarro (18, 28,
33), Robben (23), Kroos (66)*
Neuer, Dante, Ribéry (Shaqiri 72), Javi Martínez,
Robben, Pizarro, Boateng, Lahm, Müller (Kroos
61), Alaba, Schweinsteiger (Tymoshchuk 67).
Coach: Jupp Heynckes (GER)
Match 5 - Valencia CF (ESP)
A 1-1 *Müller (82)*
Neuer, Dante, Ribéry (Gomez 79), Javi
Martínez, Pizarro (Mandžukić 66), Lahm, Müller,
Alaba, Badstuber, Schweinsteiger, Kroos
(Shaqiri 66). Coach: Jupp Heynckes (GER)
Match 6 - FC BATE Borisov (BLR)
H 4-1 *Gomez (22), Müller (54), Shaqiri (65),
Alaba (83)*
Neuer, Van Buyten, Shaqiri, Rafinha,
Boateng, Müller (Dante 53), Contento,
Schweinsteiger (Ribéry 72), Gomez, Kroos
(Alaba 64), Tymoshchuk. Coach: Jupp
Heynckes (GER)
Red card: Boateng 51

Round of 16 - Arsenal FC (ENG)
A 3-1 *Kroos (7), Müller (21), Mandžukić (77)*
Neuer, Dante, Van Buyten, Ribéry (Robben
63), Javi Martínez, Mandžukić (Gomez 78),
Lahm, Müller, Alaba, Schweinsteiger, Kroos
(Luiz Gustavo 73). Coach: Jupp Heynckes
(GER)

H 0-2
Neuer, Dante, Van Buyten, Javi Martínez,
Mandžukić (Gomez 73), Robben, Lahm,
Müller, Alaba, Luiz Gustavo, Kroos
(Tymoshchuk 81). Coach: Jupp Heynckes
(GER)

Quarter-final - Juventus (ITA)
H 2-0 *Alaba (1), Müller (63)*
Neuer, Dante, Van Buyten, Ribéry (Shaqiri
90+3), Mandžukić (Gomez 90+1), Lahm, Müller,
Alaba, Luiz Gustavo, Schweinsteiger, Kroos
(Robben 16). Coach: Jupp Heynckes (GER)
A 2-0 *Mandžukić (64), Pizarro (90+1)*
Neuer, Dante, Van Buyten (Boateng 35),
Ribéry (Luiz Gustavo 80), Javi Martínez,
Mandžukić (Pizarro 83), Robben, Lahm,
Müller, Alaba, Schweinsteiger. Coach: Jupp
Heynckes (GER)

Semi-final - FC Barcelona (ESP)
H 4-0 *Müller (25, 82), Gomez (49), Robben
(73)*
Neuer, Dante, Ribéry (Shaqiri 89), Javi Martínez,
Robben, Boateng, Lahm, Müller (Pizarro 83),
Alaba, Schweinsteiger, Gomez (Luiz Gustavo
71). Coach: Jupp Heynckes (GER)
A 3-0 *Robben (49), Piqué (72og), Müller (76)*
Neuer, Van Buyten, Ribéry, Javi Martínez
(Tymoshchuk 74), Mandžukić, Robben,
Boateng, Lahm (Rafinha 77), Müller, Alaba,
Schweinsteiger (Luiz Gustavo 66). Coach:
Jupp Heynckes (GER)

Final - Borussia Dortmund (GER)
N 2-1 *Mandžukić (60), Robben (89)*
Neuer, Dante, Ribéry (Luiz Gustavo 90+1),
Javi Martínez, Mandžukić (Gomez 90+4),
Robben, Boateng, Lahm, Müller, Alaba,
Schweinsteiger. Coach: Jupp Heynckes (GER)

FC SCHALKE 04

CHAMPIONS
LEAGUE

Group B
Match 1 - Olympiacos FC (GRE)
A 2-1 *Höwedes (41), Huntelaar (59)*
Unnerstall, Höwedes, Holtby, Jones (Höger
90+1), Papadopoulos, Farfán (Draxler 90+4),
Fuchs, Huntelaar, Barnetta (Afellay 79),
Matip, Neustädter. Coach: Huub Stevens
(NED)
Match 2 - Montpellier Hérault SC (FRA)
H 2-2 *Draxler (26), Huntelaar (53p)*
Unnerstall, Höwedes, Holtby (Barnetta 84),
Höger, Papadopoulos, Pukki (Farfán 66),
Uchida, Fuchs, Huntelaar, Draxler (Afellay
55), Neustädter. Coach: Huub Stevens
(NED)
Match 3 - Arsenal FC (ENG)
A 2-0 *Huntelaar (76), Afellay (86)*
Unnerstall, Höwedes, Holtby (Barnetta 65),
Afellay, Höger (Jones 46), Farfán, Uchida,
Fuchs, Huntelaar (Marica 88), Matip,
Neustädter. Coach: Huub Stevens (NED)
Match 4 - Arsenal FC (ENG)
H 2-2 *Huntelaar (45+2), Farfán (67)*
Unnerstall, Höwedes, Holtby (Barnetta 90+3),
Afellay, Jones, Farfán, Uchida (Höger 25;
Papadopoulos 66), Fuchs, Huntelaar, Matip,
Neustädter. Coach: Huub Stevens (NED)
Match 5 - Olympiacos FC (GRE)
H 1-0 *Fuchs (77)*
Unnerstall, Höwedes, Holtby (Pukki 71), Jones,
Papadopoulos, Farfán, Fuchs, Huntelaar
(Marica 90+1), Draxler (Barnetta 89), Matip,
Neustädter. Coach: Huub Stevens (NED)
Match 6 - Montpellier Hérault SC (FRA)
A 1-1 *Höwedes (56)*
Hildebrand, Höwedes, Marica (Huntelaar
77), Holtby, Pukki (Obasi 84), Metzelder,
Uchida, Barnetta (Jones 72), Draxler,
Neustädter, Kolašinac. Coach: Huub
Stevens (NED)

Round of 16 - Galatasaray AŞ (TUR)
A 1-1 *Jones (45)*
Hildebrand, Höwedes, Michel Bastos,
Höger, Jones, Farfán, Huntelaar (Pukki 75),
Draxler (Barnetta 84), Matip, Neustädter,
Kolašinac. Coach: Jens Keller (GER)
H 2-3 *Neustädter (17), Michel Bastos (63)*
Hildebrand, Höwedes, Michel Bastos,
Höger (Meyer 85), Farfán, Pukki (Obasi 85),
Uchida, Draxler, Matip, Neustädter (Fuchs
46), Kolašinac. Coach: Jens Keller (GER)

VFL BORUSSIA MÖNCHENGLADBACH

Play-offs - FC Dynamo Kyiv (UKR)
H 1-3 *Ring (13)*
Ter Stegen, Daems, Ring (Herrmann 69), L de Jong, De Camargo (Hanke 69), Álvaro Domínguez, Nordtveit (Ciğerci 74), Arango, Jantschke, Xhaka, Stranzl. Coach:
A 2-1 *Khacheridi (70og), Arango (78)*
Ter Stegen, Daems, Brouwers, Herrmann (Ring 88), L de Jong (De Camargo 72), Nordtveit, Arango, Hanke (Hrgota 59), Jantschke, Xhaka, Stranzl. Coach: Lucien Favre (SUI)

Group C
Match 1 - AEL Limassol FC (CYP)
A 0-0
Ter Stegen, Brouwers, Ring (Rupp 79), Ciğerci, Herrmann, Álvaro Domínguez, Nordtveit, Wendt, Hanke (De Camargo 81), Jantschke, Hrgota (Xhaka 46). Coach: Lucien Favre (SUI)
Match 2 - Fenerbahçe SK (TUR)
H 2-4 *De Jong (18), De Camargo (74)*
Ter Stegen, Daems, Brouwers, Ring (Hrgota 46), Ciğerci (De Camargo 62), De Jong, Marx, Nordtveit, Arango, Xhaka (Mlapa 87), Stranzl. Coach: Lucien Favre (SUI)
Match 3 - Olympique de Marseille (FRA)
H 2-0 *Daems (33p), Mlapa (67)*
Ter Stegen, Daems, Herrmann (Hanke 80), Rupp, De Jong (Mlapa 65), Marx, Álvaro Domínguez, Nordtveit, Arango, Jantschke (Brouwers 35), Stranzl. Coach: Lucien Favre (SUI)
Match 4 - Olympique de Marseille (FRA)
A 2-2 *Hanke (20), Arango (90+3)*
Ter Stegen, Brouwers, Herrmann (Mlapa 71), Rupp, Marx (Xhaka 74), Álvaro Domínguez, Nordtveit, Wendt, Arango, Hanke (De Camargo 73), Jantschke. Coach: Lucien Favre (SUI)
Match 5 - AEL Limassol FC (CYP)
H 2-0 *De Camargo (79, 90+1)*
Ter Stegen, Ring (Mlapa 63), Herrmann, Marx (Xhaka 72), Álvaro Domínguez, Nordtveit, Wendt, Arango, Hanke (De Camargo 74), Jantschke, Stranzl. Coach: Lucien Favre (SUI)

Match 6 - Fenerbahçe SK (TUR)
A 3-0 *Ciğerci (23), Hanke (28p), De Jong (79)*
Heimeroth, Brouwers, Ring, Ciğerci (Younes 72), Álvaro Domínguez, Wendt, Hanke (De Jong 67), Mlapa (Zimmermann 80), Korb, Hrgota, Xhaka. Coach: Lucien Favre (SUI)
Round of 32 - S.S. Lazio (ITA)
H 3-3 *Stranzl (17p), Marx (84p), Arango (88)*
Ter Stegen, Brouwers, Ciğerci (Xhaka 75), Herrmann, De Jong, Álvaro Domínguez, Nordtveit (Marx 73), Wendt, Arango, Jantschke (Hanke 75), Stranzl. Coach: Lucien Favre (SUI)
A 0-2
Ter Stegen, Ciğerci (Hanke 68), Herrmann, De Jong, Marx (Xhaka 77), Álvaro Domínguez, Nordtveit, Wendt, Arango (Younes 52), Jantschke, Stranzl. Coach: Lucien Favre (SUI)

BAYER 04 LEVERKUSEN

Group K
Match 1 - FC Metalist Kharkiv (UKR)
H 0-0
Leno, Schwaab, Reinartz, Wollscheid, Rolfes, Bender (Schürrle 63), Renato Augusto (Castro 63), Kiessling (Fernandes 76), Hosogai, Ömer Toprak, Bellarabi. Coach: Sascha Lewandowski (GER)
Match 2 - Rosenborg BK (NOR)
A 1-0 *Kiessling (76)*
Leno, Schwaab, Wollscheid, Friedrich (Ömer Toprak 46), Rolfes, Fernandes (Kiessling 75), Bender, Schürrle (Sam 64), Renato Augusto, Kadlec, Castro. Coach: Sami Hyypiä (FIN)
Match 3 - SK Rapid Wien (AUT)
A 4-0 *Wollscheid (37), Castro (56, 90+2), Bellarabi (59)*
Leno, Schwaab, Wollscheid, Friedrich, Rolfes, Schürrle (Hegeler 61), Kiessling (Fernandes 70), Hosogai, Kadlec (Bender 10), Castro, Bellarabi. Coach: Sascha Lewandowski (GER)
Match 4 - SK Rapid Wien (AUT)
H 3-0 *Hegeler (4), Schürrle (53), Friedrich (66)*
Rensing, Reinartz, Friedrich, Rolfes, Fernandes, Schürrle (Renato Augusto 62), Hegeler, Hosogai, Sam (Castro 46), Carvajal (Carlinhos 74), Ömer Toprak. Coach: Sascha Lewandowski (GER)

Match 5 - FC Metalist Kharkiv (UKR)
A 0-2
Leno, Reinartz (Meffert 65), Wollscheid, Friedrich, Fernandes (Kiessling 78), Renato Augusto, Hegeler, Carlinhos, Pusch, Kohr, Steffen (Aydın 46). Coach: Sascha Lewandowski (GER)
Match 6 - Rosenborg BK (NOR)
H 1-0 *Riedel (65)*
Lomb, Reinartz (Rolfes 46), Wollscheid, Friedrich, Fernandes, Renato Augusto (Sam 46), Hegeler, Carlinhos, Kohr, Steffen (Aydın 75), Riedel. Coach: Sascha Lewandowski (GER)
Round of 32 - SL Benfica (POR)
H 0-1
Leno, Schwaab, Wollscheid, Rolfes, Bender, Schürrle (Sam 46), Kiessling, Hegeler, Hosogai (Boenisch 82), Kadlec, Castro (Milik 79). Coach: Sascha Lewandowski (GER)
A 1-2 *Söhürle (75)*
Leno, Reinartz (Milik 74), Wollscheid, Rolfes, Bender (Hegeler 57), Schürrle, Kiessling, Boenisch, Carvajal, Ömer Toprak, Castro. Coach: Sascha Lewandowski (GER)

VFB STUTTGART

Play-offs - FC Dinamo Moskva (RUS)
H 2-0 *Ibišević (72, 90+1)*
Ulreich, Kvist, Taşçı, Harnik (Tunay Torun 62), Ibišević, Rodríguez, Boka, Gentner, Hoogland, Hajnal (Cacau 77), Okazaki (Traoré 62). Coach: Bruno Labbadia (GER)
A 1-1 *Ibišević (64)*
Ulreich, Sakai, Kvist, Taşçı, Harnik (Tunay Torun 68), Ibišević (Cacau 78), Rodríguez, Boka (Molinaro 74), Gentner, Hajnal, Okazaki. Coach: Bruno Labbadia (GER)

Group E
Match 1 - FC Steaua Bucureşti (ROU)
H 2-2 *Ibišević (5), Niedermeier (85)*
Ulreich, Sakai, Kvist (Harnik 82), Niedermeier, Ibišević, Rodríguez, Boka, Tunay Torun (Okazaki 62), Cacau, Gentner, Hajnal (Traoré 82). Coach: Bruno Labbadia (GER)
Match 2 - Molde FK (NOR)
A 0-2
Ulreich, Taşçı, Niedermeier, Harnik, Kuzmanović, Ibišević, Traoré (Cacau 67), Gentner, Molinaro, Rüdiger (Boka 81), Hajnal (Holzhauser 67). Coach: Bruno Labbadia (GER)

Match 3 - FC København (DEN)
H 0-0
Ulreich, Sakai (Hajnal 84), Kvist, Taşçı, Niedermeier, Harnik, Ibišević, Traoré (Okazaki 62), Gentner, Molinaro, Holzhauser (Tunay Torun 46). Coach: Bruno Labbadia (GER)

Match 4 - FC København (DEN)
A 2-0 *Ibišević (76), Harnik (90+2)*
Ulreich, Sakai, Kvist, Taşçı, Niedermeier, Harnik, Ibišević, Traoré (Boka 63), Gentner, Molinaro, Okazaki (Kuzmanović 86). Coach: Bruno Labbadia (GER)

Match 5 - FC Steaua Bucureşti (ROU)
A 5-1 *Taşçı (5), Harnik (18), Sakai (23), Okazaki (31, 55)*
Ulreich, Sakai (Rüdiger 70), Kvist, Taşçı, Harnik (Traoré 61), Kuzmanović, Ibišević, Rodríguez, Gentner (Hajnal 46), Molinaro, Okazaki. Coach: Bruno Labbadia (GER)

Match 6 - Molde FK (NOR)
H 0-1
Ulreich, Sakai, Niedermeier, Ibišević, Rodríguez, Traoré, Tunay Torun (Harnik 30), Gentner, Molinaro, Hajnal (Röcker 88), Okazaki (Holzhauser 70). Coach: Bruno Labbadia (GER)

Round of 32 - KRC Genk (BEL)
H 1-1 *Gentner (42)*
Ulreich, Sakai, Kvist, Taşçı, Niedermeier, Harnik (Okazaki 57), Ibišević, Boka, Traoré (Maxim 74), Tunay Torun (Holzhauser 46), Gentner. Coach: Bruno Labbadia (GER)
A 2-0 *Boka (45), Gentner (59)*
Ulreich, Sakai, Kvist, Harnik, Ibišević (Macheda 83), Boka, Traoré (Maxim 75), Gentner, Rüdiger, Okazaki (Holzhauser 77). Coach: Bruno Labbadia (GER)

Round of 16 - S.S. Lazio (ITA)
H 0-2
Ulreich, Sakai, Kvist (Harnik 55), Taşçı, Boka, Traoré, Gentner, Rüdiger, Okazaki, Maxim (Hajnal 41), Macheda (Holzhauser 90+3). Coach: Bruno Labbadia (GER)
A 1-3 *Hajnal (62)*
Ulreich, Sakai, Taşçı, Niedermeier, Ibišević, Gentner, Molinaro, Holzhauser, Hajnal (Harnik 74), Okazaki, Macheda (Traoré 64). Coach: Bruno Labbadia (GER)

HANNOVER 96

Third qualifying round - Saint Patrick's Athletic FC (IRL)
A 3-0 *Andreasen (6), Pander (67), Ya Konan (80)*
Zieler, Andreasen (Schmiedebach 72), Haggui, Eggimann, Cherundolo, Pinto, Huszti (Rausch 57), Ya Konan, Schlaudraff (Abdellaoue 79), Pander, Stindl. Coach: Mirko Slomka (GER)
H 2-0 *Haggui (32), Eggimann (47)*
Zieler, Andreasen, Haggui, Cherundolo, Pinto (Schmiedebach 64), Huszti, Ya Konan (Sobiech 46), Schulz (Eggimann 39), Abdellaoue, Stindl, Rausch. Coach: Mirko Slomka (GER)

Play-offs - WKS Śląsk Wrocław (POL)
A 5-3 *Andreasen (7, 82), Schlaudraff (25), Stindl (40), Schmiedebach (85)*
Zieler, Andreasen, Haggui, Cherundolo, Pinto, Huszti (Schmiedebach 66), Ya Konan (Sobiech 75), Schlaudraff (Nikçi 85), Felipe, Pander, Stindl. Coach: Mirko Slomka (GER)
H 5-1 *Abdellaoue (22), Huszti (35, 88), Sobiech (68, 85)*
Zieler, Andreasen, Haggui, Eggimann, Cherundolo (Sakai 70), Schmiedebach, Huszti, Schlaudraff (Sobiech 63), Schulz (Rausch 39), Abdellaoue, Stindl. Coach: Mirko Slomka (GER)

Group L
Match 1 - FC Twente (NED)
A 2-2 *Sobiech (67), Wisgerhof (73og)*
Zieler, Andreasen (Schmiedebach 75), Eggimann, Cherundolo, Pinto (Nikçi 31), Huszti, Schlaudraff, Felipe, Abdellaoue (Sobiech 46), Stindl, Rausch. Coach: Mirko Slomka (GER)

Match 2 - Levante UD (ESP)
H 2-1 *Huszti (21p), Ya Konan (49)*
Zieler, Haggui, Eggimann, Cherundolo, Pinto, Sobiech (Diouf 76), Huszti (Schmiedebach 85), Ya Konan, Schlaudraff (Felipe 11), Stindl, Rausch. Coach: Mirko Slomka (GER)
Red card: Haggui 9

Match 3 - Helsingborgs IF (SWE)
A 2-1 *Diouf (12), Ya Konan (90+3)*
Zieler, Eggimann, Cherundolo, Pinto, Huszti (Pander 89), Ya Konan, Schulz, Abdellaoue (Sobiech 46), Stindl, Rausch, Diouf (Schmiedebach 75). Coach: Mirko Slomka (GER)

Match 4 - Helsingborgs IF (SWE)
H 3-2 *Diouf (3, 50), Huszti (90+1p)*
Zieler, Haggui, Eggimann, Cherundolo, Schmiedebach, Huszti, Ya Konan (Schlaudraff 72), Schulz, Stindl, Rausch (Pander 73), Diouf (Sobiech 87). Coach: Mirko Slomka (GER)

Match 5 - FC Twente (NED)
H 0-0
Zieler, Haggui, Eggimann, Cherundolo, Pinto, Sobiech, Huszti (Rausch 78), Schlaudraff (Ya Konan 62), Schulz, Nikçi (Schmiedebach 71), Pander. Coach: Mirko Slomka (GER)

Match 6 - Levante UD (ESP)
A 2-2 *Stindl (18), Ya Konan (26)*
Zieler, Haggui, Sakai, Pinto, Schmiedebach, Huszti (Cherundolo 71), Ya Konan (Abdellaoue 90), Schulz, Stindl (Nikçi 38), Rausch, Diouf. Coach: Mirko Slomka (GER)

Round of 32 - FC Anji Makhachkala (RUS)
A 1-3 *Huszti (22)*
Zieler, Pinto, Schmiedebach, Huszti, Ya Konan, Schlaudraff (Abdellaoue 67), Djourou, Pocognoli (Pander 79), Schulz, Chahed, Diouf (Sobiech 71). Coach: Mirko Slomka (GER)
H 1-1 *Pinto (70)*
Zieler, Sakai (Sobiech 83), Pinto, Schmiedebach (Schlaudraff 61), Huszti, Ya Konan, Djourou, Pocognoli (Rausch 70), Schulz, Abdellaoue, Diouf. Coach: Mirko Slomka (GER)

Domestic league club-by-club

FC AUGSBURG

Coach: Markus Weinzierl
1907 • SGL arena (30,660) • fcaugsburg.de

2012

25/08	Düsseldorf	h	0-2	
01/09	Schalke	a	1-3	Oehrl
14/09	Wolfsburg	h	0-0	
22/09	Mainz	a	0-2	
26/09	Leverkusen	h	1-3	Werner
29/09	Hoffenheim	a	0-0	
05/10	Bremen	h	3-1	Werner, Hain, Baier
21/10	Nürnberg	h	0-0	
26/10	Hamburg	h	0-2	
03/11	Hannover	a	0-2	
10/11	Dortmund	h	1-3	Mölders
17/11	Eintracht	a	2-4	Koo, Mölders
25/11	Mönchengladbach	h	1-1	Mölders
28/11	Stuttgart	a	1-2	Koo
01/12	Freiburg	h	1-1	Werner
08/12	Bayern	h	0-2	
15/12	Fürth	a	1-1	Mölders

2013

20/01	Düsseldorf	a	3-2	Mölders 2, Koo
26/01	Schalke	h	0-0	
02/02	Wolfsburg	a	1-1	Mandžukić
10/02	Mainz	h	1-1	Mölders
16/02	Leverkusen	a	1-2	Mölders
23/02	Hoffenheim	h	2-1	Ji, Mölders
02/03	Bremen	a	1-0	Werner
08/03	Nürnberg	h	1-2	Werner
16/03	Hamburg	a	1-0	Callsen-Bracker
30/03	Hannover	h	0-2	
06/04	Dortmund	a	2-4	Baier, Vogt
14/04	Eintracht	h	2-0	Ji 2
19/04	Mönchengladbach	a	0-1	
27/04	Stuttgart	h	3-0	Mölders, De Jong, Ji
05/05	Freiburg	a	0-2	
11/05	Bayern	a	0-3	
18/05	Fürth	h	3-1	Werner, Callsen-Bracker, Ji

No	Name	Nat	DoB	Pos	Aps	(s)	Gls
30	Mohamed Amsif	MAR	17/02/89	G	17		
10	Daniel Baier		18/05/84	M	33		2
23	Aristide Bancé	BFA	19/09/84	A	4	(14)	
18	Jan-Ingwer Callsen-Bracker		28/03/84	M	23	(1)	2
7	Marcel de Jong	CAN	15/10/86	D	14	(6)	1
4	André Hahn		13/08/90	M	12	(4)	
36	Stephan Hain		27/07/87	A	3	(9)	1
1	Simon Jentzsch		04/05/76	G	5		
27	Ji Dong-won	KOR	28/07/91	A	17		5
5	Ragnar Klavan	EST	30/10/85	D	29	(1)	
14	Koo Ja-cheol	KOR	27/02/89	M	18	(3)	3
15	Sebastian Langkamp		15/01/88	D	11		
21	Alex Manninger	AUT	04/06/77	G	12		
33	Sascha Mölders		22/03/85	A	23	(1)	10
5	Jan Morávek	CZE	01/11/89	M	16	(5)	1
8	Knowledge Musona	ZIM	21/06/90	M	8	(6)	
9	Torsten Oehrl		07/01/86	A	11	(16)	1
19	Matthias Ostrzolek		05/06/90	D	22	(3)	
16	Andreas Ott		01/03/85	M	10	(3)	
24	Michael Parkhurst	USA	24/01/84	A	1	(1)	
11	Milan Petržela	CZE	19/06/83	M	5	(7)	
20	Ronny Philp		28/01/89	D	4		
4	Dominik Reinhardt		19/12/84	D	2	(2)	
3	Gibril Sankoh	SLE	15/05/83	D	9	(2)	
22	Giovanni Sio	FRA	31/03/89	A		(6)	
22	Somen Tchoyi	CMR	29/03/83	M		(2)	
2	Paul Verhaegh	NED	01/09/83	D	16	(1)	
6	Kevin Vogt		23/09/91	M	20	(8)	1
13	Tobias Werner		19/07/85	M	29	(1)	6

BAYER 04 LEVERKUSEN

Coach: Sami Hyypiä (FIN) & Sascha Lewandowski
1904 • BayArena (30,210) • bayer04.de
Major honours
UEFA Cup (1) 1988;
German Cup (1) 1993

2012

25/08	Eintracht	a	1-2	Kiessling
01/09	Freiburg	h	2-0	Castro, Wollscheid
15/09	Dortmund	a	0-3	
23/09	Mönchengladbach	h	1-1	Kadlec
26/09	Augsburg	a	3-1	Kiessling, Wollscheid, Schürrle
29/09	Fürth	h	2-0	Sam 2
07/10	Stuttgart	a	2-2	Kiessling 2
20/10	Mainz	h	2-2	Kiessling, Castro
28/10	Bayern	a	2-1	Kiessling, Sam
04/11	Düsseldorf	h	3-2	Sam, Schürrle, Castro
11/11	Wolfsburg	a	1-3	Kiessling
17/11	Schalke	h	2-0	Schürrle, Kiessling
25/11	Hoffenheim	a	2-1	Bender, Carvajal
28/11	Bremen	a	4-1	Castro 2, Rolfes, Hegeler
01/12	Nürnberg	h	1-0	Kiessling
09/12	Hannover	a	2-3	Castro, Kiessling
16/12	Hamburg	h	3-0	Kiessling 2, Schürrle

2013

19/01	Eintracht	h	3-1	Boenisch, Kiessling, Schürrle
26/01	Freiburg	a	0-0	
03/02	Dortmund	h	2-3	Reinartz 2
09/02	Mönchengladbach	a	3-3	Sam, Kiessling, Schürrle
16/02	Augsburg	h	2-1	Kiessling, Bender
24/02	Fürth	a	0-0	
02/03	Stuttgart	h	2-1	Kiessling (p), Bender
09/03	Mainz	a	0-1	
16/03	Bayern	h	1-2	Rolfes
30/03	Düsseldorf	a	4-1	Kiessling 2 (1p), Schürrle 2
06/04	Wolfsburg	h	1-1	Schürrle
13/04	Schalke	a	2-2	Rolfes, Kiessling
20/04	Hoffenheim	h	5-0	Kiessling 2, Schürrle 2, Reinartz
27/04	Bremen	h	1-0	Kiessling (p)
04/05	Nürnberg	a	2-0	Ömer, Kiessling (p)
11/05	Hannover	h	3-1	Hegeler 2, Kiessling
18/05	Hamburg	a	1-0	Kiessling

No	Name	Nat	DoB	Pos	Aps	(s)	Gls
38	Karim Bellarabi		08/04/90	M	5	(3)	
8	Lars Bender		27/04/89	M	32	(1)	3
17	Sebastian Boenisch	POL	01/02/87	D	12	(3)	1
20	Daniel Carvajal	ESP	11/01/92	D	31	(1)	1
27	Gonzalo Castro		11/06/87	D	29	(2)	6
7	Junior Fernandes	CHI	04/10/88	A		(6)	
5	Manuel Friedrich		13/09/79	D	5	(6)	
13	Jens Hegeler		22/01/88	M	5	(22)	4
14	Hajime Hosogai	JPN	10/06/86	M	9	(8)	
24	Michal Kadlec	CZE	13/12/84	D	14		1
11	Stefan Kiessling		25/01/84	A	34		25
31	Dominik Kohr		31/01/94	M		(4)	
23	Bernd Leno		04/03/92	G	32		
16	Arkadiusz Milik	POL	28/02/94	A		(6)	
19	Okan Aydın	TUR	03/05/94	A		(1)	
21	Ömer Toprak	TUR	21/07/89	D	26		1
3	Stefan Reinartz		01/01/89	M	29		3
10	Renato Augusto	BRA	08/02/88	M		(6)	
33	Michael Rensing		14/05/84	G	2		
6	Simon Rolfes		21/01/82	M	26	(4)	3
18	Sidney Sam		31/01/88	M	10	(12)	5
9	André Schürrle		06/11/90	A	34		11
2	Daniel Schwaab		23/08/88	D	8	(8)	
4	Philipp Wollscheid		06/03/89	D	31		2

FC BAYERN MÜNCHEN

Coach: Jupp Heynckes
1900 • Allianz-Arena (71,137) • fcbayern.de
Major honours
European Champion Clubs' Cup/UEFA Champions League (5) 1974, 1975, 1976, 2001, 2013;
UEFA Cup Winners' Cup (1) 1967;
UEFA Cup (1) 1996;
European/South American Cup (2) 1976, 2001;
German League (23) 1932, 1969, 1972, 1973, 1974, 1980, 1981, 1985, 1986, 1987, 1989, 1990, 1994, 1997, 1999, 2000, 2001, 2003, 2005, 2006, 2008, 2010, 2013;
German Cup (16) 1957, 1966, 1967, 1969, 1971, 1982, 1984, 1986, 1998, 2000, 2003, 2005, 2006, 2008, 2010, 2013

2012

25/08	Fürth	a	3-0	Müller, Mandžukić, og (Kleine)
02/09	Stuttgart	h	6-1	Müller 2, Kroos, Luiz Gustavo, Mandžukić, Schweinsteiger
15/09	Mainz	h	3-1	Mandžukić, Schweinsteiger, Kroos
22/09	Schalke	a	2-0	Kroos, Müller
25/09	Wolfsburg	h	3-0	Schweinsteiger, Mandžukić 2
29/09	Bremen	a	2-0	Luiz Gustavo, Mandžukić
06/10	Hoffenheim	h	2-0	Ribéry 2
20/10	Düsseldorf	a	5-0	Mandžukić, Luiz Gustavo, Müller 2, Rafinha
28/10	Leverkusen	h	1-2	Mandžukić
03/11	Hamburg	a	3-0	Schweinsteiger, Müller, Kroos
10/11	Eintracht	h	2-0	Ribéry, Alaba (p)
17/11	Nürnberg	a	1-1	Mandžukić
24/11	Hannover	h	5-0	Javi Martínez, Kroos, Ribéry, Dante, Gomez
28/11	Freiburg	a	2-0	Müller (p), Tymoshchuk
01/12	Dortmund	h	1-1	Kroos
08/12	Augsburg	h	2-0	Müller (p), Gomez
14/12	Mönchengladbach	h	1-1	Shaqiri

2013

19/01	Fürth	h	2-0	Mandžukić 2
27/01	Stuttgart	a	2-0	Mandžukić, Müller
02/02	Mainz	a	3-0	Müller, Mandžukić 2
09/02	Schalke	h	4-0	Alaba 2 (1p), Schweinsteiger, Gomez
15/02	Wolfsburg	h	2-0	Mandžukić, Robben
23/02	Bremen	h	6-1	Robben, Javi Martínez, og (Gebre Selassie), Gomez 2, Ribéry
03/03	Hoffenheim	a	1-0	Gomez
09/03	Düsseldorf	h	3-2	Müller, Ribéry, Boateng
16/03	Leverkusen	a	2-1	Gomez, og (Wollscheid)
30/03	Hamburg	h	9-2	Shaqiri, Schweinsteiger, Pizarro 4, Robben 2, Ribéry
06/04	Eintracht	a	1-0	Schweinsteiger
13/04	Nürnberg	h	4-0	Boateng, Gomez, Rafinha, Shaqiri
20/04	Hannover	a	6-1	og (Stindl), Ribéry, Gomez 2, Pizarro 2
27/04	Freiburg	h	1-0	Can
04/05	Dortmund	a	1-1	Gomez
11/05	Augsburg	h	3-0	Müller, Shaqiri, Luiz Gustavo
18/05	Mönchengladbach	a	4-3	Javi Martínez, Ribéry 2, Robben

No	Name	Nat	DoB	Pos	Aps	(s)	Gls
27	David Alaba	AUT	24/06/92	D	22	(1)	3
28	Holger Badstuber		13/03/89	D	12		
17	Jérôme Boateng		03/09/88	D	25	(1)	2
36	Emre Can		12/01/94	M	2	(2)	1
26	Diego Contento		01/05/90	D	4	(1)	
4	Dante	BRA	18/10/83	D	29		1
33	Mario Gomez		10/07/85	A	9	(12)	11
34	Pierre Højbjerg	DEN	05/08/95	M		(2)	
8	Javi Martínez	ESP	02/09/88	M	19	(8)	3
39	Toni Kroos		04/01/90	M	23	(1)	6
21	Philipp Lahm		11/11/83	D	28	(1)	
30	Luiz Gustavo	BRA	23/07/87	M	16	(6)	4
9	Mario Mandžukić	CRO	21/05/86	A	22	(2)	15
25	Thomas Müller		13/09/89	M	25	(3)	13
1	Manuel Neuer		27/03/86	G	31		
14	Claudio Pizarro	PER	03/10/78	A	7	(13)	6
13	Rafinha	BRA	07/09/85	M	6	(7)	2
7	Franck Ribéry	FRA	07/04/83	M	24	(3)	10
10	Arjen Robben	NED	23/01/84	M	11	(5)	5
31	Bastian Schweinsteiger		01/08/84	M	27	(1)	7
11	Xherdan Shaqiri	SUI	10/10/91	M	13	(13)	4
22	Tom Starke		18/03/81	G	3		
44	Anatoliy Tymoshchuk	UKR	30/03/79	M	5	(11)	1
5	Daniel Van Buyten	BEL	07/02/78	D	11	(2)	

BORUSSIA DORTMUND

Coach: Jürgen Klopp
1909 • Signal-Iduna-Park (80,720) • bvb.de
Major honours
UEFA Champions League (1) 1997;
UEFA Cup Winners' Cup (1) 1966;
European/South American Cup (1) 1997;
German League (8) 1956, 1957, 1963, 1995, 1996,
2002, 2011, 2012;
German Cup (3) 1965, 1989, 2012

2012

24/08	Bremen	h	2-1	Reus, Götze
01/09	Nürnberg	a	1-1	Błaszczykowski
15/09	Leverkusen	h	3-0	Hummels, Błaszczykowski, Lewandowski
22/09	Hamburg	a	2-3	Perišić 2
25/09	Eintracht	a	3-3	Piszczek, Reus, Götze
29/09	Mönchengladbach	h	5-0	Reus 2, Subotić, Gündoğan, Błaszczykowski
07/10	Hannover	a	1-1	Lewandowski
20/10	Schalke	h	1-2	Lewandowski
27/10	Freiburg	a	2-0	Subotić, Götze
03/11	Stuttgart	h	0-0	
10/11	Augsburg	a	3-1	Reus, Lewandowski 2
17/11	Fürth	h	3-1	Lewandowski 2 (1p), Götze
24/11	Mainz	a	2-1	Lewandowski 2
27/11	Düsseldorf	h	1-1	Błaszczykowski
01/12	Bayern	a	1-1	Götze
08/12	Wolfsburg	h	2-3	Reus, Błaszczykowski (p)
16/12	Hoffenheim	a	3-1	Götze, Grosskreutz, Lewandowski

2013

19/01	Bremen	a	5-0	Reus, Götze, Felipe Santana, Lewandowski, Błaszczykowski
25/01	Nürnberg	h	3-0	Błaszczykowski 2 (1p), Lewandowski
03/02	Leverkusen	a	3-2	Reus, Błaszczykowski (p), Lewandowski
09/02	Hamburg	h	1-4	Lewandowski
16/02	Eintracht	h	3-0	Reus 3
24/02	Mönchengladbach	a	1-1	Götze (p)
02/03	Hannover	h	3-1	Lewandowski 2, Schieber
09/03	Schalke	a	1-2	Lewandowski
16/03	Freiburg	h	5-1	Lewandowski 2, Nuri 2, Bittencourt
30/03	Stuttgart	a	2-1	Piszczek, Lewandowski
06/04	Augsburg	h	4-2	Schieber 2, Subotić, Lewandowski
13/04	Fürth	a	6-1	Götze 2, Gündoğan 2, Błaszczykowski, Lewandowski
20/04	Mainz	h	2-0	Reus, Lewandowski
27/04	Düsseldorf	a	2-1	Nuri, Błaszczykowski
04/05	Bayern	h	1-1	Grosskreutz
11/05	Wolfsburg	a	3-3	Bender, Reus 2
18/05	Hoffenheim	h	1-2	Lewandowski

No	Name	Nat	DoB	Pos	Aps	(s)	Gls
12	Bálint Bajner	HUN	18/11/90	A		(1)	
22	Sven Bender		27/04/89	M	15	(5)	1
32	Leonardo Bittencourt		19/12/93	M	2	(3)	1
16	Jakub Błaszczykowski	POL	14/12/85	M	23	(4)	11
27	Felipe Santana	BRA	17/03/86	D	15	(6)	1
11	Mario Götze		03/06/92	M	23	(5)	10
19	Kevin Grosskreutz		19/07/88	M	19	(10)	2
21	İlkay Gündoğan		24/10/90	M	26	(2)	3
35	Jonas Hofmann		14/07/92	M	2	(1)	
15	Mats Hummels		16/12/88	D	28		1
5	Sebastian Kehl		13/02/80	M	19	(3)	
21	Oliver Kirch		21/08/82	D	2	(2)	
20	Mitchell Langerak	AUS	22/08/88	G	3		
7	Moritz Leitner		08/12/92	M	8	(13)	
9	Robert Lewandowski	POL	21/08/88	A	29	(2)	24
18	Nuri Şahin	TUR	05/09/88	M	9	(6)	3
14	Ivan Perišić	CRO	02/02/89	M	5	(9)	2
26	Łukasz Piszczek	POL	03/06/85	D	28	(1)	2
11	Marco Reus		31/05/89	M	27	(5)	14
23	Julian Schieber		13/02/89	A	6	(17)	3
29	Marcel Schmelzer		22/01/88	D	29		
4	Neven Subotić	SRB	10/12/88	D	25		3
1	Roman Weidenfeller		06/08/80	G	31		

VFL BORUSSIA MÖNCHENGLADBACH

Coach: Lucien Favre (SUI)
1900 • Borussia-Park (54,067) • borussia.de
Major honours
UEFA Cup (2) 1975, 1979;
German League (5) 1970, 1971, 1975, 1976, 1977;
German Cup (3) 1960, 1973, 1995

2012

25/08	Hoffenheim	h	2-1	Hanke, Arango
01/09	Düsseldorf	a	0-0	
15/09	Nürnberg	h	2-3	De Jong, Xhaka
23/09	Leverkusen	a	1-1	Herrmann
26/09	Hamburg	h	2-2	Stranzl, Álvaro Domínguez
29/09	Dortmund	a	0-5	
07/10	Eintracht	h	2-0	Arango, De Jong
20/10	Bremen	a	0-4	
28/10	Hannover	a	3-2	Álvaro Domínguez, Brouwers, Arango
03/11	Freiburg	h	1-1	De Camargo
11/11	Fürth	a	4-2	Wendt, Stranzl, Herrmann, Marx (p)
17/11	Stuttgart	h	1-2	Stranzl
25/11	Augsburg	a	1-1	Herrmann
28/11	Wolfsburg	h	2-0	Arango, Jantschke
01/12	Schalke	a	1-1	De Camargo
09/12	Mainz	h	2-0	Hanke, Arango
14/12	Bayern	a	1-1	Marx (p)

2013

19/01	Hoffenheim	a	0-0	
26/01	Düsseldorf	h	2-1	og (Juanan), Herrmann
02/02	Nürnberg	a	1-2	Herrmann
09/02	Leverkusen	h	3-3	Stranzl, De Jong, Herrmann
16/02	Hamburg	a	0-1	
24/02	Dortmund	h	1-1	Younes
01/03	Eintracht	a	1-0	De Jong
09/03	Bremen	h	1-1	Mlapa
17/03	Hannover	h	1-0	De Jong
30/03	Freiburg	a	0-2	
06/04	Fürth	h	1-0	De Jong
14/04	Stuttgart	a	0-2	
19/04	Augsburg	h	1-0	Daems (p)
27/04	Wolfsburg	a	1-3	Mlapa
03/05	Schalke	h	0-1	
11/05	Mainz	a	4-2	Hrgota 3 (p), Hanke
18/05	Bayern	h	3-4	Stranzl, Hanke, Nordtveit

No	Name	Nat	DoB	Pos	Aps	(s)	Gls
15	Álvaro Domínguez	ESP	16/05/89	D	30		2
18	Juan Arango	VEN	17/05/80	M	31		5
4	Roel Brouwers	NED	28/11/81	D	15	(6)	1
6	Tolga Ciğerci		23/03/92	M	9	(3)	
3	Filip Daems	BEL	31/10/78	D	16	(3)	1
10	Igor De Camargo	BEL	12/05/83	A	7	(7)	2
19	Luuk de Jong	NED	27/08/90	A	17	(6)	6
19	Mike Hanke		05/11/83	A	13	(19)	4
33	Christofer Heimeroth		01/08/81	G		(1)	
7	Patrick Herrmann		12/02/91	M	30	(2)	6
31	Branimir Hrgota	SWE	12/01/93	A	2	(11)	3
23	Tony Jantschke		07/04/90	D	31		1
14	Thorben Marx		01/06/81	M	23		2
22	Peniel Mlapa		20/02/91	A	3	(17)	2
16	Håvard Nordtveit	NOR	21/06/90	M	30	(1)	1
5	Alexander Ring	FIN	09/04/91	M	2	(6)	
8	Lukas Rupp		08/01/91	M	13	(8)	
39	Martin Stranzl	AUT	16/06/80	D	26		5
1	Marc-André ter Stegen		30/04/92	G	34		
17	Oscar Wendt	SWE	24/10/85	D	21		1
34	Granit Xhaka	SUI	27/09/92	M	15	(7)	1
25	Amin Younes		06/08/93	M	6	(5)	1

EINTRACHT FRANKFURT

Coach: Armin Veh
1899 • Commerzbank-Arena (51,500) • eintrachtfrankfurt.de
Major honours
UEFA-Cup (1) 1980;
German League (1) 1959;
German Cup (4) 1974, 1975, 1981, 1988

2012

25/08	Leverkusen	h	2-1	Aigner, Lanig
01/09	Hoffenheim	a	4-0	Meier 2 (1p), Schwegler, Lanig
16/09	Hamburg	h	3-2	Inui, Océan, Aigner
21/09	Nürnberg	a	2-1	Hoffer, Inui
25/09	Dortmund	h	3-3	Aigner, Inui, Anderson Bamba
30/09	Freiburg	h	2-1	Meier 2
07/10	Mönchengladbach	a	0-2	
20/10	Hannover	h	3-1	Matmour, Jung, Meier
28/10	Stuttgart	a	1-2	Meier
02/11	Fürth	h	1-1	Meier
10/11	Bayern	a	0-2	
17/11	Augsburg	h	4-2	og (Mölders), Aigner, Meier 2 (1p)
24/11	Schalke	a	1-1	Aigner
27/11	Mainz	h	1-3	og (Szalai)
30/11	Düsseldorf	a	0-4	
08/12	Bremen	h	4-1	Meier, Schwegler, Aigner, Inui
15/12	Wolfsburg	a	2-0	Meier, Inui

2013

19/01	Leverkusen	a	1-3	Meier
26/01	Hoffenheim	h	2-1	Lanig, Aigner
02/02	Hamburg	a	2-0	Lakić 2
09/02	Nürnberg	h	0-0	
16/02	Dortmund	a	0-3	
22/02	Freiburg	a	0-0	
01/03	Mönchengladbach	h	0-1	
10/03	Hannover	a	0-0	
17/03	Stuttgart	h	1-2	Aigner
31/03	Fürth	a	3-2	Inui, Aigner, Meier
06/04	Bayern	h	0-1	
14/04	Augsburg	a	0-2	
20/04	Schalke	h	1-0	Russ
28/04	Mainz	a	0-0	
04/05	Düsseldorf	h	3-1	Meier 2, Lakić
11/05	Bremen	a	1-1	Lakić
18/05	Wolfsburg	h	2-2	Meier (p), og (Rodriguez)

No	Name	Nat	DoB	Pos	Aps	(s)	Gls
16	Stefan Aigner		20/08/87	M	34		9
23	Anderson Bamba	BRA	10/01/88	D	28		1
32	Aykut Özer	TUR	01/01/93	G		(1)	
3	Heiko Butscher		28/07/80	D	2	(1)	
22	Stefano Celozzi		02/11/88	D	6	(23)	
4	Vadim Demidov	NOR	10/10/86	D	4	(1)	
15	Constant Djakpa	CIV	17/10/86	D	1	(4)	
10	Erwin Hoffer	AUT	14/04/87	A	2	(4)	1
8	Takashi Inui	JPN	02/06/88	M	33		6
24	Sebastian Jung		22/06/90	D	32		1
36	Marc-Oliver Kempf		28/01/95	D	2		
28	Sonny Kittel		06/01/93	M		(6)	
7	Benjamin Köhler		04/08/80	M		(6)	
99	Dorge Kouemaha	CMR	28/06/83	A		(2)	
11	Srdjan Lakić	CRO	02/10/83	A	9	(5)	4
13	Martin Lanig		11/07/84	M	4	(15)	3
21	Karim Matmour	ALG	25/06/85	M	12	(12)	1
14	Alexander Meier		17/01/83	M	31		16
1	Oka Nikolov	MKD	25/05/74	G	8		
9	Olivier Océan	CAN	23/10/81	A	10	(8)	1
6	Bastian Oczipka		12/01/89	D	33		
20	Sebastian Rode		11/10/90	M	33		
4	Marco Russ		04/08/85	A	7	(3)	1
27	Pirmin Schwegler	SUI	09/03/87	M	25	(2)	2
37	Marc Stendera		10/12/95	M	2	(3)	
31	Kevin Trapp		08/07/90	G	26		
2	Carlos Zambrano	PER	10/07/89	D	30		

FORTUNA DÜSSELDORF

Coach: Norbert Meier
1895 • Esprit-Arena (54,500) • fortuna-duesseldorf.de
Major honours
German League (1) 1933;
German Cup (2) 1979, 1980

2012

25/08	Augsburg	a	2-0	Schahin 2
01/09	Mönchengladbach	h	0-0	
15/09	Stuttgart	a	0-0	
22/09	Freiburg	h	0-0	
25/09	Fürth	a	2-0	Fink, Ilsø
28/09	Schalke	h	2-2	Schahin 2
06/10	Mainz	a	0-1	
20/10	Bayern	h	0-5	
27/10	Wolfsburg	h	1-4	Langeneke (p)
04/11	Leverkusen	a	2-3	Nando Rafael, Bodzek
10/11	Hoffenheim	h	1-1	Kruse
18/11	Bremen	a	1-2	Langeneke (p)
23/11	Hamburg	h	2-0	Kruse, Reisinger
27/11	Dortmund	a	1-1	Reisinger
30/11	Eintracht	h	4-0	Reisinger, Fink, Nando Rafael, Bellinghausen
08/12	Nürnberg	a	0-2	
15/12	Hannover	h	2-1	Schahin, Ilsø

2013

20/01	Augsburg	h	2-3	Reisinger 2
26/01	Mönchengladbach	a	1-2	Schahin (p)
02/02	Stuttgart	h	3-1	Kruse 2, Fink
10/02	Freiburg	a	0-1	
16/02	Fürth	a	1-0	Bellinghausen
23/02	Schalke	a	1-2	Bellinghausen
03/03	Mainz	h	1-1	og (Svensson)
09/03	Bayern	a	2-3	Bolly, Lambertz
15/03	Wolfsburg	a	1-1	Bolly
30/03	Leverkusen	h	1-4	og (Schwaab)
05/04	Hoffenheim	a	0-3	
13/04	Bremen	h	2-2	Reisinger 2
20/04	Hamburg	a	1-2	Schahin
27/04	Dortmund	h	1-2	Bodzek
04/05	Eintracht	a	1-3	Schahin
11/05	Nürnberg	h	1-2	og (Balitsch)
18/05	Hannover	a	0-3	

No	Name	Nat	DoB	Pos	Aps	(s)	Gls
1	Robert Almer	AUT	20/03/84	G		(1)	
3	Leon Balogun		28/06/88	D	16	(1)	
11	Axel Bellinghausen		17/05/83	M	25	(6)	3
13	Adam Bodzek		07/09/85	M	29		2
35	Mathis Bolly	NOR	14/11/90	A	5	(2)	2
22	Cha Du-ri	KOR	25/07/80	M	1	(9)	
7	Oliver Fink		06/06/82	M	21	(5)	3
8	André Fomitschow		07/09/90	M		(1)	
18	Ronny Garbuschewski		23/02/86	M	3	(4)	
33	Fabian Giefer		17/05/90	G	34		
10	Ken Ilsø	DEN	02/12/86	M	14	(13)	2
5	Juanan	ESP	27/04/87	D	13	(2)	
23	Robbie Kruse	AUS	05/10/88	M	29	(1)	4
17	Andreas Lambertz		15/10/84	M	26	(2)	1
6	Jens Langeneke		29/03/77	D	16		2
2	Martin Latka	CZE	28/09/84	D	13		
19	Tobias Levels		22/11/86	D	17	(2)	
4	Stilianos Malezas	GRE	11/03/85	D	21		
9	Nando Rafael	ANG	10/01/84	A	4	(7)	2
39	Genki Omae	JPN	10/12/89	M	2	(5)	
27	Ivan Paurević	CRO	01/07/91	M	2	(2)	
27	Stefan Reisinger		14/09/81	A	15	(9)	7
3	Dani Schahin		09/07/89	A	16	(15)	8
8	Robert Tesche		27/05/87	M	12	(2)	
21	Johannes van den Bergh		21/11/86	D	33		
30	Andriy Voronin	UKR	21/07/79	M	6	(4)	
22	Christian Weber		15/09/83	M	1		
16	Gerrit Wegkamp		13/04/93	A		(3)	

SC FREIBURG

Coach: Christian Streich
1904 • Mage Solar Stadium (24,000) • scfreiburg.com

2012

25/08	Mainz	h	1-1	Kruse
01/09	Leverkusen	a	0-2	
16/09	Hoffenheim	h	5-3	Guédé, Kruse, Diagne, Makiadi, Freis
22/09	Düsseldorf	a	0-0	
26/09	Bremen	h	1-2	Schmid
30/09	Eintracht	h	1-2	Kruse
06/10	Nürnberg	h	3-0	Makiadi, Caligiuri (p), Terrazzino
20/10	Wolfsburg	a	2-0	Caligiuri (p), Schuster
27/10	Dortmund	h	0-2	
03/11	Mönchengladbach	a	1-1	Caligiuri (p)
10/11	Hamburg	h	0-0	
17/11	Hannover	a	2-1	Schmid, Rosenthal
25/11	Stuttgart	h	3-0	Rosenthal, Krmaš, Kruse
28/11	Bayern	h	0-2	
01/12	Augsburg	a	1-1	Schmid
08/12	Fürth	h	1-0	Caligiuri
15/12	Schalke	a	3-1	Rosenthal 2, Schmid

2013

19/01	Mainz	a	0-0	
26/01	Leverkusen	h	0-0	
02/02	Hoffenheim	a	1-2	Kruse
10/02	Düsseldorf	h	1-0	Krmaš
16/02	Bremen	a	3-2	Kruse, Caligiuri (p), Ginter
22/02	Eintracht	h	0-0	
02/03	Nürnberg	a	1-1	Schmid
09/03	Wolfsburg	h	2-5	Kruse, Flum
16/03	Dortmund	a	1-5	Schmid
30/03	Mönchengladbach	h	2-0	Kruse 2
06/04	Hamburg	a	1-0	Schmid
12/04	Hannover	h	3-1	og (Schulz), Kruse, Schmid
21/04	Stuttgart	a	1-2	Santini
27/04	Bayern	a	0-1	
05/05	Augsburg	h	2-0	Makiadi, Schmid
11/05	Fürth	a	2-1	Schmid, Kruse
18/05	Schalke	h	1-2	Schmid

No	Name	Nat	DoB	Pos	Aps	(s)	Gls
29	Tim Albutat		23/09/92	M		(1)	
07	Oliver Baumann		02/06/90	G	31		
40	Daniel Caligiuri		15/01/88	M	27	(2)	5
11	Garra Dembélé	MLI	21/02/86	A		(3)	
13	Fallou Diagne	SEN	10/11/86	D	29	(1)	1
21	Ezequiel	ESP	12/01/91	M		(2)	
18	Johannes Flum		14/12/87	M	10	(16)	1
35	Sebastian Freis		23/04/85	A	6	(6)	1
28	Matthias Ginter		19/01/94	M	21	(2)	1
31	Karim Guédé	SVK	07/01/85	M	12	(9)	1
30	Christian Günter		28/02/93	D	3	(4)	
6	Vegar Eggen Hedenstad	NOR	26/06/91	D	9	(7)	
41	Immanuel Höhn		23/12/91	D	5	(3)	
26	Erik Jendrišek	SVK	26/10/86	A	4	(5)	
37	Sebastian Kerk		17/04/94	M	1		
2	Pavel Krmaš	CZE	03/03/80	D	16	(1)	2
20	Max Kruse		19/03/88	A	33	(1)	11
32	Max Lais		04/02/91	M		(1)	
7	Cédric Makiadi	COD	23/02/84	M	26	(3)	3
24	Mensur Mujdža	BIH	28/03/84	D	21	(2)	
14	Anton Putilo	BLR	07/06/87	M	1	(1)	
8	Jan Rosenthal		07/04/86	A	18	(2)	4
9	Ivan Santini	CRO	21/05/89	A	1	(13)	1
17	Jonathan Schmid	FRA	26/06/90	M	33		11
23	Julian Schuster		15/04/85	M	31	(1)	
25	Oliver Sorg		29/05/90	D	32		
22	Marco Terrazzino		15/04/91	A	1	(5)	1

SPVGG GREUTHER FÜRTH

Coach: Michael Büskens; (21/02/13) (Ludwig Preis); (12/03/13) Frank Kramer
1903 • Trolli-Arena (18,000) • greuther-fuerth.de
Major honours
German League (3) 1914, 1926, 1929

2012

25/08	Bayern	h	0-3	
31/08	Mainz	a	1-0	Klaus
15/09	Schalke	h	0-2	
22/09	Wolfsburg	a	1-1	og (Pogatetz)
25/09	Düsseldorf	h	0-2	
29/09	Leverkusen	a	0-2	
06/10	Hamburg	h	0-1	
19/10	Hoffenheim	a	3-3	Stieber, Prib, Sobiech
27/10	Bremen	h	1-1	Edu
02/11	Eintracht	a	1-1	Stieber
11/11	Mönchengladbach	h	2-4	Nehrig (p), Prib
17/11	Dortmund	a	1-3	Stieber
24/11	Nürnberg	h	0-0	
27/11	Hannover	a	0-2	
08/12	Stuttgart	h	0-1	
08/12	Freiburg	a	0-1	
15/12	Augsburg	h	1-1	Sobiech

2013

19/01	Bayern	a	0-2	
26/01	Mainz	a	0-3	
02/02	Schalke	a	2-1	Klaus, Djurdjić
09/02	Wolfsburg	h	0-1	
16/02	Düsseldorf	h	0-1	
24/02	Leverkusen	h	0-0	
02/03	Hamburg	a	1-1	Djurdjić
09/03	Hoffenheim	h	0-3	
16/03	Bremen	a	2-2	Fürstner, Petsos
31/03	Eintracht	a	2-3	Djurdjić, Sercan
06/04	Mönchengladbach	a	0-1	
13/04	Dortmund	h	1-6	Prib
21/04	Nürnberg	a	1-0	Geis
26/04	Hannover	h	2-3	Djurdjić 2
04/05	Stuttgart	a	2-0	og (Sakai), Azemi
11/05	Freiburg	h	1-2	Zimmermann
18/05	Augsburg	a	1-3	Trinks

No	Name	Nat	DoB	Pos	Aps	(s)	Gls
11	Gerald Asamoah		03/10/78	A	12	(5)	
33	Illir Azemi	ALB	21/02/92	A	3	(18)	1
40	Nikola Djurdjić	SRB	01/04/86	A	14	(1)	5
32	Edu	BRA	30/11/81	A	7	(3)	1
24	Baye Djiby Fall	SEN	20/04/85	A	2		
8	Stephan Fürstner		11/09/87	M	30		1
30	Johannes Geis		17/08/93	D	7	(1)	1
26	Max Grün		05/04/87	G	17		
15	Michael Hefele		01/09/90	D		(1)	
1	Wolfgang Hesl		13/01/86	G	17		
36	Felix Klaus		13/09/92	M	19	(5)	2
19	Thomas Kleine		28/12/77	D	19	(3)	
5	Mërgim Mavraj	ALB	09/06/86	D	32		
27	Tobias Mikkelsen	DEN	18/09/86	M		(6)	
7	Bernd Nehrig		28/09/86	D	24	(2)	1
9	Christopher Nöthe		03/01/88	A	5	(8)	
32	Park Jung-bin	KOR	22/02/94	M	4	(5)	
11	Milorad Peković	MNE	05/08/77	M	14	(4)	
34	Tayfun Pektürk		13/05/88	M	1	(2)	
22	Athanasios Petsos	GRE	05/06/91	M	9	(5)	1
7	Thomas Pledl		23/05/94	M	3	(4)	
14	Edgar Prib		15/12/89	M	25	(2)	3
18	Baba Rahman	GHA	02/07/94	D	18	(2)	
6	Geynrich Schmidtgal	KAZ	20/11/85	D	16	(2)	
23	Sercan Sararer	TUR	27/11/89	M	21	(1)	1
2	Lasse Sobiech		18/01/91	D	17	(2)	2
16	Zoltán Stieber	HUN	16/10/88	M	14	(2)	3
27	Florian Trinks		11/03/92	M	1	(1)	1
10	Sebastian Tyrala	POL	22/02/88	M	1		
34	Jószef Varga	HUN	06/06/88	M	6		
21	Robert Zillner		04/08/85	M	3	(3)	
38	Matthias Zimmermann		16/06/92	A	13	(2)	1

GERMANY

HAMBURGER SV

Coach: Thorsten Fink
1887 • Imtech-Arena (57,000) • hsv.de
Major honours
European Champion Clubs' Cup (1) 1983;
UEFA Cup Winners' Cup (1) 1977;
German League (6) 1923, 1928, 1960, 1979, 1982, 1983;
German Cup (3) 1963, 1976, 1987

2012

25/08	Nürnberg	h	0-1	
01/09	Bremen	a	0-2	
16/09	Eintracht	a	2-3	Westermann, Son
22/09	Dortmund	h	3-2	Son 2, Iličević
26/09	Mönchengladbach	a	2-2	Van der Vaart, Rudņevs
29/09	Hannover	h	1-0	Rudņevs
06/10	Fürth	a	1-0	Son
21/10	Stuttgart	h	0-1	
26/10	Augsburg	a	2-0	Son, Rudņevs
03/11	Bayern	h	0-3	
10/11	Freiburg	h	0-0	
17/11	Mainz	h	1-0	Son
23/11	Düsseldorf	a	0-2	
27/11	Schalke	h	3-1	Beister, Rudņevs, Badelj (p)
02/12	Wolfsburg	a	1-1	Beister
07/12	Hoffenheim	h	2-0	Rudņevs 2
15/12	Leverkusen	a	0-3	

2013

20/01	Nürnberg	a	1-1	Rudņevs
27/01	Bremen	h	3-2	Son, Aogo, Rudņevs
02/02	Eintracht	h	0-2	
09/02	Dortmund	a	4-1	Rudņevs 2, Son 2
16/02	Mönchengladbach	h	1-0	Van der Vaart
23/02	Hannover	a	1-5	Van der Vaart (p)
02/03	Fürth	h	1-1	Beister
10/03	Stuttgart	a	1-0	Rudņevs
16/03	Augsburg	h	0-1	
30/03	Bayern	a	2-9	Bruma, Westermann
06/04	Freiburg	h	0-1	
13/04	Mainz	a	2-1	Son 2
20/04	Düsseldorf	h	2-1	Van der Vaart 2
28/04	Schalke	a	1-4	Jansen
05/05	Wolfsburg	h	1-1	Westermann
11/05	Hoffenheim	a	4-1	Son, Aogo, Jiráček, Rudņevs
18/05	Leverkusen	h	0-1	

No	Name	Nat	DoB	Pos	Aps	(s)	Gls
15	René Adler		15/01/85	G	32		
6	Dennis Aogo		14/01/87	D	22	(5)	2
18	Tolgay Arslan		16/08/90	M	19	(6)	
14	Milan Badelj	CRO	25/02/89	M	30	(1)	1
21	Maximilian Beister		06/09/90	M	8	(15)	3
16	Marcus Berg	SWE	17/08/86	A	2	(9)	
5	Jeffrey Bruma	NED	13/11/91	D	10	(8)	1
2	Dennis Diekmeyer		20/10/89	D	31	(1)	
1	Jaroslav Drobný	CZE	18/10/79	G	2		
11	Ivo Iličević	CRO	14/11/86	M	4	(4)	1
7	Marcell Jansen		04/11/85	M	28		1
19	Petr Jiráček	CZE	02/03/86	M	10	(3)	1
44	Gojko Kačar	SRB	26/01/87	M		(3)	
38	Lam Zhi-Gin	CHN	04/06/91	M	4		
3	Michael Mancienne	ENG	08/01/88	D	21		
23	Slobodan Rajković	SRB	03/02/89	D	6	(7)	
8	Tomás Rincón	VEN	13/01/88	M	9	(11)	
10	Artjoms Rudņevs	LVA	13/01/88	A	26	(8)	12
22	Jacopo Sala	ITA	05/12/91	M	2	(6)	
20	Paul Scharner	AUT	11/03/80	D	1	(3)	
25	Per Ciljan Skjelbred	NOR	16/06/87	M	15	(3)	
15	Son Heung-min	KOR	08/07/92	A	31	(2)	12
13	Robert Tesche		27/05/87	M		(4)	
23	Rafael van der Vaart	NED	11/12/83	M	27		5
4	Heiko Westermann		14/08/83	D	34		3

HANNOVER 96

Coach: Mirko Slomka
1896 • AWD-Arena (49,000) • hannover96.de
Major honours
German League (2) 1938, 1954;
German Cup (1) 1992

2012

26/08	Schalke	h	2-2	Felipe, Nikçi
02/09	Wolfsburg	a	4-0	Haggui, Sobiech 2, Andreasen
15/09	Bremen	h	3-2	Huszti 2, Andreasen
23/09	Hoffenheim	a	1-3	og (Delpierre)
26/09	Nürnberg	h	4-1	Stindl, Huszti, Ya Konan 2
29/09	Hamburg	a	0-1	
07/10	Dortmund	h	1-1	Diouf
20/10	Eintracht	a	1-3	Abdellaoue
28/10	Mönchengladbach	h	2-3	Schlaudraff, Diouf
03/11	Augsburg	a	2-0	Diouf, Stindl
11/11	Stuttgart	a	4-2	Sobiech, Schlaudraff (p), Abdellaoue 2 (1p)
17/11	Freiburg	h	1-2	Abdellaoue (p)
24/11	Bayern	a	0-5	
27/11	Fürth	h	2-0	Diouf, Eggimann
01/12	Mainz	a	1-2	Schulz
09/12	Leverkusen	h	3-2	Huszti 2 (2p), Diouf
15/12	Düsseldorf	a	1-2	Diouf

2013

18/01	Schalke	a	4-5	Pinto, Huszti 2, Diouf
26/01	Wolfsburg	h	2-1	Abdellaoue, Diouf
01/02	Bremen	a	0-2	
09/02	Hoffenheim	h	1-0	Diouf
17/02	Nürnberg	a	2-2	Huszti, Ya Konan
23/02	Hamburg	h	5-1	Diouf, Huszti (p), Ya Konan 2, Abdellaoue
02/03	Dortmund	a	1-3	Abdellaoue
10/03	Eintracht	h	0-0	
17/03	Mönchengladbach	a	0-1	
30/03	Augsburg	h	2-0	Rausch 2
07/04	Stuttgart	h	0-0	
12/04	Freiburg	a	1-3	Rausch
20/04	Bayern	h	1-6	Hoffmann
26/04	Fürth	a	3-2	Abdellaoue, Hoffmann, Pinto
04/05	Mainz	h	2-2	Sobiech, Diouf
11/05	Leverkusen	a	1-3	Sobiech
18/05	Düsseldorf	h	3-0	Diouf, Ya Konan 2

No	Name	Nat	DoB	Pos	Aps	(s)	Gls
25	Mohammed Abdellaoue	NOR	23/10/85	A	12	(14)	8
2	Leon Andreasen	DEN	23/04/83	M	4	(1)	2
23	Sofian Chahed	TUN	18/04/83	M	9	(4)	
6	Steve Cherundolo	USA	19/02/79	D	20		
39	Mame Biram Diouf	SEN	16/12/87	A	24	(4)	12
5	Johan Djourou	SUI	18/01/87	A	14		
20	Felipe	BRA	15/05/87	D	3	(1)	1
3	Karim Haggui	TUN	20/01/84	D	16	(6)	1
15	André Hoffmann		28/02/93	M	14	(2)	2
10	Szabolcs Huszti	HUN	18/04/83	M	19	(2)	9
27	Deniz Kadah		28/08/83	A		(2)	
22	Adrian Nikçi	SUI	10/11/89	M	1	(3)	1
24	Christian Pander		28/08/83	M	11	(7)	
7	Sérgio Pinto		16/10/80	M	28	(2)	2
18	Sébastien Pocognoli	BEL	01/08/87	D	10	(1)	
34	Konstantin Rausch		15/03/90	M	25	(5)	3
4	Hiroki Sakai	JPN	12/04/90	D	8	(5)	
13	Jan Schlaudraff		18/07/83	A	22	(8)	2
33	Manuel Schmiedebach		05/12/88	M	14	(7)	
19	Christian Schulz		01/04/83	D	18	(1)	1
9	Artur Sobiech	POL	12/06/90	A	9	(16)	5
11	Lars Stindl		26/08/88	M	17	(1)	2
11	Didier Ya Konan	CIV	22/05/84	A	21	(7)	7
1	Ron-Robert Zieler		12/02/89	G	34		

TSG 1899 HOFFENHEIM

Coach: Markus Babbel; (03/12/12) (Frank Kramer); (18/12/12) Marco Kurz; (02/04/13) Markus Gisdol
1899 • Rhein-Neckar-Arena, Sinsheim (30,150) • achtzehn99.de

2012

25/08	Mönchengladbach	a	1-2	Roberto Firmino
01/09	Eintracht	h	0-4	
16/09	Freiburg	a	3-5	Delpierre, Vukčević, Usami
23/09	Hannover	h	3-1	Johnson, Salihović, Williams
26/09	Stuttgart	a	3-0	Usami, Joselu, Johnson
29/09	Augsburg	h	0-0	
06/10	Bayern	a	0-2	
19/10	Fürth	h	3-3	Roberto Firmino, Joselu 2
27/10	Mainz	a	0-3	
03/11	Schalke	h	3-2	Volland, Roberto Firmino (p), Schipplock
10/11	Düsseldorf	a	1-1	Joselu
18/11	Wolfsburg	h	1-3	Derdiyok
25/11	Leverkusen	a	1-2	Johnson
28/11	Nürnberg	a	2-4	Schipplock, Salihović (p)
02/12	Bremen	h	1-4	Salihović
07/12	Hamburg	a	0-2	
16/12	Dortmund	h	1-3	Schipplock

2013

19/01	Mönchengladbach	h	0-0	
26/01	Eintracht	a	1-2	Volland
02/02	Freiburg	h	2-1	Volland 2
09/02	Hannover	a	0-1	
17/02	Stuttgart	h	0-1	
23/02	Augsburg	a	1-2	De Camargo
03/03	Bayern	h	0-1	
09/03	Fürth	a	3-0	Roberto Firmino, Joselu, Weis
16/03	Mainz	h	0-0	
30/03	Schalke	a	0-3	
05/04	Düsseldorf	h	3-0	Roberto Firmino, og (Lambertz), Volland
13/04	Wolfsburg	a	2-2	Salihović (p), Beck
20/04	Leverkusen	a	0-5	
27/04	Nürnberg	h	2-1	Weis, Salihović
04/05	Bremen	a	2-2	Schipplock 2
11/05	Hamburg	h	1-4	Volland
19/05	Dortmund	a	2-1	Salihović 2 (2p)

No	Name	Nat	DoB	Pos	Aps	(s)	Gls
12	David Abraham	ARG	15/07/86	D	12		
25	Luis Advíncula	PER	02/03/90	M	1	(1)	
2	Andreas Beck		13/03/87	D	31		1
30	Koen Casteels	BEL	25/06/92	G	15	(1)	
5	Marvin Compper		14/06/85	D	16		
10	Igor De Camargo	BEL	12/05/83	A	4	(4)	1
15	Matthieu Delpierre	FRA	26/04/81	D	22	(1)	1
11	Eren Derdiyok	SUI	12/06/88	A	6	(13)	1
34	Heurelho Gomes	BRA	15/02/81	G	9		
32	Vincenzo Grifo		07/04/93	M	1	(11)	
28	Pelle Jensen		24/05/92	D	2		
16	Fabian Johnson	USA	11/12/87	D	30	(1)	3
18	Joselu	ESP	27/03/90	A	17	(8)	5
39	Andreas Ludwig		11/09/90	M		(5)	
21	Patrick Ochs		14/05/84	D	8	(4)	
42	Eugen Polanski	POL	17/03/86	M	9	(2)	
22	Roberto Firmino	BRA	02/10/91	M	29	(4)	5
6	Sebastian Rudy		28/02/90	M	21	(2)	
23	Sejad Salihović	BIH	08/10/84	M	14	(6)	7
9	Sven Schipplock		08/11/88	A	7	(9)	5
44	Patrick Schorr		13/10/94	D		(1)	
40	Stephan Schröck	PHI	21/08/86	D	6	(4)	
34	Denis Streker		06/04/91	M	2	(2)	
45	Niklas Süle		03/09/95	D	1	(1)	
43	Robin Szarka		17/09/91	D		(1)	
4	Stefan Thesker		11/04/91	D	3	(1)	
33	Takashi Usami	JPN	06/05/92	M	15	(5)	2
29	Jannik Vestergaard	DEN	03/08/92	D	14	(2)	
31	Kevin Volland		30/07/92	A	31	(3)	6
7	Boris Vukčević		16/03/90	M	4	(1)	1
17	Tobias Weis		30/07/85	M	17	(1)	2
1	Tim Wiese		17/12/81	G	10		
13	Daniel Williams	USA	08/03/89	M	17	(4)	1

1. FSV MAINZ 05

Coach: Thomas Tuchel
1905 • Coface-Arena (34,034) • mainz05.de

2012

25/08	Freiburg	a	1-1	Ivanschitz (p)
31/08	Fürth	h	0-1	
15/09	Bayern	a	1-3	Szalai (p)
22/09	Augsburg	h	2-0	Ivanschitz, Szalai
25/09	Schalke	a	0-3	
30/09	Wolfsburg	a	2-0	Júnior Díaz, Szalai
06/10	Düsseldorf	h	1-0	Noveski
20/10	Leverkusen	a	2-2	Szalai, Risse
27/10	Hoffenheim	h	3-0	Szalai 3
04/11	Bremen	a	1-2	Szalai
09/11	Nürnberg	h	2-1	N Müller, Ivanschitz
17/11	Hamburg	a	0-1	
24/11	Dortmund	h	1-2	Caligiuri
27/11	Eintracht	a	3-1	Ivanschitz, Parker, Noveski
01/12	Hannover	h	2-1	N Müller, Szalai
09/12	Mönchengladbach	a	0-2	
15/12	Stuttgart	h	3-1	N Müller 2, Soto

2013

19/01	Freiburg	h	0-0	
26/01	Fürth	a	3-0	Szalai 2, Malli
02/02	Bayern	a	0-3	
10/02	Augsburg	a	1-1	Szalai
16/02	Schalke	h	2-2	Ivanschitz, Pospěch
23/02	Wolfsburg	h	1-1	Zimling
03/03	Düsseldorf	a	1-1	Klasnić
09/03	Leverkusen	h	1-0	Ivanschitz (p)
16/03	Hoffenheim	a	0-0	
30/03	Bremen	h	1-1	Szalai
07/04	Nürnberg	a	1-2	N Müller
13/04	Hamburg	h	1-2	Parker
20/04	Dortmund	a	0-2	
28/04	Eintracht	h	0-0	
04/05	Hannover	a	2-2	N Müller 2
11/05	Mönchengladbach	a	2-4	Parker, Ivanschitz (p)
18/05	Stuttgart	a	2-2	Ede, N Müller

No	Name	Nat	DoB	Pos	Aps	(s)	Gls
14	Julian Baumgartlinger	AUT	02/01/88	M	31	(1)	
16	Stefan Bell		24/08/91	D	5	(3)	
28	Niko Bungert		24/10/86	D	8		
6	Marco Caligiuri		14/04/84	M	13	(9)	1
10	Eric Maxim Choupo-Moting	CMR	23/03/89	A	4	(4)	
37	Nejmeddin Daghfous		01/10/86	M		(1)	
17	Chinedu Ede		05/02/87	M	1	(8)	1
25	Andreas Ivanschitz	AUT	15/10/83	M	29	(2)	7
20	Júnior Díaz	CRC	12/09/83	D	15	(3)	1
21	Loris Karius		22/06/93	G		(1)	
15	Jan Kirchhoff		01/10/90	D	9	(9)	
39	Ivan Klasnić	CRO	29/01/80	A	1	(2)	1
11	Yunus Malli		24/02/92	M	7	(7)	1
33	Heinz Müller		30/05/78	G	3		
27	Nicolai Müller		25/09/87	M	26	(6)	8
4	Nikolce Noveski	MKD	28/04/79	D	32		2
31	Shawn Parker		07/03/93	A	10	(6)	3
7	Eugen Polanski	POL	17/03/86	M	9	(3)	
23	Zdeněk Pospěch	CZE	14/12/78	D	32	(1)	1
23	Marcel Risse		17/12/89	M	4	(17)	1
13	Nikita Rukavytsya	AUS	22/06/87	A	6	(2)	
5	Benedikt Saller		22/09/92	D		(1)	
35	Petar Sliškoviċ	CRO	21/02/91	A		(1)	
19	Elkin Soto	COL	04/08/80	M	24	(4)	1
2	Bo Svensson	DEN	04/08/79	D	25		
28	Ádám Szalai	HUN	09/12/87	A	26	(3)	13
29	Christian Wetklo		11/01/80	G	31		
8	Radoslav Zabavník	SVK	16/09/80	D	13	(4)	
7	Niki Zimling	DEN	19/04/85	M	10	(3)	1

1. FC NÜRNBERG

Coach: Dieter Hecking; (24/12/12) Michael Wiesinger
1900 • Grundig-Stadion (50,000) • fcn.de
Major honours
German League (9) 1920, 1921, 1924, 1925, 1927, 1936, 1948, 1961, 1968;
German Cup (4) 1935, 1939, 1962, 2007

2012

25/08	Hamburg	a	1-0	Balitsch
01/09	Dortmund	h	1-1	Pekhart
15/09	Mönchengladbach	a	3-2	Klose, Simons, Kiyotake
21/09	Eintracht	h	1-2	Polter
26/09	Hannover	a	1-4	Chandler
29/09	Stuttgart	h	0-2	
06/10	Freiburg	a	0-3	
21/10	Augsburg	h	0-0	
27/10	Schalke	a	0-1	
03/11	Wolfsburg	h	1-0	Gebhart
09/11	Mainz	a	1-2	Nilsson
17/11	Bayern	h	1-1	Feulner
24/11	Fürth	a	0-0	
28/11	Hoffenheim	h	4-2	Kiyotake 2, Nilsson, Polter
01/12	Leverkusen	a	1-3	Feulner
08/12	Düsseldorf	h	2-0	Polter, Feulner
16/12	Bremen	a	1-1	Gebhart

2013

20/01	Hamburg	h	1-1	Pekhart
25/01	Dortmund	a	0-3	
02/02	Mönchengladbach	h	2-1	Simons (p), Pekhart
09/02	Eintracht	a	0-1	
17/02	Hannover	h	2-2	Klose, Polter
23/02	Stuttgart	a	1-1	Feulner
02/03	Freiburg	h	1-1	Simons (p)
08/03	Augsburg	a	2-1	Kiyotake, Esswein
16/03	Schalke	h	3-0	Feulner, Esswein, Frantz
31/03	Wolfsburg	a	2-2	Simons, Nilsson
07/04	Mainz	h	2-1	Nilsson 2
13/04	Bayern	a	0-4	
21/04	Fürth	h	0-1	
27/04	Hoffenheim	a	1-2	Simons (p)
04/05	Leverkusen	h	0-2	
11/05	Düsseldorf	a	2-1	Mak, Plattenhardt
18/05	Bremen	h	3-2	Nilsson, Polter, Pekhart

No	Name	Nat	DoB	Pos	Aps	(s)	Gls
5	Hanno Balitsch		02/01/81	D	31	(2)	1
26	Timothy Chandler	USA	29/03/90	M	29	(1)	1
18	Almog Cohen	ISR	01/09/88	M	3	(6)	
24	Berkay Dabanlı		27/06/90	D	2	(6)	
33	Alexander Esswein		25/03/90	A	19	(8)	2
7	Markus Feulner		12/02/82	M	17	(6)	4
17	Mike Frantz		14/10/86	M	19	(8)	1
10	Timo Gebhart		12/04/89	M	12	(6)	2
20	Muhammed Ildiz	AUT	14/05/91	M		(5)	
28	Mu Kanazaki	JPN	16/02/89	M	1	(3)	
13	Hiroshi Kiyotake	JPN	12/11/89	M	30	(1)	4
15	Timm Klose	SUI	09/05/88	D	32		2
19	Noah Korczowski		08/01/94	D		(3)	
14	Róbert Mak	SVK	08/03/91	M	9	(10)	1
4	Marcos António	BRA	25/05/83	D	1		
27	Markus Mendler		07/01/93	M	2	(1)	
3	Per Nilsson	SWE	15/09/82	D	29		6
9	Tomáš Pekhart	CZE	26/05/89	A	23	(8)	4
25	Javier Pinola	ARG	24/02/83	D	27	(1)	
21	Marvin Plattenhardt		26/01/92	D	8	(6)	1
8	Sebastian Polter		01/04/91	A	10	(16)	5
22	Patrick Rakovsky		02/06/93	G	3	(1)	
1	Raphael Schäfer		30/01/79	G	31		
2	Timmy Simons	BEL	11/12/76	M	34		5
39	Niklas Stark		14/04/95	M	2	(1)	

FC SCHALKE 04

Coach: Huub Stevens (NED); (16/12/12) Jens Keller
1904 • Veltins-Arena (61,673) • schalke04.de
Major honours
UEFA Cup (1) 1997;
German League (7) 1934, 1935, 1937, 1939, 1940, 1942, 1958;
German Cup (5) 1937, 1972, 2001, 2002, 2011

2012

26/08	Hannover	a	2-2	Huntelaar, Holtby
01/09	Augsburg	h	3-1	Papadopoulos, Jones, Huntelaar
15/09	Fürth	a	2-0	Draxler, Holtby
22/09	Bayern	h	0-2	
25/09	Mainz	h	3-0	Farfán (p), Holtby, Pukki
28/09	Düsseldorf	a	2-2	Huntelaar, Matip
06/10	Wolfsburg	h	3-0	Farfán, Afellay, Neustädter
20/10	Dortmund	a	2-1	Afellay, Höger
27/10	Nürnberg	h	1-0	Farfán
03/11	Hoffenheim	a	2-3	Neustädter, Uchida
10/11	Bremen	h	2-1	Neustädter, Draxler
17/11	Leverkusen	a	0-2	
24/11	Eintracht	h	1-1	Huntelaar
01/12	Hamburg	a	1-3	Huntelaar
08/12	Mönchengladbach	h	1-1	Draxler
08/12	Stuttgart	a	1-3	Marica
15/12	Freiburg	h	1-3	Farfán

2013

18/01	Hannover	h	5-4	Farfán, Draxler, Höger, Marica, Holtby
26/01	Augsburg	a	0-0	
02/02	Fürth	h	1-2	Michel Bastos
09/02	Bayern	a	0-4	
16/02	Mainz	a	2-2	Michel Bastos 2
23/02	Düsseldorf	h	2-1	Matip 2
02/03	Wolfsburg	h	4-1	Draxler 2, Farfán, Huntelaar
09/03	Dortmund	h	2-1	Draxler, Huntelaar
16/03	Nürnberg	a	0-3	
30/03	Hoffenheim	h	3-0	Höger, Raffael, Pukki
06/04	Bremen	a	2-1	Draxler, Marica
13/04	Leverkusen	h	2-2	Pukki, Raffael (p)
20/04	Eintracht	a	0-1	
28/04	Hamburg	h	4-1	Michel Bastos, Huntelaar 3
05/05	Mönchengladbach	a	1-0	Draxler
11/05	Stuttgart	h	1-2	og (Ulreich)
18/05	Freiburg	a	2-1	Draxler, og (Schuster)

No	Name	Nat	DoB	Pos	Aps	(s)	Gls
11	Ibrahim Afellay	NED	02/04/86	M	8	(2)	2
27	Tranquillo Barnetta	SUI	22/05/85	M	2	(19)	
31	Julian Draxler		20/09/93	M	24	(6)	10
9	Edu	BRA	30/11/81	A		(1)	
17	Jefferson Farfán	PER	26/10/84	A	25	(2)	6
23	Christian Fuchs	AUT	07/04/86	D	23	(6)	
34	Timo Hildebrand		05/04/79	G	21		
12	Marco Höger		16/09/89	M	15	(7)	3
10	Lewis Holtby		18/09/90	M	18	(1)	4
4	Benedikt Höwedes		29/02/88	D	32		
25	Klaas-Jan Huntelaar	NED	12/08/83	A	26		10
13	Jermaine Jones	USA	03/11/81	M	23	(2)	1
35	Sead Kolašinac		20/06/93	D	12	(4)	
8	Ciprian Marica	ROU	02/10/85	A	8	(5)	3
32	Joël Matip	CMR	08/08/91	D	32		3
21	Christoph Metzelder		05/11/80	D	1	(3)	
29	Max Meyer		18/09/95	M		(5)	
9	Michel Bastos	BRA	27/01/90	M	14		4
28	Christoph Moritz		27/01/90	M	2	(4)	
33	Roman Neustädter		18/02/88	M	31		3
19	Chinedu Obasi	NGA	01/06/86	A	2	(2)	
14	Kyriakos Papadopoulos	GRE	23/02/92	D	9	(1)	1
20	Teemu Pukki	FIN	29/03/90	A	2	(15)	3
18	Raffael	BRA	28/03/85	M	7	(9)	2
22	Atsuto Uchida	JPN	27/03/88	D	24		1
36	Lars Unnerstall		20/07/90	G	13		

VFB STUTTGART

Coach: Bruno Labbadia
1893 • Mercedes-Benz-Arena (60,300) • vfb.de
Major honours
German League (5) 1950, 1952, 1984, 1992, 2007;
German Cup (3) 1954, 1958, 1997

2012

25/08	Wolfsburg	h	0-1	
02/09	Bayern	a	1-6	Harnik
15/09	Düsseldorf	h	0-0	
23/09	Bremen	a	2-2	Harnik, Cacau
26/09	Hoffenheim	h	0-3	
29/09	Nürnberg	a	2-0	Ibišević, Harnik
07/10	Leverkusen	h	2-2	Ibišević 2 (1p)
21/10	Hamburg	a	1-0	Ibišević
28/10	Eintracht	h	2-1	Gentner, Ibišević
03/11	Dortmund	a	0-0	
11/11	Hannover	h	2-4	Gentner, Ibišević (p)
17/11	Mönchengladbach	a	2-1	Harnik, og (Brouwers)
25/11	Freiburg	a	0-3	
28/11	Augsburg	h	2-1	Traoré, Ibišević
01/12	Fürth	a	1-0	Okazaki
08/12	Schalke	h	3-1	Ibišević 3 (1p)
15/12	Mainz	a	1-3	Harnik

2013

19/01	Wolfsburg	a	0-2	
27/01	Bayern	h	0-2	
02/02	Düsseldorf	a	1-3	Gentner
09/02	Bremen	h	1-4	Traoré
17/02	Hoffenheim	a	1-0	Harnik
23/02	Nürnberg	h	1-1	Traoré
02/03	Leverkusen	a	1-2	Ibišević (p)
10/03	Hamburg	h	0-1	
17/03	Eintracht	a	2-1	Ibišević (p), Niedermeier
30/03	Dortmund	h	1-2	Maxim
07/04	Hannover	a	0-0	
14/04	Mönchengladbach	h	2-0	og (Álvaro Domínguez), Gentner
21/04	Freiburg	h	2-1	Gentner, Ibišević
27/04	Augsburg	a	0-3	
04/05	Fürth	h	0-2	
11/05	Schalke	a	2-1	Ibišević 2
18/05	Mainz	h	2-2	og (Wetklo), Boka

No	Name	Nat	DoB	Pos	Aps	(s)	Gls
24	Mamadou Bah	GUI	25/04/88	M		(1)	
29	Soufian Benyamina		02/03/90	A		(2)	
15	Arthur Boka	CIV	02/04/83	D	23	(2)	1
18	Cacau		27/03/81	A	3	(2)	1
10	Daniel Didavi		21/02/90	M		(3)	
3	Felipe Lopes	BRA	07/08/87	D	3		
20	Christian Gentner		14/08/85	M	34		5
28	Tamás Hajnal	HUN	15/03/81	M	7	(6)	
7	Martin Harnik	AUT	10/06/87	A	29	(1)	6
26	Raphael Holzhauser	AUT	16/02/93	M	14	(7)	
23	Tim Hoogland		11/06/85	D	3	(1)	
9	Vedad Ibišević	BIH	06/08/84	A	30		15
8	Zdravko Kuzmanović	SRB	22/09/87	M	7	(5)	
4	William Kvist Jørgensen	DEN	24/02/85	M	21	(2)	
14	Federico Macheda	ITA	22/08/91	D		(14)	
44	Alexandru Maxim	ROU	08/07/90	M	8	(3)	1
3	Cristian Molinaro	ITA	30/07/83	D	19	(6)	
6	Georg Niedermeier		26/02/86	D	25	(3)	1
31	Shinji Okazaki	JPN	16/04/86	M	11	(14)	1
12	Benedikt Röcker		19/11/89	D		(2)	
14	Francisco Rodríguez	MEX	20/10/81	D	9	(5)	
30	Antonio Rüdiger		03/03/93	D	11	(5)	
2	Gotoku Sakai	JPN	14/03/91	D	27		
5	Serdar Taşçı		24/04/87	D	25		
16	Ibrahima Traoré	GUI	21/04/88	M	27	(5)	3
17	Tunay Torun	TUR	21/04/90	A	4	(5)	
1	Sven Ulreich		03/08/88	G	34		

SV WERDER BREMEN

Coach: Thomas Schaaf; (15/05/13) (Wolfgang Rolff)
1899 • Weserstadion (43,789) • werder.de
Major honours
UEFA Cup Winners' Cup (1) 1992;
German League (4) 1965, 1988, 1993, 2004;
German Cup (6) 1961, 1991, 1994, 1999, 2004, 2009

2012

24/08	Dortmund	a	1-2	Gebre Selassie
01/09	Hamburg	h	2-0	Hunt (p), Petersen
15/09	Hannover	a	2-3	Hunt (p), De Bruyne
23/09	Stuttgart	h	2-2	De Bruyne, Junuzovic
26/09	Freiburg	a	2-1	Akpala, Hunt
29/09	Bayern	a	0-2	
05/10	Augsburg	a	1-3	De Bruyne
20/10	Mönchengladbach	h	4-0	Petersen, Arnautovic, Füllkrug, Junuzovic
27/10	Fürth	a	1-1	Petersen
04/11	Mainz	h	2-1	Hunt 2
10/11	Schalke	a	1-2	Hunt
18/11	Düsseldorf	h	2-1	Petersen, De Bruyne
24/11	Wolfsburg	a	1-1	Arnautovic
28/11	Leverkusen	h	1-4	Petersen
02/12	Hoffenheim	a	4-1	Prödl, Arnautovic 3
08/12	Eintracht	a	1-4	Petersen
16/12	Nürnberg	h	1-1	Petersen

2013

19/01	Dortmund	h	0-5	
27/01	Hamburg	a	2-3	Lukimya, Papastathopoulos
01/02	Hannover	h	2-0	Petersen 2
09/02	Stuttgart	a	4-1	Mehmet 2, Hunt, De Bruyne
16/02	Freiburg	h	2-3	Petersen 2
23/02	Bayern	a	1-6	De Bruyne
02/03	Augsburg	h	0-1	
09/03	Mönchengladbach	a	1-1	Ignjovski
16/03	Fürth	h	2-2	Hunt 2 (2p)
30/03	Mainz	a	1-1	Hunt
06/04	Schalke	h	0-2	
13/04	Düsseldorf	a	2-2	Junuzovic, og (Latka)
20/04	Wolfsburg	h	0-3	
27/04	Leverkusen	a	0-1	
04/05	Hoffenheim	h	2-2	Hunt (p), De Bruyne
11/05	Eintracht	h	1-1	De Bruyne
18/05	Nürnberg	a	2-3	De Bruyne 2

No	Name	Nat	DoB	Pos	Aps	(s)	Gls
19	Joseph Akpala	NGA	24/08/86	A	3	(18)	1
7	Marko Arnautovic	AUT	19/04/89	A	21	(5)	5
44	Philipp Bargfrede		03/03/89	M	7	(6)	
6	Kevin De Bruyne	BEL	28/06/91	M	33		10
11	Eljero Elia	NED	13/02/87	A	22	(2)	
7	Clemens Fritz		07/12/80	D	18	(4)	
41	Niclas Füllkrug		09/02/93	M	1	(11)	1
23	Theodor Gebre Selassie	CZE	24/12/86	D	24	(3)	1
14	Aaron Hunt		04/09/86	M	26	(2)	11
17	Aleksandar Ignjovski	SRB	27/01/91	M	17	(3)	1
23	Zlatko Junuzovic	AUT	26/09/87	M	28	(2)	3
18	Felix Kroos		12/03/91	M	5		
5	Assani Lukimya	COD	25/01/86	D	17	(5)	1
10	Mehmet Ekici	TUR	25/03/90	M	6	(3)	2
1	Sebastian Mielitz		18/07/89	G	34		
22	Sokratis Papastathopoulos	GRE	09/06/88	D	29		1
4	Mateo Pavlović	CRO	09/06/90	D	3	(1)	
24	Nils Petersen		06/12/88	A	30	(4)	11
15	Sebastian Prödl	AUT	21/06/87	D	23	(5)	1
13	Lukas Schmitz		13/10/88	D	20	(3)	
34	Aleksandar Stevanović	SRB	16/02/92	M		(2)	
25	Tom Trybull		09/03/93	M	4		
27	Johannes Wurtz		19/06/92	A		(2)	
32	Özkan Yıldırım		10/04/93	M	3	(5)	

VFL WOLFSBURG

Coach: Felix Magath;
(25/10/12) Lorenz-Günther Köstner;
(22/12/12) Dieter Hecking
1945 • Volkswagen-Arena (30,000) • vfl-wolfsburg.de
Major honours
German League (1) 2009

2012

25/08	Stuttgart	a	1-0	Dost
02/09	Hannover	h	0-4	
14/09	Augsburg	a	0-0	
22/09	Fürth	h	1-1	Olić
25/09	Bayern	a	0-3	
30/09	Mainz	h	0-2	
06/10	Schalke	a	0-3	
20/10	Freiburg	h	0-2	
27/10	Düsseldorf	a	4-1	Dost 2, Olić, Diego (p)
03/11	Nürnberg	a	0-2	
11/11	Leverkusen	h	3-1	Diego 2, Dost
18/11	Hoffenheim	a	3-1	Hasebe, Dost, Naldo
24/11	Bremen	h	1-1	Dost
28/11	Mönchengladbach	a	0-2	
02/12	Hamburg	h	1-1	Kjær
08/12	Dortmund	a	3-2	Diego (p), Naldo, Dost
15/12	Eintracht	h	0-2	

2013

19/01	Stuttgart	h	2-0	Diego, Madlung
26/01	Hannover	a	1-2	Madlung
02/02	Augsburg	h	1-1	Naldo
09/02	Fürth	a	1-0	Dost
15/02	Bayern	h	0-2	
23/02	Mainz	a	1-1	Naldo
02/03	Schalke	h	1-4	Olić
09/03	Freiburg	a	5-2	og (Makiadi), Vieirinha, Olić 2, Diego
15/03	Düsseldorf	h	1-1	Olić
31/03	Nürnberg	a	2-2	Diego, Olić
06/04	Leverkusen	a	1-1	Kjær
13/04	Hoffenheim	h	2-2	Arnold, Naldo
20/03	Bremen	a	3-0	Arnold, Olić, Diego (p)
27/04	Mönchengladbach	h	3-1	Arnold, Olić, Diego
05/05	Hamburg	a	1-1	Hasebe
11/05	Dortmund	h	3-3	Perišić 2, Naldo
18/05	Eintracht	a	2-2	Polák, Diego

No	Name	Nat	DoB	Pos	Aps	(s)	Gls
27	Maximilian Arnold		27/05/94	M	5	(1)	3
1	Diego Benaglio	SUI	08/09/83	G	34		
24	Ashkan Dejagah	IRN	05/07/86	M	1		
10	Diego	BRA	28/02/85	M	32		10
12	Bas Dost	NED	31/05/89	A	20	(8)	8
32	Fagner	BRA	11/06/89	D	24	(2)	
3	Felipe Lopes	BRA	07/08/87	D		(1)	
37	Ferhan Hasani	MKD	18/06/90	M	1	(3)	
13	Makoto Hasebe	JPN	18/01/84	M	20	(3)	2
33	Patrick Helmes		01/03/84	A	1	(3)	
19	Rasmus Jönsson	SWE	27/01/90	A		(6)	
7	Josué	BRA	19/07/87	M	13	(3)	
38	Thomas Kahlenberg	DEN	20/03/83	M	6	(7)	
34	Simon Kjær	DEN	26/03/89	D	20	(2)	2
31	Robin Knoche		22/05/92	D	8	(3)	
16	Sotirios Kyrgiakos	GRE	23/07/79	D	1	(1)	
9	Srdjan Lakić	CRO	02/10/83	A	1	(79)	
17	Alexander Madlung		11/07/82	D	6	(9)	2
6	Slobodan Medojević	SRB	20/11/90	M	6	(2)	
25	Naldo	BRA	10/09/82	D	31		6
11	Ivica Olić	CRO	14/09/79	A	28	(4)	9
30	Yohandry Orozco	VEN	19/03/91	M	1	(1)	
9	Ivan Perišić	CRO	02/02/89	M	7	(4)	2
5	Emanuel Pogatetz	AUT	16/01/83	D	8		
29	Jan Polák	CZE	14/03/81	M	26	(1)	1
34	Ricardo Rodriguez	SUI	25/08/92	D	19	(5)	
4	Marcel Schäfer		07/06/84	D	22	(9)	
15	Christian Träsch		01/09/87	M	11	(6)	
8	Vieirinha	POR	24/01/86	A	22	(5)	1

Top goalscorers

25	Stefan Kiessling (Leverkusen)
24	Robert Lewandowski (Dortmund)
16	Alexander Meier (Eintracht)
15	Mario Mandžukić (Bayern)
	Vedad Ibišević (Stuttgart)
14	Marco Reus (Dortmund)
13	Thomas Müller (Bayern)
	Ádám Szalai (Mainz)
12	Artjoms Rudņevs (Hamburg)
	Son Heung-min (Hamburg)
	Mame Biram Diouf (Hannover)

Promoted clubs

HERTHA BSC BERLIN

Coach: Jos Luhukay (NED)
1892 • Olympiastadion (74,244) • herthabsc.de
Major honours
German League (2) 1930, 1931

EINTRACHT BRAUNSCHWEIG

Coach: Torsten Lieberknecht
1895 • Eintracht-Stadion (22,100) • eintracht.com
Major honours
German League (1) 1967

SECOND LEVEL FINAL TABLE 2012/13

		Pld	W	D	L	F	A	Pts
1	Hertha BSC Berlin	34	22	10	2	65	28	76
2	Eintracht Braunschweig	34	19	10	5	52	34	67
3	1. FC Kaiserslautern	34	16	10	0	55	33	58
4	FSV Frankfurt	34	16	6	12	55	45	54
5	1. FC Köln	34	14	12	8	43	33	54
6	TSV 1860 München	34	12	13	9	39	31	49
7	1. FC Union Berlin	34	13	10	11	50	49	49
8	FC Energie Cottbus	34	12	12	10	41	36	48
9	VfR Aalen	34	12	10	12	40	39	46
10	FC St Pauli	34	11	10	13	44	47	43
11	MSV Duisburg	34	11	10	13	37	49	43
12	SC Paderborn 07	34	11	9	14	45	45	42
13	FC Ingolstadt 04	34	10	12	12	36	43	42
14	VfL Bochum 1848	34	10	8	16	40	52	38
15	FC Erzgebirge Aue	34	9	10	15	39	46	37
16	Dynamo Dresden	34	9	10	15	35	49	37
17	SV Sandhausen	34	6	8	20	38	66	26
18	SSV Jahn Regensburg	34	4	7	23	36	65	19

PROMOTION/RELEGATION PLAY-OFFS

(23/05/13 & 27/05/13)
Hoffenheim 3-1 Kaiserslautern
Kaiserslautern 1-2 Hoffenheim
(Hoffenheim 5-2)

Domestic cup: DFB-Pokal 2012/13

FIRST ROUND

(17/08/12)
Grossaspach 1-2 FSV Frankfurt
Lübeck 0-3 Braunschweig
Wilhelmshaven 0-2 Augsburg

(18/08/12)
Aachen 0-2 Mönchengladbach
Berliner AK 4-0 Hoffenheim
Falkensee-Finkenkrug 0-5 Stuttgart
Halle 0-1 Duisburg
Heidenheim 0-2 Bochum
Jena 0-4 Leverkusen
Oberneuland 0-3 Dortmund
Offenbach 2-0 Greuther Fürth
Offenburg 0-3 St Pauli
Schönberg 0-5 Wolfsburg
Unterhaching 1-2 Köln
Victoria Hamburg 1-2 Freiburg

(19/08/12)
Aalen 3-0 Ingolstadt
Aue 3-0 Eintracht Frankfurt
Bielefeld 3-1 Paderborn
Burghausen 0-1 Düsseldorf
Havelse 3-2 Nürnberg *(aet)*
Hennef 0-6 1860 München
Karlsruhe 4-2 Hamburg
Münster 4-2 Bremen *(aet)*
Nöttingen 1-6 Hannover
Rossbach/Verscheid 0-4 Mainz
Rostock 1-3 Kaiserslautern
Saarbrücken 0-5 Schalke
Worms 2-1 Hertha BSC

(20/08/12)
Chemnitz 0-3 Dresden
Regensburg 0-4 Bayern
Rot-Weiss Essen 0-1 Union Berlin *(aet)*
Sandhausen 3-0 Cottbus

SECOND ROUND

(30/10/12)
Aalen 1-4 Dortmund
Berliner AK 0-3 1860 München
Braunschweig 0-2 Freiburg
Havelse 1-3 Bochum
Mainz 2-0 Aue
Münster 0-1 Augsburg
Schalke 3-0 Sandhausen
Worms 0-0 Köln *(aet; 3-4 on pens)*

(31/10/12)
Bayern 4-0 Kaiserslautern
Bielefeld 2-3 Leverkusen *(aet)*
Düsseldorf 1-0 Mönchengladbach *(aet)*
Hannover 1-1 Dresden *(aet; 4-3 on pens)*

Karlsruhe 1-0 Duisburg
Offenbach 2-0 Union Berlin
Stuttgart 3-0 St Pauli
Wolfsburg 2-0 FSV Frankfurt

THIRD ROUND

(18/12/12)
Augsburg 0-2 Bayern
Karlsruhe 0-1 Freiburg
Offenbach 2-0 Düsseldorf
Schalke 1-2 Mainz

(19/12/12)
Bochum 3-0 1860 München
Dortmund 5-1 Hannover
Stuttgart 2-1 Köln
Wolfsburg 2-1 Leverkusen

QUARTER-FINALS

(26/02/13)
Mainz 2-3 Freiburg *(Parker 2, Zimling 4; Santini 86, Caligiuri 90p, 108) (aet)*

Offenbach 1-2 Wolfsburg *(Stadel 81; Olić 49, Dost 71)*

(27/02/13)
Bayern 1-0 Dortmund *(Robben 43)*

Stuttgart 2-0 Bochum *(Gentner 18, Ibišević 81)*

SEMI-FINALS

(16/04/13)
Bayern 6-1 Wolfsburg *(Mandžukić 17, Robben 35, Shaqiri 50, Gomez 80, 83, 86; Diego 45)*

(17/04/13)
Stuttgart 2-1 Freiburg *(Boka 9, Harnik 29; Rosenthal 14)*

FINAL

(01/06/13)
Olympiastadion, Berlin
FC BAYERN MÜNCHEN 0 *(Müller 37p, Gomez 48, 61)*
VFB STUTTGART 2 *(Harnik 71, 80)*
Referee: *Gräfe*
BAYERN: *Neuer, Lahm, Boateng, Van Buyten, Alaba, Javi Martínez, Schweinsteiger, Robben (Tymoshchuk 83), Müller, Ribéry (Shaqiri 90+1), Gomez (Mandžukić 62)*
STUTTGART: *Ulreich, Rüdiger, Taşçı, Niedermeier, Molinaro (Sakai 67), Gentner, Boka, Harnik, Maxim (Okazaki 61), Traoré (Cacau 75), Ibišević*

Bayern striker Mario Gomez slots home the third and decisive goal against former club Stuttgart in Berlin

GREECE
Ellinikos Podosfairikos Omospondia (EPO)

Address	Goudi Park	**President**	Georgios Sarris
	PO Box 14161	**General secretary**	Pafsanias
	GR-11510 Athens		Papanikolaou
Tel	+30 210 930 6000	**Media officer**	Michalis Tsapidis
Fax	+30 210 935 9666	**Year of formation**	1926
E-mail	epo@epo.gr	**National stadium**	OACA Spyro Louis,
Website	epo.gr		Athens (72,080)

SUPERLEAGUE CLUBS

1. AEK Athens FC
2. Aris Thessaloniki FC
3. Asteras Tripolis FC
4. Atromitos FC
5. Kerkyra FC
6. Levadiakos FC
7. OFI Crete FC
8. Olympiacos FC
9. Panathinaikos FC
10. Panionios GSS
11. Panthrakikos FC
12. PAOK FC
13. PAS Giannina FC
14. Platanias FC
15. Veria FC
16. Xanthi FC

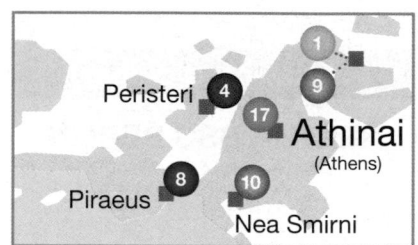

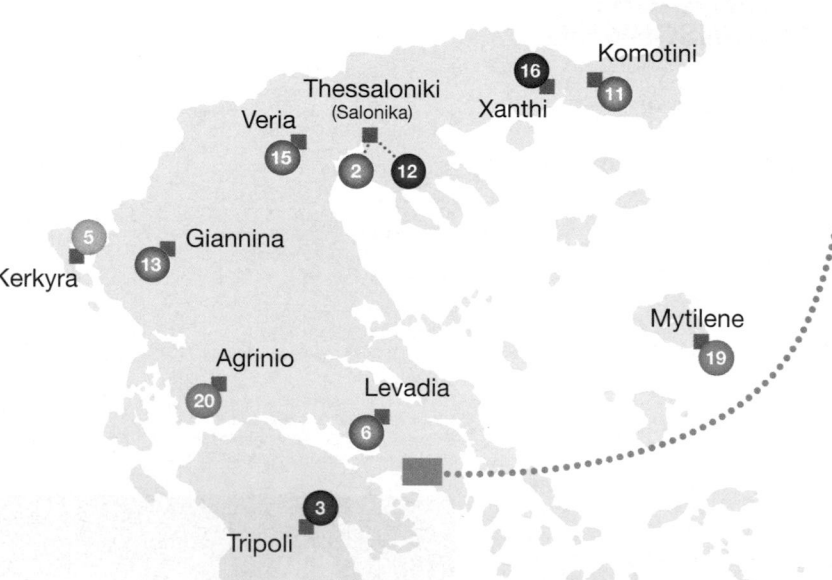

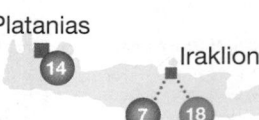

PROMOTED CLUBS

17. Apollon Smyrnis FC
18. Ergotelis FC
19. Kalloni FC
20. Panaitolikos GFS

KEY:

- ● – UEFA Champions League
- ● – UEFA Europa League
- ● – Promoted clubs
- ● – Relegated clubs

Olympiacos out on their own

While their traditional rivals underwent a season of turmoil, Olympiacos FC romped unchallenged to yet another Greek Superleague title, leaving the rest for dead as they stormed to their 40th championship crown. The Piraeus club added a 26th Greek Cup for good measure to complete a second successive double.

Equally momentous were the trials and tribulations of cash-strapped Athens giants Panathinaikos FC and AEK Athens FC, with the former failing to qualify for Europe after finishing a lowly sixth and the latter suffering relegation for the first time in their 89-year history.

Piraeus club earn fourth star with 40th title

Panathinaikos fail to qualify for Europe

AEK Athens suffer traumatic relegation

Domestic league

Olympiacos's runaway title triumph was achieved with three coaches. Leonardo Jardim, brought in from SC Braga for Ernesto Valverde, was unbeaten in 17 Superleague matches when he was surprisingly dismissed in January. Former goalkeeper Antonios Nikopolidis took charge temporarily before the club's only defeat of the league campaign – 2-3 at home to Atromitos FC – paved the way for former Real Madrid CF midfielder Míchel to take over and lead the team through the last ten matches. It was halfway through that schedule – on 10 March, the club's 88th birthday – that the title was secured with a 3-0 home win over AEK.

That Olympiacos would conclude the campaign with a fourth star to adorn the club shirt had never been in doubt from the start. Although they lost Valverde and leading scorer Kevin Mirallas from the previous campaign, they won their opening seven games and seldom looked in trouble. Algerian duo Djamel Abdoun and Rafik Djebbour came thrillingly to the fore in attack, with Greek internationals José Holebas, Ioannis Maniatis and Kostas Manolas prominent in defence. The departure of both Jardim and captain Vasilios Torosidis (to AS Roma) in January had no adverse affect quite simply

because the challenge to their supremacy was non-existent.

Panathinaikos and AEK were both torn apart by off-field battles as they struggled to stay in business. Even so, AEK's relegation was a terrible shock – as was the club's decision to drop down a further division and join the amateur ranks in 2013/14. PAOK FC won the post-season play-off for UEFA Champions League qualification – though not with Georgios Donis, their coach in the regular league campaign. He was sacked after a Greek Cup semi-final defeat to Asteras Tripolis FC, who also competed in the play-offs alongside Atromitos FC and PAS Giannina FC. The latter's European licence was revoked, however, and they were replaced in the 2013/14 UEFA Europa League by Xanthi FC.

Domestic cup

As in 2011/12, Olympiacos were taken to extra time in the cup final, but, like Atromitos a year earlier, first-time finalists Asteras had to be content with an honourable runners-up spot. Their 14th-minute lead was cancelled out by an equaliser from 2012 match-winner David Fuster before Djebbour and Abdoun both scored in the extra period to give the champions a 3-1 win.

Europe

Olympiacos's imperious domestic form was not exported to Europe, where they finished third in their UEFA Champions League group – behind FC Schalke 04 and Arsenal FC – before falling at the first hurdle of the UEFA Europa League to Spanish first-timers Levante UD. Post-Christmas European football was seen nowhere else in Greece as Panathinaikos, ousted by Málaga CF in the UEFA Champions League play-offs, managed only five points in their UEFA Europa League group campaign, during which coach Jesualdo Ferreira was given the sack.

National team

Greece's bid to reach a fourth successive major tournament remained intact despite a lack of goals and just one point from the two 2014 FIFA World Cup qualifiers against their main Group G rivals Bosnia & Herzegovina. The 0-0 draw in Piraeus and 3-1 defeat in Zenica were partly alleviated by away wins in Latvia, Slovakia and Lithuania, which enabled Fernando Santos and his players to keep the pressure on the leaders. A place in the play-offs looked to be virtually guaranteed for the UEFA EURO 2012 quarter-finalists, with three of their four remaining fixtures at home and the other in Liechtenstein.

 **GREECE**

Domestic league: Superleague 2012/13 final table

		Pld	Home					Away					Total					Pts
			W	D	L	F	A	W	D	L	F	A	W	D	L	F	A	
1	**Olympiacos FC**	30	12	2	1	34	8	12	3	0	30	8	24	5	1	64	16	77
2	PAOK FC	30	12	2	1	28	8	6	6	3	18	11	18	8	4	46	19	62
3	Asteras Tripolis FC	30	11	2	2	26	9	6	3	6	15	16	17	5	8	41	25	56
4	Atromitos FC	30	8	3	4	13	9	3	10	2	13	13	11	13	6	26	22	46
5	PAS Giannina FC	30	7	4	4	14	9	5	4	6	14	15	12	8	10	28	24	44
6	Panathinaikos FC	30	5	7	3	17	13	5	5	5	15	17	10	12	8	32	30	40
7	Xanthi FC	30	5	5	5	13	11	5	5	5	15	15	10	10	10	28	26	40
8	Panionios GSS	30	8	2	5	22	15	3	1	11	13	27	11	3	16	35	42	36
9	Platanias FC	30	7	4	4	19	18	3	2	10	10	24	10	6	14	29	42	36
10	Panthrakikos FC	30	7	1	7	18	17	3	5	7	12	16	10	6	14	30	33	36
11	Levadiakos FC	30	4	6	5	11	13	5	1	9	10	22	9	7	14	21	35	34
12	Veria FC	30	6	4	5	21	14	2	5	8	9	21	8	9	13	30	35	33
13	Aris Thessaloniki FC	30	6	7	2	22	13	1	5	9	10	27	7	12	11	32	40	33
14	OFI Crete FC	30	7	5	3	21	18	1	3	11	12	28	8	8	14	33	46	32
15	AEK Athens FC	30	6	4	5	12	17	2	2	11	9	19	8	6	16	21	36	27
16	Kerkyra FC	30	3	5	7	11	18	1	3	11	5	23	4	8	18	16	41	20

NB AEK Athens FC – 3 pts deducted; Panathinaikos FC – 2 pts deducted. For details of UEFA Champions League qualification play-offs see page 399.

Superleague play-offs 2012/13: UEFA Champions League qualification

		Pld	Home					Away					Total					Pts
			W	D	L	F	A	W	D	L	F	A	W	D	L	F	A	
2	PAOK FC	6	1	0	2	2	3	2	0	1	5	4	3	0	3	7	7	13
3	Atromitos FC	6	2	1	0	4	1	1	1	1	4	4	3	2	1	8	5	11
4	Asteras Tripolis FC	6	2	0	1	5	4	0	1	2	1	3	2	1	3	6	7	9
5	PAS Giannina FC	6	1	1	1	4	4	1	0	2	2	4	2	1	3	6	8	7

NB Points carried forward from regular league: PAOK 4 pts, Asteras Tripolis 2 pts, Atromitos 0 pts, Giannina 0 pts. Results and scorers for these matches are on page 399.

SEASON AT A GLANCE

EUROPEAN QUALIFICATION 2013/14

Champion/Cup winner: Olympiacos FC (group stage)
PAOK FC (third qualifying round)

Atromitos FC (play-offs)
Asteras Tripolis FC (third qualifying round)
Xanthi FC (second qualifying round)

Top scorer	Rafik Djebbour (Olympiacos), 20 goals
Relegated clubs	Kerkyra FC, AEK Athens FC
Promoted clubs	Apollon Smyrnis FC, Ergotelis FC, Kalloni FC, Panaitolikos GFS
Cup final	Olympiacos FC 3-1 Asteras Tripolis FC

PLAYER OF THE SEASON
Djamel Abdoun
(Olympiacos FC)

In his second season with Olympiacos, the 27-year-old Algeria winger was the team's most consistent performer. He contributed seven league goals and eight assists to the league triumph, and his right-sided runs were a constant threat. His understanding with international team-mate Rafik Djebbour was at the core of the Piraeus club's success.

NEWCOMER OF THE SEASON
Ergys Kaçe
(PAOK FC)

In a cash-strapped campaign that forced many clubs to rely on younger players from their academy, PAOK's Albanian teenager Kaçe was the pick of the new breed, excelling as the team's holding midfielder with his shrewd reading of the game, sound positional sense and marathon runner's stamina – not to mention a venomous long-range shot.

SUPERLEAGUE TEAM OF THE SEASON
(4-2-1-3)
Coach: Christopoulos *(Giannina)*

NATIONAL TEAM

Home Kit   Away Kit

INTERNATIONAL HONOURS
UEFA European Championship (1) 2004

INTERNATIONAL TOURNAMENT APPEARANCES
FIFA World Cup (2) 1994, 2010
UEFA European Championship (4) 1980, 2004 (Winners), 2008, 2012 (qtr-finals)

TOP FIVE ALL-TIME CAPS
Georgios Karagounis (125); Theodoros Zagorakis (120); **Kostas Katsouranis** (103); Angelos Basinas (100); Efstratios Apostolakis (96)

TOP FIVE ALL-TIME GOALS
Nikolaos Anastopoulos (29); Angelos Charisteas (25); **Theofanis Gekas** (24); Dimitrios Saravakos (22); Dimitrios "Mimis" Papaioannou (20)

Results 2012/13

Date	Opponent		Venue	Score	Scorers
15/08/12	Norway	A	Oslo	3-2	*Torosidis (7), K Papadopoulos (11), Mitroglou (56)*
07/09/12	Latvia (WCQ)	A	Riga	2-1	*Spyropoulos (57), Gekas (69)*
11/09/12	Lithuania (WCQ)	H	Piraeus	2-0	*Ninis (55), Mitroglou (72)*
12/10/12	Bosnia & Herzegovina (WCQ)	H	Piraeus	0-0	
16/10/12	Slovakia (WCQ)	A	Bratislava	1-0	*Salpingidis (63)*
14/11/12	Republic of Ireland	A	Dublin	1-0	*Holebas (29)*
06/02/13	Switzerland	H	Piraeus	0-0	
22/03/13	Bosnia & Herzegovina (WCQ)	A	Zenica	1-3	*Gekas (90+3)*
07/06/13	Lithuania (WCQ)	A	Vilnius	1-0	*Christodoulopoulos (20)*

Appearances 2012/13

Coach: Fernando Santos (POR) 10/10/54

Player	DOB	Club	Nor	LVA	LTU	BIH	SVK	Irl	Sui	BIH	LTU	Caps	Goals
Orestis Karnezis	11/07/85	Panathinaikos	G	G	G	G	G	G	G	G	G	10	-
Vasilios Torosidis	10/06/85	Olympiacos /Roma (ITA)	D46	D	D	D	D	D61	D	D	D	57	7
Kyriakos Papadopoulos	23/02/92	Schalke (GER)	D	D	D			D				16	4
Sokratis Papastathopoulos	09/06/88	Bremen (GER)	D	D	D	D	D	D	D	D	D	40	-
Nikolaos Spyropoulos	10/10/83	Panathinaikos /Chievo (ITA)	D80	D	D	D	D	s82	D			34	2
Ioannis Maniatis	12/10/86	Olympiacos	M46	M	M46	M80		s61	M46	s58	M	21	-
Alexandros Tziolis	13/02/85	Monaco (FRA) /APOEL (CYP)	M81	M	M	M	M	M	s46	M58	s85	41	1
Kostas Katsouranis	21/06/79	Panathinaikos /unattached /PAOK	M	M	M		M	M	M87	M	M85	103	9
Georgios Samaras	21/02/85	Celtic (SCO)	A46	s46/68		A	A	A46		A	A	65	8
Kostas Fortounis	16/10/92	Kaiserslautern (GER)	A	A80	A69	A		s46	s57			11	-
Dimitrios Salpingidis	18/08/81	PAOK	A70		s57	A		s46	A70	A73	s65	67	10
Loukas Vyntra	05/02/81	Panathinaikos	s46					s60				44	-
Sotirios Ninis	03/04/90	Parma (ITA)	s46	s68	M		M66	M60				27	3
Kostas Mitroglou	12/03/88	Olympiacos	s46	A46	s46	s80	s59	A46	A70			21	2
Lazaros Christodoulopoulos	19/12/86	Panathinaikos /Bologna (ITA)	s70							s73	M	10	1
Dimitrios Siovas	16/09/88	Olympiacos	s80				D75					2	-
Elini Dimoutsos	18/06/88	Atromitos	s81									1	-
Theofanis Gekas	23/05/80	Levante (ESP) /Akhisar (TUR)	A	A80	A57	A59			s46	A65		68	24
José Holebas	27/06/84	Olympiacos			s80	s69		M46	M57	M	D46	13	1
Charalambos Mavrias	21/02/94	Panathinaikos			s80				s87			2	-
Stilianos Malezas	11/03/85	Düsseldorf (GER)				D67						3	-
Georgios Karagounis	06/03/77	Fulham (ENG)						s67	s66	M58	M	125	9
Georgios Fotakis	29/10/81	PAOK					s75					13	2

Appearances 2012/13 (contd.)

			Nor	LVA	LTU	BIH	SVK	Irl	Sui	BIH	LTU	Caps	Goals
Kostas Stafylidis	02/12/93	PAOK						D82				1	-
Panagiotis Tachtsidis	15/02/91	Roma (ITA)						M	s58			2	-
Stefanos Athanasiadis	24/12/88	PAOK						s46	s70			5	-
Kostas Manolas	14/06/91	Olympiacos							D		D	2	-
Panagiotis Kone	26/07/87	Bologna (ITA)							s70			11	-
Avraam Papadopoulos	03/12/84	Olympiacos								D		35	-
Georgios Tzavelas	26/11/87	Monaco (FRA)								D46	s46	10	-

European club competitions 2012/13

OLYMPIACOS FC

Group B
Match 1 - FC Schalke 04 (GER)
H 1-2 *Abdoun (58)*
Megyeri, Maniatis, Modesto (Greco 69), Paulo Machado, Djebbour, Contreras, David Fuster (Ibagaza 58), Holebas, Manolas, Torosidis, Abdoun (Mitroglou 69). Coach: Leonardo Jardim (POR)
Match 2 - Arsenal FC (ENG)
A 1-3 *Mitroglou (45+1)*
Megyeri, Maniatis, Paulo Machado (Pantelić 81), Mitroglou, Contreras, David Fuster, Holebas, Siovas, Manolas, Diakité (Ibagaza 73), Greco (Abdoun 67). Coach: Leonardo Jardim (POR)
Match 3 - Montpellier Hérault SC (FRA)
A 2-1 *Torosidis (73), Mitroglou (90+1)*
Carroll, Maniatis, Modesto, Paulo Machado, Djebbour (Mitroglou 70), Contreras, David Fuster (Lykogiannis 88), Holebas, Manolas, Greco (Abdoun 60), Torosidis. Coach: Leonardo Jardim (POR)
Match 4 - Montpellier Hérault SC (FRA)
H 3-1 *Paulo Machado (4), Greco (80), Mitroglou (82)*
Carroll, Maniatis, Modesto (David Fuster 72), Paulo Machado (Fejsa 87), Mitroglou (Lykogiannis 90+3), Holebas, Siovas, Manolas, Greco, Torosidis, Abdoun. Coach: Leonardo Jardim (POR)
Match 5 - FC Schalke 04 (GER)
A 0-1
Carroll, Maniatis, Modesto (Ibagaza 81), Paulo Machado, Mitroglou (Djebbour 74), Holebas, Siovas, Manolas, Greco (David Fuster 65), Torosidis, Abdoun. Coach: Leonardo Jardim (POR)
Match 6 - Arsenal FC (ENG)
H 2-1 *Maniatis (64), Mitroglou (73)*
Carroll, Maniatis, Paulo Machado, Fejsa (David Fuster 60), Djebbour (Ibagaza 82), Contreras, Manolas, Diakité, Greco, Torosidis, Abdoun (Mitroglou 72). Coach: Leonardo Jardim (POR)

Round of 32 - Levante UD (ESP)
A 0-3
Megyeri, Maniatis, Modesto (Greco 46), Paulo Machado (Fetfatzidis 75), Fejsa, Djebbour, Contreras, Vlahodimos (Mitroglou 59), Holebas, Manolas, Abdoun. Coach: Míchel (ESP)
Red card: Abdoun 29
H 0-1
Carroll, Maniatis, Paulo Machado, Fejsa, Djebbour, Mitroglou (Ibagaza 75), Contreras, Vlahodimos, Siovas, Lykogiannis (Holebas 46), Greco (Fetfatzidis 46). Coach: Míchel (ESP)

PANATHINAIKOS FC

Third qualifying round - Motherwell FC (SCO)
A 2-0 *Christodoulopoulos (14), Mavrias (76)*
Karnezis, Sissoko, Boumsong, Vitolo, Toché (Mavrias 76), Christodoulopoulos (Fornaroli 85), Zeca, Marinos (Katsouranis 67), Vyntra, N Spyropoulos, Velázquez. Coach: Jesualdo Ferreira (POR)
H 3-0 *Christodoulopoulos (51), Mavrias (75), Sissoko (83)*
Karnezis, Sissoko, Boumsong, Vitolo, Toché (Mavrias 71), Christodoulopoulos (Petropoulos 78), Zeca, Marinos (Katsouranis 71), Vyntra, N Spyropoulos, Velázquez. Coach: Jesualdo Ferreira (POR)

Play-offs - Málaga CF (ESP)
A 0-2
Karnezis, Sissoko, Boumsong (André Pinto 64), Vitolo, Mavrias, Fornaroli (Toché 69), Zeca (Christodoulopoulos 39), Vyntra, Katsouranis, N Spyropoulos, Velázquez. Coach: Jesualdo Ferreira (POR)

H 0-0
Karnezis, Sissoko, André Pinto, Vitolo, Christodoulopoulos, Fornaroli (Toché 73), Zeca (Mavrias 46), Vyntra, Katsouranis (Marinos 71), N Spyropoulos, Velázquez. Coach: Jesualdo Ferreira (POR)

Group J
Match 1 - NK Maribor (SVN)
A 0-3
Karnezis, Sissoko, Boumsong, Vitolo, Christodoulopoulos (Fornaroli 55), Zeca, Vyntra, Katsouranis, N Spyropoulos, Velázquez, Owusu-Abeyie (Mavrias 74). Coach: Jesualdo Ferreira (POR)
Red card: N Spyropoulos 90+3
Match 2 - Tottenham Hotspur FC (ENG)
H 1-1 *Toché (77)*
Karnezis, André Pinto, Vitolo, Toché, Christodoulopoulos (Mavrias 85), Seitaridis, Zeca, Marinos (Sissoko 46), Vyntra, Triantafyllopoulos, Owusu-Abeyie (Chouchoumis 90+3). Coach: Jesualdo Ferreira (POR)
Match 3 - S.S. Lazio (ITA)
H 1-1 *Toché (90+1)*
Karnezis, Sissoko (Mavrias 79), André Pinto, Vitolo, Christodoulopoulos, Fornaroli (Toché 75), Seitaridis, Zeca, N Spyropoulos, Fourlanos (Owusu-Abeyie 68), Velázquez. Coach: Jesualdo Ferreira (POR)
Match 4 - S.S. Lazio (ITA)
A 0-3
Karnezis, Vitolo, Toché (Petropoulos 24), Christodoulopoulos, Seitaridis, Zeca (Lagos 78), Vyntra, N Spyropoulos, Chouchoumis (Mavrias 59), Velázquez, Owusu-Abeyie. Coach: Jesualdo Ferreira (POR)
Match 5 - NK Maribor (SVN)
H 1-0 *Vitolo (67p)*
Karnezis, Sissoko (Marinos 81), Vitolo, Mavrias, Toché (Petropoulos 72), Seitaridis, Zeca, Vyntra, N Spyropoulos, Velázquez, Owusu-Abeyie (Fornaroli 35). Coach: Juan Ramón Rocha (ARG)
Match 6 - Tottenham Hotspur FC (ENG)
A 1-3 *Zeca (54)*
Karnezis, Sissoko, Vitolo, Mavrias (Fornaroli 83), Toché (Petropoulos 78), Seitaridis, Zeca, Sow (Christodoulopoulos 60), Vyntra, N Spyropoulos, Triantafyllopoulos. Coach: Juan Ramón Rocha (ARG)

PAOK FC

Third qualifying round - Bnei Yehuda Tel-Aviv FC (ISR)
A 2-0 *Georgiadis (62), Athanasiadis (72)*
Glykos, Katsikas, Pablo García, Georgiadis (Salpingidis 82), Robert, Lino, Lazăr (Kaçe 75), Khumalo, Athanasiadis, Etto, Giannou (Pelkas 71). Coach: Georgios Donis (GRE)
H 4-1 *Athanasiadis (48, 52), Robert (79), Holkas (90+ 0)*
Glykos, Katsikas (Intzidis 37), Georgiadis, Salpingidis (Pelkas 71), Robert, Lino, Fotakis (Kaçe 46), Lazăr, Khumalo, Athanasiadis, Etto. Coach: Georgios Donis (GRE)

Play-offs - SK Rapid Wien (AUT)
H 2-1 *Athanasiadis (69), Katsikas (83)*
Glykos, Katsikas, Georgiadis (Lawrence 68), Robert (Fotakis 46), Lino, Lazăr, Kaçe, Khumalo, Athanasiadis, Etto, Giannou (Salpingidis 46). Coach: Georgios Donis (GRE)
Red card: Lazăr 74
A 0-3
Glykos, Pablo García, Georgiadis, Robert (Fotakis 46), Lino, Kaçe (Pelkas 70), Khumalo, Athanasiadis, Matheus, Etto, Giannou (Lawrence 46). Coach: Georgios Donis (GRE)

ATROMITOS FC

Play-offs - Newcastle United FC (ENG)
H 1-1 *Epstein (24)*
Itandje, Skondras, Giannoulis (Karagounis 86), Fitanidis, Brito, Epstein, Kuqi (Karamanos 61), Beljić (Chumbinho 61), Iglesias, Dimoutsos, Lazaridis. Coach: Dušan Bajević (SRB)
A 0-1
Itandje, Skondras, Giannoulis, Fitanidis, Brito (Kuqi 88), Epstein, Iglesias, Karamanos, Dimoutsos (Garcia 85), Lazaridis, Chumbinho (Beljić 75). Coach: Dušan Bajević (SRB)

ASTERAS TRIPOLIS FC

Second qualifying round - İnter Bakı PİK (AZE)
A 1-1 *Usero (54)*
Bantis, Juanito, Formica, Usero, Perrone (Kourbelis 90+1), Rayo (Pipinis 87), Tsabouris, Álvarez, Bartolini, Ximo Navarro, Fragoulakis (Bakasetas 53). Coach: Sakis Tsiolis (GRE)
H 1-1 *Ximo Navarro (68) (aet; 4-2 on pens)*
Bantis, Pipinis (Giannou 70), Juanito, Formica (Bakasetas 57), Usero, Perrone, Rayo, Tsabouris, Álvarez, Bartolini (Kourbelis 61), Ximo Navarro. Coach: Sakis Tsiolis (GRE)

Third qualifying round - CS Marítimo (POR)
H 1-1 *Rayo (48)*
Bantis, Pipinis, Juanito, Usero (Bakasetas 86), Perrone, Rayo, Tsabouris, Álvarez, Ximo Navarro, Kourbelis (Hegon 68), Fragoulakis (Sankaré 46). Coach: Sakis Tsiolis (GRE)
A 0-0
Fülöp, Pipinis, Juanito, Usero (Fragoulakis 74), Perrone, Rayo, Tsabouris, Álvarez (Bakasetas 6?), Sankaré, Bartolini, Ximo Navarro. Coach: Sakis Tsiolis (GRE)

AEK ATHENS FC

Coach: Evangelos Vlahos;
(01/10/12) (Emmanouil Papadopoulos);
(10/10/12) Ewald Lienen (GER);
(09/04/13) (Traianos Dellas)
1924 • OACA Spyro Louis (72,080) • aekfc.gr
Major honours
Greek League (11) 1939, 1940, 1963, 1968, 1971, 1978, 1979, 1989, 1992, 1993, 1994;
Greek Cup (14) 1932, 1939, 1949, 1950, 1956, 1964, 1966, 1978, 1983, 1996, 1997, 2000, 2002, 2011

2012

Date	Opponent		Score	Scorers
25/08	Asteras	h	0-1	
01/09	Xanthi	a	0-1	
16/09	Aris	h	1-1	Yago Fernández
23/09	OFI	a	1-2	Furtado
29/09	Panionios	a	0-1	
06/10	Kerkyra	h	1-1	Pavlis
20/10	PAOK	a	0-1	
28/10	Platanias	h	1-0	Fountas
04/11	Panathinaikos	a	0-1	
11/11	Olympiacos	h	0-4	
18/11	Veria	a	4-0	Katidis, Fountas, Roger, Stamatis
24/11	Levadiakos	h	0-1	
03/12	Giannina	h	2-1	Fountas, Stamatis
10/12	Panthrakikos	a	0-1	
16/12	Atromitos	h	1-1	Stamatis

2013

Date	Opponent		Score	Scorers
06/01	Asteras	a	1-3	Koutroumbis
12/01	Xanthi	h	1-0	Petropoulos
20/01	Aris	a	1-1	Petropoulos
26/01	OFI	h	2-1	Petropoulos, Pavlis
02/02	Panionios	h	1-0	Roger
10/02	Kerkyra	a	1-0	Roger (p)
16/02	PAOK	h	0-0	
24/02	Platanias	a	1-2	Fetsis
03/03	Panathinaikos	h	0-2	
10/03	Olympiacos	a	0-3	
16/03	Veria	h	2-1	Fountas, Katidis
31/03	Levadiakos	a	0-0	
08/04	Giannina	a	0-2	
14/04	Panthrakikos	h	0-3	(w/o; match abandoned after 87 mins at 0-1)
21/04	Atromitos	a	0-1	

No	Name	Nat	DoB	Pos	Aps	(s)	Gls
44	Dimitrios Anakoglou		06/09/91	M	2	(2)	
39	Dimitrios Anastopoulos		11/04/90	M	1	(2)	
99	Ioannis Arabatzis		28/05/84	G	6	(2)	
77	Christos Arkoudas		13/06/90	D	10	(3)	
47	Mavroudis Bougaidis		01/06/93	D	17	(1)	
23	Xenofon Fetsis		05/05/91	M	17	(2)	1
21	Taxiarhis Fountas		04/09/95	M	25	(2)	4
20	José Furtado	CPV	14/03/83	A	10	(8)	1
80	Dimitrios Grontis		21/08/94	M	4	(1)	
70	Ioannis Karalis		06/11/88	M	2	(6)	
8	Georgios Katidis		12/02/93	M	10	(10)	2
7	Nikolaos Katsikokeris		19/06/88	A	3	(4)	
1	Dimitrios Konstantopoulos		29/11/78	G	24		
2	Ioannis Kontoes		24/05/86	D	15		
12	Konstantinos Kotsaridis		12/06/92	M	2	(3)	
88	Nikolaos Kourellas		22/05/93	A	3	(1)	
91	Georgios Koutroumbis		10/02/91	D	29		1
19	Panagiotis Lagos		18/07/85	M	10		
6	Miguel Cordero	ESP	10/09/87	M	21	(2)	
82	Pavlos Mitropoulos		04/04/90	M	14		
66	Alexandros Nikolias		23/07/94	M		(1)	
63	Christos Papadimitriou		10/01/94	A	3	(2)	
11	Mihail Pavlis		22/09/89	A	4	(9)	2
33	Antonios Petropoulos		28/01/86	A	13		3
13	Antonios Rikka		03/03/86	M	13	(3)	
10	Roger Guerreiro	POL	25/05/82	M	21	(6)	3
14	Andreas Stamatis		12/05/93	A		(10)	3
9	Thomas Tsitas		30/07/91	A	1	(4)	
92	Sokratis Tsoukalas		07/07/92	D	6	(1)	
34	Anastasios Tsoumagas		22/03/91	D	13		
81	Konstantinos Tsoupros		20/07/91	D	2	(2)	
37	Valentinos Vlahos		14/01/92	M	17	(1)	
3	Yago Fernández	POR	05/01/88	D	12	(1)	1

ARIS THESSALONIKI FC

Coach: Thomas Katsavakis;
(09/10/12) (Nikolaos Passialis);
(03/12/12) Lucas Alcaraz (ESP);
(29/01/13) (Ioannis Mihalitsos);
(08/03/13) Anastasios 'Soulis' Papadopoulos)
1914 • Kleanthis Vikelidis (22,800) • arisfc.gr
Major honours
Greek League (3) 1928, 1932, 1946;
Greek Cup (1) 1970

2012
27/08	Panionios	a	0-1	
02/09	OFI	h	0-0	
16/09	AEK	a	1-1	*David Aganzo*
23/09	Kerkyra	h	1-0	*David Aganzo*
30/09	PAOK	a	1-4	*David Aganzo*
07/10	Platanias	h	0-2	
21/10	Panathinaikos	a	1-1	*Gianniotas*
29/10	Olympiacos	h	2-2	*Papasterianos, David Aganzo*
05/11	Veria	h	2-1	*David Aganzo, Ghesios*
10/11	Levadiakos	a	1-2	*Kanoulas*
17/11	Giannina	h	1-2	*Gianniotas*
26/11	Panthrakikos	a	0-4	
01/12	Atromitos	h	1-1	*Sounas*
09/12	Asteras	a	1-1	*Gianniotas (p)*
16/12	Xanthi	h	0-0	

2013
06/01	Panionios	h	2-1	*Ageloudis, David Aganzo*
13/01	OFI	a	0-2	
20/01	AEK	h	1-1	*David Aganzo*
28/01	Kerkyra	a	2-2	*Giannitsis, Karagiannis*
03/02	PAOK	h	2-2	*David Aganzo 2 (1p)*
11/02	Platanias	a	0-2	
17/02	Panathinaikos	h	1-0	*Nuno Coelho*
24/02	Olympiacos	a	1-2	*Ageloudis*
04/03	Veria	a	1-3	*Ageloudis*
10/03	Levadiakos	h	4-0	*Nuno Coelho, Gianniotas 2, Tatos*
16/03	Giannina	a	0-2	
30/03	Panthrakikos	h	0-0	
06/04	Atromitos	a	1-0	*Tatos*
14/04	Asteras	h	5-1	*Triantafyllakos, Tatos 3 (1p), Ageloudis*
21/04	Xanthi	a	0-0	

No	Name	Nat	DoB	Pos	Aps	(s)	Gls
11	Nikolaos Ageloudis		14/05/91	A	4	(8)	4
27	Pantelis Antoniadis		23/03/94	M		(1)	
32	Dimitrios Aslanidis		16/08/89	M	3	(4)	
30	Erotokritos Damarlis		13/05/92	D	6	(5)	
9	David Aganzo	ESP	10/01/81	A	19	(2)	9
33	Dimitrios Diamantakos		05/03/93	A	9	(4)	
13	Sokratis Dioudis		03/02/93	G	12		
14	Ioannis Ghesios		03/08/88	A	3	(5)	1
20	Ioannis Gianniotas		29/04/93	A	26		5
3	Mihail Giannitsis		06/02/92	D	12	(1)	1
6	Charalambos Ikonomopoulos		09/01/91	M	11	(6)	
44	Andreas Iraklis		16/05/89	D	2	(3)	
22	Athanasios Kanoulas		19/02/92	D	1	(5)	1
11	Konstantinos aKapetanos		27/10/84	M	8	(3)	
26	Alexandros Karagiannis		25/10/93	A	4	(2)	1
7	Konstantinos Kaznaferis		22/06/87	M	25		
12	Konstantinos Kotsaridis		12/06/92	M	2	(2)	
21	Georgios Margaritis		20/06/91	D	14	(6)	
66	Nuno Coelho	POR	23/11/87	M	25		2
5	Nikolaos Pantidos		04/04/91	D	7	(4)	
17	Emmanouil Papasterianos		15/08/87	M	22	(2)	1
4	Grigorios Papazaharias		20/03/85	D	22	(2)	
36	Nikolaos Psihogios		25/02/89	D	12	(1)	
28	Andi Renja	ALB	06/01/93	M		(1)	
19	Rubén Pulido	ESP	02/02/79	D	20		
24	Dimitrios Sounas		12/08/94	M	11	(7)	1
10	Andreas Tatos		11/05/89	M	11		5
8	Vasilios Triantafyllakos		16/07/91	A	9	(10)	1
35	Stilianos Tsoukanis		27/02/90	M	1	(4)	
1	Markos Vellidis		04/04/87	G	18		
34	Ioannis Zaradoukas		12/12/85	D	11	(1)	

ASTERAS TRIPOLIS FC

Coach: Athanasios 'Sakis' Tsiolis
1931 • Theodoros Kolokotronis (6,000) • asterastripolis.gr

2012
25/08	AEK	a	1-0	*Álvarez*
02/09	Kerkyra	h	3-0	*Rayo, Perrone, Pipinis*
16/09	PAOK	a	1-2	*Perrone (p)*
22/09	Platanias	h	2-1	*Rayo, Perrone*
30/09	Panathinaikos	a	0-0	
07/10	Olympiacos	a	0-1	
21/10	Veria	h	3-0	*Perrone 2, De Blasis*
27/10	Levadiakos	a	0-0	
04/11	Giannina	h	2-0	*Usero, Hegon*
11/11	Panthrakikos	a	0-1	
19/11	Atromitos	h	3-0	*Bartolini, Ximo Navarro 2*
25/11	Panionios	h	2-1	*De Blasis, Usero*
01/12	Xanthi	a	1-1	*Kalantzis*
09/12	Aris	h	1-1	*og (Giannitsis)*
15/12	OFI	a	0-2	

2013
05/01	AEK	h	3-1	*De Blasis, Rayo, Perrone*
14/01	Kerkyra	a	1-0	*Perrone*
19/01	PAOK	h	1-0	*Ximo Navarro*
27/01	Platanias	a	3-0	*Sankaré, Ximo Navarro, Perrone*
02/02	Panathinaikos	h	2-2	*Rayo, Perrone (p)*
09/02	Olympiacos	h	0-1	
17/02	Veria	a	1-0	*Rayo, Lencse*
25/02	Levadiakos	h	1-0	*Fragoulakis*
03/03	Giannina	a	2-1	*Lencse 2*
09/03	Panthrakikos	h	1-0	*Rayo*
17/03	Atromitos	a	2-0	*Usero, Rayo (p)*
01/04	Panionios	a	1-2	*De Blasis*
07/04	Xanthi	h	0-1	
14/04	Aris	a	1-5	*Caffa*
21/04	OFI	h	2-1	*Bakasetas 2*

No	Name	Nat	DoB	Pos	Aps	(s)	Gls
27	Leandro Álvarez	ARG	04/06/81	M	23	(3)	1
18	Álvaro García	ESP	07/07/86	M		(1)	
14	Anastasios Bakasetas		28/06/93	A	3	(4)	2
37	Georgios Bantis		30/04/85	G	5		
22	Sebastián Bartolini	ARG	01/02/82	D	22		1
21	Juan Pablo Caffa	ARG	30/09/84	A	3	(7)	1
21	Matías Cardaccio	URU	02/10/87	M	1	(6)	
20	Marc Castells	ESP	12/03/90	D	6	(2)	
32	Pablo De Blasis	ARG	04/02/88	A	23	(4)	4
17	Ioannis Diniotakis		14/06/94	A		(3)	
6	Lautaro Formica	ARG	27/01/86	D	18	(6)	
31	Mihail Fragoulakis		15/07/83	M	8	(9)	1
1	Márton Fülöp	HUN	03/05/83	G	24		
50	Gabriel do Carmo	BRA	12/04/90	A	4	(3)	
46	Georgios Georgakopoulos		20/05/92	G	1		
27	Eleftherios Gialousis		18/07/85	D	1	(2)	
30	Hegon	BRA	06/05/88	M	1	(7)	1
96	Christos Kalantzis		01/12/82	A	8	(10)	1
33	Ioannis Kontoes		24/05/86	D	5	(2)	
25	Dimitrios Kourbelis		02/11/93	D	9	(6)	
29	László Lencse	HUN	02/07/88	A	5	(4)	3
9	Emanuel Perrone	ARG	14/06/83	A	15	(2)	9
3	Christos Pipinis		01/11/84	D	16	(1)	1
18	Francisco Pol	VEN	17/09/87	M		(1)	
10	Rayo	ESP	21/06/86	M	28	(1)	7
88	Dimitrios Roussis		06/05/88	D	2		
19	Khalifa Sankaré	SEN	15/08/84	D	23		1
7	Sebastián Setti	ARG	15/07/86	D	3	(1)	
11	Savvas Tsabouris		16/07/86	M	26		
8	Fernando Usero	ESP	27/03/84	M	20	(2)	3
23	Ximo Navarro	ESP	12/09/88	D	27	(2)	4

ATROMITOS FC

Coach: Dušan Bajević (SRB);
(29/12/12) Nikolaos Anastopoulos;
(08/04/13) Georgios Parashos
1923 • Dimotiko Peristeriou (9,000) • atromitosfc.gr

2012
26/08	Kerkyra	a	2-0	*Chumbinho, Fitanidis*
03/09	PAOK	h	1-0	*Lazaridis*
16/09	Platanias	a	0-0	
24/09	Panathinaikos	a	1-1	*Iglesias*
29/09	Olympiacos	h	0-1	
06/10	Veria	a	2-2	*Karamanos, og (Georgeas)*
21/10	Levadiakos	a	0-0	
28/10	Giannina	a	0-0	
03/11	Panthrakikos	h	2-1	*Kuqi, Karagounis*
11/11	Panionios	h	1-0	*Karagounis*
19/11	Asteras	a	0-3	
24/11	Xanthi	h	1-0	*Fitanidis*
01/12	Aris	a	1-1	*Skondras*
08/12	OFI	h	3-2	*Skondras, Karamanos, Brito*
16/12	AEK	a	1-1	*Iglesias*

2013
06/01	Kerkyra	h	2-0	*Fitanidis, Tavlaridis*
13/01	PAOK	a	0-0	
20/01	Platanias	h	1-0	*Brito*
27/01	Panathinaikos	h	1-2	*Karamanos*
03/02	Olympiacos	a	3-2	*Brito, Karagounis, Dimoutsos*
09/02	Veria	h	0-0	
17/02	Levadiakos	a	0-0	
24/02	Giannina	h	0-0	
02/03	Panthrakikos	a	1-0	*Mantzios*
11/03	Panionios	a	0-1	
17/03	Asteras	h	0-2	
31/03	Xanthi	h	0-2	
06/04	Aris	h	0-1	
14/04	OFI	a	2-2	*Udoji 2*
21/04	AEK	h	1-0	*Giannoulis*

No	Name	Nat	DoB	Pos	Aps	(s)	Gls
16	Panagiotis Ballas		06/09/93	M	1	(3)	
11	Nikola Beljić	SRB	14/05/83	M	6	(9)	
7	Brito	BRA	21/09/82	M	23	(4)	3
86	Chumbinho	BRA	21/09/86	M	17	(7)	1
21	Elini Dimoutsos		18/06/88	M	25	(3)	1
8	Denis Epstein	GER	02/07/86	M	21	(2)	
23	Fábio	POR	26/03/88	A		(2)	
5	Sokratis Fitanidis		25/05/84	D	25	(1)	3
3	Konstantinos Giannoulis		09/12/87	D	28		1
17	Walter Iglesias	ARG	18/04/85	M	22	(2)	2
1	Charles Itandje	CMR	02/11/82	G	19		
14	Emmanouil Kallergis		05/12/90	M		(1)	
10	Athanasios Karagounis		25/09/91	A	11	(12)	3
20	Anastasios Karamanos		21/09/90	A	11	(9)	3
9	Njazi Kuqi	FIN	25/03/83	A	14	(6)	1
24	Nikolaos Lazaridis		12/07/79	D	20	(1)	1
33	Evangelos Mantzios		24/04/83	A	7		1
90	Stefano Napoleoni	ITA	26/06/86	A	5	(5)	
13	Evangelos Nastos		13/09/80	D	4	(3)	
26	Pitu	ARG	27/01/84	M	8	(16)	
30	Velimir Radman	CRO	28/05/83	G	11		
2	Ioannis Skondras		21/02/90	D	27		2
4	Efstathios Tavlaridis		25/01/80	D	17	(1)	1
5	Chigozie Udoji	NGA	16/07/86	M	8	(3)	2

KERKYRA FC

Coach: Apostolos Mantzios;
(07/02/13) Ioannis Papakostas
1967 • Ethniko Athlitiko Kentro (EAK) Kerkyras (2,685)
• aokerkyra.com.gr

2012

26/08	Atromitos	h	0-2	
02/09	Asteras	a	0-3	
16/09	Xanthi	h	1-1	*Barkoglou*
23/09	Aris	a	0-1	
29/09	OFI	h	2-1	*Agritis, Giantsis*
06/10	AEK	a	1-1	*Venetis*
20/10	Panionios	a	1-0	*Karalis*
27/10	PAOK	h	0-0	
03/11	Platanias	a	1-1	*Barkoglou (p)*
12/11	Panathinaikos	h	0-0	
17/11	Olympiacos	a	0-2	
25/11	Veria	h	1-1	*Goumas*
02/12	Levadiakos	a	0-2	
08/12	Giannina	h	0-2	
15/12	Panthrakikos	h	0-2	

2013

06/01	Atromitos	a	0-2	
14/01	Asteras	h	0-1	
20/01	Xanthi	a	0-0	
28/01	Aris	h	2-2	*Kivelidis 2*
03/02	OFI	a	0-2	
10/02	AEK	h	0-1	
16/02	Panionios	h	2-1	*Ghesios 2*
23/02	PAOK	a	1-3	*Ghesios*
02/03	Platanias	a	2-1	*Kivelidis 2*
09/03	Panathinaikos	a	0-1	
17/03	Olympiacos	h	0-1	
31/03	Veria	a	0-2	
06/04	Levadiakos	h	1-2	*Agritis*
14/04	Giannina	a	0-1	
21/04	Panthrakikos	a	1-2	*Kivelidis*

No	Name	Nat	DoB	Pos	Aps	(s)	Gls
10	Anestis Agritis		16/04/81	A	20	(4)	2
1	Nikolaos Anastasopoulos		05/08/79	G	26		
7	Kyriakos Andreopoulos		18/01/94	M		(1)	
17	Christos Armenis		22/06/93	D	3	(1)	
88	Antonios Athanasiou		21/09/92	M	7	(1)	
11	Georgios Barkoglou		08/07/78	M	14	(2)	2
2	Mihail Boukouvalas		14/01/88	D	20		
9	Dimitrios Diamantopoulos		10/11/00	A		(0)	
14	Diego Leon	ESP	18/01/84	M	25	(1)	
70	Ioannis Diniotakis		14/06/94	A		(2)	
15	Éder	BRA	21/09/83	D	26		
21	Ioannis Ghesios		03/08/88	A	9	(3)	3
19	Dimitrios Giantsis		04/03/88	A	10	(7)	1
23	Ioannis P Goumas		07/06/88	M	3	(3)	1
20	Jan Hable	CZE	04/01/89	M	4	(1)	
8	Stilianos Iliadis		03/06/86	M	17	(8)	
7	Ioannis Karalis		06/11/88	M	9	(5)	1
88	Theodoros Karapetsas		25/07/90	M		(3)	
33	Leonidas Kivelidis		08/02/86	A	10	(2)	5
21	Dimitrios Kontodimos		21/04/82	D	13		
16	Nikolaos Kritikos		01/11/94	M	8	(6)	
45	Aristidis Lottas		16/09/88	M		(1)	
25	Anestis Nastos		28/04/89	M		(1)	
3	Mauro Papadimas		26/07/91	D	1		
4	Panagiotis Petrousis		11/08/92	D	7	(3)	
77	Ioannis Simosis		13/03/91	A		(7)	
12	Nikolaos Skebis		02/11/92	D		(1)	
6	Panagiotis Stamogiannos		30/01/92	M	10	(3)	
27	Dimitrios Stamou		27/04/91	M	6	(1)	
29	Kiriakos Stratilatis		05/01/88	G	4		
24	Anastasios Tsokanis		02/05/91	M	11	(10)	
18	Nicolaos Tsoumanis		08/06/90	M	19	(1)	
71	Andreas Vasilogiannis		21/02/91	M	4	(6)	
5	Anastasios Venetis		24/03/80	D	26		1
31	Angelos Zoumboulakis		23/05/89	M	18		

LEVADIAKOS FC

Coach: Georgios Paraschoi;
(22/03/13) Jasminko Velić (BIH)
1961 • Dimotiko Livadias (6,200) • levadiakosfc.gr

2012

25/08	Panathinaikos	h	0-1	
02/09	Olympiacos	a	0-4	
15/09	Veria	h	0-0	
22/09	Panionios	h	3-0	*Vasiliou 2, Zisopoulos*
01/10	Giannina	h	0-0	
08/10	Panthrakikos	h	0-3	
21/10	Atromitos	a	0-0	
27/10	Asteras	h	0-0	
04/11	Xanthi	a	0-1	
10/11	Aris	h	2-1	*Zisopoulos, Vasiliou*
18/11	OFI	a	2-0	*Rogério Martins, og (Kourdakis)*
24/11	AEK	a	1-0	*Napoleoni*
02/12	Kerkyra	h	2-0	*Zisopoulos, Korbos*
08/12	PAOK	a	0-1	
16/12	Platanias	h	1-0	*Rogério Martins*

2013

05/01	Panathinaikos	a	2-1	*Vasiliou 2*
12/01	Olympiacos	h	0-1	
21/01	Veria	a	2-1	*Lisgaras, Vasiliou*
26/01	Panionios	a	1-2	*Vasiliou*
04/02	Giannina	h	1-1	*Zisopoulos*
10/02	Panthrakikos	a	0-0	
17/02	Atromitos	h	0-0	
24/02	Asteras	a	0-1	
03/03	Xanthi	h	1-4	*Rogério Martins*
10/03	Aris	a	0-4	
16/03	OFI	h	1-1	*Lisgaras*
31/03	AEK	h	0-0	
06/04	Kerkyra	a	2-1	*Rogério Martins, Korbos*
14/04	PAOK	h	0-1	
21/04	Platanias	a	0-2	

No	Name	Nat	DoB	Pos	Aps	(s)	Gls
39	Almir	BRA	03/03/91	M		(4)	
27	Georgios Boudopoulos		27/07/90	A		(3)	
20	Olivier Boumale	CMR	17/09/89	M		(3)	
23	Georgios Georgiou		24/09/79	D	18		
3	Josemi	ESP	15/11/79	D	25		
15	Juanmi	ESP	11/02/87	D	5	(5)	
28	Alexandros Kasmeridis		23/04/86	G	3	(2)	
82	Dimitris Kiriakidis		24/08/88	M	0		
7	Panagiotis Korbos		11/09/86	M	20		2
25	Efthimios Kotitsas		25/03/86	D		(1)	
66	Evangelos Koutsopoulos		02/02/80	D	1	(7)	
31	Christos Lisgaras		12/02/86	D	19	(1)	2
6	Dimitrios Maheras		16/08/90	M	3	(18)	
14	Kostas S Manolas		26/03/93	D	1		
76	Jackson Mendy	SEN	25/05/87	D	27		
22	Kristijan Miljević	SRB	15/07/92	A	2	(9)	
2	Athanasios Moulopoulos		09/06/85	D	26		
1	Stefano Napoleoni	ITA	26/06/86	A	7	(3)	1
21	Emmanouil Nikolakakis		19/02/91	D	4	(4)	
77	Noé Acosta	ESP	10/12/83	M	20	(3)	
19	Georgios Peppas		20/07/94	M	1		
9	Mauro Poy	ARG	07/02/81	A	29		
8	Rogério Martins	BRA	19/11/84	M	24	(5)	4
21	Romeu	BRA	13/02/85	M	6	(13)	
9	Stilianos Vasiliou		29/04/91	A	23	(3)	7
24	Thierry Zahui	CIV	22/10/87	M		(2)	
13	Georgios Zisopoulos		23/05/84	M	30		4

OFI CRETE FC

Coach: Nikolaos Anastopoulos;
(02/01/13) Ioannis Petrakis
1925 • Thodoros Vardinoyannis (8,700) • ofi.gr
Major honours
Greek Cup (1) 1987

2012

26/08	Xanthi	h	0-0	
02/09	Aris	a	0-0	
17/09	Panionios	a	1-2	*og (Koulouheris)*
23/09	AEK	h	2-1	*Šišić (p), Ioannidis (p)*
29/09	Kerkyra	a	1-2	*Dénis Souza*
06/10	PAOK	h	1-1	*Papazoglou*
22/10	Platanias	a	2-1	*Šišić, Lambropoulos*
29/10	Panathinaikos	h	2-2	*Koutsianikoulis, Papazoglou*
03/11	Olympiacos	a	0-2	
10/11	Veria	h	2-0	*Dénis Souza, Lambropoulos*
18/11	Levadiakos	h	0-2	
24/11	Giannina	a	0-1	
02/12	Panthrakikos	h	1-1	*Perogamvrakis*
08/12	Atromitos	a	2-3	*Perogamvrakis, Koutsianikoulis*
15/12	Asteras	h	2-0	*Papazoglou, Koutsianikoulis*

2013

07/01	Xanthi	a	0-3	
13/01	Aris	h	2-0	*Perogamvrakis, Papazoglou*
19/01	Panionios	h	2-1	*Lambropoulos, Perogamvrakis*
26/01	AEK	a	1-2	*Dénis Souza*
03/02	Kerkyra	h	2-0	*Papazoglou, Perogamvrakis*
09/02	PAOK	a	1-3	*Perogamvrakis*
18/02	Platanias	h	1-0	*Oarr*
23/02	Panathinaikos	a	1-3	*Koutsianikoulis*
02/03	Olympiacos	h	0-4	
10/03	Veria	a	0-0	
17/03	Levadiakos	a	1-1	*Papazoglou*
30/03	Giannina	h	2-1	*Papazoglou, Koutsianikoulis*
07/04	Panthrakikos	a	1-3	*Ioannidis*
14/04	Atromitos	h	2-2	*Papazoglou, Sarr*
21/04	Asteras	a	1-2	*Makris*

No	Name	Nat	DoB	Pos	Aps	(s)	Gls
92	Mihail Agrimakis		28/07/92	G	9		
4	Konstantinos Banousis		23/01/88	M	15	(5)	
28	Christos Bourbos		01/06/83	D	8	(6)	
5	Lazaros Charitonidis		18/12/89	D	6		
25	Stergios Chatzikosmas		18/11/92	M		(1)	
24	Dénis Souza	BRA	07/08/00	D	20		6
44	Stefanos Gounaridis		18/08/90	G	21		
19	Georgios Ioannidis		04/05/88	M	21	(1)	2
11	Athanasios Kanoulas		19/02/92	D	1	(4)	
20	Aristomenis Kapouranis		15/01/90	M	1	(5)	
12	Grigorios Kiziridis		24/10/90	M	1	(1)	
15	Panagiotis Kourdakis		15/08/88	D	12	(6)	
8	Vasilios Koutsianikoulis		09/08/88	M	26	(2)	5
18	Andreas Lambropoulos		30/07/88	A	20	(3)	3
54	Georgios Makris		15/11/84	M	5	(4)	1
6	Emmanouil Moniakis		09/11/88	D	20		
22	Nikomanolis Niktaris		04/09/92	M	1	(2)	
9	Athanasios Papazoglou		30/03/88	A	25		8
21	Alexandros Perogamvrakis		20/01/88	A	15	(8)	6
14	Emmanouil Rovithis		16/09/92	D		(4)	
2	Mohamed Adama Sarr	SEN	23/12/83	D	18	(1)	2
32	Mirnes Šišić	SVN	08/08/81	M	11		2
33	Georgios Valerianos		13/02/92	D	1		
11	Vandinho	BRA	09/06/86	D	8		
1	Ricardo Verón	ARG	22/01/81	M	28		
99	Ioannis Vitoros		12/11/92	M	9	(14)	
17	Emmanouil Zaharakis		10/08/92	D	13	(7)	
7	Panagiotis Zorbas		21/04/87	M	7	(15)	

OLYMPIACOS FC

Coach: Leonardo Jardim (POR);
(19/01/13) (Antonios Nikopolidis);
(04/02/13) Míchel (ESP)
1925 • Georgios Karaiskakis (32,130) • olympiacos.org
Major honours
*Greek League (40) 1931, 1933, 1934, 1936, 1937,
1938, 1947, 1948, 1951, 1954, 1955, 1956, 1957, 1958,
1959, 1966, 1967, 1973, 1974, 1975, 1980, 1981, 1982,
1983, 1987, 1997, 1998, 1999, 2000, 2001, 2002, 2003,
2005, 2006, 2007, 2008, 2009, 2011, 2012, 2013;
Greek Cup (26) 1947, 1951, 1952, 1953, 1954, 1957, 1958,
1959, 1960, 1961, 1963, 1965, 1968, 1971, 1973, 1975, 1981,
1990, 1992, 1999, 2005, 2006, 2008, 2009, 2012, 2013.*

2012

26/08	Veria	a	2-1	Djebbour, Modesto
02/09	Levadiakos	h	4-0	Siovas, Djebbour 2, Maniatis
15/09	Giannina	a	2-1	Mitroglou, Djebbour
23/09	Panthrakikos	h	4-1	Djebbour 2, Holebas, og (Skliopidis)
29/09	Atromitos	a	1-0	David Fuster
07/10	Asteras	h	1-0	Holebas
20/10	Xanthi	h	4-0	Manolas, Holebas, Djebbour 2
29/10	Aris	a	2-2	Abdoun (p), Holebas
03/11	OFI	h	2-0	Mitroglou, Paulo Machado
11/11	AEK	a	4-0	Abdoun (p), Mitroglou 2, David Fuster
17/11	Kerkyra	h	2-0	Mitroglou, Siovas
25/11	PAOK	a	1-1	Djebbour
01/12	Platanias	h	2-1	Abdoun (p), Torosidis
09/12	Panathinaikos	a	2-2	Djebbour 2
15/12	Panionios	a	2-1	og (Spyropoulos), Djebbour

2013

06/01	Veria	h	3-0	Mitroglou, Djebbour (p), Pantelić
12/01	Levadiakos	a	1-0	Djebbour
20/01	Giannina	h	2-0	Djebbour, Abdoun
27/01	Panthrakikos	a	1-0	Contreras
03/02	Atromitos	h	2-3	Djebbour, Abdoun
09/02	Asteras	a	1-0	Mitroglou
17/02	Xanthi	h	2-0	Paulo Machado
24/02	Aris	a	2-1	Djebbour, Maniatis
02/03	OFI	a	4-0	Djebbour 2, Vlahodimos, Papazoglou
10/03	AEK	h	3-0	Papadopoulos 2, Abdoun
17/03	Kerkyra	a	1-0	Mitroglou
31/03	PAOK	h	0-0	
07/04	Platanias	a	4-0	Abdoun, David Fuster, Mitroglou, Vlahodimos
14/04	Panathinaikos	h	1-1	Mitroglou
21/04	Panionios	h	2-1	Mitroglou, Papadopoulos

No	Name	Nat	DoB	Pos	Aps	(s)	Gls
93	Djamel Abdoun	ALG	14/02/86	M	27		7
1	Roy Carroll	NIR	30/09/77	G	16		
15	Pablo Contreras	CHI	11/09/78	D	16	(1)	1
19	David Fuster	ESP	03/02/82	M	9	(9)	3
26	Drissa Diakité	MLI	18/02/85	D	4		
87	Diogo	BRA	26/05/87	A		(1)	
10	Rafik Djebbour	ALG	08/03/84	A	23	(2)	20
8	Ljubomir Fejsa	SRB	14/08/88	M	11	(4)	
18	Ioannis Fetfatzidis		21/12/90	M	4	(8)	
27	Leandro Greco	ITA	19/07/86	M	15	(3)	
20	José Holebas		27/06/84	D	28		4
7	Ariel Ibagaza	ARG	27/10/76	M	10	(11)	
25	Charalambos Lykogiannis		22/10/93	D	2	(2)	
2	Ioannis Maniatis		12/10/86	D	25	(2)	2
24	Kostas N Manolas		14/06/91	D	24		1
42	Balázs Megyeri	HUN	31/03/90	G	14		
11	Kostas Mitroglou		12/03/88	A	10	(15)	11
3	François Modesto	FRA	19/08/78	D	18	(2)	1
9	Marko Pantelić	SRB	15/09/78	A		(6)	1
21	Avraam Papadopoulos		03/12/84	D	5		3
6	Anastasios Papazoglou		24/09/88	D	13	(2)	1
5	Paulo Machado	POR	31/03/86	M	23	(5)	2
99	Juan Pablo Pino	COL	30/03/87	M	1	(2)	
23	Dimitrios Siovas		16/09/88	D	13	(2)	2
22	Andreas Tatos		11/05/89	M	1		
35	Vasilios Torosidis		10/06/85	D	10	(2)	1
17	Panagiotis Vlahodimos		11/10/91	A	8	(4)	2
31	Ioannis Zaradoukas		12/12/85	D		(1)	

PANATHINAIKOS FC

Coach: Jesualdo Ferreira (POR);
(14/11/12) Juan Ramón Rocha (ARG);
(08/01/13) Fabri (ESP); (31/03/13) (Ioannis Vonortas)
1908 • OACA Spyro Louis (72,080) • pao.gr
Major honours
*Greek League (20) 1930, 1949, 1953, 1960, 1961,
1962, 1964, 1965, 1969, 1970, 1972, 1977, 1984, 1986,
1990, 1991, 1995, 1996, 2004, 2010;
Greek Cup (17) 1940, 1948, 1955, 1967, 1969,
1977, 1982, 1984, 1986, 1988, 1989, 1991, 1993,
1994, 1995, 2004, 2010*

2012

25/08	Levadiakos	a	1-0	Vyntra
31/08	Giannina	h	1-1	Velázquez
15/09	Panthrakikos	a	0-1	
24/09	Atromitos	h	1-1	Toché (p)
30/09	Asteras	h	0-0	
07/10	Xanthi	a	2-1	Christodoulopoulos 2
21/10	Aris	h	1-1	Christodoulopoulos (p)
29/10	OFI	a	2-2	Toché, Mavrias
04/11	AEK	h	1-0	Toché
12/11	Kerkyra	a	0-0	
18/11	PAOK	h	2-0	Zeca, Vitolo (p)
25/11	Platanias	a	1-2	Toché (p)
02/12	Panionios	a	2-1	Petropoulos, Vyntra
09/12	Olympiacos	h	2-2	Mavrias, Toché
16/12	Veria	a	0-3	

2013

05/01	Levadiakos	h	1-2	Toché
13/01	Giannina	a	0-0	
19/01	Panthrakikos	h	1-1	Toché
27/01	Atromitos	a	2-1	Zeca, Boumsong
02/02	Asteras	a	2-2	Sissoko 2
10/02	Xanthi	h	0-1	
17/02	Aris	a	0-1	
23/02	OFI	h	3-1	Marinos, Toché 2
03/03	AEK	a	2-0	Vitolo, Sow
09/03	Kerkyra	h	1-0	Figueroa (p)
17/03	PAOK	a	0-2	
30/03	Platanias	h	0-1	
07/04	Panionios	h	0-0	
14/04	Olympiacos	a	1-1	Figueroa
21/04	Veria	h	3-2	Vitolo 2 (1p), Sow

No	Name	Nat	DoB	Pos	Aps	(s)	Gls
5	André Pinto	POR	05/10/89	D	16		
36	Konstantinos Apostolopoulos		08/07/93	A		(1)	
21	Kosta Barbarouses	NZL	19/02/90	A	5	(5)	
4	Jean-Alain Boumsong	FRA	14/12/79	D	14		1
10	Lazaros Christodoulopoulos		19/12/86	M	10	(1)	3
41	Adamantios Chouchoumis		17/07/94	D	3	(5)	
26	Athanasios Dinas		12/11/89	A		(4)	
19	Luciano Figueroa	ARG	19/05/81	A	3	(4)	2
14	Bruno Fornaroli	URU	07/09/87	A	6	(10)	
34	Spiridon Fourlanos		19/11/93	M	2	(3)	
12	Jokin Arcaya	ESP	15/06/88	M	4	(4)	
49	Yohei Kajiyama	JPN	24/09/85	M	6	(1)	
40	Stefanos Kapino		18/03/94	G	11		
29	Orestis Karnezis		11/07/85	G	29		
29	Kostas Katsouranis		21/06/79	M	1		
2	Nicky Kuiper	NED	07/06/89	D	2	(1)	
23	Anastasios Lagos		12/04/92	D	3	(2)	
22	Stergos Marinos		17/09/87	D	15	(5)	1
7	Charalambos Mavrias		21/02/94	A	18	(8)	2
14	Quincy Owusu-Abeyie	GHA	15/04/86	A	2	(6)	1
28	Antonios Petropoulos		28/01/86	A	2	(6)	1
16	Giourkas Seitaridis		04/06/81	D	22		
3	Ibrahim Sissoko	CIV	29/11/91	M	25	(3)	2
20	Pape Sow	SEN	02/12/85	M	12	(3)	2
31	Nikolaos Spyropoulos		10/10/83	D	16	(1)	
18	Panagiotis Spyropoulos		21/08/92	D	3	(1)	
9	Toché	ESP	01/01/83	A	19	(4)	9
45	Kostas Triantafyllopoulos		03/04/93	D	13	(2)	
44	José Manuel Velázquez	VEN	08/09/90	D	8	(1)	1
6	Vitolo	ESP	09/09/83	M	26		4
24	Loukas Vyntra		05/02/81	D	14		2
17	Zeca	POR	31/08/88	M	24	(5)	2

PANIONIOS GSS

Coach: Dimitrios Eleftheropoulos;
(18/02/13) Konstantinos Panagopoulos
1890 • Panionios GSS (16,800) • pgss.gr
Major honours
Greek Cup (2) 1979, 1998

2012

27/08	Aris	h	1-0	Lambropoulos
01/09	Veria	a	1-0	Mendrinos
17/09	OFI	h	2-1	og (Gounaridis), og (Vandinho)
22/09	Levadiakos	a	0-3	
29/09	AEK	h	1-0	Kabadais
07/10	Giannina	a	2-1	Goundoulakis (p), Lambropoulos
20/10	Kerkyra	h	0-1	
27/10	Panthrakikos	a	2-1	Aravidis 2
04/11	PAOK	h	1-2	Aravidis
11/11	Atromitos	a	0-2	
17/11	Platanias	h	4-0	og (Argiropoulos), Rokas, Aravidis, Dounis
25/11	Asteras	a	1-2	Kolovos
02/12	Panathinaikos	h	1-2	Dounis
09/12	Xanthi	a	0-4	
15/12	Olympiacos	h	1-2	Aravidis

2013

06/01	Aris	a	1-2	Dounis
13/01	Veria	h	1-1	Kabadais
19/01	OFI	a	1-2	Aravidis
26/01	Levadiakos	h	2-1	Samaris, Goundoulakis
02/02	AEK	a	0-1	
10/02	Giannina	h	0-1	
16/02	Kerkyra	a	1-2	Kolovos
24/02	Panthrakikos	h	2-0	Samaris, Kabadais
03/03	PAOK	a	2-4	Andralas, Goundoulakis (p)
11/03	Atromitos	h	1-0	Kabadais
17/03	Platanias	a	1-2	Aravidis
01/04	Asteras	h	2-1	Samaris 2
07/04	Panathinaikos	a	0-0	
14/04	Xanthi	h	3-3	Aravidis, Kolovos, Koulouheris
21/04	Olympiacos	a	1-2	Samaris

No	Name	Nat	DoB	Pos	Aps	(s)	Gls
16	Paraskevas Andralas		02/12/78	M	8	(6)	1
88	Ioannis Anestis		09/03/91	G	1		
23	Christos Aravidis		13/03/87	A	25		8
5	Anastasios Avlonitis		01/01/90	D	21	(4)	
45	Konstantinos Beglektsis		05/01/95	A		(2)	
17	Vasilios Bouzas		30/06/93	M	1	(1)	
99	Dimitrios Diamantakos		05/03/93	A	3	(5)	
25	Markos Dounis		09/05/92	M	14	(8)	3
31	Nikolaos Giannakopoulos		19/02/93	G	14		
20	Dionisios Giannoulis		09/11/90	D	1	(2)	
	Fanourios Goundoulakis		13/07/83	M	26	(2)	3
9	Leonidas Kabadais		08/03/82	A	14	(6)	4
97	Christos Kartsabas		06/01/90	D		(1)	
7	Dimitrios Kolovos		27/04/93	M	20	(4)	3
44	Christos Kontohristos		03/01/91	M		(1)	
11	Efthimios Koulouheris		10/03/81	D	11	(2)	1
27	Alexandros Kouros		21/08/93	D	22	(1)	
27	Amir Kurdi		11/09/91	M	15	(1)	
32	Vasilios Lambropoulos		31/03/90	D	9		2
10	Konstantinos Mendrinos		28/05/85	M	12	(11)	1
8	Dejan Milovanović	SRB	21/01/84	M		(2)	
39	Emmanuel Okoye	NGA	05/04/91	A	9	(9)	
94	Konstantinos Panagiotoudis		03/12/94	M	3	(9)	
29	Nikolaos Pantidos		19/04/91	D	9		
91	Konstantinos Peristeridis		24/01/91	G	15		
21	Efstathios Rokas		18/09/84	M	15	(2)	1
4	Vasilios Rovas		06/01/84	M	1		
22	Andreas Samaris		13/06/89	M	19	(2)	5
18	Alexandros Smirlis		07/02/93	A		(1)	
2	Panagiotis Spyropoulos		21/08/92	D	15		
33	Dimitrios Toskas		13/03/91	D	10	(3)	
8	Mihail Tsamourlidis		22/03/92	M		(1)	

PANTHRAKIKOS FC

Coach: Savvas Pantelidis;
(30/10/12) Pavlos Dermitzakis
1963 • Dimotiko Komotinis (3,000) • panthrakikos.com

2012

26/08	PAOK	a	0-1	
01/09	Platanias	a	0-2	
15/09	Panathinaikos	h	1-0	Papadopoulos
23/09	Olympiacos	a	1-4	Kivelidis
30/09	Veria	h	0-1	
08/10	Levadiakos	a	3-0	Papadopoulos (p), Ladakis, Villarejo
21/10	Giannina	h	0-3	
27/10	Panionios	h	1-2	Munafo
03/11	Atromitos	a	1-2	Papadopoulos
11/11	Asteras	h	1-0	Papadopoulos
18/11	Xanthi	a	0-0	
26/11	Aris	h	4-0	Papadopoulos 2, Deniz, Lucero
02/12	OFI	a	1-1	Vahirua (p)
10/12	AEK	h	1-0	Vahirua
15/12	Kerkyra	a	2-0	Vahirua, Papadopoulos

2013

06/01	PAOK	h	1-4	og (Kaçe)
12/01	Platanias	h	1-1	Papadopoulos
13/01	Panathinaikos	a	1-1	Papadopoulos
27/01	Olympiacos	h	0-1	
03/02	Veria	a	0-2	
10/02	Levadiakos	h	3-0	Papadopoulos, Lucero 2
16/02	Giannina	h	0-0	
24/02	Panionios	a	0-2	
02/03	Atromitos	h	0-1	
09/03	Asteras	a	0-1	
18/03	Xanthi	h	0-2	
30/03	Aris	a	0-0	
07/04	OFI	h	3-1	Lucero, Deniz, Papadopoulos (p)
14/04	AEK	a	3-0	(w/o; match abandoned after 87 mins at 1-0 og (Bougaidis))
21/04	Kerkyra	h	2-1	Tzanis, Papadopoulos

No	Name	Nat	DoB	Pos	Aps	(s)	Gls
34	Adi Adilović	BIH	20/02/83	G	5	(2)	
30	Georgios Athanasiadis		07/04/93	G	1	(1)	
13	Sofyane Cherfa	ALG	13/08/84	D	29		
21	Ioannis Christou		05/03/81	D	22		
20	Deniz Baykara	TUR	13/03/84	M	28	(1)	2
32	Ioannis Goniadis		15/02/93	M	1	(3)	
15	Jordão Diogo	POR	12/11/85	D	5	(2)	
8	Mladen Kašćelan	MNE	13/02/83	M	15	(5)	
22	Nikolaos Katharios		07/10/94	M		(1)	
33	Leonidas Kivelidis		08/02/86	A	2	(14)	1
11	Evangelos Kontogoulidis		13/07/81	A	1	(12)	
1	Dimitrios Koutsopoulos		20/04/78	G	18		
84	Antonios Ladakis		25/01/82	M	23	(1)	1
10	Adrián Lucero	ARG	16/08/84	A	28		4
18	Dionisios Makridimitris		26/01/85	D	6	(5)	
2	Christos Melissis		01/12/82	D	1	(6)	
7	Ilias Mihalopoulos		15/10/85	M		(2)	
14	Christos Mingas		15/04/84	M	10	(12)	
17	Juan Manuel Munafo	ARG	20/03/83	M	22	(7)	1
22	Dimitrios Papadopoulos		20/10/81	A	25		12
55	Athanasios Prittas		09/01/79	M	1	(2)	
33	Achilleas Sarakatsanos		03/11/82	D	26		
88	Dimitrios Skliopidis		13/05/84	M	13	(4)	
5	Ioannis Stathis		20/05/87	D	5		
19	Christos Tzanis		22/04/85	A	9	(1)	1
6	Marama Vahirua	FRA	12/05/80	A	26		3
3	Miguel Villarejo	ESP	24/08/88	D	2	(4)	1
81	Spiridon Vrontaras		11/12/84	G	6		

PAOK FC

Coach: Georgios Donis;
(29/04/13) Georgios Georgiadis
1926 • Toumbas (31,060) • paokfc.gr
Major honours
Greek League (2) 1976, 1985;
Greek Cup (4) 1972, 1974, 2001, 2003

2012

26/08	Panthrakikos	h	1-0	Athanasiadis
03/09	Atromitos	a	0-1	
16/09	Asteras	h	2-1	Lawrence, Athanasiadis (p)
22/09	Xanthi	a	3-0	Athanasiadis (p), Lazăr, Robert
30/09	Aris	h	4-1	Lawrence, Katsikas, Fotakis, Athanasiadis
06/10	OFI	a	1-1	Fotakis
20/10	AEK	h	1-0	Athanasiadis
27/10	Kerkyra	a	0-0	
04/11	Panionios	a	2-1	Athanasiadis 2 (1p)
11/11	Platanias	h	2-0	Salpingidis (p), Lino
18/11	Panathinaikos	a	0-2	
25/11	Olympiacos	h	1-1	Athanasiadis
02/12	Veria	a	0-0	
08/12	Levadiakos	h	1-0	Lino
17/12	Giannina	h	3-1	Salpingidis 2, Athanasiadis

2013

06/01	Panthrakikos	a	4-1	Lazăr, Salpingidis, Giannou, Stafylidis
13/01	Atromitos	h	0-0	
19/01	Asteras	a	0-1	
27/01	Xanthi	h	0-1	
02/02	Aris	h	2-2	Athanasiadis, Carnara
09/02	OFI	h	3-1	Athanasiadis, Katsikas, Lawrence
16/02	AEK	a	0-0	
23/02	Kerkyra	h	3-1	Salpingidis 2, Athanasiadis
03/03	Panionios	h	4-2	Kaçe, Salpingidis, Katsouranis, Vukić
09/03	Platanias	a	2-1	Salpingidis 2
17/03	Panathinaikos	h	2-0	Camara, Vukić
31/03	Olympiacos	a	0-0	
06/04	Veria	h	2-0	og (Mokaké), Athanasiadis
14/04	Levadiakos	a	1-0	Robert
21/04	Giannina	h	2-0	Georgiadis, Katsouranis

No	Name	Nat	DoB	Pos	Aps	(s)	Gls
2	Alexandros Apostolopoulos		07/11/91	D	11	(4)	
33	Stefanos Athanasiadis		24/12/88	A	25	(1)	13
90	Abdoul Camara	GUI	20/02/90	A	9	(1)	2
77	Etto	BRA	08/03/81	D	10	(4)	
18	Georgios Fotakis		29/10/81	M	19	(6)	2
7	Georgios K. Georgiadis		14/11/87	A	2	(5)	1
99	Apostolos Giannou		25/01/90	A		(11)	1
71	Panagiotis Glykos		10/10/86	G	13		
39	Christos Intzidis		09/01/93	D	3	(2)	
27	Charles Itandje	CMR	02/11/82	G	9		
1	Jacobo	ESP	01/07/83	G	8	(1)	
26	Ergys Kaçe	ALB	08/07/93	M	27		1
4	Georgios Katsikas		14/06/90	D	15	(1)	2
28	Kostas Katsouranis		21/06/79	M	11	(1)	2
30	Bongani Khumalo	RSA	06/01/87	D	16	(3)	
70	Stilianos Kitsiou		28/09/93	M	2	(6)	
22	Dimitrios Konstantinidis		02/06/94	D	11	(3)	
20	Liam Lawrence	IRL	14/12/81	M	19	(3)	3
25	Costin Lazăr	ROU	24/04/81	M	24	(1)	2
16	Lino	BRA	01/07/77	D	22	(5)	2
44	Matheus	BRA	05/04/82	D	5	(2)	
62	Sekou Oliseh	LBR	05/06/90	M	4	(2)	
5	Pablo García	URU	11/05/77	M	2	(2)	
8	Konstantinos Panagiotoudis		03/12/94	M		(1)	
19	Vasilios Papadopoulos		28/01/95	A		(1)	
10	Dimitrios Pelkas		26/10/93	M	4	(6)	
95	Dimitrios Popovic		11/02/95	M		(2)	
11	Bertrand Robert	FRA	16/11/83	M	14	(5)	2
14	Dimitrios Salpingidis		18/08/81	A	23	(3)	9
13	Gordon Schildenfeld	CRO	18/03/85	D	11		
3	Kostas Stafylidis		02/12/93	D	11	(7)	1
9	Zvonimir Vukić	SRB	19/07/79	M		(3)	2

PAS GIANNINA FC

Coach: Ioannis Christopoulos
1966 • Oi Zosimades (7,652) • pasgiannina.gr

2012

25/08	Platanias	h	0-0	
31/08	Panathinaikos	a	1-1	De Vincenti
15/09	Olympiacos	h	1-2	Georgiou
23/09	Veria	a	0-1	
01/10	Levadiakos	h	1 0	Korovesis
07/10	Panionios	h	1-2	Ilić
21/10	Panthrakikos	a	3-0	Ilić, Tsoukalas, Korovesis
28/10	Atromitos	a	0-2	
04/11	Asteras	a	0-2	
10/11	Xanthi	h	1-0	De Vincenti
17/11	Aris	a	2-1	Ilić, og (Psihogios)
24/11	OFI	h	1-0	De Vincenti
03/12	AEK	a	1-2	Mihail
08/12	Kerkyra	a	2-0	Lila, De Vincenti
17/12	PAOK	h	1-3	Ilić

2013

05/01	Platanias	a	1-1	Korovesis
13/01	Panathinaikos	h	0-0	
20/01	Olympiacos	a	0-1	
27/01	Veria	h	2-0	Ilić 2
04/02	Levadiakos	a	1-1	Tzimopoulos
10/02	Panionios	a	1-0	Ilić
16/02	Panthrakikos	h	0-0	
24/02	Atromitos	a	0-0	
03/03	Asteras	h	1-2	Korovesis
10/03	Xanthi	a	1-0	Georgiou
16/03	Aris	h	2-0	Ilić, Korovesis
30/03	OFI	a	1-2	Giakos
08/04	AEK	h	2-0	Korovesis, Georgiou
14/04	Kerkyra	h	1-0	Ilić
21/04	PAOK	a	0-2	

No	Name	Nat	DoB	Pos	Aps	(s)	Gls
88	Mihail Avgenikou		25/01/93	M	1	(4)	
89	Nikolaos Babaniotis		28/06/89	G	2		
2	Georgios Dasios		12/05/83	D	5	(11)	
15	Tomás De Vincenti	ARG	09/02/89	M	22	(4)	4
1	Karim Fegrouche	MAR	14/02/82	G	22	(1)	
17	Fotios Georgiou		19/07/85	M	29	(1)	3
12	Evripidis Giakos		09/10/91	A	2	(12)	1
4	Marios Ikonomou		08/10/92	D	11	(2)	
9	Brana Ilić	SRB	16/02/85	A	30		9
24	Paul Keita	SEN	26/06/92	M	6	(15)	
26	Dimitrios Kolovetsios		16/10/91	D	26	(2)	
33	Nikolaos Korovesis		10/06/91	D	26		6
3	Andi Lila	ALB	12/02/86	D	24	(1)	1
6	Alexios Mihail		18/08/86	D	27		1
23	Georgios Niklitsiotis		23/03/91	M		(10)	
5	Anastasios Pantos		05/05/76	D	26		
7	Christos Patsatzoglou		19/03/79	D	4	(2)	
13	Charalambos Tambasis		10/05/85	G	6		
28	Stavros Tsoukalas		23/05/88	M	29	(1)	1
22	Christos Tzanis		22/04/85	A	1	(5)	
8	Themistoklis Tzimopoulos		20/11/85	M	22		1
14	Emiljano Vila	ALB	12/03/88	A	9	(19)	

PLATANIAS FC

Coach: Ioannis Hatzinikolaou;
(20/11/12) Angelos Anastasiadis
1931 • Dimotiko Perivolion (3,700) • fcplatanias.gr

2012

25/08	Giannina	a	0-0	
01/09	Panthrakikos	h	2-0	Anastasakos, Maragoudakis
16/09	Atromitos	h	0-0	
22/09	Asteras	a	1-2	Udoji
30/09	Xanthi	h	3-2	og (Gleison), Doe 2
07/10	Aris	a	2-0	Kalajdžić, Udoji
22/10	OFI	h	1-2	Anastasakos
28/10	AEK	a	0-1	
03/11	Kerkyra	h	1-1	Udoji
11/11	PAOK	a	0-2	
17/11	Panionios	a	0-4	
25/11	Panathinaikos	h	2-1	Ucar, Anastasakos (p)
01/12	Olympiacos	a	1-2	Udoji
09/12	Veria	h	0-0	
16/12	Levadiakos	a	0-1	

2013

05/01	Giannina	h	1-1	Anastasakos
12/01	Panthrakikos	a	1-1	Nazlidis
20/01	Atromitos	a	0-1	
27/01	Asteras	h	0-3	
02/02	Xanthi	a	0-2	
11/02	Aris	h	2-0	Nazlidis, Anastasakos
18/02	OFI	a	3-1	og (Moniakis), Giannou, Maragoudakis
24/02	AEK	h	2-1	Nazlidis, Anastasakos (p)
02/03	Kerkyra	a	1-2	Beljić
09/03	PAOK	h	1-2	Tetteh
17/03	Panionios	h	2-1	Tetteh, Anastasakos
30/03	Panathinaikos	a	1-0	Nazlidis
07/04	Olympiacos	h	0-4	
14/04	Veria	a	0-5	
21/04	Levadiakos	h	2-0	Beljić, Kanakoudis

No	Name	Nat	DoB	Pos	Aps	(s)	Gls
7	Ilias Anastasakos		03/03/78	A	28		7
2	Leonidas Argiropoulos		29/05/90	D	21	(1)	
8	Rubén Arocha	VEN	21/04/87	M	1	(1)	
8	Nikola Beljić	SRB	14/05/83	M	6	(2)	2
23	Cristian Castells	ESP	19/10/84	D	4		
20	Anastasios Dentsas		19/03/82	M	6	(6)	
5	Alkiviadis Dimitris		23/07/80	D	9		
24	Lawrence Doe	EQG	03/09/86	D	6	(1)	2
88	Arbër Drhami	ALB	23/06/88	A		(1)	
94	Georgios Giakoumakis		09/12/94	A		(9)	
99	Apostolos Giannou		25/01/90	A	9		1
28	Gastón González	ARG	23/02/88	M	7	(12)	
14	Juan Aguilera	ESP	13/09/85	M	23	(1)	
16	Željko Kalajdžić	SRB	11/05/78	M	27		1
6	Petros Kanakoudis		16/04/84	M	24	(1)	1
71	Fotios Kipouros		09/08/75	G	27		
3	Konstantinos Kourtesiotis		05/06/84	D	6	(3)	
30	Georgios V Lazaridis		23/07/83	G	1		
10	Markos Maragoudakis		28/01/82	A	13	(9)	2
70	Marcelo	BRA	12/08/84	M	1	(1)	
11	Stefanos Martsakis		24/05/90	A	3	(7)	
22	Igor Mirčeta	SRB	12/12/86	M	8	(13)	
9	Thomas Nazlidis		23/10/87	A	11	(11)	4
35	Chidi Onyemah	NGA	20/02/84	A		(4)	
66	Christos Paligeorgos		06/06/88	D	2	(2)	
92	Ioannis Potouridis		27/02/92	D	21		
88	Fabian Stoller	SUI	31/03/88	M	4	(3)	
52	Abdul Aziz Tetteh	GHA	25/05/90	M	11		2
4	Minas Tzanis		04/08/84	D	17		
10	Kendal Ucar	FRA	03/09/81	D	15		1
23	Chigozie Udoji	NGA	16/07/86	M	17		4
1	Vitaliy Zheludok	UKR	11/08/86	G	2		

VERIA FC

Coach: Ioakim Havos;
(05/09/12) (Nikolaos Karydas);
(20/11/12) Dimitrios Kalaitzidis
1960 • Dimotikon Verias (7,000) • veriafc.gr

2012

26/08	Olympiacos	h	1-2	Ioannou
01/09	Panionios	h	0-1	
15/09	Levadiakos	a	0-0	
23/09	Giannina	h	1-0	Olaitan
30/09	Panthrakikos	a	1-0	Kaltsas
06/10	Atromitos	h	2-2	Kafes, Bargan
21/10	Asteras	a	0-3	
28/10	Xanthi	h	0-0	
05/11	Aris	a	1-2	Kaltsas
10/11	OFI	a	0-2	
18/11	AEK	h	0-4	
25/11	Kerkyra	a	1-1	Olaitan
02/12	PAOK	h	0-0	
09/12	Platanias	a	0-0	
16/12	Panathinaikos	h	3-0	Ioannou 2, Bargan

2013

06/01	Olympiacos	a	0-3	
13/01	Panionios	a	1-1	Costly
21/01	Levadiakos	h	1-2	og (Maheras)
27/01	Giannina	a	0-2	
03/02	Panthrakikos	h	2-0	Guille 2
09/02	Atromitos	a	0-0	
17/02	Asteras	h	1-2	Orestes
23/02	Xanthi	a	2-0	Costly, Olaitan
04/03	Aris	h	3-1	Kaltsas 2, Olaitan
10/03	OFI	h	0-0	
16/03	AEK	a	1-2	Olaitan
31/03	Kerkyra	h	2-0	Costly (p), Olaitan
06/04	PAOK	a	0-2	
14/04	Platanias	h	5-0	Costly, Ioannou 3, Olaitan
21/04	Panathinaikos	a	2-3	Costly 2 (1p)

No	Name	Nat	DoB	Pos	Aps	(s)	Gls
23	Dimitrios Amarantidis		27/07/86	D	20	(1)	
6	Konstantinos Barbas		22/04/83	D	11	(1)	
11	Kenan Bargan		25/10/88	A	20	(1)	2
89	Damián Bellón	SUI	28/08/89	M	1	(6)	
93	Frantz Bertin	HAI	30/05/83	D	2	(5)	
10	Carlinos	ESP	17/02/87	A		(2)	
19	Carlos Costly	HON	18/07/82	A	17	(8)	6
78	Iosif Daskalakis		07/08/82	G	1		
26	Everton	BRA	15/06/84	D	1	(2)	
31	Nikolaos Georgeas		27/12/76	D	18		
77	Nikolaos Georgiadis		23/03/83	D	22	(1)	
5	Guille	ESP	11/01/87	M	17	(6)	2
44	Ilias Ioannou		23/10/79	A	23	(3)	6
55	Jonathan López	ESP	16/04/81	G	25		
1	Pantelis Kafes		24/06/78	M	14		1
3	Cyril Kali	FRA	21/04/84	D	17		
20	Alexandros Kalogeris		14/05/86	M	27	(2)	
7	Nikolaos Kaltsas		03/05/90	M	9	(17)	4
1	Georgios Kantimiris		19/09/82	G	2	(1)	
30	Dimitrios Kottaridis		29/05/81	G	2		
88	Dimitrios Manos		16/09/94	A		(1)	
8	Marcus Mokaké	CMR	30/11/81	M	3	(4)	
99	Michael Olaitan	NGA	01/01/93	A	28	(1)	7
14	Orestes	BRA	24/03/81	D	25	(1)	1
9	Charalambos Pavlidis		06/05/91	M	1	(3)	
12	David Reano	ARG	20/03/84	D		(2)	
17	Georgios Skatharoudis		02/11/92	A		(1)	
13	Mirosław Sznaucner	POL	09/05/79	D	11		
2	Wayne Thomas	ENG	17/05/79	D	3	(1)	
4	Nikolaos Tzimoglannis		02/11/92	M	5	(3)	
21	Alexandros Vergonis		01/12/85	M		(2)	
8	Zé Vítor	POR	11/02/82	M	5	(2)	

XANTHI FC

Coach: Marinos Ouzounidis;
(23/09/12) (Vasilios Daniel);
(28/09/12) (Ioannis Papadimitriou);
(01/10/12) Nikolaos Kostenoglou;
(03/12/12) Marinos Ouzounidis
1967 • Škoda Xanthi Arena (7,500) • skodaxanthifc.gr

2012

26/08	OFI	a	0-0	
01/09	AEK	h	1-0	Markovski
16/09	Kerkyra	a	1-1	Markovski
22/09	PAOK	h	0-3	
30/09	Platanias	a	2-3	Gleison, Vasilakakis
07/10	Panathinaikos	h	1-2	Markovski
20/10	Olympiacos	a	0-4	
28/10	Veria	a	0-0	
04/11	Levadiakos	h	1-0	og (Kiriakidis)
10/11	Giannina	a	0-1	
18/11	Panthrakikos	h	0-0	
24/11	Atromitos	a	0-0	
01/12	Asteras	h	1-1	Onwuachi
09/12	Panionios	h	4-0	Marin, Goutas, Onwuachi 2
16/12	Aris	a	0-0	

2013

07/01	OFI	h	3-0	Marin, Mantalos, Onwuachi
12/01	AEK	a	0-1	
20/01	Kerkyra	h	0-0	
27/01	PAOK	a	1-0	Onwuachi
02/02	Platanias	h	2-0	Ranos, Mantalos (p)
10/02	Panathinaikos	a	1-0	Dié
17/02	Olympiacos	h	0-2	
23/02	Veria	h	0-2	
03/03	Levadiakos	a	4-1	Soltani, Marcelinho 2, Marin
10/03	Giannina	h	0-1	
18/03	Panthrakikos	a	2-0	Goutas, Dié
31/03	Atromitos	h	0-0	
07/04	Asteras	a	1-0	Fliskas
14/04	Panionios	a	3-3	Mantalos 2, Marcelinho (p)
21/04	Aris	h	0-0	

No	Name	Nat	DoB	Pos	Aps	(s)	Gls
88	Alex Cazumba	BRA	30/06/88	D	4	(2)	
8	Marijan Altiparmakovski	MKD	18/07/91	A		(1)	
5	Dimosthenis Baxevanidis		14/04/88	M	15	(4)	
4	Emmanouil Bertos		13/05/89	D	17		
66	Dani	POR	30/01/82	M	20	(3)	
77	Serge Dié	CIV	04/10/77	M	11	(1)	2
21	Konstantinos Fliskas		22/12/80	D	20	(3)	1
24	Enea Gaqollari	ALB	14/12/92	M	1		
5	Gleison	BRA	18/08/81	D	5		1
28	Dimitrios Goutas		04/04/94	D	21	(1)	2
23	Dimitrios Komesidis		02/02/88	D	21	(1)	
19	Daniel Kutev	BUL	06/03/91	M		(1)	
27	Yuri Lodygin		26/05/90	G	22		
20	Petros Mantalos		31/08/91	M	22	(6)	4
11	Marcelinho	BRA	22/06/87	M	21	(4)	3
39	Nicolas Marin	FRA	29/08/80	M	20	(4)	3
10	Marko Markovski	SRB	26/05/86	A	11	(5)	3
94	Stilianos Nakas		27/01/94	A	1	(4)	
80	Benjamin Onwuachi	NGA	09/04/84	A	16	(5)	5
3	Paíto	MOZ	05/07/82	D	7		
17	Evangelos Platellas		01/12/88	M	6	(13)	
55	Athanasios Prittas		09/01/79	M		(6)	
99	Antonios Ranos		15/06/93	A	3	(9)	1
22	Ryan Smith	ENG	10/11/86	A	6	(5)	
9	Karim Soltani	ALG	29/08/84	A	7	(4)	1
35	Theodoros Toromanidis		08/05/93	M		(1)	
7	Panayiotis Triadis		09/09/92	A	1	(2)	
25	Spiridon Vallas		26/08/81	D	27		
16	Theodoros Vasilakakis		20/07/88	M	17	(5)	1
1	Jody Viviani	FRA	25/01/82	G	7		
91	Mihail Zaropoulos		12/07/91	G	1		

Promoted clubs

APOLLON SMYRNIS FC
Coach: Alexandros "Alekos" Vosniadis
1891 • Georgios Kamaras (14,000) • fcapollon.gr

ERGOTELIS FC
Coach: Siniša Gogić (CYP);
(16/04/13) (Stavros Lambrakis)
1929 • Pagrition (27,574) • ergotelis.gr

KALLONI FC
Coach: Timotheos Kavakas;
(11/12/12) (Loukas Karadimos);
(21/12/12) Haralampos Tennes
1994 • Dimotiko Stadio Mytilinis (4,000) • aelk.gr

PANAITOLIKOS GFS
Coach: Nikolaos Karageorgiou;
(24/01/13) Ioakim Havos
1926 • Panaitolikou (3,985) • panetolikos.gr

SECOND LEVEL FINAL TABLE 2012/13

		Pld	W	D	L	F	A	Pts
1	Apollon Smyrnis FC	40	22	9	9	50	29	75
2	Ergotelis FC	40	21	11	8	42	25	74
3	Kalloni FC	40	20	13	7	48	22	73
4	Panaitolikos GFS	40	20	13	7	55	23	73
5	Olympiacos Volou FC	40	19	16	5	49	23	73
6	Iraklis FC	40	19	14	7	49	25	71
7	Niki Volou FC	40	17	17	6	44	23	68
8	Panserraikos FC	40	19	11	10	40	29	68
9	Larissa FC	40	16	15	9	42	25	63
10	Doxa Dramas FC	40	16	12	12	35	27	60
11	Iraklis Psahnon FC	40	13	16	11	42	37	55
12	Kavala FC	40	14	11	15	35	36	53
13	Kallithea FC	40	12	14	14	42	44	50
14	Ethnikos Gazoros FC	40	9	14	17	27	35	41
15	Pierikos FC	40	9	12	19	33	61	39
16	Panachaiki FC	40	9	15	16	32	40	39
17	Fokikos FC	40	8	13	19	28	51	37
18	Anagennisis Giannitson FC	40	9	7	24	35	68	34
19	Vyzas Megara FC	40	7	11	22	22	49	32
20	Thrasivoulos Fylis FC	40	6	13	21	23	48	28
21	Anagennisis Epanomis FC	40	2	9	29	24	77	15

NB Panachaiki FC & Thrasivoulos Fylis FC – 3 pts deducted.

PROMOTION PLAY-OFF FINAL TABLE

		Pld	W	D	L	F	A	Pts
1	Panaitolikos GFS	6	4	1	1	10	6	14
2	Iraklis FC	6	3	0	3	7	8	10
3	Olympiacos Volou FC	6	2	2	2	9	6	9
4	Niki Volou FC	6	0	3	3	4	10	3

NB Points carried forward from regular league:
Panaitolikos GFS 1 pt, Olympiacos Volou FC 1 pt,
Iraklis FC 1 pt, Niki Volou FC 0 pts.

Top goalscorers

20	Rafik Djebbour (Olympiacos)
13	Stefanos Athanasiadis (PAOK)
12	Dimitrios Papadopoulos (Panthrakikos)
11	Kostas Mitroglou (Olympiacos)
9	David Aganzo (Aris)
	Emanuel Perrone (Asteras)
	Toché (Panathinaikos)
	Dimitrios Salpingidis (PAOK)
	Brana Ilić (Giannina)
8	Athanasios Papazoglou (OFI)
	Christos Aravidis (Panionios)

Superleague play-offs 2012/13: UEFA Champions League qualification

(15/05/13)
Giannina 2-1 Asteras Tripolis 1
(Tsoukalas 8, Ilić 67; Sankaré 14)
Atromitos 2-1 PAOK *(Iglesias 72, Chumbinho 90; Salpingidis 61)*

(19/05/13)
PAOK 0-1 Giannina *(Lila 88)*
Asteras Tripolis 2-1 Atromitos
(Rayo 41p, Kalantzis 63; Napoleoni 22)

(22/05/13)
Giannina 1-1 Atromitos
(Tsoukalas 34; Karagounis 3)
Asteras Tripolis 1-2 PAOK
(Perrone 89p; Athanasiadis 77, Katsouranis 80)

(26/05/13)
PAOK 1-0 Asteras Tripolis
(Oliseh 57)
Atromitos 2-0 Giannina
(Karagounis 17, Napoleoni 46)

(29/05/13)
PAOK 1-2 Atromitos *(Salpingidis 33; Napoleoni 46, 90)*
Asteras Tripolis 2-1 Giannina
(Caffa 6, Tsabouris 16; Korovesis 22p)

(02/06/13)
Giannina 1-2 PAOK *(De Vincenti 31p; Katsouranis 70, Schildenfeld 74)*
Atromitos 0-0 Asteras Tripolis

Domestic cup: Kypello Ellados 2012/13

FORTH ROUND

(28/11/12 & 19/12/12)
Fostiras 1-0, 1-2 Panionios *(2-2; Fostiras on away goal)*
Olympiacos 2-0, 3-0 (w/o) Panachaiki *(5-0)*

(28/11/12 & 20/12/12)
Levadiakos 2-0, 5-0 Pierikos *(7-0)*

(28/11/12 & 22/12/12)
OFI 1-0, 0-2 Apollon Smirnis *(aet; 1-2)*

(29/11/12 & 19/12/12)
Panathinaikos 4-0, 2-1 Proodeftiki *(6-1)*
Panthrakikos 2-0, 1-1 Niki Volou *(3-1)*

(29/11/12 & 20/12/12)
Tirnavos 0-2, 0-0 Kerkyra *(0-2)*

(29/11/12 & 23/12/12)
Giannina 1-0, 2-0 Panserraikos *(3-0)*

(12/12/12 & 20/12/12)
Veria 0-0, 2-0 Thrasivoulos *(2-0)*

(12/12/12 & 22/12/12)
Larissa 0-0, 1-4 Asteras Tripolis *(1-4)*
Olympiacos Volou 1-1, 2-2 Atromitos *(3-3; Olympiacos Volou on away goals)*

(12/12/12 & 23/12/12)
Kallithea 3-1, 1-2 Aris *(4-3)*

(13/12/12 & 20/12/12)
Kavala 0-0, 1-0 AEK *(1-0)*

(13/12/12 & 22/12/12)
Eginiakos Eginiou 1-3, 1-2 PAOK *(2-5)*

(13/12/12 & 23/12/12)
Ethnikos Gazoros 1-1, 1-1 Xanthi *(aet 1-1; 4-5 on pens)*
Platanias 3-1, 1-0 Anagennisis Karditsas *(4-1)*

FIFTH ROUND

(09/01/13 & 23/01/13)
Olympiacos Volou 1-1, 0-2 Asteras Tripolis *(1-3)*
Panathinaikos 2-1, 0-1 Platanias *(2-2; Platanias on away goal)*

(10/01/13 & 24/01/13)
Giannina 2-0, 3-2 Fostiras *(5-2)*
Kallithea 2-0, 0-6 PAOK *(2-6)*

(16/01/13 & 30/01/13)
Olympiacos 2-0, 1-0 Kavala *(3-0)*

(16/01/13 & 31/01/13)
Apollon Smirnis 1-1, 1-4 Panthrakikos *(2-5)*

(17/01/13 & 30/01/13)
Veria 2-1, 2-2 Kerkyra *(4-3)*

(17/01/13 & 31/01/13)
Levadiakos 2-1, 1-0 Kerkyra *(3-1)*

QUARTER-FINALS

(27/02/13 & 13/03/13)
Giannina 0-1 Olympiacos *(Abdoun 54)*
Olympiacos 2-0 Giannina *(Maniatis 63, Abdoun 90)*
(Olympiacos 3-0)

Veria 0-1 Panthrakikos *(Mingas 22)*
Panthrakikos 1-0 Veria *(Sarakatsanos 39)*
(Panthrakikos 2-0)

(27/02/13 & 14/03/13)
Platanias 1-2 Asteras Tripolis *(Mirčeta 16; Bartolini 31, Ximo Navarro 89)*
Asteras Tripolis 3-1 Platanias *(Fernando Usero 38, De Blasis 65, Kalantzis 88; Mirčeta 41p)*
(Asteras Tripolis 5-2)

(28/02/13 & 06/03/13)
PAOK 2-0 Levadiakos *(Athanasiadis 57, Salpingidis 60)*
Levadiakos 0-0 PAOK
(PAOK 2-0)

SEMI-FINALS

(17/04/13 & 27/04/13)
PAOK 2-1 Asteras Tripolis *(Athanasiadis 24, Salpingidis 88; Ximo Navarro 64)*
Asteras Tripolis 2-0 PAOK *(Usero 61, 85)*
(Asteras Tripolis 3-2)

(18/04/13 & 28/04/13)
Olympiacos 6-2 Panthrakikos *(David Fuster 4, 55, Ibagaza 11, Mitroglou 49, 53, Fetfatzidis 51; Tzanis 19, Lucero 32)*
Panthrakikos 1-2 Olympiacos *(Papadopoulos 83p; Mitroglou 27, 40)*
(Olympiacos 8-3)

FINAL

(11/05/13)
OACA Spyro Louis, Athens
OLYMPIACOS FC 3 *(David Fuster 44, Djebbour 98, Abdoun 119p)*
ASTERAS TRIPOLIS FC 1 *(Rayo 14)*
(aet)
Referee: Giahos
OLYMPIACOS: Carroll, Modesto *(Ibagaza 60)*, Manolas, Siovas, Holebas, Maniatis, Fejsa, Paulo Machado *(Pino 76)*, Abdoun, David Fuster, Mitroglou *(Djebbour 72)*
Sent off (from bench): Modesto *(120+6)*
ASTERAS TRIPOLIS: Fülöp, Ximo Navarro, Pipinis, Sankaré, Kourbelis *(Bartolini 67)*, Kontoes *(Kalantzis 101)*, Tsabouris, Usero, Rayo, De Blasis, Perrone *(Lencse 83)*
Sent off (from bench): Perrone *(120+6)*

HUNGARY
Magyar Labdarúgó Szövetség (MLSZ)

Address	Kánai út 2.D	**President**	Sándor Csányi
	HU-1112 Budapest	**General secretary**	Márton Vági
Tel	+36 1 577 9500	**Media officer**	László Pajor-Gyulai
Fax	+36 1 577 9503	**Year of formation**	1901
E-mail	mlsz@mlsz.hu	**National stadium**	Puskás Ferenc,
Website	mlsz.hu		Budapest (39,111)

Miskolc — 3
Eger — 4
Győr — 6
Budapest — 1
Felcsút — 18
Mezőkövesd — 17
Debrecen — 2
Szombathely — 14
Pápa — 9
5
16
10
15
Székesfehérvár
Kecskemét — 8
Siófok — 13
Paks — 11
Kaposvár — 7
Pécs — 12

0 — 100 — 200 km
0 — 100 miles

NB 1 CLUBS

 1 **Budapest Honvéd FC**

 2 **Debreceni VSC**

3 **Diósgyőri VTK**

4 **Egri FC**

5 **Ferencvárosi TC**

 6 **Győri ETO FC**

7 **Kaposvári Rákóczi FC**

8 **Kecskeméti TE**

9 **Lombard-Pápa TFC**

10 **MTK Budapest**

11 **Paksi SE**

12 **Pécsi MFC**

13 **BFC Siófok**

14 **Szombathelyi Haladás**

15 **Újpest FC**

 16 **Videoton FC**

PROMOTED CLUBS

17 **Mezőkövesd-Zsóry SE**

18 **Puskás Akadémia FC**

KEY:

● – UEFA Champions League
● – UEFA Europa League
● – Promoted clubs
● – Relegated clubs

Győr end 30-year wait

Galvanised by a 22-match unbeaten run, Győri ETO FC claimed their first Hungarian title since winning it back-to-back in 1982 and 1983. Led by coach Attila Pintér, they finished ten points clear of runners-up Videoton FC, who had a fine season in Europe.

Debreceni VSC, who won the 2011/12 championship undefeated, endured a forgettable league campaign but salvaged their season by keeping hold of the Hungarian Cup, two goals from the NB I's top scorer, Frenchman Adamo Coulibaly, giving them a 2-1 win in the final to deny double-chasing Győr.

Coach Pintér masterminds emphatic NB I triumph	Debrecen defeat champions to retain Hungarian Cup	World Cup play-off hopes in the balance

Domestic league

Despite a promising third-place finish in 2011/12, Győr's title triumph was a surprise. It was Pintér's first full season at the helm, and the squad at his disposal did not appear strong enough to end the club's 30-year wait for the title – particularly when they lost their opening game 4-1 at Debrecen. However, that result proved to be a wildly inaccurate indicator of what was to come, for while the defending champions, still led by double-winning coach Elemér Kondás, lost form alarmingly, Győr put together a run of results that would blow away the competition.

After drawing their second game, Pintér's men posted seven successive victories – the start of an eight-month unbeaten run that would open up clear daylight between Győr and the rest at the top of the table. Even when the sequence was broken by a 5-2 defeat at lowly Kecskeméti TE, and swiftly followed by another loss at Paksi SE, the leaders were too far ahead to be challenged. Indeed, there were three matches still to play when they completed the job in front of 14,000 spectators with a 1-0 home win over Ferencvárosi TC, the club that Pintér had coached to the title nine years previously.

While the champions boasted the league's best attack, scoring 57 goals, with Hungarian international Ronald Varga providing a dozen of them, second-placed Videoton had the best defence, conceding just 24. Marco Rossi's Budapest Honvéd FC were impressive in the spring, charging up the table to bypass Ferencváros and MTK Budapest and finish as the capital's top team for the second year running, in third place. Ferencváros, under Dutchman Ricardo Moniz, an Austrian double-winner with FC Salzburg in 2011/12, had an eventful season, winning the League Cup (with a 5-1 win over Videoton) and bidding farewell to their Flórián Albert Stadium in front of a capacity crowd with a 2-1 win over Újpest FC in March.

Domestic cup

Ten days after securing the league title, Győr had the opportunity to complete their first double. Victories over Honvéd and Videoton had put them in the cup final, where they faced a Debrecen side who, in contrast, had been given a relatively easy ride, avoiding top-flight opposition in every round. The newly crowned champions took an early lead, through Serbian midfielder Nemanja Andrić, but Coulibaly, a double scorer in both the quarter-finals and semi-finals,

did it again, striking in the 51st and 86th minutes to give Loki a fourth cup win in six years.

Europe

There was a rare Hungarian success in Europe as Videoton reached the group stage of the UEFA Europa League following victories over ŠK Slovan Bratislava, KAA Gent and – on penalties – Trabzonspor AŞ. For a while it looked as if they might advance further following memorable home wins over Sporting Clube de Portugal and FC Basel 1893, but three successive defeats put paid to that ambition.

National team

But for a late equaliser conceded at home to Romania, Sándor Egervári's national side would have been in a strong position to claim the runners-up spot in their 2014 FIFA World Cup qualifying group. As it was, despite the impressive feat of taking four points off Turkey, Hungary looked set for a fascinating duel with their eastern European neighbours for second place behind runaway leaders the Netherlands, with the Bucharest showdown on 6 September looming large on the horizon.

Domestic league: NB 1 2012/13 final table

		Pld	Home					Away					Total					Pts
			W	D	L	F	A	W	D	L	F	A	W	D	L	F	A	
1	Győri ETO FC	30	11	3	1	32	12	8	4	3	25	21	19	7	4	57	33	64
2	Videoton FC	30	8	3	4	25	12	8	3	4	27	12	16	6	8	52	24	54
3	Budapest Honvéd FC	30	7	5	3	26	19	8	2	5	24	17	15	7	8	50	36	52
4	MTK Budapest	30	11	2	2	29	13	4	4	7	14	17	15	6	9	43	30	51
5	Ferencvárosi TC	30	9	4	2	31	17	4	6	5	20	19	13	10	7	51	36	49
6	Debreceni VSC	30	11	0	4	32	14	3	4	8	15	22	14	4	12	47	36	46
7	Kecskeméti TE	30	6	5	4	24	22	6	3	6	18	20	12	8	10	42	42	44
8	Szombathelyi Haladás	30	6	7	2	19	11	5	4	6	17	16	11	11	8	36	27	44
9	Újpest FC	30	6	4	5	22	23	5	4	6	18	19	11	8	11	40	42	41
10	Diósgyőri VTK	30	8	5	2	23	18	1	6	8	8	21	9	11	10	31	39	38
11	Kaposvári Rákóczi FC	30	6	5	4	18	13	4	2	9	17	25	10	7	13	35	38	37
12	Pécsi MFC	30	4	3	8	12	22	6	4	5	21	22	10	7	13	33	44	37
13	Paksi SE	30	3	5	7	15	19	5	6	4	25	19	8	11	11	40	38	35
14	Lombard-Pápa TFC	30	6	3	6	18	16	1	4	10	8	30	7	7	16	26	46	28
15	BFC Siófok	30	6	2	7	17	21	1	2	12	14	40	7	4	19	31	61	25
16	Egri FC	30	2	4	9	15	29	1	2	12	10	38	3	6	21	25	67	15

SEASON AT A GLANCE

EUROPEAN QUALIFICATION 2013/14

 Champion: Győri ETO FC (second qualifying round)

 Cup winner: Debreceni VSC (second qualifying round)
Videoton FC (first qualifying round)
Budapest Honvéd FC (first qualifying round)

Top scorer Adamo Coulibaly (Debrecen), 18 goals
Relegated clubs Egri FC, BFC Siófok
Promoted clubs Mezőkövesd-Zsóry SE, Puskás Akadémia FC
Cup final Debreceni VSC 2-1 Győri ETO FC

**NB 1 TEAM
OF THE SEASON**
(4-4-2)
Coach: Pintér (Győr)

**PLAYER OF
THE SEASON
Dániel Böde**
(Ferencvárosi TC)

The striker joined Ferencvaos from Paksi SE in 2012 and was an ever-present in his first season, scoring 17 goals to finish as the NB I's second best marksman. His efforts inevitably caught the eye of Hungary coach Sándor Egervári, and he grabbed a crucial equaliser in a FIFA World Cup qualifier away to Turkey on only his second appearance.

**NEWCOMER OF
THE SEASON
István Kovács**
(Videoton FC)

The prodigiously talented attacking midfielder impressed at Videoton after his summer move from Szombathelyi Haladás, earning a first call-up for Hungary. The 21-year-old's direct running, movement and trickery left defenders chasing shadows, his fine season highlighted by a spectacular long-distance goal against Budapest Honvéd FC.

Kemenes *(Honvéd)*

Korhut *(Debrecen)* — Marco Caneira *(Videoton)* — Juhász *(Videoton)* — Bešić *(Ferencváros)*

R Varga *(Győr)* — Vécsei *(Honvéd)* — Kamber *(Győr)* — Kovács *(Videoton)*

Coulibaly *(Debrecen)* — Böde *(Ferencváros)*

HUNGARY

NATIONAL TEAM

Home Kit | Away Kit

INTERNATIONAL TOURNAMENT APPEARANCES

FIFA World Cup (9) 1934 (2nd round), 1938 (runners-up), 1954 (runners-up), 1958, 1962 (qtr-finals), 1966 (qtr finals), 1978, 1982, 1986 UEFA European Championship (2) 1964 (3rd), 1972 (4th)

TOP FIVE ALL-TIME CAPS

József Bozsik (101); László Fazekas (92); **Gábor Király** (89); Gyula Grosics (86); Ferenc Puskás (85)

TOP FIVE ALL-TIME GOALS

Ferenc Puskás (84); Sándor Kocsis (75); Imre Schlosser (59); Lajos Tichy (51); György Sárosi (42)

Results 2012/13

15/08/12	Israel	H	Budapest	1-1	*Dzsudzsák (51)*
07/09/12	Andorra (WCQ)	A	Andorra la Vella	5-0	*Juhász (12), Gera (32p), Szalai (54), Priskin (68), Koman (82)*
11/09/12	Netherlands (WCQ)	H	Budapest	1-4	*Dzsudzsák (7p)*
12/10/12	Estonia (WCQ)	A	Tallinn	1-0	*Hajnal (47)*
16/10/12	Turkey (WCQ)	H	Budapest	3-1	*Koman (31), Szalai (50), Gera (58p)*
14/11/12	Norway	A	Budapest	0-2	
06/02/13	Belarus	N	Belek (TUR)	1-1	*Szabics (32)*
22/03/13	Romania (WCQ)	H	Budapest	2-2	*Vanczák (16), Dzsudzsák (71p)*
26/03/13	Turkey (WCQ)	A	Istanbul	1-1	*Böde (71)*
06/06/13	Kuwait	H	Gyor	1-0	*Vanczák (58)*

Appearances 2012/13

Coach: Sándor Egervári 15/07/50

Name	DOB	Club	Isr	AND	NED	EST	TUR	Nor	Blr	ROU	TUR	Kuw	Caps	Goals
Ádám Bogdán	27/09/87	Bolton (ENG)	G	G	G	G	G		G			G	14	-
József Varga	06/06/88	Debrecen /Greuther Fürth (GER)	D		M	D	M	M		s58	M	M90	21	-
Roland Juhász	01/07/83	Anderlecht (BEL) /Videoton	D46	D	D	D		D74				s90	77	6
Norbert Mészáros	19/08/80	Debrecen	D			D	D		D65	D	D		8	-
Zsolt Laczkó	18/12/86	Sampdoria (ITA)	D	D									21	-
Ádám Gyurcsó	06/03/91	Videoton	M46		s61	s84		s83				M46	7	1
Ádám Pintér	12/06/88	Zaragoza (ESP)	M79				s77	M60	M	M	M		16	-
Vladimir Koman	16/03/89	Krasnodar (RUS)	M78	M	M46		M73	M59	M46	M	M	M81	29	7
Péter Szakály	17/08/86	Debrecen	M63										3	-
Balázs Dzsudzsák	23/12/86	Dinamo Moskva (RUS)	M	A	M	M		A59	M	M90	M	M	53	11
Ádám Szalai	09/12/87	Mainz (GER)	A86	A82		A	A	A69		A	A78		16	7
Zsolt Korcsmár	09/01/89	Brann (NOR)	s46	M	M	M61	D	D	D	D	D46	D	18	-
Krisztián Németh	05/01/89	Roda (NED)	s46	s82	s80			s69				s46	12	-
Vilmos Vanczák	20/06/83	Sion (SUI)	s63	D	D		D	D46	D	D	D	D	71	4
Tamás Koltai	30/04/87	Győr	s78			M84	s73	s59	s46				12	-
Péter Halmosi	25/09/79	Haladás	s79							s90			35	-
Imre Szabics	22/03/81	Sturm (AUT)	s86			s80		s59	M83	A58			34	13
Zoltán Lipták	10/12/84	Győr		D	D								12	1
Tamás Hajnal	15/03/81	Stuttgart (GER)		M75	s46	M	M77	M	M	M80	M68		55	6
Zoltán Gera	22/04/79	West Brom (ENG)		M46	M80	M80	M						77	23
Tamás Priskin	27/09/86	Alania (RUS)		s46	A							s46	42	12
Ákos Elek	21/07/88	Diósgyőr		s75	D61	s61	M45	s60	s46		s78		25	1
Tamás Kádár	14/03/90	Roda (NED) /Diósgyőr				D	D	D	D	D	D	D	11	-
Máté Pátkai	06/03/88	Győr					s45	s46				s81	3	-
Gábor Király	01/04/76	1860 München (GER)						G		G	G		89	-
Richárd Guzmics	16/04/87	Haladás					s74				s46	D	3	-
Gergely Rudolf	09/03/85	Diósgyőr						A46					24	9
Dániel Böde	24/10/86	Ferencváros						s65			s68	A46	3	1
István Kovács	27/03/92	Videoton								s80			1	-
József Kanta	24/03/84	MTK										M46	3	-
Gergő Lovrencsics	01/09/88	Lech (POL)										s46	1	-

European club competitions 2012/13

DEBRECENI VSC

Second qualifying round - KS Skënderbeu (ALB)
A 0-1
Novaković, Šimac, Rezes (Máté 90+1), Mészáros, Bódi, Nagy, J Varga, Coulibaly, Szakály, Korhut, Kulcsár (Ramos 72). Coach: Elemér Kondás (HUN)
H 3-0 *Coulibaly (12, 87), J Varga (58)*
Novaković, Šimac, Ramos (Máté 89), Nikolov, Mészáros, Yannick (Rezes 74), Bódi (Lucas 82), J Varga, Coulibaly, Szakály, Korhut. Coach: Elemér Kondás (HUN)

Third qualifying round - FC BATE Borisov (BLR)
A 1-1 *Sidibé (67)*
Verpecz, Šimac, Ramos (Sidibé 59), Nikolov, Rezes (Yannick 78), Mészáros, Bódi, J Varga, Coulibaly (Máté 86), Szakály, Korhut. Coach: Elemér Kondás (HUN)
H 0-2
Verpecz, Šimac (Máté 84), Ramos, Nikolov, Mészáros, Yannick (Rezes 65), Bódi, Nagy (Sidibé 46), Coulibaly, Szakály, Korhut. Coach: Elemér Kondás (HUN)
Red card: Nikolov 57

Play-offs - Club Brugge KV (BEL)
H 0-3
Poleksić, Šimac, Ramos, Rezes (Kulcsár 79), Mészáros, Sidibé (Bódi 66), Nagy (Lucas 87), J Varga, Coulibaly, Szakály, Mohl. Coach: Elemér Kondás (HUN)
Red card: Ramos 45+2
A 1-4 *Szakály (34)*
Verpecz, Šimac, Rezes, Mészáros, Sidibé (Korhut 54), Bódi (Kulcsár 71), Nagy, J Varga, Coulibaly, Szakály (Spitzmüller 80), Mohl. Coach: Elemér Kondás (HUN)
Red card: Rezes 40

VIDEOTON FC

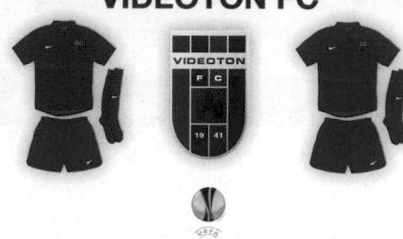

Second qualifying round - ŠK Slovan Bratislava (SVK)
A 1-1 *Filipe Oliveira (30)*
Božović, Álvaro Brachi, Paulo Vinícius, Marco Caneira, Sándor, Mitrović, Filipe Oliveira, N Nikolić (Torghelle 75), Stopira, Tóth (Szekeres 88), Gyurcsó (Walter Lee 80). Coach: Paulo Sousa (POR)
H 0-0
Božović, Paulo Vinícius, Marco Caneira, Sándor, Mitrović, Filipe Oliveira (Walter Lee 81), N Nikolić, Stopira, Tóth (Kovács 67), Szolnoki, Gyurcsó (Torghelle 86). Coach: Paulo Sousa (POR)

Third qualifying round - KAA Gent (BEL)
H 1-0 *N Nikolić (78)*
Božović, Álvaro Brachi (Szolnoki 75), Paulo Vinícius, Marco Caneira, Sándor (Kovács 61), Mitrović, Filipe Oliveira, N Nikolić, Stopira, Tóth (Renato Neto 87), Gyurcsó. Coach: Paulo Sousa (POR)
A 3-0 *Filipe Oliveira (13), N Nikolić (68, 71)*
Božović, Álvaro Brachi, Paulo Vinícius, Marco Caneira, Sándor, Mitrović, Filipe Oliveira (Renato Neto 73), N Nikolić (Torghelle 79), Stopira, Tóth (Kovács 69), Gyurcsó. Coach: Paulo Sousa (POR)

Play-offs - Trabzonspor AŞ (TUR)
A 0-0
Božović, Álvaro Brachi, Paulo Vinícius, Marco Caneira, Sándor (Renato Neto 80), Mitrović, Filipe Oliveira (U Nikolić 86), Walter Lee, Stopira, Tóth, Torghelle (N Nikolić 74). Coach: Paulo Sousa (POR)
H 0-0 *(aet; 4-2 on pens)*
Božović, Álvaro Brachi, Paulo Vinícius, Marco Caneira, Sándor, Mitrović, Filipe Oliveira (Gyurcsó 76), N Nikolić (Torghelle 70), Walter Lee (Kovács 102), Stopira, Tóth. Coach: Paulo Sousa (POR)

Group G
Match 1 - KRC Genk (BEL)
A 0-3
Božović, Álvaro Brachi, Paulo Vinícius, Marco Caneira, Sándor, Mitrović, Filipe Oliveira (Gyurcsó 58), Walter Lee, Stopira, Tóth (Kovács 65), Torghelle (N Nikolić 72). Coach: Paulo Sousa (POR)

Match 2 - Sporting Clube de Portugal (POR)
H 3-0 *Paulo Vinícius (15), Filipe Oliveira (21), N Nikolić (35)*
Božović, Álvaro Brachi, Paulo Vinícius, Marco Caneira, Sándor, Mitrović, Filipe Oliveira, N Nikolić (Torghelle 78), Walter Lee (Gyurcsó 68), Stopira (Renato Neto 89), Tóth. Coach: Paulo Sousa (POR)
Match 3 - FC Basel 1893 (SUI)
H 2-1 *Schär (2og), Marco Caneira (33)*
Božović, Álvaro Brachi, Paulo Vinícius, Marco Caneira, Renato Neto, Sándor (Tóth 73), Mitrović, N Nikolić, Walter Lee (Torghelle 86), Szolnoki, Gyurcsó (Filipe Oliveira 79). Coach: Paulo Sousa (POR)
Match 4 - FC Basel 1893 (SUI)
A 0-1
Božović, Álvaro Brachi, Paulo Vinícius, Marco Caneira, Renato Neto, Sándor (Kovács 90), Mitrović, Filipe Oliveira, Torghelle (N Nikolić 69), Szolnoki, Gyurcsó (Walter Lee 83). Coach: Paulo Sousa (POR)
Match 5 - KRC Genk (BEL)
H 0-1
Božović, Álvaro Brachi, Paulo Vinícius, Renato Neto, Sándor (Torghelle 76), Mitrović, Filipe Oliveira (Kovács 46), N Nikolić, Kaká (Walter Lee 82), Szolnoki, Gyurcsó. Coach: Paulo Sousa (POR)
Match 6 - Sporting Clube de Portugal (POR)
A 1-2 *Sándor (80p)*
Tujvel, Álvaro Brachi, Paulo Vinícius, Marco Caneira, Renato Neto, Sándor, Filipe Oliveira (Gyurcsó 57), N Nikolić (Paraiba 73), Walter Lee, Tóth (Kovács 73), Szolnoki. Coach: Paulo Sousa (POR)
Red cards: Sándor 83, Marco Caneira 90+4

BUDAPEST HONVÉD FC

First qualifying round - KS Flamurtari (ALB)
A 1-0 *Vernes (46)*
Kemenes, Ignjatović, Debreceni, Vernes (Diaby 58), Délczeg, Vidović, Ivancsics, Lovrić, Hidi (Diarra 69), Tchami (Baráth 85), Johnson. Coach: Marco Rossi (ITA)
H 2-0 *Vernes (45+1), Tchami (57)*
Kemenes, Ignjatović, Debreceni, Vernes (Diaby 71), Délczeg, Vidović, Ivancsics (Diarra 84), Lovrić, Hidi, Tchami (Faggyas 64), Johnson. Coach: Marco Rossi (ITA)

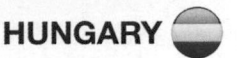
Domestic league club-by-club

Second qualifying round - FC Anji Makhachkala (RUS)

A 0-1
Kemenes, Ignjatović, Debreceni, Délczeg, Vidović, Ivancsics (Diarra 82), Diaby (Vernes 56), Lovrić, Hidi (Vécsei 61), Tchami, Johnson. Coach: Marco Rossi (ITA)

H 0-4
Kemenes, Ignjatović, Debreceni, Vernes, Délczeg (Diaby 46), Vidović, Ivancsics (Diarra 70), Lovrić, Hidi (Faggyas 58), Tchami, Johnson. Coach: Marco Rossi (ITA)
Red card: Vernes 55

MTK BUDAPEST

First qualifying round - FK Senica (SVK)

H 1-1 *Lázok (30)*
Hegedűs, Hidvégi, Kelemen, Zsidai, Csiki (Nikházi 60), Lázok (Tischler 83), Kálnoki-Kis, Kanta, Rácz (Vass 81), Vukmir, Wolfe. Coach: József Garami (HUN)
Red card: Kálnoki-Kis 56

A 1-2 *Kanta (51p)*
Hegedűs, Hidvégi, Kelemen, Zsidai, Lázok (Nikházi 74), Könyves, Kanta, Rácz (Csiki 46), Vukmir, Vadnai, Wolfe. Coach: József Garami (HUN)
Red card: Vadnai 70

BUDAPEST HONVÉD FC

Coach: Marco Rossi (ITA)
1909 • Bozsik József (13,500) • honvedfc.hu
Major honours
Hungarian League (13) 1950, 1950 (autumn), 1952, 1954, 1955, 1980, 1984, 1985, 1986, 1988, 1989, 1991, 1993;
Hungarian Cup (7) 1926, 1964, 1985, 1989, 1996, 2007, 2009

2012

29/07	Siófok	a	1-0	Ignjatović
05/08	Diósgyőr	h	2-1	Délczeg, Diaby
12/08	Videoton	a	1-0	Živanović
19/08	Paks	h	3-3	Živanović, Vernes, Délczeg
25/08	Ferencváros	a	2-0	Tchami, Délczeg
31/08	MTK	h	1-2	Diaby
16/09	Debrecen	a	1-4	Vernes
22/09	Rákóczi	h	5-3	Diarra, Johnson, Délczeg, Ivancsics, Vécsei
29/09	Kecskemét	a	1-2	Délczeg
05/10	Pécs	h	0-1	
20/10	Pápa	a	1-2	Diaby
27/10	Újpest	h	2-2	Délczeg (p), Dieng
04/11	Győr	a	0-0	
10/11	Eger	h	3-1	Délczeg (p), Baráth, Vernes
18/11	Haladás	h	1-1	Vécsei
24/11	Siófok	h	2-0	Tandia, Délczeg (p)
01/12	Diósgyőr	a	1-3	Délczeg (p)

2012

03/03	Videoton	h	0-4	
08/03	Paks	a	3-0	Vécsei 2, Vernes
30/03	MTK	a	0-1	
07/04	Debrecen	h	2-2	G Nagy, Martínez (p)
12/04	Rákóczi	a	2-1	Tchami (p), Lanzafame
16/04	Ferencváros	h	1-0	Tchami
20/04	Kecskemét	h	0-0	
28/04	Pécs	a	3-0	Lanzafame, Martínez 2 (1p)
04/05	Pápa	h	2-0	Délczeg (p), G Nagy
11/05	Újpest	a	4-2	Martínez 3 (1p), Lovrić
19/05	Győr	h	2-0	Hidi, Lanzafame
25/05	Eger	h	3-0	Lanzafame 2 (1p), G Nagy
01/06	Haladás	a	1-1	Vernes

No	Name	Nat	DoB	Pos	Aps	(s)	Gls
13	Raffaele Alcibiade	ITA	23/05/90	D	6	(1)	
99	Ustund Dánith		11/01/92	D	20	(1)	1
28	Gergely Bobál		31/08/95	A		(5)	
31	Márton Czuczi		20/05/92	G	3		
5	András Debreceni		21/04/89	D	10		
9	Gergely Délczeg		09/08/87	A	21	(1)	10
22	Souleymane Diaby	CIV	10/09/87	A	13	(5)	3
24	Drissa Diarra	MLI	07/07/85	M	9	(6)	1
17	Abass Dieng	SEN	01/01/85	A	7		1
70	Milán Faggyas		01/06/89	A	1	(11)	
26	Patrik Hidi		27/11/90	M	20	(5)	1
19	Filip Holender	SRB	27/07/94	A		(5)	
4	Aleksandar Ignjatović	SRB	11/04/88	D	29		1
8	George Ikenne	NGA	29/10/92	M	8	(6)	
20	Gellért Ivancsics		23/02/87	M	17	(2)	1
90	Marshal Johnson	NGA	12/12/89	M	12		1
71	Szabolcs Kemenes		18/05/86	G	26		
11	Davide Lanzafame	ITA	09/02/87	A	10		5
25	Ivan Lovrić	CRO	11/07/85	D	26		1
18	Attila Lőrincz		08/04/94	M		(1)	
23	Leandro Martínez	ITA	15/10/89	A	8	(3)	6
2	Sergiu Moga	ROU	07/01/92	M	2	(1)	
77	Gergő Nagy		07/01/91	M	7	(8)	3
16	Mihály Krisztián Nagy		20/06/92	A		(1)	
35	Henry Odia	NGA	03/03/91	M		(3)	
15	Claudiu Pascariu	ROU	25/09/88	D	1		
34	Norbert Szemerédi		08/12/93	G	1		
3	Souleymane Tandia	SEN	30/11/86	D	12	(1)	1
27	Hervé Tchami	CMR	20/02/88	A	9	(3)	3
30	Bálint Vécsei		13/07/93	A	20	(5)	4
7	Richárd Vernes		24/02/92	M	6	(16)	5
15	Marko Vidović	MNE	03/06/88	D	2		
33	Boris Živanović	SRB	18/07/89	D	24		2

DEBRECENI VSC

Coach: Elemér Kondás
1902 • Oláh Gábor utcai (11,500) • dvsc.hu
Major honours
Hungarian League (6) 2005, 2006, 2007, 2009, 2010, 2012;
Hungarian Cup (6) 1999, 2001, 2008, 2010, 2012, 2013

2012

28/07	Győr	h	4-1	Sidibé 2, Szakály, Kulcsár
04/08	Rákóczi	a	0-1	
11/08	Kecskemét	h	2-1	Kulcsár, Coulibaly
18/08	Pécs	a	3-2	Coulibaly 3 (1p)
26/08	Pápa	h	1-0	Szakály
02/09	Újpest	a	0-0	
16/09	Honvéd	h	4-1	Sidibé 2, Coulibaly, Szűcs
22/09	Eger	a	0-1	
29/09	Haladás	h	2-0	Rezes, Kulcsár
07/10	Siófok	a	2-0	Coulibaly (p), Bódi
21/10	Diósgyőr	h	2-0	Yannick, Coulibaly
28/10	Videoton	a	1-3	Coulibaly
03/11	Paks	h	0-1	
11/11	Ferencváros	a	1-2	Coulibaly
17/11	MTK	h	0-2	
24/11	Győr	a	0-2	
30/11	Rákóczi	h	2-1	Coulibaly 2 (1p)

2012

02/03	Kecskemét	a	0-0	
10/03	Pécs	h	4-1	Pölöskey, Sidibé 2, Szakály
31/03	Újpest	h	0-1	
07/04	Honvéd	a	2-2	Pölöskey, og (Ignjatović)
10/04	Pápa	a	0-1	
13/04	Eger	h	3-0	Sidibé, Bouadla, Coulibaly
21/04	Haladás	a	0-1	
27/04	Siófok	h	4-1	Sidibé, Coulibaly 3
04/05	Diósgyőr	a	3-3	Kulcsár, Coulibaly, Bódi
12/05	Videoton	h	2-1	Bódi, Kulcsár
17/05	Paks	a	2-1	Korhut, Mészáros
26/05	Ferencváros	h	2-3	Coulibaly 2 (2p)
01/06	MTK	a	1-3	Bódi

No	Name	Nat	DoB	Pos	Aps	(s)	Gls
22	Csaba Bernáth		26/03/79	D	15		
27	Ádám Bódi		18/10/90	M	24	(2)	4
88	Selim Bouadla	FRA	26/08/88	M	8	(6)	1
40	Ibrahima Coulibaly	FRA	11/00/91	A	24	(3)	18
14	Szabolcs Csorba		24/10/91	A	1		
77	Péter Czvitkovics		10/02/83	M	11	(6)	
7	Tibor Dombi		11/11/73	M	1	(10)	
11	János Ferenczi		03/04/91	M	9	(5)	
69	Mihály Korhut		01/12/88	D	26		1
70	Tamás Kulcsár		13/10/82	A	12	(6)	5
37	Lucas	BRA	06/05/89	M	2	(1)	
21	Bence Ludánszki		25/10/90	M	1		
18	Péter Máté		02/12/84	D	11		
17	Norbert Mészáros		19/08/80	D	24		1
28	Zoltán Nagy		25/10/85	D	15		
30	Stevo Nikolić	BIH	04/12/84	A	1		
8	Balázs Nikolov		04/07/77	M		(1)	
45	Nenad Novaković	SRB	17/07/82	G	1		
24	Gergő Oláh		18/02/89	D	1		
1	Vukašin Poleksić	MNE	30/08/82	G	3		
60	Péter Pölöskey		11/08/88	A	9	(4)	2
6	Luis Ramos	HON	11/04/85	M	10	(2)	
15	László Rezes		12/08/87	M	11	(2)	1
26	Ibrahima Sidibé	SEN	10/08/80	A	14	(13)	8
4	Dajan Šimac	GER	04/01/82	D	16	(4)	
29	István Spitzmüller		14/05/86	M	8	(5)	
55	Péter Szakály		17/08/86	M	18	(1)	3
66	Márk Szécsi		22/05/94	A	2	(9)	
2	István Szűcs		03/05/85	D	8	(3)	1
33	József Varga		06/06/88	M	14		
16	Róbert Varga		25/11/86	D		(1)	
87	István Verpecz		04/02/87	G	26	(1)	
19	Vinícius	BRA	12/08/89	A		(1)	
20	Mbengono Yannick	CMR	11/06/87	A	4	(1)	1

DIÓSGYŐRI VTK

Coach: Tibor Sisa; (22/11/12) Lázár Szentes;
(18/04/13) Zoltán Kovac (CRO)
1910 • Borsodi (12,000) • dvtk.eu
Major honours
Hungarian Cup (2) 1977, 1980

2012

27/07	Újpest	h	2-1	Fernando, Seydi
05/08	Honvéd	a	1-2	Luque
11/08	Eger	h	1-0	Seydi
18/08	Haladás	a	0-0	
25/08	Siófok	h	2-1	Fernando, Bacsa
01/09	Győr	h	0-3	
15/09	Videoton	a	0-0	
21/09	Paks	h	1-0	Bacsa
30/09	Ferencváros	a	0-2	
05/10	MTK	h	2-1	Tisza, Elek
21/10	Debrecen	a	0-2	
27/10	Rákóczi	h	0-1	
02/11	Kecskemét	a	1-1	Tisza
09/11	Pécs	h	1-1	Luque (p)
16/11	Pápa	a	2-2	Tisza 2 (2p)
25/11	Újpest	a	1-1	Tisza
01/12	Honvéd	h	3-1	Jefferson, Gohér, Bacsa

2012

01/03	Eger	a	1-0	Tisza
09/03	Haladás	h	1-1	Luque
31/03	Győr	a	0-2	
07/04	Videoton	h	2-1	Luque, Fernando
12/04	Paks	a	0-1	
16/04	Siófok	a	0-3	
21/04	Ferencváros	h	2-2	Seydi 2
27/04	MTK	a	0-2	
04/05	Debrecen	h	3-3	Fernando, Luque (p), Paco Gallardo
10/05	Rákóczi	a	1-1	Fernando
19/05	Kecskemét	h	2-1	Góhér, Luque (p)
27/05	Pécs	a	1-2	Rudolf
02/06	Pápa	h	1-1	Kádár

No	Name	Nat	DoB	Pos	Aps	(s)	Gls
10	Mohamadolu Abdouraman	CMR	24/01/85	M	8	(4)	
9	Patrik Bacsa		03/06/92	A	15	(13)	3
91	Péter Bogáti		13/03/91	M		(2)	
21	Martin Csirszki		07/01/95	M	1	(4)	
25	Ákos Elek		21/07/88	M	23	(4)	1
20	Fernando	ESP	02/06/79	M	22	(4)	5
5	Igor Gal	CRO	20/01/83	D	9	(1)	
6	Gergő Gohér		16/06/87	D	29		2
18	András Gosztonyi		07/11/90	A	16	(5)	
27	Michal Hanek	SVK	18/09/80	D	16	(2)	
11	Jefferson	BRA	29/08/86	D	2	(3)	1
4	Tamás Kádár		14/03/90	D	13		1
77	José Juan Luque	ESP	16/10/77	A	19	(3)	6
14	Tamás Nagy		18/01/87	A	4	(9)	
7	Paco Gallardo	ESP	13/01/80	M	12	(9)	1
2	Savo Rakovic	SRB	01/10/85	D	6		
17	Gergely Rudolf		09/03/85	A	12	(3)	1
12	Ladislav Rybánsky	SVK	19/12/84	G	26		
88	L'Imam Seydi	SEN	31/08/85	A	13	(9)	4
95	Balázs Szabó		28/10/95	M		(1)	
83	Norbert Tajti		07/10/83	G	4		
8	Péter Takács		25/01/90	M	21	(2)	
28	Tibor Tisza		10/11/84	A	19	(6)	6
23	Viktor Vadász		15/08/86	D	16	(1)	
15	András Vági		25/12/88	D	24	(1)	

EGRI FC

Coach: Antal Simon; (14/02/13) (Dénes Tóth);
(08/03/13) Ferenc Mészáros;
(17/05/13) (Tamás Horváth);
(31/05/13) Csaba Vojtekovszki
1907 • Szentmarjay Tibor (6,500) • egrifc.hu

2012

27/07	Haladás	a	2-4	Pisanjuk, Németh
03/08	Siófok	h	1-1	Dobrić
11/08	Diósgyőr	a	0-1	
19/08	Videoton	a	1-2	Koós
24/08	Paks	a	1-0	Pavlov
01/09	Ferencváros	h	2-2	Németh 2 (1p)
15/09	MTK	a	0-3	
22/09	Debrecen	h	1-0	Németh
29/09	Rákóczi	a	0-0	
06/10	Kecskemét	h	0-2	
20/10	Pécs	a	0-0	
26/10	Pápa	h	1-1	Farkas
02/11	Újpest	a	0-3	
10/11	Honvéd	h	1-3	Németh
17/11	Győr	a	1-2	Németh
24/11	Haladás	h	1-2	Németh
01/12	Siófok	a	3-4	Horváth, Albert, Németh

2012

01/03	Diósgyőr	h	0-1	
09/03	Videoton	h	0-4	
30/03	Ferencváros	a	0-4	
06/04	MTK	h	0-3	
09/04	Paks	h	2-2	Horváth, Koós
13/04	Debrecen	a	0-3	
20/04	Rákóczi	h	1-0	Farkas
26/04	Kecskemét	a	1-3	Zvara
05/05	Pécs	a	1-6	Lasimant, og (Gaál)
11/05	Pápa	a	1-6	Horváth
18/05	Újpest	h	1-2	Horváth
25/05	Honvéd	a	0-0	
01/06	Győr	h	2-3	Németh, Farkas (p)

No	Name	Nat	DoB	Pos	Aps	(s)	Gls
7	Ádám Albert		16/10/90	M	11	(9)	1
11	Zsolt Balog		10/11/78	D	24		
1	Darko Brljak	SVN	23/12/84	G	13	(1)	
6	Vladimir Buač	SRB	26/12/84	M	10		
22	Saša Dobrić	SRB	21/01/82	A	15	(4)	1
10	Ádám Farkas		09/11/87	M	18	(7)	3
13	Ádám Fenyvesi		01/01/96	M		(1)	
12	Josef Hamouz	CZE	08/04/80	D	6	(1)	
17	Zoltán Horváth		30/07/89	A	11	(5)	4
16	Simeon Hristov	MKD	06/04/92	A		(2)	
20	Jiří Kabele	CZE	17/02/87	A	9	(9)	
24	Dániel Kasza		01/08/94	D	5		
18	Attila Katona		16/06/81	D	7	(1)	
3	Petr Knakal	CZE	01/02/83	D	12		
4	Ismaël Koné	FRA	12/07/90	M	9	(1)	
27	Gábor Koós		09/02/84	A	15	(4)	2
4	Gábor Kovács		04/09/87	D	17		
9	Yohan Lasimant	FRA	04/09/89	A	2	(4)	1
15	Jasmin Mecinovic	MKD	22/10/90	D	20		
8	Norbert Németh		05/05/81	M	25	(3)	9
63	Dávid Palásthy		10/05/90	G		(1)	
3	Norbert Palásthy		10/02/81	A	1	(5)	
5	Čedomir Pavičević	SRB	23/05/78	M	18		
19	Dušan Pavlov	SRB	19/07/89	A	3	(7)	1
2	József Piller		16/08/88	M	6	(2)	
21	Igor Pisanjuk	CAN	28/10/89	A	8	(3)	1
14	Csaba Preklet		25/01/91	D	16	(1)	
16	Savo Rakovic	SRB	01/10/85	D	5		
6	Michael Stanislaw	AUT	05/06/87	M	10	(3)	
99	Bence Szabó		10/01/90	A	1	(6)	
26	Gábor Sztankó		18/01/85	G	17		
77	Tanque	BRA	18/07/91	A		(1)	
62	Joël Tchami	CMR	25/03/82	A		(1)	
55	Marko Vidović	MNE	03/06/88	D	5	(4)	
99	Goran Vujović	MNE	03/05/87	A	7	(1)	
23	Dávid Zvara		22/07/94	A	4	(3)	1

FERENCVÁROSI TC

Coach: Lajos Détári; (21/08/12) Ricardo Moniz (NED)
1899 • Albert Flórián (18,100); Puskás Ferenc (39,111)
• ftc.hu
Major honours
Inter Cities Fairs Cup (1) 1965;
Hungarian League (28) 1903, 1905, 1907, 1909, 1910,
1911, 1912, 1913, 1926, 1927, 1928, 1932, 1934, 1938,
1940, 1941, 1949, 1963, 1964, 1967, 1968, 1976, 1981,
1992, 1995, 1996, 2001, 2004;
Hungarian Cup (20) 1913, 1922, 1927, 1928, 1933,
1935, 1942, 1943, 1944, 1958, 1972, 1974, 1976, 1978,
1991, 1993, 1994, 1995, 2003, 2004

2012

28/07	Kecskemét	h	1-1	Alempijević
04/08	Pécs	a	0-0	
11/08	Pápa	h	4-1	Józsi 2 (1p), Klein, Máté
19/08	Újpest	a	1-2	Orosz
25/08	Honvéd	h	0-2	
01/09	Eger	a	2-2	Perić (p), Böde
14/09	Haladás	h	2-1	Somália, Čukić
23/09	Siófok	a	0-0	
30/09	Diósgyőr	h	2-0	Böde, Perić
07/10	Videoton	a	2-1	Józsi (p), Böde
19/10	Paks	h	2-2	Ionescu, Gyömbér
28/10	Győr	h	1-1	Alempijević
03/11	MTK	a	2-4	Józsi, Böde
11/11	Debrecen	h	2-1	Böde, Józsi (p)
18/11	Rákóczi	a	0-1	
24/11	Kecskemét	a	2-2	Böde, Jenner
02/12	Pécs	h	3-2	Böde 2, Perić

2012

03/03	Pápa	a	3-0	Jenner, Aborah, Böde
10/03	Újpest	h	2-1	Somália, Čukić
30/03	Eger	h	4-0	Böde 2, Jenner, Somália
06/04	Haladás	a	0-0	
13/04	Siófok	h	4-2	Böde 3, Leonardo
16/04	Honvéd	a	0-1	
21/04	Diósgyőr	a	2-2	Jenner, Gyömbér
28/04	Videoton	h	0-1	
05/05	Paks	a	3-1	Leonardo, Bešić, Klein
12/05	Győr	a	0-1	
18/05	MTK	h	2-0	Somália, Böde
26/05	Debrecen	a	3-2	Somália, Jenner, Perić
31/05	Rákóczi	h	2-2	Böde 2 (2p)

No	Name	Nat	DoB	Pos	Aps	(s)	Gls
11	Stanley Aborah	BEL	23/06/87	M	5	(2)	1
66	Aleksandar Alempijević	SRB	25/07/88	M	15	(1)	2
99	Gergő Beliczky		03/07/90	A		(4)	
21	Muhamed Bešić	BIH	10/09/92	D	20	(2)	1
15	János Birtalan		23/10/92	M		(1)	
13	Dániel Böde		24/10/86	A	29	(1)	17
5	Philipp Bönig	GER	20/03/80	D	7		
22	Attila Busai		21/01/89	M		(1)	
16	Tamás Csillus		08/05/95	M		(1)	
30	Vladan Čukić	SRB	27/06/80	M	20	(8)	2
29	Noel Fülöp		29/01/88	D	1		
18	András Gárdos		09/01/91	M		(1)	
26	Tamás Grúz		08/11/85	D	4	(1)	
19	Gábor Gyömbér		27/02/88	M	30		2
77	Juha Hakola	FIN	27/10/87	A	3	(4)	
33	Dávid Holman		17/03/93	M	2	(2)	
14	Andrei Ionescu	ROU	29/03/88	M	10	(3)	1
27	Julian Jenner	NED	28/02/84	A	17	(3)	5
55	Levente Jova		30/01/92	G	30		
7	Aleksandar Jovanović	BIH	26/10/84	M	13	(3)	
8	György Józsi		31/01/83	M	27	(1)	5
23	Júnior Fell	BRA	10/04/92	D	1		
44	Martin Klein	CZE	02/07/84	D	12	(6)	2
99	Leonardo	BRA	09/03/83	A	8	(1)	2
91	Quenten Martinus	NED	07/03/91	A	4	(3)	
11	János Máté		19/05/90	A	3	(5)	1
39	Márk Orosz		24/10/89	M	6	(14)	1
3	Mark Otten	NED	02/09/85	D	9	(2)	
10	Milan Perić	SRB	16/04/84	A	6	(10)	4
60	Péter Pölöskei		11/08/88	A	1		
88	Somália	BRA	28/09/88	A	26	(2)	5
4	Dániel Sváb		02/09/90	D	21	(1)	

GYŐRI ETO FC

Coach: Attila Pintér
1904 • ETO Park (16,000) • etofc.hu
Major honours
Hungarian League (4) 1963 (autumn), 1982, 1983, 2013;
Hungarian Cup (4) 1965, 1966, 1967, 1979

2012

28/07	Debrecen	a	1-4	*Andrić*
04/08	Haladás	h	1-1	*Kronaveter*
10/08	Rákóczi	h	2-1	*R Varga, Dina*
18/08	Siófok	a	3-2	*Kamber 2, R Varga*
25/08	Kecskemét	h	5-1	*R Varga, Koltai (p), Střeštík,*
				Kamber, Kronaveter
01/09	Diósgyőr	a	3-0	*Koltai 3*
16/09	Pécs	a	1-0	*Koltai (p)*
23/09	Videoton	a	1-0	*Koltai*
28/09	Pápa	h	6-0	*R Varga 3, Kronaveter 2, Koltai*
06/10	Paks	h	0-0	
21/10	Újpest	h	3-2	*R Varga, og (Aarab), Kamber*
28/10	Ferencváros	a	1-1	*R Varga*
04/11	Honvéd	h	0-0	
10/11	MTK	a	3-1	*R Varga, Trajković, Völgyi*
17/11	Eger	h	2-1	*Kamber, Koltai*
24/11	Debrecen	h	2-0	*R Varga, Dudás*
01/12	Haladás	a	1-1	*Trajković*

2012

02/03	Rákóczi	a	2-1	*Andrić, Kink*
09/03	Siófok	h	2-1	*Trajković 2*
31/03	Diósgyőr	h	2-0	*R Varga, Völgyi*
05/04	Pécs	a	2-0	*Trajković, Kronaveter*
14/04	Videoton	h	1-1	*Kamber*
20/04	Pápa	a	1-1	*Trajković*
23/04	Kecskemét	a	2-5	*R Varga, Kamber*
26/04	Paks	h	3-4	*Völgyi, Střeštík, Kamber*
05/05	Újpest	a	2-1	*Andrić, Střeštík*
12/05	Ferencváros	h	1-0	*Völgyi (p)*
19/05	Honvéd	a	0-2	
26/05	MTK	h	1-0	*Trajković*
01/06	Eger	a	3-2	*Kalmár, Pilibaitis, Pátkai*

No	Name	Nat	DoB	Pos	Aps	(s)	Gls
25	Jarmo Ahjupera	EST	13/04/84	A	2	(1)	
10	Rati Aleksidze	GEO	03/08/78	A		(7)	
19	Nemanja Andrić	SRB	13/06/87	M	5	(16)	3
7	Mihai Dina	ROU	15/09/85	M	4	(4)	1
3	Marko Dinjar	CRO	21/05/86	M	13	(2)	
28	Vladimir Djordjević	SRB	25/12/82	D	4		
8	Ádám Dudás		12/05/90	M	3	(13)	1
7	Balázs Farkas		24/04/88	A	1		
5	Marián Had	SVK	16/09/82	D	5		
13	Zsolt Kalmár		09/06/95	M	2		1
24	Djordje Kamber	SRB	20/11/83	M	27		8
26	Ľuboš Kamenár	SVK	17/06/87	G	3		
6	Tarmo Kink	EST	06/10/85	M	7	(3)	1
29	Tamás Koltai		30/04/87	M	18	(2)	8
9	Rok Kronaveter	SVN	07/12/86	M	11	(8)	5
25	Giorgi Kvilitaia	GEO	01/10/93	A			
18	Ádám Lang		17/01/93	D	3	(1)	
16	Zoltán Lipták		10/12/84	D	26		
31	István Matetits		06/09/93	M		(1)	
30	Péter Molnár	SVK	14/12/83	G		(1)	
20	Mihai Nicorec	ROU	24/03/86	A	3	(1)	
35	Csanád Novák		24/09/94	M		(1)	
17	Máté Pátkai		06/03/88	M	22	(4)	1
14	Linas Pilibaitis	LTU	05/04/85	M	4	(7)	1
4	Lazar Stanišić	SRB	05/07/84	M	1		
1	Saša Stevanović	SRB	04/08/74	G	27		
21	Marek Střeštík	CZE	01/02/87	M	23	(2)	3
22	Michal Švec	CZE	19/03/87	M	23		
2	Ákos Takács		14/02/82	D	23		
23	Tibor Tokody		01/09/80	M	8	(1)	
12	Nikola Trajković	SRB	05/01/81	M	20	(3)	7
11	Roland Varga		23/01/90	A	25	(2)	12
34	Tamás Varga		18/05/91	A	1		
15	Dániel Völgyi		07/06/87	M	16		4

KAPOSVÁRI RÁKÓCZI FC

Coach: László Prukner
1923 • Városi (7,000) • rakoczifc.hu

2012

29/07	MTK	a	1-3	*Waltner*
04/08	Debrecen	h	1-0	*Zámbó*
10/08	Győr	a	1-2	*Oláh*
17/08	Kecskemét	a	2-1	*Vručina 2*
25/08	Pécs	h	1-1	*Jammeh*
01/09	Pápa	a	0-3	
14/09	Újpest	h	0-0	
22/09	Honvéd	a	3-5	*Zámbó, Balázs, Jammeh*
29/09	Eger	h	0-0	
06/10	Haladás	a	0-0	
20/10	Siófok	h	3-0	*Kovács, Diallo 2*
27/10	Diósgyőr	a	1-0	*Horváth*
04/11	Videoton	h	0-2	
10/11	Paks	a	2-1	*Oláh (p), Balázs*
18/11	Ferencváros	h	1-0	*Pavlović*
23/11	MTK	h	0-0	
30/11	Debrecen	a	1-2	*Pavlović*

2012

02/03	Győr	h	1-2	*Oláh*
08/03	Kecskemét	h	2-3	*Oláh, Waltner (p)*
29/03	Pápa	a	3-2	*Waltner, Oláh (p), Balázs*
05/04	Újpest	a	0-1	
09/04	Pécs	a	2-0	*Waltner, Pavlović*
12/04	Honvéd	h	1-2	*Waltner*
20/04	Eger	a	0-1	
26/04	Haladás	h	3-2	*Hegedűs, Oláh 2 (1p)*
05/05	Siófok	a	1-0	*Oláh (p)*
10/05	Diósgyőr	h	1-1	*og (Vági)*
18/05	Videoton	a	1-2	*Thian*
25/05	Paks	h	1-0	*Balázs*
31/05	Ferencváros	a	2-2	*Okuka, Waltner (p)*

No	Name	Nat	DoB	Pos	Aps	(s)	Gls
18	Benjámin Balázs		26/04/90	M	30		4
5	István Bank		14/04/84	M	21		
4	Lukács Bőle		27/03/90	M	3	(5)	
14	Aaron Dankwah	GHA	18/08/90	M	3	(3)	
16	Moustapha Diallo	GUI	16/05/92	A		(6)	2
29	Lazaros Fotias	GRE	26/04/91	D		(1)	
21	Ľuboš Hajdúch	SVK	06/03/80	G	30		
24	Dávid Hegedűs		06/06/85	M	17	(2)	1
19	Tamás Horváth		29/04/91	M	10	(4)	1
27	Haruna Jammeh	GAM	02/06/91	A	12	(12)	2
28	Gábor Jánvári		25/04/90	D	20	(4)	
6	György Katona		23/01/88	A		(2)	
15	Olivér Kovács		22/12/90	M	21	(5)	1
13	Dražen Okuka	SRB	05/03/86	D	25	(1)	1
14	Lóránt Oláh		23/11/79	A	26	(1)	8
7	Bojan Pavlović	SRB	01/02/85	A	24	(3)	3
33	Pedro	BRA	15/09/90	M	25	(2)	
8	Nikola Šafarić	CRO	11/03/81	M	29		
25	Khaly Thian	SEN	07/01/94	M		(6)	1
17	Bojan Vručina	CRO	08/11/84	A	11	(12)	2
9	Róbert Waltner		20/09/77	A	8	(8)	6
20	Bence Zámbó		17/08/89	D	12	(6)	2

KECSKEMÉTI TE

Coach: László Török; (17/09/12) (István László Szabó);
(28/09/12) Ferenc Horváth
1911 • Széktói (6,500) • kecskemetite.hu
Major honours
Hungarian Cup (1) 2011

2012

28/07	Ferencváros	a	1-1	*Jorginho*
05/08	MTK	h	1-1	*Sós*
11/08	Debrecen	a	1-2	*Vaskó*
17/08	Rákóczi	h	1-2	*Sós*
25/08	Győr	a	1-5	*Jorginho*
31/08	Pécs	a	1-0	*Balázs*
15/09	Pápa	h	1-2	*Litsingi*
22/09	Újpest	a	1-2	*Litsingi (p)*
29/09	Honvéd	h	2-1	*Litsingi 2*
06/10	Eger	a	2-0	*og (Knakal), Burgos*
20/10	Haladás	h	2-1	*Edison, Litsingi*
26/10	Siófok	a	2-0	*Salami, Patvaros*
02/11	Diósgyőr	h	1-1	*Savić*
11/11	Videoton	a	0-2	
17/11	Paks	h	1-1	*Pekár*
24/11	Ferencváros	h	2-2	*Burgos, Forró*
01/12	MTK	a	1-2	*Litsingi*

2012

02/03	Debrecen	h	0-0	
08/03	Rákóczi	a	3-2	*Mohl, Pekár, Burgos*
30/03	Pécs	h	0-2	
06/04	Pápa	a	2-2	*Balázs, Salami*
14/04	Újpest	h	1-0	*Mogyorósi*
20/04	Honvéd	a	0-0	
23/04	Győr	h	5-2	*Mohl (p), Varga, Burgos, Salami,*
				Balázs
26/04	Eger	h	3-1	*og (Raković), Mohl, Rajczi*
03/05	Haladás	a	1-1	*Mogyorósi*
11/05	Siófok	h	3-1	*Burgos, Mohl, Salami*
19/05	Diósgyőr	a	1-2	*Rajczi*
26/05	Videoton	h	1-5	*Mohl*
31/05	Paks	a	1-0	*Bertus*

No	Name	Nat	DoB	Pos	Aps	(s)	Gls
99	Botond Antal		22/08/91	G	14		
7	Zsolt Balázs		11/08/88	A	3	(10)	3
6	Béla Balogh		30/12/84	D	10		
26	Lajos Bertus		26/09/86	M	4	(1)	1
21	Gábor Bori		16/01/84	M	5		
83	Csaba Borszéki		15/09/83	G	12	(1)	
21	Rafael Burgos	SLV	03/06/88	A	17	(3)	5
92	Edgardo Díaz	ARG	19/01/88	M	2	(2)	
19	Sindou Dosso	CIV	23/04/86	A		(3)	
20	Edison	BRA	09/12/85	A	5	(6)	1
14	Balázs Farkas		15/10/79	M	4		
23	Gyula Forró		06/08/88	D	23	(3)	1
18	Attila Hullám		11/02/87	M	3	(3)	
20	Givi Ioseliani	GEO	23/01/90	M	1	(3)	
9	Jorginho	BRA	04/12/85	A	11	(3)	2
2	Balázs Tibor Koszó		20/03/88	D	12	(2)	
18	Francis Litsingi	CGO	09/10/86	A	15	(2)	6
3	József Mogyorósi		01/11/78	D	11		2
22	Dávid Mohl		28/04/85	D	19		5
29	Patrik Nagy		16/02/91	M	3		
33	Gábor Németh		21/05/75	G	4	(1)	
8	Zsolt Patvaros		18/02/93	D	9	(6)	1
16	László Pekár		20/01/93	A	13	(10)	2
13	Krisztián Póti		28/05/89	D	18	(1)	
81	Péter Rajczi		03/04/81	A	8	(2)	2
24	Luis Ramos	HON	11/04/85	M	10		
30	Eugène Salami	NGA	05/02/89	A	13	(7)	4
10	Vladan Savić	MNE	26/07/79	D	22	(5)	1
11	Márkó Sós		29/12/90	D	10	(1)	2
88	Viktor Tölgyesi		18/01/92	M	1	(3)	
4	Róbert Varga		25/11/86	D	9		1
28	Tamás Vaskó		20/02/84	D	26		
14	Marko Vukasović	MNE	10/09/90	M	12		
27	Mbengono Yannick	CMR	11/06/87	A	1	(4)	

LOMBARD-PÁPA TFC

Coach: Ferenc Bene jr; (27/08/12) (László Kovács);
(02/09/12) Gyula Zsivóczky-Pandel;
(05/05/13) (László Kovács) ; (27/05/13) Bálint Tóth
2004 • Perutz (8,000) • lombardfcpapa.hu

2012

29/07	Videoton	a	1-1	Seye
03/08	Paks	h	0-0	
11/08	Ferencváros	a	1-4	Maróti
19/08	MTK	h	0-2	
26/08	Debrecen	a	0-1	
01/09	Rákóczi	h	3-0	Seye, Maróti, Sekour
15/09	Kecskemét	a	2-1	Marić 2 (1p)
22/09	Pécs	h	1-2	Benko
28/09	Győr	a	0-6	
06/10	Újpest	a	1-1	Marić
20/10	Honvéd	h	2-1	Marić 2 (1p)
26/10	Eger	a	1-1	og (Knakal)
03/11	Haladás	h	1-0	Marić (p)
09/11	Siófok	a	0-1	
16/11	Diósgyőr	h	2-2	Marić 2 (2p)
25/11	Videoton	h	1-0	Seye
30/11	Paks	a	0-2	

2012

03/03	Ferencváros	h	0-3	
09/03	MTK	a	0-2	
29/03	Rákóczi	a	0-3	
06/04	Kecskemét	h	0-2	
10/04	Debrecen	h	1-0	og (Szakály)
13/04	Pécs	a	0-2	
20/04	Győr	h	1-1	Griffith
27/04	Újpest	h	0-1	
04/05	Honvéd	a	0-2	
11/05	Eger	h	6-1	Griffith, Quintero 2, Marić, Arsić, Király
17/05	Haladás	a	1-2	Quintero
24/05	Siófok	h	0-1	
02/06	Diósgyőr	a	1-1	og (Vadász)

No	Name	Nat	DoB	Pos	Aps	(s)	Gls
9	Lazar Arsić	SRB	24/09/91	M	20	(6)	1
23	Balázs Balogh		21/07/82	D	8		
11	Gergő Beliczky		03/07/90	A	1	(4)	
8	Jože Benko	SVN	23/03/80	A		(9)	1
99	Aleksandrs Čekulajevs	LVA	10/09/85	A		(4)	
3	Daniel Orozco	ESP	19/02/87	D	6		
5	András Dlusztus		22/07/88	D	24	(1)	
14	Krisztián Dóczi		19/11/89	M	3	(3)	
55	József Fellai		24/06/89			(3)	
50	Georges Griffith	CIV	24/02/90	A	6	(5)	2
26	Levente Horváth		13/04/82	M	5	(3)	
31	Botond Király		26/10/94	M		(7)	1
17	Tino Lagator	CRO	14/09/87	A	4	(6)	
21	Goran Marić	SRB	23/03/84	A	22		9
25	Béla Maróti		07/05/79	M	15	(4)	2
2	Sándor Nagy		01/01/88	D	13	(2)	
29	Milán Németh		29/05/88	A	12	(6)	
32	Ádám Présinger		26/01/89	D	19	(2)	
30	César Quintero	COL	09/11/88	D	29		3
20	István Rodenbücher		22/02/84	D	25	(2)	
98	Youssef Sekour	FRA	27/02/88	M	9	(1)	1
6	Mouhamadou Seye	SEN	10/10/88	A	12	(4)	3
7	András Simon		30/03/90	A	2	(3)	
28	Ottó Szabó	SVK	01/03/81	M	17	(3)	
7	Máté Szolga		15/08/93	M		(1)	
27	Lajos Szűcs		08/08/73	G	30		
91	Tamás Tajthy		29/08/91	M	11	(1)	
10	Bence Tóth		27/07/89	M	17	(3)	
4	Gábor Tóth		26/03/87	D	20	(5)	

MTK BUDAPEST

Coach: József Garami
1888 • Hidegkuti Nándor (7,702) • mtkhungaria.hu
Major honours
Hungarian League (23) 1904, 1908, 1914, 1917, 1918,
1919, 1920, 1921, 1922, 1923, 1924, 1925, 1929, 1936,
1937, 1951, 1953, 1958, 1987, 1997, 1999, 2003, 2008;
Hungarian Cup (12) 1910, 1911, 1912, 1914, 1923,
1925, 1932, 1952, 1968, 1997, 1998, 2000

2012

29/07	Rákóczi	h	3-1	Tischler, Wolfe, Könyves
05/08	Kecskemét	a	1-1	Könyves
12/08	Pécs	h	0-0	
19/08	Pápa	a	2-0	Nikházi, Hidvégi
24/08	Újpest	h	2-1	og (landoli), Csiki
31/08	Honvéd	a	2-1	Kanta 2 (1p)
15/09	Eger	h	3-0	Tischler 3
21/09	Haladás	a	0-3	
28/09	Siófok	h	1-1	Kanta
05/10	Diósgyőr	a	1-2	Kanta (p)
19/10	Videoton	h	3-2	Tischler 2, Csiki
27/10	Paks	a	0-0	
03/11	Ferencváros	h	4-2	Csiki 2, Hidvégi, Könyves
10/11	Győr	h	1-3	Balajti
17/11	Debrecen	a	2-0	og (Korhut), Kanta
25/11	Rákóczi	a	0-0	
01/12	Kecskemét	h	3-1	Csiki 2, Vass

2012

01/03	Pécs	a	1-2	Ladányi
09/03	Pápa	h	2-0	Wolfe, Hidvégi
30/03	Honvéd	h	1-0	Pölöskei
06/04	Eger	a	3-0	Vass, Kanta 2 (1p)
13/04	Haladás	h	0-1	
19/04	Siófok	a	1-2	Tischler
27/04	Diósgyőr	h	2-0	Vass, Balajti
30/04	Újpest	a	1-1	Kanta
03/05	Videoton	a	0-2	
10/05	Paks	h	1-0	Pölöskei
18/05	Ferencváros	a	0-2	
26/05	Győr	a	0-1	
01/06	Debrecen	h	3-1	Kálnoki Kis, Kanta, Vass

No	Name	Nat	DoB	Pos	Aps	(s)	Gls
91	Ádám Balajti		07/03/91	A	5	(18)	2
18	Barnabás Bese		06/05/94	A		(12)	
8	Norbert Csiki		21/05/91	A	16	(1)	6
28	Federico Groppioni	ITA	17/06/84	G	10		
1	Lajos Hegedűs		19/12/87	G	20		
4	Sándor Hidvégi		09/04/83	D	30		3
13	Ádám Hrepka		15/04/87	A	2		
12	Dávid Kálnoki Kis		06/08/91	D	12		1
19	József Kanta		24/03/84	M	26		9
5	Dávid Kelemen		24/05/92	D	16	(1)	
15	Norbert Könyves	SRB	10/06/89	A	11	(2)	3
11	Tibor Ladányi		21/11/91	M	10	(5)	1
10	János Lázok		04/10/84	M	1	(2)	
2	Tibor Nagy		14/08/91	D	4	(1)	
25	Márk Nikházi		02/02/89	M	6	(10)	1
9	András Pál		19/08/85	A	2	(5)	
16	Zsolt Pölöskei		19/02/91	A	6	(9)	2
24	Patrik Poór		25/11/93	D	6	(2)	
20	Ferenc Rácz		28/03/91	A		(6)	
30	Patrik Tischler		30/07/91	A	22	(7)	7
23	Dániel Vadnai		19/02/88	D	27		
27	Szabolcs Varga		03/03/95	A		(1)	
17	Patrik Vass		17/01/93	A	16	(5)	4
21	Dragan Vukmir	SRB	02/08/78	D	30		
39	Rafa Wolfe	JAM	19/12/85	D	24		2
7	László Zsidai		16/07/86	M	28		

PAKSI SE

Coach: Károly Kis; (01/08/12) (Csaba Máté);
(30/08/12) Tomislav Sivić (SRB)
1952 • Városi (5,000) • paksifc.hu

2012

28/07	Pécs	h	2-3	Simon, N Heffler
03/08	Pápa	a	0-0	
12/08	Újpest	h	2-2	Simon, Éger
19/08	Honvéd	a	3-3	Simon, Sipeki, Kiss
24/08	Eger	h	0-1	
01/09	Haladás	a	2-1	Lázok, og (Kenesei)
15/09	Siófok	h	4-1	Vayer, Simon 3
21/09	Diósgyőr	a	0-1	
29/09	Videoton	h	1-1	Tököli
06/10	Győr	h	0-0	
19/10	Ferencváros	a	2-2	Simon, og (Jovanović)
27/10	MTK	h	0-0	
03/11	Debrecen	a	1-0	Tököli
10/11	Rákóczi	h	1-2	Lázok
17/11	Kecskemét	a	1-1	og (Vaskó)
23/11	Pécs	a	3-1	Eppel 2, Kulcsár
30/11	Pápa	h	2-0	Eppel, Tököli

2012

02/03	Újpest	a	6-0	Lázok 4 (1p), Tököli 2
08/03	Honvéd	h	0-3	
30/03	Haladás	a	0-2	
06/04	Siófok	a	1-1	Lázok
09/04	Eger	a	2-2	Pap, Éger (p)
12/04	Diósgyőr	h	1-0	Tököli
20/04	Videoton	a	0-2	
26/04	Győr	a	4-3	Bartha, Lázok, Eppel, Könyves
05/05	Ferencváros	h	1-3	Lázok (p)
10/05	MTK	a	0-1	
17/05	Debrecen	h	1-2	Bartha
25/05	Rákóczi	a	0-1	
31/05	Kecskemét	h	0-1	

No	Name	Nat	DoB	Pos	Aps	(s)	Gls
7	Tamás Báló		12/01/84	M	13	(1)	
39	László Bartha		09/02/87	A	18	(8)	2
21	Gábor Bori		16/01/84	M	10		
9	Tamás Csehi		06/02/84	D	6	(2)	
24	Norbert Csernyánszki		01/02/76	G	21		
63	László Éger		07/05/77	D	28		2
25	Márton Eppel		26/10/91	M	10	(13)	4
18	Attila Fiola		17/02/90	D	26		
17	Csaba János Hahn		15/05/95	M		(3)	
27	Norbert Heffler		24/05/90	M	16	(5)	1
16	Tibor Heffler		17/05/87	M	28	(1)	
7	Dániel Juhász		17/05/92	D	3		
10	Tamás Kiss		27/09/79	A	3	(4)	1
42	Norbert Könyves	SRB	10/06/89	A	8	(3)	1
8	Gábor Kovács		04/09/87	D	4	(8)	
77	Dávid Kulcsár		25/02/88	M	13	(3)	1
20	János Lázok		04/10/84	M	19	(2)	9
19	István Mészáros		03/03/80	M	1	(4)	
1	Gábor Németh		21/05/75	G	4		
89	Roland Pap		17/08/90	M		(3)	1
28	Péter Pokorni		22/11/89	G	5		
6	Tamás Sifter		03/03/81	M	24	(1)	
99	Attila Simon		04/02/83	A	10	(5)	7
22	István Sipeki		17/02/79	M	7	(2)	1
30	János Szabó		11/07/89	D	25		
55	Attila Tököli		14/05/76	A	20	(6)	6
11	Gábor Vayer		18/05/77	M	7	(14)	1
33	József Zsók		02/10/84	D	1		

PÉCSI MFC

Coach: Attila Supka; (04/01/13) Emil Lőrincz
1973 • PMFC (10,000) • pmfc.hu
Major honours
Hungarian Cup (1) 1990

2012

28/07	Paks	a	3-2	Wittrédi, Grumić, Zeljković
04/08	Ferencváros	h	0-0	
12/08	MTK	a	0-0	
18/08	Debrecen	h	2-3	Okoronkwo, Krejčí
25/08	Rákóczi	a	1-1	Wittrédi
31/08	Kecskemét	h	0-1	
16/09	Győr	a	0-1	
22/09	Pápa	a	2-1	Bajzát, Krejčí
30/09	Újpest	h	1-3	Grumić
05/10	Honvéd	a	1-0	Okoronkwo
20/10	Eger	h	0-0	
27/10	Haladás	a	1-1	Čaušić
03/11	Siófok	h	2-1	Bajzát, Okoronkwo
09/11	Diósgyőr	a	1-1	Wittrédi
17/11	Videoton	h	0-0	
23/11	Paks	h	1-3	Bajzát
02/12	Ferencváros	a	2-3	Wittrédi, Bajzát

2012

01/03	MTK	h	2-1	Grumić, Zeljković
10/03	Debrecen	a	1-1	Grumić
08/03	Kecskemét	a	2-0	Grumić, Simon
05/04	Győr	h	0-2	
09/04	Rákóczi	a	0-2	
13/04	Pápa	h	2-0	Čaušić, Lázár
19/04	Újpest	a	2-4	Wittrédi (p), Simon
28/04	Honvéd	h	0-3	
04/05	Eger	a	3-2	Simon (p), A Horváth, Wittrédi
11/05	Haladás	h	0-2	
18/05	Siófok	a	0-1	
27/05	Diósgyőr	h	2-1	Grumić, Szatmári
01/06	Videoton	a	2-1	Márkvárt, Koller

No	Name	Nat	DoB	Pos	Aps	(s)	Gls
28	Jean-Baptiste Akassou	CIV	05/11/85	M	23	(1)	
81	Péter Bajzát		22/06/81	A	12	(2)	4
6	Béla Balogh		30/12/84	D	9		
15	Péter Beke		06/12/94	A	1	(6)	
22	László Bodnár		25/02/79	D	10	(1)	
26	Andrej Čaušić	CRO	19/02/90	D	18	(4)	2
24	Nicolas Ceolin	BRA	10/04/86	A	1	(1)	
27	Gábor Demjén		01/08/88	M	2	(6)	
12	Dénes Dibusz		19/11/90	G	29		
5	Ferenc Fodor		22/03/91	D	12	(3)	
24	Miklós Gaál		13/05/81	D	5	(4)	
11	Miroslav Grumić	SRB	29/06/84	A	26	(1)	6
11	Zoltán Harsányi	SVK		A		(3)	
17	Adrián Horváth		20/11/87	M	22		1
69	Zsolt Horváth		19/05/88	A	1	(8)	
9	Krisztián Koller		08/05/83	A	8	(3)	1
27	Róbert Kővágó		23/11/95	A		(1)	
25	Jiří Krejčí	CZE	22/03/86	D	20		2
18	Levente Lantos		26/07/80	M	12		
20	Pál Lázár		11/03/88	D	8		1
8	Dávid Márkvárt		20/09/94	A	4	(3)	1
14	Dominik Nagy		08/05/95	M		(1)	
10	Olivér Nagy		30/01/89	M	10	(11)	
20	Solomon Okoronkwo	NGA	02/03/87	A	7	(3)	3
8	Leon Panikvar	SVN	28/01/83	M	5		
	András Sánta	ROU	01/06/85	G	1		
99	Attila Simon		04/02/83	A	9	(4)	3
1	Aleksandar Stojmirović	SRB	11/12/82	M	1	(3)	
13	Lóránd Szatmári		03/10/88	M	5	(12)	1
33	Eke Uzoma	NGA	11/08/89	M	25	(3)	
7	Dávid Wittrédi		17/06/87	A	28	(1)	6
21	Zoran Zeljković	SVN	09/05/80	M	16	(3)	2

BFC SIÓFOK

Coach: Károly Horváth
1921 • Városi (12,000) • bfc-siofok.hu
Major honours
Hungarian Cup (1) 1984

2012

29/07	Honvéd	h	0-1	
03/08	Eger	a	1-1	Sípos
10/08	Haladás	h	0-3	
18/08	Győr	h	2-3	Dajić, Nyári
25/08	Diósgyőr	a	1-2	Pál
02/09	Videoton	h	1-3	Zamostny
15/09	Paks	a	1-4	Pál (p)
23/09	Ferencváros	h	0-0	
28/09	MTK	a	1-1	Kiss
07/10	Debrecen	h	0-2	
20/10	Rákóczi	a	0-3	
26/10	Kecskemét	h	0-2	
03/11	Pécs	a	1-2	Pál
09/11	Pápa	h	1-0	Nyári
16/11	Újpest	a	2-4	Melczer 2
24/11	Honvéd	a	0-2	
01/12	Eger	h	4-3	Melczer 3 (3p), Dajić

2012

02/03	Haladás	a	1-2	Nagy
09/03	Győr	a	1-2	Máté
29/03	Videoton	a	0-6	
06/04	Paks	h	1-1	Pál
13/04	Ferencváros	a	2-4	Tímár, Melczer
16/04	Diósgyőr	h	3-0	Dajić, Fehér, Máté
19/04	MTK	h	2-1	Pál, Tímár
27/04	Debrecen	a	1-4	Dajić
04/05	Rákóczi	h	2-1	Windecker, Melczer
11/05	Kecskemét	a	1-3	Kiss
18/05	Pécs	h	1-0	Windecker
24/05	Pápa	a	1-0	Takács
02/06	Újpest	a	0-1	

No	Name	Nat	DoB	Pos	Aps	(s)	Gls
23	Milan Čokić	SRB	23/01/91	M	2	(1)	
9	Jusuf Dajić	BIH	21/08/84	A	16	(5)	4
16	Stefan Deák	SRB	23/03/91	D	14		
6	Tamás Egerszegi		02/08/91	M	5	(5)	
3	Zsolt Fehér		13/09/85	D	22		1
4	András Fejes		26/08/88	D	20		
15	Marcell Fodor		03/10/91	D	11	(7)	
21	Noel Fülöp		29/01/88	D		(2)	
18	András Gál		20/04/89	M	16	(7)	
1	Márk Heinrich		22/06/89	G	1		
7	Bence Horváth		12/06/86	M	5	(7)	
13	Tamás Kecskés		15/01/86	M	26		
11	Máté Kiss		30/04/91	M	11	(7)	2
21	Zoltán Kiss		12/07/86	M	1	(3)	
28	Zsolt Kiss		21/08/86	D	3	(1)	
12	Péter Kurucz		30/05/88	G	25		
21	Dániel Lengyel		01/01/89	D	2		
10	János Máté		19/05/90	A	7	(3)	2
5	Vilmos Melczer		25/02/86	M	22	(3)	7
23	Attila Menyhárt		26/11/84	A	2	(4)	
2	József Mogyorósi		01/11/78	D	11	(1)	
29	Norbert Mokánszki		08/07/89	A		(2)	
25	Marcell Molnár		26/08/90	A	2	(6)	
17	Tamás Nagy		30/07/87	M	10	(3)	1
20	Tibor Nyári		11/09/86	M	16	(4)	2
14	Szabolcs Pál		14/01/88	M	24	(2)	5
10	Norbert Sipos		21/03/81	M	7	(2)	1
29	Marián Sluka		22/07/79	M	4	(1)	
12	Zoltán Szatmári		02/05/79	G	4		
6	Zoltán Takács		26/11/83	D	12		1
2	Krisztián Tímár		04/10/79	D	9		2
8	József Windecker		02/12/92	M	14	(7)	2
21	Balázs Zamostny		31/01/92	A	7	(3)	1

SZOMBATHELYI HALADÁS

Coach: Tamás Artner
1919 • Rohonci úti (12,500) • haladasfc.nyugat.hu

2012

27/07	Eger	h	4-2	Kenesei, Halmosi, Iszlai (p), Andorka (p)
04/08	Győr	a	1-1	Radó
10/08	Siófok	a	3-0	Iszlai (p), Radó, Kenesei
18/08	Diósgyőr	h	0-0	
26/08	Videoton	a	1-2	Andorka
01/09	Paks	h	1-2	Kenesei
14/09	Ferencváros	a	1-2	Andorka
21/09	MTK	h	3-0	Iszlai (p), Kenesei, Halmosi
29/09	Debrecen	a	0-2	
06/10	Rákóczi	h	0-0	
20/10	Kecskemét	a	1-2	D Nagy
27/10	Pécs	h	1-1	Kenesei (p)
03/11	Pápa	a	0-1	
10/11	Újpest	h	2-0	Iszlai (p), Kenesei
18/11	Honvéd	a	1-1	Ugrai
24/11	Eger	a	2-1	Ugrai, Andorka
01/12	Győr	h	1-1	Radó

2012

02/03	Siófok	h	2-1	Iszlai (p), Halmosi (p)
09/03	Diósgyőr	a	1-1	Halmosi (p)
30/03	Paks	a	0-0	
06/04	Ferencváros	h	0-0	
10/04	Videoton	h	0-1	
13/04	MTK	a	1-0	Radó
21/04	Debrecen	h	1-0	Halmosi
27/04	Rákóczi	a	2-3	Andorka, Ugrai
03/05	Kecskemét	h	1-1	Andorka
11/05	Pécs	a	2-0	Radó 2 (1p)
17/05	Pápa	h	2-1	og (Dlusztus), Radó (p)
24/05	Újpest	a	1-0	Radó
01/06	Honvéd	h	1-1	Simon

No	Name	Nat	DoB	Pos	Aps	(s)	Gls
9	Péter Andorka		19/07/84	A	8	(17)	6
2	Zoltán Búrány		26/07/89	M	13	(4)	
12	Szilárd Devecseri		13/02/90	D	14	(4)	
33	Márk Farkas		13/01/92	M	1	(1)	
3	Zoltán Fehér		12/06/91	D	31	(1)	
70	Gligó Gocze		30/04/90	G	2		
22	Richard Guzmics		16/04/87	D	28		
18	Bence Gyurján		21/02/92	M	4	(6)	
13	Péter Halmosi		25/09/79	M	22	(1)	5
7	András Horváth		06/08/80	M			
90	Bence Iszlai		29/05/90	D	26	(1)	5
26	Márk Jagodics		12/04/92	M	1	(9)	
37	Milán Kalász		30/04/92	M	5	(8)	1
20	Krisztián Kenesei		07/01/77	A	9	(4)	6
5	Gábor Korolovszky		11/07/79	M	3		
10	Kornél Kulcsár		11/11/91	M	1	(5)	
91	Roland Mursits		14/03/91	G	2		
21	Dániel Nagy		22/11/84	M	9		1
8	Gábor Nagy		16/10/85	M	27		
16	Márió Németh		01/05/95	M	1	(5)	
32	András Radó		09/09/93	A	26	(1)	7
4	Gábor Rajos		17/03/84	M	11	(4)	
66	Dániel Rózsa		24/11/84	G	26		
23	Szabolcs Schimmer		24/02/84	M	26	(1)	
46	Ádám Simon		30/03/90	M	15	(2)	1
6	Attila Szakály		30/06/92	M	4	(4)	
15	Péter Tóth		25/06/77	M	14		
14	Roland Ugrai		13/11/92	A	11	(10)	3

ÚJPEST FC

Coach: Jos Daerden (BEL);
(05/03/13) Marc Leliévre (BEL)
1885 • Szusza Ferenc (13,500) • ujpestfc.hu
Major honours
Hungarian League (20) 1930, 1931, 1933, 1935, 1939,
1945, 1946, 1947, 1960, 1969, 1970, 1971, 1972, 1973,
1974, 1975, 1978, 1979, 1990, 1998;
Hungarian Cup (8) 1969, 1970, 1975, 1982, 1983, 1987,
1992, 2002

2012
27/07	Diósgyőr	a	1-2	*Vermes*
05/08	Videoton	h	0-1	
12/08	Paks	a	2-2	*Zaris, Remili*
19/08	Ferencváros	h	2-1	*Kabát, Tshibuabua*
24/08	MTK	a	1-2	*Kabát*
02/09	Debrecen	h	0-0	
14/09	Rákóczi	a	0-0	
22/09	Kecskemét	h	2-1	*Kabát, Vasiljević*
30/09	Pécs	a	3-1	*Kabát, Simon, Vasiljević*
06/10	Pápa	h	1-1	*Kabát*
21/10	Győr	a	2-3	*Kabát 2 (1p)*
27/10	Honvéd	a	2-2	*Kabát, Zaris*
02/11	Eger	h	3-0	*Vasiljević, Bruno Moraes, Balogh*
10/11	Haladás	a	0-2	
16/11	Siófok	h	4-2	*Kabát 2, Bruno Moraes, Chema Antón*
25/11	Diósgyőr	h	1-1	*Bruno Moraes*
02/12	Videoton	a	1-1	*Remili*

2012
02/03	Paks	h	0-6	
10/03	Ferencváros	a	1-2	*Kabát*
31/03	Debrecen	a	1-0	*og (Šimac)*
05/04	Rákóczi	h	1-0	*Vasiljević*
14/04	Kecskemét	a	0-1	
19/04	Pécs	h	4-2	*Kabát 2 (1p), Bruno Moraes, Vasiljević*
27/04	Pápa	a	1-0	*Chema Antón*
30/04	MTK	h	1-1	*Vasiljević*
05/05	Győr	a	1-0	*Vasiljević*
11/05	Honvéd	h	2-4	*Christ, Remili*
18/05	Eger	a	2-1	*Simon, Tshibuabua*
24/05	Haladás	h	0-1	
02/06	Siófok	a	1-0	*Zamostny*

No	Name	Nat	DoB	Pos	Aps	(s)	Gls
34	Naïm Aarab	BEL	15/05/87	D	9		
1	Szabolcs Balajcza		14/07/79	G	30		
19	Balázs Balogh		11/06/90	M	28	(1)	1
10	Dávid Barczi		01/02/89	M		(1)	
9	Bruno Moraes	BRA	07/07/84	A	8	(1)	4
17	Chema Antón	ESP	19/03/89	D	26		2
18	Grégory Christ	FRA	04/10/82	M	27		1
20	Henri Eninful	TOG	21/07/92	M		(1)	
28	Ronald Erős		27/01/93	M		(2)	
25	Richárd Horváth		11/05/92	A		(1)	
5	Alessandro Iandoli	ITA	29/04/84	M	26		
22	Péter Kabát		25/09/77	A	26		13
27	Dániel Kovács		16/06/90	M	2	(5)	
16	Bence Lázár		21/03/91	A	1	(7)	
29	Róbert Litauszki		15/03/90	D	1	(1)	
35	Bojan Mihajlović	BIH	15/09/88	D	6	(3)	
2	János Nagy		07/08/92	D	1		
20	Patrik Nagy		16/02/91	M	1		
24	Zoltán Pollák		13/01/84	D	6	(1)	
15	Nikolas Proesmans	BEL	11/05/92	M	9	(2)	
21	Mohamed Remili		30/05/86	M	17	(10)	3
7	Krisztián Simon		10/06/91	M	15	(5)	2
4	Filip Stanisavljević	SRB	20/05/87	M	5	(11)	
8	Zoltán Szélesi		22/11/81	D	26		
32	Bavon Tshibuabua	COD	17/07/91	A	4	(4)	2
6	Dušan Vasiljević	SRB	07/05/82	M	29		7
3	Krisztián Vermes		07/07/85	D	23		1
30	Balázs Zamostny		31/01/92	A		(4)	1
11	Yadin Zaris	ISR	14/05/90	A	4	(8)	2

VIDEOTON FC

Coach: Paulo Sousa (POR);
(20/01/13) José Gomes (POR)
1941 • Sóstói (15,000) • vidi.hu
Major honours
Hungarian League (1) 2011;
Hungarian Cup (1) 2006

2012
29/07	Pápa	h	1-1	*N Nikolić*
05/08	Újpest	a	1-0	*Torghelle*
12/08	Honvéd	h	0-1	
19/08	Eger	h	2-1	*Torghelle, N Nikolić (p)*
26/08	Haladás	h	2-1	*Gyurcsó 2*
02/09	Siófok	a	3-1	*Haraszti, Mitrović, Filipe Oliveira*
15/09	Diósgyőr	h	0-0	
23/09	Győr	h	0-1	
29/09	Paks	a	1-1	*Kovács*
07/10	Ferencváros	h	1-2	*N Nikolić (p)*
19/10	MTK	a	2-3	*N Nikolić (p), Sándor*
28/10	Debrecen	h	3-1	*Torghelle, Filipe Oliveira, N Nikolić*
04/11	Rákóczi	a	2-0	*N Nikolić 2*
11/11	Kecskemét	h	2-0	*N Nikolić, Mitrović*
17/11	Pécs	a	0-0	
25/11	Pápa	a	0-1	
02/12	Újpest	h	1-1	*Renato Neto*

2012
03/03	Honvéd	a	4-0	*Mitrović 2, Filipe Oliveira, Kovács*
09/03	Eger	a	4-0	*Szekeres 2, Álvaro Brachi, Kovács*
29/03	Siófok	h	6-0	*Mitrović, N Nikolić 2 (1p), Gyurcsó, Juhász, Filipe Oliveira*
07/04	Diósgyőr	a	1-2	*N Nikolić*
10/04	Haladás	a	1-0	*Álvarez*
14/04	Győr	a	1-1	*Tóth*
20/04	Paks	h	2-0	*Gyurcsó, Marco Caneira*
28/04	Ferencváros	a	1-0	*Torghelle*
03/05	MTK	h	2-0	*Mitrović, N Nikolić*
12/05	Debrecen	a	1-2	*Torghelle*
18/05	Rákóczi	h	2-1	*Álvarez, Kovács*
26/05	Kecskemét	a	5-1	*Juhász 2, Szolnoki, Torghelle, Paraiba*
01/06	Pécs	h	1-2	*N Nikolić*

No	Name	Nat	DoB	Pos	Aps	(s)	Gls
23	Arturo Álvarez	SLV	28/06/85	A	7	(4)	2
2	Álvaro Brachi	ESP	06/01/86	D	19		1
27	Mladen Božović	MNE	01/08/84	G	25		
16	Filipe Oliveira	POR	27/05/84	M	10	(7)	4
77	Ádám Gyurcsó		06/03/91	A	18	(8)	4
88	Zsolt Haraszti		04/11/91	A	6	(1)	1
24	Héctor	ESP	31/03/85	D	16		
9	Jucie Lupeta	POR	24/03/93	A		(3)	
32	Roland Juhász		01/07/83	D	8	(1)	3
23	Kaká	BRA	16/05/81	D	7	(1)	
70	István Ádám Kovács		23/03/92	M	23	(6)	4
4	Marco Caneira	POR	09/02/79	D	18	(2)	1
14	Nikola Mitrović	SRB	02/01/87	M	20	(7)	6
17	Nemanja Nikolić	SRB	31/12/87	A	17	(10)	13
99	Uroš Nikolić	SRB	14/12/93	M	3	(2)	
7	Paraiba	BRA	12/01/92	A	11	(7)	1
3	Paulo Vinícius	BRA	21/02/90	D	19	(1)	
8	Milan Perić	SRB	16/04/84	A		(1)	
10	Renato Neto	BRA	27/09/91	A	13	(1)	1
11	György Sándor		20/03/84	M	8	(3)	1
22	Stopira	CPV	20/05/88	D	7	(2)	
21	Adrián Szekeres		21/04/89	D	7	(3)	2
30	Roland Szolnoki		21/01/92	M	17	(1)	1
28	Sándor Torghelle		05/05/82	A	10	(11)	6
26	Balázs Tóth		24/05/81	M	17	(4)	1
12	Tomáš Tujvel	SVK	19/09/83	G	5		
23	Tamás Vaskó		20/02/84	D	1		
5	Vítor Gomes	POR	25/12/87	M	10	(1)	
20	Walter Lee	ESP	14/08/89	M	8	(3)	

18	Adamo Coulibaly (Debrecen)
17	Dániel Böde (Ferencváros)
13	Péter Kabát (Újpest)
	Nemanja Nikolić (Videoton)
12	Roland Varga (Győr)
10	Gergely Délczeg (Honvéd)
	Attila Simon (Paks/Pécs)
9	Norbert Németh (Eger)
	Goran Marić (Pápa)
	József Kanta (MTK)
	János Lázok (Paks)

MEZŐKÖVESD-ZSÓRY SE
Coach: György Véber
1975 • Városi Stadion (3,000) • mse-zsory.hu

PUSKÁS AKADÉMIA FC
Coach: Miklós Benczés
2012 • Aranycsapat (3,600) • pfla.hu

SECOND LEVEL FINAL TABLES 2012/13

EAST		Pld	W	D	L	F	A	Pts
1	Mezőkövesd-Zsóry SE	30	18	4	8	60	36	58
2	Vasas SC	30	17	4	9	49	34	55
3	Békéscsabai Előre SE	30	15	10	5	58	38	55
4	Balmazújvárosi FC	30	14	8	8	50	37	50
5	Nyíregyháza Spartacus FC	30	15	4	11	44	33	49
6	Szolnoki MÁV FC	30	14	6	10	54	41	48
7	Szeged 2011	30	11	9	10	43	41	42
8	Ferencvárosi TC II	30	12	5	13	49	49	41
9	Ceglédi VSE	30	11	9	10	50	47	40
10	Orosháza FC	30	12	3	15	51	57	39
11	Újpest FC II	30	11	5	14	43	49	38
12	Budapest Honvéd II	30	11	5	14	48	56	38
13	Putnok VSE	30	9	8	13	43	51	35
14	Debreceni VSC II	30	8	6	16	49	58	30
15	Kazincbarcikai SC	30	8	6	16	40	63	30
16	Dunakanyar-Vác FC	30	6	4	20	22	63	22

NB Dunakanyar-Vác FC withdrew after round 15 – their remaining matches were awarded as 0-3 defeats; Ceglédi VSE – 2 pts deducted.

WEST		Pld	W	D	L	F	A	Pts
1	Puskás Akadémia FC	30	21	7	2	57	18	70
2	Kozármislenyi SE	30	18	6	6	55	28	60
3	Gyirmót SE	30	17	5	8	57	39	56
4	Zalaegerszegi TE	30	15	6	9	50	35	51
5	FC Ajka	30	14	9	7	36	27	51
6	FC Tatabánya	30	14	8	8	46	32	50
7	Szigetszentmiklósi TK	30	14	4	12	50	43	46
8	Soproni VSE	30	13	7	10	45	39	46
9	Csákvári TK	30	13	5	12	41	40	44
10	Szombathelyi Haladás II	30	11	9	10	41	43	42
11	Veszprém FC	30	9	9	12	51	51	36
12	BKV Előre SC	30	9	6	15	36	54	33
13	Kaposvári Rákóczi FC II	30	8	6	16	29	50	26
14	Győri ETO FC II	30	6	7	17	40	51	25
15	Bajai LSE	30	5	2	23	29	75	17
16	Paksi SE II	30	4	4	22	21	59	16

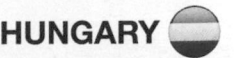

Domestic cup: Magyar Kupa 2012/13

FIRST ROUND

(08/08/12)
Dunakanyar-Vác 2-2 MTK *(aet; 3-0 on pens)*
Nyíregyháza 1-0 Eger

(11/08/12)
Bölcske 3-1 Balatonlelle
Csorna 3-1 Répcelak
Felsőtárkány 1-0 Várda
Kozármisleny 0-0 Veszprém *(aet; 5-6 on pens)*
Létavértes 2-0 Putnok
Nagybátony 3-2 Hatvan *(aet)*
Nagykőrös 0-3 Békéscsaba
Orosháza 2-0 Cegléd
Pénzügyőr 2-1 DTC Select
Sajóbábony 1-6 Balmazújváros
Tatabánya 1-2 Gyirmót
Terem 1-2 Kazincbarcika
Velence 6-6 Maglód *(aet; 5-4 on pens)*
Vésztő 1-6 Baja
Zalaszentgrót 1-2 Dunaújváros

(12/08/12)
Babót 1-0 Rábapaty
Bánk 2-4 REAC *(aet)*
Borsfa 1-14 Iváncsa
Csács-Nemesapáti 0-4 Szentlőrinc
Csanádpalota 0-0 Kalocsa *(aet; 3-2 on pens)*
ESMTK 2-1 Biatorbágy
Göd 0-8 Jászapáti
Gönyű 0-4 Kecskéd
Grund 1986 1-5 Vecsés
Gyód 0-4 Balatonfüred
Győrszemere 0-2 Ajka
Hosszúpályi 2-2 Bükkábrány *(aet; 4-5 on pens)*
Jánosháza 3-2 Lipót
JVSE 0-4 Budaörs
Kunszállás 1-4 Mórahalom
Magyarpolány 1-2 Tapolca *(aet)*
Martonvásár 2-1 Sárisáp
Nagyesztegár 0-1 Petőháza
Nagykálló 0-2 Tiszaújváros
Nyírkarász 0-8 Mezőkövesd-Zsóry
Pécsi VSK 0-0 NTF 1866 *(aet; 7-0 on pens)*
Soltvadkert 0-0 Nagyatád *(aet; 3-2 on pens)*
Szedres 0-8 Nagyatád
Szigetszentmiklós 2-1 BKV Előre
Szikszó 0-2 Tiszakanyár
Szolnok 3-1 Szeged
Uraiújfalu 0-9 Soproni VSE

SECOND ROUND

(19/09/12)
Budaörs 0-1 Siófok
ESMTK 0-2 Békéscsaba

(25/09/12)
Babót 0-12 Győr
Pénzügyőr 1-2 Vasas
Tapolca 0-9 Pápa

(26/09/12)
Ajka 4-0 Baja
Balatonfüred 0-6 Soproni VSE
Bükkábrány 2-1 Nagybátony
Csanádpalota 1-2 REAC
Csorna 1-5 Pécsi MFC
Felsőtárkány 1-1 Szigetszentmiklós *(aet; 5-4 on pens)*
Ferencváros 0-2 Haladás
Gyirmót 1-2 Rákóczi
Iváncsa 0-2 Dunaújváros
Jánosháza 1-5 Szentlőrinc
Jászapáti 0-1 Dunakanyar-Vác
Kazincbarcika 2-1 Újpest
Kecskéd 0-0 Pécsi VSK *(aet; 4-5 on pens)*
Létavértes 2-0 Mezőkövesd-Zsóry
Martonvásár 0-4 Bölcske
Nyíregyháza 4-2 Kecskemét
Orosháza 0-7 Diósgyőr
Petőháza 1-12 Zalaegerszeg
Soltvadkert 0-6 Mórahalom
Tiszaújváros 3-2 Balmazújváros
Vecsés 0-3 Szolnok
Velence 2-1 Nagyatád
Veszprém 0-2 Paks

Byes – Debrecen, Honvéd, Tiszakanyár, Videoton

THIRD ROUND

(28/10/12)
Létavértes 1-0 Pápa

(30/10/12)
Dunaújváros 1-0 Rákóczi
Kazincbarcika 1-3 Nyíregyháza
Velence 0-3 Diósgyőr

(31/10/12)
Bölcske 2-5 Győr
Bükkábrány 0-4 Zalaegerszeg
Felsőtárkány 0-1 Siófok
Mórahalom 2-3 Szolnok *(aet)*
Pécsi VSK 1-4 Honvéd

REAC 1-2 Paks
Szentlőrinc 1-3 Debrecen
Tiszakanyár 1-2 Dunakanyar-Vác
Tiszaújváros 2-1 Pécsi MFC
Vasas 3-0 Ajka
Videoton 2-0 Haladás *(aet)*

(07/11/12)
Soproni VSE 1-2 Békéscsaba *(aet)*

FOURTH ROUND

(20/11/12 & 27/11/12)
Győr 4-0, 3-2 Paks *(7-2)*

(21/11/12 & 27/11/12)
Dunaújváros 2-1, 0-1 Siófok *(2-2; Siófok on away goal)*
Nyíregyháza 3-2, 1-3 Debrecen *(4-5)*

(21/11/12 & 28/11/12)
Békéscsaba 0-1, 1-0 Vasas *(1-1; Vasas 4-3 on pens)*
Honvéd 4-0, 2-1 Diósgyőr *(6-1)*
Létavértes 0-1, 2-1 Szolnok *(2-2; Létavértes on away goal)*
Tiszaújváros 1-1, 0-5 Dunakanyar-Vác *(1-6)*

(02/02/13 & 09/02/13)
Videoton 4-0, 6-3 Zalaegerszeg *(10-3)*

QUARTER-FINALS

(03/02/13 & 06/02/13)
Létavértes 0-2 Debrecen *(Dombi 24, Šimac 32)*
Debrecen 8-0 Létavértes *(Ludánszki 10, Szakály 34, Coulibaly 56, 80, Pölöskey 69, 76, 87, Bódi 72)*
(Debrecen 10-0)

(23/02/13 & 27/02/13)
Honvéd 0-1 Győr *(Kink 80p)*
Győr 2-0 Honvéd *(Völgyi 71, Kamber 76)*
(Győr 3-0)

Vasas 3-1 Siófok *(Nikolov 37p, 56p, Popovics 64; Pál 83p)*
Siófok 2-1 Vasas *(Fehér 57, Dajić 66; Bobó 62)*
(Vasas 4-3)

Videoton – Dunakanyar-Vác
(Videoton w/o)

SEMI-FINALS

(16/04/13 & 07/05/13)
Vasas 0-3 Debrecen *(Ferenczi 9, 19, Czvitkovics 68)*
Debrecen 3-1 Vasas *(Coulibaly 55, 78, Sidibé 90; Berecz 27)*
(Debrecen 6-1)

(17/04/13 & 08/05/13)
Videoton 0-2 Győr *(Střeštík 31, Tokody 67)*
Győr 1-2 Videoton *(Kink 90+2; Kovács 57, Álvaro Brachi 73p)*
(Győr 3-2)

FINAL

(22/05/13)
Bozsik József stadium, Budapest
DEBRECENI VSC 2 *(Coulibaly 51, 86)*
GYŐRI ETO FC 1 *(Andrić 17)*
Referee: *Kassai*
DEBRECEN: *Verpecz, Bernáth, Máté, Mészáros, Korhut, Bódi, Ramos, Czvitkovics (Bouadla 81), Ferenczi (Szécsi 68), Kulcsár (Sidibé 40), Coulibaly*
GYŐR: *Molnár, Švec, Takács, Lipták (Djordjević 81), Völgyi, Pátkai, Kamber, Trajković (Dudás 62), Kink, Andrić, R Varga (Kronaveter 32)*

Debrecen players pose with the trophy after their Hungarian Cup final victory over champions Győr

ICELAND
Knattspyrnusamband Íslands (KSÍ)

Address	Laugardal	**President**	Geir Thorsteinsson
	IS-104 Reykjavík	**General secretary**	Thórir Hákonarson
Tel	+354 510 2900	**Media officer**	Ómar Smarsson
Fax	+354 568 9793	**Year of formation**	1947
E-mail	ksi@ksi.is	**National stadium**	Laugardalsvöllur,
Website	ksi.is		Reykjavik (15,182)

Akureyri
13

Ólafsvík
14

1 ~Kópavogur

2 ~Hafnarfjördur   6 Akranes

Reykjavík~ 3 4 9 12

8   10 Selfoss

Grindavík 5

Gardabær~ 11

7 Vestmannaeyjar

ÚRVALSDEILDIN CLUBS

 1 **Breidablik**

 2 **FH Hafnarfjördur**

3 **Fram Reykjavík**

4 **Fylkir**

5 **Grindavík**

6 **ÍA Akranes**

 7 **ÍBV Vestmannaeyjar**

8 **Keflavík**

 9 **KR Reykjavík**

10 **Selfoss**

11 **Stjarnan**

12 **Valur Reykjavík**

PROMOTED CLUBS

13 **Thór Akureyri**

14 **Víkingur Ólafsvík**

KEY:
● – UEFA Champions League
● – UEFA Europa League
● – Promoted clubs
● – Relegated clubs

FH freewheel to title

After a trophy-less season in 2011 – their first for eight years – FH Hafnarfjördur bounced back in impressive style to reclaim the Icelandic league title, winning it by a landslide margin of 13 points. It was the sixth championship triumph in the club's history, all of them coming within the past decade, and the third under the coaching reins of former club captain Heimir Gudjónsson.

Defending champions KR Reykjavík beat FH home and away but failed to live up to their tag of pre-season favourites, finishing a disappointing fourth. However, they did retain the Icelandic Cup, defeating Stjarnan 2-1 in the final.

Sixth league triumph in nine years for Hafnarfjordur club

Deposed champions KR find consolation in Icelandic Cup

National team in World Cup qualifying frame

Domestic league

Runners-up to Breidablik in 2010 and KR in 2011, FH were widely tipped to finish second again in 2012. KR defeated them 2-0 in the pre-season Super Cup and again in the first league meeting, but those results aside Gudjónsson's men made a solid start to the season, even registering a couple of huge wins against Fylkir (8-0 at home) and ÍA Akranes (7-2 away).

A two-horse race with KR eventually became a solitary procession as the much-fancied title holders fell away alarmingly in the closing weeks – despite completing the double against FH with a 3-1 win. With no other challengers, FH clinched the title three games from the end, freewheeling to victory thanks to eight wins in their last 11 games. Inspired from the front by the league's top marksman, 12-goal Atli Gudnason, the champions racked up league-best tallies of 15 wins – five more than any other team – and 51 goals.

As FH relaxed, a gripping battle ensued for second place. It was won, surprisingly, by Breidablik, a team that managed just ten goals at home but bagged 17 in their last five away games, four of which resulted in victory. One point behind them were ÍBV Vestmannaeyjar, who thus claimed a hat-trick of third-place finishes. The club's veteran striker Tryggvi Gudmundsson became the league's all-time top scorer during the season, ending the campaign on 128 goals.

Domestic cup

KR finished level on points with ÍBV, but they too qualified for the 2013/14 UEFA Europa League having already won the Icelandic Cup. The club's 13th victory in the competition – and third in five years – was achieved the hard way, with three narrow one-goal wins away from home en route to a final in which they had to come from behind to defeat Stjarnan 2-1 in the Laugardalsvöllur, midfielder Baldur Sigurdsson heading in a late winner after the opposition had twice struck the frame of the goal.

A first major trophy would have been a fitting way for Stjarnan to crown a season in which they drew all four league fixtures against FH and KR and scored in every game bar the last – a 2-0 defeat to Breidablik that dropped them down to fifth and out of Europe.

Europe

There were no prized scalps for Iceland's representatives in 2012/13 European competition, but Thór Akureyri, relegated from the Úrvalsdeildin in 2011 (and promoted back in 2012), did the country proud by hammering Irish club Bohemian FC 5-1. In contrast, KR's 9-1 aggregate defeat to HJK Helsinki in the UEFA Champions League was a terribly bitter pill to swallow for coach Rúnar Kristinsson and his players.

National team

With former long-serving Sweden coach Lars Lagerbäck in charge, Iceland experienced a season of conflicting emotions in the 2014 FIFA World Cup qualifying campaign. Results were encouraging but erratic, three impressive victories – against Norway (home), Albania (away) and Slovenia (away) – being followed, one after the other, by painful defeats – to Cyprus (away), Switzerland (home) and Slovenia (home).

With nine points in the bag, however, and quality individuals to call on such as Gylfi Sigurdsson, Kolbeinn Sigthórsson, Alfred Finnbogason and Birkir Bjarnason – all members of the country's 2011 UEFA European Under-21 Championship squad – Iceland's dream of reaching the play-offs remained very much alive going into their final four fixtures.

 **ICELAND**

Domestic league: Úrvalsdeildin 2012 final table

		Pld	Home					Away					Total					
			W	D	L	F	A	W	D	L	F	A	W	D	L	F	A	Pts
1	**FH Hafnarfjördur**	22	8	2	1	30	10	7	2	2	21	13	15	4	3	51	23	49
2	Breidablik	22	5	2	4	10	11	5	4	2	22	16	10	6	6	32	27	36
3	ÍBV Vestmannaeyjar	22	6	4	1	17	8	4	1	6	19	13	10	5	7	36	21	35
4	KR Reykjavík	22	7	2	2	24	15	3	3	5	15	17	10	5	7	39	32	35
5	Stjarnan	22	3	6	2	23	21	5	4	2	21	17	8	10	4	44	38	34
6	ÍA Akranes	22	5	2	4	19	22	4	3	4	13	14	9	5	8	32	36	32
7	Fylkir	22	5	3	3	16	15	3	4	4	14	24	8	7	7	30	39	31
8	Valur Reykjavík	22	5	0	6	20	18	4	1	6	14	16	9	1	12	34	34	28
9	Keflavík	22	3	2	6	17	21	5	1	5	18	17	8	3	11	35	38	27
10	Fram Reykjavík	22	5	1	5	17	15	3	2	6	14	21	8	3	11	31	36	27
11	Selfoss	22	4	1	6	15	19	2	2	7	15	25	6	3	13	30	44	21
12	Grindavík	22	1	4	6	14	28	1	2	8	17	29	2	6	14	31	57	12

SEASON AT A GLANCE

EUROPEAN QUALIFICATION 2013/14

 Champion: FH Hafnarfjördur (second qualifying round)

 Cup winner: KR Reykjavík (first qualifying round)
Breidablik (first qualifying round)
ÍBV Vestmannæyjar (first qualifying round)

Top scorer   Atli Gudnason (FH), 12 goals
Relegated clubs   Grindavík, Selfoss
Promoted clubs   Thór Akureyri, Víkingur Ólafsvík
Cup final   KR Reykjavík 2-1 Stjarnan

PLAYER OF THE SEASON
Atli Gudnason
(FH Hafnarfjördur)

FH's long-serving striker enjoyed a fabulous season, topping not just the Úrvalsdeildin's goal charts, with 12 strikes, but also providing a league-best tally of 13 assists to help his club win the championship at a canter. It was the 28-year-old's fourth Icelandic title with the club and unquestionably his most rewarding.

NEWCOMER OF THE SEASON
Jón Dadi Bödvarsson
(Selfoss)

Newcomers Selfoss were relegated, but not for the want of trying on the part of their exciting 20-year-old winger, who scored seven goals, all of them earning precious points in the club's struggle for survival. The Icelandic Under-21 international's year ended with a first senior cap and a transfer to Norwegian club Viking FK.

ÚRVALSDEILDIN TEAM OF THE SEASON
(4-2-1-3)
Coach: Gudjónsson *(FH)*

NATIONAL TEAM

Home Kit   Away Kit

TOP FIVE ALL-TIME CAPS
Rúnar Kristinsson (104); Hermann Hreidarsson (89); Gudni Bergsson (80); Brynjar Björn Gunnarsson & Birkir Kristinsson (74)

TOP FIVE ALL-TIME GOALS
Eidur Smári Gudjohnsen (24); Ríkhardur Jónsson (17); Ríkhardur Dadason & Arnór Gudjohnsen (14); Thórdur Gudjónsson (13)

Results 2012/13

15/08/12	Faroe Islands	H	Reykjavik	2-0	Sigthórsson (29, 90)
07/09/12	Norway (WCQ)	H	Reykjavik	2-0	Árnason (21), Finnbogason (81)
11/09/12	Cyprus (WCQ)	A	Larnaca	0-1	
12/10/12	Albania (WCQ)	A	Tirana	2-1	Bjarnason (19), G Sigurdsson (81)
16/10/12	Switzerland (WCQ)	H	Reykjavik	0-2	
14/11/12	Andorra	A	Sant Julia de Loria	2-0	Gudmundsson (10), Sigurjónsson (58)
06/02/13	Russia	N	Marbella (ESP)	0-2	
22/03/13	Slovenia (WCQ)	A	Ljubljana	2-1	G Sigurdsson (55, 78)
07/06/13	Slovenia (WCQ)	H	Reykjavik	2-4	Bjarnason (22), Finnbogason (26p)

Appearances 2012/13

			Fro	NOR	CYP	ALB	SUI	And	Rus	SVN	SVN	Caps	Goals
Coach: **Lars Lagerbäck (SWE)**	16/07/48												
Gunnleifur Gunnleifsson	14/07/75	FH	G					s46				24	-
Birkir Már Sævarsson	11/11/84	Brann (NOR)	D68		D	s68		D	D	D	D84	35	-
Kári Árnason	13/10/82	Rotherham (ENG)	D	D50		D	D				D	25	2
Ragnar Sigurdsson	19/06/86	København (DEN)	D46	D	D	D	D		D	D	D	27	-
Bjarni Ólafur Eiríksson	28/03/82	Stabæk (NOR)	D68	D	D63							21	-
Rúrik Gíslason	25/02/88	OB (DEN) /København (DEN)	M81	M73	M	M68	M70				s63	22	1
Aron Einar Gunnarsson	22/04/89	Cardiff (WAL)	M46	M	M	M		M46		M	M52	35	-
Gylfi Thór Sigurdsson	08/09/89	Tottenham (ENG)	M	A	A	A	A		M	M		16	4
Jóhann Berg Gudmundsson	27/10/90	AZ (NED)	M68		s77	s85	s70	M62	s60	s46		24	1
Birkir Bjarnason	27/05/88	Pescara (ITA)	A	A	A	M85	M	A	M	M	M	21	3
Kolbeinn Sigthórsson	14/03/90	Ajax (NED)	A					A60	A92	A		14	8
Indridi Sigurdsson	12/10/81	Viking (NOR)	s46					s40				64	2
Eggert Gunnthór Jónsson	18/08/88	Wolves (ENG)	s46	s91		s92	M81					19	-
Gretar Rafn Steinsson	09/01/82	unattached /Kayserispor (TUR)	s68	D		D	D					46	4
Ari Freyr Skúlason	14/05/87	Sundsvall (SWE)	s68		s63	D	D		D	D	D	11	-
Eidur Smári Gudjohnsen	15/09/78	unattached /Club Brugge (BEL)	s68					M79	s76	s52		71	24
Arnór Smárason	07/09/88	Esbjerg (DEN)	s81					s75				15	2
Hannes Thór Halldórsson	27/04/84	KR	G	G	G	G	G46	G	G	G		12	-
Helgi Valur Daníelsson	13/07/81	AIK (SWE)	M	M77			s46	s79	s92	M		27	-
Emil Hallfredsson	29/06/84	Verona (ITA)	M91	M46	M	M		M	M76	M63		37	1
Sölvi Geir Ottesen	18/02/84	København (DEN)	s50	D 87*			D		D			21	-
Alfred Finnbogason	01/02/89	Heerenveen (NED)	s73	s46	A92	A		A75	A46	A		15	4
Gudjón Baldvinsson	15/02/86	Halmstad (SWE)					s81					2	-
Hjálmar Jónsson	29/07/80	Göteborg (SWE)						D46	D			21	-
Hjörtur Logi Valgardsson	27/09/88	Göteborg (SWE)						D46				8	-
Rúnar Már Sigurjónsson	18/06/90	Valur						M				1	1
Ólafur Ingi Skúlason	01/04/83	Zulte Waregem (BEL)						M				17	1
Matthías Vilhjálmsson	30/01/87	Start (NOR)						A80				10	1
Arnór Sveinn Adalsteinsson	26/01/86	Hønefoss (NOR)						s46				12	-
Gardar Jóhannsson	01/04/80	Stjarnan						s62				8	2
Jón Dadi Bödvarsson	25/05/92	Selfoss						s80				1	-
Gunnar Heidar Thorvaldsson	01/04/82	Norrköping (SWE)									s84	24	5

ICELAND

KR REYKJAVÍK

Second qualifying round - HJK Helsinki (FIN)
A 0-7
Halldórsson, Sigurdarson, Gudjónsson
(Sigurjónsson 58), Weston, Sigurdsson,
Ragnarsson, Ó Hauksson, Snorrason
(Atlason 46), Arnarsson (E Jónsson 66),
Lúdvíksson, G R Gunnarsson. Coach: Rúnar
Kristinsson (ISL)
H 1-2 *Atlason (74)*
Thorgeirsson, Sigurdarson, H Hauksson
(Lúdvíksson 89), E Jónsson, Sigurdsson
(Gudjónsson 70), Snorrason, Atlason,
Jósepsson, G R Gunnarsson, Sigurjónsson,
B Jónsson (Ragnarsson 66). Coach: Rúnar
Kristinsson (ISL)

FH HAFNARFJÖRDUR

**First qualifying round - FC USV Eschen/
Mauren (LIE)**
H 2-1 *Ingason (44), Björnsson (81)*
Gunnleifsson, Antoníusson, Bjarnason,
Thomas (V Gudmundsson 72), Vidarsson,
Pálsson (Björnsson 62), Sverrisson,
Gudnason, Gunnlaugsson (Ingvarsson
80), Ingason, Rúnarsson. Coach: Heimir
Gudjónsson (ISL)
A 1-0 *Gudnason (12)*
Gunnleifsson, Antoníusson, Bjarnason,
Thomas, Vidarsson, Sverrisson (Pálsson
90), Gudnason, Gunnlaugsson, Ingason
(Björnsson 69), Thórisson, Rúnarsson
(Ingvarsson 90+3). Coach: Heimir
Gudjónsson (ISL)

Second qualifying round - AIK (SWE)
A 1-1 *Gudnason (40)*
Gunnleifsson, Antoníusson, Thomas,
Vidarsson, Pálsson (Snorrason 74),
Sverrisson, Gudnason, Gunnlaugsson,
Ingason (Björnsson 80), Thórisson,
Rúnarsson. Coach: Heimir Gudjónsson (ISL)
H 0-1
Gunnleifsson, Antoníusson, Thomas,
Vidarsson, Pálsson (Björnsson 64),
Sverrisson, Gudnason, Gunnlaugsson,
Ingason (Bjarnason 89), Thórisson,
Rúnarsson (Snorrason 82). Coach: Heimir
Gudjónsson (ISL)

ÍBV VESTMANNAEYJAR

**First qualifying round - Saint Patrick's
Athletic FC (IRL)**
A 0-1
Dhaira, Gudjónsson, Garner, Valdimarsson,
Thórarinsson, T Gudmundsson, Mawejje
(Arnór Ólafsson 83), Olsen (Spear
43), Baldock, Christiansen, Jeffs (V
Thorvardarson 89). Coach: Magnús
Gylfason (ISL)
H 2-1 *Garner (83), Birgisson (98) (aet)*
Dhaira, Gudjónsson, Garner, Valdimarsson,
Thórarinsson, Mawejje, Arnór Ólafsson
(T Gudmundsson 52), Olsen (Birgisson
81), Baldock, Christiansen, Jeffs (G
Gudmundsson 65). Coach: Magnús Gylfason
(ISL)

THÓR AKUREYRI

First qualifying round - Bohemian FC (IRL)
A 0-0
Rajković, Funicello, Andri Albertsson
(Björnsson 76), Atli Albertsson,
J Hannesson (Strömberg 76), Jónsson,
Hjaltalin, Hilmarsson, Vrenko, Hjaltason
(Ævarsson 66), Kristjánsson. Coach: Páll
Vidar Gíslason (ISL)
H 5-1 *Kristjánsson (36, 73, 90+3), Hjaltalin
(39), Feely (50og)*
Rajković, Funicello, Andri Albertsson,
Atli Albertsson (Olafsson 76), Ævarsson
(Strömberg 79), J Hannesson (Rosbergsson
88), Jónsson, Hjaltalin, Vrenko, Hjaltason,
Kristjánsson. Coach: Páll Vidar Gíslason
(ISL)

**Second qualifying round - FK Mladá
Boleslav (CZE)**
A 0-3
Rajković, Funicello, Andri Albertsson,
Atli Albertsson (Hilmarsson 46), Ævarsson,
J Hannesson, Jónsson (Olafsson 86),
Hjaltalin, Vrenko, Hjaltason (Björnsson 59),
Kristjánsson. Coach: Páll Vidar Gíslason
(ISL)
H 0-1
Wicks, Funicello, Andri Albertsson,
Atli Albertsson (K Hannesson 80), Ævarsson
(Hjaltason 73), Björnsson (Hilmarsson 73),
J Hannesson, Jónsson, Hjaltalin, Vrenko,
Kristjánsson. Coach: Páll Vidar Gíslason
(ISL)
Red card: J Hannesson 68

Domestic league club-by-club

BREIDABLIK

Coach: Ólafur H Kristjánsson
1950 • Kópavogsvöllur (3,009) • breidablik.is
Major honours
Icelandic League (1) 2010;
Icelandic Cup (1) 2009

2012

Date			Score	Scorers
06/05	ÍA	h	0-1	
10/05	ÍBV	a	0-0	
15/05	Valur	h	1-0	Adalsteinsson
20/05	FH	a	0-3	
24/05	Fram	h	0-2	
31/05	Selfoss	a	2-0	Vilhjálmsson, Rnkovic
16/06	Grindavík	h	2-0	Haraldsson, Pétursson
20/06	KR	h	2-1	Jónsson, Ingason
02/07	Fylkir	a	1-1	Rnkovic
05/07	Keflavík	h	0-4	
16/07	Stjarnan	a	1-1	Björgvinsson
23/07	ÍA	a	1-1	Vilhjálmsson
29/07	ÍBV	h	1-0	Rohde
08/08	Valur	a	4-3	Jónsson, Hreidarsson, Sigurgeirsson, Everson
12/08	FH	h	0-1	
20/08	Fram	a	2-3	Björgvinsson, Rohde
26/08	Selfoss	h	1-1	Haraldsson
03/09	Grindavík	a	4-2	Djorgvinsson, Jónsson, Gardarsson, Haraldsson
16/09	KR	a	4-0	Jónsson, Rohde, Adalsteinsson, Gardarsson
20/09	Fylkir	h	1-1	Ingason
23/09	Keflavík	a	3-2	Jónsson, Adalsteinsson, Rohde
29/09	Stjarnan	h	2-0	Rohde 2

No	Name	Nat	DoB	Pos	Aps	(s)	Gls
7	Elfar Árni Adalsteinsson		12/08/90	A	9	(5)	3
16	Adam Örn Arnarson		27/08/95	D		(1)	
9	Haukur Baldvinsson		05/05/90	A	8	(6)	
18	Arnar Már Björgvinsson		10/02/90	A	8	(4)	3
17	Jökull Ingason Elísabetarson		26/04/84	M	6	(5)	
8	Ben Everson	ENG	11/02/87	A	6	(3)	1
27	Tómas Óli Garvlasson		25/10/93	M	15	(3)	2
10	Rafn Andri Haraldsson		10/04/89	M	6	(12)	3
2	Gísli Páll Helgason		08/04/90	D	13	(1)	
21	Thórdur Steinar Hreidarsson		13/12/86	D	14	(3)	1
15	Sverrir Ingi Ingason		05/08/93	D	21		2
19	Kristinn Jónsson		04/08/90	D	21		5
1	Ingvar Thór Kale		08/12/83	G	14		
5	Sindri Snaer Magnússon		18/02/92	M	2	(3)	
3	Finnur Orri Margeirsson		08/03/91	D	21		
20	Stefán Thór Pálsson		31/05/95	A		(3)	
24	Gudmundur Pétursson		24/11/86	A		(3)	1
28	Petar Rnkovic	NOR	28/11/78	A	8	(1)	2
29	Nichlas Rohde	DEN	01/01/92	A	10		6
25	Sigmar Ingi Sigurdarson		25/06/83	G	8	(1)	
11	Olgeir Sigurgeirsson		22/10/82	M	6	(6)	1
4	Renee Gerard Troost	NED	06/06/88	D	21		
23	Árni Vilhjálmsson		09/05/94	A	5	(5)	2
30	Andri Rafn Yeoman		18/04/92	M	20		

FH HAFNARFJÖRDUR

Coach: Heimir Gudjónsson
1929 • Kaplakriki (6,450) • fh.is
Major honours
Icelandic League (6) 2004, 2005, 2006, 2008, 2009, 2012; Icelandic Cup (2) 2007, 2010

2012

Date			Score	Scorers
06/05	Grindavík	h	1-1	Sverrisson (p)
10/05	Fram	a	1-0	Gudnason
15/05	Selfoss	a	1-0	Sverrisson
20/05	Breidablik	h	3-0	Sverrisson (p), Snorrason 2
23/05	KR	a	0-2	
02/06	Fylkir	h	8-0	Antoníusson, Gudnason, Ingason, Sverrisson 2, Bjarnason, Björnsson,Rúnarsson
16/06	Keflavík	a	4-2	Björnsson, Antoníusson, Rúnarsson, Gudnason
20/06	Stjarnan	h	2-2	Antoníusson 2
30/06	ÍA	a	7-2	Rúnarsson, Ingason, Gudnason 3, Pálsson, Sverrisson
15/07	Valur	a	1-3	Sverrisson
22/07	Grindavík	a	1-0	Thórisson
30/07	Fram	a	1-0	Rúnarsson
08/08	Selfoss	h	3-2	Antoníusson 2, Gudnason 3
12/08	Breidablik	a	1-0	Ingason
23/08	KR	h	1-3	Rúnarsson
26/08	Fylkir	a	1-0	Ingvarsson
30/08	ÍBV	h	2-0	Sverrisson, Emilsson
03/09	Keflavík	h	3-0	Gudnason, og (Magnússon), V Gudmundsson
16/09	Stjarnan	a	2-2	Sverrisson, Gudnason
20/09	ÍA	h	2-1	Pálsson, Gudnason
23/09	ÍBV	a	2-2	Sverrisson, Ingason
29/09	Valur	h	2-1	Ingason, Snorrason

No	Name	Nat	DoB	Pos	Aps	(s)	Gls
3	Gudjón Árni Antoníusson		03/09/83	D	22		6
5	Freyr Bjarnason		30/06/77	D	18		1
17	Atli Vidar Björnsson		04/01/80	A	8	(2)	2
2	Kristján Gauti Emilsson		26/04/93	A	1	(R)	1
19	Kristján Flóki Finnbogason		12/01/95	A		(1)	
23	Brynjar Ásgeir Gudmundsson		22/06/92	D	2	(3)	
26	Viktor Örn Gudmundsson		09/11/89	D	9	(7)	1
11	Atli Gudnason		28/09/84	A	22		12
13	Bjarki Gunnlaugsson		06/03/73	M	19	(1)	
1	Gunnleifur Gunnleifsson		14/07/75	G	21		
14	Albert Brynjar Ingason		16/01/86	A	15	(6)	6
18	Einar Karl Ingvarsson		08/10/93	M	5	(4)	1
16	Jón Ragnar Jónsson		30/10/85	M	1	(4)	
20	Róbert Örn Óskarsson		27/03/87	G	1		
8	Emil Pálsson		10/06/93	M	5	(11)	2
25	Hólmar Örn Rúnarsson		10/12/81	A	14	(6)	5
22	Ólafur Páll Snorrason		22/04/82	A	9	(3)	3
10	Björn Daníel Sverrisson		29/05/90	M	21		9
6	Danny Thomas	ENG	01/05/81	D	13	(4)	
15	Gudmann Thórisson		31/01/87	D	16	(1)	1
21	Hafthór Thrastarson		14/02/90	D	1	(1)	
7	Pétur Vidarsson		25/11/87	M	19		

FRAM REYKJAVÍK

Coach: Thorvaldur Örlygsson
1908 • Laugardalsvöllur (15,182) • fram.is
Major honours
Icelandic League (18) 1913, 1914, 1915, 1916, 1917, 1918, 1921, 1922, 1923, 1925, 1939, 1946, 1947, 1962, 1972, 1986, 1988, 1990; Icelandic Cup (7) 1970, 1973, 1979, 1980, 1985, 1987, 1989

2012

Date			Score	Scorers
07/05	Valur	h	0-1	
10/05	FH	a	0-1	
15/05	Grindavík	h	4-3	Ormarsson, Ásgeirsson, Halldórsson, Lennon
21/05	Selfoss	h	0-2	
24/05	Breidablik	a	2-0	Halldórsson, Eysteinsson
02/06	KR	h	1-2	Halldórsson
14/06	Fylkir	a	0-1	
20/06	Keflavík	h	0-2	
02/07	Stjarnan	a	2-4	Jónasson, Lennon
05/07	ÍA	h	2-0	Lennon, Jónasson
15/07	ÍBV	a	2-3	Halldórsson, Lennon
23/07	Valur	a	2-0	Tillen (p), Lennon
30/07	FH	h	0-1	
08/08	Grindavík	a	2-2	Halldórsson 2
12/08	Selfoss	a	2-4	Ormarsson 2
20/08	Breidablik	h	3-2	Fridjónsson, Halldórsson, Ormarsson (p)
27/08	KR	a	1-1	Halldórsson
03/09	Fylkir	h	4-0	Halldórsson 2, Tillen, Ormarsson
16/09	Keflavík	a	0-5	
20/09	Stjarnan	h	1-1	Halldórsson
23/09	ÍA	a	1-0	og (Adolphsson)
29/09	ÍBV	h	2-1	Hewson, Ormarsson

No	Name	Nat	DoB	Pos	Aps	(s)	Gls
13	Ásgeir Gunnar Ásgeirsson		03/06/80	M	12	(4)	1
8	Jón Gunnar Eysteinsson		03/07/86	M	13	(6)	1
17	Hólmbert Aron Fridjónsson		19/04/93	A	8	(5)	1
7	Dadi Gudmundsson		11/02/81	D	9	(4)	
19	Orri Gunnarsson		05/04/92	M	4	(9)	
5	Kristinn Ingi Halldórsson		08/04/89	A	18	(1)	11
4	Kristján Hauksson		03/02/86	D	20		
21	Ingvi Thór Hermannsson		11/02/93	A		(1)	
15	Samuel Hewson	ENG	28/11/88	M	21		1
29	Stefán B. Jóhannesson		18/01/93	A		(2)	
24	Sveinbjörn Jónasson		17/07/86	A	9	(7)	2
6	Halldór Hermann Jónsson		01/10/84	M	21		
1	Ögmundur Kristinsson		19/06/89	G	22		
10	Steven Lennon	SCO	20/01/88	A	13		5
20	Alan Lowing	SCO	07/01/88	D	21		
14	Hlynur Atli Magnússon		11/09/90	D	11	(1)	
11	Almarr Ormarsson		25/02/88	M	22		6
9	Sam Tillen	ENG	16/04/85	D	18	(1)	2

FYLKIR

Coach: Ásmundur Arnarsson
1967 • Fylkisvöllur (2,780) • fylkir.com
Major honours
Icelandic Cup (2) 2001, 2002

2012

06/05	Keflavík	h	1-1	Óskarsson
10/05	Stjarnan	a	2-2	Óskarsson (p), Thórhallsson
15/05	ÍA	h	0-1	
20/05	ÍBV	a	1-1	Eythórsson
24/05	Valur	h	3-1	Gudnason 2, Ásbjörnsson
02/06	FH	a	0-8	
14/06	Fram	h	1-0	Ásbjörnsson
20/06	Selfoss	a	2-1	Óskarsson, F Ólafsson
02/07	Breidablik	h	1-1	Thórhallsson
05/07	KR	a	1-2	Elebert
16/07	Grindavík	h	2-1	Óskarsson 2 (1p)
23/07	Keflavík	a	2-0	Thórhallsson, Óskarsson
29/07	Stjarnan	h	3-3	Thórhallsson, Ásbjörnsson, Óskarsson
08/08	ÍA	a	1-2	Matthíasson
12/08	ÍBV	h	0-4	
20/08	Valur	a	2-1	og (Næs), Björnsson
26/08	FH	h	0-1	
03/09	Fram	a	0-4	
16/09	Selfoss	h	2-0	Matthíasson, Takefusa
20/09	Breidablik	a	1-1	Óskarsson
23/09	KR	h	3-2	Takefusa, Óskarsson, Ásmundsson
29/09	Grindavík	a	2-2	Óskarsson, Takefusa

No	Name	Nat	DoB	Pos	Aps	(s)	Gls
17	Ásgeir Örn Arnthórsson		02/05/90	D	1	(2)	
5	Davíd Thór Ásbjörnsson		24/02/92	M	19		3
3	Ásgeir Börkur Ásgeirsson		16/04/87	M	18	(1)	
28	Emil Ásmundsson		08/01/95	M	4	(2)	1
24	Elis Rafn Björnsson		13/10/92	M	12	(1)	1
11	Kjartan Ágúst Breiddal		20/03/86	D	18	(2)	
25	David Elebert	IRL	21/03/86	D	19		1
27	Styrmir Erlendsson		13/12/93	A		(2)	
29	Ásgeir Eythórsson		29/04/93	D	5	(8)	1
32	Kristján Finnbogason		08/05/71	G	1	(1)	
19	Oddur Ingi Gudmundsson		28/01/89	M	7	(2)	
8	Árni Freyr Gudnason		12/05/86	A	10	(8)	2
1	Bjarni Thórdur Halldórsson		26/07/83	G	21		
6	Thórir Hannesson		08/10/86	D		(1)	
22	Andri Már Hermannsson		02/03/93	M		(2)	
30	Hjörtur Hermannsson		08/02/95	M	2	(1)	
26	Andri Thór Jónsson		24/02/91	D	12		
14	Magnús Thórir Matthíasson		22/01/90	A	15	(5)	2
4	Finnur Ólafsson		30/01/84	M	14	(6)	1
21	Sigurvin Ólafsson		18/07/76	M		(4)	
7	Ingimundur Níels Óskarsson		04/02/86	A	20	(1)	10
10	Björgólfur Takefusa		11/05/80	A	13	(4)	3
23	Rúrik Andri Thorfinnsson		21/04/92	A		(4)	
16	Tómas Thorsteinsson		08/12/88	D	19		
9	Jóhann Thórhallsson		07/01/80	A	6	(8)	4
2	Kristján Valdimarsson		12/05/84	D	6		

GRINDAVÍK

Coach: Gudjón Thórdarson
1935 • Grindavíkurvöllur (1,750) • umfg.is

2012

06/05	FH	a	1-1	Ondo
10/05	Keflavík	h	0-4	
15/05	Fram	a	3-4	Ameobi, Faye, Eklund
21/05	Stjarnan	h	1-4	Morrison
24/05	Selfoss	a	3-3	Fridriksson, Magnússon, Óli Bjarnason
02/06	ÍA	h	2-2	Ameobi, Faye
16/06	Breidablik	a	0-2	
20/06	ÍBV	h	1-3	Björgvinsson
01/07	KR	a	1-4	Faye
05/07	Valur	h	2-0	Faye, Fridriksson
16/07	Fylkir	a	1-2	Grétarsson
22/07	FH	h	0-1	
30/07	Keflavík	a	1-2	Faye
08/08	Fram	h	2-2	Williamson, Vilhjálmsson
12/08	Stjarnan	a	4-3	Williamson, og (Bjarnason), Faye, Ameobi
20/08	Selfoss	h	0-4	
26/08	ÍA	a	1-2	Ramsay
03/09	Breidablik	h	2-4	Óli Bjarnason, Vilhjálmsson
16/09	ÍBV	a	1-2	Vilhjálmsson
20/09	KR	h	2-2	Björgvinsson 2
23/09	Valur	a	1-4	Vilhjálmsson
29/09	Fylkir	h	2-2	Hilmarsson, Vilhjálmsson

No	Name	Nat	DoB	Pos	Aps	(s)	Gls
11	Tomi Ameobi	ENG	16/08/88	A	14	(3)	3
18	Ólafur Örn Bjarnason		15/05/75	D	20		
19	Óli Baldur Bjarnason		31/10/89	M	14	(5)	2
17	Magnús Björgvinsson		12/09/87	A	11	(3)	3
16	Björn Berg Bryde		08/07/92	D	13	(1)	
29	Jordan Edridge	ENG	29/10/92	D	1	(2)	
21	Mikael Eklund	SWE	14/09/81	D	14		1
6	Pape Mamadou Faye		06/03/91	A	9	(8)	6
9	Matthías Örn Fridriksson		09/09/86	M	19		2
24	Daníel Leó Grétarsson		02/10/95	A	1	(5)	1
24	Páll Gudmundsson		22/10/86	M		(1)	
7	Alex Freyr Hilmarsson		26/07/93	M	8	(8)	1
3	Ray Anthony Jónsson	PHI	03/02/79	D	20	(1)	
23	Jósef Kristinn Jósefsson		12/09/89	D	3		
25	Alexander Magnússon		10/11/89	M	10		1
4	Paul McShane	SCO	13/04/78	M	1	(1)	
15	Gavin Morrison	SCO	03/01/90	M	4	(1)	1
2	Loic Mbang Ondo	GAB	05/10/90	D	12	(1)	1
1	Óskar Pétursson		26/01/89	G	22		
10	Scott Ramsay	SCO	02/10/75	M	11	(7)	1
22	Marko Valdimar Stefánsson		18/09/90	M	17	(1)	
12	Aegir Thorsteinsson		08/10/92	M		(1)	
27	Hafthór Aegir Vilhjálmsson		29/09/86	A	8	(7)	5
8	Iain Williamson	SCO	12/01/88	M	10		2

ÍA AKRANES

Coach: Thórdur Thórdarson
1946 • Akranesvöllur (5,550) • ia.is
Major honours
Icelandic League (18) 1951, 1953, 1954, 1957, 1958, 1960, 1970, 1974, 1975, 1977, 1983, 1984, 1992, 1993, 1994, 1995, 1996, 2001;
Icelandic Cup (9) 1978, 1982, 1983, 1984, 1986, 1993, 1996, 2000, 2003

2012

06/05	Breidablik	a	1-0	Ákason
10/05	KR	h	3-2	J Gudjónsson, A Gudjónsson, G Martin
15/05	Fylkir	a	1-0	Valdimarsson
20/05	Keflavík	h	3-2	G Martin, Valdimarsson, Gunnlaugsson
24/05	Stjarnan	a	1-1	Gunnlaugsson
02/06	Grindavík	a	2-2	Ákason, Doninger
15/06	ÍBV	h	0-4	
20/06	Valur	a	1-2	Gunnlaugsson
30/06	FH	h	2-7	G Martin, D Martin
05/07	Fram	a	0-2	
16/07	Selfoss	h	4-0	Ársaelsson, A Gudjónsson 2, Ákason
23/07	Breidablik	h	1-1	J Gudjónsson (p)
30/07	KR	a	0-2	
08/08	Fylkir	h	2-1	Gunnlaugsson 2
12/08	Keflavík	a	3-2	D Martin, Einarsson, J Gudjónsson (p)
23/08	Stjarnan	h	1-2	Gunnlaugsson
26/08	Grindavík	h	2-1	D Martin, Gunnlaugsson
02/09	ÍBV	a	0-0	
16/09	Valur	h	1-1	Gunnlaugsson
20/09	FH	a	1-2	D Martin
23/09	Fram	h	0-1	
29/09	Selfoss	a	3-1	Ákason, Gunnlaugsson, A Gudjónsson

No	Name	Nat	DoB	Pos	Aps	(s)	Gls
16	Andri Adolphsson		01/12/92	A	15	(5)	
24	Andri Geir Alexandersson		16/06/90	D	1		
10	Jón Vilhelm Ákason		20/11/86	M	12	(6)	4
4	Kári Ársaelsson		02/07/85	D	20		1
6	Ármann Smári Björnsson		07/01/81	D	22		
22	Mark Doninger	ENG	19/10/89	M	7		1
23	Einar Logi Einarsson		24/11/91	D	21	(1)	1
18	Hallur Flosason		01/05/93	M	4	(4)	
25	Theodore Furness	ENG	30/03/91	D	9	(2)	
11	Arnar Már Gudjónsson		20/02/87	M	21		4
15	Gudmundur Bödvar Gudjónsson		03/08/89	D	5	(2)	
8	Jóhannes Karl Gudjónsson		25/05/80	M	21		3
9	Gardar Bergmann Gunnlaugsson		25/04/83	A	16	(4)	9
17	Jesper Holdt Jensen	DEN	22/04/88	M	1	(3)	
1	Páll Gísli Jónsson		26/03/83	G	13		
19	Eggert Kári Karlsson		14/05/91	A	1	(7)	
21	Dean Martin	ENG	31/08/72	A	12	(7)	4
7	Gary Martin	ENG	10/10/90	A	11		3
12	Árni Snaer Ólafsson		16/08/90	G	9	(1)	
2	Aron Ýmir Pétursson		30/01/90	D	7	(6)	
20	Fjalar Örn Sigurdsson		23/03/94	A		(5)	
3	Gudjón Heidar Sveinsson		19/04/80	D	8	(1)	
14	Ólafur Valur Valdimarsson		13/12/90	A	6	(11)	2

ÍBV VESTMANNAEYJAR

Coach: Magnús Gylfason;
(19/09/12) (Dragan Kazić (SRB) & Ian Jeffs (ENG))
1945 • Hásteinsvöllur (3,000) • ibvsport.is
Major honours
Icelandic League (3) 1979, 1997, 1998;
Icelandic Cup (4) 1968, 1972, 1981, 1998

2012

06/05	Selfoss	a	1-2	Valdimarsson
10/05	Breidablik	h	0-0	
15/05	KR	a	2-3	Spear, Mawejje
20/05	Fylkir	h	1-1	V Thorvardarson
24/05	Keflavík	a	0-1	
29/05	Stjarnan	h	4-1	Gudjónsson, Olsen, T Gudmundsson, Jeffs
15/06	ÍA	a	4-0	Jeffs, Olsen 3
20/06	Grindavík	a	3-1	Thórarinsson, Baldock, Mawejje
29/06	Valur	h	2-0	Olsen, Mawejje
15/07	Fram	h	3-2	Olsen 2, Valdimarsson (p)
23/07	Selfoss	h	1-0	Christiansen
29/07	Breidablik	a	0-1	
08/08	KR	h	2-0	Valdimarsson (p), Thórarinsson
12/08	Fylkir	a	4-0	V Thorvardarson, Valdimarsson (p), og (Jónsson), Olsen
20/08	Keflavík	h	0-1	
26/08	Stjarnan	a	1-1	Arnór Ólafsson
30/08	FH	a	0-2	
02/09	ÍA	h	0-0	
16/09	Grindavík	h	2-1	Olsen, Andri Ólafsson (p)
20/09	Valur	a	3-0	Christiansen, Olsen, T Gudmundsson
23/09	FH	h	2-2	Valdimarsson, og (Snorrason)
29/09	Fram	a	1-2	T Gudmundsson

No	Name	Nat	DoB	Pos	Aps	(s)	Gls
27	George Baldock	ENG	09/03/93	M	16		1
23	Eythór Helgi Birgisson		24/02/89	A		(5)	
8	Yngvi Magnús Borgthórsson		26/03/75	D		(3)	
28	Rasmus Christiansen	DEN	06/01/89	D	21		2
1	Ábel Dhalra	UGA	09/09/87	G	22		
31	Jake Gallagher	ENG	06/01/93	M		(1)	
3	Matt Garner	ENG	09/04/84	D	21		
2	Brynjar Gauti Gudjónsson		27/02/92	D	21		1
4	Gunnar Már Gudmundsson		15/12/83	M	1	(4)	
9	Tryggvi Gudmundsson		30/07/74	A	9	(2)	3
16	Jón Ingason		21/09/95	M		(3)	
30	Ian Jeffs	ENG	12/10/82	M	11	(6)	3
14	Ragnar Leósson		20/03/91	M		(7)	
15	Tonny Mawejje	UGA	15/12/86	M	19	(2)	3
21	Christian Steen Olsen	DEN	09/11/83	A	21	(1)	9
6	Andri Ólafsson		26/06/85	M	5	(8)	1
19	Arnór Eyvar Ólafsson		27/11/89	D	20		1
10	Aaron Spear	ENG	29/04/93	A	2	(2)	1
22	Gauti Thorvardarson		19/02/89	A		(1)	
29	Vídir Thorvardarson		07/07/92	A	15	(4)	2
7	Gudmundur Thórarinsson		15/04/92	D	21		2
5	Thórarinn Ingi Valdimarsson		23/04/90	M	17		5

KEFLAVÍK

Coach: Zoran Daníel Ljubicic
1929 • Nettóvöllurinn (2,658) • keflavik.is
Major honours
Icelandic League (4) 1964, 1969, 1971, 1973;
Icelandic Cup (4) 1975, 1997, 2004, 2006

2012

06/05	Fylkir	a	1-1	Eidsson
10/05	Grindavík	a	4-0	Elvarsson 2, Traustason, Einarsson
14/05	Stjarnan	h	0-1	
20/05	ÍA	a	2-3	Steinarsson (p), Traustason
24/05	ÍBV	h	1-0	J Gudmundsson
31/05	Valur	a	0-4	
16/06	FH	h	2-4	Steinarsson (p), Traustason
20/06	Fram	a	2-0	Elvarsson, Steinarsson
02/07	Selfoss	h	2-2	J Gudmundsson, Traustason
05/07	Breidablik	a	4-0	Elísson, J Gudmundsson, Steinarsson, Thorsteinsson
12/07	KR	h	1-1	Steinarsson
23/07	Fylkir	h	0-2	
30/07	Grindavík	h	2-1	Elísson, Thorsteinsson
08/08	Stjarnan	a	3-1	Steinarsson, Sveinsson, J Gudmundsson
12/08	ÍA	h	2-3	J Gudmundsson 2
20/08	ÍBV	a	1-0	Steinarsson
27/08	Valur	h	0-4	
03/09	FH	a	0-3	
16/09	Fram	h	5-0	Elísson 2, Thorsteinsson, Sveinsson, Benediktsson
20/09	Selfoss	a	1-2	J Gudmundsson
23/09	Breidablik	h	2-3	Sveinsson, Vilbergsson
29/09	KR	a	0-3	

No	Name	Nat	DoB	Pos	Aps	(s)	Gls
12	Árni Freyr Ásgeirsson		10/03/92	G		(1)	
3	Jóhann Ragnar Benediktsson		30/07/80	D	21		1
15	Kristinn Björnsson		13/12/87	M	1		
10	Hilmar Geir Eidsson		05/10/85	A	10	(8)	1
6	Finar Orri Einarsson		28/10/80	M	16		1
23	Sigurbergur Elísson		10/06/92	M	12	(6)	4
25	Frans Elvarsson		14/08/90	M	20		3
26	Grétar Atli Grétarsson		05/11/88	D	13	(2)	
4	Haraldur Freyr Gudmundsson		14/12/81	D	20		
7	Jóhann Birnir Gudmundsson		05/12/77	M	19	(1)	7
13	Daníel Gylfason		30/07/93	A		(2)	
2	Viktor Smári Hafsteinsson		30/04/92	D	3		
1	Ómar Jóhannsson		02/03/81	G	22		
8	Bojan Stefán Ljubicic		22/06/92	A	4	(12)	
22	Magnús Thór Magnússon		20/02/92	D	13	(1)	
5	Gregor Mohar	SVN	22/05/85	D	8		
28	Elías Már Ómarsson		18/01/95	M		(1)	
24	Denis Selimović	SVN	22/06/79	D	12	(4)	
9	Gudmundur Steinarsson		20/10/79	A	22		7
27	Hördur Sveinsson		24/03/83	A	2	(6)	3
11	Magnús Sverrir Thorsteinsson		22/09/82	A	7	(11)	3
29	Ísak Örn Thórdarson		12/07/88	A		(2)	
17	Arnór Ingvi Traustason		30/04/93	M	14	(1)	4
14	Rafn Markús Vilbergsson		08/10/83	D	3	(3)	1

KR REYKJAVÍK

Coach: Rúnar Kristinsson
1899 • KR-völlur (2,801) • kr.is
Major honours
Icelandic League (25) 1912, 1919, 1926, 1927, 1928,
1929, 1931, 1932, 1934, 1941, 1948, 1949, 1950,
1952, 1955, 1959, 1961, 1963, 1965, 1968, 1999,
2000, 2002, 2003, 2011;
Icelandic Cup (13) 1960, 1961, 1962, 1963, 1964,
1966, 1967, 1994, 1995, 1999, 2008, 2011, 2012

2012

06/05	Stjarnan	h	2-2	Atlason, Finnbogason
10/05	ÍA	a	2-3	Ragnarsson, Finnbogason
15/05	ÍBV	h	3-2	Finnbogason 3 (3p)
20/05	Valur	a	1-0	Lúdvíksson
23/05	FH	h	2-0	Sigurdsson, og (Gunnleifsson)
02/06	Fram	a	2-1	Arnarsson, Ó Hauksson
16/06	Selfoss	h	3-1	Finnbogason (p), H Hauksson, Sigurdsson
20/06	Breidablik	a	1-2	Ragnarsson
01/07	Grindavík	h	4-1	Sigurdarson, Ragnarsson, Atlason, og (Ólafur Bjarnason)
11/07	Fylkir	h	2-1	Ó Hauksson, Ragnarsson
12/07	Keflavík	a	1-1	Atlason
21/07	Stjarnan	a	1-1	Martin
30/07	ÍA	h	2-0	Ó Hauksson, Finnbogason
08/08	ÍBV	a	0-2	
12/08	Valur	h	2-3	Martin (1p)
23/08	FH	a	3-1	Sigurdsson 2, Martin
27/08	Fram	h	1-1	Finnbogason (p)
02/09	Selfoss	a	0-1	
16/09	Breidablik	h	0-4	
20/09	Grindavík	a	2-2	Atlason 2
23/09	Fylkir	a	2-3	Arnarsson 2
29/09	Keflavík	h	3-0	og (Magnússon), Gudmundur Gunnarsson, Ragnarsson

No	Name	Nat	DoB	Pos	Aps	(s)	Gls
14	Viktor Bjarki Arnarsson		22/01/83	M	18	(2)	3
15	Emil Atlason		22/07/93	A	11	(5)	5
10	Kjartan Henry Finnbogason		09/07/86	A	12	(2)	8
4	Bjarni Gudjónsson		26/02/79	M	21		
21	Gudmundur Reynir Gunnarsson		21/01/89	D	17	(1)	1
6	Gunnar Thór Gunnarsson		04/10/85	D	4	(1)	
1	Hannes Thór Halldórsson		27/04/84	G	21		
3	Haukur Heidar Hauksson		01/09/91	D	9	(6)	1
11	Óskar Örn Hauksson		22/08/84	A	17		3
24	Björn Jónsson		07/10/90	M	1	(4)	
5	Egill Jónsson		15/02/91	M	1	(6)	
18	Aron Bjarki Jósepsson		21/11/89	D	10	(2)	
20	Magnús Már Lúdvíksson		30/05/81	D	12	(1)	1
17	Gary Martin	ENG	10/10/90	A	11		4
9	Thorsteinn Már Ragnarsson		19/04/90	A	12	(8)	5
16	Jónas Gudni Saevarsson		28/11/83	M	6	(2)	
2	Grétar Sigfinnur Sigurdarson		09/10/82	D	21		1
8	Baldur Sigurdsson		24/04/85	M	17	(3)	4
23	Atli Sigurjónsson		01/07/91	M	6	(8)	
12	Dofri Snorrason		21/07/90	D	2	(5)	
22	Fjalar Thorgeirsson		18/01/77	G	1	(1)	
7	Rhys Weston	WAL	27/10/80	D	12	(1)	

SELFOSS

Coach: Logi Ólafsson
1936 • Selfossvöllur (2,910) • umfs.is

2012

06/05	ÍBV	h	2-1	Finsen, Bödvarsson
10/05	Valur	a	1-3	Røyrane
15/05	FH	h	0-1	
21/05	Fram	a	2-0	Kjartansson (p), Tillen
24/05	Grindavík	h	3-3	Bödvarsson, Finsen, Stefán Gudlaugsson
31/05	Breidablik	h	0-2	
16/06	KR	a	1-3	Kjartansson
20/06	Fylkir	h	1-2	Finsen
02/07	Keflavík	a	2-2	Sarr, Bödvarsson
05/07	Stjarnan	h	1-3	Kjartansson
16/07	ÍA	a	0-4	
23/07	ÍBV	a	0-1	
29/07	Valur	h	0-1	
08/08	FH	a	2-5	Leifsson, Snorrason
12/08	Fram	h	4-2	Bödvarsson 2, Kjartansson, Røyrane
20/08	Grindavík	a	4-0	Bödvarsson, Røyrane, Leifsson, Kjartansson
26/08	Breidablik	a	1-1	Leifsson
02/09	KR	h	1-0	Bödvarsson
16/09	Fylkir	a	0-2	
20/09	Keflavík	h	2-1	Jónsson, Kjartansson (p)
23/09	Stjarnan	a	2-4	Kjartansson (p), Røyrane
29/09	ÍA	h	1-3	Røyrane

No	Name	Nat	DoB	Pos	Aps	(s)	Gls
6	Andri Freyr Björnsson		12/08/86	D	6	(1)	
30	Endre Ove Brenne	NOR	14/04/88	D	20		
5	Bernard Petrus Brons	NED	27/07/86	D	10		
7	Jón Dadi Bödvarsson		25/05/92	M	22		7
14	Moustapha Cissé	SEN	20/06/91	A	5	(4)	
1	Ismet Duracak	BIH	06/04/85	G	22		
25	Magnús Ingi Einarsson		12/06/94	A		(1)	
11	Ólafur Karl Finsen		30/03/92	A	12	(8)	3
2	Sigurdur Eyberg Gudlaugsson		02/10/90	D	2	(3)	
21	Stefán Ragnar Gudlaugsson		19/03/91	D	16		1
23	Markus Hermo	NOR	05/08/92	D	2	(3)	
19	Egill Jónsson		15/02/91	M	8	(1)	1
9	Vidar Örn Kjartansson		11/03/90	A	18	(3)	7
24	Tómas Leifsson		01/05/85	A	12	(6)	3
4	Agnar Bragi Magnússon		03/02/87	D	2	(1)	
15	Abdoulaye N'Diaye	SEN	07/09/91	A	4	(3)	
27	Jon André Røyrane	NOR	12/12/83	A	21	(1)	5
20	Robert Johann Sandnes	NOR	29/12/91	D	18	(1)	
8	Babacar Sarr	SEN	15/02/91	M	21		1
22	Ivar Skjerve	NOR	13/01/91	D	12	(4)	
3	Dofri Snorrason		21/07/90	A		(3)	1
10	Ingólfur Thórarinsson		31/05/86	M	3	(6)	
13	Hafthór Thrastarson		14/02/90	D	5	(1)	
17	Joseph Tillen	ENG	15/12/86	M	1	(8)	1

STJARNAN

Coach: Bjarni Jóhannsson
1960 • Stjörnuvöllur (1,400) • stjarnan.is

2012

06/05	KR	a	2-2	Árnason, A Jóhannsson
10/05	Fylkir	h	2-2	G Jónsson, Björnsson
14/05	Keflavík	a	1-0	Björnsson (p)
21/05	Grindavík	a	4-1	A Jóhannsson 2, Chopart, og (Ondo)
24/05	ÍA	h	1-1	G Jóhannsson (p)
29/05	ÍBV	a	1-4	Scholz
15/06	Valur	h	3-2	Scholz 2, Bjarnason
20/06	FH	a	2-2	Hreinsson, G Jóhannsson
02/07	Fram	h	4-2	G Jóhannsson 2, Chopart, Hreinsson
05/07	Selfoss	a	3-1	Scholz, Hreinsson, Chopart
16/07	Breidablik	h	1-1	Björnsson
21/07	KR	h	1-1	og (Gudmundur Gunnarsson)
29/07	Fylkir	a	3-3	Hreinsson, Doninger, Björnsson
08/08	Keflavík	h	1-3	Doninger
12/08	Grindavík	h	3-4	G Jóhannsson, Doninger, Björnsson
23/08	ÍA	a	2-1	Chopart, A Jóhannsson
26/08	ÍBV	h	1-1	Scholz (p)
02/09	Valur	a	2-0	G Jónsson, Chopart
16/09	FH	h	2-2	Björnsson, Doninger
20/09	Fram	a	1-1	G Jóhannsson
23/09	Selfoss	h	4-2	G Jóhannsson 2, Hreinsson, Sturluson
29/09	Breidablik	a	0-2	

No	Name	Nat	DoB	Pos	Aps	(s)	Gls
14	Hördur Árnason		19/05/89	D	17	(1)	1
3	Tryggvi Sveinn Bjarnason		16/01/83	D	7	(8)	1
10	Halldór Orri Björnsson		02/03/87	M	20	(2)	6
23	Snorri Páll Blöndal		23/03/94	D	1	(7)	
26	Kennie Knak Chopart	DEN	01/06/90	A	21	(1)	5
24	Mark Doninger	ENG	19/10/89	M	7	(4)	4
11	Bjarki Páll Eysteinsson		01/04/86	A		(8)	
6	Hilmar Thór Hilmarsson		20/09/90	M	1	(4)	
22	Ellert Hreinsson		12/10/86	A	15	(1)	5
7	Atli Jóhannsson		05/10/82	M	21		4
27	Gardar Jóhannsson		01/04/80	A	16	(2)	8
20	Gunnar Örn Jónsson		30/04/85	A	10	(6)	2
1	Ingvar Jónsson		18/10/89	G	22		
28	Darri Steinn Konrádsson		15/01/93	A		(4)	
16	Mads Thunø Laudrup	DEN	09/02/89	A	6	(1)	
9	Daníel Laxdal		22/09/86	D	21		
4	Jóhann Laxdal		27/01/90	D	20		
13	Alexander Scholz	DEN	24/10/92	D	21		5
17	Sindri Már Sigurthórsson		08/04/86	M		(3)	
21	Baldvin Sturluson		09/04/89	M	16	(4)	1

VALUR REYKJAVÍK

Coach: Kristján Gudmundsson
1911 • Vodafonevöllurinn ad Hlídarenda (2,465) • valur.is
Major honours
Icelandic League (20) 1930, 1933, 1935, 1936, 1937, 1938, 1940, 1942, 1943, 1944, 1945, 1956, 1966, 1967, 1976, 1978, 1980, 1985, 1987, 2007; Icelandic Cup (9) 1965, 1974, 1976, 1977, 1988, 1990, 1991, 1992, 2005

2012

07/05	Fram	a	1-0	Ingólfsson
10/05	Selfoss	h	3-1	Sveinsson, Gudmundsson, Sigurjónsson
15/05	Breidablik	a	0-1	
20/05	KR	h	0-1	
24/05	Fylkir	a	1-3	Gudmundsson
31/05	Keflavík	h	4-0	Kárason 2, Gudmundsson, K Sigurdsson
15/06	Stjarnan	a	2-3	og (Bjarnason), Lýdsson
20/06	ÍA	h	2-1	Sigurjónsson 2 (1p)
29/06	ÍBV	a	0-2	
05/07	Grindavík	a	0-2	
15/07	FH	h	3-1	Thórarinsson, Sigurjónsson 2 (1p)
23/07	Fram	h	0-2	
29/07	Selfoss	a	1-0	Gudmundsson
08/08	Breidablik	h	3-4	Kárason 2, Sigurjónsson (p)
12/08	KR	a	3-2	Kárason, H Sigurdsson, K Sigurdsson
20/08	Fylkir	h	1-2	Sigurjónsson
27/08	Keflavík	a	4-0	Kárason 2, Thorláksson 2
02/09	Stjarnan	h	0-2	
16/09	ÍA	a	1-1	Gudmundsson
20/09	ÍBV	h	0-3	
23/09	Grindavík	h	4-1	H Sigurdsson, Gudmundsson, Thorláksson 2
29/09	FH	a	1-2	H Sigurdsson

No	Name	Nat	DoB	Pos	Aps	(s)	Gls
6	Hafsteinn Briem		28/02/91	M	2	(6)	
15	Hilmar Rafn Emilsson		12/09/86	M		(1)	
17	Thórir Gudjónsson		07/04/91	A	5	(3)	
11	Matthías Gudmundsson		01/08/80	A	19	(2)	6
12	Ólafur Thór Gunnarsson		25/10/77	G	4		
4	Halldór Kristinn Halldórsson		13/04/88	D	19		
16	Atli Heimisson		31/08/87	A	3	(3)	
19	Ásgeir Thór Ingólfsson		31/08/90	M	10	(9)	1
12	Sindri Snær Jensson		12/08/86	G	14		
22	Matarr Jobe	GAM	22/03/92	D	13	(2)	
14	Kolbeinn Kárason		02/04/91	A	13	(7)	7
3	Brynjar Kristmundsson		19/05/92	D	8		
10	Gudjón Pétur Lýdsson		28/12/87	M	20		1
1	Ásgeir Thór Magnússon		22/05/91	G	4		
25	Jónas Tór Næs	FRO	27/12/86	D	10		
2	Úlfar Hrafn Pálsson		16/10/88	D	11	(2)	
7	Haukur Páll Sigurdsson		05/08/87	M	17	(1)	3
18	Kristinn Freyr Sigurdsson		25/12/91	A	11	(8)	2
8	Rúnar Már Sigurjónsson		18/06/90	M	22		7
23	Andri Fannar Stefánsson		22/04/91	M	5	(7)	
9	Hördur Sveinsson		24/03/83	A	8	(3)	1
20	Indridi Áki Thorláksson		02/08/95	A	2	(5)	4
5	Atli Sveinn Thórarinsson		24/01/80	D	21		1
29	Joseph Tillen	ENG	15/12/86	A	1	(1)	

Top goalscorers

12	Atli Gudnason (FH)
11	Kristinn Ingi Halldórsson (Fram)
10	Ingimundur Níels Óskarsson (Fylkir)
9	Björn Daníel Sverrisson (FH)
	Gardar Bergmann Gunnlaugsson (ÍA)
	Christian Steen Olsen (ÍBV)
8	Kjartan Henry Finnbogason (KR)
	Gardar Jóhannsson (Stjarnan)
7	Gary Martin (ÍA/KR)
	Jóhann Birnir Gudmundsson (Keflavík)
	Gudmundur Steinarsson (Keflavík)
	Jón Dadi Bödvarsson (Selfoss)
	Vidar Örn Kjartansson (Selfoss)
	Kolbeinn Kárason (Valur)
	Rúnar Már Sigurjónsson (Valur)

Promoted clubs

THÓR AKUREYRI

Coach: Páll Vidar Gíslason
1915 • Thórsvöllur (2,984) • thorsport.is

VÍKINGUR ÓLAFSVÍK

Coach: Ejub Purišević (BIH)
1928 • Ólafsvíkurvöllur (1,130) • vikingurol.bloggar.is

SECOND LEVEL FINAL TABLE 2012

		Pld	W	D	L	F	A	Pts
1	Thór Akureyri	22	16	2	4	40	20	50
2	Víkingur Ólafsvík	22	13	3	6	36	21	42
3	Thróttur Reykjavík	22	9	6	7	34	26	33
4	KA Akureyri	22	9	6	7	34	30	33
5	Haukar	22	9	6	7	23	25	33
6	Víkingur Reykjavík	22	8	7	7	34	31	31
7	Fjölnir	22	7	8	7	39	26	29
8	Tindastóll	22	8	3	11	34	42	27
9	BÍ/Bolungarvík	22	6	8	8	31	37	26
10	Leiknir Reykjavík	22	6	7	9	33	36	25
11	Höttur	22	5	6	11	30	41	21
12	ÍR Reykjavík	22	4	2	16	19	52	14

Domestic cup: Bikarkeppnin 2012

THIRD ROUND

(06/06/12)
Augnablik 1-4 Höttur
Dalvík/Reynir 1-3 Reynir Sandgerdi
Fram 1-1 Haukar *(aet; 4-3 on pens)*
Keflavík 0-1 Grindavík
KA 2-0 Fjardabyggd
Leiknir Reykjavík 1-2 Thróttur Reykjavík
Víkingur Reykjavík 2-0 Fjölnir

(07/06/12)
KFS 0-1 KB
Selfoss 2-1 Njardvík
Stjarnan 4-1 Grótta
Thróttur Vogum 1-3 Afturelding

(08/06/12)
Breidablik 5-0 BÍ/Bolungarvík
FH 1-1 Fylkir *(aet; 2-3 on pens)*
ÍA 1-2 KR
Thór 1-4 Valur

(12/06/12)
Víkingur Ólafsvík 0-2 ÍBV

FOURTH ROUND

(25/06/12)
Afturelding 2-3 Fram
ÍBV 6-1 Höttur
KA 2-3 Grindavík
Selfoss 4-0 KB
Stjarnan 1-0 Reynir Sandgerdi *(aet)*
Thróttur Reykjavík 2-1 Valur *(aet)*

(26/06/12)
KR 3-0 Breidablik
Víkingur Reykjavík 2-1 Fylkir

QUARTER-FINALS

(08/07/12)
ÍRV 1-2 KR *(Birgisson 17; Ó Hauksson 86, 88)*
Víkingur Reykjavík 0-3 Grindavík *(Faye 33, Magnússon 47, Jónsson 78)*
Thróttur Reykjavík 3-0 Selfoss *(Björnsson 50, 73, Gíslason 80)*

(09/07/12)
Stjarnan 2-1 Fram *(G Jóhannsson 6, 72; Tillen 45)*

SEMI-FINALS

(01/08/12)
Stjarnan 3-0 Thróttur Reykjavík *(Doninger 25, 66, Scholz 84)*

(02/08/12)
Grindavík 0-1 KR *(Martin 43)*

FINAL

(18/08/12)
Laugardalsvöllur, Reykjavik
KR REYKJAVÍK 2 *(Martin 32, Sigurdsson 84)*
STJARNAN 1 *(G Jóhannsson 6)*
Referee: *Hjaltalín*
KR: *Halldórsson, Lúdvíksson, Jósepsson, Sigurdarson, Gudmundur Gunnarsson, Gudjónsson, Sigurdsson, Arnarsson (Saevarsson 85), Martin, Finnbogason, Ó Hauksson (Atlason 80)*
STJARNAN: *Pétursson, J Laxdal, D Laxdal, Scholz, Chopart, Sturluson, Doninger, A Jóhannsson (Bjarnason 86), Hreinsson, G Jóhannsson, Björnsson (G Jónsson 90)*

KR pose with the trophy after successfully defending the Icelandic Cup

ISRAEL
Israel Football Association (Ifa)

Address	Ramat Gan Stadium	**President**	Avraham Luzon
	299 Aba Hillel Street	**Chief executive**	Ori Shilo
	PO Box 3591	**Media officer**	Michal Grundland
	Il-52134 Ramat Gan	**Year of formation**	1928
Tel	+972 3 617 1500	**National stadium**	Ramat Gan (41,583)
Fax	+972 3 570 2044		
E-Mail	info@football.org.il		
Website	football.org.il		

LIGAT HA'AL CLUBS

1 **FC Ashdod**

2 **Beitar Jerusalem FC**

3 **Bnei Sakhnin FC**

4 **Bnei Yehuda Tel-Aviv FC**

5 **Hapoel Akko FC**

6 **Hapoel Beer Sheva FC**

7 **Hapoel Haifa FC**

8 **Hapoel Ironi Nir Ramat HaSharon**

9 **Hapoel Kiryat Shmona FC**

10 **Hapoel Ramat Gan FC**

11 **Hapoel Tel-Aviv FC**

12 **Maccabi Haifa FC**

13 **Maccabi Netanya FC**

14 **Maccabi Tel-Aviv FC**

PROMOTED CLUBS

15 **Maccabi Petach-Tikva FC**

16 **Hapoel Raanana FC**

KEY:

● – UEFA Champions League

● – UEFA Europa League

● – Promoted clubs

● – Relegated clubs

● – Relegated club in UEFA Europa League

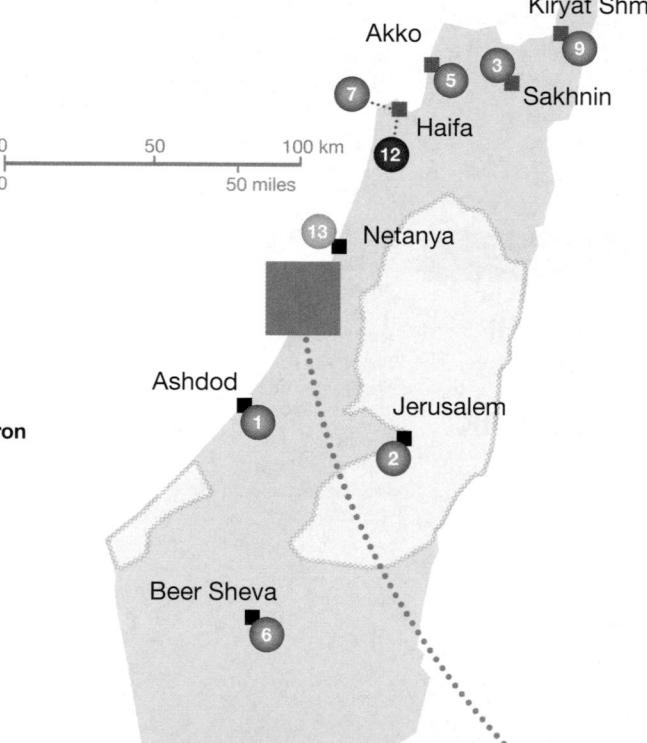

History repeats itself ten years on

In 2002/03 Maccabi Tel-Aviv FC captured the league title and Hapoel Ramat Gan FC lifted the State Cup. The same scenario occurred ten years later as each of the two clubs ended a decade-long wait to reclaim their respective trophies.

While the champions, led by Spanish coach Óscar García, celebrated a landslide triumph in the Ligat Ha'al, finishing 13 points clear of runners-up Maccabi Haifa FC, the cup winners could only savour a bittersweet victory having already finished bottom of the league and been relegated.

| Maccabi Tel-Aviv end decade-long wait for league title | Hapoel Ramat Gan go down but win State Cup | Maccabi Haifa return to Europe as league runners-up |

Domestic league

Maccabi Tel-Aviv had been through some lean times since their previous league win, but they were a class above the rest in 2012/13, the acquisition of Óscar as coach and Jordi Cruyff as general manager providing a template for success that brought the good times back to Bloomfield. Seven wins in their first eight matches, including a 4-0 victory over defending champions Hapoel Kiryat Shmona FC, signalled their intent, and although they hit a few bumps thereafter, they were imperious in the new year, a succession of wins enabling them to reach the end of the regular 26-match campaign with a ten-point cushion.

With the defence, underpinned by goalkeeper Vincent Enyeama and centre-back Shiran Yeiny, as solid as a rock and strikers Eliran Atar and Rade Prica supplying a steady stream of goals, the leaders looked unstoppable. Their fine form was carried over into the championship phase and on 22 April, with a 2-0 victory at Hapoel Ironi Nir Ramat HaSharon FC, the title was officially signed and sealed. The final table illustrated their dominance, 78 goals contributing to 80 points and a massive winning margin. Local rivals Hapoel Tel-Aviv FC finished third but they were 22 points adrift while Ramat HaSharon, the sixth-placed team, managed only half the champions' total.

Having missed out on Europe in 2011/12, Maccabi Haifa were happy enough with second place – especially after an atrocious start under their new coach, club icon Reuven Atar. His replacement in mid-November by Arik Benado, Israel's most-capped international, completely transformed the team's fortunes, and they played some splendid football thereafter, rising from the foot of the table to the runners-up spot.

Domestic cup

Hapoel Ramat Gan's league campaign had already ended in dismay when they turned up for the State Cup final against Kiryat Shmona, relegation having come just a year after promotion following a late-season collapse. However, fortune would smile on them in Netanya as they came from behind to draw 1-1 and take the trophy on penalties. Not only was it ten years since their previous win, but they claimed the trophy with the same coach, Eli Cohen. Furthermore, their goalscorer, Omer Buksenbaum, was also a veteran of the 2003 triumph.

Europe

Kiryat Shmona's scorer in the cup final, Shimon Abuhazira, struck 15 goals in the league and another five times in Europe as his club joined regular continental campaigners Hapoel Tel-Aviv in the group stage of the UEFA Europa League. While participation was a feat in itself, neither club impressed, winning just one game between them. Indeed, Kiryat Shmona's final tally of two points was the lowest of the 48 teams involved.

National team

Israel, under the command of ex-Hapoel Tel-Aviv boss Eli Guttman, played some enterprising football in their first six 2014 FIFA World Cup qualifiers, scoring 15 goals, but a 4-0 home defeat by Russia and an even more scarring 3-3 draw in the same Ramat Gan Stadium against Portugal – after they had led with seconds remaining – appeared to have left the team with too much to do to press for a place in the top two of Group F. Nevertheless, the emergence of strikers Eden Ben Basat – who scored in four successive qualifiers – and Tomer Hemed – five goals in two games against Luxembourg – augured well for the future, with further encouragement coming at the UEFA European Under-21 Championship, which the country hosted with enthusiasm and panache.

Domestic league: Ligat Ha'al 2012/13 final table

		Pld	Home					Away					Total					Pts
			W	D	L	F	A	W	D	L	F	A	W	D	L	F	A	
1	**Maccabi Tel-Aviv FC**	36	15	1	2	46	10	10	4	4	32	20	25	5	6	78	30	80
2	Maccabi Haifa FC	36	12	4	2	38	14	7	6	5	24	19	19	10	7	62	33	67
3	Hapoel Tel-Aviv FC	36	9	5	4	27	21	8	2	8	20	24	17	7	12	47	45	58
4	Bnei Yehuda Tel-Aviv FC	36	10	4	4	28	18	6	3	9	22	22	16	7	13	50	40	55
5	Hapoel Kiryat Shmona FC	36	7	5	6	18	14	7	6	5	27	24	14	11	11	45	38	53
6	Hapoel Ironi Nir Ramat HaSharon FC	36	8	2	8	18	20	4	2	12	13	30	12	4	20	31	50	40
7	FC Ashdod	33	8	3	6	25	20	4	4	8	13	20	12	7	14	38	40	43
8	Hapoel Beer Sheva FC	33	7	6	4	18	13	3	5	8	14	26	10	11	12	32	39	41
9	Hapoel Haifa FC	33	8	6	3	25	17	1	6	9	11	28	9	12	12	36	45	39
10	Beitar Jerusalem FC	33	5	7	5	24	23	4	5	7	20	31	9	12	12	44	54	39
11	Hapoel Akko FC	33	4	7	5	24	25	4	6	7	15	23	8	13	12	39	48	37
12	Bnei Sakhnin FC	33	4	5	7	14	26	4	8	5	17	23	8	13	12	31	49	37
13	Maccabi Netanya FC	33	4	4	8	21	28	4	7	6	17	22	8	11	14	38	50	35
14	Hapoel Ramat Gan FC	33	3	7	6	15	18	4	2	11	22	29	7	9	17	37	47	30

NB League splits into top 6 and bottom 8 after 26 games, after which the clubs play exclusively against teams in their group.

SEASON AT A GLANCE

EUROPEAN QUALIFICATION 2013/14

Champion: Maccabi Tel-Aviv FC (second qualifying round)

Cup winner: Hapoel Ramat Gan FC (third qualifying round)
Maccabi Haifa FC (second qualifying round)
Hapoel Tel-Aviv FC (second qualifying round)

Top scorer	Eliran Atar (M. Tel-Aviv), 22 goals
Relegated clubs	Hapoel Ramat Gan FC, Maccabi Netanya FC
Promoted clubs	Maccabi Petach-Tikva FC, Hapoel Raanana FC
Cup final	Hapoel Ramat Gan FC 1-1 Hapoel Kiryat Shmona FC (aet; 4-2 on pens)

LIGAT HA'AL TEAM OF THE SEASON
(5-4-1)
Coach: Óscar Garcia (M. Tel-Aviv)

PLAYER OF THE SEASON
Eliran Atar
(Maccabi Tel-Aviv FC)

The attacking spearhead of Maccabi's Israeli title triumph, Atar scored 22 times to finish up as the Ligat Ha'al's top marksman. A crowd favourite at Bloomfield, his name was routinely chanted three times after every goal. His third season with the club was to be his last, however, as he left for France to join Ligue 1 side Stade de Reims.

NEWCOMER OF THE SEASON
Ofir Kriaf
(Beitar Jerusalem FC)

Although it was not the best of seasons for the capital club, Kriaf seized his chance as a first-team regular and was rewarded with a place in Guy Luzon's squad for the UEFA European Under-21 Championship on home soil. The midfielder proved his worth at the tournament, scoring the winning goal against England in the hosts' final game.

NATIONAL TEAM

Home Kit | Away Kit

INTERNATIONAL TOURNAMENT APPEARANCES
FIFA World Cup (1) 1970

TOP FIVE ALL-TIME CAPS
Arik Benado (94); **Yossi Benayoun** (93); Alon Harazi (88); Amir Shelache (85); Mordechay Shpiegler (84)

TOP FIVE ALL-TIME GOALS
Mordechay Shpiegler (33); **Yossi Benayoun** & Yehushua Feigenboim (24); Ronen Harazi (23); Nahum Stelmach (22)

Results 2012/13

15/08/12	Hungary	A	Budapest	1-1	Hemed (80)
07/09/12	Azerbaijan (WCQ)	A	Baku	1-1	Natcho (50)
11/09/12	Russia (WCQ)	H	Tel-Aviv	0-4	
12/10/12	Luxembourg (WCQ)	A	Luxembourg	6-0	Radi (4), Ben Basat (12), Hemed (27, 73, 90+1), Melikson (60)
16/10/12	Luxembourg (WCQ)	H	Tel-Aviv	3-0	Hemed (14, 48), Ben Basat (36)
14/11/12	Belarus	H	Jerusalem	1-2	Damari (19)
06/02/13	Finland	H	Netanya	2-1	Ben Basat (2), Hefaelov (90+3)
22/03/13	Portugal (WCQ)	H	Tel-Aviv	3-3	Hemed (24), Ben Basat (40), Gershon (70)
26/03/13	Northern Ireland (WCQ)	A	Belfast	2-0	Refaelov (78), Ben Basat (85)
02/06/13	Honduras	N	New York (USA)	2-0	Ezra (52), Abuhazira (76)

Appearances 2012/13

Coach: Eli Guttman	24/02/58		Hun	AZE	RUS	LUX	LUX	Blr	Fin	POR	NIR	Hon	Caps	Goals
Dudu Awat	17/10/77	Mallorca (ESP)	G	G	G	G	G	G		G	G		73	-
Yuval Shpungin	03/04/87	Omonia (CYP)	D36	D	D	D		D		D	D	D	24	-
Dan Mori	08/11/88	Bnei Yehuda /Vitesse (NED)	D		D		D	D	D				7	-
Eitan Tibi	16/11/87	M. Tel-Aviv	D	D	D	D55		D	D65	D	D	D	11	-
Rami Gershon	12/08/88	Standard Liège (BEL) /Celtic (SCO)	D						D	D	D	D	16	2
Avihai Yadin	26/10/86	M. Haifa	M85					s46					10	-
Bebras Natcho	18/02/88	Rubin (RUS)	M	M	M	M77	M	M77	M	M	M		26	1
Lior Refaelov	26/04/86	Club Brugge (BEL)	M46						s61	s73	s69	M75	22	5
Maor Melikson	30/10/84	Wisła Kraków (POL) /Valenciennes (FRA)	M88	M71		M	M81		M72	M73	M69	M64	13	3
Itay Shechter	22/02/87	Kaiserslautern (GER) /Swansea (WAL)	A67	A74	A46						A86	A58	18	3
Omer Damari	24/03/89	H. Tel-Aviv	A59	s67				M46	s71				10	3
Elad Gabai	15/11/85	H. Kiryat Shmona	s36				D	s77	D			s75	6	-
Gil Vermouth	05/08/85	Kaiserslautern (GER) /H. Tel-Aviv	s46		M	s74	s57 /71						21	-
Ben Sahar	10/08/89	Hertha (GER)	s59		s46								31	6
Tomer Hemed	02/05/87	Mallorca (ESP)	s67	A67		A	A	A67	A61	A63			14	9
Beram Kayal	02/05/88	Celtic (SCO)	s85					s46		M			24	1
Tal Ben Haim	31/03/82	unattached /QPR (ENG)	s88		D				D	D	D	D	73	1
Yoav Ziv	16/03/81	M. Tel-Aviv		D	D	s57	D						32	-
Gal Alberman	17/04/83	M. Tel-Aviv		M		M	M	M46	s46			s64	33	1
Hen Ezra	19/01/89	M. Haifa		s71	M		s71	s46				s46	5	1
Yossi Benayoun	05/05/80	West Ham (ENG) /Chelsea (ENG)		s74	M74					s81	s86	M46	93	24
Almog Cohen	01/09/88	Nürnberg (GER)			M46								13	-
Maharan Radi	01/07/82	M. Tel-Aviv			M	M	M57	M46	M46		M60		6	1
Eden Ben Basat	08/09/86	Brest (FRA) /Toulouse (FRA)			s46	A	A	A67	A71	A81	A		7	5

ISRAEL

Appearances 2012/13 (contd.)

			Hun	AZE	RUS	LUX	LUX	Blr	Fin	POR	NIR	Hon	Caps	Goals
Gal Shish	28/01/89	Waasland-Beveren (BEL)				D57		D	s86				3	-
Dekel Keinan	15/09/84	M. Haifa				s55	D		D				24	-
Nir Biton	30/10/91	Ashdod				s77							6	-
Shimon Abuhazira	10/10/86	H. Kiryat Shmona					s81	s67				s58	3	1
Eliran Atar	17/02/87	M. Tel-Aviv						s67	s72	s63			3	-
Ariel Harush	08/02/88	Beitar Jerusalem							G			G	4	-
Avi Rikan	10/09/88	Beitar Jerusalem							M86			s70	2	-
Shir Tzedek	22/08/89	H. Kiryat Shmona							s65				3	-
Shiran Yeiny	08/12/86	M. Tel-Aviv								M	M	M64	3	-
Eran Zahavi	25/07/87	M. Tel-Aviv									s60	M70	13	-
Elyaniv Barda	15/12/81	Genk (BEL)										s64	31	12

European club competitions 2012/13

HAPOEL KIRYAT SHMONA FC

Second qualifying round - MŠK Žilina (SVK)
A 0-1
Amos, Tzedek, Badash (Abed 77), Gabai, Hasarma, Gerzicich, Abuhazira, Tasevski (Gazal 82), Rochet, Solari (Mresat 90+1), Matović. Coach: Gili Landau (ISR)
H 2-0 *Leitner (71og), Abuhazira (78)*
Amos, Tzedek, Badash (Vahaba 86), Gabai, Hasarma, Gerzicich, Abuhazira, Tasevski (Gazal 60), Rochet (Abed 69), Solari, Matović. Coach: Gili Landau (ISR)

Third qualifying round - Neftçi PFK (AZE)
H 4-0 *Badash (42p), Abuhazira (52), Gerzicich (70, 76)*
Amos, Tzedek, Badash (Lencse 77), Gabai, Hasarma, Gerzicich, Abuhazira, Tasevski (Abed 64), Rochet, Solari (Gazal 20), Matović. Coach: Gili Landau (ISR)
A 2-2 *Badash (50), Lencse (90+1)*
Amos, Tzedek, Gazal, Badash (Lencse 65), Gabai, Hasarma, Gerzicich (Abed 57), Abuhazira, Tasevski (Elisha 79), Rochet, Matović. Coach: Gili Landau (ISR)

Play-offs - FC BATE Borisov (BLR)
A 0-2
Amos, Vahaba (Abed 53), Tzedek, Gazal (Badash 67), Gabai, Hasarma, Abuhazira, Tasevski, Rochet, Lencse (Levi 73), Matović. Coach: Gili Landau (ISR)
Red card: Matović 70

H 1-1 *Lencse (67)*
Amos, Tzedek, Gazal, Gabai, Hasarma, Abuhazira, Levi, Tasevski (Elisha 63), Rochet (Badash 55), Sallalich (Abed 61), Lencse. Coach: Gili Landau (ISR)

Group I
Match 1 - Athletic Club (ESP)
A 1-1 *Rochet (14)*
Amos, Tzedek, Gazal, Einbinder (Vahaba 90), Gabai, Hasarma, Abuhazira (Porokara 80), Tasevski, Rochet (Elisha 74), Lencse, Matović. Coach: Gili Landau (ISR)
Match 2 - Olympique Lyonnais (FRA)
H 3-4 *Abuhazira (7, 66p), Levi (51)*
Amos, Tzedek, Einbinder, Gabai, Elisha (Gazal 89), Hasarma (Cohen 46), Gerzicich, Abuhazira, Levi, Rochet, Lencse (Abed 46). Coach: Barak Bakhar (ISR)
Match 3 - AC Sparta Praha (CZE)
A 1-3 *Abuhazira (76)*
Amos, Cohen, Tzedek , Gazal (Abed 46), Einbinder (Elisha 46), Gabai, Gerzicich (Tasevski 77), Abuhazira, Rochet, Lencse, Matović. Coach: Barak Bakhar (ISR)
Match 4 - AC Sparta Praha (CZE)
H 1-1 *Tasevski (3)*
Amos, Cohen, Gazal (Abuhazira 61), Einbinder, Hasarma (Vahaba 58), Gerzicich, Levi, Tasevski, Sallalich, Lencse (Rochet 82), Matović. Coach: Barak Bakhar (ISR)
Match 5 - Athletic Club (ESP)
H 0-2
Amos, Vahaba, Tzedek, Abed, Einbinder, Gabai, Elisha, Levi, Porokara (Abuhazira 46), Tasevski (Mizrahi 57), Sallalich (Mresat 71). Coach: Barak Bakhar (ISR)
Match 6 - Olympique Lyonnais (FRA)
A 0-2
Amos, Vahaba, Tzedek, Abed (Mizrahi 62), Einbinder, Gabai, Abuhazira (Mresat 72), Levi, Tasevski (Gazal 63), Rochet, Sallalich. Coach: Barak Bakhar (ISR)

HAPOEL TEL-AVIV FC

Play-offs - F91 Dudelange (LUX)
A 3-1 *Caillet (4og), Ben Haim (19p), Cohen (26)*
Édel, Badir, Cohen, Ben Haim (Maman 80), Toama (Bruno Coutinho 63), Damari (Mare 46), Haimovich, Djemba-Djemba, Antebi, Igiebor, Pantsil. Coach: Nitzan Shirazi (ISR)
H 4-0 *Maman (68, 84), Mare (79), Toama (88)*
Édel, Shushan, Mare, Badir, Cohen (Maman 57), Ben Haim (Atadjanov 80), Damari, Djemba-Djemba, Antebi, Bruno Coutinho (Toama 57), Pantsil. Coach: Nitzan Shirazi (ISR)

Group B
Match 1 - Club Atlético de Madrid (ESP)
H 0-3
Édel, Shushan, Maman, Badir, Ben Haim, Vermouth (Cohen 75), Djemba-Djemba, Antebi, Bruno Coutinho (Toama 58), Pantsil, Tamuz (Mare 68). Coach: Nitzan Shirazi (ISR)
Match 2 - A Académica de Coimbra (POR)
A 1-1 *Damari (90+2)*
Édel, Badir, Cohen (Damari 60), Ben Haim (Toama 67), Vermouth, Haimovich, Djemba-Djemba, Antebi, Gordana (Maman 60), Pantsil, Tamuz. Coach: Yossi Abuksis (ISR)
Match 3 - FC Viktoria Plzeň (CZE)
H 1-2 *Maman (19)*
Édel, Maman, Danin, Badir, Ben Haim, Damari, Haimovich, Djemba-Djemba (Cohen 75), Gordana (Toama 59), Khutaba, Tamuz (Pantsil 69). Coach: Yossi Abuksis (ISR)
Red card: Khutaba 64

Match 4 - FC Viktoria Plzeň (CZE)
A 0-4
Édel, Shushan, Danin, Cohen (Maman 61), Toama, Djemba-Djemba, Antebi (Badir 46), Gordana (Mare 74), Pantsil, Petković, Tamuz. Coach: Yossi Abuksis (ISR)
Red card: Djemba-Djemba 41
Match 5 - Club Atlético de Madrid (ESP)
A 0-1
Édel, Shushan, Maman, Danin, Ben Haim, Vermouth (Toama 62), Damari, Haimovich, Gordana (Mare 77), Pantsil, Petković. Coach: Yossi Abuksis (ISR)
Match 6 - A Académica de Coimbra (POR)
H 2-0 *Mare (56), Maman (80)*
Édel, Shushan, Danin, Ben Haim, Vermouth (Maman 69), Toama (Lax 86), Haimovich, Izenstein, Khutaba, Petković, Tamuz (Mare 46). Coach: Yossi Abuksis (ISR)

BNEI YEHUDA TEL-AVIV FC

Second qualifying round - FC Shirak (ARM)
H 2-0 *Ndlovu (82), Galván (90+4)*
Aiyenugba, Gal, Ndlovu, Abu Zaid (Nahum 63), Ivaškevičius, Azuz, Marinković (Agayov 77), Galván, Hadad, Edri, Menashe (Mul 46). Coach: Dror Kashtan (ISR)
Red card: Hadad 45+1
A 1-0 *Menashe (31)*
Aiyenugba, Mori, Gal, Ndlovu, Abu Zaid, Bargig, Ivaškevičius, Marinković (Nash 87), Galván (Agayov 71), Edri, Menashe (Nahum 54). Coach: Dror Kashtan (ISR)

Third qualifying round - PAOK FC (GRE)
H 0-2
Aiyenugba, Mori, Gal, Ndlovu, Ivaškevičius, Azuz, Nahum (Agayov 66), Marinković, Galván (Levi 82), Edri, Menashe (Abu Zaid 46). Coach: Dror Kashtan (ISR)
A 1-4 *Marinković (7)*
Aiyenugba, Gal, Ndlovu, Abu Zaid, Ivaškevičius, Azuz, Marinković, Galván (Nahum 56), Hadad, Edri, Menashe. Coach: Dror Kashtan (ISR)
Red card: Menashe 50

MACCABI NETANYA FC

Second qualifying round - KuPS Kuopio (FIN)
H 1-2 *Shivhon (75)*
Cennamo, Pinas, Krupnik, Sabaa, I Shriki (Akel 70), Peretz, Tchalisher, Tamir (Sarhan 71), Pietrasiak, Manzur (Shivhon 46), Shitrit. Coach: Tal Banin (ISR)
A 1-0 *Sabaa (40)*
Cennamo, Pinas, Levi, Sabaa, El-Khatib, I Shriki (Tamir 74), Peretz (Akel 64), Shivhon, Tchalisher (Sarhan 85), Pietrasiak, Shitrit. Coach: Tal Banin (ISR)

FC ASHDOD
Coach: Yossi Mizrahi
1999 • Yud Alef (7,420) • tcashdod.com

2012
Date	Opponent		Score	Scorers
25/08	H. Ramat HaSharon	h	2-0	Abu Anzeh 2
01/09	Bnei Sakhnin	a	3-1	Revivo, Makriev 2
13/09	Beitar	h	2-1	Revivo, Makriev
22/09	M. Haifa	a	1-0	Revivo
29/09	M. Netanya	h	3-0	Abu Anzeh 2, Makriev
06/10	M. Tel-Aviv	a	1-2	Makriev
20/10	H. Kiryat Shmona	h	2-0	Makriev (p), Arčon
03/11	H. Beer Sheva	a	0-0	
10/11	H. Haifa	a	1-2	Abu Anzeh
24/11	H. Ramat Gan	h	1-0	Rosh
03/12	H. Tel-Aviv	h	1-2	Revivo
08/12	Bnei Yehuda	a	0-2	
12/12	H. Akko	h	2-0	Biton 2
15/12	H. Ramat HaSharon	a	0-1	
22/12	Bnei Sakhnin	h	1-2	Makriev
31/12	Beitar	a	1-1	Biton

2013
Date	Opponent		Score	Scorers
06/01	M. Haifa	h	1-4	Hatem Elhamid
12/01	M. Netanya	a	0-2	
19/01	M. Tel-Aviv	h	1-0	Lenkebe
26/01	H. Kiryat Shmona	a	0-0	
02/02	H. Beer Sheva	h	0-1	
09/02	H. Haifa	h	1-1	Šćepović
16/02	H. Akko	a	1-3	Šćepović
01/03	H. Ramat Gan	h	2-3	Makriev, Biton
02/03	H. Tel-Aviv	a	1-1	Šćepovi
11/03	Bnei Yehuda	h	2-1	Revivo (p), Šćepović
16/03	H. Akko	h	1-2	Makriev
01/04	Beitar	h	2-2	og (Dasa), Moshal
06/04	H. Beer Sheva	a	0-2	
13/04	H. Haifa	h	1-0	Sirushtan
20/04	M. Netanya	a	1-2	Abu Anzeh
27/04	Bnei Sakhnin	h	1-1	Maymon
04/05	H. Ramat Gan	a	2-1	Šćepović 2 (1p)

No	Name	Nat	DoB	Pos	Aps	(s)	Gls
15	Murad Abu Anzeh		06/11/86	A	27	(5)	6
21	Afik Ambiose	NGA	18/10/88	D	1		
17	Sandi Arčon	SVN	06/01/91	A	8	(13)	1
12	Amir Ben Shimon		14/12/93	M	15	(4)	
19	Tom Ben Zaken		29/10/94	D		(1)	
4	Nir Biton		30/10/91	M	30	(4)	4
8	Ben Butbul		22/05/90	M	14	(7)	
8	Rahamim Checkul		08/05/88	D	13	(2)	
25	Abed Hatem Elhamid		18/03/91	M	20	(2)	1
16	Nogen Hen		09/01/95	D		(1)	
14	Gadi Kinda		23/03/94	M	3	(2)	
11	Amir Lavie		08/08/89	M		(4)	
6	Paty Yeye Lenkebe	COD	02/02/82	D	26		1
7	Dimitar Makriev	BUL	07/01/84	A	18	(4)	9
1	Offir Marciano		07/10/89	G	32		
22	Roei Mashpati		23/11/92	G	1		
23	Shay Maymon		18/03/86	D	6	(1)	1
9	Nevo Mizrahi		26/07/87	A	1		
14	Benzion Moshal		13/07/93	M	7	(6)	1
9	Itzhak Nash		23/06/89	A	1	(9)	
12	Michael Ohana		04/10/95	M		(4)	
18	Juwon Oshaniwa	NGA	14/09/90	D	18	(1)	
12	William Owusu	GHA	01/09/91	M		(1)	
10	David Revivo		05/12/77	M	26	(4)	5
2	Israel Rosh		05/03/88	D	30		1
9	Stefan Šćepović	SRB	10/01/90	A	13		6
20	Micky Sirushtan		25/04/89	M	21	(5)	1
16	Adir Tobul		03/06/79	D		(3)	
11	Zion Tzemah		19/06/90	M	5	(11)	
21	Idan Tzion		24/05/88	D	1		
3	Ofer Werta		23/05/90	D	24		
16	Niv Zrihan		24/05/94	A	2	(8)	

BEITAR JERUSALEM FC

Coach: Eli Cohen
1939 • Teddy (21,600) • beitarfc.co.il
Major honours
Israeli League (6) 1987, 1993, 1997, 1998, 2007, 2008;
Israeli Cup (7) 1976, 1979, 1985, 1986, 1989, 2008, 2009

2012

25/08	H. Kiryat Shmona	a	2-3	*Rikan, Diamant*
01/09	H. Beer Sheva	h	1-1	*Dasa*
13/09	Ashdod	a	1-2	*Levi (p)*
22/09	H. Akko	h	0-1	
29/09	H. Ramat Gan	a	2-2	*Ben Shoshan, Levi*
21/10	Bnei Yehuda	a	2-1	*Ben Shoshan, Rikan*
29/10	H. Tel-Aviv	h	3-2	*Ben Shoshan, Azriel 2*
03/11	H. Ramat HaSharon	h	1-0	*Rikan*
10/11	Bnei Yehuda	a	1-1	*Rikan*
18/11	H. Haifa	h	3-0	*Azriel, Glavina, Škvorc*
26/11	M. Haifa	a	1-2	*Moyal*
01/12	M. Netanya	a	3-2	*Rikan 2, Levi*
10/12	M. Tel-Aviv	h	1-1	*Moyal*
16/12	H. Kiryat Shmona	h	2-2	*Rikan, Azriel*
23/12	H. Beer Sheva	a	0-0	
31/12	Ashdod	h	1-1	*Azriel*

2013

05/01	H. Akko	a	3-2	*Magrelashvili, Azriel, Kriaf*
13/01	H. Ramat Gan	h	3-2	*Levi, Glavina 2*
21/01	H. Tel-Aviv	a	2-0	*Azriel, Rikan*
26/01	Bnei Yehuda	h	0-1	
03/02	H. Ramat HaSharon	a	0-1	
10/02	Bnei Sakhnin	h	2-2	*Levi, Cohen*
17/02	H. Haifa	a	0-3	
24/02	M. Haifa	a	1-4	*og (Pylyavskiy)*
03/03	M. Netanya	a	1-1	*Sadayev*
10/03	M. Tel-Aviv	a	0-5	
17/03	H. Ramat Gan	h	1-2	*Rikan*
01/04	Ashdod	a	2-2	*Ben Shoshan 2*
08/04	H. Akko	a	2-2	*Ben Shoshan, Azriel (p)*
13/04	H. Beer Sheva	h	1-0	*Rikan*
20/04	H. Haifa	a	1-3	*Ben Shoshan*
27/04	M. Netanya	h	1-3	*Rikan*
04/05	Bnei Sakhnin	a	0-0	

No	Name	Nat	DoB	Pos	Aps	(s)	Gls
20	Offir Amram		19/06/86	M		(1)	
14	Chen Azriel		26/06/88	A	24	(4)	8
7	Amit Ben Shoshan		23/05/85	A	22		7
5	Matan Brashi		06/05/88	D	32		
26	Stephen Cohen	FRA	27/02/86	M	7	(11)	1
2	Eli Dasa		03/12/92	D	13	(12)	1
10	Liron Diamant		04/04/90	A		(2)	1
17	Zahi Elihen		03/04/91	A	3	(6)	
23	Darío Fernández	ARG	24/09/78	M	28		
19	Dominik Glavina	CRO	06/12/92	A	9	(17)	3
15	Shay Hadad		02/07/87	D	22	(4)	
1	Ariel Harush		08/02/88	G	32		
44	Dzhabrail Kadiyev	RUS	21/01/94	D		(1)	
6	Tal Kahila		26/06/92	D	2	(1)	
12	Shmoel Kozokin		23/07/87	D		(3)	
24	Ofir Kriaf		17/03/91	A	25	(1)	1
10	Eran Levi		04/08/85	M	18	(7)	5
3	Haim Magrelashvili		04/07/82	D	30	(1)	1
28	Barak Moshe		19/03/91	M	3	(3)	
21	Kobi Moyal		12/06/87	M	24	(4)	2
27	Omer Nachmani		29/10/93	M	2	(6)	
26	Harel Polak		01/02/92	A		(3)	
18	Avi Rikan		10/09/88	D	30	(1)	11
13	Zaur Sadayev	RUS	06/11/89	A	4	(3)	1
22	Ohad Saydof		01/10/87	G	1		
25	Dino Škvorc	CRO	02/02/90	D	32		1

BNEI SAKHNIN FC

Coach: Shlomi Dora; (11/03/13) Marco Balbul
1993 • Doha (6,000) • skhnin.com
Major honours
Israeli Cup (1) 2004

2012

25/08	H. Beer Sheva	a	0-0	
01/09	Ashdod	h	1-3	*Kalebat*
15/09	H. Akko	a	1-5	*Viezman*
22/09	H. Ramat Gan	h	1-3	*O Zbedat*
29/09	H. Tel-Aviv	a	0-1	
06/10	Bnei Yehuda	h	2-2	*Bello, Abu Salah*
20/10	H. Ramat HaSharon	a	3-1	*H Ganaym, Abu Salah, Davidov*
03/11	H. Haifa	h	2-0	*Kasum, H Ganaym*
10/11	Beitar	h	1-1	*Bello*
19/11	M. Haifa	a	0-0	
24/11	M. Netanya	h	0-0	
01/12	M. Tel-Aviv	a	0-4	
10/12	H. Kiryat Shmona	h	1-3	*Davidov*
15/12	H. Beer Sheva	h	3-2	*Harosh, Kasum, H Ganaym*
22/12	Ashdod	a	2-1	*Halaula, Kasum*
29/12	H. Akko	h	2-1	*Bello, Osman*

2013

05/01	H. Ramat Gan	a	1-2	*Harosh*
12/01	H. Tel-Aviv	h	0-3	
19/01	Bnei Yehuda	a	0-0	
26/01	H. Ramat HaSharon	h	0-4	
02/02	H. Haifa	a	3-1	*Abu Salah, Kasum, Bello*
10/02	Beitar	a	2-2	*Kalebat 2*
16/02	M. Haifa	h	0-1	
24/02	M. Netanya	a	0-0	
02/03	M. Tel-Aviv	h	0-3	
09/03	H. Kiryat Shmona	a	0-0	
16/03	H. Beer Sheva	a	2-1	*Kalebat 2*
01/04	H. Haifa	h	0-0	
06/04	M. Netanya	a	1-1	*Mbemba*
13/04	H. Akko	a	1-1	*Bello*
23/04	H. Ramat Gan	h	1-0	*Bello*
27/04	Ashdod	a	1-1	*Bello*
04/05	Beitar	h	0-0	

No	Name	Nat	DoB	Pos	Aps	(s)	Gls
11	Mahmoud Abbas		29/07/88	M	5	(14)	
8	Allah Abu Salah		25/06/87	D	24	(3)	3
27	Siaf Alhushala		15/08/92	M		(1)	
19	Yero Bello	NGA	11/11/87	A	22	(2)	7
6	Joël Damahou	CIV	28/01/87	M	2		
9	Aleksandar Davidov	SRB	07/10/83	M	21	(1)	2
4	Arafat Djako	TOG	10/11/88	A	2	(7)	
12	Bassem Ganaym		07/10/78	D	8	(6)	
17	Hamed Ganaym		08/07/87	M	29	(3)	3
15	Haled Halaula		16/12/82	M	30		1
24	Wahil Harbawi		09/07/90	A		(1)	
23	Shimon Harosh		20/02/87	D	19		2
6	Maxime Josse	FRA	21/03/87	D	16	(1)	
10	Mohamed Kalebat		15/06/90	A	27	(4)	5
22	Mahmoud Kandil		11/08/88	G	33		
21	Ahmed Kasum		25/01/85	M	25	(7)	4
6	Imoro Lukman	GHA	04/10/84	M	7	(1)	
3	Pieter Mbemba	BEL	23/07/88	D	13	(5)	1
18	Ali Osman		08/02/87	D	19	(6)	1
25	Hasib Rokon		11/02/91	A		(2)	
24	Dia Sabaa		18/11/92	M	5	(5)	
23	Adir Tobul		03/06/79	D	12		
20	Idan Viezman		20/04/85	M	28	(1)	1
7	Mohamed Zbedat		15/11/91	D	16	(5)	
13	Obada Zbedat		30/07/90	A		(8)	1

BNEI YEHUDA TEL-AVIV FC

Coach: Dror Kashtan
1936 • Bloomfield (14,413) • bneiyehuda.com
Major honours
Israeli League (1) 1990;
Israeli Cup (2)1968, 1981

2012

25/08	H. Akko	a	1-1	*Menashe*
01/09	H. Ramat Gan	h	1-0	*Galván*
15/09	H. Tel-Aviv	a	0-2	
22/09	H. Haifa	h	3-1	*Menashe, Ivaškevičius, Marinković*
29/09	H. Ramat HaSharon	h	2-2	*Barouch, og (Lavie)*
06/10	Bnei Sakhnin	a	2-2	*og (Abu Salah), Galván*
21/10	Beitar	h	1-2	*Galván*
05/11	M. Haifa	a	1-1	*Ivaškevičius*
10/11	M. Netanya	h	3-0	*Agayov, Menashe, Rali*
17/11	M. Tel-Aviv	a	1-0	*Marinković*
25/11	H. Kiryat Shmona	h	0-2	
01/12	H. Beer Sheva	a	0-1	
08/12	Ashdod	h	2-0	*Galván 2 (1p)*
16/12	H. Akko	h	2-1	*Edri, Falach*
22/12	H. Ramat Gan	a	0-1	
29/12	H. Tel-Aviv	h	2-1	*Hrepka, Falach*

2013

05/01	H. Haifa	a	1-2	*Galván (p)*
12/01	H. Ramat HaSharon	a	1-2	*Hrepka*
19/01	Bnei Sakhnin	h	0-0	
26/01	Beitar	a	1-0	*Agayov*
03/02	M. Haifa	h	2-0	*Galván, Zamir*
09/02	M. Netanya	a	5-3	*Galván 3, Rali, Hrepka*
18/02	M. Tel-Aviv	h	2-3	*Menashe, Rali*
23/02	H. Kiryat Shmona	a	0-2	
02/03	H. Beer Sheva	h	1-0	*Marinković*
11/03	Ashdod	a	1-2	*Galván (p)*
17/03	M. Haifa	a	0-1	
30/03	H. Kiryat Shmona	h	1-1	*Marinković*
02/04	M. Tel-Aviv	a	1-2	*Marinković*
06/04	H. Ramat HaSharon	a	3-0	*Hrepka, Marinković, Dahan*
13/04	M. Tel-Aviv	h	2-2	*Hrepka, Itzhak*
21/04	M. Haifa	h	2-1	*Zamir, Hrepka*
27/04	H. Kiryat Shmona	a	1-0	*Hrepka*
06/05	H. Tel-Aviv	h	0-1	
11/05	H. Ramat HaSharon	h	2-1	*Marinković, Galván*
20/05	M. Tel-Aviv	a	3-0	*Hrepka, Edri, Agayov*

No	Name	Nat	DoB	Pos	Aps	(s)	Gls
10	Hassan Abu Zaid		04/02/91	M	3		
9	Amir Agayov		04/01/84	M	11	(18)	3
1	Bamidele Aiyenugba	NGA	20/11/83	G	36		
17	Itzhak Azuz		30/11/85	D	31		
12	Lior Bargig		07/08/91	D	3		
4	Orr Barouch		29/11/91	A	10	(8)	1
27	Roslan Barski		03/01/92	A	2	(3)	
25	Yagil Biton		16/03/92	D	3		
2	Gal Cohen		14/08/82	D	36		
11	Refael Dahan		28/09/89	M	14		1
23	Kfir Edri		12/10/76	M	26	(4)	2
5	Sari Falach		27/03/91	D	16		2
3	Stav Finish		26/03/92	M	11	(3)	
20	Pedro Galván	ARG	18/08/85	M	27	(8)	12
21	Aviv Hadad		02/04/84	D	18	(5)	
9	Ádám Hrepka	HUN	15/04/87	A	20	(9)	8
10	Gil Itzhak		29/06/93	A	7	(7)	1
16	Kęstutis Ivaškevičius	LTU	17/04/85	M	31		2
19	Nenad Marinković	SRB	28/09/88	A	28	(7)	7
26	Shalev Menashe		23/05/82	M	23	(8)	4
22	Nadav Muniss		11/10/92	D	1	(1)	
9	Nir Nahum		09/03/83	M	3	(4)	
11	Itzhak Nash		23/06/89	A		(2)	
7	Oz Rali		22/12/87	D	31	(1)	3
15	Nes Zamir		31/10/90	M	5	(14)	2

HAPOEL AKKO FC

Coach: Shimon Hadari; (01/02/13) Yuval Naim
1946 • Akko Toto (5,000) • no website

2012

Date	Opponent	H/A	Score	Scorers
25/08	Bnei Yehuda	h	1-1	Marinković
01/09	H. Ramat HaSharon	a	1-3	Kadusi
15/09	Bnei Sakhnin	h	5-1	Kahlon, Kadusi 3, Léo
22/09	Boitar	a	1-0	Taga
29/09	M. Haifa	a	1-3	
06/10	M. Netanya	a	3-1	Kadusi, Shabtay, David Gomes
20/10	M. Tel-Aviv	h	0-2	
03/11	H. Kiryat Shmona	a	0-1	
10/11	H. Beer Sheva	h	2-2	Kadusi 2 (1p)
24/11	H. Haifa	a	0-0	
01/12	H. Ramat Gan	h	0-3	
09/12	H. Tel-Aviv	a	0-0	
12/12	Ashdod	a	0-2	
16/12	Bnei Yehuda	a	1-2	Kadusi
22/12	H. Ramat HaSharon	h	0-2	
29/12	Bnei Sakhnin	a	1-2	Kahlon

2013

Date	Opponent	H/A	Score	Scorers
05/01	Beitar	h	2-3	Marinković, Mishaelov
12/01	M. Haifa	a	1-3	Abu Raya
19/01	M. Netanya	h	4-4	Kadusi 2, Kahlon, Zidane
26/01	M. Tel-Aviv	a	0-4	
02/02	H. Kiryat Shmona	h	1-1	Kadusi
09/02	H. Beer Sheva	a	0-0	
16/02	Ashdod	h	3-1	Marinković, Dayan, Arsenijević
23/02	H. Haifa	h	1-3	Jovanović
02/03	H. Ramat Gan	a	2-1	Dayan, Ben Dayan
09/03	H. Tel-Aviv	h	0-0	
16/03	Ashdod	a	2-1	Kadusi, Kahlon
30/03	M. Netanya	h	2-0	Marinković 2 (1p)
08/04	Beitar	a	2-2	Shabtay 2
13/04	Bnei Sakhnin	h	1-1	Dayan
20/04	H. Beer Sheva	h	0-0	
27/04	H. Ramat Gan	h	2-1	Dayan, Kadusi
04/05	H. Haifa	a	1-1	Kadusi

No	Name	Nat	DoB	Pos	Aps	(s)	Gls
17	Maharan Abu-Raya		22/01/83	M	7	(2)	1
10	Nemanja Arsenijević	SRB	29/03/86	A	1	(8)	1
19	Dedi Ben Dayan		22/11/78	D	24	(3)	1
17	Sagiv Cohen		20/09/87	D	12	(7)	
18	David Gomes	BRA	05/09/88	A	9	(6)	1
8	Guy Dayan		08/08/86	A	20	(8)	4
25	Dimaku Fidelis	NGA	22/04/89	D	9	(3)	
1	Dudu Goresh		01/02/80	G	33		
6	Edi Gotlib		16/08/92	D	24	(4)	
21	Branislav Jovanović	SRB	21/09/85	M	12		1
11	Ohad Kadusi		24/09/85	A	28	(4)	14
16	Tamir Kahlon		29/08/87	M	28	(1)	4
13	Lohab Kayal		03/05/88	D	3	(1)	
3	Srdja Knežević	SRB	15/04/85	D	4	(5)	
10	Léo	BRA	29/11/89	A	3	(7)	1
15	Roee Levi		04/09/87	D	4	(6)	
21	Imoro Lukman	GHA	04/10/84	M	16		
3	Din Maimoni		04/05/90	D	1	(2)	
20	Nebojša Marinković	SRB	19/06/86	M	26	(3)	5
24	Snir Mishan		13/11/88	D	24		
5	Moshe Mishaelov		14/09/83	M	27		1
7	Yuval Shabtay		18/12/86	M	25	(6)	3
15	Yuval Shawat		21/05/89	M	1	(5)	
14	Amaya Taga		04/02/85	M	21	(6)	1
23	Ammar Zidane		05/04/92	A	1	(10)	1

HAPOEL BEER SHEVA FC

Coach: Elisha Levi
1949 • Artur Vasermil (13,000) • hapoelb7.co.il
Major honours
Israeli League (2) 1975, 1976;
Israeli Cup (1) 1997

2012

Date	Opponent	H/A	Score	Scorers
25/08	Bnei Sakhnin	h	0-0	
01/09	Beitar	a	1-1	Swissa
15/09	M. Haifa	h	1-1	Swissa (p)
22/09	M. Netanya	a	1-2	Falczuk
01/10	M. Tel-Aviv	h	3-1	Naser, Marković, Njovu
20/10	M. Haifa	a	0-0	
29/10	H. Kiryat Shmona	h	1-1	Swissa
03/11	Ashdod	h	0-0	
10/11	H. Akko	a	2-2	Kehat, Swissa (p)
26/11	H. Tel-Aviv	a	1-4	Swissa
01/12	Bnei Yehuda	h	1-0	Swissa
04/12	H. Ramat Gan	h	3-2	Swissa 2 (1p), Baruchyan
08/12	H. Ramat HaSharon	a	1-0	Gavish
15/12	Bnei Sakhnin	a	2-3	Gabay 2
23/12	Beitar	h	0-0	
29/12	M. Haifa	a	0-2	

2013

Date	Opponent	H/A	Score	Scorers
05/01	M. Netanya	h	1-3	Zino
14/01	M. Tel-Aviv	a	0-5	
19/01	H. Kiryat Shmona	h	1-0	William
27/01	H. Haifa	h	2-1	Gabay, Gazal (p)
02/02	Ashdod	a	1-0	Davidaze
09/02	H. Akko	h	0-0	
16/02	H. Ramat Gan	a	0-3	
23/02	H. Tel-Aviv	h	1-2	Gabay
02/03	Bnei Yehuda	a	0-1	
09/03	H. Ramat HaSharon	a	0-1	
16/03	Bnei Sakhnin	h	1-2	Falczuk
30/03	H. Ramat Gan	a	1-1	Gabay
06/04	Ashdod	h	2-0	Gabay (p), Swissa
13/04	Beitar	a	0-1	
20/04	H. Akko	a	0-0	
27/04	H. Haifa	h	2-0	Falczuk, Gabay
04/05	M. Netanya	a	3-0	Gabay 2, Naser

No	Name	Nat	DoB	Pos	Aps	(s)	Gls
28	Riyon Aduleye	USA	28/04/87	D	1		
16	Feras Awad		09/11/91	M	1	(3)	
8	Aviram Baruchyan		20/03/85	M	20	(6)	1
1	Galil Ben Senan		27/06/82	G	6		
13	Ofir Davidaze		05/05/91	D	31		1
12	Austin Ejide	NGA	08/04/84	G	27		
27	Ido Exbrad		16/12/88	A	6	(15)	
18	Nicolás Falczuk	ARG	16/11/86	A	19	(5)	3
11	Dovev Gabay		01/04/87	A	28	(4)	9
26	Oded Gavish		23/03/89	D	30		1
20	Ravid Gazal		23/06/89	D	9	(3)	1
14	Avyatar Ilouz		04/11/83	M	19	(1)	
21	Roi Kehat		12/05/92	A	7	(15)	1
5	Bojan Marković	BIH	12/11/85	D	24		1
7	Siraj Naser		02/09/90	M	17	(13)	2
8	William Njovu	ZAM	04/03/87	M	5	(3)	1
22	Patrick Osiako	KEN	15/11/86	M	27	(1)	
17	Dia Sabaa		18/11/92	M	1	(14)	
4	Klimi Saban		17/02/80	D	6	(3)	
9	Tomer Swissa		21/12/80	A	25	(8)	9
20	Yonatan Uzan		11/02/93	A		(1)	
23	Ben Wahaba		27/03/92	D	10	(1)	
25	William	BRA	07/02/85	D	28		1
15	Lotem Zino		16/03/92	M	6	(4)	1

HAPOEL HAIFA FC

Coach: Nir Klinger
1924 • Kiriat Eliezer (17,000) • hapoel-haifa.org.il
Major honours
Israeli League (1) 1999;
Israeli Cup (3) 1963, 1966, 1974

2012

Date	Opponent	H/A	Score	Scorers
25/08	M. Netanya	h	0-0	
03/09	H. Tel-Aviv	a	0-2	
15/09	M. Tel-Aviv	h	1-3	Avidor (p)
22/09	Bnei Yehuda	a	1-3	Gluščević
29/10	H. Kiryat Shmona	h	1-1	Al Lala
06/10	H. Ramat HaSharon	a	0-2	
20/10	H. Beer Sheva	h	0-0	
03/11	Bnei Sakhnin	a	0-2	
10/11	Ashdod	h	2-1	Stoller, Gluščević
18/11	Beitar	a	0-3	
24/11	H. Akko	h	0-0	
02/12	M. Haifa	a	0-3	
08/12	H. Ramat Gan	h	1-1	Al Lala (p)
15/12	M. Netanya	a	0-0	
22/12	H. Tel-Aviv	h	2-2	Tzarfati 2 (2p)
30/12	M. Tel-Aviv	a	2-6	Avidor, Abukarat

2013

Date	Opponent	H/A	Score	Scorers
05/01	Bnei Yehuda	h	2-1	Gluščević, Avidor
12/01	H. Kiryat Shmona	a	1-1	Abukarat
19/01	H. Ramat HaSharon	h	3-0	Gluščević, Al Lala, Tzarfati (p)
27/01	H. Beer Sheva	a	1-2	Al Lala
02/02	Bnei Sakhnin	h	1-3	Brković
09/02	Ashdod	a	1-1	Cohen
17/02	Beitar	h	3-0	Gluščević 2, og (Brashi)
23/02	H. Akko	a	3-1	og (Cohen), Gluščević, og (Knežević)
04/03	M. Haifa	a	1-1	Abukarat
09/03	H. Ramat Gan	a	2-1	Cohen, Nikolić
16/03	M. Netanya	a	3-0	Al Lala, Avidor 2
01/04	Bnei Sakhnin	a	0-0	
06/04	H. Ramat Gan	h	1-0	Al Lala
13/04	Ashdod	h	0-1	
20/04	Boitar	h	4-1	Gluščević, Arel, Abukarat
27/04	H. Beer Sheva	a	0-2	
04/05	H. Akko	h	1-1	Al Lala

No	Name	Nat	DoB	Pos	Aps	(s)	Gls
20	Ran Abukarat		14/12/88	M	31		4
14	Maaran Al Lala		07/03/82	A	16	(13)	7
22	Gad Amos		24/12/88	G	1		
18	Gal Arel		09/07/84	M	30	(2)	1
27	Yuval Avidor		19/10/86	A	29	(3)	5
19	Ahad Azam		14/01/92	D	23	(7)	
17	Shlomi Azulay		30/03/90	M	1	(3)	
2	Dušan Brković	SRB	20/01/89	D	29	(1)	1
4	Liran Cohen		04/02/83	M	7	(9)	2
7	Stefan Denković	MNE	16/06/91	A	13	(10)	
26	Yossi Dora		25/08/81	M	26	(2)	
15	Eli Elbaz		21/01/92	A		(8)	
9	Vladimir Gluščević	MNE	20/10/79	A	19	(8)	8
1	Tvrtko Kale	CRO	05/06/74	G	32		
10	Hiasham Kiwan		17/05/87	M	5	(9)	
24	Guy Lipka		03/04/91	D	4		
11	Danilo Nikolić	SRB	29/07/83	D	20		1
13	Touvarno Pinas	SUR	25/11/85	D	15		
23	Ilan Rankevich		01/05/91	M	1	(6)	
21	Oshri Roash		25/07/88	D	22	(2)	
16	Kenneth Saief		17/12/93	M		(3)	
6	Adi Sheleg		06/03/87	D	4		
23	Fabian Stoller	SUI	31/03/88	M	8	(1)	1
13	Eyal Tratzki		13/09/77	D	9		
8	Guy Tzarfati		28/04/79	M	18	(9)	3

HAPOEL IRONI NIR RAMAT HASHARON FC

**Coach: Nissan Yehezkel; (04/09/12) Beni Tabak &
Meni Koretski; (12/01/13) Beni Tabak**
1995 • Yaakov Grundman (4,200) • rhfc.co.il

2012

25/08	Ashdod	a	0-2	
03/09	H. Akko	h	3-1	Itzhak, Kirovski, Lipenia
15/09	H. Ramat Gan	a	1-1	Baldut
23/09	H. Tel-Aviv	h	1-0	Fernández
29/09	Bnei Yehuda	a	2-2	Lavie, Ostaynd
06/10	H. Haifa	h	2-0	Musa, Baldut
20/10	Bnei Sakhnin	h	1-3	Abutbul
03/11	Beitar	a	0-1	
10/11	M. Haifa	h	1-1	Baldut (p)
17/11	M. Netanya	a	2-1	Itzhak, Fernández
24/11	M. Tel-Aviv	a	3-4	Itzhak 2, Baldut
01/12	H. Kiryat Shmona	a	0-2	
08/12	H. Beer Sheva	h	0-1	
15/12	Ashdod	h	1-0	Itzhak
22/12	H. Akko	a	2-0	Abutbul, Taka
29/12	H. Ramat Gan	h	1-0	Menashrov

2013

05/01	H. Tel-Aviv	a	0-1	
12/01	Bnei Yehuda	h	2-1	Nusbaum, Taka
19/01	H. Haifa	a	0-3	
26/01	Bnei Sakhnin	a	4-0	Fortune, Fernández (p), Taka, Ben Shabat
03/02	Beitar	h	1-0	Taka
09/02	M. Haifa	a	0-4	
16/02	M. Netanya	h	0-0	
23/02	M. Tel-Aviv	h	0-1	
02/03	H. Kiryat Shmona	h	0-1	
09/03	H. Beer Sheva	a	1-0	Abutbul
16/03	M. Tel-Aviv	h	0-1	
30/03	H. Tel-Aviv	h	0-1	
02/04	M. Haifa	a	0-6	
06/04	Bnei Yehuda	h	0-3	
13/04	H. Kiryat Shmona	a	0-1	
22/04	M. Tel-Aviv	a	0-2	
28/04	H. Haifa	a	0-2	
05/05	M. Haifa	h	2-1	Taka, Abutbul
11/05	Bnei Yehuda	a	1-2	Zaydan
18/05	H. Kiryat Shmona	h	0-1	

No	Name	Nat	DoB	Pos	Aps	(s)	Gls
27	Moshe Abutbul		11/08/84	D	32		4
31	Marko Andjelković	SRB	12/10/84	M	14	(1)	
8	Asi Baldut		21/10/81	M	16	(5)	4
17	Gal Barel		15/06/90	M	3	(5)	
2	Asael Ben Shabat		09/05/88	D	25	(4)	1
25	Daniel Borhel		14/06/91	D	1	(3)	
10	Cadu	BRA	23/04/82	A	3		
10	Barukh Dego		26/03/81	M	7	(6)	
11	Shalom Edri		07/04/94	M		(1)	
26	Itai Elkaslasi		15/06/88	M	2		
9	Adrián Fernández	ARG	28/11/80	M	22	(4)	3
11	Udo Fortune	NGA	02/02/88	A	6	(5)	1
26	Meir Gabay		03/07/89	D	5	(2)	
55	Hael Heshan		13/03/89	M		(4)	
10	Hugo López	ESP	15/05/88	M	8	(5)	
12	Ran Itzhak		09/10/81	A	11	(6)	5
99	Orian Jakov		26/09/92	M		(3)	
15	Liran Katzav		29/12/89	D	7	(3)	
11	Hristijan Kirovski	MKD	12/10/85	A	3	(2)	1
5	Yaniv Lavie		09/09/77	D	30	(2)	1
13	Roei Leybovich		18/07/83	G	20		
24	Savity Lipenia	COD	17/04/79	D	23	(2)	1
99	Sun Menachem		07/09/93	D	1	(1)	
21	Tom Menashrov		15/04/87	M	23	(5)	1
55	Yordan Miliev	BUL	04/10/87	D	9		
77	Kobi Musa		18/04/82	D	33		1
23	Qasim Najar		03/03/92	M	3	(4)	
22	Gal Nir		30/03/83	G	13		
6	Amir Nusbaum		09/10/80	D	34		1
11	Itay Oren		31/03/92	M		(1)	
16	Or Ostaynd		18/12/87	M	12	(17)	1
22	Ben Rahav		29/04/89	G	3	(1)	
9	Ben Reichert		04/03/94	A		(1)	
7	Efraim Taka		14/04/89	A	24	(10)	5
19	Fadi Zaydan		02/06/93	A	3	(4)	1

HAPOEL KIRYAT SHMONA FC

Coach: Gili Landau; (03/10/12) Barak Bakhar
2000 • Municipal (5,300) • iturank8.co.il
Major honours
Israeli League (1) 2012

2012

25/08	Beitar	h	3-2	Badash, Lencse, Hasarma
01/09	M. Haifa	a	3-1	Tasevski, Lencse (p), Abed
15/09	M. Netanya	h	0-1	
24/09	M. Tel-Aviv	a	0-4	
29/09	H. Haifa	a	1-1	Gerzicich
20/10	Ashdod	a	0-2	
29/10	H. Beer Sheva	h	1-1	Abuhazira (p)
03/11	H. Akko	h	1-0	Sallalich
11/11	H. Ramat Gan	a	1-1	Tzedek
17/11	H. Tel-Aviv	h	0-1	
25/11	Bnei Yehuda	a	2-0	Mizrahi, Abuhazira
01/12	H. Ramat HaSharon	h	2-0	Abuhazira 2
10/12	Bnei Sakhnin	a	3-1	Abuhazira 2, Cohen
16/12	Beitar	a	2-2	Sallalich, Mizrahi
24/12	M. Haifa	h	0-0	
29/12	M. Netanya	a	4-3	Abuhazira 2, Sallalich 2 (1p)

2013

07/01	M. Tel-Aviv	h	0-0	
12/01	H. Haifa	h	1-1	og (Denković)
19/01	H. Beer Sheva	a	0-1	
26/01	Ashdod	h	0-0	
02/02	H. Akko	a	1-1	Matović
09/02	H. Ramat Gan	h	3-1	Hasarma, Tasevski, Sallalich
16/02	H. Tel-Aviv	a	1-1	Abed
23/02	Bnei Yehuda	h	2-0	Einbinder 2 (1p)
02/03	H. Ramat HaSharon	h	1-0	Matović
09/03	Bnei Sakhnin	h	2-0	Abed, Osei
16/03	H. Tel-Aviv	h	0-1	
30/03	Bnei Yehuda	h	1-1	Tzedek
03/04	M. Tel-Aviv	h	1-3	Abuhazira (p)
06/04	M. Haifa	a	2-3	Rochet, Tzedek
13/04	H. Ramat HaSharon	h	1-0	Osei
20/04	M. Tel-Aviv	a	4-1	Abuhazira 4
27/04	Bnei Yehuda	h	0-1	
04/05	M. Tel-Aviv	a	0-1	
11/05	M. Haifa	h	1-2	Abuhazira
18/05	H. Ramat HaSharon	a	1-0	Abuhazira

No	Name	Nat	DoB	Pos	Aps	(s)	Gls
7	Ahmed Abed		30/03/90	M	16	(15)	3
16	Naor Abudi		17/07/93	M	1	(1)	
19	Shimon Abuhazira		10/10/86	A	29	(1)	15
13	Dani Amos		02/02/87	G	32		
10	Barak Badash		30/08/82	A	1		1
12	Beni Ben Zaken		18/10/82	M		(1)	
2	Itzhak Cohen		22/04/83	D	14	(2)	1
11	Dan Einbinder		16/02/89	M	28	(1)	2
16	Adi Elisha		28/01/90	M	1	(4)	
13	Elad Gabai		15/11/85	D	31	(2)	
6	Ravid Gazal		09/06/82	M	5	(8)	
18	Bryan Gerzicich	USA	20/03/84	M	25	(3)	1
17	Salah Hasarma		24/02/74	D	22		2
29	László Lencse	HUN	02/07/88	A	10		2
20	Lior Levi		26/10/87	D	14	(8)	
2	Ehud Maaravi		24/08/84	D		(3)	
81	Dušan Matović	SRB	08/07/83	D	29		2
9	Ofir Mizrahi		04/12/93	M	9	(6)	2
1	Wael Mresat		06/05/92	M	1	(16)	
25	Itamar Nitzan		19/06/87	G	4		
25	Mawuli Osei	GHA	02/10/89	A	12	(2)	2
21	Roni Porokara	FIN	12/12/83	M	1	(2)	
23	Adrian Rochet		26/05/87	M	27	(7)	1
8	Kenneth Saief		17/12/93	M		(2)	
10	Sintayehu Sallalich		09/06/91	M	15	(14)	5
24	David Solari	ARG	21/03/86	M	2	(5)	
22	Darko Tasevski	MKD	20/05/84	M	31	(2)	2
5	Shir Tzedek		22/08/89	D	34		4
4	Ben Vahaba		27/03/92	D	2	(1)	

HAPOEL RAMAT GAN FC

Coach: Fredi David; (28/11/12) Eli Cohen
1927 • Winter (4,000) • hapoelrg.co.il
Major honours
Israeli League (1) 1964;
Israeli Cup (2) 2003, 2013

2012

26/08	H. Tel-Aviv	h	0-1	
01/09	Bnei Yehuda	a	0-1	
15/09	H. Ramat HaSharon	h	1-1	Manga
22/09	Bnei Sakhnin	a	3-1	Ifrah, Manga, Zaguri
29/09	Beitar	h	2-2	Manga, Zaguri
06/10	M. Haifa	a	0-2	
20/10	M. Netanya	h	1-1	Manga
03/11	M. Tel-Aviv	a	1-3	og (Tibi)
11/11	H. Kiryat Shmona	h	1-1	Burgič
24/11	Ashdod	h	0-1	
01/12	H. Akko	a	3-0	Manga 3
04/12	H. Beer Sheva	a	2-3	Arkhipov, Onanga Itoua
08/12	H. Haifa	h	1-1	Zaguri
15/12	H. Tel-Aviv	a	2-2	Arkhipov, Zaguri (p)
22/12	Bnei Yehuda	h	1-0	Arkhipov
29/12	H. Ramat HaSharon	a	0-1	

2013

05/01	Bnei Sakhnin	h	2-1	og (Bello), Onanga Itoua
13/01	Beitar	a	2-3	Manga, Hemo
20/01	M. Haifa	h	0-3	
26/01	M. Netanya	a	1-1	Manga
02/02	M. Tel-Aviv	h	0-0	
09/02	H. Kiryat Shmona	a	1-3	Manga
16/02	H. Beer Sheva	h	3-0	Onanga Itoua, Zaguri, Hemo
23/02	Ashdod	a	3-2	Zaguri, Zandberg, Buksenbaum
02/03	H. Akko	h	1-2	Goga (p)
09/03	H. Haifa	a	1-2	Itzhak
17/03	Beitar	a	2-1	Zandberg, Zaguri
30/03	H. Beer Sheva	h	1-1	Itzhak
06/04	H. Haifa	a	0-1	
13/04	M. Netanya	h	0-0	
23/04	Bnei Sakhnin	a	0-1	
27/04	H. Akko	a	1-2	Itzhak
04/05	Ashdod	h	1-2	og (Biton)

No	Name	Nat	DoB	Pos	Aps	(s)	Gls
11	Anton Arkhipov	RUS	04/11/85	A	16	(5)	3
1	Itai Arkin		07/07/78	G	32		
77	Artur Atadjanov		30/03/91	D	18	(3)	
10	Shlomi Avisidris		14/05/89	A		(2)	
7	Aviv Azaria		02/11/91	A		(2)	
18	Tamir Ben Ami		28/02/79	D	3	(2)	
26	Yogev Ben Simon		06/04/86	D	8	(3)	
11	Ben Ben Yair		23/12/92	A		(3)	
15	Vladimir Broun		06/05/89	D	22	(4)	
20	Omer Buksenbaum		12/11/82	M	29	(2)	1
99	Miran Burgič	SVN	04/11/80	A	8	(11)	1
14	Carlos Chacana	ARG	23/06/76	A	5	(13)	
27	Lidor Cohen		14/11/91	M		(1)	
10	Dorin Goga	ROU	02/07/84	A	5	(7)	1
44	Zeev Haimovich		07/04/83	D	11	(1)	
5	Omer Hazum		18/10/92	D	1		
24	Offir Hemo		10/12/87	M	11	(17)	2
3	Tal Hen		04/08/79	D	14	(1)	
25	Oz Ifrah		10/12/82	D	13	(3)	1
12	Ran Itzhak		09/10/84	A	4	(7)	3
21	Tomer Levi		25/05/93	D		(1)	
33	Tal Maabi		15/05/85	D	12		
9	David Manga	CTA	03/02/89	A	30		10
41	Bernard Onanga Itoua	FRA	07/09/88	D	28		3
10	Miroslav Pejić	BIH	16/02/86	M		(1)	
16	Omri Perel		15/02/94	D	1	(1)	
30	Lior Reuven		12/12/80	D	26		
4	Djibril Sidibé	MLI	23/03/82	M	20	(2)	
	Guy Solomon		22/09/77	G	1		
8	Israel Zaguri		29/01/90	M	29	(1)	7
17	Michael Zandberg		16/04/80	M	16	(5)	2

HAPOEL TEL-AVIV FC

Coach: Nitzan Shirazi; (28/09/12) Yossi Abuksis; (18/02/13) Fredi David
1927 • Bloomfield (14,413) • hapoelta-fc.co.il
Major honours
Israeli League (13) 1934, 1935, 1938, 1940, 1943, 1957, 1966, 1969, 1981, 1986, 1988, 2000, 2010; Israeli Cup (15) 1928, 1934, 1937, 1938, 1939, 1960, 1972, 1983, 1990, 2000, 2006, 2007, 2010, 2011, 2012

2012
26/08	H. Ramat Gan	a	1-0	Ben Haim (p)	
02/09	H. Haifa	h	2-0	Maman, Damari (p)	
15/09	Bnei Yehuda	h	2-0	Tamuz, Damari	
23/09	H. Ramat HaSharon	a	0-1		
29/09	Bnei Sakhnin	h	1-0	Damari (p)	
22/10	M. Haifa	h	3-0	Ben Haim, Damari, Maman	
29/10	Beitar	a	2-3	Ben Haim, Tamuz	
04/11	M. Netanya	a	1-2	Damari	
11/11	M. Tel-Aviv	h	1-0	Damari (p)	
17/11	H. Kiryat Shmona	a	1-0	Tamuz	
26/11	H. Beer Sheva	h	4-1	Ben Haim, Tamuz 3	
03/12	Ashdod	a	2-1	Tamuz, Vermouth	
09/12	H. Akko	h	0-0		
15/12	H. Ramat Gan	h	2-2	Damari 2	
22/12	H. Haifa	a	2-2	Tamuz, Badir	
29/12	Bnei Yehuda	a	1-2	Shrem	

2013
05/01	H. Ramat HaSharon	h	1-0	Damari	
12/01	Bnei Sakhnin	h	3-0	Damari, Ben Haim 2	
21/01	Beitar	h	0-2		
27/01	M. Haifa	h	0-3		
02/02	M. Netanya	h	0-3		
11/02	M. Tel-Aviv	h	0-4		
16/02	H. Kiryat Shmona	h	1-1	Toama	
23/02	H. Beer Sheva	a	2-1	og (Gavish), Damari (p)	
02/03	Ashdod	h	1-1	Damari (p)	
09/03	H. Akko	a	0-0		
16/03	H. Kiryat Shmona	h	1-0	Shrem	
30/03	H. Ramat HaSharon	a	1-0	Tamuz	
02/04	Bnei Yehuda	h	2-1	Tamuz (p), Maman	
06/04	M. Tel-Aviv	a	0-2		
13/04	M. Haifa	h	2-2	Abutbul 2	
20/04	H. Kiryat Shmona	a	1-4	Sapori	
28/04	H. Ramat HaSharon	h	2-0	Damari, Toama	
06/05	Bnei Yehuda	a	1-0	A Cohen	
13/05	M. Tel-Aviv	h	2-4	Ben Haim, Édel (p)	
18/05	M. Haifa	a	2-3	Sapori, Badir	

No	Name	Nat	DoB	Pos	Aps	(s)	Gls
18	Shay Abutbul		16/01/83	M	11	(1)	2
20	Igal Antebi		01/08/74	D	15	(4)	
28	Artur Atadjanov		30/03/91	D	1		
10	Walid Badir		12/03/74	D	25	(2)	2
12	Tal Ben Haim		05/08/89	A	29	(1)	7
32	Bruno Coutinho	BRA	21/06/86	M	4	(1)	
8	Almog Cohen		01/09/88	M	12		1
11	Elroy Cohen		07/01/89	M	6	(8)	
16	Omer Damari		24/03/89	A	25	(4)	13
7	Eliran Danin		29/03/84	D	13	(5)	
25	David Rochela	ESP	19/02/90	D	13		
19	Eric Djemba-Djemba	CMR	04/05/81	M	27	(1)	
30	Apoula Edima Édel	ARM	17/06/86	G	29	(1)	1
21	Roei Gordana		06/07/90	M	18	(7)	
17	Zeev Haimovich		07/04/83	D	5		
32	Shimon Harosh		20/02/87	D	10	(1)	
28	Dor Hemo		14/06/93	D		(1)	
27	Kfir Izenstein		18/02/93	M		(1)	
29	Iyad Khutaba		20/11/87	D	16	(1)	
1	Boris Kleyman		26/10/90	G	7	(1)	
44	John Pantsil	GHA	15/06/81	D	8	(1)	
24	Savo Pavićević	MNE	11/12/80	D	12		
55	Nikola Petković	SRB	28/03/86	D	7	(1)	
28	Ramzi Sapori		21/10/85	A	4	(3)	2
8	Eden Shrem		09/03/93	A	4	(7)	2
4	Mor Shushan		04/11/88	D	12	(3)	
99	Toto Tamuz		01/04/88	A	21	(5)	10
27	Tiago Costa	POR	22/04/87	D	10	(2)	
15	Salim Toama		09/08/79	M	8	(24)	2
14	Gil Vermouth		05/08/85	M	6	(1)	1

MACCABI HAIFA FC

Coach: Reuven Atar; (17/11/12) Arik Benado
1913 • Kiriat Eliezer (17,000) • maccabi-haifafc.walla.co.il
Major honours
Israeli League (12) 1984, 1985, 1989, 1991, 1994, 2001, 2002, 2004, 2005, 2006, 2009, 2011; Israeli Cup (5) 1962, 1991, 1993, 1995, 1998

2012
27/08	M. Tel-Aviv	a	1-2	Ezra	
01/09	H. Kiryat Shmona	h	1-3	Ndlovu	
15/09	H. Beer Sheva	a	1-1	Azulay	
22/09	Ashdod	h	0-1		
29/09	H. Akko	a	0-0		
06/10	H. Ramat Gan	h	2-0	Ndlovu, Vered	
22/10	H. Tel-Aviv	a	0-3		
05/11	Bnei Yehuda	h	1-1	Ndlovu	
10/11	H. Ramat HaSharon	a	1-1	Keinan	
19/11	Bnei Sakhnin	h	0-0		
26/11	Beitar	a	2-1	og (Magrelashvili), Ezra	
02/12	H. Haifa	a	3-0	Golasa, Amasha, Ezra	
08/12	M. Netanya	h	1-0	Katan (p)	
17/12	M. Tel-Aviv	h	1-0	Amasha	
24/12	H. Kiryat Shmona	a	0-0		
29/12	H. Beer Sheva	h	2-0	Amasha, Azulay	

2013
06/01	Ashdod	a	4-1	Golasa, Ezra, Meshumar, Turgeman	
12/01	H. Akko	h	3-1	Ezra 2, Amasha	
20/01	H. Ramat Gan	a	3-0	Amasha, Tawatha, Azulay	
27/01	H. Tel-Aviv	h	3-0	Keinan 2, Turgeman	
03/02	Bnei Yehuda	a	0-2		
09/02	H. Ramat HaSharon	h	4-0	Ndlovu, Katan, Azulay 2	
16/02	Bnei Sakhnin	a	1-0	Amasha	
24/02	Beitar	h	4-1	Katan, Amasha 2 (1p), Turgeman	
04/03	H. Haifa	h	1-1	Amasha (p)	
09/03	M. Netanya	a	2-1	Turgeman, Amasha (p)	
17/03	Bnei Yehuda	h	1-0	Pylyavskiy	
30/03	M. Tel-Aviv	h	0-0		
02/04	H. Ramat Gan	h	6-0	Ndlovu 4, Tawatha, Amasha	
06/04	H. Kiryat Shmona	h	3-2	Ezra, Keinan, Azulay	
13/04	H. Tel-Aviv	a	2-2	Ndlovu, Azulay	
21/04	Bnei Yehuda	a	1-2	Ezra	
29/04	M. Tel-Aviv	h	2-2	Keinan, Ezra	
05/05	H. Ramat HaSharon	a	1-2	Haber	
11/05	H. Kiryat Shmona	a	2-1	Rian, Turgeman	
18/05	H. Tel-Aviv	h	3-2	Turgeman, Katan, Haber	

No	Name	Nat	DoB	Pos	Aps	(s)	Gls
14	Viam Amasha		08/08/85	A	19	(11)	11
9	Shlomi Azulay		18/10/89	A	13	(17)	7
25	Edin Cocalić	BIH	05/12/87	D	24	(1)	
21	Tamir Cohen		04/03/84	M	3		
6	Joël Damahou	CIV	28/01/87	M	6		
1	Nir Davidovich		17/12/76	G	2		
4	Orel Dgani		08/01/89	D	12	(3)	
22	Amir Edree		26/07/85	G	6	(1)	
18	Oded Elkayam		09/02/88	D	4	(1)	
8	Hen Ezra		19/01/89	M	32	(4)	9
15	Eyal Golasa		07/10/91	M	28	(2)	2
10	Shoval Gozlan		24/04/94	A		(1)	
7	Gustavo Boccoli	BRA	16/02/78	M	22	(2)	
19	Daniel Haber	CAN	20/05/92	A		(4)	2
2	Ayed Hbshe		10/05/95	D	1		
23	Ataa Jaber		03/10/94	M	3	(5)	
20	Yaniv Katan		27/01/81	A	32	(2)	4
24	Dekel Keinan		15/09/84	D	30		5
27	Eyal Meshumar		10/08/83	D	23		1
12	Dino Ndlovu	RSA	15/02/90	A	19	(2)	9
29	Andriy Pylyavskiy	UKR	04/12/88	D	15		1
16	Ismail Rian		24/04/94	A	2	(2)	1
33	Bojan Šaranov	SRB	22/09/87	G	28		
3	Samuel Scheimann		03/11/87	D	14	(3)	
13	Taleb Tawatha		21/06/92	D	20	(1)	2
17	Alon Turgeman		09/06/91	A	10	(11)	6
10	Idan Vered		25/05/89	M	7	(10)	1
26	Avihai Yadin		26/10/86	M	12	(4)	
11	Bamidele Yampolsky		28/07/88	A	3	(6)	
5	Liroy Zairi		02/03/89	M	6	(13)	

MACCABI NETANYA FC

Coach: Tal Banin; (19/03/13) Reuven Atar
1934 • Municipal (13,800) • fcmn.co.il
Major honours
Israeli League (5) 1971, 1974, 1978, 1980, 1983; Israeli Cup (1) 1978

2012
25/08	H. Haifa	a	0-0		
03/09	M. Tel-Aviv	h	0-1		
15/09	H. Kiryat Shmona	a	1-0	Sabaa	
22/09	H. Beer Sheva	h	2-1	I Shriki, Shivhon	
29/09	Ashdod	a	0-3		
06/10	H. Akko	h	1-3	I Shriki	
20/10	H. Ramat Gan	a	1-1	Shomovitch	
04/11	H. Tel-Aviv	h	2-1	Sabaa, El-Khatib	
10/11	Bnei Yehuda	a	0-3		
17/11	H. Ramat HaSharon	h	1-2	Sabaa (p)	
24/11	Bnei Sakhnin	a	0-0		
01/12	Beitar	h	2-3	Ćeran, Lofo	
08/12	M. Haifa	a	0-1		
15/12	H. Haifa	h	0-0		
22/12	M. Tel-Aviv	a	1-2	Ćeran	
29/12	H. Kiryat Shmona	h	3-4	Sabaa, Ćeran, Dajani	

2013
05/01	H. Beer Sheva	a	3-1	Ćeran, El-Khatib, Sabaa	
12/01	Ashdod	h	2-0	El-Khatib, Dajani	
19/01	H. Akko	a	4-4	Ćeran, Shivhon, Sabaa 2 (1p)	
26/01	H. Ramat Gan	h	1-1	Peretz	
02/02	H. Tel-Aviv	a	3-0	Ćeran, og (Abutbul), Sabaa (p)	
09/02	Bnei Yehuda	h	3-5	Ćeran, El-Khatib 2	
16/02	H. Ramat HaSharon	a	0-0		
24/02	Bnei Sakhnin	h	0-0		
03/03	Beitar	a	1-1	Ben Harush	
09/03	M. Haifa	h	1-2	Sabaa	
16/03	H. Haifa	a	0-3		
30/03	H. Akko	h	0-2		
06/04	Bnei Sakhnin	h	1-1	El-Khatib	
13/04	H. Ramat Gan	a	0-0		
20/04	Ashdod	h	2-1	Shivhon, Dajani	
27/04	Beitar	a	3-1	Mugrabi, Shivhon, Sabaa (p)	
04/05	H. Beer Sheva	h	0-3		

No	Name	Nat	DoB	Pos	Aps	(s)	Gls
20	Omri Ben Harush		07/03/90	D	27	(2)	1
8	Ben Binjamin		17/12/85	D	29		
15	Noor Bisan		17/01/95	A		(1)	
7	Bruno Pinheiro	POR	21/08/87	D	14		
1	Luigi Cennamo	ITA	07/02/80	G	31		
10	Dragan Ćeran	SRB	06/10/87	A	20	(4)	7
11	Yarden Cohen		18/09/91	M	5	(6)	
17	Kobi Dajani		05/11/84	M	24	(2)	3
23	Ali El-Khatib	PLE	18/03/89	M	19	(9)	6
21	Din Gabay		19/09/92	M		(4)	
21	Yarin Hassan		25/03/85	M	5	(1)	
21	Viki Kahlon		15/01/93	D		(3)	
5	Leonid Krupnik	UKR	15/07/79	D	8		
4	Ido Levi		31/07/90	D	23	(2)	
22	Robi Levkovic		31/08/88	G	1		
28	Serge Lofo	COD	13/10/83	A	5	(9)	1
8	Itay Manzur		02/07/94	M		(1)	
25	Firas Mugrabi		24/07/91	M	14	(2)	1
25	Omer Peretz		26/01/86	A	17	(12)	1
3	Touvarno Pinas	SUR	25/11/85	D	14		
22	Ahmed Sabaa		25/05/80	A	26	(4)	10
22	Guy Salem		23/08/84	G	1	(1)	
26	Uri Shitrit		21/01/86	D	21	(1)	
18	Yossi Shivhon		22/03/82	M	27	(6)	4
8	Amit Shomovitch		29/07/82	D	8		1
14	Idan Shriki		30/11/81	A	9	(3)	2
24	Liran Shriki		14/04/94	M	1	(2)	
23	Arnon Tamir		14/03/86	M		(3)	
19	Omer Tchalisher		22/01/93	D	14	(10)	

MACCABI TEL-AVIV FC

Coach: Óscar García (ESP)
1906 • Bloomfield (14,413) • maccabi-tlv.co.il
Major honours
Israeli League (19) 1936, 1937, 1942, 1947, 1950, 1952,
1954, 1956, 1958, 1968, 1970, 1972, 1977, 1979, 1992,
1995, 1996, 2003, 2013;
Israeli Cup (22) 1929, 1930, 1933, 1941, 1946, 1947,
1954, 1955, 1958, 1959, 1964, 1965, 1967, 1970, 1977,
1987, 1988, 1994, 1996, 2001, 2002, 2005

2012

27/08	M. Haifa	h	2-1	Dabbur 2
03/09	M. Netanya	a	1-0	Atar
15/09	H. Haifa	a	3-1	Atar 3
24/09	H. Kiryat Shmona	h	4-0	Gonzalo, Atar 2 (1p), Radi
01/10	H. Beer Sheva	a	1-3	Dabbur
06/10	Ashdod	h	2-1	Micha, Earnshaw
20/10	H. Akko	a	2-0	og (Lukman), Atar
03/11	H. Ramat Gan	h	3-1	Atar 2, Radi
11/11	H. Tel-Aviv	a	0-1	
17/11	Bnei Yehuda	h	0-1	
24/11	H. Ramat HaSharon	a	4-3	Dabbur, Gonzalo, Atar, Colautti
01/12	Bnei Sakhnin	h	4-0	Ziv, Atar 2, Dabbur
10/12	Beitar	a	1-1	Atar
17/12	M. Haifa	a	0-1	
22/12	M. Netanya	h	2-1	Atar (p), Earnshaw
30/12	H. Haifa	h	6-2	Dabbur 2, Radi, Ziv, Margoulis, Yeiny

2013

07/01	H. Kiryat Shmona	a	0-0	
14/01	H. Beer Sheva	h	5-0	Gohouri, Atar 2, Radi, Lugasi
19/01	Ashdod	a	0-1	
26/01	H. Akko	h	4-0	Micha, Yeiny, Atar 2
02/02	H. Ramat Gan	a	1-0	Radi
11/02	H. Tel-Aviv	h	4-0	Prica, Atar 2 (1p), Radi
18/02	Bnei Yehuda	a	3-2	Prica 2, Lugasi
23/02	H. Ramat HaSharon	h	1-0	Atar
02/03	Bnei Sakhnin	a	3-0	Tibi, Prica, Radi
10/03	Beitar	h	5-0	Zahavi, Prica, Atar, Dabbur 2
16/03	H. Ramat HaSharon	h	1-0	Prica
30/03	M. Haifa	h	0-0	
03/04	H. Kiryat Shmona	a	3-1	Dabbur, Prica, Zahavi (p)
06/04	H. Tel-Aviv	h	2-0	Zahavi, Micha
13/04	Bnei Yehuda	a	2-2	Zahavi 2
22/04	H. Ramat HaSharon	a	2-0	Micha, Prica
29/04	M. Haifa	a	2-2	Gonzalo 2 (1p)
04/05	H. Kiryat Shmona	h	1-0	Zahavi
13/05	H. Tel-Aviv	a	4-2	Zahavi (p), Radi, Colautti, Micha
20/05	Bnei Yehuda	h	0-3	

No	Name	Nat	DoB	Pos	Aps	(s)	Gls
20	Hassan Abu Zaid		04/02/91	M	6	(8)	
6	Gal Alberman		17/04/83	M	34		
16	Eliran Atar		17/02/87	A	31		22
29	Ben Ben Yair		23/12/92	A		(2)	
17	Yagil Biton		16/03/92	D		(1)	
31	Carlos García	ESP	29/04/84	D	29	(1)	
41	Tomer Chencinski	CAN	01/12/84	G	1		
24	Roberto Colautti		24/05/82	A	10	(9)	2
13	Munas Dabbur		14/05/92	A	14	(12)	10
26	Rafael Dahan		28/09/89	M	3	(9)	
19	Robert Earnshaw	WAL	06/04/81	A	1	(9)	2
32	Vincent Enyeama	NGA	29/08/82	G	27		
39	Ignacio Fideleff	ARG	04/07/89	D	5	(2)	
45	Steve Gohouri	CIV	08/02/81	D	8	(3)	1
10	Gonzalo	ESP	13/10/83	A	18	(8)	4
1	Barak Levi		07/01/93	G	8		
28	Moshe Lugasi		04/01/91	M	11	(10)	2
30	Gael Margoulis		03/04/94	A	2	(9)	1
15	Dor Micha		10/02/92	M	23	(5)	5
5	Reef Peretz		25/02/91	M	2		
22	Rade Prica	SWE	30/06/80	A	13	(5)	8
9	Maharan Radi		01/07/82	M	31	(2)	8
18	Eitan Tibi		16/11/87	D	34		1
27	Omer Vered		25/01/90	D	7	(2)	
21	Shiran Yeiny		08/12/86	D	33	(1)	2
7	Eran Zahavi		25/07/87	M	14	(2)	7
14	Yoav Ziv		16/03/81	D	31	(2)	2

Top goalscorers

22	Eliran Atar (M. Tel-Aviv)
15	Shimon Abuhazira (H. Kiryat Shmona)
14	Ohad Kadusi (H. Akko)
13	Omer Damari (H. Tel-Aviv)
12	Pedro Galván (Bnei Yehuda)
11	Avi Rikan (Beitar) Viam Amasha (M. Haifa)
10	David Manga (H. Ramat Gan) Toto Tamuz (H. Tel-Aviv) Ahmed Sabaa (M. Netanya) Munas Dabbur (M. Tel-Aviv)

Promoted clubs

MACCABI PETACH-TIKVA FC

Coach: Moshe Sinai
1912 • Hamoshava (11,300) • m-pt.co.il
Major honours
Israeli Cup (2) 1935, 1952

HAPOEL RAANANA FC

Coach: Tomer Kashtan; (02/04/13) Meni Koretski
1972 • Ori Karni (2,500) • no website

SECOND LEVEL FINAL TABLE 2012/13

		Pld	W	D	L	F	A	Pts
1	Maccabi Petach-Tikva FC	37	21	10	6	66	29	73
2	Hapoel Raanana FC	37	20	10	7	56	34	70
3	Hapoel Nazareth Illit FC	37	19	10	8	48	30	67
4	Hapoel Jerusalem FC	37	15	12	10	48	39	57
5	Hapoel Petach-Tikva FC	37	15	8	14	45	48	53
6	Hapoel Ironi Rishon-LeZion FC	37	11	15	11	44	43	48
7	Maccabi Herzliya FC	37	10	14	13	33	39	44
8	Hapoel Bnei Lod FC	37	10	13	14	37	42	43
9	Maccabi Yavne FC	37	13	10	14	48	52	49
10	Maccabi Ahi Nazareth FC	37	13	8	16	49	47	47
11	Hakoach Amidar Ramat Gan FC	37	12	10	15	47	59	44
12	Maccabi Um El Fahem FC	37	10	11	16	39	44	41
13	Hapoel Ashkelon FC	37	10	11	16	38	57	41
14	Beitar Tel-Aviv Ramla FC	37	9	13	15	45	58	40
15	Sektzya Ness Ziona FC	37	7	16	14	33	47	37
16	Hapoel Kfar-Saba FC	37	10	11	16	37	45	32

NB League splits into top and bottom halves after 30 games, after which the clubs play exclusively against teams in their group.
Hapoel Kfar-Saba FC – 9 pts deducted; Hakoach Amidar Ramat Gan FC – 2 pts deducted.

Domestic cup: G'Viaa Hamedina (StateCup) 2012/13

THIRD ROUND

(29/01/13)
Beitar Jerusalem 5-0 M. Um El Fahem
Beitar Tel-Aviv Ramla 0-1 H. Bnei Lod
H. Akko 1-2 H. Afula
H. Ashkelon 6-1 B. Nahariya
H. Asi Gilboa 1-0 H. Petach-Tikva
H. Ramat HaSharon 1-2 M. Yavne
H. Rishon-LeZion 2-1 M. Ahi Nazareth
M. Netanya 0-2 M. Tel-Aviv
Ness Ziona 0-5 H. Raanana

(30/01/13)
Bnei Yehuda 0-2 H. Haifa
H. Azor 0-4 M. Haifa
H. Beer Sheva 1-2 H. Tel-Aviv *(aet)*
H. Herzliya 0-3 H. Kiryat Shmona
H. Kfar-Saba 2-1 M. Herzliya *(aet)*
H. Nazareth Illit 1-1 Bnei Sakhnin *(aet; 2-4 on pens)*
H. Ramat Gan 2-0 Ashdod

FOURTH ROUND

(26/02/13)
H. Asi Gilboa 1-1 H. Ashkelon *(aet; 4-2 on pens)*
H. Kfar-Saba 0-1 H. Tel-Aviv
H. Kiryat Shmona 2-0 M. Yavne
H. Ramat Gan 5-3 H. Afula *(aet)*
H. Rishon-LeZion 2-2 H. Raanana *(aet; 4-3 on pens)*

(27/02/13)
H. Bnei Lod 2-3 Bnei Sakhnin
M. Haifa 2-1 H. Haifa
M. Tel-Aviv 0-2 Beitar Jerusalem

QUARTER-FINALS

(12/03/13)
Bnei Sakhnin 1-3 H. Kiryat Shmona *(Lukman 15; Abuhazira 46, 67, Tzedek 51)*

H. Asi Gilboa 1-2 H. Ramat Gan *(Sahfsha 58p; Manga 33, Zandberg 68)*

H. Rishon-LeZion 1-0 H. Tel-Aviv *(Zoubi 40)*

(13/03/13)
Beitar Jerusalem 0-3 M. Haifa *(Tawatha 25, Amasha 54p, Ndlovu 72)*

SEMI-FINALS

(17/04/13)
H. Kiryat Shmona 2-1 M. Haifa *(Abed 70, Osei 109; Ndlovu 22) (aet)*

H. Rishon-LeZion 1-2 H. Ramat Gan *(Azili 41; Itzhak 9, Zaguri 90)*

FINAL

(08/05/13)
Netanya stadion, Netanya
HAPOEL RAMAT GAN FC 1 *(Buksenbaum 51)*
HAPOEL KIRYAT SHMONA FC 1 *(Abuhazira 16)*
(aet; 4-2 on pens)
Referee: Tabrizi
H. RAMAT GAN: Arkin, Reuven, Onanga Itoua, Haimovich, Atadjanov, Broun (Goga 98), Buksenbaum, Sidibé (Hemo 69), Zaguri, Manga, Itzhak (Burgič 76)
Sent off: Hemo (111)
H. KIRYAT SHMONA: Amos, Gabai, Tzedek, Hasarma, Matović, Gerzicich, Einbinder, Tasevski (Abed 60), Rochet (Solari 110), Abuhazira, Osei (Sallalich 74)

ITALY

Federazione Italiana Giuoco Calcio (FIGC)

Address	Via Gregorio Allegri 14 CP 2450 IT-00198 Roma	**President** **General secretary**	Giancarlo Abete Antonio Di Sebastiano
Tel	+39 06 84 911	**Media officer**	Antonello Valentini
Fax	+39 06 84 912 620	**Year of formation**	1898
E-mail	international@figc.it	**National stadium**	Stadio Olimpico,
Website	figc.it		Rome (82,307)

SERIE A CLUBS

1. Atalanta BC
2. Bologna FC
3. Cagliari Calcio
4. Calcio Catania
5. AC Chievo Verona
6. ACF Fiorentina
7. Genoa CFC
8. FC Internazionale Milano
9. Juventus
10.  S.S. Lazio
11. AC Milan
12. SSC Napoli
13. US Città di Palermo
14. Parma FC
15. Pescara Calcio
16. AS Roma
17. UC Sampdoria
18. AC Siena
19. Torino FC
20. Udinese Calcio

PROMOTED CLUBS

21. US Sassuolo Calcio
22. Hellas Verona FC
23. AS Livorno Calcio

KEY:

● – UEFA Champions League
● – UEFA Europa League
● – Promoted clubs
● – Relegated clubs

Scudetto stays at Juventus

Juventus staged a Serie A encore in 2012/13, repeating their previous season's success with another resilient and commanding campaign. On top of the table throughout, they finished nine points clear of runners-up SSC Napoli. Third place was secured in dramatic fashion by AC Milan under pressure from a resurgent ACF Fiorentina

S.S. Lazio won the all-Rome Coppa Italia final and also became Italy's first UEFA Europa League quarter-finalists. Juve reached the equivalent stage of the UEFA Champions League, while the Italian national team, in command of their 2014 FIFA World Cup qualifying group, finished third at the FIFA Confederations Cup.

| Bianconeri secure back-to-back titles | Lazio defeat Roma in Coppa Italia final | Progress for Prandelli's Azzurri |

Domestic league

Invincible Serie A winners in 2011/12, Juventus were unable to maintain that extraordinary level of consistency, losing five times, but there was no other team in the division that could match their steady accumulation of points. Whenever their position at the top of the table appeared to be under threat, the Turin club were able to find a response, and by the closing weeks of the campaign they were unchallenged and out on their own. Indeed, their final points tally of 87 was actually three more than they had registered the previous season – a measure of the club's increasing penchant for winning matches as opposed to avoiding defeat.

Juve defended their title despite the unavailability on matchdays for the first three months of the campaign of their coach, Antonio Conte. Suspended for disciplinary reasons, he was obliged to sit in the stands in a purely observational capacity during that time, with technical director Massimo Carrera then, from mid-October, assistant Angelo Alessio serving on the bench in a caretaker capacity. There was no knock-on effect from this off-field disruption on the field of play, however, as Juve carried on where they had left off

the previous season, winning nine of their first ten games and drawing the other to prolong their unbeaten sequence to 49 matches.

That run ended on the first weekend of November when FC Internazionale Milano became the first visiting side to win at the Juventus Stadium, coming from behind to claim an impressive 3-1 victory and move to within a point of their hosts at the Serie A summit. No sooner had Inter moved within striking distance, however, than they dropped off the pace, winning just two more games before Christmas. Juve, meanwhile, recovered by winning 6-1 away at Pescara Calcio, and although they were beaten again, 1-0 at Milan, four successive wins in December ensured that they entered the new year with a healthy lead.

Lazio found form at this stage and Napoli also made a bright start to 2013, but neither could keep pace with Juventus, who, with Conte now fully operational, began to stretch their lead. A burst of wins in March and April saw off the opposition for good, and it was with a 1-0 home win over US Città di Palermo that the Bianconeri made mathematically certain of their record-extending 29th Scudetto with three games in hand. Even a last-day defeat at UC Sampdoria – who had also defeated Juve in Turin – left

them nine points clear of Napoli in the final standings.

Resilience and collective endeavour were once again the keys to Juve's success. The Bianconeri were not dependent on one person to score their goals. For the second successive season the club's top marksman managed only ten. In fact, there were two on that figure – Montenegrin striker Mirko Vučinić and Chilean midfielder Arturo Vidal, who registered half of his total during the run-in. In terms of personnel, Juve were practically unchanged from the previous campaign, with Andrea Pirlo and Claudio Marchisio dovetailing alongside Vidal in a beautifully balanced midfield and the rock-solid all-Italian three-man defence of Leonardo Bonucci, Andrea Barzagli and Giorgio Chiellini backed up by evergreen Azzurri No1 Gianluigi Buffon.

In conceding just 24 goals, Juve had by far the tightest defence in the division, but they were outscored by two other teams, Napoli and Fiorentina, and matched by a third, AS Roma. Napoli had the insatiable Edinson Cavani to thank for finishing first in that particular ranking. The Uruguayan striker topped the capocannonieri charts with 29 goals, his tally including hat-tricks at home to Lazio, Roma and Inter. With Slovakian schemer Marek Hamšík providing his

customary support from midfield, Napoli enjoyed another excellent season under coach Walter Mazzarri, taking the runners-up spot by six points after a storming finish that brought eight wins in nine games. While the club had UEFA Champions League football to look forward to for the second time in three seasons, there would be no European activity in 2013/14 for Mazzarri. He left at the end of the season to replace Andrea Stramaccioni at Inter, who lost eight of their last 11 games to plummet to ninth place, thus missing out on Europe for only the second time in two decades. Mazzarri's position in Naples was taken by Rafael Benítez, but the Spaniard would have to plan without Cavani, sold in the summer to Paris Saint-Germain FC.

Fiorentina rivalled Napoli as Serie A's most entertaining side, and Vincenzo Montella led the Viola to within a hair's breadth of a UEFA Champions League place, their bid to finish third scuppered only by two late goals from Milan at relegated AC Siena on the final day. A lowly 13th in 2011/12, Fiorentina were a team transformed under their dynamic new coach, Montella fashioning a fine team in which several imports stood out, notably Spanish midfield conductor Borja Valero, Argentinian centre-back Gonzalo Rodríguez, Colombian winger Juan Cuadrado and young Balkan strike duo Adem Ljajić and Stevan Jovetić.

Milan's return to Europe's top competition looked unlikely when, after selling star players Zlatan Ibrahimović and Thiago Silva to PSG, they began the Serie A season with five defeats in their opening eight games, including three at home, the last of them against Inter (0-1). The mid-season signing of maverick striker Mario Balotelli from Manchester City FC proved to be a shrewd piece of business, though, and whereas another young Italian international forward, Stephan El Shaarawy, had done his best to keep the Rossoneri afloat during the first half of the campaign, it was Balotelli who proved inspirational in the second, scoring 12 goals (six of them from the penalty spot) to help Massimiliano Allegri's side charge up the table. Milan lost just one of their 20 post-Christmas fixtures – 1-0 at Juventus – and ended up needing every one of those points to cling on to third place.

Udinese Calcio, the third-placed team in 2011/12, finished two places lower, securing UEFA Europa League football with a stunning late surge of eight successive victories, the last of them a 5-2 rout of Inter at San Siro. Skipper Antonio Di Natale showed that at 35 his eye for a goal was as sharp as ever, scoring eight times in that winning streak to finish second to Cavani in the goal charts with 23. It was the fourth season in a row that he had broken the 20-goal barrier – a feat not achieved for over half a century.

Pescara, Siena and Palermo were the three teams relegated, with Genoa CFC finishing one place above the drop zone for the second season running. There was a surprise in Serie B, where small-town outfit US Sassuolo Calcio finished on top of the pile to win promotion to Italy's top division for the first time. They were accompanied up by second-placed Hellas Verona FC and, after the play-offs, third-placed AS Livorno Calcio.

Domestic cup

Roma finished sixth, a point and a place above Lazio in the Serie A table, but with the two teams meeting in the final of the Coppa Italia it meant that the showdown in the Stadio Olimpico would not just determine the winners of the trophy but also the possessors of Italy's third 2013/14 UEFA Europa League berth.

Lazio had overcome Juventus in a dramatic semi-final, prevailing 3-2 on aggregate after a last-gasp winner in the second leg. They had to wait almost three months to discover who their opponents in the final would be – before Roma finished the job they had started against Inter with a 3-2 win at San Siro. The Giallorossi had a new coach for that second leg, Aurelio Andreazzoli acting as caretaker following the February dismissal of Zdeněk Zeman. He was still in situ for the final against a Lazio team led by Vladimir Petković.

Udinese striker Antonio Di Natale (No10) scores against Pescara – one of 23 Serie A goals he struck in 2012/13

It was the first time the two Rome clubs had met in the cup final, but despite all the anticipation and excitement in the capital leading up to the game, it failed to live up to expectations. Neither team produced their best form, but it was Lazio who came out on top, Senad Lulić scoring the only goal on 71 minutes when he tapped in at the far post after a cross from Antonio Candreva, the revelation of Lazio's season, was deflected into his path. It was the club's sixth victory in the competition, putting them three behind their city rivals in the all-time roll of honour.

Europe

With Italy having surrendered one of its UEFA Champions League places to Germany and Udinese failing to negotiate the play-off round – they were beaten on penalties by SC Braga – just two Serie A sides, Juventus and Milan, were among Europe's elite 32 in the 2012/13 group stage.

Juve had not played in the competition for three seasons but they made an accomplished return, topping their group and in the process knocking out holders Chelsea FC with a 2-2 draw at Stamford Bridge and an emphatic 3-0 win in Turin. Celtic FC proved easy meat for Conte's side in the round of 16, but Juve were overwhelmed themselves in the quarter-finals, losing both legs 2-0 to FC Bayern München.

Milan paid the price for finishing second in their group to debutants Málaga CF when they were paired in the round of 16 with FC Barcelona, the team that had knocked them out in the previous season's quarter-finals. Allegri's team looked set to gain their revenge when they won the first leg at San Siro 2-0, but Barça produced a brilliant performance in the return to leave the club's dreams of an eighth European crown in tatters.

The UEFA Europa League brought staggered departures for the four Italian clubs involved. Udinese dropped out at the group stage, Napoli were surprisingly crushed by Czech club FC Viktoria Plzeň in the round of 32, and Inter went down fighting in an epic tie with Tottenham Hotspur FC, losing on away goals in extra time after a San Siro fightback from a 3-0 first-leg deficit. That left just Lazio, unbeaten in 12 matches, to become the first Italian club to reach the quarter-finals of the competition. However, having knocked out two German clubs, VfL Borussia Mönchengladbach and VfB Stuttgart, Petković's side went no further, succumbing 3-1 on aggregate to Fenerbahçe SK.

National team

UEFA EURO 2012 runners-up Italy had a very busy 2012/13 season. It began in mid-August with a friendly defeat in Switzerland by England and ended on the last day of June with a penalty shoot-out victory over Uruguay in the third-place play-off of the Confederations Cup. Seventeen matches provided international caps for no fewer than 45 players – including 13 debutants – as coach Prandelli cast his net far and wide for new talent. For the matches that mattered, in the Confederations Cup and particularly the World Cup qualifiers, he was understandably more conservative, retaining the bulk of the team that had served him so well – until the final against Spain – in Poland and Ukraine.

With four wins and two draws – away to Bulgaria and the Czech Republic – in their first six World Cup games, the Azzurri were in complete control of their qualifying section, the highlight being a 3-1 home win over Denmark in October. The team's second place at UEFA EURO 2012 enabled them to sample the delights of Brazil a year in advance of the main event as they took part in the Confederations Cup. It turned out to be a tournament of mixed fortunes, with Italy displaying uncharacteristic shortcomings in defence but plenty of spirit and skill in attack during the group stage, where they defeated Mexico (2-1) and Japan (4-3) and lost to the hosts (2-4), before losing a drab goalless semi-final on penalties to bogey team Spain.

That shoot-out defeat in Fortaleza came just nine days after Italy had lost 4-2 to Spain in the final of the UEFA European Under-21 Championship – a tournament that suggested Prandelli might have an even larger pool of talent from which to choose by the time the World Cup finals come around.

All things being equal, there should still be room on the plane to Brazil for a couple of Italy's 2006 world champions. Buffon took his number of senior international appearances to 133 at the Confederations Cup – just three behind record holder Fabio Cannavaro – while Pirlo became only the fifth Italian to reach a century of caps, marking the occasion with a goal against Mexico at the same tournament.

Gianluigi Buffon – still going strong for Juventus and Italy at 35

Domestic league: Serie A 2012/13 final table

		Pld	Home					Away					Total					Pts
			W	D	L	F	A	W	D	L	F	A	W	D	L	F	A	
1	Juventus	38	14	3	2	36	10	13	3	3	35	14	27	6	5	71	24	87
2	SSC Napoli	38	14	4	1	44	18	9	5	5	29	18	23	9	6	73	36	78
3	AC Milan	38	13	2	4	33	15	8	7	4	34	24	21	9	8	67	39	72
4	ACF Fiorentina	38	13	4	2	40	19	8	3	8	32	25	21	7	10	72	44	70
5	Udinese Calcio	38	11	7	1	31	16	7	5	7	28	29	18	12	8	59	45	66
6	AS Roma	38	10	5	4	40	24	8	3	8	31	32	18	8	12	71	56	62
7	S.S. Lazio	38	13	2	4	35	16	5	5	9	16	26	18	7	13	51	42	61
8	Calcio Catania	38	12	4	3	31	15	3	7	9	19	31	15	11	12	50	46	56
9	FC Internazionale Milano	38	8	4	7	30	31	8	2	9	25	26	16	6	16	55	57	54
10	Parma FC	38	9	6	4	28	18	4	4	11	17	28	13	10	15	45	46	49
11	Cagliari Calcio	38	8	4	7	24	24	4	7	8	19	31	12	11	15	43	55	47
12	AC Chievo Verona	38	6	8	5	18	16	6	1	12	19	36	12	9	17	37	52	45
13	Bologna FC	38	6	8	5	30	24	5	3	11	16	28	11	11	16	46	52	44
14	UC Sampdoria	38	8	3	8	25	22	3	7	9	18	29	11	10	17	43	51	42
15	Atalanta BC	38	6	6	7	19	24	5	3	11	20	32	11	9	18	39	56	40
16	Torino FC	38	6	6	7	23	26	2	10	7	23	29	8	16	14	46	55	39
17	Genoa CFC	38	5	7	7	26	30	3	7	9	12	22	8	14	16	38	52	38
18	US Città di Palermo	38	5	7	7	24	26	1	7	11	10	28	6	14	18	34	54	32
19	AC Siena	38	6	5	8	16	19	3	4	12	20	38	9	9	20	36	57	30
20	Pescara Calcio	38	4	1	14	15	42	2	3	14	12	42	6	4	28	27	84	22

NB AC Siena – 6 pts deducted; Atalanta BC – 2 pts deducted; UC Sampdoria & Torino FC – 1 pt deducted.

SEASON AT A GLANCE

EUROPEAN QUALIFICATION 2013/14

Champion: Juventus (group stage)
SSC Napoli (group stage)
AC Milan (play-offs)

Cup winner: S.S. Lazio (group stage)
ACF Fiorentina (play-offs)
Udinese Calcio (third qualifying round)

Top scorer	Edinson Cavani (Napoli), 29 goals
Relegated clubs	Pescara Calcio, AC Siena, US Città di Palermo
Promoted clubs	US Sassuolo Calcio, Hellas Verona FC, AS Livorno Calcio
Cup final	S.S. Lazio 1-0 AS Roma

SERIE A TEAM OF THE SEASON
(4-2-3-1)
Coach: Montella (Fiorentina)

PLAYER OF THE SEASON
Arturo Vidal
(Juventus)

The strength of Juventus's 2012/13 Scudetto-winning side was more collective than individual, but one player who stood out was Chilean midfielder Vidal. His indefatigable box-to-box midfield play was supplemented by ten goals, including the title-clinching penalty against US Città di Palermo. He also struck three times in the UEFA Champions League.

NEWCOMER OF THE SEASON
Erik Lamela
(AS Roma)

There were many young talents on parade in the 2012/13 Serie A season, but it was Lamela, in his second season at Roma, who outshone all others. The 21-year-old Argentinian left-footer not only scored 15 league goals but thrilled spectators of all persuasions with his superb vision, immaculate technique and never-say-die spirit.

ITALY

NATIONAL TEAM

Home Kit   Away Kit

INTERNATIONAL HONOURS
FIFA World Cup (4) 1934, 1938, 1982, 2006
UEFA European Championship (1) 1968

INTERNATIONAL TOURNAMENT APPEARANCES
FIFA World Cup (17) 1934 (Winners), 1938 (Winners), 1950, 1958, 1962, 1966, 1970 (runners-up), 1974, 1978 (4th), 1982 (Winners), 1986 (2nd round), 1990 (3rd), 1994 (runners-up), 1998 (qtr-finals), 2002 (2nd round), 2006 (Winners), 2010.
UEFA European Championship (8) 1968 (Winners), 1980 (4th), 1988 (semi-finals), 1996, 2000 (runners-up), 2004, 2008 (qtr-finals), 2012 (runners-up)

TOP FIVE ALL-TIME CAPS
Fabio Cannavaro (136); **Gianluigi Buffon** (133); Paolo Maldini (126); Dino Zoff (112); **Andrea Pirlo** (102)

TOP FIVE ALL-TIME GOALS
Luigi Riva (35); Giuseppe Meazza (33); Silvio Piola (30); Roberto Baggio & Alessandro Del Piero (27)

Results 2012/13

15/08/12	England	N	Berno (SUI)	1-2	De Rossi (15)
07/09/12	Bulgaria (WCQ)	A	Sofia	2-2	Osvaldo (36, 40)
11/09/12	Malta (WCQ)	H	Modena	2-0	Destro (5), Peluso (90+2)
12/10/12	Armenia (WCQ)	A	Yerevan	3-1	Pirlo (11p), De Rossi (64), Osvaldo (81)
16/10/12	Denmark (WCQ)	H	Milan	3-1	Montolivo (33), De Rossi (37), Balotelli (54)
14/11/12	France	H	Parma	1-2	El Shaarawy (35)
06/02/13	Netherlands	A	Amsterdam	1-1	Verratti (90+1)
21/03/13	Brazil	N	Geneva (SUI)	2-2	De Rossi (54), Balotelli (57)
26/03/13	Malta (WCQ)	A	Ta' Qali	2-0	Balotelli (8p, 45)
31/05/13	San Marino	H	Bologna	4-0	Poli (28), Gilardino (34), Pirlo (50), Aquilani (79)
07/06/13	Czech Republic (WCQ)	A	Prague	0-0	
11/06/13	Haiti	N	Rio de Janeiro (BRA)	2-2	Giaccherini (1), Marchisio (73)
16/06/13	Mexico (CC)	N	Rio de Janeiro (BRA)	2-1	Pirlo (27), Balotelli (78)
19/06/13	Japan (CC)	N	Recife (BRA)	4-3	De Rossi (41), Uchida (50og), Balotelli (52p), Giovinco (86)
22/06/13	Brazil (CC)	A	Salvador	2-4	Giaccherini (51), Chiellini (71)
27/06/13	Spain (CC)	N	Fortaleza (BRA)	0-0	(aet; 6-7 on pens)
30/06/13	Uruguay (CC)	N	Salvador (BRA)	2-2	Astori (24), Diamanti (73) (aet; 3-2 on pens)

Appearances 2012/13

Coach: Cesare Prandelli			Eng	BUL	MLT	ARM	DEN	Fra	Ned	Bra	MLT	Smr	CZE	Hai	MEX	JPN	BRA	ESP	URU	Caps	Goals
Salvatore Sirigu	12/01/87	PSG (FRA)	G					G				s71		G46						6	-
Ignazio Abate	12/11/86	Milan	D86			D		D		D	s77	D			D	s59	D30			14	-
Davide Astori	07/01/87	Cagliari	D					D						D					D96	5	1
Angelo Ogbonna	23/05/88	Torino	D	D69								D								6	-
Federico Balzaretti	06/12/81	Roma	D46				D	D												15	-
Alberto Aquilani	07/07/84	Fiorentina	M68									M	s77	M72	s88	M30	M	s80	s70	30	4
Daniele De Rossi	24/07/83	Roma	M	M		M	M	M61	M81			M	s54	M	M		M	M70		90	15
Antonio Nocerino	09/04/85	Milan	M		M															15	-
Alessandro Diamanti	02/05/83	Bologna	A59	s64	M46			s73	s46	s81		A51		M54			M72		A83	14	1
Mattia Destro	20/03/91	Roma	A82	s74	A82	s89														4	1
Stephan El Shaarawy	27/10/92	Milan	A59			s60		A73	A71	s46	A76		A46	s60			s72		A	10	1
Federico Peluso	20/01/84	Atalanta	s46	s69	D															3	1
Manolo Gabbiadini	26/11/91	Atalanta	s59																	1	-
Marco Verratti	05/11/92	PSG (FRA)	s59					M50	s61											3	1
Andrea Poli	29/09/89	Sampdoria	s68							s68		M								3	1
Diego Fabbrini	31/07/90	Udinese	s82																	1	-
Ezequiel Schelotto	23/05/89	Atalanta	s86																	1	-
Gianluigi Buffon	28/01/78	Juventus	G	G	G			G	G	G	G71	G		G	G	G	G	G	G	133	-
Andrea Barzagli	08/05/81	Juventus	D	D	D	D	D46	D74	D	D		D		D	D		D46			45	-
Leonardo Bonucci	01/05/87	Juventus	D	D	D		s46		D	D		D	D			D	D	s96		31	2
Christian Maggio	11/02/82	Napoli	M		D		D		D		D77		D		D59	s30	M	D		29	-
Claudio Marchisio	19/01/86	Juventus	M	M	M	M74	M50			M		M	s72	M68	s68	M	M80			38	2
Andrea Pirlo	19/05/79	Juventus	M	M	M74	M	s50	M46	M46	M	M	M77		M	M	M		M		102	13
Emanuele Giaccherini	05/05/85	Juventus	M64		s74	s85	s50		M68	M61			M54	M88	M68	s26	M	s83		14	2
Pablo Osvaldo	12/01/86	Roma	A	A69	A	A 46*		s61	A46											8	3
Sebastian Giovinco	26/01/87	Juventus	A74	s82	A60	s70							s46		s30		s91			17	1
Mattia Cassani	26/08/83	Fiorentina		D																11	-
Lorenzo Insigne	04/06/91	Napoli		s46																1	-
Giampaolo Pazzini	02/08/84	Milan		s69																25	4
Domenico Criscito	30/12/86	Zenit (RUS)			D															20	-

Appearances 2012/13 (contd.)

			Eng	BUL	MLT	ARM	DEN	Fra	Ned	Bra	MLT	Smr	CZE	Hai	MEX	JPN	BRA	ESP	URU	Caps	Goal
Riccardo Montolivo	18/01/85	Milan				M88	M05	M50	M	M	M		M	s54	M	M	M26	s46	M 110*	50	2
Antonio Candreva	28/02/87	Lazio				s88	s74	A70	A46			s61		A		M	M	M	11	-
Morgan De Sanctis	26/03/77	Napoli					G													6	-
Giorgio Chiellini	14/08/84	Juventus					D	D					D		D	D	D	D	D	63	3
Mario Balotelli	12/08/90	Man. City (ENG)/Milan				A89	A		A01	A83	A86	s50	A 72*	s54	A86	A	A			25	10
Alessandro Florenzi	11/00/91	Roma						s50	s46											2	-
Davide Santon	02/01/91	Newcastle (ENG)							D											8	-
Alberto Gilardino	05/07/82	Bologna							s71	s83	s86	A50		A54	s86			A91	A	55	18
Andrea Ranocchia	16/02/88	Internazionale							s74			D								10	-
Mattia De Sciglio	20/10/92	Milan								D74	D	s45		D	D	D	D		D	8	-
Alessio Cerci	23/07/87	Torino								s46	s76	s51		A60	s68					5	-
Luca Antonelli	11/02/87	Genoa								s74		D45								4	-
Giacomo Bonaventura	22/08/89	Atalanta										A50								1	-
Marco Sau	03/11/87	Cagliari										s50								1	-
Federico Marchetti	07/02/83	Lazio													s46					9	-

European club competitions 2012/13

JUVENTUS

CHAMPIONS LEAGUE

Group E

Match 1 - Chelsea FC (ENG)
A 2-2 *Vidal (38), Quagliarella (80)*
Buffon, Chiellini, Marchisio, Vučinić (Matri 88), Giovinco (Quagliarella 75), Barzagli, Bonucci, Pirlo, Asamoah, Vidal, Lichtsteiner (Isla 77). Coach: Massimo Carrera (ITA)

Match 2 - FC Shakhtar Donetsk (UKR)
H 1-1 *Bonucci (25)*
Buffon, Chiellini, Marchisio, Vučinić (Giovinco 58), Barzagli, Bonucci, Pirlo, Asamoah, Vidal (Pogba 85), Lichtsteiner, Matri (Quagliarella 65). Coach: Massimo Carrera (ITA)

Match 3 - FC Nordsjælland (DEN)
A 1-1 *Vučinić (81)*
Buffon, Lúcio (Bendtner 76), Chiellini, Marchisio, De Ceglie, Giovinco, Bonucci, Pirlo, Vidal (Giaccherini 83), Matri (Vučinić 67), Isla. Coach: Angelo Alessio (ITA)

Match 4 - FC Nordsjælland (DEN)
H 4-0 *Marchisio (6), Vidal (23), Giovinco (37), Quagliarella (75)*
Buffon, Chiellini (Lúcio 69), Marchisio, Giovinco (Quagliarella 61), Barzagli, Bonucci, Pirlo, Asamoah, Vidal (Pogba 53), Matri, Isla. Coach: Angelo Alessio (ITA)

Match 5 - Chelsea FC (ENG)
H 3-0 *Quagliarella (38), Vidal (61), Giovinco (90+1)*
Buffon, Chiellini, Marchisio, Vučinić (Giovinco 83), Barzagli, Bonucci, Pirlo, Asamoah, Vidal, Lichtsteiner (Cáceres 68), Quagliarella (Pogba 89). Coach: Angelo Alessio (ITA)

Match 6 - FC Shakhtar Donetsk (UKR)
A 1-0 *Kucher (56og)*
Buffon, Chiellini, Pogba, Vučinić (Matri 00), Giovinco (Giaccherini 90+2), Barzagli, Bonucci, Pirlo, Asamoah, Vidal, Lichtsteiner. Coach: Angelo Alessio (ITA)

Round of 16 - Celtic FC (SCO)
A 3-0 *Matri (3), Marchisio (77), Vučinić (80)*
Buffon, Cáceres, Marchisio, Vučinić (Anelka 86), Peluso (Padoin 69), Barzagli, Bonucci, Pirlo, Vidal, Lichtsteiner, Matri (Pogba 81). Coach: Antonio Conte (ITA)

H 2-0 *Matri (24), Quagliarella (65)*
Buffon, Pogba, Peluso (Asamoah 59), Barzagli, Bonucci, Padoin, Pirlo (Giaccherini 69), Vidal (Isla 67), Quagliarella, Matri, Marrone. Coach: Antonio Conte (ITA)

Quarter-final - FC Bayern München (GER)
A 0-2
Buffon, Chiellini, Marchisio, Peluso (Pogba 75), Barzagli, Bonucci, Pirlo, Vidal, Lichtsteiner, Quagliarella (Giovinco 65), Matri (Vučinić 65). Coach: Antonio Conte (ITA)

H 0-2
Buffon, Chiellini, Pogba, Marchisio (Giaccherini 79), Vučinić, Barzagli, Bonucci, Padoin (Isla 69), Pirlo, Asamoah, Quagliarella (Matri 66). Coach: Antonio Conte (ITA)

AC MILAN

CHAMPIONS LEAGUE

Group C

Match 1 - RSC Anderlecht (BEL)
H 0-0
Abbiati, De Sciglio, Mexès, Nocerino, Boateng (El Shaarawy 60), Pazzini, Flamini, Bonera (Yepes 74), Emanuelson (Constant 79), De Jong, Antonini. Coach: Massimiliano Allegri (ITA)

Match 2 - FC Zenit St Petersburg (RUS)
A 3-2 *Emanuelson (13), El Shaarawy (16), Hubočan (75og)*
Abbiati, Boateng (Yepes 81), Zapata, Montolivo, Abate, Bojan (Pazzini 52), Bonera, Emanuelson (Nocerino 64), De Jong, Antonini, El Shaarawy. Coach: Massimiliano Allegri (ITA)

Match 3 - Málaga CF (ESP)
A 0-1
Amelia, De Sciglio, Mexès, Pazzini, Acerbi (Bojan 79), Montolivo, Constant (Pato 69), Ambrosini, Bonera, Emanuelson, El Shaarawy. Coach: Massimiliano Allegri (ITA)

Match 4 - Málaga CF (ESP)
H 1-1 *Pato (73)*
Abbiati, Mexès, Pato, Montolivo, Abate (De Sciglio 6), Constant, Bojan, Bonera, Emanuelson (Robinho 80), De Jong, El Shaarawy (Boateng 62). Coach: Massimiliano Allegri (ITA)

Match 5 - RSC Anderlecht (BEL)
A 3-1 El Shaarawy (47), Mexès (71), Pato (90+1)
Abbiati, De Sciglio, Mexès (Zapata 79), Nocerino, Boateng, Montolivo, Constant (Emanuelson 73), Bojan (Pato 67), De Jong, Yepes, El Shaarawy. Coach: Massimiliano Allegri (ITA)

Match 6 - FC Zenit St Petersburg (RUS)
H 0-1
Abbiati, De Sciglio, Boateng, Pazzini, Acerbi, Mesbah (Robinho 65), Flamini (El Shaarawy 80), Zapata, Bojan (Petagna 90+1), Ambrosini, Emanuelson. Coach: Massimiliano Allegri (ITA)

Round of 16 - FC Barcelona (ESP)
H 2-0 Boateng (57), Muntari (81)
Abbiati, Muntari, Mexès, Boateng, Pazzini (Niang 75), Zapata, Montolivo, Abate, Constant, Ambrosini, El Shaarawy (Traoré 88). Coach: Massimiliano Allegri (ITA)

A 0-4
Abbiati, Mexès, Boateng, Flamini (Bojan 74), Zapata, Montolivo, Niang (Robinho 60), Abate, Constant, Ambrosini (Muntari 60), El Shaarawy. Coach: Massimiliano Allegri (ITA)

UDINESE CALCIO

CHAMPIONS LEAGUE

Play-offs - SC Braga (POR)
A 1-1 Basta (23)
Brkić, Danilo, Basta, Di Natale, Domizzi, Benatia, Armero (Pasquale 85), Fabbrini (Maicosuel 72), Pereyra (Agyemang-Badu 73), Pinzi, Willians. Coach: Francesco Guidolin (ITA)

H 1-1 Armero (25) (aet; 4-5 on pens)
Brkić, Danilo, Basta, Di Natale, Domizzi, Benatia, Armero, Fabbrini (Maicosuel 81), Pereyra (Pasquale 69), Pinzi, Willians (Agyemang-Badu 46). Coach: Francesco Guidolin (ITA)

EUROPA LEAGUE

Group A
Match 1 - FC Anji Makhachkala (RUS)
H 1-1 Di Natale (90+2)
Padelli, Danilo, Faraoni, Agyemang-Badu (Di Natale 58), Domizzi, Ranégie, Benatia, Lazzari, Armero, Pereyra (Pinzi 76), Willians (Basta 59). Coach: Francesco Guidolin (ITA)

Match 2 - Liverpool FC (ENG)
A 3-2 Di Natale (46), Coates (70og), Pasquale (72)
Brkić, Danilo, Faraoni, Agyemang-Badu, Di Natale (Ranégie 85), Domizzi, Benatia, Pasquale, Armero (Lazzari 46), Pereyra, Pinzi (Willians 70). Coach: Francesco Guidolin (ITA)

Match 3 - BSC Young Boys (SUI)
A 1-3 Coda (74)
Brkić, Danilo, Faraoni, Agyemang-Badu (Pereyra 46), Ranégie (Di Natale 46), Coda, Benatia, Lazzari (Domizzi 71), Armero, Fabbrini, Willians. Coach: Francesco Guidolin (ITA)

Match 4 - BSC Young Boys (SUI)
H 2-3 Di Natale (47), Fabbrini (83)
Brkić, Danilo, Basta, Di Natale, Domizzi, Ranégie, Coda, Lazzari, Armero, Pereyra (Faraoni 64), Willians (Fabbrini 53). Coach: Francesco Guidolin (ITA)

Match 5 - FC Anji Makhachkala (RUS)
A 0-2
Brkić, Danilo, Faraoni (Basta 57; Ranégie 76), Agyemang-Badu, Di Natale, Domizzi, Armero (Pasquale 71), Fabbrini, Pereyra, Heurtaux, Willians. Coach: Francesco Guidolin (ITA)
Red card: Willians 80

Match 6 - Liverpool FC (ENG)
H 0-1
Padelli, Danilo, Faraoni, Agyemang-Badu, Ranégie (Di Natale 86), Pasquale, Armero, Fabbrini, Pereyra, Pinzi (Benatia 46; Reinthaler 65), Heurtaux. Coach: Francesco Guidolin (ITA)
Red card: Pasquale 79

SSC NAPOLI

EUROPA LEAGUE

Group F
Match 1 - AIK (SWE)
H 4-0 Vargas (6, 46, 69), Dzemaili (90+1)
Rosati, Donadel (Dzemaili 56), Aronica, Dossena, Vargas (Zúñiga 80), El Kaddouri (Hamšík 46), Mesto, Fernández, L Insigne, Gamberini, Behrami. Coach: Nicolo Frustalupi (ITA)
Red card: Hamšík 75

Match 2 - PSV Eindhoven (NED)
A 0-3
Rosati, Donadel, Aronica, Dossena (Zúñiga 72), Vargas , El Kaddouri (Cavani 46), Mesto, Dzemaili, Fernández, L Insigne (Pandev 62), Cannavaro. Coach: Walter Mazzarri (ITA)

Match 3 - FC Dnipro Dnipropetrovsk (UKR)
A 1-3 Cavani (75p)
Rosati, Donadel, Aronica, Dossena (Pandev 52), Vargas (Cavani 52), Mesto, Zúñiga, Dzemaili, Fernández, L Insigne, Gamberini (Inler 78). Coach: Walter Mazzarri (ITA)

Match 4 - FC Dnipro Dnipropetrovsk (UKR)
H 4-2 Cavani (7, 77, 88, 90+3)
Rosati, Donadel (Hamšík 55), Britos, Aronica (Pandev 72), Cavani, Dossena, Vargas (L Insigne 56), Mesto, Dzemaili, Fernández, Inler. Coach: Walter Mazzarri (ITA)

Match 5 - AIK (SWE)
A 2-1 Dzemaili (20), Cavani (90+3p)
Rosati, Donadel (Inler 62), Britos, Aronica, Cavani, Dossena, Vargas , Mesto (Zúñiga 64), Dzemaili (Hamšík 73), Gamberini, Behrami. Coach: Walter Mazzarri (ITA)
Red card: Aronica 85

Match 6 - PSV Eindhoven (NED)
H 1-3 Cavani (18)
Rosati, Uvini, Donadel, Cavani (R Insigne 66), Dossena, Vargas , Maggio (Mesto 69), El Kaddouri, Campagnaro, Fernández, Inler (Pandev 57). Coach: Walter Mazzarri (ITA)

Round of 32 - FC Viktoria Plzeň (CZE)
H 0-3
De Sanctis, Donadel (Inler 72), Britos, Cavani, Maggio, El Kaddouri (Calaiò 59), Zúñiga, Pandev, Dzemaili, Rolando, Gamberini (Hamšík 46). Coach: Walter Mazzarri (ITA)

A 0-2
De Sanctis, Donadel (Cavani 46), Maggio, Zúñiga, Pandev, Dzemaili, L Insigne, Rolando, Calaiò, Gamberini (Cannavaro 66), Behrami (Inler 46). Coach: Walter Mazzarri (ITA)

S.S. LAZIO

EUROPA LEAGUE

Play-offs - ND Mura 05 (SVN)
A 2-0 Hernanes (31), Klose (59)
Marchetti, André Dias, Mauri (Zárate 71), Hernanes (Lulić 59), Klose (Floccari 83), Biava, Onazi, Ledesma, Konko, Cavanda , Candreva. Coach: Vladimir Petković (SUI)

H 3-1 Kozák (30, 55), Zárate (42)
Bizzarri, André Dias, Scaloni, Hernanes (Konko 79), Zárate, González (Rozzi 61), Kozák, Lulić (Candreva 69), Biava, Onazi, Cavanda. Coach: Vladimir Petković (SUI)

Group J
Match 1 - Tottenham Hotspur FC (ENG)
A 0-0
Marchetti, André Dias, Mauri (Ederson 90+2), Hernanes (Ciani 90+4), Klose, González, Lulić, Biava, Onazi (Zárate 80), Ledooma, Cavanda. Coach: Vladimir Petković (SUI)
Match 2 - NK Maribor (SVN)
H 1-0 Ederson (62)
Bizzarri, Ciani, André Dias, Ederson (Onazi 69), Hernanes, González (Zárate 84), Cana, Konko, Cavanda , Candreva, Floccari (Kozák 90+2). Coach: Vladimir Petković (SUI)
Match 3 - Panathinaikos FC (GRE)
A 1-1 Seitaridis (25og)
Bizzarri, Ciani, André Dias, Mauri (Zárate 46), Hernanes (Onazi 78), González (Cana 87), Ledesma, Konko, Cavanda , Candreva, Floccari. Coach: Vladimir Petković (SUI)
Match 4 - Panathinaikos FC (GRE)
H 3-0 Kozák (23, 40), Floccari (59)
Marchetti, Ciani, Scaloni, Zárate, González (Hernanes 67), Kozák (Klose 76), Onazi, Ledesma (Lulić 80), Radu, Cana, Floccari. Coach: Vladimir Petković (SUI)
Match 5 - Tottenham Hotspur FC (ENG)
H 0-0
Marchetti, Ciani, Mauri, Hernanes (Ederson 69), González, Kozák (Floccari 79) Lulić (Candreva 79), Biava, Ledesma, Radu, Cavanda. Coach: Vladimir Petković (SUI)
Match 6 - NK Maribor (SVN)
A 4-1 Kozák (16), Radu (32), Floccari (38, 51)
Bizzarri, Ciani, Ederson, Hernanes (González 56), Kozák (Rozzi 78), Lulić, Onazi, Radu (Scaloni 56), Cana, Cavanda , Floccari. Coach: Vladimir Petković (SUI)

Round of 32 - VfL Borussia Mönchengladbach (GER)
A 3-3 Floccari (57), Kozák (64, 90+4)
Marchetti, André Dias, Hernanes, González, Lulić (Ciani 88), Biava, Ledesma (Kozák 46), Radu, Konko, Candreva (Cana 72), Floccari. Coach: Vladimir Petković (SUI)
Red card: André Dias 69
H 2-0 Candreva (10), González (33)
Marchetti, Hernanes, González (Onazi 69), Lulić, Biava, Ledesma, Radu, Cana, Konko, Candreva (Bruno Pereirinha 82), Floccari (Kozák 78). Coach: Vladimir Petković (SUI)

Round of 16 - VfB Stuttgart (GER)
A 2-0 Ederson (21), Onazi (56)
Marchetti, Ciani, Ederson (Ledesma 64), Hernanes (González 72), Bruno Pereirinha, Kozák (Floccari 84), Lulić, Onazi, Radu, Cana, Candreva. Coach: Vladimir Petković (SUI)
H 3-1 Kozák (6, 8, 87)
Marchetti (Bizzarri 43), Ciani, Mauri (Ledesma 65), Hernanes (Ederson 74), Bruno Pereirinha, Kozák, Lulić, Biava, Onazi, Radu, Candreva. Coach: Vladimir Petković (SUI)

Quarter-final - Fenerbahçe SK (TUR)
A 0-2
Marchetti, Ciani, Ederson (Ledesma 63), Hernanes (Mauri 86), González, Kozák (Klose 72), Lulić, Onazi, Radu, Cana, Candreva. Coach: Vladimir Petković (SUI)
Red card: Onazi 48
H 1-1 Lulić (60)
Marchetti, Ciani, Ederson (Floccari 73), Hernanes, Kozák (Rozzi 77), Lulić, Biava (Klose 56), Ledesma, Radu, Cana, Candreva. Coach: Vladimir Petković (SUI)

FC INTERNAZIONALE MILANO

Third qualifying round - HNK Hajduk Split (CRO)
A 3-0 Sneijder (18), Nagatomo (44), Coutinho (73)
Handanovič, Zanetti, Silvestre, Palacio, Sneijder (Coutinho 65), Guarín, Cambiasso, Milito (Livaja 76), Chivu (Samuel 46), Jonathan, Nagatomo. Coach: Andrea Stramaccioni (ITA)
H 0-2
Handanovič, Zanetti, Coutinho (Longo 64), Sneijder (Silvestre 84), Guarín, Cambiasso, Milito , Ranocchia, Samuel, Mbayé (Nagatomo 55), Jonathan. Coach: Andrea Stramaccioni (ITA)

Play-offs - FC Vaslui (ROU)
A 2-0 Cambiasso (23), Palacio (73)
Castellazzi, Zanetti, Silvestre, Palacio, Sneijder (Juan 82), Maicon, Guarín, Mudingayi (Nagatomo 21), Cambiasso, Milito (Coutinho 72), Ranocchia. Coach: Andrea Stramaccioni (ITA)
H 2-2 Palacio (76), Guarín (90+2)
Castellazzi, Zanetti, Silvestre, Coutinho, Palacio, Cambiasso, Samuel (Guarín 46), Juan, Jonathan (Ranocchia 82), Nagatomo, Cassano (Belec 34). Coach: Andrea Stramaccioni (ITA)
Red card: Castellazzi 33

Group H
Match 1 - FC Rubin Kazan (RUS)
H 2-2 Livaja (39), Nagatomo (90+2)
Handanovič, Zanetti, Coutinho, Cambiasso, Gargano, Ranocchia, Samuel, Jonathan (Guarín 46), Nagatomo, Livaja (Milito 61), Cassano (Pereira 67). Coach: Andrea Stramaccioni (ITA)

Match 2 - Neftçi PFK (AZE)
A 3-1 Coutinho (10), Obi (30), Livaja (42)
Handanovič, Silvestre, Coutinho (Garritano 75), Guarín (Gargano 82), Mudingayi, Cambiasso, Obi (Ranocchia 64), Pereira, Juan, Jonathan, Livaja. Coach: Andrea Stramaccioni (ITA)
Match 3 - FK Partizan (SRB)
H 1-0 Palacio (88)
Handanovič, Silvestre, Coutinho (Palacio 32), Guarín, Mudingayi, Cambiasso, Pereira, Juan, Jonathan, Livaja (Zanetti 52), Cassano (Milito 76). Coach: Andrea Stramaccioni (ITA)
Match 4 - FK Partizan (SRB)
A 3-1 Palacio (51, 75), Guarín (87)
Handanovič, Zanetti, Silvestre, Guarín, Mudingayi (Gargano 14), Cambiasso, Pereira, Juan, Jonathan, Nagatomo (Palacio 46), Livaja (Cassano 77). Coach: Andrea Stramaccioni (ITA)
Match 5 - FC Rubin Kazan (RUS)
A 0-3
Belec, Silvestre, Coutinho, Gargano, Ranocchia (Donkor 72), Benassi, Pereira, Juan, Jonathan, Romanò (Zanetti 46), Livaja (Palacio 46). Coach: Andrea Stramaccioni (ITA)
Match 6 - Neftçi PFK (AZE)
H 2-2 Livaja (9, 54)
Belec, Coutinho, Cambiasso, Benassi, Samuel (Cassano 46), Pasa, Pereira, Jonathan (Bandini 63), Romanò, Garritano (Nagatomo 53), Livaja. Coach: Andrea Stramaccioni (ITA)

Round of 32 - CFR 1907 Cluj (ROU)
H 2-0 Palacio (20, 87)
Handanovič, Silvestre, Guarín, Cambiasso, Obigarin, Milito (Pereira 70), Ranocchia, Mateo Kovačić (Jonathan 88), Pereira, Nagatomo, Cassano (Álvarez 74). Coach: Andrea Stramaccioni (ITA)
A 3-0 Guarín (22, 45+2), Benassi (89)
Handanovič, Zanetti, Palacio (Benassi 46), Álvarez (Pasa 54), Guarín (Mbaye 66), Cambiasso, Ranocchia, Mateo Kovačić, Pereira, Juan, Cassano. Coach: Andrea Stramaccioni (ITA)

Round of 16 - Tottenham Hotspur FC (ENG)
A 0-3
Handanovič, Zanetti, Álvarez (Jonathan 67), Cambiasso, Gargano, Ranocchia, Chivu, Mateo Kovačić (Guarín 55), Pereira, Juan (Palacio 46), Cassano. Coach: Andrea Stramaccioni (ITA)
H 4-1 Cassano (20), Palacio (52), Gallas (75og), Álvarez (110)
Handanovič, Zanetti, Palacio, Guarín (Álvarez 71), Cambiasso, Gargano, Chivu, Mateo Kovačić (Benassi 79), Juan, Jonathan (Ranocchia 107), Cassano. Coach: Andrea Stramaccioni (ITA)

Domestic league club-by-club

ATALANTA BC

Coach: Stefano Colantuono
1907 • Atleti Azzurri d'Italia (26,393) • atalanta.it
Major honours
Italian Cup (1) 1963

2012
26/08	Lazio	h	0-1	
02/09	Cagliari	a	1-1	Denis
15/09	Milan	a	1-0	Cigarini
23/09	Palermo	h	1-0	Raimondi
26/09	Catania	a	1-2	Moralez
30/09	Torino	h	1-5	Denis
07/10	Roma	a	0-2	
21/10	Siena	h	2-1	Cigarini, Bonaventura
28/10	Pescara	a	0-0	
31/10	Napoli	h	1-0	Carmona
04/11	Sampdoria	a	2-1	Bonaventura, De Luca
11/11	Internazionale	h	3-2	Bonaventura, Denis 2 (1p)
18/11	Fiorentina	a	1-4	Bonaventura
25/11	Genoa	h	0-1	
02/12	Bologna	h	2-1	Denis
08/12	Parma	h	2-1	Denis, Peluso
16/12	Juventus	a	0-3	
22/12	Udinese	h	1-1	Denis (p)

2013
06/01	Chievo	a	0-1	
13/01	Lazio	a	0-2	
20/01	Cagliari	h	1-1	Stendardo
27/01	Milan	h	0-1	
03/02	Palermo	a	2-1	Carmona, Denis
10/02	Catania	h	0-0	
17/02	Torino	a	1-2	Denis (p)
24/02	Roma	h	2-3	Livaja 2
03/03	Siena	a	2-0	Bonaventura 2
10/03	Pescara	h	2-1	Denis 2 (1p)
17/03	Napoli	a	2-3	og (Cannavaro), Denis
30/03	Sampdoria	h	0-0	
07/04	Internazionale	h	4-3	Bonaventura, Denis 3 (1p)
13/04	Fiorentina	h	0-2	
20/04	Genoa	a	1-1	Del Grosso
27/04	Bologna	h	1-1	Giorgi
05/05	Parma	a	0-2	
08/05	Juventus	h	0-1	
12/05	Udinese	a	1-2	De Luca
19/05	Chievo	h	2-2	Stendardo, Giorgi

No	Name	Nat	DoB	Pos	Aps	(s)	Gls
6	Gianpaolo Bellini		27/03/80	D	10	(1)	
88	Davide Biondini		24/01/83	M	20	(4)	
10	Giacomo Bonaventura		22/08/89	M	31	(4)	7
23	Franco Brienza		19/03/79	M	3	(3)	
28	Davide Brivio		17/03/88	M	15	(5)	
20	Igor Budan	CRO	22/04/80	A		(2)	
13	Michele Canini		05/06/85	D	10	(2)	
4	Daniele Capelli		20/06/86	D	1		
17	Carlos Carmona	CHI	21/02/87	M	19	(1)	2
44	Riccardo Cazzola		10/08/85	M	9	(13)	
21	Luca Cigarini		20/06/86	M	26	(1)	2
47	Andrea Consigli		27/01/87	G	35		
22	Matteo Contini		16/04/80	D	1	(2)	
91	Giuseppe De Luca		11/10/91	A	7	(11)	2
83	Cristiano Del Grosso		24/03/83	D	13		1
19	Germán Denis	ARG	10/09/81	A	35	(1)	15
32	Michele Ferri		29/05/81	D	7	(2)	
18	Luigi Giorgi		19/04/87	M	11	(4)	2
7	Marko Livaja	CRO	26/08/93	A	6	(5)	2
3	Stefano Lucchini		02/10/80	D	19	(1)	
5	Thomas Manfredini		27/05/80	D	15		
89	Guido Marilungo		09/08/89	A		(2)	
25	Carlos Matheu	ARG	13/05/85	D	1	(3)	
11	Maximiliano Moralez	ARG	27/02/87	M	26	(3)	1
94	Antonio Palma		03/01/94	M		(1)	
99	Facundo Parra	ARG	15/06/85	A	3	(11)	
13	Federico Peluso		20/01/84	D	13		1
16	Ciro Polito		12/04/79	G	3	(1)	
8	Ivan Radovanović	SRB	29/08/88	M	8	(8)	
77	Cristian Raimondi		30/04/81	M	22	(4)	1
5	Lionel Scaloni	ARG	16/05/78	D	6	(1)	
7	Ezequiel Schelotto		23/05/89	M	12	(4)	
23	Matteo Scozzarella		05/06/88	M		(3)	
2	Guglielmo Stendardo		06/05/81	D	29	(3)	2
9	James Troisi	AUS	03/07/88	M	2	(4)	

BOLOGNA FC

Coach: Stefano Pioli
1909 • Renato Dall'Ara (39,444) • bolognafc.it
Major honours
Italian League (7) 1925, 1929, 1936, 1937, 1939, 1941, 1964;
Italian Cup (2) 1970, 1974

2012
26/08	Chievo	a	0-2	
01/09	Milan	h	1-3	Diamanti (p)
16/09	Roma	a	3-2	Gilardino 2, Diamanti
23/09	Pescara	h	1-1	Gilardino
27/09	Siena	a	0-1	
30/09	Catania	h	4-0	Guarente, Gilardino 2, Kone
07/10	Fiorentina	a	0-1	
21/10	Cagliari	a	0-1	
28/10	Internazionale	h	1-3	Cherubin
31/10	Juventus	a	1-2	Taïder
04/11	Udinese	h	1-1	Diamanti
11/11	Torino	a	0-0	
18/11	Palermo	h	3-0	Gilardino, Gabbiadini (p), Diamanti (p)
25/11	Sampdoria	a	0-1	
02/12	Atalanta	h	2-1	Diamanti, Gabbiadini
10/12	Lazio	h	0-0	
16/12	Napoli	a	3-2	Gabbiadini, Kone, Portanova
22/12	Parma	h	1-2	Sørensen

2013
06/01	Genoa	a	0-2	
12/01	Chievo	h	4-0	Kone, Gilardino 2, Gabbiadini
20/01	Milan	a	1-2	og (Mexès)
27/01	Roma	h	3-3	Gilardino, Gabbiadini, Pasquato
03/02	Pescara	a	3-2	Diamanti (p), Gilardino, Kone
10/02	Siena	h	1-1	Kone
17/02	Catania	a	0-1	
26/02	Fiorentina	h	2-1	Motta, Christodoulopoulos
03/03	Cagliari	h	3-0	Taïder, Diamanti, Pasquato
10/03	Internazionale	a	1-0	Gilardino
16/03	Juventus	h	0-2	
30/03	Udinese	a	0-0	
06/04	Torino	h	2-2	Kone, Guarente
14/04	Palermo	a	1-1	Gabbiadini
21/04	Sampdoria	h	1-1	Gilardino
27/04	Atalanta	a	1-1	Gilardino
05/05	Lazio	a	0-6	
08/05	Napoli	h	0-3	
12/05	Parma	a	2-0	Taïder, Moscardelli
19/05	Genoa	h	0-0	

No	Name	Nat	DoB	Pos	Aps	(s)	Gls
20	Mathías Abero	URU	09/04/90	D	1	(9)	
9	Robert Acquafresca		11/09/87	A	3	(3)	
25	Federico Agliardi		11/02/83	G	20	(2)	
5	Mikael Antonsson	SWE	31/05/81	D	31		
21	Nicolò Cherubin		02/12/86	D	29		1
19	Lazaros Christodoulopoulos	GRE	19/12/86	M	7	(5)	1
1	Gianluca Curci		12/07/85	G	14		
23	Alessandro Diamanti		02/05/83	A	33	(1)	7
15	Diego Pérez	URU	18/05/80	M	23		
18	Manolo Gabbiadini		26/11/91	A	19	(11)	6
8	György Garics	AUT	08/03/84	D	21	(6)	
10	Alberto Gilardino		05/07/82	A	35	(1)	13
77	Henry Giménez	URU	13/03/86	A		(2)	
17	Tiberio Guarente		01/11/85	M	11	(9)	2
33	Panagiotis Kone	GRE	26/07/87	M	26	(5)	6
4	René Krhin	SVN	21/05/90	M	12	(9)	
28	Martí Riverola	ESP	26/01/91	M	1		
3	Archimede Morleo		26/09/83	D	28	(4)	
9	Davide Moscardelli		03/02/80	A		(9)	1
11	Marco Motta		14/05/86	D	18	(1)	1
44	Naldo	BRA	25/08/88	D	2	(3)	
14	Cesare Natali		05/04/79	D	4	(1)	
24	Daniele Paponi		16/04/88	A		(3)	
77	Cristian Pasquato		20/07/89	A	3	(12)	2
30	Michele Pazienza		05/08/82	M	10	(5)	
90	Daniele Portanova		17/12/78	D	5		1
13	Nico Pulzetti		13/02/84	M	2	(4)	
45	Roger Carvalho	BRA	10/12/86	D	4	(2)	
32	Dejan Stojanovic	AUT	11/09/93	G	4		
43	Frederik Sørensen	DEN	14/04/92	D	20	(5)	1
6	Saphir Taïder	FRA	29/02/92	M	32	(2)	3

CAGLIARI CALCIO

Coach: Massimo Ficcadenti; (02/10/12) Ivo Pulga
1920 • Is Arenas (16,200); Nereo Rocco, Trieste (32,454)
• cagliaricalcio.net
Major honours
Italian League (1) 1970

2012
26/08	Genoa	a	0-2	
02/09	Atalanta	h	1-1	Ekdal
15/09	Palermo	a	1-1	Sau
23/09	Roma	h	0-3	(w/o)
26/09	Milan	a	0-2	
30/09	Pescara	h	1-2	Pinilla (p)
07/10	Torino	a	1-0	Nenê (p)
21/10	Bologna	h	1-0	Nainggolan
28/10	Sampdoria	a	1-0	Dessena
31/10	Siena	h	4-2	Nenê 2, Sau, Thiago Ribeiro
04/11	Fiorentina	a	1-4	Casarini
10/11	Catania	h	0-0	
18/11	Internazionale	a	2-2	Sau 2
26/11	Napoli	h	0-1	
02/12	Udinese	a	1-4	Dessena
09/12	Chievo	h	0-2	
16/12	Parma	a	1-4	Sau
21/12	Juventus	h	1-3	Pinilla (p)

2013
05/01	Lazio	a	1-2	Sau
13/01	Genoa	h	2-1	Sau, Conti
20/01	Atalanta	a	1-1	og (Canini)
27/01	Palermo	h	1-1	Thiago Ribeiro
01/02	Roma	a	4-2	Nainggolan, og (Goicoechea), Sau, Pisano
10/02	Milan	h	1-1	Ibarbo
17/02	Pescara	a	2-0	Sau 2
24/02	Torino	h	4-3	Sau (p), Conti 2, Pinilla (p)
03/03	Bologna	a	0-3	
10/03	Sampdoria	h	3-1	Ibarbo 3
17/03	Siena	a	0-0	
30/03	Fiorentina	h	2-1	Pinilla 2 (1p)
07/04	Catania	a	0-0	
14/04	Internazionale	h	2-0	Pinilla 2 (1p)
21/04	Napoli	a	2-3	Ibarbo, Sau
27/04	Udinese	h	0-1	
04/05	Chievo	a	0-0	
08/05	Parma	h	0-1	
11/05	Juventus	a	1-1	Ibarbo
19/05	Lazio	h	1-0	Dessena

No	Name	Nat	DoB	Pos	Aps	(s)	Gls
1	Michael Agazzi		03/07/84	G	34		
3	Lorenzo Ariaudo		11/06/89	D	15	(2)	
13	Davide Astori		07/01/87	D	31	(1)	
25	Vlada Avramov	SRB	04/05/79	G	3	(2)	
22	Matías Cabrera	URU	16/05/86	M		(7)	
32	Federico Casarini		07/09/89	M	4	(7)	1
30	Pablo Ceppelini	URU	11/09/91	M		(1)	
5	Daniele Conti		09/01/79	M	29		3
7	Andrea Cossu		03/05/80	M	13	(11)	
8	Danilo Avelar	BRA	09/06/89	D	19	(1)	
34	Dario Del Fabro		24/03/95	D	1	(2)	
21	Daniele Dessena		10/05/87	M	28	(3)	3
20	Albin Ekdal	SWE	28/07/89	M	27	(4)	1
16	Sebastian Eriksson	SWE	31/01/89	M	1	(7)	
23	Victor Ibarbo	COL	19/05/90	A	22	(12)	6
9	Joaquín Larrivey	ARG	20/08/84	A	2	(1)	
29	Nicola Murru		16/12/94	D	13		
4	Radja Nainggolan	BEL	04/05/88	M	33	(1)	2
18	Nenê	BRA	28/07/83	A	12	(11)	3
24	Gabriele Perico		11/03/84	D	12	(4)	
51	Mauricio Pinilla	CHI	04/02/84	A	12	(11)	7
14	Francesco Pisano		29/04/86	D	28		1
15	Luca Rossettini		09/05/85	D	28		
27	Marco Sau		03/11/87	A	23	(7)	12
19	Thiago Ribeiro	BRA	24/02/86	A	17	(12)	2

CALCIO CATANIA

Coach: Rolando Maran
1946 • Angelo Massimino (23,420) • calciocatania.it

2012

26/08	Roma	a	2-2	Marchese, Gómez
02/09	Genoa	h	3-2	Bergessio 2, Lodi
16/09	Fiorentina	a	0-2	
23/09	Napoli	h	0-0	
26/09	Atalanta	h	2-1	Spolli, Barrientos
30/09	Bologna	a	0-4	
07/10	Parma	h	2-0	Gómez, Bergessio
21/10	Internazionale	a	0-2	
28/10	Juventus	a	0-1	
31/10	Udinese	a	2-2	Castro, Lodi
04/11	Lazio	h	4-0	Gómez 2, Lodi (p), Barrientos
10/11	Cagliari	a	0-0	
18/11	Chievo	h	2-1	Almirón 2
24/11	Palermo	a	1-3	Lodi
02/12	Milan	h	1-3	Legrottaglie
09/12	Siena	a	0-1	Castro, Barrientos
16/12	Sampdoria	h	3-1	Paglialunga, Bergessio, Castro
21/12	Pescara	a	1-2	Barrientos

2013

05/01	Torino	h	0-0	
13/01	Roma	h	1-0	Gómez
20/01	Genoa	a	2-0	Bergessio, Barrientos
27/01	Fiorentina	h	2-1	Legrottaglie, Castro
02/02	Napoli	a	0-2	
10/02	Atalanta	a	0-0	
17/02	Bologna	h	1-0	Almirón
24/02	Parma	a	2-1	Lodi, Keko
03/03	Internazionale	h	2-3	Bergessio, Marchese
10/03	Juventus	a	0-1	
16/03	Udinese	h	3-1	Gómez 2, Lodi
30/03	Lazio	a	1-2	Izco
07/04	Cagliari	h	0-0	
14/04	Chievo	a	0-0	
21/04	Palermo	h	1-1	Barrientos
28/04	Milan	a	1-4	Legrottaglie, Bergessio
05/05	Siena	h	3-0	Bergessio 3
08/05	Sampdoria	a	1-1	Spolli
11/05	Pescara	h	1-0	Gómez
19/05	Torino	a	2-2	Almirón, Bergessio

No	Name	Nat	DoB	Pos	Aps	(s)	Gls
4	Sergio Almirón	ARG	07/11/80	M	26	(4)	4
22	Pablo Álvarez	ARG	17/04/84	D	26	(1)	
21	Mariano Andújar	ARG	30/07/83	G	34		
25	Mirco Antenucci		08/09/84	A		(1)	
18	Błażej Augustyn	POL	26/01/88	D		(1)	
28	Pablo Barrientos	ARG	17/01/85	M	30	(1)	5
14	Giuseppe Bellusci		21/08/89	D	22	(4)	
9	Gonzalo Bergessio	ARG	20/07/84	A	32		13
27	Marco Biagianti		19/04/84	M	17	(11)	
32	Edgar Çani	ALB	22/07/89	A		(4)	
33	Ciro Capuano		10/07/81	D	9	(5)	
19	Lucas Castro	ARG	09/04/89	M	18	(18)	4
35	Souleymane Doukara	FRA	29/09/91	A	1	(11)	
1	Alberto Frison		22/01/88	G	4		
17	Alejandro Gómez	ARG	15/02/88	M	34	(2)	8
13	Mariano Izco	ARG	13/03/83	M	31	(4)	1
26	Keko	ESP	27/12/91	A	2	(2)	1
6	Nicola Legrottaglie		20/10/76	D	26	(1)	3
10	Francesco Lodi		23/03/84	M	33		6
12	Giovanni Marchese		17/10/84	D	29	(1)	2
15	Takayuki Morimoto	JPN	07/05/88	A	1	(4)	
16	Mario Paglialunga	ARG	20/04/84	M	1	(5)	1
40	Bruno Petković	CRO	16/09/94	A		(1)	
2	Alessandro Potenza		08/03/84	D		(2)	
24	Adrián Ricchiuti	ARG	30/06/78	A		(8)	
5	Alexis Rolín	URU	07/02/89	D	9	(2)	
30	Amidu Salifu	GHA	20/09/92	M	4	(6)	
8	Fabio Sciacca		16/05/89	M		(3)	
3	Nicolás Spolli	ARG	20/02/83	D	29		2

AC CHIEVO VERONA

Coach: Domenico Di Carlo; (02/10/12) Eugenio Corini
1929 • Marc'Antonio Bentegodi (39,211) •
chievoverona.tv

2012

26/08	Bologna	h	2-0	Pellissier, Cruzado
02/09	Parma	a	0-2	
16/09	Lazio	h	1-3	Pellissier (p)
22/09	Juventus	a	0-2	
26/09	Internazionale	h	0-2	
30/09	Palermo	a	1-4	M Rigoni
06/10	Sampdoria	h	2-1	Théréau, Di Michele
21/10	Fiorentina	h	1-1	Théréau
28/10	Napoli	a	0-1	
31/10	Pescara	h	2-0	Luciano (p), Stoian
03/11	Milan	a	1-5	Pellissier
11/11	Udinese	h	2-2	Andreolli, Paloschi (p)
18/11	Catania	a	1-2	Andreolli
25/11	Siena	h	0-0	
02/12	Genoa	a	4-2	Paloschi 3 (1p), Stoian
09/12	Cagliari	a	2-0	Paloschi, Théréau
16/12	Roma	h	1-0	Pellissier
22/12	Torino	a	0-0	

2013

06/01	Atalanta	h	1-0	Cofie
12/01	Bologna	a	0-4	
20/01	Parma	h	1-1	Paloschi
26/01	Lazio	a	1-0	Paloschi
03/02	Juventus	h	1-2	Théréau
10/02	Internazionale	a	1-3	L Rigoni
16/02	Palermo	h	1-1	Théréau (p)
24/02	Sampdoria	a	0-2	
03/03	Fiorentina	a	1-2	Cofie
10/03	Napoli	h	2-0	Dramé, Théréau
17/03	Pescara	a	2-0	Stoian, Théréau
30/03	Milan	h	0-1	
07/04	Udinese	a	1-3	Papp
14/04	Catania	h	0-0	
21/04	Siena	a	1-0	Pellissier
28/04	Genoa	h	0-1	
04/05	Cagliari	h	0-0	
11/05	Roma	a	1-0	Théréau
12/05	Torino	h	1-1	Théréau
19/05	Atalanta	a	2-2	Théréau 2

No	Name	Nat	DoB	Pos	Aps	(s)	Gls
51	Francesco Acerbi		10/02/88	D	5	(2)	
3	Marco Andreolli		10/06/86	D	28		2
12	Boštjan Cesar	SVN	09/07/82	D	19	(3)	
14	Isaac Cofie	GHA	05/04/91	M	23	(4)	2
8	Rinaldo Cruzado	PER	21/09/84	M	1	(4)	1
2	Dario Dainelli		09/06/79	D	34		
17	David Di Michele		06/01/76	A	6	(5)	1
93	Boukary Dramé	SEN	22/07/85	D	21	(1)	1
26	Pavol Farkaš	SVK	27/03/85	D	2	(2)	
21	Nicolas Frey	FRA	06/03/84	D	20	(1)	
5	Roberto Guana		21/01/81	M	22	(1)	
27	Gabriel Hauche	ARG	27/11/86	A		(1)	
56	Perparim Hetemaj	FIN	12/12/86	M	28	(2)	
13	Bojan Jokič	SVN	17/05/86	D	13	(7)	
95	Luciano	BRA	03/12/75	M	12	(12)	1
95	Matheus	BRA	04/01/95	M		(1)	
9	Davide Moscardelli		03/02/80	A	1	(6)	
23	Djiby N'Diaye	SEN	05/01/94	M	1		
43	Alberto Paloschi		04/01/90	A	16	(4)	7
33	Paul Papp	ROU	11/11/89	D	6	(2)	1
31	Sergio Pellissier		12/04/79	A	13	(11)	5
1	Christian Puggioni		17/01/81	G	17		
16	Luca Rigoni		07/12/84	M	31		1
6	Marco Rigoni		05/01/80	A	4	(6)	1
11	Mamadou Samassa	MLI	01/05/86	A	1	(7)	
17	Mario Sampirisi		31/10/92	M	3		
20	Gennaro Sardo		08/05/79	D	18	(5)	
7	Felipe Seymour	CHI	23/07/87	M	3	(4)	
54	Stefano Sorrentino		28/03/79	G	20		
22	Ali Sowe	GAM	14/06/94	D		(2)	
4	Nikolaos Spyropoulos	GRE	10/10/83	D		(2)	
18	Lorenzo Squizzi		20/06/74	G	1		
39	Adrian Stoian	ROU	11/02/91	A	7	(13)	3
77	Cyril Théréau	FRA	24/04/83	A	35	(2)	11
25	Kamil Vacek	CZE	18/05/87	M	7	(4)	

ACF FIORENTINA

Coach: Vincenzo Montella
1926 • Artemio Franchi (47,282) • violachannel.tv
Major honours
UEFA Cup Winners' Cup (1) 1961;
Italian League (2) 1956, 1969;
Italian Cup (6) 1940, 1961, 1966, 1975, 1996, 2001

2012

25/08	Udinese	h	2-1	Jovetić 2
02/09	Napoli	a	1-2	Jovetić
16/09	Catania	h	2-0	Jovetić, Toni
22/09	Parma	a	1-1	Roncaglia
25/09	Juventus	h	0-0	
30/09	Internazionale	h	1-2	Rômulo
07/10	Bologna	h	1-0	Jovetić
21/10	Chievo	a	1-1	Gonzalo
28/10	Lazio	h	2-0	Ljajić, Toni
01/11	Genoa	a	1-0	Pasqual
04/11	Cagliari	h	4-1	Gonzalo, Jovetić, Toni, Cuadrado
11/11	Milan	a	3-1	Aquilani, Borja Valero, El Hamdaoui
18/11	Atalanta	h	4-1	Gonzalo, Aquilani 2, Toni
25/11	Torino	a	2-2	Gonzalo (p), El Hamdaoui
02/12	Sampdoria	h	2-2	Savić 2
09/12	Torino	a	2-4	Roncaglia, El Hamdaoui
16/12	Siena	h	1-0	Toni (p), Aquilani (p), Cuadrado
22/12	Palermo	a	3-0	Jovetić 2 (1p), Gonzalo (p)

2013

06/01	Pescara	h	0-2	
13/01	Udinese	a	1-3	og (Brkić)
20/01	Napoli	h	1-1	Roncaglia
27/01	Catania	a	1-2	Migliaccio
03/02	Parma	h	2-0	Toni, Jovetić
09/02	Juventus	a	0-0	
17/02	Internazionale	h	4-1	Ljajić 2, Jovetić 2
26/02	Bologna	a	1-2	Ljajić
03/03	Chievo	h	2-1	Pasqual, Larrondo
10/03	Lazio	a	2-0	Jovetić, Ljajić
17/03	Genoa	h	3-2	Aquilani, Cuadrado, og (Cassini)
30/03	Cagliari	a	1-2	Cuadrado
07/04	Milan	h	2-2	Ljajić (p), Pizarro (p)
13/04	Atalanta	a	2-0	Pizarro (p), Larrondo
21/04	Torino	h	4-3	Cuadrado, Aquilani, Ljajić, Rômulo
28/04	Sampdoria	a	3-0	Cuadrado, Ljajić, Aquilani
04/05	Roma	h	0-1	
08/05	Siena	a	1-1	Hamdaoui
12/05	Palermo	h	1-0	Toni
19/05	Pescara	a	5-1	Ljajić 3, Fernández, Jovetić

No	Name	Nat	DoB	Pos	Aps	(s)	Gls
10	Alberto Aquilani		07/07/84	M	20	(5)	7
20	Borja Valero	ESP	12/01/85	M	37		1
16	Mattia Cassani		26/08/83	D	4	(4)	
5	Marvin Compper	GER	14/06/85	D	6	(1)	
11	Juan Cuadrado	COL	26/05/88	M	34	(2)	5
9	Mounir El Hamdaoui	MAR	14/07/84	A	3	(16)	3
14	Matías Fernández	CHI	15/05/86	M	9	(13)	1
2	Gonzalo Rodríguez	ARG	10/04/84	D	35		6
3	Ahmed Hegazy	EGY	25/01/91	D		(2)	
8	Stevan Jovetić	MNE	02/11/89	A	31		13
18	Marcelo Larrondo	ARG	16/08/88	A	2	(5)	2
22	Adem Ljajić	SRB	29/09/91	M	21	(7)	11
19	Cristian Llama	ARG	26/06/86	M	1	(4)	
12	Cristiano Lupatelli		21/06/78	G		(1)	
21	Giulio Migliaccio		23/06/81	M	9	(15)	1
15	Matija Nastasić	SRB	28/03/93	D	1		
89	Neto	BRA	19/07/89	G	6		
5	Rubén Olivera	URU	04/05/83	M	4		
23	Manuel Pasqual		13/03/82	D	35		2
7	David Pizarro	CHI	11/09/79	M	28	(1)	3
92	Rômulo	BRA	22/05/87	D	10	(10)	2
4	Facundo Roncaglia	ARG	10/02/87	D	24		3
49	Giuseppe Rossi		01/02/87	A		(1)	
15	Stefan Savić	MNE	08/01/91	D	26		2
17	Haris Seferović	SUI	22/02/92	A	1	(6)	
6	Mohamed Sissoko	MLI	22/1/85	M	1	(4)	
40	Nenad Tomović	SRB	30/08/87	D	23	(3)	
30	Luca Toni		26/05/77	A	15	(12)	8
1	Emiliano Viviano		01/12/85	G	32		
27	Rafał Wolski	POL	10/11/92	M		(1)	

GENOA CFC

Coach: Luigi De Canio; (22/10/12) Luigi Delneri; (21/01/13) Davide Ballardini

1893 • Luigi Ferraris (36,685) • genoacfc.it

Major honours

Italian League (9) 1898, 1899, 1900, 1902, 1903, 1904, 1915, 1923, 1924; Italian Cup (1) 1937

2012				
26/08	Cagliari	h	2-0	*Merkel, Immobile*
02/09	Catania	a	2-3	*Kucka, Janković*
16/09	Juventus	h	1-3	*Immobile*
23/09	Lazio	a	1-0	*Borriello*
26/09	Parma	h	1-1	*Borriello (p)*
30/09	Udinese	a	0-0	
06/10	Palermo	h	1-1	*Borriello*
21/10	Roma	h	2-4	*Kucka, Janković*
27/10	Milan	a	0-1	
01/11	Fiorentina	h	0-1	
04/11	Siena	a	0-1	
11/11	Napoli	h	2-4	*Immobile, Bertolacci*
18/11	Sampdoria	a	1-3	*Immobile*
25/11	Atalanta	a	1-0	*Bertolacci*
02/12	Chievo	h	2-4	*Said, Janković*
09/12	Pescara	a	0-2	
16/12	Torino	h	1-1	*Granqvist*
22/12	Internazionale	a	1-1	*Immobile*
2013				
06/01	Bologna	h	2-0	*Borriello 2*
13/01	Cagliari	a	1-2	*Pisano*
20/01	Catania	h	0-2	
26/01	Juventus	a	1-1	*Borriello*
03/02	Lazio	h	3-2	*Borriello, Bertolacci, Rigoni*
10/02	Parma	a	0-0	
17/02	Udinese	h	1-0	*Kucka*
23/02	Palermo	a	0-0	
03/03	Roma	a	1-3	*Borriello (p)*
08/03	Milan	h	0-2	
17/03	Fiorentina	a	2-3	*Portanova, Antonelli*
30/03	Siena	h	2-2	*Borriello, Janković*
07/04	Napoli	a	0-2	
14/04	Sampdoria	h	1-1	*Matuzalém*
20/04	Atalanta	h	1-1	*Floro Flores*
28/04	Chievo	a	1-0	*Borriello*
05/05	Pescara	h	4-1	*Floro Flores, Borriello 2, Bertolacci*
08/05	Torino	a	0-0	
12/05	Internazionale	h	0-0	
19/05	Bologna	a	0-0	

No	Name	Nat	DoB	Pos	Aps	(s)	Gls
89	Anselmo	BRA	20/02/89	M	1	(4)	
13	Luca Antonelli		11/02/87	D	32	(1)	1
91	Andrea Bertolacci		11/01/91	M	24	(5)	4
22	Marco Borriello		18/06/82	A	26	(2)	12
3	Cesare Bovo		14/01/83	D	12	(1)	
21	Michele Canini		05/06/85	D	14		
26	Mattia Cassani		26/08/83	D	3	(2)	
32	Antonio Donnarumma		07/07/90	G	1		
4	Damiano Ferronetti		01/11/84	D		(4)	
83	Antonio Floro Flores		18/06/83	A	6	(5)	2
1	Sébastien Frey	FRA	18/03/80	G	36		
5	Andreas Granqvist	SWE	16/04/85	D	32	(3)	1
16	Linus Hallenius	SWE	01/04/89	A	1		
17	Ciro Immobile		20/02/90	A	21	(12)	5
11	Boško Janković	SRB	01/03/84	M	16	(3)	4
19	Cristóbal Jorquera	CHI	04/08/88	M	4	(9)	
15	Luka Krajnc	SVN	19/09/94	D	1	(2)	
33	Juraj Kucka	SVK	26/02/87	M	32	(1)	3
21	Thomas Manfredini		27/05/80	D	14		
27	Matuzalém	BRA	10/06/80	M	15		1
9	Leonardo Melazzi	URU	04/02/91	A		(2)	
10	Alexander Merkel	GER	22/02/92	M	4	(2)	1
20	Giandomenico Mesto		25/05/82	M	1		
24	Emiliano Moretti		11/06/81	D	26	(7)	
29	Enis Nadarević	BIH	19/07/87	A		(3)	
10	Rubén Olivera	URU	04/05/83	M	2	(3)	
87	Eros Pisano		31/03/87	D	9	(1)	1
18	Giammario Piscitella		24/03/93	A		(6)	
90	Daniele Portanova		17/12/78	D	15		1
14	Marco Rigoni		05/01/80	M	7	(6)	1
7	Marco Rossi		01/04/78	M	7	(7)	
23	Ahmed Said		20/04/93	A		(5)	1
31	Mario Sampirisi		31/10/92	M	16		
14	Felipe Seymour	CHI	23/07/87	M	8	(7)	
28	Dániel Tőzsér	HUN	12/05/85	M	16	(6)	
30	Alexandros Tzorvas	GRE	12/08/82	G	1		
8	Juan Manuel Vargas	PER	05/10/83	M	15	(5)	

FC INTERNAZIONALE MILANO

Coach: Andrea Stramaccioni

1908 • Giuseppe Meazza (82,955) • inter.it

Major honours

European Champion Clubs' Cup/UEFA Champions League (3) 1964, 1965, 2010; UEFA Cup (3) 1991, 1994, 1998; European/South American Cup (2) 1964, 1965; FIFA Club World Cup (1) 2010; Italian League (18) 1910, 1920, 1930, 1938, 1940, 1953, 1954, 1963, 1965, 1966, 1971, 1980, 1989, 2006, 2007, 2008, 2009, 2010; Italian Cup (7) 1939, 1978, 1982, 2005, 2006, 2010, 2011

2012				
26/08	Pescara	a	3-0	*Sneijder, Milito, Coutinho*
02/09	Roma	h	1-3	*Cassano*
16/09	Torino	a	2-0	*Milito, Cassano*
23/09	Siena	h	0-2	
26/09	Chievo	a	2-0	*Pereira, Cassano*
30/09	Fiorentina	h	2-1	*Milito (p), Cassano*
07/10	Milan	a	1-0	*Samuel*
21/10	Catania	h	2-0	*Cassano, Palacio*
28/10	Bologna	a	3-1	*Ranocchia, Milito, Cambiasso*
31/10	Sampdoria	h	3-2	*Milito (p), Palacio, Guarín*
03/11	Juventus	a	3-1	*Milito 2 (1p), Palacio*
11/11	Atalanta	a	2-3	*Guarín, Palacio*
18/11	Cagliari	h	2-2	*Palacio, og (Astori)*
26/11	Parma	a	0-1	
02/12	Palermo	h	1-0	*og (García)*
09/12	Napoli	h	2-1	*Guarín, Milito*
15/12	Lazio	a	0-1	
22/12	Genoa	h	1-1	*Cambiasso*
2013				
06/01	Udinese	a	0-3	
12/01	Pescara	h	2-0	*Palacio, Guarín*
20/01	Roma	a	1-1	*Palacio*
27/01	Torino	h	2-2	*Chivu, Cambiasso*
03/02	Siena	a	1-3	*Cassano*
10/02	Chievo	h	3-1	*Cassano, Ranocchia, Milito*
17/02	Fiorentina	a	1-4	*Cassano*
24/02	Milan	h	1-1	*Schelotto*
03/03	Catania	a	3-2	*Álvarez, Palacio 2*
10/03	Bologna	h	0-1	
30/03	Juventus	h	1-2	*Palacio*
03/04	Sampdoria	a	2-0	*Palacio 2*
07/04	Atalanta	h	3-4	*Rocchi, Álvarez 2*
14/04	Cagliari	a	0-2	
21/04	Parma	h	1-0	*Rocchi*
28/04	Palermo	a	0-1	
05/05	Napoli	a	1-3	*Álvarez (p)*
08/05	Lazio	h	1-3	*Álvarez*
12/05	Genoa	a	0-0	
19/05	Udinese	h	2-5	*Juan, Rocchi*

No	Name	Nat	DoB	Pos	Aps	(s)	Gls
11	Ricardo Álvarez	ARG	12/04/88	M	12	(11)	5
24	Marco Benassi		08/09/94	M	3	(3)	
19	Esteban Cambiasso	ARG	18/08/80	M	26	(7)	3
30	Juan Carrizo	ARG	06/05/84	G	1		
99	Antonio Cassano		12/07/82	A	23	(5)	8
12	Luca Castellazzi		19/07/75	G	2		
26	Cristian Chivu	ROU	26/10/80	D	7	(3)	1
7	Philippe Coutinho	BRA	12/06/92	M	3	(7)	1
41	Alfred Duncan	GHA	10/03/93	M		(3)	
45	Francesco Forte		01/05/93	A		(1)	
21	Walter Gargano	URU	23/07/84	M	24	(4)	
61	Luca Garritano		11/02/94	A		(3)	
14	Fredy Guarín	COL	30/06/86	M	26	(6)	4
1	Samir Handanovič	SVN	14/07/84	G	35		
42	Jonathan	BRA	27/02/86	D	8		
40	Juan	BRA	10/06/91	D	31		1
10	Mateo Kovačić	CRO	06/05/94	M	11	(2)	
17	Zdravko Kuzmanović	SRB	22/09/87	M	10	(3)	
88	Marko Livaja	CRO	26/08/93	A	1	(5)	
17	McDonald Mariga	KEN	04/04/87	M		(1)	
22	Diego Milito	ARG	12/06/79	A	19	(1)	9
16	Gaby Mudingayi	BEL	01/10/81	M	4	(5)	
55	Yuto Nagatomo	JPN	12/09/86	D	22	(3)	
20	Joel Obi	NGA	22/05/91	M	1	(1)	
8	Rodrigo Palacio	ARG	05/02/82	A	20	(6)	12
28	Simone Pasa		21/01/94	M	2	(2)	
31	Álvaro Pereira	URU	28/11/85	D	22	(6)	1
23	Andrea Ranocchia		16/02/88	D	32		2
18	Tommaso Rocchi		19/09/77	A	8	(5)	3
25	Walter Samuel	ARG	23/03/78	D	15	(1)	1
7	Ezequiel Schelotto		23/05/89	M	5	(7)	1
6	Matías Silvestre	ARG	25/09/84	D	6	(3)	
10	Wesley Sneijder	NED	09/06/84	M	5		1
63	Lukas Spendlhofer	AUT	02/06/93	D		(1)	
5	Dejan Stanković	SRB	11/09/78	M	1	(2)	
4	Javier Zanetti	ARG	10/08/73	M	33		

JUVENTUS

Coach: (Massimo Carrera); (16/10/12) (Angelo Alessio); (09/12/12) Antonio Conte

1897 • Juventus Stadium (41,137) • juventus.com

Major honours

European Champion Clubs' Cup/UEFA Champions League (2) 1985, 1996; UEFA Cup Winners' Cup (1) 1984; UEFA Cup (3) 1977, 1990, 1993; UEFA Super Cup (2) 1984, 1997; European/South American Cup (2) 1985, 1996; Italian League (29) 1905, 1926, 1931, 1932, 1933, 1934, 1935, 1950, 1952, 1958, 1960, 1961, 1967, 1972, 1973, 1975, 1977, 1978, 1981, 1982, 1984, 1986, 1995, 1997, 1998, 2002, 2003, 2012, 2013; Italian Cup (9) 1938, 1942, 1959, 1960, 1965, 1979, 1983, 1990, 1995

2012				
25/08	Parma	h	2-0	*Lichtsteiner, Pirlo*
02/09	Udinese	a	4-1	*Vidal (p), Vučinić, Giovinco 2*
16/09	Genoa	a	3-1	*Giaccherini, Vučinić (p), Asamoah*
22/09	Chievo	h	2-0	*Quagliarella 2*
25/09	Fiorentina	a	0-0	
29/09	Roma	h	4-1	*Pirlo, Vidal (p), Matri, Giovinco*
07/10	Siena	a	2-1	*Pirlo, Marchisio*
20/10	Napoli	h	2-0	*Cáceres, Pogba*
28/10	Catania	a	1-0	*Vidal*
31/10	Bologna	h	2-1	*Quagliarella, Pogba*
03/11	Internazionale	h	1-3	*Vidal*
10/11	Pescara	a	6-1	*Vidal, Quagliarella 3, Asamoah, Giovinco*
17/11	Lazio	h	0-0	
25/11	Milan	a	0-1	
01/12	Torino	h	3-0	*Marchisio 2, Giovinco*
09/12	Palermo	a	1-0	*Lichtsteiner*
16/12	Atalanta	h	3-0	*Vučinić, Pirlo, Marchisio*
21/12	Cagliari	a	3-1	*Matri 2, Vučinić*
2013				
06/01	Sampdoria	h	1-2	*Giovinco (p)*
13/01	Parma	a	1-1	*Pirlo*
19/01	Udinese	h	4-0	*Pogba 2, Vučinić, Matri*
26/01	Genoa	h	1-1	*Quagliarella*
03/02	Chievo	a	2-1	*Matri, Lichtsteiner*
09/02	Fiorentina	h	2-0	*Vučinić, Matri*
16/02	Roma	a	0-1	
24/02	Siena	h	3-0	*Lichtsteiner, Giovinco, Pogba*
01/03	Napoli	a	1-1	*Chiellini*
10/03	Catania	h	1-0	*Giaccherini*
16/03	Bologna	a	2-0	*Vučinić, Marchisio*
30/03	Internazionale	a	2-1	*Quagliarella, Matri*
06/04	Pescara	h	2-1	*Vučinić 2 (1p)*
15/04	Lazio	a	2-0	*Vidal 2 (1p)*
21/04	Milan	h	1-0	*Vidal (p)*
28/04	Torino	a	2-0	*Vidal, Marchisio*
05/05	Palermo	h	1-0	*Vidal (p)*
08/05	Atalanta	a	1-0	*Matri*
11/05	Cagliari	h	1-1	*Vučinić*
18/05	Sampdoria	a	2-3	*Quagliarella, Giaccherini*

No	Name	Nat	DoB	Pos	Aps	(s)	Gls
18	Nicolas Anelka	FRA	14/03/79	A		(2)	
22	Kwadwo Asamoah	GHA	09/12/88	D	22	(5)	2
15	Andrea Barzagli		08/05/81	D	34		
35	Stefano Beltrame		08/02/93	A		(1)	
17	Nicklas Bendtner	DEN	16/01/88	A	2	(7)	
19	Leonardo Bonucci		01/05/87	D	33		
1	Gianluigi Buffon		28/01/78	G	32		
4	Martín Cáceres	URU	07/04/87	D	12	(6)	1
3	Giorgio Chiellini		14/08/84	D	23	(1)	1
11	Paolo De Ceglie		17/09/86	D	12	(2)	
24	Emanuele Giaccherini		05/05/85	M	10	(7)	3
12	Sebastian Giovinco		26/01/87	A	23	(8)	7
33	Mauricio Isla	CHI	12/06/88	M	8	(3)	
26	Stephan Lichtsteiner	SUI	16/01/84	D	25	(3)	4
2	Lúcio	BRA	08/05/78	D	1		
8	Claudio Marchisio		19/01/86	M	28	(1)	6
39	Luca Marrone		28/03/90	M	8	(2)	
32	Alessandro Matri		19/08/84	A	10	(12)	8
20	Simone Padoin		18/03/84	M	6	(14)	
13	Federico Peluso		20/01/84	D	7	(5)	
7	Simone Pepe		30/08/83	M		(1)	
21	Andrea Pirlo		19/05/79	M	32		5
6	Paul Pogba	FRA	15/03/93	M	18	(9)	5
34	Rubinho	BRA	04/08/82	G		(1)	
27	Fabio Quagliarella		31/01/83	A	13	(14)	9
30	Marco Storari		07/01/77	G	6		
23	Arturo Vidal	CHI	22/05/87	M	29	(2)	10
9	Mirko Vučinić	MNE	01/10/83	A	24	(7)	10

S.S. LAZIO

Coach: Vladimir Petković (SUI)
1900 • Olimpico (82,307) • sslazio.it
Major honours
UEFA Cup Winners' Cup (1) 1999;
UEFA Super Cup (1) 1999;
Italian League (2) 1974, 2000;
Italian Cup (6) 1958, 1998, 2000, 2004, 2009, 2013

2012

26/08	Atalanta	a	1-0	Hernanes
02/09	Palermo	h	3-0	Klose 2, Candreva
16/09	Chievo	a	3-1	Hernanes 2, Klose
23/09	Genoa	h	0-1	
26/09	Napoli	a	0-3	
30/09	Siena	h	2-1	Ederson, Ledesma (p)
07/10	Pescara	a	3-0	Hernanes, Klose 2
20/10	Milan	h	3-2	Hernanes, Candreva, Klose
28/10	Fiorentina	a	0-2	
31/10	Torino	h	1-1	Mauri
04/11	Catania	a	0-4	
11/11	Roma	h	3-2	Candreva, Klose, Mauri
17/11	Juventus	h	0-0	
27/11	Udinese	h	3-0	González, Klose, Hernanes
02/12	Parma	h	2-1	Biava, Klose
10/12	Bologna	a	0-0	
15/12	Internazionale	h	1-0	Klose
22/12	Sampdoria	a	1-0	Hernanes

2013

05/01	Cagliari	h	2-1	Konko, Candreva (p)
13/01	Atalanta	h	2-0	Floccari, og (Brivio)
19/01	Palermo	a	2-2	Floccari, Hernanes (p)
26/01	Chievo	h	0-1	
03/02	Genoa	a	2-3	Floccari, Mauri (p)
09/02	Napoli	h	1-1	Floccari
18/02	Siena	a	0-3	
25/02	Pescara	h	2-0	Radu, Lulić
02/03	Milan	a	0-3	
10/03	Fiorentina	h	0-2	
17/03	Torino	a	0-1	
30/03	Catania	h	2-1	og (Legrottaglie), Candreva (p)
08/04	Roma	a	1-1	Hernanes
15/04	Juventus	h	0-2	
20/04	Udinese	a	0-1	
28/04	Parma	h	0-0	
05/05	Bologna	h	6-0	Klose 5, Hernanes
08/05	Internazionale	a	3-1	og (Handanovič), Hernanes (p), Onazi
12/05	Sampdoria	h	2-0	Floccari, Candreva (p)
19/05	Cagliari	a	0-1	

No	Name	Nat	DoB	Pos	Aps	(s)	Gls
3	André Dias	BRA	15/05/79	D	25	(2)	
20	Giuseppe Biava		08/05/77	D	30	(1)	1
1	Albano Bizzarri	ARG	09/11/77	G	5		
32	Cristian Brocchi		30/01/76	M	2	(6)	
17	Bruno Pereirinha	POR	02/03/88	M	3	(5)	
27	Lorik Cana	ALB	27/07/83	D	13	(11)	
87	Antonio Candreva		28/02/87	M	32	(3)	6
39	Luis Pedro Cavanda	BEL	02/01/90	D	8	(6)	
2	Michaël Ciani	FRA	06/04/84	D	13	(5)	
4	Luca Crecco		06/09/95	A		(1)	
7	Ederson	BRA	12/11/81	A	4	(11)	1
99	Sergio Floccari		12/11/81	A	11	(11)	5
15	Álvaro González	URU	29/10/84	M	29	(5)	1
8	Hernanes	BRA	29/05/85	M	30	(4)	11
11	Miroslav Klose	GER	09/06/78	A	26	(3)	15
29	Abdoulay Konko	FRA	09/03/84	D	25		1
18	Libor Kozák	CZE	30/05/89	A	5	(14)	
24	Cristian Ledesma		24/09/82	M	35	(1)	1
19	Senad Lulić	BIH	18/01/86	M	29	(4)	1
22	Federico Marchetti		07/02/83	G	33		
6	Stefano Mauri		09/01/80	M	23	(3)	3
26	Ogenyi Onazi	NGA	25/12/92	M	8	(7)	1
26	Stefan Radu	ROU	22/10/86	D	22	(1)	1
9	Tommaso Rocchi		19/09/77	A	2	(1)	
92	Louis Saha	FRA	08/08/78	A	1	(5)	
5	Lionel Scaloni	ARG	16/05/78	D	1	(3)	
33	Marius Stankevičius	LTU	15/07/81	D	2	(1)	
10	Mauro Zárate	ARG	18/03/87	A	1		

AC MILAN

Coach: Massimiliano Allegri
1899 • Giuseppe Meazza (82,955) • acmilan.com
Major honours
European Champion Clubs' Cup/UEFA Champions League (7) 1963, 1969, 1989, 1990, 1994, 2003, 2007;
UEFA Cup Winners' Cup (2) 1968, 1973;
UEFA Super Cup (5) 1989, 1990, 1995, 2003, 2007;
European/South American Cup (3) 1969, 1989, 1990;
FIFA Club World Cup (1) 2007;
Italian League (18) 1901, 1906, 1907, 1951, 1955, 1957, 1959, 1962, 1968, 1979, 1988, 1992, 1993, 1994, 1996, 1999, 2004, 2011;
Italian Cup (5) 1967, 1972, 1973, 1977

2012

26/08	Sampdoria	h	0-1	
01/09	Bologna	a	3-1	Pazzini 3 (1p)
15/09	Atalanta	h	0-1	
23/09	Udinese	a	1-2	El Shaarawy
26/09	Cagliari	h	2-0	El Shaarawy 2
29/09	Parma	a	1-1	El Shaarawy
07/10	Internazionale	h	0-1	
20/10	Lazio	a	2-3	De Jong, El Shaarawy
27/10	Genoa	h	1-0	El Shaarawy
30/10	Palermo	a	2-2	Montolivo, El Shaarawy
04/11	Chievo	h	5-1	Emanuelson, Montolivo, El Shaarawy 2, Pazzini
11/11	Fiorentina	h	1-3	Pazzini
17/11	Napoli	a	2-2	El Shaarawy 2
25/11	Juventus	h	1-0	Robinho (p)
30/11	Catania	a	3-1	El Shaarawy 2, Boateng
09/12	Torino	a	4-2	Robinho, Nocerino, Pazzini, El Shaarawy
16/12	Pescara	h	4-1	Nocerino, og (Abbruscato), og (Jonathas), El Shaarawy
22/12	Roma	a	2-4	Pazzini (p), Bojan

2013

06/01	Siena	h	2-1	Bojan, Pazzini (p)
13/01	Sampdoria	a	0-0	
20/01	Bologna	a	2-1	Pazzini 2
27/01	Atalanta	a	1-0	El Shaarawy
03/02	Udinese	h	2-1	Balotelli 2 (1p)
10/02	Cagliari	a	1-1	Balotelli (p)
15/02	Parma	a	2-1	og (Paletta), Balotelli
24/02	Internazionale	a	1-1	El Shaarawy
02/03	Lazio	h	3-0	Pazzini 2, Boateng
08/03	Genoa	a	2-0	Pazzini, Boateng
17/03	Palermo	h	2-0	Balotelli 2 (1p)
30/03	Chievo	a	0-0	
07/04	Fiorentina	a	2-1	Montolivo, Flamini
14/04	Napoli	h	1-1	Flamini
21/04	Juventus	a	0-1	
28/04	Catania	h	4-2	Flamini, Pazzini 2, Balotelli (p)
05/05	Torino	h	1-0	Balotelli
08/05	Pescara	a	4-0	Balotelli 2 (1p), Muntari, Flamini
12/05	Roma	h	0-0	
19/05	Siena	a	2-1	Balotelli (p), Mexès

No	Name	Nat	DoB	Pos	Aps	(s)	Gls
20	Ignazio Abate		12/11/86	D	25	(2)	
32	Christian Abbiati		08/07/77	G	28		
13	Francesco Acerbi		10/02/88	D	5	(1)	
23	Massimo Ambrosini		29/05/77	M	16	(4)	
1	Marco Amelia		02/04/82	G	10	(1)	
77	Luca Antonini		04/08/82	D	5	(1)	
45	Mario Balotelli		12/08/90	A	12	(1)	12
10	Kevin-Prince Boateng	GHA	06/03/87	M	25	(4)	2
22	Bojan Krkić	ESP	28/08/90	A	5	(14)	3
25	Daniele Bonera		31/05/81	D	13		
21	Kévin Constant	GUI	15/05/87	D	20	(5)	
34	Nigel de Jong	NED	30/11/84	M	10	(2)	1
2	Mattia De Sciglio		20/10/92	D	25	(2)	
92	Stephan El Shaarawy		27/10/92	A	34	(3)	16
28	Urby Emanuelson	NED	16/06/86	M	8	(4)	1
16	Mathieu Flamini	FRA	07/03/84	M	15	(3)	4
15	Djamel Mesbah	ALG	09/10/84	D	1		
5	Philippe Mexès	FRA	30/03/82	D	25		1
18	Riccardo Montolivo		18/01/85	M	31	(1)	4
4	Sulley Ali Muntari	GHA	27/08/84	M	11	(4)	1
19	M'Baye Niang	FRA	19/12/94	A	9	(11)	
8	Antonio Nocerino		09/04/85	M	20	(6)	2
9	Pato	BRA	02/09/89	A	3	(1)	
11	Giampaolo Pazzini		02/08/84	A	15	(15)	15
7	Robinho	BRA	25/01/84	A	11	(12)	2
12	Bakaye Traoré	MLI	13/03/85	M	1	(6)	
76	Mario Yepes	COL	13/01/76	D	13	(1)	
81	Cristian Zaccardo		21/12/81	D	1	(1)	
17	Cristián Zapata	COL	30/09/86	D	22	(1)	

SSC NAPOLI

Coach: Walter Mazzarri
1926 • San Paolo (60,240) • sscnapoli.it
Major honours
UEFA Cup (1) 1989;
Italian League (2) 1987, 1990;
Italian Cup (4) 1962, 1976, 1987, 2012

2012

26/08	Palermo	a	3-0	Hamšík, Maggio, Cavani
02/09	Fiorentina	h	2-1	Hamšík, Dzemaili
16/09	Parma	h	3-1	Cavani (p), Pandev, L Insigne
23/09	Catania	a	0-0	
26/09	Lazio	h	3-0	Cavani 3
30/09	Sampdoria	a	1-0	Cavani (p)
07/10	Udinese	h	2-1	Hamšík, Pandev
20/10	Juventus	a	0-2	
28/10	Chievo	h	1-0	Hamšík
31/10	Atalanta	a	0-1	
04/11	Torino	h	1-1	Cavani
11/11	Genoa	a	4-2	Mesto, Cavani, Hamšík, L Insigne
17/11	Milan	h	2-2	Inler, L Insigne
26/11	Cagliari	a	1-0	Hamšík
02/12	Pescara	h	5-1	Inler 2, Hamšík, Cavani 2 (1p)
09/12	Internazionale	a	1-2	Cavani
16/12	Bologna	a	2-3	Gamberini, Cavani
22/12	Siena	a	2-0	Maggio, Cavani (p)

2013

06/01	Roma	h	4-1	Cavani 3, Maggio
13/01	Palermo	h	3-0	Maggio, Inler, L Insigne
20/01	Fiorentina	a	1-1	Cavani
27/01	Parma	a	1-1	Hamšík, Cavani
02/02	Catania	h	2-0	Hamšík, Cannavaro
09/02	Lazio	a	1-1	Campagnaro
17/02	Sampdoria	h	0-0	
25/02	Udinese	a	0-0	
01/03	Juventus	h	1-1	Inler
10/03	Chievo	a	0-2	
17/03	Atalanta	h	3-2	Cavani 2 (1p), Pandev
30/03	Torino	a	5-3	Dzemaili 3, Cavani 2
07/04	Genoa	h	2-0	Pandev, Dzemaili
14/04	Milan	a	1-1	Pandev
21/04	Cagliari	h	3-2	og (Astori), Cavani, L Insigne
27/04	Pescara	a	3-0	Inler, Pandev, Dzemaili
05/05	Internazionale	h	3-1	Cavani 3 (1p)
08/05	Bologna	a	3-0	Hamšík, Cavani (p), Dzemaili
12/05	Siena	h	2-1	Cavani, Hamšík
19/05	Roma	a	1-2	Cavani

No	Name	Nat	DoB	Pos	Aps	(s)	Gls
27	Pablo Armero	COL	02/11/86	D	4	(11)	
6	Salvatore Aronica		20/01/78	D	3	(2)	
85	Valon Behrami	SUI	19/04/85	M	32	(1)	
5	Miguel Britos	URU	17/07/85	D	22		
9	Emanuele Calaiò		08/01/82	A	1	(5)	
14	Hugo Campagnaro	ARG	27/06/80	D	27	(1)	1
28	Paolo Cannavaro		26/06/81	D	32		1
7	Edinson Cavani	URU	14/02/87	A	33	(1)	29
1	Morgan De Sanctis		26/03/77	G	34		
4	Marco Donadel		21/04/83	M	1	(3)	
8	Andrea Dossena		11/09/81	D	3	(4)	
20	Blerim Dzemaili	SUI	12/04/86	M	19	(15)	7
13	Omar El Kaddouri	MAR	21/08/90	M	1	(6)	
21	Federico Fernández	ARG	21/02/89	D	1	(1)	
55	Alessandro Gamberini		27/08/81	D	24	(1)	1
2	Gianluca Grava		07/03/77	D	2		
17	Marek Hamšík	SVK	27/07/87	M	37	(1)	11
88	Gökhan Inler	SUI	27/06/84	M	25	(6)	6
24	Lorenzo Insigne		04/06/91	A	16	(21)	5
42	Roberto Insigne		11/05/94	A		(1)	
11	Christian Maggio		11/02/82	M	31		4
16	Giandomenico Mesto		25/05/82	M	7	(9)	
19	Goran Pandev	MKD	27/07/83	A	25	(8)	6
6	Rolando	POR	31/08/85	D	4	(3)	
22	Antonio Rosati		26/03/83	G	4		
9	Eduardo Vargas	CHI	20/11/89	A		(9)	
18	Juan Camilo Zúñiga	COL	14/12/85	D	30	(2)	

US CITTÀ DI PALERMO

Coach: Giuseppe Sannino;
(16/09/12) Gian Piero Gasperini;
(05/02/13) Alberto Malesani;
(24/02/13) Gian Piero Gasperini;
(11/03/13) Giuseppe Sannino
1900 • Renzo Barbera (37,242) • palermocalcio.it

2012
26/08	Napoli	h	0-3	
02/09	Lazio	a	0-3	
15/09	Cagliari	h	1-1	Arévalo
23/09	Atalanta	a	0-1	
26/09	Pescara	a	0-1	
30/09	Chievo	h	4-1	Miccoli 3, Giorgi
06/10	Genoa	a	1-1	Giorgi
21/10	Torino	h	0-0	
27/10	Siena	a	0-0	
30/10	Milan	h	2-2	Miccoli (p), Brienza
04/11	Roma	a	1-4	Iličič
11/11	Sampdoria	h	0-2	Dybala 2
18/11	Bologna	a	0-3	
24/11	Catania	h	3-1	Miccoli, Iličič 2
02/12	Internazionale	a	0-0	
09/12	Juventus	h	0-1	
15/12	Udinese	a	1-1	Iličič
22/12	Fiorentina	h	0-3	

2013
06/01	Parma	a	1-2	Budan
13/01	Napoli	a	0-3	
19/01	Lazio	h	2-2	Arévalo, Dybala
27/01	Cagliari	a	1-1	Iličič
03/02	Atalanta	h	1-2	Nélson
10/02	Pescara	h	1-1	Fabbrini
16/02	Chievo	a	1-1	Formica
23/02	Genoa	h	0-0	
03/03	Torino	a	0-0	
10/03	Siena	h	1-2	Anselmo
17/03	Milan	a	0-2	
30/03	Roma	h	2-0	Iličič, Miccoli
07/04	Sampdoria	a	3-1	Von Bergen, Iličič, García
14/04	Bologna	h	1-1	Iličič
21/04	Catania	a	1-1	Iličič
28/04	Internazionale	h	1-0	Iličič
05/05	Juventus	a	0-1	
08/05	Udinese	h	2-3	Miccoli (p), Hernández
12/05	Fiorentina	a	0-1	
19/05	Parma	h	1-3	Miccoli

No	Name	Nat	DoB	Pos	Aps	(s)	Gls
14	Anselmo	BRA	20/02/89	M	2	(3)	1
20	Egidio Arévalo	URU	01/01/82	M	22	(5)	2
3	Salvatore Aronica		20/01/78	D	16		
5	Édgar Barreto	PAR	15/07/84	M	30		
99	Francesco Benussi		15/10/81	G	4	(1)	
14	Nicolás Bertolo	ARG	02/01/86	M	3	(4)	
17	Mauro Boselli	ARG	22/05/85	A	5	(3)	
21	Franco Brienza		19/03/79	M	13	(4)	1
19	Igor Budan	CRO	29/04/80	A	1	(5)	1
4	Mauro Cetto	ARG	14/04/82	D	2	(1)	
23	Massimo Donati		26/03/81	M	26	(2)	
8	Andrea Dossena		11/09/81	D	10	(1)	
9	Paulo Dybala	ARG	15/11/93	A	11	(16)	3
16	Diego Fabbrini		31/07/90	A	5	(3)	1
33	Alejandro Faurlín	ARG	09/08/86	M	3	(3)	
33	Mauro Formica	ARG	04/04/88	M	3	(5)	1
29	Santiago García	ARG	08/07/88	D	30	(2)	1
17	Luigi Giorgi		19/04/87	M	6	(4)	2
11	Abel Hernández	URU	08/08/90	A	6	(8)	1
27	Josip Iličič	SVN	29/01/88	M	29	(2)	10
28	Jasmin Kurtič	SVN	10/01/89	M	26	(5)	
18	Carlos Labrín	CHI	02/12/90	D		(1)	
24	Cephas Malele	SUI	08/01/94	A		(3)	
2	Andrea Mantovani		22/06/84	D	4	(2)	
10	Fabrizio Miccoli		27/06/79	A	22	(7)	8
8	Giulio Migliaccio		23/06/81	M		(1)	
89	Michel Morganella	SUI	17/05/89	D	30		
6	Ezequiel Muñoz	ARG	08/10/90	D	29	(3)	
22	Nélson	POR	10/06/83	D	3	(5)	1
31	Eros Pisano		31/03/87	D	7	(4)	
50	Giulio Sanseverino		10/02/94	M	2	(1)	
54	Stefano Sorrentino		28/03/79	G	15		
1	Samir Ujkani	ALB	05/07/88	G	19		
7	Nicolas Viola		12/10/89	M	1	(5)	
25	Steve Von Bergen	SUI	10/06/83	D	33	(2)	1
16	Eran Zahavi	ISR	25/07/87	M		(3)	

PARMA FC

Coach: Roberto Donadoni
1913 • Ennio Tardini (27,906) • fcparma.com
Major honours
UEFA Cup Winners' Cup (1) 1993;
UEFA Cup (2) 1995, 1999;
UEFA Super Cup (1) 1994;
Italian Cup (3) 1992, 1999, 2002

2012
25/08	Juventus	a	0-2	
02/09	Chievo	h	2-0	Belfodil, Rosi
16/09	Napoli	a	1-3	Parolo
22/09	Fiorentina	h	1-1	Valdés (p)
26/09	Genoa	a	1-1	Lucarelli
29/09	Milan	h	1-1	Galloppa
07/10	Catania	a	0-2	
21/10	Sampdoria	h	2-1	Amauri 2 (1p)
28/10	Torino	a	3-1	Sansone, Amauri, Rosi
31/10	Roma	h	3-2	Belfodil, Parolo, Zaccardo
04/11	Pescara	a	0-2	
11/11	Siena	h	0-0	
18/11	Udinese	a	2-2	Marchionni, Palladino
26/11	Internazionale	h	1-0	Sansone
02/12	Lazio	a	1-2	Belfodil
08/12	Atalanta	a	1-2	Amauri
16/12	Cagliari	h	4-1	Belfodil 2, Biabiany, Valdés (p)
22/12	Bologna	a	2-1	Valdés, Sansone

2013
06/01	Palermo	h	2-1	Belfodil, Amauri
13/01	Juventus	h	1-1	Sansone
20/01	Chievo	a	1-1	Belfodil
27/01	Napoli	h	1-2	og (Cannavaro)
03/02	Fiorentina	a	0-2	
10/02	Genoa	h	0-0	
15/02	Milan	a	1-2	Sansone
24/02	Catania	h	1-2	Amauri
03/03	Sampdoria	a	0-1	
10/03	Torino	h	4-1	Amauri 3, Sansone
17/03	Roma	a	0-2	
30/03	Pescara	h	3-0	Benalouane, Paletta, Amauri
07/04	Siena	a	0-0	
14/04	Udinese	h	0-3	
21/04	Internazionale	a	0-1	
28/04	Lazio	h	0-0	
05/05	Atalanta	h	2-0	Parolo, Biabiany
08/05	Cagliari	a	1-0	Rosi
12/05	Bologna	h	0-2	
19/05	Palermo	a	3-1	Gobbi, Valdés, Belfodil

No	Name	Nat	DoB	Pos	Aps	(s)	Gls
20	Afriyie Acquah	GHA	05/01/92	M	4	(9)	
11	Amauri		03/06/80	A	26	(7)	10
2	Álvaro Ampuero	PER	25/09/92	M	4	(1)	
91	Pavol Bajza	SVK	04/09/91	G		(1)	
9	Ishak Belfodil	ALG	19/02/92	A	22	(11)	8
28	Yohan Benalouane	FRA	29/03/87	D	18	(3)	1
7	Jonathan Biabiany	FRA	28/04/88	A	29	(4)	2
19	Filippo Boniperti		27/09/91	A		(2)	
20	Alberto Cerri		16/04/96	A		(1)	
31	Andrea Coda		25/04/85	D	6	(2)	
39	Ignacio Fideleff	ARG	04/07/89	D		(1)	
18	Daniele Galloppa		15/05/85	M	8	(4)	1
18	Massimo Gobbi		31/10/80	D	33	(1)	1
6	Alessandro Lucarelli		22/07/77	D	30	(2)	1
32	Marco Marchionni		22/07/80	M	25	(3)	1
15	McDonald Mariga	KEN	04/04/87	M	1	(1)	
5	Djamel Mesbah	ALG	09/10/84	D	3	(4)	
88	Antonio Mirante		08/07/83	G	33		
4	Stefano Morrone		26/10/78	M	1	(2)	
19	Gianluca Musacci		22/07/91	M	5	(1)	
77	Sotirios Ninis	GRE	03/04/90	M	5	(9)	
88	Dorlan Pabon	COL	24/01/88	A	5	(7)	
29	Gabriel Paletta	ARG	15/02/86	D	35		1
17	Raffaele Palladino		17/04/84	M		(8)	1
16	Marco Parolo		25/01/85	M	34	(2)	3
1	Nicola Pavarini		24/02/74	G	5	(1)	
99	Graziano Pellè		15/07/85	A		(1)	
87	Aleandro Rosi		17/05/87	D	23	(3)	3
21	Nicola Sansone		10/10/91	A	17	(9)	6
13	Fabiano Santacroce		24/08/86	D	4	(4)	
14	Rodney Strasser	SLE	30/03/90	M		(2)	
10	Jaime Valdés	CHI	11/01/81	M	28	(1)	4
5	Cristian Zaccardo		21/12/81	D	14	(1)	1

PESCARA CALCIO

Coach: Giovanni Stroppa;
(20/11/12) Cristiano Bergodi;
(05/03/13) Cristian Bucchi
1936 • Adriatico (20,681) • pescaracalcio.com

2012
26/08	Internazionale	h	0-3	
01/09	Torino	a	0-3	
16/09	Sampdoria	h	2-3	Celik, Caprari
23/09	Bologna	a	1-1	Quintero
26/09	Palermo	h	1-0	Weiss
30/09	Cagliari	a	2-1	Terlizzi, Weiss
07/10	Lazio	h	0-3	
21/10	Udinese	a	0-1	
28/10	Atalanta	h	0-0	
31/10	Chievo	a	0-2	
04/11	Parma	h	2-0	Abbruscato, Weiss
10/11	Juventus	h	1-6	Cascione
18/11	Siena	a	0-1	
25/11	Roma	h	0-1	
02/12	Napoli	a	1-5	Bjarnason
09/12	Genoa	h	2-0	Abbruscato, Vukušić
16/12	Milan	a	1-4	Terlizzi
21/12	Catania	h	2-1	Celik, Rômulo Togni

2013
06/01	Fiorentina	a	2-0	Jonathas, Celik
12/01	Internazionale	a	0-2	
20/01	Torino	h	0-2	
27/01	Sampdoria	a	0-6	
03/02	Bologna	h	2-3	Weiss (p), D'Agostino (p)
10/02	Palermo	a	1-1	Bjarnason
17/02	Cagliari	h	0-2	
25/02	Lazio	a	0-2	
03/03	Udinese	h	0-1	
10/03	Atalanta	a	1-2	D'Agostino
17/03	Chievo	h	0-2	
30/03	Parma	a	0-3	
06/04	Juventus	h	1-2	Cascione
13/04	Siena	h	2-3	Celik, Rômulo Togni
21/04	Roma	a	1-1	Caprari
27/04	Napoli	h	0-3	
05/05	Genoa	a	1-4	Sculli
08/05	Milan	h	0-4	
11/05	Catania	a	0-1	
19/05	Fiorentina	h	1-5	Vittiglio

No	Name	Nat	DoB	Pos	Aps	(s)	Gls
9	Elvis Abbruscato		14/04/81	A	11	(14)	2
14	Antonio Balzano		13/06/86	D	23	(3)	
28	Nicolás Bianchi Arce	ARG	28/01/87	D	5	(5)	
8	Birkir Bjarnason	ISL	27/05/88	M	17	(7)	2
26	Manuele Blasi		17/08/80	M	11	(1)	
15	Antonio Bocchetti		11/06/80	D	23	(1)	
99	Gianluca Caprari		30/07/93	A	14	(10)	3
5	Marco Capuano		14/10/91	D	23	(3)	
60	Milton Caraglio	ARG	01/12/88	A	3	(1)	
4	Emmanuel Cascione		22/09/83	M	23	(7)	2
45	Giovanbattista Catalano		22/01/94	A		(2)	
10	Mervan Celik	SWE	26/05/90	M	11	(12)	4
18	Giuseppe Colucci		24/08/80	M	9	(2)	
23	Uroš Cosić	SRB	24/10/92	D	20		
70	Gaetano D'Agostino		03/06/82	M	7		2
94	Federico Di Francesco		14/06/94	A	5	(2)	
49	Marco Iannascoli		06/11/94	M		(1)	
80	Jonathas	BRA	06/03/89	A	8	(4)	1
3	Per Krøldrup	DEN	31/07/79	D	5		
96	Andrea Mancini		24/09/96	A		(1)	
25	David Mbodj Mbaye	SEN	15/09/94	D		(1)	
11	Francesco Modesto		16/02/82	D	19		
20	Matti Lund Nielsen	DEN	30/05/88	M	15	(4)	
32	Ivan Pelizzoli		18/11/80	G	10	(1)	
77	Mattia Perin		10/11/92	G	28	(1)	
93	Juan Quintero	COL	18/01/93	M	12	(5)	1
18	Giuseppe Rizzo		18/03/91	M	10	(1)	
6	Simone Romagnoli		09/02/90	D	6	(1)	
21	Rômulo Togni	BRA	09/09/82	M	16	(1)	2
7	Giuseppe Sculli		23/03/81	A	8	(2)	1
33	Ferdinando Sfrozini		04/12/84	A	9	(1)	
7	Danilo Soddimo		27/09/87	M		(1)	
88	Christian Terlizzi		22/11/79	D	11		2
46	Marco Vittiglio		17/01/94	D		(1)	1
22	Ante Vukušić	CRO	04/01/91	A	13	(6)	1
17	Vladimír Weiss	SVK	30/11/89	M	16	(6)	4
2	Damiani Zanon		09/02/83	D	21	(2)	
6	Luciano Zauri		20/01/78	D	6	(2)	

AS ROMA

Coach: Zdeněk Zeman (CZE);
(02/02/13) (Aurelio Andreazzoli)
1927 • Olimpico (82,307) • asroma.it
Major honours
*Inter Cities Fairs Cup (1) 1961;
Italian League (3) 1942, 1983, 2001;
Italian Cup (9) 1964, 1969, 1980, 1981, 1984, 1986,
1991, 2007, 2008*

2012

26/08	Catania	h	2-2	Osvaldo, López
02/09	Internazionale	a	3-1	Florenzi, Osvaldo, Marquinho
16/09	Bologna	h	2-3	Florenzi, Lamela
23/09	Cagliari	a	3-0	(w/o)
26/09	Sampdoria	h	1-1	Totti
29/09	Juventus	a	1-4	Osvaldo (p)
07/10	Atalanta	h	2-0	Lamela, Bradley
21/10	Genoa	a	4-2	Totti, Osvaldo 2, Lamela
28/10	Udinese	h	2-3	Lamela 2
31/10	Parma	a	2-0	Lamela, Totti
04/11	Palermo	h	4-1	Totti, Osvaldo, Lamela, Destro
11/11	Lazio	a	2-3	Lamela, Pjanić
19/11	Torino	h	2-0	Osvaldo (p), Pjanić
25/11	Pescara	a	1-0	Destro
02/12	Siena	a	3-1	Destro 2, Perrotta
08/12	Fiorentina	h	4-2	Leandro Castán, Totti 2, Osvaldo
16/12	Chievo	a	0-1	
22/12	Milan	h	4-2	Burdisso, Osvaldo, Lamela 2

2013

06/01	Napoli	a	1-4	Osvaldo
13/01	Catania	a	0-1	
20/01	Internazionale	h	1-1	Totti (p)
27/01	Bologna	a	3-3	Florenzi, Osvaldo, Tachtsidis
01/02	Cagliari	h	2-4	Totti, Marquinho
10/02	Sampdoria	a	1-3	Lamela
16/02	Juventus	h	1-0	Totti
24/02	Atalanta	h	3-2	Marquinho, Pjanić, Totti (p)
03/03	Genoa	h	3-1	Totti (p), Romagnoli, Perrotta
09/03	Udinese	a	1-1	Lamela
17/03	Parma	h	2-0	Lamela, Totti
30/03	Palermo	a	0-2	
08/04	Lazio	h	1-1	Totti (p)
14/04	Torino	a	2-1	Osvaldo, Lamela
21/04	Pescara	h	1-1	Destro
28/04	Siena	h	4-0	Osvaldo 3, Lamela
04/05	Fiorentina	a	1-0	Osvaldo
07/05	Chievo	h	0-1	
12/05	Milan	a	0-0	
19/05	Napoli	h	2-1	Marquinho, Destro

No	Name	Nat	DoB	Pos	Aps	(s)	Gls
42	Federico Balzaretti		06/12/81	D	24	(3)	
4	Michael Bradley	USA	31/07/87	M	24	(6)	1
29	Nicolás Burdisso	ARG	12/04/81	D	25		1
16	Daniele De Rossi		24/07/83	M	21	(4)	
22	Mattia Destro		20/03/91	A	11	(10)	6
27	Dodô	BRA	06/02/92	D	7	(4)	
48	Alessandro Florenzi		11/03/91	M	25	(11)	3
13	Mauro Goicoechea	URU	27/03/88	G	13	(2)	
8	Erik Lamela	ARG	04/03/92	A	30	(3)	15
5	Leandro Castán	BRA	05/11/86	D	30		1
1	Bogdan Lobonț	ROU	18/01/78	G	5		
17	Nicolás López	URU	01/10/93	A		(6)	1
7	Marquinho	BRA	07/03/86	M	11	(15)	4
3	Marquinhos	BRA	14/05/94	D	22	(4)	
9	Pablo Osvaldo		12/01/86	A	25	(4)	16
20	Simone Perrotta		17/09/77	M	5	(11)	2
23	Iván Piris	PAR	10/03/89	D	28	(1)	
15	Miralem Pjanić	BIH	02/04/90	M	20	(7)	3
46	Alessio Romagnoli		12/01/95	D	1	(1)	1
24	Maarten Stekelenburg	NED	22/09/82	G	19		
77	Panagiotis Tachtsidis	GRE	15/02/91	M	17	(4)	1
11	Rodrigo Taddei		06/03/80	M	2	(2)	
35	Vasilios Torosidis	GRE	10/06/85	D	9	(2)	1
10	Francesco Totti		27/09/76	A	33	(1)	12

UC SAMPDORIA

Coach: Ciro Ferrara; (17/12/12) Delio Rossi
1946 • Luigi Ferraris (36,685) • sampdoria.it
Major honours
*UEFA Cup Winners' Cup (1) 1990;
Italian League (1) 1991;
Italian Cup (4) 1985, 1988, 1989, 1994*

2012

26/08	Milan	a	1-0	Costa
02/09	Siena	h	2-1	Maxi López, Gastaldello
16/09	Pescara	a	3-2	Maxi López 2, Estigarribia
23/09	Torino	h	1-1	Pozzi (p)
26/09	Roma	a	1-1	Munari
30/09	Napoli	h	0-1	
06/10	Chievo	a	1-2	Maresca
21/10	Parma	a	1-2	Éder (p)
28/10	Cagliari	h	0-1	
31/10	Internazionale	a	2-3	Munari, Éder
04/11	Atalanta	h	1-2	Maresca
11/11	Palermo	a	0-2	
18/11	Genoa	h	3-1	Poli, og (Bovo), Icardi
25/11	Bologna	h	1-0	Poli
02/12	Fiorentina	a	2-2	Icardi, og (Gonzalo)
10/12	Udinese	h	0-2	
16/12	Catania	a	1-3	Maresca (p)
22/12	Lazio	h	0-1	

2013

06/01	Juventus	a	2-1	Icardi 2
13/01	Milan	h	0-0	
20/01	Siena	a	0-1	
27/01	Pescara	h	6-0	Éder (p), Icardi 4, Pedro Obiang
02/02	Torino	a	0-0	
10/02	Roma	h	3-1	Estigarribia, Sansone, Icardi
17/02	Napoli	a	0-0	
24/02	Chievo	h	2-0	Poli, Éder
03/03	Parma	h	1-0	Icardi
10/03	Cagliari	a	1-3	Maxi López (p)
30/03	Atalanta	a	0-0	
03/04	Internazionale	h	0-2	
07/04	Palermo	h	1-3	Munari
14/04	Genoa	h	1-1	Icardi
21/04	Bologna	a	1-1	Sansone
28/04	Fiorentina	h	0-3	
05/05	Udinese	a	1-3	Éder
08/05	Catania	h	1-1	De Silvestri
12/05	Lazio	a	0-2	
18/05	Juventus	h	3-2	Éder (p), De Silvestri, Icardi

No	Name	Nat	DoB	Pos	Aps	(s)	Gls
29	Juan Antonio	ARG	05/01/88	A		(2)	
13	Gaetano Berardi	SUI	21/08/88	D	18	(3)	
32	Tommaso Berni		06/03/83	G	2	(1)	
7	Paolo Castellini		25/03/79	D	4	(3)	
3	Andrea Costa		01/02/86	D	27		1
19	Lorenzo De Silvestri		23/05/88	D	19	(5)	2
23	Éder	BRA	15/11/86	A	24	(6)	7
2	Marcelo Estigarribia	PAR	01/07/87	M	29	(5)	2
28	Daniele Gastaldello		25/06/83	D	33		1
98	Mauro Icardi	ARG	19/02/93	A	24	(7)	10
1	Júnior Costa	BRA	12/11/83	G	4		
25	Nenad Krstičić	SRB	03/07/90	M	22	(3)	1
6	Enzo Maresca		10/02/80	M	15	(1)	3
10	Maxi López	ARG	03/04/84	A	9	(8)	4
11	Gianni Munari		24/06/83	M	14	(13)	3
8	Shkodran Mustafi	GER	17/04/92	D	12	(5)	
17	Angelo Palombo		25/09/81	M	15		
14	Pedro Obiang	ESP	27/03/92	M	32	(2)	1
16	Andrea Poli		29/09/89	M	31		3
15	Simon Busk Poulsen	DEN	07/10/84	D	3	(4)	
9	Nicola Pozzi		30/06/86	A	1	(5)	1
5	Renan	BRA	19/06/86	A	3	(2)	
4	Matías Rodríguez	ARG	14/04/86	D	1		
22	Sergio Romero	ARG	22/02/87	G	32		
35	Jonathan Rossini	SUI	05/04/89	D	24	(1)	
12	Gianluca Sansone		12/05/87	A	6	(8)	2
93	Andelko Savic	SUI	11/03/93	A		(1)	
21	Roberto Soriano		08/02/91	M	8	(16)	
12	Fernando Tissone	ARG	24/07/86	M	6	(6)	

AC SIENA

Coach: Serse Cosmi; (17/12/12) Giuseppe Iachini
1904 • Artemio Franchi (15,373) • acsiena.it

2012

26/08	Torino	h	0-0	
02/09	Sampdoria	a	1-2	Vergassola
16/09	Udinese	h	2-2	Calaiò, Zé Eduardo (p)
23/09	Internazionale	a	2-0	Vergassola, Valiani
27/09	Bologna	h	1-0	Calaiò
30/09	Lazio	a	1-2	Paci
07/10	Juventus	h	1-2	Calaiò
21/10	Atalanta	a	1-2	Reginaldo
27/10	Palermo	h	0-0	
31/10	Cagliari	a	2-4	Bogdani, Calaiò
04/11	Genoa	h	1-0	Paci
11/11	Parma	a	0-0	
18/11	Pescara	h	1-0	Valiani
25/11	Chievo	h	0-0	
02/12	Roma	h	1-3	Luís Neto
09/12	Catania	h	1-3	Rosina
16/12	Fiorentina	h	1-4	Reginaldo
22/12	Napoli	h	0-2	

2013

06/01	Milan	a	1-2	Paolucci
13/01	Torino	a	2-3	Reginaldo, Paolucci
20/01	Sampdoria	h	1-0	Bogdani
27/01	Udinese	a	0-1	
03/02	Internazionale	h	3-1	Emeghara, Sestu, Rosina (p)
10/02	Bologna	a	1-1	Emeghara
18/02	Lazio	h	3-0	Emeghara 2, Rosina
24/02	Juventus	a	0-3	
03/03	Atalanta	h	0-2	
10/03	Palermo	a	2-1	Emeghara, Rosina (p)
17/03	Cagliari	h	0-0	
30/03	Genoa	a	2-2	Emeghara, Rosina (p)
07/04	Parma	h	0-0	
13/04	Pescara	h	3-2	Ângelo, og (Zanon), Emeghara
21/04	Chievo	h	0-1	
28/04	Roma	a	0-4	
05/05	Catania	a	0-3	
08/05	Fiorentina	h	0-1	
12/05	Napoli	a	1-2	Grillo
19/05	Milan	h	1-2	Terzi

No	Name	Nat	DoB	Pos	Aps	(s)	Gls
6	Ângelo	BRA	10/08/81	M	27	(1)	1
17	Nicola Belmonte		15/04/87	D	11	(1)	
81	Erjon Bogdani	ALB	14/04/77	A	4	(14)	2
36	Francesco Bolzoni		07/05/89	M	16	(9)	
11	Emanuele Calaiò		08/01/82	A	18		4
5	Adrián Calello	ARG	14/05/87	M	8	(1)	
92	Matías Campos	CHI	22/06/89	A		(1)	
22	Matteo Contini		16/04/80	D	10		
5	Manuel Coppola		11/05/82	M		(2)	
10	Gaetano D'Agostino		03/06/82	M	7	(1)	
3	Cristiano Del Grosso		23/05/83	D	13	(1)	
14	Francesco Della Rocca		14/09/87	M	16	(1)	
15	Paolo Dellafiore		02/02/85	D	2		
10	Innocent Emeghara	SUI	27/05/89	A	16	(1)	7
18	Felipe	BRA	31/07/84	D	34		
87	Fabrizio Grillo		27/08/86	D	1		1
86	Jorge Teixeira	POR	27/08/86	D	9		
63	Marcelo Larrondo	ARG	16/08/88	A	1	(2)	
13	Luís Neto	POR	26/05/88	D	20		1
70	Daniele Mannini		25/10/83	M	3	(4)	
24	Massimo Paci		09/05/78	D	20	(3)	2
9	Michele Paolucci		06/02/86	A	1	(9)	2
25	Gianluca Pegolo		25/03/81	G	38		
99	Nicola Pozzi		30/06/86	A		(3)	
91	Reginaldo	BRA	31/07/83	A	5	(14)	3
21	Ribair Rodríguez	URU	04/10/87	M	4	(2)	
27	Alessandro Rosina		31/01/84	M	29	(2)	5
33	Matteo Rubin		09/07/87	D	23	(2)	
23	Salvador Agra	POR	11/11/91	A	3	(6)	
77	Alessio Sestu		29/09/83	M	13	(15)	1
88	Christian Terlizzi		22/11/79	D	9		
19	Claudio Terzi		19/06/84	D	8		1
7	Francesco Valiani		29/10/80	M	13	(9)	2
8	Simone Vergassola		24/01/76	M	29	(1)	2
16	Valerio Verre		11/01/94	M	2	(5)	
2	Roberto Vitiello		08/05/83	D	2		
57	Zé Eduardo	BRA	29/10/87	A	6	(2)	1

TORINO FC

Coach: Giampiero Ventura
1906 • Olimpico (25,300) • torinofc.it
Major honours
Italian League (7) 1928, 1943, 1946, 1947, 1948, 1949, 1976;
Italian Cup (5) 1936, 1943, 1968, 1971, 1993

2012

26/08	Siena	a	0-0	
01/09	Pescara	h	3-0	*Sgrigna, Brighi, Bianchi*
16/09	Internazionale	h	0-2	
23/09	Sampdoria	a	1-1	*Bianchi (p)*
26/09	Udinese	h	0-0	
30/09	Atalanta	a	5-1	*Bianchi 2 (1p), Gazzi, Stevanović, D'Ambrosio*
07/10	Cagliari	h	0-1	
21/10	Palermo	a	0-0	
28/10	Parma	h	1-3	*Basha*
31/10	Lazio	a	1-1	*Glik*
04/11	Napoli	a	1-1	*Sansone*
11/11	Bologna	h	1-0	*D'Ambrosio*
19/11	Roma	a	0-2	
25/11	Fiorentina	h	2-2	*Cerci, Birsa*
01/12	Juventus	a	0-3	
09/12	Milan	h	2-4	*Santana, Bianchi*
16/12	Genoa	a	1-1	*Bianchi*
22/12	Chievo	h	2-0	*og (Sardo), Gazzi*

2013

05/01	Catania	a	0-0	
13/01	Siena	h	3-2	*Brighi, Bianchi, Cerci*
20/01	Pescara	a	2-0	*Santana, Cerci*
27/01	Internazionale	a	2-2	*Meggiorini 2*
02/02	Sampdoria	h	0-0	
10/02	Udinese	a	0-1	
17/02	Atalanta	h	2-1	*Cerci, Birsa*
24/02	Cagliari	h	3-4	*Cerci, Stevanović, Bianchi (p)*
03/03	Palermo	h	0-0	
10/03	Parma	a	1-4	*Santana*
17/03	Lazio	h	1-0	*Jonathas*
30/03	Napoli	h	3-5	*Barreto, Jonathas (p), Meggiorini*
06/04	Bologna	a	2-2	*Barreto, Bianchi*
14/04	Roma	h	1-2	*Bianchi*
21/04	Fiorentina	a	3-4	*Barreto, Santana, Cerci*
28/04	Juventus	h	0-2	
05/05	Milan	a	0-1	
08/05	Genoa	h	0-0	
12/05	Chievo	a	1-1	*Cerci (p)*
19/05	Catania	h	2-2	*Cerci, Bianchi*

No	Name	Nat	DoB	Pos	Aps	(s)	Gls
18	Marko Bakić	MNE	01/11/93	M	1		
10	Barreto	BRA	12/07/85	A	13	(3)	3
4	Migjen Basha	ALB	05/01/87	M	17	(4)	1
9	Rolando Bianchi		15/02/83	A	25	(7)	11
86	Valter Birsa	SVN	07/08/86	M	4	(13)	2
33	Matteo Brighi		14/02/81	M	18	(5)	2
15	Pablo Cáceres	URU	22/04/85	D	2		
11	Alessio Cerci		23/07/87	A	32	(3)	8
35	Ferdinando Coppola		10/06/78	G	1		
3	Danilo D'Ambrosio		09/09/88	D	22	(6)	2
36	Matteo Darmian		02/12/89	D	30		
5	Valerio Di Cesare		23/05/83	D	7	(2)	
93	Abou Diop	SEN	06/10/93	A		(3)	
14	Alessandro Gazzi		28/01/83	M	33	(1)	2
1	Jean-François Gillet	BEL	31/05/79	G	37		
25	Kamil Glik	POL	03/02/88	D	31	(1)	1
80	Jonathas	BRA	06/03/89	A	1	(10)	2
17	Salvatore Masiello		31/01/82	D	22	(2)	
69	Riccardo Meggiorini		04/09/85	A	18	(13)	3
29	Dolly Menga	BEL	02/05/93	M		(1)	
6	Angelo Ogbonna		23/05/88	D	22		
2	Guillermo Rodríguez	URU	21/03/84	D	20	(2)	
24	Gianluca Sansone		12/05/87	M	5	(9)	1
7	Mario Santana	ARG	23/12/81	M	21	(6)	4
10	Alessandro Sgrigna		24/04/80	A	7	(4)	1
19	Alen Stevanović	SRB	07/01/91	M	8	(7)	2
8	Sergiu Suciu	ROU	08/05/90	M		(1)	
77	Simone Verdi		12/07/92	A		(4)	
20	Giuseppe Vives		14/07/80	M	21	(4)	

UDINESE CALCIO

Coach: Francesco Guidolin
1896 • Friuli (41,652) • udinese.it

2012

25/08	Fiorentina	a	1-2	*Maicosuel*
02/09	Juventus	h	1-4	*Lazzari*
16/09	Siena	a	2-2	*Basta, Di Natale*
23/09	Milan	h	2-1	*Ranégie, Di Natale (p)*
26/09	Torino	a	0-0	
30/09	Genoa	h	0-0	
07/10	Napoli	a	1-2	*Pinzi*
21/10	Pescara	h	1-0	*Maicosuel*
28/10	Roma	a	3-2	*Domizzi, Di Natale 2 (1p)*
31/10	Catania	h	2-2	*Di Natale 2 (1p)*
04/11	Bologna	a	1-1	*Di Natale*
11/11	Chievo	h	2-2	*Angella 2*
18/11	Parma	h	2-2	*Di Natale, Pereyra*
27/11	Lazio	a	0-3	
02/12	Cagliari	h	4-1	*Pereyra, Angella, Danilo, Pasquale*
10/12	Sampdoria	a	2-0	*Danilo, Di Natale*
15/12	Palermo	h	1-1	*Di Natale*
22/12	Atalanta	a	1-1	*Muriel*

2013

06/01	Internazionale	h	3-0	*Di Natale 2, Muriel*
13/01	Fiorentina	h	3-1	*Di Natale 2 (1p), Muriel*
19/01	Juventus	a	0-4	
27/01	Siena	h	1-0	*Muriel*
03/02	Milan	a	1-2	*Pinzi*
10/02	Torino	h	1-0	*Pereyra*
17/02	Genoa	a	0-1	
25/02	Napoli	h	0-0	
03/03	Pescara	a	1-0	*Di Natale*
09/03	Roma	h	1-1	*Muriel*
16/03	Catania	a	1-3	*Muriel*
30/03	Bologna	h	0-0	
07/04	Chievo	h	3-1	*Di Natale 2, Benatia*
14/04	Parma	a	3-0	*Muriel 2, Pereyra*
20/04	Lazio	h	1-0	*Di Natale*
27/04	Cagliari	a	1-0	*Pereyra*
05/05	Sampdoria	h	3-1	*Di Natale 2, Muriel*
08/05	Palermo	a	3-2	*Muriel, Angella, Benatia*
12/05	Atalanta	h	2-1	*Di Natale 2*
19/05	Internazionale	a	5-2	*Pinzi, Domizzi, Di Natale, Gabriel Silva, Muriel*

No	Name	Nat	DoB	Pos	Aps	(s)	Gls
7	Emmanuel Agyemang-Badu	GHA	02/12/90	M	14	(11)	
3	Allan	BRA	08/01/91	M	33	(3)	
4	Gabriele Angella		28/04/89	D	11	(3)	4
27	Pablo Armero	COL	02/11/86	D	8	(2)	
9	Barreto	BRA	12/07/85	A	2	(2)	
8	Dušan Basta	SRB	18/08/84	D	27	(1)	1
18	Christian Battocchio		10/02/92	M	1		
17	Mehdi Benatia	MAR	17/04/87	D	19		2
1	Željko Brkić	SRB	09/07/86	G	31		
22	Matías Campos	CHI	22/06/89	A		(4)	
16	Andrea Coda		25/04/85	D	10	(1)	
5	Danilo	BRA	10/05/84	D	32		2
10	Antonio Di Natale		13/10/77	A	31	(2)	23
11	Maurizio Domizzi		28/06/80	D	29	(1)	2
31	Diego Fabbrini		31/07/90	A	4	(3)	
6	Marco Faraoni		25/10/91	M	6	(5)	
34	Gabriel Silva	BRA	13/05/91	D	13	(5)	1
75	Thomas Heurtaux	FRA	03/07/88	D	13	(4)	
21	Andrea Lazzari		03/12/84	M	21	(3)	1
77	Maicosuel	BRA	16/06/86	M	15	(5)	2
52	Alexander Merkel	GER	22/02/92	M	1	(4)	
24	Luis Muriel	COL	18/04/91	A	15	(7)	11
25	Daniele Padelli		25/10/85	G	7	(2)	
26	Giovanni Pasquale		05/01/82	D	17	(1)	1
37	Roberto Pereyra	ARG	07/01/91	M	31	(6)	5
66	Giampiero Pinzi		11/03/81	M	17	(2)	3
13	Mathias Ranégie	SWE	14/06/84	A	3	(17)	1
15	Diego Rodríguez	URU	04/09/89	M		(1)	
88	Willians	BRA	29/01/86	M	3	(2)	
94	Piotr Zieliński	POL	20/05/94	M	4	(5)	

Top goalscorers

29	Edinson Cavani (Napoli)
23	Antonio Di Natale (Udinese)
16	Stephan El Shaarawy (Milan)
	Pablo Osvaldo (Roma)
15	Germán Denis (Atalanta)
	Miroslav Klose (Lazio)
	Giampaolo Pazzini (Milan)
	Erik Lamela (Roma)
13	Alberto Gilardino (Bologna)
	Gonzalo Bergessio (Catania)
	Stevan Jovetić (Fiorentina)

Promoted clubs

US SASSUOLO CALCIO
Coach: Eusebio Di Francesco
1922 • Alberto Braglia, Modena (21,151) •
sassuolocalcio.it

HELLAS VERONA FC
Coach: Andrea Mandorlini
1903 • Marc'Antonio Bentegodi (39,211) •
hellasverona.it
Major honours
Italian League (1) 1985

AS LIVORNO CALCIO
Coach: Davide Nicola
1915 • Armando Picchi (19,238) • livornocalcio.it

SECOND LEVEL FINAL TABLE 2012/13

		Pld	W	D	L	F	A	Pts
1	US Sassuolo Calcio	42	25	10	7	78	40	85
2	Hellas Verona FC	42	23	13	6	67	32	82
3	AS Livorno Calcio	42	20	11	11	77	47	88
4	Empoli FC	42	20	13	9	69	51	73
5	Novara Calcio	42	19	10	13	73	46	64
6	Brescia Calcio	42	15	17	10	58	50	62
7	AS Varese	42	16	13	13	55	53	60
8	Modena FC	42	15	12	15	52	51	55
9	Ternana Calcio	42	12	17	13	37	38	53
10	AS Bari	42	16	12	14	55	47	53
11	Calcio Padova	42	12	17	13	47	51	53
12	FC Crotone	42	14	13	15	45	56	53
13	Spezia Calcio	42	12	15	15	52	58	51
14	AC Cesena	42	12	14	16	46	59	50
15	AS Cittadella	42	12	14	16	48	61	50
16	S.S. Juve Stabia	42	12	14	16	54	65	50
17	Reggina Calcio	42	12	15	15	42	51	49
18	S.S. Virtus Lanciano	42	9	21	12	50	60	48
19	Vicenza Calcio	42	10	12	20	41	58	42
20	Ascoli Calcio	42	11	9	22	48	67	41
21	FC Pro Vercelli	42	8	9	25	37	67	33
22	US Grosseto	42	7	13	22	44	67	28

NB AS Bari – 7 pts deducted; US Grosseto – 6 pts deducted; Novara Calcio – 3 pts deducted; FC Crotone, Modena FC & Reggina Calcio – 2 pts deducted; Ascoli Calcio & AS Varese – 1 pt deducted.

PROMOTION/RELEGATION PLAY-OFFS

(22/05/13 & 26/05/13)
Brescia 1-1 Livorno
Livorno 1-1 Brescia
(2-2; Livorno on higher position in regular season)

Novara 1-1 Empoli
Empoli 4-1 Novara
(Empoli 5-2)

(29/05/13 & 02/06/13)
Empoli 1-1 Livorno
Livorno 1-0 Empoli
(Livorno 2-1)

Domestic cup: Coppa Italia 2012/13

THIRD ROUND

(18/08/12)
Atalanta 2-0 Padova
Bologna 2-1 Varese
Cagliari 2-1 Spezia
Catania 1-0 Sassuolo
Cesena 3-2 Crotone
Chievo 4-0 Ascoli
Cittadella 1-0 Ternana
Fiorentina 2-0 Novara
Genoa 1-1 Verona *(aet; 1-4 on pens)*
Juve Stabia 1-1 Sampdoria *(aet; 4-3 on pens)*
Livorno 4-1 Perugia
Modena 1-5 Reggina *(aet)*
Palermo 3-1 Cremonese
Pescara 1-0 Carpi
Torino 4-2 Lecce
(19/08/12)
Siena 4-2 Vicenza

FOURTH ROUND

(07/11/12)
Palermo 1-2 Verona

(28/11/12)
Atalanta 3-1 Cesena
Bologna 1-0 Livorno
Chievo 0-1 Reggina
Fiorentina 2-0 Juve Stabia
Siena 2-0 Torino

(04/12/12)
Catania 3-1 Cittadella *(aet)*

(05/12/12)
Cagliari 4-2 Pescara

FIFTH ROUND

(11/12/12)
Roma 3-0 Atalanta

(12/12/12)
Juventus 1-1 Cagliari
Parma 1-1 Catania *(aet; 3-4 on pens)*

(13/12/12)
Milan 3-0 Reggina

(18/12/12)
Internazionale 2-0 Verona

(19/12/12)
Lazio 1-1 Siena *(aet; 4-1 on pens)*
Napoli 1-2 Bologna
Udinese 0-1 Fiorentina

QUARTER-FINALS

(08/01/13)
Lazio 3-0 Catania *(Radu 30, Hernanes 61, 90+1)*

(09/01/13)
Juventus 2-1 Milan *(Giovinco 13, Vučinić 96; El Shaarawy 6) (aet)*

(15/01/13)
Internazionale 3-2 Bologna *(Guarín 34, Palacio 77, Ranocchia 120; Diamanti 81, Gabbiadini 84) (aet)*

(16/01/13)
Fiorentina 0-1 Roma *(Destro 97) (aet)*

SEMI-FINALS

(22/01/13 & 29/01/13)
Juventus 1-1 Lazio *(Peluso 63; Mauri 86)*
Lazio 2-1 Juventus *(González 53, Floccari 90+3; Vidal 90+2)*
(Lazio 3-2)

(23/01/13 & 17/04/13)
Roma 2-1 Internazionale *(Florenzi 13, Destro 33; Palacio 44)*
Internazionale 2-3 Roma *(Jonathan 22, Álvarez 80; Destro 55, 69, Torosidis 74)*
(Roma 5-3)

FINAL

(26/05/13)
Stadio Olimpico, Rome
S.S. LAZIO 1 *(Lulić 71)*
AS ROMA 0
Referee: Orsato
LAZIO: Marchetti, Konko, Biava, Cana, Radu, Candreva, Onazi (Ciani 90+2), Ledesma (Mauri 54), Hernanes (González 84), Lulić, Klose
ROMA: Lobont, Marquinhos, Burdisso, Leandro Castán, Balzaretti (Osvaldo 76), De Rossi, Bradley, Lamela, Totti, Marquinho (Dodô 83), Destro

Lazio skipper Stefano Mauri lifts the Coppa Italia

KAZAKHSTAN

Kazakhstanning Futbol Federatsiyasi (KFF)

Address	29 Syganak Street
	14th floor
	KZ-010000 Astana
Tel	+7 7172 790780
Fax	+7 7172 790788
E-mail	info@kff.kz
Website	kff.kz

President	Adilbek Jaxybekov
General secretary	Sayan
	Khamitzhanov
Media officer	Izmail Bzarov
Year of formation	1992
National stadium	Astana Arena, Astana
	(30,500)

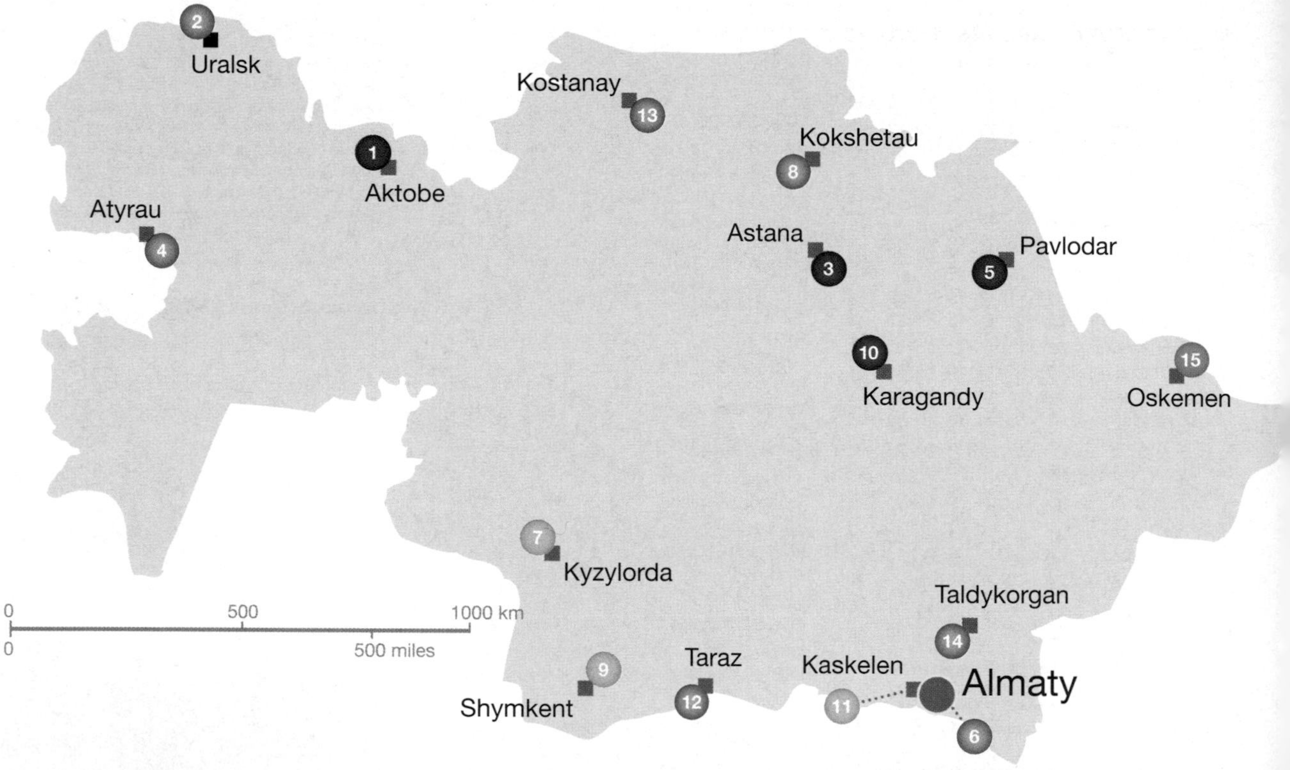

Uralsk

Kostanay

Kokshetau

Atyrau

Aktobe

Astana

Pavlodar

Karagandy

Oskemen

Kyzylorda

Taldykorgan

Taraz

Kaskelen

Almaty

Shymkent

0   500   1000 km
0   500 miles

PREMIER LIGA CLUBS

1. FC Aktobe

2. FC Akzhayik Uralsk

3. FC Astana

4. FC Atyrau

5. FC Irtysh Pavlodar

6. FC Kairat Almaty

7. FC Kaysar Kyzylorda

8. FC Okzhetpes Kokshetau

9. FC Ordabasy Shymkent

10. FC Shakhter Karagandy

11. FC Sunkar Kaskelen

12. FC Taraz

13. FC Tobol Kostanay

14. FC Zhetysu Taldykorgan

PROMOTED CLUB

15. FC Vostok Oskemen

KEY:

● – UEFA Champions League

● – UEFA Europa League

● – Promoted club

○ – Relegated clubs

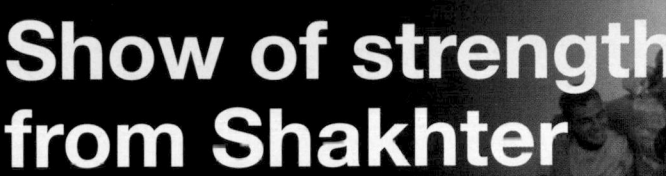

Show of strength from Shakhter

Without a major trophy until 2011, FC Shakhter Karagandy won a second successive Premier Liga title under their charismatic Russian coach Viktor Kumykov, holding off FC Irtysh Pavlodar and perennial challengers FC Aktobe to triumph with a game to spare.

Although he struggled to make an impact with the Kazakhstan national side in 2014 FIFA World Cup qualifying, Czech coach Miroslav Beránek took over at FC Astana and guided the team to domestic cup glory with a 2-0 win over Irtysh in the final.

Successful title defense for Karagandy club

National team coach leads Astana to Kazakh Cup win

Irtysh finish runners-up in league and cup

Domestic league

After an experiment with a two-tiered, 32-match system, the Premier Liga was restored to its previous format in 2012, with each side playing the other once at home and once away in a conventional 26-game campaign. The shorter season helped to produce a tighter title race, but in the end the outcome was the same as Shakhter repeated their 2011 success, recovering from a shaky start to finish up once again as worthy champions.

The Karagandy side were good to watch, scoring 48 goals in their 26 matches – more than any other team in the division – and they were also strong at the back, conceding just 15 goals – again a league-best figure – and keeping several clean sheets in a cluster of crucial victories during the run-in. They also boasted more wins at home and away than any of their rivals, and despite the lack of an out-and-out goalscorer – Lithuanian midfielder Gediminas Vičius topped the in-house rankings with just seven strikes – consistently played the most attractive and adventurous football in the land.

Irtysh, who finished second, two points behind Shakhter, after completing the double over the champions on the final day, possessed the Premier Liga's leading

marksman, which was no surprise as new signing Ulugbek Bakayev had topped the charts in each of the previous two campaigns, with different clubs. He found the target in each of Irtysh's last six matches to finish with 14 goals – four more than his closest pursuers, Astana's Tanat Nuserbayev and FC Akzhayik Uralsk's Igor Zenkovich. Akzhayik were the only one of the three newly promoted clubs to survive, FC Okzhetpes Kokshetau and FC Sunkar Kaskelen suffering immediate relegation.

Domestic cup

Nuserbayev would get his name on the scoresheet in the Kazakh Cup final, clinching Astana's 2-0 victory over Irtysh eight minutes from time after his fellow Kazakhstan international Kairat Nurdauletov had headed the team into an early lead in the club's home stadium. Astana's triumphant cup run – their second in five years – was overseen in its entirety by national team boss Beránek, the Czech having replaced Oleh Protasov in early May after a wounding start to the league campaign.

Europe

Successes for Kazakh clubs in Europe have proved elusive since the country

was admitted to UEFA in 2002, but Aktobe have emerged as stout combatants and they were the country's most impressive performers yet again in 2012/13, reaching the third qualifying round of the UEFA Europa League after ousting opposition from Georgia and Moldova.

They also put up a brave fight against Belgium's KRC Genk before returning to domestic action and finishing in the top three of the Premier Liga for the eighth season running, thus ensuring a return to Europe – also for an eighth straight campaign.

National team

Only one point from six World Cup qualifiers was a disappointing return for Beránek's Kazakhstan. They had threatened a major upset in their opening tie, at home to the Republic of Ireland, only to concede two late goals that transformed a memorable victory into a deflating 2-1 defeat. The team's only positive result was a 0-0 draw at home to Austria – a repeat of their final UEFA EURO 2012 qualifier. That at least gave them a one-point advantage over the Faroe Islands ahead of the two teams' wooden-spoon encounters in the autumn.

KAZAKHSTAN

Domestic league: Premier Liga 2012 final table

		Pld	Home					Away					Total					Pts
			W	D	L	F	A	W	D	L	F	A	W	D	L	F	A	
1	**FC Shakhter Karagandy**	26	10	1	2	32	6	7	1	5	16	9	17	2	7	48	15	53
2	FC Irtysh Pavlodar	26	9	3	1	28	6	6	3	4	18	14	15	6	5	46	20	51
3	FC Aktobe	26	9	2	2	26	11	6	3	4	18	11	15	5	6	44	22	50
4	FC Taraz	26	9	2	2	19	12	5	2	6	13	18	14	4	8	32	30	46
5	FC Astana	26	8	3	2	20	11	5	4	4	14	13	13	7	6	34	24	46
6	FC Tobol Kostanay	26	10	2	1	33	10	3	4	6	9	17	13	6	7	42	27	45
7	FC Ordabasy Shymkent	26	7	4	2	18	9	3	5	5	11	15	10	9	7	29	24	39
8	FC Akzhayik Uralsk	26	5	4	4	16	12	5	0	8	18	27	10	4	12	34	39	34
9	FC Kaysar Kyzylorda	26	7	1	5	14	12	1	5	7	7	21	8	6	12	21	33	30
10	FC Kairat Almaty	26	5	4	4	13	14	2	4	7	10	20	7	8	11	23	34	29
11	FC Atyrau	26	5	2	6	10	13	2	4	7	6	19	7	6	13	16	32	27
12	FC Zhetysu Taldykorgan	26	5	4	4	18	17	1	1	11	9	28	6	5	15	27	45	23
13	FC Sunkar Kaskelen	26	3	5	5	6	9	2	3	8	10	22	5	8	13	16	31	23
14	FC Okzhetpes Kokshetau	26	2	2	9	11	26	1	0	12	9	30	3	2	21	20	56	11

NB FC Kaysar Kyzylorda withdrew from 2013 Premier Liga.

SEASON AT A GLANCE

EUROPEAN QUALIFICATION 2013/14

Champion: FC Shakhter Karagandy (second qualifying round)

Cup winner: FC Astana (first qualifying round)
FC Irtysh Pavlodar (first qualifying round)
FC Aktobe (first qualifying round)

Top scorer	Ulugbek Bakayev (Irtysh), 14 goals
Relegated clubs	FC Okzhetpes Kokshetau, FC Sunkar Kaskelen, FC Kaysar Kyzylorda (withdrew)
Promoted club	FC Vostok Oskemen
Cup final	FC Astana 2-0 FC Irtysh Pavlodar

PREMIER LIGA TEAM OF THE SEASON
(4-4-1-1)
Coach: Kumykov (Shakhter)

PLAYER OF THE SEASON
Ulugbek Bakayev
(FC Irtysh Pavlodar)

Uzbekistan striker Bakayev finished top scorer of the Premier Liga for the third season running, his feat made all the more impressive by the fact that he achieved it with three different clubs – FC Tobol Kostanay, FC Zhetysu Taldykorgan and Irtysh. The 33-year-old's absence from the Kazakh Cup final against FC Astana was keenly felt.

NEWCOMER OF THE SEASON
Dmitri Shomko
(FC Irtysh Pavlodar)

The 22-year-old cemented his reputation as a solid, dependable wing-back, producing a level of consistency throughout the season that belied his tender years. Frequently the man for the big occasion, he helped Irtysh finish runners-up in both domestic competitions and was rewarded with a call-up to the Kazakhstan national squad.

Sidelnikov *(Aktobe)*

Nurdauletov *(Astana)* — Džidić *(Shakhter)* — Rozhkov *(Astana)* — Kenzhesariev *(Aktobe)*

Essomba *(Irtysh)* — Bogdanov *(Tobol)* — Khairullin *(Aktobe)* — Kukeyev *(Shakhter)*

Nuserbayev *(Astana)*

Bakayev *(Irtysh)*

NATIONAL TEAM

Home Kit   Away Kit

TOP FIVE ALL-TIME CAPS
Ruslan Baltiyev (73); Samat Smakov (59); Nurbol Zhumaskaliev (54); Andrei Karpovich (51); **Sergei Ostapenko** (39)

TOP FIVE ALL-TIME GOALS
Ruslan Baltiyev (13); Viktor Zubarev (12); Dmitri Byakov (8); Igor Avdeev, Oleg Litvinenko, **Sergei Ostapenko** & Nurbol Zhumaskaliev (6)

Results 2012/13

Date	Opponent		Venue	Score	Scorers
07/09/12	Republic of Ireland (WCQ)	H	Astana	1-2	*Nurdauletov (07)*
11/09/12	Sweden (WCQ)	A	Malmo	0-2	
12/10/12	Austria (WCQ)	H	Astana	0-0	
16/10/12	Austria (WCQ)	A	Vienna	0-4	
06/02/13	Moldova	N	Antalya (TUR)	3-1	*Dmitrenko (33), Dzholchiev (59, 90)*
22/03/13	Germany (WCQ)	H	Astana	0-3	
26/03/13	Germany (WCQ)	A	Nuremberg	1-4	*Schmidtgal (46)*
04/06/13	Bulgaria	H	Almaty	1-2	*Shomko (90)*

Appearances 2012/13

Coach: Miroslav Beránek (CZE)	24/04/57		IRL	SWE	AUT	AUT	Mda	GER	GER	Bu	Caps	Goals
Andrei Sidelnikov	08/03/80	Aktobe	G	G	G	G	G46	G	G	G46	18	-
Aleksandr Kislitsyn	08/03/86	Tobol	D	D							16	-
Mukhtar Mukhtarov	01/01/86	Ordabasy	D		s91	D			D		15	-
Mikhail Rozhkov	27/12/83	Astana	D	D	D						15	-
Aleksandr Kirov	04/06/84	Shakhter /Astana	D	D	D	D	D	D	D	D	29	-
Kairat Nurdauletov	06/11/82	Astana	M	M	D	D	M	M	M46	M85	32	4
Ulan Konysbayev	28/05/89	Astana	M85		M91	M	M85	s65	M78	M73	15	1
Geynrikh Schmidtgal	20/11/85	Greuther Fürth (GER)	M	M				M	M		12	1
Anatoli Bogdanov	07/08/81	Tobol	M	M	M	M					4	-
Sergei Ostapenko	23/02/86	Astana	A	A46	A		s55	A82	A64		39	6
Tanat Nuserbayev	01/01/87	Astana	A69	A68	A87		A55				15	1
Baurzhan Dzholchiev	08/05/90	Tobol	s69				M90	M	s46		6	2
Sergei Gridin	20/05/87	Shakhter /Aktobe	s85	s68	s94	A				s46	12	2
Viktor Dmitrenko	04/04/91	Astana			D	D	D74	D	D	D	7	1
Pavel Shabalin	23/10/88	Irtysh		M84					s73		2	-
Marat Shakhmetov	06/02/89	Astana		s46		M70	s67		s85		10	-
Baurzhan Islamkhan	23/02/93	Taraz		s84		s70					5	-
Marat Khairullin	26/04/84	Aktobe			M94	s83	M78	M65			10	-
Valeri Korobkin	02/07/84	Astana			M	M		s36	M	M	5	-
Azat Nurgaliyev	30/06/86	Sunkar /Ordabasy			s87	M83				M46	15	-
Mark Gurman	09/02/89	Kairat			s74		D	D	D	D	12	-
Yuri Logvinenko	22/07/88	Aktobe					D	D		M67	18	1
Maksat Baizhanov	06/08/84	Shakhter					M67	M36			15	-
Aleksandr Mokin	19/06/81	Shakhter					s46			s46	15	-
Zhambyl Kukeyev	20/09/88	Shakhter					s78		s64		27	2
Timur Baizhanov	30/03/90	Kairat					s85				1	-
Sergei Khizhnichenko	17/07/91	Shakhter					s90			A46	18	3
Kazbek Geteriev	30/06/85	Kairat						s82			6	-
Konstantin Engel	27/07/88	Cottbus (GER)							M		3	-
Dmitri Shomko	19/03/90	Irtysh							s78	s46	3	1
Aleksei Muldarov	24/04/84	Aktobe								D	1	-
Oleg Nedashkovsky	09/09/87	Kairat								s67	1	-

European club competitions 2012/13

FC SHAKHTER KARAGANDY

CHAMPIONS LEAGUE

Second qualifying round - FC Slovan Liberec (CZE)
A 0-1
Mokin, Vičius (Cañas 66), Vasiljević, Kukeyev (Višņakovs 78), Bayzhanov (Tarasov 76), Finonchenko, Poryvaev, Arsenijević, Džidić, Kirov, Gridin. Coach: Viktor Kumykov (RUS)
H 1-1 Kukeyev (40p) (aet)
Mokin, Vičius, Vasiljević, Kukeyev, Finonchenko (Tarasov 114), Poryvaev, Arsenijević (Višņakovs 120+1), Džidić, Kirov, Gridin (Bayzhanov 76), Cañas. Coach: Viktor Kumykov (RUS)

FC ORDABASY SHYMKENT

CHAMPIONS LEAGUE

First qualifying round - FK Jagodina (SRB)
A 1-0 Mansour (85)
Bekbaev, Mwesigwa, Trajković, Pakholyuk (Djilas 84), Karpovich, Ashirbekov (Beysenov 73), Mansour, Kasyanov, Tazhimbetov (Collins 66), Adyrbekov, Arouri. Coach: Viktor Pasulko (UKR)
H 0-0
Bekbaev, Mwesigwa, Trajković, Pakholyuk, Karpovich, Mansour (B Kozhabayev 90+1), Kasyanov, Tazhimbetov (Beysenov 78), Adyrbekov, Collins (Djilas 84), Arouri. Coach: Viktor Pasulko (UKR)

Second qualifying round - Rosenborg BK (NOR)
A 2-2 Pakholyuk (75), Mansour (90+3)
Bekbaev, Mwesigwa, Trajković, Karpovich, Mansour, Kasyanov, Beysenov (Pakholyuk 46), Tazhimbetov (Djilas 68), Mukhtarov, Collins (Adyrbekov 83), Arouri. Coach: Viktor Pasulko (UKR)
H 1-2 Mansour (32)
Bekbaev, Mwesigwa, Trajković, Pakholyuk (Djilas 90+3), Karpovich, Mansour, Kasyanov, Tazhimbetov (Beysenov 75), Mukhtarov, Collins (Adyrbekov 84), Arouri. Coach: Viktor Pasulko (UKR)

FC ZHETYSU TALDYKORGAN

EUROPA LEAGUE

First qualifying round - KKS Lech Poznań (POL)
A 0-2
Loginovski, Dautov, S Muzhikov (Kumysbekov 70), Skorykh (Spanov 81), Mukanov, Dobrašinović, Belić, Mihajlov, Junuzović (Shchetkin 70), Kostić, Djalovic. Coach: Branko Čavić (SRB)
H 1-1 S Muzhikov (44)
Loginovski, Dyakov, S Muzhikov, Skorykh, Spanov (Kumysbekov 84), Mukanov (Korobov 87), Dobrašinović, Belić (Shchetkin 67), Mihajlov, Junuzović, Kostić. Coach: Slobodan Krčmarević (SRB)

FC AKTOBE

EUROPA LEAGUE

First qualifying round - FC Torpedo Kutaisi (GEO)
A 1-1 Bikmaev (82)
Narzikulov, Smakov, Bajer (Lisenkov 90+3), Khairullin, Kenzhesariev, Logvinenko, Klimavičius (Badlo 76), Kovalchuk, Geynrikh (Zemlyanukhin 28), Bikmaev, Kapadze. Coach: Vladimir Mukhanov (RUS)
H 1-0 Bikmaev (75)
Sidelnikov, Badlo, Primus, Smakov, Bajer (Zemlyanukhin 90+3), Khairullin (Klimavičius 90+1), Kenzhesariev, Logvinenko, Kovalchuk, Bikmaev (Lisenkov 87), Kapadze. Coach: Vladimir Mukhanov (RUS)

Second qualifying round - FC Milsami Orhei (MDA)
A 2-4 Kapadze (8), Smakov (56)
Sidelnikov, Badlo, Smakov, Bajer, Khairullin, Kenzhesariev, Logvinenko (Primus 46), Kovalchuk, Geynrikh, Bikmaev, Kapadze. Coach: Vladimir Mukhanov (RUS)
H 3-0 Khairullin (39), Geynrikh (50), Simão (90+3og)
Sidelnikov, Badlo, Smakov, Bajer, Khairullin, Kenzhesariev, Logvinenko (Primus 46), Kovalchuk, Geynrikh (Klimavičius 78), Bikmaev (Lisenkov 71), Kapadze. Coach: Vladimir Mukhanov (RUS)

Third qualifying round - KRC Genk (BEL)
A 1-2 Badlo (25)
Sidelnikov, Badlo, Primus, Smakov, Bajer, Khairullin, Kenzhesariev, Kovalchuk, Geynrikh (Klimavičius 82), Bikmaev (Lisenkov 89), Kapadze. Coach: Vladimir Mukhanov (RUS)
Red card: Badlo 80
H 1-2 Kenzhesariev (30)
Sidelnikov, Primus, Smakov, Bajer, Khairullin, Kenzhesariev, Klimavičius, Kovalchuk, Geynrikh (Zemlyanukhin 76), Bikmaev (Lisenkov 81), Kapadze. Coach: Vladimir Mukhanov (RUS)

Domestic league club-by-club

FC AKTOBE

Coach: Vladimir Mukhanov (RUS)
1967 • Aktobe Central Stadium (13,500) • fc-aktobe.kz
Major honours
Kazakhstan League (4) 2005, 2007, 2008, 2009;
Kazakhstan Cup (1) 2008

2012

10/03	Kaysar	a	2-0	Bajer, Klimavičius
18/03	Shakhter	a	0-2	
25/03	Zhetysu	h	4-0	Maletić, Ilić 2, Lisenkov
01/04	Taraz	a	0-1	
08/04	Ordabasy	h	0-0	
15/04	Akzhayik	a	0-1	
22/04	Kairat	h	1-1	Khairullin
29/04	Irtysh	a	2-1	Khairullin (p), Ilić
06/05	Tobol	h	0-1	
12/05	Okzhetpes	a	4-1	Badlo, Smakov, Kostić, Lisenkov
20/05	Atyrau	h	1-0	Khairullin
27/05	Astana	a	0-1	
16/06	Sunkar	a	2-1	Logvinenko, Kapadze
24/06	Shakhter	h	1-0	Geynrikh
01/07	Zhetysu	a	1-1	Lisenkov
08/07	Taraz	h	4-1	Kapadze, Khairullin (p), Covalciuc, Badlo
15/07	Ordabasy	a	1-1	Bajer
19/08	Irtysh	h	1-0	Lisenkov
26/08	Tobol	a	2-2	Primus, Kenzhesariev
15/09	Okzhetpes	h	5-2	og (Martinović), Geynrikh 2, Lisenkov, Smakov
23/09	Atyrau	a	2-0	Kapadze, Kuat
26/09	Akzhayik	h	3-4	Kenzhesariev, Bajer, Geynrikh
04/10	Astana	h	2-1	Khairullin, Geynrikh
21/10	Sunkar	h	1-0	Kapadze
24/10	Kairat	a	3-0	Bajer 2, Khairullin
28/10	Kaysar	h	2-0	Geynrikh, Kenzhesarie

No	Name	Nat	DoB	Pos	Aps	(s)	Gls
95	Abat Aimbetov		07/08/95	A	5	(1)	
5	Petr Badlo		24/05/76	D	24	(1)	2
9	Lukaš Bajer	CZE	15/12/84	M	17	(7)	5
75	Marat Bikmaev	UZB	01/01/86	M	7	(2)	
39	Serghey Covalciuc	MDA	20/01/02	M	11		1
14	Aslan Darabaev		21/01/89	M	4	(5)	
21	Georgi Daskalov	BUL	03/08/81	A	2	(5)	
50	Aleksandr Geynrikh	UZB	06/10/84	A	12	(1)	6
18	Brana Ilić	SRB	16/02/85	A	9	(1)	3
80	Timur Kapadze	UZB	05/09/81	M	14		4
20	Emil Kenzhesariev		26/03/87	D	13		3
10	Marat Khairullin		26/04/84	M	23	(1)	6
28	Arūnas Klimavičius	LTU	05/10/82	D	7	(9)	1
7	Zoran Kostić	SRB	14/11/82	M	8	(2)	1
70	Islambek Kuat		12/01/93	M	7	(8)	1
91	Maksat Kurmashev		14/08/91	A	1		
22	Sergei Lisenkov		17/06/91	A	12	(8)	5
23	Yuri Logvinenko		22/07/88	M	20	(1)	1
33	Darko Maletić	BIH	20/10/80	M	12		1
77	Dmitri Miroshnichenko		26/02/92	D		(2)	
35	Stanislav Pavlov		30/05/94	G	1		
6	Robert Primus	TRI	10/11/90	D	12		1
55	Andrei Sidelnikov		08/03/80	G	25	(1)	
8	Samat Smakov		08/12/78	D	24		2
19	Murat Tleshev		12/04/80	A		(2)	
11	Vladimir Vukajlović	SRB	25/08/83	M	8	(3)	
4	Dmitri Yevstigneev		27/11/86	D	3	(1)	
88	Vitali Yevstigneev		08/05/85	M	2	(5)	
44	Anton Zemlyanukhin	KGZ	11/12/90	M	3	(7)	

FC AKZHAYIK URALSK

Coach: Saulius Širmelis (LTU)
1968 • Pyotr Atoyan (8,320) • fc-akzhayik.kz

2012

10/03	Okzhetpes	a	3-0	Zenkovich 2 (1p), Zabrodin
18/03	Atyrau	h	3-1	Azovskiy, Valkanov 2
25/03	Astana	a	1-2	Zenkovich
01/04	Sunkar	h	1-1	Zenkovich (p)
08/04	Kaysar	a	2-1	Semler 2
15/04	Aktobe	h	1-0	Erbes
22/04	Zhetysu	a	2-1	og (Marić), Chleboun
29/04	Taraz	h	3-0	Chleboun, Stojčev, Erbes
06/05	Ordabasy	a	0-2	
12/05	Shakhter	a	1-3	Zenkovich
20/05	Kairat	h	1-2	Sadjo
27/05	Irtysh	a	1-3	Semler
16/06	Tobol	h	2-1	Sadjo, Zenkovich (p)
24/06	Atyrau	a	1-0	Zenkovich
01/07	Astana	h	0-1	
08/07	Sunkar	a	0-1	
15/07	Kaysar	h	0-0	
05/08	Zhetysu	h	2-2	Chleboun, Zenkovich
19/08	Taraz	a	2-0	Semler, Chleboun
26/08	Ordabasy	h	1-1	Chleboun
15/09	Shakhter	h	0-1	
19/09	Kairat	a	1-2	Zenkovich
26/09	Aktobe	a	4-3	Zabrodin, Stojčev 3
04/10	Irtysh	h	0-1	
21/10	Tobol	a	0-6	
28/10	Okzhetpes	h	2-1	Černý, Brezinský

No	Name	Nat	DoB	Pos	Aps	(s)	Gls
11	Kanat Aliyev		09/02/85	D	22		
10	Maksim Azovskiy		04/06/86	A	15	(3)	1
87	Roman Bagautdinov		20/09/87	G	4	(2)	
90	Miloš Brezinský	SVK	02/04/84	D	9		1
20	Pavel Černý	CZE	28/01/85	A	14		1
15	Jakub Chleboun	CZE	24/03/85	D	26		5
4	Aleksei Danaev		01/09/79	D	7	(2)	
12	Vyacheslav Erbes		14/04/88	D	4	(5)	2
18	Tkachenko		18/01/90	M	3	(5)	
75	Timur Khalmuratov		29/04/86	M	9		
7	Evgeni Kostrub		27/08/82	M	23	(2)	
8	Aleksei Maltsev		25/10/86	A	4	(13)	
14	Baurzhan Omarov		03/08/90	D	22		
88	Haman Sadjo	CMR	28/11/84	D	21	(1)	2
9	Borut Semler	SVN	09/09/86	A	11	(6)	3
17	Sergei Shevtsov		29/10/90	M		(2)	
21	Miloš Stojčev	SRB	19/01/87	M	9	(11)	4
1	Anton Tsirin		10/08/87	G	22	(1)	
3	Yanko Valkanov	BUL	25/07/82	D	11		2
23	Nikolay Zabrodin		03/07/90	A	13	(11)	2
78	Igor Zenkovich	BLR	17/09/87	A	25	(1)	10
2	Konstantin Zotov		14/01/86	M	12	(10)	

FC ASTANA

Coach: Oleh Protasov (UKR);
(06/05/12) (Miroslav Beránek (CZE))
2009 • Astana Arena (30,500) • fca.kz
Major honours
Kazakhstan Cup (2) 2008, 2012

2012

10/03	Taraz	h	0-2	
25/03	Akzhayik	h	2-1	Nurdauletov, Nuserbayev
01/04	Kairat	a	2-0	Gridin, Ostapenko
08/04	Irtysh	h	2-2	Nuserbayev, Rozhkov
15/04	Tobol	a	2-3	Nuserbayev, Foxi
22/04	Okzhetpes	h	1-4	Dica
29/04	Atyrau	a	0-1	
06/05	Shakhter	h	1-0	Rozhkov
12/05	Sunkar	h	0-0	
20/05	Kaysar	a	1-0	Dmitrenko
27/05	Aktobe	h	1-0	Ostapenko
16/06	Zhetysu	a	1-1	Rozhkov
24/06	Ordabasy	h	1-0	Gridin
01/07	Akzhayik	a	1-0	Konysbayev
08/07	Kairat	h	2-1	Nuserbayev, Ostapenko (p)
15/07	Irtysh	a	0-3	
29/07	Tobol	h	1-1	Konysbayev
05/08	Okzhetpes	a	3-1	Nuserbayev, Rozhkov, Kojašević
19/08	Atyrau	h	5-0	Dmitrenko, Ostapenko, Kojašević, Konysbayev, Shakhmetov
26/08	Shakhter	a	1-0	Nuserbayev
15/09	Sunkar	a	1-0	Nuserbayev
23/09	Kaysar	h	3-0	Ostapenko, Nuserbayev, Ivanovski
04/10	Aktobe	a	1-2	Nuserbayev
21/10	Zhetysu	h	1-0	Nuserbayev
25/10	Ordabasy	a	0-0	
28/10	Taraz	a	1-1	Ostapenko

No	Name	Nat	DoB	Pos	Aps	(s)	Gls
5	Pirali Aliyev		13/01/84	D	1	(8)	
55	Aleksei Belkin		25/11/81	G	4		
15	Abzal Beysebekov		30/11/92	A	10	(3)	
19	Emil Dica	ROU	17/07/82	M	2	(6)	1
8	Viktor Dmitrenko		04/04/91	D	18		2
19	Christian Ebala	CMR	17/03/88	M	15	(1)	
1	Nenad Erić	SRB	26/05/82	G	22		
20	Foxi Kethevoama	CTA	30/05/86	A	19	(4)	1
16	Evgeni Goriachiy		02/02/91	D		(1)	
11	Sergei Gridin		20/05/87	A	9	(3)	2
28	Filip Ivanovski	MKD	01/05/85	A	4	(7)	1
90	Damir Kojašević	MNE	03/06/87	M	4	(7)	2
7	Ulan Konysbayev		28/05/89	M	20	(5)	3
3	Valeri Korobkin		02/07/84	M	14		
29	Dimitrija Lazarevski	MKD	23/09/82	D	26		
4	Mukhtar Mukhtarov		06/01/86	D	11		
6	Kairat Nurdauletov		06/11/82	D	18	(1)	1
17	Tanat Nuserbayev		01/01/87	M	23	(3)	10
9	Sergei Ostapenko		23/02/86	A	22	(4)	6
31	Dušan Petronijević	SRB	09/11/83	M	3	(6)	
40	Denis Prokopenko		05/10/91	A		(1)	
27	Mikhail Rozhkov		27/12/83	D	26		4
22	Marat Shakhmetov		06/02/89	A	15	(8)	1

FC ATYRAU

Coach: Zoran Filipović (MNE);
(16/06/12) (Yuriy Konkov)
1980 • Munayshi (8,660) • rfcatyrau.kz
Major honours
Kazakhstan Cup (1) 2009

2012

10/03	Ordabasy	h	2-3	Danilyuk, Sigurdsson
18/03	Akzhayik	a	1-3	Danilyuk
25/03	Kairat	h	2-0	Saraev, Shaff
01/04	Irtysh	a	0-0	
08/04	Tobol	h	1-0	Jonathas
15/04	Okzhetpes	a	2-1	Buač, Rodionov
22/04	Shakhter	h	0-2	
29/04	Astana	h	1-0	Rodionov
06/05	Sunkar	a	0-0	
12/05	Kaysar	h	0-1	
20/05	Aktobe	a	0-1	
27/05	Zhetysu	h	2-1	Shaff, Ovshinov
16/06	Taraz	a	1-0	Milanković
24/06	Akzhayik	h	0-1	
01/07	Kairat	a	1-1	Sigurdsson
08/07	Irtysh	h	0-2	
15/07	Tobol	a	0-1	
29/07	Okzhetpes	h	1-0	Fomin
05/08	Shakhter	a	0-4	
19/08	Astana	a	0-5	
26/08	Sunkar	h	1-0	Milanković
15/09	Kaysar	a	0-1	
23/09	Aktobe	h	0-2	
04/10	Zhetysu	a	0-1	
21/10	Taraz	h	0-0	
28/10	Ordabasy	a	1-1	Sigurdsson

No	Name	Nat	DoB	Pos	Aps	(s)	Gls
2	Yegor Azovskiy		10/01/85	D	13	(1)	
22	Mirambek Bikeev		28/12/90	M	7	(3)	
29	Sergei Boychenko		27/09/77	G	25		
34	Vladimir Buač	SRB	26/12/84	A	16	(3)	1
8	Valentin Chureev		29/08/86	D	22		
19	Taras Danilyuk		29/01/84	M	12		2
18	Fausto	POR	19/01/87	A	6	(1)	
7	Artem Fomin		08/07/88	A	7	(12)	1
25	Jonathas	BRA	05/11/87	D	5	(1)	1
23	Dauren Kayralliev		15/05/92	M	3	(2)	
9	Nikita Khokhlov		27/10/83	M	10	(4)	
20	Sergei Kutsov		23/04/77	D	17	(1)	
24	Vladislav Kuzmin		03/07/87	D	4	(2)	
44	Nursultan Madiev		08/07/93	A	1	(2)	
86	Nikola Milanković	SRB	23/04/86	M	23		2
57	Nivaldo	BRA	22/06/88	M		(5)	
13	Aybar Nuribekov		29/08/92	A	7	(2)	
4	Evgeni Ovshinov		17/10/80	D	12		1
33	Vladimir Plotnikov		03/04/86	G	1	(1)	
12	Denis Rodionov		26/07/85	M	15	(3)	2
5	Maksim Samchenko		05/05/79	D	9	(1)	
21	Sandro	BRA	13/03/83	D	2	(2)	
3	Nikolai Saraev		20/05/90	D	8	(5)	1
17	Maksim Semenyov		02/09/88	M	9	(6)	
11	Asylbek Seytkaliev		29/02/92	M		(1)	
14	Sergei Shaff		15/04/88	A	14	(8)	2
25	Sanat Shalekenov		04/04/89	D	4	(5)	
83	Hannes Sigurdsson	ISL	10/04/83	A	11	(4)	3
82	Bojan Trkulja	SRB	20/02/82	D	9		
6	Djordje Tutorić	SRB	05/03/83	D	10		

FC IRTYSH PAVLODAR

Coach: Talgat Baysufinov
1965 • Pavlodar Centralny (12,000) • fcirtysh.kz
Major honours
Kazakhstan League (5) 1993, 1997, 1999, 2002, 2003;
Kazakhstan Cup (1) 1998

2012

10/03	Shakhter	h	1-0	*Strukov*
18/03	Tobol	h	4-1	*Bakayev 2 (1p), Shabalin, Maltsev*
25/03	Okzhetpes	a	4-1	*Ivanov, Kučera, og (Bidnenko), Govedarica*
01/04	Atyrau	h	0-0	
08/04	Astana	a	2-2	*Yurin 2*
15/04	Sunkar	h	4-0	*Yurin, Strukov, Essomba, Maltsev*
22/04	Kaysar	a	0-2	
29/04	Aktobe	h	1-2	*Bakayev (p)*
06/05	Zhetysu	a	2-1	*Yurin, Ayaganov*
12/05	Taraz	h	1-1	*Maltsev*
20/05	Ordabasy	a	1-2	*Bakayev*
27/05	Akzhayik	h	3-1	*Shabalin, Ivanov, Strukov*
16/06	Kairat	a	0-0	
24/06	Tobol	a	2-2	*Yurin, Bakayev (p)*
01/07	Okzhetpes	h	3-0	*Ivanov, Yurin, Strukov*
08/07	Atyrau	a	2-0	*Essomba, Bakayev*
15/07	Astana	h	3-0	*Ivanov, Bakayev, Essomba*
29/07	Sunkar	a	1-0	*Coulibaly*
05/08	Kaysar	h	1-1	*Shabalin*
19/08	Aktobe	a	0-1	
26/08	Zhetysu	h	3-0	*Shabalin, Bakayev 2*
15/09	Taraz	a	2-3	*Bakayev (p), Govedarica*
24/09	Ordabasy	h	3-0	*Bakayev, Maltsev, Shabalin*
04/10	Akzhayik	a	1-0	*Bakayev*
21/10	Kairat	h	1-0	*Bakayev*
28/10	Shakhter	a	1-0	*Bakayev*

No	Name	Nat	DoB	Pos	Aps	(s)	Gls
19	Ali Aliyev		27/10/80	M	2	(2)	
13	Alibek Ayaganov		13/01/92	M	1	(8)	1
20	Ulugbek Bakayev	UZB	28/11/78	A	26		14
23	Timur Bayzhanov		30/03/90	A	1	(3)	
3	Vladislav Chernyshev		16/03/81	D	14	(4)	
6	Anton Chichulin		27/10/84	D	18	(1)	
8	Mamoutou Coulibaly	MLI	23/02/84	D	20	(1)	1
22	Titi Essomba	CMR	23/05/86	M	23	(1)	3
55	Predrag Govedarica	SRB	21/10/84	M	17	(4)	2
11	Sergei Ivanov		30/05/80	A	23		4
2	Igor Jugović	CRO	23/01/89	M		(2)	
33	Vyacheslav Kotlyar		03/03/82	G	12		
25	Štěpán Kučera	CZE	11/06/84	D	26		1
1	David Loria		31/10/81	G	14		
30	Darko Maletić	BIH	20/10/80	M	1	(5)	
10	Gleb Maltsev		07/03/88	A	1	(8)	4
99	Vladislav Mirchev	BUL	23/01/87	A	1	(3)	
24	Dmitri Parkhamchuk		07/03/87	M		(3)	
7	Pavel Shabalin		23/10/88	A	14	(9)	5
15	Dmitri Shomko		19/03/90	M	25		
34	Sergei Strukov	RUS	17/09/82	A	11	(4)	4
5	Kairat Utabaev		16/07/80	D	10	(6)	
27	Vladimir Yakovlev		02/08/84	M	2	(2)	
14	Igor Yurin		03/07/82	M	23	(1)	6
12	Konstantin Zarechni		14/02/84	D	1	(2)	

FC KAIRAT ALMATY

Coach: Dmitri Ogai;
(16/06/12) (José Pérez Serer (ESP))
1954 • Almaty Centralny (25,057) • fckairat.kz
Major honours
Kazakhstan League (2) 1992, 2004;
Kazakhstan Cup (5) 1992, 1996, 1999, 2001 (autumn), 2003

2012

10/03	Tobol	a	0-4	
18/03	Okzhetpes	h	3-0	*Knežević (p), Jovanović, Djordjević*
25/03	Atyrau	a	0-2	
01/04	Astana	h	0-2	
08/04	Sunkar	a	2-0	*Duff, Knežević*
15/04	Kaysar	h	1-1	*Knežević (p)*
22/04	Aktobe	a	1-1	*Mamonov*
29/04	Zhetysu	h	1-0	*Nedashkovsky*
06/05	Taraz	a	1-2	*Knežević*
12/05	Ordabasy	h	1-1	*Knežević*
20/05	Akzhayik	a	2-1	*Nedashkovsky, Jovanović*
27/05	Shakhter	a	1-4	*Nedashkovsky*
16/06	Irtysh	h	0-0	
24/06	Okzhetpes	a	0-0	
01/07	Atyrau	h	1-1	*Djordjević*
08/07	Astana	a	1-2	*Abdramanov*
15/07	Sunkar	h	1-3	*Souto*
29/07	Kaysar	a	1-1	*Kalinin*
19/08	Zhetysu	a	1-2	*Kalinin*
26/08	Taraz	h	2-1	*Knežević, Souto*
15/09	Ordabasy	a	0-0	
19/09	Akzhayik	h	2-1	*Óscar García, Sakhalbayev*
03/10	Shakhter	h	0-1	
21/10	Irtysh	a	0-1	
24/10	Aktobe	h	0-3	
28/10	Tobol	h	1-0	*Vyatkin*

No	Name	Nat	DoB	Pos	Aps	(s)	Gls
	Almat Abdramanov		12/03/90	M	2	(3)	1
37	Kanat Akhmetov		11/04/87	A	2	(3)	
19	Azamat Aubakirov		10/11/87	A	2	(2)	
10	Ruslan Baltiev		16/09/78	M		(3)	
5	Burak Akyıldız	TUR	03/01/85	D	8		
45	Aleksandr Bychenok	BLR	30/05/85	M	2	(5)	
27	Marko Djordjević	SRB	22/05/83	D	19	(1)	2
21	Stuart Duff	SCO	23/01/82	M	23	(1)	1
29	Mark Gurman		09/02/89	D	24	(1)	
16	Alberto Heredia	ESP	02/03/87	A	11	(7)	
9	Nemanja Jovanović	SRB	03/03/84	A	13	(1)	2
20	Ilya Kalinin		03/02/92	M	10	(9)	2
8	Andrei Kharabara		01/09/85	M	9		
30	Josip Knežević	CRO	03/10/88	A	14	(2)	6
15	Evgeni Levin		12/07/92	D	12	(3)	
18	Dmitri Mamonov		26/04/78	M	12	(2)	1
11	Ruslan Mansurov		23/11/90	A		(1)	
23	Oleg Nedashkovsky		09/09/87	M	6	(2)	3
35	Ramil Nurmukhametov		21/12/87	G	19		
44	Óscar García	ESP	12/07/88	A	9	(1)	1
6	Rakhimzhan Rozybakiev		02/01/91	M	6	(10)	
7	Ruslan Sakhalbayev		27/06/84	M	11	(6)	1
1	Andrei Shabanov		17/11/86	G	7		
31	Ildar Shaikheslamov		27/07/89	G		(1)	
22	Kirill Shestakov		19/06/85	M	22		
43	Gustavo Souto	ESP	29/04/83	A	9		2
50	Kasymkhan Talasbayev		27/02/93	M		(1)	
23	Nikita Utrobin		03/01/93	A	2	(4)	
88	Magomed Uzdenov		25/02/94	A	1	(2)	
4	Ilya Vorotnikov		01/02/86	D	16		
14	Vladimir Vyatkin		30/04/91	M	11	(2)	1
17	Vladimir Yakovlev		02/08/84	M	3	(2)	
14	Nursayuin Zholdasov		11/05/91	M	1	(1)	

FC KAYSAR KYZYLORDA

Coach: Sergei Kogay;
(01/04/12) (Vladimir Nikitenko)
1968 • Gany Muratbayev (7,300) • fc-kaysar.kz
Major honours
Kazakhstan Cup (1) 1999

2012

10/03	Aktobe	h	0-2	
18/03	Zhetysu	a	2-5	*Narzildaev, Sytnik*
25/03	Taraz	h	1-2	*Crnogorac*
01/04	Ordabasy	a	0-1	
08/04	Akzhayik	h	1-2	*Sytnik*
15/04	Kairat	a	1-1	*Vagner*
22/04	Irtysh	h	2-0	*Malkov, Moldakaraev*
29/04	Tobol	a	0-2	
06/05	Okzhetpes	h	1-0	*Crnogorac*
12/05	Atyrau	a	1-0	*Crnogorac*
20/05	Astana	h	0-1	
27/05	Sunkar	a	0-0	
16/06	Shakhter	h	1-0	*Marković*
24/06	Zhetysu	h	1-0	*Fachtali*
01/07	Taraz	a	0-1	
15/07	Akzhayik	a	0-0	
29/07	Kairat	h	1-1	*Moldakaraev*
05/08	Irtysh	a	1-1	*Mamić*
10/08	Ordabasy	h	2-1	*Mamić 2*
19/08	Tobol	h	1-2	*Moldakaraev*
26/08	Okzhetpes	a	2-2	*Tagybergen, Parkhachev*
15/09	Atyrau	h	1-0	*Tagybergen*
23/09	Astana	a	0-3	
04/10	Sunkar	h	2-1	*Crnogorac, Baltaev*
21/10	Shakhter	a	0-3	
28/10	Aktobe	a	0-2	

No	Name	Nat	DoB	Pos	Aps	(s)	Gls
8	Renat Abdulin		14/04/82	D	25		
22	Aziz Anarmetov		30/07/82	M	19	(4)	
3	Aldan Baltaev		15/01/89	D	17	(2)	1
4	Adrian Cascaval	MDA	10/06/87	D	2	(4)	
5	Gradimir Crnogorac	BIH	14/11/82	D	23		4
82	Serik Dosmanbetov		08/03/82	A	11		
1	Nemanja Džodžo	SRB	12/12/86	G	17		
50	Philip Edeipo	NGA	04/11/86	A	1	(6)	
12	Ruslan Esatov		31/10/84	M	23	(2)	
99	Abdelkarim Fachtali	NED	30/03/88	A	4	(5)	1
14	Anatoli Malkov		08/07/81	A	19	(3)	1
81	Bojan Mamić	SRB	13/09/81	A	9	(3)	3
20	Marjan Marković	SRB	28/09/81	M	9	(1)	1
77	Aset Menlykozha		13/03/89	M		(1)	
17	Zhasulan Moldakaraev		07/05/87	A	5	(13)	3
93	Duman Narzildaev		06/09/93	M	4	(6)	1
85	Dmitri Parkhachev	BLR	02/01/85	A	13		1
13	Kirill Pryadkin		06/07/77	G	9	(1)	
18	Serik Sagyndykov		09/01/84	D	11	(7)	
2	Yevgeniy Shmakov	UKR	07/06/85	M	12		
6	Aleksandr Stakhiv		13/01/81	M	4	(4)	
9	Olexandr Sytnik	UKR	07/07/84	M	10	(2)	2
10	Talgat Syzdykov		23/02/78	A	9	(6)	
7	Askhat Tagybergen		09/08/90	M	23	(1)	2
11	Vagner	BRA	01/06/87	M	7		1

FC OKZHETPES KOKSHETAU

Coach: Viktor Dogadaylo (UKR);
(06/05/12) (Vladimir Cheburin)
1968 • Torpedo (6,000) • okzhetpes.kz

2012

10/03	Akzhayik	h	0-3
18/03	Kairat	a	0-3
25/03	Irtysh	h	1-4 *Chagelishvili*
01/04	Tobol	a	1-3 *Mikhaylyuk*
08/04	Shakhter	h	0-2
15/04	Atyrau	h	1-2 *Chagelishvili*
22/04	Astana	a	4-1 *Chagelishvili 3, og (Beysebekov)*
29/04	Sunkar	h	0-2
06/05	Kaysar	a	0-1
12/05	Aktobe	h	1-4 *Dosmagombetov*
20/05	Zhetysu	a	0-1
27/05	Taraz	h	3-1 *Makhambetov 2, Dyak (p)*
16/06	Ordabasy	a	0-1
24/06	Kairat	h	0-0
01/07	Irtysh	a	0-3
08/07	Tobol	h	0-1
29/07	Atyrau	a	0-1
05/08	Astana	h	1-3 *Grigoruţă*
10/08	Shakhter	a	0-4
19/08	Sunkar	a	1-0 *Grigoruţă*
26/08	Kaysar	h	2-2 *Dosmagombetov 2 (1p)*
15/09	Aktobe	a	2-5 *Grigoruţă, Goloveshkin*
23/09	Zhetysu	h	1-0 *Amanow (p)*
04/10	Taraz	a	0-2
21/10	Ordabasy	h	1-2 *Dosmagombetov (p)*
28/10	Akzhayik	a	1-2 *Chagelishvili*

No	Name	Nat	DoB	Pos	Aps	(s)	Gls
10	Kuanysh Abdualyev		04/11/88	M		(2)	
7	Khasan Abdukarimov		10/03/90	M		(2)	
21	Ruslan Abzhanov		28/04/90	G	6	(1)	
19	Emil Aliyev		16/06/88	A		(8)	
75	Arslanmyrat Amanow	TKM	28/03/90	A	10	(1)	1
1	Yaroslav Baginsky		03/10/87	G	4		
18	Ruslan Bidnenko	UKR	20/07/81	M	3	(1)	
15	Maxim Cebotari	MDA	16/11/82	D	7	(1)	
25	David Chagelishvili	GEO	10/01/87	A	14	(7)	6
24	Ihor Chuchman	UKR	15/02/85	D	24	(1)	
4	Maksim Chudinov		12/09/88	D	12	(5)	
23	Timur Dosmagombetov		01/05/89	M	23	(1)	4
5	Yuri Dyak		04/07/84	M	14	(3)	1
91	Boris Fomenkov		29/09/91	D	7		
66	Vitali Goloveshkin		10/11/89	M	8	(4)	1
26	Adrian Grigoruţă	ROU	08/08/83	M	10		3
70	Yerzat Kenbaev		22/04/88	A	5	(4)	
9	Ruslan Kenetayev		21/03/88	M	2	(7)	
35	Artem Kirbyatev		16/08/84	G	5		
8	Viktor Kozhushko		03/02/81	M	12	(2)	
46	Anton Kuchma		09/12/80	M	2	(2)	
14	Ablaykhan Makhambetov		03/08/91	M	13		2
76	Dejan Martinović	BIH	19/07/83	M	9		
77	Ovidiu Mendizov	ROU	09/08/86	M	13		
27	Aleksei Mikhaylyuk		23/07/82	D	17		1
33	Marko Milovanović	SRB	12/06/82	D	17	(1)	
22	Igor Osipchuk		02/08/75	G	11	(2)	
92	Igor Pikalkin		19/03/92	M	8		
88	Vasili Prosekov		31/10/83	A	3	(3)	
11	Evgeni Samokhin		03/09/90	A	2	(6)	
2	Anuar Tokenov		28/05/91	D			
28	Aleksandr Ulshin		15/10/92	M	1	(1)	
20	Olexandr Yakymenko	UKR	05/09/88	A	3	(3)	
17	Armand Yankep	CMR	17/12/85	M	15		
3	Maksim Zabelin		04/02/77	D	6		

FC ORDABASY SHYMKENT

Coach: Viktor Pasulko (UKR)
1998 • Kazhimukan (17,000) • fcordabasy.kz
Major honours
Kazakhstan Cup (1) 2011

2012

10/03	Atyrau	a	3-2 *Karpovich, Tazhimbetov, Djilas*
25/03	Sunkar	a	0-0
01/04	Kaysar	h	1-0 *Pakholyuk*
08/04	Aktobe	a	0-0
15/04	Zhetysu	h	4-1 *Ashirbekov, Mwesigwa, Mansour, Kasyanov (p)*
22/04	Taraz	a	1-2 *Tazhimbetov*
29/04	Shakhter	a	1-1 *Mansour*
06/05	Akzhayik	h	2-0 *Tazhimbetov 2*
12/05	Kairat	a	1-1 *og (Gurman)*
20/05	Irtysh	h	2-1 *Mwesigwa 2*
27/05	Tobol	a	0-1
16/06	Okzhetpes	h	1-0 *Imanov*
24/06	Astana	a	0-1
01/07	Sunkar	h	3-1 *Tazhimbetov 2, Collins*
15/07	Aktobe	h	1-1 *Mansour*
29/07	Zhetysu	a	1-0 *Pakholyuk*
05/08	Taraz	h	1-3 *Kasyanov*
10/08	Kaysar	a	1-2 *Mansour*
19/08	Shakhter	h	0-1
26/08	Akzhayik	a	1-1 *Suyumbayev*
15/09	Kairat	h	0-0
24/09	Irtysh	a	0-3
04/10	Tobol	h	2-0 *Mansour 2*
21/10	Okzhetpes	a	2-1 *Ashirbekov (p), Mansour*
23/10	Astana	h	0-0
28/10	Atyrau	h	1-2 *Tazhimbetov*

No	Name	Nat	DoB	Pos	Aps	(s)	Gls
77	Talgat Adyrbekov		26/01/89	A	8	(11)	
99	Mohamed Arouri	TUN	13/05/83	D	19		
10	Kayrat Ashirbekov		21/10/82	M	23	(1)	2
16	Almat Bekbaev		14/07/84	G	24		
15	Bekzat Beysenov		18/02/87	M	7	(10)	
88	Baba Collins	NGA	02/12/88	A	13		1
91	Vladimir Djilas	SRB	03/03/83	A	1	(15)	1
11	Mansour Gueye	SEN	30/12/85	A	16	(10)	7
33	Kanat Imanov		23/03/91	M	1	(2)	1
2	Farhadbek Irismetov		10/08/81	D	5	(2)	
8	Andrei Karpovich		18/01/81	M	22		1
12	Artem Kasyanov	UKR	20/04/83	M	24		2
21	Ayeskhan Kozhabayev		19/05/94	D	2		
14	Bakdaulet Kozhabayev		19/06/92	D	18	(3)	
86	Mukhtar Mukhtarov		01/01/86	D	9		
3	Andrew Mwesigwa	UGA	24/04/84	D	22		3
1	Roman Nesterenko		22/03/77	G	2		
7	Roman Pakholyuk		03/10/79	M	19	(3)	2
9	Mato Simunovic	AUT	27/09/85	M	2		
5	Gafurzhan Suyumbayev		19/08/90	A	7	(7)	1
18	Daurenbek Tazhimbetov		02/07/85	A	22	(2)	7
17	Mardan Tolebek		18/12/90	D		(3)	
6	Aleksandar Trajković	SRB	16/01/81	D	20		
4	Maksim Zhalmagambetov		11/07/83	D		(4)	

FC SHAKHTER KARAGANDY

Coach: Viktor Kumykov (RUS)
1958 • Shakhter (19,500) • shahter.kz
Major honours
Kazakhstan League (2) 2011, 2012

2012

10/03	Irtysh	a	0-1
18/03	Aktobe	h	2-0 *Khizhnichenko, Vičius*
25/03	Tobol	a	1-3 *Bayzhanov*
01/04	Zhetysu	h	5-1 *Džidić, Cañas 3, Finonchenko*
08/04	Okzhetpes	a	2-0 *Arsenijević, Finonchenko*
15/04	Taraz	h	1-0 *Vičius*
22/04	Atyrau	a	2-0 *Khizhnichenko, Finonchenko*
29/04	Ordabasy	h	1-1 *Vasiljević*
06/05	Astana	a	0-1
12/05	Akzhayik	h	3-1 *Kukeyev 2 (1p), Vičius*
20/05	Sunkar	a	2-0 *Finonchenko, Kukeyev (p)*
27/05	Kairat	h	4-1 *Khizhnichenko, Finonchenko 2, Lunin*
16/06	Kaysar	a	0-1
24/06	Aktobe	a	0-1
01/07	Tobol	h	3-0 *Bayzhanov, og (Šljivić), Vasiljević*
09/07	Zhetysu	a	5-1 *Lunin, og (Mihajlov), Vičius, Višņakovs, Makhambetov*
29/07	Taraz	a	1-1 *Bayzhanov*
05/08	Atyrau	h	4-0 *Vičius 2, Lunin, Vasiljević*
10/08	Okzhetpes	h	4-0 *Višņakovs, Kukeyev, Lunin, Makhambetov*
19/08	Ordabasy	a	1-0 *Višņakovs*
26/08	Astana	h	0-1
15/09	Akzhayik	a	1-0 *Kukeyev*
23/09	Sunkar	h	2-0 *Poryvayev, Vičius*
03/10	Kairat	a	1-0 *Vasiljević*
21/10	Kaysar	h	3-0 *Bayzhanov 2, Kukeyev*
28/10	Irtysh	h	0-1

No	Name	Nat	DoB	Pos	Aps	(s)	Gls
18	Filip Arsenijević	SRB	02/09/83	A	12	(7)	1
11	Maksat Bayzhanov		06/08/84	M	14	(10)	5
7	Askhat Borantayev		22/08/78	M	4	(3)	
13	Vadim Borovskiy		30/10/86	A	1	(2)	
88	Roger Cañas	COL	27/03/90	M	21	(5)	3
8	Serik Dosmanbetov		08/03/82	A		(5)	
20	Aldin Džidić	BIH	30/08/83	M	24		2
14	Andrei Finonchenko		21/06/82	A	18	(2)	6
5	Mikhail Gabyshev		02/01/90	D	7	(3)	
55	Sergei Gridin		20/05/87	A	8	(2)	
1	Aleksandr Grigorenko		06/02/85	G	1	(1)	
91	Sergei Khizhnichenko		17/07/91	A	9	(3)	3
21	Aleksandr Kirov		04/09/84	D	22		
10	Zhambyl Kukeyev		20/09/88	M	23	(1)	6
9	Vitali Li		13/03/94	M		(2)	
77	Stanislav Lunin		02/05/93	A	13	(2)	3
6	Danijel Majkić	BIH	16/12/87	M	2	(4)	
8	Ablaykhan Makhambetov		03/08/91	M	1	(5)	2
35	Aleksandr Mokin		19/06/81	G	25		
17	Andrei Poryvayev	BLR	03/01/82	D	23	(1)	1
19	Evgeni Tarasov		04/04/85	D	12	(3)	
4	Nikola Vasiljević	SRB	19/12/83	D	23		4
3	Gediminas Vičius	LTU	05/07/85	M	20	(3)	7
15	Eduards Višņakovs	LVA	10/05/90	A	3	(9)	3

FC SUNKAR KASKELEN

Coach: Almas Kulshinbayev;
(06/05/12) (Askar Kozhabergenov)
2009 • 10 let Nezavisimosti RK (3,000) • sunkarfc.kz

2012

10/03	Zhetysu	h	1-0	Amirseitov
18/03	Taraz	a	0-1	
25/03	Ordabasy	h	0-0	
01/04	Akzhayik	a	1-1	Adamović (p)
08/04	Kairat	h	0-2	
15/04	Irtysh	a	0-4	
22/04	Tobol	h	0-0	
29/04	Okzhetpes	a	2-0	Rodríguez 2
06/05	Atyrau	h	0-0	
12/05	Astana	a	0-0	
20/05	Shakhter	h	0-0	
27/05	Kaysar	h	0-0	
16/06	Aktobe	a	1-2	Turysbek
24/06	Taraz	h	0-1	
01/07	Ordabasy	a	1-3	Baytana
08/07	Akzhayik	h	1-0	Savénas (p)
15/07	Kairat	a	3-1	Djokić, Savénas (p), Nedashkovsky
29/07	Irtysh	h	0-1	
05/08	Tobol	a	0-4	
19/08	Okzhetpes	h	3-1	Djokić, Nurgaliyev, Ovseannicov
26/08	Atyrau	a	0-1	
15/09	Astana	h	1-1	Nurgaliyev
23/09	Shakhter	a	0-2	
04/10	Kaysar	a	1-2	Djokić
21/10	Aktobe	h	0-1	
28/10	Zhetysu	a	1-1	Nedashkovsky

No	Name	Nat	DoB	Pos	Aps	(s)	Gls
91	Miloš Adamović	SRB	19/06/88	D	8	(2)	1
13	Ilyas Amirseitov		22/10/89	D	16		1
30	Aleksandr Andreev		09/09/86	D	3	(4)	
97	Baurzhan Baytana		06/06/92	M	10	(3)	1
27	Alibek Buleshev		09/04/81	A	13	(1)	
77	Goran Cvetković	SRB	09/12/82	M	23		
60	Rade Djokić	BIH	23/06/83	A	11		3
81	Farhadbek Irismetov		10/08/81	D	6	(1)	
10	Timur Khalmuratov		29/04/86	M	14		
58	Andrei Kharabara		01/03/85	M	8		
7	Zhiger Kukeev		09/08/84	D	1	(3)	
35	Dauren Kusaynov		10/04/84	A	1	(2)	
20	Timur Moldagaliev		29/09/84	D	2	(4)	
21	Askhat Mynbayev		21/02/91	D		(5)	
10	Aysultan Nazarbayev		26/08/90	M	1		
71	Oleg Nedashkovsky		09/09/87	M	10	(1)	2
25	Miloš Nikezić	MNE	02/03/87	A		(6)	
5	Stanislav Nohýnek	CZE	02/08/83	D	26		
86	Azat Nurgaliyev		30/06/86	M	9		2
4	Daulet Oskenbaev		15/01/87	D	6	(1)	
79	Gheorgii Ovseannicov	MDA	12/10/85	A	5	(6)	1
22	Andrei Pasechenko		09/08/87	G	25		
44	Luis Rodríguez	ARG	04/03/85	D	10	(2)	2
3	Oleg Sabirov		13/03/81	D	20	(3)	
79	Mantas Savénas	LTU	27/08/82	M	9	(3)	2
85	Akzhol Serikzhanov		06/05/90	M	1	(8)	
88	Aleksei Shapurin		20/09/87	A	1	(6)	
8	Anton Shurygin		03/12/88	M		(1)	
14	Dauren Suyunov		06/08/90	M	7	(9)	
17	Nikola Tonev	MKD	12/11/85	D	22		
9	Baurzhan Turysbek		15/10/91	A	9	(4)	1
12	Tomislav Vranjić	CRO	12/02/83	G	1		
90	Dragomir Vukobratović	SRB	12/05/88	M	8	(1)	

FC TARAZ

Coach: Ljupko Petrović (SRB)
1961 • Taraz Centralny (12,000) • fctaraz.kz
Major honours
Kazakhstan League (1) 1996; Kazakhstan Cup (1) 2004

2012

10/03	Astana	a	2-0	Perić, Prtenjak
18/03	Sunkar	h	1-0	Lečić
25/03	Kaysar	a	2-1	Islamkhan, Perić
01/04	Aktobe	h	1-0	Lečić
08/04	Zhetysu	a	0-2	
15/04	Shakhter	a	0-1	
22/04	Ordabasy	h	2-1	Lečić 2
29/04	Akzhayik	a	0-3	
06/05	Kairat	h	2-1	Lečić, Perić
12/05	Irtysh	a	1-1	Islamkhan
20/05	Tobol	h	1-0	Perić
27/05	Okzhetpes	a	1-3	Diakhate
16/06	Atyrau	h	0-1	
24/06	Sunkar	a	1-0	Diakhate
01/07	Kaysar	h	1-0	Islamkhan
08/07	Aktobe	a	1-4	Odita
15/07	Zhetysu	h	1-3	Mehmedović
29/07	Shakhter	h	1-1	Odita
05/08	Ordabasy	a	3-1	Muminov, Vukman, Odita
19/08	Akzhayik	h	3-2	Odita 2, Diakhate (p)
26/08	Kairat	a	1-2	Kuchma
15/09	Irtysh	h	3-2	Lečić 2, Diakhate
24/09	Tobol	a	1-0	Diakhate (p)
04/10	Okzhetpes	h	2-0	Odita, Islamkhan
21/10	Atyrau	a	0-0	
28/10	Astana	h	1-1	Diakhate

No	Name	Nat	DoB	Pos	Aps	(s)	Gls
2	Eldos Akhmetov		01/06/90	D	9	(3)	
20	Maksat Amirkhanov		10/02/92	D	8	(5)	
25	Berik Aytbaev		26/06/91	D		(1)	
11	Sherkhan Bauyrzhan		28/08/92	A	3	(9)	
16	Azat Bitabarov		14/01/90	G	3		
15	Abdoulaye Diakhate	SEN	16/01/88	M	26		6
9	Baurzhan Islamkhan		23/02/93	M	18	(4)	4
8	Yerzat Kenbaev		22/04/88	A		(9)	
24	Ognjen Krasić	SRB	10/04/88	M	11	(2)	
3	Aleksandr Kuchma		09/12/80	D	24		1
5	Nurtas Kurgulin		20/09/86	D	9		
19	Miroslav Lečić	SRB	20/04/85	A	18	(2)	7
4	Ersin Mehmedović	SRB	10/05/81	D	25	(1)	1
80	Madiyar Muminov		18/10/80	M	16	(5)	1
26	Obiora Odita	NGA	14/05/83	A	11	(1)	6
13	Senedin Oštraković	BIH	13/04/87	G	1		
55	Ivan Perić	SRB	05/05/82	A	14	(6)	4
14	Nebojša Prtenjak	SRB	10/05/83	M	6	(5)	1
22	Eduard Sergienko		18/02/83	M	22	(1)	
27	Andrei Shabaev		15/02/87	D	14	(1)	
6	Vyacheslav Sobolev		13/10/84	D	1	(2)	
7	Murat Suyumagambetov		14/10/83	A		(6)	
30	Andrei Tsvetkov		20/03/80	G	22		
17	Neven Vukman	CRO	11/04/85	D	15	(3)	1
	Dmitri Yevstigneev		27/11/86	D	7	(1)	
18	Vitali Yevstigneev		08/05/85	M	2	(2)	
32	Konstantin Zarechni		14/02/84	D	1	(6)	

FC TOBOL KOSTANAY

Coach: Vyacheslav Hrozniy (UKR)
1967 • Kostanay Centralny (5,720) • fc-tobol.kz
Major honours
Kazakhstan League (1) 2010;
Kazakhstan Cup (1) 2007

2012

10/03	Kairat	h	4-0	Dzholchiev 2, Golovskoy, Jhonnes
18/03	Irtysh	a	1-4	Jhonnes
25/03	Shakhter	h	3-1	Kontsevoi, Dzholchiev 2
01/04	Okzhetpes	h	3-1	Bogdanov, Jhonnes, Kurtisi
08/04	Atyrau	a	1-1	Dzholchiev
15/04	Astana	h	3-2	Dzholchiev, Kostyuk, Bogdanov
22/04	Sunkar	a	0-0	
29/04	Kaysar	a	2-0	Zhumaskaliyev, Dzholchiev
06/05	Aktobe	a	1-0	Kontsevoi
12/05	Zhetysu	h	2-1	Kurtisi, Bugaiov
20/05	Taraz	a	0-1	
27/05	Ordabasy	h	1-0	og (Mwesigwa)
16/06	Akzhayik	a	1-2	Kostyuk
24/06	Irtysh	h	2-2	Zhumaskaliyev, Bogdanov
01/07	Shakhter	a	0-3	
08/07	Okzhetpes	a	1-0	Šljivić
15/07	Atyrau	h	1-0	Jovanović
29/07	Astana	a	1-1	Zhumaskaliyev
05/08	Sunkar	h	4-0	Zhumaskaliyev, Strukov, Kuantayev, Dzholchiev
19/08	Kaysar	a	2-1	Bugaiov, Kostyuk (p)
26/08	Aktobe	a	2-2	Strukov, Bogdanov
15/09	Zhetysu	a	1-1	Zhumaskaliyev
24/09	Taraz	h	0-1	
04/10	Ordabasy	a	0-2	
21/10	Akzhayik	h	6-0	Strukov, Bogdanov, Jovanović, Zhumaskaliyev, Andreev 2
28/10	Kairat	a	0-1	

No	Name	Nat	DoB	Pos	Aps	(s)	Gls
80	Ali Aliyev		27/10/80	M		(2)	
77	Pirali Aliyev		13/01/84	D	6	(2)	
86	Aleksandr Andreev		09/09/86	A	3		2
	Evgeni Averchenko		06/04/82	M	8	(2)	
14	Radoslav Batak	SRB	15/08/77	D	3		
5	Anatoli Bogdanov		07/08/81	M	21	(2)	5
7	Igor Bugaiov	MDA	26/06/84	A	7	(13)	2
23	Artem Deli		02/03/89	M		(1)	
22	Baurzhan Dzholchiev		08/05/90	A	16	(4)	8
17	Konstantin Golovskoy		25/04/75	M	17		1
40	Olzhas Ilyasov		09/09/94	M		(1)	
4	Jhonnes	BRA	22/04/84	D	22		3
84	Nemanja Jovanović	SRB	03/03/84	A	9		2
13	Aleksandr Kislitsyn		03/03/86	D	25		
2	Sergei Kontsevoi	BLR	21/06/86	D	16	(3)	2
18	Sergei Kostyuk		30/11/78	A	5	(15)	3
20	Yermek Kuantayev		13/10/90	M	12	(8)	1
10	Mensur Kurtisi	MKD	25/03/86	A	6	(2)	2
21	Aleksei Malyshev		24/06/89	M		(5)	
25	Aleksandr Petukhov		11/01/85	G	13		
16	Daniil Rikhard		27/02/74	G	13		
58	Vladimir Sedelnikov		15/10/91	D	2	(2)	
8	Nenad Šljivić	SRB	08/06/85	M	22		1
91	Sergei Strukov	RUS	17/09/82	A	9	(1)	3
95	Alisher Suley		01/11/95	A		(4)	
11	Vitali Volkov	RUS	22/03/81	M	25		
9	Nurbol Zhumaskaliyev		11/05/81	M	26		6

FC ZHETYSU TALDYKORGAN

Coach: Serik Abdualiyev;
(06/05/12) Slobodan Krčmarević (SRB)
1981 • Zhetysu (4,000) • fc-zhetisu.kz

2012

10/03	Sunkar	a	0-1	
18/03	Kaysar	h	5-2	Junuzović 3, Nurgaliyev, S Muzhikov
25/03	Aktobe	a	0-4	
01/04	Shakhter	a	1-5	Nurgaliyev
08/04	Taraz	h	2-0	Junuzović 2
15/04	Ordabasy	a	1-4	Nurgaliyev (p)
22/04	Akzhayik	h	1-2	Nurgaliyev (p)
29/04	Kairat	a	0-1	
06/05	Irtysh	h	1-2	Kusaynov
12/05	Tobol	a	1-2	Skorykh
20/05	Okzhetpes	h	1-0	Marić
27/05	Atyrau	a	1-2	Junuzović
16/06	Astana	h	1-1	Djalović
24/06	Kaysar	a	0-1	
01/07	Aktobe	h	1-1	Belić
09/07	Shakhter	h	1-5	og (Kirov)
15/07	Taraz	a	3-1	Belić, Mihajlov, Tleshev
29/07	Ordabasy	h	0-1	
05/08	Akzhayik	a	2-2	Junuzović, Shchetkin
19/08	Kairat	a	2-1	Junuzović, Dobrašinović
26/08	Irtysh	a	0-3	
15/09	Tobol	h	1-1	Mihajlov
23/09	Okzhetpes	a	0-1	
04/10	Atyrau	h	1-0	Tleshev
21/10	Astana	a	0-1	
28/10	Sunkar	h	1-1	Tleshev (p)

No	Name	Nat	DoB	Pos	Aps	(s)	Gls
30	Evgeni Averchenko		06/04/82	M	9		
20	Danilo Belić	SRB	10/11/80	A	5	(1)	2
11							
31	Ivan Cvetković	SRB	12/02/81	M	10	(1)	
5	Damir Dautov		03/03/80	D	14	(2)	
86	Marko Djalović	SRB	19/06/86	M	21	(3)	1
19	Siniša Dobrašinović	CYP	17/02/77	M	13		1
3	Tanko Dyakov	BUL	18/08/84	D	7		
28	Edin Junuzović	CRO	28/04/86	A	19	(4)	8
23	Zakhar Korobov		18/05/88	D	14	(4)	
70	Zoran Kostić	SRB	14/11/82	M	10	(2)	
24	Viktor Kovalev		25/08/80	D	3	(4)	
2	Aydar Kumysbekov		09/02/79	D	1	(1)	
8	Dauren Kusaynov		10/04/84	A		(3)	1
1	Vladimir Loginovski		08/10/85	G	14		
9	Goran Marić	SRB	23/04/84	A	8	(4)	1
21	Miloš Mihajlov	SRB	15/02/88	D	24	(1)	2
18	Daniyar Mukanov		26/09/76	M	18	(2)	
60	Marlan Muzhikov		01/12/86	M		(2)	
7	Serikzhan Muzhikov		17/06/89	M	18		1
77	Amir Murzabaev		00/00/00	M	0	(0)	1
22	Sauyat Sariyev		15/10/92	M	2	(12)	
11	Aleksei Shchetkin		21/05/91	A	18	(8)	1
10	Sergei Skorykh		25/05/84	M	23	(2)	1
14	Olzhas Spanov		30/11/89	M	5	(3)	
16	Sergei Stepanenko		25/01/81	G	12	(2)	
79	Murat Tleshev		12/04/80	A	3	(7)	3
6	Vule Trivunović	BIH	13/03/83	D	7	(2)	

Top goalscorers

14	Ulugbek Bakayev (Irtysh)	
10	Igor Zenkovich (Akzhayik) Tanat Nuserbayev (Astana)	
8	Baurzhan Dzholchiev (Tobol) Edin Junuzović (Zhetysu)	
7	Sergei Strukov (Irtysh/Tobol) Mansour Gueye (Ordabasy) Daurenbek Tazhimbetov (Ordabasy) Gediminas Vičius (Shakhter) Miroslav Lečić (Taraz)	

Promoted club

FC VOSTOK OSKEMEN

Coach: Pavel Saliy
1963 • Vostok (8,500) • fc-vostok.kz
Major honours
Kazakhstan Cup (1) 1994

SECOND LEVEL FINAL TABLE 2012

		Pld	W	D	L	F	A	Pts
1	FC Ile-Saulet Almatinskaya oblast	30	17	10	3	52	20	61
2	FC Vostok Oskemen	30	16	9	5	40	21	57
3	FC Astana-64	30	16	5	9	52	37	53
4	FC Bayterek Astana	30	14	11	5	39	19	53
5	FC Kyran Shymkent	30	14	6	10	51	38	48
6	FC Spartak Semey	30	14	4	12	38	45	46
7	FC Bolat-AMT Temirtau	30	12	10	8	30	23	46
8	FC Kaspiy Aktau	30	12	7	11	39	31	43
9	FC Ak-Bulak Talgar	30	11	8	11	34	29	41
10	FC Lashyn Taraz	30	11	8	11	33	28	41
11	FC Kyzylzhar Petropavlovsk	30	11	7	12	35	42	40
12	FC Ekibastuz	30	11	4	15	45	43	37
13	FC Kairat Academy Almaty	30	8	5	17	37	44	29
14	FC Aktobe-Jas	30	8	2	20	31	62	26
15	CSKA Almaty	30	4	6	20	18	55	18
16	FC BIIK Shymkent	30	3	4	23	20	66	13

NB FC Ile-Saulet Almatinskaya oblast declined promotion.

Domestic cup: Kubok Kazakhstana 2012

FIRST ROUND

(15/05/12)
Kyzylzhar 0-2 Taraz

(16/05/12)
Ak-Bulak 2-1 Bolat-AMT
Aktobe-Jas 0-2 Kaysar
Astana-64 0-1 Astana
BIIK 1-4 Aktobe
CSKA Almaty 5-3 Bayterek
Ekibastuz 1-4 Irtysh
Ile-Saulet 0-3 Okzhetpes
Kairat Academy 1-0 Atyrau
Kaspiy 1-3 Akzhayik
Kyran 2-4 Kairat
Lashyn 2-0 Sunkar
Spartak Semey 0-2 Shakhter
Vostok 1-3 Zhetysu

Byes – Ordabasy, Tobol

SECOND ROUND

(20/06/12 & 27/06/12)
Ak-Bulak 1-1; 0-2 Astana (1-3)
Aktobe 5-0; 2-0 Lashyn (7-0)
Akzhayik 1-2; 0-5 Ordabasy (1-7)
CSKA Almaty 0-4; 0-3 Shakhter (0-7)
Kairat Academy 1-4; 0-4 Irtysh (1-8)
Kaysar 2-0; 0-1 Kairat (2-1)
Okzhetpes 1-3; 1-0 Tobol (2-3)
Zhetysu 1-1; 2-0 Taraz (3-1)

QUARTER-FINALS

(19/09/12 & 29/09/12)
Kaysar 1-0 Astana (Stakhiv 89)
Astana 4-1 Kaysar (Ostapenko 16, Foxi 44, Kojašević 77, 82; Parkhachev 56)
(Astana 4-2)

Zhetysu 1-1 Shakhter (Mihajlov 56p; Cañas 76p)
Shakhter 1-0 Zhetysu (Ostapenko 9)
(Shakhter 2-1)

(19/09/12 & 30/09/12)
Aktobe 0-0 Ordabasy
Ordabasy 0-1 Aktobe (Khairullin 84)
(Aktobe 1-0)

(20/09/12 & 29/09/12)
Irtysh 3-0 Tobol (Bakayev 50, 87p; Yurin 61)
Tobol 1-0 Irtysh (Jovanović 72)
(Irtysh 3-1)

SEMI-FINALS

(01/11/12 & 05/11/12)
Irtysh 5-0 Aktobe (Yurin 7, Shabalin 46, Bakayev 48, 61p, Maletić 49)
Aktobe 3-1 Irtysh (Primus 19, Geynrikh 61, Bajer 78; Yurin 80)
(Irtysh 6-3)

Shakhter 2-1 Astana (Kirov 66, Višņakovs 72; Primus 90p)
Astana 2-0 Shakhter (Rozhkov 41, Foxi 57)
(Astana 3-2)

FINAL

(11/11/12)
Astana Arena, Astana
FC ASTANA 2 (Nurdauletov 5, Nuserbayev 82)
FC IRTYSH PAVLODAR 0
Referee: Slambekov
ASTANA: Erić, Nurdauletov, Beysebekov, Lazarevski, Rozhkov, Foxi (Goriachiy 90+2), Korobkin, Shakhmetov, Kojašević (Konysbayev 89), Ostapenko, Nuserbayev (Ivanovski 87)
IRTYSH: Kotlyar, Chernyshev, Shornko, Coulibaly, Chichulin (Yakovlev 75), Shabalin (Bayzhanov 80), Yurin, Kučera, Govedarica, Maletić, Essomba (Maltsev 83)

LATVIA
Latvijas Futbola Federācija (LFF)

Address	Olympic Sports Centre	**President**	Guntis Indriksons
	Grostonas Street 6b	**General secretary**	Jānis Mežeckis
	LV-1013 Rīga	**Media officer**	Viktors Sopirins
Tel	+371 67 292988	**Year of formation**	1921
Fax	+371 67 315604	**National stadium**	Skonto, Riga (9,500)
E-mail	futbols@lff.lv		
Website	lff.lv		

Ventspils · Gulbene · Rīga · Jūrmala · Jelgava · Liepāja · Ilūkste · Daugavpils

0 ___ 50 ___ 100 km
0 ___ 50 miles

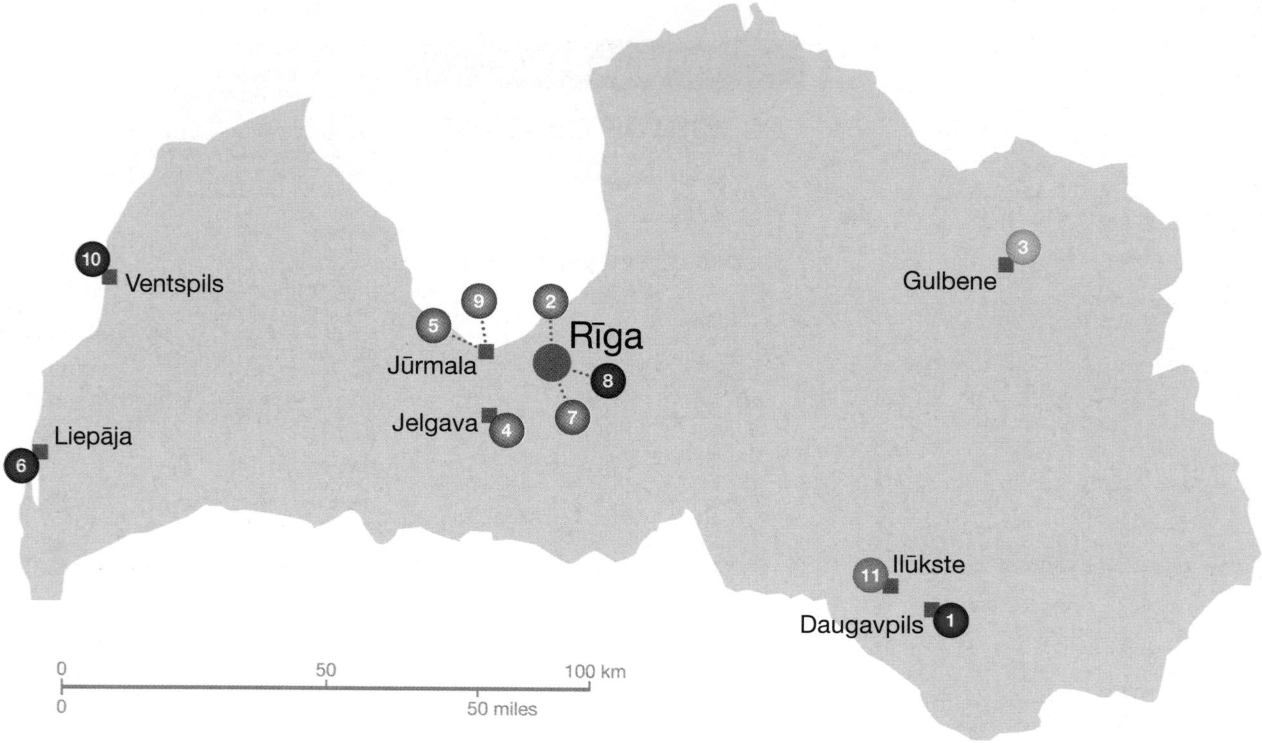

VIRSLĪGA CLUBS

1. FC Daugava Daugavpils
2. FK Daugava Rīga
3. FB Gulbene 2005
4. FK Jelgava
5. FC Jūrmala

6. SK Liepājas Metalurgs
7. FS Metta/LU
8. Skonto FC
9. FK Spartaks Jūrmala
10. FK Ventspils

PROMOTED CLUB

11. Ilūkstes NSS

KEY:
● – UEFA Champions League
● – UEFA Europa League
● – Promoted club
● – Relegated club

First title for Daugava

An absorbing tussle for the 2012 Virslīga title ended in jubilation for FC Daugava Daugavpils, who held firm under challenge from perennial title contenders Skonto FC, FK Ventspils and SK Liepājas Metalurgs to become the champions of Latvia for the first time.

It was a change of coach early in the season, with Moldovan Ivan Tabanov coming in for Russian Ravil Sabitov, that proved decisive in Daugava's triumph. The champions did not always prosper against their three direct rivals but they won just about every other game and ended the campaign unbeaten at home.

| Switch to Moldovan coach Tabanov pays dividends | Ventspils beat Metalurgs to capture sixth Latvian Cup | International results cause growing concern |

Domestic league

Placed third in 2011, Daugava made a quiet start under new coach Sabitov, but when in round seven the team were thrashed 6-1 at FC Jūrmala, the club's administrators decided to replace the Russian with Tabanov, a former coach of FC Zimbru Chisinau. He settled into his task straight away, three successive wins incorporating a vital 2-1 success at defending champions Ventspils.

Daugava would lose their next two big games, away at Skonto and Liepājas Metalurgs, then draw at home to the same two opponents, but against the league's lesser lights they demonstrated a ruthless streak that kept them firmly in contention for that first Virslīga crown, with Georgian striker Mamuka Gongadze – the league's top scorer – and Nigerian import Stanley Ibe providing a steady supply of goals. The team also boasted a formidable defence that grew in strength as the season progressed. Indeed, in the run-in Tabanov's men kept five consecutive clean sheets before nailing their most important win of the campaign, 3-1 at Metalurgs. Two weeks later, with another 3-1 away win, at bottom club FB Gulbene 2005, the championship was theirs.

Ventspils and Metalurgs also changed their coach around the same time as Daugava, the former surprisingly letting go of their 2011 title-winning boss Sergei Podpali in mid-May. However, neither reaped the same dividends as Daugava. All four title contenders took points off each other, but in a mini-league between them it was Skonto who fared best – albeit with just 19 points accrued from a possible 36. The country's record champions bucked the common trend by staying loyal to their coach, Marians Pahars, and he steered them home to second place, level on points with Ventspils but ahead of them thanks to their superior head-to-head record.

Domestic cup

The 2013 Latvian Cup final brought together local rivals Ventspils and Metalurgs, the former having routed champions Daugava 4-0 in the semi-finals. The two finalists had very different records in the fixture. Ventspils had won on five of their previous six appearances, whereas their opponents had lifted the trophy just once in seven attempts. Indeed, Metalurgs were hoping to avoid a hat-trick of defeats, but once again lady luck deserted them as Ventspils came from behind to win 2-1, an extra-time winner from defender Kaspars Dubra – who had never previously scored

for the club – deciding the contest and rewarding Ventspils coach Jurgis Pučinskis with a trophy almost a year to the day after his appointment.

Europe

It was another dismal season for Latvian clubs in Europe, with three of the four entrants losing their opening tie and the other, Metalurgs, progressing only at the expense of opposition from San Marino. Against that, only one of five home games were lost. Sadly for Daugava, that 3-2 defeat came after a 1-0 win at Lithuanian side FC Sūduva and eliminated them on away goals.

National team

A decade on from Latvia's historic qualification for UEFA EURO 2004, fortunes were very different for Aleksandrs Starkovs' team as they made a hash of their 2014 FIFA World Cup qualifying group, taking just four points from their first six matches, all of those from Liechtenstein. Growing concerns about the team's competitiveness came to a head in June when – albeit without star players Aleksandrs Cauņa and Artjoms Rudņevs – they crashed 5-0 at home to Bosnia & Herzegovina.

LATVIA

Domestic league: Virslīga 2012 final table

		Pld	Home					Away					Total					Pts
			W	D	L	F	A	W	D	L	F	A	W	D	L	F	A	
1	**FC Daugava Daugavpils**	**36**	**12**	**6**	**0**	**27**	**4**	**11**	**3**	**4**	**37**	**21**	**23**	**9**	**4**	**64**	**25**	**78**
2	Skonto FC	36	13	3	2	34	8	8	8	2	24	14	21	11	4	58	22	74
3	FK Ventspils	36	12	3	3	31	10	11	2	5	32	12	23	5	8	63	22	74
4	SK Liepājas Metalurgs	36	12	2	4	31	15	9	5	4	29	18	21	7	8	60	33	70
5	FK Spartaks Jūrmala	36	5	8	5	30	31	8	2	8	31	25	13	10	13	61	56	49
6	FC Jūrmala	36	4	6	8	27	26	6	3	9	20	23	10	9	17	47	49	39
7	FK Jelgava	36	1	4	13	16	36	6	6	6	16	20	7	10	19	32	56	31
8	FS Metta/LU	36	4	5	9	21	39	3	3	12	18	43	7	8	21	39	82	29
9	FK Daugava Rīga	36	2	6	10	19	41	3	6	9	23	38	5	12	19	42	79	27
10	FB Gulbene 2005	36	3	2	13	14	34	2	7	9	14	36	5	9	22	28	70	24

SEASON AT A GLANCE

EUROPEAN QUALIFICATION 2013/14

Champion: FC Daugava Daugavpils (second qualifying round)

Cup winner: FK Ventspils (first qualifying round)
Skonto FC (first qualifying round)
SK Liepājas Metalurgs (first qualifying round)

Top scorer Mamuka Gongadze (Daugava Daugavpils), 18 goals
Relegated club FB Gulbene 2005
Promoted club Ilūkstes NSS
Cup final FK Ventspils 2-1 SK Liepājas Metalurgs

PLAYER OF THE SEASON
Mihails Ziziļevs
(FC Daugava Daugavpils)

The 38-year-old midfielder proved his durability with a string of combative performances and capped a formidable season by scoring the goal that earned Daugava their first league title. Challenged by the exuberance of youth, he seldom shirked a tackle and used his superior know-how to come out on top in many midfield battles.

NEWCOMER OF THE SEASON
Vladimirs Kamešs
(SK Liepājas Metalurgs)

The 24-year-old winger lit up the Virslīga with his dazzling pace and skill. He was his club's joint-top marksman with ten league goals and also added another couple in Europe. A call-up for Latvia was inevitable, and he registered his first international goal against Liechtenstein before launching a new career in Russia with FC Amkar Perm.

VIRSLĪGA TEAM OF THE SEASON
(4-4-2)
Coach: Tabanov *(Daugava Daugavpils)*

NATIONAL TEAM

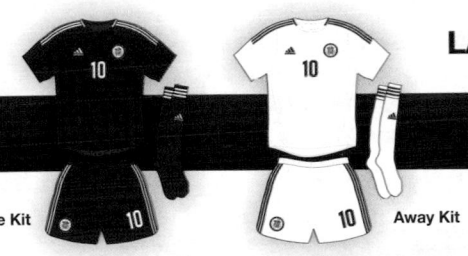

Home Kit   Away Kit

INTERNATIONAL TOURNAMENT APPEARANCES
UEFA European Championship (1) 2004

TOP FIVE ALL-TIME CAPS
Vitālijs Astafjevs (167); Andrejs Rubins (117); Juris Laizāns (108); Imants Bleidelis (106); Mihails Zemļinskis (105)

TOP FIVE ALL-TIME GOALS
Māris Verpakovskis (29); Eriks Petersons (24); Vitālijs Astafjevs (16); Juris Laizāns & Marians Pahars (15)

Results 2012/13

Date	Opponent		Venue	Score	Scorers
15/08/12	Montenegro	A	Podgorica	0-2	
07/09/12	Greece (WCQ)	H	Riga	1-2	Cauņa (42p)
11/09/12	Bosnia & Herzegovina (WCQ)	A	Zenica	1-4	Gorkšs (5)
12/10/12	Slovakia (WCQ)	A	Bratislava	1-2	Verpakovskis (84p)
16/10/12	Liechtenstein (WCQ)	H	Riga	2-0	Kamešs (29), Gauračs (77)
06/02/13	Japan	A	Kobe	0-3	
22/03/13	Liechtenstein (WCQ)	A	Vaduz	1-1	Cauņa (90)
24/05/13	Qatar	H	Līga	1-3	Žigajevs (22)
28/05/13	Turkey	N	Duisburg (GER)	3-3	Gauračs (53), Šabala (68, 84)
07/06/13	Bosnia & Herzegovina (WCQ)	H	Riga	0-5	

Appearances 2012/13

Coach: Aleksandrs Starkovs /(Jurijs Ševļakovs)		Club	Mne	GRE	BIH SVK		LIE	Jpn	LIE	Qat	Tur	BIH	Caps	Goals
	26/07/55 24/01/59													
Andris Vaņins	30/04/80	Sion (SUI)	G	G	G	G	G	G	G			G	56	-
Oskars Kļava	08/08/83	Olimpik-Şüvälan (AZE)	D	D	D	D			D	s74	M	M	65	1
Vitālijs Smirnovs	28/06/86	Ventspils	D							D			7	1
Deniss Ivanovs	11/01/84	Bakı (AZE)	D	D	D	D	D	D	D	D	D	D	60	2
Ritus Krjauklis	23/04/86	Golden Arrows (RSA)	D	D	D	D							22	-
Oļegs Laizāns	28/03/87	Yenisey (RUS)	M	M80	M	M70	M65	M65	M46	M74	s67		18	-
Aleksandrs Fertovs	10/06/87	Skonto	M	M75		M	M	M		M80	M	M 11*	20	-
Aleksejs Višņakovs	03/02/84	unattached /Baltika (RUS)	M63		M75	M61	M	s74	M65	s46		M46	51	7
Artūrs Zjuzins	18/06/91	Baltika (RUS)	M46		s80			s85	s65				7	-
Ivans Lukjanovs	24/01/87	Metalurh Zaporizhya (UKR)	M75	M	M80	M53							14	-
Artjoms Rudņevs	13/01/88	Hamburg (GER)	A63	A	A61	A	A		A				24	1
Ritvars Rugins	17/10/89	Skonto	s46	s75	M	s70	D	D	D	M74			15	-
Vladimirs Kamešs	28/10/88	Liepājas Metalurgs /Amkar (RUS)	s63		s61		M74	M72	M56		s46	M59	10	1
Edgars Gauračs	10/03/88	Torpedo Moskva (RUS)	s63	s80		s53	s65	A71	s66		A67	A64	18	5
Māris Verpakovskis	15/10/79	Bakı (AZE) /Ergotelis (GRE)	s75	s75	s61	s77	A85		s71	A66		A15	98	29
Kaspars Gorkšs	06/11/81	Reading (ENG) /Wolves (ENG)	D	D	D	D	D		D	D	D	D	52	5
Aleksandrs Cauņa	19/01/88	CSKA Moskva (RUS)	M	M	M77	M	M88	M					38	11
Nauris Bulvītis	15/03/87	Spartaks Jūrmala					D	D		D	D	D	7	-
Jurijs Žigajevs	14/11/85	Ventspils					s65	s56	M	M46			30	2
Vitālijs Maksimenko	08/12/90	Brighton (ENG)					s72		D	D46			3	-
Alans Siņeļņikovs	14/05/90	Skonto					s88		M	M63	M		6	-
Artis Lazdiņš	03/05/86	Piast (POL)						M			s15		11	-
Pāvels Doroševs	09/10/80	Liepājas Metalurgs							G	G			3	-
Valērijs Šabala	12/10/94	Skonto							A74	s46	s64		3	2
Gļebs Kļuškins	01/10/92	Daugava Rīga							s74				1	-
Vladislas Gabovs	13/07/87	Skonto							s74	s63	s59		3	-
Igors Tarasovs	16/10/88	Ventspils							s80				4	-
Pāvels Mihadjuks	27/05/80	Daugava Rīga								s46	D		16	1

LATVIA

European club competitions 2012/13

FK VENTSPILS

CHAMPIONS LEAGUE

Second qualifying round - Molde FK (NOR)
A 0-3
Uvarenko, Kurakins, Smirnovs, Gilmanov, Turkovs, Kozlovs (Žatkins 81), Martínez, Saito, Paulius, Timofejevs, Badyautdinov (Barinovs 78). Coach: Jurģis Pučinskis (LVA)
H 1-1 *Kurakins (24)*
Uvarenko, Kurakins, Smirnovs, Gilmanov, Turkovs (Žatkins 68), Kozlovs (Agoh 88), Martínez, Saito, Paulius, Timofejevs, Badyautdinov. Coach: Jurģis Pučinskis (LVA)

SKONTO FC

EUROPA LEAGUE

Second qualifying round - HNK Hajduk Split (CRO)
A 0-2
Māliņš, Savčenkovs, Ibragimov (Rode 72), Fertovs, Gjorgievski, Blanks (Šabala 49), Amirkhanov, Segundo, Maksimenko, Labukas, Siņeļņikovs. Coach: Marians Pahars (LVA)
H 1-0 *Siņeļņikovs (90+3)*
Māliņš, Rode, Savčenkovs, Ibragimov, Mingazov, Fertovs, Šabala, Segundo (Siņeļņikovs 87), Maksimenko, Labukas (Blanks 62), Kukanos. Coach: Marians Pahars (LVA)

SK LIEPĀJAS METALURGS

EUROPA LEAGUE

First qualifying round - SP La Fiorita (SMR)
A 2-0 *Leliūga (40), Soloņicins (90)*
Šteinbors, Kļava, Zirņis (Leliūga 34), Kamešs (Gucs 75), Savaļnieks, Surņins, Mihadjuks, Afanasjevs (Šadčins 90), Soloņicins, Bagužis, Krjauklis. Coach: Jānis Intenbergs (LVA)
H 4-0 *Kamešs (1), Afanasjevs (72), Soloņicins (82p), Äsgärov (85)*
Šteinbors, Kļava, Kamešs (Äsgärov 79), Leliūga (Šadčins 66), Savaļnieks, Surņins, Mihadjuks, Afanasjevs (Hmizs 86), Soloņicins, Bagužis, Krjauklis. Coach: Jānis Intenbergs (LVA)

Second qualifying round - Legia Warszawa (POL)
H 2-2 *Leliuga (43), Kļava (81p)*
Doroševs, Kļava, Zirņis, Kamešs (Hmizs 90+1), Tamošauskas, Savaļnieks, Surņins (Leliūga 34), Mihadjuks, Afanasjevs (Mežs 70), Soloņicins, Bagužis. Coach: Dzintars Kazaks (LVA)
Red card: Zirņis 68
A 1-5 *Kamešs (45+1)*
Doroševs, Kamešs, Tamošauskas, Leliūga (Flaksis 81), Savaļnieks, Hmizs (Ikaunieks 88), Mihadjuks, Afanasjevs (Šadčins 67), Soloņicins, Bagužis, Mežs. Coach: Jānis Intenbergs (LVA)
Red card: Soloņicins 54

FC DAUGAVA DAUGAVPILS

EUROPA LEAGUE

First qualifying round - FK Sūduva (LTU)
A 1-0 *Kovaļovs (87)*
Ikstens, Tsintsadze, Kovaļovs (Silagailis 88), Ibe, Ziziļevs, Sokolovs, Mihalj, Polovinchuk, Logins, Gongadze (Volkovs 67), Mamaev (Yashin 59). Coach: Ivan Tabanov (MDA)
H 2-3 *Ibe (52, 54)*
Ikstens, Tsintsadze, Kovaļovs, Ibe, Ziziļevs (Gongadze 87), Sokolovs, Volkovs (Uļyanov 86), Mihalj, Polovinchuk, Logins, Mamaev (Yashin 56). Coach: Ivan Tabanov (MDA)

Domestic league club-by-club

FC DAUGAVA DAUGAVPILS

Coach: Ravil Sabitov (RUS);
(30/04/12) Ivan Tabanov (MDA)
1944 • Celtnieks (4,070); Daugava (3,480) • fcdaugava.lv
Major honours
Latvian League (1) 2012;
Latvian Cup (1) 2008

2012

Date	Opponent		Score	Scorers
24/03	Daugava Rīga	a	4-0	Ulyanov, Sokolovs, Silagailis, Kokins
31/03	Spartaks	h	1-0	Kovaļovs
08/04	Metta/LU	a	1-1	Gongadze
15/04	Skonto	h	1-1	Gongadze (p)
18/04	Jelgava	a	2-1	Kokins, Gongadze
22/04	Liepājas Metalurgs	h	0-0	
28/04	Jūrmala	a	1-6	Streltsov
02/05	Gulbene	h	3-0	Gongadze, Kovaļovs, Mihalj
06/05	Ventspils	a	2-1	Gongadze (p), Sokolovs
13/05	Daugava Rīga	h	3-1	Gongadze 3
16/05	Spartaks	a	2-2	Gongadze (p), Ulyanov
27/05	Metta/LU	h	2-0	Volkovs, Mihalj
07/06	Skonto	a	0-3	
16/06	Jelgava	h	2-0	Ziziļevs, Gongadze
21/06	Liepājas Metalurgs	a	0-2	
26/06	Jūrmala	h	2-0	Ziziļevs, Ulyanov
30/06	Gulbene	a	2-0	Gongadze 2
08/07	Ventspils	h	3-0	Silagailis, Ibe 2
15/07	Daugava Rīga	a	3-0	Yashin 2, Tsintsadze
29/07	Spartaks	h	3-2	Yashin 2, Kovaļovs
04/08	Metta/LU	a	5-0	Tsintsadze, Halvitovs, Ibe, Kovaļovs, Gongadze
11/08	Skonto	h	0-0	
18/08	Jelgava	a	2-0	Ibe 2
22/08	Liepājas Metalurgs	h	0-0	
26/08	Jūrmala	a	4-2	Gongadze 2, Yashin, Rafaļskis
01/09	Gulbene	h	1-0	Ibe
16/09	Ventspils	a	0-1	
19/09	Daugava Rīga	h	3-0	Sokolovs (p), Kovaļovs, Jermolajevs
22/09	Spartaks	a	3-0	Ola, Gongadze, Ibe
26/09	Metta/LU	h	1-0	Ibe
30/09	Skonto	a	0-0	
06/10	Jelgava	h	0-0	
20/10	Liepājas Metalurgs	a	3-1	Mihalj, Gongadze, Ibe
27/10	Jūrmala	h	2-0	Gongadze, Ola
04/11	Gulbene	a	3-1	Ibe, Ziziļevs, og (Gluško)
10/11	Ventspils	h	0-0	

No	Name	Nat	DoB	Pos	Aps	(s)	Gls
33	Mamuka Gongadze	GEO	25/11/85	A	27	(6)	18
19	Dmitrijs Halvitovs		03/04/86	D	14		1
8	Stanley Ibe	NGA	19/07/84	A	16	(2)	10
12,88	Kaspars Ikstens		05/06/88	G	18		
14,7	Edgars Jermolajevs		16/06/92	M	11	(9)	1
16	Ēriks Kokins		11/01/91	A	9	(11)	2
6	Andrejs Kovaļovs		23/03/89	A	30	(4)	5
30	Vadims Logins		30/12/81	D	18		
8,39	Pavel Mamaev	RUS	03/02/84	M	13	(2)	
26,23	Matija Mihalj	CRO	06/01/87	D	21	(4)	3
1,81	Jevgeņijs Nerugals		26/02/89	G	18		
13	Daniel Ola	NGA	26/11/82	D	14		2
25	Dmitri Polovinchuk	RUS	27/09/82	M	24	(3)	
36	Jans Radevičs		14/03/89	M	4	(6)	
5,14	Maksims Rafaļskis		24/05/84	M	14	(6)	1
2,20	Ričards Raščevskis		02/04/92	M		(2)	
10	Guntars Silagailis		31/08/84	M	14	(11)	2
22	Jevgeņijs Simonovs		29/03/84	D	11	(6)	
11	Jurijs Sokolovs		12/09/83	M	30	(3)	3
7	Andrei Streltsov	RUS	18/03/84	A	3	(4)	1
5	Andrei Tcaciuc	MDA	10/02/82	M	2	(1)	
13,4	Badzina Tsintsadze	GEO	04/06/89	D	24	(1)	2
3,17,19	Georgi Ulyanov	RUS	09/09/85	D	11	(2)	3
15	Vladimirs Volkovs		10/08/84	A	9	(9)	1
18	Sergei Yashin	RUS	03/01/81	A	9	(4)	5
9	Mihails Ziziļevs		27/12/73	M	32	(3)	3

FK DAUGAVA RĪGA

Coach: Jurijs Popkovs
2003 • Vidusskolas Sporta Komplekss (1,000);
Daugava (5,083) • daugavariga.com

2012

24/03	Daugava Daugavpils	h	0-4	
31/03	Metta/LU	h	1-0	Kārkliņš
07/04	Jelgava	a	4-3	Gospodars, Kārkliņš, Diakvishvili, Ziļs
14/04	Jūrmala	h	1-1	Alekseev
18/04	Ventspils	a	0-2	
21/04	Spartaks	h	1-2	Kārkliņš
28/04	Skonto	a	0-1	
02/05	Liepājas Metalurgs	h	1-3	Diakvishvili (p)
06/05	Gulbene	a	0-0	
13/05	Daugava Daugavpils	a	1-3	Ziļs
18/05	Metta/LU	h	3-0	Mežs, Ziļs, og (Priedēns)
26/05	Jelgava	h	1-0	Ziļs
07/06	Jūrmala	a	1-1	Grippa (p)
17/06	Ventspils	h	1-1	
01/07	Spartaks	a	2-2	Kārkliņš, Ziļs
26/06	Skonto	h	1-1	Sokoļskis
01/07	Liepājas Metalurgs	a	0-1	
07/07	Gulbene	h	2-2	Grippa, Diakvishvili
15/07	Daugava Daugavpils	h	0-3	
28/07	Metta/LU	h	1-1	Solovich
04/08	Jelgava	a	2-2	Grippa (p), Gramovičs
11/08	Jūrmala	h	1-2	Solovich
18/08	Ventspils	a	0-5	
22/08	Spartaks	h	2-5	Ziļs, Gospodars
26/08	Skonto	a	1-1	Grippa
01/09	Liepājas Metalurgs	h	3-3	Diakvishvili, Ziļs, Grippa (p)
15/09	Gulbene	a	1-2	Korban
19/09	Daugava Daugavpils	a	0-5	
23/09	Metta/LU	a	3-4	Ziļs 2, Gramovičs
26/09	Jelgava	h	1-2	Gramovičs
30/09	Jūrmala	a	3-2	Solovich, Ziļs, Kļuškins
06/10	Ventspils	h	0-4	
20/10	Spartaks	a	2-2	Grippa, Diakvishvili
27/10	Skonto	h	1-0	Diakvishvili
04/11	Liepājas Metalurgs	a	0-4	
10/11	Gulbene	h	1-1	Kļuškins

No	Name	Nat	DoB	Pos	Aps	(s)	Gls
10	Aleksei Alekseev	RUS	14/04/89	M	7	(4)	1
16	Vitālijs Artjomenko		26/08/90	G	1		
22	Aleksandrs Baturinskis		15/12/91	D	8	(5)	
2,20	Reinis Broders		17/07/92	M	15	(8)	
7,20,23	Giorgi Diakvishvili	GEO	21/11/87	M	32	(1)	7
8	Vadims Gospodars		25/12/83	M	30	(4)	2
10	Aleksandrs Gramovičs		25/03/89	M	17		3
22,7	Vadym Grippa	UKR	09/01/92	M	27	(2)	6
17	Stepan Hlubokiy	UKR	06/03/92	M	14		
12	Deividas Kapustas	LTU	16/02/93	M	5	(7)	
11	Edgars Kārkliņš		21/07/91	A	23	(11)	4
9	Glebs Kļuškins		01/10/92	A	10	(5)	2
3,24	Kirill Korban	RUS	12/06/89	D	34		1
32	Romāns Maksimovs		03/01/95	G	1		
7	Volodymyr Melnyk	UKR	21/11/79	M	4	(2)	
4	Toms Mežs		07/09/89	D	16		1
21	Artis Novickis		09/11/86	M		(2)	
26	Vladislavs Pavļučenko		14/03/92	M		(6)	
9	Bogdans Petruks		23/03/92	D	10	(6)	
6	Ernests Pilats		15/03/93	M		(1)	
27	Otto Rihters		15/05/92	M	1	(5)	
5,3	Dmitrijs Šiļuks		21/06/87	D	35		
6,5	Deniss Sokoļskis		25/08/81	D	31	(1)	1
4	Oleh Solovich	UKR	27/09/91	M	13		3
18	Aleksandrs Šumilovs		04/08/85	M		(1)	
14	Artjoms Uljanovs		09/08/89	M	1	(8)	
1	Artūrs Vaičulis		26/02/90	G	34		
19	Andriy Zadoyko	UKR	11/03/92	M	1	(2)	
12,13	Vitālijs Ziļs		19/08/87	A	26	(8)	10

FB GULBENE 2005

Coach: Mihails Koņevs
2005 • Municipal (2,000) • fbgulbene.com

2012

25/03	Metta/LU	a	0-0	
31/03	Jelgava	h	1-2	Saito
07/04	Jūrmala	a	2-2	Saito 2 (1p)
15/04	Ventspils	a	0-3	
18/04	Spartaks	a	1-3	Saito
22/04	Skonto	h	0-1	
28/04	Liepājas Metalurgs	a	1-0	Saito
02/05	Daugava Daugavpils	a	0-3	
06/05	Daugava Rīga	h	0-0	
13/05	Metta/LU	h	5-1	Mišins 2, Saito 2, Lapss
16/05	Jelgava	a	1-0	Saito
26/05	Jūrmala	h	2-0	Saito, Irie
07/05	Ventspils	h	0-5	
16/06	Spartaks	h	0-3	
17/06	Skonto	a	1-4	Ishikawa
27/06	Liepājas Metalurgs	h	1-1	Maksimenko
30/06	Daugava Daugavpils	h	0-2	
07/07	Daugava Rīga	a	2-2	Ivanovs, Mišins
15/07	Metta/LU	a	1-1	Ishikawa
27/07	Jelgava	h	0-1	
05/08	Jūrmala	a	0-4	
11/08	Ventspils	h	1-2	Takeda
18/08	Spartaks	a	2-2	Takeda 2
22/08	Skonto	h	0-4	
26/08	Liepājas Metalurgs	a	1-0	Takeda
01/09	Daugava Daugavpils	a	0-1	
09/09	Jūrmala	h	0-1	
15/09	Daugava Rīga	h	2-1	Takeda, Gluško (p)
19/09	Metta/LU	h	0-3	
23/09	Jelgava	a	0-0	
30/09	Ventspils	a	0-4	
06/10	Spartaks	h	0-1	
21/10	Skonto	a	1-3	Gluško
27/10	Liepājas Metalurgs	h	1-3	Lapss
04/11	Daugava Daugavpils	h	1-3	Karašauskas
10/11	Daugava Rīga	a	1-1	Takeda

No	Name	Nat	DoB	Pos	Aps	(s)	Gls
11	Shoma Akuta	JPN	13/09/91	M	1	(3)	
20	Lado Datunashvili	GEO	06/03/87	M	2	(5)	
6	Ivans Gluško		25/09/84	D	32	(1)	2
20,19	Kirils Grigorovs		19/10/92	M	13	(1)	
11	Arevšats Hačatrjans		24/07/90	A	4		
10	Toshikazu Irie	JPN	11/11/84	M	14	(1)	1
5	Ryota Ishikawa	JPN	11/02/88	M	25	(3)	2
2	Aleksandrs Ivanovs		16/11/85	D	32		1
14,19	Edijs Ivaško		15/02/85	D	17		
3	Kirils Jeļkins		01/09/87	D	19	(2)	
11	Artūrs Karašauskas		29/01/92	A	13	(2)	1
18	Igors Korabļovs		23/11/74	M	35	(1)	
20	Damian Kostkowski	POL	14/09/93	M	1		
9	Ryoki Kozawa	JPN	25/06/88	M	8	(1)	
22	Mareks Kozlovskis		19/11/96	M		(1)	
21	Igors Labuts		07/06/90	G	8		
17	Jānis Lapss		16/09/86	A	21	(9)	2
4	Anatolijs Maksimenko		09/05/93	D	17	(12)	1
7	Sergejs Mišins		04/06/87	M	34		3
1	Alberts Nikoļskis		05/12/80	G	28		
12	Deniss Ostrovskis		05/02/92	M		(5)	
9	Yosuke Saito	JPN	07/04/88	A	14		9
8	Seung Ki-yoo	KOR	22/07/87	M	15		
15	Nils Sitenkovs		30/01/89	M	14	(4)	
22,16,9	Edijs Skurjats		05/02/92	M	2	(2)	
10	Hideaki Takeda	JPN	22/05/86	A	15		6
15	David Tsiskarishvili	GEO	05/02/92	M	2	(5)	
12	Shohei Tsushiya	JPN	02/08/89	M	4	(1)	
16,8	Shota Yanagi	JPN	25/12/93	A	6	(7)	

FK JELGAVA

Coach: Dainis Kazakevičs
2004 • Zemgales Olimpiskā centra (2,560) • fkjelgava.lv
Major honours
Latvian Cup (1) 2010

2012

24/03	Liepājas Metalurgs	h	0-2	
31/03	Gulbene	a	2-1	Kozlovs, Redjko (p)
07/04	Daugava Rīga	h	3-4	Kozlovs, Žatkins 2
15/04	Metta/LU	a	1-1	Kozlovs
18/04	Daugava Daugavpils	h	1-2	Kozlovs
22/04	Jūrmala	h	0-2	
28/04	Ventspils	a	1-0	Lukošius
02/05	Spartaks	h	1-3	Baturinskis
06/05	Skonto	a	3-2	Kozlovs, Bogdaškins, Kazura
16/05	Gulbene	h	0-1	
26/05	Daugava Rīga	a	0-1	
07/05	Metta/LU	h	1-4	Žatkins
16/06	Daugava Daugavpils	a	0-2	
21/06	Jūrmala	a	0-0	
27/06	Ventspils	h	0-2	
01/07	Spartaks	h	3-2	Redjko (p), Petrenko, Kozlovs
15/07	Liepājas Metalurgs	h	1-2	R Bespalovs
27/07	Gulbene	a	1-0	R Bespalovs
01/08	Liepājas Metalurgs	a	1-1	Ilin
04/08	Daugava Rīga	h	2-2	Redjko, Grigaravičius
08/08	Skonto	h	1-2	A Bespalovs
11/08	Metta/LU	a	3-1	Redjko (p), Ilin, A Bespalovs
18/08	Daugava Daugavpils	h	0-2	
22/08	Jūrmala	h	1-3	Ilin
26/08	Ventspils	a	0-0	
31/08	Spartaks	a	0-2	
15/09	Skonto	h	0-2	
19/09	Liepājas Metalurgs	a	0-2	
23/09	Gulbene	h	0-0	
26/09	Daugava Rīga	a	2-1	Ošs, R Bespalovs
30/09	Metta/LU	h	1-1	Malašenoks
16/10	Daugava Daugavpils	a	0-0	
21/10	Jūrmala	a	1-3	Ilin
27/10	Ventspils	h	0-1	
04/11	Spartaks	a	1-1	Keita
10/11	Skonto	h	1-1	Kļimovs

No	Name	Nat	DoB	Pos	Aps	(s)	Gls
92	Edgars Andrejevs		21/10/92	G		(1)	
22	Igors Barinovs		01/06/94	D	3	(1)	
15	Aleksandrs Baturinskis		15/12/91	D	10	(3)	1
24	Alberts Bārbalis		05/03/88	D		(3)	
9	Aleksejs Bespalovs		04/12/85	M	12	(11)	2
37	Romans Bespalovs		18/10/88	A	15	(1)	3
81	Marks Bogdanovs		02/12/86	G	17		
11	Boriss Bogdaškins		21/12/90	M	14	(2)	1
5	Dmitrijs Danilovs		25/01/91	D	26		
13	Mindaugas Grigaravičius	LTU	15/07/92	A	23	(8)	1
16	Dmitrijs Grigorjevs		13/05/92	G	4		
77	Aleksandrs Gubins		16/05/88	D	29	(3)	
10	Pāvels Hohlovs		19/12/89	D	7	(8)	
19,34	Serhiy Ilin	UKR	10/01/87	A	15	(1)	4
10	Rey Ishikawa	JPN	10/02/87	M	2	(4)	
35,4	Darius Jankauskas	LTU	27/04/92	M	5	(4)	
4	Jevgenijs Kazura		24/01/88	D	12		1
14,21	Soumaïla Keita	FRA	02/02/90	M	12	(1)	1
23	Kārlis Kinderevičs		03/08/89	M		(3)	
20	Arturs Klimovics		31/08/91	M		(1)	
18	Aleksandrs Kļimovs		16/11/91	M	16	(16)	1
21	Vladislavs Kozlovs		30/11/87	A	15		6
3	Jurijs Ksenzovs		05/06/81	D		(1)	
17	Igors Lapkovskis		24/02/87	M	10	(6)	
20	Artis Lazdiņš		03/05/86	M	16		
99	Deividas Lukošius	LTU	24/01/91	M	7	(9)	1
15,33,30	Oļegs Malašenoks		27/04/86	A	17	(1)	1
27	Okechukwu Onyeulo	NGA	12/08/88	M	1	(4)	
24,25	Mārcis Ošs		25/07/91	D	19	(6)	1
2	Deniss Petrenko		14/03/88	D	29		1
7	Valērijs Redjko		10/03/83	M	31	(1)	4
1	Jevgenijs Sazonovs		31/07/88	G	15		
15,37	Nils Sitenkovs		30/01/89	M	1	(4)	
14	Aldis Trukšāns		19/07/90	M		(2)	
22	Oļegs Žatkins		13/04/87	M	13	(1)	3

 **LATVIA**

FC JŪRMALA

Coach: Vladimir Pachko (RUS)
2008 • Sloka (2,000); Arkādija artificial, Riga (650)
• jurmalafc.lv

2012

25/03	Skonto	h	3-3	Halvitovs, Ola, Osipovs (p)
31/03	Liepājas Metalurgs	a	0-2	
07/04	Gulbene	h	2-2	Žuļevs, Osipovs
14/04	Daugava Rīga	a	1-1	Aleksejevs
18/04	Metta/LU	a	2-0	Rečickis, Sputajs
22/04	Jelgava	a	2-0	Rečickis, Sputajs
28/04	Daugava Daugavpils	h	6-1	Osipovs 2 (1p), Sputajs 2 (1p), Daņilovs, Golubevs
02/05	Ventspils	h	1-2	Osipovs
06/05	Spartaks	a	0-0	
18/05	Liepājas Metalurgs	h	0-2	
26/05	Gulbene	a	0-2	
07/06	Daugava Rīga	h	1-1	Sputajs
16/06	Metta/LU	h	0-0	
21/06	Jelgava	h	0-0	
26/06	Daugava Daugavpils	a	0-2	
01/07	Ventspils	a	1-1	Daņilovs
05/07	Skonto	a	0-1	
14/07	Skonto	h	0-0	
19/07	Spartaks	h	0-1	
29/07	Liepājas Metalurgs	a	2-3	Šlampe, Osipovs (p)
05/08	Gulbene	h	4-0	Solovjovs 2 (1p), Mysin, Daņilovs
11/08	Daugava Rīga	a	2-1	Osipovs (p), Solovjovs
19/08	Metta/LU	h	3-0	Šlampe, Joksts, Mysin
22/08	Jelgava	a	3-1	Daņilovs, Mysin 2 (1p)
26/08	Daugava Daugavpils	a	2-4	Daņilovs, Seletski
01/09	Ventspils	h	0-1	
09/09	Gulbene	a	1-0	Solovjovs
15/09	Spartaks	a	2-4	Aleksejevs, Sputajs
19/09	Skonto	a	0-1	
23/09	Liepājas Metalurgs	h	0-2	
30/09	Daugava Rīga	h	2-3	Mysin, Solovjovs
06/10	Metta/LU	a	3-0	Sputajs 2, Mysin
21/10	Jelgava	h	3-1	Žuļevs, Daņilovs, Osipovs
27/10	Daugava Daugavpils	a	0-2	
04/11	Ventspils	a	1-2	Aleksejevs
10/11	Spartaks	h	0-3	

No	Name	Nat	DoB	Pos	Aps	(s)	Gls
27	Igors Aleksejevs		31/07/88	M	32		3
23	Artūrs Burņins		27/12/89	D		(1)	
11	Igor Byrlov	RUS	10/07/86	M	4	(2)	
17	Maksims Daņilovs		02/08/86	A	26	(2)	6
77	Pāvels Davidovs		30/12/80	G	14		
12,14	Ulvi Gaibov	RUS	22/04/91	M		(5)	
3	Sergejs Golubevs		24/02/88	D	34	(1)	1
24	Kirils Grigorovs		19/10/92	M		(6)	
13	Dmitrijs Halvitovs		03/04/86	D	17		1
91	Oskars Ikstens		23/01/91	M	7	(12)	
21	Edijs Joksts		21/07/92	D	18	(8)	1
12	Deniss Kačanovs		27/11/79	D	13		
67	Jānis Krūmiņš		09/01/92	G	6	(2)	
22	Jevgeņijs Laizāns		30/05/83	G	16		
23	Mikhail Milshin	RUS	28/01/91	M	1	(6)	
28	Mikhail Mysin	RUS	24/05/79	M	12	(1)	6
28	Daniel Ola	NGA	26/11/82	D	15		1
7	Artjoms Osipovs		08/01/89	A	26	(7)	8
12	Deniss Ostrovskis		05/02/92	M		(1)	
9	Dmitrijs Paplavskis		10/04/88	A	3	(20)	
69,23	Staņislavs Pihockis		09/08/88	M	25	(4)	
20	Vitālijs Rečickis		14/07/88	M	25	(3)	2
11	Vyacheslav Seletski	RUS	31/03/88	M	1	(7)	1
5	Ingus Šlampe		31/01/89	M	34		2
69	Aleksandrs Solovjovs		25/02/88	M	10	(3)	5
10	Ivans Sputajs		09/04/87	A	30	(3)	8
8	Vadims Žuļevs		01/03/88	M	27	(1)	2

SK LIEPĀJAS METALURGS

Coach: Vladimirs Osipovs;
(30/04/12) Dmitrijs Kalašņikovs;
(02/07/12) Jānis Intenbergs
1997 • Daugava (6,000) • sport.metalurgs.lv
Major honours
Latvian League (2) 2005, 2009;
Latvian Cup (1) 2006

2012

24/03	Jelgava	a	2-0	Kamešs, Afanasjevs
31/03	Jūrmala	h	2-0	Krjauklis, Kalns (p)
14/04	Spartaks	h	1-2	Afanasjevs
18/04	Skonto	a	1-0	Kamešs
22/04	Daugava Daugavpils	a	0-0	
28/04	Gulbene	h	0-1	
02/05	Daugava Rīga	a	3-1	Prohorenkovs (p), Kalns, Äsgārov
06/05	Metta/LU	a	1-4	Kalns
18/05	Jūrmala	a	2-0	Kamešs 2
27/05	Ventspils	h	0-0	
06/06	Spartaks	a	2-2	Mihadjuks, Kļava
17/06	Skonto	h	0-1	
21/06	Daugava Daugavpils	h	2-0	Afanasjevs, Kļava (p)
27/06	Gulbene	a	1-1	Afanasjevs
01/07	Daugava Rīga	h	1-0	Mihadjuks
15/07	Jelgava	a	2-1	Soloņicins, Savaļnieks
29/07	Jūrmala	h	3-2	Kamešs, Afanasjevs, Šadčins
01/08	Jelgava	h	1-1	Karlsons
05/08	Ventspils	a	0-1	
08/08	Metta/LU	h	3-2	Karlsons 2, Soloņicins (p)
11/08	Spartaks	h	2-1	Leliūga 2
18/08	Skonto	h	1-0	Leliūga
22/08	Daugava Daugavpils	a	0-0	
26/08	Gulbene	h	3-1	Leliūga 2 (1p), Soloņicins
01/09	Daugava Rīga	a	3-3	Soloņicins, Karlsons 2
15/09	Metta/LU	h	4-1	Soloņicins 2 (1p), Karlsons, Savaļnieks
19/09	Jelgava	h	2-0	Kamešs, Soloņicins
23/09	Jūrmala	a	2-0	Afanasjevs 2
26/09	Ventspils	h	1-0	Karlsons
29/09	Spartaks	a	3-0	Leliūga, Afanasjevs 2
03/10	Ventspils	a	3-0	Karlsons, og (Tarasovs), Soloņicins (p)
06/10	Skonto	a	1-3	Kamešs
20/10	Daugava Daugavpils	h	1-3	Kamešs
27/10	Gulbene	a	3-1	Kamešs, Kalns, Karlsons
04/11	Daugava Rīga	h	4-0	Kamešs, Kalns 2, Afanasjevs
10/11	Metta/LU	a	0-1	

No	Name	Nat	DoB	Pos	Aps	(s)	Gls
19	Valērijs Afanasjevs		20/09/82	M	28	(6)	10
23	Vüqar Äsgärov	AZE	14/05/85	A	3	(13)	1
26	Mindaugas Bagužis	LTU	10/04/83	D	27		
12	Pāvels Doroševs		09/10/80	G	21		
2	Reinis Flaksis		05/04/94	M		(1)	
25	Toms Gucs		28/04/92	M	1	(5)	
16	Dmitrijs Hmizs		31/07/92	D	19	(5)	
87	Dāvis Ikaunieks		07/01/94	M		(3)	
8	Jurģis Kalns		05/10/82	M	22	(2)	6
7	Vladimirs Kamešs		28/10/88	A	27	(2)	10
5	Ģirts Karlsons		07/06/81	A	17	(2)	9
3	Oskars Kļava		08/08/83	D	14		2
25	Lukas Kočanauskas	LTU	27/02/90	A	1	(11)	
87	Ritus Krjauklis		23/04/86	D	14		1
6	Jurijs Kučma		09/07/93	M		(2)	
5	Artjoms Kuzņecovs		30/05/86	D		(2)	
10	Rytis Leliūga	LTU	04/01/87	M	19	(1)	6
28	Toms Mežs		07/09/89	D	14	(2)	
18	Pāvels Mihadjuks		27/05/80	D	11	(1)	2
17	Andrejs Prohorenkovs		05/02/77	M	13	(2)	1
14	Ilja Šadčins		02/07/94	A	6	(11)	1
11	Roberts Savaļnieks		06/05/87	M	28	(4)	2
20	Genādijs Soloņicins		03/01/80	M	29	(3)	8
21	Pāvels Šteinbors		21/09/85	G	14		
13	Pāvels Surņins		05/09/86	M	9	(1)	
9	Tomas Tamošauskas	LTU	22/05/83	M	29	(1)	
1	Raivo Varažinskis		07/03/93	G	1	(1)	
4	Dzintars Zirņis		25/04/77	D	29	(2)	

FS METTA/LU

Coach: Andris Riherts
2006 • Vidusskolas Sporta Komplekss (1,000);
Arkādija (1,000) • fsmetta.lv

2012

25/03	Gulbene	h	0-0	
31/03	Daugava Rīga	a	0-1	
08/04	Daugava Daugavpils	h	1-1	Kalniņš
15/04	Jelgava	h	1-1	Rožkovskis
18/04	Jūrmala	h	0-2	
22/04	Ventspils	h	1-6	Vardanjans
28/04	Spartaks	a	1-3	Kalniņš
02/05	Skonto	h	0-5	Puķītis (p)
06/05	Liepājas Metalurgs	h	4-1	Kalniņš 2, Māris Savinovs, Priedēns
13/05	Gulbene	a	1-5	Milašēvičs
18/05	Daugava Rīga	h	0-3	
27/05	Daugava Daugavpils	a	0-2	
07/06	Jelgava	a	4-1	Milašēvičs, Parfjonovs, Kamkins, Puķītis (p)
16/06	Jūrmala	a	0-0	
21/06	Ventspils	a	0-1	
27/06	Spartaks	h	2-1	Zotovs, Loginovs
30/06	Skonto	a	0-5	
15/07	Gulbene	h	1-1	Puķītis
28/07	Daugava Rīga	a	1-1	Grāveris
04/08	Daugava Daugavpils	h	0-5	
08/08	Liepājas Metalurgs	a	2-3	Lonščakovs, Loginovs
11/08	Jelgava	a	1-3	Milašēvičs
19/08	Jūrmala	a	0-3	
22/08	Ventspils	h	0-2	
25/08	Spartaks	a	4-3	Puķītis 2 (1p), Loginovs (p), Kalniņš
01/09	Skonto	h	1-2	Loginovs
15/09	Liepājas Metalurgs	a	1-4	Rožkovskis
19/09	Gulbene	a	3-0	Milašēvičs 2, Skābardis
23/09	Daugava Rīga	h	4-3	Loginovs, Pallo, Milašēvičs 2
26/09	Daugava Daugavpils	a	0-1	
30/09	Jelgava	a	1-1	Māris Savinovs
06/10	Jūrmala	h	0-3	
21/10	Ventspils	a	0-4	
28/10	Spartaks	h	3-3	Milašēvičs 3
04/11	Skonto	a	0-5	
10/11	Liepājas Metalurgs	h	1-0	Zuntners

No	Name	Nat	DoB	Pos	Aps	(s)	Gls
1	Artūrs Biezais		08/11/86	G	26		
13	Vladislavs Gabovs		13/07/87	D	22		
21	Kalvis Grāveris		21/11/87	M	5	(7)	1
11	Gatis Kalniņš		12/08/88	A	28	(3)	5
18	Maksims Kamkins		17/05/88	M		(6)	1
8	Artjoms Loginovs		20/07/93	M	9	(19)	5
18	Artjoms Lonščakovs		11/06/92	M	3	(8)	1
26	Mārtiņš Milašēvičs		12/02/92	A	22	(8)	10
17	Artūrs Pallo		27/02/89	M	31	(3)	1
23	Ņikita Parfjonovs		14/03/93	M	14	(12)	1
14	Kristaps Priedēns		12/01/90	A	19	(11)	1
2	Rūdolfs Puķītis		14/02/91	D	27		5
24	Kristers Putniņš		16/07/93	G	10		
92	Māris Riherts		11/02/92	M	19	(5)	
20	Romans Rožkovskis		03/12/90	D	31	(1)	2
33	Mārcis Savinovs		03/05/87	D	16	(1)	
34	Māris Savinovs		03/05/87	D	28		2
89	Juris Skābardis		17/07/89	D	26	(4)	1
6	Vents Vanags		24/12/91	M		(3)	
77	Marsels Vapne		02/10/81	M	2		
7	Edgars Vardanjans		09/05/91	M	24	(3)	1
9	Jurijs Višņakovs		16/01/87	M	1	(4)	
5	Artjoms Zotovs		02/10/91	M	20	(4)	1
25	Mareks Zuntners		13/02/83	A	13		1

SKONTO FC

Coach: Marians Pahars
1991 • Skonto (9,500) • skontofc.lv
Major honours
Latvian League (15) 1991, 1992, 1993, 1994, 1995, 1996, 1997, 1998, 1999, 2000, 2001, 2002, 2003, 2004, 2010; Latvian Cup (8) 1992, 1995, 1997, 1998, 2000, 2001, 2002, 2012

2012

25/03	Jūrmala	a	3-3	*Siņicins 2 (2p), Siņeļņikovs*
01/04	Ventspils	h	1-0	*Siņeļņikovs*
07/04	Spartaks	h	1-0	*Labukas (p)*
15/04	Daugava Daugavpils	a	1-1	*Siņicins (p)*
18/04	Liepājas Metalurgs	h	0-1	
22/04	Gulbene	a	1-0	*Labukas*
28/04	Daugava Rīga	h	1-0	*Labukas*
02/05	Metta/LU	a	2-1	*Siņicins (p), Fertovs*
06/05	Jelgava	h	2-3	*Shmatovalenko (p), Savčenkovs*
18/05	Ventspils	a	0-0	
26/05	Spartaks	a	2-2	*Labukas, Šabala*
07/06	Daugava Daugavpils	h	3-0	*Savčenkovs, Mingazov, og (Logins)*
17/06	Liepājas Metalurgs	a	1-0	*Šabala*
21/06	Gulbene	h	4-1	*Šabala, Maksimenko, Mingazov, Siņeļņikovs (p)*
26/06	Daugava Rīga	a	1-1	*Šabala*
30/06	Metta/LU	h	5-0	*Šabala 3, Segundo, Blanks*
05/07	Jūrmala	h	1-0	*Siņeļņikovs (p)*
14/07	Jūrmala	a	0-0	
30/07	Ventspils	h	1-0	*Labukas*
04/08	Spartaks	a	1-0	*Mingazov*
08/08	Jelgava	a	2-1	*Blanks, Siņeļņikovs*
11/08	Daugava Daugavpils	a	0-0	
18/08	Liepājas Metalurgs	a	0-1	
22/08	Gulbene	a	4-0	*Savčenkovs, Rode, Siņeļņikovs, Šabala*
26/08	Daugava Rīga	h	1-1	*Mingazov*
01/09	Metta/LU	a	2-1	*Siņeļņikovs 2 (1p)*
15/09	Jelgava	h	2-0	*Siņeļņikovs (p), Labukas*
19/09	Jūrmala	h	1-0	*Mingazov*
22/09	Ventspils	a	0-1	
26/09	Spartaks	h	0-0	
30/09	Daugava Daugavpils	h	0-0	
06/10	Liepājas Metalurgs	h	3-1	*Labukas 2, Amirkhanov*
21/10	Gulbene	h	3-1	*Šabala 2, Labukas*
27/10	Daugava Rīga	a	3-1	*Fertovs, Šabala, og (Rihters)*
04/11	Metta/LU	h	5-0	*Labukas 2, Mingazov, Maksimenko, Pētersons*
10/11	Jelgava	a	1-1	*Kukanos (p)*

No	Name	Nat	DoB	Pos	Aps	(s)	Gls
13	Roman Amirkhanov	RUS	13/05/89	D	20	(3)	1
9	Kristaps Blanks		30/01/86	A	21	(3)	2
30	Oskars Darģis		03/06/93	G	3		
7	Aleksandrs Fertovs		16/06/87	M	29	(1)	2
8	Bojan Gjorgievski	MKD	25/01/92	D	15	(2)	
4,24	Adil Ibragimov	RUS	23/04/89	D	12	(1)	
21	Aleksandr Kukanos	RUS	30/05/83	D	18	(3)	1
19,8,24	Tadas Labukas	LTU	10/01/84	A	26	(2)	11
5	Jurijs Laizāns		06/01/79	M	1	(5)	
17	Vitālijs Maksimenko		08/12/90	D	30	(2)	2
1	Germans Māliņš		12/10/87	G	33		
6	Ruslan Mingazov	TKM	23/11/91	M	27	(2)	6
11	Armands Pētersons		05/12/90	A	1	(8)	1
24	Toms Rajeckis		16/10/94	D	1		
2	Renārs Rode		06/04/89	M	17	(1)	1
22	Ritvars Rugins		17/10/89	M	18		
14	Valērijs Šabala		12/10/94	A	17	(14)	11
10	Minori Sato	JPN	02/03/91	M	17	(7)	
3	Igors Savčenkovs		03/11/82	D	34	(1)	3
15	Julio Segundo	PAN	21/09/93	A	15	(9)	1
18	Kirils Ševeļovs		02/06/90	D	5	(2)	
5,4	Serhiy Shmatovalenko	UKR	15/01/89	D	9	(13)	1
23	Alans Siņeļņikovs		14/05/90	M	21	(7)	9
20	Andrejs Siņicins		30/01/91	D	5	(5)	4
12	Elvis Stuglis		04/07/93	A	1	(3)	

FK SPARTAKS JŪRMALA

Coach: Oļegs Blagonadeždins; (01/07/12) Arminas Narbekovas (LTU)
2007 • Sloka (2,000) • spartaks.lv

2012

25/03	Ventspils	a	2-3	*Mosquera, Twumasi*
31/03	Daugava Daugavpils	a	0-1	
07/04	Skonto	a	0-1	
14/04	Liepājas Metalurgs	a	2-1	*Twumasi, Mosquera*
18/04	Gulbene	h	3-1	*Twumasi, Mickevičs, Cortés*
21/04	Daugava Rīga	a	2-1	*Jemeļins (p), Cortés*
28/04	Metta/LU	h	3-1	*Cortés, Mosquera, Twumasi*
02/05	Jelgava	a	3-1	*Mosquera, Cortés, Twumasi*
06/05	Jūrmala	h	0-0	
13/05	Ventspils	h	2-0	*Bulvītis, og (Smirnovs)*
16/05	Daugava Daugavpils	h	2-2	*Jemeļins, Mosquera (p)*
26/05	Skonto	h	2-2	*Cortés, Jemeļins*
06/06	Liepājas Metalurgs	h	2-2	*Cortés, og (Mihadjuks)*
16/06	Gulbene	a	3-0	*Mickevičs, Jemeļins, Cortés*
20/06	Daugava Rīga	h	2-2	*Mosquera, Jemeļins*
27/06	Metta/LU	a	1-2	*Jemeļins*
01/07	Jelgava	a	2-3	*Kolomijcevs, Jemeļins (p)*
14/07	Ventspils	a	0-2	
19/07	Jūrmala	a	1-0	*Jemeļins (p)*
29/07	Daugava Daugavpils	a	2-3	*Castañeda, Agudelo*
04/08	Skonto	h	0-1	
11/08	Liepājas Metalurgs	a	1-2	*Jemeļins*
18/08	Gulbene	h	2-2	*Twumasi, Cortés*
22/08	Daugava Rīga	a	5-2	*Bulvītis, Cortés, Uļimbaševs, Morozs, Twumasi*
25/08	Metta/LU	h	3-4	*Mickevičs, Uļimbaševs, Agudelo*
31/08	Jelgava	h	2-0	*Cortés 2*
15/09	Jūrmala	h	4-2	*Twumasi 2, Bulvītis, Cortés*
19/09	Ventspils	h	0-3	
22/09	Daugava Daugavpils	h	0-3	
26/09	Skonto	a	0-0	
29/09	Liepājas Metalurgs	h	0-3	
06/10	Gulbene	a	1-0	*Jemeļins (p)*
20/10	Daugava Rīga	h	2-2	*Morozs, Jemeļins (p)*
28/10	Metta/LU	a	3-3	*Tarasovs, Agudelo, Bulvītis*
04/11	Jelgava	h	1-1	*Agudelo*
10/11	Jūrmala	a	3-0	*Morozs, Agudelo, Twumasi*

No	Name	Nat	DoB	Pos	Aps	(s)	Gls
13	Diego Agudelo	COL	30/03/92	A	15	(4)	5
19	Alexsandro	BRA	20/08/88	M	1		
13	Aleksandrs Briļs		05/02/89	A		(1)	
12	Konstantīns Budilovs		21/03/91	M	13	(5)	
3	Nauris Bulvītis		15/03/87	D	32		4
8	Deniels Calkovskis		23/01/93	M	4	(4)	
26	Andrea Casimirri	ITA	20/01/90	D		(2)	
20	Duvan Castañeda	COL	03/01/91	M	30		1
10	David Cortés	COL	01/05/92	A	22	(3)	12
26	Moustapha Dabo	SEN	27/02/86	A	3	(1)	
24	Vafoumbé Dosso	CIV	11/01/90	A		(1)	
29	Romāns Geiko		19/11/93	A	1	(2)	
10	Geraldo	BRA	20/03/91	A	1		
6	Jevgenijs Golovins		06/03/89	M	8	(2)	
8	Aleksandrs Gramovičs		25/03/89	M	9	(5)	
14	Joseph Gyawu	GHA	01/01/94	M	15	(3)	
28	Antons Jemeļins		19/02/84	D	33		11
11	Stanislavs Kolomijcevs		19/06/88	M	2	(7)	1
4	Maksims Lukaševičs		31/03/92	D		(1)	
5	Jose Luís Meza	COL	05/04/92	M	12	(4)	
21	Romāns Mickevičs		23/03/93	D	24	(5)	3
2,18	Viktors Morozs		30/07/80	M	23	(1)	3
13	Jairo Mosquera	COL	20/05/86	D	14		6
37	Pāvels Naglis		29/04/87	G	4	(1)	
30	Aleksandr Nevokshonov	RUS	29/12/84	G	4		
15	Andrejs Panasjuks		26/05/87	D	27		
23	Andrejs Pavlovs		22/02/79	G	13		
32	Vīts Rimkus		21/06/73	A	1		
9	Romāns Rjabinskis		19/05/89	M		(2)	
4	Carlos Rúa	COL	31/05/92	M	15		
2	Francisco Serna	COL	10/06/90	A	12	(2)	
27	Jānis Skābardis		27/07/87	G	8	(2)	
18	Yaroslav Sokol	UKR	03/01/91	M	2	(2)	
7	Deniss Tarasovs		14/10/90	M	13	(6)	1
17	Patrick Twumasi	GHA	09/05/94	A	22		10
4	Daniils Uļimbaševs		12/03/92	M	6	(7)	2
37	Aleksandrs Vlasovs		07/05/86	G	7	(1)	

FK VENTSPILS

Coach: Sergei Podpali (RUS); (15/05/12) Jurģis Pučinskis
1997 • OSC Ventspils (3,200) • fkventspils.lv
Major honours
Latvian League (4) 2006, 2007, 2008, 2011; Latvian Cup (6) 2003, 2004, 2005, 2007, 2011, 2013

2012

25/03	Spartaks	h	3-2	*Tukura, Tigirlas, Martínez*
01/04	Skonto	a	0-1	
15/04	Gulbene	h	3-0	*Sukhanov, Turkovs, Martínez*
18/04	Daugava Rīga	h	2-0	*Višņakovs, Tukura*
22/04	Metta/LU	a	6-1	*Smirnovs, Tukura, Martínez, Turkovs, Višņakovs 2*
28/04	Jelgava	h	0-1	
02/05	Jūrmala	a	2-1	*R Bespalovs, Višņakovs*
06/05	Daugava Daugavpils	h	1-2	*Turkovs*
13/05	Spartaks	a	0-2	
18/05	Skonto	h	0-0	
27/05	Liepājas Metalurgs	a	0-0	
07/06	Gulbene	a	5-0	*og (Ivanovs), Tigirlas, Turkovs, R Bespalovs, Svārups*
17/06	Daugava Rīga	a	4-1	*Smirnovs, Turkovs 2, Martínez*
21/06	Metta/LU	h	1-0	*Turkovs*
27/06	Jelgava	a	2-0	*Gilmanov, Tigirlas*
01/07	Jūrmala	h	1-1	*Turkovs (p)*
08/07	Daugava Daugavpils	a	0-3	
14/07	Spartaks	h	2-0	*Kurakins, Martínez*
30/07	Skonto	a	0-1	
05/08	Liepājas Metalurgs	h	1-0	*Kurakins*
11/08	Gulbene	a	2-1	*Turkovs, Martínez*
18/08	Daugava Rīga	h	5-0	*Saito 2, Paulius 2, Tarasovs*
22/08	Metta/LU	a	2-0	*Paulius, Saito (p)*
26/08	Jelgava	h	0-0	
01/09	Jūrmala	a	1-0	*Žatkins*
16/09	Daugava Daugavpils	h	1-0	*Paulius*
19/09	Spartaks	a	3-0	*Abdultaofik (p), Tarasovs, Kozlovs*
22/09	Skonto	h	1-0	*Saito*
26/09	Liepājas Metalurgs	a	0-1	
30/09	Gulbene	h	4-0	*Turkovs 2, Tarasovs, Martínez*
03/10	Liepājas Metalurgs	h	0-3	
06/10	Daugava Rīga	a	4-0	*Turkovs, Abdultaofik 2, Yanchuk*
21/10	Metta/LU	h	4-0	*Tarasovs, Žigajevs 2, Abdultaofik*
27/10	Jelgava	a	1-0	*Martínez*
04/11	Jūrmala	h	2-1	*Saito 2*
10/11	Daugava Daugavpils	a	0-0	

No	Name	Nat	DoB	Pos	Aps	(s)	Gls
22	Ahmed Abdultaofik	NGA	25/04/92	A	15	(7)	4
24	Christian Agoh	NGA	24/10/92	M	1	(3)	
57	Mikhail Badyautdinov	RUS	11/10/89	D	5	(4)	
5	Vitālijs Barinovs		04/05/93	D	4		
21	Romāns Bespalovs		18/10/88	A	7	(4)	2
23	Vladimirs Bespalovs		22/06/86	D	1		
2	Kaspars Dubra		20/12/90	D	17		
6	Igor Gilmanov	RUS	11/04/91	M	23	(5)	1
34	Raivis Hščanovičs		15/02/87	D	14	(2)	
8	Visvaldis Ignatāns		03/08/91	M	1	(1)	
9,21	Vladislavs Kozlovs		30/11/87	A	11	(7)	1
3	Antons Kurakins		01/01/90	D	33	(1)	2
13	Federico Martínez	URU	28/11/84	A	26	(7)	8
99	Vitālijs Meļņičenko		11/11/87	G	15		
28	Vladimirs Mukins		28/01/93	M		(1)	
21	Simonas Paulius	LTU	12/05/91	M	16		4
19	Yosuke Saito	JPN	07/04/88	A	12	(5)	6
4	Vitālijs Smirnovs		28/06/86	D	33		2
17	Eduard Sukhanov	RUS	22/04/91	M	9	(6)	1
33	Kaspars Svārups		28/01/94	A	3	(10)	1
23	Igors Tarasovs		16/10/88	M	16		4
10	Igor Tigirlas	MDA	24/02/84	M	17		3
32	Oļegs Timofejevs		28/11/88	D	33		
25	Michael Tukura	NGA	19/10/88	M	13	(1)	3
7	Danils Turkovs		17/02/88	A	23	(9)	12
30	Maksims Uvarenko		17/01/87	G	19		
9	Eduards Višņakovs		10/05/90	A	9	(5)	4
1	Aleksandrs Vlasovs		07/05/86	G	2		
20	Vadim Yanchuk	RUS	16/07/82	A	1	(7)	1
15	Oļegs Žatkins		13/04/87	M	7	(3)	1
10	Jurijs Žigajevs		14/11/85	M	10	(5)	2

Top goalscorers

18	Mamuka Gongadze (Daugava Daugavpils)
15	Yosuke Saito (Gulbene/Ventspils)
12	David Cortés (Spartaks)
	Danils Turkovs (Ventspils)
11	Tadas Labukas (Skonto)
	Valērijs Šabala (Skonto)
	Antons Jemeļins (Spartaks)
10	Stanley Ibe (Daugava Daugavpils)
	Vitālijs Ziļs (Daugava Rīga)
	Valērijs Afanasjevs (Liepājas Metalurgs)
	Vladimirs Kamešs (Liepājas Metalurgs)
	Mārtiņš Milaševičs (Metta/LU)
	Patrick Twumasi (Spartaks)

Promoted club

ILŪKSTES NSS
Coach: Alens Vinokurovs

2012 • NSS (1,000) • no website

SECOND LEVEL FINAL TABLE 2012

		Pld	W	D	L	F	A	Pts
1	SK Liepājas Metalurgs II	25	21	4	0	92	20	67
2	Ilūkstes NSS	26	18	3	5	87	38	57
3	Skonto FC II	26	17	5	4	56	32	56
4	BFC Daugava Daugavpils	26	15	7	4	49	20	52
5	Rīgas Futbola skola	26	16	3	7	62	33	51
6	FK Ventspils II	26	15	3	8	57	37	48
7	SFK Varavīksne Liepāja	26	11	7	8	47	45	40
8	Valmieras FK/BJSS	26	8	3	15	39	53	27
9	JPFS/FK Spartaks II	26	7	5	14	48	71	26
10	Rēzeknes BJSS	25	8	1	16	49	57	25
11	FS Metta II/ Salaspils SS	26	7	3	16	33	52	24
12	FK Auda Rīga	26	6	3	17	36	51	21
13	FK Tukums-2000/ TSS	26	4	1	21	28	116	13
14	FK Jelgava II	26	3	2	21	29	87	11

NB SK Liepājas Metalurgs II & Skonto FC II ineligible for promotion; Ilūkstes NSS promoted directly; BFC Daugava Daugavpils entered play-offs; SK Liepājas Metalurgs II - Rēzeknes BJSS match in round 26 cancelled.

PROMOTION/RELEGATION PLAY-OFFS
(14/11/12 & 18/11/12)
Daugava Rīga 1-0 BFC Daugava Daugavpils
BFC Daugava Daugavpils 1-3 Daugava Rīga
(Daugava Rīga 4-1)

Domestic cup: Latvijas Kauss 2012/13

FOURTH ROUND

(21/07/12)
BFC Daugava Daugavpils 0-3 Ventspils
Rīgas Futbola skola 0-11 FC Daugava Daugavpils

(22/07/12)
Auda Rīga 0-2 Spartaks Jūrmala
Ilūkstes 1-4 Gulbene
Jelgava 1-2 Liepājas Metalurgs
Metta/LU 1-7 Jūrmala
Tukums-2000/TSS 0-6 Skonto

(23/07/12)
Rīnūži/Strong 0-6 Daugava Rīga

QUARTER-FINALS

(16/03/13)
FC Daugava Daugavpils 2-1 Jūrmala *(Babatunde 35, Jermolajevs 49; Belov 90+2p)*

Liepājas Metalurgs 3-1 Skonto *(Hmizs 21, D Ikaunieks 40, Āsgärov 74; Sineļņikovs 9)*

(17/03/13)
Spartaks Jūrmala 1-1 Ventspils *(Solovjovs 62; Smirnovs 69) (aet; 5-6 on pens)*

(18/03/13)
Gulbene 0-7 Daugava Rīga *(Tamošauskas 13, Veliulis 22, Surač 45, 49, 61, Kozačuks 58, Klimavičius 73)*

SEMI-FINALS

(04/05/13)
Daugava Rīga 1-1 Liepājas Metalurgs *(Savénas 40p; Kačanovs 74og) (aet; 2-4 on pens)*

Ventspils 4-0 FC Daugava Daugavpils *(Žigajevs 16, 39, Abdultaofik 42, 70)*

FINAL

(18/05/13)
Skonto Stadium, Riga
FK VENTSPILS 2 *(Yanchuk 72, Dubra 93)*
SK LIEPĀJAS METALURGS 1 *(Jemeļins 42)*
(aet)
Referee: *Treimanis*
VENTSPILS: *Meļņičenko, Timofejevs, Dubra, Smirnovs, Kurakins, Sukhanov (Paulius 97), Tarasovs, Žigajevs, Turkovs (Yanchuk 62), Kozlovs, Abdultaofik (Ignatāns 113)*
LIEPĀJAS METALURGS: *Doroševs, Hmizs, Mežs, Zirņis, Jemeļins, I Šlampe, Prohorenkovs, Afanasjevs, Zuntners (J Ikaunieks 46), Šadčins (D Ikaunieks 95), Kalns*
Sent off: *Prohorenkovs (106)*

Ventspils show off the Latvian Cup

LIECHTENSTEIN
Liechtensteiner Fussballverband (FLV)

Address Landstrasse 149
FL-9494 Schaan
Tel +423 237 4747
Fax +423 237 4748
E-mail nfo@lfv.li
Website lfv.li

President Matthias Voigt
General secretary Roland Ospelt
Media officer Judith Frommelt
Year of formation 1934
National stadium Rheinpark, Vaduz
(7,789)

CLUBS

1 **FC Balzers**

2 **FC USV Eschen/Mauren**

3 **FC Ruggell**

4 **FC Schaan**

5 **FC Triesen**

6 **FC Triesenberg**

7 **FC Vaduz**

KEY:

● – UEFA Europa League

Ruggell
3

Mauren
2
Eschen

Schaan
4

Vaduz
7

Triesenberg
6

Triesen
5

0   5   10 km
0   10 miles

Balzers
1

Vaduz avenge penalty defeat

Defeated on penalties in the 2012 FL1 Cup final, by FC USV Eschen/Mauren, FC Vaduz avoided the same pitfall 12 months on, converting all three of their kicks while opponents FC Balzers missed all three of theirs to reclaim Liechtenstein's only domestic silverware for a record 41st time.

A change of national team coach proved beneficial to Liechtenstein in the 2014 FIFA World Cup qualifiers as René Pauritsch came in for Hans-Peter Zaugg and oversaw draws in his first two competitive outings following four straight defeats under his predecessor.

Capital club win 41st domestic cup

Vaduz, competing in the Swiss Challenge League (second tier), were firm favourites – as ever – to win the Liechtenstein Cup. Giorgio Contini's side gained due revenge on Eschen/Mauren for ending their 14-year winning run in the competition by defeating them 2-0 in the semi-finals before overcoming Balzers on penalties after a

Perfect shoot-out denies Balzers

keenly contested 1-1 draw at the Rheinparkstadion. Ivan Quintans, Robin Gubser and Thomas Beck all missed for Balzers while Amin Tighazoui, Nico Abegglen and Mario Sara all scored for Vaduz.

An 8-1 humbling at home by Bosnia & Herzegovina got Liechtenstein's World Cup

New national coach off to promising start

campaign off to a dismal start, and when that was followed by three further defeats, all by 2-0, Zaugg, a Swiss, was replaced by Pauritsch, an Austrian. Deploying record cap holder/goalscorer Mario Frick in an unfamiliar defensive role, the new man steered the team to a pair of 1-1 draws at home to Latvia and Slovakia.

European club competitions 2012/13

FC USV ESCHEN/ MAUREN

EUROPA LEAGUE

First qualifying round - FH Hafnarfjördur (ISL)

A 1-2 *Fässler (48)*
Büchel, Simma, Barandun, Christen, Batir, Manojlović, Dulundu (Kuster 88), Fässler, Istrefi (Ospelt 90+2), Fisch, Huber (Giger 46). Coach: Uwe Wegmann (GER)

H 0-1
Büchel, Simma, Barandun, Christen, Batir, Manojlović, Giger, Dulundu, Fässler, Istrefi, Fisch (Huber 73). Coach: Uwe Wegmann (GER)

Domestic cup: FL1 Cup 2012/13

FIRST ROUND

(21/08/12)
Vaduz II 1-0 Triesenberg II

(22/08/12)
Balzers III 2-4 Eschen/Mauren II
Eschen/Mauren III 0-5 Ruggell
Ruggell II 5-0 Triesen II

SECOND ROUND

(26/09/12)
Eschen/Mauren II 1-4 Schaan
Ruggell 0-0 Schaan Azzurri *(aet; 5-3 on pens)*

(02/10/12)
Vaduz II 0-3 Ruggell II

(03/10/12)
Triesen 2-1 Balzers II

QUARTER-FINALS

(06/11/12)
Ruggell II 0-5 Triesenberg

(07/11/12)
Ruggell 0-2 Balzers
Schaan 0-3 Vaduz
Triesen 0-5 Eschen/Mauren

SEMI-FINALS

(30/03/13)
Balzers 2-0 Triesenberg *(Beck 73, Akyer 78)*

(17/04/13)
Eschen/Mauren 0-2 Vaduz *(Abegglen 14, Tighazoui 66)*

FINAL

(01/05/13)
Rheinparkstadion, Vaduz
FC VADUZ 1 *(Guilherme 22)*
FC BALZERS 1 *(Akyer 31)*
(aet; 3-0 on pens)
Referee: *Hänni*
VADUZ: *Klaus, Oehri (Milosevic 80), Kaufmann, Sara, Burgmeier, Bader, Baron (Tighazoui 55), Cecchini, N Hasler (Cecchini 33), Abegglen, Guilherme*
BALZERS: *Zuvic, Nuhija, Rechsteiner, Caluori (Tinner 79), Gubser, Quintans, Hermann, Frick (Christen 16), Nsingui (Sen 71), Akyer, T Beck*

EUROPEAN QUALIFICATION 2013/14

EUROPA LEAGUE

Cup winner: FC Vaduz (first qualifying round)

NATIONAL TEAM

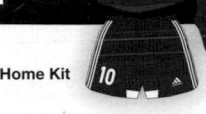 

Home Kit Away Kit

TOP FIVE ALL-TIME CAPS
Mario Frick (109); Martin Stocklasa (107);
Peter Jehle (99); Thomas Beck (90);
Daniel Hasler (78)

TOP FIVE ALL-TIME GOALS
Mario Frick (16); Franz Burgmeier (7);
Thomas Beck & Martin Stocklasa (5);
Michele Polverino (4)

Results 2012/13

Date	Opponent	H/A	Venue	Score	Scorers
14/08/12	Andorra	H	Vaduz	1-0	D Hasler (45)
07/09/12	Bosnia & Herzegovina (WCQ)	H	Vaduz	1-8	M Christen (61)
11/09/12	Slovakia (WCQ)	A	Bratislava	0-2	
12/10/12	Lithuania (WCQ)	H	Vaduz	0-2	
16/10/12	Latvia (WCQ)	A	Riga	0-2	
14/11/12	Malta	H	Vaduz	0-1	
06/02/13	Azerbaijan	N	Dubai (UAE)	0-1	
22/03/13	Latvia (WCQ)	H	Vaduz	1-1	Polverino (17)
04/06/13	Poland	A	Krakow	0-2	
07/06/13	Slovakia (WCQ)	H	Vaduz	1-1	M Büchel (13)

Appearances 2012/13

Coach:
Hans-Peter Zaugg (SUI) 02/12/52
/(29/10/12) René Pauritsch (AUT) 04/02/64

Player	DOB	Club	And	BIH	SVK	LTU	LVA	Mlt	Aze	LVA	Pol	SVK	Caps	Goals
Peter Jehle	22/01/82	Vaduz /Luzern (SUI)	G40	G	G			G	G	G	G46	G	99	-
Ivan Quintans	15/10/89	Balzers	D	D	D		D	D82	D85	s46	D81	D	11	-
Martin Stocklasa	29/05/79	St Gallen (SUI)	D	D	D	D	D	D			D	D	107	5
Daniel Kaufmann	22/12/90	Vaduz	D	D	D	D	D 60*	D67	D88		s46	D	15	-
Yves Oehri	15/03/87	Vaduz	D	D	D	D	D	D		D46	D46	D	37	-
Nicolas Hasler	04/05/91	Vaduz	M	M89	M	M74	M85	M90	M	M	M	M	21	-
Michele Polverino	26/09/84	Wolfsberg (AUT)	M	M	M	M	M	M	M	M			33	4
Thomas Beck	21/02/81	Balzers	M46	s71	M70	A		M67	M64	s72	M59	s90	90	5
Mario Frick	07/09/74	Balzers	M81							D	D46	D24	109	16
Franz Burgmeier	07/04/82	Vaduz	M	M	D	M	M	M	D	D			77	7
David Hasler	04/05/90	Vaduz	A90	A	M			A	M	M	M		24	1
Benjamin Büchel	04/07/89	Eschen/Mauren /Bournemouth (ENG)	s46			G							5	-
Philippe Erne	14/12/86	Vaduz /Balzers	s46	M71	M	M87	M80	s67	M 74*		M93		16	1
Mathias Christen	18/08/87	Eschen/Mauren /unattached /Singhtarua (THA)	s81	s46	A84		A	s82	A88	A72	A	A90	27	1
Vinzenz Flatz	05/07/94	Young Boys (SUI)	s90	M46	s84								3	-
Fabian Eberle	27/07/92	Balzers		s89	s70								4	-
Sandro Wieser	03/02/93	Hoffenheim (GER)				M84	M	M		M	M83	M95	17	-
Niklas Kieber	04/03/93	St Gallen (SUI)				s74	s80						2	-
Lucas Eberle	13/10/90	Balzers /Triesenberg				s84	s85	s67	s64				11	-
Philipp Ospelt	07/10/92	Eschen/Mauren				s87							1	-
Cengiz Biçer	11/12/87	Mersin (TUR)					G				s46		4	-
Andreas Christen	29/08/89	Balzers					s90		D85			M	5	-
Franz-Josef Vogt	30/10/85	Eschen/Mauren							s85		s46	s24	29	-
Seyhan Yildiz	30/04/89	Schaan							s85		s59		2	-
Burak Eris	17/07/89	Schaan							s88				1	-
Olcay Gür	27/03/91	Chur (SUI)							s88	s93	s81		3	-
Martin Büchel	19/02/87	Unterföhring (GER)									M	M	41	2
Robin Gubser	17/04/91	Balzers									s83	s95	2	-

LITHUANIA

Lietuvos futbolo federacija (LFF)

Address	Stadiono g. 2	**President**	Julius Kvedaras
	LT-02106 Vilnius	**General secretary**	Edvinas Eimontas
Tel	+370 5 2638741	**Media officer**	Vaiva Zizaitė
Fax	+370 5 2638740	**Year of formation**	1922
E-mail	v.zizaite@lff.lt	**National stadium**	S. Darius & S.
Website	lff.lt		Girėnas, Kaunas
			(8,248)

Pakruojis
⑦
⑤

Šiauliai

Gargždai
①
Klaipėda
②

④
Panevėžys

Tauragė
⑨

Vilnius

Marijampolė
⑧
⑥
③
⑩
Alytus

0   50   100 km
0   50 miles

A LYGA CLUBS

① **FK Atlantas**

② **FK Banga**

③ **FK Dainava**

④ **FK Ekranas**

⑤ **FK Kruoja**

⑥ **FK REO Vilnius**

⑦ **FC Šiauliai**

 ⑧ **FK Sūduva**

⑨ **FK Tauras**

 ⑩ **VMFD Žalgiris**

KEY:

● – UEFA Champions League

● – UEFA Europa League

● – Relegated club

Fifth straight title for Ekranas

Valdas Urbonas maintained his flawless record as coach of FK Ekranas, his fifth season in charge ending in exactly the same way as the previous four as he steered his hometown club to yet another A Lyga title.

There were no easy pickings, however, for Urbonas and his players as they were challenged all the way to the finishing line by a dogged VMFD Žalgiris, having to win each of their last four matches to resist the sustained challenge of the club from the capital and take the title by a solitary point.

Perennial A Lyga champions prevail on final day

Penalty kings Žalgiris retain Lithuanian Cup

Goalscoring record for Šiauliai striker Rimkevičius

Domestic league

Although there were two teams fewer in the 2012 A Lyga compared to 2011, the ten participants had to play four additional games, 36 in total. In the event, with the withdrawal after 24 rounds of FK REO Vilnius, Ekranas and Žalgiris actually played only 34. Both clubs won 25 of those matches, receiving another two 3-0 wins by forfeit, but in the final analysis it was a bona fide result against REO, Žalgiris's shock 1-0 derby defeat at home in June, that, to all intents and purposes, decided the title.

Ekranas lost their opening fixture, 3-1 at FK Sūduva, which handed Žalgiris the early initiative, but the defending champions responded with 11 successive victories, the first nine of them without conceding, including a 1-0 home win over Žalgiris. That result put the two teams level on points, and 11 days later Ekranas were out in front on their own. They would increase their advantage to eight points by August, at which juncture Žalgiris changed their coach, replacing Croatian Damir Petravić with Marek Zub – who had only just taken up a job as assistant coach to the Polish national team.

Zub's first game in charge was a 0-0 draw against the league leaders, but

when he led Žalgiris to a 2-1 home win in the title rivals' next meeting, Ekranas's advantage was down to just one point. Four matches remained, but while Žalgiris took maximum points from them, so too, under considerable pressure, did Ekranas, their fifth successive title – and seventh in all – being sealed on the final day as two goals from Vitalijus Kavaliauskas brought a 2-0 win at fourth-placed FK Kruoja. That double enabled Kavaliauskas to end the season as the champions' top scorer, but his ten-goal tally was dwarfed by that of Šiauliai striker Artūras Rimkevičius, who set a new A Lyga record by finding the net 35 times.

Domestic cup

Žalgiris had denied Ekranas a hat-trick of calendar-year doubles by beating them on penalties to win the 2012 Lithuanian Cup final, and they were at it again a year later to defeat Šiauliai on spot-kicks after an epic 3-3 draw in Kaunas. Šiauliai overcame Ekranas home and away in the semi-final but their valiant bid for a first major trophy was scuppered at the end of a marathon shoot-out when Deivydas Lunskis had his effort saved by Armantas Vitkauskas and Žalgiris defender Egidijus Vaitkūnas duly converted the winning kick. Šiauliai's defeat enabled Kruoja to

qualify for Europe – for the first time - at their expense, joining Žalgiris and Sūduva in the UEFA Europa League.

Europe

There was little cheer for the A Lyga's continental taskforce in 2012/13, although Ekranas's victory over Shamrock Rovers FC – UEFA Europa League group participants in 2011/12 – enabled them to get in some useful practice against heavyweight European opposition in the shape of RSC Anderlecht and FC Steaua Bucureşti. Not unexpectedly, they were heavily beaten in both ties.

National team

The national team's new head coach, Csaba László, did no better nor worse than expected in the first six matches of Lithuania's 2014 FIFA World Cup qualifying campaign. A victory over Liechtenstein and two 1-1 draws against Slovakia were offset by defeats to Greece (twice) and Bosnia & Herzegovina. The two ties that would arguably determine the success or failure of the Hungarian's first qualifying campaign – against neighbours Latvia – were still to come.

 # LITHUANIA

Domestic league: A Lyga 2012 final table

		Pld	Home					Away					Total					
			W	D	L	F	A	W	D	L	F	A	W	D	L	F	A	Pts
1	**FK Ekranas**	**36**	**15**	**3**	**0**	**51**	**9**	**12**	**4**	**2**	**32**	**16**	**27**	**7**	**2**	**83**	**25**	**88**
2	VMFD Žalgiris	36	14	2	2	47	0	13	4	1	33	13	27	6	3	80	22	87
3	FK Sūduva	36	12	3	3	40	14	9	4	5	37	23	21	7	8	77	37	70
4	FK Kruoja	36	13	1	4	32	15	7	4	7	24	16	20	5	11	56	31	65
5	FC Šiauliai	36	10	3	5	52	29	7	1	10	27	28	17	4	15	79	57	55
6	FK Banga	36	8	5	5	23	14	5	3	10	20	27	13	8	15	43	41	47
7	FK Dainava	36	6	3	9	20	28	3	2	13	22	43	9	5	22	42	71	32
8	FK Atlantas	36	4	4	10	21	38	3	2	13	12	54	7	6	23	33	92	27
9	FK Tauras	36	4	2	12	17	41	3	0	15	18	56	7	2	27	35	97	23
10	FK REO Vilnius	36	4	1	13	16	38	1	3	14	10	43	5	4	27	26	81	19

NB FK REO Vilnius withdrew after round 24 – their remaining matches were awarded as 0-3 defeats.

SEASON AT A GLANCE

EUROPEAN QUALIFICATION 2013/14

 Champion: FK Ekranas (second qualifying round)

 Cup winner: VMFD Žalgiris (first qualifying round)
FK Sūduva (first qualifying round)
FK Kruoja (first qualifying round)

Top scorer Artūras Rimkevičius (Šiauliai), 35 goals
Relegated club FK REO Vilnius
Promoted clubs None
Cup final VMFD Žalgiris 3-3 FC Šiauliai (aet; 8-7 on pens)

**A LYGA TEAM
OF THE SEASON**
(4-4-2)
Coach: Urbonas (Ekranas)

Zubas
(Ekranas)

Samusiovas (Ekranas) Skerla (Žalgiris) Dedura (Ekranas) Freidgeimas (Žalgiris)

Radavičius (Ekranas/ Žalgiris) Lukša (Ekranas) Rafael Ledesma (Sūduva) Vertelis (Ekranas)

Rimkevičius (Šiauliai) Biliński (Žalgiris)

 **PLAYER OF
THE SEASON
Artūras Rimkevičius**
(FC Šiauliai)

Long-standing concerns over the Šiauliai striker's inability to fulfil his potential were emphatically laid to rest in 2012 as the 29-year-old plundered 35 goals to shatter a 56-year-old Lithuanian top-flight record. The A Lyga's official player of the year ended the year with a brace of goals for the national team before signing a contract with national champions FK Ekranas.

 **NEWCOMER OF
THE SEASON
Emilijus Zubas**
(FK Ekranas)

The departure of Vytautas Černiauskas in 2010 had left a goalkeeping void at Ekranas, but Zubas filled it with a magnificent second season in 2012. Displaying maturity beyond his 22 years, he conceded just 23 goals in 32 appearances in the club's title triumph, earning himself a transfer to Polish Ekstraklasa side GKS Bełchatów and a debut for Lithuania.

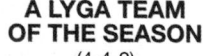

NATIONAL TEAM

Home Kit

Away Kit

TOP FIVE ALL-TIME CAPS
Andrius Skerla (84); **Deividas Šemberas** (82); **Tomas Danilevičius** (71); Aurelijus Skarbalius (65); **Žydrūnas Karčemarskas** (64)

TOP FIVE ALL-TIME GOALS
Tomas Danilevičius (19); Antanas Lingis (12); Edgaras Jankauskas & Robertas Poškus (10); Virginijus Baltušnikas (9)

Results 2012/13

15/08/12	FYROM	A	Skopje	0-1	
07/09/12	Slovakia (WCQ)	H	Vilnius	1-1	Žaliūkas (18)
11/09/12	Greece (WCQ)	A	Piraeus	0-2	
12/10/12	Liechtenstein (WCQ)	A	Vaduz	2-0	E Česnauskis (51, 75)
16/10/12	Bosnia & Herzegovina (WCQ)	A	Zenica	0-3	
14/11/12	Armenia	A	Yerevan	2-4	Rimkevičius (66, 82p)
22/03/13	Slovakia (WCQ)	A	Zilina	1-1	Šernas (19)
26/03/13	Albania	A	Tirana	1-4	Razulis (74)
07/06/13	Greece (WCQ)	H	Vilnius	0-1	

Appearances 2012/13

Coach: Csaba László (HUN) 13/02/64

			Mkd	SVK	GRE	LIE	BIH	Arm	SVK	Alb	GRE	Caps	Goals
Žydrūnas Karčemarskas	24/05/83	Gaziantepspor (TUR)	G46	G	G	G	G		G46			64	-
Vytautas Andriuškevičius	08/10/90	Lechia Gdańsk (POL)	D80	D			D			D85		8	-
Arūnas Klimavičius	05/10/82	Aktobe (KAZ)	D	D	D	D	D					41	3
Marius Žaliūkas	10/11/83	Leeds (ENG)	D	D	D	D	D					20	1
Valdemar Borovskij	02/05/84	Sūduva /Daugava Rīga (LVA)	D	D	D46		D				D	9	-
Edgaras Česnauskis	05/02/84	Rostov (RUS)	M62	M58	M	M		M	M	M	M	43	5
Mindaugas Panka	01/05/84	Ruch (POL)	M				M85	M	M		M	24	-
Ramūnas Radavičius	20/01/81	Žalgiris	M	M		M91	M46					21	1
Saulius Mikoliūnas	02/05/84	Arsenal Kyiv (UKR) /Sevastopol (UKR)	M46	M75	M	D		D46	D	s85	D73	58	3
Tomas Danilevičius	18/07/78	Juve Stabia (ITA)	A72			A87						71	19
Darvydas Šernas	22/07/84	Zagłębie Lubin (POL) /Gaziantepspor (TUR)	A79	A	A56	s58	s46		A90			32	5
Giedrius Arlauskis	01/12/87	Rubin (RUS)	s46					G46	s46			8	-
Deividas Česnauskis	30/06/81	Bakı (AZE)	s46	s67	s46	M58				M	s86	54	4
Deividas Šemberas	02/08/78	Alania (RUS)	s62	M	M	M	M		D			82	-
Tadas Labukas	10/01/84	Skonto (LVA)	s72	s75 96*			A66					18	-
Arturas Rimkevičius	14/04/83	Šiauliai	s79	s56	s07	s06	s61					7	3
Tadas Kijanskas	06/09/85	Korona (POL)	s80			D	D	s59	D		D	24	-
Gediminas Vičius	05/07/85	Shakhter (KAZ)		M67	M							6	-
Arvydas Novikovas	18/12/90	Hearts (SCO)		s58	s76	A	A		s69	M		12	-
Egidijus Vaitkūnas	08/08/88	Žalgiris			D							5	-
Andrius Velička	05/04/79	Olimpik-Şüvälan (AZE)			A76							27	2
Marius Stankevičius	15/07/81	Lazio (ITA)				s91	M	D			M	63	5
Linas Pilibaitis	05/04/85	Győr (HUN)					s85	M61		M64		28	-
Aurimas Vilkaitis	11/02/93	Lazio (ITA)						D59				1	-
Karolis Chvedukas	21/04/91	Sūduva						M72				1	-
Fedor Černych	21/05/91	Naftan (BLR) /Dnepr (BLR)						A56		A46		2	-
Deivydas Matulevičius	08/04/89	Pandurii (ROU)						A	A	A	A86	8	-
Ernestas Šetkus	25/05/85	Botev Plovdiv (BUL) /Gomel (BLR)						s46		G61		7	-
Georgas Freidgeimas	10/08/87	Žalgiris						s46		D		4	-
Vytautas Lukša	14/08/84	Ekranas /Polonia Warszawa (POL)						s56	s90			14	-
Tadas Eliošius	01/03/90	Sūduva /Atlantas						s72			s86	5	-
Tomas Mikuckis	13/01/83	SKA-Energia (RUS)							D		D	7	-
Kęstutis Ivaškevičius	17/04/85	Bnei Yehuda (ISR)							M		M86	25	-

Appearances 2012/13 (contd.)

			Mkd	SVK	GRE	LIE	BIH	Arm	SVK	Alb	GRE	Caps	Goals
Mindaugas Kalonas	28/02/84	Rävan (AZE)							M69	s64	M	38	2
Markus Palionis	12/05/87	Paderborn (GER)								D		2	-
Andrius Bartkus	21/01/86	Atlantas								D73		1	-
Evaldas Razulis	03/04/86	Atlantas								s46		1	1
Emilijus Zubas	10/07/90	Bełchatów (POL)								s61	G	2	-
Martynas Dapkus	16/02/93	H. Nazareth Illit (ISR)								s73		1	-
Artūras Žulpa	10/06/90	Žalgiris									s73	1	-

European club competitions 2012/13

FK EKRANAS

Second qualifying round - Shamrock Rovers FC (IRL)
A 0-0
Zubas, Urdinov, Lukša, Kučys, Kymantas, Varnas, Dedura, Andjelković (Norvilas 90+2), Vertelis, Tomkevičius, Samusiovas. Coach: Valdas Urbonas (LTU)
H 2-1 Andjelković (45+1), Kymantas (63)
Zubas, Urdinov, Lukša (Kavaliauskas 90), Kučys, Kymantas (Girdvainis 87), Varnas, Dedura, Andjelković, Vertelis (Umeh 80), Tomkevičius, Samusiovas. Coach: Valdas Urbonas (LTU)

Third qualifying round - RSC Anderlecht (BEL)
A 0-5
Zubas, Urdinov, Lukša, Kučys, Kymantas (Buinickij 60), Varnas, Dedura, Andjelković, Vertelis (Kavaliauskas 83), Tomkevičius (Gleveckas 90+2), Samusiovas. Coach: Valdas Urbonas (LTU)
H 0-6
Zubas, Urdinov (Umeh 70), Lukša, Kučys, Buinickij (Kauneckas 28), Kymantas (Kavaliauskas 60), Varnas, Dedura, Andjelković, Vertelis, Samusiovas. Coach: Valdas Urbonas (LTU)
Red card: Zubas 25

Play-offs - FC Steaua Bucureşti (ROU)
H 0-2
Kauneckas, Urdinov, Lukša, Kučys (Girdvainis 78), Buinickij (Varnas 63), Kymantas (Norvilas 76), Dedura, Andjelković, Vertelis, Tomkevičius, Samusiovas. Coach: Valdas Urbonas (LTU)
A 0-3
Zubas, Urdinov, Lukša, Kučys, Kymantas (Markevičius 77), Varnas (Buinickij 89), Dedura, Andjelković, Vertelis (Kavaliauskas 70), Tomkevičius, Girdvainis. Coach: Valdas Urbonas (LTU)

VMFD ŽALGIRIS

Second qualifying round - FC Admira Wacker Mödling (AUT)
H 1-1 Radavičius (72)
Vitkauskas, Skerla, Radavičius, Vaitkūnas, Elliot, Švrljuga (Biliński 46), Perić, Pek, Šilėnas (Komolov 84), Nagumanov (Grgurović 83), Kuklys. Coach: Damir Petravić (CRO)
A 1-5 Kuklys (22)
Vitkauskas, Skerla, Freidgeimas, Jankauskas, Radavičius, Vaitkūnas (Švrljuga 42), Elliot, Perić, Pek, Biliński (Komolov 74), Kuklys (Nagumanov 57). Coach: Damir Petravić (CRO)

FK SŪDUVA

First qualifying round - FC Daugava Daugavpils (LVA)
H 0-1
Davidovs, Radžius, Borovskij, Lukšys (Beniušis 61), Eliošius, Leimonas, Chvedukas, Loginov, Urbšys (Šoblinskas 68), Slavickas, Rafael Ledesma. Coach: Virginijus Liubšys (LTU)
A 3-2 Šoblinskas (8), Rafael Ledesma (45+1, 84)
Davidovs, Beniušis, Eliošius (Breivė 83), Leimonas, Chvedukas, Loginov, Urbšys, Slavickas, Urba (Lukšys 78), Rafael Ledesma (Lasevičius 90+1), Šoblinskas. Coach: Darius Gvildys (LTU)

Second qualifying round - FK Vojvodina (SRB)
A 1-1 Beniušis (56)
Davidovs, Radžius (Urba 79), Lukšys, Beniušis (Borovskij 71), Eliošius (Urbšys 68), Leimonas, Chvedukas, Loginov, Slavickas, Ledesma, Šoblinskas. Coach: Darius Gvildys (LTU)
H 0-4
Davidovs, Radžius, Borovskij (Breive 83), Lukšys, Tad Eliošius (Šoblinskas 46), Leimonas, Chvedukas, Loginov, Slavickas, Urba (Beniušis 55), Rafael Ledesma. Coach: Darius Gvildys (LTU)

FC ŠIAULIAI

First qualifying round - FC Levadia Tallinn (EST)
A 0-1
Jurevičius, Juvenal, Bartkus (Hvorosteanov 69), Kozlovs, Rimkevičius, Kirhners, Lunskis, Cesanelli, Rimavičius, Vėževičius (Jasaitis 83). Coach: Gediminas Jarmalavičius (LTU)
H 2-1 Rimkevičius (40p), Kozlovs (80)
Jurevičius, Juvenal (Urbelis 87), Bartkus, Kozlovs, Rimkevičius, Kirhners, Lunskis, Birškys (Eliošius 67), Cesanelli, Rimavičius, Vėževičius (Jasaitis 83). Coach: Gediminas Jarmalavičius (LTU)

Domestic league club-by-club

FK ATLANTAS
Coach: Romualdas Norkus;
(22/07/12) Sébastien Roques (FRA)
1962 • Centrinis (4,940); Miesto, Gargzdai (3,250) •
atlantas.lt
Major honours
Lithuanian Cup (2) 2001, 2003

2012

17/03	Žalgiris	a	0-7
25/04	Dainava	h	0-0
01/04	Banga	a	1-0 *Razulis*
07/04	REO	h	0-0
14/04	Kruoja	a	0-1
17/04	Sūduva	a	0-6
21/04	Ekranas	h	0-3
28/04	Tauras	a	0-0
01/05	Šiauliai	a	I-5 *Kymantas*
07/05	Žalgiris	h	0-1
12/05	Dainava	a	0-1
18/05	Banga	h	1-1 *Peištaras*
26/05	REO	a	0-3
13/06	Sūduva	h	0-4
17/06	Ekranas	a	0-2
21/06	Kruoja	a	1-5 *Vilavičius*
26/06	Tauras	h	0-5
29/06	Šiauliai	h	1-2 *Taciano*
22/07	Žalgiris	a	1-3 *Gordej*
28/07	Dainava	h	2-1 *Smith, Lagator*
03/08	Banga	a	0-1
11/08	REO	h	4-2 *Basić, Lagator 3*
18/08	Kruoja	h	2-1 *Lagator (p), Razulis*
21/08	Sūduva	a	0-2
26/08	Ekranas	h	1-2 *Lagator*
01/09	Tauras	a	1-1 *N'Diaye*
13/09	Šiauliai	a	0-6
18/09	Banga	h	3-4 *Kruša, Lagator 2*
24/09	Dainava	a	2-1 *Razulis, Lagator*
01/10	Banga	h	2-2 *Lagator, Taciano*
06/10	REO	a	3-0 (w/o)
20/10	Kruoja	a	0-5
27/10	Sūduva	h	1-5 *Laukžemis*
02/11	Ekranas	a	2-6 *Razulis, Žukauskas*
11/11	Tauras	h	4-1 *Khadraoui, Kruša 2, Lagator*

No	Name	Nat	DoB	Pos	Aps	(s)	Gls
27	Ernestas Alekna		11/04/90	M	6	(1)	
5	Davydas Arlauskis		18/11/86	D	18	(1)	
19	Modestas Atmanavičius		06/06/87	D		(1)	
13	Karolis Atutis		18/04/91	M	3	(5)	
29	Aleksandr Babachin		06/01/90	D	3		
10	Žilvinas Banys		25/02/86	M	2		
29	Petar Basić	CRO	27/07/84	M	11		1
8	Ivo Begić	CRO	24/03/82	D	18		
14	Markas Beneta		08/07/93	M	5		
27	Franck Boissier	FRA	13/05/93	M	1	(3)	
31	Marjan Choruži		29/03/80	M	1	(1)	
14	Osvaldas Derinsis		28/10/95	D		(1)	
23	Artiomas Drozdovas		25/05/92	M		(1)	
12	Mantas Gintalas		04/04/88	G	11		
15	Denis Gordej		20/07/89	D	29		1
26	Giga Imnadze	GEO	08/07/87	M	4	(9)	
34	Artem Jerošenko		06/01/91	M	11	(0)	
11	Filimonas Jesipovas		08/11/94	M		(1)	
18	Deividas Kapustas		06/02/93	M	7	(1)	
28	Walid Khadraoui	FRA	31/10/87	M	15		1
39	Gediminas Kruša		31/10/90	M	9	(3)	3
9	Žilvinas Kymantas		18/01/90	M	13		1
9	Tino Lagator	CRO	14/09/87	A	13		11
11	Karolis Laukžemis		13/03/92	M	17	(11)	1
25	Maximir Luburic	CAN	14/09/89	G	5		
10	Ramūnas Macežinskas		11/10/88	A		(1)	
18	Edgar Mastianica		26/10/88	M	18	(1)	
13	Malik N'Diaye	FRA	17/08/87	D	7	(1)	1
21	Deivydas Peištaras		28/02/92	M	1	(3)	1
37	Mantas Perepliotovas		15/10/92	D	1		
31	Ernestas Razonas		09/04/92	M		(4)	
19	Evaldas Razulis		03/04/86	A	23		4
2	Julian Rullier	FRA	04/04/90	D	14		
6	Povilas Šarūnas		14/11/85	D	2		
7	Valdas Šaulėnas		06/03/91	M		(1)	
4	Dmitrij Šiškin		17/07/87	D	13	(1)	
16	Nathan Smith	CAN	29/12/93	M	1	(4)	1
1	Giedrius Štreimikis		14/10/76	G	18		
30	Mantas Šumskis		18/08/82	G	1	(1)	
2	Donatas Surblys		15/07/87	M	6	(1)	
3	Taciano	BRA	04/08/87	D	7	(4)	2
24	Evaldas Užkuraitis		29/06/85	D	12	(1)	
35	Justinas Vilavičius		20/12/92	M	20	(4)	1
4	Gabrielius Zagurskas		04/07/95	D	5	(4)	
35	Edgaras Žarskis		04/08/91	M	3	(9)	
20	Erikas Žilinskas		20/03/93	M	8		
14	Vygantas Zubavičius		14/11/84	M	7	(1)	
7	Gerardas Žukauskas		07/07/94	M	10	(4)	

FK BANGA
Coach: Vaidotas Žutautas
1966 • Miesto (3,250) • fkbanga.lt

2012

10/03	Žalgiris	h	1-2 *Gailius*
18/03	Dainava	a	0-0
25/03	REO	h	2-2 *Tatiefang, Staponka*
01/04	Atlantas	h	0-1
06/04	Kruoja	a	0-1
14/04	Sūduva	h	0-1
18/04	Ekranas	a	0-3
22/04	Tauras	h	1-0 *Nikabadze*
27/04	Šiauliai	a	2-1 *Nikabadze, Grigaltis*
03/05	Žalgiris	a	0-2
06/05	Dainava	h	2-1 *Kura, Mgeladze*
11/05	REO	a	0-1
18/05	Atlantas	a	1-1 *Nikabadze*
27/05	Kruoja	h	1-1 *Staponka*
12/06	Ekranas	h	1-1 *Mgeladze*
16/06	Tauras	a	2-3 *Nikabadze, Staponka*
19/06	Sūduva	a	1-3 *Nikabadze*
26/06	Šiauliai	h	0-1
29/06	Žalgiris	h	0-0
20/07	Dainava	a	4-0 *Staponka 2, Alaverdashvili 2*
27/07	REO	h	2 1 *Kura, Staponka*
03/08	Atlantas	h	1-0 *Staponka*
10/08	Kruoja	h	1-0 *Ivanauskas*
17/08	Sūduva	h	0-0
26/08	Tauras	h	4-0 *Alaverdashvili 2, Banys, Butkus*
01/09	Šiauliai	a	1-0 *Alaverdashvili*
11/09	Žalgiris	a	0-1
20/09	Dainava	h	5-0 *Staponka, Alaverdashvili, Tatiefang 2, Masiuk*
23/09	REO	a	3-0 (w/o)
29/09	Ekranas	a	0-2
01/10	Atlantas	a	2-2 *Alaverdashvili 2*
06/10	Kruoja	a	1-2 *Borusas*
21/10	Sūduva	a	0-3
27/10	Ekranas	h	0-2
03/11	Tauras	a	3-1 *Alaverdashvili 2, Borusas*
11/11	Šiauliai	h	2-1 *Banys, Alaverdashvili*

No	Name	Nat	DoB	Pos	Aps	(s)	Gls
20	Giorgi Alaverdashvili	GEO	21/11/87	A	15		11
15	Žilvinas Banys		25/02/86	M	14		2
37	Mindaugas Bitinas		24/12/92	D	8	(2)	
90	Rokas Borusas		03/01/90	D	7	(11)	2
17	Andrius Butkus		05/04/91	M	3	(9)	1
15	Gytis Gailius		20/11/90	M	5	(5)	1
11	Evaldas Grigaitis		28/09/87	M	23	(1)	1
91	Ernestas Grigiun		11/01/91	D	8	(1)	
13	Mantas Gudanskas		04/01/89	D	21	(9)	
12	Aleksandras Ivanauskas		05/12/87	D	24		1
18	Andrius Jokšas		12/01/79	D	28		
10	Mika Kura		01/04/89	M	33	(1)	2
16	Mandinho	BRA	28/01/84	M	18	(9)	
33	Andrius Marcinkevičius		07/01/93	A		(6)	
9	Roman Masiuk	UKR	15/05/92	M	19	(5)	1
7	Nika Mgeladze	GEO	20/12/85	D	31		2
1	Vitaliy Myrniy	UKR	03/04/92	G	35		
27	Giorgi Nikabadze	GEO	10/01/91	A	11	(14)	5
5	Anatol Ostap	MDA	22/11/79	M	2	(4)	
32	Deividas Padaigis		02/02/86	D	31		
38	Alvydas Ruškys		05/06/90	M		(4)	
11	Aurelijus Staponka		09/11/83	A	28	(1)	8
55	Moshe Sulimanov	ISR	11/01/91	M	6	(5)	
8	Serge Tatiefang	CMR	25/08/87	M	20	(6)	3
4	Sigitas Urbys		07/11/95	M		(1)	
28	Simonas Urbys		07/11/95	M	3	(1)	

FK DAINAVA
Coach: Rimvydas Kochanauskas
2011 • Centrinis (4,000); ARVI Arena,
Marijampole (2,500) • fkdainava.lt

2012

11/03	REO	h	3-2 *Mikaitis, Baranovskij, Buinickij (p)*
18/03	Banga	h	0-0
25/03	Atlantas	a	0-0
30/03	Kruoja	h	0-0
07/04	Sūduva	a	1-3 *Biržinis*
15/04	Ekranas	h	0-1
18/04	Tauras	a	4-2 *Buinickij, Stankevičius, Kochanauskas, Biržinis*
22/04	Šiauliai	h	1-0 *Kochanauskas*
29/04	Žalgiris	a	0-4
06/05	Banga	a	1-2 *Buinickij*
12/05	Atlantas	h	1-0 *Buinickij*
17/05	Kruoja	a	0-2
21/05	REO	a	0-1
25/05	Sūduva	h	2-4 *Buinickij 2*
09/06	Tauras	h	3-1 *Buinickij 3*
15/06	Šiauliai	a	2-4 *Buinickij (p), Cibulskas*
20/06	Ekranas	a	2-3 *Kochanauskas, Buinickij*
25/06	Žalgiris	h	1-3 *Kochanauskas*
30/06	REO	h	2-0 *Blinovas, Biržinis*
20/07	Banga	h	0-4
28/07	Atlantas	a	1-2 *Strauka*
04/08	Kruoja	h	1-2 *Sakalis*
12/08	Sūduva	a	2-3 *Stankevičius, Sakalis*
19/08	Ekranas	h	2-2 *Sakalin, og (Cemisianas)*
23/08	Tauras	a	1-3 *Sakalis 2, Biržinis*
26/08	Šiauliai	h	0-2
02/09	Žalgiris	a	0-3
15/09	REO	a	3-0 (w/o)
20/09	Banga	a	0-5
24/09	Atlantas	h	1-2 *Sakalis*
29/09	Kruoja	a	0-2
06/10	Sūduva	h	0-3
21/10	Ekranas	a	0-3
28/10	Tauras	h	2-0 *Strauka, Baranauskas*
03/11	Šiauliai	a	3-3 *Baranauskas, Sakalis (p), Strauka*
11/11	Žalgiris	h	1-2 *Cibulskas*

No	Name	Nat	DoB	Pos	Aps	(s)	Gls
20	Lukas Baranauskas		02/12/72	A	3	(9)	2
2	Valentin Baranovskij		15/10/86	M	18		1
19	Nerijus Bartkevičius		13/11/85	M	32	(2)	
17	Martynas Biržinis		22/03/79	M	23	(5)	4
5	Ruslanas Blinovas		29/07/82	D	24	(7)	1
26	Aurimas Botyrius		05/07/91	D	1	(1)	
91	Alvaras Bražinskas		07/11/90	G	18		
11	Arsenij Buinickij		10/10/85	A	19		11
18	Ervinas Chvesko		02/02/94	D	1	(3)	
16	Darius Cibulskas		23/05/88	M	34		2
44	Aurimas Dubickas		20/08/90	G	12		
30	Povilas Gavėnas		07/07/92	M	1	(7)	
27	Dominykas Grižas		24/04/92	M		(1)	
14	Nerijus Kavaliauskas		27/10/88	D	9	(12)	
23	Ruslan Kliukoitis		02/07/83	D	33		
8	Lukas Kochanauskas		28/11/84	A	12	(3)	4
13	Teisis Loskauskas		05/04/95	M	1	(2)	
3	Arnas Mikaitis		21/07/92	D	10		1
91	Donatas Mikučionis		23/04/91	G	1		
1	Aurimas Miniauskas		02/12/79	D	18	(11)	
7	Marius Miškinis		19/02/92	M	5		
5	Simonas Paulius		12/05/91	D	15		
24	Tomas Rakauskas		17/12/94	M		(1)	
13	Rinaldo	BRA	23/02/86	M	2	(1)	
4	Vaidotas Rutkauskas		09/03/85	D	34	(1)	
9	Paulius Sakalis		03/06/87	A	17	(5)	7
20	Marius Šarkelis		24/05/86	M		(2)	
12	Renaldas Stankevičius		04/04/91	M	18	(8)	2
10	Mindaugas Strauka		29/06/90	M	17	(2)	3
99	Gintaras Štreimikis		14/10/76	G	6		
7	Giedrius Vaitulevičius		24/10/85	A	1		
21	Titas Vitukynas		23/10/94	M	1	(1)	

FK EKRANAS

Coach: Valdas Urbonas
1964 • Aukštaitija (4,000); PFA (1,089) • fkekranas.lt
Major honours
Lithuanian League (7) 1993, 2005, 2008, 2009,
2010, 2011, 2012;
Lithuanian Cup (4) 1998, 2000, 2010, 2011

2012

11/03	Sūduva	a	1-3	Lukša
17/03	REO	a	1-0	Radavičius (p)
25/03	Tauras	h	5-0	Andjelković, Vertelis, Savénas, Lukša, Samusiovas
31/03	Šiauliai	a	1-0	Fofana
07/04	Žalgiris	h	1-0	Savénas
15/04	Dainava	a	1-0	Savénas
18/04	Banga	h	3-0	Kavaliauskas, Radavičius 2 (2p)
21/04	Atlantas	a	3-0	Radavičius, Savénas, Velička
29/04	Kruoja	h	1-0	Kučys
02/05	Sūduva	h	2-0	Velička, Vertelis
06/05	REO	h	6-1	Radavičius 3, Kučys, Savénas, Kavaliauskas
12/05	Tauras	a	2-1	Savénas, Velička
16/05	Šiauliai	h	2-2	Andjelković, Savénas
25/05	Žalgiris	a	0-0	
12/06	Banga	a	1-1	Velička
17/06	Atlantas	h	2-0	Varnas, Lukša
20/06	Dainava	h	3-2	Samusiovas, Umeh, Varnas
25/06	Kruoja	a	1-1	Velička
01/07	Sūduva	a	3-2	Velička 3
21/07	REO	h	3-0	(w/o)
28/07	Tauras	h	5-0	Kymantas, Kavaliauskas 2, Kučys, Buinickij
05/08	Šiauliai	a	4-3	Vertelis, Dedura, Buinickij 2
12/08	Žalgiris	h	0-0	
19/08	Dainava	a	2-2	Vertelis, Markevičius
26/08	Atlantas	a	2-1	Buinickij, Tomkevičius
03/09	Kruoja	h	2-0	Kučys, Buinickij (p)
16/09	Sūduva	h	2-2	Dedura, Markevičius
18/09	REO	h	3-0	(w/o)
22/09	Tauras	a	2-0	Kučys, Kavaliauskas
26/09	Banga	a	2-0	Urdinov, Lukša
30/09	Šiauliai	h	3-0	Kavaliauskas, Lukša, Vertelis
07/10	Žalgiris	a	1-2	Umeh
21/10	Dainava	h	3-0	Lukša, Andjelković, Varnas
27/10	Banga	a	2-0	Vertelis, Buinickij
02/11	Atlantas	h	6-2	Vertelis 2, Kavaliauskas 2 (1p), Samusiovas, Lukša
11/11	Kruoja	a	2-0	Kavaliauskas 2 (1p)

No	Name	Nat	DoB	Pos	Aps	(s)	Gls
31	Marko Andjelković	SRB	12/10/84	M	25	(1)	3
71	Andrius Arlauskas		16/01/86	M	1	(3)	
2	Edgaras Baranauskas		12/03/93	D	3	(4)	
13	Arsenij Buinickij		10/10/85	A	12	(3)	6
20	Ignas Dedura		01/06/78	D	31		2
24	Adama Fofana	CIV	20/12/89	A	3	(8)	1
93	Edvinas Girdvainis		17/01/93	D	3	(1)	
3	Dainius Gleveckas		05/03/77	D	7	(2)	
12	Tadas Kauneckas		31/03/86	G	1		
8	Vitalijus Kavaliauskas		02/07/83	A	12	(13)	10
10	Aurimas Kučys		22/02/81	M	27	(1)	5
18	Žilvinas Kymantas		16/01/90	A	5	(1)	1
5	Vytautas Lukša		14/08/84	M	28	(4)	7
28	Tadas Markevičius		10/04/85	A		(15)	2
7	Jevgenij Moroz		20/01/90	M		(4)	
23	Dovydas Norvilas		05/04/93	M	2	(3)	
88	Rytis Pilotas		17/12/92	D	2	(2)	
7	Ramūnas Radavičius		20/01/81	M	18		7
9	Arnas Ribokas		14/01/93	M	3	(8)	
78	Mantas Samusiovas		08/09/78	D	31		3
82	Mantas Savénas		27/08/82	M	13		7
27	Rokas Stanulevičius		10/02/94	M		(1)	
77	Giedrius Tomkevičius		09/02/84	D	25	(2)	1
32	Uchenna Umeh	NGA	10/10/91	A	12	(5)	2
4	Yani Urdinov	MKD	28/03/91	D	24	(1)	1
19	Egidijus Varnas		31/07/75	A	15	(5)	3
17	Andrius Velička		05/04/79	A	15	(2)	8
70	Aurimas Vertelis		06/09/86	M	23	(6)	8
21	Emilijus Zubas		10/07/90	G	33		

FK KRUOJA

Coach: Aidas Dambrauskas
2001 • City Pakruojis (2,000); PFA, Panevezys (1,089)
• fkkruoja.lt

2012

10/03	Tauras	h	1-0	Miklinevičius
18/03	Šiauliai	a	1-2	Zelmikas
24/03	Žalgiris	h	0-1	
30/03	Dainava	a	0-0	
06/04	Banga	h	1-0	Miklinevičius
14/04	Atlantas	a	1-0	Veliulis
17/04	REO	h	2-1	Zhygalov, Žulpa
21/04	Sūduva	h	2-1	Žulpa 2
29/04	Ekranas	a	0-1	
02/05	Tauras	a	4-0	Juška, Čistjakovs, Zhygalov, Filatov
05/05	Šiauliai	h	0-4	
13/05	Žalgiris	a	2-0	Petrauskas, Dyakiv
17/05	Dainava	h	2-0	Zhygalov, Veliulis
27/05	Banga	a	1-1	Zhygalov
10/06	REO	a	2-2	Žulpa, Zhygalov
16/06	Sūduva	a	1-0	Zhygalov
21/06	Atlantas	h	5-1	Pocevičius, Zhygalov 2, Juška, Slavickas
25/06	Ekranas	h	1-1	og (Dedura)
30/06	Tauras	h	3-1	Zhygalov, Juška 2
22/07	Šiauliai	a	0-1	
30/07	Žalgiris	h	0-1	
04/08	Dainava	a	2-1	og (Rutkauskas), Žulpa
10/08	Banga	a	0-1	
18/08	Atlantas	a	1-2	Zhygalov
21/08	REO	h	3-0	(w/o)
25/08	Sūduva	h	2-1	Miklinevičius (p), Zelmikas
03/09	Ekranas	a	0-2	
15/09	Tauras	a	4-0	Veikutis, Veliulis, Zelmikas, Čistjakovs
18/09	Šiauliai	h	1-0	Mačiulis
22/09	Žalgiris	a	1-2	Zhygalov
29/09	Dainava	h	2-0	Zhygalov (p), Žulpa
06/10	Banga	a	2-1	Veliulis, Zhygalov
20/10	Atlantas	h	5-0	Žulpa, Zhygalov (p), Savastas, Petrauskas, Mačiulis
29/10	REO	a	3-0	(w/o)
04/11	Sūduva	a	1-1	Zhygalov
11/11	Ekranas	h	0-2	

No	Name	Nat	DoB	Pos	Aps	(s)	Gls
11	Vadym Antipov	UKR	08/09/88	M	9	(4)	
25	Maxym Bilyk	UKR	10/06/90	D	14	(1)	
14	Valerijs Čistjakovs	LVA	27/11/92	M	14	(17)	2
60	Rostislav Dyakiv	UKR	17/09/90	M	1	(16)	1
16	Māris Eltermanis	LVA	16/10/81	G	33		
6	Mykyta Filatov	UKR	24/06/92	M	2	(2)	1
22	Mantas Galdikas		22/06/89	G		(1)	
5	Karolis Jarmalavičius		12/01/91	D	4	(6)	
17	Gvidas Juška		17/08/82	A	12	(7)	4
2	Giedrius Kvedaras		09/07/91	G	1		
77	Roman Kysliakov	UKR	02/05/88	M		(1)	
11	Nerijus Mačiulis		01/04/83	M	9	(2)	2
55	Konstyantyn Matsion	UKR	09/02/82	D	25		
24	Tomas Miklinevičius		09/02/79	M	24		3
28	Donatas Petrauskas		16/03/84	M	26	(1)	2
4	Valdas Pocevičius		16/05/86	D	17	(1)	1
19	Linas Savastas		24/01/86	M	3	(21)	1
84	Alfredas Skroblas		11/03/84	D	28		
99	Giedrius Slavickas		03/10/82	M	19		1
28	Donatas Strockis		23/03/87	M	7	(1)	
19	Valdas Trakys		20/03/79	A	3	(7)	
87	Arvydas Veikutis		19/03/87	M	6	(1)	1
7	Ernestas Veliulis		22/08/92	M	29	(1)	4
39	Irmantas Zelmikas		03/01/80	D	32		3
10	Serhiy Zhygalov	UKR	06/01/83	M	27	(2)	15
8	Artūras Žulpa		10/06/90	M	29	(3)	7

FK REO VILNIUS

Coach: Stasys Baranauskas
2005 • Žalgiris (15,030);
Vilniaus Sportimos maniežas (3,157) • no website

2012

11/03	Dainava	a	2-3	Grigalevičius, Kulbis
17/03	Ekranas	h	0-1	
25/03	Banga	a	2-2	Solomin, Moroz
31/03	Tauras	h	0-1	
07/04	Atlantas	a	0-0	
14/04	Šiauliai	h	3-1	Moroz 3
17/04	Kruoja	a	1-2	Romeiko
21/04	Žalgiris	h	1-2	Dzhioev
29/04	Sūduva	a	0-0	
06/05	Ekranas	a	1-6	Grigalevičius
11/05	Banga	h	0-2	Grigalevičius
15/05	Tauras	a	0-2	
21/05	Dainava	h	0-0	Ražanauskas (p)
26/05	Atlantas	h	3-0	Dzhioev 2, Ražanauskas (p)
10/06	Kruoja	h	2-2	Lipskis, og (Zelmikas)
17/06	Žalgiris	a	1-0	Lipskis
20/06	Šiauliai	a	0-2	
24/06	Sūduva	h	0-2	
30/06	Dainava	a	0-2	
21/07	Ekranas	a	0-3	(w/o)
27/07	Banga	a	1-2	Makutunovič
04/08	Tauras	h	2-3	Moroz, Makutunovič
11/08	Atlantas	a	2-4	Kulbis 2 (1p)
18/08	Šiauliai	h	3-5	Lipskis, Kulbis (p), Ražanauskas
21/08	Kruoja	a	0-3	(w/o)
26/08	Žalgiris	h	0-3	(w/o)
31/08	Sūduva	h	0-3	(w/o)
15/09	Dainava	h	0-3	(w/o)
19/09	Ekranas	a	0-3	(w/o)
22/09	Banga	h	0-3	(w/o)
29/09	Tauras	a	0-3	(w/o)
05/10	Atlantas	h	0-3	(w/o)
19/10	Šiauliai	a	0-3	(w/o)
29/10	Kruoja	h	0-3	(w/o)
04/11	Žalgiris	a	0-3	(w/o)
11/11	Sūduva	h	0-3	(w/o)

No	Name	Nat	DoB	Pos	Aps	(s)	Gls
19	Ignas Bagdonas		21/05/92	A		(8)	
80	Soslan Dzhioev	RUS	25/05/77	A	15	(2)	3
11	Mindaugas Grigalevičius		03/12/81	A	15	(2)	3
3	Vikentij Ivanov		24/04/86	D	6	(2)	
55	Valdas Jakimavičius		19/07/83	G	19		
5	Karolis Jasaitis		01/11/82	M	16		
21	Martyn Jefišov		29/06/93	D	1		
88	Marius Kazlauskas		01/05/84	D	20		
8	Gajus Kulbis		05/07/89	M	11	(8)	4
33	Andrius Lipskis		16/02/88	M	23		3
17	Mantas Makutunovič		29/04/91	M	10	(3)	2
17	David Malkevičius		16/02/91	M	10	(3)	
24	Albert Masiuk		01/06/94	M	1	(1)	
6	Andrius Miliškevičius		28/11/83	M	3	(1)	
13	Jevgenij Moroz		20/01/90	M	15	(4)	5
2	Audrius Račkus		27/12/88	D	14		
10	Tomas Ražanauskas		07/01/76	M	21		3
10	Andžej Romeiko		11/06/82	D	10		1
4	Edgaras Rukštelė		28/03/83	D	2	(1)	
1	Marius Šalankauskas		22/05/89	G	4		
14	Paulius Širvys		31/03/96	D	3		
26	Liutauras Smilga		28/04/94	A	3		
9	Ronald Solomin		23/03/91	M	6	(8)	1
16	Marius Stanaitis		26/12/87	M	6	(6)	
18	Darius Zacharževskij		13/12/91	D	19		
25	Vainius Žukauskas		22/09/94	M		(2)	

FC ŠIAULIAI

Coach: Doivis Kančelskis;
(01/05/12) Gedeminas Jarmalavičius
1995 • Savivaldybės (3,000); Gytariai (1,500) •
fcsiauliai.lt

2012

10/03	Atlantas	a	3-0	Cesanelli, Rimkevičius, Kozlovs
18/03	Kruoja	h	2-1	og (Bilyk), Bartkus
24/03	Sūduva	a	1-4	Bezykornovas
31/03	Ekranas	h	0-1	
09/04	Tauras	a	0-1	
14/04	REO	a	1 3	Bezykornovas
18/04	Žalgiris	h	2-2	Eliošius, Rimavičius
22/04	Dainava	a	0-1	
27/04	Banga	h	1-2	Vėževičius
01/05	Atlantas	h	5-1	Rimkevičius, Lunskis, Cesanelli, Kozlovs, Vėževičius
05/05	Kruoja	a	4-0	Rimkevičius 3, Vėževičius
13/05	Sūduva	h	3-3	Cesanelli, Vėževičius, Kozlovs
16/05	Ekranas	a	2-2	Kozlovs, Urbelis
26/05	Tauras	h	7-3	Rimkevičius 6 (2p), Cesanelli
12/06	Žalgiris	a	0-2	
15/06	Dainava	h	4-2	Bartkus, Rimkevičius 3 (1p)
20/06	REO	h	2-0	Kozlovs 2
26/06	Banga	a	1-0	Cesanelli
29/06	Atlantas	a	2-1	Cesanelli, Kozlovs
22/07	Kruoja	h	1-0	Rimkevičius
01/08	Sūduva	a	0 1	
05/08	Ekranas	h	3-4	Rimkevičius 3, Vėževičius
11/08	Tauras	a	4-0	Cesanelli, Rimkevičius 2 (1p), Kozlovs
18/08	REO	a	5-3	Vėževičius 3, Kozlovs (p), Cesanelli
22/08	Žalgiris	h	2-4	Bartkus, Biršys
26/08	Dainava	a	2-0	Rimkevičius 2
01/09	Banga	h	0-1	
13/09	Atlantas	h	6-0	Rimkevičius 6 (2p)
18/09	Kruoja	a	0-1	
23/09	Sūduva	h	1-0	Rimkevičius (p)
30/09	Ekranas	a	0-3	
07/10	Tauras	h	7-2	Cesanelli, Biršys, Rimkevičius 4, Lipskis
19/10	REO	h	3-0	(w/o)
28/10	Žalgiris	a	1-4	Cesanelli
03/11	Dainava	h	3-3	Rimkevičius 3 (1p)
11/11	Banga	h	1-2	Snapkauskas

No	Name	Nat	DoB	Pos	Aps	(s)	Gls
0	Andrius Bartkus		21/01/86	M	34		3
17	Mariuč Bezykornovas		22/08/76	M	2	(11)	2
21	Tomas Biršys		05/11/92	M	13	(9)	2
22	Santiago Cesanelli	ARG	01/02/90	A	34	(1)	10
8	Tautvydas Eliošius		03/11/91	M	13	(6)	1
34	Rokas Gedminas		13/04/93	M		(6)	
4	Klimas Gusočenko		09/03/89	M	4	(2)	
17	Petru Hvorosteanov	MDA	28/08/86	M	4	(1)	
7	Edvinas Jasaitis		11/04/90	M	1	(8)	
20	Giga Jeladze	GEO	01/01/90	D		(1)	
20	Artūras Jeršovas		10/07/86	A	2		
1	Šarūnas Jurevičius		03/12/80	G	9		
5	Juvenal	BRA	05/06/79	D	28		
14	Intars Kirhners	LVA	09/04/83	D	29	(1)	
10	Igors Kozlovs	LVA	26/03/87	M	31		9
18	Andrius Lipskis		16/02/88	M	8		1
15	Deivydas Lunskis		12/07/77	D	31		1
27	Mindaugas Malinauskas		11/08/83	G	14	(1)	
43	Leonid Mushnikov	RUS	30/12/92	M	6	(17)	
66	Ernestas Pilypas		17/05/90	D	19	(3)	
81	Paulius Pocius		09/11/88	G	12		
31	Laurynas Rimavičius		21/10/85	D	26		1
11	Artūras Rimkevičius		14/04/83	A	29		35
23	Lukas Sendžikas		19/11/81	M		(1)	
13	Tomas Snapkauskas		13/06/92	M	9	(8)	1
9	Rokas Urbelis		27/01/90	A	1	(12)	1
32	Robertas Vėževičius		05/01/86	M	26		8

FK SŪDUVA

Coach: Virginijus Liubšys, (05/07/12) Darius Gvildys
1968 • ARVI (6,250); ARVI Arena (2,500) • fksuduva.lt
Major honours
Lithuanian Cup (2) 2006, 2009

2012

11/03	Ekranas	h	3-1	Šoblinskas, Loginov, Rafael Ledesma
17/03	Tauras	a	4-1	Beniušis, Radžius, Thomson, Borovskij
24/03	Šiauliai	h	4-1	Beniušis, Eliošius, Urbšys, Lukšys (p)
01/04	Žalgiris	a	0-4	
07/04	Dainava	h	3-1	Rafael Ledesma 2, Eliošius
14/04	Banga	a	1-0	Lukšys
17/04	Atlantas	h	6-0	og (Šiškin), Šoblinskas, Slavickas, Beniušis, Eliošius, Lukšys
21/04	Kruoja	a	1-2	og (Zelmikas)
29/04	REO	h	0-0	
02/05	Ekranas	a	0-2	
05/05	Tauras	h	1-0	Lukšys
13/05	Šiauliai	a	3-3	Rafael Ledesma, Loginov, Šoblinskas
16/05	Žalgiris	h	0-0	
25/05	Dainava	a	4-2	Thomson, Lukšys, Urbšys, Chvedukas
13/06	Atlantas	a	4-0	Leimonas, Thomson, Šoblinskas, Rafael Ledesma
16/06	Banga	h	0 1	
19/06	Banga	h	3-1	Rafael Ledesma (p), Lukšys 2
24/06	REO	a	2-0	Lukšys, Rafael Ledesma
01/07	Ekranas	h	2-3	Chvedukas, Loginov
22/07	Tauras	a	2-1	Rafael Ledesma 2
30/07	Šiauliai	h	1-0	Lukšys
05/08	Žalgiris	a	2-2	Beniušis 2
12/08	Dainava	h	3-2	Freidgelmas 2, Šoblinskas
17/08	Banga	a	0-0	
21/08	Atlantas	h	2-0	Rafael Ledesma (p), Urbšys
25/08	Kruoja	a	1-2	Rafael Ledesma
31/08	REO	h	3-0	(w/o)
16/09	Ekranas	a	2-2	Rafael Ledesma, Lukšys
19/09	Tauras	h	4-1	Rafael Ledesma 2, Valskis 2
23/09	Šiauliai	a	0-1	
30/09	Žalgiris	h	1-2	Rafael Ledesma
06/10	Dainava	a	3-0	Eliošius, Rafael Ledesma 2
21/10	Banga	h	3-0	Rafael Ledesma 2, Eliošius
27/10	Atlantas	a	5-1	Rafael Ledesma, Chvedukas, Loginov 2, Lukšys
04/11	Kruoja	h	1-1	Rafael Ledesma
11/11	REO	a	0-0	(w/o)

No	Name	Nat	DoB	Pos	Aps	(s)	Gls
25	Valentin Baranovskij		15/10/86	M	9	(3)	
31	Džiugas Bartkus		07/11/89	G	10		
8	Ričardas Beniušis		23/04/80	A	13	(15)	5
3	Valdemar Borovskij		02/05/84	D	31		1
23	Armandas Breivė		04/03/94	M		(5)	
16	Audrius Brokas		20/08/90	M	1	(8)	
13	Karolis Chvedukas		21/04/91	M	22	(4)	3
77	Pāvels Davidovs	LVA	30/12/80	G	16		
9	Tadas Eliošius		01/03/90	M	20	(8)	5
45	Robertas Freidgelmas		21/02/89	M	8	(3)	2
10	Povilas Kiselevskis		05/07/94	M	2	(5)	
4	Vytautas Lasevičius		07/06/90	D	2	(1)	
12	Povilas Leimonas		16/11/87	M	28	(2)	1
15	Serhiy Loginov	UKR	24/08/90	M	28	(3)	5
7	Povilas Lukšys		07/07/79	A	18	(12)	11
1	Martynas Matuzas		28/08/89	G	8		
2	Nerijus Radžius		27/08/76	D	30	(1)	1
82	Rafael Ledesma	BRA	31/12/82	M	24	(8)	21
19	Vaidas Slavickas		26/02/86	D	31		1
88	Marius Šoblinskas		23/08/87	M	26	(1)	5
21	Craig Thomson	SCO	17/04/91	A	9	(7)	3
22	Gytis Urba		31/03/91	D	10	(3)	
17	Andrius Urbšys		22/08/86	M	20	(7)	3
21	Nerijus Valskis		04/08/87	M	8		2

FK TAURAS

Coach: Giovanni Scanu (ITA)
1942 • Vytautas (3,200); Tauragė (2,000) • fktauras.lt

2012

10/03	Kruoja	a	0-1	
17/03	Sūduva	h	1-4	Kuzin
25/03	Ekranas	a	0-5	
31/03	REO	a	1-0	Mascia
09/04	Šiauliai	h	1-0	Martišauskis
15/04	Žalgiris	a	0-2	
18/04	Dainava	h	2-4	Solovjovs, og (Rutkauskas)
22/04	Banga	a	0-1	
28/04	Atlantas	h	0-0	
02/05	Kruoja	h	0-4	
05/05	Sūduva	a	0-1	
12/05	Ekranas	h	1-2	Sirevičius
15/05	REO	h	2-0	Mascia (p), Petkevičius
26/05	Šiauliai	a	3-7	Mascia, Petkevičius, Freidgelmas
09/06	Dainava	a	1-3	Kižys
16/06	Banga	h	3-2	Kuzin, Mascia, og (Jokšas)
20/06	Žalgiris	h	0-2	
26/06	Atlantas	a	5-0	Vyšniauskas, Solovjovs, Kižys, Petkevičius 2
30/06	Kruoja	a	1-3	Babilius
22/07	Sūduva	h	1-2	Demurtas
28/07	Ekranas	a	0-5	
04/08	REO	a	3-2	Kuzin, Sirevičius 2 (1p)
11/08	Šiauliai	h	0-4	
17/08	Žalgiris	h	0-0	
23/08	Dainava	h	1-3	Kuzin
26/08	Banga	a	0-4	
01/09	Atlantas	h	1-1	Petkevičius (p)
15/09	Kruoja	a	0-4	
19/09	Sūduva	a	1-4	Martišauskis
22/09	Ekranas	a	0-2	
29/09	REO	h	3 0	(w/o)
07/10	Šiauliai	a	2-7	Rimas, Kižys
20/10	Žalgiris	a	0-4	
28/10	Dainava	a	0-2	
03/11	Banga	h	1-3	Kuzin
11/11	Atlantas	a	1-4	Meištininkas

Nu	Name	Nat	DoB	Pos	Aps	(s)	Gls
33	Lukas Ankudinovas		10/08/95	M	4	(7)	
32	Egidijus Auryla		26/07/92	D	15	(9)	
25	Simonas Babilius		16/09/91	A	7	(16)	1
70	Titi Belle	CMR	10/03/85	A	8	(3)	
15	Lukas Bielskis		11/05/92	M	1	(2)	
16	Olexandr Borysenko	UKR	01/01/85	G	27		
1	Vladimir Brekun	BUG	30/03/92	G	2	(1)	
	Francesco Callide	ITA	01/09/85	A	7		
87	Nicola Cutolo	ITA	27/09/87	D	7	(2)	
7	Giampietro Demurtas	ITA	06/04/92	M	6	(12)	1
9	Michele Di Piedi	ITA	21/12/80	A	6	(1)	
26	Mantvydas Eiza		15/06/93	M	18	(4)	
27	Robertas Freidgelmas		02/02/89	D	9		1
1	Mantas Gintalas		04/04/88	G	1		
13	Marius Kižys		21/02/82	M	20	(1)	3
93	Karolis Kuliešius		14/10/93	S	5	(2)	
39	Roman Kuzin	RUS	20/03/89	M	29	(2)	5
3	Mantas Lėkis		15/11/86	D	29		
8	Luca Marongiu	ITA	01/09/87	M	11	(3)	
22	Lukas Martišauskis		03/01/90	M	22	(8)	2
4	Alessandro Mascia	ITA	06/08/86	M	13		4
21	Julius Meištininkas		21/06/95	D	1	(3)	1
10	Manuel Perra	ITA	21/01/89	A	10		
23	Vladas Petkevičius		02/08/89	M	27	(5)	5
11	Tomas Rimas		02/05/78	D	29	(1)	1
19	Tomas Sirevičius		23/03/79	D	30	(2)	3
14	Aleksandrs Solovjovs	LVA	25/02/88	D	14	(1)	2
90	Renat Taibov	RUS	11/08/90	M		(1)	
4	Federico Vela	ARG	05/02/82	D	4	(1)	
6	Tomas Vyšniauskas		07/03/88	M	23	(1)	1

VMFD ŽALGIRIS

Coach: Damir Petravić (CRO);
(08/08/12) Marek Zub (POL)
1947 • Vilniaus LFF (8,000) • zalgiris-vilnius.lt
Major honours
Lithuanian League (3) 1991, 1992, 1999;
Lithuanian Cup (7) 1991, 1993, 1994, 1997,
2003 (autumn), 2012, 2013

2012

10/03	Banga	a	2-1	Grgurović (p), Elliott
17/03	Atlantas	h	7-0	Elliott 4, Kazlauskas, Jankauskas, Šilėnas
24/03	Kruoja	a	1-0	Elliott
01/04	Sūduva	h	4-0	Pek, Kuklys 2, Elliott
07/04	Ekranas	a	0-1	
15/04	Tauras	h	2-0	og (Rimas), Perić
18/04	Šiauliai	a	2-2	Komolov, Kuklys (p)
21/04	REO	a	2-1	Elliott, Pek
29/04	Dainava	h	4-0	Elliott 2, Šilėnas, Grgurović
03/05	Banga	h	2-0	Elliott, Grgurović
07/05	Atlantas	a	1-0	Elliott
13/05	Kruoja	h	0-2	
16/05	Sūduva	a	0-0	
25/05	Ekranas	h	0-0	
12/06	Šiauliai	h	2-0	Pek, Kuklys
17/06	REO	h	0-1	
20/06	Tauras	a	2-0	Kuklys (p), Grgurović
25/06	Dainava	a	3-1	Elliott, Janušauskas, Kuklys
29/06	Banga	a	0-0	
22/07	Atlantas	h	3-1	Kuklys (p), Biliński, Janušauskas
30/07	Kruoja	a	1-0	Skerla
05/08	Sūduva	h	2-2	Biliński 2
12/08	Ekranas	a	0-0	
19/08	Tauras	h	5-0	Komolov, Pek, Elliott 2, Kuklys (p)
22/08	Šiauliai	a	4-2	Komolov 2, Nagumanov, Biliński
26/08	REO	a	3-0	(w/o)
02/09	Dainava	h	3-0	Jankauskas, Radavičius, og (Botyrius)
14/09	Banga	h	2-0	Elliott (p), Biliński
18/09	Atlantas	a	4-3	Komolov, Biliński 2, og (N'Diaye)
22/09	Kruoja	h	2-1	Freidgeimas, Biliński
30/09	Sūduva	a	2-1	Radavičius (p), Švrljuga
07/10	Ekranas	h	2-1	Biliński 2
20/10	Tauras	a	4-0	Komolov (p), Perić, Skerla, Radavičius
28/10	Šiauliai	h	4-1	Biliński 2, Perić, Švrljuga
04/11	REO	h	3-0	(w/o)
11/11	Dainava	a	2-1	Skerla, Radavičius

No	Name	Nat	DoB	Pos	Aps	(s)	Gls
19	Kamil Biliński	POL	23/01/88	A	10	(5)	12
9	Calum Elliot	SCO	30/03/87	A	29	(4)	16
3	Georgas Freidgeimas		10/08/87	D	30		1
50	Mario Grgurović	CRO	02/02/85	M	15	(2)	4
5	Algis Jankauskas		27/09/82	D	24		2
16	Paulius Janušauskas		28/02/89	M	14	(10)	2
23	Jaunius Juozaitis		30/01/90	D	1	(1)	
11	Donatas Kazlauskas		31/03/94	A	3	(4)	1
10	Pavel Komolov	RUS	10/03/89	M	22	(10)	6
29	Povilas Krasnovskis		29/04/89	M	3	(8)	
88	Mantas Kuklys		10/06/87	M	26	(7)	8
38	Andrey Nagumanov	RUS	21/02/87	M	23	(6)	1
18	Tomislav Pek	CRO	22/10/84	A	18	(3)	4
14	Luka Perić	CRO	14/12/87	D	27	(1)	3
7	Ramūnas Radavičius		20/01/81	M	13	(1)	4
31	Marius Rapalis		22/05/89	G	14		
20	Vaidas Šilėnas		16/07/85	M	25	(4)	2
2	Andrius Skerla		29/04/77	D	16		3
11	Andro Švrljuga	CRO	24/10/85	M	7	(5)	2
4	Karolis Urbaitis		12/12/90	D	7	(3)	
8	Egidijus Vaitkūnas		08/08/88	D	24	(2)	
21	Arminas Vaskéla		12/08/90	M	1	(5)	
17	Raimondas Vilėniškis		10/06/76	M	2	(14)	
1	Armantas Vitkauskas		23/03/89	G	20		

480 | The European Football Yearbook 2013/14

Top goalscorers

35	Artūras Rimkevičius (Šiauliai)
21	Rafael Ledesma (Sūduva)
17	Arsenij Buinickij (Dainava/Ekranas)
16	Calum Elliott (Žalgiris)
15	Serhiy Zhygalov (Kruoja)
12	Kamil Biliński (Žalgiris)
11	Tino Lagator (Atlantas)
	Giorgi Alaverdashvili (Banga)
	Ramūnas Radavičius (Ekranas/Žalgiris)
	Povilas Lukšys (Sūduva)

Second level

SECOND LEVEL FINAL TABLE 2012

		Pld	W	D	L	F	A	Pts
1	FK Lietava	27	19	5	3	68	18	62
2	FK Nevėžis	27	18	4	5	65	23	58
3	FK Granitas	27	15	7	5	56	33	52
4	FK Trakai	27	14	6	7	57	29	48
5	FK Polonija	27	12	1	14	50	48	37
6	NFA	27	10	3	14	66	61	33
7	FK Šilutė	27	8	8	11	39	33	32
8	FK Palanga	27	8	6	13	38	55	30
9	FK Venta	27	8	1	18	44	70	25
10	FK Kėdainiai	27	1	3	23	15	128	6

NB No promotion.

Domestic cup: LFF Taurė 2012/13

FOURTH ROUND

(19/09/12)
Trakai 1-2 Venta

(26/09/12)
Atlantas 3-0 Kėdainiai *(w/o)*
Ave.Ko 0-15 Nevėžis
Granitas 3-0 United *(w/o)*
Palanga 2-0 Ipūkis
Spyris 6-2 Polonija

(28/09/12)
Šilute 2-0 Prelegentai

FIFTH ROUND

(22/10/12)
Spyris 2-3 Šilute *(aet)*

(23/10/12)
Granitas 4-0 Venta
Kruoja 5-0 Palanga
Nevėžis 0-1 Lietava
Tauras 0-3 Žalgiris

(24/10/12)
Atlantas 1-0 Sūduva
Dainava 0-3 Ekranas
Šiauliai 1-0 Banga

QUARTER-FINALS

(06/11/12)
Granitas 1-6 Žalgiris *(Sadovskij 87; Biliński 1, 40, 42, 69, Janušauskas 58, Freidgeimas 77)*

(07/11/12)
Atlantas 4-1 Šilute *(Begić 38, 99, Razulis 107, Laukžemis 119; Užkuraitis 44) (aet)*

Kruoja 0-2 Ekranas *(Vertelis 10, Buinickij 75)*

Šiauliai 4-1 Lietava *(Lipskis 45, Rimkevičius 53, 80, Cesanelli 55; Bezykornovas 61)*

SEMI-FINALS

(16/04/13 & 01/05/13)
Ekranas 1-2 Šiauliai *(Fernando 40; Alaverdashvili 15, Gedminas 38)*
Šiauliai 2-1 Ekranas *(Alaverdashvili 75, Urbelis 79; Rimkevičius 82)*
(Šiauliai 4-2)

(17/04/13 & 30/04/13)
Atlantas 0-0 Žalgiris
Žalgiris 1-0 Atlantas *(Gerc 90)*
(Žalgiris 1-0)

FINAL

(19/05/13)
S. Darius ir S. Girėnas SK, Kaunas
VMFD ŽALGIRIS 3 *(Švrljuga 13, Skerla 45+1, Gerc 91)*
FC ŠIAULIAI 3 *(Vaskéla 5, Rašo 34, Birškys 98)*
(aet; 8-7 on pens)
Referee: Dunauskas
ŽALGIRIS: Vitkauskas, Vaitkūnas, Skerla, Perić, Radavičius (Janušauskas 80), Žulpa, Švrljuga, Kuklys, Wilk, Komolov (Šilėnas 87), Biliński (Gerc 73)
ŠIAULIAI: Pocius, Lunskis, Fridrikas, Pšelenskis (Rašo 32), Žderić, Eliošius (Birškys 94), Snapkauskas, Mushnikov, Vaskéla, Alaverdashvili (Jankauskas 102), Tokić

Žalgiris players bask in the sun with the Lithuanian Cup

LUXEMBOURG
Fédération Luxembourgeoise de Football (FLF)

Address	BP5, Rue de Limpach	**President**	Paul Philipp
	LU-3901 Mondercange	**General secretary**	Joël Wolff
Tel	+352 488 665 1	**Media officer**	Marc Diederich
Fax	+352 488 665 82	**Year of formation**	1908
E-mail	flf@football.lu	**National stadium**	Josy Barthel,
Website	football.lu		Luxembourg (8,000)

BGL LIGUE CLUBS

1. FC Differdange 03
2. F91 Dudelange
3. FC Etzella Ettelbruck

4. CS Fola Esch
5. CS Grevenmacher
6. FC RM Hamm Benfica
7. FC Jeunesse Canach

8. AS Jeunesse Esch
9. UN Käerjéng 97
10. CS Pétange
11. FC Progrès Niedercorn
12. Racing FC Union Lëtzebuerg
13. Union 05 Kayl-Tétange
14. FC Wiltz 71

PROMOTED CLUBS

15. FC Swift Hesper
16. US Rumelange

KEY:

- – UEFA Champions League
- – UEFA Europa League
- – Promoted clubs
- – Relegated clubs

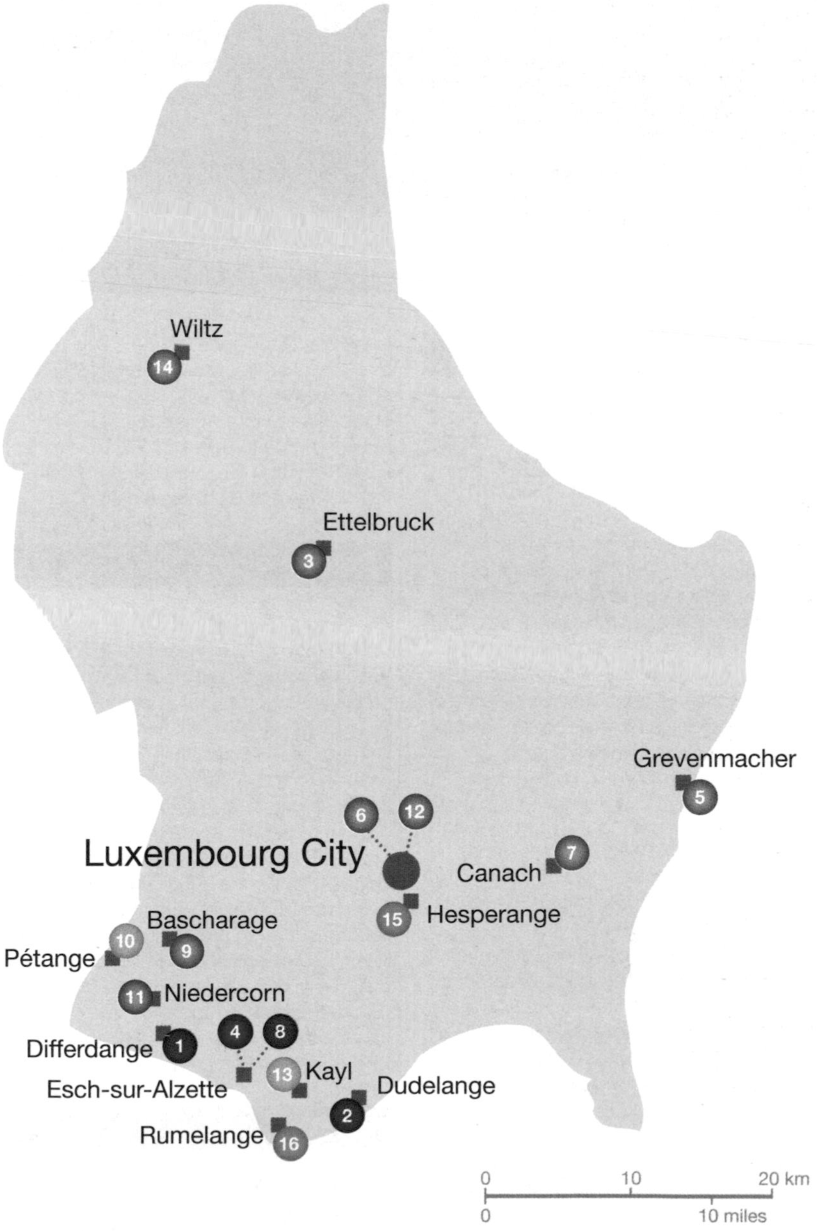

Wiltz
14

Ettelbruck
3

Grevenmacher
5

6 12

Luxembourg City

Canach 7

15 Hesperange

Bascharage

Pétange 10

9

11 Niedercorn

Differdange 1 4 8

13 Kayl

Esch-sur-Alzette Dudelange

2

Rumelange 16

0	10	20 km
0		10 miles

Strasser steers Fola to victory

The town of Esch-sur-Alzette, close to the French border, is the second most populous in Luxembourg, and it became the country's football capital in 2012/13 as its two top-flight clubs, CS Fola Esch and AS Jeunesse Esch, shared the two domestic trophies.

While for Jeunesse, the country's most decorated club, a 13th domestic cup win was most welcome, it could hardly be celebrated with the same fervour as Fola's title triumph, which finally arrived after an 83-year wait, Luxembourg's record cap-holder Jeff Strasser leading the club to the promised land in his second season as coach.

Esch club's 83-year wait for title ends

Local rivals Jeunesse scoop domestic cup

Dudelange cause major upset in Europe

Domestic league

Promoted back to the top flight only in 2008 and a mere sixth in 2011/12, Fola got off to a blistering start, opening the new campaign with a 6-1 win at Union 05 Kayl-Tétange and dropping just two points in their first eight matches, in which new signing from F91 Dudelange, Stefano Bensi, scored 11 goals. Strasser, a former German Bundesliga professional with 1. FC Kaiserslautern and VfL Borussia Mönchengladbach, clearly had the magic touch, his players consistently delivering the goods to maintain their position at the top of the table – despite a double challenge from defending champions Dudelange and 28-time winners Jeunesse.

The climax to Fola's exceptional campaign was perfectly scripted, the title being wrapped up with a scintillating 5-1 win at Jeunesse's Stade de la Frontière in the penultimate round. A 4-2 home win over relegated Kayl-Tétange four days later cemented the club's historic achievement, leaving them four points clear of Dudelange at the summit with a final tally of 67 goals that dwarfed those of all the other teams in the division. Although it had been a long time in coming, the title was the sixth in Fola's history. Very few, if any, of their fans, however, would have had any memory of the previous five.

Like Fola, Dudelange lost only three of their 26 matches, and only one away from home, but they fell short of claiming their eighth league title in nine years, a 0-0 draw at home to Fola and a 2-1 defeat at FC Differdange 03 combining to derail their hopes in the closing weeks.

Domestic cup

The Stade Josy Barthel welcomed Differdange and Jeunesse Esch for the final of the Luxembourg Cup. Jeunesse had eliminated both Fola – 2-1 in the last 16 – and holders Dudelange – on penalties in the quarter-finals – whereas Differdange, seeking a third cup win in four years, had been given a much more straightforward passage. Having not won the trophy since 2000, Jeunesse seized control with two goals in three minutes from their leading scorer in the league, Sanel Ibrahimović, and although Differdange pulled a goal back from the penalty spot before the interval, the scoreline did not change in the second half and Jeunesse held on to win 2-1.

Europe

Successes in Europe for teams from Luxembourg are rare, but Dudelange produced one of the country's biggest upsets when they eliminated Austrian double winners FC Salzburg from the UEFA Champions League in the second qualifying round. A 1-0 victory at home – courtesy of Luxembourg international Aurélien Joachim's 75th-minute winner – was followed by an amazing second leg, which Didier Philippe's side lost 4-3 to sneak through on away goals.

That guaranteed Dudelange four more European matches, but although they lost them all, to NK Maribor and Hapoel Tel-Aviv FC, nothing could tarnish the memory of their earlier exploit. Indeed, Joachim, a scorer of eight goals in Dudelange's European campaign – a national record – was rewarded for his efforts with a professional contract at Dutch Eredivisie club Willem II.

National team

There were no giant-killing acts from the Luxembourg national team in the 2014 FIFA World Cup qualifying campaign but, with the exception of a couple of heavy defeats by Israel, Luc Holtz's side gave a creditable account of themselves, losing narrowly at home to Portugal, holding Northern Ireland to a 1-1 draw in Belfast and sharing the spoils home and away against Azerbaijan.

Domestic league: BGL Ligue 2012/13 final table

		Pld	Home					Away					Total					Pts
			W	D	L	F	A	W	D	L	F	A	W	D	L	F	A	
1	CS Fola Esch	26	9	2	2	31	13	9	3	1	36	10	18	5	3	67	23	59
2	F91 Dudelange	26	9	2	2	28	10	7	5	1	25	10	16	7	3	53	20	55
3	AS Jeunesse Esch	26	5	2	6	26	24	11	0	2	27	7	16	2	8	53	31	50
4	FC Differdange 03	26	8	3	2	27	15	6	2	5	27	19	14	5	7	54	34	47
5	FC RM Hamm Benfica	26	8	3	2	28	19	5	4	4	25	19	13	7	6	53	38	46
6	CS Grevenmacher	26	7	4	2	27	18	4	5	4	16	14	11	9	6	43	32	42
7	FC Jeunesse Canach	26	4	4	5	22	19	6	3	4	18	16	10	7	9	40	35	37
8	Racing FC Union Lëtzebuerg	26	5	2	6	16	19	4	4	5	27	25	9	6	11	43	44	33
9	UN Käerjéng 97	26	7	2	4	30	25	2	2	9	14	28	9	4	13	44	53	31
10	FC Wiltz 71	26	4	2	7	18	35	5	1	7	24	31	9	3	14	42	66	30
11	FC Etzella Ettelbruck	26	3	6	4	18	28	3	3	7	23	33	6	9	11	41	61	27
12	FC Progrès Niedercorn	26	4	1	8	14	22	3	3	7	15	23	7	4	15	29	45	25
13	CS Pétange	26	1	4	8	7	23	2	1	10	14	34	3	5	18	21	57	14
14	Union 05 Kayl-Tétange	26	1	1	11	10	40	2	2	9	19	33	3	3	20	29	73	12

SEASON AT A GLANCE

EUROPEAN QUALIFICATION 2013/14

Champion: CS Fola Esch (second qualifying round)

Cup winner: AS Jeunesse Esch (first qualifying round)
F91 Dudelange (first qualifying round)
FC Differdange 03 (first qualifying round)

Top scorer Edis Osmanović (Wiltz), 21 goals
Relegated clubs Union 05 Kayl-Tétange, CS Pétange
Promoted clubs FC Swift Hesper, US Rumelange
Cup final AS Jeunesse Esch 2-1 FC Differdange 03

BGL LIGUE TEAM OF THE SEASON
(4-4-2)
Coach: Strasser (Fola)

PLAYER OF THE SEASON
Stefano Bensi
(CS Fola Esch)

A new signing from F91 Dudelange, Bensi scored 20 league goals – second only to FC Wiltz 71's Edis Osmanović – and played a huge part in Fola's long-awaited title triumph. Four days after officially being declared Luxembourg's player of the year, he opened his international account, earning his country a 1-1 draw against Azerbaijan in Baku.

NEWCOMER OF THE SEASON
David Turpel
(FC Etzella Ettelbruck)

Newly promoted Etzella only just avoided the relegation play-offs, and for that they owed a considerable debt to 20-year-old local lad Turpel, who scored 15 goals and was a consistent menace to opposition defences. His efforts not only earned him a first senior international cap but also sparked transfer interest from Germany.

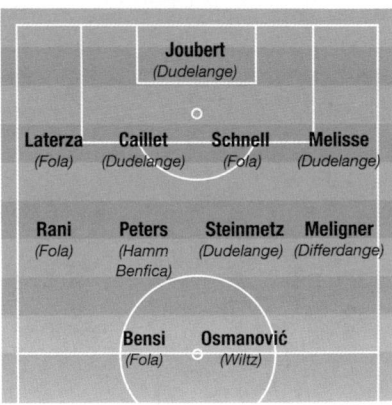

Joubert (Dudelange)
Laterza (Fola) **Caillet** (Dudelange) **Schnell** (Fola) **Melisse** (Dudelange)
Rani (Fola) **Peters** (Hamm Benfica) **Steinmetz** (Dudelange) **Meligner** (Differdange)
Bensi (Fola) **Osmanović** (Wiltz)

LUXEMBOURG

NATIONAL TEAM

Home Kit   Away Kit

TOP FIVE ALL-TIME CAPS
Jeff Strasser (98); **René Peters** (90);
Carlo Weis (88); **Eric Hoffmann** (86);
François Konter (77)

TOP FIVE ALL-TIME GOALS
Léon Mart (16); Gusty Kemp (15);
Camille Libar (14); Nicolas Kettel (13);
François Müller (12)

Results 2012/13

Date	Opponent		Venue	Score	Scorer
15/08/12	Georgia	H	Obercorn	1-2	Joachim (84p)
07/09/12	Portugal (WCQ)	H	Luxembourg	1-2	Da Mota (14)
11/09/12	Northern Ireland (WCQ)	A	Belfast	1-1	Da Mota (87)
12/10/12	Israel (WCQ)	H	Luxembourg	0-6	
16/10/12	Israel (WCQ)	A	Tel-Aviv	0-3	
14/11/12	Scotland	H	Luxembourg	1-2	Gerson (47)
05/02/13	Armenia	N	Valence (FRA)	1-1	Mutsch (15)
22/03/13	Azerbaijan (WCQ)	H	Luxembourg	0-0	
26/03/13	Finland	H	Luxembourg	0-3	
07/06/13	Azerbaijan (WCQ)	A	Baku	1-1	Bensi (79)

Appearances 2012/13

Coach: Luc Holtz	14/06/69		Geo	POR	NIR	ISR	ISR	Sco	Arm	AZE	Fin	AZE	Caps	Goals
Jonathan Joubert	12/09/79	Dudelange	G	G	G	G	G	G	G	G	G	G	62	-
Tom Schnell	08/10/85	Fola	D67	D	D	D18		D	D	D	D		36	-
Guy Blaise	12/12/80	Virton (BEL)	D	D	D		D	D	s90				30	-
Eric Hoffmann	21/06/84	Jeunesse Esch	D46		s93	s78	D		D	D	D	D	86	-
René Peters	15/06/81	Hamm Benfica	D46				D81	s46	s23		s46		90	3
Mario Mutsch	03/09/84	St Gallen (SUI)	M72	M	M	M	M	M	M23	M94	M46	M	66	2
Gilles Bettmer	31/03/89	Differdange	M	M	M93	M	M	M71	M56	s94	M59		58	1
Charles Leweck	19/07/83	Etzella	M75			s18	M	M76			s41		39	-
Ben Payal	08/09/88	Dudelange	M	M	M	M78	M	M46				s46	53	-
Lars Gerson	05/02/90	Norrköping (SWE)	M46	M	M50	M		M		M		M	28	2
Aurélien Joachim	10/08/86	Dudelange /Willem II (NED)	A	A	A46	A61	A46		A90	A93	A	A	42	3
Ante Bukvic	14/11/87	Differdange	s46	D	D	D		D					9	-
Daniel Da Mota	11/09/85	Dudelange	s46	M79	M	M	M86	s53	M84	M67	M	s78	47	4
Maurice Deville	31/07/92	Elversberg (GER)	s46	s79	s46	s61	s46	A63		s93	s59	A27	12	2
Tom Laterza	09/05/92	Fola	s67				s86	s76	M63	s67		s27 /78	22	-
Mathias Jänisch	27/08/90	Differdange	s72	D	D	D		D53	D	D	s55		27	-
Stefano Bensi	11/08/88	Fola	s75					s63		M	M41	M	14	1
Chris Philipps	08/03/94	Metz (FRA)			s50	D	s81		M	M	M 53*	M46	9	-
Laurent Jans	05/08/92	Fola					D		D	D	D	D	5	-
David Turpel	19/10/92	Etzella						s71	s56				2	-
Massimo Martino	18/09/90	Dudelange							s63			D	14	-
Dan Collette	02/04/85	Jeunesse Esch							s84				32	-
Billy Bernard	09/04/91	Fola									D55		2	-
Maxime Chanot	21/11/89	Beerschot (BEL)										D	1	-

European club competitions 2012/13

F91 DUDELANGE

First qualifying round - SP Tre Penne (SMR)
H 7-0 Melisse (25), Benzouien (29, 53), Legros (47), Joachim (51, 90+3), D'Orsi (78og)
Joubert, Prempeh, Martino (Zeghdane 65), Tournut, Payal (Hug 57), Joachim, Kitenge (Gomez 57), Benzouien, Legros, Melisse, Steinmetz. Coach: Didier Philippe (FRA)

A 4-0 Joachim (28, 34), Benzouien (41), Gomez (45+1)
Joubert, Martino (Prempeh 62), Caillet, Joachim (Kitenge 62), Da Mota, Benzouien (Touray 62), Gomez, Legros, Haddadji, Melisse, Beltorangal. Coach: Didier Philippe (FRA)

Second qualifying round - FC Salzburg (AUT)
H 1-0 Joachim (75)
Joubert, Prempeh, Tournut, Caillet, Payal, Joachim (Kitenge 87), Da Mota, Benzouien (Zeghdane 90+2), Legros, Melisse, Steinmetz (Haddadji 88). Coach: Didier Philippe (FRA)

A 3-4 *Steinmetz (26, 57), Joachim (48)*
Joubert, Prempeh, Tournut, Caillet,
Payal (Zeghdane 89), Joachim, Da Mota
(Beltorangal 87), Benzouien, Legros,
Melisse, Steinmetz (Haddadji 79). Coach:
Didier Philippe (FRA)
Red card: Benzouien 74

Third qualifying round - NK Maribor (SVN)
A 1-4 *Joachim (90+2)*
Joubert, Prempeh, Tournut, Caillet, Payal
(Hug 64), Joachim, Da Mota, Idazza
(Beltorangal 64), Legros, Melisse, Steinmetz
(Kitenge 73). Coach: Didier Philippe (FRA)
H 0-1
Joubert, Tournut, Caillet, Joachim, Hug
(Kitenge 67), Da Mota, Benzouien (Idazza
87), Payal, Melisse, Zeghdane (Beltorangal
75), Steinmetz. Coach: Didier Philippe (FRA)

Play-offs - Hapoel Tel-Aviv FC (ISR)
H 1-3 *Joachim (20)*
Joubert, Prempeh, Tournut (Da Mota 46),
Caillet, Payal (Zeghdane 46), Joachim,
Hug, Idazza (Kitenge 75), Legros, Melisse,
Steinmetz. Coach: Didier Philippe (FRA)
A 0-4
Joubert, Prempeh, Martino, Caillet, Payal
(Malget 88), Hug (Touray 85), Da Mota,
Kitenge (Pedro 73), Benzouien, Legros,
Melisse, Coach: Didier Philippe (FRA)

AS JEUNESSE ESCH

**First qualifying round - NK Olimpija
Ljubljana (SVN)**
A 0-3
Oberweis, Moreira, Hoffmann, Portier,
Benichou (Ibrahimović 64), Miceli, Agović,
Benajiba (Agović 87), Collette, Quéré,
Ndongala (Ramdedović 82). Coach:
Sébastian Grandjean (BEL)
H 0-3
Oberweis, Moreira, Hoffmann, Portier, Miceli
(Quéré 61), Agović, Benajiba, Collette (Vitali
46), Ibrahimović, Ramdedović (Delgado 46),
Ndongala. Coach: Sébastian Grandjean
(BEL)

CS GREVENMACHER

First qualifying round - KF Tirana (ALB)
A 0-2
Schaab, Brzyski, Bechtold, Battaglia, Huss
(Gaspar 69), Louadj, Hoffmann, Schiltz
(Jaures 88), Fürst, Heinz, Steffen (Mimalla
38). Coach: Marc Thomé (LUX)
H 0-0
Schaab, Brzyski, Bechtold, Battaglia (Huss
67), Braun, Almeida (Brandao 79), Louadj,
Hoffmann, Schiltz (Gaspar 83), Fürst, Heinz.
Coach: Marc Thomé (LUX)

FC DIFFERDANGE 03

First qualifying round - NSÍ Runavík (FRO)
H 3-0 *Kettenmeyer (31), Bettmer (41), Er
Rafik (47)*
Weber, Almeida Rodrigues, Siebenaler
(Pedro Ribeiro 71), Bastos, Er Rafik, Caron
(Piskor 80), Franzoni, Bukvic, Kettenmeyer,
Bettmer, Lebresne (Jänisch 53). Coach:
Michel Leflochmoan (FRA)
A 3-0 *Er Rafik (14, 45), Albanese (73)*
Weber, Almeida Rodrigues (Meligner 69),
Siebenaler, Er Rafik, Albanese, Franzoni
(Afoun 76), Bukvic, Bettmer, Jänisch,
Lebresne (Pedro Ribeiro 76), Piskor. Coach:
Michel Leflochmoan (FRA)

Second qualifying round - KAA Gent (BEL)
H 0-1
Weber, Almeida Rodrigues, Siebenaler,
Pedro Ribeiro (Meligner 69), Er Rafik,
Franzoni, Bukvic, Kettenmeyer, Bettmer
(Caron 57), Jänisch (May 71), Lebresne.
Coach: Michel Leflochmoan (FRA)
Red card: Kettenmeyer 36
A 2-3 *Er Rafik (24), Bettmer (37)*
Weber, Siebenaler, May, Er Rafik (Piskor
77), Caron (Albanese 79), Franzoni, Bukvic,
Meligner, Bettmer, Jänisch, Afoun (Bastos
74). Coach: Michel Leflochmoan (FRA)

FC DIFFERDANGE 03
Coach: Michel Leflochmoan (FRA)
2003 • Parc des Sports, Obercorn (1,800) • fcd03.lu
Major honours
Luxembourg Cup (2) 2010, 2011

2012

05/08	Progrès	h	2-1	*Er Rafik 2*
11/08	Pétange	h	3-0	*Piskor 2, Meligner*
19/08	Käerjéng	a	2-2	*Bettmer, Piskor*
26/08	Etzella	h	0-0	
16/09	Jeunesse Canach	a	3-1	*Er Rafik 3*
22/09	Jeunesse Esch	h	0-3	
30/09	Fola	a	1-2	*Piskor*
04/10	Kayl-Tétange	h	3-1	*Piskor, Kettenmeyer, og (Ollé-Nicolle)*
20/10	Wiltz	a	4-0	*Er Rafik 2, Franzoni, Pedro Ribeiro*
28/10	Grevenmacher	h	2-3	*Bukvic, Piskor*
04/11	Dudelange	a	0-3	
10/11	Hamm Benfica	h	4-2	*Bukvic, Caron, Bastos, Er Rafik*
25/11	Racing Union	a	3-1	*Meligner, Lebresne, Er Rafik*

2013

03/03	Etzella	a	4-0	*Lebresne, Meligner, Piskor, Bettmer*
06/03	Pétange	a	1-1	*Franzoni (p)*
10/03	Jeunesse Canach	h	3-1	*Bettmer, Meligner, Piskor*
30/03	Fola	h	1-0	*May*
07/04	Käerjéng	h	0-0	
13/04	Jeunesse Esch	a	4-2	*Pedro Ribeiro, Meligner, Bastos, Caron*
17/04	Kayl-Tétange	a	0-1	
21/04	Wiltz	h	1-1	*Caron*
28/04	Grevenmacher	a	2-3	*Caron, Er Rafik*
05/05	Dudelange	a	2-1	*Er Rafik 2*
19/05	Hamm Benfica	a	1-2	*Caron*
22/05	Racing Union	h	6-2	*Caron, Pedro Ribeiro 2, Lebresne, Er Rafik, Piskor*
26/05	Progrès	a	2-1	*Jänisch, Piskor*

No	Name	Nat	DoB	Pos	Aps	(s)	Gls
3	Yannick Afoun		16/06/86	D	1	(2)	
22	Mirko Albanese		04/09/89	A	2	(3)	
10	André Almeida Rodrigues		06/12/87	D	11	(1)	
9	Yannick Bastos		30/05/93	M	16	(4)	2
28	Claudio Beretta		19/10/93	M		(1)	
13	Gilles Bettmer		31/03/89	M	18	(8)	3
4	Ante Bukvic		14/11/87	D	25		2
24	Gauthier Caron	FRA	27/12/89	A	7	(11)	6
14	Omar Er Rafik	FRA	07/01/86	M	23	(3)	13
23	Geoffrey Franzoni	FRA	18/02/91	A	24		2
1	Yann Heil		05/09/90	G	15		
16	Mathias Jänisch		27/08/90	D	21	(2)	1
17	Michel Kettenmeyer		07/02/89	M	12	(2)	1
	Kim Kintziger		02/04/87	D	11	(2)	
18	Philippe Lebresne	FRA	09/07/78	M	16	(5)	3
8	Andy May		02/09/89	D	16	(2)	1
26	Jérémy Meligner	FRA	11/06/91	M	17	(4)	5
20	Pedro Ribeiro	POR	07/01/89	M	12	(4)	4
25	Pierre Piskor	FRA	02/05/87	A	10	(11)	10
11	Tom Siebenaler		28/09/90	D	18	(1)	
27	Dejvid Sinani	ALB	02/04/93	M		(4)	
2	Julien Weber	FRA	12/10/85	G	11		

F91 DUDELANGE

Coach: Didier Philippe (FRA);
(12/11/12) Patrick Hesse
1991 • Jos Nosbaum (4,500) • f91.lu
Major honours
Luxembourg League (10) 2000, 2001, 2002, 2005,
2006, 2007, 2008, 2009, 2011, 2012;
Luxembourg Cup (5) 2004, 2006, 2007, 2009, 2012

2012

05/08	Etzella	a	1-0	Steinmetz
19/08	Kayl-Tétange	a	5-1	Legros, Idazza 3, Kitenge
26/08	Grevenmacher	h	1-1	Melisse
16/09	Hamm Benfica	a	1-1	Steinmetz
23/09	Progrès	h	3-0	Idazza 2, Caillet
26/09	Jeunesse Esch	h	0-1	
30/09	Käerjéng	a	3-1	Da Mota (p), Idazza, Steinmetz
03/10	Jeunesse Canach	h	0-1	
21/10	Fola	a	2-1	Kitenge, Malget
28/10	Wiltz	h	7-1	Kitenge 2, Steinmetz 3, Malget, Da Mota
04/11	Differdange	h	3-0	Pedro 2, Steinmetz
10/11	Racing Union	a	1-1	Steinmetz
25/11	Pétange	a	2-1	Steinmetz 2

2013

03/03	Grevenmacher	a	0-0	
06/03	Jeunesse Esch	a	3-0	Karapetyan 2, Benzouien
10/03	Hamm Benfica	h	1-0	Caillet
30/03	Käerjéng	h	2-1	Malget, Kitenge
07/04	Kayl-Tétange	h	3-0	Kitenge 2, Pedro
13/04	Progrès	a	1-0	Da Mota
17/04	Jeunesse Canach	a	1-1	Prempeh
21/04	Fola	h	0-0	
27/04	Wiltz	a	2-1	Steinmetz (p), Melisse (p)
05/05	Differdange	a	1-2	Caillet
12/05	Racing Union	h	2-1	Steinmetz, Haddadji (p)
22/05	Pétange	a	4-0	Kitenge, Benzouien, Maury, Jäger
26/05	Etzella	h	4-3	Jäger 2, Betorangal, Benzouien

No	Name	Nat	DoB	Pos	Aps	(s)	Gls
13	Morgan Beltorangal	FRA	25/08/88	M	5		1
12	Sofian Benzouien	BEL	11/08/86	M	19	(2)	3
4	Jean-Philippe Caillet	FRA	24/06/77	D	12	(3)	3
22	Daniel Da Mota		11/09/85	A	16	(6)	3
25	Daniel Gomez	FRA	16/03/79	A	5	(7)	
14	Ilies Haddadji	FRA	09/04/90	M	19	(1)	1
16	Gaël Hug	FRA	08/01/80	M	5	(1)	
27	Saïd Idazza	MAR	25/04/89	A	8	(2)	6
32	Jonathan Jäger	FRA	25/03/76	A	1	(2)	3
24	Aurélien Joachim		10/08/86	A	2		
3	Jonathan Joubert		12/09/79	G	26		
31	Alexander Karapetyan	GEO	23/12/87	A	4		2
28	Joël Kitenge		12/11/87	A	14	(5)	8
17	Jean-Sébastien Legros	BEL	16/02/81	M	8	(3)	1
7	Kevin Malget		15/01/91	D	15	(3)	3
9	Massimo Martino		18/09/90	D	12	(4)	
29	Donovan Maury	BEL	08/05/81	D	10		1
15	Bryan Melisse	FRA	25/03/89	A	20		2
16	Ben Payal		08/09/88	M	12	(4)	
18	Joël Pedro de Almeida		10/04/92	M	16	(4)	3
22	Mike Post		16/03/93	A		(5)	
5	Jerry Prempeh	FRA	29/12/88	D	25		1
30	Delvin Skenderovic		23/01/94	D		(5)	
19	Thierry Steinmetz	FRA	09/07/83	M	22		12
6	Ibrahim Touray	FRA	10/07/89	D	1		
10	Julien Tournut	FRA	02/07/82	D	2		
12	Lehit Zeghdane	FRA	03/10/77	D	7	(7)	

FC ETZELLA ETTELBRUCK

Coach: Patrick Grettnich
1917 • Stade du Centre Sportif "Deich" (2,024) •
fc-etzella.lu
Major honours
Luxembourg Cup (1) 2001

2012

05/08	Dudelange	h	0-1	
11/08	Racing Union	a	3-1	Theis, Bassing, Turpel
19/08	Pétange	h	2-2	Moos, Frederico
26/08	Differdange	a	0-0	
16/09	Jeunesse Esch	a	2-3	Turpel 2
23/09	Kayl-Tétange	h	3-3	Nílton, Holtz, Bassing
30/09	Grevenmacher	a	1-4	Reeff
04/10	Hamm Benfica	h	2-2	Turpel, Frederico
21/10	Progrès	a	1-5	A Leweck
28/10	Käerjéng	h	3-1	Turpel 2, Bassing
03/11	Jeunesse Canach	a	2-1	Moos, Frederico
10/11	Fola	h	0-5	
25/11	Wiltz	a	0-0	

2013

03/03	Differdange	h	0-4	
06/03	Racing Union	h	2-2	Turpel 2
10/03	Jeunesse Esch	h	0-4	
30/03	Grevenmacher	h	1-0	Nílton (p)
07/04	Pétange	a	1-1	C Leweck
14/04	Kayl-Tétange	a	4-1	Pietrasik, A Leweck, Nílton, Theis
17/04	Hamm Benfica	a	2-3	Turpel, Da Mota
21/04	Progrès	h	1-1	Turpel
28/04	Käerjéng	a	3-5	Turpel, Nílton (p), Dany Fernandes
05/05	Jeunesse Canach	h	1-1	Nílton
12/05	Fola	a	1-5	Moos
22/05	Wiltz	h	3-2	Turpel 2 (1p), C Leweck
26/05	Dudelange	a	3-4	Turpel 2, Pietrasik

No	Name	Nat	DoB	Pos	Aps	(s)	Gls
19	Michaël Barrela Rodrigues		12/05/88	A	7	(5)	
20	Pit Bassing		27/06/94	A	4	(16)	3
9	Randy Chionna	ITA	08/09/89	M	2	(4)	
10	David Da Mota		12/05/89	M	15	(3)	1
22	Dany Fernandes	POR	09/05/94	A	8	(6)	1
4	Gilles Engeldinger		04/05/84	D	19		
1	Joé Flick		16/07/79	G	1	(1)	
21	Frederico	POR	28/12/92	A	11	(6)	3
3	Gilson Delgado	CPV	19/10/92	D	24		
2	Philippe Hahm		13/01/90	G	25		
12	Kevin Holtz		06/03/93	M	2	(2)	1
25	Almin Kocan	MNE	10/10/92	M	3		
15	Alphonse Leweck		16/12/81	M	14	(6)	2
14	Charles Leweck		19/07/83	M	25		2
16	Paulo Mendes		27/09/88	M	13	(1)	
17	Jeff Moos		02/09/94	M	19	(2)	3
5	Nílton	CPV	19/01/79	M	11	(3)	5
5	Bartłomiej Pietrasik	POL	25/05/84	D	22	(2)	2
7	Alain Reeff		29/10/86	D	11		1
6	Michaël Sarfati	FRA	19/07/87	D	6	(1)	
23	Andreas Theis	GER	03/12/82	A	14	(7)	2
24	David Turpel		19/10/92	A	21	(2)	15
8	Nicolas Valletta		28/03/94	D	9	(3)	

CS FOLA ESCH

Coach: Jeff Strasser
1906 • Emile Mayrisch (6,000) • csfola.lu
Major honours
Luxembourg League (6) 1918, 1920, 1922, 1924, 1930, 2013;
Luxembourg Cup (3) 1923, 1924, 1955

2012

05/08	Kayl-Tétange	a	6-1	Boulahfari, Ronny (p), Hornuss 2, Bensi 2
11/08	Grevenmacher	h	1-1	Rani
19/08	Hamm Benfica	a	3-2	Bensi 3 (1p)
26/08	Progrès	h	4-0	Bensi 3, Boulahfari
16/09	Käerjéng	a	4-1	Bensi 2, Rani, Hornuss
23/09	Jeunesse Canach	a	3-1	Hornuss 2, Boulahfari
30/09	Differdange	h	2-1	Schnell (p), Boulahfari
04/10	Wiltz	a	3-0	Bensi (p), Dallevedove, Hornuss
21/10	Dudelange	h	1-2	Bernard
28/10	Racing Union	a	1-0	Laterza
04/11	Pétange	h	3-0	Rani, Bensi, Dallevedove
10/11	Etzella	a	5-1	Rani, Hadji 2, Bensi, Schnell
25/11	Jeunesse Esch	h	0-2	

2013

06/03	Grevenmacher	a	3-3	Renouard, Bensi 2
10/03	Käerjéng	h	4-1	Renouard, Bensi 2, Rani
30/03	Differdange	a	0-1	
03/04	Progrès	a	3-0	Rani 2, Hadji
07/04	Hamm Benfica	h	2-1	Schnell, Laterza
14/04	Jeunesse Canach	a	1-1	Ronny (p)
17/04	Wiltz	h	1-0	Laterza
21/04	Dudelange	a	0-0	
28/04	Racing Union	h	1-1	Rani
05/05	Pétange	a	2-0	Laterza, Hadji
12/05	Etzella	h	5-1	Hornuss 2, Laterza, Ronny 2, Bensi
22/05	Jeunesse Esch	a	5-1	Hornuss, Bensi 2, Laterza, Dallevedove
26/05	Kayl-Tétange	h	4-2	Pazos, Hadji 2, Maikel Veloso

No	Name	Nat	DoB	Pos	Aps	(s)	Gls
13	Assim Alomerovic		15/01/83	M	8	(4)	
15	Alessandro Alunni		19/12/91	M	2	(13)	
24	Stefano Bensi		11/08/88	A	18	(3)	20
5	Billy Bernard		09/04/91	D	21		1
14	Rachid Boulahfari	FRA	17/04/84	M	14	(6)	4
22	Jakob Dallevedove	GER	21/11/87	A	16	(2)	3
28	Samir Hadji	FRA	12/09/89	D	8	(16)	6
24	Julien Hornuss	FRA	01/01/87	A	21	(4)	9
2	Thomas Hym	FRA	29/08/87	G	12		
16	Laurent Jans		05/08/92	M	12	(10)	
32	João Freitas	POR	06/07/96	A	1		
7	Mehdi Kirch	FRA	27/01/90	D	23		
2	Julien Klein	FRA	07/04/87	M	21	(3)	
6	Tom Laterza		09/05/92	D	16	(4)	6
31	Dany Loureiro da Cunha		10/03/96	M		(1)	
30	Maikel Veloso	POR	29/04/93	A	1		1
18	Sébastien Mazurier	FRA	13/04/81	M	3	(4)	
19	Christophe Pazos	ESP	19/05/90	M	3	(2)	1
27	Ahmed Rani	FRA	20/08/87	M	23	(2)	8
29	Sébastien Renouard	FRA	11/07/84	A	6	(1)	2
20	Ronny	CPV	07/12/78	M	25	(1)	5
3	Rui Peixoto	POR	03/12/93	G	1		
8	Tom Schnell		08/10/85	D	18		3
4	Pit Theis		25/01/79	G	13		
11	David Veiga		12/06/91	D		(1)	

CS GREVENMACHER

Coach: Marc Thomé
1909 • Op Flohr (4,000) • csg.lu
Major honours
Luxembourg League (1) 2003;
Luxembourg Cup (4) 1995, 1998, 2003, 2008

2012

05/08	Jeunesse Canach	h	0-0		
11/08	Fola	a	1-1	*F Gaspar*	
19/08	Wiltz	h	4-1	*Battaglia 2, Huss 2 (1p)*	
26/08	Dudelange	a	1-1	*Louadj*	
16/09	Racing Union	h	3-3	*Huss 3*	
23/09	Pétange	a	1-1	*Mikael Pinto*	
30/09	Etzella	h	4-1	*Huss 2, Mota, Louadj*	
04/10	Jeunesse Esch	a	0-0		
21/10	Kayl-Tétange	h	2-1	*Hoffmann (p), Dragolovcanin*	
28/10	Differdange	a	3-2	*Louadj, F Gaspar, Herres*	
04/11	Hamm Benfica	a	1-1	*H...*	
11/11	Progrès	h	3-2	*Louadj, Huss, F Gaspar*	
25/11	Käerjéng	a	0-2		

2013

03/03	Dudelange	h	0-0		
06/03	Fola	h	3-3	*Battaglia, Huss (p), Herres*	
10/03	Racing Union	a	1-2	*Daniel Lopes*	
30/03	Etzella	a	0-1		
07/04	Wiltz	a	4-0	*Schiltz 3, Steinmetz*	
14/04	Pétange	h	3-1	*Louadj, Heinz, F Gaspar*	
17/04	Jeunesse Esch	a	1-1		
21/04	Kayl-Tétange	a	2-1	*Heinz, og (I lugo Gonçalves)*	
28/04	Differdange	h	3-2	*og (Bukvic), Hoffmann, Huss*	
05/05	Hamm Benfica	h	1-2	*F Gaspar*	
12/05	Progrès	a	0-2		
22/05	Käerjéng	h	1-0	*Battaglia*	
26/05	Jeunesse Canach	a	2-0	*Huss, Louadj*	

No	Name	Nat	DoB	Pos	Aps	(s)	Gls
10	Gonçalo Almeida		26/11/90	M	14	(3)	
3	Thomas Battaglia	FRA	05/08/92	D	22		4
29	Michel Bechtold		01/07/95	D	17	(3)	
12	Christian Braun		12/08/86	M	19	(1)	
4	Dariusz Brzyski	POL	06/09/86	D	16		
25	Hamza Cherit	ALG	02/06/93	M	5	(2)	
18	Daniel Lopes	POR	31/08/87	M	4	(11)	1
23	Denis Dragolovcanin		17/12/90	A	1	(8)	1
32	Gilles Feltes		06/12/95	M		(2)	
6	Jonathan Furst	FRA	23/03/87	D	19	(3)	
14	Florian Gaspar	GER	07/07/87	M	13	(7)	5
30	Gabriel Gaspar		20/07/90	M	9	(1)	
7	Tim Heinz		05/02/84	D	24		2
17	Patrick Herres	GER	11/10/89	M	6	(10)	2
21	Sébastien Hoffmann	FRA	18/12/78	A	24	(1)	2
22	Daniel Huss		08/10/79	A	14	(8)	12
11	Sidney Loes		21/10/93	M		(1)	
19	Samir Louadj	FRA	09/12/85	M	21	(2)	6
9	Mikael Pinto	POR	10/11/90	D	4	(2)	1
20	André Mota		02/08/92	M	7	(3)	1
2	Arnaud Schaab	FRA	03/09/90	G	26		
24	Laurent Schiltz		17/02/82	A	10	(3)	3
9	Vic Speller		03/07/93	D	8		
26	Andreas Steffen	GER	29/03/88	A	2	(1)	
31	Damian Steinmetz		04/02/95	A	1	(3)	1

FC RM HAMM BENFICA

Coach: Carlo Weis
2004 • Cents (3,000) • benficafcluxembourg.com

2012

05/08	Käerjéng	h	2-1	*Di Domenico, Kehal*	
11/08	Jeunesse Canach	a	2-2	*Benhamza, Peters*	
19/08	Fola	h	2-3	*Kehal, Papadopoulos*	
26/08	Wiltz	a	2-2	*Kitenge, Thior*	
16/09	Dudelange	h	1-1	*Augusto*	
23/09	Racing Union	a	1-1	*Peters (p)*	
30/09	Pétange	h	5-2	*Do Rosario, Stojadinovic, Augusto 2, Kitenge*	
04/10	Etzella	a	2-2	*Peters (p), Gonçalves da Silva*	
21/10	Jeunesse Esch	h	1-0	*Augusto*	
28/10	Kayl-Tétange	a	5-1	*Niabaly, Stojadinovic, Augusto 3*	
04/11	Grevenmacher	h	1-1	*Augusto*	
11/11	Differdange	a	3-0	*Niabaly, Pereira Fereira*	
25/11	Progrès	a	0-1		

2013

03/03	Wiltz	h	2-0	*Bruno Matias, Do Rosario*	
06/03	Jeunesse Canach	h	0-4		
10/03	Dudelange	a	0-1		
20/03	Pétange	a	3-0	*Bruno Matias, Bastos Silva, Do Rosario*	
07/04	Fola	a	1-2	*Schneider*	
14/04	Racing Union	h	4-1	*Kehal, Schneider 2, Pereira Fereira*	
17/04	Etzella	h	3-2	*Pereira Fereira 2, Bellanger*	
21/04	Jeunesse Esch	a	1-0	*Augusto*	
28/04	Kayl-Tétange	h	3-1	*Peters 2, Augusto*	
05/05	Grevenmacher	a	2-1	*Augusto, Bruno Matias*	
12/05	Differdange	h	2-1	*Bruno Matias, Kehal*	
22/05	Progrès	h	2-2	*Bruno Matias, Kehal*	
26/05	Käerjéng	a	4-2	*Augusto 2, Peters 2*	

No	Name	Nat	DoB	Pos	Aps	(s)	Gls
8	André Gonçalves	POR	26/00/88	D	1	(0)	
17	François Augusto		02/06/88	A	16	(9)	13
11	André Bastos Silva		18/03/91	M	14	(4)	1
13	Robin Bellanger	FRA	20/02/92	D	12	(2)	1
10	Nabil Benhamza	FRA	22/08/88	M	24	(1)	1
2	Alex Boukhetaia	FRA	19/11/79	G	13		
22	Bruno Matias	POR	04/03/89	A	5	(7)	5
25	Nicolas Desgranges	FRA	19/06/96	M		(3)	
12	Sven Di Domenico		15/03/82	M	4		1
3	Sébastien Do Rosario	FRA	12/01/84	D	23	(1)	3
15	Nelson Gonçalves da Silva		17/06/91	M		(7)	1
19	Djilali Kehal	FRA	01/10/78	A	15	(4)	5
14	Dimitri Kitenge		02/01/91	M	6	(4)	2
7	Jérôme Marcolino Rodrigues		27/03/89	D	2		
21	Ousmane Niabaly	FRA	25/06/79	A	11	(1)	2
4	Wilfried Ntede	FRA	12/04/90	D	8		
5	Thomas Papadopoulos		11/12/93	A	3	(6)	1
20	Cristiano Pereira Fereira		21/11/89	A	16	(6)	4
18	René Peters		15/06/81	M	25		4
24	Chris Sagramola		25/02/88	A	1	(6)	
23	Mike Schneider		01/02/95	M	9	(5)	3
1	Kevin Sommer	FRA	11/08/89	G	13		
16	Igor Stojadinovic		18/11/85	M	20	(1)	2
9	François Thior	FRA	11/02/85	D	22		1
6	Ben Vogel		22/12/94	D	23	(2)	

FC JEUNESSE CANACH

Coach: Patrick Maurer
1957 • Stade rue de Lenningen (1,000) • fccanach.lu

2012

05/08	Grevenmacher	a	0-0		
11/08	Hamm Benfica	h	2-2	*Oséias 2 (1p)*	
19/08	Progrès	a	2-0	*Marcão 2*	
25/08	Käerjéng	h	3-1	*Oséias (p), Kalabic, Augusto Cravo*	
16/09	Differdange	h	1-3	*Augusto Cravo*	
23/09	Fola	a	1-3	*Oséias*	
30/09	Wiltz	h	6-2	*Pedro Ferro 3, Marco Semedo, Dimitri, Oséias*	
03/10	Dudelange	a	1-0	*Kalabic*	
21/10	Racing Union	h	1-1	*Oséias*	
28/10	Pétange	h	2-1	*Pedro Ferro 2*	
03/11	Etzella	h	1-2	*Oséias*	
10/11	Jeunesse Esch	a	1-5	*Oséias*	
25/11	Kayl-Tétange	h	2-0	*Augusto Cravo, Pedro Ferro*	

2013

03/03	Käerjéng	a	1-1	*Amartey*	
06/03	Hamm Benfica	a	4-0	*Teixeira Caçador, Dervisevic 2, Kettels*	
10/03	Differdange	a	1-3	*Dimitri*	
30/03	Wiltz	a	2-1	*Marco Semedo, Amartey*	
07/04	Progrès	h	0-2		
14/04	Fola	h	1-1	*Oséias*	
17/04	Dudelange	h	1-1	*Marcão*	
21/04	Racing Union	a	0-1		
27/04	Pétange	h	1-2	*Pedro Ferro*	
05/05	Etzella	a	1-1	*Dervisevic*	
12/05	Jeunesse Esch	h	3-0	*Pedro Ferro 2, Oséias*	
22/05	Kayl-Tétange	a	2-0	*Oséias 2 (1p)*	
26/05	Grevenmacher	h	0-2		

No	Name	Nat	DoB	Pos	Aps	(s)	Gls
20	Mohamed Akab	FRA	18/02/89	M	3	(1)	
9	Luis Alvites		09/11/87	M		(1)	
31	George Amartey	GHA	22/02/80	A	12	(1)	5
17	Arthur	BRA	08/03/77	M	1	(6)	
22	Augusto Cravo	BRA	06/09/80	A	22		3
2	Cadabra	CPV	26/06/84	G	26		
32	Yves Candida Lima		06/11/79	D	1	(1)	
34	Noureddine Danhach	FRA	30/10/73	M	1		
11	Din Dervisevic		19/05/91	M	8	(14)	3
6	Dimitri	BRA	18/06/79	D	25		2
15	Laurent Hoeser		20/10/86	M	8	(8)	
16	Emko Kalabic		30/03/89	M	6	(5)	2
34	Kalú	CPV	08/09/84	M	1		
12	Karl Ferro	BRA	31/07/83	M	15	(3)	
30	Gilles Kettels	GER	28/06/98	M	3	(3)	1
7	Gueton Kremer	FRA	25/04/85	D	16		
8	Renaud Kremer	FRA	05/04/84	D	16	(1)	
21	Marcão	BRA	19/07/76	M	18	(1)	3
29	Marco Semedo	POR	08/10/87	D	19		2
14	Steve Oliveira		01/07/84	M	1	(8)	
25	Oséias	POR	13/06/72	A	20	(5)	12
28	Patrick Ossamba	FRA	25/09/86	M	1		
24	Pedro Ferro	POR	21/07/87	A	24	(1)	9
1	Pit Rauen		05/05/82	G		(1)	
35	Roger Sousa	BRA	30/08/71	A		(2)	
33	Tomasz Sajdak	POL	10/11/84	A		(1)	
18	Admir Skrijelj		03/06/92	M	19	(3)	
19	David Teixeira Caçador		17/12/86	M	21		1
10	Waldino Borges	CPV	01/10/80	M		(4)	

AS JEUNESSE ESCH

Coach: Sébastien Grandjean (BEL); (18/10/12)
Lionel Zanini; (02/04/13) Dan Theis
1907 • Stade de la Frontière (7,000) • jeunesse-esch.lu
Major honours
Luxembourg League (28) 1921, 1937, 1951, 1954,
1958, 1959, 1960, 1963, 1967, 1968, 1970, 1973, 1974,
1975, 1976, 1977, 1980, 1983, 1985, 1987, 1988, 1995,
1996, 1997, 1998, 1999, 2004, 2010;
Luxembourg Cup (13) 1935, 1937, 1946, 1954, 1973,
1974, 1976, 1981, 1988, 1997, 1999, 2000, 2013

2012

05/08	Wiltz	h	0-2	
19/08	Racing Union	h	3-4	Moreira, Benajiba, Agović
25/08	Pétange	a	2-0	Wang, Benajiba
16/09	Etzella	h	3-2	Ibrahimović 2, Benajiba (p)
22/09	Differdange	a	3-0	Ndongala, Ibrahimović, Benajiba
26/09	Dudelange	a	1-0	Benajiba
30/09	Kayl-Tétange	a	2-0	Benajiba, Quéré
04/10	Grevenmacher	h	0-0	
21/10	Hamm Benfica	a	0-1	
28/10	Progrès	h	0-0	
04/11	Käerjéng	a	3-2	Miceli, Benajiba 2
10/11	Jeunesse Canach	h	5-1	Delgado, Quéré, Ramdedović, Benichou, Ibrahimović
25/11	Fola	a	2-0	Ndongala, Hoffmann

2013

03/03	Pétange	h	3-0	Dufoor 2, Benajiba (p)
06/03	Dudelange	h	0-3	
10/03	Etzella	a	4-0	Ibrahimović 3, Dufoor
30/03	Kayl-Tétange	h	4-1	Ibrahimović, Collette, Dufoor, og (Mendes Pina)
07/04	Racing Union	a	2-0	Ibrahimović 2
13/04	Differdange	h	2-4	Benajiba (p), Ramdedović
17/04	Grevenmacher	a	2-0	Benichou, Ibrahimović
21/04	Hamm Benfica	h	0-1	
28/04	Progrès	a	4-0	Collette 2, Ibrahimović, Benajiba
05/05	Käerjéng	h	5-1	Miceli 2, Deidda 2, Wang
12/05	Jeunesse Canach	a	0-3	
22/05	Fola	h	1-5	Benichou
26/05	Wiltz	a	2-1	Ibrahimović 2 (1p)

No	Name	Nat	DoB	Pos	Aps	(s)	Gls
11	Denis Agović	MNE	12/07/93	M	9	(4)	1
19	Yassine Benajiba	MAR	01/11/84	M	22		11
5	Khalid Benichou	FRA	28/03/88	M	24		3
32	Amar Catić	BIH	07/08/95	D		(2)	
6	Dan Collette		02/04/85	A	24	(1)	3
28	Andrea Deidda		15/12/93	A	3	(2)	2
29	Ricardo Delgado		22/02/94	D	4	(5)	1
27	Sébastien Dufoor	BEL	07/07/81	A	7	(5)	4
31	Glenn Gomes Borges		16/05/95	A		(2)	
26	Nabil Guelsifi	FRA	27/11/86	M	2	(3)	
8	Eric Hoffmann		21/06/84	D	26		1
20	Sanel Ibrahimović	BIH	24/11/87	A	20	(5)	14
25	Damien Miceli	BEL	17/10/84	M	21	(2)	3
7	Clayton de Sousa Moreira		24/02/88	D	25		1
24	Dieumerci Ndongala	BEL	14/06/91	A	6	(3)	2
2	Marc Oberweis		06/11/82	G	26		
16	Adrien Portier	FRA	02/02/88	D	20		
23	Frankie Quéré	FRA	25/02/80	A	4	(5)	2
9	Dzenid Ramdedović	MNE	25/02/92	D	12	(10)	2
30	Milos Todorovic		18/08/95	M	1	(3)	
10	Alexandre Vitali	FRA	17/01/89	D	14	(7)	
14	Wang Chu	CHN	10/01/91	M	16	(7)	2

UN KÄERJÉNG 97

Coach: Roland Schaack
1997 • Käerjénger Dribbel (2,000) • un-kaerjeng.lu

2012

05/08	Hamm Benfica	a	1-2	Guthleber
12/08	Progrès	h	2-0	Fiorani, Sabotic (p)
19/08	Differdange	a	2-2	Teixeira Soares, Zewe
25/08	Jeunesse Canach	a	1-3	Sabotic (p)
16/09	Fola	h	1-4	Sabotic (p)
22/09	Wiltz	a	2-3	Da Cruz, Piron
30/09	Dudelange	h	1-3	Zewe
21/10	Pétange	h	3-0	Teixeira Soares, Fiorani, Piron
28/10	Etzella	a	1-3	Piron
04/11	Jeunesse Esch	h	2-3	Andres, Sabotic (p)
11/11	Kayl-Tétange	a	1-1	Zewe
25/11	Grevenmacher	h	2-0	Piron, Brix
06/12	Racing Union	a	0-3	

2013

03/03	Jeunesse Canach	h	1-1	Piron
06/03	Progrès	a	2-0	Piron, Corral Garcia
10/03	Fola	a	1-4	Fiorani
30/03	Dudelange	a	1-2	Sabotic (p)
07/04	Differdange	a	0-0	
14/04	Wiltz	h	4-3	Hess, Teixeira Soares, Piron, Zewe
17/04	Racing Union	h	2-0	Corral Garcia, Sabotic (p)
21/04	Pétange	a	3-1	Teixeira Soares, Binsfeld, Corral Garcia
28/04	Etzella	h	5-3	Zewe 2, Piron 2, Fiorani
05/05	Jeunesse Esch	a	1-5	Cunha da Fonseca
12/05	Kayl-Tétange	h	3-2	Piron, Rolandi, Sabotic (p)
22/05	Grevenmacher	a	0-1	
26/05	Hamm Benfica	h	2-4	Da Cruz 2

No	Name	Nat	DoB	Pos	Aps	(s)	Gls
11	Romain Andres	FRA	20/01/88	M	17	(3)	1
12	Marc Binsfeld		30/04/87	M	13	(2)	1
4	Jérôme Brix		22/09/92	D	13	(3)	1
17	Cleyton	CPV	20/08/90	M	4	(8)	
21	Ken Corral Garcia		08/05/92	A	11	(1)	3
34	Christophe Cunha da Fonseca		08/01/95	A	2	(3)	1
22	Stéphane Da Cruz	FRA	01/03/88	A	12	(5)	3
27	Jeff Feller		18/04/85	M	6		
14	Alessandro Fiorani		16/02/89	M	23	(1)	4
7	Alexis Grégoire	FRA	29/04/88	D	12	(4)	
26	Laurent Guthleber	FRA	26/10/80	D	9		1
32	Pit Hess		17/01/92	D	12	(1)	1
29	Sam Loes		25/04/94	M	1	(3)	
30	Jérôme Marcolino Rodrigues		27/03/89	D	8	(1)	
23	Stéphane Piron	BEL	17/01/84	M	18	(3)	10
9	Henid Ramdedović		20/07/87	D	12	(1)	
24	Jeff Reichling		27/10/93	A	7	(5)	
33	Julien Rolandi	FRA	28/03/86	M	10	(2)	1
19	Ernad Sabotic		13/10/79	M	24		7
2	Philippe Stelletta	FRA	24/02/84	G	20		
28	Chris Stumpf		28/08/94	M		(3)	
18	Sergio Teixeira Soares		03/01/92	M	15	(10)	4
1	Tom Weiland		27/07/94	G	1		
31	Cyrille Welter		24/02/91	M	1	(3)	
3	Jérôme Winckel		20/12/85	G	5		
25	Romain Zewe	FRA	21/04/88	A	12	(9)	6
20	Jonathan Zydko	FRA	12/01/84	D	18	(2)	

CS PÉTANGE

Coach: Michel Renquin (BEL);
(25/09/12) (Mourad Boukellal (ALG));
(31/10/12) Paulo Gomes (POR)
1910 • Stade Municipal (2,400) • cspetange.lu
Major honours
Luxembourg Cup (1) 2005

2012

05/08	Racing Union	h	1-0	N'Diaye
11/08	Differdange	a	0-3	
19/08	Etzella	a	2-2	Wang, Nissan
25/08	Jeunesse Esch	h	0-2	
16/09	Kayl-Tétange	a	3-1	Maïa, Camara 2
23/09	Grevenmacher	h	1-1	Bahin
30/09	Hamm Benfica	a	2-5	N'Diaye, Bahin
07/10	Progrès	h	0-2	
21/10	Käerjéng	a	0-3	
28/10	Jeunesse Canach	h	1-2	Thonon
04/11	Fola	a	0-3	
11/11	Wiltz	h	0-1	
25/11	Dudelange	a	1-2	N'Diaye

2013

03/03	Jeunesse Esch	a	0-3	
06/03	Differdange	h	1-1	Mutuale
10/03	Kayl-Tétange	h	1-1	Makela
29/03	Hamm Benfica	h	0-3	
07/04	Etzella	h	1-1	Hodzic
14/04	Grevenmacher	a	1-3	N'Diaye
17/04	Progrès	a	0-1	
21/04	Käerjéng	h	1-3	Basić
27/04	Jeunesse Canach	a	2-1	og (Dimitri), Pedro Pinto
05/05	Fola	h	0-2	
12/05	Wiltz	a	2-4	og (Sène), Michael Barbosa
22/05	Dudelange	h	0-4	
26/05	Racing Union	a	1-3	Dione

No	Name	Nat	DoB	Pos	Aps	(s)	Gls
36	Patrick Abreu	POR	26/12/90	A		(1)	
13	Gaël Arend	BEL	13/06/89	M	12	(1)	
5	Aristide Bahin	CIV	21/11/87	A	6	(3)	2
35	Ernest Basić	SRB	26/10/95	A	1	(4)	1
20	Claudio Beretta		19/10/93	A	2	(5)	
4	Bastien Borel	FRA	11/01/92	D	7		
21	Soriba Camara	GUI	05/02/74	A	8	(8)	2
36	Yannick da Graça Dias		13/07/96	M	3	(1)	
6	Aldi Dervisevic		19/08/84	D	16	(3)	
4	Papa Aye Dione	SEN	08/03/86	D	19		1
34	Michael Gaspar		22/07/94	A		(2)	
31	Jasmin Hodzic		26/08/88	D	7	(2)	1
1	Bob Kirsch		18/02/87	G	1		
8	Tim Lehnen		17/06/86	D	21	(2)	
7	Nawfel Loudifa	FRA	16/06/92	D	9		
15	Gaël Maïa	FRA	02/01/84	M	21	(1)	1
25	Andrely Makela	FRA	24/10/91	A	7	(4)	1
35	Steven Martins		15/03/92	M	1	(3)	
33	Michael Barbosa	POR	31/10/84	M	10		1
10	Grégory Molitor		12/03/80	D	13	(3)	
11	Yamukile Mutuale	FRA	25/08/87	M	19	(1)	1
22	Abdoulaye N'Diaye	FRA	14/09/91	A	16	(4)	4
12	Jérémy Neves		18/08/93	D	6	(1)	
17	Dylan Nissan	IRQ	07/11/88	M	3	(6)	1
30	Pedro Fernandes	POR	17/01/85	G	9		
32	Pedro Pinto	POR	03/01/84	M	17	(4)	1
23	Anel Pjanić	BIH	26/12/83	A	5	(4)	
2	Samin Redzepagic		01/10/91	G	10		
2	Joé Reuter		24/08/91	G	6		
27	Thibaut Thonon	FRA	05/02/87	A	11	(5)	1
16	Juncai Wang		05/04/90	M	20	(4)	1

FC PROGRÈS NIEDERCORN

Coach: Henri Bossi; (02/10/12) Paolo Amodio
1919 • Jos Haupert (4,000) • progres.lu
Major honours
Luxembourg League (3) 1953, 1978, 1981; Luxembourg Cup (4) 1933, 1945, 1977, 1978

2012

05/08	Differdange	a	1-2	Rougeaux
12/08	Käerjéng	a	0-2	
19/08	Jeunesse Canach	h	0-2	
26/08	Fola	a	0-4	
16/09	Wiltz	h	2-3	Menaï, Thill
23/09	Dudelange	a	0-3	
30/09	Racing Union	h	0-1	
07/10	Pétange	a	2-0	Thill, Menaï
21/10	Etzella	h	5-1	Gruszczynski 3, Fabbro, Menaï
28/10	Jeunesse Esch	a	0-0	
03/11	Kayl-Tétange	h	1-3	Thill
11/11	Grevenmacher	a	2-3	Gruszczynski, Rougeaux
25/11	Hamm Benfica	h	1-0	Rougeaux

2013

06/03	Käerjéng	h	0-2	
10/03	Wiltz	a	1-2	Rougeaux
30/03	Racing Union	a	1-3	Gilgemann (p)
03/04	Fola	h	0-3	
07/04	Jeunesse Canach	a	2-0	Caldieri, Gilgemann (p)
13/04	Dudelange	h	1-1	Caldieri
17/04	Pétange	h	2-0	Rougeaux
21/04	Etzella	a	1-1	Rougeaux
28/04	Jeunesse Esch	h	0-4	
05/05	Kayl-Tétange	a	3-1	De Sousa, Thill 2
12/05	Grevenmacher	h	2-0	Menaï 2
22/05	Hamm Benfica	a	2-2	Caldieri, Rougeaux
26/05	Differdange	h	1-2	Nouidra

No	Name	Nat	DoB	Pos	Aps	(s)	Gls
1	Jérémie Bandel	FRA	03/04/85	G	1		
04	Ben Bossi		11/06/94	M		(2)	
21	Paul Bossi		22/07/91	A	17	(5)	
22	Nicolas Broquard	FRA	17/01/84	D	23	(1)	
7	Bruno Pinto	POR	03/10/94	D	1	(1)	
30	Nicolas Caldieri	FRA	01/12/82	A	11	(1)	3
2	Fabiano Castellani		11/05/89	G	21	(1)	
33	Danielson	CPV	09/07/93	A		(4)	
12	David Soares	POR	20/02/91	D	21	(1)	
14	Marco De Sousa		17/08/86	M	15	(3)	1
3	Vincent Degré	FRA	03/09/85	D	3		
4	El Hadji Dione	GER	25/03/73	D	3		
31	Moreno Fabbro		27/01/95	M	7	(8)	1
6	Thomas Gilgemann	FRA	15/09/83	D	26		2
28	Thomas Gruszczynski	FRA	04/12/80	A	11	(6)	4
19	Jorge Ribeiro	POR	24/10/92	M	4	(12)	
26	Angoua Lambert Kabran	CIV	18/10/89	A	1	(5)	
25	Hakim Menaï	FRA	27/03/86	A	17		5
15	Kevin Molinero Linares	FRA	09/01/85	M	1	(3)	
35	Neves Dias	CPV	11/10/95	A		(1)	
18	Tarek Nouidra	FRA	09/05/87	M	21	(2)	1
27	Michael Oliveira Martins		21/09/93	A		(1)	
13	Paulo da Costa	POR	24/04/81	D	7	(1)	
23	Jacques Plein		17/02/87	M	8		
10	Jonathan Rigo	FRA	16/09/87	D	23		
16	Lévy Rougeaux	FRA	05/05/85	M	21	(1)	7
32	Andy Theves		09/11/94	G	1		
20	Sébastien Thill		29/12/93	M	22	(4)	5

RACING FC UNION LËTZEBUERG

Coach: Claude Origer
2005 • Achille Hammerel (6,000) • racing-fc.lu

2012

05/08	Pétange	a	0-1	
11/08	Etzella	h	1-3	Romero
19/08	Jeunesse Esch	a	4-3	Lukic 2, Romero, Bellini
26/08	Kayl-Tétange	h	0-2	
16/09	Grevenmacher	a	3-3	Lukic, Luisi, Romero
23/09	Hamm Benfica	h	1-1	Lukic
30/09	Progrès	a	1-0	Luisi
21/10	Jeunesse Canach	a	1-1	Bellini
28/10	Fola	h	0-1	
04/11	Wiltz	a	9-0	Lukic 4, Bellini, Simion, Luisi 3
10/11	Dudelange	h	1-1	Bellini
25/11	Differdange	h	1-3	Klapp
06/12	Käerjéng	h	3-0	Lukic, Carlos, Luisi

2013

03/03	Kayl-Tétange	a	2-0	Bellini, Hammami
06/03	Etzella	a	2-2	Hammami, Klapp
10/03	Grevenmacher	h	2-1	Klapp, Dragovic
30/03	Progrès	h	3-1	Klapp, og (Gilgemann), Hammami (p)
07/04	Jeunesse Esch	h	0-2	
14/04	Hamm Benfica	a	1-4	Bellini (p)
17/04	Käerjéng	a	0-2	
21/04	Jeunesse Canach	h	1-0	Djellal
28/04	Fola	a	1-1	Luisi
05/05	Wiltz	h	0-3	
12/05	Dudelange	a	1-2	Klapp
22/05	Differdange	a	2-6	Lukic 2
26/05	Pétange	h	3-1	Lukic 2, Klapp

No	Name	Nat	DoB	Pos	Aps	(s)	Gls
1	Alexandre Abello	FRA	22/08/82	G	17		
13	Johan Bellini	FRA	02/06/83	M	25		6
25	Carlos	CPV	29/12/85	A	8	(2)	1
15	Ricardo Centrone		03/06/90	M		(9)	
2	Dany Rodrigues	POR	10/02/94	A	9		
7	Karim Djellal	FRA	27/01/82	D	19	(1)	1
17	Nenad Dragovic		04/06/94	D	21		1
16	Nasreddine Hammami	TUN	05/12/81	M	21	(1)	7
31	Amine Hamouni		29/09/94	A	1	(4)	
35	Juliano Jackson		23/09/94	M	18	(2)	
20	Jimmy Karemanns	BEL	23/05/95	A		(1)	
18	Ryan Klapp		10/01/93	M	21	(4)	6
28	Antonio Luisi		07/10/94	A	15	(8)	7
29	Zarko Lukic		22/05/83	A	20	(5)	13
24	Marco Simões	BRA	01/08/86	D	11	(8)	
30	Christopher Martins Pereira		19/02/97	A	7	(2)	
3	Loïc Mouny	FRA	28/03/81	D	14		
22	Damir Muhovic		19/02/85	M	12	(4)	
8	Jonathan Rodrigues Monteiro		08/01/91	D	14	(9)	
23	Nicolas Romero	FRA	18/08/88	A	7	(2)	3
9	Pit Siebenaler		23/06/93	D	6	(5)	
19	Dany Simion	FRA	17/09/92	D	20	(1)	1

UNION 05 KAYL-TÉTANGE

Coach: Manuel Correia
2005 • Stade Victor Marchal "An der Gonnerwiss" (1,000) & Stade rue de Dudelange (1,000) • union05.lu

2012

05/08	Fola	h	1-6	Muni (p)
11/08	Wiltz	a	2-4	Muni (p), Mokkedem
19/08	Dudelange	h	1-5	Lopes
26/08	Racing Union	a	0-2	Lopes, Kevin Lourenço
16/09	Pétange	h	1-3	Ricardo Sousa
23/09	Etzella	a	3-3	Lopes, Mokrani, Ricardo Sousa
30/09	Jeunesse Esch	h	0-2	
04/10	Differdange	a	1-3	Lopes
21/10	Grevenmacher	a	1-2	Kevin Lourenço
28/10	Hamm Benfica	h	1-5	Mokkedem
03/11	Progrès	a	3-1	Lopes, Mokkedem (p), Mokrani
11/11	Käerjéng	h	1-1	Ramdedovic
25/11	Jeunesse Canach	a	0-2	

2013

03/03	Racing Union	h	0-2	
06/03	Wiltz	h	1-5	Lopes
10/03	Pétange	a	1-1	Lopes
30/03	Jeunesse Esch	a	1-1	Lopes
07/04	Dudelange	a	0-0	
14/04	Etzella	h	1-4	Lopes (p)
17/04	Differdange	h	1-0	Lopes
21/04	Grevenmacher	h	1-0	Lopes
28/04	Hamm Benfica	a	1-3	Ollé-Nicolle
05/05	Progrès	h	1-3	Deidda
12/05	Käerjéng	a	2-3	Lopes, Deidda
22/05	Jeunesse Canach	h	0-2	
26/05	Fola	a	2-4	Geisbusch, Agović (p)

No	Name	Nat	DoB	Pos	Aps	(s)	Gls
32	Edis Agović	MNE	13/07/93	A	8	(2)	1
12	Cédric Bastos		07/05/89	M	12	(6)	
1	Rick Carreira	CAN	12/04/90	G	19		
25	Nedim Cirikovic		13/06/88	A	2	(1)	
33	Albino da Conceicao		03/11/82	A	3	(2)	
23	Ilario Deidda	ITA	18/12/89	A	3	(14)	2
34	Geoffrey Dépré	FRA	15/04/90	G	1		
7	Eduardo Lopes	POR	15/01/89	D	19	(1)	
3	Dániel Faoui	ROU	29/07/90	D	5	(3)	
30	Jonathan Gadroy	FRA	02/02/07	D	11		
5	Gérard Geisbusch		04/05/88	D	13	(2)	1
4	Hugo Gonçalves	POR	10/02/84	D	8	(2)	
36	Nedim Jasarović	MNE	15/10/93	A		(1)	
16	Kevin Lourenço	POR	12/05/92	M	14	(4)	2
24	Tony Lopes	FRA	04/11/81	A	23		12
10	Flavio Miguel Mendes Pina		05/05/89	M	14	(5)	
17	Jalil Mokkedem	FRA	04/06/90	M	14	(4)	3
29	Idir Mokrani	ALG	23/01/91	A	14	(4)	2
8	Andrea Moro		27/01/94	D	1	(2)	
26	Hajrullah Muni	GER	24/02/90	A	7	(4)	2
9	Romain Ollé-Nicolle	FRA	18/08/87	D	24	(1)	1
35	Sven Pauly		29/11/91	D	1		
34	Paulo Peixoto		02/05/92	M	2	(1)	
11	Meris Ramdedovic		03/10/90	M	15		1
14	Ricardo Ferreira	POR	27/06/82	M	2	(1)	
13	Ricardo Sousa	POR	14/04/81	M	11	(2)	2
2	Kim Rohmann		21/01/84	G	6		
18	Fahret Selimovic		26/09/93	M	6	(6)	
31	Eddy Shamavu	BEL	31/07/90	M	10	(2)	
19	Roméo Wétié Tchumou	CMR	11/10/91	M	18	(3)	

FC WILTZ 71

Coach: Pascal Lebrun (BEL);
(06/11/12) Samir Kalabic
1971 • Stade Géitzt (2,000) • fcwiltz.lu

2012

05/08	Jeunesse Esch	a	2-0	Osmanović 2
11/08	Kayl-Tétange	h	4-2	Osmanović 2, Yasan, Scolas
19/08	Grevenmacher	a	1-4	Osmanović
26/08	Hamm Benfica	h	2-2	Scolas, Osmanović
16/09	Progrès	a	3-2	Touré, Thiombiano, Yasan
22/09	Käerjéng	a	3-2	Amel Cosic, Osmanović 2
30/09	Jeunesse Canach	a	2-6	Sérgio Oliveira, Osmanović
04/10	Fola	h	0-3	
20/10	Differdange	h	0-4	
28/10	Dudelange	a	1-7	Osmanović
04/11	Racing Union	h	0-9	
11/11	Pétange	a	1-0	Osmanović
25/11	Etzella	h	0-0	

2013

03/03	Hamm Benfica	a	0-2	
06/03	Kayl-Tétange	a	5-1	Amel Cosic, Osmanović, Touré, M Mujkic, Thiombiano
10/03	Progrès	h	2-1	Osmanović, Hentz
30/03	Jeunesse Canach	h	1-2	Osmanović (p)
07/04	Grevenmacher	h	0-4	
14/04	Käerjéng	a	3-4	Amel Cosic 2, Osmanović
17/04	Fola	a	0-1	
21/04	Differdange	a	1-1	M Mujkic
27/04	Dudelange	h	1-2	Osmanović (p)
05/05	Racing Union	a	3-0	Cossalter 2, Osmanović
12/05	Pétange	h	4-2	Osmanović 2 (1p), Civic, Cossalter
22/05	Etzella	a	2-3	Amel Cosic, Osmanović
26/05	Jeunesse Esch	h	1-2	Osmanović (p)

No	Name	Nat	DoB	Pos	Aps	(s)	Gls
9	Adaílton	BRA	11/06/77	M	12		
1	Nils Beerens	NED	27/08/92	G	2	(1)	
18	Adis Civic		26/11/94	A	1	(6)	1
19	Jason Conrad	BEL	03/01/90	A	6	(10)	
3	Adis Cosic		04/06/91	D	2		
20	Amel Cosic		19/11/89	A	24		5
26	Maid Ćosić	BIH	10/08/94	A		(1)	
25	Kevin Cossalter	BEL	19/04/85	A	5	(3)	3
2	Dorian Delcour	BEL	11/03/88	G	20		
22	Denis Teixeira	POR	29/05/71	A	1	(7)	
10	Haris Faljic		01/06/91	D	10	(4)	
4	Ben Heiderscheid		09/04/89	D	12	(4)	
12	Claude Hentz		09/06/85	M	16	(2)	1
5	Tom Kopecky		16/05/82	D	10	(2)	
6	Besim Krdžalić	BIH	07/11/83	D	24		
26	Manuel Cardoso	POR	23/05/91	M		(1)	
14	Mehmet Mujkic		26/09/83	M	13	(3)	2
7	Sevad Mujkic		13/06/85	D	11		
21	Edis Osmanović	BIH	30/06/88	A	25		21
16	Grégory Scolas	BEL	24/01/90	M	20	(2)	2
24	Babacar Sené	SEN	01/01/83	M	12		
15	Sérgio Oliveira	POR	17/01/94	M	15		1
17	Mamadou Thiombiano	BFA	31/12/92	M	14	(6)	2
8	Amadou Touré	BFA	27/09/82	D	18	(2)	2
23	Fred Van de Sande	BEL	20/11/70	G	4	(1)	
13	Yasan Karaca	TUR	16/12/83	M	9	(1)	2

Top goalscorers

21	Edis Osmanović (Wiltz)
20	Stefano Bensi (Fola)
15	David Turpel (Etzella)
14	Sanel Ibrahimović (Jeunesse Esch)
13	Omar Er Rafik (Differdange)
	François Augusto (Hamm Benfica)
	Zarko Lukic (Racing Union)
12	Thierry Steinmetz (Dudelange)
	Daniel Huss (Grevenmacher)
	Oséias (Jeunesse Canach)
	Tony Lopes (Kayl-Tétange)

Promoted clubs

FC SWIFT HESPER

Coach: Serge Wolf
1916 • Alphonse Theis (4,100) • swifthesper.lu
Major honours
Luxembourg Cup (1) 1990

US RUMELANGE

Coach: Manuel Cardoni; (02/10/12) Jean-Marc Klein
1908 • Municipal (2,950) • usrumelange.lu
Major honours
Luxembourg Cup (2) 1968, 1975

SECOND LEVEL FINAL TABLE 2012/13

		Pld	W	D	L	F	A	Pts
1	FC Swift Hesper	26	18	6	2	67	19	60
2	US Rumelange	26	17	5	4	55	31	56
3	FC Una Strassen	26	17	4	5	57	30	55
4	FC Victoria Rosport	26	16	4	6	64	30	52
5	US Sandweiler	26	14	4	8	64	40	46
6	US Hostert	26	14	2	10	48	42	44
7	FC Erpeldange 72	26	11	5	10	54	55	38
8	FF Norden 02	26	9	6	11	38	49	33
9	FC Alliance Äischdall	26	8	5	13	34	49	29
10	US Mondorf-les-Bains	26	6	10	10	43	37	28
11	CS Obercorn	26	7	5	14	38	55	26
12	FC Mondercange	26	6	5	15	29	56	23
13	FC Marner 32	26	5	5	16	29	58	20
14	FC Young Boys Diekirch	26	1	0	25	18	87	3

PROMOTION/RELEGATION PLAY-OFF

(30/05/13)
Progrès 1-0 Strassen *(aet)*

Domestic cup: Coupe de Luxembourg 2012/13

FIFTH ROUND

(16/11/12)
Hostert 3-3 Pétange *(aet; 5-3 on pens)*

(18/11/12)
Berdorf-Consdorf 0-7 Hamm Benfica
Bertrange 3-4 Weiler *(aet)*
Bissen 1-0 Sandweiler
Cebra 0-3 Kayl-Tétange *(aet)*
CS Obercorn 0-2 Grevenmacher
Diekirch 0-3 Progrès
Erpeldange 3-2 Jeunesse Canach *(aet)*
Feulen 0-4 Wiltz
Hesper 1-2 Fola
Mersch 0-3 Differdange
Mertert-Wasserbuillig 0-2 Etzella
Mondorf 0-2 Racing Union
Rosport 2-2 Käerjéng *(aet; 3-5 on pens)*
Rumelange 1-3 Jeunesse Esch
US Esch 1-4 Dudelange

SIXTH ROUND

(01/12/12)
Dudelange 4-1 Kayl-Tétange *(aet)*

(02/12/12)
Erpeldange 1-4 Hostert
Etzella 0-7 Differdange
Fola 1-2 Jeunesse Esch
Grevenmacher 4-2 Wiltz *(aet)*
Käerjéng 1-0 Hamm Benfica
Progrès 2-1 Racing Union
Weiler 2-3 Bissen

QUARTER-FINALS

(01/05/13)
Differdange 2-0 Bissen *(Caron 16, Er Rafik 51)*
Hostert 1-2 Grevenmacher *(Pintar 26; Hoffmann 87, Huss 100) (aet)*
Jeunesse Esch 0-0 Dudelange *(aet; 3-1 on pens)*
Käerjéng 1-0 Progrès *(Sabotic 89p)*

SEMI-FINALS

(08/05/13)
Käerjéng 0-2 Jeunesse Esch *(Ibrahimović 43, Hoffmann 79)*

(09/05/13)
Differdange 1-0 Grevenmacher *(Er Rafik 65)*

FINAL

(17/05/13)
Stade Josy Barthel, Luxembourg
AS JEUNESSE ESCH 2 *(Ibrahimović 17, 19)*
FC DIFFERDANGE 03 1 *(Franzoni 37p)*
Referee: Durieux
JEUNESSE ESCH: Oberweis, Delgado, Portier, Hoffmann, Ramdedovic, Benichou, Wang (Dufoor 90), Moreira (Todorovic 93), Miceli (Agović 70), Collette, Ibrahimović
DIFFERDANGE: Heil, Bukvic, Siebenaler, Jänisch (Piskor 84), May, Lebresne (Bettmer 72), Kettenmeyer (Caron 48), Bastos, Meligner, Er Rafik, Franzoni

Former Yugoslav Republic of

MACEDONIA
Futbalska Federacija na Makedonija (FFM)

Address	Osma Udarna Brigada 31 A MK-1000 Skopje	**President**	Ilco Gjorgioski
Tel	+389 23 129 291	**General secretary**	Dimitar Zisovski
Fax	+389 23 165 448	**Media officer**	Zoran Nikolovski
E-mail	ffm@ffm.com.mk	**Year of formation**	1948
Website	ffm.com.mk	**National stadium**	Phillp II Arena, Skopje (33,000)

PRVA LIGA CLUBS

1 FK Bregalnica Stip

2 FK Drita

 3 FK Metalurg Skopje

4 FK Napredok

5 FK Pelister

6 FK Rabotnicki

7 FK Renova

8 FK Shkëndija 79

9 FK Sileks

 10 FK Teteks

 11 FK Turnovo

 12 FK Vardar

PROMOTED CLUBS

13 FK Makedonija GP Skopje

14 FK Gostivar

15 FK Gorno Lisice

KEY:

⬤ – UEFA Champions League

⬤ – UEFA Europa League

⬤ – Promoted clubs

⬤ – Relegated clubs

◯ – Relegated club in
UEFA Europa League

Back-to-back titles for Vardar

For the first time in a decade FK Vardar, the Former Yugoslav Republic of Macedonia's most decorated club, claimed back-to-back league titles. They did it the hard way, however, with Blagoja Milevski, the coach they sacked in mid-season, returning to mastermind a late revival that culminated with a last-day 5-0 win over title rivals FK Turnovo.

While FK Metalurg Skopje finished runners-up for the third season in a row, the Macedonian Cup was claimed by the Prva Liga's bottom club, FK Teteks, who beat local rivals FK Shkëndija 79 on penalties in the final.

Coach Milevski returns to steer Skopje club home

Final-day win wraps up seventh title

Relegated Teteks win cup on penalties

Domestic league

With 2011/12 championship-winning coach Ilco Gjorgioski having departed to become president of the Football Federation of Macedonia (FFM), Vardar appointed a rookie, Blagoja Milevski, as his replacement. It was a gamble but it looked to be paying off when the club won five of their first six matches and, following a further run of seven games without conceding a goal, reached the winter break holding a three-point lead. Despite his record, Milevski was relieved of his duties in January as the Vardar board opted to go for the far greater experience of former FYROM national coach Nikola Ilievski.

It proved an ill-fated decision. Although Ilievski oversaw a 6-1 win over Shkëndija in his first home game, the 58-year-old struggled to inspire the team thereafter, and after his third defeat in five games, the call went out for Milevski to return. At once harmony was restored and Vardar reeled off six straight wins to return to the top of the table. A 1-1 draw against Metalurg left Milevski's men still requiring a point in their final fixture, at home to village club Turnovo, to secure the title. A defeat would have given their opponents, fired by in-form goalgetters Dejan Blazevski and Zoran Baldovaliev, a remarkable first championship triumph, but on the day of judgment Vardar blew their challengers away, romping to a magnificent 5-0 win that gave them the title by five points.

Metalurg also won their final fixture to pip Turnovo to second place on goal difference. Like Vardar, they benefited from a change of coach, former FYROM international Srgjan Zaharievski losing just one of his 19 games in charge after replacing Georgi Hristov in November. Both clubs qualified for the UEFA Europa League, Turnovo entering European competition for the first time.

Domestic cup

The third UEFA Europa League berth was decided by the Macedonian Cup final, which had to be abandoned after ten minutes because of crowd trouble and replayed in an empty Philip II Arena four days later. It went to Teteks, who put the disappointment of relegation behind them by repeating their 2010 success, at the expense of city rivals Shkëndija. Muzafer Ejupi, Shkëndija's top scorer in the league – his 19-goal tally was second only to Vardar's Jovan Kostovski (23) – gave his side an early lead before they lost goalkeeper Hadis Velii to a red card. Teteks eventually capitalised through a Darko Micevski equaliser before the game went to penalties, where Teteks keeper Vance Mancevski put his name up in lights by saving two spot kicks.

Europe

The modest quality of the Prva Liga was once again emphasised by its representatives' struggles in Europe. The only ties won were against opposition from San Marino and Malta, but by the end of July all interest in both competitions was at an end.

National team

The FYROM national team was led into 2014 FIFA World Cup qualification by former defender Cedomir Janevski. He made a reasonable start, with two narrow defeats against Croatia supplemented by a 1-1 draw in Scotland and a wildly celebrated 1-0 win over northern neighbours Serbia. Attacking midfielder Agim Ibraimi's winner against Serbia was one of four the NK Maribor player struck in successive home games, including the team's best performance of the season, a 3-0 win against Denmark in a February friendly. Unfortunately, the next four games all ended in defeats without goals, including back-to-back qualifying matches against Belgium.

Domestic league: Prva Liga 2012/13 final table

		Pld	Home						Away						Total						Pts
			W	D	L	F	A		W	D	L	F	A		W	D	L	F	A	
1	**FK Vardar**	**33**	**14**	**1**	**2**	**53**	**11**		**6**	**7**	**3**	**18**	**10**		**20**	**8**	**5**	**71**	**21**	**68**
2	FK Metalurg Skopje	33	10	5	2	28	13		8	4	4	20	15		18	9	6	48	28	63
3	FK Turnovo	33	12	4	1	34	12		5	8	3	15	19		17	12	4	49	31	63
4	FK Rabotnicki	33	11	3	2	27	12		5	2	10	20	30		16	5	12	47	42	53
5	FK Shkëndija 79	33	9	3	5	28	18		4	5	7	24	31		13	8	12	52	49	44
6	FK Bregalnica Stip	33	8	5	3	22	11		4	2	11	15	24		12	7	14	37	35	43
7	FK Napredok	33	8	4	5	17	16		4	3	9	12	23		12	7	14	29	39	43
8	FK Renova	33	9	4	4	20	15		3	3	10	15	31		12	7	14	35	46	43
9	FK Drita	33	7	3	6	21	18		4	4	9	14	32		11	7	15	35	50	40
10	FK Pelister	33	7	6	3	19	14		2	4	11	8	22		9	10	14	27	36	37
11	FK Teteks	33	6	4	6	17	16		0	3	14	5	31		6	7	20	22	47	25
12	FK Sileks	33	5	4	7	21	22		1	1	10	12	39		6	5	22	33	61	23

NB FK Shkëndija 79 – 3 pts deducted.

SEASON AT A GLANCE

EUROPEAN QUALIFICATION 2013/14

 Champion: FK Vardar (second qualifying round)

 Cup winner: FK Teteks (first qualifying round)
FK Metalurg Skopje (first qualifying round)
FK Turnovo (first qualifying round)

Top scorer Jovan Kostovski (Vardar), 23 goals
Relegated clubs FK Sileks, FK Teteks, FK Drita
Promoted clubs FK Makedonija GP Skopje, FK Gostivar, FK Gorno Lisice
Cup final FK Teteks 1-1 FK Shkëndija 79 *(aet; 6-5 on pens)*

**PRVA LIGA TEAM
OF THE SEASON**
(3-5-2)
Coach: Milevski *(Vardar)*

**PLAYER OF
THE SEASON
Dejan Blazevski**
(FK Turnovo)

The 27-year-old attacking midfielder enjoyed a fabulous season back home following four seasons in Greece. Exceptionally consistent, Blazevski was Turnovo's talisman on the pitch, registering 17 goals and 12 assists in 32 matches to drive the club's title challenge. He also scored his first international goal, on his first start, in a friendly against Poland.

**NEWCOMER OF
THE SEASON
Marko Simonovski**
(FK Metalurg Skopje)

Metalurg promoted a number of their talented youth players into the starting XI, and it was 21-year-old Simonovski who proved the pick of the bunch after returning in mid-season from a loan spell at Napredok. An attacker with fine technical skills, good movement and aerial prowess, he made his senior FYROM debut in the December friendly against Poland.

Former Yugoslav Republic of **MACEDONIA**

NATIONAL TEAM

Home Kit   Away Kit

Results 2012/13

Date	Opponent		Venue	Score	Scorers
15/08/12	Lithuania	H	Skopje	1-0	*Pandev (54)*
07/09/12	Croatia (WCQ)	A	Zagreb	0-1	
11/09/12	Scotland (WCQ)	A	Glasgow	1-1	*Noveski (11)*
12/10/12	Croatia (WCQ)	H	Skopje	1-2	*Ibraimi (16)*
16/10/12	Serbia (WCQ)	H	Skopje	1-0	*Ibraimi (59p)*
14/11/12	Slovenia	H	Skopje	3-2	*Tasevski (27), Jahovic (41), Ibraimi (51)*
14/12/12	Poland	N	Antalya (TUR)	1-4	*Blazevski (87)*
06/02/13	Denmark	H	Skopje	3-0	*Pandev (9), Ibraimi (17), Noveski (24)*
22/03/13	Belgium (WCQ)	H	Skopje	0-2	
26/03/13	Belgium (WCQ)	A	Brussels	0-1	
03/06/13	Sweden	A	Malmo	0-1	
11/06/13	Norway	A	Oslo	0-2	

Appearances 2012/13

Coach:
(Goce Sedloski) 10/04/74
/(20/08/12)
Cedomir Janevski 03/07/61

Player	DOB	Club	Ltu	CRO	SCO	CRO	SRB	Svn	Pol	Den	BEL	BEL	Swe	Nor	Caps	Goals
Martin Bogatinov	26/04/86	Karpaty (UKR)	G46	G	G	G	s46			s46					15	-
Stefan Ristovski	12/02/92	Bari (ITA)	D60					s91			D70	D			6	-
Nikolce Noveski	28/04/79	Mainz (GER)	D	D	D	D	D			D89	D	D	D		59	5
Boban Grncarov	12/08/82	Botev Plovdiv (BUL)	D		s75	D	D			D	D			D 60*	31	1
Vance Sikov	19/07/85	Volyn (UKR)	D	D	D	D75		D				D	D		28	3
Yani Urdinov	28/03/91	Ekranas (LTU)	M												3	-
Stefan Spirovski	23/08/90	Borac Čačak (SRB)	M74												4	-
Velice Sumulikoski	24/04/81	Tianjin Teda (CHN) /Slovácko (CZE)	M		s70	M54	s86							M	84	1
Agim Ibraimi	29/08/88	Maribor (SVN)	M65	M	M89	M	M	M		M80	M	M	M		20	4
Goran Pandev	27/07/83	Napoli (ITA)	A89	M	M	M				M65	M	M			71	26
Ivan Trickovski	18/04/87	Club Brugge (BEL)	A46	M73	M38	M	s73			M	M82	M65	M46	M46	28	3
Tomislav Pacovski	28/06/82	Mechelen (BEL)	s46				G	G46		G46	G	G	G46	G46	30	-
Ferhan Hasani	18/06/90	Wolfsburg (GER)	s46		s38	s82	M	M87			M82	s46	s46	M83	18	1
Daniel Georgievski	17/02/88	Steaua (ROU)	s60		D	D	D	D	s80		D				14	-
Nikola Gligorov	15/08/83	Alki (CYP)	s65	M82	M70	s54	M			M73	M	M	M46		16	-
Mirko Ivanovski	31/10/89	Astra (ROU)	s74	s80	A		A91	A55		s89	s58	A	s69	A	16	1
Daniel Mojsov	25/12/87	Vojvodina (SRB) /Brann (NOR)	s89						D	s89			s50	D	21	-
Goran Popov	02/10/84	West Brom (ENG)		D	D	D82									44	2
Muhamed Demiri	20/11/85	Thun (SUI)		M	M	M	M86	M		M	M				19	-
Stevica Ristic	23/05/82	Suwon Bluewings (KOR)		A80	A										17	1
Dragan Georgiev	16/12/90	Vardar		s73				s87	A61						3	-
Darko Tasevski	20/05/84	H. Kiryat Shmona (ISR)		s82	s89		M73	M60		s65	s82	M46	M50		42	1
Aleksandar Lazevski	21/01/88	Partizan (SRB)				D	D80			D	D		D80		13	-
Aleksandar Todorovski	26/02/84	Polonia Warszawa (POL)							D	D	D	s70		D	13	-
Adis Jahovic	18/03/87	Zürich (SUI)					A75			A89	A58			s46	4	1
Aleksandar Trajkovski	05/09/92	Zulte Waregem (BEL)						s55		s80	s82	s65	s46		9	-
Ostoja Stjepanovic	17/01/85	Vardar						s60	M	s73				s46	4	-
Dejan Blazevski	06/12/85	Turnovo						s75	A						2	1
Kristijan Naumovski	17/09/88	Dinamo București (ROU)							G				s46		3	-
Vladica Brdarovski	07/02/90	Rabotnicki								D83					1	-
Sedat Berisha	23/09/89	Shkëndija								D80					1	-
Mite Cikarski	06/01/93	Vardar								D					1	-
Riste Markoski	30/04/86	Napredok								M61					1	-
Nderim Nedzipi	22/05/84	Shkëndija								M75					1	-
Jovan Kostovski	19/04/87	Vardar								A61					1	-
Predrag Randjelovic	02/03/90	Vardar								s61					1	-
Muzafer Ejupi	16/09/88	Shkëndija								s61					1	-

Appearances 2012/13

			Ltu	CRO	SCO	CRO	SRB	Svn	Pol	Den	BEL	BEL	Swe	Nor	Caps	Goals
Ivan Mitrov	24/10/88	Bregalnica Stip							s61						1	
Marko Simonovski	02/01/92	Napredok							s75						1	-
Vladimir Dimitrovski	30/11/88	Rabotnicki							s80						3	-
Tome Kitanovski	21/05/89	Pelister							s83						1	-
Bajram Fetai	07/09/85	Denizlispor (TUR)											M46		4	-
Samir Fazli	22/04/91	Helmond (NED)											A69	A63	7	-
Darko Glisic	23/09/91	Dinamo Tbilisi (GEO)											s80	D46	2	-
Darko Tofiloski	13/01/86	Košice (SVK)												s46	1	-
Blagoja Ljamcevski	07/04/87	Metalurg Skopje												s46	1	-
Daniel Ivanovski	27/06/83	Mjällby (SWE)												s63	3	-
Dusan Savic	01/10/85	Volyn (UKR)												s83	9	-

European club competitions 2012/13

FK VARDAR

Second qualifying round - FC BATE Borisov (BLR)
A 2-3 Kostovski (54), Stjepanovic (62)
Zahov, Alechenwu, Tanevski, Randjelovic (Manevski 86), Stojaković (Guobadia 83), Georgiev (Petrov 59), Stjepanovic, Kostovski, Temelkov, Ilievski, Vajs. Coach: Ilco Gjorgjioski (MKD)
H 0-0
Zahov, Tanevski, Randjelovic (Bojović 90), Georgiev, Stjepanovic (Manevski 75), Giménez (Stojaković 46), Kostovski, Temelkov, Cikarski, Ilievski, Vajs. Coach: Ilco Gjorgjioski (MKD)

FK RENOVA

First qualifying round - AC Libertas (SMR)
H 4-0 Bajrami (10p, 14p, 83), Skenderi (60)
Zendeli, Bajrami, V Emini (Skenderi 55), Andonov (Ismaili 50), Nuhiu, Stepanovski, Gafuri, Siljanovski, Pandev (Fetai 85), Simovski, Ristov. Coach: Vlatko Kostov (MKD)

A 4-0 Nuhiu (10), Jancevski (61, 64p), Ismaili (87)
Zendeli, Bilal Velija, Bajrami, Nuhiu, Stepanovski, Gafuri (Skenderi 65), Siljanovski, Pandev (Ismaili 59), Jancevski, Simovski, Ristov (Asani 67). Coach: Vlatko Kostov (MKD)

Second qualifying round - FC Gomel (BLR)
H 0-2
Zendeli, Skenderi, Bajrami, Nuhiu, Stepanovski, Gafuri, Siljanovski, Pandev (Ismaili 46), Jancevski (Andonov 63), Simovski, Ristov (Asani 46). Coach: Vlatko Kostov (MKD)
A 1-0 Asani (56)
Zendeli, Bilal Velija, Bajrami, Asani, V Emini (Ukundori 56), Andonov, Nuhiu, Stepanovski, Gafuri (Ismaili 77), Siljanovski, Simovski (Fetai 85). Coach: Vlatko Kostov (MKD)

FK METALURG SKOPJE

First qualifying round - Birkirkara FC (MLT)
A 2-2 Nestorovski (2), Curlinov (54)
Pavlović, Alomerovic, Kralevski, P Ljamcevski (Tenekedziev 52), B Ljamcevski, Nestorovski (Naumovski 65), Dimoski, Krstev, Petkovski, Curlinov (Peev 81), Stevanović. Coach: Aleksandar Vlaho (MKD)
H 0-0
Pavlović, Alomerovic (Memedi 80), Kralevski, B Ljamcevski, Nestorovski (Naumovski 76), Dragović, Dimoski (Dodevski 86), Krstev, Petkovski, Curlinov, Stevanović. Coach: Aleksandar Vlaho (MKD)

Second qualifying round - Ruch Chorzów (POL)
A 1-3 Memedi (69)
Pavlović, Alomerovic (Nestorovski 50), Kralevski, B Ljamcevski, Memedi, Dragović, Dimoski (Dalcevski 90+2), Krstev, Petkovski, Curlinov (Dodevski 86), Stevanović. Coach: Aleksandar Vlaho (MKD)
H 0-3
Pavlović, Kralevski, B Ljamcevski, Memedi (Alomerovic 58), Dragović, Dimoski (P Ljamcevski 46), Ristovski (Nestorovski 65), Krstev, Petkovski, Curlinov, Stevanović. Coach: Aleksandar Vlaho (MKD)
Red card: Dragović 88

FK SHKËNDIJA 79

First qualifying round - Portadown FC (NIR)
H 0-0
Nikov, Mustafi, Neziri, Cuculi, Ejupi (Redzepi 82), Emini (Hasan 76), Selmani, Elmazovski (Aliu 55), Demiri, Taipi, Berisha. Coach: Catip Osmani (MKD)
A 1-2 Cuculi (4)
Velii, Mustafi, Neziri, Cuculi, Ejupi (Emini 61), Selmani, Miskovski, Demiri, Taipi, Berisha (Hasan 84), Aliu (Redzepi 80). Coach: Catip Osmani (MKD)

Domestic league club-by-club

FK BREGALNICA STIP

Coach: Nikola Spasov (BUL);
(03/02/13) Dobrinko Ilievski
1921 • City, Stip (6,000) • no website

2012

Date	Opp	H/A	Score	Scorers
12/08	Drita	a	1-0	Naumov
19/08	Sileks	h	2-0	Naumov, Mandak
26/08	Pelister	a	0-1	
29/08	Shkëndija	h	0-0	
02/09	Metalurg	a	1-2	Mitrov
16/09	Turnovo	a	0-2	
23/09	Rabotnicki	h	2-0	Mitrov, Iliev
30/09	Napredok	a	1-2	Naumov
07/10	Teteks	h	2-0	Naumov, Vučetić
20/10	Renova	a	0-2	
28/10	Vardar	h	1-1	Naumov
31/10	Drita	h	3-0	Zdravkov, Mitrov, Naumov
04/11	Sileks	a	1-2	Naumov
11/11	Pelister	h	1-0	Naumov (p)
18/11	Shkëndija	a	3-0	Mitrov 3
25/11	Metalurg	h	0-1	
02/12	Turnovo	h	1-1	Trajcev
08/12	Rabotnicki	a	1-3	Mitrov

2013

Date	Opp	H/A	Score	Scorers
06/03	Napredok	h	0-1	
10/03	Teteks	a	2-0	Zdravkov, Vučetić
17/03	Renova	h	0-0	
30/03	Vardar	a	0-3	
03/04	Turnovo	a	1-2	Blazevski
07/04	Vardar	h	1-1	Zdravkov (p)
14/04	Rabotnicki	a	1-1	Zdravkov
21/04	Pelister	a	0-0	
28/04	Drita	h	1-0	Mandak
04/05	Sileks	a	1-0	Zlatkovski
12/05	Teteks	h	2-0	Zdravkov (p), Zlatkovski
15/05	Renova	a	1-2	Zdravkov (p)
19/05	Shkëndija	h	4-3	Mitrov, Zlatkovski 2, Zdravkov
29/05	Napredok	a	1-2	Mandak
02/06	Metalurg	h	2-3	Zdravkov 2 (1p)

Name	Nat	DoB	Pos	Aps	(s)	Gls
Dusko Andonov		06/02/87	D	24	(5)	
Marjan Andonov		20/12/85	A	5	(4)	
Marjan Belcev		22/10/82	D	16		
Tomislav Blazevski		30/08/89	D	21	(8)	1
Darko Bozinov		06/01/89	D	14	(3)	
Aleksandar Čanović	SRB	18/02/83	G	29		
Vlado Danilov		31/08/79	D	4	(2)	
Goran Dimovski		14/10/82	D	8	(4)	
Dušan Dunjić	SRB	29/03/87	D	12	(2)	
Saso Gjoreski		18/09/82	D	17	(1)	
Lazar Iliev		23/05/87	A	6	(11)	1
Ljupco Kolev		06/12/78	G	1		
Elmir Mandak		11/11/84	M	25	(5)	3
Ivan Mitrov		24/10/88	M	25	(5)	8
Angel Nacev		10/10/89	A	3	(6)	
Riste Naumov		14/04/81	A	19	(1)	8
Vladimir Nikitović	SRB	04/12/80	D	10	(1)	
Ilce Petrovski		22/07/89	G	3	(1)	
Darko Stojanov		11/02/90	D	14	(1)	
Igorce Stojanov		12/02/76	D	23	(2)	
Jovica Trajcev		09/01/81	M	7	(11)	1
Slavce Velkovski		05/07/87	M	16	(8)	
Marko Vučetić	SRB	24/06/86	M	28	(1)	2
Goran Zdravkov		11/11/80	A	25	(3)	9
Zoran Zlatkovski		05/04/87	A	8	(6)	4

FK DRITA

Coach: Ane Andovski; (19/03/13) Nedzat Husein
1994 • Bogovinje (600) • no website

2012

Date	Opp	H/A	Score	Scorers
12/08	Bregalnica	h	0-1	
18/08	Rabotnicki	a	2-2	Nuhiji 2 (1p)
26/08	Napredok	h	3-0	Tunevski, Stankovski, Miftari
30/08	Teteks	a	2-1	Miftari, Ramadani
02/09	Renova	h	2-0	Tunevski, Nuhiji
16/09	Vardar	a	0-4	
22/09	Turnovo	h	0-0	
30/09	Sileks	h	2-1	Mustafi (p), Miftari
07/10	Pelister	a	1-1	Nuhiji
21/10	Shkëndija	h	2-2	Nuhiji, Mustafi (p)
28/10	Metalurg	a	1-0	Nuhiji
31/10	Bregalnica	a	0-3	
04/11	Rabotnicki	h	1-0	Sakiri
11/11	Napredok	a	1-1	Stankovski
16/11	Teteks	h	1-0	Alili
24/11	Renova	a	0-2	
04/12	Vardar	h	0-1	
09/12	Turnovo	a	1-2	Idrizi

2013

Date	Opp	H/A	Score	Scorers
03/03	Sileks	a	0-4	
10/03	Pelister	h	1-1	Jonuzi
17/03	Shkëndija	a	1-2	Stankovski
31/03	Metalurg	h	1-2	Tunevski
03/04	Napredok	a	2-1	Nuhiji, Barać
09/04	Metalurg	h	0-2	
14/04	Turnovo	a	0-4	
21/04	Vardar	h	1-3	Ramadani
28/04	Bregalnica	a	0-1	
04/05	Pelister	h	2-0	Mustafi, Barać
12/05	Rabotnicki	a	0-2	
15/05	Sileks	a	2-1	Stankovski 2
19/05	Teteks	h	2-0	Jonuzi, Nuhiji
29/05	Renova	a	1-1	Tunevski
02/06	Shkëndija	h	3-1	Miftari, Nuhiji, Mustafi

Name	Nat	DoB	Pos	Aps	(s)	Gls
Besim Adili		18/10/87	G	9		
Zejdan Alili		11/10/90	M	3	(4)	1
Amir Aliu		09/12/81	D	23	(6)	
Domagoj Barać	CRO	28/06/90	M	6	(5)	2
Petar Basnarkov		10/07/80	G	19		
Rufat Chelik		19/04/89	M	1	(6)	
Aleksandar Donev		26/04/82	D	9		
Iliknur Dzaferi		01/11/86	D	25	(2)	
Toni Gjorgievski		15/09/86	D	10		
Mensur Idrizi		03/08/83	M	15	(2)	1
Valmir Jonuzi		23/05/94	M	3	(14)	2
Aleksandar Krsteski		09/03/83	D	11	(1)	
Marko Lukić	SRB	10/08/91	D	6		
Betim Miftari		08/10/90	M	20	(3)	4
Kjahil Muaremi		29/02/92	D	18	(4)	
Dzhenis Munishi		14/09/92	M		(1)	
Burhan Mustafa		22/07/90	G	5		
Nebi Mustafi		21/08/76	M	27		4
Blertan Nafija		26/07/89	M	6	(3)	
Ardijan Nuhiji		17/12/78	M	29	(1)	9
René Osei	NED	31/12/91	D		(1)	
Minas Osmani		22/02/85	D	22	(2)	
Daniel Radevski		17/01/85	D	7	(11)	
Zivorad Radonjic		02/10/84	A		(1)	
Ardzent Ramadani		30/10/87	M	23	(1)	2
Brendim Rusiti		23/06/92	M		(2)	
Burim Sadiki		05/08/89	M	12	(2)	
Ardit Sakiri		04/05/85	M	3	(3)	1
Imer Shaipi		05/06/94	D		(1)	
Goran Stankovski		20/11/76	A	27	(1)	5
Nikola Tripunovski		19/12/82	M	3	(2)	
Vladimir Tunevski		08/03/83	M	21		4

FK METALURG SKOPJE

Coach: Georgi Hristov;
(20/11/12) Srgjan Zaharievski
1964 • Zelezarnica (3,000) • fcmetalurg.com.mk
Major honours
Macedonian Cup (1) 2011

2012

Date	Opp	H/A	Score	Scorers
12/08	Sileks	a	2-0	Krstev, P Ljamcevski
19/08	Pelister	h	1-0	Krstev (p)
26/08	Shkëndija	a	0-1	
29/08	Turnovo	a	0-2	
02/09	Bregalnica	h	2-1	Krstev, Maznov
15/09	Rabotnicki	a	0-3	
22/09	Napredok	h	3-2	Krstev, Curlinov, Stevanović
30/09	Teteks	a	1-0	Maznov
07/10	Renova	h	4-0	Curlinov, Maznov, Dimoski, P Ljamcevski
21/10	Vardar	a	1-1	Dalcevski
28/10	Drita	h	0-1	
31/10	Sileks	h	1-1	Curlinov
04/11	Pelister	a	1-0	Stevanović
11/11	Shkëndija	h	0-1	
18/11	Turnovo	h	1-1	Dimoski
25/11	Bregalnica	a	1-0	Krstev
02/12	Rabotnicki	h	2-1	Alomerovic, Krstev
16/12	Napredok	a	1-1	Stevanović

2013

Date	Opp	H/A	Score	Scorers
03/03	Teteks	h	0-0	
10/03	Renova	a	0-1	
17/03	Vardar	h	3-2	Radeski, Simonovski 2
31/03	Drita	a	2-1	Stevanović, Maznov
03/04	Pelister	h	1-0	Krstev
09/04	Drita	a	2-0	Stevanović, Mitrevski
14/04	Sileks	h	3-0	Curlinov 2, Stevanović
21/04	Teteks	a	1-1	Krstev
28/04	Renova	h	3-1	Krstev 2, Ignatov
07/05	Shkëndija	a	1-0	Dragović
12/05	Napredok	h	2-0	Krstev, Ignatov (p)
15/05	Rabotnicki	h	1-1	Peev
19/05	Turnovo	a	4-2	B Ljamcevski, Alomerovic, Simonovski 2
29/05	Vardar	h	1-1	Krstev
02/06	Bregalnica	a	3-2	Mitrevski, Simonovski, Krstev

Name	Nat	DoB	Pos	Aps	(s)	Gls
Kemal Alomerovic		08/12/80	M	18	(5)	2
Cvetan Curlinov		24/07/86	A	16	(12)	5
Aleksandar Dalcevski		18/04/91	M	19	(5)	1
Hristijan Dimoski		29/06/85	A	11	(3)	2
Ninoslav Dodevski		29/11/91	D	12	(3)	
Goran Dragović	SRB	20/10/81	D	25	(2)	1
Andreja Efremov		02/09/92	G	16	(1)	
Bojan Gjorgjievski		25/01/92	D	12	(1)	
Stojan Ignatov		22/12/79	M	16	(10)	2
Mile Krstev		13/05/79	M	15	(11)	13
Blagoja Ljamcevski		07/04/87	D	25	(1)	1
Petar Ljamcevski		08/08/91	M	6	(1)	2
Goran Maznov		22/04/81	A	25	(4)	4
Vasko Mitrev		23/05/84	M	20	(1)	
Risto Mitrevski		05/10/91	D	12		2
Blagoja Naumovski		24/11/93	M		(5)	
Igor Pavlović	MNE	24/02/82	G	17		
Oliver Peev		08/06/87	M	20	(4)	1
Mile Petkovski		19/09/88	D	20		
Marjan Radeski		10/02/95	A	10	(1)	1
Milan Ristovski		01/03/89	A	1	(6)	
Marko Simonovski		02/01/92	A	6	(6)	5
Martin Siskov		17/07/87	M	10	(4)	
Ljubomir Stevanović	SRB	08/08/86	M	31		6

MALTA
Malta Football Association (MFA)

Address	Millennium Stand, Floor 2
	National Stadium
	MT-Ta' Qali ATD 4000
Tel	+356 21 232 581
Fax	+356 21 245 136
E-mail	info@mfa.com.mt
Website	mfa.com.mt

President	Norman Darmanin Demajo
General secretary	Joseph Gauci
Media officer	Alex Vella
Year of formation	1900
National stadium	National, Ta' Qali (17,797)

KEY:
- ● – UEFA Champions League
- ● – UEFA Europa League
- ● – Promoted clubs
- ● – Relegated clubs

PREMIER LEAGUE CLUBS

1. Balzan Youths FC
2. Birkirkara FC
3. Floriana FC
4. Hamrun Spartans FC
5. Hibernians FC
6. Melita FC
7. Mosta FC
8. Qormi FC
9. Rabat Ajax FC
10. Sliema Wanderers FC
11. Tarxien Rainbows FC
12. Valletta FC

PROMOTED CLUBS

13. Naxxar Lions FC
14. Vittoriosa Stars FC

Birkirkara triumph in tie break

For the first time in 41 years the Maltese championship had to be decided by a play-off. Birkirkara FC defeated Hibernians FC 3-1 at Ta' Qali to capture their fourth Premier League title after the two sides had finished the regular campaign on the same number of points, some distance ahead of defending champions Valletta FC, who had led at the end of the 22-match first phase.

Eleven days later Hibernians won the FA Trophy by the same scoreline, defeating Qormi FC 3-1 in the final for the second successive season to claim domestic cup honours for the tenth time.

Premier League title race goes to play-off

League runners-up Hibernians retain cup

Mifsud strikes again as Malta win in Armenia

Domestic league

Led again by Paul Zammit, the coach who had steered them to the 2009/10 title, Birkirkara came from behind in the play-off. 1-0 down at half-time, they stormed back after the interval with goals from Edward Herrera, Nikola Vukanac and Rowen Muscat to see off Hibernians in some style. It was their fifth meeting of the season with the Paola side and their third victory, the other two games having ended all square. The Stripes were the toughest team to beat in the division, losing just four of their 32 matches. Their defence became tighter as the season progressed, conceding just three goals in the ten games of the second phase, which yielded seven wins and 23 points.

Hibernians, under coach Michael Woods, also found form in the second phase, winning six of their last seven matches to force the play-off. Their final-day victory over Valletta completed a miserable second phase for the club from the capital, who looked on course for a hat-trick of Premier League titles when they topped the table at the 22-game cut-off. Led by new coach Mark Miller, recruited from Hibernians, Valletta lost only two of their first phase matches but five thereafter, back-to-back defeats against Birkirkara (0-2) and Hibernians (2-4) marking the beginning of the end of their challenge.

Of the teams that made the championship pool, Tarxien Rainbows FC provided the top scorer in Brazilian Daniel Bueno (20 goals). The Premier League's leading marksman outright was Spaniard José Luis Negrin, who had a major bearing on the relegation battle, effectively condemning Melita FC and rescuing Rabat Ajax FC when he switched allegiance in mid-season. The latter failed to win any of their first 21 games but staged a dramatic recovery thanks to his 17 goals.

Domestic cup

History repeated itself in the final of the FA Trophy as Hibernians shrugged off the disappointment of their defeat in the Premier League decider to beat Qormi 3-1 for the second year in succession. After a goalless first half, Hibernians took charge with a couple of goals from recently-signed Brazilian striker Edison – his six league strikes had all come in doubles – and each side registered in added time to ensure yet another 3-1 scoreline. Hibernians had also lost the Super Cup to Valletta by that same margin at the start of the campaign.

Europe

Michael Mifsud was the top indigenous marksman in the Premier League scoring charts, with 18 goals, and he warmed up for the domestic campaign by finding the net six times for Valletta in Europe, four of them in the Citizens' opening 8-0 win against Andorran champions FC Lusitans and the other two against Serbia's FK Partizan.

Malta had three teams in the UEFA Europa League – one more than in 2011/12 – but none of them survived the first qualifying round.

National team

Mifsud was also the main man once again for the Maltese national team, his 37th international goal – on his 96th appearance – proving to be one of his most important as it earned the side a sensational 1-0 victory away to Armenia in the 2014 FIFA World Cup qualifying campaign – the country's first win in the competition for 20 years.

The five previous qualifiers had all ended in defeat, although new coach Pietro Ghedin was entitled to feel satisfied with a couple of 2-0 defeats against Italy, his country of birth.

Domestic league: Premier League 2012/13 final tables

FIRST PHASE

		Pld	W	D	L	F	A	Pts	
1	Valletta FC	22	13	7	2	49	15	46	(23)
2	Hibernians FC	22	14	3	5	47	24	45	(23)
3	Birkirkara FC	22	12	7	3	47	19	43	(22)
4	Tarxien Rainbows FC	22	11	5	6	39	32	38	(19)
5	Sliema Wanderers FC	22	11	4	7	34	22	37	(19)
6	Mosta FC	22	11	1	10	39	33	34	(17)
7	Qormi FC	22	9	3	10	32	34	30	(15)
8	Balzan Youths FC	22	7	6	9	34	36	27	(14)
9	Floriana FC	22	5	9	8	26	31	24	(12)
10	Hamrun Spartans FC	22	4	4	14	24	58	16	(8)
11	Melita FC	22	3	5	14	18	56	14	(7)
12	Rabat Ajax FC	22	1	8	13	16	45	11	(6)

NB Figures in brackets indicate points carried forward to the Second Phase

SECOND PHASE

Championship Pool		Pld	W	D	L	F	A	Pts
1	**Birkirkara FC**	32	19	9	4	62	22	45
2	Hibernians FC	32	21	4	7	72	34	45
3	Valletta FC	32	17	8	7	70	29	36
4	Sliema Wanderers FC	32	16	6	10	48	32	36
5	Tarxien Rainbows FC	32	14	6	12	53	51	29
6	Mosta FC	32	11	2	19	45	72	18

Relegation Pool		Pld	W	D	L	F	A	Pts
7	Floriana FC	32	14	10	8	48	38	38
8	Qormi FC	32	15	4	13	61	50	34
9	Balzan Youths FC	32	9	9	14	48	61	23
10	Rabat Ajax FC	32	6	9	17	70	60	22
11	Hamrun Spartans FC	32	6	5	21	39	88	14
12	Melita FC	32	4	8	20	31	78	13

NB Floriana FC – 2 pts deducted, Hamrun Spartans FC – 1 pt deducted.

CHAMPIONSHIP PLAY-OFF

(11/05/13)
National Stadium, Ta' Qali
BIRKIRKARA FC 3 (Herrera 56, Vukanac 67, R Muscat 74)
HIBERNIANS FC 1 (Failla 33p)
Referee: Sant

BIRKIRKARA: Haber, Herrera, Vukanac, Moreno, R Muscat (Scicluna 84), Mifsud Triganza (Camenzuli 77), Z Muscat, Fenech, Sciberras, Jhonnattann (Shodiya 34), Rodrigo

HIBERNIANS: M Muscat, Camilleri, Farrugia (Pulis 74), Pearson, Rodolfo Soares (Obiefule 74), Failla, Kristensen, Jackson, Cohen, Marcelo (Allan Kardeck 85), Edison

SEASON AT A GLANCE

EUROPEAN QUALIFICATION 2013/14

Champion: Birkirkara FC (second qualifying round)

Cup winner: Hibernians FC (first qualifying round)
Valletta FC (first qualifying round)
Sliema Wanderers FC (first qualifying round)

Top scorer	José Luis Negrin (Melita/Rabat Ajax), 22 goals
Relegated clubs	Melita FC, Hamrun Spartans FC
Promoted club	Naxxar Lions FC, Vittoriosa Stars FC
Cup final	Hibernians FC 3-1 Qormi FC

PLAYER OF THE SEASON
Gareth Sciberras
(Birkirkara FC)

A regular in Malta's FIFA World Cup qualifying campaign, the captain of Birkirkara enjoyed an outstanding second season with the club, his drive and determination proving decisive in the Stripes' Premier League title triumph. The 30-year-old midfielder's influence was especially profound in a number of narrow wins during the championship phase.

NEWCOMER OF THE SEASON
Zach Muscat
(Birkirkara FC)

Having turned 19 just two days into the season, Muscat showed maturity beyond his years to assist Birkirkara over the line in the title race. The holding midfielder returned home after a trial in England at Barnsley FC and, despite failing to command a regular place at first, eventually racked up 19 starts plus another in the title decider against Hibernians FC.

PREMIER LEAGUE TEAM OF THE SEASON
(4-4-1-1)
Coach: Zammit *(Birkirkara)*

Haber *(Birkirkara)*
Herrera *(Birkirkara)* — Rodolfo Soares *(Hibernians)* — Vukanac *(Birkirkara)* — Failla *(Hibernians)*
Jackson *(Hibernians)* — Sciberras *(Birkirkara)* — Fenech *(Birkirkara)* — Briffa *(Valletta)*
Cohen *(Hibernians)*
Mifsud *(Valletta)*

MALTA

NATIONAL TEAM

Home Kit   Away Kit

TOP FIVE ALL-TIME CAPS
David Carabott (121); Gilbert Agius (120);
Carmel Busuttil (111); Joe Brincat (103);
Michael Mifsud (96)

TOP FIVE ALL-TIME GOALS
Michael Mifsud (37); Carmel Busuttil (23);
David Carabott (12); Gilbert Agius &
Hubert Suda (8)

Results 2012/13

14/08/12	San Marino	A	Serravalle	3-2	*Mifsud (13, 84), Agius (21)*
07/09/12	Armenia (WCQ)	H	Ta' Qali	0-1	
11/09/12	Italy (WCQ)	A	Modena	0-2	
12/10/12	Czech Republic (WCQ)	A	Plzen	1-3	*Briffa (38)*
14/11/12	Liechtenstein	A	Vaduz	1-0	*Caruana (38)*
06/02/13	Northern Ireland	H	Ta' Qali	0-0	
22/03/13	Bulgaria (WCQ)	A	Sofia	0-6	
26/03/13	Italy (WCQ)	H	Ta' Qali	0-2	
07/06/13	Armenia (WCQ)	A	Yerevan	1-0	*Mifsud (8)*

Appearances 2012/13

Coach:
Pietro Ghedin (ITA) 21/11/52

			Smr	ARM	ITA	CZE	Lie	Nir	BUL	ITA	ARM	Caps	Goals
Andrew Hogg	02/03/85	Paralimni (CYP)	G	G	G	G		G	G			31	-
Steve Borg	15/05/88	Valletta	D62	D	D	D						8	-
Ryan Camilleri	22/05/88	Hibernians	D54		s86			s46	s56	D	D	6	-
Andrei Agius	12/08/86	Latina (ITA)	D	D	D	D	D	D46	D56			33	1
Alex Muscat	14/12/84	Sliema	D86		D86	D	s90	D		D	D	22	-
Roderick Briffa	24/08/81	Valletta	M46	M85	M	M	M69		M	M	M85	72	1
Gareth Sciberras	29/03/83	Birkirkara	M	M	M	M	M84	M		M	M57	36	-
André Schembri	27/05/86	unattached /Omonia (CYP)	M46	M	M	M87	M	M90	M	M	M	50	3
Andrew Cohen	13/05/81	Hibernians	M	M74	s69		M46	M		s82		54	1
Daniel Bogdanovic	26/03/80	Mosta	M	M	M69							41	1
Michael Mifsud	17/04/81	Valletta	A86	A	A	A		A89	A	A88	A93	96	37
Shaun Bajada	19/10/83	Valletta /Sliema	s46	s85		M89	s69	s90				33	-
Etienne Barbara	10/06/82	Vancouver (CAN)	s46									30	3
Luke Dimech	11/01/77	Mosta /Valletta	s54	D	D	D	D	D	D	D	D	76	1
Ryan Fenech	20/04/86	Valletta	s62	s74					M			30	-
Paul Fenech	20/12/86	Birkirkara	s86			s87	s46	M	M70		s57	16	-
John Mintoff	23/08/88	Sliema	s86									1	-
Edward Herrera	14/07/86	Birkirkara				M	M	M	M	M	M	11	-
Ayrton Azzopardi	12/09/93	Hibernians				s89						1	-
Justin Haber	09/06/81	Mosta /Birkirkara					G			G	G	46	-
Jonathan Caruana	24/07/86	Valletta						D		D	D	27	1
Clayton Failla	08/01/86	Hibernians					D90	D	D	M82	M	26	-
Terence Vella	20/04/90	Hamrun					A	s89		s88	s93	4	-
Rowen Muscat	05/06/91	Birkirkara						s84	s70		s85	3	-

European club competitions 2012/13

VALLETTA FC

CHAMPIONS LEAGUE

First qualifying round - FC Lusitans (AND)
H 8-0 *Caruana (4), Mifsud (10, 18, 45, 70), Jhonnattann (17, 23), E Agius (72)*
Krul, Caruana, Azzopardi (Falzon 69), Borg, Mifsud, Briffa, Barbosa, Ricardo Rocha (Fenech 46), Jhonnattann (E Agius 71), Denni, Donizete. Coach: Mark Miller (ENG)
A 1-0 *Jhonnattann (16)*
Krul, Caruana, Azzopardi (Falzon 59), Borg, Mifsud, Briffa, Barbosa, Ricardo Rocha, Jhonnattann (E Agius 66), Denni, Donizete (Fenech 61). Coach: Mark Miller (ENG)

Second qualifying round - FK Partizan (SRB)
H 1-4 *Mifsud (65)*
Krul, Caruana, Azzopardi (João Gabriel 46), Borg (E Agius 80), Fenech (Jhonnattann 66), Mifsud, Briffa, Barbosa, Ricardo Rocha, Denni, Falzon. Coach: Mark Miller (ENG)
A 1-3 *Mifsud (60)*
Krul, Caruana (E Agius 46), Azzopardi, Borg, Mifsud, Briffa, Barbosa, Ricardo Rocha, João Gabriel, Denni (Fenech 51), Falzon (G Agius 85). Coach: Mark Miller (ENG)

HIBERNIANS FC

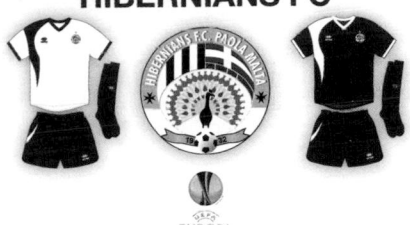

EUROPA LEAGUE

First qualifying round - FK Sarajevo (BIH)
A 2-5 *Farrugia (20), Rodolfo Soares (33)*
M Muscat, Herrera, Pulis, Camilleri, Rodolfo Soares, Marcelo (Pisani 77), Cohen (Caruana 85), Kristensen, Jackson, Vandelannoite, Farrugia. Coach: Michael Woods (MLT)
Red card: Rodolfo Soares 52
H 4-4 *Marcelo (22, 35), Farrugia (40, 44)*
M Muscat, Herrera, Pulis, Camilleri, Pisani (Bezzina 74), Marcelo, Cohen, Kristensen, Jackson, Vandelannoite, Farrugia. Coach: Michael Woods (MLT)

BIRKIRKARA FC

EUROPA LEAGUE

First qualifying round - FK Metalurg Skopje (MKD)
H 2-2 *Jorge Silva (53), Mifsud Triganza (87)*
Gauci, Rodrigo, Fenech, Shodiya, Vukanac, Camenzuli, Joselito (Mifsud Triganza 76), Zerafa, Scicluna (F Zammit 89), Jorge Silva, R Muscat. Coach: Paul Zammit (MLT)
A 0-0
Gauci, Rodrigo, Fenech, Shodiya, Vukanac (Mifsud Triganza 77), Camenzuli (Sciberras 56), Joselito, Zerafa, Scicluna (Camilleri 87), Jorge Silva, R Muscat. Coach: Paul Zammit (MLT)

FLORIANA FC

EUROPA LEAGUE

First qualifying round - IF Elfsborg (SWE)
A 0-8
Jurgen Borg, B Farrugia, Paris, Micallef, Caruana (Brincat 84), Woods (Darmanin 78), D Pisani, Joseph Borg (S Borg 17), Gusman, T Farrugia, C Borg. Coach: Ivan Woods (MLT)
Red card: T Farrugia 25
H 0-4
Jurgen Borg, B Farrugia, Paris, Micallef, Caruana (Brincat 72), S Borg, Woods, D Pisani, Darmanin, Gusman, C Borg. Coach: Ivan Woods (MLT)

Domestic league club-by-club

BALZAN YOUTHS FC
Coach: Ivan Zammit;
(04/04/13) Riccardo Tumiatti (ITA)
1937 • balzanyouthsfc.com

2012

19/08	Hamrun	2-2	Mendy, Pedrinho
26/08	Birkirkara	1-2	Licari
02/09	Floriana	1-3	Alex
17/09	Tarxien	1-2	Pedrinho
23/09	Hibernians	2-3	Alex 2 (1p)
28/09	Qormi	2-1	Alex 2 (1p)
07/10	Melita	2-1	Deyanov, Pedrinho
19/10	Sliema	1-0	Caruana
28/10	Mosta	0-0	
02/11	Valletta	1-1	Pedrinho
09/11	Rabat Ajax	2-0	Pace, Alex
17/11	Hamrun	3-2	Alex, Pedrinho (p), Licari
23/11	Birkirkara	2-2	Alex, Forace
10/12	Floriana	1-3	Caruana
16/12	Tarxien	3-4	Y Camilleri, Alex 2
22/12	Mosta	0-2	

2013

04/01	Qormi	2-1	Alex (p), Pedrinho
11/01	Melita	4-0	Renato, Pedrinho 2, Alex
20/01	Rabat Ajax	1-1	Alex (p)
27/01	Hibernians	0-2	
03/02	Valletta	1-1	N'Dekre
09/02	Sliema	2-3	Darmanin, Alex
24/02	Hamrun	3-1	Darmanin, Caruana, N'Dekre
03/03	Floriana	1-1	Darmanin
12/03	Melita	0-0	
18/03	Qormi	4-4	Renato 2, N'Dekre, Darmanin
01/04	Rabat Ajax	0-3	
08/04	Hamrun	2-3	Aboulezz, N'Dekre
12/04	Floriana	0-2	
21/04	Melita	2-1	Aboulezz, Darmanin
26/04	Qormi	2-5	Agius, Darmanin
02/05	Rabat Ajax	0-5	

Name	Nat	DoB	Pos	Aps	(s)	Gls
Firas Aboulezz	LIB	26/07/90	A	9	(3)	2
Aaron Agius		25/12/86	A	16	(8)	1
Alex	BRA	20/09/85	A	20		14
Bjorn Bondin		28/05/88	M	15	(12)	
Jacob Borg	AUS	02/05/91	D	17	(7)	
Michael Borg		18/10/92	M		(2)	
Shaun Bugeja		03/08/95	M	1	(1)	
Kevin Camilleri		13/06/93	M	2		
Matthew Camilleri		09/04/79	A	6	(1)	
Yessous Camilleri		27/11/91	D	24	(1)	1
Christian Caruana		21/10/86	D	19	(7)	3
Andrew Cassar		14/02/97	M		(1)	
Juan Carlos Corbalan		13/03/97	M		(1)	
Dani Miguéles	ESP	23/04/85	G	13		
Ryan Darmanin		12/12/85	A	13	(1)	6
Martin Deyanov	BUL	17/01/80	M	7	(5)	1
Rennie Forace		08/06/80	D	14	(4)	1
Jonathan Francica		19/06/85	D	5	(5)	
Stefan Giglio		26/02/79	M	27	(1)	
Dylan Grima		18/07/90	M	25	(1)	
Cryuff Grixti		21/05/93	D		(2)	
Malcolm Licari		18/04/78	A	3	(12)	2
Matthew Mendy	GAM	13/06/83	M	27		1
Clint Micallef		24/08/81	D	2	(4)	
Gianfranco Micallef		13/02/97	M		(1)	
Matthew Mifsud		29/05/93	M		(1)	
Elie N'Dekre	CIV	01/01/92	A	10		4
Jamie Pace		30/10/82	M	25		1
Pedrinho	BRA	04/08/86	A	16		8
Renato	BRA	14/06/81	M	23		3
Rodrigo	BRA	15/06/91	M		(3)	
Shaun Spiteri		01/01/97	M		(1)	
Fredrick Tabone		08/11/88	G	13		

BIRKIRKARA FC
Coach: Paul Zammit
1950 • birkirkarafc.com
Major honours
Maltese League (4) 2000, 2006, 2010, 2013;
Maltese Cup (4) 2002, 2003, 2005, 2008

2012

20/08	Melita	4-0	Joselito 2, Shodiya, Jhonnattann
26/08	Balzan	2-1	Shodiya, Z Muscat
31/08	Rabat Ajax	2-0	Vukanac, Mifsud Triganza
15/09	Floriana	3-0	Jhonnattann 3
22/09	Sliema	1-3	R Muscat
30/09	Tarxien	4-1	Mifsud Triganza 3, Camenzuli
06/10	Valletta	1-1	Fenech
19/10	Hamrun	1-3	Shodiya (p)
27/10	Hibernians	1-0	Mifsud Triganza
04/11	Qormi	1-1	Vukanac
11/11	Mosta	1-0	Jhonnattann (p)
17/11	Melita	3-0	Camenzuli, Sciberras 2
23/11	Balzan	2-2	Mifsud Triganza, Z Muscat
08/12	Rabat Ajax	3-3	Fenech, Jhonnattann, Vukanac
15/12	Floriana	1-1	Vukanac
22/12	Hibernians	0-0	

2013

06/01	Tarxien	5-0	Fenech, Shodiya 2, Vukanac, Herrera
12/01	Valletta	0-1	
19/01	Mosta	7-1	Jhonnattann 3, Shodiya 2, Herrera, Mifsud Triganza
27/01	Sliema	0-0	
02/02	Qormi	2-1	Joselito, Jhonnattann
13/02	Hamrun	3-0	Mifsud Triganza, Herrera, Camenzuli
24/02	Sliema	0-1	
02/03	Hibernians	1-0	Mifsud Triganza
13/03	Mosta	7-1	Vukanac, Rodrigo, Jhonnattann 2, Zerafa, R Muscat, Joselito
17/03	Valletta	2-0	Jhonnattann, R Muscat
30/03	Tarxien	1-0	Jhonnattann
07/04	Sliema	1-0	og (Mintoff)
14/04	Hibernians	1-1	Shodiya
20/04	Mosta	0-0	
27/04	Valletta	1-0	Mifsud Triganza
04/05	Tarxien	1-0	Shodiya

Name	Nat	DoB	Pos	Aps	(s)	Gls
Ini Etim Akpan	NGA	03/08/84	G	3	(1)	
Brandon Attard		05/07/93	A		(1)	
Antoine Borg		04/04/94	M		(2)	
Bernard Borg		01/03/95	D		(1)	
Ryan Camenzuli		08/09/94	D	15	(9)	3
Paul Fenech		20/12/86	M	29		3
Reuben Gauci		28/10/83	G	17		
Justin Haber		09/06/81	G	12		
Edward Herrera		14/07/86	D	24	(3)	3
Jhonnattann	BRA	27/07/89	A	26	(4)	14
Joselito	BRA	06/02/91	A	3	(9)	4
Godwin Mackay		20/06/95	M		(2)	
Jean Pierre Mifsud Triganza		20/11/81	A	23	(8)	10
Alejandro Moreno	ESP	17/05/86	D	30	(1)	
Rowen Muscat		05/06/91	M	24	(5)	3
Zach Muscat		22/08/93	M	19	(6)	2
Rodrigo	BRA	15/06/91	M	11	(3)	1
Gareth Sciberras		29/03/83	M	27		2
Ryan Scicluna		30/07/93	M	14	(7)	
Shola Shodiya	NGA	17/06/91	A	18	(6)	9
David Spiteri		22/08/93	M		(2)	
Nikola Vukanac	SRB	14/01/86	D	26		6
Yosimar	ESP	31/05/88	M	5	(6)	
Fabian Zammit		21/01/93	M		(2)	
Kurt Zammit		21/01/93	M		(3)	
Joseph Zerafa		31/05/88	D	26	(3)	1

MALTA

FLORIANA FC

Coach: Mark Wright (ENG);
(15/09/12) (Alan Lewer (ENG));
(18/10/12) (Stephen Azzopardi);
(31/01/13) Iain Brunskill (ENG)
1894 • florianafc.org
Major honours
Maltese League (25) 1910, 1912, 1913, 1921, 1922, 1925,
1927, 1928, 1929, 1931, 1935, 1937, 1950, 1951, 1952, 1953,
1955, 1958, 1962, 1968, 1970, 1973, 1975, 1977, 1993;
Maltese Cup (19) 1938, 1945, 1947, 1949, 1950, 1953,
1954, 1955, 1957, 1958, 1961, 1966, 1967, 1972, 1976,
1981, 1993, 1994, 2011

2012
18/08	Sliema	1-1	Valdo Alhinho
24/08	Hamrun	1-1	Darmanin
02/09	Balzan	3-1	Darmanin, Verma, Cilia
15/09	Birkirkara	0-3	
22/09	Rabat Ajax	3-0	Brown, Cilia, Darmanin
29/09	Mosta	1-3	Wasiu
05/10	Qormi	2-2	Verma, Wasiu
20/10	Valletta	0-2	
27/10	Tarxien	2-3	Darmanin, Jeffers
03/11	Hibernians	0-1	
10/11	Melita	2-2	Darmanin 2
19/11	Sliema	2-0	Verma, Darmanin
25/11	Hamrun	2-0	M Spiteri, Darmanin
10/12	Balzan	3-1	Wasiu 2, Coronado
15/12	Birkirkara	1-1	Verma
23/12	Tarxien	1-1	Bugeja
2013
06/01	Mosta	1-2	Coronado
12/01	Qormi	0-0	
20/01	Melita	0-0	
26/01	Rabat Ajax	1-1	Coronado
01/02	Hibernians	0-3	(w/o; original result 1-0 Coronado)
13/02	Valletta	0-3	
22/02	Melita	2-1	Coronado, Nwoko
03/02	Balzan	2-1	Coronado
12/03	Rabat Ajax	2-1	Coronado 2
16/03	Hamrun	3-0	Coronado 3
02/04	Qormi	4-2	Coronado, S Pisani 2, Joseph Borg
08/04	Melita	2-0	Joseph Borg, Coronado
12/04	Balzan	2-0	Cilia, S Pisani
19/04	Rabat Ajax	2-1	Roberts 2 (1p)
28/04	Hamrun	3-1	Coronado, Casha 2
03/05	Qormi	1-0	Tremarco

Name	Nat	DoB	Pos	Aps	(s)	Gls
Clyde Borg		20/03/92	D	27	(3)	
Joseph Borg		26/01/87	M	9	(3)	2
Jurgen Borg		08/08/94	G	3		
Sacha Borg		26/04/93	A	15	(5)	
Aaron Brown	ENG	23/06/83	D	5		1
Owen Bugeja		20/02/90	D	23	(2)	1
Christian Caruana		21/10/86	M	2		
Luca Casha		05/07/93	A	1	(8)	2
Trevor Cilia		02/01/83	A	26	(2)	3
Igor Coronado	BRA	18/08/92	M	21		14
Ryan Darmanin		12/12/85	A	11	(3)	8
Jonathan Debono		17/07/85	G	5		
Brooke Farrugia		17/07/93	D	14	(5)	
Kane Farrugia		24/03/90	D	28	(1)	
Tyrone Farrugia		22/02/89	D	14		
Isaac Galea		31/08/95	M		(1)	
Francesco Gusman		13/01/94	D		(3)	
Henrique	BRA	30/10/91	M	3		
Francis Jeffers	ENG	25/01/81	A	2		1
Udochukwu Nwoko		15/11/86	D	10	(1)	1
Thomas Paris		15/11/86	D	16	(5)	
Duncan Pisani		25/05/88	D	16	(1)	
Steve Pisani		07/08/92	A	9	(1)	3
Gary Roberts	ENG	02/02/87	M	13		2
Rodrigo Branco	BRA	14/07/91	A	1		
Luke Scorfna		24/07/93	A		(1)	
Mark Spiteri		25/04/92	M	7	(9)	1
Carl Tremarco	ENG	11/10/85	D	19	(3)	1
Valdo Alhinho	POR	17/12/88	M	7	(6)	1
Aman Verma	ENG	03/01/87	M	14		4
Tony Warner	TRI	11/05/74	G	24		
Akanni-Sunday Wasiu	NGA	18/03/84	A	7	(3)	4

HAMRUN SPARTANS FC

Coach: Stefan Sultana
1907 • hamrunspartansfc.com
Major honours
Maltese League (7) 1914, 1918, 1947, 1983, 1987,
1988, 1991;
Maltese Cup (6) 1983, 1984, 1987, 1988, 1989, 1992

2012
19/08	Balzan	2-2	Grima, Scerri
24/08	Floriana	1-1	Calabretta
02/09	Tarxien	1-1	Grima (p)
17/09	Mosta	1-4	Bozhov
24/09	Valletta	2-8	Zerafa, Grima
28/09	Melita	3-1	og (Gribbon), Calabretta, Vella
05/10	Rabat Ajax	1-1	Grima (p)
19/10	Birkirkara	3-1	Vella 2, Grima
28/10	Qormi	1-0	Spiteri
04/11	Sliema	1-2	Camilleri (p)
10/11	Hibernians	1-2	Yoshev
17/11	Balzan	2-3	Calabretta, Vella
25/11	Floriana	0-2	
07/12	Tarxien	1-4	Fenech
14/12	Mosta	0-3	
23/12	Qormi	0-4	
2013
05/01	Melita	0-1	
13/01	Rabat Ajax	3-1	Lumbilla-Kandja 3 (1p)
19/01	Hibernians	1-6	Vella
26/01	Valletta	0-6	
02/02	Sliema	0-2	
13/02	Birkirkara	0-3	
24/02	Balzan	1-3	Lattes
01/03	Rabat Ajax	2-1	Borg, Camilleri
12/03	Qormi	0-2	
16/03	Floriana	0-3	
01/04	Melita	2-2	Grima, Camilleri
08/04	Balzan	3-2	Favero, Fenech, Lattes
12/04	Rabat Ajax	1-3	Fenech
19/04	Qormi	2-6	Spiteri, Vella
28/04	Floriana	1-3	Grima
04/05	Melita	3-5	Favero 2, Grima (p)

Name	Nat	DoB	Pos	Aps	(s)	Gls
Glenn Azzopardi		08/08/93	M	13	(5)	
Adrian Borg		20/05/89	D	16	(3)	1
Nikolay Bozhov	BUL	18/07/77	A	8	(3)	1
Richard Brightwell		09/06/86	M	3	(1)	
Melvin Buzuttil		05/05/95	A	1	(1)	
Gianluca Calabretta		14/10/87	M	16	(1)	3
David Camilleri		21/08/74	M	22	(7)	3
Andrea Cassar		19/12/92	G	21		
Christian Cassar		20/06/93	M		(4)	
César Clemente	ESP	15/08/83	D	2		
Anthony Curmi		20/11/82	G	11	(4)	
Gianluca Debattista		14/10/87	D		(2)	
Giacomo Favero	ITA	01/01/91	M	12		3
Roderick Fenech		19/12/87	D	26	(1)	3
Luke Grech		06/01/94	D	10	(17)	
Massimo Grima		05/07/79	M	28	(1)	8
Bledjon Guga		19/12/91	D	12	(1)	
Emiliano Lattes	ARG	28/01/85	A	13		2
Loïc Lumbilla-Kandja	FRA	12/05/87	A	8	(1)	3
Ayrton Micallef		27/08/94	D	2	(8)	
Adrian Olegov	BUL	01/05/85	D	16		
Rodney Refalo		08/01/95	M		(5)	
Terence Scerri		03/04/84	A	5	(2)	1
Ryan Spiteri		02/02/95	M	21	(9)	2
Terence Vella		20/04/90	A	29	(1)	6
Anton Vergilov	BUL	31/01/85	D	10	(2)	
Lyubomir Vitanov	BUL	11/05/81	M	14		
Angel Yoshev	BUL	01/01/85	D	13		1
Daniel Zerafa		08/04/94	D	20	(5)	1

HIBERNIANS FC

Coach: Michael Woods
1922 • hiberniansfc.org
Major honours
Maltese League (10) 1961, 1967, 1969, 1979, 1981,
1982, 1994, 1995, 2002, 2009;
Maltese Cup (10) 1962, 1970, 1971, 1980, 1982, 1998,
2006, 2007, 2012, 2013

2012
20/08	Mosta	3-2	Marcelo 2, Pisani
25/08	Qormi	4-2	Rodolfo Soares, Cohen, Marcelo, Jackson
01/09	Melita	3-1	Cohen, Jackson 2
16/09	Rabat Ajax	3-0	Levnajić, Pulis, Jackson (p)
23/09	Balzan	3-2	Pulis, Cohen, Nwoba
30/09	Valletta	0-1	
06/10	Sliema	0-4	
21/10	Tarxien	2-2	Farrugia, Jackson (p)
27/10	Birkirkara	0-1	
03/11	Floriana	1-0	Jackson
10/11	Hamrun	2-1	Cohen, Anderson Ribeiro
19/11	Mosta	1-0	Failla
24/11	Qormi	0-1	
07/12	Melita	5-1	Cohen, Failla 2, Pulis, Farrugia
14/12	Rabat Ajax	6-0	Failla, Kristensen, Anderson Ribeiro 2, Camilleri, Jackson
22/12	Birkirkara	0-0	
2013
05/01	Valletta	1-4	Bezzina
13/01	Sliema	2-1	Failla, Allan Kardeck
19/01	Hamrun	6-1	Failla, og (Guga), Cohen 2, Jackson, Farrugia
27/01	Balzan	2-0	og (Giglio), Farrugia
01/02	Floriana	3-0	(w/o; original result 0-1)
11/02	Tarxien	0-0	
23/02	Tarxien	3-0	Rodolfo Soares, Farrugia, Failla
02/03	Birkirkara	0-1	
13/03	Sliema	0-2	
16/03	Mosta	3-1	Failla, Edison 2
30/03	Valletta	4-2	og (Vandelannotie), Failla, Farrugia, Jackson
07/04	Tarxien	3-0	Rodolfo Soares, Edison 2
14/04	Birkirkara	1-1	Failla
20/04	Sliema	3-2	Pearson, Jackson, Failla
28/04	Mosta	6-0	Cohen, Edison 2, Failla, Farrugia, Bezzina
05/05	Valletta	2-1	Failla, Jackson

Name	Nat	DoB	Pos	Aps	(s)	Gls
Allan Kardeck	BRA	22/02/80	A	6	(7)	1
Anderson Ribeiro	BRA	02/07/81	M	7	(6)	3
Ayrton Azzopardi		12/09/93	M	1	(11)	
Daniel Balzan		08/05/91	G	3	(3)	
Johann Bezzina		30/05/94	A	6	(14)	2
Ryan Camilleri		22/05/88	D	31		1
Scott Chircop		17/02/94	D	3	(3)	
Andrew Cohen		13/05/81	M	31		8
Edison	BRA	09/12/85	A	7	(1)	6
Clayton Failla		08/01/86	M	24		13
Jean Paul Farrugia		21/03/92	D	16	(8)	7
Jackson	BRA	09/07/82	M	25	(3)	11
Bjorn Kristensen		05/04/93	M	31		1
Zoran Levnajić	CRO	04/04/87	M	21	(3)	1
Marcelo	BRA	29/09/85	A	26		3
Brandon Muscat		03/11/94	M	3	(4)	
Mario Muscat		18/08/76	G	29		
John Nwoba	NGA	18/08/89	A	3	(5)	1
Udochukwu Nwoko		15/10/84	M	6	(2)	
Polycarp Obiefule	NGA	07/01/88	A	1	(3)	
Jonathan Pearson		13/01/87	D	16	(1)	1
Steve Pisani		07/08/92	A	4	(5)	1
Adrian Pulis		30/03/79	D	21	(2)	3
Rodolfo Soares	BRA	25/05/85	D	28		3
Keith Tanti		11/05/93	D	1	(1)	
Jason Vandelannoite	BEL	06/11/86	D	2		

MELITA FC

Coach: Martin Gregory;
(08/11/12) Patxi Salinas (ESP)
1933 • no website
Major honours
Maltese Cup (1) 1939

2012

20/08	Birkirkara	0-4	
25/08	Rabat Ajax	3-3	L Micallef, Negrin 2
01/09	Hibernians	1-3	J Galea
16/09	Valletta	1-5	Vukanić (p)
24/09	Tarxien	0-2	
28/09	Hamrun	1-3	L Micallef
07/10	Balzan	1-2	og (Pace)
21/10	Qormi	3-2	Negrin 2, Sammut
26/10	Sliema	0-4	
02/11	Mosta	0-5	
10/11	Floriana	2-2	J Galea, Negrin
17/11	Birkirkara	0-3	
23/11	Rabat Ajax	0-0	
07/12	Hibernians	1-5	Sierra
16/12	Valletta	2-1	L Micallef 2
21/12	Sliema	0-0	

2013

05/01	Hamrun	1-0	Dani Cabanillas
11/01	Balzan	0-4	
20/01	Floriana	0-0	
28/01	Tarxien	0-0	
01/02	Mosta	1-3	Tufegdžić
09/02	Qormi	1-2	Dani Cabanillas
22/02	Floriana	1-2	J Galea
01/03	Qormi	0-2	
12/03	Balzan	0-0	
18/03	Rabat Ajax	2-2	Borg, Tufegdžić
01/04	Hamrun	2-2	I Micallef, J Galea
08/04	Floriana	0-2	
13/04	Qormi	1-3	J Galea
21/04	Balzan	1-2	A Attard
26/04	Rabat Ajax	1-4	J Galea
04/05	Hamrun	5-3	J P Attard, Valenzia (p), J Galea 2, Sierra

Name	Nat	DoB	Pos	Aps	(s)	Gls
Andrew Abela		09/01/90	G	1		
Alhinho	POR	12/01/90	D	14	(6)	
Antoine Attard		18/01/96	A		(2)	1
Jean Pierre Attard		07/08/93	M	7	(9)	1
Marc Attard		25/11/92	A		(3)	
Orland Nicolo						
Baldacchino		09/07/93	A	1	(1)	
Maxime Batel	FRA	02/03/87	A		(2)	
Luke Bianco		12/07/92	D	9		
Matthew Borg		19/11/84	M	21		1
Alan Borg Olivier		12/08/92	M	5	(4)	
Michael Cachia		11/01/92	M		(2)	
Marco Calleja		07/04/91	M		(1)	
Andrew Caruana Scicluna		30/09/89	D	15	(7)	
Dani Cabanillas	ESP	01/02/87	A	14	(2)	2
Guillermo Gabilondo	ESP	28/01/92	G	12		
Julian Galea		09/02/89	A	24		8
Michael Galea		01/02/79	A	1		
Simon Galea		19/12/87	A	1	(2)	
Daniel Gravino		01/10/84	D	2	(1)	
George Gribbon		23/05/89	D	25	(1)	
Michael Martin		11/04/84	D	16	(3)	
Kane Micallef		06/02/89	M	3	(2)	
Luke Micallef		08/11/90	D	27	(4)	5
José Luis Negrin	ESP	15/12/86	A	12		5
Nigel Rizzo		30/09/91	M	16	(4)	
Luke Sammut		23/01/92	M	14	(7)	1
Matthew Sapiano		25/09/82	G	10		
Philippe Schranz		14/07/96	G	4		
Manuel Sierra	ESP	29/08/81	D	26		2
Tobias Terpougoff		27/04/81	M	2	(4)	
Ivan Tufegdžić	SRB	12/07/83	M	26	(1)	2
Michael Valenzia		22/03/82	A	10	(8)	1
Karl Vella Petroni		25/11/81	M	13	(7)	
Jorge Veloso	ESP	03/06/90	A	2	(3)	
Jovan Vukanić	SRB	22/06/90	D	14		1
Karl Zahra		19/02/89	G	5		

MOSTA FC

Coach: Steve D'Amato; (16/02/13) Danilo Dončić (SRB)
1935 • mpstafc.com

2012

20/08	Hibernians	2-3	Bajada, Mitev
26/08	Valletta	1-3	Obiefule
31/08	Sliema	2-0	Obiefule 2
17/09	Hamrun	4-1	Carlinhos, Mitev 2, Aboulezz
23/09	Qormi	4-2	Mitev, og (Bello-Osagie), Aboulezz, Zongo
29/09	Floriana	3-1	Obiefule 2 (1p), Apap
07/10	Tarxien	0-2	
20/10	Rabat Ajax	2-0	Mitev, Obiefule
28/10	Balzan	0-0	
02/11	Melita	5-0	Obiefule 2, Bogdanovic 2 (1p), Zongo (p)
11/11	Birkirkara	0-1	
19/11	Hibernians	0-1	
24/11	Valletta	1-0	Obiefule
10/12	Sliema	0-2	
14/12	Hamrun	3-0	Obiefule 2, Bogdanovic
22/12	Balzan	2-0	Carlinhos, Bogdanovic

2013

06/01	Floriana	2-1	Chiemeka, Bogdanovic
11/01	Tarxien	1-3	Apap
19/01	Birkirkara	1-7	Mitev
28/01	Qormi	1-2	David Maia
01/02	Melita	3-1	M'Bonu, Mitev, Micallef
11/02	Rabat Ajax	2-3	Mitev 2 (1p)
23/02	Valletta	0-5	
03/03	Tarxien	0-3	
13/03	Birkirkara	1-7	Mitev
16/03	Hibernians	1-3	Apap
02/04	Sliema	0-1	
06/04	Valletta	1-6	Mitev
14/04	Tarxien	2-4	Vignaroli, Mitev
20/04	Birkirkara	0-0	
28/04	Hibernians	0-6	
03/05	Sliema	1-4	Bezzina

Name	Nat	DoB	Pos	Aps	(s)	Gls
Firas Aboulezz	LIB	25/07/86	A	10	(1)	2
Bryan Agius		12/07/82	D	24	(2)	
Ferdinando Apap		29/07/92	D	21	(2)	3
Noel Attard		04/10/91	G	2	(2)	
Jonathan Bajada		01/02/91	D	12	(12)	1
Stephen Bezzina		05/01/87	D	10	(6)	1
Daniel Bogdanovic		26/03/80	A	10	(3)	5
Carlinhos	BRA	09/06/87	M	26	(2)	2
Wayne Chetcuti		01/09/93	M		(1)	
Steve Chiemeka	NGA	01/05/87	A	10	(3)	1
Alex Cini		28/10/91	D	14	(4)	
David Maia	BRA	20/11/91	A	2	(8)	1
Luke Dimech		11/01/77	D	14		
Adrian Farrugia		20/09/81	M		(3)	
Jeffrey Farrugia		13/06/81	G	12		
Tyrone Farrugia		22/02/89	D	15		
Ryan Grech		03/04/85	M	26	(3)	
Justin Haber		09/06/81	G	18		
Samuel Kehinde	NGA	07/12/87	A		(2)	
Bruno M'Bonu	NGA	30/11/93	A	8	(3)	1
Kurt Magro		04/06/86	A	11	(1)	
Manolito Micallef		16/11/83	M	30		1
Danail Mitev	BUL	11/01/84	M	28	(1)	12
Polycarp Obiefule	NGA	07/01/88	A	17		11
Emmanuel Okafor	NGA	29/04/89	M	1	(1)	
Ugochukwo Okoro	ENG	11/11/86	A	1	(4)	
Giancarlo Sammut		30/10/92	M	3	(3)	
Steve Schembri		30/07/94	M		(2)	
Fabio Vignaroli	ITA	07/06/76	M	13		1
Kurt Zammit		01/12/95	A	3	(16)	
Ousseni Zongo	BUR	06/08/84	M	11	(2)	2

QORMI FC

Coach: Stephen Azzopardi;
(18/10/12) Jesmond Zerafa
1961 • qormifc.com

2012

18/08	Rabat Ajax	1-0	Chetcuti
25/08	Hibernians	2-4	Spiteri 2
01/09	Valletta	0-3	
15/09	Sliema	2-1	V Pisani, Bello-Osagie
22/09	Mosta	2-4	Spiteri, Thackray
28/09	Balzan	1-2	Bello-Osagie
05/10	Floriana	2-2	V Pisani 2
21/10	Melita	2-3	Thackray, Bello-Osagie
28/10	Hamrun	0-1	
04/11	Birkirkara	1-1	Bello-Osagie
11/11	Tarxien	2-1	Moisés Pérez, V Pisani
18/11	Rabat Ajax	3-0	Moisés Pérez, Bello-Osagie 2 (1p)
24/11	Hibernians	1-0	Grech
08/12	Valletta	0-2	
15/12	Sliema	1-2	Chetcuti
23/12	Hamrun	4-0	Zárate 2, Moisés Pérez, Chetcuti

2013

04/01	Balzan	1-2	Bello-Osagie
12/01	Floriana	0-0	
19/01	Tarxien	2-1	Effiong, Moisés Pérez
28/01	Mosta	2-1	Bello-Osagie, Effiong
02/02	Birkirkara	1-2	Effiong
09/02	Melita	2-1	og (Tufegdžić), Moisés Pérez
22/02	Rabat Ajax	1-2	Zárate
01/03	Melita	2-0	Moisés Pérez, Zarate
12/03	Hamrun	2-0	Sciberras, Grech
18/03	Balzan	4-4	Chetcuti, Effiong 2, C Cassar
02/04	Floriana	2-4	Effiong, Moisés Pérez
06/04	Rabat Ajax	4-0	Moisés Pérez, Chetcuti, Thackray, Effiong (p)
13/04	Melita	3-1	Moisés Pérez, Grech, Effiong
19/04	Hamrun	6-2	Zárate, Moisés Pérez 2 (1p), Bondin, Effiong 2
26/04	Balzan	5-2	Moisés Pérez 2 (1p), Zárate, Thackray, og (Bondin)
03/05	Floriana	0-1	

Name	Nat	DoB	Pos	Aps	(s)	Gls
Gilmore Azzopardi		09/11/96	M		(1)	
Matthew Bartolo		14/06/86	M	14	(9)	
Abubakar Bello-Osagie	NGA	11/08/88	A	19		8
Jonathan Bondin		11/10/82	D	29		1
Ismael Borg		30/10/96	M		(1)	
Gabriel Buttigieg		12/04/79	M	2	(5)	
Clyde Camoin		31/07/87	M		(1)	
Triston Caruana		15/06/90	M		(2)	
Alessio Cassar		27/02/92	M	13	(7)	
Christian Cassar		20/06/83	M	6	(4)	1
Joseph Chetcuti		16/08/82	M	24	(6)	5
Alfred Effiong	NGA	29/11/85	A	13	(1)	10
Carmelo Farrugia		17/06/92	M		(3)	
Matthew Farrugia		17/04/81	G	23		
Matthew Gauci		02/09/91	M	23	(5)	
Leighton Grech		23/03/90	A	18	(10)	3
Moisés Pérez	ESP	13/07/88	A	12	(2)	13
Dylan Pirotta		31/01/94	A	1	(1)	
Duncan Pisani		25/05/88	D	9		
Vincenzo Pisani	ITA	08/09/90	A	9	(4)	4
Roderick Sammut		07/12/83	D	22	(1)	
Luke Sciberras		15/09/89	A	22	(5)	1
Sebastian Sirito	ITA	04/06/84	M	8	(5)	
Gaetan Spiteri		05/06/81	A	6	(2)	3
Steve Sultana		07/09/90	G	9	(1)	
Kris Thackray	ENG	27/04/88	D	31		4
Stephen Wellman		31/08/82	D	12	(2)	
Shamison Zammit		02/05/97	M		(2)	
Edison Zárate	CHI	03/06/87	M	27		6

RABAT AJAX FC

Coach: Silvio Vella
1930 • rabatajaxsc.com
Major honours
Maltese League (2) 1985, 1986;
Maltese Cup (1) 1986

2012

18/08	Qormi	0-1	
25/08	Melita	3-3	*Astrauskas 2, Manu Moral*
31/08	Birkirkara	0-2	
16/09	Hibernians	0-3	
22/09	Floriana	0-3	
29/09	Sliema	0-2	
05/10	Hamrun	1-1	*Smeir*
20/10	Mosta	0-2	
26/10	Valletta	1-1	*Čarapić*
03/11	Tarxien	1-3	*W Borg*
09/11	Balzan	0-2	
18/11	Qormi	0-3	
23/11	Melita	0-0	
08/12	Birkirkara	3-3	*Manu Moral, Felice, Negrin*
14/12	Hibernians	0-6	
21/12	Valletta	1-1	*Negrin*

2013

04/01	Sliema	0-1	
13/01	Hamrun	1-3	*Felice*
20/01	Balzan	1-1	*Negrin*
26/01	Floriana	1-1	*Negrin (p)*
03/02	Tarxien	0-1	
11/02	Mosta	3-2	*Negrin 3 (2p)*
22/02	Qormi	2-1	*Licari, Y Cauchi*
01/03	Hamrun	1-2	*Licari*
12/03	Floriana	1-2	*D Azzopardi*
18/03	Melita	2-2	*Manu Moral, Negrin (p)*
01/04	Balzan	3-0	*Negrin 2, D Azzopardi*
06/04	Qormi	0-4	
12/04	Hamrun	3-1	*Negrin, Licari, Manu Moral*
19/04	Floriana	1-2	*Negrin*
26/04	Melita	4-1	*Negrin (p), Diego Carrillo 2, Licari*
02/05	Balzan	5-0	*Felice, Negrin 4*

Name	Nat	DoB	Pos	Aps	(s)	Gls
Nerijus Astrauskas	LTU	18/10/80	A	8	(1)	2
Adrian Azzopardi		02/05/97	M		(1)	
David Azzopardi		08/01/91	M	30	(1)	2
Jonathan Azzopardi		04/02/82	G	12	(1)	
Heiner Backhaus	GER	04/02/82	D	7	(2)	
Patrick Borg		13/08/87	D	12	(4)	
Wayne Borg		14/05/93	M	2	(6)	1
Clive Brincat		31/05/83	D	20	(1)	
Ivan Čarapić	MNE	19/02/81	D	30		1
Joseph Caruana		01/02/87	M	25	(4)	
Luke Cauchi		18/07/94	M		(1)	
Yan Cauchi		23/07/91	D	19	(4)	1
Diego Carrillo	ESP	25/09/82	M	16	(1)	2
Dylan Falzon		24/04/86	D	30		
Neil Farrugia		22/03/92	A		(1)	
Justin Felice		27/04/85	A	17	(7)	3
Clifford Gauci		08/04/92	M	24	(2)	
Shaun Gauci		30/04/92	D		(3)	
Gaetano Gesualdi		15/02/92	D	12	(7)	
Malcolm Licari		18/04/78	A	3	(8)	4
Manu Moral	ESP	27/12/87	M	28	(1)	4
Ryan Micallef		18/07/92	A	3		
Sean Mintoff		13/10/85	G	20		
Christian Muscat		01/04/79	D	1	(2)	
Kurt Muscat		10/04/94	M		(4)	
José Luis Negrin	ESP	15/12/86	A	19		17
Christopher Schembri		19/04/84	D	6	(1)	
Adam Smeir		04/08/85	A	8		1
Chris Vella		19/03/94	A		(6)	

SLIEMA WANDERERS FC

Coach: Alfonso Greco (ITA)
1909 • sliemawfc.org
Major honours
Maltese League (26) 1920, 1923, 1924, 1926, 1930,
1933, 1934, 1936, 1938, 1939, 1940, 1949, 1954, 1956,
1957, 1964, 1965, 1966, 1971, 1972, 1976, 1989, 1996,
2003, 2004, 2005;
Maltese Cup (20) 1935, 1936, 1937, 1940, 1946, 1948,
1951, 1952, 1956, 1959, 1963, 1965, 1968, 1969, 1974,
1979, 1990, 2000, 2004, 2009

2012

18/08	Floriana	1-1	*Woods*
24/08	Tarxien	3-2	*Ciantar, Barbetti, El Ghaouti*
31/08	Mosta	0-2	
15/09	Qormi	1-2	*Ciantar*
22/09	Birkirkara	3-1	*Woods, Muchardi, A Muscat*
29/09	Rabat Ajax	2-0	*Ruggiero 2*
06/10	Hibernians	4-0	*Woods 3 (1p), Muchardi*
19/10	Balzan	0-1	
26/10	Melita	4-0	*Woods 2 (1p), Ruggiero, Faccini*
04/11	Hamrun	2-1	*Faccini, Ciantar*
09/11	Valletta	1-1	*Timotić*
19/11	Floriana	0-2	
25/11	Tarxien	1-2	*Gatt Baldacchino*
10/12	Mosta	2-0	*Laudisi, Mifsud*
15/12	Qormi	3-1	*Woods (p), Faccini 2*
21/12	Melita	0-0	

2013

04/01	Rabat Ajax	1-0	*Martinelli*
13/01	Hibernians	1-2	*Woods*
19/01	Valletta	0-2	
27/01	Birkirkara	0-0	
02/02	Hamrun	2-0	*Muchardi 2*
09/02	Balzan	3-2	*Muchardi, Ohawuchi, A Muscat*
24/02	Birkirkara	1-0	*Woods*
02/03	Valletta	0-0	
13/03	Hibernians	2-0	*Muchardi, I Zammit*
17/03	Tarxien	0-0	
02/04	Mosta	1-0	*Woods*
07/04	Birkirkara	0-1	
13/04	Valletta	0-2	
20/04	Hibernians	2-3	*Bajada, Ciantar*
27/04	Tarxien	4-3	*Ohawuchi 4*
03/05	Mosta	4-1	*Bajada, B Muscat, og (Apap), Ohawuchi*

Name	Nat	DoB	Pos	Aps	(s)	Gls
James Abela		18/05/88	G	1		
Shaun Bajada		19/10/83	M	13	(1)	2
Paltemio Barbetti	ITA	25/10/89	M	29		1
Stefano Bianciardi	ITA	15/03/85	D	26		
Henry Bonello		13/10/88	G	12		
Marlon Briffa		31/10/83	M		(1)	
Miguel Ciantar		17/10/90	A	9	(10)	4
Ryan Dalli		18/03/93	M		(1)	
Andrew Decesare		04/03/84	D	5	(6)	
Omar El Ghaouti	MAR	15/02/90	A	2	(5)	1
Alain Faccini	ITA	18/10/91	A	7	(7)	4
David Fenech		17/06/88	M		(1)	
Clifford Gatt Baldacchino		09/02/88	D	28		1
Pablo González	ARG	18/04/83	M	2		
Ariel Laudisi	ARG	03/10/91	M	7	(4)	1
Luca Martinelli		03/12/91	M	19	(1)	1
Josef Mifsud		07/09/84	D	8	(11)	1
John Mintoff		23/08/88	M	17	(6)	
Matías Muchardi	ARG	09/02/88	M	25	(2)	6
Alex Muscat		14/12/84	D	30		2
Beppe Muscat		13/04/89	D	15	(6)	1
Stanley Ohawuchi	NGA	27/05/90	A	5	(3)	6
Diego Ortega	ARG	05/09/91	M		(2)	
Luigi Ruggiero	ITA	16/09/90	A	14	(7)	3
Ian Scerri		03/06/93	M	1		
Mark Scerri		16/01/90	M	21	(2)	
Branislav Timotić	SRB	23/02/81	D	3		1
Ivan Woods		31/12/76	M	26	(1)	11
Glenn Zammit		05/08/87	G	19	(3)	
Ian Zammit		09/12/86	A	8		1

TARXIEN RAINBOWS FC

Coach: Danilo Dončić (SRB); (27/08/12) Clive Mizzi
1944 • tarxiensupportersclub.webs.com

2012

19/08	Valletta	0-1	
24/08	Sliema	2-3	*Danilo Santos 2*
02/09	Hamrun	1-1	*Daniel Bueno*
17/09	Balzan	2-1	*Evaldo, Daniel Bueno*
24/09	Melita	2-0	*Evaldo, Andrezinho*
30/09	Birkirkara	1-4	*Tanti*
07/10	Mosta	2-0	*Daniel Bueno (p), Danilo Santos*
21/10	Hibernians	2-2	*Danilo Santos, Andrezinho*
27/10	Floriana	3-2	*Pulo, Danilo Santos 2*
03/11	Rabat Ajax	3-1	*Bonnici, Danilo Santos, Daniel Bueno*
11/11	Qormi	1-2	*Daniel Bueno*
18/11	Valletta	1-1	*Evaldo*
25/11	Sliema	2-1	*Anonam, Tanti*
07/12	Hamrun	4-1	*Daniel Bueno (p), Anonam, Andrezinho, Evaldo*
16/12	Balzan	4-3	*Evaldo, Andrezinho, Daniel Bueno 2*
23/12	Floriana	1-1	*Danilo Santos*

2013

06/01	Birkirkara	0-5	
11/01	Mosta	3-1	*Daniel Bueno 2, Bajada*
19/01	Qormi	1-2	*Andrezinho*
28/01	Melita	3-0	*Daniel Bueno 2, Marco Túlio*
03/02	Rabat Ajax	1-0	*Marco Túlio*
11/02	Hibernians	0-0	
23/02	Hibernians	0-3	
03/03	Mosta	3-0	*Daniel Bueno 3*
12/03	Valletta	3-2	*Andrezinho, Daniel Bueno, Marco Túlio*
17/03	Sliema	0-0	
30/03	Birkirkara	0-1	
07/04	Hibernians	0-3	
14/04	Mosta	4-2	*Tanti, Daniel Bueno 2, Mamo*
21/04	Valletta	1-3	*Andrezinho*
27/04	Sliema	3-4	*Andrezinho, Daniel Bueno 2*
04/05	Birkirkara	0-1	

Name	Nat	DoB	Pos	Aps	(s)	Gls
Andrew Agius		01/06/91	D	12	(9)	
Andrezinho	BRA	11/01/84	M	27		8
Orosco Anonam		15/06/79	M	24	(2)	2
Roderick Bajada		04/01/83	M	21	(4)	1
Steve Bonnici		02/02/89	D	22	(3)	1
Gianluca Calabretta		14/10/87	A	2	(2)	
Manuel Caruana		17/02/85	D	17	(7)	
David Cassar		24/11/87	G	16		
Warren Chircop		15/09/88	A		(1)	
Daniel Bueno	BRA	15/12/83	A	31		20
Danilo Santos	BRA	12/11/83	A	13	(1)	8
Evaldo	BRA	04/01/83	D	11		5
Clive Fenech		13/04/94	M		(6)	
David Fenech		17/06/88	M	10	(9)	
Lee Galea		14/02/88	D		(1)	
Justin Grioli		20/09/87	M	23	(3)	
Leandro	BRA	23/02/84	A	11	(4)	
Carlo Mamo		23/04/79	D	22	(1)	1
Marco Túlio	BRA	28/02/81	M	6	(3)	3
Karl Pulo		30/07/89	M	10	(3)	1
Rômulo	BRA	09/12/87	M	5	(5)	
Steven Sadowski		21/01/82	D	7	(6)	
Ryan Sammut		06/04/92	M	21	(1)	
James Shead		27/12/91	A	1	(1)	
Mark Tanti		20/04/81	M	15	(12)	3
Branislav Timotić	SRB	23/02/81	D	9		
Nicholas Vella		27/08/80	G	16		
Nigel Vella		08/02/95	A		(1)	

VALLETTA FC

Coach: Mark Miller (ENG)
1943 • vallettafc.net
Major honours
Maltese League (21) 1915, 1932, 1945, 1946, 1948,
1959, 1960, 1963, 1974, 1978, 1980, 1984, 1990, 1992,
1997, 1998, 1999, 2001, 2008, 2011, 2012;
Maltese Cup (12) 1960, 1964, 1975, 1977, 1978, 1991,
1995, 1996, 1997, 1999, 2001, 2010

2012

19/08	Tarxien	1-0	Caruana
26/08	Mosta	3-1	Mifsud, Ricardo Rocha, Borg
01/09	Qormi	3-0	Fenech 2, Briffa
16/09	Melita	5-1	João Gabriel 2, Mifsud 2, og (Tufegdžić)
24/09	Hamrun	8-2	Mifsud 6 (1p), Fenech, Denni
30/09	Hibernians	1-0	João Gabriel
06/10	Birkirkara	1-1	Briffa
20/10	Floriana	2-0	Mifsud, João Gabriel
26/10	Rabat Ajax	1-1	João Gabriel
02/11	Balzan	1-1	Denni
09/11	Sliema	1-1	William
18/11	Tarxien	1-1	Mifsud
24/11	Mosta	0-1	
08/12	Qormi	2-0	Denni, Leandro
16/12	Melita	1-2	Leandro
21/12	Rabat Ajax	1-1	Ogunnupe

2013

05/01	Hibernians	4-1	Denni 2, Zammit (p), William (p)
12/01	Birkirkara	1-0	Zammit
19/01	Sliema	2-0	Touré, Caruana
26/01	Hamrun	6-0	Toure 2, Mifsud 2, Vandelannotie, Dimech
03/02	Balzan	1-1	Bello-Osagie
13/02	Floriana	3-0	Touré, Fenech, Caruana
23/02	Mosta	5-0	William 2, Mifsud 3
02/03	Sliema	0-0	
12/03	Tarxien	2-3	Denni, Fenech
17/03	Birkirkara	0-2	
30/03	Hibernians	2-4	William, Touré
06/04	Mosta	6-1	William 2 (1p), Mifsud 2, Denni 2
13/04	Sliema	2-0	Falzon, Touré
21/04	Tarxien	3-1	Denni, Bello-Osagie, William (p)
27/04	Birkirkara	0-1	
05/05	Hibernians	1-2	Dimech

Name	Nat	DoB	Pos	Aps	(s)	Gls
Edmond Agius		23/02/87	M	12	(9)	
Gilbert Agius		21/02/74	A		(2)	
Ian Azzopardi		12/08/82	D	23	(2)	
Shaun Bajada		19/10/83	M	11	(1)	
Manuel Bartolo		26/08/83	G	22		
Abubakar Bello-Osagie	NGA	11/08/88	A	5	(4)	2
Daniel Bogdanovic		26/03/80	A	3	(6)	
Steve Borg		15/05/88	D	9		1
Roderick Briffa		24/08/81	M	24	(1)	2
Jonathan Caruana		24/07/86	D	27	(1)	3
Yenz Cini		04/01/94	G	10	(1)	
Llywelyn Cremona		07/05/95	A		(2)	
Denni	BRA	21/08/82	M	25	(3)	9
Luke Dimech		11/01/77	D	14		2
Dyson Falzon		09/03/86	M	15	(8)	1
Ryan Fenech		20/04/86	M	26	(1)	5
João Gabriel	BRA	04/07/84	M	20	(10)	5
Leandro	BRA	23/02/84	A	9	(7)	2
Kurt Magro		04/06/86	M	6	(4)	
Michael Mifsud		17/04/81	A	20	(8)	18
Joseph Ogunnupe	NGA	23/02/92	A		(10)	1
Ricardo Rocha	BRA	06/02/86	A	12	(1)	1
Demba Touré	SEN	31/12/84	A	12	(2)	6
Jason Vandelannotie	BEL	06/11/86	D	14	(1)	1
William	BRA	02/06/87	A	28	(1)	8
Ian Zammit		09/12/86	A	5	(6)	2

Stadiums

Ta' Qali National Stadium (17,797)
Hibernians Ground (2,000)
Victor Tedesco Stadium (2,000)
MFA Centenary Stadium (2,000)

Top goalscorers

22	José Luis Negrin (Melita/Rabat Ajax)
20	Daniel Bueno (Tarxien)
18	Michael Mifsud (Valletta)
14	Alex (Balzan)
	Jhonnattann (Birkirkara)
	Igor Coronado (Floriana)
	Ryan Darmanin (Floriana/Balzan)
13	Clayton Failla (Hibernians)
	Moisés Pérez (Qormi)
12	Danail Mitev (Mosta)

Promoted clubs

NAXXAR LIONS FC

Coach: Winston Muscat
1920 • naxxarlions.com

VITTORIOSA STARS FC

Coach: Marlon Galea
1906 • vittoriosastars.com

SECOND LEVEL FINAL TABLE 2012/13

		Pld	W	D	L	F	A	Pts
1	Naxxar Lions FC	22	13	5	4	47	22	44
2	Vittoriosa Stars FC	22	13	5	4	41	28	44
3	Pietà Hotspurs FC	22	13	4	5	46	22	43
4	Lija Athletics FC	22	13	3	6	42	30	42
5	St Andrews FC	22	11	5	6	43	32	38
6	Marsaxlokk FC	22	9	5	8	38	44	32
7	Gudja United FC	22	8	6	8	33	36	30
8	Gzira United FC	22	5	9	8	26	29	24
9	Birzebbuga St Peter's FC	22	6	5	11	38	43	23
10	Zejtun Corinthians FC	22	5	6	11	21	35	21
11	Dingli Swallows FC	22	4	4	14	21	50	16
12	Mqabba FC	22	1	5	16	24	51	8

Domestic cup: FA Trophy 2012/13

THIRD ROUND

(30/11/12)
Gudja 2-0 Sengiea
Lija 2-1 Gharghur
Marsaskala 3-1 St Venera
Naxxar 3-4 Balzan *(aet)*

(01/12/12)
Birkirkara 1-0 Tarxien
Hibernians 2-1 Mosta
Melita 0-2 Floriana
Msida 0-2 St Andrews
Qormi 5-2 Pembroke 2 *(aet)*
Sliema 1-1 Zebbug *(aet; 6-7 on pens)*

(02/12/12)
Gzira 1-0 Victoria
Hamrun 1-3 Valletta
Pieta 0-1 Rabat Ajax
St Patrick 1-2 Sannat
Zejtun 1-3 Nadur
Zurrieq 1-2 Mqabba

FOURTH ROUND

(20/01/13)
Marsaskala 0-3 Zebbug
St Andrews 4-1 Mqabba *(aet)*

(22/01/13)
Gudja 0-4 Hibernians

(23/01/13)
Balzan 3-2 Gzira *(aet)*
Lija 1-0 Floriana
Qormi 2-1 Birkirkara
Sannat 0-5 Rabat Ajax
Valletta 2-0 Nadur

QUARTER-FINALS

(17/02/13)
Balzan 0-1 Qormi *(Giglio 12og)*
Hibernians 3-0 Zebbug *(Cohen 17, Failla 71p, Farrugia 81)*
Rabat Ajax 0-3 Valletta *(Ogunnupe 27, Bello-Osagie 50, William 75)*
St Andrews 0-1 Lija *(Fleri Soler 15)*

SEMI-FINALS

(17/05/13)
Qormi 1-0 Lija *(Zárate 67)*

(18/05/13)
Valletta 2-3 Hibernians *(Touré 45p, Briffa 90; Failla 38, 45, Edison 66)*

FINAL

(22/05/13)
National Stadium, Ta' Qali
HIBERNIANS FC 3 *(Edison 53, 67, Jackson 90+3)*
QORMI FC 1 *(Moisés Pérez 90+1)*
Referee: *Azzopardi*
HIBERNIANS: *Balzan, Camilleri, Farrugia, Pearson (Pulis 63), Rodolfo Soares, Cohen, Failla, Kristensen, Levnajić, Marcelo (Jackson 58), Edison (Obiefule 89)*
QORMI: *M Farrugia, Thackray, Sammut, D Pisani, Bondin, Sciberras, Gauci, Zárate, Grech (Bartolo 80), Effiong (Chetcuti 14), Moisés Pérez*
Sent off: *Gauci (74)*

MOLDOVA

Federatia Moldoveneasca de Fotbal (FMF)

Address	Str. Tricolorului 39 MD-2012 Chisinau	**President**	Pavel Cebanu
Tel	+373 22 210 413	**General secretary**	Nicolai Cebotari
Fax	+373 22 210 432	**Media officer**	Victor Daghi
E-mail	fmf@fmf.md	**Year of formation**	1990
Website	fmf.md	**National stadium**	Zimbru, Chisinau (10,400)

DIVIZIA NATIONALA CLUBS

1. FC Academia Chisinau
2. FC Costuleni
3. FC Dacia Chisinau
4. FC Iskra-Stal
5. FC Milsami Orhei
6. FC Nistru Otaci
7. FC Olimpia Balti
8. FC Rapid Ghidighici
9. FC Sheriff
10. FC Speranta Crihana Veche
11. FC Tiraspol
12. FC Zimbru Chisinau

PROMOTED CLUBS

13. FC Veris
14. FC Dinamo-Auto Tiraspol

KEY:
- UEFA Champions League
- UEFA Europa League
- Promoted clubs
- Relegated clubs

Another stroll for Sheriff

A season in which FC Sheriff further strengthened their status as the dominant force in Moldova with a 12th Divizia Nationala title in 13 years was spiced up by the exploits of unheralded FC Veris, who won the second division by a landslide and also reached the final of the Moldovan Cup, which they lost on penalties to FC Tiraspol.

A first major trophy for Sheriff's city rivals was supplemented by an impressive league campaign in which they challenged FC Dacia Chisinau for the runners-up spot. That battle was won – just – by the team from the capital, led again by their 2010/11 title-winning coach Igor Dobrovolski.

Easy title triumph for perennial champions

Second-tier champions Veris reach cup final

FC Tiraspol capture first major silverware

Domestic league

Championship-winning teams tend to benefit from stability and a settled side, but Sheriff danced to a very different tune as they swept all before them to claim yet another Moldovan title. Although they were a class apart from the other teams in the league, racking up 25 wins and 80 points and securing the title with four fixtures in hand, the search for perfection led them to use three coaches and no fewer than 45 players, representing 14 different nations.

The season started with new Serbian coach Milan Milanović in charge, but in less than a month he was gone, the previous season's championship-winning boss Vitali Rashkevich stepping in for a few days before Romanian Mihai Stoichiță, a double-winning coach with Sheriff in 2001/02, was summoned. His reign lasted until the following April when, with the title virtually wrapped up, he was dismissed following a pair of goalless draws at home to Dacia.

Back in for the final few weeks came Rashkevich, and despite defeats in his first two games he was there at the finish. There was a sense of anti-climax, however, as the title was wrapped up with a walkover win, their opponents FC

Iskra-Stal having withdrawn from the competition a couple of weeks earlier.

While Sheriff made changes on the bench, Dacia and Tiraspol, who aped the champions' fine home form but were nowhere near as impressive away, stuck with the same coach from start to finish. They were the only two clubs in the division to do so. FC Nistru Otaci, who finished rock bottom with just 12 points, used five of them.

Domestic cup

Nistru were replaced in the 2013/14 Divizia Nationala by Veris, who romped to the Divizia A (second division) title, scoring 103 goals and conceding just five. Even more impressive were the club's exploits in the Moldovan Cup, where they eliminated three top-flight teams, including holders FC Milsami Orhei in the semi-finals, to become the first second-tier club to reach the final of the competition.

They gave it their best shot against Vlad Goian's Tiraspol, also appearing in the fixture for the first time, and were five minutes away from glory in extra time, but whereas Veris had needed a penalty shoot-out to defeat Milsami, they were to fall by the same method against

Tiraspol, Bulgarian goalkeeper Georgi Georgiev breaking their hearts with two decisive saves.

Europe

Heavily beaten by GNK Dinamo Zagreb in the third qualifying round of the UEFA Champions League – a result that cost coach Milanović his job – Sheriff gave a decent account of themselves against Olympique de Marseille in the UEFA Europa League play-offs before bowing out 2-1 on aggregate. Two rounds earlier FC Zimbru had put up a fine show against BSC Young Boys but were eliminated on penalties after two 1-0 home wins.

National team

With Ion Caras back in charge after a 15-year gap, Moldova made a troubled start to their 2014 FIFA World Cup qualifying campaign, losing 5-0 at home to England. A month later they held Ukraine to a 0-0 draw at the same venue, and the season ended with another draw, 1-1 at home to Poland, but otherwise there was not much to celebrate. The only World Cup win was away to San Marino, the 2-0 scoreline no different from the one Moldova managed there in the qualifying series for UEFA EURO 2012.

MOLDOVA

Domestic league: Divizia Nationala 2012/13 final table

		Pld	Home					Away					Total					Pts
			W	D	L	F	A	W	D	L	F	A	W	D	L	F	A	
1	**FC Sheriff**	**33**	**12**	**4**	**1**	**30**	**6**	**13**	**1**	**2**	**35**	**11**	**25**	**5**	**3**	**65**	**17**	**80**
2	FC Dacia Chisinau	33	12	4	1	29	10	6	8	2	18	9	18	12	3	47	19	66
3	FC Tiraspol	33	12	4	1	41	11	6	6	4	13	9	18	10	5	54	20	64
4	FC Milsami Orhei	33	12	3	2	29	7	6	1	9	19	23	18	4	11	48	30	58
5	FC Rapid Ghidighici	33	7	2	8	17	20	8	2	6	19	18	15	4	14	36	38	49
6	FC Zimbru Chisinau	33	7	5	4	27	17	5	5	7	26	21	12	10	11	53	38	46
7	FC Academia Chisinau	33	7	3	7	36	30	5	5	6	19	22	12	8	13	55	52	44
8	FC Costuleni	33	4	6	6	17	18	5	5	7	21	30	9	11	13	38	48	38
9	FC Iskra-Stal	33	5	4	7	22	29	5	4	8	15	26	10	8	15	37	55	38
10	FC Olimpia Balti	33	4	3	9	16	22	6	2	9	15	28	10	5	18	31	50	35
11	FC Speranta Crihana Veche	33	2	3	11	12	31	2	4	11	23	39	4	7	22	35	70	19
12	FC Nistru Otaci	33	2	4	10	11	32	0	2	15	10	51	2	6	25	21	83	12

NB FC Iskra-Stal withdrew after round 28 – their remaining matches were awarded as 0-3 defeats.

SEASON AT A GLANCE

EUROPEAN QUALIFICATION 2013/14

 Champion: FC Sheriff (second qualifying round)

 Cup winner: FC Tiraspol (first qualifying round)
FC Dacia Chisinau (first qualifying round)
FC Milsami Orhei (first qualifying round)

Top scorer   Gheorghe Bogiu (Milsami), 16 goals
Relegated clubs   FC Nistru Otaci , FC Iskra-Stal (withdrew)
Promoted clubs   FC Veris, FC Dinamo-Auto Tiraspol
Cup final   FC Tiraspol 2-2 FC Veris (aet; 4-2 on pens)

DIVIZIA NATIONALA TEAM OF THE SEASON
(3-4-1-2)
Coach: Goian (Tiraspol)

PLAYER OF THE SEASON
Georgi Georgiev
(FC Tiraspol)

The 24-year-old Bulgarian goalkeeper, signed by FC Tiraspol from OFC Sliven 2000 in 2011, performed with bravery and skill throughout his second season, inspiring the team to a third-place finish in the league and a first ever major trophy with victory in the Moldovan Cup. His ability was noted by champions FC Sheriff, who signed him up in the summer.

NEWCOMER OF THE SEASON
Artem Khachaturov
(FC Sheriff)

A product of Sheriff's academy, Khachaturov won his third title with the club in 2012/13 and was one of the most consistent performers in an ever-changing starting XI. A Moldovan Under-21 international, he decided to pursue his senior international career with Armenia, the land of his ancestors, making his debut in February against Luxembourg.

Georgiev (Tiraspol)
Metoua (Sheriff) — Ilescu (Dacia) — Paye (Tiraspol)
Ginsari (Academia) — Dragun (Onica) — Guira (Dacia) — Guilherme (Milsami)
Stanojević (Sheriff)
Popovici (Tiraspol) — Boghiu (Milsami)

MOLDOVA

NATIONAL TEAM

Home Kit — Away Kit

Results 2012/13

15/08/12	Albania	A	Tirana	0-0	
07/09/12	England (WCQ)	H	Chisinau	0-5	
11/09/12	Poland (WCQ)	A	Wroclaw	0-2	
12/10/12	Ukraine (WCQ)	H	Chisinau	0-0	
16/10/12	San Marino (WCQ)	A	Serravalle	2-0	Dadu (72p), Epureanu (78)
06/02/13	Kazakhstan	N	Antalya (TUR)	1-3	Doros (86)
22/03/13	Montenegro (WCQ)	H	Chisinau	0-1	
26/03/13	Ukraine (WCQ)	A	Odessa	1-2	Suvorov (80)
07/06/13	Poland (WCQ)	H	Chisinau	1-1	Sidorenco (37)
14/06/13	Kyrgyzstan	H	Tiraspol	2-1	Sidorenco (29, 78)

Appearances 2012/13

Coach: Ion Caras	11/09/50		Alb	ENG	POL	UKR	SMR	Kaz	MNE	UKR	POL	Kgz	Caps	Goals
Stanislav Namasco	10/11/86	Kuban (RUS) /Volgar (RUS)	G	G	G	G	G			G	G		37	-
Igor Armas	14/07/87	Kuban (RUS)	D	D	D						D		29	1
Petru Racu	17/07/87	unattached	D		D	D		D					17	-
Alexandru Epureanu	27/09/86	Krylya Sovetov (RUS) /Dinamo Moskva (RUS)	D	D	D	D	D	D	D	D	D		55	4
Semion Bulgaru	26/05/85	Alania (RUS) /unattached /Volga (RUS)	D	D		D	D	D		D	D		24	1
Alexandru Suvorov	02/02/87	Cracovia (POL) /unattached /Academia	M57	M46	M81	M79	M59	M46		s78	M74	M53	46	5
Alexandru Gatcan	27/03/84	Rostov (RUS)	M	M	M	M	M	M59	M 90*		M		31	1
Alexandru Onica	29/07/84	Sheriff	M	M	s73	M	M	s59		s67			17	-
Artur Patras	10/01/88	Olimpik-Şüvälan (AZE) /Academia	M77	M	M46		s59					M69	11	-
Serghey Covalciuc	20/01/82	Aktobe (KAZ)	M88	M	M	M61							41	2
Igor Picusciac	27/03/83	Amkar (RUS)	A63	A76	A	A84	A82	A51					16	2
Anatol Doros	21/03/83	Rapid Chisinau	s57			s84		s51		s69		s53	26	3
Gheorgii Ovseannicov	12/10/85	Sunkar (KAZ) /Rapid Chisinau	s63	s85	s46	s79					s82		22	2
Alexandr Dedov	26/07/89	Sheriff /Academia	s77	s46		M	M71	M73	M	M78	M	M74	9	-
Alexandr Pascenco	28/05/89	Sheriff	s88			s61		M76	M	M67	s74		6	-
Victor Golovatenco	28/04/84	Sibir (RUS)		D	D	D	D	D	D	D	D	D	52	3
Eugen Sidorenco	19/03/89	H. Nazareth Illit (ISR)		s76 /85					A	M	A	A	10	3
Stanislav Ivanov	07/10/80	Sheriff /Tiraspol			M73			M65					43	-
Serghey Alexeev	31/05/86	Yenisey (RUS)			s81	A							24	5
Vitalie Bordian	11/08/84	Hoverla (UKR) /Volga (RUS)				D			D	D	D71		30	1
Serghey Dadu	23/01/81	Sheriff					s71	s73					30	8
Evgheny Cebotari	16/10/84	Spartak Nalchik (RUS)					s82				s71		33	-
Serghey Pascenco	18/12/82	Malavan (IRN)						G	G				15	-

Appearances 2012/13 (contd.)

				Alb	ENG	POL	UKR	SMR	Kaz	MNE	UKR	POL	Kgz	Caps	Goals
Serghei Gheorghiev	20/10/91	Sheriff							s46	M77	M		M	5	-
Artur Ionita	17/08/90	Aarau (SUI)							s65	M	M	M		5	-
Igor Bugaiov	26/06/84	Tobol (KAZ)							s76		A69			43	8
Nicolae Josan	18/09/83	Tiraspol								s77				17	2
Alexandru Antoniuc	23/05/89	Zimbru										M82	M	3	-
Andrian Negai	28/01/85	Milsami											G	1	-
Oleg Clonin	04/02/88	Rapid Chisinau											D	1	-
Ion Jardan	10/01/90	Rapid Chisinau											D	1	-
Veaceslav Posmac	07/11/90	Dacia											D	1	-
Radu Catan	30/05/89	Zimbru											s69	3	-
Maxim Antoniuc	15/01/91	unattached											s74	1	-

European club competitions 2012/13

FC SHERIFF

Second qualifying round - Ulisses FC (ARM)
A 1-0 Gheorghiev (60)
Stoyanov, João Pereira, Onica, Gheorghiev (Pajović 87), Ríos (Dima 69), Dedov (Zamaliev 79), Marjanović, Metoua, Apatič, Samardžič, Stanojević. Coach: Milan Milanović (SRB)
H 1-0 Samardžič (66p)
Stoyanov, João Pereira, Onica, Gheorghiev (Balima 76), Pešić (Dima 90+2), Dedov, Marjanović, Metoua, Apatič, Samardžič, Stanojević (Rouamba 59). Coach: Milan Milanović (SRB)

Third qualifying round - GNK Dinamo Zagreb (CRO)
H 0-1
Stoyanov, João Pereira, Onica (Cheptine 79), Gheorghiev (Balima 57), Pešić, Dedov (Ivanov 69), Marjanović, Metoua, Apatič, Samardžič, Stanojević. Coach: Milan Milanović (SRB)
A 0-4
Stoyanov, João Pereira (Pajović 37), Onica, Gheorghiev, Pešić, Marjanović (Ivanov 66), Metoua, Apatič, Samardžič, Stanojević, Henrique Luvannor (Balima 46). Coach: Milan Milanović (SRB)

Play-offs - Olympique de Marseille (FRA)
H 1-2 Pajović (27)
Stoyanov, Onica (Ivanov 75), Pešić, Dedov (Henrique Luvannor 79), Balima, Metoua, Morales, Rouamba, Pajović, Samardžič, Stanojević (Pascenco 71). Coach: Mihai Stoichiță (ROU)
A 0-0
Stoyanov, Onica, Pešić (Dadu 75), Dedov (Henrique Luvannor 85), Balima, Metoua, Morales, Rouamba, Pajović, Samardžič, Stanojević (Ivanov 70). Coach: Mihai Stoichiță (ROU)

FC MILSAMI ORHEI

Second qualifying round - FC Aktobe (KAZ)
H 4-2 Boghiu (16, 51), Wellington (33), Gheți (87)
Negai, Wellington, Sosnovschi, Bruno Simão, Gârlă, Boghiu, Guilherme, Rassulov, Elias (Gheți 68), Casabella, Stoleru (Nurudeen 59). Coach: Serghey Clescenco (MDA)
A 0-3
Negai, Wellington, Sosnovschi, Bruno Simão, Gârlă, Boghiu (Traoré 72), Nurudeen, Rassulov, Elias, Casabella (Furdui 56), Stoleru (Guilherme 47). Coach: Serghey Clescenco (MDA)

FC DACIA CHISINAU

First qualifying round - NK Celje (SVN)
H 1-0 Sow (42)
Matiughin, Popovici, Guira, Mihaliov (Stjepanović 81), Cojocari, Sow (Sali 90), Krkotić, Caraus (Orbu 61), Mamah, Célio, Dimovski. Coach: Igor Dobrovolski (RUS)
Red card: Orbu 85
A 1-0 Mihaliov (32p)
Gaiduchevici, Popovici, Guira (Grosu 66), Josan (Stjepanović 80), Mihaliov, Cojocari, Sow (Sali 59), Krkotić, Mamah, Célio, Dimovski. Coach: Igor Dobrovolski (RUS)
Red card: Sali 77

Second qualifying round - IF Elfsborg (SWE)
H 1-0 Mihaliov (32)
Matiughin, Ilescu, Lucas, Guira, Josan (Stjepanović 61), Mihaliov, Cojocari, Sow (Cairo 90+1), Krkotić, Mamah, Dimovski. Coach: Igor Dobrovolski (RUS)
A 0-2
Gaiduchevici, Ilescu, Lucas, Guira, Josan (Cairo 46), Mihaliov (Orbu 22), Cojocari, Sow, Krkotić, Mamah, Dimovski (Pavlov 83). Coach: Igor Dobrovolski (RUS)

Domestic league club-by-club

FC ZIMBRU CHISINAU

EUROPA LEAGUE

First qualifying round - Bangor City FC (WAL)
A 0-0
Calancea, Korgalidze (Sischin 70), Bălaşa, Tumbasević (Iavorschi 46), Zastavniy, Cuznetov, Molla, Catan, Derkach, Barakhoev (Slivca 77), Gorceac. Coach: Oleg Bejenari (MDA)
H 2-1 *Molla (29, 31)*
Calancea, Sischin (Korgalidze 71), Nikolaev (Gafina 82), Bălaşa, Zastavniy (Tumbasević 55), Cuznetov, Molla, Catan, Derkach, Barakhoev, Gorceac. Coach: Oleg Bejenari (MDA)

Second qualifying round - BSC Young Boys (SUI)
A 0-1
Calancea, Sischin (Iavorschi 57), Bălaşa, Tumbasević (Anton 82), Zastavniy, Cuznetov, Molla, Catan (Cucu 65), Derkach, Barakhoev, Gorceac. Coach: Serghey Sirbu (MDA)
H 1-0 *Barakhoev (42) (aet; 1-4 on pens)*
Calancea, Korgalidze, Sischin (Anton 75), Bălaşa, Tumbasević, Zastavniy, Cuznetov, Molla, Catan, Derkach, Barakhoev (Spataru 83). Coach: Serghey Sirbu (MDA)

FC ACADEMIA CHISINAU

Coach: Veaceslav Rusnac;
(04/09/12) Volodymyr Knysh (UKR)
2006 • Satesc, Ghidighici (1,500); CPSM, Vadul lui Voda (1,000) • academia.md

2012
14/07	Milsami	a	0-1	
21/07	Sheriff	h	1-4	*Livandovschi (p)*
28/07	Iskra-Stal	a	0-1	
05/08	Zimbru	h	2-2	*Ginsari 2*
10/08	Rapid	a	2-0	*Erhan, Ojog*
18/08	Olimpia	h	1-2	*Andronic*
25/08	Nistru	a	2-1	*Caraulan, Cascaval*
01/09	Tiraspol	h	1-0	*Demerji*
16/09	Speranta	a	3-1	*Ginsari, D Bogdan, Leagu*
22/09	Dacia	h	0-4	
30/09	Costuleni	a	2-1	*Livandovschi (p), Ginsari*
05/10	Milsami	h	3-1	*Erhan, Livandovschi (p), Demerji*
21/10	Sheriff	a	0-3	
26/10	Iskra-Stal	h	3-2	*Livandovschi (p), Ginsari, Ojog*
03/11	Zimbru	a	0-4	
11/11	Rapid	h	5-0	*Ginsari 4 (1p), Leagu*
18/11	Olimpia	a	1-1	*P Stinga*
24/11	Nistru	h	6-0	*Ginsari 2 (1p), Potlog, Livandovschi (p), Solomin, Demerji*
28/11	Tiraspol	a	0-1	
02/12	Speranta	h	3-5	*Vremea, D Bogdan, Ginsari (p)*

2013
03/03	Dacia	a	1-1	*Truhanov*
10/03	Costuleni	h	1-1	*Prokuror*
16/03	Iskra-Stal	h	0-2	
30/03	Olimpia	a	3-0	*Chuperka, Prokuror, Suvorov*
06/04	Zimbru	h	0-1	
13/04	Costuleni	a	2-2	*Suvorov, Potlog*
21/04	Nistru	h	5-1	*Vremea, Suvorov (p), Potlog, Patras, Prokuror*
27/04	Sheriff	a	1-1	*Chuperka*
02/05	Dacia	h	1-2	*Focsa*
11/05	Tiraspol	a	1-1	*E Avram*
17/05	Milsami	h	2-1	*Suvorov, Dedov*
21/05	Rapid	a	1-3	*Chuperka*
31/05	Speranta	h	2-2	*E Avram 2*

No	Name	Nat	DoB	Pos	Aps	(s)	Gls
20	Igor Andronic		11/03/88	D	8	(1)	1
26	Mihai Apostol		21/01/97	M		(0)	
12	Cristian Avram		07/07/94	G	10		
33	Eduard Avram		05/01/90	M	4	(13)	3
13	Dumitru Berbinschi		23/02/88	D	3	(3)	
1	Andrian Bogdan		27/08/76	G	1		
21	Dumitru Bogdan		04/03/89	D	26		2
15	Ion Burlacu		03/02/95	M	1	(6)	
22	Stefan Caraulan		02/02/89	D	17	(5)	1
2	Adrian Cascaval		10/06/87	D	22	(2)	1
16	Alexandru Cheltuiala		05/02/83	D	24		
13	Cristian Chetrus		08/02/94	M		(1)	
10	Valeri Chuperka	RUS	12/06/92	M	9		3
9	Ion Cocebanu		20/02/92	A	2	(1)	
17	Efim Cojuhari		19/03/88	M		(5)	
11	Alexandr Dedov		26/07/89	M	8		1
6	Ion Demerji		28/04/89	M	24	(2)	3
1	Victor Dimov		19/01/90	G	8	(1)	
8	Iulian Erhan		01/07/86	D	16		2
29	Maxim Focsa		21/04/92	D	8	(1)	1
14	Radu Ginsari		10/12/91	A	18		12
17	Veaceslav Gorban		05/01/97	M		(3)	
10	Ion Leagu		15/05/90	A	6	(3)	2
7	Iurie Livandovschi		17/02/88	A	17	(7)	5
3	Alexandru Mardari		01/09/91	D	12	(11)	
19	Petr Ojog		17/07/90	M	2	(12)	2
8	Artur Patras		10/01/88	M	7	(3)	1
25	Vladimir Potlog		04/04/88	A	19	(12)	3
19	Ihor Prokuror	UKR	05/03/91	D	13		3
10	Denis Reveachin		15/08/94	A	1	(3)	
9	Alexei Solomin		05/06/93	M	9	(9)	1
18	Igor Soltanici		04/05/84	D	1	(2)	
1	Andrei Stinca		16/06/89	G	6		
11	Petru Stinga		17/04/87	M	10		1
10	Alexandru Suvorov		02/02/87	M	8	(1)	4
14	Victor Truhanov		30/01/91	M	9	(2)	1
15	Alexandru Vremea		03/11/91	M	26	(1)	3

FC COSTULENI

Coach: Vitalie Mostovoi; (22/01/13) Lilian Popescu
1983 • Municipal, Orhei (3,000); Buiucani, Chisinau (1,200) • fccostuleni.md

2012
13/07	Sheriff	a	0-5	
21/07	Iskra-Stal	h	0-0	
29/07	Zimbru	a	3-3	*Valcu, Mocanu, Sinitchih*
04/08	Rapid	h	0-2	
11/08	Olimpia	a	1-0	*Kouadio (p)*
18/08	Nistru	h	1-1	*Gonta*
25/08	Tiraspol	a	0-4	
31/08	Speranta	h	2-2	*Ivanov, Gonta (p)*
16/09	Dacia	a	2-4	*Onofrei 2*
22/09	Milsami	h	0-3	
30/09	Academia	h	1-2	*Ivanov*
06/10	Sheriff	h	0-3	
20/10	Iskra-Stal	a	2-2	
26/10	Zimbru	h	1-0	*Onofrei*
04/11	Rapid	a	2-1	*Onofrei, Valcu*
10/11	Olimpia	h	0-1	
17/11	Nistru	a	2-0	*Mocanu, Ivanov*
24/11	Tiraspol	h	1-1	*Egwatu*
28/11	Speranta	a	0-0	
02/12	Dacia	h	0-0	

2013
02/03	Milsami	h	0-1	
10/03	Academia	a	1-1	*Ivanov*
16/03	Tiraspol	a	1-3	*Solodchi*
31/03	Milsami	h	1-2	*Ivanov*
07/04	Rapid	a	0-0	
13/04	Academia	h	2-2	*Bugneac, Cemirtan*
20/04	Iskra-Stal	a	3-0	*(w/o)*
27/04	Olimpia	h	4-0	*Ivanov, Cemirtan 2, Pisla*
03/05	Zimbru	a	1-1	*Ivanov*
10/05	Speranta	a	4-1	*Bugneac, Cemirtan, Pisla, Solodchi*
17/05	Nistru	h	2-0	*Bugneac, Cemirtan*
21/05	Sheriff	a	1-1	*Cemirtan*
31/05	Dacia	h	2-1	*Cemirtan, Bugneac*

No	Name	Nat	DoB	Pos	Aps	(s)	Gls
20	Iury Aseev		23/10/92	A	1	(9)	
3	Dumitru Berbinschi		23/02/88	D	11		
16	Andrei Bugneac		30/03/88	A	11	(1)	4
10	Vadim Cemirtan		21/07/87	A	9	(3)	7
28	Alexandru Chirilov		28/01/78	G	1		
15	Cristian Efros		06/01/92	M		(2)	
15	Maxwell Egwatu	NGA	20/08/91	A	9	(4)	1
18	Victor Gonta		21/09/90	A	11	(6)	2
19	Pavel Gurau		05/02/01	D	2	(4)	
22	Petru Hvprosteanov		28/08/86	M	15	(1)	
17	Vladislav Ivanov		07/05/90	A	25	(6)	7
7	Pacôme Kouadio	CIV	25/12/88	M	17	(4)	1
18	Evgheny Lavrinovici		15/09/88	D	1	(10)	
22	Vitalie Mardari		28/07/79	D	7	(1)	
8	Sergiu Mocanu		24/10/87	M	26		2
2	Mihai Moraru		22/10/79	G	13		
10	Ilie Mostovoi		26/10/89	D	10	(1)	
18	Vitalie Negru		15/01/87	D	13	(4)	
6	Yusif Nurudeen	GHA	28/08/92	D	5	(1)	
11	Octavian Onofrei	ROU	16/05/91	A	17	(12)	4
5	Dan Pisla		14/06/86	A	18	(4)	2
19	Maxim Repinetschi		02/07/89	M		(6)	
3	Ion Sandu		09/03/93	D	11	(5)	
5	Alexei Savinov		19/04/79	D	6		
21	Iurii Sinitchih		09/02/91	M	15	(2)	1
16	Sergiu Sirbu		01/04/86	D	14		
9	Andrei Solodchi		14/12/85	A	20	(7)	2
6	Alphonse Soppo	CMR	15/05/85	M	11		
1	Gheorghe Tonu		25/11/89	G	18		
22	Pavel Trofin		10/11/91	A	4	(17)	
4	Timur Valcu		16/01/91	D	31		2

FC DACIA CHISINAU

Coach: Igor Dobrovolski (RUS)
1999 • Zimbru (10,400); Baza Zimbru artificial (2,142); Buiucani, Chisinau (1,200) • fcdacia.md
Major honours
Moldovan League (1) 2011

2012
15/07	Iskra-Stal	a	2-2	*Sow, Orbu*
22/07	Zimbru	h	3-2	*og (Barakhoev), Pavlov, Cairo*
29/07	Rapid	a	1-0	*Sow*
05/08	Olimpia	h	1-0	*Krkotić*
11/08	Nistru	a	2-0	*Orbu 2 (1p)*
19/08	Tiraspol	h	1-1	*Krkotić*
26/08	Speranta	a	1-1	*Orbu*
01/09	Milsami	a	0-0	

MONTENEGRO

Futbalski savez Crne Gore (FSCG)

Address	Ulica "19. decembra" 13	**President**	Dejan Savićević
	ME-81000 Podgorica	**General secretary**	Momir Djurdjevac
Tel	+382 20 445 600	**Media officer**	Ivan Radović
Fax	+382 20 445 660	**Year of formation**	1931
E-mail	info@fscg.co.me	**National stadium**	Pod Goricom,
Website	fscg.co.me		Podgorica (12,000)

PRVA LIGA CLUBS

1. FK Budućnost Podgorica
2. FK Čelik Nikšić
3. FK Grbalj
4. FK Jedinstvo Bijelo Polje
5. FK Lovćen
6. FK Mladost Podgorica
7. FK Mogren
8. FK Mornar
9. OFK Petrovac
10. FK Rudar Pljevlja
11. FK Sutjeska
12. FK Zeta

PROMOTED CLUB

13. FK Dečić

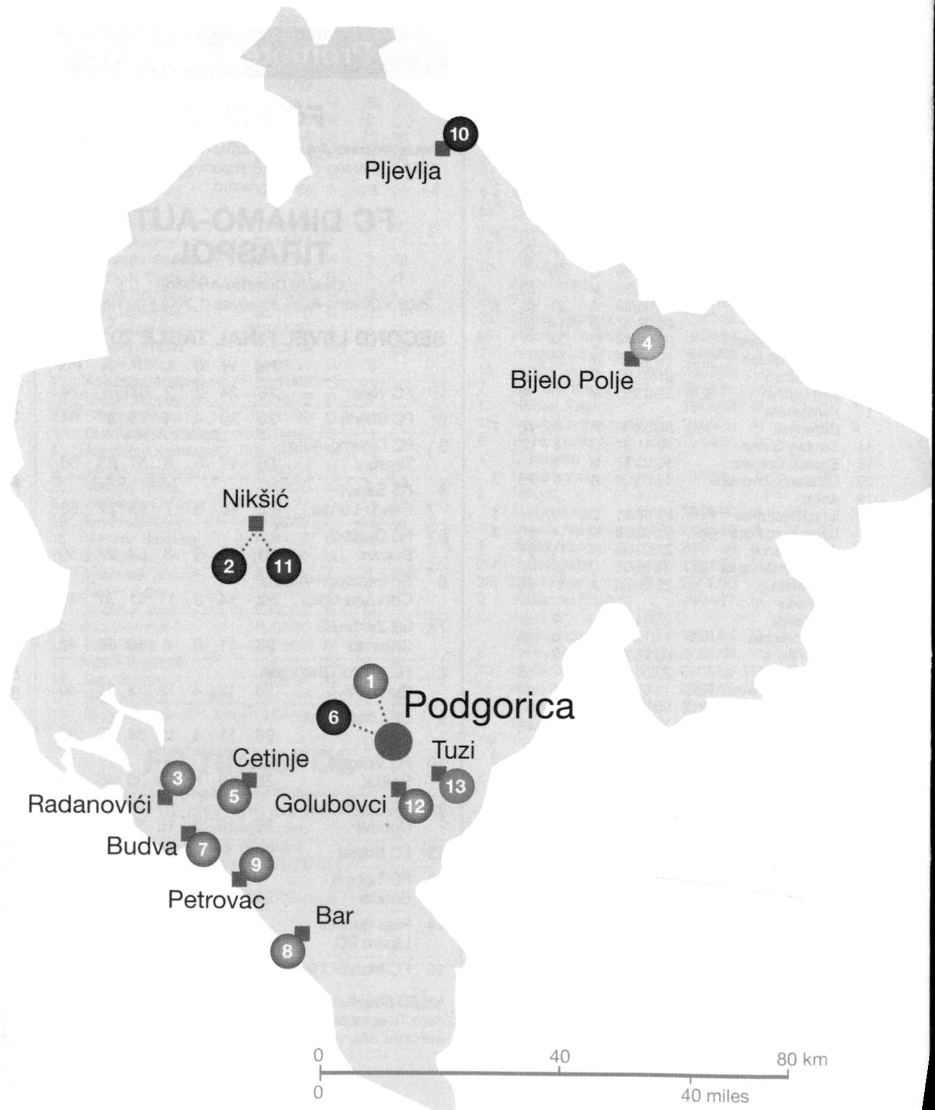

KEY:

- ● – UEFA Champions League
- ● – UEFA Europa League
- ● – Promoted club
- ● – Relegated club

Pljevlja **10**

Bijelo Polje **4**

Nikšić
2 ⋯ **11**

1
6 **Podgorica**
Cetinje Tuzi
3 **13**
Radanovići **5** Golubovci **12**
Budva **7**
9
Petrovac
Bar
8

0		40		80 km
0			40 miles	

Sutjeska reach the summit

There were new names on both of Montenegro's main domestic trophies at the end of the 2012/13 season as FK Sutjeska, from Niksic, won the league title and two-time champions FK Budućnost Podgorica lifted the cup.

Relegation strugglers in each of the previous two seasons, Sutjeksa benefited from the arrival of former player Dragan Radojićić, who transformed the team's fortunes. Another coach, Branko Brnović, continued to work wonders with the Montenegro national side as they topped their 2014 FIFA World Cup group heading into the summer.

Niksic side hold on for first title after late stumble

Budućnost beat holders Čelik in fractious cup final

National team top World Cup qualifying group

Domestic league

Sutjeska were not among the title candidates at the start of the campaign. They had finished eighth in 2011/12, 44 points behind champions Budućnost. But with Radojićić, recruited from runners-up FK Rudar Pljevlja, back at the club where he began his playing career, Sutjeska made an incredible start, registering six straight wins to storm clear at the top of the table.

It was not all plain sailing thereafter, but the leaders were never toppled from their perch, going into the winter break with a one-point advantage over Budućnost and forging clear – despite the return of top-scoring loanee Djordje Šušnjar to FK Vojvodja – with a remarkable run in the spring.

Sutjeska won eight of their first nine games on the resumption, and with seven fixtures left had chiselled out a 12-point lead. A first championship triumph was within touching distance, but it was then that nerves took hold, a horrible six-match winless run whittling Sutjeska's advantage down to just two points with a game to play. The pressure was intense ahead of that final fixture, away to FK Lovćen, but to great relief they survived the ordeal to win 2-1 and,

with challengers Budućnost losing, take the title by five points.

Sutjeska's final tally of 65 points was 15 down on Budućnost's winning 2011/12 total, and with eight defeats and just 50 goals scored it was not, ultimately, the most emphatic of triumphs, but having almost let it slip, the relief and joy were boundless. Sutjeska had become the fifth side to win the Montenegrin title in seven seasons.

Domestic cup

The teams that finished second and third in the league, Budućnost and FK Čelik Nikšić, met in the Montenegrin Cup final. Čelik, the holders, had to cede home advantage to Budućnost, but their 'hosts' had won only two matches in the Pod Goricom Stadium since the turn of the year. An evenly-poised contest turned, however, into a sour and controversial affair and was ultimately decided by a single goal, scored in added time by Budućnost defender Mitar Peković.

But while the capital club celebrated a first cup win, both they and FK Grbalj, the league's fourth-placed side, were refused a licence to compete in Europe, their places going instead to Rudar and FK Mladost Podgorica.

Europe

FK Zeta had a poor season domestically but they preceded it by negotiating three qualifying rounds of the UEFA Europa League, eliminating opposition from Armenia, Finland and Bosnia & Herzegovina. Unfortunately their run was ended brutally by PSV Eindhoven, who put 14 goals past them without reply.

National team

Montenegro have a number of players plying their trade in Europe's top leagues, and those called into action during the opening bouts of the World Cup qualifying campaign did their country proud. Maximum points from three away games, including a 1-0 win in Kyiv, enabled Montenegro to top their group – a position they retained by holding England to a 1-1 draw with an excellent second-half fightback in Podgorica.

Next time out, however, at home to Ukraine, the second 45 minutes proved disastrous as Brnović's men conceded four goals and had two players sent off, falling to their first defeat. Although they still held a two-point lead, England and Ukraine, each with a game in hand, were now both within striking distance.

MONTENEGRO

Domestic league: Prva Liga 2012/13 final table

		Pld	Home					Away					Total					
			W	D	L	F	A	W	D	L	F	A	W	D	L	F	A	Pts
1	FK Sutjeska	33	13	1	3	30	15	7	4	5	20	16	20	5	8	50	31	65
2	FK Budućnost Podgorica	33	7	4	6	24	24	10	5	1	32	15	17	9	7	56	39	60
3	FK Čelik Nikšić	33	8	5	4	24	17	7	3	6	17	18	15	8	10	41	35	53
4	FK Grbalj	33	9	6	2	30	11	4	6	6	11	10	13	12	8	41	21	51
5	FK Rudar Pljevlja	33	8	3	6	24	22	7	3	6	18	18	15	6	12	42	40	51
6	FK Mladost Podgorica	33	6	7	4	25	22	3	5	8	14	26	9	12	12	39	48	39
7	OFK Petrovac	33	3	8	5	15	17	5	6	6	21	25	8	14	11	36	42	38
8	FK Zeta	33	7	4	5	22	17	1	9	7	21	28	8	13	12	43	45	37
9	FK Lovćen	33	6	2	8	18	23	5	2	10	20	28	11	4	18	38	51	37
10	FK Mogren	33	5	3	8	16	22	5	4	8	17	20	10	7	16	33	42	36
11	FK Mornar	33	5	6	5	17	16	4	3	10	19	31	9	9	15	36	47	36
12	FK Jedinstvo Bijelo Polje	33	4	5	7	15	20	5	4	8	16	25	9	9	15	31	45	36

NB FK Mogren – 1 pt deducted.

SEASON AT A GLANCE

EUROPEAN QUALIFICATION 2013/14

Champion: FK Sutjeska (second qualifying round)

FK Čelik Nikšić (first qualifying round)
FK Rudar Pljevlja (first qualifying round)
FK Mladost Podgorica (first qualifying round)

Top scorers	Admir Adrović (Budućnost) & Žarko Korać (Zeta), 15 goals
Relegated club	FK Jedinstvo Bijelo Polje
Promoted club	FK Dečić
Cup final	FK Budućnost Podgorica 1-0 FK Čelik Nikšić

PRVA LIGA TEAM OF THE SEASON
(3-4-1-2)
Coach: Radojičić (Sutjeska)

PLAYER OF THE SEASON
Blažo Igumanović
(FK Rudar Pljevlja)

Named Montenegrin player of the year at the end of 2012, the versatile left-sided player maintained an excellent performance level throughout the season. One of the few national team players operating in the domestic league, the 27-year-old scored six goals and made ten assists, his free-kicks and crosses providing a constant source of danger.

NEWCOMER OF THE SEASON
Aleksandar Boljević
(FK Zeta)

Despite a tough season for his club, who finished eighth in the league, 17-year-old Boljević announced himself as a player of prodigious talent. With lightning pace he terrorised defences and ended the season with five goals in 23 league appearances. A regular member of the national Under-21 side, his future clearly lies at senior international level.

NATIONAL TEAM

Home Kit   Away Kit

TOP FIVE ALL-TIME CAPS
Simon Vukčević (41); Elsad Zverotić (38);
Mirko Vučinić (35); Savo Pavićević (34);
Vladimir Božović, Milan Jovanović &
Milorad Peković (33)

TOP FIVE ALL-TIME GOALS
Mirko Vučinić (14); Stevan Jovetić (10);
Radomir Djalović (7); Andrija Delibašić (6);
Dejan Damjanović & Elsad Zverotić (4)

Results 2012/13

Date	Opponent	H/A	Venue	Score	Scorers
15/08/12	Latvia	H	Podgorica	2-0	Jovetić (36), Kasalica (76)
07/09/12	Poland (WCQ)	H	Podgorica	2-2	Drinčić (27), Vučinić (45+3)
11/09/12	San Marino (WCQ)	A	Serravalle	6-0	Djordjević (24), Bećiraj (26, 51), Zverotić (69), Delibašić (78, 82)
16/10/12	Ukraine (WCQ)	A	Kyiv	1-0	Damjanović (45)
14/11/12	San Marino (WCQ)	H	Podgorica	3-0	Delibašić (14, 31), Zverotić (68)
22/03/13	Moldova (WCQ)	A	Chisinau	1-0	Vučinić (78)
26/03/13	England (WCQ)	H	Podgorica	1-1	Damjanović (76)
07/06/13	Ukraine (WCQ)	H	Podgorica	0-4	

Appearances 2012/13

Coach: Branko Brnović	08/08/67		Lva	POL	SMR	UKR	SMR	MDA	ENG	UKR	Caps	Goals
Mladen Božović	01/08/84	Videoton (HUN)	G	U	G	G	G	G	G	G	32	-
Savo Pavićević	11/12/80	Omonia (CYP)	D	D 69*			D					
		/H. Tel-Aviv (ISR)						D		D 81*	34	-
Stefan Savić	08/01/91	Man. City (ENG)	D									
		/Fiorentina (ITA)		D	D	D	D46	D	D		21	2
Marko Baša	29/12/82	LOSC (FRA)	D46	D	D	D	D71	D	D	D	23	1
Milan Jovanović	21/07/83	Crvena zvezda (SRB)	D77	D65		D					33	
Elsad Zverotić	31/10/86	Young Boys (SUI)	M	M	s66	M88	M	M	M	M	38	4
Vladimir Volkov	06/06/86	Partizan (SRB)	M	M	D	M	D	M	M	M 66*	9	-
Nikola Drinčić	07/09/84	Krasnodar (RUS)	M60	M84		M					29	3
Simon Vukčević	29/01/86	Blackburn (ENG)	M73	M71	M66	s72	M					
		/Karpaty (UKR)						s64	M63		41	2
Stevan Jovetić	02/11/89	Fiorentina (ITA)	A79	A	M	A86	A	A	A	A43	27	10
Andrija Delibašić	24/04/81	Rayo Vallecano (ESP)	A65		s66		A		s75	s63	21	6
Filip Kasalica	17/12/88	Crvena zvezda (SRB)	s46	s65	s75		A77	A45		M75	6	1
Milorad Peković	05/08/77	Greuther Fürth (GER)	s60	s71	M	M		M 61*		M	33	-
Mirko Vučinić	01/10/83	Juventus (ITA)	s65	A		s86		A80	A	A	35	14
Fatos Bećiraj	05/05/88	Dinamo Zagreb (CRO)	s73	A75		A				s75	20	3
Miodrag Džudović	06/09/79	Spartak Nalchik (RUS)	s77	s84	D	D			D		24	1
Marko Bakić	01/11/93	Mogren	s79								1	-
Dejan Damjanović	27/07/81	Seoul (KOR)			A	A72		s45	s46	s43	19	4
Luka Djordjević	09/07/94	Zenit (RUS)			A66		s46				2	1
Mitar Novaković	27/09/81	Amkar (RUS)				s88	M	s80	M46		24	-
Ivan Kecojević	10/04/88	Gaziantepspor (TUR)					s71			D	2	-
Blažo Igumanović	19/01/86	Rudar Pljevlja					s77				1	-
Vladimir Božović	13/11/81	Mordovia (RUS)						D64	D75	D63	33	-
Miloš Krkotić	29/09/87	Dacia (MDA)								s63	1	-

European club competitions 2012/13

FK BUDUĆNOST PODGORICA

Second qualifying round - WKS Śląsk Wrocław (POL)
H 0-2
Agović, Radunović, Peković, Djikanović, Golubović, Bošković (Radonjić 59), Kurbegović, N Vukčević (Flávio Beck 75), Kamberović, Adrović (M Vukčević 85), Kalezić. Coach: Radislav Dragićević (MNE)
Red card: Flávio Beck 79
A 1-0 N Vukčević (15)
Agović, Radunović, Peković, Djikanović (Nikač 86), Bošković, M Vukčević, Kurbegović (Golubović 70), N Vukčević, Kamberović, Adrović, Kalezić (Mugoša 79). Coach: Radislav Dragićević (MNE)

FK ČELIK NIKŠIĆ

First qualifying round - FK Borac Banja Luka (BIH)
A 2-2 Bojić (36p), Agović (83)
Banović, Dubljević, Radović, Adrović, Ivanović, Simić (Agović 63), Zorić (Nikolić 90+2), Bulatović, Jovović (Brnović 46), Bojić, Bulajić. Coach: Slavoljub Bubanja (MNE)
H 1-1 Milić (54og)
Banović, Dubljević, Radović, Adrović, Ivanović, Kasapi (Simić 65), Zorić (Nikolić 90+1), Bulatović, Jovović (Agović 46), Bojić, Bulajić. Coach: Slavoljub Bubanja (MNE)

Second qualifying round - FC Metalurh Donetsk (UKR)
A 0-7
Banović, Dubljević, Radović, Adrović, Ivanović (Agović 64), Simić (Brnović 86), Zorić, Nikolić, Videkanić (Drinčić 88), Jovović, Bulajić. Coach: Slavoljub Bubanja (MNE)
H 2-4 Jovović (23), Zorić (50p)
Banović, Dubljević, Radović, Adrović, Ivanović (Agović 80), Simić (Kasapi 60), Zorić, Nikolić, Bulatović (Videkanić 60), Jovović, Bulajić. Coach: Slavoljub Bubanja (MNE)

FK RUDAR PLJEVLJA

First qualifying round - FC Shirak (ARM)
H 0-1
Vukliš, Alić, Igumanović (Bakoč 80), Ivanović, Kaludjerović, Adžić, Stojanović (Nerić 64), M Jovanović, I Jovanović, Nestorović, Vlahović. Coach: Nikola Rakojevic (MNE)
A 1-1 Mkoyan (11og)
Vukliš, Alić, Popović, Igumanović (Rustemović 85), Ivanović, Kaludjerović (Stojanović 46), Adžić, Brnović, I Jovanović (Bakoč 78), Nestorović, Vlahović. Coach: Nikola Rakojevic (MNE)

FK ZETA

First qualifying round - FC Pyunik (ARM)
A 3-0 Vujačić (61), Peličić (81), Orlandić (90+2)
Bulatović, M M Radulović, Vujačić, Zlatičanin, Boljević (Z Peličić 80), Novović, Božović (Kalačević 89), Došljak, Burzanović, Orlandić, M B Radulović. Coach: Rade Vešović (MNE)
H 1-2 M B Radulović (16)
Bulatović, M M Radulović, Vujačić, Zlatičanin (Z Peličić 60), Boljević, Novović, Božović (Kalačević 77), Došljak, Burzanović, M B Radulović, Knežević (Orlandić 68). Coach: Rade Vešović (MNE)

Second qualifying round - JJK Jyväskylä (FIN)
A 2-3 Došljak (17), M B Radulović (38)
Bulatović, M M Radulović, Vujačić, Boljević, Z Peličić (Zlatičanin 68), Novović, Božović (Kalačević 90), Došljak (Dabić 70), Burzanović, Korać, M B Radulović. Coach: Rade Vešović (MNE)
H 1-0 Došljak (82)
Brnović, M M Radulović (Knežević 67), Vujačić (V Peličić 58), Zlatičanin (Z Peličić 46), Boljević, Novović, Božović, Došljak, Burzanović, Korać, M B Radulović. Coach: Rade Vešović (MNE)

Third qualifying round - FK Sarajevo (BIH)
A 1-2 Božović (45)
Brnović, M M Radulović, V Peličić, Zlatičanin, Boljević (Dabić 53), Novović, Božović (Kalačević 81), Došljak, Burzanović, Korać, M B Radulović. Coach: Rade Vešović (MNE)
Red card: V Peličić 71
H 1-0 Burzanović (9)
Bulatović, M M Radulović, Kaludjerović, Zlatičanin, Boljević (Dabić 73), Novović, Božović (Ajković 60), Došljak, Burzanović, Korać (Knežević 80), M B Radulović. Coach: Rade Vešović (MNE)

Play-offs - PSV Eindhoven (NED)
H 0-5
Bulatović, M M Radulović, Vujačić, Zlatičanin (Z Peličić 81), Boljević, Novović, Božović (Ajković 46), Došljak, Burzanović, Korać, M B Radulović. Coach: Rade Vešović (MNE)
A 0-9
Bulatović, M M Radulović, Kaludjerović, Boljević, Z Peličić (Ajković 46), Novović, Božović (Zlatičanin 71), Došljak, Burzanović, Korać, M B Radulović (Vujačić 30). Coach: Rade Vešović (MNE)

Domestic league club-by-club

FK BUDUĆNOST PODGORICA

Coach: Radislav Dragićević
1925 • Pod Goricom (12,000) • fkbuducnost.co.me
Major honours
Montenegrin League (2) 2008, 2012;
Montenegrin Cup (1) 2013

2012

11/08	Sutjeska	a	0-1	
18/08	Lovćen	h	3-1	Kurbegović, Golubović, Mugoša
22/08	Grbalj	a	2-1	og (Djalac), Mugoša
25/08	Mogren	h	0-2	
01/09	Mladost	a	1-1	Adrović (p)
15/09	Petrovac	h	4-1	Adrović 2, M Vukčević, Flávio Beck
23/09	Čelik	a	0-0	
29/09	Zeta	a	3-1	Adrović, Bošković, M Vukčević
06/10	Rudar	h	1-4	Adrović
13/10	Mornar	a	4-1	Adrović 2, Bošković, Raičković
20/10	Jedinstvo	h	0-0	
28/10	Sutjeska	h	2-0	Bošković, Adrović
03/11	Lovćen	a	2-1	Peković, Adrović
10/11	Grbalj	h	1-0	Flávio Beck
17/11	Mogren	h	2-1	Bošković, Adrović
24/11	Mladost	h	1-0	Bošković (p)
01/12	Petrovac	a	1-1	Nikač

2013

26/02	Čelik	h	1-1	Nikač
02/03	Zeta	h	3-3	Golubović, Radonjić, Cmiljanić
09/03	Rudar	a	0-0	
16/03	Mornar	h	4-1	Adrović 2 (1p), Nikač, Golubović
20/03	Jedinstvo	a	5-0	Nikač 2, Radonjić, M Vukčević, Mugoša
30/03	Jedinstvo	h	3-2	Adrović, Flávio Beck, Orahovac
06/04	Petrovac	h	1-1	Adrović
13/04	Zeta	a	0-0	
20/04	Mogren	h	1-2	Mugoša
27/04	Mladost	a	2-1	Adrović, M Vukčević
01/05	Grbalj	h	1-4	Mugoša
05/05	Rudar	a	4-3	Mugoša 2, Raičković, M Vukčević
11/05	Čelik	h	1-0	Flávio Beck
18/05	Lovćen	h	0-3	(w/o)
25/05	Sutjeska	a	3-1	Radonjić, M Vukčević, Kalezić
01/06	Mornar	h	0-1	

Name	Nat	DoB	Pos	Aps	(s)	Gls
Admir Adrović		08/05/88	A	24	(2)	15
Jasmin Agović		13/02/91	D	28		
Dragan Bošković		27/12/85	M	13	(?)	5
Boris Cmiljanić		17/03/96	A	2	(13)	1
Djordje Djikanović		18/08/84	D	4		
Flávio Beck	BRA	14/03/87	M	24	(3)	4
Radivoje Golubović		22/04/90	D	11	(8)	3
Miloš Kalezić		09/08/93	M	9	(12)	1
Radenko Kamberović	SRB	13/02/83	D	27		
Marko Kažić		16/11/95	M	2	(5)	
Boris Kopitović		17/05/94	D	11	(1)	
Selmo Kurbegović	SRB	13/01/85	M	6	(2)	1
Damir Ljuljanović		23/02/92	G	4		
Stefan Mugoša		26/02/92	A	18	(11)	7
Darko Nikač		15/09/90	A	17	(9)	5
Adnan Orahovac		05/02/91	D	13	(1)	1
Mitar Peković	SRB	28/09/81	D	30		1
Srdjan Radonjić		08/05/81	A	9	(2)	3
Risto Radunović		04/05/92	D	17		
Milos Raičković		02/12/93	M	4	(5)	2
Momcilo Raspopović		18/03/94	D	5	(4)	
Vladislav Rogošić		21/05/94	M		(7)	
Mihailo Tomković		10/06/91	D	20		
Marko Vukčević		07/06/93	M	27	(3)	6
Nikola Vukčević		13/12/91	M	27		

FK ČELIK NIKŠIĆ

Coach: Slavoljub Bubanja
1957 • Željezare (2,000) • no website
Major honours
Montenegrin Cup (1) 2012

2012

11/08	Lovćen	a	3-0	Račić, Ivanović, Agović
18/08	Grbalj	h	0-3	
22/08	Mogren	a	2-1	Radović, Videkanić
25/08	Mladost	h	3-0	Račić, Zorić (p), Ivanović
01/09	Petrovac	a	0-0	
15/09	Zeta	a	1-3	Račić
23/09	Budućnost	h	0-0	
30/09	Rudar	a	3-1	Adrović, Simić, Kasapi
06/10	Mornar	h	3-0	Račić 3
13/10	Jedinstvo	a	1-0	Agović
21/10	Sutjeska	h	3-0	Zorić (p), Kasapi, Račić
28/10	Lovćen	h	1-1	Kasapi
03/11	Grbalj	a	0-2	
10/11	Mogren	h	0-0	
17/11	Mladost	a	1-0	Bulajić
24/11	Petrovac	h	0-2	
01/12	Zeta	h	2-2	Vuković, Ilić

2013

26/02	Budućnost	a	1-1	Kolev
02/03	Rudar	h	1-0	Račić
09/03	Mornar	a	0-0	
16/03	Jedinstvo	h	2-0	Zorić (p), Račić
20/03	Sutjeska	a	0-1	
30/03	Petrovac	a	0-0	
06/04	Zeta	h	4-3	Zorić 2 (1p), Marjanović, Radović
13/04	Mogren	a	1-0	Dubljević
20/04	Mladost	h	1-0	Račić
27/04	Grbalj	a	3-2	Ivanović, Zorić (p), Račić
01/05	Rudar	a	1-0	Ivanović
04/05	Lovćen	h	1-3	Račić
11/05	Budućnost	a	0-1	
18/05	Sutjeska	h	1-0	Videkanić
25/05	Mornar	a	1-4	Bakoč
01/06	Jedinstvo	h	2-0	Ivanović

Name	Nat	DoB	Pos	Aps	(s)	Gls
Zijad Adrović		17/02/86	D	20	(8)	1
Semir Agović		27/04/92	A	1	(9)	2
Luka Bakoč		23/11/86	M	3	(8)	1
Zoran Banović		14/10/77	G	33		
Nemanja Bubanja		01/08/84	D		(1)	
Boris Bulajić		27/05/88	M	30		1
Darko Bulatović		05/09/90	D	17	(1)	
Ilija Bulatović		11/08/91	D	2		
Djordje Djikanović		18/08/84	D	14		
Bojan Drinčić		01/02/93	D		(2)	
Aleksandar Dubljević		09/03/85	D	23	(1)	1
Marko Dževerdanović		03/11/81	M		(1)	
Boško Guzina		30/04/96	M		(1)	
Milan Ilić	SRB	15/05/87	D	6		1
Ivan Ivanović		14/09/89	M	27	(2)	5
Vasilije Jovović		12/05/86	A	13	(8)	
Marko Kasalica		09/11/88	M		(5)	
Fetim Kasapi	ALB	08/10/83	M	11	(2)	3
Dilyan Kolev	BUL	09/11/88	M	24	(1)	1
Dejan Kovačević		04/04/95	D		(1)	
Rodoljub Marjanović	CRO	27/01/88	A	5	(3)	1
Ivan Mirković		09/08/81	M		(4)	
Milovan Nikolić		05/09/93	D	5	(4)	
Stevan Račić		17/01/84	A	27		12
Ilija Radović		05/09/85	D	23		2
Bratislav Ristić	SRB	21/01/80	M	5	(1)	
Nikola Simić	SRB	30/07/81	M	14	(12)	1
Predrag Videkanić		23/08/86	D	13	(4)	2
Vojislav Vranković	SRB	01/01/83	M	3		
Danilo Vuković		01/05/89	D	17	(5)	1
Darko Zorić		12/09/93	A	27		6

FK GRBALJ

Coach: Aleksandar Nedović
1970 • Pod Sutvarom (1,500) • no website

2012

11/08	Petrovac	h	0-0	
18/08	Čelik	a	3-0	Janković, N Nikolić, Ragipović
22/08	Budućnost	h	1-2	D Nikolić
25/08	Rudar	a	0-1	
01/09	Mornar	h	2-0	Djalac, Carević
15/09	Jedinstvo	a	0-0	
22/09	Sutjeska	h	0-0	
29/09	Lovćen	a	0-0	
06/10	Zeta	h	2-0	N Nikolić, Janković
13/10	Mogren	h	0-0	
20/10	Mladost	a	0-0	
27/10	Petrovac	a	0-0	
03/11	Čelik	h	2-0	Matić, N Nikolić
10/11	Budućnost	a	0-1	
17/11	Rudar	h	4-0	Radulović (p), Djalac, Merdović, N Nikolić (p)
24/11	Mornar	a	0-1	
01/12	Jedinstvo	h	2-1	Djalac, Merdović

2013

26/02	Sutjeska	a	0-1	
02/03	Lovćen	h	1-0	Ašćerić
09/03	Zeta	a	0-0	
16/03	Mogren	a	0-0	
20/03	Mladost	h	1-1	Ašćerić
30/03	Mogren	h	1-0	Ašćerić
06/04	Mladost	a	4-1	N Bogdanović, Djalac 2, Luković
13/04	Lovćen	h	3-0	Milojko, Ašćerić 2
20/04	Rudar	a	2-0	Pepić 2
27/04	Čelik	h	2-3	Carević, Pepić
01/05	Budućnost	a	4-1	Djalac, Ašćerić, Glavan, Martinović (p)
04/05	Sutjeska	h	1-1	Ašćerić
11/05	Mornar	a	0-3	
18/05	Jedinstvo	h	4-1	Ašćerić 2, Djalac, Martinović
25/05	Petrovac	a	1-1	Ašćerić
01/06	Zeta	h	1-1	Ašćerić

Name	Nat	DoB	Pos	Aps	(s)	Gls
Nikola Ašćerić	SRB	19/04/91	A	15		11
Ilija Bogdanović		14/03/92	M	27	(1)	
Nikola Bogdanović		22/03/87	M	30		1
Milan Carević		05/10/93	D	17	(3)	2
Miloš Djalac		17/10/82	A	26	(4)	7
Nebojša Djalović		27/03/94	A	3	(6)	
Ljubomir Djurović	SRB	00/01/89	G	1	(1)	
Ilija Glavan	BIH	03/07/90	D	23		1
Dragan Grivić		12/02/96	D		(1)	
Takeshi Ito	JPN	11/09/87	D	2		
Branislav Janković		08/02/92	M	24	(4)	2
Stevan Luković	SRB	16/03/93	D	13		1
Aleksandar Macanović		16/04/93	M	1	(1)	
Djuro Magud		18/01/92	M	9		
Ćetko Manojlović		03/01/91	D		(6)	
Lazar Martinović		03/07/89	M	16	(8)	2
Vladimir Matić	SRB	12/07/83	M	12	(2)	1
Dražen Medjedović		15/10/81	M	2	(4)	
Luka Merdović		14/03/89	A	16	(11)	2
Zoran Mikijelj		13/12/91	D	3	(4)	
Goran Milojko		05/01/94	D	12	(4)	1
Dragan Nikolić		20/01/93	M	1	(17)	1
Nemanja Nikolić		19/10/92	A	16		4
Dejan Pepić		27/07/93	A	4	(12)	3
Mileta Radulović		29/01/81	G	32		1
Igor Radusinović		15/03/84	D	29		
Kenan Ragipović	SRB	16/11/82	M	27		1
Nikola Raičević		18/11/93	M		(1)	
Ilija Tučević		18/10/95	D	2	(2)	

FK JEDINSTVO BIJELO POLJE

Coach: Sreten Avramović
1922 • Gradski (5,000) • no website

2012

11/08	Rudar	h	0-2
18/08	Mornar	a	0-0
25/08	Sutjeska	h	0-1
01/09	Lovćen	a	1-0	Rosić
06/09	Zeta	h	0-0
15/09	Grbalj	h	0-0
22/09	Mogren	a	1-0	Radulović
29/09	Mladost	h	0-0
06/10	Petrovac	a	3-0	Kajević, Boričić 2
13/10	Čelik	h	0-1
20/10	Budućnost	a	0-0
28/10	Rudar	a	1-1	Mihailo Petrović
03/11	Mornar	h	1-3	Boričić
10/11	Zeta	a	1-2	Kajević
17/11	Sutjeska	a	0-3
24/11	Lovćen	h	3-0	Sseppuya 2, Boričić
01/12	Grbalj	a	1-2	Sseppuya

2013

26/02	Mogren	h	1-2	Miloš Petrović
02/03	Mladost	a	3-3	Radulović, Miloš Petrović, Rosić
09/03	Petrovac	h	2-0	Raičević, Miloš Petrović
16/03	Čelik	a	0-2
20/03	Budućnost	h	0-5
30/03	Budućnost	h	2-3	Miloš Petrović, Rosić
06/04	Sutjeska	a	1-4	Mihailo Petrović
13/04	Mornar	a	2-1	Miloš Petrović (p), Kalezić
20/04	Lovćen	a	0-2
27/04	Petrovac	a	1-0	Raičević
01/05	Zeta	h	1-1	Raičević
04/05	Mogren	a	0-1
11/05	Mladost	h	1-1	Kalezić
18/05	Grbalj	a	1-4	Miloš Petrović
25/05	Rudar	h	2-0	Djurović, Kalezić
01/06	Čelik	a	2-1	Raičević, Radulović

Name	Nat	DoB	Pos	Aps	(s)	Gls
Zoran Aković		26/12/85	G	32		
Sead Babača		30/10/81	M	1	(10)	
Denis Banda		01/05/94	A		(1)	
Adnan Bećirović		19/07/91	A	3	(5)	
Dino Bećirović		14/12/89	M	1	(1)	
Vladimir Boričić		09/01/85	D	11	(14)	4
Amel Brzać		17/01/94	D	1		
Edis Čindrak		15/10/81	A	17	(5)	
Vladan Čujović		24/12/94	A		(4)	
Nemanja Djurović	SRB	20/12/86	A	13		1
Mihailo Drašković		10/07/83	M	28		
Denis Fetahović		29/12/79	D	16		
Milenko Garić	SRB	08/05/88	M	11	(2)	
Nemanja Gojačanin		27/10/90	D	22	(2)	
Vladan Gordić		27/07/90	D	23	(2)	
Andrija Janketić		10/10/93	A		(2)	
Demir Kajević		20/05/89	A	13	(1)	2
Bojan Kalezić		11/03/88	M	9	(1)	3
Nemanja Kalić		06/08/83	D		(2)	
Emin Kasumović		07/02/93	A	2	(9)	
Stefan Kljajević		19/05/90	M	2	(1)	
Miloš Ljujić		01/10/94	D	3	(3)	
Mihailo Luković		31/05/95	D	1		
Haris Mahmutović		29/11/94	M		(1)	
Saša Medenica		25/07/93	M	11	(11)	
Mihailo Petrović		12/12/89	D	27		2
Miloš Petrović	SRB	14/04/86	M	14		6
Jasmin Pućurica		15/03/93	G	1	(1)	
Nikola Radulović		17/12/85	M	20	(1)	3
Mileta Raičević		02/11/90	A	12	(3)	4
Vladislav Rosić	SRB	20/04/84	M	12	(2)	3
Eugene Sseppuya	UGA	01/04/83	A	7	(4)	3
Lamin Sesay	SLE	14/07/91	M	4	(3)	
Aleksandar Šćekić		12/12/91	D	11	(1)	
Bojan Ušumović	SRB	24/06/88	D	3	(1)	
Stefan Vojinović		21/10/90	M	17	(2)	
Zoran Vuković		07/07/79	D	15		

FK LOVĆEN

Coach: Slobodan Halilović (SRB)
1913 • Obilića poljana (2,000) • no website

2012

11/08	Čelik	h	0-3
18/08	Budućnost	a	1-3	Djurišić
22/08	Rudar	h	0-1
25/08	Mornar	a	2-1	Stevović 2
01/09	Jedinstvo	h	0-1
15/09	Sutjeska	a	0-2
22/09	Zeta	h	2-0	Turković, Djurišić
29/09	Grbalj	h	0-0
06/10	Mogren	a	1-3	Novović
13/10	Mladost	h	2-3	Djurišić, Radović
20/10	Petrovac	a	1-2	Radović
28/10	Čelik	a	1-1	Bogdanović
03/11	Budućnost	h	1-2	Djurišić (p)
10/11	Rudar	a	0-3
17/11	Mornar	h	1-2	Sjekloća
24/11	Jedinstvo	a	0-3
01/12	Sutjeska	h	1-6	Todorović

2013

26/02	Zeta	a	0-2
02/03	Grbalj	a	0-1
09/03	Mogren	h	1-0	G Vujović
16/03	Mladost	a	0-0
20/03	Petrovac	h	1-1	G Vujović
30/03	Mladost	a	5-0	G Vujović, Mirković, Djurišić 3 (1p)
06/04	Mornar	h	2-0	Mirković, G Vujović (p)
13/04	Grbalj	a	0-3
20/04	Jedinstvo	h	2-0	Djurišić, og (Mihailo Petrović)
27/04	Rudar	a	2-1	G Vujović, Djurišić
01/05	Petrovac	h	0-1
04/05	Čelik	a	3-1	Halilović, og (Dubljević), Djurišić
11/05	Zeta	h	3-2	D Marković, G Vujović 2
18/05	Budućnost	a	3-0	(w/o)
25/05	Mogren	h	2-1	D Marković, Djurišić
01/06	Sutjeska	a	1-2	G Vujović

Name	Nat	DoB	Pos	Aps	(s)	Gls
Dejan Bogdanović		08/08/90	M	7	(3)	1
Filip Borozan		11/09/95	D		(4)	
Jovan Bošković		18/07/95	D	4		
Mirko Djaković		14/09/94	M		(1)	
Milan Djurišić		11/04/87	A	28		11
Marko Draganić		19/09/94	M	7	(5)	
Nikola Draganić		19/09/94	M	7	(9)	
Andrija Dragojević		25/12/91	G	14		
Bogdan Drinčić		29/07/95	D		(2)	
Marko Dušak	CRO	29/06/89	D	14		
Mirko Džaković		14/09/94	M	1	(3)	
Alen Halilović	SRB	26/04/93	M	7	(6)	1
Deni Hočko		22/04/94	M	25	(1)	
Jovan Kaludjerović		26/11/94	M	3		
Danko Kovačević	SRB	10/07/91	M		(1)	
Darko Marković		15/05/87	M	12	(2)	2
Igor Marković		05/11/95	D	4		
Mirko Marković		25/10/88	D	1	(1)	
Ilija Martinović		31/01/94	D	7		
Vuk Martinović		19/09/89	D	27	(1)	
Nikola Mijanović		05/04/95	M	4		
Luka Mirković		01/11/90	D	23	(1)	2
Andrija Mudreša		28/06/95	M		(2)	
Milivoje Novović		29/02/84	D	11		1
Ivan Pejaković		22/08/92	M	6	(7)	
Jovan Perović		28/12/89	G	1		
Blažo Perutović		08/09/83	A	8	(1)	
Miloš Petrović	SRB	14/04/86	M		(1)	
Saša Petrović		31/12/96	A	1		
Balša Radović		04/01/91	M	19	(4)	2
Miloš Radunović		07/07/90	D	15	(7)	
Vladimir Sjekloća		20/10/95	A	3	(1)	1
Miloš Stevović		14/09/89	M	5	(3)	2
Marko Tanović		21/07/94	G	4		
Vladan Tatar		28/01/84	D	11		
Gorčin Todorović		28/05/95	M	1		1
Nedo Turković	BIH	21/03/84	A	5	(4)	1
Vukan Vujačić		15/03/95	D	2	(1)	
Branko Vujović		24/11/80	G	13		
Goran Vujović		03/05/87	A	14		8
Nenad Vujović		02/01/89	D	8	(3)	
Stevan Vujović		13/12/89	A		(1)	
Luka Vušurović		24/02/90	D	16	(2)	
Milan Vušurović		18/04/95	M	11		
Gojko Žižić		27/01/89	D	3	(5)	

FK MLADOST PODGORICA

Coach: Miodrag Vukotić
1950 • na Starom Aerodromu (2,000) • no website

2012

11/08	Mogren	a	3-0	(w/o)
18/08	Zeta	a	0-0
22/08	Petrovac	h	2-0	Rotković, Šćepanović
25/08	Čelik	a	0-3
01/09	Budućnost	h	1-1	Božović
15/09	Rudar	a	0-1
22/09	Mornar	a	2-1	Rotković, Šćepanović (p)
29/09	Jedinstvo	a	0-0
06/10	Sutjeska	h	1-2	Caicedo
13/10	Lovćen	a	3-2	Šćepanović 2 (1p), Pavićević
20/10	Grbalj	h	0-0
27/10	Mogren	h	3-1	Šćepanović 2, Caicedo
03/11	Zeta	h	1-1	Mandič
10/11	Petrovac	a	1-3	Šćepanović
17/11	Čelik	h	0-1
24/11	Budućnost	a	0-1
01/12	Rudar	h	2-0	Tatar, Šćepanović (p)

2013

26/02	Mornar	a	0-0
02/03	Jedinstvo	h	3-3	Šćepanović (p), Seratlić, Orahovac
09/03	Sutjeska	a	1-2	Božović
16/03	Lovćen	h	0-0
20/03	Grbalj	a	1-1	Orahovac (p)
30/03	Lovćen	h	0-5
06/04	Grbalj	a	1-4	Kalezić
13/04	Rudar	h	2-0	Seratlić, Mitrović
20/04	Čelik	a	0-1
27/04	Budućnost	h	1-2	Šćepanović (p)
01/05	Sutjeska	a	3-2	Marković, Pavićević, og (Ognjanović)
04/05	Mornar	h	3-3	Šćepanović 2, Tomić
11/05	Jedinstvo	a	1-1	Seratlić
18/05	Petrovac	h	1-1	Tomić (p)
25/05	Zeta	a	0-3
01/06	Mogren	h	3-1	Savićević, Šćepanović 2

Name	Nat	DoB	Pos	Aps	(s)	Gls
Arben Adžović		31/01/92	A	2	(7)	
Matija Božanović		13/04/94	M		(1)	
Draško Božović		30/06/88	D	17	(2)	2
Eber Caicedo	ECU	03/05/91	A	9	(5)	2
Nikola Cerović		22/10/94	G		(1)	
Saša Četković		29/05/82	D	9	(1)	
Obren Čučković	SRB	11/08/92	G	11		
Taku Ishihara	JPN	03/10/88	M	10	(4)	
Vasko Kalezić		14/03/94	M		(2)	1
Bojan Kaljević		02/08/83	M	6	(2)	
Predrag Kašćelan		30/06/90	M	7	(1)	
Ivan Knežević		22/02/86	A	5	(6)	
Šaleta Kordić		19/04/93	A	2	(3)	
Vladimir Mandič	SVN	05/07/87	M	20		1
Nikola Marčelja		30/11/85	G	8		
Božo Marković		26/10/89	A	9	(4)	1
Ivan Mijušković		15/07/88	M	3	(2)	
Filip Mitrović		17/11/93	D	18	(2)	1
Miladin Nelević		15/03/86	D	1	(2)	
Sanibal Orahovac		12/12/78	A	6	(2)	2
Elvis Ozegovic	AUT	18/06/90	D		(2)	
Miloš Pavićević		09/02/94	M	8	(15)	2
Dragiša Prelević		06/10/94	D	3		
Milan Radulović		18/08/81	D	8		
Ognjen Rolović		12/06/88	A		(2)	
Luka Rotković		05/06/88	A	7	(2)	2
Bojan Sanković		21/11/93	M	27	(1)	
Vladimir Savićević		27/11/89	M	11	(10)	1
Ermin Seratlić		21/08/90	M	28		3
Marko Šćepanović		02/08/82	A	26	(2)	14
Aleksandar Šofranac		21/10/90	D	25	(2)	
Boris Tatar		17/03/93	D	8	(3)	1
Danilo Tomić		23/06/86	M	16	(6)	2
Novak Tomović		05/06/96	M		(1)	
Branko Vujović		24/11/80	G	10		
Nemanja Vuković		13/04/84	D	13	(1)	
Radule Živković		20/10/90	D	19		

FK MOGREN

Coach: Branislav Milačić
1920 • Mogren (3,500) • no website
Major honours
Montenegrin League (2) 2009, 2011;
Montenegrin Cup (1) 2008

2012

11/08	Mladost	h	0-3	*(w/o)*
18/08	Petrovac	a	0-0	
22/08	Čelik	h	1-2	*Bojić*
25/08	Budućnost	a	2-0	*Djoković 2*
01/09	Rudar	h	0-0	
15/09	Mornar	a	1-0	*Ivanović*
22/09	Jedinstvo	h	0-1	
29/09	Sutjeska	a	2-0	*Vujović 2*
06/10	Lovćen	h	3-1	*Vujović 2, Grbović*
13/10	Grbalj	a	0-0	
20/10	Zeta	h	1-1	*Vujović*
27/10	Mladost	a	1-3	*Vujović*
03/11	Petrovac	h	3-1	*Brnović, Vujović, Božović*
10/11	Čelik	a	0-0	
17/11	Budućnost	h	1-2	*Pržica*
24/11	Rudar	a	0-1	
02/12	Mornar	h	2-1	*Grbović, Ivanović*

2013

26/02	Jedinstvo	a	2-1	*Vujović (p), Pržica*
02/03	Sutjeska	h	0-2	
09/03	Lovćen	a	0-1	
16/03	Grbalj	h	0-0	
20/03	Zeta	a	0-1	
30/03	Grbalj	h	0-1	
06/04	Rudar	a	2-3	*Djurović, Radišić*
13/04	Čelik	h	0-1	
20/04	Budućnost	a	2-1	*Djurović, Vujović*
27/04	Sutjeska	h	3-2	*Djoković 2, Djurović (p)*
01/05	Mornar	a	1-2	*Vujović*
04/05	Jedinstvo	h	1-0	*Djurović (p)*
11/05	Petrovac	a	2-2	*Djurović (p), Djoković*
18/05	Zeta	h	1-4	*Vujović*
25/05	Lovćen	a	1-2	*Djoković*
01/06	Mladost	a	1-3	*R Zec*

Name	Nat	DoB	Pos	Aps	(s)	Gls
Marko Bakić		01/11/93	A	3		
Jovan Baošić		07/07/95	D	10	(2)	
Veselin Bojić		16/06/77	D	22	(2)	1
Nebojša Božović		05/02/93	D	4	(3)	1
Nenad Brnović		18/01/80	M	13	(2)	1
Ivan Butorović		23/11/92	G	24		
Marko Ćosić		18/02/95	M	2	(8)	
Adis Djoković		25/08/91	A	22	(5)	6
Marko Djurović		08/05/88	A	16	(5)	5
Sava Gardašević		27/01/93	A		(12)	
Žarko Grbović		20/05/95	M	10	(10)	2
Bojan Ivanović		03/12/81	D	30		2
Aleksandar Kapisoda	CRO	17/09/89	D	4		
Dušan Lagator		29/03/94	M	21	(4)	
Velimir Lončar		02/05/90	D	6	(2)	
Ivan Mijušković		15/07/88	D	13	(1)	
Dejan Milošević		18/08/93	D	5	(3)	
Miloš Milović		22/12/95	M	8	(3)	
Andrija Mirković		13/12/83	M	9		
Stefan Nedović		24/02/95	M	1	(6)	
Amar Nuhodžić		12/09/90	M	1	(1)	
Zarija Pelićić		22/01/89	M	8	(3)	
Bracan Popović		31/03/82	D	25		
Dejan Pržica		19/01/92	M	24	(6)	2
Ivan Racković		13/09/94	D	4	(9)	
Mirko Radišić		01/10/90	D	27		1
Agrzim Redžović		26/02/92	D		(1)	
Andjelo Rudović		03/05/96	M		(1)	
Miodrag Todorović		01/04/88	D	8		
Nikola Vujović		23/06/81	A	28	(1)	11
Miodrag Zec		04/10/82	M	2		
Ratko Zec		24/03/77	A	2	(3)	1

FK MORNAR

Coach: Obren Sarić; (16/09/12) (Zoran Pešić);
(25/09/12) (Zoran Djurašković);
(30/09/12) Saša Petrović; (24/04/13) Obren Sarić
1923 • Topolica (5,000) • no website

2012

14/08	Zeta	h	2-1	*B Marković, Ćulafić*
18/08	Jedinstvo	h	0-0	
22/08	Sutjeska	a	1-2	*Ćulafić*
25/08	Lovćen	h	1-2	*Bogdanović*
01/09	Grbalj	a	0-2	
15/09	Mogren	h	0-1	
22/09	Mladost	a	1-2	*Ćulafić*
29/09	Petrovac	h	1-2	*Obradović*
06/10	Čelik	a	0-3	
13/10	Budućnost	h	1-4	*Ćulafić*
20/10	Rudar	a	2-2	*Gačević, Metović*
27/10	Zeta	a	1-0	*Sekulić*
03/11	Jedinstvo	a	3-1	*Ćulafić 2, Vojvodić*
10/11	Sutjeska	h	0-0	
17/11	Lovćen	a	2-1	*Radovanović, B Marković*
24/11	Grbalj	h	1-0	*Gačević*
02/12	Mogren	a	1-2	*Bogdanović*

2013

26/02	Mladost	h	0-0	
02/03	Petrovac	a	1-1	*Rotković (p)*
09/03	Čelik	h	0-0	
16/03	Budućnost	a	1-2	*Ćulafić (p)*
20/03	Rudar	h	0-2	
30/03	Sutjeska	h	1-1	*Ćulafić*
06/04	Lovćen	a	0-2	
13/04	Jedinstvo	h	1-2	*Bogdanović*
20/04	Petrovac	h	1-1	*Krstović*
27/04	Zeta	a	0-0	
30/04	Mogren	h	2-1	*Bogdanović, Divanović*
04/05	Mladost	a	3-3	*Ćulafić 2, Metović*
11/05	Grbalj	h	3-0	*Rotković 2, Ćulafić*
18/05	Rudar	a	1-3	*Rotković*
25/05	Čelik	h	4-1	*Rotković 3, og (Jovović)*
01/06	Budućnost	a	1-0	*Rotković (p)*

Name	Nat	DoB	Pos	Aps	(s)	Gls
Bogdan Bogdanović		05/03/89	A	16	(10)	4
Nenad Bubanja		01/07/84	D	8	(4)	
Danilo Ćulafić		01/08/86	M	22	(7)	11
Slavko Damjanović		02/11/90	D		(4)	
Mehmed Divanović		12/12/84	M	10	(5)	1
Denis Džanović		03/06/93	M	1	(7)	
Nikola Gačević		14/05/87	M	22	(2)	2
Aleksandar Jelenić		06/12/89	D	12	(4)	
Dejan Jovančov	SRB	28/09/87	A	7	(9)	
Saša Jovović		06/09/86	A		(1)	
Benjamin Kacić		28/06/91	M	16	(7)	
Demir Kajević		20/04/89	M	8	(1)	
Željko Krstović	SRB	15/10/89	D	16		1
Božo Marković		26/10/89	A	12	(3)	2
Stevan Marković		31/01/88	D	3		
Nenad Matić		20/11/91	D	10		
Boris Merdović		08/12/94	M	11	(4)	
Mustafa Metović		03/04/92	M	21	(3)	2
Boban Obradović	BIH	04/06/79	M	23	(2)	1
Miloš Radanović		05/11/80	G	33		
Stefan Radovanović		19/02/92	M	9	(3)	1
Novak Rajković		05/10/89	M	10	(2)	
Marko Rašović		04/06/92	D	3	(3)	
Luka Rotković		05/06/88	A	8	(4)	8
Nikola Sekulić		10/04/81	M	15	(1)	1
Andrija Simunović		21/03/91	D	1	(1)	
Nebojša Skopljak	SRB	12/05/87	D	16		
Petar Stanišić		23/09/84	D	14		
Djordje Vojvodić		31/05/86	D	30		1
Nino Vukmarković		15/04/93	M	5	(8)	
Miomir Vuković		27/05/87	A	1	(1)	

OFK PETROVAC

Coach: Milorad Malovrazić
1969 • Pod Malim Brdom (1,000) • ofkpetrovac.com
Major honours
Montenegrin Cup (1) 2009

2012

11/08	Grbalj	a	0-0	
18/08	Mogren	h	0-0	
22/08	Mladost	a	0-0	
26/08	Zeta	a	4-3	*Živković, Jovanović, Jablan, Radulović*
01/09	Čelik	h	0-0	
15/09	Budućnost	a	1-4	*Gazivoda*
22/09	Rudar	h	1-2	*Vujačić*
29/09	Mornar	a	2-1	*Grbović, Leverda*
06/10	Jedinstvo	h	0-3	
13/10	Sutjeska	a	1-2	*Jablan*
20/10	Lovćen	h	2-1	*Mihailović, Jovanović*
27/10	Grbalj	h	0-0	
03/11	Mogren	a	1-3	*Jablan*
10/11	Mladost	h	3-1	*Golubović, Jovanović, Marković*
17/11	Zeta	h	0-0	
24/11	Čelik	a	2-0	*Djukić 2 (1p)*
01/12	Budućnost	h	1-1	*Jovanović*

2013

26/02	Rudar	a	2-0	*Jablan 2*
02/03	Mornar	h	1-1	*Leverda*
09/03	Jedinstvo	a	0-2	
16/03	Sutjeska	h	1-2	*Djukić*
20/03	Lovćen	a	1-1	*Vujačić*
30/03	Čelik	h	2-0	*Grbović, Muhović*
06/04	Budućnost	a	1-2	*Mrvaljević*
13/04	Sutjeska	h	1-2	*Zvicer*
20/04	Mornar	a	1-1	*Muhović*
27/04	Jedinstvo	h	0-1	
01/05	Lovćen	h	1-0	*Muhović*
04/05	Zeta	a	2-2	*Vujačić, Muhović*
11/05	Mogren	h	2-2	*Muhović, Leverda*
18/05	Mladost	a	1-1	*Jablan*
25/05	Grbalj	a	1-1	*Muhović*
01/06	Rudar	a	1-2	*Leverda*

Name	Nat	DoB	Pos	Aps	(s)	Gls
Nikola Čelebić		04/07/89	D	13		
Petar Djordjević	SRB	26/01/88	M		(1)	
Dalibor Djukić		16/09/86	M	18	(5)	3
Savo Gazivoda		18/07/94	M		(4)	1
Bojan Golubović		28/11/86	M	26	(3)	1
Siniša Graovac	BIH	01/09/84	D	8	(1)	
Boris Grbović		31/01/80	D	27		2
Ivan Jablan		18/07/79	A	24	(2)	6
Nenad Jovanović		12/05/88	M	14	(1)	4
Stefan Kruščić		20/11/93	A	1	(1)	
Miloš Lakić		21/12/85	D	20	(4)	
Nemanja Leverda		07/06/92	M	4	(13)	4
Marko Marković		05/09/87	M	16	(8)	1
Luka Medigović		03/04/95	M		(1)	
Nikola Mihailović		15/09/84	D	13		1
Željko Mrvaljević		08/04/81	D	23	(2)	1
Jasmin Muhović		02/04/89	A	17	(7)	6
Nikola Osmajić		05/03/94	M		(1)	
Ivan Pejaković		22/08/92	M	11	(4)	
Rijad Pepić		19/09/91	M	8	(16)	
Blažo Perutović		08/12/83	M	4	(5)	
Nemanja Popović		20/05/84	G	33		
Marko Radulović		17/06/85	D	29	(1)	1
Nenad Šofranc		20/04/83	M	26	(4)	
Aleksandar Vujačić		19/03/90	A	17	(9)	3
Krsto Zvicer		10/06/87	A	3	(2)	1
Tihomir Živković	CRO	28/10/85	A	8	(3)	1

FK RUDAR PLJEVLJA

Coach: Nikola Rakojević
1920 • Pod Golubinjom (10,000) • fcrudarpljevlja.com
Major honours
Montenegrin League (1) 2010;
Montenegrin Cup (3) 2007, 2010, 2011

2012

11/08	Jedinstvo	a	2-0	Nerić, Ivanović
18/08	Sutjeska	h	0-1	
22/08	Lovćen	a	1-0	Igumanović
25/08	Grbalj	h	1-0	Vlahović
01/09	Mogren	a	0-0	
15/09	Mladost	h	1-0	Nerić
22/09	Petrovac	a	2-1	Vlahović 2 (1p)
30/09	Čelik	h	1-3	Jovanović
06/10	Budućnost	a	4-1	Brnović, Igumanović, Ivanović 2
13/10	Zeta	a	3-1	Brnović, Jovanović, Rustemović
20/10	Mornar	h	3-2	Igumanović 2, Krkeljić
28/10	Jedinstvo	h	1-1	Vlahović (p)
04/11	Sutjeska	a	0-2	
10/11	Lovćen	h	3-0	Jovanović, Krkeljić 2
17/11	Grbalj	a	0-4	
24/11	Mogren	h	1-0	Brnović
01/12	Mladost	a	0-2	

2013

26/02	Petrovac	h	0-2	
02/03	Čelik	a	0-1	
09/03	Budućnost	h	0-0	
16/03	Zeta	h	1-1	Vlahović
20/03	Mornar	a	2-0	Jovanović, Bambur
30/03	Zeta	a	2-0	Jovanović, Vlahović (p)
06/04	Mogren	h	3-2	Stojanović, Petrović 2
13/04	Mladost	a	0-2	
20/04	Grbalj	a	0-2	
27/04	Lovćen	h	1-2	Jovanović
01/05	Čelik	a	1-1	Igumanović (p)
05/05	Budućnost	h	3-4	Stojanović 2, Nerić
12/05	Sutjeska	h	1-1	Stojanović
18/05	Mornar	h	3-1	Brnović, Jovanović, Igumanović
25/05	Jedinstvo	a	0-2	
01/06	Petrovac	h	2-1	Stojanović, Jovanović

Name	Nat	DoB	Pos	Aps	(s)	Gls
Ermin Alić		23/02/92	D	29		
Siniša Bajić	SRB	24/02/94	D	1		
Luka Bakoč		23/11/86	M		(4)	
Adi Bambur		14/09/92	M	2	(5)	1
Predrag Brnović		22/10/86	M	28		4
Dejan Damjanović		08/07/86	D	19	(2)	
Milija Golubović		25/04/96	M			
Blažo Igumanović		19/01/86	M	30		6
Igor Ivanović		09/09/90	M	8		3
Vojin Jeknić		24/05/94	M	12	(11)	
Miroje Jovanović		10/03/87	M	30		8
Andrija Kaludjerović		29/10/93	M	29		
Djordje Krkeljić		10/09/90	A	7	(14)	3
Boris Lakićević		24/10/88	G	13	(1)	
Milenko Nerić		09/02/88	A	12	(11)	3
Dušan Nestorović	SRB	26/06/86	D	30		
Gavrilo Petrović		21/05/84	D	13		2
Miloš Popović		05/06/84	M	15	(5)	
Edi Rustemović	SRB	06/09/88	M	6	(14)	1
Nikola Sekulić		10/04/81	M	3	(7)	
Nenad Stojanović	SRB	22/10/79	A	13	(1)	5
Srdjan Šćepanović		20/10/94	D	1		
Jovan Šljivančanin		08/03/94	M	6	(15)	
Željko Tomašević		05/04/88	D	7	(4)	
Nedjeljko Vlahović		15/01/84	M	29		6
Goran Vukliš	BIH	24/09/87	G	20		
Marko Vuković		20/03/96	M		(1)	

FK SUTJESKA

Coach: Dragan Radojičić
1927 • Kraj Bistrice (11,000) • fksutjeska.me
Major honours
Montenegrin League (1) 2013

2012

11/08	Budućnost	h	1-0	Šušnjar
18/08	Rudar	a	1-0	Šušnjar
22/08	Mornar	h	2-1	Šušnjar, V Karadžić
25/08	Jedinstvo	a	1-0	Isidorović
02/09	Zeta	h	2-1	B Nikolić, Pejović
15/09	Lovćen	h	2-0	og (L Vušurović), Šušnjar
22/09	Grbalj	a	0-0	
29/09	Mogren	h	0-2	
06/10	Mladost	a	2-1	Šušnjar, D Karadžić
13/10	Petrovac	a	2-1	Pejović, Šušnjar
21/10	Čelik	a	0-3	
28/10	Budućnost	a	0-2	
04/11	Rudar	h	2-0	Šušnjar 2
10/11	Mornar	a	0-0	
17/11	Jedinstvo	h	3-0	Jovović, Ćuković 2
24/11	Zeta	a	0-1	
01/12	Lovćen	a	6-1	Šušnjar, Perošević 2, Jovović, D Karadžić, Poček

2013

26/02	Grbalj	h	1-0	J Nikolić
02/03	Mogren	a	2-0	Ćetković 2
09/03	Mladost	h	2-1	Isidorović, Poček
16/03	Petrovac	a	2-1	J Nikolić, D Karadžić
20/03	Čelik	h	1-0	Isidorović
30/03	Mornar	a	1-1	Čolaković
06/04	Jedinstvo	h	4-1	Isidorović 2, Ćetković, D Karadžić
13/04	Petrovac	a	2-1	D Karadžić 2
20/04	Zeta	a	2-0	D Karadžić (p), Jovović
27/04	Mogren	a	2-3	D Karadžić 2
01/05	Mladost	h	2-3	Ćuković, D Karadžić
04/05	Grbalj	a	1-1	Isidorović
11/05	Rudar	a	1-1	D Karadžić
18/05	Čelik	a	0-1	
25/05	Budućnost	h	1-3	Perošević
01/06	Lovćen	h	2-1	Ćetković, D Karadžić (p)

Name	Nat	DoB	Pos	Aps	(s)	Gls
Srdjan Bečelić	SRB	08/06/92	D	22	(4)	
Boris Bulajić		25/12/90	G	1		
Djordjije Ćetković		03/01/83	M	11	(5)	4
Petar Čolaković		19/07/84	M	2	(6)	1
Igor Ćuković		06/06/93	D	27		3
Stefan Djajić		24/12/94	A		(1)	
Nenad Djurović		17/01/86	D	8		
Darko Isidorović	SRB	17/04/87	M	24	(1)	6
Božidar Janjušević		30/03/94	A	2		
Ivan Janjušević		11/07/87	G	32		
Vladimir Jovović		26/10/94	M	30		3
Darko Karadžić		17/04/87	M	18	(11)	12
Vladan Karadžić		04/02/95	A	1	(13)	1
Nemanja Kosović		15/05/93	D	3	(8)	
Milorad Krivokapić		14/05/85	D	11		
Baćo Nikolić		19/01/86	M	17		1
Jovan Nikolić		21/07/91	M	27		2
Dejan Ognjanović		21/06/78	D	15		
Andrija Pejović		21/11/91	M	12	(10)	2
Petar Perošević		14/01/89	A	27	(1)	3
Igor Poček		23/12/94	A	2	(12)	2
Stefan Stefanović	SRB	22/08/91	M	5	(9)	
Miloš Stevović		14/09/89	M	14	(1)	
Nikola Stijepović		02/11/93	D	24	(5)	
Djordje Šušnjar		18/02/92	A	16		9
Vojkan Višnjić		08/03/93	D		(1)	
Miloš Vučić		26/08/94	M		(3)	
Jovan Vujović		20/01/96	M		(1)	
Dejan Zarubica		11/04/93	A		(3)	
Stefan Zogović		17/04/90	D	12		

FK ZETA

Coach: Rade Vešović;
(13/10/12) Darko Šuškavčević;
(22/04/13) Mladen Vukićević
1927 • Trešnjica (6,000) • fkzeta.me
Major honours
Montenegrin League (1) 2007

2012

14/08	Mornar	a	1-2	Miloš B Radulović
18/08	Mladost	h	0-0	
26/08	Petrovac	h	3-4	Korać, Božović, Boljević
02/09	Sutjeska	a	1-2	Božović
06/09	Jedinstvo	a	0-0	
15/09	Čelik	h	3-1	Orlandić, Boljević, Došljak
22/09	Lovćen	a	0-2	
29/09	Budućnost	h	1-3	og (Adrović)
06/10	Grbalj	a	0-2	
13/10	Rudar	h	1-3	Orlandić
20/10	Mogren	a	1-1	Korać (p)
27/10	Mornar	h	0-1	
03/11	Mladost	a	1-1	Orlandić
10/11	Jedinstvo	h	2-1	Orlandić, Korać
17/11	Petrovac	a	0-0	
24/11	Sutjeska	h	1-0	Korać
01/12	Čelik	a	2-2	Korać, Kalačević

2013

26/02	Lovćen	h	2-0	Vlaisavljević, Novović
02/03	Budućnost	a	3-3	Kaludjerović, Vlaisavljević, Orlandić (p)
09/03	Grbalj	h	1-0	Burzanović
16/03	Rudar	a	1-1	og (Vukliš)
20/03	Mogren	h	1-0	Korać
30/03	Rudar	h	0-2	
06/04	Čelik	h	3-4	Korać 2, Došljak
13/04	Budućnost	h	0-0	
20/04	Sutjeska	a	0-2	
27/04	Mornar	a	0-0	
01/05	Jedinstvo	h	1-1	Kukuličić
04/05	Petrovac	h	2-2	Korać 2
11/05	Lovćen	a	2-3	Orlandić, Burzanović
18/05	Mogren	a	4-1	Došljak, Korać 3
25/05	Mladost	h	5-0	Boljević 3, Burzanović, Korać
01/06	Grbalj	a	1-1	Korać

Name	Nat	DoB	Pos	Aps	(s)	Gls
Dražen Ajković		25/08/85	D	4	(1)	
Bojan Aligrudić		30/11/95	M		(1)	
Luka Bojić		09/04/92	M		(1)	
Aleksandar Boljević		12/12/95	A	21	(2)	5
Balša Božović		01/05/87	M	16	(5)	2
Nenad Brnović		18/01/80	M	14		
Miloš Bulatović		17/05/89	G	3		
Goran Burzanović		04/08/84	M	27	(1)	3
Nemanja Cavnić		05/09/95	D	18	(2)	
Aleksandar Dabić	SRB	01/05/91	D	4	(2)	
Milorad Dabić	SRB	01/05/91	M	7	(2)	
Boris Došljak		04/06/89	M	27	(2)	3
Saša Ivanović		26/06/84	G	13		
Filip Kalačević		12/03/94	M	8	(6)	1
Miroslav Kaludjerović		04/02/86	D	27	(1)	1
Ivan Klikovac		01/06/93	M		(7)	
Ivan Knežević		22/02/86	A	4		
Žarko Korać		11/06/87	A	30		15
Miroslav Kovačević		03/05/94	M	2	(4)	
Koča Krstović		27/03/95	A	3	(2)	
Filip Kukuličić		13/02/96	M		(8)	1
Ivan Novović		26/04/89	D	28		1
Petar Orlandić		06/08/90	A	10	(12)	6
Stefan Otašević		17/08/94	M	5	(8)	
Vladan Peličić		24/06/89	D	4		
Zarija Peličić		22/01/89	M	6	(4)	
Vojin Perazić		14/01/93	A	2	(1)	
Jovan Prenkić		11/09/92	A	1	(4)	
Vuk Radović		28/02/93	G	17		
Miloš B Radulović		23/02/90	D	10	(2)	1
Miloš M Radulović		06/08/90	D	23		
Marko Rašović		21/04/90	M		(4)	
Miljan Vlaisavljević		16/04/91	A	13	(2)	2
Igor Vujačić		08/08/94	D	10		
Stefan Vukčević		11/04/97	M		(1)	
Velimir Vukćević		17/05/95	M		(1)	
Miroslav Zlatićanin	SRB	26/05/85	M	6	(3)	

Top goalscorers

15 Admir Adrović (Budućnost)
Žarko Korać (Zeta)

14 Marko Šćepanović (Mladost)

12 Stevan Račić (Čelik)
Darko Karadžić (Sutjeska)

11 Nikola Ašćerić (Grbalj)
Milan Djurišić (Lovćen)
Nikola Vujović (Mogren)
Danilo Ćulafić (Mornar)

10 Luka Rotković (Mladost/Mornar)

Promoted club

FK DEČIĆ

Coach: Fuad Krkanović
1926 • Tuško polje (2,000) • fkdecictuzi.com

SECOND LEVEL FINAL TABLE 2012/13

		Pld	W	D	L	F	A	Pts
1	FK Dečić	30	21	3	6	46	19	66
2	FK Bokelj	30	16	8	6	39	20	56
3	FK Zabjelo	30	15	8	7	40	29	53
4	FK Bratstvo	30	14	5	11	41	32	47
5	OSK Igalo	30	11	9	10	39	35	39
6	FK Jezero	30	8	12	10	26	29	36
7	FK Berane	30	10	8	12	38	56	35
8	FK Ibar	30	7	12	11	33	36	33
9	FK Zora	30	8	6	16	28	32	29
10	FK Arsenal	30	5	14	11	24	38	29
11	FK Iskra	30	5	5	20	29	57	20

*ND FK Berane & OSK Igalo – 3 pts deducted;
FK Zora – 1 pt deducted. OFK Bar withdrew after round
22 – their matches were annulled.*

PROMOTION/RELEGATION PLAY-OFFS

(05/06/13 & 09/06/13)
Zabjelo 1-6 Mogren
Mogren 3-1 Zabjelo
(Mogren 9-2)

Bokelj 1-0 Mornar
Mornar 2-0 Bokelj
(Mornar 2-1)

Domestic cup: Kup Crne Gore 2012/13

FIRST ROUND

(18/09/12)
Tekstilac 0-6 Sutjeska

(19/09/12)
Budućnost Podgorica 3-0 Bratstvo
Cetinje 1-4 Mornar
Gorštak 1-0 Bar
Grbalj 6-0 Dečić
Igalo 3-1 Arsenal
Iskra 1-7 Mogren
Jedinstvo 1-1 Zabjelo *(4-1 on pens)*
Jezero 0-2 Lovćen
Kom 1-2 Berane
Mladost Podgorica 6-0 Ibar
Petrovac 3-0 Bokelj
Sloga 1-3 Pljevlja
Zeta 3-2 Zora

Byes – Čelik, Rudar Pljevlja

SECOND ROUND

(02/10/12 & 24/10/12)
Pljevlja 1-2, 1 10 Mladost Podgorica *(2-12)*

(03/10/12 & 24/10/12)
Budućnost Podgorica 2-1, 1-0 Jedinstvo *(3-1)*

Grbalj 2-0, 3-0 Gorštak *(5-0)*

Igalo 1-1, 0-5 Lovćen *(1-6)*

Mornar 4-0, 2-1 Berane *(6-1)*

Petrovac 4-0, 0-0 Mogren *(4-0)*

Zeta 1-0, 0-0 Sutjeska *(1-0)*

(03/10/12 & 25/10/12)
Rudar Pljevlja 1-1, 0-1 Čelik *(1-2)*

QUARTER-FINALS

(07/11/12 & 21/11/12)
Čelik 2-0 Lovćen *(Zorić 17, Bulajić 25)*
Lovćen 1-1 Čelik *(Kaludjerović 87; Kolev 30)*
(Čelik 3-1)

Grbalj 1-0 Mornar *(Djalac 55)*
Mornar 1-1 Grbalj *(Bogdanović 88; N Nikolić 56)*
(Grbalj 2-1)

Petrovac 0-1 Mladost Podgorica *(Pavićević 35)*
Mladost Podgorica 1-1 Petrovac *(Šćepanović 45p; Jablan 83)*
(Mladost Podgorica 2-1)

(21/11/12 & 28/11/12)
Budućnost Podgorica 2-0 Zeta *(Adrović 39, Bošković 52p)*
Zeta 0-2 Budućnost Podgorica *(N Vukčević 26, Nikač 67)*
(Budućnost Podgorica 4-0)

SEMI-FINALS

(03/04/13 & 17/04/13)
Grbalj 0-0 Čelik
Čelik 2-0 Grbalj *(Zorić 49p, 74)*
(Čelik 2-0)

Mladost Podgorica 1-1 Budućnost Podgorica *(Tomić 12; Adrović 23)*
Budućnost Podgorica 3-2 Mladost Podgorica *(Nikač 10, Orahovac 78, Adrović 88; Orahovac 45p, Ishihara 90)*
(Budućnost Podgorica 4-3)

FINAL

(22/05/13)
Stadion Pod Goricom, Podgorica
FK BUDUĆNOST PODGORICA 1 *(Peković 90+1)*
FK ČELIK NIKŠIĆ 0
Referee: *Dabanović*
BUDUĆNOST: *Agović, Peković, Kamberović, Raspopović, Kopitović, Tomković, Flávio Beck (Adrović 90), M Vukčević, N Vukčević (Kalezić 90), Radonjić, Mugoša (Nikač 90)*
ČELIK: *Banović, Radović, Djikanović, Dubljević, Videkanić (Simić 90), Bulajić, Kolev (Bakoč 90), Zorić (Adrović 65), Ivanović, Račić, Jovović*
Sent off: *Dubljević (66)*

Budućnost players celebrate the club's first Montenegrin Cup triumph

NETHERLANDS
Koninklijke Nederlandse Voetbalbond (KNVB)

Address	Woudenbergseweg 56-58	**President**	Michael van Praag
	Postbus 515	**General secretary**	Bert van Oostveen
	NL-3700 AM Zeist	**Media officer**	Kees Jansma
Tel	+31 343 499 201	**Year of formation**	1889
Fax	+31 343 499 189		
E-mail	concern@knvb.nl		
Website	knvb.nl		

EREDIVISIE CLUBS

1. ADO Den Haag
2. AFC Ajax
3. AZ Alkmaar
4. Feyenoord
5. FC Groningen
6. sc Heerenveen
7. Heracles Almelo
8. NAC Breda
9. NEC Nijmegen
10. PEC Zwolle
11. PSV Eindhoven
12. RKC Waalwijk
13. Roda JC
14. FC Twente
15. FC Utrecht
16. Vitesse
17. VVV-Venlo
18. Willem II

PROMOTED CLUBS

19. SC Cambuur
20. Go Ahead Eagles

KEY:

- – UEFA Champions League
- – UEFA Europa League
- – Promoted clubs
- – Relegated clubs

Map labels:
Leeuwarden 19
Groningen 5
Heerenveen 6
Alkmaar 3
Zwolle 10
Amsterdam 2
Den Haag (The Hague) 1
Utrecht 15
Deventer 20
Almelo 7
Enschede 14
Rotterdam 4
Arnhem 16
Nijmegen 9
Breda 8
Waalwijk 12
Tilburg 18
Eindhoven 11
Venlo 17
Kerkrade 13

Scale: 0 — 50 — 100 km / 0 — 50 miles

Hat-trick for De Boer's Ajax

For the third season running AFC Ajax came up with a powerful late run of form to win the Dutch Eredivisie. As in the previous two campaigns, the architect of their triumph was coach Frank de Boer, who thus joined Rinus Michels (1966-68) and Louis van Gaal (1994-96) as the only Ajax bosses to capture a hat-trick of league wins.

As Van Gaal enjoyed a successful return to the Dutch national team in 2012/13, Dick Advocaat had a frustrating season back at PSV Eindhoven, with second place in the league accompanied by a runners-up spot in the Dutch Cup to AZ Alkmaar.

Amsterdam giants retain Eredivisie crown	AZ cup win leaves PSV as double runners-up	One foot in Brazil for Van Gaal's Oranje

Domestic league

For much of the season the top of the Eredivisie table was tightly congested, with Ajax accompanied by PSV, Feyenoord, FC Twente and surprise challengers Vitesse. Indeed at Christmas there was only five points separating those five teams, with PSV leading the way on goal difference from Twente. It was anybody's title, but Ajax had proved their mettle during the run-in in each of the previous two campaigns, and they were to do so again in 2012/13, reaching the summit in the early spring and staying there thanks to a brilliant unbeaten run punctuated by several high-scoring victories.

The most important of those wins came in mid-April at PSV. A victory for Advocaat's free-scoring team would have enabled them to leapfrog the Amsterdammers to the top of the table, but Ajax won 3-2, a 77th-minute strike from Derk Boerrigter deciding the contest after the home side had twice come back to equalise, through striker Jeremain Lens. With Feyenoord and Vitesse both drawing that weekend – Twente's challenge had long since evaporated, culminating in the dismissal of coach Steve McClaren – Ajax now had clear daylight between themselves and the chasing group, and although they were held 1-1 at home by sc Heerenveen in their

next game, on 5 May they sealed their record-extending 32nd national title with a thumping 5-0 win at home to Willem II, a result that also relegated their opponents.

Ajax ended the campaign with the same number of points as in 2011/12 (76), and although their goal tally was down by ten (83 from 93), they suffered only half the number of defeats, their two losses both coming against Vitesse, who won 2-0 in Amsterdam and 3-2 in Arnhem. The toughest team to beat in the division by far, De Boer's men were just as productive on the road as they were in the Amsterdam ArenA, winning 11 games and drawing five. As usual, it was a collective effort, with significant contributors throughout the team. Christian Eriksen had another superb season as the team's central playmaker, while his Danish compatriot, Viktor Fischer, emerged as the hottest of prospects in attack. Siem de Jong was the team's only ever-present and also their top scorer, with 12 goals, while Toby Alderweireld and Daley Blind (son of former Ajax player and coach Danny) were consistency personified in defence and the ever-improving Kenneth Vermeer a solid, occasionally spectacular, presence in goal.

PSV, branded pre-season favourites following the return of both Advocaat and former skipper Mark van Bommel to

Eindhoven, played entertaining football and were never short of goals, scoring 103 in total, but a fragile defence ultimately proved their undoing – that and an inability to win the big games, their only victory against the other teams in the top four coming early in the season when they defeated Feyenoord 3-0 at home. Lens was their standout player, scoring 15 goals, and Van Bommel also performed with distinction in what was to be the final season of his illustrious career. Both he and Advocaat announced their retirement at the end of the campaign. There were no trophies to sign off with, but they did leave a place in the UEFA Champions League third qualifying round as a parting gift.

PSV edged out Feyenoord for the runners-up spot thanks to their huge goal difference, thus finishing in their highest position since their last title triumph in 2007/08. The Rotterdammers finished one place lower than in 2011/12, but they again impressed under coach Ronald Koeman and a first Eredivisie crown for 14 years looked on the cards at one stage for an ebullient young side that drew inspiration from their magnificent fans – who cheered them to 14 wins and three draws in an unbeaten home record – as well as the consistent goalscoring of striker Graziano Pellè. The Italian struck 27 times, but it was not enough to earn him the Eredivisie golden boot. That prize went to Vitesse's

NETHERLANDS

Ruben Schaken lets fly to score the Netherlands' third goal at home to Estonia

Ivorian striker Wilfried Bony, who scored 31 of his team's 68 goals, many of them set up by the young revelation of the season, Marco van Ginkel.

Domestic cup

Another winning striker-midfielder combination was that of AZ Alkmaar's Jozy Altidore and Adam Maher. Despite the pair's best efforts AZ had a ropey season in the league, finishing down in tenth place, but that disappointment was counterbalanced by a brilliant campaign in the KNVB-Beker. Gertjan Verbeek's side scored 20 goals en route to the final, climaxing in a 3-0 semi-final win at Ajax. Holders PSV also won their semi-final 3-0, away to PEC Zwolle, having earlier eliminated Feyenoord, but there would be no tenth cup win for the club, two strikes in three minutes at De Kuip from Maher and Altidore putting AZ in early command and en route to a 2-1 win that returned the trophy to Alkmaar for the first time in 31 years.

Europe

2012/13 was a shabby season for Dutch clubs in Europe. Of the seven Eredivisie representatives on show, only three were involved in the autumn group stages and

just one made it beyond Christmas, Ajax's round of 32 involvement in the UEFA Europa League coming after they had failed to reach the knockout phase of the UEFA Champions League. Admittedly, De Boer's side could hardly have been drawn in a tougher group – alongside the champions of Germany, Spain and England – but there was considerable dismay when they fell to FC Steaua Bucureşti on penalties, their bid to reach the UEFA Europa League final in their own Amsterdam ArenA lasting just two games.

PSV and Twente were familiar participants in that competition but for the first time neither progressed beyond the group stage. PSV's double over SSC Napoli proved in vain as they took just one point from their other four games, while Respect Fair Play qualifiers Twente, having negotiated four preliminary rounds, failed to win any of their group encounters. Vitesse, Heerenveen, AZ and Feyenoord all dropped out in the early stages, the latter having previously lost both legs of their UEFA Champions League qualifier against FC Dynamo Kyiv.

National team

While the Netherlands' clubs struggled, the national team made a stunning recovery from their UEFA EURO 2012

whitewash, winning all six of their 2014 FIFA World Cup qualifiers and scoring 20 goals in the process while conceding just two. It was a fanfare return to the team for Van Gaal, reappointed to replace Bert van Marwijk despite his failure to qualify the Oranje for the 2002 World Cup in his first spell in charge. His bold selection policy, drawing on a number of new faces, especially from Feyenoord and Ajax, paid handsome dividends – albeit after an opening 4-2 friendly defeat by neighbours Belgium. Potential Group D rivals were all soundly beaten in the opening autumn exchanges, Turkey going down 2-0 in Amsterdam and both Hungary and Romania losing 4-1 to Van Gaal's rampant charges at home.

Another big win against Romania in the spring, 4-0, made it 18 points out of 18 and 14 successive World Cup qualifying victories. It also virtually guaranteed the Oranje's safe passage to Brazil, where stalwarts Robin van Persie, Arjen Robben and Wesley Sneijder will in all probability be joined by promising newcomers such as Blind, Van Ginkel, Maher, Lens, Bruno Martins Indi, Ruben Schaken and Daryl Janmaat plus, perhaps, some of the members of the Jong Oranje side that reached the semi-finals of the UEFA European Under-21 Championship in Israel, memorably defeating arch-rivals Germany en route.

Domestic league: Eredivisie 2012/13 final table

		Pld	Home					Away					Total					Pts
			W	D	L	F	A	W	D	L	F	A	W	D	L	F	A	
1	**AFC Ajax**	**34**	**11**	**5**	**1**	**40**	**10**	**11**	**5**	**1**	**43**	**21**	**22**	**10**	**2**	**83**	**31**	**76**
2	PSV Eindhoven	34	14	0	3	58	17	8	3	6	45	26	22	3	9	103	43	69
3	Feyenoord	34	14	3	0	42	12	7	3	7	22	26	21	6	7	64	38	69
4	Vitesse	34	9	6	2	34	18	10	1	6	34	24	19	7	8	68	42	64
5	FC Utrecht	34	11	3	3	27	12	8	3	6	28	29	19	6	9	55	41	63
6	FC Twente	34	10	4	3	33	17	7	7	3	27	16	17	11	6	60	33	62
7	FC Groningen	34	6	5	6	20	25	6	2	9	16	28	12	7	15	36	53	43
8	sc Heerenveen	34	8	3	6	29	30	3	6	8	21	33	11	9	14	50	63	42
9	ADO Den Haag	34	6	6	5	25	28	3	7	7	24	35	9	13	12	49	63	40
10	AZ Alkmaar	34	5	4	8	29	23	5	5	7	27	31	10	9	15	56	54	39
11	PEC Zwolle	34	5	4	8	23	29	5	5	7	19	26	10	9	15	42	55	39
12	Heracles Almelo	34	6	6	5	38	32	3	5	9	20	39	9	11	14	58	71	38
13	NAC Breda	34	7	3	7	25	27	3	5	9	15	29	10	8	16	40	56	38
14	RKC Waalwijk	34	7	5	5	24	19	2	5	10	15	29	9	10	15	39	48	37
15	NEC Nijmegen	34	4	6	7	19	30	6	1	10	25	36	10	7	17	44	66	37
16	Roda JC	34	6	8	3	29	18	1	4	12	22	51	7	12	15	51	69	33
17	VVV-Venlo	34	3	1	10	22	42	3	0	8	11	20	6	10	18	33	62	28
18	Willem II	34	5	3	9	23	35	0	5	12	10	41	5	8	21	33	76	23

SEASON AT A GLANCE

EUROPEAN QUALIFICATION 2013/14

Champion: AFC Ajax (group stage)
PSV Eindhoven (third qualifying round)

Cup winner: AZ Alkmaar (play-offs)
Feyenoord (play-offs)
Vitesse (third qualifying round)
FC Utrecht (second qualifying round)

Top scorer	Wilfried Bony (Vitesse), 31 goals
Relegated clubs	Willem II, VVV-Venlo
Promoted clubs	SC Cambuur, Go Ahead Eagles
Cup final	AZ Alkmaar 2-1 PSV Eindhoven

EREDIVISIE TEAM OF THE SEASON
(4-3-3)
Coach: De Boer (Ajax)

PLAYER OF THE SEASON
Wilfried Bony
(Vitesse)

Despite playing for Ivory Coast at the 2013 Africa Cup of Nations, Bony claimed the Eredivisie top scorer prize with 31 goals for Vitesse, 14 of them coming in the nine games that followed his return from South Africa. Strong, skilful and a clinical finisher, he now has the chance to display those qualities in the English Premier League with Swansea City AFC.

NEWCOMER OF THE SEASON
Marco van Ginkel
(Vitesse)

Voted Eredivisie talent of the year by a judging panel headed by Johan Cruyff, the 20-year-old was a key midfielder in Fred Rutten's side, his sustained excellence over the season earning a summer move to Chelsea FC. A talented box-to-box midfielder, he set up and scored a number of goals to help Vitesse challenge for the title and qualify for Europe.

Vermeer *(Ajax)*

Janmaat *(Feyenoord)* · Alderweireld *(Ajax)* · Van Dijk *(Groningen)* · Blind *(Ajax)*

Van Ginkel *(Vitesse)* · Eriksen *(Ajax)* · Djuričić *(Heerenveen)*

Altidore *(AZ)* · Pellè *(Feyenoord)* · Bony *(Vitesse)*

NETHERLANDS

NATIONAL TEAM

Home Kit Away Kit

INTERNATIONAL HONOURS
UEFA European Championship (1) 1988

INTERNATIONAL TOURNAMENT APPEARANCES
FIFA World Cup (9) 1934, 1938, 1974 (runners-up), 1978 (runners-up), 1990 (2nd round), 1994 (qtr-finals), 1998 (4th), 2006 (2nd round), 2010 (runners-up)
UEFA European Championship (9) 1976 (3rd), 1980, 1988 (Winners), 1992 (semi-finals), 1996 (qtr-finals), 2000 (semi-finals), 2004 (semi-finals), 2008 (qtr-finals), 2012

TOP FIVE ALL-TIME CAPS
Edwin van der Sar (130); Frank de Boer (112); Giovanni van Bronckhorst (106); **Rafael van der Vaart** (105); Phillip Cocu (101)

TOP FIVE ALL-TIME GOALS
Patrick Kluivert (40); Dennis Bergkamp (37); Ruud van Nistelrooy, **Robin van Persie** & Faas Wilkes (35); **Klaas-Jan Huntelaar** (34)

Results 2012/13

Date	Opponent		Venue	Score	Scorers
15/08/12	Belgium	A	Brussels	2-4	*Narsingh (54), Huntelaar (55)*
07/09/12	Turkey (WCQ)	H	Amsterdam	2-0	*Van Persie (17), Narsingh (90+3)*
11/09/12	Hungary (WCQ)	A	Budapest	4-1	*Lens (3, 53), Martins Indi (19), Huntelaar (74)*
12/10/12	Andorra (WCQ)	H	Rotterdam	3-0	*Van der Vaart (7), Huntelaar (15), Schaken (50)*
16/10/12	Romania (WCQ)	A	Bucharest	4-1	*Lens (9), Martins Indi (29), Van der Vaart (45+2p), Van Persie (86)*
14/11/12	Germany	H	Amsterdam	0-0	
06/02/13	Italy	H	Amsterdam	1-1	*Lens (33)*
22/03/13	Estonia (WCQ)	H	Amsterdam	3-0	*Van der Vaart (47), Van Persie (72), Schaken (84)*
26/03/13	Romania (WCQ)	H	Amsterdam	4-0	*Van der Vaart (12), Van Persie (56, 65p), Lens (90+1)*
07/06/13	Indonesia	A	Jakarta	3-0	*S de Jong (57, 67), Robben (90)*
11/06/13	China	A	Beijing	2-0	*Van Persie (11p), Sneijder (66)*

Appearances 2012/13

Coach: Louis van Gaal 08/08/51

Player	DOB	Club	Bel	TUR	HUN	AND	ROU	Ger	Ita	EST	ROU	Idn	Chn	Caps	Goals
Maarten Stekelenburg	22/09/82	Roma (ITA)	G		G	G	G							54	-
Ricardo van Rhijn	13/06/91	Ajax	D	s46	D		D	D46	s85					6	-
Joris Mathijsen	05/04/80	Feyenoord	D46		s64									84	3
John Heitinga	15/11/83	Everton (ENG)	D46	D86		D	D	D46				s46	D	87	7
Jetro Willems	30/03/94	PSV	D46	D	D									8	-
Nigel de Jong	30/11/84	Man. City (ENG)/Milan (ITA)	M			M	M	M						67	1
Wesley Sneijder	09/06/84	Internazionale (ITA)/Galatasaray (TUR)	M	M	M					M36		M46	s46	93	25
Rafael van der Vaart	11/02/83	Tottenham (ENG)/Hamburg (GER)	M46			M71	M76	M72		s36	M79			105	23
Arjen Robben	23/01/84	Bayern (GER)	A	A				A46	s46	A	A	s14	A	68	18
Klaas-Jan Huntelaar	12/08/83	Schalke (GER)	A		s46	A								59	34
Luciano Narsingh	13/09/90	PSV	A68	A	A		A							6	2
Stefan de Vrij	05/02/92	Feyenoord	s46					s46	D	D	D			5	-
Nick Viergever	03/08/89	AZ	s46											1	-
Bruno Martins Indi	08/02/92	Feyenoord	s46	D	D64	D	D	D	D	D	D			9	2
Adam Maher	20/07/93	AZ	s46		s78				M		s73			4	-
Jeremain Lens	24/11/87	PSV	s68		A	A71	A89	A		A73	A	A14	A70	13	6
Tim Krul	03/04/88	Newcastle (ENG)		G				G						5	-
Daryl Janmaat	22/07/89	Feyenoord		D46	D			s46	D85	D	D	D66	s46	8	-
Jordy Clasie	27/06/91	Feyenoord		M50	M			M46	s86	s79				5	-
Kevin Strootman	13/02/90	PSV	M	M78	M75	M		M	M	M				18	1
Robin van Persie	06/08/83	Man. United (ENG)	A	A46		A		A46	A	A86		A46	A	76	35
Leroy Fer	05/01/90	Twente	s50											2	-
Ron Vlaar	16/02/85	Aston Villa (ENG)	s86	D	D	D	D	D			D		D	16	1
Ruben Schaken	03/04/82	Feyenoord			A		A			s73		A	s70	5	2
Ibrahim Afellay	02/04/86	Schalke (GER)				s71	s76	M59						44	5
Dirk Kuyt	22/07/80	Fenerbahçe (TUR)				s71	A		s60				s70	94	24
Urby Emanuelson	16/06/86	Milan (ITA)				s75		s72						17	-
Eljero Elia	13/02/87	Bremen (GER)					s89	s46						28	2
Kenneth Vermeer	10/01/86	Ajax						G	G	G		s46		4	-
Marco van Ginkel	01/12/92	Vitesse						s59						1	-
Daley Blind	09/03/90	Ajax							D	D	D			3	-
Ola John	19/05/92	Benfica (POR)						A60						1	-
Jonathan de Guzmán	13/09/87	Swansea (WAL)							s46	M86	M73	M	M	5	-
Siem de Jong	28/01/89	Ajax									s86	s46	M70	4	2
Jasper Cillessen	22/04/89	Ajax										G46		1	-
Erik Pieters	07/08/88	PSV										D46	s46	17	-
Miquel Nelom	22/09/90	Feyenoord										D	D46	2	-
Jens Toornstra	04/04/89	Utrecht										M	M46	2	-
Ricky van Wolfswinkel	27/01/89	Sporting (POR)										s46		2	-
Dwight Tiendalli	21/10/85	Swansea (WAL)										s66	D46	2	-
Michel Vorm	20/10/83	Swansea (WAL)											G	10	-

European club competitions 2012/13

AFC AJAX

Group D
Match 1 - Borussia Dortmund (GER)
A 0-1
Vermeer, Alderweireld, Moisander, Poulsen, Eriksen, De Jong, Blind, Sana (Sulejmani 89), Boerrigter, Van Rhijn, Babel (Schøne 79). Coach: Frank de Boer (NED)
Match 2 - Real Madrid CF (ESP)
H 1-4 *Moisander (56)*
Vermeer, Alderweireld, Moisander, Poulsen (Sporkslede 69), Eriksen, De Jong, Blind, Sana (Hoesen 66), Boerrigter, Van Rhijn, Babel (Lukoki 81). Coach: Frank de Boer (NED)
Match 3 - Manchester City FC (ENG)
H 3-1 *De Jong (45), Moisander (57), Eriksen (68)*
Vermeer, Alderweireld, Moisander, Poulsen, Eriksen, De Jong, Blind, Sana (Enoh 74), Schøne (Boerrigter 89), Van Rhijn, Babel. Coach: Frank de Boer (NED)
Match 4 - Manchester City FC (ENG)
A 2-2 *De Jong (10, 17)*
Vermeer, Alderweireld, Moisander, Poulsen (Fischer 87), Eriksen, De Jong, Blind, Schøne (Enoh 78), Boerrigter (Sana 90+3), Van Rhijn, Babel. Coach: Frank de Boer (NED)
Match 5 - Borussia Dortmund (GER)
H 1-4 *Hoesen (87)*
Vermeer, Alderweireld, Moisander, Poulsen (Schøne 46), Enoh (Hoesen 64), Eriksen, De Jong, Blind, Boerrigter (Fischer 73), Van Rhijn, Lukoki. Coach: Frank de Boer (NED)
Match 6 - Real Madrid CF (ESP)
A 1-4 *Boerrigter (59)*
Vermeer, Alderweireld, Moisander, Poulsen (Schøne 40), Eriksen, De Jong, Blind, Boerrigter, Hoesen (Enoh 77), Van Rhijn, Fischer (Sana 77). Coach: Frank de Boer (NED)

Round of 32 - FC Steaua Bucureşti (ROU)
H 2-0 *Alderweireld (28), Van Rhijn (48)*
Vermeer (Cillessen 46), Alderweireld, Moisander, Eriksen, Sigthórsson (Boerrigter 82), De Jong, Blind, Schøne, Van Rhijn, Isaac Cuenca (Poulsen 73), Fischer. Coach: Frank de Boer (NED)
A 0-2 *(aet; 2-4 on pens)*
Vermeer, Alderweireld, Moisander, Poulsen, Eriksen, Sigthórsson (Schøne 71), De Jong, Blind, Van Rhijn, Isaac Cuenca (Boerrigter 70), Fischer (Serero 82). Coach: Frank de Boer (NED)

FEYENOORD

Third qualifying round - FC Dynamo Kyiv (UKR)
A 1-2 *Schaken (49)*
Mulder, Janmaat (Singh 33), De Vrij, Martins Indi, Clasie (Kongolo 90), Leerdam, Vormer (Trindade de Vilhena 71), Immers, Nelom, Cissé, Schaken. Coach: Ronald Koeman (NED)
H 0-1
Mulder, Janmaat (Vormer 76), De Vrij, Martins Indi, Clasie, Leerdam, Fernandez (Cabral 67), Immers, Nelom (Singh 86), Cissé, Schaken. Coach: Ronald Koeman (NED)

Play-offs - AC Sparta Praha (CZE)
H 2-2 *Nelom (60), Achahbar (90+3)*
Mulder, Janmaat, Mathijsen, Martins Indi, Clasie, Leerdam (Vormer 63), Fernandez (Achahbar 81), Immers, Nelom, Cissé (Elabdellaoui 63), Schaken. Coach: Ronald Koeman (NED)
A 0-2
Mulder, Janmaat, De Vrij (Nelom 18), Mathijsen, Martins Indi, Clasie, Leerdam (Fernandez 73), Vormer, Immers, Cissé (Achahbar 80), Schaken. Coach: Ronald Koeman (NED)

PSV EINDHOVEN

Play-offs - FK Zeta (MNE)
A 5-0 *Toivonen (2), Matavž (74), Strootman (77), Lens (83), Van Bommel (90)*
Tytoń, Marcelo, Van Bommel, Toivonen, Strootman, Matavž, Lens, Hutchinson, Mertens, Derijck, Ritzmaier. Coach: Dick Advocaat (NED)
H 9-0 *Jørgensen (5), Van Ooijen (12, 74), Matavž (15, 27, 63), Wijnaldum (39, 66, 83)*
Waterman, Jørgensen, Matavž, Wijnaldum, Willems (Ritzmaier 46), Engelaar, Narsingh, Derijck, Van Ooijen, Depay, Manolev. Coach: Dick Advocaat (NED)

Group F
Match 1 - FC Dnipro Dnipropetrovsk (UKR)
A 0-2
Waterman, Marcelo, Van Bommel, Toivonen, Strootman, Lens, Hutchinson, Mertens (Depay 74), Willems (Engelaar 46), Narsingh (Matavž 74), Derijck. Coach: Dick Advocaat (NED)
Match 2 - SSC Napoli (ITA)
H 3-0 *Lens (19), Mertens (41), Marcelo (52)*
Waterman, Bouma, Marcelo, Van Bommel, Toivonen, Strootman, Lens, Hutchinson, Mertens, Narsingh, Derijck. Coach: Dick Advocaat (NED)
Match 3 - AIK (SWE)
H 1-1 *Lens (80)*
Waterman (Tytoń 57), Marcelo, Strootman, Matavž, Wijnaldum, Lens, Hutchinson, Mertens, Willems, Derijck, Van Ooijen (Narsingh 55). Coach: Dick Advocaat (NED)
Match 4 - AIK (SWE)
A 0-1
Waterman, Marcelo, Matavž, Wijnaldum, Hutchinson, Mertens, Willems, Engelaar, Narsingh (Locadia 65), Derijck, Manolev (Depay 75). Coach: Dick Advocaat (NED)
Match 5 - FC Dnipro Dnipropetrovsk (UKR)
H 1-2 *Wijnaldum (18)*
Waterman, Bouma, Marcelo, Matavž, Wijnaldum, Lens, Hutchinson, Mertens, Engelaar (Depay 66), Derijck, Manolev (Locadia 87). Coach: Dick Advocaat (NED)
Match 6 - SSC Napoli (ITA)
A 3-1 *Matavž (30, 41, 60)*
Waterman, Jørgensen, Bouma, Marcelo, Matavž, Wijnaldum, Lens, Engelaar, Van Ooijen (Brenet 87), Depay, Manolev. Coach: Dick Advocaat (NED))

AZ ALKMAAR

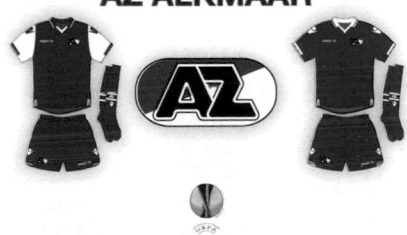

Play-offs - FC Anji Makhachkala (RUS)
A 0-1
Alvarado, Marcellis, Viergever, Gorter, Reijnen, Maher, Falkenburg, Martens, Elm, Altidore, Beerens (Berghuis 74). Coach: Gertjan Verbeek (NED)
H 0-5
Alvarado, Marcellis, Viergever, Gorter, Reijnen, Maher, Falkenburg, Martens (Gudmundsson 41), Elm, Altidore (Boymans 60), Beerens (Rosheuvel 72). Coach: Gertjan Verbeek (NED)

SC HEERENVEEN

Third qualifying round - FC Rapid Bucureşti (ROU)
H 4-0 *Djuričić (9, 64), De Roon (69), Fazli (89)*
Nordfeldt, Zuiverloon, Gouweleeuw, Van la Parra, Djuričić (Fazli 86), Kums, De Roon, Raitala, Zomer, Tannane (Valpoort 71), Ziyech (Van Anholt 53). Coach: Marco van Basten (NED)
A 0-1
Nordfeldt, Zuiverloon, Gouweleeuw, Van la Parra (Assaidi 46), Djuričić (El Akchaoui 74), Kums, De Roon, Raitala, Zomer, Tannane, Ziyech (Van Anholt 46). Coach: Marco van Basten (NED)

Play-offs - Molde FK (NOR)
A 0-2
Nordfeldt, Zuiverloon, Gouweleeuw, El Akchaoui, Van la Parra (Fazli 85), Djuričić, Kums, De Roon, Zomer (Kruiswijk 58), Tannane (Valpoort 46), Van Anholt. Coach: Marco van Basten (NED)
H 1-2 *Valpoort (90+2)*
Nordfeldt, Zuiverloon, El Akchaoui (Raitala 71), Van la Parra (De Ridder 76), Kruiswijk, Djuričić, Kums, De Roon, Zomer, Valpoort, Van Anholt (Gouweleeuw 60). Coach: Marco van Basten (NED)

VITESSE

Second qualifying round - PFC Lokomotiv Plovdiv 1936 (BUL)
A 4-4 *Jonathan Reis (23), Van Ginkel (31, 77), Bony (53)*
Velthuizen, Kalas, Van der Heijden, Hofs (Pröpper 62), Van Ginkel, Bony, Jonathan Reis, Yasuda, Ibarra (Chanturia 80), Kashia, Van Aanholt (Van der Struijk 70). Coach: Fred Rutten (NED)

H 3-1 *Van Ginkel (25), Van Aanholt (45+2), Bony (48)*
Velthuizen, Kalas, Van der Heijden, Van der Struijk, Hofs (Pröpper 77), Van Ginkel, Bony (Havenaar 69), Jonathan Reis, Ibarra (Chanturia 73), Kashia, Van Aanholt. Coach: Fred Rutten (NED)
Red card: Kalas 79

Third qualifying round - FC Anji Makhachkala (RUS)
A 0-2
Velthuizen, Van der Heijden (Cziommer 78), Van der Struijk, Van Ginkel, Bony, Pröpper (Havenaar 71), Jonathan Reis, Yasuda, Ibarra, Kashia, Van Aanholt. Coach: Fred Rutten (NED)
H 0-2
Velthuizen, Kalas, Van der Heijden (Pröpper 78), Van Ginkel, Bony, Jonathan Reis (Havenaar 74), Cziommer, Yasuda, Ibarra (Chanturia 74), Kashia, Van Aanholt. Coach: Fred Rutten (NED)
Red card: Cziommer 59

FC TWENTE

First qualifying round - UE Santa Coloma (AND)
H 6-0 *Schilder (28, 29), Tadić (63), John (71), Plet (77, 79)*
Boschker, Kuiper (Fer 64), Wisgerhof, Schilder, Brama, Verhoek (Tadić 46), Janssen (Chadli 46), Breukers, Röseler, Plet, John. Coach: Steve McClaren (ENG)
A 3-0 *Janssen (19p), Wisgerhof (29), Plet (34)*
Boschker, Kuiper, Wisgerhof (Gortemaker 71), Brama (Hölscher 62), Verhoek, Janssen, Breukers, Röseler, Plet (Born 46), John, Promes. Coach: Steve McClaren (ENG)

Second qualifying round - FC Inter Turku (FIN)
H 1-1 *Tadić (66)*
Mihaylov, Wisgerhof, Schilder, Fer, Tadić, Rosales, Bengtsson (Brama 46), Douglas, Plet, Chadli, Gyasi (Janssen 62). Coach: Steve McClaren (ENG)
A 5-0 *Fer (4, 37), Plet (7), Chadli (77, 89)*
Mihaylov, Wisgerhof (Bjelland 78), Schilder (Breukers 72), Brama, Fer, Tadić, Janssen, Rosales, Douglas, Plet (Verhoek 76), Chadli. Coach: Steve McClaren (ENG)

Third qualifying round - FK Mladá Boleslav (CZE)
H 2-0 *Fer (52), Chadli (58)*
Mihaylov, Bjelland, Schilder, Brama, Fer, Tadić, Janssen (Gutiérrez 73), Rosales, Douglas, Plet (Bulykin 46), Chadli. Coach: Steve McClaren (NED)
A 2-0 *Chadli (9), Fer (31)*
Daniel Fernandes, Bjelland, Schilder (Wisgerhof 77), Brama, Fer, Tadić (Gutiérrez 60), Janssen, Rosales, Douglas, Chadli, Bulykin (Verhoek 64). Coach: Steve McClaren (ENG)

Play-offs - Bursaspor (TUR)
A 1-3 *Chadli (31)*
Mihaylov, Bjelland, Schilder, Brama (Gutiérrez 62), Fer, Tadić, Janssen, Rosales, Douglas, Chadli (Bulykin 80), Castaignos (Verhoek 72). Coach: Steve McClaren (ENG)
H 4-1 *Fer (26p, 116), Schilder (61), Gutiérrez (62) (aet)*
Mihaylov, Wisgerhof, Schilder, Brama, Fer, Tadić, Janssen (Gutiérrez 60), Rosales, Douglas, Castaignos (Landzaat 118), Bulykin (Verhoek 60). Coach: Steve McClaren (ENG)

Group L
Match 1 - Hannover 96 (GER)
H 2-2 *Janssen (7), Chadli (54)*
Mihaylov, Wisgerhof, Schilder (Landzaat 46), Brama, Tadić, Janssen, Rosales, Douglas, Chadli (Gutiérrez 77), Braafheid (Boyata 50), Castaignos. Coach: Steve McClaren (ENG)
Match 2 - Helsingborgs IF (SWE)
A 2-2 *Bengtsson (74), Douglas (88)*
Mihaylov, Schilder, Brama, Tadić, Rosales (Bengtsson 62), Douglas, Gutiérrez (Cabral 62), Chadli, Braafheid (Landzaat 84), Castaignos, Boyata. Coach: Steve McClaren (ENG)
Match 3 - Levante UD (ESP)
A 0-3
Mihaylov, Brama, Landzaat (Janssen 69), Tadić, Rosales, Bengtsson, Douglas, Gutiérrez (Schilder 62), Chadli, Braafheid (Cabral 62), Castaignos. Coach: Steve McClaren (ENG)
Match 4 - Levante UD (ESP)
H 0-0
Mihaylov, Schilder (Bulykin 62), Brama, Tadić, Janssen, Rosales, Bengtsson, Douglas, Cabral (Gutiérrez 77), Braafheid, Castaignos. Coach: Steve McClaren (ENG)
Match 5 - Hannover 96 (GER)
A 0-0
Boschker, Brama, Tadić, Janssen, Rosales (Breukers 77), Bengtsson, Douglas, Gutiérrez , Braafheid, Bulykin (Castaignos 71), Pelupessy (Fer 63). Coach: Steve McClaren (ENG)
Red card: Bengtsson 84
Match 6 - Helsingborgs IF (SWE)
H 1-3 *Tadić (74)*
Bednarek, Wisgerhof, Landzaat (Brama 72), Breukers, Chadli (Bulykin 60), Braafheid, Castaignos, Boyata, Hölscher, Born (Tadić 72), Pelupessy. Coach: Steve McClaren (ENG)

Domestic league club-by-club

ADO DEN HAAG

Coach: Maurice Steijn
1971 • ADO Den Haag (15,000) • adodenhaag.nl
Major honours
Dutch Cup (1) 1975

2012

12/08	Vitesse	a	2-2	Chery, Holla
19/08	RKC	h	2-2	Wormgoor, Holla
25/08	VVV	a	4-2	Chery 2, Van Duinen, Toornstra
31/08	Groningen	h	0-1	
15/09	Heerenveen	a	3-1	Poepon, Toornstra, Chery
23/09	Ajax	h	1-1	Beugelsdijk
29/09	Heracles	a	3-3	og (Duarte), Holla 2 (1p)
05/10	NEC	a	1-1	Van Duinen
21/10	Utrecht	h	1-2	Holla (p)
27/10	Willem II	h	2-0	Holla (p), Van Duinen
02/11	Roda	a	0-0	
10/11	AZ	h	2-2	Vicento, Holla (p)
17/11	PSV	h	1-6	Vicento
23/11	NAC	a	3-0	Beugelsdijk, Chery, Poepon (p)
01/12	Twente	h	0-2	
08/12	Zwolle	h	1-1	Toornstra
16/12	Feyenoord	a	2-3	Van Duinen, Holla (p)
22/12	NEC	h	2-0	Toornstra 2

2013

20/01	Willem II	a	1-1	Jansen
26/01	Roda	h	2-2	Van Duinen, Holla (p)
02/02	PSV	a	0-7	
09/02	NAC	h	2-1	Vicento, Chery
17/02	Heerenveen	h	2-1	Holla, Kolk
24/02	Ajax	a	1-1	Chery
03/03	Heracles	h	3-1	Van Duinen 2, Chery
09/03	AZ	a	1-1	Van Duinen
16/03	Vitesse	h	0-4	
31/03	RKC	a	0-4	
07/04	Utrecht	a	0-1	
13/04	Twente	h	1-3	Van Duinen
20/04	Groningen	a	1-2	Jansen
27/04	VVV	h	1-1	Van Duinen
05/05	Feyenoord	h	2-0	Van Duinen, Holla (p)
12/05	Zwolle	a	2-4	Kolk, Poepon

No	Name	Nat	DoB	Pos	Aps	(s)	Gls
18	Tom Beugelsdijk		07/08/90	D	25	(2)	2
11	Tjaronn Chery		04/06/88	M	32		8
1	Gino Coutinho		05/08/82	G	26		
24	Martijn de Zwart		08/11/90	G	2		
17	Stanley Elbers		14/05/92	M		(6)	
6	Danny Holla		31/12/87	M	28		11
33	Gábor Horváth	HUN	10/07/83	D	2	(1)	
7	Kevin Jansen		08/04/92	M	31		2
13	Santi Kolk		02/10/81	A	6	(7)	2
2	Dico Koppers		31/01/92	D	14		
23	Giovanni Korte		01/08/93	A		(1)	
20	Ramon Leeuwin		01/09/87	M	1	(3)	
15	Dion Malone		13/02/89	D	18	(8)	
8	Aaron Meijers		13/10/87	M	30	(1)	
4	Kenneth Omeruo	NGA	17/10/93	D	26	(1)	
9	Rydell Poepon		28/08/87	A	22	(5)	3
5	Christian Supusepa		02/04/89	D	12	(8)	
10	Jens Toornstra		01/01/89	M	20		5
19	Mike van Duinen		06/11/91	A	31	(2)	11
36	Charlton Vicento		19/01/91	A	7	(21)	3
14	Kevin Visser		19/07/88	M	3	(16)	
3	Vito Wormgoor		16/11/88	D	32		1
22	Robert Zwinkels		04/05/83	G	6	(1)	

AFC AJAX

Coach: Frank de Boer
1900 • Amsterdam ArenA (51,638) • ajax.nl
Major honours
European Champion Clubs' Cup/UEFA Champions
League (4) 1971, 1972, 1973, 1995;
UEFA Cup Winners' Cup (1) 1987; UEFA Cup (1) 1992;
UEFA Super Cup (3) 1972, 1973, 1995;
European/South American Cup (2) 1972, 1995;
Dutch League (32) 1918, 1919, 1931, 1932, 1934, 1937,
1939, 1947, 1957, 1960, 1966, 1967, 1968, 1970, 1972,
1973, 1977, 1979, 1980, 1982, 1983, 1985, 1990, 1994,
1995, 1996, 1998, 2002, 2004, 2011, 2012, 2013;
Dutch Cup (18) 1917, 1943, 1961, 1967, 1970, 1971,
1972, 1979, 1983, 1986, 1987, 1993, 1998, 1999, 2002,
2006, 2007, 2010

2012

12/08	AZ	h	2-2	Van der Wiel, Sigthórsson
19/08	NEC	a	6-1	Lukoki, Eriksen, Sana 2, Janssen, De Jong
25/08	NAC	h	5-0	De Jong 2, Moisander, Sana, Serero
02/09	Heerenveen	a	2-2	Serero 2
15/09	RKC	h	2-0	Schøne, Lukoki
23/09	Den Haag	a	1-1	Babel
29/09	Twente	h	1-0	Eriksen
07/10	Utrecht	h	1-1	Babel
20/10	Heracles	a	3-3	og (Rienstra), Schøne, Sana
28/10	Feyenoord	a	2-2	Eriksen, De Jong
03/11	Vitesse	h	0-2	
11/11	Zwolle	a	4-2	Alderweireld, Fischer 2, De Jong
17/11	VVV	h	2-0	Boerrigter, Hoesen
25/11	Roda	a	2-1	Eriksen, Schøne
01/12	PSV	h	3-1	De Jong, Hoesen, Fischer
08/12	Groningen	h	2-0	Boerrigter, Schøne (p)
16/12	Willem II	a	4-2	De Jong, Hoesen, Moisander, Lukoki
23/12	Utrecht	a	0-0	

2013

20/01	Feyenoord	h	3-0	Fischer 2, Eriksen
27/01	Vitesse	a	2-3	Schøne, Eriksen
03/02	VVV	h	3-0	De Jong, Fischer, Boerrigter
10/02	Roda	h	1-1	Blind
17/02	RKC	a	2-0	Moisander, Eriksen
24/02	Den Haag	h	1-1	Schøne
02/03	Twente	a	2-0	Moisander, Alderweireld
10/03	Zwolle	h	3-0	Sigthórsson, De Jong, Boerrigter
17/03	AZ	a	3-2	De Jong 2, Blind
31/03	NEC	h	4-1	Fischer 2, og (Van Eijden), Babel
07/04	Heracles	a	4-0	Schøne, Sigthórsson, Babel, Eriksen
14/04	PSV	a	3-2	Sigthórsson, Eriksen, Boerrigter
19/04	Heerenveen	h	1-1	Fischer
27/04	NAC	a	2-0	Sigthórsson, og (Gillissen)
05/05	Willem II	h	5-0	Sigthórsson, Eriksen, Fischer, De Jong, Hoesen
12/05	Groningen	a	2-0	Sigthórsson, Hoesen

No	Name	Nat	DoB	Pos	Aps	(s)	Gls
3	Toby Alderweireld	BEL	02/03/89	D	33		2
16	Lucas Andersen	DEN	13/09/94	M		(1)	
5	Vurnon Anita		04/04/89	D	1		
49	Ryan Babel		19/12/86	A	9	(7)	4
17	Daley Blind		09/03/90	D	32	(2)	2
43	Ilan Boccara		14/05/93	M		(1)	
21	Derk Boerrigter		16/10/86	A	17	(13)	5
22	Jasper Cillessen		22/04/89	G	4	(1)	
10	Siem de Jong		28/01/89	M	34		12
37	Lesley de Sa		02/04/93	M		(1)	
34	Stefano Denswil		07/05/93	D	2	(2)	
35	Mitchell Dijks		09/02/93	D	3	(3)	
6	Eyong Enoh	CMR	23/03/86	M	1	(2)	
8	Christian Eriksen	DEN	14/02/92	M	33		10
39	Viktor Fischer	DEN	09/06/94	A	21	(2)	10
23	Danny Hoesen		15/01/91	A	4	(13)	5
11	Isaac Cuenca	ESP	27/04/91	A	2	(5)	
16	Theo Janssen		27/07/81	M	1	(1)	1
18	Davy Klaassen		21/02/93	A		(2)	
32	Ruben Ligeon		24/05/92	A	1		
27	Jody Lukoki		15/11/92	A	7	(9)	3
4	Niklas Moisander	FIN	29/09/85	D	29		4
5	Christian Poulsen	DEN	28/02/80	M	21	(4)	
19	Tobias Sana	SWE	11/07/89	M	9	(4)	4
20	Lasse Schøne	DEN	27/05/86	M	28	(4)	7
25	Thulani Serero	RSA	11/04/90	M	4	(5)	3
9	Kolbeinn Sigthórsson	ISL	14/03/90	A	12	(3)	7
40	Fabian Sporkslede		03/08/93	D		(2)	
7	Miralem Sulejmani	SRB	05/12/88	A		(5)	
2	Gregory van der Wiel		03/02/88	D	3		1
24	Ricardo van Rhijn		13/06/91	D	31		
33	Joël Veltman		15/01/92	D	2	(5)	
1	Kenneth Vermeer		10/01/86	G	30		

AZ ALKMAAR

Coach: Gertjan Verbeek
1967 • DSB (17,150) • az.nl
Major honours
Dutch League (2) 1981, 2009;
Dutch Cup (4) 1978, 1981, 1982, 2013

2012

12/08	Ajax	a	2-2	Altidore 2
19/08	Heracles	h	3-1	Altidore 2, Martens
26/08	Heerenveen	h	0-0	
02/09	PSV	a	1-5	Maher
16/09	Roda	h	4-0	Altidore 3, Falkenburg
23/09	NAC	a	1-2	Maher
30/09	RKC	h	3-3	Elm, Altidore, Maher
07/10	Twente	a	0-3	
20/10	NEC	h	0-2	
28/10	Vitesse	a	2-1	Beerens, Gudmundsson
04/11	VVV	h	1-2	Falkenburg
10/11	Den Haag	a	2-2	Falkenburg, Altidore
17/11	Groningen	a	1-1	Maher
25/11	Feyenoord	h	0-2	
02/12	Utrecht	a	1-2	Reijnen
08/12	Willem II	h	0-0	
15/12	Zwolle	a	2-1	Altidore 2
22/12	Twente	h	0-3	

2013

19/01	Vitesse	h	4-1	Altidore 3, Beerens
26/01	VVV	a	4-1	Maher, Görter (p), Altidore, Reijnen
02/02	Groningen	h	0-1	
10/02	Feyenoord	a	1-3	Beerens
16/02	Roda	a	2-2	Altidore, Overtoom
24/02	NAC	h	0-1	
03/03	RKC	a	1-2	Altidore
09/03	Den Haag	h	1-1	Elm
17/03	Ajax	h	2-3	Henriksen, Altidore
31/03	Heracles	a	2-1	Henriksen, og (Te Wierik)
07/04	NEC	a	1-1	Maher
14/04	Utrecht	h	6-0	Altidore 3 (2p), og (Van der Hoorn), Henriksen, Jóhannsson
20/04	PSV	h	1-3	Jóhannsson
26/04	Heerenveen	a	4-0	Altidore 2, Beerens, Gudmundsson
05/05	Zwolle	h	4-0	Elm, Beerens, Jóhannsson, Maher
12/05	Willem II	a	0-2	

No	Name	Nat	DoB	Pos	Aps	(s)	Gls
17	Jozy Altidore	USA	06/11/89	A	33		23
1	Esteban Alvarado	CRC	28/04/89	G	34		
23	Roy Beerens		22/12/87	A	34		5
22	Steven Berghuis		19/12/91	M	10	(12)	
9	Ruud Boymans		28/04/89	A	1	(4)	
12	Viktor Elm	SWE	13/11/85	M	30		3
10	Erik Falkenburg		05/05/88	M	7	(7)	3
8	Donny Gorter		15/06/88	D	21	(2)	1
7	Jóhann Berg Gudmundsson	ISL	27/10/90	A	18	(12)	2
19	Markus Henriksen	NOR	25/07/92	M	27	(2)	3
20	Aron Jóhannsson	ISL	10/11/90	A		(5)	3
2	Mattias Johansson	SWE	16/02/92	D	2	(10)	
28	Thomas Lam	FIN	18/12/93	D	5	(1)	
8	Adam Maher		20/07/93	M	31		7
3	Dirk Marcellis		13/04/88	D	31		
11	Maarten Martens	BEL	02/07/84	M	6		1
36	Ali Messaoud		13/04/91	M		(1)	
25	Niklas Moisander	FIN	29/09/85	D	2		
26	Celso Ortíz	PAR	26/01/89	M	1	(3)	
10	Willy Overtoom	CMR	02/09/86	M	6	(3)	1
6	Etiënne Reijnen		05/04/87	D	28	(3)	2
18	Mikhail Rosheuvel		10/08/90	A		(14)	
4	Nick Viergever		03/08/89	D	31		
32	Giliano Wijnaldum		31/08/92	D	16	(3)	

FEYENOORD

Coach: Ronald Koeman
1908 • De Kuip (51,137) • feyenoord.nl
Major honours
European Champion Clubs' Cup (1) 1970;
UEFA Cup (2) 1974, 2002;
European/South American Cup (1) 1970;
Dutch League (14) 1924, 1928, 1936, 1938, 1940, 1961,
1962, 1965, 1969, 1971, 1974, 1984, 1993, 1999;
Dutch Cup (11) 1930, 1935, 1965, 1969, 1980, 1984,
1991, 1992, 1994, 1995, 2008

2012

12/08	Utrecht	a	1-0	Cissé
18/08	Heerenveen	h	1-1	Schaken
26/08	Heracles	a	2-1	Janmaat, Immers
02/09	Vitesse	a	0-1	
15/09	Zwolle	h	2-1	og (Broerse), Immers (p)
23/09	PSV	a	0-3	
29/09	NEC	h	5-1	Pellè 2, Immers 3 (1p)
07/10	Groningen	a	2-2	Cissé, Martins Indi
21/10	VVV	a	3-2	Immers (p), Verhoek, Pellè
28/10	Ajax	h	2-2	Boëtius, Pellè
04/11	Twente	a	0-3	
11/11	Roda	h	5-2	Pellè 2, Immers, Clasie, Janmaat
18/11	Willem II	h	3-0	Immers, Pellè 2
25/11	AZ	a	2-0	Trindade de Vilhena, Schaken
01/12	RKC	h	2-0	Pellè 2
09/12	NAC	a	2-2	Pellè, Immers (p)
16/12	Den Haag	h	3-2	Pellè, Immers (p), og (Chery)
23/12	Groningen	h	2-1	Pellè 2

2013

20/01	Ajax	a	0-3	
27/01	Twente	h	0-0	
03/02	Willem II	a	3-1	Pellè, Trindade de Vilhena 2
10/02	AZ	h	3-1	Boëtius, Clasie, Trindade de Vilhena
17/02	Zwolle	a	2-3	Pellè 2
24/02	PSV	h	2-1	Schaken, Pellè
03/03	NEC	a	3-0	Boëtius 2, Pellè
10/03	Roda	a	1-0	Pellè
17/03	Utrecht	h	2-1	Pellè, Janmaat
30/03	Heerenveen	a	0-2	
05/04	VVV	h	1-0	Pellè
14/04	RKC	a	1-0	Pellè (p)
21/04	Vitesse	h	2-0	Pellè (p), Immers
28/04	Heracles	h	6-0	Goossens 2, Pellè 2 (1p), Immers, Schaken
05/05	Den Haag	a	0-2	
12/05	NAC	h	1-0	Pellè

No	Name	Nat	DoB	Pos	Aps	(s)	Gls
29	Anass Achahbar		13/01/94	A	1	(6)	
28	Jean-Paul Boëtius		22/03/94	A	17	(3)	4
11	Jerson Cabral		03/01/91	A		(1)	
23	Sekou Cissé	CIV	23/05/85	A	6	(4)	2
6	Jordy Clasie		27/06/91	M	33		2
3	Stefan de Vrij		05/02/92	D	26		
17	Omar Elabdellaoui	NOR	05/12/91	A	1	(4)	
9	Guyon Fernandez		18/04/86	A	4	(5)	
20	John Goossens		25/07/88	M	5	(5)	2
10	Lex Immers		08/06/86	M	31	(1)	12
2	Daryl Janmaat		22/07/89	D	33		3
25	Terence Kongolo		14/02/94	D	3	(2)	
33	Kostas Lamprou	GRE	18/09/91	G	12		
7	Kelvin Leerdam		24/06/90	D	7	(4)	
5	Bruno Martins Indi		08/02/92	D	32		1
4	Joris Mathijsen		05/04/80	D	29		
15	Kamohelo Mokotjo	SFA	11/03/91	M		(1)	
1	Erwin Mulder		03/03/89	G	22		
18	Miguel Nelom		22/09/90	D	12	(8)	
19	Graziano Pellè	ITA	15/07/85	A	29		27
27	Ruben Schaken		03/04/82	A	27	(4)	4
16	Harmeet Singh	NOR	12/11/90	M	1	(6)	
22	Mitchell te Vrede		07/08/91	A		(1)	
21	Tonny Trindade de Vilhena		03/01/95	M	24	(3)	4
11	Wesley Verhoek		25/09/86	A	12	(13)	1
8	Ruud Vormer		11/05/88	M	7	(13)	

FC GRONINGEN

Coach: Robert Maaskant
1926 • Euroborg (22,329) • fcgroningen.nl

2012

12/08	Twente	a	1-4	Bacuna
19/08	Willem II	h	1-1	Texeira
26/08	PSV	h	1-3	Schet
31/08	Den Haag	a	1-0	Sparv
16/09	Vitesse	h	0-3	
22/09	Zwolle	a	2-1	Zeefuik, De Leeuw
30/09	Roda	h	3-2	De Leeuw 3
07/10	Feyenoord	h	2-2	Bacuna, Van Dijk
21/10	Heerenveen	a	0-3	
26/10	Utrecht	a	0-1	
04/11	NEC	h	1-2	De Leeuw
09/11	NAC	a	1-0	De Leeuw
17/11	AZ	h	1-3	Sparv
24/11	RKC	a	1-1	Kwakman
02/12	Heracles	h	2-0	og (Vejinovic), De Leeuw
08/12	Ajax	a	0-2	
15/12	VVV	h	0-0	
23/12	Feyenoord	a	1-2	Van Dijk

2013

20/01	Utrecht	h	0-2	
27/01	NEC	a	1-2	Burnet
02/02	AZ	h	1-0	Kirm
09/02	RKC	h	2-1	Zeefuik 2 (2p)
17/02	Vitesse	a	0-2	
23/02	Zwolle	h	1-0	De Leeuw
03/03	Roda	a	1-4	Texeira
08/03	NAC	h	1-1	Kieftenbeld
17/03	Twente	h	0-3	
30/03	Willem II	h	2-1	Bacuna (p), Texeira
07/04	Heerenveen	h	3-1	og (Raitala), Bacuna (p), De Leeuw
13/04	Heracles	a	2-1	Texeira, Bacuna (p)
20/04	Den Haag	h	2-1	Zeefuik, Texeira
27/04	PSV	a	2-5	De Leeuw 2
05/05	VVV	a	0-0	
12/05	Ajax	h	0-2	

No	Name	Nat	DoB	Pos	Aps	(s)	Gls
7	Leandro Bacuna		21/08/91	M	26	(7)	5
34	Nick Bakker		21/02/92	M	2	(3)	
39	Hilal Ben Moussa		22/05/92	M		(2)	
1	Marco Bizot		10/03/91	G	16		
27	Henk Bos		12/11/92	M	3	(8)	
18	Lorenzo Burnet		11/01/91	D	26		1
42	Alexander Christovao		14/03/93	A		(3)	
21	Michael de Leeuw		07/10/86	A	30		11
24	Tom Hiariej		25/07/88	D		(3)	
3	Jonas Ivens	BEL	14/10/84	D		(1)	
5	Emil Johansson	SWE	11/08/86	D	3		
2	Johan Kappelhof		05/08/90	D	21		
17	Maikel Kieftenbeld		26/06/90	M	18	(9)	1
17	Andraž Kirm	SVN	06/09/84	M	30	(1)	1
10	Filip Kostić	SRB	01/11/92	M		(5)	
14	Kees Kwakman		10/06/83	D	33		1
32	Timo Letschert		25/05/93	M	2	(1)	
23	Rasmus Lindgren	SWE	29/11/84	M	14		
26	Luciano	BRA	16/03/80	G	18	(1)	
29	Stefano Magnasco	CHI	28/09/92	D	14	(1)	
15	Ajilore Oluwafemi	NGA	18/01/85	M	9	(9)	
19	Mitchell Schet		28/01/88	A	18	(4)	1
8	Tim Sparv	FIN	20/02/87	M	17	(5)	2
11	Suk Hyun-jun	KOR	29/06/91	A		(7)	
4	David Texeira	URU	27/02/91	A	13	(14)	5
4	Virgil van Dijk		08/07/91	D	32		2
20	Paco van Moorsel		15/12/89	M	3	(4)	
9	Yoell van Nieff		17/06/93	D	1		
36	Género Zeefuik		05/04/90	A	25	(2)	4
30	Richairo Zivkovic		05/09/96	A		(4)	

SC HEERENVEEN

Coach: Marco van Basten
1920 • Abe Lenstra (26,100) • sc-heerenveen.nl
Major honours
Dutch Cup (1) 2009

2012

12/08	NEC	h	0-2	
18/08	Feyenoord	a	1-1	Djuričić (p)
26/08	AZ	a	0-0	
02/09	Ajax	h	2-2	Finnbogason 2
15/09	Den Haag	h	1-3	Gouweleeuw
23/09	Twente	a	0-1	
29/09	NAC	h	2-0	Finnbogason, De Ridder
06/10	Vitesse	a	3-3	Finnbogason 2, Kums
21/10	Groningen	h	3-3	Van La Parra 2, Finnbogason (p)
28/10	Heracles	a	3-6	Djuričić, Finnbogason 2
04/11	Zwolle	h	2-1	Finnbogason, De Ridder
11/11	PSV	a	1-5	De Ridder
17/11	RKC	h	0-2	
24/11	VVV	a	1-1	Finnbogason
01/12	Willem II	h	1-3	Finnbogason
09/12	Roda	h	4-4	Djuričić, Van La Parra 2, Finnbogason
16/12	Utrecht	a	1-3	Finnbogason (p)
22/12	Vitesse	h	2-1	Djuričić, Finnbogason

2013

19/01	Heracles	h	0-1	
26/01	Zwolle	a	1-1	Finnbogason
01/02	RKC	a	1-0	Djuričić (p)
09/02	VVV	h	2-2	Mareček, Finnbogason
17/02	Den Haag	a	1-2	Kums
23/02	Twente	h	2-1	Van La Parra, Finnbogason
02/03	NAC	a	2-1	Finnbogason 2
09/03	PSV	h	2-1	De Roon, El Ghanassy
16/03	NEC	a	3-1	Finnbogason, Djuričić 2
30/03	Feyenoord	h	2-0	Finnbogason, El Ghanassy
07/04	Groningen	a	1-3	Mareček
14/04	Willem II	a	3-2	El Ghanassy, Finnbogason 2 (1p)
19/04	Ajax	a	1-1	Finnbogason
26/04	AZ	h	0-4	
05/05	Utrecht	h	2-4	El Ghanassy 2
12/05	Roda	a	0-1	

No	Name	Nat	DoB	Pos	Aps	(s)	Gls
22	Oussama Assaidi	MAR	05/08/88	A	1		
6	Daniël de Ridder		06/03/84	A	9	(6)	3
15	Marten de Roon		29/03/91	M	22	(2)	1
9	Filip Djuričić	SRB	30/01/92	A	32		7
5	Youssef El Akchaoui	MAR	18/02/81	D	4	(1)	
12	Yassine El Ghanassy	BEL	12/07/90	A	10	(2)	5
19	Samir Fazli	MKD	22/04/91	A		(4)	
11	Alfred Finnbogason	ISL	01/02/89	A	31		24
3	Jeffrey Gouweleeuw		10/07/91	D	26	(4)	1
8	Arnold Kruiswijk		02/11/84	D	17	(2)	
4	Christian Kum		13/09/85	D	18	(2)	
18	Sven Kums	BEL	26/02/88	M	31	(1)	2
18	Lukáš Mareček	CZE	17/04/90	M	22	(6)	2
1	Kristoffer Nordfeldt	SWE	23/06/89	G	31		
34	Kenny Otigba	HUN	29/08/92	D		(3)	
16	Marco Pappa	GUA	15/11/87	M	2	(10)	
20	Jukka Raitala	FIN	15/09/88	D	15	(3)	
30	Doke Schmidt		07/04/92	M		(1)	
37	Luciano Slagveer		05/10/93	A		(2)	
30	Oussama Tannane		23/03/94	A	3	(5)	
31	Mark Uth	GER	24/08/91	A	1	(2)	
29	Arsenio Valpoort		05/08/92	M	2	(3)	
46	Pele van Anholt		23/04/91	M	26	(5)	
21	Joey van den Berg		13/02/86	M	12	(1)	
21	Rajiv van La Parra		04/06/91	M	20	(9)	5
25	Brian Vandenbussche	BEL	24/09/81	G	3	(1)	
33	Hakim Ziyech		19/03/93	A	1	(2)	
23	Ramon Zomer		13/04/83	D	28	(1)	
2	Gianni Zuiverloon		30/12/86	D	7	(3)	

HERACLES ALMELO

Coach: Peter Bosz
1903 • Polman (8,500) • heracles.nl

2012

11/08	VVV	h	1-1	Everton	
19/08	AZ	a	1-3	Armenteros	
26/08	Feyenoord	a	1-2	Duarte	
01/09	RKC	a	1-1	Overtoom	
16/09	NAC	h	2-1	Overtoom, Everton	
22/09	Vitesse	a	0-1	Gouriye	
29/09	Den Haag	h	3-3	Overtoom 2 (2p), Gouriye	
06/10	Zwolle	a	3-0	Armenteros, Gouriye 2	
20/10	Ajax	h	3-3	Te Wierik, Bruns, Pedro	
28/10	Heerenveen	h	6-3	Gouriye 3, Armenteros, Everton, Bruns	
03/11	PSV	a	0-4		
10/11	NEC	a	2-3	Armenteros 2	
18/11	Roda	h	5-1	Duarte 2, Overtoom (p), Castillion, Armenteros	
24/11	Willem II	a	2-2	Armenteros 2	
02/12	Groningen	a	0-2		
07/12	Utrecht	h	1-1	Duarte	
14/12	Twente	a	2-3	Vejinovic, Bruns	
22/12	Zwolle	h	1-1	Armenteros	

2013

19/01	Heerenveen	a	1-0	Everton	
26/01	PSV	h	1-5	Everton	
02/02	Roda	a	3-3	Vejinovic, Gouriye, Vujičević	
09/02	Willem II	h	4-1	Vejinovic, Bruns 2, Duarte	
16/02	NAC	a	1-1	Everton	
23/02	Vitesse	a	3-5	Duarte, Castillion, Gouriye	
03/03	Den Haag	a	1-3	Castillion	
09/03	NEC	h	1-0	Everton	
16/03	VVV	a	2-0	Everton, Te Wierik	
31/03	AZ	h	1-2	Te Wierik	
07/04	Ajax	a	0-4		
13/04	Groningen	h	0-2		
20/04	RKC	h	4-0	Quansah (p), Vejinovic, Everton 2	
28/04	Feyenoord	a	0-6		
05/05	Twente	h	1-1	Bruns	
12/05	Utrecht	a	0-3		

No	Name	Nat	DoB	Pos	Aps	(s)	Gls
9	Samuel Armenteros	SWE	27/05/90	A	17	(1)	9
33	Joey Belterman		18/08/93	M	4	(2)	
20	Thomas Bruns		07/01/92	M	23	(4)	6
21	Geoffrey Castillion		25/05/91	A	17	(13)	3
29	Jason Alan Davidson	AUS	29/06/91	D	6	(4)	
5	Christian Dorda	GER	06/12/88	D	24		
8	Lerin Duarte		11/08/90	M	29	(1)	6
11	Everton	BRA	08/06/83	A	28	(4)	10
7	Ninos Gouriye		14/01/91	A	17	(9)	9
2	Milano Koenders		31/07/86	D	16	(7)	
15	Jaroslav Navrátil	CZE	30/12/91	A	1	(3)	
23	Willie Overtoom	CMR	02/09/86	A	18		5
13	Dragan Paljic	GER	08/04/83	M	12	(6)	
22	Remko Pasveer		08/03/83	G	33		
19	Luis Pedro		27/04/90	A	8	(5)	1
17	Kwame Quansah	GHA	24/11/82	M	32		1
14	Ben Rienstra		05/06/90	M	31	(1)	
18	Mathias Schamp	BEL	18/06/88	A	1	(4)	
3	Bart Schenkeveld		28/08/91	D	12		
32	Mike te Wierik		08/06/92	D	15	(3)	3
30	Leon van Dijk		09/03/92	D		(1)	
16	Brian van Loo		02/04/75	G	1	(1)	
27	Daryl van Mieghem		05/12/89	A		(2)	
10	Marko Vejinovic		03/02/90	M	19	(6)	4
4	Jeroen Veldmate		08/11/88	D	2	(1)	
6	Dario Vujičević	CRO	01/04/90	M	8		1

NAC BREDA

Coach: John Karelse; (23/10/12) (Adrie Bogers); (21/11/12) Nebojša Gudelj (SRB)
1912 • Rat Verlegh (17,254) • nac.nl
Major honours
Dutch League (1) 1921;
Dutch Cup (1) 1973

2012

10/08	Willem II	a	1-1	Lurling	
18/08	Twente	h	0-1		
25/08	Ajax	a	0-5		
01/09	Utrecht	h	1-1	Schalk	
16/09	Heracles	a	1-2	Schalk	
23/09	AZ	h	2-1	Luijckx, De Roover	
29/09	Heerenveen	a	0-2		
07/10	PSV	a	0-4		
20/10	Vitesse	h	0-1		
27/10	VVV	a	4-1	Luijckx, Hooi, Verbeek, Lurling	
04/11	RKC	h	2-1	Verbeek, Gudelj	
09/11	Groningen	h	0-1		
17/11	Zwolle	a	0-2		
23/11	Den Haag	h	0-3		
02/12	NEC	a	1-1	Lurling	
09/12	Feyenoord	h	2-2	Luijckx, Gudelj	
15/12	Roda	a	0-0		
22/12	PSV	h	1-6	Buijs	

2013

19/01	VVV	h	1-0	Botteghin	
26/01	Ajax	a	4-0	Verbeek, Buijs, Schalk, Botteghin	
02/02	Zwolle	h	3-0	Buijs (p), Gudelj, Hadouir	
09/02	Den Haag	a	1-2	Ten Voorde	
16/02	Heracles	h	1-1	Ten Voorde	
24/02	AZ	a	1-0	Gudelj	
02/03	Heerenveen	h	1-2	Gudelj	
08/03	Groningen	a	1-1	Buijs (p)	
17/03	Willem II	h	4-0	Luijckx, Seuntjens, Hooi, Verbeek	
30/03	Twente	a	1-1	Van der Weg	
06/04	Vitesse	a	0-3		
13/04	NEC	h	2-0	Lurling, Hooi	
21/04	Utrecht	a	0-3		
27/04	Ajax	h	0-2		
05/05	Roda	h	5-3	Botteghin, Ten Voorde, Lurling 2, Hooi	
12/05	Feyenoord	a	0-1		

No	Name	Nat	DoB	Pos	Aps	(s)	Gls
3	Eric Botteghin	BRA	31/00/07	D	32		3
23	Jordy Buijs		28/12/88	M	32		4
2	Sepp De Roover	BEL	12/11/84	D	29	(1)	1
22	Steven Edwards		15/01/91	D		(2)	
6	Tim Gilissen		04/06/82	M	20	(3)	
24	Peter Gommeren		09/03/92	M		(3)	
16	Nemanja Gudelj	SRB	16/11/91	M	34		5
17	Anouar Hadouir		14/09/82	A	17	(4)	1
25	Elson Hooi		01/10/91	A	25	(4)	4
11	Jens Janse		01/07/86	D	21	(3)	
14	Andreas Lasnik	AUT	09/11/83	M		(6)	
8	Thilo Leugers	GER	09/01/91	D	6	(8)	
4	Mark Looms		24/03/81	D	8		
7	Kees Luijckx		11/02/86	D	33	(1)	4
10	Anthony Lurling		22/04/77	A	28	(2)	6
18	Nadir Çiftçi	TUR	12/02/92	A		(7)	
9	Alex Schalk		07/08/92	A	12	(8)	3
20	Mats Seuntjens		17/05/92	A	8	(14)	1
1	Jelle Rouwelaar		24/12/80	G	34		
14	Rick ten Voorde		20/06/91	A	5	(8)	3
28	Kenny van der Weg		19/02/91	D	11	(4)	1
15	Danny Verbeek		15/08/90	A	19	(6)	4

NEC NIJMEGEN

Coach: Alex Pastoor
1900 • Goffert (12,500) • nec-nijmegen.nl

2012

12/08	Heerenveen	a	2-0	Platje, Čmovš	
19/08	Ajax	h	1-6	Nuytinck	
26/08	Twente	h	1-3	Sno	
01/09	Zwolle	a	4-0	Koolwijk 2 (2p), Sno, Platje	
15/09	VVV	a	2-2	Breuer, Platje	
22/09	Willem II	h	0-0		
29/09	Feyenoord	a	1-5	Rieks	
05/10	Den Haag	h	1-1	George	
20/10	AZ	a	2-0	Koolwijk 2 (1p)	
27/10	Roda	h	0-0		
04/11	Groningen	a	2-1	Pálsson, Roorda	
10/11	Heracles	h	3-2	Ten Voorde 2, George	
18/11	Vitesse	a	1-4	Platje	
24/11	Utrecht	h	2-0	Ten Voorde, Platje	
02/12	NAC	h	1-1	Platje	
08/12	RKC	a	0-2		
15/12	PSV	h	1-1	Pálsson	
22/12	Den Haag	a	0-2		

2013

20/01	Roda	a	0-2		
27/01	Groningen	h	2-1	Van Eijden, Rieks	
03/02	Vitesse	h	2-1	Amieux, Boymans	
10/02	Utrecht	a	3-0	Platje, Falkenburg, Boymans	
15/02	VVV	h	1-2	Van der Velden	
22/02	Willem II	a	3-2	og (Cornelisse), Platje 2	
03/03	Feyenoord	a	0-3		
09/03	Heracles	a	0-1		
16/03	Heerenveen	h	1-3	Boymans	
01/00	Ajax	a	1-4	Van der Velden	
07/04	AZ	h	1-1	Conboy	
13/04	NAC	a	0-2		
21/04	Zwolle	h	1-3	George	
28/04	Twente	a	2-5	Van der Velden, Falkenburg	
05/05	PSV	a	2-4	Van der Velden, Amieux	
12/05	RKC	h	1-2	Conboy	

No	Name	Nat	DoB	Pos	Aps	(s)	Gls
5	Rémy Amieux	FRA	05/09/86	D	16	(5)	2
1	Gábor Babos	HUN	24/10/74	G	28		
4	Daan Bovenberg		25/04/88	D	6	(1)	
26	Ruud Boymans		28/04/89	A	2	(5)	3
21	Michel Breuer		25/05/80	D	27	(1)	1
17	Pavel Čmovš	CZE	29/06/90	D	16	(4)	1
14	Kevin Conboy	DEN	15/10/87	D	20	(2)	2
16	Erik Falkenburg		05/05/88	M	10	(4)	2
25	Navarone Foor		04/02/92	M	24	(5)	
7	Leroy George		21/04/87	A	16	(14)	3
32	Karl-Johan Johnsson	SWE	28/01/90	G		(1)	
8	Ryan Koolwijk		08/08/85	M	31		4
4	Bram Nuytinck		04/05/90	D	1	(1)	1
19	Victor Pálsson	ISL	30/04/91	M	24	(3)	2
11	Melvin Platje		16/12/88	A	27	(6)	9
31	Søren Rieks	DEN	07/04/87	M	23	(5)	2
10	Geert Arend Roorda		02/03/88	M	7	(7)	1
22	Khalid Sinouh	MAR	02/05/75	G	6		
6	Evander Sno		09/04/87	M	7		2
27	Marcel Stutter	GER	06/03/88	M	3	(9)	
16	Rick ten Voorde		20/06/91	A	11	(7)	3
28	Jordi Tutuarima		28/04/93	A		(2)	
15	Danny van den Meiracker		27/03/89	A		(5)	
23	Nick van der Velden		16/12/81	M	18	(5)	4
3	Rens van Eijden		03/03/88	D	34		1
33	Kevin Wattamaleo		25/01/89	M		(3)	
2	Nathaniel Will		16/02/89	D	17	(2)	

PEC ZWOLLE

Coach: Art Langeler
1990 • FC Zwolle Stadion (12,500) • peczwolle.nl

2012

11/08	Roda	a	1-1	Broerse
18/08	Vitesse	h	0-1	
25/08	Utrecht	a	1-1	Lachman
01/09	NEC	h	0-4	
15/09	Feyenoord	a	0-2	
22/09	Groningen	h	1-2	Mokhtar
30/09	Willem II	a	1-0	Van Hintum
06/10	Heracles	h	0-3	
21/10	RKC	a	2-1	Benson, Reniers
28/10	PSV	h	1-2	Van den Berg
04/11	Heerenveen	a	1-2	Van den Berg (p)
11/11	Ajax	h	2-4	Avdic, Drost
17/11	NAC	h	2-0	Reniers, Avdic
25/11	Twente	a	2-2	Avdic, Van den Berg
30/11	VVV	h	0-0	
08/12	Den Haag	a	1-1	Achenteh
15/12	AZ	h	1-2	Avdic
22/12	Heracles	a	1-1	Mokhtar

2013

18/01	PSV	a	3-1	Benson 2, Pluim
26/01	Heerenveen	h	1-1	Avdic
02/02	NAC	a	0-3	
10/02	Twente	h	1-1	Avdic (p)
17/02	Feyenoord	h	3-2	og (Pellè), Lachman, Avdic
24/02	Groningen	a	0-1	
02/03	Willem II	h	2-0	Valpoort, Klich
10/03	Ajax	a	0-3	
15/03	Roda	h	3-2	Van Hintum, Mokhtar, Avdic
31/03	Vitesse	a	1-1	Valpoort
06/04	RKC	h	1-1	Mokhtar
12/04	VVV	a	2-0	Benson 2
21/04	NEC	a	3-1	Mokhtar, Benson, Klich
28/04	Utrecht	a	1-1	Broerse
05/05	AZ	a	0-4	
12/05	Den Haag	h	4-2	Benson 2, Saymak, Mokhtar

No	Name	Nat	DoB	Pos	Aps	(s)	Gls
30	Gerard Aafjes		27/01/85	D	7	(2)	
8	Rochdi Achenteh		07/03/88	M	33		1
44	Denni Avdic	SWE	05/09/88	A	17	(6)	8
9	Fred Benson		10/04/84	A	26	(5)	8
1	Diederik Boer		24/09/80	G	26		
14	Joost Broerse		08/05/79	D	33		2
11	Jesper Drost		11/01/93	A	13	(13)	1
18	Mimoun Eloisghiri		15/09/89	A		(1)	
12	Giovanni Gravenbeek		11/08/88	M	20	(4)	
43	Mateusz Klich	POL	13/06/90	M	12	(1)	2
3	Darryl Lachman		11/11/89	D	33		2
36	Youness Mokhtar		29/08/91	A	30	(2)	6
7	Furdjel Narsingh		13/03/88	A	4	(9)	
17	Norichio Nieveld		25/04/89	D		(4)	
6	Frank Olijve		07/03/80	M	1		
23	Wiljan Pluim		04/01/89	M	34		1
15	Ronnie Reniers		08/11/87	A	4	(8)	2
20	Mustafa Saymak		11/02/93	M	5	(12)	1
10	Arne Slot		17/09/78	M	4	(8)	
24	Ricardo Talu		21/07/93	M		(1)	
21	Leon ter Wielen		31/08/88	G	5		
29	Arsenio Valpoort		05/08/92	A	4	(5)	2
4	Joey van den Berg		13/02/86	M	16		3
4	Maikel van der Werff		22/04/89	D	1	(5)	
5	Bart van Hintum		16/01/87	D	10	(2)	2
2	Bram van Polen		11/10/85	D	33		
33	Danny Wintjens		30/09/83	G	3	(1)	

PSV EINDHOVEN

Coach: Dick Advocaat
1913 • Philips (35,000) • psv.nl
Major honours
European Champion Clubs' Cup (1) 1988;
UEFA Cup (1) 1978;
Dutch League (21) 1929, 1935, 1951, 1963, 1975, 1976,
1978, 1986, 1987, 1988, 1989, 1991, 1992, 1997, 2000,
2001, 2003, 2005, 2006, 2007, 2008;
Dutch Cup (9) 1950, 1974, 1976, 1988, 1989, 1990,
1996, 2005, 2012

2012

11/08	RKC	a	2-3	Lens, Matavž
18/08	Roda	h	5-0	Strootman, Toivonen, og (Tamata), Lens, Wijnaldum
26/08	Groningen	a	3-1	Hutchinson, Mertens, Depay
02/09	AZ	h	5-1	Matavž 2, Van Bommel, Marcelo, Hutchinson
16/09	Utrecht	a	0-1	
23/09	Feyenoord	h	3-0	Toivonen, Wijnaldum, Narsingh
30/09	VVV	a	6-0	Mertens 3, Locadia 3
07/10	NAC	h	4-0	Lens, Toivonen, Van Bommel, Wijnaldum
20/10	Willem II	h	3-2	Strootman 2, Matavž
28/10	Zwolle	a	2-1	Derijck, og (Van den Berg)
03/11	Heracles	h	4-0	Mertens, Narsingh, Strootman, Matavž
11/11	Heerenveen	h	5-1	Narsingh, Mertens, Wijnaldum, Matavž 2
17/11	Den Haag	a	6-1	Narsingh, Strootman, Mertens, Wijnaldum, Derijck, Engelaar
25/11	Vitesse	h	1-2	Derijck
01/12	Ajax	a	1-3	Lens
09/12	Twente	h	3-0	Wijnaldum, Matavž, Narsingh
15/12	NEC	a	1-1	Jørgensen
22/12	NAC	a	6-1	Lens 2, Wijnaldum, Jørgensen, Narsingh, Locadia

2013

18/01	Zwolle	h	1-3	Matavž
26/01	Heracles	a	5-1	Matavž, Lens, Wijnaldum 2, Mertens
02/02	Den Haag	h	7-0	Wijnaldum 2, og (Supusepa), Mertens 2, Lens, Locadia
09/02	Vitesse	a	2-2	Mertens (p), Wijnaldum
17/02	Utrecht	h	2-1	Mertens, Wijnaldum
24/02	Feyenoord	a	1-2	Lens
02/03	VVV	h	2-0	Depay, Van Bommel
09/03	Heerenveen	a	1-2	Toivonen
16/03	RKC	h	2-0	Mertens (p), Wijnaldum
31/03	Roda	a	2-2	Toivonen 2
06/04	Willem II	a	3-1	Van Bommel, Toivonen, Derijck
14/04	Ajax	h	2-3	Lens 2
20/04	AZ	a	3-1	Van Bommel, Mertens, Lens
27/04	Groningen	h	5-2	Matavž, Mertens (p), Lens 2, Van Bommel
05/05	NEC	h	4-2	og (Bovenberg), Toivonen, Lens, Locadia
12/05	Twente	a	1-3	Mertens (p)

No	Name	Nat	DoB	Pos	Aps	(s)	Gls
3	Wilfred Bouma		15/06/78	D	17	(6)	
22	Memphis Depay		13/02/94	A	2	(18)	2
18	Timothy Derijck	BEL	25/05/87	D	22	(1)	4
16	Orlando Engelaar		24/08/79	M	1	(3)	1
27	Oscar Hiljemark	SWE	28/06/92	M	6	(5)	
13	Atiba Hutchinson	CAN	08/02/83	D	33		2
2	Mathias "Zanka" Jørgensen	DEN	23/04/90	D	4	(1)	2
11	Jeremain Lens		24/11/87	A	29	(1)	15
19	Jürgen Locadia		07/11/93	A	4	(11)	6
23	Stanislav Manolev	BUL	16/12/85	D	2		
4	Marcelo	BRA	20/05/87	D	32		1
9	Tim Matavž	SVN	13/01/89	A	16	(11)	11
23	Dries Mertens	BEL	06/05/87	A	29		16
17	Luciano Narsingh		13/09/90	A	14	(4)	6
5	Erik Pieters		07/08/88	D	1	(1)	
24	Marcel Ritzmaier	AUT	22/04/93	M	3	(1)	
8	Kevin Strootman		13/02/90	M	32		5
7	Ola Toivonen	SWE	03/07/86	A	15	(2)	8
1	Przemysław Tytoń	POL	04/01/87	G	5	(1)	
6	Mark van Bommel		22/04/77	M	28		6
21	Boy Waterman		24/01/84	G	29		
10	Georginio Wijnaldum		11/11/90	M	25	(8)	14
15	Jetro Willems		30/03/94	D	25	(1)	

RKC WAALWIJK

Coach: Erwin Koeman
1940 • Mandemakers (7,500) • rkcwaalwijk.nl

2012

11/08	PSV	h	3-2	Sneijder 2, og (Bouma)
19/08	Den Haag	a	2-2	Chevalier 2
24/08	Roda	h	1-0	Braber
01/09	Heracles	h	1-1	Jozefzoon
15/09	Ajax	a	0-2	
22/09	VVV	h	1-1	Chevalier
30/09	AZ	a	3-3	Chevalier, Van Mosselveld, Drost
06/10	Willem II	a	0-1	
21/10	Zwolle	h	1-2	Chevalier
28/10	Twente	h	0-1	
04/11	NAC	a	1-2	Chevalier
10/11	Utrecht	h	4-0	Chevalier, Jozefzoon, Najah, Duits
17/11	Heerenveen	a	2-0	Jozefzoon 2
24/11	Groningen	h	1-1	Van Peppen
01/12	Feyenoord	a	0-2	
08/12	NEC	h	2-0	Martina, Jozefzoon
16/12	Vitesse	a	2-0	Chevalier, Duits
23/12	Willem II	h	0-0	

2013

19/01	Twente	a	0-0	
26/01	NAC	h	0-4	
01/02	Heerenveen	h	0-1	
09/02	Groningen	a	1-2	Braber (p)
17/02	Ajax	h	0-2	
23/02	VVV	a	0-1	
03/03	AZ	h	2-1	Lieder 2
10/03	Utrecht	a	0-1	
16/03	PSV	a	0-2	
31/03	Den Haag	h	4-0	Lieder, og (Wormgoor), Braber, Drost
06/04	Zwolle	a	1-1	Jozefzoon
14/04	Feyenoord	h	1-1	Duits
20/04	Heracles	a	0-4	
27/04	Roda	a	1-3	Boukhari
05/05	Vitesse	h	3-2	Braber, Lieder, Duits (p)
12/05	NEC	a	2-1	Anderson, Jozefzoon

No	Name	Nat	DoB	Pos	Aps	(s)	Gls
15	Furkan Alakmak		07/05/91	A		(1)	
22	Kenny Anderson		14/02/92	M	1	(2)	1
2	Sigourney Bandjar		18/08/84	D	8	(2)	
23	Nourdin Boukhari	MAR	30/06/80	M	22	(4)	1
10	Robert Braber		09/11/82	A	32	(2)	4
9	Teddy Chevalier	FRA	28/06/87	A	25	(4)	8
3	Henrico Drost		21/01/87	D	34		2
17	Sander Duits		29/08/83	M	31		4
7	Florian Jozefzoon		09/02/91	A	32	(2)	7
6	Peter Jungschläger		22/05/84	M	3	(1)	
29	Michael Lamey		29/11/79	D	7	(1)	
11	Mart Lieder		01/05/90	A	13	(16)	4
12	Cuco Martina		25/09/89	D	34		1
21	Imad Najah	MAR	19/02/91	D	13	(6)	1
18	Guy Ramos	CPV	16/08/85	D	11	(4)	
14	Denzel Slager		02/05/93	A		(5)	
8	Rodney Sneijder		31/03/91	M	12	(14)	2
13	Jeff Stans		20/03/90	M	16	(4)	
22	Arjan van Dijk		17/01/87	G	1	(2)	
4	Frank van Mosselveld		02/01/84	D	13	(9)	1
5	Ard van Peppen		26/06/85	D	33		1
15	Furhgill Zeldenrust		21/07/89	M		(6)	
1	Jeroen Zoet		06/01/91	G	33		

RODA JC

Coach: Ruud Brood
1962 • Parkstad Limburg (19,979) • rodajc.nl
Major honours
Dutch Cup (2) 1997, 2000

2012

11/08	Zwolle	h	1-1	*Malki*
18/08	PSV	a	0-5	
24/08	RKC	a	0-1	
01/09	Willem II	h	3-0	*Malki, Németh, Ramzi*
16/09	AZ	a	0-4	
21/09	Utrecht	h	0-1	
30/09	Groningen	a	2-3	*Fledderus, Affane*
06/10	VVV	h	3-0	*Malki 2, Fledderus*
20/10	Twente	h	1-1	*Hupperts*
27/10	NEC	a	0-0	
02/11	Den Haag	h	0-0	
11/11	Feyenoord	a	2-5	*Malki, Biemans*
18/11	Heracles	a	1-5	*Malki*
25/11	Ajax	h	1-2	*Hupperts*
02/12	Vitesse	a	0-3	
09/12	Heerenveen	h	4-4	*Malki 2, Biemans, Hupperts*
15/12	NAC	h	0-0	
23/12	VVV	a	4-2	*Lebedyński, Delorge, Fledderus, Sutchuin*

2013

20/01	NEC	h	2-0	*Malki, Lebedyński*
26/01	Den Haag	a	2-2	*Lebedyński, Fledderus*
02/02	Heracles	h	3-3	*Malki, Danilo Pereira, og (Dorda)*
10/02	Ajax	a	1-1	*Ramzi*
16/02	AZ	h	2-2	*Malki, Demouge*
24/02	Utrecht	a	0-4	
03/03	Groningen	a	4-1	*Demouge 2, Hupperts, Malki*
10/03	Feyenoord	h	0-1	
15/03	Zwolle	a	2-3	*Malki, Biemans*
31/03	PSV	h	2-2	*Demouge, Malki*
06/04	Twente	a	0-2	
13/04	Vitesse	h	3-3	*Malki (p), Demouge, Donald*
20/04	Willem II	a	1-2	*Malki*
27/04	RKC	h	3-1	*og (Zoet), Malki, og (Ramos)*
05/05	NAC	a	3-5	*Demouge, Bonevacia, Donald*
12/05	Heerenveen	h	1-0	*Németh*

No	Name	Nat	DoB	Pos	Aps	(s)	Gls
19	Amin Affane	SWE	21/01/94	A	8	(7)	1
3	Bart Biemans	BEL	14/03/88	D	28	(3)	3
28	Roly Bonevacia		08/10/91	M	16		1
6	Danilo Pereira	POR	09/09/91	M	29	(2)	1
10	Davy De Beule	BEL	07/11/81	M	11	(4)	
26	Laurent Delorge	BEL	21/07/79	M	8	(7)	1
12	Frank Demouge		25/06/82	A	10	(1)	6
14	Mitchell Donald		10/12/88	M	26	(4)	2
8	Mark-Jan Fledderus		14/12/82	M	33		4
15	Jimmy Hempte	BEL	24/03/82	D	5	(5)	
20	Guus Hupperts		25/04/92	A	24	(8)	4
23	Tamás Kádár	HUN	14/03/90	D	10	(1)	
1	Filip Kurto	POL	14/06/91	G	31		
17	Mikołaj Lebedyński	POL	14/10/90	A	5	(19)	3
16	Sanharib Malki	SYR	01/01/84	A	30	(2)	17
2	Martijn Monteyne	BEL	12/11/84	D	28		
9	Krisztián Németh	HUN	05/01/89	A	16	(5)	2
25	Mitchell Paulissen		21/04/93	M		(2)	
21	Mateusz Prus	POL	09/03/90	G	3	(1)	
11	Adil Ramzi	MAR	14/07/77	A	7	(6)	2
18	Arnaud Sutchuin	BEL	02/05/89	M	9	(11)	1
5	Abel Tamata		05/12/90	D	22		
4	Rob Wielaert		29/12/78	D	15	(5)	

FC TWENTE

Coach: Steve McClaren (ENG);
(26/02/13) (Alfred Schreuder)
1965 • De Grolsch Veste (24,244) • fctwente.nl
Major honours
Dutch League (1) 2010;
Dutch Cup (3) 1977, 2001, 2011

2012

12/08	Groningen	h	4-1	*Chadli 2, Tadić 2*
18/08	NAC	a	1-0	*Fer*
26/08	NEC	a	3 1	*Castaignos, Bulykin, Fer (p)*
02/09	VVV	h	1-0	*Fer (p)*
15/09	Willem II	a	6-2	*Gutiérrez, Castaignos, Schilder 2, Janssen, og (Haastrup)*
23/09	Heerenveen	h	1-0	*Tadić (p)*
29/09	Ajax	a	0-1	
07/10	AZ	h	3-0	*Chadli, Tadić (p), Castaignos*
20/10	Roda	a	1-1	*Castaignos*
28/10	RKC	a	1-0	*Tadić*
04/11	Feyenoord	h	3-0	*Chadli, Castaignos, Tadić*
11/11	Vitesse	a	0-0	
18/11	Utrecht	a	1-1	*Janssen*
25/11	Zwolle	h	2-2	*Tadić (p), Castaignos*
01/12	Den Haag	h	2-0	*Tadić, Bulykin*
09/12	PSV	a	0-3	
14/12	Heracles	h	3-2	*Chadli, Gyasi, Castaignos*
21/12	AZ	a	3-0	*Chadli 2, Castaignos*

2013

19/01	RKC	h	0-0	
27/01	Feyenoord	a	0-0	
03/02	Utrecht	h	2-4	*Tadić 2 (1p)*
10/02	Zwolle	a	1-0	*Tadić*
16/02	Willem II	h	1-1	*Douglas*
23/02	Heerenveen	a	1-2	*Bulykin*
02/03	Ajax	h	1-1	
10/03	Vitesse	h	0-1	
17/03	Groningen	a	3-0	*Fer, Tadić (p), Castaignos*
30/03	NAC	h	1-1	*Brama*
06/04	Roda	h	2-0	*Castaignos, Chadli*
13/04	Den Haag	a	3-1	*Douglas, Bulykin 2*
22/04	VVV	a	2-2	*Bengtsson, Castaignos*
28/04	NEC	h	5-2	*Douglas, Castaignos, Chadli, Bengtsson, Gutiérrez*
05/05	Heracles	a	1-1	*Fer*
12/05	PSV	h	3-1	*Castaignos, Chadli, Janssen*

No	Name	Nat	DoB	Pos	Aps	(s)	Gls
17	Rasmus Bengtsson	SWE	26/06/86	D	20	(1)	2
2	Andreas Bjelland	DEN	11/07/88	D	4	(2)	
38	Mirco Born	GER	28/06/94	A		(1)	
1	Sandor Boschker		20/10/70	G	7		
18	Dedryck Boyata	BEL	08/09/90	D	1	(4)	
20	Edson Braafheid		08/04/83	D	22	(3)	
6	Wout Brama		21/08/86	M	25		1
4	Tim Breukers		04/11/87	D	10		
9	Dmitri Bulykin	RUS	20/11/79	A	12	(10)	5
11	Jerson Cabral		03/01/91	A	1	(8)	
30	Luc Castaignos		27/09/92	A	25	(9)	13
22	Nacer Chadli	BEL	02/08/89	M	20	(2)	10
19	Douglas	BRA	12/01/88	D	31		3
26	Shadrach Kwesi Eghan	GHA	04/07/94	M		(2)	
8	Leroy Fer		05/01/90	M	25	(1)	5
21	Felipe Gutiérrez	CHI	08/10/90	M	14	(9)	2
45	Edwin Gyasi		01/07/91	A	8	(4)	1
37	Tim Hölscher	GER	21/02/95	M	7	(5)	
14	Willem Janssen		04/07/86	M	24	(6)	3
7	Denny Landzaat		06/05/76	M		(7)	
13	Nikolay Mihaylov	BUL	28/06/88	G	26		
39	Joey Pelupessy		15/05/93	A	2	(1)	
35	Timo Plattel		12/03/94	G	1		
15	Roberto Rosales	VEN	20/11/88	D	23	(4)	
5	Robbert Schilder		18/04/86	M	27	(1)	2
10	Dušan Tadić	SRB	20/11/88	M	32	(1)	12
12	Wesley Verhoek		25/09/86	A		(3)	
4	Peter Wisgerhof		19/11/79	D	7	(4)	
46	Felitciano Zschusschen		24/01/92	M		(3)	

FC UTRECHT

Coach: Jan Wouters
1970 • Galgenwaard (24,600) • fcutrecht.nl
Major honours
Dutch Cup (3) 1985, 2003, 2004

2012

12/08	Feyenoord	h	0-1	
18/08	VVV	a	3-1	*Asare, Van der Gun, Gerndt*
25/08	Zwolle	h	1-1	*Duplan*
01/09	NAC	a	1-1	*Gerndt*
16/09	PSV	h	1-0	*Bulthuis*
21/09	Roda	a	1-0	*Bulthuis*
29/09	Vitesse	h	1-2	*Mulenga*
07/10	Ajax	a	1-1	*og (Sporkslede)*
21/10	Den Haag	a	2-1	*Gerndt, Mulenga*
26/10	Groningen	h	1-0	*Asare*
03/11	Willem II	a	5-1	*Van der Gun, Mulenga 2, Gerndt 2*
10/11	RKC	a	0-4	
18/11	Twente	h	1-1	*Mulenga*
24/11	NEC	a	0-2	
02/12	AZ	h	2-1	*De Kogel, Mulenga*
07/12	Heracles	a	1-1	*og (Dorda)*
16/12	Heerenveen	h	3-1	*De Kogel 2, Mulenga*
23/12	Ajax	h	0-0	

2013

20/01	Groningen	a	2-0	*Gerndt (p), Van der Hoorn*
27/01	Willem II	h	3-1	*Kali, Duplan, Schepers*
03/02	Twente	a	4-2	*Toornstra, Mulenga (p), Bulthuis, Van der Hoorn*
10/02	NEC	h	0-3	
16/02	PSV	a	1-2	*Mulenga*
24/02	Roda	h	4-0	*Mulenga 2 (1p), Wuytens, Oar*
01/03	Vitesse	a	0-2	
10/03	RKC	h	1-0	*Mulenga*
17/03	Feyenoord	a	1-2	*Van der Gun*
30/03	VVV	h	2-1	*Duplan, De Kogel*
07/04	Den Haag	h	1-0	*Toornstra*
14/04	AZ	a	0-6	
21/04	NAC	h	3-0	*Van der Hoorn, Toornstra, Duplan*
28/04	Zwolle	a	2-1	*Asare, Pappot*
05/05	Heerenveen	a	4-2	*Toornstra, Mulenga, Wuytens, Van der Hoorn*
12/05	Heracles	h	3-0	*Van der Gun, Mulenga (p), Toornstra*

No	Name	Nat	DoB	Pos	Aps	(s)	Gls
15	Nana Asare	GHA	11/07/86	M	28	(2)	3
16	Yassine Ayoub		06/03/94	M		(2)	
49	Cédric Badjeck	CMR	25/01/95	M		(2)	
2	Daan Bovenberg		25/10/88	D	1		
28	Davy Bulthuis		28/06/90	D	30		3
12	Leon de Kogel		13/11/91	A	5	(13)	4
7	Édouard Duplan	FRA	13/05/83	A	18	(4)	4
9	Alexander Gerndt	SWE	14/07/86	A	16	(1)	6
21	Kai Heerings		12/01/90	D	3	(10)	
20	Anouar Kali		03/06/91	M	25	(2)	1
35	Gévero Markiet		08/04/91	D	2	(1)	
41	Soufian Moro		21/02/93	A		(1)	
8	Jacob Mulenga	ZAM	12/02/84	A	23	(5)	14
6	Johan Mårtensson	SWE	16/02/89	M	11	(5)	
23	Marcus Nilsson	SWE	26/02/88	D	2	(1)	
10	Tommy Oar	AUS	10/12/91	A	22	(5)	1
40	Elroy Pappot		20/04/93	M	1	(1)	1
1	Robbin Ruiter		25/03/87	G	33		
19	Adam Sarota	AUS	28/12/88	M	18		
24	Bob Schepers		30/03/92	A		(8)	1
18	Yoshiaki Takagi	JPN	09/12/92	M	1	(6)	
22	Jens Toornstra		04/04/89	M	12		5
4	Cedric van der Gun		05/05/79	M	22	(4)	4
3	Mike van der Hoorn		15/10/92	D	31		4
14	Mark van der Maarel		12/08/89	D	31	(1)	
48	Romano van der Stoep		11/11/94	A		(2)	
26	Jeroen Verhoeven		30/04/80	G	1	(1)	
29	Jan Wuytens	BEL	09/06/85	D	32	(1)	2
5	Michael Zullo	AUS	11/09/88	D	6	(7)	

VITESSE

Coach: Fred Rutten
1892 • Gelredome (26,600) • vitesse.nl

2012

12/08	Den Haag	h	2-2	*Bony, Jonathan Reis*
18/08	Zwolle	a	1-0	*Ibarra*
26/08	Willem II	a	2-0	*Jonathan Reis 2*
02/09	Feyenoord	h	1-0	*Bony*
16/09	Groningen	a	3-0	*Havenaar, Kalas, Bony*
22/09	Heracles	h	1-1	*Bony (p)*
29/09	Utrecht	a	2-1	*Van Ginkel, Bony*
06/10	Heerenveen	h	3-3	*Bony 3 (1p)*
20/10	NAC	a	3-0	*Jonathan Reis, Bony 2*
28/10	AZ	h	1-2	*Van Ginkel*
03/11	Ajax	a	2-0	*Bony 2*
11/11	Twente	h	0-0	
18/11	NEC	h	4-1	*Bony 2, Kashia, Havenaar*
25/11	PSV	a	2-1	*Jonathan Reis, Bony*
02/12	Roda	h	3-0	*Van Ginkel, Jonathan Reis 2*
09/12	VVV	a	1-3	*Van Ginkel*
16/12	RKC	h	2-2	*Bony, Cziommer*
22/12	Heerenveen	a	1-2	*Kashia*

2013

19/01	AZ	a	1-4	*Kakuta*
27/01	Ajax	h	3-2	*Janssen, Van Aanholt, Ibarra*
03/02	NEC	a	1-2	*Havenaar*
09/02	PSV	h	2-2	*Bony 2 (1p)*
17/02	Groningen	h	2-0	*Havenaar, Bony (p)*
23/02	Heracles	a	5-3	*Bony 3, Van Ginkel 2*
01/03	Utrecht	h	2-0	*Havenaar, Bony*
10/03	Twente	a	1-0	*Bony*
16/03	Den Haag	h	4-0	*Bony 2, Van Ginkel, Havenaar*
31/03	Zwolle	h	2-1	*Bony, Havenaar*
06/04	NAC	h	3-0	*Bony 2, Ibarra*
13/04	Roda	a	3-3	*Havenaar 2, Bony*
21/04	Feyenoord	a	0-2	
28/04	Willem II	h	3-1	*Havenaar, Bony, Van Ginkel*
05/05	RKC	a	2-3	*Van der Heijden, Havenaar*
12/05	VVV	h	0-1	

No	Name	Nat	DoB	Pos	Aps	(s)	Gls
9	Wilfried Bony	CIV	10/12/88	A	30		31
11	Giorgi Chanturia	GEO	11/04/93	A	1		
15	Simon Cziommer	GER	06/11/80	M	8	(13)	1
44	Brahim Darri		14/09/94	A	1	(1)	
14	Mike Havenaar	JPN	20/05/87	A	18	(14)	11
7	Nicky Hofs		17/05/83	M		(6)	
30	Renato Ibarra	ECU	20/01/90	A	30	(2)	3
5	Theo Janssen		27/07/81	M	27		1
13	Jonathan Reis	BRA	06/06/89	A	25	(3)	7
20	Gaël Kakuta	FRA	21/06/91	M	21	(1)	1
2	Tomáš Kalas	CZE	15/05/93	D	33	(1)	1
37	Guram Kashia	GEO	04/07/87	D	33		2
18	Valeri Kazaishvili	GEO	29/01/93	A	1	(4)	
3	Dan Mori	ISR	08/11/88	D	2	(4)	
10	Davy Pröpper		02/09/91	A	5	(8)	
1	Eloy Room		06/02/89	G		(2)	
38	Patrick van Aanholt		29/08/90	D	31		1
4	Jan-Arie van der Heijden		03/03/88	M	30		1
6	Frank van der Struijk		28/03/85	D	7	(5)	
8	Marco van Ginkel		01/12/92	M	33		8
22	Piet Velthuizen		03/11/86	G	34		
16	Michihiro Yasuda	JPN	20/12/87	D	4	(2)	

VVV-VENLO

Coach: Ton Lokhoff
1903 • Seacon (7,500) • vvv-venlo.nl
Major honours
Dutch Cup (1) 1959

2012

11/08	Heracles	a	1-1	*Linssen*
18/08	Utrecht	h	1-3	*Wildschut*
25/08	Den Haag	h	2-4	*Seip, Vorstermans*
02/09	Twente	a	0-1	
15/09	NEC	h	2-2	*Nwofor 2*
22/09	RKC	a	1-1	*Seip*
30/09	PSV	h	0-6	
06/10	Roda	a	0-3	
21/10	Feyenoord	h	2-3	*Türk, Joppen*
27/10	NAC	h	1-4	*Nwofor*
04/11	AZ	a	2-4	*Maguire, Radosavljević*
10/11	Willem II	a	4-1	*Seip, Cullen, Linssen, Türk*
17/11	Ajax	a	0-2	
24/11	Heerenveen	h	1-1	*Linssen*
30/11	Zwolle	a	0-0	
09/12	Vitesse	h	3-1	*Otsu, Linssen, Cullen*
15/12	Groningen	a	0-0	
23/12	Roda	h	2-4	*Linssen, Maguire*

2013

19/01	NAC	a	0-1	
25/01	AZ	h	1-4	*Nwofor*
03/02	Ajax	h	0-3	
09/02	Heerenveen	a	2-2	*Nwofor, Seip*
15/02	NEC	a	2-1	*Nwofor, Linssen*
23/02	RKC	h	1-0	*Seip*
02/03	PSV	a	0-2	
09/03	Willem II	a	0-1	
16/03	Heracles	h	0-2	
30/03	Utrecht	a	1-2	*Linssen*
05/04	Feyenoord	a	0-1	
12/04	Zwolle	h	0-2	
21/04	Twente	h	2-2	*Röseler, Nwofor*
27/04	Den Haag	a	1-1	*Nwofor*
05/05	Groningen	h	0-0	
12/05	Vitesse	a	1-0	*Linssen*

No	Name	Nat	DoB	Pos	Aps	(s)	Gls
25	Jeffrey Altheer		09/03/87	M		(2)	
2	Ahmed Ammi	MAR	19/01/81	D	5	(3)	
55	Roland Bergkamp		03/04/91	A	3	(7)	
10	Robert Cullen	JPN	07/06/85	A	14	(12)	2
5	Niels Fleuren		01/11/86	D	16	(3)	
1	Niclas Heimann	GER	12/03/91	G	1		
24	Guus Joppen		14/11/89	D	33		1
17	Quin Kruijsen		27/11/90	M	2		
26	Jeffrey Leiwakabessy		23/02/81	D	18		
11	Bryan Linssen		19/01/91	M	30	(4)	8
12	Niki Mäenpää	FIN	23/01/85	G	33		
18	Barry Maguire		27/10/89	M	17	(5)	2
8	Marcel Meeuwis		31/10/80	M	7	(2)	
9	Uche Nwofor	NGA	17/09/91	A	17	(8)	8
17	Yuki Otsu	JPN	24/03/90	M	8	(14)	1
6	Aleksandar Radosavljević	SVN	25/04/79	M	25	(2)	1
20	Kaj Ramsteijn		17/01/90	D	11	(1)	
7	Jules Reimerink		30/09/89	A		(1)	
3	Nils Röseler	GER	10/02/92	D	26		1
19	Marcel Seip		05/04/82	D	31		5
14	Oğuzhan Türk		17/05/86	M	26	(3)	2
21	Ricky van Haaren		21/01/91	M	25	(6)	
4	Ismo Vorstermans		30/03/89	D	9	(1)	1
30	Yanic Wildschut		01/11/91	A	16	(16)	1
3	Maya Yoshida	JPN	24/08/88	D	1	(1)	

WILLEM II

Coach: Jürgen Streppel
1896 • Koning Willem II Stadion (14,500) • willem-ii.nl
Major honours
Dutch League (3) 1916, 1952, 1955;
Dutch Cup (2) 1944, 1963

2012

10/08	NAC	h	1-1	*Podevijn*
19/08	Groningen	a	1-1	*Höcher*
26/08	Vitesse	h	0-2	
01/09	Roda	a	0-3	
15/09	Twente	h	2-6	*Höcher, Lumu*
22/09	NEC	a	0-0	
30/09	Zwolle	h	0-1	
06/10	RKC	h	1-0	*Joachim*
20/10	PSV	a	2-3	*Podevijn, Vossebelt*
27/10	Den Haag	a	0-2	
03/11	Utrecht	h	1-5	*og (Mulenga)*
10/11	VVV	h	1-4	*Misidjan*
18/11	Feyenoord	a	0-3	
24/11	Heracles	h	2-2	*Vossebelt, Peters*
01/12	Heerenveen	h	3-1	*Misidjan, Mulder, Joachim*
08/12	AZ	a	0-0	
16/12	Ajax	h	2-4	*Joachim, Snijders*
23/12	RKC	a	0-0	

2013

20/01	Den Haag	h	1-1	*Mulder*
27/01	Utrecht	a	1-3	*Haemhouts*
03/02	Feyenoord	h	1-3	*Misidjan (p)*
09/02	Heracles	a	1-4	*Vossebelt*
16/02	Twente	a	1-1	*Ippel*
22/02	NEC	h	2-3	*Haemhouts, Joachim*
02/03	Zwolle	a	0-2	
09/03	VVV	h	1-0	*Guijt*
17/03	NAC	a	0-4	
30/03	Groningen	h	1-2	*Haemhouts*
06/04	PSV	h	1-3	*Peters*
14/04	Heerenveen	a	2-3	*Ippel, Joachim*
20/04	Roda	h	2-1	*Haastrup, Joachim (p)*
28/04	Vitesse	a	1-3	*Snijders*
05/05	Ajax	a	0-5	
12/05	AZ	h	2-0	*Misidjan, og (Wijnaldum)*

No	Name	Nat	DoB	Pos	Aps	(s)	Gls
18	Sofian Akouili		28/02/89	D	10	(7)	
20	Kevin Brands		28/03/88	M	4	(9)	
21	Arjan Christianen		19/12/82	G	1		
13	Tim Cornelisse		03/04/78	D	14		
29	Stijn Derkx		03/02/95	A		(1)	
16	Danny Guijt		07/02/81	M	14	(7)	1
14	Philipp Haastrup	GER	05/03/82	D	31		1
8	Robbie Haemhouts	BEL	09/12/83	M	16	(6)	3
10	Marc Höcher		09/09/84	A	22	(10)	2
30	Nicky Hofs		17/05/83	M	7	(2)	
12	Ricardo Ippel		31/08/90	M	15	(5)	2
23	Gaby Jallo		01/09/89	D	13	(2)	
9	Aurélien Joachim	LUX	10/08/86	A	25		6
17	Jeroen Lumu		27/05/95	A	3	(9)	1
1	David Meul	BEL	03/07/81	G	33		
11	Virgil Misidjan		24/07/93	A	28	(6)	4
26	Sanny Monteiro		11/12/89	M		(1)	
6	Hans Mulder		27/04/87	M	22		2
4	Jordens Peters		03/05/87	D	27	(1)	2
5	Mitchell Pique		20/11/79	D	14	(1)	
22	Jens Podevijn	BEL	18/07/89	A	11	(6)	2
24	Ryan Sanusi	BEL	05/01/92	M		(2)	
7	Genaro Snijders		29/07/89	A	14	(9)	2
2	Kees van Buuren		27/07/86	D	21	(4)	
3	Ruud van der Rijt		17/11/88	D	4		
28	Jonas van Kerckhoven	BEL	04/02/94	M		(2)	
19	Simon van Zeelst		23/02/94	M	4	(2)	
15	Niek Vossebelt		07/08/91	M	21	(1)	3

Top goalscorers

31	Wilfried Bony (Vitesse)
27	Graziano Pellè (Feyenoord)
24	Alfred Finnbogason (Heerenveen)
23	Jozy Altidore (AZ)
17	Sanharib Malki (Roda)
16	Dries Mertens (PSV)
15	Jeremain Lens (PSV)
14	Georginio Wijnaldum (PSV)
	Jacob Mulenga (Utrecht)
13	Luc Castaignos (Twente)

UEFA Europa League play-offs

FIRST ROUND

(16/05/13 & 19/05/13)
Heerenveen 0-1 Utrecht *(Van der Gun 60)*
Utrecht 2-1 Heerenveen *(Toornstra 9, 82; Uth 89)*
(Utrecht 3-1)

Groningen 0-1 Twente *(Gutiérrez 22)*
Twente 3-2 Groningen *(Braafheid 12, Gutiérrez 83, Chadli 90+1; Braafheid 23og, Kirm 26)*
(Twente 4-2)

SECOND ROUND

(23/05/13 & 26/05/13)
Twente 0-2 Utrecht *(Van der Gun 9, Duplan 59)*
Utrecht 1-2 Twente *(Duplan 40, Tadic 34, Chadli 36)*
(Utrecht 3-2)

Domestic cup: KNVB Beker 2012/13

SECOND ROUND

(25/09/12)
ADO 20 4-1 Almere City
AFC 0-1 Den Bosch *(aet)*
Go Ahead Eagles 4-4 VVV *(aet; 4-3 on pens)*
Hollandia 1-0 Fortuna Sittard
JVC 2-4 Eindhoven *(aet)*
Lisse 0-5 RKC
ONS 1-1 Excelsior *(aet; 5-4 on pens)*
Roda 0-1 Zwolle *(aet)*
Bolnevellingen 2-1 Oss *(aet)*
Sparta Nijkerk 2-3 De Graafschap
Sparta Rotterdam 3-2 AGOVV
Staphorst 2-0 Montfoort
VVOG 0-0 Emmen *(aet; 4-5 on pens)*

(26/09/12)
Capelle 3-4 HBS *(aet)*
Gemert 0-3 Vitesse
GVVV 1-2 Groningen
IJsselmeervogels 0-2 Den Haag
Kloetinge 0-4 Telstar
Kozakken Boys 0-4 Heerenveen
Lienden 0-4 Heracles
MVV 1-3 NAC
NEC 2-3 Feyenoord *(aet)*
Rijnsburgse Boys 1-0 Volendam
RKVV 1-5 Cambuur
RVVH 0-1 Twente
SWZ 2-1 Noordwijk *(aet)*
Utrecht 0-3 Ajax
Willem II 0-2 Dordrecht
Venlon 0-3 Helmond Sport *(aet; 6-5 on pens)*

(27/09/12)
Achilles 29 2-3 PSV
AZ 4-1 Veendam
Zouaven 0-1 EHC

THIRD ROUND

(30/10/12)
ADO 20 6-1 Eindhoven
Cambuur 1-1 Telstar *(aet; 4-3 on pens)*
De Graafschap 0-3 Go Ahead Eagles
Dordrecht 2-1 Scheveningen
Groningen 1-0 Den Haag
Rijnsburgse Boys 0-0 Emmen *(aet; 7-6 on pens)*

(31/10/12)
Heracles 2-0 Sparta Rotterdam
NAC 1-1 HBS *(aet; 4-2 on pens)*
ONS 0-2 Ajax
PSV 3-1 EHC
RKC 2-4 Zwolle
Vitesse 4-0 Staphorst

(01/11/12)
Heerenveen 1-0 Hollandia
SWZ 1-4 AZ
Twente 1-2 Den Bosch
Xerxes 0-4 Feyenoord

FOURTH ROUND

(18/12/12)
Den Bosch 1-0 Cambuur
Dordrecht 2-4 AZ
Rijnsburgse Boys 0-4 PSV

(19/12/12)
Go Ahead Eagles 2-3 Zwolle *(aet)*
Heerenveen 2-2 Feyenoord *(aet; 6-7 on pens)*
NAC 1-3 Heracles
Vitesse 10-1 ADO 20

(20/12/12)
Groningen 0-3 Ajax

QUARTER-FINALS

(29/01/13)
Den Bosch 0-5 AZ *(Elm 5, Gudmundsson 23, Maher 35, 60, Altidore 39p)*

(30/01/13)
PSV 2-1 Feyenoord 1 *(Mertens 20, Van Bommel 78; Pellè 29)*
Zwolle 3-2 Heracles 2 *(Slot 16, Benson 44, Drost 58; Vejinovic 9, Everton 68)*

(31/01/13)
Vitesse 0-4 Ajax *(Hoesen 7, Schøne 59, Sigthórsson 81,86)*

SEMI-FINALS

(27/02/13)
Ajax 0-3 AZ *(Altidore 74, 90+3, Gudmundsson 88)*
Zwolle 0-3 PSV *(Locadia 16, 34, 85)*

FINAL

(09/05/13)
De Kuip, Rotterdam
AZ ALKMAAR 2 *(Maher 12, Altidore 14)*
PSV EINDHOVEN 1 *(Locadia 31)*
Referee: *Kuipers*
AZ: *Alvarado, Marcellis (Johansson 67), Reijnen, Viergever, Wijnaldum, Henriksen, Maher, Elm, Beerens, Altidore (Jóhannsson 88), Gudmundsson (Berghuis 74)*
PSV: *Waterman, Hutchinson, Marcelo, Bouma (Matavž 79), Willems, Van Bommel, Toivonen (Wijnaldum 68), Strootman, Lens, Locadia, Mertens (Depay 85)*

Promoted clubs

SC CAMBUUR
Coach: Alfons Arts; (22/03/13) (Henk de Jong)
1964 • Cambuur Stadion (10,500) • cambuur.nl

GO AHEAD EAGLES
Coach: Erik ten Hag
1902 • De Adelaarshorst (6,750) • ga-eagles.nl

SECOND LEVEL FINAL TABLE 2012/13

		Pld	W	D	L	F	A	Pts
1	SC Cambuur	30	19	4	7	50	00	61
2	FC Volendam (*4)	30	19	3	8	70	43	60
3	Sparta Rotterdam (*2)	30	16	7	7	59	36	55
4	Helmond Sport (*1)	30	15	10	5	55	45	55
5	MVV Maastricht	30	14	8	8	56	44	50
6	Go Ahead Eagles	30	13	9	8	60	46	48
7	Fortuna Sittard	30	13	7	10	39	33	46
8	De Graafschap (*3)	30	12	9	9	57	41	45
9	FC Dordrecht	30	11	7	12	56	56	40
10	FC Oss	30	10	7	13	40	57	37
11	FC Den Bosch	30	10	5	15	38	49	35
12	FC Emmen	30	8	8	14	38	52	32
13	Almere City FC	30	10	1	19	41	67	31
14	Telstar	30	7	8	15	31	46	29
15	SBV Excelsior	30	4	9	17	39	63	21
16	FC Eindhoven	30	5	6	19	40	67	21

NB (*) period champions; AGOVV Apeldoorn withdrew after round 18; BV Veendam withdrew after round 25 – all their matches annulled.

PROMOTION/RELEGATION PLAY-OFFS

FIRST ROUND
(08/05/13 & 11/05/13)
De Graafschap 2-1 Fortuna Sittard
Fortuna Sittard 1-3 De Graafschap
(De Graafschap 5-2)

Dordrecht 3-3 Go Ahead Eagles
Go Ahead Eagles 3-0 Dordrecht
(Go Ahead Eagles 6-3)

SECOND ROUND
(16/05/13 & 19/05/13)
De Graafschap 1-1 Roda
Roda 6-1 De Graafschap
(Roda 7-2)

Go Ahead Eagles 1-0 VVV
VVV 0-3 Go Ahead Eagles
(Go Ahead Eagles 4-0)

Helmond Sport 2-4 Sparta
Sparta 1-1 Helmond Sport
(Sparta 5-3)

MVV 0-1 Volendam
Volendam 3-1 MVV
(Volendam 4-1)

THIRD ROUND
(23/05/13 & 26/05/13)
Go Ahead Eagles 3-0 Volendam
Volendam 1-0 Go Ahead Eagles
(Go Ahead Eagles 3-1)

Sparta 0-0 Roda
Roda 2-1 Sparta
(Roda 2-1)

NORTHERN IRELAND

Irish Football Association (IFA)

Address	20 Windsor Avenue	**President**	Jim Shaw
	GB-Belfast BT9 6EG	**Chief executive**	Patrick Nelson
Tel	+44 2890 669 458	**Media officer**	Sueann Harrison
Fax	+44 2890 667 620	**Year of formation**	1880
E-mail	info@irishfa.com	**National stadium**	Windsor Park, Belfast
Website	irishfa.com		(12,950)

0   50   100 km

0   50 miles

Coleraine ④

Ballymena ②

⑤
③ Belfast
Newtownards
⑥
⑬
Dungannon
⑦ Lisburn ⑨
⑧ ⑪
⑫ ⑩
Portadown Lurgan

① Ballinamallard

⑭ Warrenpoint

PREMIERSHIP CLUBS

① Ballinamallard United FC
② Ballymena United FC
③ Cliftonville FC
④ Coleraine FC
⑤ Crusaders FC
⑥ Donegal Celtic FC

⑦ Dungannon Swifts FC
⑧ Glenavon FC
⑨ Glentoran FC
⑩ Linfield FC
⑪ Lisburn Distillery FC
⑫ Portadown FC

PROMOTED CLUBS

⑬ Ards FC
⑭ Warrenpoint Town FC

KEY:

● – UEFA Champions League
● – UEFA Europa League
● – Promoted clubs
● – Relegated clubs

Cliftonville change the script

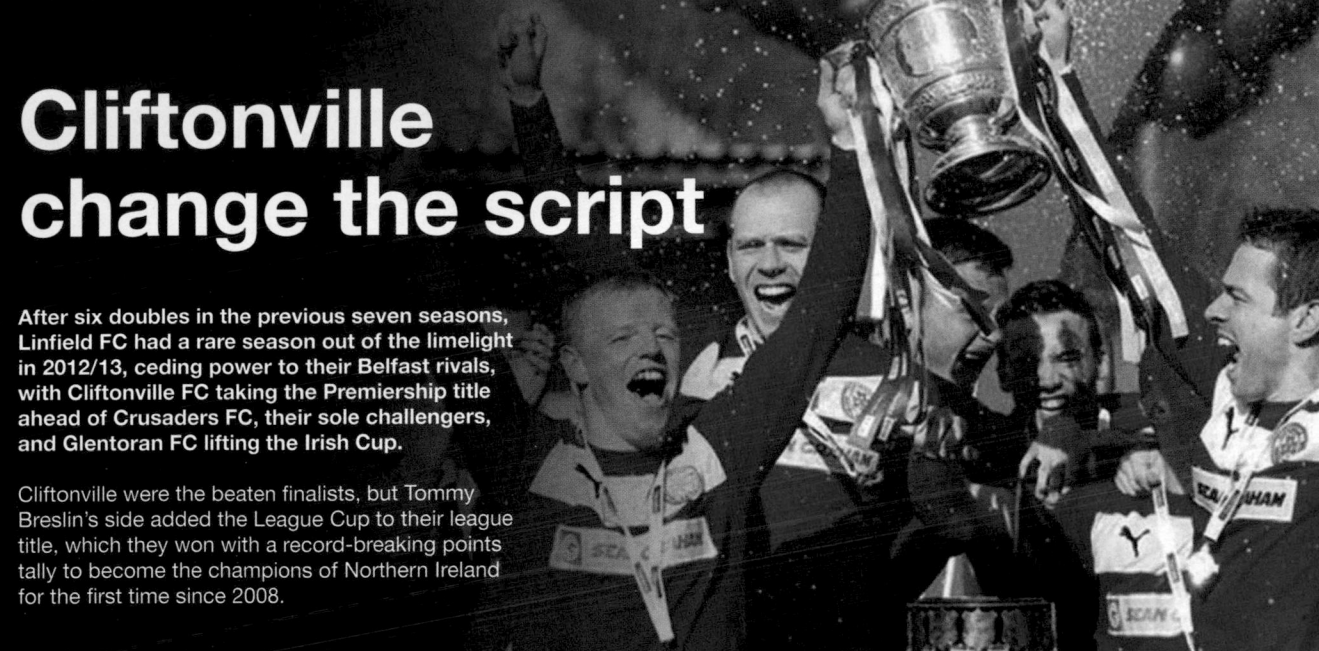

After six doubles in the previous seven seasons, Linfield FC had a rare season out of the limelight in 2012/13, ceding power to their Belfast rivals, with Cliftonville FC taking the Premiership title ahead of Crusaders FC, their sole challengers, and Glentoran FC lifting the Irish Cup.

Cliftonville were the beaten finalists, but Tommy Breslin's side added the League Cup to their league title, which they won with a record-breaking points tally to become the champions of Northern Ireland for the first time since 2008.

North Belfast club end 15-year wait for title

Serial champions Linfield 29 points adrift

Glentoran deny Cliftonville a domestic treble

Domestic league

Fittingly it was with a 3-2 home win over outgoing champions Linfield, thanks to two goals from the league's top scorer, Liam Boyce, and an added-time penalty from skipper George McMullan, that Cliftonville secured the Premiership title. It was the Reds' 11th successive victory, the tenth of those wins coming against North Belfast rivals Crusaders, 3-1 at their Solitude home. The Crues had been on an impressive run of their own leading up to that encounter, recording nine wins in ten games, but they had spent the whole season trying in vain to catch Cliftonville, and that result ended their chances of a fifth title for good.

Third in 2011/12, the first season with Breslin at the helm, Cliftonville were on top of the table for practically the entire campaign. They won 18 of their 20 matches at Solitude and scored 95 goals, 29 of them belonging to the irrepressible Boyce and another 17 to his attacking partner Joe Gormley. The oldest club in the country, it was only their fourth league title in 134 years, the first of them, back in 1906, having been shared.

Crusaders, led by Stephen Baxter, played entertaining football and finished 21 points clear in the runners-up spot, three

places higher than the previous season. There was pleasure too for the supporters of Premiership debutants Ballinamallard United FC, who surprised everyone by finishing fifth. In contrast, third-placed Linfield had a desperately disappointing campaign, three defeats in their first seven games denting confidence to such an extent that they were never able to challenge the top two. By the end of the season David Jeffrey's' team had won less than half of their matches.

Domestic cup

Having defeated Crusaders 4-0 to win the League Cup in January, Cliftonville returned to Windsor Park in early May bidding to complete the treble. They had defeated Crusaders yet again to win their semi-final, and were favourites to overcome a Glentoran side that had finished fourth in the league, but a first Irish Cup win since 1979 was not to be. The Glens, whose season had been overshadowed by financial problems, came from behind to win 3-1 after extra time, their 20-goal marksman in the league, Andrew Waterworth, proving the hero of the day with a decisive double. It was to be the 27-year-old's swansong performance as he left for Linfield in the summer.

Europe

As usual, Northern Ireland's interest in UEFA club competition did not last very long. The best and worst performance belonged to Portadown FC, who defeated FK Shkëndija 79 in the first qualifying round of the UEFA Europa League before going down 10-2 on aggregate to NK Slaven Koprivnica. Ports boss Ronnie McFall would become Europe's longest-serving active manager at the end of the season following the retirement of Manchester United FC's Sir Alex Ferguson.

National team

The appointment of a new manager, Michael O'Neill, did nothing to improve the fortunes of the Northern Ireland national side, whose failure to overcome any of their seven opponents in 2012/13 – including Luxembourg and Azerbaijan at home in FIFA World Cup qualifiers and Malta away in a friendly – stretched their winless run to two years.

The only bright spot was a gutsy and totally unexpected 1-1 draw away to UEFA EURO 2012 semi-finalists Portugal, which rather spoiled the occasion of Cristiano Ronaldo's 100th cap.

Domestic league: Premiership 2012/13 final table

		Pld	Home					Away					Total					Pts
			W	D	L	F	A	W	D	L	F	A	W	D	L	F	A	
1	**Cliftonville FC**	38	18	1	1	56	15	11	3	4	39	23	29	4	5	95	38	91
2	Crusaders FC	38	15	4	0	45	14	11	1	7	37	27	26	5	7	82	41	83
3	Linfield FC	38	10	4	5	34	20	7	7	5	35	28	17	11	10	69	48	62
4	Glentoran FC	38	9	6	4	37	21	6	6	7	26	23	15	12	11	63	44	57
5	Ballinamallard United FC	38	6	6	7	21	22	9	2	8	28	21	15	8	15	49	43	53
6	Coleraine FC	38	8	5	5	26	27	5	9	6	24	30	13	14	11	50	57	53
7	Portadown FC	38	9	5	5	32	27	6	5	8	23	28	15	10	13	55	55	55
8	Ballymena United FC	38	6	7	6	30	31	5	6	8	24	37	11	13	14	54	68	46
9	Glenavon FC	38	8	4	8	44	30	4	2	12	20	32	12	6	20	64	62	42
10	Dungannon Swifts FC	38	5	7	6	21	23	4	6	10	21	35	9	13	16	42	58	40
11	Donegal Celtic FC	38	5	3	11	16	39	1	6	12	16	41	6	9	23	32	80	27
12	Lisburn Distillery FC	38	2	4	13	12	41	2	3	14	17	49	4	7	27	29	90	19

NB League splits into top and bottom halves after 33 games, after which the clubs play exclusively against teams in their group

SEASON AT A GLANCE

EUROPEAN QUALIFICATION 2013/14

Champion: Cliftonville FC (second qualifying round)

CHAMPIONS LEAGUE

Cup winner: Glentoran FC (first qualifying round)
Crusaders FC (first qualifying round)
Linfield FC (first qualifying round)

EUROPA LEAGUE

Top scorer	Liam Boyce (Cliftonville), 29 goals
Relegated clubs	Lisburn Distillery FC, Donegal Celtic FC
Promoted clubs	Ards FC, Warrenpoint Town FC
Cup final	Glentoran FC 3-1 Cliftonville FC *(aet)*

PREMIERSHIP TEAM OF THE SEASON
(4-4-2)
Coach: Breslin *(Cliftonville)*

PLAYER OF THE SEASON
Liam Boyce
(Cliftonville FC)

The 22-year-old striker was the inspiration behind Cliftonville's charge to the Premiership title, scoring in 23 matches and topping the division's goal charts by a distance with 29 goals. His tally of 36 in all competitions broke an 81-year-old club record held by Norman McCaw, who struck 35 for the Reds during the 1931/32 campaign.

NEWCOMER OF THE SEASON
Conor Devlin
(Cliftonville FC)

Devlin was named young player of the year following an impressive debut season in the Premiership. The 21-year-old goalkeeper, who started his career as a trainee with Manchester United FC, kept 12 clean sheets in 34 league matches, conceding an average of less than a goal a game and making a major contribution to Cliftonville's league triumph.

Devlin *(Cliftonville)*

McMullan *(Cliftonville)* Smyth *(Cliftonville)* Magowan *(Crusaders)* McClean *(Crusaders)*

Caddell *(Crusaders)* Johnston *(Cliftonville)* Catney *(Cliftonville)* Heatley *(Crusaders)*

Boyce *(Cliftonville)* Gormley *(Cliftonville)*

NATIONAL TEAM

Home Kit   Away Kit

INTERNATIONAL TOURNAMENT APPEARANCES
FIFA World Cup (3) 1958 (qtr-finals), 1982 (2nd phase), 1986

TOP FIVE ALL-TIME CAPS
Pat Jennings (119); **David Healy (95);** Mal Donaghy (91), Sammy McIlroy & Maik Taylor (88)

TOP FIVE ALL-TIME GOALS
David Healy (36); Colin Clarke & Billy Gillespie (13); Gerry Armstrong, Joe Bambrick, Ian Dowie & Jimmy Quinn (12)

Results 2012/13

16/08/12	Finland	H	Belfast	3-3	*Ferguson (7), K Lafferty (19), Paterson (84p)*
07/09/12	Russia (WCQ)	A	Moscow	0-2	
11/09/12	Luxembourg (WCQ)	H	Belfast	1-1	*Shiels (14)*
16/10/12	Portugal (WCQ)	A	Porto	1-1	*McGinn (30)*
14/11/12	Azerbaijan (WCQ)	H	Belfast	1-1	*Healy (90+6)*
06/02/13	Malta	A	Ta' Qali	0-0	
26/03/13	Israel (WCQ)	H	Belfast	0-2	

Appearances 2012/13

Coach: Michael O'Neill	05/07/69		Fin	RUS	LUX	POR	AZE	Mlt	ISR	Caps	Goals
Roy Carroll	30/09/77	Olympiacos (GRE)	G46	G	G	G	G		G	26	-
Lee Hodson	02/10/91	Watford (ENG)	D84							9	-
Gareth McAuley	05/12/79	West Brom (ENG)	D	D	D		D	D	D	42	2
Craig Cathcart	06/02/89	Blackpool (ENG)	D	D		D	D82	s46		14	-
Ryan McGivern	08/01/90	Man. City (ENG) /Hibernian (SCO)	D		D	D				19	-
Chris Brunt	14/12/84	West Brom (ENG)	M46	M	M		s67	M	M	42	1
Chris Baird	25/02/82	Fulham (ENG)	M	M	M	M	M			61	-
Steven Davis	01/01/85	Southampton (ENG)	M	M	M	M	M	M	M	59	4
Shane Ferguson	12/07/91	Newcastle (ENG) /Birmingham (ENG)	M84		M74		M	M63	M73	8	1
Dean Shiels	01/02/85	Rangers (SCO)	A	s84	M83		M55			14	1
Kyle Lafferty	16/09/87	Sion (SUI)	A63	A	A	A	A			35	9
Lee Camp	22/08/84	Nottingham Forest (ENG)	s46							9	-
Jamie Ward	12/05/86	Derby (ENG)	s46	M76	s74					4	-
Martin Paterson	10/05/87	Burnley (ENG)	s63						A84	15	1
Josh Carson	03/06/93	Ipswich (ENG)	s84							4	-
Oliver Norwood	12/04/91	Huddersfield (ENG)	s84		s83	M				9	-
Aaron Hughes	08/11/79	Fulham (ENG)		D	D	D	D	D	D	86	1
Jonny Evans	03/01/88	Man. United (ENG)		D	D	D		D46	D	34	1
Corry Evans	30/07/90	Hull (ENG)		M84		M				18	1
Andrew Little	12/05/89	Rangers (SCO)		s76						9	-
Niall McGinn	20/07/87	Aberdeen (SCO)				M	M67	M	M	22	1
Daniel Lafferty	18/05/89	Burnley (ENG)					D	D	D	4	-
Paddy McCourt	16/12/83	Celtic (SCO)					s55	s72	s78	13	2
David Healy	05/08/79	Bury (ENG)					s82		s84	95	36
Alan Mannus	19/05/82	St Johnstone (SCO)						G		5	-
Alex Bruce	28/09/84	Hull (ENG)						M72		1	-
Will Grigg	03/07/91	Walsall (ENG)						A86		2	-
Billy McKay	22/10/88	Inverness (SCO)						s63		1	-
Josh Magennis	15/08/90	Aberdeen (SCO)						s86	s73	5	-
Sammy Clingan	13/01/84	Kilmarnock (SCO)							M78	34	-

European club competitions 2012/13

LINFIELD FC

First qualifying round - B36 Tórshavn (FRO)
H 0-0
Ross Glendinning, Douglas, Curran, Thompson (Tipton 75), Fordyce, Garrett, Ervin, Mulgrew, Watson (Armstrong 46), McCaul (Carvill 65), McAllister. Coach: David Jeffrey (NIR)
A 0-0 *(aet; 4-3 on pens)*
Ross Glendinning, Douglas, Armstrong, Curran, Thompson (Browne 77), Carvill, Fordyce (McCaul 65), Garrett, Ervin, Mulgrew, McAllister. Coach: David Jeffrey (NIR)

Second qualifying round - AEL Limassol FC (CYP)
A 0-3
Blayney, Douglas, Armstrong, Curran, Thompson (McCaul 73), Carvill, Burns, Garrett, Ervin, Mulgrew (Henderson 77), McAllister (Browne 78). Coach: David Jeffrey (NIR)
H 0-0
Blayney, Douglas, Armstrong, Murphy, Henderson (Carvill 78), Thompson, Burns, Garrett (Fordyce 83), Ervin, Mulgrew, McAllister (Browne 84). Coach: David Jeffrey (NIR)

PORTADOWN FC

First qualifying round - FK Shkëndija 79 (MKD)
A 0-0
Miskelly, Mackle, Redman, Breen, Tomelty (Lecky 30), Murray, Braniff, McNeill, Casement, Gartland, McCafferty. Coach: Ronnie McFall (NIR)
H 2-1 *Lecky (58), Redman (80)*
Miskelly, Mackle (O'Hara 84), Redman, Breen, Murray, Braniff, McNeill, Casement, Lecky, Gartland, McCafferty. Coach: Ronnie McFall (NIR)

Second qualifying round - NK Slaven Koprivnica (CRO)
A 0-6
McArdle, Mackle, Redman, Breen (Andrew Burns 78), Murray (O'Hara 64), Braniff, McNeill, Casement, Lecky, Gartland, McCafferty. Coach: Ronnie McFall (NIR)
H 2-4 *Lecky (45+2), McCafferty (67p)*
Miskelly, Mackle, Redman, O'Hara, Breen, Braniff, McNeill, Casement, Lecky (Murray 81), Gartland, McCafferty. Coach: Ronnie McFall (NIR)

CLIFTONVILLE FC

First qualifying round - Kalmar FF (SWE)
H 1-0 *Boyce (71)*
Brown, McGovern, R Scannell, Caldwell (O'Carroll 69), McMullan, Garrett (Lynch 90), Donnelly, Smyth, Catney, Gormley (Boyce 69), Cosgrove. Coach: Tommy Breslin (NIR)
A 0-4
Brown, McGovern, R Scannell, Caldwell, McMullan, Garrett (Boyce 59), Donnelly (Gormley 78), O'Carroll (C Scannell 65), Smyth, Catney, Cosgrove. Coach: Tommy Breslin (NIR)

CRUSADERS FC

First qualifying round - Rosenborg BK (NOR)
H 0-3
O'Neill, McKeown, McBride, Leeman, Magowan, Adamson, Rainey (Snoddy 86), Caddell, Watson, Owens (McAllister 83), Heatley (McClean 72). Coach: Charlie Murphy (NIR)
Red card: Caddell 74
A 0-1
O'Neill, Magowan, Coates, Adamson, Rainey, McCutcheon (McAllister 76), Watson (Snoddy 81), McClean, Owens, Gibson, Heatley (Gargan 75). Coach: Stephen Baxter (NIR)

Domestic league club-by-club

BALLINAMALLARD UNITED FC

Manager: Whitey Anderson
1975 • Ferney Park (2,000) • no website

2012

11/08	Dungannon	h	2-2	Crawford, Curran
18/08	Distillery	a	5-0	McCartney 3, Curran, Crawford
25/08	Ballymena	h	0-0	
01/09	Crusaders	a	1-2	Stafford
04/09	Glentoran	h	1-4	Stafford
08/09	Cliftonville	a	1-0	McCartney
15/09	Portadown	h	2-0	Campbell, Curran
22/09	Donegal Celtic	a	3-0	Campbell, Crawford, Martin
28/09	Glenavon	h	2-1	Campbell, McCartney
06/10	Linfield	a	3-1	Campbell, Curran, Martin
13/10	Coleraine	h	1-0	Campbell
20/10	Crusaders	h	0-2	
27/10	Ballymena	a	1-1	Feeney
02/11	Distillery	h	2-0	Feeney, Curran
10/11	Portadown	a	1-2	Crawford
16/11	Donegal Celtic	h	0-0	
24/11	Glenavon	a	1-0	Kee
01/12	Glentoran	a	1-2	McKenna
08/12	Linfield	h	1-3	Crawford
15/12	Cliftonville	h	1-3	Kee
26/12	Dungannon	a	1-0	Hill
29/12	Crusaders	h	1-3	Kee

2013

01/01	Distillery	a	2-0	McCartney, Kee
04/01	Ballymena	h	0-3	
15/01	Coleraine	a	5-1	McCartney (p), og (Ogilby), Curran 2, Campbell
19/01	Glenavon	h	2-1	Feeney 2, Carters
25/01	Portadown	h	0-1	
02/02	Coleraine	a	0-0	
16/02	Donegal Celtic	a	0-1	
23/02	Cliftonville	h	0-1	
09/03	Dungannon	h	4-0	McCartney 3, Crawford
16/03	Glentoran	a	0-3	
30/03	Linfield	h	0-0	
02/04	Coleraine	h	1-1	Stafford
13/04	Glentoran	h	0-0	
16/04	Crusaders	a	1-3	Sheridan
20/04	Linfield	a	1-0	Campbell
27/04	Cliftonville	a	1-2	Campbell

No	Name	Nat	DoB	Pos	Aps	(s)	Gls
20	Ryan Campbell		08/07/81	A	30	(7)	8
4	Leon Carters		23/07/84	D	33		1
15	Nathan Cashel		18/12/90	M		(6)	
10	Andy Crawford		06/08/77	A	24	(10)	6
7	Chris Curran		05/01/91	M	36	(2)	7
27	John Currie		10/09/93	M	2		
9	Steve Feeney	IRL	16/05/84	D	20	(11)	4
15	Ciaran Harper		31/10/91	M	3		
22	Michael Haveron		16/06/92	A		(2)	
21	Craig Hill		01/07/91	D	17	(2)	1
8	Stuart Hutchinson		10/05/91	M	11	(4)	
5	David Kee		09/08/88	A	33		4
3	Daniel Keohane	IRL	30/11/88	D	35	(1)	
12	Gareth Liggett		22/05/79	D	2		
19	Liam Martin		23/01/94	M	6	(18)	2
11	Jason McCartney	IRL	06/09/86	M	28	(4)	10
2	Mark McConkey		14/06/82	M	15	(1)	
13	James McGrath		19/04/88	G	2		
14	James McKenna		20/07/84	M	21	(10)	1
29	Colm McLaughlin	IRL	01/08/93	M	1		
8	Duwayne McManus		20/01/87	M	5	(8)	
18	Conor O'Grady	IRL	27/05/80	M	15	(11)	
25	Gary Phair		24/01/94	D	7		
1	Alvin Rouse	BRB	07/01/80	G	36		
29	Stephen Sheridan		30/09/88	A	1	(10)	1
5	Mark Stafford		20/08/87	D	35		3

BALLYMENA UNITED FC

Manager: Glenn Ferguson
1928 • The Showgrounds (4,390) •
ballymenaunitedfc.com
Major honours
Irish Cup (6) 1929, 1940, 1958, 1981, 1984, 1989

2012

11/08	Linfield	h	2-0	J Davidson 2
18/08	Crusaders	a	0-0	
25/08	Ballinamallard	a	0-0	
31/08	Distillery	h	2-0	og (Harkness), Lowry
04/09	Cliftonville	a	1-2	Thompson
08/09	Donegal Celtic	h	3-3	Jenkins (p), Taylor, J Davidson
15/09	Dungannon	h	1-1	Cushley
22/09	Coleraine	a	1-4	Thompson
28/09	Glentoran	h	1-1	Thompson
06/10	Portadown	h	2-2	Surgenor, Teggart (p)
13/10	Glenavon	h	2-1	og (McCashin), Teggart
20/10	Distillery	a	4-0	J Davidson, Cushley, McCabe 2
27/10	Ballinamallard	h	1-1	Teggart (p)
02/11	Dungannon	a	3-1	A Davidson, J Davidson, Surgenor
10/11	Crusaders	h	2-1	A Davidson, Costello
17/11	Cliftonville	h	0-8	
24/11	Linfield	a	1-2	Stewart
01/12	Donegal Celtic	a	0-1	
08/12	Portadown	h	1-2	Rodgers
15/12	Glenavon	a	1-4	J Davidson
26/12	Coleraine	h	0-2	
29/12	Distillery	h	3-3	Taggart, Cushley, Surgenor

2013

04/01	Ballinamallard	a	3-0	Rodgers, Dolan, Cushley
15/01	Glentoran	a	2-1	Teggart (p), Kane
19/01	Crusaders	a	1-3	Teggart
29/01	Dungannon	a	0-0	
02/02	Linfield	a	2-2	Cushley 2
16/02	Coleraine	a	0-1	
23/02	Glenavon	a	0-7	
02/03	Donegal Celtic	h	2-2	Cushley, Kane
09/03	Glentoran	h	0-0	
16/03	Portadown	a	0-0	
30/03	Cliftonville	a	0-5	
02/04	Portadown	h	6-1	Cushley 3, Surgenor, Liggett 2
13/04	Donegal Celtic	a	4-1	og (M Burns), Liggett, Dolan, Teggart
16/04	Distillery	a	2-0	Liggett, A Davidson
20/04	Glenavon	h	0-2	
27/04	Dungannon	h	1-2	Taylor

No	Name	Nat	DoB	Pos	Aps	(s)	Gls
18	Stuart Addis		05/07/79	G	4		
	Jordan Baker		05/09/88	A		(2)	
25	William Bingham		27/04/93	M	2	(1)	
3	Ross Black		10/05/88	D	16		
	James Costello		09/06/86	A	5	(4)	1
11	David Cushley		22/07/89	M	35	(1)	10
19	Alan Davidson	SCO	19/03/88	M	11	(12)	3
23	Jamie Davidson		30/12/93	A	14	(5)	6
14	Shane Dolan		06/02/88	M	10	(1)	2
22	Peter Duffin		23/03/94	A	1	(6)	
5	Denver Gage		03/05/87	D		(1)	
10	Allan Jenkins	SCO	07/10/81	M	25	(2)	1
2	Tony Kane		29/08/87	M	30	(3)	2
9	Gary Liggett		28/09/87	A	12	(3)	4
24	Neil Lowry		09/08/93	A	3	(12)	1
27	Shaun Maher	IRL	10/06/78	D	5	(2)	
26	James McCabe		19/02/83	A	6	(11)	2
25	Mark McCullagh		10/05/87	D	7		
16	David Munster		24/02/79	M	31	(2)	
1	Dwayne Nelson		05/09/84	G	34		
25	Corey Price		23/02/94	D		(1)	
20	Chris Rodgers		03/01/91	A	10	(4)	2
17	Michael Ruddy		05/08/93	D	15	(1)	
6	Aaron Stewart		03/12/89	D	30	(1)	1
15	Mark Surgenor		19/12/85	D	14	(12)	4
8	Gavin Taggart		15/11/84	M	21	(4)	1
21	Johnny Taylor		30/06/88	D	12	(4)	2
12	Alan Teggart		24/11/86	A	26	(5)	6
7	Gary Thompson		26/05/90	A	31	(1)	3
4	Richard Vauls		22/09/90	D	8	(2)	

CLIFTONVILLE FC

Manager: Tommy Breslin
1879 • Solitude (2,552) • cliftonvillefc.net
Major honours
Irish League (4) 1906 (shared), 1910, 1998, 2013;
Irish Cup (8) 1883, 1888, 1897, 1900, 1901, 1907, 1909, 1979

2012

11/08	Glenavon	h	2-1	Boyce, C Scannell
18/08	Dungannon	a	1-1	og (McMinn)
25/08	Glentoran	h	1-1	Gormley
01/09	Coleraine	a	5-1	Gormley, Boyce, Garrett, Johnston, O'Carroll
04/09	Ballymena	h	2-1	Donnelly, Boyce
08/09	Ballinamallard	h	0-1	
15/09	Linfield	a	2-1	Boyce, McMullan
22/09	Portadown	h	3-2	Lynch, Boyce, Gormley
28/09	Donegal Celtic	h	3-1	McMullan (p), og (L Bradley), Gormley
06/10	Distillery	a	2-1	Boyce, Holland
13/10	Crusaders	a	1-3	Boyce
20/10	Dungannon	h	4-1	Gormley, Boyce 2, Donnelly
27/10	Glenavon	a	2-0	McMullan (p), og (McCallion)
03/11	Glentoran	a	1-1	Boyce
10/11	Linfield	h	3-0	Caldwell, Boyce, og (Watson)
17/11	Ballymena	a	8-0	Garrett 2, McMullan, Boyce 2, Knowles, Gormley, O'Carroll
26/11	Distillery	h	4-0	Gormley, Boyce, Johnston, Knowles
01/12	Portadown	a	3-3	Gormley, Johnston, McMullan (p)
08/12	Coleraine	h	3-1	Boyce, Gormley 2
15/12	Ballinamallard	a	3-1	Smyth 2, Garrett
20/12	Crusaders	h	1-0	Gormley
29/12	Dungannon	h	2-0	Boyce, McMullan (p)

2013

01/01	Linfield	a	1-3	Boyce
07/01	Glentoran	h	4-1	McMullan 2, Boyce, Cosgrove
15/01	Donegal Celtic	a	1-0	Garrett
19/01	Portadown	a	3-1	O'Carroll, Gormley, Boyce
02/02	Distillery	h	4-0	Gormley 3, Garrett
05/02	Coleraine	h	5-0	og (Canning), Boyce, Gormley, Garrett, Seydak
23/02	Ballinamallard	a	1-0	Gormley
09/03	Donegal Celtic	h	2-1	Garrett, Caldwell
16/03	Glenavon	a	3-1	Caldwell 2, Boyce
30/03	Ballymena	h	5-0	Boyce 2, R Scannell, Garrett, Caldwell
02/04	Crusaders	h	3-1	Boyce 2, Johnston
13/04	Linfield	h	3-2	Boyce 2, McMullan (p)
16/04	Glentoran	a	0-3	
20/04	Coleraine	a	2-0	Boyce 2 (1p)
22/04	Crusaders	a	0-3	
27/04	Ballinamallard	h	2-1	O'Carroll, Caldwell

No	Name	Nat	DoB	Pos	Aps	(s)	Gls
27	Liam Boyce		08/04/91	A	36		29
1	Ryan Brown		27/11/80	G	4		
7	Ciaran Caldwell		10/10/89	M	11	(6)	6
17	Ryan Catney		17/02/87	M	30	(1)	
23	Tomas Cosgrove		11/12/92	M	10	(9)	1
12	Conor Devlin		23/09/91	G	34		
11	Martin Donnelly		28/08/88	M	24	(12)	2
10	Stephen Garrett		13/04/87	A	27	(10)	9
19	Joe Gormley		26/11/89	A	25	(6)	17
5	Barry Holland		10/05/84	D	13		1
4	Barry Johnston		28/10/79	M	27	(7)	4
26	James Knowles		06/04/93	M	10	(11)	2
21	Jody Lynch		23/07/89	M	7	(6)	1
14	Ryan McCloskey		26/02/90	D		(1)	
30	Anthony McGonnell		12/06/91	M	1		
2	Jamie McGovern		29/05/89	D	37		
31	Conor McGrandles		12/01/94	M		(1)	
8	George McMullan		04/08/81	D	33		9
10	Jonathan McMurray		19/09/94	A	1		
25	Dermot McVeigh		24/07/90	D	3		
14	Diarmuid O'Carroll	IRL	16/03/87	A	12	(14)	4
20	Anthony O'Hanlon		02/07/94	M		(2)	
32	Gerard Reynolds		01/05/95	D	1	(2)	
9	Chris Scannell		07/09/77	A		(3)	1
3	Ronan Scannell		11/05/79	D	24	(2)	1
15	Eamon Seydak		25/02/86	D	14	(10)	1
16	Marc Smyth	SCO	27/12/82	D	32		2
22	Darren Stuart		31/03/92	M	2	(3)	
18	Emmett Templeton		29/10/92	D		(1)	

COLERAINE FC

Manager: Oran Kearney
1927 • The Showgrounds (3,960) • colerainefc.com
Major honours
Irish League (1) 1974;
Irish Cup (5) 1965, 1972, 1975, 1977, 2003

2012

11/08	Crusaders	h	3-1	Allen, Owens, Ogilby
18/08	Linfield	a	0-0	
24/08	Portadown	a	4-3	Boyce, Canning, Allen, Gillan
01/09	Cliftonville	h	1-5	Owens
04/09	Donegal Celtic	a	3-1	McVey 2, Allen
08/09	Distillery	h	2-1	Ogilby, Lowry
15/09	Glentoran	a	0-0	
22/09	Ballymena	h	4-1	Boyce, Hegarty, Scullion, Allen
29/09	Dungannon	h	2-0	Lowry, Owens
06/10	Glenavon	a	1-1	Lowry
13/10	Ballinamallard	a	0-1	
22/10	Linfield	h	3-2	Boyce, Allen, Lowry
27/10	Crusaders	a	1-1	Allen
03/11	Portadown	h	1-1	Allen
10/11	Distillery	a	1-1	Lowry
17/11	Dungannon	a	1-1	Allen
24/11	Glentoran	h	1-0	Jennings
01/12	Glenavon	h	0-2	
08/12	Cliftonville	a	1-3	Allen
15/12	Donegal Celtic	h	2-1	Allen, Boyce
26/12	Ballymena	a	2-0	Scullion, Allen
29/12	Portadown	a	0-2	

2013

01/01	Glentoran	h	1-1	Jennings
05/01	Linfield	a	2-5	Allen, Harkin
15/01	Ballinamallard	h	1-5	Scullion
19/01	Distillery	h	3-1	Lowry, Harkin, McVey
02/02	Ballinamallard	h	0-0	
05/02	Cliftonville	a	0-5	
16/02	Ballymena	h	1-0	Allen
23/02	Donegal Celtic	h	0-0	
09/03	Crusaders	h	1-3	Allen
16/03	Dungannon	a	3-1	Tommons, Lowry, Allen
30/03	Glenavon	a	1-1	Tommons
02/04	Ballinamallard	a	1-1	Allen
13/04	Crusaders	a	1-2	Scullion
16/04	Linfield	h	1-1	Allen
20/04	Cliftonville	h	0-2	
27/04	Glentoran	a	1-1	Lowry

No	Name	Nat	DoB	Pos	Aps	(s)	Gls
9	Curtis Allen		22/02/88	A	35	(2)	17
2	Howard Beverland		30/03/90	D	35		
19	Darren Boyce		25/01/86	A	15	(6)	4
23	Aaron Boyd		12/02/91	A		(9)	
21	Joel Bradley		16/02/95	A	8	(8)	
12	Aaron Canning		07/03/92	D	34	(1)	1
18	Ciaran Clarke		28/01/93	M	3	(1)	
22	Lee Colligan		21/11/80	D	8	(1)	
1	Gavin Cullen		21/11/80	G	5		
20	Michael Doherty		19/10/83	G	32		
17	Mark Gillan		17/01/90	A	1	(8)	1
10	Ruairi Harkin	IRL	11/10/89	M	34	(3)	2
4	Michael Hegarty		09/12/83	M	30	(5)	1
26	Hugo Batista	POR	22/01/89	A	1		
15	Shane Jennings		21/01/92	A	6	(7)	2
8	Stephen Lowry		14/10/86	M	37		8
11	Ryan McIlmoyle		12/12/84	M	37		
25	Stuart McMullan		30/05/89	D	6	(1)	
5	Kyle McVey		07/07/86	D	16	(1)	3
26	Craig Moore		28/12/84	M	1	(3)	
6	David Ogilby		02/06/84	D	25	(1)	2
24	Paul Owens		11/11/82	M	10	(14)	3
7	David Scullion		27/04/84	A	19	(6)	4
30	Greg Shannon		15/02/81	G	1		
27	Jamie Tomelty		16/09/83	M	11	(1)	
16	Gareth Tommons		18/05/89	M	5	(1)	2
14	John Watt		20/03/86	D	3	(4)	

CRUSADERS FC

Manager: Stephen Baxter
1898 • Seaview (3,330) • crusadersfc.com
Major honours
Irish League (4) 1973, 1976, 1995, 1997;
Irish Cup (3) 1967, 1968, 2009

2012

11/08	Coleraine	a	1-3	Rainey
18/08	Ballymena	h	0-0	
25/08	Distillery	a	3-1	McMaster, Adamson, Heatley
01/09	Ballinamallard	h	2-1	Adamson 2
04/09	Linfield	a	2-1	McCutcheon (p), Caddell
08/09	Glenavon	a	0-1	
15/09	Donegal Celtic	h	2-0	Morrow, McCutcheon (p)
22/09	Dungannon	a	0-2	
28/09	Portadown	a	0-1	
06/10	Glentoran	h	2-0	Owens 2
13/10	Cliftonville	h	3-1	Adamson, Owens, McCutcheon
20/10	Ballinamallard	a	2-0	Heatley 2
27/10	Coleraine	h	1-1	Owens
03/11	Glenavon	h	5-1	Adamson 2, McCutcheon, Owens, Heatley
10/11	Ballymena	a	1-2	McCutcheon
17/11	Portadown	h	2-0	Owens, Adamson
24/11	Donegal Celtic	a	5-2	Heatley, Adamson 3, McKeown
01/12	Dungannon	h	2-1	Owens 2
08/12	Glentoran	a	1-1	Coates
15/12	Distillery	h	3-1	Owens, Coates, Caddell
22/12	Linfield	h	2-2	McCutcheon, Rainey
26/12	Cliftonville	a	0-1	
29/12	Ballinamallard	a	3-1	McCutcheon, Owens, Caddell

2013

01/01	Portadown	h	1-0	McKeown
05/01	Glenavon	a	3-2	McCutcheon, Heatley, Caddell
19/01	Ballymena	h	5-1	McCutcheon 2, Heatley, Morrow, Coates
02/02	Donegal Celtic	a	3-0	Rainey 2, Adamson
23/02	Dungannon	h	1-1	Owens
09/03	Coleraine	a	3-1	McAllister 2, Adamson
18/03	Linfield	h	3-0	Owens 2, Caddell
27/03	Distillery	a	2-0	Rainey 2
30/03	Glentoran	h	5-4	Morrow, Adamson 2, Heatley, McMaster
02/04	Cliftonville	a	1-3	Adamson
13/04	Coleraine	h	2-1	Rainey, Snoddy
16/04	Ballinamallard	h	3-1	Owens 2, McCutcheon
20/04	Glentoran	a	3-2	McCutcheon, Caddell, McAllister
22/04	Cliftonville	h	3-0	Coates 2 (1p), Owens
27/04	Linfield	a	2-1	McCutcheon, Rainey

No	Name	Nat	DoB	Pos	Aps	(s)	Gls
9	Timmy Adamson		05/01/83	A	29	(2)	15
12	Declan Caddell		13/04/88	M	29	(4)	6
6	Colin Coates		26/10/85	D	18	(4)	5
	Ciaran Gargan		09/02/86	M	1		
20	David Gibson		15/02/90	D	7	(5)	
15	Aaron Harris		04/01/91	M		(1)	
22	Paul Heatley		30/06/87	A	27	(1)	8
28	David Johnston		26/12/92	M	1		
38	Matthew King		03/02/92	D	4		
1	Yohann Lacroix	FRA	01/02/85	G	7		
4	Paul Leeman		21/01/78	D	16	(2)	
5	David Magowan		04/10/83	D	32	(2)	
7	Eamon McAllister		19/11/87	M	6	(2)	3
3	Stephen McBride		06/04/83	D	5	(3)	
57	Craig McClean		06/07/85	D	33	(3)	
21	Jack McCrea		20/05/94	G	1		
27	Ryan McCready		23/03/94	M		(3)	
14	Gary McCutcheon	SCO	08/10/78	A	31	(2)	13
2	Gareth McKeown		14/07/83	D	20		2
15	David McMaster		29/12/88	M	12	(13)	2
26	James Mitchell		15/07/94	M		(1)	
8	Chris Morrow		20/09/85	M	17	(6)	3
30	Sean O'Neill		11/04/88	G	30		
18	Jordan Owens		09/07/89	A	25	(8)	16
10	David Rainey		06/04/76	A	8	(19)	8
11	Joshua Robinson		30/06/93	D	31		
19	Matthew Snoddy		02/06/93	M	11	(9)	1
16	Aidan Watson		19/08/86	M	17	(3)	

DONEGAL CELTIC FC

Manager: Stephen Small;
(11/10/12) (Declan McGreevey);
(21/10/12) Pat McAllister
1970 • Suffolk Road (3,000) • no website

2012

11/08	Glentoran	a	1-3	Miskimmin
18/08	Portadown	h	1-1	Miskimmin
24/08	Linfield	a	0-4	
31/08	Glenavon	h	1-1	Miskimmin
04/09	Coleraine	h	1-3	Miskimmin
08/09	Ballymena	a	3-3	Miskimmin, Deans, S Cleary
15/09	Crusaders	a	0-2	
22/09	Ballinamallard	h	0-3	
28/09	Cliftonville	a	1-3	Miskimmin
06/10	Dungannon	h	1-1	McCann
13/10	Distillery	h	0-3	
20/10	Portadown	a	0-1	
27/10	Glentoran	h	2-1	Dolan 2
03/11	Linfield	h	0-3	
10/11	Glenavon	a	2-4	McAllister, McVeigh
16/11	Ballinamallard	a	0-0	
24/11	Crusaders	h	2-5	S Cleary, McCann
01/12	Ballymena	h	1-0	Dolan
08/12	Dungannon	a	0-3	
15/12	Coleraine	a	1-2	Gargan
26/12	Distillery	a	3-3	Deans, McVeigh, Gargan
29/12	Glentoran	a	0-5	

2013

01/01	Glenavon	h	1-0	McVeigh
05/01	Portadown	a	0-1	
15/01	Cliftonville	h	0-1	
29/01	Linfield	h	1-4	Miskimmin
02/02	Crusaders	h	0-3	
16/02	Ballinamallard	h	1-0	C Burns
23/02	Coleraine	a	0-0	
02/03	Ballymena	a	2-2	K Hughes, S Cleary (p)
09/03	Cliftonville	a	1-2	Deans
16/03	Distillery	h	0-3	(w/o; original result 2-1 O'Neill, S Cleary)
30/03	Dungannon	a	0-0	
02/04	Distillery	a	1-0	O'Neill
13/04	Ballymena	h	1-4	S Cleary
16/04	Dungannon	h	2-1	M Burns, K Hughes
20/04	Portadown	h	1-2	K Hughes
27/04	Glenavon	a	1-3	McVeigh (p)

No	Name	Nat	DoB	Pos	Aps	(s)	Gls
2	Jason Bannon		07/09/89	D	3	(2)	
8	Liam Bradley		21/09/81	M	3		
4	Paul Bradley		04/10/79	D	17	(1)	
5	Ciaran Burns		14/06/87	D	14		1
24	Mark Burns		16/01/88	M	28	(4)	1
23	Ciaran Carson		14/06/87	M	5	(1)	
21	Andrew Cleary		06/04/86	D	3	(3)	
17	Sean Cleary		26/02/83	M	24	(1)	5
23	Liam Conlon		08/04/95	A	1	(1)	
1	John Connolly	IRL	01/02/77	G	31		
6	Ryan Deans		14/09/89	M	25	(6)	3
19	Pearse Devine		23/10/90	M	11	(5)	
	Shane Dolan		06/02/88	M	8	(7)	3
16	Conor Downey		12/03/82	M	29	(2)	
14	Harry Dyer		03/04/92	M	1		
18	Ciaran Gargan		09/02/86	M	22	(5)	2
12	James Haughey		16/06/91	M	1	(1)	
13	Eamon Hughes		18/08/92	M	17	(1)	
10	Kevin Hughes		23/11/88	A	6	(6)	3
7	Kevin Keegan		01/01/80	M	27	(2)	
5	Anto Lagan		13/01/83	A	6	(3)	
12	Kevin Lynch		23/09/91	A		(2)	
15	David McAllister		01/09/94	D	3	(12)	1
8	Paul McAreavey		03/12/80	M	9	(3)	
25	Peter McCann		18/01/81	D	13	(4)	2
22	Patrick McIlkenny		03/12/92	M		(4)	
2	Darren McNamee		17/10/85	D	13	(4)	
3	Pat McShane		28/11/74	D	32		
11	Paul McVeigh		11/03/77	A	14	(9)	4
9	Mark Miskimmin		11/06/88	A	30	(3)	7
20	Niall Murphy		14/05/91	G	1		
12	Stephen O'Neill		31/12/84	A	9		2
21	Joe Todd		03/05/93	M	4	(5)	

DUNGANNON SWIFTS FC
Manager: Darren Murphy
1949 • Stangmore Park (2,154) • dungannonswifts.co.uk

2012
11/08	Ballinamallard	a	2-2	Harpur, Topley
18/08	Cliftonville	h	1-1	S O'Neill
24/08	Glenavon	a	1-0	S Friars
31/08	Portadown	h	1-1	Cahoon
04/09	Distillery	a	1-2	S Friars
08/09	Glentoran	h	1-0	S O'Neill
15/09	Ballymena	a	1-1	Cahoon
22/09	Crusaders	h	2-0	E Friars, Cahoon
29/09	Coleraine	a	0-2	
06/10	Donegal Celtic	a	1-1	S Lavery
13/10	Linfield	h	1-1	Cahoon
20/10	Cliftonville	a	1-4	S O'Neill
27/10	Distillery	h	1-1	Harpur
02/11	Ballymena	h	1-3	Cahoon
10/11	Glentoran	a	1-2	Cahoon
17/11	Coleraine	h	1-1	Cahoon
24/11	Portadown	a	1-1	Cahoon
01/12	Crusaders	a	1-2	Cahoon
08/12	Donegal Celtic	h	3-0	Gawley, Topley, Cahoon (p)
15/12	Linfield	a	1-2	S Lavery
26/12	Ballinamallard	h	0-1	
29/12	Cliftonville	a	0-2	

2013
05/01	Distillery	h	1-0	E Friars
15/01	Glenavon	h	2-1	Hazley 2
29/01	Ballymena	h	0-0	
02/02	Glenavon	a	1-3	Costello
09/02	Linfield	h	1-4	Harpur
16/02	Portadown	a	2-0	Topley, og (Ramsey)
23/02	Crusaders	a	1-1	Gawley
09/03	Ballinamallard	a	0-4	
16/03	Coleraine	a	1-3	Hazley
19/03	Glentoran	a	3-2	Costello 2, McKerr
30/03	Donegal Celtic	h	0-0	
02/04	Glenavon	h	2-3	Hazley (p), Costello
13/04	Portadown	a	1-1	S Lavery
16/04	Donegal Celtic	a	1-2	og (McShane)
20/04	Distillery	a	1-0	Costello
27/04	Ballymena	a	2-1	P Lavery, Devlin

No	Name	Nat	DoB	Pos	Aps	(s)	Gls
25	Francis Brennan		11/09/91	M	18	(2)	
15	Joshua Cahoon		26/06/91	A	10	(13)	10
12	James Costello		09/06/86	A	12	(1)	5
21	Jonathan Curran		26/10/86	G	16		
9	Rian Devlin		03/04/95	M	1		1
10	Jamie Douglas		04/07/92	M	3	(2)	
6	Terry Fitzpatrick		23/03/82	M	18	(6)	
31	Emmett Friars		14/09/85	D	28	(1)	2
29	Sean Friars		15/05/79	M	5	(6)	2
30	John-Paul Gallagher		28/07/82	D	1		
11	Neal Gawley		20/02/86	M	17	(2)	2
27	Jamie Glackin		16/02/95	M	2	(5)	
19	Cameron Grieve		22/12/81	A	28		
26	Ryan Harpur		01/12/88	M	19	(4)	3
8	Matt Hazley		25/02/87	M	32		4
18	Grant Hutchinson		11/11/89	M	21	(4)	
7	Chris Lavery		20/01/91	A	15	(10)	
17	Patrick J. Lavery		03/05/89	M	4	(12)	1
20	Stefan Lavery		20/07/93	A	18	(8)	3
	Kris Lowe		06/01/96	M		(1)	
11	Daryl Magee		07/08/94	M		(2)	
16	Michael McKerr		23/02/90	D	20	(4)	1
5	Adam McMinn		15/01/84	D	24	(1)	
4	Johnny Montgomery		06/04/74	D	22	(1)	
1	Niall Morgan		17/07/91	G			
3	Darren Murphy		23/01/75	M	1	(1)	
14	Tuda Murphy	CAY	04/11/80	G	4		
22	Ryan O'Neill		14/01/90	D	29	(3)	
9	Stephen O'Neill		31/12/84	A	14	(6)	3
2	Jarlath O'Rourke		13/02/95	D	2		
24	Johnny Topley		12/07/80	M	16	(4)	3

GLENAVON FC
Manager: Gary Hamilton
1889 • Mourneview Park (4,160) • glenavonfc.com
Major honours
Irish League (3) 1952, 1957, 1960;
Irish Cup (5) 1957, 1959, 1961, 1992, 1997

2012
11/08	Cliftonville	a	1-2	McCashin
18/08	Glentoran	h	1-1	Burrows
24/08	Dungannon	h	0-1	
31/08	Donegal Celtic	a	1-1	Bates
03/09	Portadown	h	2-2	Doherty, og (Miskelly)
08/09	Crusaders	h	1-0	Bates
15/09	Distillery	h	1-0	Doherty
22/09	Linfield	h	2-3	Doherty, Hamilton
28/09	Ballinamallard	a	1-2	Neill (p)
06/10	Coleraine	h	1-1	McGrory
13/10	Ballymena	h	1-2	Hagan
20/10	Glentoran	a	1-2	Brown
27/10	Cliftonville	h	0-2	
03/11	Crusaders	a	1-5	McGrory
10/11	Donegal Celtic	h	4-2	Hamilton, McGrory, Neill, Bennett
17/11	Linfield	a	1-1	Martyn
24/11	Ballinamallard	h	0-1	
01/12	Coleraine	a	2-0	Martyn, McGrory
08/12	Distillery	h	4-1	Hamilton, McGrory, Mitchell 2
15/12	Ballymena	h	4-1	Bates 2, Lindsay, Martyn
26/12	Portadown	a	0-2	
29/12	Linfield	h	0-0	

2013
01/01	Donegal Celtic	a	0-1	
05/01	Crusaders	h	2-3	Haughey, Martyn
15/01	Dungannon	a	1-2	Farren
19/01	Ballinamallard	a	1-3	Bates
02/02	Dungannon	h	3-1	Bates 2 (1p), Farren
16/02	Distillery	a	1-1	Farren
23/02	Ballymena	h	7-0	Shannon, Martyn, Farren, og (Liggett), Brown, Neill, Bates
26/02	Glentoran	a	1-2	Martyn
09/03	Portadown	a	1-3	Martyn
16/03	Cliftonville	h	1-3	Farren
30/03	Coleraine	h	1-1	Shannon
02/04	Dungannon	a	3-2	Brown, Farren, Martyn
13/04	Distillery	h	7-0	Bates, Farren 2, Martyn, Hamilton 2, Neill
16/04	Portadown	h	1-3	Farren
20/04	Ballymena	a	1-2	Farren, Bates
27/04	Donegal Celtic	h	3-1	Gardiner, Rooney 2

No	Name	Nat	DoB	Pos	Aps	(s)	Gls
45	Jude Ballard		25/11/94	A		(2)	
9	Guy Bates	ENG	31/10/85	A	36		10
29	Brendan Bennett		07/07/94			(4)	1
14	Marc Brown		18/04/88	M	22	(3)	3
	Matthew Burrows		15/10/85	A	3	(11)	1
1	Andy Coleman		13/06/85	G	29		
25	Jordan Dane		21/04/95	M	2	(1)	
8	Ciaran Doherty		25/01/90	A	20	(4)	3
10	Mark Farren	IRL	12/05/81	A	15		10
88	Grant Gardiner		13/09/88	M	7	(2)	1
31	Jason Greenway		03/06/97	D	1		
16	Conor Hagan		31/03/82	M	12	(6)	1
80	Gary Hamilton		06/10/80	A	21	(10)	5
6	Mark Haughey		23/01/91	D	30	(4)	1
26	Niall Henderson		07/02/88	M	10	(3)	
44	Michael Hynes		20/01/93	M		(1)	
7	Andy Kilmartin		08/01/83	M	37		
	Gary Lavery		04/07/97	A		(1)	
11	Kris Lindsay		05/02/84	D	21		1
24	Ciaran Martyn	IRL	25/03/80	M	20		9
4	Eddie McCallion		25/01/79	D	29	(1)	
15	Sean McCashin		29/09/90	D	15	(4)	1
51	Robbie McDaid		23/10/86	A		(5)	
17	Andrew McGrory		15/12/91	M	15	(14)	5
19	Andrew Mitchell		25/01/94	A	4	(10)	2
3	Kyle Neill		30/03/78	M	28	(3)	4
22	Davy O'Hare		02/03/70	G	9		
12	Matthew Rooney		18/02/90	A		(4)	2
2	Brendan Shannon		27/09/88	A	14	(2)	2
13	James Singleton		22/08/95	D	1	(2)	
18	Mark Turkington		20/03/84	A	14	(3)	
21	Robbie White		01/10/85	A	3	(2)	

GLENTORAN FC
Manager: Eddie Patterson
1882 • The Oval (9,400) • glentoran.com
Major honours
Irish League (23) 1894, 1897, 1905, 1912, 1913, 1921, 1925, 1931, 1951, 1953, 1964, 1967, 1968, 1970, 1972, 1977, 1981, 1988, 1992, 1999, 2003, 2005, 2009;
Irish Cup (21) 1914, 1917, 1921, 1932, 1933, 1935, 1951, 1966, 1973, 1983, 1985, 1986, 1987, 1988, 1990, 1996, 1998, 2000, 2001, 2004, 2013

2012
11/08	Donegal Celtic	h	3-1	Magee, Waterworth, O'Hanlon
18/08	Glenavon	a	1-1	Waterworth
25/08	Cliftonville	a	1-1	Carson
01/09	Linfield	h	1-1	Waterworth
04/09	Ballinamallard	a	4-1	Waterworth, Magee, og (Carters), M Murray
08/09	Dungannon	a	3-1	Magee (p), Waterworth 2
15/09	Coleraine	h	0-0	
22/09	Distillery	h	3-0	R Clarke, Waterworth 2
28/09	Ballymena	a	1-1	Howland
06/10	Crusaders	a	0-2	
13/10	Portadown	h	0-1	
20/10	Glenavon	h	2-1	R Clarke, M Clarke
27/10	Donegal Celtic	a	1-2	Ward
03/11	Cliftonville	h	1-1	Callacher
10/11	Dungannon	h	2-1	R Clarke, Waterworth
17/11	Distillery	a	2-0	Waterworth 2
24/11	Coleraine	a	0-1	
01/12	Ballinamallard	a	2-1	R Clarke, Howland
08/12	Crusaders	h	1-1	Howland
15/12	Portadown	a	4-2	Waterworth, R Clarke, Magee (p), McComb
26/12	Linfield	a	1-2	Magee
29/12	Donegal Celtic	h	5-0	R Clarke, Callacher, M Clarke, Carson, Waterworth (p)

2013
01/01	Coleraine	a	1-1	Kane
07/01	Cliftonville	a	1-4	Carson
15/01	Ballymena	h	1-2	Hill (p)
02/02	Portadown	a	1-0	R Clarke
16/02	Linfield	h	1-1	Magee (p)
23/02	Distillery	a	3-0	Ward, R Clarke, Waterworth
26/02	Glenavon	h	2-1	Waterworth, Carson
09/03	Ballymena	a	0-0	
16/03	Ballinamallard	h	3-0	R Clarke, M Murray, Waterworth
19/03	Dungannon	h	2-3	Waterworth, Howland
30/03	Crusaders	h	4-5	Waterworth, R Clarke, O'Hanlon, Carson
02/04	Linfield	a	0-1	
13/04	Ballinamallard	a	0-0	
16/04	Cliftonville	h	3-0	Waterworth 2, McComb
20/04	Crusaders	a	2-3	Howland, M Clarke
27/04	Coleraine	h	1-1	Nixon

No	Name	Nat	DoB	Pos	Aps	(s)	Gls
22	Calum Birney		19/04/93	D	12		
27	Kevin Bradley		29/04/92	D	4	(4)	
11	Jimmy Callacher		11/06/91	M	33	(3)	2
11	Stephen Carson		06/10/80	M	29	(5)	5
12	Mark Clarke		23/08/89	M	29	(1)	3
4	Richard Clarke		28/11/85	M	28	(8)	10
10	Stuart Elliott		23/07/78	M	3	(4)	
24	William Garrett		31/08/91	D	1	(1)	
14	Richard Gibson		11/01/85	A		(4)	
26	Steven Gordon		27/07/93	D		(1)	
15	Jason Hill		24/02/82	D	24	(6)	1
18	Aaron Hogg		14/01/90	G	3		
8	David Howland		17/09/86	M	25	(4)	5
3	Marcus Kane		08/12/91	M	21	(6)	1
6	Jay Magee		04/05/88	D	27	(1)	6
16	Stephen McAlorum		11/06/86	M	15	(8)	
21	Carl McComb		14/08/92	A	1	(13)	2
28	Steven McCullough		30/08/94	M		(2)	
23	John McGuigan		26/08/93	M	12	(6)	
1	Elliott Morris		04/05/81	G	35		
5	Eamon Murray		11/05/88	D	4	(1)	
19	Martin Murray		18/08/93	A	9	(15)	4
25	Ryan Newbury		01/11/89	M	1		
2	Colin Nixon		08/09/78	D	14	(3)	1
20	Jim O'Hanlon		14/03/93	M	20	(9)	2
7	Sean Ward		12/01/84	D	34	(2)	2
9	Andrew Waterworth		11/04/86	A	34		20

LINFIELD FC

Manager: David Jeffrey
1886 • Windsor Park (12,950) • linfieldfc.com
Major honours
Irish League (51) 1891, 1892, 1893, 1895, 1898, 1902, 1904, 1907, 1908, 1909, 1911, 1914, 1922, 1923, 1930, 1932, 1934, 1935, 1949, 1950, 1954, 1955, 1956, 1959, 1961, 1962, 1966, 1969, 1971, 1975, 1978, 1979, 1980, 1982, 1983, 1984, 1985, 1986, 1987, 1989, 1993, 1994, 2000, 2001, 2004, 2006, 2007, 2008, 2010, 2011, 2012; Irish Cup (42) 1891, 1892, 1893, 1895, 1898, 1899, 1902, 1904, 1912, 1913, 1915, 1916, 1919, 1922, 1923, 1930, 1931, 1934, 1936, 1939, 1942, 1945, 1946, 1948, 1950, 1953, 1960, 1962, 1963, 1970, 1978, 1980, 1982, 1994, 1995, 2002, 2006, 2007, 2008, 2010, 2011, 2012

2012

11/08	Ballymena	a	0-2	
18/08	Coleraine	h	0-0	
24/08	Donegal Celtic	h	4-0	Browne, McCaul, Thompson 2 (1p)
01/09	Glentoran	a	1-1	Burns
04/09	Crusaders	h	1-2	McAllister
08/09	Portadown	a	4-2	og (Casement), Murphy 2, Henderson
15/09	Cliftonville	h	1-2	McAllister
22/09	Glenavon	a	3-2	Watson, Fordyce 2
28/09	Distillery	h	4-0	Quinn, og (Hunter), McCaul, Henderson
06/10	Ballinamallard	h	1-3	McCaul
13/10	Dungannon	a	1-1	Armstrong
22/10	Coleraine	a	2-3	Carvill, Henderson
27/10	Portadown	h	1-0	og (Murray)
03/11	Donegal Celtic	a	3-0	McAllister, Thompson, Mulgrew
10/11	Cliftonville	a	0-3	
17/11	Glenavon	h	1-1	Fordyce
24/11	Ballymena	h	2-1	Hanley, Browne (p)
01/12	Distillery	a	1-1	Browne
08/12	Ballinamallard	a	3-1	Gault, Carvill 2
15/12	Dungannon	h	2-1	Thompson, McCaul (p)
22/12	Crusaders	a	2-2	Burns, McCaul
26/12	Glentoran	h	2-1	McAllister, Clarke
29/12	Glenavon	a	3-0	McCaul (p), Tipton, Clarke

2013

01/01	Cliftonville	h	3-1	Tipton 2, Carvill
05/01	Coleraine	h	5-2	Tipton 3, McCaul (p), McAllister
29/01	Donegal Celtic	a	4-1	Lowry, McCaul 2 (1p), Tipton
02/02	Ballymena	h	2-2	Tipton, McCaul
09/02	Dungannon	a	4-1	McCaul, Browne, Lowry, McAllister
16/02	Glentoran	a	1-1	Lowry
23/02	Portadown	h	2-0	Gault, McAllister
09/03	Distillery	h	1-1	Gault
18/03	Crusaders	a	0-3	
30/03	Ballinamallard	h	0-0	
02/04	Glentoran	h	1-0	Thompson
13/04	Cliftonville	a	2-3	Lowry, Carvill
16/04	Coleraine	a	1-1	Carvill
20/04	Ballinamallard	a	0-1	
27/04	Crusaders	h	1-2	Carvill

No	Name	Nat	DoB	Pos	Aps	(s)	Gls
3	David Armstrong		23/01/87	D	17	(2)	1
26	Jonny Black		26/02/88	D	13		
1	Alan Blayney		09/10/81	G	24		
17	Gary Browne		17/01/83	A	8	(9)	4
12	Billy Joe Burns		24/04/89	D	34	(1)	2
10	Michael Carvill		03/04/88	M	32	(5)	7
32	Ross Clarke		17/05/93	A	3	(12)	2
7	Damien Curran		17/10/81	D	3		
35	Gareth Deane		14/06/94	G	1		
2	Steven Douglas		27/09/77	D	4	(2)	
21	Jim Ervin		05/06/85	D	19	(3)	
16	Daryl Fordyce		02/01/87	M	6	(15)	3
20	Robert Garrett		05/05/88	M	12	(8)	
4	Michael Gault		15/04/83	M	18	(1)	3
14	Reece Glendinning		09/06/95	D	4	(1)	
19	Ross Glendinning		18/05/93	G	13		
15	Nathan Hanley		18/07/90	M	3	(2)	1
6	Ryan Henderson		26/10/84	M	7	(7)	3
8	Philip Lowry		15/07/89	M	16	(5)	4
25	Mark McAllister		26/04/88	A	25	(3)	7
24	Brian McCaul		06/08/90	M	33	(2)	11
28	Conor McMenamin		24/08/95	M	1	(3)	
22	Jamie Mulgrew		05/06/86	M	33	(2)	1
5	William Murphy		29/01/74	D	34		2
31	Niall Quinn		02/08/93	D	18	(1)	1
9	Peter Thompson		02/05/84	A	19	(8)	5
18	Matthew Tipton	WAL	29/06/80	A	14	(2)	8
23	Albert Watson		08/09/85	D	14	(1)	1

LISBURN DISTILLERY FC

Manager: Tim McCann
1879 • New Grosvenor (2,220) • lisburn-distillery.net
Major honours
Irish League (6) 1896, 1899, 1901, 1903, 1906 (shared), 1963; Irish Cup (12) 1884, 1885, 1886, 1889, 1894, 1896, 1903, 1905, 1910, 1925, 1956, 1971

2012

11/08	Portadown	a	2-4	Forsythe, Halliday
18/08	Ballinamallard	h	0-5	
25/08	Crusaders	h	1-3	Traynor
31/08	Ballymena	a	0-2	
04/09	Dungannon	h	2-1	McCullough, Liggett
08/09	Coleraine	a	1-2	Liggett
15/09	Glenavon	h	0-1	
22/09	Glentoran	a	0-3	
28/09	Linfield	a	0-4	
06/10	Cliftonville	h	1-2	Liggett
13/10	Donegal Celtic	a	3-0	Halliday, Davidson, Liggett
20/10	Ballymena	h	0-4	
27/10	Dungannon	a	1-1	Davidson
02/11	Ballinamallard	a	0-2	
10/11	Coleraine	h	1-1	Simpson
17/11	Glentoran	h	0-2	
26/11	Cliftonville	a	0-4	
01/12	Linfield	h	1-1	Forsythe
08/12	Glenavon	a	1-4	McCullough
15/12	Crusaders	a	1-3	Liggett
26/12	Donegal Celtic	h	3-3	Davidson, McCann, Hughes (p)
29/12	Ballymena	a	3-3	Hughes 2, Liggett

2013

01/01	Ballinamallard	h	0-2	
05/01	Dungannon	a	0-1	
19/01	Coleraine	a	1-3	Beggs
02/02	Cliftonville	h	0-4	
16/02	Glenavon	h	2-1	Davidson, Boyd
23/02	Glentoran	h	0-3	
09/03	Linfield	a	1-1	Boyd
16/03	Donegal Celtic	a	3-0	(w/o; original result 1-2 Harkness)
20/03	Portadown	h	0-5	
27/03	Crusaders	h	0-2	
30/03	Portadown	h	1-1	Davidson
02/04	Donegal Celtic	h	0-1	
13/04	Glenavon	a	0-7	
16/04	Ballymena	h	0-2	
20/04	Dungannon	a	0-1	
27/04	Portadown	a	0-1	

No	Name	Nat	DoB	Pos	Aps	(s)	Gls
20	Owain Beggs		30/07/92	M	4	(11)	1
19	Aaron Boyd		12/02/91	A	11	(1)	2
1	Billy Brennan	IRL	06/03/85	G	14		
7	Scott Davidson		27/09/91	M	31	(4)	5
29	Michael Fegan		05/03/93	A		(2)	
14	Andrew Ferguson		22/02/89	D	20	(2)	
17	Jordan Forsythe		11/02/91	M	24	(8)	2
17	William Garrett		31/08/91	D	7		
18	Steven Gordon		27/07/93	D	3	(5)	
	Andy Hall		19/09/89	M	4	(7)	
10	Michael Halliday		28/05/79	A	24	(9)	2
3	Johnny Harkness		18/11/85	D	24	(1)	1
15	Jordan Hughes		27/01/91	M	26	(8)	3
4	Andy Hunter		19/01/81	D	20		
24	Ryan Irwin		03/04/94	D	1	(1)	
18	Artur Kopyt	POL	31/07/85	M	2	(2)	
	Gary Liggett		28/09/87	A	24		6
8	Ryan McCann		15/09/82	M	29	(3)	1
6	David McCullough		24/04/87	M	30	(5)	2
	Dermot McVeigh		24/07/90	D	11	(1)	
13	Dominic Melly		19/07/87	M	12	(5)	
	Michael Moore		21/03/85	A	2	(2)	
19	Bradley Morton		22/12/92	M	1		
5	Philip Simpson		21/10/86	D	22	(2)	1
2	Aaron Smyth		25/05/87	D	31	(2)	
12	Aaron Traynor		24/07/90	M	15	(3)	1
16	Lee Windrum		14/08/85	G	24		
20	Mikey Withers		23/05/94	A	2	(9)	

PORTADOWN FC

Manager: Ronnie McFall
1924 • Shamrock Park (15,800) • portadownfc.co.uk
Major honours
Irish League (4) 1990, 1991, 1996, 2002; Irish Cup (3) 1991, 1999, 2005

2012

11/08	Distillery	h	4-2	R Burns, McNeill, Breen, Tomelty
18/08	Donegal Celtic	a	1-1	Breen
24/08	Coleraine	h	3-4	McNeill, Braniff, Mackle
31/08	Dungannon	a	1-1	Murray
03/09	Glenavon	a	2-2	O'Hara, og (Shannon)
08/09	Linfield	h	2-4	McCafferty (p), Lecky
15/09	Ballinamallard	a	0-2	
22/09	Cliftonville	a	2-3	Murray, Gartland
28/09	Crusaders	h	1-0	Murray
06/10	Ballymena	h	2-2	Murray 2
13/10	Glentoran	a	1-0	Murray (p)
20/10	Donegal Celtic	h	1-0	Gartland
27/10	Linfield	a	0-1	
03/11	Coleraine	a	1-1	Murray (p)
10/11	Ballinamallard	h	2-1	Patton, Mackle
17/11	Crusaders	a	0-2	
24/11	Dungannon	h	1-1	Murray
01/12	Cliftonville	h	3-3	Braniff 2, Murray
08/12	Ballymena	a	2-1	Braniff 2
15/12	Glentoran	h	2-4	Murray 2
26/12	Glenavon	h	2-0	Redman, Lecky
29/12	Coleraine	h	2-0	Lecky, Gartland

2013

01/01	Crusaders	a	0-1	
05/01	Donegal Celtic	h	1-0	Twigg
19/01	Cliftonville	h	1-3	Mackle
25/01	Ballinamallard	a	1-0	Twigg
02/02	Glentoran	h	0-1	
16/02	Dungannon	a	0-2	
23/02	Linfield	a	0-2	
09/03	Glenavon	h	3-1	Mackle, Murray, Braniff
16/03	Ballymena	h	0-0	
20/03	Distillery	a	5-0	Murray 3, Mackle, Braniff
30/03	Distillery	a	1-1	Twigg
02/04	Ballymena	a	1-6	Twigg
13/04	Dungannon	h	1-1	Twigg
16/04	Glenavon	a	3-1	Murray 2, Breen
20/04	Donegal Celtic	a	2-1	Twigg, Murray
27/04	Distillery	h	1-0	Mackle

No	Name	Nat	DoB	Pos	Aps	(s)	Gls
10	Kevin Braniff		04/03/83	A	31		7
6	Gary Breen	IRL	17/03/89	D	23	(1)	3
23	Matthew Brown		20/02/92	A		(1)	
7	Aaron Burns		29/05/92	D	8	(2)	
21	Andrew Burns		29/05/92	D	6	(1)	
14	Ryan Burns		08/09/92	A	13	(4)	1
17	Chris Casement		12/01/88	D	29		
19	Brian Gartland	IRL	04/11/86	D	29	(2)	3
18	Richard Lecky		13/05/84	A	7	(20)	3
2	Sean Mackle	SCO	10/04/88	D	30	(5)	6
13	Jamie McArdle		12/06/93	G	1	(1)	
22	Neil McCafferty		19/07/84	M	24	(4)	1
16	Michael McLellan		22/01/93	A	5	(3)	
12	Joe McNeill		23/08/88	A	27	(6)	2
1	David Miskelly		03/09/79	G	37		
11	Tim Mouncey		27/04/82	M	17	(2)	
9	Darren Murray		24/10/91	A	26	(5)	18
4	Keith O'Hara		03/02/81	D	17	(2)	1
26	Mark Patton		21/06/89	M	13	(5)	1
5	Chris Ramsey		24/05/90	D	22	(3)	
3	Ross Redman		23/11/89	D	36	(1)	1
4	Ciaran Rooney		05/08/95	M	1		
20	Sammy Stewart		25/11/90	M		(2)	
	Jamie Tomelty		16/09/83	M	6	(6)	1
27	Gary Twigg	SCO	19/03/84	A	10	(1)	6

Top goalscorers

29	Liam Boyce (Cliftonville)
20	Andrew Waterworth (Glentoran)
18	Darren Murray (Portadown)
17	Joe Gormley (Cliftonville)
	Curtis Allen (Coleraine)
16	Jordan Owens (Crusaders)
15	Timmy Adamson (Crusaders)
13	Gary McCutcheon (Crusaders)
11	Brian McCaul (Linfield)
10	Jason McCartney (Ballinamallard)
	David Cushley (Ballymena)
	Gary Liggett (Ballymena/Distillery)
	Joshua Cahoon (Dungannon)
	Guy Bates (Glenavon)
	Mark Farren (Glenavon)
	Richard Clarke (Glentoran)

Promoted clubs

ARDS FC

Coach: Niall Currie
1900 • Clandeboye Park (2,850) • ardsfc.co.uk
Major honours
Irish League (1) 1958;
Irish Cup (4) 1927, 1952, 1969, 1974

WARRENPOINT TOWN FC

Coach: Barry Gray
1988 • Stangmore Park (2,154) • warrenpointtownfc.co.uk

SECOND LEVEL FINAL TABLE 2012/13

		Pld	W	D	L	F	A	Pts
1	Ards FC	24	18	5	1	56	19	59
2	Warrenpoint Town FC	24	15	5	4	46	23	50
3	Institute FC	24	14	5	5	50	23	47
4	Dundela FC	24	13	4	7	62	51	43
5	Carrick Rangers FC	24	11	6	7	48	32	39
6	Harland & Wolff Welders FC	24	10	4	10	37	35	34
7	Dergview FC	24	7	6	11	27	39	27
8	Larne FC	24	5	9	10	24	40	24
9	Coagh United FC	24	6	5	13	35	51	23
10	Bangor FC	24	6	5	13	23	42	23
11	Loughgall FC	24	6	5	13	27	48	23
12	Limavady United FC	24	5	6	13	34	49	21
13	Tobermore United FC	24	6	3	15	38	55	21

NB Newry City FC withdrew after round 5 – their matches were annulled.

PROMOTION/RELEGATION PLAY-OFFS

(07/05/13 & 10/05/13)
Warrenpoint 1-0 Donegal Celtic
Donegal Celtic 2-1 Warrenpoint
(2-2; Warrenpoint on away goal)

Domestic cup: Irish Cup 2012/13

FIFTH ROUND

(12/01/13)
Ards 4-0 Immaculata
Ballyclare 2-3 Bangor
Ballymena 2-1 Warrenpoint Town
Cliftonville 4-2 Ballinamallard
Coleraine 7-0 Ballynahinch United
Distillery 5-1 Coagh United
Dundela 4-3 Queens University
Glenavon 5-1 Harland & Wolff Welders
Institute 2-1 Rathfriland Rangers
Killymoon Rangers 1-4 Glentoran
Knockbreda 5-1 Rosario Youth Club
Larne 1-1 Lurgan Celtic
Linfield 2-2 Crusaders
Loughgall 1-3 Donegal Celtic
Portadown 2-1 Dungannon
Tobermore United 2-2 Kilmore Recreation

Replays
(22/01/13)
Crusaders 2-1 Linfield
Tobermore United 0-1 Kilmore Recreation

(04/02/13)
Larne 1-4 Lurgan Celtic

SIXTH ROUND

(09/02/13)
Ballymena 2-3 Coleraine
Bangor 2-5 Glentoran
Cliftonville 2-0 Donegal Celtic
Crusaders 4-1 Glenavon
Institute 0-2 Kilmore Recreation
Lurgan Celtic 0-3 Knockbreda
Portadown 1-0 Ards

(26/02/13)
Distillery 2-1 Dundela

QUARTER-FINALS

(02/03/13)
Cliftonville 2-0 Kilmore Recreation *(Seydak 56, Donnelly 85)*
Coleraine 0-3 Portadown *(Braniff 34, 87, Murray 68)*
Crusaders 1-1 Distillery *(Adamson 18; Boyd 12)*
Knockbreda 1-3 Glentoran *(McClean 18; Magee 12p, McMenamin 53og, Waterworth 68)*

Replay
(12/03/13)
Distillery 1-1 Crusaders *(Withers 74; Owens 52)*
(aet; 3-4 on pens)

SEMI-FINALS

(06/04/13)
Crusaders 0-2 Cliftonville *(McMullan 67p, Gormley 68)*
Portadown 0-1 Glentoran *(Kane 79)*

FINAL

(04/05/13)
Windsor Park, Belfast
GLENTORAN FC 3 *(Waterworth 64, 103, Callacher 99)*
CLIFTONVILLE FC 1 *(Gormley 34)*
(aet)
Referee: *Hunter*
GLENTORAN: *Morris, R Clarke, Hill (Nixon 109), Magee, Ward, Howland, Carson, M Clarke (O'Hanlon 70), McAlorum (Kane 100), Callacher, Waterworth*
CLIFTONVILLE: *Devlin, McGovern (O'Carroll 60), McMullan, Seydak, Smyth, Johnston, Caldwell, Garrett (Cosgrove 82), Catney, Gormley (Donnelly 70), Boyce*

Andrew Waterworth, a double goalscorer for Glentoran in the final against Cliftonville, holds aloft the Irish Cup

NORWAY
Norges Fotballforbund (NFF)

Address	Serviceboks 1
	Ullevaal stadion
	NO-0840 Oslo
Tel	+47 210 29300
Fax	+47 210 29301
E-mail	nff@fotball.no
Website	fotball.no

President	Yngve Hallén
General secretary	Kjetil P Siem
Media officer	Svein Graff
Year of formation	1902
National stadium	Ullevaal, Oslo
	(25,572)

TIPPELIGAEN CLUBS

1. Aalesunds FK
2. SK Brann
3. Fredrikstad FK
4. FK Haugesund
5. Hønefoss BK
6. Lillestrøm SK
7. Molde FK
8. Odd Grenland
   NB Renamed Odds BK for 2013 season.
9. Rosenborg BK
10. Sandnes Ulf
11. Sogndal IL Fotball
12. Stabæk Fotball
13. Strømsgodset IF
14. Tromsø IL
15. Viking FK
16. Vålerenga Fotball

PROMOTED CLUBS

17. IK Start
18. Sarpsborg 08 FF

OTHER CLUB

19. IL Hødd Fotball

KEY:
- – UEFA Champions League
- – UEFA Europa League
- – Promoted clubs
- – Relegated clubs
- – Second level club in UEFA Europa League

Molde defend Tippeligaen title

Having steered Molde FK to their first ever championship in 2011, former Manchester United FC and Norway striker Ole Gunnar Solskjær proved it was no fluke by repeating the trick in 2012. But while the league went the same way as the previous year, arguably the biggest shock in the country's football history was provided by second-tier IL Hødd Fotball in the Norwegian Cup.

On the international front, Molde and Rosenborg BK reached the UEFA Europa League group stage, but there were mixed fortunes in the 2014 FIFA World Cup qualifying campaign for Egil Olsen's national side.

| Successive championship wins for Solskjær's team | Giant-killers Hødd provide domestic cup shock | National team record cap-holder Riise retires |

Domestic league

Molde retained the Tippeligaen title, securing the silverware with one game to go. A 1-0 victory over Hønefoss BK proved enough to seal the title ahead of Strømsgodset IF, their eventual winning margin amounting to four points. Record champions Rosenborg BK were also in the hunt, but they fell away sharply at the tail end of the season.

Molde owed their triumph in particular to consistent home form, winning 14 of their 15 fixtures at the Aker Stadium, the only faux pas coming in the middle of the campaign when visitors Viking FK claimed a 2-1 victory. Solskjær's men kept their cool despite a prolonged run in Europe and boasted outstanding performers in defender Vegard Forren, midfielder Magnus Wolff Eikrem and Ivory Coast striker Davy Claude Angan, the club's top scorer with 13 goals.

That left the African one goal shy of the league's joint two best marksmen – the eastern European pair of Péter Kovács, Strømsgodset's 34-year-old Hungarian striker, and Zdeněk Ondrášek, Tromsø IL's new signing from the Czech Republic. Kovács was especially prolific in the closing weeks to help his team secure an unexpected second place. The

Drammen club were the league's top-scoring team, with 62 goals, and the only club undefeated at home.

Domestic cup

Hødd, who only avoided relegation from the second division on the last day, completed a fairytale cup run in a closely-fought final at the Ullevaal Stadium. Having already accounted for top-flight FK Haugesund and SK Brann, Hødd led Tromsø, fourth in the Tippeligaen, through Kjell Rune Sellin's 62nd-minute strike before Saliou Ciss claimed a late equaliser. Hødd goalkeeper Ørjan Håskjold Nyland then produced brilliant saves in extra time and the penalty shoot-out before midfielder Andreas Rekdal converted the decisive spot-kick to secure the club's first major trophy and a European debut in 2013/14.

Europe

Between them Norway's five European representatives clocked up 38 matches in 2012/13 thanks to the efforts of Molde and Rosenborg, who both participated in the group stage of the UEFA Europa League. The two clubs took very different routes to get there, Molde dropping out of the UEFA Champions League at the third qualifying

stage and Rosenborg progressing through four successive preliminary rounds. Both clubs picked up six points in their respective groups, in each case doing the double over German-speaking opposition as Molde twice claimed the prized scalp of VfB Stuttgart and Rosenborg won home and away against SK Rapid Wien.

National team

Having narrowly missed out on a UEFA EURO 2012 play-off spot, Norway set about the task of qualifying for the World Cup in Brazil in an inviting group for which they were drawn as top seeds. However, they got off to a calamitous start with a 2-0 defeat in Iceland, and further misery beckoned four days later at home to Slovenia until John Arne Riise secured a 2-1 win with an added-time penalty.

Riise would retire from international duty, with a record tally of 110 caps, at the end of the season, by which time Norway were down in fourth place in Group E – though still in contention for a play-off berth – after taking just one point from two games against Albania. Considerable encouragement for the future, however, was provided by Tor Ole Skullerud's Under-21 side, who not only qualified against the odds for the 2013 European finals but went on to beat England and reach the last four in Israel.

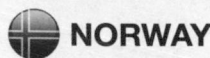 **NORWAY**

Domestic league: Tippeligaen 2012 final table

		Pld	Home W	D	L	F	A	Away W	D	L	F	A	Total W	D	L	F	A	Pts
1	**Molde FK**	30	14	0	1	33	16	5	5	5	18	15	19	5	6	51	31	62
2	Strømsgodset IF	30	12	3	0	39	12	5	4	6	23	28	17	7	6	62	40	58
3	Rosenborg BK	30	8	5	2	28	11	7	5	3	25	15	15	10	5	53	26	55
4	Tromsø IL	30	10	4	1	32	8	4	3	8	13	24	14	7	9	45	32	49
5	Viking FK	30	10	1	4	25	16	4	6	5	16	20	14	7	9	41	36	49
6	SK Brann	30	10	1	4	36	20	3	2	10	21	30	13	3	14	57	50	42
7	FK Haugesund	30	8	4	3	26	16	3	5	7	20	24	11	9	10	46	40	42
8	Vålerenga Fotball	30	7	4	4	22	16	5	1	9	20	28	12	5	13	42	44	41
9	Lillestrøm SK	30	3	8	4	23	19	6	4	5	23	28	9	12	9	46	47	39
10	Odd Grenland	30	6	4	5	23	21	5	3	7	17	22	11	7	12	40	43	39
11	Aalesunds FK	30	8	5	2	29	15	1	6	8	11	26	9	11	10	40	41	38
12	Sogndal IL Fotball	30	6	5	4	15	14	2	5	8	14	23	8	10	12	29	37	34
13	Hønefoss BK	30	4	8	3	17	19	3	4	8	13	23	7	12	11	30	42	33
14	Sandnes Ulf	30	6	5	4	25	19	2	3	10	19	37	8	8	14	44	56	32
15	Fredrikstad FK	30	5	1	9	30	30	4	2	9	12	29	9	3	18	42	59	30
16	Stabæk Fotball	30	3	1	11	10	28	2	1	12	15	41	5	2	23	25	69	17

NB Odd Grenland – 1 pt deducted

SEASON AT A GLANCE

EUROPEAN QUALIFICATION 2013/14

Champion: Molde FK (second qualifying round)

Cup winner: IL Hødd Fotball (second qualifying round)
Strømsgodset IF (second qualifying round)
Rosenborg BK (first qualifying round)
Tromsø IL (first qualifying round)

Top scorers Péter Kovács (Strømsgodset) & Zdeněk Ondrášek (Tromsø), 14 goals
Relegated clubs Stabæk Fotball, Fredrikstad FK
Promoted clubs IK Start, Sarpsborg 08 FF
Cup final IL Hødd Fotball 1-1 Tromsø IL *(aet; 4-2 on pens)*

**TIPPELIGAEN TEAM
OF THE SEASON**
(4-4-2)
Coach: Solskjær *(Molde)*

**PLAYER OF
THE SEASON
Vegard Forren**
(Molde FK)

Pivotal to each of Molde's two Norwegian title successes, and the club's only ever-present in 2012, the powerful centre-back also began to forge a solid partnership with Brede Hangeland at the heart of the Norwegian national team's defence. Forren's growing reputation earned him a January 2013 transfer to English Premier League side Southampton FC.

**NEWCOMER OF
THE SEASON
Ørjan Håskjold Nyland**
(IL Hødd Fotball)

Man of the match in the Norwegian Cup final, this young goalkeeper is tipped for stardom. His heroics in Hødd's giant-killing cup run made bigger clubs sit up and take notice, and he eventually signed for champions Molde FK. A Norwegian Under-21 international, he helped his team eliminate France to qualify unexpectedly for the 2013 finals in Israel.

Hirschfeld *(Vålerenga)*
Vilsvik *(Strømsgodset)* — Semb *(Odd Grenland)* — Forren *(Molde)* — Dorsin *(Rosenborg)*
Eikrem *(Molde)* — Johansen *(Strømsgodset)* — Fellah *(Vålerenga)* — Henriksen *(Rosenborg)*
Djurdjić *(Haugesund)* — Angan *(Molde)*

NATIONAL TEAM

NORWAY

Home Kit 10   10 Away Kit

INTERNATIONAL TOURNAMENT APPEARANCES

FIFA World Cup (3) 1938, 1994, 1998 (2nd round)
UEFA European Championship (1) 2000

TOP FIVE ALL-TIME CAPS

John Arne Riise (110); Thorbjørn Svenssen (104); Henning Berg (100); Erik Thorstvedt (97); John Carew (91)

TOP FIVE ALL-TIME GOALS

Jørgen Juve (33); Einar Gundersen (26); Harald Hennum (25); John Carew (24); Tore André Flo & Ole Gunnar Solskjær (23)

Results 2012/13

15/08/12	Greece	H	Oslo	2-3	Hangeland (13), J A Riise (75)
07/09/12	Iceland (WCQ)	A	Reykjavik	0-2	
11/09/12	Slovenia (WCQ)	H	Oslo	2-1	Henriksen (26), J A Riise (90+4p)
12/10/12	Switzerland (WCQ)	A	Berne	1-1	Hangeland (81)
16/10/12	Cyprus (WCQ)	A	Larnaca	3-1	Hangeland (44), Elyounoussi (81p), King (83)
14/11/12	Hungary	A	Budapest	2-0	Nielsen (38), Abdellaoue (79)
08/01/13	South Africa	A	Cape Town	1-0	Elyounoussi (41)
12/01/13	Zambia	A	Ndola	0-0	
06/02/13	Ukraine	N	Seville (ESP)	0-2	
22/03/13	Albania (WCQ)	H	Oslo	0-1	
07/06/13	Albania (WCQ)	A	Tirana	1-1	Høgli (87)
11/06/13	FYROM	H	Oslo	2-0	Skjelbred (9), Braaten (79)

Appearances 2012/13

Coach: Egil Olsen	22/04/42		Gre	ISL	SVN	SUI	CYP	Hun	Rsa	Zam	Ukr	ALB	ALB	Mkd	Caps	Goals
Rune Almenning Jarstein	29/09/84	Viking	G		G	G	G	G	G		G	G	G		30	-
Tom Høgli	24/02/84	Club Brugge (BEL)	D					D			s85	D	D	D72	31	2
Vadim Demidov	10/10/86	Eintracht Frankfurt (GER)	D37												16	-
Brede Hangeland	20/06/81	Fulham (ENG)	D79	D	D	D	D	D			D46	D	D		84	4
John Arne Riise	24/09/80	Fulham (ENG)	D	D	D	D	D				D85	D			110	16
Markus Henriksen	25/07/92	Rosenborg /AZ (NED)	M46	s90	M	M	M	M61			M	M	M		17	1
Håvard Nordtveit	21/06/90	Mönchengladbach (GER)	M	M	M53	M		M46				M	M		10	1
Tarik Elyounoussi	23/02/88	Rosenborg	M	M	M89	M92	M		M81	M	M	M62	M46	M	21	6
Morten Gamst Pedersen	08/09/81	Blackburn (ENG)	M46												74	16
Erik Huseklepp	05/09/84	Brann	M63					M46	s67		s62			M84	34	7
Mohammed Abdellaoue	23/10/85	Hannover (GER)	A63	A67	A46			s77				A			25	6
Thomas Rogne	29/06/90	Celtic (SCO)	s37												2	-
Magnus Wolff Eikrem	08/08/90	Molde	s46	M		s80	M92	s46			M46				9	-
Christian Grindheim	17/07/83	København (DEN) /Vålerenga	s46											M	53	2
Alexander Søderlund	03/08/87	Haugesund	s63	s67	s89	A64	A46	A77	A63			M75	s70	s84	14	-
Daniel Omoya Braaten	25/05/82	Toulouse (FRA)	s63	M67	M	M	M	M90			A		M	A	45	3
Espen Ruud	26/02/84	OB (DEN)	s79	D	D	D	D		D	D			D	s46	30	1
Espen Bugge Pettersen	10/05/80	Molde		G											7	-
Kjetil Wæhler	16/03/76	Göteborg (SWE)	D	D									D38		32	1
Bjørn Helge Riise	21/06/83	Lillestrøm		M90	s53				M46	s77					35	1
Joshua King	15/01/92	Man. United (ENG) /Blackburn (ENG)		s67	s46	s64	s46					s62	A70		6	1
Ruben Yttergård Jenssen	04/05/88	Tromsø			M	M80	M75	M84	M	s46	M62	M	M86	s72	25	-
Vegard Forren	16/02/88	Molde /Southampton (ENG)				D	D	D			s46	D			7	-
Jonathan Parr	21/10/88	Crystal Palace (ENG)				s92		s62			s73				9	-
Valon Berisha	07/02/93	Salzburg (AUT)					s75	s61				s75	s46		10	-
Ardian Gashi	20/06/81	Helsingborg (SWE)					s92		M	M46	s46			M	12	-

Appearances 2012/13 (contd.)

			Gre	ISL	SVN	SUI	CYP	Hun	Rsa	Zam	Ukr	ALB	ALB	Mkd	Caps	Goals
Vegar Eggen Hedenstad	26/06/91	Freiburg (GER)						D			D73				4	-
Håvard Nielsen	15/07/93	Salzburg (AUT)						M62			M62				2	1
Anders Konradsen	18/07/90	Strømsgodset /Rennes (FRA)						s84			s62				2	-
Tore Reginiussen	10/04/86	Rosenborg						s90			D		D	s38	16	2
Fredrik Semb Berge	06/02/90	Odd							D	D46					2	-
Kim André Madsen	12/03/89	Strømsgodset							D64	s46				D	5	-
Lars-Christopher Vilsvik	18/10/88	Strømsgodset							D87	s90					4	-
Yann-Erik de Lanlay	14/05/92	Viking							s46	s73					2	-
Mohammed Fellah	24/05/89	Vålerenga							s46	M77					2	-
Marcus Pedersen	08/06/90	OB (DEN)							s63	A73					2	-
Jørgen Horn	07/06/87	Strømsgodset							s64	D					2	-
Jo Inge Berget	11/09/90	Molde							s81	M67					3	-
Ruben Kristiansen	20/02/88	Tromsø							s87	D				D46	3	-
André Hansen	17/12/89	Odd								G				G89	2	-
Magnus Lekven	13/01/88	Esbjerg (DEN)								M90				s62	4	-
Per Ciljan Skjelbred	16/06/87	Hamburg (GER)											s86	M62	18	1
Sten Grytebust	25/10/89	Aalesund												s89	1	-

European club competitions 2012/13

MOLDE FK

EUROPA
LEAGUE

Play-offs - sc Heerenveen (NED)
H 2-0 *Eikrem (31), Moström (90)*
Pettersen, Vatshaug, Forren, Berg Hestad (Hussain 70), Eikrem, Moström, Berget (Diouf 70), Linnes, Gatt (Simonsen 82), Rindarøy, Chima. Coach: Ole Gunnar Solskjær (NOR)
A 2-1 *Berget (54), Diouf (73)*
Pettersen, Vatshaug, Forren, Berg Hestad, Eikrem (Hoseth 77), Moström, Berget (Chima 57), Linnes, Gatt (Hussain 74), Rindarøy, Diouf. Coach: Ole Gunnar Solskjær (NOR)

Group E
Match 1 - FC København (DEN)
A 1-2 *Diouf (45+1)*
Pettersen, Vatshaug, Forren, Berg Hestad, Moström, Hoseth (Hussain 41), Berget (Ekpo 82), Linnes, Angan (Chima 83), Rindarøy, Diouf. Coach: Ole Gunnar Solskjær (NOR)
Match 2 - VfB Stuttgart (GER)
H 2-0 *Berget (58), Chima (88)*
Pettersen, Steenslid, Forren, Berg Hestad, Eikrem, Linnes, Stamnestrø (Moström 46), Hussain (Gatt 81), Simonsen, Chima, Diouf (Berget 30). Coach: Ole Gunnar Solskjær (NOR)

CHAMPIONS LEAGUE

Second qualifying round - FK Ventspils (LVA)
H 3-0 *Angan (53, 83), Forren (74p)*
Pettersen, Hovland, Forren, Eikrem, Moström (Chima 74), Hoseth (Berg Hestad 42), Berget (Tripic 82), Linnes, Angan, Gatt, Rindarøy. Coach: Ole Gunnar Solskjær (NOR)
A 1-1 *Eikrem (37)*
Pettersen, Vatshaug, Hovland, Berg Hestad, Eikrem (Camara 74), Moström (Tripic 59), Linnes, Stamnestrø, Angan (Viní Dantas 72), Rindarøy, Chima. Coach: Ole Gunnar Solskjær (NOR)

Third qualifying round - FC Basel 1893 (SUI)
H 0-1
Pettersen, Vatshaug, Hovland, Forren, Berg Hestad (Hoseth 79), Eikrem, Moström, Linnes (Simonsen 64), Angan, Rindarøy, Chima. Coach: Ole Gunnar Solskjær (NOR)
Red card: Angan 27
A 1-1 *Berget (32)*
Pettersen, Vatshaug, Hovland (Simonsen 26), Forren, Berg Hestad, Eikrem (Stamnestrø 70), Moström, Berget, Linnes, Rindarøy (Hoseth 57), Chima. Coach: Ole Gunnar Solskjær (NOR)

Match 3 - FC Steaua Bucureşti (ROU)
A 0-2
Söderberg, Steenslid, Stamnestrø, Hussain (Furu 90), Ekpo, Simonsen, Angan, Gatt (Hestad 69), Ødegaard, Hollingen (Camara 46), Johansen. Coach: Ole Gunnar Solskjær (NOR)
Match 4 - FC Steaua Bucureşti (ROU)
H 1-2 *Chima (56)*
Söderberg, Vatshaug, Forren, Berg Hestad, Eikrem, Linnes, Hussain (Angan 77), Simonsen, Gatt (Moström 46), Chima, Diouf (Berget 46). Coach: Ole Gunnar Solskjær (NOR)
Match 5 - FC København (DEN)
H 1-2 *Chima (62)*
Pettersen, Vatshaug, Forren, Berg Hestad (Hussain 46), Eikrem (Angan 85), Moström, Berget (Diouf 55), Linnes, Gatt, Rindarøy, Chima. Coach: Ole Gunnar Solskjær (NOR)
Match 6 - VfB Stuttgart (GER)
A 1-0 *Angan (45+1)*
Pettersen, Forren, Eikrem, Moström, Berget (Simonsen 79), Linnes, Angan (Chima 64), Gatt (Hussain 68), Rindarøy, Ødegaard, Diouf. Coach: Ole Gunnar Solskjær (NOR)

AALESUNDS FK

Second qualifying round - KF Tirana (ALB)
A 1-1 *Stewart (57)*
Grytebust, Skiri (Ulvestad 34), Skagestad (Sellin 87), Tollås, Morrison, Carlsen (Barrantes 68), Stewart, Arnefjord, Wembangomo, Matland, Fuhre. Coach: Kjetil Rekdal (NOR)
H 5-0 *Barrantes (45+1), Tollås (48), James (64, 77), Stewart (83)*
Grytebust, Tollås, Carlsen, Post (James 46), Stewart, Arnefjord, Wembangomo, Matland (Skagestad 67), Ulvestad, Fuhre (Myklebust 68), Barrantes. Coach: Kjetil Rekdal (NOR)

Third qualifying round - APOEL FC (CYP)
A 1-2 *Stewart (16)*
Grytebust, Tollås, Morrison, Carlsen (Skagestad 90), Stewart, James (Sellin 79), Arnefjord, Wembangomo, Ulvestad, Fuhre (Matland 70), Jääger. Coach: Kjetil Rekdal (NOR)
H 0-1
Grytebust, Tollås, Morrison, Carlsen (Wembangomo 46), Stewart, James, Arnefjord, Matland, Fuhre (Post 46), Jääger, Barrantes. Coach: Kjetil Rekdal (NOR)

TROMSØ IL

Second qualifying round - NK Olimpija Ljubljana (SVN)
A 0-0
Sahlman, Björck, Koppinen, Drage (Nyström 79; Kristiansen 88), Yttergård Jenssen, Ondrášek (Årst 88), Norbye, Andersen, Yndestad, Johansen, Bendiksen. Coach: Per-Mathias Høgmo (NOR)
H 1-0 *Koppinen (108) (aet)*
Sahlman, Björck, Koppinen, Drage (Lysvoll 100), Yttergård Jenssen, Ondrášek, Norbye (Kristiansen 45), Andersen, Yndestad, Johansen, Bendiksen (Årst 74). Coach: Per-Mathias Høgmo (NOR)

Third qualifying round - FC Metalurh Donetsk (UKR)
H 1-1 *Ondrášek (43)*
Sahlman, Björck, Kristiansen, Koppinen, Drage (Yndestad 79), Yttergård Jenssen, Ondrášek, Norbye, Andersen, Bendiksen, Årst (Lysvoll 66). Coach: Per-Mathias Høgmo (NOR)
A 1-0 *Prijovic (9)*
Sahlman, Kara, Björck, Kristiansen, Koppinen, Drage (Andersen 81), Yttergård Jenssen, Ondrášek (Ciss 86), Yndestad, Bendiksen, Prijovic (Årst 62). Coach: Per-Mathias Høgmo (NOR)

Play-offs - FK Partizan (SRB)
H 3-2 *Prijovic (37), Björck (77), Kara (82)*
Sahlman, Kara, Björck, Kristiansen, Koppinen, Drage, Yttergård Jenssen, Ondrášek, Andersen (Bendiksen 72), Ciss (Yndestad 78), Prijovic (Johansen 62). Coach: Per-Mathias Høgmo (NOR)
A 0-1
Lekström, Kara, Björck, Kristiansen, Koppinen, Drage, Yttergård Jenssen, Ondrášek (Årst 78), Bendiksen (Norbye 78), Ciss, Prijovic (Andersen 59). Coach: Per-Mathias Høgmo (NOR)

ROSENBORG BK

First qualifying round - Crusaders FC (NIR)
A 3-0 *Dorsin (19, 76), Dočkal (71)*
Örlund, Ankersen, Dorsin, Rønning, Issah, Dočkal, Chibuike (Midtsjø 77), Iversen (Prica 55), Wangberg (Høiland 68), Henriksen, Svensson. Coach: Jan Jönsson (SWE)
H 1-0 *Ankersen (81)*
Örlund, Ankersen, Rønning, Issah (Svensson 61), Prica, Høiland, Wangberg, Berntsen, Henriksen (Strandberg 46), Midtsjø, Fredheim Holm (Chibuike 70). Coach: Jan Jönsson (SWE)

Second qualifying round - FC Ordabasy Shymkent (KAZ)
H 2-2 *Dočkal (33, 45+2p)*
Örlund, Ankersen, Dorsin, Rønning, Issah, Dočkal, Prica, Chibuike (Fredheim Holm 45+1), Henriksen, Svensson (Iversen 70), Strandberg. Coach: Jan Jönsson (SWE)
A 2-1 *Fredheim Holm (67), Dočkal (90+4)*
Örlund, Ankersen (Wangberg 46), Dorsin, Rønning, Issah (Selnæs 67), Dočkal, Prica (Iversen 82), Henriksen, Svensson, Strandberg, Fredheim Holm. Coach: Jan Jönsson (SWE)
Red cards: Wangberg 77, Prica 83

Third qualifying round - Servette FC (SUI)
A 1-1 *Dočkal (81)*
Örlund, Dorsin, Rønning, Issah, Dočkal, Chibuike (Alas 90+3), Høiland, Henriksen, Svensson, Strandberg, Fredheim Holm (Selnæs 77). Coach: Jan Jönsson (SWE)
H 0-0
Örlund, Dorsin, Rønning, Issah, Dočkal, Prica, Høiland, Henriksen, Svensson, Strandberg, Fredheim Holm (Selnæs 83). Coach: Jan Jönsson (SWE)

Play-offs - Legia Warszawa (POL)
A 1-1 *Dočkal (80)*
Örlund, Dorsin, Reginiussen, Dočkal, Høiland, Elyounoussi, Henriksen, Svensson, Strandberg, Fredheim Holm (Prica 74), Diskerud. Coach: Jan Jönsson (SWE)
H 2-1 *Reginiussen (69), Diskerud (87)*
Örlund, Dorsin, Reginiussen, Rønning, Dočkal, Prica, Høiland, Elyounoussi, Svensson, Fredheim Holm, Diskerud (Iversen 90+2). Coach: Jan Jönsson (SWE)

Group K
Match 1 - SK Rapid Wien (AUT)
A 2-1 *Elyounoussi (18), Dorsin (60)*
Örlund, Gamboa, Dorsin, Reginiussen, Rønning, Dočkal, Prica, Elyounoussi, Svensson, Fredheim Holm (Selnæs 81), Diskerud (Iversen 90+1). Coach: Jan Jönsson (SWE)
Match 2 - Bayer 04 Leverkusen (GER)
H 0-1
Örlund, Gamboa, Dorsin, Rønning, Dočkal (Chibuike 79), Prica, Elyounoussi, Selnæs (Iversen 88), Svensson, Strandberg, Fredheim Holm (Issah 69). Coach: Jan Jönsson (SWE)
Match 3 - FC Metalist Kharkiv (UKR)
H 1-2 *Elyounoussi (46)*
Örlund, Gamboa, Dorsin, Reginiussen, Dočkal, Prica, Chibuike (Fredheim Holm 77), Elyounoussi, Svensson, Strandberg, Diskerud. Coach: Jan Jönsson (SWE)
Match 4 - FC Metalist Kharkiv (UKR)
A 1-3 *Dočkal (42)*
Lund Hansen, Gamboa, Dorsin, Reginiussen, Issah, Dočkal, Iversen (Høiland 84), Selnæs (Diskerud 63), Svensson, Strandberg (Rønning 79), Fredheim Holm. Coach: Jan Jönsson (SWE)
Match 5 - SK Rapid Wien (AUT)
H 3-2 *Chibuike (28), Elyounoussi (76), Prica (79)*
Lund Hansen, Gamboa, Dorsin, Reginiussen, Dočkal (Iversen 75), Chibuike (Prica 75), Elyounoussi, Svensson, Strandberg, Fredheim Holm (Selnæs 60), Diskerud. Coach: Jan Jönsson (SWE)
Match 6 - Bayer 04 Leverkusen (GER)
A 0-1
Lund Hansen, Gamboa, Dorsin, Reginiussen, Rønning, Prica (Issah 46), Chibuike, Elyounoussi, Selnæs (Iversen 72), Svensson (Alas 82), Diskerud. Coach: Jan Jönsson (SWE)

NORWAY

STABÆK FOTBALL

EUROPA
LEAGUE

First qualifying round - JJK Jyväskylä (FIN)
A 0-2
Sayouba, Eiríksson, Cunningham, Hammer, Brustad, Haidar (Stengel 68), Boli (Stokkelien 83), Haugsdal, Hedenstad, Clark (Sortevik 79), Kleiven. Coach: Petter Belsvik (NOR)
H 3-2 *Kleiven (37), Stokkelien (45+2), Haugsdal (64)*
Sayouba, Eiríksson, Cunningham, Hammer, Brustad, Haugsdal, Stengel (Hanssen 59), Stokkelien (Boli 78), Hedenstad, Clark (Haidar 42), Kleiven. Coach: Petter Belsvik (NOR)

Domestic league club-by-club

AALESUNDS FK
Coach: Kjetil Rekdal
1914 • Color Line (10,778) • aafk.no
Major honours
Norwegian Cup (2) 2009, 2011

2012

25/03	Stabæk	a 0-0	
02/04	Tromsø	h 0-0	
09/04	Sandnes Ulf	a 1-1	*Arnefjord*
15/04	Odd Grenland	h 2-1	*Phillips, Tollås*
22/04	Hønefoss	a 1-3	*Matland*
27/04	Rosenborg	h 2-2	*Fuhre, Tollås*
06/05	Molde	h 1-2	*Arnefjord*
13/05	Strømsgodset	h 3-1	*Barrantes, Fuhre 2*
16/05	Haugesund	a 2-4	*Stewart, Arnefjord*
20/05	Brann	h 2-0	*Barrantes, Post*
24/05	Lillestrøm	a 0-2	
24/06	Sogndal	h 2-2	*Post, Arnefjord*
02/07	Vålerenga	a 0-0	
08/07	Viking	h 1-1	*Arnefjord*
15/07	Fredrikstad	h 3-0	*Barrantes 2, Post*
22/07	Brann	a 1-2	*Fuhre*
29/07	Stabæk	h 3-1	*Arnefjord, Stewart, Ulvestad (p)*
05/08	Rosenborg	a 0-3	
12/08	Molde	h 0-1	
27/08	Fredrikstad	a 3-1	*Stewart 2, Barrantes*
02/09	Hønefoss	h 2-0	*Barrantes, Tollås*
15/09	Strømsgodset	a 0-4	
22/09	Lillestrøm	h 1-2	*Ulvestad (p)*
30/09	Tromsø	a 0-1	
06/10	Viking	a 0-1	
21/10	Vålerenga	h 3-1	*Barrantes 2, James*
28/10	Sogndal	a 1-1	*James*
04/11	Haugesund	h 2-2	*Barrantes, James*
11/11	Odd Grenland	a 0-3	
18/11	Sandnes Ulf	h 3-1	*James, Matland, Fuhre*

No	Name	Nat	DoB	Pos	Aps	(s)	Gls
15	Daniel Arnefjord	SWE	21/03/79	D	23		6
31	Michael Barrantes	CRC	04/10/83	M	28		9
8	Fredrik Carlsen		01/12/89	M	5	(6)	
25	Lars Fuhre		29/09/89	A	8	(9)	5
13	Sten Grytebust		25/10/89	G	30		
37	Torbjørn Grytten		06/04/95	A		(1)	
27	Enar Jääger	EST	18/11/84	D	24	(1)	
5	Ville Jalasto	FIN	19/04/86	D	5	(4)	
14	Leke James	NGA	01/11/92	A	12		4
10	Peter Orry Larsen		25/02/89	M	12	(6)	
36	Thomas Martinussen		05/02/95	M		(3)	
22	Jo Nymo Matland		21/04/87	D	20	(1)	3
7	Jason Morrison	JAM	07/06/84	M	23		
18	Christian Myklebust		11/03/92	A	10	(2)	
6	Magnus Sylling Olsen		02/07/83	A	7	(5)	
17	Demar Phillips	JAM	23/09/83	A	19	(1)	1
9	Sander Post	EST	10/09/84	A	9	(13)	3
19	Kjell Rune Sellin		01/06/89	A	6	(2)	
3	Edvard Skagestad		06/07/88	D	12	(12)	
2	Amund Skiri		25/02/78	D	3	(7)	
11	Tremaine Stewart	JAM	01/05/88	A	13	(8)	4
4	Jonatan Tollås		01/07/90	D	29		3
23	Fredrik Ulvestad		19/05/92	M	24	(1)	2
16	Hugues Wembangomo		10/05/92	D	8	(4)	

SK BRANN
Coach: Rune Skarsfjord
1908 • Brann (17,232) • brann.no
Major honours
Norwegian League (3) 1962, 1963, 2007;
Norwegian Cup (6) 1923, 1925, 1972, 1976, 1982, 2004

2012

25/03	Rosenborg	a 1-3	*Askar*
30/03	Sandnes Ulf	h 3-1	*Austin (p), Askar, Ojo*
09/04	Molde	a 1-2	*Askar*
15/04	Strømsgodset	h 1-2	*Barmen*
21/04	Haugesund	a 1-2	*Ojo*
29/04	Vålerenga	h 1-2	*Ojo*
07/05	Viking	h 0-0	
13/05	Lillestrøm	a 4-3	*Akabueze 3, Mjelde*
16/05	Sogndal	h 5-0	*Akabueze, Mjelde, Ojo, Barmen, Askar*
20/05	Aalesund	a 0-2	
23/05	Fredrikstad	h 2-0	*Akabueze, Sævarsson*
28/05	Tromsø	a 0-2	
30/06	Stabæk	h 2-1	*Austin (p), Ojo*
07/07	Hønefoss	a 1-2	*Sokolowski*
15/07	Odd Grenland	h 6-2	*Jonsson, Korcsmár 2, Sokolowski, Austin, Ojo*
22/07	Aalesund	h 2-1	*Austin, Akabueze*
30/07	Vålerenga	a 1-1	*Askar*
06/08	Stabæk	a 4-0	*Akabueze 2, Sævarsson, Huseklepp*
11/08	Haugesund	h 3-2	*Askar 2, Nordkvelle*
24/08	Odd Grenland	a 0-1	
02/09	Molde	h 4-1	*Askar, Wangberg, Ojo 2*
16/09	Sandnes Ulf	a 3-3	*Akabueze, Ojo 2*
23/09	Rosenborg	h 2-1	*Finne 2*
30/09	Strømsgodset	a 0-2	
08/10	Hønefoss	h 3-2	*og (Sigurdsson), Finne, Larsen*
22/10	Fredrikstad	a 4-3	*Ojo, Huseklepp (p), Larsen, og (Landgren)*
29/10	Lillestrøm	h 2-3	*Huseklepp 2 (1p)*
04/11	Viking	a 1-2	*og (Bjørdal)*
11/11	Tromsø	h 0-2	
18/11	Sogndal	a 0-2	

No	Name	Nat	DoB	Pos	Aps	(s)	Gls
11	Chukwuma Akabueze	NGA	06/05/89	A	20	(8)	9
22	Amin Askar		01/10/85	M	22	(1)	8
5	Rodolph Austin	JAM	01/06/85	M	12		4
29	Kristoffer Barmen		19/08/83	M	10	(8)	2
15	Eirik Birkelund		13/01/94	M		(3)	
27	Erdin Demir	SWE	27/03/90	D	20	(2)	
7	Hassan El Fakiri		18/04/77	D	9	(2)	
28	Bård Finne		13/02/95	A	1	(6)	3
4	Lars Grorud		02/07/83	D	7		
30	Jonas Grønner		11/04/94	D	2	(3)	
33	Hannes Thór Halldórsson	ISL	27/04/84	G	1		
8	Fredrik Haugen		13/06/92	M	16	(9)	
13	Erik Huseklepp		05/09/84	A	11	(1)	4
18	Markus Jonsson	SWE	09/03/81	D	16	(1)	1
20	Kjetil Kalve		10/03/94	M		(1)	
3	Christian Kalvenes		08/03/77	D	5	(2)	
21	Zsolt Korcsmár	HUN	09/01/89	D	26		2
19	Kristoffer Larsen		19/01/92	A	8	(13)	2
24	Piotr Leciejewski	POL	23/03/85	G	23		
10	Erik Mjelde		06/03/84	M	18	(7)	2
1	Jørgen Mohus		05/09/91	G	3		
17	Oumar Niasse	SEN	18/04/90	A		(3)	
14	Fredrik Nordkvelle		13/09/85	M	15	(9)	1
9	Kim Ojo	NGA	02/12/88	A	29		11
26	Kasper Skaanes		19/03/95	A		(1)	
23	Tomasz Sokolowski		25/06/85	M	13		2
2	Birkir Már Sævarsson	ISL	11/11/84	D	30		2
4	Simen Wangberg		06/05/91	D	10		1
12	Øystein Øvretveit		25/06/94	G	3	(2)	

FREDRIKSTAD FK

Coach: Tom Freddy Aune;
(10/05/12) Trond Amundsen
1903 • Fredrikstad (12,565) • fredrikstadfk.no
Major honours
Norwegian League (9) 1938, 1939, 1949, 1951, 1952,
1954, 1957, 1960, 1961;
Norwegian Cup (11) 1932, 1935, 1936, 1938, 1940,
1950, 1957, 1961, 1966, 1984, 2006

2012

25/03	Tromsø	a 0-1	
01/04	Stabæk	h 5-1	*Elyounoussi, Hussain, Valencia, Landgren, Hagen*
09/04	Hønefoss	a 1-1	*Elyounoussi*
13/04	Rosenborg	h 1-2	*Holm*
22/04	Odd Grenland	a 1-1	*Dure*
28/04	Sandnes Ulf	h 3-4	*Valencia, Hussain, Elyounoussi (p)*
06/05	Vålerenga	a 2-3	*Elyounoussi 2*
13/05	Haugesund	h 0-0	
16/05	Molde	a 0-2	
19/05	Strømsgodset	h 2-3	*Strømsborg, Horn*
23/05	Brann	a 0-2	
29/05	Viking	h 3-0	*Halvorsen, Rafn, Gueye*
29/06	Sogndal	a 3-1	*Jabbie, Ruud Tveter, Halvorsen*
09/07	Lillestrøm	h 3-4	*Elyounoussi, Hagen, Hussain*
15/07	Aalesund	a 0-3	
22/07	Hønefoss	h 0-2	
27/07	Strømsgodset	a 0-5	
05/08	Tromsø	h 2-0	*Srećković, Elyounoussi*
12/08	Viking	a 0-3	
27/08	Aalesund	h 1-3	*Gueye*
01/09	Lillestrøm	a 2-1	*Tripic, Pusic (p)*
16/09	Sogndal	h 2-1	*og (Karadas), Pusic*
23/09	Stabæk	a 1-0	*Pusic*
01/10	Vålerenga	h 1-2	*Stene*
07/10	Haugesund	a 0-1	
22/10	Brann	h 3-4	*Stene, Pusic, Halvorsen*
27/10	Sandnes Ulf	a 1-5	*og (Bertolt)*
02/11	Odd Grenland	h 4-2	*Halvorsen 2, Srećković, Pusic*
11/11	Rosenborg	a 1-0	*Stene*
18/11	Molde	h 0-2	

No	Name	Nat	DoB	Pos	Aps	(s)	Gls
2	Haitam Aleesami		31/07/91	D	12	(1)	
18	Daniel Berntsen		04/04/93	M	3	(3)	
13	Kevin Dure		08/03/93	D	6		1
10	Tarik Elyounoussi		23/02/88	A	16		7
26	Lars Grorud		02/07/93	D	10		
16	Mouhamed Gueye	SEN	05/12/93	A	4	(16)	2
2	Benjamin Dahl Hagen		09/01/88	D	17		2
9	Ole Jørgen Halvorsen		02/07/87	M	27	(1)	5
11	Mads Hansen		02/02/84	M	11	(4)	
22	Thomas Holm		19/02/81	M	10	(3)	1
3	Jørgen Horn		07/06/87	D	19	(1)	1
20	Etzaz Hussain		27/01/93	M	12		3
14	Khalifa Jabbie	SLE	20/01/93	M	22	(5)	1
1	Jon Knudsen		20/11/84	G	16		
5	Andreas Landgren	SWE	17/03/89	D	26	(1)	1
4	Vidar Martinsen		11/03/82	D	23		
25	Jon Masalin	FIN	29/01/86	G	14		
10	Martin Pusic	AUT	24/10/87	A	10		5
21	Simen Rafn		16/02/92	M	4	(7)	1
6	Hans Erik Ramberg		08/08/76	M	17	(1)	
23	Alexander Ruud Tveter		07/03/91	M	10	(10)	1
18	Nenad Srećković	SRB	11/04/88	M	10	(2)	2
19	Simen Standerholen		15/10/93	M		(2)	
13	Robert Stene		06/01/83	A	10		3
24	Ole Strømsborg		22/08/93	D	8	(5)	1
20	Zlatko Tripic		02/12/92	A	4	(6)	1
7	Alex Valencia		22/09/79	A	9	(8)	2

FK HAUGESUND

Coach: Jostein Grindhaug
1993 • Haugesund (5,000) • fkh.no

2012

25/03	Vålerenga	a 1-2	*Djurdjić (p)*
01/04	Molde	h 2-0	*Søderlund 2*
09/04	Strømsgodset	a 3-3	*Djurdjić 2, Andreassen*
15/04	Sogndal	a 1-1	*Søderlund*
21/04	Brann	h 2-1	*Søderlund, Djurdjić*
28/04	Viking	a 2-0	*Søderlund, Fevang*
06/05	Lillestrøm	h 1-1	*Sema*
13/05	Fredrikstad	a 0-0	
16/05	Aalesund	h 4-2	*Djurdjić 3 (1p), Haukås*
20/05	Stabæk	a 2-0	*Søderlund 2*
24/05	Hønefoss	h 1-1	*Sema*
28/05	Sandnes Ulf	a 2-0	*Søderlund, Djurdjić*
30/06	Tromsø	h 1-1	*Djurdjić*
08/07	Odd Grenland	a 1-2	*Decamps*
15/07	Rosenborg	h 0-1	
20/07	Sogndal	h 0-0	
29/07	Hønefoss	a 2-3	*Fevang, Djurdjić*
03/08	Vålerenga	h 4-2	*Osmanagić, Mæland, Søderlund, Engblom*
11/08	Brann	a 2-3	*Djurdjić 2*
26/08	Stabæk	h 4-1	*Søderlund, Fevang, Myrestam, Storbæk*
02/09	Odd Grenland	h 0-1	
15/09	Molde	a 0-1	
23/09	Sandnes Ulf	h 3-2	*Storbæk, Johansen, Myrestam*
28/09	Rosenborg	a 2-5	*Fevang 2*
07/10	Fredrikstad	h 1-0	*Fevang*
21/10	Tromsø	a 0-2	
26/10	Strømsgodset	h 2-3	*Engblom, Haukås*
04/11	Aalesund	a 2-2	*Haukås, Fevang*
11/11	Viking	h 1-0	*Andreassen*
18/11	Lillestrøm	a 0-0	

No	Name	Nat	DoB	Pos	Aps	(s)	Gls
11	Tor Arne Andreassen		16/03/83	M	10	(4)	2
16	Ugonna Anyora	NGA	29/04/91	M	17	(5)	
10	Umaru Bangura	SLE	07/10/87	D	29		
15	Martin Bjørnbak		22/03/92	D	16	(1)	
3	Derek Decamps	FRA	26/05/85	D	11	(2)	1
44	Nikola Djurdjić	SRB	01/04/86	A	18		12
21	Pontus Engblom	SWE	03/11/91	A	9	(3)	2
17	Geir Ludvig Fevang		17/11/80	M	21	(2)	7
19	Kristoffer Haraldseid		17/01/94	M	3	(5)	
8	Michael Haukås		21/11/86	M	14	(8)	3
14	Andrés Már Jóhannesson	ISL	21/12/88	D	8	(2)	
25	Henrik Kjelsrud Johansen		22/02/93	A	2	(7)	1
1	Per Morten Kristiansen		14/07/81	G	30		
3	David Myrestam	SWE	04/04/87	D	9		2
13	Eirik Mæland		15/02/89	M	8	(7)	1
5	Trygve Nygaard		19/08/75	M	19	(1)	
22	Amer Osmanagić	BIH	07/05/89	M	2		1
4	Chris Pozniak	CAN	10/01/81	D	1		
20	Maic Sema	SWE	02/12/88	M	18	(5)	2
7	Oddbjørn Skartun		28/01/89	A	1	(8)	
18	Vegard Skjerve		22/05/88	D	27		
6	Håvard Storbæk		25/05/86	M	11	(12)	2
9	Alexander Søderlund		03/08/87	A	29		10
2	Joakim Våge Nilsen		24/04/91	D	17	(3)	

HØNEFOSS BK

Coach: Leif Gunnar Smerud
1895 • AKA Arena (4,373) • honefossbk.no

2012

24/03	Lillestrøm	h 0-0	
01/04	Sogndal	a 0-0	
09/04	Fredrikstad	h 1-1	*Sigurdsson*
16/04	Stabæk	a 2-0	*Riku Riski 2 (1p)*
22/04	Aalesund	h 3-1	*Bolseth, Riku Riski 2*
28/04	Tromsø	a 0-0	
06/05	Sandnes Ulf	a 0-1	
13/05	Odd Grenland	h 1-4	*Beugre*
16/05	Rosenborg	a 1-0	*Dahl*
19/05	Vålerenga	h 1-0	*Kaland*
24/05	Haugesund	a 1-1	*Riku Riski*
28/05	Molde	h 1-1	*Bolseth*
30/06	Strømsgodset	a 0-4	
07/07	Brann	h 2-1	*Mendy, Riku Riski*
15/07	Viking	a 1-2	*Riku Riski*
22/07	Fredrikstad	a 2-0	*Hovda, Larsen*
29/07	Haugesund	h 3-2	*Groven, Sigurdsson, Mora*
04/08	Strømsgodset	h 1-1	*Riku Riski*
12/08	Lillestrøm	a 2-2	*Sigurdsson, Riku Riski*
26/08	Tromsø	h 0-1	
02/09	Aalesund	a 0-2	
16/09	Viking	h 2-2	*Kaland, Beugre*
24/09	Vålerenga	a 2-3	*Kaland, Larsen*
30/09	Sogndal	h 0-0	
08/10	Brann	a 2-3	*Vendelbo, Beugre*
21/10	Stabæk	h 0-0	
28/10	Odd Grenland	a 0-4	
04/11	Sandnes Ulf	h 1-1	*Mora*
11/11	Molde	a 0-1	
18/11	Rosenborg	h 1-4	*Riku Riski*

No	Name	Nat	DoB	Pos	Aps	(s)	Gls
22	Arnór Svein Adalsteinsson	ISL	26/01/86	D	29		
27	Kevin Beugre	CIV	23/08/92	A	9	(5)	3
18	Rune Bolseth		04/07/80	M	18	(5)	2
26	Steve Clark	USA	14/04/86	G	30		
7	Christoffer Dahl		08/01/84	M	7	(7)	1
5	Vegar Gjermundstad		14/03/90	D	2	(2)	
23	Alexander Groven		02/01/92	D	23	(2)	1
4	Helge Haugen		15/02/82	M	27		
16	Tor Øyvind Hovda		24/09/89	M	9	(8)	1
24	Kenneth Di Vita Jensen		22/07/90	A	4	(5)	
19	Magnus Johannessen		27/01/93	M		(1)	
20	Mats-André Kaland		09/05/89	A	6	(14)	3
13	Toni Kolehmainen	FIN	20/07/88	M	6	(2)	
2	Frode Lafton		03/03/76	D	30		
3	Kevin Larsen		10/05/86	D	19	(7)	2
11	Joachim Magnussen		18/06/87	A	9	(4)	
21	Remond Mendy	SEN	10/10/85	A	12	(12)	1
14	Heiner Mora	CRC	20/06/84	M	26		2
17	Leo Olsen		25/09/81	M	1	(1)	
10	Riku Riski	FIN	16/08/89	A	25	(1)	10
9	Roope Riski	FIN	16/08/91	A		(1)	
6	Kristján Örn Sigurdsson	ISL	07/10/80	D	28		3
7	Mikkel Vendelbo	DEN	15/08/87	M	10		1

LILLESTRØM SK

Coach: Magnus Haglund (SWE)
1917 • Åråsen (12,000) • lsk.no
Major honours
Norwegian League (5) 1959, 1976, 1977, 1986, 1989;
Norwegian Cup (5) 1977, 1978, 1981, 1985, 2007

2012

24/03	Hønefoss	a	0-0	
01/04	Rosenborg	h	2-2	Andersson, Rodgers
09/04	Odd Grenland	a	0-2	
15/04	Vålerenga	h	1-1	Vaagan Moen (p)
23/04	Molde	a	2-3	Pálmason, Kippe
28/04	Strømsgodset	h	0-1	
06/05	Haugesund	a	1-1	Sigurdarson
13/05	Brann	h	3-4	Sigurdarson 3 (1p)
16/05	Viking	a	2-1	Sigurdarson 2
20/05	Sogndal	h	1-0	Sigurdarson
24/05	Aalesund	h	0-0	
28/05	Stabæk	a	1-4	Knudtzon
30/06	Sandnes Ulf	h	1-3	Knudtzon
09/07	Fredrikstad	a	4-3	Knudtzon 2, Vaagan Moen, Pálmason
13/07	Tromsø	h	4-2	Knudtzon, Omoijuanfo, Toindouba, Pálmason
23/07	Rosenborg	a	1-1	Vaagan Moen
28/07	Molde	h	1-1	Nystuen
05/08	Sandnes Ulf	a	1-0	Kippe
12/08	Hønefoss	h	2-2	Knudtzon, Andersson
25/08	Strømsgodset	a	3-3	Helstad, Knudtzon, Riise (p)
01/09	Fredrikstad	h	1-2	Helstad
17/09	Tromsø	a	1-5	Vaagan Moen
22/09	Aalesund	a	2-1	Riise, Bolly
28/09	Viking	h	0-0	
07/10	Sogndal	a	0-1	
20/10	Odd Grenland	h	1-1	Vaagan Moen
29/10	Brann	a	3-2	Bolly 2, Østli
04/11	Stabæk	h	6-0	Vaagan Moen, Helstad, Pálmason 2, Bolly, Gulbrandsen
11/11	Vålerenga	a	2-1	Knudtzon, Pálmason
18/11	Haugesund	h	0-0	

No	Name	Nat	DoB	Pos	Aps	(s)	Gls
7	Johan Andersson	SWE	22/08/83	M	19	(8)	2
26	Mathis Bolly		14/11/90	A	13	(11)	4
29	Jakob Faye-Lund		15/09/94	G		(2)	
21	Moryké Fofana	CIV	23/11/91	M		(2)	
28	Ruben Gabrielsen		03/03/92	D	13	(3)	
9	Fredrik Gulbrandsen		10/09/92	A	3	(7)	1
23	Henning Hauger		17/07/85	M	8	(1)	
22	Thorstein Helstad		28/04/77	A	10	(2)	3
13	Frode Kippe		17/01/78	D	21	(1)	2
11	Erling Knudtzon		15/12/88	A	25	(4)	8
1	Stefán Logi Magnússon	ISL	05/09/80	G	2		
4	Espen Nystuen		19/12/81	D	15	(3)	1
16	Ohi Omoijuanfo		30/11/93	M	12	(5)	1
33	Joachim Osvold		23/09/94	A		(3)	
14	Pálmi Rafn Pálmason	ISL	09/11/84	M	27	(1)	6
2	Steinar Pedersen		06/06/75	D	11	(1)	
12	Sead Ramović	BIH	14/03/79	G	26		
8	Bjørn Helge Riise		21/06/83	M	11		2
20	Stian Ringstad		29/08/91	D	14	(6)	
23	Luke Rodgers	ENG	01/01/82	A	1	(6)	1
3	Isak Scheel		19/06/90	D	4		
8	Björn Bergmann Sigurdarson	ISL	26/02/91	A	13		7
1	Lasse Staw		01/01/88	G	2		
27	Fredrik Stoor	SWE	28/02/84	D	21		
6	Espen Søgård		10/10/79	M	1	(3)	
25	Guy Roger Toindouba	CMR	14/11/88	M	12	(6)	1
10	Petter Vaagan Moen		05/02/84	M	23		6
5	Jesper Westerberg	SWE	01/02/86	D	10	(2)	
19	Anders Østli		08/01/83	D	13		1

MOLDE FK

Coach: Ole Gunnar Solskjær
1911 • Aker (11,167) • moldefk.no
Major honours
Norwegian League (2) 2011, 2012;
Norwegian Cup (2) 1994, 2005

2012

23/03	Strømsgodset	h	2-1	Angan, Gatt
01/04	Haugesund	a	0-2	
09/04	Brann	h	2-1	Berget, Angan
16/04	Viking	a	0-1	
23/04	Lillestrøm	h	3-2	Angan, Moström, Chima
28/04	Sogndal	a	1-2	Moström
06/05	Aalesund	h	2-1	Moström, Hoseth (p)
12/05	Stabæk	a	5-0	Berg Hestad, Angan 2, Gatt, Berget
16/05	Fredrikstad	h	2-0	Angan 2
20/05	Sandnes Ulf	a	2-0	Moström, Berget
24/05	Tromsø	h	3-2	Berget, Angan, Hovland
28/05	Hønefoss	a	1-1	Angan
30/06	Odd Grenland	h	3-1	Berget, Hoseth 2 (1p)
08/07	Rosenborg	a	0-1	
14/07	Vålerenga	a	2-1	Gatt, Angan
21/07	Viking	h	1-2	Gatt
28/07	Lillestrøm	a	1-1	Simonsen
04/08	Sogndal	h	2-1	Linnes, Chima
12/08	Aalesund	a	1-0	Hussain
26/08	Vålerenga	h	2-0	Gatt, Angan
02/09	Brann	a	1-4	Angan
15/09	Haugesund	h	1-0	Berget
23/09	Odd Grenland	a	0-0	
30/09	Stabæk	h	3-2	Chima 3, Stamnestrø
07/10	Sandnes Ulf	h	3-2	Moström, Berget (p), Forren
21/10	Strømsgodset	a	1-1	Berget
28/10	Rosenborg	h	2-0	Diouf, Hussain
03/11	Tromsø	a	1-1	Chima
11/11	Hønefoss	h	1-0	Chima
18/11	Fredrikstad	a	2-0	Angan (p), Berg Hestad

No	Name	Nat	DoB	Pos	Aps	(s)	Gls
20	Davy Claude Angan	CIV	20/09/87	A	22	(4)	13
6	Daniel Berg Hestad		30/07/75	M	15	(9)	2
11	Jo Inge Berget		11/09/90	A	23	(5)	8
32	Abdou Karim Camara	SEN	27/10/92	M	1	(5)	
27	Daniel Chima	NGA	04/04/91	A	10	(14)	7
29	Pape Paté Diouf	SEN	04/04/86	A	8	(1)	1
7	Magnus Wolff Eikrem		08/08/90	M	26	(1)	
17	Emmanuel Ekpo	NGA	20/12/87	M	7	(6)	
5	Vegard Forren		16/02/88	D	30		1
22	Joshua Gatt	USA	29/08/91	A	14	(5)	5
10	Magne Hoseth		13/10/80	M	13	(3)	3
4	Even Hovland		14/02/89	D	18		1
16	Etzaz Hussain		27/01/93	M	6	(4)	2
14	Martin Linnes		20/09/91	D	23	(1)	1
9	Mattias Moström	SWE	25/02/83	A	23	(5)	5
1	Espen Bugge Pettersen		10/05/80	G	23		
23	Knut Olav Rindarøy		17/07/85	D	26		
18	Magne Simonsen		13/07/88	D	10	(4)	1
15	Magnus Stamnestrø		18/04/92	M	6	(3)	1
3	Børre Steenslid		25/06/85	D	1	(4)	
12	Ole Söderberg	SWE	20/07/90	G	7		
30	Zlatko Tripic		02/12/92	A	3	(9)	
2	Kristoffer Paulsen Vatshaug		03/06/81	D	13		
19	Viní Dantas	BRA	04/08/89	A	1		
24	Magnar Ødegaard		11/05/93	D	1	(1)	

ODD GRENLAND

Coach: Dag-Eilev Fagermo
1894 • Skagerak Arena (13,500) • odd.no
Major honours
Norwegian Cup (12) 1903, 1904, 1905, 1906, 1913, 1915, 1919, 1922, 1924, 1926, 1931, 2000

2012

25/03	Sogndal	h	0-4	
01/04	Viking	a	0-1	
09/04	Lillestrøm	h	2-0	Børven, Eriksen
15/04	Aalesund	a	1-2	Krogsgård
22/04	Fredrikstad	h	1-1	Fevang (p)
28/04	Stabæk	a	2-0	Johnsen, Børven
05/05	Tromsø	h	2-2	Johnsen, Brenne
13/05	Hønefoss	a	4-1	Güven 2, Krogsgård, Brenne
16/05	Sandnes Ulf	h	2-2	Børven, Fevang (p)
20/05	Rosenborg	a	0-0	
23/05	Strømsgodset	a	0-1	
30/06	Molde	a	1-3	Børven
08/07	Haugesund	h	2-1	Güven, Børven
11/07	Vålerenga	h	2-3	Brenne, Børven (p)
15/07	Brann	a	2-6	Semb, Andersson
22/07	Strømsgodset	h	2-1	Børven, og (Aas)
29/07	Sogndal	a	1-0	Børven (p)
05/08	Viking	h	1-4	Johnsen
10/08	Vålerenga	a	1-3	Rashani
24/08	Brann	h	1-0	Shala
02/09	Haugesund	a	1-0	Gunnarsson
16/09	Stabæk	h	1-2	Shala
23/09	Molde	h	0-0	
30/09	Sandnes Ulf	a	0-0	
07/10	Rosenborg	h	0-1	
20/10	Lillestrøm	a	1-1	Olsen
28/10	Hønefoss	h	4-0	Shala, Güven, Krogsgård, White
02/11	Fredrikstad	a	2-4	Güven, Brenne
11/11	Aalesund	h	3-0	Brenne, Fevang, Johnsen
18/11	Tromsø	a	1-0	Fevang (p)

No	Name	Nat	DoB	Pos	Aps	(s)	Gls
5	Paul Addo	GHA	14/06/90	D	9	(2)	
9	Mattias Andersson	SWE	07/10/81	A	8	(4)	1
6	Simen Brenne		17/03/81	M	23	(2)	5
22	Torgeir Børven		03/12/91	A	17	(2)	8
23	Lars-Kristian Eriksen		28/06/83	D	7	(2)	1
4	Morten Fevang		06/03/75	D	23	(3)	4
17	Niklas Gunnarsson		27/04/91	D	16	(6)	1
7	Adem Güven		11/10/85	A	20	(7)	5
21	Steffen Hagen		08/03/86	D	30		
1	André Hansen		17/12/89	G	29		
11	Frode Johnsen		17/03/74	A	23	(6)	4
2	Emil Jonassen		17/02/93	D	22		
19	Snorre Krogsgård		25/05/91	A	18	(10)	3
10	Magnus Lekven		13/01/88	M	11	(1)	
13	Andreas Lie		31/08/87	G	1	(2)	
20	Fredrik Oldrup Jensen		18/05/93	M	5	(3)	
28	Dag Alexander Olsen		09/09/89	A	1	(5)	1
15	Elba Rashani		09/05/93	A	10	(6)	1
8	Jone Samuelsen		06/07/84	M	23	(2)	
3	Fredrik Semb Berge		06/02/90	D	21		1
18	Herolind Shala		01/02/92	M	12	(14)	3
14	George White	NGA	13/01/93	A	1	(4)	1

ROSENBORG BK

Coach: Jan Jönsson (SWE)
1917 • Lerkendal (21,166) • rbk.no
Major honours
Norwegian League (22) 1967, 1969, 1971, 1985, 1988,
1990, 1992, 1993, 1994, 1995, 1996, 1997, 1998, 1999,
2000, 2001, 2002, 2003, 2004, 2006, 2009, 2010;
Norwegian Cup (9) 1960, 1964, 1971, 1988, 1990,
1992, 1995, 1999, 2003

2012

25/03	Brann	h	3-1	*Iversen, Larsen, Prica*
01/04	Lillestrøm	a	2-2	*Iversen, Dorsin*
09/04	Sogndal	h	0-0	
13/04	Fredrikstad	a	2-1	*Iversen, Larsen*
22/04	Tromsø	h	3-0	*Henriksen, Dorsin, Svensson*
27/04	Aalesund	a	2-2	*Prica, Iversen*
04/05	Stabæk	h	3-1	*Midtsjø, Dočkal, Svensson*
13/05	Sandnes Ulf	a	1-1	*Prica*
16/05	Hønefoss	h	0-1	
20/05	Odd Grenland	h	0-0	
23/05	Vålerenga	a	0-0	
24/06	Strømsgodset	h	3-3	*og (Sætra), Dočkal 2 (1p)*
30/06	Viking	a	4-1	*Fredheim Holm, Dočkal, Chibuike, Prica*
08/07	Molde	h	1-0	*Svensson*
15/07	Haugesund	a	1-0	*Dočkal*
23/07	Lillestrøm	h	1-1	*Rønning*
29/07	Tromsø	a	1-1	*Fredheim Holm*
05/08	Aalesund	h	3-0	*Dočkal, Prica, Strandberg*
12/08	Sogndal	a	3-0	*Dočkal 2 (2p), Chibuike*
26/08	Viking	h	1-1	*Dorsin*
03/09	Stabæk	a	2-0	*Iversen 2*
16/09	Vålerenga	h	3-0	*Prica 2, Selnæs*
23/09	Brann	a	1-2	*Chibuike*
28/09	Haugesund	h	5-2	*og (Søderlund), Dočkal, Prica, Chibuike, Diskerud*
07/10	Odd Grenland	a	1-0	*Prica*
19/10	Sandnes Ulf	a	2-0	*Dočkal (p), Dorsin*
28/10	Molde	a	0-2	
04/11	Strømsgodset	a	1-2	*Prica*
11/11	Fredrikstad	h	0-1	
18/11	Hønefoss	a	4-1	*Strandberg, Fredheim Holm, Prica, Rønning*

No	Name	Nat	DoB	Pos	Aps	(s)	Gls
13	Jaime Alas	SLV	30/07/89	M		(3)	
2	Peter Ankersen	DEN	22/09/90	D	4	(6)	
18	Daniel Berntsen		04/04/93	M		(1)	
10	John Chibuike	NGA	10/10/88	A	17	(6)	4
42	Mikkel Diskerud	USA	02/10/90	M	10	(1)	1
8	Bořek Dočkal	CZE	30/09/88	M	27		10
3	Mikael Dorsin	SWE	06/10/81	D	28		4
17	Tarik Elyounoussi		23/02/88	A	10	(1)	
28	Daniel Fredheim Holm		30/07/85	A	22	(6)	3
2	Cristian Gamboa	CRC	24/10/89	D	9	(1)	
19	Markus Henriksen		25/07/92	M	18		1
14	Jon Inge Høiland		20/09/77	D	18	(1)	
7	Mohammed-Awal Issah	GHA	04/04/86	M	10	(2)	
11	Steffen Iversen		10/11/76	A	12	(9)	6
4	Jim Larsen	DEN	06/11/85	D	11		2
12	Alexander Lund Hansen		06/10/82	G	2	(1)	
21	Fredrik Midtsjø		11/08/93	M	2	(6)	1
9	Rade Prica	SWE	30/06/80	A	16	(10)	11
4	Tore Reginiussen		10/04/86	D	9	(2)	
5	Per Verner Rønning		09/01/83	D	12	(2)	2
20	Ole Kristian Selnæs		07/07/94	M	12	(10)	1
24	Stefan Strandberg		25/07/90	D	23		2
22	Jonas Svensson		06/03/93	M	24	(3)	3
16	Simen Wangberg		06/05/91	D	6	(4)	
1	Daniel Örlund	SWE	23/06/80	G	28		

SANDNES ULF

Coach: Asle Andersen
1911 • Sandnes Idrettspark (4,969) • sandnesulf.no

2012

26/03	Viking	h	2-2	*Ondo, Aanestad*
30/03	Brann	a	1-3	*Saaliti*
09/04	Aalesund	h	1-1	*Raskaj*
15/04	Tromsø	a	1-3	*Torsteinbø*
22/04	Stabæk	h	2-1	*Thorsteinsson, Skjølsvik (p)*
28/04	Fredrikstad	a	4-3	*Høiland 2, Skjølsvik (p), og (Hagen)*
06/05	Hønefoss	h	1-0	*og (Lafton)*
13/05	Rosenborg	h	1-1	*Skjølsvik (p)*
16/05	Odd Grenland	a	2-2	*Saaliti, Skjølsvik (p)*
20/05	Molde	h	0-2	
23/05	Sogndal	a	0-0	
28/05	Haugesund	h	0-2	
30/06	Lillestrøm	a	3-1	*Saaliti, Thorsteinsson, Ondo*
08/07	Vålerenga	h	0-2	
16/07	Strømsgodset	a	1-2	*Aanestad*
29/07	Viking	a	0-5	
05/08	Lillestrøm	h	0-1	
12/08	Stabæk	a	1-2	*og (Helgason)*
26/08	Sogndal	h	3-1	*Gytkjær, Thorsteinsson, Torsteinbø*
31/08	Vålerenga	a	0-4	
16/09	Brann	h	3-3	*Gytkjær 2, Torsteinbø*
23/09	Haugesund	a	2-3	*Gytkjær, Thorsteinsson*
30/09	Odd Grenland	h	0-0	
07/10	Molde	a	2-3	*Høiland, Raskaj*
19/10	Rosenborg	a	0-2	
27/10	Fredrikstad	h	5-1	*Gytkjær 2 (2p), Raskaj, Torsteinbø, Thorsteinsson*
04/11	Hønefoss	a	1-1	*Skjølsvik (p)*
07/11	Tromsø	h	5-1	*Skjølsvik (p), Gytkjær (p), Thorsteinsson, Torsteinbø, Helle*
11/11	Strømsgodset	h	2-1	*Gytkjær, Pepa*
18/11	Aalesund	a	1-3	*Bertolt*

No	Name	Nat	DoB	Pos	Aps	(s)	Gls
19	Vegard Aanestad		12/06/87	D	23	(3)	2
17	Andreas Ulland Andersen		06/05/89	M	9	(2)	
1	Bo Andersen	DEN	26/03/76	G	14		
28	Morten Bertolt	DEN	12/02/84	M	10	(1)	1
25	Zymer Bytyqi		14/09/96	M		(5)	
22	Morten Eriksen		26/04/83	A	1	(1)	
4	Ronny Espedal		09/05/75	D	24		
24	Aslak Falch		25/05/92	G	10		
5	Edier Frejd	SWE	16/12/79	D	26		
29	Christian Gytkjær	DEN	06/05/90	A	12		8
14	Steffen Haugland		11/08/87	D	2	(1)	
11	Óskar Örn Hauksson	ISL	22/08/84	A	1	(7)	
18	Marius Helle		11/08/83	A	5	(7)	1
10	Bjørnar Holmvik		02/06/85	D	18	(3)	
77	Tommy Høiland		11/04/89	A	15	(10)	3
12	Sean McDermott	IRL	30/05/93	G	6		
7	Vetle Myhre		15/02/91	A		(5)	
20	Mobi Okoli	NGA	18/10/87	M		(2)	
18	Gilles Mbang Ondo	GAB	10/10/85	A	5	(8)	2
6	Avni Pepa		14/11/88	D	17		1
21	Anel Raskaj	ALB	02/08/89	M	19	(2)	3
11	Kamal Saaliti		02/08/79	A	17	(2)	3
8	Aksel Berget Skjølsvik		15/05/87	M	25		6
26	Kenneth Sola		25/08/85	D	15	(1)	
23	Steinthór Thorsteinsson	ISL	29/07/85	M	29		6
7	Fredrik Torsteinbø		13/03/91	A	19	(10)	5
27	Arnór Ingvi Traustason	ISL	30/04/93	A	4	(6)	
15	Harald Vindenes		01/06/87	D	3	(4)	
16	Andreas Haukland Westlye		17/08/86	M	1	(3)	

SOGNDAL IL FOTBALL

Coach: Jonas Olsson (SWE)
1926 • Fosshaugane Campus (5,500) • sogndalfotball.no

2012

25/03	Odd Grenland	a	4-0	*Brochmann 2, Hopen, Furebotn*
01/04	Hønefoss	h	0-0	
09/04	Rosenborg	a	0-0	
15/04	Haugesund	h	1-1	*Mané*
20/04	Vålerenga	a	2-0	*Valsvik, Brochmann*
28/04	Molde	h	2-1	*og (Linnes), U Flo*
06/05	Strømsgodset	a	0-3	
13/05	Viking	h	1-2	*Patronen*
16/05	Brann	a	0-5	
20/05	Lillestrøm	a	0-1	
23/05	Sandnes Ulf	h	0-0	
24/06	Aalesund	a	2-2	*U Flo 2*
29/06	Fredrikstad	h	1-3	*U Flo*
07/07	Tromsø	a	1-1	*Valsvik*
15/07	Stabæk	h	3-1	*U Flo 2, Brochmann*
20/07	Haugesund	a	0-0	
29/07	Odd Grenland	h	0-1	
04/08	Molde	a	1-2	*Brochmann*
12/08	Rosenborg	h	0-3	
26/08	Sandnes Ulf	a	1-3	*Ricardo Santos*
02/09	Strømsgodset	h	1-1	*Ricardo Santos*
16/09	Fredrikstad	a	1-2	*U Flo*
23/09	Tromsø	h	1-0	*og (Ciss)*
30/09	Hønefoss	a	0-0	
07/10	Lillestrøm	h	1-0	*Mané*
21/10	Viking	a	1-2	*U Flo*
28/10	Aalesund	h	1-1	*Dyngeland*
05/11	Vålerenga	h	1-0	*Patronen*
11/11	Stabæk	a	1-2	*U Flo*
18/11	Brann	h	2-0	*U Flo, Hopen*

No	Name	Nat	DoB	Pos	Aps	(s)	Gls
27	Peter Aase		27/03/95	M		(2)	
12	Stéphane Diarra Badji	SEN	29/05/90	M	24		
9	Eirik Bakke		13/09/77	M	8	(11)	
27	Tonny Brochmann	DEN	27/11/90	M	24	(1)	5
18	Stian Dyngeland		13/02/91	A	4	(9)	1
6	Ahyee Aye Elvis	CIV	12/12/83	M	2	(12)	
24	Per Egil Flo		18/01/89	D	16		
19	Tore André Flo		15/06/73	A		(13)	
8	Ulrik Flo		06/10/88	A	27		10
7	Henrik Furebotn		11/02/86	M	25	(1)	1
25	Ruben Holsæter		20/04/91	M	4	(10)	
10	Ørjan Hopen		19/03/92	M	17	(9)	2
3	Azar Karadas		09/08/81	A	5	(2)	
21	Leif Lysne		09/04/92	G			
26	Malick Mané	SEN	14/10/88	A	30		2
28	Jasmin Mecinovic	MKD	22/10/90	D	2		
23	Espen Næss Lund		07/05/85	D			
4	Hannu Patronen	FIN	23/05/84	D	28		2
11	Ricardo Santos	BRA	13/02/87	A	12	(1)	2
24	Eirik Skaasheim		22/01/93	D	24	(1)	
2	Taijo Teniste	EST	31/01/88	D	24		
1	Nils Kenneth Udjus		02/07/83	G	30		
17	Gustav Valsvik		26/05/93	D	24	(3)	2

STABÆK FOTBALL

Coach: Petter Belsvik
1912 • Nadderud (7,000) • stabak.no
Major honours
Norwegian League (1) 2008;
Norwegian Cup (1) 1998

2012

Date	Opponent		Score	Scorers
25/03	Aalesund	h	0-0	
01/04	Fredrikstad	a	1-5	*Boli*
09/04	Tromsø	a	0-3	
16/04	Hønefoss	h	0-2	
22/04	Sandnes Ulf	a	1-2	*Brustad*
28/04	Odd Grenland	h	0-2	
04/05	Rosenborg	a	1-3	*Boli*
12/05	Molde	h	0-5	
20/05	Haugesund	h	0-2	
23/05	Viking	a	0-1	
28/05	Lillestrøm	h	4-1	*Aase, Brustad 2, Hedenstad*
24/06	Vålerenga	a	2-1	*Hedenstad, Kleiven*
30/06	Brann	a	1-2	*Kleiven*
08/07	Strømsgodset	h	1-2	*Haugsdal*
15/07	Sogndal	a	1-3	*Stokkelien*
22/07	Vålerenga	h	1-3	*Brustad*
29/07	Aalesund	a	1-3	*Boli*
06/08	Brann	h	0-4	
12/08	Sandnes Ulf	h	2-1	*Kleiven, Hammer*
26/08	Haugesund	a	1-4	*Haugsdal*
03/09	Rosenborg	h	0-2	
16/09	Odd Grenland	a	2-1	*Eiríksson, Brustad*
23/09	Fredrikstad	h	0-1	
30/09	Molde	a	3-4	*Boli, Gunnarsson, Haugsdal*
07/10	Tromsø	h	0-1	
21/10	Hønefoss	a	0-0	
28/10	Viking	h	0-1	
04/11	Lillestrøm	a	0-6	
11/11	Sogndal	h	2-1	*Boli, Eiríksson*
18/11	Strømsgodset	a	1-3	*Gunnarsson*

No	Name	Nat	DoB	Pos	Aps	(s)	Gls
27	Torstein Andersen Aase		24/10/91	A	4	(3)	1
25	Erik Benjaminsen		03/09/92	M		(4)	
11	Franck Boli	CIV	07/12/93	A	19	(9)	5
6	Fredrik Brustad		22/06/89	A	25	(2)	5
26	Ricardo Clark	USA	10/02/83	M	12		
4	Sean Cunningham	USA	24/01/94	D	18		
2	Bjarni Ólafur Eiríksson	ISL	28/03/82	D	28		2
16	Tor Marius Gromstad		08/07/89	D	6		
20	Veigar Páll Gunnarsson	ISL	21/03/80	A	10		2
10	Adnan Haidar	LIB	03/08/89	M	20	(4)	
5	Jørgen Hammer		02/04/85	M	23	(2)	1
27	David Hanssen		13/11/76	M	15	(2)	
13	Bjarte Haugsdal		09/03/90	M	17	(4)	3
23	Vegar Eggen Hedenstad		26/06/91	D	14		2
3	Elfar Freyr Helgason	ISL	27/07/89	D	7		
17	Kim-André Hunstad		07/12/84	D	7	(2)	
15	Ville Jalasto	FIN	19/04/86	D	11		
28	Luc Kassi	CIV	20/08/94	M		(5)	
81	Christer Kleiven		09/04/88	M	30		3
21	Abdurahim Laajab		25/05/85	A		(5)	
22	Jan Kjell Larsen		24/06/83	G	12	(1)	
1	Mandé Sayouba	CIV	15/06/93	G	18		
8	Stian Sortevik		17/07/88	A	11	(8)	
14	Herman Stengel		26/08/95	M	15	(5)	
18	Mads Stokkelien		15/03/90	A	8	(10)	1
21	Ståle Sæthre		02/04/93	A		(3)	
24	Anders Trondsen		30/03/95	M		(3)	

STRØMSGODSET IF

Coach: Ronny Deila
1907 • Marienlyst (7,500) • godset.no
Major honours
Norwegian League (1) 1970;
Norwegian Cup (5) 1969, 1970, 1973, 1991, 2010

2012

Date	Opponent		Score	Scorers
23/03	Molde	a	1-2	*Wikheim*
31/03	Vålerenga	h	3-2	*Storflor, Diomande, Strand*
09/04	Haugesund	h	3-3	*Diomande, Kamara (p), Kovács*
15/04	Brann	a	2-1	*Aas, Kovács*
22/04	Viking	h	1-0	*Vilsvik (p)*
28/04	Lillestrøm	a	1-0	*Diomande*
06/05	Sogndal	h	3-0	*Sankoh, Aas, Diomande*
13/05	Aalesund	a	1-3	*Diomande*
16/05	Tromsø	h	2-0	*Konradsen, Storflor*
19/05	Fredrikstad	a	3-2	*Kovács, Abu 2*
23/05	Odd Grenland	h	1-0	*Aas*
24/06	Rosenborg	a	3-3	*Kamara 3*
30/06	Hønefoss	h	4-0	*Keita, Kamara 2, og (Lafton)*
08/07	Stabæk	a	2-1	*Storflor, Kovács*
16/07	Sandnes Ulf	h	2-1	*Johansen, Keita*
22/07	Odd Grenland	a	1-2	*Diomande*
27/07	Fredrikstad	h	5-0	*Johansen, Kovács 2, Diomande, Kamara*
04/08	Hønefoss	a	1-1	*Storflor*
12/08	Tromsø	a	0-4	
25/08	Lillestrøm	h	3-3	*Kovács 2, Kamara (p)*
02/09	Sogndal	a	1-1	*Keita*
15/09	Aalesund	h	4-0	*Kovács, Johansen, Nuhu, Wikheim*
21/09	Viking	a	2-3	*Ibrahim, Vilsvik*
30/09	Brann	h	2-0	*Vilsvik (p), Kamara*
05/10	Vålerenga	a	1-1	*Ibrahim*
21/10	Molde	h	1-1	*Storbæk*
26/10	Haugesund	a	3-2	*Kovács 2, Storbæk*
04/11	Rosenborg	h	2-1	*Kamara, Kovács*
11/11	Sandnes Ulf	a	1-2	*Ibrahim*
18/11	Stabæk	h	3-1	*Kamara, Kovács 2*

No	Name	Nat	DoB	Pos	Aps	(s)	Gls
6	Alexander Aas		14/09/78	D	12		3
21	Mohammed Abu	GHA	14/11/91	M	11		2
22	Bismarck Adjei-Boateng	GHA	10/05/94	D	2	(6)	
24	Lars Cramer		25/05/91	G	1		
15	Adama Diomande		14/02/90	A	8	(13)	7
50	Karanveer Grewal		23/04/93	D		(1)	
2	Mounir Hamoud		01/02/85	D	7	(5)	
16	Abdisalam Ibrahim		04/05/91	M	9	(2)	3
8	Stefan Johansen		08/01/91	M	21	(6)	3
11	Ola Kamara		15/10/89	A	19	(11)	11
7	Muhamed Keita		02/09/90	A	16	(3)	3
23	Anders Konradsen		18/07/90	M	24	(5)	1
10	Péter Kovács	HUN	07/02/78	A	22	(6)	14
12	Adam Larsen Kwarasey	GHA	12/12/87	G	29		
4	Kim André Madsen		12/03/89	D	27		
25	Tokmac Nguen		20/10/93	A		(1)	
28	Razak Nuhu	GHA	01/05/91	D	23	(2)	1
18	Martin Rønning Ovenstad		18/04/94	M		(3)	
27	Alfred Sankoh	SLE	22/10/88	M	10	(1)	1
27	Jarl-André Storbæk		21/09/78	D	10		2
9	Øyvind Storflor		18/12/79	A	27		4
14	Lars Iver Strand		07/05/83	M	8	(12)	1
29	Ole Amund Sveen		05/01/90	D		(2)	
3	Lars Sætra		24/07/91	D	11	(2)	
26	Lars Christopher Vilsvik		18/10/88	D	30		3
19	Gustav Wikheim		18/03/93	M	3	(7)	2

TROMSØ IL

Coach: Per-Mathias Høgmo
1920 • Alfheim (6,859) • til.no
Major honours
Norwegian Cup (2) 1986, 1996

2012

Date	Opponent		Score	Scorers
25/03	Fredrikstad	h	1-0	*Ondrášek*
02/04	Aalesund	a	0-0	
09/04	Stabæk	h	3-0	*Andersen, Kara, Norbye*
15/04	Sandnes Ulf	h	3-1	*Ondrášek, Drage (p), og (Aanestad)*
22/04	Rosenborg	a	0-3	
28/04	Hønefoss	h	0-0	
05/05	Odd Grenland	a	2-2	*Kara, Norbye*
12/05	Vålerenga	h	3-1	*Ondrášek, Andersen 2*
16/05	Strømsgodset	a	0-2	
20/05	Viking	h	5-1	*Johansen, Andersen, Koppinen, Nystrøm, Ondrášek*
24/05	Molde	a	2-3	*Ondrášek, Johansen*
28/05	Brann	h	2-0	*Ondrášek 2*
30/06	Haugesund	a	1-1	*Norbye*
07/07	Sogndal	h	1-1	*Ondrášek*
11/07	Lillestrøm	a	2-4	*Norbye, Nystrøm*
29/07	Rosenborg	h	1-1	*Ondrášek*
05/08	Fredrikstad	a	0-2	
12/08	Strømsgodset	h	4-0	*Kristiansen, Ciss, Drage (p), Ondrášek*
26/08	Hønefoss	a	1-0	*Johansen*
02/09	Viking	a	1-0	*Årst*
17/09	Lillestrøm	h	5-1	*Björck 2, Bendiksen, Ondrášek 2*
23/09	Sogndal	a	0-1	
30/09	Aalesund	h	1-0	*Kara*
07/10	Stabæk	a	0-1	*Årst*
21/10	Haugesund	h	2-0	*Prijovic, Årst*
28/10	Vålerenga	a	0-1	
03/11	Molde	h	1-1	*Prijovic*
07/11	Sandnes Ulf	a	1-5	*Prijovic*
11/11	Brann	a	2-0	*Ondrášek 2 (1p)*
18/11	Odd Grenland	h	0-1	

No	Name	Nat	DoB	Pos	Aps	(s)	Gls
15	Magnus Andersen		28/05/86	M	23	(7)	4
18	Thomas Kind Bendiksen		08/08/89	A	19	(4)	1
3	Fredrik Björck	SWE	22/10/79	D	30		2
22	Saliou Ciss	SEN	15/09/89	D	20	(3)	1
10	Thomas Drage		20/02/92	M	26	(4)	2
19	William Frantzen		13/06/93	M		(1)	
17	Remi Johansen		04/09/90	M	13	(11)	3
2	Sérigne Modou Kara	SEN	11/11/89	A	21	(1)	3
7	Miika Koppinen	FIN	05/07/78	D	17	(2)	1
4	Ruben Kristiansen		20/02/88	D	13	(3)	1
27	Benny Lekström	SWE	19/02/81	G	19	(1)	
21	Vegard Lysvoll		16/08/89	A		(4)	
14	Hans Julius Norbye		16/01/87	D	27	(1)	4
9	Steffen Nystrøm		01/07/84	A	7	(10)	2
13	Zdeněk Ondrášek	CZE	22/12/88	A	27	(2)	14
28	Aleksandar Prijovic	SUI	21/04/90	A	11	(2)	3
1	Marcus Sahlman	SWE	02/01/85	G	9		
35	Henri Sillanpää	FIN	04/06/79	G	2		
16	Hans Åge Yndestad		24/07/80	D	13	(9)	
11	Ruben Yttergård Jenssen		04/05/88	M	29		
25	Ole Martin Årst		19/07/74	A	4	(21)	3

VIKING FK

Coach: Åge Hareide; (09/06/12) (Gary Goodchild (ENG));
(25/06/12) Kjell Jonevret (SWE)
1899 • Viking (16,300) • viking-fk.no
Major honours
Norwegian League (8) 1958, 1972, 1973, 1974,
1975, 1979, 1982, 1991;
Norwegian Cup (5) 1953, 1959, 1979, 1989, 2001

2012

26/03	Sandnes Ulf	a	2-2	*og (Skjølsvik), Nevland*
01/04	Odd Grenland	h	1-0	*Danielsen*
10/04	Vålerenga	a	0-1	
16/04	Molde	h	1-0	*Ørnskov*
22/04	Strømsgodset	a	0-1	
28/04	Haugesund	h	0-2	
07/05	Brann	a	0-0	
13/05	Sogndal	a	2-1	*Danielsen, Sigurdsson*
16/05	Lillestrøm	h	1-2	*Andersson*
20/05	Tromsø	a	1-5	*Lanlay*
23/05	Stabæk	h	1-0	*Nisja*
29/05	Fredrikstad	a	0-3	
30/06	Rosenborg	h	1-4	*Danielsen*
08/07	Aalesund	a	1-1	*Olsen*
15/07	Hønefoss	h	2-1	*Olsen, Veton Berisha*
21/07	Molde	a	2-1	*Veton Berisha, og (Forren)*
29/07	Sandnes Ulf	h	5-0	*Veton Berisha, Nisja, Lanlay, Skogseid, Landu Landu*
05/08	Odd Grenland	a	4-1	*Veton Berisha 2, Nisja, Ørnskov*
12/08	Fredrikstad	h	3-0	*Lanlay, Olsen, Nisja*
26/08	Rosenborg	a	1-1	*Nisja*
02/09	Tromsø	h	0-1	
16/09	Hønefoss	a	2-2	*Nevland, Thioune (p)*
21/09	Strømsgodset	h	3-2	*Olsen, Thioune (p), Veton Berisha*
28/09	Lillestrøm	a	0-0	
06/10	Aalesund	h	1-1	*Veton Berisha*
21/10	Sogndal	h	2-1	*Bjørdal, Nisja*
28/10	Stabæk	a	1-0	*Olsen*
04/11	Brann	h	2-1	*Nisja, Ørnskov*
11/11	Haugesund	a	0-1	
18/11	Vålerenga	h	2-1	*Ørnskov, Gyan*

No	Name	Nat	DoB	Pos	Aps	(s)	Gls
4	Björn Andersson	SWE	13/02/82	A	2	(9)	1
21	Henri Anier	EST	17/12/90	A	9	(7)	
22	Valon Berisha		07/02/93	M	16		
26	Veton Berisha		13/04/94	A	13	(8)	7
2	Trond Erik Bertelsen		05/06/84	D	29		
3	Johan Lædre Bjørdal		05/05/86	D	21		1
29	Henrik Breimyr		20/07/93	D		(1)	
14	André Danielsen		20/01/85	M	20	(7)	3
11	Jóan Símun Edmundsson	FRO	26/07/91	M	1	(1)	
19	King Osei Gyan	GHA	22/12/88	M	12	(3)	1
9	Patrik Ingelsten	SWE	25/01/82	A	1	(8)	
17	Eirik Jakobsen		19/07/92	A	1	(3)	
1	Rune Almenning Jarstein		29/09/84	G	30		
13	Christian Landu Landu		25/01/92	D	10	(3)	1
16	Yann-Erik de Lanlay		14/05/92	A	28	(2)	3
10	Erik Nevland		10/11/77	A	5	(9)	2
8	Vidar Nisja		21/08/86	A	16	(11)	7
27	Trond Olsen		05/02/84	A	16	(8)	5
20	Indridi Sigurdsson	ISL	12/10/81	D	24		
6	Håkon Skogseid		14/01/88	D	26	(1)	1
15	El Hadji Makhtar Thioune	SEN	05/08/84	M	10	(2)	2
18	Jon-Helge Tveita		27/01/92	D	12	(2)	
7	Martin Ørnskov Nielsen	DEN	10/10/85	M	28		4

VÅLERENGA FOTBALL

Coach: Martin Andresen
1913 • Ullevaal (25,572) • vif-fotball.no
Major honours
Norwegian League (5) 1965, 1981, 1983, 1984, 2005;
Norwegian Cup (4) 1980, 1997, 2002, 2008

2012

25/03	Haugesund	h	2-1	*Nielsen, Pusic*
31/03	Strømsgodset	a	2-3	*Pedersen, Hæstad*
10/04	Viking	h	1-0	*og (Sigurdsson)*
15/04	Lillestrøm	a	1-1	*Pusic*
20/04	Sogndal	h	0-2	
29/04	Brann	a	2-1	*Pedersen, Zajić (p)*
06/05	Fredrikstad	h	3-2	*Pedersen 2, Berre*
12/05	Tromsø	a	1-3	*Fellah*
19/05	Hønefoss	a	0-1	
23/05	Rosenborg	h	0-0	
24/06	Stabæk	h	1-2	*Nielsen*
02/07	Aalesund	h	0-0	
08/07	Sandnes Ulf	a	2-0	*Nielsen, Nordvik*
11/07	Odd Grenland	a	3-2	*Nielsen 3*
14/07	Molde	h	1-2	*Pedersen*
22/07	Stabæk	a	3-1	*Larsen, Pedersen 2*
30/07	Brann	h	1-1	*Pedersen*
03/08	Haugesund	a	2-4	*Fellah, Pusic*
10/08	Odd Grenland	h	3-1	*Berre, Fellah, og (Hansen)*
26/08	Molde	a	0-2	
31/08	Sandnes Ulf	h	4-0	*Larsen, Børven, Fellah, Samuel*
16/09	Rosenborg	a	0-3	
24/09	Hønefoss	h	3-2	*og (Olsen), Fellah, Anene*
01/10	Fredrikstad	a	2-1	*Berre, Børven (p)*
05/10	Strømsgodset	h	1-1	*Anene*
21/10	Aalesund	a	1-3	*Fellah*
28/10	Tromsø	h	1-0	*Berre*
05/11	Sogndal	a	0-1	
11/11	Lillestrøm	h	1-2	*og (Ringstad)*
18/11	Viking	a	1-2	*Ricketts*

No	Name	Nat	DoB	Pos	Aps	(s)	Gls
33	Akinsola Akinyemi		12/07/93	M		(3)	
27	Chuma Anene		14/05/93	A	7	(7)	2
19	Chad Barrett	USA	30/04/85	A	5		
11	Morten Berre		10/08/75	A	21	(6)	4
10	Torgeir Børven		03/12/91	A	7	(3)	2
16	Pape Maly Diamanka	SEN	10/01/90	M	8	(1)	
17	Mohammed Fellah		24/05/89	M	22	(3)	6
18	Giancarlo González	CRC	08/02/88	D	12		
10	Veigar Páll Gunnarsson	ISL	21/03/80	A	6	(1)	
2	Benjamin Dahl Hagen		09/01/88	D	7	(2)	
1	Lars Hirschfeld	CAN	17/10/78	G	28		
23	Kristofer Hæstad		09/12/83	M	22	(2)	1
34	Gudmund Kongshavn		23/01/91	G	2	(2)	
8	Abdurahim Laajab		25/05/85	A	1	(5)	
6	Simon Larsen		01/06/88	D	27		2
20	Dawda Leigh		27/06/86	A	10	(2)	
4	André Muri		22/04/81	D	25		
16	Håvard Nielsen		15/07/93	A	14	(2)	6
3	Andreas Nordvik		18/03/87	D	17	(1)	1
24	Nicolai Næss		19/01/93	D	2	(3)	
13	Fegor Ogude	NGA	29/07/87	M	8		
19	Marcus Pedersen		08/06/90	A	13	(2)	8
22	Martin Pusic	AUT	24/10/87	A	14	(2)	3
30	Kamer Qaka		11/04/95	M	2	(4)	
25	Tosaint Ricketts	CAN	06/08/87	A	2	(1)	1
28	Aaron Samuel	NGA	30/11/93	A		(5)	1
28	Harmeet Singh		12/11/90	M	8	(2)	
5	Aleksander Solli		16/03/90	D		(7)	
21	Ahmed Suleiman	NGA	18/08/92	A	2	(8)	
15	Joachim Thomassen		04/05/88	D	16	(2)	
40	Ghayas Zahid		18/11/94	M	1	(3)	
26	Bojan Zajić	SRB	17/06/80	M	21	(5)	4

Top goalscorers

14	Péter Kovács (Strømsgodset)
	Zdeněk Ondrášek (Tromsø)
13	Davy Claude Angan (Molde)
12	Nikola Djurdjić (Haugesund)
11	Kim Ojo (Brann)
	Rade Prica (Rosenborg)
	Ola Kamara (Strømsgodset)
10	Alexander Søderlund (Haugesund)
	Riku Riski (Hønefoss)
	Torgeir Børven (Odd Grenland/Vålerenga)
	Bořek Dočkal (Rosenborg)
	Ulrik Flo (Sogndal)

Promoted clubs

IK START

Coach: Mons Ivar Mjelde
1905 • Sør Arena (14,563) • ikstart.no
Major honours
Norwegian League (2) 1978, 1980

SARPSBORG 08 FF

Coach: Roar Johansen
2000 • Sarpsborg (5,500) • sarpsborg08.no

SECOND LEVEL FINAL TABLE 2012

		Pld	W	D	L	F	A	Pts
1	IK Start	30	20	6	4	71	35	66
2	Sarpsborg 08 FF	30	19	6	5	73	43	63
3	Sandefjord Fotball	30	16	7	7	44	29	55
4	Mjøndalen IF	30	16	7	7	52	43	55
5	FK Bodø/Glimt	30	13	9	8	59	36	48
6	Ullensaker/Kisa IL	30	14	2	14	45	39	44
7	Ranheim Fotball	30	11	10	9	55	40	43
8	HamKam Fotball	30	13	6	11	51	49	43
9	Kongsvinger IL	30	12	3	15	44	48	39
10	Bryne FK	30	10	8	12	41	53	38
11	Strømmen IF	30	10	7	13	39	51	37
12	IL Hødd Fotball	30	10	5	15	43	52	35
13	Tromsdalen UIL	30	10	5	15	51	62	35
14	Bærum SK	30	5	7	18	49	73	22
15	Notodden FK	30	6	4	20	38	71	22
16	Alta IF	30	4	10	16	30	61	21

NB HamKam Fotball – 2 pts deducted; Alta IF – 1 pt deducted

PROMOTION/RELEGATION PLAY-OFFS

(14/11/12)
Mjøndalen 1-2 Bodø/Glimt
Sandefjord 3-4 Ullensaker/Kisa

(17/11/12)
Ullensaker/Kisa 2-0 Bodø/Glimt

(21/11/12 & 24/11/12)
Ullensaker/Kisa 0-4 Sandnes Ulf
Sandnes Ulf 3-1 Ullensaker/Kisa
(Sandnes Ulf 7-1)

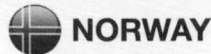
Domestic cup: Norgesmesterskapet 2012

FIRST ROUND

(01/05/12)
Askim 1-3 Fredrikstad
Avaldsnes 1-7 Haugesund
Bjarg 1-2 Brann
Donn 2-4 Start
Drammen 0-2 Bærum
Eidsvold Turn 1-3 Kongsvinger
Faaberg 3-5 HamKam
Flekkefjord 1-4 Viking
Florø 3-0 Sogndal
Gvarv 0-4 Odd Grenland
Hauerseter 0-6 Ullensaker/Kisa
Herd 0-1 Aalesund
Holmlia 1-3 Sarpsborg
Høland 0-7 Strømmen
KIL/Hemne 1-3 Nardo
Kristiansund 5-0 Buvik
Lommedalen 0-3 Stabæk
Lyn 1-2 Vålerenga
Lyngen/Karnes 1-3 Alta
Porsanger 0-2 Tromsø
Rosseland 1-4 Bryne
Runar 0-6 Sandefjord
Røa 1-6 Hønefoss
Salangen 1-3 Tromsdalen
Skjetten 0-8 Lillestrøm
Solberg 0-9 Strømsgodset
Spjelkavik 1-1 Træff *(aet; 2-4 on pens)*
Sprint-Jeløy 0-2 Mjøndalen
Staal Jørpeland 2-1 Sandnes Ulf
Stjørdals-Blink 4-2 Levanger
Strindheim 1-2 Byåsen
Sunndal 0-4 Molde
Tiller 0-8 Rosenborg
Tornado Måløy 0-3 Hødd
Tverlandet 0-5 Bodø/Glimt
Urædd 0-9 Notodden
Verdal 2-1 Ranheim
Voss 0-7 Fana

(02/05/12)
Arendal 3-2 Fløy
Arna-Bjørnar 2-1 Fyllingsdalen
Austevoll 2-2 Nest-Sotra *(aet; 2-3 on pens)*
Egersund 4-3 Mandalskameratene *(aet)*
Follo 1-2 Raufoss
Fram Larvik 0-3 Pors Grenland
Gjøvik 1-1 Nesodden *(aet; 7-6 on pens)*
Harstad 3-2 Senja *(aet)*
Jevnaker 2-3 Asker
Kjelsås 4-1 Birkebeineren
Kvik Halden 4-1 Ørn-Horten *(aet)*
Lillehammer 3-3 Lørenskog *(aet; 3-4 on pens)*
Mjølner 5-0 Finnsnes
Moss 2-0 Elverum *(aet)*
Namsos 2-5 Mo
Os 1-3 Åsane
Oslo City 2-4 Nybergsund
Ottestad 4-3 Brumunddal
Stavanger 0-1 Ålgård
Tønsberg 1-2 KFUM Oslo
Valdres 2-0 Frigg
Vidar 0-0 Randaberg *(aet; 4-3 on pens)*
Vindbjart 3-4 Jerv
Østsiden 0-1 Skeid
Øystese 2-5 Vard Haugesund

(03/05/12)
Skarbøvik 0-0 Grorud *(aet; 4-3 on pens)*

SECOND ROUND

(09/05/12)
Arendal 0-5 Odd Grenland
Arna-Bjørnar 0-1 Hødd
Asker 5-3 Bærum
Egersund 3-3 Vidar *(aet; 8-7 on pens)*
Fana 1-4 Stabæk *(aet)*
Gjøvik 0-2 Strømsgodset
HamKam 5-1 Valdres
Harstad 0-7 Rosenborg
Kvik Halden 2-2 Fredrikstad *(aet; 5-3 on pens)*
Lørenskog 1-2 Kongsvinger
Nybergsund 1-4 Hønefoss
Nardo 0-1 Bodø/Glimt
Notodden 4-3 Kjelsås
Ottestad 0-2 Lillestrøm
Pors Grenland 0-2 Sandefjord
Raufoss 2-0 Strømmen
Skeid 0-3 Vålerenga
Staal Jørpeland 1-5 Haugesund
Start 5-0 Vard Haugesund
Stjørdals-Blink 1-2 Tromsø
Tromsdalen 3-2 Mjølner *(aet)*
Træff 0-1 Ullensaker/Kisa
Verdal 0-2 Molde *(aet)*
Ålgård 0-2 Nest-Sotra
Åsane 1-0 Bryne

(10/05/12)
Byåsen 1-1 Kristiansund *(aet; 5-4 on pens)*
Florø 1-6 Brann
Jerv 1-4 Viking *(aet)*
KFUM Oslo 0-2 Mjøndalen
Mo 0-1 Alta
Sarpsborg 6-1 Moss
Skarbøvik 0-1 Aalesund

THIRD ROUND

(20/06/12)
Aalesund 4-0 Byåsen
Alta 2-2 Bodø/Glimt *(aet; 4-5 on pens)*
Asker 2-1 Stabæk
Haugesund 8-2 Egersund
Hødd 2-1 Sarpsborg *(aet)*
Kongsvinger 0-1 Start
Mjøndalen 2-2 Hønefoss *(aet; 3-0 on pens)*
Molde 3-2 HamKam
Nest-Sotra 0-3 Brann
Raufoss 2-3 Odd Grenland
Rosenborg 4-0 Kvik Halden
Sandefjord 3-1 Vålerenga *(aet)*
Strømsgodset 3-2 Notodden
Tromsø 4-0 Tromsdalen
Ullensaker/Kisa 0-3 Lillestrøm
Åsane 0-2 Viking

FOURTH ROUND

(27/06/12)
Molde 4-3 Rosenborg

(04/07/12)
Bodø/Glimt 4-0 Lillestrøm
Odd Grenland 0-2 Haugesund
Start 1-1 Tromsø *(aet; 1-4 on pens)*
Strømsgodset 6-1 Mjøndalen
Viking 2-3 Brann *(aet)*

(05/07/12)
Hødd 7-0 Asker
Sandefjord 2-1 Aalesund *(aet)*

QUARTER-FINALS

(18/08/12)
Haugesund 2-2 Hødd *(Djurdjić 45p, 62; Helland 32, 49) (aet; 4-5 on pens)*
Molde 2-1 Sandefjord *(Angan 82, Hoseth 90+2; Aas 65)*

(19/08/12)
Brann 4-3 Strømsgodset *(Jonsson 44, Nordkvelle 67, Akabueze 71, Huseklepp 86p; Kovács 22, Storflor 58, Diomande 90+3)*
Tromsø 1-0 Bodø/Glimt *(Ondrášek 23)*

SEMI-FINALS

(26/09/12)
Tromsø 2-1 Molde *(Ondrášek 3, Årst 72; Chima 83)*
(27/09/12)
Hødd 3-1 Brann *(Aursnes 40, Helland 66, Sellin 81; Korcsmár 17)*

FINAL

(25/11/12)
Ullevaal stadion, Oslo
IL HØDD FOTBALL 1 *(Sellin 62)*
TROMSØ IL 1 *(Ciss 87)*
(aet; 4-2 on pens)
Referee: *Sælen*
HØDD: *Nyland, Latifu, Klock, Moltu, Grodås, Aursnes (Torset 120), Sandal, Nilsen, Helland, Sellin (Standal 96), V Heltne (Rekdal 85)*
TROMSØ: *Lekström, Norbye, Björck, Ciss, Kristiansen, Bendiksen (Andersen 81), Kara (Johansen 67), Yttergård Jenssen, Drage, Prijovic (Årst 54), Ondrášek*

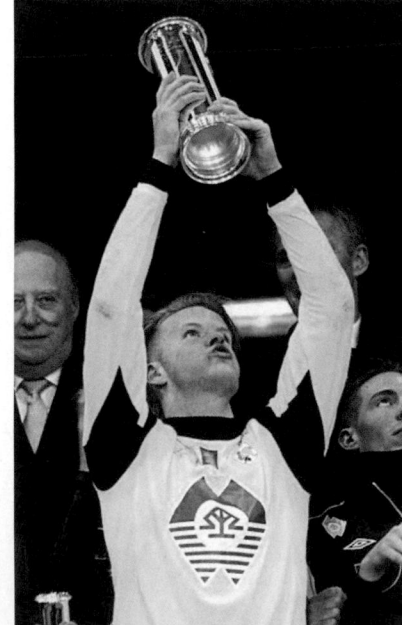

Hødd's Ørjan Håskjold Nyland lifts the Norwegian Cup

POLAND

Polski Związek Piłki Nożnej (PZPN)

Address	Bitwy Warszawskiej 1920 r.7 PL-02 366 Warszawa	**President**	Zbigniew Boniek
		General secretary	Maciej Sawicki
Tel	+48 22 551 2300	**Media officer**	Agnieszka Olejkowska
Fax	+48 22 551 2240	**Year of formation**	1919
E-mail	pzpn@pzpn.pl	**National stadium**	National Stadium, Warsaw (58,145)
Website	pzpn.pl		

EKSTRAKLASA CLUBS

1. GKS Bełchatów
2. Górnik Zabrze
3. Jagiellonia Białystok
4. Korona Kielce
5. KKS Lech Poznań
6. KS Lechia Gdańsk
7. Legia Warszawa
8. GKS Piast Gliwice
9. TS Podbeskidzie Bielsko-Biała
10. MKS Pogoń Szczecin
11. KSP Polonia Warszawa
12. Ruch Chorzów
13. WKS Śląsk Wrocław
14. RTS Widzew Łódź
15. Wisła Kraków
16. Zagłębie Lubin

PROMOTED CLUBS

17. Zawisza Bydgoszcz
18. MKS Cracovia Kraków

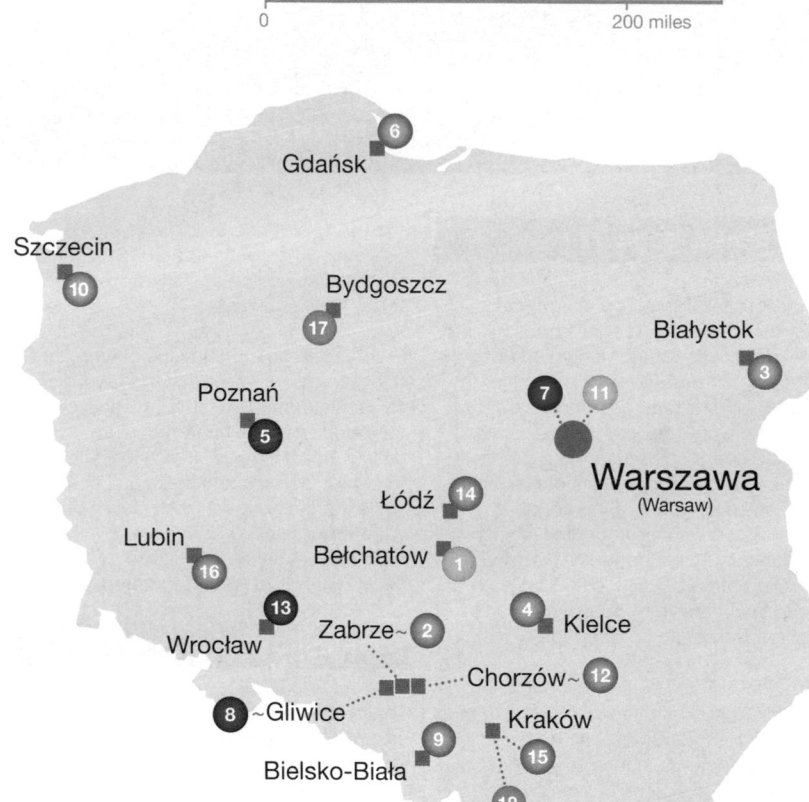

KEY:
- – UEFA Champions League
- – UEFA Europa League
- – Promoted clubs
- – Relegated clubs

Double joy for Urban's Legia

Dismissed as Legia Warszawa coach in March 2010 after failing to win the Polish title in nearly three seasons at the helm, Jan Urban made a triumphant return in 2012/13, leading the club to victory not just in the Ekstraklasa but also in the Polish Cup.

Legia were the dominant force in the league from start to finish, with only KKS Lech Poznań applying any pressure. Defending champions WKS Śląsk Wrocław finished third, 20 points in arrears of their successors, and also lost to them in the cup final, which Legia won for the third season in a row.

Returning coach claims both domestic trophies	Lech provide sole title challenge to Warsaw club	No joy for new national team coach Fornalik

Domestic league

With victories in their opening three Ekstraklasa fixtures, Legia established an early dominance that they would not relinquish en route to their ninth title. It was November before Urban's side lost, and there would be just three defeats over the entire campaign. Four points clear of Lech at the winter break, Legia found another gear in the spring, powering on with a run of nine wins in ten games, the exception a 0-0 draw at newly promoted GKS Piast Gliwice, who would finish fourth to qualify for a first crack at European competition.

Lech, cleverly led by rookie coach Mariusz Rumak, stayed with Legia thanks to an impressive run of their own, but after posting ten successive away wins they lost the big game in Warsaw on 18 May, an 86th-minute penalty from Ivica Vrdoljak delighting most of the 29,416 spectators. That win put Legia five points clear, and the title was sealed seven days later when a lacklustre Lech lost 2-0 at home to relegation strugglers TS Podbeskidzie Bielsko-Biała. Their victors, who supplied the league's top marksman in Slovakian striker Róbert Demjan, would also win their next two games to avoid the drop, sending GKS Bełchatów and Ruch Chorzów down instead. Ruch,

the 2011/12 runners-up, were saved, however, when debt-ridden KSP Polonia Warszawa were denied a licence for the 2013/14 Ekstraklasa.

Polonia had sold off several players in mid-campaign, one of whom, Georgian striker Vladimer Dvalishvili, went on to star for Legia. The champions' top scorer, with 12 goals, was another foreigner, Serbian striker Danijel Ljuboja, while the pick of the Polish contingent were winger Jakub Kosecki and international defenders Jakub Wawrzyniak and Artur Jędrzejczyk.

Domestic cup

The first of Legia's two trophies was secured in early May when they won the Polish Cup for a record 16th time. The Puchar Polski specialists had never previously completed a hat-trick of victories, but they rectified that in the two-legged final against Śląsk. A double from striker Marek Saganowski gave them a 2-0 lead in Wrocław, but an early own goal conceded in the return led to a tight encounter in Warsaw, and it was with some relief that Legia greeted the final whistle. With the pressure off, Urban's men would end the league season a few weeks later by hammering the same opponents 5-0 at the same venue.

Europe

Legia's domestic dominance might have been partially explained by their failure to make progress in Europe. Having reached the UEFA Europa League round of 32 – in the company of Wisła Kraków – the previous season, they were eliminated in the play-offs by Rosenborg BK. With Śląsk also dropping out at the same stage, conceding ten goals to Hannover 96, Polish interest in Europe ended in August.

National team

Franciszek Smuda stepped down as Poland coach after UEFA EURO 2012, handing the reins on to Waldemar Fornalik. But while his former club Ruch clearly missed him, Fornalik found good results hard to come by in the 2014 FIFA World Cup qualifying campaign. The team's only wins were at home to Moldova and San Marino, the other games in Warsaw bringing a 1-1 draw against England – following a one-day postponement because of torrential rain – and a damaging 3-1 defeat by Ukraine. Despite the presence of celebrated Borussia Dortmund trio Robert Lewandowski, Łukasz Piszczek and skipper Jakub Błaszczykowski, Poland's chances of a top-two finish looked pretty remote as they headed into the autumn.

Domestic league: Ekstraklasa 2012/13 final table

		Pld	Home					Away					Total					Pts
			W	D	L	F	A	W	D	L	F	A	W	D	L	F	A	
1	Legia Warszawa	30	12	2	1	33	8	8	5	2	26	14	20	7	3	59	22	67
2	KKS Lech Poznań	30	7	3	5	24	15	12	1	2	22	7	19	4	7	46	22	61
3	WKS Śląsk Wrocław	30	9	4	2	23	15	4	4	7	21	27	13	8	9	44	42	47
4	GKS Piast Gliwice	30	5	5	5	18	19	8	2	5	23	22	13	7	10	41	41	46
5	Górnik Zabrze	30	7	2	6	19	15	5	5	5	16	16	12	7	11	35	31	43
6	KSP Polonia Warszawa	30	5	5	5	20	17	6	4	5	25	17	11	9	10	45	34	42
7	Wisła Kraków	30	6	3	6	15	14	4	5	6	13	21	10	8	12	28	35	38
8	KS Lechia Gdańsk	30	3	5	7	23	27	7	3	5	19	16	10	8	12	42	43	38
9	Zagłębie Lubin	30	7	2	6	24	18	4	5	6	14	19	11	7	12	38	37	37
10	Jagiellonia Białystok	30	4	6	5	13	19	4	7	4	18	26	8	13	9	31	45	37
11	Korona Kielce	30	9	4	2	24	10	0	5	10	8	27	9	9	12	32	37	36
12	MKS Pogoń Szczecin	30	7	2	6	17	17	3	3	9	12	22	10	5	15	29	39	35
13	RTS Widzew Łódź	30	6	4	5	19	16	2	5	8	11	25	8	9	13	30	41	33
14	TS Podbeskidzie Bielsko-Biała	30	2	6	7	21	24	6	2	7	18	19	8	8	14	39	43	32
15	Ruch Chorzów	30	4	5	6	17	21	4	2	9	18	27	8	7	15	35	48	31
16	GKS Bełchatów	30	4	5	6	12	21	3	5	7	12	17	7	10	13	24	38	31

NB KSP Polonia Warszawa excluded for 2013/14 season – Ruch Chorzów therefore avoid relegation; Zagłębie Lubin – 3 pts deducted.

SEASON AT A GLANCE

EUROPEAN QUALIFICATION 2013/14

 Champion/Cup winner: Legia Warszawa (second qualifying round)

 KKS Lech Poznań (second qualifying round)
WKS Śląsk Wrocław (second qualifying round)
GKS Piast Gliwice (second qualifying round)

Top scorer	Róbert Demjan (Podbeskidzie), 14 goals
Relegated clubs	GKS Bełchatów, KSP Polonia Warszawa (excluded)
Promoted club	Zawisza Bydgoszcz, MKS Cracovia Kraków
Cup final	WKS Śląsk Wrocław 0-2; 1-0 Legia Warszawa (agg 1-2)

EKSTRAKLASA TEAM OF THE SEASON
(4-4-2)
Coach: **Urban** (Legia)

 **PLAYER OF THE SEASON**
Jakub Kosecki
(Legia Warszawa)

The Ekstraklasa's discovery of the year was the son of former Poland striker Roman Kosecki, and he achieved what his father never managed by winning the Polish title with Legia. The 22-year-old winger scored a number of vital goals for the capital club and his sterling performances were recognised with a first cap for the national side.

NEWCOMER OF THE SEASON
Gergő Lovrencsics
(KKS Lech Poznań)

The Hungarian winger was signed on loan from Lombard-Pápa TFC at the beginning of the season, but he played so well that Lech put up the cash to buy him outright. Easily distinguishable by his outlandish hairstyles, the 24-year-old also caught the eye with a number of spectacular goals, quickly becoming a firm favourite with the Poznan fans.

Kuciak (Legia)

Broź (Widzew) | Jędrzejczyk (Legia) | Kamiński (Lech) | Wawrzyniak (Legia)

Kosecki (Legia) | Łukasik (Legia) | Mila (Śląsk) | Tonev (Lech)

Demjan (Podbeskidzie) | Dvalishvili (Polonia/Legia)

POLAND

NATIONAL TEAM

Home Kit   Away Kit

INTERNATIONAL TOURNAMENT APPEARANCES
FIFA World Cup (7) 1938, 1974 (3rd), 1978 (2nd phase), 1982 (3rd), 1986 (2nd round), 2002, 2006
UEFA European Championship (2) 2008, 2012

TOP FIVE ALL-TIME CAPS
Michał Żewłakow (102); Grzegorz Lato (100); Kazimierz Deyna (97); Jacek Bąk & Jacek Krzynówek (96)

TOP FIVE ALL-TIME GOALS
Włodzimierz Lubański (48); Grzegorz Lato (45); Kazimierz Deyna (41); Ernest Pol (39); Andrzej Szarmach (32)

Results 2012/13

Date	Opponent		Venue	Score	Scorers
15/08/12	Estonia	A	Tallinn	0-1	
07/09/12	Montenegro (WCQ)	A	Podgorica	2-2	Błaszczykowski (6p), Mierzejewski (55)
11/09/12	Moldova (WCQ)	H	Wroclaw	2-0	Błaszczykowski (33p), Wawrzyniak (81)
12/10/12	South Africa	H	Warsaw	1-0	Komorowski (82)
17/10/12	England (WCQ)	H	Warsaw	1-1	Glik (70)
14/11/12	Uruguay	H	Gdansk	1-3	Obraniak (64)
14/12/12	FYROM	N	Antalya (TUR)	4-1	Milik (11), Pawłowski (23), Jędrzejczyk (64), Sobota (79)
02/02/13	Romania B	N	Malaga (ESP)	4-1	Pawłowski (15), Teodorczyk (24, 27), Łukasik (33)
06/02/13	Republic of Ireland	A	Dublin	0-2	
22/03/13	Ukraine (WCQ)	H	Warsaw	1-3	Piszczek (18)
26/03/13	San Marino (WCQ)	H	Warsaw	5-0	Lewandowski (21p, 50p), Piszczek (28), Teodorczyk (61), Kosecki (90+2)
04/06/13	Liechtenstein	H	Krakow	2-0	Sobiech (53), Rybus (72)
07/06/13	Moldova (WCQ)	A	Chisinau	1-1	Błaszczykowski (7)

Appearances 2012/13

Coach: Waldemar Fornalik 11/04/63			Est	MNE	MDA	Rsa	ENG	Uru	Mkd	Rou	Irl	UKR	SMR	Lie	MDA	Caps	Goals
Wojciech Szczęsny	18/04/90	Arsenal (ENG)	G								s46					13	-
Łukasz Piszczek	03/06/85	Dortmund (GER)	D	D	D		D	D				D	D			34	2
Marcin Wasilewski	09/06/80	Anderlecht (BEL)	D	D	D	D	D	D			s46	D	s87			60	2
Damien Perqius	10/04/84	Sochaux (FRA) /Betis (ESP)	D			D		s46			D					14	1
Jakub Wawrzyniak	07/07/83	Legia	D	D	D	D84	D			D	D		D	D46	D	36	1
Jakub Błaszczykowski	14/12/85	Dortmund (GER)	M84	M	M			s73			M	M			M	61	13
Ariel Borysiuk	29/07/91	Kaiserslautern (GER)	M68	M69	M75	M	s90						M			9	-
Eugen Polanski	17/03/86	Mainz (GER) /Hoffenheim (GER)	M	M	M		M	M72					M		M79	18	-
Maciej Rybus	19/08/89	Terek (RUS)	M57									M46		M79	M64	26	2
Artur Sobiech	12/06/90	Hannover (GER)	A46		s71	A75								A	s79	10	2
Robert Lewandowski	21/08/88	Dortmund (GER)	A	A92	A		A	A			A	A	A		A	54	17
Adrian Mierzejewski	06/11/86	Trabzonspor (TUR)	s46	s46	M71	M58	s63	M59			s77		M	M68	M62	35	2
Kamil Grosicki	08/06/88	Sivasspor (TUR)	s57	M46		s46	M83	M73			s46		M	M46		22	-
Janusz Gol	11/11/85	Legia	s68													8	-
Arkadiusz Piech	07/06/85	Ruch	s84			A46		s75								4	-
Przemysław Tytoń	04/01/87	PSV (NED)		G	G	G	G	G46								13	-
Kamil Glik	03/02/88	Torino (ITA)		D	D		D	D46			D	D	D46			18	2
Ludovic Obraniak	10/11/84	Bordeaux (FRA)		M 73*		s84	M90	M			M60	s59				32	6
Rafał Murawski	09/10/81	Lech		s69		s65										48	1
Marek Saganowski	31/10/78	Legia		s92	A46											35	5
Waldemar Sobota	19/05/87	Śląsk			s46	s46			s46	M84						5	2
Grzegorz Krychowiak	29/01/90	Reims (FRA)			s75	M65	M	M83			M	M	M		M	10	-
Grzegorz Wojtkowiak	26/01/84	1860 München (GER)				D										20	-
Paweł Wszołek	30/04/92	Polonia Warszawa				M46	M63		M46	M46						4	-
Arkadiusz Milik	28/02/94	Górnik Zabrze /Leverkusen (GER)				s58	s83	s83	A		s60		A59			6	1
Marcin Komorowski	17/04/84	Terek (RUS)				s75		D					D	D	D	10	1
Tomasz Kuszczak	20/03/82	Brighton (ENG)						s46								11	-
Szymon Pawłowski	04/11/86	Zagłębie Lubin						s59	M75	M55	M46					15	2
Łukasz Trałka	11/05/84	Lech						s72								7	-
Łukasz Skorupski	05/05/91	Górnik Zabrze												G		1	-

Appearances 2012/13 (contd.)

			Est	MNE	MDA	Rsa	ENG	Uru	Mkd	Rou	Irl	UKR	SMR	Lie	MDA	Caps	Goals
Łukasz Broź	17/12/85	Widzew							D	D						2	-
Artur Jędrzejczyk	04/11/87	Legia							D84	D46				D	D	5	1
Tomasz Jodłowiec	08/09/85	Śląsk /Legia							D	s46						27	-
Jakub Rzeźniczak	26/10/86	Legia							D46							8	-
Daniel Łukasik	28/04/91	Legia							M46	M67	M77	M59		s79		5	1
Przemysław Kaźmierczak	05/05/82	Śląsk							M	M						11	1
Jakub Kosecki	29/08/90	Legia							M59			s46	s46	s68	s64	5	1
Dominik Furman	06/07/92	Legia							s46	s67						2	-
Bartosz Rymaniak	13/11/89	Zagłębie Lubin							s46							1	-
Tomasz Kupisz	02/01/90	Jagiellonia							s59	s55						4	-
Adam Danch	15/12/87	Górnik Zabrze							s84							2	-
Jakub Słowik	31/08/91	Jagiellonia								G						1	-
Piotr Celeban	25/06/85	Vaslui (ROU)								D						6	-
Łukasz Teodorczyk	03/06/91	Lech								A		s76	s59			3	3
Michał Kucharczyk	20/03/91	Legia								s46						6	-
Mariusz Stępiński	12/05/95	Widzew								s84						1	-
Artur Boruc	20/02/80	Southampton (ENG)									G46	G	G	s34	G	51	-
Sebastian Boenisch	01/02/87	Leverkusen (GER)									D46	D		s46		12	-
Radosław Majewski	15/12/86	Nottingham Forest (ENG)										M76				9	-
Bartosz Salamon	01/05/91	Milan (ITA)											D87	D46	D	3	-
Jerzy Dudek	23/03/73	unattached												G34		60	-
Adam Matuszczyk	14/02/89	Köln (GER)												M		21	1
Bartosz Bereszyński	12/07/92	Legia												s46		1	-
Piotr Zieliński	20/05/94	Udinese (ITA)												s46	s62	2	-

European club competitions 2012/13

WKS ŚLĄSK WROCŁAW

Second qualifying round - FK Budućnost Podgorica (MNE)
A 2-0 *Elsner (19), Mila (49p)*
Kelemen, Sobota (Stevanovič 88), Mráz, Cetnarski (Patejuk 71), Mila, Kowalczyk, Pawelec, Socha, Kaźmierczak (Díaz 82), Elsner. Coach: Orest Lenczyk (POL)
H 0-1
Kelemen, Spahić, Mráz (Patejuk 38), Cetnarski (Sobota 46), Mila, Kowalczyk, Grodzicki, Pawelec, Kaźmierczak, Ł Gikiewicz, Elsner. Coach: Orest Lenczyk (POL)

Third qualifying round - Helsingborgs IF (SWE)
H 0-3
Kelemen, Spahić, Sobota, Patejuk (Ł Gikiewicz 73), Mila, Kowalczyk, Grodzicki, Pawelec, Voskamp (Díaz 66), Kaźmierczak (Stevanovič 73), Elsner. Coach: Orest Lenczyk (POL)
Red card: Elsner 90
A 1-3 *Díaz (31)*
Kelemen, Jodłowiec (Cetnarski 73), Sobota, Mráz, Patejuk (Voskamp 73), Mila, Kowalczyk, Stevanovič, Pawelec, Díaz (Ł Gikiewicz 74), Kaźmierczak. Coach: Orest Lenczyk (POL)

Play-offs - Hannover 96 (GER)
H 3-5 *Jodłowiec (34), Patejuk (54), Kaźmierczak (61)*
R Gikiewicz, Jodłowiec, Sobota, Mráz, Mila, Kowalczyk, Stevanovič, Pawelec, Kaźmierczak, Ł Gikiewicz (Voskamp 46), Elsner (Patejuk 46). Coach: Orest Lenczyk (POL)
A 1-5 *Kaźmierczak (10)*
Kelemen, Jodłowiec, Spahić, Sobota, Patejuk (Voskamp 65), Mila, Kowalczyk, Díaz (Pawelec 46), Socha, Kaźmierczak, Elsner (Stevanovič 82). Coach: Orest Lenczyk (POL)
Red card: Jodłowiec 21

LEGIA WARSZAWA

Second qualifying round - SK Liepājas Metalurgs (LVA)
A 2-2 *Kucharczyk (20), Kosecki (47)*
Kuciak, Jędrzejczyk, Gol (Ljuboja 76), Żewłakow, Wawrzyniak, Iñaki Astiz, Kucharczyk, Kosecki, Radović, Żyro (Saganowski 69), Łukasik (Furman 90). Coach: Jan Urban (POL)
H 5-1 *Saganowski (4, 39, 79), Gol (57), Żyro (61)*
Kuciak, Jędrzejczyk, Gol, Żewłakow (Šuler 78), Saganowski, Wawrzyniak, Iñaki Astiz, Kucharczyk (Żyro 61), Kosecki, Radović, Łukasik (Furman 64). Coach: Jan Urban (POL)

 **POLAND**

Third qualifying round - SV Ried (AUT)
A 1-2 *Ljuboja (85)*
Kuciak, Jędrzejczyk, Gol (Saganowski 46), Żewłakow, Wawrzyniak, Iñaki Astiz, Kucharczyk (Rzeźniczak 64), Kosecki, Ljuboja, Radović, Łukasik (Vrdoljak 72). Coach: Jan Urban (POL)
Red card: Wawrzyniak 61
H 3-1 *Saganowski (41), Radović (55), Ljuboja (63)*
Kuciak, Jędrzejczyk, Żewłakow (Šuler 12), Saganowski, Iñaki Astiz, Kosecki, Vrdoljak, Rzeźniczak, Ljuboja (Žyro 79), Radović, Łukasik (Gol 59). Coach: Jan Urban (POL)
Red card: Vrdoljak 71

Play-offs - Rosenborg BK (NOR)
H 1-1 *Kosecki (42)*
Kuciak, Jędrzejczyk, Saganowski, Wawrzyniak, Iñaki Astiz, Kucharczyk (Žyro 76), Kosecki, Rzeźniczak, Ljuboja, Radović, Łukasik (Furman 90). Coach: Jan Urban (POL)
A 1-2 *Ljuboja (36)*
Kuciak, Gol, Żewłakow, Saganowski, Wawrzyniak, Iñaki Astiz, Kosecki (Salinas 90), Rzeźniczak, Ljuboja, Radović (Žyro 68), Łukasik (Furman 87). Coach: Jan Urban (POL)

RUCH CHORZÓW

Second qualifying round - FK Metalurg Skopje (MKD)
H 3-1 *Piech (74, 83), Stawarczyk (90+1)*
Peškovič, Stawarczyk, Djokić, Zieńczuk, Jankowski (Kuświk 78), Janoszka (Šultes 63), Piech, Szyndrowski, Sadlok, Straka (Starzyński 57), Malinowski. Coach: Tomasz Fornalik (POL)
A 3-0 *Janoszka (9), Straka (15), Piech (63)*
Peškovič, Stawarczyk, Djokić (Lewczuk 53), Zieńczuk, Jankowski, Janoszka (Starzyński 76), Piech, Szyndrowski, Sadlok, Straka, Malinowski (Lisowski 65). Coach: Tomasz Fornalik (POL)

Third qualifying round - FC Viktoria Plzeň (CZE)
H 0-2
Peškovič, Stawarczyk, Djokić, Zieńczuk, Jankowski, Janoszka (Starzyński 61), Piech (Niedzielan 81), Szyndrowski, Sadlok, Straka (Lisowski 57), Malinowski. Coach: Tomasz Fornalik (POL)

A 0-5
Peškovič, Stawarczyk, Djokić, Zieńczuk, Jankowski (Janoszka 64), Piech (Kuświk 78), Panka, Szyndrowski, Sadlok, Lisowski (Lewczuk 81), Malinowski. Coach: Tomasz Fornalik (POL)

KKS LECH POZNAŃ

First qualifying round - FC Zhetysu Taldykorgan (KAZ)
H 2-0 *Murawski (61), Lovrencsics (65)*
Kotorowski, Trałka (Murawski 54), Krivets (Ubiparip 46), Lovrencsics, Drewniak, Ślusarski, Wołąkiewicz, Tonev (Kiełb 85), Henriquez, Możdżeń, Kamiński. Coach: Mariusz Rumak (POL)
A 1-1 *Ślusarski (13)*
Kotorowski, Djurdjević (Tonev 79), Lovrencsics (Kiełb 66), Ubiparip, Murawski, Drewniak, Ślusarski (Kędziora 90), Wołąkiewicz, Henriquez, Możdżeń, Kamiński. Coach: Mariusz Rumak (POL)

Second qualifying round - Xäzär Länkäran FK (AZE)
A 1-1 *Możdżeń (19)*
Burić, Arboleda, Ubiparip (Lovrencsics 87), Murawski, Drewniak, Ślusarski (Djurdjević 60), Wołąkiewicz, Tonev (Wilk 73), Henriquez, Możdżeń, Kamiński. Coach: Mariusz Rumak (POL)
Red card: Drewniak 90+1
H 1-0 *Tonev (16)*
Burić, Arboleda, Trałka (Djurdjević 90+3), Ubiparip (Lovrencsics 63), Murawski, Ślusarski (Bereszyński 87), Wołąkiewicz, Tonev, Henriquez, Możdżeń, Kamiński. Coach: Mariusz Rumak (POL)

Third qualifying round - AIK (SWE)
A 0-3
Burić, Arboleda, Trałka, Lovrencsics, Murawski, Ślusarski, Wołąkiewicz (Drewniak 83), Tonev (Bereszyński 85), Henriquez, Możdżeń (Ubiparip 72), Kamiński. Coach: Mariusz Rumak (POL)
H 1-0 *Możdżeń (72)*
Burić, Arboleda, Trałka (Bereszyński 60), Lovrencsics (Wilk 85), Murawski, Drewniak, Wołąkiewicz, Ceesay, Tonev (Ubiparip 60), Henriquez, Możdżeń. Coach: Mariusz Rumak (POL)

Domestic league club-by-club

GKS BEŁCHATÓW
Coach: Kamil Kiereś; (25/09/12) Jan Złomańczuk; (14/11/12) Michał Probierz; (09/01/13) Kamil Kiereś
1977 • GKS (5,238) • gksbelchatow.com

2012

19/08	Wisła	a	1-2	Szmatiuk
26/08	Legia	h	0-2	
01/09	Widzew	a	0-1	
17/09	Lech	h	0-1	
23/09	Śląsk	a	1-2	Wróbel
29/09	Korona	h	1-1	Wróbel
05/10	Ruch	a	1-2	Buzała
20/10	Podbeskidzie	h	2-1	Buzała, Wacławczyk
27/10	Polonia	h	0-5	
02/11	Górnik	a	0-2	
12/11	Pogoń	h	0-1	
16/11	Zagłębie	a	0-1	
24/11	Lechia	h	1-1	Madej
30/11	Jagiellonia	a	2-2	Wróbel, Wacławczyk
08/12	Piast	h	1-3	Buzała

2013

24/02	Wisła	h	0-0	
02/03	Legia	a	0-0	
09/03	Widzew	h	0-0	
16/03	Lech	a	0-0	
30/03	Śląsk	h	1-0	Madej (p)
07/04	Korona	a	0-1	
13/04	Ruch	h	0-3	
20/04	Podbeskidzie	a	1-1	Michalski
27/04	Polonia	h	1-0	Wacławczyk
04/05	Górnik	h	2-0	Bartosiak, Poźniak
11/05	Pogoń	a	1-0	Mateusz Mak
19/05	Zagłębie	h	3-2	Mateusz Mak (p), Sawala, Madej
25/05	Lechia	a	1-1	Bartosiak
30/05	Jagiellonia	h	1-1	Sawala
02/06	Piast	a	3-2	Michał Mak 2, Michalski

No	Name	Nat	DoB	Pos	Aps	(s)	Gls
3	Grzegorz Baran		23/12/82	M	22	(4)	
45	Bartłomiej Bartosiak		26/02/91	M	8	(4)	2
17	Adrian Basta		01/12/88	D	12		
15	Miroslav Božok	SVK	19/10/84	M	12	(2)	
20	Paweł Buzała		27/12/85	A	8	(3)	3
65	Marcin Flis		10/02/94	D	1		
31	Paweł Giel		08/12/89	M	1	(5)	
27	Raúl González	VEN	28/06/85	D	19	(3)	
22	Mikołaj Grzelak		20/06/91	D		(2)	
11	Łukasz Grzeszczyk		29/07/87	M	2	(2)	
11	Kamil Kosowski		30/08/77	M	8	(1)	
2	Rafał Kosznik		17/12/83	D	14		
14	Mate Lačić	CRO	12/09/80	M	7		
18	Łukasz Madej		14/04/82	M	23	(1)	3
16	Mateusz Mak		14/11/91	M	14	(2)	2
8	Michał Mak		14/11/91	A	2	(8)	2
15	Krzysztof Michalak		15/04/87	D	1	(6)	
42	Seweryn Michalski		12/09/94	D	15		2
9	Dawid Nowak		30/11/84	A	1	(3)	
48	Piotr Piekarski		26/06/93	M	1	(3)	
19	Kamil Poźniak		11/12/89	M	1	(3)	1
20	Patryk Rachwał		27/01/81	M	8	(3)	
6	Szymon Sawala		25/09/82	D	24	(3)	2
19	Marko Šimić	CRO	23/01/88	A	2	(3)	
1	Adam Stachowiak		18/12/86	G	15		
10	Alan Stulin		05/06/90	M	2	(4)	
32	Maciej Szmatiuk		09/05/80	D	13		1
99	Mouhamadou Traoré	SEN	16/04/82	A	4	(5)	
30	Kamil Wacławczyk		29/03/87	M	27	(1)	3
24	Maciej Wilusz		25/09/88	D	23		
66	Piotr Witasik		04/12/92	D	4		
23	Tomasz Wróbel		10/07/82	M	14		3
55	Łukasz Wroński		13/01/94	M	4	(7)	
1	Emilijus Zubas	LTU	10/07/90	G	15		
7	Bartosz Żurek		15/03/93	M	3	(7)	

GÓRNIK ZABRZE

Coach: Adam Nawałka
1948 • Ernesta Pohla (3,500) • gornikzabrze.pl
Major honours
*Polish League (14) 1957, 1959, 1961, 1963, 1964,
1965, 1966, 1967, 1971, 1972, 1985, 1986, 1987, 1988;
Polish Cup (6) 1965, 1968, 1969, 1970, 1971, 1972*

2012

17/08	Piast	a	2-1	Przybylski, Milik
24/08	Jagiellonia	a	1-1	Milik
02/09	Lech	a	0-0	
16/09	Legia	h	2-2	Oziębała, Danch
24/09	Widzew	a	1-1	Shevelyukhin
30/09	Śląsk	h	4-1	Kwiek, Nakoulma 2, Milik
06/10	Podbeskidzie	a	3-1	Milik 2, Nakoulma
19/10	Korona	a	2-0	Milik, Nakoulma
20/10	Ruch	a	0-0	
02/11	Bełchatów	h	2-0	Przybylski, Kwiek
11/11	Zagłębie	h	0-2	
17/11	Polonia	a	1-1	og (Kokoszka)
24/11	Pogoń	h	0-0	
01/12	Wisła	a	3-1	Danch, Mączyński, Milik
08/12	Lechia	h	2-0	Zachara, Łuczak

2013

25/02	Piast	h	1-0	Zahorski
03/03	Jagiellonia	h	1-2	Przybylski
10/03	Lech	h	0-1	
15/03	Legia	a	0-3	
28/03	Widzew	h	3-1	Jeleń, Kwiek, Danch
06/04	Śląsk	a	1-2	Nakoulma
14/04	Podbeskidzie	h	0-1	
19/04	Korona	a	0-1	
28/04	Ruch	h	2-0	Kopacz, Jeleń
04/05	Bełchatów	a	0-2	
13/05	Zagłębie	a	2-1	Kwiek, Bonin
18/05	Polonia	h	0-4	
26/05	Pogoń	a	0-1	
30/05	Wisła	h	0-1	
02/06	Lechia	a	2-0	Mośnikov, Bonin

No	Name	Nat	DoB	Pos	Aps	(s)	Gls
7	Maciej Bębenek		22/09/84	M		(2)	
24	Michael Bemben	GER	28/01/76	D	17	(1)	
15	Grzegorz Bonin		02/12/83	M	6	(9)	2
26	Adam Danch		15/12/87	D	29		3
22	Seweryn Gancarczyk		22/11/81	D	24	(1)	
38	Bartosz Iwan		18/04/84	M	16	(9)	
30	Ireneusz Jeleń		09/04/81	A	6	(6)	2
2	Bartosz Kopacz		21/05/92	D	6		1
6	Aleksander Kwiek		13/01/83	M	25	(1)	4
89	Wojciech Łuczak		28/07/89	M	6	(3)	1
3	Antoni Łukasiewicz		26/06/83	D	1	(4)	
29	Krzysztof Mączyński		23/05/87	M	22	(4)	1
21	Mariusz Magiera		25/08/84	D	6		
99	Arkadiusz Milik		28/02/94	A	13	(1)	7
7	Sergei Mośnikov	EST	07/01/88	M	3	(5)	1
14	Préjuce Nakoulma	BFA	21/04/87	M	23	(5)	5
10	Konrad Nowak		07/11/94	M	2	(16)	
17	Paweł Olkowski		13/02/90	D	28	(1)	
8	Przemysław Oziębała		24/08/86	A	1	(9)	1
19	Mariusz Przybylski		19/01/82	M	25	(1)	3
5	Olexandr Shevelyukhin	UKR	27/08/82	D	28		1
28	Łukasz Skorupski		05/05/91	G	29		
33	Norbert Witkowski		05/08/81	G	1		
11	Marcin Wodecki		14/01/88	A		(2)	
20	Mateusz Zachara		27/03/90	A	8	(5)	1
23	Tomasz Zahorski		22/11/84	A	5	(3)	1

JAGIELLONIA BIAŁYSTOK

Coach: Tomasz Hajto
1932 • Miejski (6,000) • jagiellonia.pl
Major honours
Polish Cup (1) 2010

2012

18/08	Podbeskidzie	h	2-1	Plizga, Norambuena
24/08	Górnik	h	1-1	Makuszewski
01/09	Zagłębie	h	0-0	
15/09	Polonia	a	1-1	Frankowski
22/09	Piast	h	0-2	
29/09	Pogoń	a	1-1	Dzalamidze
08/10	Lechia	h	0-2	
20/10	Wisła	h	0-1	
27/10	Lech	a	2-0	Pazdan, Norambuena
03/11	Widzew	h	2-2	Dzalamidze 2
10/11	Legia	a	2-1	Plizga, Frankowski
17/11	Korona	h	0-0	
25/11	Śląsk	a	3-3	Kupisz (p), Plizga, Smolarek
30/11	Bełchatów	h	2-2	Frankowski, Dzalamidze
07/12	Ruch	a	1-1	Smolarek

2013

23/02	Podbeskidzie	a	0-4	
03/03	Górnik	a	2-1	Dani Quintana, Dźwigała
08/03	Zagłębie	a	1-2	Dani Quintana
15/03	Polonia	h	2-0	Frankowski, Plizga
30/03	Piast	a	1-1	Frankowski
06/04	Pogoń	h	1-0	Frankowski (p)
14/04	Lechia	a	3-2	Dani Quintana, Gajos, Smolarek
20/04	Wisła	h	2-2	Gajos, Plizga
29/04	Lech	h	0-1	
04/05	Widzew	a	0-3	
11/05	Legia	h	0-3	
19/05	Korona	a	0-5	
26/05	Śląsk	h	0-3	
30/05	Bełchatów	a	1-1	Smolarek
02/06	Ruch	h	1-0	Dani Quintana

No	Name	Nat	DoB	Pos	Aps	(s)	Gls
5	Tomasz Bandrowski		18/09/84	M	12	(5)	
99	Dani Quintana	ESP	08/03/87	M	14	(1)	4
10	Nika Dzalamidze	GEO	06/01/92	M	13	(2)	4
14	Adam Dźwigała		25/09/95	D	11	(3)	1
25	Michał Fidziukiewicz		08/02/91	A		(1)	
21	Tomasz Frankowski		16/08/74	A	21	(2)	6
20	Maciej Gajos		19/03/91	M	12	(8)	2
22	Rafał Grzyb		16/01/83	M	29	(1)	
16	Luka Gusić	CRO	30/07/85	D	4	(1)	
18	Ľuboš Hanzel	SVK	07/05/87	D	5	(1)	
23	Damian Kądzior		16/06/92	M		(2)	
77	Kim Min-kyun	KOR	30/11/88	M	3	(2)	
92	Tomasz Kowalski		14/09/92	M	1	(8)	
8	Tomasz Kupisz		02/01/90	M	29	(1)	1
11	Karol Mackiewicz		01/06/92	A	1	(2)	
7	Maciej Makuszewski		29/09/89	M	3		1
28	Filip Modelski		28/09/92	D	15	(3)	
17	Alexis Norambuena	PLE	31/03/84	D	28		2
4	Michał Pazdan		21/09/87	D	26	(1)	1
16	Luka Pejović	MNE	30/07/85	D	6	(5)	
6	Dawid Plizga		17/11/85	M	22	(7)	5
32	Tomasz Porębski		12/01/92	D	2		
30	Łukasz Skowron		17/03/91	M	7	(1)	
1	Jakub Słowik		31/08/91	G	23		
7	Euzebiusz Smolarek		09/01/81	A	6	(14)	4
3	Jonatan Straus		30/06/94	D	3	(1)	
28	Paweł Tarnowski		21/09/88	M	2	(5)	
18	Thiago Rangel	BRA	21/04/86	D	2		
18	Łukasz Tymiński		08/11/90	M	8	(4)	
19	Ugochukwu Ukah	NGA	18/01/84	D	21	(2)	
9	Tomasz Zahorski		22/11/84	A	1	(3)	

KORONA KIELCE

Coach: Leszek Ojrzyński
1973 • Miejski Arena Kielc (15,550) • korona-kielce.pl

2012

19/08	Legia	a	0-4	
26/08	Śląsk	a	0-2	
01/09	Lechia	h	0-1	
15/09	Ruch	a	1-1	Staňo
21/09	Podbeskidzie	h	2-1	Żewłakow, Korzym
29/09	Bełchatów	h	1-0	Sobolewski (p)
06/10	Zagłębie	h	1-0	Korzym
19/10	Górnik	a	0-2	
27/10	Pogoń	h	2-1	Lenartowski, Korzym
04/11	Polonia	a	0-2	
11/11	Wisła	h	1-1	Korzym
17/11	Jagiellonia	a	0-0	
23/11	Piast	h	4-0	Székely, Staňo, Lenartowski, Jovanović
01/12	Widzew	a	0-1	
09/12	Lech	h	0-1	

2013

23/02	Legia	h	3-2	Korzym, Lenartowski, Kijanskas
03/03	Śląsk	h	1-1	Korzym
11/03	Lechia	a	2-3	Janota, Staňo
16/03	Ruch	h	2-1	Korzym, Golański (p)
28/03	Podbeskidzie	a	1-1	Korzym
07/04	Bełchatów	a	1-0	Jovanović
12/04	Zagłębie	a	1-2	Staňo
19/04	Górnik	h	1-0	Malarczyk
26/04	Pogoń	a	1-2	Malarczyk
03/05	Polonia	h	1-1	Korzym
11/05	Wisła	a	0-3	
19/05	Jagiellonia	h	5-0	Golański 2 (1p), Lenartowski, Janota, Staňo
23/05	Piast	a	1-1	Adamek
30/05	Widzew	h	0-0	

No	Name	Nat	DoB	Pos	Aps	(s)	Gls
23	Kamil Adamek		09/02/89	A	1	(5)	1
58	Karol Angielski		20/03/96	A	1	(4)	
18	Marcin Cebula		06/12/95	M		(2)	
6	Tomasz Foszmańczyk		07/02/86	M	6	(9)	
44	Paweł Golański		12/10/82	D	23		3
19	Łukasz Jamróz		18/02/90	A	4	(3)	
10	Michał Janota		29/07/90	M	20	(4)	2
8	Vlastimir Jovanović	BIH	03/04/85	M	28		2
13	Krzysztof Kierc		16/02/89	D	4		
2	Tadas Kijanskas	LTU	06/09/85	D	15	(5)	1
20	Maciej Korzym		02/05/88	A	23		9
3	Kamil Kuzera		11/03/83	D	10	(6)	
39	Bartosz Kwiecień		07/05/94	D	3		
22	Grzegorz Lech		10/01/83	M	6	(3)	
16	Artur Lenartowski		17/03/88	M	25	(2)	4
7	Tomasz Lisowski		04/04/85	D	26		
4	Piotr Malarczyk		01/08/91	D	23	(2)	2
26	Wojciech Małecki		11/10/90	G	2		
1	Zbigniew Małkowski		19/01/78	G	24		
27	Vanja Marković	SRB	20/06/94	M		(1)	
37	Bartosz Papka		12/09/93	A		(1)	
24	Olexiy Shlyakotin	UKR	02/09/89	G	4	(1)	
14	Łukasz Sierpina		23/03/88	M	10	(15)	
29	Paweł Sobolewski		20/06/79	M	18	(3)	1
17	Pavol Staňo	SVK	29/09/77	D	27		5
99	Mateusz Stąporski		28/01/88	M	4	(7)	
88	Kamil Sylwestrzak		16/07/88	D	2		
11	Janos Székely	ROU	13/05/83	M	4	(4)	1
5	Aleksandar Vuković	SRB	25/08/79	M	4		
11	Paweł Zawistowski		04/06/84	M	3	(3)	
21	Marcin Żewłakow		22/04/76	A	9	(4)	1
15	Michał Zieliński		06/05/84	A	1	(6)	

 **POLAND**

KKS LECH POZNAŃ

Coach: Mariusz Rumak
1922 • Miejski (41,609) • lechpoznan.pl
Major honours
Polish League (6) 1983, 1984, 1990, 1992, 1993, 2010;
Polish Cup (5) 1982, 1984, 1988, 2004, 2009

2012
18/08	Ruch	h	4-0	*Ceesay, Ślusarski, Lovrencsics, Ubiparip*
25/08	Polonia	a	2-1	*Trałka, Tonev*
02/09	Górnik	h	0-0	
17/09	Bełchatów	a	1-0	*Ślusarski*
23/09	Pogoń	h	1-1	*Ślusarski*
30/09	Lechia	a	0-2	
06/10	Piast	h	4-0	*Ceesay, Ślusarski, Tonev, Wolski*
19/10	Zagłębie	a	1-0	*Ubiparip*
27/10	Jagiellonia	a	0-2	
02/11	Wisła	a	1-0	*Drewniak*
09/11	Widzew	a	1-0	*Murawski*
18/11	Legia	h	1-3	*Ślusarski*
26/11	Podbeskidzie	a	3-2	*Ślusarski 2, Bereszyński*
30/11	Śląsk	h	0-3	
09/12	Korona	a	1-0	*Ślusarski*

2013
24/02	Ruch	a	4-0	*Ślusarski, Kamiński, og (Baszczyński), Hämäläinen*
01/03	Polonia	h	0-1	
10/03	Górnik	a	1-0	*Wołąkiewicz (p)*
16/03	Bełchatów	h	0-0	
01/04	Pogoń	a	2-0	*Kamiński, Tonev*
05/04	Lechia	h	4-2	*Kamiński, Wołąkiewicz (p), Lovrencsics, Ślusarski*
15/04	Piast	a	3-0	*Lovrencsics, Tonev, Murawski*
21/04	Zagłębie	a	3-1	*Lovrencsics, Hämäläinen, Reiss*
29/04	Jagiellonia	a	1-0	*Lovrencsics*
04/05	Wisła	h	1-0	*Teodorczyk*
10/05	Widzew	a	4-0	*Możdżeń, Hämäläinen, Ślusarski, Lovrencsics*
18/05	Legia	a	0-1	
25/05	Podbeskidzie	h	0-2	
30/05	Śląsk	a	1-1	*Murawski*
02/06	Korona	h	2-0	*Djurdjević, Lovrencsics*

No	Name	Nat	DoB	Pos	Aps	(s)	Gls
5	Manuel Arboleda	COL	02/08/79	D	10		
28	Bartosz Bereszyński		12/07/92	A	4	(7)	1
1	Jasmin Burić	BIH	18/02/87	G	22		
21	Kebba Ceesay	GAM	14/11/87	D	25		2
3	Ivan Djurdjević	SRB	05/02/77	D	5	(6)	1
17	Szymon Drewniak		11/07/93	M	12	(3)	1
19	Kasper Hämäläinen	FIN	08/08/86	M	12	(2)	3
25	Luis Henríquez	PAN	23/11/81	D	23	(2)	
35	Marcin Kamiński		15/01/92	D	22	(1)	3
4	Tomasz Kędziora		11/06/94	D	5	(3)	
27	Krzysztof Kotorowski		12/09/76	G	8	(1)	
23	Karol Linetty		02/02/95	M	8	(6)	
11	Gergő Lovrencsics	HUN	01/09/88	A	22	(5)	7
32	Mateusz Możdżeń		14/03/91	M	13	(12)	1
16	Rafał Murawski		09/10/81	M	28	(1)	3
9	Piotr Reiss		20/06/72	A	1	(7)	1
18	Bartosz Ślusarski		11/12/81	A	20	(3)	11
10	Łukasz Teodorczyk		03/06/91	A	8	(6)	1
24	Alexander Tonev	BUL	03/02/90	M	22	(4)	4
6	Łukasz Trałka		11/05/84	M	27	(1)	1
14	Vojo Ubiparip	SRB	10/05/88	A	6	(13)	2
7	Jakub Wilk		11/07/85	M	1	(4)	
20	Hubert Wołąkiewicz		21/10/85	D	26		2
13	Patryk Wolski		12/04/93	A		(3)	1

KS LECHIA GDAŃSK

Coach: Bogusław Kaczmarek
1945 • PGE Arena (43,165) • lechia.pl
Major honours
Polish Cup (1) 1983

2012
20/08	Polonia	h	1-3	*Wiśniewski*
27/08	Pogoń	a	2-0	*Traoré, Surma*
01/09	Korona	a	1-0	*Ricardinho*
15/09	Piast	h	1-2	*Traoré*
22/09	Wisła	a	0-1	
30/09	Lech	h	2-0	*Wiśniewski, Traoré*
08/10	Jagiellonia	a	2-0	*Machaj, Ricardinho*
21/10	Śląsk	h	2-3	*Traoré 2 (1p)*
26/10	Podbeskidzie	a	3-2	*Rasiak, Ricardinho, Traoré (p)*
04/11	Legia	h	1-2	*Traoré*
09/11	Ruch	a	1-0	*Łazaj*
16/11	Widzew	h	2-0	*Traoré (p), Ricardinho*
24/11	Bełchatów	a	1-0	*Ricardinho (p)*
02/12	Zagłębie	h	2-2	*Traoré, Deleu*
08/12	Górnik	a	0-2	

2013
22/02	Polonia	a	1-1	*Wiśniewski*
01/03	Pogoń	h	1-1	*Brożek (p)*
11/03	Korona	h	3-2	*Buzała, Pietrowski, Duda*
18/03	Piast	a	0-0	
01/04	Wisła	h	0-0	
05/04	Lech	a	2-4	*Wiśniewski, Duda*
14/04	Jagiellonia	h	2-3	*Duda, Ricardinho (p)*
21/04	Śląsk	a	1-1	*Wiśniewski*
27/04	Podbeskidzie	h	1-2	*Frankowski*
05/05	Legia	a	0-1	
12/05	Ruch	h	4-4	*Wiśniewski, Ricardinho, Duda, Rasiak*
20/05	Widzew	a	2-1	*Duda, Machaj*
25/05	Bełchatów	h	1-1	*Rasiak*
30/05	Zagłębie	a	3-0	*og (Banaś), Buzała, Rasiak*
02/06	Górnik	h	0-2	

No	Name	Nat	DoB	Pos	Aps	(s)	Gls
16	Andreu	ESP	17/06/83	M	4	(4)	
3	Vytautas Andriuškevičius	LTU	08/10/90	D	2		
5	Krzysztof Bąk		22/06/82	D	15	(2)	
6	Jarosław Bieniuk		04/06/79	D	29		
4	Piotr Brożek		21/04/83	D	23	(1)	1
1	Michał Buchalik		03/02/89	G	24	(1)	
20	Paweł Buzała		27/12/85	A	14		2
34	Paweł Dawidowicz		20/05/95	D		(2)	
26	Deleu	BRA	01/03/84	D	18	(3)	1
15	Adam Duda		29/04/91	A	5	(12)	5
35	Przemysław Frankowski		12/04/95	M	3	(5)	1
9	Piotr Grzelczak		02/03/88	A	2	(4)	
20	Levon Hayrapetyan	ARM	17/04/89	D	2	(1)	
2	Rafał Janicki		05/07/92	D	22	(2)	
29	Łukasz Kacprzycki		29/04/94	M	4	(8)	
12	Bartosz Kaniecki		11/07/88	G	5	(1)	
30	Maciej Kostrzewa		16/05/91	M		(1)	
31	Damian Kugiel		30/05/95	A		(3)	
18	Kacper Łazaj		24/07/95	M	1	(10)	1
21	Mateusz Machaj		28/06/89	M	19	(6)	2
13	Sebastian Madera		30/05/87	D	10		
33	Sebastian Małkowski		02/03/87	G	1		
22	Paweł Nowak		27/01/79	M	1	(2)	
28	Christopher Oualembo	COD	31/01/87	D	3	(4)	
17	Marcin Pietrowski		01/03/88	M	24		1
22	Mohammed Rahoui	ALG	02/11/88	M	2	(1)	
11	Grzegorz Rasiak		12/01/79	A	11	(2)	4
19	Ricardinho	BRA	03/09/89	M	24	(3)	7
8	Łukasz Surma		28/06/77	M	25	(3)	1
7	Abdou Razack Traoré	BFA	28/12/88	M	13		9
14	Piotr Wiśniewski		11/08/82	M	21	(3)	6
25	Wojciech Zyska		08/01/94	M	3	(1)	

LEGIA WARSZAWA

Coach: Jan Urban
1916 • Pepsi Arena (31,284) • legia.com
Major honours
Polish League (9) 1955, 1956, 1969, 1970, 1994, 1995, 2002, 2006, 2013;
Polish Cup (16) 1955, 1956, 1964, 1966, 1973, 1980, 1981, 1989, 1990, 1994, 1995, 1997, 2008, 2011, 2012, 2013

2012
19/08	Korona	h	4-0	*Ljuboja 3 (1p), og (Staňo)*
26/08	Bełchatów	a	2-0	*Saganowski, Żyro*
03/09	Podbeskidzie	h	3-1	*Żyro, Furman, Radović*
16/09	Górnik	a	2-2	*Saganowski, Furman*
21/09	Polonia	h	1-1	*Ljuboja (p)*
29/09	Zagłębie	a	2-2	*Saganowski 2*
05/10	Wisła	h	2-1	*Kosecki 2*
22/10	Pogoń	a	3-0	*Ljuboja 2, Kosecki*
28/10	Piast	h	3-2	*Ljuboja 2, Radović*
04/11	Lechia	a	2-1	*Radović, Ljuboja*
10/11	Jagiellonia	h	1-2	*Rzeźniczak*
18/11	Lech	a	3-1	*Kosecki, Wawrzyniak, Radović*
23/11	Widzew	h	1-0	*Kosecki*
02/12	Ruch	h	3-0	*Kosecki 2, Ljuboja*
07/12	Śląsk	a	0-1	

2013
23/02	Korona	a	2-3	*Kosecki, Iñaki Astiz*
02/03	Bełchatów	h	0-0	
08/03	Podbeskidzie	a	2-1	*Saganowski, Wawrzyniak*
15/03	Górnik	h	3-0	*Saganowski, Ljuboja, Dvalishvili*
30/03	Polonia	a	2-1	*Ljuboja, Furman*
06/04	Zagłębie	h	2-0	*Radović, Dvalishvili*
13/04	Wisła	a	2-1	*Dvalishvili, Jędrzejczyk*
20/04	Pogoń	h	3-1	*Vrdoljak (p), Dvalishvili (p), Brzyski*
27/04	Piast	a	0-0	
05/05	Lechia	h	1-0	*Kosecki*
11/05	Jagiellonia	a	3-0	*Jodłowiec, Kucharczyk, Dvalishvili (p)*
18/05	Lech	h	1-0	*Vrdoljak (p)*
24/05	Widzew	a	1-1	*Saganowski*
30/05	Ruch	a	0-0	
02/06	Śląsk	h	5-0	*Saganowski 3 (1p), Kucharczyk, Radović*

No	Name	Nat	DoB	Pos	Aps	(s)	Gls
19	Bartosz Bereszyński		12/07/92	D	9	(3)	
17	Tomasz Brzyski		10/01/82	D	5	(4)	1
4	Dickson Choto	ZIM	19/03/81	D	2	(1)	
13	Vladimer Dvalishvili	GEO	20/04/86	A	8	(5)	5
37	Dominik Furman		06/07/92	M	10	(18)	3
5	Janusz Gol		11/11/85	M	10	(9)	
15	Iñaki Astiz	ESP	05/11/83	D	26		1
2	Artur Jędrzejczyk		04/11/87	D	25		2
3	Tomasz Jodłowiec		08/09/85	D	7		1
11	Tomasz Kiełbowicz		21/02/76	D		(1)	
9	Michał Kopczyński		15/06/92	M		(1)	
20	Jakub Kosecki		29/08/90	M	23	(2)	9
18	Michał Kucharczyk		20/03/91	A	13	(10)	2
12	Dušan Kuciak	SVK	21/05/85	G	30		
28	Danijel Ljuboja	SRB	04/09/78	A	24	(2)	12
35	Daniel Łukasik		28/04/91	M	19	(3)	
32	Miroslav Radović	SRB	16/01/84	M	25	(2)	5
25	Jakub Rzeźniczak		26/10/86	D	10	(2)	1
7	Marek Saganowski		31/10/78	A	17	(2)	10
7	Jorge Salinas	PAR	06/05/92	M	2	(11)	
8	Marko Šuler	SVN	09/03/83	D	3	(1)	
14	Ivica Vrdoljak	CRO	19/09/83	M	19	(1)	2
14	Jakub Wawrzyniak		07/07/83	D	25		2
6	Michał Żewłakow		22/04/76	D	13	(3)	
33	Michał Żyro		20/09/92	M	5	(4)	2

GKS PIAST GLIWICE

Coach: Marcin Brosz
1945 • Miejski (10,037) • piast-gliwice.eu

2012

17/08	Górnik	h	1-2	og (Skorupski)
24/08	Zagłębie	a	1-2	Rubén Jurado
31/08	Pogoń	h	1-0	Kędziora
15/09	Lechia	a	2-1	Rubén Jurado, Podgórski
22/09	Jagiellonia	a	2-0	Podgórski, Zganiacz
01/10	Wisła	h	2-0	Podgórski, Kędziora
06/10	Lech	a	0-4	
20/10	Widzew	h	1-2	Kędziora
28/10	Legia	a	2-3	Fernando Cuerda, Kędziora
03/11	Ruch	h	1-3	Ižvolt
10/11	Śląsk	h	3-1	Kędziora (p), Rubén Jurado, Zbozień
17/11	Podbeskidzie	h	1-0	Rubén Jurado
23/11	Korona	a	0-4	
03/12	Polonia	h	1-1	Rubén Jurado
08/12	Bełchatów	a	3-1	Podgórski 2, Sikora

2013

25/02	Górnik	a	0-1	
02/03	Zagłębie	h	1-1	Dočekal
10/03	Pogoń	a	2-0	Dočekal 2
18/03	Lechia	h	2-0	Podgórski, Robak
30/03	Jagiellonia	h	1-1	Lazdiņš
07/04	Wisła	a	2-1	Zbozień, Urban
15/04	Lech	h	0-3	
19/04	Widzew	a	1-1	Robak
27/04	Legia	h	0-0	
06/05	Ruch	a	2-1	Matras, Podgórski
12/05	Śląsk	h	3-2	Rubén Jurado (p), Oleksy, Murawski
18/05	Podbeskidzie	a	2-1	og (Konieczny), Robak
23/05	Korona	h	1-1	Cicman
30/05	Polonia	a	1-1	Robak
02/06	Bełchatów	h	2-3	Cicman, Rubén Jurado (p)

No	Name	Nat	DoB	Pos	Aps	(s)	Gls
19	Álvaro Jurado	ESP	05/09/81	M	3	(1)	
20	Jan Buryán	CZE	17/02/77	D		(3)	
7	Tomasz Bzdęga		18/03/85	A	1	(4)	
16	Pavol Cicman	SVK	30/01/85	A	13	(8)	2
13	Tomáš Dočekal	CZE	24/05/89	A	8	(8)	3
3	Fernando Cuerda	ESP	06/03/84	D	6	(3)	1
18	Matej Ižvolt	SVK	05/06/86	M	16	(5)	1
24	Wojciech Kędziora		20/12/80	A	15		5
14	Adrian Klepczyński		01/04/81	D	26	(3)	
15	Łukasz Krzycki		10/01/84	D	6	(4)	
27	Artis Lazdiņš	LVA	03/05/86	M	14	(8)	1
21	Wojciech Lisowski		08/10/91	M		(1)	
4	Mateusz Matras		23/01/91	M	24	(1)	1
9	Radosław Murawski		22/04/94	M	6	(3)	1
23	Paweł Oleksy		01/04/91	D	22	(1)	1
28	Kornel Osyra		07/02/93	D		(1)	
17	Tomasz Podgórski		30/12/85	M	30		7
5	Jan Polák	CZE	26/03/89	D	26	(1)	
30	Marcin Robak		29/11/82	A	7	(4)	4
22	Rubén Jurado	ESP	25/04/86	M	24	(5)	7
2	El Mehdi Sidqy	MAR	06/01/84	D	8	(1)	
11	Adrian Sikora		19/03/80	A	1	(8)	1
26	Bartosz Szeliga		10/01/93	M	1	(1)	
1	Jakub Szmatuła		22/03/81	G	1	(1)	
10	Jakub Świercok		28/12/92	A		(1)	
12	Dariusz Trela		05/12/89	G	29		
8	Rudolf Urban	SVK	01/03/80	M	2	(7)	1
25	Damian Zbozień		25/04/89	D	25	(2)	2
6	Mariusz Zganiacz		31/01/84	M	16	(1)	1

TS PODBESKIDZIE BIELSKO-BIAŁA

Coach: Robert Kasperczyk;
(22/10/12) (Andrzej Wyroba); (29/10/12) Marcin Sasal;
(04/01/13) Dariusz Kubicki;
(22/03/13) Czesław Michniewicz
1995 • Miejski (4,279) • ts.podbeskidzie.pl

2012

18/08	Jagiellonia	a	1-2	Pawela
25/08	Wisła	h	1-1	Demjan
03/09	Legia	a	1-3	Demjan
14/09	Śląsk	h	1-1	Adamek
21/09	Korona	a	1-2	Chmiel
28/09	Ruch	h	1-1	Demjan
06/10	Górnik	h	1-3	Chmiel
20/10	Bełchatów	a	1-2	Adamek
26/10	Lechia	a	2-3	Cohen, Pawela
03/11	Zagłębie	a	2-1	Chmiel, Cohen
10/11	Polonia	h	0-1	
17/11	Piast	a	0-1	
26/11	Lech	h	2-3	Demjan, Adamek
01/12	Pogoń	a	0-2	
09/12	Widzew	h	2-2	Pawela, Chmiel

2013

23/02	Jagiellonia	h	4-0	Demjan 2, Telichowski, Sokołowski
04/03	Wisła	a	0-0	
08/03	Legia	h	1-2	Demjan
17/03	Śląsk	a	1-1	Sloboda
28/03	Korona	h	1-1	Demjan
05/04	Ruch	a	3-1	Sokołowski (p), Demjan 2
14/04	Górnik	a	1-0	Demjan
20/04	Bełchatów	h	1-1	Pawela
27/04	Lechia	h	2-1	Górkiewicz, Chmiel
03/05	Zagłębie	h	1-1	Demjan
10/05	Polonia	a	1-2	Wodecki
18/05	Piast	h	1-2	Demjan
25/05	Lech	a	2-2	Pawela 2 (1p)
30/05	Pogoń	h	2-1	Konieczny, Pawela
02/06	Widzew	a	2-1	Chmiel, Demjan (p)

No	Name	Nat	DoB	Pos	Aps	(s)	Gls
16	Kamil Adamek		09/02/89	A	4	(7)	3
12	Mateusz Bąk		24/02/83	G	3		
3	Damian Byrtek		07/03/91	D	8		
19	Marko Ćetković	MNE	10/07/86	M	3	(6)	
8	Damian Chmiel		06/05/87	M	24	(2)	6
18	Sławomir Cienciała		19/03/83	D	7		
4	Liran Cohen	ISR	14/02/83	M	4	(11)	2
7	Juraj Dančík	SVK	21/02/82	D	5	(1)	
27	Adam Deja		24/06/93	M	6	(4)	
23	Róbert Demjan	SVK	26/10/82	A	30		14
2	Tomasz Górkiewicz		28/01/82	D	12	(1)	1
29	Mateusz Janeczko		30/11/94	A		(6)	
31	Ireneusz Jeleń		09/04/81	A	7		
9	Dariusz Kołodziej		17/04/82	M		(3)	
21	Piotr Koman		25/06/85	M	2		
26	Bartłomiej Konieczny		09/06/81	D	14		1
25	Krzysztof Król		06/02/87	D	14		
28	Dariusz Łatka		14/09/78	M	24	(1)	
13	Piotr Malinowski		24/03/84	M	11	(15)	
22	Matej Náther	SVK	23/07/85	M	8	(1)	
20	Fabian Pawela		30/11/85	A	13	(11)	7
17	Dariusz Pietrasiak		12/02/80	D	22		
2	Michal Piter-Bučko	SVK	28/12/85	D	16	(7)	
11	Wojciech Reiman		05/08/88	M	1	(1)	
5	Mariusz Sacha		19/07/87	M	4		
11	Anton Sloboda	SVK	10/07/87	M	10	(3)	1
10	Marek Sokołowski		11/03/78	D	23	(2)	2
21	Damian Szczęsny		26/12/86	A	3	(3)	
6	Błażej Telichowski		06/06/84	D	7	(1)	1
22	Marcin Wodecki		14/01/88	A	6	(4)	1
1	Richard Zajac	SVK	16/08/76	G	27		
11	Sebastian Ziajka		15/12/82	M	12		

MKS POGOŃ SZCZECIN

Coach: Artur Skowronek;
(20/03/13) Dariusz Wdowczyk
1948 • im. Floriana Krygiera (15,717) • pogonszczecin.pl

2012

17/08	Zagłębie	h	4-0	Edi Andradina, Traoré, Bonin, Djoussé
27/08	Lechia	h	0-2	
31/08	Piast	a	0-1	
14/09	Wisła	h	2-0	Edi Andradina (p), Kolendowicz
23/09	Lech	a	1-1	Djoussé
29/09	Jagiellonia	h	1-1	Akahoshi
07/10	Widzew	a	3-1	Frączczak, Kolendowicz, Dąbrowski
22/10	Legia	h	0-3	
27/10	Korona	a	1-2	Noll
05/11	Śląsk	h	0-3	
12/11	Bełchatów	a	1-0	Rogalski
19/11	Ruch	h	1-0	Frączczak
24/11	Górnik	a	0-0	
01/12	Podbeskidzie	h	2-0	Frączczak, Budka
10/12	Polonia	a	0-2	

2013

22/02	Zagłębie	a	0-3	
01/03	Lechia	h	1-1	Edi Andradina (p)
10/03	Piast	h	0-2	
17/03	Wisła	a	0-2	
01/04	Lech	h	0-2	
06/04	Jagiellonia	a	0-1	
12/04	Widzew	h	1-1	Edi Andradina (p)
20/04	Legia	a	1-3	Ława
26/04	Korona	h	2-1	Hernâni 2
05/05	Śląsk	a	0-1	
11/05	Bełchatów	h	0-1	
17/05	Ruch	a	3-2	Akahoshi, Dąbrowski, Chałas
26/05	Górnik	h	1-0	og (Bemben)
30/05	Podbeskidzie	a	1-2	Rogalski
02/06	Polonia	h	3-1	Frączczak 2, Chałas

No	Name	Nat	DoB	Pos	Aps	(s)	Gls
27	Takafumi Akahoshi	JPN	27/05/86	M	22	(5)	2
15	Grzegorz Bonin		02/12/83	M	4	(1)	1
16	Adrian Budka		26/01/80	M	8	(5)	1
7	Tomasz Chałas		20/07/88	A	5	(5)	2
3	Maciej Dąbrowski		20/04/87	D	25		2
10	Donald Djoussé	CMR	18/03/90	A	10	(7)	2
5	Edi Andradina	BRA	13/09/74	M	25	(3)	4
9	Adam Frączczak		07/08/87	M	25	(3)	5
14	Wojciech Golla		12/01/92	M	13	(5)	
44	Hernâni	BRA	03/02/84	D	19	(1)	2
8	Peter Hricko	SVK	25/07/81	D	18	(1)	
84	Radosław Janukiewicz		05/05/84	G	19	(1)	
11	Robert Kolendowicz		26/09/80	M	19	(5)	2
30	Dawid Kort		29/04/95	M		(1)	
20	Bartosz Ława		26/02/79	M	10	(5)	1
28	Mateusz Lewandowski		18/03/93	M	9	(7)	
24	Sergei Mošnikov	EST	07/01/88	M		(2)	
13	Takuya Murayama	JPN	08/08/89	A	11	(2)	
29	Norbert Neumann		24/02/94	A		(1)	
19	Emil Noll	COD	21/11/78	D	20	(1)	1
12	Dušan Perniš	SVK	28/11/84	G	11	(1)	
6	Przemysław Pietruszka		18/03/84	D	22	(2)	
17	Maksymilian Rogalski		24/06/83	M	25	(2)	2
25	Sebastian Rudol		21/02/95	M	1	(2)	
13	Mateusz Szałek		16/10/91	D	1	(3)	
23	Julien Tadrowski		17/05/93	D	2		
99	Mouhamadou Traoré	SEN	16/04/82	A	3	(6)	1
18	Radosław Wiśniewski		10/09/92	A	3	(11)	
7	Łukasz Zwoliński		24/02/93	A		(1)	

KSP POLONIA WARSZAWA

Coach: Piotr Stokowiec
1911 • Polonii (7,150) • ksppolonia.pl
Major honours
Polish League (2) 1946, 2000;
Polish Cup (2) 1952, 2001

2012

20/08	Lechia	a	3-1	Gołębiewski, Wszołek, Kiełb
25/08	Lech	h	1-2	Teodorczyk
31/08	Wisła	a	3-1	Teodorczyk, Dvalishvili, Wszołek
15/09	Jagiellonia	h	1-1	Brzyski
21/09	Legia	a	1-1	Dvalishvili
28/09	Widzew	h	3-1	Teodorczyk, Wszołek, Gołębiewski
07/10	Śląsk	a	1-2	Wszołek
21/10	Ruch	h	2-1	Dvalishvili, Brzyski
27/10	Bełchatów	a	5-0	Wszołek, Brzyski, og (Basta), Dvalishvili, Gołębiewski
04/11	Korona	h	2-0	Teodorczyk 2
10/11	Podbeskidzie	a	1-0	Piątek
17/11	Górnik	h	1-1	Dvalishvili
24/11	Zagłębie	h	0-1	
03/12	Piast	a	1-1	Dvalishvili
10/12	Pogoń	h	2-0	og (Dąbrowski), Dvalishvili

2013

22/02	Lechia	h	1-1	Przybecki
01/03	Lech	a	1-0	Piątek
09/03	Wisła	h	1-2	Przybecki
15/03	Jagiellonia	a	0-2	
30/03	Legia	h	1-2	Piątek
08/04	Widzew	a	2-3	og (Kaczmarek), Hołota
13/04	Śląsk	h	2-2	Kiełb, og (Kelemen)
22/04	Ruch	h	1-2	Wszołek
27/04	Bełchatów	h	0-1	
03/05	Korona	a	1-1	Todorovski (p)
10/05	Podbeskidzie	h	2-1	Wszołek, Grzelczak
18/05	Górnik	a	4-0	Przybecki, Kiełb, Gołębiewski 2
27/05	Zagłębie	a	0-0	
30/05	Piast	h	1-1	Todorovski (p)
02/06	Pogoń	a	1-3	Tarnowski

No	Name	Nat	DoB	Pos	Aps	(s)	Gls
37	Martin Baran	SVK	03/01/88	D	11	(1)	
8	Aviram Baruchyan	ISR	20/03/85	M		(1)	
4	Marcin Baszczyński		07/06/77	D	12		
22	Tomasz Brzyski		10/01/82	D	14		3
9	Edgar Çani	ALB	22/07/89	A		(5)	
5	Djordje Čotra	SRB	13/09/84	D	11	(1)	
21	Vladimer Dvalishvili	GEO	20/04/86	A	13	(2)	7
23	Mateusz Gliński		03/06/91	M		(1)	
33	Sergei Golatkin	RUS	04/05/88	D		(1)	
19	Daniel Gołębiewski		15/07/87	A	15	(14)	5
27	Piotr Grzelczak		02/03/88	A	9	(2)	1
20	Tomasz Hołota		27/01/91	M	19	(3)	1
6	Dimitrije Injac	SRB	12/08/80	M	4	(3)	
25	José Isidoro	ESP	01/08/86	D	1	(3)	
33	Maciej Joczys		11/03/92	D	1		
11	Jacek Kiełb		10/01/88	M	8	(7)	3
13	Adam Kokoszka		06/10/86	D	11		
22	Krzysztof Kopciński		14/07/92	M	2	(2)	
29	Andrzej Krajewski		22/09/95	D		(1)	
9	Vytautas Lukša	LTU	14/08/84	M	2	(1)	
16	Mateusz Michalski		29/06/91	M	1	(5)	
4	Igor Morozov	EST	27/05/89	D	13		
21	Michał Olczak		12/02/96	G	1		
18	Sebastian Olczak		30/11/91	D	1	(3)	
31	Mariusz Pawełek		17/03/81	G	16	(1)	
32	Adam Pazio		25/03/91	D	22	(5)	
28	Łukasz Piątek		21/09/85	M	28		3
5	Piotr Piekarski		26/06/93	M		(1)	
14	Miłosz Przybecki		02/01/91	M	12	(4)	3
81	Sebastian Przywarski		30/11/81	G	13		
15	Borys Rusak		05/05/91	M		(1)	
2	Wojciech Szymanek		01/03/82	D	7	(1)	
8	Paweł Tarnowski		28/06/90	M	3	(7)	1
10	Łukasz Teodorczyk		03/06/91	A	12	(1)	5
26	Aleksandar Todorovski	MKD	26/02/84	D	24	(1)	2
24	Jakub Tosik		21/05/87	D	12		
3	Tomasz Wełna		27/01/91	D	2		
25	Konrad Wrzesiński		10/09/93	M	1	(2)	
7	Paweł Wszołek		30/04/92	M	23	(4)	7
17	Diemé Yahiya	SEN	10/12/90	M	5	(1)	

RUCH CHORZÓW

Coach: Tomasz Fornalik; (05/09/12) Jacek Zieliński
1920 • Miejski (9,300) • ruchchorzow.com.pl
Major honours
Polish League (14) 1933, 1934, 1935, 1936, 1938, 1951, 1952, 1953, 1960, 1968, 1974, 1975, 1979, 1989;
Polish Cup (3) 1951, 1974, 1996

2012

18/08	Lech	a	0-4	
25/09	Widzew	a	0-2	
02/09	Śląsk	a	0-1	
15/09	Korona	h	1-1	Piech
22/09	Zagłębie	h	2-1	Piech, Smektała
28/09	Podbeskidzie	a	2-1	Jankowski, Piech
05/10	Bełchatów	h	2-1	Piech, Jankowski
21/10	Polonia	a	1-2	Piech
29/10	Górnik	h	0-0	
03/11	Piast	a	3-1	Kuświk 2, Šultes
09/11	Lechia	h	0-1	
19/11	Pogoń	a	0-1	
25/11	Wisła	h	1-2	Niedzielan
02/12	Legia	a	0-3	
07/12	Jagiellonia	h	1-1	og (Grzyb)

2013

24/02	Lech	h	0-4	
02/03	Widzew	h	3-0	Jankowski, Zieńczuk (p), Panka
09/03	Śląsk	h	1-1	Panka
16/03	Korona	a	1-2	Starzyński
01/04	Zagłębie	a	3-2	og (Čotra), Janoszka, Smektała
05/04	Podbeskidzie	h	1-3	Zieńczuk
13/04	Bełchatów	a	3-0	Jankowski 2, Janoszka
22/04	Polonia	a	2-1	og (Hołota), Jankowski
28/04	Górnik	a	0-2	
06/05	Piast	h	1-2	Starzyński
12/05	Lechia	a	4-4	Janoszka, Šultes 2, Zieńczuk
17/05	Pogoń	h	2-3	Janoszka, og (Frączczak)
24/05	Wisła	a	1-1	Starzyński (p)
30/05	Legia	h	0-0	
02/06	Jagiellonia	a	0-1	

No	Name	Nat	DoB	Pos	Aps	(s)	Gls
44	Marcin Baszczyński		07/06/77	D	9		
24	Robert Chwastek		11/09/88	M	1	(1)	
4	Željko Djokić	BIH	10/05/82	D	19	(1)	
7	Maciej Jankowski		04/01/90	M	23	(5)	6
14	Łukasz Janoszka		18/03/87	M	16	(3)	4
12	Krzysztof Kamiński		26/11/90	G	6		
10	Marcin Kikut		25/06/83	D	13	(1)	
11	Martin Konczkowski		14/09/93	D	9	(1)	
9	Grzegorz Kuświk		23/05/87	A	3	(16)	2
11	Mateusz Kwiatkowski		23/11/92	A	1	(2)	
3	Igor Lewczuk		30/05/85	D	17	(2)	
22	Arkadiusz Lewiński		18/08/90	D	5		
31	Paweł Lisowski		08/10/91	M	2	(3)	
32	Marcin Malinowski		06/11/75	M	19	(3)	
23	Andrzej Niedzielan		27/02/79	A	3	(6)	1
19	Mindaugas Panka	LTU	01/05/84	M	14	(5)	2
30	Matko Perdijić	CRO	26/05/82	G	1		
33	Michal Peškovič	SVK	08/02/82	G	23		
18	Arkadiusz Piech		07/06/85	A	11	(2)	5
22	Maciej Sadlok		29/06/89	D	10	(1)	
8	Jakub Smektała		26/08/87	A	6	(14)	2
34	Filip Starzyński		27/05/91	M	22	(6)	3
7	Piotr Stawarczyk		23/08/83	D	25	(1)	
28	Gábor Straka	SVK	18/12/81	M	5		
29	Pavel Šultes	CZE	15/09/85	A	15	(5)	3
20	Marek Szyndrowski		30/10/80	D	21	(1)	
4	Łukasz Tymiński		08/11/90	M	8	(1)	
27	Kamil Włodyka		11/10/94	M	1	(4)	
5	Marek Zieńczuk		24/09/78	M	22	(2)	3

WKS ŚLĄSK WROCŁAW

Coach: Orest Lenczyk; (31/08/12) (Paweł Barylski); (03/09/12) Stanislav Levý (CZE)
1947 • Miejski (42,771) • slaskwroclaw.pl
Major honours
Polish League (2) 1977, 2012;
Polish Cup (2) 1976, 1987

2012

18/08	Widzew	a	1-2	Kaźmierczak
26/08	Korona	h	2-0	Cetnarski 2 (1p)
02/09	Ruch	h	1-0	Cetnarski (p)
14/09	Podbeskidzie	a	1-1	Sobota
23/09	Bełchatów	h	2-1	Jodłowiec, Ł Gikiewicz
30/09	Górnik	h	1-4	Ćwielong
07/10	Polonia	h	2-1	Ł Gikiewicz, Sobota
21/10	Lechia	a	3-2	Mila 2, Elsner
28/10	Zagłębie	h	0-2	
05/11	Pogoń	a	3-0	Elsner, Jodłowiec, Mila
10/11	Piast	h	1-3	Mila
18/11	Wisła	a	0-1	
25/11	Jagiellonia	h	3-3	Díaz (p), Kaźmierczak, Ćwielong
30/11	Lech	a	3-0	Díaz, Sobota, Ćwielong
07/12	Legia	h	1-0	Jodłowiec

2013

23/02	Widzew	h	2-1	Wasiluk, Sobota
03/03	Korona	a	1-1	Ćwielong
09/03	Ruch	a	1-1	Kaźmierczak
17/03	Podbeskidzie	h	1-1	Ł Gikiewicz
30/03	Bełchatów	a	0-1	
06/04	Górnik	h	2-1	Mila, Ćwielong
13/04	Polonia	a	2-2	Kokoszka, Mila
21/04	Lechia	h	1-1	Ćwielong
28/04	Zagłębie	a	0-4	
05/05	Pogoń	h	1-0	Ćwielong
12/05	Piast	a	2-3	Stevanović 2 (1p)
17/05	Wisła	h	3-0	Patejuk, Ł Gikiewicz 2
26/05	Jagiellonia	a	3-0	Sobota, Mila, Ćwielong
30/05	Lech	h	1-1	Mouloungui
02/06	Legia	a	0-5	

No	Name	Nat	DoB	Pos	Aps	(s)	Gls
10	Mateusz Cetnarski		06/07/88	M	5	(10)	3
20	Piotr Ćwielong		23/04/86	M	18	(10)	8
21	Cristián Díaz	ARG	03/11/86	A	8	(2)	2
29	Rok Elsner	SVN	25/01/86	M	17	(6)	2
30	Paweł Garyga		22/12/91	M		(2)	
27	Łukasz Gikiewicz		26/10/87	A	14	(9)	5
33	Rafał Gikiewicz		26/10/87	G	9	(1)	
15	Rafał Grodzicki		28/10/83	D	17		
3	Tomasz Jodłowiec		08/09/85	D	15		3
26	Przemysław Kaźmierczak		05/05/82	M	23	(1)	3
25	Marián Kelemen	SVK	07/12/79	G	21		
3	Adam Kokoszka		06/10/86	D	12	(1)	1
14	Marcin Kowalczyk		09/04/85	D	23	(1)	
31	Robert Menzel		14/02/91	D	2		
11	Sebastian Mila		10/07/82	M	26		7
8	Éric Mouloungui	GAB	01/04/84	A	2	(8)	1
6	Patrik Mráz	SVK	01/02/87	D	3	(2)	
2	Krzysztof Ostrowski		03/05/82	M	12		
9	Sylwester Patejuk		30/11/82	A	13	(6)	1
17	Mariusz Pawelec		14/04/86	D	16	(4)	
5	Waldemar Sobota		19/05/87	M	28	(1)	5
24	Tadeusz Socha		15/02/88	D	13	(6)	
4	Amir Spahić	BIH	13/09/83	D	11	(1)	
16	Dalibor Stevanović	SVN	27/09/84	M	16	(2)	2
18	Johan Voskamp	NED	15/10/84	A	3	(4)	
28	Marek Wasiluk		03/06/87	D	4		1
23	Jakub Więzik		15/07/91	M	1	(2)	

RTS WIDZEW ŁÓDŹ

Coach: Radosław Mroczkowski
1922 • Widzew (10,500) • widzew.pl
Major honours
Polish League (4) 1981, 1982, 1996, 1997;
Polish Cup (1) 1985

2012

18/08	Śląsk	h	2-1	*Dudek, Broź*
25/08	Ruch	h	2-0	*Ben Dhifallah (p), Rybicki*
01/09	Bełchatów	h	1-0	*Alex Bruno*
16/09	Zagłębie	a	1-0	*Alex Bruno*
24/09	Górnik	h	1-1	*M Stępiński*
28/09	Polonia	a	1-3	*Broź (p)*
07/10	Pogoń	h	1-3	*Kaczmarek*
20/10	Piast	a	2-1	*Kaczmarek, Broź (p)*
26/10	Wisła	h	1-2	*Ben Dhifallah*
03/11	Jagiellonia	a	2-2	*Rybicki, M Stępiński*
09/11	Lech	h	0-1	
16/11	Lechia	a	0-2	
23/11	Legia	a	0-1	
01/12	Korona	h	1-0	*M Stępiński*
09/12	Podbeskidzie	a	2-2	*Broź (p), Nowak*

2013

23/02	Śląsk	a	1-2	*Pawłowski*
02/03	Ruch	a	0-3	
09/03	Bełchatów	a	0-0	
16/03	Zagłębie	h	0-0	
28/03	Górnik	a	1-3	*Pawłowski*
08/04	Polonia	h	3-2	*Batrović, Pawłowski, Broź (p)*
12/04	Pogoń	a	1-1	*M Stępiński*
19/04	Piast	h	1-1	*Pawłowski*
26/04	Wisła	a	0-1	
04/05	Jagiellonia	h	3-0	*Okachi, M Stępiński, Broź*
10/05	Lech	a	0-4	
20/05	Lechia	h	1-2	*Broź (p)*
24/05	Legia	h	1-1	*Broź (p)*
30/05	Korona	a	0-0	
02/06	Podbeskidzie	h	1-2	*Rybicki*

No	Name	Nat	DoB	Pos	Aps	(s)	Gls
30	Hachem Abbès	TUN	01/12/86	D	24	(1)	
29	Alex Bruno	BRA	07/10/93	M	16	(5)	2
23	Adam Banasiak		07/12/89	D	2	(3)	
2	Jakub Bartkowski		07/11/91	D	19		
14	Radosław Bartoszewicz		09/05/83	M	19	(2)	
94	Veljko Batrović	MNE	05/03/94	M	2	(4)	1
7	Mehdi Ben Dhifallah	TUN	06/05/83	A	11	(5)	2
28	Łukasz Broź		17/12/85	D	28		8
24	Miloš Dragojević	MNE	03/02/89	G	7		
27	Sebastian Duda		15/04/93	D	3	(1)	
77	Sebastian Dudek		19/01/80	M	24	(3)	1
31	Emerson Carvalho	BRA	16/06/93	M		(1)	
4	Dino Gavrić	CRO	11/04/89	D	9		
16	Michał Jonczyk		11/03/92	M		(3)	
9	Marcin Kaczmarek		03/12/79	M	27	(2)	2
33	Bartłomiej Kasprzak		12/01/93	M	5	(2)	
6	Jakub Kowalski		09/10/87	M	2	(3)	
23	Maciej Krakowiak		07/09/92	G	3	(1)	
3	Denis Kramar	SVN	07/11/91	D	3		
16	Aleksandr Lebedev	BLR	14/04/85	A	2	(1)	
13	Maciej Mielcarz		15/10/80	D	20		
18	Krystian Nowak		01/04/94	M	7	(10)	1
8	Princewill Okachi	NGA	20/06/91	M	25	(1)	1
19	Bartłomiej Pawłowski		13/11/92	A	14	(1)	4
5	Thomas Phibel	FRA	31/05/86	D	29		
19	Adrian Pietrowski		20/09/90	A		(3)	
20	Michał Płotka		11/06/88	D	7	(2)	
22	Sebastian Radzio		02/04/91	M	3	(2)	
17	Mariusz Rybicki		13/03/93	A	8	(18)	3
15	Mariusz Stępiński		12/05/95	A	11	(14)	5
95	Patryk Stępiński		16/01/95	D		(1)	

WISŁA KRAKÓW

Coach: Michał Probierz; (03/10/12) Tomasz Kulawik
1906 • Miejski im. Henryka Reymana (33,326) •
wisla.krakow.pl
Major honours
Polish League (13) 1927, 1928, 1949, 1950, 1978,
1999, 2001, 2003, 2004, 2005, 2008, 2009, 2011;
Polish Cup (4) 1926, 1967, 2002, 2003

2012

19/08	Bełchatów	h	2-1	*Melikson (p), Genkov*
25/08	Podbeskidzie	a	1-1	*Burliga*
31/08	Polonia	h	1-3	*Iliev*
14/09	Pogoń	a	0-2	
22/09	Lechia	h	1-0	*Genkov*
01/10	Piast	a	0-2	
05/10	Legia	a	1-2	*Garguła*
20/10	Jagiellonia	h	0-0	
26/10	Widzew	a	2-1	*Boguski 2*
02/11	Lech	h	0-1	
11/11	Korona	a	1-1	*Genkov*
18/11	Śląsk	h	1-0	*Iliev*
25/11	Ruch	a	2-1	*Garguła 2*
01/12	Górnik	h	1-3	*Chávez*
08/12	Zagłębie	h	1-4	*Garguła (p)*

2013

24/02	Bełchatów	a	0-0	
04/03	Podbeskidzie	h	0-0	
09/03	Polonia	a	2-1	*Wilk, Chrapek*
17/03	Pogoń	a	2-0	*Sobolewski, Genkov*
01/04	Lechia	a	0-0	
07/04	Piast	h	1-2	*Iliev*
13/04	Legia	h	1-2	*Sikorski*
20/04	Jagiellonia	a	2-2	*Sarki, Boguski*
26/04	Widzew	h	1-0	*Małecki*
04/05	Lech	a	0-1	
11/05	Korona	h	3-0	*Chrapek 2, Małecki*
17/05	Śląsk	a	0-3	
24/05	Ruch	h	1-1	*Chávez*
30/05	Górnik	a	1-0	*Chrapek*
02/06	Zagłębie	h	0-1	

No	Name	Nat	DoB	Pos	Aps	(s)	Gls
30	Gerard Bieszczad		05/02/93	G		(1)	
9	Rafał Boguski		09/06/84	A	17	(9)	3
17	Daniel Brud		20/05/89	M		(1)	
3	Gordan Bunoza	BIH	05/02/88	D	17	(2)	
21	Łukasz Burliga		10/05/88	D	16		1
4	Osman Chávez	HON	29/07/84	D	17	(1)	2
20	Michał Chrapek		03/04/92	M	15	(10)	4
33	Michał Czekaj		13/02/92	D	8		
55	Jan Frederiksen	DEN	20/06/82	D	9	(2)	
10	Łukasz Garguła		25/02/81	M	16	(6)	4
8	Tsvotan Genkov	BUL	08/02/84	A	12	(9)	4
6	Arkadiusz Głowacki		13/03/79	D	19	(1)	
77	Ivica Iliev	SRB	27/10/79	M	15	(5)	3
2	Kew Jaliens	NED	15/09/78	D	15		
22	Marko Jovanović	SRB	26/03/88	D	15	(1)	
54	Dawid Kamiński		13/02/95	A	1		
17	Andraž Kirm	SVN	06/09/84	M		(1)	
5	Kamil Kosowski		30/08/77	M	7	(3)	
19	Patryk Małecki		01/08/88	M	13		2
10	Maor Melikson	ISR	30/10/84	M	13		1
12	Michał Miśkiewicz		20/01/89	G	8		
25	Sergei Pareiko	EST	31/01/77	G	22		
31	Romell Quioto	HON	09/08/91	A	2	(7)	
15	Emmanuel Sarki	NGA	26/12/87	M	7	(5)	1
23	Daniel Sikorski	AUT	02/11/87	A	10	(9)	1
7	Radosław Sobolewski		13/12/76	M	17	(2)	1
41	Paweł Stolarski		28/01/96	M	4	(1)	
42	Michał Szewczyk		17/10/92	A	3	(4)	
34	Alan Uryga		19/02/94	M	5	(5)	
28	Cezary Wilk		12/02/86	M	27	(1)	1

ZAGŁĘBIE LUBIN

Coach: Pavel Hapal (CZE)
1945 • Dialog Arena (16,100) • zaglebie-lubin.pl
Major honours
Polish League (2) 1991, 2007

2012

17/08	Pogoń	a	0-4	
24/08	Piast	h	2-1	*Jeż, Woźniak*
01/09	Jagiellonia	a	0-0	
16/09	Widzew	h	0-1	
22/09	Ruch	a	1-2	*Pawłowski*
29/09	Legia	h	2-2	*Papadopulos, Jeż*
06/10	Korona	a	0-1	
19/10	Lech	h	0-1	
28/10	Śląsk	a	2-0	*Papadopulos, Pawłowski*
03/11	Podbeskidzie	h	1-2	*Papadopulos*
11/11	Górnik	a	2-0	*Pawłowski 2*
16/11	Bełchatów	h	1-0	*Hanzel*
24/11	Polonia	a	1-0	*Papadopulos*
02/12	Lechia	h	2-2	*Pawłowski, Nhamoinesu*
08/12	Wisła	a	4-1	*Papadopulos, Pawłowski, Jeż, Trochim*

2013

22/02	Pogoń	h	3-0	*Rymaniak, Pawłowski (p), Papadopulos*
02/03	Piast	a	1-1	*Banaś*
08/03	Jagiellonia	h	2-1	*Papadopulos, Godál*
16/03	Widzew	a	0-0	
01/04	Ruch	h	2-3	*Błąd 2*
06/04	Legia	a	0-2	
12/04	Korona	h	2-1	*Rakowski, Błąd*
21/04	Lech	a	1-3	*Pawłowski*
28/04	Śląsk	h	4-0	*Małkowski 2, Papadopulos, Jeż*
03/05	Podbeskidzie	a	1-1	*Papadopulos*
13/05	Górnik	h	1-2	*Papadopulos*
19/05	Bełchatów	a	2-3	*Woźniak, Papadopulos*
27/05	Polonia	h	0-0	
30/05	Lechia	a	0-3	
02/06	Wisła	a	1-0	*Woźniak (p)*

No	Name	Nat	DoB	Pos	Aps	(s)	Gls
20	David Abwo	NGA	10/05/86	M	5	(8)	
5	Adam Banaś		25/12/82	D	21		1
7	Jiří Bilek	CZE	04/11/83	M	29		
15	Adrian Błąd		16/04/91	M	7	(7)	3
85	Djordje Čotra	SRB	13/09/84	D	6	(3)	
85	Martins Ekwueme	NGA	02/10/85	M		(1)	
6	Élton	BRA	21/09/86	D	4	(9)	
24	Michał Gliwa		08/04/88	G	28		
37	Boris Godál	SVK	27/05/87	D	5	(1)	1
25	Łukasz Hanzel		16/09/86	M	13	(7)	1
3	Csaba Horváth	SVK	02/05/82	D	1	(1)	
31	Róbert Jeż	SVK	10/07/81	M	27		4
38	Damian Kowalczyk		03/08/95	A		(7)	
94	Maciej Kowalski-Haberek		16/05/94	M		(3)	
1	Marek Kozioł		01/06/88	G	2		
19	Maciej Małkowski		19/03/85	M	20	(5)	2
2	Costa Nhamoinesu	ZIM	06/01/86	D	22	(1)	1
27	Michał Papadopulos	CZE	14/04/85	A	24	(2)	11
23	Szymon Pawłowski		04/11/86	M	23		8
17	Adrian Rakowski		07/10/90	M	7	(6)	1
33	Sergio Reina	COL	26/01/85	D	3		
21	Bartosz Rymaniak		13/11/89	D	20	(2)	1
9	Darvydas Šernas	LTU	22/07/84	A	2	(8)	
77	Wojciech Trochim		31/03/89	M		(1)	1
33	Alexander Tunchev	BUL	10/07/81	D	19		1
4	Pavel Vidanov	BUL	08/01/88	D	26		
88	Kamil Wilczek		14/01/88	M	2	(8)	
11	Arkadiusz Woźniak		01/06/90	A	14	(8)	3

Top goalscorers

14	Róbert Demjan (Podbeskidzie)
12	Danijel Ljuboja (Legia)
	Vladimer Dvalishvili (Polonia/Legia)
11	Bartosz Ślusarski (Lech)
	Michal Papadopulos (Zagłębie)
10	Marek Saganowski (Legia)
9	Maciej Korzym (Korona)
	Abdou Razack Traoré (Lechia)
	Jakub Kosecki (Legia)
8	Piotr Ćwielong (Śląsk)
	Łukasz Broż (Widzew)
	Szymon Pawłowski (Zagłębie)

Promoted clubs

ZAWISZA BYDGOSZCZ

Coach: Yuriy Shatalov (UKR);
(27/04/13) Ryszard Tarasiewicz
1946 • im. Zdzisława Krzyszkowiaka (20,247) •
wkszawisza.pl

MKS CRACOVIA KRAKÓW

Coach: Wojciech Stawowy
1906 • im. Jana Pawła II (15,016) • cracovia.pl
Major honours
Polish League (5) 1921, 1930, 1932, 1937, 1948

SECOND LEVEL FINAL TABLE 2012/13

		Pld	W	D	L	F	A	Pts
1	Zawisza Bydgoszcz	34	19	9	6	69	26	66
2	MKS Cracovia Kraków	34	19	7	8	48	35	64
3	LKS Termalica Bruk-Bet Nieciecza	34	19	6	9	54	28	63
4	MKS Flota Świnoujście	34	19	6	9	57	33	63
5	Arka Gdynia	34	17	6	11	46	29	57
6	GKS Tychy	34	15	10	9	44	28	55
7	MKS Dolcan Ząbki	34	16	6	12	52	41	54
8	Miedź Legnica	34	15	8	11	49	42	53
9	GKS Olimpia Grudziądz	34	13	12	9	39	34	51
10	GKS Katowice	34	14	8	12	43	36	50
11	KS Kolejarz Stróże	34	14	8	12	47	45	50
12	GKS Bogdanka Łęczna	34	11	13	10	37	42	46
13	Stomil Olsztyn	34	8	14	12	37	45	38
14	MKS Sandecja Nowy Sącz	34	10	7	17	35	54	37
15	Okocimski KS Brzesko	34	7	11	16	38	54	32
16	KS Warta Poznań	34	7	7	20	34	57	28
17	KS Polonia Bytom	34	5	7	22	29	64	22
18	ŁKS Łódź	34	3	5	26	17	82	14

Domestic cup: Puchar Polski 2012/13

FIRST ROUND

(31/07/12)
Arka Gdynia 0-1 Olimpia Elbląg
Okocimski KS Brzesko 1-1 Polonia Bytom *(aet; 4-2 on pens)*
Pelikan Łowicz 2-1 Kolejarz Stróże
Stomil Olsztyn 2-3 Bogdanka Łęczna
(01/08/12)
Fogo Luboń 4-2 GKS Katowice
Górnik Wałbrzych 4-1 Sandecja Nowy Sącz
Kotwica Kołobrzeg 0-4 Warta Poznań
Legia II Warszawa 2-4 KS Polkowice *(aet)*
Limanovia Limanowa 0-1 Piast Gliwice
Łysica II Bodzentyn 1-2 Wisła Płock
Miedź Legnica 2-1 Dolcan Ząbki
Olimpia Grudziądz 1-0 Pogoń Szczecin *(aet)*
Ruch Zdzieszowice 0-5 Flota Świnoujście
Sokół Aleksandrów Łódzki 0-5 Zawisza Bydgoszcz
Sokół Ostróda 3-0 Ruch Radzionków *(w/o)*
Wigry Suwałki 1-2 Termalica Nieciecza

SECOND ROUND

(04/08/12)
KS Polkowice 0-1 Śląsk Wrocław
(05/08/12)
Okocimski KS Brzesko 0-4 Legia Warszawa
(11/08/12)
Bogdanka Łęczna 1-2 Lechia Gdańsk *(aet)*
Flota Świnoujście 2-1 Górnik Zabrze
Fogo Luboń 0-5 Wisła Kraków
Górnik Wałbrzych 2-1 ŁKS Łódź
Olimpia Elbląg 1-2 Korona Kielce *(aet)*
Piast Gliwice 1-0 Widzew Łódź
Sokół Ostróda 1-8 Jagiellonia Białystok
Termalika Nieciecza 0-2 GKS Bełchatów
Warta Poznań 1-0 Podbeskidzie Bielsko-Biała
Wisła Płock 2-4 Zagłębie Lubin
Zawisza Bydgoszcz 0-2 Cracovia Kraków
(12/08/12)
Miedź Legnica 1-3 Polonia Warszawa
Olimpia Grudziądz 2-1 Lech Poznań *(aet)*
Pelikan Łowicz 0-1 Ruch Chorzów

1/8 FINALS

(25/09/12)
Ruch Chorzów 3-1 Korona Kielce *(aet)*
Warta Poznań 0-1 Wisła Kraków
(26/09/12)
Piast Gliwice 1-2 Legia Warszawa
Śląsk Wrocław 3-0 GKS Bełchatów
(27/09/12)
Górnik Wałbrzych 1-3 Olimpia Grudziądz (aet)
(02/10/12)
Zagłębie Lubin 2-1 Polonia Warszawa
(03/10/12)
Flota Świnoujście 2-2 Cracovia Kraków *(aet; 8-7 on pens)*
Jagiellonia Białystok 2-2 Lechia Gdańsk *(aet; 5-4 on pens)*

QUARTER-FINALS

(26/02/13 & 26/03/13)
Legia Warszawa 4-1 Olimpia Grudziądz *(Saganowski 51, 89, Jędrzejczyk 63, Dvalishvili 90+1; Ruszkul 35)*
Olimpia Grudziądz 1-2 Legia Warszawa *(Banasiak 89; Dvalishvili 73, Saganowski 78)*
(Legia 6-2)
(27/02/13 & 13/03/13)
Zagłębie Lubin 2-2 Ruch Chorzów *(Pawłowski 42, Wilczek 59; Jankowski 13, Tymiński 70)*
Ruch Chorzów 1-0 Zagłębie Lubin *(Janoszka 57)*
(Ruch 3-2)

(27/02/13 & 27/03/13)
Śląsk Wrocław 3-2 Flota Świnoujście *(Ostrowski 23, Sobota 56, Ćwielong 90+5; Niedziela 6p, Bodziony 26)*
Flota Świnoujście 0-2 Śląsk Wrocław *(Ł Gikiewicz 6, Sobota 35)*
(Śląsk 5-2)
(28/02/13 & 12/03/13)
Wisła Kraków 2-0 Jagiellonia Białystok *(Boguski 39, 45+1)*
Jagiellonia Białystok 2-4 Wisła Kraków *(Dani Quintana 56, 70; Burliga 21, Boguski 35, Sobolewski 48, Małecki 89)*
(Wisła 6-2)

SEMI-FINALS

(09/04/13 & 16/04/13)
Ruch Chorzów 0-0 Legia Warszawa
Legia Warszawa 2-1 Ruch Chorzów *(Dvalishvili 52, 60p; Starzyński 55p)*
(Legia 2-1)
(10/04/13 & 17/04/13)
Śląsk Wrocław 2-1 Wisła Kraków *(Sobota 10, Mila 13; Małecki 50)*
Wisła Kraków 2-3 Śląsk Wrocław *(Wilk 27, Iliev 68; Stevanovič 23, Sobota 54, Mila 80)*
(Śląsk 5-3)

FINAL

(02/05/13)
Stadion Miejski, Wroclaw
WKS ŚLĄSK WROCŁAW 0
LEGIA WARSZAWA 2 *(Saganowski 32, 44)*
Referee: *Marciniak*
ŚLĄSK: R Gikiewicz, Socha (Ostrowski 83), Kowalczyk, Wasiluk, Pawelec, Sobota, Kaźmierczak (Ł Gikiewicz 53), Stevanovič, Mila, Ćwielong, Mouloungui (Cetnarski 46)
LEGIA: Skaba, Jędrzejczyk, Iñaki Astiz, Jodłowiec, Šuler, Brzyski (Jagiełło 84), Kucharczyk, Vrdoljak, Furman, Dvalishvili, Saganowski (Łukasik 77)

(08/05/13)
Pepsi Arena, Warsaw
LEGIA WARSZAWA 0
WKS ŚLĄSK WROCŁAW 1 *(Żewłakow 2og)*
Referee: *Gil*
LEGIA: Skaba, Jędrzejczyk, Żewłakow, Jodłowiec, Šuler, Brzyski (Radović 74), Kosecki, Vrdoljak, Gol (Łukasik 33), Dvalishvili, Saganowski (Furman 87)
ŚLĄSK: R Gikiewicz, Socha, Grodzicki, Kokoszka, Kowalczyk, Ostrowski, Sobota, Stevanovič (Ł Gikiewicz 87), Mila, Ćwielong (Więzik 87), Cetnarski (Patejuk 65)

(agg LEGIA 2-1)

Legia celebrate a hat-trick of Polish Cup successes

PORTUGAL

Federação Portuguesa de Futebol (FPF)

Address	Rua Alexandre Herculano 58	**President**	Fernando Gomes
	Apartado 24013	**General secretary**	Paulo Manuel
	PT-1250-012 Lisboa		Lourenço
Tel	+351 21 325 2700	**Media officer**	Onofre Costa
Fax	+351 21 325 2780	**Year of formation**	1914
E-mail	ceo@fpf.pt		
Website	fpf.pt		

PRIMEIRA LIGA CLUBS

1. A. Académica de Coimbra
2. SC Beira-Mar
3. SL Benfica
4. SC Braga
5. GD Estoril-Praia
6. Gil Vicente FC
7. CS Marítimo
8. Moreirense FC
9. CD Nacional
10. SC Olhanense
11. FC Paços de Ferreira
12. FC Porto
13. Rio Ave FC
14. Sporting Clube de Portugal
15. Vitória FC (Setúbal)
16. Vitória SC (Guimarães)

PROMOTED CLUBS

17. CF OS Belenenses
18. FC Arouca

KEY:

- ● – UEFA Champions League
- ● – UEFA Europa League
- ● – Promoted clubs
- ● – Relegated clubs

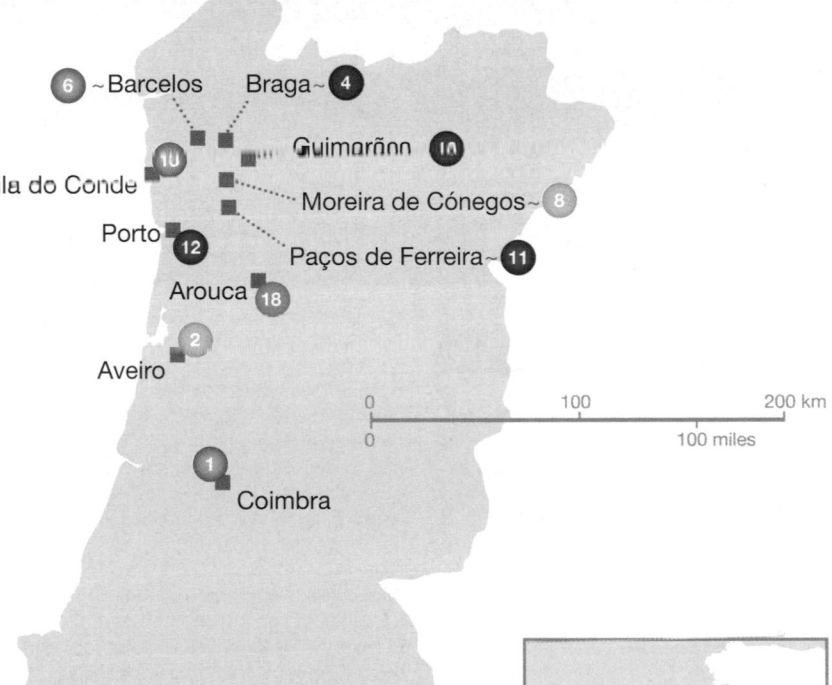

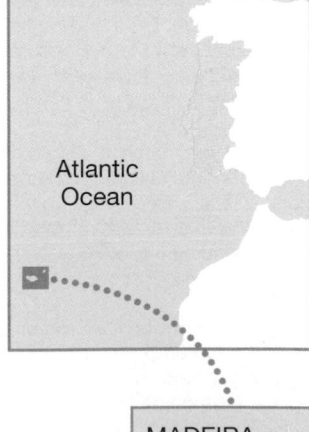

Agony for Benfica, ecstasy for Porto

SL Benfica went into the closing stages of the 2012/13 season with their sights fixed firmly on emulating FC Porto's 2010/11 treble success. Through to the finals of the UEFA Europa League and Portuguese Cup and with a four-point lead in the Primeira Liga, Jorge Jesus's team would ultimately end up with nothing.

Porto edged them out in the Portuguese title race thanks to a last-gasp winner in the head-to-head encounter, and after Chelsea FC had scored an added-time winner to beat them in Amsterdam, Benfica allowed underdogs Vitória SC to come from behind and claim the domestic cup for the first time.

Dragons pip Eagles to take title undefeated

Lisbon giants squander treble chance

100th international cap for Cristiano Ronaldo

Domestic league

There were only ever two candidates for the 2012/13 Liga crown. Porto and Benfica stalked each other from pillar to post, victories coming each team's way in large clusters. With both teams avoiding defeat, draws became major setbacks. Porto, the defending champions, suffered a couple in the early weeks, but so too did their rivals, and by the time the two sides came face to face in mid-January, there was nothing to choose between them, Benfica's three-point lead down solely to the fact that Porto had a game in hand on them.

When the big match in Lisbon ended 2-2, it was honours even in every respect, Porto winning their catch-up fixture ten days later to ensure that the sides remained locked together – with similar goal differences - at the top of the table.

Both clubs drew on 10 February, but the next team to drop points were Porto. Held in successive away fixtures by Sporting Clube de Portugal and CS Marítimo, they allowed Benfica to break into a four-point lead, which they maintained, with a nine-match winning run, all the way through to round 27, when, against all odds, they were held 1-1 at home by newly promoted GD

Estoril-Praia. A tenth straight win would have preserved the Eagles' four-point cushion going into the head-to-head clash at the Estádio do Dragão. Instead they had no margin for error. They simply had to avoid a first defeat of the season, otherwise Vítor Pereira's side would leapfrog them into a one-point lead.

A full house of over 50,000 saw Benfica take an early lead through their top scorer, Brazilian striker Lima, but a Maxi Pereira own goal on 26 minutes restored the equilibrium, and it was anyone's game from there on in.

Chances were made and squandered at both ends, but just as it looked as if Benfica had got the point they craved, Porto's 19-year-old Brazilian substitute Kelvin turned the title race on its head with a superb low cross-shot past Benfica keeper Artur. The home fans went understandably wild as Benfica boss Jesus dropped to his knees in despair. There were 92 minutes on the clock and the visitors had no time to respond.

With that dramatic 2-1 win, Porto were firmly in control going into the final game. It was not the easiest fixture, away to an FC Paços de Ferreira side that had already secured third place – the club's highest ever Liga position – to qualify for

the 2013/14 UEFA Champions League. But having done the hard bit by beating Benfica, Porto were not going to let their advantage slip away, and, sure enough, a goal in each half from Lucho González – a penalty – and Jackson Martínez – the 26th of the campaign from the Liga's top scorer – clinched the club's ninth title in 11 seasons and 27th in all.

It was the second time in three seasons that Porto had completed their 30-match league campaign without a defeat. Furthermore, they had lost just once in 2011/12. It was a remarkable record, and great credit was due to the team for their remarkable stamina and belief – as exemplified by that last-gasp win against Benfica.

Stars of the show were Martínez, a jewel of a signing who could not stop scoring; string-pulling midfield general João Moutinho; winger James Rodríguez; and, at the back, experienced goalkeeper Helton and young French central defender Eliaquim Mangala.

Benfica could take no consolation from having the league's best attack, spearheaded by Lima and Óscar Cardozo, and scoring in every game, but, for all the agony they would ultimately suffer, their season was considerably more memorable than that of local rivals

Sporting, who had a catastrophic campaign, employing four coaches, dicing with relegation and eventually finishing seventh, 36 adrift of the champions, to miss out on European qualification for the first time in 35 years.

Into the breach vacated by Sporting stepped the unlikely lads of Paços Ferreira and Estoril, the latter qualifying for Europe for the first time, with SC Braga, who defeated Porto to win the League Cup, also making it through to the UEFA Europa League.

Equally happy with their season were CF Os Belenenses, who not only returned to the elite after romping to the second division title but also reached the semi-finals of the Portuguese Cup – at the expense of the club that accompanied them up, FC Arouca.

Domestic cup

Belenenses were defeated 3-0 on aggregate in the last four by Guimarães. A mere ninth in the Liga, the northern club had never won a major trophy and were not expected to defeat a Benfica side desperate to avoid yet another runners-up spot. But the curse seemingly hanging over the Lisbon giants was not lifted at the Estádio Nacional.

Despite taking a first-half lead, with a fortuitous goal from Nicolás Gaitán, they fell to another excruciating 2-1 defeat, conceding two goals in three minutes late in the game, the second via a heavy deflection from a cross by Guimarães's 19-year-old winger Ricardo, who had not scored in the league all season.

Europe

Porto outlasted Benfica in the UEFA Champions League, reaching the last 16, where they fell, somewhat unexpectedly, to competition debutants Málaga CF. But it was the Lisbon side, eliminated at the group stage by FC Barcelona and Celtic FC, who went on to distinguish themselves in Europe after Christmas, reaching the final of the UEFA Europa League at the expense of Bayer 04 Leverkusen, FC Girondins de Bordeaux, Newcastle United FC and Fenerbahçe SK.

Benfica had not won a European trophy in over half a century, losing several finals in the interim, and Chelsea were to prolong their misery with a 2-1 win in Amsterdam, their winning goal coming from the head of defender Branislav Ivanović deep into added time.

All three of Portugal's original UEFA Europa League entrants made it into the group stage, but not one of them – Sporting, Marítimo or A. Académica de Coimbra – joined Benfica in the knockout phase. It was a similar tale in the UEFA Champions League for Braga, who finished bottom of their group after defeating Udinese Calcio on penalties in the play-offs.

National team

Paulo Bento's UEFA EURO 2012 semi-finalists made heavy weather of their bid to reach the 2014 FIFA World Cup finals. They ended the season on top of their group after a crucial 1-0 home win over Russia, but their opponents, two points behind but with two games in hand, remained better placed to take the direct route to Brazil. Seven points dropped in three games threatened to send Portugal into a third successive qualifying play-off. Indeed it could have been nine given that they were behind until late on in both of their drawn games at home to Northern Ireland (1-1) and away to Israel (3-3).

It was in the first of those two matches that Cristiano Ronaldo won his 100th international cap, becoming only the third Portuguese player – after Fernando Couto and Luís Figo – to reach that milestone. The Real Madrid CF superstar's 39th international goal – in a June friendly win over Croatia – put him eight behind the country's record scorer Pauleta and just two behind the great Eusébio. He was outscored for his country in 2012/13, however, by the ever-reliable Hélder Postiga, who struck six goals, five of them in the World Cup campaign including the all-important winner at home to Russia.

Cristiano Ronaldo (left) and Hélder Postiga – Portugal's main men in attack

PORTUGAL

Domestic league: Primeira Liga 2012/13 final table

		Pld	Home W	D	L	F	A	Away W	D	L	F	A	Total W	D	L	F	A	Pts
1	**FC Porto**	30	14	1	0	38	5	10	5	0	32	9	24	6	0	70	14	78
2	SL Benfica	30	12	3	0	42	9	12	2	1	35	11	24	5	1	77	20	77
3	FC Paços de Ferreira	30	8	5	2	20	13	6	7	2	22	16	14	12	4	42	29	54
4	SC Braga	30	9	1	5	34	23	7	3	5	26	21	16	4	10	60	44	52
5	GD Estoril-Praia	30	9	2	4	31	18	4	4	7	16	19	13	6	11	47	37	45
6	Rio Ave FC	30	5	4	6	14	17	7	2	6	21	25	12	6	12	35	42	42
7	Sporting Clube de Portugal	30	7	4	4	16	14	4	5	6	20	22	11	9	10	36	36	42
8	CD Nacional	30	6	5	4	26	25	5	2	8	19	26	11	7	12	45	51	40
9	Vitória SC	30	6	4	5	18	22	5	3	7	18	25	11	7	12	36	47	40
10	CS Marítimo	30	4	8	3	14	14	5	3	7	20	31	9	11	10	34	45	38
11	A. Académica de Coimbra	30	4	5	6	22	27	2	5	8	11	18	6	10	14	33	45	28
12	Vitória FC	30	6	1	8	18	25	1	4	10	12	30	7	5	18	30	55	26
13	Gil Vicente FC	30	4	3	8	18	24	2	4	9	13	30	6	7	17	31	54	25
14	SC Olhanense	30	3	4	8	13	20	2	6	7	13	22	5	10	15	26	42	25
15	Moreirense FC	30	3	5	7	16	24	2	4	9	14	27	5	9	16	30	51	24
16	SC Beira-Mar	30	3	6	6	21	26	2	2	11	14	29	5	8	17	35	55	23

SEASON AT A GLANCE

EUROPEAN QUALIFICATION 2013/14

Champion: FC Porto (group stage)
SL Benfica (group stage)
FC Paços de Ferreira (play-offs)

Cup winner: Vitória SC (group stage)
SC Braga (play-offs)
GD Estoril-Praia (third qualifying round)

Top scorer	Jackson Martínez (Porto), 26 goals
Relegated clubs	SC Beira-Mar, Moreirense FC
Promoted club	CF Os Belenenses, FC Arouca
Cup final	Vitória SC 2-1 SL Benfica

PRIMEIRA LIGA TEAM OF THE SEASON
(4-4-2)
Coach: Paulo Fonseca (Paços Ferreira)

**PLAYER OF
THE SEASON
Jackson Martínez**
(FC Porto)

Recruited by Porto from Mexican club Chiapas FC, Martínez ended his debut campaign in Portugal with 26 Liga goals – one more than Colombian compatriot Radamel Falcao managed in 2009/10, and the best in the division. He hit the ground running with the winner in the Portuguese Super Cup and never lost his scoring touch.

**NEWCOMER OF
THE SEASON
Eliaquim Mangala**
(FC Porto)

The imposing central defender matured into a key member of Vítor Pereira's title-winning side. In addition to his defensive excellence, he endeared himself to the Porto faithful by scoring against SL Benfica in the 2-2 draw in Lisbon. His rapid progress continued in June when he was awarded his first senior international cap for France.

Helton
(Porto)

Danilo *(Porto)* · Garay *(Benfica)* · Mangala *(Porto)* · Alex Sandro *(Porto)*

Salvio *(Benfica)* · Matić *(Benfica)* · João Moutinho *(Porto)* · Gaitán *(Benfica)*

Martínez *(Porto)* · Lima *(Benfica)*

PORTUGAL

NATIONAL TEAM

Home Kit   Away Kit

INTERNATIONAL TOURNAMENT APPEARANCES
FIFA World Cup (5) 1966 (3rd), 1986, 2002, 2006 (4th), 2010 (2nd round)
UEFA European Championship (6) 1984 (semifinals), 1996 (qtr-finals), 2000 (semi-finals), 2004 (runners-up), 2008 (qtr-finals), 2012 (semi-finals)

TOP FIVE ALL-TIME CAPS
Luís Figo (127); Fernando Couto (110); **Cristiano Ronaldo** (104) Rui Costa (95); Pauleta (88)

TOP FIVE ALL-TIME GOALS
Pauleta (47); Eusébio (41); **Cristiano Ronaldo** (39); Luís Figo (32); Nuno Gomes (29)

Results 2012/13

Date	Opponent	H/A	Venue	Score	Scorers
15/08/12	Panama	H	Faro	2-0	Nélson Oliveira (30), Cristiano Ronaldo (51)
07/09/12	Luxembourg (WCQ)	A	Luxembourg	2-1	Cristiano Ronaldo (27), Hélder Postiga (54)
11/09/12	Azerbaijan (WCQ)	H	Braga	3-0	Varela (64), Hélder Postiga (85), Bruno Alves (88)
12/10/12	Russia (WCQ)	A	Moscow	0-1	
16/10/12	Northern Ireland (WCQ)	H	Porto	1-1	Hélder Postiga (79)
14/11/12	Gabon	A	Libreville	2-2	Pizzi (36p), Hugo Almeida (60)
06/02/13	Ecuador	H	Guimaraes	2-3	Cristiano Ronaldo (23), Hélder Postiga (60)
22/03/13	Israel (WCQ)	A	Tel-Aviv	3-3	Bruno Alves (2), Hélder Postiga (72), Fábio Coentrão (90+3)
26/03/13	Azerbaijan (WCQ)	A	Baku	2-0	Bruno Alves (63), Hugo Almeida (79)
07/06/13	Russia (WCQ)	H	Lisbon	1-0	Hélder Postiga (9)
10/06/13	Croatia	N	Geneva (SUI)	1-0	Cristiano Ronaldo (36)

Appearances 2012/13

Coach: Paulo Bento 20/06/69

Name	Date	Club	Pan	LUX	AZE	RUS	NIR	Gab	Ecu	ISR	AZE	RUS	CRO	Caps	Goals
Eduardo	19/09/82	İstanbul BB (TUR)	G61						G				G	31	-
Miguel Lopes	19/12/86	Porto	D			s20	D46							4	-
Ricardo Costa	16/05/81	Valencia (ESP)	D					D					D	14	-
Rolando	31/08/85	Porto	D											18	-
Fábio Coentrão	11/03/88	Real Madrid (ESP)	D	D	D	D20			D	D	D	D	D61	36	2
João Moutinho	08/09/86	Porto	M73	M	M	M	M	M74	M	M	M	M	M82	59	2
Raul Meireles	17/03/83	Chelsea (ENG) /Fenerbahçe (TUR)	M73	M67	M				M80	M	M58	M73		68	8
Hugo Viana	15/01/83	Braga	M46				s74							29	1
Cristiano Ronaldo	05/02/85	Real Madrid (ESP)	A61	A	A	A	A		A62	A		A	A46	104	39
Nani	17/11/86	Man. United (ENG)	A	A81	A76	A	A		A73			s66		66	13
Nélson Oliveira	08/08/91	Deportivo (ESP)	A61						s80			s75		10	1
Rúben Micael	19/08/86	Braga	s46	s81		M67	M61	M46				s61		14	2
Beto	01/05/82	Braga	s61					G						4	-
Silvestre Varela	02/02/85	Porto	s61	s46	s63	s67	s61	A67	s62	A60	s73		A84	19	3
Hugo Almeida	23/05/84	Beşiktaş (TUR)	s61				s55			s74	s58	A75		49	17
Carlos Martins	29/04/82	Benfica	s73							s60				17	2
Miguel Veloso	11/05/86	Dynamo Kyiv (UKR)	s73	M46	M63	M	M	M73	M60	M	M			38	2
Rui Patrício	15/02/88	Sporting	G	G	G	G			G	G	G			23	-
João Pereira	25/02/84	Valencia (ESP)	D	D	D	D74		D80	D	D	D		s84	28	-
Bruno Alves	27/11/81	Zenit (RUS)	D	D	D	D	s46	D	D74	D	D	D46		65	8
Pepe	26/02/83	Real Madrid (ESP)	D	D	D	D	D46		D			D		51	3
Hélder Postiga	02/08/82	Zaragoza (ESP)	A	A87	A75	A			A62	A	A82	A66		61	26
Custódio	24/05/83	Braga		s67				M79	s73		s82	s92	M	10	-
Rùben Amorim	27/01/85	Braga			s76		s46	s46	s80			s73	M	7	-
Éder	22/12/87	Braga			s87	s75	s74	A55	s62					5	-
Nélson	10/06/83	Betis (ESP)						D						4	-
Sílvio	28/09/87	Atlético (ESP) /Deportivo (ESP)						D					D	7	-
Pizzi	06/10/89	Deportivo (ESP)						A						1	1
Paulo Machado	31/03/86	Olympiacos (GRE)						s67						5	-
Hélder Barbosa	25/05/87	Braga						s79						1	-
Luís Neto	26/05/88	Zenit (RUS)								D		D		2	-
Danny	07/08/83	Zenit (RUS)							s73		A73			25	4
Vieirinha	24/01/86	Wolfsburg (GER)								s60	A	A92	s46	4	-
Henrique Sereno	18/05/85	Valladolid (ESP)											s46	1	-
André Martins	21/01/90	Sporting											s82	1	-

European club competitions 2012/13

FC PORTO

CHAMPIONS LEAGUE

Group A
Match 1 - GNK Dinamo Zagreb (CRO)
A 2-0 *Lucho González (41), Defour (90+2)*
Helton, Lucho González, Maicon, João Moutinho, Martínez (Kléber 78), Rodríguez (Mangala 88), Miguel Lopes, Varela (Atsu 72), Alex Sandro, Otamendi, Defour. Coach: Vítor Pereira (POR)
Match 2 - Paris Saint-Germain FC (FRA)
H 1-0 *Rodríguez (83)*
Helton, Danilo, Lucho González (Defour 81), Maicon, João Moutinho, Martínez, Rodríguez (Mangala 90+1), Varela (Atsu 73), Fernando, Alex Sandro, Otamendi. Coach: Vítor Pereira (POR)
Match 3 - FC Dynamo Kyiv (UKR)
H 3-2 *Varela (15), Martínez (36, 78)*
Helton, Danilo, Lucho González, Maicon, João Moutinho (Defour 75), Martínez, Rodríguez (Miguel Lopes 90+2), Varela (Atsu 64), Mangala, Fernando, Otamendi. Coach: Vítor Pereira (POR)
Match 4 - FC Dynamo Kyiv (UKR)
A 0-0
Helton, Danilo, Lucho González, João Moutinho, Martínez, Rodríguez (Kléber 90+1), Varela (Atsu 76), Mangala, Ba, Otamendi, Defour (André Castro 79). Coach: Vítor Pereira (POR)
Match 5 - GNK Dinamo Zagreb (CRO)
H 3-0 *Lucho González (20), João Moutinho (67), Varela (85)*
Helton, Danilo, Lucho González (Atsu 75), João Moutinho, Martínez, Rodríguez, Varela, Mangala, Ba (Alex Sandro 66), Otamendi, Defour (Fernando 66). Coach: Vítor Pereira (POR)
Match 6 - Paris Saint-Germain FC (FRA)
A 1-2 *Martínez (33)*
Helton, Danilo, Lucho González, João Moutinho, Martínez, Rodríguez, Varela (Atsu 85), Mangala, Fernando (Defour 70), Alex Sandro (Ba 86), Otamendi. Coach: Vítor Pereira (POR)

Round of 16 - Málaga CF (ESP)
H 1-0 *João Moutinho (56)*
Helton, Danilo, Lucho González (André Castro 90+1), João Moutinho, Martínez, Izmailov (Atsu 70), Varela (Rodríguez 58), Mangala, Fernando, Alex Sandro, Otamendi. Coach: Vítor Pereira (POR)
A 0-2
Helton, Danilo, Lucho González, João Moutinho (Rodríguez 46), Martínez, Varela (Maicon 58), Mangala, Fernando, Alex Sandro (Atsu 70), Otamendi, Defour. Coach: Vítor Pereira (POR)
Red card: Defour 49

SL BENFICA

CHAMPIONS LEAGUE

Group G
Match 1 - Celtic FC (SCO)
A 0-0
Artur, Aimar (Cardozo 63), Salvio, Rodrigo (Bruno César 70), Gaitán (Nolito 83), Matić, Garay, Melgarejo, Jardel, André Almeida, Pérez. Coach: Jorge Jesus (POR)
Match 2 - FC Barcelona (ESP)
H 0-2
Artur, Bruno César (Carlos Martins 46), Lima, Maxi Pereira, Salvio, Gaitán (Nolito 75), Matić, Garay, Melgarejo, Jardel, Pérez (Aimar 60). Coach: Jorge Jesus (POR)
Match 3 - FC Spartak Moskva (RUS)
A 1-2 *Lima (33)*
Artur, Bruno César (Gaitán 65), Lima, Maxi Pereira, Salvio, Rodrigo (Cardozo 65), Matić (John 89), Garay, Melgarejo, Jardel, Pérez. Coach: Jorge Jesus (POR)
Match 4 - FC Spartak Moskva (RUS)
H 2-0 *Cardozo (55, 69)*
Artur, Lima (Bruno César 74), Maxi Pereira (André Gomes 82), John, Salvio, Rodrigo (Cardozo 46), Garay, Melgarejo, Jardel, André Almeida, Pérez. Coach: Jorge Jesus (POR)
Match 5 - Celtic FC (SCO)
H 2-1 *John (7), Garay (71)*
Artur, Luisão, Cardozo, Lima (Gaitán 75), John, Salvio (Jardel 90+2), Matić (Maxi Pereira 78), Garay, Melgarejo, André Almeida, Pérez. Coach: Jorge Jesus (POR)
Match 6 - FC Barcelona (ESP)
A 0-0
Artur, Luisão, Nolito (Bruno César 63), Lima (Cardozo 74), Maxi Pereira, John, Rodrigo (André Almeida 74), Matić, Garay, Melgarejo, André Gomes. Coach: Jorge Jesus (POR)

EUROPA LEAGUE

Round of 32 - Bayer 04 Leverkusen (GER)
A 1-0 *Cardozo (61)*
Artur, Luisão, Cardozo (Lima 72), John, Gaitán, Matić, Urreta (Salvio 57), Garay, Melgarejo, André Almeida, André Gomes (Pérez 42). Coach: Jorge Jesus (POR)
H 2-1 *John (60), Matić (77)*
Artur, Luisão, Cardozo (Lima 64), John (Jardel 90+4), Carlos Martins (Salvio 53), Gaitán, Matić, Garay, Melgarejo, André Almeida, Pérez. Coach: Jorge Jesus (POR)

Round of 16 - FC Girondins de Bordeaux (FRA)
H 1-0 *Carrasso (21og)*
Artur, Roderick, Luisão, Cardozo (Salvio 63), John (Lima 74), Carlos Martins (Pérez 64), Rodrigo, Gaitán, Garay, Melgarejo, André Almeida. Coach: Jorge Jesus (POR)
A 3-2 *Jardel (30), Cardozo (75, 90+2)*
Artur, Roderick, John (Carlos Martins 84), Salvio (Maxi Pereira 88), Rodrigo (Cardozo 66), Gaitán, Matić, Melgarejo, Jardel, André Almeida, Peréz. Coach: Jorge Jesus (POR)

Quarter-final - Newcastle United FC (ENG)
H 3-1 *Rodrigo (25), Lima (65), Cardozo (71p)*
Artur, Luisão, Cardozo (Maxi Pereira 77), John, Rodrigo (Lima 61), Gaitán, Matić, Garay, Melgarejo, André Almeida, André Gomes (Pérez 61). Coach: Jorge Jesus (POR)
A 1-1 *Salvio (90+2)*
Artur, Luisão, Lima (Cardozo 72), John (Rodrigo 76), Salvio (Jardel 90+3), Gaitán, Matić, Garay, Melgarejo, André Almeida, Pérez. Coach: Jorge Jesus (POR)

Semi-final - Fenerbahçe SK (TUR)
A 0-1
Artur, Cardozo, Aimar (Gaitán 46), Maxi Pereira, John (Rodrigo 64), Salvio, Matić, Garay, Melgarejo, Jardel, André Gomes (Carlos Martins 81). Coach: Jorge Jesus (POR)
H 3-1 *Gaitán (9), Cardozo (35, 66)*
Artur, Luisão, Cardozo (Urreta 87), Lima, Maxi Pereira, Salvio, Gaitán (Roderick 90+3), Matić, Garay, André Almeida, Pérez. Coach: Jorge Jesus (POR)

Final - Chelsea FC (ENG)
N 1-2 *Cardozo (68p)*
Artur, Luisão, Cardozo, Salvio, Rodrigo (Lima 66), Gaitán, Matić, Garay (Jardel 78), Melgarejo (John 66), André Almeida, Pérez. Coach: Jorge Jesus (POR)

SC BRAGA

Play-offs - Udinese Calcio (ITA)
H 1-1 *Ismaily (68)*
Beto, Mossoró (Zé Luis 87), Hélder Barbosa (Rúben Micael 58), Lima, Ismaily, Leandro Salino, Paulo Vinícius, Custódio, Alan (Rúben Amorim 85), Douglão, Hugo Viana. Coach: José Peseiro (POR)
A 1-1 *Rúben Micael (72) (aet; 5-4 on pens)*
Beto, Rúben Amorim (Rúben Micael 60), Mossoró (Éder 107), Lima, Ismaily, Leandro Salino, Paulo Vinícius, Custódio, Alan (Paulo César 94), Douglão, Hugo Viana. Coach: José Peseiro (POR)

Group H
Match 1 - CFR 1907 Cluj (ROU)
H 0-2
Beto, Nuno André Coelho, Mossoró, Rúben Micael, Éder, Ismaily, Leandro Salino (Paulo César 70), Paulo Vinícius, Custódio, Alan (Hélder Barbosa 46), Hugo Viana (Zé Luis 64). Coach: José Peseiro (POR)
Match 2 - Galatasaray AŞ (TUR)
A 2-0 *Rúben Micael (27), Alan (90+4)*
Beto, Rúben Amorim, Rúben Micael (Nuno André Coelho 90+2), Éder, Ismaily (Hélder Barbosa 84), Leandro Salino, Paulo Vinícius, Custódio, Alan, Douglão, Hugo Viana (Djamal 78). Coach: José Peseiro (POR)
Match 3 - Manchester United FC (ENG)
A 2-3 *Alan (2, 20)*
Beto, Nuno André Coelho, Rúben Amorim (Hélder Barbosa 80), Rúben Micael (Zé Luis 88), Éder, Elderson, Leandro Salino, Paulo Vinícius, Custódio, Alan (Mossoró 86), Hugo Viana. Coach: José Peseiro (POR)
Match 4 - Manchester United FC (ENG)
H 1-3 *Alan (49p)*
Beto, Nuno André Coelho, Rúben Amorim (Hélder Barbosa 85), Rúben Micael, Éder, Elderson (Zé Luis 90+1), Leandro Salino, Custódio, Alan, Douglão, Hugo Viana (Mossoró 86). Coach: José Peseiro (POR)
Match 5 - CFR 1907 Cluj (ROU)
A 1-3 *Alan (17)*
Beto, Nuno André Coelho, Rúben Amorim, Rúben Micael, Éder (Zé Luis 57), Ismaily, Leandro Salino (Hélder Barbosa 33), Custódio, Alan, Douglão, Hugo Viana (Mossoró 68). Coach: José Peseiro (POR)
Red card: Douglão 45+1

Match 6 - Galatasaray AŞ (TUR)
H 1-2 *Mossoró (32)*
Quim, Nuno André Coelho, Rúben Amorim, Mossoró, Éder (Carlão 86), Elderson, Ismaily, Leandro Salino, Paulo Vinícius, Custódio (Hugo Viana 79), Alan. Coach: José Peseiro (POR)

A ACADÉMICA DE COIMBRA

Group B
Match 1 - FC Viktoria Plzeň (CZE)
A 1-3 *Wilson Eduardo (19)*
Ricardo, Flávio Ferreira, Halliche (Bruno China 47), Keita (Ogu 63), Marinho, Makelele (Edinho 73), Rodrigo Galo, Nivaldo, Wilson Eduardo, Reiner Ferreira, Cissé. Coach: Pedro Emanuel (POR)
Match 2 - Hapoel Tel-Aviv FC (ISR)
H 1-1 *Cissé (47)*
Ricardo, João Dias, Flávio Ferreira, Marinho (Afonso 85), Bruno China, Cleyton (Makelele 69), Wilson Eduardo, Ogu, Reiner Ferreira, Hélder Cabral, Cissé (Edinho 58). Coach: Pedro Emanuel (POR)
Match 3 - Club Atlético de Madrid (ESP)
A 1-2 *Cissé (85)*
Ricardo, João Dias, Flávio Ferreira, Halliche (Júnior Lopes 22), Marinho, Makelele (Cissé 60), Bruno China, Nivaldo, Wilson Eduardo, Ogu (Cleyton 60), Edinho. Coach: Pedro Emanuel (POR)
Match 4 - Club Atlético de Madrid (ESP)
H 2-0 *Wilson Eduardo (28, 70p)*
Ricardo, João Dias, Flávio Ferreira, Keita (Bruno China 79), Marinho (Afonso 71), Makelele, João Real, Cleyton, Nivaldo, Wilson Eduardo, Cissé (Edinho 84). Coach: Pedro Emanuel (POR)
Match 5 - FC Viktoria Plzeň (CZE)
H 1-1 *Edinho (88p)*
Ricardo, João Dias, Flávio Ferreira, Keita, Marinho, João Real, Cleyton, Wilson Eduardo (Afonso 81), Ogu (Cissé 70), Reiner Ferreira, Edinho. Coach: Pedro Emanuel (POR)
Match 6 - Hapoel Tel-Aviv FC (ISR)
A 0-2
Peiser, João Dias, Flávio Ferreira, Keita, Marinho (Afonso 82), João Real, Cleyton, Nivaldo (Cissé 71), Wilson Eduardo, Ogu (Makelele 71), Edinho. Coach: Pedro Emanuel (POR)

SPORTING CLUBE DE PORTUGAL

Play-offs - AC Horsens (DEN)
A 1-1 *Carrillo (79)*
Rui Patrício, Boulahrouz, Jeffren (Diego Capel 66), Schaars (Labyad 58), Van Wolfswinkel, Rojo, Carrillo, Adrien Silva, Cédric, Insúa, Elías (André Martins 78). Coach: Ricardo Sá Pinto (POR)
H 5-0 *Van Wolfswinkel (8, 54), Kortegaard (23og), Carrillo (57), Elías (63)*
Rui Patrício, Boulahrouz, Van Wolfswinkel, Diego Capel, Rojo, Carrillo (André Martins 65), Adrien Silva (Jeffren 65), Pranjić, Cédric, Elías, Fernandes (Daniel Carriço 73). Coach: Ricardo Sá Pinto (POR)

Group G
Match 1 - FC Basel 1893 (SUI)
H 0-0
Rui Patrício, Xandão, Van Wolfswinkel, Izmailov (André Martins 67), Diego Capel, Rojo, Carrillo (Labyad 77), Pranjić, Cédric, Elías (Daniel Carriço 56), Fernandes. Coach: Ricardo Sá Pinto (POR)
Red card: Xandão 50
Match 2 - Videoton FC (HUN)
A 0-3
Rui Patrício, Boulahrouz (Adrien Silva 71), Jeffren, Izmailov, Rojo, Viola, Labyad (Schaars 46), Rinaudo (Van Wolfswinkel 30), André Martins, Pranjić, Fernandes. Coach: Ricardo Sá Pinto (POR)
Match 3 - KRC Genk (BEL)
A 1-2 *Hamalainen (7og)*
Rui Patrício, Boulahrouz, Jeffren (Viola 61), Schaars, Van Wolfswinkel, Rojo, Rinaudo, Adrien Silva (Xandão 79), Pranjić (Diego Capel 58), Cédric, Insúa. Coach: Oceano da Cruz (POR)
Red card: Boulahrouz 76
Match 4 - KRC Genk (BEL)
H 1-1 *Van Wolfswinkel (64)*
Rui Patrício, Xandão, Schaars, Van Wolfswinkel, Diego Capel (Carrillo 87), Rojo, Viola (Fernandes 63), Labyad (Tiago Ilori 84), Cédric, Insúa, Elías. Coach: Frank Vercauteren (BEL)
Red card: Schaars 59
Match 5 - FC Basel 1893 (SUI)
A 0-3
Rui Patrício, Xandão, Van Wolfswinkel, Diego Capel, Rojo, Labyad (Carrillo 60), Pranjić, Cédric, Insúa, Elías, Fernandes (Betinho 67). Coach: Frank Vercauteren (BEL)

PORTUGAL

Match 6 - Videoton FC (HUN)
H 2-1 *Labyad (65), Viola (82)*
Marcelo, Xandão, Boulahrouz, Diego Capel (Pranjić 85), Viola, Labyad, Rinaudo, Cédric, Ricardo Esgaio, Insúa, Fernandes. Coach: Frank Vercauteren (BEL)

CS MARÍTIMO

EUROPA
LEAGUE

Third qualifying round - Asteras Tripolis FC (GRE)
A 1-1 *Fidélis (71)*
Salin, Rafael Miranda, Fidélis (Adilson 85), Héldon (Rodrigo Antônio 74), Roberge, Sami, João Luiz, Briguel, Danilo Dias (Igor Rossi 87), Rúben Ferreira, João Guilherme. Coach: Pedro Martins (POR)
H 0-0
Salin, Rafael Miranda, Fidélis (Adilson 77), Héldon (Igor Rossi 73), Roberge, Sami, João Luiz, Briguel, Danilo Dias (Rodrigo Antônio 61), Rúben Ferreira, João Guilherme. Coach: Pedro Martins (POR)
Red card: Rúben Ferreira 69

Play-offs - FC Dila Gori (GEO)
H 1-0 *Fidélis (64)*
Salin, Rafael Miranda, Héldon (Danilo Dias 55), Roberge, Sami, Luís Olim, João Luiz (Rodrigo Antônio 81), Briguel, Adilson (Fidélis 54), João Guilherme, David Simão. Coach: Pedro Martins (POR)
A 2-0 *Héldon (42), Danilo Dias (90+3)*
Salin, Rafael Miranda, Fidélis, Héldon (Igor Rossi 67), Roberge, Sami (Danilo Dias 73), Luís Olim, Briguel, Rodrigo Antônio, João Guilherme, David Simão (Márcio Rosário 58). Coach: Pedro Martins (POR)
Red card: Rodrigo Antônio 55

Group D
Match 1 - Newcastle United FC (ENG)
H 0-0
Salin, Rafael Miranda, Héldon (Fidélis 54), Roberge, Sami, Luís Olim, João Luiz, Briguel, Danilo Dias (Adilson 82), João Guilherme, David Simão (Gonçalo Abreu 75). Coach: Pedro Martins (POR)
Match 2 - Club Brugge KV (BEL)
A 0-2
Salin, Rafael Miranda, Fidélis, Héldon (David Simão 80), Roberge, Sami, João Luiz (Adilson 85), Briguel, Rodrigo Antônio (Danilo Dias 67), Rúben Ferreira, João Guilherme. Coach: Pedro Martins (POR)
Match 3 - FC Girondins de Bordeaux (FRA)
H 1-1 *Roberge (36)*
Salin, Rafael Miranda, Fidélis (Ibrahim 74), Héldon (Rodrigo Antônio 58), Roberge, Sami, João Luiz (David Simão 77), Briguel, Danilo Dias, Rúben Ferreira, João Guilherme. Coach: Pedro Martins (POR)
Match 4 - FC Girondins de Bordeaux (FRA)
A 0-1
Salin, Márcio Rosário, Rafael Miranda, Fidélis, Olberdam (David Simão 67), Roberge, Sami, João Luiz (Danilo Dias 80), Briguel, Rúben Ferreira, João Guilherme (Héldon 56). Coach: Pedro Martins (POR)
Match 5 - Newcastle United FC (ENG)
A 1-1 *Fidélis (79)*
Salin, João Diogo, Márcio Rosário, Rafael Miranda, Roberge, Sami, João Luiz, Adilson (Fidélis 59), Danilo Dias, Rúben Ferreira, David Simão (Rúben Brígido 73). Coach: Pedro Martins (POR)
Match 6 - Club Brugge KV (BEL)
H 2-1 *Gonçalo Abreu (18), Héldon (87)*
Salin, Igor Rossi, Semedo, Gonçalo Abreu (Héldon 55), Sami (Rafael Miranda 63), Luís Olim, Briguel, Adilson, Rodrigo Antônio, Rúben Brígido (Danilo Dias 75), João Guilherme. Coach: Pedro Martins (POR)

Domestic league club-by-club

A. ACADÉMICA DE COIMBRA

Coach: Pedro Emanuel;
(10/04/13) Sérgio Conceição
1876 • Cidade de Coimbra (30,075) • academica-oaf.pt
Major honours
Portuguese Cup (2) 1939, 2012

2012
20/08	Beira-Mar	a	3-3	Cissé, Edinho 2
24/09	Olhanense	h	1-1	Edinho
02/09	Rio Ave	a	0-0	
23/09	Benfica	h	2-2	Cissé (p), Wilson Eduardo (p)
30/09	Marítimo	a	2-0	Wilson Eduardo, Marinho
07/10	Guimarães	h	1-2	Marinho
29/10	Sporting	h	0-0	
04/11	Estoril	h	0-2	
11/11	Porto	a	1-2	Wilson Eduardo
25/11	Gil Vicente	h	2-2	Flávio Ferreira, Edinho
10/12	Braga	h	1-4	Cissé
16/12	Moreirense	a	2-2	Edinho, Cissé

2013
05/01	Setúbal	h	4-2	Cissé, Edinho 3
13/01	Paços Ferreira	a	0-1	
21/01	Nacional	h	2-1	Makelele, Edinho
25/01	Beira-Mar	h	3-1	Marinho, Edinho, Cleyton
03/02	Olhanense	a	0-0	
10/02	Rio Ave	h	1-2	Cissé
17/02	Benfica	a	0-1	
25/02	Marítimo	h	2-3	Edinho, Wilson Eduardo
04/03	Guimarães	a	0-2	
09/03	Sporting	a	1-1	Wilson Eduardo (p)
17/03	Estoril	a	0-2	
30/03	Porto	h	0-3	
07/04	Gil Vicente	a	1-2	Wilson Eduardo
19/04	Braga	a	0-1	
28/04	Moreirense	h	1-0	Marinho
05/05	Setúbal	a	1-0	Ogu
11/05	Paços Ferreira	h	1-1	Edinho (p)
19/05	Nacional	a	1-2	Edinho (p)

No	Name	Nat	DoB	Pos	Aps	(s)	Gls
77	Afonso	BRA	14/11/91	A	5	(8)	
88	Rodolph Amessan	CIV	27/09/90	A		(7)	
14	Bruno China		05/08/82	M	16	(4)	
39	Carlos Saleiro		25/02/86	A	1	(6)	
92	Salim Cissé	GUI	24/12/92	A	14	(11)	6
59	Cleyton	BRA	24/02/90	A	18	(7)	1
36	Edinho		07/07/82	A	18	(9)	13
4	Flávio Ferreira		19/10/91	M	24		1
5	Rafik Halliche	ALG	02/09/86	D	8	(1)	
55	Hélder Cabral		07/05/84	D	18	(1)	
23	Henrique		19/10/86	M	1	(1)	
2	João Dias		23/12/86	D	16	(1)	
13	João Real		13/05/83	D	13	(1)	
3	Júnior Lopes	BRA	19/10/87	D	1	(1)	
6	Alphousseyni Keita	MLI	13/11/85	A	11	(5)	
8	Makelele	BRA	26/02/85	M	24	(2)	1
21	Marcos Paulo	BRA	13/07/88	M	9	(3)	
20	Marinho		26/04/83	A	24	(3)	4
9	Serge N'Gal	CMR	13/01/86	A		(1)	
26	Nivaldo	CPV	10/07/88	M	6	(1)	
30	John Ogu	NGA	20/04/88	A	11	(9)	1
35	Reiner Ferreira	BRA	17/11/85	D	20	(1)	
12	Ricardo		06/07/82	G	30		
22	Rodrigo Galo	BRA	19/09/86	D	21		
28	Wilson Eduardo		08/07/90	A	21	(5)	6

SC BEIRA-MAR

Coach: Ulisses Morais; (18/02/13) Costinha
1922 • Municipal de Aveiro (31,100) • beiramar.pt
Major honours
Portuguese Cup (1) 1999

2012

Date	Opp		Score	Scorers
20/08	Académica	h	3-3	Balboa (p), Abel Camará 2
25/08	Braga	a	1-3	Nildo
02/09	Moreirense	h	1-1	Al-Shehri
22/09	Porto	a	0-4	
30/09	Setúbal	h	1-1	Abel Camará
06/10	Benfica	a	1-2	Sasso
27/10	Paços Ferreira	h	0-2	
04/11	Nacional	a	4-2	Balboa, Rúben Ribeiro, Jaime, Sasso
11/11	Olhanense	a	0-1	
23/11	Guimarães	h	2-2	Al-Shehri, Abel Camará
09/12	Gil Vicente	a	2-1	Serginho, Balboa
15/12	Rio Ave	h	3-1	Serginho, Balboa, Joãozinho

2013

Date	Opp		Score	Scorers
06/01	Marítimo	a	1-1	Serginho
14/01	Estoril	h	0-1	
18/01	Sporting	a	0-1	
25/01	Académica	a	1-3	Rúben Ribeiro (p)
03/02	Braga	h	3-3	Yazalde, Rui Sampaio, Rúben Ribeiro
10/02	Moreirense	a	0-3	
15/02	Porto	h	0-2	
23/02	Setúbal	a	0-1	
03/03	Benfica	h	0-1	
10/03	Paços Ferreira	a	1-1	Rúben Ribeiro
17/03	Nacional	h	2-2	Rúben Ribeiro, Abel Camará
30/03	Olhanense	h	0-1	
07/04	Guimarães	a	1-2	Bura
21/04	Gil Vicente	h	0-1	Yazalde
28/04	Rio Ave	a	1-2	Yazalde
05/05	Marítimo	h	4-2	Nildo 2, Balboa (p), Dani Abalo
11/05	Estoril	a	1-2	Dani Abalo
19/05	Sporting	h	1-4	Rúben Ribeiro

No	Name	Nat	DoB	Pos	Aps	(s)	Gls
77	Abel Camará		06/01/90	A	10	(11)	5
15	Saleh Al-Shehri	KSA	01/11/93	A	2	(5)	2
28	André Sousa		09/07/90	M	1	(3)	
21	Javier Balboa	EQG	13/05/85	A	17	(4)	5
3	Bura		17/12/88	M	14	(3)	1
19	Cédric Collet	FRA	07/03/84	A	7	(2)	
8	Dani Abalo	ESP	29/09/87	M	6	(2)	2
26	Felipe Desco	BRA	29/06/89	D			
6	David Fleurival	FRA	19/02/84	M	22	(1)	
22	Hélder Lopes		04/01/89	M	19	(2)	
5	Hugo		11/08/76	D	17	(3)	
14	Jaime		11/06/89	M	19	(6)	1
23	Joãozinho		02/07/89	D	14		1
16	Nildo	BRA	01/05/86	D	28		3
33	Nuno Lopes		19/12/86	M	14	(5)	
18	Pedro Moreira		23/10/83	D	14	(1)	
11	Rafael Batatinha	BRA	09/02/90	A	5	(6)	
27	Ricardo Dias		25/02/91	M	14	(5)	
7	Rúben Ribeiro		01/08/87	M	23	(2)	6
1	Rui Rêgo		05/07/80	G	30		
2	Rui Sampaio		29/05/87	D	11	(1)	1
4	Vincent Sasso	FRA	16/02/91	D	15		2
10	Serginho		21/02/91	A	12	(11)	3
19	Tiago Cintra		05/07/89	M		(2)	
13	Tonel		13/04/80	D	3	(1)	
25	Tozé Marreco		25/07/87	A		(2)	
24	Yazalde		21/09/88	A	13	(2)	3

SL BENFICA

Coach: Jorge Jesus
1904 • Sport Lisboa e Benfica (65,647) • slbenfica.pt
Major honours
European Champion Clubs' Cup (2) 1961, 1962; Portuguese League (32) 1936, 1937, 1938, 1942, 1943, 1945, 1950, 1955, 1957, 1960, 1961, 1963, 1964, 1965, 1967, 1968, 1969, 1971, 1972, 1973, 1975, 1976, 1977, 1981, 1983, 1984, 1987,1989, 1991, 1994, 2005, 2010; Portuguese Cup (27) 1930, 1931, 1935, 1940, 1943, 1944, 1949, 1951, 1952, 1953, 1955, 1957, 1959, 1962, 1964, 1969, 1970, 1972, 1980, 1981, 1983, 1985, 1986, 1987, 1993, 1996, 2004

2012

Date	Opp		Score	Scorers
18/08	Braga	h	2-2	Salvio, Cardozo (p)
26/08	Setúbal	a	5-0	Rodrigo 2, Salvio, Pérez, Nolito
02/09	Nacional	h	3-0	Cardozo 2, Rodrigo
23/09	Académica	a	2-2	Cardozo (p), Lima
28/09	Paços Ferreira	a	2-1	Lima 2
06/10	Beira-Mar	h	2-1	Maxi Pereira, Rodrigo
27/10	Gil Vicente	a	3-0	Lima, Luisinho, André Gomes
03/11	Guimarães	h	3-0	Cardozo 2 (1p), Lima
11/11	Rio Ave	a	1-0	Lima
24/11	Olhanense	h	2-0	Cardozo (p), Luisão
10/12	Sporting	a	3-1	og (Rojo), Cardozo 2 (1p)
15/12	Marítimo	h	4-1	Cardozo 3 (1p), Rodrigo

2013

Date	Opp		Score	Scorers
06/01	Estoril	a	3-1	Gaitán, Lima, Salvio
13/01	Porto	h	2-2	Matić, Gaitán
21/01	Moreirense	a	2-0	Salvio, Lima
26/01	Braga	a	2-1	Salvio, Lima
03/02	Setúbal	h	3-0	Pérez, Lima, Rodrigo
10/02	Nacional	a	2-2	og (Mexer), Urreta
17/02	Académica	h	1-0	Lima (p)
24/02	Paços Ferreira	h	3-0	Pérez, Cardozo, Salvio
03/03	Beira-Mar	a	1-0	Cardozo (p)
10/03	Gil Vicente	h	5-0	Maxi Pereira, Salvio, Melgarejo, Lima, Gaitán
17/03	Guimarães	a	4-0	Cardozo (p), Garay, Salvio, Rodrigo
30/03	Rio Ave	h	6-1	Melgarejo, Matić, Lima 3, Pérez
07/04	Olhanense	a	2-0	Salvio, Matić
21/04	Sporting	h	2-0	Salvio, Lima
29/04	Marítimo	a	2-1	Lima (p), og (Igor Rossi)
06/05	Estoril	h	1-1	Maxi Pereira
11/05	Porto	a	1-2	Lima
19/05	Moreirense	h	3-1	Cardozo, Lima 2 (1p)

No	Name	Nat	DoB	Pos	Aps	(s)	Gls
10	Pablo Aimar	ARG	03/11/79	M		(13)	
31	Alan Kardec	BRA	12/01/89	A		(3)	
34	André Almeida		10/09/90	M	7	(7)	
89	André Gomes		30/07/93	M	4	(3)	1
1	Artur	BRA	25/01/81	G	30		
8	Bruno César	BRA	03/11/88	M	2	(4)	
7	Óscar Cardozo	PAR	20/05/83	A	20	(4)	16
17	Carlos Martins		29/04/82	M	3	(10)	
20	Nicolás Gaitán	ARG	23/02/88	M	11	(12)	3
24	Ezequiel Garay	ARG	10/10/86	D	27		1
33	Jardel	BRA	29/03/86	D	15	(1)	
6	Javi García	ESP	08/02/87	M	2		
15	Ola John	NED	19/05/92	A	15	(7)	
11	Lima	BRA	11/08/83	A	24	(3)	20
4	Luisão	BRA	13/02/81	D	18		1
5	Luisinho		05/05/85	D	5		1
21	Nemanja Matić	SRB	01/08/88	M	25	(1)	3
14	Maxi Pereira	URU	08/06/84	D	28		3
25	Lorenzo Melgarejo	PAR	10/08/90	D	21		2
27	Miguel Vítor		30/06/89	D		(1)	
9	Nolito	ESP	15/10/86	A	1	(5)	1
35	Enzo Pérez	ARG	22/02/86	M	25	(3)	4
3	Roderick		30/03/91	D		(2)	
19	Rodrigo	ESP	06/03/91	A	14	(6)	7
18	Eduardo Salvio	ARG	13/07/90	A	29		10
23	Jonathan Urreta	URU	19/01/90	A	1	(3)	1
28	Axel Witsel	BEL	12/01/89	M	3		

SC BRAGA

Coach: José Peseiro
1921 • Municipal de Braga (30,286) • scbraga.pt
Major honours
Portuguese Cup (1) 1966

2012

Date	Opp		Score	Scorers
18/08	Benfica	a	2-2	og (Melgarejo), Mossoró
25/08	Beira-Mar	h	3-1	Rúben Micael 2, Rúben Amorim
02/09	Paços Ferreira	a	0-2	
23/09	Rio Ave	h	4-1	Éder 2, Rúben Amorim, Custódio (p)
28/09	Guimarães	a	2-0	Éder, Hugo Viana
07/10	Olhanense	h	4-4	Hélder Barbosa, Douglão 2, Éder
28/10	Marítimo	a	2-0	Éder 2
03/11	Gil Vicente	h	3-1	Zé Luís, Alan (p), Hugo Viana
11/11	Sporting	a	0-1	
25/11	Porto	h	0-2	
10/12	Académica	h	4-1	Ismaily, Rúben Amorim, Mossoró, Carlão
16/12	Estoril	h	3-0	Hugo Viana, Mossoró, Éder

2013

Date	Opp		Score	Scorers
06/01	Moreirense	h	1-0	Éder
12/01	Nacional	a	2-3	Hélder Barbosa, Éder
20/01	Setúbal	h	4-1	Mossoró, Custódio, Rúben Amorim, Rúben Micael
26/01	Benfica	h	1-2	João Pedro
03/02	Beira-Mar	a	3-3	Éder, Alan, João Pedro
11/02	Paços Ferreira	h	2-3	Leandro Salino, Éder
18/02	Rio Ave	a	1-1	Alan (p)
23/02	Guimarães	h	3-2	Éder 2, Paulo Vinícius
04/03	Olhanense	a	1-0	Leandro Salino
09/03	Marítimo	h	2-0	Hugo Viana, Alan
15/03	Gil Vicente	h	3-1	Hugo Viana 2, Zé Luís
01/04	Sporting	h	2-3	Elderson, Carlão
08/04	Porto	a	1-3	Alan
19/04	Académica	h	1-0	Rúben Micael
26/04	Estoril	a	1-2	Mossoró
03/05	Moreirense	a	3-2	Carlão, Santos, Zé Luís
11/05	Nacional	h	1-3	Hugo Viana
19/05	Setúbal	a	1-0	Zé Luís

No	Name	Nat	DoB	Pos	Aps	(s)	Gls
30	Alan	BRA	19/09/79	A	22	(4)	5
15	Baiano	BRA	23/02/87	D	12	(2)	
33	Beto		01/05/82	G	15		
83	Carlão	BRA	01/08/86	A	8	(7)	3
23	Cristiano		29/11/90	G	1		
27	Custódio		24/05/83	M	27	(1)	2
44	Douglão	BRA	15/08/86	D	13		2
20	Elderson	NGA	20/01/88	D	17	(1)	1
17	Éder		22/12/87	A	17	(1)	13
6	Emídio Rafael		24/01/86	D		(1)	
3	Maximilian Haas	GER	07/12/85	D	4	(1)	
10	Hélder Barbosa		25/05/87	M	12	(8)	2
45	Hugo Viana		15/01/83	M	27	(1)	7
21	Ismaily	BRA	11/01/90	D	10	(2)	1
7	João Pedro		04/04/86	A	6	(8)	2
25	Leandro Salino	BRA	22/04/85	D	21		2
18	Lima	BRA	11/05/83	A	2		
22	Djamal Mahamat	LBY	26/04/83	M	1	(5)	
63	Mauro	BRA	31/10/90	M	4	(3)	
12	Michel	BRA	22/08/86	A	3		
8	Mossoró	BRA	04/07/83	M	23	(5)	5
4	Nuno André Coelho		07/01/86	D	7	(1)	
77	Palmeira		24/08/89	D	2		
9	Paulo César	BRA	05/01/80	A	1	(3)	
26	Paulo Vinícius	BRA	12/08/84	D	19	(1)	1
12	Quim		13/11/75	G	14		
90	Rúben Amorim		27/01/85	M	17	(5)	4
14	Rúben Micael		19/08/86	M	11	(8)	4
75	Santos	BRA	09/04/89	D	9		1
2	Vincent Sasso	FRA	16/02/91	D	5		
27	Zé Luís	CPV	24/01/91	A	3	(12)	4

GD ESTORIL-PRAIA

Coach: Marco Silva
1939 • António Coimbra da Mota (5,015) • estorilpraia.pt

2012

17/08	Olhanense	a	1-2	*Steven Vitória (p)*
26/08	Paços Ferreira	h	1-1	*Steven Vitória (p)*
01/09	Guimarães	a	2-2	*Licá, Bruno Miguel*
24/09	Marítimo	h	3-1	*Luís Leal 3*
29/09	Sporting	a	2-2	*Steven Vitória (p), Luís Leal*
07/10	Rio Ave	h	1-3	*og (Lionn)*
28/10	Porto	h	1-2	*Steven Vitória*
04/11	Académica	a	2-0	*Bruno Nascimento, Licá*
11/11	Moreirense	h	2-0	*Jefferson, Luís Leal*
25/11	Nacional	a	0-1	
07/12	Setúbal	h	3-0	*Luís Leal, Evandro, Jefferson*
16/12	Braga	a	0-3	

2013

06/01	Benfica	h	1-3	*Gonçalo Santos*
14/01	Beira-Mar	a	1-0	*Licá*
20/01	Gil Vicente	h	1-2	*Luís Leal*
27/01	Olhanense	h	3-3	*Steven Vitória 2 (2p), Evandro*
05/02	Paços Ferreira	a	0-1	
09/02	Guimarães	h	2-0	*Luís Leal, Carlitos*
17/02	Marítimo	a	1-2	*Evandro*
22/02	Sporting	h	3-1	*Jefferson, Steven Vitória (p), Carlos Eduardo*
03/03	Rio Ave	a	2-0	*Licá, Steven Vitória (p)*
08/03	Porto	a	0-2	
17/03	Académica	h	2-0	*Licá, Carlos Eduardo*
30/03	Moreirense	a	1-1	*Taylor*
07/04	Nacional	h	4-0	*Carlitos, Carlos Eduardo 2, Luís Leal*
21/04	Setúbal	a	0-1	
26/04	Braga	h	2-1	*og (Douglão), Steven Vitória*
06/05	Benfica	a	1-1	*Jefferson*
11/05	Beira-Mar	h	2-1	*Licá, og (Rui Rêgo)*
19/05	Gil Vicente	a	3-1	*Steven Vitória 2 (1p), Luís Leal*

No	Name	Nat	DoB	Pos	Aps	(s)	Gls
5	Ânderson Luís	BRA	31/07/88	D	22		
27	Bruno Miguel		24/09/82	D	3	(2)	1
3	Bruno Nascimento		30/05/91	M	14		1
70	Carlitos		06/09/82	M	22		2
30	Carlos Eduardo	BRA	17/10/89	M	16	(13)	4
45	Dieguinho	BRA	07/06/92	M		(2)	
25	Diogo Amado		21/01/90	M	15	(7)	
7	Elizeu	BRA	28/05/89	A	1	(1)	
15	Evandro	BRA	23/08/86	M	23	(2)	3
10	Gerso	GNB	23/02/91	M	7	(20)	
13	Gonçalo Santos		15/11/86	M	29		1
20	Hugo Leal		21/05/80	M	3	(3)	
4	Jefferson	BRA	05/07/80	D	27	(1)	4
23	João Coimbra		24/05/86	A	5	(9)	
8	João Paulo		08/04/80	A	2	(5)	
14	João Pedro		29/12/87	D	5		
88	Licá		08/09/88	A	30		6
9	Luís Leal		29/05/87	A	25	(5)	10
12	Mano		09/04/87	D	8	(2)	
21	Frédéric Mendy	FRA	18/09/88	M		(1)	
11	Pedro Henrique	BRA	28/03/91	A		(2)	
22	Renan	BRA	12/12/90	G	2		
19	Steven Vitória		11/01/87	D	27		11
77	Tony Taylor	USA	13/07/89	A	2	(12)	1
6	Tiago Gomes		20/07/86	M	3	(2)	
1	Vagner	BRA	06/06/86	G	28		
2	Yohan		02/03/88	D	11		

GIL VICENTE FC

Coach: Paulo Alves
1924 • Cidade Barcelos (13,350) • gilvicentefc.pt

2012

19/08	Porto	h	0-0	
26/08	Marítimo	a	0-0	
02/09	Setúbal	h	0-0	
24/09	Sporting	h	1-2	*Luís Carlos*
30/09	Moreirense	h	4-3	*André Cunha 2, Cláudio, Halisson*
07/10	Nacional	a	1-0	*Rafael Silva*
27/10	Benfica	h	0-3	
03/11	Braga	a	1-3	*Yero*
09/11	Paços Ferreira	h	0-1	
25/11	Académica	a	2-2	*Pio, Cláudio*
09/12	Beira-Mar	h	1-2	*Cláudio (p)*
15/12	Olhanense	a	2-2	*Yero, Luís Carlos*

2013

05/01	Guimarães	h	0-0	
13/01	Rio Ave	h	0-1	
20/01	Estoril	a	2-1	*Cláudio (p), Luís Carlos*
28/01	Porto	a	0-5	
03/02	Marítimo	h	4-2	*João Vilela (p), Luís Carlos, Hugo Vieira 2*
10/02	Setúbal	a	0-1	
16/02	Sporting	h	2-3	*Hugo Vieira 2*
24/02	Moreirense	a	0-0	
03/03	Nacional	h	1-2	*Luís Carlos*
10/03	Benfica	a	0-5	
15/03	Braga	h	1-3	*Hugo Vieira*
29/03	Paços Ferreira	a	2-3	*Hugo Vieira, Yero*
07/04	Académica	h	2-1	*Brito, Yero*
21/04	Beira-Mar	a	0-1	
28/04	Olhanense	h	2-0	*Hugo Vieira, César Peixoto (p)*
05/05	Guimarães	a	1-3	*Hugo Vieira*
11/05	Rio Ave	a	1-2	*João Vilela*
19/05	Estoril	h	1-3	*Sandro*

No	Name	Nat	DoB	Pos	Aps	(s)	Gls
1	Adriano	BRA	12/03/83	G	24	(1)	
10	André Cunha		16/02/78	M	26	(2)	2
13	Brito		16/11/87	A	12	(12)	1
2	Bruno Pinheiro		21/08/87	M		(1)	
25	César Peixoto		12/05/80	M	20	(2)	1
44	Cláudio	BRA	17/08/77	D	23	(1)	4
6	Daniel		27/03/87	D	4		
28	Djalma	BRA	15/04/88	A		(6)	
20	Éder	BRA	25/09/85	D	9	(7)	
54	Halisson	BRA	18/06/85	D	23	(1)	1
70	Hugo Vieira		25/07/88	A	13	(1)	8
3	João Pedro		15/08/80	D	5		
77	João Vilela		09/09/85	A	14		2
12	Leonardo	BRA	09/04/88	A	1	(3)	
83	Luciano Amaral	BRA	20/10/82	D	8		
58	Luís Carlos	BRA	15/06/87	A	21	(6)	5
66	Luís Manuel		25/06/81	M	22	(1)	
5	Luís Martins		10/06/92	D	15	(2)	
79	Murta		21/07/79	G	6	(1)	
22	Paulo Arantes		15/11/86	D	11	(3)	
81	Paulo Jorge		05/05/81	D	8		
23	Pecks	CPV	10/04/93	D	5	(1)	
7	Pedro Pereira		01/03/84	A	7	(5)	
21	Pio	BRA	23/01/88	D	9	(3)	1
17	Rafael Silva	BRA	23/03/91	A	5	(1)	1
99	Ramazotti	BRA	09/08/88	A		(3)	
9	Gabriel Rodríguez	ARG	05/02/89	A		(2)	
4	Sandro		05/12/82	D	12	(3)	1
80	William Tiero	GHA	03/12/80	M	5	(7)	
11	Valdinho	ANG	06/10/89	M	2	(7)	
19	Vítor Vinha		11/11/86	A	8		
13	Kalidou Yero	SEN	19/08/91	A	12	(6)	4

CS MARÍTIMO

Coach: Pedro Martins
1910 • Barreiros (8,922) • csmaritimo.pt
Major honours
Portuguese Cup (1) 1926

2012

18/08	Rio Ave	a	1-0	*João Guilherme*
26/08	Gil Vicente	h	0-0	
16/09	Sporting	h	1-1	*João Guilherme*
24/09	Estoril	a	1-3	*Adilson*
30/09	Académica	h	0-2	
08/10	Moreirense	a	1-0	*Rafael Miranda*
28/10	Braga	h	0-2	
02/11	Porto	a	0-5	
12/11	Setúbal	h	1-1	*David Simão (p)*
27/11	Paços Ferreira	a	2-2	*Rafael Miranda, David Simão (p)*
09/12	Nacional	h	2-0	*Fidélis, Sami*
15/12	Benfica	a	1-4	*Rodrigo António*

2013

06/01	Beira-Mar	h	1-1	*Fidélis*
12/01	Guimarães	a	1-1	*Danilo Dias*
20/01	Olhanense	h	1-0	*Adilson*
27/01	Rio Ave	h	1-0	*Roberge*
03/02	Gil Vicente	a	2-4	*David Simão (p), Rafael Miranda*
10/02	Sporting	a	1-0	*Suk*
17/02	Estoril	h	2-1	*Sami, David Simão (p)*
25/02	Académica	a	3-2	*Danilo Dias, Artur, Sami*
03/03	Moreirense	h	1-1	*Kukula*
09/03	Braga	a	0-2	
17/03	Porto	h	1-1	*Suk*
30/03	Setúbal	a	4-2	*Artur, Héldon, Suk, Sami*
05/04	Paços Ferreira	h	1-1	*Héldon*
21/04	Nacional	a	1-2	*Suk*
29/04	Benfica	h	1-2	*Igor Rossi*
05/05	Beira-Mar	a	2-4	*Sami 2*
11/05	Guimarães	h	1-0	*Danilo Dias*
19/05	Olhanense	a	0-0	

No	Name	Nat	DoB	Pos	Aps	(s)	Gls
18	Adilson	BRA	01/01/82	A	2	(8)	2
84	Artur		18/02/84	A	13	(4)	2
21	Briguel		08/03/79	D	22	(1)	
30	Danilo Dias	BRA	06/11/85	M	19	(10)	3
90	David Simão		15/05/90	M	22	(4)	4
9	Fidélis	BRA	14/06/89	A	11	(6)	2
8	Gonçalo Abreu		25/06/86	A	1	(2)	
20	Héldon	CPV	14/11/88	A	17	(4)	2
91	Suk Hyun-jun	KOR	29/06/91	A	12	(2)	4
11	Ibrahim	NGA	09/09/92	A	1		
15	Igor Rossi	BRA	10/03/89	M	5	(1)	1
2	João Diogo		28/02/88	D	9	(1)	
44	João Guilherme	BRA	21/04/86	D	10	(2)	2
20	João Luiz	BRA	24/04/85	D	10		
74	Kukula	CPV	22/01/93	A	2	(9)	1
18	Luís Olim		22/08/81	M	7	(6)	
6	Marakis		11/11/81	M	6	(1)	
3	Márcio Rosário	BRA	21/11/83	D	20		
13	Olberdam	BRA	06/02/85	M		(7)	
5	Rafael Miranda	BRA	11/08/84	A	27	(1)	3
37	Ricardo		03/12/89	G	8		
16	Valentin Roberge	FRA	09/06/87	M	26	(1)	1
27	Rodrigo António	BRA	27/07/87	M	5	(3)	1
28	Rúben Brígido		23/06/91	M	2		
41	Rúben Ferreira		17/02/90	D	23	(1)	
77	Romain Salin	FRA	29/07/84	G	22		
17	Sami	GNB	18/12/88	A	26	(3)	6
7	Semedo		23/02/88	M	4	(6)	
33	Ytalo	BRA	12/01/88	M		(3)	

MOREIRENSE FC

Coach: Jorge Casquilha; (30/01/13) Augusto Inácio
1938 • Comendador Joaquim Almeida Freitas (6,151) •
moreirensefc.pt

2012

19/08	Paços Ferreira	a	1-1	Fábio Espinho
26/08	Nacional	h	3-1	Ghilas 2, Diego Gaúcho
02/09	Beira-Mar	a	1-1	Ricardo Pessoa (p)
21/09	Guimarães	h	0-1	
30/09	Gil Vicente	a	3-4	Ghilas 2, Vinícius
08/10	Marítimo	h	0-1	
27/10	Olhanense	a	2-2	Olivera, Ghilas
04/11	Rio Ave	h	0-1	
11/11	Estoril	a	0-2	
26/11	Sporting	h	2-2	Olivera, Ghilas
08/12	Porto	a	0-1	
16/12	Académica	h	2-2	Ghilas, Wagner

2013

06/01	Braga	a	0-1	
13/01	Setúbal	a	0-5	
21/01	Benfica	h	0-2	
27/01	Paços Ferreira	h	0-5	
03/02	Nacional	a	2-1	Ghilas, Renatinho
10/02	Beira-Mar	h	3-0	Aníbal Capela, Ghilas 2
17/02	Guimarães	a	0-1	
24/02	Gil Vicente	h	0-0	
03/03	Marítimo	a	1-1	Filipe Gonçalves
10/03	Olhanense	h	1-1	Ricardo Pessoa (p)
17/03	Rio Ave	a	1-0	Filipe Gonçalves
30/03	Estoril	h	1-1	Ghilas
06/04	Sporting	a	2-3	Ghilas, Aníbal Capela
20/04	Porto	h	0-3	
28/04	Académica	a	0-1	
03/05	Braga	h	2-3	Fábio Espinho, Ghilas
11/05	Setúbal	h	2-1	Olivera, Vinícius
19/05	Benfica	a	1-3	Vinícius

No	Name	Nat	DoB	Pos	Aps	(s)	Gls
18	André Luiz	BRA	18/09/85	M		(3)	
80	Aníbal Capela		08/05/91	D	13	(1)	2
3	Anílton Júnior	BRA	10/07/80	D	27		
24	Augusto		30/08/87	D	18	(1)	
21	Tijani Belaïd	TUN	15/01/86	A	1	(3)	
8	Castro		03/06/79	M		(2)	
33	Diego Gaúcho	BRA	15/11/81	D	12	(4)	1
10	Fábio Espinho		18/08/85	M	22	(1)	2
6	Filipe Gonçalves		12/08/84	M	27		2
11	Nabil Ghilas	ALG	20/04/90	A	30		13
14	Florent Hanin	FRA	04/02/00	D	12		
20	Jô	BRA	19/09/88	A		(1)	
27	Jorge Chula		13/02/90	M	3	(2)	
88	Júlio César		13/12/83	M	3	(4)	
19	Christian Kinkela	COD	25/05/82	M	4	(4)	
7	Pablo Olivera	URU	28/12/87	A	7	(9)	3
2	Paulinho		13/07/91	D	7	(2)	
17	Pintassilgo		30/06/85	M	23	(2)	
9	Rafael Lopes		28/07/91	A		(21)	
22	Renatinho	BRA	29/01/93	A	14	(7)	1
25	Ricardo Andrade	BRA	22/06/77	G	11	(1)	
23	Ricardo Fernandes		14/01/78	D	8	(3)	
5	Ricardo Pessoa		05/02/82	D	23		2
1	Ricardo Ribeiro		27/01/90	G	19	(1)	
29	Tales	BRA	11/06/83	M		(7)	
15	Vinícius	BRA	16/05/86	A	28		3
28	Wagner	BRA	03/04/87	A	18	(8)	1

CD NACIONAL

Coach: Pedro Caixinha; (13/10/12) Manuel Machado
1910 • Madeira (5,132) • cdnacional.pt

2012

19/08	Setúbal	h	2-2	Claudemir (p), Isael
26/08	Moreirense	a	1-3	Isael
02/09	Benfica	a	0-3	
23/09	Paços Ferreira	h	0-3	Claudemir, Mateus, Manuel da Costa
30/09	Olhanense	a	2-1	og (Maurício), Rondón
07/10	Gil Vicente	h	0-1	
28/10	Rio Ave	a	1-2	Diego Barcellos
04/11	Beira-Mar	h	2-4	Revson 2
10/11	Guimarães	a	3-1	Diego Barcellos, Mateus, Keita
25/11	Estoril	h	1-0	Mateus
09/12	Marítimo	a	0-2	
15/12	Sporting	h	1-1	Isael

2013

05/01	Porto	a	0-1	
12/01	Braga	h	3-2	Mexer, Diego Barcellos, og (Ismaily)
21/01	Académica	a	1-2	Rondón
27/01	Setúbal	a	2-0	Rondón, Candeias
03/02	Moreirense	h	1-2	og (Ricardo Andrade)
10/02	Benfica	h	2-2	Diego Barcellos, Mateus
17/02	Paços Ferreira	a	1-1	Bruno Moreira
24/02	Olhanense	h	3-1	Rondón, Moreno, Revson (p)
03/03	Gil Vicente	a	2-1	Mexer, Manuel da Costa
10/03	Rio Ave	h	1-1	Claudemir (p)
17/03	Beira-Mar	a	2-1	Mateus 2
01/04	Guimarães	h	2-1	Claudemir (p), Mateus
07/04	Estoril	a	0-4	
21/04	Marítimo	h	2-1	Claudemir (p), Candeias
28/04	Sporting	a	1-2	Candeias
04/05	Porto	h	1-3	Candeias (p)
11/05	Braga	a	3-1	Keita, João Aurélio, Mateus
19/05	Académica	h	2-1	Candeias, Keita

No	Name	Nat	DoB	Pos	Aps	(s)	Gls
90	Bruno Moreira		06/09/87	A	7	(5)	1
11	Candeias	BRA	25/02/88	M	18	(10)	5
2	Claudemir	BRA	17/08/84	D	28	(2)	5
50	David Crespo		14/02/94	D	1		
10	Diego Barcellos	BRA	05/04/85	M	16	(5)	4
20	Edgar Costa		14/04/87	A	2	(4)	
91	Eliandro	BRA	23/04/90	M		(2)	
27	Ali Ghazal	EGY	01/02/92	M	9	(2)	
24	Vladan Giljen	MNE	07/12/89	G	9		
12	Gottardi	BRA	18/10/85	G	21		
20	Isael	BRA	13/05/88	M	9	(3)	3
22	João Aurélio		17/08/88	A	18	(6)	1
15	Jota	BRA	03/07/93	M	7	(9)	
99	Ladji Keita	SEN	29/04/83	A	10	(9)	3
55	Kim	BRA	10/09/87	D	1		
3	Manuel da Costa		06/05/86	D	16		2
50	Marçal	BRA	19/02/89	D	27		
9	Mateus	ANG	19/06/84	M	16	(9)	8
4	Mexer	MOZ	08/09/87	D	28		2
30	Miguel Rodrigues		16/03/93	M	13	(4)	
7	René Mihelič	SVN	05/07/88	M	2	(4)	
6	Moreno		19/08/81	D	24	(3)	1
31	Nuno Campos		13/06/93	D	3	(4)	
23	Oliver	BRA	29/08/92	A		(1)	
44	Revson	BRA	20/12/87	M	17	(3)	3
18	Mario Rondón	VEN	26/03/86	A	26	(2)	4
66	Sérgio Duarte		11/01/93	M		(1)	
8	Dejan Školnik	CRO	01/01/89	M	2	(1)	

SC OLHANENSE

Coach: Sérgio Conceição; (08/01/13) Manuel Cajuda;
(02/05/13) Bruno Saraiva
1912 • José Arcanjo (11,622) • scolhanense.com

2012

17/00	Estoril	h	2-1	Yontcha , Fernando Alexandre
24/09	Académica	a	1-1	David Silva
01/09	Porto	h	2-3	Abdi, Tiago Targino
23/09	Setúbal	a	0-1	
30/09	Nacional	h	1-2	Abdi
07/10	Braga	a	4-4	Abdi, Ivanildo 2, og (Rúben Amorim)
27/10	Moreirense	h	2-2	Rui Duarte 2 (2p)
04/11	Paços Ferreira	a	0-0	
11/11	Beira-Mar	h	1-0	Abdi
24/11	Benfica	a	0-2	
09/12	Guimarães	a	0-2	
15/12	Gil Vicente	h	2-2	Nuno Piloto, Evandro Brandão

2013

05/01	Rio Ave	a	1-0	Tiago Targino
13/01	Sporting	h	0-2	
20/01	Marítimo	a	0-1	
27/01	Estoril	a	0-3	Tiago Targino, Maurício, Rui Duarte (p)
03/02	Académica	h	0-0	
10/02	Porto	a	1-1	Tiago Targino
17/02	Setúbal	h	0-1	
24/02	Nacional	a	1-3	André Micael
04/03	Braga	h	0-1	
10/03	Moreirense	a	1-1	Lucas
16/03	Paços Ferreira	h	1-2	og (Nuno Santos)
30/03	Beira-Mar	a	1-0	Lucas
07/04	Benfica	h	0-2	
22/04	Guimarães	h	1-2	Djalmir
28/04	Gil Vicente	a	0-2	
05/05	Rio Ave	h	1-0	og (Tarantini)
11/05	Sporting	a	0-1	
19/05	Marítimo	h	0-0	

No	Name	Nat	DoB	Pos	Aps	(s)	Gls
14	Liban Abdi	SOM	05/10/88	A	14	(2)	4
3	André Micael		04/02/89	D	23	(1)	1
55	Babanco	CPV	27/07/85	D	22		
26	François D'Onofrio	BEL	06/10/90	D	3	(3)	
7	David Silva	CPV	11/10/86	A	7	(11)	1
99	Djalmir	BRA	22/03/76	A	1	(8)	1
19	Djaniny	CPV	21/03/91	A	9	(9)	
47	Evandro Brandão		07/05/91	A	8	(10)	1
20	José Luis Fernández	ARG	26/10/87	A		(1)	
65	Fernando Alexandre		02/08/85	M	22		1
10	Ivanildo	GNB	09/01/86	A	10	(5)	2
13	Jander	BRA	08/07/88	M	23	(1)	
17	Leandro	BRA	04/03/88	M	2	(6)	
88	Lucas	BRA	04/06/90	M	9	(2)	2
21	Luís Filipe		14/06/79	D	17		
5	Maurício	BRA	05/07/76	D	12		1
6	Nuno Piloto		19/03/82	M	9	(4)	1
4	Nuno Reis		31/01/91	D	20	(1)	
23	Nuno Silva		15/07/86	A		(1)	
92	Pedro Paz		20/12/94	D		(3)	
81	Rafael Bracalli	BRA	05/05/81	G	25		
76	Ricardo		11/02/76	G	5		
16	Rui Duarte		16/09/78	M	29		3
13	Rui Sampaio		29/05/87	M	1		
59	Thalles	BRA	08/01/91	M		(2)	
96	Tiago Targino		06/06/86	A	18	(11)	4
8	Tiago Terroso		13/01/88	M	13		
33	Vasco Fernandes		12/11/86	D	20	(1)	
99	Jean Paul Yontcha	CMR	26/03/84	A	8	(4)	1

FC PAÇOS DE FERREIRA

Coach: Paulo Fonseca
1950 • Mata Real (5,172) • fcpf.pt

2012

19/08	Moreirense	h	1-1		André Leão
26/08	Estoril	a	1-1		Antunes
02/09	Braga	h	2-0		Cohene, Hurtado
23/09	Nacional	a	3-3		Manuel José, Vítor, Cícero
28/09	Benfica	h	1-2		Cícero
07/10	Setúbal	a	0-0		
27/10	Beira-Mar	a	2-0		Vítor, Arturo Álvarez
04/11	Olhanense	h	0-0		
09/11	Gil Vicente	a	1-0		Antunes
27/11	Marítimo	h	2-2		Antunes, Luiz Carlos
09/12	Rio Ave	a	0-0		
16/12	Guimarães	h	2-1		Cícero 2

2013

05/01	Sporting	a	1-0		Hurtado
13/01	Académica	h	1-0		Hurtado
19/01	Porto	a	0-2		
27/01	Moreirense	a	5-0		Hurtado 2, Vítor 2, Luiz Carlos
05/02	Estoril	h	1-0		Manuel José
11/02	Braga	a	3-2		Hurtado 2, Cícero
17/02	Nacional	h	1-1		Cícero
24/02	Benfica	a	0-3		
02/03	Setúbal	h	2-0		Cícero 2
10/03	Beira-Mar	h	1-1		Manuel José (p)
16/03	Olhanense	a	2-1		Manuel José 2
29/03	Gil Vicente	h	3-2		Manuel José 2 (1p), Vítor
05/04	Marítimo	a	1-1		Cícero
20/04	Rio Ave	h	2-1		Hurtado, André Leão
28/04	Guimarães	a	2-2		Luiz Carlos, Caetano
05/05	Sporting	h	1-0		Tony
11/05	Académica	a	1-1		Manuel José
19/05	Porto	h	0-2		

No	Name	Nat	DoB	Pos	Aps	(s)	Gls
8	André Leão		20/05/85	M	29		2
33	Vinício Angulo	ECU	26/07/88	M	1	(4)	
55	Antunes		01/04/87	M	14		3
21	Arturo Álvarez	SLV	28/06/85	A	1	(1)	1
11	Caetano		20/04/91	A	4	(21)	1
1	Cássio	BRA	12/08/80	G	30		
9	Cícero	GNB	08/05/86	A	28	(1)	9
5	Javier Cohene	PAR	03/05/87	D	6	(5)	1
23	Diego Figueiras		01/07/91	D	18	(1)	
96	Filipe Anunciação		27/05/79	M	4	(13)	
16	Paolo Hurtado	PER	27/07/90	A	22	(6)	8
25	Christian Irobiso	NGA	28/05/93	A		(3)	
14	Jaime Poulson		22/06/89	M	1	(6)	
7	Josué		17/09/90	M	18	(5)	
10	Luiz Carlos	BRA	23/05/85	M	25	(2)	3
81	Manuel José		25/09/83	M	19	(10)	8
17	Nuno Santos		19/05/80	A	7	(1)	
19	Ricardo	CPV	19/08/80	D	29		
2	Tiago Valente		24/04/85	D	25	(1)	
80	Tony		20/12/80	D	21		1
6	Vítor		07/01/84	M	28	(1)	5

FC PORTO

Coach: Vítor Pereira
1893 • Dragão (50,476) • fcporto.pt

Major honours
European Champion Clubs' Cup/UEFA Champions League (2) 1987, 2004; UEFA Cup (1) 2003; UEFA Europa League (1) 2011; UEFA Super Cup (1) 1987; European/South American Cup (2) 1987, 2004; Portuguese League (27) 1935, 1939, 1940, 1956, 1959, 1978, 1979, 1985, 1986, 1988, 1990, 1992, 1993, 1995, 1996, 1997, 1998, 1999, 2003, 2004, 2006, 2007, 2008, 2009, 2011, 2012, 2013; Portuguese Cup (20) 1922, 1925, 1932, 1937, 1956, 1958, 1968, 1977, 1984, 1988, 1991, 1994, 1998, 2000, 2001, 2003, 2006, 2009, 2010, 2011

2012

19/08	Gil Vicente	a	0-0		
25/08	Guimarães	h	4-0		Lucho González 2, Hulk, Martínez (p)
01/09	Olhanense	a	3-2		Rodríguez, Martínez, Hulk
22/09	Beira-Mar	h	4-0		Martínez, Varela, Rodríguez, Maicon
29/09	Rio Ave	a	2-2		Miguel Lopes, Martínez
07/10	Sporting	h	2-0		Martínez, Rodríguez (p)
28/10	Estoril	a	2-1		Varela, Martínez
02/11	Marítimo	h	5-0		Martínez 2, Varela, Rodríguez 2
11/11	Académica	h	2-1		Rodríguez, João Moutinho
25/11	Braga	a	2-0		Rodríguez, Martínez
08/12	Moreirense	h	1-0		Martínez

2013

05/01	Nacional	h	1-0		Martínez
13/01	Benfica	a	2-2		Mangala, Martínez
19/01	Paços Ferreira	h	2-0		Alex Sandro, Izmailov
23/01	Setúbal	a	3-0		Martínez 2 (1p), Lucho González
28/01	Gil Vicente	h	5-0		Danilo, og (Vítor Vinha), Defour, Varela, Martínez
02/02	Guimarães	a	4-0		Mangala, Martínez 3
10/02	Olhanense	h	1-1		Martínez
15/02	Beira-Mar	a	2-0		Atsu, Martínez
23/02	Rio Ave	h	2-1		Martínez 2 (1p)
02/03	Sporting	a	0-0		
08/03	Estoril	h	2-0		Maicon, Martínez (p)
17/03	Marítimo	a	1-1		Rodríguez
30/03	Académica	a	3-0		Mangala, Danilo, André Castro
08/04	Braga	h	3-1		Rodríguez, Kelvin 2
20/04	Moreirense	a	3-0		Martínez 2, Fernando
27/04	Setúbal	h	2-0		Lucho González, Defour
04/05	Nacional	a	3-1		Rodríguez, Mangala, Lucho González
11/05	Benfica	h	2-1		og (Maxi Pereira), Kelvin
19/05	Paços Ferreira	a	2-0		Lucho González (p), Martínez

No	Name	Nat	DoB	Pos	Aps	(s)	Gls
26	Alex Sandro	BRA	26/01/91	D	24	(1)	1
6	André Castro		02/04/88	M		(17)	1
27	Christian Atsu	GHA	10/01/92	M	9	(8)	1
23	Abdoulaye Ba	SEN	01/01/91	D	2	(4)	
2	Danilo	BRA	15/07/91	D	28		2
35	Steven Defour	BEL	15/04/88	M	14	(11)	2
24	Fabiano	BRA	29/02/88	G		(1)	
25	Fernando	BRA	25/07/87	M	23	(1)	1
1	Helton	BRA	18/05/78	G	30		
12	Hulk	BRA	25/07/86	A	3		2
27	Juan Manuel Iturbe	ARG	04/06/93	M		(1)	
15	Marat Izmailov	RUS	21/09/82	M	6	(7)	1
8	João Moutinho		08/09/86	M	27		1
28	Kelvin	BRA	01/06/93	A	1	(8)	3
11	Kléber	BRA	02/05/90	A		(4)	
19	Liedson		17/12/77	A		(6)	
3	Lucho González	ARG	19/01/81	M	29		6
4	Maicon	BRA	14/09/88	D	12	(3)	2
22	Eliaquim Mangala	FRA	13/02/91	D	22	(1)	4
9	Jackson Martínez	COL	03/10/86	A	30		26
13	Miguel Lopes		19/12/86	D	2	(1)	1
30	Nicolás Otamendi	ARG	12/02/88	D	29		
5	Héctor Quiñonez	COL	18/02/92	D	1		
19	James Rodríguez	COL	12/07/91	M	19	(5)	10
14	Rolando		31/08/85	D		(1)	
57	Sebá	BRA	08/06/92	A		(4)	
70	Tozé		14/01/93	A		(1)	
17	Silvestre Varela		02/02/85	A	19	(6)	4

RIO AVE FC

Coach: Nuno Espírito Santo
1939 • Rio Ave (12,815) • rioave-fc.pt

2012

18/08	Marítimo	h	0-1		
27/08	Sporting	a	1-0		Edimar
02/09	Académica	h	0-0		
23/09	Braga	a	1-4		Edimar
29/09	Porto	h	2-2		Tarantini 2
07/10	Estoril	a	3-1		João Tomás 2, Tarantini
28/10	Nacional	h	2-1		João Tomás (p), Tarantini
04/11	Moreirense	a	1-0		João Tomás
11/11	Benfica	h	0-1		
25/11	Setúbal	a	5-3		João Tomás 3, Del Valle 2
09/12	Paços Ferreira	h	0-0		
15/12	Beira-Mar	h	1-3		Tarantini

2013

05/01	Olhanense	h	0-1		
13/01	Gil Vicente	a	1-0		Marcelo
20/01	Guimarães	h	1-3		Hassan
27/01	Marítimo	a	1-1		Hassan
02/02	Sporting	h	2-1		og (Joãozinho), Ukra
10/02	Académica	a	1-1		Hassan, Bebé
18/02	Braga	h	1-1		Hassan
23/02	Porto	a	1-2		Braga
03/03	Estoril	h	0-2		
10/03	Nacional	a	1-1		Hassan (p)
17/03	Moreirense	h	0-1		
30/03	Benfica	a	1-6		Hassan
07/04	Setúbal	h	2-1		Hassan (p), Braga
20/04	Paços Ferreira	a	1-2		Tarantini
28/04	Beira-Mar	h	2-1		Braga, Rodríguez
05/05	Olhanense	a	0-1		
11/05	Gil Vicente	h	2-1		Rodríguez, Hassan (p)
19/05	Guimarães	a	1-0		Braga

No	Name	Nat	DoB	Pos	Aps	(s)	Gls
40	André Costa		27/11/92	D	2	(1)	
22	André Dias		18/04/92	D	1	(1)	
23	André Vilas Boas		04/06/83	M	3	(9)	
33	Bebé		12/07/90	A	13	(3)	1
11	Braga		17/06/83	M	22	(7)	4
28	Yonathan del Valle	VEN	28/05/90	A	10	(13)	2
20	Diego Lopes	BRA	03/05/94	A	8	(13)	
93	Ederson	BRA	17/08/93	G	2		
6	Edimar	BRA	21/05/86	D	28		2
77	Esmaël Gonçalves	GNB	25/06/91	A	5	(1)	
25	Feliz		09/04/89	A		(1)	
16	Filipe Augusto		12/08/93	M	22	(4)	
18	Ahmed Hassan	EGY	05/03/93	A	12	(5)	8
5	Jeferson	BRA	15/01/86	D	1		
9	João Tomas		27/05/75	A	9	(2)	7
23	Lionn	BRA	29/01/89	D	25		
46	Marcelo	BRA	27/07/89	D	28		1
3	Nivaldo	BRA	23/06/80	D	20		
29	Tope Obadeyi	ENG	10/09/89	A	1	(11)	
1	Jan Oblak	SVN	07/01/93	G	28		
2	Alberto Rodríguez	PER	31/03/84	D	11	(1)	2
8	Tarantini		07/10/83	M	28	(1)	6
30	Ukra		16/03/88	A	23	(1)	1
10	Vítor Gomes		25/12/87	M	1	(9)	
30	Wires	BRA	30/12/82	M	27	(1)	

SPORTING CLUBE DE PORTUGAL

Coach: Ricardo Sá Pinto; (02/10/12) Oceano Cruz;
(24/10/12) Frank Vercauteren (BEL);
(06/01/13) Jesualdo Ferreira
1906 • José Alvalade (50,466) • sporting.pt
Major honours
UEFA Cup Winners' Cup (1) 1964;
Portuguese League (18) 1941, 1944, 1947, 1948, 1949,
1951, 1952, 1953, 1954, 1958, 1962, 1966, 1970, 1974,
1980, 1982, 2000, 2002;
Portuguese Cup (19) 1923, 1934, 1936, 1938, 1941,
1945, 1946, 1948, 1954, 1963, 1971, 1973, 1974, 1978,
1982, 1995, 2002, 2007, 2008

2012

19/08	Guimarães	a	0-0	
27/08	Rio Ave	h	0-1	
16/09	Marítimo	a	1-1	Van Wolfswinkel
24/09	Gil Vicente	h	2-1	Diego Capel, Van Wolfswinkel
29/09	Estoril	h	2-2	og (Ânderson Luís), Van Wolfswinkel
07/10	Porto	a	0-2	
29/10	Académica	h	0-0	
04/11	Setúbal	a	1-2	Jeffrén
11/11	Braga	h	1-0	Van Wolfswinkel
26/11	Moreirense	a	2-2	Xandão, Dier
10/12	Benfica	h	1-3	Van Wolfswinkel
15/12	Nacional	a	1-1	Cédric

2013

05/01	Paços Ferreira	h	0-1	
13/01	Olhanense	a	2-0	Labyad, Adrien Silva
18/01	Beira-Mar	h	1-0	Carrillo
27/01	Guimarães	h	1-1	Van Wolfswinkel
02/02	Rio Ave	a	1-2	Jeffrén
10/02	Marítimo	h	0-1	
16/02	Gil Vicente	a	3-2	Bruma, Tiago Ilori, Diego Capel
22/02	Estoril	a	1-3	Van Wolfswinkel
02/03	Porto	h	0-0	
09/03	Académica	a	1-1	Van Wolfswinkel
16/03	Setúbal	h	2-1	og (Amoreirinha), Labyad (p)
01/04	Braga	a	3-2	Van Wolfswinkel 3
06/04	Moreirense	h	3-2	Diego Capel 2, Van Wolfswinkel, Viola
21/04	Benfica	a	0-2	
28/04	Nacional	h	2-1	Diego Capel, Rojo
05/05	Paços Ferreira	a	0-1	
11/05	Olhanense	h	1-0	Diego Capel
19/05	Beira-Mar	a	4-1	Adrien Silva 2 (1p), Van Wolfswinkel 2

No	Name	Nat	DoB	Pos	Aps	(s)	Gls
23	Adrien Silva		15/03/89	M	15	(4)	3
28	André Martins		21/01/90	M	7	(8)	
19	Santiago Arias	COL	13/01/92	D	1		
87	Betinho		21/07/93	A		(2)	
6	Khalid Boulahrouz	NED	28/12/81	D	10	(1)	
51	Bruma		24/10/94	A	11	(2)	1
18	André Carrillo	PER	14/06/91	A	13	(10)	1
41	Cédric		31/08/91	D	13		1
3	Daniel Carriço		04/08/88	D		(1)	
11	Diego Capel	ESP	16/02/88	M	23	(3)	5
54	Eric Dier	ENG	15/01/94	D	12	(1)	1
77	Elías	BRA	16/05/85	M	8	(1)	
86	Gelson Fernandes	SUI	02/09/86	M	4	(2)	
71	Fabrice Fokobo	CMR	25/01/94	D	1	(1)	
48	Emiliano Insúa	ARG	07/01/89	D	13		
10	Marat Izmailov	RUS	21/09/82	M	5	(2)	
17	Jeffrén	ESP	20/01/88	A	5	(8)	2
49	João Mário		19/01/93	M		(1)	
5	Joãozinho		02/07/89	D	13		
20	Zakaria Labyad	MAR	09/03/93	A	11	(8)	2
13	Miguel Lopes		19/12/86	D	14		
50	Pedro Mendes		01/10/90	D	2	(1)	
60	Nii Plange	BFA	28/06/89	A		(1)	
30	Danijel Pranjić	CRO	02/12/81	M	9		
47	Ricardo Esgaio		16/05/93	M		(3)	
21	Fabián Rinaudo	ARG	08/05/87	M	22	(1)	
15	Marcos Rojo	ARG	20/03/90	D	24		1
33	Diego Rubio	CHI	15/05/93	A		(2)	
1	Rui Patrício		15/02/88	G	30		
8	Stijn Schaars	NED	11/01/84	M	7	(4)	
34	Tiago Ilori		26/02/93	D	11		1
9	Ricky van Wolfswinkel	NED	27/01/89	A	30		14
16	Valentín Viola	ARG	28/08/91	A	3	(15)	1
4	Xandão	BRA	23/02/88	M	11	(2)	1
90	Zézinho	GNB	23/09/92	M	2	(3)	

VITÓRIA FC (SETÚBAL)

Coach: José Mota
1910 • Bonfim (18,694) • vfc.pt
Major honours
Portuguese Cup (3) 1965, 1967, 2005

2012

19/08	Nacional	a	2-2	Meyong (p), Cristiano
26/08	Benfica	h	0-5	
02/09	Gil Vicente	h	0-0	
23/09	Olhanense	h	1-0	Meyong (p)
30/09	Beira-Mar	a	1-1	Meyong
07/10	Paços Ferreira	h	0-0	
26/10	Guimarães	a	1-2	Meyong (p)
04/11	Sporting	h	2-1	Pedro Santos, Meyong
12/11	Marítimo	a	1-1	Makukula
25/11	Rio Ave	h	3-5	Meyong 3 (1p)
07/12	Estoril	a	0-3	

2013

05/01	Académica	a	2-4	Cristiano, Meyong (p)
13/01	Moreirense	h	5-0	Meyong 3, Pedro Santos, Bruninho
20/01	Braga	a	1-4	Jorginho
23/01	Porto	h	0-3	
27/01	Nacional	h	0-2	
03/02	Benfica	a	0-3	
10/02	Gil Vicente	h	1-0	Pedro Santos
17/02	Olhanense	a	1-0	Paulo Tavares
23/02	Beira-Mar	h	1-1	Miguel Lourenço
02/03	Paços Ferreira	h	0-2	
11/03	Guimarães	h	2-3	Makukula, Pedro Santos
16/03	Sporting	a	1-2	Makukula
30/03	Marítimo	h	2-4	José Pedro 2
07/04	Rio Ave	a	1-2	Venâncio
21/04	Estoril	h	1-0	Paulo Tavares (p)
27/04	Porto	a	0-2	
05/05	Académica	h	0-1	
11/05	Moreirense	a	1-2	Bruninho
19/05	Braga	h	0-1	

No	Name	Nat	DoB	Pos	Aps	(s)	Gls
6	Amoreirinha		05/08/84	D	7	(1)	
12	Bruninho		30/09/88	M	3	(11)	2
37	Bruno Amaro		17/02/83	M	29		
7	Bruno Gallo	BRA	07/05/88	M	5	(11)	
5	Bruno Turco	BRA	30/07/91	M	3	(2)	
87	Cristiano	BRA	28/09/83	A	17	(6)	2
13	Igor		03/05/84	M	1		
4	Jorge Luiz	BRA	22/04/82	D	28		
90	Jorginho		18/03/88	A	14	(11)	1
11	José Pedro		18/10/78	M	10	(7)	2
31	Paweł Kieszek	POL	16/04/84	G	27		
91	Kiko		20/01/93	M	5	(1)	
99	Makukula		04/03/81	A	2	(8)	2
18	Albert Meyong	CMR	19/10/80	A	16		13
44	Miguel Lourenço		27/05/92	D	16	(1)	1
10	Miguel Pedro		06/11/83	A	16	(9)	
15	Nélson Pedroso		10/06/85	D	22	(1)	
68	Ney	BRA	23/02/81	D	25		
1	Caleb Patterson-Sewell	AUS	20/05/87	G	3		
8	Paulo Tavares		09/12/85	M	21	(5)	2
24	Pedro Queirós		08/08/84	D	29		
9	Pedro Santos		22/04/88	M	21	(7)	4
77	Ricardo Horta		15/09/94	A		(6)	
3	Ricardo Silva		26/09/75	D	3	(2)	
2	Peter Suswam	NGA	05/09/91	D	1		
14	Venâncio		04/02/93	M	6	(1)	1

VITÓRIA SC (GUIMARÃES)

Coach: Rui Vitória
1922 • D. Afonso Henriques (30,146) • vitoriasc.pt
Major honours
Portuguese Cup (1) 2013

2012

19/08	Sporting	h	0-0	
25/08	Porto	a	0-4	
01/09	Estoril	h	2-2	N'Diaye, João Ribeiro
21/09	Moreirense	a	1-0	Addy
28/09	Braga	h	0-2	
07/10	Académica	a	2-1	Soudani 2
26/10	Setúbal	h	2-1	Toscano, João Ribeiro (p)
03/11	Benfica	a	0-3	
10/11	Nacional	h	1-3	João Ribeiro (p)
23/11	Beira-Mar	a	2-2	Freire, Baldé
09/12	Olhanense	h	2-0	Baldé, André
16/12	Paços Ferreira	a	1-2	Barrientos

2013

05/01	Gil Vicente	a	0-0	
12/01	Marítimo	h	1-1	Baldé
20/01	Rio Ave	a	3-1	Baldé 2, Tiago Rodrigues (p)
27/01	Sporting	a	1-1	og (Xandão)
02/02	Porto	h	0-4	
09/02	Estoril	a	0-2	
17/02	Moreirense	h	1-0	Leonel Olímpio (p)
23/02	Braga	a	2-3	Paulo Oliveira, Soudani
04/03	Académica	h	2-0	Tiago Rodrigues, Soudani
11/03	Setúbal	a	3-2	Soudani, El Adoua, Baldé
17/03	Benfica	h	0-4	
01/04	Nacional	a	1-2	Baldé
07/04	Beira-Mar	h	2-1	Baldé, Soudani
22/04	Olhanense	a	2-1	Soudani 2
28/04	Paços Ferreira	h	2-2	Tiago Rodrigues, Baldé
05/05	Gil Vicente	h	3-1	Soudani, Leonel Olímpio (p), Tiago Rodrigues
11/05	Marítimo	a	0-1	
19/05	Rio Ave	h	0-1	

No	Name	Nat	DoB	Pos	Aps	(s)	Gls
30	David Addy	GHA	21/02/90	M	22		1
79	Alex		06/09/79	D	17		
11	André		26/08/89	M	20	(4)	1
13	Assis	BRA	04/10/89	G	1		
17	Baldé		16/05/91	A	19	(8)	9
16	Siaka Bamba	CIV	24/08/89	M	7	(1)	
14	Jean Pierre Barrientos	URU	16/09/90	M	11	(6)	1
6	Bruno Teles	BRA	01/05/86	D	3		
50	Crivellaro	BRA	02/03/89	A		(14)	
3	Defendi	BRA	17/06/86	D	10		
83	Douglas	BRA	09/03/83	G	29		
5	Issam El Adoua	MAR	09/12/86	D	19	(5)	1
2	Freire	BRA	21/08/89	D	9		1
40	Gonçalo		28/12/90	M		(1)	
57	Hernâni		20/08/91	M		(3)	
31	Indío	BRA	10/12/90	A		(1)	
28	João Gonçalves		18/01/88	D	3		
7	João Ribeiro		13/08/87	A	7	(7)	3
29	Jona	ESP	07/01/89	M		(2)	
32	Josué Sá		17/06/92	M		(3)	
51	Kanu	BRA	05/03/92	D	9		
23	Milan Lalkovič	SVK	09/12/92	M		(8)	
18	Leonel Olímpio	BRA	07/07/82	M	21	(2)	2
53	Luís Rocha		27/06/93	M	5	(1)	
27	Darwin Machis	VEN	07/02/93	M		(3)	
9	Marco Matias		10/05/89	A	13	(7)	
44	Mahamadou N'Diaye	MLI	21/07/90	D	13	(1)	1
15	Paulo Oliveira		08/01/92	D	18		1
39	Pedro Lemos		17/03/93	D	1		
41	Preto		18/04/93	G		(1)	
21	Ricardo		06/10/93	M	26	(1)	
22	El Arbi Soudani	ALG	25/11/87	A	20	(1)	9
42	Tiago Rodrigues		29/01/92	M	17	(3)	4
8	Toscano	BRA	12/05/85	A	10		

Top goalscorers

26	Jackson Martínez (Porto)
20	Lima (Benfica)
16	Óscar Cardozo (Benfica)
14	Ricky van Wolfswinkel (Sporting)
13	Edinho (Académica)
	Éder (Braga)
	Nabil Ghilas (Moreirense)
	Albert Meyong (Setúbal)
11	Steven Vitória (Estoril)
10	Eduardo Salvio (Benfica)
	Luís Leal (Estoril)
	James Rodríguez (Porto)

Promoted clubs

CF OS BELENENSES

Coach: **Mitchell van der Gaag (NED)**
1919 • Restelo (12,164) • osbelenenses.com
Major honours
Portuguese League (1) 1946;
Portuguese Cup (6) 1927, 1929, 1933, 1942, 1960, 1989

FC AROUCA

Coach: **Vitor Oliveira**
1951 • Municipal (1,470) • fcarouca.aroucanet.com

SECOND LEVEL FINAL TABLE 2012/13

		Pld	W	D	L	F	A	Pts
1	CF Os Belenenses	42	29	7	6	75	41	94
2	FC Arouca	42	21	10	11	65	48	73
3	Leixões SC	42	18	14	10	49	36	68
4	Sporting Clube de Portugal B	42	17	15	10	62	47	66
5	CD Aves	42	16	17	9	47	42	65
6	Portimonense SC	42	17	13	12	61	50	64
7	SL Benfica B	42	15	17	10	71	54	62
8	UD Oliveirense	42	16	12	14	52	49	60
9	FC Penafiel	42	16	12	14	48	44	60
10	CD Tondela	42	16	11	15	55	60	59
11	CD Santa Clara	42	15	14	13	55	48	59
12	CF União Madeira	42	13	17	12	47	46	56
13	CD Feirense	42	15	11	16	61	59	56
14	FC Porto B	42	13	15	14	49	49	54
15	CS Marítimo B	42	14	7	21	40	46	49
16	SC Braga B	42	12	13	17	39	51	47
17	A. Naval 1º Maio	42	13	18	11	51	50	45
18	Atlético CP	42	12	8	22	45	63	44
19	CD Trofense	42	9	13	20	41	60	40
20	SC Covilhã	42	7	17	18	37	52	38
21	Vitória SC B	42	7	15	20	30	56	36
22	SC Freamunde	42	7	12	23	46	75	33

NB A. Naval 1º Maio – 12 pts deducted;
SC Braga B – 3 pts deducted.

Domestic cup: Taça de Portugal 2012/13

THIRD ROUND

(18/10/12)
Freamunde 0-4 Benfica

(19/10/12)
Braga 3-0 Leixões *(aet)*

(20/10/12)
Beira-Mar 0-0 Penafiel *(aet; 4-2 on pens)*
Gondomar 0-2 Gil Vicente *(aet)*
Naval 1-3 Arouca *(aet)*
Olhanense 3-0 1º Dezembro
Santa Eulália 0-1 Porto
Setúbal 1-0 Tondela

(21/10/12)
Aguiar Beira 1-0 União Lamas *(aet)*
Aliados Lordelo 0-2 UD Oliveirense
Anadia 2-5 Belenenses *(aet)*
Atlético Reguengos 0-1 Farense
Aves 3-1 Tirsense 1 *(aet)*
Estoril 1-2 Paços Ferreira
Fabril Barreiro 3-1 Eléctrico Ponte de Sôr
Fátima 0-0 Penalva Castelo *(aet; 3-4 on pens)*
Feirense 3-0 Fafe
Guimarães 6-1 Vilaverdense
Limianos 0-1 Tourizense
Maritimo 2-1 AD Oliveirense *(aet)*
Moreirense 3-2 Sporting *(aet)*
Nacional 4-0 Espinho
Nogueirense 1-3 Santa Clara
Oliveira Hospital 1-1 Ribeirão *(aet; 4-2 on pens)*
Pampilhosa 5-5 Covilhã *(aet; 4-3 on pens)*
Pedras Rubras 3-2 União Madeira *(aet)*
Pinhalnovense 0-3 Lourinhanense
Ponte da Barca 1-3 Académica
Rio Ave 2-1 Portimonense
Sacavenense 2-2 União Leiria *(aet; 2-3 on pens)*
Varzim 1-1 Mirandela *(aet; 2-3 on pens)*

(02/12/12)
Caldas 0-0 Coimbrões *(aet; 2-4 on pens)*

FOURTH ROUND

(16/11/12)
Moreirense 0-2 Benfica
Pampilhosa 1-3 Braga

(17/11/12)
Aguiar Beira 0-3 Maritímo
Farense 1-1 Beira-Mar *(aet; 4-5 on pens)*
Nacional 0-3 Porto

(18/11/12)
Académica 1-0 Penalva Castelo *(aet)*
Arouca 2-1 Rio Ave *(aet)*
Belenenses 3-0 Pedras Rubras
Lourinhanense 3-2 Feirense
Mirandela 1-2 Gil Vicente *(aet)*
Oliveira Hospital 0-2 Fabril Barreiro
Oliveirense 1-0 União Leiria
Paços Ferreira 2-1 Olhanense
Setúbal 2-2 Guimarães *(aet; 3-5 on pens)*
Tourizense 1-0 Santa Clara *(aet)*

(12/12/12)
Aves 2-1 Coimbrões

FIFTH ROUND

(30/11/12)
Braga 2-1 Porto

(01/12/12)
Académica 3-0 Tourizense

(02/12/12)
Arouca 2-1 Beira-Mar
Belenenses 4-0 Fabril Barreiro
Gil Vicente 1-0 Oliveirense
Lourinhanense 0-6 Paços Ferreira
Maritímo 1-1 Guimarães *(aet; 3-4 on pens)*

(02/01/13)
Benfica 6-0 Aves

QUARTER-FINALS

(16/01/13)
Guimarães 2-1 Braga *(Barrientos 1, 93; Éder 86) (aet)*
Paços Ferreira 2-1 Gil Vicente *(Yero 17og, Caetano 90; João Vilela 73)*

(17/01/13)
Académica 0-4 Benfica *(John 5, Lima 9, 27, Salvio 71)*
Arouca 1-4 Belenenses *(André Claro 8; Tiago Silva 56, Diakité 65, Kay 76, Fernando Ferreira 90)*

SEMI-FINALS

(30/01/13 & 15/04/13)
Paços Ferreira 0-2 Benfica *(Lima 58, John75)*
Benfica 1-1 Paços Ferreira *(Cardozo 54; Cícero 80)*
(Benfica 3-1)

(27/03/13 & 17/04/13)
Belenenses 0-2 Guimarães *(Ricardo 29, 76)*
Guimarães 1-0 Belenenses *(Marco Matias 13)*
(Guimarães 3-0)

FINAL

(26/05/13)
Estádio Nacional, Lisbon
VITÓRIA SC 2 *(Soudani 79, Ricardo 81)*
SL BENFICA 1 *(Gaitán 30)*
Referee: *Jorge Sousa*
GUIMARÃES: *Douglas, Kanu (Marco Matias 64), Paulo Oliveira, El Adoua, Addy, André, Leonel Olímpio (Crivellaro 77), Tiago Rodrigues, Ricardo, Soudani, Baldé (N'Diaye 90)*
BENFICA: *Artur, Maxi Pereira, Luisão, Garay, André Almeida, Matić, Salvio, Pérez (Aimar 87), Gaitán (Rodrigo 83), Lima, Cardozo (Urreta 69)*

Guimarães youngster Ricardo celebrates his cup final winner against Benfica

REPUBLIC OF IRELAND

Cumann Peile na héireann/Football Association of Ireland (FAI)

Address	National Sports Campus	**President**	Paddy McCaul
	Abbotstown	**Chief executive**	John Delaney
	IE-Dublin 15	**Media officer**	Peter Sherrard
Tel	+353 1 8999500	**Year of formation**	1921
Fax	+353 1 8999501	**National stadium**	Dublin Arena, Dublin
E-mail	info@fai.ie		(51,700)
Website	fai.ie		

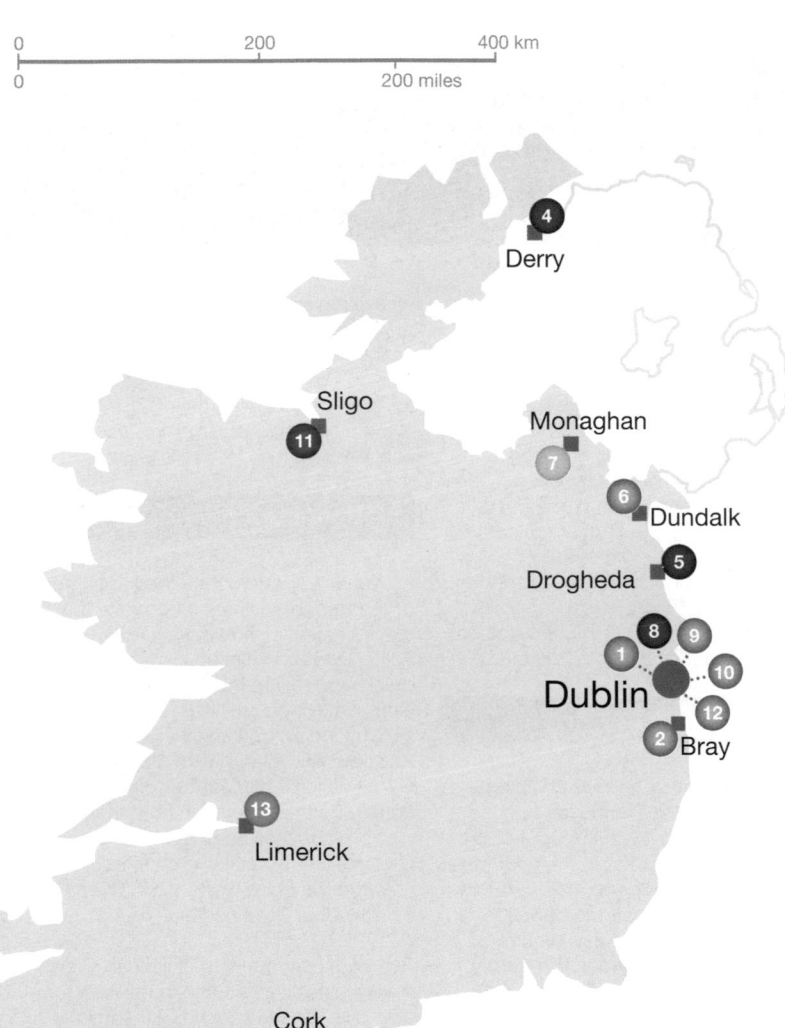

LEAGUE OF IRELAND CLUBS

1. **Bohemian FC**
2. **Bray Wanderers AFC**
3. **Cork City FC**
4. **Derry City FC**
5. **Drogheda United FC**
6. **Dundalk FC**
7. **Monaghan United FC**
8. **Saint Patrick's Athletic FC**
9. **Shamrock Rovers FC**
10. **Shelbourne FC**
11. **Sligo Rovers FC**
12. **University College Dublin AFC**

PROMOTED CLUB

13. **Limerick FC**

KEY:

● – UEFA Champions League
● – UEFA Europa League
● – Promoted club
● – Relegated club

Long wait over for Sligo

Obliged to change manager on the eve of the season when Paul Cook, who had led the club to back-to-back FAI Cup wins, returned home to England, Sligo Rovers FC found a worthy successor in Cook's compatriot, Ian Baraclough, who would bring the League of Ireland title back to the Showgrounds for the first time in 35 years.

Sligo's hold on the FAI Cup was ended early by Premier Division newcomers Monaghan United FC, who went into liquidation soon afterwards and quit the league, leaving it with just 11 participants. Derry City FC won the cup, defeating Saint Patrick's Athletic FC 3-2 in an entertaining Dublin final.

Provincial club land first league title since 1977	**Derry inherit Sligo's FAI Cup crown**	**Rocky road for Republic in World Cup campaign**

Domestic league

Runners-up to Shamrock Rovers FC in 2011, Sligo were a growing force under manager Cook, so when he left for Accrington Stanley FC in late February, the club's challenge for the 2012 title was expected to suffer as a consequence. But Baraclough, a former English lower-league defender with brief managerial experience at Scunthorpe United FC, ensured a virtually seamless transition.

Sligo began well, avoiding defeat until round 13 and taking command of the title race thanks to the consistent goalscoring of striker Danny North. When the Englishman suffered a season-ending knee injury in July, Sligo's title ambitions took a painful hit, but fortunately they had a ready-made replacement in Mark Quigley, who assumed the goalscoring mantle with aplomb as Sligo continued to pile up the points in the second half of the campaign. Fittingly it was the Dubliner's tenth goal of the season, a penalty, that confirmed the Bit O'Red's title win with a 3-2 victory over St Patrick's.

With the pressure off, Sligo lost their last two games but still finished four points clear of surprise runners-up Drogheda United FC, whose excellent Premier Division campaign was supplemented by

victory in the League Cup, which they claimed with a 3-1 win over Shamrock Rovers FC. The defending champions never looked likely to match their fabulous 2011 campaign under manager Michael O'Neill, when they also reached the UEFA Europa League group stage. O'Neill's replacement, Stephen Kenny, did not see out the season, and fourth place was a major disappointment. Further concern for Rovers fans was the post-season departure – to Portadown FC – of resident marksman Gary Twigg, whose 22 goals brought him the Premier League's golden boot for the third time in four years.

Domestic cup

Rovers would have qualified for Europe had St Patrick's, third in the league, ended a 51-wait for the FAI Cup, but the Dubliners' sterling efforts in the final were undone by Derry's supersub striker Rory Patterson, who came off the bench to score two goals, the second in extra time, as the Ulster club took the trophy for the sixth time with a 3-2 victory.

Europe

Unlike in 2011/12, there was no extended Irish presence in Europe. Only six ties were played, half of them featuring St Patrick's,

whose reward for reaching the third qualifying round of the UEFA Europa League was a plum tie against the previous season's quarter-finalists Hannover 96. As for Shamrock Rovers, their UEFA Champions League campaign lasted just one round as they fell to FK Ekranas.

National team

Giovanni Trapattoni remained in charge of the Republic of Ireland despite the team's hapless showing at UEFA EURO 2012, but there was no evidence of a quick recovery in the 2014 FIFA World Cup qualifying campaign. After somehow scrambling an opening win in Kazakhstan, Ireland were mauled by Germany in Dublin, falling to a record 6-1 defeat. Further agony on home turf came with the concession of a late equaliser against Austria (2-2), which effectively negated the good work of a 0-0 draw in Sweden four days earlier.

Two wins over the Faroe Islands nevertheless kept Ireland in the hunt for a play-off spot, the second of them, in Dublin, featuring a Robbie Keane hat-trick on the day he became his country's most-capped international – in addition, of course, to being its record scorer, his goal haul rising to a remarkable 59 with that treble against the Group C minnows.

Domestic league: League of Ireland 2012 final table

		Pld	Home					Away					Total					Pts
			W	D	L	F	A	W	D	L	F	A	W	D	L	F	A	
1	**Sligo Rovers FC**	30	11	4	1	37	13	6	6	2	16	10	17	10	3	53	23	61
2	Drogheda United FC	30	9	4	3	22	15	8	2	4	29	21	17	6	7	51	36	57
3	Saint Patrick's Athletic FC	30	9	2	3	23	8	6	8	2	21	14	15	10	5	44	22	55
4	Shamrock Rovers FC	30	6	7	2	33	14	8	3	4	23	23	14	10	6	56	37	52
5	Derry City FC	30	6	1	8	17	17	5	5	5	19	19	11	6	13	36	36	39
6	Cork City FC	30	5	6	4	23	18	3	6	6	15	18	8	12	10	38	36	36
7	Bohemian FC	30	4	6	4	16	16	5	3	8	19	22	9	9	12	35	38	36
8	Shelbourne FC	30	4	3	8	19	23	5	5	5	16	20	9	8	13	35	43	35
9	University College Dublin AFC	30	5	5	5	18	18	3	2	10	14	30	8	7	15	32	48	31
10	Bray Wanderers AFC	30	2	5	8	19	34	3	5	7	14	20	5	10	15	33	54	25
11	Dundalk FC	30	2	5	8	12	21	2	3	10	11	42	4	8	18	23	63	20

NB Monaghan United FC withdrew from the league after 14 games. All matches annulled. No automatic relegation.

SEASON AT A GLANCE

EUROPEAN QUALIFICATION 2013/14

Champion: Sligo Rovers FC (second qualifying round)

Cup winner: Derry City FC (second qualifying round)

Drogheda United FC (first qualifying round)
Saint Patrick's Athletic FC (first qualifying round)

Top scorer	Gary Twigg (Shamrock Rovers), 22 goals
Relegated club	Monaghan United FC (withdrew)
Promoted club	Limerick FC
Cup final	Derry City FC 3-2 Saint Patrick's Athletic FC (aet)

LEAGUE OF IRELAND TEAM OF THE SEASON
(4-4-2)
Coach: Baraclough (Sligo)

PLAYER OF THE SEASON
Mark Quigley
(Sligo Rovers FC)

The Dublin-born forward had a frustrating start to the season but a cruciate ligament injury to top marksman Danny North in July returned Quigley to the side, which triggered a glut of goals from him in the second half of the campaign. His ten strikes not only helped Sligo to the title but also secured him the players' player of the year award.

NEWCOMER OF THE SEASON
Christopher Forrester
(Saint Patrick's Athletic FC)

The talented young winger made his senior debut with Bohemian FC in the 2011 season but he really blossomed in 2012 after a move to Dublin rivals St Patrick's. The Irish Under-21 international struck seven top-flight goals, including an exquisite lob in a 5-1 success against outgoing champions Shamrock Rovers FC that became an online hit.

NATIONAL TEAM

Home Kit

Away Kit

INTERNATIONAL TOURNAMENT APPEARANCES

FIFA World Cup (3) 1990 (qtr-finals), 1994 (2nd round), 2002 (2nd round)
UEFA European Championship (2) 1988, 2012

TOP FIVE ALL-TIME CAPS

Robbie Keane (127); Shay Given (125); Kevin Kilbane (110); Stephen Staunton (102); Damien Duff (100)

TOP FIVE ALL-TIME GOALS

Robbie Keane (59); Niall Quinn (21); Frank Stapleton (20); John Aldridge, Tony Cascarino & Don Givens (19)

Results 2012/13

Date	Opponent		Venue	Score	Scorers
15/08/12	Serbia	A	Belgrade	0-0	
07/09/12	Kazakhstan (WCQ)	A	Astana	2-1	Keane (89p), Doyle (90)
11/09/12	Oman	N	London (ENG)	4-1	Long (7), Brady (23), Doyle (35), Pearce (85)
12/10/12	Germany (WCQ)	H	Dublin	1-6	A Keogh (90+2)
16/10/12	Faroe Islands (WCQ)	A	Torshavn	4-1	Wilson (46), Walters (53), P J Justinussen (73og), O'Dea (88)
14/11/12	Greece	H	Dublin	0-1	
06/02/13	Poland	H	Dublin	2-0	Clark (35), Hoolahan (76)
22/03/13	Sweden (WCQ)	A	Solna	0-0	
26/03/13	Austria (WCQ)	H	Dublin	2-2	Walters (25p, 45+1)
29/05/13	England	A	London	1-1	Long (13)
02/06/13	Georgia	H	Dublin	4-0	R Keogh (42), Cox (48), Keane (77, 88)
07/06/13	Faroe Islands (WCQ)	H	Dublin	3-0	Keane (5, 56, 81)
11/06/13	Spain	N	New York (USA)	0-2	

Appearances 2012/13

Coach: Giovanni Trapattoni (ITA) 17/3/39			Srb	KAZ	Oma	GER	FRO	Gre	Pol	SWE	AUT	Eng	Geo	FRO	Esp	Caps	Goals
Keiren Westwood	23/10/84	Sunderland (ENG)	G	G	·	G	G						G			15	-
Paul McShane	06/01/86	Hull (ENG)	D						D				D		D	31	-
John O'Shea	30/04/81	Sunderland (ENG)	D	D		D	D	D	D	D	D	D		D		89	1
Darren O'Dea	04/02/87	Toronto (CAN)	D	D		D	D								D	19	1
Stephen Kelly	06/09/83	Fulham (ENG)/Reading (ENG)	D		D							D		s82	D88	35	-
Aiden McGeady	04/04/86	Spartak Moskva (RUS)	M79	M	s70	M68	M					M68	s65	M77		60	2
James McCarthy	12/11/90	Wigan (ENG)	M	M	M65	M	M	M70	M71	M	M	M	M71		M85	15	-
Glenn Whelan	13/01/84	Stoke (ENG)	M60	M				M33	M46			M74		M		49	2
James McClean	22/04/89	Sunderland (ENG)	M69		s61			M	M81	M83	M	s68	M65	s77	s73	13	-
Jonathan Walters	20/09/83	Stoke (ENG)	A79	A70		A	A		s71	M	M	M82		M73		19	4
Simon Cox	28/04/87	Nottingham Forest (ENG)	A	M58	s65	A83	s46	A60	s81			s66	A	A	s56	26	4
Paul Green	10/04/83	Leeds (ENG)	s60						s46	M	s83					16	1
Andy Keogh	16/05/86	Millwall (ENG)	s69		M	s68		s60		s83			M46		M73	29	2
Joey O'Brien	17/02/86	West Ham (ENG)	s79		s73											5	-
Séamus Coleman	11/10/88	Everton (ENG)	s79		D	D	D	D		D	D	D		D	M	14	-
Stephen Ward	20/08/85	Wolves (ENG)	D			D		D								18	2
Sean St Ledger	28/12/84	Leicester (ENG)	D	D						s72		D		D	D	36	3
Robbie Keane	08/07/80	LA Galaxy (USA)	A			A80			A77			A66	s46	A	A56	127	59
Kevin Doyle	18/09/83	Wolves (ENG)		s58	A61			s46								53	12
Shane Long	22/01/87	West Brom (ENG)		s70	A73	s51	s80	A46	A62	A87	A83	A	A71			37	9
David Forde	20/12/79	Millwall (ENG)			G46			G	G	G	G	G		G	G73	10	-
Marc Wilson	17/08/87	Stoke (ENG)			D46		D			D	D		D65	D82		7	1
Robbie Brady	14/01/92	Man. United (ENG)/Hull (ENG)			M70	s83	M46	M46	M71							5	1
David Meyler	29/05/89	Sunderland (ENG)/Hull (ENG)			M	s91		s70								4	-
Darren Randolph	12/05/87	Motherwell (SCO)			s46										s73	2	-
Alex Pearce	09/11/88	Reading (ENG)			s46											1	1
Keith Andrews	13/09/80	Bolton (ENG)				M	M91	s33								35	3
Keith Fahey	15/01/83	Birmingham (ENG)				M51										16	3
Ciaran Clark	26/09/89	Aston Villa (ENG)						D	D85	D	D72					6	1

Appearances 2012/13 (contd.)

			Srb	KAZ	Oma	GER	FRO	Gre	Pol	SWE	AUT	Eng	Geo	FRO	Esp	Caps	Goals
Wes Hoolahan	20/05/82	Norwich (ENG)						s46	s62	s77			M76	M		6	1
Greg Cunningham	31/01/91	Bristol City (ENG)							D							4	-
Conor Sammon	06/11/86	Derby (ENG)							A	s87	A	s02	s71	s73	A	7	-
Joff Hendrick	31/01/92	Derby (ENG)							s71			s74	s71		M46	4	-
Richard Keogh	11/08/86	Derby (ENG)							s85				D			2	1
Damien Delaney	20/07/81	Crystal Palace (ENG)											D		s88	7	-
Richard Dunne	21/09/79	unattached											s65			77	8
Stephen Quinn	01/04/86	Hull (ENG)											s76		s46	2	-

European club competitions 2012/13

SHAMROCK ROVERS FC

Second qualifying round - FK Ekranas (LTU)
H 0-0
Jansson, Powell, Sives, Oman, Rice, McCabe (Turner 74), Twigg, Brennan (O'Donnell 83), Kavanagh (Dennehy 70), Finn, Sullivan. Coach: Stephen Kenny (IRL)
A 1-2 *McCabe (90+2p)*
Jansson, Powell, Sives, Oman, Rice (Kavanagh 73), McCabe, Twigg, Brennan (Turner 65), Dennehy (Kilduff 79), Finn, Sullivan. Coach: Stephen Kenny (IRL)

SLIGO ROVERS FC

Second qualifying round - FC Spartak Trnava (SVK)
A 1-3 *Peers (68)*
Rogers, Peers, Ventre, Boco, Cretaro (Millien 77), Gaynor (Henderson 90), Ndo, McGuinness, Cawley, North, Conneely. Coach: Ian Baraclough (ENG)
H 1-1 *McGuinness (90+2)*
Rogers, Peers, Ventre (Lynch 72), Boco, Gaynor, Millien (Connolly 77), Ndo, McGuinness, Cawley, North (Quigley 50), Conneely. Coach: Ian Baraclough (ENG)

SAINT PATRICK'S ATHLETIC FC

First qualifying round - ÍBV Vestmannaeyjar (ISL)
H 1-0 *Fagan (39)*
Clarke, O'Brien, Kenna, Bolger, Meenan, Chambers, Fagan (D Kelly 48), O'Connor (Flood 87), Bermingham, Browne, Russell. Coach: Liam Buckley (IRL)
A 1-2 *O'Flynn (99)*
Clarke, O'Brien, Kenna, Bolger, Meenan (J Kelly 58), Chambers, O'Connor, Bermingham, Browne, Forrester (Carroll 81), Flood (O'Flynn 68). Coach: Liam Buckley (IRL)

Second qualifying round - NK Široki Brijeg (BIH)
A 1-1 *Fagan (12)*
Clarke, O'Brien, Kenna, Bolger, Chambers, Fagan, O'Connor (Meenan 75), Bermingham, Browne, Forrester (J Kelly 86), Russell. Coach: Liam Buckley (IRL)
H 2-1 *Russell (39), Fagan (105) (aet)*
Clarke, O'Brien, Kenna, Bolger, Chambers, Fagan (Flood 111), O'Connor (Meenan 89), Bermingham, Browne, Forrester (J Kelly 106), Russell. Coach: Liam Buckley (IRL)

Third qualifying round - Hannover 96 (GER)
H 0-3
Clarke, O'Brien, Kenna, Bolger (Flood 83), Chambers, Fagan, O'Connor (Meenan 79), Bermingham, Browne, Forrester (Carroll 87), Russell. Coach: Liam Buckley (IRL)
A 0-2
Clarke, O'Brien, Kenna, Bolger, Chambers, Fagan (Flood 79), O'Connor, Bermingham, Browne, Forrester (Meenan 58), Russell (Carroll 64). Coach: Liam Buckley (IRL)

BOHEMIAN FC

First qualifying round - Thór Akureyri (ISL)
H 0-0
McNulty, Heary, McMillan, Feely, Buckley, McEvoy, Ward, Mulcahy (Traynor 84), Wilson (Moore 77), L Byrne, McMahon (Scully 58). Coach: Aaron Callaghan (IRL)
A 1-5 *Scully (23)*
McNulty, Heary, McMillan, Feely, Buckley (Wilson 60), McEvoy, Ward (Moore 67), L Byrne, McMahon (Traynor 61), Scully, Martin. Coach: Aaron Callaghan (IRL)

Domestic league club-by-club

BOHEMIAN FC

Manager: Aaron Callaghan
1890 • Dalymount Park (6,000) • bohemians.ie
Major honours
League of Ireland (11) 1924, 1928, 1930, 1934, 1936,
1975, 1978, 2001, 2003 (spring), 2008, 2009;
Irish Cup (1) 1908;
FAI Cup (7) 1928, 1935, 1970, 1976, 1992, 2001, 2008

2012

02/03	Derry	a	0-1	
09/03	Shelbourne	h	0-2	
16/03	Sligo	a	0-1	
25/03	St Patrick's	h	0-0	
30/03	Shamrock Rovers	a	0-2	
06/04	Cork	h	1-0	Corcoran
13/04	UCD	a	2-1	Ward, Corcoran
20/04	Monaghan	h	1-2	McEvoy (match annulled)
27/04	Dundalk	a	2-0	McEvoy, McMahon
04/05	Bray	a	1-2	Corcoran
11/05	Drogheda	h	1-1	McEvoy
18/05	Derry	h	1-2	Ward
21/05	Shelbourne	a	2-1	McMahon, McEvoy
01/06	Sligo	h	0-0	
22/06	St Patrick's	a	1-2	Joyce
29/06	Shamrock Rovers	h	4-0	McMahon 2, Moore 2
08/07	Cork	a	1-1	Ward (p)
15/07	UCD	h	1-0	McMillan
27/07	Dundalk	h	2-1	McMillan 2
03/08	Bray	h	0-0	
10/08	Drogheda	a	0-1	
17/08	Derry	a	0-2	
20/08	Shelbourne	h	2-2	McMillan, Ward (p)
03/09	Sligo	a	1-3	Pender
07/09	St Patrick's	h	2-3	McMillan, Feely
10/09	Shamrock Rovers	a	1-0	Devaney
21/09	Cork	h	1-1	McMillan
28/09	UCD	a	2-2	Scully 2
13/10	Dundalk	a	2-2	McMillan, Corcoran
19/10	Bray	a	4-1	Mulcahy, Buckley, Mulligan, McEvoy
26/10	Drogheda	h	1-4	McMillan

No	Name	Nat	DoB	Pos	Aps	(s)	Gls
33	Michael Barker		16/08/93	D	11	(4)	
7	Keith Buckley		17/06/92	M	15	(5)	1
21	David Byrne		01/03/91	A	2	(2)	
19	Luke Byrne		08/07/93	D	17		
12	Ken Carr		04/03/86	A	2	(2)	
21	Dylan Connolly		02/05/95	M		(1)	
24	Daniel Corcoran		13/02/89	A	14	(8)	4
26	Correy Davidson		11/06/93	M		(1)	
14	Kevin Devaney		26/09/90	M	5	(2)	1
6	Kevin Feely		30/08/92	D	23		1
22	Neil Harney		20/02/91	D	2	(2)	
2	Owen Heary		04/10/76	D	18		
28	Danny Joyce		05/06/92	D	8		1
4	Roberto Lopes		17/06/92	D	13	(2)	
34	Dan Mahon		12/02/93	A		(1)	
27	Adam Martin	ENG	18/03/89	M	10	(2)	
39	Philip McCabe		04/08/93	D	1		
9	Ryan McEvoy		19/07/90	M	18	(1)	5
20	Peter McMahon		20/04/89	M	9	(2)	4
5	Evan McMillan		20/11/86	D	29		8
25	Andy McNulty		16/01/89	G	15		
8	Karl Moore		09/11/88	M	20	(6)	2
15	Dave Mulcahy		28/01/78	M	21	(3)	1
18	Andy Mulligan		07/07/93	M	5	(9)	1
30	Greg Murray		30/08/93	G	6		
17	John O'Connor		26/06/92	M	4	(7)	
3	Derek Pender		02/10/84	D	20	(3)	1
23	Dave Scully		20/01/85	A	5	(9)	2
1	Craig Sexton		23/01/92	G	10	(1)	
11	Stephen Traynor		25/10/91	M	10	(6)	
10	Keith Ward		12/10/90	M	18	(7)	4
16	Dwayne Wilson		14/06/87	M	10	(6)	

BRAY WANDERERS AFC

Manager: Pat Devlin
1942 • Carlisle Grounds (3,000) • braywanderers.ie
Major honours
FAI Cup (2) 1990, 1999

2012

02/03	St Patrick's	a	0-1	
09/03	Derry	h	0-4	
16/03	UCD	a	3-2	Byrne, D O'Connor 2
23/03	Drogheda	h	2-4	Byrne, Zambra
30/03	Cork	a	1-1	Byrne
06/04	Sligo	h	1-2	Waters
13/04	Shelbourne	a	1-2	Byrne
20/04	Shamrock Rovers	h	2-2	Waters 2
27/04	Monaghan	a	1-0	Byrne (match annulled)
04/05	Bohemians	h	2-1	Byrne, D O'Connor
11/05	Dundalk	a	2-0	Byrne 2 (2p)
18/05	St Patrick's	h	3-3	Byrne, Mulroy
21/05	Derry	a	2-3	Waters, D O'Connor
01/06	UCD	h	3-1	Byrne 2, Mulroy
22/06	Drogheda	a	1-3	Houston
29/06	Cork	h	0-3	
07/07	Sligo	a	1-1	Byrne
13/07	Shelbourne	h	2-3	Waters, Mulroy
20/07	Shamrock Rovers	a	0-0	
03/08	Bohemians	a	0-0	
10/08	Dundalk	h	1-1	Webster
17/08	St Patrick's	a	1-0	Waters
20/08	Derry	h	0-0	
31/08	UCD	a	1-3	Houston
07/09	Drogheda	h	1-3	Marshall
10/09	Cork	a	0-2	
21/09	Sligo	h	0-0	
28/09	Shelbourne	a	0-0	
05/10	Shamrock Rovers	h	1-3	Waters
19/10	Bohemians	h	1-4	Byrne
26/10	Dundalk	a	1-2	Waters

No	Name	Nat	DoB	Pos	Aps	(s)	Gls
23	Ismahil Akinade	NGA	11/02/94	A		(5)	
9	Anthony Bolger		05/04/92	A		(8)	
19	Conor Butler		20/12/92	D	1		
10	Jason Byrne		23/02/78	A	26		14
15	Lee Dixon		01/05/91	M	1	(3)	
8	Daire Doyle		18/10/80	M	8	(9)	
27	Conor Earley		28/05/93	M	1	(1)	
30	Yani Georgiev	BUL	18/06/92	A		(4)	
21	Adam Hanlon		03/06/92	M	20	(6)	
20	Sean Houston		29/10/89	M	24	(3)	2
28	Sean Hurley		17/11/95	M		(2)	
25	Brian Kane		06/07/90	G	1	(1)	
14	Graham Kelly		31/10/91	M	2	(4)	
17	Jonathan Kelty		18/09/91	M		(9)	
30	Brendan King	USA	25/02/90	M		(1)	
12	Kevin Knight		13/02/93	M	13	(3)	
24	Stephen Last		05/10/91	D		(1)	
17	Dean Marshall		15/03/90	M	4	(6)	1
3	Dane Massey		17/04/88	D	26	(2)	
5	Adam Mitchell		23/06/83	D	14	(4)	
9	Paul Moffatt		28/08/93	M	1	(2)	
18	John Mulroy		27/12/87	A	25	(2)	3
6	Danny O'Connor		28/09/80	M	30		4
7	Kevin O'Connor		19/10/85	M	13		
26	Shane O'Connor		19/06/90	D	14		
1	Darren Quigley		10/06/86	G	30		
22	Patrick Seery		03/06/92	D	1		
22	Pierce Sweeney		11/09/94	D	12		
4	Colm Tresson		29/06/71	M		(1)	
11	Kieran Marty Waters		05/05/90	A	29		8
2	David Webster		08/09/89	D	18	(3)	1
16	Dean Zambra		30/07/88	M	27		1

CORK CITY FC

Manager: Tommy Dunne
1984 • Turner's Cross (7,365) • corkcityfc.net
Major honours
League of Ireland (2) 1993, 2005;
FAI Cup (2) 1998, 2007

2012

02/03	UCD	a	0-1	
09/03	Drogheda	h	2-3	D Horgan, Sullivan
16/03	Shamrock Rovers	h	1-1	Kavanagh
23/03	Derry	a	0-2	
30/03	Bray	h	1-1	Purcell
06/04	Bohemians	a	0-1	
13/04	Monaghan	h	6-0	D Horgan, O'Neill 3 (1p), Sullivan, Purcell (match annulled)
20/04	Sligo	h	0-1	
27/04	Shelbourne	a	2-1	Sullivan 2
04/05	Dundalk	h	3-2	O'Neill 2, Sullivan
11/05	St Patrick's	a	0-0	
18/05	UCD	h	4-2	D Horgan, O'Neill 3 (1p)
21/05	Drogheda	a	1-1	D Horgan
01/06	Shamrock Rovers	a	1-1	Dunleavy
22/06	Derry	h	2-2	Sullivan, Duggan
29/06	Bray	a	3-0	Purcell, Duggan, Sullivan
08/07	Bohemians	h	1-1	D Horgan
22/07	Sligo	a	2-2	Turner, Sullivan
27/07	Shelbourne	h	0-0	
03/08	Dundalk	a	1-1	Turner
13/08	St Patrick's	h	0-1	
17/08	UCD	a	1-3	Parker
20/08	Drogheda	h	3-2	Sullivan, K Murray, O'Neill
31/08	Shamrock Rovers	h	1-2	Turner
07/09	Derry	a	1-0	Buckley
10/09	Bray	h	2-0	Parker, Kavanagh
21/09	Bohemians	a	1-1	Sullivan
05/10	Sligo	h	0-0	
13/10	Shelbourne	a	2-3	Sullivan, K Murray
19/10	Dundalk	h	3-0	G Morrissey, Sullivan, Duggan
26/10	St Patrick's	a	0-1	

No	Name	Nat	DoB	Pos	Aps	(s)	Gls
26	Garry Buckley		19/08/93	M	2	(1)	1
25	Kevin Burns		28/07/90	G	1	(1)	
8	Shane Duggan		11/03/89	M	29		3
16	John Dunleavy		03/07/91	D	23		1
7	Colin Healy		14/03/80	M	18	(3)	
23	Daryl Horgan		10/08/92	M	29		5
22	Neal Horgan		29/11/79	D	3	(3)	
5	Gavin Kavanagh		22/11/87	D	19	(1)	2
30	Stephen Kenny		14/05/93	A	1	(13)	
33	Brian Lenihan		08/06/94	M	1	(2)	
19	Cathal Lordan		23/03/87	M		(3)	
1	Mark McNulty		13/10/80	G	30		
15	Danny Morrissey		13/12/93	M		(2)	
6	Gearóid Morrissey		17/11/91	M	25	(2)	1
2	Danny Murphy		04/12/82	D	29		
20	Jamie Murphy		07/01/91	A	1	(2)	
17	Dan Murray	ENG	16/05/82	D	15	(2)	
21	Kevin Murray		16/11/93	D	12	(2)	2
20	Andy O'Connell		09/03/93	M	1	(3)	
11	Shane O'Connor		14/04/90	D	4	(1)	
9	Davin O'Neill		22/06/83	A	20	(9)	9
14	Keigan Parker	SCO	08/06/82	A	4	(4)	2
14	Tadhg Purcell		02/09/85	A	10	(6)	3
11	Keith Quinn		22/09/88	M		(4)	
18	Kalen Spillane		09/08/91	D	20	(1)	
10	Vinny Sullivan		19/04/81	A	26	(3)	12
2	Ian Turner		19/04/89	D	18	(7)	3

DERRY CITY FC

Manager: Declan Devine (NIR)
1928 • The Brandywell (8,200) • derrycityfc.net
Major honours
Irish League (1) 1965;
League of Ireland (2) 1989, 1997;
Irish Cup (3) 1949, 1954, 1964;
FAI Cup (5) 1989, 1995, 2002 (autumn), 2006, 2012

2012

02/03	Bohemians	h	1-0	McLaughlin
09/03	Bray	a	4-0	Patterson 2, Greacen, McDaid
16/03	Shelbourne	a	0-1	
23/03	Cork	h	2-0	Farren, McLaughlin
30/03	Drogheda	a	0-2	
06/04	UCD	h	0-0	
13/04	Sligo	a	1-1	McDaid (p)
20/04	Dundalk	h	1-2	Higgins
27/04	Shamrock Rovers	a	1-1	McDaid
04/05	St Patrick's	h	0-2	
15/05	Monaghan	a	4-1	McDaid, McLaughlin, P McEleney, Patterson (match annulled)
18/05	Bohemians	a	2-1	McLaughlin, P McEleney (p)
21/05	Bray	h	3-2	McLaughlin 2, McBride
01/06	Shelbourne	h	0-1	
22/06	Cork	a	2-2	Patterson 2
29/06	Drogheda	h	0-3	
06/07	UCD	a	1-0	McLaughlin
13/07	Sligo	h	1-2	McDaid
20/07	Dundalk	a	1-0	McDaid
27/07	Shamrock Rovers	h	0-1	
17/08	Bohemians	h	2-0	Murphy, McLaughlin
20/08	Bray	a	0-0	
31/08	Shelbourne	a	2-0	McDaid, McLaughlin
03/09	St Patrick's	a	0-3	
07/09	Cork	h	0-1	
10/09	Drogheda	a	1-2	McDaid (p)
21/09	UCD	h	1-2	Deery
29/09	Sligo	a	1-4	McDaid
02/10	Dundalk	h	4-0	McDaid, P McEleney, Curran, McCaffrey
13/10	Shamrock Rovers	a	3-1	McLaughlin, Patterson (p), McNamee
19/10	St Patrick's	h	2-1	Madden, McDaid

No	Name	Nat	DoB	Pos	Aps	(s)	Gls
24	Michael Barr		28/06/93	D	1	(2)	
27	Caoimhin Bonner	NIR	15/01/93	D	1		
21	Marc Brolly		11/09/86	M	5	(3)	
16	Matt Crossan		23/09/86	D	1	(1)	
23	Ryan Curran		13/10/93	A	1	(12)	1
8	Kevin Deery		06/12/84	M	5	(3)	1
1	Gerard Doherty		24/08/81	G	31		
29	Michael Duffy		28/07/94	A		(5)	
18	Mark Farren		01/05/82	A	10	(8)	1
5	Stewart Greacen	SCO	31/03/82	D	13	(1)	1
7	Ruaidhri Higgins	NIR	23/10/84	M	28	(1)	1
17	Simon Madden		01/05/88	D	29		1
12	Ryan McBride		15/12/89	D	20	(3)	1
3	Dermot McCaffrey	NIR	29/03/86	D	29		1
2	Eddie McCallion	NIR	25/01/79	D	9	(3)	
9	David McDaid	NIR	03/12/90	A	24	(5)	11
10	Patrick McEleney		26/09/92	A	25	(2)	3
6	Shane McEleney		31/01/91	D	21	(5)	
14	Brian McGroary		01/02/93	M		(6)	
15	Stephen McLaughlin		14/06/90	A	24		10
25	Barry McNamee		17/02/92	D	9	(4)	1
4	Barry Molloy		28/11/83	M	23		
19	Owen Morrison		08/12/81	M	12	(6)	
16	Conor Murphy		11/11/92	A	7	(5)	1
11	Rory Patterson	NIR	16/07/84	A	13	(1)	6

DROGHEDA UNITED FC

Manager: Mick Cooke
1919 • Hunky Dorys Park (2,500) • droghedaunited.ie
Major honours
League of Ireland (1) 2007;
FAI Cup (1) 2005

2012

02/03	Shamrock Rovers	h	1-2	Marshall
09/03	Cork	a	3-2	Mulvenna, Hynes (p), og (Kavanagh)
16/03	Dundalk	h	0-0	
23/03	Bray	a	4-2	Marshall, Gannon, S Brennan, D O'Brien
30/03	Derry	h	2-0	R Brennan, Gannon
06/04	Monaghan	a	2-0	D O'Brien (match annulled)
13/04	St Patrick's	h	0-0	
20/04	Shelbourne	h	3-1	Gannon, R Brennan, Hynes
27/04	UCD	a	1-1	McNally
04/05	Sligo	h	1-3	D O'Brien
11/05	Bohemians	a	1-1	McNally
18/05	Shamrock Rovers	a	1-3	D O'Brien
21/05	Cork	h	1-1	D O'Brien
01/06	Dundalk	a	2-1	S Brennan, Crowley
22/06	Bray	h	3-1	D O'Brien, Crowley, Hynes
29/06	Derry	a	3-0	G Brennan 2, D O'Brien
15/07	St Patrick's	a	2-0	G Brennan, Hynes
20/07	Shelbourne	a	2-1	Brady, G Brennan
27/07	UCD	h	1-0	D O'Brien
04/08	Sligo	a	1-4	Hynes
10/08	Bohemians	h	1-0	D O'Brien (p)
17/08	Shamrock Rovers	h	0-2	
20/08	Cork	a	2-3	Foley, D O'Brien (p)
31/08	Dundalk	h	3-2	Hynes 2, Sullivan
07/09	Bray	a	3-1	Foley, D O'Brien (p), Marks
10/09	Derry	h	2-1	D O'Brien (p), McNally
28/09	St Patrick's	h	0-0	
01/10	Shelbourne	h	2-1	D O'Brien (p), R Brennan
13/10	UCD	a	0-1	
19/10	Sligo	h	2-1	McNally, Gannon
26/10	Bohemians	a	4-1	Mulvenna 3, McNally

No	Name	Nat	DoB	Pos	Aps	(s)	Gls
7	Cathal Brady		24/03/85	M	4	(11)	1
21	Johnny Breen		25/02/91	A		(7)	
11	Gavin Brennan		23/01/88	M	22		4
8	Ryan Brennan		11/11/91	M	21	(3)	3
10	Seán Brennan		01/01/86	M	16	(9)	2
28	Alan Byrne		21/07/83	D	12	(1)	
16	Paul Crowley		13/08/80	M	21	(1)	2
18	Jack Flynn		21/08/89	M	1	(1)	
22	Eric Foley		30/01/90	M	21	(1)	2
17	Brian Gannon		20/07/84	D	21	(2)	4
12	Shane Grimes		09/03/87	D	12		
3	Philip Hand		17/06/90	D	19	(1)	
15	Peter Hynes		28/11/83	A	20	(7)	7
23	Chris Kerr		08/06/91	M		(1)	
23	Jason Marks		02/05/89	M	1	(6)	1
14	Dean Marshall		15/03/90	M	2	(5)	2
18	Conor McMahon		04/12/86	D	6		
5	Alan McNally		15/09/82	D	27		5
9	Tiarnán Mulvenna		10/12/88	A	11	(11)	4
19	Declan O'Brien		16/06/79	A	24	(3)	13
6	Mark O'Brien		13/05/84	M	3	(5)	
4	Derek Prendergast		17/10/84	D	28		
2	Stephen Quigley		13/01/85	D	16		
1	Gabriel Sava	ITA	15/01/86	G	30		
20	Michael Schlingermann		23/06/91	G	1		
6	John Sullivan		06/01/91	M	2	(8)	1

DUNDALK FC

Manager: Sean McCaffrey;
(12/07/12) (Darius Kierans)
1903 • Oriel Park (4,000) • dundalkfc.com
Major honours
League of Ireland (9) 1933, 1963, 1967, 1976, 1979,
1982, 1988, 1991, 1995;
FAI Cup (9) 1942, 1949, 1952, 1958, 1977, 1979, 1981,
1988, 2002 (spring)

2012

02/03	Monaghan	a	0-0	(match annulled)
09/03	St Patrick's	h	0-2	
16/03	Drogheda	a	0-0	
23/03	UCD	h	2-1	Shields, O'Neill
31/03	Sligo	a	0-3	
06/04	Shelbourne	h	0-0	
13/04	Shamrock Rovers	a	0-6	
20/04	Derry	a	2-1	Rafter, O'Neill
27/04	Bohemians	h	0-2	
04/05	Cork	a	2-3	Rafter, Shanahan
11/05	Bray	h	0-2	
18/05	Monaghan	h	1-2	Rafter (match annulled)
21/05	St Patrick's	a	2-1	Griffin 2
01/06	Drogheda	h	1-2	Shanahan
22/06	UCD	a	1-1	Murphy
29/06	Sligo	h	1-2	Rafter
06/07	Shelbourne	a	0-4	
13/07	Shamrock Rovers	h	1-1	Shanahan
20/07	Derry	h	1-1	Shields
27/07	Bohemians	a	1-2	Rafter
03/08	Cork	h	1-1	Shanahan
10/08	Bray	a	1-1	Shanahan
20/08	St Patrick's	h	0-1	
31/08	Drogheda	a	2-3	Griffin 2
07/09	UCD	h	1-2	Rafter
10/09	Sligo	a	0-3	
21/09	Shelbourne	h	0-1	
28/09	Shamrock Rovers	a	0-7	
02/10	Derry	a	0-4	
13/10	Bohemians	h	2-2	Maher, McKenna
19/10	Cork	a	0-3	
26/10	Bray	h	2-1	Rafter, Conlon

No	Name	Nat	DoB	Pos	Aps	(s)	Gls
26	Gareth Brady		24/02/94	M	1	(2)	
5	Liam Burns	NIR	30/10/78	D	21	(2)	
27	Cian Byrne		28/08/93	D	1	(1)	
1	Peter Cherrie	SCO	01/10/83	G	31	(1)	
24	Barry Conlon		01/10/78	A	1	(5)	1
10	Gareth Coughlan		24/11/89	M	1	(6)	
3	Dan Cunningham		31/01/91	D	4	(2)	
4	Luke Danville	ENG	04/09/91	D	7		
17	Derek Foran		10/09/89	D	25		
27	Robbie Gaul		11/03/92	A	5	(2)	
11	Mark Griffin		16/06/91	A	15	(3)	4
20	Ger Hanley		04/04/91	G	1		
30	Mark Leavy		30/08/93	M		(1)	
19	Stephen Maher		03/03/88	M	8		1
3	Philip McCabe		04/08/93	D		(1)	
22	Conor McDonald		14/06/95	M	3	(1)	
16	Stephen McDonnell		28/03/92	M	23	(3)	
15	Bob McKenna		16/05/94	A	2	(6)	1
17	Ben McLaughlin		15/04/95	D	12	(1)	
29	Ger McSorley		26/05/93	A		(1)	
8	John Mountney		22/02/93	M	28		
21	Nathan Murphy		01/11/92	D	13		1
7	Mark Griffin		13/05/84	M	9		
7	Shane O'Neill		09/01/89	M	10	(2)	2
25	Eoghan Osbourne		25/03/92	D	16		
28	Michael Osobe	NGA		M		(1)	
9	Michael Rafter		19/06/92	A	25	(2)	7
13	Chris Reilly		06/08/93	M	1	(15)	
18	Gary Shanahan		15/02/93	A	18	(4)	5
10	Lorcan Shannon		10/11/93	M	5	(3)	
6	Chris Shields		27/12/90	M	26		2
23	Peter Thomas		11/07/93	M	4	(10)	
14	Paul Walsh		07/10/88	M	16	(4)	
19	Robert Waters		26/09/90	M	11	(4)	
4	Paul Whelan		29/06/87	D	10		
29	William Woods		05/07/91	A	2	(4)	

MONAGHAN UNITED FC

Manager: Roddy Collins
1979 • Gortakeegan (3,000) • monaghanunited.tv

2012

02/03	Dundalk	h	0-0	
09/03	Shamrock Rovers	a	1-3	McDonagh
16/03	St Patrick's	a	1-1	Murphy
23/03	Sligo	h	0-1	
30/03	UCD	a	2-3	Murphy, Keegan
06/04	Drogheda	h	0-1	
13/04	Cork	a	0-6	
20/04	Bohemians	a	2-1	Stephen Maher, Marks
27/04	Bray	h	0-1	
04/05	Shelbourne	a	1-2	McDonagh (p)
15/05	Derry	h	1-4	Murphy
18/05	Dundalk	a	2-1	Keegan 2
21/05	Shamrock Rovers	h	0-0	
01/06	St Patrick's	h	0-4	

NB Monaghan United withdrew from the league after 14 games; all matches were annulled.

No	Name	Nat	DoB	Pos	Aps	(s)	Gls
6	Robert Bayly		22/02/88	M	7	(1)	
1	Chris Bennion	SCO	30/08/80	G	10		
5	Alan Byrne		21/07/83	D	8		
22	Aidan Collins		22/03/84	D	5		
2	Roddy Collins		06/08/94	D	3	(3)	
20	Shane Dunne		04/04/93	M	1	(1)	
9	Tony Griffiths		19/03/86	A	7	(4)	
10	Owen Humphrey		03/08/94	A	5	(8)	
12	Michael Isichei		14/05/91	A	1	(3)	
3	Jordan Keegan		05/02/92	A	13		3
17	Shaun Maher		10/06/78	D	13		
18	Stephen Maher		03/03/88	M	5		1
23	Jason Marks		02/05/89	M	5	(6)	1
14	Willo McDonagh		14/03/83	M	9	(2)	2
15	Daniel McGuinness		19/02/93	A	4	(4)	
4	Conor McMahon		04/12/86	D	12		
7	Conor Murphy		11/11/92	A	10	(3)	3
19	Garreth O'Connor		10/11/78	M	5	(1)	
8	Keith Quinn		22/09/88	M	8		
11	Darragh Reynor		14/02/93	M	9	(2)	
16	Bobby Ryan		01/05/79	M	3	(3)	
21	Michael Schlingermann		23/06/91	G	4	(1)	
24	Paul Whelan		29/06/87	D	7		

SAINT PATRICK'S ATHLETIC FC

Manager: Liam Buckley
1929 • Richmond Park (5,000) • stpatsfc.com
Major honours
League of Ireland (7) 1952, 1955, 1956, 1990, 1996, 1998, 1999;
FAI Cup (2) 1959, 1961

2012

02/03	Bray	h	1-0	D Kelly
09/03	Dundalk	a	2-0	O'Flynn, Russell
16/03	Monaghan	h	1-1	D Kelly (match annulled)
25/03	Bohemians	a	0-0	
30/03	Shelbourne	a	1-1	Fagan
06/04	Shamrock Rovers	h	5-1	Forrester 2, Russell, Fagan 2
13/04	Drogheda	a	0-0	
20/04	UCD	h	2-0	Fagan, Bolger
27/04	Sligo	a	1-1	O'Connor
04/05	Derry	a	2-0	Meenan, O'Connor
11/05	Cork	h	0-0	
18/05	Bray	a	3-3	Fagan 2, Russell
21/05	Dundalk	h	1-2	Forrester
01/06	Monaghan	a	4-0	Fagan, J Kelly 2, Bolger (match annulled)
22/06	Bohemians	h	2-1	Fagan 2
29/06	Shelbourne	h	1-0	Bolger
08/07	Shamrock Rovers	a	1-1	Flynn
15/07	Drogheda	h	0-2	
22/07	UCD	a	1-1	Forrester
13/08	Cork	a	1-0	Fagan
17/08	Bray	h	0-1	
20/08	Dundalk	a	1-0	O'Connor
24/08	Sligo	h	0-0	
03/09	Derry	h	3-0	O'Connor, J Kelly, Faherty
07/09	Bohemians	a	3-2	Chambers, Forrester, O'Connor
10/09	Shelbourne	a	2-0	Fagan, Faherty
25/09	Shamrock Rovers	h	2-1	O'Connor (p), Carroll
28/09	Drogheda	a	0-0	
05/10	UCD	h	5-0	J Kelly, Faherty 3, Flood
13/10	Sligo	a	2-3	Fagan, Forrester
19/10	Derry	a	1-2	Forrester
26/10	Cork	h	1-0	Fagan

No	Name	Nat	DoB	Pos	Aps	(s)	Gls
12	Ian Bermingham		16/06/89	D	28		
6	Greg Bolger		09/09/88	M	24	(4)	3
31	Gavin Boyne		17/04/95	M		(1)	
15	Kenny Browne		07/08/86	D	28	(2)	
3	Jake Carroll		11/08/91	D	17	(2)	1
8	James Chambers		14/02/87	M	25	(1)	1
1	Brendan Clarke		17/09/85	G	21	(1)	
22	Ryan Coombes		30/01/94	M	3	(5)	
10	Ian Daly		29/03/90	A		(8)	
9	Christy Fagan		11/05/89	A	24	(2)	13
26	Vinny Faherty		13/06/87	A	4	(7)	5
25	Anto Flood		31/12/84	A	3	(5)	1
13	Pat Flynn		13/01/85	D	8		1
17	Chris Forrester		17/12/92	M	23	(3)	7
30	Hernany Macedo	BRA	15/02/87	D	1	(1)	
21	Dean Kelly		18/09/85	A	5	(8)	2
19	Jake Kelly		18/06/90	M	15	(11)	4
4	Conor Kenna		21/11/84	D	29		
7	Darren Meenan	NIR	16/11/86	M	7	(11)	1
16	Barry Murphy		08/06/85	G	11		
2	Ger O'Brien		02/07/84	D	30		
11	Sean O'Connor		21/10/83	M	19	(6)	6
20	Stephen O'Flynn		27/04/82	A	4	(2)	1
5	Aidan Price		08/12/81	D	2		
14	Mark Rossiter		27/05/83	M	2	(1)	
18	John Russell		18/05/85	M	19	(2)	3

SHAMROCK ROVERS FC

Manager: Stephen Kenny;
(11/09/12) (Stephen Glass (SCO));
(17/09/12) (Brian Laws (ENG))
1901 • Tallaght Stadium (6,500) • shamrockrovers.ie
Major honours
League of Ireland (17) 1923, 1925, 1927, 1932, 1938, 1939, 1954, 1957, 1959, 1964, 1984, 1985, 1986, 1987, 1994, 2010, 2011;
FAI Cup (24) 1925, 1929, 1930, 1931, 1932, 1933, 1936, 1940, 1944, 1945, 1948, 1955, 1956, 1962, 1964, 1965, 1966, 1967, 1968, 1969, 1978, 1985, 1986, 1987

2012

02/03	Drogheda	a	2-1	Twigg 2
09/03	Monaghan	h	3-1	Brennan, Dennehy, Greene (match annulled)
16/03	Cork	a	1-1	Twigg
23/03	Shelbourne	h	4-0	Twigg (p), og (Hurley), Finn, Greene
30/03	Bohemians	h	2-0	Twigg, Dennehy
06/04	St Patrick's	a	1-5	Oman
13/04	Dundalk	h	6-0	Turner, Twigg 3, Dennehy, Kavanagh
20/04	Bray	a	2-2	Finn, Twigg
27/04	Derry	h	1-1	Twigg
04/05	UCD	h	2-2	Dennehy, Kavanagh
12/05	Sligo	a	0-3	
18/05	Drogheda	h	3-1	McCabe, Twigg 2
21/05	Monaghan	a	0-0	(match annulled)
01/06	Cork	h	1-1	Twigg
21/06	Shelbourne	a	3-2	Twigg 2, McCabe
29/06	Bohemians	a	0-4	
08/07	St Patrick's	h	1-1	Sives
13/07	Dundalk	a	1-1	Kavanagh
20/07	Bray	h	0-0	
27/07	Derry	a	1-0	Finn
03/08	UCD	a	2-0	Twigg, McCabe
13/08	Sligo	h	1-1	Finn
17/08	Drogheda	a	2-0	Kilduff, Finn
31/08	Cork	a	2-1	Finn, McCabe
07/09	Shelbourne	h	2-2	Kilduff, Finn
10/09	Bohemians	h	0-1	
25/09	St Patrick's	a	1-2	McCabe
28/09	Dundalk	h	7-0	Finn, Oman, Kilduff, McCabe 2 (2p), Twigg 2
05/10	Bray	a	3-1	Brennan, Oman, McCabe (p)
13/10	Derry	h	1-3	Stewart
19/10	UCD	h	2-1	Twigg 2
26/10	Sligo	a	2-0	Twigg 2

No	Name	Nat	DoB	Pos	Aps	(s)	Gls
15	Killian Brennan		31/01/84	M	17	(7)	2
20	Billy Dennehy		17/02/87	M	23	(6)	4
32	Dean Ebbe		16/07/94	A		(1)	
21	Ronan Finn		21/12/87	M	26		8
19	Sean Gannon		11/07/91	D	5	(3)	
17	Graham Gartland		13/07/83	D	8	(2)	
2	Kerrea Gilbert	ENG	28/02/87	D	12	(2)	
14	Aaron Greene		02/01/90	A	6	(18)	2
13	Colin Hawkins		17/08/77	D	10	(2)	
1	Oscar Jansson	SWE	23/12/90	G	31		
16	Daryl Kavanagh		11/08/86	A	7	(10)	3
11	Ciaran Kilduff		29/09/88	A	7	(3)	3
7	Gary McCabe		01/08/88	M	24	(4)	8
22	Conor McCormack		18/05/90	M	10	(4)	
28	Shane O'Connor		14/04/90	D	2	(1)	
8	Stephen O'Donnell		15/01/86	M	2	(2)	
10	Gary O'Neill		30/01/82	A	10	(6)	
5	Ken Oman		29/07/82	D	20	(1)	3
30	Reyaad Pieterse	RSA	17/02/92	G	1		
3	Conor Powell		26/08/87	D	27	(1)	
6	Stephen Rice		06/10/84	M	23		
4	Craig Sives	SCO	09/04/86	D	26		1
24	Thomas Stewart	NIR	12/11/86	A	4	(3)	1
27	Pat Sullivan		30/10/82	D	11		
18	Chris Turner	NIR	03/01/87	M	12	(7)	1
9	Gary Twigg	SCO	19/03/84	A	28	(1)	22

SHELBOURNE FC

Manager: Alan Mathews
1895 • Tolka Park (9,000) • shelbournefc.ie
Major honours
League of Ireland (13) 1926, 1929, 1931, 1944, 1947, 1953, 1962, 1992, 2000, 2002, 2003 (autumn), 2004, 2006;
Irish Cup (3) 1906, 1911, 1920; FAI Cup (7) 1939, 1960, 1963, 1993, 1996, 1997, 2000

2012

02/03	Sligo	h	1-1	Hughes
09/03	Bohemians	a	2-0	Kavanagh, Hughes
16/03	Derry	h	1-0	Hughes
23/03	Shamrock Rovers	a	0-4	
30/03	St Patrick's	h	1-1	og (Clarke)
06/04	Dundalk	a	0-0	
13/04	Bray	h	2-1	Hughes, Gorman
20/04	Drogheda	a	1-3	Hughes (p)
27/04	Cork	h	1-2	Kavanagh
04/05	Monaghan	h	2-1	Kavanagh, Cassidy (match annulled)
11/05	UCD	a	2-0	Gorman, Cassidy
18/05	Sligo	a	0-3	
21/05	Bohemians	h	1-2	Cronin (p)
01/06	Derry	a	1-0	Hughes
21/06	Shamrock Rovers	h	2-3	P Byrne, Hughes
29/06	St Patrick's	a	0-1	
06/07	Dundalk	h	4-0	Gorman 2, Dawson, og (McLaughlin)
13/07	Bray	a	3-2	Cassidy, Gorman, Kavanagh
20/07	Drogheda	h	1-2	C Byrne
27/07	Cork	a	0-0	
10/08	UCD	h	1-2	Hughes
17/08	Sligo	h	1-3	Kavanagh
20/08	Bohemians	a	2-2	Hughes (p), Dawson
31/08	Derry	h	0-2	
07/09	Shamrock Rovers	a	2-2	Kavanagh, Gorman
10/09	St Patrick's	h	0-2	
21/09	Dundalk	a	1-0	Kavanagh
28/09	Bray	h	0-0	
01/10	Drogheda	a	1-2	Hughes
13/10	Cork	h	3-2	Cassidy, Hughes (p), C Byrne
26/10	UCD	a	1-1	Cassidy

No	Name	Nat	DoB	Pos	Aps	(s)	Gls
30	Chris Bennion	SCO	30/08/80	G	14		
4	Andy Boyle		07/03/91	D	22	(1)	
7	Conan Byrne		10/07/85	M	11	(12)	2
18	Paul Byrne		19/05/86	A	5	(6)	1
17	Sean Byrne		13/07/89	D	13	(1)	
8	David Cassidy		23/05/85	M	25	(1)	5
15	Barry Clancy		20/04/85	M	11	(5)	
6	Glenn Cronin		14/09/81	M	22	(1)	1
10	Kevin Dawson		30/06/90	M	19	(6)	2
1	Dean Delany		15/09/80	G	12		
3	Lorcan Fitzgerald		03/01/89	D	15		
19	Philip Gorman		07/08/81	A	12	(12)	6
9	Philip Hughes		30/08/80	A	26	(3)	11
16	Stephen Hurley		20/12/85	M	16	(3)	
14	Patrick Kavanagh		29/12/85	M	27	(2)	7
2	Gareth Matthews		13/02/90	D	15	(1)	
11	Brendan McGill		22/05/81	M	7	(3)	
24	Anto Murphy		01/08/82	M	8	(10)	
5	Stephen Paisley		28/07/83	D	15	(3)	
23	Ian Ryan		09/06/87	D	15	(2)	
12	Brian Shortall		28/05/85	D	22	(1)	
13	Paul Skinner		03/02/89	G	5	(1)	
35	John Sullivan		06/01/91	M	4	(2)	

SLIGO ROVERS FC

Manager: Ian Baraclough (ENG)
1928 • The Showgrounds (5,500) • sligorovers.com
Major honours
League of Ireland (3) 1937, 1977, 2012;
FAI Cup (4) 1983, 1994, 2010, 2011

2012

02/03	Shelbourne	a	1-1	McGuinness
10/03	UCD	h	2-1	North, McGuinness
16/03	Bohemians	h	1-0	Lynch
23/03	Monaghan	a	1-0	North (match annulled)
31/03	Dundalk	h	3-0	North 2, Peers
06/04	Bray	a	2-1	Cretaro, North
13/04	Derry	h	1-1	North
20/04	Cork	a	1-0	North
27/04	St Patrick's	h	1-1	og (Browne)
04/05	Drogheda	a	3-1	Peers, North 2
12/05	Shamrock Rovers	h	3-0	North 2, Cawley
18/05	Shelbourne	h	3-0	North 2, Millien
21/05	UCD	a	0-1	
01/06	Bohemians	a	0-0	
29/06	Dundalk	a	2-1	North 2
07/07	Bray	h	1-1	Keane
13/07	Derry	a	2-1	Cawley, Quigley
22/07	Cork	h	2-2	Quigley 2 (1p)
04/08	Drogheda	h	4-1	Quigley, Conneely, Boco, Ndo
13/08	Shamrock Rovers	a	1-1	Quigley
17/08	Shelbourne	a	3-1	McGuinness, Peers, Quigley (p)
20/08	UCD	h	3-0	Quigley, Millien, Boco
24/08	St Patrick's	a	0-0	
03/09	Bohemians	h	3-1	Quigley, Cretaro, Lynch
10/09	Dundalk	h	3-0	Quigley, Peers, Buchanan
21/09	Bray	a	0-0	
29/09	Derry	h	4-1	og (McBride), Cretaro 2, Lynch
05/10	Cork	a	0-0	
13/10	St Patrick's	h	3-2	Cretaro 2, Quigley (p)
19/10	Drogheda	a	1-2	Buchanan
26/10	Shamrock Rovers	h	0-2	

No	Name	Nat	DoB	Pos	Aps	(s)	Gls
8	Romuald Boco	BEN	08/07/85	M	22		2
12	Richard Brush	ENG	26/11/84	G	1		
39	Liam Buchanan	SCO	27/03/85	A	1	(9)	2
22	David Cawley		17/09/91	M	16	(10)	2
29	Seamus Conneely		09/07/88	D	11	(2)	1
26	Ryan Connolly		13/01/92	M	1	(5)	
10	Rafael Cretaro		15/10/81	A	20	(8)	6
3	Iarfhlaith Davoren		12/05/86	D	12	(2)	
7	John Dillon	ENG	02/08/88	M	8	(11)	
24	Jake Dykes		30/06/95	D		(2)	
11	Ross Gaynor		09/09/87	M	26	(2)	
6	Jeff Henderson	ENG	19/12/91	D	4		
2	Alan Keane		23/09/84	D	17		1
16	Lee Lynch		27/11/91	M	18	(10)	3
18	Liam Martin		23/01/94	A		(1)	
17	Mark McGoldrick		27/11/91	A		(1)	
20	Jason McGuinness		08/08/82	D	26		3
14	Pascal Millien	HAI	03/05/86	M	11	(9)	2
15	Joesph Ndo	CMR	28/04/76	M	24		1
27	Danny North	ENG	07/09/87	A	17		15
28	Martin Owens		12/02/93	D		(5)	
4	Gavin Peers		10/11/85	D	29		4
9	Mark Quigley		27/10/85	A	21	(4)	10
1	Gary Rogers		25/09/81	G	30		
5	Danny Ventre	ENG	23/01/86	M	26		

UNIVERSITY COLLEGE DUBLIN AFC

Manager: Martin Russell
1895 • UCD Bowl (2,500) • ucdsoccer.com
Major honours
FAI Cup (1) 1984

2012

02/03	Cork	h	1-0	Langtry
10/03	Sligo	a	1-2	O'Connor
16/03	Bray	h	2-3	Rusk 2 (2p)
23/03	Dundalk	a	1-2	Rusk (p)
30/03	Monaghan	h	3-2	Ledwith, Morrison, O'Conor (match annulled)
06/04	Derry	a	0-0	
13/04	Bohemians	h	1-2	Rusk (p)
20/04	St Patrick's	a	0-2	
27/04	Drogheda	h	1-1	Ledwith
04/05	Shamrock Rovers	a	2-2	Rusk (p), O'Conor
11/05	Shelbourne	h	0-2	
18/05	Cork	a	2-4	Rusk (p), O'Conor
21/05	Sligo	h	1-0	Rusk
01/06	Bray	a	1-3	Ledwith
22/06	Dundalk	h	1-1	Benson
06/07	Derry	h	0-1	
15/07	Bohemians	a	0-1	
22/07	St Patrick's	h	1-1	Benson
27/07	Drogheda	a	0-1	
03/08	Shamrock Rovers	h	0-2	
10/08	Shelbourne	a	2-1	McMillan, Corry
17/08	Cork	h	3-1	Leahy, og (O'Connell), Benson
20/08	Sligo	a	0-3	
31/08	Bray	h	3-1	McMillan (p), og (Quigley), Lyons
07/09	Dundalk	a	2-1	McMillan 2 (1p)
21/09	Derry	a	2-1	McCabe, McMillan
28/09	Bohemians	h	2-2	Ledwith, O'Conor
05/10	St Patrick's	a	0-5	
13/10	Drogheda	h	1-0	McMillan (p)
19/10	Shamrock Rovers	a	1-2	McMillan
26/10	Shelbourne	h	1-1	Douglas

No	Name	Nat	DoB	Pos	Aps	(s)	Gls
1	Ger Barron		03/06/89	G	9		
25	Samir Belhout		15/07/91	A	5	(7)	
10	Robbie Benson		07/05/92	A	28	(3)	3
12	Tomás Boyle		10/08/91	D		(1)	
9	Gary Burke		27/03/91	M	5	(8)	
21	Dean Clarke		29/03/93	M	12	(8)	
6	Paul Corry		03/02/91	M	17		1
13	Hugh Douglas		22/06/93	M	23	(2)	1
22	Stephen Doyle		04/07/91	M		(1)	
14	James Kavanagh		12/01/93	M	10	(7)	
28	John Kelly		24/12/91	G	2		
2	Mark Langtry		09/12/87	D	7	(8)	1
5	Michael Leahy		30/04/89	D	27	(1)	1
17	Danny Ledwith		17/08/91	M	25	(1)	4
26	Chris Lyons		08/05/93	A	13	(10)	1
18	Barry McCabe		12/01/92	M	7	(5)	1
16	Mark McGinley		26/03/90	G	20		
23	David McMillan		14/12/88	A	15		7
15	Tyrone McNelis		02/06/90	M	4	(3)	
27	Cillian Morrison		25/07/91	A	5	(4)	1
11	Chris Mulhall		09/02/88	M	10	(3)	
3	Ciaran Nangle		23/03/90	D	25	(1)	
4	David O'Connor		24/08/91	D	27		1
8	Paul O'Conor		10/08/87	M	31		4
9	Graham Rusk		13/12/89	A	13	(1)	7
19	Sean Russell		10/12/93	M	1	(4)	

NB Appearances and goals for all clubs include those from the annulled matches against Monaghan United FC.

Top goalscorers

22	Gary Twigg (Shamrock Rovers)
15	Danny North (Sligo)
14	Jason Byrne (Bray)
13	Declan O'Brien (Drogheda)
	Christy Fagan (St Patrick's)
12	Vinny Sullivan (Cork)
11	David McDaid (Derry)
	Philip Hughes (Shelbourne)
10	Stephen McLaughlin (Derry)
	Mark Quigley (Sligo)

Promoted club

LIMERICK FC

Manager: Pat Scully
1937 • Jackman Park (2,000) • limerickfc.ie
Major honours
League of Ireland (2) 1960, 1980;
FAI Cup (2) 1971, 1982

SECOND LEVEL FINAL TABLE 2012

		Pld	W	D	L	F	A	Pts
1	Limerick FC	28	20	2	6	51	20	6
2	Waterford United FC	28	18	4	6	46	29	58
3	Longford Town FC	28	15	5	8	42	33	50
3	FC Vitebsk	28	19	2	7	57	30	59
4	Wexford Youths FC	28	11	6	11	45	40	39
5	Finn Harps FC	28	10	6	12	40	43	36
6	Athlone Town FC	28	8	5	15	25	41	29
7	Mervue United FC	28	6	5	17	34	49	23
8	SD Galway FC	28	5	5	18	23	51	20

NB Salthill Devon FC renamed SD Galway FC prior to 2012 season.

PROMOTION/RELEGATION PLAY-OFFS

(20/10/12 & 26/10/12)
Longford 0-2 Waterford
Waterford 1-1 Longford
(Waterford 3-1)

(30/10/12 & 02/11/12)
Dundalk 2-2 Waterford
Waterford 0-2 Dundalk
(Dundalk 4-2)

Domestic cup: FAI Cup 2012

SECOND ROUND

(25/05/12)
Blarney 1-4 Malahide
Bohemians 5-0 Drumkeen
Bray 1-1 Shelbourne
Cork 6-1 Athlone
Derry 4-0 Finn Harps
Drogheda 6-1 Mayfield
Dundalk 1-0 St Patrick's CY
SD Galway 0-2 Mervue
Sligo 1-3 Monaghan
Shamrock Rovers 1-0 Limerick
UCD 3-1 Phoenix

(27/05/12)
Cherry Orchard 2-0 Longford
Crumlin 0-3 St Patrick's
Douglas Hall 1-1 Wexford
Everton 0-1 Waterford
Kildrum 1-3 Avondale

Replays
(28/05/12)
Shelbourne 1-0 Bray

(29/05/12)
Wexford 3-2 Douglas Hall

THIRD ROUND

(24/08/12)
Bohemians 1-0 Avondale
Drogheda 1-0 Wexford
Malahide 0-4 Dundalk
Shamrock Rovers 2-0 Cork
Shelbourne 3-2 Cherry Orchard
UCD 0-1 Derry

(03/09/12)
Waterford 0-4 Mervue

Bye - St Patrick's
NB: Monaghan withdrew before the third round; St Patrick's were awarded a bye

QUARTER-FINALS

(14/09/12)
Bohemians 0-1 Dundalk *(Griffin 75)*
Derry 7-1 Mervue *(McDaid 15, 56, Farren 35, 60, 61, P McEleney 40, Curran 77; Hoban 52)*
St Patrick's 0-0 Drogheda
Shelbourne 2-1 Shamrock Rovers *(Hughes 30, 71; Gannon 90+2)*

Replay
(17/09/12)
Drogheda 1-1 St Patrick's *(Prendergast 79; Faherty 90) (aet; 2-3 on pens)*

SEMI-FINALS

(07/10/12)
Derry 1-1 Shelbourne *(McDaid 58; Cassidy 5)*
Dundalk 0-3 St Patrick's *(Browne 20, Bolger 52, O'Connor 85)*

Replay
(10/10/12)
Shelbourne 0-3 Derry *(McLaughlin 44, 62, McDaid 68)*

FINAL

(04/11/12)
Aviva Stadium, Dublin
DERRY CITY FC 3 *(Greacen 55, Patterson 69p, 105)*
SAINT PATRICK'S ATHLETIC FC 2 *(O'Connor 53, Fagan 87)*
(aet)
Referee: *Doyle*
DERRY: Doherty, S McEleney, McCaffrey, Madden, Greacen (McBride 98), Molloy, McNamee (Higgins 81), McLaughlin, P McEleney (Patterson 59), Deery, McDaid
ST PATRICK'S: Clarke, Browne, Bermingham, Kenna, O'Brien (Flynn 105), Forrester, Chambers, Carroll (Russell 23), J Kelly (Faherty 46), O'Connor, Fagan

Joy for FAI Cup winners Derry

ROMANIA
Federaţia Română de Fotbal (FRF)

Address	Casa Fotbalului	**President**	Mircea Sandu
	Str. Serg. Serbanica	**General secretary**	Adalbert Kassai
	Vasile 12	**Media officer**	Paul-Daniel Zaharia
	RO-022186 Bucureşti	**Year of formation**	1909
Tel	+40 21 325 0678	**National stadium**	National Arena,
Fax	+40 21 325 0679		Bucharest (55,611)
E-mail	frf@frf.ro		
Website	frf.ro		

KEY:
● – UEFA Champions League
● – UEFA Europa League
● – Promoted clubs
○ – Relegated clubs

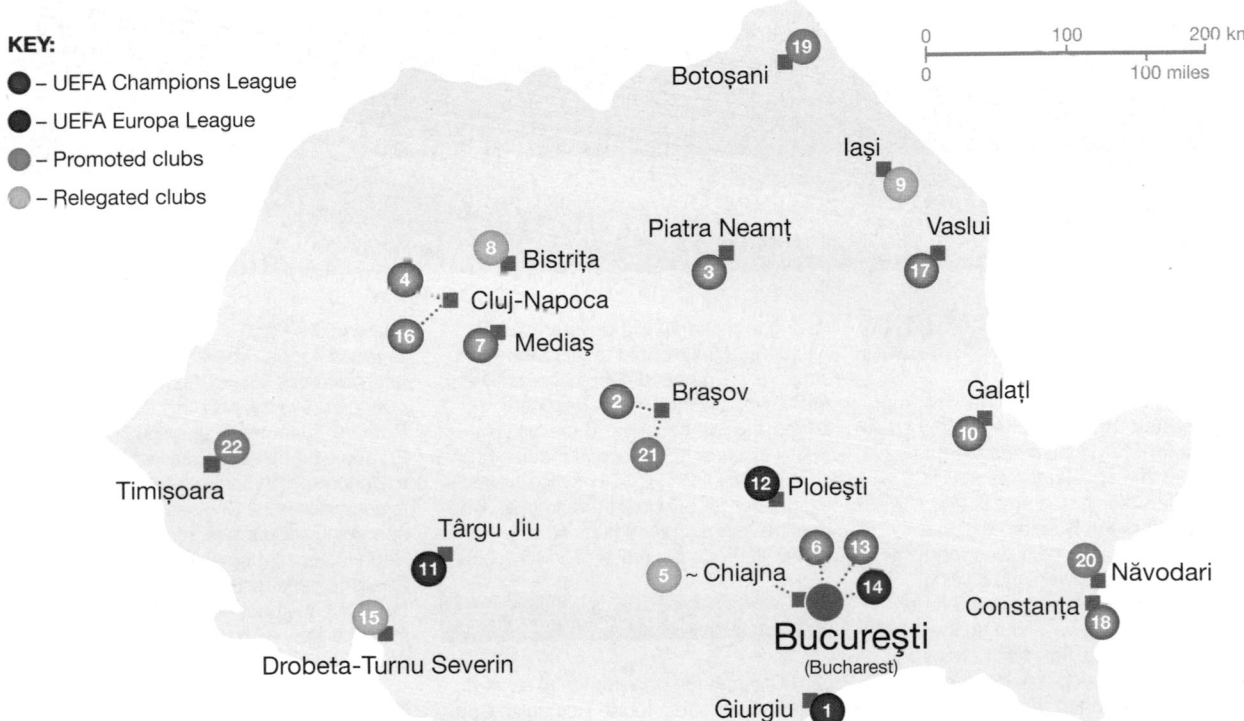

LIGA I CLUBS

 1 FC Astra

2 FC Braşov

3 FC Ceahlăul Piatra Neamţ

4 CFR 1907 Cluj

5 CS Concordia Chiajna

6 FC Dinamo Bucureşti

7 CS Gaz Metan Mediaş

8 ACF Gloria 1922 Bistriţa

9 CSMS Iaşi

10 FC Oţelul Galaţi

11 CS Pandurii Târgu Jiu

12 FC Petrolul Ploieşti

13 FC Rapid Bucureşti

14 FC Steaua Bucureşti

15 CS Turnu Severin

16 FC Universitatea Cluj

17 FC Vaslui

18 FC Viitorul Constanţa

PROMOTED CLUBS

19 FC Botoşani

20 AFC Săgeata Năvodari

21 ASC Corona 2010 Braşov

22 ACS Poli Timişoara

Steaua storm back to power

FC Steaua Bucureşti ended a seven-year wait for the Liga I title with an emphatic triumph in 2012/13. Impressive also in Europe under new coach Laurenţiu Reghecampf, they blitzed their way to domestic glory, finishing with a 16-point winning margin and scoring 74 goals, the league's highest total for 13 years.

Although no other club could live with Steaua, it was a memorable campaign for the three teams that finished directly beneath them in the table, with CS Pandurii Târgu Jiu and FC Astra qualifying for a first crack at European football and FC Petrolul Ploieşti winning the Romanian Cup.

Runaway Liga I triumph for record champions	Petrolul defeat CFR Cluj to win Romanian Cup	First European qualification for Pandurii and Astra

Domestic league

The arrival of former player Reghecampf reinvigorated Steaua after a lengthy spell in the doldrums. His first league game was a 1-0 win against former club CS Concordia Chiajna, the first of 24 three-pointers the Bucharest giants would post over the next ten months as they returned to power with a bang. Having hit the front in mid-September, they accelerated away, leaving the other 17 teams for dead. Ten points ahead at the winter break with a perfect record at home, they stretched their lead in the spring and celebrated their record 24th title with five matches to spare, winning 2-0 at home to Pandurii, the early leaders who would eventually finish second.

Steaua found goals easy to come by and boasted the league's top scorer in Raul Rusescu (21). Operating chiefly as the team's lone striker, he found strong support in attack from Cristian Tănase and Adi Sobrinho, while elsewhere there were excellent contributions from centre-back Vlad Chircheş, left-back Iasmin Latovlevici and midfield linchpin Alexandru Bourceanu. Pandurii changed coach in mid-season, with Cristian Pustai replacing Petre Grigoraş, but both men deserved praise for steering the club to their highest league position, Pustai

having to make do without star player Alexandru Maxim, sold to VfB Stuttgart in January. A European debut also beckoned Astra, who finished fourth despite employing five coaches. There was no return to Europe, however, for defending champions CFR 1907 Cluj, who finished eighth, nor for FC Dinamo Bucureşti, who thus missed out on continental competition for the first time in 15 years.

Domestic cup

CFR Cluj had the opportunity to salvage their season with a fourth Romanian Cup win in seven years, but instead it was Petrolul, third in the league, who captured the trophy for the first time since 1995 and third in all. They took the honours in the Naţional Arena thanks to a solitary early strike from regular marksman Jeremy Bokila, who, with 16 goals, was the second highest scorer in Liga I.

Europe

Cluj had a fine season in Europe. They qualified for the UEFA Champions League group stage with a play-off win over FC Basel 1893 and claimed ten points, finishing off with a famous 1-0 win over Manchester United FC at Old Trafford. That was only enough for third place, however,

and a mid-season cross-over to the UEFA Europa League, where they lost to FC Internazionale Milano, FC Vaslui's conquerors in the play-offs. Steaua were Romania's last team standing, their UEFA Europa League adventure lasting 14 matches and ending at the home of the eventual winners, Chelsea FC, after two absorbing encounters, the first of which Reghecampf's men won 1-0 with a Rusescu penalty. Spot-kicks had also taken Steaua past AFC Ajax in the previous round as they won the UEFA Europa League's first ever penalty shoot-out.

National team

Despite two heavy defeats by the Netherlands, Romania's hopes of reaching the 2014 FIFA World Cup qualifying play-offs remained intact going into their final four fixtures thanks to two excellent away results in Turkey and Hungary. Petrolul's Gheorghe Grozav, a rising star in midfield alongside Gabriel Torje, scored the only goal in Istanbul and Steaua's Alexandru Chipciu grabbed an added-time equaliser in Budapest to earn a potentially decisive 2-2 draw. Coach Victor Piţurcă selected heavily from Steaua but also recalled Adrian Mutu, whose penalty in Budapest was his 35th international goal, matching the national record set by the great Gheorghe Hagi.

Domestic league: Liga I 2012/13 final table

		Pld	Home					Away					Total					Pts
			W	D	L	F	A	W	D	L	F	A	W	D	L	F	A	
1	FC Steaua Bucureşti	34	15	1	1	41	12	9	6	2	33	17	24	7	3	74	20	79
2	CS Pandurii Târgu Jiu	34	11	4	2	40	20	8	2	7	17	23	19	6	9	57	43	63
3	FC Petrolul Ploieşti	34	10	6	1	35	12	6	8	3	25	22	16	14	4	60	34	62
4	FC Astra	34	10	5	2	42	20	7	4	6	22	17	17	9	8	64	37	60
5	FC Vaslui	34	12	5	0	33	12	4	5	8	17	22	16	10	8	50	34	58
6	FC Dinamo Bucureşti	34	10	2	5	30	19	6	6	5	18	21	16	8	10	48	40	56
7	FC Braşov	34	11	3	3	30	16	3	6	8	20	35	14	9	11	50	51	51
8	CFR 1907 Cluj	34	5	6	6	28	21	7	7	3	28	18	12	13	9	56	39	49
9	FC Rapid Bucureşti	34	8	4	5	23	20	5	6	6	12	15	13	10	11	35	35	49
10	CS Gaz Metan Mediaş	34	8	5	4	26	18	4	5	8	16	28	12	10	12	42	46	46
11	FC Oţelul Galaţi	34	7	5	5	19	17	4	5	8	19	25	11	10	13	38	42	41
12	FC Universitatea Cluj	34	6	3	8	20	25	4	5	8	19	30	10	8	16	39	55	38
13	FC Viitorul Constanţa	34	3	6	8	19	24	5	4	8	26	33	8	12	14	45	57	36
14	FC Ceahlăul Piatra Neamţ	34	9	3	5	25	20	0	4	13	16	39	9	7	18	41	59	34
15	CS Concordia Chiajna	34	3	8	6	12	22	4	4	9	17	27	7	12	15	29	49	33
16	CS Turnu Severin	34	5	7	5	20	20	2	4	11	16	27	7	11	16	36	47	32
17	CSMS Iaşi	34	4	3	10	16	23	3	2	12	15	27	7	5	22	31	50	26
18	ACF Gloria 1922 Bistriţa	34	2	7	8	11	25	1	2	14	10	44	3	9	22	21	69	18

NB: FC Oţelul Galaţi – 2 pts deducted

SEASON AT A GLANCE

EUROPEAN QUALIFICATION 2013/14

Champion: FC Steaua Bucureşti (second qualifying round)

Cup winner: FC Petrolul Ploieşti (second qualifying round)
CS Pandurii Târgu Jiu (second qualifying round)
FC Astra (first qualifying round)

Top scorer   Raul Rusescu (Steaua), 21 goals

Relegated clubs   ACF Gloria 1922 Bistriţa, CSMS Iaşi, CS Turnu Severin, CS Concordia Chiajna

Promoted clubs   FC Botoşani, AFC Săgeata Năvodari, ASC Corona 2010 Braşov, ACS Poli Timişoara

Cup final   FC Petrolul Ploieşti 1-0 CFR 1907 Cluj

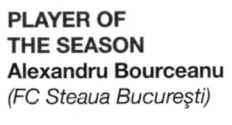

PLAYER OF THE SEASON
Alexandru Bourceanu
(FC Steaua Bucureşti)

A natural leader of men, the 28-year-old Steaua captain was a pivotal figure in both the team's Liga I triumph and their extended run in Europe. A regular figure also at international level for Romania, the midfielder had a busy season, but despite the heavy workload he was invariably influential and never less than fully committed

NEWCOMER OF THE SEASON
Gabriel Iancu
(FC Steaua Bucureşti)

The Bucharest-born 19-year-old rose through the ranks at the Gheorghe Hagi Academy and joined Steaua from FC Viitorul Constanţa in January. A tricky, adventurous left-winger with an eye for goal, the Romanian Under-21 international signed a five-year contract with Steaua, but his talent seems bound to draw interest from Europe's elite.

LIGA I TEAM OF THE SEASON
(4-4-2)
Coach: Reghecampf *(Steaua)*

Mário Felgueiras *(CFR Cluj)*

Măţel *(Astra)* — Chiricheş *(Steaua)* — Viera *(Pandurii)* — Latovlevici *(Steaua)*

Chipciu *(Steaua)* — Bourceanu *(Steaua)* — Nistor *(Pandurii)* — Alexe *(Dinamo)*

Rusescu *(Steaua)* — Bokila *(Petrolul)*

ROMANIA

NATIONAL TEAM

Home Kit

Away Kit

INTERNATIONAL TOURNAMENT APPEARANCES
FIFA World Cup (7) 1930, 1934, 1938, 1970, 1990 (2nd round), 1994 (qtr-finals), 1998 (2nd round)
UEFA European Championship (4) 1984, 1996, 2000 (qtr-finals), 2008.

TOP FIVE ALL-TIME CAPS
Dorinel Munteanu (134); Gheorghe Hagi (124); Gheorghe Popescu (115); László Bölöni (102); Dan Petrescu (95)

TOP FIVE ALL-TIME GOALS
Gheorghe Hagi & **Adrian Mutu** (35); Iuliu Bodola (30); Viorel Moldovan (25); László Bölöni (23)

Results 2012/13

Date	Opponent		Venue	Score	Scorers
15/08/12	Slovenia	A	Ljubljana	3-4	Papp (56), Torje (68p), Grozav (80)
07/09/12	Estonia (WCQ)	A	Tallinn	2-0	Torje (55), Marica (75)
11/09/12	Andorra (WCQ)	H	Bucharest	4-0	Torje (29), Lazăr (44), Găman (90+1), Maxim (90+3)
12/10/12	Turkey (WCQ)	A	Istanbul	1-0	Grozav (45+1)
16/10/12	Netherlands (WCQ)	H	Bucharest	1-4	Marica (40)
14/11/12	Belgium	H	Bucharest	2-1	Maxim (32), Torje (66p)
06/02/13	Australia	N	Malaga (ESP)	3-2	Tănase (34), Stancu (79), Torje (83)
22/03/13	Hungary (WCQ)	A	Budapest	2-2	Mutu (68p), Chipciu (90+2)
26/03/13	Netherlands (WCQ)	A	Amsterdam	0-4	
04/06/13	Trinidad & Tobago	H	Bucharest	4-0	Marica (31, 33, 81), Cyrus (49og)

Appearances 2012/13

Coach: Victor Piţurcă 08/05/56			Svn	EST	AND	TUR	NED	Bel	Aus	HUN	NED	Tri	Caps	Goals
Bogdan Lobonţ	18/01/78	Roma (ITA)	G	G	G46							G	83	-
Paul Papp	11/11/89	Chievo (ITA)	D74										11	1
Valerică Găman	25/02/89	Astra	D46	s92	D			D46				D	11	1
Vlad Chiricheş	14/11/89	Steaua	D	D	D	D	D	D61	D	D	D		18	-
Răzvan Raţ	26/05/81	Shakhtar Donetsk (UKR)	D80	D	D	D	D		D46		D	D	89	1
Răzvan Cociş	19/02/83	Rostov (RUS)	M			s50							49	2
Costin Lazăr	24/04/81	PAOK (GRE)	M46	M66	M		s61	s46	s56			M65	25	1
Gabriel Torje	22/11/89	Granada (ESP)	M	M	M	M	M66	s46	M89	M66	s63	M	28	9
Cristian Tănase	18/02/87	Steaua	M	M	M80			s46	M71		M60		27	5
Bogdan Stancu	28/06/87	Orduspor (TUR)	M46			M82	M	s46	A	M	A	M81	22	3
Ciprian Marica	02/10/85	Schalke (GER)	A65	A85	A54	A79	A	A				A	61	21
Gabriel Tamaş	09/11/83	West Brom (ENG)	s46			D	D		D	D	D		63	3
Alexandru Bourceanu	24/04/85	Steaua	s46	M	M	M	M61	s46	M56	M	M		20	-
Gheorghe Grozav	29/09/90	Petrolul	s46	M	M	M50	M75	M46	M62	M71	M68	s46	12	3
Marius Niculae	16/05/81	Vaslui	s65	s85									43	15
Srdjan Luchin	04/03/86	Dinamo Bucureşti	s74					s61	s84			s46	8	1
Iasmin Latovlevici	11/05/86	Steaua	s80					D69					6	-
Alexandru Măţel	17/10/89	Astra		D	D							D46	5	-
Dorin Goian	12/12/80	Spezia (ITA)		D92		D	D	s46	D84	D		D46	52	5
Mihai Pintilii	09/11/84	Steaua		s66		M	M	M46	M	M86	M		12	-
Ciprian Tătăruşanu	09/02/86	Steaua			s46	G	G	G	G				17	-
Raul Rusescu	09/07/88	Steaua			s54				s71				2	-
Alexandru Maxim	08/07/90	Pandurii /Stuttgart (GER)			s80			M46	s71	s66			6	2
Alexandru Chipciu	18/05/89	Steaua				s79		M46		s86	s60		9	2
Adrian Mutu	08/01/79	Ajaccio (FRA)				s82	s75		A	s68			77	35
Adrian Popa	24/07/88	Steaua				s66					M63		2	-
Florin Gardoş	29/10/88	Steaua						D			D		9	-
Dan Nistor	06/05/88	Pandurii						M46				s65	2	-
Ştefan Radu	22/10/86	Lazio (ITA)						s69	s46	D			14	-
Costel Pantilimon	01/02/87	Man. City (ENG)							G		G		16	-
Marius Alexe	22/02/90	Dinamo Bucureşti							s62				7	-
Aurelian Chiţu	25/03/91	Viitorul							s89			M46	2	-
Nicolae Grigore	19/07/83	Rapid Bucureşti										M46	4	-
Dragoş Grigore	07/09/86	Dinamo Bucureşti										s46	3	-
Ovidiu Hoban	27/12/82	Petrolul										s46	1	-
Adrian Stoian	11/02/91	Chievo (ITA)										s81	1	-

European club competitions 2012/13

CFR 1907 CLUJ

Third qualifying round - FC Slovan Liberec (CZE)
H 1-0 *Cadú (53p)*
Mário Felgueiras, Ivo Pinto, Mureşan (Sare 46), Deac, Kapetanos, Rafael Bastos (Diogo Valente 80), Vass (Edimar 77), Cadú, Rada, Camora, Modou Sougou. Coach: Ioan Andone (ROU)
A 2-1 *Kapetanos (45+1), Modou Sougou (90+4)*
Mário Felgueiras, Ivo Pinto, Sare, Kapetanos, Rafael Bastos (Mureşan 61), Vass (Ronny 78), Cadú, Rada, Camora, Edimar (Nicoară 83), Modou Sougou. Coach: Ioan Andone (ROU)

Play-offs - FC Basel 1893 (SUI)
A 2-1 *Modou Sougou (66, 71)*
Mário Felgueiras, Ivo Pinto, Sare, Kapetanos (Ronny 50), Rafael Bastos, Cadú, Godemèche (Mureşan 67), Rada, Rui Pedro (Nicoară 72), Camora, Modou Sougou. Coach: Ioan Andone (ROU)
H 1-0 *Kapetanos (20)*
Mário Felgueiras, Ivo Pinto, Sare (Godemèche 51), Mureşan, Kapetanos (Rui Pedro 82), Diogo Valente (Nicoară 73), Rafael Bastos, Cadú, Rada, Camora, Modou Sougou. Coach: Ioan Andone (ROU)

Group H
Match 1 - SC Braga (POR)
A 2-0 *Rafael Bastos (19, 34)*
Mário Felgueiras, Ivo Pinto, Mureşan, Sepsi, Kapetanos, Rafael Bastos (Rui Pedro 79), Cadú, Rada, Luís Alberto (Godemèche 65), Camora, Modou Sougou (Aguirregaray 46). Coach: Ioan Andone (ROU)
Match 2 - Manchester United FC (ENG)
H 1-2 *Kapetanos (14)*
Mário Felgueiras, Ivo Pinto, Mureşan, Sepsi, Kapetanos (Bjelanović 61), Rafael Bastos, Cadú, Rada, Aguirregaray (Nicoară 80), Camora, Modou Sougou (Luís Alberto 24). Coach: Ioan Andone (ROU)
Match 3 - Galatasaray AŞ (TUR)
A 1-1 *Nounkeu (19og)*
Mário Felgueiras, Ivo Pinto, Sepsi (Rada 53), Kapetanos (Mureşan 78), Piccolo, Rafael Bastos (Nicoară 72), Cadú, Godemèche, Luís Alberto, Aguirregaray, Camora. Coach: Ioan Andone (ROU)
Red card: Aguirregaray 28

Match 4 - Galatasaray AŞ (TUR)
H 1-3 *Modou Sougou (53)*
Mário Felgueiras, Ivo Pinto, Mureşan, Sepsi (Rafael Bastos 31), Kapetanos (Diogo Valente 77), Piccolo, Cadú, Godemèche (Bjelanović 46), Luís Alberto, Camora, Modou Sougou. Coach: Paulo Sérgio (POR)
Match 5 - SC Braga (POR)
H 3-1 *Rui Pedro (7, 15, 33)*
Mário Felgueiras, Ivo Pinto, Mureşan, Piccolo, Rafael Bastos (Godemèche 83), Cadú, Rada, Luís Alberto, Rui Pedro (Kapetanos 81), Camora, Modou Sougou (Aguirregaray 74). Coach: Paulo Sérgio (POR)
Match 6 - Manchester United FC (ENG)
A 1-0 *Luís Alberto (56)*
Mário Felgueiras, Ivo Pinto, Mureşan, Piccolo, Rafael Bastos (Maftei 78), Cadú, Rada, Luís Alberto, Rui Pedro (Aguirregaray 71), Camora, Modou Sougou (Kapetanos 90+2). Coach: Paulo Sérgio (POR)

Round of 32 - FC Internazionale Milano (ITA)
A 0-2
Mário Felgueiras, Ivo Pinto, Mureşan, Sepsi, Piccolo, Maah (Hora 79), Cadú, Godemèche (Maftei 39), Rada, Rui Pedro (Bjelanović 84), Camora. Coach: Paulo Sérgio (POR)
H 0-3
Mário Felgueiras, Ivo Pinto, Mureşan (Hora 9), Sepsi, Piccolo, Maah, Cadú, Godemèche, Rada (Kapetanos 36), Rui Pedro (Diogo Valente 71), Camora. Coach: Paulo Sérgio (POR)
Red card: Camora 80

FC VASLUI

Third qualifying round - Fenerbahçe SK (TUR)
A 1-1 *Antal (75)*
Coman, Varela, Antal (Buhăescu 88), Stanciu (Sburlea 60), Cauê, Sânmărtean, Milanov, Sălăgeanu, Niculae (Costin 81), Charalambous, N'Doye. Coach: Marius Şumudică (ROU)
H 1-4 *Niculae (14)*
Coman, Varela, Antal (Zsiga 83), Stanciu, Cauê (Sburlea 74), Sânmărtean, Milanov, Sălăgeanu, Niculae, Charalambous, N'Doye (Costin 79). Coach: Marius Şumudică (ROU)

Play-offs - FC Internazionale Milano (ITA)
H 0-2
Coman, Varela, Celeban (Cauê 73), Antal, Stanciu (Varga 46), Sânmărtean, Milanov, Sălăgeanu, Niculae (Sburlea 61), Charalambous, N'Doye. Coach: Marius Şumudică (ROU)
A 2-2 *Stanciu (35p), Varela (79)*
Straton, Varela, Celeban, Antal, Sburlea, Stanciu (Buhăescu 78), Cauê (Sânmărtean 58), Sălăgeanu, Tukura, Cordoş, N'Doye. Coach: Marius Şumudică (ROU)

ROMANIA

FC DINAMO BUCUREŞTI

Play-offs - FC Metalist Kharkiv (UKR)
H 0-2
Bălgrădean, Pulhac, Matei, Munteanu (Axente 78), Alexe (Curtean 66), Ba (Galchev 60), Mansaly, Grigore, Luchin, Țucudean, Koulibaly. Coach: Dario Bonetti (ITA)
A 1-2 *Curtean (52)*
Bălgrădean, Nica, Matei, Munteanu, Galchev (Filip 46), Mansaly (Dănciulescu 71), Curtean, Grigore, Luchin, Țucudean (Alexe 46), Koulibaly. Coach: Dario Bonetti (ITA)
Red card: Filip 82

FC STEAUA BUCUREŞTI

Third qualifying round - FC Spartak Trnava (SVK)
H 0-1
Tătăruşanu, Pintilii, Gardoş, Chipciu, Tănase, Latovlevici (M Costea 46), Georgievski (Bălan 62), Chiricheş, Rusescu, Bourceanu, Nikolić (Adi Sobrinho 46). Coach: Laurențiu Reghecampf (ROU)
Red card: Tănase 81
A 3-0 *Adi Sobrinho (8), Rusescu (77), Nikolić (84)*
Stanca, Pintilii, Gardoş, Chipciu, Georgievski, Chiricheş, Pârvulescu, Rusescu (Bălan 89), F Costea (Latovlevici 80), Bourceanu, Adi Sobrinho (Nikolić 60). Coach: Laurențiu Reghecampf (ROU)

Play-offs - FK Ekranas (LTU)
A 2-0 *Martinović (36), Popa (76)*
Stanca, Pintilii, Chipciu (Rusescu 57), M Costea, Latovlevici, Georgievski, Martinović, Chiricheş, Bourceanu (Filip 53), Popa, Nikolić (Adi Sobrinho 62). Coach: Laurențiu Reghecampf (ROU)

H 3-0 *Adi Sobrinho (21, 86), Dumitraş (31)*
Tătăruşanu, Pintilii, Gardoş, Chipciu (Prepeliță 46), Filip, Latovlevici, Martinović (Puşcaş 57), Dumitraş, Rusescu (M Costea 46), Popa, Adi Sobrinho. Coach: Laurențiu Reghecampf (ROU)

Group E
Match 1 - VfB Stuttgart (GER)
A 2-2 *Chipciu (6), Rusescu (80p)*
Tătăruşanu, Szukała, Chipciu, Filip (Rusescu 46), Prepeliță (Pintilii 46), Georgievski, Chiricheş, Pârvulescu (Latovlevici 81), Bourceanu, Popa, Nikolić. Coach: Laurențiu Reghecampf (ROU)
Match 2 - FC København (DEN)
H 1-0 *Sigurdsson (83og)*
Tătăruşanu, Matei (Rusescu 64), Pintilii, Gardoş, Tănase, Prepeliță (Chipciu 46), Chiricheş, Pârvulescu, Bourceanu, Popa, Adi Sobrinho (Nikolić 46). Coach: Laurențiu Reghecampf (ROU)
Match 3 - Molde FK (NOR)
H 2-0 *Chiricheş (30), Rusescu (32)*
Tătăruşanu, Szukała, Pintilii (Bălan 64), Chipciu, Tănase, Latovlevici, Georgievski, Chiricheş, Rusescu (Popa 46), Bourceanu, Adi Sobrinho (M Costea 55). Coach: Laurențiu Reghecampf (ROU)
Match 4 - Molde FK (NOR)
A 2-1 *Chipciu (21), Latovlevici (37)*
Tătăruşanu, Szukała, Gardoş, Chipciu, M Costea, Tănase, Prepeliță (Pintilii 70), Chiricheş, Pârvulescu (Latovlevici 16), Bourceanu, Adi Sobrinho (Nikolić 56). Coach: Laurențiu Reghecampf (ROU)
Match 5 - VfB Stuttgart (GER)
H 1-5 *M Costea (83)*
Tătăruşanu, Szukała, Pintilii (Prepeliță 58), Gardoş (M Costea 32), Chipciu, Tănase (Adi Sobrinho 62), Latovlevici, Chiricheş, Rusescu, Bourceanu, Popa. Coach: Laurențiu Reghecampf (ROU)
Match 6 - FC København (DEN)
A 1-1 *Rusescu (72)*
Tătăruşanu, Pintilii, Gardoş, Chipciu, Tănase, Latovlevici, Chiricheş, Rusescu (Filip 85), Bourceanu, Popa (Prepeliță 88), Nikolić (Martinović 62). Coach: Laurențiu Reghecampf (ROU)
Red card: Tănase 49

Round of 32 - AFC Ajax (NED)
A 0-2
Tătăruşanu, Pintilii, Gardoş, Chipciu, Latovlevici, Râpă, Chiricheş, Rusescu (Adi Sobrinho 70), Bourceanu, Popa (M Costea 82), Nikolić (Leandro Tatu 53). Coach: Laurențiu Reghecampf (ROU)
Red card: Pintilii 90
H 2-0 *Latovlevici (38), Chiricheş (76) (aet; 4-2 on pens)*
Tătăruşanu, Gardoş, Chipciu, Tănase (Nikolić 66), Prepeliță (Filip 46), Latovlevici, Râpă, Leandro Tatu (Pârvulescu 77), Chiricheş, Rusescu, Popa. Coach: Laurențiu Reghecampf (ROU)

Round of 16 - Chelsea FC (ENG)
H 1-0 *Rusescu (34p)*
Tătăruşanu, Szukała, Pintilii (Prepeliță 58), Chipciu, Tănase (Leandro Tatu 82), Latovlevici, Râpă, Chiricheş, Rusescu (Gardoş 90+2), Bourceanu, Popa. Coach: Laurențiu Reghecampf (ROU)
A 1-3 *Chiricheş (45+1)*
Tătăruşanu, Szukała, Pintilii, Chipciu, Tănase (Leandro Tatu 78), Latovlevici, Râpă (Adi Sobrinho 84), Chiricheş, Rusescu, Bourceanu, Popa. Coach: Laurențiu Reghecampf (ROU)

FC RAPID BUCUREŞTI

Second qualifying round - Myllykosken Pallo-47 (FIN)
H 3-1 *Filipe Teixeira (8), Grigore (40), Pancu (45)*
Albuț, Rui Duarte, Abrudan, Milisavljević, Grigore, Pancu, Roman (Goga 57), Oros, Grigorie (Ilijoski 46), Surdu, Filipe Teixeira (Voicu 72). Coach: Ioan Ovidiu Sabău (ROU)
A 2-0 *Surdu (19), Ilijoski (42)*
Albuț, Rui Duarte (Coman 73), Abrudan, Milisavljević, Ilijoski (Božović 46), Oros, Grigorie, Goga, Surdu, Voicu, Filipe Teixeira (Ciolacu 66). Coach: Ioan Ovidiu Sabău (ROU)

Third qualifying round - sc Heerenveen (NED)
A 0-4
Albuț, Rui Duarte, Milisavljević (Filipe Teixeira 58), Grigore, Ilijoski (Goga 63), Roman (Ciolacu 76), Oros, Božović, Grigorie, Surdu, Constantin. Coach: Ioan Ovidiu Sabău (ROU)
H 1-0 *Herea (20p)*
Albuț, Rui Duarte (Goga 48), Herea (Milisavljević 73), Roman, Oros, Ciolacu (Ilijoski 46), Božović, Grigorie, Surdu, Gláuber, Filipe Teixeira. Coach: Ioan Ovidiu Sabău (ROU)

Domestic league club-by-club

FC ASTRA

Coach: Bogdan Stelea;
(14/08/12) Gheorghe Mulțescu;
(29/10/12) Valentin Sinescu; (06/04/13) Marin Barbu;
(14/04/13) Daniel Isăilă
1937 • Marin Anastasovici (7,000);
Astra, Ploiesti (7,000) • fcastraploiesti.ro

2012

22/07	Gloria	a	2-1	Fatai 2
28/07	Steaua	h	3-4	Enache 2, Júnior Morais
05/08	Viitorul	a	0-0	
10/08	Turnu Severin	h	1-1	Bukari
20/08	Brașov	a	2-1	Găman, Fatai
27/08	Concordia	h	6-3	og (Belica), Ivanovski 3, Fatai 2 (1p)
02/09	Dinamo	h	1-0	Tembo
17/09	U Cluj	a	3-1	Seto, Budescu 2
23/09	Gaz Metan	h	4-0	Distéfano, Dudescu, Tembo, Seto
01/10	Ceahlăul	a	2-3	Júnior Morais 2
08/10	Vaslui	h	1-1	Tembo
20/10	Oțelul	a	1-2	Fatai
26/10	Iași	h	1-0	Bukari
05/11	Rapid	a	2-0	Tembo 2
10/11	Petrolul	h	1-1	Seto
16/11	CFR Cluj	a	2-0	Budescu, Ivanovski
25/11	Pandurii	h	4-1	Seto, Mureșan, Budescu, Fatai
03/12	Gloria	h	4-0	Fatai, Distéfano 2, Dudescu
10/12	Steaua	a	0-2	

2013

25/02	Viitorul	h	2-0	Budescu, Fatai
04/03	Turnu Severin	a	0-0	
09/03	Brașov	h	3-0	Budescu, Seto, Fatai
15/03	Concordia	a	2-0	Tembo (p), Găman
31/03	Dinamo	a	0-1	
05/04	U Cluj	h	1-2	Budescu (p)
12/04	Gaz Metan	a	1-2	Budescu
21/04	Ceahlăul	h	4-2	Fatai 2, Ben Youssef, Bukari
27/04	Vaslui	a	1-2	Budescu (p)
04/05	Oțelul	h	0-0	
09/05	Iași	a	2-0	Budescu, Ivanovski
12/05	Rapid	h	3-2	Seto, Yahaya, Bukari
18/05	Petrolul	a	1-1	Ben Youssef
26/05	CFR Cluj	h	3-3	Fatai 2, Seto
29/05	Pandurii	a	1-1	Bukari

No	Name	Nat	DoB	Pos	Aps	(s)	Gls
20	Ștefan Bărboianu		24/01/88	D	14	(6)	
3	Selim Ben Djemia	TUN	29/01/89	D	4	(1)	
5	Syam Ben Youssef	TUN	31/03/89	D	17	(6)	2
20	Constantin Budescu		19/02/89	A	22	(4)	12
19	Sadat Bukari	GHA	12/04/89	A	3	(13)	5
11	David Distéfano	ARG	10/07/87	M	22	(5)	3
9	Gabriel Enache		18/08/90	M	19	(7)	3
21	Kehinde Fatai	NGA	07/09/90	A	30	(3)	14
33	George Florescu		21/05/84	M	5	(1)	
12	George Gavrilaș		15/12/90	G	4	(1)	
25	Valerică Găman		25/02/89	D	26	(1)	2
23	Alexandru Giurgiu		25/09/92	D		(1)	
22	Mirko Ivanovski	MKD	31/10/89	A	14	(14)	5
13	Júnior Morais	BRA	22/07/86	D	32	(1)	3
32	Marián Kello	SVK	05/09/82	G	1	(1)	
55	Omri Kende	ISR	07/06/86	D		(1)	
1	Silviu Lung jr		04/06/89	G	29		
77	Alexandru Mățel		17/10/89	D	17	(4)	
29	Cristian Melinte		09/05/88	D	4	(2)	
27	Andrei Mureșan		01/08/85	M	26	(1)	1
8	Takayuki Seto	JPN	05/02/86	M	32	(1)	7
7	Fwayo Tembo	ZAM	02/05/89	M	21	(5)	6
14	Daniel Vădrariu		25/06/90	A	1	(3)	
91	William	BRA	15/12/91	M	10	(11)	
6	Seidu Yahaya	GHA	31/12/89	M	21	(4)	1

FC BRAȘOV

Coach: Ionuț Badea; (22/09/12) (Adrian Szabo);
(10/10/12) Sorin Cârțu; (12/11/12) Adrian Szabo
1937 • Silviu Ploeșteanu (12,670) • fcbrasov.ro

2012

23/07	Viitorul	a	2-2	Buga 2
27/07	Turnu Severin	h	2-1	Buga, I Popa
06/00	Dinamo	h	2-2	Batin, Buga
13/08	Concordia	a	1-2	Hadnagy
20/08	Astra	h	1-2	Munteanu (p)
25/08	U Cluj	a	1-1	Păun
01/09	Gaz Metan	h	3-1	I Popa 2, Batin
14/09	Ceahlăul	a	1-2	Bruno Madeira
23/09	Vaslui	h	2-1	I Popa, Batin
30/09	Oțelul	a	0-0	
08/10	Iași	h	1-0	Munteanu
19/10	Rapid	a	2-1	Buga, Ionescu
26/10	Petrolul	h	0-1	
03/11	CFR Cluj	a	0-5	
11/11	Pandurii	h	0-1	
16/11	Gloria	a	1-1	Ricardo Machado
26/11	Steaua	h	3-1	Batin (p), Păun, Buga (p)
01/12	Viitorul	h	3-1	Mateiu, Buga (p), Păun
10/12	Turnu Severin	a	1-2	Tameș

2013

24/02	Dinamo	a	1-2	Păun
04/03	Concordia	h	3-2	Buga, Oltean, Batin
09/03	Astra	a	0-3	
18/03	U Cluj	h	0-0	
29/03	Gaz Metan	a	0-0	
05/04	Ceahlăul	h	1-0	Mateiu
15/04	Vaslui	a	1-1	Danquah
22/04	Oțelul	h	3-2	Buga, Ricardo Machado, Păun
29/04	Iași	a	2-1	Tătar, Ricardo Machado
04/05	Rapid	h	2-0	Buga, Batin
08/05	Petrolul	a	4-6	Batin 2, I Popa, Mateiu
13/05	CFR Cluj	h	0-0	
18/05	Pandurii	a	3-2	Tătar, I Popa, Ricardo Machado
24/05	Gloria	h	4-1	Enceanu 2, Buga, Ricardo Machado
28/05	Steaua	a	0-4	

No	Name	Nat	DoB	Pos	Aps	(s)	Gls
3	Radu Barbu		29/08/89	D		(1)	
10	Paul Batin		29/06/87	A	24	(5)	8
9	Ciprian Brata		24/03/91	M	2	(7)	
26	Bruno Madeira	POR	17/09/84	M	25	(1)	1
29	Mugurel Buga		16/12/77	A	26	(3)	11
4	Alin Damian		11/04/94	A		(1)	
89	Frank Danquah	GHA	14/10/89	M	2	(4)	1
21	Alexandru David		15/06/91	D	6	(3)	
21	Davide Dias		12/04/83	M	12	(2)	
55	Florin Dumbravă		19/02/95	D		(1)	
20	Rareș Enceanu		05/08/94	M	1	(5)	2
27	Ayhan Guclu	TUR	28/03/90	A		(2)	
80	Attila Hadnagy		08/09/80	A	1	(10)	1
12	Cristian Ionescu		01/03/78	D	25		1
5	Florin Lazăr		15/01/80	D	4	(1)	
30	Andrei Marinescu		11/02/85	G	5		
8	Alexandru Mateiu		10/12/89	M	28	(2)	3
5	Șerban Moraru		09/02/86	D	2	(4)	
17	Cristian Munteanu		17/10/80	D	27		2
13	Daniel Mutu		11/09/87	G	13	(1)	
5	Menassel Nasser	FRA	06/01/83	D	5	(1)	
16	Nuno Viveiros	POR	22/06/83	M	25	(4)	
17	Vasile Olariu		22/07/87	M	2	(3)	
6	Sergiu Oltean		24/07/87	D	11		1
14	Georgian Păun		24/10/85	A	6	(18)	5
14	Dorin Popa		29/11/88	M		(1)	
7	Iulian Popa		20/07/84	M	27	(2)	6
6	Vlad Potecu		06/05/86	D	1	(1)	
23	Ricardo Machado	POR	13/09/88	D	28	(1)	5
25	Bogdan Strauț		28/04/86	D	3		
99	Manuel Taborda	POR	22/06/78	G	16		
27	Iulian Tameș		06/12/78	M	7	(9)	1
17	Daniel Tătar		21/10/87	M	6	(6)	2
25	Alexandru Vagner		19/08/89	D	7		
2	Javier Velayos	ESP	06/04/87	D	27	(1)	

FC CEAHLĂUL PIATRA NEAMȚ

Coach: Constantin Enache; (12/05/13) Viorel Hizo
1919 • Ceahlăul (16,880) • fcceahlaul.ro

2012

21/07	Petrolul	a	0-5	
27/07	CFR Cluj	h	2-2	Ichim, Tolimir
03/08	Pandurii	a	1-3	Margină
13/08	Gloria	h	2-0	Golubović (p), Lukanovic
19/08	Steaua	a	0-3	
27/08	Viitorul	h	0-3	
03/09	Turnu Severin	a	1-1	Velici
14/09	Brașov	h	2-1	Velici, Golubović
21/09	Concordia	a	1-2	Cazan
01/10	Astra	h	3-2	Golubović 2, Stana
08/10	U Cluj	a	0-1	
19/10	Gaz Metan	h	2-1	Ichim, Golubović (p)
27/10	Dinamo	h	0-0	
03/11	Vaslui	a	3-4	Ichim, Lukanovic, Achim
10/11	Oțelul	h	4-1	Bădescu, Aloisio, Stana 2
17/11	Iași	a	0-1	
24/11	Rapid	h	0-0	
02/12	Petrolul	h	0-2	
09/12	CFR Cluj	a	2-3	Golubović, Achim

2013

23/02	Pandurii	h	0-1	
01/03	Gloria	a	0-0	
10/03	Steaua	h	3-4	Gheorghiu, Golubović (p), Constantinescu
17/03	Viitorul	a	2-2	Ichim, Constantinescu
31/03	Turnu Severin	h	1-0	Marc
05/04	Brașov	a	0-1	
13/04	Concordia	h	3-0	Golubović, Aitor Monroy, Rusu
21/04	Astra	a	2-4	Golubović (p), Pavel
26/04	U Cluj	h	2-1	Achim, Constantinescu
03/05	Gaz Metan	a	1-3	Golubović
07/05	Dinamo	a	1-1	Lukanovic
11/05	Vaslui	h	0-2	
17/05	Oțelul	a	2-3	Stana, Constantinescu
27/05	Iași	h	1-0	Golubović
30/05	Rapid	a	0-2	

No	Name	Nat	DoB	Pos	Aps	(s)	Gls
10	Alexandru Achim		07/04/89	M	23	(4)	3
21	Aitor Monroy	ESP	18/10/87	M	29	(1)	1
26	Aloisio	ESP	25/03/79	D	10		1
2	Daniel Barna		22/09/86	M	13	(3)	
15	Ionuț Bădescu		25/01/78	M	14	(17)	1
4	Lucian Cazan		25/12/89	D	15	(2)	1
7	Cătălin Chiș		06/01/88	M		(2)	
17	Sebastian Chitoșcă		02/10/92	M	1	(1)	
20	Marian Constantinescu		08/08/81	A	29	(2)	4
6	Constantin Drugă		27/02/90	D	2		
23	Andrei Dumitraș		23/01/88	D	12	(1)	
24	Alexandru Forminte		19/09/82	D	2		
9	Cristinel Gafița		14/06/87	A	1		
25	Adrian Gheorghiu		30/11/81	M	11		1
14	Bojan Golubović	BIH	22/08/83	A	33		11
5	Alexandru Ichim		16/01/89	D	27	(2)	4
1	Bojan Jović	SRB	01/04/82	G	10		
34	Sergei Lepmets	EST	05/04/87	G	3		
52	Lucas García	ARG	13/01/88	M	2	(4)	
23	Darko Lukanovic	SWE	01/06/84	A	7	(18)	3
3	Andrei Marc		29/04/93	D	16		1
16	Alexandru Margină		08/03/83	D	1	(5)	1
82	Bogdan Miron		02/01/82	G	21		
33	Aitor Moreno	ESP	13/02/83	D	14	(1)	
18	Marius Onciu		23/04/87	M	12	(4)	
19	Andrei Pavel		29/07/92	A	2	(3)	1
13	Marius Rusu		22/02/90	D	13	(4)	1
11	Ionel Stana		02/12/82	M	26	(2)	4
31	Cătălin Ștefănescu		30/11/94	M	2	(3)	
29	Mario Titone	ITA	14/10/88	A	2	(1)	
9	Nikola Tolimir	SVN	01/04/89	M	3	(5)	1
25	Andrei Țepeș		23/02/91	D	6		
32	Gelu Velici		22/04/92	A	7	(8)	2
28	Andrei Vițelaru		02/03/85	D	3	(3)	

CFR 1907 CLUJ

Coach: Ioan Andone; (29/10/12) Paulo Sérgio (POR);
(13/04/13) Eugen Trică
1907 • Dr Constantin Rădulescu (23,200) • cfr1907.ro
Major honours
Romanian League (3) 2008, 2010, 2012;
Romanian Cup (3) 2008, 2009, 2010

2012

Date		Loc	Score	Scorers
21/07	Gaz Metan	h	1-1	Kapetanos
27/07	Ceahlăul	a	2-2	Kapetanos, Maftei
04/08	Vaslui	h	3-0	Cadú, Rafael Bastos 2
13/08	Oțelul	a	2-1	Mureșan (p), Ronny
17/08	Iași	h	2-2	Cadú (p), Hora
25/08	Rapid	a	2-3	Ronny, Maftei
02/09	Petrolul	h	2-2	Kapetanos, Mureșan
14/09	Dinamo	a	1-0	Rui Pedro
23/09	Pandurii	a	1-2	Rafael Bastos
29/09	Gloria	h	5-1	Kapetanos, Mureșan 2 (1p), Bjelanović, Luís Alberto
07/10	Steaua	a	0-1	
18/10	Viitorul	h	0-1	
27/10	Turnu Severin	a	3-1	Hora, Rui Pedro, Cadú (p)
03/11	Brașov	h	5-0	Kapetanos, Mureșan, Cadú (p), Rui Pedro, Aguirregaray
11/11	Concordia	a	2-1	Rui Pedro, Modou Sougou
16/11	Astra	h	0-2	
24/11	U Cluj	a	2-1	Rui Pedro, Bjelanović
01/12	Gaz Metan	a	1-1	Diogo Valente
09/12	Ceahlăul	h	3-2	Rui Pedro, Deac (p), Kapetanos

2013

Date		Loc	Score	Scorers
25/02	Vaslui	a	0-0	
02/03	Oțelul	h	0-1	
09/03	Iași	a	1-1	Rada
18/03	Rapid	h	0-0	
31/03	Petrolul	a	1-1	Weldon
06/04	Dinamo	h	0-1	
12/04	Pandurii	h	2-3	Rada, Bjelanović
21/04	Gloria	a	5-0	Hora, Cadú (p), Weldon, Deac (p), Buș
28/04	Steaua	h	0-0	
05/05	Viitorul	a	2-0	Deac, Buș
09/05	Turnu Severin	h	1-3	Rui Pedro
13/05	Brașov	a	0-0	
17/05	Concordia	h	1-1	Bjelanović
26/05	Astra	a	3-3	Mureșan (p), Maah 2
29/05	U Cluj	h	3-1	Maah 3

No	Name	Nat	DoB	Pos	Aps	(s)	Gls
31	Matías Aguirregaray	URU	01/04/89	M	6	(2)	1
19	Saša Bjelanović	CRO	11/06/79	A	4	(10)	4
17	Sergiu Buș		02/11/92	A	1	(5)	2
20	Cadú	POR	21/12/81	D	19	(1)	5
45	Camora	POR	10/11/86	M	23	(2)	
26	Celestino	POR	02/01/87	M	3		
7	Ciprian Deac		16/02/86	M	14	(4)	3
10	Diogo Valente	POR	23/09/84	M	15	(3)	1
66	Edimar	BRA	21/05/86	A	1	(1)	
88	Liviu Ganea		23/02/88	A		(1)	
23	Nicolas Godemèche	FRA	22/06/84	M	12	(1)	
22	Ioan Hora		21/08/88	M	16	(5)	3
3	Ivo Pinto	POR	07/01/90	D	26	1	
9	Pantelis Kapetanos	GRE	08/06/83	A	17	(3)	6
25	Luís Alberto	BRA	17/11/83	M	5	(3)	1
11	Robert Maah	FRA	25/03/85	A	9	(4)	5
12	Vasile Maftei		01/01/81	D	18	(2)	2
1	Mário Felgueiras	POR	12/12/86	G	28		
99	Modou Sougou	SEN	18/12/84	A	8	(3)	1
48	Sulley Muniru	GHA	25/09/92	M	6	(2)	
6	Gabriel Mureșan		13/02/82	M	18	(2)	6
11	Viorel Nicoară		27/09/87	A	3	(5)	
55	Nuno Diogo	POR	13/06/81	D	2		
40	Nwankwo Obiora	NGA	12/07/91	M	5	(2)	
4	Cristian Panin		09/06/78	D	5	(1)	
13	Felice Piccolo	ITA	27/08/83	D	23		
24	Ionuț Rada		06/07/82	D	13	(3)	2
16	Rafael Bastos	BRA	01/01/85	A	13	(3)	3
27	Ronny	BRA	25/02/83	A	3	(4)	2
30	Rui Pedro	POR	02/07/88	A	16	(3)	7
5	BakarySare	CIV	05/04/90	M	7	(1)	
8	Laszlo Sepsi		07/06/86	D	15	(2)	
44	Eduard Stăncioiu		03/03/81	G	6		
18	Ádám Vass	HUN	09/09/88	M	7	(8)	
99	Weldon	BRA	06/08/80	A	7	(5)	2

CS CONCORDIA CHIAJNA

Coach: Ilie Stan
1957 • Concordia (4,123) • csconcordia.ro

2012

Date		Loc	Score	Scorers
23/07	Steaua	a	0-1	
30/07	Viitorul	h	1-1	Wellington
04/08	Turnu Severin	a	1-0	Popa
13/08	Brașov	h	2-1	Popa 2
17/08	Dinamo	h	0-0	
27/08	Astra	a	3-6	Ghionea, Pană, og (Lung)
02/09	U Cluj	h	0-2	
15/09	Gaz Metan	a	3-1	Wellington, Leca, Zuluf
21/09	Ceahlăul	h	2-1	Ghionea, Purece
29/09	Vaslui	a	0-3	
08/10	Oțelul	h	0-0	
22/10	Iași	a	1-0	Wellington
27/10	Rapid	h	0-0	
05/11	Petrolul	a	0-0	
11/11	CFR Cluj	h	1-2	Pană
19/11	Pandurii	a	1-2	Wellington
23/11	Gloria	h	2-1	Ibrić, Belu
30/11	Steaua	h	0-6	
10/12	Viitorul	a	1-1	Pană

2013

Date		Loc	Score	Scorers
23/02	Turnu Severin	h	1-1	Ispir (p)
04/03	Brașov	a	2-3	Belu, Popovici
11/03	Dinamo	a	0-2	
15/03	Astra	h	0-2	
29/03	U Cluj	a	0-1	
08/04	Gaz Metan	h	0-1	
13/04	Ceahlăul	a	0-3	
21/04	Vaslui	h	1-1	Wellington
29/04	Oțelul	a	1-2	Serediuc
06/05	Iași	h	1-1	Purece (p)
09/05	Rapid	a	0-0	
12/05	Petrolul	h	1-1	Ghionea
17/05	CFR Cluj	a	1-1	Bambara
27/05	Pandurii	h	0-1	
31/05	Gloria	a	3-1	Savin, Ilie, Balgiu

No	Name	Nat	DoB	Pos	Aps	(s)	Gls
22	George Apostol		09/06/92	M	1	(1)	
9	Cristian Balgiu		03/08/94	A		(2)	1
5	Narcisse Bambara	BFA	23/06/89	D	22		1
3	Egzon Belica	MKD	03/09/90	D	10	(1)	
77	Claudiu Belu		07/01/93	D	19	(4)	2
21	Bogdan Bucurică		11/02/86	D	4	(1)	
16	Paul Butucel		22/05/93	A		(1)	
21	Rover Cârstea		24/08/89	A		(1)	
13	Radu Ciupitu		10/10/89	M		(1)	
90	Alberto Cobrea		01/11/90	G	9		
6	Valentin Coșereanu		17/07/91	M	11	(2)	
2	Valentin Crețu		02/01/89	D	12	(2)	
28	Andrei Damian		30/11/92	M	1	(3)	
24	Sorin Ghionea		11/05/79	D	27		3
16	Damir Ibrić	BIH	30/03/84	A	1	(6)	1
8	Florin Ilie		18/06/92	D	10	(4)	1
6	Sorin Ispir		26/07/87	M	18	(2)	1
15	Mihai Leca		14/04/92	D	27	(1)	1
12	Sergei Lepmets	EST	05/04/87	G	7		
16	Florin Maxim		02/03/81	D	6		
1	Florin Niță		03/07/87	G	18		
19	Daniel Novac		26/09/87	M	5	(4)	
8	Silviu Pană		24/09/91	M	22	(4)	3
22	Sorin Paraschiv		17/06/81	M	15	(2)	
7	Adrian Popa		24/07/88	M	4		3
18	Adrian Popovici		06/09/88	A	18	(12)	1
11	Florin Purece		06/11/91	M	21	(5)	2
10	Rafael Rocha	BRA	04/03/86	A	2	(1)	
20	Neluț Roșu		05/07/93	M	1	(2)	
2	Cătălin Savin		08/11/90	D	4	1	1
23	Tiberiu Serediuc		02/07/92	A	28	(4)	1
9	Valentin Simion		04/03/86	A	4	(8)	
17	Andrei Stan		31/12/95	M	1		
30	Daniel Stan		04/01/92	M	2	(10)	
17	Wellington	BRA	05/10/87	D	29	(3)	5
10	Nicolae Zuluf		03/04/88	M	15	(8)	1

FC DINAMO BUCUREȘTI

Coach: Dario Bonetti (ITA);
(14/11/12) Dorinel Munteanu;
(28/12/12) Cornel Țălnar
1948 • Dinamo (15,300); Național Arena (55,611) • fcdinamo.ro
Major honours
Romanian League (18) 1955, 1962, 1963, 1964, 1965, 1971, 1973, 1975, 1977, 1982, 1983, 1984, 1990, 1992, 2000, 2002, 2004, 2007;
Romanian Cup (13) 1959, 1964, 1968, 1982, 1984, 1986, 1990, 2000, 2001, 2003, 2004, 2005, 2012

2012

Date		Loc	Score	Scorers
20/07	Turnu Severin	a	2-1	Axente, Dănciulescu
29/07	Iași	h	5-2	Țucudean 4, Rus
06/08	Brașov	a	2-2	Grigore, Matei
17/08	Concordia	a	0-0	
26/08	Petrolul	h	2-1	Luchin, Țucudean
02/09	Astra	a	0-1	
14/09	CFR Cluj	h	0-1	
22/09	U Cluj	a	2-1	Dănciulescu (p), Curtean
01/10	Pandurii	h	3-0	Curtean, Alexe, Dănciulescu
06/10	Gaz Metan	a	2-2	Alexe, og (Trtovac)
19/10	Gloria	h	1-2	Matei
22/10	Rapid	h	2-1	Alexe 2 (1p)
27/10	Ceahlăul	a	0-0	
04/11	Steaua	a	1-3	Alexe
10/11	Vaslui	h	0-1	
17/11	Viitorul	a	1-1	Ba
23/11	Oțelul	h	2-1	Alexe (p), Matei (p)
03/12	Turnu Severin	h	4-2	Matei, Dănciulescu, Alexe (p), Țucudean
09/12	Iași	a	1-1	og (Tincu)

2013

Date		Loc	Score	Scorers
24/02	Brașov	h	2-1	Alexe 2 (1p)
03/03	Rapid	a	1-0	Dănciulescu
11/03	Concordia	h	2-0	Axente, Matei
16/03	Petrolul	a	1-2	Axente
31/03	Astra	h	1-0	Alexe
06/04	CFR Cluj	a	1-0	Dănciulescu
13/04	U Cluj	h	1-1	Mușat
21/04	Pandurii	a	0-2	
28/04	Gaz Metan	h	2-0	Alexe, Cristea
03/05	Gloria	a	2-1	Alexe 2 (2p)
07/05	Ceahlăul	h	1-1	Alexe
10/05	Steaua	h	0-2	
18/05	Vaslui	a	1-4	Strătilă
24/05	Viitorul	h	2-3	Dănciulescu, Alexe
28/05	Oțelul	a	1-0	Axente

No	Name	Nat	DoB	Pos	Aps	(s)	Gls
10	Marius Alexe		22/02/90	A	30	(1)	15
27	Edgar Álvarez	HON	09/10/80	M	4	(1)	
15	Mircea Axente		14/03/87	A	4	(10)	4
18	Issa Ba	SEN	07/10/81	A	4	(3)	1
34	Cristian Bălgrădean		21/03/88	G	24		
17	Andrei Cristea		15/05/84	A	3	(16)	1
20	Alexandru Curtean		27/03/87	M	25	(7)	2
30	Alexandru Dandea		23/01/88	M	9	(5)	
25	Ionel Dănciulescu		06/12/76	A	20	(7)	7
33	Steliano Filip		15/05/94	M	1	(8)	
8	Boris Galchev	BUL	31/10/83	M	3	(1)	
21	Dragoș Grigore		07/09/86	D	30	(2)	1
30	Paul Koulibaly	BFA	24/03/86	D	6	(2)	
24	Srdjan Luchin		04/02/86	D	29		1
19	Boubacar Mansaly	SEN	04/02/88	M	26		
4	Cosmin Matei		30/09/91	M	27	(1)	5
7	Cătălin Munteanu		26/01/79	M	22	(1)	
32	Nicolae Mușat		04/12/86	D	16		1
23	Kristijan Naumovski	MKD	17/09/88	G	10		
2	Constantin Nica		18/03/93	D	15	(4)	
5	Cristian Pulhac		17/08/84	M	17		
16	Andrei Radu		21/06/96	D		(1)	
27	Alin Roman		27/01/94	M		(1)	
3	Dorin Rotariu		29/07/95	M	1	(6)	
26	Laurențiu Rus		07/05/85	D	27	(4)	1
6	Cristian Scutaru		13/04/87	D	4		
1	Raphael Schneider		27/06/93	M	1		
22	Sorin Strătilă		20/10/86	M	4	(6)	1
29	George Țucudean		30/04/91	A	9	(9)	6
18	Alexandru Tudose		03/04/87	D	3	(2)	

CS GAZ METAN MEDIAŞ

Coach: Cristian Pustai; (23/01/13) Gheorghe Mulţescu
1945 • Gaz Metan (7,800) • gaz-metan-medias.ro

2012

21/07	CFR Cluj	a	1-1	Vasilache
28/07	Pandurii	h	0-2	
03/08	Gloria	a	1-1	Roman
12/08	Steaua	h	1-1	Astafei
20/08	Viitorul	a	1-0	Astafei
24/08	Turnu Severin	h	2-0	Avram, Astafei
01/09	Braşov	a	1-3	Astafei (p)
15/09	Concordia	h	1-3	Astafei
23/09	Astra	a	0-4	
29/09	U Cluj	h	2-1	Bawab 2
06/10	Dinamo	h	2-2	Astafei, Bawab
19/10	Ceahlăul	a	1-2	Eric
28/10	Vaslui	h	1-0	Astafei (p)
04/11	Oţelul	a	0-2	
09/11	Iaşi	h	0-1	
19/11	Rapid	a	1-2	Eric (p)
23/11	Petrolul	h	2-0	Astafei, Bawab (p)
01/12	CFR Cluj	h	1-1	Llullaku
07/12	Pandurii	a	1-1	og (Rusu)

2013

22/02	Gloria	h	3-1	Llullaku, Bawab 2
02/03	Steaua	a	0-3	
08/03	Viitorul	h	4-1	Bawab 2, Llullaku 2
15/03	Turnu Severin	a	0-2	
29/03	Braşov	h	0-0	
08/04	Concordia	a	1-0	Llullaku (p)
12/04	Astra	h	2-1	Eric, Roman
19/04	U Cluj	h	4-3	Roman, Bawab, Petre, Gheorghe
28/04	Dinamo	a	0-2	
03/05	Ceahlăul	h	3-1	Avram, Bawab, Breeveld
07/05	Vaslui	a	1-1	Roman
11/05	Oţelul	h	1-2	Vitinho
20/05	Iaşi	h	2-0	Eric (p), Munteanu
24/05	Rapid	h	1-1	Breeveld
29/05	Petrolul	a	1-1	Vitinho

No	Name	Nat	DoB	Pos	Aps	(s)	Gls
6	Victor Astafei		06/07/87	A	16		8
14	Răzvan Avram		12/10/86	M	12	(7)	2
10	Thaer Bawab	JOR	01/03/85	A	18	(7)	10
18	Nicandro Breeveld	NED	07/10/86	M	20	(2)	2
30	Miloš Buchta	SVK	19/07/80	G	8		
7	Cristian Bud		26/06/85	A	5	(4)	
9	Sergiu Buş		02/11/92	A	2	(1)	
8	Ionuţ Buzean		18/09/82	D	22	(1)	
4	Marius Ciucă		04/11/82	D	5	(8)	
17	Sebastian Cojocnean		11/07/89	M	1	(1)	
6	Florin Dan		01/04/79	M	7	(4)	
9	Octavian Drăghici		26/11/85	A	2	(3)	
27	Eric	BRA	05/12/85	M	22		4
28	Fabio Bravo	ITA	04/09/89	A	1		
85	Cosmin Frăsinescu		10/02/85	D	28	(3)	
89	Costin Gheorghe		08/01/89	M	1	(2)	1
1	Alexandru Greab		26/05/92	G	3		
13	Akaki Khubutia	GEO	17/03/86	D	7		
7	Azdren Llullaku	ALB	15/02/88	A	16	(4)	5
82	Filip Loncarić	CRO	17/09/86	G	3		
25	Žarko Marković	SRB	31/01/87	D	24		
5	Alex Munteanu		31/10/87	M	3	(3)	1
23	Sergiu Muth		24/07/90	D	11	(2)	
15	Valentin Negru		04/09/82	D	8	(8)	
2	Ciprian Petre		10/12/80	M	25	(3)	1
12	Răzvan Pleşca		25/11/82	G	20		
6	Aleksandar Radovici	MNE	30/03/87	D	7	(2)	
20	Dan Roman		22/12/85	A	7	(7)	4
22	Aymen Tahar	ALG	02/10/89	M	17	(2)	
21	Cristian Todea		18/10/78	M	17	(9)	
3	Jasmin Trtovac	SRB	27/12/86	D	15	(1)	1
17	Ciprian Vasilache		14/09/83	M	4	(3)	1
11	Vitinho	BRA	20/02/89	A	6	(6)	2
28	Ivan Vukadinović	SRB	21/08/84	D	6	(2)	
16	Radu Zaharia		25/01/89	D	6	(4)	

ACF GLORIA 1922 BISTRIŢA

Coach: Nicolae Manea
1922 • Gloria (7,967) • cfgloria.ro
Major honours
Romanian Cup (1) 1994

2012

22/07	Astra	h	1-2	Predescu
29/07	U Cluj	a	0-1	
03/08	Gau Metan	h	1-1	Predescu
13/08	Ceahlăul	a	0-2	
18/08	Vaslui	h	0-3	
25/08	Oţelul	a	1-1	Markísio
31/08	Iaşi	h	1-0	Bratu
15/09	Rapid	a	1-3	Predescu
21/09	Petrolul	h	1-1	Laio
29/09	CFR Cluj	a	1-5	Zahiri
07/10	Pandurii	h	1-3	Predescu
19/10	Dinamo	a	2-1	Jaime Bragança, Predescu
28/10	Steaua	a	0-4	
02/11	Viitorul	h	1-1	Predescu
09/11	Turnu Severin	a	0-1	
16/11	Braşov	h	1-1	Curtuiuş (p)
23/11	Concordia	a	1-2	Anton
03/12	Astra	a	0-4	
07/12	U Cluj	h	0-0	

2013

22/02	Gaz Metan	a	1-3	Antonache
01/03	Ceahlăul	h	0-0	
11/03	Vaslui	h	1-1	Bucur
15/03	Oţelul	h	2-1	Radu, Feher
01/04	Iaşi	a	1-2	Radu (p)
07/04	Rapid	h	0-1	
13/04	Petrolul	a	0-4	
21/04	CFR Cluj	h	0-5	
29/04	Pandurii	a	0-4	
03/05	Dinamo	h	1-2	Enescu
07/05	Steaua	h	0-1	
13/05	Viitorul	a	0-2	
20/05	Turnu Severin	h	0-0	
23/05	Braşov	a	1-4	Feher (p)
31/05	Concordia	h	1-3	Cubilla

No	Name	Nat	DoB	Pos	Aps	(s)	Gls
22	Călin Albuţ		23/05/81	G	1	(1)	
29	Paul Anton		10/05/91	M	17	(1)	1
15	Bogdan Antonache		13/05/95	D	8		1
26	Andrei Berceanu		29/04/89	D	1	(6)	
22	Alin Bota		29/04/83	G	3		
19	Florin Bratu		02/01/80	A	4	(5)	1
15	Daniel Brumă		15/09/94	A	1		
10	Cătălin Bucur		25/03/88	A	7		1
15	Fernando Cafasso	ARG	09/02/83	D	11		
16	Marian Chiţu		19/08/86	M	10		
16	Valerian Ciofu		12/08/86	D		(2)	
23	Paul Colţa		04/08/94	D		(1)	
20	Walter Cubilla	ARG	05/03/89	A	6	(4)	1
22	Marius Curtuiuş		13/08/89	A	14	(13)	1
22	Emilian Dolha		03/11/79	G	26		
28	Andrei Enescu		12/10/87	M	16	(6)	1
11	Marius Feher		08/06/89	M	10	(7)	2
23	Daniel Guţ		17/05/94	D	1		
27	Roberto Hasnaş		02/08/97	M		(1)	
6	Ionuţ Hlinca		05/06/88	M	14		
4	Octavian Ionescu		15/03/90	D	6	(3)	
4	Gheorghe Iordache		12/09/80	D	11		
17	Jaime Bragança	POR	09/06/83	A	9	(1)	1
18	Traian Jarda		24/01/94	D	1	(1)	
3	Wilfried Kanon	CIV	06/07/93	D	25		
7	Laio	BRA	02/05/89	A	6	(8)	1
25	Markísio	BRA	21/01/91	M	7	(2)	1
4	Valentin Năstase		04/10/74	D	4	(1)	
1	Costin Oghinciuc		25/01/88	G	4		
28	Bogdan Oprea		29/09/82	A	6	(4)	
25	Vlăduţ Peica		29/05/95	D		(3)	
23	Andrei Peteleu		20/08/92	D	16		
29	Vasile Pop		21/11/94	M	2	(2)	
25	Fooye Mor Pouye	SEN	21/11/94	M	7	(1)	
10	Cornel Predescu		21/12/87	M	18		6
17	Răzvan Radu		25/11/84	A	12	(1)	2
21	David Reano	ARG	20/03/84	D	9	(3)	
18	Roberto Ayza	BRA	19/05/81	M	12	(1)	
8	Romário	BRA	16/01/89	M	18		
9	Otniel Sighiartău		19/01/85	A	1	(3)	
17	Daniel Stan		28/08/78	M	1	(3)	
30	Mădălin Stancu		06/01/92	M	4	(2)	
8	Lucian Stroe		04/01/88	D	5	(1)	
16	Iulian Şiplăcan		05/04/94	D	1		
2	Caudiu Traşcă		13/11/85	D	2		
2	Valentin Trestenicu		15/05/93	M	4	(4)	
20	Alexandru Tudose		03/04/87	D	11		
20	Florin Ţircă		01/02/84	D	15	(6)	
16	Yedi Zahiri	CIV	02/09/85	M	7	(3)	1

CSMS IAŞI

Coach: Ionuţ Popa;
(30/08/12) Liviu Ciobotariu; (22/04/13) Sorin Cârţu
2010 • Emil Alexandrescu (11,481) • csmsiasi.ro

2012

22/07	Oţelul	h	1-2	Ionescu
29/07	Dinamo	a	2-5	Onofraş, Vladu
06/08	Rapid	a	0-1	
10/08	Petrolul	h	2-2	Straton, Pătulea
17/08	CFR Cluj	a	2-2	Milea, Herghelegiu
26/08	Pandurii	h	0-1	
31/08	Gloria	a	0-1	
16/09	Steaua	h	0-3	
24/09	Viitorul	a	0-1	
30/09	Turnu Severin	h	1-0	Petrović
08/10	Braşov	a	0-1	
22/10	Concordia	a	0-1	
26/10	Astra	a	0-1	
03/11	U Cluj	h	4-0	Keita, Tincu (p), Straton, Ţigănaşu
09/11	Gaz Metan	a	1-0	Pătulea
17/11	Ceahlăul	h	1-0	Milea
26/11	Vaslui	a	0-3	
03/12	Oţelul	a	3-0	Onofraş 3
09/12	Dinamo	h	1-1	Straton

2013

23/02	Rapid	h	0-1	
03/03	Petrolul	a	1-2	Pătulea
09/03	CFR Cluj	h	1-1	Milea
16/03	Pandurii	a	1-3	Mihălăchioaie
01/04	Gloria	h	2-1	Pătulea, Onofraş
07/04	Steaua	a	1-3	Tudor (p)
15/04	Viitorul	h	1-2	Milea
20/04	Turnu Severin	a	1-2	Onofraş
29/04	Braşov	h	1-2	Pătulea
06/05	Concordia	a	1-1	Hugo Moutinho
09/05	Astra	h	0-2	
13/05	U Cluj	a	2-0	Ţigănaşu, Pătulea
20/05	Gaz Metan	a	0-1	
27/05	Ceahlăul	a	0-1	
30/05	Vaslui	h	1-2	Mitrea

No	Name	Nat	DoB	Pos	Aps	(s)	Gls
4	Adrian Avrămia		31/01/92	D	15	(2)	
5	Narcis Bădic		01/07/91	M		(2)	
7	Alexandru Ciucur		01/03/90	M	12	(11)	
2	Alexandru Creţu		24/04/92	D	25	(1)	
27	Cătălin Curiliuc		25/07/89	A		(1)	
19	Ramses Gado		09/05/82	M		(3)	
9	Andrei Herghelegiu		21/03/92	A	14	(11)	1
13	Hugo Moutinho	POR	01/01/82	M	11	(2)	1
8	Claudiu Ionescu		18/08/84	A	7	(12)	1
23	Ionuţ Irimia		17/05/79	G	26		
77	Petar Jovanović	BIH	12/07/82	D	11		
28	Souleymane Keita	SEN	04/11/87	A	11	(6)	1
33	Cezar Lungu		06/04/88	G	8		
31	Ionuţ Mihălăchioaie		31/01/91	D	6	(2)	1
25	Ciprian Milea		12/07/84	M	29	(1)	4
22	Milan Mitić	SRB	22/01/84	D	10		
3	Bogdan Mitrea		29/09/87	D	13	(6)	1
21	Adrian Nalaţi		21/05/83	M	1	(2)	
11	Marius Onofraş		17/08/80	M	20	(9)	6
24	Adrian Pătulea		10/11/84	A	20	(9)	6
17	Ivan Petrović	SRB	17/07/86	M	6	(2)	1
13	Artem Semenenko	UKR	02/09/88	M	6	(4)	
14	Bogdan Straton		23/08/83	D	22	(1)	3
6	Răzvan Tincu		15/07/87	D	31		1
10	Claudiu Tudor		29/04/85	M	22	(9)	1
30	Alexandru Ţigănaşu		12/06/90	M	21	(3)	2
20	Iulian Vladu		02/02/82	M	27		1

FC OȚELUL GALAȚI

Coach: Dorinel Munteanu; (30/08/12) Viorel Tănase;
(24/02/13) (Ioan Balaur); (05/03/13) Petre Grigoraș;
(22/04/13) Marian Dinu
1964 • Oțelul (13,500) • otelul-galati.ro
Major honours
Romanian League (1) 2011

2012

22/07	Iași	a	2-1	Iorga (p), Viglianti	
30/07	Rapid	h	1-1	Viglianti	
04/08	Petrolul	h	1-2	Inkango	
13/08	CFR Cluj	h	1-2	Inkango	
20/08	Pandurii	a	2-3	Iorga (p), Inkango	
25/08	Gloria	h	1-1	Štromajer	
02/09	Steaua	a	1-2	Viglianti	
15/09	Viitorul	h	1-1	Viglianti	
22/09	Turnu Severin	a	1-1	Punoševac	
30/09	Brașov	h	0-0		
08/10	Concordia	a	0-0		
20/10	Astra	h	2-1	Pena (p), Inkango	
26/10	U Cluj	a	1-1	Paraschiv	
04/11	Gaz Metan	h	2-0	Giurgiu, Pena	
10/11	Ceahlăul	a	1-4	Giurgiu	
19/11	Vaslui	h	2-0	Iorga, Viglianti	
23/11	Dinamo	a	1-2	og (Rus)	
03/12	Iași	h	0-3		
08/12	Rapid	a	3-2	Pena 3	

2013

24/02	Petrolul	h	0-1		
02/03	CFR Cluj	a	1-0	Paraschiv	
10/03	Pandurii	h	1-0	Iorga (p)	
15/03	Gloria	a	1-2	Paraschiv	
01/04	Steaua	h	1-1	Sârghi	
08/04	Viitorul	a	0-0		
13/04	Turnu Severin	h	2-0	Štromajer, Astafei	
22/04	Brașov	a	2-2	Sârghi, Filip	
29/04	Concordia	h	2-1	Sârghi, Iorga (p)	
04/05	Astra	a	0-0		
08/05	U Cluj	h	0-2		
11/05	Gaz Metan	a	2-1	Benga, Vancea	
17/05	Ceahlăul	h	3-2	Neagu, Astafei, Iorga	
24/05	Vaslui	a	0-1		
28/05	Dinamo	h	0-1		

No	Name	Nat	DoB	Pos	Aps	(s)	Gls
21	Victor Astafei		06/07/87	A	10	(4)	2
30	Liviu Băjenaru		06/05/83	M	9	(4)	
6	Alexandru Benga		15/06/89	D	19		1
1	Cristian Brăneț		14/07/77	G	14	(1)	
17	Laurențiu Buș		27/08/87	M	4	(2)	
2	Marian Cârjă		03/05/87	D	8		
8	Bogdan Chipirliu		21/07/92	A		(2)	
20	Samoel Cojoc		08/07/87	D	13		
18	Sergiu Costin		21/11/78	D	18	(1)	
24	Sorin Cucu		17/06/90	D	7		
9	Didy	BRA	10/09/82	A	6	(8)	
4	Ioan Filip		20/05/89	M	13	(5)	1
9	Daúd Gazale	CHI	10/08/84	A	1	(5)	
29	Gabriel Giurgiu		03/09/82	M	27		2
12	Branko Grahovac	BIH	08/07/83	G	19	(1)	
14	Silviu Ilie		27/06/88	D	1		
88	Bruce Inkango	FRA	18/05/84	A	7	(5)	4
7	Cătălin Iorga		17/03/88	M	29	(2)	6
3	João Felipe	BRA	11/03/92	D		(4)	
5	Zoran Ljubinković	SRB	04/07/82	D	17	(3)	
8	Marquinhos	BRA	28/05/92	M	2	(7)	
23	Lucian Murgoci		25/03/92	D	6	(3)	
77	Ionuț Neagu		26/10/89	M	26	(2)	1
10	Gabriel Paraschiv		27/03/78	M	13	(3)	3
27	Marius Pena		02/05/85	A	13	(3)	5
55	Milan Perendija	SRB	05/01/86	D	12		
24	Daniel Popescu		20/02/88	D	5		
19	Bratislav Punoševac	SRB	09/07/87	A	2	(9)	1
3	Corneliu Râpă		16/01/90	D	13	(1)	
16	Cristian Sârghi		22/02/87	D	20	(1)	3
88	Tadas Simaitis	LTU	29/12/90	G	1	(1)	
69	Enes Šipović	BIH	11/09/90	D	6		
11	Jaka Štromajer	SVN	27/07/83	A	21	(9)	2
96	Alexandru Tudorie		19/03/96	A		(1)	
23	Cosmin Vancea		24/12/84	A	4	(5)	1
37	Gabriel Viglianti	ARG	12/06/79	M	8	(7)	5

CS PANDURII TÂRGU JIU

Coach: Petre Grigoraș; (19/01/13) Cristian Pustai
1974 • Tudor Vladimirescu (10,000) • pandurii-tg-jiu.ro

2012

20/07	U Cluj	h	6-2	Ibeh 2, Viera, Răduț, Matulevičius, Boutadjine	
28/07	Gaz Metan	a	2-0	Nistor, Ibeh	
03/08	Ceahlăul	h	3-1	Răduț 2, Maxim	
12/08	Vaslui	h	0-0		
20/08	Oțelul	h	3-2	Maxim (p), Boutadjine 2	
26/08	Iași	a	1-0	Nistor	
01/09	Rapid	h	2-1	Voiculeț, Ibeh	
16/09	Petrolul	a	0-4		
23/09	CFR Cluj	h	2-1	Maxim (p), Răduț (p)	
01/10	Dinamo	a	0-3		
07/10	Gloria	a	3-1	Răduț, Matulevičius, Nistor	
21/10	Steaua	h	0-0		
29/10	Viitorul	a	0-2		
05/11	Turnu Severin	h	2-2	Cristea, Viera	
11/11	Brașov	a	1-0	Lemnaru	
19/11	Concordia	h	2-1	Voiculeț, Maxim	
25/11	Astra	a	1-4	Maxim	
30/11	U Cluj	a	1-1	Rusu	
07/12	Gaz Metan	h	1-1	Viera	

2013

23/02	Ceahlăul	a	1-0	Matulevičius	
04/03	Vaslui	h	2-1	Matulevičius 2	
10/03	Oțelul	a	0-1		
16/03	Iași	h	3-1	Nistor, Lemnaru, Matulevičius	
30/03	Rapid	a	0-2		
06/04	Petrolul Ploiești	h	1-3	Nicoară	
12/04	CFR Cluj	a	3-2	Ibeh, Matulevičius, Voiculeț	
21/04	Dinamo	h	2-0	Ibeh, Nistor	
29/04	Gloria	h	4-0	Predescu, Ibeh, Matulevičius, Nicoară	
03/05	Steaua	a	0-2		
09/05	Viitorul	h	4-1	Matulevičius 2, Mamele, Anton	
12/05	Turnu Severin	a	3-1	Anton 2 (1p), Ibeh	
18/05	Brașov	h	2-3	Nistor, Viera	
27/05	Concordia	a	1-0	Răduț	
29/05	Astra	h	1-1	Lemnaru	

No	Name	Nat	DoB	Pos	Aps	(s)	Gls
19	Paul Anton		10/05/91	D	13		3
19	Alexandru Avramescu		03/06/91	M		(1)	
7	Cosmin Băcilă		10/09/83	M		(7)	
21	Karim Boutadjine	FRA	23/03/89	M	3	(15)	3
8	Călin Cristea		06/05/88	D	13	(9)	1
30	Alexandru Dan		30/01/94	D	1	(2)	
9	Alexandru Grigoraș		05/07/89	A	7	(9)	
14	John Ike Ibeh	NGA	16/04/86	M	18	(1)	8
30	Alin Ignea		28/04/86	M		(1)	
1	David Lazăr		08/08/91	G	8	(1)	
27	Valentin Lemnaru		24/06/84	A	10	(13)	3
6	Iulian Mamele		17/02/85	M	28		1
99	Deivydas Matulevičius	LTU	08/04/89	A	23	(8)	10
28	Alexandru Maxim		08/07/90	M	19		5
17	Viorel Nicoară		27/09/87	M	10	(2)	2
16	Dan Nistor		06/05/88	M	33		6
20	Konyeha Godwin Onyeka	NGA	22/06/92	M		(1)	
80	Pedro Mingote	POR	06/08/80	G	26		
25	Marian Pleașcă		06/02/90	D	9	(4)	
29	Saša Popin	SRB	28/10/89	A	1	(2)	
20	Cornel Predescu		21/12/87	M	3	(2)	1
23	Ionuț Rada		16/03/90	D	8	(5)	
90	Mihai Răduț		18/03/90	M	25	(5)	6
4	Adrian Rusu		28/07/84	D	7	(11)	1
18	Bogdan Ungurușan		20/02/83	D	22	(1)	
3	Ousmane Viera	CIV	21/12/86	M	31		4
2	Alexandru Vlad		06/12/89	D	30		
10	Claudiu Voiculeț		08/08/85	M	26	(2)	3

FC PETROLUL PLOIEȘTI

Coach: Mircea Rednic; (29/10/12) Cosmin Contra
1952 • Ilie Oană (15,500) • fcpetrolul.ro
Major honours
Romanian League (3) 1958, 1959, 1966;
Romanian Cup (3) 1963, 1995, 2013

2012

21/07	Ceahlăul	h	5-0	Younès 3, Grozav, Szukała	
28/07	Vaslui	a	0-3		
04/08	Oțelul	a	2-1	Boudjemaa 2	
10/08	Iași	a	2-2	Younès, Marinescu (p)	
18/08	Rapid	h	0-0		
26/08	Dinamo	h	1-2	Grozav	
02/09	CFR Cluj	a	2-2	Bokila, og (Cadú)	
16/09	Pandurii	h	4-0	Younès, Cristescu, Bokila 2	
21/09	Gloria	a	1-1	Cristescu	
30/09	Steaua	h	1-2	Bokila	
06/10	Viitorul	h	2-1	Younès, Morar	
20/10	Turnu Severin	h	1-0	Bokila	
26/10	Brașov	a	1-0	Grozav	
05/11	Concordia	h	0-0		
10/11	Astra	a	1-1	Grozav	
16/11	U Cluj	h	2-0	Neag, Grozav	
23/11	Gaz Metan	a	0-2		
02/12	Ceahlăul	a	2-0	Bokila, Hoban	
08/12	Vaslui	h	0-0		

2013

24/02	Oțelul	a	1-0	Bokila	
03/03	Iași	h	2-1	Hoban, Grozav	
09/03	Rapid	a	0-0		
16/03	Dinamo	a	2-1	Bokila, Sauvadet	
31/03	CFR Cluj	h	1-1	Younès	
06/04	Pandurii	a	3-1	Younès, Bokila 2	
13/04	Gloria	h	4-0	Sauvadet, Bokila, Morar, Mojica (p)	
22/04	Steaua	a	2-2	Hoban, og (Chiricheș)	
27/04	Viitorul	h	3-0	Younès, Bokila 2	
04/05	Turnu Severin	a	2-2	Bokila, Younès	
08/05	Brașov	h	6-4	Younès 2 (1p), Marinescu 2, Sony, Grozav	
12/05	Concordia	a	1-1	Grozav	
18/05	Astra	h	1-1	Bokila (p)	
26/05	U Cluj	a	4-2	Grozav, Bokila, Sauvadet, Mojica	
29/05	Gaz Metan	h	1-1	Younès (p)	

No	Name	Nat	DoB	Pos	Aps	(s)	Gls
32	Sebastian Achim		02/07/86	D	19		
26	Stefano Avogadri	ITA	11/08/85	D	1		
11	Jeremy Bokila	COD	14/11/88	A	23	(8)	16
23	Mircea Bornescu		03/05/80	G	32		
8	Damien Boudjemaa	FRA	07/06/85	M	25	(3)	2
14	Césinha	BRA	12/03/80	A		(2)	
20	Sebastian Cojocnean		14/02/88	M	1	(1)	
10	Adrian Cristea		30/11/83	M	12	(3)	
18	Marian Cristescu		17/03/85	M	13	(11)	2
4	Manassé Enza-Yamissi	CTA	28/09/89	D	27	(1)	
6	George Galamaz		05/04/81	D	16		
3	Geraldo Alves	POR	08/11/80	D	18		
29	Constantin Grecu		08/06/88	D	2		
7	Gheorghe Grozav		29/09/90	A	24	(7)	9
21	Guilherme	BRA	01/04/90	D	31	(1)	
33	Ovidiu Hoban		27/12/82	M	18	(6)	3
33	Vasili Khomutovski	BLR	30/08/78	G	2	(1)	
30	Laurențiu Marinescu		25/08/84	M	21	(7)	3
45	Gaston Mendy	SEN	22/11/85	M	1		
14	Gualberto Mojica	BOL	07/10/84	M	7	(6)	2
93	Vlăduț Morar		01/08/93	A	4	(6)	2
5	Sony Mustivar	FRA	12/02/90	M	18	(7)	
16	Elhad Năziri	AZE	29/12/92	D		(3)	
16	Ionuț Neag		18/02/94	M	5		1
99	Anthony Nwakaema	NGA	04/04/83	A		(3)	
19	Daniel Oprița		10/08/81	M	7	(6)	
5	Renan Silva	BRA	02/01/89	M	5	(7)	
52	Romário	BRA	16/01/89	M		(3)	
31	Florent Sauvadet	FRA	31/01/89	M	6	(2)	3
2	Jean Sony Alcenat	HAI	23/01/86	D	14	(2)	1
3	Łukasz Szukała	POL	26/05/84	D	2		1
9	Hamza Younès	TUN	16/04/86	A	20	(8)	13

FC RAPID BUCUREŞTI

Coach: Ioan Ovidiu Sabău; (21/10/12) Marian Rada
1923 • Valentin Stănescu (19,100) • fcrapid.ro

Major honours
Romanian League (3) 1967, 1999, 2003;
Romanian Cup (13) 1935, 1937, 1938, 1939, 1940, 1941, 1942, 1972, 1975, 1998, 2002, 2006, 2007

2012

22/07	Vaslui	h	2-2	*Pancu, Filipe Teixeira*
30/07	Oţelul	a	1-1	*N Grigore*
06/08	Iaşi	h	1-0	*Goga*
18/08	Petrolul	a	0-0	
25/08	CFR Cluj	h	3-2	*Ilijoski, N Grigore 2 (1p)*
01/09	Pandurii	a	0-2	
15/09	Gloria	h	3-1	*Herea 2 (2p), Goga*
24/09	Steaua	a	0-1	
30/09	Viitorul	h	2-1	*Ioniţă (I), N Grigore*
06/10	Turnu Severin	a	1-0	*Filipe Teixeira*
19/10	Braşov	h	1-2	*Ilijoski*
22/10	Dinamo	a	1-2	*Pancu*
27/10	Concordia	a	0-0	
05/11	Astra	h	0-2	
12/11	U Cluj	a	2-1	*Herea, Grigorie*
19/11	Gaz Metan	h	2-1	*Ioniţă (I), Herea (p)*
24/11	Ceahlăul	a	0-0	
02/12	Vaslui	a	0-1	
08/12	Oţelul	h	2-3	*Herea, Ioniţă (I)*

2013

23/02	Iaşi	a	1-0	*og (Creţu)*
03/03	Dinamo	h	0-1	
09/03	Petrolul	h	0-0	
18/03	CFR Cluj	a	0-0	
30/03	Pandurii	h	2-0	*N Grigore, Coman*
07/04	Gloria	a	1-0	*Grigorie*
14/04	Steaua	h	1-1	*Herea*
20/04	Viitorul	a	2-1	*Roman, Oros*
20/04	Turnu Severin	h	1-0	*Ioniţă (I)*
04/05	Braşov	a	0-2	
09/05	Concordia	h	0-0	
12/05	Astra	a	2-3	*Dică, Herea*
20/05	U Cluj	h	1-4	*Ciolacu*
24/05	Gaz Metan	a	1-1	*Herea*
30/05	Ceahlăul	h	2-0	*Ciolacu, Herea*

No	Name	Nat	DoB	Pos	Aps	(s)	Gls
4	Octavian Abrudan		16/03/84	D	19		
22	Călin Albuţ		23/05/81	G	6		
9	Marius Bilaşco		13/07/81	M	2	(2)	
19	Vladimir Božović	MNE	13/11/81	D	11	(2)	
33	Ovidiu Burcă		16/03/80	D	3	(2)	
33	Florin Călin		16/08/93	M		(1)	
18	Andrei Ciolacu		09/08/92	A	7	(6)	2
6	Paul Codrea		04/04/81	M	8	(3)	
17	Alexandru Coman		16/10/91	M	14	(4)	1
84	Marius Constantin		25/10/84	D	3		
23	Alexandru Dăescu		05/09/91	D		(1)	
7	Emil Dică		17/07/82	M	14		1
90	Virgil Drăghia		31/07/90	G	3		
80	Filipe Teixeira	POR	02/10/80	M	15		2
27	Gláuber	BRA	05/08/83	D	11	(1)	
21	Dorin Goga		02/07/84	D	8	(6)	2
2	Adrian Grigore		27/05/90	M		(1)	
8	Nicolae Grigore		19/07/83	M	22	(4)	5
20	Ştefan Grigorie		31/01/82	M	17	(8)	2
10	Nicolae Herea		26/03/85	M	24	(1)	9
9	Blaze Ilijoski	MKD	09/07/84	A	7	(4)	2
25	Alexandru Ioniţă (I)		05/08/89	A	12	(6)	4
29	Alexandru Ioniţă (II)		14/12/94	M	5	(6)	
84	Ştefan Mardare		03/12/87	D	6	(2)	
80	Mădălin Martin		21/06/92	A	3	(4)	
3	Andrei Matei		03/08/90	M		(3)	
7	Nemanja Milisavljević	SRB	01/11/84	D	14	(4)	
15	Cristian Oros		15/10/84	D	27	(1)	1
11	Daniel Pancu		17/08/77	A	16	(4)	2
23	Miloš Pavlović	SRB	27/11/83	M	9		
33	Cătălin Păun		03/01/88	D		(3)	
1	Peçanha	BRA	11/01/80	G	25		
30	Renan Silva	BRA	02/01/89	M	1	(2)	
14	Mihai Roman		16/10/84	M	21	(5)	1
2	Rui Duarte	POR	11/10/80	D	5	(1)	
30	Stefan	BRA	16/04/88	A	1	(1)	
21	Marian Stoica		26/08/89	M	2	(2)	
24	Romeo Surdu		12/01/84	A	3	(6)	
19	Nicolae Vasile		29/12/95	D	12		
28	Ionuţ Voicu		02/08/84	D	15		
5	Wallace	BRA	20/10/89	D	3	(1)	

FC STEAUA BUCUREŞTI

Coach: Laurenţiu Reghecampf
1947 • Steaua (28,000); Naţional Arena (55,611) • steauafc.ro

Major honours
European Champion Clubs' Cup (1) 1986;
UEFA Super Cup (1) 1986;
Romanian League (24) 1951, 1952, 1953, 1956, 1960, 1961, 1968, 1976, 1978, 1985, 1986, 1987, 1988, 1989, 1993, 1994, 1995, 1996, 1997, 1998, 2001, 2005, 2006, 2013;
Romanian Cup (22) 1949, 1950, 1951, 1952, 1955, 1962, 1966, 1967, 1969, 1970, 1971, 1976, 1979, 1985, 1987, 1988, 1989, 1992, 1996, 1997, 1999, 2011

2012

23/07	Concordia	h	1-0	*Rusescu*
28/07	Astra	a	4-3	*Tănase, Martinović, Rusescu, Adi Sobrinho*
05/08	U Cluj	h	5-1	*Adi Sobrinho 2, Rusescu, Tănase 2 (1p)*
12/08	Gaz Metan	a	1-1	*Rusescu*
19/08	Ceahlăul	h	3-0	*Rusescu 2, Adi Sobrinho*
27/08	Vaslui	a	1-3	*Chipciu*
02/09	Oţelul	h	2-1	*Adi Sobrinho, Pintilii*
16/09	Iaşi	a	3-0	*Chipciu 2, Adi Sobrinho*
24/09	Rapid	h	1-0	*Bourceanu*
30/09	Petrolul	a	2-1	*Nikolić, Latovlevici*
07/10	CFR Cluj	h	1-0	*Rusescu*
21/10	Pandurii	a	0-0	
28/10	Gloria	h	4-0	*M Costea 2, Rusescu 2*
04/11	Dinamo	h	3-1	*Rusescu 2 (1p), Szukała*
11/11	Viitorul	a	4-0	*Chipciu, Rusescu 2 (1p), Gardoş*
18/11	Turnu Severin	h	2-1	*Tănase, Rusescu*
26/11	Braşov	a	1-3	*Rusescu (p)*
30/11	Concordia	a	6-0	*Chiricheş, Rusescu 2, Nikolić, Tănase, Adi Sobrinho*
10/12	Astra	h	2-0	*Tănase, Prepeliţă*

2013

25/02	U Cluj	a	1-0	*Rusescu*
02/03	Gaz Metan	h	3-0	*Nikolić, Pintilii 2*
10/03	Ceahlăul	a	4-3	*Bourceanu, Adi Sobrinho, Pintilii, Leandro Tatu*
17/03	Vaslui	h	1-0	*Chipciu*
01/04	Oţelul	a	1-1	*Szukała*
07/04	Iaşi	h	3-1	*Chipciu, Pintilii, Leandro Tatu*
14/04	Rapid	a	1-1	*Bourceanu*
22/04	Petrolul	h	2-2	*Rusescu (p), Latovlevici (p)*
28/04	CFR Cluj	a	0-0	
03/05	Pandurii	h	2-0	*Rusescu, Szukała*
07/05	Gloria	a	1-0	*Iancu*
10/05	Dinamo	a	2-0	*og (Mansaly), Tănase*
19/05	Viitorul	h	2-5	*Nikolić (p), Adi Sobrinho*
26/05	Turnu Severin	a	1-1	*Iancu*
28/05	Braşov	h	4-0	*Rusescu, Szukała, Nikolić, Tănase*

No	Name	Nat	DoB	Pos	Aps	(s)	Gls
99	Adi Sobrinho	BRA	15/12/85	M	11	(5)	9
30	Tiberiu Bălan		17/02/81	M	1	(4)	
55	Alexandru Bourceanu		24/04/85	M	32		3
3	Dorin Bratu		27/05/89	D	2		
7	Alexandru Chipciu		18/05/89	M	26	(1)	6
21	Vlad Chiricheş		14/11/89	D	26		1
95	Valentin Cojocaru		01/10/95	G	2	(1)	
29	Florin Costea		16/05/85	A	1		
9	Mihai Costea		29/05/88	A	5	(7)	2
23	Andrei Dumitraş		23/01/88	D	3	(2)	
8	Lucian Filip		25/09/90	D	7	(10)	
6	Florin Gardoş		29/10/88	D	18	(3)	1
17	Daniel Georgievski	MKD	17/02/88	D	17	(2)	
80	Gabriel Iancu		15/04/94	M	5	(5)	2
14	Iasmin Latovlevici		11/05/86	D	22	(2)	2
20	Leandro Tatu	BRA	26/04/82	A	4	(5)	2
19	Valeriu Lupu		24/01/91	D	2		
18	Novak Martinović	SRB	31/01/85	D	5		1
2	Gabriel Matei		26/02/90	D	1		
27	Ionuţ Năstăsie		07/01/92	M	1	(1)	
90	Stefan Nikolić	MNE	16/04/90	A	11	(13)	5
22	Paul Pârvulescu		11/08/88	D	10	(2)	
5	Mihai Pintilii		09/11/84	M	21	(9)	5
77	Adrian Popa		24/07/88	M	19	(11)	
11	Andrei Prepeliţă		08/12/85	M	7	(11)	1
2	Corneliu Râpă		16/01/90	D	7	(1)	
24	Raul Rusescu		09/07/88	A	29	(5)	21
1	Răzvan Stanca		18/01/80	G	4		
4	Łukasz Szukała	POL	26/05/84	D	20		4
10	Cristian Tănase		18/02/87	M	27	(2)	8
12	Ciprian Tătăruşanu		09/02/86	G	28		

CS TURNU SEVERIN

Coach: Marian Bondrea; (03/09/12) (Ionel Gane); (05/09/12) Nicolò Napoli (ITA); (04/01/13) Ionel Gane
2011 • Municipal (20,028) • csseverin.ro

2012

20/07	Dinamo	h	1-2	*Vancea*
27/07	Braşov	a	1-2	*Thomas*
04/08	Concordia	h	0-1	
10/08	Astra	a	1-1	*Vancea*
17/08	U Cluj	h	1-1	*Abba*
24/08	Gaz Metan	a	0-2	
03/09	Ceahlăul	h	1-1	*Dandea*
17/09	Vaslui	a	1-2	*Hugo Moutinho*
22/09	Oţelul	h	1-1	*Thomas*
30/09	Iaşi	a	0-1	
06/10	Rapid	h	0-1	
20/10	Petrolul	a	0-1	
27/10	CFR Cluj	h	1-3	*Arnăutu*
05/11	Pandurii	a	2-2	*Zaharia 2*
09/11	Gloria	h	1-0	*Neacşa*
18/11	Steaua	a	1-2	*Vancea*
26/11	Viitorul	h	2-2	*Vancea 2*
03/12	Dinamo	a	2-4	*Neacşa (p), Thomas*
10/12	Braşov	h	2-1	*Dandea, Thomas*

2013

23/02	Concordia	a	1-1	*Costea (p)*
04/03	Astra	h	0-0	
11/03	U Cluj	a	0-1	
15/03	Gaz Metan	h	2-0	*Costea, Roman*
31/03	Ceahlăul	a	0-1	
05/04	Vaslui	h	2-0	*Hasanović, Neacşa*
13/04	Oţelul	a	0-2	
20/04	Iaşi	h	2-1	*Costea, Thomas*
26/04	Rapid	a	0-1	
04/05	Petrolul	h	2-2	*Thomas, Stoica*
09/05	CFR Cluj	a	3-1	*Costea 2, Vranjković*
12/05	Pandurii	h	1-3	*Costea*
20/05	Gloria	a	0-0	
26/05	Steaua	h	1-1	*Roman*
30/05	Viitorul	a	4-3	*Roman, Costea 2, Vranjković*

No	Name	Nat	DoB	Pos	Aps	(s)	Gls
14	Paul Abba	NGA	20/12/90	A	1	(6)	1
27	Sergiu Arnăutu		27/05/90	A	4	(4)	1
21	Antonio Asanović	CRO	30/11/91	D	12	(1)	
17	Silviu Bălace		13/11/78	M	4		
29	Marius Bălău		12/06/80	D	11	(7)	
5	Alexandros Biris	GRE	30/10/86	D		(1)	
17	Ciprian Brata		24/03/91	M	9	(1)	
4	Florian Buleică		12/09/91	D	11	(3)	
10	Florin Costea		16/05/85	A	14		8
35	Cătălin Crăciun		26/08/91	A	1	(3)	
20	Alexandru Dandea		23/01/88	D	16		2
18	Ovidiu Dănănae		26/08/85	D	13		
21	Dragoş Dragalina		12/10/87	A	4	(2)	
2	Alexandre Durimel	FRA	16/03/90	D	17		
16	Iskandar Dzhalilov	RUS	01/06/92	D	11		
34	Cosmin Fruntelată		25/09/87	M		(1)	
3	Alexandru Giurgiu		25/09/92	D	13	(1)	
5	Jovan Golić	SRB	18/09/86	M	11	(2)	
6	Costinel Gugu		20/05/92	D	3	(3)	
8	Mirza Hasanović	BIH	16/09/90	M	9	(2)	1
12	Dumitru Hotoboc		23/12/78	G	3		
13	Hugo Moutinho	POR	01/01/82	M	18		1
23	Alexandru Iordan		17/08/88	G		(1)	
32	Barry Kader	CIV	26/03/86	M	2	(2)	
1	Andrei Marinescu		11/02/85	G	15		
23	Marian Mecea		05/03/90	G		(1)	
22	Milan Mitić	SRB	14/01/84	D	18		
7	Sergiu Neacşă		03/09/91	M	13	(13)	3
16	Răzvan Neagu		25/05/87	A		(1)	
19	Emil Ninu		23/08/86	D	1	(1)	
10	Adrian Olah		30/04/81	M	26	(2)	
8	Alexandru Ologu		16/07/89	M	1	(1)	
1	Leonidas Panagopoulos	GRE	03/01/87	G	12		
18	Florin Pătraşcu		12/04/86	M	4	(5)	
20	Cristian Poiană		23/12/88	M	1	(3)	
11	Mihai Roman		31/05/92	A	4	(8)	3
6	Dorel Stoica		15/12/78	M	9	(1)	1
12	Mihai Ştetca		07/03/81	G	4		
25	Ionuţ Tătaru		05/10/89	D	10		
25	Joël Thomas	FRA	30/06/87	A	15	(12)	6
77	Georgian Tobă		23/05/89	M	1	(1)	
13	Oliver Tole	CRO	16/06/90	A	4	(1)	
9	Cosmin Vancea		24/12/84	A	14	(2)	5
22	Gabriel Velcovici		02/10/84	D	4		
30	Vojislav Vranjković	SRB	01/01/83	M	13		2
11	Alexandru Zaharia		25/05/90	M	18	(1)	2
15	Nicolae Zuluf		03/04/88	M		(2)	

FC UNIVERSITATEA CLUJ

Coach: Claudiu Niculescu; (26/07/12) Cristian
Dulca; (01/10/12) (Marius Popescu);
(10/11/12) Marius Şumudică;
(16/11/12) Marius Popescu;
(31/01/13) Ioan Viorel Ganea
1919 • Cluj Arena (32,000) • universitateacluj.ro
Major honours
Romanian Cup (1) 1965

2012

Date	Opp	H/A	Score	Scorers
20/07	Pandurii	a	2-6	Pătraşcu, Păcurar
29/07	Gloria	h	1-0	Szilagyi
05/08	Steaua	a	1-5	Dinu
12/08	Viitorul	h	2-1	Dinu, Cleiton
17/08	Turnu Severin	a	1-1	Dinu
25/08	Braşov	h	1-1	Dinu (p)
02/09	Concordia	a	2-0	Paulinho 2
17/09	Astra	h	1-3	Dinu (p)
22/09	Dinamo	h	1-2	Dinu (p)
29/09	Gaz Metan	a	1-2	Paulinho (p)
08/10	Ceahlăul	h	1-0	Alex
21/10	Vaslui	a	0-1	
26/10	Oţelul	h	1-1	Cleiton
03/11	Iaşi	a	0-4	
12/11	Rapid	h	1-2	Drăghici
16/11	Petrolul	a	0-1	
24/11	CFR Cluj	h	1-2	Dinu (p)
30/11	Pandurii	h	1-1	Dinu
07/12	Gloria	a	0-0	

2013

Date	Opp	H/A	Score	Scorers
25/02	Steaua	h	0-1	
02/03	Viitorul	a	1-1	Dinu (p)
11/03	Turnu Severin	h	1-0	Buleică
18/03	Braşov	h	0-0	
29/03	Concordia	h	1-0	Buleică
05/04	Astra	a	2-1	Borza, Muzac (p)
13/04	Dinamo	a	1-1	Nwakaema
19/04	Gaz Metan	h	3-4	Hidişan, Nwakaema (p), Apostu
26/04	Ceahlăul	a	1-2	Nicola
04/05	Vaslui	h	2-1	Buleică, Nicola
08/05	Oţelul	a	2-0	Borza, Apostu
13/05	Iaşi	h	0-2	
20/05	Rapid	a	4-1	Székely 2, Apostu, Muzac
26/05	Petrolul	h	2-4	Buleică, Borza
29/05	CFR Cluj	a	1-3	Székely

No	Name	Nat	DoB	Pos	Aps	(s)	Gls
24	Alex Bráz	BRA	20/05/90	M	17		1
5	Alex Bráz	BRA	14/09/84	D		(2)	
11	Bogdan Apostu		20/04/82	A	4	(9)	3
12	Dragoş Balauru		11/11/89	G	17		
20	Adrian Borza		18/02/85	M	11	(3)	3
12	Ionuţ Boşneag		15/02/82	G	8		
5	Dan Bucşa		23/06/88	M	14		
14	Florian Buleică		12/09/91	D	14		4
30	Paraskevas Christou	CYP	02/02/84	D	16	(1)	
2	Raul Ciupe		24/11/83	D	22	(2)	
14	Cleiton	BRA	02/01/84	A	11	(4)	2
21	Rareş Cucui		30/10/93	D	1		
26	Cătălin Dedu		16/05/87	A	4	(8)	
29	Viorel Dinu		17/03/80	A	20	(1)	9
11	Octavian Drăghici		26/11/85	A	8	(5)	1
26	Erico	BRA	20/07/89	D	13	(2)	
27	Dragoş Firţulescu		15/05/89	M	1	(1)	
18	Vasile Gheorghe		05/09/85	M	17	(1)	
17	Florin Hidişan		24/06/82	M	9	(1)	1
8	Roberto Iancu		14/06/93	M	1	(6)	
27	Lorant Kovacs		06/06/93	D	1		
77	Plamen Krumov	BUL	04/11/85	D	10	(3)	
3	Valeriu Lupu		24/01/91	D	7	(2)	
3	Gaston Mendy	SEN	22/11/85	D	6	(1)	
12	Dinu Moldovan		03/05/90	G	1		
23	Apostol Muzac		06/07/87	M	17	(7)	2
17	Ionuţ Năstăsie		07/01/92	M	2	(8)	
16	Eduard Nicola		23/05/83	D	18	(7)	2
1	Vladimir Niculescu		26/09/87	G	7	(1)	
22	Emil Ninu		28/08/86	D	12	(1)	
15	Anthony Nwakaema	NGA	04/04/83	A	5	(5)	2
20	Paulinho	POR	30/01/85	M	17		3
10	Alexandru Păcurar		20/01/82	M	1		1
7	Bogdan Pătraşcu		07/05/79	M	12	(2)	1
6	Adrian Popa		07/04/90	M	15	(2)	
24	Alin Raţiu		14/09/82	D	13	(1)	
22	Mihai Roman		31/05/92	A		(1)	
1	Cătălin Samoilă		12/01/90	G	1		
8	János Székely		13/05/83	M	3	(5)	3
4	Zsolt Szilagyi		29/06/81	D	13	(6)	1
21	Rareş Takacs		10/12/91	M	4		
27	Georgian Tobă		23/05/89	M		(4)	
3	Lucian Turcu		03/10/86	D	4		

FC VASLUI

Coach: Marius Şumudică; (28/09/12) Viorel Hizo;
(09/04/13) Gabriel Balint
2001 • Municipal (15,000) • vasluifc.ro

2012

Date	Opp	H/A	Score	Scorers
22/07	Rapid	a	2-2	Wesley 2
28/07	Petrolul	h	3-0	Sânmărtean, Sburlea, Niculae
04/08	CFR Cluj	a	0-3	
12/08	Pandurii	h	0-0	
18/08	Gloria	a	3-0	Milanov, Niculae, Sburlea
27/08	Steaua	h	3-1	Celeban, Sânmărtean, Niculae
02/09	Viitorul	a	2-2	Sânmărtean (p), Celeban
17/09	Turnu Severin	h	2-1	Niculae, N'Doye
23/09	Braşov	a	1-2	Varga
29/09	Concordia	h	3-0	Niculae 3
08/10	Astra	a	1-1	Varga
21/10	U Cluj	h	1-0	Niculae
28/10	Gaz Metan	a	1-1	
03/11	Ceahlăul	h	4-3	Celeban 2, Cauê, Niculae
10/11	Dinamo	a	1-0	Sânmărtean
19/11	Oţelul	a	0-2	
26/11	Iaşi	h	3-0	Varela, Niculae 2
02/12	Rapid	h	1-0	Jumisse
08/12	Petrolul	a	0-0	

2013

Date	Opp	H/A	Score	Scorers
25/02	CFR Cluj	h	0-0	
04/03	Pandurii	a	1-2	Jumisse
11/03	Gloria	h	1-1	Sânmărtean (p)
17/03	Steaua	a	0-2	
01/04	Viitorul	h	3-2	Celeban 2, Antal
05/04	Turnu Severin	a	0-2	
15/04	Braşov	h	1-1	Charalambous
21/04	Concordia	a	1-1	Buhăescu
27/04	Astra	h	2-1	Sânmărtean, Temwanjera
01/05	U Cluj	a	1-2	Sânmărtean (p)
07/05	Gaz Metan	h	1-1	Buhăescu
11/05	Ceahlăul	a	2-0	Temwanjera, Antal
18/05	Dinamo	h	4-1	Antal, Celeban, Stanciu, Temwanjera
24/05	Oţelul	h	1-0	Antal
30/05	Iaşi	a	2-1	Antal, Buhăescu

No	Name	Nat	DoB	Pos	Aps	(s)	Gls
8	Liviu Antal		02/06/89	M	23	(8)	5
88	Vasile Buhăescu		02/02/88	M	10	(7)	3
40	Alex Buziuc		15/03/94	A		(2)	
16	Cauê	BRA	24/05/89	M	26	(4)	1
28	Gabriel Cânu		18/01/81	D	1		
5	Piotr Celeban	POL	25/06/85	D	27	(1)	7
12	Vytautas Černiauskas	LTU	12/03/89	G	8		
33	Ilias Charalambous	CYP	25/09/80	D	17	(2)	1
1	Dănuţ Sânmărtean		28/03/79	G	18		
67	Andrei Cordoş		06/06/88	D	5	(7)	
30	Raul Costin		29/01/85	D	13	(10)	
7	Davide	POR	12/04/83	M		(5)	
17	Adrian Gheorghiu		30/11/81	M		(1)	
6	Valter Heil		11/02/90	D	1		
77	Eduardo Jumisse	MOZ	06/06/84	M	17	(1)	2
20	Zhivko Milanov	BUL	15/07/84	D	30	1	1
78	Ousmane N'Doye	SEN	21/03/78	M	14	(3)	1
70	Nderim Nedzipi	MKD	22/05/84	M	1	(6)	
15	Adrian Neniţă		02/11/96	M		(1)	
29	Marius Niculae		16/05/81	A	19		11
17	Sergiu Popovici		23/03/93	M	3	(3)	
23	Adrian Sălăgeanu		09/04/83	D	22	(1)	
3	Lucian Sânmărtean		13/03/80	M	29		7
9	Sabrin Sburlea		12/05/89	A	7	(6)	2
10	Nicolae Stanciu		07/05/93	M	21	(10)	1
89	Cătălin Straton		18/12/89	G	8		
19	Mike Temwanjera	ZIM	21/05/82	A	9	(5)	3
11	Emile Paul Tendeng	SEN	09/03/92	A	2	(4)	
25	Michael Tukura	NGA	19/08/88	D	3	(2)	
3	Fernando Varela	CPV	26/11/87	D	32		1
40	Dacian Varga		15/10/84	M	7	(8)	2
80	Wesley	BRA	10/11/80	A	1		2
11	Ervin Zsiga		07/11/91	M		(1)	

FC VIITORUL CONSTANŢA

Coach: Cătălin Anghel
2009 • Oţelul, Galaţi (13,500); Farul (15,500) •
academiahagi.ro

2012

Date	Opp	H/A	Score	Scorers
23/07	Braşov	h	2-2	Rusu, Cristea
30/07	Concordia	a	1-1	Iancu
05/08	Astra	h	0-0	
12/08	U Cluj	a	1-2	Dică
20/08	Gaz Metan	h	0-1	
27/08	Ceahlăul	a	3-0	Iancu, Chiţu, Alibec
02/09	Vaslui	h	2-2	Iancu, Dică (p)
15/09	Oţelul	a	1-1	Dică (p)
24/09	Iaşi	h	1-0	Dică
30/09	Rapid	a	1-2	Bejan
06/10	Petrolul	h	1-2	og (Galamaz)
18/10	CFR Cluj	a	1-0	Iancu
29/10	Pandurii	h	2-0	Iancu (p), Chiţu
02/11	Gloria	a	1-1	Iancu
11/11	Steaua	h	0-4	
17/11	Dinamo	h	1-1	Benzar
26/11	Turnu Severin	a	2-2	Benzar, Dică
01/12	Braşov	a	1-3	Chiţu
10/12	Concordia	h	1-1	Alibec

2013

Date	Opp	H/A	Score	Scorers
25/02	Astra	a	0-2	
02/03	U Cluj	h	1-1	Chiţu
08/03	Gaz Metan	a	1-4	Chiţu
17/03	Ceahlăul	h	2-2	Dică 2 (1p)
01/04	Vaslui	a	2-3	Dică, Alibec
08/04	Oţelul	h	0-0	
15/04	Iaşi	a	2-1	Alibec 2
20/04	Rapid	h	1-2	og (Voicu)
27/04	Petrolul	a	0-1	
05/05	CFR Cluj	h	0-2	
09/05	Pandurii	a	1-4	Benzar
13/05	Gloria	h	2-0	Lazăr, Dică
19/05	Steaua	a	5-2	Chiţu 2, Dică (p), Larie, Nikolov
24/05	Dinamo	a	3-2	Lazăr, Chiţu, Bălaşa
30/05	Turnu Severin	h	3-4	Puţanu, Rusu 2 (1p)

No	Name	Nat	DoB	Pos	Aps	(s)	Gls
91	Marius Albu		20/02/91	M	1	(9)	
9	Denis Alibec		05/01/91	A	21	(2)	5
27	Mihai Bălaşa		14/01/95	D	20	(2)	1
4	Florin Bejan		28/03/91	D	29		1
30	Romario Benzar		26/03/92	M	20	(4)	3
31	Alexandru Buzbuchi		31/10/93	G	17		
7	George Călinţaru		26/02/89	A		(1)	
11	Aurelian Chiţu		25/03/91	A	33		8
92	Alin Cîrstocea		16/01/92	M	15	(8)	
99	Cristian Cristea		31/05/88	A	3	(1)	1
2	Vasilică Cristocea		27/09/80	M	1	(9)	
20	Nicolae Dică		09/05/80	M	25	(1)	10
17	Cristian Gavra		03/04/93	A	1	(12)	
7	Claudiu Herea		16/03/90	M	2	(13)	
28	Alexandru Iacob		14/04/89	M	1		
10	Gabriel Iancu		15/04/94	M	17	(1)	6
6	Ionuţ Larie		16/01/87	D	30		1
8	Alexandru Lazăr		20/02/91	M	26	(4)	2
28	Alexandru Mitriţă		08/02/95	M	2	(5)	
41	Sebastian Mladen		11/12/91	D	19	(1)	
24	Boban Nikolov	MKD	28/07/94	M	2	(3)	1
18	Mihai Onicaş		27/01/90	M	2	(4)	
3	Adrian Puţanu		09/01/94	D	9	(4)	1
19	Vlad Rusu		22/06/90	A	8	(2)	3
15	Alexandru Tîrnovan		27/07/95	M	5	(1)	
3	Alin Toşca		14/03/92	D	24	(1)	
3	Lucian Turcu		03/10/86	D	6	(1)	
14	Bogdan Ţiru		15/03/94	M	1		
66	Andrei Vaştag		21/03/94	M	10	(10)	
95	Ionuţ Vînă		20/02/95	A		(3)	
12	Cosmin Vîtcă		12/05/82	G	17		

Top goalscorers

21	Raul Rusescu (Steaua)
16	Jeremy Bokila (Petrolul)
15	Marius Alexe (Dinamo)
14	Kehinde Fatai (Astra)
13	Hamza Younès (Petrolul)
12	Constantin Budescu (Astra)
11	Mugurel Buga (Braşov)
	Bojan Golubović (Ceahlăul)
	Marius Niculae (Vaslui)
10	Thaer Bawab (Gaz Metan)
	Deivydas Matulevičius (Pandurii)
	Nicolae Dică (Viitorul)

Domestic cup: Cupa României 2012/13

FIRST ROUND

(25/09/12)
Ceahlăul 4-0 Gloria Bistriţa
Dinamo Bucureşti 2-1 Voinţa Sibiu *(aet)*
Petrolul 2-0 Damila
Şoimii Pâncota 2-3 Concordia
(26/09/12)
Berceni 0-2 CFR Cluj
Braşov 1-0 Farul
Delta 2-1 U Cluj
Gaz Metan 2-1 Caracal
Pandurii 7-1 FC Zagon
Sportul Studenţesc 0-1 Oţelul
Turnu Severin 2-1 Mioveni
Vaslui 0-1 Botoşani
(27/09/12)
Brăila 0-0 Viitorul Constanţa *(aet; 6-5 on pens)*
CSMS Iaşi 1-4 Astra
Rapid Bucureşti 6-0 Olimpia
Steaua 3-1 Târgu-Mureş

SECOND ROUND

(30/10/12)
Astra 5-1 Turnu Severin
Braşov 0-2 Petrolul
Rapid Bucureşti 4-1 Delta
(31/10/12)
Ceahlăul 2-0 Gaz Metan
CFR Cluj 2-0 Botoşani
Concordia 0-0 Steaua *(aet; 4-3 on pens)*
(01/11/12)
Oţelul 3-0 Brăila
Pandurii 1-2 Dinamo Bucureşti

QUARTER-FINALS

(27/11/12)
Petrolul 2-1 Concordia *(Bokila 44, 55; Purece 82p)*
(28/11/12)
Ceahlăul 0-2 Oţelul *(Iorga 11, Băjenaru 65)*
CFR Cluj 2-1 Dinamo Bucureşti *(Rafael Bastos 66, Mureşan 101; Alexe 62) (aet)*
(29/11/12)
Rapid Bucureşti 2-3 Astra *(Oros 65, Bărboianu 75og; Budescu 4, Fatai 49, Mureşan 111) (aet)*

SEMI-FINALS

(16/04/13 & 22/05/13)
CFR Cluj 0-0 Astra
Astra 0-2 CFR Cluj *(Hora 19, Diogo Valente 90)*
(CFR Cluj 2-0)
(18/04/13 & 21/05/13)
Oţelul 0-3 Petrolul *(Geraldo Alves 3, Morar 60, Bokila 71)*
Petrolul 1-2 Oţelul *(Bokila 56; Paraschiv 8, Iorga 90p)*
(Petrolul 4-2)

FINAL

(01/06/13)
Naţional Arena, Bucharest
FC PETROLUL PLOIEŞTI 1 *(Bokila 9)*
CFR 1907 CLUJ 0
Referee: *Balaj*
PETROLUL: *Khomutovski, Sony, Hoban, Enza-Yamissi, Guilherme, Mustivar, Boudjemaa (Achim 80), Mojica (Romário 82), Younès, Grozav (Morar 72), Bokila*
CFR CLUJ: *Mário Felgueiras, Ivo Pinto, Cadú, Piccolo, Camora, Mureşan, Sare, Deac (Weldon 81), Diogo Valente (Kapetanos 61), Rui Pedro, Maah*

Promoted clubs

FC BOTOŞANI
Coach: Cristian Popovici
2001 • Municipal (12,000) • fcbotosani.ro

AFC SĂGEATA NĂVODARI
Coach: Aurel Şunda;
(24/01/13) Constantin Gache;
(26/04/13) (Gheorghe Mina)
2010 • Flacăra (5,000) • sageata-navodari.ro

ASC CORONA 2010 BRAŞOV
Coach: Daniel Bona
2010 • Carpaţi (2,000) • asccorona.ro

ACS POLI TIMIŞOARA
Coach: Valentin Velcea
2012 • Dan Păltinişanu (32,972) • acspoli.ro

SECOND LEVEL FINAL TABLES 2012/13

SERIA I

		Pld	W	D	L	F	A	Pts
1	FC Botoşani	24	17	2	5	47	19	53
2	AFC Săgeata Năvodari	24	14	4	6	43	29	46
3	FC Delta Tulcea	24	12	6	6	45	22	42
4	CS Otopeni	24	12	5	7	37	27	41
5	CF Brăila	24	12	4	8	39	35	40
6	CS Buftea	24	9	5	10	34	38	32
7	CSM Unirea 04 Slobozia	24	7	9	8	35	38	30
8	FCM Dunărea Galaţi	24	8	4	12	23	30	28
9	FC Sportul Studenţesc Bucureşti	24	9	1	14	28	58	28
10	ACS Rapid CFR Suceava	24	7	6	11	31	35	27
11	FC Farul Constanţa	24	8	3	13	35	41	27
12	CF Chindia Târgovişte	24	7	5	12	33	41	26
13	FC Dinamo II Bucureşti	24	5	4	15	27	44	19

NB FCM Bacău withdrew after round 1 – their match was annulled.

SERIA II

		Pld	W	D	L	F	A	Pts
1	ASC Corona 2010 Braşov	24	14	6	4	41	22	48
2	ACS Poli Timişoara	24	12	9	3	39	19	45
3	FC Damila Măciuca	24	13	5	6	38	22	44
4	FC UTA Arad	24	11	7	6	29	17	38
5	FCM Târgu Mureş	24	10	5	9	31	29	35
6	CSM Râmnicu Vâlcea	24	10	4	10	27	28	34
7	FC Bihor Oradea	24	8	9	7	35	31	33
8	FC Argeş Piteşti	24	9	4	11	34	40	31
9	CS Mioveni	24	7	11	6	27	23	28
10	CS Luceafărul Oradea	24	6	8	10	25	32	26
11	CS ALRO Slatina	24	4	10	10	27	29	22
12	FC Maramureş Universitar Baia Mare	24	5	8	11	21	36	21
13	FC Unirea 2006 Alba Iulia	24	3	2	19	12	58	11

NB CS Mioveni – 4 pts deducted; FC UTA Arad & FC Maramureş Universitar Baia Mare – 2 pts deducted; CSU Voinţa Sibiu withdrew after round 11 – their matches were annulled; FC Unirea 2006 Alba Iulia withdrew after round 13 – their remaining matches were awarded as 0-3 defeats.

RUSSIA
Russian Football Union (RFS)

Address	Ulitsa Narodnaya 7	**President**	Nikolai Tolstykh
	RU-115172 Moskva	**General secretary**	Ekaterlna Fedyshina
Tel	+7 495 9261300	**Media officer**	Igor Vladimirov
Fax	+7 495 9261305	**Year of formation**	1912
E-mail	info@rfs.ru	**National stadium**	Luzhniki, Moscow
Website	rfs.ru		(78,360)

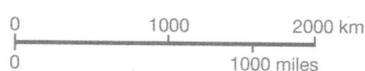

St Peterburg
(St Petersburg)

16

4 5 9 13

Moskva
(Moscow)

Nizhny Novgorod

15 Kazan Perm

Saransk

10 12 2

Rostov-na-Donu

17

6 11 Samara 7 Yekaterinburg

8 Krasnodar

Tomsk

18

Grozny~ 14

1 ~Vladikavkaz

3 Makhachkala

PREMIER-LIGA CLUBS

1. FC Alania Vladikavkaz
2. FC Amkar Perm
3. FC Anji Makhachkala
4. PFC CSKA Moskva
5. FC Dinamo Moskva
6. FC Krasnodar
7. PFC Krylya Sovetov Samara
8. FC Kuban Krasnodar

9. FC Lokomotiv Moskva
10. FC Mordovia Saransk
11. FC Rostov
12. FC Rubin Kazan
13. FC Spartak Moskva
14. FC Terek Grozny
15. FC Volga Nizhny Novgorod
16. FC Zenit St Petersburg

PROMOTED CLUBS

17. FC Ural Yekaterinburg
18. FC Tom Tomsk

KEY:

● – UEFA Champions League
● – UEFA Europa League
● – Promoted clubs
● – Relegated clubs

New calendar suits CSKA

The first staging of the Russian Premier-Liga in its new autumn-to-spring schedule found favour with PFC CSKA Moskva, who won the title for the first time since 2006. Leonid Slutski's well-drilled team also completed the double with a sixth Russian Cup triumph in nine years, edging FC Anji Makhachkala on penalties in the final.

Neither Anji nor equally ambitious FC Zenit St Petersburg, therefore, won a trophy, and although the two clubs enjoyed extended European campaigns, both were outlasted in the UEFA Europa League by quarter-finalists FC Rubin Kazan.

Moscow club beat Zenit to Premier-Liga title

Slutski's team complete double with cup win

Ambitious Anji miss out on first trophy

Domestic league

An early elimination from Europe, in the UEFA Europa League play-offs, enabled CSKA to concentrate exclusively on domestic matters. They would use that to their advantage to dethrone Zenit, top dogs in the previous two Premier-Liga seasons, and become champions of Russia for the fourth time. With just 30 matches to play, rather than the 44 of the previous, transitional, campaign, CSKA were never threatened by the burn-out that had caused their 2011/12 challenge to unravel in the closing stages, when they won just three of their last 15 games.

Slutski, the club's head coach since October 2009, was retained for the 2012/13 campaign despite coming under pressure for his position in the summer, and although further questions were asked after a couple of early league defeats, one of them 3-1 at home to Zenit, and the shock European elimination by Swedish club AIK, the CSKA board's faith in him was to be amply rewarded.

The Army Men marched to the top of the table with a brilliant burst of form in the autumn that brought them 12 wins in 13 games, including six on the trot away from home. By the winter break – all

three months of it – they held a two-point advantage over Anji, with Zenit three points further back. These three teams looked set for an intriguing tussle in the spring, but Guus Hiddink's expensively-assembled Anji fell away quickly and by the start of April, following four successive wins – all without conceding – CSKA found themselves eight points ahead of Zenit.

It was then that Slutski's side, with the finishing line in sight, began to get nervous, shedding seven points in their next three games to allow Luciano Spalletti's in-form title holders back in with a shout.

A vital 1-0 win at home to FC Terek Grozny, with Swedish midfielder Pontus Wernbloom scoring the only goal, settled the leaders down, however, and a week later a thumping 4-1 win at local rivals FC Lokomotiv Moskva re-established a five-point lead with two games to go. Because of their greater number of victories – the deciding factor in the Premier-Liga when teams are level on points – a 0-0 draw at FC Kuban Krasnodar next time out was sufficient to clinch the title with a game to spare.

CSKA's strength throughout the campaign was their rock-solid spine of goalkeeper Igor Akinfeev, central

defenders Sergei Ignashevich and Vasili Berezutski, Swedish midfield duo Wernbloom and Rasmus Elm and 11-goal Nigerian striker Ahmed Musa. It was generally recognised that there were superior playing squads at Anji – captained by reportedly the world's highest paid footballer, Samuel Eto'o – and Zenit – who spent a vast sum on new recruits Hulk and Axel Witsel – but CSKA's was the most harmonious and homogenous of the three, and that was often evident on the field of play.

Zenit finished just two points behind the champions to secure a UEFA Champions League qualifying place (CSKA's prize was direct access to the group stage). The four UEFA League qualifiers were headed by third-placed Anji and included European first-timers FC Kuban Krasnodar, who, assisted by the league's biggest average home attendances (20,934), went unbeaten throughout the spring under new coach Leonid Kuchuk to finish fifth, one place below FC Spartak Moskva and one above Rubin. Spartak sacked their new Spanish coach Unai Emery after less than half a season, restoring Valeri Karpin to the role, whereas Rubin's Kurban Berdyev completed his 11th season in charge of the Tatarstan outfit.

Continued on page 620

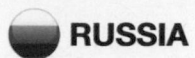
Domestic league: Premier-Liga 2012/13 final table

		Pld	Home					Away					Total					Pts
			W	D	L	F	A	W	D	L	F	A	W	D	L	F	A	
1	**PFC CSKA Moskva**	30	11	2	2	23	9	9	2	4	26	16	20	4	6	49	25	64
2	FC Zenit St Petersburg	30	10	3	2	26	9	8	5	2	27	16	18	8	4	53	25	62
3	FC Anji Makhachkala	30	10	5	0	30	15	5	3	7	15	19	15	8	7	45	34	53
4	FC Spartak Moskva	30	9	3	3	26	18	6	3	6	25	21	15	6	9	51	39	51
5	FC Kuban Krasnodar	30	8	6	1	27	13	6	3	6	21	15	14	9	7	48	28	51
6	FC Rubin Kazan	30	10	2	3	21	8	5	3	7	18	19	15	5	10	39	27	50
7	FC Dinamo Moskva	30	8	3	4	20	14	6	3	6	21	20	14	6	10	41	34	48
8	FC Terek Grozny	30	9	2	4	21	17	5	4	6	17	23	14	6	10	38	40	48
9	FC Lokomotiv Moskva	30	6	3	6	21	21	6	4	5	18	15	12	7	11	39	36	43
10	FC Krasnodar	30	10	1	4	28	12	2	5	8	17	27	12	6	12	45	39	42
11	FC Amkar Perm	30	4	5	6	22	25	3	3	9	12	26	7	8	15	34	51	29
12	FC Volga Nizhny Novgorod	30	2	6	7	12	22	5	2	8	16	24	7	8	15	28	46	29
13	FC Rostov	30	6	3	6	20	20	1	5	9	10	21	7	8	15	30	41	29
14	PFC Krylya Sovetov Samara	30	3	3	9	14	27	4	4	7	17	25	7	7	16	31	52	28
15	FC Mordovia Saransk	30	3	4	8	17	27	2	1	12	13	30	5	5	20	30	57	20
16	FC Alania Vladikavkaz	30	4	3	8	19	23	0	4	11	7	30	4	7	19	26	53	19

SEASON AT A GLANCE

EUROPEAN QUALIFICATION 2013/14

Champion/Cup winner: PFC CSKA Moskva (group stage)

FC Zenit St Petersburg (third qualifying round)

FC Anji Makhachkala (group stage)
FC Spartak Moskva (play-offs)
FC Kuban Krasnodar (third qualifying round)
FC Rubin Kazan (second qualifying round)

Top scorers	Yura Movsisyan (Krasnodar/Spartak) & Wanderson (Krasnodar), 13 goals
Relegated clubs	FC Alania Vladikavkaz, FC Mordovia Saransk
Promoted club	FC Ural Yekaterinburg, FC Tom Tomsk
Cup final	PFC CSKA Moskva 1-1 FC Anji Makhachkala (aet; 4-3 on pens)

PREMIER-LIGA TEAM OF THE SEASON
(4-4-2)
Coach: Slutski (CSKA)

PLAYER OF THE SEASON
Igor Akinfeev
(PFC CSKA Moskva)

After suffering a serious knee injury the previous season, Akinfeev returned to peak form in 2012/13. Ever-present in the Premier-Liga until the final-day dead rubber, he conceded only 22 goals in 29 outings and was also pivotal to CSKA's cup success. Furthermore, he kept clean sheets in each of Russia's first four FIFA World Cup qualifying outings.

NEWCOMER OF THE SEASON
Aleksei Miranchuk
(FC Lokomotiv Moskva)

Lokomotiv had a miserable campaign, but out of the gloom emerged, albeit belatedly, a beaming ray of light in the shape of this hugely gifted Russian Under-17 international midfielder. Miranchuk made his top-flight debut in April and scored his first goal in May. He only played six games but the potential was there for all to see.

NATIONAL TEAM

Home Kit   Away Kit

INTERNATIONAL HONOURS*
UEFA European Championship (1) 1960

INTERNATIONAL TOURNAMENT APPEARANCES*
FIFA World Cup (9) 1958 (qtr-finals), 1962 (qtr-finals), 1966 (4th), 1970 (qtr-finals), 1982 (2nd phase), 1986 (2nd round), 1990, 1994, 2002
UEFA European Championship (10) 1960 (Winners), 1964 (runners-up), 1968 (4th), 1972 (runners-up), 1988 (runners-up), 1992, 1996, 2004, 2008 (semi-finals), 2012

TOP FIVE ALL-TIME CAPS
Viktor Onopko (113); Oleh Blokhin (112); Rinat Dasaev (91); Albert Shesternyov (90); **Sergei Ignashevich** (87)

TOP FIVE ALL-TIME GOALS
Oleh Blokhin (42); Oleh Protasov (29); Vladimir Beschastnykh & Valentin Ivanov (26); Eduard Streltsov (25)

(* before 1992 as USSR; 1992 as CIS)

Results 2012/13

15/08/12	Ivory Coast	H	Moscow	1-1	*Dzagoev (55)*
07/09/12	Northern Ireland (WCQ)	H	Moscow	2-0	*Fayzulin (30), Shirokov (78p)*
11/09/12	Israel (WCQ)	A	Tel-Aviv	4-0	*Kerzhakov (7, 64), Kokorin (18), Fayzulin (77)*
12/10/12	Portugal (WCQ)	H	Moscow	1-0	*Kerzhakov (6)*
16/10/12	Azerbaijan (WCQ)	H	Moscow	1-0	*Shirokov (84p)*
14/11/12	United States	H	Krasnodar	2-2	*Smolov (9), Shirokov (84p)*
06/02/13	Iceland	N	Marbella (ESP)	2-0	*Shirokov (43), Shatov (66)*
25/03/13	Brazil	N	London (ENG)	1-1	*Fayzulin (73)*
07/06/13	Portugal (WCQ)	A	Lisbon	0-1	

Appearances 2012/13

Coach: Fabio Capello (ITA)	18/06/46		Civ	NIR	ISR	POR	AZE	Usa	Isl	Bra	POR	Caps	Goals
Igor Akinfeev	08/04/86	CSKA Moskva	G59	G	G	G	G		G46		G	59	-
Aleksandr Anyukov	28/09/82	Zenit	D30	D	D50	D		D59	D46	D46	D31	76	1
Vasili Berezutski	20/06/82	CSKA Moskva	D	D	D	D	D	D	D	D	D	70	2
Sergei Ignashevich	14/07/79	CSKA Moskva	D	D	D	D	D	D	D	D	D	87	5
Georgi Schennikov	27/04/91	CSKA Moskva	D									1	-
Igor Denisov	17/05/84	Zenit	M	M	M	M	M	M	M		M	37	-
Denis Glushakov	27/01/87	Lokomotiv Moskva	M	s85	M	s46	s46	s46	s57	M	s21	19	1
Alan Dzagoev	17/06/90	CSKA Moskva	M59	M58			s79	s46				27	8
Vladimir Bystrov	31/01/84	Zenit	M74	M	M23	M83	s62		M75	M46	M	43	4
Viktor Fayzulin	22/04/86	Zenit	M	M85	s34	M46	M46		M57	M	M21	8	3
Roman Pavlyuchenko	15/12/81	Lokomotiv Moskva	A46									51	21
Arseni Logashov	20/08/91	Anji	s30									1	-
Aleksandr Kokorin	19/03/91	Dinamo Moskva	s46	s58	A34	A	A	A65		A46		13	1
Andrey Arshavin	29/05/81	Arsenal (ENG)	s59									75	17
Vyacheslav Malafeev	04/03/79	Zenit	s59									29	-
Aleksandr Samedov	19/07/84	Lokomotiv Moskva	s74		s23	s83	M62					6	-
Dmitri Kombarov	22/01/87	Spartak Moskva		D	D	D	D	M46	s46	s46	D	12	-
Roman Shirokov	06/07/81	Zenit		M	M	M	M	M	M	M	M	33	11
Aleksandr Kerzhakov	27/11/82	Zenit		A	A	A65	A79	A46	A46	A	A68	72	22
Andrei Eschenko	09/02/84	Lokomotiv Moskva /Anji			s50	s65	D	D	D	D		6	-
Vladimir Gabulov	19/10/83	Anji						G	s46	G		10	-
Fedor Smolov	09/02/90	Anji						M11	s46		s68	3	1
Maksim Grigoryev	06/07/90	Lokomotiv Moskva						s11/80		s85		2	-
Renat Yanbaev	07/04/84	Zenit						s59				12	-
Artem Dzyuba	22/08/88	Spartak Moskva						s65				2	-
Denis Cheryshev	26/12/90	Real Madrid (ESP)						s80				1	-
Yuri Zhirkov	20/08/83	Anji							M46	s46/85	M	58	-
Oleg Shatov	29/07/90	Anji							s46	s46		2	1
Kirill Nababkin	08/09/86	CSKA Moskva							s75			2	-
Aleksei Kozlov	25/12/86	Kuban									s31	1	-

RUSSIA

Domestic cup

CSKA's seventh appearance in the Russian Cup final since the turn of the century ended like all of the others – in victory. However, like most of those previous triumphs, they had to fight tooth and nail for their win. Anji dominated for long periods in Grozny after Musa had given the champions an early lead, equalising through Frenchman Lassana Diarra and eventually taking the competition specialists all the way to penalties, where keeper Akinfeev was at his resilient best, making a decisive save from his Russian international team-mate Yuri Zhirkov before Seydou Doumbia struck the final blow with an audacious chip.

Europe

It was a fallow season in the UEFA Champions League for Russia, with both Zenit and Spartak Moskva failing to make it through the group stage – a year after Zenit and CSKA had both reached the knockout phase – but there was a strong and sustained Premier-Liga presence in the UEFA Europa League as three teams reached the last 16, with Rubin going all the way to the quarter-finals, where they were eliminated by eventual winners Chelsea FC.

Berdyev's side claimed a notable scalp in the round of 32 when they ousted holders

Club Atlético de Madrid (after a 2-0 first-leg win in Spain), while competition latecomers Zenit used the away-goals rule to eliminate Liverpool FC, with whom Anji had shared a couple of 1-0 home wins in the group stage before knocking out 2011/12 quarter-finalists Hannover 96. Hiddink's side would, like Berdyev's, eventually fall to English opposition in Newcastle United FC, but there was considerable disappointment in St Petersburg when Zenit came a cropper against FC Basel 1893, missing a host of chances, including a penalty, in the home leg against a team reduced to ten men for more than half the game.

National team

The frustration of Russia's early exit from UEFA EURO 2012 was quickly forgotten as new coach Fabio Capello led the team to victory in each of their opening four 2014 FIFA World Cup qualifiers. Deploying virtually the same side in each game, not that dissimilar from the one selected in Poland by his predecessor, Dick Advocaat, the Italian was rewarded with not just 12 points but four clean sheets. The hardest earned of those was the 1-0 win at home to Portugal, in which the CSKA trio of Akinfeev, Ignashevich and Berezutski were especially impressive. Zenit striker Aleksandr Kerzhakov, a frustrated figure at UEFA EURO 2012, scored the early winner in that game, having also been on target twice in the previous qualifier – a magnificent 4-0 win in Israel.

Fabio Capello – enjoying life as head coach of Russia

Russia were hoping to make it five wins out of five when they visited Northern Ireland in March, but heavy snow forced the postponement of that fixture, so they had to wait until June for their next qualifier, away to Portugal. As in the teams' first meeting in Moscow, an early goal decided the contest, and again it came from the home side, Hélder Postiga's strike resulting in Capello's first defeat – in his ninth match at the helm. With half of their fixtures still to complete, Russia's fate was still in their own hands, but having failed to qualify for the previous two World Cups, the pressure on the 2018 tournament hosts to ensure themselves a dress rehearsal in Brazil intensified significantly with that 1-0 defeat in Lisbon.

European club competitions 2012/13

FC ZENIT ST PETERSBURG

CHAMPIONS LEAGUE

Group C
Match 1 - Málaga CF (ESP)
A 0-3
Malafeev, Anyukov, Bruno Alves, Lombaerts, Kerzhakov, Shirokov (Lumb 86), Zyryanov (Djordjević 75), Fayzulin, Luković (Bystrov 40), Denisov, Hulk. Coach: Luciano Spalletti (ITA)

Match 2 - AC Milan (ITA)
H 2-3 *Hulk (45+2), Shirokov (49)*
Malafeev, Anyukov, Criscito, Lombaerts (Bukharov 90), Kerzhakov, Hubočan, Shirokov, Fayzulin (Kanunnikov 79), Hulk, Bystrov (Zyryanov 72). Coach: Luciano Spalletti (ITA)

Match 3 - RSC Anderlecht (BEL)
H 1-0 *Kerzhakov (72p)*
Malafeev, Anyukov, Criscito, Lombaerts, Kerzhakov, Hubočan, Shirokov (Bruno Alves 76), Fayzulin (Bystrov 58), Semak (Zyryanov 67), Witsel, Hulk. Coach: Luciano Spalletti (ITA)

Match 4 - RSC Anderlecht (BEL)
A 0-1
Malafeev, Anyukov, Criscito, Lombaerts (Bruno Alves 69), Kerzhakov, Hubočan, Shirokov, Semak (Danny 46), Denisov, Witsel, Bystrov (Kanunnikov 77). Coach: Luciano Spalletti (ITA)

Match 5 - Málaga CF (ESP)
H 2-2 *Danny (49), Fayzulin (87)*
Malafeev, Anyukov (Bystrov 81), Bruno Alves, Lombaerts, Danny, Kerzhakov, Hubočan, Shirokov (Fayzulin 72), Denisov, Witsel, Hulk. Coach: Luciano Spalletti (ITA)
Red card: Bystrov 90+5

Match 6 - AC Milan (ITA)
A 1-0 *Danny (35)*
Malafeev, Anyukov, Bruno Alves, Lombaerts, Danny, Hubočan, Shirokov (Kanunnikov 88), Semak (Lumb 90+1), Denisov, Witsel, Hulk (Zyryanov 80). Coach: Luciano Spalletti (ITA)

EUROPA LEAGUE

Round of 32 - Liverpool FC (ENG)
H 2-0 *Hulk (69), Semak (72)*
Malafeev, Anyukov, Lombaerts, Danny (Semak 54), Kerzhakov (Fayzulin 82), Luís Neto, Hubočan, Shirokov, Denisov, Witsel, Hulk. Coach: Luciano Spalletti (ITA)

A 1-3 *Hulk (19)*
Malafeev, Anyukov, Lombaerts (Criscito 46),
Danny (Fayzulin 46), Luís Neto, I lubočan,
Shirokov, Semak (Rodić 84), Denisov,
Witsel, Hulk. Coach: Luciano Spalletti (ITA)

Round of 16 - FC Basel 1893 (SUI)
A 0-2
Malafeev, Lombaerts, Danny (Kerzhakov
82), Luís Neto, Hubočan, Shirokov, Rodić,
Semak (Fayzulin 46), Denisov, Witsel, Hulk.
Coach: Luciano Spalletti (ITA)
Red card: Luís Neto 90+3
H 1-0 *Witsel (30)*
Zhevnov, Anyukov, Bruno Alves (Bystrov 73),
Lombaerts, Danny (Fayzulin 83), Kerzhakov,
Hubočan, Shirokov, Denisov, Witsel (Bukharov
90), Hulk. Coach: Luciano Spalletti (ITA)

FC SPARTAK MOSKVA

Play-offs - Fenerbahçe SK (TUR)
H 2-1 *Emenike (59), D Kombarov (69)*
Dykan, Pareja, Rafael Carioca, McGeady,
Ari (Dzyuba 77), Suchý, D Kombarov,
Bilyaletdinov, Emenike (Welliton 72),
Makeev, Rômulo (De Zeeuw 43). Coach:
Unai Emery (ESP)
A 1-1 *Ari (6)*
Dykan, Insaurralde, K Kombarov
(Bilyaletdinov 66), McGeady, Ari (Rafael
Carioca 51), Suchý, De Zeeuw, D
Kombarov, Emenike (Dzyuba 74), Makeev,
Rômulo. Coach: Unai Emery (ESP)
Red card: De Zeeuw 81

Group G
Match 1 - FC Barcelona (ESP)
A 2-3 *Dani Alves (29og), Rômulo (59)*
Dykan, Insaurralde, Rafael Carioca, K
Kombarov (Makeev 46), McGeady, Ari
(Dzyuba 83), Suchý, Källström (Jurado 78),
D Kombarov, Emenike, Rômulo. Coach:
Unai Emery (ESP)
Match 2 - Celtic FC (SCO)
H 2-3 *Emenike (41, 48)*
Pesyakov, Insaurralde, Pareja, Rafael
Carioca, McGeady (Dzyuba 76), Ari (Kozlov
87), De Zeeuw (Bryzgalov 66), Källström, D
Kombarov, Emenike, Makeev. Coach: Unai
Emery (ESP)
Red card: Insaurralde 63
Match 3 - SL Benfica (POR)
H 2-1 *Rafael Carioca (3), Jardel (43og)*
Rebrov, Pareja, Rafael Carioca, Ari,
Suchý, Jurado, Källström (Bryzgalov 79),
D Kombarov, Bilyaletdinov (Welliton 73),
Makeev, Ananidze (K Kombarov 58). Coach:
Unai Emery (ESP)

Match 4 - SL Benfica (POR)
A 0-2
Rebrov, Insaurralde, Pareja, Rafael Carioca,
K Kombarov (Ananidze 62), Ari, Jurado,
Källström (Dzyuba 71), D Kombarov,
Bilyaletdinov (Suchý 79), Makeev. Coach:
Unai Emery (ESP)
Red card: Pareja 76
Match 5 - FC Barcelona (ESP)
H 0-3
Dykan, Insaurralde, Rafael Carioca
(Bryzgalov 75), K Kombarov (Welliton 63),
Ari, Suchý, Jurado, Källström, D Kombarov,
Emenike (Ananidze 63), Makeev. Coach:
Unai Emery (ESP)
Match 6 - Celtic FC (SCO)
A 1-2 *Ari (39)*
Pesyakov, Insaurralde, Rafael Carioca,
K Kombarov, Ari (McGeady 61), Dzyuba,
Suchý, Jurado, Källström, D Kombarov,
Emenike. Coach: Valeri Karpin (RUS)
Red card: Källström 88

FC RUBIN KAZAN

Group H
Match 1 - FC Internazionale Milano (ITA)
A 2-2 *Ryazantsev (17), Rondón (84)*
Ryzhikov, Kuzmin, César Navas, Ryazantsev
(Orbaiz 70), R Eremenko, Marcano,
Bocchetti (Kaleshin 81), Gökdeniz Karadeniz
(Kasaev 85), Natcho, Sharonov, Rondón.
Coach: Kurban Berdyev (RUS)
Match 2 - FK Partizan (SRB)
H 2-0 *Gökdeniz Karadeniz (45),
Ryazantsev (48)*
Ryzhikov, Kuzmin, César Navas, Orbaiz,
Ryazantsev (Carlos Eduardo 83),
R Eremenko, Marcano, Bocchetti, Gökdeniz
Karadeniz (Kasaev 77), Natcho, Rondón
(Davydov 81). Coach: Kurban Berdyev
(RUS)
Match 3 - Neftçi PFK (AZE)
H 1-0 *Kasaev (16)*
Ryzhikov, Kuzmin, Ansaldi, César Navas,
Orbaiz, Kasaev, Kaleshin, Marcano,
Gökdeniz Karadeniz (Dyadyun 70), Natcho,
Rondón. Coach: Kurban Berdyev (RUS)
Match 4 - Neftçi PFK (AZE)
A 1-0 *Dyadyun (16)*
Ryzhikov, Ansaldi, César Navas, Orbaiz,
Kasaev (Gökhan Töre 83), Kaleshin,
Dyadyun (Davydov 77), Marcano, Gökdeniz
Karadeniz, Natcho, Rondón (R Eremenko
80). Coach: Kurban Berdyev (RUS)

Match 5 - FC Internazionale Milano (ITA)
H 3-0 *Gökdeniz Karadeniz (2), Rondón (85,
90+2)*
Ryzhikov, Kuzmin, Ansaldi, Orbaiz, Kasaev
(Gökhan Töre 61), Dyadyun (Rondón 59),
R Eremenko (Carlos Eduardo 8), Bocchetti,
Gökdeniz Karadeniz, Natcho, Sharonov.
Coach: Kurban Berdyev (RUS)
Match 6 - FK Partizan (SRB)
A 1-1 *Rondón (59)*
Arlauskis, Kuzmin, Ansaldi, Orbaiz, Kasaev
(Davydov 62), Carlos Eduardo (A Eremenko
75), Marcano, Bocchetti, Gökdeniz
Karadeniz, Sharonov, Rondón. Coach:
Kurban Berdyev (RUS)

**Round of 32 - Club Atlético de Madrid
(ESP)**
A 2-0 *Gökdeniz Karadeniz (6), Orbaiz (90+5)*
Ryzhikov, Ansaldi, César Navas, Orbaiz,
Kislyak, R Eremenko, Marcano, Gökdeniz
Karadeniz (Kuzmin 88), Natcho, Sharonov,
Rondón (Dyadyun 85). Coach: Kurban
Berdyev (RUS)
Red card: Sharonov 45
H 0-1
Ryzhikov, Kuzmin, Ansaldi, César Navas,
Orbaiz, Kislyak (Kaleshin 77), R Eremenko,
Marcano, Gökdeniz Karadeniz, Natcho
(Ryazantsev 88), Rondón. Coach: Kurban
Berdyev (RUS)
Red card: César Navas 89

Round of 16 - Levante UD (ESP)
A 0-0
Ryzhikov, Kuzmin, Ansaldi, Orbaiz, Kasaev
(Kaleshin 53), R Eremenko, Marcano,
Gökdeniz Karadeniz, Natcho, Sharonov,
Rondón (Dyadyun 85). Coach: Kurban
Berdyev (RUS)
Red card: Ansaldi 52
H 2-0 *Rondón (100), Dyadyun (112) (aet)*
Ryzhikov, Kuzmin, Orbaiz, Kasaev (Dyadyun
100), Kaleshin, R Eremenko, Marcano,
Gökdeniz Karadeniz (Kislyak 116), Natcho,
Sharonov, Rondón. Coach: Kurban Berdyev
(RUS)

Quarter-final - Chelsea FC (ENG)
A 1-3 *Natcho (41p)*
Ryzhikov, Kuzmin (Kasaev 82), Ansaldi,
César Navas, Orbaiz, Kaleshin, Dyadyun
(Rondón 46), R Eremenko, Gökdeniz
Karadeniz, Natcho, Sharonov. Coach:
Kurban Berdyev (RUS)
H 3-2 *Marcano (51), Gökdeniz Karadeniz (62),
Natcho (75p)*
Ryzhikov, Kuzmin (Kaleshin 46), Ansaldi,
César Navas, Orbaiz (Dyadyun 66), Kasaev
(Ryazantsev 72), R. Eremenko, Marcano,
Gökdeniz Karadeniz, Natcho, Rondón.
Coach: Kurban Berdyev (RUS)

RUSSIA

PFC CSKA MOSKVA

Play-offs - AIK (SWE)
A 1-0 *Honda (61)*
Akinfeev, Ignashevich, Honda, Dzagoev, Mário Fernandes (Nababkin 71), Musa, Cauņa (Wernbloom 66), Elm, Tošić (Mark González 76), V Berezutski, Schennikov. Coach: Leonid Slutski (RUS)
H 0-2
Akinfeev, Ignashevich, Honda, Dzagoev, Mário Fernandes, Nababkin, Musa, Cauņa (Wernbloom 12), Elm, Tošić (Mark González 85), V Berezutski. Coach: Leonid Slutski (RUS)

FC DINAMO MOSKVA

EUROPA LEAGUE

Third qualifying round - Dundee United FC (SCO)
A 2-2 *Semshov (50), Kokorin (90+3)*
Shunin, Schildenfeld, Dzsudzsák, Misimović, Kokorin, Semshov, Yusupov (Sapeta 90+1), Kuranyi, Wilkshire, Lomić, Rykov. Coach: Sergei Silkin (RUS)
H 5-0 *Semshov (2), Kokorin (23), Yusupov (40), Sapeta (83, 89)*
Berezovski, Fernández, Dzsudzsák (Bakkal 63), Misimović, Kokorin, Semshov, Yusupov (Sapeta 64), Kuranyi, Wilkshire, Lomić, Rykov (Schildenfeld 63). Coach: Dmitri Khokhlov (RUS)

Play-offs - VfB Stuttgart (GER)
A 0-2
Shunin, Schildenfeld, Fernández, Dzsudzsák, Misimović (Semshov 38), Nekhaichik (Granat 85), Yusupov, Noboa, Kuranyi (Panyukov 75), Wilkshire, Lomić. Coach: Dan Petrescu (ROU)
H 1-1 *Kokorin (77)*
Shunin, Schildenfeld, Fernández, Dzsudzsák (Nekhaichik 68), Kokorin, Granat, Noboa, Kuranyi (Misimović 68), Lomić, Sapeta (Semshov 61), Chicherin. Coach: Dan Petrescu (ROU)

FC ANJI MAKHACHKALA

EUROPA LEAGUE

Second qualifying round - Budapest Honvéd FC (HUN)
H 1-0 *Jucilei (22)*
V Gabulov, Samba, João Carlos, Ahmedov , Jucilei, Eto'o, Shatov (Lahiyalov 69), Logashov, Zhirkov (Tagirbekov 77), Traoré (Smolov 83), Boussoufa. Coach: Guus Hiddink (NED)
A 4-0 *Eto'o (7, 81), Traoré (53), Shatov (68)*
V Gabulov, Samba (G Gabulov 66), João Carlos, Ahmedov , Jucilei, Eto'o, Tagirbekov, Shatov, Logashov, Traoré (Smolov 73), Boussoufa (Zhirkov 54). Coach: Guus Hiddink (NED)

Third qualifying round - Vitesse (NED)
H 2-0 *Shatov (63), Smolov (74)*
V Gabulov, Samba, João Carlos (Gadzhibekov 15), Boussoufa, Jucilei, Eto'o, Tagirbekov, Shatov (Carcela-González 88), Logashov, Smolov, Ahmedov (G Gabulov 19). Coach: Guus Hiddink (NED)
A 2-0 *Eto'o (48, 84p)*
V Gabulov, Samba, João Carlos, Boussoufa (Lahiyalov 77), Agalarov, Jucilei, Eto'o (Smolov 85), Tagirbekov, Carcela-González, Zhirkov (Shatov 74), G Gabulov. Coach: Guus Hiddink (NED)

Play-offs - AZ Alkmaar (NED)
H 1-0 *Traoré (51)*
V Gabulov, Samba, João Carlos, Boussoufa, Agalarov, Jucilei, Eto'o, Tagirbekov, Shatov, Carcela-González, Traoré (Smolov 78). Coach: Guus Hiddink (NED)
A 5-0 *Boussoufa (17), Eto'o (45+2), Traoré (79), Carcela-González (83), Lahiyalov (90+4)*
V Gabulov, Samba, João Carlos, Boussoufa, Agalarov, Jucilei, Eto'o (Lahiyalov 85), Shatov (Smolov 72), Logashov (Zhirkov 54), Carcela-González, Traoré. Coach: Guus Hiddink (NED)

Group A
Match 1 - Udinese Calcio (ITA)
A 1-1 *Padelli (45og)*
Pomazan, Samba, João Carlos, Boussoufa, Agalarov, Jucilei, Eto'o, Shatov, Zhirkov, Traoré (Carcela-González 61), L Diarra. Coach: Guus Hiddink (NED)

Match 2 - BSC Young Boys (SUI)
H 2-0 *Eto'o (62p, 90)*
V Gabulov, Samba, João Carlos (G Gabulov 78), Boussoufa, Agalarov, Jucilei, Eto'o, Tagirbekov (Zhirkov 17), Shatov, Traoré (Carcela-González 63), L Diarra. Coach: Guus Hiddink (NED)
Match 3 - Liverpool FC (ENG)
A 0-1
V Gabulov, Samba, João Carlos, Boussoufa (Lahiyalov 77), Agalarov (Logashov 62), Eto'o, Shatov, Carcela-González, Zhirkov, Smolov (Traoré 64), G Gabulov. Coach: Guus Hiddink (NED)
Match 4 - Liverpool FC (ENG)
H 1-0 *Traoré (45+1)*
V Gabulov, Samba, João Carlos, Boussoufa, Jucilei, Eto'o, Tagirbekov, Logashov, Zhirkov, Traoré (Smolov 80), Ahmedov (Carcela-González 29; Lahiyalov 92). Coach: Guus Hiddink (NED)
Match 5 - Udinese Calcio (ITA)
H 2-0 *Samba (72), Eto'o (75)*
V Gabulov, Samba (Lahiyalov 87), João Carlos, Boussoufa, Jucilei, Eto'o, Tagirbekov, Shatov, Logashov, Carcela-González (Traoré 68), Zhirkov. Coach: Guus Hiddink (NED)
Match 6 - BSC Young Boys (SUI)
A 1-3 *Ahmedov (45+2)*
V Gabulov, Samba (Agalarov 46), João Carlos, Jucilei, Eto'o, Tagirbekov, Shatov, Logashov, Traoré, Ahmedov (Carcela-González 79), L Diarra (Lahiyalov 85). Coach: Guus Hiddink (NED)
Red card: Traoré 69

Round of 32 - Hannover 96 (GER)
H 3-1 *Eto'o (34), Ahmedov (48), Boussoufa (64)*
V Gabulov, Eschenko, João Carlos, Boussoufa, Jucilei, Eto'o, Zhirkov, Ahmedov, Ewerton, L Diarra (Carcela-González 85). Coach: Guus Hiddink (NED)
A 1-1 *Traoré (90+9)*
V Gabulov, Eschenko, João Carlos, Boussoufa (Carcela-González 79), Jucilei, Eto'o, Logashov, Ahmedov (Shatov 90+10), Ewerton, L Diarra, Willian (Traoré 67). Coach: Guus Hiddink (NED)

Round of 16 - Newcastle United FC (ENG)
H 0-0
V Gabulov, Eschenko (Logashov 90), João Carlos, Jucilei, Eto'o, Shatov (Carcela-González 84), Zhirkov, Ahmedov , Ewerton, L Diarra, Willian (Traoré 23). Coach: Guus Hiddink (NED)
A 0-1
V Gabulov, Eschenko, João Carlos, Boussoufa, Jucilei, Eto'o, Carcela-González, Zhirkov, Ahmedov , Ewerton, L Diarra (Shatov 74). Coach: Guus Hiddink (NED)
Red card: Carcela-González 55

Domestic league club-by-club

FC ALANIA VLADIKAVKAZ

Coach: Vladimir Gazzaev; (14/11/12) Valeri Gazzaev
1921 • Spartak (32,464) • fc-alania.ru
Major honours
Russian League (1) 1995

2012

21/07	Spartak	h	1-2	Khubulov
29/07	Rubin	a	1-3	Danilo Neco
04/08	Terek	h	5-0	Danilo Neco 2 (1p), Priskin, Khozin, Khubulov
11/08	Lokomotiv	a	2-2	Grigoryev, Priskin
20/08	Kuban	h	2-1	Danilo Neco 2 (1p)
25/08	Rostov	a	1-3	Danilo Neco
01/09	Amkar	h	1-1	Priskin
16/09	CSKA	a	0-2	
24/09	Anji	h	0-1	
01/10	Mordovia	a	1-1	Danilo Neco
06/10	Krylya Sovetov	h	2-2	Danilo Neco 2
20/10	Krasnodar	a	0-2	
27/10	Zenit	h	2-3	Khozin 2
05/11	Volga	a	0-2	
10/11	Dinamo	a	0-2	
17/11	Rubin	a	0-2	
24/11	Terek	a	0-1	
01/12	Lokomotiv	h	0-1	
08/12	Kuban	a	0-0	

2013

09/03	Rostov	h	0-0	
16/03	Amkar	a	1-5	Vranješ
01/04	CSKA	h	0-4	
07/04	Anji	a	0-0	
15/04	Mordovia	h	3-1	Drenthe 3 (1p)
20/04	Krylya Sovetov	a	1-2	Priskin
29/04	Krasnodar	h	2-3	Vranješ, Welinton
04/05	Zenit	a	0-1	
11/05	Volga	a	0-1	
19/05	Dinamo	h	1-0	Priskin
26/05	Spartak	a	0-2	

No	Name	Nat	DoB	Pos	Aps	(s)	Gls
48	Azat Bairyev		17/02/89	M	17	(2)	
8	Mikhail Bakaev		05/08/87	M	8	(13)	
3	Semion Bulgaru	MDA	26/05/85	D	10	(2)	
21	Carlos Cardoso	BRA	11/09/84	D	7	(1)	
39	Giorgi Chanturia	GEO	11/04/93	A	4	(2)	
11	Danilo Neco	BRA	27/01/86	A	22	(1)	9
49	Diego Maurício	BRA	25/06/91	A	3	(9)	
87	Royston Drenthe	NED	08/04/87	M	6		3
4	Aslan Dudiev		15/06/90	D	13	(5)	
35	Soslan Dzhanaev		12/03/87	G	10	(1)	
7	Georgi Gabulov		04/09/88	M	3		
13	Kazbek Geteriev	KAZ	30/06/85	M	2		
29	Roland Gigolaev		04/01/90	D	1	(6)	
18	Dmitri Golubov		24/06/85	A	1	(3)	
20	Akès Goore	CIV	31/12/84	D	8	(2)	
36	Dmitri Grachyov		06/10/83	D	5	(1)	
13	Shota Grigalashvili	GEO	21/06/86	M	8	(1)	
23	Anton Grigoryev		13/12/85	D	19	(3)	1
33	Vitali Gudiev		22/04/95	G	3		
14	Zaurbek Kambolov		04/03/92	M		(3)	
98	Igor Khaimanov		26/03/94	D		(1)	
27	Dzambolat Khastsaev		22/02/95	A		(1)	
1	Dmitri Khomich		04/10/84	G	17		
2	Vladimir Khozin		03/07/89	M	24	(3)	3
9	Arsen Khubulov		13/12/90	M	9	(5)	2
25	Ioan Mera	ROU	05/01/87	D	2	(1)	
95	Edik Pliev		24/11/95	D	2		
3	Zaurbek Pliev		27/09/91	D	16	(2)	
10	Tamás Priskin	HUN	27/09/86	A	19	(4)	5
19	Aleksandr Prudnikov		26/02/89	A	2	(1)	
31	Renan Bressan	BLR	03/11/88	M	9	(1)	
84	Rudnei	BRA	07/10/84	M	18	(1)	
18	Deividas Šemberas	LTU	02/08/78	D	26	(1)	
17	Taras Tsarikaev		17/06/89	M	16	(1)	
7	Sanjar Tursunov	UZB	29/12/86	M	5	(5)	
15	Ognjen Vranješ	BIH	24/10/89	D	5	(2)	2
13	Welinton	BRA	10/04/89	D	9	(1)	1
22	Rodolfo Zelaya	SLV	03/07/88	A	1		

FC AMKAR PERM

Coach: Nikolai Trubachev; (17/01/13) Rustem Khuzin
1993 • Zvezda (17,000) • fc-amkar.org

2012

22/07	Zenit	a	0-2	
28/07	CSKA	h	3-1	Burmistrov, Rebko 2
05/08	Anji	a	0-1	
12/08	Mordovia	h	0-0	
20/08	Krylya Sovetov	a	2-0	Burmistrov, Vassiljev (p)
25/08	Krasnodar	h	2-2	Burmistrov, Ryabokobylenko
01/09	Alania	a	1-1	Ignatovich
17/09	Volga	h	3-2	Peev 2, Picusciac
22/09	Dinamo	a	2-3	Jakubko, Breznanik
29/09	Spartak	h	1-3	Ignatovich
07/10	Rubin	a	1-0	Ignatovich
21/10	Terek	h	0-1	
26/10	Lokomotiv	a	2-1	Peev, Picusciac
03/11	Kuban	h	0-3	
09/11	Rostov	a	0-3	
18/11	CSKA	a	0-3	
26/11	Anji	h	1-2	Semyonov
03/12	Mordovia	a	1-1	Picusciac
08/12	Krylya Sovetov	h	0-2	

2013

08/03	Krasnodar	a	1-2	Burmistrov
16/03	Alania	h	5-1	Kolomeitsev, Jakubko 2, Vassiljev (p), Kanunnikov
31/03	Volga	a	1-1	Peev (p)
05/04	Dinamo	h	1-1	Peev (p)
14/04	Spartak	a	0-2	
19/04	Rubin	h	1-1	Kanunnikov
27/04	Terek	a	1-2	Burmistrov
05/05	Lokomotiv	h	2-4	Georgiev, Sirakov
11/05	Kuban	a	0-4	
17/05	Rostov	h	3-2	Kolomoitsev, Jakubko, Georgiev (p)
26/05	Zenit	h	0-0	

No	Name	Nat	DoB	Pos	Aps	(s)	Gls
21	Dmitri Belorukov		24/03/83	D	15		
6	Marko Blažić	SRB	02/08/85	M	2	(3)	
85	Michal Breznanik	SVK	16/12/85	M	5	(2)	1
81	Nikita Burmistrov		06/07/89	A	14	(3)	5
23	Ivan Cherenchikov		25/08/84	D	24	(2)	
27	Vadim Gagloev		18/01/89	M	8	(2)	
14	Serhiy Garaschenko	UKR	16/05/90	D	1	(2)	
9	Blagoy Georgiev	BUL	21/12/81	M	10		2
1	Roman Gerus		14/09/89	G	9	(2)	
5	Vitali Grishin		09/09/80	M	3	(4)	
11	Pavel Ignatovich		24/05/89	A	12	(7)	3
26	Martin Jakubko	SVK	26/02/80	A	17	(4)	4
15	Vladimirs Kameš	LVA	28/10/88	A	3	(7)	
99	Maksim Kanunnikov		14/07/91	A	10	(1)	2
2	Nikolaos Karelis	GRE	24/02/92	A	1	(8)	
19	Aleksandr Kolomeitsev		21/02/89	M	25		2
63	Stanislav Matyash		23/04/91	A	1	(2)	
3	Nikola Mijailović	SRB	15/02/82	D	20		
42	Sergei Narubin		05/12/81	G	21		
32	Gianluca Nijholt	NED	14/02/90	M	6	(4)	
13	Mitar Novaković	MNE	27/09/81	M	9	(3)	
7	Georgi Peev	BUL	11/03/79	M	23	(1)	5
83	Igor Picusciac	MDA	27/03/83	A	6	(16)	3
24	Aleksei Popov	KAZ	07/07/78	D	8	(1)	
10	Aleksei Rebko		23/04/86	M	2	(1)	2
66	Artur Ryabokobylenko		05/04/91	M	7	(3)	1
22	Andrei Semyonov		24/03/89	D	9		1
33	Makhmadnaim Sharifi		03/06/92	D	1	(1)	
14	Zahari Sirakov	BUL	08/10/77	D	27		1
50	Mikhail Smirnov		03/06/90	D	4		
46	Aleksandr Subbotin		20/10/91	A	1	(2)	
43	Evgeni Tyukalov		07/08/92	A		(3)	
17	Konstantin Vassiljev	EST	16/08/84	M	23	(4)	2
8	Sergei Volkov		27/09/80	A	3	(6)	

FC ANJI MAKHACHKALA

Coach: Guus Hiddink (NED)
1991 • Dinamo (16,863); Anji-Arena (30,000) • fc-anji.ru

2012

22/07	Kuban	h	2-1	Eto'o, Traoré
29/07	Rostov	a	2-2	Tagirbekov 2
05/08	Amkar	h	1-0	G Gabulov
12/08	CSKA	a	0-1	
19/08	Zenit	h	1-1	Shatov
26/08	Mordovia	h	4-2	Traoré, Agalarov, Eto'o 2
02/09	Krylya Sovetov	a	2-1	Samba, Traoré
16/09	Krasnodar	h	5-2	Shatov, João Carlos, Eto'o 2, Boussoufa
24/09	Alania	a	1-0	Traoré
30/09	Volga	h	2-1	Eto'o, Traoré
07/10	Dinamo	a	2-0	Zhirkov, Eto'o
20/10	Spartak	a	2-1	Traoré, og (Insaurralde)
28/10	Rubin	h	1-2	Traoré
04/11	Terek	h	3-1	Boussoufa, Traoré, Samba
11/11	Lokomotiv	a	1-1	Carcela-González
18/11	Rostov	h	0-0	
26/11	Amkar	a	2-1	Ahmedov, Shatov
02/12	CSKA	h	2-0	Traoré, Boussoufa
10/12	Zenit	a	1-1	João Carlos

2013

10/03	Mordovia	a	0-2	
17/03	Krylya Sovetov	h	1-1	Traoré
31/03	Krasnodar	a	0-4	
07/04	Alania	h	0-0	
14/04	Volga	a	3-0	Spahić, Traoré, Willian
21/04	Dinamo	h	3-3	Boussoufa, Zhirkov, Eto'o
28/04	Spartak	a	0-2	
04/05	Rubin	h	2-1	Traoré, Eto'o
12/05	Terek	a	0-1	
20/05	Lokomotiv	h	2-1	og (Ćorluka), Eto'o
26/05	Kuban	a	0-1	

No	Name	Nat	DoB	Pos	Aps	(s)	Gls
7	Kamil Agalarov		11/06/88	M	14		1
25	Odil Ahmedov	UZB	25/11/87	M	11	(5)	1
6	Mbark Boussoufa	MAR	15/08/84	M	24	(2)	4
18	Nikita Burmistrov		06/07/89	A	1	(2)	
16	Mehdi Carcela-González	MAR	01/07/89	M	9	(11)	1
85	Lassana Diarra	FRA	10/03/85	M	14		
2	Andrei Eschenko		09/02/84	D	2		
9	Samuel Eto'o	CMR	10/03/81	A	24	(1)	10
37	Ewerton	BRA	23/03/89	D	7		
21	Georgi Gabulov		04/09/88	M	2	(5)	1
1	Vladimir Gabulov		19/10/83	G	26	(1)	
3	Ali Gadzhibekov		06/08/89	D	7	(1)	
27	Aleksei Ivanov		01/09/81	M	1		
5	João Carlos	BRA	01/01/82	D	25		2
8	Jucilei	BRA	06/04/88	M	27		
13	Shamil Lahiyalov		28/10/79	M	2	(6)	
15	Arseni Logashov		20/08/91	D	15	(4)	
17	Sharif Muhammad		21/03/91	M	1	(2)	
22	Evgeni Pomazan		31/01/89	G	4	(1)	
4	Christopher Samba	CGO	28/03/84	D	17		2
28	Serder Serderov		10/03/94	A	1	(3)	
14	Oleg Shatov		29/07/90	M	18	(5)	3
20	Fedor Smolov		09/02/90	A	4	(11)	
33	Emir Spahić	BIH	18/08/80	D	7		1
13	Rasim Tagirbekov		04/05/84	D	22		2
19	Lacina Traoré	CIV	20/05/90	A	20	(4)	12
10	Willian	BRA	09/08/88	M	6	(1)	1
18	Yuri Zhirkov		20/08/83	M	19	(4)	2

RUSSIA

PFC CSKA MOSKVA

Coach: Leonid Slutski
1911 • Luzhniki (78,360); Arena Khimki (18,636) •
pfc-cska.ru
Major honours
UEFA Cup (1) 2005;
USSR League (7) 1946, 1947, 1948, 1950, 1951,
1970, 1991;
Russian League (4) 2003, 2005, 2006, 2013;
USSR Cup (5) 1945, 1948, 1951, 1955, 1991;
Russian Cup (7) 2002, 2005, 2006, 2008, 2009, 2011, 2013

2012

Date	Opponent	H/A	Score	Scorers
21/07	Rostov	h	1-0	Doumbia
28/07	Amkar	a	1-3	Honda
04/08	Zenit	h	1-3	Honda
12/08	Anji	h	1-0	Tošić
19/08	Mordovia	a	3-0	Tošić, Dzagoev, Cauņa
26/08	Krylya Sovetov	h	3-0	Cauņa, Tošić, Musa
02/09	Krasnodar	a	1-0	Musa
16/09	Alania	h	2-0	Honda 2
22/09	Volga	a	3-2	Dzagoev 2, Musa
30/09	Dinamo	h	0-2	
07/10	Spartak	a	2-0	Musa, Honda
21/10	Rubin	h	2-0	Elm (p), Musa
28/10	Terek	a	2-1	Honda, Wernbloom
04/11	Lokomotiv	h	2-1	Elm, Wernbloom
10/11	Kuban	a	3-1	Musa 2, Elm
18/11	Amkar	h	3-0	Elm (p), Musa, Cauņa
26/11	Zenit	h	1-1	Elm (p)
02/12	Anji	a	0-2	
09/12	Mordovia	h	2-1	Honda, Mamaev

2013

Date	Opponent	H/A	Score	Scorers
09/03	Krylya Sovetov	a	2-0	Wernbloom, Musa
17/03	Krasnodar	h	1-0	Dzagoev
01/04	Alania	a	4-0	Dzagoev, Vágner Love 2 (1p), Doumbia
06/04	Volga	h	2-0	Dzagoev, Vágner Love
12/04	Dinamo	a	0-0	
21/04	Spartak	h	2-2	Musa, Dzagoev (p)
28/04	Rubin	a	0-2	
04/05	Terek	h	1-0	Wernbloom
12/05	Lokomotiv	a	4-1	Vágner Love 2, Musa, Doumbia
18/05	Kuban	h	0-0	
26/05	Rostov	a	0-3	

No	Name	Nat	DoB	Pos	Aps	(s)	Gls
35	Igor Akinfeev		08/04/86	G	29		
6	Aleksei Berezutski		20/06/82	D	3	(2)	
24	Vasili Berezutski		20/06/82	D	29		
19	Aleksandrs Cauņa	LVA	19/01/88	M	19	(6)	3
1	Sergei Chepchugov		15/07/85	G	1		
88	Seydou Doumbia	CIV	31/12/87	A	4	(3)	3
10	Alan Dzagoev		17/06/90	M	24		7
20	Rasmus Elm	SWE	17/03/88	M	26		5
7	Keisuke Honda	JPN	13/06/86	M	21	(2)	7
4	Sergei Ignashevich		14/07/79	D	28		
29	Kim In-sung	KOR	09/09/89	M		(1)	
17	Pavel Mamaev		17/09/88	M	4	(15)	1
2	Mário Fernandes	BRA	19/09/90	D	27	(1)	
11	Mark González	CHI	10/07/84	M	1	(10)	
18	Ahmed Musa	NGA	14/10/92	A	26	(2)	11
14	Kirill Nababkin		08/09/86	D	17	(2)	
89	Tomáš Necid	CZE	13/08/89	A		(1)	
52	Ravil Netfullin		03/03/93	M	1	(7)	
26	Sekou Oliseh	LBR	05/06/90	A		(11)	
42	Georgi Schennikov		27/04/91	D	16	(2)	
92	Petr Ten		12/07/92	D		(1)	
21	Zoran Tošić	SRB	28/04/87	M	22	(3)	3
9	Vágner Love	BRA	11/06/84	A	9		5
3	Pontus Wernbloom	SWE	25/06/86	M	23	(3)	4
15	Dmitri Yefremov		01/04/95	A		(3)	

FC DINAMO MOSKVA

**Coach: Sergei Silkin; (06/08/12) (Dmitri Khokhlov);
(14/08/12) Dan Petrescu (ROU)**
1923 • Arena Khimki (18,636) • fcdynamo.ru
Major honours
USSR League (11) 1936 (spring), 1937, 1940, 1945,
1949, 1954, 1955, 1957, 1959, 1963, 1976 (spring);
USSR Cup (6) 1937, 1953, 1967, 1970, 1977, 1984;
Russian Cup (1) 1995

2012

Date	Opponent	H/A	Score	Scorers
21/07	Volga	a	0-1	
28/07	Zenit	a	0-2	
05/08	Spartak	h	0-4	
12/08	Rubin	h	0-2	
19/08	Terek	h	1-2	Dzsudzsák
25/08	Lokomotiv	a	3-2	Kokorin, Dzsudzsák, Noboa
02/09	Kuban	h	1-2	Noboa
16/09	Rostov	a	0-1	
22/09	Amkar	h	3-2	Jantscher, Kuranyi, Kokorin
30/09	CSKA	a	2-0	Dzsudzsák, Kokorin
07/10	Anji	h	0-2	
21/10	Mordovia	a	2-1	Kokorin 2
28/10	Krylya Sovetov	h	1-0	Kokorin
04/11	Krasnodar	a	0-2	
10/11	Alania	h	2-0	Kuranyi 2
17/11	Zenit	h	3-0	(w/o; original match 1-0 Granat)
25/11	Spartak	a	5-1	Kokorin 2, Noboa, Semshov 2
01/12	Rubin	h	3-0	Yusupov, Dzsudzsák, Kuranyi
09/12	Terek	a	2-1	Kuranyi 2

2013

Date	Opponent	H/A	Score	Scorers
09/03	Lokomotiv	h	1-0	Solovyov
16/03	Kuban	a	1-1	Kokorin
30/03	Rostov	h	1-0	Kuranyi
05/04	Amkar	a	1-1	Noboa
12/04	CSKA	h	0-0	
21/04	Anji	a	3-3	Noboa, Gatagov, Kuranyi
27/04	Mordovia	h	3-1	Yusupov, Kuranyi 2
05/05	Krylya Sovetov	a	2-1	Dzsudzsák, Solomatin
11/05	Krasnodar	h	1-1	Kokorin
19/05	Alania	a	0-1	
26/05	Volga	h	0-0	

No	Name	Nat	DoB	Pos	Aps	(s)	Gls
28	Otman Bakkal	NED	27/02/85	M		(4)	
18	Roman Berezovski	ARM	05/08/74	G	7		
44	Nikita Chicherin		18/08/90	D	12	(3)	
8	Sergei Davydov		22/07/85	A		(8)	
7	Balázs Dzsudzsák	HUN	23/12/86	M	27		5
15	Alexandru Epureanu	MDA	27/09/86	D	5	(2)	
6	Leandro Fernández	ARG	30/01/83	D	28		
19	Evgeni Frolov		05/02/88	M		(1)	
17	Alan Gatagov		23/01/91	M		(3)	1
13	Vladimir Granat		22/03/87	D	25		1
21	Pavel Ignatovich		24/05/89	A	3	(4)	
21	Jakob Jantscher	AUT	08/01/89	M	14	(6)	1
9	Aleksandr Kokorin		19/03/91	A	22		10
5	Denis Kolodin		11/01/82	D		(2)	
22	Kevin Kuranyi	GER	02/03/82	A	24	(3)	10
32	Marko Lomić	SRB	13/09/83	D	26		
8	Zvjezdan Misimović	BIH	05/06/82	M	5	(4)	
12	Pavel Nekhaichik	BLR	15/07/88	M		(6)	
16	Christian Noboa	ECU	09/04/85	M	21	(6)	5
93	Andrei Panyukov		25/09/94	A		(3)	
19	Adrian Ropotan	ROU	08/05/86	M	2	(4)	
33	Vladimir Rykov		13/11/87	D	7		
41	Aleksandr Sapeta		28/06/89	M	13	(7)	
3	Gordon Schildenfeld	CRO	18/03/85	D	5	(1)	
10	Igor Semshov		06/04/78	M	10	(6)	2
14	Igor Shitov	BLR	24/10/86	D		(1)	
1	Anton Shunin		27/01/87	G	23		
78	Pavel Solomatin		04/04/93	M	3	(5)	1
90	Ivan Solovyov		29/03/93	M	8	(4)	1
23	Luke Wilkshire	AUS	02/10/81	D	17		
14	Artur Yusupov		01/09/89	M	23	(2)	

FC KRASNODAR

Coach: Slavoljub Muslin (SRB)
2007 • Kuban (35,200) • fckrasnodar.ru

2012

Date	Opponent	H/A	Score	Scorers
23/07	Rubin	h	2-1	Movsisyan 2
30/07	Terek	a	0-1	
04/08	Lokomotiv	h	3-1	og (Pavlyuchenko), Joãozinho, Movsisyan
10/08	Kuban	a	1-2	Movsisyan
18/08	Rostov	h	0-0	
26/08	Amkar	a	2-2	Movsisyan 2
02/09	CSKA	h	0-1	
16/09	Anji	a	2-5	Márcio Abreu, Vranješ
21/09	Mordovia	h	6-1	Movsisyan 2, Martynovich, Andjelković, Ignatiev, Wanderson
01/10	Krylya Sovetov	a	2-2	Movsisyan, Wanderson
07/10	Zenit	h	0-2	
20/10	Alania	h	2-0	Shipitsin, Drinčić
27/10	Volga	a	1-1	Koman
04/11	Dinamo	h	2-0	Wanderson, Konaté
11/11	Spartak	a	0-2	
19/11	Terek	h	3-0	Joãozinho (p), Wanderson, Shipitsin
24/11	Lokomotiv	a	2-3	Shipitsin, Wanderson
30/11	Kuban	h	2-1	Shipitsin, Martynovich
07/12	Rostov	a	3-2	Wanderson 2, Shipitsin

2013

Date	Opponent	H/A	Score	Scorers
08/03	Amkar	h	2-1	Márcio Abreu, Wanderson
17/03	CSKA	a	0-1	
31/03	Anji	h	4-0	Wanderson 3, Joãozinho
08/04	Mordovia	a	0-0	
13/04	Krylya Sovetov	h	0-3	
21/04	Zenit	a	0-1	
29/04	Alania	a	3-2	Joãozinho, Wanderson 2
05/05	Volga	h	2-0	Petrov, Isael
11/05	Dinamo	a	1-1	Pereira
18/05	Spartak	h	0-1	
26/05	Rubin	a	0-2	

No	Name	Nat	DoB	Pos	Aps	(s)	Gls
5	Aleksandre Amisulashvili	GEO	20/08/82	D	14	(3)	
3	Dušan Andjelković	SRB	15/06/82	D	16	(5)	1
20	Khazyr Appaev		27/01/90	A	1	(2)	
18	Nikola Drinčić	MNE	07/09/84	M	17		1
23	Aleksandr Filtsov		02/01/90	G	11		
10	Pavel Golyshev		07/07/87	M		(1)	
7	Vladislav Ignatiev		20/01/87	M	18	(9)	1
19	Isael	BRA	13/05/88	M	6	(2)	1
22	Joãozinho	BRA	25/12/88	M	30		4
15	Sergei Kislyak	BLR	06/08/87	M	3	(8)	
77	Vladimir Koman	HUN	16/03/89	M	12	(14)	1
11	Moussa Konaté	SEN	03/04/93	A		(10)	1
20	Igor Lambarschi	MDA	26/11/92	M	2	(5)	
26	Márcio Abreu	POR	25/04/80	M	25	(3)	2
2	Nikolai Markov		20/04/85	D	13		
4	Aleksandr Martynovich	BLR	26/08/87	D	20	(1)	2
12	Yura Movsisyan	ARM	02/08/87	A	12	(1)	9
6	Ruslan Nakhushev		05/09/84	D	13	(2)	
33	Mauricio Pereira	URU	15/03/90	M	9		1
98	Sergei Petrov		02/01/91	M	10		1
5	Nukri Revishvili	GEO	02/03/87	G	4		
25	Evgeni Shipitsin		16/01/85	M	12	(6)	5
88	Andrei Sinitsyn		23/06/88	G	15		
28	Igor Smolnikov		08/08/88	D	24	(2)	
36	Adolphe Teikeu	CMR	23/06/90	D	2	(3)	
55	Nemanja Tubić	SRB	08/04/84	D	15	(1)	
15	Ognjen Vranješ	BIH	24/10/89	D	7		1
14	Wanderson	BRA	18/02/86	A	19	(3)	13
19	Aleksandr Yerokhin		13/10/89	M		(2)	

PFC KRYLYA SOVETOV SAMARA

Coach: Andrei Kobelev;
(15/11/12) (Aleksandr Tsygankov);
(27/01/13) Gadzhi Gadzhiev
1942 • Metallurg (33,001) • kc-camapa.ru

2012

22/07	Terek	h	1-1	Caballero
28/07	Lokomotiv	a	0-2	
05/08	Kuban	h	2-1	Kornilenko, Joseph-Reinette
12/08	Rostov	a	2-1	Caballero, Verkhovtsov
20/08	Amkar	h	0-2	
26/08	CSKA	a	0-3	
02/09	Anji	h	1-2	Zeballos
17/09	Mordovia	a	3-2	Epureanu, Nemov, Grigoryan
22/09	Zenit	h	2-2	Kornilenko, Caballero
01/10	Krasnodar	h	2-2	Caballero 2
06/10	Alania	a	2-2	Grigoryan, Bruno Teles
22/10	Volga	h	0-1	
28/10	Dinamo	a	0-1	
03/11	Spartak	h	0-5	
11/11	Rubin	a	0-2	
19/11	Lokomotiv	h	0-1	
25/11	Kuban	a	1-4	og (Özbiliz)
02/12	Rostov	h	0-2	
08/12	Amkar	a	2-0	og (Cherenchikov), Fliseev

2013

09/03	CSKA	h	0-2	
17/03	Anji	a	1-1	Kornilenko
30/03	Mordovia	h	0-2	
07/04	Zenit	a	0-1	
13/04	Krasnodar	a	3-0	Goreux, Maksimov 2
20/04	Alania	h	2-1	Goreux, Angbwa
26/04	Volga	a	1-1	Caballero (p)
05/05	Dinamo	a	1-1	Taranov
10/05	Spartak	a	1-1	Nemov
19/05	Rubin	h	3-1	Caballero, Maksimov 2 (1p)
26/05	Terek	a	1-4	Caballero

No	Name	Nat	DoB	Pos	Aps	(s)	Gls
5	Aleksandre Amisulashvili	GEO	20/08/82	D	10		
19	Benoît Angbwa	CMR	01/01/82	D	11		1
23	Evgeni Balyaikin		19/05/88	M	18	(1)	
16	Bruno Teles	BRA	01/05/86	D	22		1
9	Luis Caballero	PAR	22/04/90	A	21	(6)	8
63	Artyom Delkin		02/08/90	A	5	(7)	
2	Stanislav Dragun	BLR	04/06/88	M	8		
32	Aleksandr Eliseev		15/11/91	M	1	(10)	1
15	Alexandru Epureanu	MDA	27/09/86	D	17		1
21	Dmitri Golubev		01/03/92	D	3	(3)	
2	Réginal Goreux	HAI	31/12/87	D	11		2
11	Roman Grigoryan	ARM	14/09/82	M	4	(6)	2
83	Steeve Joseph-Reinette	FRA	02/12/83	D	15		1
44	Konstantin Kertanov		22/07/91	M		(1)	
45	Aleksei Kontsedalov		24/07/90	D	12	(1)	
8	Sergei Kornilenko	BLR	14/06/83	A	19	(3)	3
13	Shamil Lahiyalov		28/10/79	M	4		
87	Iliya Maksimov		02/02/87	M	8	(1)	4
7	Petr Nemov		18/10/83	M	20		2
98	Sergei Petrov		02/01/91	M	13		
14	Igor Portnyagin		07/01/89	A		(5)	
51	Viktor Svezhov		17/05/91	M	8	(6)	
4	Ivan Taranov		22/06/86	D	18		1
15	Ibragim Tsallagov		12/12/90	M	12	(4)	
1	Denis Vavilin		04/07/82	G	1		
82	Sergei Veremko	BLR	16/10/82	G	29		
18	Dmitri Verkhovtsov	BLR	10/10/86	D	11	(3)	1
84	Roman Vorobyov		24/03/84	M	16	(10)	
10	Pablo Zeballos	PAR	04/03/86	A	13	(2)	1

FC KUBAN KRASNODAR

Coach: Dan Petrescu (ROU);
(16/08/12) Yuri Krasnozhan;
(09/01/13) Leonid Kuchuk (BLR)
1928 • Kuban (35,200) • fckuban.ru

2012

22/07	Anji	a	1-2	og (João Carlos)
27/07	Mordovia	h	1-0	Bucur
05/08	Krylya Sovetov	a	1-2	Tsorayev
10/08	Krasnodar	h	2-1	og (Amisulashvili), Ionov
20/08	Alania	a	1-2	Dealbert
27/08	Volga	h	6-2	Tsorayev, Pizzelli 2, Baldé 2, Niculae
02/09	Dinamo	a	2-1	Fidler, Özbiliz
15/09	Spartak	h	2-2	Fidler, Özbiliz
23/09	Rubin	a	0-1	
29/09	Terek	h	2-1	Ionov, Özbiliz
06/10	Lokomotiv	a	1-0	Bucur
20/10	Zenit	a	0-1	
26/10	Rostov	h	1-0	Popov
03/11	Amkar	a	3-0	Baldé, Özbiliz (p), Pizzelli
10/11	CSKA	h	1-3	Özbiliz (p)
18/11	Mordovia	a	3-0	og (Stepanets), Baldé, Özbiliz
25/11	Krylya Sovetov	h	4-1	Baldé, Popov 2, Pizzelli (p)
30/11	Krasnodar	a	1-2	Özbiliz
08/12	Alania	h	0-0	

2013

08/03	Volga	a	2-0	Özbiliz, Tlisov
16/03	Dinamo	h	1-1	Baldé
31/03	Spartak	a	2-2	Özbiliz (p), Bucur
07/04	Rubin	h	0-0	
13/04	Terek	a	2-2	Bucur, Popov
20/04	Lokomotiv	h	0-0	
28/04	Zenit	h	2-2	Niculae, Popov
04/05	Rostov	a	2-0	Popov 2
11/05	Amkar	h	4-0	Baldé 2, Popov, Pizzelli (p)
18/05	CSKA	a	0-0	
26/05	Anji	h	1-0	Popov

No	Name	Nat	DoB	Pos	Aps	(s)	Gls
3	Ayodele Adeleye	NGA	25/12/88	D			
14	Abdulwaheed Afolabi	NGA	30/11/91	A	1	(1)	
2	Igor Armas	MDA	14/07/87	D	14	(2)	
28	Ibrahima Baldé	SEN	01/09/90	A	21	(2)	8
23	Aleksandr Belenov		13/09/86	G	30		
11	Gheorghe Bucur	ROU	08/04/80	A	5	(15)	4
43	Roman Bugaev		11/02/89	D	7		
5	Ángel Dealbert	ESP	01/01/83	D	28		1
17	Artem Fidler		14/07/83	M	11	(4)	2
10	Aleksei Ionov		18/02/89	M	29	(1)	2
34	Charles Kaboré	BFA	09/02/88	M	11		
73	Mikhail Komkov		01/10/84	M		(1)	
25	Aleksei Kozlov		25/12/86	D	25		
7	Vladislav Kulik		27/02/85	M	25	(1)	
31	Leandro	BRA	26/06/85	M	7		
27	Igor Lolo	CIV	22/07/82	D	16		
20	Daniel Niculae	ROU	06/10/82	A	6	(5)	2
24	Aras Özbiliz	ARM	09/03/90	M	16	(6)	9
30	Marcos Pizzelli	ARM	03/11/84	M	12	(9)	5
71	Ivelin Popov	BUL	26/10/87	M	18	(5)	9
19	Aleksandr Prudnikov		26/02/89	A		(2)	
23	Anton Rogochi		23/01/82	A		(1)	
19	Anton Sekret		23/01/92	A	1		
22	Anton Sosnin		27/01/90	M	1	(1)	
8	Artur Tlisov		10/06/82	M	15	(9)	1
6	David Tsorayev		07/05/83	M	8	(7)	2
21	Marcos Ureña	CRC	05/03/90	A		(6)	
4	Xandão	BRA	23/02/88	D	10		
26	Zelão	BRA	12/11/84	D	9	(2)	
15	Maksim Zhavnerchik	BLR	09/02/85	D	4	(6)	

FC LOKOMOTIV MOSKVA

Coach: Slaven Bilić (CRO)
1923 • Lokomotiv (28,800) • fclm.ru
Major honours
Russian League (2) 2002, 2004;
USSR Cup (2) 1936, 1957;
Russian Cup (5) 1996, 1997, 2000, 2001, 2007

2012

20/07	Mordovia	a	3-2	Torbinski, Ozdoev, Ćorluka
28/07	Krylya Sovetov	h	2-0	Pavlyuchenko, Caicedo
04/08	Krasnodar	a	1-3	Caicedo
11/08	Alania	h	2-2	Pavlyuchenko, Maicon
18/08	Volga	a	2-0	Caicedo, Glushakov
25/08	Dinamo	h	2-3	Maicon, N'Doye
02/09	Spartak	h	2-1	N'Doye, Pavlyuchenko
15/09	Rubin	h	1-0	Tarasov
22/09	Terek	a	3-0	Grigoryev, Obinna, Maicon
29/09	Zenit	a	1-1	N'Doye
06/10	Kuban	h	0-1	
21/10	Rostov	a	0-0	
26/10	Amkar	h	1-2	Pavlyuchenko
04/11	CSKA	a	1-2	Eschenko
11/11	Anji	h	1-1	N'Doye
19/11	Krylya Sovetov	a	1-0	N'Doye
24/11	Krasnodar	h	3-2	N'Doye 2, Obinna
01/12	Alania	a	1-0	Grigoryev
08/12	Volga	h	0-1	

2013

09/03	Dinamo	a	0-1	
16/03	Spartak	a	0-0	
30/03	Rubin	a	0-2	
06/04	Terek	h	1-1	Đurica
13/04	Zenit	h	0-1	
20/04	Kuban	a	0-0	
27/04	Rostov	h	3-1	N'Doye, Caicedo, Torbinski
05/05	Amkar	a	4-2	Miranchuk, N'Doye (p), Torbinski, Yanbaev
12/05	CSKA	h	1-4	Tarasov
20/05	Anji	a	1-2	Samedov
26/05	Mordovia	h	2-1	Samedov (p), N'Doye

No	Name	Nat	DoB	Pos	Aps	(s)	Gls
30	Maksim Belyaev		01/09/91	D	1		
5	Taras Burlak		22/02/90	D	15	(2)	
25	Felipe Caicedo	ECU	05/09/88	A	11	(11)	4
14	Vedran Ćorluka	CRO	05/02/86	D	27		1
29	Vitali Denisov	UZB	23/02/87	D	8		
28	Ján Ďurica	SVK	10/12/81	D	18	(2)	1
2	Andrei Eschenko		09/02/84	D	17		1
8	Denis Glushakov		27/01/87	M	26	(1)	1
6	Maksim Grigoryev		06/07/90	M	12	(8)	2
1	Guilherme	BRA	12/12/85	G	11		
22	Dario Krešić	CRO	11/01/84	G	16		
41	Miroslav Lobantsev		27/05/95	G	3		
79	Vitali Lystsov			D		(1)	
90	Maicon	BRA	18/02/90	A	12	(5)	3
59	Aleksei Miranchuk		10/07/95	M	6		1
33	Dame N'Doye	SEN	21/02/85	A	21	(4)	10
13	Victor Obinna	NGA	25/03/87	A	14	(12)	2
27	Magomed Ozdoev		05/11/92	M	5	(5)	1
18	Roman Pavlyuchenko		15/12/81	A	9	(10)	4
65	Vyacheslav Podberyozkin		21/06/92	M		(1)	
19	Aleksandr Samedov		19/07/84	M	20	(6)	2
49	Roman Shishkin		27/01/87	D	19	(1)	
11	Dmitri Sychev		26/10/83	A		(3)	
23	Dmitri Tarasov		18/03/87	M	17	(1)	2
26	Yan Tigorev	BLR	10/03/84	M	16		
21	Dmitri Torbinski		28/04/84	M	7	(8)	3
55	Renat Yanbaev		07/04/84	D	11		1
4	Alberto Zapater	ESP	13/06/85	M	4	(1)	
33	Reto Ziegler	SUI	16/01/86	D	4	(2)	

FC MORDOVIA SARANSK

Coach: Fedor Shcherbachenko;
(19/11/12) (Vladimir Bibikov);
(27/12/12) Dorinel Munteanu (ROU)
1961 • Start (11,581) • fc-mordovia.ru

2012

20/07	Lokomotiv	h	2-3	Panchenko, Osipov
27/07	Kuban	a	0-1	
03/08	Rostov	h	3-0	Osipov, og (Dyakov), Ruslan Mukhametshin
12/08	Amkar	a	0-0	
19/08	CSKA	h	0-3	
26/08	Anji	a	2-4	Ruslan Mukhametshin, Rogov
31/08	Zenit	h	0-3	
17/09	Krylya Sovetov	h	2-3	Osipov, Bober (p)
21/09	Krasnodar	a	1-6	Bober
01/10	Alania	h	1-1	og (Bairyev)
06/10	Volga	a	2-0	Ruslan Mukhametshin (p), Panchenko
21/10	Dinamo	h	1-2	Ruslan Mukhametshin (p)
27/10	Spartak	a	0-2	
03/11	Rubin	h	1-3	Panchenko
10/11	Terek	a	1-2	Ruslan Mukhametshin
18/11	Kuban	h	0-3	
23/11	Rostov	a	0-2	
03/12	Amkar	h	1-1	Panchenko
09/12	CSKA	a	1-2	Bober

2013

10/03	Anji	h	2-0	Perendija, Rustem Mukhametshin
17/03	Zenit	a	0-1	
30/03	Krylya Sovetov	a	2-0	Opriţa, Ruslan Mukhametshin
08/04	Krasnodar	h	0-0	
15/04	Alania	a	1-3	Ruslan Mukhametshin
20/04	Volga	a	1-3	Ruslan Mukhametshin
27/04	Dinamo	a	1-3	Panchenko
03/05	Spartak	h	2-1	Pazin, Opriţa
10/05	Rubin	a	1-2	Ruslan Mukhametshin
18/05	Terek	h	1-1	Ruslan Mukhametshin
26/05	Lokomotiv	a	1-2	Pazin

No	Name	Nat	DoB	Pos	Aps	(s)	Gls
1	Dmitri Abakumov		08/07/89	G	10		
10	Evgeni Aldonin		22/01/80	M	20	(1)	
7	Anton Bober		28/09/82	M	14	(12)	3
12	Vladimir Božović	MNE	13/11/81	M	10		
2	Maksim Budnikov		31/05/83	D	2	(3)	
20	Tomislav Dujmović	CRO	26/02/81	M	22	(3)	
27	Aleksei Ivanov		01/09/81	M	17	(1)	
35	Akaki Khubutia	GEO	17/03/86	D	11		
7	Roman Kontsegalov		11/05/86	M	3	(5)	
4	Yuri Kuleshov		12/04/81	M	19	(4)	
22	Sergei Kuznetsov		07/05/86	M	1	(2)	
13	Mikhail Markin		21/11/93	A		(7)	
23	Ruslan Mukhametshin		29/10/81	A	27	(3)	10
9	Rustem Mukhametshin		02/04/84	M	9	(15)	1
3	Aleksei Muldarov	KAZ	24/04/84	D	18		
32	Daniel Opriţa	ROU	10/08/81	M	10	(1)	2
19	Evgeni Osipov		29/10/86	D	18	(2)	3
8	Kirill Panchenko		16/10/89	A	19	(9)	5
24	Andrei Pazin		20/01/86	M	10	(2)	2
40	Milan Perendija	SRB	05/01/86	D	7		1
13	Vladimir Ponomaryov		22/04/87	D	1		
11	Maksim Rogov		11/02/86	A	10	(4)	1
14	Igor Shitov	BLR	24/10/86	D	20		
87	Aleksandar Simčević	SRB	15/02/87	D	15	(1)	
18	Pavlo Stepanets	UKR	26/05/87	M	17	(1)	
73	Maksim Terentiev		09/08/92	M		(1)	
17	Dalibor Volaš	SVN	27/02/87	A		(6)	
31	David Yurchenko		27/03/86	G	20	(1)	

FC ROSTOV

Coach: Miodrag Božović (MNE)
1930 • Olimp 2 (17,023) • fc-rostov.ru

2012

21/07	CSKA	a	0-1	
29/07	Anji	h	2-2	Kirichenko (p), Holenda
03/08	Mordovia	a	0-3	
12/08	Krylya Sovetov	h	1-2	Saláta
18/08	Krasnodar	a	0-0	
25/08	Alania	h	3-1	Holenda 3
01/09	Volga	a	1-1	Blatnjak
16/09	Dinamo	h	1-0	Holenda
23/09	Spartak	a	1-3	Sinama-Pongolle
30/09	Rubin	h	0-4	
05/10	Terek	a	1-2	Kalachev
21/10	Lokomotiv	h	0-0	
26/10	Kuban	a	0-1	
02/11	Zenit	a	1-2	Holenda
09/11	Amkar	h	3-0	Cociş, Saláta, Kirichenko (p)
18/11	Anji	a	0-0	
23/11	Mordovia	h	2-0	Dyakov (p), Kirichenko
02/12	Krylya Sovetov	a	2-0	Blatnjak, Česnauskis
07/12	Krasnodar	h	2-3	Poloz, Kirichenko

2013

09/03	Alania	a	0-0	
15/03	Volga	h	1-2	Kirichenko
30/03	Dinamo	a	0-1	
06/04	Spartak	h	1-0	Lazović (p)
14/04	Rubin	a	1-1	Poloz
22/04	Terek	h	0-3	
27/04	Lokomotiv	a	1-3	Kalachev
04/05	Kuban	h	0-2	
12/05	Zenit	h	1-1	Dyakov (p)
17/05	Amkar	a	2-3	Starikov 2
26/05	CSKA	h	3-0	Poloz, Kanga, Kalachev

No	Name	Nat	DoB	Pos	Aps	(s)	Gls
9	Roman Adamov		21/06/82	A	5	(1)	
19	Benoît Angbwa	CMR	01/01/82	D	14		
47	Sergei Belousov		04/05/90	M		(2)	
30	Maksim Belyaev		30/09/91	D	5		
21	David Bentley	ENG	27/08/84	M	7		
19	Dragan Blatnjak	BIH	01/08/81	M	7	(8)	2
88	Edgaras Česnauskis	LTU	05/02/84	M	19	(6)	1
81	Răzvan Cociş	ROU	19/02/83	A	13	(2)	1
5	Vitali Dyakov		31/01/89	D	24	(1)	2
84	Alexandru Gatcan	MDA	27/03/84	M	27		
33	Inal Getigezhev		23/05/87	D	28		
11	Jan Holenda	CZE	22/08/85	A	14	(14)	6
22	Andrei Ivanov		08/10/88	D	1	(3)	
2	Timofei Kalachev	BLR	01/05/81	M	20	(1)	3
27	Guélor Kanga	GAB	01/09/90	M	8	(2)	1
10	Dmitri Kirichenko		17/01/77	A	2	(20)	5
18	Vladimir Kisenkov		08/10/81	D	12	(1)	
70	Magomed Kurbanov		11/04/92	A		(1)	
77	Danko Lazović	SRB	17/05/83	A	8	(1)	1
63	Maksim Lepski		08/04/92	M		(2)	
8	Dmitri Malyaka		15/01/90	M		(2)	
34	Timofei Margasov		12/06/92	D	7		
4	Isaac Okoronkwo	NGA	01/05/78	D	4	(1)	
21	Stipe Pletikosa	CRO	08/01/79	G	30		
14	Dmitri Poloz		12/07/91	A	8	(9)	3
3	Kornel Saláta	SVK	24/01/85	D	18		2
17	Aleksandr Sheshukov		15/04/83	M	27		
24	Florent Sinama-Pongolle	FRA	20/10/84	A	10		1
87	Evgeni Starikov	USA	17/01/88	A	3	(5)	2
55	Siyanda Xulu	RSA	30/12/91	D	9	(2)	
25	Nikolai Zabolotni		16/04/90	A		(1)	

FC RUBIN KAZAN

Coach: Kurban Berdyev
1936 • Central (27,756) • rubin-kazan.ru
Major honours
Russian League (2) 2008, 2009;
Russian Cup (1) 2012

2012

23/07	Krasnodar	a	1-2	Natcho (p)
29/07	Alania	h	3-1	Natcho 2 (1p), Dyadyun
06/08	Volga	a	2-1	Gökdeniz, R Eremenko
12/08	Dinamo	h	2-0	Natcho, R Eremenko
18/08	Spartak	a	1-2	Natcho (p)
25/08	Zenit	a	2-1	Natcho (p), R Eremenko
01/09	Terek	h	1-2	Rondón
15/09	Lokomotiv	a	0-1	
23/09	Kuban	h	1-0	Bocchetti
30/09	Rostov	a	4-0	Rondón 2, Bocchetti, Dyadyun
07/10	Amkar	h	0-1	
21/10	CSKA	a	0-2	
28/10	Anji	h	2-1	Kuzmin, Kasaev
03/11	Mordovia	a	3-1	Dyadyun 2, Rondón
11/11	Krylya Sovetov	h	2-0	Sharonov, Natcho (p)
17/11	Alania	a	2-0	Marcano, Kasaev
26/11	Volga	h	0-0	
01/12	Dinamo Moskva	a	0-3	
10/12	Spartak	h	0-1	

2013

10/03	Zenit	h	1-0	Rondón
17/03	Terek	a	0-0	
30/03	Lokomotiv	h	2-0	Natcho, Dyadyun
07/04	Kuban	a	0-0	
14/04	Rostov	h	1-1	Gökdeniz
19/04	Amkar	a	1-0	Rondón
28/04	CSKA	h	2-0	Rondón, R Eremenko
04/05	Anji	a	1-2	R Eremenko
10/05	Mordovia	h	2-1	Gökdeniz, Dyadyun
19/05	Krylya Sovetov	a	1-3	Dyadyun
26/05	Krasnodar	h	2-1	R Eremenko, Natcho

No	Name	Nat	DoB	Pos	Aps	(s)	Gls
87	Ruslan Abışov	AZE	10/10/87	D	1		
3	Cristian Ansaldi	ARG	20/09/86	D	24	(1)	
24	Giedrius Arlauskis	LTU	01/12/87	G	1	(1)	
33	Salvatore Bocchetti	ITA	30/11/86	D	13		2
7	Petr Bystrov		15/07/79	M	3	(2)	
11	Carlos Eduardo	BRA	18/07/87	M	2		
4	César Navas	ESP	14/02/80	D	21		
5	Sergei Davydov		22/07/85	A	1	(8)	
22	Vladimir Dyadyun		12/07/88	A	12	(11)	7
20	Alexei Eremenko	FIN	24/03/83	M	1	(2)	
23	Roman Eremenko	FIN	19/03/87	A	23	(2)	6
61	Gökdeniz Karadeniz	TUR	11/01/80	M	23	(5)	3
55	Gökhan Töre	TUR	20/01/92	M	2	(3)	
19	Vitali Kaleshin		03/10/80	D	10	(1)	
10	Alan Kasaev		08/04/86	M	11	(9)	2
15	Sergei Kislyak	BLR	06/08/87	M		(2)	
2	Oleg Kuzmin		09/05/81	D	25	(1)	1
62	Solomon Kvirkvelia	GEO	06/02/92	D	3		
90	Yann M'Vila	FRA	29/06/90	M	5		
25	Iván Marcano	ESP	23/06/87	D	20	(1)	1
66	Bebras Natcho	ISR	18/02/88	M	30		9
6	Pablo Orbaiz	ESP	06/02/79	M	20	(3)	
99	José Salomón Rondón	VEN	16/09/89	A	20	(5)	7
8	Aleksandr Ryazantsev		05/09/86	M	16	(3)	
1	Sergei Ryzhikov		19/09/80	G	29		
76	Roman Sharonov		08/09/76	D	12	(3)	1
35	Ivan Temnikov		28/01/89	M		(1)	
16	Nelson Valdez	PAR	28/11/83	A	2	(1)	

FC SPARTAK MOSKVA

Coach: Unai Emery (ESP); (26/11/12) Valeri Karpin
1922 • Luzhniki (78,360) • spartak.com
Major honours
USSR League (12) 1936 (autumn), 1938, 1939, 1952,
1953, 1956, 1958, 1962, 1969, 1979, 1987, 1989;
Russian League (9) 1992, 1993, 1994, 1996, 1997,
1998, 1999, 2000, 2001;
USSR Cup (10) 1938, 1939, 1946, 1947, 1950, 1958,
1963, 1965, 1971, 1992;
Russian Cup (3) 1994, 1998, 2003

2012

21/07	Alania	a	2-1	Emenike, og (Grigoryev)
29/07	Volga	h	2-1	McGeady, D Kombarov (p)
05/08	Dinamo	a	4-0	Bilyaletdinov, Pareja, Ananidze, Rafael Carioca
11/08	Zenit	a	0-5	
18/08	Rubin	h	2-1	Rômulo, D Kombarov (p)
25/08	Terek	a	1-2	Insaurralde
02/09	Lokomotiv	a	1-2	D Kombarov
15/09	Kuban	a	2-2	McGeady, Emenike
23/09	Rostov	h	3-1	Emenike 2, Ari
29/09	Amkar	a	3-1	Källström, Ari, Dzyuba
07/10	CSKA	h	0-2	
20/10	Anji	a	1-2	Bilyaletdinov
27/10	Mordovia	h	2-0	Jurado, Bilyaletdinov
03/11	Krylya Sovetov	a	5-0	Jurado, Pareja, D Kombarov, Dzyuba, Ananidze
11/11	Krasnodar	h	2-0	Ari, D Kombarov (p)
17/11	Volga	a	1-1	D Kombarov
25/11	Dinamo	h	1-5	Dzyuba
30/11	Zenit	h	2-4	Dzyuba, Emenike
10/12	Rubin	a	1-0	McGeady

2013

10/03	Terek	h	3-1	Movsisyan 3
16/03	Lokomotiv	h	0-0	
31/03	Kuban	h	2-2	og (Kaboré), Jurado
06/04	Rostov	a	0-1	
14/04	Amkar	h	2-0	Yakovlev, Movsisyan
21/04	CSKA	a	2-2	McGeady, Ari
28/04	Anji	a	2-0	Källström, D Kombarov (p)
03/05	Mordovia	a	1-2	McGeady
10/05	Krylya Sovetov	h	1-1	Suchý
18/05	Krasnodar	a	1-0	Yakovlev
26/05	Alania	h	2-0	Bryzgalov, Ananidze

No	Name	Nat	DoB	Pos	Aps	(s)	Gls
49	Jano Ananidze	GEO	10/10/92	A	6	(9)	3
9	Ari	BRA	11/12/85	A	21	(6)	4
25	Diniyar Bilyaletdinov		27/02/85	M	10	(4)	3
33	Salvatore Bocchetti	ITA	30/11/86	D	10		
3	Sergei Bryzgalov		15/11/92	D	10	(1)	1
20	Demy de Zeeuw	NED	26/05/83	M	9	(3)	
31	Andriy Dykan	UKR	16/07/77	G	19		
10	Artem Dzyuba		22/08/88	A	18	(7)	4
29	Emmanuel Emenike	NGA	10/05/87	A	10	(6)	5
44	Soslan Gatagov		29/09/92	D	1		
39	Igor Gorbatenko		13/02/89	M	3	(1)	
2	Juan Insaurralde	ARG	03/10/84	D	10	(1)	1
19	José Manuel Jurado	ESP	29/06/86	M	15	(3)	3
21	Kim Källström	SWE	24/08/82	M	16	(4)	2
51	Dmitri Kayumov		11/05/92	M		(1)	
23	Dmitri Kombarov		22/01/87	D	29		7
7	Kirill Kombarov		22/01/87	D	11	(7)	
54	Aleksandr Kozlov		19/03/93	A		(1)	
57	Vyacheslav Krotov		14/02/93	A		(1)	
18	Ilya Kutepov		29/07/93	D		(1)	
28	Waris Majeed	GHA	19/09/91	A	2	(5)	
34	Evgeni Makeev		24/07/89	M	21	(1)	
67	Emin Makhmudov		27/04/92	M		(1)	
8	Aiden McGeady	IRL	04/04/86	M	14	(3)	5
12	Yura Movsisyan	ARM	02/08/87	A	6	(2)	4
77	Vladimir Obukhov		08/02/92	A		(1)	
5	Nicolás Pareja	ARG	19/01/84	D	12		2
30	Sergei Pesyakov		16/12/88	G	7	(1)	
6	Rafael Carioca	BRA	18/06/89	M	24	(3)	1
32	Artem Rebrov		04/03/84	G	4		
37	Rômulo	BRA	19/09/90	M	4		1
17	Marek Suchý	CZE	29/03/88	D	20	(1)	1
90	Ognjen Vukojević	CRO	20/12/83	M	7	(2)	
11	Welliton	BRA	22/10/86	A	4	(4)	
14	Pavel Yakovlev		07/04/91	A	7	(9)	2

FC TEREK GROZNY

Coach: Stanislav Cherchesov
1946 • Ahmat-Arena (30,597) • fc-terek.ru
Major honours
Russian Cup (1) 2004

2012

22/07	Krylya Sovetov	a	1-1	Ivanov
30/07	Krasnodar	h	1-0	Ivanov
04/08	Alania	a	0-5	
11/08	Volga	h	2-0	Lebedenko 2
19/08	Dinamo	a	2-1	Rybus 2
25/08	Spartak	h	2-1	Lebedenko, Ferreira
01/09	Rubin	a	2-1	N'Douassel, Mitrishev
14/09	Zenit	a	2-0	Ailton, Lebedenko
22/09	Lokomotiv	h	0-3	
29/09	Kuban	a	1-2	Jiránek
05/10	Rostov	h	2-1	Komorowski, Ailton
21/10	Amkar	a	1-0	Lebedenko
28/10	CSKA	h	1-2	Ailton
04/11	Anji	a	1-3	Georgiev (p)
10/11	Mordovia	h	2-1	Legear, Ailton
19/11	Krasnodar	a	0-3	
24/11	Alania	h	1-0	Lebedenko
01/12	Volga	a	1-1	Ivanov
09/12	Dinamo	h	1-2	Ailton

2013

10/03	Spartak	a	1-3	Maurício
17/03	Rubin	h	0-0	
31/03	Zenit	h	0-3	
06/04	Lokomotiv	a	1-1	Maurício
13/04	Kuban	h	2-2	Utsiyev, N'Douassel (p)
22/04	Rostov	a	3-0	Ailton, og (Holenda), Adílson
27/04	Amkar	h	2-1	Rybus 2
04/05	CSKA	a	0-1	
12/05	Anji	h	1-0	Píriz
18/05	Mordovia	a	1-1	Mitrishev
26/05	Krylya Sovetov	h	4-1	N'Douassel, og (Angbwa), Ferreira, Kanu

No	Name	Nat	DoB	Pos	Aps	(s)	Gls
6	Adílson	BRA	16/01/87	M	24		1
9	Ailton	BRA	20/08/84	A	16	(6)	6
85	Anton Amelchenko	BLR	27/03/85	G	9		
35	Soslan Dzhanaev		13/03/87	G		(1)	
9	António Ferreira	BRA	24/08/84	D	17		2
9	Blagoy Georgiev	BUL	21/12/81	M	19		1
12	Yaroslav Hodzyur	UKR	03/09/82	G	21		
19	Oleg Ivanov		04/08/86	M	26		3
52	Martin Jiránek	CZE	25/05/79	D	22	(3)	1
20	Kanu	BRA	23/09/87	A	3	(3)	1
10	Adlan Katsaev		20/02/88	M		(2)	
24	Marcin Komorowski	POL	17/04/84	D	21	(6)	1
87	Fedor Kudryashov		05/04/87	D	14	(1)	
55	Igor Lebedenko		27/05/83	A	26	(1)	6
99	Jonathan Legear	BEL	13/04/87	A	6	(2)	1
89	Maciej Makuszewski	POL	29/09/89	M	2	(7)	
8	Maurício	BRA	21/10/88	M	19	(4)	2
11	Magomed Mitrishev		10/09/92	M	3	(15)	2
77	Stanislav Murikhin		21/01/92	M		(2)	
80	Ezechiel N'Douassel	CHA	22/04/88	A	10	(5)	3
4	Juhani Ojala	FIN	19/06/89	D	3		
15	Aleksandr Pavlenko		20/01/85	M	2	(1)	
7	Facundo Píriz	URU	27/03/90	M	6		1
25	Piotr Polczak	POL	25/09/86	D		(2)	
31	Maciej Rybus	POL	19/08/89	M	15	(4)	4
13	Zayr Sadaev		06/11/89	A	1	(6)	
90	Murad Tagilov		27/01/90	D	1		
40	Rizvan Utsiyev		07/02/88	D	24	(1)	1
21	Oleg Vlasov		10/12/84	M		(2)	
3	Dmitri Yatchenko		25/08/86	D	20	(5)	

FC VOLGA NIZHNY NOVGOROD

Coach: Gadzhi Gadzhiev;
(19/01/13) Yuriy Kalitvintsev (UKR)
1998 • Lokomotiv (17,856) • fcvolgann.ru

2012

21/07	Dinamo	h	1-0	Shulenin
29/07	Spartak	a	1-2	Sapogov
06/08	Rubin	h	1-2	Kharitonov
11/08	Terek	a	0-2	
18/08	Lokomotiv	h	0-2	
27/08	Kuban	a	2-6	Asildarov (p), Sapogov
01/09	Rostov	h	1-1	Sapogov
17/09	Amkar	a	2-3	Sapogov, Grigalava
22/09	CSKA	a	2-3	Maksimov, Sapogov
30/09	Anji	h	1-2	Maksimov
06/10	Mordovia	h	0-2	
22/10	Krylya Sovetov	a	1-0	Belozyorov
27/10	Krasnodar	h	1-1	Bibilov
05/11	Alania	a	2-0	Sapogov, Maksimov
11/11	Zenit	h	1-2	Maksimov
17/11	Spartak	h	1-1	Salugin
26/11	Rubin	a	0-0	
01/12	Terek	h	1-1	Asildarov
08/12	Lokomotiv	a	1-0	Asildarov

2013

08/03	Kuban	h	0-2	
15/03	Rostov	a	2-1	Sarkisov 2
31/03	Amkar	h	1-1	Sapogov (p)
06/04	CSKA	a	0-2	
14/04	Anji	a	0-3	
20/04	Mordovia	a	3-1	Sapogov (p), Belozyorov, Sarkisov
26/04	Krylya Sovetov	h	1-1	Karyaka (p)
05/05	Krasnodar	a	0-2	
11/05	Alania	h	1-0	Karyaka (p)
19/05	Zenit	a	1-3	Shulenin
26/05	Dinamo	a	0-0	

No	Name	Nat	DoB	Pos	Aps	(s)	Gls
31	Ilya Abayev		02/08/81	G	11		
21	Ruslan Adjindjal		22/06/74	M	28	(1)	
90	Mersudin Ahmetović	BIH	19/02/85	A	3	(3)	
4	Aleksei Aidov		10/04/82	D	15		
11	Shamil Asildarov		18/05/83	A	6	(7)	3
63	Aleksandr Belozyorov		27/10/81	D	25	(3)	2
29	Shota Bibilov		06/08/90	M	12	(9)	1
37	Vitalie Bordian	MDA	11/08/84	D	9		
25	Andrei Buivolov		12/01/87	D	7	(1)	
2	Semion Bulgaru	MDA	26/05/85	D	6	(1)	
10	Romeo Castelen	NED	03/05/83	M		(2)	
17	Matija Dvorneković	CRO	01/01/89	M	5	(5)	
8	Gia Grigalava	GEO	05/08/89	D	19		1
5	Andrei Karyaka		01/04/78	M	23	(3)	2
41	Mikhail Kerzhakov		28/01/87	G	19		
83	Aleksandr Kharitonov		04/04/83	M	13	(8)	1
2	Valeri Kichin	KGZ	12/10/92	D	3		
13	Dmitri Kudryashov		13/05/83	M	5	(10)	
87	Ilya Maksimov		02/02/87	M	13		4
23	Mihăiță Pleşan	ROU	19/02/83	M	6	(3)	
26	Piotr Polczak	POL	25/09/86	D	5		
6	Dmitri Polyanin		30/03/80	M	18		
16	Anton Putilo	BLR	10/06/87	M	10	(1)	
19	Adrian Ropotan	ROU	08/05/86	M	6		
77	Aleksandr Salugin		23/10/88	A	7	(9)	1
27	Aleksei Sapogov		24/04/88	A	20	(2)	8
14	Artur Sarkisov	ARM	19/01/87	A	10	(8)	3
9	Aleksandr Shulenin		31/10/79	M	15	(1)	2
33	Nikolai Zaitsev		01/06/89	D	11	(1)	

FC ZENIT ST PETERSBURG

Coach: Luciano Spalletti (ITA)
1925 • Petrovski (21,405) • fc-zenit.ru
Major honours
UEFA Cup (1) 2008;
UEFA Super Cup (1) 2008;
USSR League (1) 1984;
Russian League (3) 2007, 2010, 2012;
USSR Cup (1) 1944;
Russian Cup (2) 1999, 2010

2012

22/07	Amkar	h	2-0	Kerzhakov 2 (1p)
28/07	Dinamo	h	2-0	Kerzhakov, Criscito
03/08	CSKA	a	3-1	Semak 2, Kerzhakov (p)
11/08	Spartak	h	5-0	Kanunnikov, Bystrov, Shirokov, Fayzulin 2
19/08	Anji	a	1-1	Zyryanov
25/08	Rubin	h	1-2	Fayzulin
31/08	Mordovia	a	3-0	Zyryanov, Kerzhakov 2
14/09	Terek	h	0-2	
22/09	Krylya Sovetov	a	2-2	Hulk, Shirokov
29/09	Lokomotiv	h	1-1	Criscito
07/10	Krasnodar	a	2-0	Zyryanov, Fayzulin
20/10	Kuban	h	1-0	Kerzhakov (p)
27/10	Alania	a	3-2	Bystrov, Kerzhakov 2
02/11	Rostov	h	2-1	Bystrov, Shirokov
11/11	Volga	a	2-1	Anyukov, Kerzhakov
17/11	Dinamo	a	0-3	(w/o; original match 0-1)
26/11	CSKA	h	1-1	Yanbaev
30/11	Spartak	a	4-2	Hulk, Witsel 2, Shirokov
10/12	Anji	h	1-1	Zyryanov
2013				
10/03	Rubin	a	0-1	
17/03	Mordovia	h	1-0	Hulk
31/03	Terek	a	3-0	Witsel, Bruno Alves, Zyryanov
07/04	Krylya Sovetov	h	1-0	Hulk (p)
13/04	Lokomotiv	a	1-0	Fayzulin
21/04	Krasnodar	h	1-0	Danny
28/04	Kuban	a	2-2	Zyryanov, Danny
04/05	Alania	h	4-0	Hulk 3 (1p), Bukharov
12/05	Rostov	a	1-1	Witsel
19/05	Volga	h	3-1	Luís Neto, Fayzulin, Shirokov
26/05	Amkar	a	0-0	

No	Name	Nat	DoB	Pos	Aps	(s)	Gls
2	Aleksandr Anyukov		28/09/82	D	22		1
71	Yegor Baburin		09/08/93	G	2	(2)	
3	Bruno Alves	POR	27/11/81	D	20	(1)	1
9	Aleksandr Bukharov		12/03/85	A	2	(7)	1
34	Vladimir Bystrov		31/01/84	M	13	(11)	3
50	Igor Cheminava		23/03/91	D		(1)	
4	Domenico Criscito	ITA	30/12/86	D	12		2
10	Danny	POR	07/08/83	A	10	(2)	2
27	Igor Denisov		17/05/84	M	22	(1)	
77	Luka Djordjević	MNE	09/07/94	A	2	(5)	
94	Aleksei Evseev		30/03/94	M		(1)	
20	Viktor Fayzulin		22/04/86	M	23	(1)	6
48	Aleksei Gasilin		01/03/96	A		(1)	
14	Tomáš Hubočan	SVK	17/09/85	D	24		
29	Hulk	BRA	25/07/86	A	17	(1)	7
99	Maksim Kanunnikov		14/07/91	A	3	(6)	1
11	Aleksandr Kerzhakov		27/11/82	A	20	(3)	10
6	Nicolas Lombaerts	BEL	20/03/85	D	21	(1)	
13	Luís Neto	POR	26/05/88	D	9		1
24	Aleksandar Luković	SRB	23/10/82	D	3	(6)	
82	Michael Lumb	DEN	09/01/88	D		(1)	
16	Vyacheslav Malafeev		04/03/79	G	26		
85	Pavel Mogilevets		25/01/93	M	1	(1)	
21	Milan Rodić	SRB	02/04/91	D	3	(1)	
25	Sergei Semak		27/02/76	M	9	(7)	2
15	Roman Shirokov		06/07/81	M	24	(1)	5
28	Axel Witsel	BEL	12/01/89	M	16	(3)	4
55	Renat Yanbaev		07/04/84	D	8	(3)	1
65	Danila Yaschuk		13/03/95	M		(1)	
30	Yuri Zhevnov	BLR	17/04/81	G	2		
68	Vyacheslav Zinkov		26/05/93	M		(1)	
18	Konstantin Zyryanov		05/10/77	M	16	(11)	6

Top goalscorers

13	Yura Movsisyan (Krasnodar/Spartak)
	Wanderson (Krasnodar)
12	Lacina Traoré (Anji)
11	Ahmed Musa (CSKA)
10	Samuel Eto'o (Anji)
	Aleksandr Kokorin (Dinamo)
	Kevin Kuranyi (Dinamo)
	Dame N'Doye (Lokomotiv)
	Ruslan Mukhametshin (Mordovia)
	Aleksandr Kerzhakov (Zenit)

Promoted clubs

FC URAL YEKATERINBURG

Coach: Pavel Gusev
1930 • Central (27,500) • fc-ural.ru

FC TOM TOMSK

Coach: Sergei Peredhya
1957 • Trud (15,000) • fctomtomsk.ru

SECOND LEVEL FINAL TABLE 2012/13

		Pld	W	D	L	F	A	Pts
1	FC Ural Yekaterinburg	32	19	11	2	61	18	68
2	FC Tom Tomsk	32	19	8	5	57	34	65
3	PFC Spartak Nalchik	32	15	8	9	32	27	53
4	FC SKA-Energia Khabarovsk	32	13	13	6	36	26	52
5	FC Baltika Kaliningrad	32	14	8	10	40	33	50
6	FC Ufa	32	13	9	10	31	30	48
7	FC Neftekhimik Nizhnekamsk	32	13	8	11	44	40	47
8	FC Sibir Novosibirsk	32	12	9	11	34	38	45
9	FC Rotor Volgograd	32	11	8	13	27	26	41
10	FC Yenisey Krasnoyarsk	32	9	12	11	30	31	39
11	FC Shinnik Yaroslavl	32	9	12	11	28	33	39
12	FC Petrotrest St Petersburg	32	10	5	17	28	43	35
13	FC Salyut Belgorod	32	8	11	13	25	31	35
14	FC Torpedo Moskva	32	6	15	11	29	38	33
15	FC Metallurg-Kuzbass Novokuznetsk	32	8	6	18	19	40	30
16	FC Khimki	32	6	10	16	23	40	28
17	FC Volgar Astrakhan	32	5	11	16	23	39	26

PROMOTION/RELEGATION PLAY-OFFS

(30/05/13 & 03/06/13)
Krylya Sovetov 2-0 Spartak Nalchik
Spartak Nalchik 2-5 Krylya Sovetov
(Krylya Sovetov 7-2)

Rostov 2-0 SKA-Energia
SKA-Energia 0-1 Rostov
(Rostov 3-0)

Domestic cup: Kubok Rossii 2012/13

1/16 FINALS

(25/09/12)
Baltika Kaliningrad 1-2 Zenit
SKA-Energia 2-1 Amkar *(aet)*
Spartak Nalchik 1-3 Terek

(26/09/12)
Astrakhan 1-3 Rostov
Khimik Dzerzhinsk 1-2 Krasnodar
Khimki 2-0 Volga Nizhny Novgorod
Lokomotiv Moskva-2 0-1 Mordovia
Salyut Belgorod 1-2 Spartak Moskva
Tom 0-1 CSKA Moskva
Torpedo Armavir 0-3 Lokomotiv Moskva
Torpedo Moskva 0-3 Dinamo Moskva
Volga Ulyanovsk 0-1 Kuban
Yenisey Krasnoyarsk 2-1 Rubin

(27/09/12)
Gazovik Orenburg 2-4 Krylya Sovetov *(aet)*
Tyumen 2-1 Alania
Ural Yekaterinburg 0-0 Anji *(aet; 2-4 on pens)*

1/8 FINALS

(30/10/12)
Kuban 1-0 Krasnodar
Mordovia 0-2 Zenit
Rostov 0-0 Spartak Moskva *(aet; 3-2 on pens)*
Yenisey Krasnoyarsk 1-0 SKA-Energia

(31/10/12)
Anji 2-1 Krylya Sovetov
CSKA Moskva 3-0 Tyumen
Dinamo Moskva 2-1 Khimki
Terek 3-1 Lokomotiv Moskva *(aet)*

QUARTER-FINALS

(17/04/13)
Anji 1-0 Dinamo Moskva *(Eto'o 98) (aet)*
CSKA Moskva 3-0 Yenisey Krasnoyarsk *(Vágner Love 12, Musa 65, Mamaev 82)*
Zenit 0-0 Kuban *(aet; 4-3 on pens)*

(18/04/13)
Rostov 0-0 Terek *(aet; 4-3 on pens)*

SEMI-FINALS

(07/05/13)
Rostov 0-2 CSKA Moskva *(Doumbia 105, Musa 120) (aet)*

(08/05/13)
Zenit 0-1 Anji *(Eto'o 60)*

FINAL

(01/06/13)
Ahmat-Arena, Grozny
PFC CSKA MOSKVA 1 *(Musa 9)*
FC ANJI MAKHACHKALA 1 *(Diarra 74)*
(aet; 4-3 on pens)
Referee: Yegorov
CSKA MOSKVA: Akinfeev, Schennikov, A Berezutski, V Berezutski, Nababkin, Honda *(Cauņa 67)*, Elm *(Doumbia 78)*, Wernbloom, Dzagoev *(Mamaev 99)*, Musa, Vágner Love
Sent off: *Wernbloom (87)*
ANJI: V Gabulov, Tagirbekov *(Shatov 63)*, João Carlos *(Traoré 46)*, Ewerton, Gadzhibekov, Zhirkov, Diarra *(Ahmedov 115)*, Jucilei, Boussoufa, Willian, Eto'o

SAN MARINO
Federazione Sammarinese Giuoco Calcio (FSGC)

Address	Strada di Montecchio 17 SM-47890 San Marino	**President**	Giorgio Crescentini
Tel	+378 0549 990 515	**General secretary**	Luciano Casadei
Fax	+378 0549 992 348	**Media officer**	Elisa Felici
E-mail	fsgc@omniway.sm	**Year of formation**	1931
Website	fsgc.sm	**National stadium**	Stadio Olimpico, Serravalle (6,664)

CAMPIONATO SAMMARINESE CLUBS

1. SP Cailungo
2. SS Cosmos
3. Domagnano FC
4. SC Faetano
5. SS Fiorentino
6. SS Folgore/Falciano
7. AC Juvenes-Dogana
8. SP La Fiorita
9. AC Libertas
10. SS Murata
11. SS Pennarossa
12. SS San Giovanni
13. SP Tre Fiori
14. SP Tre Penne
15. SS Virtus

KEY:

- – UEFA Champions League
- – UEFA Europa League

0		5		10 km
0			5 miles	

Same again for trophy holders

The 2012/13 season in San Marino was practically a re-run of the previous campaign, with the championship title claimed by SP Tre Penne after a play-off final victory over AC Libertas and the Coppa Titano retained by SP La Fiorita.

A penalty shoot-out was required to decide a goalless championship final, while there was just one goal in the cup final, scored by a 42-year-old. Meanwhile, Giampaolo Mazza's national team continued to pile up the defeats in unenviable record-breaking fashion.

Tre Penne defend league crown	Libertas lose out on penalties in play-off final	La Fiorita keep hold of Coppa Titano

Domestic league

History repeated itself as Tre Penne and Libertas contested a second successive play-off for the championship title. The two clubs finished in the same positions at the end of the group phase as they had done in 2011/12, with Libertas topping Group A and Tre Penne taking third place in Group B. Thereafter Libertas won two further play-off matches to reach the final while their opponents in Serravalle were obliged to compete in every round, playing five games and eliminating all of the other four teams en route.

Such are the complexities of the Campionato Sammarinese that by the time the two teams met for the decider, Libertas had lost just one league game all season whereas Tre Penne had lost nine. Furthermore, although the two teams had come through different first phase groups, they had actually met each other in a cross-over fixture, with Libertas triumphing 3-1. A meeting in the Coppa Titano quarter-final had also gone Libertas's way (1-0).

On the big day, however, the form book went out of the window, and it was Tre Penne once again who carried off the trophy. There were no goals in regulation play, nor in extra time, but despite the

presence in the Libertas goal of San Marino's first-choice goalkeeper Aldo Simoncini, Tre Penne converted all five of their spot-kicks, and it was Simoncini's opposite number, Federico Valentini, also a San Marino international, who made the decisive save, from Daniele Rocchi. Although it was the club's second title in succession, it was the first for coach Moris Tamburini.

Domestic cup

The first major silverware of the season was claimed by La Fiorita, who defended the Coppa Titano with a 1-0 win in Serravalle against first-time finalists SS San Giovanni. The holders needed a penalty shoot-out to get past Libertas in the semi-final, but it was a conventional goal, scored by veteran striker Sossio Aruta two minutes into the second half, that saw off San Giovanni, who had kept clean sheets in each of their previous four ties. It was the second time Aruta had scored the match-winner in the Coppa Titano final, having done the same in 2009/10 for SP Tre Fiori.

Europe

First qualifying round eliminations are commonplace for European

representatives from San Marino, and there were three more in 2012/13, with Tre Penne, La Fiorita and Libertas all losing both of their matches without scoring a goal.

National team

It was another season of predictable woe for Giampaolo Mazza's team as they lost all of their opening six 2014 FIFA World Cup qualifying ties, conceding 29 goals and scoring none. The good news came in an early-season friendly at home to Malta, in which they actually found the net – not once but twice. It was not enough to prevent a 3-2 defeat, but it ended a run of 20 matches without scoring and enabled Manuel Marani to become only the second player – after Andy Selva – to register more than once for the team, his second international goal coming five and a half years after his first, in a UEFA EURO 2008 qualifier against the Republic of Ireland.

On the negative side, however, San Marino became the first international side to lose 50 matches in a row when they went down 3-0 in Montenegro in November 2012. By the end of the season, following a 4-0 defeat to Italy in nearby Bologna, they had stretched that unwanted run to 53.

Domestic league: Campionato Sammarinese 2012/13 final tables

FIRST PHASE

Group A		Pld	W	D	L	F	A	Pts
1	AC Libertas	20	13	6	1	36	13	45
2	SP La Fiorita	20	13	3	4	35	21	42
3	SS Murata	20	11	3	6	31	19	36
4	SP Cailungo	20	6	5	9	30	37	23
5	SC Faetano	20	5	6	9	20	26	21
6	AC Juvenes-Dogana	20	5	3	12	24	36	18
7	SS Virtus	20	3	3	14	15	35	12

Group B		Pld	W	D	L	F	A	Pts
1	SS Folgore/Falciano	21	10	9	2	25	17	39
2	SS Cosmos	21	9	8	4	27	19	35
3	SP Tre Penne	21	11	2	8	24	18	35
4	SS Fiorentino	21	7	8	6	36	25	29
5	SS San Giovanni	21	6	9	6	35	39	27
6	Domagnano FC	21	5	8	8	24	30	23
7	SS Pennarossa	21	5	5	11	23	38	20
8	SP Tre Fiori	21	5	2	14	22	34	17

CHAMPIONSHIP PLAY-OFFS

FIRST ROUND
(06/05/13)
La Fiorita 1-1 Cosmos *(F Rinaldi 89; Lazzarini 94)*
(aet; 6-5 on pens)
Tre Penne 1-2 Murata *(Cibelli 67; Protti 78, Tellinai 96) (aet)*

SECOND ROUND
(10/05/13)
La Fiorita 1-1 Murata *(Aruta 78; Casadei 90+1)*
(aet; 5-3 on pens)
(11/05/13)
Cosmos 0-0 Tre Penne *(aet; 3-4 on pens)*
(Cosmos eliminated)

THIRD ROUND
(13/05/13)
Folgore/Falciano 0-2 Libertas *(Fantani 65, Morelli 83)*
(14/05/13)
Tre Penne 2-0 Murata *(Cardini 12, Cibelli 60p)*
(Murata eliminated)

FOURTH ROUND
(17/05/13)
Libertas 1-0 La Fiorita *(Morelli 81)*
(18/05/10)
Tre Penne 2-0 Folgore/Falciano *(Cibelli 82, Valli 89)*
(Folgore/Falciano eliminated)

SEMI-FINAL
(23/05/13)
La Fiorita 0-1 Tre Penne *(Mikhaylovski 81)*
(La Fiorita eliminated)

FINAL
(27/05/13)
Stadio Olimpico, Serravalle
SP TRE PENNE 0
SP LIBERTAS 0
(aet; 5-3 on pens)
Referee: *Guidi*
TRE PENNE: *Valentini, Capicchioni (M Rossi 80), Baschetti, Bonini, Mikhaylovski, A Rossi, Cibelli, Cardini (Tamburini 96), Valli, Di Giuli (Pignieri 58), Chiaruzzi*
Sent off: *A Rossi (99)*
LIBERTAS: *A Simoncini, Molinari, Benvenuti (Vagnetti 76), Torelli (Angeli 120), Morelli, D Simoncini, Rocchi, Facondini, Fantini, Antonelli, De Luigi (Polidori 67)*
Sent off: *D Simoncini (74)*

SEASON AT A GLANCE

EUROPEAN QUALIFICATION 2013/14

 Champion: SP Tre Penne (first qualifying round)

 Cup winner: SP La Fiorita (first qualifying round)
AC Libertas (first qualifying round)

Top scorers	Denis Iencinella (Fiorentino) & Alberto Cannini (Juvenes-Dogana), 17 goals
Cup final	SP La Fiorita 1-0 SS San Giovanni

PLAYER OF THE SEASON
Aldo Simoncini
(AC Libertas)

The San Marino goalkeeper, impressive against England at Wembley, conceded only 13 goals for Libertas in the regular season and none at all in the play-offs. Unarguably one of the best keepers in the country's history, he made a series of fine saves against SP Tre Penne to send the championship final to penalties but was powerless in the shoot-out.

NEWCOMER OF THE SEASON
Vladimir Mikhaylovski
(SP Tre Penne)

The Russian centre-back was a key player in the Tre Penne team that clinched back-to-back titles. In 2012/13 he scored three goals, including a crucial one in the play-off semi-final against SP La Fiorita. Dominant in the air and always dangerous from set pieces, he also showed great composure when converting one of the penalties in the final.

CAMPIONATO SAMMARINESE TEAM OF THE SEASON
(4-3-1-2)
Coach: Venturi *(San Giovanni)*

Simoncini *(Libertas)*

Benvenuti *(Libertas)* — Mikhaylovski *(Tre Penne)* — Bollini *(La Fiorita)* — Rocchi *(Libertas)*

Bollini *(La Fiorita)* — Mottola *(La Fiorita)* — Cibelli *(Tre Penne)*

Morelli *(Libertas)*

Iencinella *(Fiorentino)* — Cannini *(Juvenes-Dogana)*

NATIONAL TEAM

Home Kit | Away Kit

TOP FIVE ALL-TIME CAPS
Damiano Vannucci (68); **Andy Selva** (61);
Simone Bacciocchi (60); Mirco Gennari (48);
Paolo Montagna (47)

TOP FIVE ALL-TIME GOALS
Andy Selva (8); **Manuel Marani** (2)

NB No other player has scored more than one goal.

Results 2012/13

14/08/12	Malta	H	Serravalle	2-3	*Marani (7), D Rinaldi (90+3p)*
11/09/12	Montenegro (WCQ)	H	Serravalle	0-6	
12/10/12	England (WCQ)	A	London	0-5	
16/10/12	Moldova (WCQ)	H	Serravalle	0-2	
14/11/12	Montenegro (WCQ)	A	Podgorica	0-3	
22/03/13	England (WCQ)	H	Serravalle	0-8	
26/03/13	Poland (WCQ)	A	Warsaw	0-5	
31/05/13	Italy	A	Bologna	0-4	

Appearances 2012/13

Coach: Giampaolo Mazza (ITA) 26/02/56			Mlt	MNE	ENG	MDA	MNE	ENG	POL	Ita	Caps	Goals
Aldo Simoncini	30/08/86	Libertas	G46	G	G	G	G	G	G	G46	34	-
Fabio Vitaioli	05/04/84	Murata/Sammaurese (ITA)	D63	D	D84	D		D	D	D79	29	-
Davide Simoncini	30/08/86	Libertas	D	D	D	D		D		D	30	-
Alessandro Della Valle	08/06/82	Folgore/Sanvitese (ITA)	D46	D	D	D	D	D	D	D72	45	-
Mirko Palazzi	24/03/87	Rimini (ITA)	D		D	D46	D	D	D		10	-
Michele Cervellini	14/04/88	Pennarossa	M	M	M	M	M	M		M	19	-
Enrico Cibelli	14/07/87	Tre Penne	M46	s64	M	s61	M89	M67		s46	9	-
Alex Gasperoni	30/06/84	Tre Penne	M	M	M		s89	M	M	M60	29	1
Matteo Vitaioli	27/10/89	Fiorentino/San Marino (ITA)	M71	M80		M	M74	M	M	M	28	-
Danilo Rinaldi	18/04/86	La Fiorita	A	A	A79		A	s75	s51	s79	11	1
Manuel Marani	07/06/84	Murata/Sammaurese (ITA)	A79	A64		A67					33	2
Federico Valentini	22/01/82	Tre Penne	s46							s46	12	-
Cristian Brolli	28/02/92	Folgore/Cattolica (ITA)	s46	D84	D						3	-
Alessandro Bianchi	19/07/89	Tre Villaggi (ITA)	s46								1	-
Damiano Vannucci	30/07/77	La Fiorita	s63	s84		s46	D				68	-
Marco Muraccini	25/02/91	Verucchio (ITA)	s71								1	-
Simone Bacciocchi	22/01/77	San Giovanni	s79		s84				s57		60	-
Matteo Coppini	05/05/89	Campitello (ITA)		M	M76		M		M	M46	11	-
Pier Filippo Mazza	20/08/88	Juvenes-Dogana/Sant'Ermete (ITA)		s80		M61					10	-
Lorenzo Buscarini	27/05/91	Cailungo /Murata			s76	M	s74	s67	s80	s68	6	-
Andy Selva	23/05/76	La Fiorita/Fidene (ITA)			s79	s67		A75	A51	A	61	8
Gian Luca Bollini	24/03/80	La Fiorita				D	D		D57	s72	8	-
Giacomo Benedettini	07/10/82	Tre Fiori					D83				7	-
Alex Della Valle	13/06/90	Faetano					s83		D80		4	-
Fabio Bollini	19/09/83	La Fiorita						M81	M	M68	15	-
Carlo Valentini	15/03/82	Murata						s81			39	-
Federico Rinaldi	13/11/89	La Fiorita								D	1	-
Maicol Berretti	01/05/89	Pennarossa								s60	20	-

NB The Sanmarinese amateur players can appear for more than one club at the same time.

European club competitions 2012/13

SP TRE PENNE

First qualifying round - F91 Dudelange (LUX)
A 0-7
Valentini, Bonini, Baschetti, D'Orsi, Tamburini (L Nanni 85), Cibelli, Chiaruzzi, Pignieri (Valli 57), Cardini, Gasperoni (Rossi 76), Marani. Coach: Stefano Ceci (ITA)
H 0-4
Valentini, Bonini, Baschetti, D'Orsi, Mikhaylovski, Tamburini (L Nanni 50), Cibelli, Pignieri, Cardini (Rossi 35), Valli (F Nanni 69), Gasperoni. Coach: Stefano Ceci (ITA)

SP LA FIORITA

  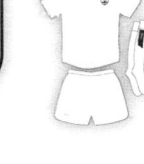

First qualifying round - SK Liepājas Metalurgs (LVA)
H 0-2
Montanari, Confalone, Parma (Forcellini 89), Mazzola, Cavalli, G Bollini, Enakarhire, F Bollini (Bellocchi 53), Bucchi, Perrotta, Guidi (Fucili 68). Coach: Nicola Berardi (SMR)
A 0-4
Montanari, Confalone, Parma (Zanotti 88), Mazzola, Cavalli, D Rinaldi (Fucili 82), G Bollini, Enakarhire, F Bollini (Bellocchi 63), Bucchi, Perrotta. Coach: Nicola Berardi (SMR)
Red card: Bellocchi 73

AC LIBERTAS

First qualifying round - FK Renova (MKD)
A 0-4
Ceccoli, Benvenuti, Torelli, D Simoncini, Facondini, Fantini (Zennaro 76), Antonelli, Molinari (Vagnetti 65), Mastronicola, Rocchi, De Luigi (Morelli 61). Coach: Michele Ceccoli (SMR)
H 0-4
A Simoncini, Torelli, Morelli, D Simoncini, Facondini (Santarini 78), Antonelli, Zennaro (Fantini 65), Polidori (Angeli 85), Molinari, Mastronicola, Rocchi. Coach: Michele Ceccoli (SMR)

Domestic cup: Coppa Titano 2012/13

FIRST PHASE

(Played in Groups)

Group A

(01/09/12)
Cailungo 0-1 Folgore/Falciano
Tre Fiori 3-2 San Giovanni
(05/09/12)
San Giovanni 3-1 Cosmos
Tre Fiori 1-1 Cailungo
(21/11/12)
Cosmos 1-1 Tre Fiori
San Giovanni 1-1 Folgore/Falciano
(28/11/12)
Cosmos 5-0 Cailungo
Folgore/Falciano 1-0 Tre Fiori
(05/12/12)
Cailungo 1-2 San Giovanni
Folgore/Falciano 0-1 Cosmos
(20/01/13)
Folgore/Falciano 1-1 Cailungo
San Giovanni 1-0 Tre Fiori
(26/01/13)
Cailungo 0-2 Tre Fiori
(27/01/13)
Cosmos 1-2 San Giovanni
(20/02/13)
Folgore/Falciano 0-0 San Giovanni
Tre Fiori 3-2 Cosmos
(02/04/13)
Cailungo 1-2 Cosmos
Tre Fiori 1-0 Folgore/Falciano
(10/04/13)
Cosmos 4-1 Folgore/Falciano
San Giovanni 1-0 Cailungo

Final standings
1 San Giovanni 17 pts;
2 Tre Fiori 14 pts;
3 Cosmos 13 pts *(qualified)*;
4 Folgore/Falciano 9 pts;
5 Cailungo 2 pts *(eliminated)*

Group B

(02/09/12)
Domagnano 3-0 Pennarossa
Faetano 0-2 Libertas
(05/09/12)
Domagnano 0-0 Murata
Pennarossa 2-1 Faetano
(21/11/12)
Libertas 0-0 Domagnano
Pennarossa 2-1 Murata
(28/11/12)
Libertas 2-0 Pennarossa
Murata 2-1 Faetano
(05/12/12)
Faetano 1-0 Domagnano
Murata 2-1 Libertas
(19/01/13)
Libertas 2-1 Faetano
Pennarossa 2-2 Domagnano
(26/01/13)
Faetano 0-2 Pennarossa
(27/01/13)
Murata 3-1 Domagnano
(20/02/13)
Domagnano 0-0 Libertas
Murata 4-1 Pennarossa
(02/04/13)
Faetano 2-4 Murata
Pennarossa 3-1 Libertas
(10/04/13)
Domagnano 1-2 Faetano
Libertas 0-1 Murata

Final standings
1 Murata 19 pts;
2 Pennarossa 13 pts;
3 Libertas 11 pts *(qualified)*;
4 Domagnano 7 pts;
5 Faetano 6 pts *(eliminated)*

Group C

(01/09/12)
Fiorentino 0-3 La Fiorita
(02/09/12)
Virtus 1-4 Juvenes-Dogana
(05/09/12)
Juvenes-Dogana 2-2 Fiorentino
Virtus 0-3 Tre Penne
(21/11/12)
Juvenes-Dogana 0-1 Tre Penne
La Fiorita 3-0 Virtus
(28/11/12)
La Fiorita 3-1 Juvenes-Dogana
Tre Penne 1-2 Fiorentino
(05/12/12)
Fiorentino 2-1 Virtus
Tre Penne 4-1 La Fiorita
(19/01/13)
Juvenes-Dogana 2-2 Virtus
(20/01/13)
La Fiorita 1-0 Fiorentino
(26/01/13)
Fiorentino 1-2 Juvenes-Dogana
(27/01/13)
Tre Penne 5-1 Virtus
(20/02/13)
Tre Penne 0-1 Juvenes-Dogana
Virtus 1-4 La Fiorita
(02/04/13)
Fiorentino 2-3 Tre Penne
(03/04/13)
Juvenes-Dogana 1-5 La Fiorita
(10/04/13)
La Fiorita 0-2 Tre Penne
Virtus 1-2 Fiorentino

Final standings
1 Tre Penne 18 pts;
2 La Fiorita 18 pts *(qualified)*;
3 Juvenes-Dogana 11 pts;
4 Fiorentino 10 pts;
5 Virtus 1 pt *(eliminated)*

QUARTER-FINALS

(20/04/13)
La Fiorita 2-1 Tre Fiori *(D Rinaldi 48, Aruta 66; Lisi 70)*
Murata 2-3 Cosmos *(Rais 27, 81; Grigore 34, 56, 90+2)*
San Giovanni 1-0 Pennarossa *(Ugolini 84)*
Tre Penne 0-1 Libertas *(Morelli 61)*

SEMI-FINALS

(25/04/13)
Cosmos 0-4 San Giovanni *(Cuttone 4, 7, 85, Bacciocchi 14)*
Libertas 1-1 La Fiorita *(Polidori 54; Perrotta 34)*
(aet; 3-5 on pens)

FINAL

(29/04/13)
Stadio Olimpico, Serravalle
SP LA FIORITA 1 *(Aruta 47)*
SS SAN GIOVANNI 0
Referee: Casanova
LA FIORITA: Montanari, Mazzola, Vannucci, Bucchi, G Bollini, Bellocchi, Perrotta, F Bollini, D Rinaldi *(Ceci 46)*, Mottola *(Parma 66)*, Aruta
SAN GIOVANNI: Manzaroli, Zafferani, M Zanotti, Bacciocchi, Cuttone, Baiardi, Ugolini, Henrique, Pasquali *(Mariani 58)*, Bianchi, Duarte
Sent off: Bacciocchi *(79)*

Top goalscorers

(excluding Play-offs)

17	Denis Iencinella (Fiorentino)
	Alberto Cannini (Juvenes-Dogana)
11	Franklin (Domagnano)
10	Valentin Grigore (Cosmos)
	Giorgio Mariotti (Juvenes-Dogana)
	Marco Ugolini (San Giovanni)
9	Andrea Moroni (Faetano)
	Adnan Rais (Murata)
8	Nicolò Zennaro (Libertas)
	Omar Tomassoni (Pennarossa)

SCOTLAND
Scottish Football Association (SFA)

Address	Hampden Park GB-Glasgow G42 9AY	**President**	Campbell Ogilvie
Tel	+44 141 616 6000	**General secretary**	Stewart Regan
Fax	+44 141 616 6001	**Media officer**	Darryl Broadfoot
E-mail	info@scottishfa.co.uk	**Year of formation**	1873
Website	scottishfa.co.uk	**National stadium**	Hampden Park, Glasgow (52,063)

PREMIER LEAGUE CLUBS

1. Aberdeen FC
2. Celtic FC
3. Dundee FC
4. Dundee United FC
5. Heart of Midlothian FC
6. Hibernian FC
7. Inverness Caledonian Thistle FC
8. Kilmarnock FC
9. Motherwell FC
10. Ross County FC
11. Saint Johnstone FC
12. Saint Mirren FC

PROMOTED CLUB

13. Partick Thistle FC

KEY:
- – UEFA Champions League
- – UEFA Europa League
- – Promoted club
- – Relegated club

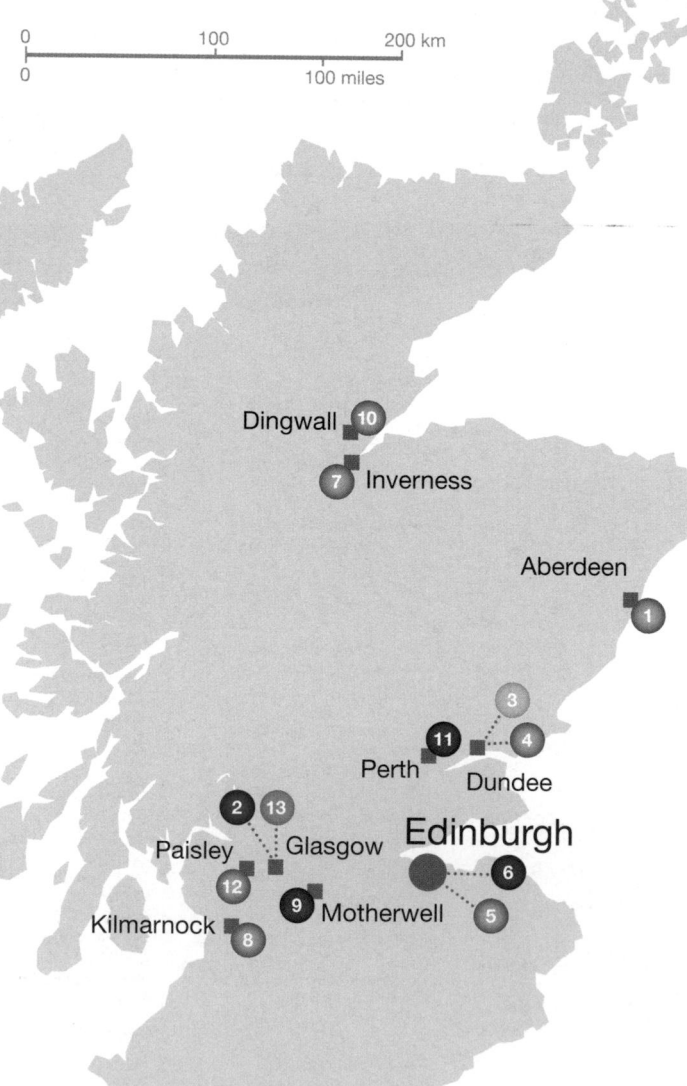

No contest for Celtic

With Old Firm rivals Rangers FC having to start afresh in the fourth tier after going into liquidation, Celtic FC predictably won their 44th Scottish title at a canter.

Although put under some pressure during the autumn, when their main focus was on the UEFA Champions League, the Bhoys breezed clear in the second half of the season and ended the campaign with a record 06th victory in the Scottish Cup. It enabled Neil Lennon to become the third man to win the Scottish double with Celtic as both player and manager.

Lennon steers Glasgow giants to domestic double

Rangers begin long climb back to elite

Early World Cup elimination for national team

Domestic league

It was a strange sensation for Scottish football followers when the 2012/13 season kicked off with just one half of the Old Firm involved. Rangers' absence meant that Celtic were overwhelming favorites to retain the SPL trophy, but with important matters to attend to in the UEFA Champions League, it took them the best part of three months before they established a significant lead at the top of the table.

Once Lennon's side picked up the pace, the victories began to accumulate and the destiny of the SPL trophy soon became a foregone conclusion. Celtic eventually secured their crown with four games in hand after rocketing into a 15-point lead over Motherwell FC, who, fuelled by the 26 goals of SPL hot shot Michael Higdon, ended the campaign in second place. Celtic's top marksman, once again, was Gary Hooper, another Englishman, who struck 19 times. His compatriot, goalkeeper Fraser Forster, also had a fine season, and there were consistent contributions also from defender Charlie Mulgrew and all-purpose Kenyan midfielder Victor Wanyama.

Saint Johnstone FC re-qualified for the UEFA Europa League after a late surge carried them past Highland duo Inverness Caledonian Thistle FC and newly-promoted Ross County FC. Dundee FC, late additions to the SPL to replace Rangers, went straight back down to the First Division, ending up one level above the Ibrox club, who, with Ally McCoist still in charge, won the Third Division by a 24-point margin to make their first step back towards the elite.

Domestic cup

Saint Mirren FC endured a tough season in the league but ended a 26-year wait for silverware with a first victory in the League Cup. They ended Celtic's treble hopes with a momentous 3-2 win in the semi-final before defeating financially beleaguered Heart of Midlothian FC by the same scoreline in the Hampden final.

Celtic did manage the double, denying Hibernian their first Scottish Cup win in over a century thanks to a 3-0 win at Hampden in which Hooper scored the first two goals before Joe Ledley added a late third. As both player and manager of double-winning teams, Lennon joined the hitherto exclusive two-man band of Jock Stein and Billy McNeill in the Celtic hall of fame.

Europe

It was not just a joyous season domestically for Lennon and his players.

Reaching the last 16 of the UEFA Champions League arguably eclipsed anything else. Fourth seeds in a group containing FC Barcelona, FC Spartak Moskva and SL Benfica, they defied the odds to qualify in second place, the highlights a rare away win in Moscow and a thrilling 2-1 victory over the mighty Barça at Celtic Park.

Juventus proved too strong in the round of 16, but it was nonetheless a European campaign to treasure. In stark contrast, the other four Scottish representatives all fell at the first hurdle in their respective competitions.

National team

The Scottish national side ended a dreadful season on a high note with an unlikely 1-0 win over Croatia in Split. In terms of qualification for the 2014 FIFA World Cup it was far too little too late, the team having already been eliminated after collecting just two points from their opening six matches, which included a brace of defeats to Wales.

Manager Craig Levein was dismissed in the autumn and subsequently replaced by the Tartan Army's popular choice, Gordon Strachan, whose mission is to qualify Scotland for the 24-team finals of UEFA EURO 2016.

Domestic league: Scottish Premier League 2012/13 final table

		Pld	Home					Away					Total					Pts
			W	D	L	F	A	W	D	L	F	A	W	D	L	F	A	
1	**Celtic FC**	38	15	2	2	52	14	9	5	5	40	21	24	7	7	92	35	79
2	Motherwell FC	38	9	6	4	35	24	9	3	7	32	27	18	9	11	67	51	63
3	Saint Johnstone FC	38	9	7	3	25	17	5	7	7	20	27	14	14	10	45	44	56
4	Inverness Caledonian Thistle FC	38	7	8	4	35	27	6	7	6	29	33	13	15	10	64	60	54
5	Ross County FC	38	8	8	3	22	15	5	6	8	25	33	13	14	11	47	48	53
6	Dundee United FC	38	4	9	6	30	33	7	5	7	21	29	11	14	13	51	62	47
7	Hibernian FC	38	7	7	5	26	22	6	5	8	23	30	13	12	13	49	52	51
8	Aberdeen FC	38	6	9	4	18	15	5	6	8	23	28	11	15	12	41	43	48
9	Kilmarnock FC	38	5	4	10	25	29	6	8	5	27	24	11	12	15	52	53	45
10	Heart of Midlothian FC	38	9	3	7	27	25	2	8	9	13	24	11	11	16	40	49	44
11	Saint Mirren FC	38	6	6	7	25	31	3	8	8	22	29	9	14	15	47	60	41
12	Dundee FC	38	4	4	11	17	34	3	5	11	11	32	7	9	22	28	66	30

NB League split into top and bottom halves after 33 games, with each team playing a further five matches exclusively against clubs from its half of the table.

SEASON AT A GLANCE

EUROPEAN QUALIFICATION 2013/14

Champion/Cup winner: Celtic FC (second qualifying round)

Motherwell FC (third qualifying round)
Saint Johnstone FC (second qualifying round)
Hibernian FC (second qualifying round)

Top scorer	Michael Higdon (Motherwell), 26 goals
Relegated club	Dundee FC
Promoted club	Partick Thistle FC
Cup final	Celtic FC 3-0 Hibernian FC
League Cup final	Saint Mirren FC 3-2 Heart of Midlothian FC

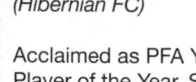

PLAYER OF THE SEASON
Leigh Griffiths
(Hibernian FC)

Acclaimed as PFA Young Player of the Year, SPL Player of the Year and Football Writers' Player of the Year, Griffiths completed a remarkable hat-trick of individual awards, his 28 goals in all competitions for Hibernian holding sway with all three voting panels. The young striker's only disappointment was Hibs' Scottish Cup final defeat to Celtic FC.

NEWCOMER OF THE SEASON
Alex Harris
(Hibernian FC)

The 18-year-old burst on to the scene during Hibs' epic 4-3 Scottish Cup semi-final triumph over Falkirk FC. The Easter Road side trailed their second-tier opponents 3-0 after 30 minutes, but the teenage winger grabbed the game by the scruff of the neck to score early in the second half and inspire his side to a memorable extra-time victory.

SCOTTISH PREMIER LEAGUE TEAM OF THE SEASON
(4-4-2)
Coach: Lennon *(Celtic)*

Forster *(Celtic)*

Matthews *(Celtic)* · Wilson *(Celtic)* · Hutchinson *(Motherwell)* · Hammell *(Motherwell)*

Commons *(Celtic)* · Wanyama *(Celtic)* · Ledley *(Celtic)* · Law *(Motherwell)*

Higdon *(Motherwell)* · Griffiths *(Hibernian)*

NATIONAL TEAM

Home Kit   Away Kit

INTERNATIONAL TOURNAMENT APPEARANCES

FIFA World Cup (8) 1954, 1958, 1974, 1978, 1982, 1986, 1990, 1998
UEFA European Championship (2) 1992, 1996

TOP FIVE ALL-TIME CAPS

Kenny Dalglish (102); Jim Leighton (91); Alex McLeish (77); Paul McStay (76); Tommy Boyd (72)

TOP FIVE ALL-TIME GOALS

Kenny Dalglish & Denis Law (30); Hughie Gallacher (24); Lawrie Reilly (22); Ally McCoist (19)

Results 2012/13

Date	Opponent		Venue	Score	Scorers
15/08/12	Australia	H	Edinburgh	3-1	Rhodes (29), Davidson (62og), McCormack (75)
08/09/12	Serbia (WCQ)	H	Glasgow	0-0	
11/09/12	FYROM (WCQ)	H	Glasgow	1-1	Miller (43)
12/10/12	Wales (WCQ)	A	Cardiff	1-2	Morrison (28)
16/10/12	Belgium (WCQ)	A	Brussels	0-2	
14/11/12	Luxembourg	A	Luxembourg	2-1	Rhodes (11, 24)
06/02/13	Estonia	H	Aberdeen	1-0	Mulgrew (39)
22/03/13	Wales (WCQ)	H	Glasgow	1-2	Hanley (45+2)
26/03/13	Serbia (WCQ)	A	Novi Sad	0-2	
07/06/13	Croatia (WCQ)	A	Zagreb	1-0	Snodgrass (26)

Appearances 2012/13

Coach:
Craig Levein — 22/10/64
/(05/11/12) (Billy Stark) — 01/12/56
/(15/01/13) Gordon Strachan — 09/02/57

Player	DOB	Club	Aus	SRB	MKD	WAL	BEL	Lux	Est	WAL	SRB	CRO	Caps	Goals
Allan McGregor	31/01/82	Beşiktaş (TUR)	G22	G	G	G	G		G	G		G	29	-
Alan Hutton	30/11/84	Aston Villa (ENG) /Mallorca (ESP)	D67	D	D	D	D		D	D	D	D	32	-
Andy Webster	23/04/82	Hearts	D	D	D				D				28	1
Christophe Berra	31/01/85	Wolves (ENG)	D	D	D	D	D	D	D				27	2
Danny Fox	29/05/86	Southampton (ENG)	D69			D	D						4	-
Gary Caldwell	12/04/82	Wigan (ENG)	M87	M	M	M	D			D	D		55	2
Charlie Adam	10/12/85	Liverpool (ENG) /Stoke (ENG)	M	M	s58	s46			M61	s64	s46		23	-
James Morrison	25/05/86	West Brom (ENG)	M27	M81	M66	M87	M80		s62		M		27	2
Robert Snodgrass	07/09/87	Norwich (ENG)	M	M69					s46	M 71*	M		10	2
Steven Naismith	14/09/86	Everton (ENG)	M	M	s77			M	A75		M	s63	22	2
Jordan Rhodes	05/02/90	Huddersfield (ENG) /Blackburn (ENG)	A67	s81	s66			A90	s46	s86	A80	s64	9	3
Matt Gilks	04/07/82	Blackpool (ENG)	s22					G					2	-
Shaun Maloney	24/01/83	Wigan (ENG)	s27		M	M	M		M46	M	M80	M75	28	1
Russell Martin	04/01/86	Norwich (ENG)	s67									D	5	-
Ross McCormack	18/08/86	Leeds (ENG)	s67										8	2
Charlie Mulgrew	06/03/86	Celtic	s69					M46	D				6	1
Ian Black	14/03/85	Rangers	s87										1	-
Paul Dixon	22/11/86	Huddersfield (ENG)		D	D			D					3	-
Kenny Miller	23/12/79	Vancouver (CAN)		A81	A58	s87	s76	A	s67	s5	s80		68	17
James Forrest	07/07/91	Celtic		s69	M								7	-
Jamie Mackie	22/09/85	QPR (ENG)		s81	M77	s87	s46						9	2
Darren Fletcher	01/02/84	Man. United (ENG)				M	M	M					61	5
Scott Brown	25/06/85	Celtic				M46			M62				30	2
Kris Commons	30/08/83	Celtic				M87	M46		s75				12	2
Steven Fletcher	26/03/87	Sunderland (ENG)					A	A76	A67	A5			12	1
James McArthur	07/10/87	Wigan (ENG)					M		s61	M	M46	M	12	1
Matt Phillips	13/03/91	Blackpool (ENG)					s80						2	-
Steven Whittaker	16/06/84	Norwich (ENG)						D			D	D	18	-

Appearances 2012/13 (contd.)

			Aus	SRB	MKD	WAL	BEL	Lux	Est	WAL	SRB	CRO	Caps	Goals
Grant Hanley	20/11/91	Blackburn (ENG)						D		D	D	D	7	1
Andrew Shinnie	17/07/89	Inverness						M69					1	-
Liam Kelly	10/02/90	Kilmarnock						s46					1	-
Leigh Griffiths	20/08/90	Hibernian						s69				A64	2	-
Murray Davidson	07/03/88	St Johnstone						s90					1	-
Chris Burke	02/12/83	Birmingham (ENG)							M46	M86	s80		5	2
Graham Dorrans	05/05/87	West Brom (ENG)								M64			9	-
David Marshall	05/03/85	Cardiff (WAL)									G		6	-
George Boyd	02/10/85	Hull (ENG)									M		1	-
Liam Bridcutt	08/05/89	Brighton (ENG)									M		1	-
Barry Bannan	01/12/89	Aston Villa (ENG)										M63	12	-
Craig Conway	02/05/85	Cardiff (WAL)										s75	4	-

European club competitions 2012/13

CELTIC FC

Third qualifying round - HJK Helsinki (FIN)
H 2-1 *Hooper (54), Mulgrew (61)*
Forster, Matthews, Izaguirre, Brown, Samaras (Lustig 87), Commons (Stokes 65), Ledley, Mulgrew, Forrest, Wanyama, Hooper (McCourt 87). Coach: Neil Lennon (NIR)
A 2-0 *Ledley (67), Samaras (86)*
Forster, Matthews, Izaguirre, Brown, Samaras (Murphy 88), Commons (Forrest 75), Ledley, Mulgrew, Rogne, Wanyama, Hooper (Kayal 75). Coach: Neil Lennon (NIR)
Red card: Wanyama 71

Play-offs - Helsingborgs IF (SWE)
A 2-0 *Commons (2), Samaras (75)*
Forster, Matthews, Izaguirre, Brown, Samaras, Commons (Watt 90), Ledley (Wilson 66), Mulgrew, Rogne, Kayal (Forrest 46), Hooper. Coach: Neil Lennon (NIR)
H 2-0 *Hooper (30), Wanyama (88)*
Forster, Matthews (Lustig 76), Izaguirre, Wilson, Brown, Samaras (Watt 70), Commons, Mulgrew, Forrest, Wanyama, Hooper (McCourt 90+1). Coach: Neil Lennon (NIR)

Group G
Match 1 - SL Benfica (POR)
H 0-0
Forster, Matthews, Izaguirre (Hooper 66), Wilson, Miku, Brown, Commons, Mulgrew, Lustig (Rogne 63), Forrest, Wanyama. Coach: Neil Lennon (NIR)
Match 2 - FC Spartak Moskva (RUS)
A 3-2 *Hooper (12), D Kombarov (71og), Samaras (90)*
Forster, Izaguirre, Ambrose, Wilson, Brown, Samaras, Commons, Mulgrew (Ledley 80), Lustig, Wanyama (Forrest 70), Hooper. Coach: Neil Lennon (NIR)
Match 3 - FC Barcelona (ESP)
A 1-2 *Samaras (18)*
Forster, Izaguirre, Ambrose, Wilson, Brown (Commons 63), Samaras (Forrest 43), Ledley, Mulgrew (Kayal 76), Lustig, Wanyama, Hooper. Coach: Neil Lennon (NIR)
Match 4 - FC Barcelona (ESP)
H 2-1 *Wanyama (21), Watt (83)*
Forster, Matthews, Ambrose, Wilson, Miku, Samaras (Kayal 79), Commons, Ledley, Mulgrew, Lustig (Watt 72), Wanyama. Coach: Neil Lennon (NIR)
Match 5 - SL Benfica (POR)
A 1-2 *Samaras (32)*
Forster, Matthews, Ambrose, Wilson, Brown (Commons 64), Samaras, Ledley (Watt 80), Mulgrew (Kayal 46), Lustig, Wanyama, Hooper. Coach: Neil Lennon (NIR)
Match 6 - FC Spartak Moskva (RUS)
H 2-1 *Hooper (21), Commons (81p)*
Forster, Izaguirre, Ambrose, Wilson, Brown (Ledley 85), Samaras, Commons, Mulgrew, Lustig (Matthews 71), Kayal (Nouioui 73), Hooper. Coach: Neil Lennon (NIR)

Round of 16 - Juventus (ITA)
H 0-3
Forster, Izaguirre, Ambrose, Wilson, Brown (Kayal 80), Commons (Watt 73), Mulgrew, Lustig (Matthews 59), Forrest, Wanyama, Hooper. Coach: Neil Lennon (NIR)
A 0-2
Forster, Matthews (Forrest 52), Izaguirre, Wilson, Samaras, Commons (Nouioui 73), Ledley, Mulgrew, Kayal, Wanyama (Ambrose 46), Hooper. Coach: Neil Lennon (NIR)

MOTHERWELL FC

Third qualifying round - Panathinaikos FC (GRE)
H 0-2
Randolph, Hammell, Law, Hutchinson, Hateley, Humphrey, Ojamaa (Daley 79), Higdon, Murphy, Lasley, Ramsden. Coach: Stuart McCall (SCO)
A 0-3
Randolph, Hammell, Law, Hutchinson, Hateley, Ojamaa (McHugh 71), Murphy, Lasley, Ramsden, Daley (Higdon 76), Cummins (Francis-Angol 76). Coach: Stuart McCall (SCO)

Play-offs - Levante UD (ESP)

H 0-2
Randolph, Hammell, Law (Carswell 86),
Hutchinson, Hateley, Humphrey (Kerr 68),
Ojamaa (McHugh 68), Higdon, Murphy,
Lasley, Cummins. Coach: Stuart McCall
(SCO)
Red card: Hutchinson 77

A 0-1
Randolph, Hammell (Francis-Angol 74),
Ojamaa (McHugh 67), Higdon, Murphy,
Lasley, Carswell (Humphrey 68), Kerr, Page,
Hetherington, Cummins. Coach: Stuart
McCall (SCO)

HEART OF MIDLOTHIAN FC

Play-offs - Liverpool FC (ENG)

H 0-1
MacDonald, Grainger, R McGowan, Barr
(Robinson 87), Webster, Templeton (Driver
78), Sutton, Taouil, Novikovas (Carrick 84),
Žaliūkas, Paterson. Coach: John McGlynn
(SCO)

A 1-1 *Templeton (85)*
MacDonald, Grainger, R McGowan, Barr,
Webster, Templeton, Sutton (Driver 66),
Taouil, Novikovas (Carrick 76), Žaliūkas,
Paterson. Coach: John McGlynn (SCO)

DUNDEE UNITED FC

Third qualifying round - FC Dinamo Moskva (RUS)

H 2-2 *Flood (37), Watson (76)*
Cierzniak, Dillon, Douglas, Gunning, Flood,
Russell, Rankin, Daly, Ryan, Mackay-
Steven, Watson. Coach: Peter Houston
(SCO)

A 0-5
Cierzniak, Douglas, McLean, Gunning,
Flood, Russell (Gardyne 78), Rankin
(Armstrong 59), Daly, Ryan, Mackay-Steven
(Dow 86), Watson. Coach: Peter Houston
(SCO)

SAINT JOHNSTONE FC

Second qualifying round - Eskişehirspor (TUR)

A 0-2
Mannus, C Davidson, Cregg (Moon 85),
Wright, Millar, M Davidson, Craig, Higgins
(Hasselbaink 69), McCracken, Miller, Adams
(May 78). Coach: Steve Lomas (NIR)

H 1-1 *Tadé (35)*
Mannus, C Davidson, Cregg, Wright, Millar,
M Davidson, Tadé (Higgins 67), Craig,
Hasselbaink (May 84), McCracken, Miller
(MacKay 60). Coach: Steve Lomas (NIR)

SCOTLAND

Domestic league club-by-club

ABERDEEN FC

Coach: Craig Brown; (06/04/13) Derek McInnes
1903 • Pittodrie (22,199) • afc.co.uk
Major honours
UEFA Cup Winners' Cup (1) 1983;
UEFA Super Cup (1) 1983;
Scottish League (4) 1955, 1980, 1984, 1985;
Scottish Cup (7) 1947, 1970, 1982, 1983, 1984, 1986, 1990;
Scottish League Cup (5) 1956, 1977, 1986, 1990, 1996

2012

Date	Opponent		Score	Scorers
04/08	Celtic	a	0-1	
11/08	Ross County	h	0-0	
18/08	St Johnstone	a	2-1	Osbourne, Hayes
26/08	Hearts	h	0-0	
01/09	St Mirren	h	0-0	
15/09	Inverness	a	1-1	Smith
23/09	Motherwell	h	3-3	Rae, McGinn, Magennis
29/09	Hibernian	a	2-1	McGinn, Rae
06/10	Kilmarnock	a	3-1	Rae, McGinn, Vernon
20/10	Dundee United	a	1-1	McGinn
27/10	Dundee	h	2-0	McGinn, Hayes
03/11	Ross County	a	1-2	McGinn
10/11	St Mirren	a	4-1	Hayes, McGinn, Clark, Reynolds
17/11	Celtic	h	0-2	
24/11	Hibernian	a	1-0	McGinn
27/11	Inverness	h	2-3	Magennis 2
08/12	Hearts	a	0-2	
15/12	Kilmarnock	h	0-2	
22/12	St Johnstone	h	2-0	McGinn 2
26/12	Motherwell	a	1-4	Hayes
29/12	Dundee	a	3-1	McGinn 3

2013

Date	Opponent		Score	Scorers
02/01	Dundee United	h	2-2	Vernon, McGinn
19/01	Inverness	a	0-3	
27/01	Hibernian	h	0-0	
30/01	St Johnstone	a	1-3	McGinn
09/02	St Mirren	h	0-0	
15/02	Dundee	h	1-0	McGinn
23/02	Kilmarnock	a	1-1	Fallon
26/02	Ross County	h	0-1	
09/03	Motherwell	h	0-0	
16/03	Celtic	a	3-4	Vernon, Magennis 2
30/03	Hearts	h	2-0	McGinn 2
06/04	Dundee United	a	0-1	
22/04	Hibernian	a	0-0	
27/04	Kilmarnock	h	1-0	McGinn
05/05	Dundee	a	1-1	McGinn (p)
11/05	St Mirren	a	0-0	
18/05	Hearts	h	1-1	og (Hamill)

No	Name	Nat	DoB	Pos	Aps	(s)	Gls
4	Russell Anderson		25/10/78	D	30	(1)	
32	Jason Brown	WAL	18/05/82	G	1	(1)	
24	Jordon Brown		28/11/92	M		(2)	
7	Christopher Clark		15/08/80	M	6	(4)	1
6	Andrew Considine		01/04/87	D	17	(1)	
14	Rory Fallon	NZL	20/03/82	A	8	(7)	1
20	Ryan Fraser		24/02/94	M	13	(3)	
11	Jonny Hayes	IRL	09/07/87	M	29	(6)	4
18	Stephen Hughes		14/11/82	M	22	(1)	
2	Ryan Jack		27/02/92	M	18		
1	Jamie Langfield		22/12/79	G	37		
13	Nicky Low		06/01/92	M	1	(4)	
21	Josh Magennis	NIR	15/08/90	A	18	(17)	5
25	Jamie Masson		05/04/93	M	1	(5)	
10	Niall McGinn	NIR	20/07/87	M	33	(2)	20
34	Declan McManus		03/08/94	A		(7)	
19	Mitchel Megginson		27/07/92	M	1	(2)	
8	Robert Milsom	ENG	02/01/87	M	3	(10)	
35	Craig Murray		17/04/94	M		(1)	
17	Gary Naysmith		16/11/78	D	7	(2)	
16	Isaac Osbourne	ENG	22/06/86	M	21	(2)	1
15	Peter Pawlett		18/06/91	M	4	(8)	
5	Gavin Rae		28/11/77	M	34	(1)	3
22	Mark Reynolds		07/05/87	D	34	(1)	1
3	Clark Robertson		05/09/93	D	21	(2)	
23	Joe Shaughnessy	IRL	06/07/92	D	22	(1)	
38	Cameron Smith		24/08/95	A	7	(11)	1
39	Craig Storie		13/01/96	M	1		
9	Scott Vernon	ENG	13/12/83	A	29	(6)	3

CELTIC FC

Coach: Neil Lennon (NIR)
1888 • Celtic Park (60,832) • celticfc.net
Major honours
European Champion Clubs' Cup (1) 1967;
Scottish League (44) 1893, 1894, 1896, 1898, 1905,
1906, 1907, 1908, 1909, 1910, 1914, 1915, 1916, 1917,
1919, 1922, 1926, 1936, 1938, 1954, 1966, 1967, 1968,
1969, 1970, 1971, 1972, 1973, 1974, 1977, 1979, 1981,
1982, 1986, 1988, 1998, 2001, 2002, 2004, 2006, 2007,
2008, 2012, 2013;
Scottish Cup (36) 1892, 1899, 1900, 1904, 1907, 1908,
1911, 1912, 1914, 1923, 1925, 1927, 1931, 1933, 1937,
1951, 1954, 1965, 1967, 1969, 1971, 1972, 1974, 1975,
1977, 1980, 1985, 1988, 1989, 1995, 2001, 2004, 2005,
2007, 2011, 2013;
Scottish League Cup (14) 1957, 1958, 1966, 1967,
1968, 1969, 1970, 1975, 1983, 1998, 2000, 2001,
2006, 2009

2012

04/08	Aberdeen	h	1-0	Commons
18/08	Ross County	a	1-1	Commons
25/08	Inverness	a	4-2	Wanyama, Watt 2, Mulgrew
01/09	Hibernian	h	2-2	Lustig, og (McPake)
15/09	St Johnstone	a	1-2	Commons
22/09	Dundee	h	2-0	Hooper, Wanyama
29/09	Motherwell	a	2-0	Hooper, og (Cummins)
07/10	Hearts	h	1-0	Samaras
20/10	St Mirren	a	5-0	Hooper, Ambrose, Wanyama 2, Watt
27/10	Kilmarnock	h	0-2	
04/11	Dundee United	a	2-2	Miku, Watt
11/11	St Johnstone	h	1-1	Watt
17/11	Aberdeen	a	2-0	Nouioui, Mulgrew
24/11	Inverness	h	0-1	
28/11	Hearts	a	4-0	Nouioui, Lustig, og (Stevenson), Hooper
08/12	Kilmarnock	a	3-1	Brown, Ledley, Samaras
15/12	St Mirren	h	2-0	Wanyama, Hooper
22/12	Ross County	h	4-0	Brown, Hooper 2, Forrest
26/12	Dundee	a	2-0	Samaras, Hooper
29/12	Hibernian	a	0-1	

2012

02/01	Motherwell	h	1-0	Hooper
19/01	Hearts	h	4-1	Hooper 2, Samaras, Nouioui
22/01	Dundee United	h	4-0	Hooper 2, Wanyama, Brown
30/01	Kilmarnock	h	4-1	Ledley, Matthews 2, Stokes
09/02	Inverness	a	3-1	Commons, Gershon, Miku
16/02	Dundee United	h	6-2	Ambrose, Commons 2 (1p), Ledley, Stokes 2
19/02	St Johnstone	a	1-1	Ambrose
24/02	Dundee	h	5-0	Ledley 2, Forrest (p), McGeouch, Hooper
27/02	Motherwell	a	1-2	Samaras
09/03	Ross County	a	2-3	Mulgrew, Hooper
16/03	Aberdeen	h	4-3	Commons, Mulgrew, Hooper, Samaras
31/03	St Mirren	a	1-1	Commons
06/04	Hibernian	h	3-0	Commons 2, Lustig
21/04	Inverness	h	4-1	Hooper 2, Ledley, Samaras
28/04	Motherwell	a	1-3	Hooper
05/05	Ross County	a	1-1	Stokes
11/05	St Johnstone	h	4-0	Ledley, Mulgrew, Forrest, og (Wright)
19/05	Dundee United	a	4-0	Commons, Samaras 2, Stokes

No	Name	Nat	DoB	Pos	Aps	(s)	Gls
4	Efe Ambrose	NGA	18/10/88	D	24	(3)	3
37	Bahrudin Atajić	BIH	16/11/93	A		(1)	
14	Mohamed Bangura	SLE	27/07/89	A		(1)	
8	Scott Brown		25/06/85	M	14	(3)	3
43	Joe Chalmers		03/01/94	D		(2)	
15	Kris Commons		30/08/83	M	25	(2)	11
49	James Forrest		07/07/91	A	10	(5)	3
1	Fraser Forster	ENG	17/03/88	G	34		
44	Marcus Fraser		23/06/94	D	1		
5	Rami Gershon	ISR	12/08/88	D	3		1
31	John Herron		01/02/94	M		(1)	
88	Gary Hooper	ENG	26/01/88	A	30	(2)	19
36	Jackson Irvine	AUS	07/03/93	M		(1)	
3	Emilio Izaguirre	HON	10/05/86	D	29	(2)	
33	Beram Kayal	ISR	02/05/88	M	19	(8)	
16	Joe Ledley	WAL	23/01/87	M	21	(4)	7
23	Mikael Lustig	SWE	13/12/86	D	21	(2)	3
2	Adam Matthews	WAL	13/01/92	M	19	(3)	2
20	Paddy McCourt	NIR	16/12/83	M	4	(11)	
46	Dylan McGeouch		15/01/93	M	4	(8)	1
7	Miku	VEN	19/08/85	A	5	(6)	2
21	Charlie Mulgrew		06/03/86	D	30		5
27	Daryl Murphy	IRL	15/03/83	A		(1)	
11	Lassad Nouioui	TUN	08/03/86	A	8	(6)	3
18	Tom Rogić	AUS	16/12/92	M	3	(5)	
25	Thomas Rogne	NOR	29/06/90	D	8	(5)	
9	Georgios Samaras	GRE	21/02/85	A	18	(7)	9
30	Paul Slane		25/11/91	M		(1)	
10	Anthony Stokes	IRL	25/07/88	A	11	(6)	5
56	Filip Twardzik	CZE	10/02/93	M	2		
67	Victor Wanyama	KEN	25/06/91	M	31	(1)	6
32	Tony Watt		29/12/93	A	9	(11)	5
6	Kelvin Wilson	ENG	03/09/85	D	31	(1)	
24	Łukasz Załuska	POL	16/06/82	G	4		

DUNDEE FC

Coach: Barry Smith; (20/02/13) (Ray Farningham);
(23/02/13) John Brown
1893 • Dens Park (12,085) • dundeefc.co.uk
Major honours
Scottish League (1) 1962;
Scottish Cup (1) 1910;
Scottish League Cup (3) 1952, 1953, 1974

2012

04/08	Kilmarnock	a	0-0	
11/08	St Mirren	h	0-2	
19/08	Dundee United	a	0-3	
25/08	Ross County	h	0-1	
02/09	Hearts	a	1-0	Conroy
15/09	Motherwell	h	1-2	Nish
22/09	Celtic	a	0-2	
29/09	St Johnstone	h	1-3	Conroy (p)
06/10	Hibernian	a	0-3	
19/10	Inverness	h	1-4	Nish
27/10	Aberdeen	a	0-2	
03/11	Hearts	a	1-0	Lockwood
10/11	Motherwell	a	1-1	Riley
17/11	Hibernian	h	3-1	Benedictus, Milne, McBride (p)
24/11	St Mirren	a	1-3	Conroy (p)
09/12	Dundee United	h	0-3	
15/12	Ross County	a	1-1	Davidson
22/12	Inverness	a	1-4	Riley
26/12	Celtic	h	0-2	
29/12	Aberdeen	a	1-3	Stewart

2013

02/01	St Johnstone	a	0-1	
19/01	Hibernian	a	1-1	Baird
27/01	Kilmarnock	h	0-0	
30/01	Hearts	a	0-1	
08/02	Ross County	h	0-2	
15/02	Aberdeen	a	0-1	
24/02	Celtic	a	0-5	
27/02	St Johnstone	h	2-2	Baird, Stewart
06/03	St Mirren	h	2-1	Baird, McAlister
09/03	Inverness	h	1-1	Baird
17/03	Dundee United	a	1-1	Conroy
30/03	Motherwell	h	0-3	
06/04	Kilmarnock	a	2-1	Harkins 2
20/04	St Mirren	a	2-1	McAlister, Finnigan
27/04	Hearts	h	1-0	Conroy
05/05	Aberdeen	h	1-1	McAlister
11/05	Kilmarnock	h	2-3	Conroy, Stewart
18/05	Hibernian	a	0-1	

No	Name	Nat	DoB	Pos	Aps	(s)	Gls
12	John Baird		22/08/85	A	29	(8)	4
47	Andrew Barrowman		27/11/84	A		(1)	
16	Kyle Benedictus		07/12/91	D	24	(3)	1
23	Martin Boyle		25/04/93	M	1	(8)	
11	Ryan Conroy		28/04/87	M	19	(14)	6
46	Don Cowan	IRL	16/11/89	M		(2)	
6	Iain Davidson		14/01/84	M	35	(1)	1
1	Rab Douglas		24/04/72	G	30		
26	Brian Easton		05/03/88	D	17		
9	Carl Finnigan	ENG	01/10/86	A	1	(7)	1
18	Declan Gallagher		13/02/91	D	24		
21	Davide Grassi	ITA	13/01/86	D	10	(1)	
29	Gary Harkins		02/01/85	M	14		2
2	Gary Irvine		17/03/85	D	34		
28	Mark Kerr		02/03/82	M	6	(2)	
3	Matt Lockwood	ENG	17/10/76	D	21	(2)	1
20	Jim McAlister		02/11/85	M	38		3
8	Kevin McBride		14/06/81	M	20	(4)	1
5	Neil McGregor		17/07/85	D	5		
14	Leighton McIntosh		06/02/93	A		(1)	
10	Steven Milne		05/05/80	A	11	(3)	1
22	David Morgan	NIR	04/07/94	M		(1)	
24	Colin Nish		03/07/81	A	21	(3)	2
4	Stephen O'Donnell		10/07/83	M	6		
17	Nicky Riley		10/05/86	M	19	(9)	2
45	Steve Simonsen	ENG	03/04/79	G	8		
27	Mark Stewart		22/06/88	M	5	(10)	3
32	James Thomson		07/11/94	D		(1)	
25	Lewis Toshey		26/04/92	D	20	(3)	
16	Graham Webster		15/05/92	M		(3)	

DUNDEE UNITED FC

Coach: Peter Houston; (30/01/13) Jackie McNamara
1909 • Tannadice (14,209) • dundeeunitedfc.co.uk
Major honours
Scottish League (1) 1983;
Scottish Cup (2) 1994, 2010;
Scottish League Cup (2) 1980, 1981

2012

05/08	Hibernian	h	3-0	Russell, Daly, Gardyne
19/08	Dundee	h	3-0	Gunning, Russell 2
25/08	Kilmarnock	a	1-3	Daly
01/09	St Johnstone	a	0-0	
14/09	Ross County	h	0-0	
22/09	Hearts	h	0-3	
29/09	Inverness	a	0-4	
20/10	Aberdeen	h	1-1	Rankin
27/10	St Mirren	a	1-0	Russell (p)
04/11	Celtic	h	2-2	Mackay-Steven, og (Ambrose)
07/11	Motherwell	a	0-1	Russell
11/11	Hibernian	a	1-2	Mackay-Steven
16/11	Kilmarnock	h	3-3	Mackay-Steven, Daly 2
24/11	Ross County	a	2-1	Russell, Armstrong
27/11	Motherwell	a	0-1	Daly
09/12	Dundee	a	3-0	Watson, Daly (p), Flood
15/12	Inverness	h	4-4	og (Meekings), Daly 2 (1p), Skácel
23/12	Hearts	a	1-2	Watson
26/12	St Johnstone	h	1-1	Gunning
30/12	St Mirren	h	3-4	Daly (p), Armstrong, Douglas

2013

02/01	Aberdeen	a	2-2	Gunning, og (Langfield)
19/01	Kilmarnock	a	3-2	Russell 3
22/01	Celtic	a	0-4	
26/01	Ross County	h	1-1	Mackay-Steven
09/02	Hearts	a	3-1	Russell, Flood, Gardyne
16/02	Celtic	a	2-6	Armstrong, Russell
19/02	Motherwell	a	1-0	Russell
24/02	Hibernian	h	2-2	Rankin, Russell (p)
27/02	Inverness	a	0-0	
09/03	St Mirren	a	0-0	
18/03	Dundee	h	1-1	Gardyne
01/04	St Johnstone	a	1-1	Gauld
06/04	Aberdeen	h	1-0	Boulding
19/04	Motherwell	h	1-3	Daly
26/04	Ross County	a	0-1	
04/05	St Johnstone	h	0-1	
11/05	Inverness	a	2-1	Dow, Mackay-Steven
19/05	Celtic	h	0-4	

No	Name	Nat	DoB	Pos	Aps	(s)	Gls
16	Stuart Armstrong		30/03/92	M	30	(6)	3
19	Rory Boulding	ENG	21/07/88	A	3	(5)	1
1	Radosław Cierzniak	POL	24/04/83	G	38		
9	Jon Daly	IRL	02/05/85	A	35	(1)	10
2	Seán Dillon	IRL	30/07/83	D	31		
3	Barry Douglas		04/09/89	D	27	(1)	1
18	Ryan Dow		07/06/91	A	3	(9)	1
6	Willo Flood	IRL	10/04/85	M	37		2
15	Michael Gardyne		23/01/86	M	10	(20)	3
38	Ryan Gauld		16/12/95	M	5	(5)	1
5	Gavin Gunning	IRL	26/01/91	D	25		3
23	Dale Hilson		23/12/92	A		(1)	
33	Luke Johnston		03/09/93	D	1	(1)	
20	Miloš Lačný	SVK	08/03/88	A		(2)	
11	Gary Mackay-Steven		31/08/90	A	19	(4)	5
4	Brian McLean		28/02/85	D	25	(4)	
14	Mark Millar		23/02/88	M	11	(7)	
40	Darren Petrie		26/07/95	M		(1)	
8	John Rankin		27/06/83	M	35		2
7	Johnny Russell		08/04/90	A	30	(2)	13
10	Richie Ryan	IRL	06/01/85	M	12	(10)	
51	Rudolf Skácel	CZE	17/07/79	M	5	(9)	1
44	Jon Souttar		25/09/96	D	7	(1)	
27	Robert Thomson		28/05/93	A		(2)	
17	Marcus Törnstrand	SWE	10/01/90	D		(1)	
12	Keith Watson		14/11/89	D	29		2

HEART OF MIDLOTHIAN FC

Coach: John McGlynn; (28/02/13) Gary Locke
1874 • Tynecastle Stadium (17,420) • heartsfc.co.uk
Major honours
Scottish League (4) 1895, 1897, 1958, 1960;
Scottish Cup (8) 1891, 1896, 1901, 1906, 1956, 1998, 2006, 2012;
Scottish League Cup (4) 1955, 1959, 1960, 1963

2012

04/08	St Johnstone	h	2-0	Sutton (p), Templeton
12/08	Hibernian	a	1-1	Driver
18/08	Inverness	h	2-2	Novikovas, Sutton (p)
26/08	Aberdeen	a	0-0	
02/09	Dundee	a	0-1	
15/09	St Mirren	a	0-2	
22/09	Dundee United	h	3-0	Paterson 2, Novikovas
29/09	Kilmarnock	h	1-3	Žaliūkas
07/10	Celtic	a	0-1	
21/10	Motherwell	h	1-0	Grainger
27/10	Ross County	a	2-2	Novikovas, Sutton
03/11	Dundee	a	0-1	
10/11	Inverness	a	1-1	Žaliūkas (p)
17/11	St Mirren	h	1-0	Grainger
24/11	Motherwell	a	0-0	
28/11	Celtic	h	0-4	
08/12	Aberdeen	h	2-0	Stevenson (p), Paterson
15/12	St Johnstone	a	2-2	Sutton, Driver
23/12	Dundee United	h	2-1	Stevenson 2 (1p)
26/12	Kilmarnock	a	0-1	

2013

03/01	Hibernian	h	0-0	
19/01	Celtic	a	1-4	Holt
30/01	Dundee	h	1-0	Sutton
02/02	Ross County	a	2-2	Ngoo, Walker
09/02	Dundee United	a	1-3	Ngoo
16/02	Kilmarnock	h	0-3	
23/02	Inverness	h	2-3	Holt, Webster
02/03	St Mirren	a	0-2	
27/02	Motherwell	h	1-2	Sutton
05/03	St Johnstone	h	2-0	Stevenson, Sutton
10/03	Hibernian	a	0-0	
30/03	Aberdeen	a	0-2	
06/04	Ross County	h	4-2	Ngoo 2, Holt, og (Ikonomou)
20/04	Kilmarnock	a	1-0	Sutton
27/04	Dundee	a	0-1	
04/05	St Mirren	h	3-0	Walker, McHattie, Hamill (p)
12/05	Hibernian	h	1-2	Barr
18/05	Aberdeen	a	1-1	Stevenson

No	Name	Nat	DoB	Pos	Aps	(s)	Gls
5	Darren Barr		17/03/85	D	30	(2)	1
37	Dale Carrick		07/01/94	M	5	(11)	
11	Andrew Driver	ENG	12/11/87	M	15	(7)	2
21	Peter Enckelman	FIN	10/03/77	G		(1)	
3	Danny Grainger	ENG	28/07/86	D	13		2
2	Jamie Hamill		29/07/86	D	6	(1)	1
15	Jason Holt		19/02/93	M	16	(5)	3
32	Billy King		12/05/94	A	4	(4)	
1	Jamie MacDonald		17/04/86	G	38		
44	Jordan McGhee		24/07/96	D		(1)	
19	Dylan McGowan	AUS	19/10/91	D	11	(8)	
7	Ryan McGowan	AUS	15/08/89	M	20		
29	Kevin McHattie		15/07/93	D	21	(1)	
28	Brad McKay		26/03/93	D	1	(1)	
30	Fraser Mullen		08/11/93	D	7	(1)	
21	Michael Ngoo	ENG	23/03/93	A	15	(4)	4
18	Arvydas Novikovas	LTU	18/12/90	A	16	(14)	3
33	Callum Paterson		13/10/94	M	18	(4)	3
16	Denis Prychynenko	GER	17/02/92	M	1	(3)	
8	Scott Robinson		12/03/92	A	7	(6)	
17	David Smith		01/03/93	A	1	(2)	
12	Gordon Smith		14/02/91	M	4	(5)	
7	Ryan Stevenson		01/01/83	M	28	(1)	5
9	John Sutton	ENG	26/12/83	A	20	(15)	8
10	Mehdi Taouil	MAR	20/05/83	M	23	(6)	
27	Calum Tapping		05/06/93	M	10	(1)	
7	David Templeton		07/01/89	A	2		1
9	Jamie Walker		25/06/93	A	16	(8)	2
6	Andy Webster		23/04/82	D	33		1
4	Danny Wilson		27/12/91	D	13		
26	Marius Žaliūkas	LTU	10/11/83	D	24	(1)	2

HIBERNIAN FC

Coach: Pat Fenlon (IRL)
1875 • Easter Road (20,421) • hibernianfc.co.uk
Major honours
Scottish League (4) 1903, 1948, 1951, 1952;
Scottish Cup (2) 1887, 1902;
Scottish League Cup (3) 1973, 1992, 2007

2012

05/08	Dundee United	a	0-3	
12/08	Hearts	h	1-1	Griffiths
18/08	St Mirren	a	2-1	Griffiths 2
25/08	St Johnstone	h	2-0	Hanlon, Doyle
01/09	Celtic	a	2-2	Clancy, Cairney
15/09	Kilmarnock	a	2-1	Griffiths 2 (1p)
22/09	Inverness	h	2-2	Doyle, Wotherspoon
29/09	Aberdeen	a	1-2	Doyle
06/10	Dundee	h	3-0	Doyle, Griffiths (p), Wotherspoon
20/10	Ross County	a	2-3	Griffiths, McPake
26/10	Motherwell	a	4-0	Wotherspoon, Griffiths 2 (2p), Handling
03/11	St Mirren	h	2-1	Griffiths 2
11/11	Dundee United	h	2-1	Griffiths, Doyle
17/11	Dundee	a	1-3	Griffiths
24/11	Aberdeen	h	0-1	
28/11	St Johnstone	a	1-0	Cairney
08/12	Inverness	a	0-3	
15/12	Motherwell	h	2-3	Doyle 2
23/12	Kilmarnock	a	1-1	Doyle
26/12	Ross County	h	0-1	
29/12	Celtic	h	1-0	Griffiths

2013

03/01	Hearts	a	0-0	
19/01	Dundee	a	1-1	Griffiths
27/01	Aberdeen	a	0-0	
30/01	Ross County	a	0-1	
11/02	St Johnstone	a	1-3	Griffiths
16/02	St Mirren	a	1-0	Griffiths (p)
24/02	Dundee United	a	2-2	McPake, Griffiths
27/02	Kilmarnock	h	2-2	McGivern, Griffiths
10/03	Hearts	h	0-0	
15/03	Motherwell	a	1-4	Taiwo
30/03	Inverness	h	1-2	Griffiths
06/04	Celtic	a	0-3	
22/04	Aberdeen	h	0-0	
27/04	St Mirren	h	3-3	Griffiths 2, Caldwell
12/05	Hearts	a	2-1	Griffiths, Caldwell
15/05	Kilmarnock	a	3-1	Robertson, Doyle 2
18/05	Dundee	h	1-0	Wotherspoon

No	Name	Nat	DoB	Pos	Aps	(s)	Gls
11	Paul Cairney		29/08/87	M	26	(3)	2
29	Ross Caldwell		26/10/93	A	3	(14)	2
2	Tim Clancy	IRL	08/06/84	D	19		1
8	Jorge Claros	HON	08/01/86	M	29	(5)	
7	Gary Deegan	IRL	28/09/88	M	19	(1)	
17	Matt Done	ENG	22/07/88	M	6	(1)	
10	Eoin Doyle	IRL	12/03/88	A	28	(8)	10
37	Jordon Forster		23/09/93	D	3		
9	Leigh Griffiths		20/08/90	A	36		23
24	Danny Handling		06/02/94	A	4	(11)	1
4	Paul Hanlon		20/01/90	D	34		1
33	Alex Harris		31/08/94	M	6	(5)	
34	Dean Horribine		14/01/93	M		(1)	
32	Sňefki Kuqi	FIN	10/11/76	A	1	(12)	
18	Alan Maybury	IRL	08/08/78	D	24	(3)	
3	Ryan McGivern	NIR	08/01/90	D	25	(2)	1
6	James McPake	NIR	24/06/84	D	29		2
31	Seán Murdoch		31/07/86	G	1		
5	Seán O'Hanlon	ENG	02/01/83	D		(1)	
28	Scott Robertson		07/04/85	M	8	(4)	1
17	Ivan Sproule	NIR	18/02/81	M	2	(8)	
26	Sam Stanton		19/04/94	M		(1)	
20	David Stephens	WAL	18/10/91	D	1		
16	Lewis Stevenson		05/01/88	M	22	(7)	
20	Tom Taiwo	ENG	27/02/90	M	24	(2)	1
38	Kevin Thomson		14/10/84	M	5	(1)	
1	Ben Williams	ENG	27/08/82	G	37		
14	David Wotherspoon		16/01/90	M	26	(8)	4

INVERNESS CALEDONIAN THISTLE FC

Coach: Terry Butcher (ENG)
1994 • Caledonian Stadium (7,918) • ictfc.com

2012

04/08	St Mirren	a	2-2	Ross, McKay
11/08	Kilmarnock	h	1-1	A Shinnie
18/08	Hearts	a	2-2	A Shinnie (p), Pepper
25/08	Celtic	h	2-4	Draper 2
02/09	Motherwell	a	1-4	Foran
15/09	Aberdeen	h	1-1	Foran (p)
22/09	Hibernian	a	2-2	Pepper, Foran
29/09	Dundee United	h	4-0	Foran 2, A Shinnie, Roberts
05/10	Ross County	h	3-1	Draper, A Shinnie, Doran
19/10	Dundee	a	4-1	McKay 2, Warren, A Shinnie (p)
27/10	St Johnstone	h	1-1	McKay
03/11	Kilmarnock	a	2-1	A Shinnie, McKay (p)
10/11	Hearts	h	1-1	Tudur-Jones
18/11	Motherwell	h	1-5	Foran
24/11	Celtic	a	1-0	McKay
27/11	Aberdeen	a	3-2	McKay 2, Warren
08/12	Hibernian	h	3-0	Draper, Foran, McKay
15/12	Dundee United	a	4-4	McKay 3 (1p), Warren
22/12	Dundee	a	4-1	McKay 2 (1p), Tudur-Jones, A Shinnie
26/12	St Mirren	h	2-2	A Shinnie, Foran
29/12	St Johnstone	a	0-0	

2013

19/01	Aberdeen	h	3-0	A Shinnie, McKay 2
30/01	St Mirren	h	1-2	McKay (p)
09/02	Celtic	h	1-3	Ross
13/02	Kilmarnock	h	1-1	Ross
16/02	Motherwell	a	0-3	
23/02	Hearts	h	3-2	Warren 2, McKay
27/02	Dundee United	h	0-0	
02/03	Ross County	a	0-0	
09/03	Dundee	a	1-0	McKay
16/03	Ross County	h	2-1	A Shinnie, McKay (p)
30/03	Hibernian	a	2-1	Draper, A Shinnie
05/04	St Johnstone	h	0-0	
21/04	Celtic	a	1-4	Doran
27/04	St Johnstone	a	0-1	
04/05	Motherwell	h	4-3	McKay 3, A Shinnie
11/05	Dundee United	h	1-2	Doran
19/05	Ross County	a	0-1	

No	Name	Nat	DoB	Pos	Aps	(s)	Gls
12	Antonio Reguero	ESP	04/07/82	G	23	(1)	
25	Andre Doran	ENG	10/11/90	D	2		
32	Matthew Cooper		01/07/94	M	2	(1)	
27	Daniel Devine	IRL	07/09/92	D	8	(2)	
23	Aaron Doran	IRL	13/05/91	A	38		3
8	Ross Draper	ENG	20/10/88	M	33	(1)	5
1	Ryan Esson		19/03/80	G	15		
9	Richie Foran	IRL	16/06/80	A	25	(3)	8
26	Jordan Gibbons	ENG	18/11/93	M		(1)	
6	Chris Hogg	ENG	12/03/85	D	3		
15	Simon King	ENG	11/04/83	D	4		
21	Billy McKay	NIR	22/10/88	A	33	(5)	23
26	Josh Meekings	ENG	02/09/92	D	31	(3)	
19	Gavin Morrison		03/01/90	M	2	(7)	
16	Jason Oswell	ENG	07/10/92	A		(2)	
22	Conor Pepper	IRL	04/05/94	M	2	(10)	2
31	Liam Polworth		12/10/94	M		(3)	
2	David Raven	ENG	10/03/85	D	36		
23	Philip Roberts	IRL	07/04/94	A	8	(9)	1
11	Nick Ross		11/11/91	M	8	(13)	3
10	Andrew Shinnie		17/07/89	M	37	(1)	12
3	Graeme Shinnie		04/08/91	D	37		
18	Shane Sutherland		23/10/90	A	5	(64)	
28	Charlie Taylor	ENG	18/09/93	D	4	(3)	
4	Owain Tudur-Jones	WAL	15/10/84	M	31	(2)	2
5	Gary Warren	ENG	16/08/84	D	31		5

KILMARNOCK FC

Coach: Kenny Shiels (NIR)
1869 • Rugby Park (18,128) • kilmarnockfc.co.uk
Major honours
Scottish League (1) 1965;
Scottish Cup (3) 1920, 1929, 1997;
Scottish League Cup (1) 2012

2012

04/08	Dundee	h	0-0	
11/08	Inverness	a	1-1	Pascali
18/08	Motherwell	h	1-2	Harkins
25/08	Dundee United	h	3-1	McKenzie, Borja Pérez (p), Winchester
01/09	Ross County	a	0-0	
15/09	Hibernian	a	1-2	Racchi
22/09	St Mirren	h	3-1	Sheridan, Fowler, Dayton
29/09	Hearts	a	3-1	Sheridan 3
06/10	Aberdeen	h	1-3	O'Leary
20/10	St Johnstone	h	1-2	Fowler
27/10	Celtic	a	2-0	Sheridan, Kelly (p)
03/11	Inverness	h	1-2	Kelly
10/11	Ross County	h	3-0	Heffernan 2, Harkins
16/11	Dundee United	a	3-3	Sheridan 2, Heffernan
24/11	St Johnstone	h	1-2	Nelson
08/12	Celtic	h	1-3	Sheridan
15/12	Aberdeen	a	2-0	Kelly 2 (1p)
23/12	Hibernian	h	1-1	Heffernan
26/12	Hearts	h	1-0	Kelly (p)
29/12	Motherwell	a	2-2	Borja Pérez, Heffernan

2013

02/01	St Mirren	a	1-1	Kelly (p)
18/01	Dundee United	h	2-3	Pascali 2
27/01	Dundee	h	0-0	
30/01	Celtic	a	1-4	Sheridan
09/02	Motherwell	h	2-0	og (Hammell), Gros
13/02	Inverness	a	1-1	Borja Pérez
16/02	Hearts	h	3-0	Heffernan 3
23/02	Aberdeen	h	1-1	Heffernan
27/02	Hibernian	a	2-2	Clingan, Winchester
09/03	St Johnstone	a	0-2	
30/03	Ross County	a	1-0	Fowler
03/04	St Mirren	h	1-1	Boyd
06/04	Dundee	h	1-2	Boyd
20/04	Hearts	h	0-1	
27/04	Aberdeen	a	0-1	
11/05	Dundee	a	3-2	McKenzie, Johnston, Clingan
15/05	Hibernian	h	1-3	Ashcroft
18/05	St Mirren	h	1-3	Boyd

No	Name	Nat	DoB	Pos	Aps	(s)	Gls
35	Lee Ashcroft		29/08/93	D	2	(1)	1
25	Ross Barbour		01/02/93	D	16		
1	Cameron Bell		18/09/86	G	30		
15	Borja Pérez	ESP	14/01/81	M	19	(6)	3
16	Rory Boulding	ENG	21/07/88	A	1	(3)	
11	Kris Boyd		18/08/83	A	6	(2)	3
8	Sammy Clingan	NIR	13/01/84	M	13	(1)	2
31	Ross Davidson		28/10/93	A	2		
10	James Dayton	IRL	12/12/88	M	23	(4)	1
4	James Fowler		26/10/80	D	33	(1)	3
9	William Gros	FRA	31/03/92	A	9	(8)	1
11	Gary Harkins		02/01/85	M	14	(2)	2
3	Garry Hay		07/08/77	D	4	(4)	
14	Paul Heffernan	IRL	29/12/81	A	22	(5)	9
19	Rabiu Ibrahim	NGA	15/03/91	M	2	(4)	
30	Chris Johnston		03/09/94	A	4	(7)	1
18	Lee Johnson	ENG	07/06/81	M	7	(4)	
8	Liam Kelly		10/02/90	M	19		6
33	Matthew Kennedy		01/11/94	A	3		
46	Greg Kiltie		18/01/97	M		1	
17	Kyle Letheren	WAL	26/12/87	G	8	(1)	
24	Rory McKenzie		07/10/93	A	8	(14)	2
23	Rory McKeown	NIR	08/04/93	D	16		
39	Robbie Muirhead		08/03/96	A		(1)	
6	Michael Nelson	ENG	23/03/80	D	21		1
38	Mark O'Hara		12/12/95	M	13	(4)	
5	Ryan O'Leary		24/08/87	D	22	(6)	1
29	Manuel Pascali	ITA	09/09/81	M	24		3
26	Alex Pursehouse	ENG	06/05/92	D	1		
7	Danny Racchi	ENG	22/11/88	M	8	(8)	1
12	Cillian Sheridan	IRL	23/02/89	A	19	(7)	9
88	Mahamadou Sissoko	FRA	08/08/88	D	18	(2)	
36	Craig Slater		26/04/94	M	1	(1)	
2	Jeroen Tesselaar	NED	16/01/89	D	25	(1)	
28	Jude Winchester	NIR	13/04/93	M	5	(3)	2

MOTHERWELL FC

Coach: Stuart McCall
1886 • Fir Park (13,742) • motherwellfc.co.uk
Major honours
Scottish League (1) 1932;
Scottish Cup (2) 1952, 1991;
Scottish League Cup (1) 1951

2012

04/08	Ross County	a	0-0	
11/08	St Johnstone	h	1-1	McHugh
18/08	Kilmarnock	a	2-1	Murphy 2
26/08	St Mirren	h	1-1	Higdon
02/09	Inverness	h	4-1	Hateley, Higdon 3
15/09	Dundee	a	2-1	Higdon 2
23/09	Aberdeen	h	3-3	Higdon, Hutchinson, Law
29/09	Celtic	h	0-2	
21/10	Hearts	a	0-1	
26/10	Hibernian	h	0-4	
03/11	St Johnstone	a	3-1	Murphy 2, Law
07/11	Dundee United	h	0-1	
10/11	Dundee	h	1-1	Higdon
18/11	Inverness	a	5-1	Higdon, Murphy, Cummins, Ojamaa, Daley
24/11	Hearts	h	0-0	
27/11	Dundee United	a	2-1	Higdon, Humphrey
08/12	Ross County	h	3-2	Higdon, Law, Lasley
15/12	Hibernian	a	3-2	Murphy 2, McHugh
21/12	St Mirren	a	1-2	McHugh
26/12	Aberdeen	h	4-1	Hateley, Murphy 2, Higdon
29/12	Kilmarnock	h	2-2	Murphy, Ojamaa

2013

02/01	Celtic	a	0-1	
20/01	St Johnstone	h	3-2	Higdon 3
09/02	Kilmarnock	a	0-2	
16/02	Inverness	h	3-0	Higdon 2, Law
19/02	Dundee United	h	0-1	
23/02	Ross County	a	0-3	
27/02	Celtic	h	2-1	Humphrey, Higdon
02/03	Hearts	a	2-1	Higdon, og (D McGowan)
09/03	Aberdeen	a	0-0	
15/03	Hibernian	h	4-1	Higdon, McFadden, Higginbotham, Hateley
30/03	Dundee	a	3-0	Higdon, Law 2
06/04	St Mirren	h	2-2	Higdon, McFadden
19/04	Dundee United	a	3-1	Higdon 2, Ojamaa
28/04	Celtic	h	3-1	Ojamaa, Higdon (p), og (Forster)
04/05	Inverness	a	3-4	McFadden 2, Higdon (p)
12/05	Ross County	h	2-0	McFadden, Humphrey
19/05	St Johnstone	a	0-2	

No	Name	Nat	DoB	Pos	Aps	(s)	Gls
18	Stewart Carswell		09/09/92	M	8	(16)	
30	Adam Cummins	ENG	03/03/93	A	15	(5)	1
17	Omar Daley	JAM	25/04/81	M	2	(12)	1
26	Zaine Francis-Angol	ATG	30/06/93	D	8	(12)	
5	Steven Hammell		18/02/82	D	31		
6	Tom Hateley	ENG	12/09/89	D	34		3
27	Steven Hetherington	ENG	09/03/93	D	1	(2)	
9	Michael Higdon	ENG	02/09/83	A	37		26
11	Kallum Higginbotham	ENG	15/06/89	A	3	(7)	1
12	Lee Hollis		12/03/86	G	2	(1)	
7	Chris Humphrey	JAM	19/09/87	M	32	(1)	3
5	Shaun Hutchinson	ENG	23/11/90	D	31		1
19	Fraser Kerr		17/01/93	D	10	(6)	
14	Keith Lasley		21/09/79	M	36		1
4	Nicky Law	ENG	29/03/88	M	38		6
40	James McFadden		14/04/83	A	11	(2)	5
16	Robert McHugh		16/07/91	A	2	(22)	3
11	Jamie Murphy		28/08/89	A	20	(2)	10
8	Henrik Ojamaa	EST	20/05/91	A	32	(5)	4
20	Jonathan Page	ENG	08/02/90	D	1		
15	Simon Ramsden	ENG	17/12/81	D	28	(1)	
1	Darren Randolph	IRL	12/05/87	G	36		
2	Steven Saunders		23/02/91	D		(1)	
43	Ross Stewart		16/04/95	G		(1)	

ROSS COUNTY FC

Coach: Derek Adams
1929 • Victoria Park (6,300) •
rosscountyfootballclub.co.uk

2012

04/08	Motherwell	h	0-0	
11/08	Aberdeen	a	0-0	
18/08	Celtic	h	1-1	Brittain
25/08	Dundee	a	1-0	Brittain (p)
01/09	Kilmarnock	h	0-0	
14/09	Dundee United	a	0-0	
22/09	St Johnstone	h	1-2	Morrow
29/09	St Mirren	a	4-5	Vigurs, Munro, Quinn 2
05/10	Inverness	a	1-3	Vigurs
20/10	Hibernian	h	3-2	Kettlewell, Vigurs, McMenamin
27/10	Hearts	a	2-2	Brittain (p), Kettlewell
03/11	Aberdeen	h	2-1	og (Reynolds), Ross
10/11	Kilmarnock	a	0-3	
17/11	St Johnstone	a	1-1	og (Craig)
24/11	Dundee United	h	1-2	Vigurs
27/11	St Mirren	h		
08/12	Motherwell	a	2-3	Quinn 2
15/12	Dundee	h	1-1	Glen
22/12	Celtic	a	0-4	
26/12	Hibernian	a	1-0	Brittain

2013

19/01	St Mirren	a	4-1	Brittain, Morrow, Sproule 2
26/01	Dundee United	a	1-1	Brittain
30/01	Hibernian	h	1-0	Sproule
02/02	Hearts	h	2-2	Quinn, Vigurs
08/02	Dundee	a	1-2	Lawson, Glen
16/02	St Johnstone	h	1-0	Sproule
23/02	Motherwell	h	3-0	Sproule, Brittain, Vigurs
26/02	Aberdeen	a	1-0	Glen
02/03	Inverness	h	0-0	
09/03	Celtic	h	3-2	Munro, Morrow, Wohlfarth
16/03	Inverness	a	1-2	Lawson
30/03	Kilmarnock	h	0-1	
06/04	Hearts	a	2-4	Wohlfarth 2
21/04	St Johnstone	a	2-2	Brittain 2 (2p)
26/04	Dundee United	h	1-0	Sproule
05/05	Celtic	h	1-1	Vigurs
12/05	Motherwell	a	0-2	
19/05	Inverness	h	1-0	Hainault

No	Name	Nat	DoB	Pos	Aps	(s)	Gls
5	Scott Boyd		06/04/86	D	34	(1)	
10	Richard Brittain		24/09/83	M	34		9
25	Mark Brown		28/02/81	G	13		
21	Alex Cooper		04/11/91	M	7	(8)	
15	Mark Corcoran		30/11/80	M	2	(3)	
18	Russell Duncan		15/09/80	M	1	(2)	
3	Marc Fitzpatrick		11/05/86	M	18	(2)	
29	Mark Fotheringham		22/10/83	M	12	(2)	
1	Michael Fraser		08/10/83	G	24		
19	Paul Gallacher		16/08/79	G	1		
20	Gary Glen		22/03/90	A	6	(20)	3
13	André Hainault	CAN	17/06/86	D	5	(3)	1
18	Evangelos Ikonomou	GRE	18/07/87	D	18		
7	Stuart Kettlewell		04/06/84	M	19	(6)	2
22	Mihael Kovacevic	SUI	03/03/88	M	28	(2)	
8	Paul Lawson		15/05/84	M	20	(2)	2
9	Colin McMenamin		12/02/81	A	10	(9)	1
3	Branislav Micic	SUI	17/04/90	D		(1)	
17	Sam Morrow	NIR	03/03/85	A	17	(6)	3
4	Grant Munro		15/09/80	D	36	(1)	2
12	Rocco Quinn		07/09/86	M	31		5
24	Steven Ross		29/08/93	M	4	(6)	1
14	Martin Scott		15/02/86	M	8	(7)	
16	Ivan Sproule	NIR	18/02/81	M	14		6
6	Ross Tokely		08/03/79	D	13	(4)	
11	Iain Vigurs		07/05/88	M	37		7
15	Steffen Wohlfarth	GER	14/09/83	A	6	(10)	3

SAINT JOHNSTONE FC

Coach: Steve Lomas (NIR)
1884 • McDiarmid Park (10,456) •
perthstjohnstonefc.co.uk

2012

04/08	Hearts	a	0-2	
11/08	Motherwell	a	1-1	M Davidson
18/08	Aberdeen	h	1-2	Hasselbaink
25/08	Hibernian	a	0-2	
01/09	Dundee United	h	0-0	
15/09	Celtic	h	2-1	Tadé, Vine
22/09	Ross County	a	2-1	Craig, Wright
29/09	Dundee	a	3-1	Tadé, Craig, MacLean
06/10	St Mirren	h	2-1	Hasselbaink, M Davidson
20/10	Kilmarnock	h	2-1	M Davidson, Hasselbaink
27/10	Inverness	a	1-1	Robertson
03/11	Motherwell	h	1-3	Robertson
11/11	Celtic	a	1-1	Hasselbaink
17/11	Ross County	h	1-1	MacKay
24/11	Kilmarnock	a	2-1	M Davidson, Vine
28/11	Hibernian	h	0-1	
08/12	St Mirren	a	1-1	M Davidson
15/12	Hearts	h	2-2	Vine, MacLean
22/12	Aberdeen	a	0-0	
26/12	Dundee United	a	1-1	og (McLean)
29/12	Inverness	h	0-0	

2013

02/01	Dundee	h	1-0	Craig
20/01	Motherwell	a	2-3	Hasselbaink, Craig
30/01	Aberdeen	h	3-1	Tadé, Vine, MacKay
11/02	Hibernian	a	3-1	Vine 2, Cregg
16/02	Ross County	a	0-1	
19/02	Celtic	h	1-1	Hasselbaink
23/02	St Mirren	h	1-0	Vine
27/02	Dundee	a	2-2	MacLean, MacKay
05/03	Hearts	a	0-2	
09/03	Kilmarnock	h	2-0	M Davidson, Tadé
01/04	Dundee United	h	1-1	Craig
05/04	Inverness	a	0-0	
21/04	Ross County	h	2-2	MacLean, M Davidson
27/04	Inverness	h	1-0	MacLean
04/05	Dundee United	a	1-0	Craig
11/05	Celtic	a	0-4	
19/05	Motherwell	h	2-0	Craig, Hasselbaink

No	Name	Nat	DoB	Pos	Aps	(s)	Gls
21	Mehdi Abeid	ALG	06/08/92	M	9	(3)	
20	Jamie Adams		26/08/87	M		(4)	
6	Steven Anderson		19/12/85	M	28	(2)	
16	Craig Beattie		16/01/84	A		(2)	
26	Liam Caddis		20/09/93	M		(1)	
10	Liam Craig		27/12/86	D	37		7
4	Patrick Cregg	IRL	21/02/86	M	19	(5)	1
17	Callum Davidson		25/06/76	D	20	(1)	
8	Murray Davidson		07/03/88	M	31	(1)	7
16	Michael Doughty	WAL	20/11/92	M	1	(4)	
14	Gwion Edwards	WAL	01/03/93	M		(6)	
11	Nigel Hasselbaink	NED	21/11/90	A	15	(21)	7
17	Sean Higgins		29/10/84	A	1	(2)	
2	David MacKay		02/05/80	D	32		3
17	Steven MacLean		23/08/82	A	27	(4)	5
1	Alan Mannus	NIR	19/05/82	G	38		
27	Stevie May		02/11/92	M		(3)	
18	David McCracken		16/10/81	D	15	(1)	
7	Chris Millar		30/03/83	M	25	(1)	
12	Gary Miller		15/04/87	D	13	(4)	
14	Kevin Moon		08/06/87	M		(1)	
22	Peter Pawlett		03/02/91	M	7	(2)	
12	David Robertson		23/09/86	M	1	(6)	2
33	Tam Scobbie		31/03/88	D	11	(7)	
9	Grégory Tadé	FRA	02/09/86	A	25	(11)	4
23	Rowan Vine	ENG	21/09/82	A	28	(7)	7
5	Frazer Wright		23/12/79	D	35		1

SAINT MIRREN FC

Coach: Danny Lennon (NIR)
1877 • St Mirren Park (8,023) • saintmirren.net
Major honours
Scottish Cup (3), 1926, 1959, 1987;
Scottish League Cup (1) 2013

2012

04/08	Inverness	h	2-2	Guy, McGregor
11/08	Dundee	a	2-0	McLean, Parkin
18/08	Hibernian	h	1-2	Thompson
26/08	Motherwell	a	1-1	Reilly
01/09	Aberdeen	a	0-0	
15/09	Hearts	h	2-0	Goodwin, Guy
22/09	Kilmarnock	a	1-3	McGowan
29/09	Ross County	h	5-4	Thompson 2, Guy (p), Parkin, McLean
06/10	St Johnstone	a	1-2	Guy
20/10	Celtic	h	0-5	
27/10	Dundee United	h	0-1	
03/11	Hibernian	a	1-2	McLean
10/11	Aberdeen	h	1-4	Thompson
17/11	Hearts	a	0-1	
24/11	Dundee	h	3-1	Thompson 2, Imrie
27/11	Ross County	a	1-1	Dummett
08/12	St Johnstone	h	1-1	Dummett
15/12	Celtic	a	0-2	
21/12	Motherwell	h	2-1	Thompson 2
26/12	Inverness	a	2-2	Imrie, Thompson
30/12	Dundee United	a	4-3	Dummett, Thompson, McAusland, Van Zanten

2013

02/01	Kilmarnock	h	1-1	McGowan (p)
19/01	Ross County	h	1-4	Thompson
30/01	Inverness	a	2-1	Esmaël Gonçalves, Thompson
09/02	Aberdeen	a	0-0	
16/02	Hibernian	a	0-0	
23/02	St Johnstone	a	0-1	
27/02	Hearts	h	2-0	McGowan (p), Carey
06/03	Dundee	a	1-2	Imrie
09/03	Dundee United	h	0-0	
31/03	Celtic	h	1-1	McGowan (p)
03/04	Kilmarnock	a	1-1	Esmaël Gonçalves
06/04	Motherwell	a	2-2	Newton, Guy
20/04	Dundee	h	1-2	Thompson
27/04	Hibernian	a	3-3	Esmaël Gonçalves, McAusland 2
04/05	Hearts	a	0-3	
11/05	Aberdeen	h	0-0	
18/05	Kilmarnock	a	3-1	McGinn, McGowan (p), Newton

No	Name	Nat	DoB	Pos	Aps	(s)	Gls
23	David Barron		10/09/87	M	8	(4)	
34	Anton Brady		07/02/94	M		(1)	
11	Graham Carey	IRL	20/05/89	D	18	(8)	1
3	Paul Dummett	WAL	26/09/91	D	29	(1)	2
77	Esmaël Gonçalves	GNB	25/06/91	A	11	(1)	3
6	Jim Goodwin	IRL	20/11/81	M	29		1
27	Lewis Guy	ENG	22/09/85	A	17	(12)	5
7	Dougie Imrie		03/08/83	M	13	(14)	3
5	Lee Mair		09/12/80	D	21	(3)	
14	Marc McAusland		13/08/88	D	35	(1)	3
297	John McGinn		18/10/94	M	15	(7)	1
10	Paul McGowan		07/10/87	M	25		5
4	Darren McGregor		07/08/85	D	3		1
17	Kenny McLean		08/01/92	M	26	(3)	3
24	Conor Newton	ENG	17/10/91	M	16		2
19	Sam Parkin	ENG	14/03/81	A	12	(15)	2
88	Sander Puri	EST	07/05/88	M	1	(1)	
20	Thomas Reilly		05/09/94	A	2	(7)	1
8	Jon Robertson		25/04/89	M	11	(8)	
1	Craig Samson		01/04/84	G	38		
28	Jack Smith		27/12/94	A		(2)	
21	Gary Teale		21/07/78	M	23	(7)	
9	Steven Thompson		14/10/78	A	33	(1)	13
2	David van Zanten	IRL	08/05/82	D	32	(2)	1
33	Mo Yaqub		07/01/94	M		(1)	

SCOTLAND

Top goalscorers

26	Michael Higdon (Motherwell)
23	Leigh Griffiths (Hibernian)
	Billy McKay (Inverness)
20	Niall McGinn (Aberdeen)
19	Gary Hooper (Celtic)
13	Johnny Russell (Dundee United)
	Steven Thompson (St Mirren)
12	Andrew Shinnie (Inverness)
11	Kris Commons (Celtic)
10	Jon Daly (Dundee United)
	Eoin Doyle (Hibernian)
	Jamie Murphy (Motherwell)

Promoted club

PARTICK THISTLE FC

Coach: Jackie McNamara; (30/01/13) Alan Archibald
1876 • Firhill Stadium (13,079) • ptfc.co.uk
Major honours
Scottish Cup (1) 1921;
Scottish League Cup (1) 1972

SECOND LEVEL FINAL TABLE 2012/13

		Pld	W	D	L	F	A	Pts
1	Partick Thistle FC	36	23	9	4	76	28	78
2	Greenock Morton FC	36	20	7	9	73	47	67
3	Falkirk FC	36	15	8	13	52	48	53
4	Livingston FC	36	14	10	12	58	56	52
5	Hamilton Academical FC	36	14	9	13	52	45	51
6	Raith Rovers FC	36	11	13	12	45	48	46
7	Dumbarton FC	36	13	4	19	58	83	43
8	Cowdenbeath FC	36	8	12	16	51	65	36
9	Dunfermline Athletic FC	36	14	7	15	62	59	34
10	Airdrie United FC	36	5	7	24	41	89	22

NB Dunfermline Athletic FC – 15 pts deducted.

Domestic cup: Scottish Cup 2012/13

FOURTH ROUND

(01/12/12)
Aberdeen 1-1 Motherwell
Celtic 1-1 Arbroath
Forfar 2-1 Ayr United
Kilmarnock 2-1 Queen of the South
Livingston 0-2 Dundee
Partick Thistle 0-1 Dunfermline
Raith Rovers 2-1 Deveronvale
Ross County 3-3 Inverness
St Mirren 2-0 Brechin
Stenhousemuir 0-1 Falkirk
Stranraer 0-5 Dundee United
Turriff United 1-1 Greenock Morton
(02/12/12)
Hibernian 1-0 Hearts
Rangers 3-0 Elgin
(17/12/12)
Cowdenbeath 0-3 St Johnstone
Dumbarton 1-3 Hamilton

Replays
(11/12/12)
Inverness 2-1 Ross County
Motherwell 1-2 Aberdeen
(12/12/12)
Arbroath 0-1 Celtic
(17/12/12)
Greenock Morton 6-0 Turriff United

FIFTH ROUND

(02/02/13)
Dundee United 3-0 Rangers
Dunfermline 0-2 Hamilton
Falkirk 4-1 Forfar
Kilmarnock 2-0 Inverness
St Mirren 2-0 St Johnstone
(03/02/13)
Dundee 5-1 Greenock Morton
Hibernian 1-0 Aberdeen
Raith Rovers 0-3 Celtic

QUARTER-FINALS

(02/03/13)
Hamilton 1-2 Falkirk (Ryan 74; Alston 44, 71)
St Mirren 1-2 Celtic (Esmaël Gonçalves 13; Ledley 5, Stokes 21)
(03/03/13)
Dundee 1-2 Dundee United (McAlister 19; McLean 11, Mackay-Steven 35)
Kilmarnock 2-4 Hibernian (Dayton 26, Heffernan 72p; Griffiths 15, 82, 89p, Done 39)

SEMI-FINALS

(13/04/13)
Hibernian 4-3 Falkirk (Harris 52, Griffiths 78, 115, Doyle 83; Sibbald 6, Fulton 18, Alston 30) (aet)
(14/04/13)
Dundee United 3-4 Celtic (Mackay-Steven 23, Daly 30, 72; Commons 2, 59, Wanyama 31, Stokes 103) (aet)

FINAL

(26/05/13)
Hampden Park, Glasgow
CELTIC FC 3 (Hooper 9, 31, Ledley 80)
HIBERNIAN FC 0
Referee: *Collum*
CELTIC: *Forster, Izaguirre, Wilson, Mulgrew, Lustig, Brown (Ambrose 81), Commons (Samaras 76), Ledley, Forrest (McCourt 88), Stokes, Hooper*
HIBERNIAN: *Williams, McGivern, Hanlon, Maybury, Forster, Claros, Taiwo, Harris, Thomson (Caldwell 76), Griffiths (Stevenson 84), Doyle (Handling 71)*

Domestic cup: League Cup 2012/13

QUARTER-FINALS

(30/10/12)
Aberdeen 2-2 St Mirren (Vernon 22, Magennis 90; Parkin 6, McLean 69) (aet; 2-4 on pens)
Celtic 5-0 St Johnstone (Commons 28, 32, 57p, Hooper 38, Mulgrew 61)
(31/10/12)
Dundee United 1-1 Hearts (Russell 35; Paterson 21) (aet; 4-5 on pens)
Rangers 0-3 Inverness (A Shinnie 27, Warren 59, G Shinnie 79p)

SEMI-FINALS

(26/01/13)
Inverness 1-1 Hearts (A Shinnie 49; Ngoo 66) (aet; 4-5 on pens)
(27/01/13)
St Mirren 3-2 Celtic (Esmaël Gonçalves 8, McGowan 63p, Thompson 69; Hooper 45, Mulgrew 90)

FINAL

(17/03/13)
Hampden Park, Glasgow
SAINT MIRREN FC 3 (Esmaël Gonçalves 37, Thompson 46, Newton 66)
HEART OF MIDLOTHIAN FC 2 (Stevenson 10, 85)
Referee: *Thompson*
ST MIRREN: *Samson, Van Zanten, McAusland, Goodwin, Dummett, Newton, McGinn (Carey 81), Teale, McGowan, Esmaël Gonçalves (Mair 90+1), Thompson (Parkin 77)*
HEARTS: *MacDonald, D McGowan, Webster, Wilson, McHattie, Stevenson, Taouil (Carrick 80), Barr (Holt 70), Walker (Novikovas 64), Sutton, Ngoo*

SERBIA

Fudbalski savez Srbije (FSS)

Address	Terazije 35, CP 263
	RS-11000 Beograd
Tel	+381 11 323 4253
Fax	+381 11 323 3433
E-mail	office@fss.rs
Website	fss.org.rs

President	Tomislav Karadžić
General secretary	Zoran Laković
Media officer	Aleksandar Bošković
Year of formation	1919

SUPERLIGA CLUBS

1. FK BSK Borča
2. FK Crvena zvezda
3. FK Donji Srem
4. FK Hajduk Kula
5. FK Jagodina
6. FK Javor
7. FK Novi Pazar
8. OFK Beograd
9. FK Partizan
10. FK Rad
11. FK Radnički 1923
12. FK Radnički Niš
13. FK Sloboda Užice
14. FK Smederevo
15. FK Spartak Zlatibor voda
16. FK Vojvodina

PROMOTED CLUBS

17. FK Napredak
18. FK Čukarički

KEY:

- – UEFA Champions League
- – UEFA Europa League
- – Promoted clubs
- – Relegated clubs

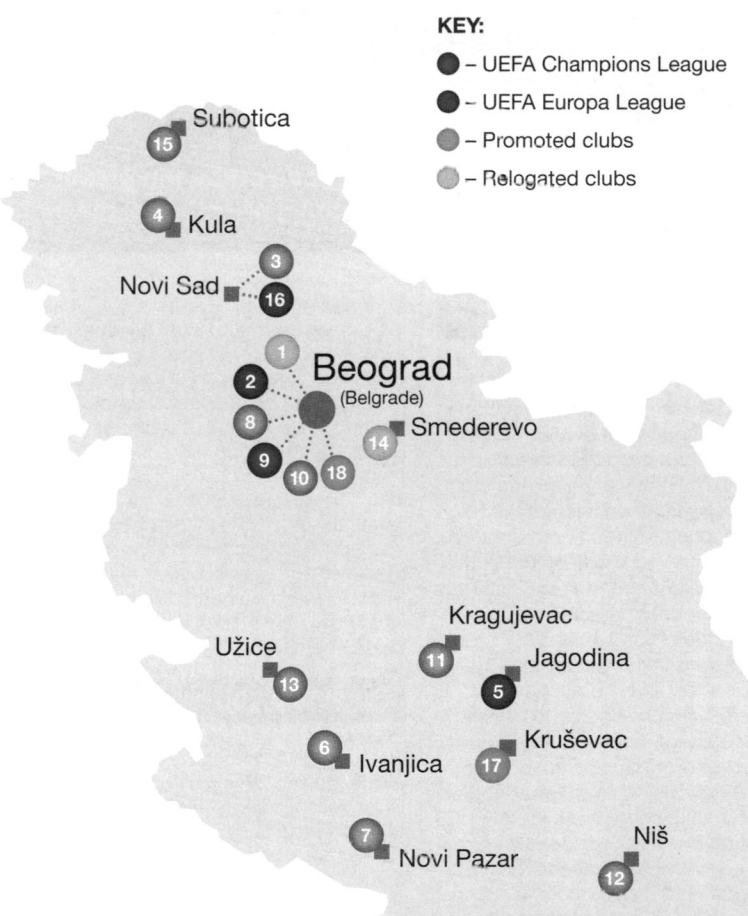

Six in a row for Partizan

FK Partizan won a sixth successive national title to make it 25 in total (Serbia and Yugoslavia combined) and match the all-time record of Belgrade rivals FK Crvena zvezda.

The club's historic achievement was effectively sealed with a 1-0 win in the Eternal Derby three rounds from the end, Crvena zvezda having reduced Partizan's large lead to just two points before that pivotal encounter. For once, neither of the big two reached the cup final, enabling FK Jagodina to take the trophy for the first time at the expense of FK Vojvodina.

25th title ties Crvena zvezda record

Belgrade derby win proves pivotal

Jagodina prolong Vojvodina cup jinx

Domestic league

Vladimir Vermezović, who coached Partizan to the last 16 of the UEFA Cup in 2004/05, returned to the club at the start of the season, but despite steering them to the top of the table, and keeping them there, he was jettisoned following a dry spell in the spring, during which the team allowed Crvena zvezda back into the title race after they had at one stage fallen 11 points behind.

Ten straight wins in the autumn got Vermezović off to an excellent start, but as the big match at home to Crvena zvezda loomed, he was shunted aside and replaced by the club's former youth coach Vuk Rašović, who led Partizan to wins in each of their last five games. It was a dramatic last-minute free-kick from 21-year-old Miloš Jojić that brought victory at home to Crvena zvezda in front of 30,000 fans. Four days later a 2-0 win at bottom-of-the-table FK Smederevo clinched the title, and with Crvena zvezda, now coached by ex-Portugal striker Ricardo Sá Pinto, also losing their last two games, that 11-point cushion was restored in the Superliga's final standings.

Sá Pinto had come in for Aleksandar Janković, the early-season replacement for Robert Prosinečki, in mid-March and led Crvena zvezda to eight successive wins. A 3-2 victory at home to the defending champions in November had kept alive hopes of a first championship triumph since 2007, but ultimately it was Partizan's greater consistency that saw them home. At the heart of their effort was 35-year-old skipper Saša Ilić, as influential as ever in midfield. He had able young lieutenants in winger Lazar Marković and central striker Aleksandar Mitrović, while Bulgarian Ivan Ivanov was the league's most consistent central defender.

Domestic cup

The top five clubs in the Superliga were unchanged from the previous season, which meant another third place for Vojvodina and fourth spot for Jagodina. Furthermore, both clubs reached the final of the Serbian Cup. It was the first time since the break–up of the federal Yugoslavia that neither Partizan nor Crvena zvezda were involved in the fixture. But while it was Jagodina's first appearance, Vojvodina had been to five previous finals and lost the lot. That hoodoo continued as Simo Krunić's fluent side took the trophy – the first in Jagodina's 51-year history – thanks to an early penalty converted by Milan Djurić after a shot from the Superliga's top scorer, 19-goal Miloš Stojanović, had struck a hand.

Europe

For the fifth time in seven seasons Partizan reached a European group stage. As in all their previous outings, however, they failed to make further progress. Indeed, they posted no wins in the UEFA Europa League proper, having squeezed through the play-offs against Tromsø IL. Crvena zvezda were unable to accompany them into the group stage following a narrow play-off defeat by FC Girondins de Bordeaux.

National team

Siniša Mihajlović's first season as Serbia coach was something of a letdown as the team's hopes of qualifying for the 2014 FIFA World Cup were effectively extinguished by four defeats in seven matches. The 6-1 win at home to Wales in September proved to be a flash in the pan as Mihajlović's men subsequently lost at home to Belgium and away to regional rivals FYROM and Croatia. The painful 2-0 defeat in Zagreb was partially remedied by a 2-0 win at home to Scotland, in which rising star Filip Djuričić bagged a brace, but another defeat by Belgium – 2-1 in Brussels – closed the door on any potential recovery.

Domestic league: Superliga 2012/13 final table

		Pld	Home					Away					Total					Pts
			W	D	L	F	A	W	D	L	F	A	W	D	L	F	A	
1	FK Partizan	30	14	0	1	45	7	9	4	2	26	9	23	4	3	71	16	73
2	FK Crvena zvezda	30	11	1	3	36	18	9	1	5	19	17	20	2	8	55	35	62
3	FK Vojvodina	30	8	5	2	19	11	9	5	1	21	9	17	10	3	40	20	61
4	FK Jagodina	30	10	1	4	20	9	5	4	6	15	17	15	5	10	35	26	50
5	FK Sloboda Užice	30	7	6	2	23	15	4	6	5	16	22	11	12	7	39	37	45
6	OFK Beograd	30	8	4	3	19	13	5	2	8	15	19	13	6	11	34	32	45
7	FK Rad	30	10	4	1	22	6	2	4	9	10	24	12	8	10	32	30	44
8	FK Hajduk Kula	30	7	5	3	23	12	3	3	9	13	20	10	8	12	36	32	38
9	FK Spartak Zlatibor voda	30	6	5	4	25	17	3	4	8	11	22	9	9	12	36	39	36
10	FK Javor	30	7	2	6	21	17	2	5	8	17	23	9	7	14	38	40	34
11	FK Donji Srem	30	6	4	5	16	11	3	3	9	10	23	9	7	14	26	34	34
12	FK Radnički Niš	30	6	5	4	16	13	3	2	10	14	31	9	7	14	30	44	34
13	FK Radnički 1923	30	5	5	5	16	16	0	5	8	9	19	7	10	13	25	35	31
14	FK Novi Pazar	30	6	6	3	21	13	1	3	11	8	27	7	9	14	29	40	30
15	FK BSK Borča	30	6	2	7	16	24	2	4	9	10	33	8	6	16	26	57	30
16	FK Smederevo	30	2	3	10	8	22	1	3	11	10	31	3	6	21	18	53	15

SEASON AT A GLANCE

EUROPEAN QUALIFICATION 2013/14

 Champion: FK Partizan (second qualifying round)

 Cup winner: FK Jagodina (second qualifying round)
FK Crvena zvezda (second qualifying round)
FK Vojvodina (first qualifying round)

Top scorer	Miloš Stojanović (Jagodina), 19 goals
Relegated clubs	FK Smederevo, FK BSK Borča
Promoted clubs	FK Napredak, FK Čukarički
Cup final	FK Jagodina 1-0 FK Vojvodina

SUPERLIGA TEAM OF THE SEASON
(4-4-2)
Coach: Krunić (Jagodina)

Stojković (Partizan)

Vulićević (Vojvodina) Trajković (Vojvodina) Ivanov (Partizan) Josimov (Donji Srem)

Oumarou (Vojvodina) Milivojević (Crvena zvezda) Ilić (Partizan) L Marković (Partizan)

Mitrović (Partizan) L Veselinović (Hajduk)

PLAYER OF THE SEASON
Saša Ilić
(FK Partizan)

The 35-year-old midfielder ended the season with 626 appearances for Partizan over two spells, placing him second on the all-time list. Harnessing that know-how, Ilić rolled back the years to collect his ninth championship medal. It was just reward for another stirring season, in which he continued to enrapture the Partizan fans with his array of passing skills.

NEWCOMER OF THE SEASON
Aleksandar Mitrović
(FK Partizan)

After years of searching for a traditional No9, Partizan looked to have unearthed a jewel in Mitrović. Strong, aerially dominant and two-footed, the 18-year-old exhibited all the qualities of a complete centre-forward, striking ten goals in 23 games. His youthful prowess caught the eye of Serbia boss Siniša Mihajlović, who gave him his first cap in June.

NATIONAL TEAM

Home Kit   Away Kit

INTERNATIONAL TOURNAMENT APPEARANCES*

FIFA World Cup (11) 1930 (semi-finals), 1950, 1954 (qtr-finals), 1958 (qtr-finals), 1962 (4th), 1974 (2nd phase), 1982, 1990 (qtr-finals), 1998 (2nd round), 2006, 2010 UEFA European Championship (5) 1960 (runners-up), 1968 (runners-up), 1976 (4th), 1984, 2000 (qtr-finals).

TOP FIVE ALL-TIME CAPS*

Savo Milošević & Dejan Stanković (102); Dragan Džajić (85); Dragan Stojković (84); Predrag Mijatović (73)

TOP FIVE ALL-TIME GOALS*

Stjepan Bobek (38); Milan Galić & Savo Milošević (37); Blagoje Marjanović (36); Rajko Mitić (32)

before 2006 as Yugoslavia; 2006 as Serbia & Montenegro.

Results 2012/13

Date	Opponent		Venue	Score	Scorers
15/08/12	Republic of Ireland	H	Belgrade	0-0	
08/09/12	Scotland (WCQ)	A	Glasgow	0-0	
11/09/12	Wales (WCQ)	H	Novi Sad	6-1	Kolarov (16), Tošić (24), Djuričić (39), Tadić (55), Ivanović (80), Sulejmani (90)
12/10/12	Belgium (WCQ)	H	Belgrade	0-3	
16/10/12	FYROM (WCQ)	A	Skopje	0-1	
14/11/12	Chile	N	St Gallen (SUI)	3-1	Marković (23), Djordjević (48), Djuričić (59)
06/02/13	Cyprus	A	Nicosia	3-1	Tadić (23, 47), Basta (70)
22/03/13	Croatia (WCQ)	A	Zagreb	0-2	
26/03/13	Scotland (WCQ)	H	Novi Sad	2-0	Djuričić (60, 65)
07/06/13	Belgium (WCQ)	A	Brussels	1-2	Kolarov (87)

Appearances 2012/13

Coach: Siniša Mihajlović — 20/02/69

Player	DOB	Club	Irl	SCO	WAL	BEL	MKD	Chi	Cyp	CRO	SCO	BEL	Caps	Goals
Vladimir Stojković	28/07/83	Partizan	G	G	G				G		G	G	45	-
Branislav Ivanović	22/02/84	Chelsea (ENG)	D	D	D	D	s68	D46	D46	D	D	D	61	7
Milan Biševac	31/08/83	Lyon (FRA)	D46	D	D	D	D					D	15	-
Matija Nastasić	28/03/93	Fiorentina (ITA) /Man. City (ENG)	D		D	D	D		D	D	D		9	-
Aleksandar Kolarov	10/11/85	Man. City (ENG)	D	D	D	D	D	D46	D	D		D	41	2
Srdjan Mijailović	10/11/93	Crvena zvezda	M64	M46	s85	M							5	-
Zdravko Kuzmanović	22/09/87	Stuttgart (GER) /Internazionale (ITA)	M82						M73				47	6
Zoran Tošić	28/04/87	CSKA Moskva (RUS)	M82	M	M70	M67	M		M46	M	M93		49	8
Aleksandar Ignjovski	27/01/91	Bremen (GER)	M	M	M85	M	M	s85		M75			11	-
Dušan Tadić	20/11/88	Twente (NED)	M63	s58	M	M81	M68	s60	M53	s57	M69	M	15	3
Dejan Lekić	07/06/85	Gençlerbirliği (TUR)	A46	s84	s81	s81	s61						10	-
Nikola Maksimović	25/11/91	Crvena zvezda	s46					D					4	-
Lazar Marković	02/03/94	Partizan	s46		A	A	A74	M				M	7	1
Filip Djuričić	30/01/92	Heerenveen (NED)	s63	A84	M81	M56	M61	M60	M	M	A		11	4
Miloš Ninković	25/12/84	Dynamo Kyiv (UKR)	s64	M									28	-
Dušan Basta	18/08/84	Udinese (ITA)	s82						s53		M	M	8	1
Nemanja Tomić	21/01/88	Partizan	s82										5	1
Darko Lazović	15/09/90	Crvena zvezda		M58									4	-
Ljubomir Fejsa	14/08/88	Olympiacos (GRE)		s46	M		M				M85	M	12	-
Miralem Sulejmani	05/12/88	Ajax (NED)			s70		s74	A60	s46				13	1
Željko Brkić	09/07/86	Udinese (ITA)				G	G	G		G			10	-
Marko Šćepović	23/05/91	Partizan			s56			A46		A9		s69	4	-
Alen Stevanović	07/01/91	Torino (ITA)				s67				M57	s93		3	-
Nenad Tomović	30/08/87	Fiorentina (ITA)					D 59*	D	D		D		13	-
Radosav Petrović	08/03/89	Gençlerbirliği (TUR)						M	M46	s75	s85	s69	32	1
Luka Milivojević	07/04/91	Crvena zvezda						M85			M	M69	3	-
Antonio Rukavina	26/01/84	Valladolid (ESP)						s46	s46				24	-
Marko Lomić	13/09/83	Dinamo Moskva (RUS)						s46					3	-
Filip Djordjević	28/09/87	Nantes (FRA)						s46	s46	s9	s69		4	1
Ivan Radovanović	29/08/88	Atalanta (ITA)						s60	s46	M			6	-
Nikola Djurdjić	01/04/86	Greuther Fürth (GER)							A46				1	-
Nenad Krstičić	03/07/90	Sampdoria (ITA)							s73				1	-
Neven Subotić	10/12/88	Dortmund (GER)								D	D	D	34	2
Aleksandar Mitrović	16/09/94	Partizan										A69	1	-

European club competitions 2012/13

FK PARTIZAN

CHAMPIONS LEAGUE

Second qualifying round - Valletta FC (MLT)
A 4-1 Tomić (6), Ivanov (33), S Šćepović (42), Ostojić (71)
Stojković, Volkov, Tomić (Zubya 76), Lovre (S Ilić 39), S Šćepović, Aksentijević, Ivanov, S Marković, Babović, Ostojić, L Marković (Ninković 57). Coach: Vladimir Vermezović (SRB)
H 3-1 Tomić (10, 67), Mitrović (70)
Petrović, Volkov, Tomić (Ninković 77), S Šćepović (Mitrović 64), Aksentijević, Ivanov, S Marković, S Ilić, Babović (Vukić 66), Ostojić, L Marković. Coach: Vladimir Vermezović (SRB)

Third qualifying round - AEL Limassol FC (CYP)
A 0-1
Stojković, Volkov, Tomić (L Marković 85), Lovre, S Šćepović (Zubya 70), Aksentijević, Ivanov, S Marković, S Ilić (Vukić 74), Babović, Ostojić. Coach: Vladimir Vermezović (SRB)
H 0-1
Stojković, Volkov, Tomić, S Šćepović (Mitrović 73), Aksentijević, Ivanov, S Marković, S Ilić (Zubya 62), Babović (Ninković 46), Ostojić, L Marković. Coach: Vladimir Vermezović (SRB)

EUROPA LEAGUE

Play-offs - Tromsø IL (NOR)
A 2-3 S Marković (43), Mitrović (84)
Stojković, Miljković, Volkov, Medo, Tomić, S Šćepović (Mitrović 58), Aksentijević, Ivanov, S Marković (Smiljanić 90+3), Babović (S Ilić 81), L Marković. Coach: Vladimir Vermezović (SRB)
H 1-0 Ivanov (75)
Stojković, Miljković, Volkov, Medo, Tomić, Ivanov, S Marković (Smiljanić 78), S Ilić (Ninković 72), Ostojić, Mitrović, L Marković (Zubya 46). Coach: Vladimir Vermezović (SRB)

Group H
Match 1 - Neftçi PFK (AZE)
H 0-0
Stojković, Miljković, Medo, Tomić, Ivanov, Lazevski, S Marković (Jojić 63), S Ilić, Ostojić, Mitrović (S Šćepović 73), L Marković. Coach: Vladimir Vermezović (SRB)
Match 2 - FC Rubin Kazan (RUS)
A 0-2
Stojković, Miljković, Volkov, Medo, Ninković (Mitrović 61), Ivanov, Volkov, S Marković, S Ilić (S Šćepović 74), Jojić, Ostojić, L Marković. Coach: Vladimir Vermezović (SRB)
Match 3 - FC Internazionale Milano (ITA)
A 0-1
Petrović, Miljković, Volkov, Medo, Tomić (S Marković 80), Ivanov, S Ilić (Jojić 76), Ostojić, Mitrović (M Šćepović 68), L Marković, Smiljanić. Coach: Vladimir Vermezović (SRB)

Match 4 - FC Internazionale Milano (ITA)
H 1-3 Tomić (90+1)
Petrović, Miljković, Medo (M Šćepović 55), Tomić, S Šćepović (Mitrović 69), Ivanov, Lazevski, S Ilić (Jojić 30), Ostojić, L Marković, Smiljanić. Coach: Vladimir Vermezović (SRB)
Match 5 - Neftçi PFK (AZE)
A 1-1 Mitrović (67)
Petrović, Miljković, Volkov, Tomić, S Šćepović (M Šćepović 66), Ivanov, S Ilić, Jojić (S Marković 83), Ostojić, L Marković (Mitrović 46), Smiljanić. Coach: Vladimir Vermezović (SRB)
Red card: Mitrović 76
Match 6 - FC Rubin Kazan (RUS)
H 1-1 S Marković (53)
Petrović, Miljković, Volkov, Tomić (Jojić 74), S Šćepović (M Šćepović 72), Ivanov, S Marković, S Ilić, Ostojić, L Marković (Knežević 90), Smiljanić. Coach: Vladimir Vermezović (SRB)

FK CRVENA ZVEZDA

EUROPA LEAGUE

Second qualifying round - FC Naftan Novopolotsk (BLR)
A 4-3 Kasalica (9, 69), Milunović (18, 34)
Bajković, Krneta, Dimitrijević, Lazović, Evandro (Cadú 71), Maksimović, Mikić, Milunović (Vešović 77), Kasalica, Milivojević, Mladenović. Coach: Robert Prosinečki (CRO)
H 3-3 Kasalica (9), Dimitrijević (15), Vešović (90+1)
Bajković, Krneta, Dimitrijević (Cadú 77), Lazović, Evandro, Maksimović, Mikić, Milunović (Vešović 85), Kasalica, Milivojević (Mijailović 62), Mladenović. Coach: Robert Prosinečki (CRO)
Third qualifying round - AC Omonia (CYP)
H 0-0
Bajković, Mijailović, Dimitrijević (Cadú 88), Lazović (Milivojević 81), Evandro, Maksimović, Jovanović, Milunović, Kasalica, Mladenović, Vešović. Coach: Robert Prosinečki (CRO)
Red card: Vešović 90+3
A 0-0 (aet; 6-5 on pens)
Bajković, Mijailović, Dimitrijević, Lazović (Milunović 102), Evandro (Mirić 119), Maksimović, Mikić, Jovanović, Kasalica, Milivojević, Mladenović. Coach: Robert Prosinečki (CRO)
Play-offs - FC Girondins de Bordeaux (FRA)
H 0-0
Bajković, Mijailović, Dimitrijević, Lazović (Asamoah 79), Maksimović, Mikić, Jovanović (Spajić 85), Milunović, Milivojević, Mladenović, Vešović (Mirić 69). Coach: Aleksandar Janković (SRB)
A 2-3 Mladenović (45+2), Mikić (90)
Bajković, Mijailović, Dimitrijević, Lazović, Maksimović, Mikić, Jovanović (Babalj 85), Milunović (Mirić 63), Kasalica, Mladenović, Vešović (Asamoah 76). Coach: Aleksandar Janković (SRB)

FK VOJVODINA

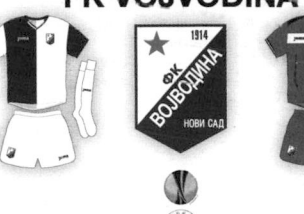

EUROPA LEAGUE

Second qualifying round - FK Sūduva (LTU)
H 1-1 Oumarou (90+3)
Supić, Trajković, Moreira, Bilbija (Škuletić 71), Mitošević, Oumarou, Stevanović, Vulićević (Smiljanić 87), Djurić, Ajuru (Bojović 60), Pavlović. Coach: Zlatomir Zagorčić (BUL)
A 4-0 Moreira (4), Škuletić (37), Stevanović (40), Oumarou (48)
Supić, Trajković, Škuletić, Moreira, Mitošević (Ajuru 31), Oumarou (Bojović 63), Stevanović, Poletanović (Bilbija 81), Vulićević, Djurić, Pavlović. Coach: Zlatomir Zagorčić (BUL)
Red card: Trajković 90+1

Third qualifying round - SK Rapid Wien (AUT)
H 2-1 Oumarou (75), Bojović (90+4)
Supić, Greene, Škuletić (Bilbija 66), Moreira, Oumarou (Bojović 89), Stevanović, Poletanović (Ajuru 84), Vulićević, Djurić, Pavlović, Jokić. Coach: Zlatomir Zagorčić (BUL)
A 0-2
Supić, Greene (Jokić 87), Trajković, Moreira, Oumarou, Stevanović, Poletanović (Bojović 90+3), Vulićević, Djurić, Ajuru (Mitošević 73), Pavlović. Coach: Zlatomir Zagorčić (BUL)
Red card: Pavlović 83

FK JAGODINA

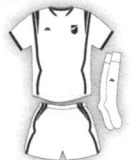

EUROPA LEAGUE

First qualifying round - FC Ordabasy Shymkent (KAZ)
H 0-1
Bondžulić, Tomić, Mudrinski (Kostić 68), Stojković (Milenković 83), Dukić, Projić, Stojkov, M Stojanović, Živanović, Djenić (Nikodijević 71), Gogić. Coach: Simo Krunić (BIH)
A 0-0
Bondžulić, Tomić, Mudrinski, Stojković (Vukmirović 88), Dukić (Nikodijević 87), Projić, Stojkov, M Stojanović, Živanović, Djenić (Kostić 74), Gogić. Coach: Simo Krunić (BIH)
Red card: Živanović 90+4

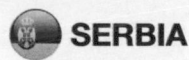

Domestic league club-by-club

FK BSK BORČA

Coach: Goran Milojević;
(25/12/12) Nebojša Milošević;
(15/05/13) Miodrag Radanović
1937 • FK BSK (3,900) • fkbskborca.rs

2012

11/08	Partizan	a	0-7	
18/08	Sloboda	h	1-0	Savković
25/08	Vojvodina	a	0-1	
01/09	Javor	h	1-0	Savković
15/09	Rad	a	0-3	
22/09	Novi Pazar	h	2-3	Simović, Bošković
29/09	Radnički Niš	a	1-4	Sotirović
07/10	Radnički 1923	h	2-0	Petrović, Nuhi
20/10	Crvena zvezda	a	2-7	Sotirović, Bulatović
27/10	Smederevo	h	1-1	Djukić
03/11	Spartak	a	1-2	Živković
10/11	Hajduk	a	1-1	Sotirović
17/11	Donji Srem	h	2-1	Djukić, Savković
25/11	Jagodina	a	0-2	
01/12	OFK Beograd	h	0-2	

2013

02/03	Sloboda	a	0-1	
06/03	Partizan	h	0-4	
09/03	Vojvodina	h	3-3	Ajković, Ademović, Nuhi (p)
17/03	Javor	a	2-1	Novaković, Božičić
30/03	Rad	h	1-0	N Jovanović
03/04	Novi Pazar	a	1-1	Ademović
06/04	Radnički Niš	h	2-1	Živanović, Rogač
13/04	Radnički 1923	a	0-0	
21/04	Crvena zvezda	h	0-1	
27/04	Smederevo	a	0-2	
04/05	Spartak	h	0-3	
11/05	Hajduk	h	0-3	
17/05	Donji Srem	a	1-0	Nuhi (p)
22/05	Jagodina	h	1-2	Nuhi
26/05	OFK Beograd	a	1-1	Ajković

No	Name	Nat	DoB	Pos	Aps	(s)	Gls
17	Edin Ademović		02/10/87	M	13		2
7	Srdjan Ajković	MNE	15/10/91	A	13	(1)	2
8	Dražen Andjušić	MNE	03/07/92	M		(2)	
24	Marko Bošković		15/04/82	D	2	(2)	1
33	Dario Božičić		30/08/89	D	13		1
18	Blažo Bulatović		18/09/90	M	2	(6)	1
2	Nikola Čelebić	MNE	04/07/89	D	8		
25	Nikola Česarević		03/10/83	M	13	(1)	
30	Branislav Danilović		24/06/88	G	11		
14	Aleksandar Djukić		30/11/80	A	18	(5)	2
17	Nenad Djurdjević		14/07/87	A	1	(3)	
31	Dušan Dunjić		29/03/87	D	11	(1)	
33	Miroslav Gegić		27/08/84	D	3		
11	Miroslav Grujičić		17/06/94	G	4		
5	Jordan Jovanović		27/01/92	M	5	(14)	
32	Nenad Jovanović		12/05/88	M	7	(2)	1
34	Ljubo Kovačević		08/09/78	G	11		
11	Aleksandar Marinković		13/07/90	G	4		
1	Vladimir Matić		12/07/83	M	6	(6)	
23	Stefan Milojević		20/02/91	D	13		
29	Branislav Milošević		13/05/88	D	3		
33	Ivica Milutinović		20/10/83	D	10		
26	Milko Novaković	MNE	21/01/88	A	15		1
20	Ajazdin Nuhi		10/10/79	M	26	(1)	4
4	Aleksandar Petrović		01/02/85	D	12	(1)	1
69	Petar Planić		16/03/89	D	21	(2)	
28	Miloš Radivojević		05/04/90	M	2	(3)	
6	Aleksandar Radunović		09/05/80	D	12	(1)	
4	Ivan Rogač		30/11/91	M	12	(1)	1
21	Mile Savković		11/03/92	M	26		3
10	Aleksandar Simović		30/01/92	D		(16)	1
1	Vuk Sotirović		13/07/82	A	10	(1)	3
15	Miloš Stamenković		01/06/90	D	11		
32	Perica Stanceski	MKD	29/01/85	D	2	(4)	
9	Miloš Živanović		24/07/88	A	6	(6)	1
9	Nenad Živković		10/03/89	A	4	(8)	1

FK CRVENA ZVEZDA

Coach: Robert Prosinečki (CRO);
(21/08/12) Aleksandar Janković;
(18/03/13) Ricardo Sá Pinto (POR)
1945 • FK Crvena zvezda (51,328) • crvenazvezdafk.com

Major honours
European Champion Clubs' Cup (1) 1991;
European/South American Cup (1) 1991;
Yugoslav/Serbian League (25) 1951, 1953, 1956, 1957,
1959, 1960, 1964, 1968, 1969, 1970, 1973, 1977, 1980,
1981, 1984, 1988, 1990, 1991, 1992, 1995, 2000, 2001,
2004, 2006, 2007;
Yugoslav/Serbian Cup (24) 1948, 1949, 1950, 1958, 1959,
1964, 1968, 1970, 1971, 1982, 1985, 1990, 1993, 1995, 1996,
1997, 1999, 2000, 2002, 2004, 2006, 2007, 2010, 2012

2012

19/08	Rad	h	2-2	Milivojević, Lazović
26/08	Novi Pazar	a	2-1	Kasalica, Milunović
02/09	Radnički Niš	h	3-2	Mudrinski 3
16/09	Radnički 1923	a	3-0	Miljaš, Kasalica, Milivojević
22/09	Hajduk	a	1-0	Mudrinski
29/09	Smederevo	h	3-1	Milunović, Mikić, Babalj
03/10	Javor	a	2-1	Mudrinski, Lazović
07/10	Spartak	a	0-3	
20/10	BSK Borča	h	7-2	Dimitrijević, Mikić, Mudrinski, Milunović, Asamoah, Pantić, Maksimović
27/10	Donji Srem	a	2-1	Milivojević 2
03/11	Jagodina	h	1-2	Mudrinski
11/11	OFK Beograd	a	0-1	
17/11	Partizan	h	3-2	Kasalica, Milivojević, Milijaš
25/11	Sloboda	a	2-1	Mudrinski 2
01/12	Vojvodina	h	0-3	

2013

27/02	Javor	h	2-1	Savićević, Milunović
03/03	Rad	a	1-1	Miljaš 2
09/03	Novi Pazar	h	3-0	Milivojević, Mudrinski, Milijaš
17/03	Radnički Niš	a	1-2	Kasalica
30/03	Radnički 1923	h	2-0	Cadú, Miljaš
03/04	Hajduk	h	3-0	Dauda 2, Lazović
07/04	Smederevo	a	1-0	Dauda
13/04	Spartak	h	4-1	Miljaš 3 (1p), Lazović
21/04	BSK Borča	a	1-0	Milunović
27/04	Donji Srem	h	1-0	Mikić
02/05	Jagodina	a	3-2	Cadú, Dauda, Milunović
11/05	OFK Beograd	h	1-0	Miljaš (p)
18/05	Partizan	a	0-1	
22/05	Sloboda	h	1-2	Mudrinski
26/05	Vojvodina	a	0-3	

No	Name	Nat	DoB	Pos	Aps	(s)	Gls
77	Nathaniel Asamoah	GHA	22/02/90	A	2	(9)	1
9	Eli Babalj	AUS	21/02/92	A		(6)	1
1	Boban Bajković		15/03/85	G	28		
34	Miloš Brajović		02/08/96	D		(1)	
11	Cadú	BRA	31/08/86	M	9	(4)	2
9	Abiola Dauda	NGA	03/02/88	A	8	(3)	4
7	Miloš Dimitrijević		16/02/84	M	9	(3)	1
10	Evandro	BRA	23/08/86	M	1		
20	Luis Garrido	HON	05/11/90	M	10		
35	Marko Grujić		13/04/96	M	1		
21	Nemanja Jakšić		11/07/95	D	1		
15	Nikola Karaklajić	MNE	21/07/83	D	8	(1)	
24	Nikola Karaklajić		05/02/95	M		(1)	
17	Filip Kasalica	MNE	17/12/88	A	22	(2)	4
32	Aleksandar Kirovski		25/12/90	G	1		
6	Jovan Krneta		04/05/92	D	1		
33	Darko Lazić		19/07/94	D	1		
8	Darko Lazović		15/09/90	M	20	(3)	4
13	Nikola Maksimović		25/11/91	D	11	(2)	1
27	Stefan Mihajlović		24/06/94	A		(3)	
4	Srdjan Mijajlović		10/11/93	M	9	(9)	
14	Nikola Mikić		13/09/85	D	21		3
10	Nenad Milijaš		30/04/83	M	26		9
19	Luka Milivojević		07/04/91	M	20	(5)	6
16	Luka Milunović		21/12/92	A	16	(11)	6
27	Marko Mirić		26/03/87	M		(2)	
25	Filip Mladenović		15/08/91	D	23	(3)	
91	Ognjen Mudrinski		19/11/91	A	20	(3)	11
18	Ognjen Ožegović		09/06/94	A	2	(2)	
2	Aleksandar Pantić		11/04/92	D	12	(1)	1
3	Nikola Petković		28/03/86	D	10	(1)	
28	Vukan Savićević		29/01/94	M	3	(7)	1
5	Uroš Spajić		13/02/93	D	15	(1)	
55	Nikola Stojković		02/02/95	M		(1)	
22	Miloš Vesić		23/07/89	G	1		
29	Marko Vešović	MNE	28/08/91	M	19	(6)	

FK DONJI SREM

Coach: Bogić Bogićević; (19/05/13) Vladimir Naić
1927 • Karadjordje, Novi Sad (15,754) • fkdonjisrem.com

2012

11/08	OFK Beograd	a	1-0	Milutinović
18/08	Partizan	h	2-1	Čordašić, Damnjanović
25/08	Sloboda	a	2-2	Damnjanović, Petković (p)
01/09	Vojvodina	h	0-1	
15/09	Javor	a	1-0	Damnjanović
22/09	Rad	h	1-2	Damnjanović
29/09	Novi Pazar	a	0-2	
07/10	Radnički Niš	h	1-1	Damnjanović (p)
20/10	Radnički 1923	a	0-2	
27/10	Crvena zvezda	h	1-2	Janković
03/11	Smederevo	a	1-0	Putinčanin
11/11	Spartak	h	0-0	
17/11	BSK Borča	a	1-2	Lakić-Pešić
24/11	Hajduk	a	2-3	Josimov, N Tošić
01/12	Jagodina	h	0-2	

2013

27/02	OFK Beograd	h	0-0	
02/03	Partizan	a	0-2	
09/03	Sloboda	h	0-0	
19/03	Vojvodina	a	0-3	
30/03	Javor	h	3-0	Josimov, Lakić-Pešić, Krunić
03/04	Rad	a	0-2	
06/04	Novi Pazar	h	3-0	Janković (p), Krunić, Damnjanović
13/04	Radnički Niš	a	1-1	Vukobrat
20/04	Radnički 1923	h	2-0	Janković, Damnjanović
27/04	Crvena zvezda	a	0-1	
04/05	Smederevo	h	2-1	Damnjanović, Škorić
11/05	Spartak	a	1-1	Damnjanović (p)
17/05	BSK Borča	h	0-1	
22/05	Hajduk	h	1-0	Josimov
26/05	Jagodina	a	0-2	

No	Name	Nat	DoB	Pos	Aps	(s)	Gls
38	Nemanja Belić		24/04/87	G	20	(1)	
8	Stefan Bukorac		15/02/91	M	22		
15	Matthew Byrne	AUS	05/06/92	D	3	(2)	
22	Marjan Ćirić		21/04/85	A	3	(3)	
20	Lazar Čordašić		21/01/88	M	24		1
21	Ognjen Damnjanović		20/04/85	A	25	(3)	9
40	Andjelko Djuričić		21/11/80	G	2		
19	Goran Janković		10/12/78	M	15	(10)	3
13	Žarko Jeličić		12/10/83	M		(9)	
3	Miloš Josimov		27/09/84	D	28		3
18	Dejan Jovanović		17/04/86	A	1	(1)	
16	Uroš Košutić		11/11/91	M	12		
12	Ljubo Kovačević		08/09/78	G	3		
17	Rade Krunić	BIH	07/10/93	M	11	(2)	2
14	Nemanja Lakić-Pešić		22/09/91	D	21	(4)	2
24	Ivan Lakićević		27/07/93	M	8	(1)	
15	Nenad Lukić		02/09/92	M	4	(8)	
99	Damjan Marčeta		11/05/94	D	1	(1)	
25	Igor Miladinović		25/06/89	M	5	(4)	
5	Boris Milekić		29/09/88	D	3	(4)	
30	Uroš Milosavljević		13/06/82	M	5		
88	Milan Milutinović		20/04/83	A	10	(9)	1
10	Miša Petković		16/10/83	A	1	(7)	1
6	Marko Prljević		02/08/88	D	12	(2)	
17	Marko Putinčanin		16/12/87	D	13		1
11	Aleksandar Radišić		03/11/89	D	1		
7	Denis Ristov		24/06/90	M	1	(3)	
12	Dragan Starčević		01/07/77	G	4		
23	Matija Šegavac		01/02/95	G	1		
18	Ognjen Škorić	BIH	02/03/93	A	6	(8)	1
1	Saša Teofanov		03/04/90	M	2	(1)	
22	Branislav Terzić		01/11/91	D	12		
25	Branislav Tošić		28/09/87	M	12		
99	Nemanja Tošić		01/04/86	A		(3)	1
44	Igor Urošević		04/04/92	A	3	(2)	
4	Djordje Vukobrat		05/05/84	D	21	(2)	1
13	Djuro Zec		06/03/90	A	13		
9	Damir Zeljko		13/07/92	M	2		

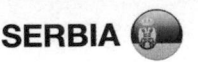

FK HAJDUK KULA

Coach: Veličko Kaplanović; (16/09/12) Milan Milanović
1925 • SPC Hajduk (11,710) • fkhajduk.rs

2012

11/08	Jagodina	a	0-1	
18/08	Radnički Niš	h	1-2	L Veselinović (p)
25/08	OFK Beograd	a	0-0	
01/09	Radnički 1923	h	0-0	
15/09	Partizan	a	2-5	Sekulić, L Veselinović (p)
22/09	Crvena zvezda	h	0-1	
29/09	Sloboda	a	1-2	L Veselinović
07/10	Smederevo	h	2-1	L Veselinović (p), Ćulum
20/10	Vojvodina	a	1-1	Cvetković
27/10	Spartak	h	0-1	
03/11	Javor	a	1-2	L Veselinović
10/11	BSK Borča	h	1-1	Adamović
17/11	Rad	a	0-1	
24/11	Donji Srem	h	3-2	Lalić, Obrovac, L Veselinović
01/12	Novi Pazar	a	2-0	Adamović 2

2013

27/02	Jagodina	h	3-0	L Veselinović 3
02/03	Radnički Niš	a	0-1	
09/03	OFK Beograd	h	3-0	Rusmir, Adamović, Sekulić
17/03	Radnički 1923	a	2-3	L Veselinović, Tošić
31/03	Partizan	h	1-1	L Veselinović
03/04	Crvena zvezda	a	0-3	
07/04	Sloboda	h	3-3	L Veselinović, Adamović, Kiš
13/04	Smederevo	a	1-0	Ćulum
20/04	Vojvodina	h	0-0	
27/04	Spartak	a	0-0	
04/05	Javor	h	2-0	Kiš, L Veselinović
11/05	BSK Borča	h	3-0	Sekulić, L Veselinović, Adamović
18/05	Rad	h	2-0	L Veselinović 2
22/05	Donji Srem	a	0-1	
26/05	Novi Pazar	h	2-0	L Veselinović, Vuković

No	Name	Nat	DoB	Pos	Aps	(s)	Gls
7	Nenad Adamović		12/01/89	M	26		6
23	Nemanja Bošković		08/05/90	M	1	(3)	
1	Bojan Brać		28/02/89	G	16	(1)	
99	Milan Bubalo		08/05/90	A	2		
4	Radoš Bulatović		05/06/84	D	13		
23	Davor Cavrić		11/07/89	M	1	(3)	
14	Nemanja Crnoglavac		13/01/90	D	9		
11	Aleksandar Ćovin		23/11/88	A	5	(3)	
8	Milan Ćulum		28/10/84	M	21	(2)	2
19	Miloš Cvetković		06/01/90	D	25		1
5	Boris Grozdić		07/02/96	D	1	(2)	
22	Predrag Jerinić		05/12/88	M		(1)	
22	Marko Jevtović		24/07/93	M	3	(7)	
17	Saša Kiš		07/04/89	M	12	(10)	2
13	Miloš Kovačević		31/03/91	M	4	(3)	
32	Aleksandar Kršić		17/06/90	D		(1)	
15	Slobodan Lalić		18/02/92	D	20	(2)	1
24	Nemanja Latinović		21/02/94	G	1		
22	Novica Maksimović		04/04/88	M	2		
2	Miroslav Milutinović		01/02/85	D	15	(3)	
33	Milan Mirosavljev		24/04/95	A	2	(6)	
6	Ivan Obrovac		08/12/86	M	17	(4)	1
18	Nino Pekarić		16/08/82	D	12		
12	Nikola Perić		04/02/92	G	13		
18	Mladen Popović		29/08/88	A	5	(2)	
20	Dejan Rusmir		28/01/80	M	11	(3)	1
10	Danilo Sekulić		18/04/90	A	28	(1)	3
25	Aleksandar Stojković		15/08/90	M	4	(4)	
26	Ognjen Šveljo		27/03/94	A		(2)	
11	Jacques Tabi	CMR	22/01/88	M	1		
13	Branislav Tošić		28/09/87	M	3	(8)	1
16	Boris Varga		14/08/93	M	3	(7)	
9	Lazar Veselinović		04/08/86	A	28		17
3	Mladen Veselinović		15/03/92	D	14	(3)	
4	Slobodan Vuković		23/01/86	D	9	(2)	1
28	Milan Zorica		07/01/92	M	1	(5)	
25	Dragan Žarković		16/04/86	D	2		

FK JAGODINA

Coach: Simo Krunić (BIH)
1918 • Pod Djurdjevim brdom (15,000) • fkjagodina.org.rs
Major honours
Serbian Cup (1) 2013

2012

11/08	Hajduk	h	1-0	M Stojanović
19/08	OFK Beograd	h	1-0	M Stojanović
26/08	Partizan	a	0-1	
01/09	Sloboda	h	2-0	M Stojanović, Lepović
16/09	Vojvodina	a	1-1	Živanović
22/09	Javor	a	1-0	Živanović
30/09	Rad	a	0-1	
07/10	Novi Pazar	h	2-1	M Stojanović, Cvetković
20/10	Radnički Niš	a	0-0	
28/10	Radnički 1923	h	2-1	Lepović, M Stojanović
03/11	Crvena zvezda	a	2-1	Djurić (p), Djenić
10/11	Smederevo	h	0-1	
17/11	Spartak	a	1-3	M Stojanović
25/11	BSK Borča	h	2-0	Djenić 2
01/12	Donji Srem	a	2-0	M Stojanović 2

2013

27/02	Hajduk	a	0-3	
02/03	OFK Beograd	a	3-1	Ilić, M Stojanović, Djurić
09/03	Partizan	h	0-1	
23/03	Sloboda	a	1-1	Živanović
30/03	Vojvodina	h	0-1	
03/04	Javor	h	1-0	M Stojanović
06/04	Rad	h	3-0	M Stojanović 3
13/04	Novi Pazar	a	1-2	M Stojanović
21/04	Radnički Niš	h	1-0	Lepović
27/04	Radnički 1923	a	0-0	
02/05	Crvena zvezda	h	2-3	M Stojanović, Djurić
11/05	Smederevo	a	1-2	M Stojanović (p)
18/05	Spartak	h	1-1	M Stojanović
22/05	BSK Borča	a	2-1	Arsenijević, Lepović
26/05	Donji Srem	h	2-0	M Stojanović 2

No	Name	Nat	DoB	Pos	Aps	(s)	Gls
77	Filip Arsenijević		02/09/83	A	11	(4)	1
11	Igor Bondžulić		05/10/80	A	28		
3	Francis Bossman	GHA	24/06/84	M	1		
31	Ivan Cvetković		12/02/81	M	23	(1)	1
13	Dario Damjanović	BIH	23/07/81	M	10	(1)	
24	Dejan Djenić		02/06/86	A	12	(11)	3
7	Milan Djurić		03/10/87	M	19	(6)	3
27	Duško Dukić		21/06/86	D	18	(4)	
32	Mohamed El Monir	LBY	08/04/92	M	13	(5)	
25	Goran Gogić		24/04/86	M	27		
26	Vladimir Ilić		23/03/82	D	8	(3)	1
8	Miroljub Kostić		05/06/88	M	2	(10)	
23	Miloš Lepović		03/10/87	M	23	(2)	4
30	Márcio Teruel	BRA	11/03/86	M		(2)	
10	Danijel Mihajlović		02/06/85	D	5	(2)	
29	Vladimir Milenković		22/06/82	A		(4)	
4	Milan Milinković		04/05/92	D	3	(1)	
91	Ognjen Mudrinski		19/11/91	A	3		
20	Saša Nikodijević		16/07/87	M	1	(1)	
1	Predrag Rajković		31/10/95	G	2		
18	Miloš Stojanović		25/12/84	A	29	(1)	19
39	Slaviša Stojanović		27/01/89	A		(15)	
17	Dragan Stojkov	MKD	23/02/88	M	14	(8)	
10	Aleksandar Stojanović		15/08/90	M		(1)	
5	Vukašin Tomić		08/04/87	D	18		
3	Nikola Valentić		06/09/83	D	9		
19	Aleksandar Živanović		08/04/87	D	29		3

FK JAVOR

Coach: Mladen Dodić
1912 • Kraj Moravice (5,000) • fkjavor.com

2012

18/08	Smederevo	a	5-0	Radivojević 3, Jakimovski, Lazetić
25/08	Spartak	h	2-0	Eliomar, Jakimovski (p)
01/09	BSK Borča	a	0-1	
15/09	Donji Srem	a	0-1	
22/09	Jagodina	h	0-1	
29/09	OFK Beograd	h	3-1	Eliomar 3
03/10	Crvena zvezda	a	1-2	Onyilo
07/10	Partizan	a	1-2	Onyilo
20/10	Sloboda	h	1-1	og (Marić)
28/10	Vojvodina	a	0-1	
03/11	Hajduk	h	2-1	Onyilo, Milovanović
10/11	Rad	h	1-0	Eliomar
17/11	Novi Pazar	a	2-2	Eliomar, Vidić
24/11	Radnički Niš	h	2-0	Onyilo, Vidić
01/12	Radnički 1923	a	2-1	Milovanović, Eliomar

2013

27/02	Crvena zvezda	a	1-2	Momčilović
02/03	Smederevo	h	4-0	Radivojević, Stojaković, Onyilo, Mišić
09/03	Spartak	a	1-1	Djordjević
17/03	BSK Borča	a	1-2	Mišić
30/03	Donji Srem	a	0-3	
03/04	Jagodina	a	0-1	
06/04	OFK Beograd	a	1-1	Radivojević
13/04	Partizan	h	0-1	
21/04	Sloboda	a	2-2	Momčilović (p), Radivojević
27/04	Vojvodina	h	0-4	
04/05	Hajduk	a	0-2	
11/05	Rad	a	2-2	Onyilo, Josović
18/05	Novi Pazar	h	3-2	Radivojević, Veselinović, Onyilo
22/05	Radnički Niš	a	0-2	
26/05	Radnički 1923	h	1-1	Veselinović

No	Name	Nat	DoB	Pos	Aps	(s)	Gls
19	Jovan Djokić		13/08/92	M	10	(11)	
2	Predrag Djordjević		30/06/90	A	26	(1)	1
10	Eliomar	BRA	16/03/88	M	14	(1)	7
30	Nikola Ivanovic		22/03/89	A		(3)	
7	Nikola Jakimovski	MKD	26/02/90	M	12		2
3	Ivan Josović		27/12/89	D	9	(7)	1
7	Patrick Kamgaing	CMR	11/11/90	M	1	(4)	
14	Aleksandar Keljević		14/06/89	M		(1)	
31	Marko Kolaković		09/02/93	D		(1)	
9	Filip Kostić		08/10/93	A	1	(8)	
13	Žarko Lazetić		22/02/82	A	1	(5)	1
12	Djordje Lazović		16/11/92	G	7		
22	Milan Milinković		04/05/92	D	4	(2)	
18	Marko Milosavljević		13/11/91	M		(1)	
30	Dragan Milovanović		03/01/86	A	5	(8)	2
20	Milovan Milovan		24/10/80	D	26		
25	Živorad Mišić		01/10/86	A	8	(13)	2
17	Marko Momčilović		11/06/87	M	27		2
1	Milorad Nikolić		06/02/84	G	23		
21	Milko Novaković	MNE	21/05/88	D	10	(3)	
11	Ifeanyi Onyilo	NGA	31/10/90	A	25		7
5	Branko Ostojić		03/01/84	M	24	(1)	
6	Ognjen Petrović	BIH	18/10/93	D	3	(2)	
8	Vladimir Radivojević		04/02/86	M	25	(2)	7
32	Vujica Radosavljević		21/01/94	D		(1)	
9	Bojan Spasojević		18/01/92	M	1		
10	Igor Stojaković		27/05/80	M	3	(1)	1
4	Borko Veselinović		06/01/86	A	10	(4)	2
26	Nemanja Vidić		06/08/89	M	27		2
24	Radoslav Vlašić		11/03/87	D	19	(4)	
22	Ibrahim Walidjo	CMR	02/04/89	D	10	(1)	

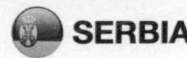

FK NOVI PAZAR

Coach: Dragoljub Bekvalac;
(27/12/12) Slavenko Kuzeljević;
(01/04/13) (Izet Ljajić); (13/04/13) Nebojša Vučićević
1928 • Gradski stadion – Abdulah Gegić Duce (6,500) •
fknovipazar.rs

2012

11/08	Radnički Niš	h	3-0	Alivodić, Damjanović, Ristović
17/08	Radnički 1923	a	1-1	Raščić
26/08	Crvena zvezda	h	1-2	Bogunović
01/09	Smederevo	a	0-0	
15/09	Spartak	h	1-1	Damjanović (p)
22/09	BSK Borča	a	3-2	Alivodić, Popin, Vusljanin
29/09	Donji Srem	h	2-0	Bogunović, Damjanović (p)
07/10	Jagodina	a	1-2	Alivodić
20/10	OFK Beograd	h	0-0	
28/10	Partizan	a	1-3	Alivodić
03/11	Sloboda	h	2-2	Damjanović, Bogunović
10/11	Vojvodina	a	0-1	
17/11	Javor	h	2-2	Alivodić, Vusljanin
24/11	Rad	a	0-2	
01/12	Hajduk	h	0-2	

2013

27/02	Radnički Niš	a	0-0	
02/03	Radnički 1923	h	1-0	Bulatović
09/03	Crvena zvezda	a	0-3	
17/03	Smederevo	h	2-1	Mutavdžić (p), Bulatović
30/03	Spartak	a	0-2	
03/04	BSK Borča	h	1-1	Kecap
06/04	Donji Srem	a	0-1	
13/04	Jagodina	h	2-1	Kecap, Popović
20/04	OFK Beograd	a	0-1	
28/04	Partizan	h	0-0	
04/05	Sloboda	a	0-2	
12/05	Vojvodina	h	0-1	
18/05	Javor	a	2-3	Vidaković 2
22/05	Rad	h	4-0	Mutavdžić 2 (1p), Popović, Vidaković
26/05	Hajduk	a	0-2	

No	Name	Nat	DoB	Pos	Aps	(s)	Gls
11	Enver Alivodić		27/12/84	A	15		5
23	Ibrahim Arifović		22/03/90	D	4	(4)	
33	Ljubo Baranin		25/08/86	D	1	(2)	
18	Faruk Bihorac		12/06/96	M	2	(1)	
9	Miloš Bogunović		10/06/85	A	15	(5)	3
25	Dejan Boljević	MNE	30/05/90	M	11	(2)	
1	Miloš Budaković		10/07/91	G	1	(1)	
44	Radoš Bulatović		05/06/84	D	11		2
13	Dario Damjanović	BIH	23/07/81	M	12		4
24	Vladan Djogatović		03/11/84	G	23		
29	Ivan Djoković		20/12/82	D		(3)	
22	Semir Hadžibulić		16/08/86	M	5	(3)	
6	Slobodan Jakovljević		26/05/89	D	5	(3)	
22	Marko Janković		15/01/88	G	1		
77	Igor Jelić		28/12/89	M		(1)	
14	Admir Kecap		25/11/87	A	10	(6)	2
4	Emir Lotinac		25/09/87	D	24		
50	Slavko Lukić		14/03/89	D	4		
86	Miloš Marković		10/12/86	D	10		
55	Marko Milić		06/11/87	D	4	(4)	
5	Ahmed Mujdragić	BIH	13/03/86	D	12		
1	Denis Mujkić	BIH	02/09/83	G	5		
5	Miljan Mutavdžić		03/02/86	M	11	(1)	3
33	Ljubo Nenadić		29/04/86	D	6	(1)	
12	Zoran Pešić		25/09/83	D		(1)	
28	Saša Popin		28/10/89	A	1	(11)	1
99	Mladen Popović		29/08/88	A	9	(4)	2
88	Haris Radžepi	BIH	20/07/88	M	2	(1)	
21	Amar Rahmanović	BIH	13/05/94	M	11	(1)	
30	Admir Raščić	BIH	16/09/81	A	12	(1)	1
10	Risto Ristović		05/05/88	M	9	(5)	1
3	Miloš Rnić		24/01/89	D	14	(1)	
10	Edin Selimović		28/01/91	M	1	(3)	
15	Branislav Stanić		30/07/88	M	15	(2)	
8	Filip Stojanović		19/05/88	M	2	(3)	
32	Borislav Topić		22/05/84	M	1	(2)	
3	Aleksandar Vasiljević		19/06/82	D	14		
11	Vladan Vidaković		29/09/85	A	8	(5)	3
7	Vladimir Vujović		20/12/85	A	3	(3)	
64	Zoran Vujović		07/01/86	M	9	(3)	
7	Irfan Vusljanin		07/01/86	M	15		2
25	Dragan Žarković		16/04/86	D	10		

OFK BEOGRAD

Coach: Stevica Kuzmanovski;
(16/09/12) Zoran Milinković
1911 • Omladinski stadion (13,900) • ofkbeograd.co.rs
Major honours
Yugoslav League (5) 1931, 1933, 1935, 1936, 1939;
Yugoslav Cup (4) 1953, 1955, 1962, 1966

2012

11/08	Donji Srem	h	0-1	
19/08	Jagodina	a	0-1	
25/08	Hajduk	h	0-0	
02/09	Partizan	h	1-3	Brkić
15/09	Sloboda	a	3-4	Jovanović 2, Tufegdžić
22/09	Vojvodina	h	0-0	
29/09	Javor	a	1-3	Jovanović
07/10	Rad	h	1-0	Trivunović
20/10	Novi Pazar	a	0-0	
27/10	Radnički Niš	h	5-1	Bogavac 2, Adžić, Milić, Pavlović
03/11	Radnički 1923	a	2-3	Trivunović (p), Jovanović
11/11	Crvena zvezda	h	1-0	Grbić
17/11	Smederevo	a	2-0	Pavlović, Jovanović
24/11	Spartak	h	1-0	Adžić
01/12	BSK Borča	a	2-0	Grbić, Bogavac

2013

27/02	Donji Srem	a	0-0	
02/03	Jagodina	h	1-3	Škrbić
09/03	Hajduk	a	0-3	
17/03	Partizan	a	0-2	
30/03	Sloboda	h	1-0	Vasiljević
03/04	Vojvodina	a	1-0	Grbić
06/04	Javor	h	1-1	Grbić
13/04	Rad	a	0-0	
20/04	Novi Pazar	h	1-0	Pavlovski
27/04	Radnički Niš	a	2-1	Jovanović, Nikolić (p)
02/05	Radnički 1923	h	1-0	Grbić
11/05	Crvena zvezda	a	0-1	
18/05	Smederevo	h	4-3	Grbić 2 (1p), Nikolić (p), Ivanović
22/05	Spartak	a	2-0	Mijić, Pavlovski
26/05	BSK Borča	h	1-1	Pavlovski

No	Name	Nat	DoB	Pos	Aps	(s)	Gls
5	Vladan Adžić	MNE	05/07/87	D	26	(1)	2
28	Bojan Aleksić		12/04/91	A		(1)	
32	Nemanja Antonov		06/05/95	D	1		
14	Augusto Batioja	ECU	04/05/90	A	9	(14)	
7	Dragan Bogavac	MNE	07/04/80	A	8	(1)	3
20	Ivan Bogavac		26/05/90	D	1		
30	Goran Brkić		28/04/91	M	9	(2)	1
11	Aleksandar Cavrić		18/05/94	M	11	(9)	
25	Stefan Čupić		07/05/94	G	1		
12	Andrija Dragojević	MNE	25/12/91	G	2		
4	Danijel Gašić		19/01/87	D	18		
15	Petar Golubović		13/07/94	D	2		
18	Petar Grbić	MNE	07/08/88	M	19	(3)	7
28	Igor Ivanović	MNE	09/09/90	A	10	(3)	1
23	Aleksandar Ješić		13/09/94	M	3	(3)	
16	Ivica Jovanović	MNE	04/12/87	A	15	(5)	6
5	Ivan Kecojević	MNE	10/04/88	D	1		
1	Milan Lukač		04/10/85	G	27		
24	Miloš Milić		22/11/89	M	8	(8)	1
9	Nemanja Milić		25/05/90	A	8	(1)	1
20	Nemanja Nikolić	MNE	01/01/88	M	27		2
26	Predrag Pavlović		16/06/86	M	14	(7)	2
10	Marko Pavlovski		07/02/94	M	9	(4)	3
2	Marko Petković		03/09/92	D	21		
31	Dušan Punoševac		28/07/91	D	4	(1)	
3	Milan Rodić		02/04/91	D	13		
3	Edin Rustemović	MNE	06/01/93	M	1	(1)	
22	Igor Stanojević		24/10/91	D	1		
29	Miljan Škrbić	MNE	18/09/95	A	2	(3)	1
18	Tamás Takács	HUN	20/02/91	A		(1)	
8	Veseljko Trivunović		13/01/80	M	18	(1)	2
19	Vladimir Tufegdžić		12/06/91	A	3	(13)	1
6	Nikola Vasiljević		30/06/91	D	20	(1)	1
27	Saša Zdjelar		20/03/95	M	10	(5)	
36	Miloš Zeravica		22/07/88	M	2	(1)	

FK PARTIZAN

Coach: Vladimir Vermezović; (29/04/13) Vuk Rašović
1945 • FK Partizan (30,900) • partizan.rs
Major honours
Yugoslav/Serbian League (25) 1947, 1949, 1961, 1962, 1963, 1965, 1976, 1978, 1983, 1986, 1987, 1993, 1994, 1996, 1997, 1999, 2002, 2003, 2005, 2008, 2009, 2010, 2011, 2012, 2013;
Yugoslav/Serbian Cup (12) 1947, 1952, 1954, 1957, 1989, 1992, 1994, 1998, 2001, 2008, 2009, 2011

2012

11/08	BSK Borča	h	7-0	Ivanov, Ilić, Zubya, Ninković, S Šćepović, L Marković, Stojković (p)
18/08	Donji Srem	a	1-2	S Marković
26/08	Jagodina	h	1-0	Mitrović
02/09	OFK Beograd	a	3-1	L Marković, S Šćepović 2
15/09	Hajduk	h	5-2	og (Kovačević), Tomić, Jojić, Marković, S Šćepović 2, Ivanov
23/09	Sloboda	h	5-0	L Marković, Ninković, S Šćepović 2, Ivanov
29/09	Vojvodina	a	3-0	Ostojić, Ilić, S Marković
07/10	Javor	h	2-1	M Šćepović, Mitrović
20/10	Rad	a	1-0	Ivanov
28/10	Novi Pazar	h	3-1	S Šćepović, L Marković, M Šćepović
03/11	Radnički Niš	a	4-0	og (Kolarević), S Šćepović, Jojić, Ninković
11/11	Radnički 1923	h	2-0	Ivanov, L Marković
17/11	Crvena zvezda	a	3-1	Mitrović, og (Jovanović)
25/11	Smederevo	h	4-0	Tomić 2, Mitrović, Smiljanić
01/12	Spartak	a	2-2	L Marković, M Šćepović

2013

02/03	Donji Srem	h	2-0	Luka, M Šćepović
06/03	BSK Borča	a	4-0	Kojić 2, Mitrović, Brašanac
09/03	Jagodina	a	1-0	Kojić
17/03	OFK Beograd	h	2-0	Mitrović, Luka
31/03	Hajduk	a	1-0	Mitrović
04/04	Sloboda	a	0-0	
07/04	Vojvodina	h	1-2	Jojić
13/04	Javor	a	1-0	Ilić (p)
20/04	Rad	h	2-0	Ilić, Kojić
28/04	Novi Pazar	a	0-0	
02/05	Radnički Niš	h	3-1	Volkov, Mitrović 2
11/05	Radnički 1923	a	1-0	Ilić
18/05	Crvena zvezda	h	1-0	Jojić
22/05	Smederevo	a	1-0	Jojić
26/05	Spartak	h	5-0	L Marković, M Šćepović, Kojić, Ninković, Kojić, Luka

No	Name	Nat	DoB	Pos	Aps	(s)	Gls
13	Nikola Aksentijević		09/03/93	D	3		
37	Stefan Askovski	MKD	24/02/92	D		(1)	
20	Dejan Babić		20/04/89	M		(2)	
14	Darko Brašanac		12/02/92	M	9	(2)	1
10	Eliomar	BRA	16/03/88	M	1	(6)	
22	Saša Ilić		30/12/77	M	24	(1)	5
15	Ivan Ivanov	BUL	25/02/88	D	29		4
39	Miloš Jojić		19/03/92	M	12	(8)	4
77	Filip Knežević		08/11/91	A	1		
9	Nemanja Kojić		03/02/90	A	8	(5)	6
18	Aleksandar Lazevski	MKD	21/01/88	D	15	(2)	
8	Goran Lovre		23/03/82	M	3	(1)	
7	Predrag Luka		11/05/88	M	12	(2)	3
50	Lazar Marković		02/03/94	A	15	(4)	7
21	Saša Marković		13/03/91	M	7	(10)	2
4	Medo	SLE	16/11/87	M	7	(1)	
2	Aleksandar Miljković		26/02/90	D	24		
45	Aleksandar Mitrović		16/09/94	A	17	(8)	10
1	Nikola Milinković		19/12/94	M	11	(10)	4
40	Miloš Ostojić		03/08/91	D	13		1
23	Tomislav Pajović		25/03/86	D	12		
55	Danilo Pantić		26/10/96	M		(1)	
19	Branko Pauljević		01/05/87	D	5		
30	Nikola Petrović		10/04/88	G	8	(2)	
44	Marko Šćepović		23/05/91	A	12	(5)	6
2	Stefan Šćepović		10/01/90	A	7	(7)	8
99	Milan Smiljanić		19/11/86	M	22	(2)	1
6	Sreten Sretenović		12/01/85	D	1		
2	Vojislav Stanković		22/09/87	D	5		
88	Vladimir Stojković		28/07/83	G	21		1
7	Nemanja Tomić		21/01/88	M	9	(4)	3
3	Vladimir Volkov	MNE	06/06/86	D	11	(1)	1
24	Andrija Živković		11/07/96	M		(1)	
24	Marko Živković		17/05/94	D	2		
1	Živko Živković		14/04/89	G	1		
27	Mohamed Zubya	LBY	20/03/89	A	3	(1)	1

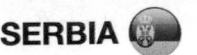

FK RAD

Coach: Marko Nikolić
1958 • Kralj Petar I (6,000) & Stadion na Vračaru (4,506)
• fcrad.co.rs

2012

10/08	Radnički 1923	h	2-0	Luka, Čaušić
19/08	Crvena zvezda	a	2-2	Kojić 2
25/08	Smederevo	h	0-0	
01/09	Spartak	a	3-2	Kojić 2, Luka
15/09	BSK Borča	h	3-0	Perović, Luka, Pršo
22/09	Donji Srem	a	2-1	Milošević, Čaušić
30/09	Jagodina	h	1-0	Luka
07/10	OFK Beograd	a	0-1	
20/10	Partizan	h	0-1	
27/10	Sloboda	a	0-1	
04/11	Vojvodina	h	1-1	Kojić
10/11	Javor	a	0-1	
17/11	Hajduk	h	1-0	Djurdjević
24/11	Novi Pazar	h	2-0	Mitrović, Perović
01/12	Radnički Niš	a	1-1	Djurdjević

2013

27/02	Radnički 1923	a	1-1	Djurdjević
03/03	Crvena zvezda	h	1-1	Djurdjević
09/03	Smederevo	a	1-1	Luković
30/03	BSK Borča	a	0-2	
03/04	Donji Srem	h	2-0	Djurdjević, Čirković
06/04	Jagodina	a	0-3	
13/04	OFK Beograd	h	1-0	Djurdjević
17/04	Spartak	h	1-0	Luković
20/04	Partizan	a	0-2	
27/04	Sloboda	h	2-0	Luković, Djurdjević
02/05	Vojvodina	a	0-1	
11/05	Javor	h	2-2	Milošević, Djurdjević (p)
18/05	Hajduk	a	0-2	
22/05	Novi Pazar	a	0-4	
26-05	Radnički Niš	h	3-1	Perović, Djurdjević, S Jovanović

No	Name	Nat	DoB	Pos	Aps	(s)	Gls
7	Marko Adamović		11/03/91	M	10	(3)	
3	Nikola Antić		04/01/94	D	6	(2)	
10	Goran Čaušić		05/05/92	M	15		2
4	Lazar Čirković		22/08/92	D	21	(1)	1
18	Uroš Damnjanović		08/02/95	M	1	(9)	
1	Branislav Danilović		24/06/88	G	5		
9	Uroš Djurdjević		02/03/94	A	14	(9)	9
19	Ognjen Gnjatić	BIH	16/10/91	M	12	(3)	
8	Milan Jagodić		11/03/91	D	3	(5)	
26	Aleksandar Jovanović		06/12/92	G	1	(1)	
8	Branislav Jovanović		21/09/85	M	4	(2)	
6	Saša Jovanović		30/08/93	M	8	(3)	1
12	Filip Kljajić		16/08/90	G	24		
27	Nemanja Kojić		03/02/90	A	14	(1)	5
30	Nikola Leković		19/12/89	D	23	(2)	
22	Marko Ljubinković		07/12/81	M	3	(5)	
20	Predrag Luka		11/05/88	M	14	(1)	4
17	Andrija Luković		24/10/94	M	7	(5)	3
25	Mikola Maraš		19/12/95	D		(1)	
20	Nemanja Mihajlović		19/01/96	A		(4)	
29	Branislav Milošević		13/05/88	D	21		2
25	Milan Mitrović		02/07/88	D	13	(1)	1
7	Andrej Mrkela		09/04/92	M		(11)	
18	Dušan Pantelić		15/04/93	M		(2)	
2	Aleksandar Pantić		11/04/92	D	2		
14	Andrija Pavlović		16/11/93	M		(2)	
23	Slavko Perović		09/06/89	A	28	(1)	3
16	Miroljub Pešić		23/10/93	D	1		
11	Milan Pršo		29/06/90	A	24		1
2	Boris Radunović		26/05/96	G		(1)	
21	Nikola Raspopović		18/10/89	M	15		
4	Ivan Rogač		30/11/91	M	1	(4)	
2	Miloš Stanojević		20/11/93	M	7	(3)	
17	Nikola Stojiljković		17/08/92	A		(1)	
28	Slobodan Urošević		15/04/94	D	2		
24	Saša Varga		19/02/93	M	1	(5)	
22	Anto Vasović		15/06/95	A		(2)	
10	Uroš Vico		28/02/95	D	2		
5	Uroš Vitas		06/07/92	D	28		

FK RADNIČKI 1923

Coach: Slavenko Kuzeljević; (04/10/12); Dejan Djurdjević; (23/04/13) Dragoljub Bekvalac
1923 • Čika Dača (22,100) • fkradnicki.com

2012

10/08	Rad	a	0-2	
17/08	Novi Pazar	h	1-1	Tintor
24/08	Radnički Niš	a	1-1	Tintor
01/09	Hajduk	h	0-0	
16/09	Crvena zvezda	h	0-3	
22/09	Smederevo	a	2-2	Spalević, Milošković
29/09	Spartak	h	1-1	Simović
07/10	BSK Borča	a	0-2	
20/10	Donji Srem	h	2-0	Milošković, Spalević
28/10	Jagodina	a	1-2	Spalević
03/11	OFK Beograd	h	3-2	Spalević, Milošković 2
11/11	Partizan	a	0-2	
18/11	Sloboda	h	0-2	
24/11	Vojvodina	a	0-0	
01/12	Javor	h	1-2	Milošević

2013

27/02	Rad	h	1-1	Otašević
02/03	Novi Pazar	a	0-1	
10/03	Radnički Niš	h	0-1	
17/03	Hajduk	h	3-2	og (Crnoglavac), Beljić, Fejsa
30/03	Crvena zvezda	a	0-2	
03/04	Smederevo	h	2-0	Beljić, Milošković
06/04	Spartak	a	2-1	Spalević, Marić
13/04	BSK Borča	h	0-0	
20/04	Donji Srem	a	0-2	
27/04	Jagodina	h	0-0	
02/05	OFK Beograd	a	0-1	
11/05	Partizan	h	0-1	
18/05	Sloboda	a	2-0	Kovačević, Milošković
22/05	Vojvodina	h	2-0	Spalević, I Petrović
26/05	Javor	a	1-1	Spalević

No	Name	Nat	DoB	Pos	Aps	(s)	Gls
9	Komnen Andrić		01/07/95	A		(5)	
14	Bojan Beljić		08/05/85	A	13		2
19	Vladimir Bubanja		02/08/89	D	8	(1)	
22	Ognjen Čančarević		25/09/89	G	22		
21	Petar Djurićković		20/06/91	M	5	(10)	
3	Darko Fejsa		27/08/87	D	19		1
1	Marko Knežević		29/03/89	G	8	(1)	
23	Aleksandar Kosorić	BIH	30/01/87	D	8	(1)	
15	Nikola Kovačević		14/04/94	D	1	(2)	1
77	Slavko Marić		07/03/84	D	11	(1)	1
5	Željko Milošević		25/01/76	D	7		1
10	Stanimir Milošković		21/12/83	A	25	(2)	6
33	Dragan Milovanović		03/01/86	A	5	(4)	
23	Marko Mirić		26/03/87	M	9	(2)	
5	Miljan Mutavdžić		03/02/86	M	9	(2)	
6	Stefan Nedović		12/01/88	M	13	(7)	
6	Ivan Obrovac		08/12/86	M	2	(1)	
28	Vladimir Otašević		08/06/86	D	15		1
24	Petar Pavlović		03/03/87	D	26		
11	Ivan Pejčić		11/09/82	A	5	(4)	
7	Dušan Petronijević		09/11/83	M	13	(4)	
32	Ivan Petrović		03/07/93	M	23		1
20	Stefan Petrović		24/01/90	M	1	(1)	
33	Dragan Radosavljević		24/10/82	D	7		
4	Marko Ristić		09/03/87	D	2		
29	Lazar Rosić		29/06/93	D	4	(2)	
19	Predrag Sikimić		29/08/82	A	2	(9)	
31	Srdjan Simović		17/06/85	M	12	(4)	1
18	Darko Spalević		24/03/77	A	22	(3)	7
8	Milan Svojić		09/10/85	M	13	(10)	
4	Miloš Tintor		21/08/86	D	17		2
17	Aleksandar Varjačić		23/05/91	A	1	(5)	
16	Bojan Zoranović		12/04/90	A	2	(5)	

FK RADNIČKI NIŠ

Coach: Aleksandar Ilić; (23/02/13) Saša Mrkić; (16/05/13) Miodrag Stefanović
1923 • Čair (18,151) • fcradnicki-nis.com

2012

11/08	Novi Pazar	a	0-3	
18/08	Hajduk	h	2-1	S Petrović 2
24/08	Radnički 1923	h	1-1	Binić
02/09	Crvena zvezda	a	2-3	A Jovanović 2
15/09	Smederevo	h	1-0	Kolarević
22/09	Spartak	a	1-4	Pejčić
29/09	BSK Borča	h	4-1	Randjelović, S Petrović, M Jovanović, Stojanović
07/10	Donji Srem	a	1-1	M Jovanović (p)
20/10	Jagodina	h	0-0	
27/10	OFK Beograd	a	1-5	M Jovanović
03/11	Partizan	h	0-4	
10/11	Sloboda	a	0-0	
17/11	Vojvodina	h	0-1	
24/11	Javor	a	0-2	
01/12	Rad	h	1-1	Stojanović

2013

27/02	Novi Pazar	h	0-0	
02/03	Hajduk	a	1-0	Mitrović
10/03	Radnički 1923	a	1-0	Škuletić
17/03	Crvena zvezda	h	2-1	Ljubinković, Škuletić
30/03	Smederevo	a	1-0	Binić
03/04	Spartak	h	2-0	Pejčić, A Jovanović
06/04	BSK Borča	a	1-2	A Jovanović
13/04	Donji Srem	h	1-1	Ljubinković
21/04	Jagodina	a	0-1	
27/04	OFK Beograd	h	1-2	Stojanović
02/05	Partizan	a	1-3	Binić
11/05	Sloboda	h	0-1	
18/05	Vojvodina	a	2-3	Ljubinković (p), Mitrović
22/05	Javor	h	2-0	Škuletić, A Jovanović
26/05	Rad	a	1-3	M Jovanović

No	Name	Nat	DoB	Pos	Aps	(s)	Gls
9	Aleksandar Bajevski	MKD	08/12/79	A	1	(3)	
8	Vladan Binić		25/01/87	M	14	(6)	3
58	Stefan Cicmil	MNE	16/08/90	D	6	(1)	
2	Bojan Djordjević		05/04/84	D	17	(4)	
55	Ivan Dragićević		21/10/81	D	6	(3)	
12	Dušan Ivanov		17/02/91	M		(1)	
24	Aleksandar Jovanović		17/12/84	M	26	(3)	5
9	Jovan Jovanović		02/10/85	A	1	(2)	
15	Milan Jovanović		14/10/83	A	9	(12)	4
40	Kojo Kankam	GHA	16/11/92	D		(1)	
23	Aleksandar Kesić		18/08/87	G	12		
19	Dušan Kolarević		19/04/87	M	26	(2)	1
48	Marko Ljubinkobić		07/12/81	M	12		3
4	Nikola Lukić		14/05/90	M	6	(8)	
18	Ivan Milenković		04/07/83	M	1	(2)	
22	Dalibor Mitrović		04/11/77	A	4	(9)	2
7	Milan Pavličić	CRO	20/12/80	A	1	(6)	
17	Bratislav Pejčić		17/01/83	M	24	(2)	2
1	Miloš Perić		27/07/90	G	17		
16	Zoran Pešić		25/09/83	D	3		
14	Miloš Petrović		05/05/90	D	26	(1)	
21	Strahinja Petrović		14/06/92	A	13	(2)	3
11	Marko Randjelović		16/08/84	D	14		1
3	Aleksandar Simov		05/02/87	D	2	(1)	
20	Predrag Stamenković		07/07/77	D	18	(1)	
5	Stevan Stefanović		28/03/84	M	12	(2)	
25	Saša Stojanović		21/01/83	A	16	(1)	3
11	Petar Škuletić		29/06/90	A	12		3
23	Zoran Vasković		14/02/79	G	1		
3	Branislav Vukomanović		29/12/81	D	13	(1)	
6	Miloš Živković		01/12/84	D	17	(3)	

FK SLOBODA UŽICE

Coach: Ljubiša Stamenković
1925 • Gradski stadion kraj Djetinje (9,800) • fksloboda.rs

2012

11/08	Spartak	h	2-0	Kovačević, Randjelović
18/08	BSK Borča	a	0-1	
25/08	Donji Srem	h	2-2	Randjelović, Stajić
01/09	Jagodina	a	0-2	
15/09	OFK Beograd	h	4-3	Thiago Galvão 2, Randjelović, Beljić
23/09	Partizan	a	0-5	
29/09	Hajduk	h	2-1	Thiago Galvão 2
07/10	Vojvodina	h	1-1	Thiago Galvão
20/10	Javor	a	1-1	Knežević
27/10	Rad	h	1-0	Randjelović
03/11	Novi Pazar	a	2-2	Pilipović, Randjelović
10/11	Radnički Niš	h	0-0	
18/11	Radnički 1923	a	2-0	Randjelović, Purić
25/11	Crvena zvezda	h	1-2	Purić
01/12	Smederevo	a	1-0	Randjelović (p)

2013

27/02	Spartak	a	2-2	Randjelović 2 (1p)
02/03	BSK Borča	h	1-0	Gojković
09/03	Donji Srem	a	0-0	
23/03	Jagodina	h	1-1	Thiago Galvão
30/03	OFK Beograd	a	0-1	
04/04	Partizan	h	0-0	
07/04	Hajduk	a	3-3	Randjelović 2, Krstić
13/04	Vojvodina	a	2-2	Pilipović, Vasilić
21/04	Javor	h	2-2	Randjelović, Thiago Galvão (p)
27/04	Rad	a	0-2	
04/05	Novi Pazar	h	2-0	Randjelović 2
11/05	Radnički Niš	a	1-0	Krstić
18/05	Radnički 1923	h	0-2	
22/05	Crvena zvezda	a	2-1	Randjelović 2
26/05	Smederevo	h	4-1	Thiago Galvão, Randjelović 2, Krstić

No	Name	Nat	DoB	Pos	Aps	(s)	Gls
55	Delimir Bajić	BIH	28/03/83	D	15		
10	Bojan Beljić		08/05/85	A	13		1
55	Slavko Ćulibrk		21/03/86	D	6	(2)	
6	Nemanja Cvetković		24/06/96	D		(1)	
10	Nuriddin Davronov	TJK	16/01/91	M	1	(7)	
15	Aleksandar Gojković		18/08/88	D	19	(4)	1
14	Miloš Janićijević		21/03/89	M	5	(6)	
33	Lazar Jovanović		13/07/93	M	1	(10)	
5	Zoran Knežević		15/08/88	D	24		1
23	Savo Kovačević		15/08/88	A	5	(3)	1
18	Vladimir Krstić		28/06/87	M	11	(7)	3
44	Mladen Lazarević		16/01/84	D	3	(2)	
31	Darko Lovrić		24/11/80	D	28		
7	Slavko Marić		07/03/84	D	13		
11	Marko Memedović		18/01/91	A	3	(17)	
23	Daniel Olerum	NGA	13/03/87	A	2	(4)	
13	Aleksandar Pejović		28/12/90	M	24		
16	Stojan Pilipović		02/02/87	M	23		2
17	Dario Purić	BIH	18/05/86	A	18	(7)	2
9	Predrag Randjelović		13/09/76	A	28		18
1	Dejan Ranković		25/07/76	G	29		
8	Duško Stajić	BIH	11/07/82	A	4	(8)	1
25	Nikola Tasić		07/09/94	G	1		
20	Thiago Galvão	BRA	15/08/87	M	30		8
21	Kalla Touré	GUI	28/12/91	M		(1)	
2	Jovica Vasilić		08/07/90	D	28		1

FK SMEDEREVO

Coach: Aleksandar Janjić; (11/10/12) Miloš Velebit; (08/04/13) Ljubomir Ristovski
1924 • FK Smederevo (17,200) • fksmederevo.com
Major honours
Yugoslav Cup (1) 2003

2012

12/08	Vojvodina	a	0-0	
18/08	Javor	h	0-5	
25/08	Rad	a	0-0	
01/09	Novi Pazar	h	0-0	
15/09	Radnički Niš	a	0-1	
22/09	Radnički 1923	h	2-2	D Živković 2
29/09	Crvena zvezda	a	1-3	Momić
07/10	Hajduk	a	1-2	Nikolić
20/10	Spartak	h	0-2	
27/10	BSK Borča	a	1-1	Veljović
03/11	Donji Srem	h	0-1	
10/11	Jagodina	a	1-0	D Živković
17/11	OFK Beograd	h	0-2	
25/11	Partizan	a	0-4	
01/12	Sloboda	h	0-1	

2013

27/02	Vojvodina	h	1-2	Ristić
02/03	Javor	a	0-4	
09/03	Rad	h	1-1	Sikimić
17/03	Novi Pazar	a	1-2	Sikimić (p)
30/03	Radnički Niš	h	0-1	
03/04	Radnički 1923	a	0-2	
07/04	Crvena zvezda	h	0-1	
13/04	Hajduk	h	0-1	
21/04	Spartak	a	0-2	
27/04	BSK Borča	h	2-0	Sikimić, Krmar
04/05	Donji Srem	a	1-2	Sikimić
11/05	Jagodina	h	2-1	Milosavljević 2
18/05	OFK Beograd	a	3-4	M Radosavljević 2, Sikimić
22/05	Partizan	h	0-2	
26/05	Sloboda	a	1-4	D Živković

No	Name	Nat	DoB	Pos	Aps	(s)	Gls
19	Branislav Atanacković		05/08/83	D	9		
16	Saša Blagojević		01/02/89	D	12		
25	Nikola Bogić		30/06/81	M	9	(1)	
20	Ivan Božović		26/05/90	D	14		
10	Bojan Čukić		05/02/88	M	8	(3)	
99	Miloš Djordjević		07/06/92	A	2	(7)	
33	Miroslav Gegić		07/08/84	D	3	(3)	
27	Marko Jovanović		07/02/89	M			
7	Igor Krmar		14/01/91	M	16	(7)	1
14	Vlade Lazarevski	MKD	09/06/83	D	13		
15	Lucas	BRA	02/05/90	M	2	(1)	
21	Aleksandar Miljković		23/08/82	M	19	(5)	
12	Nikola Milojević		16/04/81	G		(1)	
14	Marko Milosavljević		20/12/87	M	9	(3)	2
55	Igor Miović		31/03/86	D	11	(1)	
20	Uroš Momić		26/03/92	A	8	(4)	1
5	Miloš Nikolić		22/02/89	M	9	(2)	1
4	Dejan Ognjanović	MNE	21/06/78	D	11		
23	Darko Opančina		27/07/90	D	18	(3)	
11	Filip Osman		21/12/91	M	15	(6)	
25	Lazar Pavić		02/02/94	M		(4)	
55	Dragan Radosavljević		24/10/82	D	6	(1)	
29	Miloš Radosavljević		20/05/88	M	8	(3)	2
33	Mirko Radovanović		05/04/86	D	10		
3	Marko Ristić		09/03/87	D	14		1
44	Omega Roberts	LBR	02/02/89	D	14		
8	Predrag Sikimić		29/08/82	A	14		5
31	Srdjan Soldatović		10/01/74	G	1		
66	Marko Stanovčić		09/05/90	D		(1)	
10	Nenad Stojaković		04/04/80	M	6		
17	Stefan Stojanović		25/04/92	A	4	(8)	
8	Luka Tiodorović	MNE	21/01/86	M	1	(6)	
6	Srdjan Urošević		30/03/84	M		(1)	
32	Rade Veljović		09/08/86	A	17	(5)	1
19	Milan Vukašinović		31/05/92	A	2	(3)	
4	Bojan Živanović		27/06/89	D		(1)	
13	Dejan Živković		28/04/82	M	16	(4)	4
1	Mladen Živković		26/08/89	G	29		

FK SPARTAK ZLATIBOR VODA

Coach: Zoran Milinković; (04/09/12) Zoran Marić; (10/09/12) Petar Kurćubić
1921 • Gradski stadion (25,000) • fkspartakzlatiborvoda.com

2012

11/08	Sloboda	a	0-2	
18/08	Vojvodina	h	0-1	
25/08	Javor	a	0-2	
01/09	Rad	h	2-3	Novaković, Bratić
15/09	Novi Pazar	a	1-1	Despotović
22/09	Radnički Niš	h	4-1	Despotović 2, Novaković, Torbica (p)
29/09	Radnički 1923	a	1-1	Despotović
07/10	Crvena zvezda	h	3-0	Novaković 2, Despotović
20/10	Smederevo	a	2-0	Puškarić, og (Radovanović)
27/10	Hajduk	a	1-0	Novaković
03/11	BSK Borča	h	2-1	og (Stamenković), Despotović
11/11	Donji Srem	a	0-0	
17/11	Jagodina	h	3-1	Nosković 3
24/11	OFK Beograd	a	0-1	
01/12	Partizan	h	2-2	Nosković, Bratić

2013

27/02	Sloboda	h	2-2	Torbica, Novaković
02/03	Vojvodina	a	1-2	Despotović
09/03	Javor	h	1-1	Čović
30/03	Novi Pazar	h	2-0	Despotović, Torbica (p)
03/04	Radnički Niš	a	0-2	
06/04	Radnički 1923	h	1-2	Šarac
13/04	Crvena zvezda	a	1-4	Čović
17/04	Rad	a	0-1	
21/04	Smederevo	h	2-0	Despotović, Kovačević
27/04	Hajduk	h	0-0	
04/05	BSK Borča	a	3-0	Despotović 2, Milivojev
11/05	Donji Srem	h	1-1	Despotović (p)
18/05	Jagodina	a	1-1	Nosković
22/05	OFK Beograd	h	0-2	
26/05	Partizan	a	0-5	

No	Name	Nat	DoB	Pos	Aps	(s)	Gls
24	Goran Adamović		24/04/87	D	22		
7	Marko Adamović		11/03/91	M	14		
12	Branimir Aleksić		24/12/90	G	29		
17	Goran Antonić		05/11/90	D	24	(1)	
6	Vidak Bratić		20/10/76	D	26		2
9	Nemanja Čović		18/06/91	A	12	(7)	2
2	Djordje Despotović		04/03/92	A	24	(3)	12
21	Danijel Farkaš		13/01/93	D	14	(1)	
19	Fahrudin Gjurgjevic	MKD	17/02/92	M	1	(7)	
4	Milan Joksimović		09/02/90	D		(1)	
4	Aleksandar Kovačević		09/01/92	M	28		1
14	Nebojša Mezei		15/02/91	D	5	(5)	
14	Novica Milenović		14/01/89	D	2		
18	Miljan Milivojev		21/11/88	A	4	(17)	1
11	Aleksandar Nosković		12/12/88	M	25	(17)	5
13	Slobodan Novaković		15/10/86	M	25		6
28	Vladimir Otašević		08/06/86	D	2		
22	Nikola Popara		08/03/92	M	8	(12)	
20	Darko Puškarić		13/07/85	D	25	(1)	1
2	Siniša Stevanović		12/01/89	D		(2)	
1	Nikola Stijaković		10/03/89	G	1	(1)	
15	Dino Šarac		06/09/90	M	25		1
8	Vladimir Torbica		20/09/80	M	26	(1)	3
16	Borko Veselinović		06/01/86	A	3	(3)	
23	Milan Vojvodić		20/01/94	M	2	(6)	

FK VOJVODINA

Coach: Zlatomir Zagorčić (BUL);
(13/09/12) Nebojša Vignjević
1914 • Karadjordje (15,754) • fcvojvodina.co.rs
Major honours
Yugoslav League (2) 1966, 1989

2012

12/08	Smederevo	h	0-0	
18/08	Spartak	a	1-0	Stevanović
25/08	BSK Borča	h	1-0	Moreira
01/09	Donji Srem	a	1-0	Bojović
16/09	Jagodina	h	1-1	Djurić
22/09	OFK Beograd	a	0-0	
29/09	Partizan	h	0-3	
07/10	Sloboda	a	1-1	Bojović
20/10	Hajduk	h	1-1	Bojović
28/10	Javor	h	1-0	Oumarou (p)
04/11	Rad	a	1-1	Trajković
10/11	Novi Pazar	h	1-0	Katai
17/11	Radnički Niš	a	1-0	Oumarou
24/11	Radnički 1923	h	0-0	
01/12	Crvena zvezda	a	3-0	Oumarou 2, Stevanović

2013

27/02	Smederevo	a	2-1	Vulićević, Vranješ
02/03	Spartak	h	2-1	Alivodić, Katai
09/03	BSK Borča	a	3-3	Oumarou 2 (1p), Kosović
19/03	Donji Srem	h	3-0	Vranješ, Katai 2
30/03	Jagodina	a	1-0	Oumarou
03/04	OFK Beograd	h	0-1	
07/04	Partizan	a	2-1	Oumarou, Alivodić
13/04	Sloboda	h	2-2	Alivodić, Vranješ
20/04	Hajduk	a	0-0	
27/04	Javor	a	4-0	Oumarou, Alivodić, Katai, Deletić
02/05	Rad	h	1-0	Vulićević
12/05	Novi Pazar	a	1-0	Djurić
18/05	Radnički Niš	h	3-2	Gačinović, Vulićević, Oumarou (p)
22/05	Radnički 1923	a	0-2	
26/05	Crvena zvezda	h	3-0	Oumarou (p), Alivodić, Trajković

No	Name	Nat	DoB	Pos	Aps	(s)	Gls
28	Nnaemeka Ajuru	NGA	28/09/86	M	16	(3)	
13	Enver Alivodić		27/12/84	A	13		5
8	Yaw Antwi	GHA	15/06/85	A		(3)	
11	Nemanja Bilbija	BIH	02/11/90	A	5	(4)	
9	Milan Bojović		13/04/87	A	6	(6)	3
3	Vladimir Branković		22/09/85	D	1	(3)	
21	Miloš Deletić		13/10/93	A	2	(5)	1
23	Igor Djurić		22/02/85	D	21		2
11	Mijat Gačinović		08/02/95	M	2	(3)	1
4	Serginho Greene	NED	24/06/82	M	7		
34	Georgije Ilić		13/05/95	M		(1)	
37	Djordje Jokić		20/01/81	D	20		
33	Aleksandar Katai		06/02/91	A	15	(5)	5
17	Nebojša Kosović		24/02/95	M	10	(9)	1
32	Dejan Meleg		01/10/94	M	4	(3)	
13	Vuk Mitošević		12/02/91	M	4	(6)	
10	Almami Moreira	GNB	16/06/78	M	10	(3)	1
15	Bojan Nastić		06/07/94	D	14		
14	Aboubakar Oumarou	CMR	04/01/87	A	27	(2)	11
31	Vladan Pavlović		24/02/84	D	15		
18	Marko Poletanović		20/07/93	M	15	(4)	
2	Nemanja Radoja		06/02/93	D	16	(6)	
26	Nemanja Sekulić	MNE	29/03/94	M		(2)	
29	Goran Smiljanić		31/01/90	M	5	(6)	
16	Miroslav Stevanović	BIH	29/07/90	A	14	(1)	2
27	Nemanja Supić	BIH	12/01/82	G	28		
7	Petar Škuletić		29/06/90	A	1	(2)	
9	Djordje Šušnjar	MNE	18/02/92	A	4	(4)	
6	Branislav Trajković		29/08/89	D	17		2
10	Stojan Vranješ	BIH	11/10/86	M	8	(5)	3
5	Igor Vujačić	MNE	08/08/94	D	2		
22	Miroslav Vulićević		29/05/85	D	26		3
1	Srdjan Žakula		22/03/79	G	2	(1)	

19	Miloš Stojanović (Jagodina)
18	Predrag Randjelović (Sloboda)
17	Lazar Veselinović (Hajduk)
12	Djordje Despotović (Spartak)
11	Ognjen Mudrinski (Crvena zvezda) Nemanja Kojić (Rad/Partizan) Aboubakar Oumarou (Vojvodina)
10	Enver Alivodić (Novi Pazar/Vojvodina) Aleksandar Mitrović (Partizan)
9	Nenad Milijaš (Crvena zvezda) Ognjen Damnjanović (Donji Srem) Uroš Djurdjević (Rad)

Promoted clubs

FK NAPREDAK
Coach: Nenad Milovanović
1946 • Mladost (10,800) • fknapredak.rs

FK ČUKARIČKI
Coach: Vladan Milojević
1926 • FK Čukarički (3,500) • fkcukaricki.rs

SECOND LEVEL FINAL TABLE 2012/13

		Pld	W	D	L	F	A	Pts
1	FK Napredak	34	25	5	4	74	25	80
2	FK Čukarički	34	19	10	5	52	26	67
3	FK Voždovac	34	17	12	5	49	22	63
4	FK Proleter Novi Sad	34	16	9	9	53	43	57
5	FK Metalac	34	17	5	12	48	32	56
6	FK Jedinstvo Putevi	34	15	11	8	40	32	56
7	FK Borac Čačak	34	16	6	12	47	25	54
8	FK Bežanija	34	11	11	12	41	32	44
9	FK Mladost Lučani	34	10	13	11	31	35	43
10	FK Sloga Kraljevo	34	10	13	11	32	39	43
11	FK Timok	34	11	10	13	37	48	43
12	FK Indjija	34	10	12	12	27	35	42
13	FK Teleoptik	34	8	12	14	25	43	36
14	FK Radnički Nova Pazova	34	9	8	17	35	44	35
15	FK Banat Zrenjanin	34	9	8	17	29	47	35
16	OFK Mladenovac	34	8	8	18	21	41	32
17	FK Kolubara	34	8	9	19	30	48	27
18	RFK Novi Sad	34	5	6	23	17	71	21

FIRST ROUND

(26/09/12)
Bežanija 0-2 Jagodina
Borac Čačak 0-0 Kolubara *(5-4 on pens)*
Čukarički 1-0 BSK Borča
Dunav 1-4 Metalac
Kovačevac 2-4 Hajduk Kula
Mladenovac 0-1 Spartak Zlatibor voda
Mladost Lučani 2-2 Novi Pazar *(2-4 on pens)*
Novi Sad 1-0 Radnički 1923
OFK Beograd 5-0 Sloga Kraljevo
Partizan 4-1 Proleter
Radnički Niš 1-2 Crvena zvezda
Sloboda Užice 0-1 Indjija
Smederevo 0-0 Napredak *(5-4 on pens)*
Teleoptik 0-0 Javor *(7-8 on pens)*
Timok 0-2 Rad
Vojvodina 1-0 Donji Srem

SECOND ROUND

(24/10/12)
Čukarički 0-1 Vojvodina
Hajduk Kula 0-2 Crvena zvezda
Indjija 2-3 OFK Beograd
Jagodina 1-0 Novi Sad
Javor 2-0 Smederevo
Novi Pazar 0-1 Rad
Spartak Zlatibor voda 0-0 Metalac *(8-7 on pens)*

(31/10/12)
Partizan 1-2 Borac

QUARTER-FINALS

(21/11/12)
Borac 0-0 Javor *(4-5 on pens)*

Crvena zvezda 1-3 OFK Beograd *(Lazović 30; Grbić 12, 62, Bogavac 63)*

Rad 0-1 Jagodina *(Lepović 61)*

Spartak Zlatibor voda 1-1 Vojvodina *(Puškarić 31; Oumarou 89) (3-5 on pens)*

SEMI-FINALS

(13/03/13 & 17/04/13)
Javor 1-0 Jagodina *(Stojaković 54)*
Jagodina 4-1 Javor *(Gogić 13, Vlašić 22og, M Stojanović 34, Lepović 61; Momčilović 19) (Jagodina 4-1)*

Vojvodina 1-0 OFK Beograd *(Oumarou 71)*
OFK Beograd 1-1 Vojvodina *(Mijić 54; Radoja 60) (Vojvodina 2-1)*

FINAL

(08/05/13)
FK Partizan, Belgrade
FK JAGODINA 1 *(Djurić 16p)*
FK VOJVODINA 0
Referee: *Mažić*
JAGODINA: *Bondžulić, Dukić, Živanović, Mihajlović, Projić, Gogić, Djurić, Cvetković (Kostić 83), Arsenijević (Stojkov 81), Lepović (Petričević 90), M Stojanović*
VOJVODINA: *Supić, Vulićević, Jokić, Trajković, Pavlović, Vranješ (Kosović 78), Ajuru (Poletanović 65), Radoja, Alivodić, Oumarou, Katai (Šušnjar 65)*

SLOVAKIA
Slovenský futbalový zväz (SFZ)

Address Trnavská 100/II
SK-821 01 Bratislava
Tel +421 2 4820 6000
Fax +421 2 4820 6099
E-mail office@futbalsfz.sk
Website futbalsfz.sk

President Ján Kováčik
General secretary Jozef Kliment
Media officer Juraj Čurný
Year of formation 1938

1. LIGA CLUBS

1. Dukla Banská Bystrica
2. MFK Košice
3. FC Nitra
4. MFK Ružomberok
5. FK Senica
 6. ŠK Slovan Bratislava
7. TJ Spartak Myjava
8. FC Spartak Trnava
9. 1. FC Tatran Prešov
 10. FK AS Trenčín
11. FC ViOn Zlaté Moravce
 12. MŠK Žilina

PROMOTED CLUB

 13. DAC 1904 Dunajská Streda

KEY:

● – UEFA Champions League
● – UEFA Europa League
● – Promoted club
● – Relegated club

Slovák's Slovan stand tall

For the third successive season the champions of Slovakia also won the domestic cup. 2010/11 double winners ŠK Slovan Bratislava repeated the feat in 2012/13 after surrendering both trophies to MŠK Žilina in 2011/12.

The country's most famous club reaped the benefits of a brave decision made in the early weeks of the campaign, when they replaced Vladimír Weiss with inexperienced reserve team coach Samuel Slovák. FK Senica finished second to Slovan in the league, while Žilina partly compensated for an ill-starred title defence by reaching another cup final.

Second double in three seasons for Bratislava club	**Rookie coach hits jackpot in debut season**	**Defending champions Žilina in shock decline**

Domestic league

Less than two years after hanging up his boots as a Slovan player, Slovák was handed the coaching reins at the age of 36. Despite a few hiccups early on, he proved his worth when he steered the side to seven wins and a draw in the eight matches straddling the winter break. The title race had been a closely contested affair until then, with five teams clustered within three points of each other in early November, but that mid-season surge propelled Slovan into a ten-point lead with ten games remaining.

The club's 11th Slovakian title appeared to be a formality at that stage, but no sooner had Slovák's charges run up a big lead than they seemed intent on frittering it away. Suddenly victories became hard to come by, and after a run of four successive draws, which ended with a pivotal 3-2 success over Senica, Slovan could only manage one win in their last five matches. Fortunately, they had plenty of points in the bag, and with no other team able to sustain a winning run of any significant length, the championship was wrapped up without undue distress.

Although there was something of an anti-climax to Slovan's title triumph, the battle to avoid relegation was gripping to the end, with the two candidates for the drop, 1. FC Tatran Prešov and 2011/12 runners-up FC Spartak Trnava, meeting on the final day. Trnava, the visitors, needed a win, and they got it, 1-0, despite the second-half dismissal of their esteemed captain, Miroslav Karhan.

As Trnava struggled, newly promoted TJ Spartak Myjava finished fourth despite having the lowest budget in the 1. Liga. They just missed out on a place in the UEFA Europa League, finishing behind Senica and third-placed FK AS Trenčín, who provided the league's top scorer in 16-goal Argentinian-born striker David Depetris.

Domestic cup

The Slovakian Cup was concluded on May Day, and Slovan celebrated it by collecting the first of their two trophies with a 2-0 win over Žilina in Ruzomberok. Although Žilina's presence virtually guaranteed them a ticket to Europe – confirmed when Slovan won the league – their sixth defeat in seven finals brought further disappointment in a season of continuous trouble and strife. Slovan's goals were scored, fittingly, by two of their most consistent performers in 2012/13 – captain Igor Žofčák and Trinidad & Tobago striker Lester Peltier.

Europe

It was a European season of few highlights for Slovakian clubs, with interest ended in early August after Trnava blew a 1-0 first-leg lead away to FC Steaua Bucureşti in the UEFA Europa League third qualifying round. A round earlier Slovan had been eliminated on away goals by Hungarian club Videoton FC.

National team

Hopes of a second successive appearance at the FIFA World Cup finals were intact after Slovakia made a decent start to the 2014 qualifying series, taking seven points from their opening nine, with midfielder Marek Sapara scoring in all three games. By the end of term, however, they had become forlorn, three damaging results in a row, the last of them a 1-1 draw against Liechtenstein, not only leaving the team lagging behind Bosnia & Herzegovina and Greece in the Group G standings but also ending the short spell in charge of joint coaches Stanislav Griga and Michal Hipp. The pair were replaced in the summer by 59-year-old former Czechoslovakia midfielder Ján Kozák, who had just led MFK Košice to a fifth-place finish in the 1. Liga.

SLOVAKIA

Domestic league: 1. Liga 2012/13 final table

		Pld	Home					Away					Total					
			W	D	L	F	A	W	D	L	F	A	W	D	L	F	A	Pts
1	ŠK Slovan Bratislava	33	12	4	1	41	16	4	7	5	15	17	16	11	6	56	33	59
2	FK Senica	33	8	4	5	21	17	8	3	5	19	17	16	7	10	40	34	55
3	FK AS Trenčín	33	8	7	2	36	14	6	4	6	16	20	14	11	8	52	34	53
4	TJ Spartak Myjava	33	7	4	5	20	17	6	5	6	23	20	13	9	11	43	37	48
5	MFK Košice	33	9	5	2	26	11	3	6	8	12	22	12	11	10	38	33	47
6	MFK Ružomberok	33	10	3	4	27	21	2	6	8	9	25	12	9	12	36	46	45
7	MŠK Žilina	33	5	7	5	20	11	4	8	4	17	17	9	15	9	37	28	42
8	FC ViOn Zlaté Moravce	33	9	3	4	22	13	2	5	10	20	30	11	8	14	42	43	41
9	FC Nitra	33	6	4	6	25	21	5	2	10	14	33	11	6	16	39	54	39
10	Dukla Banská Bystrica	33	5	8	3	15	10	4	3	10	13	22	9	11	13	28	32	38
11	FC Spartak Trnava	33	5	5	7	16	22	3	6	7	18	29	8	11	14	34	51	35
12	1. FC Tatran Prešov	33	7	5	4	15	9	1	4	12	6	32	8	9	16	21	41	33

SEASON AT A GLANCE

EUROPEAN QUALIFICATION 2013/14

Champion/Cup winner: ŠK Slovan Bratislava (second qualifying round)

FK Senica (second qualifying round)
FK AS Trenčín (second qualifying round)
MŠK Žilina (first qualifying round)

Top scorer	David Depetris (Trenčín), 16 goals
Relegated club	1. FC Tatran Prešov
Promoted club	DAC 1904 Dunajská Streda
Cup final	ŠK Slovan Bratislava 2-0 MŠK Žilina

1. LIGA TEAM OF THE SEASON
(3-4-3)
Coach: Slovák (Slovan)

Putnocký (Slovan)

Gorosito (Slovan) — Adámik (Tatran/Banská Bystrica) — Černáček (Spartak Myjava)

Pich (Žilina) — Žofčák (Slovan) — Ďubek (Ružomberok) — Matić (Košice)

Hodek (Zlaté Moravce) — Depetris (Trenčín) — Sládek (Spartak Myjava)

PLAYER OF THE SEASON
Igor Žofčák
(ŠK Slovan Bratislava)

Whenever captain Žofčák was on the field, Slovan were at their best. Whether supporting attacks, scoring goals or infusing his side with spirit, the 30-year-old proved the team's key figure. Alongside midfielder Marko Milinkovič's technical ability and forward Lester Peltier's ferocity, it was a recipe for success that spurred Slovan on towards the double.

NEWCOMER OF THE SEASON
Tomáš Ďubek
(MFK Ružomberok)

Pavol Masaryk's move to Senica deprived Ružomberok of their main goal supply, but they discovered a more than worthy replacement in Ďubek, a long-serving unsung 26-year-old midfielder, who suddenly struck the form of his life, hitting nine goals after the winter break and 13 in total – more than he had managed in his six previous seasons combined.

Home Kit

Away Kit

INTERNATIONAL TOURNAMENT APPEARANCES
FIFA World Cup (1) 2010 (2nd round)

TOP FIVE ALL-TIME CAPS
Miroslav Karhan (107); Róbert Vittek (80);
Marek Hamšík (64); Filip Hološko (62);
Martin Škrtel (61)

TOP FIVE ALL-TIME GOALS
Róbert Vittek (23); Szilárd Németh (22);
Miroslav Karhan & Marek Mintál (14);
Peter Dubovský (12)

Results 2012/13

Date	Opponent		Venue	Score	Scorers
15/08/12	Denmark	A	Odense	3-1	Jakubko (63), Hamšík (72), Guldan (83)
07/09/12	Lithuania (WCQ)	A	Vilnius	1-1	Sapara (41)
11/09/12	Liechtenstein (WCQ)	H	Bratislava	2-0	Sapara (36), Jakubko (78)
12/10/12	Latvia (WCQ)	H	Bratislava	2-1	Hamšík (6p), Sapara (10)
16/10/12	Greece (WCQ)	H	Bratislava	0-1	
14/11/12	Czech Republic	A	Olomouc	0-3	
06/02/13	Belgium	A	Bruges	1-2	Lásik (00)
22/03/13	Lithuania (WCQ)	H	Zilina	1-1	Jakubko (40)
26/03/13	Sweden	H	Zilina	0-0	
07/06/13	Liechtenstein (WCQ)	A	Vaduz	1-1	Ďurica (73)

Appearances 2012/13

Coach: Stanislav Griga & Michal Hipp	04/11/61 13/03/63		Den	LTU	LIE	LVA	GRE	Cze	Bel	LTU	Swe	LIE	Caps	Goals
Ján Mucha	05/12/82	Everton (ENG)	G	G									35	-
Peter Pekarík	30/10/86	Wolfsburg (GER) /Hertha (GER)	D	D	D	D		D17					44	1
Martin Škrtel	15/12/84	Liverpool (ENG)	D	D	D	D00	D		D	D	D46		61	5
Tomáš Hubočan	17/09/85	Zenit (RUS)	D	D				D	D77	D	s79	D46	24	-
Lukáš Pauschek	09/12/92	Slovan Bratislava	D						s46		D79	s46	4	-
Juraj Kucka	26/02/87	Genoa (ITA)	M46	s86	s82		M82		M87	M	s46		29	1
Marek Sapara	31/07/82	Trabzonspor (TUR)	M90	M	M	M	M	M	M			M	38	5
Vladimír Weiss	30/11/89	Pescara (ITA)	M46		M63	M44	s69						28	2
Marek Hamšík	27/07/87	Napoli (ITA)	M76	M86	M82	M	M	M	M	M	M46	M	64	10
Miroslav Stoch	19/10/89	Fenerbahçe (TUR)	M88	M61	M	M	M69	M46	M61			M	37	4
Marek Bakoš	15/04/83	Plzeň (CZE)	A61	A79	A60	A61		s46		s70	A71	s70	11	-
Viktor Pečovský	24/05/83	Žilina	s46	M 55*		M	M	M	M	M70			7	-
Michal Ďuriš	01/06/88	Plzeň (CZE)	s46	M		s44	A72	s46	s15	s64	A71		8	-
Martin Jakubko	26/02/80	Amkar (RUS)	s61	s79	s60					A	s71		30	7
Ľubomír Guldan	30/01/83	Ludogorets (BUL)	s76		M			s46			M		5	1
Michal Breznaník	16/12/85	Liberec (CZE) /Amkar (RUS)	s88	s61	s63	D	D						8	-
Kornel Saláta	24/01/85	Rostov (RUS)	s90		D	D	D	D46	s87				24	-
Radoslav Zabavník	16/09/80	Mainz (GER)		D	D		D	D					58	1
Dušan Kuciak	21/05/85	Legia (POL)			G	G	G	G	G			G	10	-
Filip Hološko	17/01/84	Beşiktaş (TUR)				s61	s72	s76			A	A70	62	7
Ján Ďurica	10/12/81	Lokomotiv Moskva (RUS)				s90			D	D	s46	D	57	3
Karim Guédé	07/01/85	Freiburg (GER)					s82	M76					8	-
Jakub Sylvestr	02/02/89	Erzgebirge Aue (GER)						A46					2	-
Marián Čišovský	02/11/79	Plzeň (CZE)						s17			D	D	11	-
Dušan Švento	01/08/85	Salzburg (AUT)							D46	D	s57	D	26	1
Róbert Vittek	01/04/82	İstanbul BB (TUR)							A15				80	23
Róbert Mak	08/03/91	Nürnberg (GER)							s61	M64	s71	M	4	-
Richard Lásik	18/08/92	Brescia (ITA)							s77		M	M24	3	1
Dušan Perniš	28/11/84	Pogoń (POL)									G		6	-
Marek Čech	26/01/83	Trabzonspor (TUR)									D57		52	5
Tomáš Ďubek	22/01/87	Ružomberok									s24		1	-

 **SLOVAKIA**

European club competitions 2012/13

MŠK ŽILINA

Second qualifying round - Hapoel Kiryat Shmona FC (ISR)
H 1-0 *Piaček (82)*
Dúbravka, Leitner, Barčík (Angelovič 90+2), Pečovský, Piaček, Pich, Ceesay (Deza 70), Šulek, Guima (Majtán 58), Mabouka, Ricardo Nunes. Coach: Frans Adelaar (NED)
A 0-2
Dúbravka, Angelovič, Leitner, Majtán (Deza 66), Barčík, Pečovský, Piaček, Pich, Ceesay (Guima 46), Šulek (Paur 81), Mabouka. Coach: Frans Adelaar (NED)

FC SPARTAK TRNAVA

Second qualifying round - Sligo Rovers FC (IRL)
H 3-1 *Karhan (38), Mikovič (45, 45+1)*
Filipko, Čvirik, Stožický, Habánek, Janečka, Mikovič (Schranz 70), Tomaček (Pavelka 60), Gross, Karhan, Bicák (Koubský 84), Gašparík. Coach: Pavel Hoftych (CZE)
A 1-1 *Čvirik (70)*
Filipko, Čvirik, Stožický, Janečka, Vyskočil (Čarnota 62), Mikovič (Gašparík 67), Hanzel, Gross, Karhan, Schranz (Koubský 85), Bicák. Coach: Pavel Hoftych (CZE)

Third qualifying round - FC Steaua București (ROU)
A 1-0 *Mikovič (6)*
Filipko, Čvirik, Stožický, Janečka, Mikovič (Gašparík 87), Čarnota (Tomaček 61), Hanzel, Gross, Karhan, Sabo, Bicák (Kaščák 79). Coach: Pavel Hoftych (CZE)
H 0-3
Filipko, Čvirik (Tomaček 24), Stožický, Janečka, Mikovič, Čarnota (Mikinič 82), Hanzel, Gross, Karhan, Sabo, Bicák (Koubský 87). Coach: Pavel Hoftych (CZE)

FK SENICA

First qualifying round - MTK Budapest (HUN)
A 1-1 *Blackburn (58)*
Kamesch, Pavlík, Kóňa, Blackburn, Brabec, Ďurica (Ventúra 90+2), Hošek (Janso 90), Wijlaars, Diviš (Bolinha 75), Kalabiška, Križko. Coach: Zdeněk Psotka (CZE)
H 2-1 *Blackburn (72), Kalabiška (87)*
Kamesch, Pavlík, Kóňa, Blackburn, Brabec, Ďurica (Bolinha 90), Hošek (Diarrassouba 60), Wijlaars, Diviš (Janso 90+2), Kalabiška, Križko. Coach: Zdeněk Psotka (CZE)

Second qualifying round - APOEL FC (CYP)
A 0-2
Švenger, Krajčík, Kóňa, Brabec, Wijlaars, Diviš (Blackburn 59), Varadi, Kalabiška (Frýdek 65), Masaryk, Križko (Babic 84), Koutný. Coach: Zdeněk Psotka (CZE)
H 0-1
Švenger, Krajčík, Kóňa, Blackburn, Brabec, Diviš (Frýdek 78), Kalabiška, Masaryk, Križko (Štěpánek 81), Babic (Varadi 74), Koutný. Coach: Zdeněk Psotka (CZE)

ŠK SLOVAN BRATISLAVA

Second qualifying round - Videoton FC (HUN)
H 1-1 *Šebo (26)*
Kováč, Lukšík, Grendel (Mészáros 78), Halenár (Szarka 87), Milinković, Gorosito, Kladrubský (Sabo 67), Bagayoko, Peltier, Pauschek, Šebo. Coach: Vladimír Weiss (SVK)
A 0-0
Putnocký, Lukšík, Grendel (Szarka 83), Halenár (Hlohovský 78), Milinković, Kopúnek, Gorosito, Bagayoko (Jánošík 88), Peltier, Pauschek, Šebo. Coach: Vladimír Weiss (SVK)

Domestic league club-by-club

DUKLA BANSKÁ BYSTRICA

Coach: Norbert Hrnčár
1965 • Na Štiavničkách (9,881) • fkdukla.sk
Major honours
Slovakian Cup (1) 2005

2012

15/07	Senica	a	3-2	Hlinka, Turňa, Slančík
21/07	Trenčín	h	2-0	Slančík, Ferenčík
28/07	Ružomberok	a	0-1	
04/08	Zlaté Moravce	h	0-0	
11/08	Nitra	a	1-1	Brašeň
18/08	Spartak Myjava	a	1-0	Pančík
25/08	Tatran	h	0-0	
01/09	Košice	a	0-1	
16/09	Žilina	h	2-2	Hučko, Turňa
22/09	Spartak Trnava	a	0-1	
29/09	Slovan	h	1-1	Sakhnyuk
06/10	Senica	h	1-2	Ferenčík
20/10	Trenčín	a	1-1	Ferenčík
20/11	Ružomberok	h	0-0	
03/11	Zlaté Moravce	a	0-2	
10/11	Nitra	h	2-0	Turňa, Hučko (p)
17/11	Spartak Myjava	h	1-1	Hučko
24/11	Tatran	a	0-1	
01/12	Košice	h	1-2	Považanec

2013

02/03	Žilina	a	1-0	Peňaška
08/03	Spartak Trnava	h	2-0	Hlinka, Vrána
16/03	Slovan	a	0-2	
23/03	Senica	a	1-1	Turňa
02/04	Trenčín	h	0-0	
06/04	Ružomberok	a	2-3	Peňaška, Turňa
13/04	Zlaté Moravce	h	1-0	Adámik
20/04	Nitra	a	1-3	Turňa
27/04	Spartak Myjava	a	1-2	Šovčík
04/05	Tatran	h	0-0	
11/05	Košice	a	0-1	
18/05	Žilina	h	1-2	Šovčík
22/05	Spartak Trnava	a	1-0	Slančík
26/05	Slovan	h	1-0	Chrien

No	Name	Nat	DoB	Pos	Aps	(s)	Gls
25	Jozef Adámik		10/04/85	D	13		1
16	Radoslav Augustín		05/01/87	A	2	(6)	
1	Tomáš Belic		02/07/78	G	10		
13	Peter Boroš		17/02/80	G	23		
21	Jakub Brašeň		02/05/89	M	25	(2)	1
2	Peter Chrappan		21/12/84	D	8	(1)	
18	Martin Chrien		08/09/95	M	1	(1)	1
8	Dionatan	BRA	24/07/92	D	13		
23	Michal Faško		24/08/94	M		(4)	
17	Milan Ferenčík		13/02/91	A	12	(2)	3
14	Norbert Gyömbér		03/07/92	D	25	(1)	
33	Marek Hlinka		04/10/90	D	29	(2)	2
3	Tomáš Hučko		03/10/85	M	28	(2)	3
26	Lukáš Laksík		21/01/90	A		(3)	
30	Branislav Ľupták		05/06/91	D	6	(3)	
25	Martin Matúš		09/03/82	A	3	(3)	
14	Michal Pančík		18/08/82	M	18	(12)	1
26	Michal Peňaška		30/08/86	A	11	(2)	2
5	Matej Podstavek		21/02/91	D	2	(2)	
4	Martin Poljovka		09/01/75	D	20	(1)	
11	Jakub Považanec		11/01/91	M	22	(5)	1
24	Jozef Rejdovjan		21/12/84	M	8	(4)	
8	Viktor Sakhnyuk	UKR	04/06/90	A	5	(6)	1
34	Saša Savić	SRB	05/02/84	D	16	(5)	
22	Fabian Slančík		22/09/91	A	14	(13)	3
9	Marek Šovčík		08/01/93	A	5	(11)	2
19	Matúš Turňa		11/05/86	D	32		6
27	Patrik Vajda		20/03/89	D	4	(2)	
28	Pavel Vrána	CZE	13/06/85	A	8	(2)	1

MFK KOŠICE

Coach: Ján Kozák
2005 • Lokomotívy v Čermeli (10,787) • mfkkosice.sk
Major honours
Slovakian League (2) 1997, 1998 (as 1. FC Košice);
Slovakian Cup (1) 2009

2012

14/07	Spartak Trnava	a	0-0	
22/07	Slovan	h	1-0	Škutka
29/07	Senica	a	1-2	Škutka
04/08	Trenčín	h	3-0	Novák (p), Škutka 2
11/08	Ružomberok	a	1-3	Novák
18/08	Zlaté Moravce	h	2-1	Škutka, Šinglár
25/08	Nitra	a	1-4	Škutka
01/09	Banská Bystrica	h	1-0	Hovančík
15/09	Tatran	a	0-0	
22/09	Spartak Myjava	a	1-3	Škutka
29/09	Žilina	h	1-1	Matić
05/10	Spartak Trnava	h	1-0	Škutka
21/10	Slovan	a	1-3	Škutka
27/10	Senica	h	2-2	Novák, Škutka
03/11	Trenčín	a	0-0	
10/11	Ružomberok	h	3-0	Ostojić, Novák, Kuzma
16/11	Zlaté Moravce	a	0-0	
24/11	Nitra	h	4-0	Škutka 3, Matić
01/12	Banská Bystrica	a	2-1	Viazanko, Novák

2013

02/03	Tatran	h	3-0	O Diaby, Bukata 2
09/03	Spartak Myjava	h	1-2	Matić
17/03	Žilina	a	1-0	K Diaby
23/03	Spartak Trnava	a	3-2	Viazanko, Ostojić, O Diaby
02/04	Slovan	h	1-1	O Diaby (p)
06/04	Senica	a	0-0	
13/04	Trenčín	h	0-0	
20/04	Ružomberok	a	1-1	Matić
27/04	Zlaté Moravce	h	0-2	
11/05	Banská Bystrica	h	1-0	Viazanko
14/05	Nitra	a	0-1	
18/05	Tatran	a	0-0	
22/05	Spartak Myjava	a	0-1	
26/05	Žilina	h	2-2	Karaš, Matić

No	Name	Nat	DoB	Pos	Aps	(s)	Gls
38	Peter Bašista		06/04/85	D	29		
28	Martin Bukata		02/10/93	M	13	(13)	2
26	Juraj Chupáč		17/03/88	D	5	(2)	
27	Karim Diaby	FRA	25/12/89	A	4	(13)	1
11	Oumar Diaby	FRA	07/02/90	A	13		3
8	Ondrej Duda		15/12/94	M		(14)	
17	Peter Gál-Andrezly		13/05/90	M	2	(16)	
40	Juraj Hovančík		22/11/90	M	25	(5)	1
5	Tomáš Huk		22/12/94	D		(4)	
24	Kamil Karaš		01/03/91	M	17	(7)	1
16	Peter Kavka		20/11/90	M	17	(4)	
7	Kamil Kuzma		08/03/88	M	12	(1)	1
23	Uroš Matić	SRB	23/05/90	A	31	(1)	5
18	Ján Novák		06/03/85	A	11	(1)	5
4	Ivan Ostojić	SRB	26/06/89	D	29	(1)	2
41	František Pavúk		21/07/93	D		(3)	
1	Matúš Ružinský		15/01/92	G	2		
2	Boris Sekulić	SRB	21/10/91	D	32		
6	Jozef Skvašík		08/09/91	M		(4)	
10	Peter Šinglár		24/07/79	M	29	(2)	1
39	Dávid Škutka		25/05/88	A	16		13
25	Darko Tofiloski	MKD	13/01/86	G	31		
15	Mikuláš Tóth		15/03/88	D	15	(2)	
14	Miroslav Viazanko		27/10/81	M	30	(1)	3

FC NITRA

Coach: Ladislav Jurkemik; (06/11/12) Jozef Vukušič
1909 • Pod Zoborom (11,384) • fcnitra.sk

2012

14/07	Trenčín	a	0-5	
21/07	Ružomberok	h	1-1	Šimonek
28/07	Zlaté Moravce	a	2-0	Soumah, Cléber
04/08	Spartak Myjava	a	2-0	Šimončič, Soumah
11/08	Banská Bystrica	h	1-1	Soumah
18/08	Tatran	a	0-1	
25/08	Košice	h	4-1	Soumah, Boszorád, Cléber 2 (1p)
01/09	Žilina	a	1-1	Gajdoš (p)
14/09	Spartak Trnava	h	1-3	Cléber
21/09	Slovan	a	2-5	Boszorád, Cléber
30/09	Senica	h	0-1	
06/10	Trenčín	h	1-2	Cléber
20/10	Ružomberok	a	1-2	Ivančík
27/10	Zlaté Moravce	h	1-1	Mikuš
03/11	Spartak Myjava	h	0-2	
10/11	Banská Bystrica	a	0-2	
17/11	Tatran	h	4-1	Cléber 2, Mikúš 2 (1p)
24/11	Košice	a	0-4	
30/11	Žilina	h	2-0	Mikúš (p), Cléber

2013

02/03	Spartak Trnava	a	0-2	
10/03	Slovan	h	0-3	
15/03	Senica	a	1-2	Gajdoš (p)
23/03	Trenčín	a	0-3	
02/04	Ružomberok	h	3-0	Benčík, Mičic, Cléber (p)
06/04	Zlaté Moravce	a	2-1	Šimončič, Tawamba
14/04	Spartak Myjava	a	0-0	
20/04	Banská Bystrica	h	3-1	Zošák, Gajdoš, Tawamba
27/04	Tatran	a	1-0	Struhár
11/05	Žilina	a	2-1	Cicman, Benčík
14/05	Košice	h	1-0	Tawamba
18/05	Spartak Trnava	h	3-3	Danáili, Šimončič, Obradovic
22/05	Slovan	a	0-4	
26/05	Senica	h	0-1	

No	Name	Nat	DoB	Pos	Aps	(s)	Gls
19	Henrich Benčík		04/10/78	A	11	(1)	3
4	Martin Boszorád		13/11/89	M	9	(9)	2
1	Martin Chudý		23/04/89	G	25	(1)	
17	Róbert Cicman		03/09/84	D	11		1
10	Cléber	BRA	03/06/86	A	30	(1)	10
8	Denis Čery		01/08/94	M	8	(1)	
18	Marek Dubeň		11/07/94	M		(3)	
13	Vratislav Gajdoš		13/01/86	M	24	(1)	3
23	Pavol Grman		10/02/92	D		(2)	
6	Ján Harbuľák		15/11/88	D	11	(1)	
31	Lukáš Hrošso		19/04/87	G	1		
15	Andrej Ivančík		25/05/90	M	3	(5)	1
9	Martin Jackuliak		13/09/91	M	2	(3)	
16	Petr Kašpřák	CZE	17/01/84	D	19		
29	Filip Kinček		24/08/91	M	3		
7	Ľuboš Kolár		01/09/89	M	1	(4)	
22	Marián Kolmokov		23/03/91	D	19	(1)	
22	Matej Kopecký		09/06/90	G	7		
26	Igor Kotora		13/07/89	D	3	(4)	
25	Matej Kráľ		28/12/90	M		(4)	
21	Karel Kroupa	CZE	27/04/80	A	7	(7)	
20	Lukáš Kutra	CZE	05/08/91	M	6	(2)	
28	Peter Mičic		30/04/86	D	23		1
9	Matúš Mikuš		08/07/91	A	7		4
12	Filip Moravčík		27/07/91	M	2	(9)	
3	Miloš Obradović	SRB	30/03/87	D	2	(5)	1
77	Róbert Oravec		07/10/94	M		(2)	
24	Matúš Paukner		20/06/91	A		(1)	
23	Seydouba Soumah	GUI	11/06/91	M	9		4
16	Peter Struhár		17/01/84	D	27	(1)	1
3	Marek Szabo		14/02/89	M	15		
14	Miloš Šimončič		27/05/87	M	31		3
19	Arnold Šimonek		19/09/90	A	10	(5)	1
27	Šimon Šmehyl		20/06/91	A		(9)	
21	Léandre Tawamba	CMR	20/12/89	M	14		3
23	Boris Turčák		21/02/93	M	2	(7)	
11	Lukáš Zelenický		10/04/90	D	3	(6)	
24	Štefan Zošák		03/04/84	M	9	(1)	1

MFK RUŽOMBEROK

Coach: Ladislav Šimčo
1906 • Mestský štadión (4,817) • mfkruzomberok.sk
Major honours
Slovakian League (1) 2006;
Slovakian Cup (1) 2006

2012

14/07	Zlaté Moravce	h	3-1	Ďubek 2 (1p), Serečin
21/07	Nitra	a	1-1	Serečin
28/07	Banská Bystrica	h	1-0	Pekár
04/08	Tatran	a	0-2	
11/08	Košice	h	3-1	Lupták, Mukendi, Ďubek
18/08	Žilina	a	0-0	
25/08	Spartak Trnava	h	2-2	og (Gross), Ďubek (p)
01/09	Slovan	a	1-2	Práznovský
15/09	Senica	h	0-2	
22/09	Trenčín	a	0-0	
29/09	Spartak Myjava	h	0-4	
05/10	Zlaté Moravce	a	0-0	
20/10	Nitra	h	2-1	Mukendi 2
20/11	Banská Bystrica	a	0-0	
03/11	Tatran	h	2-0	Mukendi, Serečin
10/11	Košice	a	0-3	
17/11	Žilina	h	1-0	Bielák
24/11	Spartak Trnava	a	1-0	Mukendi
01/12	Slovan	h	2-2	Mukendi, Bielák

2013

03/03	Senica	a	3-0	Ďubek, Almaský, Pekár
09/03	Trenčín	h	1-2	Ďubek (p)
16/03	Spartak Myjava	a	0-1	
23/03	Zlaté Moravce	h	2-1	Almaský, Ďubek
02/04	Nitra	a	0-3	
06/04	Banská Bystrica	h	3-2	Zrelák, Serečin, Ďubek
13/04	Tatran	a	1-3	Ďubek
20/04	Košice	h	1-1	Ďubek
27/04	Žilina	a	0-3	
04/05	Spartak Trnava	h	1-0	og (Čarnota)
11/05	Slovan	a	2-2	Lovás, Ďubek
18/05	Senica	h	3-1	Pekár, Ďubek 2 (1p)
22/05	Trenčín	a	0-5	
26/05	Spartak Myjava	h	0-1	

No	Name	Nat	DoB	Pos	Aps	(s)	Gls
7	Mário Almaský		25/06/91	M	17	(15)	2
3	Richard Bartoš		28/06/92	M	6	(2)	
5	Lukáš Bielák		14/12/86	M	20	(7)	2
26	Tomáš Ďubek		22/01/87	M	31		13
18	Štefan Gerec		10/11/92	A		(3)	
6	Lukáš Greššák		23/01/89	D	33		
15	Jakub Janso		27/12/89	D	2		
8	Martin Jurkemik		14/11/89	D	6	(4)	
23	Ivan Kotora		27/06/91	M	6	(2)	
30	Tomáš Lešňovský		07/10/93	G		(2)	
12	Andrej Lovás		28/05/91	A	12	(11)	1
14	Lukáš Lupták		28/07/90	M	20	(12)	1
17	Peter Maslo		02/02/87	D	31	(1)	
22	Mulumba Mukendi	CGO	27/05/85	A	13	(7)	6
10	Martin Nagy		05/09/90	D	28	(3)	
12	Martin Nosek		26/01/87	D	22	(2)	
2	Patrick Oboya	KEN	19/02/87	A		(1)	
16	Lukáš Ondrek		11/01/93	D	7	(2)	
19	Štefan Pekár		03/12/88	A	21	(6)	3
18	Dejan Pesevski	MKD	05/08/93	M		(1)	
21	Oliver Práznovský		15/02/91	D	30	(1)	1
25	Filip Serečin		04/10/89	A	15	(9)	4
1	Lukáš Zich	CZE	10/01/85	G	33		
9	Adam Zrelák		05/05/94	A	10	(1)	1

FK SENICA

Coach: Zdeněk Psotka (CZE);
(03/01/13) Vladimír Koník
1921 • Mestský štadión (4,165) • Website: fksenica.eu

2012

15/07	Banská Bystrica	h	2-3	Kóňa (p), Varadi
22/07	Tatran	a	0-2	
29/07	Košice	h	2-1	Babic, Diviš
04/08	Žilina	a	0-2	
12/08	Spartak Trnava	h	3-0	Kóňa, Diviš, Masaryk (p)
19/08	Slovan	a	0-1	
24/08	Spartak Myjava	h	0-1	
01/09	Trenčín	h	1-1	Masaryk
15/09	Ružomberok	a	2-0	Diviš, Piroska (p)
22/09	Zlaté Moravce	h	3-0	Piroska (p), Černý 2
30/09	Nitra	a	1-0	Diviš
06/10	Banská Bystrica	a	1-0	Blackburn 2
20/10	Tatran	h	2-0	Pavlík, Diarrassouba
27/10	Košice	a	2-2	Piroska (p), Varadi
03/11	Žilina	h	0-0	
10/11	Spartak Trnava	a	1-1	Piroska
17/11	Slovan	h	0-1	
25/11	Spartak Myjava	a	2-1	Štepanovský, Piroska (p)
02/12	Trenčín	a	1-1	Blackburn

2013

03/03	Ružomberok	h	0-3	
08/03	Zlaté Moravce	a	2-0	Štepanovský, Kalabiška
15/03	Nitra	h	2-1	Blackburn 2
23/03	Banská Bystrica	h	1-1	Diviš
02/04	Tatran	a	1-0	Štepanovský
06/04	Košice	h	0-0	
13/04	Žilina	a	1-0	Blackburn
21/04	Spartak Trnava	h	3-2	Štepanovský, Wijlaars, Kalabiška
27/04	Slovan	a	2-3	Blackburn 2
04/05	Spartak Myjava	h	0-3	
11/05	Trenčín	h	1-0	Piroska (p)
18/05	Ružomberok	a	1-3	Blackburn
22/05	Zlaté Moravce	h	1-0	Blackburn
26/05	Nitra	h	1-0	Pillár

No	Name	Nat	DoB	Pos	Aps	(s)	Gls
23	Martin Babic		27/07/82	M	7	(3)	1
7	Rolando Blackburn	PAN	09/01/90	A	18	(9)	10
8	Erich Brabec	CZE	24/02/77	D	32		
26	Jaroslav Černý	CZE	26/06/79	M	7		2
13	Lamine Diarrassouba	CIV	01/01/86	A	3	(16)	1
14	Jaroslav Diviš	CZE	09/07/86	M	24	(8)	5
9	Martin Ďurica		11/07/81	M	5	(5)	
28	Martin Frýdek	CZE	24/03/92	D	13	(2)	
11	Petr Hošek	CZE	12/04/89	A		(3)	
19	Jan Kalabiška	CZE	22/12/86	A	23	(6)	2
10	Jakub Kosorín		27/04/95	A	1		
6	Tomáš Kóňa		01/03/84	M	28		2
24	Václav Koutný	CZE	04/10/91	D	9	(1)	
5	Matej Krajčík		19/03/78	D	18	(6)	
23	Juraj Križko		20/09/85	M	15	(8)	
20	Pavol Masaryk		11/02/80	A	6	(2)	2
2	Patrik Mráz		01/02/87	D	12		
4	Petr Pavlík	CZE	22/02/87	D	26	(1)	1
17	Róbert Pillár		27/05/91	D	2	(1)	1
33	Juraj Piroska		27/02/87	A	19	(2)	6
2	Peter Šenk		19/05/94	D	1		
2	Miroslav Štěpánek	CZE	15/01/90	D	1		
21	Peter Štepanovský		12/01/88	D	16	(6)	4
1	Michal Šulla		15/07/91	G	1	(1)	
29	Milan Švenger	CZE	06/07/86	G	32		
16	Adam Varadi	CZE	30/04/85	M	5	(9)	2
25	Denis Ventúra		01/08/95	M	1		
23	Tomáš Vrťo	CZE	06/09/86	A		(2)	
12	Stef Wijlaars	NED	19/01/88	M	28	(2)	1

ŠK SLOVAN BRATISLAVA

Coach: Vladimír Weiss; (03/08/12) Samuel Slovák
1919 • Pasienky (13,295) • slovanfutbal.com
Major honours
UEFA Cup Winners'Cup (1) 1969;
Czechoslovakian League (8) 1949, 1950, 1951, 1955, 1970, 1974, 1975, 1992;
Slovakian League (11) 1940, 1941, 1942, 1944, 1994, 1995, 1996, 1999, 2009, 2011, 2013;
Czechoslovakian Cup (5) 1962, 1963, 1968, 1974, 1982;
Slovakian Cup (6) 1994, 1997, 1999, 2010, 2011, 2013

2012

14/07	Tatran	h	2-1	Gorosito, Peltier
22/07	Košice	a	0-1	
29/07	Žilina	h	1-1	Šebo
05/08	Spartak Trnava	a	1-0	Hlohovský
11/08	Spartak Myjava	h	2-1	Hlohovský 2
19/08	Senica	h	1-0	Kolčák
25/08	Trenčín	a	2-2	Šebo (p), Milinković
01/09	Ružomberok	h	2-1	Milinković, Halenár
15/09	Zlaté Moravce	a	1-3	Grendel
21/09	Nitra	h	5-2	Halenár 2, Gorosito, Hlohovský, Peltier
29/09	Banská Bystrica	a	1-1	Grendel
06/10	Tatran	a	0-0	
21/10	Košice	h	3-1	Gorosito, Peltier, Milinković
28/10	Žilina	a	0-0	
02/11	Spartak Trnava	h	0-1	
10/11	Spartak Myjava	a	2-1	Hlohovský, Žofčák
17/11	Senica	a	1-0	Milinković
24/11	Trenčín	h	3-1	Peltier, Gorosito, Žofčák (p)
01/12	Ružomberok	a	2-2	Peltier, Hlohovský

2013

01/03	Zlaté Moravce	h	4-1	Hlohovský, Peltier 2, Kladrubský
10/03	Nitra	a	3-0	Žofčák, Halenár, Pauschek
16/03	Banská Bystrica	h	2-0	Žofčák, Milinković (p)
22/03	Tatran	h	5-0	Halenár 2 (1p), Hlohovský, Grendel 2
02/04	Košice	a	1-1	Peltier
06/04	Žilina	h	1-1	Kladrubský
13/04	Spartak Trnava	a	0-0	
20/04	Spartak Myjava	h	1-1	Peltier
27/04	Senica	h	3-2	Kladrubský, Peltier, Grendel
05/05	Trenčín	a	1-4	Gorosito
11/05	Ružomberok	h	2-2	Niňaj, Halenár
19/05	Zlaté Moravce	a	0-1	
22/05	Nitra	h	4-0	Halenár (p), Kolčák, Pauschek, Grendel
26/05	Banská Bystrica	a	0-1	

No	Name	Nat	DoB	Pos	Aps	(s)	Gls
18	Mamadou Bagayoko	CIV	31/12/89	D	26	(3)	
12	Adrián Čermák		01/07/93	M		(1)	
4	Erik Čikoš		31/07/88	D	2	(1)	
16	Nicolás Gorosito	ARG	17/08/88	D	32		5
19	Patrik Gregora		06/03/93	M		(1)	
8	Erik Grendel		13/10/88	M	28	(2)	6
7	Juraj Halenár		28/06/83	A	21	(10)	8
7	Filip Hlohovský		13/06/88	M	22	(7)	8
5	Dávid Hudák		21/03/93	D	7		
17	Jiří Kladrubský	CZE	19/11/85	D	18	(1)	3
23	Kristián Kolčák		30/01/90	D	27	(3)	2
29	Milan Kopic		23/11/85	D		(3)	
14	Kamil Kopúnek		18/05/84	M	15	(6)	
1	Pavel Kováč		12/08/74	G	3		
26	Marek Kuzma		22/06/88	M	2	(6)	
2	Leandro Ledesma	ARG	15/03/87	A	2	(1)	
2	Filip Lukšík		03/02/85	D	20	(2)	
13	Karol Mészáros		25/07/93	M	1	(8)	
3	Marko Milinković	SRB	16/04/88	M	27	(1)	5
3	Branislav Niňaj		17/05/94	D	4	(1)	1
25	Lukáš Pauschek		09/12/92	D	20	(6)	2
23	Lester Peltier	TRI	13/09/88	A	22	(7)	10
7	Juraj Piroska		27/02/87	A	3	(1)	
30	Matúš Putnocký		01/11/84	G	30		
15	Patrik Sabo		09/03/93	M	1	(3)	
20	Seydouba Soumah	GUI	11/06/91	A	7	(4)	
14	Ákos Szarka		24/11/90	A	2	(13)	
33	Filip Šebo		24/02/84	A	8		2
6	Martin Vrablec		13/01/92	M		(2)	
16	Igor Žofčák		10/04/83	M	18	(1)	4

TJ SPARTAK MYJAVA

Coach: Ladislav Hudec
1920 • Mestský štadión (2,800) • spartakmyjava.sk

2012

13/07	Žilina	a	1-4	Častulín
21/07	Zlaté Moravce	h	2-2	Sládek, Sabo
29/07	Spartak Trnava	a	1-1	Sládek (p)
04/08	Nitra	h	0-2	
11/08	Slovan	a	1-2	Kuračka
18/08	Banská Bystrica	a	0-1	
24/08	Senica	a	1-0	Černáček
01/09	Tatran	h	2-0	Sládek, Dian
15/09	Trenčín	a	2-3	Siva, Kukoľ
22/09	Košice	h	3-1	Černáček 2, Harsányi
29/09	Ružomberok	a	4-0	Sládek 2 (1p), Častulín, Kosík
06/10	Žilina	h	1-1	Častulín
20/10	Zlaté Moravce	a	1-3	Siva
27/10	Spartak Trnava	h	2-2	Sládek 2
03/11	Nitra	a	2-0	Kuračka 2
10/11	Slovan	h	1-2	Harsányi
17/11	Banská Bystrica	h	1-1	Kuračka
25/11	Senica	h	1-2	Černáček
01/12	Tatran	a	1-2	Harsányi

2013

02/03	Trenčín	a	0-1	
09/03	Košice	a	2-1	Sládek, Kuračka
16/03	Ružomberok	h	1-0	Urgela
23/03	Žilina	a	0-0	
06/04	Spartak Trnava	a	1-1	Kosík
14/04	Nitra	h	0-0	
20/04	Slovan	h	1-1	Kukoľ
27/04	Banská Bystrica	h	2-1	Sládek, Urgela
04/05	Senica	a	3-0	Sládek, og (Pavlik), Kuračka
07/05	Zlaté Moravce	h	2-1	og (Chren), Pelegríni
11/05	Tatran	h	2-2	Harsányi, Kosík
18/05	Trenčín	h	0-2	
22/05	Košice	h	1-0	Šulek
26/05	Ružomberok	a	1-0	Kosík

No	Name	Nat	DoB	Pos	Aps	(s)	Gls
21	Tomáš Bruško		21/02/83	M	10	(8)	
15	Roman Častulín		03/04/85	D	29		3
10	Martin Černáček		09/11/79	D	33		4
23	Erik Daniel	CZE	04/02/92	M	3	(8)	
8	Michal Dian		13/11/81	M	4	(11)	1
19	Miroslav Duga		29/01/89	D	4		
18	Peter Ďuriš		10/04/81	M	14	(9)	
9	Zoltán Harsányi		01/06/87	A	8	(12)	4
2	Marek Jastráb		10/05/93	M		(1)	
23	Matúš Jurík		11/09/93	A		(1)	
7	Pavol Kosík		02/07/80	A	19	(10)	4
11	Vladimír Kukoľ		08/05/86	M	22	(2)	2
6	Peter Kumančík		21/07/85	D	9		
13	Peter Kuračka		13/07/78	M	28	(1)	6
5	Peter Majerník		31/12/78	D	10	(3)	
20	Tomáš Marček		10/03/87	M	26	(2)	
22	Tomáš Mrva		06/04/89	M	17	(1)	
16	Ondrej Neoveský		10/09/86	D	2	(1)	
8	Lukáš Pelegríni		10/05/88	M	2	(8)	1
17	Ján Petráš		18/02/86	M	4	(5)	
24	Erik Sabo		22/11/91	M	3		1
10	Matej Siva		10/10/84	D	26		2
26	Peter Sládek		07/07/89	A	31		10
1	Peter Solnička		14/06/82	G	26		
9	Pavol Straka		13/12/80	A		(2)	
25	Matej Székely		12/05/91	G	1		
27	Lukáš Šebek		10/10/88	A	2	(8)	
6	Zdeno Štrba		09/06/76	M	4		
14	Peter Šulek		21/09/88	M	13		1
28	Michal Šulla		15/07/91	G	6		
16	Ľubomír Urgela		23/01/90	A	7	(4)	2

FC SPARTAK TRNAVA

Coach: Pavel Hoftych (CZE);
(19/11/12) Peter Zelenský; (23/04/13) Vladimír Ekhardt
1923 • Antona Malatinského (18,448) • spartakas.eu
Major honours
Czechoslovakian League (5) 1968, 1969, 1971, 1972, 1973;
Czechoslovakian Cup (4) 1967, 1971,1975, 1986;
Slovakian Cup (1) 1998

2012

14/07	Košice	h	0-0	
29/07	Spartak Myjava	h	1-1	Gašparík
05/08	Slovan	a	0-1	
12/08	Senica	a	0-3	
19/08	Nitra	h	0-3	
21/08	Žilina	a	1-1	Gross
25/08	Ružomberok	a	2-2	Karhan, Nikolić
02/09	Zlaté Moravce	h	0-5	
14/09	Nitra	a	3-1	Bicák, Sabo, Ciprys
22/09	Banská Bystrica	h	1-0	Čvirik
29/09	Tatran	a	1-2	Sabo (p)
05/10	Košice	a	0-1	
20/10	Žilina	h	1-2	Karhan
27/10	Spartak Myjava	a	2-2	Gašparík, Janečka
02/11	Slovan	a	1-0	Gašparík
10/11	Senica	h	1-1	Vyskočil
17/11	Trenčín	h	0-6	
24/11	Ružomberok	h		Vyskočil
01/12	Zlaté Moravce	a	1-1	Vyskočil

2013

02/03	Nitra	h	2-0	Schranz, Tomaček
08/03	Banská Bystrica	a	0-2	
16/03	Tatran	h	2-1	Schranz, Kaščák
23/03	Košice	h	2-3	Schranz, Mikovič
02/04	Žilina	a	1-1	Ciprys
06/04	Spartak Myjava	h	1-1	Tomaček
13/04	Slovan	h	0-0	
21/04	Senica	a	2-3	Mikovič, Vyskočil
27/04	Trenčín	a	2-1	Schranz, Vyskočil
05/05	Ružomberok	a	0-1	
11/05	Zlaté Moravce	h	3-2	Vyskočil, Augustíni, Kaščák
18/05	Nitra	a	3-3	Vlasko, Kaščák, Vyskočil (p)
22/05	Banská Bystrica	h	0-1	
26/05	Tatran	a	1-0	Vlasko (p)

No	Name	Nat	DoB	Pos	Aps	(s)	Gls
13	Oliver Augustíni		12/06/90	M	6	(1)	1
5	Patrik Banovič		13/11/91	D	1		
27	Mário Bicák		21/10/79	M	8		1
19	Radoslav Ciprys		24/06/87	M	10	(10)	2
17	Patrik Čarnota		10/10/86	D	25	(5)	
2	Peter Čvirik		13/06/79	D	12		1
18	Filip Deket		01/05/93	D	1	(2)	
24	Samy Derras	FRA	07/06/88	M	1		
1	Miroslav Filipko		23/09/73	G	7		
33	Michal Gašparík		19/12/81	M	10	(3)	3
5	Srdjan Grabež	SRB	02/04/91	D	13		
20	Patrik Gross	CZE	06/05/78	D	11	(2)	1
4	Michal Habánek		12/04/94	D	9		
18	Ľuboš Hanzel		07/05/87	D	16		
30	Ivan Hodúr		10/07/79	M	8	(3)	
40	Jakub Jakubov		01/02/89	G	4		
6	Marek Janečka		09/06/83	D	32		1
21	Miroslav Karhan		21/06/76	M	29	(1)	2
29	Marek Kaščák		22/05/82	M	16	(4)	3
3	Martin Klabník		22/11/91	D	6		
5	Jiří Koubský	CZE	05/08/82	D	6		
39	Ivan Lietava		20/07/83	A	5	(3)	
10	Tomáš Mikinič		22/11/92	M		(8)	
8	Martin Mikovič		12/09/90	M	19	(4)	2
15	Stevo Nikolić	BIH	04/12/84	A	4	(2)	1
11	Karol Pavelka		31/07/83	A	1	(11)	
22	Martin Raška	CZE	31/01/77	G	5	(1)	
28	Marek Rehák		15/02/90	M		(1)	
31	Dobrivoj Rusov		13/01/93	M	17		
25	Erik Sabo		22/11/91	M	23	(7)	2
26	Ivan Schranz		13/09/93	M	16	(5)	4
3	Vlastimil Stožický	CZE	19/08/83	D	5	(3)	
12	Ladislav Tomaček		26/09/82	A	3	(13)	2
16	Ján Vlasko		11/01/90	M	15	(4)	2
7	Martin Vyskočil	CZE	15/09/82	M	19	(3)	6

1. FC TATRAN PREŠOV

Coach: Angel Chervenkov (BUL);
(20/11/12) Ladislav Totkovič;
(16/04/13) Jozef Bubenko
1898 • Tatran (5,410) • fctatran.sk

2012

14/07	Slovan	a	1-2	og (Kolčák)
22/07	Senica	h	2-0	Guba, Marcin
20/07	Trenčín	a	1-2	og (Ramon)
04/08	Ružomberok	h	2-0	Kostadinov, Adámik
11/08	Zlaté Moravce	a	0-2	
18/08	Nitra	h	1-0	og (Šimončič)
25/08	Banská Bystrica	a	0-0	
01/09	Spartak Myjava	a	0-2	
15/09	Košice	h	0-0	
22/09	Žilina	a	0-3	
29/09	Spartak Trnava	h	2-1	Shevchuk 2
06/10	Slovan	h	0-0	
20/10	Senica	a	0-2	
27/10	Trenčín	h	1-2	Shevchuk
03/11	Ružomberok	a	0-1	
10/11	Zlaté Moravce	h	1-1	og (Bortel)
17/11	Nitra	a	1-4	Macko
24/11	Banská Bystrica	h	1-0	Lipták
01/12	Spartak Myjava	h	2-1	Marcin, Petráš

2013

02/03	Košice	a	0-3	
09/03	Žilina	ň	0-0	
16/03	Spartak Trnava	a	1-2	Petráš
22/03	Slovan	a	0-5	
02/04	Senica	h	0-1	
06/04	Trenčín	a	1-1	Gergel
13/04	Ružomberok	h	3-1	Yakovlev, Hruška, Novák
20/04	Zlaté Moravce	a	0-0	
27/04	Nitra	a	0-1	
04/05	Banská Bystrica	a	0-1	
11/05	Spartak Myjava	a	0-2	
18/05	Košice	h	0-0	
23/05	Žilina	a	1-0	Marcin
26/05	Spartak Trnava	h	0-1	

No	Name	Nat	DoB	Pos	Aps	(s)	Gls
7	Marián Adam		20/09/81	M	12	(7)	
25	Jozef Adámik		10/04/85	D	14		1
8	Radoslav Augustín		05/01/87	M	3	(2)	
2	Jakub Bartek		01/07/92	D	15	(4)	
88	Bernardo	BRA	07/11/88	A	1	(5)	
77	Dejan Boljević	SRB	30/05/90	M	2	(1)	
84	Miloš Brezinský		02/04/84	D	7	(1)	
23	Jakub Diviš	CZE	27/12/86	G	32		
10	Jozef Dolný		13/05/92	M	6	(10)	
42	Roman Gergel		22/02/88	M	11		1
29	Dávid Guba		29/06/91	A	7	(6)	1
36	Lukáš Hruška		02/03/92	M	1	(7)	1
4	Patrik Jacko		26/09/92	M	7	(2)	
14	Richard Kačala		01/03/91	M	2	(1)	
15	Michal Kamenčík		12/01/93	M		(1)	
11	Peter Katona		12/04/88	M	2	(6)	
9	Jaroslav Kolbas		10/01/85	M	31		
8	Branimir Kostadinov	BUL	24/07/89	A	4	(6)	1
5	Michal Krajník		05/04/88	D	21		
87	Jan Krob	CZE	27/04/87	D	9		
17	Peter Lipták		07/09/89	M	28		1
55	Anton Lysyuk	UKR	26/02/87	M		(1)	
6	Viliam Macko		22/10/91	M	2	(2)	1
16	Matúš Marcin		06/04/94	M	27	(2)	3
33	Ján Novák		06/03/85	A	11	(1)	1
24	Ján Papaj		16/06/79	M	22	(4)	
18	Peter Petráš		07/05/79	D	30		2
30	Jakub Plánička	CZE	25/12/84	G	1		
19	Miroslav Poliaček		13/07/83	M	19	(3)	
20	Martin Pribula		29/11/85	M	9	(1)	
99	Rafael	BRA	26/10/89	A		(3)	
22	Andriy Shevchuk	UKR	12/08/85	A	8	(1)	3
44	Andriy Yakovlev	UKR	20/02/89	D	11	(12)	1
18	Štefan Zošák		03/04/84	M	8		

FK AS TRENČÍN

Coach: Adrián Guľa
1992 • Na Sihoti (4,200) • astn.sk

2012

14/07	Nitra	h	5-0	Depetris 4, Štefánik
21/07	Banská Bystrica	a	0-2	
28/07	Tatran	h	2-1	Depetris 2
04/08	Košice	a	0-3	
11/08	Žilina	h	0-2	
18/08	Spartak Trnava	a	3-0	Holúbek, Štefánik, Depetris
25/08	Slovan	h	2-2	Depetris 2 (1p)
01/09	Senica	a	1-1	Depetris (p)
15/09	Spartak Myjava	h	3-2	Depetris 2, Malec
22/09	Ružomberok	h	0-0	
29/09	Zlaté Moravce	a	1-4	Mazan
06/10	Nitra	a	2-1	Mazan, Depetris
20/10	Banská Bystrica	a	1-1	Díaz
27/10	Tatran	a	2-1	Mondek, Štefánik
03/11	Košice	h	0-0	
11/11	Žilina	a	0-0	
17/11	Spartak Trnava	h	6-0	Depetris 2, og (Čvirik), Godál, Adi, Lobotka
24/11	Slovan	a	1-3	Depetris
02/12	Senica	h	1-1	Díaz

2013

02/03	Spartak Myjava	h	1-0	Mazan (p)
09/03	Ružomberok	a	2-1	Holúbek (p), Kubík
16/03	Zlaté Moravce	h	1-1	Willian
23/03	Nitra	a	3-0	Kubík, Bednárik, Lobotka (p)
02/04	Banská Bystrica	a	0-0	
06/04	Tatran	h	1-1	Mazan
13/04	Košice	a	0-0	
20/04	Žilina	h	1-2	Willian
27/04	Spartak Trnava	a	0-2	
05/05	Slovan	h	4-1	Willian 2, Holúbek, Kubík
11/05	Senica	a	0-1	
18/05	Spartak Myjava	a	2-0	Holúbek, Adi
22/05	Ružomberok	h	5-0	Kubík 2, Štefánik, Holúbek, Adi
26/05	Zlaté Moravce	a	2-1	Kubík, Štefánik

No	Name	Nat	DoB	Pos	Aps	(s)	Gls
12	Fanendo Adi	NGA	10/10/90	A	6	(10)	3
8	Aldo Baéz	ARG	05/09/88	M	23	(1)	
30	Peter Bartalský		27/01/78	G		(1)	
4	Daniel Bednárik		10/03/94	D	8		1
5	Samuel Čéntéš		19/02/94	M		(2)	
17	Peter Čögley		11/08/88	D	22	(6)	
10	David Depetris	ARG	11/11/88	A	18	(1)	16
20	Iván Díaz	ARG	23/01/93	M	19		2
3	Lukáš Ďuriška		16/08/92	M		(5)	
13	Marek Frimmel		10/11/92	M	1	(9)	
21	Boris Godál		27/05/87	D	13	(1)	1
14	Jakub Holúbek		12/01/91	M	30	(1)	5
19	Peter Kleščík		18/09/88	D	23		
9	František Kubík		14/03/89	A	18	(1)	6
29	Stanislav Lobotka		25/11/94	M	21	(10)	2
6	Tomáš Malec		05/01/93	A		(8)	1
15	Peter Mazan		13/05/90	M	15	(13)	4
27	Róbert Mazáň		09/02/94	D	27	(3)	
16	Karol Mondek		02/06/91	M	18	(5)	1
23	Adam Morong		16/06/93	M		(3)	
22	Ramon	BRA	22/08/90	D	30		
26	Samuel Štefánik		16/11/91	M	29	(4)	5
1	Miloš Volešák		20/04/84	G	33		
11	Willian	BRA	07/12/91	A	9	(5)	4

FC VION ZLATÉ MORAVCE

Coach: Juraj Jarábek
1995 • ViOn (5,000) • fcvion.sk
Major honours
Slovakian Cup (1) 2007

2012

14/07	Ružomberok	a	1-3	Kováč
21/07	Spartak Myjava	a	2-2	Hodek, Bernáth
28/07	Nitra	h	0-2	
04/08	Banská Bystrica	a	0-0	
11/08	Tatran	h	2-0	Hodek, Žilák
18/08	Košice	a	1-2	Bernáth
25/08	Žilina	h	1-0	Škvarka
02/09	Spartak Trnava	a	5-0	Hodek 3, Škvarka, Mihálik
15/09	Slovan	h	3-1	Hodek, Kováč, Žilák
22/09	Senica	a	0-3	
29/09	Trenčín	h	4-1	og (Ramon), Škvarka, Hodek, Bernáth
05/10	Ružomberok	h	0-0	
20/10	Spartak Myjava	h	3-1	Bernáth, Kováč, Candrák
27/10	Nitra	a	1-1	Hodek
03/11	Banská Bystrica	h	2-0	Janič 2
10/11	Tatran	a	1-1	Janič
16/11	Košice	h	1-0	Chren
23/11	Žilina	a	1-4	Orávik
01/12	Spartak Trnava	h	1-1	Pavlovič (p)

2013

01/03	Slovan	a	1-4	Hodek
08/03	Senica	h	0-2	
16/03	Trenčín	a	1-1	Hodek
23/03	Ružomberok	a	1-2	Mészáros
06/04	Nitra	a	1-2	Bernáth
13/04	Banská Bystrica	a	0-1	
20/04	Tatran	h	0-0	
27/04	Košice	a	2-0	Hodek, Orávik
07/05	Spartak Myjava	a	1-2	Orávik
11/05	Spartak Trnava	a	2-3	og (Grabež), Mészáros
15/05	Žilina	h	2-1	Hodek 2
19/05	Slovan	h	1-0	Obročník
22/05	Senica	a	0-1	
26/05	Trenčín	h	1-2	Bolinha (p)

No	Name	Nat	DoB	Pos	Aps	(s)	Gls
15	Ľubomír Bernáth		03/09/85	A	22	(10)	5
28	Bolinha	BRA	29/11/90	M	10	(12)	1
13	Milan Bortel		07/04/87	D	15		
9	Adrian Candrák		18/12/82	A	20	(11)	1
12	Martin Chren		02/01/84	D	29		1
23	Peter Farkaš		11/11/82	D	1	(4)	
10	Andrej Hodek		24/05/81	A	29	(1)	13
25	Lukáš Janič		30/12/86	M	5	(8)	3
13	Dmitrij Korman		25/12/89	D	1	(1)	
25	Lukáš Kováč		21/06/87	M	15	(6)	3
22	Martin Kuciak		15/03/82	G	33		
19	Pavol Majerník		31/12/78	D	31		
17	Karol Mészáros		25/07/93	A	9	(3)	2
18	Lukáš Mihálik		12/02/94	M		(13)	1
20	Michal Obročník		04/06/91	M	31		1
26	Marcel Ondráš		20/09/85	D	11		
8	Martin Ondrejka		08/01/83	M		(4)	
14	Peter Orávik		18/12/88	M	29	(3)	3
5	Patrik Pavlenda		03/05/82	D	27		
17	Milan Pavlovič		22/11/80	D	6	(6)	1
11	Michal Pintér		04/02/94	D	8	(4)	
6	Milan Škriniar		11/02/95	M	5	(2)	
26	Michal Škvarka		19/08/92	M	15	(3)	3
24	Adam Žilák		07/12/91	M	11		2

MŠK ŽILINA

Coach: Frans Adelaar (NED);
(04/01/13) Štefan Tarkovič
1908 • Pod Dubňom (11,181) • mskzilina.sk
Major honours
Slovakian League (6) 2002, 2003, 2004, 2007, 2010, 2012;
Slovakian Cup (1) 2012

2012

13/07	Spartak Myjava	h	4-1	Guima, Pich, Káčer, Barčík
29/07	Slovan	a	1-1	Pich
04/08	Senica	h	2-0	Pich 2
11/08	Trenčín	a	2-0	Akakpo, Guima
18/08	Ružomberok	h	0-0	
21/08	Spartak Trnava	h	1-1	Piaček
25/08	Zlaté Moravce	a	0-1	
01/09	Nitra	h	1-1	Leitner
16/09	Banská Bystrica	a	2-2	Mihálik, Paur
22/09	Tatran	h	3-0	Paur, Ricardo Nunes, Ceesay
29/09	Košice	a	1-1	Akakpo
06/10	Spartak Myjava	a	1-1	Pečovský
20/10	Spartak Trnava	a	2-1	Pich, Ceesay
28/10	Slovan	h	0-0	
03/11	Senica	a	0-0	
11/11	Trenčín	h	0-0	
17/11	Ružomberok	a	0-1	
23/11	Zlaté Moravce	h	4-1	Pich 2, Škriniar, Ricardo Nunes (p)
30/11	Nitra	a	0-2	

2013

02/03	Banská Bystrica	h	0-1	
09/03	Tatran	a	0-0	
17/03	Košice	h	0-1	
23/03	Spartak Myjava	h	0-0	
02/04	Spartak Trnava	h	1-1	Pich
06/04	Slovan	a	1-1	Pich
13/04	Senica	h	0-1	
20/04	Trenčín	a	2-1	Guba, Majtán
23/04	Nitra	h	1-2	Škvarka
27/04	Ružomberok	h	3-0	Paur, Majtán, Škvarka
15/05	Zlaté Moravce	a	1-2	Majtán
18/05	Banská Bystrica	a	2-1	Pich 2
22/05	Tatran	h	0-1	
26/05	Košice	a	2-2	Paur, Guba

No	Name	Nat	DoB	Pos	Aps	(s)	Gls
5	Serge Akakpo	TOG	15/10/87	D	25		2
2	Stanislav Angelovič		26/03/82	D	20	(8)	
14	Bello Babatunde	BEN	06/10/89	M	4	(2)	
11	Miroslav Barčík		26/05/78	M	19	(13)	1
18	Mamadou Ceesay	GAM	24/12/88	A	9	(2)	2
16	Lukáš Čmelík		13/04/96	M	1	(6)	
4	Jean Deza	PER	09/06/93	M		(7)	
30	Martin Dúbravka		15/01/89	G	26		
42	Roman Gergel		22/02/88	M	6	(3)	
11	Dávid Guba		29/06/91	A	7	(5)	2
21	Guima	POR	11/03/86	A	7	(4)	2
6	Miroslav Káčer		09/06/96	M	5	(6)	1
22	Martin Krnáč		30/01/85	G	3		
89	Patrik Le Giang		08/09/92	G	4		
7	Vladimír Leitner		28/06/74	D	10	(3)	1
4	Peter Lupčo		21/04/95	M	3	(4)	
45	Ernest Mabouka	CMR	16/06/88	D	21	(1)	
10	Tomáš Majtán		30/03/87	A	18	(3)	3
23	Jaroslav Mihálik		27/07/94	M	11	(4)	1
25	Michal Mravec		19/06/87	D	4	(3)	
29	Jakub Paur		04/07/92	M	20	(8)	4
12	Viktor Pečovský		24/05/83	M	29	(1)	1
15	Jozef Piaček		20/06/83	D	30		1
17	Róbert Pich		12/11/88	A	31	(2)	11
77	Ricardo Nunes	RSA	11/06/86	D	25	(1)	2
3	Milan Škriniar		11/02/95	M	9	(1)	1
20	Michal Škvarka		19/08/92	M	11		2
20	Peter Šulek		21/09/88	M	2	(3)	
19	Denis Vavro		10/04/96	D	3	(1)	

Top goalscorers

16	David Depetris (Trenčín)
13	Dávid Škutka (Košice)
	Tomáš Ďubek (Ružomberok)
	Andrej Hodek (Zlaté Moravce)
11	Róbert Pich (Žilina)
10	Cléber (Nitra)
	Rolando Blackburn (Senica)
	Lester Peltier (Slovan)
	Peter Sládek (Spartak Myjava)
8	Juraj Halenár (Slovan)
	Filip Hlohovský (Slovan)

Promoted club

DAC 1904 DUNAJSKÁ STREDA

Coach: Mikuláš Radványi
1904 • DAC (16,410) • fcdac1904.com
Major honours
Czechoslovakian Cup (1) 1987

SECOND LEVEL FINAL TABLE 2012/13

		Pld	W	D	L	F	A	Pts
1	DAC 1904 Dunajská Streda	33	19	8	6	41	26	65
2	ŽP Šport Podbrezová	33	16	13	4	45	20	61
3	ŠK SFM Senec	33	16	9	8	48	32	57
4	Partizán Bardejov	33	16	5	12	41	36	53
5	MFK Zemplín Michalovce	33	12	7	14	41	43	43
6	MFK Dubnica	33	11	8	14	31	38	41
7	FC ŠTK 1914 Šamorín	33	10	11	12	29	32	41
8	FK Slovan Duslo Šaľa	33	12	5	16	41	45	41
9	MFK Rimavská Sobota	33	11	7	15	39	47	40
10	MFK Tatran Liptovský Mikuláš	33	9	9	15	26	39	36
11	MFK Dolný Kubín	33	7	13	13	34	42	34
12	TJ Baník Ružiná	33	7	9	17	38	54	30

Domestic cup: Slovenský Pohár 2012/13

SECOND ROUND

(28/08/12)
Bardejov 3-0 Lipany
Dunajská Lužná 0-2 Spartak Myjava
Lokomotíva Košice 1-1 Lučenec *(aet; 4-3 on pens)*
Námestovo 0-1 Banská Bystrica
Nemšová 0-4 Trenčín
Petržalka 0-3 Nitra
Podbrezová 0-0 Zlaté Moravce *(aet; 4-5 on pens)*
Poprad 1-2 MFK Košice
Ružomberok 4-1 Rimavská Sobota
Senec 0-4 Slovan Bratislava
Senica 7-1 Dunajská Streda
Žilina 2-0 Ružiná

(29/08/12)
Kalinovo 1-3 Tatran Prešov
Moravany 1-2 Sereď
Pohronie 0-1 Domino
Spartak Trnava 3-1 Nové Mesto nad Váhom

THIRD ROUND

(25/09/12)
Banská Bystrica 4-1 Bardejov
MFK Košice 3-1 Lokomotíva Košice
Sereď 2-3 Spartak Trnava
Slovan Bratislava 3-2 Zlaté Moravce
Spartak Myjava 2-1 Nitra
Žilina 3-1 Trenčín

(26/09/12)
Domino 0-4 Senica
Tatran Prešov 1-1 Ružomberok *(aet; 3-4 on pens)*

QUARTER-FINALS

(23/10/12 & 06/11/12)
Banská Bystrica 2-1 Spartak Trnava *(Pančík 82, Hlinka 86; Karhan 80p)*
Spartak Trnava 3-1 Banská Bystrica *(Čarnota 8, Vlasko 46, Schranz 88; Brašeň 54)*
(Spartak Trnava 4-3)
Senica 1-2 Žilina *(Diarrassouba 55; Ricardo Nunes 62p, Pich 79)*
Žilina 1-2 Senica *(Ceesay 12; Blackburn 35, Babic 41)*
(3-3; Žilina 4-2 on pens)

(24/10/12 & 06/11/12)
MFK Košice 2-0 Spartak Myjava *(Novák 31p, Duda 90)*
Spartak Myjava 3-1 MFK Košice *(Harsányi 2p, Černáček 8, Šebek 90; Bašista 10)*
(3-3; MFK Košice on away goal)
Slovan Bratislava 2-0 Ružomberok *(Peltier 10, Hlohovský 55)*
Ružomberok 3-1 Slovan Bratislava *(Serečin 24, Lovás 71, 90; Mészáros 34)*
(3-3; Slovan Bratislava on away goal)

SEMI-FINALS

(09/04/13 & 16/04/13)
MFK Košice 0-3 Slovan Bratislava *(Milinković 48, Halenár 73p, Grendel 90)*
Slovan Bratislava 3-1 MFK Košice *(Milinković 23, Kuzma 32, Žofčák 45p; Gál-Andrezly 20)*
(Slovan Bratislava 6-1)
Žilina 3-2 Spartak Trnava *(Leitner 3, Majtán 34, Piaček 41; Vlasko 9, Kaščák 81)*
Spartak Trnava 1-1 Žilina *(Hodúr 52; Leitner 49)*
(Žilina 4-3)

FINAL

(01/05/13)
Mestský štadión, Ruzomberok
ŠK SLOVAN BRATISLAVA 2 *(Žofčák 27, Peltier 49)*
MŠK ŽILINA 0
Referee: *Kralovič*
SLOVAN: *Kováč, Bağayoko, Gorosito, Kolčák, Pauschek, Kladrubský (Kopúnek 71), Grendel, Žofčák, Milinković (Kuzma 80), Soumah (Halenár 72), Peltier*
ŽILINA: *Krnáč, Mabouka, Piaček, Leitner, Ricardo Nunes, Akakpo, Barčík, Paur (Babatunde 55), Škvarka (Guba 55), Pich (Lupčo 81), Majtán*

Action from the Slovakian Cup final as Slovan's Jiří Kladrubský (No17) contests an aerial duel with Tomáš Majtán of Žilina

SLOVENIA
Nogometna zveza Slovenije (NZS)

Address	Cerinova 4, PP 3986	**President**	Aleksander Čeferin
	SI-1001 Ljubljana	**General secretary**	Aleš Zavrl
Tel	+386 1 530 0400	**Media officer**	Matjaž Krajnik
Fax	+386 1 530 0410	**Year of formation**	1920
E-mail	nzs@nzs.si	**National stadium**	Ljudski vrt, Maribor
Website	nzs.si		(12,432)

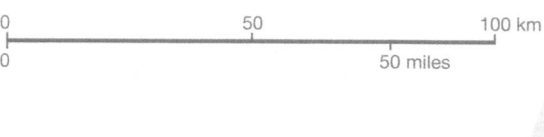

Murska Sobota

Maribor

Velenje

Kidričevo

Zavrč

Kranj

Domžale

Celje

Nova Gorica

Ljubljana

Novo Mesto

Koper

PROMOTED CLUBS

11 NK Zavrč

12 NK Krka

PRVA LIGA CLUBS

1 NK Aluminij

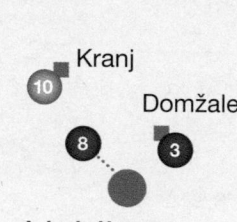 2 NK Celje

 3 NK Domžale

4 ND Gorica

5 FC Koper

 6 NK Maribor

7 ND Mura 05

 8 NK Olimpija Ljubljana

9 NK Rudar Velenje

10 NK Triglav

KEY:

● – UEFA Champions League

● – UEFA Europa League

● – Promoted clubs

● – Relegated clubs

More of the same from Maribor

For the second season in a row NK Maribor won both of the domestic prizes on offer and also competed in the group stage of the UEFA Europa League. It enabled departing coach Darko Milanič to sign off on a high after five successful years at the helm.

As in 2011/12, the runners-up to Maribor in the league were NK Olimpija Ljubljana, with NK Celje again succumbing to Milanič's men in the final of the Slovenian Cup. A poor start to the 2014 FIFA World Cup qualifying campaign heralded the return of Srečko Katanec as Slovenia national team coach.

Successive doubles for Milanič's men

Olimpija finish runners-up again

Katanec back in charge of national team

Domestic league

Not quite as dominant as in the previous season, when they won the Prva Liga by 20 points, Maribor were nevertheless a class apart once again, and although Olimpija put up a decent fight, the club from the capital were never able to recover from a poor start and apply enough pressure on the defending champions to induce doubt or anxiety. Although Milanič had to make do without his two principal goalscorers in 2011/12, Dalibor Volaš and Etien Velikonja having both been transferred abroad, the depth of his squad was still strong, with goalkeeper Jasmin Handanovič, midfielders Agim Ibraimi and Goran Cvijanovič, and ever-reliable Brazilian Marcos Tavares, the league's top scorer with 17 goals, the team's standout individuals.

Maribor hit the front early, courtesy of ten wins in their opening 12 games, and stayed there. Although less consistent and prolific than in 2011/12, they never went longer than two matches without a win. Olimpija, in fact, picked up more points than Maribor from September onwards, after they had replaced coach Ermin Šiljak with former youth team boss Andrej Razdrh, but by that stage, with seven matches played, they had already fallen nine points behind.

Olimpija might have made up the ground but for their inability to beat Maribor, losing both away fixtures and drawing twice at home. Eight points separated the top two, and the gap was even greater between the next two positions, with NK Domžale surprisingly finishing third – and claiming a place in Europe – under Serbian coach Stevan Mojsilović.

Domestic cup

Fifth-placed Celje booked a return ticket to the UEFA Europa League by reaching the Slovenian Cup final for the second successive season. The 2005 winners had taken Maribor to penalties in 2011/12 but despite another worthy effort they were again unable to prevent the champions from completing their double.

Ibraimi scored the only goal in Koper to provide a fitting send-off for coach Milanič, who decided to cross the border to Austria and take over at SK Sturm Graz, where he won two league titles and three cups as a player from 1993-2000.

Europe

Maribor failed to reach the group stage of the UEFA Champions League, where they had last competed in 1999/2000, but their play-off defeat by GNK Dinamo Zagreb put them back into the equivalent stage of the UEFA Europa League, and this time they registered a victory, 3-0 at home to Panathinaikos FC in their opening game. It would be their only one, however, and they ended up bottom of their group. They lost home and away to S.S. Lazio, the same fate incurred in the play-offs by ND Mura 05, who reached that round after unexpectedly eliminating PFC CSKA Sofia and FC Arsenal Kyiv.

National team

Slaviša Stojanovič's reign as Slovenia coach lasted a little over a year. He was dismissed after overseeing a poor start to the World Cup qualifying campaign, during which the 2010 final tournament participants lost three of their opening four matches. His replacement was none other than Katanec, the man who had led the country to the finals of UEFA EURO 2000 and the 2002 World Cup.

There was no fanfare start for the returning hero as a friendly against Bosnia & Herzegovina and a qualifier against Iceland, both in Ljubljana, ended in defeat, but two good results in the early summer, notably a revenge 4-2 win over Iceland in Reykjavik, offered the promise of better times to come.

Domestic league: Prva Liga 2012/13 final table

		Pld	Home					Away					Total					Pts
			W	D	L	F	A	W	D	L	F	A	W	D	L	F	A	
1	**NK Maribor**	36	14	2	2	42	14	10	4	4	38	21	24	6	6	80	35	78
2	NK Olimpija Ljubljana	36	10	5	3	39	20	11	2	5	34	15	21	7	8	73	35	70
3	NK Domžale	36	5	6	7	19	21	12	3	3	23	13	17	9	10	42	34	60
4	FC Koper	36	9	5	4	31	15	5	8	5	21	27	14	13	9	52	42	55
5	NK Celje	36	5	8	5	20	18	7	5	6	19	21	12	13	11	39	39	49
6	ND Gorica	36	6	6	6	24	26	4	5	9	21	34	10	11	15	45	60	41
7	NK Rudar Velenje	36	9	2	7	22	22	2	5	11	20	37	11	7	18	42	59	40
8	NK Triglav	36	8	5	5	21	17	1	6	11	14	33	9	11	16	35	50	38
9	ND Mura 05	36	6	4	8	27	28	3	2	13	16	38	9	6	21	43	66	33
10	NK Aluminij	36	5	3	10	24	37	2	6	10	12	30	7	9	20	36	67	30

SEASON AT A GLANCE

EUROPEAN QUALIFICATION 2013/14

Champion/Cup winner: NK Maribor (second qualifying round)

NK Olimpija Ljubljana (second qualifying round)
NK Domžale (first qualifying round)
NK Celje (first qualifying round)

Top scorer	Marcos Tavares (Maribor), 17 goals
Relegated clubs	NK Aluminij, ND Mura 05
Promoted clubs	NK Zavrč, NK Krka
Cup final	NK Maribor 1-0 NK Celje

PRVA LIGA TEAM OF THE SEASON
(4-3-3)
Coach: Milanič (Maribor)

PLAYER OF THE SEASON
Agim Ibraimi
(NK Maribor)

The classy midfielder gave a string of eye-catching displays for Maribor and proved a player for the big occasion by scoring the winner in the cup final. He also weighed in with six league goals and encapsulated the team spirit of the double winners. Ibraimi was named 2012 Macedonian player of the year and scored four times for his country during the season.

NEWCOMER OF THE SEASON
Miha Zajc
(NK Olimpija/NK Celje)

Touted as a player of vast potential, the teenager lived up to expectations in 2012/13 and emerged as one of the most prized talents in Slovenia. The attacking midfielder spent the first half of the campaign on loan at Olimpija, scoring twice on his only appearance, before exploding into life back at Celje and playing in the cup final.

NATIONAL TEAM

Home Kit   Away Kit

INTERNATIONAL TOURNAMENT APPEARANCES
FIFA World Cup (2) 2002, 2010
UEFA European Championship (1) 2000

TOP FIVE ALL-TIME CAPS
Zlatko Zahovič (80), Milenko Ačimovič & Aleš Čeh (74); Džoni Novak (71);
Boštjan Cesar (70)

TOP FIVE ALL-TIME GOALS
Zlatko Zahovič (35); **Milivoje Novakovič** (21); Sašo Udovič (16); Ermin Šiljak (14); Milenko Ačimovič (13)

Results 2012/13

Date	Opponent		Venue	Score	Scorers
15/08/12	Romania	H	Ljubljana	4-3	*Cesar (4), Dedič (51p, 60), Kirm (70)*
07/09/12	Switzerland (WCQ)	H	Ljubljana	0-2	
11/09/12	Norway (WCQ)	A	Oslo	1-2	*Šuler (17)*
12/10/12	Cyprus (WCQ)	H	Maribor	2-1	*Matavž (38, 61)*
16/10/12	Albania (WCQ)	A	Tirana	0-1	
14/11/12	FYROM	A	Skopje	2-3	*Pečnik (49, 63)*
06/02/13	Bosnia & Herzegovina	H	Ljubljana	0-3	
22/03/13	Iceland (WCQ)	H	Ljubljana	1-2	*Novakovič (34)*
31/05/13	Turkey	N	Bielefeld (GER)	2-0	*Novakovič (11), Matavž (65)*
07/06/13	Iceland (WCQ)	A	Reykjavik	4-2	*Kirm (11), Birsa (31p), Cesar (61), Krhin (85)*

Appearances 2012/13

Coach:
Slaviša Stojanovič 06/12/69
/(04/01/13) Srečko Katanec 16/07/63

Name	DOB	Club	Rou	SUI	NOR	CYP	ALB	Mkd	Bih	ISL	Tur	ISL	Caps	Goals
Jasmin Handanovič	28/01/78	Maribor	G	G									8	-
Mišo Brečko	01/05/84	Köln (GER)	D	D	D	D	D		D	D	D90	D	60	-
Marko Šuler	09/03/83	Legia (POL)	D90	D	D	D	D	s64	D46				39	3
Boštjan Cesar	09/07/82	Chievo (ITA)	D	D	D	D89*			D	D	D	D	70	6
Andraz Struna	20/04/80	Cracovia (POL)	D						D	s80	s70	c90	5	-
Andraž Kirm	06/09/84	Wisła Kraków (POL) /Groningen (NED)	M88		M	M	M	s46	M		M	M	53	6
Aleksandar Radosavljevič	25/04/79	Den Haag (NED) /VVV (NED)	M	M80		M91	M77			M	s56	s73	39	1
Jasmin Kurtič	10/01/89	Palermo (ITA)	M72	s80	M	M		M46	s46	M	M	M	10	1
Valter Birsa	07/08/86	Genoa (ITA) /Torino (ITA)	M80		M61	M7			M60	M52	M70	M90	61	4
Zlatko Dedič	05/10/84	Bochum (GER)	A72	A55		A68	A59	s80		s79	s83		47	8
Tim Matavž	13/01/89	PSV (NED)	A84	A	A	A	A	A	A72	s65	s58	s87	23	10
Josip Iličič	29/01/88	Palermo (ITA)	s72	s61	M	M84	M73	s75					22	-
Aleš Mertelj	22/03/87	Maribor	s72				M	s66					4	-
Mirnes Šišič	08/08/81	OFI (GRE)	s80				s73						15	2
Etien Velikonja	26/12/88	Cardiff (WAL)	s84										3	-
Armin Bačinovič	24/10/89	Hellas Verona (ITA)	s88	M	M60				s46				13	-
Dominic Maroh	04/03/87	Köln (GER)	s90			s91	D	D64					4	-
Bojan Jokič	17/05/86	Chievo (ITA)		D	D	D	D	D	M86	D	D	D	63	1
Zlatan Ljubijankič	15/12/83	Omiya Ardija (JPN)		s55	A91					A65			38	6
Jan Oblak	07/01/93	Rio Ave (POR)			G						G		2	-
Nejc Pečnik	03/01/86	Sheffield Wed (ENG)			s7		s46						17	4
Darijan Matič	28/05/83	Kryvbas (UKR)			s60								10	-
Dejan Kelhar	05/04/84	Qäbälä (AZE)			s91		D						4	-
Samir Handanovič	14/07/84	Internazionale (ITA)				G	G	G	G	G		G	63	-
Kevin Kampl	09/10/90	Salzburg (AUT)				s68	s77	M46			M83	M73	5	-
Goran Cvijanovič	09/09/86	Maribor				s84	M80		M46				3	-
Džengis Čavuševič	26/11/87	St Gallen (SUI)					s59						1	-
Rene Krhin	21/05/90	Bologna (ITA)						M66	M46	M79	M56	M	12	1
Robert Berič	17/06/91	Maribor						A75	s72				2	-
Branko Ilič	06/02/83	Anorthosis (CYP)							D	D	D	D	46	-
Aleksander Rajčevič	17/11/86	Maribor							s46				1	-
Dejan Lazarevič	15/02/90	Modena (ITA)							s60	s52	s90		4	-
Milivoje Novakovič	18/05/79	Omiya Ardija (JPN)							A	A58	A87		57	21

European club competitions 2012/13

NK MARIBOR

Second qualifying round - FK Željezničar (BIH)
H 4-1 *Berič (47, 76), Mezga (67p), Marcos Tavares (90+2)*
Handanovič, Mejač, Mezga (Lesjak 81), Marcos Tavares, Ibraimi, Cvijanovič, Trajkovski, Rajčevič, Berič (Velikonja 90+4), Arghus, Mertelj (Filipovič 72). Coach: Darko Milanič (SVN)
A 2-1 *Ibraimi (20), Marcos Tavares (86)*
Handanovič, Filipovič, Mejač, Marcos Tavares, Ibraimi (Mezga 45+3), Cvijanovič, Potokar (Trajkovski 78), Rajčevič, Berič, Arghus, Mertelj (Lesjak 87). Coach: Darko Milanič (SVN)

Third qualifying round - F91 Dudelange (LUX)
H 4-1 *Mezga (13, 47), Marcos Tavares (38), Berič (77)*
Handanovič, Mejač (Potokar 58), Mezga, Marcos Tavares, Ibraimi (Filipovič 67), Cvijanovič, Trajkovski, Rajčevič, Berič (Komazec 85), Arghus, Mertelj. Coach: Darko Milanič (SVN)
A 1-0 *Mertelj (79)*
Handanovič, Filipovič, Mejač, Mezga, Marcos Tavares, Cvijanovič (Ibraimi 67), Potokar, Rajčevič, Berič (Komazec 78), Arghus, Mertelj (Dodlek 89). Coach: Darko Milanič (SVN)

Play-offs - GNK Dinamo Zagreb (CRO)
A 1-2 *Badelj (39og)*
Handanovič, Filipovič, Mejač, Marcos Tavares, Ibraimi (Mezga 78), Cvijanovič, Potokar, Rajčevič, Berič (Komazec 82), Arghus, Mertelj. Coach: Darko Milanič (SVN)
H 0-1
Handanovič, Filipovič (Mezga 46), Milec, Mejač, Marcos Tavares, Ibraimi (Komazec 70), Cvijanovič, Rajčevič, Berič, Arghus, Mertelj. Coach: Darko Milanič (SVN)
Red card: Arghus 84

Group J
Match 1 - Panathinaikos FC (GRE)
H 3-0 *Berič (25), Ibraimi (62), Marcos Tavares (88p)*
Handanovič, Milec, Mejač, Mezga (Dodlek 85), Marcos Tavares (Filipovič 90+1), Ibraimi, Cvijanovič, Potokar (Vidovič 81), Rajčevič, Berič, Mertelj. Coach: Darko Milanič (SVN)
Match 2 - S.S. Lazio (ITA)
A 0-1
Handanovič, Vidovič, Filipovič, Milec, Mejač, Marcos Tavares (Mezga 61), Ibraimi, Cvijanovič (Komazec 86), Rajčevič, Berič, Mertelj. Coach: Darko Milanič (SVN)
Red card: Vidovič 76
Match 3 - Tottenham Hotspur FC (ENG)
H 1-1 *Berič (42)*
Handanovič, Milec, Mejač, Mezga (Filipovič 73), Marcos Tavares (Komazec 89), Ibraimi, Cvijanovič, Rajčevič, Berič, Arghus, Mertelj. Coach: Darko Milanič (SVN)
Match 4 - Tottenham Hotspur FC (ENG)
A 1-3 *Berič (40)*
Handanovič, Filipovič, Milec, Mejač, Marcos Tavares (Komazec 76), Ibraimi, Cvijanovič (Mezga 70), Rajčevič, Berič, Arghus, Mertelj (Dodlek 88). Coach: Darko Milanič (SVN)
Match 5 - Panathinaikos FC (GRE)
A 0-1
Handanovič, Filipovič, Milec (Viler 69), Mejač, Marcos Tavares (Dodlek 77), Ibraimi, Cvijanovič (Potokar 46), Rajčevič, Berič, Arghus, Mertelj. Coach: Darko Milanič (SVN)
Red card: Mejač 45
Match 6 - S.S. Lazio (ITA)
H 1-4 *Marcos Tavares (84)*
Handanovič, Filipovič (Dodlek 56), Mezga (Črnic 80), Marcos Tavares, Ibraimi, Cvijanovič (Arghus 80), Potokar, Trajkovski, Rajčevič, Berič, Mertelj. Coach: Darko Milanič (SVN)

NK OLIMPIJA LJUBLJANA

First qualifying round - AS Jeunesse Esch (LUX)
H 3-0 *Ivelja (53), Franklin (76, 90+3)*
Džafič, Zarifovič, Trifkovič, Škerjanc (Franklin 52), Šporar, Nikezić (Valenčič 84), Ivelja, Delamea Mlinar (Jovič 46), Radujko, Sretenović, Salkič. Coach: Ermin Šiljak (SVN)
A 3-0 *Bešič (25), Sretenović (38), Omladič (66)*
Šeliga, Jovič, Zarifovič, Franklin, Trifkovič, Valenčič (Omladič 64), Bešič (Šporar 75), Radujko (Božič 46), Lovrečič, Sretenović, Salkič. Coach: Ermin Šiljak (SVN)

Second qualifying round - Tromsø IL (NOR)
H 0-0
Džafič, Jovič, Zarifovič, Franklin, Trifkovič, Šporar (Nikezić 81), Omladič (Valenčič 62), Radujko, Lovrečič (Salkič 90), Sretenović, Iñigo Sarasola. Coach: Ermin Šiljak (SVN)
A 0-1 *(aet)*
Džafič, Jovič, Zarifovič, Franklin (Nikezić 105+2), Trifkovič, Škerjanc (Omladič 78), Šporar, Fink, Radujko, Lovrečič, Sretenović. Coach: Ermin Šiljak (SVN)
Red card: Radujko 120+1

ND MURA 05

First qualifying round - Bakı FK (AZE)
A 0-0
Luk, Kramar, Janža, Sreš, Fajić, Bohar, Horvat, Cipot, Jelić (Gruškovnjak 77), Maruško, Eterović. Coach: Franc Cifer (SVN)
H 2-0 *Eterović (26), Fajić (83)*
Drakovič, Cipot, Sreš (Gruškovnjak 80), Bohar, Horvat, Kramar, Janža, Kouter (Botjak 90+2), Jelić (Fajić 50), Eterović, Maruško. Coach: Franc Cifer (SVN)

Second qualifying round - PFC CSKA Sofia (BUL)
H 0-0
Drakovič, Cipot, Majer, Bohar (Kouter 90+4), Horvat, Kramar, Fajić, Janža, Jelić, Eterović (Sreš 54), Maruško. Coach: Franc Cifer (SVN)
Red card: Horvat 37
A 1-1 *Fajić (76)*
Drakovič, Cipot, Sreš (Gruškovnjak 90), Majer, Bohar, Kramar, Fajić, Janža, Jelić, Eterović (Kouter 75), Maruško. Coach: Franc Cifer (SVN)

Third qualifying round - FC Arsenal Kyiv (UKR)
A 3-0 *(w/o; original result 0-3)*
Drakovič, Cipot, Sreš (Vaš 84), Majer, Bohar (Gruškovnjak 90+1), Kramar, Janža, Kouter (Buzeti 62), Jelić, Eterović, Maruško. Coach: Franc Cifer (SVN)
H 0-2
Drakovič, Cipot, Majer, Bohar (Sreš 71), Horvat, Kramar, Fajić, Janža, Jelić (Kouter 90), Eterović (Vaš 66), Maruško. Coach: Franc Cifer (SVN)

Play-offs - S.S. Lazio (ITA)
H 0-2
Drakovič, Bohar (Majer 86), Horvat, Kramar (Sreš 62), Buzeti, Vaš, Travner, Fajić, Janža, Eterović (Kouter 78), Maruško. Coach: Franc Cifer (SVN)
A 1-3 *Travner (88)*
Drakovič, Majer, Bohar (Buzeti 46), Horvat (Kouter 84), Kramar, Vaš (Kozar 88), Travner, Fajić, Janža, Eterović, Maruško. Coach: Oliver Bogatinov (SVN)

NK CELJE

First qualifying round - FC Dacia Chisinau (MDA)
A 0-1
Kotnik, Vrhovec, Krajcer, Bajde (Romih 59), Močič, Bezjak, Kolsi, Mučivnik (Verbič 43), Gobec, Gaber (Centrih 76), Žitko. Coach: Marijan Pušnik (SVN)
H 0-1
Kotnik, Vrhovec, Krajcer, Centrih (Gaber 60), Romih (Verbič 46), Bajde (Močivnik 70), Močič, Bezjak, Kolsi, Gobec, Žitko. Coach: Marijan Pušnik (SVN)

Domestic league club-by-club

NK ALUMINIJ
Coach: Bojan Flis; (11/03/13) Edin Osmanovič
1947 • Športni park Aluminij (2,570) • nkaluminij.net

2012

Date	Opponent		Score	Scorers
22/07	Triglav	a	0-1	
29/07	Domžale	h	0-1	
01/08	Koper	h	0-3	
04/08	Rudar	a	2-1	*Kurež 2*
12/08	Gorica	h	2-1	*Kmetec, Kurež*
19/08	Mura	a	3-1	*Bešič, Kurež, D Hesek*
26/08	Olimpija	h	2-1	*Kurež, Bingo*
01/09	Celje	a	1-2	*Kurež*
15/09	Maribor	h	1-5	*Drevenšek (p)*
22/09	Koper	a	0-0	
26/09	Triglav	h	1-0	*Drevenšek*
30/09	Domžale	a	0-2	
07/10	Rudar	h	3-0	*Bingo, Kurež, Drevenšek (p)*
20/10	Gorica	a	1-4	*Jeleč*
03/11	Olimpija	a	0-0	
07/11	Celje	h	1-2	*Kurež*
11/11	Maribor	a	1-2	*Bingo*
18/11	Koper	h	1-1	*Kurež*
21/11	Mura	h	0-2	
25/11	Triglav	a	0-0	
01/12	Domžale	h	1-4	*Jeleč*

2013

Date	Opponent		Score	Scorers
03/03	Rudar	a	0-3	
10/03	Gorica	h	1-3	*Jeleč*
17/03	Mura	a	1-1	*Žagar*
30/03	Celje	h	0-0	
07/04	Maribor	h	1-2	*Kurež*
13/04	Koper	a	0-3	
17/04	Olimpija	h	2-0	*Kurež, Topolovec*
21/04	Triglav	a	2-2	*Žagar, Drevenšek (p)*
27/04	Domžale	a	1-1	*Bloudek*
05/05	Rudar	h	3-5	*Jovanovič, Bloudek, Črnic*
11/05	Gorica	a	0-2	
14/05	Mura	h	2-2	*Zajc, Kurež*
18/05	Olimpija	a	0-2	
22/05	Celje	h	1-3	*Kurež*
26/05	Maribor	a	2-2	*M Rešek, Kurež*

No	Name	Nat	DoB	Pos	Aps	(s)	Gls
28	Adnan Bešič		28/03/91	A	9	(4)	1
4	Klemen Bingo		23/05/80	D	34		3
10	Sandro Bloudek		16/02/86	M	14		2
32	Blaž Brezovački		29/04/87	M	5		
26	Blaž Cesar		01/07/93	D		(1)	
32	Matic Črnic		12/06/92	M	12	(2)	1
2	Blaž Dolinar		14/10/86	D		(1)	
17	Marko Drevenšek		10/09/87	M	30	(1)	4
2	Emir Hodžurda	BIH	12/11/90	D	9		
31	Jurica Jeleč	CRO	14/11/86	A	9	(6)	3
21	Rade Jovanovič		08/01/91	A	5	(6)	1
20	David Kašnik		16/01/87	D	14		
13	Luka Kirič		23/12/94	A		(1)	
9	Marko Kmetec		03/01/76	A	2	(10)	1
19	Tomaž Kožar		02/06/88	M	15	(5)	
7	Robert Kurež		20/07/91	A	34		14
12	Kristian Lipovac		03/12/89	G	3	(1)	
5	David Lonzarič		20/02/92	D	7	(1)	
18	Aljaž Medved		05/10/87	M	22	(4)	
1	Tomaž Murko		07/02/79	G	33		
14	Dorijan Ožvald	CRO	22/09/87	D	2	(1)	
6	Nejc Pečovnik		06/03/92	M	5	(9)	
8	Timotej Petek		02/05/92	M	3	(5)	
16	Denis Rešek		01/11/90	A	5	(13)	1
30	Mitja Rešek		15/01/91	D	19	(7)	1
10	Gregor Režonja		15/01/81	M	7	(5)	
15	Semir Spahič		26/01/91	M	26	(2)	
27	Almir Sulejmanovič		26/01/78	D	12		
3	Denis Topolovec		11/09/83	D	32		1
24	Marcel Vindiš		05/06/92	M		(1)	
14	Žiga Vraničar		26/11/90	M	4	(4)	
9	Matic Vrbanec		28/10/96	A		(2)	
27	Gorazd Zajc		28/12/87	A	4	(7)	1
11	Tadej Žagar		12/08/91	A	20	(3)	2

NK CELJE

Coach: Marijan Pušnik; (07/01/13) Miloš Rus
1919 • Petrol Arena (13,400) • nkcelje.si
Major honours
Slovenian Cup (1) 2005

2012

15/07	Triglav	h	1-0	Bezjak	
22/07	Domžale	a	1-0	Bezjak	
28/07	Rudar	h	1-1	Bezjak	
04/08	Gorica	a	1-1	Bajde	
12/08	Mura	h	1-0	Vrhovec	
18/08	Olimpija	a	2-2	Bezjak, Bilali	
25/08	Maribor	h	0-2		
01/09	Aluminij	h	2-1	Močič, Ivanović	
16/09	Koper	a	0-1		
23/09	Triglav	a	0-0		
26/09	Domžale	h	0-0		
30/09	Rudar	a	0-1		
06/10	Gorica	h	0-0		
21/10	Mura	a	2-2	Žitko, Gobec	
27/10	Olimpija	h	1-2	Bajde	
03/11	Maribor	a	2-1	Bajde, Krajcer	
07/11	Aluminij	a	2-1	Ivanović, Žurej	
10/11	Koper	h	0-1		
17/11	Triglav	h	1-2	Ivanović	
24/11	Domžale	a	2-1	Bajde, Bilali	
01/12	Rudar	h	1-1	Ivanović	

2013

02/03	Gorica	a	0-0		
09/03	Mura	h	4-0	Verbič 2, Žurej, Gobec	
16/03	Olimpija	a	1-3	Srdić	
30/03	Aluminij	h	0-0		
06/04	Koper	a	1-0	Srdić	
14/04	Triglav	a	0-1		
17/04	Maribor	h	2-1	Žurej, Srdić	
21/04	Domžale	a	0-0		
27/04	Rudar	a	1-0	Bajde	
04/05	Gorica	h	2-3	Tomažič Šeruga, Gobec (p)	
11/05	Mura	a	0-1		
14/05	Olimpija	h	2-2	Gobec 2 (1p)	
18/05	Maribor	a	1-5	Bajić	
22/05	Aluminij	a	3-1	Verbič, Tomažič Šeruga, og (Hodžurda)	
26/05	Koper	h	2-2	Bajić, Gobec	

No	Name	Nat	DoB	Pos	Aps	(s)	Gls
9	Gregor Bajde		29/04/94	A	30	(4)	5
13	Aleksandar Bajić	SRB	25/08/87	A	4	(8)	2
11	Roman Bezjak		21/02/89	A	6	(4)	
25	Lutfi Bilali	MKD	14/04/92	A		(12)	2
11	Stefan Cebara	CRO	12/04/91	A	6	(11)	
6	Matej Centrih		05/09/88	D	13	(1)	
23	Tadej Gaber		22/01/92	D	3	(1)	
18	Sebastjan Gobec		06/12/79	M	28		6
27	Žan Horvat		08/02/92	A		(12)	
28	Nikola Ivanović	SRB	22/03/89	A	7	(8)	4
14	Marko Kolsi	FIN	20/01/85	M	20		
16	Miha Korošec		11/08/91	D	26	(2)	
12	Matic Kotnik		23/07/90	G	36		
5	Marko Krajcer		06/06/85	D	35		1
20	Klemen Medved		10/11/88	M	15	(13)	
10	Marijo Močič		04/05/89	M	9	(1)	1
17	Iztok Močivnik		22/01/92	A	3	(3)	
19	Nejc Plesec		13/03/94	M	14	(8)	
15	Matej Rapnik		24/02/90	D	5		
21	Stefan Ristovski	MKD	21/12/92	D		(1)	
8	Alen Romih		16/06/90	M		(4)	
14	Alexander Srdić	SRB	30/05/92	A	9	(3)	3
26	David Tomažič Šeruga		30/04/86	M	22	(2)	2
7	Benjamin Verbič		27/11/93	A	22	(4)	3
30	Tadej Vidmajer		10/03/92	D	8		
4	Blaž Vrhovec		20/02/92	M	26	(1)	1
28	Miha Zajc		01/07/94	M	12		
24	Matic Žitko		21/02/90	D	26		1
29	Andraž Žurej		17/05/93	A	11	(5)	3

NK DOMŽALE

Coach: Stevan Mojsilović (SRB)
1921 • Športni park (3,212) • nkdomzale.si
Major honours
Slovenian League (2) 2007, 2008;
Slovenian Cup (1) 2011

2012

15/07	Olimpija	a	2-1	Živec 2	
22/07	Celje	h	0-1		
29/07	Aluminij	a	1-0	Balkovec	
04/08	Koper	a	0-1		
12/08	Triglav	a	1-0	Požeg Vancaš	
18/08	Maribor	h	1-2	Knezović	
25/08	Rudar	h	2-0	Majer, Osmanaj	
01/09	Gorica	a	2-1	Požeg Vancaš, Papež	
16/09	Mura	h	0-2		
23/09	Olimpija	h	0-2		
26/09	Celje	a	0-0		
30/09	Aluminij	h	2-0	Kovjenič, Balkovec	
06/10	Koper	a	2-1	Halilovič, Husmani	
20/10	Triglav	h	2-1	Požeg Vancaš 2	
03/11	Rudar	a	0-1		
07/11	Gorica	h	0-1		
11/11	Mura	a	2-1	G Vuk, S Vuk	
17/11	Olimpija	a	2-1	S Vuk, Požeg Vancaš	
24/11	Celje	h	1-2	Korun	
28/11	Maribor	h	2-2	Ihbeisheh 2	
01/12	Aluminij	a	4-1	Simunovic, Kous, og (Bešić), Dobrovoljc	

2013

03/03	Koper	h	1-1	Zec	
16/03	Maribor	a	3-1	S Vuk 2, Balkovec	
30/03	Gorica	a	1-0	Kous	
06/04	Mura	h	1-1	Zec	
13/04	Olimpija	h	0-4		
17/04	Rudar	h	2-0	Dobrovoljc, S Vuk	
21/04	Celje	a	0-0		
24/04	Triglav	a	0-0		
27/04	Aluminij	h	1-1	Cadikovski	
08/05	Koper	a	0-3		
11/05	Triglav	h	1-1	og (Zolič)	
14/05	Maribor	h	1-1	G Vuk	
18/05	Rudar	a	1-0	Cadikovski	
22/05	Gorica	h	3-0	G Vuk 3	
26/05	Mura	a	1-0	Halilovič	

No	Name	Nat	DoB	Pos	Aps	(s)	Gls
22	Vjekoslav Andrič		05/08/92	G		(1)	
29	Jure Balkovec		09/09/94	D	20	(2)	3
21	Michel Balokog	CMR	10/09/86	M	8	(6)	
8	Dragan Cadikovski	MKD	13/01/82	A	11	(2)	2
27	Gaber Dobrovoljc		27/01/93	D	15	(2)	2
4	Dejan Gerič		03/05/88	M	4	(1)	
15	Jon Gorenc Stankovič		14/01/96	M	6		
19	Denis Halilovič		02/03/86	D	19	(1)	2
90	Zeni Husmani	CRO	28/11/90	M	17	(7)	1
23	Jaka Ihbeisheh		29/08/86	M	6	(2)	2
64	Erik Janža		21/06/93	D	11	(1)	
13	Ivan Knezović	CRO	25/09/82	D	18	(4)	1
25	Uroš Korun		25/05/87	D	19	(3)	1
7	Charis Kostakis	GRE	12/07/90	M	1	(4)	
92	Žiga Kous		27/10/92	D	26	(3)	2
17	Marko Kovjenič		02/02/93	M	8	(8)	1
37	Žan Majer		25/07/92	M	18	(3)	1
11	Liridon Osmanaj		04/01/92	A	7	(5)	1
14	Jernej Papež		13/01/94	A	3	(3)	1
14	Aleks Pihler		15/01/94	M	5	(5)	
77	Rudi Požeg Vancaš		15/03/94	M	16	(10)	5
24	Tadej Rems		31/07/93	D	7	(3)	
28	Mato Simunovic	AUT	27/09/85	M	17	(7)	1
2	Nejc Skubič		13/06/89	M	32		
50	Jure Škafar		15/06/90	M	1		
3	Lan Tirc		17/11/94	D		(1)	
3	Darko Topič		01/03/85	D	8		
41	Nejc Vidmar		31/03/89	G	25		
91	Luka Vrhunc		11/03/91	A		(1)	
9	Goran Vuk	CRO	11/10/87	A	18	(10)	5
10	Slobodan Vuk		15/09/89	A	14	(9)	5
39	Gregor Zabret		18/08/95	G	11		
5	Darko Zec		21/02/89	D	17		2
7	Saša Aleksander Živec		02/04/91	A	8	(2)	2

ND GORICA

Coach: Miran Srebrnič
1947 • Športni park (5,000) • nd-gorica.com
Major honours
Slovenian League (4) 1996, 2004, 2005, 2006;
Slovenian Cup (2) 2001, 2002

2012

114/07	Maribor	h	1-3	Žigon	
22/07	Mura	h	3-1	Žigon 3	
29/07	Olimpija	a	3-1	A Jogan, Arčon 2	
04/08	Celje	h	1-1	N'Diaye	
12/08	Aluminij	a	1-2	Žigon	
18/08	Koper	h	2-0	Celcer (p), Žigon	
26/08	Triglav	a	1-2	og (M Poplatnik)	
01/09	Domžale	h	1-2	K Jogan	
15/09	Rudar	a	2-2	Vetrih, Žigon	
23/09	Maribor	a	0-4		
26/09	Mura	a	1-3	N'Diaye	
30/09	Olimpija	h	0-1		
06/10	Celje	a	0-0		
20/10	Aluminij	h	4-1	Praprotnik 2, Kadrija, N'Diaye	
27/10	Koper	a	0-4		
03/11	Triglav	h	2-2	Vetrih, A Jogan	
07/11	Domžale	a	1-0	Bremec	
11/11	Rudar	h	0-4		
17/11	Maribor	h	1-6	Širok	
24/11	Mura	a	2-0	Žigon 2	
01/12	Olimpija	a	2-2	K Jogan, Širok	

2013

02/03	Celje	h	0-0		
10/03	Aluminij	a	3-1	Žigon, Šturm, Mbida	
16/03	Koper	h	1-1	Vetrih	
30/03	Domžale	h	0-1		
06/04	Rudar	a	0-1		
13/04	Maribor	a	1-2	Bremec	
17/04	Triglav	a	0-2		
21/04	Mura	a	1-1	Praprotnik	
27/04	Olimpija	h	1-1	Žigon	
04/05	Celje	a	3-2	Žigon, N'Diaye, Vetrih	
11/05	Aluminij	h	2-0	Žigon, Frelih	
14/05	Koper	a	2-2	Žigon 2	
18/05	Triglav	h	0-0		
22/05	Domžale	a	0-3		
26/05	Rudar	h	3-2	Dornik, Živec 2	

No	Name	Nat	DoB	Pos	Aps	(s)	Gls
11	Sandi Arčon		06/01/91	A	6		2
21	Sandi Bremec		06/10/93	A	7	(20)	2
3	Uroš Celcer		07/04/89	D	33	(2)	1
24	Jan Dornik		04/02/93	M	5	(9)	1
13	Nedim Durić	BIH	24/07/93	M	2	(3)	
6	Boštjan Frelih		10/02/93	M	1	(6)	1
19	Miha Gregorič		22/08/89	M	29		
20	Robi Jakovljević		07/05/93	M	1	(7)	
27	Alen Jogan		24/08/85	D	31	(1)	2
9	Kris Jogan		14/09/91	A	13	(3)	2
2	Taulant Kadrija		18/05/93	D	14	(7)	1
15	Tine Kavčič		16/02/94	M		(1)	
15	Dino Martinovič		20/07/90	M	4		
14	Jean Mbida	CMR	09/04/90	M	16	(3)	1
17	Miha Mevlja		12/06/90	M	30	(3)	
25	Welle N'Diaye	SEN	05/04/90	A	23	(3)	4
8	Alen Pavič		18/03/93	M	3	(16)	
14	Vito Plut		08/07/88	A	3		
29	Aleksandar Popovič		28/08/92	D	2		
16	Nejc Praprotnik		17/01/93	M	15	(8)	3
4	Marko Rojc		05/03/93	M	1	(1)	
12	Vasja Simčič		01/07/83	G	35		
8	Matija Širok		31/05/91	D	34		2
30	Januš Štrukelj		08/04/91	G	1		
7	Jani Šturm		20/03/82	A	12	(1)	1
7	Amedej Vetrih		16/09/90	M	32	(1)	4
10	Dejan Žigon		30/03/89	M	32	(1)	15
11	Saša Aleksander Živec		02/04/91	A	11	(2)	2

FC KOPER

Coach: Milivoj Bračun (CRO);
(04/10/12) Rodolfo Vanoli (ITA)
1955 • Bonifika (10,000) • fckoper.si
Major honours
Slovenian League (1) 2010;
Slovenian Cup (2) 2006, 2007

2012
21/07	Maribor	a	0-0	
28/07	Triglav	h	0-0	
01/08	Aluminij	a	3-0	Pučko, Guberac, Bubalo
04/08	Domžale	a	1-0	Guberac
11/08	Rudar	h	1-0	Mavrič Rožič (p)
18/08	Gorica	a	0-2	
26/08	Mura	h	4-1	Djukić, Brečević 2, Cadikovski
01/09	Olimpija	a	1-4	Popovič
16/09	Celje	h	1-0	Cadikovski
22/09	Aluminij	h	0-0	
26/09	Maribor	h	2-3	Cadikovski, Žibert
30/09	Triglav	a	0-4	
06/10	Domžale	h	1-2	Pučko
20/10	Rudar	a	0-2	
27/10	Gorica	h	4-0	Pučko, Čovilo, Brečević 2
04/11	Mura	a	3-2	Cadikovski 2, Popovič
07/11	Olimpija	h	2-0	Bradaschia, Brečević
10/11	Celje	a	1-0	Djukič
18/11	Aluminij	a	1-1	Pučko
25/11	Maribor	a	0-3	
01/12	Triglav	h	1-1	Brečević

2013
03/03	Domžale	a	1-1	Pučko
10/03	Rudar	h	2-2	Blažič, Brečević
16/03	Gorica	a	1-1	Brečević
30/03	Olimpija	a	2-2	Guberac, Mendy
06/04	Celje	h	0-1	
13/04	Aluminij	a	3-0	Mendy, Bagarić, Brečević
17/04	Mura	h	3-1	Štulac, Galešić 2
20/04	Maribor	h	2-1	Galešić, Čovilo
28/04	Triglav	a	1-0	Guberac
08/05	Domžale	h	3-0	Mavrič Rožič (p), Brečević, Štulac
11/05	Rudar	a	4-1	Čovilo, Mendy, Pučko, Guberac
14/05	Gorica	h	2-2	Bradaschia, Bagarić (p)
18/05	Mura	a	0-3	
22/05	Olimpija	h	0-1	
26/05	Celje	a	2-2	Pučko, Bagarić (p)

No	Name	Nat	DoB	Pos	Aps	(s)	Gls
25	Davor Bagarić	CRO	08/09/85	D	13		3
5	Miha Blažič		08/05/93	D	20	(2)	1
17	Daniel Bradaschia	ITA	02/03/89	A	15	(4)	2
9	Ivan Brečević	CRO	28/07/87	A	17	(11)	10
77	Milan Bubalo	SRB	08/05/90	M	10	(1)	1
99	Dragan Cadikovski	MKD	13/01/82	A	8	(3)	5
33	Miroslav Čovilo	SRB	06/05/86	M	24		3
20	Domen Črnigoj		18/11/95	M	17	(4)	
28	Bojan Djukić		06/11/86	D	23		2
14	Romeo Filipovic	GER	31/03/86	M	6	(2)	
13	Goran Galešić	BIH	11/03/89	M	13		3
7	Ivica Guberac		05/07/88	M	30		5
27	Damir Hadžić		01/10/84	D	27	(1)	
1	Ermin Hasič		19/05/75	G	14		
8	Mitja Lotrič		03/09/94	A		(8)	
11	Luka Majcen		25/07/89	A	6	(16)	
24	Matej Mavrič Rožič		29/01/79	D	28	(1)	2
14	Jean-Philippe Mendy	FRA	04/03/87	A	6	(7)	3
4	Andrea Migliorini	ITA	22/03/88	M	2	(3)	
21	Igor Nenezić		23/03/84	G	22		
29	Matej Palčič		21/06/93	A	24	(1)	
23	Denis Perger		10/06/93	D	12	(5)	
10	Denis Popovič		15/10/89	M	15	(7)	2
49	Matej Pučko		06/10/93	A	24	(11)	7
19	Žiga Smrtnik		01/02/94	A		(3)	
18	Leo Štulac		26/09/94	M	8	(2)	2
22	Tom	BRA	21/06/88	M	3	(5)	
3	Urban Žibert		08/05/92	M	9	(6)	1

NK MARIBOR

Coach: Darko Milanič
1960 • Ljudski vrt (12,432) • nkmaribor.com
Major honours
Slovenian League (11) 1997, 1998, 1999, 2000, 2001, 2002, 2003, 2009, 2011, 2012, 2013;
Slovenian Cup (8) 1992, 1994, 1997, 1999, 2004, 2010, 2012, 2013

2012
14/07	Gorica	a	3-1	Mezga 2, og (Vetrih)
21/07	Koper	h	0-0	
29/07	Mura	a	3-1	Vidovič, Ploj, Komazec
04/08	Triglav	h	1-0	Marcos Tavares (p)
11/08	Olimpija	a	0-0	
18/08	Domžale	h	2-1	Marcos Tavares 2
25/08	Celje	a	2-0	Ploj, Črnic
01/09	Rudar	h	4-0	Berič, Cvijanovič, Marcos Tavares, Ploj
15/09	Aluminij	a	5-1	Rajčević, Berič, Cvijanovič 2, Ploj
23/09	Gorica	h	4-0	Ploj, Berič 2, Vidovič
26/09	Koper	a	3-2	Cvijanovič, Mejač, Marcos Tavares
30/09	Mura	h	1-0	Cvijanovič
07/10	Triglav	a	0-1	
20/10	Olimpija	h	1-0	Marcos Tavares
03/11	Celje	h	1-2	Mezga (p)
11/11	Aluminij	h	2-1	Ploj, Komazec
17/11	Gorica	a	6-1	Cvijanovič, Ibraimi 2, Marcos Tavares 3
25/11	Koper	h	3-0	Ibraimi 2, Komazec
28/11	Domžale	a	2-2	Berič, Marcos Tavares
02/12	Mura	a	2-1	Mezga, Cvijanovič

2013
02/03	Triglav	h	4-1	Berič, Cvijanovič, Marcos Tavares, Milec
10/03	Olimpija	a	1-1	Fajić
13/03	Rudar	a	3-0	Fajić, Berič, og (Bubalovic)
16/03	Domžale	h	1-3	Fajić
30/03	Rudar	h	3-1	Mezga, Marcos Tavares, Berič
07/04	Aluminij	a	2-1	Fajić, Cvijanovič
13/04	Gorica	h	2-1	Milec, Arghus
17/04	Celje	a	1-2	Berič
20/04	Koper	a	1-2	Marcos Tavares
27/04	Mura	h	4-0	Ibraimi 2, Cvijanovič, Berič
05/05	Triglav	a	2-2	Mezga, Berič
11/05	Olimpija	h	2-1	Cvijanovič, Berič
14/05	Domžale	a	1-1	Mertelj
18/05	Celje	h	5-1	Mezga, Marcos Tavares 3, Cvijanovič
22/05	Rudar	a	1-3	og (Dedič)
26/05	Aluminij	h	2-2	Berič, Marcos Tavares

No	Name	Nat	DoB	Pos	Aps	(s)	Gls
44	Arghus	BRA	19/01/88	D	12	(2)	1
32	Robert Berič		17/06/91	A	24	(8)	13
20	Goran Cvijanovič		09/09/86	M	26	(6)	12
92	Matic Črnic		12/06/92	M	6	(6)	1
29	Timotej Dodlek		23/11/89	M	11	(8)	
5	Nusmir Fajić	BIH	12/01/87	A	6	(2)	4
5	Željko Filipovič		03/10/88	M	16	(10)	
23	Jasmin Handanovič		28/01/78	G	33		
23	Dino Hotič		26/07/95	M	2	(1)	
10	Agim Ibraimi	MKD	29/08/88	A	23	(2)	6
31	Nikola Komazec	SRB	15/11/87	A	8	(5)	3
31	Zoran Lesjak	CRO	01/02/88	M	5	(1)	
7	Marcos Tavares	BRA	30/03/84	A	21	(8)	17
7	Aleš Mejač		18/03/83	M	16	(2)	1
70	Aleš Mertelj		22/03/87	M	22	(5)	1
45	Nejc Mevlja		12/06/90	M	8	(3)	
8	Dejan Mezga	CRO	16/07/85	M	27	(1)	7
9	Martin Milec		20/09/91	M	23	(2)	2
25	Ranko Moravac	SRB	25/01/95	M	3	(1)	
27	Alen Ploj		30/06/92	A	7	(7)	6
22	Nejc Potokar		02/12/88	D	21	(2)	
12	Marko Pridigar		18/05/85	G	3		
26	Aleksander Rajčević		17/11/86	D	23		1
55	Rajko Rep		20/06/90	M	3	(1)	
35	Mitja Rešek		15/01/91	D	1		
57	Matija Smrekar	CRO	08/04/89	A	6	(4)	
30	Petar Stojanović		07/10/95	M		(2)	
14	Bian Paul Šauperl		15/04/95	A		(1)	
7	Dejan Trajkovski		14/04/92	D	10	(1)	
11	Etien Velikonja		26/12/88	A	1	(1)	1
4	Jovan Vidovič		01/09/86	D	20	(1)	
28	Mitja Viler		01/09/86	D	9	(1)	
11	Luka Zahovič		15/11/95	A		(1)	

ND MURA 05

Coach: (Franc Cifer); (22/08/12) Oliver Bogatinov;
(04/02/13) Ante Šimundža
2005 • Fazanerija (3,716) • mura05.si

2012
15/07	Rudar	h	1-1	Eterović
22/07	Gorica	a	1-3	Fajić
29/07	Maribor	h	1-3	Fajić
05/08	Olimpija	h	1-2	Fajić
12/08	Celje	a	0-1	
19/08	Aluminij	h	1-3	Eterović
26/08	Koper	a	1-4	Bohar
02/09	Triglav	h	2-1	Fajić, Bohar
16/09	Domžale	a	2-0	Bohar, Eterović
22/09	Rudar	a	1-2	Cipot
26/09	Gorica	h	3-1	Fajić, Kramar, Jelić
30/09	Maribor	a	0-1	
06/10	Olimpija	a	1-3	Jelić
21/10	Celje	h	2-2	Bohar, Jelić
04/11	Koper	h	2-3	Bohar, Matusiwa
07/11	Triglav	a	1-3	Aborah
11/11	Domžale	h	1-1	Eterović
18/11	Rudar	h	4-0	Eterović 2 (1p), Travner, Bohar
21/11	Aluminij	a	2-0	Eterović, Jelić
24/11	Gorica	a	0-2	
02/12	Maribor	h	1-2	Bohar

2013
09/03	Celje	a	0-4	
13/03	Olimpija	h	0-4	
17/03	Aluminij	h	1-1	Sačer
30/03	Triglav	h	2-1	Kurbus, Sačer
06/04	Domžale	a	1-1	Vinko
13/04	Rudar	a	0-3	
17/04	Koper	a	1-3	Šimić
21/04	Gorica	h	1-1	Ploj
27/04	Maribor	a	0-4	
04/05	Olimpija	a	1-2	Vaš
11/05	Celje	h	1-0	Bohar
14/05	Aluminij	a	2-2	Rep, Vinko
18/05	Koper	h	3-0	Vinko, Majer, Maruško
22/05	Triglav	a	2-0	Maruško, Bohar
26/05	Domžale	h	0-1	

No	Name	Nat	DoB	Pos	Aps	(s)	Gls
26	Stanley Aborah	BEL	23/06/87	M	12		1
42	Darko Atanasov	MKD	05/09/90	D	3	(1)	
24	Denis Barbič		14/03/93	D	8	(2)	
2	Emmanuel Boakye	GHA	25/03/85	D	1		
9	Damjan Bohar		18/10/91	M	31	(2)	9
14	Rok Buzeti		10/02/88	M	14	(2)	
5	Fabijan Cipot		25/08/76	D	15		1
1	Filip Drakovič		31/03/91	G	32		
32	Mate Eterović	CRO	13/07/84	A	18	(2)	7
17	Nusmir Fajić	BIH	12/01/87	A	10	(5)	5
23	Rok Gruškovnjak		05/02/92	D		(4)	
11	Leon Horvat		29/08/86	M	12	(5)	
18	Erik Janža		21/06/93	D	20		
25	Dragan Jelić		27/02/86	A	14	(5)	4
21	Nino Kouter		19/12/93	D	4	(3)	
7	Alen Kozar		07/04/95	M	1	(1)	
13	Denis Kramar		07/11/91	D	14	(2)	1
33	Denis Kurbus		16/01/93	D	12	(3)	1
8	Aleš Majer		02/08/89	D	23	(3)	1
13	Amadej Maroša		07/02/94	M		(2)	
90	Matic Maruško		30/11/90	M	29	(4)	2
31	Diangi Matusiwa	ANG	21/12/85	A	2	(5)	1
92	Josip Mlinarič	CRO	21/12/92	M	4	(3)	
20	Mitja Mörec		21/02/83	D	14	(2)	
27	Alen Ploj		30/06/92	A	10	(5)	1
14	Kevin Poredoš		16/03/95	A		(2)	
10	Rajko Rep		20/06/90	M	11		1
77	Matic Sačer	CRO	17/11/90	A	13	(7)	2
6	Leon Sreš		27/04/92	M	3	(6)	
22	Jaka Šafer		15/09/94	G	4		
17	Marko Šimić	CRO	23/01/88	A	6	(1)	1
16	Jure Travner		09/09/85	D	27	(1)	1
15	Arpad Vaš		31/07/89	M	22	(8)	1
19	Vedran Vinko		22/02/90	A	7	(8)	3

NK OLIMPIJA LJUBLJANA

Coach: Ermin Šiljak; (27/08/12) Andrej Razdrh
2005 • Stožice (16,038) • nkolimpija.si

2012

15/07	Domžale	h	1-2	Franklin
22/07	Rudar	a	5-0	Šporar, Škerjanc, Lovrečič, Franklin, Jovič (p)
29/07	Gorica	h	1-3	Božič
05/08	Mura	a	2-1	Trifkovič 2
11/08	Maribor	h	0-0	
18/08	Celje	h	2-2	Delamea Mlinar, Jovič (p)
26/08	Aluminij	a	1-2	Valenčič
01/09	Koper	h	4-1	Jovič 2 (1p), Šporar, Nikezić
16/09	Triglav	a	3-0	Zarifovič, Trifkovič, Nikezić
23/09	Domžale	a	2-0	Nikezić, Omladič
26/09	Rudar	h	2-1	Nikezić (p), Omladič
30/09	Gorica	a	1-0	Franklin
06/10	Mura	h	3-1	Omladič, Zajc 2
20/10	Maribor	a	0-1	
27/10	Celje	a	2-1	Šporar 2
03/11	Aluminij	h	3-0	Šporar, Božič, Zorc
07/11	Koper	a	0-2	
10/11	Triglav	h	5-1	Zorc, Nikezić 2 (1p), Lovrečič, Valenčič
17/11	Domžale	h	1-2	Šporar
25/11	Rudar	a	1-0	Šporar
01/12	Gorica	h	2-2	Valenčič, Zarifovič

2013

10/03	Maribor	h	1-1	Nikezić
13/03	Mura	a	4-0	Nikezić, Valenčič, Omladič, Fink
16/03	Celje	h	3-1	og (Centrih), Nikezić, Baskera
30/03	Koper	h	2-2	Omladič, Fink
07/04	Triglav	a	4-1	Lovrečič 2, Nikezić 2
13/04	Domžale	a	4-0	og (Skubič), Omladič, Nikezić 2
17/04	Aluminij	a	0-2	
20/04	Rudar	h	1-0	Nikezić
27/04	Gorica	a	1-1	Nikezić (p)
04/05	Mura	h	2-1	Omladič, Valenčič
11/05	Maribor	a	1-2	Lovrečič
14/05	Celje	a	2-2	Šporar 2
18/05	Aluminij	h	2-0	Mitrovič, Zorc
22/05	Koper	a	1-0	Kapun
26/05	Triglav	h	4-0	Valenčič, Franklin, Šporar 2 (2p)

No	Name	Nat	DoB	Pos	Aps	(s)	Gls
24	Kenan Bajrič		20/12/94	D	1	(1)	
29	Rok Baskera		26/05/93	M	8	(14)	1
15	Adnan Bešič		28/03/91	A	2	(4)	
16	Blaž Božič		23/10/90	M	17	(4)	2
20	Antonio Delamea Mlinar		10/06/91	D	28		1
30	Elvis Džafič		19/12/90	G	18	(1)	
17	Matic Fink		27/02/90	M	18	(3)	2
7	Franklin	BRA	12/06/89	A	15	(12)	4
4	Dejan Gerič		03/05/88	M	2	(5)	
31	Iñigo Sarasola	ESP	10/06/87	D	7	(2)	
19	Djordje Ivelja	SRB	30/06/84	M	11	(2)	
5	Boban Jovič		25/06/91	D	27		4
23	Nik Kapun		09/01/94	M	4	(5)	1
3	Mitja Kovačevič		12/04/91	D	4	(2)	
25	Anej Lovrečič		10/05/87	M	26		5
32	Nemanja Mitrovič		15/10/92	D	7	(1)	1
18	Nikola Nikezić	MNE	13/06/81	A	26	(2)	15
27	Marko Nunič		16/03/93	A		(1)	
21	Nik Omladič		21/08/89	M	33	(1)	7
23	Dalibor Radujko		17/06/85	M			
33	Erik Salkič		10/04/87	D	17	(3)	
26	Sreten Sretenović	SRB	12/01/85	D	5		
1	Aleksander Šeliga		01/02/80	G	18		
9	Davor Škerjanc		07/01/86	A	1	(5)	1
10	Andraž Šporar		27/02/94	A	22	(6)	11
26	Aleksander Topič		11/02/93	M		(2)	
8	Damjan Trifkovič		22/07/87	M	30		3
11	Filip Valenčič		07/01/92	A	11	(13)	6
4	Miha Zajc		01/07/94	M	1		1
6	Aris Zarifovič		02/06/88	D	30	(1)	2
14	Anže Zorc		06/02/94	M	4	(8)	3

NK RUDAR VELENJE

Coach: Milan Djuričić (CRO);
(12/08/12) (Andrej Goršek); (14/09/12) Aleš Čeh;
(07/01/13) Jernej Javornik
1948 • Ob Jezeru (7,000) • nkrudar.com
Major honours
Slovenian Cup (1) 1998

2012

15/07	Mura	a	1-1	Podlogar
22/07	Olimpija	h	0-5	
28/07	Celje	a	1-1	Rošer (p)
04/08	Aluminij	h	1-2	Bubalovic
11/08	Koper	a	0-1	
18/08	Triglav	h	1-0	Rošer (p)
25/08	Domžale	a	0-2	
01/09	Maribor	a	0-4	
15/09	Gorica	h	2-2	Podlogar, Bratanovič
22/09	Mura	h	2-1	Bratanovič 2
26/09	Olimpija	a	1-2	Rošer
30/09	Celje	h	1-0	Črnčič
07/10	Aluminij	a	0-3	
20/10	Koper	h	0-0	
03/11	Domžale	h	1-0	Klinar
11/11	Gorica	a	4-0	Radujko, Berko, Bratanovič, Čonka
18/11	Mura	a	0-4	
21/11	Triglav	a	2-2	Rošer, Črnčič
25/11	Olimpija	h	0-1	
01/12	Celje	a	1-1	Bratanovič

2013

03/03	Aluminij	h	3-0	Eterović 2, Firer
10/03	Koper	a	2-2	Firer, Eterović (p)
13/03	Maribor	h	0-3	
17/03	Triglav	h	3-1	Bratanovič 2, Bubalovic
30/03	Maribor	a	1-3	Podlogar
06/04	Gorica	a	1-0	Eterović
13/04	Mura	h	3-0	Kašnik, Eterović, Podlogar
17/04	Domžale	a	0-2	
20/04	Olimpija	a	0-1	
27/04	Celje	a	0-1	
05/05	Aluminij	a	5-3	Eterović, Bratanovič 2, Radujko, Podlogar
11/05	Koper	h	1-4	Firer
14/05	Triglav	a	0-2	
18/05	Domžale	h	0-1	
22/05	Maribor	h	3-1	Kašnik, Firer, Eterović
26/05	Gorica	a	2-3	Rotman, Bratanovič

No	Name	Nat	DoB	Pos	Aps	(s)	Gls
24	Saša Bakarič		18/03/87	M	7	(7)	
16	Sebastjan Berko		20/06/84	D	21	(2)	1
29	Jaka Bizjak		09/04/91	M	4	(6)	
25	Klemen Bolha		19/03/93	M		(3)	
21	Elvis Bratanovič		21/08/92	M	27	(3)	10
2	Christian Bubalovic	AUT	09/08/91	D	28	(1)	2
10	Branislav Čonka	SRB	28/01/89	A	4	(5)	1
10	Leon Črnčič		02/03/90	M	19	(14)	2
27	Rusmin Dedič		11/09/82	D	7		
32	Mate Eterović	CRO	13/07/84	A	16		7
7	Ivan Firer		19/11/84	A	23	(8)	4
19	Senad Jahič		13/05/87	D	27	(2)	
4	Aleš Jeseničnik		28/06/84	D	25		
20	David Kašnik		16/01/87	D	13		2
23	Denis Klinar		21/02/92	M	22	(7)	1
20	Aljaž Krefl		20/02/94	M	3	(3)	
18	Almedin Muharemovič		22/04/92	M		(1)	
1	Alen Pašagić		16/06/89	G	6	(1)	
17	Matej Podlogar		23/02/91	A	17	(15)	5
28	Dalibor Radujko		17/06/85	M	27		2
28	Uroš Rošer		27/06/86	M	19	(5)	4
15	Rajko Rotman		19/03/89	M	29	(4)	1
22	Matjaž Rozman		03/01/87	G	30		
4	Dragoslav Stakić	BIH	20/09/85	D	12	(4)	
5	Nemanja Stjepanović	BIH	07/02/84	M	8	(7)	
11	Lovro Šindik	CRO	12/01/92	M	2	(3)	

NK TRIGLAV

Coach: Siniša Brkič
2000 • Stanko Mlakar (5,000) • nktriglav.com

2012

15/07	Celje	a	0-1	
22/07	Aluminij	h	1-0	M Poplatnik
28/07	Koper	a	0-0	
04/08	Maribor	a	0-1	
12/08	Domžale	h	0-1	
18/08	Rudar	a	0-1	
26/08	Gorica	h	2-1	Djurkovič, Šujica
02/09	Mura	a	1-2	Jelar
16/09	Olimpija	h	0-3	
23/09	Celje	h	0-0	
26/09	Aluminij	a	0-1	
30/09	Koper	h	4-0	M Poplatnik, Djurkovič 2 (1p), Zolič
07/10	Maribor	h	1-0	M Poplatnik
20/10	Domžale	a	1-2	Djurkovič
03/11	Gorica	a	2-2	Djurkovič 2
07/11	Mura	h	3-1	A Poplatnik, M Poplatnik, Bubanja
10/11	Olimpija	a	1-5	Djurkovič
17/11	Celje	a	2-1	Djurkovič 2
21/11	Rudar	h	2-2	Djurkovič, Bubanja
25/11	Aluminij	h	0-0	
01/12	Koper	a	1-1	Jelar

2013

02/03	Maribor	a	1-4	Djurkovič
17/03	Rudar	a	1-3	Bubanja
30/03	Mura	a	1-2	Bubanja
07/04	Olimpija	h	1-4	Bubanja (p)
14/04	Celje	a	1-0	Diallo
17/04	Gorica	h	2-0	Djurkovič, A Poplatnik
21/04	Aluminij	a	2-2	Diallo, Djurkovič
24/04	Domžale	a	0-0	
28/04	Koper	h	1-1	Stojnič
04/05	Maribor	a	1-2	M Poplatnik
11/05	Domžale	a	1-1	Šmit
14/05	Rudar	h	2-0	Jelar, Djurkovič
18/05	Gorica	a	0-0	
22/05	Mura	h	0-2	
26/05	Olimpija	a	0-4	

No	Name	Nat	DoB	Pos	Aps	(s)	Gls
13	Rok Brajič		13/01/85	D	3	(4)	
33	Davor Bubanja		26/09/87	A	20	(2)	5
27	Igor Bukara		02/12/95	M		(5)	
1	Darjan Curanovič		05/04/86	G	9	(1)	
5	Lamin Diallo		31/08/91	D	6	(1)	2
14	Bojan Djuric		08/05/89	M		(4)	
9	Enis Djurkovič		24/05/89	M	26	(1)	14
11	Rok Dolžan		21/09/85	M	12	(4)	
8	Anže Jelar		18/08/91	A	31	(3)	3
32	Tim Kern		23/03/93	M		(1)	
6	Tilen Klemenčič		28/08/95	D	23	(2)	
7	Dinnyuy Kongnyuy	CMR	24/01/88	M	16	(6)	
11	Alen Krcič		19/11/88	M	12		
30	Jasmin Nazič		18/01/92	M	1	(1)	
4	Dragan Ovčina		13/05/82	M	8	(11)	
28	Žan Pelko		28/09/90	G	27		
29	Matej Peternel		22/08/92	M	2	(2)	
21	Matej Pirc		18/05/91	M		(1)	
3	Jalen Pokorn		07/06/79	M	30		
19	Aleš Poplatnik		25/06/87	A	11	(7)	2
15	Matej Poplatnik		15/07/92	A	23	(11)	5
18	Ajdin Redžič		05/12/89	A	1		
5	Marko Roškar		21/10/92	D	18		
7	Matic Sever		04/01/90	M	11	(7)	
2	Petar Stojnič		29/09/81	D	30		1
20	Vlado Šmit	SRB	06/04/80	M	12	(1)	1
3	Klemen Šturm		27/06/94	D	29	(1)	
26	Blaž Šujica		05/08/93	A	1	(15)	1
26	Martin Šušteršič		30/11/92	M	8	(4)	
26	Aleksander Topič		11/02/93	M		(1)	
16	Gašper Udovič		22/05/95	A		(1)	
4	Edvin Zolič		06/11/88	D	26		1

Top goalscorers

17	Marcos Tavares (Maribor)
15	Dejan Žigon (Gorica)
	Nikola Mikezić (Olimpija)
14	Robert Kurež (Aluminij)
	Mate Eterović (Mura/Rudar)
	Enis Djurković (Triglav)
13	Robert Berić (Maribor)
12	Goran Cvijanović (Maribor)
11	Andraž Šporar (Olimpija)
10	Ivan Brečević (Koper)
	Elvis Bratanović (Rudar)

Promoted clubs

NK ZAVRČ

Coach: Miran Emeršič; (26/09/12) Zlatko Onbari
(02/01/13) Viktor Trenevski (MKD)
1998 • Športni park (300) • nkzavrc.si

NK KRKA

Coach: Borivoje Lučić
1922 • Portoval (1,500) • nkkrka.com

SECOND LEVEL FINAL TABLE 2012/13

		Pld	W	D	L	F	A	Pts
1	NK Zavrč	27	20	4	3	69	25	64
2	NK Dob	27	18	3	6	63	27	57
3	NK Krka	27	16	5	6	63	24	53
4	NK Krško	27	10	7	10	39	41	37
5	NK Radomlje	27	9	7	11	38	42	34
6	NK Šenčur	27	8	8	11	37	46	32
7	NK Šampion Celje	27	10	2	15	32	50	32
8	NK Šmartno 1928	27	9	3	15	31	51	30
9	NK Bela Krajina	27	7	4	16	24	56	25
10	ND Dravinja	27	4	5	18	32	66	17

NB NK Dob denied licence for 2013/14 Prva Liga;
NK Krka promoted instead.

Domestic cup: Pokal NZS 2012/13

FIRST ROUND

(21/08/12)
Jesenice 0-3 Zavrč *(w/o)*
Šalovci 1-6 Gorica

(22/08/12)
Brda 1-1 Šenčur *(aet; 8-7 on pens)*
Cerknica 0-3 Triglav
Kamnik 1-3 Dravinja
Koroška Dravograd 1-3 Rudar
Odranci 3-2 Bela Krajina
Pesnica 1-2 Domžale
Šmarje pri Jelšah 2-4 Aluminij
Tromejnik 0-2 Koper
Turnišče 0-8 Ankaran Hrvatini

Byes – Celje, Maribor, Mura, Olimpija, Tolmin

SECOND ROUND

(19/09/12)
Aluminij 1-1 Rudar *(aet; 5-4 on pens)*
Ankaran Hrvatini 0-3 Koper
Brda 0-3 Celje
Dravinja 2-1 Domžale
Mura 0-3 Olimpija
Odranci 0-2 Triglav *(aet)*
Tolmin 1-4 Gorica *(aet)*

(31/10/12)
Zavrč 0-2 Maribor

QUARTER-FINALS

(24/10/12 & 31/10/12)
Aluminij 1-2 Gorica *(Režonja 52; Žigon 2, Vetrih 44)*
Gorica 0-2 Aluminij *(Jeleč 82, Kurež 89)*
(Aluminij 3-2)

Triglav 0-1 Koper *(Brečević 74)*
Koper 0-2 Triglav *(Zolič 90+3, Jelar 115) (aet)*
(Triglav 2-1)

(24/10/12 & 21/11/12)
Celje 2-0 Dravinja *(Verbič 2, 90+1)*
Dravinja 0-1 Celje *(Medved 48)*
(Celje 3-0)

(27/02/13 & 06/03/13)
Olimpija 1-3 Maribor *(Omladič 61; Mezga 69, 87p, Rajčevič 90)*
Maribor 0-1 Olimpija *(Valenčič 5)*
(Maribor 3-2)

SEMI-FINALS

(01/05/13 & 08/05/13)
Aluminij 1-1 Celje *(Petek 66; Verbič 41)*
Celje 0-0 Aluminij
(1-1; Celje on away goal)

Triglav 2-2 Maribor *(Bubanja 14, Djurković 76; Mezga 8, Marcos Tavares 90)*
Maribor 3-0 Triglav *(Marcos Tavares 50, 73, 77)*
(Maribor 5-2)

FINAL

(29/05/13)
Bonifika, Koper
NK MARIBOR 1 *(Ibraimi 44)*
NK CELJE 0
Referee: Jug
MARIBOR: Handanovič, Potokar, Viler, Arghus, Mertelj, Milec, Mezga, Cvijanović (Filipovič 79), Berič, Ibraimi, Marcos Tavares
CELJE: Kotnik, Korošec, Žitko, Krajcer, Gobec, Zajc, Vrhovec, Bajde (Bajić 76), Srdić (Plesec 61), Verbič, Žurej

Maribor pose with the trophy after their Slovenian Cup win against Celje

SPAIN
Real Federación Española de Fútbol (RFEF)

Address	Ramón y Cajal s/n
	Apartado postal 385
	ES-28230 Las Rozas
	(Madrid)
Tel	+34 91 495 9800
Fax	+34 91 495 9801
E-mail	rfef@rfef.es
Website	rfef.es

President	Ángel María Villar Llona
General secretary	Jorge Juan Pérez Arias
Media officer	Antonio Bustillo Abella
Year of formation	1909

LIGA CLUBS

1 Athletic Club
 2 Club Atlético de Madrid
 3 FC Barcelona
4 Real Betis Balompié
5 RC Celta de Vigo
6 RC Deportivo La Coruña
7 RCD Espanyol
8 Getafe CF
9 Granada CF
10 Levante UD
11 Málaga CF
12 RCD Mallorca
13 CA Osasuna
14 Rayo Vallecano de Madrid
 15 Real Madrid CF
 16 Real Sociedad de Fútbol
 17 Sevilla FC
 18 Valencia CF
19 Real Valladolid CF
20 Real Zaragoza

PROMOTED CLUBS

21 Elche CF
22 Villarreal CF
23 UD Almería

KEY:
– UEFA Champions League
– UEFA Europa League
– Promoted clubs
– Relegated clubs

Messi-inspired Barça regain Liga crown

Another glorious goal-laden season from Lionel Messi enabled FC Barcelona to regain the Spanish Liga title they had surrendered the previous season to arch-rivals Real Madrid CF. Despite serious health problems for their new coach, Tito Vilanova, the Catalans led from start to finish and racked up a century of points.

Barça and Madrid both crashed out of the UEFA Champions League semi-finals for the second successive season, each falling to German opposition, and there was no trophy for departing Merengues boss José Mourinho as Club Atlético de Madrid ended their long-standing derby jinx with victory in the final of the Copa del Rey.

| Relentless Catalans romp to 22nd Spanish title | Atlético defeat Real Madrid to win Copa del Rey | More European semi-final anguish for Big Two |

Domestic league

The destiny of the 2012/13 Liga title was effectively settled in the early weeks of the campaign, when Barcelona, with Vilanova having stepped up from assistant coach to replace the departed Josep Guardiola, roared off to a perfect start with six wins out of six and Madrid stuttered and spluttered, drawing their opening home game 1-1 against Valencia CF and losing each of their first two away fixtures, at Getafe CF and Sevilla FC. By the time the two teams met at the Camp Nou in early October, there was an eight-point gap between them, and while Madrid managed to check Barça's stride by holding them to a 2-2 draw, with Cristiano Ronaldo's double matching one from Messi, the result was clearly of greater benefit to the Catalans.

Barcelona were not alone at the top the table, Diego Simeone's Atlético having followed an opening-day draw at Levante UD with a surge of victories that kept the two teams level on points throughout October. By Christmas, however, Barça were out on their own, ten successive victories giving them a nine-point advantage over Atlético, defeated in each of their big away fixtures at Valencia (0-2), Real Madrid (0-2) and Barcelona (1-4). Mourinho's men, meanwhile, had

fallen further behind, defeats at Real Betis Balompié and Málaga CF leaving them 16 points adrift at the festive break.

Barcelona won their first two fixtures of 2013 to end the first half of the campaign with a record-breaking tally of 55 points from 57. Their unbeaten streak ended a week later when they lost 3-2 at Real Sociedad de Fútbol, but that game came in the middle of an astonishing run of goalscoring form from the uncontainable Messi. From the mid-November 4-2 win at RCD Mallorca through to a 2-2 draw at RC Celta de Vigo on the final weekend of March, he found the net in every game, scoring 30 goals in total over that 19-game stretch. Although injury would sideline him in April, he returned to score on his next two appearances as well, taking his final tally for the season to 46.

Barcelona's title triumph was heavily Messi-dependent, but they managed to win the last three games without him to match the 100-point total achieved by Madrid 12 months earlier. Their goal tally of 115 was six shy of Madrid's 2011/12 mark, but they scored at least once in every game. Vilanova was unable to oversee the entire campaign. He was absent for two spells, the longest of them between late January and early April, when he underwent cancer treatment in New York. His assistant Jordi Roura was

given temporary charge of the team during that time, and although Vilanova returned to supervise the closing weeks of the season, and share in the title celebrations, his health remained a subject of concern and in the summer it was agreed that he would step down. His place was taken, somewhat surprisingly, by ex-Paraguay coach Gerardo Martino, an Argentinian hailing from Messi's home town, Rosario. Another major new summer recruit from South America was 21-year-old Brazilian forward Neymar, outstanding during his country's 2013 FIFA Confederations Cup triumph.

There was a change of regime too at Madrid, with Mourinho departing after three seasons and returning to former club Chelsea FC as another ex-Stamford Bridge boss, Carlo Ancelotti, moved in to the Bernabéu. Having claimed the Spanish Cup in his first season and the Liga in his second, Mourinho won only the pre-season Spanish Super Cup in his third. That was achieved with an away-goals triumph over Barcelona, and the Portuguese was to enjoy his best season yet against the Catalans, taking four points off them in the league and also dumping them out of the Copa del Rey. However, a 15-point deficit in the final standings painted an ugly picture for Madrid and their fans. Although imperious at home, where they won 17 games and

drew two, they dropped points in over half of their away fixtures. As ever, Ronaldo was their most consistent attacking force, contributing 34 of the team's 103 goals and much more besides. New signing Luka Modrić had less of an impact than anticipated, and skipper Iker Casillas became a frustrated bystander during the second half of the campaign, injured first of all, then dropped by Mourinho in favour of deputy keeper Diego López.

Atlético had the Liga's most consistent goalkeeper in giant young Belgian Thibaut Courtois and also the best defence, conceding just 31 goals. They were unable to maintain sufficient momentum to finish above their city rivals – a feat last accomplished in their 1995/96 double-winning season – but they were always assured of qualifying for the UEFA Champions League, the consistent marksmanship of 28-goal Radamel Falcao – third in the Liga listings once again – keeping their points total ticking along to consolidate that blistering start. The tussle for fourth place – and a UEFA Champions League play-off berth – was fought out to the finish, with Real Sociedad leapfrogging Valencia on the final day.

With Athletic Club having a miserable season, Basque honour was maintained by the San Sebastián outfit, whose French coach Philippe Montanier got the best out of an unheralded group of players featuring right-back Carlos Martínez, holding midfielder Asier Illarramendi and classy forwards Antoine Griezmann and Carlos Vela. Valencia had to be content with UEFA Europa League qualification after losing 4-3 at Sevilla, who – with Málaga and Rayo Vallecano de Madrid both banned from Europe – made it into the same competition despite finishing ninth. They were joined there by city rivals Betis, who finished six points and two places above them.

A riveting relegation battle was not resolved until the final day, when Real Zaragoza, RC Deportivo La Coruña and RCD Mallorca all dropped out of the division and Celta, courtesy of a 1-0 home win over RCD Espanyol, stayed up. As Deportivo followed promotion with immediate relegation, Villarreal enjoyed the reverse outcome, returning to the elite in the company of Segunda División champions Elche CF and play-off winners UD Almería.

Domestic cup

The fifth all-Madrid Copa del Rey final was staged at Real's Bernabéu home, but Atlético had won four finals there before – including two against their city rivals, in 1960 and 1961 – and once again the stadium would be the venue for a red-and-white party as Simeone's underdogs got the better of Mourinho's favourites, coming from behind to win 2-1 after extra time. The result ended Atlético's 14-year wait for a win over Madrid – a sequence of 25 matches, the last ten of which had all been won by the men in white.

A turn up for the books looked unlikely when Ronaldo put Madrid in front on 14 minutes, but Atlético were level by half-time when Diego Costa converted a brilliant Falcao through ball. Mourinho's team had ample opportunity to restore their advantage, but a combination of the woodwork and Courtois's defiant goalkeeping kept them at bay, and nine minutes into extra time Atlético defender Miranda soared high to head in the winning goal. It was the club's tenth Spanish Cup win and the third major piece of silverware claimed by Simeone in just 18 months in charge following the previous year's UEFA Europa League and UEFA Super Cup triumphs.

Europe

Atlético had got the European club season off to a cracking start with a magnificent Falcao-inspired 4-1 victory over Chelsea FC in Monaco, but the UEFA Super Cup was the only European trophy Spanish sides would win in 2012/13. For the third season in a row Barcelona and Real Madrid made up half of the UEFA Champions League's semi-final quartet, but as in 2011/12 neither reached the final. Barça unearthed a vintage display to beat AC Milan 4-0 at home in the round of 16 – after a 2-0 first-leg defeat – but once Messi injured his hamstring in the first leg of the quarter-final against Paris Saint-Germain FC, they looked ill at ease, and FC Bayern München destroyed them 7-0 on aggregate in the semi-final.

Madrid also fell victim to Bundesliga opposition, although they at least put up a

Atlético's Thibaut Courtois, in action here against Betis, won the Zamora Trophy awarded to the Liga's top goalkeeper

Continued on page 681

Domestic league: Liga 2012/13 final table

		Pld	Home W	D	L	F	A	Away W	D	L	F	A	Total W	D	L	F	A	Pts
1	FC Barcelona	38	18	1	0	63	15	14	3	2	52	25	32	4	2	115	40	100
2	Real Madrid CF	38	17	2	0	67	21	9	5	5	36	21	26	7	5	103	42	85
3	Club Atlético de Madrid	38	14	2	3	42	12	9	5	5	23	19	23	7	8	65	31	76
4	Real Sociedad de Fútbol	38	10	7	2	41	22	8	5	6	29	27	18	12	8	70	49	66
5	Valencia CF	38	13	3	3	42	25	6	5	8	25	29	19	8	11	67	54	65
6	Málaga CF	38	10	5	4	33	18	6	4	9	20	32	16	9	13	53	50	57
7	Real Betis Balompié	38	9	5	5	28	18	7	3	9	29	38	16	8	14	57	56	56
8	Rayo Vallecano de Madrid	38	9	3	7	27	29	7	2	10	23	37	16	5	17	50	66	53
9	Sevilla FC	38	13	1	5	41	21	1	7	11	17	33	14	8	16	58	54	50
10	Getafe CF	38	9	4	6	25	23	4	4	11	18	34	13	8	17	43	57	47
11	Levante UD	38	8	4	7	25	26	4	6	9	15	31	12	10	16	40	57	46
12	Athletic Club	38	8	3	8	22	27	4	6	9	22	38	12	9	17	44	65	45
13	RCD Espanyol	38	6	7	6	25	28	5	4	10	18	24	11	11	16	43	52	44
14	Real Valladolid CF	38	7	6	6	29	26	4	4	11	20	32	11	10	17	49	58	43
15	Granada CF	38	6	6	7	21	21	5	3	11	16	33	11	9	18	37	54	42
16	CA Osasuna	38	7	5	7	15	14	3	4	12	10	36	10	9	19	33	50	39
17	RC Celta de Vigo	38	7	6	6	23	21	3	1	15	14	31	10	7	21	37	52	37
18	RCD Mallorca	38	7	5	7	26	30	2	4	13	17	42	9	9	20	43	72	36
19	RC Deportivo La Coruña	38	6	5	8	23	26	2	6	11	24	44	8	11	19	47	70	35
20	Real Zaragoza	38	5	4	10	23	27	4	3	12	14	35	9	7	22	37	62	34

SEASON AT A GLANCE

EUROPEAN QUALIFICATION 2013/14

Champion: FC Barcelona (group stage)
Real Madrid CF (group stage)
Cup winner: Club Atlético de Madrid (group stage)
Real Sociedad de Fútbol (play-offs)

Valencia CF (group stage)
Real Betis Balompié (play-offs)
Sevilla FC (third qualifying round)

Top scorer	Lionel Messi (Barcelona), 46 goals
Relegated clubs	Real Zaragoza, RC Deportivo La Coruña, RCD Mallorca
Promoted clubs	Elche CF, Villarreal CF, UD Almería
Cup final	Club Atlético de Madrid 2-1 Real Madrid CF *(aet)*

PLAYER OF THE SEASON
Lionel Messi
(FC Barcelona)

The Argentinian's astonishing goalscoring feats continued in 2012/13. Of Barcelona's club-record 115 league goals, Messi contributed 46. Before succumbing to injury, he became the first player to score against every opponent in the division consecutively and also registered in 21 successive Liga games – obliterating the previous club record of ten.

NEWCOMER OF THE SEASON
Isco
(Málaga CF)

Following on from an impressive 2011/12 season, Isco's stock rose even higher during a campaign that brought several eye-catching performances from him in Málaga's run to the UEFA Champions League quarter-finals. The tricky attacking midfielder also played a starring role in Spain's UEFA European Under-21 Championship triumph in Israel.

LIGA TEAM OF THE SEASON
(4-4-2)
Coach: Simeone *(Atlético)*

Courtois *(Atlético)*

Carlos Martínez *(Real Sociedad)* — Sergio Ramos *(Real Madrid)* — Miranda *(Atlético)* — Jordi Alba *(Barcelona)*

Iniesta *(Barcelona)* — Isco *(Málaga)* — Özil *(Real Madrid)* — Vela *(Real Sociedad)*

Cristiano Ronaldo *(Real Madrid)* — Messi *(Barcelona)*

SPAIN

NATIONAL TEAM

Home Kit   Away Kit

INTERNATIONAL HONOURS
FIFA World Cup (1) 2010
UEFA European Championship (3) 1964, 2008, 2012

INTERNATIONAL TOURNAMENT APPEARANCES
FIFA World Cup (13) 1934, 1950 (4th), 1962, 1966, 1978, 1982 (2nd phase), 1986 (qtr-finals), 1990 (2nd round), 1994 (qtr-finals), 1998, 2002 (qtr-finals), 2006 (2nd round), 2010 (Winners)
UEFA European Championship (9) 1964 (Winners), 1980, 1984 (runners-up), 1988, 1996 (qtr-finals), 2000 (qtr-finals), 2004, 2008 (Winners), 2012 (Winners)

TOP FIVE ALL-TIME CAPS
Iker Casillas (148); **Xavi Hernández** & Andoni Zubizarreta (126); **Sergio Ramos** (108); **Xabi Alonso** (107)

TOP FIVE ALL-TIME GOALS
David Villa (56); Raúl González (44); **Fernando Torres** (36); Fernando Hierro (29); Fernando Morientes (27)

Results 2012/13

Date	Opponent		Venue	Score	Scorers
15/08/12	Puerto Rico	A	Bayamon	2-1	Santi Cazorla (41), Fàbregas (44)
07/09/12	Saudi Arabia	H	Pontevedra	5-0	Santi Cazorla (23), Pedro (26, 73), Xavi (46), David Villa (62p)
11/09/12	Georgia (WCQ)	A	Tbilisi	1-0	Soldado (86)
12/10/12	Belarus (WCQ)	A	Minsk	4-0	Jordi Alba (12), Pedro (21, 69, 72)
16/10/12	France (WCQ)	H	Madrid	1-1	Sergio Ramos (25)
14/11/12	Panama	A	Panama City	5-1	Pedro (15, 42), David Villa (29), Sergio Ramos (81), Susaeta (84)
06/02/13	Uruguay	N	Doha (QAT)	3-1	Fàbregas (16), Pedro (51, 74)
22/03/13	Finland (WCQ)	H	Gijon	1-1	Sergio Ramos (49)
26/03/13	France (WCQ)	A	Paris	1-0	Pedro (58)
08/06/13	Haiti	N	Miami (USA)	2-1	Santi Cazorla (8), Fàbregas (18)
11/06/13	Republic of Ireland	N	New York (USA)	2-0	Soldado (68), Mata (87)
16/06/13	Uruguay (CC)	N	Recife (BRA)	2-1	Pedro (20), Soldado (32)
20/06/13	Tahiti (CC)	N	Rio de Janeiro (BRA)	10-0	Fernando Torres (5, 33, 57, 78), Silva (31, 89), David Villa (39, 49, 64), Mata (66)
23/06/13	Nigeria (CC)	N	Fortaleza (BRA)	3-0	Jordi Alba (3, 88), Fernando Torres (62)
27/06/13	Italy (CC)	N	Fortaleza (BRA)	0-0	(aet; 7-6 on pens)
30/06/13	Brazil (CC)	A	Rio de Janeiro	0-3	

Appearances 2012/13

Coach: Vicente del Bosque 23/12/50

Player	DOB	Club	Pur	Ksa	GEO	BLR	FRA	Pan	Uru	FIN	FRA	Hai	Irl	URU	TAH	NGA	ITA	BRA	Caps	Goals
Pepe Reina	31/08/82	Liverpool (ENG)	G70										s46		G				28	-
Juanfran	09/01/85	Atlético	D18	D			s50	D											5	-
Gerard Piqué	02/02/87	Barcelona	D46	D46	D				s46	D	D	D46	D	D		D	D	D68*	57	4
Raúl Albiol	04/09/85	Real Madrid	D	D		s70		D				D			D				40	-
Nacho Monreal	26/02/86	Málaga /Arsenal (ENG)	D55	M					s78	D	D				D				13	-
Jesús Navas	21/11/85	Sevilla	M					s46			s61	A46	s46		s46		s53	s52	28	2
Xabi Alonso	25/11/81	Real Madrid	M46		M	M	M				M								107	15
Santi Cazorla	13/12/84	Arsenal (ENG)	M	A60	s64	M	s13		M70	M46		M	s79	s65	M76				56	9
Andrés Iniesta	11/05/84	Barcelona	A46	s60	A	s56	M75	M46	M60	A	A93	s59	M59	A	s76				87	10
Cesc Fàbregas	04/05/87	Barcelona	A	M46	s80	A	A	s46	A		M76	s76	A59	s59	M65	s69	A54		83	13
Fernando Torres	20/03/84	Chelsea (ENG)	A	A52			s75					A59			A	s60	A94	A59	106	36
Álvaro Arbeloa	17/01/83	Real Madrid	s18	D80	D	D50				D	D	D	D			D	D	D46	52	-
Sergio Ramos	30/03/86	Real Madrid	s46	s46	D	D70	D	s59	D	D	D	D46	D	D	D46	D	D	D	108	9
Sergio Busquets	16/07/88	Barcelona	s46	M60	M57	D	D	M	M	M	M	M	M		M	M	M	M	59	-
Fernando Llorente	26/02/85	Athletic	s46																21	7
David Silva	08/01/86	Man. City (ENG)	s55	s60	A64	A56	A13				A	s46	A46		M	s54	A53		75	20
Iker Casillas	20/05/81	Real Madrid	s70	s71	G	G	G	s59					G46	s59	G		G	G	148	-
Víctor Valdés	14/01/82	Barcelona		G71				G59	G	G	G		G59		G				15	-
Beñat Etxebarria	19/02/87	Betis		D				M											4	-
Pedro Rodríguez	28/07/87	Barcelona		A	s57	A	A	A46	A75	s46	A76		A79	A81		A75	A79	A	31	13
Xavi Hernández	25/01/80	Barcelona		s46	M	M76	M				M	s71	M69	M77		M	M	M	126	12
David Villa	03/12/81	Barcelona		s52	s76		A72	s46	A65	A61		A59			A	s75		s59	92	56
Jordi Alba	21/03/89	Barcelona			D	D	D	D59	D78	D		D			D	D	D	D	22	4
Roberto Soldado	27/05/85	Valencia			A			s46				s59	s59	A		A60			11	6
Javi Martínez	02/09/88	Bayern (GER)						D				M		s77	M		s94		13	-
Juan Mata	28/04/88	Chelsea (ENG)					A46	A46	s76	s93	M71	s69	s81	A69			s79	A52	29	8
Markel Susaeta	14/12/87	Athletic					s72												1	1
César Azpilicueta	28/08/89	Chelsea (ENG)							D			D		D				s46	4	-
Carles Puyol	13/04/78	Barcelona							D46										100	3
Isco	21/04/92	Málaga							s60										1	-
Mario Suárez	24/02/87	Atlético							s70										1	-
Álvaro Negredo	20/08/85	Sevilla							s75	s65									14	6

fight against Borussia Dortmund before losing 4-3 on aggregate to a team that had taken four points off them in the group stage. The highlight of Madrid's campaign was a 2-1 win against Manchester United FC at Old Trafford, although that was only achieved after their opponents had been reduced to ten men. Galatasaray AŞ were easier to shift in the quarter-finals, but Dortmund, thanks to their 4-1 first-leg win, were to make it three semi-final defeats in as many seasons for Mourinho, Madrid's only consolation being the competition's top scorer prize claimed by Ronaldo with his dozen goals.

Málaga came within seconds of joining the Big Two in the last four, the concession of two added-time goals to Dortmund ending their debut campaign in the most agonising fashion. Manuel Pellegrini's team exceeded all expectations, winning their first three matches, topping their group, and eliminating FC Porto before putting Dortmund through the wringer. They

lasted a round longer than Valencia, eliminated by PSG, and there was a similar tale of the unexpected in the UEFA Europa League, where the two 2011/12 finalists dropped out early – Athletic in the group stage, Atlético in the round of 32 – to leave European debutants Levante as the last Spanish team standing.

National team

Vicente del Bosque's Spain were unable to add the Confederations Cup to their FIFA World Cup and UEFA European Championship crowns. Outclassed in the final by host nation Brazil, their 3-0 defeat in the Maracanã was so emphatic that it inevitably sparked debate about whether the 'golden generation' might have passed its peak.

Up until the final Spain had conceded just one goal in four matches, but they needed penalties to defeat Italy in a goalless semi-final – a far cry from the

splendour of their 4-0 win in Kyiv a year earlier – and in the qualifying campaign for the 2014 World Cup they had also surprisingly dropped points in each of their first two home fixtures, 1-1 draws against France and Finland.

Maximum points from their three away qualifiers – the last of them, critically, against France – meant that Spain were on course to defend their global title in Brazil, but that heavy defeat in Rio de Janeiro may lead Del Bosque to make a few adjustments to his side before the big kick-off next summer. Of course, he still has a super-abundance of talent to draw upon, and Spain's victory at the 2013 UEFA European Under-21 Championship in Israel, where they successfully defended the trophy won two years earlier in Denmark, showcased a few more Spanish jewels in Isco, Illarramendi, Álvaro Morata and 2011 survivors David de Gea and Thiago Alcántara, the latter skippering the team to victory with a hat-trick in the final against Italy.

European club competitions 2012/13

REAL MADRID CF

Group D
Match 1 - Manchester City FC (ENG)
H **3-2** Marcelo (76), Benzema (87), Cristiano Ronaldo (90)
Casillas, Varane, Pepe, Khedira (Modrić 73), Cristiano Ronaldo, Marcelo, Xabi Alonso, Essien (Özil 65), Arbeloa, Higuaín (Benzema 73), Di María. Coach: José Mourinho (POR)
Match 2 - AFC Ajax (NED)
A **4-1** Cristiano Ronaldo (42, 79, 81), Benzema (48)
Casillas, Pepe, Sergio Ramos, Cristiano Ronaldo, Kaká (Özil 75), Benzema, Marcelo, Xabi Alonso, Essien (Khedira 78), Arbeloa, Callejón (Di María 61). Coach: José Mourinho (POR)
Match 3 - Borussia Dortmund (GER)
A **1-2** Cristiano Ronaldo (38)
Casillas, Varane, Pepe, Sergio Ramos, Khedira (Modrić 20), Cristiano Ronaldo, Benzema (Higuaín 73), Özil, Xabi Alonso, Essien, Di María. Coach: José Mourinho (POR)

Match 4 - Borussia Dortmund (GER)
H **2-2** Pepe (34), Özil (89)
Casillas, Varane, Pepe, Sergio Ramos, Cristiano Ronaldo, Özil, Xabi Alonso, Arbeloa (Kaká 77), Modrić (Essien 46), Higuaín (Callejón 46), Di María. Coach: José Mourinho (POR)
Match 5 - Manchester City FC (ENG)
A **1-1** Benzema (10)
Casillas, Pepe, Sergio Ramos, Fábio Coentrão, Khedira, Cristiano Ronaldo, Benzema (Varane 75), Xabi Alonso, Arbeloa, Modrić (Callejón 68), Di María (Albiol 87). Coach: José Mourinho (POR)
Red card: Arbeloa 73
Match 6 - AFC Ajax (NED)
H **4-1** Cristiano Ronaldo (13), Callejón (28, 88), Kaká (49)
Adán, Varane, Fábio Coentrão (Pepe 23), Khedira, Cristiano Ronaldo, Kaká (José Rodriguez 72), Benzema (Morata 80), Ricardo Carvalho, Modrić, Callejón, Nacho. Coach: José Mourinho (POR)

Round of 16 - Manchester United FC (ENG)
H **1-1** Cristiano Ronaldo (30)
Diego López, Varane, Sergio Ramos, Fábio Coentrão, Khedira, Cristiano Ronaldo, Benzema (Higuaín 60), Özil, Xabi Alonso (Pepe 84), Arbeloa, Di María (Modrić 75). Coach: José Mourinho (POR)
A **2-1** Modrić (66), Cristiano Ronaldo (69)
Diego López, Varane, Sergio Ramos, Fábio Coentrão, Khedira, Cristiano Ronaldo, Özil (Pepe 71), Xabi Alonso, Arbeloa (Modrić 59), Higuaín, Di María (Kaká 45+1). Coach: José Mourinho (POR)

Quarter-final - Galatasaray AŞ (TUR)
H **3-0** Cristiano Ronaldo (9), Benzema (29), Higuaín (73)
Diego López, Varane, Sergio Ramos, Fábio Coentrão, Khedira, Cristiano Ronaldo, Benzema (Higuaín 65), Özil (Modrić 80), Xabi Alonso, Essien, Di María (Pepe 86). Coach: José Mourinho (POR)
A **2-3** Cristiano Ronaldo (7, 90+2)
Diego López, Varane, Pepe, Fábio Coentrão, Khedira, Cristiano Ronaldo, Özil (Albiol 81), Essien (Arbeloa 31), Modrić, Higuaín (Benzema 73), Di María. Coach: José Mourinho (POR)
Red card: Arbeloa 90

Semi-final - Borussia Dortmund (GER)
A **1-4** Cristiano Ronaldo (43)
Diego López, Varane, Pepe, Sergio Ramos, Fábio Coentrão, Khedira, Cristiano Ronaldo, Özil, Xabi Alonso (Kaká 80), Modrić (Di María 68), Higuaín (Benzema 68). Coach: José Mourinho (POR)
H **2-0** Benzema (83), Sergio Ramos (88)
Diego López, Varane, Sergio Ramos, Fábio Coentrão (Kaká 57), Cristiano Ronaldo, Özil, Xabi Alonso (Khedira 67), Essien, Modrić, Higuaín (Benzema 57), Di María. Coach: José Mourinho (POR)

FC BARCELONA

Group G
Match 1 - FC Spartak Moskva (RUS)
H 3-2 *Tello (14), Messi (72, 80)*
Víctor Valdés, Dani Alves (Alexis Sánchez 64), Piqué (Song 12), Fàbregas, Xavi, Messi, Mascherano, Busquets, Pedro, Adriano, Tello (David Villa 74). Coach: Tito Vilanova (ESP)
Match 2 - SL Benfica (POR)
A 2-0 *Alexis Sánchez (6), Fàbregas (55)*
Víctor Valdés, Dani Alves, Fàbregas (Iniesta 72), Puyol (Song 78), Xavi, Alexis Sánchez, Messi, Mascherano, Busquets, Pedro (David Villa 82), Jordi Alba. Coach: Tito Vilanova (ESP)
Red card: Busquets 88
Match 3 - Celtic FC (SCO)
H 2-1 *Iniesta (45), Jordi Alba (90+4)*
Víctor Valdés, Xavi, Iniesta, Alexis Sánchez (David Villa 80), Messi, Mascherano, Bartra, Pedro (Tello 76), Jordi Alba, Adriano, Song. Coach: Tito Vilanova (ESP)
Match 4 - Celtic FC (SCO)
A 1-2 *Messi (90+1)*
Víctor Valdés, Dani Alves, Xavi, Iniesta, Alexis Sánchez (David Villa 65), Messi, Mascherano, Bartra (Piqué 72), Pedro, Jordi Alba, Song (Fàbregas 71). Coach: Tito Vilanova (ESP)
Match 5 - FC Spartak Moskva (RUS)
A 3-0 *Dani Alves (16), Messi (27, 39)*
Víctor Valdés, Dani Alves, Piqué, Fàbregas, Xavi (Song 81), Iniesta, Messi, Mascherano, Busquets, Pedro (Gerard 85), Jordi Alba (Montoya 87). Coach: Tito Vilanova (ESP)
Match 6 - SL Benfica (POR)
H 0-0
Pinto, Puyol, David Villa, Thiago, Montoya, Adriano (Piqué 66), Song, Sergi Roberto, Planas, Rafinha (Messi 58), Tello (Gerard 78). Coach: Tito Vilanova (ESP)

Round of 16 - AC Milan (ITA)
A 0-2
Víctor Valdés, Dani Alves, Piqué, Fàbregas (Alexis Sánchez 62), Puyol (Mascherano 88), Xavi, Iniesta, Messi, Busquets, Pedro, Jordi Alba. Coach: Jordi Roura (ESP)
H 4-0 *Messi (5, 40), David Villa (55), Jordi Alba (90+2)*
Víctor Valdés, Dani Alves, Piqué, Xavi, David Villa (Alexis Sánchez 75), Iniesta, Messi, Mascherano (Puyol 77), Busquets, Pedro (Adriano 84), Jordi Alba. Coach: Jordi Roura (ESP)

Quarter-final - Paris Saint-Germain FC (FRA)
A 2-2 *Messi (38), Xavi (89p)*
Víctor Valdés, Dani Alves, Piqué, Xavi, David Villa (Tello 81), Iniesta, Alexis Sánchez, Messi (Fàbregas 46), Mascherano (Bartra 84), Busquets, Jordi Alba. Coach: Tito Vilanova (ESP)
H 1-1 *Pedro (71)*
Víctor Valdés, Dani Alves, Piqué, Fàbregas (Messi 62), Xavi, David Villa (Song 84), Iniesta, Busquets, Pedro, Jordi Alba, Adriano (Bartra 62). Coach: Tito Vilanova (ESP)

Semi-final - FC Bayern München (GER)
A 0-4
Víctor Valdés, Dani Alves, Piqué, Xavi, Iniesta, Alexis Sánchez, Messi, Bartra, Busquets, Pedro (David Villa 83), Jordi Alba. Coach: Tito Vilanova (ESP)
H 0-3
Víctor Valdés, Dani Alves, Piqué, Fàbregas, Xavi (Alexis Sánchez 55), David Villa, Iniesta (Thiago 64), Bartra (Montoya 87), Pedro, Adriano, Song. Coach: Tito Vilanova (ESP)

VALENCIA CF

Group F
Match 1 - FC Bayern München (GER)
A 1-2 *Valdez (90+1)*
Diego Alves, Cissokho, Rami, Jonas (Valdez 63), Feghouli, Soldado (Barragán 88), João Pereira, Guardado (Jonathan Viera 71), Ricardo Costa, Parejo, Tino Costa. Coach: Mauricio Pellegrino (ARG)
Red card: Rami 90+3
Match 2 - LOSC Lille (FRA)
H 2-0 *Jonas (38, 75)*
Guaita, Cissokho, Gago, Jonas (Parejo 81), Feghouli (João Pereira 87), Soldado (Valdez 84), Barragán, Guardado, Víctor Ruiz, Tino Costa, Delgado. Coach: Mauricio Pellegrino (ARG)
Match 3 - FC BATE Borisov (BLR)
A 3-0 *Soldado (45+1p, 55, 69)*
Diego Alves, Cissokho, Rami, Gago, Albelda (Éver Banega 72), Feghouli (Barragán 82), Soldado (Jonas 77), João Pereira, Guardado, Ricardo Costa, Tino Costa. Coach: Mauricio Pellegrino (ARG)
Match 4 - FC BATE Borisov (BLR)
H 4-2 *Jonas (26), Soldado (29p), Feghouli (51, 86)*
Guaita, Cissokho, Rami, Gago, Jonas (Éver Banega 67), Feghouli, Soldado (Valdez 79), João Pereira, Guardado (Albelda 88), Ricardo Costa, Tino Costa. Coach: Mauricio Pellegrino (ARG)
Match 5 - FC Bayern München (GER)
H 1-1 *Feghouli (77)*
Guaita, Cissokho, Rami, Feghouli, Soldado, Éver Banega (Albelda 80), Barragán, Guardado (Valdez 86), Ricardo Costa, Parejo (Jonas 75), Tino Costa. Coach: Mauricio Pellegrino (ARG)
Red card: Barragán 33
Match 6 - LOSC Lille (FRA)
A 1-0 *Jonas (36p)*
Guaita, Cissokho, Rami, Albelda (Gago 74), Jonas, Feghouli (Piatti 61), Valdez, Guardado, Víctor Ruiz (Jonathan Viera 83), Ricardo Costa, Tino Costa. Coach: Voro (ESP)

Round of 16 - Paris Saint-Germain FC (FRA)
H 1-2 *Rami (90)*
Guaita, Rami, Jonas (Valdez 46), Feghouli (Jonathan Viera 84), Soldado, Éver Banega (Canales 46), João Pereira, Guardado, Ricardo Costa, Parejo, Tino Costa. Coach: Ernesto Valverde (ESP)
A 1-1 *Jonas (55)*
Guaita, Cissokho, Albelda (Éver Banega 46), Jonas (Valdez 76), Feghouli (Piatti 63), Soldado, Barragán, Víctor Ruiz, Parejo, Mathieu, Tino Costa. Coach: Ernesto Valverde (ESP)

MÁLAGA CF

Play-offs - Panathinaikos FC (GRE)
H 2-0 *Demichelis (17), Eliseu (34)*
Caballero, Jesús Gámez, Weligton, Demichelis, Joaquín, Toulalan, Monreal, Maresca (Camacho 70), Eliseu (Duda 78), Isco, Olinga (Buonanotte 70). Coach: Manuel Pellegrini (CHI)
A 0-0
Caballero, Jesús Gámez, Weligton, Demichelis, Camacho, Joaquín (Portillo 90+2), Toulalan, Monreal, Eliseu (Duda 88), Isco, Olinga (Juanmi 63). Coach: Manuel Pellegrini (CHI)

Group C
Match 1 - FC Zenit St Petersburg (RUS)
H 3-0 *Isco (3, 76), Saviola (13)*
Caballero, Jesús Gámez, Weligton, Demichelis, Camacho, Joaquín (Duda 85), Saviola (Santa Cruz 62), Monreal, Eliseu, Isco, Portillo (Iturra 46). Coach: Manuel Pellegrini (CHI)

Match 2 - RSC Anderlecht (BEL)
A 3-0 *Eliseu (45+1, 64), Joaquín (57p)*
Caballero, Weligton, Demichelis, Camacho, Joaquín (Duda 74), Saviola (Santa Cruz 66), Monreal, Iturra, Eliseu, Sergio Sánchez, Isco (Seba Fernández 81). Coach: Manuel Pellegrini (CHI)

Match 3 - AC Milan (ITA)
H 1-0 *Joaquín (64)*
Caballero, Jesús Gámez, Weligton, Demichelis, Camacho, Joaquín (Duda 85), Saviola (Santa Cruz 70), Iturra, Eliseu, Isco, Portillo (Onyewu 90+3). Coach: Manuel Pellegrini (CHI)

Match 4 - AC Milan (ITA)
A 1-1 *Eliseu (40)*
Caballero, Jesús Gámez, Weligton, Demichelis, Camacho, Joaquín (Seba Fernández 82), Saviola (Santa Cruz 69), Iturra (Toulalan 75), Eliseu, Sergio Sánchez, Isco. Coach: Manuel Pellegrini (CHI)

Match 5 - FC Zenit St Petersburg (RUS)
A 2-2 *Buonanotte (8), Seba Fernández (9)*
Caballero, Jesús Gámez, Demichelis (Weligton 46), Camacho, Toulalan, Seba Fernández (Juanmi 76), Duda (Portillo 63), Eliseu, Buonanotte, Onyewu, Santa Cruz. Coach: Manuel Pellegrini (CHI)

Match 6 - RSC Anderlecht (BEL)
H 2-2 *Duda (45, 61)*
Kameni, Weligton (Jesús Gámez 54), Toulalan (Camacho 16), Seba Fernández, Iturra, Duda (Portillo 80), Eliseu, Buonanotte, Sergio Sánchez, Onyewu, Santa Cruz. Coach: Manuel Pellegrini (CHI)

Round of 16 - FC Porto (POR)
A 0-1
Caballero, Weligton, Demichelis, Joaquín (Portillo 63), Toulalan, Júlio Baptista (Lucas Piazón 78), Iturra (Camacho 78), Sergio Sánchez, Isco, Santa Cruz, Antunes. Coach: Manuel Pellegrini (CHI)

H 2-0 *Isco (43), Santa Cruz (77)*
Caballero, Jesús Gámez, Weligton, Demichelis, Joaquín (Camacho 88), Toulalan, Saviola (Lucas Piazón 78), Júlio Baptista (Santa Cruz 74), Iturra, Isco, Antunes. Coach: Manuel Pellegrini (CHI)

Quarter-final - Borussia Dortmund (GER)
H 0-0
Caballero, Jesús Gámez, Weligton, Demichelis, Joaquín, Toulalan, Saviola (Portillo 68), Júlio Baptista (Santa Cruz 76), Iturra, Isco (Duda 87), Antunes. Coach: Manuel Pellegrini (CHI)

A 2-3 *Joaquín (25), Eliseu (82)*
Caballero, Jesús Gámez, Demichelis, Camacho, Joaquín (Portillo 87), Toulalan, Júlio Baptista (Santa Cruz 83), Duda (Eliseu 74), Sergio Sánchez, Isco, Antunes. Coach: Manuel Pellegrini (CHI)

CLUB ATLÉTICO DE MADRID

Group B
Match 1 - Hapoel Tel-Aviv FC (ISR)
A 3-0 *Rodríguez (37), Diego Costa (40), Raúl García (63)*
Asenjo, Mario Suárez, Adrián López (Koke 69), Raúl García, Rodríguez (Juanfran 74), Cisma, Sílvio, Cata Díaz, Diego Costa (Saúl 78), Emre Belözoğlu, Miranda. Coach: Diego Simeone (ARG)

Match 2 - FC Viktoria Plzeň (CZE)
H 1-0 *Rodríguez (90+3)*
Asenjo, Koke (Tiago 64), Adrián López, Rodríguez, Pulido, Gabi, Cisma, Cata Díaz, Diego Costa (Raúl García 61), Emre Belözoğlu, Oueslati (Saúl 85). Coach: Diego Simeone (ARG)

Match 3 - A Académica de Coimbra (POR)
H 2-1 *Diego Costa (48), Emre Belözoğlu (67)*
Asenjo, Filipe Luís, Tiago, Koke (Rodríguez 61), Adrián López (Saúl 81), Pulido, Gabi, Sílvio, Cata Díaz, Diego Costa, Emre Belözoğlu (Raúl García 75). Coach: Diego Simeone (ARG)

Match 4 - A Académica de Coimbra (POR)
A 0-2
Asenjo, Filipe Luís, Mario Suárez (Emre Belözoğlu 58), Tiago (Oueslati 71), Koke, Adrián López, Raúl García, Pulido, Sílvio, Cata Díaz, Saúl (Pedro Martín 46). Coach: Diego Simeone (ARG)

Match 5 - Hapoel Tel-Aviv FC (ISR)
H 1-0 *Raúl García (7)*
Asenjo, Mario Suárez, Adrián López, Raúl García, Rodríguez (Pedro Martín 87), Pulido, Cisma, Sílvio, Cata Díaz, Diego Costa (Koke 58), Emre Belözoğlu. Coach: Diego Simeone (ARG)

Match 6 - FC Viktoria Plzeň (CZE)
A 0-1
Asenjo, Tiago, Adrián López, Raúl García, Pulido, Cisma (Saúl 87), Diego Costa, Juanfran (Koke 59), Emre Belözoğlu, Miranda, Javi Manquillo (Pedro Martín 89). Coach: Diego Simeone (ARG)
Red card: Diego Costa 90+1

Round of 32 - FC Rubin Kazan (RUS)
H 0-2
Asenjo, Godín, Filipe Luís (Saúl 65), Mario Suárez (Koke 46), Tiago, Adrián López, Falcao, Arda Turan, Rodríguez, Cata Díaz (Raúl García 60), Juanfran. Coach: Diego Simeone (ARG)

A 1-0 *Falcao (84)*
Asenjo, Mario Suárez, Adrián López, Raúl García, Falcao, Rodríguez, Cisma, Cata Díaz, Miranda, Javi Manquillo, Saúl. Coach: Diego Simeone (ARG)

LEVANTE UD

Play-offs - Motherwell FC (SCO)
A 2-0 *Juanlu (42), El Zhar (62)*
Navas, David Navarro, Barkero, Iborra, Karabelas (El Zhar 40), Gekas, Ballesteros, Pedro López, Juanlu (Serrano 76), Míchel (Pallardó 66), Lell. Coach: Juan Ignacio Martínez (ESP)

H 1-0 *Gekas (72)*
Navas, David Navarro, Barkero (Míchel 61), El Zhar, Iborra (Pallardó 80), Juanfran, Gekas, Ballesteros (Héctor Rodas 76), Pedro López, Juanlu, Diop. Coach: Juan Ignacio Martínez (ESP)

Group L
Match 1 - Helsingborgs IF (SWE)
H 1-0 *Juanfran (40)*
Navas, David Navarro, Ángel (Rubén García 72), Iborra, Juanfran, Pedro Ríos (Pallardó 87), Ballesteros, Pedro López, Juanlu, Míchel (Barkero 60), Diop. Coach: Juan Ignacio Martínez (ESP)

Match 2 - Hannover 96 (GER)
A 1-2 *Míchel (10p)*
Navas, Héctor Rodas, Iborra, Dudka (Ángel 70), Karabelas, Pedro Ríos, Gekas (Rubén García 70), Ballesteros, Pedro López, Míchel, Lell (El Zhar 33). Coach: Juan Ignacio Martínez (ESP)

Match 3 - FC Twente (NED)
H 3-0 *Míchel (59p), Pedro Ríos (78, 88)*
Navas, Héctor Rodas, Iborra, Karabelas, Pedro Ríos, Gekas (Ángel 63), Ballesteros, Juanlu (Rubén García 73), Míchel (Barkero 76), Lell, Diop. Coach: Juan Ignacio Martínez (ESP)

Match 4 - FC Twente (NED)
A 0-0
Navas, Héctor Rodas, Iborra, Karabelas, Pedro Ríos, Gekas (Ángel 74), Ballesteros, Míchel (Barkero 84), Lell, Diop, Rubén García (Juanlu 77). Coach: Juan Ignacio Martínez (ESP)

Match 5 - Helsingborgs IF (SWE)
A 3-1 *Ángel (8), Diop (37), Iborra (81)*
Navas, Héctor Rodas, Ángel, Iborra (Pallardó 83), Karabelas, Pedro Ríos, Ballesteros, Míchel (Pedro López 86), Lell, Diop, Rubén García (Barkero 73). Coach: Juan Ignacio Martínez (ESP)

Match 6 - Hannover 96 (GER)
H 2-2 *Ángel (49), Iborra (90+4)*
Navas, David Navarro, Héctor Rodas, El
Zhar (Juanlu 59), Ángel, Iborra, Karabelas,
Pedro López, Míchel, Diop (Pallardó 74),
Rubén García (Barkero 59). Coach: Juan
Ignacio Martínez (ESP)

Round of 32 - Olympiacos FC (GRE)
H 3-0 *Pedro Ríos (10), Barkero (40p),
Martins (56)*
Navas, David Navarro, Héctor Rodas,
Barkero, Iborra, Juanfran, Pedro Ríos (Valdo
67), Pedro López, Diop (Míchel 61), Martins
(Acquafresca 83), Rubén García. Coach:
Juan Ignacio Martínez (ESP)
A 1-0 *Martins (9)*
Navas, David Navarro, Héctor Rodas,
Barkero, Iborra, Juanfran, Pedro Ríos (Valdo
66), Ballesteros, Míchel (Dudka 84), Martins
(Acquafresca 82), Rubén García. Coach:
Juan Ignacio Martínez (ESP)

Round of 16 - FC Rubin Kazan (RUS)
H 0-0
Navas, David Navarro, Barkero, Iborra,
Juanfran, Ballesteros, Pedro López, Míchel,
Diop (Pedro Ríos 68), Martins, Rubén García
(Juanlu 80). Coach: Juan Ignacio Martínez
(ESP)
Red card: Míchel 54
A 0-2 *(aet)*
Navas, David Navarro, Barkero, El
Zhar (Pedro Ríos 76), Iborra, Juanfran,
Ballesteros, Lell, Diop, Rubén García
(Juanlu 91), Acquafresca (Valdo 66). Coach:
Juan Ignacio Martínez (ESP)

ATHLETIC CLUB

Third qualifying round - NK Slaven Koprivnica (CRO)
H 3-1 *Isma López (16, 68), Susaeta (20)*
Iraizoz, Toquero (Ruiz de Galarreta 63),
Iturraspe, De Marcos, Ibai Gómez (Llorente
46), Susaeta, Iraola, Isma López, Íñigo
Pérez, Gurpegui, Ramalho (Ekiza 46).
Coach: Marcelo Bielsa (ARG)
A 1-2 *Muniain (47)*
Iraizoz, Toquero (Llorente 46), Iturraspe,
De Marcos, Ibai Gómez (Ruiz de Galarreta
46), Susaeta, Iraola, Isma López, Íñigo
Pérez, Gurpegui, Ekiza (Muniain 46). Coach:
Marcelo Bielsa (ARG)

Play-offs - HJK Helsinki (FIN)
H 6-0 *Aduriz (25, 51), Susaeta (31, 57),
Íñigo Pérez (42), Iraola (85)*
Iraizoz, San José, Iturraspe, De Marcos,
Susaeta (Muniain 69), Iraola, Isma López,
Íñigo Pérez, Gurpegui, Aduriz (Ibai Gómez
59), Ander Herrera (Ruiz de Galarreta 74).
Coach: Marcelo Bielsa (ARG)
A 3-3 *San José (67), Hakanpää (77og), Igor
Martínez (88)*
Raúl, Toquero, San José, Iturraspe (Íñigo
Pérez 46), De Marcos (Ramalho 46), Ibai
Gómez, Susaeta (Igor Martínez 46), Muniain,
Xabi Castillo, Ekiza, Ruiz de Galarreta.
Coach: Marcelo Bielsa (ARG)

Group I
Match 1 - Hapoel Kiryat Shmona FC (ISR)
H 1-1 *Susaeta (40)*
Iraizoz, Amorebieta, Iturraspe, De Marcos,
Susaeta, Iraola, Isma López (Llorente 46),
Gurpegui, Muniain, Aduriz (Ibai Gómez 59),
Xabi Castillo (Ruiz de Galarreta 81). Coach:
Marcelo Bielsa (ARG)
Match 2 - AC Sparta Praha (CZE)
A 1-3 *De Marcos (73)*
Iraizoz, Amorebieta, Iturraspe, De Marcos,
Ibai Gómez (Isma López 57), Susaeta,
Iraola, Gurpegui, Muniain, Aduriz (Llorente
64), Xabi Castillo (Ander Herrera 62). Coach:
Marcelo Bielsa (ARG)
Match 3 - Olympique Lyonnais (FRA)
A 1-2 *Ibai Gómez (79)*
Iraizoz, Aurtenetxe, Amorebieta, Iturraspe,
De Marcos, Susaeta, Iraola, Gurpegui,
Muniain (Ibai Gómez 66), Aduriz (Llorente
60), Ander Herrera. Coach: Marcelo Bielsa
(ARG)
Match 4 - Olympique Lyonnais (FRA)
H 2-3 *Ander Herrera (48), Aduriz (55p)*
Iraizoz, Aurtenetxe (Ibai Gómez 46),
Amorebieta, Iturraspe, De Marcos, Susaeta,
Iraola, Gurpegui, Muniain (Isma López 85),
Aduriz (Llorente 70), Ander Herrera. Coach:
Marcelo Bielsa (ARG)
Match 5 - Hapoel Kiryat Shmona FC (ISR)
A 2-0 *Llorente (34), Toquero (76)*
Raúl, Toquero, San José, Llorente, Isma
López (Ibai Gómez 64), Xabi Castillo, Igor
Martínez (Undabarrena 77), Ramalho,
Laporte, Morán, Peña (Vidal 85). Coach:
Marcelo Bielsa (ARG)
Match 6 - AC Sparta Praha (CZE)
H 0-0
Raúl, Toquero (Morán 46), San José,
Iturraspe, Llorente (Aduriz 46), Isma
López, Muniain (Peña 46), Xabi Castillo,
Igor Martínez, Ramalho, Laporte. Coach:
Marcelo Bielsa (ARG)

Domestic league club-by-club

ATHLETIC CLUB
Coach: Marcelo Bielsa (ARG)
1898 • San Mamés (40,000) • athletic-club.net
Major honours
Spanish League (8) 1930, 1931, 1934, 1936, 1943,
1956, 1983, 1984;
Spanish Cup (23) 1903, 1904, 1910, 1911, 1914, 1915,
1916, 1921, 1923, 1930, 1931, 1932, 1933, 1943, 1944,
1945, 1950, 1955, 1956, 1958, 1969, 1973, 1984

2012

Date	Opponent		Score	Scorers
19/08	Betis	h	3-5	De Marcos, San José 2
27/08	Atlético	a	0-4	
02/09	Valladolid	h	2-0	Aduriz, Susaeta
16/09	Espanyol	a	3-3	Aduriz 2, Llorente
23/09	Málaga	h	0-0	
29/09	Real Sociedad	a	0-2	
07/10	Osasuna	h	1-0	Aduriz
20/10	Valencia	a	2-3	Aduriz 2
28/10	Getafe	h	1-2	San José
04/11	Granada	a	2-1	Aduriz 2 (1p)
11/11	Sevilla	h	2-1	De Marcos, Susaeta
17/11	Real Madrid	a	1-5	Ibai Gómez
25/11	Deportivo	h	1-1	De Marcos
01/12	Barcelona	a	1-5	Ibai Gómez
09/12	Celta	h	1-0	Aduriz
15/12	Mallorca	h	1-0	Aduriz
22/12	Zaragoza	h	0-2	

2013

Date	Opponent		Score	Scorers
05/01	Levante	a	1-3	Aduriz
11/01	Rayo Vallecano	h	1-2	San José
21/01	Betis	a	1-1	Aduriz
27/01	Atlético	h	3-0	San José, Susaeta, De Marcos
01/02	Valladolid	a	2-2	De Marcos, Susaeta
10/02	Espanyol	h	0-4	
16/02	Málaga	a	0-1	
22/02	Real Sociedad	h	1-3	Ibai Gómez
02/03	Osasuna	a	1-0	Susaeta
10/03	Valencia	h	1-0	Muniain
16/03	Getafe	a	0-1	
01/04	Granada	h	1-0	Aduriz
08/04	Sevilla	h	1-2	Gurpegui
14/04	Real Madrid	h	0-3	
21/04	Deportivo	a	1-1	Llorente
27/04	Barcelona	h	2-2	Susaeta, Ander Herrera
03/05	Celta	a	1-1	De Marcos
11/05	Mallorca	h	2-1	Aduriz, Llorente
19/05	Zaragoza	a	2-1	Llorente, Ibai Gómez
26/05	Levante	h	0-1	
01/06	Rayo Vallecano	a	2-2	Susaeta, Aurtenetxe

No	Name	Nat	DoB	Pos	Aps	(s)	Gls
20	Aritz Aduriz		11/02/81	A	33	(3)	14
5	Fernando Amorebieta	VEN	29/03/85	D	10	(1)	
21	Ander Herrera		14/08/89	M	29		1
3	Jon Aurtenetxe		03/01/92	D	24	(3)	1
10	Óscar De Marcos		14/04/89	M	36		6
23	Borja Ekiza		06/03/88	D	23	(1)	
18	Carlos Gurpegui		19/08/80	M	24	(3)	1
11	Ibai Gómez		11/11/89	A	17	(18)	4
26	Igor Martínez		19/07/89	M		(3)	
17	Íñigo Pérez		18/01/88	M	5		
1	Gorka Iraizoz		06/03/81	G	35		
15	Andoni Iraola		22/06/82	D	34	(1)	
16	Isma López		29/01/90	A	6	(2)	
8	Ander Iturraspe		08/03/89	M	27	(3)	
38	Aymeric Laporte	FRA	27/05/94	D	14	(1)	
9	Fernando Llorente		26/02/85	A	4	(22)	4
39	Erik Morán		25/05/91	M		(1)	
19	Iker Muniain		19/12/92	M	27	(6)	1
28	Jonás Ramalho		10/06/93	D	4	(2)	
13	Raúl		13/03/88	G	3		
27	Íñigo Ruiz de Galarreta		06/08/93	M		(3)	
6	Mikel San José		30/05/89	D	23	(11)	5
14	Markel Susaeta		14/12/87	M	36		7
2	Gaizka Toquero		09/08/84	M	1	(15)	
22	Xabi Castillo		29/03/86	D	3	(4)	

CLUB ATLÉTICO DE MADRID

Coach: Diego Simeone (ARG)
1903 • Vicente Calderón (54,851) • clubatleticodemadrid.com

Major honours
UEFA Cup Winners' Cup (1) 1962;
UEFA Europa League (2) 2010, 2012;
UEFA Super Cup (2) 2010, 2012;
European/South American Cup (1) 1974;
Spanish League (9) 1940, 1941, 1950, 1951, 1966, 1970, 1973, 1977, 1996;
Spanish Cup (10) 1960, 1961, 1965, 1972, 1976, 1985, 1991, 1992, 1996, 2013

2012

19/08	Levante	a	1-1	*Arda*
27/08	Athletic	h	4-0	*Falcao 3 (1p), Tiago*
16/09	Rayo Vallecano	h	4-3	*Mario Suárez, Koke, Arda, Falcao (p)*
23/09	Valladolid	h	2-1	*Godín, Falcao (p)*
26/09	Betis	a	4-2	*Falcao 2 (1p), Diego Costa, Raúl García*
30/09	Espanyol	a	1-0	*Raúl García*
07/10	Málaga	h	2-1	*Falcao, og (Weligton)*
21/10	Real Sociedad	a	1-0	*Falcao*
28/10	Osasuna	h	3-1	*Miranda, Raúl García, Falcao*
03/11	Valencia	a	0-2	
11/11	Getafe	h	2-0	*Adrián López, Arda*
18/11	Granada	a	1-0	*Arda*
25/11	Sevilla	h	4-0	*Falcao (p), og (Spahić), Koke, Miranda*
01/12	Real Madrid	a	0-2	
09/12	Deportivo	h	6-0	*Diego Costa, Falcao 5 (1p)*
16/12	Barcelona	a	1-4	*Falcao*
21/12	Celta	h	1-0	*Adrián López*

2013

06/01	Mallorca	a	1-1	*Raúl García*
13/01	Zaragoza	h	2-0	*Tiago, Falcao (p)*
20/01	Levante	h	2-0	*Adrián López, Koke*
27/01	Athletic	a	0-3	
03/02	Betis	h	1-0	*Diego Costa*
10/02	Rayo Vallecano	a	1-2	*Falcao*
17/02	Valladolid	a	3-0	*Falcao, Diego Costa, Rodríguez*
24/02	Espanyol	h	1-0	*Falcao (p)*
03/03	Málaga	a	0-0	
10/03	Real Sociedad	h	0-1	
17/03	Osasuna	a	2-0	*Diego Costa 2*
31/03	Valencia	h	1-1	*Falcao*
07/04	Getafe	a	0-0	
14/04	Granada	h	5-0	*Diego Costa, Falcao 2, Raúl García, Filipe Luís*
21/04	Sevilla	a	1-0	*Falcao*
27/04	Real Madrid	h	1-2	*Falcao*
04/05	Deportivo	a	0-0	
08/05	Celta	a	3-1	*Diego Costa, Juanfran, Falcao*
12/05	Barcelona	h	1-2	*Falcao*
26/05	Mallorca	h	0-0	
01/06	Zaragoza	a	3-1	*Arda, Diego Costa 2*

No	Name	Nat	DoB	Pos	Aps	(s)	Gls
7	Adrián López		08/01/88	M	15	(17)	3
10	Arda Turan	TUR	30/01/87	M	26	(6)	5
1	Sergio Asenjo		28/06/89	G	1		
18	Cata Díaz	ARG	13/03/79	D	7	(2)	
15	Domingo Cisma		09/02/82	D	2		
13	Thibaut Courtois	BEL	11/05/92	G	37		
36	Dani Aquino		27/07/90	A		(1)	
19	Diego Costa	BRA	07/10/88	A	24	(7)	10
21	Emre Belözoğlu	TUR	07/09/80	M	4	(3)	
9	Radamel Falcao	COL	10/02/86	A	34		28
3	Filipe Luís	BRA	09/08/85	D	32		1
14	Gabi		10/07/83	M	34	(1)	
2	Diego Godín	URU	16/02/86	D	35		1
22	Emiliano Insúa	ARG	07/01/89	D	2	(1)	
26	Javi Manquillo		05/05/94	D	2	(1)	
20	Juanfran		09/01/85	D	35		1
6	Koke		08/01/92	M	29	(4)	3
4	Mario Suárez		24/02/87	M	23	(6)	1
23	João Miranda	BRA	07/09/84	D	35		2
30	Óliver Torres		10/11/94	M		(8)	
42	Abdelkader Oueslati	TUN	07/10/91	D		(1)	
12	Jorge Pulido		08/04/91	D	1		
8	Raúl García		11/07/86	M	13	(17)	5
11	Cristian Rodríguez	URU	30/09/85	M	12	(21)	1
28	Saúl Ñíguez		21/11/94	M		(2)	
17	Sílvio	POR	28/09/87	D	1		
5	Tiago	POR	02/05/81	M	14	(8)	2

FC BARCELONA

Coach: Tito Vilanova; (18/12/12) (Jordi Roura); (04/01/13) Tito Vilanova; (23/01/13) (Jordi Roura); (01/04/13) Tito Vilanova
1899 • Camp Nou (98,772) • fcbarcelona.com

Major honours
European Champion Clubs' Cup/UEFA Champions League (4) 1992, 2006, 2009, 2011;
UEFA Cup Winners' Cup (4) 1979, 1982, 1989, 1997;
Inter Cities Fairs Cup (3) 1958, 1960, 1966;
UEFA Super Cup (4) 1992, 1997, 2009, 2011;
FIFA Club World Cup (2) 2009, 2011;
Spanish League (22) 1929, 1945, 1948, 1949, 1952, 1953, 1959, 1960, 1974, 1985, 1991, 1992, 1993, 1994, 1998, 1999, 2005, 2006, 2009, 2010, 2011, 2013;
Spanish Cup (26) 1910, 1912, 1913, 1920, 1922, 1925, 1926, 1928, 1942, 1951, 1952, 1953, 1957, 1959, 1963, 1968, 1971, 1978, 1981, 1983, 1988, 1990, 1997, 1998, 2009, 2012

2012

19/08	Real Sociedad	h	5-1	*Puyol, Messi 2, Pedro, David Villa*
26/08	Osasuna	a	2-1	*Messi 2*
02/09	Valencia	h	1-0	*Adriano*
15/09	Getafe	a	4-1	*Adriano, Messi 2 (1p), David Villa*
22/09	Granada	h	2-0	*Xavi, og (Borja Gómez)*
29/09	Sevilla	a	3-2	*Fàbregas 2, David Villa*
07/10	Real Madrid	a	2-2	*Messi 2*
20/10	Deportivo	a	5-4	*Jordi Alba, Tello, Messi 3*
27/10	Rayo Vallecano	a	5-0	*David Villa, Messi 2, Xavi, Fàbregas*
03/11	Celta	h	3-1	*Adriano, David Villa, Jordi Alba*
11/11	Mallorca	a	4-2	*Xavi, Messi 2, Tello*
17/11	Zaragoza	h	3-1	*Messi 2, Song*
25/11	Levante	a	4-0	*Messi 2, Iniesta, Fàbregas*
01/12	Athletic	h	5-1	*Piqué, Messi 2, Adriano, Fàbregas*
09/12	Betis	a	2-1	*Messi 2*
16/12	Atlético	h	4-1	*Adriano, Busquets, Messi 2*
22/12	Valladolid	a	3-1	*Xavi, Messi, Tello*

2013

06/01	Espanyol	h	4-0	*Xavi, Pedro 2, Messi (p)*
13/01	Málaga	a	3-1	*Messi, Fàbregas, Thiago*
19/01	Real Sociedad	a	2-3	*Messi, Pedro*
27/01	Osasuna	h	5-1	*Messi 4 (1p), Pedro*
03/02	Valencia	a	1-1	*Messi (p)*
10/02	Getafe	h	6-1	*Alexis Sánchez, Messi, David Villa, Tello, Iniesta, Piqué*
16/02	Granada	a	2-1	*Messi 2*
23/02	Sevilla	h	2-1	*David Villa, Messi*
02/03	Real Madrid	a	1-2	*Messi*
09/03	Deportivo	h	2-0	*Alexis Sánchez, Messi*
17/03	Rayo Vallecano	h	3-1	*David Villa, Messi 2*
30/03	Celta	a	2-2	*Tello, Messi*
06/04	Mallorca	h	5-0	*Fàbregas 3, Alexis Sánchez 2*
14/04	Zaragoza	a	3-0	*Thiago, Tello 2*
20/04	Levante	h	1-0	*Fàbregas*
27/04	Athletic	a	2-2	*Messi, Alexis Sánchez*
05/05	Betis	h	4-2	*Alexis Sánchez, David Villa, Messi 2*
12/05	Atlético	a	2-1	*Alexis Sánchez, og (Gabi)*
19/05	Valladolid	h	2-1	*Pedro, og (Marc Valiente)*
26/05	Espanyol	a	2-0	*Alexis Sánchez, Pedro*
01/06	Málaga	h	4-1	*David Villa, Fàbregas, Montoya, Iniesta*

No	Name	Nat	DoB	Pos	Aps	(s)	Gls
22	Éric Abidal	FRA	11/09/79	D	2	(3)	
21	Adriano	BRA	26/10/84	D	18	(5)	5
9	Alexis Sánchez	CHI	19/12/88	A	18	(11)	8
15	Marc Bartra		15/01/91	D	3		
16	Sergio Busquets		16/07/88	M	25	(6)	1
2	Dani Alves	BRA	06/05/83	D	26	(4)	
7	David Villa		03/12/81	A	17	(11)	10
4	Cesc Fàbregas		04/05/87	M	30	(2)	11
27	Gerard Deulofeu		13/03/94	A		(1)	
8	Andrés Iniesta		11/05/84	M	24	(7)	3
12	Jonathan dos Santos	MEX	26/04/90	M		(3)	
18	Jordi Alba		21/03/89	D	27	(2)	2
14	Javier Mascherano	ARG	08/06/84	M	21	(4)	
10	Lionel Messi	ARG	24/06/87	A	28	(4)	46
19	Martín Montoya		14/04/91	D	11	(4)	1
17	Pedro Rodríguez		28/07/87	A	23	(5)	7
13	José Manuel Pinto		08/11/75	G	7		
3	Gerard Piqué		02/02/87	D	27	(1)	2
5	Carles Puyol		13/04/78	D	12	(1)	1
28	Sergi Roberto		07/02/92	M		(1)	
25	Alex Song	CMR	09/09/87	M	17	(3)	1
37	Cristian Tello		11/08/91	A	12	(10)	7
11	Thiago Alcántara		11/04/91	M	15	(12)	2
1	Víctor Valdés		14/01/82	G	31		
6	Xavi Hernández		25/01/80	M	24	(6)	5

REAL BETIS BALOMPIÉ

Coach: José Mel
1907 • Benito Villamarín (55,500) • realbetisbalompie.es

Major honours
Spanish League (1) 1935;
Spanish Cup (2) 1977, 2005

2012

19/08	Athletic	a	5-3	*Rubén Castro, Jorge Molina 2, Beñat, Pozuelo*
25/08	Rayo Vallecano	h	1-2	*Jorge Molina*
17/09	Valladolid	a	1-0	*Rubén Castro*
22/09	Espanyol	h	1-0	*Paulão*
26/09	Atlético	h	2-4	*Salvador, og (Juanfran)*
29/09	Málaga	a	0-4	
06/10	Real Sociedad	h	2-0	*Paulão, Rubén Castro*
21/10	Osasuna	a	0-0	
27/10	Valencia	h	1-0	*Salva Sevilla*
05/11	Getafe	a	4-2	*Jorge Molina, Beñat, Rubén Castro, Salva Sevilla*
09/11	Granada	h	1-2	*Rubén Castro*
18/11	Sevilla	a	1-5	*Rubén Castro*
24/11	Real Madrid	h	1-0	*Beñat*
02/12	Deportivo	a	3-2	*Rubén Castro 2, Campbell*
09/12	Barcelona	h	1-2	*Rubén Castro*
17/12	Celta	a	1-0	*Jorge Molina*
22/12	Mallorca	h	1-2	*Beñat*

2013

04/01	Zaragoza	a	2-1	*Rubén Castro, Jorge Molina*
13/01	Levante	h	2-0	*Campbell, Rubén Castro*
21/01	Athletic	h	1-1	*Rubén Castro (p)*
27/01	Rayo Vallecano	a	0-3	
03/02	Atlético	a	0-1	
11/02	Valladolid	h	0-0	
17/02	Espanyol	a	0-1	
24/02	Málaga	h	3-0	*Jorge Molina, Mario, Pabón*
03/03	Real Sociedad	a	3-3	*Jorge Molina, Pabón 2*
08/03	Osasuna	h	2-1	*Jorge Molina, Rubén Castro*
16/03	Valencia	a	0-3	
01/04	Getafe	h	0-0	
05/04	Granada	a	5-1	*Rubén Castro 2, og (Íñigo López), Pabón, Ángel*
12/04	Sevilla	h	3-3	*Pabón, Rubén Castro (p), Nosa*
20/04	Real Madrid	a	1-3	*Jorge Molina (p)*
29/04	Deportivo	h	1-1	*Jorge Molina*
05/05	Barcelona	a	2-4	*Pabón, Rubén Pérez*
12/05	Celta	h	1-0	*Rubén Castro*
20/05	Mallorca	a	0-1	
26/05	Zaragoza	h	4-0	*Rubén Castro, Pabón 2, Jorge Molina*
01/06	Levante	a	1-1	*Jorge Molina*

No	Name	Nat	DoB	Pos	Aps	(s)	Gls
13	Adrián		03/01/87	G	31	(1)	
6	Álex Martínez		12/08/90	D	11	(2)	
4	Antonio Amaya		31/05/83	D	26	(2)	
7	Ángel		10/03/81	D	8	(3)	1
10	Beñat Etxebarria		19/02/87	M	33	(1)	4
15	Joel Campbell	CRC	26/06/92	A	21	(7)	2
21	José Cañas		27/05/87	M	26	(1)	
34	Carlos García		17/09/93	M		(1)	
1	Casto		18/06/82	G	5		
2	Javier Chica		17/05/85	D	21	(1)	
5	José Antonio Dorado		10/07/82	D	5	(2)	
25	Fabricio		31/12/87	G	2		
27	Fausto Tienza		08/01/90	M		(1)	
9	Jonathan Pereira		12/05/87	A	1	(5)	
19	Jorge Molina		22/04/82	A	22	(10)	13
17	Juan Carlos		30/03/90	A	21	(4)	
3	Mario		02/02/82	D	19	(1)	1
18	Guillermo Molins	SWE	26/09/88	M		(4)	
23	Nacho		24/06/80	D	26	(4)	
22	Nélson	POR	10/06/83	D	10		
29	Nono		30/03/93	M	4	(11)	
20	Emmanuel Nosa Igiebor	NGA	09/11/90	M	7	(9)	1
22	Dorlan Pabón	COL	24/01/88	M	14	(3)	8
12	Paulão	BRA	06/08/82	M	19	(3)	2
16	Damien Perquis	POL	10/04/84	D	7	(3)	
11	Alejandro Pozuelo		20/09/91	A	4	(7)	1
24	Rubén Castro		27/06/81	A	32	(2)	18
8	Rubén Pérez		26/04/89	M	18	(7)	1
14	Salva Sevilla		18/03/84	M	15	(2)	2
18	Salvador Agra	POR	11/11/91	A	7	(3)	1
39	Sergio Rodríguez		07/09/92	A		(1)	
27	Álvaro Vadillo		12/09/94	A	3	(11)	
32	Eder Vilarchao		09/02/90	M		(1)	

RC CELTA DE VIGO

Coach: Paco Herrera; (18/02/13) Abel Resino
1923 • Balaídos (31,800) • celtavigo.net

2012

18/08	Málaga	h	0-1	
25/08	Real Sociedad	a	1-2	De Lucas
01/09	Osasuna	h	2-0	Iago Aspas, Mario Bermejo
15/09	Valencia	a	1-2	Cabral
22/09	Getafe	h	2-1	Fernández, Park
30/09	Granada	a	1-0	Iago Aspas
05/10	Sevilla	h	2-0	Iago Aspas (p), De Lucas
20/10	Real Madrid	a	0-2	
27/10	Deportivo	h	1-1	Mario Bermejo
03/11	Barcelona	a	1-3	Mario Bermejo
10/11	Rayo Vallecano	a	2-3	Iago Aspas 2
18/11	Mallorca	h	1-1	Park
26/11	Zaragoza	a	1-0	Iago Aspas
02/12	Levante	h	1-1	De Lucas
09/12	Athletic	a	0-1	
17/12	Betis	h	0-1	
21/12	Atlético	a	0-1	

2013

06/01	Valladolid	h	3-1	Iago Aspas 2 (1p), Álex López
12/01	Espanyol	a	0-1	
19/01	Málaga	a	1-1	Fernández
26/01	Real Sociedad	h	1-1	Krohn-Dehli
02/02	Osasuna	a	0-1	
09/02	Valencia	h	0-1	
16/02	Getafe	a	1-3	Fernández
24/02	Granada	h	2-1	Iago Aspas, Mario Bermejo
04/03	Sevilla	a	1-4	Fernández
10/03	Real Madrid	h	1-2	Iago Aspas
15/03	Deportivo	a	1-3	Park
30/03	Barcelona	h	2-2	Natxo Insa, Oubiña
07/04	Rayo Vallecano	h	0-2	
15/04	Mallorca	a	0-1	
22/04	Zaragoza	h	2-1	Álex López, Mario Bermejo
27/04	Levante	a	1-0	Fernández
03/05	Athletic	h	1-1	Iago Aspas
08/05	Atlético	a	1-3	Fernández
12/05	Betis	a	0-1	
26/05	Valladolid	a	2-0	Cabral, Iago Aspas (p)
01/06	Espanyol	h	1-0	Natxo Insa

No	Name	Nat	DoB	Pos	Aps	(s)	Gls
8	Álex López		11/01/88	M	30	(3)	2
16	Carlos Bellvís		24/04/85	D	8	(4)	
12	Gustavo Cabral	ARG	14/10/85	D	26	(1)	2
14	Cristian Bustos		25/03/83	M	2	(5)	
22	Enrique De Lucas		17/08/78	A	6	(18)	3
15	Vadim Demidov	NOR	10/10/86	D	12		
24	Augusto Fernández	ARG	10/04/86	M	36		6
2	Hugo Mallo		22/06/91	D	17		
10	Iago Aspas		01/08/87	A	34		12
13	Javi Varas		10/09/82	G	35		
17	Joan Tomás		17/05/85	M		(3)	
6	Jonathan Vila		06/03/86	M	10	(4)	
28	Jonny		03/03/94	D	19		
23	Michael Krohn-Dehli	DEN	06/06/83	M	32	(2)	1
29	Levy Madinda	GAB	22/06/92	M	1	(4)	
9	Mario Bermejo		07/10/78	A	16	(17)	5
31	Santiago Mina		07/12/95	A		(1)	
25	Natxo Insa		09/06/86	M	14	(4)	2
19	Fabián Orellana	CHI	27/01/86	A	7	(7)	
4	Borja Oubiña		17/05/82	M	36		1
18	Park Chu-young	KOR	10/07/85	A	8	(14)	3
11	Danijel Pranjić	CRO	02/12/81	M	4	(6)	
3	Roberto Lago		30/08/85	D	32	(2)	
26	Rubén Blanco		25/07/95	G	1	(1)	
21	Samuel		26/04/85	D		(1)	
1	Sergio Álvarez		03/08/86	G	2		
20	Toni		04/04/90	M		(14)	
5	Andrés Túñez	VEN	15/03/87	D	30		

RC DEPORTIVO LA CORUÑA

Coach: José Luis Oltra;
(30/12/12) Domingos Paciência (POR);
(11/02/13) Fernando Vázquez
1906 • Riazor (34,600) • canaldeportivo.com
Major honours
Spanish League (1) 2000;
Spanish Cup (2) 1995, 2002

2012

20/08	Osasuna	h	2-0	Riki, Nélson Oliveira
26/08	Valencia	a	3-3	Aguilar 2, Pizzi (p)
01/09	Getafe	h	1-1	Riki
16/09	Granada	a	1-0	Nélson Oliveira
24/09	Sevilla	h	0-2	
30/09	Real Madrid	a	1-5	Riki
06/10	Rayo Vallecano	h	1-1	Pizzi (p)
20/10	Barcelona	h	4-5	Pizzi 2 (1p), Álex Bergantiños, og (Jordi Alba)
27/10	Celta	a	1-1	Juan Domínguez
04/11	Mallorca	h	1-0	Bruno Gama
10/11	Zaragoza	a	3-5	Bruno Gama, Riki, Bodipo
18/11	Levante	h	0-2	
25/11	Athletic	a	1-1	Aguilar
02/12	Betis	h	2-3	Riki 2
09/12	Atlético	a	0-6	
17/12	Valladolid	h	0-0	
20/12	Espanyol	a	0-2	

2013

05/01	Málaga	h	1-0	Pizzi
13/01	Real Sociedad	a	1-1	Pizzi
20/01	Osasuna	a	1-2	Camuñas
26/01	Valencia	h	2-3	Riki 2
02/02	Getafe	a	1-2	Pizzi (p)
09/02	Granada	h	0-3	
15/02	Sevilla	a	1-3	Riki
23/02	Real Madrid	h	1-2	Riki
02/03	Rayo Vallecano	h	1-0	
09/03	Barcelona	a	0-2	
15/03	Celta	h	3-1	Riki, Sílvio, Diogo Salomão
31/03	Mallorca	a	3-2	Sílvio, Marchena, Riki
06/04	Zaragoza	h	3-2	Bruno Gama, Marchena, og (Abraham)
13/04	Levante	a	4-0	Valerón, Pizzi, Nélson Oliveira, Bruno Gama
21/04	Athletic	h	1-1	Bruno Gama
29/04	Betis	a	1-1	Riki
04/05	Atlético	h	0-0	
11/05	Valladolid	a	0-1	
19/05	Espanyol	h	2-0	Bruno Gama, Nélson Oliveira
26/05	Málaga	a	1-3	Diogo Salomão
01/06	Real Sociedad	h	0-1	

No	Name	Nat	DoB	Pos	Aps	(s)	Gls
14	Abel Aguilar	COL	06/01/85	M	27	(1)	3
4	Álex Bergantiños		07/06/85	M	21	(7)	1
8	André Santos	POR	02/03/89	M	4	(9)	
1	Daniel Aranzubia		18/09/79	G	35		
17	Ayoze		25/05/82	D	11	(3)	
6	Aythami		02/04/86	D	24	(2)	
23	Rodolfo Bodipo	EQG	25/10/77	A		(6)	1
16	Bruno Gama	POR	15/11/87	A	38		6
18	Javier Camuñas		17/07/80	M	4	(19)	1
22	Diogo Salomão	POR	14/09/88	A	2	(12)	2
3	Evaldo	BRA	18/03/82	D	14	(1)	
28	Pablo Insúa		09/09/93	D	2	(1)	
20	Jesús Vázquez		01/05/84	D	2	(1)	
10	Juan Domínguez		08/01/90	M	21	(3)	1
23	Kaká	BRA	16/05/81	D	5	(1)	
15	Laure		22/03/85	D	10	(1)	
13	Germán Lux	ARG	07/06/82	G	3	(1)	
2	Manuel Pablo		25/01/76	D	24		
24	Carlos Marchena		31/07/79	D	22		2
25	Nélson Oliveira	POR	08/08/91	A	2	(28)	4
12	Paulo Assunção	BRA	25/01/80	M	7	(2)	
9	Pizzi	POR	06/10/89	A	35		8
11	Riki		11/08/80	A	36		13
19	Roderick	POR	30/03/91	D	3		
19	Sílvio	POR	28/09/87	D	16	(1)	2
29	Tiago Pinto	POR	01/02/88	D	1		
21	Juan Carlos Valerón		17/06/75	M	29	(5)	1
5	Zé Castro	POR	13/01/83	D	20	(4)	

RCD ESPANYOL

Coach: Mauricio Pochettino (ARG);
(28/11/12) Javier Aguirre (MEX)
1900 • Cornellá-El Prat (40,500) • rcdespanyol.com
Major honours
Spanish Cup (4) 1929, 1940, 2000, 2006

2012

18/08	Mallorca	a	1-2	Mubarak
25/08	Zaragoza	h	1-2	Álvaro Vázquez
02/09	Levante	a	2-3	Longo, Tejera
16/09	Athletic	h	3-3	Javi López, Verdú, Longo
22/09	Betis	a	0-1	
30/09	Atlético	h	0-1	
06/10	Valladolid	a	1-1	Verdú (p)
21/10	Rayo Vallecano	h	3-2	Verdú 2, Stuani
27/10	Málaga	h	0-0	
04/11	Real Sociedad	a	1-0	Colotto
10/11	Osasuna	h	0-3	
17/11	Valencia	a	1-2	Longo
25/11	Getafe	h	0-2	
02/12	Granada	a	0-0	
07/12	Sevilla	h	2-2	Verdú (p), Simão
16/12	Real Madrid	a	2-2	Sergio García, Albín
20/12	Deportivo	h	2-0	Simão, Stuani

2013

06/01	Barcelona	a	0-4	
12/01	Celta	h	1-0	Sergio García
18/01	Mallorca	h	3-2	Simão, Verdú (p), Baena
26/01	Zaragoza	a	0-0	
02/02	Levante	h	3-2	og (Iborra), Stuani, Sergio García
10/02	Athletic	a	4-0	Moreno, Víctor Sánchez, Stuani, Verdú
17/02	Betis	h	1-0	Sergio García
24/02	Atlético	a	0-1	
03/03	Valladolid	h	0-0	
09/03	Rayo Vallecano	a	0-2	
17/03	Málaga	a	2-0	Colotto, Sergio García
31/03	Real Sociedad	h	2-2	Sergio García, Stuani
07/04	Osasuna	h	2-0	Moreno, Mubarak
13/04	Valencia	h	3-3	Mubarak, Verdú, Sergio García
21/04	Getafe	a	2-0	Verdú, Stuani
28/04	Granada	h	0-1	
05/05	Sevilla	a	0-3	
11/05	Real Madrid	h	1-1	Stuani
19/05	Deportivo	a	0-2	
26/05	Barcelona	h	0-2	
01/06	Celta	a	0-1	

No	Name	Nat	DoB	Pos	Aps	(s)	Gls
17	Juan Albín	URU	17/07/86	A	2	(5)	1
8	Álvaro Vázquez		27/04/91	A	2		1
7	Raúl Baena		02/03/89	M	11	(8)	1
18	Joan Capdevila		03/02/78	D	25	(1)	
13	Francisco Casilla		02/10/86	G	20	(1)	
19	Diego Colotto	ARG	10/03/81	D	28		2
24	Cristian Alfonso		02/05/89	M	2	(11)	
1	Cristian Álvarez	ARG	13/11/85	G	18		
23	Cristian Gómez		27/07/89	M	8	(8)	
6	Felipe Mattioni	BRA	15/10/88	D	4	(2)	
6	Juan Forlín	ARG	10/01/88	D	32	(1)	
16	Javi López		21/01/86	M	28	(4)	1
12	Samuel Longo	ITA	12/01/92	A	11	(7)	3
15	Héctor Moreno	MEX	17/01/88	D	31	(1)	2
22	Wakaso Mubarak	GHA	25/07/90	M	23	(3)	3
17	Martin Petrov	BUL	15/01/79	M		(8)	
3	Raúl Rodríguez		22/09/87	D	17	(5)	
11	Rui Fonte	POR	23/04/90	A	5	(5)	
9	Sergio García		09/06/83	A	27	(1)	7
8	Simão Sabrosa	POR	31/10/79	A	18	(8)	3
8	Christian Stuani	URU	12/10/86	A	21	(11)	7
5	Sergio Tejera		28/05/90	M	3	(9)	1
10	Joan Verdú		05/05/83	M	36	(1)	9
27	Víctor Álvarez		14/03/93	D	13	(5)	
4	Víctor Sánchez		08/09/87	D	33		1

GETAFE CF

Coach: Luis García Plaza
1983 • Coliseum Alfonso Pérez (17,000) • getafecf.com

2012

18/08	Sevilla	a	1-2	*Alexis*
26/08	Real Madrid	h	2-1	*Valera, Barrada*
01/09	Deportivo	a	1-1	*Barrada*
15/09	Barcelona	h	1-4	*og (Mascherano)*
22/09	Celta	a	1-2	*Barrada*
01/10	Mallorca	h	1-0	*Diego Castro*
06/10	Zaragoza	a	1-0	*Diego Castro (p)*
21/10	Levante	h	0-1	
28/10	Athletic	a	2-1	*Juan Rodríguez, Álvaro Vázquez*
05/11	Betis	h	2-4	*Diego Castro, Pedro León*
11/11	Atlético	a	0-2	
18/11	Valladolid	h	2-1	*Alexis, Lafita*
25/11	Espanyol	a	2-0	*Pedro León, Mané*
01/12	Málaga	h	1-0	*Lopo*
08/12	Real Sociedad	a	1-1	*Lafita*
15/12	Osasuna	h	1-1	*Diego Castro (p)*
21/12	Valencia	a	2-1	*Álvaro Vázquez, Alexis*

2013

07/01	Rayo Vallecano	a	1-3	*Paco Alcácer*
14/01	Granada	h	2-2	*Juan Rodríguez, Paco Alcácer*
19/01	Sevilla	h	1-1	*Adrián Colunga*
27/01	Real Madrid	a	0-4	
02/02	Deportivo	h	3-1	*Diego Castro (p), Álvaro Vázquez, Adrián Colunga*
10/02	Barcelona	a	1-6	*Álvaro Vázquez*
16/02	Celta	h	3-1	*Adrián Colunga, Diego Castro, Fernández*
23/02	Mallorca	a	3-1	*Diego Castro (p), Adrián Colunga 2*
01/03	Zaragoza	h	2-0	*Adrián Colunga, Sergio Escudero*
10/03	Levante	a	0-0	
16/03	Athletic	h	1-0	*Borja*
01/04	Betis	h	0-0	
07/04	Atlético	h	0-0	
13/04	Valladolid	a	1-2	*Paco Alcácer*
21/04	Espanyol	h	0-2	
28/04	Málaga	a	1-2	*Valera*
06/05	Real Sociedad	h	2-1	*Pedro León, Barrada*
11/05	Osasuna	a	0-1	
18/05	Valencia	h	0-1	
26/05	Rayo Vallecano	h	1-2	*Rafa*
01/06	Granada	a	0-2	

No	Name	Nat	DoB	Pos	Aps	(s)	Gls
16	David Abraham	ARG	15/07/86	D	9		
11	Adrián Colunga		17/11/84	A	15	(7)	6
2	Alexis		04/08/85	D	25	(1)	3
7	Álvaro Vázquez		27/04/91	A	14	(15)	4
19	Abdelaziz Barrada	MAR	19/06/89	M	30	(2)	4
23	Borja		14/01/81	M	14	(2)	1
13	Jordi Codina		27/04/82	G	6	(1)	
17	Diego Castro		02/07/82	A	30	(4)	7
12	Federico Fernández	ARG	21/02/89	D	13	(1)	1
10	Jaime Gavilán		12/05/85	M	10	(12)	
24	Hugo Fraile		16/03/87	A		(3)	
22	Juan Rodríguez		01/04/82	M	7	(2)	2
5	Mehdi Lacen	ALG	15/03/84	M	10	(10)	
18	Ángel Lafita		07/08/84	M	17	(9)	2
6	Alberto Lopo		05/05/80	D	17	(4)	1
3	Mané		21/12/81	D	11	(2)	1
21	Míchel		08/11/85	M	13	(4)	
4	Miguel Torres		28/01/86	D	20	(1)	
7	Miku	VEN	19/08/85	A			
1	Miguel Ángel Moyá		02/04/84	G	32		
9	Paco Alcácer		30/08/93	A	6	(14)	3
14	Pedro León		24/11/86	M	26	(3)	3
15	Rafa López		09/04/85	D	16	(3)	1
8	Pablo Sarabia		11/05/92	M	3	(10)	
16	Sergio Escudero		02/09/89	D	10		1
20	Juan Valera		21/12/84	D	30		2
25	Xavi Torres		21/11/86	M	32	(3)	

GRANADA CF

Coach: Juan Antonio Anquela;
(30/01/13) Lucas Alcaraz
1931 • Nuevo Los Cármenes (16,200) • granadacf.es

2012

20/08	Rayo Vallecano	a	0-1	
26/08	Sevilla	h	1-1	*Mikel Rico*
02/09	Real Madrid	a	0-3	
16/09	Deportivo	h	1-1	*Floro Flores*
22/09	Barcelona	a	0-2	
30/09	Celta	h	2-1	*Guilherme Siqueira (p), Torje*
07/10	Mallorca	a	2-1	*El-Arabi (p), Torje*
21/10	Zaragoza	h	1-2	*El-Arabi*
28/10	Levante	a	1-3	*El-Arabi*
04/11	Athletic	h	1-2	*El-Arabi*
09/11	Betis	a	2-1	*Torje, Mikel Rico*
18/11	Atlético	h	0-1	
24/11	Valladolid	a	0-1	
02/12	Espanyol	h	0-0	
09/12	Málaga	a	0-4	
15/12	Real Sociedad	h	0-0	
22/12	Osasuna	a	2-1	*Mainz, Dani Benítez*

2013

05/01	Valencia	h	1-2	*Angulo*
14/01	Getafe	a	2-2	*Guilherme Siqueira 2 (2p)*
19/01	Rayo Vallecano	h	2-0	*og (Jordi Amat), Recio*
28/01	Sevilla	a	0-3	
02/02	Real Madrid	h	1-0	*og (Cristiano Ronaldo)*
09/02	Deportivo	a	3-0	*og (Marchena), Ighalo, Guilherme Siqueira (p)*
16/02	Barcelona	h	1-2	*Ighalo*
24/02	Celta	a	1-2	*Ighalo*
03/03	Mallorca	h	1-2	*Nolito*
11/03	Zaragoza	a	0-0	
17/03	Levante	h	1-1	*Guilherme Siqueira (p)*
01/04	Athletic	a	0-1	
05/04	Betis	h	1-5	*Aranda*
14/04	Atlético	a	0-5	
20/04	Valladolid	h	1-1	*El-Arabi*
28/04	Espanyol	a	1-0	*Nolito*
04/05	Málaga	h	1-0	*Ighalo*
13/05	Real Sociedad	a	2-2	*El-Arabi, Recio*
18/05	Osasuna	h	3-0	*El-Arabi, Guilherme Siqueira (p), Buonanotte*
26/05	Valencia	a	0-1	
01/06	Getafe	h	2-0	*Nolito, El-Arabi*

No	Name	Nat	DoB	Pos	Aps	(s)	Gls
16	Brayan Angulo	COL	02/11/89	D	4	(11)	1
7	Carlos Aranda		27/07/80	A	9	(8)	1
20	Borja Gómez		14/05/88	D	12	(1)	
3	Yacine Brahimi	ALG	08/02/90	M	21	(6)	
12	Diego Buonanotte	ARG	19/04/88	M	4	(11)	1
11	Dani Benítez		04/04/87	M	9		1
15	Pape Diakhaté	SEN	21/06/84	D	17	(1)	
9	Youssef El-Arabi	MAR	03/02/87	A	23	(8)	8
7	Antonio Floro Flores	ITA	18/06/83	A	5	(5)	1
6	Guilherme Siqueira	BRA	28/04/86	D	35		6
25	Odion Ighalo	NGA	16/06/89	A	19	(9)	4
8	Íñigo López		23/07/82	D	21	(2)	
24	Iriney	BRA	23/04/81	M	21	(3)	
10	Jaime Romero		31/07/90	M	2	(9)	
21	Juanma Ortiz		01/03/82	M	5	(17)	
18	Manuel Lucena		18/11/82	D	2		
12	Darwin Machís	VEN	07/02/93	A		(4)	
5	Diego Mainz		29/12/82	D	26	(1)	1
14	Mikel Rico		04/11/84	M	38		2
23	Moisés Hurtado		20/02/81	M	1		
10	Nolito		15/11/86	A	17		3
2	Allan Nyom	CMR	10/05/88	D	35		
19	Fabián Orellana	CHI	27/01/86	A	12	(5)	
28	Recio		11/01/91	M	14	(1)	2
13	Roberto		25/01/79	G	14		
1	Toño		17/12/79	G	24		
22	Gabriel Torje	ROU	22/11/89	A	28	(6)	3
17	Hassan Yebda	ALG	14/05/84	D		(2)	

LEVANTE UD

Coach: Juan Ignacio Martínez
1939 • Ciutat de València (25,354) • levanteud.com

2012

19/08	Atlético	h	1-1	*El Zhar*
27/08	Valladolid	a	0-2	
02/09	Espanyol	h	3-2	*Juanlu, Lell, og (Raúl Rodríguez)*
15/09	Málaga	a	1-3	*Míchel*
23/09	Real Sociedad	h	2-1	*Barkero (p), Martins*
30/09	Osasuna	a	0-4	
07/10	Valencia	h	1-0	*Martins*
21/10	Getafe	a	1-0	*Míchel*
28/10	Granada	h	3-1	*Martins 2, Pedro Ríos*
04/11	Sevilla	a	0-0	
11/11	Real Madrid	h	1-2	*Ángel*
18/11	Deportivo	a	2-0	*Martins, Barkero*
25/11	Barcelona	h	0-4	
02/12	Celta	a	1-1	*Roger*
09/12	Mallorca	h	4-0	*Martins, David Navarro, Rubén García, Iborra*
16/12	Zaragoza	a	1-0	*Rubén García*
20/12	Rayo Vallecano	h	0-3	

2013

05/01	Athletic	h	3-1	*Lell, Iborra, El Zhar*
13/01	Betis	a	0-2	
20/01	Atlético	a	0-2	
26/01	Valladolid	h	2-1	*Barkero, og (Rukavina)*
02/02	Espanyol	a	2-3	*Rubén García, Martins*
09/02	Málaga	h	1-2	*Barkero (p)*
17/02	Real Sociedad	a	1-1	*Míchel (p)*
25/02	Osasuna	h	0-2	
02/03	Valencia	a	2-2	*Iborra, Barkero*
10/03	Getafe	h	0-0	
17/03	Granada	a	1-1	*Acquafresca*
30/03	Sevilla	h	1-0	*Rubén García*
06/04	Real Madrid	a	1-5	*Míchel*
13/04	Deportivo	h	0-4	
20/04	Barcelona	a	0-1	
27/04	Celta	h	0-0	
05/05	Mallorca	a	1-1	*Acquafresca*
10/05	Zaragoza	h	0-0	
19/05	Rayo Vallecano	h	2-3	*Acquafresca, Iborra*
26/05	Athletic	a	1-0	*Juanlu*
01/06	Betis	h	1-1	*Pedro Ríos*

No	Name	Nat	DoB	Pos	Aps	(s)	Gls
9	Robert Acquafresca	ITA	11/09/87	A	12	(1)	3
9	Ángel		26/04/87	A	2	(8)	1
18	Sergio Ballesteros		04/09/75	D	26		
7	José Barkero		27/04/79	M	25	(3)	5
4	David Navarro		25/05/80	D	35		1
23	Pape Diop	SEN	19/03/86	M	32		
14	Dariusz Dudka	POL	09/12/83	M		(2)	
8	Nabil El Zhar	MAR	27/08/86	M	21	(10)	2
17	Theofanis Gekas	GRE	23/05/80	A	2	(2)	
5	Héctor Rodas		07/03/88	D	5	(5)	
10	Vicente Iborra		16/01/88	M	35		4
12	Juanfran		15/07/76	D	28	(1)	
20	Juanlu		08/05/80	M	14	(11)	2
15	Nikolaos Karabelas	GRE	20/12/84	D	8	(2)	
22	Christian Lell	GER	29/08/84	D	20	(1)	
24	Obafemi Martins	NGA	28/10/84	A	18	(3)	7
21	Míchel		29/07/88	M	20	(17)	4
1	Gustavo Munúa	URU	27/01/78	G	29		
13	Keylor Navas	CRC	15/12/86	G	9		
6	Miguel Pallardó		05/09/86	M		(5)	
19	Pedro López		01/11/83	D	16	(1)	
16	Pedro Ríos		12/12/81	M	15	(10)	2
27	Roger Martí		03/01/91	A	2	(13)	1
29	Rubén García		14/07/93	A	21	(10)	4
24	Simão	MOZ	23/07/88	M	2	(2)	
17	Valdo	CPV	23/04/81	M	6	(7)	
6	Loukas Vyntra	GRE	05/02/81	D	15		

MÁLAGA CF

Coach: Manuel Pellegrini (CHI)
1994 • La Rosaleda (28,963) • malagacf.com

2012

18/08	Celta	a	1-0	Olinga
25/08	Mallorca	h	1-1	Juanmi
01/09	Zaragoza	a	1-0	Camacho
15/09	Levante	h	3-1	Saviola, Joaquín, Portillo
23/09	Athletic	a	0-0	
29/09	Betis	h	4-0	Joaquín (p), Saviola, og (Amaya), Isco
07/10	Atlético	a	1-2	Santa Cruz
20/10	Valladolid	h	2-1	Isco, Joaquín
27/10	Espanyol	a	0-0	
03/11	Rayo Vallecano	h	1-2	Demichelis
10/11	Real Sociedad	h	1-2	Saviola
17/11	Osasuna	a	0-0	
24/11	Valencia	h	4-0	Portillo, Saviola, Santa Cruz, Isco
01/12	Getafe	a	0-1	
08/12	Granada	h	4-0	Joaquín, Saviola, Camacho, Santa Cruz
15/12	Sevilla	a	2-0	Demichelis, Eliseu (p)
22/12	Real Madrid	h	3-2	Isco, Santa Cruz 2

2013

05/01	Deportivo	a	0-1	
13/01	Barcelona	h	1-3	Buonanotte
19/01	Celta	h	1-1	Demichelis
27/01	Mallorca	a	3-2	Saviola, Isco, Monreal
03/02	Zaragoza	h	1-1	Isco (p)
09/02	Levante	a	2-1	Isco 2 (1p)
16/02	Athletic	h	1-0	Saviola
24/02	Betis	a	0-3	
03/03	Atlético	h	0-0	
09/03	Valladolid	a	1-1	Demichelis
17/03	Espanyol	h	0-2	
30/03	Rayo Vallecano	a	3-1	Weligton, Júlio Baptista, Morales
06/04	Real Sociedad	a	2-4	Morales, Santa Cruz
13/04	Osasuna	h	1-0	Júlio Baptista
20/04	Valencia	a	1-5	Júlio Baptista
28/04	Getafe	h	2-1	Santa Cruz, Weligton
04/05	Granada	a	0-1	
08/05	Real Madrid	a	2-6	Santa Cruz, Antunes
12/05	Sevilla	h	0-0	
26/05	Deportivo	h	3-1	Saviola, Júlio Baptista, Isco
01/06	Barcelona	a	1-4	Morales

No	Name	Nat	DoB	Pos	Aps	(s)	Gls
25	Antunes	POR	01/04/87	D	10	(1)	1
20	Diego Buonanotte	ARG	19/04/88	A	2	(7)	1
13	Willy Caballero	ARG	28/09/81	G	36		
6	Ignacio Camacho		04/05/90	M	30	(3)	2
5	Martín Demichelis	ARG	20/12/80	D	31		4
17	Duda	POR	27/06/80	M	3	(14)	
18	Eliseu	POR	01/10/83	M	25	(3)	1
22	Isco		21/04/92	A	36	(1)	9
16	Manuel Iturra	CHI	23/06/84	M	15	(10)	
2	Jesús Gámez		10/04/85	D	28		
7	Joaquín		21/07/81	A	29	(5)	4
26	Juanmi		20/05/93	A		(1)	1
10	Júlio Baptista	BRA	01/10/81	A	11	(3)	4
1	Carlos Kameni	CMR	18/02/84	G	2	(1)	
12	Lucas Piazón	BRA	20/01/94	M	4	(7)	
4	Diego Lugano	URU	02/11/80	D	10	(1)	
15	Nacho Monreal		26/02/86	D	14		1
14	Pedro Morales	CHI	25/05/85	M	5	(2)	3
45	Fabrice Olinga	CMR	12/05/96	A	1	(1)	1
23	Oguchi Onyewu	USA	13/05/82	D	1	(1)	
19	Francisco Portillo		13/06/90	M	20	(7)	2
28	Recio		11/01/91	M	1	(3)	
24	Roque Santa Cruz	PAR	16/08/81	A	15	(16)	8
9	Javier Saviola	ARG	11/12/81	A	19	(8)	8
11	Seba Fernández	URU	23/05/85	A	5	(12)	
21	Sergio Sánchez		03/04/86	D	14	(4)	
8	Jérémy Toulalan	FRA	10/09/83	M	18	(1)	
3	Weligton	BRA	26/08/79	D	33		2

RCD MALLORCA

Coach: Joaquín Caparrós;
(05/02/13) Gregorio Manzano
1916 • Iberostar Estadio (23,142) • rcdmallorca.es
Major honours
Spanish Cup (1) 2003

2012

18/08	Espanyol	h	2-1	Hemed 2
25/08	Málaga	a	1-1	Hemed
01/09	Real Sociedad	h	1-0	Víctor
16/09	Osasuna	a	1-1	Hemed
23/09	Valencia	h	2-0	Víctor, Arizmendi
01/10	Getafe	a	1-1	Hemed
07/10	Granada	h	1-2	Hemed
22/10	Sevilla	a	2-3	Bigas, Hemed
28/10	Real Madrid	h	0-5	
04/11	Deportivo	h	1-1	
11/11	Barcelona	h	2-4	Pereira, Víctor (p)
18/11	Celta	a	1-1	Hemed
24/11	Rayo Vallecano	a	0-2	
02/12	Zaragoza	h	1-1	Víctor
09/12	Levante	a	0-2	
15/12	Athletic	h	0-1	
22/12	Betis	a	2-1	Víctor, Javi Márquez (p)

2013

06/01	Atlético	h	1-1	Kevin
12/01	Valladolid	a	1-3	Víctor
18/01	Espanyol	a	2-3	Giovani, Javi Márquez
27/01	Málaga	h	2-3	Víctor, Giovani
03/02	Real Sociedad	a	0-3	
09/02	Osasuna	h	1-1	Pedro Geromel
17/02	Valencia	a	0-2	
23/02	Getafe	h	1-3	Giovani
03/03	Granada	a	2-1	Alfaro, Hemed
09/03	Sevilla	h	2-1	Alfaro 2
16/03	Real Madrid	a	2-5	Nsue, Alfaro
31/03	Deportivo	h	2-3	Víctor, Nsue
06/04	Barcelona	a	0-5	
15/04	Celta	h	1-0	Giovani
19/04	Rayo Vallecano	h	1-1	Alfaro
27/04	Zaragoza	a	2-3	Hemed, Arizmendi
05/05	Levante	h	1-1	Hemed
11/05	Athletic	a	1-2	Giovani
20/05	Betis	h	1-1	Hemed
26/05	Atlético	a	0-0	
01/06	Valladolid	h	4-2	Alfaro, Martí, Giovani, Javi Márquez

No	Name	Nat	DoB	Pos	Aps	(s)	Gls
21	Alejandro Alfaro		23/11/86	M	13	(14)	6
30	Álvaro		19/05/91	A		(1)	
4	Anderson Conceição	BRA	24/10/89	D	14	(2)	
6	Antonio López		13/09/81	D	7	(1)	
22	Javier Arizmendi		03/03/84	A	5	(16)	2
13	Dudu Awat	ISR	17/10/77	G	35		
17	Pedro Bigas		15/05/90	M	24		1
38	Brandon		04/02/95	A		(1)	
1	Juan Jesús Calatayud		21/12/79	G	3		
24	Andreu Fontàs		14/11/89	D	5	(4)	
9	Giovani dos Santos	MEX	11/05/89	A	27	(2)	6
10	Tomer Hemed	ISR	02/05/87	A	28	(9)	11
2	Alan Hutton	SCO	30/11/84	D	17		
11	Javi Márquez		11/05/86	M	19	(6)	3
3	João Víctor	BRA	07/11/88	M	2		
23	Kevin García		08/09/89	D	8	(3)	1
20	Antonio Luna		17/03/91	D	11		
35	Marc Fernández		29/04/90	M		(6)	
19	José Luis Martí		28/04/75	M	18	(11)	1
25	Rubén Miño		18/01/89	G		(1)	
8	Emilio Nsue	EQG	30/09/89	A	25	(7)	2
16	José Nunes	POR	07/03/77	D	21	(2)	
14	Pedro Geromel	BRA	21/09/85	D	29	(1)	1
7	Michael Pereira	FRA	08/12/87	A	17	(8)	1
12	Fernando Tissone	ARG	24/07/86	M	12	(3)	
5	Tomás Pina		14/10/87	M	34	(2)	
32	Charlie Took Essome	CMR	25/05/93	D		(1)	
18	Víctor		28/02/85	A	31	(2)	9
27	Ximo Navarro		23/01/90	D	13	(3)	

CA OSASUNA

Coach: José Luis Mendilíbar
1920 • Reyno de Navarra (19,800) • osasuna.es

2012

20/08	Deportivo	a	0-2	
26/08	Barcelona	h	1-2	Llorente
01/09	Celta	a	0-2	
16/09	Mallorca	h	1-1	Kike Sola
22/09	Zaragoza	a	1-3	Armenteros
30/09	Levante	h	4-0	Armenteros, Lamah, Timor (p), Nino
07/10	Athletic	a	0-1	
21/10	Betis	h	0-0	
28/10	Atlético	a	1-3	Lamah
04/11	Valladolid	h	0-1	
10/11	Espanyol	a	3-0	Álvaro Cejudo, Kike Sola, Onwu
17/11	Málaga	h	0-0	
23/11	Real Sociedad	a	0-0	
30/11	Rayo Vallecano	h	1-0	Kike Sola
08/12	Valencia	h	0-0	
15/12	Getafe	a	1-1	Kike Sola
22/12	Granada	h	1-2	Nino

2013

05/01	Sevilla	a	0-1	
12/01	Real Madrid	h	0-0	
20/01	Deportivo	h	2-0	Kike Sola, Nino
27/01	Barcelona	a	1-5	Loé
02/02	Celta	h	1-0	Armenteros
09/02	Mallorca	a	1-1	Lolo
16/02	Zaragoza	h	1-0	Kike Sola
25/02	Levante	a	2-0	Shojaei, Kike Sola
02/03	Athletic	h	0-1	
08/03	Betis	h	1-2	Silva
17/03	Atlético	a	0-2	
31/03	Valladolid	a	3-1	Kike Sola 2, De las Cuevas
07/04	Espanyol	h	0-2	
13/04	Málaga	a	0-1	
21/04	Real Sociedad	h	0-2	
26/04	Rayo Vallecano	a	2-2	Loé, Arribas
04/05	Valencia	a	0-4	
11/05	Getafe	h	1-0	Arribas
18/05	Granada	a	0-3	
26/05	Sevilla	h	2-1	Puñal, Álvaro Cejudo
01/06	Real Madrid	a	2-4	Roberto Torres, Álvaro Cejudo

No	Name	Nat	DoB	Pos	Aps	(s)	Gls
16	Álvaro Cejudo		29/01/84	M	25	(7)	3
13	Andrés Fernández		17/12/86	G	37		
11	Anthony Annan	GHA	21/07/86	M	5	(1)	
9	Emiliano Armenteros	ARG	18/01/86	A	30		3
14	Alejandro Arribas		01/05/89	D	32	(2)	2
24	Damià		15/04/82	D	29		
6	Miguel De las Cuevas		19/06/86	M	15	(1)	1
8	Ion Echaide		05/01/88	D	1		
7	Kike Sola		25/02/86	A	24	(7)	9
20	Roland Lamah	BEL	31/12/87	A	7	(8)	2
12	Joseba Llorente		24/11/79	A	10	(14)	1
23	Raoul Loé	FRA	31/01/89	M	18	(5)	2
5	Lolo		22/08/84	M	17	(5)	1
2	Marc Bertrán		22/05/82	D	20	(3)	
36	Maikel Mesa		04/06/91	M		(1)	
4	Miguel Flaño		19/08/84	D	22		
19	Nano		20/04/82	M	16	(2)	
17	Nino		10/06/80	A	17	(8)	3
15	Oier		25/05/86	D	25	(6)	
18	Manuel Onwu		11/01/88	A		(6)	1
10	Francisco Puñal		06/09/75	M	13	(6)	1
25	Ricardo		30/12/71	G		(1)	
	Asier Riesgo		06/10/83	G	1		
21	Roberto Torres		07/03/89	M	1	(4)	1
3	Rubén González		29/01/82	D	15	(1)	
30	Masoud Shojaei	IRN	09/06/84	M	2	(12)	1
20	Francisco Silva	CHI	11/02/86	M	14	(1)	
11	Sisi		22/04/86	M	11		
22	David Timor		17/01/89	M	10	(6)	
35	Unai García		03/09/92	D	1		

RAYO VALLECANO DE MADRID

Coach: Paco Jémez
1924 • Vallecas (15,500) • rayovallecano.es

2012

20/08	Granada	h	1-0	Trashorras
25/08	Betis	a	2-1	Piti, Léo Baptistão
02/09	Sevilla	h	0-0	
16/09	Atlético	a	3-4	Delibašić 2, Léo Baptistão
24/09	Real Madrid	h	0-2	
30/09	Valladolid	a	1-6	Domínguez
06/10	Deportivo	h	2-1	Piti, José Carlos
21/10	Espanyol	a	2-3	Léo Baptistão 2
27/10	Barcelona	h	0-5	
03/11	Málaga	a	2-1	Piti 2
10/11	Celta	h	3-2	Léo Baptistão, Tito, Piti (p)
19/11	Real Sociedad	a	0-4	
24/11	Mallorca	h	2-0	Léo Baptistão, Delibašić
30/11	Osasuna	a	0-1	
10/12	Zaragoza	h	0-2	
16/12	Valencia	a	1-0	Domínguez (p)
20/12	Levante	h	3-0	Nacho, Piti, Vázquez

2013

07/01	Getafe	h	3-1	Bangoura, Piti 2
11/01	Athletic	a	2-1	Bangoura, Piti (p)
19/01	Granada	a	0-2	
27/01	Betis	h	3-0	Piti (p), Delibašić, José Carlos
03/02	Sevilla	a	1-2	Domínguez (p)
10/02	Atlético	h	2-1	Bangoura, Léo Baptistão
17/02	Real Madrid	a	0-2	
24/02	Valladolid	h	1-2	Jordi Amat
02/03	Deportivo	a	0-0	
09/03	Espanyol	h	2-0	Domínguez, Piti
17/03	Barcelona	a	1-3	Tamudo
30/03	Málaga	h	1-3	Piti (p)
07/04	Celta	a	2-0	Piti, Delibašić
14/04	Real Sociedad	h	0-2	
19/04	Mallorca	a	1-1	Piti
26/04	Osasuna	h	2-2	Delibašić, Piti
05/05	Zaragoza	a	0-3	
12/05	Valencia	h	0-4	
19/05	Levante	a	3-2	Piti 2 (1p), Vázquez
26/05	Getafe	a	2-1	Domínguez, og (Diego Castro)
01/06	Athletic	h	2-2	Vázquez, Piti

No	Name	Nat	DoB	Pos	Aps	(s)	Gls
21	Mohamed Abu	GHA	14/11/91	M	1		
8	Adrián		25/05/88	M	8	(13)	
33	Alberto Perea		19/12/90	M	1	(3)	
7	Manuel Arana		03/12/84	M		(2)	
14	Anaitz Arbilla		15/05/87	D	8	(3)	
19	Alhassane "Lass" Bangoura	GUI	30/03/92	A	20	(12)	3
3	José Manuel Casado		09/08/86	D	28		
25	David Cobeño		06/04/82	G	8		
13	Dani		30/07/83	G	1	(1)	
23	Andrija Delibašić	MNE	24/04/81	A	11	(21)	6
11	Alejandro Domínguez	ARG	10/06/81	M	32	(1)	5
5	Alejandro Gálvez		06/06/89	D	24	(4)	
39	Isi		28/10/95	M		(1)	
18	Javi Fuego		04/01/84	M	36		
16	Jordi Amat		21/03/92	D	26	(1)	1
22	Jordi Figueras		16/05/87	D	13	(1)	
9	José Carlos		17/07/87	M	21	(11)	2
4	Mikel Labaka		10/08/80	D	7	(3)	
29	Léo Baptistão	BRA	26/08/92	A	26	(2)	7
38	Nacho		07/03/89	D	8	(2)	1
14	Nicki Bille Nielsen	DEN	07/02/88	A	4	(5)	
10	Piti		26/05/81	A	33	(2)	18
37	Rubén Ramiro		16/04/93	A		(1)	
6	Rodri		17/08/84	D	3	(1)	
1	Rubén		22/06/84	G	29	(1)	
15	Raúl Tamudo		19/10/77	A		(4)	1
2	Tito		11/07/85	D	31	(2)	1
17	Roberto Trashorras		28/02/81	M	31	(4)	1
20	Franco Vázquez	ARG	22/02/89	M	8	(10)	3

REAL MADRID CF

Coach: José Mourinho (POR)
1902 • Santiago Bernabéu (80,354) • realmadrid.com

Major honours

European Champion Clubs' Cup/UEFA Champions League (9) 1956, 1957, 1958, 1959, 1960, 1966, 1998, 2000, 2002;
UEFA Cup (2) 1985, 1986;
UEFA Super Cup (1) 2002;
European/South American Cup (3) 1960, 1998, 2002;
Spanish League (32) 1932, 1933, 1954, 1955, 1957, 1958, 1961, 1962, 1963, 1964, 1965, 1967, 1968, 1969, 1972, 1975, 1976, 1978, 1979, 1980, 1986, 1987, 1988, 1989, 1990, 1995, 1997, 2001, 2003, 2007, 2008, 2012;
Spanish Cup (18) 1905, 1906, 1907, 1908, 1917, 1934, 1936, 1946, 1947, 1962, 1970, 1974, 1975, 1980, 1982, 1989, 1993, 2011

2012

19/08	Valencia	h	1-1	Higuaín
26/08	Getafe	a	1-2	Higuaín
02/09	Granada	h	3-0	Cristiano Ronaldo 2, Higuaín
15/09	Sevilla	a	0-1	
24/09	Rayo Vallecano	a	2-0	Benzema, Cristiano Ronaldo (p)
30/09	Deportivo	h	5-1	Cristiano Ronaldo 3 (2p), Di María, Pepe
07/10	Barcelona	a	2-2	Cristiano Ronaldo 2
20/10	Celta	h	2-0	Higuaín, Cristiano Ronaldo (p)
28/10	Mallorca	a	5-0	Higuaín 2, Cristiano Ronaldo 2, Callejón
03/11	Zaragoza	a	4-0	Higuaín, Di María, Essien, Modrić
11/11	Levante	a	2-1	Cristiano Ronaldo, Morata
17/11	Athletic	h	5-1	og (Aurtenetxe), Sergio Ramos, Benzema, Özil, Khedira
24/11	Betis	a	0-1	
01/12	Atlético	h	2-0	Cristiano Ronaldo, Özil
08/12	Valladolid	a	3-2	Benzema, Özil 2
16/12	Espanyol	h	2-2	Cristiano Ronaldo, Fábio Coentrão
22/12	Málaga	a	2-3	og (Sergio Sánchez), Benzema

2013

06/01	Real Sociedad	h	4-3	Benzema, Khedira, Cristiano Ronaldo 2
12/01	Osasuna	a	0-0	
20/01	Valencia	a	5-0	Higuaín, Di María 2, Cristiano Ronaldo 2
27/01	Getafe	h	4-0	Sergio Ramos, Cristiano Ronaldo 3 (1p)
02/02	Granada	a	0-1	
09/02	Sevilla	h	4-1	Benzema, Cristiano Ronaldo 3
17/02	Rayo Vallecano	h	2-0	Morata, Sergio Ramos
23/02	Deportivo	a	2-1	Kaká, Higuaín
02/03	Barcelona	a	2-1	Benzema, Sergio Ramos
10/03	Celta	a	2-1	Cristiano Ronaldo 2 (1p)
16/03	Mallorca	h	5-2	Higuaín 2, Cristiano Ronaldo, Modrić, Benzema
30/03	Zaragoza	a	1-1	Cristiano Ronaldo
06/04	Levante	h	5-1	Higuaín, Kaká (p), Cristiano Ronaldo, Özil 2
14/04	Athletic	a	3-0	Cristiano Ronaldo 2, Higuaín
20/04	Betis	h	3-1	Özil 2, Benzema
27/04	Atlético	a	2-1	og (Juanfran), Di María
04/05	Valladolid	h	4-3	og (Marc Valiente), Cristiano Ronaldo 2, Kaká
08/05	Málaga	h	6-2	Albiol, Cristiano Ronaldo, Özil, Benzema, Modrić, Di María
11/05	Espanyol	a	1-1	Higuaín
26/05	Real Sociedad	a	3-3	Higuaín, Callejón, Khedira
01/06	Osasuna	h	4-2	Higuaín, Essien, Benzema, Callejón

No	Name	Nat	DoB	Pos	Aps	(s)	Gls
13	Antonio Adán		13/05/87	G	3		
18	Raúl Albiol		04/09/85	D	14	(4)	1
17	Álvaro Arbeloa		19/01/83	D	25	(1)	
9	Karim Benzema	FRA	19/12/87	A	19	(11)	11
21	José Callejón		11/02/87	M	15	(15)	0
38	Casemiro	BRA	23/02/92	M	1		
1	Iker Casillas		20/05/81	G	18	(1)	
35	Jesús Collado		11/06/88	G	1		
7	Cristiano Ronaldo	POR	05/02/85	A	30	(4)	34
22	Ángel Di María	ARG	14/02/88	A	22	(10)	6
24	Lassana Diarra	FRA	10/03/85	M	2		
25	Diego López		03/11/81	G	16		
15	Michael Essien	GHA	03/12/82	M	19	(2)	2
33	Fabinho	BRA		D		(1)	
5	Fábio Coentrão	POR	11/03/88	D	16		1
20	Gonzalo Higuaín	ARG	10/12/87	A	19	(9)	16
34	José Rodríguez		16/12/94	M		(1)	
8	Kaká	BRA	22/04/82	M	12	(7)	3
6	Sami Khedira	GER	04/04/87	M	19	(6)	3
37	Diego Llorente		16/08/93	D		(1)	
12	Marcelo	BRA	12/05/88	D	13	(1)	
19	Luka Modrić	CRO	09/09/85	M	25	(8)	3
29	Álvaro Morata		23/10/92	A	5	(7)	2
27	Nacho		18/01/90	D	6	(3)	
39	Omar Mascarell		02/02/93	M		(1)	
10	Mesut Özil	GER	15/10/88	M	23	(9)	9
3	Pepe	POR	26/02/83	D	26	(2)	1
11	Ricardo Carvalho	POR	18/05/78	D	9		
4	Sergio Ramos		30/03/86	D	26		4
2	Raphael Varane	FRA	25/04/93	D	12	(3)	
14	Xabi Alonso		25/11/81	M	22	(0)	

REAL SOCIEDAD DE FÚTBOL

Coach: Philippe Montanier (FRA)
1909 • Anoeta (32,000) • realsociedad.com
Major honours
Spanish League (2) 1981, 1982;
Spanish Cup (2) 1909, 1987

2012

19/08	Barcelona	a	1-5	Castro
25/08	Celta	h	2-1	Agirretxe 2
01/09	Mallorca	a	0-1	
16/09	Zaragoza	h	2-0	Íñigo Martínez, Vela (p)
23/09	Levante	a	1-2	Zurutuza
29/09	Athletic	h	2-0	Griezmann, Vela (p)
06/10	Betis	a	0-2	
21/10	Atlético	h	0-1	
29/10	Valladolid	a	2-2	Griezmann 2
04/11	Espanyol	h	0-1	
10/11	Málaga	a	2-1	Vela, Xabi Prieto
19/11	Rayo Vallecano	h	4-0	Vela 2, Mikel González, Castro
23/11	Osasuna	h	0-0	
01/12	Valencia	a	5-2	De la Bella, Mikel González, Ifrán, Agirretxe, Vela (p)
08/12	Getafe	h	1-1	Carlos Martínez
15/12	Granada	a	0-0	
20/12	Sevilla	h	2-1	Vela, De la Bella

2013

06/01	Real Madrid	a	3-4	Xabi Prieto 3 (1p)
13/01	Deportivo	h	1-1	Vela
19/01	Barcelona	h	3-2	Castro 2, Agirretxe
26/01	Celta	a	1-1	Elustondo
02/02	Mallorca	h	3-0	Castro, Vela, Ifrán
10/02	Zaragoza	a	2-1	Griezmann, Agirretxe
17/02	Levante	h	1-1	Vela (p)
22/02	Athletic	a	3-1	Griezmann, Agirretxe, Vela
03/03	Betis	h	3-3	Vela, Íñigo Martínez, Xabi Prieto (p)
10/03	Atlético	a	1-0	Xabi Prieto
16/03	Valladolid	h	4-1	Griezmann 2, Agirretxe, Xabi Prieto
31/03	Espanyol	a	2-2	Zurutuza, og (Javi López)
06/04	Málaga	h	4-2	Vela, De la Bella, Griezmann, Íñigo Martínez
14/04	Rayo Vallecano	a	2-0	Agirretxe 2
21/04	Osasuna	a	0-0	
28/04	Valencia	h	4-2	Íñigo Martínez, Castro, Agirretxe 2
06/05	Getafe	a	1-2	Vela
13/05	Granada	h	2-2	Agirretxe 2
18/05	Sevilla	a	2-1	og (Rakitić), Agirretxe
26/05	Real Madrid	h	3-3	Xabi Prieto 2 (1p), Griezmann
01/06	Deportivo	a	1-0	Griezmann

No	Name	Nat	DoB	Pos	Aps	(s)	Gls
9	Imanol Agirretxe		24/02/87	A	22	(12)	14
15	Ion Ansotegi		13/07/82	D	4	(3)	
1	Claudio Bravo	CHI	13/04/83	G	31		
19	Liassine Cadamuro	ALG	05/03/88	D	2	(2)	
2	Carlos Martínez		09/04/86	D	29		1
18	Gonzalo Castro	URU	14/09/84	M	13	(17)	6
24	Alberto De la Bella		02/12/85	D	36		3
4	Gorka Elustondo		18/03/87	M	5	(3)	1
22	Daniel Estrada		03/01/87	M	10	(9)	
7	Antoine Griezmann	FRA	21/03/91	A	32	(1)	10
21	Diego Ifrán	URU	08/06/87	A	9	(17)	2
8	Asier Illarramendi		08/03/90	M	32	(1)	
5	Íñigo Martínez		17/05/91	D	34		4
23	Javi Ros		16/02/90	M		(6)	
20	José Ángel		05/09/89	D	2	(9)	
5	Markel Bergara		05/05/85	M	27	(1)	
3	Mikel González		24/09/85	D	34		2
14	Rubén Pardo		22/10/92	M	10	(15)	
11	Carlos Vela	MEX	01/03/89	A	32	(3)	14
10	Xabi Prieto		29/08/83	M	33	(2)	9
13	Eñaut Zubikarai		26/02/84	G	7		
17	David Zurutuza	FRA	19/07/86	M	14	(7)	6

SEVILLA FC

Coach: Míchel; (14/01/13) Unai Emery
1905 • Ramón Sánchez Pizjuán (45,500) • sevillafc.es
Major honours
UEFA Cup (2) 2006, 2007;
UEFA Super Cup (1) 2006;
Spanish League (1) 1946;
Spanish Cup (5) 1935, 1939, 1948, 2007, 2010

2012

18/08	Getafe	h	2-1	Fazio, Negredo (p)
26/08	Granada	a	1-1	Negredo
02/09	Rayo Vallecano	a	0-1	
15/09	Real Madrid	h	1-0	Trochowski
24/09	Deportivo	a	2-0	Negredo, Rakitić
29/09	Barcelona	a	2-3	Trochowski, Negredo
05/10	Celta	a	0-2	
22/10	Mallorca	h	3-2	Negredo 2, Cicinho
28/10	Levante	a	2-1	Medel
04/11	Levante	h	0-0	
11/11	Athletic	a	1-2	Negredo (p)
18/11	Betis	h	5-1	Reyes 2, Fazio 2, Rakitić
25/11	Atlético	a	0-4	
03/12	Valladolid	h	1-2	og (Manucho)
07/12	Espanyol	a	2-2	Rakitić (p), Negredo
15/12	Málaga	h	0-2	
20/12	Real Sociedad	a	1-2	Medel

2013

05/01	Osasuna	h	1-0	Spahić
12/01	Valencia	a	0-2	
19/01	Getafe	a	1-1	Reyes
28/01	Granada	h	3-0	Kondogbia, Negredo, Medel
03/02	Rayo Vallecano	h	2-1	Rakitić, Negredo
09/02	Real Madrid	a	1-4	Manu del Moral
15/02	Deportivo	h	3-1	Rakitić, Medel 2
23/02	Barcelona	a	1-2	Botía
04/03	Celta	h	4-1	Negredo 3, Medel
09/03	Mallorca	a	1-2	Negredo
17/03	Zaragoza	h	4-0	Coke 2, Reyes, Negredo
30/03	Levante	a	0-1	
08/04	Athletic	h	2-1	Negredo 2
12/04	Betis	a	3-3	Rakitić 2, Negredo
21/04	Atlético	h	0-1	
28/04	Valladolid	a	1-1	Negredo (p)
05/05	Espanyol	h	3-0	og (Capdevila), Coke, Negredo
12/05	Málaga	a	0-0	
18/05	Real Sociedad	h	1-2	Rakitić
26/05	Osasuna	a	1-2	Negredo
01/06	Valencia	h	4-3	Negredo 4 (1p)

No	Name	Nat	DoB	Pos	Aps	(s)	Gls
28	Álex Rubio		27/03/93	A		(2)	
20	Baba Diawara	SEN	01/01/88	A	5	(14)	
13	Beto	POR	01/05/82	G	14		
24	Alberto Botía		27/01/89	D	14	(4)	1
5	Cala		26/11/89	D	8	(2)	
6	José Campaña		31/05/93	M	3	(2)	
21	Cicinho	BRA	04/08/86	D	19	(8)	1
23	Coke		26/04/87	D	19	(2)	3
13	Diego López		03/11/81	G	8		
2	Federico Fazio	ARG	17/03/87	D	25	(1)	3
3	Fernando Navarro		25/06/82	D	35		
17	Javi Hervás		09/06/89	M	1	(8)	
7	Jesús Navas		21/11/85	M	37		
29	Julián Cuesta		28/03/91	G	1		
22	Geoffrey Kondogbia	FRA	15/02/93	M	23	(8)	1
16	Antonio Luna		17/03/91	D	1	(3)	
12	Hedwiges Maduro	NED	13/02/85	M	16	(10)	
14	Manu del Moral		25/02/84	A	7	(15)	1
8	Gary Medel	CHI	03/08/87	M	31	(1)	6
35	Alberto Moreno		05/07/92	D	12	(3)	
9	Álvaro Negredo		20/08/85	A	34	(2)	25
1	Andrés Palop		22/10/73	G	15	(1)	
10	Diego Perotti	ARG	26/07/88	A	8	(10)	
34	Israel Puerto		15/06/93	D		(2)	
30	Bryan Rabello	CHI	16/05/94	M		(3)	
11	Ivan Rakitić	CRO	10/03/88	M	34		8
19	José Antonio Reyes		01/09/83	M	20	(6)	4
4	Emir Spahić	BIH	18/08/80	D	22		1
18	Miroslav Stevanović	BIH	29/07/90	A		(7)	
15	Piotr Trochowski	GER	22/03/84	M	6		2

VALENCIA CF

Coach: Mauricio Pellegrino (ARG);
(03/12/12) Ernesto Valverde
1919 • Mestalla (52,000) • valenciacf.com
Major honours
UEFA Cup Winners' Cup (1) 1980;
UEFA Cup (1) 2004;
Inter Cities Fairs Cup (2) 1962, 1963;
UEFA Super Cup (2) 1980, 2004;
Spanish League (6) 1942, 1944, 1947, 1971, 2002, 2004;
Spanish Cup (7) 1941, 1949, 1954, 1967, 1979, 1999, 2008

2012

19/08	Real Madrid	a	1-1	Jonas
26/08	Deportivo	h	3-3	Soldado 2, Feghouli
02/09	Barcelona	a	0-1	
15/09	Celta	h	2-1	Feghouli, Cissokho
23/09	Mallorca	a	0-2	
29/09	Zaragoza	h	2-0	Feghouli, Jonathan Viera
07/10	Levante	a	0-1	
20/10	Athletic	h	3-2	Soldado (p), Tino Costa, Valdez
27/10	Betis	a	0-1	
03/11	Atlético	h	2-0	Soldado, Valdez
11/11	Valladolid	a	1-1	Cissokho
17/11	Espanyol	h	3-1	Jonathan Viera, Soldado (p)
24/11	Málaga	a	0-4	
01/12	Real Sociedad	h	2-5	Soldado 2
08/12	Osasuna	a	1-0	Soldado
16/12	Rayo Vallecano	h	0-1	
21/12	Getafe	h	4-2	Soldado, Jonas, Ricardo Costa, Valdez

2013

05/01	Granada	a	2-1	Jonas, Piatti
12/01	Sevilla	h	2-0	Soldado 2
20/01	Real Madrid	h	0-5	
26/01	Deportivo	a	3-2	Jonas, Valdez, Ricardo Costa
03/02	Barcelona	h	1-1	Éver Banega
09/02	Celta	a	1-0	Valdez
17/02	Mallorca	h	2-0	Ricardo Costa, Soldado
23/02	Zaragoza	a	2-2	Jonas 2
02/03	Levante	h	2-2	Jonas, Soldado
10/03	Athletic	a	0-1	
16/03	Betis	h	3-0	Soldado (p), og (Paulão), Jonas
31/03	Atlético	a	1-1	Jonas
07/04	Valladolid	h	2-1	og (Balenziaga), Jonas
13/04	Espanyol	a	3-3	Canales, Jonas, Soldado
20/04	Málaga	h	5-1	Parejo, Soldado 2 (1p), Canales, Éver Banega
28/04	Real Sociedad	a	2-4	Soldado, Jonas
04/05	Osasuna	h	4-0	Soldado, Ricardo Costa, Éver Banega, Jonas (p)
12/05	Rayo Vallecano	a	4-0	Soldado 2 (1p), Guardado, Valdez
18/05	Getafe	a	1-0	Mathieu
26/05	Granada	h	1-0	Soldado
01/06	Sevilla	a	3-4	Éver Banega, Soldado 2

No	Name	Nat	DoB	Pos	Aps	(s)	Gls
6	David Albelda		01/09/77	M	16	(2)	
14	Antonio Barragán		12/06/87	D	9	(5)	
28	Juan Bernat		01/03/93	D	6	(6)	
23	Sergio Canales		16/02/91	M	7	(6)	2
3	Aly Cissokho	FRA	15/09/87	D	18	(7)	2
1	Diego Alves	BRA	24/06/85	G	24		
10	Éver Banega	ARG	29/06/88	M	22	(7)	4
8	Sofiane Feghouli	ALG	26/12/89	M	23	(4)	3
5	Fernando Gago	ARG	10/04/86	M	11	(2)	
13	Vicente Guaita		18/02/87	G	14		
17	Andrés Guardado	MEX	28/09/86	M	26	(6)	1
12	João Pereira	POR	25/02/84	D	28	(2)	
7	Jonas	BRA	01/04/84	A	30	(5)	13
15	Jonathan Viera		21/10/89	M	7	(10)	2
22	Jérémy Mathieu	FRA	29/10/83	D	16	(1)	1
21	Daniel Parejo		16/04/89	M	20	(7)	1
11	Pablo Piatti	ARG	31/03/89	A	14	(1)	1
4	Adil Rami	FRA	27/12/85	D	24	(1)	
20	Ricardo Costa	POR	16/05/81	D	25	(1)	4
9	Roberto Soldado		27/05/85	A	33	(2)	24
24	Tino Costa	ARG	09/01/85	M	26	(5)	1
16	Nélson Valdez	PAR	28/11/83	A	6	(22)	6
18	Víctor Ruiz		25/01/89	D	17	(9)	

REAL VALLADOLID CF

Coach: Miroslav Djukić (SRB)
1928 • Nuevo José Zorrilla (26,512) • realvalladolid.es

2012

20/08	Zaragoza	a	1-0	Óscar
27/08	Levante	h	2-0	Víctor Pérez 2 (2p)
02/09	Athletic	a	0-2	
17/09	Betis	h	0-1	
23/09	Atlético	a	1-2	Bueno
30/09	Rayo Vallecano	h	6-1	Bueno, Manucho 2, Óscar 2, Rukavina
06/10	Espanyol	h	1-1	Óscar
20/10	Málaga	a	1-2	Manucho
29/10	Real Sociedad	h	2-2	Ebert, Óscar
04/11	Osasuna	a	1-0	Ebert
11/11	Valencia	h	1-1	Víctor Pérez (p)
18/11	Getafe	a	1-2	Óscar
24/11	Granada	h	1-0	Manucho
03/12	Sevilla	a	2-1	Ebert, Óscar
08/12	Real Madrid	h	2-3	Manucho 2
17/12	Deportivo	a	0-0	
22/12	Barcelona	h	1-3	Javi Guerra

2013

06/01	Celta	a	1-3	Bueno (p)
12/01	Mallorca	h	3-1	Ebert 2, Óscar
20/01	Zaragoza	h	2-0	Javi Guerra, Óscar
26/01	Levante	a	1-2	Baraja
01/02	Athletic	h	2-2	Javi Guerra, Bueno
11/02	Betis	a	0-0	
17/02	Atlético	h	0-3	
24/02	Rayo Vallecano	a	2-1	og (Jordi Amat), Manucho
03/03	Espanyol	a	0-0	
09/03	Málaga	h	1-1	Manucho
16/03	Real Sociedad	a	1-4	Javi Guerra
31/03	Osasuna	h	1-3	og (Rubén González)
07/04	Valencia	a	1-2	Óscar
13/04	Getafe	h	2-1	Óscar, Javi Guerra
20/04	Granada	a	1-1	Ebert
28/04	Sevilla	h	1-1	Javi Guerra
04/05	Real Madrid	a	3-4	Óscar, Javi Guerra, Lluís Sastre
11/05	Deportivo	h	1-0	Javi Guerra
19/05	Barcelona	a	1-2	Víctor Pérez
26/05	Celta	h	0-2	
01/06	Mallorca	a	2-4	Bueno, Omar Ramos

No	Name	Nat	DoB	Pos	Aps	(s)	Gls
18	Álvaro Rubio		18/04/79	M	34	(1)	
24	Mikel Balenziaga		29/02/88	D	32		
8	Javier Baraja		24/08/80	D	3	(9)	1
15	Alberto Bueno		20/03/88	A	14	(19)	5
13	Dani Hernández	VEN	21/10/85	G	24		
20	Patrick Ebert	GER	17/03/87	M	22	(1)	6
1	Jaime		10/12/80	G	14		
9	Javi Guerra		15/03/82	A	17	(13)	8
6	Jesús Rueda		19/02/87	D	26	(2)	
11	Daniel Larsson	SWE	25/01/87	A	17	(1)	
16	Lluís Sastre		26/03/86	M	13	(16)	1
27	Lolo		17/04/93	A		(7)	
25	Manucho	ANG	07/03/83	A	19	(6)	8
4	Marc Valiente		29/03/87	D	28		
7	Juan Neira	ARG	24/08/87	A	1	(6)	
14	Omar Ramos		26/01/88	A	29	(5)	1
10	Óscar		12/11/82	M	33	(2)	12
17	Carlos Peña		28/07/87	D	11	(9)	
23	Valdet Rama	ALB	20/11/87	M	1	(4)	
28	Rubén Peña		18/07/91	M		(1)	
2	Antonio Rukavina	SRB	26/01/84	D	37		1
5	Henrique Sereno	POR	18/05/85	D	19	(1)	
22	Víctor Pérez		12/01/88	M	24	(1)	4

REAL ZARAGOZA

Coach: Manuel Jiménez
1932 • La Romareda (34,594) • realzaragoza.com
Major honours
UEFA Cup Winners' Cup (1) 1995;
Inter Cities Fairs Cup (1) 1964;
Spanish Cup (6) 1964, 1966, 1986, 1994, 2001, 2004.

2012

20/08	Valladolid	h	0-1	
25/08	Espanyol	a	2-1	Apoño (p), Hélder Postiga
01/09	Málaga	h	0-1	
16/09	Real Sociedad	a	0-2	
22/09	Osasuna	h	3-1	Hélder Postiga, og (Timor), Apoño (p)
29/09	Valencia	a	0-2	
06/10	Getafe	h	0-1	
21/10	Granada	a	2-1	Hélder Postiga, Víctor Rodríguez
28/10	Sevilla	h	2-1	Hélder Postiga, Săpunaru
03/11	Real Madrid	a	0-4	
10/11	Deportivo	h	5-3	Apoño (p), Paco Montañés, Álvaro, Hélder Postiga 2
17/11	Barcelona	a	1-3	Paco Montañés
26/11	Celta	h	0-1	
02/12	Mallorca	a	1-1	Hélder Postiga
10/12	Rayo Vallecano	a	2-0	Zuculini, Apoño
16/12	Levante	h	0-1	
22/12	Athletic	a	2-0	Apoño (p), Hélder Postiga

2013

04/01	Betis	h	1-2	Paco Montañés
13/01	Atlético	a	0-2	
20/01	Valladolid	a	0-2	
26/01	Espanyol	h	0-0	
03/02	Málaga	a	1-1	Hélder Postiga
10/02	Real Sociedad	h	1-2	Apoño (p)
16/02	Osasuna	a	0-1	
23/02	Valencia	h	2-2	Apoño (p), Hélder Postiga
01/03	Getafe	a	0-2	
11/03	Granada	h	0-0	
17/03	Sevilla	a	0-4	
30/03	Real Madrid	h	1-1	Rodri
06/04	Deportivo	a	2-3	Hélder Postiga (p), Paco Montañés
14/04	Barcelona	h	0-3	
22/04	Celta	a	1-2	Săpunaru
27/04	Mallorca	h	3-2	Paco Montañés, Hélder Postiga, Rubén Rochina
05/05	Rayo Vallecano	h	3-0	Apoño 2 (1p), Rodri
10/05	Levante	a	0-0	
19/05	Athletic	h	1-2	Hélder Postiga
26/05	Betis	a	0-4	
01/06	Atlético	h	1-3	Hélder Postiga

No	Name	Nat	DoB	Pos	Aps	(s)	Gls
21	Abraham Minero		22/02/86	D	35		
30	Pablo Alcolea		23/03/89	G	1	(1)	
4	Álvaro González		08/01/90	D	33		1
10	Apoño		13/02/84	M	29	(3)	9
7	Carlos Aranda		27/07/80	A	2	(9)	
17	Stefan Babović	SRB	07/01/87	M	3	(6)	
7	Henri Bienvenu	CMR	05/07/88	A	1	(3)	
25	Adrià Carmona		12/10/88	D	4		
6	Raúl Goni		12/10/88	D	4		
27	Héctor		23/05/91	D	1		
9	Hélder Postiga	POR	02/08/82	A	36	(1)	14
23	Javi Álamo		18/08/88	A		(7)	
14	José Fernández		11/11/89	D	7	(4)	
15	José Mari		06/12/87	M	16	(8)	
5	Maurizio Lanzaro	ITA	14/03/82	D		(1)	
13	Leo Franco	ARG	20/05/77	G	4		
16	Glenn Loovens	NED	22/09/83	D	21		
2	José María Movilla		08/02/75	M	23	(6)	
24	Ivan Obradović	SRB	25/07/88	D	1		
8	Eduard Oriol		05/11/86	A	8	(11)	
26	Jorge Ortí		28/04/93	A	1	(5)	
11	Paco Montañés		08/10/86	M	38		5
3	Javier Paredes		05/07/82	M	16	(4)	
22	Ádám Pintér	HUN	12/06/88	D	16	(2)	
1	Roberto		10/02/86	G	33		
6	Rodri		06/06/90	A	8	(4)	2
12	Romarić	CIV	04/06/83	M	7	(5)	
24	Rubén Rochina		23/03/91	A	5	(10)	1
19	Cristian Săpunaru	ROU	05/04/84	D	29		2
28	Tarsi		16/10/94	M		(1)	
32	Víctor Rodríguez		19/03/89	A	26	(7)	1
18	Lucas Wilchez	ARG	31/08/83	M	1	(4)	
20	Franco Zuculini	ARG	05/09/90	M	13	(3)	1

Domestic cup: Copa del Rey 2012/13

FOURTH ROUND

(30/10/12 & 28/11/12)
Alavés 0-3, 1-3 Barcelona *(1-6)*
Llagostera 0-2, 1-3 Valencia *(1-5)*

(31/10/12 & 27/11/12)
Alcoyano 1-4, 0-3 Real Madrid *(1-7)*
Cacereño 3-4, 1-0 Málaga *(4-4; Málaga on away goals)*
Las Palmas 1-0, 0-0 Rayo Vallecano *(1-0)*

(31/10/12 & 28/11/2012)
Jaén 0-3, 0-1 Atlético *(0-4)*

(31/10/12 & 29/11/12)
Almería 2-0, 0-3 Celta *(aet; 2-3)*
Zaragoza 1-0, 1-2 Granada *(2-2; Zaragoza on away goal)*

(01/11/12 & 27/11/12)
Córdoba 2-0, 2-2 Real Sociedad *(4-2)*
Sporting 1-0, 0-2 Osasuna *(1-2)*
Valladolid 1-0, 0-3 Betis *(1-3)*

(01/11/12 & 28/11/12)
Melilla 1-0, 1-4 Levante *(2-4)*
Ponferradina 0-4, 0-0 Getafe *(0-4)*
Sevilla 3-1, 3-0 Espanyol *(6-1)*

(01/11/12 & 29/11/12)
Deportivo 1-1, 0-0 Mallorca *(1-1; Mallorca on away goal)*

(01/11/12 & 12/12/12)
Éibar 0-0, 1-1 Athletic *(1-1; Éibar on away goal)*

FIFTH ROUND

(11/12/12 & 08/01/13)
Osasuna 0-2, 1-2 Valencia *(1-4)*

(12/12/12 & 09/01/13)
Celta 2-1, 0-4 Real Madrid *(2-5)*
Mallorca 0-5, 2-1 Sevilla *(2-6)*

(12/12/12 & 10/01/13)
Atlético 3-0, 0-0 Getafe *(3-0)*
Córdoba 0-2, 0-5 Barcelona *(0-7)*

(13/12/12 & 09/01/13)
Levante 0-1, 0-2 Zaragoza *(0-3)*

(13/12/12 & 10/01/13)
Las Palmas 1-1, 0-1 Betis *(1-2)*

(18/12/12 & 08/01/13)
Éibar 1-1, 1-4 Málaga *(2-5)*

QUARTER-FINALS

(15/01/13 & 23/01/13)
Real Madrid 2-0 Valencia *(Benzema 37, Guardado 73og)*
Valencia 1-1 Real Madrid *(Tino Costa 52; Benzema 44)*
(Real Madrid 3-1)

(16/01/13 & 23/01/13)
Zaragoza 0-0 Sevilla
Sevilla 4-0 Zaragoza *(Negredo 36, 66p, Rakitić 45+3, Manu del Moral 90+2)*
(Sevilla 4-0)

(16/01/13 & 24/01/13)
Barcelona 2-2 Málaga *(Messi 29, Puyol 30; Iturra 25, Camacho 89)*
Málaga 2-4 Barcelona *(Joaquín 12, Santa Cruz 68; Pedro 9, Piqué 49, Iniesta 76, Messi 80)*
(Barcelona 6-4)

(17/01/13 & 24/01/13)
Atlético 2-0 Betis *(Falcao 10, Filipe Luís 23)*
Betis 1-1 Atlético *(Jorge Molina 88p; Diego Costa 44)*
(Atlético 3-1)

SEMI-FINALS

(30/01/13 & 26/02/13)
Real Madrid 1-1 Barcelona *(Varane 81; Fàbregas 50)*
Barcelona 1-3 Real Madrid *(Jordi Alba 89; Cristiano Ronaldo 13p, 58, Varane 68)*
(Real Madrid 4-2)

(31/01/13 & 27/02/13)
Atlético 2-1 Sevilla *(Diego Costa 49p, 71p; Negredo 56p)*
Sevilla 2-2 Atlético *(Jesús Navas 39, Rakitić 90; Diego Costa 6, Falcao 29)*
(Atlético 4-3)

FINAL

(18/05/13)
Santiago Bernabéu, Madrid
CLUB ATLÉTICO DE MADRID 2 *(Diego Costa 35, Miranda 99)*
REAL MADRID CF 1 *(Cristiano Ronaldo 14)*
(aet)
Referee: *Clos Gómez.*
ATLÉTICO: *Courtois, Juanfran, Miranda, Godín, Filipe Luís, Arda (Rodríguez 110), Mario Suárez, Gabi, Koke (Raúl García 112), Diego Costa (Adrián López 106), Falcao*
Sent off: *Gabi (119)*
REAL MADRID: *Diego López, Essien, Sergio Ramos, Albiol, Fábio Coentrão (Arbeloa 91), Khedira, Xabi Alonso, Modrić (Di María 91), Özil, Cristiano Ronaldo, Benzema (Higuaín 91)*
Sent off: *Cristiano Ronaldo (115)*

Atlético defender Miranda towers over Real Madrid goalkeeper Diego López to head home the winner in the final of the Copa del Rey

SWEDEN

Svenska Fotbollförbundet (SvFF)

Address	Evenemangsgatan 31	**President**	Karl-Erik Nilsson
	SE-171 23 Solna	**General secretary**	Mikael Santoft
Tel	+46 8 7350900	**Media officer**	Jonas Nystedt
Fax	+46 8 7350901	**Year of formation**	1904
E-Mail	svff@svenskfotboll.se	**National stadium**	Friends Arena, Solna
Website	svenskfotboll.se		(50,000)

ALLSVENSKAN CLUBS

1. AIK
2. Djurgårdens IF
3. IF Elfsborg
4. GAIS Göteborg
5. Gefle IF
6. IFK Göteborg
7. Helsingborgs IF
8. BK Häcken
9. Kalmar FF
10. Malmö FF
11. Mjällby AIF
12. IFK Norrköping
13. GIF Sundsvall
14. Syrianska FC
15. Åtvidabergs FF
16. Örebro SK

PROMOTED CLUBS

17. Östers IF
18. IF Brommapojkarna
19. Halmstads BK

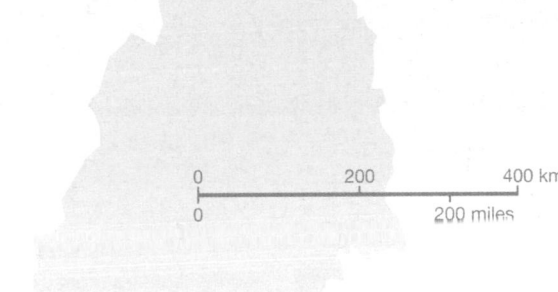

KEY:

- ● – UEFA Champions League
- ● – UEFA Europa League
- ● – Promoted clubs
- ● – Relegated clubs

Elfsborg hold their nerve

From 2005 to 2011 the Allsvenskan title was claimed by seven different clubs, but that sequence came to an end as IF Elfsborg, the 2006 champions, regained the trophy that had repeatedly eluded them – and their long-serving coach Magnus Haglund – since their previous triumph.

Haglund was replaced for the 2012 campaign by Jörgen Lennartsson, and the move brought immediate success as the former Sweden Under-21 boss masterminded a triumph rooted in outstanding home form. High-scoring BK Häcken were unlikely runners-up, finishing just ahead of AIK and Malmö FF as 2011 champions Helsingborgs IF dropped to sixth.

SVENSKA MÄSTARE 2012

Johan Valkonen

SVEN

| Boras club claim Allsvenskan title on final day | Häcken spring a surprise to finish second | Amazing World Cup comeback in Berlin |

Domestic league

Top-four finishers in each of the five previous campaigns, Elfsborg got off to a blistering start under their new coach, winning ten of their first 12 matches, including all six at home on the artificial surface of the Borås Arena. That gave them an eight-point lead at the top of the table as the Allsvenskan shut down for UEFA EURO 2012.

The break did Elfsborg no favours. On the resumption they lost 5-1 at Åtvidabergs FF and surrendered their first points in Boras, but while they quickly rediscovered their home form, poor results on the road became commonplace, and they went five months without an away win until rock-bottom GAIS Göteborg obliged them in October. This allowed other clubs back into contention, but just as it seemed that another title would escape their clutches, Elfsborg climbed back to the summit and squeezed home on the final day with a nervy 1-1 draw against earlier conquerors Åtvidaberg as Malmö lost 2-0 at AIK – in the last match played at the Råsundastadion.

Having held top spot for 23 rounds and remained unbeaten at home, Elfsborg's triumph was well merited. Runners-up Häcken, with a monster tally of 67 goals,

had the league's most potent attack, and AIK, with just 27 conceded, the best defence, but Lennartsson's team boasted the most effective and energetic midfield, where the experienced duo of skipper Anders Svensson and Stefan Ishizaki blended superbly with youngsters Oscar Hiljemark and Niklas Hult.

Domestic cup

The Svenska Cupen was switched to a different timetable, with no winners in 2012 but an extended competition, involving a lengthy group phase, ending at the newly constructed Friends Arena in May 2013. Several feats of giant-killing were witnessed en route before Djurgårdens IF and IFK Göteborg assembled for the final. An even contest ended 1-1 before Göteborg came good in the penalty shoot-out to take the trophy for the sixth time.

Europe

Mediocre in domestic competition, Helsingborg partly redeemed themselves in Europe, where they reached the group stage of the UEFA Europa League and took four points off FC Twente. AIK joined them there after a rousing play-off victory over PFC CSKA Moskva and also got the better of Dutch opposition,

registering a win and a draw against PSV Eindhoven. A disappointing earlier effort against Danish club AC Horsens put paid to Elfsborg's hopes.

National team

2012/13 was an up-and-down season for the Swedish national team but it featured two glorious highs that will be remembered forever and a day. The first was an extraordinary 4-4 draw against Germany in Berlin, a 2014 FIFA World Cup qualifier in which Erik Hamrén's side made the impossible possible, coming back from 4-0 down to score four goals themselves in the last half-hour. The second came a few weeks later at the grand opening of the new national stadium, where the talismanic Zlatan Ibrahimović scored all four goals, the last of them a sensational long-distance overhead kick, as Sweden defeated England 4-2 in a friendly.

The unlikely World Cup draw in Germany looked even more precious when Hamrén's men shed five points in their next two qualifiers, against the Republic of Ireland (0-0) and Austria (1-2). Sweden have not missed back-to-back World Cups since the 1980s, but those results left Ibrahimović and co – absentees from South Africa in 2010 – having to fight tooth and nail simply to reach the play-offs.

Domestic league: Allsvenskan 2012 final table

		Pld	Home					Away					Total					
			W	D	L	F	A	W	D	L	F	A	W	D	L	F	A	Pts
1	IF Elfsborg	30	12	3	0	24	5	6	2	7	24	24	18	5	7	48	29	59
2	BK Häcken	30	9	3	3	44	19	8	3	4	23	17	17	6	7	67	36	57
3	Malmö FF	30	10	4	1	26	6	6	4	5	23	27	16	8	6	49	33	56
4	AIK	30	7	6	2	23	12	8	4	3	18	15	15	10	5	41	27	55
5	IFK Norrköping	30	7	5	3	29	21	8	2	5	21	22	15	7	8	50	43	52
6	Helsingborgs IF	30	8	6	1	32	13	5	5	5	20	20	13	11	6	52	33	50
7	IFK Göteborg	30	6	7	2	21	15	3	5	7	15	26	9	12	9	36	41	39
8	Åtvidabergs FF	30	7	4	4	27	16	2	6	7	21	32	9	10	11	48	48	37
9	Djurgårdens IF	30	5	6	4	19	19	3	7	5	18	21	8	13	9	37	40	37
10	Kalmar FF	30	5	4	6	23	19	5	3	7	13	26	10	7	13	36	45	37
11	Gefle IF	30	3	5	7	13	16	6	4	5	13	21	9	9	12	26	37	36
12	Mjällby AIF	30	5	4	6	18	18	3	6	6	15	21	8	10	12	33	39	34
13	Syrianska FC	30	5	4	6	20	22	4	3	8	15	23	9	7	14	35	45	34
14	GIF Sundsvall	30	4	3	8	22	25	2	8	5	13	21	6	11	13	35	46	29
15	Örebro SK	30	3	3	9	18	22	2	6	7	14	24	5	9	16	32	46	24
16	GAIS Göteborg	30	1	5	9	16	26	0	4	11	8	35	1	9	20	24	61	12

SEASON AT A GLANCE

EUROPEAN QUALIFICATION 2013/14

Champion: IF Elfsborg (second qualifying round)

Cup winner: IFK Göteborg (second qualifying round)
BK Häcken (second qualifying round)
Malmö FF (first qualifying round)
Gefle IF (first qualifying round)

Top scorer Waris Majeed (Häcken), 23 goals
Relegated clubs GAIS Göteborg, Örebro SK, GIF Sundsvall
Promoted clubs Östers IF, IF Brommapojkarna, Halmstads BK
Cup final IFK Göteborg 1-1 Djurgårdens IF *(aet; 3-1 on pens)*

ALLSVENSKAN TEAM OF THE SEASON
(4-4-2)
Coach: Gerhardsson *(Häcken)*

Turina *(AIK)*

Lorentzson *(AIK)* — Jansson *(Malmö)* — Backman *(AIK)* — Arkivuo *(Häcken)*

Hamad *(Malmö)* — Hult *(Elfsborg)* — Ishizaki *(Elfsborg)* — Bergström *(Åtvidaberg)*

Majeed *(Häcken)* — Thorvaldsson *(Norrköping)*

PLAYER OF THE SEASON
Stefan Ishizaki
(IF Elfsborg)

While Zlatan Ibrahimović picked up Swedish football's top individual prize, the Guldbollen, for a sixth consecutive year, Ishizaki had no equals on the domestic front. Elfsborg's title-winning season relied heavily on the long-serving midfielder's assists and goals, one of them a spectacular volley from his own half against Örebro SK in April.

NEWCOMER OF THE SEASON
Waris Majeed
(BK Häcken)

Häcken's free-scoring attack was led by the 21-year-old Ghanaian, who finished as the league's top scorer with 23 goals, five of them coming in one glorious game against IFK Norrköping. Allsvenskan defenders were entitled to breathe a sigh of relief when the razor-sharp striker completed a transfer to FC Spartak Moskva at the end of the season.

SWEDEN

NATIONAL TEAM

Home Kit   Away Kit

INTERNATIONAL TOURNAMENT APPEARANCES

FIFA World Cup (11) 1934 (2nd round), 1938 (4th), 1950 (3rd), 1958 (runners-up), 1970, 1974 (2nd phase), 1978, 1990, 1994 (3rd), 2002 (2nd round), 2006 (2nd round)

UEFA European Championship (5) 1992 (semi-finals), 2000, 2004 (qtr-finals), 2008, 2012

TOP FIVE ALL-TIME CAPS

Thomas Ravelli (143); **Anders Svensson** (141); Olof Mellberg (117); Roland Nilsson (116); Björn Nordqvist (115)

TOP FIVE ALL-TIME GOALS

Sven Rydell (49); Gunnar Nordahl (43); **Zlatan Ibrahimović** (41); Henrik Larsson (37); Gunnar Gren (32)

Results 2012/13

Date	Opponent		Venue	Score	Scorers
15/08/12	Brazil	H	Solna	0-3	
06/09/12	China	H	Helsingborg	1-0	*Elmander (47)*
11/09/12	Kazakhstan (WCQ)	H	Malmo	2-0	*Elm (37), Berg (90+4)*
12/10/12	Faroe Islands (WCQ)	A	Torshavn	2-1	*Kacaniklic (65), Ibrahimović (75)*
16/10/12	Germany (WCQ)	A	Berlin	4-4	*Ibrahimović (62), Lustig (64), Elmander (76), Elm (90+3)*
14/11/12	England	H	Solna	4-2	*Ibrahimović (20, 78, 84, 90+1)*
23/01/13	North Korea	N	Chiang Mai (THA)	1-1	*Fejzullahu (56) (4-1 on pens)*
26/01/13	Finland	N	Chiang Mai (THA)	3-0	*Hysén (23), Quaison (73), Svensson (90)*
06/02/13	Argentina	H	Solna	2-3	*J Olsson (18), Elm (90+5)*
22/03/13	Republic of Ireland (WCQ)	H	Solna	0-0	
26/03/13	Slovakia	A	Zilina	0-0	
03/06/13	FYROM	H	Malmo	1-0	*Kacaniklic (39)*
07/06/13	Austria (WCQ)	A	Vienna	1-2	*Elmander (82)*
11/06/13	Faroe Islands (WCQ)	H	Solna	2-0	*Ibrahimović (35, 82p)*

Appearances 2012/13

Coach: Erik Hamrén	27/06/57		Bra	Chn	KAZ	FRO	GER	Eng	Prk	Fin	Arg	IRL	Svk	Mkd	AUT	FRO	Caps	Goals
Andreas Isaksson	03/10/81	Kasımpaşa (TUR)	G	G	G	G	G	G			G	G		G	G		106	-
Sebastian Larsson	06/06/85	Sunderland (ENG)	D	M	M	M	M78	M86			M	M87		M74	M	M63	55	6
Andreas Granqvist	16/04/85	Genoa (ITA)	D	D	D	D	D	D73			D	D		D74	D	D 79*	32	2
Jonas Olsson	10/03/83	West Brom (ENG)	D	D	D	D	D	D			D	D	D46	D89	D	s83	22	1
Behrang Safari	09/02/85	Anderlecht (BEL)	D	D88	D		D	s46			D	D					31	-
Pontus Wernbloom	25/06/86	CSKA Moskva (RUS)	M	M88	M	M	M46	s89			s77		s46				32	2
Samuel Holmén	28/06/84	İstanbul BB (TUR)	M	s84			M46						M46				32	2
Rasmus Elm	17/03/88	CSKA Moskva (RUS)	M64	M84	M64		M	M			s61	M	s46		M60		35	4
Ola Toivonen	03/07/86	PSV (NED)	M	M	M56						s73	M	s60	s70	A83		34	6
Christian Wilhelmsson	08/12/79	unattached /LA Galaxy (USA)	M64			M62											79	9
Marcus Berg	17/08/86	Hamburg (GER)	A73	s74	s85	s77											23	6
Anders Svensson	17/07/76	Elfsborg	s64	s88	s64	s62		s61	M	M	M61		M46		s60	s58	141	19
Alex Kacaniklic	13/08/91	Fulham (ENG)	s64			s62	s46	M			M77	M	M62	M80	M	M	10	2
Tobias Hysén	09/03/82	Göteborg	s73						A	A79	A	A73	A61				29	8
Mikael Lustig	13/12/86	Celtic (SCO)		D20	D	D	D	D74			D60	D46		D46	D	D	36	2
Zlatan Ibrahimović	03/10/81	PSG (FRA)		M46	M	M	M	M			M46	M		M	M	A	90	41
Johan Elmander	27/05/81	Galatasaray (TUR)		A74	A85		A							A60	A84		70	19
Adam Johansson	21/02/83	Seattle (USA)		s20				D86	s56	s60							15	-
Albin Ekdal	28/07/89	Cagliari (ITA)		s46									M		M		4	-
Pierre Bengtsson	12/04/88	København (DEN)		s88					D				s74		D		7	-
Emir Bajrami	07/03/88	Monaco (FRA)			s56												18	2
Martin Olsson	17/05/88	Blackburn (ENG)				D		D46			D						15	4
Kim Källström	24/08/82	Spartak Moskva (RUS)				M62	s46	M61			M77	M		M	M70	M58	103	16
Mathias Ranégie	14/06/84	Udinese (ITA)				A77		A89			s46						5	1
Tobias Sana	11/07/89	Ajax (NED)				s78	s74										2	-
Mikael Antonsson	31/05/81	Bologna (ITA)					s73						s46	D			8	-
Pontus Jansson	13/02/91	Malmö					s86	D	s47								4	-
Pär Hansson	22/06/86	Helsingborg							G	G						G	5	-

Appearances 2012/13 (contd.)

			Bra	Chn	KAZ	FRO	GER	Eng	Prk	Fin	Arg	IRL	Svk	Mkd	AUT	FRO	Caps	Goals
Daniel Majstorovic	05/04/77	AIK							D	D47							50	2
Jakob Johansson	21/06/90	Göteborg							M84								1	-
Jiloan Hamad	06/11/90	Malmö							M	M69							6	-
Simon Thern	18/09/92	Malmö							M73								2	1
Erton Fejzullahu	09/04/88	Djurgården							M64	M			s01				3	1
Viktor Claesson	02/01/92	Elfsborg							s64	M							4	1
Robin Quaison	09/10/93	AIK							s73	s68							2	1
Ivo Pekalski	03/11/90	Malmö							s84	M68							2	-
Erdin Demir	27/03/90	Brann (NOR)							s86	D							4	-
Niklas Backman	13/11/88	AIK								D79							4	-
Martin Lorentzson	21/07/84	AIK								D56							1	-
Viktor Prodell	29/02/88	Åtvidaberg								s69							1	-
Christoffer Nyman	05/10/92	Norrköping								s79							1	-
Alexander Milosevic	30/01/92	AIK								s79							1	-
Jimmy Durmaz	22/03/89	Gönçlerbirliği (TUR)									s77	s87	s62	s74	s84	s63	9	1
Kristoffer Nordfeldt	23/06/89	Heerenveen (NED)										G					2	-
Oscar Wendt	24/10/85	Mönchengladbach (GER)											D	D	D		21	-
Erkan Zengin	05/08/85	Eskişehirspor (TUR)											M	s80			2	-
Per Nilsson	15/09/82	Nürnberg (GER)												s46	s46	D	8	-
Rasmus Bengtsson	26/06/86	Twente (NED)													s89		2	-

European club competitions 2012/13

HELSINGBORGS IF

CHAMPIONS LEAGUE

Second qualifying round - The New Saints FC (WAL)
A 0-0
Hansson, Sadiku, Atta, Mahlangu, Gashi, Sørum (Sundin 79), Bouaouzan (Nordmark 46), Edman, Finnbogason, C Andersson, Hanstveit. Coach: Åge Hareide (NOR)
H 3-0 *Atta (8), Sørum (27), Álvaro (89)*
Hansson, Sadiku, Atta, Nordmark, Mahlangu, Lindström, Gashi (Wahlstedt 85), Sørum (Sundin 46), Finnbogason (Álvaro 70), C Andersson, Uronen. Coach: Åge Hareide (NOR)

Third qualifying round - WKS Śląsk Wrocław (POL)
A 3-0 *Finnbogason (36), C Andersson (72), Nordmark (85)*
Hansson, Sadiku, Atta, Mahlangu, Lindström, Gashi, Sørum (Álvaro 66), Finnbogason (Sundin 90+1), C Andersson, Wahlstedt (Nordmark 81), Uronen. Coach: Åge Hareide (NOR)

H 3-1 *Sørum (43, 49, 68)*
Hansson, Sadiku, Atta, Mahlangu, Lindström (Nordmark 28), Gashi, Sørum (Álvaro 71), Finnbogason, C Andersson, Wahlstedt (Bergholtz 84), Uronen. Coach: Åge Hareide (NOR)

Play-offs - Celtic FC (SCO)
H 0-2
Hansson, Sadiku, Atta, Mahlangu, Gashi, Sørum (Álvaro 65), Djurdjić, Bedoya, C Andersson, Wahlstedt (Accam 63), Uronen. Coach: Åge Hareide (NOR)
A 0-2
Hansson, Atta (Nordmark 81), Mahlangu, Gashi, Sørum (Accam 62), Baffo, Djurdjić, Bedoya, C Andersson, Wahlstedt (Lindström 75), Uronen. Coach: Åge Hareide (NOR)

EUROPA LEAGUE

Group L
Match 1 - Levante UD (ESP)
A 0-1
Hansson, Mahlangu (Álvaro 85), Lindström (Bouaouzan 73), Gashi, Baffo, Djurdjić, Bedoya, C Andersson, Accam (Sørum 64), Larsson, Uronen. Coach: Åge Hareide (NOR)

Match 2 - FC Twente (NED)
H 2-2 *Djurdjić (7, 43)*
Hansson, Atta, Mahlangu, Lindström (Wahlstedt 78), Gashi, Bouaouzan, Djurdjić, Bedoya (Accam 41), C Andersson, Larsson (Baffo 46), Uronen. Coach: Åge Hareide (NOR)
Match 3 - Hannover 96 (GER)
H 1-2 *Álvaro (90+1)*
Hansson, Atta, Mahlangu, Lindström (Accam 46), Gashi, Bouaouzan (Álvaro 66), Djurdjić, C Andersson, Larsson, Uronen. Coach: Åge Hareide (NOR)
Match 4 - Hannover 96 (GER)
A 2-3 *Djurdjić (59), Bedoya (67)*
Hansson, Atta, Mahlangu, Lindström (Accam 90+4), Gashi, Bouaouzan (Álvaro 46), Djurdjić, Bedoya, C Andersson, Larsson, Uronen (Hanstveit 84). Coach: Åge Hareide (NOR)
Red cards: Atta 89, Larsson 89
Match 5 - Levante UD (ESP)
H 1-3 *Sørum (89)*
Hansson, Mahlangu, Lindström (Accam 68), Gashi, Álvaro (Sørum 78), Baffo, Djurdjić, Bedoya, C Andersson (Krafth 25), Hanstveit, Uronen. Coach: Åge Hareide (NOR)
Match 6 - FC Twente (NED)
A 3-1 *Djurdjić (6), Bedoya (21), Sørum (67)*
Hansson, Mahlangu, Gashi, Sørum (Álvaro 75), Bouaouzan (Accam 85), Edman (Wahlstedt 75), Krafth, Djurdjić, Bedoya, Hanstveit, Larsson. Coach: Åge Hareide (NOR)

AIK

EUROPA LEAGUE

Second qualifying round - FH Hafnarfjördur (ISL)
H 1-1 *Lundberg (56)*
Turina, Backman, Johansson, Åhman Persson, Daníelsson, Borges, Atakora (Kayongo-Mutumba 72), Quaison (Kamara 80), Lorentzson, Gustavsson, Lundberg. Coach: Andreas Alm (SWE)
A 1-0 *Lorentzson (40)*
Turina, Backman, Karlsson, Johansson, Åhman Persson, Daníelsson, Borges, Atakora (Kayongo-Mutumba 62), Lorentzson, Gustavsson, Lundberg. Coach: Andreas Alm (SWE)

Third qualifying round - KKS Lech Poznań (POL)
H 3-0 *Lorentzson (60), Borges (78), Lundberg (86)*
Turina, Backman, Karlsson, Johansson, Åhman Persson (Daníelsson 79), Tjernström, Kayongo-Mutumba, Borges, Lorentzson, Gustavsson (Atakora 79), Lundberg. Coach: Andreas Alm (SWE)
A 0-1
Turina, Backman, Karlsson, Johansson, Åhman Persson, Daníelsson, Kayongo-Mutumba (Tjernström 81), Borges, Atakora, Lorentzson, Lundberg (Karikari 72). Coach: Andreas Alm (SWE)

Play-offs - PFC CSKA Moskva (RUS)
H 0-1
Turina, Backman, Karlsson, Johansson, Daníelsson (Moro 79), Kayongo-Mutumba, Borges, Lorentzson, Karikari (Tjernström 62), Gustavsson, Lundberg. Coach: Andreas Alm (SWE)
A 2-0 *Karikari (6), Lorentzson (90+3)*
Turina, Backman, Karlsson, Johansson, Daníelsson, Kayongo-Mutumba (Tjernström 68), Borges, Atakora, Quaison (Lundberg 68), Lorentzson, Karikari. Coach: Andreas Alm (SWE)

Group F
Match 1 - SSC Napoli (ITA)
A 0-4
Turina, Karlsson, Johansson, Daníelsson (Lundberg 81), Kayongo-Mutumba (Quaison 70), Borges, Atakora, Lorentzson, Karikari (Goitom 76), Majstorovic, Bangura. Coach: Andreas Alm (SWE)
Match 2 - FC Dnipro Dnipropetrovsk (UKR)
H 2-3 *Daníelsson (5), Goitom (45+1)*
Turina, Backman, Karlsson, Johansson, Daníelsson, Atakora, Lorentzson, Moro, Karikari (Bangura 74), Gustavsson (Kayongo-Mutumba 65), Goitom (Borges 65). Coach: Andreas Alm (SWE)
Match 3 - PSV Eindhoven (NED)
A 1-1 *Karikari (61)*
Turina, Karlsson, Johansson, Daníelsson, Kayongo-Mutumba (Lundberg 71), Borges, Atakora (Gustavsson 46), Quaison (Bangura 64), Lorentzson, Karikari, Majstorovic. Coach: Andreas Alm (SWE)
Match 4 - PSV Eindhoven (NED)
H 1-0 *Bangura (12)*
Turina, Backman, Karlsson, Johansson, Daníelsson, Borges, Quaison (Lundberg 69), Lorentzson, Moro, Gustavsson (Tjernström 75), Bangura. Coach: Andreas Alm (SWE)
Match 5 - SSC Napoli (ITA)
H 1-2 *Daníelsson (35)*
Turina, Backman, Karlsson, Johansson, Daníelsson, Borges, Quaison (Karikari 76), Lorentzson, Moro, Lundberg, Bangura. Coach: Andreas Alm (SWE)
Match 6 - FC Dnipro Dnipropetrovsk (UKR)
A 0-4
Turina, Backman, Karlsson, Johansson, Daníelsson, Borges, Quaison (Åhman Persson 90+1), Lorentzson, Moro (Karikari 65), Lundberg (Gustavsson 65), Bangura. Coach: Andreas Alm (SWE)

IF ELFSBORG

EUROPA LEAGUE

First qualifying round - Floriana FC (MLT)
H 8-0 *Hult (5, 24, 26p), Jawo (10), Nilsson (37), Claesson (51), Frick (54), J Larsson (62)*
Stuhr Ellegaard, Jørgensen, Jönsson, J Larsson, Svensson, Nilsson (Frick 46), Klarström (Wede 58), Claesson, Jawo, Hult (Holmén 66), Rohdén. Coach: Jörgen Lennartsson (SWE)
A 4-0 *Mobaeck (19), Hiljemark (50), Frick (67), Claesson (77)*
A Andersson, M Andersson, Mobaeck, Holmén, Hiljemark (Ishizaki 65), Frick, Abdulrahman, Hedlund, Jawo, Wede, Rohdén (Claesson 68). Coach: Jörgen Lennartsson (SWE)

Second qualifying round - FC Dacia Chisinau (MDA)
A 0-1
Stuhr Ellegaard, Jørgensen, Jönsson, J Larsson, Svensson, Nilsson, Hiljemark, Klarström, Claesson (Elm 76), Hult, Ishizaki. Coach: Jörgen Lennartsson (SWE)
H 2-0 *Nilsson (9, 40)*
Stuhr Ellegaard, Jönsson, J Larsson, Svensson, Nilsson (Claesson 83), Mobaeck, Elm, Hiljemark (Rohdén 68), Klarström, Hult, Ishizaki. Coach: Jörgen Lennartsson (SWE)

Third qualifying round - AC Horsens (DEN)
A 1-1 *Nilsson (65)*
Stuhr Ellegaard, Jönsson, J Larsson, Svensson, Nilsson (Jawo 74; Augustsson 86), Mobaeck, Elm, Hiljemark, Klarström, Hult (Claesson 80), Ishizaki. Coach: Jörgen Lennartsson (SWE)
H 2-3 *Nilsson (6), Elm (18)*
Stuhr Ellegaard, Jönsson (Augustsson 69), J Larsson, Svensson, Nilsson, Mobaeck, Elm, Hiljemark (Ishizaki 61), Klarström, Claesson, Hult. Coach: Jörgen Lennartsson (SWE)

Domestic league club-by-club

KALMAR FF

EUROPA LEAGUE

First qualifying round - Cliftonville FC (NIR)

A 0-1
Berisha, Thorbjörnsson (Hallberg 79), Israelsson, Arajuuri, Rydström, Dauda (Andersson 70), Skjelvik, McDonald (Söderqvist 70), Diouf, Öhman, Djordjević. Coach: Nanne Bergstrand (SWE)

H 4-0 *Israelsson (10), Djordjević (16), Dauda (38), Berisha (90+1p)*
Berisha, Israelsson, Arajuuri, Rydström, Dauda (Andersson 46), Nouri, Skjelvik, Gutu (Thorbjörnsson 85), Hallberg, Söderqvist (Daniel Mendes 90+1), Djordjević. Coach: Nanne Bergstrand (SWE)

Second qualifying round - NK Osijek (CRO)

A 3-1 *Daniel Mendes (34), Dauda (66), Gutu (68)*
Berisha, Thorbjörnsson (Gutu 46), Arajuuri, Rydström, Andersson, Dauda, Nouri, Skjelvik, Daniel Mendes (Hallberg 77), Diouf (Israelsson 46), Djordjević. Coach: Nanne Bergstrand (SWE)

H 3-0 *Dauda (25), Ibriks (45+1og), Nouri (90+3)*
Berisha, Israelsson (McDonald 85), Arajuuri, Rydström, Andersson, Dauda (Söderqvist 72), Nouri, Daniel Mendes (Diouf 75), Gutu, Öhman, Djordjević. Coach: Nanne Bergstrand (SWE)

Third qualifying round - BSC Young Boys (SUI)

H 1-0 *Andersson (18)*
Berisha, Israelsson, Arajuuri, Rydström, Andersson (McDonald 90), Nouri, Skjelvik, Gutu, Diouf (Öhman 86), Söderqvist (Dauda 46), Djordjević. Coach: Nanne Bergstrand (SWE)

A 0-3
Berisha, Israelsson, Arajuuri, Rydström, Andersson (McDonald 79), Dauda, Nouri, Gutu (Eriksson 56), Diouf, Öhman (Skjelvik 46), Djordjević. Coach: Nanne Bergstrand (SWE)

AIK

Coach: Andreas Alm
1891 • Råsundastadion (36,608) • aik.se
Major honours
Swedish League (11) 1900, 1901, 1911, 1914, 1916, 1923, 1932, 1937, 1992, 1998, 2009;
Swedish Cup (8) 1949, 1950, 1976, 1985, 1996, 1997, 1999, 2009

2012

01/04	Mjällby	h	0-0	
09/04	Kalmar	a	2-1	Kayongo-Mutumba, Borges
12/04	Göteborg	h	1-1	Engblom
15/04	Syrianska	a	1-0	Atakora
22/04	Sundsvall	h	1-1	Milosevic
26/04	Gefle	a	1-0	Borges
02/05	Helsingborg	a	0-0	
08/05	Djurgården	h	1-1	og (Pedersen)
13/05	Elfsborg	a	0-1	
16/05	Örebro	a	2-2	Borges, Lundberg
20/05	Norrköping	h	5-2	Gustavsson 2, Lundberg, Lorentzson, Quaison
24/05	GAIS	h	1-0	Lundberg
02/07	Malmö	a	0-4	
08/07	Häcken	h	3-1	Borges 2, Quaison
14/07	Åtvidaberg	a	0-2	
22/07	Ålvidaberg	h	1-0	Lorentzson
29/07	Mjällby	a	1-0	Åhman Persson (p)
05/08	Kalmar	h	1-2	Karikari
12/08	Örebro	h	3-0	Karikari, Kayongo-Mutumba, Gustavsson
26/08	GAIS	a	1-0	Karikari
02/09	Helsingborg	h	2-1	Lorentzson, Borges
16/09	Djurgården	a	3-0	Karikari, Bangura, Borges
23/09	Norrköping	a	2-2	Borges, Karikari
26/09	Elfsborg	h	1-1	Lorentzson
30/09	Sundsvall	a	3-2	Bangura 2, Lundberg
07/10	Gefle	h	0-1	
21/10	Göteborg	a	1-0	Backman
28/10	Syrianska	h	1-1	Goitom
01/11	Häcken	a	1-1	Danielsson
04/11	Malmö	h	2-0	Bangura, Lundberg

No	Name	Nat	DoB	Pos	Aps	(s)	Gls
11	Lalawélé Atakora	TOG	09/11/90	M	10	(12)	1
2	Niklas Backman		13/11/88	D	28		1
75	Mohamed Bangura	SLE	27/07/89	A	10		4
10	Celso Borges	CRC	27/05/88	M	29		8
7	Helgi Valur Danielsson	ISL	13/07/81	M	16	(3)	1
21	Pontus Engblom		11/11/91	A	3	(3)	1
36	Henok Goitom		22/09/84	A	3	(6)	1
24	Daniel Gustavsson		29/08/90	M	20	(5)	3
4	Nils-Eric Johansson		13/01/80	D	30		
19	Alhassan Kamara	SLE	13/01/93	A	3	(8)	
22	Kwame Karikari	GHA	21/01/92	A	6	(6)	5
3	Per Karlsson		02/01/86	D	22	(1)	
9	Martin Kayongo-Mutumba	UGA	15/06/85	M	25	(2)	2
12	Christian Kouakou		20/04/95	A		(3)	
16	Martin Lorentzson		21/07/84	D	29		4
28	Viktor Lundberg		04/03/91	M	19	(8)	5
45	Daniel Majstorovic		05/04/77	D	4		
18	Niklas Maripuu		02/03/92	D		(2)	
6	Alexander Milosevic		30/01/92	D	6		1
20	Ibrahim Moro	GHA	10/11/93	M	4	(1)	
15	Robin Quaison		09/10/93	A	13	(5)	2
13	Kenny Stamatopoulos	CAN	28/08/79	G	6		
8	Daniel Tjernström		19/02/74	M	7	(5)	
27	Ivan Turina	CRO	03/10/81	G	24		
5	Robert Åhman Persson		26/03/87	M	12	(4)	1
29	Gabriel Özkan		23/05/86	M	1	(6)	

DJURGÅRDENS IF

Coach: Magnus Pehrsson
1891 • Stockholms stadion (14,417) • dif.se
Major honours
Swedish League (11) 1912, 1915, 1917, 1920, 1955, 1959, 1964, 1966, 2002, 2003, 2005;
Swedish Cup (4) 1990, 2002, 2004, 2005

2012

31/03	Elfsborg	a	1-2	Pedersen
08/04	Sundsvall	h	1-0	Rajalakso
11/04	GAIS	a	0-0	
16/04	Malmö	h	2-3	Keene, Hämäläinen
20/04	Mjällby	a	3-4	Keene, Toivio, Hämäläinen
29/04	Kalmar	h	1-1	Hämäläinen
03/05	Örebro	h	2-1	Keene, Youssef
08/05	AIK	a	1-1	Gustafsson
12/05	Åtvidaberg	h	1-1	Ricardo Santos
17/05	Gefle	a	1-1	Ricardo Santos
20/05	Häcken	a	1-1	Ricardo Santos
23/05	Helsingborg	a	1-1	Span
03/07	Göteborg	h	3-2	Keene 2, Sjölund
07/07	Syrianska	a	1-1	Keene
16/07	Norrköping	h	1-1	Sjölund
23/07	Norrköping	a	1-1	Nymann
29/07	Elfsborg	h	0-0	
06/08	Sundsvall	a	1-0	Sjölund
10/08	Gefle	h	1-0	Fejzullahu
25/08	Helsingborg	h	3-1	Fejzullahu 3
31/08	Örebro	a	3-2	Hämäläinen, Hellquist, Fejzullahu
16/09	AIK	h	0-3	
21/09	Häcken	h	0-3	
26/09	Åtvidaberg	a	1-2	Bergström
01/10	Mjällby	h	0-1	
07/10	Kalmar	a	2-2	Toivio, Gustafsson
22/10	GAIS	h	3-0	Fejzullahu 2, Tibbling
26/10	Malmö	a	1-3	Nymann
31/10	Syrianska	h	1-1	Rajalakso
04/11	Göteborg	a	0-1	

No	Name	Nat	DoB	Pos	Aps	(s)	Gls
13	Emil Bergström		19/05/93	D	17	(6)	1
7	Martin Broberg		24/09/90	M	5	(4)	
14	Kebba Ceesay		14/11/87	D	13		
4	Yussif Chibsah	GHA	30/12/83	M	14	(9)	
20	Andreas Dahlén		11/12/82	D	16	(3)	
10	Erton Fejzullahu		09/04/88	A	13		7
5	Petter Gustafsson		01/01/85	D	24	(4)	2
22	Philip Hellquist		21/05/91	M	4	(7)	1
16	Kasper Hämäläinen	FIN	08/08/86	M	30		4
12	Kenneth Høie	NOR	11/09/79	G	13		
27	Kennedy Igboananike	NGA	26/02/89	A	1	(4)	
24	Daniel Jarl		13/04/92	D		(1)	
21	Kasper Jensen	DEN	07/10/82	G	5		
28	Alhaji Kamara	SLE	16/04/94	A	1	(4)	
8	James Keene	ENG	26/12/85	A	22	(4)	6
6	Petter Nymann Mikkelsen	DEN	22/08/82	M	29		2
19	Nahir Oyal		17/12/90	M	3	(6)	
3	Marc Pedersen	DEN	31/07/89	D	10		1
25	Sebastian Rajalakso		23/09/88	M	16	(8)	2
9	Ricardo Santos	BRA	13/02/87	A	9	(5)	3
17	Joel Riddez		21/05/80	D	1	(1)	
11	Daniel Sjölund	FIN	22/04/83	M	25	(2)	3
15	Brian Span	USA	23/02/92	M	2	(7)	1
36	Philip Sparrdal Mantilla		11/08/93	D		(1)	
31	Simon Tibbling		07/12/94	M	14	(1)	1
2	Joona Toivio	FIN	10/03/83	D	30		2
23	Tommi Vaiho		19/05/93	G	12		
10	Christer Youssef		24/09/90	A	1	(5)	1
14	Mattias Östberg		14/11/87	D		(2)	

IF ELFSBORG

Coach: Jörgen Lennartsson
1904 • Borås Arena (16,284) • elfsborg.se
Major honours
Swedish League (6) 1936, 1939, 1940, 1961, 2006,
2012; Swedish Cup (2) 2001, 2003

2012

31/03	Djurgården	h	2-1	Svensson 2
08/04	Helsingborg	a	1-2	Hult
12/04	Norrköping	h	2-0	Nilsson, Claesson
16/04	Gefle	a	2-1	J Larsson, Nilsson
23/04	Örebro	a	2-0	Ishizaki, Jawo
26/04	GAIS	h	2-1	Ishizaki, Jawo
02/05	Syrianska	a	4-1	Ishizaki 2, Elm, Jönsson
07/05	Göteborg	h	1-0	Nilsson (p)
13/05	AIK	h	1-0	Elm
17/05	Malmö	a	0-1	
21/05	Sundsvall	a	3-0	Ishizaki, Hult, og (Danielsson)
24/05	Häcken	h	2-0	Ishizaki, Nilsson (p)
30/06	Åtvidaberg	a	1-5	J Larsson
08/07	Mjällby	h	0-0	
15/07	Kalmar	a	1-2	Svensson
22/07	Kalmar	h	3-0	Nilsson, Elm, Claesson
29/07	Djurgården	a	0-0	
12/08	Malmö	h	4-1	J Larsson, Elm, Hult, Mobaeck
18/08	Helsingborg	h	2-1	Augustsson, Claesson
26/08	Häcken	a	2-4	Elm, Rohdén
02/09	Syrianska	h	1-0	Svensson
16/09	Göteborg	a	1-2	Rohdén
23/09	Sundsvall	h	0-0	
26/09	AIK	a	1-1	Claesson
30/09	Örebro	h	1-0	Ishizaki
07/10	GAIS	a	2-1	Hiljemark 2
21/10	Norrköping	a	1-2	Jönsson
29/10	Gefle	h	2-0	Nilsson, Svensson
01/11	Mjällby	a	3-2	Nilsson, Svensson, Claesson
04/11	Åtvidaberg	h	1-1	Ishizaki

No	Name	Nat	DoB	Pos	Aps	(s)	Gls
22	Andreas Augustsson		26/11/76	D	10	(7)	1
16	Viktor Claesson		02/01/92	M	19	(8)	5
13	David Elm		10/01/83	A	15	(11)	5
17	Per Frick		14/04/92	A		(1)	
2	Skúli Jón Fridgeirsson	ISL	30/07/88	A	1	(4)	
19	Simon Hedlund		11/03/93	M		(7)	
14	Oscar Hiljemark		28/06/92	M	27	(1)	2
23	Niklas Hult		13/02/90	M	26	(1)	3
30	Kenneth Høie	NOR	11/09/79	G	11		
24	Stefan Ishizaki		15/05/82	M	23	(2)	8
20	Amadou Jawo		26/09/84	A	9	(5)	2
6	Jon Jönsson		08/07/83	D	26	(1)	2
4	Joackim Jørgensen	NOR	20/09/88	M	18	(4)	
15	Andreas Klarström		23/12/77	M	21	(3)	
7	Johan Larsson		05/05/90	M	28	(2)	3
3	Stefan Larsson		21/01/83	D	9		
11	Daniel Mobaeck		22/05/80	D	9	(3)	1
9	Lars Nilsson		03/01/82	A	24	(5)	7
25	Marcus Rohdén		11/05/91	M	7	(15)	2
1	Kevin Stuhr Ellegaard	DEN	23/05/83	G	19		
8	Anders Svensson		17/07/76	M	27	(1)	6
21	Carl Wede		20/04/90	D	1	(1)	

GAIS GÖTEBORG

Coach: Alexander Axén;
(23/07/12) (Kjell Pettersson);
(31/07/12) Jan Mak (NED);
(03/10/12) Benjamin Westman & Jonas Lundén
1894 • Nya Gamla Ullevi (19,000) • gais.se
Major honours
Swedish League (4) 1919, 1922, 1931, 1954;
Swedish Cup (1) 1942

2012

31/03	Häcken	h	0-0	
06/04	Åtvidaberg	a	1-2	Olsson
11/04	Djurgården	h	0-0	
16/04	Helsingborg	a	1-1	Celik
22/04	Norrköping	h	2-0	Wanderson, Ayarna
26/04	Elfsborg	a	1-2	Tornblad
04/05	Kalmar	a	2-2	Wanderson, Olsson
07/05	Mjällby	h	2-2	Ijeh, Olsson
11/05	Syrianska	a	0-2	
17/05	Sundsvall	h	1-2	Celik
21/05	Göteborg	h	1-1	M Gustafsson
24/05	AIK	a	0-1	
05/07	Örebro	h	0-1	
08/07	Gefle	a	0-0	
16/07	Malmö	a	0-2	
23/07	Malmö	h	2-3	Tornblad, Johansson
30/07	Häcken	a	1-3	Romarinho
04/08	Åtvidaberg	h	2-2	Ijeh, Aubynn (p)
11/08	Sundsvall	a	0-2	
26/08	AIK	h	0-1	
02/09	Kalmar	h	1-2	Johansson
15/09	Mjällby	a	0-4	
24/09	Göteborg	a	0-0	
28/09	Syrianska	h	1-4	Romarinho
01/10	Norrköping	a	2-7	Romarinho, Olsson
07/10	Elfsborg	h	1-2	Johansson
22/10	Djurgården	a	0-3	
28/10	Helsingborg	h	1-3	Olsson
01/11	Gefle	h	2-3	Romarinho, Johansson
04/11	Örebro	a	0-4	

No	Name	Nat	DoB	Pos	Aps	(s)	Gls
19	Alexander Angelin		30/01/90	M	2	(1)	
13	Calum Angus	ENG	15/04/86	D	17	(2)	
22	Jeffrey Aubynn		12/05/77	M	10	(5)	1
6	Reuben Ayarna	GHA	22/10/85	M	27	(2)	1
21	Eric Bassombeng	CMR	02/11/83	M	9	(5)	
27	Mervan Celik		26/05/90	M	13	(1)	2
12	Joakim Edström		27/11/92	A	1	(7)	
2	Richard Ekunde	COD	04/08/82	D	24		
10	Jesper Florén		11/09/90	D	10	(4)	
20	Kenneth Gustafsson		15/09/83	D	20		
31	Markus Gustafsson		06/03/89	M	21	(5)	1
35	Oliver Gustafsson		15/05/93	G		(1)	
28	August Gustafsson Lohaprasert		03/09/93	A	1	(3)	
9	Peter Ijeh	NGA	28/03/77	A	8	(10)	2
11	Gzim Istrefi		18/09/91	M		(2)	
1	Dime Jankulovski		18/09/77	G	15	(1)	
17	Erik Johansson		30/12/88	M	27		4
15	Fredrik Lundgren		26/10/79	D	18	(2)	
16	Enis Majlici		05/04/94	M		(1)	
26	Malkom Moenza		15/11/93	M	7		
4	Mirza Mujcic		01/04/89	D	8		
7	Jakob Olsson		14/08/91	M	14	(13)	5
29	Romarinho	BRA	15/04/86	M	19	(5)	4
32	Henri Sillanpää	FIN	04/06/79	G	15	(1)	
8	Richard Spong		23/09/83	M	6	(1)	
18	Linus Tornblad		02/07/93	M	20	(6)	2
25	Wanderson	BRA	26/05/90	A	18	(1)	2

GEFLE IF

Coach: Per Olsson
1882 • Strömvallen (7,302) • geflefffotboll.se

2012

02/04	Malmö	a	0-0	
06/04	Syrianska	h	1-1	Orlov
10/04	Åtvidaberg	a	1-6	Dahlberg
16/04	Elfsborg	h	1-2	Orlov
21/04	Kalmar	a	1-0	Orlov
26/04	AIK	h	0-1	
03/05	Norrköping	h	0-2	
10/05	Häcken	a	0-3	
14/05	Sundsvall	h	0-0	
17/05	Djurgården	a	1-1	og (Broberg)
20/05	Mjällby	a	0-2	
23/05	Örebro	h	2-1	Orlov, Larsson
02/07	Helsingborg	a	1-4	Dahlberg
08/07	GAIS	h	0-0	
14/07	Göteborg	a	1-1	Faltsetas
21/07	Göteborg	h	5-0	Bernhardsson, Orlov, Dahlberg, Faltsetas 2
28/07	Malmö	h	0-2	
04/08	Syrianska	a	0-1	
10/08	Djurgården	h	0-1	
24/08	Örebro	a	2-1	Dahlberg (p), Orlov
02/09	Norrköping	a	1-0	Lantto
17/09	Häcken	h	0-2	
23/09	Mjällby	h	1-0	Orlov
26/09	Sundsvall	a	1-0	Dahlberg
30/09	Kalmar	h	0-2	
07/10	AIK	a	1-0	Orlov
20/10	Åtvidaberg	h	1-2	Oremo
29/10	Elfsborg	a	0-2	
01/11	GAIS	a	3-2	Lantto, Mård, Dahlberg (p)
04/11	Helsingborg	h	2-2	Orlov, Lantto

No	Name	Nat	DoB	Pos	Aps	(s)	Gls
5	Zakaria Abdullai	GHA	17/11/89	M	4	(7)	
25	Joachim Adukor	GHA	02/05/93	M		(3)	
6	Pär Asp		14/08/82	D	27		
12	Daniel Bernhardsson		31/01/78	D	24		1
15	Mikael Dahlberg		06/03/85	A	28	(1)	6
7	Alexander Faltsetas		04/07/87	M	27	(2)	3
16	David Fällman		04/02/90	D	22	(1)	
19	Marcus Hansson		12/02/90	M	29		
9	Jonathan Hellström		09/08/88	D	10	(7)	
1	Mattias Hugosson		24/01/74	G	30		
17	Jonas Lantto		22/05/87	A	29		3
21	Eric Larsson		15/07/91	D	8	(16)	1
8	Simon Lundevall		23/09/88	M		(2)	
3	Linus Malmborg		16/02/88	D	13	(1)	
2	Olof Mård		31/01/89	D	24		1
24	Johan Oremo		24/10/86	A	4	(17)	1
10	Jakob Orlov		15/03/86	A	28	(1)	9
14	Jens Portin	FIN	13/12/84	D	17		
4	Sebastian Senatore		17/12/85	D	5	(1)	
23	Johan Svantesson		13/09/92	A		(4)	
18	Erik Törnros		11/06/93	A		(4)	
11	Hjalmar Öhagen		17/05/85	M	1	(6)	

IFK GÖTEBORG

Coach: Mikael Stahre
1904 • Nya Gamla Ullevi (19,000) • ifkgoteborg.se
Major honours
UEFA Cup (2) 1982, 1987;
Swedish League (18) 1908, 1910, 1918, 1935, 1942,
1958, 1969, 1982, 1983, 1984, 1987, 1990, 1991, 1993,
1994, 1995, 1996, 2007;
Swedish Cup (6) 1979, 1982, 1983, 1991, 2008, 2013

2012

01/04	Syrianska	a	1-2	Daniel Sobralense	
09/04	Norrköping	h	1-2	Hysén	
12/04	AIK	a	1-1	Jónsson	
15/04	Örebro	h	2-2	Sana, Farnerud	
23/04	Häcken	a	2-1	Sana, Selakovic (p)	
28/04	Åtvidaberg	h	2-1	Stiller 2	
02/05	Sundsvall	h	2-0	Stiller, Allansson	
07/05	Elfsborg	a	0-1		
14/05	Malmö	h	2-2	Söder, Dyrestam	
17/05	Mjällby	a	1-1	Söder	
21/05	GAIS	a	1-1	Hysén	
24/05	Kalmar	h	1-1	Allansson	
03/07	Djurgården	a	2-3	Daniel Sobralense, Hysén	
09/07	Helsingborg	h	1-1	Selakovic	
14/07	Gefle	a	1-1	Farnerud	
21/07	Gefle	a	0-5		
31/07	Syrianska	h	1-0	Hysén	
06/08	Norrköping	a	0-0		
12/08	Mjällby	h	4-2	Daniel Sobralense 2, Farnerud, Selakovic (p)	
26/08	Kalmar	a	0-3		
02/09	Sundsvall	a	3-3	Gerzic, Stiller, Bjärsmyr	
16/09	Elfsborg	h	2-1	Hysén, Farnerud	
24/09	GAIS	h	0-0		
27/09	Malmö	a	2-1	Hysén, Stiller	
01/10	Häcken	h	1-2	Stiller	
06/10	Åtvidaberg	a	2-1	Gerzic, Stiller	
21/10	AIK	h	0-1		
28/10	Örebro	a	0-0		
31/10	Helsingborg	a	0-2		
04/11	Djurgården	h	1-0	Selakovic	

No	Name	Nat	DoB	Pos	Aps	(s)	Gls
27	Joel Allansson		03/11/92	M	10	(10)	2
1	John Alvbåge		10/08/82	G	23		
20	Jonathan Azulay		05/05/93	D		(1)	
30	Mattias Bjärsmyr		03/01/86	D	8		1
6	Niklas Bärkroth		19/01/92	A		(3)	
25	Erik Dahlin		28/04/89	G	7		
9	Daniel Sobralense	BRA	10/02/82	A	21		4
24	Mikael Dyrestam		10/12/91	D	7		1
21	Pontus Farnerud		04/06/80	M	28		4
8	Nordin Gerzic		09/11/83	M	12	(11)	2
5	Philip Haglund		22/03/87	M	20	(4)	
7	Tobias Hysén		09/03/82	M	30		6
15	Jakob Johansson		21/06/90	M	19	(3)	
14	Hjálmar Jónsson	ISL	29/07/80	D	16	(1)	1
17	Sam Larsson		10/04/93	M		(2)	
16	Erik Lund		06/11/83	D	1		
26	David Moberg Karlsson		20/03/94	M	5	(13)	
2	Emil Salomonsson		28/04/89	M	27		
22	Tobias Sana		11/07/89	M	9	(2)	2
10	Stefan Selakovic		09/01/77	A	20	(4)	4
19	Hannes Stiller		03/07/78	A	9	(18)	7
11	Robin Söder		01/04/91	A	15	(8)	2
3	Hjörtur Logi Valgardsson	ISL	27/09/88	D	19	(3)	
4	Kjetil Wæhler	NOR	16/03/76	D	24		

HELSINGBORGS IF

Coach: Conny Karlsson;
(14/06/12) Åge Hareide (NOR)
1907 • Olympia (17,200) • hif.se
Major honours
Swedish League (5) 1933, 1934, 1941, 1999, 2011;
Swedish Cup (5) 1941, 1998, 2006, 2010, 2011

2012

02/04	Norrköping	a	0-1		
08/04	Elfsborg	h	2-1	Finnbogason 2	
11/04	Örebro	a	0-0		
16/04	GAIS	h	1-1	og (Angus)	
21/04	Åtvidaberg	a	2-1	Sundin 2	
27/04	Mjällby	h	1-1	Finnbogason	
02/05	AIK	h	0-0		
05/05	Sundsvall	a	1-0	Sørum	
10/05	Malmö	a	0-3		
13/05	Häcken	h	3-2	Finnbogason, Nordmark 2	
16/05	Kalmar	h	1-1	Finnbogason	
23/05	Djurgården	h	1-1	Nordmark	
02/07	Gefle	h	4-1	Atta, Finnbogason 3	
09/07	Göteborg	a	1-1	Finnbogason	
14/07	Syrianska	h	1-0	Atta	
21/07	Syrianska	a	3-1	Sundin, Álvaro (p), Nordmark	
28/07	Norrköping	h	1-2	Finnbogason	
12/08	Kalmar	h	7-2	Finnbogason 2, Sørum, Uronen, Bouaouzan, Nordmark, Álvaro	
18/08	Elfsborg	a	1-2	Bedoya	
25/08	Djurgården	a	1-3	Djurdjić	
02/09	AIK	a	1-2	Accam	
15/09	Sundsvall	h	4-0	Accam, Djurdjić 3	
24/09	Malmö	h	1-1	Uronen	
27/09	Häcken	a	2-2	Accam, Djurdjić	
30/09	Åtvidaberg	h	3-0	Atta, Álvaro, Djurdjić	
07/10	Mjällby	a	2-0	C Andersson, Atta	
21/10	Örebro	h	1-1	Djurdjić	
28/10	GAIS	a	3-1	Björkman, Bouaouzan, Djurdjić	
31/10	Göteborg	h	2-0	Djurdjić, Álvaro (p)	
04/11	Gefle	a	2-2	Lindström, Djurdjić	

No	Name	Nat	DoB	Pos	Aps	(s)	Gls
25	David Accam	GHA	28/09/90	M	7	(3)	3
10	Álvaro	BRA	30/01/80	A	2	(17)	4
21	Christoffer Andersson		22/10/78	M	22	(1)	1
1	Daniel Andersson		18/12/72	G	1		
4	Walid Atta		28/08/86	D	16	(2)	4
16	Joseph Baffo		07/04/92	D	13	(3)	
18	Alejandro Bedoya	USA	29/04/87	M	8	(1)	1
2	Marcus Bergholtz		15/12/89	M	1	(3)	
29	Jesper Björkman		29/04/93	D	2		1
13	Rachid Bouaouzan	NED	20/02/84	M	17	(6)	2
18	Nikola Djurdjić	SRB	01/04/86	A	11		10
14	Erik Edman		11/11/78	D	7	(1)	
19	Alfred Finnbogason	ISL	01/02/89	A	14	(3)	12
8	Ardian Gashi	NOR	20/06/81	M	27		
30	Pär Hansson		22/06/86	G	29		
24	Erlend Hanstveit	NOR	28/01/81	D	15	(1)	
15	Emil Krafth		02/08/94	D	7	(2)	
26	Peter Larsson		30/04/84	D	7		
7	Mattias Lindström		18/04/80	M	20	(4)	1
9	May Mahlangu	RSA	01/01/89	M	28	(2)	
5	Daniel Nordmark		04/01/88	M	14	(12)	5
3	Loret Sadiku		28/07/91	M	18	(1)	
3	Erik Sundin		01/03/79	A	7	(8)	3
11	Thomas Sørum	NOR	17/11/82	A	17	(6)	2
28	Jere Uronen	FIN	13/07/94	D	15	(2)	2
23	Erik Wahlstedt		16/04/76	D	5	(5)	

BK HÄCKEN

Coach: Peter Gerhardsson
1940 • Rambergsvallen (8,480) • bkhacken.se

2012

31/03	GAIS	a	0-0		
07/04	Malmö	h	5-0	Anklev, Majeed 2, Makondele 2 (1p)	
12/04	Mjällby	h	4-2	Makondele, Söderberg, Majeed 2	
16/04	Kalmar	a	1-3	Söderberg	
23/04	Göteborg	h	1-2	Östberg	
28/04	Syrianska	a	2-1	Ericsson, Makondele	
02/05	Åtvidaberg	a	3-0	Makondele, Drugge, Majeed	
10/05	Gefle	a	3-0	Makondele 2 (1p), Majeed	
13/05	Helsingborg	a	2-3	Anklev, Majeed	
16/05	Norrköping	h	6-0	Majeed 5, Ericsson	
20/05	Djurgården	h	1-1	Makondele	
24/05	Elfsborg	a	0-2		
30/06	Sundsvall	h	1-2	Ericsson (p)	
08/07	AIK	a	1-3	Majeed	
15/07	Örebro	h	2-1	Williams, Makondele	
19/07	Örebro	h	2-1	Makondele, Johansson	
30/07	GAIS	h	3-1	Ericsson 2 (1p), Majeed	
05/08	Malmö	a	0-0		
12/08	Norrköping	a	2-1	Anklev, Söderberg	
26/08	Elfsborg	h	4-2	Anklev, Mohammed 2, Majeed	
31/08	Åtvidaberg	h	5-2	Makondele 2, Majeed 2, Mohammed	
17/09	Gefle	a	2-0	Majeed, Mohammed	
21/09	Djurgården	a	3-0	Anklev, Williams, Majeed	
27/09	Helsingborg	h	2-2	Williams 2	
01/10	Göteborg	a	1-1	Ericsson	
06/10	Syrianska	h	5-1	Majeed 3 (1p), Ericsson 2	
20/10	Mjällby	a	2-1	Khan, og (Ivanovski)	
27/10	Kalmar	h	1-2	Williams	
01/11	AIK	h	1-1	Lewicki	
04/11	Sundsvall	a	2-1	Majeed, Söderberg	

No	Name	Nat	DoB	Pos	Aps	(s)	Gls
17	Björn Anklev		13/04/79	A	18	(11)	5
15	Kari Arkivuo	FIN	23/06/83	M	24	(1)	
7	Jonas Bjurström		24/03/79	M	2	(4)	
20	Dominic Chatto	NGA	12/07/85	M	24	(3)	
3	Jimmy Dixon	LBR	10/10/81	D		(2)	
10	Andreas Drugge		20/01/83	A	6	(8)	1
8	Josef Elvby		13/07/82	M	7	(11)	
14	Martin Ericsson		04/09/80	M	26	(1)	8
22	Daniel Forssell		04/01/82	D	4	(2)	
6	Daniel Frölund		04/06/79	D	22	(3)	
21	Jonas Henriksson		24/03/79	M		(1)	
23	Joel Johansson		16/01/86	A		(11)	1
16	Tibor Joza		10/08/86	D	1	(4)	
4	Mohammed Ali Khan		21/01/86	D	24	(2)	1
1	Christoffer Källqvist		26/08/83	G	30		
12	Oscar Lewicki		14/07/92	D	24		1
18	Waris Majeed	GHA	19/09/91	M	29		23
24	René Makondele	COD	20/04/82	M	28		12
41	Nasiru Mohammed	GHA	06/06/94	M	3	(8)	4
27	Tom Söderberg		25/08/87	D	22	(3)	4
5	Emil Wahlström		02/03/87	D	8		
25	Jesper Westermark		25/07/93	A		(2)	
9	Dioh Williams	LBR	08/10/84	A	15	(8)	5
19	Leonard Zuta		09/08/92	M		(1)	
3	Mattias Östberg		24/08/77	D	13	(1)	1

SWEDEN

KALMAR FF

Coach: Nanne Bergstrand
1910 • Guldfågeln Arena (12,105) • kalmarff.se
Major honours
Swedish League (1) 2008;
Swedish Cup (3) 1981, 1987, 2007

2012

31/03	Sundsvall	a	1-0	Daniel Mendes
09/04	AIK	h	1-2	Söderqvist
13/04	Malmö	a	0-2	
16/04	Häcken	h	3-1	Dauda 3
21/04	Gefle	h	0-1	
29/04	Djurgården	a	1-1	Daniel Mendes
04/05	GAIS	h	2-2	Dauda 2
07/05	Örebro	a	1-0	Israelsson
12/05	Mjällby	h	1-2	Daniel Mendes
16/05	Helsingborg	h	1-1	McDonald
20/05	Åtvidaberg	a	0-3	
24/05	Göteborg	a	1-1	McDonald
30/06	Syrianska	h	3-0	Israelsson, Andersson, Thorbjörnsson
08/07	Norrköping	a	1-2	Dauda
15/07	Elfsborg	h	2-1	Daniel Mendes, Hallberg
22/07	Elfsborg	a	0-3	
29/07	Sundsvall	h	1-1	Diouf
05/08	AIK	a	2-1	Arajuuri, Dauda
12/08	Helsingborg	a	2-7	Berisha (p), Diouf
26/08	Göteborg	h	3-0	Dauda 2, McDonald
02/09	GAIS	a	2-1	Israelsson, Dauda
17/09	Örebro	h	1-2	Dauda
23/09	Åtvidaberg	h	2-0	Dauda 2
26/09	Mjällby	a	0-1	
30/09	Gefle	a	0-0	
07/10	Djurgården	h	2-2	McDonald, Skjelvik
21/10	Malmö	h	1-2	Israelsson
27/10	Häcken	a	1-1	og (Frölund), Dauda
31/10	Norrköping	h	0-2	
04/11	Syrianska	a	0-3	

No	Name	Nat	DoB	Pos	Aps	(s)	Gls
9	Sebastian Andersson		15/07/91	A	7	(18)	1
6	Paulus Arajuuri	FIN	15/06/88	D	21		1
99	Etrit Berisha	ALB	10/03/89	G	30		
18	Johan Bertilsson		15/02/88	M	3	(1)	
17	Daniel Mendes	BRA	18/01/81	A	17	(1)	4
11	Abiola Dauda	NGA	03/02/88	A	22	(3)	14
27	Papa Alioune Diouf	SEN	22/06/89	A	11	(10)	2
80	Nenad Đorđević	SRB	07/08/79	D	14	(3)	
25	Tobias Eriksson		19/03/85	M	20	(1)	
10	Kristoffer Fagercrantz		09/10/86	M	5	(2)	
20	Archford Gutu	ZIM	05/08/93	M	10	(10)	
22	Melker Hallberg		20/10/95	M	5	(6)	1
4	Erik Israelsson		25/02/89	M	24	(2)	4
19	Jonathan McDonald	CRC	16/02/92	A	16	(11)	4
13	Emin Nouri		22/07/85	D	23		
8	Henrik Rydström		16/02/76	M	26	(2)	
35	Rasmus Sjöstedt		28/02/92	D	6		
14	Jørgen Skjelvik	NOR	05/07/91	D	29		1
34	Måns Söderqvist		08/02/93	M	8	(9)	1
2	Markus Thorbjörnsson		01/10/87	D	17	(5)	1
30	Ludvig Öhman		10/10/91	D	16		

MALMÖ FF

Coach: Rikard Norling
1910 • Swedbank Stadion (24,000) • mff.se
Major honours
Swedish League (16) 1944, 1949, 1950, 1951, 1953, 1965, 1967, 1970, 1971, 1974, 1975, 1977, 1986, 1988, 2004, 2010;
Swedish Cup (14) 1944, 1946, 1947, 1951, 1953, 1967, 1973, 1974, 1975, 1977, 1980, 1984, 1986, 1989

2012

02/04	Gefle	h	0-0	
07/04	Häcken	a	0-5	
13/04	Kalmar	h	2-0	Larsson, Durmaz
16/04	Djurgården	a	3-2	Wilton Figueiredo, Hamad, Ranégie
23/04	Syrianska	h	2-0	Wilton Figueiredo, Durmaz
29/04	Norrköping	a	2-3	Durmaz, Hamad
03/05	Mjällby	a	2-2	Durmaz, Hamad
06/05	Åtvidaberg	h	2-1	Ranégie 2
10/05	Helsingborg	h	3-0	Larsson, Pekalski, Ranégie
14/05	Göteborg	a	2-2	Thern, Nilsson
17/05	Elfsborg	h	1-0	Ranégie
24/05	Sundsvall	a	1-1	Nilsson
02/07	AIK	h	4-0	Wilton Figueiredo 2, Durmaz 2
09/07	Örebro	a	1-0	Hamad
16/07	GAIS	h	2-0	Larsson, Ranégie
23/07	GAIS	a	3-2	Ranégie, Andersson (p), Jansson
28/07	Gefle	a	2-0	Ranégie 2 (1p)
05/08	Häcken	h	0-0	
12/08	Elfsborg	a	1-4	Ranégie
27/08	Sundsvall	h	2-0	Albornoz, Rantie
01/09	Mjällby	h	1-1	Rantie
17/09	Åtvidaberg	a	1-0	Ricardinho (p)
24/09	Helsingborg	a	1-1	Wilton Figueiredo
27/09	Göteborg	h	1-2	Rantie
01/10	Syrianska	a	2-0	og (Felic), Thern
05/10	Norrköping	h	2-0	Hamad, Albornoz (p)
21/10	Kalmar	a	2-1	Ricardinho, Larsson
26/10	Djurgården	h	3-1	Thern, Halsti, Hamad
01/11	Örebro	h	1-1	Albornoz
04/11	AIK	a	0-2	

No	Name	Nat	DoB	Pos	Aps	(s)	Gls
14	Miiko Albornoz		30/11/90	D	25	(2)	3
4	Daniel Andersson		28/08/77	D	16		1
23	Matias Concha		31/03/80	D		(2)	
21	Johan Dahlin		08/09/86	G	29		
21	Jimmy Durmaz		21/12/81	M	15		6
8	Erik Friberg		10/02/86	M	20	(4)	
6	Markus Halsti	FIN	19/03/84	D	7	(6)	1
10	Jiloan Hamad		06/11/90	M	30		6
15	Filip Helander		22/04/93	D	12		
5	Pontus Jansson		13/02/91	D	30		1
31	Simon Kroon		16/06/93	M		(1)	
7	Daniel Larsson		25/01/87	A	26	(4)	4
32	Tobias Lewicki		02/05/93	M		(1)	
24	David Löfquist		06/08/86	A	2	(2)	
18	Amin Nazari		26/04/93	M		(1)	
28	Alexander Nilsson		23/10/92	A	2	(15)	2
25	Robin Olsen	DEN	08/01/90	G	1		
19	Ivo Pekalski		03/11/90	M	10	(11)	1
13	Mathias Ranégie		14/06/84	A	19		10
29	Tokelo Rantie	RSA	08/09/90	A	10	(1)	3
19	Dardan Rexhepi		16/01/92	A		(13)	
20	Ricardinho	BRA	09/09/84	D	28		2
22	Filip Stenström		03/07/91	D		(1)	
3	Jasmin Sudic		24/11/90	D	3	(6)	
11	Simon Thern		18/09/92	M	22	(6)	3
2	Ulrich Vinzents	DEN	04/11/76	D	6	(2)	
9	Wilton Figueiredo	BRA	17/03/82	A	17	(5)	5

MJÄLLBY AIF

Coach: Peter Swärdh
1939 • Strandvallen (7,000) • maif.se

2012

01/04	AIK	a	0-0	
07/04	Örebro	h	0-0	
12/04	Häcken	a	2-4	Ericsson, Kivuvu
15/04	Åtvidaberg	h	2-0	Ericsson, Radetinac
20/04	Djurgården	h	4-3	Ericsson 2, Ekenberg, Kivuvu
27/04	Helsingborg	a	1-1	Pode
03/05	Malmö	h	2-2	Fejzullahu 2
07/05	GAIS	a	2-2	Fejzullahu (p), Kivuvu
12/05	Kalmar	a	2-1	Nicklasson, Fejzullahu
17/05	Göteborg	h	1-1	Fejzullahu
20/05	Gefle	h	0-0	
23/05	Syrianska	a	1-2	Ericsson
30/06	Norrköping	h	0-2	
08/07	Elfsborg	a	0-0	
14/07	Sundsvall	h	1-0	Fejzullahu
21/07	Sundsvall	a	1-3	Ericsson
29/07	AIK	h	0-1	
06/08	Örebro	a	1-0	Ekenberg
12/08	Göteborg	a	2-4	Ericsson, Ekenberg
27/08	Syrianska	h	0-2	
01/09	Malmö	a	1-1	Ericsson
15/09	GAIS	h	4-0	Ericsson 2, Agardius, El Kabir
23/09	Gefle	a	0-1	
26/09	Kalmar	h	1-0	Ericsson
01/10	Djurgården	a	1-0	Ericsson
07/10	Helsingborg	h	0-2	
20/10	Häcken	h	1-2	Radetinac
28/10	Åtvidaberg	a	0-0	
01/11	Elfsborg	h	2-3	Henderson 2
04/11	Norrköping	a	1-2	Ericsson

No	Name	Nat	DoB	Pos	Aps	(s)	Gls
12	Viktor Agardius		23/10/89	D	14	(7)	1
33	Gbenga Arokoyo	NGA	01/11/92	M	9	(1)	
1	Mattias Asper		20/03/74	G	30		
11	Adam Berner		25/01/87	A		(1)	
23	Andreas Blomqvist		05/05/92	M	7	(4)	
15	Robin Cederberg		25/02/83	D	16	(7)	
25	Anton Dahlström		27/08/90	D		(1)	
10	Marcus Ekenberg		16/06/80	A	16	(11)	3
88	Moestafa El Kabir	NED	05/10/88	A	3	(2)	1
18	Pär Ericsson		21/07/88	A	24	(6)	13
19	Erton Fejzullahu		19/04/88	A	11	(4)	6
19	Craig Henderson	NZL	24/06/87	M	8	(4)	2
24	Mattias Håkansson		20/02/93	M		(1)	
4	Daniel Ivanovski	MKD	27/06/83	D	27		
7	Dominique Kivuvu	ANG	16/09/87	M	16		3
5	William Leandersson		09/01/84	D	26		
14	Daniel Nicklasson		23/04/81	M	15	(3)	1
13	Daniel Nilsson		21/09/82	M	28		
21	Simon Nilsson		01/07/92	M	1	(6)	
22	Marcus Pode		27/03/86	A	8	(14)	1
8	Haris Radetinac	SRB	28/10/85	M	29		2
7	Juan Robledo	CHI	21/08/79	D		(5)	
6	Patrik Rosengren		25/07/71	D	22	(1)	
17	Robin Strömberg		23/01/92	M		(2)	
3	Anders Wikström		14/12/81	D	17		
20	Pavel Zavadil	CZE	30/04/78	M		(3)	
2	Mahmut Özen		01/09/88	D	3	(2)	

IFK NORRKÖPING

Coach: Jan Andersson
1897• Nya Parken (17,234) • ifknorrkoping.se
Major honours
Swedish League (12) 1943, 1945, 1946, 1947, 1948,
1952, 1956, 1957, 1960, 1962, 1963, 1989;
Swedish Cup (6) 1943, 1945, 1969, 1988, 1991, 1994

2012

02/04	Helsingborg	h	1-0	Thorvaldsson
09/04	Göteborg	a	2-1	Hasani 2 (1p)
12/04	Elfsborg	a	0-2	
16/04	Sundsvall	h	2-2	Nyman, Thorvaldsson
22/04	GAIS	a	0-2	
29/04	Malmö	h	3-2	Thorvaldsson 2, Frempong
03/05	Gefle	a	2-0	Nyman, Smedberg Dalance
06/05	Syrianska	h	1-4	Hasani
13/05	Örebro	h	3-0	Nyman, Khalili 2
16/05	Häcken	a	0-6	
20/05	AIK	a	2-5	Thorvaldsson, Ajdarevic
23/05	Åtvidaberg	h	2-2	Ajdarevic, Nyman
30/06	Mjällby	a	2-0	Thorvaldsson, Hasani
08/07	Kalmar	a	2-1	Thorvaldsson 2
16/07	Djurgården	a	1-1	Nyman
23/07	Djurgården	h	1-1	Khalili
28/07	Helsingborg	a	2-1	Thorvaldsson, Hasani
06/08	Göteborg	h	0-0	
12/08	Häcken	h	1-2	Smedberg Dalance
27/08	Åtvidaberg	a	1-1	Nyman
02/09	Gefle	h	0-1	
14/09	Syrianska	a	2-1	Gerson, Khalili
23/09	AIK	h	2-2	Thorvaldsson 2
26/09	Örebro	a	1-0	Tkalčić
01/10	GAIS	h	7-2	Thorvaldsson 2, Nyman, Tkalčić 2, og (M Gustafsson), Thelin
05/10	Malmö	a	0-2	
21/10	Elfsborg	h	2-1	og (Ishizaki), Frempong
28/10	Sundsvall	a	4-0	Thorvaldsson 3, Gerson
31/10	Kalmar	a	2-0	Thelin, Falk-Olander
04/11	Mjällby	h	2-1	Thorvaldsson, Nyman

No	Name	Nat	DoB	Pos	Aps	(s)	Gls
8	Astrit Ajdarevic		17/04/90	M	12		2
19	Modou Barrow	GAM	13/10/92	A		(7)	
15	Marcus Falk-Olander		21/05/87	M	5	(2)	1
6	Mathias Florén		11/08/76	D	27		
14	James Frempong		11/01/89	M	7	(12)	2
17	Bobbie Friberg da Cruz		16/02/82	D	20	(1)	
12	Lars Gerson	LUX	05/02/90	M	20	(8)	2
16	Shpëtim Hasani	ALB	10/08/82	M	13	(4)	5
29	Abbas Hassan		10/05/85	G	11		
4	Andreas Johansson		10/03/82	M	29		
9	Imad Khalili		03/04/87	A	12	(8)	4
1	Andreas Lindberg		14/12/80	G		(1)	
91	David Nilsson		12/01/91	G	19		
5	Christoffer Nyman		05/10/92	A	16	(13)	8
3	Morten Morisbak Skjønsberg	NOR	12/02/83	D	28		
84	Martin Smedberg Dalence		10/05/84	D	29	(1)	2
21	Joonas Tamm	EST	09/02/92	A		(2)	
22	Armin Tankovic		22/03/90	M		(6)	
11	Christopher Telo		04/11/89	M	10	(8)	
20	Isaac Kiese Thelin		24/06/92	A	1	(10)	2
10	Gunnar Heidar Thorvaldsson	ISL	01/04/82	A	29		17
13	Nikola Tkalčić	CRO	03/12/89	D	14	(3)	3
23	David Wiklander		03/10/84	M	28		

GIF SUNDSVALL

Coach: Sören Åkeby
1903 • Norrporten Arena (8,500) • gifsundsvall.se

2012

31/03	Kalmar	h	0-1	
08/04	Djurgården	a	0-1	
12/04	Syrianska	h	4-0	Walker, Holster, Dibba 2
16/04	Norrköping	a	2-2	og (Friberg da Cruz), Eklund
22/04	AIK	a	1-1	Walker
29/04	Örebro	h	3-1	Brink, Holster, Risholt
02/05	Göteborg	a	0-2	
05/05	Helsingborg	h	0-1	
14/05	Gefle	a	0-0	
17/05	GAIS	a	2-1	Eklund, Skúlason (p)
21/05	Elfsborg	h	0-3	
24/05	Malmö	h	1-1	Eklund
30/06	Häcken	a	2-1	Helg, Holster
07/07	Åtvidaberg	h	3-3	Holster, Helg, Eklund
14/07	Mjällby	a	0-1	
21/07	Mjällby	h	3-1	Forsberg, og (Cederberg), Helg
29/07	Kalmar	a	1-1	Danielsson
06/08	Djurgården	h	0-1	
11/08	GAIS	h	2-0	Eklund, Sliper
27/08	Malmö	a	0-2	
02/09	Göteborg	h	3-3	Forsberg 2, Sellin
15/09	Helsingborg	a	0-4	
23/09	Elfsborg	a	0-1	
26/09	Gefle	h	0-1	
30/09	AIK	h	2-3	Skúlason, Forsberg
07/10	Örebro	a	2-2	Helg, Skúlason
22/10	Syrianska	a	1-1	Forsberg
28/10	Norrköping	h	0-4	
01/11	Åtvidaberg	a	2-2	Risholt, Forsberg
04/11	Häcken	h	1-2	Holster

No	Name	Nat	DoB	Pos	Aps	(s)	Gls
1	Oscar Berglund		13/04/84	G	28	(1)	
2	Christian Brink		17/03/83	D	5	(5)	1
22	Markus Danielsson		08/04/89	D	29		1
14	Pa Amat Dibba		15/10/87	A	12	(10)	2
9	Johan Eklund		30/05/84	A	16	(10)	5
31	Jón Gudni Fjóluson	ISL	10/04/89	D	4	(2)	
33	Emil Forsberg		23/10/91	A	20	(1)	6
16	Simon Helg		10/04/90	M	24	(2)	4
12	Fredrik Holster		10/03/88	M	29		5
8	Fredric Jonson		15/07/87	D	22	(1)	
15	Robert Lundström		01/11/89	D	17	(8)	
21	Michel Pires	BRA	25/06/89	M	3	(4)	
25	Nuri Mustafi	MKD	16/03/83	M	1	(9)	
3	David Myrestam		04/04/87	D	15		
17	Tommy Naurin		17/05/84	G	2		
6	Patrik Rikama-Hinnenberg	FIN	08/02/83	D	1	(4)	
5	Roger Risholt	NOR	10/04/79	M	13	(8)	2
32	Robin Sellin		12/04/90	D	7	(3)	1
11	Ari Freyr Skúlason	ISL	14/05/87	M	26		3
7	Daniel Sliper		23/04/87	M	8	(13)	1
23	Kevin Walker		03/08/89	M	25	(2)	2
4	Stefan Ålander		25/04/83	D	23	(1)	

SYRIANSKA FC

Coach: Özkan Melkemichel
1977 • Södertälje Fotbollsarena (6,400) •
syrianskafc.com

2012

01/04	Göteborg	h	2-1	Touma, Aganović
06/04	Gefle	a	1-1	og (Malmborg)
12/04	Sundsvall	a	0-4	
15/04	AIK	h	0-1	
23/04	Malmö	a	0-2	
28/04	Häcken	h	1-2	Chanko
02/05	Elfsborg	h	1-4	Felic
06/05	Norrköping	a	4-1	Touma 3, Bååth
11/05	GAIS	h	2-0	Felic, Chanko
16/05	Åtvidaberg	a	0-1	
20/05	Örebro	a	1-0	Aganović
23/05	Mjällby	h	2-1	Felic, Bååth
30/06	Kalmar	a	0-3	
07/07	Djurgården	h	1-1	Mourad
14/07	Helsingborg	a	0-1	
21/07	Helsingborg	h	1-3	Felic
31/07	Göteborg	a	0-1	
04/08	Gefle	h	1-0	Aganović
11/08	Åtvidaberg	h	2-2	Aganović, og (Tinnerholm)
27/08	Mjällby	a	2-0	Yasar, Michel
02/09	Elfsborg	a	0-1	
14/09	Norrköping	h	1-2	Massi
22/09	Örebro	h	2-2	Felic, Touma
28/09	GAIS	a	4-1	Skenderović, Mourad, Felic, Saleh
01/10	Malmö	h	0-2	
06/10	Häcken	a	1-5	Massi
22/10	Sundsvall	h	1-1	Felic
28/10	AIK	a	1-1	Touma
31/10	Djurgården	a	1-1	Touma
04/11	Kalmar	h	3-0	Felic, Touma, Bååth

No	Name	Nat	DoB	Pos	Aps	(s)	Gls
11	Admir Aganović	BIH	25/08/86	A	17	(8)	4
4	Alex	BRA	15/05/82	D	18	(2)	
6	Johan Arneng		14/06/79	M	28		
18	Anders Bååth		13/04/91	M	13	(7)	3
77	Louay Chanko	SYR	29/11/79	M	27		2
5	Christian Demirtas	GER	25/05/84	D	3		
16	Rabi Elia		19/04/87	D	19	(2)	
23	Dinko Felic	NOR	10/11/83	A	28	(1)	8
1	Dejan Garaca		21/07/91	G	3	(2)	
50	Labinot Harbuzi	ALB	04/04/86	M		(3)	
8	Josef Ibrahim		13/03/91	M		(2)	
19	Lawal Ismail	NGA	05/09/91	A	2	(4)	
13	Omar Jawo	GAM	10/11/81	D	10	(3)	
8	Marcos Gondra Krug	ESP	01/01/87	M	2	(3)	
99	Besim Kunić	BIH	13/02/86	M	1	(4)	
7	Robert Massi		02/01/87	M	9	(4)	2
50	Matthew Mbuta	CMR	21/12/85	M	4	(5)	
26	Samir Mete		27/10/87	A		(1)	
22	Alexander Michel		14/11/92	M	18	(5)	1
21	Dwayne Miller	JAM	14/07/87	G	22		
17	George Mourad	SYR	18/09/82	A	4	(14)	2
14	Yussuf Saleh	ETH	22/03/84	M	21	(3)	1
24	Haris Skenderović	BIH	03/11/81	D	24	(1)	1
2	Suleyman Sleyman		28/12/79	D	12	(2)	
20	Gabriel Somi		24/08/91	D	13	(2)	
30	Lasse Staw	NOR	01/01/88	G	5	(3)	
10	Sharbel Touma		25/03/79	M	25		8
9	Özgur Yasar		26/11/81	A	2	(4)	1

ÅTVIDABERGS FF

Coach: Andreas Thomsson
1907 • Kopparvallen (8,600) • atvidabergsff.se
Major honours
Swedish League (2) 1972, 1973;
Swedish Cup (2) 1970, 1971

2012

02/04	Örebro	a	4-3	Prodell 2, Suljić, Arvidsson
06/04	GAIS	h	2-1	Hallingström, Arvidsson
10/04	Gefle	h	6-1	Prodell 2, Eriksson 2, Álberis Silva, Bergström
15/04	Mjällby	a	0-2	
21/04	Helsingborg	h	1-2	Prodell
28/04	Göteborg	a	1-2	Arvidsson
02/05	Häcken	h	0-3	
06/05	Malmö	a	1-2	Möller
12/05	Djurgården	a	1-1	Zhubi
16/05	Syrianska	h	1-0	Eriksson
20/05	Kalmar	h	3-0	Prodell, Eriksson (p), Zhubi
23/05	Norrköping	a	2-2	Prodell, Mete
30/06	Elfsborg	h	5-1	Prodell 2, Pettersson, Eriksson (p), Tinnerholm
07/07	Sundsvall	a	3-3	Eriksson, Prodell 2
14/07	AIK	h	2-0	Eriksson, Prodell
22/07	AIK	a	0-1	
27/07	Örebro	h	1-1	Pettersson
04/08	GAIS	a	2-2	Eriksson 2
11/08	Syrianska	a	2-2	Eriksson, Mete
27/08	Norrköping	h	1-1	Eriksson
31/08	Häcken	a	2-5	Abubakari, Mete
17/09	Malmö	h	0-1	
23/09	Kalmar	a	0-2	
26/09	Djurgården	h	2-1	Bergström, Möller
30/09	Helsingborg	a	0-3	
06/10	Göteborg	h	1-2	Prodell
20/10	Gefle	a	2-1	Zatara, Pettersson
28/10	Mjällby	h	0-0	
01/11	Sundsvall	h	2-2	Prodell, Mete
04/11	Elfsborg	a	1-1	Prodell

No	Name	Nat	DoB	Pos	Aps	(s)	Gls
6	Mohamed Abubakari	GHA	15/01/86	M	12		1
13	Álberis Silva	BRA	02/12/84	D	18	(5)	1
18	Jesper Arvidsson		01/01/85	D	29		3
7	Kristian Bergström		08/01/74	M	30		2
32	Martin Christensen	DEN	23/12/87	M	4	(4)	
22	Magnus Eriksson		08/04/90	A	20		11
1	Henrik Gustavsson		21/10/76	G	16		
5	Daniel Hallingström		10/02/81	D	29		1
20	Gustav Jansson		24/02/86	G	14	(1)	
8	Christoffer Karlsson		27/01/88	M		(2)	
12	Marinho	BRA	05/07/84	M	21	(1)	
15	Mattias Mete		30/05/87	A	2	(15)	4
3	Erik Moberg		05/07/86	D	1	(4)	
14	Oscar Möller		15/04/87	A	11	(15)	2
2	Tobias Nilsson		20/02/86	M	12	(10)	
2	Allan Olesen	DEN	20/05/82	D	11	(8)	
16	Alain Junior Ollé Ollé	CMR	11/04/87	M	3	(4)	
24	Tom Pettersson		25/03/90	D	17	(5)	3
11	Viktor Prodell		29/02/88	A	26	(3)	15
19	Amir Suljić	BIH	08/02/89	M	15		1
23	Anton Tinnerholm		26/02/91	D	23	(2)	1
25	Imad Zatara	PLE	01/10/84	M	7	(2)	1
9	Petrit Zhubi	ALB	08/05/88	M	9	(6)	2

ÖREBRO SK

Coach: Sixten Boström (FIN);
(08/06/12) Per-Ola Ljung
1908 • Behrn Arena (14,500) • oskfotboll.se

2012

02/04	Åtvidaberg	h	3-4	Atashkadeh 2, Daniel Bamberg
07/04	Mjällby	a	0-0	
11/04	Helsingborg	h	0-0	
15/04	Göteborg	a	2-2	Atashkadeh, Grahn
23/04	Elfsborg	h	0-2	
29/04	Sundsvall	a	1-3	Atashkadeh
03/05	Djurgården	a	1-2	Rama (p)
07/05	Kalmar	h	0-1	
13/05	Norrköping	a	0-3	
16/05	AIK	h	2-2	Saeid, Atashkadeh (p)
20/05	Syrianska	h	0-1	
23/05	Gefle	a	1-2	Grahn
05/07	GAIS	a	1-0	Daniel Bamberg
09/07	Malmö	h	2-1	Lumbana, Berisha
15/07	Häcken	h	1-2	Astvald
19/07	Häcken	a	1-2	Lumbana
27/07	Åtvidaberg	a	1-1	Astvald
06/08	Mjällby	h	0-1	
12/08	AIK	a	0-3	
24/08	Gefle	h	1-2	Berisha
31/08	Djurgården	h	2-3	Holmberg, Wikström
17/09	Kalmar	a	2-1	Kamara, Atashkadeh (p)
22/09	Syrianska	a	2-2	Hasani, Kamara
26/09	Norrköping	h	0-1	
30/09	Elfsborg	a	0-1	
07/10	Sundsvall	h	2-2	og (Ålander), Holmberg
21/10	Helsingborg	a	1-1	Rama
28/10	Göteborg	h	1-0	Hasani
01/11	Malmö	a	1-1	Kamara
04/11	GAIS	h	4-0	Berisha, Kamara, Hasani 2 (1p)

No	Name	Nat	DoB	Pos	Aps	(s)	Gls
30	Armend Alimi	MKD	11/12/87	M	11	(6)	
3	Patrik Anttonen		06/03/80	D	13	(2)	
18	Markus Astvald		03/09/90	M	15	(5)	2
28	William Atashkadeh		12/04/92	A	14	(2)	6
6	Emil Berger		23/05/91	M	12	(2)	
5	Ilir Berisha	ALB	25/06/91	D	18	(1)	3
14	Tomer Chencinski	CAN	01/12/84	G	14		
22	Daniel Bamberg	BRA	23/04/84	M	17	(4)	2
7	Tobias Grahn		05/03/80	M	16	(3)	2
9	Andreas Haddad		05/05/82	A	1	(2)	
2	Patrik Haginge		02/04/85	D	25	(2)	
16	Shpëtim Hasani	ALB	10/08/82	A	11		4
17	Karl Holmberg		03/03/93	M	15	(10)	2
15	Josef Ibrahim		13/03/91	M		(2)	
93	Alhassan Kamara	SLE	13/01/93	A	6	(2)	4
44	Simon Leonidsson		25/10/73	M		(1)	
27	Boris Lumbana		16/09/91	D	8	(3)	2
32	Kushtrim Lushtaku	ALB	08/09/89	M		(9)	
29	Valdet Rama	ALB	20/11/87	M	12	(9)	2
8	Mohammed Saeid		24/12/90	M	20	(4)	1
10	Peter Samuelsson		20/11/81	A	3	(3)	
1	Jonas Sandqvist		06/05/81	G	16		
4	Magnus Wikström		07/12/77	D	28		1
21	Christoffer Wiktorsson		22/03/89	D	10	(4)	
11	Tommi Wirtanen	FIN	19/01/83	M	10		
20	Samuel Wowoah		17/06/76	D	27	(1)	
19	Ahmed Yasin	IRQ	21/04/91	A	8	(5)	

Promoted clubs

ÖSTERS IF

Coach: Roar Hansen
1930 • Myresjöhus Arena (12,000) • ostersif.se
Major honours
Swedish League (4) 1968, 1978, 1980, 1981;
Swedish Cup (1) 1977

IF BROMMAPOJKARNA

Coach: Robert Björknesjö
1942 • Grimsta IP (8,000) • brommapojkarna.se

HALMSTADS BK

Coach: Jens Gustafsson
1914 • Örjans Vall (15,500) • hbk.se
Major honours
Swedish League (4) 1976, 1979, 1997, 2000;
Swedish Cup (1) 1995

SECOND LEVEL FINAL TABLE 2012

		Pld	W	D	L	F	A	Pts
1	Östers IF	30	20	6	4	57	28	66
2	IF Brommapojkarna	30	20	1	9	61	40	61
3	Halmstads BK	30	16	8	6	61	33	56
4	Hammarby Fotboll	30	13	10	7	40	33	49
5	Ljungskile SK	30	11	9	10	36	36	42
6	Landskrona BoIS	30	12	5	13	35	43	41
7	Jönköpings Södra IF	30	10	10	10	52	47	40
8	Assyriska FF	30	11	6	13	44	49	39
9	Ängelholms FF	30	10	9	11	40	46	39
10	IK Brage	30	10	9	11	35	45	39
11	Varbergs BoIS FC	30	8	13	9	49	52	37
12	Degerfors IF	30	9	8	13	46	53	35
13	Falkenbergs FF	30	8	10	12	45	47	34
14	IFK Värnamo	30	8	6	16	47	54	30
15	Trelleborgs FF	30	8	5	17	40	55	29
16	Umeå FC	30	6	5	19	34	61	23

PROMOTION/RELEGATION PLAY-OFFS

(10/11/12 & 17/11/12)
Halmstad 3-0 Sundsvall
Sundsvall 4-3 Halmstad
(Halmstad 6-4)

Domestic cup: Svenska Cupen 2012/13

SECOND ROUND

(16/08/12)
Sirius 1-1 Hammarby *(aet; 5-4 on pens)*

(18/08/12)
Arameiska-Syrianska 1-3 Sundsvall
Enskede 0-1 Landskrona
Frej Täby 2-1 Trelleborg
Hässleholm 0-2 Umeå

Karlstad 0-0 Gefle *(aet; 3-4 on pens)*
Kristianstad 1-2 Falkenberg
Lärje-Angered 1-1 Öster *(aet; 0-3 on pens)*
Nyköping 5-3 Brommapojkarna *(aet)*
Ramlösa Södra 0-7 Assyriska
Ronneby 2-5 Halmstad
Rynninge 0-2 Norrköping
Uddevalla 0-7 Syrianska
Valsta Syrianska 0-1 Brage
Östersund 0-3 Mjällby

(19/08/12)
Mariehem 0-2 Örebro
Motala 1-2 Varberg
Råslätt 2-3 Värnamo
Selånger 0-6 Ljungskile
Skövde 0-3 Åtvidaberg
Sleipner 0-2 Jönköping Södra *(aet)*
Torn 1-2 Ängelholm
Utsikten 0-3 GAIS
Åkarp 0-3 Häcken
Örgryte 3-0 Degerfors

(20/08/12)
Dalstorp 1-5 Djurgården
Gute 0-4 Kalmar
Långholmen 0-9 Göteborg
Sandviken 3-6 Malmö *(aet)*

(12/09/12)
Torslanda 0-1 AIK

(11/11/12)
Hovslätt 0-4 Elfsborg
Höllviken 1-2 Helsingborg

THIRD ROUND

Group 1
(02/03/13)
Elfsborg 5-1 Ljungskile
Sirius 0-2 GAIS

(09/03/13)
GAIS 2-1 Ljungskile
Sirius 2-1 Elfsborg

(16/03/13)
Ljungskile 1-7 Sirius

(17/03/13)
Elfsborg 3-1 GAIS

Final standings
1 Sirius 6 pts *(qualified)*
2 Elfsborg 6 pts; 3 GAIS 6 pts; 4 Ljungskile 0 pts
(eliminated)

Group 2
(02/03/13)
Häcken 1-2 Falkenberg
Örebro 2-0 Värnamo

(09/03/13)
Värnamo 0-3 Häcken
Örebro 0-1 Falkenberg

(13/03/13)
Falkenberg 4-1 Värnamo

(16/03/13)
Häcken 2-0 Örebro

Final standings
1 Falkenberg 9 pts *(qualified)*
2 Häcken 6 pts; 3 Örebro 3 pts 4 Värnamo 0 pts
(eliminated)

Group 3
(02/03/13)
Frej 2-1 Sundsvall
Malmö 1-1 Öster

(09/03/13)
Sundsvall 0-2 Öster

(10/03/13)
Frej 0-2 Malmö

(14/03/13)
Öster 5-0 Frej

(16/03/13)
Malmö 4-1 Sundsvall

Final standings
1 Öster 7 pts *(qualified)*
2 Malmö 7 pts; 3 Frej 3 pts; 4 Sundsvall 0 pts
(eliminated)

Group 4
(03/03/13)
AIK 1-2 Halmstad
Örgryte 2-1 Syrianska

(10/03/13)
Syrianska 2-1 Halmstad
Örgryte 4-1 AIK

(16/03/13)
AIK 2-0 Syrianska
Halmstad 2-1 Örgryte

Final standings
1 Örgryte 6 pts *(qualified)*
2 Halmstad 6 pts; 3 AIK 3 pts; 4 Syrianska 3 pts
(eliminated)

Group 5
(02/03/13)
Mjällby 1-1 Ängelholm
Norrköping 0-0 Landskrona

(09/03/13)
Mjällby 3-0 Landskrona

(10/03/13)
Ängelholm 0-4 Norrköping

(16/03/13)
Landskrona 3-1 Ängelholm
Norrköping 2-0 Mjällby

Final standings
1 Norrköping 7 pts *(qualified)*
2 Mjällby 4 pts; 3 Landskrona 4 pts; 4 Ängelholm 1
pt *(eliminated)*

Group 6
(02/03/13)
Gefle 3-2 Varberg

(03/03/13)
Helsingborg 1-1 Assyriska

(10/03/13)
Gefle 5-1 Assyriska
Varberg 0-5 Helsingborg

(16/03/13)
Assyriska 1-1 Varberg

(17/03/13)
Helsingborg 3-1 Gefle

Final standings
1 Helsingborg 7 pts *(qualified)*
2 Gefle 6 pts; 3 Assyriska 2 pts; 4 Varberg 1 pt
(eliminated)

Group 7
(02/03/13)
Göteborg 2-0 Brage

(03/03/13)
Nyköping 2-1 Kalmar

(10/03/13)
Kalmar 3-0 Brage
Nyköping 1-4 Göteborg

(16/03/13)
Brage 3-1 Nyköping

(17/03/13)
Göteborg 0-1 Kalmar

Final standings
1 Göteborg 6 pts *(qualified)*
2 Kalmar 6 pts; 3 Brage 3 pts; 4 Nyköping 3 pts
(eliminated)

Group 8
(03/03/13)
Djurgården 3-0 Umeå
Åtvidaberg 3-1 Jönköping Södra

(10/03/13)
Djurgården 3-1 Jönköping Södra
Umeå 2-1 Åtvidaberg

(16/03/13)
Jönköping Södra 3-0 Umeå

(17/03/13)
Åtvidaberg 1-1 Djurgården

Final standings
1 Djurgården 7 pts
2 Åtvidaberg 4 pts; 3 Jönköping Södra 3 pts;
4 Umeå 3 pts (eliminated)

QUARTER-FINALS

(03/04/13)
Falkenberg 0-1 Örgryte *(Wallén 50)*
Helsingborg 0-1 Göteborg *(Haglund 4)*

(04/04/13)
Norrköping 0-0 Djurgården *(aet; 4-5 on pens)*
Öster 2-1 Sirius *(Persson 16, Söderberg 77;
Björkebaum 79)*

SEMI-FINALS

(01/05/13)
Djurgården 1-0 Örgryte *(Johansson 59)*
Öster 1-4 Göteborg *(Robledo 50; Hysén 9, 52,
Moberg Karlsson 69, 81)*

FINAL

(26/05/13)
Friends Arena, Solna
IFK GÖTEBORG 1 *(Hysén 6)*
DJURGÅRDENS IF 1 *(Amartey 52)*
(aet; 3-1 on pens)
Referee: Johannesson
GÖTEBORG: Alvbåge, Dyrestam, Wæhler, Bjärsmyr,
A Johansson, Larsson (Farnerud 59), J Johansson,
Haglund, Salomonsson (Daniel Sobralense 59),
Hysén, Söder (Moberg Karlsson 83)
DJURGÅRDEN: Høie, Andriuškevičius (Arvidsson
43; Chibsah 63), Bergström, Östberg, Nymann,
Tibbling, Amartey, Johansson, Broberg (Solignac
76), Fejzullahu, Jawo

SWITZERLAND

Schweizerischer Fussballverband/Association Suisse de Football (SFV/ASF)

Address	Worbstrasse 48, Postfach CH-3000 Bern 15	**President**	Peter Gilliéron
Tel	+41 31 950 8111	**General secretary**	Alex Miescher
Fax	+41 31 950 8181	**Media officer**	Marco von Ah
E-mail	sfv.asf@football.ch	**Year of formation**	1895
Website	football.ch	**National stadium**	Stade de Suisse, Berne (32,000)

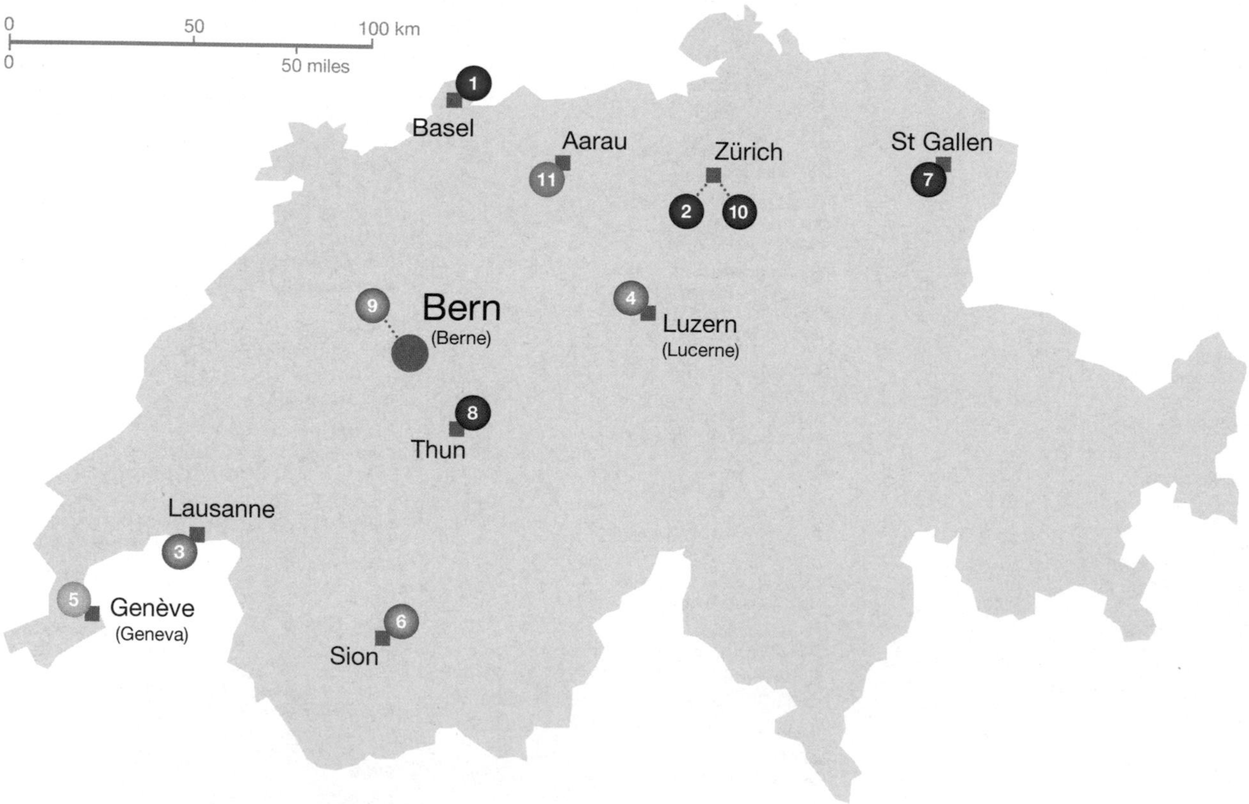

0 — 50 — 100 km
0 — 50 miles

SUPER LEAGUE CLUBS

 1 FC Basel 1893

 2 Grasshopper Club

3 FC Lausanne-Sport

4 FC Luzern

 5 Servette FC

 6 FC Sion

 7 FC St Gallen

 8 FC Thun

9 BSC Young Boys

 10 FC Zürich

PROMOTED CLUB

11 FC Aarau

KEY:

● – UEFA Champions League

● – UEFA Europa League

● – Promoted club

● – Relegated club

Basel maintain their grip

FC Basel 1893 captured the Swiss Super League title for the fourth season running, coming from behind under new coach Murat Yakin to overtake halfway leaders Grasshopper Club, who denied the champions a double by defeating them on penalties in the final of the Swiss Cup.

It was a memorable season also for Basel in Europe, where they broke new ground by reaching the semi-finals of the UEFA Europa League. The Swiss national team had much to celebrate too as they dominated their 2014 FIFA World Cup qualifying group.

| Super League title remains at St Jakob-Park | Perennial champions reach European semi-final | Resurgent Grasshoppers win the cup |

Domestic league

Basel became the first team to win four consecutive Swiss league titles since BSC Young Boys in 1957-60, but it was nothing like the cakewalk of the previous season. Indeed, they made such a stuttering start that double-winning coach Heiko Vogel was removed in October – a year after his appointment – and replaced by former defender Murat Yakin, dismissed by FC Luzern a few weeks earlier. Basel were off the pace at the time, with FC Sion, FC St Gallen and Grasshoppers in turn making the early running, but at the winter break they were just four points in arrears of Grasshoppers, a team undergoing a startling resurgence under coach Uli Forte.

Basel increased the pressure in the early weeks of the spring campaign, and by mid-March they had ascended to the Super League summit. Once there, they remained. Despite a heavy workload in Europe, their focus remained undimmed, and when they met Grasshoppers for the fourth time in the campaign – having won one and drawn two of the previous three encounters – they required just a point to effectively seal their 16th Swiss title. They would come within seconds of achieving it, only for the home side to deny them with a dramatic added-time winner. Basel, however, held their nerve and won their

last two matches – as did Grasshoppers – to finish with a three-point advantage.

With average gates of 28,751, Basel were once again the best supported club in the land, and the St Jakob-Park faithful were treated to some fine entertainment, with skipper Marco Streller, goalkeeper Yann Sommer, defender Aleksandar Dragovic and midfield starlet Valentin Stocker particularly excelling, and local hero Alex Frei ending his fabulous career with a fourth championship medal. Newly promoted St Gallen finished 13 points behind Basel, but their third-place finish, made possible by a league-best 21-goal haul from Argentinian midfielder Ezequiel Scarione, was one of the surprises of the season.

Domestic cup

Grasshoppers collected their first major silverware for a decade as they ended Basel's dreams of a third double in four years with a penalty shoot-out win in the Swiss Cup final. Izet Hajrovic, GC's semi-final match-winner against FC Zürich, provided a quick equaliser to Markus Steinhöfer's 71st-minute opener before Milan Vilotić struck the decisive kick in the shoot-out. Whereas Basel had won the previous season's final on penalties, against Luzern, it was a second successive shoot-out defeat in the fixture for coach Yakin.

Europe

Basel's busy season comprised 20 matches in Europe, extending from the second qualifying round of the UEFA Champions League to the semi-finals of the UEFA Europa League. Bidding to become the first Swiss club to reach a European final, Yakin's men battled heroically before going out to Chelsea FC. Earlier rounds had brought unforgettable and unexpected victories over FC Dnipro Dnipropetrovsk, FC Zenit St Petersburg and Tottenham Hotspur FC, the latter on penalties.

National team

As Basel flew the Swiss flag proudly in club competition, the national team did likewise in the World Cup, a place in Brazil seemingly theirs for the taking at the end of a season in which they won four and drew two of their six qualifiers to take a commanding lead at the top of Group E.

Experienced coach Ottmar Hitzfeld was fortunate in being able to select virtually the same team from one game to the next, but he pooled his resources well, notably in defence, leaving Switzerland odds-on to qualify directly for a third successive World Cup.

 **SWITZERLAND**

Domestic league: Super League 2012/13 final table

		Pld	Home W	D	L	F	A	Away W	D	L	F	A	Total W	D	L	F	A	Pts
1	**FC Basel 1893**	36	14	3	1	36	10	7	6	5	25	21	21	9	6	61	31	72
2	Grasshopper Club	36	11	4	3	25	13	9	5	4	23	19	20	9	7	48	32	69
3	FC St Gallen	36	10	5	3	35	17	7	3	8	19	19	17	8	11	54	36	59
4	FC Zürich	36	9	1	8	32	22	7	6	5	30	26	16	7	13	62	48	55
5	FC Thun	36	8	6	4	30	23	5	3	10	14	23	13	9	14	44	46	48
6	FC Sion	36	7	6	5	20	22	6	3	9	20	32	13	9	14	40	54	48
7	BSC Young Boys	36	9	4	5	34	19	2	6	10	14	31	11	10	15	48	50	43
8	FC Luzern	36	6	8	4	18	19	4	4	10	23	33	10	12	14	41	52	42
9	FC Lausanne-Sport	36	6	4	8	24	23	2	5	11	8	28	8	9	19	32	51	33
10	Servette FC	36	4	4	10	18	22	2	4	12	14	40	6	8	22	32	62	26

SEASON AT A GLANCE

EUROPEAN QUALIFICATION 2013/14

 Champion: FC Basel 1893 (third qualifying round)
Cup winner: Grasshopper-Club (third qualifying round)

 FC St Gallen (play-offs)
FC Zürich (third qualifying round)
FC Thun (second qualifying round)

Top scorer Ezequiel Scarione (St Gallen), 21 goals
Relegated club Servette FC
Promoted club FC Aarau
Cup final Grasshopper Club 1-1 FC Basel (aet; 4-3 on pens)

SUPER LEAGUE TEAM OF THE SEASON
(4-4-2)
Coach: Yakin (Basel)

PLAYER OF THE SEASON
Valentin Stocker
(FC Basel 1893)

Stocker's impressive technique and pace was not new to the Swiss Super League, but the left-sided midfielder stepped up a level in 2012/13, not least in the goalscoring department. Eleven goals in all competitions, many of them at crucial times, helped the 24-year-old work his way back into the thoughts of Swiss national team coach Ottmar Hitzfeld.

NEWCOMER OF THE SEASON
Izet Hajrovic
(Grasshopper Club)

Hajrovic was Grashoppers' top scorer in the league with eight goals, but there could have been many more from one of the discoveries of the season, who ignited the Zurich club's title challenge and also scored important goals in the cup semi-final and final. The midfielder's reward was a first cap for Switzerland in an autumn friendly against Tunisia.

SWITZERLAND

NATIONAL TEAM

Home Kit   Away Kit

Results 2012/13

15/08/12	Croatia	A	Split	4-2	Xhaka (11), Barnetta (37), Gavranovic (52, 81)
07/09/12	Slovenia (WCQ)	A	Ljubljana	2-0	Xhaka (20), Inler (51)
11/09/12	Albania (WCQ)	H	Lucerne	2-0	Shaqiri (22), Inler (68p)
12/10/12	Norway (WCQ)	H	Berne	1-1	Gavranovic (79)
16/10/12	Iceland (WCQ)	A	Reykjavik	2-0	Barnetta (66), Gavranovic (79)
14/11/12	Tunisia	A	Sousse	2-1	Derdiyok (40), Shaqiri (90+6)
06/02/13	Greece	A	Piraeus	0-0	
23/03/13	Cyprus (WCQ)	A	Nicosia	0-0	
08/06/13	Cyprus (WCQ)	H	Geneva	1-0	Seferovic (90)

Appearances 2012/13

Coach: Ottmar Hitzfeld (GER)	12/01/49		Cro	SVN	ALB	NOR	ISL	Tun	Gre	CYP	CYP	Caps	Goals
Diego Benaglio	08/09/83	Wolfsburg (GER)	G	G	G	G	G				G	49	-
Stephan Lichtsteiner	16/01/84	Juventus (ITA)	D46	D	D	D	D	D46	D30	D	D	57	2
Steve von Bergen	10/06/83	Genoa (ITA) /Palermo (ITA)	D		D	D	D	s68	D74	D	D	35	-
Johan Djourou	18/01/87	Arsenal (ENG) /Hannover (GER)	D	D	D	D	D	D	D46	D52	D	41	1
Ricardo Rodriguez	25/08/92	Wolfsburg (GER)	D62	D	D	D	D	s46	D	D	D	14	-
Xherdan Shaqiri	10/10/91	Bayern (GER)	M	M74	M	M	M80	M		M	M	26	7
Gökhan Inler	27/06/84	Napoli (ITA)	M46	M	M	M	M	M46	s46	M	M	66	6
Valon Behrami	19/04/85	Napoli (ITA)	M46	M	M73	M92	M	s46	M46	M76	M67	41	2
Tranquillo Barnetta	22/05/85	Schalke (GER)	M46	M 75*		M71	M91	M83	M46		s77	68	10
Granit Xhaka	27/09/92	Mönchengladbach (GER)	M	M85	M91	M	M	M72	M	s46		17	3
Admir Mehmedi	16/03/91	Dynamo Kyiv (UKR)	A88		s79		s83		M			14	1
Gelson Fernandes	02/09/86	Sporting (POR) /Sion	s46	s85				s46	s74			42	2
Blerim Dzemaili	12/04/86	Napoli (ITA)	s46	s74	s73	s92	s80	M46			s67	25	-
Valentin Stocker	12/04/89	Basel	s46		M79				s46	M	M77	17	3
Mario Gavranovic	24/11/89	Zürich	s46			s71	A83		A68		A	7	4
Reto Ziegler	16/01/86	Juventus (ITA) /Lokomotiv Moskva (RUS)	s62					D				32	1
Innocent Emeghara	27/05/89	Lorient (FRA) /Siena (ITA)	s88							M46		9	-
Eren Derdiyok	12/06/88	Hoffenheim (GER)		A	A	A		A		s76		45	8
Josip Drmic	08/08/92	Zürich			s91						A74	2	-
Timm Klose	09/05/88	Nürnberg (GER)					s91	D68	s46			6	-
Yann Sommer	17/12/88	Basel						G	G	G		4	-
Nassim Ben Khalifa	13/01/92	Grasshoppers						s72				4	-
Izet Hajrovic	04/08/91	Grasshoppers						s83				1	-
Pirmin Schwegler	09/03/87	Eintracht Frankfurt (GER)							M			12	-
Michel Morganella	17/05/89	Palermo (ITA)							s30			2	-
Haris Seferovic	22/02/92	Novara (ITA)							s68	A	s74	3	1
Philippe Senderos	14/02/85	Fulham (ENG)								s52		48	5

SWITZERLAND

FC BASEL 1893

CHAMPIONS LEAGUE

Second qualifying round - FC Flora Tallinn (EST)
A 2-0 *A Frei (64, 87p)*
Sommer, Park, P Degen, Dragovic, D Degen (Vuleta 73), Streller, Yapi Yapo, A Frei (Andrist 87), Díaz, Sauro, Zoua (Stocker 62). Coach: Heiko Vogel (GER)
H 3-0 *Zoua (9, 31), Díaz (63)*
Vailati, Dragovic, D Degen, Streller (A Frei 73), Voser, Díaz (Grether 80), Cabral, Sauro, Steinhöfer (Andrist 67), Vuleta, Zoua. Coach: Heiko Vogel (GER)

Third qualifying round - Molde FK (NOR)
A 1-0 *Zoua (79)*
Sommer, Park, Dragovic, D Degen (Zoua 61), Streller, Yapi Yapo, Stocker, Díaz, Cabral, Sauro, Steinhöfer. Coach: Heiko Vogel (GER)
H 1-1 *D Degen (75)*
Sommer, Park, Dragovic, D Degen (F Frei 89), Streller, Yapi Yapo (Salah 74), Stocker (Zoua 84), Díaz, Cabral, Sauro, Steinhöfer. Coach: Heiko Vogel (GER)

Play-offs - CFR 1907 Cluj (ROU)
H 1-2 *Streller (44)*
Sommer, Park, Dragovic, D Degen (F Frei 72), Streller, Stocker (A Frei 79), Díaz, Salah, Cabral, Sauro (Kováč 86), Steinhöfer. Coach: Heiko Vogel (GER)
A 0-1
Sommer, Park (Schär 85), Dragovic, D Degen (Zoua 46), Streller, A Frei, F Frei, Díaz (Andrist 69), Cabral, Sauro, Steinhöfer. Coach: Heiko Vogel (GER)

EUROPA LEAGUE

Group G
Match 1 - Sporting Clube de Portugal (POR)
A 0-0
Sommer, Park, Dragovic, Streller, A Frei, Stocker (D Degen 90+1), Díaz (F Frei 83), Salah (Zoua 75), Cabral, Sauro, Steinhöfer. Coach: Heiko Vogel (GER)
Match 2 - KRC Genk (BEL)
H 2-2 *Streller (70p, 85)*
Sommer, Park, P Degen, Dragovic (Schär 53), Streller, A Frei (Zoua 46), Stocker, Díaz (F Frei 69), Salah, Cabral, Sauro. Coach: Heiko Vogel (GER)
Match 3 - Videoton FC (HUN)
A 1-2 *Schär (90+1)*
Sommer, Park (Voser 46), Dragovic, D Degen (F Frei 72), Streller, Stocker, Schär, Díaz, Salah (Pak 57), Cabral, Steinhöfer. Coach: Murat Yakin (SUI)
Match 4 - Videoton FC (HUN)
H 1-0 *Streller (80)*
Sommer, P Degen, Dragovic, D Degen (Zoua 90+1), Streller, A Frei (Salah 66), Stocker, Schär, Díaz (F Frei 75), Cabral, Steinhöfer. Coach: Murat Yakin (SUI)
Match 5 - Sporting Clube de Portugal (POR)
H 3-0 *Schär (23), Stocker (66), D Degen (71)*
Sommer, P Degen, Dragovic, D Degen, A Frei (Salah 64), Stocker (Zoua 81), Schär, F Frei (Ajeti 90), Díaz, Cabral, Steinhöfer. Coach: Murat Yakin (SUI)
Red card: Cabral 58
Match 6 - KRC Genk (BEL)
A 0-0
Sommer, P Degen, Dragovic, D Degen (Salah 68), Streller, Yapi Yapo, Stocker, Schär, F Frei, Díaz, Steinhöfer. Coach: Murat Yakin (SUI)

Round of 32 - FC Dnipro Dnipropetrovsk (UKR)
H 2-0 *Stocker (23), Streller (67)*
Sommer, Park, P Degen, Dragovic, D Degen (Salah 68), Serey Die, Streller, Stocker (Zoua 88), Schär, F Frei (Elneny 77), Cabral. Coach: Murat Yakin (SUI)
A 1-1 *Schär (81p)*
Sommer, Park, Dragovic, D Degen (Zoua 82), Serey Die, Stocker, Schär, F Frei, Salah (Elneny 89), Cabral, Steinhöfer. Coach: Murat Yakin (SUI)
Red card: F Frei 75

Round of 16 - FC Zenit St Petersburg (RUS)
H 2-0 *Díaz (83), A Frei (90+4p)*
Sommer, Park, P Degen, Dragovic, D Degen (Steinhöfer 62), Serey Die (Elneny 69), Schär, Díaz, Salah, Cabral, Zoua (A Frei 79). Coach: Murat Yakin (SUI)

A 0-1
Sommer, Park, P Degen (Steinhöfer 90+1), Dragovic, Streller (Sauro 66), Stocker (F Frei 18), Schär, Díaz, Salah, Cabral, Elneny. Coach: Murat Yakin (SUI)
Red card: Díaz 45+1

Quarter-final - Tottenham Hotspur FC (ENG)
A 2-2 *Stocker (30), F Frei (34)*
Sommer, Dragovic, Serey Die (Cabral 66), Streller (Zoua 71), Stocker, Voser, Schär, F Frei, Salah (D Degen 84), Steinhöfer, Elneny. Coach: Murat Yakin (SUI)
H 2-2 *Salah (27), Dragovic (49) (aet; 4-1 on pens)*
Sommer, Park, P Degen, Dragovic, Serey Die (Díaz 58), Streller, Stocker (Steinhöfer 71), Schär, F Frei, Salah (A Frei 111), Elneny. Coach: Murat Yakin (SUI)

Semi-final - Chelsea FC (ENG)
H 1-2 *Schär (87p)*
Sommer, Park, P Degen, Dragovic, Serey Die (Díaz 61), Streller, Stocker, Schär, F Frei, Salah (D Degen 78), Elneny (Zoua 65). Coach: Murat Yakin (SUI)
A 1-3 *Salah (45+1)*
Sommer, Serey Die, Streller (Zoua 62), Stocker (D Degen 62), Voser, Schär, F Frei (Díaz 75), Salah, Sauro, Steinhöfer, Elneny. Coach: Murat Yakin (SUI)

FC LUZERN

EUROPA LEAGUE

Play-offs - KRC Genk (BEL)
H 2-1 *Rangelov (7), Winter (71)*
Zibung, Puljić, Lustenberger, Rangelov, Gygax, Stahel, Muntwiler, Lezcano (Kryeziu 83), Winter (Hochstrasser 90+3), Sarr, Wiss. Coach: Ryszard Komornicki (POL)
A 0-2
Zibung, Puljić, Lustenberger, Rangelov, Gygax (Pacar 73), Stahel (Hochstrasser 79), Muntwiler, Lezcano (Hyka 39), Winter, Sarr, Wiss. Coach: Ryszard Komornicki (POL)
Red card: Rangelov 37

BSC YOUNG BOYS

Second qualifying round - FC Zimbru Chisinau (MDA)
H 1-0 Frey (53)
Wölfli, González (Frey 46) Ojala, Nef, Silberbauer, Vitkieviez, Farnerud (Costanzo 72), Raimondi (Nuzzolo 63), Spycher, Sutter, Mayuka. Coach: Martin Rueda (SUI)
A 0-1 (aet; 4-1 on pens)
Wölfli, Nef, Silberbauer (González 67), Vitkieviez (Schneuwly 75), Farnerud, Spycher, Frey (Costanzo 91), Veškovac, Sutter, Mayuka, Lecjaks. Coach: Martin Rueda (SUI)

Third qualifying round - Kalmar FF (SWE)
A 0-1
Wölfli, Ojala, Nef, Farnerud, Costanzo (Frey 68), Schneuwly, Raimondi, Spycher, Sutter, Mayuka (Bobadilla 46), Nuzzolo (González 81). Coach: Martin Rueda (SUI)
H 3-0 Mayuka (7), Raimondi (69), Bobadilla (82)
Wölfli, Ojala, Nef, Farnerud, Bobadilla (Frey 84), Schneuwly, Raimondi, Spycher, Sutter, Mayuka (González 89), Nuzzolo (Costanzo 81). Coach: Martin Rueda (SUI)

Play-offs - FC Midtjylland (DEN)
A 3-0 Bobadilla (42), Farnerud (81), Costanzo (90+3)
Wölfli, Ojala, Nef, Farnerud (Silberbauer 84), Bobadilla, Zverotić, Schneuwly (Costanzo 73), Raimondi, Spycher, Mayuka (Frey 84), Nuzzolo. Coach: Martin Rueda (SUI)
H 0-2
Wölfli, Ojala, Nef, Vitkieviez (Zverotić 85), Farnerud, Bobadilla, Schneuwly, Raimondi (Lecjaks 34), Spycher (Silberbauer 66), Sutter, Nuzzolo. Coach: Martin Rueda (SUI)
Red card: Nef 74

Group A
Match 1 - Liverpool FC (ENG)
H 3-5 Nuzzolo (38), Ojala (53), Zárate (63)
Wölfli, Ojala, Farnerud, Bobadilla, Zverotić (Frey 81), Raimondi, Spycher, Zárate (González 65), Veškovac, Sutter, Nuzzolo (Schneuwly 68). Coach: Martin Rueda (SUI)
Match 2 - FC Anji Makhachkala (RUS)
A 0-2
Wölfli, Ojala, Nef, Vitkieviez (González 77), Bobadilla, Costanzo, Zverotić, Schneuwly (Frey 67), Zárate (Nuzzolo 67), Veškovac, Lecjaks. Coach: Martin Rueda (SUI)

Match 3 - Udinese Calcio (ITA)
H 3-1 Bobadilla (4, 71, 81p)
Wölfli, Ojala, Nef, Farnerud (Veškovac 87), Bobadilla, Costanzo (Schneuwly 71), Zverotić, Raimondi, Zárate (González 80), Sutter, Nuzzolo. Coach: Martin Rueda (SUI)
Match 4 - Udinese Calcio (ITA)
A 3-2 Bobadilla (27), Farnerud (65), Nuzzolo (73)
Wölfli, Nef, Farnerud, Bobadilla (Frey 88), Zverotić, Schneuwly (P Doubaï 74), Raimondi, Zárate (González 81), Veškovac, Sutter, Nuzzolo. Coach: Martin Rueda (SUI)
Match 5 - Liverpool FC (ENG)
A 2-2 Bobadilla (52), Zverotić (88)
Wölfli, Nef, Farnerud, Bobadilla, Zverotić, Schneuwly (Vitkieviez 82), Zárate, Veškovac (Ojala 23), Sutter, Nuzzolo (Frey 77), Lecjaks. Coach: Martin Rueda (SUI)
Match 6 - FC Anji Makhachkala (RUS)
H 3-1 Zárate (38), Costanzo (52), González (90)
Wölfli, Ojala, Nef, Farnerud, Bobadilla (Frey 87), Costanzo (P Doubaï 72), Schneuwly, Raimondi, Zárate (González 77), Sutter, Nuzzolo. Coach: Martin Rueda (SUI)

SERVETTE FC

Second qualifying round - FC Gandzasar (ARM)
H 2-0 Karanovic (48), Gissi (79)
Gonzalez, Pizzinat (Pasche 46), Kouassi, Karanovic, Lang (Gissi 74), Tréand, Mfuyi, Rüfli, De Azevedo (Moutinho 63), Moubandje, Schneider. Coach: João Alves (POR)
A 3-1 De Azevedo (47), Pont (64, 68)
Barroca, Pizzinat (Poceiro Lopes 67), Pont, Kouassi, Karanovic, Lang (Moutinho 75), Mfuyi (Gissi 73), Pasche, De Azevedo, Moubandje, Schneider. Coach: João Alves (POR)

Third qualifying round - Rosenborg BK (NOR)
H 1-1 Schneider (68)
Barroca, Pizzinat, Kouassi, Karanovic, Lang (Poceiro Lopes 58), Gomes, Grippo, Pasche (Gissi 82), De Azevedo, Moubandje (Pont 84), Schneider. Coach: João Alves (POR)
A 0-0
Barroca, Pizzinat, Moutinho, Kouassi, Karanovic, Gomes, Paratte (Lang 63), Grippo, Pasche (De Azevedo 71), Moubandje (Rüfli 83), Schneider. Coach: João Alves (POR)
Red card: De Azevedo 90+4

FC BASEL 1893

Coach: Heiko Vogel (GER); (15/10/12) Murat Yakin
1893 • St Jakob-Park (38,500) • fcb.ch
Major honours
Swiss League (16) 1953, 1967, 1969, 1970, 1972, 1973, 1977, 1980, 2002, 2004, 2005, 2008, 2010, 2011, 2012, 2013; Swiss Cup (11) 1933, 1947, 1963, 1967, 1975, 2002, 2003, 2007, 2008, 2010, 2012

2012
13/07	Servette	a	1-0	D Degen
21/07	Luzern	h	2-2	A Frei, Streller
28/07	Grasshoppers	a	2-2	A Frei, Yapi Yapo
04/08	Sion	a	1-1	Kováč
12/08	Thun	h	3-1	Streller 2 (1p), Stocker
18/08	Lausanne	h	2-0	Streller, Salah
25/08	St Gallen	a	1-2	Zoua
02/09	Zürich	h	0-0	
23/09	Young Boys	a	1-1	Streller
26/09	Sion	h	4-1	P Degen 2, Stocker, Sauro
29/09	Lausanne	a	1-1	Salah
07/10	Servette	h	3-2	Schär, D Degen, Streller
21/10	Luzern	a	0-1	
28/10	Zürich	a	2-1	Schär, A Frei
03/11	Young Boys	h	2-0	Yapi Yapo, Streller
18/11	Grasshoppers	h	4-0	D Degen, Streller (p), A Frei 2
25/11	Thun	a	2-3	F Frei, Streller
01/12	St Gallen	h	1-0	Streller

2012
10/02	Sion	h	3-0	Streller, Salah, Stocker
17/02	Lausanne	a	2-1	Stocker, Díaz
24/02	Grasshoppers	h	0-0	
03/03	Servette	a	2-1	Dragovic 2
10/03	Young Boys	h	3-0	A Frei, Streller, Schär
17/03	Thun	h	1-0	Streller
01/04	Luzern	a	4-0	Serey Die, Díaz, Salah, P Degen
07/04	St Gallen	a	1-1	Streller
14/04	Zürich	h	3-1	A Frei, Schär (p), Salah
21/04	Thun	a	2-2	Park, Díaz
28/04	Luzern	h	0-3	
05/05	Sion	a	1-0	Díaz
08/05	Zürich	a	1-3	Stocker
12/05	Servette	h	2-0	Stocker, Dragovic
18/05	Lausanne	h	2-0	F Frei 2
26/05	Grasshoppers	a	0-1	
29/05	Young Boys	h	1-0	F Frei
01/06	St Gallen	h	1-0	Bobadilla

No	Name	Nat	DoB	Pos	Aps	(s)	Gls
11	Endogan Adili		03/08/94	M		(1)	
5	Arlind Ajeti		25/09/93	D	2	(2)	
28	Stephan Andrist		12/12/87	M		(1)	
17	Raúl Bobadilla	ARG	18/06/87	A	6	(4)	1
24	Cabral		22/10/88	M	23	(4)	
7	David Degen		15/02/83	M	17	(9)	3
4	Philipp Degen		15/02/83	D	19	(2)	1
21	Marcelo Díaz	CHI	30/12/86	M	19	(7)	4
6	Aleksandar Dragovic	AUT	06/03/91	D	32		3
33	Mohamed Elneny	EGY	11/07/92	M	7	(8)	
13	Alexander Frei		15/07/79	A	16	(2)	7
20	Fabian Frei		08/01/89	M	24	(3)	4
19	Simon Grether		20/05/92	M		(2)	
25	Darko Jevtic		08/02/93	M	1	(1)	
29	Radoslav Kováč	CZE	27/11/79	D	4	(1)	1
3	Park Joo-ho	KOR	16/01/87	D	19	(2)	1
22	Mohamed Salah	EGY	15/06/92	M	12	(17)	5
26	Gastón Sauro	ARG	23/02/90	D	14	(2)	1
16	Fabian Schär		20/12/91	D	21		4
8	Serey Die	CIV	07/11/84	M	12	(2)	1
1	Yann Sommer		17/12/88	G	36		
27	Markus Steinhöfer	GER	07/03/86	D	23	(6)	
14	Valentin Stocker		12/04/89	M	29	(2)	6
9	Marco Streller		18/06/81	A	30	(2)	14
15	Kay Voser		04/01/87	D	11	(2)	
30	Stjepan Vuleta		29/10/93	A		(2)	
10	Gilles Yapi Yapo	CIV	30/01/82	M	12		2
31	Jacques Zoua	CMR	06/09/91	A	7	(17)	1

GRASSHOPPER CLUB

Coach: Uli Forte
1886 • Letzigrund (26,000) • gcz.ch
Major honours
Swiss League (27) 1898, 1900, 1901, 1905, 1921, 1927,
1928, 1931, 1937, 1939, 1942, 1943, 1945, 1952, 1956,
1971, 1978, 1982, 1983, 1984, 1990, 1991, 1995, 1996,
1998, 2001, 2003;
Swiss Cup (19) 1926, 1927, 1932, 1934, 1937, 1938,
1940, 1941, 1942, 1943, 1946, 1952, 1956, 1983, 1988,
1989, 1990, 1994, 2013

2012

15/07	Sion	h	0-2	
22/07	Young Boys	a	1-0	Salatic
28/07	Basel	h	2-2	Ben Khalifa, Brahimi
04/08	St Gallen	a	1-1	Hajrovic
12/08	Servette	h	1-0	Ben Khalifa
19/08	Luzern	a	2-0	Zuber, Abrashi
25/08	Thun	h	1-0	Hajrovic
01/09	Lausanne	a	2-0	Vilotić, Abrashi
22/09	Zürich	a	1-0	Zuber
27/09	Luzern	h	2-0	Nzuzi, Lang
01/10	St Gallen	h	1-0	Ben Khalifa
06/10	Thun	a	3-2	Zuber, Ben Khalifa, Nzuzi
21/10	Young Boys	h	3-2	Hajrovic 2, Zuber
28/10	Servette	a	0-2	
03/11	Lausanne	h	1-1	Hajrovic
18/11	Basel	a	0-4	
24/11	Sion	h	1-1	Gashi
02/12	Zürich	h	1-0	Hajrovic (p)

2013

09/02	Servette	a	1-0	Brahimi
16/02	Young Boys	h	2-0	Ngamukol 2
24/02	Basel	a	0-0	
03/03	Lausanne	a	0-0	
09/03	St Gallen	h	3-1	Ngamukol, Salatic, Gashi
17/03	Luzern	h	0-0	
30/03	Thun	a	0-1	
06/04	Zürich	a	4-2	Hajrovic (p), Lang, Salatic, Vilotić
14/04	Sion	h	1-1	Feltscher
21/04	Luzern	a	1-1	Lang
27/04	Thun	h	0-2	
04/05	Servette	h	2-0	Gashi, Ben Khalifa
07/05	Young Boys	a	0-4	
12/05	Zürich	h	0-1	
18/05	Sion	a	4-0	Gashi, Zuber, Ngamukol, Brahimi
26/05	Basel	h	1-0	Ngamukol
29/05	St Gallen	a	2-1	Hajrovic (p), Abrashi
01/06	Lausanne	h	4-1	Zuber (p), Gashi (p), Ngamukol, Ben Khalifa

No	Name	Nat	DoB	Pos	Aps	(s)	Gls
8	Amir Abrashi	ALB	27/03/90	M	22	(5)	3
25	Endogan Adili		03/08/94	A		(1)	
34	Moritz Bauer		25/01/92	D	11	(2)	
15	Nassim Ben Khalifa		13/01/92	A	26	(7)	6
27	Mergim Brahimi	ALB	08/08/92	M		(16)	3
1	Roman Bürki		14/11/90	G	34		
32	Mohamed Coulibaly	FRA	08/08/88	M		(5)	
11	Frank Feltscher	VEN	17/05/88	M	14	(20)	1
10	Shkelzen Gashi		15/07/88	M	17	(11)	5
3	Stéphane Grichting		30/03/79	D	33		
14	Izet Hajrovic		04/08/91	M	31	(2)	8
22	Gianluca Hossmann		25/03/91	D	1		
9	João Paiva	POR	08/02/83	A	2	(10)	
5	Michael Lang		08/02/91	D	33		3
35	Orhan Mustafi		04/04/90	A		(4)	
17	Anatole Ngamukol	FRA	15/01/88	A	13	(3)	6
28	Toko Nzuzi	COD	20/11/90	M	22	(4)	2
20	Daniel Pavlovic		22/04/88	D	22	(1)	
6	Veroljub Salatic		14/11/85	M	31		3
18	Davide Taini		07/12/76	G	2		
4	Milan Vilotić	SRB	21/10/86	D	31		2
2	Willian Rocha	BRA	01/04/89	D	2	(3)	
13	Taulant Xhaka		28/03/91	D	19	(6)	
7	Steven Zuber		17/08/91	M	30	(2)	5

FC LAUSANNE-SPORT

Coach: Laurent Roussey (FRA)
1896 • Olympique de la Pontaise (15,850) •
lausanne-sport.ch
Major honours
Swiss League (7) 1913, 1932, 1935, 1936, 1944, 1951, 1965;
Swiss Cup (9) 1935, 1939, 1944, 1950, 1962, 1964, 1981,
1998, 1999

2012

14/07	Thun	a	0-0	
21/07	St Gallen	h	0-1	
29/07	Servette	h	5-1	Sanogo 2, Malonga, Roux, Moussilou
05/08	Zürich	a	0-4	
11/08	Sion	h	0-2	
18/08	Basel	a	0-2	
26/08	Young Boys	a	0-0	
01/09	Grasshoppers	h	0-2	
23/09	Luzern	h	1-0	Malonga
26/09	Servette	a	1-0	Malonga
29/09	Basel	h	1-1	Moussilou
06/10	St Gallen	h	1-2	Malonga
20/10	Zürich	h	0-2	
27/10	Sion	a	1-1	Marazzi
03/11	Grasshoppers	a	1-1	Guié
17/11	Thun	h	3-0	Moussilou, Tafer, Khelifi
25/11	Young Boys	h	2-1	Gabri, Malonga (p)
01/12	Luzern	a	0-0	

2013

10/02	Zürich	a	0-2	
17/02	Basel	h	1-2	Malonga
23/02	Servette	a	0-1	
03/03	Grasshoppers	h	0-0	
10/03	Sion	a	1-0	Malonga
16/03	St Gallen	a	1-3	Moussilou
24/03	Young Boys	h	0-0	
07/04	Thun	h	2-4	Moussilou, Sonnerat
13/04	Luzern	a	0-1	
20/04	St Gallen	h	1-3	Moussilou (p)
28/04	Young Boys	a	1-3	Roux
03/05	Zürich	h	1-1	Martin
08/05	Sion	h	1-3	Sonnerat
12/05	Thun	a	0-2	
18/05	Basel	a	0-2	
25/05	Luzern	h	3-0	og (Zibung), Marazzi, Malonga
29/05	Servette	h	3-0	Roux 2, Meoli
01/06	Grasshoppers	a	1-4	Avanzini

No	Name	Nat	DoB	Pos	Aps	(s)	Gls
13	Michel Avanzini		28/03/89	M	11	(6)	1
28	Mehmed Begzadić	BIH	05/01/93	A		(1)	
23	Abdelouahed Chakhsi	MAR	01/10/86	D	32	(1)	
30	Mathieu Debonnaire		26/04/87	G	8	(1)	
28	Romain Dessarzin		09/11/93	M		(2)	
3	Mickaël Facchinetti		15/02/91	D	28	(1)	
1	Anthony Favre		01/02/84	G	27		
5	Gabri	ESP	10/02/79	M	21	(1)	
21	Abraham Gneki Guié	CIV	25/07/86	A	6	(4)	1
2	Janick Kamber		26/02/92	D	6	(8)	
6	Guillaume Katz		14/02/89	D	33	(1)	
7	Salim Khelifi		26/01/94	M	13	(14)	1
10	Chris Malonga	CGO	11/07/87	M	30		8
20	Nicolas Marazzi		13/07/81	M	21	(11)	2
4	Malaury Martin	FRA	25/08/88	M	10	(2)	1
14	Sébastien Meoli		02/08/80	D	6	(3)	1
29	Matt Moussilou	CGO	01/06/82	A	21	(9)	6
8	Rodrigo	BRA	06/10/80	M	20		
9	Jocelyn Roux		28/08/86	M	14	(14)	4
25	Sékou Sanogo	CIV	05/05/89	M	25	(6)	2
22	Antonio Signori	ANG	25/07/94	G	1		
24	Jérôme Sonnerat	FRA	19/02/85	D	27	(1)	2
19	Bashkim Sukaj		20/03/92	A		(1)	
11	Yannis Tafer	FRA	11/02/91	A	15	(8)	1
12	Ibrahim Tall	SEN	23/06/81	D	21	(1)	
17	Kevin Tapoko	FRA	13/04/94	A		(2)	
26	Adam Waidi		05/08/94	A		(1)	

FC LUZERN

Coach: Murat Yakin;
(20/08/12) Ryszard Komornicki (POL);
(02/04/13) (Gerardo Seoane);
(07/04/13) Carlos Bernegger (ARG)
1901 • Swissporarena (17,800) • fcl.ch
Major honours
Swiss League (1) 1989;
Swiss Cup (2) 1960, 1992

2012

15/07	Zürich	h	1-1	Winter
21/07	Basel	a	2-2	Lezcano 2
29/07	Sion	h	0-3	
05/08	Thun	a	1-2	Gygax
11/08	St Gallen	h	1-1	Rangelov (p)
19/08	Grasshoppers	h	0-2	
26/08	Servette	a	2-0	Stahel, Gygax
02/09	Young Boys	h	1-2	Puljić
23/09	Lausanne	a	0-1	
27/09	Grasshoppers	a	0-2	
30/09	Thun	h	2-1	Winter, Andrist
07/10	Sion	a	2-3	Andrist (p), Puljić
21/10	Basel	h	1-0	og (Ajeti)
04/11	Servette	h	1-0	Andrist
17/11	Zürich	a	2-0	Wiss, Andrist
25/11	St Gallen	a	1-1	Winter
28/11	Young Boys	a	1-0	og (Sutter)
01/12	Lausanne	h	0-0	

2013

09/02	Young Boys	a	2-3	Otele (p), Wiss
17/02	Zürich	h	1-1	Wiss
24/02	St Gallen	a	0-4	
02/03	Thun	a	0-0	
09/03	Servette	h	1-1	Muntwiler
17/03	Grasshoppers	a	0-0	
01/04	Basel	h	0-4	
06/04	Sion	a	1-2	Wiss
13/04	Lausanne	h	1-0	Stahel
21/04	Grasshoppers	h	1-1	Andrist
28/04	Basel	a	3-0	Gygax, Hochstrasser, Winter
05/05	Thun	h	2-0	Muntwiler
08/05	St Gallen	h	2-0	Hochstrasser, Winter
11/05	Young Boys	h	3-1	Hochstrasser, Gygax, Andrist
18/05	Zürich	a	1-4	Sarr
25/05	Lausanne	a	0-3	
29/05	Sion	h	2-0	Gygax 2
01/06	Servette	a	4-3	Renggli (p), Gygax, Kasami, Neziraj

No	Name	Nat	DoB	Pos	Aps	(s)	Gls
27	Stephan Andrist		12/12/87	M	17	(7)	6
29	Mario Bühler		05/01/92	D	3		
11	Daniel Gygax		28/08/81	M	22	(7)	7
20	Xavier Hochstrasser		01/07/88	M	16	(7)	3
8	Jahmir Hyka	ALB	08/03/88	M	17	(12)	
33	Peter Jehle	LIE	22/01/82	G	2		
10	Pajtim Kasami		02/06/92	M	14	(2)	1
31	Hekuran Kryeziu		12/02/93	M	8	(9)	
17	Dario Lezcano	PAR	30/06/90	A	13	(1)	2
34	Adekunle Lukmon	NGA	10/10/84	D	2		
7	Claudio Lustenberger		06/01/87	D	29		
15	Philipp Muntwiler		25/02/87	M	21	(10)	2
35	Haxhi Neziraj		16/03/93	M		(2)	1
22	Mouangue Otele	CMR	05/02/89	A	2	(8)	1
32	Janko Pacar			A		(4)	
6	Tomislav Puljić	CRO	21/03/83	D	33	(1)	2
18	Michael Räber		04/11/92	G		(1)	
9	Dimitar Rangelov	BUL	09/02/83	A	22	(6)	
3	Michel Renggli		19/03/80	M	12	(2)	1
4	Enzo Ruiz	URU	31/08/88	D	1	(1)	
23	Sally Sarr	FRA	06/05/86	D	22	(4)	
23	Nico Siegrist		09/06/91	A	1	(4)	
26	Dejan Sorgić	SRB	15/09/89	A		(2)	
13	Florian Stahel		10/03/85	D	31		2
19	Jérôme Thiesson		06/08/87	D	22	(1)	
19	Adrian Winter		08/07/86	M	27	(6)	5
24	Alain Wiss		21/08/90	M	25	(4)	3
1	David Zibung		10/01/84	G	34		

SERVETTE FC

Coach: João Alves (POR);
(04/09/12) (Anthony Braizat (FRA) &
Ricardo Dionísio (POR)); (13/09/12) Sébastien Fournier
1890 • Stade de Genève (30,084) • servettefc.ch
Major honours
Swiss League (17) 1907, 1918, 1922, 1925, 1926, 1930, 1933,
1934, 1940, 1946, 1950, 1961, 1962, 1979, 1985, 1994, 1999;
Swiss Cup (7) 1928, 1949, 1971, 1978, 1979, 1984, 2001

2012
13/07	Basel	h	0-1	
22/07	Sion	a	0-1	
29/07	Lausanne	a	1-5	og (Katz)
05/08	Young Boys	h	1-1	Karanovic (p)
12/08	Grasshoppers	a	0-1	
19/08	Zürich	h	1-1	Eudis
26/08	Luzern	a	0-2	
02/09	Thun	a	0-3	
23/09	St Gallen	a	0-2	
26/09	Lausanne	a	0-1	
30/09	Young Boys	a	2-6	Pont, Kouassi
07/10	Basel	a	2-3	Tréand, Lang
20/10	St Gallen	h	1-1	Pont
28/10	Grasshoppers	h	2-0	Lang, Pasche
04/11	Luzern	a	1-1	Eudis
18/11	Sion	h	0-2	
24/11	Zürich	a	2-0	Tréand, Eudis
02/12	Thun	h	0-0	

2013
09/02	Grasshoppers	h	0-1	
17/02	Thun	a	1-1	Tréand
23/02	Lausanne	h	1-0	Vitkieviez
03/03	Basel	h	1-2	Karanovic
09/03	Luzern	a	1-1	Karanovic
16/03	Zürich	h	1-2	Karanovic (p)
30/03	Sion	a	1-1	De Azevedo
07/04	Young Boys	a	2-0	Vitkieviez, Karanovic
13/04	St Gallen	a	1-3	Eudis
20/04	Zürich	a	0-4	
04/05	Grasshoppers	a	0-2	
09/05	Thun	h	2-0	Tréand, Kouassi
12/05	Basel	a	0-2	
18/05	Young Boys	h	0-1	
22/05	Sion	h	4-0	Vitkieviez, Tréand, Karanovic 2
26/05	St Gallen	a	1-4	Eudis
29/05	Lausanne	a	0-3	
01/06	Luzern	h	3-4	Tréand, Pont, Pasche

No	Name	Nat	DoB	Pos	Aps	(s)	Gls
18	Barroca	POR	29/07/86	G	25		
23	De Azevedo	BRA	23/11/81	M	18	(12)	1
4	Issaga Diallo	FRA	26/01/87	D	10	(6)	
10	Julian Esteban		16/09/86	A	3	(4)	
31	Eudis	BRA	05/08/83	A	16	(9)	5
27	Kevin Gissi		10/09/92	M	1	(2)	
12	Mike Gomes		19/09/88	D	3	(1)	
1	David Gonzalez		09/11/86	G	11		
9	Simone Grippo		12/12/88	M	6	(3)	
9	Goran Karanovic		13/10/87	A	18	(10)	7
10	Omar Kossoko	FRA	12/03/88	M	8	(1)	
8	Xavier Kouassi	CIV	28/12/89	M	27	(2)	2
29	Genséric Kusunga		12/03/88	D	18	(1)	
11	Steven Lang		03/09/87	M	20	(4)	2
2	Kevin Mbabu		19/04/95	D		(1)	
27	Mario Meireles		27/04/94	M		(2)	
19	Christopher Mfuyi	COD	03/07/89	D	25		
24	François Moubandje		21/06/90	D	17	(2)	
7	Thierry Moutinho	POR	26/02/91	M	2	(7)	
13	Ludovic Paratte		01/02/92	M	1		
21	Alexandre Pasche		31/05/91	M	31	(3)	2
5	Lionel Pizzinat		09/08/77	M	6	(6)	
16	Poceiro Lopes		09/11/91	D		(1)	
6	Tibert Pont		23/01/84	M	15	(9)	3
28	Samir Ramizi	ALB	24/07/91	A	1	(3)	
3	Christopher Routis	FRA	03/03/90	D	16	(6)	
22	Vincent Rüfli		22/01/88	D	26	(1)	
20	Christian Schlauri		30/03/85	D	1	(4)	
25	Jérôme Schneider		04/11/81	D	27	(1)	
14	Geoffrey Tréand	FRA	16/01/86	M	30		6
17	Matías Vitkieviez		16/05/85	A	14	(2)	3

FC SION

Coach: Sébastien Fournier; (04/09/12) Michel Decastel;
(30/10/12) Pierre-André Schürmann;
(12/12/12) Víctor Muñoz (ESP);
(25/02/13) Gennaro Gattuso (ITA) & Luigi Riccio (ITA);
(25/03/13) Gennaro Gattuso (ITA) & Arno Rossini (ITA);
(15/05/13) Michel Decastel
1909 • Tourbillon (16,500) • fc-sion.ch
Major honours
Swiss League (2) 1992, 1997;
Swiss Cup (12) 1965, 1974, 1980, 1982, 1986, 1991,
1995, 1996, 1997, 2006, 2009, 2011

2012
15/07	Grasshoppers	a	2-0	Léo Itaperuna 2
22/07	Servette	h	1-0	Manset (p)
29/07	Luzern	a	3-0	Margairaz, Serey Die, Lafferty
04/08	Basel	h	1-1	Léo Itaperuna
11/08	Lausanne	a	2-0	Bühler, Margairaz
19/08	Young Boys	h	1-0	Crettenand
26/08	Zürich	a	0-1	
01/09	St Gallen	h	0-3	
22/09	Thun	h	2-1	Léo Itaperuna 2
26/09	Basel	a	1-4	Gattuso
30/09	Zürich	h	2-2	Lafferty, Margairaz
07/10	Luzern	h	3-2	Margairaz, Lafferty, Bühler
20/10	Thun	a	1-1	Margairaz
27/10	Lausanne	h	1-1	Vanczák
04/11	St Gallen	a	3-0	Bühler, Crettenand, Wüthrich
18/11	Servette	a	2-0	Lafferty (p), Léo Itaperuna
24/11	Grasshoppers	h	1-1	Léo Itaperuna
02/12	Young Boys	a	1-3	Dingsdag

2013
10/02	Basel	a	0-3	
16/02	St Gallen	h	1-0	og (Montandon)
24/02	Thun	a	0-4	
02/03	Zürich	a	1-3	N'Djeng
10/03	Lausanne	a	0-1	
17/03	Young Boys	h	0-0	
30/03	Servette	h	1-1	Léo Itaperuna
06/04	Luzern	h	2-1	Lacroix, Lafferty
14/04	Grasshoppers	a	1-1	Yoda
21/04	Young Boys	a	0-0	
05/05	Basel	h	0-1	
08/05	Lausanne	a	3-1	N'Djeng (p), Kololli, Darragi
11/05	St Gallen	a	0-5	
16/05	Grasshoppers	h	0-4	
22/05	Servette	a	0-4	
25/05	Thun	h	0-1	
29/05	Luzern	a	0-2	
01/06	Zürich	h	4-2	Vanczák, Kololli, Karlen, Veloso

No	Name	Nat	DoB	Pos	Aps	(s)	Gls
4	Adaílton	BRA	16/04/83	D	14		
6	Joaquim Adão	ANG	14/07/92	M		(12)	
3	Aislan	BRA	11/01/88	D	13	(1)	
5	André Marques	POR	01/08/87	D	14	(7)	
14	Vullnet Basha	ALB	11/07/90	M	18	(7)	
31	Arnaud Bühler		17/01/85	D	33		3
16	Didier Crettenand		24/02/86	M	20	(9)	2
10	Oussama Darragi	TUN	03/04/87	M	20	(4)	1
15	Michael Dingsdag	NED	18/10/82	D	29		1
17	Matteo Fedele	ITA	20/07/92	M	1	(3)	
33	Edimilson Fernandes		15/04/96	M	1		
26	Gelson Fernandes		02/09/86	M	14		
8	Gennaro Gattuso	ITA	09/01/78	M	25	(2)	1
4	Gonçalves	POR	17/09/85	D		(1)	
19	Gaëtan Karlen		07/06/93	A		(3)	1
2	Benjamin Kololli	ALB	19/01/92	M	5	(2)	2
27	Léo Lacroix		27/02/92	D	9	(1)	1
12	Kyle Lafferty	NIR	16/09/87	A	16	(9)	5
11	Léo Itaperuna	BRA	12/04/89	A	25	(8)	8
19	Mathieu Manset	FRA	05/08/89	A	2	(3)	1
23	Xavier Margairaz		07/01/84	M	17	(3)	5
25	Evan Melo		31/05/93	A	1	(1)	
22	Dragan Mrdja	SRB	23/01/84	A		(5)	
21	Yannick N'Djeng	CMR	11/03/90	A	13	(3)	2
34	Birama N'Doye	SEN	27/03/94	M	3		
29	Alberto Regazzoni		04/05/83	M	9	(2)	
32	Anthony Sauthier		05/02/91	D	10	(4)	
26	Serey Die	CIV	07/11/84	M	10	(1)	1
20	Vilmos Vanczák	HUN	20/06/83	D	30	(1)	2
1	Andris Vaņins	LVA	30/04/80	G	36		
24	Veloso	POR	27/03/92	M	3		1
7	Sébastien Wüthrich		29/05/90	M	3	(10)	1
9	Abdoul Yoda	FRA	25/10/88	M	2	(5)	1

FC ST GALLEN

Coach: Jeff Saibene (LUX)
1879 • AFG Arena (18,026) • fcsg.ch
Major honours
Swiss League (2) 1904, 2000;
Swiss Cup (1) 1969

2012
15/07	Young Boys	h	1-1	Abegglen
21/07	Lausanne	a	1-0	Scarione
28/07	Zürich	h	3-1	Scarione, Čavuševič 2
04/08	Grasshoppers	a	1-1	Abegglen
11/08	Luzern	a	1-1	Janjatovic
18/08	Thun	h	1-0	Scarione (p)
25/08	Basel	h	2-1	Čavuševič, Regazzoni
01/09	Sion	a	3-0	Mathys 2, Scarione
23/09	Servette	h	2-0	og (Moubandje), Etoundi
26/09	Zürich	a	2-0	Scarione, Čavuševič
01/10	Grasshoppers	a	0-1	
06/10	Lausanne	h	2-1	Scarione, Montandon
20/10	Servette	a	1-1	Scarione
28/10	Thun	a	1-0	Mathys
04/11	Sion	h	0-3	
18/11	Young Boys	h	0-0	
25/11	Luzern	h	1-1	Martić
01/12	Basel	a	0-1	

2013
16/02	Sion	a	0-1	
24/02	Luzern	h	4-0	Scarione 3 (2p), Ishak
03/03	Young Boys	a	0-2	
09/03	Grasshoppers	h	1-3	Nushi
13/03	Thun	h	0-0	
16/03	Lausanne	h	3-1	Wüthrich, Besle 2
30/03	Zürich	a	3-1	Wüthrich, Scarione 2
07/04	Basel	h	1-1	Wüthrich
13/04	Servette	h	3-1	Besle, Scarione, Etoundi
20/04	Lausanne	a	3-1	Besle, Scarione, Nushi
28/04	Zürich	h	1-2	Scarione
04/05	Young Boys	a	3-1	Scarione 2 (1p), Nushi
08/05	Luzern	a	0-2	
11/05	Sion	h	5-0	Wüthrich, Scarione 3 (1p), Modou
17/05	Thun	a	0-3	
26/05	Servette	h	4-1	Nushi, Ishak 2, Scarione (p)
29/05	Grasshoppers	h	1-2	Janjatovic
01/06	Basel	a	0-1	

No	Name	Nat	DoB	Pos	Aps	(s)	Gls
26	Nico Abegglen		16/02/90	A	4	(10)	2
15	Stéphane Besle	FRA	23/01/84	D	23	(1)	4
20	Džengis Čavuševič	SVN	26/11/87	A	11	(9)	4
11	Franck Etoundi	CMR	30/08/90	A	13	(9)	2
24	Marco Hämmerli		07/05/85	D	1	(2)	
18	Marcel Herzog		28/06/80	G	1		
16	Mikael Ishak	SWE	31/03/93	A	11	(2)	3
4	Ilija Ivić	CRO	16/07/91	M	5	(1)	
31	Dejan Janjatovic	GER	25/02/92	M	32		2
23	Sven Lehmann		18/12/91	A		(1)	
28	Ermir Lenjani		05/08/89	A	2	(5)	
1	Daniel Lopar		19/04/85	G	35		
21	Ivan Martić	CRO	02/10/90	D	9	(6)	1
27	Marco Mathys		05/07/87	M	24	(10)	3
9	Pa Modou	GAM	26/12/89	D	33	(1)	1
6	Philippe Montandon		15/07/82	D	31		1
19	Mario Mutsch	LUX	03/09/84	D	27	(4)	
5	Stéphane Nater		20/01/84	M	33		
7	Kristian Nushi	ALB	21/07/82	M	22	(9)	4
32	Alberto Regazzoni		04/05/83	M	11	(1)	1
10	Ezequiel Scarione	ARG	14/07/85	M	36		21
14	Mario Schönenberger		19/05/86	M	5	(7)	
5	Martin Stocklasa	LIE	29/05/79	D	16	(2)	
13	Manuel Sutter	AUT	08/03/91	M	2	(12)	
33	Igor Tadic		04/07/86	A		(8)	
22	Sébastien Wüthrich		29/05/90	M	9	(2)	4

FC THUN

Coach: Bernard Challandes; (20/11/12) (Mauro Lustrinelli); (29/11/12) Urs Fischer
1898 • Arena Thun (10,000) • fcthun.ch

2012

Date	Opponent		Score	Scorers
14/07	Lausanne	h	0-0	
22/07	Zürich	a	2-0	Demiri, Ngamukol
29/07	Young Boys	a	0-3	
05/08	Luzern	h	2-1	Cassio, Schirinzi (p)
12/08	Basel	a	1-3	Schirinzi
18/08	St Gallen	h	0-1	
25/08	Grasshoppers	a	0-1	
01/09	Servette	h	3-0	Schneuwly, Nélson Ferreira, Ngamukol
22/09	Sion	a	1-2	Ngamukol
27/09	Young Boys	h	2-1	Ngamukol, Salamand
30/09	Luzern	a	1-2	Schirinzi (p)
06/10	Grasshoppers	h	2-3	Steffen, Schneuwly
20/10	Sion	h	1-1	Ghezal
28/10	St Gallen	a	0-1	
04/11	Zürich	h	1-4	Schneuwly
17/11	Lausanne	a	0-3	
25/11	Basel	h	3-2	Ngamukol 2, Wittwer
02/12	Servette	a	0-0	

2013

Date	Opponent		Score	Scorers
17/02	Servette	h	1-1	Steffen
24/02	Sion	h	4-0	Salamand, Nélson Ferreira, Schneuwly, Sadik
02/03	Luzern	a	0-0	
10/03	Zürich	h	0-4	
13/03	St Gallen	a	0-0	
17/03	Basel	a	0-1	
30/03	Grasshoppers	h	1-0	Schneuwly
07/04	Lausanne	a	4-2	Schirinzi 2 (1p), Schneuwly 2
14/04	Young Boys	a	2-1	Schneuwly 2
21/04	Basel	h	2-2	Demiri, Zuffi
27/04	Grasshoppers	a	2-0	Steffen, Schneuwly
05/05	Luzern	h	1-1	Schneuwly
09/05	Servette	a	0-2	
12/05	Lausanne	h	2-0	Sadik, Hediger
17/05	St Gallen	h	3-0	Schneuwly, Wittwer, Siegfried
25/05	Sion	a	1-0	Schneuwly
29/05	Zürich	a	0-2	
01/06	Young Boys	h	2-2	Steffen, Matić

No	Name	Nat	DoB	Pos	Aps	(s)	Gls
6	Roland Bättig		28/07/79	M	18	(2)	
16	Cassio	BRA	20/08/90	A	2	(8)	1
8	Muhamed Demiri	MKD	20/11/85	M	27	(1)	2
1	Guillaume Faivre		20/02/87	G	35		
31	David Frey		08/02/91	M	1	(3)	
34	Cyril Gasser		11/03/92	M		(1)	
5	Saïf Ghezal	TUN	30/06/81	D	22		1
17	Dennis Hediger		22/09/86	M	18	(1)	1
10	Miloš Krstić	SRB	05/03/87	M	9	(11)	
33	Benjamin Lüthi		30/11/88	D	32	(1)	
29	Jérémy Manière	CRO	26/07/91	M	1	(2)	
24	Stipe Matić	CRO	06/02/79	D	10	(3)	1
22	David Moser		24/03/89	G	1	(1)	
21	Nélson Ferreira	POR	26/05/82	M	21	(5)	2
9	Anatole Ngamukol	FRA	15/01/88	A	17		6
26	Thomas Reinmann		09/04/83	D	28	(2)	
9	Berat Sadik	FIN	14/09/86	A	3	(15)	2
32	Mathieu Salamand	FRA	17/04/91	M	12	(9)	2
14	Nicolas Schindelholz		12/02/88	D	14	(2)	
27	Enrico Schirinzi	ITA	14/11/84	D	31	(2)	5
23	Marc Schneider		23/07/80	D	1		
15	Marco Schneuwly		27/03/85	A	29	(5)	13
4	Michael Siegfried		18/02/88	D	6	(6)	1
11	Renato Steffen		03/11/91	M	14	(5)	4
30	Mirson Volina	ALB	08/01/90	M		(5)	
28	Andreas Wittwer		05/10/90	M	26	(5)	2
7	Luca Zuffi		27/03/90	M	19	(7)	1

BSC YOUNG BOYS

Coach: Martin Rueda; (07/04/13) Bernard Challandes
1898 • Stade de Suisse (32,000) • bscyb.ch
Major honours
Swiss League (11) 1903, 1909, 1910, 1911, 1920, 1929, 1957, 1958, 1959, 1960, 1986;
Swiss Cup (6) 1930, 1945, 1953, 1958, 1977, 1987

2012

Date	Opponent		Score	Scorers
15/07	St Gallen	a	1-1	Mayuka
22/07	Grasshoppers	h	0-1	
29/07	Thun	h	3-0	Schneuwly, Spycher (p), Mayuka
05/08	Servette	a	1-1	Farnerud
12/08	Zürich	h	4-1	Bobadilla 2, Farnerud, Nuzzolo
19/08	Sion	a	0-1	
26/08	Lausanne	h	0-0	
02/09	Luzern	a	2-1	Farnerud, González
23/09	Basel	h	1-1	Zárate
27/09	Thun	a	1-2	Nuzzolo
30/09	Servette	h	6-2	Nuzzolo, Frey, Bobadilla 2, Costanzo, Lecjaks
07/10	Zürich	a	1-1	Costanzo (p)
21/10	Grasshoppers	a	2-3	Martínez, Bobadilla
03/11	Basel	a	0-2	
18/11	St Gallen	h	0-0	
25/11	Lausanne	a	1-2	Frey
28/11	Luzern	h	2-1	Farnerud, Zárate
02/12	Sion	h	3-1	Nef, Nuzzolo 2 (1p)

2013

Date	Opponent		Score	Scorers
09/02	Luzern	h	3-2	Costanzo 2, Nuzzolo
16/02	Grasshoppers	a	0-2	
23/02	Zürich	a	0-4	
03/03	St Gallen	h	2-0	Frey, Nuzzolo
10/03	Basel	a	0-3	
17/03	Sion	h	0-0	
01/04	Lausanne	h	0-0	
07/04	Servette	h	0-2	
14/04	Thun	h	1-2	Nuzzolo
21/04	Sion	a	0-0	
28/04	Lausanne	h	3-1	Costanzo (p), Zverotić, Afum
04/05	St Gallen	a	1-3	Costanzo (p)
07/05	Grasshoppers	h	4-0	Afum, Farnerud, Nuzzolo, Gerndt
11/05	Luzern	a	1-3	Gerndt
18/05	Servette	a	1-0	Afum
26/05	Zürich	h	2-4	Afum, Farnerud
29/05	Basel	h	0-1	
01/06	Thun	a	2-2	Afum, Frey

No	Name	Nat	DoB	Pos	Aps	(s)	Gls
35	François Affolter		13/03/91	D	3	(1)	
7	Samuel Afum	GHA	24/12/90	A	13	(3)	5
32	Leonardo Bertone		14/03/94	M	1	(1)	
9	Raúl Bobadilla	ARG	18/06/87	A	10	(1)	5
28	Marco Bürki		10/07/93	D	14	(2)	
30	Moreno Costanzo		20/02/88	M	21	(3)	6
30	Pascal Doubaï	CIV	22/05/92	M	8	(4)	
8	Alexander Farnerud	SWE	01/05/84	M	32	(2)	6
20	Michael Frey		19/07/94	A	13	(18)	4
20	Alexander Gerndt	SWE	14/07/86	A	13	(3)	2
2	Alexander González	VEN	13/09/92	D	9	(12)	1
33	Jan Lecjaks	CZE	09/08/90	D	5	(2)	1
25	Josef Martínez	VEN	19/05/93	A	1	(7)	1
24	Emmanuel Mayuka	ZAM	21/11/90	A	7		2
4	Alain Nef		06/02/82	D	34		1
29	Raphael Nuzzolo		04/07/83	M	29	(1)	9
3	Juhani Ojala	FIN	19/06/89	D	11	(1)	
16	Mario Raimondi		10/07/80	M	23	(5)	
14	Christian Schneuwly		07/12/88	M	20	(7)	1
34	Hélios Sessolo		26/05/93	M		(1)	
6	Michael Silberbauer	DEN	07/07/81	M	2	(1)	
17	Christoph Spycher		30/03/78	D	12	(2)	1
23	Scott Sutter		13/05/86	D	20	(5)	
31	Haris Tabakovic		20/06/94	A	1	(6)	
22	Dušan Veškovac	SRB	16/05/86	D	18	(1)	
7	Matías Vitkievez		16/05/85	A	2	(11)	
1	Marco Wölfli		22/08/82	G	36		
19	Gonzalo Zárate	ARG	06/08/84	A	12	(4)	2
13	Elsad Zverotić	MNE	31/10/86	M	26	(2)	1

FC ZÜRICH

Coach: Rolf Fringer (AUT); (26/11/12) Urs Meier
1896 • Letzigrund (26,000) • fcz.ch
Major honours
Swiss League (12) 1902, 1924, 1963, 1966, 1968, 1974, 1975, 1976, 1981, 2006, 2007, 2009;
Swiss Cup (7) 1966, 1970, 1972, 1973, 1976, 2000, 2005

2012

Date	Opponent		Score	Scorers
15/07	Luzern	a	1-1	Gavranovic
22/07	Thun	h	0-2	
28/07	St Gallen	a	1-3	Gavranovic
05/08	Lausanne	h	4-0	Drmic, Chermiti 2 (1p), Schönbächler
12/08	Young Boys	a	1-4	Drmic
19/08	Servette	h	1-1	Chiumiento
26/08	Sion	h	1-0	Chiumiento (p)
02/09	Basel	a	0-0	
22/09	Grasshoppers	h	0-1	
26/09	St Gallen	a	0-2	
30/09	Sion	a	2-2	Gavranovic, Jorge Teixeira
07/10	Young Boys	h	1-1	Schönbächler
21/10	Lausanne	a	2-0	Schönbächler, Drmic
28/10	Basel	h	1-2	Gavranovic (p)
04/11	Thun	a	4-1	Jorge Teixeira, Kukuruzović 2, Jahovic
17/11	Luzern	h	0-2	
24/11	Servette	h	0-2	
02/12	Grasshoppers	a	0-1	

2013

Date	Opponent		Score	Scorers
10/02	Lausanne	h	2-0	Chermiti, Drmic
17/02	Luzern	a	1-1	Béda (p)
23/02	Young Boys	h	4-0	Drmic, Chermiti, Gavranovic, Jahovic
02/03	Sion	h	3-1	Drmic 2, Schönbächler
10/03	Thun	a	4-0	og (Schindelholz), Buff, Drmic, Chermiti (p)
16/03	Servette	a	2-1	Chermiti, Jahovic
30/03	St Gallen	h	1-3	R Koch
06/04	Grasshoppers	h	2-4	Gajić 2
14/04	Basel	a	1-3	Drmic
20/04	Servette	h	4-0	Kukuruzović 2, Chikhaoui, Jahovic
28/04	St Gallen	a	2-1	Kukuruzović, Chermiti
03/05	Lausanne	a	1-1	Drmic (p)
08/05	Basel	h	3-1	Gajić, Schönbächler, Pedro Henrique
12/05	Grasshoppers	a	1-0	Chermiti
18/05	Luzern	h	4-1	Gavranovic, Schönbächler, Drmic, Chikhaoui
26/05	Young Boys	a	4-2	Drmic, Chermiti, Gajić (p), Gavranovic
29/05	Thun	h	2-0	Gavranovic, Chermiti
01/06	Sion	a	2-4	Gavranovic, Drmic

No	Name	Nat	DoB	Pos	Aps	(s)	Gls
19	Armin Alesevic		06/03/94	D	1		
25	Joetex Asamoah Frimpong	GHA	17/04/82	A		(7)	
28	Mathieu Béda	FRA	28/07/81	D	17		1
3	Loris Benito		07/01/92	D	28		
18	Yanick Brecher		25/05/93	G	1		
24	Maurice Brunner		29/01/91	M	1	(6)	
15	Oliver Buff		03/08/92	M	22	(2)	1
10	Amine Chermiti	TUN	26/12/87	A	17	(8)	10
17	Yassine Chikhaoui	TUN	22/09/86	M	5	(8)	2
29	David Chiumiento		22/11/84	M	16	(2)	2
1	David Da Costa		19/04/86	G	35		
5	Berat Djimsiti		19/02/93	D	32	(2)	
11	Josip Drmic		08/08/92	A	28	(3)	13
14	Milan Gajić	SRB	17/11/86	M	15	(1)	4
7	Mario Gavranovic		24/11/89	A	29	(3)	9
2	Stefan Glarner		21/11/87	D	20	(5)	
26	André Gonçalves		23/01/92	D		(1)	
21	Adis Jahovic	MKD	18/03/87	A	5	(11)	4
6	Jorge Teixeira	POR	27/08/86	D	12		2
22	Asmir Kajević	MNE	15/02/90	M	3	(2)	
34	Mike Kleiber		04/02/93	M	1		
16	Philippe Koch		02/09/91	D	27	(1)	
4	Raphael Koch		20/01/90	D	15	(5)	1
20	Burim Kukeli	ALB	16/01/84	M	12		
8	Stjepan Kukuruzović	CRO	07/06/89	M	18	(10)	5
23	Ludovic Magnin		20/04/79	D	3		
33	Davide Mariani	ITA	19/05/91	M	7	(9)	
10	Pedro Henrique	BRA	16/06/90	A	6	(11)	1
27	Marco Schönbächler		11/01/90	M	21	(9)	6

Top goalscorers

21	Ezequiel Scarione (St Gallen)	
14	Marco Streller (Basel)	
13	Marco Schneuwly (Thun)	
	Josip Drmic (Zürich)	
12	Anatole Ngamukol (Thun/Grasshoppers)	
10	Amine Chermiti (Zürich)	
9	Raphael Nuzzolo (Young Boys)	
	Mario Gavranovic (Zürich)	
8	Izet Hajrovic (Grasshoppers)	
	Chris Malonga (Lausanne)	
	Léo Itaperuna (Sion)	

Promoted club

FC AARAU

Coach: René Weiler
1902 • Brügglifeld (9,250) • fcaarau.ch
Major honours
Swiss League (3) 1912, 1914, 1993;
Swiss Cup (1) 1985

SECOND LEVEL FINAL TABLE 2012/13

		Pld	W	D	L	F	A	Pts
1	FC Aarau	36	24	6	6	76	40	78
2	AC Bellinzona	36	21	8	7	62	37	64
3	FC Winterthur	36	19	5	12	61	43	62
4	FC Wil 1900	36	15	6	15	59	65	51
5	FC Biel/Bienne	36	13	8	15	59	59	47
6	FC Chiasso	36	13	8	15	42	51	47
7	FC Lugano	36	11	11	14	52	50	44
8	FC Wohlen	36	9	12	15	39	58	39
9	FC Vaduz	36	10	7	19	41	52	37
10	FC Locarno	36	5	9	22	32	68	24

*NB AC Bellinzona – 7 pts deducted and excluded for
2013/14 season; FC Locarno therefore avoid relegation.*

Domestic cup: Schweizer Cup/Coupe de Suisse 2012/13

FIRST ROUND

(14/09/12)
Le Mont 1-4 Biel/Bienne

(15/09/12)
Altstetten 0-7 St Gallen
Amriswil 1-6 Basel
Arlesheim 1-3 Chiasso
Colombier 2-4 Hergiswil
CS Italien 1-5 Schaffhausen
Diessenhofen 0-5 Baden
Düdingen 3-4 Thun
Eschenbach 0-1 Winterthur
Étoile Carouge 1-1 Wohlen *(aet; 5-6 on pens)*
Hochdorf 0-4 Lausanne
Ibach 1-2 Black Stars *(aet)*
Köniz 3-1 Tuggen
Langenthal 1-3 Kriens
Monthey 2-4 Brühl (aet)
Moutier 0-4 Grenchen
Olten 0-4 Lugano
Saxon 2-3 La Sarraz/Eclépens *(aet)*
Schönbühl 2-1 Aarberg
Thierrens 2-3 Locarno
Vallemaggia 3-1 Bümpliz *(aet)*
Wettswil-Bonstetten 1-5 Young Boys
Zofingen 1-3 Schötz *(aet)*

(16/09/12)
Cham 2-1 Servette
Delémont 1-1 Luzern *(aet; 7-6 on pens)*
Echallens 0-6 Zürich
Ems 0-5 Bellinzona
Linth 2-3 Muttenz
Pully 1-4 Aarau
Richemond 0-1 Sion
Vedeggio 0-5 Grasshoppers
Windisch 0-7 Wil

SECOND ROUND

(10/11/12)
Baden 0-5 Schaffhausen
Black Stars 1-3 Zürich
Köniz 2-2 Winterthur *(aet; 4-2 on pens)*
Lugano 0-2 Thun
Schönbühl 0-4 Kriens
Schötz 1-4 Wil
Vallemaggia 0-6 Grasshoppers

(11/11/12)
Aarau 2-0 Bellinzona
Biel/Bienne 0-3 St Gallen
Cham 2-2 Locarno *(aet; 4-5 on pens)*
Chiasso 1-4 Basel
Delémont 0-4 Lausanne
Grenchen 0-4 Wohlen
Hergiswil 0-3 Sion
La Sarraz/Eclépens 0-3 Brühl *(aet)*
Muttenz 1-5 Young Boys

THIRD ROUND

(08/12/12)
Brühl 1-3 Lausanne
Schaffhausen 1-1 Grasshoppers *(aet; 2-3 on pens)*

(09/12/12)
Köniz 1-5 Zürich
Locarno 2-3 Basel *(aet)*
Wil 4-3 Young Boys

(03/02/13)
Aarau 2-0 St Gallen *(aet)*
Kriens 0-4 Sion
Wohlen 1-2 Thun

QUARTER-FINALS

(27/02/13)
Aarau 1-4 Grasshoppers *(Ionita 66; Feltscher 16, 74, Zuber 89, Ngamukol 90)*
Lausanne 0-2 Sion *(Vanczák 29, N'Djeng 90p)*

Thun 1-2 Basel *(Schneuwly 79; A Frei 12, 115) (aet)*
Wil 2-4 Zürich *(Muslin 28, Audino 95; Gavranovic 5, Gajić 92, Drmic 114, Schönbächler 119) (aet)*

SEMI-FINALS

(17/04/13)
Sion 0-1 Basel *(Stocker 73)*
Zürich 1-2 Grasshoppers *(Benito 22; Feltscher 39, Hajrovic 94) (aet)*

FINAL

(20/05/13)
Stade de Suisse, Berne
GRASSHOPPER CLUB 1 *(Hajrovic 75)*
FC BASEL 1893 1 *(Steinhöfer 71)*
(aet; 4-3 on pens)
Referee: Studer
GRASSHOPPERS: *Bürki, Lang, Vilotić, Grichting, Bauer, Salatic, Hajrovic, Abrashi (Nzuzi 95), Gashi (Ben Khalifa 100), Zuber (Feltscher 66), Ngamukol*
BASEL: *Sommer, Voser (Steinhöfer 60), Schär, Dragovic, Park, F Frei, Díaz, Serey Die (D Degen 106), Elneny, Stocker, Streller (Bobadilla 69)*

The champagne flows for Swiss Cup winners Grasshoppers

TURKEY
Türkiye Futbol Federasyönü (TFF)

Address Istinye Mahallesi
Darüşşafaka Caddesi
No. 45 Kat 2, Sarıyer
TR-34330 İstanbul
Tel +90 212 362 2222
Fax +90 212 323 4968
E-mail intdept@tff.org
Website tff.org

President Yıldırım Demirören
General secretary Emre Alkin
Media officer Türker Tozar
Year of formation 1923

SÜPER LIG CLUBS

1. Akhisar Belediyespor
2. Antalyaspor
 3. Beşiktaş JK
 4. Bursaspor
5. Elaziğspor
6. Eskişehirspor
 7. Fenerbahçe SK
8. Galatasaray AŞ
9. Gaziantepspor

10. Gençlerbirliği SK
11. İstanbul BB SK
12. Kardemir Karabükspor
13. Kasımpaşa SK
14. Kayserispor
15. Mersin İdman Yurdu
16. Orduspor
17. Sivasspor
 18. Trabzonspor AŞ

PROMOTED CLUBS

19. Kayseri Erciyesspor
20. Rizespor
21. Konyaspor

KEY:
● – UEFA Champions League
● – UEFA Europa League
● – Promoted clubs
○ – Relegated clubs

Galatasaray remain in charge

After a one-season experiment with play-offs, the Süper Lig returned to its conventional 34-match format in 2012/13. There was no change to the outcome of the title race, however, with Fatih Terim's Galatasaray AŞ holding off Fenerbahçe SK to overtake their arch-rivals in the league's all-time roll of honour with a record 19th victory.

Both Istanbul giants enjoyed excellent European campaigns, while Fenearbahçe retained the Turkish Cup, defeating Trabzonspor AŞ in the final. It was a poor season, however, for the Turkish national team, who struggled in the 2014 FIFA World Cup qualifiers.

Record 19th league title for Cimbom	Runners-up Fenerbahçe retain Turkish Cup	Big Two make big impression in Europe

Domestic league

A ten-point winning margin in the final standings did not tell the full story of Galatasaray's Süper Lig triumph. Although they topped the table from the third round onwards and were never shifted from their perch, for most of the campaign the defending champions had one or more teams breathing heavily down their neck. Like a marathon runner whose strategy is to lead from the front and gradually break the pack with a series of sustained bursts, Galatasaray were ultimately rewarded for their stamina and durability, burning off the opposition one by one and then seeing off the challenge of Fenerbahçe, their last remaining challengers, with a sprint-finish in the spring that brought seven successive victories.

Although coach Terim and midfield playmaker Selçuk İnan were both as influential as they had been in the 2011/12 title win, Galatasaray's successful title defence would not have been possible without the addition of several key new elements. The most significant of these was striker Burak Yılmaz, newly arrived from Trabzonspor, who scored 24 goals to retain the Süper Lig golden boot. He was well supported in attack by another newcomer, Umut Bulut, and although the team hardly

needed strengthening in that area, the mid-season acquisition of Didier Drogba ensured that the goals kept flowing during the season's critical phase. The Ivory Coast striker was not the only marquee signing in January, his arrival accompanied by that of another UEFA Champions League winner, Dutch international midfielder Wesley Sneijder.

Fenerbahçe inflicted on Galatasaray their fourth defeat of the season in round 33, winning 2-1 at the Şükrü Saracoğlu Stadium, but by then the game was up. Defeats in each of their previous two away fixtures, at Gençlerbirliği SK and İstanbul BB SK, had ended the aspirations of Aykut Kocaman's side, and another one at Kayserispor on the final day dropped them ten points behind the champions and just three points above Beşiktaş. Like the top two, the Black Eagles were also led by a Turkish coach, Saymet Aybaba, but despite a decent season at the helm, his first campaign turned out to be his last, with ex-Croatia coach Slaven Bilić taking over for 2013/14. Fener also made a summer change, bringing in Ersun Yanal from Eskişehirspor.

Fourth-placed Burasapor qualified for the UEFA Europa League, but there was no continental prize for fifth-placed Kayserispor, coached by Robert

Prosinečki, nor for Antalyaspor, who plummeted to seventh after a fine autumn during which they were often Galatasaray's closest pursuers. Their season was a mirror image of Akhisar Belediyespor's. The newly promoted, low-budget club looked doomed to an immediate relegation at the halfway point, but the arrival in January of Greek sharpshooter Theofanis Gekas transformed their fortunes, and with nine wins after Christmas they managed to stay up, condemning İstanbul BB to follow bottom two Mersin İdman Yurdu and Orduspor through the trapdoor.

Domestic cup

Having waited 29 years to break their Turkish Cup jinx in 2012, Fenerbahçe made it two wins in as many years, with Kocaman becoming the only coach in the club's history to claim the trophy back-to-back. The competition was a long drawn-out affair, with an extended group stage played over the winter months replacing the traditional quarter-finals.

Fenerbahçe and Trabzonspor topped their respective groups before coming through their semi-finals in contrasting fashion, Fener requiring penalties to see off

Continued on page 720

Domestic league: Süper Lig 2012/13 final table

		Pld	Home					Away					Total					
			W	D	L	F	A	W	D	L	F	A	W	D	L	F	A	Pts
1	Galatasaray AŞ	34	13	2	2	38	17	8	6	3	28	18	21	8	5	66	35	71
2	Fenerbahçe SK	34	12	2	3	35	18	6	5	6	21	21	18	7	9	56	39	61
3	Beşiktaş JK	34	8	7	2	36	22	8	3	6	27	27	16	10	8	63	49	58
4	Bursaspor	34	8	7	2	24	12	6	6	5	28	29	14	13	7	52	41	55
5	Kayserispor	34	9	5	3	25	14	6	2	9	23	31	15	7	12	48	45	52
6	Kasımpaşa SK	34	7	5	5	23	18	7	3	7	25	19	14	8	12	48	37	50
7	Antalyaspor	34	11	1	5	37	28	3	4	10	13	24	14	5	15	50	52	47
8	Eskişehirspor	34	7	6	4	28	20	4	7	6	20	20	11	13	10	48	40	46
9	Trabzonspor AŞ	34	9	4	4	23	17	4	3	10	16	23	13	7	14	39	40	46
10	Gaziantepspor	34	8	2	7	23	20	4	8	5	19	29	12	10	12	42	49	46
11	Gençlerbirliği SK	34	6	8	3	26	21	4	7	6	20	26	10	15	9	46	47	45
12	Sivasspor	34	9	5	3	30	20	3	3	11	12	26	12	8	14	42	46	44
13	Elazığspor	34	6	7	4	14	17	4	6	7	17	29	10	13	11	31	46	43
14	Akhisar Belediyespor	34	5	5	7	16	21	6	4	7	20	23	11	9	14	36	44	42
15	Kardemir Karabükspor	34	6	4	7	14	21	5	3	9	27	32	11	7	16	41	53	40
16	İstanbul BB SK	34	5	6	6	24	24	4	3	10	19	26	9	9	16	43	50	36
17	Orduspor	34	6	4	7	26	28	0	7	10	9	23	6	11	17	35	51	29
18	Mersin İdman Yurdu	34	4	5	8	17	10	0	5	12	14	33	4	10	20	31	53	22

SEASON AT A GLANCE

EUROPEAN QUALIFICATION 2013/14

Champion: Galatasaray AŞ (group stage)
Cup winner: Fenerbahce SK (third qualifying round)

Beşiktaş JK (play-offs)
Bursaspor (third qualifying round)
Trabzonspor AŞ (second qualifying round)

Top scorer	Burak Yılmaz (Galatasaray) 24 goals
Relegated clubs	Mersin İdman Yurdu, Orduspor, İstanbul BB SK
Promoted clubs	Kayseri Erciyesspor, Rizespor, Konyaspor
Cup final	Fenerbahçe SK 1-0 Trabzonspor AŞ

SÜPER LIG TEAM OF THE SEASON
(4-3-3)
Coach: Terim (Galatasaray)

PLAYER OF THE SEASON
Burak Yılmaz
(Galatasaray AŞ)

The Süper Lig's top scorer for the second season running, Burak replicated his domestic prowess in the UEFA Champions League, notching eight goals in Galatasaray's run to the quarter-finals. Combining speed of thought, movement and fearsome finishing, his first season at the club could not have turned out much better.

NEWCOMER OF THE SEASON
Salih Uçan
(Fenerbahçe SK)

Plucked from second-tier Bucaspor, the 19-year-old made a seamless transition to top-flight football. With a sound understanding of the game and a studious eye for a pass, Salih has all the tools to flourish at the highest level. The midfielder especially came to the fore in the latter stages of Fenerbahçe's run to the UEFA Europa League semi-finals.

Muslera (Galatasaray)
Gökhan (Fenerbahçe) — Diego Ângelo (Eskişehirspor) — Aykut (Gençlerbirliği) — Tošić (Gençlerbirliği)
Olcay (Beşiktaş) — Selçuk (Galatasaray) — Černáček (Bursaspor)
Burak (Galatasaray) — Gekas (Akhisar) — Webó (Fenerbahçe)

NATIONAL TEAM

Home Kit

Away Kit

INTERNATIONAL TOURNAMENT APPEARANCES

FIFA World Cup (2) 1954, 2002 (3rd)
UEFA European Championship (3) 1996, 2000 (qtr-finals), 2008 (semi-finals)

TOP FIVE ALL-TIME CAPS

Rüştü Reçber (120); Hakan Şükür (112); Bülent Korkmaz (102); Tugay Kerimoğlu (94); Alpay Özalan & **Emre Belözoğlu** (90)

TOP FIVE ALL-TIME GOALS

Hakan Şükür (51); Tuncay Şanlı (22); Lefter Küçükandonyadis (21), Cemil Turan, Metin Oktay & Nihat Kahveci (19)

Results 2012/13

15/08/12	Austria	A	Vienna	0-2	
07/09/12	Netherlands (WCQ)	A	Amsterdam	0-2	
11/09/12	Estonia (WCQ)	H	Istanbul	3-0	*Emre Belözoğlu (44), Umut (60), Selçuk (75)*
12/10/12	Romania (WCQ)	H	Istanbul	0-1	
16/10/12	Hungary (WCQ)	A	Budapest	1-3	*Mevlüt (22)*
14/11/12	Denmark	H	Istanbul	1-1	*Mevlüt (69)*
06/02/13	Czech Republic	H	Manisa	0-2	
22/03/13	Andorra (WCQ)	A	Andorra la Vella	2-0	*Selçuk (30), Burak (45+2)*
26/03/13	Hungary (WCQ)	H	Istanbul	1-1	*Burak (63)*
28/05/13	Latvia	N	Duisburg (GER)	3-3	*Olcay (8), Selçuk (23p), Veysel (59)*
31/05/13	Slovenia	N	Bielefeld (GER)	0-2	

Appearances 2012/13

Coach: Abdullah Avcı	31/07/63		Aut	NED	EST	ROU	HUN	Den	Cze	AND	HUN	Lva	Svn	Caps	Goals
Mert Günok	01/03/89	Fenerbahçe	G46									s46		5	-
Hamit Altıntop	08/12/82	Galatasaray	D	D		M61	M		s46		s70			79	7
Ömer Toprak	21/07/89	Leverkusen (GER)	D	D	D	D	D		D			D	D	14	2
Semih Kaya	24/02/91	Galatasaray	D62	D	D	D		D		D	D			10	-
Caner Erkin	04/10/88	Fenerbahçe	D				D76	M65				D	M69	20	1
Emre Belözoğlu	07/09/80	Atlético (ESP) /Fenerbahçe	M60	M60	M82	M81	M		s68					90	9
Selçuk İnan	10/02/85	Galatasaray	M60		s68			s46	M	M	M	M46	M81	28	4
Serdar Sururer	27/11/89	Greuther Fürth (GER)	M	M70	M68	M69	s64		M68	M58				11	-
Arda Turan	30/01/87	Atlético (ESP)	A46	A	A	A		M78	A	M	M			64	12
Umut Bulut	15/03/83	Galatasaray	A	A	A68	A	s75	s83	s61	A82	A80			23	3
Burak Yılmaz	15/07/85	Galatasaray	A46	s70	A			A46	s46	A	A		s60	26	8
Tunay Torun	21/04/90	Stuttgart (GER)	s46	M81	s68		M45							9	-
Mevlüt Erdinç	25/02/87	Rennes (FRA)	s46	s81		s61	A	A83	A46		s80		A76	22	3
Tolga Zengin	10/10/83	Trabzonspor	s46	G	G									5	-
Nuri Şahin	05/09/88	Real Madrid (ESP) /Liverpool (ENG) /Dortmund (GER)	s60	s60	s82	s81	M	M83	M61	M91	M90	M		41	2
Mehmet Topal	03/03/86	Fenerbahçe	s60	M	M	M		M46	M68			s46	M	35	-
Bekir İtegün	20/04/84	Fenerbahçe	s62					D	D	D	D	D		9	-
Hasan Ali Kaldırım	09/12/89	Fenerbahçe		D	D	D	D	D	D	D	D		D	14	-
Gökhan Gönül	04/01/85	Fenerbahçe		D	D			D	D46	D	D			34	1
Volkan Demirel	27/10/81	Fenerbahçe				G	G							57	-
Emre Çolak	20/05/91	Galatasaray				s69								1	-
Egemen Korkmaz	03/11/82	Fenerbahçe					D							9	-
Mehmet Ekici	25/03/90	Bremen (GER)					M64					s61		9	-
Aydın Yılmaz	29/01/88	Galatasaray					s45							1	-
Onur Kıvrak	01/01/88	Trabzonspor						G	G	G	G			7	-
Alper Potuk	08/04/91	Eskişehirspor					s46		s58	M70		M60		5	-
Kerim Frei	19/11/93	Cardiff (WAL) /Fulham (ENG)					s65		s91	s90	s61			4	-
Gökhan Töre	20/01/92	Rubin (RUS)					s78					s86	s69	13	-
Soner Aydoğdu	05/01/91	Trabzonspor					s83							2	-
Ahmet İlhan Özek	01/01/88	Karabükspor					s68							1	-
Olcay Şahan	26/05/87	Beşiktaş							s82			M86	M69	3	1
Sinan Bolat	03/09/88	Standard Liège (BEL)										G46	G	6	-
Serdar Kurtuluş	23/07/87	Gaziantepspor										D46	D46	6	-
Oğuzhan Özyakup	23/09/92	Beşiktaş										M61	s81	2	-
Mustafa Pektemek	11/08/88	Beşiktaş										A	s76	7	1
Sefa Yılmaz	14/02/90	Kayserispor										A61	s69	2	-
Veysel Sarı	25/07/88	Eskişehirspor										s46	s46	2	1
Gökhan Zan	07/09/81	Galatasaray											D	36	-

TURKEY

Eskişehirspor while Trabzonspor hammered Sivasspor 6-0 in the second leg of their tie. The final, staged in Ankara, went the way of the team from Istanbul thanks to an early goal scored by the team's top marksman in the league, Senegalese striker Moussa Sow, who finished off a counterattack, clinically converting Mehmet Topal's pass.

Europe

Galatasaray reached the quarter-finals of the UEFA Champions League for the first time since 2000/01, and once again it was Real Madrid CF who barred their route to the last four – although not before a rousing second leg 3-2 win in Istanbul. Terim's team reached that stage thanks to the eight goals of Burak, who inspired his colleagues to a three-game winning sequence in the group stage – after they had taken just one point from their opening three fixtures – and to a dramatic last-16 win against FC Schalke 04.

Fenerbahçe were unable to join Galatasaray in the premier competition, narrowly losing out to FC Spartak Moskva in the play-offs, but their European campaign was to last 18 matches in total as they made amends

Caner Erkin (centre) celebrates the goal against Lazio that put Fenerbahçe into the UEFA Europa League semi-finals

with an outstanding effort in the UEFA Europa League, reaching a European semi-final for the first time in the club's history following a 3-1 aggregate victory over S.S. Lazio. Excellent away form and a tight defence were the keys to the team's run, but both of those attributes deserted them in the second leg of the semi-final as SL Benfica overturned a 1-0 first-leg deficit with a 3-1 win in Lisbon.

National team

If 2012/13 was a season full of positives for Turkish clubs in the international arena, it was negative in the extreme for the national team, who appeared to have lost all hope of qualifying for the 2014 World Cup after collecting just seven points from their opening six matches. While Estonia were defeated 3-0 at home and Andorra 2-0 away, the games against the major opposition in Group E all ended in disappointment. Having played well but lost in their first fixture, 2-0 against the Netherlands in Amsterdam, Abdullah Avcı's team were defeated 1-0 at home by Romania and, four days later, 3-1 by Hungary in Budapest.

A home win over the Hungarians was imperative when the teams met again in Istanbul in March, but despite taking the lead, through Burak, Turkey were unable to hold on to it and dropped two further points in a 1-1 draw. With no wins either in the team's five friendly matches, the last two against Latvia (3-3) and Slovenia (0-2) in May, confidence was not exactly flowing through the side as they approached the final set of World Cup fixtures in the early autumn.

European club competitions 2012/13

GALATASARAY AŞ

Group H
Match 1 - Manchester United FC (ENG)
A 0-1
Muslera, Hamit Altıntop, Selçuk İnan, Felipe Melo (Aydın Yılmaz 79), Nounkeu, Burak Yılmaz, Umut Bulut (Elmander 16), Hakan Balta, Semih Kaya, Eboué, Amrabat (Emre Çolak 63). Coach: Fatih Terim (TUR)
Match 2 - SC Braga (POR)
H 0-2
Muslera, Selçuk İnan, Felipe Melo (Elmander 76), Riera, Nounkeu, Burak Yılmaz, Umut Bulut, Semih Kaya, Eboué, Emre Çolak (Yekta Kurtuluş 78), Amrabat (Aydın Yılmaz 46). Coach: Fatih Terim (TUR)

Match 3 - CFR 1907 Cluj (ROU)
H 1-1 Burak Yılmaz (77)
Muslera, Hamit Altıntop (Burak Yılmaz 39), Selçuk İnan, Elmander, Emre Çolak 42), Felipe Melo, Riera, Nounkeu, Umut Bulut, Semih Kaya, Eboué (Sabri Sarıoğlu 68), Amrabat. Coach: Fatih Terim (TUR)
Match 4 - CFR 1907 Cluj (ROU)
A 3-1 Burak Yılmaz (18, 61, 74)
Muslera, Cris, Hamit Altıntop (Semih Kaya 90+1), Selçuk İnan, Riera, Nounkeu, Burak Yılmaz, Umut Bulut (Amrabat 76), Eboué, Yekta Kurtuluş (Sabri Sarıoğlu 89), Emre Çolak. Coach: Fatih Terim (TUR)
Match 5 - Manchester United FC (ENG)
H 1-0 Burak Yılmaz (53)
Muslera, Hamit Altıntop, Selçuk İnan, Elmander (Engin Baytar 63), Felipe Melo, Riera, Nounkeu, Burak Yılmaz (Umut Bulut 90+1), Semih Kaya, Eboué, Amrabat (Emre Çolak 81). Coach: Fatih Terim (TUR)
Match 6 - SC Braga (POR)
A 2-1 Burak Yılmaz (58), Aydın Yılmaz (78)
Muslera, Hamit Altıntop (Aydın Yılmaz 46), Selçuk İnan, Elmander (Amrabat 46), Felipe Melo, Riera, Nounkeu, Burak Yılmaz, Semih Kaya, Eboué, Emre Çolak (Umut Bulut 69). Coach: Fatih Terim (TUR)

Round of 16 - FC Schalke 04 (GER)
H 1-1 Burak Yılmaz (12)
Muslera, Hamit Altıntop (Eboué 66), Selçuk İnan, Felipe Melo, Riera, Drogba, Nounkeu, Sneijder (Amrabat 46), Burak Yılmaz, Semih Kaya, Sabri Sarıoğlu (Umut Bulut 83). Coach: Fatih Terim (TUR)
A 3-2 Hamit Altıntop (37), Burak Yılmaz (42), Umut Bulut (90+5)
Muslera, Hamit Altıntop, Selçuk İnan, Felipe Melo, Riera, Drogba, Nounkeu, Sneijder (Amrabat 70), Burak Yılmaz (Umut Bulut 86), Semih Kaya (Gökhan Zan 79), Eboué. Coach: Fatih Terim (TUR)

Quarter-final - Real Madrid CF (ESP)
A 0-3
Muslera, Hamit Altıntop (Umut Bulut 78), Selçuk İnan, Felipe Melo, Riera (Amrabat 83), Drogba, Nounkeu, Sneijder (Gökhan Zan 46), Burak Yılmaz, Semih Kaya, Eboué. Coach: Fatih Terim (TUR)
H 3-2 Eboué (57), Sneijder (70), Drogba (72)
Muslera, Hamit Altıntop (Amrabat 46), Gökhan Zan, Selçuk İnan, Felipe Melo, Riera, Drogba, Sneijder, Umut Bulut (Sabri Sarıoğlu 63), Semih Kaya, Eboué (Elmander 80). Coach: Fatih Terim (TUR)

FENERBAHÇE SK

CHAMPIONS LEAGUE

Third qualifying round - FC Vaslui (ROU)
H 1-1 *Bekir İrtegün (90)*
Volkan Demirel, Egemen Korkmaz, Hasan Ali Kaldırım, Bekir İrtegün, Mehmet Topal (Sow 79), Stoch (Caner Erkin 62), Alex, Kuyt, Cristian, Semih Şentürk (Mehmet Topuz 46), Gökhan Gönül. Coach: Aykut Kocaman (TUR)
A 4-1 *Caner Erkin (12), Kuyt (71, 76), Sow (90+2)*
Volkan Demirel, Egemen Korkmaz, Hasan Ali Kaldırım, Bekir İrtegün, Alex (Mehmet Topal 81), Kuyt (Sow 86), Cristian, Selçuk Şahin, Mehmet Topuz, Gökhan Gönül, Caner Erkin (Stoch 61). Coach: Aykut Kocaman (TUR)

Play-offs - FC Spartak Moskva (RUS)
A 1-2 *Kuyt (65)*
Mert Günok, Egemen Korkmaz, Hasan Ali Kaldırım, Mehmet Topal (Bienvenu 83), Yobo, Sow (Krasić 77), Kuyt, Cristian, Selçuk Şahin, Mehmet Topuz (Caner Erkin 88), Gökhan Gönül. Coach: Aykut Kocaman (TUR)
H 1-1 *Sow (69)*
Mert Günok, Egemen Korkmaz, Hasan Ali Kaldırım, Mehmet Topal, Yobo, Sow, Kuyt, Selçuk Şahin (Alex 59), Krasić (Stoch 16), Mehmet Topuz (Cristian 79), Gökhan Gönül. Coach: Aykut Kocaman (TUR)

EUROPA LEAGUE

Group C
Match 1 - Olympique de Marseille (FRA)
H 2-2 *Caner Erkin (28), Alex (57)*
Volkan Demirel, Hasan Ali Kaldırım, Bekir İrtegün, Mehmet Topal, Yobo, Sow (Bienvenu 74), Alex (Cristian 67), Raul Meireles, Mehmet Topuz, Gökhan Gönül, Caner Erkin (Stoch 88). Coach: Aykut Kocaman (TUR)
Match 2 - VfL Borussia Mönchengladbach (GER)
A 4-2 *Cristian (25, 87), Raul Meireles (40), Kuyt (71)*
Volkan Demirel, Egemen Korkmaz, Hasan Ali Kaldırım, Bekir İrtegün, Mehmet Topal, Sow (Krasić 78), Kuyt (Selçuk Şahin 90+4), Raul Meireles, Cristian, Gökhan Gönül, Caner Erkin. Coach: Aykut Kocaman (TUR)

Match 3 - AEL Limassol FC (CYP)
A 1-0 *Egemen Korkmaz (72)*
Volkan Demirel, Egemen Korkmaz, Hasan Ali Kaldırım, Bekir İrtegün, Mehmet Topal, Sow (Serdar Kesimal 90+3), Kuyt (Stoch 85), Cristian, Selçuk Şahin, Gökhan Gönül, Caner Erkin (Krasić 68). Coach: Aykut Kocaman (TUR)
Match 4 - AEL Limassol FC (CYP)
H 2-0 *Kuyt (11), Sow (41)*
Volkan Demirel, Hasan Ali Kaldırım (Caner Erkin 73), Bekir İrtegün, Mehmet Topal, Yobo, Sow, Stoch, Kuyt, Raul Meireles (Recep Niyaz 83), Cristian (Selçuk Şahin 73), Gökhan Gönül. Coach: Aykut Kocaman (TUR)
Match 5 - Olympique de Marseille (FRA)
A 1-0 *Bekir İrtegün (39)*
Volkan Demirel, Hasan Ali Kaldırım, Bekir İrtegün, Mehmet Topal, Yobo, Sow (Mehmet Topuz 79), Kuyt, Raul Meireles, Cristian (Selçuk Şahin 89), Gökhan Gönül, Caner Erkin (Stoch 85). Coach: Aykut Kocaman (TUR)
Match 6 - VfL Borussia Mönchengladbach (GER)
H 0-3
Mert Günok, Egemen Korkmaz, Mehmet Topal (Caner Erkin 75), Stoch (Kuyt 60), Bienvenu, Recep Niyaz (Cristian 60), Selçuk Şahin, Krasić, Serdar Kesimal, Özgür Çek, Orhan Şam. Coach: Aykut Kocaman (TUR)

Round of 32 - FC BATE Borisov (BLR)
A 0-0
Volkan Demirel, Egemen Korkmaz, Bekir İrtegün, Mehmet Topal, Sow (Salih Uçan 90), Kuyt, Raul Meireles, Cristian (Selçuk Şahin 85), Ziegler, Gökhan Gönül, Webó (Caner Erkin 72). Coach: Aykut Kocaman (TUR)
Red card: Raul Meireles 4
H 1-0 *Cristian (45+1p)*
Volkan Demirel, Egemen Korkmaz, Mehmet Topal, Yobo, Sow (Caner Erkin 85), Kuyt, Cristian, Ziegler, Salih Uçan (Selçuk Şahin 63), Gökhan Gönül, Webó (Semih Şentürk 78). Coach: Aykut Kocaman (TUR)

Round of 16 - FC Viktoria Plzeň (CZE)
A 1-0 *Webó (81)*
Volkan Demirel, Bekir İrtegün, Mehmet Topal, Yobo, Sow (Caner Erkin 83), Kuyt, Cristian, Selçuk Şahin, Ziegler, Gökhan Gönül, Webó (Mehmet Topuz 85). Coach: Aykut Kocaman (TUR)
H 1-1 *Salih Uçan (44)*
Volkan Demirel, Bekir İrtegün, Mehmet Topal (Salih Uçan 35), Yobo, Sow (Mehmet Topuz 82), Kuyt, Cristian (Egemen Korkmaz 90+1), Selçuk Şahin, Ziegler, Gökhan Gönül, Caner Erkin. Coach: Aykut Kocaman (TUR)

Quarter-final - S.S. Lazio (ITA)
H 2-0 *Webó (78p), Kuyt (90+1)*
Volkan Demirel, Egemen Korkmaz, Mehmet Topal (Caner Erkin 71), Yobo, Sow (Mehmet Topuz 86), Kuyt, Raul Meireles, Cristian (Salih Uçan 75), Ziegler, Gökhan Gönül, Webó. Coach: Aykut Kocaman (TUR)
A 1-1 *Caner Erkin (73)*
Volkan Demirel, Egemen Korkmaz, Yobo, Kuyt, Raul Meireles, Cristian (Salih Uçan 73), Selçuk Şahin, Ziegler, Gökhan Gönül, Caner Erkin (Krasić 87), Webó (Mehmet Topuz 80). Coach: Aykut Kocaman (TUR)

Semi-final - SL Benfica (POR)
H 1-0 *Egemen Korkmaz (72)*
Volkan Demirel, Egemen Korkmaz, Mehmet Topal, Yobo, Sow (Krasić 87), Kuyt, Raul Meireles (Salih Uçan 64), Cristian (Selçuk Şahin 86), Ziegler, Gökhan Gönül, Webó. Coach: Aykut Kocaman (TUR)
A 1-3 *Kuyt (23p)*
Volkan Demirel, Egemen Korkmaz, Yobo (Stoch 75), Sow, Kuyt, Cristian, Selçuk Şahin (Mehmet Topuz 45), Ziegler, Salih Uçan, Gökhan Gönül (Bekir İrtegün 61), Caner Erkin. Coach: Aykut Kocaman (TUR)

TRABZONSPOR AŞ

EUROPA LEAGUE

Play-offs - Videoton FC (HUN)
H 0-0
Onur Kıvrak, Bamba, Zokora, Colman (Alanzinho 46), Halil Altıntop, Giray Kaçar (Mustafa Yumlu 74), Sapara, Čelůstka, Serkan Balcı, Volkan Şen (Yasin Öztekin 42), Olcan Adın. Coach: Şenol Güneş (TUR)
A 0-0 *(aet; 2-4 on pens)*
Onur Kıvrak, Bamba, Yasin Öztekin (Vittek 82), Paulo Henrique, Soner Aydoğdu, Zokora, Mustafa Yumlu, Alanzinho (Sapara 111), Čelůstka, Serkan Balcı, Volkan Şen (Halil Altıntop 60). Coach: Şenol Güneş (TUR)

TURKEY

ESKİŞEHİRSPOR

Second qualifying round - Saint Johnstone FC (SCO)
H 2-0 *Alper Potuk (41), Wright (65og)*
Boffin, Batuhan Karadeniz (Tello 69), Diego Ângelo, Dedê, Alper Potuk, Erkan Zengin (Nuhiu 85), Kamara, Małecki (Burhan Eşer 78), Hürriyet Gücer, Servet Çetin, Veysel Sarı. Coach: Ersun Yanal (TUR)
A 1-1 *Veysel Sarı (52)*
Boffin, Diego Ângelo, Dedê, Alper Potuk, Erkan Zengin (Małecki 61), Tello, Kamara, Burhan Eşer (Nuhiu 73), Hürriyet Gücer (Mehmet Güven 81), Servet Çetin, Veysel Sarı. Coach: Ersun Yanal (TUR)

Third qualifying round - Olympique de Marseille (FRA)
H 1-1 *Nuhiu (62)*
Boffin, Diego Ângelo, Dedê, Alper Potuk, Nuhiu, Erkan Zengin (Mehmet Güven 46), Kamara, Małecki (Burhan Eşer 68), Hürriyet Gücer, Servet Çetin, Veysel Sarı (Mikail Albayrak 81). Coach: Ersun Yanal (TUR)
A 0-3
Boffin, Diego Ângelo, Dedê, Alper Potuk, Mehmet Güven (Tello 46), Nuhiu, Erkan Zengin (Małecki 46), Kamara, Hürriyet Gücer, Servet Çetin, Veysel Sarı. Coach: Ersun Yanal (TUR)

BURSASPOR

Third qualifying round - KuPS Kuopio (FIN)
A 0-1
Carson, N'Diaye, Batalla, Pinto, Chrétien, Serdar Aziz, Ozan İpek (Ferhat Kiraz 60), Musa Çağıran (Adem Koçak 88), İbrahim Öztürk, Hakan Aslantaş, İsmail Haktan Odabaşı (Turgay Bahadır 60). Coach: Ertuğrul Sağlam (TUR)
H 6-0 *İbrahim Öztürk (23), Pinto (28, 49), Batalla (36), N'Diaye (47), Ozan Tufan (72)*
Carson, N'Diaye, Šesták (İsmail Haktan Odabaşı 73), Batalla, Pinto (Bangura 76), Chrétien, Serdar Aziz, Ozan İpek, Musa Çağıran, İbrahim Öztürk, Hakan Aslantaş (Ozan Tufan 63). Coach: Ertuğrul Sağlam (TUR)

Play-offs - FC Twente (NED)
H 3-1 *Batalla (40, 82), Šesták (53)*
Carson, Gökçek Vederson, N'Diaye, Šesták (Forsell 69), Batalla (Ferhat Kiraz 90), Pinto, Chrétien, Serdar Aziz (Ömer Erdoğan 10), Ozan İpek, Musa Çağıran, İbrahim Öztürk. Coach: Ertuğrul Sağlam (TUR)
A 1-4 *Pinto (45+4) (aet)*
Carson, Gökçek Vederson, N'Diaye (Adem Koçak 82), Šesták, Batalla (Ferhat Kiraz 112), Pinto, Ömer Erdoğan, Chrétien, Ozan İpek (Hakan Aslantaş 40), Musa Çağıran, İbrahim Öztürk. Coach: Ertuğrul Sağlam (TUR)
Red card: Chrétien 89

Domestic league club-by-club

AKHİSAR BELEDİYESPOR
Coach: Hamza Hamzaoğlu
1970 • Akhisar (2,918) • akhisarspor.com

2012

Date	Opponent		Score	Scorers
17/08	Eskişehirspor	a	1-0	Güray
25/08	Gençlerbirliği	h	0-0	
01/09	Kayserispor	a	1-1	Sertan (p)
16/09	İstanbul BB	h	0-4	
23/09	Galatasaray	a	0-3	
29/09	Karabükspor	h	1-3	Emrah
06/10	Elazığspor	a	0-0	
22/10	Gaziantepspor	h	0-0	
27/10	Sivasspor	a	2-1	Kenan, Sertan
03/11	Fenerbahçe	h	1-2	Çağdaş
10/11	Trabzonspor	a	1-3	Bruno Mezenga
18/11	Kasımpaşa	h	0-2	
23/11	Beşiktaş	a	1-3	Mustafa
01/12	Bursaspor	h	2-2	Mustafa, Bruno Mezenga
15/12	Mersin	a	1-2	Kenan
21/12	Orduspor	h	0-0	

2013

Date	Opponent		Score	Scorers
09/01	Antalyaspor	h	1-0	Uğur
21/01	Eskişehirspor	h	1-1	Kenan
26/01	Gençlerbirliği	a	0-1	
01/02	Kayserispor	h	1-2	Gekas
09/02	İstanbul BB	a	2-0	Gekas 2
15/02	Galatasaray	h	1-2	Sertan
24/02	Karabükspor	a	2-0	Bilal, Gekas (p)
02/03	Elazığspor	h	0-1	
09/03	Gaziantepspor	a	2-2	Gekas, Bruno Mezenga
17/03	Sivasspor	h	2-1	Kenan, Gekas
31/03	Fenerbahçe	a	0-2	
07/04	Trabzonspor	h	1-0	Gekas
14/04	Kasımpaşa	a	1-0	Gekas
20/04	Beşiktaş	h	4-1	Gekas 2, Uğur, Emin
27/04	Bursaspor	a	1-1	Gekas
05/05	Antalyaspor	a	3-4	Ahmet, Uğur, og (Koray)
13/05	Mersin	h	1-0	Gekas
18/05	Orduspor	a	2-0	Bruno Mezenga 2

No	Name	Nat	DoB	Pos	Aps	(s)	Gls
20	Ahmet Cebe		02/03/83	M	15	(13)	1
10	Anıl Taşdemir		01/01/88	D	8	(2)	
24	Severin Bikoko	CMR	24/09/88	A	2	(1)	
35	Bilal Kısa		22/06/83	M	14	(2)	1
80	Bruno Mezenga	BRA	08/08/88	A	26	(5)	5
4	Çağdaş Atan		28/02/80	D	31		1
30	Diego Lima	BRA	30/09/88	M	1	(7)	
14	Emin Aladağ		25/02/83	M	22	(5)	1
34	Emrah Eren		13/11/78	D	34		1
17	Theofanis Gekas	GRE	23/05/80	A	14	(1)	12
22	Güray Vural		11/06/88	M	17	(8)	1
7	Kenan Özer		16/08/87	M	19	(6)	4
99	Kerem Bulut		03/02/92	A	1	(11)	
5	Kürşat Duymuş		01/02/79	D	6		
61	Mahmet Yılmaz		22/05/79	M	4	(3)	
9	Mert Kaytankaş		09/03/80	A	1	(6)	
6	Merter Yüce		18/02/85	M	23	(3)	
21	Mustafa Aşan		11/09/88	M	13	(11)	2
18	Oğuz Dağlaroğlu		18/08/79	G	34		
8	Gideon Sani	NGA	08/06/90	A		(6)	
3	Serkan Yalçın		02/11/82	D	6		
11	Sertan Vardar		13/03/82	M	27	(4)	3
19	Ibrahima Sonko	SEN	22/01/81	D	30		
15	Uğur Demirok		08/07/88	D	26	(2)	3
28	Paweł Wojciechowski	POL	24/04/90	D	11	(1)	5

ANTALYASPOR

Coach: Mehmet Özdilek
1966 • Mardan (7,428) • antalyaspor.com.te

2012

20/08	Gençlerbirliği	a	1-3	Uğur
27/08	Kayserispor	h	3-0	Tita 2, Emrah
01/09	İstanbul BB	a	1-0	Promise
15/09	Galatasaray	h	0-4	
21/09	Karabükspor	a	0-1	
30/09	Elazığspor	h	4-0	Uğur 2, Ömer 2
05/10	Gaziantepspor	a	1-0	Diarra
20/10	Sivasspor	h	4-2	Aissati, Promise 2, Diarra
29/10	Fenerbahçe	a	3-1	Diarra 2, Deniz
05/11	Trabzonspor	h	2-1	Ömer, Murat Duruer
10/11	Kasımpaşa	a	1-1	Aissati (p)
18/11	Beşiktaş	h	3-5	Promise, Diarra, Ömer
24/11	Bursaspor	a	1-1	Aissati
02/12	Mersin	h	1-0	Ömer
16/12	Orduspor	a	1-1	Tita
23/12	Eskişehirspor	h	2-1	Diarra 2

2013

09/01	Akhisar	a	0-1	
20/01	Gençlerbirliği	h	3-5	Murat Duruer, Diarra, Promise
27/01	Kayserispor	a	0-2	
02/02	İstanbul BB	h	1-0	Diarra
10/02	Galatasaray	a	0-2	
16/02	Karabükspor	h	0-0	
23/02	Elazığspor	a	1-2	Promise
03/03	Gaziantepspor	h	5-2	Diarra, Tita 2, Promise, Ömer
10/03	Sivasspor	a	1-2	Diarra
17/03	Fenerbahçe	h	1-2	Tita
31/03	Trabzonspor	a	0-2	
05/04	Kasımpaşa	h	3-2	Diarra 2, Tita
15/04	Beşiktaş	a	0-1	
21/04	Bursaspor	h	0-1	
28/04	Mersin	a	1-1	Murat Duruer
05/05	Akhisar	h	4-3	Koray, Promise, og (Merter), Tita
11/05	Orduspor	h	1-0	Ömer
19/05	Eskişehirspor	a	1-3	Ömer

No	Name	Nat	DoB	Pos	Aps	(s)	Gls
6	Ismail Aissati	MAR	16/08/88	M	28	(3)	3
2	Ali Tandoğan		25/12/77	D	10	(2)	
24	Deniz Barış		02/07/77	D	27	(1)	1
26	Lamine Diarra	SEN	20/12/83	A	32	(1)	13
11	Emrah Başşan		17/04/92	M	9	(12)	1
3	Emre Güngör		01/08/84	D	22		
9	Emre Torun		02/06/93	A		(1)	
15	Ergün Teber		01/09/85	D	23	(3)	
1	Hakan Arıkan		17/08/82	G	19		
4	İbrahim Dağaşan		15/06/84	M	16	(6)	
22	Petr Janda	CZE	05/01/87	M	7	(11)	
51	Koray Arslan		01/10/83	D	24	(1)	1
59	Mehmet Sedef		05/08/87	D	9	(1)	
67	Mehmet Eren Boyraz		11/10/81	M	3	(8)	
14	Veselin Minev	BUL	14/10/80	D	4		
32	Murat Akın		22/10/86	M	1		
21	Murat Duruer		15/01/88	M	15	(11)	3
7	Musa Nizam		08/09/90	D	14	(2)	
33	Sammy N'Djock	CMR	25/02/90	G	14	(1)	
27	Okan Özçelik		10/05/82	A		(1)	
77	Ömer Şişmanoğlu		01/08/89	A	3	(21)	8
17	Polat Keser		04/12/85	G	1		
20	Isaac Promise	NGA	02/12/87	A	29	(1)	8
10	Tita	BRA	20/07/81	A	27	(1)	8
8	Uğur İnceman		25/05/81	M	30		3
18	Zeki Yıldırım		15/01/91	M	4	(8)	
28	Nikola Žižić	CRO	23/01/88	D	3	(4)	

BEŞİKTAŞ JK

Coach: Samet Aybaba
1903 • İnönü (32,086) • bjk.com.tr
Major honours
Turkish League (13) 1957, 1958, 1960, 1966, 1967,
1982, 1986, 1990, 1991, 1992, 1995, 2003, 2009;
Turkish Cup (9) 1975, 1989, 1990, 1994, 1998, 2006,
2007, 2009, 2011

2012

19/08	İstanbul BB	a	1-1	Hugo Almeida
26/08	Galatasaray	h	3-3	og (Felipe Melo), Hološko 2
01/09	Karabükspor	a	3-0	Manuel Fernandes 2, Uğur
17/09	Elazığspor	h	3-0	Necip, Sivok, Hilbert
22/09	Gaziantepspor	a	2-3	Olcay, Hugo Almeida
01/10	Sivasspor	h	0-1	
07/10	Fenerbahçe	a	0-3	
22/10	Trabzonspor	h	1-1	Manuel Fernandes
26/10	Kasımpaşa	a	3-1	Hugo Almeida, Manuel Fernandes, Sivok
04/11	Mersin	h	3-0	Hugo Almeida (p), Oğuzhan, Hološko
09/11	Bursaspor	a	3-3	Olcay, Hološko, Hugo Almeida (p)
18/11	Antalyaspor	a	5-3	Hugo Almeida 3, Olcay, Manuel Fernandes
23/11	Akhisar	h	3-1	Hološko 2, Hilbert
01/12	Orduspor	a	2-1	İbrahim, Oğuzhan
07/12	Eskişehirspor	h	2-2	Hološko, Hugo Almeida
15/12	Gençlerbirliği	a	1-1	Olcay
21/12	Kayserispor	h	3-1	Hološko, Sivok, Olcay

2013

19/01	İstanbul BB	h	2-2	Sivok, Olcay
27/01	Galatasaray	a	1-2	Sivok
01/02	Karabükspor	h	2-2	İbrahim, Olcay
09/02	Elazığspor	a	3-1	Hološko, İbrahim, Manuel Fernandes
16/02	Gaziantepspor	h	1-1	Ersan
23/02	Sivasspor	a	1-0	Hilbert
03/03	Fenerbahçe	h	3-2	og (Kuyt), Niang, Olcay
09/03	Trabzonspor	a	0-0	
16/03	Kasımpaşa	h	1-3	Olcay
01/04	Mersin	a	2-1	Manuel Fernandes, og (Mert Nobre)
08/04	Bursaspor	a	0-3	
15/04	Antalyaspor	h	1-0	Olcay
20/04	Akhisar	a	1-4	Mustafa
27/04	Orduspor	h	2-0	Niang, og (Ömer)
05/05	Eskişehirspor	a	2-1	Niang, Mustafa
11/05	Gençlerbirliği	h	3-0	Kavlak, Olcay, Hološko
19/05	Kayserispor	a	0-2	

No	Name	Nat	DoB	Pos	Aps	(s)	Gls
34	Batuhan Karadeniz		24/04/91	A	3	(8)	
1	Cenk Gönen		21/02/88	G	8		
7	Dentinho	BRA	19/01/89	A	1	(5)	
24	Emre Özkan		24/12/88	M	7	(2)	
39	Erkan Kaş		10/09/91	M	1	(8)	
22	Ersan Gülüm		17/05/87	D	17	(3)	1
14	Julien Escudé	FRA	17/08/79	D	10	(4)	
19	Gökhan Süzen		12/07/87	D	11	(1)	
30	Hasan Türk		20/03/93	A	1	(7)	
13	Roberto Hilbert	GER	16/10/84	D	32		3
37	Filip Hološko	SVK	17/01/84	A	28	(4)	10
9	Hugo Almeida	POR	23/05/84	A	17	(3)	9
5	İbrahim Toraman		20/11/81	D	25	(1)	3
18	Kadir Ari		27/11/94	A		(1)	
8	Veli Kavlak	AUT	03/11/88	M	24	(6)	1
4	Manuel Fernandes	POR	05/02/86	M	26	(1)	7
23	Allan McGregor	SCO	31/01/82	G	26		
28	Mehmet Akgün		06/08/86	M	4	(3)	
17	Mehmet Akyüz		02/01/95	M	1	(7)	
80	Muhammed Demirci		03/01/95	M		(4)	
11	Mustafa Pektemek		11/08/88	A	9		2
20	Necip Uysal		24/01/91	M	20	(6)	1
53	Mamadou Niang	SEN	13/10/79	A	8	(2)	3
15	Oğuzhan Özyakup		23/09/92	M	18	(10)	2
10	Olcay Şahan		26/05/87	M	33	(1)	11
26	Sinan Kurumuş		02/08/94	D	1	(1)	
6	Tomáš Sivok	CZE	15/09/83	D	27	(1)	5
25	Uğur Boral		14/04/92	D	16	(2)	1

BURSASPOR

Coach: Ertuğrul Sağlam; (07/02/13) Hikmet Karaman
1963 • Atatürk (25,661) • bursaspor.org.tr
Major honours
Turkish League (1) 2010;
Turkish Cup (1) 1986

2012

19/08	Kayserispor	a	1-0	Pinto
26/08	İstanbul BB	h	0-1	
02/09	Galatasaray	a	2-3	Musa, Ömer
15/09	Karabükspor	h	4-1	Pinto 2 (1p), Batalla 2
23/09	Elazığspor	a	1-1	Pinto (p)
29/09	Gaziantepspor	h	1-1	Šesták
07/10	Sivasspor	a	2-2	Okan, Belluschi
20/10	Fenerbahçe	h	1-1	og (Serdar)
28/10	Trabzonspor	a	1-0	Batalla
05/11	Kasımpaşa	h	1-2	Batalla
09/11	Beşiktaş	h	3-3	Šesták, İbrahim, Batalla
18/11	Mersin	h	3-0	Ferhat, N'Diaye (p), Belluschi (p)
24/11	Antalyaspor	h	1-1	Ferhat
01/12	Akhisar	a	2-2	Šesták, Gökçek Vederson
08/12	Orduspor	h	1-0	Šesták
14/12	Eskişehirspor	a	2-2	Belluschi, Ferhat
23/12	Gençlerbirliği	h	0-0	

2013

19/01	Kayserispor	h	2-1	Pinto, Belluschi
26/01	İstanbul BB	a	1-4	Batalla
02/02	Galatasaray	h	1-1	Pinto
09/02	Karabükspor	a	3-0	Tuncay, Chrétien, Batalla
17/02	Elazığspor	h	1-2	Batalla
22/02	Gaziantepspor	a	1-2	Batalla
03/03	Sivasspor	h	1-0	Batalla
10/03	Fenerbahçe	a	1-4	Šesták
15/03	Trabzonspor	h	3-2	Batalla 2, Şener
31/03	Kasımpaşa	a	0-2	
08/04	Beşiktaş	h	3-0	Pinto, Batalla, Ferhat
13/04	Mersin	h	1-0	Pinto
21/04	Antalyaspor	a	1-0	Batalla
27/04	Akhisar	h	1-1	Batalla
04/05	Orduspor	a	4-2	Pinto, Belluschi, Šesták 2
13/05	Eskişehirspor	h	0-0	
19/05	Gençlerbirliği	a	2-2	Ferhat, Murat

No	Name	Nat	DoB	Pos	Aps	(s)	Gls
66	Adem Koçak		01/09/83	M	1	(1)	
19	Ibrahim "Teteh" Bangura	SLE	27/12/89	M	2	(8)	
52	Barış Örücü		10/05/92	D		(1)	
10	Pablo Batalla	ARG	16/01/84	M	32	(1)	15
2	Aziz Behiç	AUS	16/12/90	D		(1)	
5	Fernando Belluschi	ITA	10/09/83	M	28	(2)	5
17	Scott Carson	ENG	03/09/85	G	29		
20	Michaël Chrétien	MAR	10/07/84	D	22	(5)	1
96	Doğanay Kılıç		08/06/96	M	1		
21	Maurice Edu	USA	18/04/86	M	10	(1)	
3	Anton Ferdinand	ENG	18/02/85	D	6	(1)	
39	Ferhat Kiraz		02/01/89	A	14	(7)	5
7	Petteri Forsell	FIN	16/10/90	M		(2)	
26	Furkan Soyalp		12/06/95	M		(1)	
6	Gökçek Vederson		22/07/81	D	25	(3)	1
42	Hakan Aslantaş		26/08/85	D	10	(2)	
14	Harun Tekin		17/06/89	G	5	(1)	
38	İbrahim Öztürk		21/06/81	D	32		1
91	İsmail Haktan Odabaşı		07/08/91	D	1	(1)	
55	Murat Yıldırım		18/05/87	M	11	(15)	1
35	Musa Çağıran		17/11/92	M	14	(11)	1
27	Mustafa Batuhan Altıntaş		14/03/96	A		(3)	
8	Alfred N'Diaye	FRA	06/03/90	M	13	(1)	1
14	Okan Deniz		20/05/94	M	3	(7)	1
33	Ozan İpek		10/10/86	M	5	(1)	
28	Ozan Tufan		23/03/95	M		(1)	
16	Ömer Erdoğan		05/03/77	D	11	(4)	1
11	Sebastián Pinto	CHI	05/02/86	A	24	(2)	9
23	Serdar Aziz		23/10/90	D	18	(1)	
22	Şener Özbayraklı		23/01/90	D	16		1
9	Stanislav Šesták	SVK	16/12/82	A	17	(12)	7
15	Taha Can Velioğlu		21/02/94	A	1		
4	Tuncay Şanlı		16/01/82	A	23	(4)	1

ELAZIĞSPOR

Coach – Bülent Uygun; (10/10/12) Yılmaz Vural
1967 • Atatürk (13,923) • elazigspor.org.tr

2012

18/08	Fenerbahçe	h	1-1	Tum
26/08	Trabzonspor	a	0-2	
01/09	Kasımpaşa	h	0-3	
17/09	Beşiktaş	a	0-3	
23/09	Bursaspor	h	1-1	Gökhan
30/09	Antalyaspor	a	0-4	
06/10	Akhisar	h	0-0	
20/10	Orduspor	a	2-2	Faubert, Köksal
26/10	Eskişehirspor	h	1-1	Göksu
04/11	Gençlerbirliği	a	2-1	Sedat, Sinan
11/11	Kayserispor	h	0-4	
17/11	İstanbul BB	a	1-1	Serdar
24/11	Galatasaray	h	0-1	
01/12	Karabükspor	a	1-0	Sinan
07/12	Mersin	h	1-0	Sinan
15/12	Gaziantepspor	h	0-0	
23/12	Sivasspor	a	1-3	Feindouno

2013

20/01	Fenerbahçe	a	2-2	Jervis, Köksal
27/01	Trabzonspor	h	3-1	Sinan, Köksal, Serdar
02/02	Kasımpaşa	a	0-0	
09/02	Beşiktaş	h	1-3	Görkem
17/02	Bursaspor	a	0-1	
23/02	Antalyaspor	h	2-1	Serdar, Mehmet
02/03	Akhisar	a	1-0	Serdar
10/03	Orduspor	h	1-0	Sane
15/03	Eskişehirspor	a	2-2	Köksal, Serdar
31/03	Gençlerbirliği	h	1-1	Sane
06/04	Kayserispor	a	1-4	Sinan
14/04	İstanbul BB	h	1-0	Volkan
19/04	Galatasaray	a	1-3	Serdar
27/04	Karabükspor	h	1-0	Sedat
05/05	Mersin	a	2-0	Sane 2
10/05	Gaziantepspor	a	1-1	Sinan
19/05	Sivasspor	h	0-0	

No	Name	Nat	DoB	Pos	Aps	(s)	Gls
22	Adem Alkaşi		14/04/84	D	27		
78	Ahmet Şahin		22/03/78	G		(1)	
40	Roland Alberg	NED	06/08/80	M		(2)	
48	Alper Kalemci		22/07/91	M		(2)	
10	Arif Şahin		22/12/85	M	1	(2)	
21	Aydın Karabulut		25/01/88	M	19	(5)	
20	Bülent Ertuğrul		17/09/78	M	15	(1)	
3	Caner Bulut		03/03/89	D		(1)	
34	Eren Aydın		16/01/82	D	3	(3)	
58	Fábio Bilica	BRA	14/01/79	D	31		
81	Julien Faubert	FRA	01/08/83	D	16		1
2	Pascal Feindouno	GUI	27/02/81	M	1	(9)	1
8	Gökhan Emreciksin		10/09/84	M	6	(2)	1
15	Göksu Türkdoğan		15/04/85	A	2	(4)	1
14	Görkem Görk		30/06/83	D	9	(2)	1
1	Vanja Iveša	CRO	21/07/77	G	34		
19	Jake Jervis	ENG	17/09/81	A	3	(1)	1
11	Köksal Yedek		17/01/85	M	34		4
50	Emir Kujovic	SWE	22/06/88	A	1	(2)	
6	Mehmet Çakır		04/01/84	M	3	(10)	1
71	Murat Akyüz		13/08/81	D	6		
23	Murat Kayalı		13/08/89	M	9	(6)	
16	Mustafa Sarp		05/11/80	M	9	(3)	
4	Orhan Ak		29/09/79	D	24	(1)	
31	Tidiane Sane	SEN	10/07/85	M	15	(2)	4
61	Sedat Bayrak		10/04/81	D	22	(2)	2
67	Serdar Gürler		14/09/91	A	16	(7)	6
39	Ivan Sesar	BIH	29/08/89	M	10	(4)	
26	Sezer Badur		20/06/84	M	11	(2)	
17	Sinan Kaloğlu		10/06/81	A	13	(8)	6
7	Sinan Özkan		22/03/85	A		(1)	
27	Hrvoje Spahija	CRO	23/03/88	D	1	(1)	
18	Hervé Tum	CMR	15/02/79	A	13		1
88	Volkan Yılmaz		01/09/87	M	1	(5)	1
9	Amr Zaki	EGY	01/04/83	A	5	(3)	
90	Marvin Zeegelaar	NED	12/08/90	M	14	(5)	

ESKİŞEHİRSPOR

Coach: Ersun Yanal
1965 • Atatürk (13,520) • eskisehirspor.org
Major honours
Turkish Cup (1) 1971

2012

17/08	Akhisar	h	0-1	
25/08	Orduspor	a	0-2	
31/08	Mersin	h	2-1	Kamara 2, Zengin
16/09	Gençlerbirliği	h	4-2	Dedê, Kamara, Necati, Tello
22/09	Kayserispor	a	2-3	Necati, Tello
30/09	İstanbul BB	h	1-0	Alper
06/10	Galatasaray	a	1-1	Zengin
21/10	Karabükspor	h	5-2	Necati, Kamara 2, Alper, Małecki
26/10	Elazığspor	a	1-1	Kamara
03/11	Gaziantepspor	h	4-0	Necati 2, Servet, Alper
09/11	Sivasspor	a	0-1	
17/11	Fenerbahçe	h	1-1	Necati (p)
26/11	Trabzonspor	a	3-0	Kamara, Necati, Servet
02/12	Kasımpaşa	h	2-2	Kamara, Burhan
07/12	Beşiktaş	a	2-2	Necati (p), Nuhiu
14/12	Bursaspor	h	2-2	Necati, Zengin
23/12	Antalyaspor	a	1-2	Nuhiu

2013

21/01	Akhisar	a	1-1	og (Uğur)
28/01	Orduspor	h	1-0	Necati (p)
03/02	Mersin	a	0-0	
09/02	Gençlerbirliği	a	2-0	Diego Ângelo, Necati
15/02	Kayserispor	h	0-3	
23/02	İstanbul BB	a	2-2	Akaminko, Zengin
02/03	Galatasaray	h	0-0	
10/03	Karabükspor	a	0-0	
15/03	Elazığspor	h	2-2	Kamara, Necati (p)
30/03	Gaziantepspor	a	0-0	
07/04	Sivasspor	h	2-1	Veysel, Kamara
14/04	Fenerbahçe	a	0-1	
22/04	Trabzonspor	h	0-1	
28/04	Kasımpaşa	a	2-2	Diego Ângelo 2
05/05	Beşiktaş	h	1-2	Özgür
13/05	Bursaspor	a	0-0	
19/05	Antalyaspor	h	3-1	Özgür 2, Kamara

No	Name	Nat	DoB	Pos	Aps	(s)	Gls
30	Jerry Akaminko	GHA	02/05/88	D	21	(3)	1
6	Alper Potuk		08/04/91	M	29	(1)	4
35	Aytaç Kara		28/03/93	M		(2)	
25	Ruud Boffin	BEL	05/11/87	G	33		
21	Burhan Eşer		01/01/85	M	2	(10)	1
99	Goran Čaušić	SRB	05/05/92	M	10	(3)	
4	Dedê	BRA	18/04/78	D	31		1
3	Diego Ângelo	BRA	17/02/86	D	32	(1)	3
2	Ediz Bahtiyaroğlu		02/01/86	D	1	(1)	
18	Erkut Şentürk		06/05/94	M		(2)	
50	Hürriyet Güçer		25/10/81	M	30		
15	Diomansy Kamara	SEN	08/11/80	A	28	(2)	11
33	Kayacan Erdoğan		21/03/88	G	1		
10	Patryk Małecki	POL	01/08/88	M	1	(4)	1
8	Mehmet Güven		30/07/87	M	8	(11)	
20	Necati Ateş		03/01/80	A	26	(1)	12
60	Atdhe Nuhiu	AUT	29/07/89	A	6	(22)	2
60	Özgür Çek		03/01/91	M	4	(10)	3
17	Serol Demirhan		05/12/88	M	3	(3)	
76	Servet Çetin		17/03/81	D	26		2
1	Sezgin Coşkun		23/08/84	D	1		
77	Tarık Çamdal		24/03/91	M	4	(4)	
14	Rodrigo Tello	CHI	14/10/79	M	24	(3)	2
88	Veysel Sarı		25/07/88	D	25	(6)	1
10	Erkan Zengin	SWE	05/08/85	M	28	(2)	4

FENERBAHÇE SK

Coach: Aykut Kocaman
1907 • Şükrü Saracoğlu (50,509) • fenerbahce.org
Major honours
Turkish League (18) 1959, 1961, 1964, 1965, 1968, 1970, 1974, 1975, 1978, 1983, 1985, 1989, 1996, 2001, 2004, 2005, 2007, 2011;
Turkish Cup (6) 1968, 1974, 1979, 1983, 2012, 2013

2012

18/08	Elazığspor	a	1-1	Kuyt
25/08	Gaziantepspor	h	3-0	Mehmet Topal, Sow, Kuyt
02/09	Sivasspor	a	0-0	
16/09	Mersin	h	2-1	Mehmet Topal, Cristian
24/09	Trabzonspor	h	0-0	
29/09	Kasımpaşa	a	0-2	
07/10	Beşiktaş	h	3-0	Sow, Gökhan 2
20/10	Bursaspor	a	1-1	Sow
29/10	Antalyaspor	h	1-3	Sow
03/11	Akhisar	a	2-1	Kuyt, Selçuk
11/11	Orduspor	h	2-1	Sow, Sezer
17/11	Eskişehirspor	a	1-1	Sow
25/11	Gençlerbirliği	h	4-1	Sow, Raul Meireles, Kuyt, Sezer
02/12	Kayserispor	a	1-1	Kuyt
09/12	İstanbul BB	h	2-1	Cristian, Bekir
16/12	Galatasaray	a	1-2	Hasan Ali
22/12	Karabükspor	h	1-3	Kuyt

2013

20/01	Elazığspor	h	2-2	Sow, Mehmet Topal
26/01	Gaziantepspor	a	2-1	Sow, Semih
03/02	Sivasspor	h	1-2	Webó
10/02	Mersin	a	1-0	Webó
17/02	Trabzonspor	a	3-0	og (Bamba), Cristian, Gökhan
24/02	Kasımpaşa	h	3-1	Webó, Emre (p), Sow
03/03	Beşiktaş	a	2-3	Sow 2
10/03	Bursaspor	h	4-1	Emre, Raul Meireles, Kuyt, Sow
17/03	Antalyaspor	a	2-1	Salih, Sow
31/03	Akhisar	h	2-0	Webó, Sow
07/04	Orduspor	a	2-0	Salih 2
14/04	Eskişehirspor	h	1-0	Cristian
21/04	Gençlerbirliği	a	0-2	
28/04	Kayserispor	h	2-1	Kuyt, Cristian
05/05	İstanbul BB	a	0-2	
12/05	Galatasaray	h	2-1	Webó 2
18/05	Karabükspor	a	2-3	Mehmet Topuz, Webó

No	Name	Nat	DoB	Pos	Aps	(s)	Gls
10	Alex	BRA	14/09/77	M	5		
4	Bekir Irtegün		20/04/84	D	25	(1)	1
28	Beykan Şimşek		01/01/95	A		(1)	
15	Henri Bienvenu	CMR	05/07/88	A		(2)	
88	Caner Erkin		04/10/88	D	13	(17)	
16	Cristian	BRA	25/06/83	M	23	(7)	5
2	Egemen Korkmaz		03/11/82	D	18	(2)	
25	Emre Belözoğlu		07/09/80	M	10		2
22	Gökhan Gönül		04/01/85	D	27		3
3	Hasan Ali Kaldırım		09/12/89	D	25		1
27	Miloš Krasić	SRB	01/11/84	M	7	(7)	
11	Dirk Kuyt	NED	22/07/80	A	29	(2)	8
5	Mehmet Topal		03/03/86	M	25	(3)	3
38	Mehmet Topuz		07/09/83	M	12	(10)	1
34	Mert Günok		01/03/89	G	6		
67	Orhan Şam		01/06/86	D	4	(1)	
14	Raul Meireles	POR	17/03/83	M	22		2
17	Recep Niyaz		01/01/95	M		(2)	
48	Salih Uçan		06/01/94	M	4	(6)	3
21	Selçuk Şahin		31/01/81	M	7	(6)	1
23	Semih Şentürk		29/04/83	A	1	(16)	1
53	Serdar Kesimal		24/01/89	D	5		
20	Sezer Öztürk		03/11/85	M	1	(8)	2
7	Moussa Sow	SEN	19/01/86	A	28	(3)	15
9	Miroslav Stoch	SVK	19/10/89	A	9	(7)	
1	Volkan Demirel		27/10/81	G	28		
99	Pierre Webó	CMR	20/01/82	A	13		7
6	Joseph Yobo	NGA	06/09/80	D	20		
33	Reto Ziegler	SUI	16/01/86	D	7		

GALATASARAY AŞ

Coach: Fatih Terim
1905 • Türk Telecom Arena (52,600) • galatasaray.org
Major honours
UEFA Cup (1) 2000;
UEFA Super Cup (1) 2000;
Turkish League (19) 1962, 1963, 1969, 1971, 1972,
1973, 1987, 1988, 1993, 1994, 1997, 1998, 1999, 2000,
2002, 2006, 2008, 2012, 2013;
Turkish Cup (14) 1963, 1964, 1965, 1966, 1973, 1976,
1982, 1985, 1991, 1993, 1996, 1999, 2000, 2005

2012
20/08	Kasımpaşa	h	2-1	Umut 2
26/08	Beşiktaş	a	3-3	Elmander, Umut, Selçuk (p)
02/09	Bursaspor	h	3-2	Umut, og (Musa), Burak
15/09	Antalyaspor	a	4-0	Elmander, Amrabat, Burak, Umut
23/09	Akhisar	h	3-0	Burak 2, Sercan
28/09	Orduspor	a	0-2	
06/10	Eskişehirspor	h	1-1	Burak
19/10	Gençlerbirliği	a	3-3	Umut, Elmander, Hakan
27/10	Kayserispor	h	3-0	Umut, Cris, Burak
02/11	İstanbul BB	a	3-1	Umut, Selçuk, og (Zayatte)
11/11	Mersin	a	1-1	Umut
16/11	Karabükspor	h	1-3	Burak
24/11	Elazığspor	h	1-0	Yekta
30/11	Gaziantepspor	h	1-1	Burak
08/12	Sivasspor	a	3-1	Umut 2, Burak
16/12	Fenerbahçe	h	2-1	og (Bekir), Selçuk
23/12	Trabzonspor	a	0-0	

2013
18/01	Kasımpaşa	a	1-2	Elmander
27/01	Beşiktaş	h	2-1	Emre, Riera
02/02	Bursaspor	a	1-1	Umut
10/02	Antalyaspor	h	2-0	Burak 2
15/02	Akhisar	a	2-1	Drogba, Burak
25/02	Orduspor	h	4-2	Sneijder, Burak 2, Selçuk
02/03	Eskişehirspor	a	0-0	
08/03	Gençlerbirliği	h	0-1	
17/03	Kayserispor	a	3-1	Sneijder, Burak 2
30/03	İstanbul BB	h	2-0	Burak 2
06/04	Mersin	h	3-1	Felipe Melo, Drogba 2
13/04	Karabükspor	a	1-0	Sneijder
19/04	Elazığspor	h	3-1	Burak, Drogba 2
28/04	Gaziantepspor	a	1-0	Burak
05/05	Sivasspor	h	4-2	Selçuk 2, Burak 2
12/05	Fenerbahçe	a	1-2	Burak
18/05	Trabzonspor	h	2-0	Riera, Burak

No	Name	Nat	DoB	Pos	Aps	(s)	Gls
53	Nordin Amrabat	MAR	31/03/87	A	13	(17)	1
7	Aydın Yılmaz		29/01/88	A	3	(14)	
17	Burak Yılmaz		15/07/85	A	27	(3)	24
6	Ceyhun Gülselam		25/12/87	M		(1)	
3	Cris	BRA	03/06/77	D	9	(1)	1
33	Çağlar Birinci		02/10/85	D		(1)	
12	Didier Drogba	CIV	11/03/78	A	11	(2)	5
27	Emmanuel Eboué	CIV	04/06/83	D	26	(2)	
9	Johan Elmander	SWE	27/05/81	A	11	(5)	4
52	Emre Çolak		20/05/91	M	14	(10)	1
50	Engin Baytar		11/07/83	M	2	(5)	
67	Eray İşcan		19/07/91	G		(1)	
10	Felipe Melo	BRA	26/06/83	M	24	(2)	1
5	Gökhan Zan		07/09/81	D	9	(1)	
22	Hakan Balta		23/03/83	D	12	(1)	1
4	Hamit Altıntop		08/12/82	M	29		
25	Fernando Muslera	URU	16/06/86	G	33		
13	Dany Nounkeu	CMR	11/04/86	D	24		
11	Albert Riera	ESP	15/04/82	D	22	(4)	2
55	Sabri Sarıoğlu		26/07/84	D	8	(8)	
8	Selçuk İnan		10/02/85	M	31		6
26	Semih Kaya		24/02/91	D	24	(1)	
90	Sercan Yıldırım		05/04/90	A	1	(2)	1
14	Wesley Sneijder	NED	09/06/84	M	10	(2)	3
86	Ufuk Ceylan		23/06/86	G	1		
30	Tomáš Ujfaluši	CZE	24/03/78	D	2		
19	Umut Bulut		15/03/83	A	17	(10)	12
35	Yekta Kurtuluş		11/12/85	M	11	(7)	1

GAZİANTEPSPOR

Coach: Hikmet Karaman; (08/02/13) Bülent Uygun
1969 • Kamil Ocak (16,981) • gaziantepspor.org.tr

2012
18/08	Sivasspor	h	0-1	
25/08	Fenerbahçe	a	0-3	
02/09	Trabzonspor	h	1-0	Ibričić (p)
15/09	Kasımpaşa	a	0-3	
22/09	Beşiktaş	h	3-2	Sosa, Cenk (p), Orhan
29/09	Bursaspor	a	1-1	Ekrem
05/10	Antalyaspor	h	0-1	
12/10	Akhisar	a	0-0	
28/10	Orduspor	h	3-0	Medunjanin 2, Sosa
03/11	Eskişehirspor	a	0-4	
11/11	Gençlerbirliği	h	2-3	Serdar Özbayraktar, Muhammet
18/11	Kayserispor	a	1-1	Cenk
25/11	İstanbul BB	h	2-1	Cenk, Kecojević
30/11	Galatasaray	a	1-1	Ibričić
08/12	Karabükspor	h	0-2	
15/12	Elazığspor	a	0-0	
23/12	Mersin	h	2-1	Turgut Doğan, Cenk

2013
19/01	Sivasspor	a	0-0	
26/01	Fenerbahçe	h	1-2	Šernas
03/02	Trabzonspor	a	1-4	Kouemaha
11/02	Kasımpaşa	a	2-1	Cenk, Šernas
16/02	Beşiktaş	h	1-1	Kouemaha
22/02	Bursaspor	a	2-1	Šernas, Cenk (p)
03/03	Antalyaspor	a	2-5	Serdar Kurtuluş, Kouemaha
09/03	Akhisar	h	2-2	Traoré, Wilton Figueiredo
17/03	Orduspor	a	3-2	Medunjanin, Šernas 2
30/03	Eskişehirspor	h	2-0	Medunjanin, Cenk
07/04	Gençlerbirliği	a	2-2	Turgut Doğan, Kouemaha
14/04	Kayserispor	h	0-1	
21/04	İstanbul BB	a	3-1	Kouemaha, Šernas, Traoré
28/04	Galatasaray	h	0-1	
05/05	Karabükspor	a	2-0	Cenk 2
10/05	Elazığspor	h	1-1	Bekir Ozan
17/05	Mersin	a	2-1	Turgut Doğan, Cenk

No	Name	Nat	DoB	Pos	Aps	(s)	Gls
8	Bekir Ozan Has		18/02/85	M	24	(5)	1
28	Gilles Binya	CMR	29/08/84	D	30		
23	Cenk Tosun		07/06/91	A	29	(3)	10
47	Ekrem Dağ	AUT	05/12/80	D	18	(3)	1
34	Eray Birniçan		20/07/88	G	1		
10	Senijad Ibričić	BIH	26/09/85	M	12	(1)	2
6	Ivan	BRA	18/01/82	D	2	(1)	
27	İbrahim Halil Keser		02/07/97	M		(1)	
20	İbrahim Halil Yaşar		21/01/94	M		(1)	
1	Žydrūnas Karčemarskas	LTU	24/05/83	G	25		
50	Ivan Kecojević	MNE	10/04/88	D	27	(2)	1
13	Kemal Tokat		25/04/89	M	12	(2)	
99	Dorge Kouemaha	CMR	28/06/83	A	7	(8)	5
91	Mahmut Bezgin		01/03/86	G	8		
4	Haris Medunjanin	BIH	08/03/85	M	28	(3)	4
11	Muhammet Demir		10/01/92	A	5	(5)	1
77	Oktay Delibalta		27/10/85	M	5	(8)	
61	Orhan Gülle		15/01/92	M	8	(5)	1
55	Yasin Pehlivan	AUT	05/01/89	M	10	(4)	
16	Serdar Kurtuluş		23/07/87	M	32		1
15	Serdar Özbayraktar		22/11/81	M	11	(6)	1
18	Ismael Sosa	ARG	18/01/87	M	7	(6)	2
35	Süleyman Özdamar		25/02/93	D	1		
3	Şenol Can		01/01/92	D	29	(3)	
9	Darvydas Šernas	LTU	22/07/84	A	16		6
81	Taşkın Çalış		25/07/93	M	10	(10)	
12	Abdou Razack Traoré	BFA	28/12/88	M	2	(9)	2
93	Tufan Kelleci		24/10/93	D		(2)	
7	Turgut Doğan Şahin		02/02/88	A	14	(10)	4
90	Wilton Figueiredo	BRA	17/03/82	A	1	(2)	1

GENÇLERBİRLİĞİ SK

Coach: Fuat Çapa
1923 • 19 Mayıs (19,209) • genclerbirligi.org.tr
Major honours
Turkish Cup (2) 1987, 2001

2012
20/08	Antalyaspor	h	3-1	Oktay, Zec 2
25/08	Akhisar	a	0-0	
31/08	Orduspor	h	1-1	Hurşut
16/09	Eskişehirspor	a	2-4	Özgür, Lekić
22/09	Mersin	a	1-1	Kulusić
30/09	Kayserispor	h	4-0	Petrović, Zec (p), Azofeifa, Durmaz
06/10	İstanbul BB	a	2-0	Aykut, Hurşut
19/10	Galatasaray	h	3-3	Azofeifa, Aykut, Durmaz
28/10	Karabükspor	a	0-0	
04/11	Elazığspor	h	1-2	Aykut
11/11	Gaziantepspor	a	3-2	Petrović, Azofeifa, Tošić
17/11	Sivasspor	h	1-1	Hurşut (p)
25/11	Fenerbahçe	a	1-4	Aykut
03/12	Trabzonspor	h	0-4	
08/12	Kasımpaşa	a	2-2	Durmaz, Lekić
15/12	Beşiktaş	h	1-1	Kulusić
23/12	Bursaspor	a	0-0	

2013
20/01	Antalyaspor	a	5-3	Vleminckx 4, og (Musa)
26/01	Akhisar	h	1-0	Kulusić
03/02	Orduspor	a	1-2	Lekić
09/02	Eskişehirspor	h	0-2	
17/02	Mersin	h	3-1	Vleminckx, Durmaz, Zec
24/02	Kayserispor	a	0-1	
01/03	İstanbul BB	h	0-0	
08/03	Galatasaray	a	1-0	Vleminckx
16/03	Karabükspor	h	2-1	Petrović, Vleminckx
31/03	Elazığspor	a	1-1	Kulusić
07/04	Gaziantepspor	h	2-2	Durmaz, Vleminckx
12/04	Sivasspor	a	1-1	Zec
21/04	Fenerbahçe	h	2-0	Aykut, Vleminckx
27/04	Trabzonspor	a	0-2	
03/05	Kasımpaşa	h	0-0	
11/05	Beşiktaş	a	0-3	
19/05	Bursaspor	h	2-2	Özgür, Zec

No	Name	Nat	DoB	Pos	Aps	(s)	Gls
94	Ahmet Çalık		26/02/94	D	5		
99	Artun Akçakın		06/05/93	A	5	(10)	
4	Aykut Demir		22/10/88	D	31		5
8	Randall Azofeifa	CRC	30/12/84	M	27	(1)	3
40	Cem Can		01/04/81	M	30		
20	Debatik Curri	ALB	28/12/83	D	6	(7)	
5	Doğa Kaya		30/06/84	M	1	(6)	
21	Jimmy Durmaz	SWE	22/03/89	M	22	(7)	5
12	Ekigho Ehiosun	NGA	25/06/90	A	1	(11)	
35	Ferhat Kaplan		07/01/89	G	2		
17	Hurşut Meriç		31/07/83	M	25	(3)	3
19	Kerim Zengin		13/04/85	D	1	(1)	
6	Ante Kulusić	CRO	06/06/86	D	24	(1)	4
3	Dejan Lekić	SRB	07/06/85	A	10	(11)	3
7	Mehmet Kara		24/01/83	M	4	(3)	
59	Mehmet Sedef		05/08/87	D	8	(3)	
14	Mustafa Kayabaşı		15/03/88	A		(2)	
24	Oktay Delibalta		27/10/85	M	21	(9)	2
58	Özkan Karabulut		16/01/91	G	3	(1)	
11	Radosav Petrović	SRB	08/03/89	M	25	(2)	3
10	Ramazan Köse		12/05/88	G	29		
16	Serkan Kurtuluş		01/01/90	D	12	(2)	
30	Tayfur Bingöl		11/01/93	M		(1)	
77	Nemanja Tomić	SRB	21/01/88	M	5	(3)	
3	Duško Delibala	SRB	19/01/85	D	33		1
18	Björn Vleminckx	BEL	01/12/85	A	16		9
93	Yusuf Emre Gültekin		12/03/93	A		(1)	
10	Ermin Zec	BIH	18/02/88	A	26	(2)	6

İSTANBUL BB SK

Coach: Carlos Carvalhal (POR);
(14/11/12) Bülent Korkmaz
1990 • Atatürk Olimpiyat (76,092) • istanbulbbsk.org

2012

19/08	Beşiktaş	h	1-1	Cihan
26/08	Bursaspor	a	1-0	Webó
01/09	Antalyaspor	h	0-1	
16/09	Akhisar belediye	a	4-0	Holmén, Webó 3
22/09	Orduspor	h	1-1	Webó
30/09	Eskişehirspor	a	0-1	
06/10	Gençlerbirliği	h	0-2	
23/10	Kayserispor	a	1-0	Holmén
27/10	Mersin	a	0-2	
02/11	Galatasaray	h	1-3	Turgay
10/11	Karabükspor	a	1-3	Webó
17/11	Elazığspor	h	1-1	Ömer Can
25/11	Gaziantepspor	a	1-2	Gökhan
02/12	Sivasspor	h	2-0	Holmén, Viśća
09/12	Fenerbahçe	a	1-2	Webó
16/12	Trabzonspor	h	2-1	Ekrem, Webó
22/12	Kasımpaşa	a	2-0	Webó (p), Holmén

2013

19/01	Beşiktaş	a	2-2	Holmén, Doka Madureira
26/01	Bursaspor	h	4-1	Doka Madureira, Holmén, Ekrem, Viśća
02/02	Antalyaspor	a	0-1	
09/02	Akhisar	h	0-2	
17/02	Orduspor	a	2-2	Viśća, Ömer Can
23/02	Eskişehirspor	h	2-2	Holmén 2 (1p)
01/03	Gençlerbirliği	a	0-0	
09/03	Kayserispor	h	0-0	
16/03	Mersin	h	4-2	Zenke, Wellington, Mahmut, Holmén
30/03	Galatasaray	a	0-2	
06/04	Karabükspor	h	2-2	Doka Madureira, Holmén
14/04	Elazığspor	a	0-1	
21/04	Gaziantepspor	h	1-3	Holmén
27/04	Sivasspor	a	1-4	Doka Madureira
05/05	Fenerbahçe	h	2-0	Ömer Can, og (Mehmet Topuz)
13/05	Trabzonspor	a	3-4	Doka Madureira, Zayatte, Zenke
18/05	Kasımpaşa	h	1-2	Tevfik

No	Name	Nat	DoB	Pos	Aps	(s)	Gls
18	André Geraldes	POR	02/05/81	D	30		
2	Can Arat		21/01/84	D	18	(2)	
67	Cenk Şahin		22/09/94	M		(5)	
20	Cihan Haspolatlı		04/01/80	M	20	(3)	1
22	Doka Madureira	BRA	11/02/84	A	20	(5)	5
1	Eduardo	POR	19/09/82	G	33		
6	Efe İnanç		24/03/90	M	11	(8)	
17	Ekrem Ekşioğlu		15/01/78	D	33		2
9	Gökhan Süzen		12/07/87	D	5	(7)	1
23	Samuel Holmén	SWE	28/06/84	M	33		11
5	Mahmut Tekdemir		20/01/88	D	23	(5)	1
3	Metin Depe		10/01/81	D	27		
61	Oğuzhan Bahadır		24/12/79	G	1		
14	Ömer Can Sokullu		14/08/88	M	10	(11)	3
53	Rızvan Şahin		30/10/81	D	5		
4	Serhat Gülpınar		01/01/79	M	1	(2)	
10	Taner Yalçın		18/02/90	M		(5)	
34	Tayfun Pektürk		13/05/88	M	3	(2)	
7	Tevfik Köse		12/07/88	A	7	(8)	1
19	Turgay Bahadır		15/01/84	M	2	(6)	1
13	Edin Viśća	BIH	17/02/90	M	14	(14)	3
81	Pierre Webó	CMR	20/01/82	A	18		9
88	Wellington	BRA	23/07/85	A	12	(9)	1
86	Kamil Zayatte	GUI	07/03/85	D	22	(3)	1
8	Zeki Korkmaz		01/09/88	M	15	(2)	
32	Simon Zenke	NGA	24/12/88	A	11	(4)	2

KARDEMİR KARABÜKSPOR

Coach: Michael Skibbe (GER); (07/11/12) Mesut
Bakkal; (06/05/13) Suat Sarıcan
1969 • Necmettin Şeyhoğlu (7,593) •
kardemirkarabukspor.org.tr

2012

17/08	Trabzonspor	h	1-1	Shelton
24/08	Kasımpaşa	a	1-2	Cernat
01/08	Beşiktaş	h	0-3	
15/09	Bursaspor	a	1-4	İlhan
21/09	Antalyaspor	h	1-0	Ahmet İlhan
29/09	Akhisar	a	3-1	Cernat, LuaLua, İlhan
05/10	Orduspor	h	1-1	Shelton
21/10	Eskişehirspor	a	2-5	İlhan, Ahmet İlhan
28/10	Gençlerbirliği	h	1-0	
03/11	Kayserispor	a	0-3	
10/11	İstanbul BB	h	3-1	Cernat (p), İlhan, LuaLua
16/11	Galatasaray	a	3-1	Ahmet İlhan, Mehmet, İlhan
23/11	Mersin	a	1-2	İlhan
01/12	Elazığspor	h	0-1	
08/12	Gaziantepspor	a	2-0	Deumi, LuaLua
16/12	Sivasspor	h	1-0	Shelton
22/12	Fenerbahçe	a	3-1	İlhan, LuaLua 2

2013

20/01	Trabzonspor	a	3-1	Hakan Özmert, İlhan (p), Ahmet İlhan
25/01	Kasımpaşa	h	0-3	
01/02	Beşiktaş	a	2-2	Ahmet İlhan, LuaLua
09/02	Bursaspor	h	0-3	
16/02	Antalyaspor	a	0-0	
24/02	Akhisar	h	0-0	
02/03	Orduspor	a	2-3	İlhan, LuaLua
10/03	Eskişehirspor	h	0-0	
16/03	Gençlerbirliği	a	1-2	Shelton
01/04	Kayserispor	h	3-1	İlhan, Shelton, LuaLua
06/04	İstanbul BB	a	2-2	Ahmet İlhan, Gökhan
13/04	Galatasaray	h	0-1	
20/04	Mersin	h	1-0	LuaLua
27/04	Elazığspor	a	0-1	
05/05	Gaziantepspor	h	0-2	
13/05	Sivasspor	a	1-2	Gökhan
18/05	Fenerbahçe	h	3-2	LuaLua 2, Ahmet İlhan

No	Name	Nat	DoB	Pos	Aps	(s)	Gls
1	Abdülaziz Demircan		05/02/91	G		(1)	
9	Ahmet İlhan Özek		01/01/88	A	24	(3)	7
17	Anıl Karaer		04/07/88	D	7	(2)	
11	Aybars Garhan		12/05/91	A		(2)	
78	Bertül Kocabaş		15/02/92	A	1	(4)	
8	Bilal Kısa		22/06/83	M	3	(2)	
5	Birol Hikmet		24/03/82	M	20	(7)	
35	Bora Körk		09/06/80	G	12		
10	Florin Cernat	ROU	10/03/80	M	9	(5)	3
71	Ceyhun Yazar		16/05/92	A		(1)	
12	Armand Deumi	CMR	12/03/79	D	21	(1)	1
2	Erdem Özgenç		22/08/84	D	25	(2)	
99	Gökhan Ünal		23/07/82	A	5	(7)	2
14	Güven Varol		02/06/81	M	3	(1)	
70	Hakan Özmert		03/06/85	M	5	(5)	1
68	Hakan Söyler		06/04/83	M	10	(7)	
39	Jugurtha Hamroun	ALG	27/01/89	M	9	(11)	
23	İlhan Parlak		18/01/87	A	30	(3)	10
86	İshak Doğan		09/06/90	D	7	(6)	
81	Sanel Jahić	BIH	10/12/81	D	6	(1)	
6	Kağan Söylemezgiller		04/03/88	M	15	(5)	
32	Lomana LuaLua	COD	28/12/80	A	26	(4)	11
25	Larrys Mabiala	COD	08/10/87	D	29		
58	Mehmet Yıldız		14/09/81	A	9	(1)	1
61	Muhammet Özdin		10/09/78	M	5		
30	Selim Teber		07/03/81	M	2	(6)	
20	Ante Serić	CRO	15/01/79	D	25	(1)	
21	Luton Shelton	JAM	11/11/85	A	12	(7)	5
19	Vjekoslav Tomić	CRO	19/07/83	G	22	(1)	
3	Uğur Uçar		05/04/87	D	4		
90	Umut Sözen		27/01/90	M		(2)	
4	Yiğit İncedemir		09/03/85	M	28		

KASIMPAŞA SK

Coach: Metin Diyadin; (25/09/12) (Fuat Kılıç);
(10/10/12) Shota Arveladze (GEO)
1921 • Recep Tayyip Erdoğan (14,234) •
kasimpasaspor.org.tr

2012

20/08	Galatasaray	a	1-2	İlhan
24/08	Karabükspor	h	2-1	Hakan, Hüseyin
01/09	Elazığspor	a	3-0	Uche 3 (1p)
15/09	Gaziantepspor	h	3-0	Özer, Uche, Pintos
23/09	Sivasspor	a	0-1	
29/09	Fenerbahçe	h	2-0	Uche, Hüseyin
05/10	Trabzonspor	a	0-1	
21/10	Mersin	h	2-2	Viudez, Adem
26/10	Beşiktaş	h	1-3	Özer
05/11	Bursaspor	a	0-1	Özer 2 (1p)
10/11	Antalyaspor	h	1-1	Uche (p)
18/11	Akhisar	a	2-0	Özer, Djalma
24/11	Orduspor	h	1-1	Uche
02/12	Eskişehirspor	a	2-2	Uche, Adem
08/12	Gençlerbirliği	h	2-2	Uche, Yalçın
17/12	Kayserispor	a	0-1	
22/12	İstanbul BB	h	0-2	

2013

18/01	Galatasaray	h	2-1	Ibričić, Viudez
25/01	Karabükspor	a	3-0	Viudez, Halil, Uche
02/02	Elazığspor	h	0-0	
11/02	Gaziantepspor	a	1-2	Uche (p)
18/02	Sivasspor	h	1-0	Uche
24/02	Fenerbahçe	a	1-3	Uche (p)
03/03	Trabzonspor	h	2-0	Viudez, Uche
10/03	Mersin	a	1-1	Uche
16/03	Beşiktaş	a	3-1	Viudez, Djalma, Halil
31/03	Bursaspor	h	2-0	Ibričić, Uche
05/04	Antalyaspor	a	2-3	Özer, Uche
14/04	Akhisar	h	0-0	
20/04	Orduspor	a	2-0	Uche 2
28/04	Eskişehirspor	h	1-2	Ibričić
05/05	Gençlerbirliği	a	0-0	
10/05	Kayserispor	h	1-2	Ibričić
18/05	İstanbul BB	a	2-1	Djalma, Halil

No	Name	Nat	DoB	Pos	Aps	(s)	Gls
61	Abdurrahman Dereli		15/02/81	D	28		
10	Adem Büyük		30/08/87	A	10	(16)	2
6	Ali Bilgin		17/02/81	A		(6)	
22	Barış Başdaş		17/01/90	D	13	(2)	
14	Kafoumba Coulibaly	CIV	26/10/85	M	1		
14	Nikolay Dimitrov	BUL	15/10/87	M	1	(1)	
30	Djalma	ANG	30/05/87	A	19	(3)	3
49	Elyasa Süme		13/08/83	D	24		
93	Erhan Kartal		01/03/93	D	2	(1)	
24	Fabian Ernst	GER	30/05/79	M	30		
33	Matías Fritzler	ARG	23/08/86	M	5	(4)	
23	Santiago García	URU	14/09/90	A		(1)	
70	Hakan Özmert		03/06/85	M	8	(2)	1
7	Halil Çolak		29/01/88	A	3	(13)	3
31	Hüseyin Kala		05/05/87	M	5	(9)	2
28	Senijad Ibričić	BIH	26/09/85	M	12	(2)	4
4	İlhan Eker		01/03/83	D	8	(5)	1
15	Andreas Isaksson	SWE	03/10/81	G	34		
20	Kerem Şeras		01/01/84	M	18	(7)	
18	Özer Hurmacı		20/11/86	M	27		6
21	Pablo Pintos	URU	01/07/87	D		(7)	1
5	Sancak Kaplan		25/05/82	D	30		
8	Georgi Sarmov	BUL	07/09/85	M	14	(8)	
17	Şahin Aygüneş		01/10/90	A		(2)	
9	Kalu Uche	NGA	15/11/82	A	34		19
19	Tabaré Viudez	URU	08/09/89	A	17	(6)	5
2	Yalçın Ayhan		01/05/82	D	31		1

KAYSERİSPOR

Coach: Shota Arveladze (GEO);
(15/10/12) Robert Prosinečki (CRO)
1966 • Kadir Has (32,864) • kayserispor.org.tr
Major honours
Turkish Cup (1) 2008

2012

19/08	Bursaspor	h	0-1	
27/00	Antalyaspor	a	0-3	
01/09	Akhisar	h	1-1	og (Sertan)
17/09	Orduspor	a	2-3	og (Miguel Garcia), Biseswar
22/09	Eskişehirspor	h	3-2	Bobô 2, Mouche
30/09	Gençlerbirliği	a	0-4	
07/10	Mersin	a	2-1	Cleyton, Steinsson
23/10	İstanbul BB	h	0-1	
27/10	Galatasaray	a	0-3	
03/11	Karabükspor	h	3-0	Sefa, Bobô 2
11/11	Elazığspor	a	4-0	Sefa, Bobô 2 (1p), Cleyton
18/11	Gaziantepspor	h	1-1	Sefa
25/11	Sivasspor	a	2-4	Bobô, Cleyton
02/12	Fenerbahçe	h	1-1	Bobô
09/12	Trabzonspor	a	1-1	Salih
17/12	Kasımpaşa	h	1-0	Mouche
21/12	Beşiktaş	a	1-3	Mouche

2013

18/01	Bursaspor	a	1-2	Bobô
27/01	Antalyaspor	h	2-0	Sefa, Bobô
01/02	Akhisar	a	2-1	Bobô, Mouche
10/02	Orduspor	h	0-0	
16/02	Eskişehirspor	a	3-0	Cleyton, Sefa 2
24/02	Gençlerbirliği	h	1-0	Salih
03/03	Mersin	h	2-1	Salih, Bobô
09/03	İstanbul BB	a	0-0	
17/03	Galatasaray	h	1-3	Biseswar
01/04	Karabükspor	a	1-3	Ceyhun
06/04	Elazığspor	h	4-1	Bobô, og (Fábio Bilica), Mouche 2
14/04	Gaziantepspor	a	1-0	Bobô
21/04	Sivasspor	h	1-1	Mouche
28/04	Fenerbahçe	a	1-2	Cleyton
04/05	Trabzonspor	h	2-1	Biseswar, Bobô
10/05	Kasımpaşa	a	2-1	Sefa, Bobô
19/05	Beşiktaş	h	2-0	Yener, Bobô

No	Name	Nat	DoB	Pos	Aps	(s)	Gls
8	Abdullah Durak		01/04/87	M	20	(3)	
4	Berkay Dabanlı		27/06/90	M	6	(2)	
21	Diego Biseswar	NED	08/03/88	M	6	(16)	3
9	Bobô	BRA	09/06/85	A	31		17
18	Franco Cángele	ARG	16/07/84	M		(5)	
54	Ceyhun Gülselam		25/12/87	M	16		1
19	Cleyton	BRA	08/03/83	M	29	(3)	5
13	Babacar Diop	SEN	21/10/93	A	2	(3)	
28	Engin Bekdemir		07/02/92	M	6	(6)	
27	Erdal Akdan		05/06/93	D	4	(1)	
5	Eren Güngör		02/04/88	D	20	(4)	
1	Ertuğrul Taşkıran		05/11/89	G	30		
3	Malik Fathi	GER	29/10/83	M	16		
12	Gökhan Değirmenci		21/03/89	G	4	(1)	
26	Kamil Ahmet Çörekçi		01/02/92	D	4	(2)	
6	Zurab Khizanishvili	GEO	06/10/81	D	29		
11	Emir Kujovic	SWE	22/06/88	A		(4)	
17	Pablo Mouche	ARG	11/10/87	A	27	(1)	7
25	Nurettin Kayaoğlu		08/01/92	D	3	(1)	
30	Okay Yokuşlu		09/03/94	M	6	(18)	
38	Ömer Bayram		27/07/91	M	11	(11)	
16	Cristian Riveros	PAR	16/10/82	M	30		
24	Salih Dursun		12/07/91	M	22	(3)	3
7	Sefa Yılmaz		14/02/90	M	24	(3)	7
33	Marko Simić	SRB	16/06/87	D	15		
2	Grétar Rafn Steinsson	ISL	09/01/82	D	9		1
14	Yener Arıca		28/02/92	M	4	(4)	1

MERSİN İDMAN YURDU

Coach: Nurullah Sağlam; (20/12/12) Giray Bulak;
(08/03/13) Hakan Kutlu
1925 • Tevfik Sırrı Gür (10,128) • mersinidmanyurdu.org.tr

2012

19/08	Orduspor	h	0-0	
25/08	Sivasspor	a	3-3	Culio, Stepanov, Ben Yahia
31/08	Eskişehirspor	h	1-3	Culio
16/09	Fenerbahçe	h	1-2	Ben Yahia
22/09	Gençlerbirliği	h	1-1	Mert Nobre
30/09	Trabzonspor	a	1-1	Mert Nobre
07/10	Kayserispor	h	1-2	Mert Nobre
21/10	Kasımpaşa	a	2-2	Mert Nobre, Mustafa Keçeli
27/10	İstanbul BB	h	2-0	Mert Nobre 2
04/11	Beşiktaş	a	0-3	
11/11	Galatasaray	h	1-1	Mert Nobre
18/11	Bursaspor	a	0-3	
23/11	Karabükspor	a	2-1	Mert Nobre (p), Stepanov
02/12	Antalyaspor	a	0-1	
07/12	Elazığspor	a	0-1	
15/12	Akhisar	h	2-1	Ömer Aysan, Mert Nobre
23/12	Gaziantepspor	a	1-2	Murat Ceylan

2013

21/01	Orduspor	a	1-1	Ozokwo
27/01	Sivasspor	h	3-0	Culio 2 (1p), Can
03/02	Eskişehirspor	a	0-0	
10/02	Fenerbahçe	a	0-1	
17/02	Gençlerbirliği	a	1-3	Culio (p)
23/02	Trabzonspor	h	0-1	
03/03	Kayserispor	a	1-2	Burhan
10/03	Kasımpaşa	h	1-1	Mert Nobre (p)
16/03	İstanbul BB	a	2-4	Mert Nobre 2
01/04	Beşiktaş	h	1-2	Mert Nobre
06/04	Galatasaray	a	1-3	Burhan
13/04	Bursaspor	h	0-1	
20/04	Karabükspor	a	0-1	
26/04	Antalyaspor	h	1-1	Stepanov
05/05	Elazığspor	h	0-2	
13/05	Akhisar	a	0-1	
17/05	Gaziantepspor	h	1-2	Ben Yahia

No	Name	Nat	DoB	Pos	Aps	(s)	Gls
25	Aydın Toscalı		14/08/80	D	8	(2)	
13	Wissem Ben Yahia	TUN	09/09/84	M	23	(5)	3
35	David Bičík	CZE	06/04/81	G	11		
3	Joseph Boum	CMR	26/09/89	D	15	(1)	
95	Burak Kalender		24/06/95	M		(1)	
21	Burhan Eşer		01/01/85	M	16		2
19	Can Erdem		08/06/87	A		(4)	1
38	Cengiz Biçer		11/12/87	G	1		
10	Emmanuel Culio	ARG	30/08/83	M	30	(1)	5
8	Danilo Bueno	BRA	07/12/83	M		(7)	
17	Erdal Kılıçaslan		23/08/84	A		(1)	
28	Eren Tozlu		27/12/90	A	4	(11)	
9	Ergin Keleş		01/01/87	A	3	(8)	
47	Jean Jacques Gosso	CIV	15/03/83	M	6		
55	Hakan Bayraktar		11/02/76	M	23	(3)	
15	Hasan Üçüncü		16/11/80	M		(1)	
6	Ivan	BRA	18/01/82	D	27		
24	Tanju Kayhan	AUT	22/07/89	D	7	(4)	
88	Raheem Lawal	NGA	04/05/90	M	6	(5)	
58	Mehmet Yıldız		14/09/81	A	3	(3)	
93	Mert Can		09/10/93	D		(1)	
11	Mert Nobre	BRA	06/11/80	A	30		13
30	Milan Mitrović	SRB	02/07/88	D	14		
4	Murat Ceylan		02/03/88	M	16	(3)	1
33	Murat Erdoğan		01/08/76	M	5	(8)	
23	Mustafa Keçeli		15/09/78	D	19	(1)	1
16	Mustafa Sarp		05/01/80	M	7	(4)	
20	Nurullah Kaya		20/07/86	A		(2)	
54	Orkun Uşak		05/11/80	G	5		
77	Ozan İpek		10/10/86	M	3	(1)	
7	Nduka Ozokwo	NGA	25/12/88	A	19	(10)	1
41	Ömer Aysan Barış		23/07/82	D	4	(3)	1
1	Özden Öngün		10/09/78	G	3		
87	Serkan Sanlı		02/04/87	D	25		
5	Milan Stepanov	SRB	02/04/83	D	24	(2)	3
12	Ibrahim Šehić	BIH	02/09/88	G	14		
18	Ibrahima Yattara	GUI	03/06/80	A	3	(1)	

ORDUSPOR

Coach: Héctor Cúper (ARG); (17/04/13) Cevat Güler
1967 • 19 Eylül (11,024) • orduspor.org.tr

2012

19/08	Mersin	a	0-0	
25/08	Eskişehirspor	h	2-0	David Barral, Hasan
31/08	Gençlerbirliği	a	1-1	og (Mehmet Sedef)
17/00	Kayserispor	h	3-2	David Barral, Hasan, Stancu
22/09	İstanbul BB	a	1-1	Stancu
28/09	Galatasaray	h	2-0	Hasan, Stancu
05/10	Karabükspor	a	1-1	Stancu
20/10	Elazığspor	h	2-2	Nizamettin, Stancu (p)
28/10	Gaziantepspor	a	0-3	
04/11	Sivasspor	h	2-0	Stancu (p), Hasan
11/11	Fenerbahçe	a	1-2	Şamil
19/11	Trabzonspor	a	1-2	Stancu
24/11	Kasımpaşa	a	1-1	Rovérsio
01/12	Beşiktaş	h	1-2	Hasan
08/12	Bursaspor	a	0-1	
16/12	Antalyaspor	h	1-1	Şamil
21/12	Akhisar	a	0-0	

2013

21/01	Mersin	h	1-1	Şamil
28/01	Eskişehirspor	a	0-1	
03/02	Gençlerbirliği	h	2-1	Umbides, Müslüm
10/02	Kayserispor	a	0-0	
17/02	İstanbul BB	a	2-2	Umbides, Yussuf
25/02	Galatasaray	h	2-4	og (Selçuk), Stancu (p)
02/03	Karabükspor	h	3-2	Ali 2, Şamil
10/03	Elazığspor	a	0-1	
17/03	Gaziantepspor	h	2-3	Stancu (p), Atila
30/03	Sivasspor	a	2-3	David Barral 2
07/04	Fenerbahçe	h	0-2	
12/04	Trabzonspor	a	0-1	
20/04	Kasımpaşa	h	0-2	
27/04	Beşiktaş	a	0-1	
04/05	Bursaspor	h	2-4	Ali, Stancu
11/05	Antalyaspor	a	0-1	
18/05	Akhisar	h	0-2	

No	Name	Nat	DoB	Pos	Aps	(s)	Gls
20	Abdülkadir Kayalı		30/01/91	M		(10)	
14	Agus	ESP	03/05/85	D	23	(1)	
8	Ali Çamdalı		22/02/84	M	32		3
21	Anıl Taşdemir		01/01/88	D	3	(3)	
89	Atila Turan		10/04/92	D	17	(4)	1
46	Burak Demireğen		03/08/93	M		(1)	
23	David Barral	ESP	10/05/83	A	16	(11)	4
92	Erdal Pekdemir		13/06/92	M		(1)	
85	Ferhat Çökmüş		14/02/85	D	17	(3)	
18	Ferhat Öztorun		08/05/87	D	13	(1)	
17	Fevzi Elmas		09/06/83	G	4		
32	Sašo Fornezzi	SVN	11/12/82	G	30		
10	Hasan Kabze		26/05/82	A	23	(2)	5
3	Hüsamettin Tut		01/01/91	D		(1)	
78	İbrahim Kaş		20/09/86	D	13	(2)	
75	Jaime Romero	ESP	31/07/90	M	7	(4)	
15	Miguel Garcia	POR	04/02/83	D	26		
26	Vicente Monje	ARG	22/06/81	M	13	(3)	
19	Murat Torun		27/05/94	M	1	(3)	
9	Müslüm Yelken		28/11/88	A	5	(10)	1
11	Nizamettin Çalışkan		20/03/87	M	29		1
5	Ömer Kulga	BEL	08/01/89	D	4		
84	Rovérsio	BRA	17/01/84	D	8	(3)	1
27	Selçuk Şahin		26/03/83	D	1	(1)	
9	Bogdan Stancu	ROU	28/06/87	A	28	(2)	10
6	Şamil Çinaz		08/03/86	D	23	(6)	4
22	Javier Umbides	ARG	09/02/82	M	28	(3)	2
25	Yasin Kocatepe	GER	08/09/91	A		(1)	
91	Yasin Öztop		25/05/91	D		(1)	
39	Yiğit Gökoğlan		05/06/89	M	2	(10)	
37	Ayila Yussuf	NGA	04/11/84	M	8		1

SİVASSPOR

Coach: Rıza Çalımbay
1967 • 4 Eylül (14,998) • sivasspor.org.tr

2012

18/08	Gaziantepspor	a	1-0	Pedriel
25/08	Mersin	h	3-3	Chahéchouche, Eneramo 2
02/09	Fenerbahçe	h	0-0	
16/09	Trabzonspor	a	0-1	
23/09	Kasımpaşa	h	1-0	Chahéchouche
01/10	Beşiktaş	a	1-0	Chahéchouche
07/10	Bursaspor	h	2-2	Navrátil, Eneramo
20/10	Antalyaspor	a	2-4	Grosicki (p), Eneramo
27/10	Akhisar	h	1-2	Ziya
04/11	Orduspor	a	0-2	
09/11	Eskişehirspor	h	1-0	Rajnoch
17/11	Gençlerbirliği	a	1-1	Pedriel
25/11	Kayserispor	h	4-2	Grosicki, Erman, Eneramo, Chahéchouche
02/12	İstanbul BB	a	0-2	
08/12	Galatasaray	h	1-3	Erman
16/12	Karabükspor	a	0-1	
23/12	Elazığspor	h	3-1	Erman 2, Mehmet

2013

19/01	Gaziantepspor	h	0-0	
27/01	Mersin	a	0-3	
03/02	Fenerbahçe	a	2-1	Eneramo 2
10/02	Trabzonspor	h	2-0	Hakan, Chahéchouche
18/02	Kasımpaşa	a	0-1	
23/02	Beşiktaş	h	0-1	
03/03	Bursaspor	a	0-1	
10/03	Antalyaspor	a	2-1	Rajnoch, Erman
17/03	Akhisar	a	1-2	Hakan
30/03	Orduspor	h	3-2	Eneramo, Hakan, Pedriel
07/04	Eskişehirspor	a	1-2	Piech
12/04	Gençlerbirliği	h	1-1	og (Ramazan)
21/04	Kayserispor	a	1-1	Mehmet
27/04	İstanbul BB	h	4-1	Adem, Eneramo 3
05/05	Galatasaray	a	2-4	Kadir, Özkara
13/05	Karabükspor	h	2-1	og (Uğur), Chahéchouche
19/05	Elazığspor	a	0-0	

No	Name	Nat	DoB	Pos	Aps	(s)	Gls
9	Abdülkadir Özgen		08/09/86	A		(7)	
66	Adem Koçak		01/09/83	M	17	(9)	1
29	Atilla Koca		16/07/80	G	1	(1)	
18	Milan Borjan	CAN	23/10/87	G	29		
92	Aatif Chahéchouche	FRA	02/07/86	M	26	(2)	6
16	Milan Černý	CZE	16/03/88	M	2	(3)	
20	Doğa Kaya		30/06/84	M	8		
14	Michael Eneramo	NGA	20/11/85	A	30		11
44	Erhan Güven		15/05/82	D	19	(5)	
11	Erman Kılıç		20/09/83	M	33		5
19	Jacques Faty	SEN	25/02/84	D	1		
10	Kamil Grosicki	POL	08/06/88	M	23	(5)	2
37	Hakan Arslan		18/07/88	D	11	(1)	3
58	Hayrettin Yerlikaya		13/08/81	D	2	(11)	
8	Kadir Bekmezci		05/07/85	M	30	(2)	1
1	Korcan Çelikay		31/12/87	G	4		
6	Mehmet Nas		20/11/79	M	5	(15)	2
4	Murat Akça		13/07/90	D	3	(2)	
21	Jakub Navrátil	CZR	01/02/84	D	30	(1)	1
17	Cihan Özkara	AZE	14/07/91	A		(3)	1
3	Ricardo Pedriel	BOL	19/01/87	A	15	(16)	3
22	Arkadiusz Piech	POL	07/06/85	A	3	(4)	1
33	Jan Rajnoch	CZE	30/09/81	D	18	(7)	2
99	Sercan Yıldırım		05/04/90	A		(5)	
67	Uğur Kavuk		11/09/79	D	22	(3)	
80	Ümit Kurt		02/05/91	M	11		
5	Ziya Erdal		05/01/88	D	31		1

TRABZONSPOR AŞ

Coach: Şenol Güneş; (28/01/13) Tolunay Kafkas
1967 • Hüseyin Avni Aker (24,169) • trabzonspor.org.tr

Major honours
Turkish League (6) 1976, 1977, 1979, 1980, 1981, 1984;
Turkish Cup (8) 1977, 1978, 1984, 1992, 1995, 2003, 2004, 2010

2012

17/08	Karabükspor	a	1-1	Volkan
26/08	Elazığspor	h	2-0	Vittek, Paulo Henrique
02/09	Gaziantepspor	a	0-1	
16/09	Sivasspor	h	1-0	Halil
24/09	Fenerbahçe	a	0-0	
30/09	Mersin	h	1-1	Soner
05/10	Kasımpaşa	h	1-0	Olcan
22/10	Beşiktaş	a	1-1	Sapara
28/10	Bursaspor	h	0-1	
05/11	Antalyaspor	a	1-2	Mierzejewski
10/11	Akhisar	h	3-1	Mierzejewski 2, Emerson
19/11	Orduspor	a	2-1	Janko, Olcan
26/11	Eskişehirspor	h	0-3	
03/12	Gençlerbirliği	h	4-0	Emerson, Halil, Olcan, Yasin
09/12	Kayserispor	a	1-0	Olcan
16/12	İstanbul BB	h	1-2	Paulo Henrique
23/12	Galatasaray	h	0-0	

2013

20/01	Karabükspor	h	1-3	Vittek
27/01	Elazığspor	a	1-3	Sapara
03/02	Gaziantepspor	h	4-1	Mierzejewski, Alanzinho, Colman, Halil
10/02	Sivasspor	a	0-2	
17/02	Fenerbahçe	h	0-3	
23/02	Mersin	a	1-0	Paulo Henrique
03/03	Kasımpaşa	a	0-2	
09/03	Beşiktaş	h	0-0	
15/03	Bursaspor	a	2-3	Paulo Henrique, Halil
31/03	Antalyaspor	h	2-0	Volkan, Yasin
07/04	Akhisar	a	0-1	
12/04	Orduspor	h	1-0	Halil
22/04	Eskişehirspor	a	1-0	Mierzejewski
27/04	Gençlerbirliği	a	2-0	Halil, Olcan
04/05	Kayserispor	a	1-2	Olcan
13/05	İstanbul BB	h	4-3	Olcan, Volkan, Halil, Yasin
18/05	Galatasaray	a	0-2	

No	Name	Nat	DoB	Pos	Aps	(s)	Gls
3	Abdullah Karmil		22/01/88	D	3		
25	Alanzinho	BRA	22/02/83	M	12	(14)	1
18	Aykut Akgün		18/09/87	M	5	(5)	
6	Souleymane Bamba	CIV	13/01/85	D	17	(1)	
8	Barış Özbek		14/09/86	M		(7)	
20	Gustavo Colman	ARG	18/04/85	M	10	(2)	1
5	Marek Čech	SVK	26/01/83	M	13	(1)	
28	Ondřej Čelůstka	CZE	18/06/89	D	18	(1)	
86	Emerson	BRA	23/02/86	D	17		2
9	Emre Güral		05/04/89	A	1	(7)	
63	Ferhat Öztorun		08/05/87	D		(2)	
23	Giray Kaçar		15/03/85	D	17	(1)	
21	Halil Altıntop		08/12/82	A	20	(7)	7
83	Marc Janko	AUT	25/06/83	A	7	(7)	1
10	Adrian Mierzejewski	POL	06/11/86	M	19	(2)	5
22	Mustafa Yumlu		25/09/87	D	26		
92	Olcan Adın		30/09/85	M	26	(4)	7
1	Onur Kıvrak		01/01/88	G	29	(1)	
12	Paulo Henrique	BRA	13/03/89	A	15	(5)	4
27	Marek Sapara	SVK	31/07/82	M	15	(7)	2
30	Serkan Balcı		22/08/83	D	24	(1)	
14	Soner Aydoğdu		05/01/91	M	15	(5)	1
29	Tolga Zengin		10/10/83	G	5		
7	Róbert Vittek	SVK	01/04/82	A	4	(1)	2
40	Volkan Şen		07/07/87	M	6	(8)	3
11	Yasin Öztekin		19/03/87	M	18	(8)	3
91	Zeki Yavru		05/09/91	M	6	(1)	
15	Didier Zokora	CIV	14/12/80	M	26	(1)	

Promoted clubs

KAYSERİ ERCİYESSPOR

Coach: Osman Özköylü
1966 • Kadir Has (32,864) • erciyesspor.org.tr

RİZESPOR

Coach: Engin Korukır; (14/12/12) Mustafa Denizli
1953 • Yeni Rize Şehir (15,558) • caykurrizespor.org.tr

KONYASPOR

Coach: Hüsnü Özkara; (30/11/12) Uğur Tütüneker
1981 • Atatürk (22,459) • konyaspor.org.tr

SECOND LEVEL FINAL TABLE 2012/13

		Pld	W	D	L	F	A	Pts
1	Kayseri Erciyesspor	34	19	6	9	59	37	63
2	Rizespor	34	17	8	9	53	35	59
3	1461 Trabzon	34	15	8	11	47	31	53
4	Manisaspor	34	14	11	9	41	28	53
5	Bucaspor	34	14	10	10	48	33	52
6	Konyaspor	34	14	10	10	38	35	52
7	Adana Demirspor	34	14	9	11	54	53	51
8	Adanaspor	34	13	10	11	42	42	49
9	Karşıyaka SK	34	12	11	11	37	39	47
10	Boluspor	34	13	7	14	41	45	46
11	Denizlispor	34	11	10	13	35	37	43
12	Şanlıurfaspor	34	10	13	11	32	38	43
13	Gaziantep BBK	34	11	8	15	37	43	41
14	Samsunspor	34	7	18	9	38	39	39
15	Tavşanlı Linyitspor	34	9	11	14	34	47	38
16	Göztepe SK	34	10	7	17	28	40	37
17	Kartalspor	34	7	17	33	44	37	
18	MKE Ankaragücü	34	7	8	19	31	62	29

NB 1461 Trabzon ineligible for promotion.

PROMOTION/RELEGATION PLAY-OFFS

(19/05/13 & 23/05/13)
Konyaspor 0-1 Bucaspor
Bucaspor 1-2 Konyaspor
(2-2; Konyaspor on away goals)

Adana Demirspor 0-2 Manisaspor
Manisaspor 1-1 Adana Demirspor
(Manisaspor 3-1)

(26/05/13)
Konyaspor 2-0 Manisaspor

Domestic cup: Türkiye Kupası 2012/13

SECOND ROUND

(25/09/12)
Dersim 0-7 Gençlerbirliği
Niğde Belediye 1-2 Beşiktaş

(26/09/12)
Akhisar Belediye 5-2 Aydınspor 1923
Ankaragücü 5-1 Iğdır Üniversitesi *(aet)*
Antalyaspor 5-3 Menemen Belediye
Çorum Beldiye 2-1 Adana Demirspor *(aet)*
Gaziantepspor 1-0 Emrespor *(aet)*
İstanbulspor AŞ 1-3 Kasımpaşa
Karabükspor 3-2 Gümüşhanespor
Konyaspor 2-0 Kırıkhanspor
Orhangazi 2-1 İstanbul BB *(aet)*
Patnos 1-2 Kartal
Samsunspor 0-2 Dört Eylül Belediye
Ümraniye 1-2 Kayseri Erciyesspor *(aet)*
(27/09/12)
Adanaspor 2-1 Erzurum BB *(aet)*
Alanyaspor 0-3 Yeni Malatya
Anadolu Selçuklu 1-2 Pendik
Ankara Demirspor 0-1 Elazığspor
Arsinspor 4-2 Bucaspor
Balıkesirspor 4-0 İskenderunspor 1967
Bandırmaspor 1-0 Kilimli Belediye
Batman Petrol 2-1 Körfez
Boluspor 1-2 Yozgatspor
BUGSAŞ 2-1 Silivrispor
Çankırı 1-2 Nazilli Belediye
Darıca Gençlerbirliği 2-1 Kırklareli
Denizlispor 1-2 Dardanel
Eyüpspor 3-2 Ünyespor *(aet)*
Fethiyespor 5-0 Cizre Basra
Gaziantep BB 2-0 Keçiörengücü
Gaziosmanpaşa 0-1 Bayrampaşa *(aet)*
Göztepe 3-0 Gölcük
İnegölspor 0-2 Giresunspor
İskenderun DÇ 2-3 Ofspor
Kahramanmaraş 1-2 Sakaryaspor
Kanuni 0-3 Sivasspor
Karaman Belediye 1-2 Bozüyükspor
Kızılcahamam 1-0 Kütahyaspor
Manisaspor 3-1 Kayseri Şekerspor *(aet)*
Mersin İdman Yurdu 3-0 Siirtspor
Muğlaspor 2-3 Tavşanlı Linyitspor *(aet)*
Şekerspor 1-2 Güngörenspor
Tarsus İdman Yurdu 2-0 Sarıyer
Tepecikspor 3-0 Beylerbeyi
Tokatspor 3-2 Hatayspor
Turgutluspor 1-0 Beyköy Belediye
Uşak Belediye 1-10 Denizli Belediye

(02/10/12)
Diyarbakır BB 1-0 Rizespor
Kastamonuspor 2-3 Orduspor

(03/10/12)
Kocaelispor 1-0 Karşıyaka
Sancaktepe Belediye 3-1 Kayserispor

(04/10/12)
1461 Trabzon 4-1 Belediye Vanspor
Tekirova Belediye 2-4 Altay

(11/10/12)
Kadirlispor 0-3 Şanlıurfa

THIRD ROUND

(30/10/12)
Konyaspor 0-3 Nazilli Belediye
Tepecikspor 1-3 Gençlerbirliği

(31/10/12)
Ankaragücü 2-0 Çorum Belediye *(aet)*
Bandırmaspor 4-1 Yozgatspor
Batman Petrol 1-2 Adanaspor
Beşiktaş 2-1 Ofspor
Dardanel 1-1 Manisaspor *(aet;5-6 on pens)*

Diyarbakır BB 0-1 BUGSAŞ
Giresunspor 0-3 Mersin İdman Yurdu
Göztepe 2-1 Sakaryaspor
Güngören 0-2 Sivasspor
Karabükspor 1-0 Yeni Malatya
Kızılcahamam 2-3 1462 Trabzon *(aet)*
Şanlıurfa 1-1 Orhangazi *(aet; 3-1 on pens)*
Tokatspor 1-0 Akhisar Belediye

(01/11/12)
Altay 1-0 Fethiyespor
Antalyaspor 7-0 Eyupspor
Balıkesirspor 2-1 Turgutluspor
Denizli Belediye 0-3 Bozüyükspor
Gaziantep BB 3-3 Darıca Gençlerbirliği *(aet; 5-4 on pens)*
Kasımpaşa 5-0 Kocaelispor
Orduspor 3-0 Sancaktepe Belediye
Tavşanlı Linyitspor 1-0 Dört Eylül Belediye

(07/11/12)
Arsinspor 0-1 Gaziantepspor
Kayseri Erciyesspor 4-1 Sarıyer

(08/11/12)
Bayrampaşa 1-0 Kartal
Pendik 3-2 Elazığ

FOURTH ROUND

(27/11/12)
Altay 1-0 Kayseri Erciyesspor *(aet)*
Galatasaray 4-1 Balıkesirspor
Tokatspor 0-1 Mersin İdman Yurdu

(28/11/12)
Adanaspor 1-1 1461 Trabzon *(aet; 2-4 on pens)*
Beşiktaş 3-2 Ankaragücü
Fenerbahçe 1-0 Pendik
Göztepe 1-0 Orduspor
Tavşanlı Linyitspor 0-5 Antalyaspor

(29/11/12)
BUGSAŞ 0-4 Eskişehirspor
Gençlerbirliği 5-1 Bandırmaspor
Sivasspor 3-0 Manisaspor
Trabzonspor 4-0 Şanlıurfa

(04/12/12)
Bozüyükspor 1-2 Gaziantepspor
Nazilli Belediye 0-3 Bursaspor

(05/12/12)
Gaziantep BB 1-2 Karabükspor *(aet)*
Kasımpaşa 3-1 Bayrampaşa

FIFTH ROUND

(11/12/12)
Altay 0-2 Bursaspor
Eskişehirspor 5-1 Karabükspor
Galatasaray 1-2 1461 Trabzon
Gaziantepspor 0-1 Sivasspor *(aet)*

(12/12/12)
Antalyaspor 2-1 Beşiktaş
Fenerbahçe 4-0 Göztepe
Gençlerbirliği 2-3 Mersin İdman Yurdu

(13/12/12)
Kasımpaşa 1-1 Trabzonspor *(aet; 2-4 on pens)*

GROUP STAGE

GROUP A

(19/12/12)
Bursaspor 2-0 1461 Trabzon
Fenerbahçe 2-0 Sivasspor

(13/01/13)
Sivasspor 2-1 Bursaspor
1461 Trabzon 0-2 Fenerbahçe

(16/01/13)
1461 Trabzon 1-1 Sivasspor
Bursaspor 2-3 Fenerbahçe

(23/01/13)
Fenerbahçe 3-0 Bursaspor
Sivasspor 2-1 1461 Trabzon

(29/01/13)
1461 Trabzon 0-0 Bursaspor

(30/01/13)
Sivasspor 0-0 Fenerbahçe

(27/02/13)
Fenerbahçe 2-3 1461 Trabzon

(28/02/13)
Bursaspor 0-1 Sivasspor

Final standings
1 Fenerbahçe 13 pts; 2 Sivasspor 11 pts *(qualified)*
3 1461 Trabzon 5 pts; 4 Bursaspor 4 pts
(eliminated)

GROUP B

(20/12/12)
Mersin İdman Yurdu 0-5 Antalyaspor
Trabzonspor 2-0 Eskişehirspor

(11/01/13)
Eskişehirspor 3-1 Mersin İdman Yurdu

(12/01/13)
Antalyaspor 2-3 Trabzonspor

(15/01/13)
Mersin İdman Yurdu 0-2 Trabzonspor

(17/01/13)
Antalyaspor 1-0 Eskişehirspor

(24/01/13)
Eskişehirspor 2-1 Antalyaspor
Trabzonspor 3-0 Mersin İdman Yurdu

(30/01/13)
Antalyaspor 4-2 Mersin İdman Yurdu

(31/01/13)
Eskişehirspor 1-0 Trabzonspor

(27/02/13)
Mersin İdman Yurdu 0-3 Eskişehirspor
Trabzonspor 1-0 Antalyaspor

Final standings
1 Trabzonspor 15 pts; 2 Eskişehirspor 12 pts
(qualified)
3 Antalyaspor 9 pts; 4 Mersin İdman Yurdu 0 pts
(eliminated)

SEMI-FINALS

(17/04/13 & 08/05/13)
Eskişehirspor 1-1 Fenerbahçe *(Zengin 13; Mehmet Topal 20)*
Fenerbahçe 1-1 Eskişehirspor *(Webó 32; Tello 17)*
(aet)
(2-2; Fenerbahçe 4-1 on pens)

Sivasspor 2-1 Trabzonspor *(Chahéchouche 44, Erman 76; Sapara 90)*
Trabzonspor 6-0 Sivasspor *(Mierzejewski 38, 47, 53, Olcan 65, Volkan 72, Aykut 77)*
(Trabzonspor 7-2)

FINAL

(22/05/13)
19 Mayıs Stadium, Ankara
FENERBAHÇE SK 1 *(Sow 9)*
TRABZONSPOR AŞ 0
Referee: *Aydınus*
FENERBAHÇE: *Mert, Gökhan, Egemen (Bekir 51), Yobo, Hasan Ali, Mehmet Topal, Emre (Mehmet Topuz 76), Kuyt, Cristian (Caner 85), Sow, Webó*
TRABZONSPOR: *Tolga, Serkan, Giray, Mustafa, Čech, Soner (Sapara 83), Zokora (Aykut 46), Volkan (Paulo Henrique 69), Mierzejewski, Olcan, Halil*

UKRAINE

Federatsiya Futbola Ukrainy (FFU)

Address Provulok Laboratorniy 7-A
PO Box 55
UA-01133 Kyiv
Tel +380 44 521 0521
Fax +380 44 521 0550
E-mail info@ffu.org.ua
Website ffu.org.ua

President Anatoliy Konkov
General secretary Maksym Bondarev
Media officer Pavlo Ternovoy
Year of formation 1989
National stadium NSK Olimpiyskiy,
Kyiv (70,050)

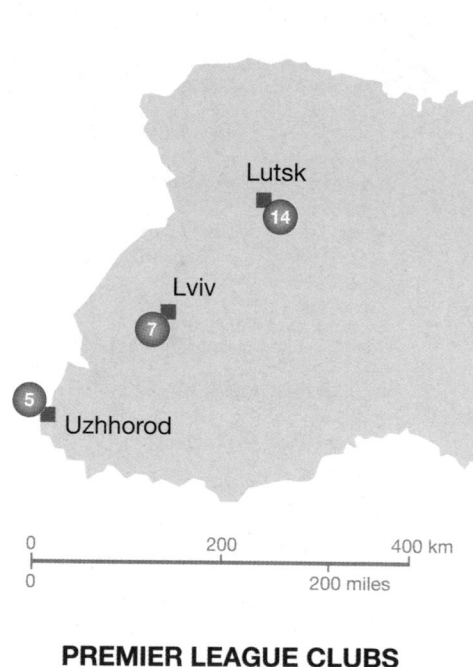

PREMIER LEAGUE CLUBS

1 FC Arsenal Kyiv

2 FC Chornomorets Odesa

3 FC Dnipro Dnipropetrovsk

4 FC Dynamo Kyiv

5 FC Hoverla Uzhhorod

6 FC Illychivets Mariupil

7 FC Karpaty Lviv

8 FC Kryvbas Kryvyi Rih

9 FC Metalist Kharkiv

10 FC Metalurh Donetsk

11 FC Metalurh Zaporizhya

12 FC Shakhtar Donetsk

13 SC Tavriya Simferopol

14 FC Volyn Lutsk

15 FC Vorskla Poltava

16 FC Zorya Luhansk

PROMOTED CLUB

17 PFC Sevastopol

KEY:
 – UEFA Champions League
 – UEFA Europa League
 – Promoted club
 – Relegated club

Another double for Shakhtar

FC Shakhtar Donetsk's domination of Ukrainian football ascended to a new level in 2012/13 as they won the double for a third successive season. Coach Mircea Lucescu's seventh Premier League title in nine seasons was arguably the most emphatic, fuelled by a remarkable opening run of 15 straight victories.

As Shakhtar left the rest in their wake, an intriguing battle for second place ensued, with FC Metalist Kharkiv eventually claiming it ahead of FC Dynamo Kyiv, who endured a torrid season under new coach Oleh Blokhin. FC Chornomorets Odesa were Shakhtar's victims in the final of the Ukrainian Cup.

Lucescu's team a class apart in league and cup

Markevych's Metalist take runners-up spot

Forgettable season for Blokhin's Dynamo Kyiv

Domestic league

Shakhtar's fourth successive Premier League title was effectively wrapped up by Christmas. Having closed the previous season with nine successive victories, they extended that sequence to 24 by beating every one of the division's other 15 teams. It was a stunning run, in which just six goals were conceded and 45 scored, with Armenian attacking midfielder Henrikh Mkhitaryan alone contributing 15. A 2-0 defeat at FC Arsenal Kyiv finally brought things to a halt, but it was just a temporary blip. Two wins later Lucescu's men were entering the winter break with a 13-point lead.

Despite the January sale of star winger Willian to FC Anji Makhachkala, Shakhtar maintained that comfortable cushion through to the finish. There were no further defeats, and although their 100% home record was ended by Metalist, one of three draws in succession, this was just a statistical footnote to a comprehensive triumph. Mkhitaryan, who ended up with a league-best tally of 25 goals, was just one of several outstanding contributors, among them skipper Darijo Srna, centre-back Yaroslav Rakitskiy and midfielder Fernandinho – the pick of the team's large Brazilian contingent.

Metalist, another club with a strong South American connection, finally achieved their mission of qualifying for the UEFA Champions League, taking the runners-up spot after six consecutive third-place finishes. Long-serving coach Myron Markevych steered the team through 16 matches unbeaten to pip Dynamo Kyiv and FC Dnipro Dnipropetrovsk to that coveted second spot, home wins over both rivals in the final month proving decisive. With eight defeats Dynamo could hardly complain about finishing third, their season failing to ignite at any stage despite the goals of Nigerian striker Ideye Brown. Blokhin's impact was lessened by health issues – a factor the club could not legislate for when they appointed him to replace Yuri Semin in October.

Domestic cup

Semin was in charge when Dynamo, not for the first time, were knocked out of the Ukrainian Cup by Shakhtar. That was in the third round. Four matches and four wins later Lucescu's team were celebrating their third successive cup success – and ninth in all. Chornomorets were no match for them in the final, three unanswered goals made in Brazil – from Fernandinho, Alex Teixeira and Taison, a mid-season signing from Metalist – securing a straightforward victory in Kharkiv.

Europe

A fine effort in the UEFA Champions League from Shakhtar, who helped to eliminate holders Chelsea FC, ended with a 3-0 defeat in the last 16 at Borussia Dortmund. Lucescu's men were the last Ukrainian side to depart the European scene, all three of the country's UEFA Europa League round of 32 participants having unexpectedly been eliminated.

Dynamo Kyiv did well to join Shakhtar in the UEFA Champions League group stage, overcoming Feyenoord and VfL Borussia Mönchengladbach, but by the new year they had joined Metalist and Dnipro in the UEFA Europa League.

National team

Blokhin's departure for Dynamo left the Ukrainian national side in a turbulent state, and the dust did not settle until the appointment in December of Mykhailo Fomenko as his permanent replacement.

By that stage Ukraine's bid to qualify for the 2014 FIFA World Cup looked doomed, with just two points taken from their first three fixtures, albeit one of those from England at Wembley. But Fomenko, who had not held a major coaching post for several years, revived the campaign with three wins out of three, the first in Poland (3-1), the last in Montenegro, where four second-half goals without reply completely reconfigured the qualifying picture in Group H.

UKRAINE

Domestic league: Premier League 2012/13 final table

		Pld	Home					Away					Total					Pts
			W	D	L	F	A	W	D	L	F	A	W	D	L	F	A	
1	FC Shakhtar Donetsk	30	14	1	0	48	7	11	3	1	34	11	25	4	1	82	18	79
2	FC Metalist Kharkiv	30	12	1	2	31	10	8	5	2	28	15	20	6	4	59	25	66
3	FC Dynamo Kyiv	30	12	1	2	30	9	8	1	6	25	14	20	2	8	55	23	62
4	FC Dnipro Dnipropetrovsk	30	11	2	2	35	10	5	6	4	19	17	16	8	6	54	27	56
5	FC Metalurh Donetsk	30	8	5	2	28	12	6	2	7	17	23	14	7	9	45	35	49
6	FC Chornomorets Odesa	30	6	5	4	18	18	6	2	7	14	18	12	7	11	32	36	43
7	FC Kryvbas Kryvyi Rih	30	8	4	3	25	12	4	3	8	11	29	12	7	11	36	41	43
8	FC Arsenal Kyiv	30	6	4	5	20	14	4	5	6	14	27	10	9	11	34	41	39
9	FC Illychivets Mariupil	30	6	4	5	12	10	4	4	7	18	22	10	8	12	30	32	38
10	FC Zorya Luhansk	30	6	3	6	22	24	4	4	7	10	19	10	7	13	32	43	37
11	SC Tavriya Simferopol	30	7	2	6	18	17	3	3	9	9	29	10	5	15	27	46	32
12	FC Vorskla Poltava	30	6	3	6	19	14	2	4	9	12	22	8	7	15	31	36	31
13	FC Volyn Lutsk	30	4	5	6	14	21	3	3	9	12	24	7	8	15	26	45	29
14	FC Karpaty Lviv	30	6	3	6	24	19	1	3	11	13	33	7	6	17	37	52	27
15	FC Hoverla Uzhhorod	30	4	5	6	17	23	1	2	12	12	34	5	7	18	29	57	22
16	FC Metalurh Zaporizhya	30	1	5	9	9	31	0	3	12	3	33	1	8	21	12	64	11

NB SC Tavriya Simferopol – 3 pts deducted.

SEASON AT A GLANCE

EUROPEAN QUALIFICATION 2013/14

Champion/Cup winner: FC Shakhtar Donetsk (group stage)

FC Metalist Kharkiv (third qualifying round)

FC Dynamo Kyiv (play-offs)
FC Dnipro Dnipropetrovsk (play-offs)
FC Metalurh Donetsk (third qualifying round)
FC Chornomorets Odesa (second qualifying round)

Top scorer	Henrikh Mkhitaryan (Shakhtar), 25 goals
Relegated club	FC Kryvbas Kryvyi Rih (withdrew)
Promoted club	PFC Sevastopol
Cup final	FC Shakhtar Donetsk 3-0 FC Chornomorets Odesa

PLAYER OF THE SEASON
Henrikh Mkhitaryan
(FC Shakhtar Donetsk)

The attacking midfielder set a Premier League scoring record with 25 goals, missing out by just one on matching Vitaliy Starukhin's 1979 club record mark. The Armenian international was in particularly irrepressible form during Shakhtar's hot streak at the start of the season but held back a couple of goals for a 2-1 win at FC Dynamo Kyiv in the spring.

NEWCOMER OF THE SEASON
Maxym Koval
(FC Dynamo Kyiv)

The 20-year-old goalkeeper, an unused member of Ukraine's UEFA EURO 2012 squad, used the 2012/13 season to usurp long-serving Olexandr Shovkovskiy as Dynamo's first choice between the posts. The quality and consistency of his displays suggested that Andriy Pyatov might be the next keeper to make way for him – in the national team.

PREMIER LEAGUE TEAM OF THE SEASON
(4-4-1-1)
Coach: Lucescu *(Shakhtar)*

Goryainov *(Metalist)*

Srna *(Shakhtar)* — Kucher *(Shakhtar)* — Rakitskiy *(Shakhtar)* — Márcio Azevedo *(Metalist)*

Yarmolenko *(Dynamo)* — Fernandinho *(Shakhtar)* — Cleiton Xavier *(Metalist)* — Konoplyanka *(Dnipro)*

Mkhitaryan *(Shakhtar)*

Zozulya *(Dnipro)*

NATIONAL TEAM

Home Kit   Away Kit

INTERNATIONAL TOURNAMENT APPEARANCES
FIFA World Cup (1) 2006 (qtr-finals)
UEFA European Championship (1) 2012

TOP FIVE ALL-TIME CAPS
Anatoliy Tymoshchuk (128); Andriy Shevchenko (111); Olexandr Shovkovskiy (92); **Oleh Gusev** (83); Serhiy Rebrov (75)

TOP FIVE ALL-TIME GOALS
Andriy Shevchenko (48); Serhiy Rebrov (15); **Oleh Gusev** (13); **Serhiy Nazarenko** (12); **Andriy Yarmolenko** (11)

Results 2012/13

Date	Opponent		Venue	Score	Scorers
15/08/12	Czech Republic	H	Lviv	0-0	
11/09/12	England (WCQ)	A	London	1-1	Konoplyanka (38)
12/10/12	Moldova (WCQ)	A	Chisinau	0-0	
16/10/12	Montenegro (WCQ)	H	Kyiv	0-1	
14/11/12	Bulgaria	A	Sofia	1-0	Kucher (33)
06/02/13	Norway	N	Seville (ESP)	2-0	Morozyuk (17), Yarmolenko (42)
22/03/13	Poland (WCQ)	A	Warsaw	3-1	Yarmolenko (2), Gusev (7), Zozulya (45)
26/03/13	Moldova (WCQ)	H	Odessa	2-1	Yarmolenko (61), Khacheridi (70)
02/06/13	Cameroon	H	Kyiv	0-0	
07/06/13	Montenegro (WCQ)	A	Podgorica	4-0	Garmash (52), Konoplyanka (77), Fedetskiy (85), Bezus (90+3)

Appearances 2012/13

Coach:
Oleh Blokhin 05/11/52
/(06/10/12) (Andriy Bal) 16/02/58
/(01/11/12) (Olexandr Zavarov) 26/04/61
/(26/12/12) Mykhailo Fomenko 19/09/48

Player	DOB	Club	Cze	ENG	MDA	MNE	Bul	Nor	POL	MDA	Cmr	MNE	Caps	Goals
Andriy Pyatov	28/06/84	Shakhtar Donetsk	G	G	G	G	G	G	G	G	G	G	39	-
Bohdan Butko	13/01/91	Illychivets	D		D	D62	D						15	-
Yevhen Khacheridi	28/07/87	Dynamo Kyiv	D	D	D		D	D46	D	D	D		22	1
Yaroslav Rakitskiy	03/08/89	Shakhtar Donetsk	D	D							D	D	22	3
Yevhen Selin	09/05/88	Vorskla	D	D75	D	D	s90						14	1
Anatoliy Tymoshchuk	30/03/79	Bayern (GER)	M46	M	M	M	s46	M64	s60	M		D	128	4
Denys Garmash	19/04/90	Dynamo Kyiv	M72	M	M60		M	M64	M92		M76	M69	14	1
Yevhen Konoplyanka	29/09/89	Dnipro	M46	M		M		s46/85			M	M	28	7
Roman Zozulya	17/11/89	Dnipro	A	A89	A74	s52		A76	A	A	A87	A45*	10	2
Marko Dević	27/10/83	Shakhtar Donetsk	A71	s89	s79	A52		s76					29	2
Yevhen Seleznyov	20/07/85	Shakhtar Donetsk /Dnipro	A46		s60	A82	A75	s64		A62	A46		36	5
Ruslan Rotan	29/10/81	Dnipro	s46	M92	M	M	M90	M	M		M	M91	68	6
Oleh Gusev	25/04/83	Dynamo Kyiv	s46	D	M79	M			M93	M90	s46	D	83	13
Andriy Yarmolenko	23/10/89	Dynamo Kyiv	s46	M	M	s62		M64	M	M	M46	M92	32	11
Taras Stepanenko	08/08/89	Shakhtar Donetsk	s71				M46	s64	M60	M92*	s46		10	-
Roman Bezus	26/09/90	Vorskla /Dynamo Kyiv	s72				A	s64	s92	s62		s91	7	1
Vyacheslav Shevchuk	13/05/79	Shakhtar Donetsk		s75			D	D	D	D	D		27	-
Serhiy Nazarenko	16/02/80	Tavriya		s92		s82	s62						56	12
Taras Mikhalik	28/10/83	Dynamo Kyiv			D	D	s46/62						32	-
Artem Milevskiy	12/01/85	Dynamo Kyiv			s74								50	8
Olexandr Kucher	22/10/82	Shakhtar Donetsk				D	D46		D	D			33	2
Artem Fedetskiy	26/04/85	Dnipro					M55	D	D	D	s46	D	23	1
Vitaliy Mandzyuk	24/01/86	Dnipro					s55	D84*					21	-
Anton Shinder	13/06/87	Tavriya					s75						2	-
Mykola Morozyuk	17/01/88	Metalurh Donetsk						M	s93	D46			6	1
Andriy Bogdanov	21/01/90	Dynamo Kyiv						s85					1	-
Dmytro Grechishkin	22/09/91	Shakhtar Donetsk								s90			1	-
Edmar	16/06/80	Metalist									s76	M	3	-
Olexandr Kovpak	02/02/83	Sevastopol									s87	s92	2	-
Serhiy Kravchenko	24/04/83	Dnipro										s69	10	1

European club competitions 2012/13

FC SHAKHTAR DONETSK

Group E
Match 1 - FC Nordsjælland (DEN)
H 2-0 *Mkhitaryan (44, 76)*
Pyatov, Hübschman, Kucher, Fernandinho, Luiz Adriano (Dević 75), Willian (Douglas Costa 81), Mkhitaryan, Raţ, Srna, Rakitskiy, Ilsinho (Alex Teixeira 70). Coach: Mircea Lucescu (ROU)

Match 2 - Juventus (ITA)
A 1-1 *Alex Teixeira (23)*
Pyatov, Hübschman, Kucher, Fernandinho, Luiz Adriano, Willian, Mkhitaryan, Raţ, Alex Teixeira (Ilsinho 84), Srna, Rakitskiy. Coach: Mircea Lucescu (ROU)

Match 3 - Chelsea FC (ENG)
H 2-1 *Alex Teixeira (3), Fernandinho (52)*
Pyatov, Hübschman, Kucher, Fernandinho, Luiz Adriano, Willian (Douglas Costa 88), Mkhitaryan, Raţ, Alex Teixeira (Ilsinho 82), Srna, Rakitskiy. Coach: Mircea Lucescu (ROU)

Match 4 - Chelsea FC (ENG)
A 2-3 *Willian (9, 47)*
Pyatov, Hübschman, Kucher, Fernandinho, Luiz Adriano, Willian, Mkhitaryan, Raţ, Alex Teixeira (Ilsinho 78), Srna, Rakitskiy. Coach: Mircea Lucescu (ROU)

Match 5 - FC Nordsjælland (DEN)
A 5-2 *Luiz Adriano (26, 53, 81), Willian (44, 50)*
Pyatov, Kucher, Stepanenko, Fernandinho, Luiz Adriano (Eduardo 82), Willian (Ilsinho 86), Mkhitaryan, Raţ, Alex Teixeira (Douglas Costa 78), Srna, Rakitskiy. Coach: Mircea Lucescu (ROU)

Match 6 - Juventus (ITA)
H 0-1
Pyatov, Kucher, Stepanenko, Fernandinho, Willian, Eduardo (Dević 46), Mkhitaryan, Raţ, Alex Teixeira (Ilsinho 65), Srna, Rakitskiy. Coach: Mircea Lucescu (ROU)

Round of 16 - Borussia Dortmund (GER)
H 2-2 *Srna (31), Douglas Costa (68)*
Pyatov, Hübschman, Fernandinho, Luiz Adriano, Mkhitaryan, Raţ, Chygrynskiy, Taison (Douglas Costa 62), Alex Teixeira (Eduardo 84), Srna, Rakitskiy. Coach: Mircea Lucescu (ROU)

A 0-3
Pyatov, Hübschman (Stepanenko 82), Kucher, Fernandinho, Luiz Adriano, Mkhitaryan, Raţ, Taison (Douglas Costa 46), Alex Teixeira, Srna, Rakitskiy. Coach: Mircea Lucescu (ROU)

FC DYNAMO KYIV

Third qualifying round - Feyenoord (NED)
H 2-1 *Immers (56og), Ideye (69)*
Koval, Danilo Silva, Betão, Miguel Veloso, Vukojević (Milevskiy 55), Popov, Yarmolenko, Ideye, Mikhalik, Kranjčar (Gusev 46), Ninković. Coach: Yuri Semin (RUS)

A 1-0 *Ideye (90+6)*
Koval, Danilo Silva, Betão, Miguel Veloso, Vukojević, Popov, Yarmolenko, Ideye, Mikhalik, Gusev (Milevskiy 81), Ninković (Garmash 90+1). Coach: Yuri Semin (RUS)

Play-offs - VfL Borussia Mönchengladbach (GER)
A 3-1 *Mikhalik (28), Yarmolenko (36), De Jong (81og)*
Koval, Danilo Silva, Betão, Miguel Veloso, Yarmolenko, Ideye (Mehmedi 90+3), Mikhalik, Garmash, Kranjčar (Vukojević 65), Taiwo, Ninković (Raffael 78). Coach: Yuri Semin (RUS)

H 1-2 *Ideye (88)*
Koval, Danilo Silva, Betão, Miguel Veloso, Yarmolenko, Ideye (Marco Ruben 90+3), Garmash, Gusev, Taiwo, Khacheridi, Ninković (Vukojević 46). Coach: Yuri Semin (RUS)

Group A
Match 1 - Paris Saint-Germain FC (FRA)
A 1-4 *Miguel Veloso (87)*
Koval, Danilo Silva, Miguel Veloso, Yarmolenko, Ideye, Mikhalik (Betão 46), Garmash (Vukojević 53), Kranjčar (Gusev 77), Taiwo, Khacheridi, Raffael. Coach: Yuri Semin (RUS)

Match 2 - GNK Dinamo Zagreb (CRO)
H 2-0 *Gusev (3), Pivarić (33og)*
Shovkovskiy, Danilo Silva, Miguel Veloso, Vukojević, Yarmolenko (Mehmedi 80), Ideye, Mikhalik, Gusev (Raffael 83), Kranjčar (Garmash 46), Taiwo, Khacheridi. Coach: Oleh Blokhin (UKR)

Match 3 - FC Porto (POR)
A 2-3 *Gusev (21), Ideye (72)*
Shovkovskiy, Betão, Miguel Veloso, Vukojević (Kranjčar 84), Yarmolenko, Ideye, Mikhalik, Garmash, Gusev, Taiwo, Khacheridi. Coach: Olexiy Mykhaylychenko (UKR)

Match 4 - FC Porto (POR)
H 0-0
Koval, Betão, Miguel Veloso, Vukojević (Kranjčar 88), Yarmolenko, Milevskiy (Haruna 58), Marco Ruben (Ideye 67), Mikhalik, Gusev, Taiwo, Khacheridi. Coach: Oleh Blokhin (UKR)

Match 5 - Paris Saint-Germain FC (FRA)
H 0-2
Koval, Danilo Silva, Betão, Miguel Veloso, Ideye, Garmash (Bogdanov 78), Gusev (Yarmolenko 67), Haruna (Milevskiy 67), Taiwo, Khacheridi, Dudu. Coach: Oleh Blokhin (UKR)

Match 6 - GNK Dinamo Zagreb (CRO)
A 1-1 *Yarmolenko (45+1)*
Koval, Betão, Miguel Veloso, Vukojević, Yarmolenko, Ideye (Marco Ruben 76), Mikhalik, Garmash, Haruna (Bogdanov 90+1), Taiwo, Dudu (Mehmedi 82). Coach: Oleh Blokhin (UKR)

Round of 32 - FC Girondins de Bordeaux (FRA)
H 1-1 *Haruna (20)*
Koval, Miguel Veloso, Yarmolenko, Mehmedi (Marco Ruben 78), Mikhalik, Bezus (Garmash 69), Kranjčar (Gusev 61), Haruna, Taiwo, Khacheridi, Vida. Coach: Oleh Blokhin (UKR)

A 0-1
Koval, Miguel Veloso, Yarmolenko, Mehmedi (Ideye 46), Mikhalik, Bezus (Gusev 46), Kranjčar (Garmash 81), Haruna, Taiwo, Khacheridi, Vida. Coach: Oleh Blokhin (UKR)

FC METALIST KHARKIV

Play-offs - FC Dinamo Bucureşti (ROU)
A 2-0 *Cleiton Xavier (9), Cristaldo (57)*
Goryainov, Torsiglieri, Edmar, Cleiton Xavier (Marlos 83), Sosa, Fininho, Torres, Cristaldo (Rebenok 69), Obradović, Gueye, Willian (Blanco 58). Coach: Myron Markevych (UKR)
Red card: Fininho 68

H 2-1 *Blanco (29), Cristaldo (60)*
Goryainov, Torsiglieri, Cleiton Xavier, Sosa (Willian 77), Barvinko, Torres, Cristaldo, Obradović, Blanco (Edmar 57), Marlos (Taison 57), Gueye. Coach: Myron Markevych (UKR)

Group K
Match 1 - Bayer 04 Leverkusen (GER)
A 0-0
Goryainov, Villagra, Torsiglieri, Taison (Willian 65), Edmar, Cleiton Xavier, Sosa (Pshenychnykh 88), Fininho, Torres, Cristaldo (Marlos 76), Gueye. Coach: Myron Markevych (UKR)

Match 2 - SK Rapid Wien (AUT)
H 2-0 *Edmar (66), Cleiton Xavier (80)*
Goryainov, Villagra, Torsiglieri, Taison, Cleiton Xavier, Sosa (Marlos 83), Fininho, Torres, Cristaldo (Willian 74), Blanco (Edmar 51), Gueye. Coach: Myron Markevych (UKR)

Match 3 - Rosenborg BK (NOR)
A 2-1 *Marlos (81), Cleiton Xavier (89)*
Goryainov, Villagra, Torsiglieri, Taison, Cleiton Xavier, Fininho, Torres, Blanco (Edmar 72), Marlos (Rebenok 90+2), Gueye, Willian (Cristaldo 46). Coach: Myron Markevych (UKR)

Match 4 - Rosenborg BK (NOR)
H 3-1 *Taison (4), Cleiton Xavier (70), Torres (90+3)*
Dišljenković (Goryainov 46), Villagra, Torsiglieri, Taison (Blanco 82), Edmar, Cleiton Xavier, Fininho, Torres, Cristaldo (Willian 75), Marlos, Gueye. Coach: Myron Markevych (UKR)

Match 5 - Bayer 04 Leverkusen (GER)
H 2-0 *Cristaldo (46), Cleiton Xavier (85)*
Goryainov, Villagra, Torsiglieri, Taison (Sharpar 88), Edmar, Cleiton Xavier, Fininho, Torres, Cristaldo (Blanco 82), Gueye, Willian (Marlos 71). Coach: Myron Markevych (UKR)

Match 6 - SK Rapid Wien (AUT)
A 0-1
Goryainov, Villagra, Torsiglieri, Sosa, Fininho (Edmar 72), Torres, Cristaldo, Blanco, Marlos, Gueye, Willian. Coach: Myron Markevych (UKR)

Round of 32 - Newcastle United FC (ENG)
A 0-0
Goryainov, Villagra, Torsiglieri, Edmar, Cleiton Xavier, Sosa, Fininho, Torres, Cristaldo (Jajá 82), Marlos (Willian 73), Gueye. Coach: Myron Markevych (UKR)
H 0-1
Goryainov, Villagra, Torsiglieri, Edmar (Blanco 82), Cleiton Xavier, Sosa, Fininho, Torres (Willian 67), Cristaldo, Marlos (Jajá 67), Gueye. Coach: Myron Markevych (UKR)

FC DNIPRO DNIPROPETROVSK

Play-offs - FC Slovan Liberec (CZE)
A 2-2 *Konoplyanka (43), Matheus (49)*
Laštůvka, Mazuch, Mandzyuk, Giuliano, Konoplyanka (Oliynyk 66), Cheberyachko, Strinić, Zozulya, Rotan, Aliyev (Odibe 74), Matheus. Coach: Juande Ramos (ESP)

H 4-2 *Aliyev (12p, 59p), Konoplyanka (76), Kalinić (87)*
Laštůvka, Mazuch, Giuliano, Konoplyanka, Cheberyachko, Strinić, Zozulya (Kravchenko 72), Odibe, Rotan, Aliyev (Mandzyuk 88), Matheus (Kalinić 56). Coach: Juande Ramos (ESP)

Group F
Match 1 - PSV Eindhoven (NED)
H 2-0 *Matheus (50), Hutchinson (58og)*
Laštůvka, Mazuch, Giuliano, Konoplyanka (Denisov 85), Cheberyachko, Strinić, Zozulya (Kankava 85), Seleznyov, Rotan, Matheus (Odibe 90+1). Coach: Juande Ramos (ESP)

Match 2 - AIK (SWE)
A 3-2 *Kalinić (41), Mandzyuk (74), Seleznyov (83)*
Laštůvka, Mazuch (Matheus 66), Mandzyuk, Giuliano, Kalinić, Konoplyanka, Cheberyachko (Fedetskiy 46), Strinić, Seleznyov, Rotan, Aliyev (Kravchenko 78). Coach: Juande Ramos (ESP)

Match 3 - SSC Napoli (ITA)
H 3-1 *Fedetskiy (2), Matheus (42), Giuliano (64)*
Laštůvka, Mazuch, Mandzyuk, Giuliano, Cheberyachko, Strinić, Zozulya (Kankava 37), Seleznyov (Kalinić 59), Rotan, Fedetskiy (Denisov 82), Matheus. Coach: Juande Ramos (ESP)

Match 4 - SSC Napoli (ITA)
A 2-4 *Fedetskiy (34), Zozulya (52)*
Laštůvka, Mazuch, Mandzyuk, Kankava, Konoplyanka (Cheberyachko 81), Zozulya, Denisov, Odibe, Rotan, Fedetskiy (Matheus 86), Aliyev (Giuliano 56). Coach: Juande Ramos (ESP)

Match 5 - PSV Eindhoven (NED)
A 2-1 *Seleznyov (24), Konoplyanka (74)*
Laštůvka, Mazuch, Mandzyuk, Kankava, Giuliano, Konoplyanka (Fedetskiy 85), Cheberyachko, Strinić (Denisov 69), Seleznyov (Zozulya 77), Rotan, Matheus. Coach: Juande Ramos (ESP)
Red card: Kankava 84

Match 6 - AIK (SWE)
H 4-0 *Kalinić (20p), Zozulya (39, 52), Kravchenko (86)*
Laštůvka, Mazuch (Fedetskiy 46), Kravchenko, Mandzyuk, Giuliano, Kalinić (Aliyev 57), Konoplyanka, Cheberyachko, Strinić (Denisov 57), Zozulya, Rotan. Coach: Juande Ramos (ESP)

Round of 32 - FC Basel 1893 (SUI)
A 0-2
Laštůvka, Mazuch, Kravchenko (Matheus 53), Mandzyuk, Giuliano, Kalinić (Seleznyov 53), Konoplyanka, Cheberyachko, Strinić, Zozulya (Kankava 68), Rotan. Coach: Juande Ramos (ESP)
H 1-1 *Seleznyov (76p)*
Laštůvka, Mazuch, Mandzyuk, Giuliano, Cheberyachko, Strinić, Zozulya, Seleznyov, Rotan, Douglas (Kalinić 53), Fedetskiy (Konoplyanka 31), Matheus (Kravchenko 53). Coach: Juande Ramos (ESP)
Red card: Kalinić 63

FC ARSENAL KYIV

Third qualifying round - ND Mura 05 (SVN)
H 0-3 *(w/o; original result 3-0 Mazilu (6), Kovpak (61), Matoukou (83))*
Borovyk, Mazilu, Maximov, Matoukou, Shatskikh, Gitchenko, Kobakhidze (Mikoliūnas 77), Adiyiah (Kovpak 57), Polyoviy, Leandro, Shakhov (Starhorodskiy 67). Coach: Leonid Kuchuk (BLR)
A 2-0 *Kobakhidze (2), Homenyuk (61)*
Pankiv, Symonenko, Mazilu (Homenyuk 61), Maximov, Mikoliūnas, Shatskikh, Gitchenko, Kobakhidze (Kovpak 81), Adiyiah (Simović 35), Polyoviy, Shakhov. Coach: Leonid Kuchuk (BLR)

FC METALURH DONETSK

Second qualifying round - FK Čelik Nikšić (MNE)
H 7-0 *Makrides (17, 49), Ghazaryan (36, 61, 86), Danilo (51), Júnior Moraes (78)*
Bandura, Checher, Morozyuk, Lazić, Ghazaryan, Danilo (Júnior Moraes 54), Makrides, Volovyk, Zé Soares (Nelson 64), Priyma (Gryshschenko 76), Golaydo. Coach: Volodymyr Pyatenko (UKR)
A 4-2 *Danilo (15), Júnior Moraes (53), Volovyk (72), Zé Soares (84)*
Bandura, Checher, Nelson, Lazić (Makrides 72), Ghazaryan (Zé Soares 60), Danilo, Volovyk, Dimitrov, Yedigaryan, Golaydo (Morozyuk 46), Júnior Moraes. Coach: Volodymyr Pyatenko (UKR)

Third qualifying round - Tromsø IL (NOR)
A 1-1 *Björck (88og)*
Bandura, Checher, Morozyuk, Lazić, Ghazaryan, Makrides (Nelson 66), Volovyk, Dimitrov, Yedigaryan, Priyma, Júnior Moraes (Danilo 75). Coach: Volodymyr Pyatenko (UKR)
H 0-1
Bandura, Checher, Morozyuk, Lazić, Ghazaryan, Makrides, Volovyk, Zé Soares (Nelson 46), Yedigaryan, Priyma (Dimitrov 72), Júnior Moraes (Traoré 58). Coach: Volodymyr Pyatenko (UKR)

Domestic league club-by-club

FC ARSENAL KYIV

Coach: Leonid Kuchuk (BLR);
(10/01/13) Yuriy Bakalov
2001 • Dynamo im. Valeriy Lobanovskiy (16,873) •
fcarsenal.com.ua

2012
15/07	Shakhtar	a	0-6	
22/07	Dynamo	h	0-1	
29/07	Zorya	a	3-1	Shatskikh 2 (1p), Homenyuk
05/08	Dnipro	h	1-1	Kobakhidze
12/08	Metalist	a	1-0	Kovpak
17/08	Illychivets	h	2-1	Shatskikh, Homenyuk
26/08	Tavriya	a	1-1	Mikoliūnas
02/09	Metalurh Zaporizhya	h	3-0	Kovpak, Adiyiah, Shatskikh
16/09	Metalurh Donetsk	a	0-5	
30/09	Karpaty	a	1-1	Adiyiah
06/10	Hoverla	h	2-0	Homenyuk, Kovpak
21/10	Kryvbas	a	1-1	Mikoliūnas
26/10	Volyn	h	1-1	Adiyiah
04/11	Vorskla	a	0-1	
11/11	Chornomorets	h	0-1	
17/11	Shakhtar	h	2-0	Shatskikh, Kobakhidze
25/11	Dynamo	a	0-4	
02/12	Zorya	h	0-1	

2013
02/03	Dnipro	a	0-3	
10/03	Metalist	h	1-2	Martynyuk
17/03	Illychivets	a	1-2	Arzhanov
30/03	Tavriya	h	1-1	Bogdanov (p)
06/04	Metalurh Zaporizhya	a	0-0	
14/04	Metalurh Donetsk	h	0-2	
22/04	Karpaty	h	4-1	Arzhanov (p), Adiyiah, Bogdanov, Romanchuk
27/04	Hoverla	a	3-1	Homenyuk, Sharpar, Tkachuk
04/05	Kryvbas	h	1-1	Herasymyuk
11/05	Volyn	a	3-1	Sharpar, Arzhanov 2
18/05	Vorskla	a	2-1	Bogdanov, Arzhanov
26/05	Chornomorets	a	0-0	

No	Name	Nat	DoB	Pos	Aps	(s)	Gls
20	Dominic Adiyiah	GHA	29/11/89	M	18	(8)	4
27	Volodymyr Arzhanov		29/11/85	M	12		5
17	Andriy Bogdanov		21/01/90	M	11		3
12	Yevhen Borovyk		02/03/85	G	7		
44	Ihor Brovko		13/08/92	M		(1)	
9	Yuriy Bushman		14/05/90	M	2	(4)	
21	Olexandr Filippov		23/10/92	A		(3)	
10	George Florescu	ROU	21/05/87	M	10		
99	Oleh Herasymyuk		25/09/86	M	6	(3)	1
17	Andriy Hitchenko		02/10/84	D	7	(2)	
22	Volodymyr Homenyuk		19/07/85	A	20	(4)	4
33	Andriy Khomyn		02/01/82	D	2	(2)	
19	Aleksandre Kobakhidze	GEO	11/02/87	A	8	(8)	2
9	Olexandr Kovpak		02/02/83	A	14	(1)	3
2	Veli Lampi	FIN	18/07/84	D	3		
31	Leandro	BRA	26/06/85	D	16	(1)	
9	Yaroslav Martynyuk		20/02/89	M	8	(2)	1
14	Eric Matoukou	CMR	08/07/83	D	13		
8	Olexandr Maximov		13/02/85	M	2	(1)	
7	Ionuţ Maziu	ROU	09/02/82	A	2	(3)	
13	Saulius Mikoliūnas	LTU	02/05/84	M	8	(7)	2
29	Milan Obradović	SRB	03/08/77	D	11		
4	Michael Odibe	NGA	23/07/88	D	8		
77	Yuriy Pankiv		03/11/84	G	11		
25	Pelé	POR	29/09/91	M	1	(4)	
28	Volodymyr Polyoviy		28/07/85	M	16		
18	Abeiku Quansah	GHA	02/11/90	M		(6)	
6	Rafael Santos	BRA	10/11/84	D	10	(2)	
1	Vitaliy Reva		19/11/74	G	9	(1)	
31	Olexandr Romanchuk		21/10/84	D	8	(1)	1
23	Bohdan Sarnavskiy		29/01/95	G	3		
52	Yevhen Shakhov		30/11/90	M	9	(2)	
13	Vyacheslav Sharpar		02/06/87	M	7	(2)	2
16	Maksim Shatskikh	UZB	30/08/78	A	16	(2)	5
27	Serhiy Starenkiy		20/09/84	M	5	(2)	
11	Artem Starhorodskiy		17/01/82	M	12	(4)	
5	Kyrylo Sydorenko		25/07/85	D	7		
4	Serhiy Symonenko		12/06/81	M	12	(1)	
8	Andriy Tkachuk		18/11/87	M	6	(1)	1
28	Vyacheslav Turchanov		03/08/91	M		(1)	
78	Serhiy Valyayev		16/09/78	M	10	(2)	

FC CHORNOMORETS ODESA

Coach: Roman Hryhorchuk
1935 • Chornomorets (34,164) • chernomorets.odessa.ua
Major honours
Ukrainian Cup (2) 1992, 1994

2012
14/07	Hoverla	h	3-2	Léo Matos 2, og (Yeliseyev)
20/07	Kryvbas	a	0-1	
28/07	Volyn	h	0-2	
05/08	Vorskla	a	1-0	Bakaj
11/08	Karpaty	h	1-1	Bakaj
19/08	Shakhtar	h	1-5	Didenko
25/08	Dynamo	a	0-2	
01/09	Zorya	h	2-1	Didenko, Burdujan
15/09	Dnipro	a	0-1	
29/09	Metalist	h	1-1	Anderson (p)
06/10	Illychivets	a	1-2	Politylo
21/10	Tavriya	h	1-0	Bakaj
26/10	Metalurh Zaporizhya	a	1-0	Burdujan
04/11	Metalurh Donetsk	h	3-0	og (Lazić), Dja Djédjé, Anderson (p)
11/11	Arsenal	a	1-0	Bakaj
17/11	Hoverla	a	1-1	Politylo
23/11	Kryvbas	h	2-0	Bobko, Didenko
02/12	Volyn	a	2-0	Bakaj, Anderson (p)

2013
03/03	Vorskla	h	1-0	Léo Matos
09/03	Karpaty	a	2-1	Burdujan, Dja Djédjé
16/03	Shakhtar	a	0-3	
31/03	Dynamo	h	0-2	
05/04	Zorya	a	1-1	Fontanello
12/04	Dnipro	h	1-2	Dja Djédjé
21/04	Metalist	a	1-3	Burdujan
27/04	Illychivets	h	1-1	Politylo
03/05	Tavriya	a	3-1	Burdujan, Dja Djédjé, Didenko
12/05	Metalurh Zaporizhya	h	1-1	og (Sakhnevych)
19/05	Metalurh Donetsk	a	0-2	
26/05	Arsenal	h	0-0	

No	Name	Nat	DoB	Pos	Aps	(s)	Gls
5	Anderson	BRA	24/04/86	D	26		3
25	Artur	POR	18/02/84	M		(5)	
8	Elis Bakaj	ALB	25/06/87	A	16	(3)	5
4	Vitaliy Balashov		07/02/91	A	7	(6)	
11	Markus Berger	AUT	21/01/85	D	25		
12	Dmytro Bezotosniy		15/11/83	G	29		
11	Ivan Bobko		10/12/90	M	17	(12)	1
20	Lucien Burdujan	ROU	02/02/84	A	22	(1)	5
9	Anatoliy Didenko		09/06/82	A	6	(22)	4
23	Franck Dja Djédjé	CIV	02/06/86	A	19	(3)	4
29	Pablo Fontanello	ARG	26/09/84	D	28		1
8	Kyrylo Kovalchuk		11/06/86	M	24	(1)	
2	Pavlo Kovalchuk		28/05/84	D	6		
77	Pavlo Kutas		03/09/82	D	15	(2)	
8	Léo Matos	BRA	02/04/86	M	27	(1)	3
1	Yevhen Past		16/03/88	G	1		
89	Serhiy Politylo		09/01/89	M	28		3
16	Maksim Shatskikh	UZB	30/08/78	A	2	(4)	
14	Ihor Silantiyev		03/01/91	A		(1)	
99	Sito Riera	ESP	05/01/87	M	9	(3)	
33	Andriy Slinkin		19/02/81	D		(1)	
39	Artem Starhorodskiy		17/01/82	M	2	(4)	
8	Borys Tashchi		26/07/93	M		(1)	
17	Tiago Terroso	POR	13/01/88	M	3	(2)	
32	Kristi Vangjeli	ALB	05/09/85	D	3	(3)	
39	Denys Vasin		04/03/89	A		(3)	
42	Yevhen Zubeiko		30/09/89	M	15	(1)	

FC DNIPRO DNIPROPETROVSK

Coach: Juande Ramos (ESP)
1918 • Dnipro-Arena (31,003) • fcdnipro.ua
Major honours
USSR League (2) 1983, 1988;
USSR Cup (1) 1989

2012
15/07	Tavriya	h	3-1	Giuliano 2, Denisov
22/07	Metalurh Zaporizhya	a	4-0	Zozulya, Giuliano, Aliyev (p), Matheus
29/07	Metalurh Donetsk	h	2-0	Konoplyanka 2
05/08	Arsenal	a	1-1	Matheus (p)
11/08	Hoverla	h	4-1	Zozulya 2, Rotan, Giuliano
18/08	Kryvbas	a	0-0	
26/08	Volyn	h	2-1	Kalinić, Aliyev
02/09	Vorskla	a	2-2	Oliynyk, Giuliano
15/09	Chornomorets	h	1-0	Seleznyov
28/09	Shakhtar	a	1-2	Rotan
07/10	Dynamo	h	2-1	Seleznyov, Matheus
20/10	Zorya	a	0-3	(w/o; original result 2-3 Kalinić 2)
28/10	Karpaty	h	2-0	Seleznyov (p), Odibe
03/11	Metalist	a	2-0	Rotan, Giuliano
11/11	Illychivets	h	0-0	
18/11	Tavriya	a	2-1	Kalinić, Giuliano
26/11	Metalurh Zaporizhya	h	3-0	Kravchenko 2, Kalinić
01/12	Metalurh Donetsk	a	0-0	

2013
02/03	Arsenal	h	3-0	Zozulya, Matheus (p), Fedetskiy
10/03	Hoverla	a	1-0	og (Petrov)
17/03	Kryvbas	h	1-2	Kankava
31/03	Volyn	a	1-1	Giuliano
06/04	Vorskla	a	1-2	Giuliano
12/04	Chornomorets	a	2-1	Matheus, Zozulya
21/04	Shakhtar	h	1-1	Matheus
27/04	Dynamo	a	0-2	
03/05	Zorya	h	1-1	Seleznyov
12/05	Karpaty	a	4-2	Kravchenko, Seleznyov, Kalinić, Kobakhidze
19/05	Metalist	a	1-2	Seleznyov
26/05	Illychivets	h	7-0	Zozulya 3, Seleznyov, Rotan, Shakhov, Oliynyk

No	Name	Nat	DoB	Pos	Aps	(s)	Gls
88	Olexandr Aliyev		03/02/85	M	6	(6)	2
36	Ruslan Babenko		08/07/92	M		(2)	
20	Derek Boateng	GHA	02/05/83	M	2		
14	Yevhen Cheberyachko		19/06/83	D	25	(1)	
23	Vitali Denisov	UZB	23/02/87	D	7	(3)	1
23	Douglas	BRA	04/04/90	D	8		
44	Artem Fedetskiy		26/04/85	D	13	(4)	1
8	Giuliano	BRA	31/05/90	M	28		9
9	Nikola Kalinić	CRO	05/01/88	A	13	(7)	6
6	Jaba Kankava	GEO	18/03/86	M	10	(7)	1
19	Aleksandre Kobakhidze	GEO	11/02/87	A	1	(4)	1
10	Yevhen Konoplyanka		29/09/89	A	15	(5)	2
4	Serhiy Kravchenko		24/04/83	M	15	(5)	3
7	Denys Kulakov		01/05/86	M	2	(7)	
16	Jan Laštůvka	CZE	07/07/82	G	24		
5	Vitaliy Mandzyuk		24/01/86	D	23	(3)	
99	Matheus	BRA	15/01/83	A	19	(9)	6
3	Ondřej Mazuch	CZE	15/03/89	D	19		
23	Michael Odibe	NGA	23/07/88	A	7	(2)	1
11	Denys Oliynyk		16/06/87	M	10	(3)	2
29	Ruslan Rotan		29/10/81	M	24	(1)	4
21	Yevhen Seleznyov		20/07/85	A	14	(8)	7
28	Yevhen Shakhov		30/11/90	M	1	(3)	1
77	Denys Shelikhov		23/06/89	G	4		
17	Ivan Strinić	CRO	17/07/87	D	21	(2)	
91	Ihor Vartsaba		28/01/91	G	2		
18	Roman Zozulya		17/11/89	M	17	(6)	8

FC DYNAMO KYIV

Coach: Yuri Semin (RUS); (25/09/12) Oleh Blokhin
1927 • Dynamo im. Valeriy Lobanovskiy (16,873);
NSK Olimpiyskiy (70,050) • fcdynamo.kiev.ua
Major honours
UEFA Cup Winners' Cup (2) 1975, 1986;
UEFA Super Cup (1) 1975;
USSR League (13) 1961, 1966, 1967, 1968, 1971, 1974,
1975, 1977, 1980, 1981, 1985, 1986, 1990;
Ukrainian League (13) 1993, 1994, 1995, 1996, 1997,
1998, 1999, 2000, 2001, 2003, 2004, 2007, 2009;
USSR Cup (9) 1954, 1964, 1966, 1974, 1978, 1982,
1985, 1987, 1990;
Ukrainian Cup (9) 1993, 1996, 1998, 1999, 2000, 2003,
2005, 2006, 2007

2012

14/07	Metalurh Donetsk	h	1-0	Ideye
22/07	Arsenal	a	1-0	Ideye
27/07	Hoverla	h	3-1	Gusev, Ideye 2
03/08	Kryvbas	a	1-0	Yarmolenko
12/08	Volyn	h	4-1	Kranjčar 2, Ideye 2
18/08	Vorskla	a	0-1	
25/08	Chornomorets	h	2-0	Ninković, Ideye
02/09	Shakhtar	a	1-3	Yarmolenko
14/09	Karpaty	h	3-1	Ideye, Kranjčar 2
28/09	Zorya	h	1-0	Raffael
07/10	Dnipro	a	1-2	Miguel Veloso
20/10	Metalist	h	1-3	Yarmolenko
28/10	Illychivets	h	0-0	
03/11	Tavriya	h	2-0	Marco Ruben, Mikhalik
10/11	Metalurh Zaporizhya	a	5-0	Miguel Veloso, Garmash, Ideye 2, Yarmolenko
17/11	Metalurh Donetsk	a	0-1	
25/11	Arsenal	h	4-0	Khacheridi, Ideye 2, Gusev
30/11	Hoverla	a	4-2	Haruna, Ideye, Dudu, Yarmolenko

2013

03/03	Kryvbas	h	1-1	Haruna
10/03	Volyn	a	2-0	Yarmolenko, Garmash
17/03	Vorskla	h	1-0	Vida
31/03	Chornomorets	a	2-0	Gusev, Yarmolenko
07/04	Shakhtar	h	1-2	Yarmolenko
13/04	Karpaty	a	1-0	Ideye
20/04	Zorya	a	5-0	Yarmolenko, Ideye 2, Bezus, Gusev
27/04	Dnipro	h	2-0	Haruna 2
04/05	Metalist	a	0-2	
11/05	Illychivets	h	1-0	Haruna
19/05	Tavriya	a	2-3	Ideye, Yarmolenko
26/05	Metalurh Zaporizhya	h	3-0	Yarmolenko, Kravets 2

No	Name	Nat	DoB	Pos	Aps	(s)	Gls
8	Olexandr Aliyev		03/02/85	M		(3)	
3	Betão	BRA	11/11/83	D	12	(1)	
9	Roman Bezus		26/09/90	M	3	(6)	1
23	Andriy Bogdanov		21/01/90	M	1	(6)	
71	Denys Boiko		29/01/88	G	1	(1)	
23	Vitaliy Buyalskiy		06/01/93	M	1		
2	Danilo Silva	BRA	24/11/86	D	21		
99	Dudu	BRA	07/01/92	M	9	(4)	1
19	Denys Garmash		19/04/90	M	18	(5)	2
20	Oleh Gusev		25/04/83	M	25	(3)	4
25	Lukman Haruna	NGA	04/12/90	M	17	(1)	5
11	Ideye Brown	NGA	10/10/88	A	24	(4)	17
45	Vladyslav Kalitvintsev		04/01/93	M	1		
34	Yevhen Khacheridi		28/07/87	D	23		1
29	Dmytro Khlebas		09/05/94	A		(1)	
35	Maxym Koval		09/12/92	G	23		
21	Niko Kranjčar	CRO	13/08/84	M	11	(2)	4
22	Artem Kravets		03/06/89	A	1		2
15	Marco Ruben	ARG	26/10/86	A	5	(6)	1
13	Admir Mehmedi	SUI	16/03/91	A	8	(8)	
4	Miguel Veloso	POR	11/05/86	M	23	(1)	2
17	Taras Mikhalik		28/10/83	M	16		1
10	Artem Milevskiy		12/01/85	A	3	(7)	
36	Miloš Ninković	SRB	25/12/84	M	1	(4)	1
6	Goran Popov	MKD	02/10/84	M	1		
85	Raffael	BRA	28/03/85	A	4	(5)	1
3	Yevhen Selin		09/05/88	D	5	(1)	
1	Olexandr Shovkovskiy		02/01/75	G	6		
16	Serhiy Sydorchuk		02/05/91	M	2	(5)	
33	Taye Taiwo	NGA	16/04/85	D	19	(1)	
77	Andriy Tsurikov		05/10/92	M	1	(2)	
24	Domagoj Vida	CRO	29/04/89	D	12		1
5	Ognjen Vukojević	CRO	20/12/83	M	9	(3)	
9,10	Andriy Yarmolenko		23/10/89	A	23	(4)	11
37	Ayila Yussuf	NGA	04/11/84	M	1	(1)	

FC HOVERLA UZHHOROD

Coach: Olexandr Sevidov
1925 • Avanhard (12,000) • fcgoverla.uz.ua

2012

14/07	Chornomorets	a	2-3	Mishchenko, Trukhin
21/07	Shakhtar	h	1-3	Raičević
27/07	Dynamo	a	1-3	Kosyrin
03/08	Zorya	h	0-1	
11/08	Dnipro	a	1-4	Melikyan
18/08	Metalist	h	0-3	
25/08	Illychivets	h	0-2	
31/08	Tavriya	h	2-1	Mishchenko, Odonkor
16/09	Metalurh Zaporizhya	a	1-1	Mishchenko
30/09	Metalurh Donetsk	h	2-1	Odonkor, Mališič
06/10	Arsenal	a	0-2	
21/10	Karpaty	a	1-1	Raičević
27/10	Kryvbas	h	1-1	Raičević
04/11	Volyn	a	1-2	Le Tallec
09/11	Vorskla	h	1-1	Le Tallec
17/11	Chornomorets	h	1-1	Jordi López
24/11	Shakhtar	a	1-5	Le Tallec
30/11	Dynamo	h	2-4	Balafas, Raičević

2013

03/03	Zorya	a	1-2	Lysenko
10/03	Dnipro	h	0-1	
18/03	Metalist	a	0-1	
30/03	Illychivets	h	1-1	Lysenko
07/04	Tavriya	a	2-0	Le Tallec, Balafas
14/04	Metalurh Zaporizhya	h	2-0	Makarenko, og (Nesterov)
20/04	Metalurh Donetsk	a	1-2	Jordi López
27/04	Arsenal	h	1-3	Petrov
03/05	Karpaty	h	2-1	Le Tallec, Trukhin
12/05	Kryvbas	a	0-3	
18/05	Volyn	h	1-1	Raičević
26/05	Vorskla	a	0-3	

No	Name	Nat	DoB	Pos	Aps	(s)	Gls
33	Dmytro Babenko		28/06/78	G	21		
44	Sotirios Balatas	GRE	19/08/86	M	19	(2)	2
28	Vitalie Bordian	MDA	11/08/84	D	10		
23	Vyacheslav Churko		10/05/93	M	6	(5)	
2	Oleh Dopilka		12/03/86	D	8	(3)	
29	Andriy Hrinchenko		23/01/86	D	2		
29	Mykola Hybalyuk		23/01/86	M	2	(1)	
88	Jordi López	ESP	28/02/81	M	7	(10)	2
10	Olexandr Kosyrin		18/06/77	A	3	(7)	1
18	Serhiy Kurta		30/06/93	A		(1)	
76	Damien Le Tallec	FRA	19/04/90	A	15	(5)	5
10	Volodymyr Lysenko		20/04/88	A	6	(2)	2
19	Yevhen Makarenko		21/05/91	D	24	(1)	1
34	Bojan Mališić	SRB	14/01/85	D	23		1
7	Yegishe Melikyan	ARM	13/08/79	D	4	(1)	1
9	Oleh Mishchenko		10/10/89	A	12	(13)	3
77	Robert Molnar		24/06/91	M	1		
23	Vladyslav Mykulyak		30/08/84	M	4	(2)	
1	Olexandr Nagy		02/09/85	G	9		
37	David Odonkor	GER	21/02/84	M	13	(1)	2
11	Stanislav Pechenkin		02/03/88	M	12	(5)	
2	Kyrylo Petrov		22/06/90	D	12		1
7	Mirko Raičević	MNE	22/03/82	M	21	(1)	5
21	Nemanja Rnić	SRB	30/09/84	D	9		
17	Viktor Ryashko		27/11/92	M		(1)	
25	Pavlo Shchedrakov		17/01/85	D	22		
18	Olexandr Sytnyk		02/01/85	M	4	(5)	
99	Svetoslav Todorov	BUL	30/08/78	A	4	(5)	
8	Aleksandar Trišović	SRB	25/11/83	M	1	(5)	
15	Dmytro Trukhin		29/06/83	M	26	(1)	2
77	Serhiy Valyayev		16/09/78	M		(1)	
22	Artur Yedigaryan	ARM	26/06/87	M	16	(3)	
13	Yevhen Yeliseyev		06/03/89	D	14		

FC ILLYCHIVETS MARIUPIL

Coach: Mykola Pavlov
2003 • Illychivets (12,460) • fcilich.com

2012

14/07	Metalist	a	0-2	
21/07	Karpaty	a	5-1	Kravchenko 2, Fedotov 2, Butko
28/07	Tavriya	h	0-1	
05/08	Metalurh Zaporizhya	a	3-0	Pukanych, Kravchenko, Yaroshenko
12/08	Metalurh Donetsk	h	0-1	
17/08	Arsenal	a	1-2	Okriashvili
25/08	Hoverla	h	2-0	Grechishkin, Fedotov
01/09	Kryvbas	a	2-1	Kravchenko, Targamadze
15/09	Volyn	h	0-0	
30/09	Vorskla	a	0-1	
06/10	Chornomorets	h	2-1	Chizhov, Fedotov
19/10	Shakhtar	a	1-2	Fomin
28/10	Dynamo	h	0-0	
04/11	Zorya	a	2-2	Yaroshenko 2
11/11	Dnipro	h	0-0	
18/11	Metalist	h	0-2	
25/11	Karpaty	h	2-0	Fomin, Fedotov
02/12	Tavriya	a	0-1	

2013

02/03	Metalurh Zaporizhya	h	1-0	Fomin
08/03	Metalurh Donetsk	a	0-0	
17/03	Arsenal	h	2-1	Okriashvili 2 (1p)
30/03	Hoverla	a	1-1	Fomin
06/04	Kryvbas	h	0-1	
12/04	Volyn	a	2-0	Polyanskiy, Ordets
19/04	Vorskla	h	1-0	Mandzyuk
27/04	Chornomorets	a	1-1	Okriashvili (p)
04/05	Shakhtar	h	1-1	Mandzyuk
11/05	Dynamo	a	0-1	
19/05	Zorya	h	1-2	Polyanskiy
26/05	Dnipro	a	0-7	

No	Name	Nat	DoB	Pos	Aps	(s)	Gls
91	Bohdan Butko		13/01/91	D	29		1
36	Olexandr Chizhov		10/08/86	D	20		1
4	Olexiy Dovhiy		02/11/89	M	1		
11	Vitaliy Fedotov		16/07/91	M	26	(4)	5
11	Ruslan Fomin		02/03/86	A	13	(3)	4
22	Dmytro Grechishkin		22/09/91	M	13	(2)	1
32	Mykola Ishchenko		09/03/83	D	25		
12	Rustam Khudzhamov		05/10/82	G	30		
14	Ruslan Kisil		23/10/91	A	1	(4)	
29	Denys Kozhanov		13/06/87	M	5	(6)	
24	Kostyantyn Kravchenko		24/09/86	M	9	(3)	4
16	Olexandr Mandzyuk		10/01/83	A	7	(13)	2
80	Tornike Okriashvili	GEO	12/02/92	M	25	(3)	4
44	Ivan Ordets		08/07/92	D	12		1
2	Olexiy Polyanskiy		12/04/86	M	12		2
5	Adrian Pukanych		22/06/83	M	1	(5)	1
77	Artem Putivtsev		29/08/88	D	26		
7	Serhiy Shevchuk		18/06/85	D	7	(5)	
99	David Targamadze	GEO	22/08/89	M	20	(8)	1
93	Ivan Tsyupa		25/06/93			(1)	
39	Vitaliy Vitsenets		03/08/90	M	10	(4)	
9	Kostyantyn Yaroshenko		12/09/86	M	15	(8)	3
13	Serhiy Yavorskiy		05/07/89	M	9	(10)	
33	Roman Yemeliyanov	RUS	08/05/92	M	14	(6)	

FC KARPATY LVIV

Coach: Pavel Kucherov (RUS);
(20/1/12) Nikolay Kostov (BUL);
(06/05/13) (Yuriy Dyachuk-Stavytskiy)
1963 • Ukraina (27,925) • fckarpaty.lviv.ua
Major honours
USSR Cup (1) 1969

2012

13/07	Volyn	a	1-1	Lucas	
21/07	Illychivets	h	1-5	Ksionz	
28/07	Vorskla	a	1-3	Oshchypko	
04/08	Tavriya	h	2-0	Ksionz, Lucas	
11/08	Chornomorets	a	1-1	Lucas	
19/08	Metalurh Zaporizhya	a	2-1	Ksionz, Kasiyan	
26/08	Shakhtar	a	0-3		
01/09	Metalurh Donetsk	h	0-1		
14/09	Dynamo	a	1-3	Lucas (p)	
30/09	Arsenal	h	1-1	Balažič	
06/10	Zorya	a	1-2	Oshchypko	
21/10	Hoverla	h	1-1	Hladkiy	
28/10	Dnipro	a	0-2		
04/11	Kryvbas	h	6-0	Kenia, Hladkiy, Lucas 3, Štilić	
11/11	Metalist	a	1-2	Kopolovets	
18/11	Volyn	h	2-0	Lucas, Kenia	
25/11	Illychivets	a	0-2		
01/12	Vorskla	h	2-0	Khudobyak, Hladkiy	

2013

03/03	Tavriya	a	2-0	Zenjov, Hladkiy	
09/03	Chornomorets	h	1-2	Khudobyak	
15/03	Metalurh Zaporizhya	a	1-1	Kopolovets	
30/03	Shakhtar	h	1-2	Zhovtyuk	
07/04	Metalurh Donetsk	a	0-4		
13/04	Dynamo	h	0-1		
22/04	Arsenal	a	1-4	Kenia	
28/04	Zorya	h	2-0	Plastun, Holodyuk	
03/05	Hoverla	a	1-2	Hladkiy	
12/05	Dnipro	h	2-4	og (Douglas), Milošević	
18/05	Kryvbas	a	2-3	Zenjov 2	
26/05	Metalist	h	1-1	Ozarkiv	

No	Name	Nat	DoB	Pos	Aps	(s)	Gls
21	Gregor Balažič	SVN	12/02/88	D	17		1
33	Volodymyr Bidlovskiy		31/05/88	D	4		
83	Oleh Biliy		29/05/93	M	1		
1	Martin Bogatinov	MKD	26/04/86	G	22		
88	Murtaz Daushvili	GEO	01/05/89	D	21	(1)	
14	Serhiy Gerashchenkov		16/05/90	D	1	(3)	
41	Stepan Hirskiy		08/01/91	D	3	(1)	
10	Olexandr Hladkiy		24/08/87	A	16	(7)	5
17	Oleh Holodyuk		02/01/88	M	17	(2)	1
36	Volodymyr Hudyma		20/07/90	A	1	(3)	
28	Olexandr Kasiyan		27/01/89	A	6	(5)	1
20	Levan Kenia	GEO	18/10/90	M	16	(4)	3
16	Ihor Khudobyak		20/02/85	M	26	(3)	2
18	Mykhailo Kopolovets		29/01/84	M	9	(16)	2
7	Pavlo Ksionz		02/01/87	M	28		3
77	Lucas	ESP	10/09/88	A	17		8
19	Marcelinho	BRA	28/03/90	M	4	(7)	
19	Yaroslav Martynyuk		20/02/89	M	2	(2)	
4	Ivan Milošević	SRB	03/11/84	D	18		1
23	Roman Mysak		09/09/91	G	8	(2)	
8	Ihor Oshchypko		25/10/85	D	15		2
43	Ihor Ozarkiv		21/01/92	M	16	(5)	1
32	Ihor Plastun		20/08/90	D	24	(1)	1
62	Taras Puchkovskiy		23/08/94	A	2	(1)	
22	Semir Štilić	BIH	08/10/87	M	12	(10)	1
25	Andriy Tkachuk		18/11/87	M	10	(3)	
3	Jakub Tosik	POL	21/05/87	D	3	(1)	
3	Simon Vukčević	MNE	29/01/86	M		(2)	
51	Serhiy Zagidulin		26/03/92	A		(3)	
73	Taras Zaviyskiy		12/04/95	M	1	(1)	
11	Sergei Zenjov	EST	20/04/89	A	7	(3)	3
39	Mykola Zhovtyuk		21/05/92	D	3	(4)	1

FC KRYVBAS KRYVYI RIH

Coach: Oleh Taran
1959 • Metalurh (29,734) • fckryvbas.com.ua

2012

15/07	Vorskla	a	1-0	Antonov	
20/07	Chornomorets	h	1-0	Kankava	
29/07	Shakhtar	a	0-1		
03/08	Dynamo	h	0-1		
11/08	Zorya	a	1-0	Bartulović	
18/08	Dnipro	h	0-0		
26/08	Metalist	a	1-3	Kankava	
01/09	Illychivets	h	1-2	Bartulović	
16/09	Tavriya	a	0-1		
30/09	Metalurh Zaporizhya	h	5-0	Samodin 2, Liopa, Valeyev, Antonov	
05/10	Metalurh Donetsk	a	2-6	Antonov (p), Samodin	
21/10	Arsenal	h	1-1	Antonov (p)	
27/10	Hoverla	a	1-1	Bartulović	
04/11	Karpaty	a	0-6		
10/11	Volyn	h	1-0	Samodin	
18/11	Vorskla	h	3-2	Antonov 2, Priyomov	
23/11	Chornomorets	a	0-2		
30/11	Shakhtar	h	0-2		

2013

03/03	Dynamo	a	1-1	Priyomov	
09/03	Zorya	h	3-0	Samodin 2, og (Vernydub)	
17/03	Dnipro	a	2-1	Antonov, Dedechko	
31/04	Metalist	h	1-1	Priyomov	
06/04	Illychivets	a	1-0	Fedorchuk	
13/04	Tavriya	h	2-0	Shershun, Samodin	
20/04	Metalurh Zaporizhya	a	0-2		
28/04	Metalurh Donetsk	h	1-1	Antonov (p)	
04/05	Arsenal	a	1-1	Samodin	
12/05	Hoverla	h	3-0	Antonov 2, Bartulović	
18/05	Karpaty	h	3-2	Samodin 2, Lysytskiy	
26/05	Volyn	a	0-3	(w/o)	

No	Name	Nat	DoB	Pos	Aps	(s)	Gls
86	Olexiy Antonov		08/05/86	A	18	(6)	10
17	Michel Babatunde	NGA	24/12/92	M	2	(9)	
47	Saša Balić	MNE	29/01/90	D	3	(6)	
11	Mladen Bartulović	CRO	05/10/86	M	24		4
12	Yevhen Borovyk		02/03/85	G	11		
15	Denys Dedechko		02/07/87	M	16	(8)	1
7	Valeriy Fedorchuk		05/10/88	M	10	(1)	1
5	Vitaliy Fedoriv		21/10/87	D	6		
5	Andriy Hitchenko		02/10/84	D	10	(1)	
77	Olexandr Ivashchenko		19/02/85	A		(6)	
33	Antonio Jakoliš	CRO	18/02/92	A	1	(3)	
9	Jiří Jeslínek	CZE	30/09/87	M	8	(8)	
20	Jaba Kankava	GEO	18/03/86	M	7		2
39	Dmytro Liopa		23/11/88	M	8	(4)	1
23	Ucha Lobjanidze	GEO	23/02/87	D	21	(2)	
22	Vitaliy Lysytskiy		16/04/82	M	23	(1)	1
28	Darijan Matić	SVN	28/05/83	M	11	(5)	
94	Denys Miroshnychenko		11/10/94	D	2	(7)	
24	Pavlo Pashayev		04/01/88	D	24		
18	Kyrylo Petrov		22/06/90	M	11	(2)	
10	Volodymyr Priyomov		02/01/86	M	13	(3)	3
1	Vitaliy Reva		19/11/74	G	6		
8	Sergei Samodin	RUS	14/02/85	A	24	(2)	10
3	Vyacheslav Serdyuk		28/01/85	D	16	(2)	
4	Bohdan Shershun		14/05/81	D	16	(2)	1
55	Artem Shtanko		06/09/80	G	12	(1)	
88	Rinar Valeyev		22/08/87	M	16	(4)	1

FC METALIST KHARKIV

Coach: Myron Markevych
1925 • Metalist Stadium (41,307) • metalist.ua
Major honours
USSR Cup (1) 1988

2012

14/07	Illychivets	h	2-0	Sosa, Rebenok	
21/07	Tavriya	a	1-0	Sosa	
28/07	Metalurh Zaporizhya	h	1-1	Cristaldo	
05/08	Metalurh Donetsk	a	2-2	Cleiton Xavier 2	
12/08	Arsenal	h	0-1		
18/08	Hoverla	a	3-0	Cristaldo 2 (1p), Willian	
26/08	Kryvbas	h	3-1	Cleiton Xavier (p), Marlos, Edmar	
02/09	Volyn	a	1-2	Willian	
15/09	Vorskla	h	4-0	Cleiton Xavier 2, Taison, Marlos	
29/09	Chornomorets	a	1-1	Willian	
07/10	Shakhtar	h	0-2		
20/10	Dynamo	a	3-1	Taison, Cleiton Xavier (p), Torres	
28/10	Zorya	h	2-0	Willian, Edmar	
03/11	Dnipro	a	0-2		
11/11	Karpaty	h	2-1	Cristaldo 2	
18/11	Illychivets	a	2-0	Cristaldo 2	
26/11	Tavriya	h	5-0	Blanco 2, Taison, Cristaldo, Marlos	
01/12	Metalurh Zaporizhya	a	3-1	Edmar, Cleiton Xavier, Berezovchuk	

2013

02/03	Metalurh Donetsk	h	3-2	Marlos, og (Morozyuk), Dević	
10/03	Arsenal	a	2-1	Sosa, Jajá	
18/03	Hoverla	h	1-0	Cleiton Xavier	
31/03	Kryvbas	a	1-1	Cleiton Xavier	
06/04	Volyn	h	1-0	Cleiton Xavier	
14/04	Vorskla	a	4-1	Villagra, Cristaldo, Marlos, Cleiton Xavier	
21/04	Chornomorets	h	3-1	Cleiton Xavier 2, Sosa	
28/04	Shakhtar	a	1-1	Dević	
04/05	Dynamo	h	2-0	Dević, Cleiton Xavier	
10/05	Zorya	a	3-1	Sosa 2, Cleiton Xavier (p)	
19/05	Dnipro	h	2-1	Dević 2	
26/05	Karpaty	a	1-1	Sosa	

No	Name	Nat	DoB	Pos	Aps	(s)	Gls
65	Olexandr Andriyevskiy		25/06/94	M		(1)	
16	Denys Barvinko		16/02/94	D	6		
4	Andriy Berezovchuk		16/04/81	D	13		1
23	Sebastián Blanco	ARG	15/03/88	M	9	(17)	2
10	Cleiton Xavier	BRA	23/03/83	M	28	(1)	15
9	Jonathan Cristaldo	ARG	05/03/89	A	16	(6)	9
18	Marko Dević		27/10/83	M	7	(3)	5
81	Vladimir Dišljenković	SRB	02/07/81	G	5		
8	Edmar		16/06/80	M	24	(1)	3
5	Fininho	BRA	03/11/83	A	9	(2)	
29	Olexandr Goryainov		29/06/75	G	23	(1)	
30	Papa Gueye	SEN	07/06/84	D	25		
50	Jajá	BRA	28/02/86	A	3		1
32	Oleh Krasnoperov		25/07/80	M	9	(2)	
32	Volodymyr Lysenko		20/04/88	M	2	(1)	
20	Márcio Azevedo	BRA	05/02/86	D	8		
25	Marlos	BRA	07/06/88	M	24	(3)	6
22	Milan Obradović	SRB	03/08/77	D		(1)	
17	Serhiy Pshenychnykh		19/11/81	D	20	(2)	
46	Artem Radchenko		02/01/95	A	1		
82	Pavlo Rebenok		23/07/85	M		(7)	1
13	Vyacheslav Sharpar		02/06/87	M	2	(7)	
5	Oleh Shelayev		05/11/76	M	10	(5)	
99	Ihor Shukhovtsev		13/07/71	G	1		
35	Bohdan Shust		04/03/86	G	1		
11	José Ernesto Sosa	ARG	19/06/85	M	21		7
7	Taison	BRA	13/01/88	A	12	(1)	3
19	Juan Manuel Torres	ARG	20/06/85	M	10	(7)	1
3	Cristian Villagra	ARG	27/12/85	D	24		1
9	Andriy Vorobei		29/11/78	A			
86	Willian	BRA	19/11/86	A	6	(19)	4
6	Marco Torsiglieri	ARG	12/01/88	M	10	(1)	

FC METALURH DONETSK

Volodymyr Pyatenko; (23/08/12) Yuriy Maximov
1996 • Metalurh (5,094) • metallurg.donetsk.ua

2012

14/07	Dynamo	a	0-1	
22/07	Zorya	h	1-2	Zé Soares
29/07	Dnipro	a	0-2	
05/08	Metalist	h	2-2	Baranovskiy, Traoré
12/08	Illychivets	a	1-0	Volovyk
18/08	Tavriya	h	1-1	Júnior Moraes (p)
26/08	Metalurh Zaporizhya	a	2-1	Ghazaryan, Júnior Moraes
01/09	Karpaty	a	1-0	Júnior Moraes
16/09	Arsenal	h	5-0	Júnior Moraes 2 (1p), Ghazaryan, Traoré 2
30/09	Hoverla	a	1-2	Ghazaryan
05/10	Kryvbas	h	6-2	Golaydo, Volovyk (p), Traoré 3, Danilo
20/10	Volyn	a	1-1	Júnior Moraes (p)
27/10	Vorskla	h	0-0	
04/11	Chornomorets	a	0-3	
11/11	Shakhtar	h	0-4	
17/11	Dynamo	h	1-0	Dimitrov
24/11	Zorya	a	2-1	Nelson, og (Ignjatijević)
01/12	Dnipro	h	0-0	

2013

03/03	Metalist	a	2-3	Júnior Moraes 2
08/03	Illychivets	h	0-0	
16/03	Tavriya	a	3-4	Nelson 2, Volovyk (p)
30/03	Metalurh Zaporizhya	h	2-0	Traoré, Nelson
07/04	Karpaty	h	4-0	Júnior Moraes 2, Leonardo, Polyoviy
14/04	Arsenal	a	2-0	Traoré 2
20/04	Hoverla	h	2-1	Morozyuk, Dimitrov
28/04	Kryvbas	a	1-1	Júnior Moraes
03/05	Volyn	a	2-0	Checher, Volovyk
11/05	Vorskla	a	1-0	Volovyk
19/05	Chornomorets	h	2-0	Polyoviy, Dimitrov
26/05	Shakhtar	a	0-4	

No	Name	Nat	DoB	Pos	Aps	(s)	Gls
12	Olexandr Bandura		30/05/86	G	20		
2	Artem Baranovskiy		17/03/90	D	12	(4)	1
4	Vyacheslav Checher		15/12/80	D	15		1
11	Danilo	BEL	13/01/90	M	25	(2)	1
18	Velizar Dimitrov	BUL	13/04/79	M	20		3
21	Lorenzo Ebecilio	NED	24/09/91	M	4	(2)	
10	Gevorg Ghazaryan	ARM	05/04/88	M	12	(9)	3
84	Denys Golaydo		03/06/84	M	17	(9)	1
43	Pavlo Gryshchenko		06/07/90	M		(2)	
19	Vitaliy Ivanko		09/04/92	A	2	(6)	
91	Júnior Moraes	BRA	04/04/87	A	21	(2)	11
55	Vitaliy Kvashuk		01/04/93	M		(1)	
9	Djordje Lazić	SRB	18/06/83	M	14	(6)	
42	Leonardo	BRA	18/03/93	M	2	(7)	1
13	Konstantinos Makrides	CYP	13/01/82	M	22	(2)	
6	Karlen Mkrtchyan	ARM	25/11/88	M	15	(1)	
27	Gaetano Monachello	ITA	03/03/94	A		(4)	
7	Mykola Morozyuk		17/01/88	M	27		1
8	Gregory Nelson	NED	31/01/88	A	21	(6)	4
26	Kyrylo Nesterenko		01/03/92	M		(1)	
79	Yuriy Pankiv		03/11/84	G	10		
5	Volodymyr Polyoviy		28/07/85	D	10	(1)	2
44	Vasyl Priyma		10/06/91	D	6	(1)	
15	Dramane Traoré	MLI	17/10/85	A	20	(5)	9
35	Yevhen Troyanovskiy		02/07/93	M		(2)	
90	Vitaliy Tymofeyenko		04/12/93	M		(1)	
14	Olexandr Volovyk		28/10/85	D	26		5
21	Artak Yedigaryan	ARM	18/03/90	D	2	(6)	
17	Zé Soares	BRA	27/07/83	M	7	(6)	1

FC METALURH ZAPORIZHYA

Coach: Ihor Luchkevych; (24/07/12) Serhiy Kovalets;
(06/09/12) Vitaliy Kvartsyanyi;
(31/12/12) Serhiy Zaitsev
1935 • Slavutych Arena (11,756) • fcmetalurg.com

2012

14/07	Zorya	a	0-2	
22/07	Dnipro	h	0-4	
28/07	Metalist	a	1-1	Tsurikov
05/08	Illychivets	h	0-3	
10/08	Tavriya	a	0-1	
19/08	Karpaty	a	1-2	Matyazh
26/08	Metalurh Donetsk	h	1-2	Lazarovych
02/09	Arsenal	a	0-3	
16/09	Hoverla	h	1-1	Teikeu
30/09	Kryvbas	a	0-5	
06/10	Volyn	h	0-3	
21/10	Vorskla	a	0-5	
26/10	Chornomorets	h	0-1	
03/11	Shakhtar	a	0-2	
10/11	Dynamo	h	0-5	
17/11	Zorya	h	0-0	
26/11	Dnipro	a	0-3	
01/12	Metalist	h	1-3	Pisotskiy

2013

02/03	Illychivets	a	0-1	
09/03	Tavriya	h	0-1	
15/03	Karpaty	h	1-1	Matheus
30/03	Metalurh Donetsk	a	0-2	
06/04	Arsenal	h	0-0	
14/04	Hoverla	a	0-2	
20/04	Kryvbas	h	2-0	Rudyka 2
27/04	Volyn	a	0-0	
04/05	Vorskla	h	0-4	
12/05	Chornomorets	a	1-1	Shturko
19/05	Shakhtar	h	3-3	Jokić, Júnior, Pisotskiy
26/05	Dynamo	a	0-3	

No	Name	Nat	DoB	Pos	Aps	(s)	Gls
9	Olexiy Belik		15/02/81	A	8		
50	Andriy Boiko		27/04/81	D	4		
11	Andriy Haidash		16/01/89	A	1	(2)	
9	Vitaliy Havrysh		18/03/86	D	8	(2)	
6	Yuriy Hlushko		05/02/91	A	1	(2)	
12	Libor Hrdlička	SVK	02/01/86	G	10		
8	Besart Ibraimi	MKD	17/12/86	A	7	(4)	
27	Milan Ilić	SRB	23/01/91	D	1		
44	Maxym Imerekov		23/01/91	D	1		
5	Miloš Jokić	SRB	07/06/87	M	6	(4)	1
10	Júnior	BRA	20/09/78	A	25	(2)	1
30	Artur Kaskov		18/11/91	A	1	(3)	
9	Vitaliy Kaverin		04/09/90	A	1	(4)	
7	Mohamed Khalfaoui	TUN	24/10/80	M	9	(1)	
25	Volodymyr Korobka		22/07/89	M		(3)	
13	Ihor Korotetskiy		13/09/87	D	9	(1)	
23	Taras Lazarovych		22/04/82	A	2	(13)	1
23	Ivans Lukjanovs	LVA	24/01/87	M	3	(1)	
4	Matheus	BRA	08/03/85	D	20	(1)	1
17	Ivan Matyazh		15/02/88	M	14	(6)	1
17	Andriy Nesterov		02/07/90	D	16	(3)	
77	Andriy Oberemko		18/03/84	M	4		
39	Yevhen Opanasenko		25/08/90	M	27		
91	Temur Partsvania		06/07/91	D	7		
31	Yevhen Pisotskiy		22/04/87	M	25	(2)	2
90	Milan Purović	MNE	07/05/85	A	3	(1)	
25	Ante Rožić	CRO	08/03/86	D	1		
1	Vitaliy Rudenko		26/01/81	G	11		
19	Serhiy Rudyka		14/06/88	M	20	(5)	2
2	Andriy Sakhnevych		17/04/89	D	11	(1)	
4	Olexiy Shevchenko		24/02/92	G	9		
21	Yuriy Shturko		08/10/84	M	10	(3)	1
8	Maxym Skorokhodov		03/12/86	M	1	(2)	
18	Mohamed Slim	TUN	18/11/89	M	5	(6)	
2	Eduard Sobol		04/05/95	D	8	(1)	
34	Serhiy Sydorchuk		02/05/91	M	9	(1)	
3	Adolphe Teikeu	CMR	23/06/90	D	15		1
27	Andriy Tsurikov		05/10/92	M	12	(3)	1
23	Dmytro Ulyanov		01/12/93	D		(1)	
80	Andriy Voronkov		08/02/89	A	5	(4)	
36	Dmytro Yusov		11/05/93	M		(2)	
88	Yevhen Zadoya		05/01/91	M		(1)	

FC SHAKHTAR DONETSK

Coach: Mircea Lucescu (ROU)
1936 • Donbass Arena (50,149) • shakhtar.com
Major honours
UEFA Cup (1) 2009; Ukrainian League (8) 2002, 2005, 2006, 2008, 2010, 2011, 2012, 2013;
USSR Cup (4) 1961, 1962, 1980, 1983;
Ukrainian Cup (9) 1995, 1997, 2001, 2002, 2004, 2008, 2011, 2012, 2013

2012

15/07	Arsenal	h	6-0	Mkhitaryan 2, Seleznyov, Ilsinho, Dević (p)
21/07	Hoverla	a	3-1	Mkhitaryan, Ilsinho, Seleznyov
29/07	Kryvbas	h	1-0	Fernandinho
06/08	Volyn	a	4-0	Dević, Mkhitaryan 2, Alex Teixeira
12/08	Vorskla	h	4-1	Mkhitaryan 2, Dević, Alex Teixeira
19/08	Chornomorets	a	5-1	Mkhitaryan 3, Alex Teixeira, Willian
26/08	Karpaty	h	3-0	Dentinho, Luiz Adriano, Mkhitaryan
02/09	Dynamo	h	3-1	Kucher 2, Luiz Adriano
15/09	Zorya	a	3-0	Alex Teixeira, Mkhitaryan, Luiz Adriano
28/09	Dnipro	h	2-1	Mkhitaryan, Srna
07/10	Metalist	a	2-0	Mkhitaryan, Ilsinho
19/10	Illychivets	h	2-1	Ilsinho, Chygrynskiy
27/10	Tavriya	a	1-0	Alex Teixeira
03/11	Metalurh Zaporizhya	h	2-0	Douglas Costa (p), Luiz Adriano
11/11	Metalurh Donetsk	a	4-0	Eduardo, Mkhitaryan 2, Alex Teixeira
17/11	Arsenal	a	0-2	
24/11	Hoverla	h	5-1	Ilsinho, Willian, Mkhitaryan, Douglas Costa, Dević
30/11	Kryvbas	a	2-0	Mkhitaryan, Alex Teixeira

2013

01/03	Volyn	h	4-1	og (Shandruk), Kucher, Douglas Costa, Eduardo
10/03	Vorskla	a	1-0	Luiz Adriano
16/03	Chornomorets	h	3-0	Fernandinho, Mkhitaryan, Luiz Adriano
30/03	Karpaty	a	2-1	Alex Teixeira, Rakitskiy
07/04	Dynamo	a	2-1	Mkhitaryan 2
13/04	Zorya	h	3-0	Kryvtsov, Mkhitaryan, Luiz Adriano
21/04	Dnipro	a	1-1	Srna (p)
28/04	Metalist	h	1-1	Ilsinho
04/05	Illychivets	a	1-1	Alan Patrick
11/05	Tavriya	h	5-0	Douglas Costa, Alex Teixeira, Maicon, Mkhitaryan 2 (1p)
19/05	Metalurh Zaporizhya	a	3-3	Ismaily, Eduardo, Taison
26/05	Metalurh Donetsk	h	4-0	Douglas Costa, Mkhitaryan, Taison, Eduardo

No	Name	Nat	DoB	Pos	Aps	(s)	Gls
10	Alan Patrick	BRA	13/02/82	M	1	(3)	1
29	Alex Teixeira	BRA	06/01/90	M	16	(11)	10
27	Dmytro Chygrynskiy		07/11/86	D	10	(1)	1
18	Dentinho	BRA	04/05/85	M	2	(2)	1
18	Marko Dević		27/10/83	A	3	(9)	4
20	Douglas Costa	BRA	14/09/90	M	17	(10)	5
11	Eduardo	CRO	25/02/83	A	12	(8)	4
7	Fernandinho	BRA	04/05/85	M	23	(1)	2
30	Olexiy Gai		06/11/82	M	4	(2)	
24	Dmytro Grechishkin		22/09/91	M	5	(2)	
3	Tomáš Hübschman	CZE	04/09/81	M	8	(1)	
31	Ilsinho	BRA	12/10/85	M	10	(9)	6
31	Ismaily	BRA	11/01/90	D	1		1
32	Anton Kanibolotskiy		16/05/88	G	9		
14	Vasyl Kobin		24/05/85	M	4	(1)	
38	Serhiy Kryvtsov		15/03/91	D	12	(3)	1
5	Olexandr Kucher		22/10/82	D	14	(1)	3
9	Luiz Adriano	BRA	12/04/87	A	17	(2)	7
47	Maicon	BRA	08/05/88	A	3	(1)	1
22	Henrikh Mkhitaryan	ARM	21/01/89	A	27	(2)	25
30	Andriy Pyatov		28/06/84	G	21	(1)	
44	Yaroslav Rakitskiy		03/08/89	D	23	(1)	1
26	Răzvan Raţ	ROU	26/05/81	D	15	(1)	
7	Yevhen Seleznyov		20/07/85	A	1	(2)	2
13	Vyacheslav Shevchuk		13/05/79	D	14		
95	Eduard Sobol		04/05/95	D		(5)	
33	Darijo Srna	CRO	01/05/82	D	25	(1)	2
6	Taras Stepanenko		08/08/89	D	17	(1)	
28	Taison	BRA	13/01/88	A	7	(4)	2
10	Willian	BRA	09/08/88	M	9	(5)	2

SC TAVRIYA SIMFEROPOL

Coach: Oleh Luzhniy
1958 • Lokomotyv (19,978) • sctavriya.com
Major honours
Ukrainian League (1) 1992;
Ukrainian Cup (1) 2010

2012

15/07	Dnipro	a	1-3	*Feshchuk*
21/07	Metalist	h	0-1	
28/07	Illychivets	a	1-0	*Putrash*
04/08	Karpaty	a	0-2	
10/08	Metalurh Zaporizhya	h	1-0	*Nazarenko*
18/08	Metalurh Donetsk	a	1-1	*Nazarenko (p)*
26/08	Arsenal	h	1-1	*Kalynychenko*
31/08	Hoverla	a	1-2	*Kalynychenko*
16/09	Kryvbas	h	2-0	*Shinder, Nazarenko*
29/09	Volyn	a	1-0	*Nazarenko*
07/10	Vorskla	h	0-0	
21/10	Chornomorets	a	0-1	
27/10	Shakhtar	h	0-1	
03/11	Dynamo	a	0-2	
10/11	Zorya	h	1-0	*Nazarenko*
18/11	Dnipro	h	1-2	*Feshchuk*
26/11	Metalist	a	0-5	
02/12	Illychivets	h	1-0	*Shinder*

2013

03/03	Karpaty	h	0-2	
09/03	Metalurh Zaporizhya	a	1-0	*Humenyuk*
16/03	Metalurh Donetsk	h	4-3	*Humenyuk 2, Shinder, Nazarenko*
30/03	Arsenal	a	1-1	*Gadzhiyev*
07/04	Hoverla	h	0-2	
13/04	Kryvbas	a	0-2	
21/04	Volyn	h	3-0	*Humenyuk, Gadzhiyev, Shinder*
26/04	Vorskla	a	2-2	*Nazarenko (p), Feshchuk*
03/05	Chornomorets	h	1-3	*Eduardo*
11/05	Shakhtar	a	0-5	
19/05	Dynamo	h	3-2	*Nazarenko (p), Gadzhiyev, Né*
26/05	Zorya	a	0-3	

No	Name	Nat	DoB	Pos	Aps	(s)	Gls
3	Ayodele Adeleye	NGA	25/12/88	D	2		
20	Anis Boussaïdi	TUN	10/04/81	D	26		
15	Célio	BRA	20/07/87	D	22		
8	Eduardo	BRA	24/10/88	D	18	(1)	1
10	Maxym Feshchuk		25/11/85	A	13	(14)	3
90	Makhach Gadzhiyev	RUS	18/10/87	M	10	(6)	3
27	Rubén Gómez	ARG	26/01/84	M	29		
7	Yuriy Habovda		06/05/89	M	6	(8)	
30	Oleh Humenyuk		03/05/83	D	17	(11)	4
1	Damir Kahriman	SRB	19/11/84	G	15	(1)	
25	Maxym Kalynychenko		26/01/79	M	11	(2)	2
11	František Kubík	SVK	14/03/89	M	2		
4	Marin Ljubičić	CRO	15/06/88	M	16	(4)	
11	Dmytro Matviyenko		25/05/92	D	1	(3)	
93	Serhiy Melnyk		25/06/93	A	1	(2)	
18	Serhiy Nazarenko		16/02/80	M	28	(1)	8
16	Marco Né	CIV	17/07/83	M	3	(6)	1
21	Vladyslav Pavlenko		05/04/94	M	6	(1)	
23	Serhiy Pohoriliy		28/07/86	G	14		
92	Maxym Prikhodnoi		27/10/92	M	1		
9	Stanislav Prychynenko		26/06/91	M		(2)	
44	Yuriy Putrash		29/01/90	D	19	(6)	1
2	Olexandr Romanchuk		21/10/84	D	9	(3)	
17	Anton Shinder		13/06/87	A	26		4
31	Serhiy Sitalo		20/12/86	G	1		
6	Gustav Svensson	SWE	07/02/87	M	11		
5	Volodymyr Yezerskiy		15/11/76	D	23	(1)	

FC VOLYN LUTSK

Coach: Anatoliy Demyanenko;
(23/04/13) (Anatoliy Piskovets);
(07/05/13) Vitaliy Kvartsyanyi
1960 • Avanhard (10,792) • fcvolyn.net

2012

13/07	Karpaty	h	1-1	*Ramon Lopes*
22/07	Vorskla	h	1-0	*Subotic*
28/07	Chornomorets	a	2-0	*Izvoranu, Bicfalvi*
06/08	Shakhtar	h	0-4	
12/08	Dynamo	a	1-4	*Ramon Lopes*
19/08	Zorya	h	2-2	*Pylypchuk, Ramon Lopes*
26/08	Dnipro	a	1-2	*Subotic*
02/09	Metalist	h	2-1	*Bicfalvi, Subotic*
15/09	Illychivets	a	0-0	
29/09	Tavriya	h	0-1	
06/10	Metalurh Zaporizhya	h	3-0	*Pylypchuk, Bicfalvi, Arzhanov*
20/10	Metalurh Donetsk	h	1-1	*Savic*
26/10	Arsenal	a	1-1	*Owonikoko*
04/11	Hoverla	h	2-1	*Arzhanov, Savic*
10/11	Kryvbas	a	0-1	
18/11	Karpaty	a	0-2	
24/11	Vorskla	a	1-0	*Savic*
02/12	Chornomorets	h	0-2	

2013

01/03	Shakhtar	a	1-4	*Bicfalvi*
10/03	Dynamo	h	0-2	
16/03	Zorya	a	1-3	*Savic*
31/03	Dnipro	h	1-1	*Bicfalvi (p)*
06/04	Metalist	a	0-1	
12/04	Illychivets	h	0-2	
21/04	Tavriya	a	0-3	
27/04	Metalurh Zaporizhya	h	0-0	
03/05	Metalurh Donetsk	a	0-2	
11/05	Arsenal	h	1-3	*Subotic*
18/05	Hoverla	a	1-1	*Savic*
26/05	Kryvbas	h	3-0	*(w/o)*

No	Name	Nat	DoB	Pos	Aps	(s)	Gls
21	Volodymyr Arzhanov		29/11/85	M	12		2
19	Olexiy Babyr		15/03/90	A	7	(10)	
10	Eric Bicfalvi	ROU	05/02/88	M	23	(1)	5
9	Oleh Herasymyuk		25/09/86	M	1	(4)	
4	Valentin Iliev	BUL	11/07/80	D	17	(1)	
24	Silviu Izvoranu	ROU	03/12/83	M	16	(1)	1
40	Viktor Khomchenko		11/11/94	A		(1)	
29	Yaroslav Kinash		16/04/88	M	3	(2)	
78	Serhiy Lytovchenko		04/10/87	G	12	(2)	
14	Ján Maslo	SVK	05/02/86	D	11	(3)	
38	Olexandr Nasonov		28/04/92	M	15	(4)	
42	Vitaliy Nedilko		21/08/82	G	1		
2	Abayomi Owonikoko	NGA	13/09/92	A	4	(11)	1
17	Yevhen Pavlov		12/03/91	A	2	(9)	
18	Vitaliy Pryndeta		02/02/93	M	10	(4)	
90	Serhiy Pylypchuk		26/11/84	M	22	(2)	2
89	Ramon Lopes	BRA	07/08/89	M	11	(1)	3
11	Dusan Savic	MKD	01/10/85	A	14	(6)	5
7	Schumacher	BRA	31/03/86	A	2	(4)	
15	Oleh Shandruk		30/01/83	D	15	(3)	
57	Artem Shchedriy		09/11/92	D	1		
6	Vance Sikov	MKD	19/07/85	D	21	(1)	
3	Serhiy Siminin		09/10/87	M	26		
8	Ihor Skoba		21/05/82	M	6	(3)	
1	Maxym Startsev		20/01/80	G	16		
35	Saša Stević	SRB	31/05/81	M	8	(6)	
31	Danijel Subotic	SUI	31/01/89	A	21	(2)	4
5	Petar Zanev	BUL	18/10/85	D	22		

FC VORSKLA POLTAVA

Coach: Vadym Yevtushenko;
(15/08/12) Serhiy Svystun
1984 • Vorskla im. Olexiy Butovskiy (24,795) •
vorskla.com.ua
Major honours
Ukrainian Cup (1) 2009

2012

15/07	Kryvbas	h	0-1	
22/07	Volyn	a	0-1	
28/07	Karpaty	h	3-1	*Liyetava, Bezus, Yeremenko*
05/08	Chornomorets	h	0-1	
12/08	Shakhtar	a	1-4	*Januzi*
18/08	Dynamo	h	1-0	*Gromov*
24/08	Zorya	a	1-1	*Bezus*
02/09	Dnipro	h	2-2	*Selin, Januzi*
15/09	Metalist	a	0-4	
30/09	Illychivets	h	1-0	*Kryvosheyenko*
07/10	Tavriya	h	0-0	
21/10	Metalurh Zaporizhya	h	5-0	*Kryvosheyenko, Budnyk, Bezus 2, Gromov*
27/10	Metalurh Donetsk	a	0-0	
04/11	Arsenal	h	1-0	*Gromov*
09/11	Hoverla	a	1-1	*Bezus (p)*
18/11	Kryvbas	a	2-3	*Januzi, Bezus*
24/11	Volyn	h	0-1	
01/12	Karpaty	a	0-2	

2013

03/03	Chornomorets	a	0-1	
10/03	Shakhtar	h	0-1	
17/03	Dynamo	a	0-1	
29/03	Zorya	h	0-0	
06/04	Dnipro	a	2-1	*og (Mazuch), Gromov*
14/04	Metalist	h	1-4	*Budnyk (p)*
19/04	Illychivets	a	0-1	
26/04	Tavriya	h	2-2	*Gromov (p), Budnyk*
04/05	Metalurh Zaporizhya	a	4-0	*Chesnakov, Gromov, Budnyk 2*
11/05	Metalurh Donetsk	h	0-1	
18/05	Arsenal	a	1-2	*Gromov*
26/05	Hoverla	h	3-0	*Budnyk, Sklyar, Kryvosheyenko*

No	Name	Nat	DoB	Pos	Aps	(s)	Gls
24	Oleh Barannyk		20/03/92	A		(5)	
9	Roman Bezus		26/09/90	M	15	(1)	6
8	Yevhen Budnyk		04/09/90	M	14	(11)	6
28	Serhiy Chenbai		06/11/92	M		(2)	
17	Volodymyr Chesnakov		12/02/88	D	27		1
18	Olexiy Chichikov		30/09/87	A	1	(7)	
4	Armend Dallku	ALB	16/06/83	D	28		
1	Serhiy Dolhanskiy		15/09/74	G	23		
19	Artem Gromov		14/01/90	M	20	(6)	7
27	Ahmed Januzi	ALB	08/07/88	A	9	(3)	3
51	Olexiy Kazakov		22/02/90	G	2		
5	Oleh Krasnoperov		25/07/80	M	18		
11	Ivan Kryvosheyenko		11/05/84	A	21	(6)	3
20	Roman Kunev		20/09/90	A		(4)	
45	Valeriy Kurelekh		12/08/91	D		(1)	
78	Olexiy Kurilov		24/04/88	D	6	(2)	
22	Valeriy Kutsenko		02/06/91	D	6	(4)	
33	Panagiotis Lagos	GRE	05/06/85	M	10		
39	Ivan Liyetava		30/07/83	A	3	(5)	1
10	Jovan Markoski	SRB	23/06/80	M	24	(2)	
2	Olexandr Metveyev		11/02/89	D	12	(2)	
20	Vadym Milko		22/08/86	M		(2)	
12	Dmytro Nepogodov		17/02/88	G	5		
13	Yevhen Peskov		22/09/81	D	2	(1)	
77	Yevhen Pichkur		30/08/79	M	2	(1)	
40	Ihor Preduta		15/11/90	D	10	(1)	
82	Pavlo Rebenok		23/07/85	M	8	(4)	
23	Vadym Sapai		07/02/86	D	16	(4)	
33	Yevhen Selin		09/05/88	D	16		1
6	Olexandr Sklyar		26/02/91	M	8	(6)	1
5	Serhiy Sylyuk		05/06/85	M	7	(2)	
34	Yevhen Tkachuk		27/06/91	M	13	(2)	
3	Serhiy Vovkodav		02/07/88	D	1	(1)	
19	Dmytro Yeremenko		20/06/90	M	3	(3)	1

FC ZORYA LUHANSK

Coach: Yuriy Vernydub
1923 • Avanhard (22,288) • zarya-lugansk.com
Major honours
USSR League (1) 1972

2012

14/07	Metalurh Zaporizhya	h	2-0	Galyuza, Idahor
22/07	Metalurh Donetsk	a	2-1	Ljubenović, Galyuza
29/07	Arsenal	h	1-3	Galyuza
03/08	Hoverla	a	1-0	Lipartia (p)
11/08	Kryvbas	h	0-1	
19/08	Volyn	a	2-2	Idahor, Hrytsai
24/08	Vorskla	h	1-1	Galyuza (p)
01/09	Chornomorets	a	1-2	Khudzik
15/09	Shakhtar	h	0-3	
28/09	Dynamo	a	0-1	
06/10	Karpaty	h	2-1	Galyuza (p), Khudzik
20/10	Dnipro	h	3-0	(w/o; original result 3-2 Danilo, Hrytsai, Idahor)
28/10	Metalist	a	0-2	
04/11	Illychivets	h	2-2	Ljubenović, Danilo
10/11	Tavriya	a	0-1	
17/11	Metalurh Zaporizhya	a	0-0	
24/11	Metalurh Donetsk	h	1-2	Khudzik
02/12	Arsenal	a	1-0	Hrytsai

2013

03/03	Hoverla	h	2-1	Idahor, Vernydub
09/03	Kryvbas	a	0-3	
16/03	Volyn	h	3-1	Danilo 2 (1p), Boli
29/03	Vorskla	a	0-0	
05/04	Chornomorets	h	1-1	Khomchenovskiy
13/04	Shakhtar	a	0-3	
20/04	Dynamo	h	0-5	
28/04	Karpaty	a	0-2	
03/05	Dnipro	a	1-1	Danilo
09/05	Metalist	h	1-3	Boli
19/05	Illychivets	a	2-1	Galyuza, Khomchenovskiy
26/05	Tavriya	h	3-0	Danilo, Ljubenović, Khudzik

No	Name	Nat	DoB	Pos	Aps	(s)	Gls
25	Maxym Ihorovych Biliy		21/06/90	D	15	(10)	
94	Yannick Boli	CIV	13/01/88	A	2	(8)	2
4	Ihor Chaikovskiy		07/10/91	M	14		
9	Danilo	BRA	11/11/86	A	20		6
18	Serhiy Ferenchak		27/04/84	M	3	(3)	
2	Illya Galyuza		16/11/79	M	20	(3)	6
45	Artem Hordiyenko		04/03/91	D	1		
30	Olexandr Hrytsai		30/09/77	M	29		3
11	Lucky Idahor	NGA	30/08/80	A	19	(6)	4
17	Nikola Ignjatijević	SRB	12/12/83	D	25		
6	Mykyta Kamenyuka		03/06/85	M	19	(1)	
37	Dmytro Khomchenovskiy		16/04/90	M	11	(3)	2
9	Pavlo Khudzik		29/04/85	M	17	(7)	4
5	Ihor Korotetskiy		13/09/87	D	7	(2)	
30	Dmytro Kozachenko		11/01/82	G	4	(2)	
91	Ihor Levchenko		23/02/91	G	2		
10	Jaba Lipartia	GEO	16/11/87	A	10	(15)	1
22	Željko Ljubenović	SRB	09/07/81	M	22	(6)	3
88	Maicon	BRA	08/05/88	A	1	(3)	
19	Yaroslav Oliynyk		14/03/91	D	3	(4)	
34	Ivan Petryak		13/03/94	M		(3)	
12	Vitaliy Postranskiy		02/08/77	G	16	(1)	
23	Ivan Rodić	CRO	11/11/85	A	1	(9)	
1	Krševan Santini	CRO	11/04/87	G	8		
14	Toni Šunjić	BIH	15/12/88	D	28		
27	Serhiy Sylyuk		05/06/85	A		(1)	
15	Vitaliy Vernydub		17/10/87	D	15		1
16	Hryhoriy Yarmash		04/01/85	D	18	(3)	

Top goalscorers

25	Henrikh Mkhitaryan (Shakhtar)
17	Ideye Brown (Dynamo)
15	Cleiton Xavier (Metalist)
11	Andriy Yarmolenko (Dynamo)
	Júnior Moraes (Metalurh Donetsk)
10	Olexiy Antonov (Kryvbas)
	Sergei Samodin (Kryvbas)
	Alex Teixeira (Shakhtar)
9	Giuliano (Dnipro)
	Jonathan Cristaldo (Metalist)
	Dramane Traoré (Metalurh Donetsk)
	Marko Dević (Shakhtar/Metalist)
	Yevhen Seleznyov (Shakhtar/Dnipro)

Promoted club

PFC SEVASTOPOL

Coach: Oleg Kononov (BLR)
2002 • SC Sevastopol (5,576) • fcsevastopol.com

SECOND LEVEL FINAL TABLE 2012/13

		Pld	W	D	L	F	A	Pts
1	PFC Sevastopol	34	22	8	4	71	22	74
2	FC Stal Alchevsk	34	20	6	8	58	35	66
3	PFC Olexandriya	34	17	9	8	48	35	60
4	FC Bukovyna Chernivtsiy	34	16	10	8	49	33	58
5	FC Naftovyk-Ukrnafta Okhtyrka	34	15	9	10	39	31	54
6	MFK Mykolaiv	34	16	9	9	45	41	54
7	FC Avanhard Kramatorsk	34	15	8	11	37	26	53
8	FC Zirka Kirovohrad	34	14	10	10	46	37	52
9	FC Sumy	34	14	8	12	32	35	50
10	FC Helios Kharkiv	34	12	13	9	33	21	49
11	FC Olimpik Donetsk	34	15	4	15	34	37	49
12	FC Tytan Armyansk	34	13	9	12	44	40	48
13	FC Poltava	34	11	12	11	35	45	45
14	FC Krymteplytsya Molodizhne	34	9	8	17	30	45	35
15	FC Dynamo-2 Kyiv	34	8	6	20	31	55	30
16	FK Odesa	34	7	3	24	21	63	22
17	FC Obolon Kyiv	34	5	7	22	19	28	22
18	FC Arsenal Bila Tserkva	34	5	5	24	23	76	20

NB FC Obolon Kyiv withdrew at winter break – their remaining matches were awarded as goalless defeats. MFK Mykolaiv – 3 pts deducted; FC Stal Alchevsk declined promotion.

Domestic cup: Kubok Ukraïny 2012/13

THIRD ROUND

(22/09/12)
Chornomorets Odesa 2-0 Metalurh Donetsk
Stal Alchevsk 2-3 Arsenal Kyiv *(aet)*

(23/09/12)
Avanhard Kramatorsk 1-1 Zorya Luhansk *(aet; 4-3 on pens)*
Desna Chernihiv 1-2 Vorskla Poltava
Helios Kharkiv 0-1 Hoverla Uzhhorod
Hirnyk-Sport Komsomolsk 0-2 Tavriya Simferopol
Kremin Kremenchuk 0-2 Nyva Ternopil
Krymteplytsya Molodizhne 0-2 Karpaty Lviv
PFC Sevastopol 2-1 Kryvbas Kryvyi Rih
Shakhtar Donetsk 4-1 Dynamo Kyiv
Shakhtar Sverdlovsk 2-1 FC Odesa
Slavutych Cherkasy 1-3 Volyn Lutsk *(aet)*
Stal Dniprodzerzhynsk 0-6 Illychivets Mariupil
Ukrahrokom Holovkivka 1-1 Metalurh Zaporizhya *(aet; 5-4 on pens)*
Zhemchuzhyna Yalta 0-1 Dnipro Dnipropetrovsk
Obolon Kyiv 1-4 Metalist Kharkiv

FOURTH ROUND

(31/10/12)
Avanhard Kramatorsk 0-1 Arsenal Kyiv
Dnipro Dnipropetrovsk 2-0 Illychivets Mariupil
Hoverla Uzhhorod 1-4 Shakhtar Donetsk
Karpaty Lviv 2-1 Metalist Kharkiv *(aet)*
Nyva Ternopil 0-2 PFC Sevastopol
Shakhtar Sverdlovsk 0-2 Volyn Lutsk
Ukrahrokom Holovkivka 1-2 Chornomorets Odesa
Vorskla Poltava 2-3 Tavriya Simferopol

QUARTER-FINALS

(17/04/13)
Arsenal Kyiv 1-2 Chornomorets Odesa *(Tkachuk 45+1; Burdujan 6, Fontanello 77)*
PFC Sevastopol 1-1 Tavriya Simferopol *(Kovpak 23; Gadzhiyev 55) (aet; 3-1 on pens)*
Shakhtar Donetsk 2-1 Karpaty Lviv *(Gai 32, Alex Teixeira 42; Zenjov 79p)*
Volyn Lutsk 0-2 Dnipro Dnipropetrovsk *(Kravchenko 45+3, Matheus 90+4)*

SEMI-FINALS

(08/05/13)
Chornomorets Odesa 2-1 Dnipro Dnipropetrovsk *(Fontanello 62, Léo Matos 68; Matheus 6)*
PFC Sevastopol 2-4 Shakhtar Donetsk *(Tkachov 37, 71; Luiz Adriano 9, 65, Mkhitaryan 19, 53)*

FINAL

(22/05/13)
Metalist Stadium, Kharkiv
FC SHAKHTAR DONETSK 3 *(Fernandinho 40, Alex Teixeira 53, Taison 74)*
FC CHORNOMORETS ODESA 0
Referee: *Aranovskiy*
SHAKHTAR DONETSK: *Kanibolotskiy, Srna, Rakitskiy, Kucher, Shevchuk, Hübschman (Stepanenko 78), Alex Teixeira, Taison, Fernandinho (Douglas Costa 67), Mkhitaryan, Luiz Adriano (Eduardo 78)*
CHORNOMORETS: *Bezotosniy, Zubeiko, Berger, Vangjeli, Fontanello, Starhorodskiy (Didenko 46), Burdujan, Bakaj, K Kovalchuk, Dja Djédjé (Sito Riera 67), Léo Matos (Slinkin 84)*

WALES

Cymdeithas Bêl-droed Cymru / Football Association of Wales (FAW)

Address	11/12 Neptune Court, Vanguard Way GB-Cardiff CF24 5PJ	**President**	Trefor Hughes
Tel	+44 29 2043 5830	**General secretary**	Jonathan Ford
Fax	+44 29 2049 6953	**Media officer**	Ceri Stennett
E-mail	info@faw.co.uk	**Year of formation**	1876
Website	faw.org.uk	**National stadium**	Millennium Stadium, Cardiff (74,500)

PREMIER LEAGUE CLUBS

1. Aberystwyth Town FC
2. Afan Lido FC

3. AUK Broughton FC
4. Bala Town FC
5. Bangor City FC
6. Carmarthen Town AFC
7. Connah's Quay FC
8. Llanelli AFC
9. Newtown AFC
10. Port Talbot Town FC

11. Prestatyn Town FC

12. The New Saints FC

PROMOTED CLUB

13. Rhyl FC

KEY:
- – UEFA Champions League
- – UEFA Europa League
- – Promoted club
- – Relegated club

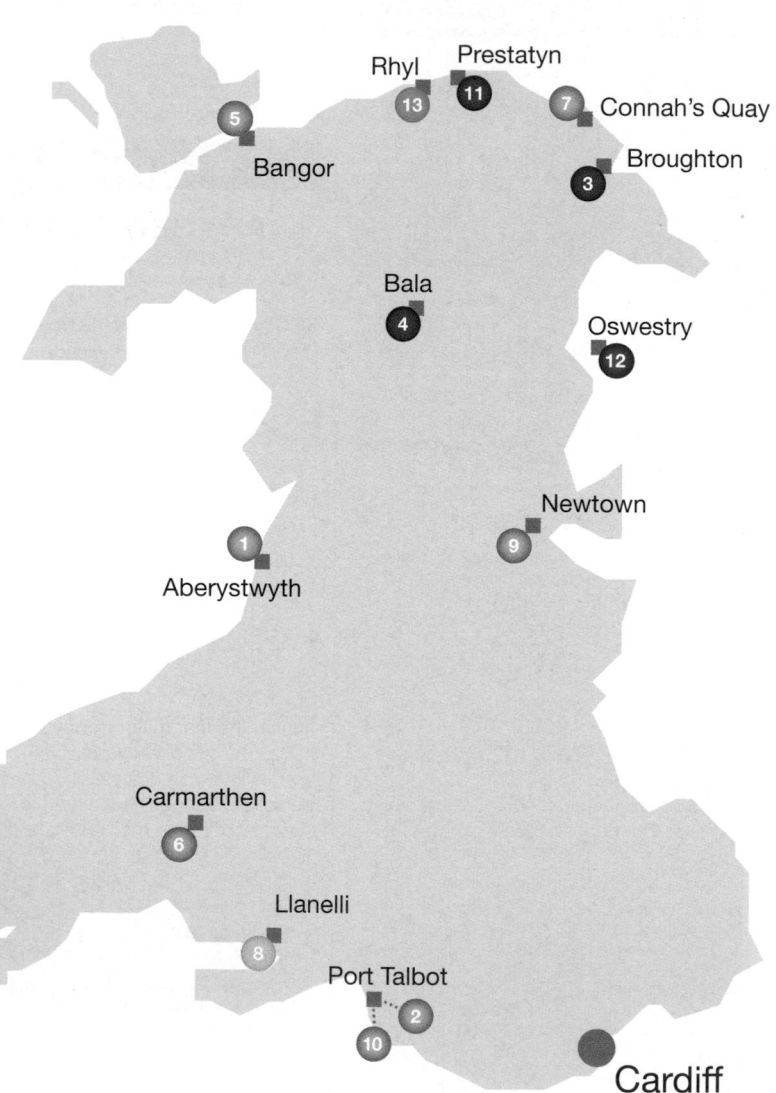

TNS in total control

The New Saints FC won the Welsh Premier League by a record-breaking margin of 22 points. It was the club's seventh national title, equalling the feat of Barry Town FC, and their third in four seasons. There was no second successive double, however, for TNS as the Welsh Cup was won, for the first time, by Prestatyn FC.

It was a wonderful season for Welsh teams competing in England, with Swansea City AFC capturing the League Cup and Cardiff City FC winning promotion to join their local rivals in the Premier League.

| Record margin of victory for Oswestry-based side | Extra-time cup win for Prestatyn | Joy across border for Swansea and Cardiff |

Domestic league

In each of the previous two Welsh Premier League campaigns the title had been decided on the final day, but there was no late drama in 2012/13, TNS romping to victory with four games to spare thanks to a scintillating burst of form that brought them 15 wins and two draws in their last 17 fixtures. Ordinary during the first half of the campaign, they were a class apart after Christmas, when the goals of Michael Wilde, who finished as the league's top scorer with 25, fired them to a succession of high-scoring victories.

Ironically it was with a 3-0 win at home to Carmarthen Town AFC that TNS's record-equalling seventh title was secured. Carmarthen had been the last team to defeat them – both in the league, with a 3-0 win at The Venue in late November, and in the League Cup final in January, which they won on penalties after a 3-3 draw. It was a traumatic season for Carmarthen's local rivals, Llanelli AFC. Although they avoided relegation on the pitch, the 2008 champions were wound up two days after their final fixture, enabling bottom club Afan Lido FC to survive.

It was a memorable campaign for AUK Broughton FC, who finished runners-up and qualified for Europe for the first time.

Bala Town FC ended up in the relegation pool but won all ten second-phase fixtures and maintained that winning run in the post-season play-offs for UEFA Europa League qualification, defeating Connah's Quay FC, Bangor City FC and Port Talbot Town FC on successive weekends to claim a first ever ticket to Europe.

Domestic cup

Yet another first-time European qualifier emerged from the Welsh Cup, with Prestatyn Town FC, fifth in the league, winning the first major trophy in their 103-year history thanks to a 3-1 extra-time win in the final against competition specialists Bangor. Prestatyn had a couple of thirtysomething midfielders to thank for their win, Jason Price scoring twice and Andy Parkinson once as the eight-time winners paid the penalty for going down to ten men in extra time.

Europe

All four Welsh clubs were dumped out of Europe at the first attempt, although in every case they drew their home game. In the UEFA Champions League TNS held Helsingborgs IF 0-0 before losing the second leg 3-0 in Sweden.

National team

Home and away wins over Scotland were all Wales had to show for their efforts in the 2014 FIFA World Cup qualifying campaign as dreams of making the journey to Brazil were shattered early on by a 2-0 home defeat against Belgium and a 6-1 crushing in Serbia. Two further losses against Croatia rendered the pair of 2-1 wins over Scotland largely academic, although nothing could erase from Welsh fans' memory the joyous moment of Gareth Bale's 90th-minute wonder strike that enabled his team to come from behind and defeat their British rivals in Cardiff.

Bale scored five of Wales' eight goals in 2012/13 and was the Footballer of the Year across the border after a brilliant season with Tottenham Hotspur FC. His was not the only Welsh success story in England as Swansea, under new manager Michael Laudrup, won the League Cup with a 5-0 win at Wembley over fourth-tier Bradford City AFC (having ousted European champions Chelsea FC in the semis) and Cardiff, led by Scottish manager Malky Mackay, won the Championship (second tier) to secure promotion to the Premier League and set up a couple of tasty south Wales derbies in 2013/14.

 **WALES**

Domestic league: Premier League 2012/13 final table

SECOND PHASE

Championship Pool

		Pld	Home					Away					Total					
			W	D	L	F	A	W	D	L	F	A	W	D	L	F	A	Pts
1	**The New Saints FC**	32	13	1	2	45	9	11	3	2	41	13	24	4	4	86	22	76
2	AUK Broughton FC	32	11	2	3	40	15	6	1	9	36	27	17	3	12	76	42	54
3	Bangor City FC	32	8	5	3	42	23	6	4	6	23	30	14	9	9	65	53	51
4	Port Talbot Town FC	32	9	3	4	34	23	4	5	7	17	29	13	8	11	51	52	47
5	Prestatyn Town FC	32	8	2	6	33	34	3	5	8	29	45	11	7	14	62	79	40
6	Carmarthen Town AFC	32	7	5	4	20	16	3	2	11	16	34	10	7	15	36	50	37

Relegation Pool

		Pld	Home					Away					Total					
			W	D	L	F	A	W	D	L	F	A	W	D	L	F	A	Pts
7	Bala Town FC	32	10	2	4	37	24	7	3	6	25	17	17	5	10	62	41	56
8	Connah's Quay FC	32	7	3	6	33	33	5	2	9	29	36	12	5	15	62	69	40
9	Newtown AFC	32	3	5	8	17	29	7	2	7	27	25	10	7	15	44	54	37
10	Aberystwyth Town FC	32	7	4	5	23	25	2	6	8	17	34	9	10	13	40	59	37
11	Llanelli AFC	32	3	3	10	20	44	7	3	6	21	24	10	6	16	41	68	36
12	Afan Lido FC	32	5	2	9	18	31	3	1	12	25	48	8	3	21	43	79	27

NB League split into top and bottom halves after First Phase of 22 games, with each team playing a further ten matches (home and away) exclusively against clubs from its half of the table. Connah's Quay FC – 1 pt deducted; Llanelli AFC withdrew from 2013/14 Premier League.

SEASON AT A GLANCE

EUROPEAN QUALIFICATION 2013/14

 Champion: The New Saints FC (second qualifying round)

 Cup winner: Prestatyn Town FC (first qualifying round)
AUK Broughton FC (first qualifying round)
Bala Town FC (first qualifying round)

Top scorer	Michael Wilde (TNS), 25 goals
Relegated club	Llanelli AFC (withdrew)
Promoted club	Rhyl FC
Cup final	Prestatyn Town FC 3-1 Bangor City FC *(aet)*

PREMIER LEAGUE TEAM OF THE SEASON
(4-4-2)
Coach: Darlington *(TNS)*

 **PLAYER OF THE SEASON**
Michael Wilde
(The New Saints FC)

Wilde returned to TNS after three years away and enjoyed a magnificent season, scoring 25 league goals, 18 of them after Christmas including two in the title-clinching 3-0 triumph over Carmarthen Town AFC. In addition to winning the Premier League's golden boot, the striker was officially named as the player of the year.

 **NEWCOMER OF THE SEASON**
Ryan Fraughan
(The New Saints FC)

The Saints winger was named young player of the year in the Welsh League annual awards. His hard-working displays, allied to a return of seven goals, were highly influential in TNS's title triumph. The Liverpool-born 22-year-old has already played in the English Football League with Tranmere Rovers FC and Stockport County FC.

Harrison *(TNS)*

Owens *(Airbus)*   K Edwards *(TNS)*   Kearney *(Airbus)*   Marriott *(TNS)*

Riley *(Airbus)*   M Jones *(Bala)*   Fraughan *(TNS)*   Darlington *(TNS)*

Wilde *(TNS)*   Parkinson *(Prestatyn)*

NATIONAL TEAM

Home Kit   Away Kit

INTERNATIONAL TOURNAMENT APPEARANCES
FIFA World Cup (1) 1958 (qtr-finals)

TOP FIVE ALL-TIME CAPS
Neville Southall (92), Gary Speed (85); Dean Saunders (75); **Craig Bellamy,** Peter Nicholas & Ian Rush (73)

TOP FIVE ALL-TIME GOALS
Ian Rush (28); Ivor Allchurch & Trevor Ford (23); Dean Saunders (22); **Craig Bellamy (19)**

Results 2012/13

15/08/12	Bosnia & Herzegovina	H	Llanelli	0-2	
07/09/12	Belgium (WCQ)	H	Cardiff	0-2	
11/09/12	Serbia (WCQ)	A	Novi Sad	1-6	*Bale (31)*
12/10/12	Scotland (WCQ)	H	Cardiff	2-1	*Bale (81p, 90)*
16/10/12	Croatia (WCQ)	A	Osijek	0-2	
06/02/13	Austria	H	Swansea	2-1	*Bale (21), Vokes (52)*
22/03/13	Scotland (WCQ)	A	Glasgow	2-1	*Ramsey (72p), Hobson-Kanu (74)*
26/03/13	Croatia (WCQ)	H	Swansea	1-2	*Bale (21p)*

Appearances 2012/13

Coach:			Bih	BEL	SRB	SCO	CRO	Aut	SCO	CRO	Caps	Goals
Chris Coleman	10/06/70											
Boaz Myhill	09/11/82	West Brom (ENG)	G	G	G			G	G	G	16	-
Chris Gunter	21/07/89	Reading (ENG)	D69	D	D	D	D	s73	D	D	45	-
Darcy Blake	13/12/88	Crystal Palace (ENG)	D78	D	D	D	D				14	1
Ashley Williams	23/08/84	Swansea	D	M	D	D	D	D	D	D	41	1
Neil Taylor	07/02/89	Swansea	D								10	-
Gareth Bale	16/07/89	Tottenham (ENG)	M62	M	M	M	M	M60	A46	A	41	11
Joe Allen	14/03/90	Liverpool (ENG)	M		M71	M	M	M			13	-
Andrew Crofts	29/05/84	Brighton (ENG)	M88								24	-
Aaron Ramsey	26/12/90	Arsenal (ENG)	M	M	M	M			M95*		26	6
Simon Church	12/12/88	Reading (ENG)	A64	A72	A		s61	s84	s89	s84	22	1
Sam Vokes	21/10/89	Burnley (ENG)	A69	s72			s72	s46			25	5
Hal Robson-Kanu	21/05/89	Reading (ENG)	s62	s72		s72	s82	s60	A	A64	14	1
Craig Bellamy	13/07/79	Cardiff	s64					A46	A	A	73	19
Sam Ricketts	11/10/81	Bolton (ENG)	s69		s46			D	D		48	-
Steve Morison	29/08/83	Norwich (ENG)	s69	A72	A	A66	A61				20	1
Joel Lynch	03/10/87	Huddersfield (ENG)	s78								1	-
Robert Earnshaw	06/04/81	Cardiff	s88								59	16
James Collins	23/08/83	West Ham (ENG)		D25*						D	41	2
Adam Matthews	13/01/92	Celtic (SCO)		D	D46			D73			10	-
David Edwards	03/02/86	Wolves (ENG)		M80	M46						26	3
Andy King	29/10/88	Leicester (ENG)			s80	s71		M72	s46	s58	M	18	1
David Vaughan	18/02/83	Sunderland (ENG)			s46	M	M	M46			33	1
Lewis Price	19/07/84	Crystal Palace (ENG)				G	G				11	-
Ben Davies	24/04/93	Swansea				D	D	D	D	D	5	-
Joe Ledley	23/01/87	Celtic (SCO)				M72	M82	M	M89	M	46	3
Craig Davies	09/01/86	Barnsley (ENG)					s66				6	-
Jack Collison	02/10/88	West Ham (ENG)						M84	M58		13	-
Jonathan Williams	09/10/93	Crystal Palace (ENG)							s46	M84	2	-
Ashley Richards	12/04/91	Swansea								s64	2	-

European club competitions 2012/13

THE NEW SAINTS FC

CHAMPIONS LEAGUE

Second qualifying round - Helsingborgs IF (SWE)
H 0-0
Harrison, Spender, Marriott, Baker, Evans, Draper (Ward 89), Seargeant (Finley 68), Craig Jones, Chris Jones (Ruscoe 86), Darlington, A Edwards. Coach: Carl Darlington (WAL) & Craig Harrison (WAL)
A 0-3
Harrison, Spender, Marriott, Baker, Evans, Draper (Fraughan 75), Seargeant (Finley 69), Craig Jones, Chris Jones, Darlington (K Edwards 87), A Edwards. Coach: Carl Darlington (WAL) & Craig Harrison (WAL)

BANGOR CITY FC

EUROPA LEAGUE

First qualifying round - FC Zimbru Chisinau (MDA)
H 0-0
Idzi, Roberts, Brewerton, Johnston, Garside, L Davies, Simm (Corey Jones 68), S Edwards (Bull 68), Smyth (Morley 77), Brownhill, Allen. Coach: Nev Powell (WAL)
A 1-2 *Smyth (44)*
Idzi, Roberts, Brewerton, Johnston, Chris Jones (Simm 60), Garside (Morley 66), L Davies, S Edwards (Bull 55), Smyth, Brownhill, Allen. Coach: Nev Powell (WAL)

CEFN DRUIDS AFC

EUROPA LEAGUE

First qualifying round - Myllykosken Pallo-47 (FIN)
H 0-0
Mullock, Harris, Hesp, James, Hughes, Burke (Duckett 89), Quinn, Dures (Price 74), Darlington, Edwards, S Jones (Cann 80). Coach: Huw Griffiths (WAL)
A 0-5
Mullock, Harris, Hesp (Duckett 73), James, Hughes, Burke, Quinn (Price 60), Dures (McElmeel 56), Darlington, Edwards, S Jones. Coach: Huw Griffiths (WAL)

LLANELLI AFC

EUROPA LEAGUE

First qualifying round - KuPS Kuopio (FIN)
A 1-2 *J Bowen (45+1)*
Morris, Thomas, Grist, Venables, Ashley Evans, Surman, J Bowen, Corbisiero, Rose, L Bowen (S Evans 90), Kellaway (Williams 55). Coach: Gary Lloyd (WAL)
H 1-1 *L Bowen (50p)*
Morris, Thomas, Grist, Venables, Ashley Evans, Surman, J Bowen, Corbisiero, Rose, L Bowen (Kellaway 64), Williams (S Evans 71). Coach: Andy Legg (WAL)

Domestic league club-by-club

ABERYSTWYTH TOWN FC

Manager: Tomi Morgan
1884 • Park Avenue (3,000) • atfc.org.uk
Major honours
Welsh Cup (1) 1900

2012

18/08	Carmarthen	a	0-2	
24/08	Bala	h	1-1	*Follows*
01/09	Bangor	a	1-7	*Follows*
04/09	Bangor	h	0-0	
08/09	Port Talbot	h	0-5	
15/09	Connah's Quay	a	2-1	*Collins, Follows (p)*
21/09	Llanelli	h	0-2	
29/09	Airbus	a	1-5	*Follows*
05/10	Afan Lido	h	4-2	*Thomas, Follows, Cadwallader, Hughes*
13/10	Prestatyn	a	2-2	*Collins, Hughes*
19/10	TNS	h	1-4	*Collins*
27/10	Carmarthen	h	1-0	*og (Hanford)*
03/11	Bala	a	2-3	*Collins, Carroll*
17/11	Port Talbot	a	4-2	*Collins, Hughes, Follows 2*
24/11	Connah's Quay	h	3-0	*C Davies, Follows, Carroll*
30/11	Llanelli	a	0-0	
21/12	Afan Lido	a	0-0	
26/12	Newtown	h	0-2	

2013

01/01	Newtown	a	1-3	*M Jones*
05/01	Prestatyn	h	4-1	*M Jones 3, Follows*
12/01	Airbus	h	1-0	*M Jones*
02/02	TNS	a	0-3	
15/02	Bala	h	1-3	*og (Davies)*
23/02	Newtown	a	0-0	
02/03	Connah's Quay	h	1-1	*C Davies*
09/03	Afan Lido	h	4-3	*Thomas 2, Corbisiero, M Jones*
16/03	Llanelli	a	3-4	*Thomas, M Jones 2*
06/04	Llanelli	h	2-1	*Venables, C Davies*
09/04	Connah's Quay	h	1-1	*M Jones*
13/04	Newtown	h	0-0	
19/04	Afan Lido	a	0-0	
23/04	Bala	a	0-1	

No	Name	Nat	DoB	Pos	Aps	(s)	Gls
25	Ifan Burrell		18/03/95	D		(2)	
12	Gavin Cadwallader		18/04/86	D	25	(5)	1
15	Declan Carroll		04/07/93	M	19	(9)	2
4	Matty Collins		31/03/86	M	21	(1)	5
3	Antonio Corbisiero	ENG	17/11/84	M	9		1
11	Cledan Davies		10/03/90	M	29	(1)	3
19	Rhydian Davies		05/10/95	M	7	(12)	
9	Jordan Follows		23/03/90	A	29	(3)	9
29	Christy Gale		18/01/95	M		(2)	
14	Darren Griffiths		15/09/87	A		(1)	
16	Glyndwr Hughes		05/12/76	M	14	(9)	3
18	Liam James		19/05/95	D	3	(8)	
2	Sion James		03/02/80	D	21	(5)	
22	Mark Jones		05/01/89	A	14		9
5	Stuart Jones		14/03/84	D	32		
1	Mike Lewis		04/04/89	G	22		
7	Josh MacAuley	ENG	02/03/91	M	14	(1)	
17	Bari Morgan		13/08/80	M	13	(3)	
40	Ed Powl-Jones		18/09/96	M		(2)	
6	Wyn Thomas		11/01/79	D	29	(1)	4
7	Chris Venables		23/07/85	M	10		1
10	Michael Walsh	ENG	30/05/86	M	16	(2)	
20	James Wood		11/04/91	G	10		
3	Adam Worton	ENG	10/04/87	D	15	(2)	

AFAN LIDO FC

Manager: Paul Reid; (24/01/13) Paul Evans; (01/04/13) Paul Reid
1967 • Marston's Stadium (4,200) • afanlidofc.com

2012

18/08	Prestatyn	a	2-4	*Borrelli, M Jones*
24/08	TNS	h	1-3	*Borrelli*
31/08	Carmarthen	a	1-1	*M Jones*
04/09	Carmarthen	h	2-1	*Howard, M Jones*
08/09	Bala	h	1-0	*Rawlings*
15/09	Bangor	a	1-4	*Borrelli*
22/09	Connah's Quay	a	4-6	*Borrelli 2, M Jones 2*
29/09	Newtown	h	2-3	*Howard, Paul Evans*
05/10	Aberystwyth	a	2-4	*Hartland, Rawlings*
13/10	Airbus	h	1-5	*Hartland*
19/10	Llanelli	a	2-3	*Hartshorn, Hartland*
27/10	Prestatyn	h	2-4	*Rawlings 2*
03/11	TNS	a	1-2	*Hartland*
18/11	Bala	a	2-3	*Hartland, Hartshorn*
24/11	Bangor	a	2-3	*Hartland, Howard*
01/12	Connah's Quay	h	2-1	*Hartland, M Jones (p)*
15/12	Newtown	a	2-1	*M Jones, Paul Evans*
21/12	Aberystwyth	h	0-0	
26/12	Port Talbot	h	0-3	
29/12	Port Talbot	a	1-6	*M Jones*

2013

19/01	Llanelli	h	0-1	
02/02	Airbus	a	1-3	*Howard*
09/02	Llanelli	a	2-0	*Borrelli, Hartland*
23/02	Bala	h	0-2	
09/03	Aberystwyth	a	3-4	*Borrelli, Prangley, Rawlings*
23/03	Llanelli	h	1-3	*Hartland*
01/04	Newtown	h	2-1	*Prangley, Borrelli*
06/04	Connah's Quay	h	2-1	*Hartland 2*
13/04	Bala	a	0-4	
16/04	Connah's Quay	a	0-3	
19/04	Aberystwyth	h	0-0	
27/04	Newtown	a	1-0	*Hartland*

No	Name	Nat	DoB	Pos	Aps	(s)	Gls
14	Luke Borrelli		28/03/91	A	27	(5)	8
28	Callan Bowden		16/05/94	D	1	(2)	
4	Mark Crutch		17/10/83	D	8		
1	Christopher Curtis		13/09/82	G	20		
19	Joshua Doyle		13/12/93	D	12	(1)	
25	Paul Evans		25/05/82	D	20		2
4	Paul J Evans		21/11/73	D	1	(1)	
17	Alex Gammond		26/08/94	M	11	(16)	
15	Kyle Graves	ENG	01/04/89	D	4		
29	Jackson Hall		14/02/95	A	5	(3)	
7	Christopher Hartland		20/06/90	M	23	(5)	12
6	Lee Hartshorn		12/03/87	D	20	(1)	2
3	Samuel Hodge		14/10/93	D	5	(1)	
22	Aaron Houlihan		29/12/93	M		(4)	
11	Kieran Howard		17/01/91	M	32		4
2	Dean Hudson		01/03/91	D	29	(3)	
6	Adam James		11/01/84	M	4		
5	Kristian James		05/02/82	D	22	(2)	
15	Gavin Jefferies		24/12/83	D	2	(3)	
9	Craig Jones		28/03/87	M		(1)	
9	Mark Jones		05/01/89	A	20		8
24	Jamie Latham		08/12/96	A		(1)	
21	Adam Llewellyn		27/10/93	A		(2)	
13	Rory McCreesh		05/09/90	G	6		
18	Rameer Outlaw		12/06/90	A		(3)	
12	Gareth Phillips		19/08/79	M	22	(1)	
9	Simon Prangley		10/01/90	A	10	(1)	2
3	Michael Pursey		17/02/90	D		(1)	
10	Anthony Rawlings		23/11/85	A	22	(6)	5
1	Kristian Rogers		02/10/80	G	6		
16	Damon Thomas		09/09/89	A	2	(5)	
20	Daniel Thomas		28/04/84	M	2		
8	Matthew Thompson		29/05/88	M	16	(7)	
19	Jack Underwood		15/07/95	A		(3)	
3	Remi Whitelock		08/11/90	D		(1)	

AUK BROUGHTON FC

Manager: Andy Preece (ENG)
1946 • The Airfield (3,000) • airbusfc.com

2012

17/08	TNS	a	0-1	
25/08	Carmarthen	h	1-2	*Lewis*
31/08	Bala	h	1-0	*Tomassen*
04/09	Bala	a	2-0	*Wade 2*
08/09	Bangor	h	2-3	*Budrys, Wade*
15/09	Port Talbot	h	4-4	*Riley, Rule, Roddy, Johnson*
22/09	Newtown	a	7-1	*Abbott 3, Field, Kearney, Tomassen, Budrys*
29/09	Aberystwyth	h	5-1	*Abbott 3, Riley, Wade*
06/10	Llanelli	h	1-1	*Riley*
13/10	Afan Lido	a	5-1	*Johnson 2, Abbott, Lewis, Hayes*
19/10	Prestatyn	h	5-0	*Kearney, Riley, Tomassen, Johnson, Budrys*
26/10	TNS	h	2-1	*Budrys 2*
03/11	Carmarthen	a	1-2	*Abbott*
16/11	Bangor	a	0-2	
24/11	Port Talbot	h	5-0	*Riley 2, Johnson, Hayes, Abbott*
30/11	Newtown	h	2-1	*Hayes, Budrys*
23/12	Llanelli	a	4-2	*Field, Riley 2, Johnson*
26/12	Connah's Quay	h	2-2	*Tomassen, og (Wynne)*

2013

01/01	Connah's Quay	a	1-4	*Hart*
12/01	Aberystwyth	a	0-1	
19/01	Prestatyn	a	6-1	*Wade, Rule, Budrys 2, Bolland, Riley*
02/02	Afan Lido	h	3-1	*Riley, Tomassen, Bolland*
15/02	Prestatyn	h	4-0	*Budrys, Bolland, Kearney, Wade*
23/02	TNS	h	1-2	*Budrys*
08/03	Bangor	a	0-2	
16/03	Port Talbot	h	2-0	*Jarrett, Abbott*
29/03	Prestatyn	h	4-1	*Riley, Roddy, Wade 2*
06/04	Carmarthen	a	0-1	
09/04	Carmarthen	h	2-0	*Johnson, Kearney*
12/04	TNS	a	2-4	*Kearney, Roddy*
20/04	Bangor	h	2-0	*Riley, Tomassen*
27/04	Port Talbot	a	0-1	

No	Name	Nat	DoB	Pos	Aps	(s)	Gls
29	Steve Abbott	ENG	31/07/82	A	21	(8)	10
8	Kyle Armstrong	ENG	24/02/86	M	7	(9)	
12	Phil Bolland	ENG	26/08/76	D	6		3
9	Chris Budrys	ENG	13/08/85	A	24	(4)	10
11	Mark Cadwallader	ENG	08/07/88	M	2	(2)	
1	Ben Chapman	ENG	03/05/91	G	15		
2	Zyiac Edwards		25/05/94	M		(1)	
6	Tom Field	ENG	02/08/85	M	27		2
15	Sam Hart	ENG	29/11/91	D	13	(3)	1
19	Mike Hayes	ENG	21/11/87	A	5	(10)	3
16	Tommy Holmes	ENG	01/09/79	D	2	(1)	
24	Jason Jarrett	ENG	14/09/79	M	6	(4)	1
32	Max Jenks-Gilbert	ENG	04/09/95	A			
18	Jordan Johnson	ENG	09/10/86	A	14	(13)	7
20	Toby Jones		25/08/92	A	2	(4)	
5	Ian Kearney	ENG	15/06/87	D	26		5
3	Jack Lewis		18/05/88	D	14		2
11	Luke McCarthy	ENG	07/07/93	M	1	(2)	
22	Aaron Morrison	ENG	27/04/93	G	4		
20	Lee Owens	ENG	29/06/86	D	28	(1)	
17	Richie Partridge	IRL	12/09/80	A		(1)	
14	Wayne Riley	ENG	26/09/89	M	29	(2)	12
4	Michael Roddy	ENG	22/09/88	M	21	(9)	3
7	Glenn Rule	ENG	30/11/89	M	14	(11)	2
3	Lewis Short	ENG	11/06/90	D	7		
1	Jamie Stephens	ENG	24/08/93	G	13		
25	Steve Tomassen	ENG	03/10/93	A	28		6
10	Ryan Wade	ENG	22/01/88	A	23	(4)	8

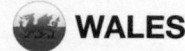

BALA TOWN FC

Manager: Colin Caton
1880 • Maes Tegid (2,000) • balatownfc.co.uk

2012

17/08	Newtown	h	4-4	Murtagh, Sheridan 3
24/08	Aberystwyth	a	1-1	Connolly (p)
31/08	Airbus	a	0-1	
04/09	Airbus	h	0-2	
08/09	Afan Lido	a	0-1	
15/09	Prestatyn	h	1-2	Hunt
22/09	Carmarthen	h	3-0	Hunt 2, Lunt
29/09	Llanelli	a	4-1	Connolly, Lunt, Sheridan, Codling
05/10	Bangor	a	0-5	
14/10	Port Talbot	h	2-0	Lunt, Hunt
19/10	Connah's Quay	a	1-0	Hunt
27/10	Newtown	a	1-1	og (A Jones)
03/11	Aberystwyth	h	3-2	Sheridan, Hunt 2
18/11	Afan Lido	h	3-2	S Jones, Connolly 2
24/11	Prestatyn	a	0-1	
01/12	Carmarthen	a	1-1	Hunt (p)
15/12	Llanelli	h	1-2	M Jones
26/12	TNS	a	0-1	

2013

02/01	TNS	h	2-2	Connolly, Davies
05/01	Port Talbot	a	1-2	Brown
11/01	Bangor	h	2-1	Lunt, M Jones
02/02	Connah's Quay	h	3-6	Codling, Hunt (p), S Jones
08/02	Newtown	h	3-1	Hunt 2, S Jones
15/02	Aberystwyth	a	3-1	Davies, Hunt, Brown
23/02	Afan Lido	a	2-0	Hunt, Connolly
10/03	Llanelli	h	4-0	S Jones, Hunt, M Jones, Connolly
15/03	Connah's Quay	a	5-0	Hunt 2, Sheridan, Brown, S Jones
13/04	Afan Lido	h	4-0	Sheridan, S Jones, Irving, M Jones
16/04	Newtown	a	1-0	S Jones
20/04	Llanelli	a	5-1	Sheridan 3 (1p), Hunt (p), Brown
23/04	Aberystwyth	h	1-0	Lunt
27/04	Connah's Quay	h	1-0	Connolly

No	Name	Nat	DoB	Pos	Aps	(s)	Gls
17	Stephen Brown	ENG	11/08/84	M	23	(5)	4
5	Mike Byron	ENG	16/08/87	D	5	(1)	
18	Lewis Codling	ENG	01/11/90	A	13	(12)	2
3	Ben Collins	ENG	13/06/88	D	16	(4)	
7	Mark Connolly	ENG	02/07/84	M	18	(12)	8
16	Tony Davies	ENG	23/11/84	D	29		2
11	Steffan Edwards		10/10/89	M	22	(3)	
21	Stephen Fisher	ENG	11/08/84	D		(1)	
9	Lee Hunt	ENG	05/06/82	A	27		17
2	John Irving	ENG	17/09/88	D	24		1
15	Ross Jefferies		05/08/79	M	12	(4)	
4	Mark Jones		15/08/84	M	30	(2)	4
8	Ryan Jones		17/01/96	M		(15)	
22	Stuart Jones	ENG	28/08/86	D	26	(3)	7
20	Kenny Lunt	ENG	20/11/79	M	31		5
1	Ashley Morris		31/03/84	G	32		
6	Conall Murtagh	NIR	29/06/85	M	14	(4)	1
10	Ian Sheridan	ENG	12/03/89	A	30	(2)	10
12	Mike Thompson	ENG	05/01/84	A		(4)	

BANGOR CITY FC

Manager: Nev Powell
1876 • Nantporth (1,800) • bangorcityfc.com
Major honours
Welsh League (3) 1994, 1995, 2011;
Welsh Cup (8) 1889, 1896, 1962, 1998, 2000, 2008, 2009, 2010

2012

17/08	Connah's Quay	h	2-1	Simm, Morley (p)
25/08	Newtown	a	2-3	Simm, Smyth
01/09	Aberystwyth	h	7-1	Chris Jones, S Edwards 3, og (S Jones), og (Thomas), Simm
04/09	Aberystwyth	a	0-0	
08/09	Airbus	a	3-2	Simm 3
15/09	Afan Lido	h	4-1	Chris Jones 2, L Davies, Allen
22/09	TNS	a	0-3	
29/09	Carmarthen	a	1-0	Simm
05/10	Bala	h	5-0	S Edwards, Chris Jones, Brownhill, Simm 2 (1p)
13/10	Llanelli	h	1-2	Simm
20/10	Port Talbot	a	1-1	Roberts
26/10	Connah's Quay	h	6-2	Hoy, Simm, Chris Jones 2, L Davies 2
02/11	Newtown	h	3-0	Simm, S Edwards, Bull
16/11	Airbus	h	2-0	Simm, Brewerton
24/11	Afan Lido	a	3-2	S Edwards, Brownhill, og (Curtis)
01/12	TNS	h	0-1	
15/12	Carmarthen	h	2-2	R Edwards, Chris Jones
28/12	Prestatyn	h	3-3	S Edwards, L Davies, Hoy

2013

01/01	Prestatyn	a	1-4	L Davies
05/01	Llanelli	a	2-2	Simm 2
11/01	Bala	a	1-2	Morley
02/02	Port Talbot	h	2-2	Simm 2
09/02	Prestatyn	h	3-3	Mackin, Simm, L Davies
16/02	Port Talbot	a	1-1	Simm
23/02	Carmarthen	a	1-0	L Davies
08/03	Airbus	h	2-0	O'Toole, Booth
16/03	TNS	a	0-6	
30/03	Port Talbot	h	3-3	Chris Jones, R Edwards, L Davies
09/04	Prestatyn	a	1-0	Simm
13/04	Carmarthen	h	2-0	Simm, S Edwards
20/04	Airbus	a	0-2	
27/04	TNS	h	1-4	L Davies

No	Name	Nat	DoB	Pos	Aps	(s)	Gls
19	Damien Allen	ENG	01/08/86	M	28	(1)	1
8	Robbie Booth	ENG	30/12/85	A	5	(7)	1
5	James Brewerton		17/11/79	D	19		1
18	Liam Brownhill	ENG	28/11/86	D	27	(1)	2
14	Alan Bull	ENG	25/11/87	A	3	(12)	1
6	Les Davies		29/10/84	A	31		9
22	Sean Davies		22/05/91	M		(1)	
11	Ryan Edwards		22/06/88	D	29		2
20	Sion Edwards		01/08/87	M	26	(6)	8
8	Craig Garside		11/01/85	M	3	(1)	
2	Peter Hoy	ENG	16/05/82	D	9	(7)	2
1	Lee Idzi		08/02/88	G	32		
6	Michael Johnston		16/12/87	D	30		
7	Chris Jones		09/10/85	M	26	(5)	8
22	Corey Jones		28/11/94	M		(1)	
24	Levi Mackin		04/04/86	M	3	(6)	1
21	Jamie McDaid		29/03/94	M		(2)	
4	David Morley	ENG	25/09/77	M	18	(10)	2
16	Gary O'Toole	ENG	29/01/87	A		(7)	1
17	John Owen		18/08/92	A		(12)	
3	Chris Roberts		14/08/85	D	23		1
19	Chris Simm	ENG	10/04/84	M	30		21
16	Marc Smyth	ENG	09/01/85	A	2	(10)	1
15	Chris Thomas		16/01/83	D	6		
15	Clive Williams		01/01/91	D	2	(1)	

CARMARTHEN TOWN AFC

Manager: Mark Aizlewood
1896 • Richmond Park (3,000) •
carmarthentownafc.com
Major honours
Welsh Cup (1) 2007

2012

18/08	Aberystwyth	h	2-0	Christopher, L Thomas
25/08	Airbus	a	2-1	Corey Thomas, L Thomas
31/08	Afan Lido	h	1-1	Christopher
04/09	Afan Lido	a	1-2	Hicks
08/09	Prestatyn	a	1-7	Hicks
15/09	TNS	h	0-0	
22/09	Bala	a	0-3	
29/09	Bangor	h	0-1	
05/10	Port Talbot	a	1-2	Jeanne (p)
13/10	Connah's Quay	h	2-4	L Thomas, Hood
20/10	Newtown	a	2-1	Casey Thomas, L Thomas
27/10	Aberystwyth	a	0-1	
03/11	Airbus	h	2-1	L Thomas 2
17/11	Prestatyn	h	2-2	L Thomas 2 (2p)
24/11	TNS	a	3-0	Fowler, Palmer, L Thomas
01/12	Bala	h	1-1	L Thomas (p)
15/12	Bangor	a	2-2	Hughes, L Thomas
21/12	Port Talbot	h	1-0	Hood
26/12	Llanelli	h	1-0	C Evans
29/12	Llanelli	a	2-4	L Thomas 2

2013

05/01	Connah's Quay	a	1-1	Hughes
02/02	Newtown	h	4-2	Kellaway 2, Doidge 2
23/02	Bangor	h	0-1	
08/03	Port Talbot	a	0-1	
16/03	Prestatyn	h	3-2	Corey Thomas, McCreesh, Casey Thomas
30/03	TNS	a	0-3	
06/04	Airbus	h	1-0	Corey Thomas
09/04	Airbus	a	0-2	
13/04	Bangor	a	0-2	
16/04	TNS	h	0-1	
20/04	Port Talbot	h	0-0	
27/04	Prestatyn	a	1-2	Kellaway

No	Name	Nat	DoB	Pos	Aps	(s)	Gls
23	Julian Alsop	ENG	28/05/73	A	2	(2)	
1	Steve Cann		20/01/88	G	24		
10	Jack Christopher		18/05/87	A	5	(1)	2
26	Luke Cummings		25/10/91	A	8	(2)	
30	Christian Doidge		24/08/92	M	5	(7)	2
21	Carl Evans		13/06/86	D	18	(2)	1
6	Iestyn Evans		07/02/95	D	4	(1)	
14	Anthony Finselbach		05/01/91	M	1		
8	Paul Fowler		08/02/84	M	23	(4)	1
12	Kyle Graves		01/04/89	D		(1)	
24	Craig Hanford		08/07/84	D	27		
4	Tim Hicks		05/04/83	A	22	(5)	2
3	Ian Hillier		26/12/79	D	23	(4)	
7	Jonathan Hood		07/02/91	M	12	(4)	2
9	Craig Hughes		18/12/78	A	8	(3)	2
11	Leon Jeanne		17/11/80	A	7	(1)	1
11	Geoff Kellaway		07/04/86	M	11		3
25	Liam McCreesh		09/09/85	M	22	(1)	1
35	Kerry Nicholas		24/10/92	G	4		
	Finton O'Brien		05/07/91	M		(1)	
16	Nicky Palmer		11/06/81	M	17	(3)	1
	Namir Queni	POR	16/12/93	G	1		
12	Scott Quigley	ENG	02/09/92	A	4	(1)	
7	Matthew Rees		02/09/82	D	23	(3)	
15	Neil Smothers		08/12/77	M	8	(3)	
17	Casey Thomas		14/11/90	M	13	(8)	2
36	Corey Thomas		30/11/89	D	28	(3)	3
18	Danny Thomas		13/05/85	M	4	(5)	
2	Liam Thomas		06/11/91	M	24	(3)	13
22	Rhys Wilson		11/06/92	G	3		
20	Sam Wilson		13/05/95	A	1	(5)	

CONNAH'S QUAY FC
Manager: Mark McGregor (ENG)
1946 • Deeside Stadium (4,000) • the-nomads.co.uk

2012

17/08	Bangor	a	1-2	Canning
25/08	Port Talbot	h	2-0	Thompson, O'Toole
01/09	Llanelli	h	3-1	O'Toole, Evans, Thompson
08/09	Newtown	a	3-1	Petrie 2, Healey
15/09	Aberystwyth	h	1-2	Petrie
22/09	Afan Lido	h	6-4	Petrie, Canning 2, O'Toole 2, Healey
28/09	Prestatyn	a	1-4	Healey
06/10	TNS	h	1-3	Robinson
13/10	Carmarthen	a	4-2	McGregor, Healey, Evans, Petrie
19/10	Bala	h	0-1	
26/10	Bangor	h	2-6	Robinson, Petrie
03/11	Port Talbot	a	1-6	Healey
11/11	Llanelli	a	6-1	Healey 3, Petrie 3
16/11	Newtown	h	2-1	Robert Jones, Healey
24/11	Aberystwyth	a	0-3	
01/12	Afan Lido	a	1-2	Hooley
21/12	TNS	a	1-5	Healey
26/12	Airbus	a	2-2	Robert Jones, Petrie

2013

01/01	Airbus	h	4-1	Evans 2 (2p), Wynne, Petrie
05/01	Carmarthen	h	1-1	Forde
11/01	Prestatyn	h	3-3	Healey 2, Rowntree
02/02	Bala	a	6-3	og (Collins), Edwards, Hayes 4
23/02	Llanelli	a	1-0	Robinson
02/03	Aberystwyth	h	1-1	Evans
09/03	Newtown	a	0-1	
15/03	Bala	h	0-5	
06/04	Afan Lido	a	1-2	Hayes
09/04	Aberystwyth	a	1-1	Petrie
13/04	Llanelli	h	4-2	Hayes 2, Forde, Petrie
16/04	Afan Lido	h	3-0	Forde, Hayes 2
20/04	Newtown	h	0-2	
27/04	Bala	a	0-1	

No	Name	Nat	DoB	Pos	Aps	(s)	Gls
15	Jordon Beck		17/02/94	D		(3)	
32	Sean Breen	ENG	26/10/92	A	1	(5)	
20	Dean Canning		12/09/86	A	9	(5)	3
30	Lee Davey	ENG	20/02/87	A		(1)	
16	Daniel Dobbins	ENG	30/04/87	D	22	(5)	
23	Ryan Edwards		25/05/94	M	16	(7)	1
10	Ricky Evans		24/09/76	M	30	(1)	5
8	Daniel Forde	ENG	08/01/86	M	11	(3)	3
31	John Hardiker	ENG	07/07/82	D	12	(1)	
9	Mike Hayes	ENG	21/11/87	A	9		9
14	Rhys Healey		06/12/94	A	12	(8)	12
3	Alan Hooley	ENG	13/10/78	M	25		1
6	Craig Jones	ENG	07/11/84	M	24	(2)	
11	Robert Jones	ENG	23/06/89	M	20	(8)	2
22	Ryan Jones		20/02/94	D			
4	Mark McGregor	ENG	16/02/77	D	31	(1)	1
9	Gary O'Toole	ENG	29/01/87	A	5	(1)	4
7	Jamie Petrie	ENG	15/05/86	A	32		13
5	Michael Robinson	ENG	02/06/89	D	21	(1)	3
24	Jack Rowlands		11/09/89	D		(1)	
12	Chris Rowntree		14/04/88	D	22	(1)	1
1	John Rushton		17/05/90	G	32		
2	Mike Thompson	ENG	05/01/84	A	11	(4)	2
19	Jamie Wynne		07/03/94	M	7	(7)	1

LLANELLI AFC
Manager: Andy Legg; (10/11/12) Bob Jeffrey (SCO)
1892 • Stebonheath Park (3,000) • llanelliafc.org
Major honours
Welsh League (1) 2008; Welsh Cup (1) 2011

2012

18/08	Port Talbot	a	2-1	L Bowen, Moses
25/08	Prestatyn	h	2-2	Rose, Surman
01/09	Connah's Quay	a	1-3	Rose
08/09	TNS	a	0-0	
15/09	Newtown	h	0-3	
21/09	Aberystwyth	a	2-0	Rose 2
29/09	Bala	h	1-4	Rose
06/10	Airbus	a	1-1	Venables
13/10	Bangor	a	2-1	Rose, L Bowen
19/10	Afan Lido	h	3-2	L Bowen 2 (1p), Rose
27/10	Port Talbot	h	0-1	
03/11	Prestatyn	a	1-3	Kellaway
11/11	Connah's Quay	h	1-6	Rose
17/11	TNS	h	0-6	
24/11	Newtown	a	1-1	Grist
30/11	Aberystwyth	h	0-0	
15/12	Bala	a	2-1	Corbisiero, Rose
23/12	Airbus	h	2-4	Moses 2
26/12	Carmarthen	a	0-1	
29/12	Carmarthen	h	4-2	Batley, Rose, Corbisiero (p), L Bowen

2013

05/01	Bangor	h	2-2	Rose, Corbisiero (p)
19/01	Afan Lido	a	1-0	L Bowen
09/02	Afan Lido	h	0-2	
16/02	Newtown	a	2-1	Lloyd, Moses
23/02	Connah's Quay	h	0-1	
10/03	Bala	a	0-4	
16/03	Aberystwyth	h	4-3	White, Alex Evans 2, Williams
23/03	Afan Lido	a	3-1	Moses, Smith, McKenna
30/03	Newtown	h	0-1	
06/04	Aberystwyth	a	1-2	Williams
13/04	Connah's Quay	a	2-4	Blain, Holland
20/04	Bala	h	1-5	Williams (p)

No	Name	Nat	DoB	Pos	Aps	(s)	Gls
20	Dan Barnard		14/11/93	M		(3)	
18	Ryan Batley	ENG	17/11/91	D	19	(2)	1
4	Dylan Blain		10/11/92	M	9		1
7	Jason Bowen		24/08/72	M	8	(6)	
10	Luke Bowen		07/03/88	A	12	(3)	6
8	Antonio Corbisiero	ENG	17/11/84	M	19	(2)	3
22	Adam Davies		15/10/93	D	23	(2)	
15	Mamadou Diallo	GUI	18/05/93	M	5	(2)	
5	Alex Evans		17/09/92	D	9		2
5	Ashley Evans		18/07/89	M	18		
17	Scott Evans		06/01/89	M		(1)	
3	Lloyd Grist		13/11/85	D	24		1
6	Lee Hartshorn		12/03/87	D	9		
10	Nicky Holland		24/04/89	M	7	(3)	1
20	Corey Jenkins		14/02/91	A	8	(5)	
19	Dafydd Jones		22/06/95	G		(1)	
11	Geoff Kellaway	ENG	07/04/86	M	15	(1)	1
21	Andy Legg		28/07/66	D		(4)	
14	Steffan Lloyd		21/09/94	M	8	(5)	1
14	Jack McKenna	ENG	31/12/92	M	9	(1)	1
1	Craig Morris		27/07/84	G	27		
12	Craig Moses		12/04/88	A	18	(5)	5
15	Ariel Mrowinski	POL	22/02/86	M		(2)	
25	Dave Richards		31/12/93	G	5		
9	Martin Rose	ENG	29/02/84	A	19		11
14	James Secker		25/02/92	M		(3)	
8	Jordan Smith		24/04/93	M	10		1
6	Lee Surman		03/04/86	D	20		1
2	Chris Thomas		16/01/83	D	20		
4	Chris Venables		23/07/85	M	12		1
9	Jeff White		18/01/86	A	8	(1)	1
16	Craig Williams		28/01/83	M	11	(4)	3

NEWTOWN AFC
Manager: Bernard McNally
1896 • GF Grigg Latham Park (6,000) • newtownafc.co.uk
Major honours
Welsh Cup (2) 1879, 1895

2012

17/08	Bala	a	4-4	Boundford, Whitfield, Sutton, A Jones
25/08	Bangor	h	3-2	Boundford 2, Blenkinsop
31/08	Port Talbot	a	0-1	
04/09	Port Talbot	h	1-1	og (Belle)
08/09	Connah's Quay	h	1-3	Sutton
15/09	Llanelli	a	3-0	Edmunds, Ward, Partridge
22/09	Airbus	h	1-7	Whitfield
29/09	Afan Lido	a	3-2	Blenkinsop, Evans (p), og (M Jones)
06/10	Prestatyn	h	1-4	Evans (p)
13/10	TNS	a	1-0	Williams
20/10	Carmarthen	h	1-2	Ward
27/10	Bala	h	1-1	Boundford
02/11	Bangor	a	0-3	
16/11	Connah's Quay	a	1-2	Boundford
24/11	Llanelli	h	1-1	A Jones
30/11	Airbus	a	1-2	Mills-Evans
15/12	Afan Lido	h	1-2	Ward
22/12	Prestatyn	a	5-2	A Jones 3, Evans, Whitfield
26/12	Aberystwyth	a	2-0	Evans, Mills-Evans

2013

01/01	Aberystwyth	h	3-1	A Jones, Boundford, Partridge
05/01	TNS	h	1-1	Williams
02/02	Carmarthen	a	2-4	Boundford, Sutton
08/02	Bala	a	1-3	Boundford
16/02	Llanelli	h	1-2	Boundford
23/02	Aberystwyth	h	0-0	
09/03	Connah's Quay	h	1-0	Cook
30/03	Llanelli	a	1-0	Whitfield
01/04	Afan Lido	a	1-2	Evans
13/04	Aberystwyth	a	0-0	
16/04	Bala	h	0-1	
20/04	Connah's Quay	a	2-0	Hearsey, Williams
27/04	Afan Lido	h	0-1	

No	Name	Nat	DoB	Pos	Aps	(s)	Gls
10	Steve Blenkinsop	ENG	03/02/89	A	6	(7)	2
9	Luke Boundford		30/01/88	A	26	(2)	9
8	Matthew Cook	ENG	07/09/85	M	27	(2)	1
15	Ian Edmunds		12/01/93	D	24	(3)	1
17	Zac Evans		03/05/91	M	24	(6)	5
12	Josh Hartrick		20/12/91	M		(1)	
7	Matthew Hearsey	ENG	25/02/91	A	9	(1)	1
18	Barry Hogan	ENG	15/02/83	M	9		
14	Andrew Jones	ENG	23/03/85	A	28	(1)	6
21	Elliot Jones		28/12/93	A	2	(5)	
5	Kieran Mills-Evans	ENG	11/10/92	D	29		2
2	Gareth Partridge		25/09/91	A	8	(11)	2
3	Max Penk		17/02/93	D	15	(2)	
7	Jamie Price		22/07/88	M	7	(3)	
21	Connell Rawlinson		22/09/91	D			
1	Dave Roberts	ENG	10/12/88	G	32		
6	Shane Sutton		31/01/89	D	32		3
20	Nicky Ward		30/11/77	M	23	(2)	3
22	Aaron Warwick	GER	20/11/84	G		(1)	
16	Craig Whitfield	ENG	16/08/89	A	11	(10)	4
19	Craig Williams		21/12/87	M	30	(2)	3
14	Adam Worton	ENG	10/04/87	D	5	(1)	

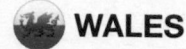

PORT TALBOT TOWN FC

Manager: Mark Jones; (26/11/12) Scott Young
1901 • GenQuip Stadium (3,000) • porttalbottown.co.uk
Major honours
Welsh Cup (1) 1900

2012

18/08	Llanelli	h	1-2	Belle (p)
25/08	Connah's Quay	a	0-2	
31/08	Newtown	h	1-0	Brooks
04/09	Newtown	a	1-1	Belle (p)
08/09	Aberystwyth	a	5-0	Brooks, John, Crowell (p), White 2
15/09	Airbus	h	4-4	White 2, Brooks 2 (1p)
22/09	Prestatyn	a	1-1	Brooks
29/09	TNS	a	0-5	
05/10	Carmarthen	h	2-1	Payne, John
14/10	Bala	a	0-2	
20/10	Bangor	h	1-1	John
27/10	Llanelli	a	1-0	Thomas
03/11	Connah's Quay	h	6-1	White 2, Belle (p), Blain, Wright 2
17/11	Aberystwyth	h	2-4	Brooks, White
24/11	Airbus	a	0-5	
01/12	Prestatyn	h	1-0	Thomas
15/12	TNS	h	1-3	Brooks (p)
21/12	Carmarthen	a	0-1	
26/12	Afan Lido	a	3-0	Brooks, Payne, Harling
29/12	Afan Lido	h	6-1	Harling, Brooks 2, Payne, Green, De Vulgt

2013

05/01	Bala	h	2-1	Brooks, Bond
02/02	Bangor	a	2-2	Evans 2
09/02	TNS	a	0-5	
16/02	Bangor	h	1-1	Bloom
23/02	Prestatyn	a	1-0	Bond
08/03	Carmarthen	h	1-0	Rose
16/03	Airbus	a	0-2	
24/03	TNS	h	0-3	
30/03	Bangor	a	3-3	Bond, Brooks 2
13/04	Prestatyn	h	4-1	Brooks (p), Rose 2, Payne
20/04	Carmarthen	a	0-0	
27/04	Airbus	h	1-0	Brooks

No	Name	Nat	DoB	Pos	Aps	(s)	Gls
10	Cortez Belle	ENG	27/08/83	D	14	(2)	3
16	Dylan Blain		10/11/82	M	7	(9)	1
6	James Bloom		11/08/91	D	29	(1)	1
31	Chad Bond		20/04/87	A	9	(3)	3
39	David Brooks		19/05/89	M	26	(2)	15
25	Dave Burnett		28/01/90	G	5		
23	Matty Crowell		03/07/84	M	18	(6)	1
12	Leigh De Vulgt		10/03/81	D	13	(3)	1
4	Ashley Evans		18/07/89	M	9	(1)	2
24	Ryan Green		20/10/80	D	26	(1)	1
11	Lloyd Grist		13/11/85	M	7		
29	Steven Hall		11/04/85	G	10		
5	Liam Hancock		27/09/82	D	1		
8	Lewis Harling		11/06/92	M	25	(4)	2
15	Nicky Holland		24/04/89	D	1	(1)	
7	Lee John		05/02/83	M	25	(3)	3
4	Craig Jones		28/03/87	M		(5)	
3	Paul Keddle		18/11/83	D	5		
26	Jake Parry		15/12/93	M	2	(2)	
14	Carl Payne		05/09/90	M	24	(1)	4
27	Joshua Pike		03/03/94	D		(2)	
1	Craig Richards		25/01/91	G	17		
9	Martin Rose	ENG	29/02/84	A	9		3
17	Duane Saunders		22/09/86	M		(1)	
2	Dan Sheehan		22/12/90	D	20		
5	Lee Surman		03/04/86	D	8		
11	Daniel Thomas		28/04/84	M	17	(1)	2
21	Sasha Walters		20/06/84	M	3	(9)	
19	Jeff White		18/01/86	A	17	(2)	7
18	Adam Wright		30/05/91	A	5	(24)	2

PRESTATYN TOWN FC

Manager: Lee Jones & Neil Gibson
1910 • Bastion Road (3,000) • ptfconline.co.uk
Major honours
Welsh Cup (1) 2013

2012

18/08	Afan Lido	h	4-2	Parkinson 3, Parker
25/08	Llanelli	a	2-2	Price, O'Neill
31/08	TNS	a	1-4	Price
08/09	Carmarthen	h	7-1	Parkinson, Price 2, Parker 2 (2p), Gibson 2
12/09	TNS	h	1-0	Price
15/09	Bala	a	2-1	Parkinson, R Stephens
22/09	Port Talbot	h	1-1	Price
28/09	Connah's Quay	h	4-1	Parker, Parkinson, R Stephens 2
06/10	Newtown	a	4-1	Price, Stones, Parkinson 2
13/10	Aberystwyth	h	2-2	R Stephens (p), Wilson
19/10	Airbus	a	0-5	
27/10	Afan Lido	a	4-2	Parkinson 2, Price, Hayes
03/11	Llanelli	h	3-1	Wilson, Parkinson, Gibson
17/11	Carmarthen	a	2-2	R Stephens, Parker (p)
24/11	Bala	h	1-0	Parker
01/12	Port Talbot	a	0-1	
22/12	Newtown	h	2-5	Parkinson, R Stephens
28/12	Bangor	a	3-3	Price 2, Parker

2013

01/01	Bangor	h	4-1	Parkinson, Parker, Price, R Stephens
05/01	Aberystwyth	a	1-4	Parkinson
11/01	Connah's Quay	a	3-3	A Stephens, Parkinson 2
19/01	Airbus	h	1-6	Parker
09/02	Bangor	a	3-3	Parkinson 2, Parker
15/02	Airbus	h	0-4	
23/02	Port Talbot	h	0-1	
08/03	TNS	a	0-3	
16/03	Carmarthen	a	2-3	Smyth, Stones
29/03	Airbus	a	1-4	Parkinson
09/04	Bangor	h	0-1	
13/04	Port Talbot	a	1-4	Smyth
20/04	TNS	h	1-7	R Stephens (p)
27/04	Carmarthen	h	2-1	Hayes, A Stephens

No	Name	Nat	DoB	Pos	Aps	(s)	Gls
1	Gareth Barker	ENG	08/09/91	G		(1)	
18	Martyn Beattie	ENG	18/01/83	D	3		
2	Chris Davies		21/10/90	M	27	(2)	
16	Daniel Davies		28/06/95	M		(1)	
12	Dan Evans		01/03/87	M	5	(11)	
32	Jon Fisher-Cooke		13/05/82	A		(1)	
14	Adam France		18/08/87	D		(1)	
8	Neil Gibson		11/10/79	M	26	(1)	3
4	David Hayes		15/01/82	D	25	(2)	2
25	Jon Hill-Dunt		13/05/86	G	29		
24	Tommy Holmes	ENG	01/09/79	D	6		
3	Guto Hughes		29/05/92	A	1	(1)	
7	Tom Kemp		30/12/94	D	4	(4)	
1	Lee Kendall		08/01/81	G	3		
21	Rhys Lewis		21/04/94	M	2	(2)	
17	Carl Murray		24/09/90	M	4	(10)	
5	Paul O'Neill	ENG	17/06/82	D	18		1
20	Rhys Owen		10/06/93	M	4	(5)	
7	Michael Parker		31/10/87	M	28		10
9	Andy Parkinson	ENG	27/05/79	M	31		19
10	Jason Price		12/04/77	A	28		11
15	Mark Smyth	ENG	09/01/85	M	8	(1)	2
11	Anthony Stephens		23/08/90	D	27		2
22	Ross Stephens		28/05/85	M	25	(3)	8
23	Greg Stones	ENG	04/05/82	D	24		2
6	Gareth Wilson		23/05/78	M	24		2

THE NEW SAINTS FC

Manager: Carl Darlington & Craig Harrison
1959 • The Venue (3,000) • tnsfc.co.uk
Major honours
Welsh League (7) 2000, 2005, 2007, 2010, 2012, 2013;
Welsh Cup (3) 1996, 2005, 2012

2012

17/08	Airbus	h	1-0	Spender
24/08	Afan Lido	a	3-1	Fraughan, Evans, Draper
31/08	Prestatyn	h	4-1	Draper, Fraughan 2, Finley
08/09	Llanelli	h	0-0	
12/09	Prestatyn	a	0-1	
15/09	Carmarthen	h	0-0	
22/09	Bangor	h	3-0	Darlington, Wilde, Seargeant
29/09	Port Talbot	h	5-0	Darlington 3 (1p), Seargeant, Wilde
06/10	Connah's Quay	a	3-1	og (Dobbins), Wilde, A Edwards
13/10	Newtown	h	0-1	
19/10	Aberystwyth	a	4-1	Finley, Seargeant, Wilde, Darlington
26/10	Airbus	a	1-2	A Edwards
03/11	Afan Lido	h	2-1	Draper, Seargeant
17/11	Llanelli	a	6-0	Jones 2, Darlington 2, Wilde 2
24/11	Carmarthen	h	0-3	
01/12	Bangor	a	1-0	Jones
15/12	Port Talbot	a	3-1	Darlington (p), og (Bloom), Fraughan
21/12	Connah's Quay	h	5-1	Wilde, Baker, Finley, Marriott, Draper
26/12	Bala	h	1-0	Wilde

2013

02/01	Bala	a	2-2	Wilde 2 (1p)
05/01	Newtown	a	1-1	Wilde
02/02	Aberystwyth	h	3-0	Darlington 2, K Edwards
09/02	Port Talbot	h	5-0	Wilde 2, Darlington, Draper, Fraughan
23/02	Airbus	a	2-1	Fraughan, Darlington (p)
08/03	Prestatyn	h	3-0	Wilde 2, Williams
16/03	Bangor	h	6-0	Wilde 2, Darlington 3, Williams
24/03	Port Talbot	a	3-0	Wilde, A Edwards, Mullan
30/03	Carmarthen	h	3-0	Ruscoe, Wilde 2
12/04	Airbus	h	4-2	Fraughan, Wilde 2, Marriott
16/04	Carmarthen	a	1-0	Wilde
20/04	Prestatyn	a	7-1	Williams 3, A Edwards, Darlington, Wilde 2 (1p)
27/04	Bangor	a	4-1	A Edwards, og (Johnston), Darlington 2

No	Name	Nat	DoB	Pos	Aps	(s)	Gls
4	Phil Baker	ENG	04/11/82	D	21	(1)	1
20	Alex Darlington		26/12/88	A	20	(10)	18
9	Greg Draper	NZL	13/08/89	A	10	(10)	5
6	Aeron Edwards		16/02/88	M	25	(3)	5
23	Kai Edwards		29/01/91	D	23	(3)	1
5	Steve Evans		26/02/79	D	19		1
14	Sam Finley	ENG	04/08/92	M	19	(4)	3
11	Ryan Fraughan	ENG	11/02/91	M	21	(6)	7
1	Paul Harrison	ENG	18/12/84	G	32		
19	Chris Jones		12/09/89	M	31		3
15	Jason Lampkin	ENG	24/04/94	M	2	(4)	
3	Chris Marriott	ENG	24/09/89	D	32		2
14	Jamie Mullan	ENG	10/02/88	A	4	(5)	1
22	Scott Quigley	ENG	02/09/92	A		(6)	
16	Connell Rawlinson		22/09/91	D	3	(1)	
7	Scott Ruscoe		15/12/77	M	7	(7)	1
12	Christian Seargeant	ENG	13/09/86	M	26	(2)	4
26	Aaron Simms		01/12/94	D	1		
2	Simon Spender		15/11/85	D	29		1
18	Michael Wilde	ENG	27/08/83	A	24	(6)	25
10	Matty Williams		05/11/82	A	3	(11)	5

Top goalscorers

25	Michael Wilde (TNS)
21	Chris Simm (Bangor)
19	Andy Parkinson (Prestatyn)
18	Alex Darlington (TNS)
17	Mark Jones (Afan Lido/Aberystwyth)
	Lee Hunt (Bala)
15	David Brooks (Port Talbot)
14	Martin Rose (Llanelli/Port Talbot)
13	Liam Thomas (Carmarthen)
	Jamie Petrie (Connah's Quay)

UEFA Europa League play-offs

FIRST ROUND

(04/05/13)
Bala 1-0 Connah's Quay *(Hunt 75p)*

SEMI-FINALS

(11/05/13)
Bangor 2-4 Bala *(Chris Jones 57, Hoy 79; S Jones 29, M Jones 34, Sheridan 43, 47)*
Port Talbot 1-0 Carmarthen *(Brooks 71)*

FINAL

(18/05/13)
Port Talbot 0-1 Bala *(Irving 88)*

Promoted club

RHYL FC

Manager: Greg Strong
1883 • Belle Vue Stadium (3,000) • rhylfc.co.uk
Major honours
Welsh League (2) 2004, 2009;
Welsh Cup (4) 1952, 1953, 2004, 2006

SECOND LEVEL FINAL TABLES 2012/13

NORTH		Pld	W	D	L	F	A	Pts
1	Rhyl FC	30	24	6	0	100	24	78
2	Cefn Druids FC	30	22	3	5	79	32	69
3	Conwy Borough FC	30	18	7	5	57	37	61
4	Caersws FC	30	18	3	9	90	42	57
5	Buckley Town FC	30	13	10	7	60	35	49
6	Flint Town United FC	30	14	6	10	61	51	48
7	Holyhead Hotspur FC	30	13	4	13	51	55	43
8	Guilsfield FC	30	12	6	12	61	54	42
9	CPD Porthmadog	30	11	5	14	48	52	38
10	CPD Penrhyncoch	30	9	7	14	50	63	34
11	Rhayader Town FC	30	9	6	15	44	66	33
12	Llandudno FC	30	8	8	14	36	59	32
13	Penycae FC	30	7	5	18	49	84	26
14	Rhydymwyn FC	30	6	8	16	49	96	26
15	Llanrhaeadr-ym-Mochnant FC	30	4	7	19	29	87	19
16	Ruthin Town FC	30	3	7	20	47	74	16

SOUTH		Pld	W	D	L	F	A	Pts
1	West End FC	28	18	4	6	64	29	58
2	Cambrian & Clydach Vale BGC	28	17	5	6	56	26	56
3	Taffs Well AFC	28	14	7	7	57	39	49
4	Haverfordwest County AFC	28	13	8	7	63	35	47
5	Aberdare Town FC	28	13	8	7	45	35	47
6	AFC Porth	28	13	7	8	39	34	46
7	Monmouth Town FC	28	13	6	9	54	43	42
8	Bryntirion Athletic FC	28	10	9	9	38	40	39
9	Ton Pentre AFC	28	9	9	10	39	30	36
10	Pontardawe Town FC	28	10	5	13	34	39	35
11	Goytre United FC	28	10	4	14	33	51	34
12	Cwmbran Celtic FC	28	9	5	14	41	52	32
13	Bridgend Town AFC	28	8	7	13	28	51	31
14	Tata Steel FC	28	5	6	17	28	61	21
15	Caerleon AFC	28	1	4	23	18	63	7

NB Monmouth Town FC – 3 pts deducted; Barry Town FC withdrew after round 28 – their matches annulled; No promotion as neither of the top two clubs obtained a domestic licence.

Domestic cup: Welsh Cup 2012/13

THIRD ROUND

(08/12/12)
Aberystwyth 2-5 Rhyl
Afan Lido 3-4 Prestatyn
Airbus 3-0 Port Talbot
Bangor 4-1 Aberdare
Barry 3-1 Ely *(aet)*
Connah's Quay 4-2 Llanelli
Flint 1-0 Llanidloes
Gwalchmai 0-2 Chepstow
Holyhead 1-2 Carmarthen
Holywell 0-2 Caerau Ely
Llandudno Junction 2-3 Haverfordwest
Llanrug 0-5 West End
Monmouth 2-3 Bala Town
Newtown 2-0 Cefn Druids
TNS 3-1 Conwy *(aet)*

(05/01/13)
Goytre (Gwent) 0-2 Pontardawe

FOURTH ROUND

(26/01/13)
Barry 2-1 Pontardawe
Carmarthen 3-2 Bala *(aet)*
Chepstow 3-4 Haverfordwest
Connah's Quay 0-2 Bangor
Prestatyn 2-0 West End

(02/02/13)
Flint 3-1 Caerau Ely

(05/02/13)
Newtown 1-1 Airbus *(aet; 4-5 on pens)*
TNS 5-1 Rhyl

QUARTER-FINALS

(01/03/13)
Haverfordwest 0-1 TNS *(Williams 57)*

(02/03/13)
Bangor 1-0 Airbus *(Simm 30)*
Carmarthen 2-3 Prestatyn *(Kellaway 65, Hughes 77; Parker 76, Parkinson 81, Hayes 115) (aet)*
Flint 0-2 Barry *(Evans 27, Jenkins 54)*

SEMI-FINALS

(06/04/13)
Bangor 1-0 TNS *(Chris Jones 90+4)*
Barry 1-2 Prestatyn *(Nagy 20; Parkinson 18, Price 78)*

FINAL

(06/05/13)
Racecourse Ground, Wrexham
PRESTATYN TOWN FC 3 *(Price 2, 111, R Stephens 103)*
BANGOR CITY FC 1 *(C Davies 60og)*
(aet)
Referee: *Morgan*
PRESTATYN: *Hill-Dunt, C Davies, Stones, Hayes, A Stephens, Parker, Wilson (Owen 106), Gibson, Parkinson, R Stephens, Price (Murray 119)*
BANGOR: *Idzi, R Edwards, Roberts, Brewerton, Johnston, Morley (Booth 65), Chris Jones (S Edwards 59), Brownhill (Hoy 105), L Davies, Allen, Simm*
Sent off: *Johnston (102)*

Prestatyn celebrate their Welsh Cup win

UEFA.com

education
women's
football GRASSROOTS striker heatmaps

media
referee

facebook The OFFICIAL classics
unity website for
assists UEFA EUROPEAN
Europa
League FOOTBALL

Michel
Platini

teams

profiles

video news WOMEN'S UNDER-19 Women's Under-17

STATISTICS

UEFA comparisons UEFA CHAMPIONS
FUTSAL
Live EURO twitter
match PHOTOS FUTSAL CUP LEAGUE
streaming match UNDER-21 mobile NO TO
UEFA YOUTH app
EURO corner LEAGUE RESPECT RACISM
2016 executive corporate
committee coach FINAL events excellence FANS
UEFA Super squad TURIN fair play AREA
WOMEN'S Cup leadership 2014 player MatchCentre
CHAMPIONS kits rater
LEAGUE match history
FINAL goal
Lisbon 2014 stars
openness

exclusive UNDER-17 care live community

GAMES LIVE

CLUBS formations DATA

assists MIDFIELDER ranking PITCH